Best Books for Young Teen Readers

Best Books for Young Teen Readers™
Grades 7 to 10

John T. Gillespie

EDITOR

R. R. BOWKER®

A business unit of Reed Elsevier Inc.

New Providence, New Jersey

Published by R. R. Bowker, a business unit of Reed Elsevier Inc.
Copyright © 2000 by Reed Elsevier Inc.
All rights reserved
Printed and bound in the United States of America
Bowker® is a registered trademark of Reed Elsevier Inc.

Library of Congress Cataloging-in-Publication Data

Best books for young teen readers, grades 7 to 10 / John T. Gillespie, editor
p. cm.
Includes index.
ISBN 0-8352-4264-1
1. Children's literature, English—Bibliography. 2. Young adult literature, English—Bibliography. I. Gillespie, John Thomas, 1928–

Z1037 .B55 2000
011.62'5—dc21   99-089583

ISBN 0-8352-4264-1

9 780835 242646

Contents

CONTENTS

Guidance and Personal Development

CONTENTS

Recreation and Sports

Major Subjects Arranged Alphabetically

Preface

Best Books for Young Teen Readers is intended to be a continuation of *Best Books for Children* (Bowker, 6th edition, 1998), supplying information on recommended books for readers in grades 7 through 10 or roughly ages 12 through 16. As every librarian knows, there is no such thing as, for example, a seventh-grade book; instead there are only seventh-grade readers who, in their diversity, can represent a wide range of reading abilities and interests. This bibliography contains a liberal selection of entries that, one hopes, will accommodate readers in these grades and make allowance for their great range of tastes and reading competencies. By the ninth and tenth grades, a high percentage of the books read should be at the adult level. Keeping this in mind, about one third of the entries in this volume are adult books suitable for young adult readers (they are designated by the reading level grades of 9–12 and 10–12 within the entries). At the other end of the spectrum, there are also many titles that are suitable for readers below the seventh grade (indicated by using grade level designations such as 5–8 or 6–8 within the entries). This has resulted in a slight duplication of titles (under 5 percent) in this book with those in *Best Books for Children*, particularly those recommended for grades 6 and up.

Because of the breadth of this selection policy, it is hoped that this work will be of value not only in junior high schools but also in middle and senior high schools.

In selecting books for inclusion, deciding on their arrangement, and collecting the information supplied on each, it was the editor's intention to reflect the current needs and interests of young readers while keeping in mind the latest trends and curricular emphases in today's schools.

General Scope and Criteria for Inclusion

Of the 11,730 titles listed in *Best Books for Young Teen Readers*, 11,147 are individually numbered entries and 583 are cited within the annotations as additional recommended titles by the same author (often these are titles that are part of an extensive series). If these titles do not have separate entries elsewhere in the volume, publication dates are generally given. However, some popular titles may have been published in several editions (and some may be out of print); in these cases the year of publication is not given. It should also be noted that some series are so extensive that, because of space limitations, only representative titles are included.

Excluded from this bibliography are general reference works, such as dictionaries and encyclopedias, except for a few single-volume works that are so heavily illustrated and attractive that they can also be used in the general circulation collection. Also excluded are professional books for librarians and teachers and mass market series books.

For most fiction and nonfiction, a minimum of two recommendations were required from the current reviewing sources consulted for a title to be considered for listing. However, there were a number of necessary exceptions. For example, in some reviewing journals only a few representative titles from extensive nonfiction series are reviewed even though others in the series will also be recommended. In such cases a single favorable review was enough for inclusion. This also held true for some of the adult titles suitable for young adult readers where, it has been found, reviewing journals tend to be less inclusive than with juvenile titles. As well as favorable reviews, additional criteria such as availability, up-to-dateness, accuracy, usefulness, and relevance were considered. All titles were in print as of December 1999.

Sources Used

A number of current and retrospective sources were used in compiling this bibliography. Of the retrospective sources, three were used extensively. They were *Best Books for Junior High Readers* (Bowker, 1991), *Best Books for Senior High Readers* (Bowker, 1991), and *Best Books for Young Adult Readers* (Bowker, 1997). After out-of-print titles were removed, remaining entries in these bibliographies were evaluated for content and suitability before inclusion was recommended.

Current book reviewing journals were consulted to obtain entries published after March 1996, when coverage in *Best Books for Young Adult Readers* ended. These current sources were *Booklist, Book Report, School Library Journal,* and *VOYA (Voice of Youth Advocates).* Reviews in these journals were read and tabulated from March 1996 through August 1999, when this book's coverage ends.

Uses of This Book

Best Books for Young Teen Readers was designed to help librarians and media specialists with four vital tasks: (1) evaluating the adequacy of existing collections; (2) building new collections or strengthening existing holdings; (3) providing reading guidance to young adults; and (4) preparing bibliographies and reading lists. To increase the book's usefulness, particularly in preparation of bibliographies or suggested reading lists, titles are arranged under broad areas of interest or, in the case of nonfiction works, by curriculum-oriented subjects rather than the Dewey Decimal classification (suggested Dewey classification numbers are nevertheless provided within nonfiction entries). The subject arrangement corresponds roughly to the one used in *Best Books for Children*, minus its large section on picture books.

Some arbitrary decisions were made concerning placement of books under specific subjects. For example, books of experiments and projects in general science are placed under "Physical and Applied Sciences—Experiments and Projects," whereas books of experiments and projects on a specific branch of science (e.g., physics) appear under that branch. It is hoped that use of the many "see" and "see also" references in the Subject/Grade Level Index will help guide the user in this regard.

Arrangement

In the Table of Contents, subjects are arranged by the order in which they appear in the book. Following the Table of Contents is a listing of Major Subjects Arranged Alphabetically, which provides entry numbers as well as page numbers for easy access. Following the main body of the text, there are three indexes. The Author Index cites authors and editors, titles, and entry numbers (joint authors and editors are listed separately). The Title Index gives the book's entry number. Works of fiction in both of these indexes are indicated by (F) following the entry number. Finally, an extensive Subject/Grade Level Index lists entry numbers under hundreds of subject headings with specific grade-level suitability given for each entry. The following codes are used to identify general grade levels:

IJ (Intermediate-Junior High) suitable for grades 4–8, 4–9, 5–8, and 6–8

J (Junior High) suitable for grades 5–9, 5–10, 6–9, and 7–9

JS (Junior-Senior High) suitable for grades 6–10, 6–12, 7–10, 7–12, 8–10, 8–12, and 9–12

S (Senior High) suitable for grades 10–12

Entries

A typical entry contains the following information when applicable: (1) author, joint author, or editor; (2) title and subtitle; (3) specific grade levels, given in parentheses; (4) adapter or translator; (5) indication of illustrations; (6) publication date; (7) publisher and price of hardbound edition (LB = library binding); (8) International Standard Book Number

(ISBN) of hardbound edition; (9) paperback publisher (paper) and price (if no publisher is listed it is the same as the hardbound edition); (10) ISBN of paperback edition: (11) annotation; (12) review citations; (13) Dewey Decimal classification number.

Review Citations

Review citations are given for books published and reviewed from 1985 through August 1999. These citations can be used to find more detailed information about each of the books listed. The four periodical sources identified are:

BL   *Booklist*
BR   *Book Report*
SLJ   *School Library Journal*
VOYA   *VOYA (Voice of Youth Advocates)*

Acknowledgments

Many people were involved in the preparation of this bibliography. I am particularly indebted to Megan Jackson, Director of Web Vendor Sales, formerly Project Director for this title, R. R. Bowker; Catherine Barr (publisher, Rock Hill Press); Julie Miller (Database Coordinator, Rock Hill Press); and especially Nancy Bucenec, Bowker Managing Editor, who so ably coordinated all our efforts. I thank them for their suggestions, assistance, and, above all, patience.

Best Books for Young Teen Readers

Literary Forms

Fiction

Adventure and Survival Stories

1 Aaron, Chester. *Lackawanna* (6–9). 1986, Harper-Collins LB $11.89 (0-397-32058-2). In Depression New York, the youthful Lackawanna gang sets out to find a member who has been kidnapped. (Rev: BL 2/15/86; BR 9–10/86; SLJ 4/86; VOYA 6/86)

2 Aaron, Chester. *Out of Sight, Out of Mind* (6–9). 1985, HarperCollins LB $11.89 (0-397-32101-5). Twins with psychic powers are being pursued by foreign agents who want their secret. (Rev: BR 3–4/86; VOYA 12/85)

3 Aiken, Joan. *Is Underground* (6–8). 1993, 1995, Dell paper $3.99 (0-440-41068-1). Is Twite seeks the whereabouts of Arun, her cousin, and Davy Suart, the king's son, who vanished in London under suspicious circumstances. Part of a long, entertaining series about the Twites. (Rev: BL 4/1/93)

4 Aiken, Joan. *Midnight Is a Place* (7–10). 1974, Demco $8.05 (0-606-05466-9); Scholastic paper $2.95 (0-590-45496-X). In Victorian England 2 young waifs are cast adrift in a hostile town when their guardian's house burns.

5 Alcock, Vivien. *Singer to the Sea God* (6–12). 1995, Dell paper $3.99 (0-440-41003-7). Weaves together epic tales—from Scylla and Charybdis to Perseus and the Gorgon—with the story of a group of runaway slaves who act out scary travelers' tales they've only half-believed. (Rev: BL 5/1/93)

6 Alexander, Lloyd. *Gypsy Rizka* (5–8). 1999, Dutton $16.99 (0-525-46121-3). A delightful adventure story featuring Rizka, a young gypsy who lives alone in her wagon and becomes involved in a series of hilarious situations with the neighboring townspeople. (Rev: SLJ 3/99)

7 Alexander, Lloyd. *The Illyrian Adventure* (6–9). 1986, Dell paper $3.99 (0-440-40297-2). Vesper Holly and her companion Brinnie get involved in an archaeological expedition and unforeseen adventure in this, the first of a recommended series. (Rev: BL 4/1/86; BR 11–12/86; SLJ 5/86; VOYA 12/86)

8 Alexander, Lloyd. *Westmark* (7–10). 1981, Dell paper $4.50 (0-440-99731-3). In this first of 3 volumes, Theo, in the imaginary kingdom of Westmark, joins revolutionaries intent on establishing a democracy. Also in this series: *The Beggar Queen* (1984). (Rev: BL 12/15/89)

9 Amato, Angela, and Joe Sharkey. *Lady Gold* (10–12). 1998, St. Martin's $23.95 (0-312-18541-3). A tense, realistic tale of 2 undercover policemen, a man and a woman, and their efforts to arrest a top Mafia boss. (Rev: BL 5/15/98; SLJ 3/99)

10 Anderson, Scott. *Unknown Rider* (6–9). 1995, Dennoch Pr. paper $12.50 (0-9644521-0-3). Combining fact and fiction, this is the story of fighter pilot Rick Wedon—his training, experiences in officer school, and his missions. (Rev: VOYA 8/96)

11 Antal, John F. *Proud Legions: A Novel of America's Next War* (10–12). 1999, Presidio Pr. $24.95 (0-89141-667-6). An adventure thriller set in the near future about an American tank battalion that faces an invasion of South Korea by North Korean forces. (Rev: BL 2/1/99; SLJ 5/99)

12 Archer, Jeffrey. *A Matter of Honor* (10–12). 1993, HarperCollins paper $6.50 (0-06-100713-7). For better readers, a tense thriller about a chase across Europe to secure a priceless icon. (Rev: BL 6/15/86)

13 Archer, Jeffrey. *Shall We Tell the President?* (10–12). 1987, Pocket Books paper $5.50 (0-671-63305-8). Someone is out to kill the president in this exciting tale told with a dash of humor.

14 Ashley, Bernard. *Break in the Sun* (6–9). Illus. 1980, Phillips $25.95 (0-87599-230-7). Patsy Bleigh runs away on a ship belonging to a theatrical company.

15 Ashley, Bernard. *A Kind of Wild Justice* (6–9). Illus. 1978, Phillips $25.95 (0-87599-229-3). Ronnie is threatened by the same gang that made his father a criminal.

16 Bacon, Katharine Jay. *Finn* (5–9). 1998, Simon & Schuster paper $16.00 (0-689-82216-2). After a traumatizing plane crash that killed his family, 15-year-old Finn refuses to talk until encounters with drug dealers force him to choose between remaining silent or saving his few remaining loved ones. (Rev: BL 12/1/98; SLJ 11/98; VOYA 12/98)

17 Baillie, Allan. *Secrets of Walden Rising* (6–8). 1997, Viking paper $13.99 (0-670-87351-9). Murder and adventure mix in this story about 2 boys and their quest for gold in a part of Australia stricken with a severe drought. (Rev: BL 4/1/97; BR 1–2/98; SLJ 5/97)

18 Bainbridge, Beryl. *The Birthday Boys* (9–12). 1994, Carroll & Graf $18.95 (0-7867-0071-8). A fictional account of an early 20th-century expedition to Antarctica, narrated by Captain Robert Scott and 4 fellow explorers who were doomed to die. (Rev: BL 4/1/94; SLJ 10/94)

19 Baird, Thomas. *Finding Fever* (6–8). 1982, HarperCollins $12.95 (0-06-020353-6). Kidnappers make off with Benny's sister's dog, and so Benny sets out to investigate.

20 Barr, Nevada. *Firestorm* (10–12). 1996, Putnam $22.95 (0-399-14126-X). A combination murder mystery and survival story featuring a gallant female sleuth that takes place during a firestorm in Northern California. (Rev: BL 3/15/96; SLJ 9/96)

21 Bawden, Nina. *Rebel on a Rock* (6–8). 1978, HarperCollins LB $13.89 (0-397-32140-6). Jo reluctantly believes that her stepfather is a spy for a cruel dictator.

22 Bernardo, Anilu. *Jumping Off to Freedom* (7–10). 1996, Arte Publico $14.95 (1-55885-087-2); paper $9.95 (1-55885-088-0). The story of 4 refugees, including teenage David, on a harrowing voyage from Cuba to Florida on a raft. (Rev: BL 5/1/96; BR 9–10/96; SLJ 7/96; VOYA 6/96)

23 Blades, Ann. *A Boy of Tache* (6–9). 1995, Tundra paper $7.95 (0-88776-350-2). A Canadian novel of a boy's trek through the wilderness to save his grandfather's life.

24 Bodett, Tom. *Williwaw* (5–8). 1999, Knopf LB $17.99 (0-679-99030-5). The story of 2 youngsters, 13-year-old September Crane and her 12-year-old brother, Ivan, and their life in the wilds of Alaska where they are often left alone by their fisherman father. (Rev: BL 4/1/99; SLJ 5/99)

25 Brand, Max. *Dan Barry's Daughter* (7–12). 1976, Amereon LB $25.95 (0-88411-516-X). Harry is an accused murderer who, though innocent, is forced to hide. One of many recommended westerns by this prolific author.

26 Brand, Max. *Way of the Lawless* (10–12). 1985, Warner paper $2.50 (0-446-32665-8). In this western by the prolific writer Brand, a basically decent young man finds himself on the wrong side of the law.

27 Bridal, Tessa. *The Tree of Red Stars* (10–12). 1997, Milkweed $21.95 (1-57131-013-4). In a series of flashbacks, Magdalena tells of her secret work with the Tupamaro rebels in Uruguay, her imprisonment and torture, and her subsequent life in Europe. (Rev: BL 6/1–15/97; SLJ 10/97)

28 Brown, Sam. *The Trail to Honk Ballard's Bones* (9–12). 1990, Walker $27.95 (0-8027-4101-0). In this western adventure, Honk Ballard discovers that his new trail buddy is really a bank robber. (Rev: BL 1/15/90)

29 Bunting, Eve. *Someone Is Hiding on Alcatraz Island* (7–9). 1984, Berkley paper $4.99 (0-425-10294-7). A young boy is trapped by a ruthless gang of hoodlums when he seeks shelter on Alcatraz Island. (Rev: BL 7/88)

30 Bunting, Eve. *SOS Titanic* (6–9). 1996, Harcourt $13.00 (0-15-200271-5); paper $6.00 (0-15-201305-9). During his voyage on the *Titanic*, 15-year-old Barry O'Neill learns about the inequities of the class system and the true meaning of heroism. (Rev: BL 3/15/96; SLJ 4/96; VOYA 6/96)

31 Burgess, Melvin. *The Baby and Fly Pie* (7–10). 1996, Simon & Schuster paper $16.00 (0-689-80489-X). This novel, set in a bleak London of the future, tells how a street waif, Fly Pie, his sharp sister, Jane, and sidekick, Sham, become involved in a kidnapping scheme. (Rev: BL 5/15/96; BR 1–2/97; SLJ 7/96; VOYA 8/96)

32 Burks, Brian. *Wrango* (5–8). 1999, Harcourt $16.00 (0-15-201815-8). A story about a young African American cowboy and his adventures riding the range. (Rev: BL 9/1/99)

33 Burroughs, Edgar Rice. *Tarzan of the Apes* (9–12). 1988, NAL paper $4.95 (0-451-52423-3). The beginning of the famous saga of the Ape Man, a series of more than 20 titles.

34 Butler, Geoff. *The Hangashore* (6–8). Illus. 1998, Tundra $15.95 (0-88776-444-4). A picture book for older children set in Newfoundland about a stubborn, self-righteous magistrate from England who changes his mind about a slow-witted local boy and his own role in the community after the boy saves his life. (Rev: SLJ 2/99)

35 Butler, William. *The Butterfly Revolution* (7–12). 1961, Ballantine paper $5.99 (0-345-33182-6). A frightening story of problems in a boy's camp told in diary form by one of the campers.

36 Byars, Betsy. *Coast to Coast* (5–8). 1994, Dell paper $3.99 (0-440-40926-8). The adventures of Birch, 13, and her grandfather, who fly a Piper Cub from South Carolina to California. (Rev: BL 12/1/92; SLJ 1/93)

37 Cage, Elizabeth. *Spy Girls: License to Thrill* (6–9). (Spy Girls) 1998, Pocket Books paper $4.50 (0-671-02286-5). Three young women are recruited by the Tower, a part of the CIA, to find a document in the U.S. Embassy in London that lists the location of leftover Soviet nuclear warheads. (Rev: BL 3/1/99; SLJ 2/99)

38 Campbell, Eric. *The Place of Lions* (6–9). 1991, Harcourt $17.00 (0-15-262408-2). When their plane crashes over the Serengeti, Chris and his injured father must learn a lesson in survival while surrounded by a pride of lions and poachers. (Rev: BL 11/15/91; SLJ 11/91)

39 Campbell, Eric. *The Shark Callers* (7–10). 1994, Harcourt $10.95 (0-15-200007-0); paper $4.95 (0-15-200010-0). Parallel stories of 2 boys' survival in Papua New Guinea during a volcanic eruption and tidal wave. (Rev: BL 11/15/94; SLJ 9/94; VOYA 10/94)

40 Carey, D. L. *Distress Call 911: Twist of Fate #1* (5–9). (Distress Call 911) 1996, Archway paper $3.99 (0-671-55306-2). A lightweight adventure story about 3 teenagers who are involved in the emergency medical volunteer program at a local hospital. (Rev: VOYA 8/96)

41 Carter, Alden R. *Between a Rock and a Hard Place* (6–9). 1995, Scholastic $14.95 (0-590-48684-5). An exciting survival novel involving 2 boys on a ten-day canoe trip through the Minnesota lake country. (Rev: BL 1/1–15/96*; BR 3–4/96; SLJ 12/95; VOYA 4/96)

42 Casanova, Mary. *Wolf Shadows* (5–8). 1997, Hyperion LB $14.89 (0-7868-2269-4). After Matt shoots a wolf in the north Minnesota woods, his friend Seth is so disgusted that he leaves Matt, endangering his life. (Rev: BL 10/1/97; SLJ 10/97)

43 Castelli, Alfredo. *The Snowman* (9–12). Illus. 1990, Catalan Communications paper $9.95 (0-87416-124-X). A reporter on an Everest expedition encounters huge figures in the snow and later awakens in a lamasery, where, after terrifying dreams, he discovers the monks' secret. (Rev: BL 9/1/91)

44 Cavanagh, Helen. *Panther Glade* (5–8). 1993, Simon & Schuster paper $16.00 (0-671-75617-6). Bill spends a summer in Florida with his great-aunt Cait. He's afraid of the Everglades and alligators, but he comes to appreciate Indian history and crafts. (Rev: BL 6/1–15/93; SLJ 6/93; VOYA 10/93)

45 Childress, Mark. *V for Victor* (9–12). 1990, Ballantine paper $5.99 (0-345-35427-3). In 1942, a 16-year-old boy living on the coast of Alabama gets involved in a spy plot. (Rev: BL 11/15/88; BR 9–10/89; SLJ 7/89; VOYA 2/90)

46 Clancy, Tom. *Clear and Present Danger* (9–12). 1989, Putnam $25.95 (0-399-13440-9). An intricate spy thriller that deals with the drug war in Colombia. (Rev: SLJ 1/90)

47 Clancy, Tom. *Patriot Games* (9–12). 1987, Putnam $25.95 (0-399-13241-4); Berkley paper $7.50 (0-425-10972-0). In this large adventure novel for better readers, hero Jack Ryan tries to prevent a terrorist plan to kidnap Princess Diana and Prince Charles. Also recommended by Clancy are *Red Storm Rising* (1986) and *The Hunt for Red October* (1984). (Rev: BL 6/1/87; SLJ 11/87)

48 Clavell, James. *Children's Story* (9–12). 1981, Delacorte $7.95 (0-385-28135-8); 1989, Dell paper $5.99 (0-440-20468-2). After a terrible war has been lost, thought control is introduced in the schools.

49 Clavell, James. *Noble House* (10–12). 1981, Dell paper $7.99 (0-440-16484-2). An action-filled story about a China trading firm in Hong Kong. Also use: *Tai-Pan* (1983).

50 Coleman, Michael. *Weirdo's War* (5–8). 1998, Orchard $16.95 (0-531-30103-6). Noted for being the class misfit, Daniel is paired with Tozer, his nemesis, on a class excursion in this life-or-death survival story. (Rev: BL 8/98; BR 5–6/99; SLJ 10/98; VOYA 4/99)

51 Cook, Robin. *Sphinx* (9–12). 1983, NAL paper $7.99 (0-451-15949-7). Set in Egypt, this thriller involves a young art specialist from Boston and an antique statue in a tale of danger and romance.

52 Cook, Robin. *Vital Signs* (10–12). 1992, Berkley paper $7.99 (0-425-13176-9). A medical thriller that combines murder and infertility therapy. (Rev: BL 11/15/90)

53 Cooney, Caroline B. *Flash Fire* (7–10). 1995, Scholastic $14.95 (0-590-25253-4). A girl's wish for a more exciting life comes true when a fire sweeps the wealthy Los Angeles neighborhood where she lives. (Rev: BL 11/1/95; SLJ 12/95; VOYA 12/95)

54 Cooney, Caroline B. *Flight No. 116 Is Down* (7–10). 1992, Scholastic $14.95 (0-590-44465-4). With a lightning pace, the author depicts the drama and human interest inherent in disaster. (Rev: BL 1/15/92; SLJ 2/92)

55 Cooney, Caroline B. *The Terrorist* (6–10). 1997, Scholastic $15.95 (0-590-22853-6). Teenage Laura devotes all her energies to finding the terrorist whose bomb was responsible for her young brother's death in London. (Rev: BL 7/97; BR 9–10/97; SLJ 9/97; VOYA 10/97)

56 Coonts, Stephen. *Fortunes of War* (10–12). 1998, St. Martin's $24.95 (0-312-18583-9); paper $7.99 (0-312-96941-4). A modern military thriller about 2 friends, one an American colonel in the Air Force and the other a Japanese fighter pilot, who find themselves on opposing sides when Japanese radicals attempt to take over Siberian oil fields. (Rev: BL 3/15/98; SLJ 9/98)

57 Cormier, Robert. *After the First Death* (7–12). 1979, Pantheon LB $14.99 (0-394-94122-5). A busload of school children become the victims of a terrorist plot.

58 Crichton, Michael. *Airframe* (10–12). 1996, Knopf $26.00 (0-679-44648-6). Casey Singleton leads an investigation into a mysterious airplane disaster in which 3 people are killed. (Rev: BL 11/15/96; SLJ 3/97)

59 Cross, Gillian. *Born of the Sun* (7–10). 1984, Holiday House $11.95 (0-8234-0528-1). On an expedition in Peru with her archaeologist father, Paula finds the glamour gone and her relationship with her father changing. (Rev: BL 2/15/85)

60 Cunningham, Julia. *Dorp Dead* (6–8). Illus. 1993, Random paper $2.99 (0-679-84718-9). Gilly seeks freedom as an apprentice of Kobalt and finds instead he's a prisoner.

61 Cussler, Clive. *Cyclops* (9–12). 1986, Pocket Books paper $7.99 (0-671-70464-8). A thriller involving hero Dirk Pitt and such elements as a missing blimp and a secret mission to the moon. (Rev: BL 1/15/86)

62 Cussler, Clive. *Flood Tide* (10–12). 1997, Simon & Schuster $26.00 (0-684-80298-8). A page-turner that involves the adventurer Dick Pitt, who finds a lost treasure, destroys an evil villain, and saves a woman's life while protecting the country from possible economic collapse. (Rev: BL 8/97; SLJ 12/97)

63 Cussler, Clive. *Inca Gold* (5–9). 1998, Archway paper $4.99 (0-671-02056-0). In this successful adaption of the adult novel, Dirk Pitt and sidekick Al Giordino look for 2 scientists who disappeared in an Inca sacrificial well, and not only find them in an unexpected place, but discover a new dead body and an old one as well. Also use another Dirk Pitt adventure, *Shock Wave* (1998). (Rev: VOYA 6/99)

64 Cussler, Clive. *Raise the Titanic* (9–12). 1990, Pocket Books paper $7.99 (0-671-72519-X). A thriller about trying to recover riches from the sunken *Titanic*.

65 Cussler, Clive. *Shock Wave* (5–9). 1999, Pocket Books paper $4.99 (0-671-02055-2). An abridgement for younger readers of Cussler's adult title about a plot to shatter the diamond market, and a mysterious plague that kills thousands of people and animals. (Rev: SLJ 4/99; VOYA 6/99)

66 Cussler, Clive. *Treasure* (9–12). 1989, Pocket Books paper $7.99 (0-671-70465-6). Adventurer Dirk Pitt combats terrorists to rescue hostages in a frozen wilderness in Greenland. (Rev: BL 3/15/88)

67 DeFelice, Cynthia. *Nowhere to Call Home* (5–8). 1999, Farrar $16.00 (0-374-35552-5). During the Great Depression and after her father has committed suicide, 12-year-old Frances decides to dress as a boy and ride the rails like the hobos she has heard about. (Rev: BL 4/1/99; BR 9–10/99; SLJ 4/99; VOYA 10/99)

68 Delaney, Mark. *The Vanishing Chip* (6–9). 1998, Peachtree paper $5.95 (1-56145-176-2). Four gifted but unpopular high school friends form Misfits, Inc., and catch a gang of computer chip thieves. (Rev: BL 12/15/98; SLJ 2/99)

69 Disher, Garry. *Ratface* (5–9). 1994, Ticknor $14.95 (0-395-69451-5). Kidnapped by a racist Australian cult known as the White League, Max, Christina, and Stefan escape captivity and are pursued by Ratface, a cult deputy. (Rev: BL 11/1/94; SLJ 12/94; VOYA 2/95)

70 Doyle, Brian. *Spud Sweetgrass* (5–8). 1996, Douglas & McIntyre $14.95 (0-88899-164-9). In this adventure story, John Sweetgrass, nicknamed Spud, and two friends set out to find the culprits who are dumping grease into the Ottawa River. A sequel is *Spud in Winter* (1996). (Rev: BL 6/1–15/96; SLJ 9/96)

71 Doyon, Stephanie. *Leaving Home* (8–12). (On the Road) 1999, Simon & Schuster paper $3.99 (0-689-82107-7). High school graduate Miranda and friend Kirsten decide to postpone college for a year to travel cross-country. (Rev: BL 6/1–15/99; SLJ 9/99)

72 Dygard, Thomas J. *River Danger* (7–12). 1998, Morrow $15.00 (0-688-14852-2). While on a hiking trip 2 brothers encounter a gang of car thieves, and one of the brothers is taken captive. (Rev: BL 3/15/98; BR 11–12/98; SLJ 5/98)

73 Dygard, Thomas J. *Wilderness Peril* (7–12). 1991, Puffin paper $4.99 (0-14-034785-2). Two teenage campers find money hidden by a hijacker and soon find they are being trailed by him. (Rev: BL 4/15/85; SLJ 8/85)

74 Elmer, Robert. *Follow the Star* (5–8). (The Young Underground) 1997, Bethany House paper $5.99 (1-55661-660-0). Thirteen-year-old twins Peter and Ellise of Denmark, and their friend, Henrik, attempt to rescue Henrik's mother and a family friend held as spies on a Danish island by the Russians after World War II. (Rev: SLJ 2/98)

75 Ewing, Lynne. *Drive-By* (5–8). 1996, HarperCollins $13.95 (0-06-027125-6). When Tito's brother is killed in a gang-related shooting, he is bullied and threatened by the gang to reveal where his brother has hidden a cache of stolen money. (Rev: SLJ 8/96)

76 Ferris, Jean. *All That Glitters* (7–10). 1996, Farrar $16.00 (0-374-30204-9). In this adventure, Brian, 16, goes on a scuba-diving expedition with his father and an archaeologist investigating a shipwrecked Spanish galleon. (Rev: BL 2/15/96; SLJ 3/96; VOYA 6/96)

77 Ferris, Jean. *Song of the Sea* (7–9). (American Dreams) 1996, Avon paper $3.99 (0-380-78199-9). In the second title of this adventure series, set on the sea and in the Yucatan in 1814, privateer Raider Lyons lies near death as a result of wounds inflicted by the evil Captain Lawrence of the British navy and longs for the love of Rosie. (Rev: VOYA 10/96)

78 Fleischman, Sid. *The Ghost in the Noonday Sun* (6–8). 1989, Greenwillow $16.00 (0-688-08410-9). In this reissue of a 1965 title, Oliver is kidnapped by the pirate Captain Scratch. (Rev: VOYA 8/89)

79 Follett,. Ken. *Eye of the Needle* (9–12). 1979, NAL paper $4.95 (0-451-15524-6). A story of suspense and mounting horror involving a German spy and a family on a remote Scottish island.

80 Forester, C. S. *The African Queen* (9–12). 1935, Little, Brown paper $13.95 (0-316-28910-8). An English spinster and a cockney male friend decide, as an act of revenge, to blow up a German boat in this novel set in Africa.

81 Forsyth, Frederick. *The Day of the Jackal* (9–12). 1971, Bantam paper $7.50 (0-553-26630-6). A rousing thriller about an attempted assassination of Charles de Gaulle.

82 Forsyth, Frederick. *The Devil's Alternative* (9–12). 1980, Bantam paper $6.99 (0-553-26490-7). The rescue of a man from drowning in the Mediterranean Sea begins a series of events that almost leads to nuclear disaster in this thriller.

83 Forsyth, Frederick. *The Dogs of War* (9–12). 1982, Bantam paper $6.99 (0-553-26846-5). An adventure story about greed and an attempt to seize power in a small West African country.

84 Forsyth, Frederick. *The Fist of God* (9–12). 1994, Bantam paper $6.99 (0-553-57242-3). Two British brothers who are espionage experts organize an elaborate mission to find a secret weapon that's in Saddam Hussein's possession. (Rev: BL 3/1/94)

85 Forsyth, Frederick. *The Odessa File* (9–12). 1983, Bantam paper $6.99 (0-553-27198-9). A German reporter infiltrates an organization of former Nazis and is discovered.

86 Fox, Paula. *How Many Miles to Babylon?* (5–8). 1980, Bradbury $13.95 (0-02-735590-X). James is

kidnapped by older boys to help their dog-stealing racket.

87 Freedman, Benedict, and Nancy Freedman. *Mrs. Mike* (7–12). 1968, Berkley paper $4.99 (0-425-10328-5). Based on a true story, this tells of Kathy, her love for her Mountie husband Mike, and her hard life in the Canadian Northwest.

88 Funderburk, Robert. *Winter of Grace* (10–12). 1998, Bethany House paper $8.99 (1-55661-616-3). Deputy Dylan St. John investigates a string of robberies and murders that lead him to a troubled Vietnam vet, his small daughter, and his younger brother. (Rev: SLJ 3/99)

89 Gann, Ernest K. *Fate Is the Hunter* (9–12). 1986, Simon & Schuster paper $14.00 (0-671-63603-0). A thrilling adventure story that was the basis of a successful movie.

90 Garretson, James D. *The Deadwood Conspiracy* (10–12). 1996, DeHart $23.75 (0-9649706-0-0). Complete with a surprise ending, this thrilling adult novel combines international intrigue, murder, romance, and a conspiracy involving top-ranking government officials. (Rev: SLJ 9/96)

91 George, Jean Craighead. *The Case of the Missing Cutthroats: An Ecological Mystery* (4–8). 1996, HarperCollins LB $13.89 (0-06-025466-1). A mystery adventure story involving a 13-year-old girl and the discovery of a cutthroat trout in an unusual habitat. (Rev: SLJ 6/96; VOYA 8/96)

92 George, Jean Craighead. *Julie of the Wolves* (6–9). Illus. 1972, HarperCollins LB $14.89 (0-06-021944-0); paper $5.95 (0-06-440058-1). An Eskimo girl travels across Alaska alone to find a new life. Newbery Medal, 1973.

93 George, Jean Craighead. *Julie's Wolf Pack* (5–8). Illus. 1997, HarperCollins $15.89 (0-06-027407-7). A continuation of the story of Julie and Kapu, the wolf pack leader whose life Julie saved when he was a pup. This book chronicles six years in the lives of Kapu and his pack, who come in touch with Julie again when Kapu is captured by researchers. (Rev: BL 9/1/97; BR 1–2/98; SLJ 9/97; VOYA 6/98)

94 George, Jean Craighead. *My Side of the Mountain* (6–9). 1959, Dutton $15.99 (0-525-44392-4); paper $4.95 (0-525-44395-9). In this survival story, young Sam Gribley decides to spend a year alone in the Catskill Mountains. (Rev: BL 9/1/89)

95 George, Jean Craighead. *One Day in the Alpine Tundra* (6–8). Illus. 1984, HarperCollins LB $15.89 (0-690-04326-0). A boy spends a day examining the life in a tundra region of the Wyoming Tetons.

96 George, Jean Craighead. *Shark Beneath the Reef* (7–9). 1989, HarperCollins $13.95 (0-06-021992-0); paper $4.95 (0-06-440-308-4). The story of a young Mexican boy who is torn between becoming a shark fisherman like his father or going to college to be a marine biologist. (Rev: BL 6/1/89; BR 11–12/89; SLJ 6/89; VOYA 6/89)

97 George, Jean Craighead. *The Talking Earth* (6–9). 1983, HarperCollins LB $15.89 (0-06-021976-9); paper $4.95 (0-06-440212-6). A Seminole girl is forced to survive alone in the Everglades. (Rev: BL 11/1/88)

98 George, Jean Craighead. *Water Sky* (6–8). 1987, HarperCollins LB $14.89 (0-06-022199-2); paper $4.95 (0-06-440202-9). A boy is sent by his father to an Eskimo whaling camp to learn survival techniques. (Rev: BL 2/1/87; BR 9–10/87)

99 Gerritsen, Tess. *Bloodstream* (10–12). 1998, Pocket Books $23.00 (0-671-01675-X). In this gory medical thriller, Dr. Claire Elliot becomes involved in a mysterious epidemic of teen violence at her son's high school in a small town. (Rev: BL 7/97; SLJ 1/99)

100 Gilman, Dorothy. *Mrs. Pollifax and the Hong Kong Buddha* (9–12). 1985, Fawcett paper $5.99 (0-449-20983-0). This unlikely CIA agent gets involved in a plan by terrorists to destroy Hong Kong. Another in this series is *Mrs. Pollifax on the China Station* (1983). (Rev: BL 11/1/85)

101 Glenn, Mel. *Foreign Exchange* (7–12). 1999, Morrow $16.00 (0-688-16472-2). Through free-verse reflections of teens and adults, the murder of a small-town girl is explored and, with it, the underlying prejudices, anger, and secrets of the town are revealed. (Rev: BL 4/15/99; SLJ 6/99; VOYA 12/99)

102 Glenn, Mel. *The Taking of Room 114* (8–12). 1997, Dutton paper $16.99 (0-525-67548-5). A story told in poetry form about the teacher, villainous M. Wiedermayer, how he held his history class hostage at gunpoint, and the backgrounds of the young people in his class. (Rev: BL 3/1/97; BR 11–12/97; SLJ 4/97; VOYA 2/98)

103 Golding, William. *Lord of the Flies* (8–12). 1999, Viking paper $12.95 (0-14-028333-1). When they are marooned on a deserted island, a group of English schoolboys soon lose their civilized ways.

104 Gourley, Catherine, ed. *Read for Your Life: Tales of Survival from the Editors of Read Magazine* (5–8). (Best of Read) 1998, Millbrook paper $5.95 (0-7613-0344-8). This is a collection of excellent survival stories from 50 years of *Read,* a literary magazine for middle and high school students. (Rev: BL 8/98)

105 Grimes, Martha. *Biting the Moon* (10–12). 1999, Holt $25.00 (0-8050-5621-1). This is a riveting, fast moving story about a teenager with amnesia who names herself Andi, a girl who befriends her, and their quest to uncover Andi's past. (Rev: BL 1/1–15/99; SLJ 7/99)

106 Grisham, John. *The Street Lawyer* (10–12). 1998, Doubleday $27.95 (0-385-49099-2); Dell paper $7.99 (0-440-22570-1). In this fast-moving plot, a successful young lawyer's investigations raise serious questions about his firm's role in evicting homeless people during a cold winter. (Rev: BL 2/15/98; SLJ 6/98)

107 Hafen, Lyman. *Over the Joshua Slope* (6–8). 1994, Bradbury paper $14.95 (0-02-741100-1). A gritty, fast-paced adventure where a father and son come to an understanding after an accident caused by the boy cripples his father. (Rev: BL 5/1/94; SLJ 6/94; VOYA 6/94)

108 Haggard, H. Rider. *King Solomon's Mines* (9–12). 1982, Amereon LB $20.95 (0-89190-703-3). First published in 1885, this is a story of old-fashioned adventure and romance and the search for the source of King Solomon's wealth in Africa.

109 Haldeman, Joe. *Tool of the Trade* (9–12). 1988, Avon paper $3.95 (0-380-70438-2). A thriller about a Russian spy being pursued by both the CIA and the KGB. (Rev: BL 4/15/87)

110 Harrison, Michael. *It's My Life* (6–8). 1998, Holiday House $15.95 (0-8234-1363-2). Martin's mother and her lover conspire to "kidnap" Martin to collect a ransom in this British thriller that is told alternately by Martin and his friend, Hannah. (Rev: BL 3/1/98; SLJ 4/98; VOYA 8/98)

111 Hemingway, Ernest. *The Old Man and the Sea* (9–12). 1977, Macmillan $30.00 (0-684-15363-7). A deceptively simple novel about an old Gulf fisherman and his encounter with a giant marlin.

112 Heneghan, James. *Torn Away* (7–10). 1994, Viking paper $14.99 (0-670-85180-9). A teenager, forced to leave his home in Northern Ireland where he wants to stay and fight with the IRA, must join his uncle's family in Canada. (Rev: BL 2/15/94; SLJ 9/94; VOYA 4/94)

113 Hernon, Peter. *8.4* (10–12). 1999, Putnam $24.95 (0-399-14400-5). A thriller about attempts to prevent a major earthquake in the Midwest by detonating an atomic bomb underground. (Rev: BL 2/15/99; SLJ 8/99)

114 Higgins, Jack. *Cold Harbour* (9–12). 1990, Pocket Books paper $6.50 (0-671-68426-4). A fast-paced thriller set during World War II about a submarine that takes agents to occupied France. (Rev: BL 1/1/90)

115 Higgins, Jack. *The Eagle Has Landed* (9–12). 1990, Pocket Books paper $6.99 (0-671-72773-7). In this thriller, a group of German paratroopers land in England during World War II to kidnap Churchill.

116 Higgins, Jack. *Flight of Eagles* (10–12). 1998, Putnam $24.95 (0-399-14376-9). Identical twins, separated as children, are on opposite sides during

World War II in this action-packed novel filled with intrigue and danger. (Rev: SLJ 11/98)

117 Higgins, Jack. *Solo* (9–12). 1989, Pocket Books paper $6.99 (0-671-67617-2). A tough Welshman sets out to find out the identity of a terrorist who has murdered his child.

118 Higgins, Jack. *Touch the Devil* (10–12). 1983, NAL paper $6.99 (0-451-16677-9). A retired agent must stop a killer whose target is Margaret Thatcher.

119 Hill, David. *Take It Easy* (7–10). 1997, Dutton paper $14.99 (0-525-45763-1). After an argument with his father, Rob Kennedy joins a hiking trip in a remote part of New Zealand that turns into a nightmare survival story. (Rev: BL 9/1/97; BR 1–2/98; SLJ 6/97; VOYA 10/97)

120 Hinton, S. E. *The Outsiders* (7–10). 1967, Viking paper $16.99 (0-670-53257-6). Two rival gangs—the "haves" and "have-nots"—fight it out on the streets of an Oklahoma city. (Rev: BL 11/15/97)

121 Hinton, S. E. *Rumble Fish* (7–10). 1975, Dell paper $5.50 (0-440-97534-4). Rusty-James loses everything he loves most including his brother.

122 Hinton, S. E. *Tex* (7–10). 1979, Dell paper $4.99 (0-440-97850-5). Tex and his 17-year-old older brother encounter problems with family, sex, and drugs.

123 Hinton, S. E. *That Was Then, This Is Now* (7–10). 1971, Viking $15.99 (0-670-69798-2). Bryon discovers that his "brother' Mark is a drug pusher.

124 Hobbs, Will. *The Big Wander* (7–10). 1992, Atheneum $16.00 (0-689-31767-0); 1994, Avon paper $4.99 (0-380-72140-6). Clay Lancaster, 14, and his brother Mike are on a "big waner," their last trip together before Mike goes away to college. (Rev: BL 10/15/92*; SLJ 11/92)

125 Hobbs, Will. *Downriver* (9–12). 1991, Atheneum $17.00 (0-689-31690-9). Jessie, 15, is one of 8 problem teens in an outdoor survival program that almost ends in disaster. (Rev: BL 3/1/91; SLJ 3/91)

126 Hobbs, Will. *Far North* (7–12). 1996, Morrow $15.00 (0-688-14192-7). Fifteen-year old Gabe, his school roommate, and an elderly Native American are stranded in the Canadian wilderness. The boys survive even after the death of the wise old man. (Rev: BL 7/96; BR 9–10/96; SLJ 9/96; VOYA 2/97)

127 Hobbs, Will. *Ghost Canoe* (6–8). 1997, Morrow $15.00 (0-688-14193-5); Avon paper $4.99 (0-380-72537-1). Mystery, plenty of action, murder, Spanish treasure, and a dangerous villain are some of the elements in this historical adventure set on the northwest coast of Washington state. (Rev: BL 5/1/97; SLJ 4/97; VOYA 8/97)

128 Hobbs, Will. *The Maze* (6–12). 1998, Morrow $15.00 (0-688-15092-6). After living in a series of foster homes and detention centers, Rick escapes to Canyonlands National Park in Utah where he is befriended by a loner who helps him find himself. (Rev: BL 9/1/98; SLJ 10/98; VOYA 2/99)

129 Hobbs, Will. *River Thunder* (8–12). 1997, Delacorte $15.95 (0-385-32316-6). In this sequel to *Downriver* (1996), Troy and his troubled teenage friends undertake an adventure-filled rafting trip through the Grand Canyon. (Rev: BL 9/1/97; BR 3–4/98; SLJ 9/97; VOYA 10/97)

130 Holman, Felice. *Slake's Limbo* (7–9). 1974, Macmillan $16.00 (0-684-13926-X); paper $4.50 (0-689-71066-6). A 13-year-old boy escapes to New York City's subways, which he learns to call his home. (Rev: BL 6/1/88)

131 Holt, Victoria. *The Demon Lover* (9–12). 1983, Fawcett paper $3.50 (0-449-20098-1). This gothic novel is set in England of the mid-1800s. Some others by this author are *Lord of the Far Islands* (1986), *The Judas Kiss, Menfreya in the Morning*, and *King of the Castle* (all 1982).

132 Holt, Victoria. *The Road to Paradise Island* (9–12). 1985, Fawcett paper $5.99 (0-449-20888-5). While investigating her ancestral home in England, Annalice finds a map of a Utopia-like island and a diary that reveals a murder. (Rev: BL 8/85)

133 Holt, Victoria. *Shivering Sands* (9–12). 1986, Fawcett paper $5.99 (0-449-21361-7). This is one of the author's exciting gothic romances using historical settings and dealing with damsels in distress and dashing heroes. Others are: *The Devil on Horseback* (1987) and *House of a Thousand Lanterns* (1974).

134 Holt, Victoria. *The Time of the Hunter's Moon* (9–12). 1984, Fawcett paper $0.05 (0-449-20511-8). In 19th-century England a young schoolteacher is caught up in romance, adventure, and mystery.

135 Houston, James. *Frozen Fire: A Tale of Courage* (6–9). Illus. 1977, Macmillan $16.99 (0-689-50083-1). An Eskimo boy, Kayak, and his white friend set out to find Kayak's father, a prospector who has disappeared. A sequel is: *Black Diamond*. (Rev: BL 9/1/89)

136 Hubert, Cam. *Dreamspeaker* (9–12). 1981, Avon paper $3.50 (0-380-56622-2). A boy who escapes from an institution finds friendship in a British Columbia forest.

137 Innes, Hammond. *The Wreck of the Mary Deare* (9–12). 1985, Carroll & Graf paper $3.50 (0-88184-152-8). Gideon Patch boards what appears to be a ghost ship and his adventures begin. Also use: *The Doomed Oasis* (1986).

138 Judson, William. *Cold River* (9–12). 1976, NAL paper $3.50 (0-451-16164-5). A survival story involving a brother and sister lost in the Adirondacks.

139 Kalpakian, Laura. *Caveat* (10–12). 1998, Blair $19.95 (0-89587-223-4). In this novel set in a small, drought-stricken California town in 1916, rainmaker Hank Beecham vows revenge when the city fathers refuse to pay him when his efforts result in life-destroying floods. (Rev: BL 6/1–15/98; SLJ 1/99)

140 Kehret, Peg. *Danger at the Fair* (5–8). 1995, Dutton paper $15.99 (0-525-65182-9). Ellen and Corey are back, this time sharing a thrill-a-minute adventure set at a county fair, where a fortune-teller tells Ellen that her brother Corey is in danger. (Rev: BL 12/1/94; SLJ 2/95)

141 Kehret, Peg. *Night of Fear* (6–10). 1994, Dutton paper $14.99 (0-525-65136-5). This suspense novel for reluctant readers concerns the escape attempts of a boy who is abducted and taken on the road by a man who fits the description of a bank robber. (Rev: BL 2/15/94; SLJ 4/94; VOYA 2/94)

142 Kehret, Peg. *Searching for Candlestick Park* (5–8). 1997, Dutton paper $14.99 (0-525-65256-6). An adventure story about a boy who sets out from Seattle with his cat to find his father in San Francisco. (Rev: BL 8/97; BR 3–4/98; SLJ 9/97)

143 Kerrigan, Philip. *Survival Game* (9–12). 1987, Avon paper $3.95 (0-380-70682-2). A simulated war game turns serious when a gunman begins picking off the participants. (Rev: SLJ 12/87)

144 King, Stephen. *The Girl Who Loved Tom Gordon* (9–12). 1999, Scribners $16.45 (0-684-86762-1). This is a vivid novel about the terrors experienced by a 9-year-girl who is lost in the Maine woods for 9 days when she wanders away from her parents. (Rev: BL 4/1/99; VOYA 8/99)

145 Kinsolving, William. *Mister Christian: The Further Adventures of Fletcher Christian, the Legendary Leader of the Bounty Mutiny* (10–12). 1996, Simon & Schuster $23.00 (0-684-81303-3). In this sequel to *Mutiny on the Bounty*, Fletcher Christian continues his worldwide wandering and reluctantly becomes involved in sea battles between France and England. (Rev: BL 3/15/96; SLJ 11/96)

146 Klaveness, Jan O'Donnell. *Ghost Island* (7–10). 1987, Dell paper $2.95 (0-440-93097-9). Delia, her mother, and new stepfather encounter both family trauma and a murder involving poachers when they vacation on a remote Canadian lake. (Rev: BL 5/15/85; BR 11–12/85; SLJ 9/85; VOYA 2/86)

147 Konigsburg, E. L. *From the Mixed-Up Files of Mrs. Basil E. Frankweiler* (6–8). 1967, Macmillan $16.00 (0-689-20586-4); Dell paper $5.50 (0-440-93180-0). Two resourceful kids live for a week in the Metropolitan Museum of Art. Newbery Medal, 1968.

148 Koontz, Dean. *Seize the Night* (9–12). 1998, Bantam $26.95 (0-553-10665-1). While investigating the kidnapping of a young boy, Chris Snow uncovers a plot to alter time and space in this enthralling adventure novel. (Rev: BL 12/1/98; VOYA 4/99)

149 Koontz, Dean. *Sole Survivor* (10–12). 1997, Knopf $25.95 (0-679-42526-8). When Joe Carpenter discovers that the airplane crash in which his wife and 2 daughters were killed was not an accident, he sets out on a dangerous mission to find the truth. (Rev: BL 1/1–15/97; SLJ 7/97)

150 Lamensdorf, Len. *The Crouching Dragon* (6–9). 1999, Seascape $19.95 (0-9669741-5-8). In this novel set in a French coastal town in 1959, 14-year-old William and his friends secretly renovate a crumbling castle called the Crouching Dragon. (Rev: BL 9/1/99; VOYA 12/99)

151 L'Amour, Louis. *Bendigo Shafter* (9–12). 1983, Bantam paper $5.50 (0-553-26446-X). An old-fashioned western by a master of the genre. There are approximately 100 other westerns by this author available in paperback.

152 Lee, Stan, ed. *The Ultimate Spider-Man* (10–12). 1996, Berkley paper $5.99 (1-57297-103-7). Twelve short stories by different authors continue the adventures of the Amazing Spider-Man, the crime fighting comic book hero. (Rev: SLJ 5/96)

153 Leib, Franklin Allen. *The House of Pain* (10–12). 1999, Forge $23.95 (0-312-86616-X). In this legal thriller, a Vietnam veteran suffering from post-traumatic stress disorder rescues his goddaughter, 15-year-old Sally Collins, from kidnappers, and is then put on trial for his vigilante killings. (Rev: SLJ 5/99)

154 L'Engle, Madeleine. *The Arm of the Starfish* (7–10). 1965, Farrar $18.00 (0-374-30396-7); Dell paper $4.99 (0-440-90183-9). A young scientist becomes involved in intrigue and the disappearance of Polly O'Keefe in this tale of danger.

155 L'Engle, Madeleine. *The Young Unicorns* (7–10). 1968, Farrar $16.00 (0-374-38778-8); Dell paper $4.99 (0-440-99919-7). In this novel set in New York City and involving the Austin family, a young gang threatens the lives of an ex-member and a blind musician.

156 Leonard, Elmore. *Cuba Libre: A Novel* (10–12). 1998, Delacorte $23.95 (0-385-32383-2); Dell paper $7.50 (0-440-22559-0). An action-filled historical novel that includes a bank robbery, cattle rustling, suspense, and romance between an attractive hero and heroine, set at the time of the Spanish-American War and Cuba's fight for independence. (Rev: BL 11/15/97; SLJ 8/98)

157 Leonard, Elmore. *Out of Sight* (10–12). 1996, Delacorte $22.95 (0-385-30848-5). Deputy U. S. Marshal Karen Sisco is pitted against 2 convicts, one of whom is attracted to her. (Rev: SLJ 3/97)

158 Levin, Ira. *The Boys from Brazil* (9–12). 1976, Random House $8.95 (0-394-40267-7). The story of a group of ex-Nazis and their diabolical plan to create a Fourth Reich.

159 London, Jack. *Best Short Stories of Jack London* (9–12). 1953, Amereon LB $15.50 (0-89190-656-8). These stories of action and adventure represent locales ranging from the South Seas to the Far North.

160 Lopez, Barry. *Winter Count* (9–12). 1982, Avon paper $4.95 (0-380-58107-8). This group of stories deals with survival in the wilds and man's battle with nature.

161 Lourie, Peter. *The Lost Treasure of Captain Kidd* (5–8). Illus. 1996, Shawangunk Pr. paper $10.95 (1-885482-03-5). Friends Killiam and Alex set out to discover Captain Kidd's treasure buried on the banks of the Hudson River centuries ago. (Rev: BL 2/15/96; SLJ 6/96)

162 Ludlum, Robert. *The Bourne Identity* (9–12). 1984, Bantam paper $7.99 (0-553-26011-1). A man wakens to find that in spite of having no memory, he is the target of a killer's plot. Followed by *The Bourne Supremacy*.

163 MacInnes, Helen. *Above Suspicion* (9–12). 1954, Harcourt $24.95 (0-15-102707-2). This is one of the many novels of intrigue and suspense by this writer. Some others are: *The Salzburg Connection*, *Snare of the Hunter*, *Decision at Delphi* (1984), *Agent in Place*, and *Assignment in Brittany*.

164 Macken, Walter. *Island of the Great Yellow Ox* (5–8). 1991, Simon & Schuster paper $14.00 (0-671-73800-3). An Irish boy and 2 American friends are shipwrecked on an uninhabited island, where they are held captive by ruthless archeologists and must solve a mystery to survive. (Rev: BL 10/15/91; SLJ 10/91)

165 MacLean, Alistair. *Circus* (9–12). 1984, Amereon $24.95 (0-89190-672-X). In this spy thriller, an aerialist is sent on a secret mission by the CIA into Eastern Europe. Other recommended adventures by MacLean include *Secret Ways* and *South by Java Head*.

166 MacLean, Alistair. *H.M.S. Ulysses* (9–12). 1985, Fawcett paper $5.95 (0-449-12929-2). This is an exciting story of a British light cruiser's treacherous voyage to Murmansk during World War II. Other adventure stories by MacLean include *Athabasca* (1986) and *Way to Dusty Death* (1985).

167 MacLean, Norman. *A River Runs Through It and Other Stories* (10–12). 1979, Univ. of Chicago Pr. $20.00 (0-226-50055-1); paper $11.00 (0-226-50057-8). These stories convey the grandeur of our western mountain wilderness and the ways in which man has adjusted to this environment. (Rev: BL 3/87)

168 Marsden, John. *Darkness, Be My Friend* (9–12). 1999, Houghton $15.00 (0-395-92274-7). In this sequel to *A Killing Frost*, Ellie, Fi, and their other teenage combatants continue their struggle against the forces that have invaded Australia. (Rev: BL 6/1–15/99; SLJ 7/99; VOYA 10/99)

169 Marsden, John. *The Dead of Night* (6–10). 1997, Houghton $16.00 (0-395-83734-0). In this sequel to *Tomorrow, When the War Began* (1996), the teenage group continues its guerrilla activities against their enemy, a country that has invaded their homeland, Australia. (Rev: SLJ 11/97; VOYA 2/98)

170 Marsden, John. *A Killing Frost* (7–12). 1998, Houghton $15.00 (0-395-83735-9). In this third episode of an adventure series about a group of Australian teens who fight an enemy that has occupied their country, 5 young people carry out a plan to sink a container ship. (Rev: BL 5/15/98; SLJ 6/98; VOYA 6/98)

171 Martin, Les. *X Marks the Spot* (6–9). 1995, HarperCollins paper $4.50 (0-06-440613-X). Based on an episode of the *X-Files*, 2 FBI agents investigate a series of mysterious deaths in Oregon. Also use *Darkness Falls* (1995). (Rev: VOYA 2/96)

172 Martini, Steve. *Critical Mass* (10–12). 1998, Putnam $25.99 (0-399-143629). Jocelyn Cole, an attorney living on a remote island in Puget Sound, is taken prisoner by an arms smuggling militia group that her client is involved with and which is assembling a nuclear device to destroy Washington, D.C. (Rev: SLJ 2/99)

173 Mazer, Harry. *The Island Keeper* (7–10). 1981, Dell paper $3.99 (0-440-94774-X). Feeling completely alone in this world, Cleo decides to run away to a desolate island that her father owns.

174 Mazer, Harry. *Snow Bound* (7–10). 1975, Dell paper $4.50 (0-440-96134-3). A boy and girl survive for several days after being trapped in a snow storm. (Rev: BL 9/1/89)

175 Mazer, Harry, and Norma Fox Mazer. *The Solid Gold Kid* (7–10). 1989, Bantam paper $4.50 (0-553-27851-7). A millionaire's son and 4 other teenagers are kidnapped.

176 Meltzer, Brad. *The Tenth Justice* (10–12). 1997, Morrow $23.00 (0-688-15089-6). Ben, a clerk for a Supreme Court justice, is being blackmailed and he thinks one of his friends is supplying information to the blackmailer in this thriller that also supplies lots of information about the Supreme Court. (Rev: BL 2/1/97; SLJ 11/97)

177 Mendelsohn, Jane. *I Was Amelia Earhart* (9–12). 1996, Knopf $18.00 (0-679-45054-8). A fictionalized account of what might have happened had Amelia Earhart's plane landed on an island rather than crashing into the ocean. (Rev: BL 4/15/96; SLJ 10/96)

178 Miklowitz, Gloria D. *After the Bomb* (7–12). 1987, Scholastic paper $2.50 (0-590-40568-3). This novel describes the experiences of a group of young people after an atomic bomb falls on Los Angeles. (Rev: BL 6/15/86; SLJ 9/85; VOYA 8/85)

179 Miklowitz, Gloria D. *Camouflage* (8–10). 1998, Harcourt $16.00 (0-15-201467-5). When 14-year-old Kyle visits northern Michigan to spend a summer with his father, he becomes involved in a government-hating militia movement in which his father is a general. (Rev: SLJ 4/98; VOYA 10/98)

180 Miller, Frances A. *The Truth Trap* (7–10). 1986, Fawcett paper $4.50 (0-449-70247-2). When Matt's parents are killed in a car accident, he leaves town only to be accused of a murder.

181 Morey, Walt. *Angry Waters* (6–9). 1990, Blue Heron $7.95 (0-936085-10-X). A hostile 15-year-old boy is unwillingly paroled to a family farm, where he comes to terms with himself. (Rev: VOYA 8/90)

182 Morey, Walt. *Death Walk* (6–10). 1991, Blue Heron $13.95 (0-936085-18-5). After being stranded in the Alaskan wilderness, a teenage boy must learn to survive in the harsh climate while on the run from killers. (Rev: BL 6/1/91; SLJ 6/91)

183 Morpurgo, Michael. *The Butterfly Lion* (4–8). 1997, Viking $14.99 (0-670-87461-2). A ghost narrates a touching adventure story about a boy in Africa and his lion pet, who are separated and reunited years later during World War I in France. (Rev: BL 6/1–15/97; SLJ 8/97)

184 Morrison, Dorothy Nafus. *Whisper Again* (6–8). 1987, Troll paper $2.95 (0-8167-1307-3). Stacey is unhappy when her family has to rent part of their ranch land to a summer camp. This is a sequel to *Whisper Goodbye* (1985). (Rev: BL 9/15/87; SLJ 12/87; VOYA 10/87)

185 Mowat, Farley. *Lost in the Barrens* (7–9). 1985, Bantam paper $5.50 (0-553-27525-9). Two boys lost in the wilderness of Northern Canada must fight for survival.

186 Murphy, Jim. *Death Run* (7–10). 1982, Clarion $12.95 (0-89919-065-0). Four teenage boys try to escape from the police after they accidentally cause the death of a fellow student.

187 Myers, Walter Dean. *The Mouse Trap* (6–8). 1990, HarperCollins LB $14.89 (0-06-024344-9). A group of boys in Harlem form a gang to explore a deserted building they believe contains hidden loot. (Rev: BL 4/15/90; SLJ 7/90; VOYA 6/90)

188 Nordhoff, Charles, and James N. Hall. *The Bounty Trilogy* (9–12). Illus. 1982, Little, Brown paper $21.95 (0-316-61166-2). An adventure story based on fact concerning a mutiny aboard the Bounty and its aftermath. The three individual books are *Mutiny on the Bounty, Men against the Sea,* and *Pitcairn's Island.* These books were originally published in 1932, 1934, and 1934, respectively.

189 O'Dell, Scott. *The Black Pearl* (7–9). 1967, Houghton $17.00 (0-395-06961-0). Young Ramon dives into a forbidden cave to collect a fabulous black pearl that in time seems to bring a curse to his family.

190 O'Dell, Scott. *Black Star, Bright Dawn* (5–9). 1988, Houghton $15.95 (0-395-47778-6). An Eskimo girl faces alone the challenge of running the famous Alaskan dog race, the Iditarod. (Rev: BL 4/1/88; BR 9–10/88; SLJ 5/88; VOYA 6/88)

191 O'Dell, Scott. *Island of the Blue Dolphins* (6–9). 1960, Houghton $16.00 (0-395-06962-9); Dell paper $5.99 (0-440-43988-4). Karana must fend for herself when she is left on a remote California island. Newbery Medal, 1961. Continued in *Zia* (1976). (Rev: BL 3/1/88)

192 Patneaude, David. *The Last Man's Reward* (5–8). 1996, Albert Whitman LB $14.95 (0-8075-4370-5). In this adventure, a group of boys agree to a pact rewarding the last to leave the neighborhood. (Rev: BL 6/1–15/96; SLJ 7/96)

193 Paulsen, Gary. *Brian's Winter* (5–9). 1996, Delacorte $15.95 (0-385-32198-8). In a reworking of the ending of *Hatchet,* in which Brian Robeson is rescued after surviving a plane crash, this novel tells what would have happened had Brian had to survive a harsh winter in the wilderness. (Rev: BL 12/15/95; BR 5–6/96; SLJ 2/96; VOYA 2/97)

194 Paulsen, Gary. *Canyons* (7–10). 1991, Dell paper $4.99 (0-440-21023-2). Blennan becomes obsessed with the story of a young Indian boy murdered by white men 100 years before. (Rev: SLJ 9/90)

195 Paulsen, Gary. *Dogsong* (8–10). 1985, Bradbury LB $16.00 (0-02-770180-8). An Eskimo youth faces hardship and danger when he ventures alone by dogsled into the wilderness. (Rev: BL 4/1/85; SLJ 4/85; VOYA 12/85)

196 Paulsen, Gary. *Hatchet* (6–9). 1987, Macmillan $16.95 (0-02-770130-1). Teenage Brian survives a plane crash in the Canadian wilderness but then must fend for himself. (Rev: BL 11/15/87; SLJ 12/87; VOYA 2/88)

197 Paulsen, Gary. *The Haymeadow* (6–9). Illus. 1992, 1994, Dell paper $4.99 (0-440-40923-3). A 14-year-old boy takes sheep out to pasture for the summer in this story about a boy who is trying to gain acceptance by his father. (Rev: BL 5/15/92*; SLJ 6/92)

198 Paulsen, Gary. *The River* (5–10). 1991, Delacorte $14.95 (0-385-30388-2). In this sequel to *Hatchet*, Paulsen takes the wilderness adventure beyond self-preservation and makes teen Brian responsible for saving someone else. (Rev: BL 5/15/91)

199 Paulsen, Gary. *The Voyage of the Frog* (6–8). 1989, Orchard $16.95 (0-531-05805-0); Dell paper $4.99 (0-440-40364-2). Alone on a 22-foot sailboat, a 14-year-old boy survives a 9-day sea ordeal. (Rev: BL 3/1/89; BR 9–10/89; SLJ 1/89; VOYA 2/89)

200 Peck, Richard. *Secrets of the Shopping Mall* (7–10). 1979, Dell paper $3.99 (0-440-98099-2). Two eighth graders find they are not alone when they take up residence in a shopping mall.

201 Peck, Robert Newton. *Arly's Run* (6–9). 1991, Walker $25.95 (0-8027-8120-9). Orphaned Arly escapes from an early 19th-century Florida work farm and journeys to Moore Haven, where shelter has been arranged for him. (Rev: BL 12/15/91; SLJ 2/92)

202 Peck, Robert Newton. *The Cowboy Ghost* (5–9). 1999, HarperCollins LB $15.89 (0-06-028211-8). In order to prove his maturity to his overly critical father, 16-year-old Titus decides to help his brother on a grueling cattle drive across Florida. (Rev: BL 6/1–15/99; SLJ 3/99)

203 Peck, Robert Newton. *Nine Man Tree* (5–8). 1998, Random LB $18.99 (0-679-99257-X). Two children of a kind mother and an abusive father become involved in a hunt for a wild 500-pound boarhog in this novel set in the Florida wetlands. (Rev: BL 8/98; SLJ 11/98)

204 Philbrick, Rodman. *Max the Mighty* (6–9). 1998, Scholastic $16.95 (0-590-18892-5); paper $3.99 (0-590-57964-9). Maxwell Kane and his new friend Worm, who is being abused by her stepfather, run away in a cross-country search for Worm's real father. (Rev: BL 6/1–15/98; BR 9–10/98; SLJ 4/98; VOYA 6/98)

205 Phleger, Marjorie. *Pilot Down, Presumed Dead* (7–9). 1988, HarperCollins paper $5.95 (0-06-440067-0). A survival story involving a pilot whose plane crashes off the Baja California coast. A reissue.

206 Preston, Douglas, and Lincoln Child. *Riptide* (10–12). 1998, Warner $25.00 (0-446-52364-4). A classic struggle between good and evil emerges in this adventure yarn after a group of treasure seekers tries to recover buried booty worth billions of dollars. (Rev: BL 5/15/98; SLJ 12/98; VOYA 12/98)

207 Pullman, Philip. *The Tiger in the Well* (8–12). 1996, Demco $10.09 (0-606-09969-7). This conclusion of the rich historical trilogy that began with *The Ruby in the Smoke* (1987) and *The Shadow in the North* (1988) completes the adventures of Victorian heroine Sally Lockhart who, in this novel, encounters a man who wants passionately to destroy her. (Rev: BL 10/15/90)

208 Puzo, Mario. *The Godfather* (10–12). 1969, Putnam $24.95 (0-399-10342-2); NAL paper $5.95 (0-451-15736-2). The story of a fictional crime family in New York led by Vito Corleone and then by his son Michael.

209 Repp, Gloria. *Mik-Shrok* (4–8). 1998, Bob Jones Univ. Pr. paper $6.49 (1-57924-069-0). A married missionary couple journey to a remote Alaska village in 1950 where they begin their work and, in time, acquire a dog team lead by Mik-Shrok. (Rev: BL 3/1/99)

210 Roberts, Willo Davis. *Megan's Island* (6–8). 1988, Macmillan LB $14.95 (0-689-31397-7). Two children are the victims of a custody battle that involves an attempted kidnapping. (Rev: BL 5/1/88; BR 9–10/88; SLJ 4/88; VOYA 6/88)

211 Roberts, Willo Davis. *What Could Go Wrong?* (6–9). 1989, Macmillan $15.00 (0-689-31438-8). A seemingly innocent plane trip from Seattle to San Francisco leads 3 cousins into danger and a confrontation with a gang of money launderers. (Rev: BL 4/15/89; SLJ 3/89; VOYA 8/89)

212 Rochman, Hazel, and Darlene Z. McCampbell, eds. *Leaving Home* (7–12). 1997, HarperCollins LB $16.89 (0-06-024874-2). These 16 stories by well known writers describe various forms of leaving home, from immigration to a new country to running away or taking a trip. (Rev: BL 1/1–15/97; SLJ 3/97*)

213 Ross, Rhea Beth. *The Bet's On, Lizzie Bingman!* (6–9). 1992, Houghton paper $4.95 (0-395-64375-9). A 14-year-old girl vows to remain completely independent for one summer. (Rev: BL 6/1/88; BR 9–10/88; SLJ 4/88)

214 Ruckman, Ivy. *Night of the Twisters* (6–8). 1984, HarperCollins paper $4.95 (0-06-440176-6). An account based on fact about children who survive a devastating series of tornadoes.

215 Salisbury, Graham. *Shark Bait* (7–12). 1997, Delacorte $15.95 (0-385-32237-2). Set in Hawaii, this novel deals with Eric Chock and his friends, one of whom is determined to kill a sailor like the one his mother ran away with. (Rev: BL 9/1/97; SLJ 9/97; VOYA 6/98)

216 Shusterman, Neal. *Dissidents* (7–10). 1989, Little, Brown $13.95 (0-316-78904-6). A teenage boy joins his mother, the American ambassador in Moscow, and becomes involved in a spy caper. (Rev: BL 8/89; BR 11–12/89; SLJ 10/89)

217 Skurzynski, Gloria, and Alane Ferguson. *Cliff-Hanger* (6–9). (National Parks Mystery) 1999, National Geographic $15.95 (0-7922-7036-3). A solid adventure story about Jack Landon, age 12, his younger sister, Ashley, and a foster child, Lucky, who find themselves in a life-threatening situation involving a cougar when they visit Mesa Verde National Park with Jack's parents. (Rev: BL 4/15/99; SLJ 5/99)

218 Smith, Cotton. *Dark Trail to Dodge* (7–10). 1997, Walker $29.95 (0-8027-4158-4). Eighteen-year-old Tyrel Bannon faces unusual problems on his first cattle drive when rustlers attack and plan on taking no prisoners. (Rev: BL 6/1–15/97; VOYA 8/97)

219 Smith, Roland. *Jaguar* (5–8). 1997, Hyperion LB $16.49 (0-7868-2226-0); Disney paper $5.95 (0-7868-1312-1). While visiting his zoologist father in Brazil's jungle, Jake becomes involved in battling the environment as well as some vicious fortune hunters. A sequel to *Thunder Cave*. (Rev: BL 5/15/97; BR 1–2/98; SLJ 6/97)

220 Smith, Roland. *Sasquatch* (5–8). Illus. 1998, Hyperion LB $16.49 (0-7868-2315-1). When Dylan and his father join an expedition to track down a Sasquatch specimen, the youngster discovers a plot to kill both of them. (Rev: SLJ 6/98; VOYA 10/98)

221 Smith, Wilbur. *A Time to Die* (10–12). 1990, Random $19.95 (0-394-58475-9). An adventure novel set in Africa about a big game hunter and an expedition into territory where 2 rival tribes are fighting. (Rev: SLJ 7/90)

222 Steele, Mary Q. *Journey Outside* (6–8). 1984, Peter Smith $18.25 (0-8446-6169-4); Puffin paper $4.99 (0-14-030588-2). Dilar and his family are following an underground river looking for a better place to live.

223 Stewart, A. C. *Ossian House* (6–8). 1976, Phillips LB $25.95 (0-87599-219-6). An 11-year-old boy inherits a mansion in Scotland and sets out alone to live there for the summer.

224 Strasser, Todd. *Kidnap Kids* (5–8). 1998, Putnam $15.99 (0-399-23111-0). Steven and younger brother, Benjy, find unexpected excitement when they and their parents are pursued by villains during a camping trip. (Rev: BL 1/1–15/98; SLJ 3/98)

225 Strasser, Todd. *Shark Bite* (5–8). (Against the Odds) 1998, Scholastic paper $3.99 (0-671-02309-8). After a freak storm in the Gulf of Mexico, 12-year-old Ian and friends must abandon their sinking sailboat. (Rev: BL 2/15/99; SLJ 12/98)

226 Strickland, Brad. *The Hand of the Necromancer* (5–8). 1996, Dial paper $14.89 (0-8037-1830-6). In a continuation of the series begun by John Bellairs, Johnny Dixon and Professor Childermass combat a wicked magician, Mattheus Mergel. (Rev: SLJ 9/96)

227 Strieber, Whitley. *Wolf of Shadows* (6–8). 1985, Knopf LB $9.99 (0-394-97224-4). A pack of wolves and a mother and daughter develop a relationship of trust after a nuclear war. (Rev: BL 1/1/86; SLJ 10/85; VOYA 4/86)

228 Sullivan, Paul. *The Unforgiving Land* (7–10). 1996, Royal Fireworks paper $7.00 (0-88092-256-7). In this story of the Inuit people and a white trader who gives them guns and bullets, the delicate harmony between nature and humankind is broken and their way of life dies. (Rev: VOYA 8/96)

229 Svee, Gary. *Incident at Pishkin Creek* (9–12). 1989, Walker $28.95 (0-8027-4095-2). Max Bass exaggerated in the advertisement for a bride as poor Catherine O'Dowd discovers when she arrives in Montana. (Rev: BL 7/89)

230 Swarthout, Glendon, and Kathryn Swarthout. *Whichaway* (7–10). 1997, Rising Moon/Northland LB $12.95 (0-87358-675-1); paper $6.95 (0-87358-676-X). A reissue of an exciting story about a boy whose character is tested when he is trapped on top of a windmill with 2 broken legs in an isolated area of Texas. (Rev: BR 11–12/98; VOYA 2/98)

231 Sweeney, Joyce. *Free Fall* (9–12). 1996, Delacorte $15.95 (0-385-32211-9). Trapped in a cave in Ocala National Park, 4 boys plot their escape and in the process learn about themselves, their families, and personal tragedies. (Rev: BL 7/96; BR 9–10/96; SLJ 11/96; VOYA 6/96)

232 Taylor, Theodore. *The Cay* (6–9). 1969, Doubleday $15.95 (0-385-07906-0). A blinded boy and an old black sailor are shipwrecked on a coral island. (Rev: BL 9/1/89)

233 Taylor, Theodore. *Rogue Wave and Other Red-Blooded Sea Stories* (6–10). 1996, Harcourt $16.00 (0-15-201408-X). Eight sea stories that involve such subjects as sharks, a cruel captain, and a captured U-boat commander. (Rev: BL 11/1/96; BR 3–4/97; SLJ 4/97; VOYA 4/97)

234 Taylor, Theodore. *The Weirdo* (9–12). 1991, Harcourt $15.95 (0-15-294952-6). After his friend mysteriously disappears, Chip assumes leadership of the fight to protect bears living in the local swamp. (Rev: BL 12/15/91; SLJ 1/92)

235 Thomas, Rob. *Green Thumb* (6–8). 1999, Simon & Schuster paper $16.00 (0-689-81780-0). While trying to unmask an unscrupulous scientist in the Amazon rain forest, 13-year-old science genius Grady Jacobs becomes a target for murder. (Rev: BL 4/15/99; SLJ 6/99; VOYA 8/99)

236 Thompson, Julian. *A Band of Angels* (9–12). 1986, Scholastic $12.95 (0-590-33780-7). Jordan, his suitcase of money, and 2 friends hit the road to escape government agents who are searching for them. (Rev: BL 3/87; SLJ 8/86; VOYA 6/86)

237 Thompson, Julian. *Brothers* (7–12). 1998, Random LB $18.99 (0-679-99082-8). Chris trails his unstable brother to an eastern Montana militia camp, where there is a standoff between the zealots and local authorities. (Rev: BL 11/1/98; BR 5–6/99; SLJ 11/98; VOYA 10/98)

238 Thompson, Julian. *The Grounding of Group Six* (8–12). 1983, Avon paper $3.99 (0-380-83386-7). Five 16-year-olds think they are being sent to an exclusive school but actually they have been slated for murder.

239 Thompson, Julian. *The Taking of Mariasburg* (9–12). 1988, Scholastic paper $12.95 (0-590-41247-7). Maria buys a ghost town with her inheritance and populates it with teenagers. (Rev: BL 4/1/88; BR 9–10/88; SLJ 5/88; VOYA 4/88)

240 Townsend, John Rowe. *The Islanders* (7–10). 1981, HarperCollins $11.95 (0-397-31940-1). Two strangers washed up on a remote island are regarded as enemies by the inhabitants.

241 Townsend, John Rowe. *Kate and the Revolution* (7–10). 1983, HarperCollins LB $12.89 (0-397-32016-7). A 17-year-old girl is attracted to a visiting prince and then the adventure begins.

242 Ullman, James R. *Banner in the Sky* (7–9). 1988, HarperCollins LB $12.89 (0-397-30264-9); paper $5.95 (0-06-447048-2). The thrilling story of a boy's determination to conquer a challenging Swiss mountain. (Rev: SLJ 2/88)

243 Uris, Leon. *Exodus* (9–12). Illus. 1958, Bantam paper $7.99 (0-553-25847-8). An adventure novel set in the days of the establishment of Israel. Also use *The Haj* (1984).

244 Vanasse, Deb. *Out of the Wilderness* (5–8). 1999, Clarion $15.00 (0-395-91421-3). Fifteen-year-old Josh, his father, and his older half-brother move to Willow Creek, Alaska, where they build a cabin and try to live off the land. (Rev: BL 3/15/99; SLJ 4/99; VOYA 8/99)

245 Voigt, Cynthia. *On Fortune's Wheel* (7–12). 1990, Macmillan $17.00 (0-689-31636-4). In this historical adventure, a young runaway couple are captured by pirates and sold into slavery. (Rev: BL 2/15/90; SLJ 3/90; VOYA 4/90)

246 Waddell, Martin. *The Kidnapping of Suzie Q* (7–10). 1996, Candlewick $15.99 (1-56402-530-6). A tense adventure story involving the plight of Suzi Quinn, who witnesses a robbery and is kidnapped by the robbers, who are fearful she can identify them. (Rev: BL 5/1/96; BR 11–12/96; SLJ 4/96)

247 Wallace, Irving. *The Seventh Secret* (9–12). 1986, NAL paper $4.95 (0-451-14557-7). Emily Ashcroft is convinced that Hitler is still alive and sets out to find him. (Rev: BL 10/15/85)

248 Whittaker, Dorothy Raymond. *Angels of the Swamp* (6–8). 1991, Walker $27.95 (0-8027-8129-2). Two teenage orphans survive on an island off the Florida coast, then discover they're not alone. (Rev: BL 1/15/92; SLJ 4/92)

249 Williams, Barbara. *Titanic Crossing* (5–8). 1995, Dial paper $15.89 (0-8037-1791-1). A 13-year-old boy is aboard the *Titanic* with his mother and sister when it sinks. (Rev: BL 5/15/95; SLJ 6/95)

250 Williams, Michael. *The Genuine Half-Moon Kid* (7–10). 1994, Dutton $15.99 (0-525-67479-5). Like questing Jason in Greek mythology, 18-year-old South African Jay Watson sets out with some friends to find a yellow wood box left him by his grandfather. (Rev: BL 6/1–15/94)

251 Wynne-Jones, Tim. *The Maestro* (6–8). 1996, Orchard LB $17.99 (0-531-08894-4). As well as a survival story, this moving novel tells of a boy's maturation in the wilderness of northern Ontario and of a gifted musician who befriends him. (Rev: BL 12/15/96*; SLJ 1/97; VOYA 4/97)

252 Yep, Laurence. *The Case of the Goblin Pearls* (4–8). 1997, HarperCollins LB $14.89 (0-06-024446-1). Lily and her Aunt Tiger Lil solve the mystery of the stolen pearls. (Rev: BR 9–10/97; SLJ 3/97)

253 Yolen, Jane, and Bruce Coville. *Armageddon Summer* (7–12). 1998, Harcourt $17.00 (0-15-201767-4). When truckloads of artillery suddenly appear, events turn deadly for teenagers Marina and Jed, who are at a meeting of a millennial cult known as the Believers on a mountain in Massachusetts. (Rev: BL 8/98; SLJ 10/98; VOYA 10/98)

254 Zindel, Paul. *Raptor* (5–9). 1998, Hyperion LB $15.49 (0-7868-2374-7); paper $4.99 (0-7868-1224-9). While on a paleontology dig, two friends discover a mysterious egg that hatches into a raptor, and mayhem follows when its mother attempts to save her baby—and herself—from the mercenary director of the dig. (Rev: BL 9/1/98; SLJ 10/98; VOYA 8/99)

255 Zindel, Paul. *Reef of Death* (7–12). 1998, HarperCollins $15.95 (0-06-024728-2). A tale of terror about two teens, a monster creature that lives on an Australian reef, and a mad geologist who has a torture chamber on her freighter. (Rev: BL 3/1/98; SLJ 3/98; VOYA 4/98)

Animal Stories

256 Adler, C. S. *That Horse Whiskey!* (6–8). 1996, Avon paper $3.99 (0-380-72601-7). Lainey, 13, disappointed that she didn't get a horse for her birthday, works at a stable training a stubborn horse and falls for a city boy. (Rev: BL 11/1/94; SLJ 11/94; VOYA 12/94)

257 Alter, Judith. *Callie Shaw, Stable Boy* (5–8). 1996, Eakin $15.95 (1-57168-092-6). During the Great Depression, Callie, disguised as a boy, works in a stable and uncovers a race-fixing racket. (Rev: BL 2/1/97; SLJ 8/97)

258 Bagnold, Enid. *National Velvet* (7–10). 1991, Avon paper $4.99 (0-380-71235-0). The now-classic story of Heather Brown and her struggle to ride in the Grand National. A reissue.

259 Bauer, Marion Dane. *Face to Face* (5–9). 1993, Dell paper $3.99 (0-440-40791-5). This novel of a troubled father-son relationship describes their reunion on a failed whitewater rafting trip and the painful aftermath when they separate again. (Rev: BL 9/15/91; SLJ 10/91)

260 Benchley, Peter. *The Beast* (9–12). 1992, Fawcett paper $5.99 (0-449-22089-3). *Jaws* (1973) revisited, this time with a giant squid as villain. (Rev: BL 5/15/91; SLJ 11/91)

261 Benchley, Peter. *White Shark* (9–12). 1995, St. Martin's paper $6.50 (0-312-95573-1). An evil Nazi scientist creates a water-breathing superkiller that is sunk in a U-boat at the end of World War II and gets loose 50 years later. (Rev: BL 1/15/94; SLJ 11/94)

262 Branford, Henrietta. *White Wolf* (7–12). 1999, Candlewick $16.99 (0-7636-0748-7). Kept as a pet, Snowy, a wolf cub, escapes, searches for a pack, and eventually has a family of its own in this tale set in the Pacific Northwest. (Rev: BL 8/99; SLJ 6/99; VOYA 10/99)

263 Bryant, Bonnie. *The Long Ride* (6–9). (Pine Hollow) 1998, Bantam paper $4.50 (0-553-49242-X). A terrible accident revives the friendship of 3 horse-loving girls who have grown apart as they developed new interests in high school. (Rev: BL 11/15/98; SLJ 2/99)

264 Campbell, Eric. *Papa Tembo* (7–12). 1998, Harcourt $16.00 (0-15-201727-5). This story set in Tanzania creates a fatal encounter between Papa Tembo, the father of elephants, and his arch enemy, Laurens Van Der Wel, the evil poacher. (Rev: BL 8/98; SLJ 10/98; VOYA 10/98)

265 Caras, Roger A. *Roger Caras' Treasury of Great Cat Stories* (9–12). 1990, Galahad Books $10.98 (0-88365-763-5). A fine collection of short stories from internationally known writers, all about the mysterious creature, the cat. (Rev: BL 4/1/87)

266 Caras, Roger A. *Roger Caras' Treasury of Great Dog Stories* (9–12). 1987, Dutton paper $12.50 (0-525-48428-0). An anthology of dog stories written by great authors. (Rev: BL 4/1/87)

267 Cavanna, Betty. *Going on Sixteen* (6–9). 1998, Morrow paper $5.95 (0-688-16324-6). This story of a shy girl's love for her dog has become a young adult classic. (Rev: BL 12/15/85; BR 1–2/86)

268 Cleary, Beverly. *Strider* (5–9). Illus. 1991, Morrow LB $13.88 (0-688-09901-7). In this sequel to *Dear Mr. Henshaw,* the hero is now 4 years older, beginning high school and still writing in his diary, with his beloved dog, Strider, by his side. (Rev: BL 7/91*; SLJ 9/91)

269 Corcoran, Barbara. *Wolf at the Door* (6–8). 1993, Atheneum $16.00 (0-689-31870-7). Lee, age 13, feels inferior to her beautiful sister until Lee rescues a young wolf and opposition from neighbors unites them. (Rev: BL 10/1/93; VOYA 12/93)

270 Crompton, Anne E. *The Snow Pony* (5–9). 1994, Simon & Schuster paper $3.99 (0-671-78507-9). New in town, a lonely eighth-grade girl is offered a job by her shy, misunderstood neighbor taming and grooming a pony for his grandson. (Rev: BL 9/15/91)

271 Cross, Gillian. *Wolf* (6–12). 1991, Holiday House $13.95 (0-8234-0870-1). Cassy, 13, learns all about wolves, in both animal and human form, while growing up in London. (Rev: BL 1/15/91; SLJ 4/91)

272 Curwood, James Oliver. *The Bear—A Novel* (8–12). 1989, Newmarket Pr. paper $6.95 (1-55704-053-2). A reissue of the 1916 novel about a grizzly and an orphaned black bear cub in the wilds of British Columbia. (Rev: VOYA 4/90)

273 Evans, Nicholas. *The Horse Whisperer* (9–12). 1995, Delacorte $24.95 (0-385-31523-6). After a teenager loses her leg in a riding accident, her mother moves them to Montana, where the "horse whisperer," a man of mystical powers, tries to rebuild their lives. (Rev: BL 8/95*)

274 Farley, Walter. *The Black Stallion* (5–8). 1977, Random LB $11.99 (0-394-90601-2). First published in 1941, this is the first of a lengthy series of horse stories by this author.

275 Farley, Walter, and Steven Farley. *The Young Black Stallion* (5–9). 1989, Random $10.95 (0-394-84562-5); paper $2.99 (0-517-11121-7). In this sequel to *The Black Stallion,* the reader learns about the early life of Shêtân. (Rev: BR 5–6/90; SLJ 12/89)

276 Gallico, Paul. *The Snow Goose* (7–12). Illus. 1941, Knopf $15.00 (0-394-44593-7); Tundra paper $9.99 (0-7710-3250-1). A hunchbacked artist and a young child nurse a wounded snow goose back to health, and it later returns to protect them in this large, illustrated fiftieth-anniversary edition of this classic. (Rev: BL 9/15/92)

277 George, Jean Craighead. *Frightful's Mountain* (5–8). 1999, Dutton $15.99 (0-525-46166-3). The falcon Frightful from *My Side of the Mountain* tells her story of how she escaped from kidnappers, survived a series of adventures, raised her own family, and finally returned to Delhi. (Rev: BL 9/1/99; SLJ 9/99)

278 George, Jean Craighead. *Summer of the Falcon* (7–9). 1979, HarperCollins paper $4.95 (0-06-440095-6). A young woman matures as she traces 3 years in the life of a falcon.

279 Gipson, Fred. *Old Yeller* (6–10). Illus. 1956, HarperCollins $23.00 (0-06-011545-9); paper $5.50 (0-06-080971-X). A boy and his dog in Texas of 1860. A sequel is *Savage Sam.*

280 Graeber, Charlotte. *Grey Cloud* (6–8). Illus. 1979, Macmillan $8.95 (0-02-736690-2). Tom and Orville become friends when they train pigeons for a big race.

281 Grey, Zane. *The Wolf Tracker and Other Animal Tales* (10–12). 1984, Santa Barbara Pr. paper $7.95 (0-915643-01-4). This collection of tales includes 4 stories about animals and the outdoors.

282 Griffith, Helen V. *Foxy* (6–8). 1984, Greenwillow $15.00 (0-688-02567-6). Jeff doesn't like outdoor life but finding a homeless dog helps him fit in.

283 Haas, Jessie. *Unbroken: A Novel* (5–8). 1999, Greenwillow $15.00 (0-688-16260-6). In this turn-of-the-century story, Harriet is moved to her stern aunt's farm after the death of her mother, and is given a colt to train. (Rev: BL 3/15/99; SLJ 4/99; VOYA 8/99)

284 Hall, Lynn. *The Soul of the Silver Dog* (5–8). 1992, Harcourt $16.95 (0-15-277196-4). A handicapped dog bonds with his new teenage owner living in a troubled family. (Rev: BL 4/15/92; SLJ 6/92)

285 Hart, Alison. *Shadow Horse* (4–8). 1999, Random $15.00 (0-679-88642-7). When Jas begins caring for Shadow, a neglected horse, she uncovers suspicious facts about her old horse, which died a mysterious death. (Rev: BL 7/99; SLJ 10/99)

286 Hermes, Patricia. *Fly Away Home: The Novel and Story Behind the Film* (5–8). 1996, Newmarket Pr. paper $6.95 (1-55704-303-5). Based on a true story that later became a film and was featured on the television show *20/20,* this is the story of a girl who raised 16 geese and her father, who taught the geese to migrate south by using an airplane. (Rev: VOYA 2/97)

287 Herriot, James. *James Herriot's Favorite Dog Stories* (10–12). Illus. 1996, St. Martin's $17.95 (0-312-14841-0). A collection of 10 stories written by the famous veterinarian and author. (Rev: SLJ 5/97)

288 High, Linda O. *Hound Heaven* (5–8). 1995, Holiday House $15.95 (0-8234-1195-8). More than anything in the world, Silver Iris wants a dog, but her

grandfather won't allow it. (Rev: SLJ 11/95; VOYA 2/96)

289 Hillerman, Tony. *Finding Moon* (9–12). 1996, HarperCollins paper $6.99 (0-06-109261-4). In Vietnam in 1975, Moon Mathias, a newspaper editor, searches for the daughter of his younger brother, who died in the war. (Rev: BL 9/15/95*)

290 Hobbs, Will. *Beardance* (7–12). 1993, Atheneum $16.00 (0-689-31867-7). Prospector Cloyd Atcity stays the winter in the Colorado mountains to ensure the survival of the last 2 grizzly cubs in the state after their mother and sibling die. (Rev: BL 11/15/93; SLJ 12/93; VOYA 12/93)

291 Holland, Isabelle. *Toby the Splendid* (6–8). 1987, Walker $13.95 (0-8027-6674-9). An intense argument arises between mother and daughter when young Janet buys a horse and wants to start riding. (Rev: BL 4/1/87; BR 9–10/87; SLJ 4/87; VOYA 8/89)

292 Howard, Jean G. *Half a Cage* (6–8). Illus. 1978, Tidal Pr. $5.50 (0-930954-07-6). Ann's pet monkey causes so many problems she wonders if she should give it away.

293 Jones, Adrienne. *The Hawks of Chelney* (7–9). Illus. 1978, HarperCollins $13.95 (0-06-023057-6). A young outcast and his girlfriend try to understand the hawks and their habits.

294 Kamida, Vicki. *Night Mare* (5–8). 1997, Random $17.00 (0-679-88628-1). In this horse story combining supernatural and natural elements, Janet dreams of riding a magnificent white mare, and her dream comes true. (Rev: BL 11/1/97; BR 1–2/98; SLJ 11/97)

295 Katz, Welwyn W. *Whalesinger* (7–10). 1991, Macmillan paper $14.95 (0-689-50511-6). Two Vancouver teens spending their summer on the California coast encounter a corrupt research scientist, endangered whales, and natural disasters. (Rev: BL 2/1/91; SLJ 5/91)

296 Keehn, Sally M. *The First Horse I See* (5–9). 1999, Philomel $17.99 (0-399-23351-2). Willo adopts a bony ex-racehorse and is determined to keep him despite her father's objections in this novel set in Chesapeake Bay. (Rev: BL 9/1/99; SLJ 7/99; VOYA 10/99)

297 Kendall, Sarita. *Ransom for a River Dolphin* (5–8). 1993, Lerner LB $19.95 (0-8225-0735-8). The story of a Colombian girl who discovers her stepfather's harpoon head in a wounded Amazon River dolphin and nurses the dolphin back to health. (Rev: BL 2/1/94; SLJ 3/94)

298 Kennedy, Barbara. *The Boy Who Loved Alligators* (7–9). 1994, Atheneum $15.00 (0-689-31876-6). When young Jim's "friend," an alligator, eats the neighbor's dog, he's forced to face some hard truths. (Rev: BL 4/1/94; SLJ 6/94)

299 Kincaid, Beth. *Back in the Saddle* (5–9). (Silver Creek Riders) 1994, Berkley paper $3.99 (0-515-11480-4). This first book in the series focuses on 4 girls attending a summer riding camp and their relationships with each other and their horses. (Rev: BL 1/1/95; SLJ 12/94)

300 Kjelgaard, James A. *Big Red* (6–9). 1956, Holiday House $16.95 (0-8234-0007-7); Bantam paper $4.99 (0-553-15434-6). This is the perennial favorite about Danny and his Irish setter. Continued in *Irish Red* and *Outlaw Red*. (Rev: BL 9/1/89)

301 Kjelgaard, James A. *Snow Dog* (6–8). 1983, Bantam paper $4.99 (0-553-15560-1). In the wilderness, a snow dog fights for survival. A sequel is: *Wild Trek*.

302 Kjelgaard, James A. *Stormy* (6–8). 1983, Bantam paper $4.50 (0-553-15468-0). Alan is helped to accept his father's being sent to prison through love for a retriever named Stormy.

303 Knight, Eric. *Lassie Come Home* (6–9). 1978, Holt $16.95 (0-8050-0721-0). The classic story of how a faithful collie returns to the boy who was his first master.

304 Levin, Betty. *Look Back, Moss* (5–8). 1998, Greenwillow $15.00 (0-688-15696-7). Young Moss, disturbed by his mother's lack of attention and his own weight problems, welcomes an injured sheepdog into the family. (Rev: BL 8/98; SLJ 11/98)

305 Lippincott, Joseph W. *Wilderness Champion* (7–9). 1944, HarperCollins $11.95 (0-397-30099-9). This novel, now almost 50 years old, tells about a most unusual hound dog.

306 Lowry, Lois. *Stay! Keeper's Story* (5–8). Illus. 1997, Houghton $15.00 (0-395-87048-8). A dog named Keeper narrates this story about his puppyhood and the 3 different homes he has had. (Rev: BL 11/1/97; SLJ 10/97)

307 Mazer, Harry. *The Dog in the Freezer* (6–9). 1997, Simon & Schuster paper $16.00 (0-689-80753-8). Three short novels about boys and dogs. In one, a dog changes places with his master, in another a fatherless boy finds love with his puppy, and in the title story, a boy wants to bury the dead dog of a neighbor. (Rev: BL 3/15/97; BR 9–10/97; SLJ 7/97)

308 Michener, James A. *Creatures of the Kingdom: Stories of Animals and Nature* (9–12). 1995, Fawcett paper $6.99 (0-449-22092-3). Sections from Michener's novels that deal with animals and other aspects of nature, such as the volcanoes of Hawaii, the habits of the diplodocus dinosaur, and the life of the salmon. (Rev: BL 7/93; SLJ 5/94)

309 Mikaelsen, Ben. *Rescue Josh McGuire* (6–9). 1991, Hyperion LB $14.89 (1-56282-100-8). Josh, 13, rescues an orphaned bear cub; when he is told it must be turned over to game authorities, he runs away into the mountains. (Rev: BL 12/15/91)

310 Mikaelsen, Ben. *Stranded* (6–8). 1995, Hyperion LB $15.89 (0-7868-2059-4). Koby, a 12-year-old girl who feels as isolated and stranded as the wounded pilot whales she helps rescue, learns about emotional barriers and reconciliation. (Rev: BL 8/95*; SLJ 6/95; VOYA 12/95)

311 Morey, Walt. *Gentle Ben* (5–8). Illus. 1976, Dutton paper $15.99 (0-525-30429-0). Mark befriends a captive brown bear but eventually he must give him up.

312 Morey, Walt. *Kavik the Wolf Dog* (7–9). 1977, Dutton paper $15.99 (0-525-33093-3). This is a story of survival and courage set in the Far North.

313 Morey, Walt. *The Year of the Black Pony* (6–8). 1976, Blue Heron paper $6.95 (0-936085-14-2). Christopher's love for the black stallion turns to tragedy and bitterness.

314 Mukerji, Dhan Gopal. *Gay-Neck: The Story of a Pigeon* (6–8). Illus. 1968, Dutton paper $15.99 (0-525-30400-2). Gay-Neck, a carrier pigeon, is selected to perform dangerous missions during World War I. Newbery Medal, 1928.

315 Naylor, Phyllis Reynolds. *Shiloh* (5–8). 1991, Atheneum $15.00 (0-689-31614-3). Set in the West Virginia hills, this novel of an 11-year-old and a neighbor's abused beagle that he loves explores the complex nature of right and wrong. Newbery Medal, 1992. (Rev: BL 12/1/91*; SLJ 9/91)

316 Naylor, Phyllis Reynolds. *Shiloh Season* (4–8). 1996. Simon & Schuster $15.00 (0-689-80647-7). The evil Judd Travers wants his dog back from the Prestons in this sequel to 1992's Newbery Medal winner, *Shiloh*. (Rev: BL 11/15/96*; BR 9–10/97; SLJ 11/96)

317 O'Hara, Mary. *My Friend Flicka* (7–12). 1988, HarperCollins paper $6.00 (0-06-080902-7). This story about Ken McLaughlin and the filly named Flicka is continued in *Thunderhead, Son of Flicka*.

318 Peck, Robert Newton. *The Horse Hunters* (7–10). 1988, Random $15.95 (0-394-56980-6). A 15-year-old boy reaches manhood through capturing a white stallion in this novel set in Florida of the 1930s. (Rev: BL 2/15/89; BR 5–6/89; VOYA 6/89)

319 Pevsner, Stella. *Jon, Flora, and the Odd-Eyed Cat* (6–8). 1997, Pocket Books paper $3.99 (0-671-56105-7). Jon, 14, moves with his family to South Carolina, where he receives late-night visits from a cat. Soon he meets Flora, 12, the cat's crazy owner. (Rev: BL 11/1/94; SLJ 10/94; VOYA 12/94)

320 Peyton, K. M. *Darkling* (9–12). 1989, Doubleday $16.95 (0-385-26963-3). Jenny's unusual grandfather buys her a horse but it is her lover, Goddard, who gives her the help that this responsibility requires. (Rev: BL 5/1/90; SLJ 5/90; VOYA 6/90)

321 Peyton, K. M. *The Team* (7–9). Illus. 1976, HarperCollins $12.00 (0-690-01083-4). Ruth is determined to own the special show pony that is for sale.

322 Rawlings, Marjorie Kinnan. *The Yearling* (6–9). Illus. 1983, Macmillan paper $5.95 (0-02-044931-3). The classic story of Joss and the orphaned fawn he adopts. (Rev: BL 9/1/89)

323 Rylant, Cynthia. *Every Living Thing* (6–9). Illus. 1985, Bradbury LB $14.00 (0-02-777200-4). In each of these 12 stories, the lives of humans change because of their relationship with animals. (Rev: SLJ 12/85; VOYA 4/86)

324 Sachs, Marilyn. *Another Day* (6–9). 1997, NAL paper $15.99 (0-525-45787-9). Olivia faces problems after her grandfather's death and the divorce of her parents, including poor grades at school, but finds new energy and joy in her struggle to adopt a dog that is being mistreated. (Rev: BL 6/1–15/97; BR 11–12/97; SLJ 6/97; VOYA 12/97)

325 Savage, Deborah. *To Race a Dream* (6–9). 1994, Houghton $16.00 (0-395-69252-0). In early 20th-century Minnesota, young Theodora dreams of being a harness-racing driver. She disguises herself as a boy and works as a stable hand. (Rev: BL 11/1/94*; SLJ 12/94; VOYA 10/94)

326 Schinto, Jeanne, ed. *The Literary Dog: Great Contemporary Dog Stories* (9–12). 1991, Grove Atlantic paper $15.00 (0-87113-504-3). Over 30 dog stories by such present-day writers as Doris Lessing and John Updike. (Rev: BL 9/1/90)

327 Sewell, Anna. *Black Beauty* (7–9). 1974, Airmont paper $1.50 (0-8049-0023-X). The classic sentimental story about the cruelty and kindness experienced by a horse in Victorian England.

328 Sherlock, Patti. *Four of a Kind* (5–9). 1991, Holiday House $13.95 (0-8234-0913-9). Andy's grandfather agrees to lend him money to buy a pair of horses, and he sets his sights on winning the horse-pulling contest at a state fair. (Rev: BL 12/1/91; SLJ 10/91)

329 Snelling, Lauraine. *The Winner's Circle* (5–8). 1995, Bethany House paper $5.99 (1-55661-533-7). In this horse story, Trish Evanston, a high school senior who is also a Triple Crown winner, is being stalked by a mystery man who sends her threatening notes. (Rev: SLJ 10/95; VOYA 4/96)

330 Springer, Nancy. *The Boy on a Black Horse* (6–9). 1994, Atheneum $14.95 (0-689-31840-5). A story about a gypsy youth (a rom, as they prefer to be called) who has run off from his abusive father. (Rev: BL 4/15/94; SLJ 6/94; VOYA 6/94)

331 Springer, Nancy. *A Horse to Love* (4–8). 1987, HarperCollins $11.95 (0-06-025824-1). Erin's parents buy her a horse hoping that this will help cure her shyness. (Rev: BL 3/87; SLJ 3/87)

332 Steinbeck, John. *The Red Pony* (9–12). 1986, Viking paper $8.95 (0-14-018739-1). These stories about a young boy growing up on a farm in California involve such elements as a loving family, a colt, and an old hired hand.

333 Sullivan, Paul. *Legend of the North* (7–12). 1995, Royal Fireworks paper $7.00 (0-88092-308-3). Set in northern Canada, this novel contains 2 narratives, the first about a young wolf's struggle for dominance within the pack, and the second about an elderly Inuit and his survival in the harsh tundra regions. (Rev: BL 1/1–15/96; VOYA 4/96)

334 Taylor, Theodore. *The Trouble with Tuck* (5–8). 1989, Doubleday $15.95 (0-385-17774-7); Avon paper $4.99 (0-380-62711-6). An easily read story about a girl's concern for her dog who is going blind.

335 Temple, Frances. *Tonight, by Sea* (6–10). 1995, Orchard LB $16.99 (0-531-08749-2). A docunovel about Haitian boat people who struggle for social justice after harrowing escapes to freedom. (Rev: BL 3/15/95; SLJ 4/95)

336 Terhune, Albert Payson. *Lad: A Dog* (7–9). 1978, NAL paper $2.50 (0-451-14626-3). The classic story of a beautiful collie. The beginning of a lengthy series now all out of print.

337 Wallace, Bill. *A Dog Called Kitty* (7–9). 1980, Holiday House $15.95 (0-8234-0376-9); paper $3.50 (0-671-63969-2). On an Oklahoma farm a young boy adopts an abandoned puppy.

338 Wilbur, Frances. *The Dog with Golden Eyes* (5–8). Illus. 1998, Milkweed $14.95 (1-57131-614-0); paper $6.95 (1-57131-615-9). Thirteen-year-old Cassie Beasley's life is beset with problems until she begins caring for a stray dog she believes to be an Alaskan sled dog—but this becomes another problem when she finds it is actually a wolf. (Rev: BL 9/1/98; BR 9–10/98; SLJ 7/98; VOYA 8/98)

Classics

Europe

GENERAL AND MISCELLANEOUS

339 Dumas, Alexandre. *The Count of Monte Cristo* (8–12). Illus. 1996, Random $25.95 (0-679-60199-6); NAL paper $6.95 (0-451-52195-1). The classic French novel about false imprisonment, escape, and revenge.

340 Dumas, Alexandre. *The Man in the Iron Mask* (9–12). 1976, Lightyear LB $35.95 (0-89968-146-8). This rousing French adventure story continues the exploits of the 3 Musketeers.

341 Dumas, Alexandre. *The Three Musketeers* (8–12). 1984, Dodd paper $5.95 (0-553-21337-7). A novel of daring and intrigue in France. Sequels are *The Man in the Iron Mask* and *Twenty Years After* (available in various editions).

342 Hudson, W. H. *Green Mansions: A Romance of the Tropical Forest* (10–12). 1982, Buccaneer LB $25.95 (0-89966-374-5). The haunting novel of a naturalist's encounter with the bird-girl, Rima, in a South American jungle.

343 Hugo, Victor. *The Hunchback of Notre-Dame* (6–9). Illus. (Eyewitness Classics) 1997, DK Publg. $14.95 (0-7894-1491-0). This is a heavily illustrated abridgment of Hugo's tale with supplementary material on the time and everyday life of the people. (Rev: SLJ 9/97)

344 Hugo, Victor. *The Hunchback of Notre Dame* (10–12). 1981, Buccaneer LB $31.95 (0-89966-382-6); NAL paper $5.95 (0-451-52222-2). The world of medieval Paris, from nobility to paupers, comes alive in this sprawling novel whose central characters are Quasimodo, a hunchback, and a gypsy named Esmeralda.

345 Hugo, Victor. *Les Miserables* (10–12). 1980, Random $16.95 (0-394-60489-X); Pocket Books paper $5.99 (0-671-50439-8). This lengthy novel describes the flight of Jean Valjean from the law in France during the first half of the 19th century. First published in 1862.

346 Maupassant, Guy de. *The Best Short Stories of Guy de Maupassant* (7–12). 1968, Amereon $21.95 (0-88411-589-5). The French master is represented by 19 tales including "The Diamond Necklace."

347 Osborne, Mary P. *Favorite Medieval Tales* (4–9). Illus. 1997, Scholastic $17.95 (0-590-60042-7). This collection of tales about medieval heroes such as Beowulf, King Arthur, Roland, Robin Hood, and Gawain is also a good introduction to the art and literature of the Middle Ages and the development of the English language. (Rev: BL 5/1/98; SLJ 8/98)

348 Remarque, Erich Maria. *All Quiet on the Western Front* (10–12). 1929, Little, Brown $24.95 (0-316-73992-8); Fawcett paper $5.99 (0-449-21394-3). The touching story of four young German boys and their army life during World War I. (Rev: BL 6/1/88)

349 Sienkiewicz, Henryk. *Quo Vadis* (10–12). 1981, Amereon LB $29.95 (0-89190-484-0). The contrast between the hedonistic pagans and the early Christians is highlighted in this novel set in ancient Rome.

350 Verne, Jules. *Around the World in Eighty Days* (7–12). 1996, Puffin paper $4.99 (0-14-036711-X). Phileas Fogg and servant Passepartout leave on a world trip in this 1873 classic adventure. (Rev: SLJ 7/96)

351 Verne, Jules. *A Journey to the Center of the Earth* (7–12). Illus. 1984, Penguin paper $4.95 (0-14-002265-1). A group of adventurers enter the earth through a volcano in Iceland. First published in French in 1864.

352 Verne, Jules. *Twenty Thousand Leagues under the Sea* (7–12). 1990, Troll LB $19.95 (0-8167-1879-2); Viking paper $3.99 (0-14-036721-7). Evil Captain Nemo captures a group of underwater explorers. First published in 1869. A sequel is: *The Mysterious Island* (1988 Macmillan).

353 Wallace, Lew. *Ben Hur* (10–12). 1987, Buccaneer LB $35.95 (0-89966-289-7). The story of a Jewish slave who escapes a life on the galleys and later is converted to Christianity after an encounter with Christ's healing powers.

354 Wyss, Johann. *The Swiss Family Robinson* (6–9). 1999, Bantam paper $4.50 (0-440-41594-2). One of many editions of the classic survival story, first published in 1814, of a family marooned on a deserted island.

GREAT BRITAIN AND IRELAND

355 Austen, Jane. *Pride and Prejudice* (9–12). 1984, Putnam paper $2.25 (0-451-52226-5). Mrs. Bennet's fondest wish is to marry off her daughters but Elizabeth won't cooperate.

356 Barrie, J. M. *Peter Pan* (5–8). Illus. 1995, Holt $19.95 (0-8050-0276-6); NAL paper $4.95 (0-451-52088-2). The classic tale of the boy who wouldn't grow up and of his adventures with the Darling children. (Rev: BL 12/15/87)

357 Blishen, Edward. *Stand Up, Mr. Dickens: A Dickens Anthology* (7–10). Illus. 1996, Houghton $16.95 (0-395-75656-1). An illustrated anthology of classic passages from such Dickens works as *David Copperfield, Oliver Twist,* and *Christmas Carol,* all of which are suitable for public readings. (Rev: BL 3/1/96)

358 Brontë, Charlotte. *Jane Eyre* (8–12). 1964, Airmont paper $3.95 (0-8049-0017-5). Jane finds terror and romance when she becomes a governess for Mr. Rochester.

359 Brontë, Emily. *Wuthering Heights* (9–12). 1959, Signet paper $4.95 (0-451-52338-5). The love between Catherine and Heathcliff that even death cannot destroy.

360 Burnett, Frances Hodgson. *The Secret Garden* (5–8). 1999, Scholastic paper $3.99 (0-439-09939-

0). An easily read classic about a spoiled girl relocated to England and of the unusual friendship she finds there.

361 Cohen, Barbara. *Canterbury Tales* (5–9). Illus. 1988, Lothrop $20.00 (0-688-06201-6). Several of the popular stories are retold with handsome illustrations by Trina Schart Hyman. (Rev: BL 9/1/88; SLJ 11/88) [821.1]

362 Collins, Wilkie. *The Moonstone* (9–12). 1984, Demco $12.30 (0-606-01905-7). Often called the first detective story in English, this mystery story revolves around the disappearance of a diamond named the Moonstone.

363 Collins, Wilkie. *The Woman in White* (10–12). 1998, Oxford paper $7.95 (0-19-283429-0). This mystery story first appeared in 1860 and tells of a plot to illegally obtain the inheritance of the heroine of the novel.

364 Defoe, Daniel. *Robinson Crusoe* (7–12). Illus. 1983, Macmillan $27.00 (0-684-17946-6); NAL paper $5.95 (0-451-52236-2). The classic survival story with illustrations by N. C. Wyeth.

365 Dickens, Charles. *A Christmas Carol* (7–12). 1983, Pocket Books paper $3.99 (0-671-47369-7). Scrooge discovers the true meaning of Christmas after some trying experiences.

366 Dickens, Charles. *David Copperfield* (8–12). Illus. 1997, Viking paper $7.95 (0-14-043494-1). Includes some little-known episodes that Dickens excerpted from his book for public readings, information about dramatic performance, and illustrations. (Rev: BL 12/15/95)

367 Dickens, Charles. *Great Expectations* (8–12). 1998, NAL paper $4.95 (0-451-52671-6). The story of Pip and his slow journey to maturity and fortune.

368 Dickens, Charles. *Martin Chuzzlewit* (10–12). 1968, Viking paper $10.95 (0-14-043031-8). In order to placate his grandfather, Martin emigrates from England in this novel largely set in the United States. First published in 1844.

369 Dickens, Charles. *The Mystery of Edwin Drood* (9–12). Illus. 1987, Oxford $25.95 (0-19-254516-7). The last novel of Dickens, left unfinished at his death.

370 Dickens, Charles. *Oliver Twist* (7–12). 1961, NAL paper $4.95 (0-451-52351-2). In probably the most accessible of Dickens' works, readers meet such immortals as Fagin, Nancy, and Oliver himself.

371 Dickens, Charles. *A Tale of Two Cities* (7–12). 1960, NAL paper $3.95 (0-451-52441-1). The classic novel of sacrifice during the French Revolution. A reissue.

372 Doyle, Arthur Conan. *Adventures of Sherlock Holmes* (7–12). 1981, Avon paper $2.95 (0-380-

78105-0). A collection of 12 of the most famous stories about this famous sleuth.

373 Doyle, Arthur Conan. *The Complete Sherlock Holmes* (7–12). 1998, Bantam paper $13.00 (0-553-32825-5). In 2 volumes, all the stories and novels involving Holmes and foil Watson.

374 Doyle, Arthur Conan. *The Hound of the Baskervilles* (9–12). 1983, Buccaneer LB $19.95 (0-89966-229-3). These are 2 of the many editions available of this Sherlock Holmes mystery about strange deaths on the moors close to the Baskerville estate.

375 Doyle, Arthur Conan. *Sherlock Holmes: The Complete Novels and Stories* (8–12). 1986, Bantam paper $6.50 each (Vol. 1: 0-553-21241-9; Vol. 2: 0-553-21242-7). A handy collection in 2 volumes of all the writings about Holmes and Watson. (Rev: BL 3/15/87)

376 Doyle, Arthur Conan. *The Sign of the Four* (9–12). 1989, Buccaneer LB $15.95 (0-89966-230-7). This is one of the 4 full-length novels featuring Sherlock Holmes.

377 Doyle, Arthur Conan. *A Study in Scarlet* (9–12). 1982, Penguin paper $6.95 (0-14-005707-2). In this, Holmes's first appearance in a full-length novel, historical material involving the Mormons plays an important part.

378 Doyle, Arthur Conan. *Tales of Terror and Mystery* (9–12). 1982, Buccaneer LB $16.95 (0-89966-429-6). From the creator of Sherlock Holmes, 13 stories of mystery and the supernatural.

379 Eliot, George. *The Mill on the Floss* (10–12). 1965, NAL paper $3.95 (0-451-51922-1). The tragic story of Maggie, her brother, and the events that separate their love. First published in 1860.

380 Eliot, George. *Silas Marner* (8–12). 1960, NAL paper $3.95 (0-451-52427-6). The love of an old man for a young child brings redemption in this classic English novel.

381 Kipling, Rudyard. *Captains Courageous* (7–10). 1964, Amereon LB $20.95 (0-88411-818-5). The story of a spoiled teenager who learns about life from common fishermen who save him when he falls overboard from an ocean liner.

382 Kipling, Rudyard. *The Jungle Book* (5–8). Illus. (The Whole Story) 1996, Viking paper $22.99 (0-670-86919-8). Along with plenty of background information that introduces the reader to the India of Kipling's time, this edition contains the complete text of the story of Mowgli, the jungle boy, and his animal friends and enemies. (Rev: SLJ 7/96)

383 Kipling, Rudyard. *The Jungle Books* (6–9). 1961, NAL paper $4.95 (0-451-52340-7). The complete 15 stories that make up the original 2 volumes of jungle books.

384 Kipling, Rudyard. *Kim* (10–12). 1997, Bantam paper $3.95 (0-553-21332-6). Beginning in Lahore, this novel follows a young street urchin through many adventures in British-controlled India.

385 Stevenson, Robert Louis. *The Black Arrow* (7–12). 1998, Tor paper $3.99 (0-8125-6562-2). Set against the War of the Roses, this is an adventure story involving a young hero, Dick Shelton. First published in 1888.

386 Stevenson, Robert Louis. *Dr. Jekyll and Mr. Hyde* (7–12). 1990, Buccaneer LB $16.95 (0-89968-552-8); NAL paper $3.95 (0-451-52393-8). This 1886 classic of horror involves a drug-induced change of personality. One of several editions.

387 Stevenson, Robert Louis. *Kidnapped* (7–12). Illus. 1886, NAL paper $2.50 (0-451-52333-4). David Balfour escapes death to claim his inheritance. One of several editions. A sequel is *Master of Ballantrae*.

388 Stevenson, Robert Louis. *The Strange Case of Dr. Jekyll and Mr. Hyde* (9–12). Illus. 1993, Oxford paper $11.95 (0-19-585429-2). An edition of this classic that includes comments by Joyce Carol Oates and engravings by Barry Moser. (Rev: BL 5/1/90)

389 Stevenson, Robert Louis. *Treasure Island* (6–10). Illus. (The Whole Story) 1996, Viking paper $23.99 (0-670-86920-1). Along with the complete text of this novel, illustrations are used to explain details of life during this period, particularly life at sea. (Rev: SLJ 7/96)

390 Stoker, Bram. *Dracula* (6–9). Illus. 1997, DK Publg. $14.95 (0-7894-1489-9). This abridged version of the classic horror story gives supplementary material about the story, characters, and locale, primarily through the heavy use of illustrations. (Rev: SLJ 9/97)

391 Stoker, Bram. *Dracula* (10–12). 1985, Amereon LB $27.95 (0-88411-131-8). In epistolary form, this novel involves a baron who is a vampire and his mysterious castle in Transylvania.

392 Swift, Jonathan. *Gulliver's Travels* (7–12). 1947, Putnam $15.95 (0-448-06010-8); NAL paper $3.95 (0-451-52219-2). The 4 fantastic voyages of Lemuel Gulliver. First published in 1726.

United States

393 Alcott, Louisa May. *Little Women* (6–10). 1947, Putnam $18.99 (0-448-06019-1). The beginning of the story of the March family and their 4 daughters—Jo, Amy, Beth, and Meg. Also use sequels *Good Wives, Little Men,* and *Jo's Boys* (available in many editions).

394 Cather, Willa. *My Antonia* (10–12). 1973, Houghton $24.95 (0-395-07514-9); paper $5.95 (0-395-75514-X). A novel set in Nebraska about pioneering Bohemian farmers and of the courageous heroine, Antonia. First published in 1918.

395 Cooper, James Fenimore. *The Last of the Mohicans* (8–12). 1986, Macmillan $28.00 (0-684-18711-6); paper $4.95 (0-553-21329-6). This is the second of the classic Leatherstocking Tales. The others are *The Pioneers, The Prairie, The Pathfinder,* and *The Deerslayer* (all available in various editions). (Rev: BL 1/87)

396 Crane, Stephen. *The Red Badge of Courage* (8–12). 1991, Random $9.99 (0-517-66844-0); Airmont paper $2.50 (0-8049-0003-5). The classic novel of a young man who explored the meanings of courage during the Civil War.

397 Hale, E. E. *The Man without a Country and Other Stories* (7–10). 1977, Buccaneer LB $18.95 (0-89966-253-6). A man is doomed to wander the world because he has denied his country. Five other stories are included in this volume.

398 Hawthorne, Nathaniel. *The Scarlet Letter* (9–12). 1977, Cambridge Univ. Pr. paper $8.50 (0-521-56783-1). Set in New England during Colonial times, this is a novel of adultery and expiation.

399 Henry, O. *The Gift of the Magi* (5–10). Illus. 1988, Simon & Schuster paper $14.00 (0-671-64706-7). A beautifully illustrated edition of this classic story of Christmas and true love. (Rev: BL 12/15/88)

400 Irving, Washington. *The Legend of Sleepy Hollow and Other Selections* (7–12). 1963, Washington Square Pr. paper $3.99 (0-671-46211-3). The story of Ichabod Crane, the ill-fated schoolteacher, and his encounter with the headless horseman.

401 Lewis, Sinclair. *Babbitt* (10–12). 1949, Harcourt $18.00 (0-15-110421-2); NAL paper $6.95 (0-451-52366-0). A satire on the shallow life led by members of the middle-class in an American city named Zenith.

402 Lewis, Sinclair. *Main Street* (10–12). 1950, NAL paper $4.50 (0-451-52147-1). A woman marries a small town doctor and decides to change things in Gopher Prairie, Minnesota. First published in 1920.

403 London, Jack. *The Call of the Wild* (5–10). Illus. 1996, Viking paper $21.99 (0-670-86918-X). Along with the full text of this novel about the heroic dog Buck, this edition supplies background material on the Klondike, the gold rush, sled dogs, and the author. (Rev: SLJ 7/96)

404 London, Jack. *The Call of the Wild, White Fang, and Other Stories* (9–12). 1993, Viking paper $7.95 (0-14-018651-4). In addition to 2 complete novels, this collection contains 2 other stories with settings in the Arctic.

405 London, Jack. *The Sea-Wolf* (7–12). 1958, Macmillan $15.95 (0-02-574630-8); Oxford paper $10.95 (0-19-282931-9). Wolf Larsen helps a ne'er-do-well and a female poet find their destinies in the classic that was originally published in 1904.

406 London, Jack. *White Fang* (7–12). 1996, NAL paper $10.95 (0-14-086220-X). A dog sacrifices himself to save his master in the classic that was first published in 1906.

407 Poe, Edgar Allan. *The Complete Tales and Poems of Edgar Allan Poe* (9–12). 1938, Modern Library $15.95 (0-394-60408-3); Random paper $16.00 (0-394-71678-7). In addition to 63 stories, this volume includes 53 poems and some nonfiction works.

408 Poe, Edgar Allan. *The Fall of the House of Usher and Other Tales* (9–12). 1960, NAL paper $2.95 (0-451-52174-9). A collection of 14 of the best known horror stories by Poe.

409 Poe, Edgar Allan. *Tales of Edgar Allan Poe* (7–12). 1991, Morrow $22.00 (0-688-07509-6). Eerie watercolor paintings illustrate 14 of Poe's most unsettling stories. (Rev: BL 8/91)

410 Stowe, Harriet Beecher. *Uncle Tom's Cabin* (10–12). Illus. 1982, Buccaneer LB $27.95 (0-89966-378-8); NAL paper $5.95 (0-451-52302-4). The American classic about slavery and racial violence in the old South.

411 Twain, Mark. *The Adventures of Huckleberry Finn* (7–12). 1959, NAL paper $1.75 (0-451-51912-4). The classic 1885 story of Huck and Jim on the Mississippi.

412 Twain, Mark. *The Adventures of Tom Sawyer* (7–12). 1998, Oxford paper $4.95 (0-19-283389-8). The story of Tom, Aunt Polly, Becky Thatcher, and the villianous Injun Joe. First published in 1876.

413 Twain, Mark. *The Adventures of Tom Sawyer* (5–10). Illus. (The Whole Story) 1996, Viking paper $23.99 (0-670-86984-8). In addition to the full text of Twain's novel, captioned illustrations are used to portray life in the 1800s. One of many editions. (Rev: SLJ 1/97)

414 Twain, Mark. *The Complete Short Stories of Mark Twain* (9–12). 1957, Bantam paper $6.95 (0-553-21195-1). A total of 60 stories are included and arranged chronologically.

415 Twain, Mark. *A Connecticut Yankee in King Arthur's Court* (7–12). 1988, Morrow $23.00 (0-688-06346-2); Bantam paper $4.95 (0-553-21143-

9). Through a time travel fantasy, a swaggering Yankee is plummeted into the age of chivalry. First published in 1889. (Rev: BL 2/15/89)

416 Twain, Mark. *The Prince and the Pauper* (7–12). 1996, Andre Deutsch $9.95 (0-233-99081-1); Airmont paper $3.47 (0-8049-0032-9). A king and a poor boy switch places in 16th-century England. First published in 1881.

417 Twain, Mark. *Pudd'nhead Wilson* (7–12). 1966, Airmont paper $2.50 (0-8049-0124-4). In the Midwest of over 100 years ago, a black servant switches her baby with a white couple's child to ensure that he gets a fair chance at life.

418 Twain, Mark. *Tom Sawyer Abroad [and] Tom Sawyer, Detective* (7–12). 1981, Univ. of California Pr. $45.00 (0-520-04560-2); paper $13.95 (0-520-04561-0). Two sequels to *The Adventures of Tom Sawyer*, both involving Tom and Huck.

419 Wharton, Edith. *Ethan Frome* (9–12). 1911, Macmillan $30.00 (0-684-15326-2). A love triangle involving Ethan, his wife Zeena, and her young cousin Mattie.

Contemporary Life and Problems

General and Miscellaneous

420 Bell, William. *Zack* (7–12). 1999, Simon & Schuster $16.95 (0-689-82248-0). Zack Lane, a biracial teenager growing up in Ontario, travels to rural Mississippi to find his African American grandfather in this disturbing novel that explores bigotry and prejudice. (Rev: BL 5/15/99; SLJ 7/99; VOYA 8/99)

421 Binchy, Maeve. *Evening Class* (10–12). 1997, Delacorte $24.95 (0-385-31807-3). This novel set in Dublin brings together a diverse group of students who are attending a night school course in Italian taught by the intriguing Signora and supervised by an unhappy Latin teacher, Aidan Dunne. (Rev: SLJ 11/97)

422 Butcher, Kristin. *The Runaways* (5–8). 1998, Kids Can $14.95 (1-55074-413-5). During an unsuccessful attempt to run away from home, young Nick Battle meets Luther, a homeless man, and through this friendship gains insights into poverty in America. (Rev: SLJ 4/98)

423 Cardillo, Joe. *Pulse* (7–10). 1996, Dutton paper $15.99 (0-525-45396-2). Jason and his girlfriend, Kris, organize a protest to prevent the destruction of a wilderness area to build a shopping mall. (Rev: BL 11/15/96; BR 5–6/97; SLJ 5/97; VOYA 6/97)

424 Craven, Margaret. *I Heard the Owl Call My Name* (7–12). 1973, Dell paper $6.50 (0-440-34369-0). A terminally ill Anglican priest and his assignment in a coastal Indian community in British Columbia. The nonfiction story behind this book is told in *Again Calls the Owl*.

425 Ewing, Lynne. *Party Girl* (6–9). 1998, Random LB $17.99 (0-679-99285-5). A nightmarish look at Southern California gang culture is provided in this powerful novel about a girl who plots revenge when her closest friend is gunned down. (Rev: BL 8/98; SLJ 9/98; VOYA 4/99)

426 Garcia, Cristina. *The Aguero Sisters: A Novel* (10–12). 1997, Knopf $24.00 (0-679-45090-4). Two half-sisters, one in the United States and the other in Cuba, try to forget their hatred of one another to find the truth about their parentage. (Rev: BL 5/1/97; SLJ 9/97)

427 Haddix, Margaret P. *Leaving Fishers* (6–9). 1997, Simon & Schuster $17.00 (0-689-81125-X). High-schooler Dorrie becomes innocently involved in a religious cult called Fishers of Men and soon finds that getting out is difficult. (Rev: BL 12/15/97; BR 5–6/98; SLJ 10/97; VOYA 2/98)

428 Holtwijk, Ineke. *Asphalt Angels* (8–12). Trans. by Wanda Boeke. 1999, Front Street $15.95 (1-886910-24-3). When a homeless boy in the slums of Rio de Janeiro joins a street gang, the Asphalt Angels, for protection from corrupt police officers, pedophiles, and other homeless people, he finds himself being drawn into a life of crime. (Rev: BL 8/99; SLJ 9/99; VOYA 12/99)

429 Klass, David. *California Blue* (7–10). 1994, Scholastic $13.95 (0-590-46688-7). A 17-year-old California boy who cares about track and butterflies finds a chrysalis that turns out to be an unknown species. (Rev: BL 3/1/94; SLJ 4/94*; VOYA 6/94)

430 McCorkle, Jill. *Carolina Moon* (10–12). 1996, Algonquin $29.95 (1-56512-136-8). Quee opens a no-smoking clinic in Fulton, North Carolina, and finds that her staff and clients have a number of problems in addition to smoking in this novel that combines romance, mystery, and humor. (Rev: BL 5/1/98; SLJ 1/97)

431 Rosen, Roger, and Patra McSharry, eds. *Border Crossings: Emigration and Exile* (8–12). (Icarus World Issues) 1992, Rosen LB $16.95 (0-8239-1364-3); paper $8.95 (0-8239-1365-1). Twelve fiction and nonfiction selections that illustrate the lives of those affected by geopolitical change. (Rev: BL 11/1/92)

432 Stoehr, Shelley. *Wannabe* (9–12). 1997, Delacorte $15.95 (0-385-32223-2). Streetwise 17-year-old Cat falls for a young mobster but tries to save her brother, a wannabe gangster, from going in that direction in this harsh portrayal of lives on the skids. (Rev: BR 5–6/97; SLJ 1/97; VOYA 4/97)

433 Thomas, Rob. *Doing Time: Notes from the Undergrad* (8–10). 1997, Simon & Schuster $16.00 (0-689-80958-1). The 10 short stories in this fine collection deal with various aspects of volunteerism, why people participate, and their rewards. (Rev: BL 10/1/97; SLJ 11/97*; VOYA 12/97)

434 Westall, Robert. *Echoes of War* (7–12). 1991, Farrar $13.95 (0-374-31964-2). Five short stories about ordinary people caught up in war and its aftermath. (Rev: BL 8/91; SLJ 8/91)

Ethnic Groups and Problems

435 Alcala, Kathleen. *The Flower in the Skull* (10–12). 1998, Chronicle $22.95 (0-8118-1916-7). This adult novel set in the Southwest, told by 3 Latina women and spanning over 100 years, tells of the assimilation of Mexicans into Anglo culture and of their hardships, inner conflicts, survival, and loss. (Rev: BL 6/1–15/98; SLJ 1/99)

436 Allen, Paula Gunn, ed. *Song of the Turtle: American Indian Literature 1974–1994* (10–12). 1997, Ballantine $25.00 (0-345-37525-4). After a brief history of Native American literature, this volume anthologizes 33 stories, many by well-known writers, that tell about being a Native American in today's world. (Rev: BL 8/96; SLJ 6/97)

437 Aparicio, Frances R., ed. *Latino Voices* (8–12). (Writers of America) 1994, Millbrook LB $23.90 (1-56294-388-X). Poetry, fiction, and true stories by 24 Latino writers describing experiences with immigration, family, work, discrimination, and love. (Rev: BL 10/1/94; SLJ 12/94; VOYA 2/95)

438 Armstrong, William H. *Sounder* (6–10). Illus. 1969, HarperCollins LB $14.89 (0-06-020144-4); paper $4.95 (0-06-440020-4). The moving story of a black sharecropper, his family, and his devoted coon dog, Sounder. A sequel is *Sour Land* (1971). Newbery Medal, 1970.

439 Augenbraum, Harold, and Ilan Stavans, eds. *Growing Up Latino: Memoirs and Stories* (9–12). 1993, Houghton paper $13.95 (0-395-66124-2). The "Hispanic journey from darkness to light, from rejection to assimilation, from silence to voice," in 25 diverse, eloquent voices. (Rev: BL 2/1/93)

440 Baldwin, James. *If Beale Street Could Talk* (9–12). 1986, Dell paper $6.99 (0-440-34060-8). Fonny is sent to jail for a crime he didn't commit before he can marry his pregnant girlfriend, Tish.

441 Balgassi, Haemi. *Tae's Sonata* (5–8). 1997, Clarion $14.00 (0-395-84314-6). When Tae, a Korean American, is given a school assignment on Korea she must come to terms with her native culture and the memories she has of her homeland. (Rev: BL 10/15/97; BR 5–6/98; SLJ 9/97)

442 Barrett, William E. *The Lilies of the Field* (8–12). Illus. 1988, Warner paper $5.99 (0-446-31500-1). A young black man, Homer Smith, helps a group of German nuns to achieve their dream.

443 Beake, Lesley. *Song of Be* (6–12). 1993, Holt $14.95 (0-8050-2905-2); 1995, Penguin paper $3.99 (0-14-037498-1). The tragedy of Namibian natives who are caught in a changing world is told by the character Be, a 15-year-old girl working on a white man's ranch. (Rev: BL 12/1/93*; SLJ 3/94; VOYA 4/94)

444 Bedford, Simi. *Yoruba Girl Dancing* (9–12). 1994, Viking paper $10.95 (0-14-023293-1). A semi-autobiographical novel about a Nigerian girl's adjustment to life at an English boarding school in the 1950s. (Rev: BL 10/1/92; SLJ 3/93*)

445 Bertrand, Diane Gonzales. *Sweet Fifteen* (8–12). 1995, Arte Publico $12.95 (1-55885-122-4); paper $9.95 (1-55885-133-X). While making a party dress for Stefanie Bonilla, age 14, Rita Navarro falls in love with her uncle and befriends her widowed mother, maturing in the process. (Rev: BL 6/1–15/95; SLJ 9/95)

446 Bolden, Tonya, ed. *Rites of Passage: Stories about Growing Up by Black Writers from Around the World* (7–12). 1994, Hyperion $16.95 (1-56282-688-3). A collection of 17 stories that focus on growing up black in the United States, Africa, Australia, Great Britain, the Caribbean, and Central America. (Rev: BL 3/1/94; SLJ 6/94)

447 Bosse, Malcolm. *Ganesh* (7–9). 1981, Harper-Collins LB $11.89 (0-690-04103-9). A young boy from India has difficulty fitting into the American Midwest and its ways.

448 Brown, John Gregory. *The Wrecked, Blessed Body of Shelton LaFleur* (10–12). 1996, Houghton $21.95 (0-395-72988-2). Life in the South during the 1930s Depression is presented in this novel about a poor black child who was deformed from a fall off a tree, and his search for his family. (Rev: BL 3/1/96; SLJ 8/96)

449 Brown, Linda Beatrice. *Crossing over Jordon* (9–12). 1996, One World paper $11.00 (0-345-40231-6). From the time of slavery to the early 21st century, the women of an African American family experience love, suffering, and the struggle to be free. (Rev: BL 2/15/95; SLJ 9/95)

450 Brown, Wesley, and Amy Ling, eds. *Imagining America: Stories from the Promised Land* (9–12). 1992, Persea paper $11.95 (0-89255-167-4). A multicultural anthology of 37 stories by distinguished writers about emigration to and migration within the United States during the 20th century. (Rev: BL 12/15/91*; SLJ 6/92)

451 Bruchac, Joseph. *The Heart of a Chief* (5–8). 1998, Dial $15.99 (0-8037-2276-1). Eleven-year-old Chris, a Native American, tries to hold on to and defend his people's culture in spite of problems they face involving racism, alcoholism, and the lure of casino gambling. (Rev: BL 10/15/98; SLJ 12/98)

452 Bush, Lawrence. *Rooftop Secrets: And Other Stories of Anti-Semitism* (6–9). Illus. 1986, American Hebrew Cong. paper $8.95 (0-8074-0314-8). In each of these 8 short stories, some form of anti-Semitism is encountered by a young person. (Rev: SLJ 11/86)

453 Carlson, Lori M., ed. *American Eyes: New Asian-American Short Stories for Young Adults* (8–12). 1994, Holt $14.95 (0-8050-3544-3). These stories present widely varied answers to the question, What does it mean to Asian American adolescents to grow up in a country that views them as aliens? (Rev: BL 1/1/95; SLJ 1/95; VOYA 5/95)

454 Childress, Alice. *A Hero Ain't Nothin' but a Sandwich* (7–10). 1973, Avon paper $4.50 (0-380-00132-2). Benjie's life in Harlem, told from many viewpoints, involves drugs and rejection. (Rev: BL 10/15/88)

455 Childress, Alice. *Rainbow Jordan* (7–10). 1982, Avon paper $3.99 (0-380-58974-5). Rainbow is growing up alternately in a foster home and with a mother who is too preoccupied to care for her. (Rev: BL 10/15/88)

456 Cofer, Judith O. *An Island Like You* (7–12). 1995, Orchard LB $16.99 (0-531-08747-6). Stories of Puerto Rican immigrant kids experiencing the tensions between 2 cultures. (Rev: BL 2/15/95*; SLJ 7/95)

457 Cofer, Judith O. *The Latin Deli* (9–12). 1993, Univ. of Georgia Pr. $19.95 (0-8203-1556-7). At the heart of this collection of Ortiz Coffer's stories, essays, and poems is the conflict of her childhood as a first-generation immigrant. (Rev: BL 11/15/93*)

458 Cofer, Judith O. *The Year of Our Revolution* (9–12). 1998, Arte Publico $16.95 (1-55885-224-7). This collection of short stories and poetry highlights cultural differences between Puerto Rican immigrant parents and their children. (Rev: BL 7/98; VOYA 6/99)

459 Cooney, Caroline B. *Burning Up* (7–10). 1999, Delacorte $15.95 (0-385-32318-2). Macey uncovers shabby family secrets and learns about herself when she investigates the senseless murder of an African American teen and a long-ago incident in her town that nearly killed an African American teacher. (Rev: BL 12/1/98; BR 9–10/99; SLJ 2/99; VOYA 2/99)

460 Curtis, Christopher Paul. *The Watsons Go to Birmingham-1963* (5–8). 1995, Delacorte $15.95 (0-385-32175-9). Fourth-grader Kenny Watson tells of conflicts in his African American family, especially with his tough older brother, that cause them to return to the South during the 1960s civil rights movement. (Rev: BL 8/95; SLJ 10/95; VOYA 12/95)

461 Davis, Ossie. *Just Like Martin* (5–8). 1992, Simon & Schuster paper $15.00 (0-671-73202-1). A docunovel of 13-year-old Isaac's struggles with family problems and a vow of nonviolence during the 1960s civil rights movement. (Rev: BL 9/1/92; SLJ 10/92)

462 Deberry, Virginia, and Donna Grant. *Tryin' to Sleep in the Bed You Made* (10–12). 1997, St. Martin's $24.95 (0-312-15233-7). This novel describes the friendship, from a childhood meeting to adulthood, of 3 African Americans, one who loses her rich husband and becomes homeless, another who finds her destiny in the corporate world, and the third a successful baseball player haunted by his brother's death. (Rev: BL 11/1/96; SLJ 8/97)

463 Dorris, Michael. *A Yellow Raft in Blue Water* (10–12). 1987, Holt $16.95 (0-8050-0045-3); Warner paper $14.00 (0-446-38787-8). A stirring novel dealing with 3 generations of females in an American Indian family, beginning in the present and moving back. (Rev: BL 3/1/87; BR 11–12/87; SLJ 11/87; VOYA 8/87)

464 Doyle, Brian. *Uncle Ronald* (6–8). 1997, Groundwood $16.95 (0-88899-266-1). This novel, set in Ontario in 1895, tells about Mickey who, with his mother, flees an abusive alcoholic father to her family's farm run by her brother and twin sisters. (Rev: SLJ 5/97)

465 Ellison, Ralph. *Flying Home and Other Stories* (10–12). Ed. by John F. Callahan. 1996, Random $23.00 (0-679-45704-6). A collection of 13 short stories written between the 1930s and 1950s by the African American writer best known for *Invisible Man*. (Rev: BL 10/15/96; SLJ 6/97)

466 English, Karen. *Francie* (5–8). 1999, Farrar $16.00 (0-374-32456-5). Francie, a black girl growing up in segregated Alabama, places her family in danger when she helps a friend who is escaping a racist employer. (Rev: BL 10/15/99; SLJ 9/99)

467 Fleischman, Paul. *Seedfolks* (4–8). Illus. 1997, HarperCollins LB $14.89 (0-06-027472-7). Thirteen people from many cultures explain why they have planted their gardens in a vacant lot in Cleveland, Ohio. (Rev: BL 5/15/97; BR 11–12/97; SLJ 5/97*; VOYA 6/97)

468 Flores, Bettina R. *Chiquita's Diary* (6–9). Illus. 1995, Pepper Vine paper $13.50 (0-962-5777-7-4). Twelve-year-old Chiquita is determined to break out of the poverty that her widowed Mexican American mother endures and she makes a start by becoming a mother's helper. (Rev: BL 2/15/96)

469 Gaines, Ernest J. *The Autobiography of Miss Jane Pittman* (9–12). 1971, Bantam paper $5.99 (0-553-26357-9). This novel, supposedly the memoirs of a 110-year-old ex-slave, is a stirring tribute to survival and courage.

470 Gaines, Ernest J. *A Gathering of Old Men* (10–12). 1983, Knopf $17.95 (0-394-51468-8). A group of old black men protect their own but assume collective guilt for a crime none of them committed.

471 Gallo, Donald R., ed. *Join In: Multiethnic Short Stories by Outstanding Writers for Young Adults* (7–12). 1995, Bantam paper $5.50 (0-440-21957-4). Seventeen stories concerning the problems teenagers of other ethnic backgrounds have living in the United States. (Rev: BL 1/15/94; SLJ 11/93; VOYA 10/93)

472 Gardner, Mary. *Boat People* (9–12). 1995, Norton $21.00 (0-393-03738-X). A sympathetic fictional portrait of Vietnamese refugees in Galveston, Texas. (Rev: BL 2/15/95*)

473 Garland, Sherry. *Shadow of the Dragon* (6–12). 1993, Harcourt $10.95 (0-15-273530-5); paper $6.00 (0-15-273532-1). Danny Vo has grown up American since he emigrated from Vietnam as a child. Now traditional Vietnamese ways, the new American culture, and skinhead prejudice clash, resulting in his cousin's death. (Rev: BL 11/15/93*; SLJ 11/93; VOYA 12/93)

474 Gordon, Sheila. *Waiting for the Rain: A Novel of South Africa* (7–12). 1996, Bantam paper $5.50 (0-440-22698-8). The story of the friendship between a black boy and a white boy in apartheid-ridden South Africa. (Rev: BL 8/87; SLJ 8/87; VOYA 12/87)

475 Green, Richard G. *Sing, like a Hermit Thrush* (6–9). 1995, Ricara paper $12.95 (0-911737-01-4). A young Native American teenager growing up on the Six Nations Reserve is confused by his gift of seeing events before they happen. (Rev: BL 4/15/96)

476 Grimes, Nikki. *Jazmin's Notebook* (6–10). 1998, Dial $15.99 (0-8037-2224-9). The journal of 14-year-old Jazmin, who writes about her tough, tender, and angry life in Harlem in the 1960s, living with her sister after her mother is hospitalized with a breakdown and her father has died. (Rev: BL 9/15/98; BR 1–2/99; SLJ 7/98; VOYA 10/98)

477 Grove, Vicki. *The Starplace* (6–8). 1999, Putnam $17.99 (0-399-23207-9). In this story set in 1961, eighth-grader Frannie defies the prejudice of her classmates and becomes friends with Celeste, the first black student in her junior high school. (Rev: BL 6/1–15/99; SLJ 6/99; VOYA 12/99)

478 Guy, Rosa. *The Music of Summer* (9–12). 1992, Doubleday $12.00 (0-385-30704-7). Sarah, age 17, weighs the pain of peer pressure against the excitement of first love during one summer on Cape Cod. (Rev: BL 4/15/92; SLJ 2/92)

479 Hale, Janet Campbell. *The Owl's Song* (10–12). 1976, Avon paper $2.50 (0-380-00605-7). An American Indian boy faces new problems when he leaves his reservation to live with a half-sister in Los Angeles.

480 Haley, Alex, and David Stevens. *Mama Flora's Family* (10–12). 1998, Scribners $25.00 (0-684-83471-5). This novel traces an African American family from 1929 through 1968 and tells of the indomitable Flora and her struggle to keep her 3 children and their offspring intact through the troubled days of integration. (Rev: BL 8/98; SLJ 3/99)

481 Hamanaka, Sheila. *The Journey* (5–9). Illus. 1990, Watts LB $20.99 (0-531-08449-3). A picture book with text that deals with the injustices suffered by Japanese Americans at the beginning of World War II. (Rev: BL 3/15/90; VOYA 6/90)

482 Hamilton, Virginia. *Arilla Sundown* (7–9). 1995, Scholastic paper $4.99 (0-590-22223-6). Arilla is part Indian and part black and growing up in a unique family situation.

483 Hamilton, Virginia. *Zeely* (6–9). 1967, Macmillan $17.00 (0-02-742470-7). A beautiful, statuesque woman enters Geeder's life and he is convinced she is an African queen.

484 Harris, Marilyn. *Hatter Fox* (9–12). 1986, Ballantine paper $5.99 (0-345-33157-5). A touching novel about a young Navaho girl and her many problems.

485 Hazelgrove, William Elliot. *Tobacco Sticks* (9–12). 1995, Pantonne Pr. $18.95 (0-9630052-8-6). Racial tensions come to a peak in 1945 Richmond, Virginia, when 13-year-old Lee Hartwell's lawyer father defends an African American maid in court. (Rev: BL 7/95; SLJ 9/95)

486 Hernandez, Irene B. *Across the Great River* (7–10). 1989, Arte Publico paper $9.95 (0-934770-96-4). The harrowing story of a young Mexican girl and her family who illegally enter the United States. (Rev: BL 8/89; SLJ 8/89)

487 Hernandez, Jo Ann Y. *White Bread Competition* (7–12). 1997, Arte Publico paper $9.95 (1-55885-210-7). The effects of winning a spelling bee on Luz Rios and her Hispanic American family in San Antonio are explored in a series of vignettes. (Rev: BL 1/1–15/98; BR 9–10/98; SLJ 8/98; VOYA 4/98)

488 Hewett, Lorri. *Dancer* (7–10). 1999, Dutton $15.99 (0-525-45968-5). A 16-year-old African American ballet student faces several obstacles, including hostile classmates and a father who doesn't approve of her career choice. (Rev: BL 8/99)

489 Hewett, Lorri. *Lives of Our Own* (6–9). 1998, Dutton $15.99 (0-525-45959-6). Shawna Riley, an African American teen new to her high school in Georgia, confronts the informal segregation she finds by writing an editorial in the school paper. (Rev: BL 2/15/98; SLJ 4/98; VOYA 8/98)

490 Hewett, Lorri. *Soulfire* (7–12). Illus. 1996, Dutton $15.99 (0-525-45559-0). Todd Williams, 16 and growing up in the Denver projects, begins to take responsibility for his actions and seeks direction for his life in this coming-of-age novel. (Rev: BL 5/1/96; BR 9–10/96; SLJ 6/96*; VOYA 10/96)

491 Hobbs, Will. *Bearstone* (7–10). 1989, Macmillan $17.00 (0-689-31496-5). A hostile, resentful Indian teenager is sent to live with a rancher in Colorado. (Rev: BL 11/1/89; BR 3–4/90; SLJ 9/89; VOYA 12/89)

492 Hodge, Merle. *For the Life of Laetitia* (5–9). 1993, Farrar $15.00 (0-374-32447-6). Rooted in Caribbean culture and language, this novel celebrates place and community as it confronts divisions of race, class, and gender. (Rev: BL 12/1/92; SLJ 1/93)

493 Hong, Maria, ed. *Growing Up Asian American* (9–12). 1995, Avon paper $12.50 (0-380-72418-9). This collection of stories and essays looks at the Asian American experience through such issues as education stratification, kinship, beauty standards, and intraethnic conflicts. (Rev: BL 12/15/93)

494 Hooks, William H. *Circle of Fire* (6–8). 1982, Macmillan LB $15.00 (0-689-50241-9). In rural North Carolina of 1936, a white boy wonders if his father is a member of the Ku Klux Klan. (Rev: BL 3/1/88)

495 Hurston, Zora Neale. *Their Eyes Were Watching God* (10–12). 1990, Demco $18.85 (0-606-04401-9). A novel about black Americans in Florida that centers on the life of Janie and her 3 marriages. First published in 1937.

496 Hyppolite, Joanne. *Ola Shakes It Up* (4–8). Illus. 1998, Delacorte $14.95 (0-385-32235-6). A spunky girl tries to prevent her parents from moving to a neighborhood where she will be the only African American in her school. (Rev: BL 2/15/98; SLJ 2/98)

497 Irwin, Hadley. *Kim/Kimi* (7–10). 1987, Macmillan $16.00 (0-689-50428-4); Penguin paper $3.99 (0-14-032593-X). A half-Japanese teenager brought up in an all-white small town sets out to explore her Oriental roots. (Rev: BL 3/15/87; SLJ 5/87; VOYA 6/87)

498 Irwin, Hadley. *Sarah with an H* (6–8). 1996, Simon & Schuster $16.00 (0-689-80949-2). Newcomer Sarah, who is rich, bright, and pretty, is blocked from joining the "in" crowd partly because she is Jewish. (Rev: BL 9/1/96; SLJ 2/97; VOYA 12/96)

499 Jackson, Brian Keith. *The View from Here* (10–12). 1998, Pocket Books paper $14.00 (0-671-56896-5). Set in rural Mississippi in the 1960s, this emotion-charged novel, told from various points of view, tells of a black family's struggle to succeed. (Rev: BL 2/15/97; SLJ 3/97)

500 Jimenez, Francisco. *The Circuit: Stories from the Life of a Migrant Child* (5–10). 1997, Univ. of New Mexico Pr. paper $10.95 (0-8263-1797-9). Eleven moving stories about the lives, fears, hopes, and problems of children in Mexican migrant worker families. (Rev: BL 12/1/97)

501 Johnson, Angela. *Toning the Sweep* (7–12). 1993, 1994, Scholastic paper $4.99 (0-590-48142-8). This novel captures the innocence, vulnerability, and love of human interaction, as well as the melancholy, self-discovery, and introspection of an African American adolescent. (Rev: BL 4/1/93*; SLJ 4/93*)

502 Johnson-Coleman, Lorraine. *Just Plain Folks* (10–12). 1998, Little, Brown $22.00 (0-316-46084-2). Rural blacks from the South are introduced in these short stories about ordinary people who lived during the periods of slavery, Reconstruction, the Depression, and the Civil Rights era, based on interviews conducted by the author as she traveled through her home state of North Carolina. (Rev: SLJ 5/99)

503 Jukes, Mavis. *Planning the Impossible* (6–8). 1999, Delacorte $14.95 (0-385-32243-7). In this companion to *Expecting the Unexpected*, sixth-grader River has problems with sex education, understanding adult behavior, her mother's pregnancy, and manipulative classmates trying to come between her and a boy she likes. (Rev: BL 6/1–15/99; SLJ 4/99; VOYA 4/99)

504 Killens, John Oliver, and Jerry W. Ward, eds. *Black Southern Voices: An Anthology of Fiction, Poetry, Drama, Nonfiction, and Critical Essays* (9–12). 1992, NAL paper $15.00 (0-452-01096-9). Essays, poetry, drama, and fiction by such familiar names as Arna Bontemps, Alice Walker, and Nikki Giovanni, as well as less-well-known writers. (Rev: BL 10/15/92)

505 Killingsworth, Monte. *Circle Within a Circle* (7–9). 1994, Macmillan paper $14.95 (0-689-50598-1). A runaway teenage boy and a Chinook Indian join a crusade to save a stretch of sacred land from commercial development. (Rev: BL 3/1/94; SLJ 6/94; VOYA 6/94)

506 Kincaid, Jamaica. *The Autobiography of My Mother* (9–12). 1996, Farrar $20.00 (0-374-10731-9); NAL paper $10.95 (0-452-27466-4). Kincaid's essay *A Small Place* is expanded into this novel about a woman's search for identity as she searches for her mother. (Rev: BL 12/1/95*)

507 Laird, Elizabeth. *Kiss the Dust* (6–10). 1992, 1994, Penguin paper $4.99 (0-14-036855-8). A docunovel about a refugee Kurdish teen caught up in the 1984 Iran-Iraq War. (Rev: BL 6/15/92)

508 Lee, Gus. *China Boy* (9–12). 1994, NAL paper $11.95 (0-452-27158-4). Kai—or "China Boy," as he is called by the neighborhood bullies—turns his life around when he learns to stand his ground and fight back. (Rev: BL 3/1/91)

509 Lee, Gus. *Honor and Duty* (9–12). 1994, Knopf $24.00 (0-679-41258-1). A Chinese American cadet at West Point demonstrates honor and devotion to duty by implicating classmates and friends in a cheating incident. (Rev: BL 1/1/94*)

510 Lee, Harper. *To Kill a Mockingbird* (8–12). 1977, HarperCollins $23.00 (0-397-00151-7). A small Southern town lawyer defends a black man wrongfully accused of rape.

511 Lee, Marie G. *F Is for Fabuloso* (6–9). 1999, Avon $15.00 (0-380-97648-X). A sensitive story about Jin-Ha, a Korean girl, and the troubles she and her parents face in the United States. (Rev: BL 9/15/99)

512 Lee, Marie G. *Finding My Voice* (7–12). 1994, Demco $9.09 (0-606-06979-8). Pressured by her strict Korean parents to get into Harvard, high-school senior Ellen Sung tries to find time for friendship, romance, and fun in her small Minnesota town. (Rev: BL 9/1/92; SLJ 10/92)

513 Lee, Marie G. *Necessary Roughness* (7–12). 1996, HarperCollins LB $14.89 (0-06-025130-1). Chan, a football enthusiast, and his twin sister, Young, Korean Americans, encounter prejudice when their family moves to a small Minnesota community. (Rev: BL 1/1–15/97; BR 5–6/97; SLJ 1/97; VOYA 6/97)

514 Lester, Julius. *This Strange New Feeling* (9–12). 1985, Scholastic paper $4.50 (0-590-44047-0). Based on fact, this is a group of 3 short stories about slaves who react in different ways to gaining freedom.

515 Lipsyte, Robert. *The Brave* (8–12). 1991, 1993, HarperCollins paper $4.95 (0-06-447079-2). A Native American heavyweight boxer is rescued from drugs, pimps, and hookers by a tough but tender ex-boxer/New York City cop. (Rev: BL 10/15/91; SLJ 10/91*)

516 Lipsyte, Robert. *The Chief* (7–10). 1995, HarperCollins paper $4.95 (0-06-447097-0). Sonny Bear can't decide whether to go back to the reservation, continue boxing, or become Hollywood's new Native American darling. Sequel to *The Brave*. (Rev: BL 6/1–15/93; VOYA 12/93)

517 Lipsyte, Robert. *The Contender* (9–12). 1967, HarperCollins LB $14.89 (0-06-023920-4); paper $4.95 (0-06-447039-3). A black teenager hopes to get out of Harlem through a boxing career. (Rev: BL 3/1/90)

518 López, Tiffany Ana, ed. *Growing Up Chicana/o* (9–12). 1995, Avon paper $12.50 (0-380-72419-7). This anthology presents the writings of 20 current Chicano authors, including Rudolfo Anaya and Sandra Cisneros, on multicultural issues. (Rev: BL 12/1/93)

519 Lord, Bette Bao. *In the Year of the Boar and Jackie Robinson* (6–8). Illus. 1984, HarperCollins paper $4.95 (0-06-440175-8). A young Chinese girl finds that the world of baseball helps her adjust to her new home in America.

520 McGahan, Jerry. *A Condor Brings the Sun* (10–12). 1996, Sierra Club $25.00 (0-87156-354-1). This is the story of Pilar, a Peruvian girl who is consumed with curiosity about her Inca heritage but leaves her homeland to live with an American zoologist in Montana, where she tries to free a bear and 3 cubs from captivity. (Rev: SLJ 2/97)

521 McKay, Kathleen C. *Hearts of Rosewood* (5–10). 1997, Tudor $18.95 (0-936389-46-X). In this novel based on an incident in U.S. history, two elderly sisters recall the murders they witnessed as children when a mob of angry white men attacked a black community in Rosewood, Florida, in 1923. (Rev: SLJ 10/97)

522 McLaren, Clemence. *Dance for the Land* (4–8). 1999, Simon & Schuster $16.00 (0-689-82393-2). A half-Hawaiian girl experiences prejudice when her family relocates from the mainland to her father's home in Hawaii after her mother dies. (Rev: BL 2/15/99; SLJ 6/99)

523 Major, Clarence, ed. *Calling the Wind: Twentieth-Century African-American Short Stories* (9–12). 1993, HarperCollins paper $17.00 (0-06-098201-2). Includes stories by Langston Hughes, Zora Neale Hurston, James Baldwin, Toni Morrison, and dozens more. (Rev: BL 12/1/92*)

524 Marino, Jan. *The Day That Elvis Came to Town* (7–10). 1993, Avon paper $3.50 (0-380-71672-0). In this tale of southern blacks, Wanda is thrilled when a room in her parents' boarding house is rented to Mercedes, who makes her feel pretty and smart—and who once went to school with Elvis Presley. (Rev: BL 12/15/90*; SLJ 1/91*)

525 Markle, Sandra. *The Fledglings* (6–9). 1998, Boyds Mills paper $9.95 (1-56397-696-X). With her parents dead, Kate, 14, runs away to live with her Cherokee grandfather and immerses herself happily in his world. (Rev: BL 6/1/92)

526 Martinez, Victor. *Parrot in the Oven: Mi Vida* (7–10). 1996, HarperCollins LB $15.89 (0-06-026706-2). Through a series of vignettes, the story of Manuel, a teenage Mexican American, unfolds as he grows up in the city projects with an abusive father and a loving mother. (Rev: BL 10/15/96; SLJ 11/96)

527 Mazzio, Joann. *The One Who Came Back* (7–10). 1992, Houghton $15.00 (0-395-59506-1). A New Mexico teen must prove he didn't kill his best friend. (Rev: BL 4/1/92; SLJ 5/92)

528 Meriwether, Louise. *Daddy Was a Numbers Runner* (7–12). 1986, Feminist Pr. paper $10.95 (0-935312-57-9). The story of Frances, a black girl, growing up in Harlem during the Depression.

529 Meyer, Carolyn. *Gideon's People* (6–9). 1996, Harcourt $12.00 (0-15-200303-7); paper $6.00 (0-15-200304-5). Similarities and differences in religious practices become apparent when an Orthodox Jewish boy spends time on an Amish farm in 1911. (Rev: BL 5/1/96; SLJ 4/96; VOYA 6/96)

530 Meyer, Carolyn. *Jubilee Journey* (5–9). 1997, Harcourt $13.00 (0-15-201377-6); paper $6.00 (0-15-201591-4). This sequel to *White Lilacs* begins 75 years later and tells about Emily Rose, a biracial girl, who finds her spiritual identity when she visits her African American relatives in Texas. (Rev: BL 9/1/97; SLJ 1/98; VOYA 12/97)

531 Mikaelsen, Ben. *Countdown* (6–9). 1996, Hyperion LB $15.89 (0-7868-2207-4). Two 14-year-old boys (one who lives in a remote village in Kenya and the other whose home is at the Johnson Space Center) face similar personal problems, particularly the conflict each has with his father. (Rev: BL 1/1–15/97; BR 5–6/97; SLJ 3/97; VOYA 6/97)

532 Miklowitz, Gloria D. *The War Between the Classes* (7–10). 1986, Dell paper $4.99 (0-440-99406-3). A Japanese American girl finds that hidden prejudices and bigotry emerge when students in school are divided into 4 socioeconomic groups. (Rev: BL 4/15/85; SLJ 8/85; VOYA 6/85)

533 Mohr, Nicholasa. *El Bronx Remembered: A Novella and Stories* (7–9). 1993, HarperCollins paper $4.95 (0-06-447100-4). These 12 stories set in the Bronx reflect the general Puerto Rican experience in New York.

534 Mohr, Nicholasa. *Felita* (7–9). 1995, Bantam paper $4.50 (0-440-41295-1). Felita, a Puerto Rican girl, encounters problems when her family moves to a non-Spanish-speaking neighborhood.

535 Mohr, Nicholasa. *Going Home* (6–8). 1986, Dial LB $13.89 (0-8037-0338-4). The young heroine finds a boyfriend and spends a summer in her family's home in Puerto Rico in this sequel to *Felita*. (Rev: BL 7/86; SLJ 8/86)

536 Mohr, Nicholasa. *Nilda* (7–9). 1986, Publico paper $11.95 (0-934770-61-1). The story of a 12-year-old Puerto Rican girl growing up in the New York barrio.

537 Moore, Yvette. *Freedom Songs* (6–12). 1991, 1992, Penguin paper $4.99 (0-14-036017-4). In 1968, Sheryl, 14, witnesses and then experiences acts of prejudice while visiting relatives in North Carolina. (Rev: BL 4/15/91; SLJ 3/91)

538 Mowry, Jess. *Way Past Cool* (9–12). 1992, Farrar $17.00 (0-374-28669-8). Kids struggle to survive in a violent California ghetto. (Rev: BL 3/15/92)

539 Mullane, Deirdre. *Crossing the Danger Water: Three Hundred Years of African-American Writing* (9–12). 1993, Doubleday paper $16.00 (0-385-42243-1). The history of African Americans is explored in their writings, narratives, letters, editorials, speeches, lyrics, and folktales, from U.S. colonial times to today. (Rev: BL 11/1/93) [810.8]

540 Myers, Walter Dean. *Fast Sam, Cool Clyde, and Stuff* (7–10). 1995, Peter Smith $18.75 (0-8446-6798-6); Puffin paper $4.99 (0-14-032613-8). Three male friends in Harlem join forces to found the 116th Street Good People.

541 Myers, Walter Dean. *The Glory Field* (7–10). 1994, Scholastic $14.95 (0-590-45897-3). This novel follows a family's 200-year history, from the capture of an African boy in the 1750s through the lives of his descendants on a small plot of South Carolina land called the Glory Field. (Rev: BL 10/1/94)

542 Myers, Walter Dean. *Monster* (9–12). 1999, HarperCollins LB $15.89 (0-06-028078-6). Told in a film script format written by the protagonist, this is 16-year-old Steve's story and his trial for felony murder because he acted as a lookout for a robbery that lead to murder. (Rev: BL 5/1/99; BR 9–10/99; SLJ 7/99; VOYA 8/99)

543 Myers, Walter Dean. *Motown and Didi: A Love Story* (7–9). 1984, Dell paper $4.50 (0-440-95762-1). In the midst of trouble and despair in Harlem, this is a tender love story.

544 Myers, Walter Dean. *Scorpions* (7–9). 1988, HarperCollins LB $15.89 (0-06-024365-1). Gang warfare, death, and despair are the elements of this story set in present-day Harlem. (Rev: BL 9/1/88; BR 11–12/88; SLJ 9/88; VOYA 8/88)

545 Myers, Walter Dean. *Slam!* (8–12). 1996, Scholastic $15.95 (0-590-48667-5). Although Slam is successful on the school's basketball court, his personal life has problems caused by difficulties fitting into an all-white school, a very sick grandmother, and a friend who is involved in drugs. Coretta Scott King Award, 1997. (Rev: BL 11/15/96; BR 11–12/96; SLJ 11/96; VOYA 2/97)

546 Myers, Walter Dean. *The Young Landlords* (7–10). 1979, Penguin paper $4.99 (0-14-034244-3). A group of black teenagers take over a slum building in Harlem.

547 Namioka, Lensey. *April and the Dragon Lady* (7–12). 1994, Harcourt $10.95 (0-15-276644-8). A Chinese American high school junior must relinquish important activities to care for her ailing grandmother and struggles with the constraints of a traditional female role. (Rev: BL 3/1/94; SLJ 4/94; VOYA 6/94)

548 Naylor, Gloria, ed. *Children of the Night: The Best Short Stories by Black Writers, 1967 to the Present* (9–12). 1996, Little, Brown $24.95 (0-316-59926-3). A short-story collection, balanced thematically, from the editorial hands of one of the finest black female writers. (Rev: BL 12/1/95)

549 Neufeld, John. *Edgar Allan* (6–8). 1968, Phillips $27.25 (0-87599-149-1). Michael's family adopts a 3-year-old black boy and the signs of bigotry begin.

550 Ng, Fae Myenne. *Bone* (9–12). 1993, Hyperion $19.95 (1-56282-944-0). A look at the barriers and the love between generations in a Chinese American family. (Rev: BL 9/15/92*)

551 Okimoto, Jean D. *Talent Night* (6–10). 1995, Scholastic $14.95 (0-590-47809-5). In this story, Rodney Suyama, 17, wants to be the first Japanese American rapper and to date beautiful Ivy Ramos. (Rev: BL 6/1–15/95; SLJ 5/95)

552 Oughton, Jerrie. *Music from a Place Called Half Moon* (6–10). 1995, Houghton $13.95 (0-395-70737-4). Small-town bigotry and personal transformation in the 1950s figure in this novel about Native Americans. (Rev: BL 5/1/95; SLJ 4/95)

553 Parks, Gordon. *The Learning Tree* (10–12). 1987, Fawcett paper $5.99 (0-449-21504-0). The story of a black boy's coming of age in a small town in Kansas in the 1920s.

554 Perkins, Mitali. *The Sunita Experiment* (7–10). 1993, 1994, Hyperion paper $4.50 (1-56282-671-9). An Asian American eighth-grade teen is confused about self-identity as she tries to fit into a "normal" high school. (Rev: BL 5/1/93; SLJ 6/93; VOYA 10/93)

555 Pinkney, Andrea D. *Hold Fast to Dreams* (5–8). 1995, Morrow $16.00 (0-688-12832-7). A young African American girl moves from her neighborhood into an all-white suburb, where she is challenged by her new situation and referred to as "the other." (Rev: BL 2/15/95; SLJ 4/95)

556 Potok, Chaim. *The Promise* (10–12). 1969, Fawcett paper $6.99 (0-449-20910-5). The friendship between 2 Jewish boys in Brooklyn becomes strained because of family problems.

557 Power, Susan. *The Grass Dancer* (9–12). 1995, Berkley paper $6.99 (0-425-14962-5). Anna Thunder, a Sioux living in North Dakota, is the central character in this novel that tells the generational stories of Anna's family. (Rev: BL 8/94; SLJ 5/95; VOYA 12/94)

558 Pullman, Philip. *The Broken Bridge* (8–12). 1992, Knopf LB $15.99 (0-679-91972-4). A biracial girl learns the truth about her heritage. (Rev: BL 2/15/92; SLJ 3/92*)

559 Qualey, Marsha. *Revolutions of the Heart* (7–12). 1993, Houghton $15.00 (0-395-64168-3). Cory lives in a small Wisconsin town that is torn by bigotry when Chippewa Indians reclaim their hunting and fishing rights. (Rev: BL 4/1/93; SLJ 5/93*)

560 Rana, Indi. *The Roller Birds of Rampur* (7–12). 1993, Holt $15.95 (0-8050-2670-3); 1994, Ballantine paper $3.99 (0-449-70434-3). This coming-of-age story of a young woman caught between British and Indian cultures is a lively account of the immigration experience and of Indian culture. (Rev: BL 7/93; SLJ 5/93; VOYA 2/94)

561 Rebolledo, Tey Diana, and Eliana S. Rivero, eds. *Infinite Divisions: An Anthology of Chicana Literature* (9–12). 1993, Univ. of Arizona Pr. paper $22.50 (0-8165-1384-8). A collection that spans the history of prose and poetry by Mexican American women and the settlement of the "New World." (Rev: BL 6/1–15/93)

562 Rosen, Sybil. *Speed of Light* (5–9). 1999, Simon & Schuster $16.00 (0-689-82437-8). When Audrey's father, a Jewish worker in a small Virginia town in 1956, supports the appointment of the first black police officer in town, it unleashes a flood of anti-Semitism. (Rev: BL 8/99; SLJ 8/99; VOYA 10/99)

563 Santiago, Danny. *Famous All Over Town* (10–12). 1984, NAL paper $12.95 (0-452-25974-6). An honest, realistic novel about a young Mexican American growing up in a California barrio. (Rev: BL 12/15/89)

564 Savage, Deborah. *A Stranger Calls Me Home* (9–12). 1992, Houghton $14.95 (0-395-59424-3). A mystical tale of 3 friends' search for cultural identity. (Rev: BL 3/15/92; SLJ 5/92)

565 Sebestyen, Ouida. *On Fire* (6–9). 1985, Little, Brown $12.95 (0-87113-010-6). Tater leaves home with his brother Sammy and takes a mining job where he confronts labor problems in this sequel to the author's powerful *Words by Heart.* (Rev: BL 5/15/85; SLJ 4/85; VOYA 8/85)

566 Sebestyen, Ouida. *Words by Heart* (7–12). 1979, Little, Brown $15.95 (0-316-77931-8). A black girl unknowingly arouses racial conflicts in a southwestern white town at the turn of the century. (Rev: BL 6/1/88)

567 Senna, Danzy. *Caucasia* (10–12). 1998, Berkley paper $24.95 (1-57322-091-4). Two sisters, the products of a biracial marriage, are separated when their parents divorce, and the younger, named Birdie, is forced to go underground with her mother for political reasons and pass as white, all the while hoping to some day be reunited with her sister. (Rev: BL 2/15/98; SLJ 9/98)

568 Sherman, Eileen B. *The Violin Players* (6–10). 1998, Jewish Publication Soc. $14.95 (0-8276-0595-1). When Melissa leaves New York City to spend part of her junior year in a small Missouri town, she encounters the ugliness of anti-Semitism for the first time. (Rev: BL 12/1/98; SLJ 3/99)

569 Singer, Isaac Bashevis. *The Power of Light: Eight Stories for Hanukkah* (7–10). Illus. 1980, Avon paper $2.50 (0-380-60103-6). Eight stories of the Festival of Lights that span centuries of Jewish history.

570 Smothers, Ethel Footman. *Down in the Piney Woods* (5–8). 1992, 1994, Random paper $4.99 (0-679-84714-6). The daily life of a strong African American sharecropper family in 1950s rural Georgia is described in a colloquial voice. (Rev: BL 12/15/91; SLJ 1/92)

571 Soto, Gary. *Jesse* (10–12). 1994, Harcourt $14.95 (0-15-240239-X). Mexican American Jesse, 17, leaves high school in 1968, moves in with his poor older brother, takes college classes, worries about the draft, and faces racism. (Rev: BL 10/1/94; SLJ 12/94; VOYA 2/95)

572 Soto, Gary. *Petty Crimes* (5–8). 1998, Harcourt $16.00 (0-15-201658-9). Ten short stories about Mexican American teenagers in California's Central Valley that deal with some humorous situations but more often with gangs, violence, and poverty. (Rev: BL 3/15/98; SLJ 5/98)

573 Soto, Gary. *Taking Sides* (6–9). 1991, Harcourt $17.00 (0-15-284076-1). Lincoln Mendoza moves from his inner-city San Francisco neighborhood to a middle-class suburb and must adjust to life in a new high school. (Rev: BL 12/1/91; SLJ 11/91)

574 Spinelli, Jerry. *Maniac Magee* (6–10). 1990, Little, Brown $15.95 (0-316-80722-2). A white boy runs away from home and suddenly becomes aware of the racism in his town. Newbery Medal, 1991. (Rev: SLJ 6/90)

575 Stepto, Michele, ed. *African-American Voices* (7–12). (Writers of America) 1995, Millbrook LB $23.90 (1-56294-474-6). Selections by W. E. B. Du Bois, Toni Morrison, Ralph Ellison, and others, plus traditional chants, speeches, and poetry. (Rev: BL 5/15/95; SLJ 3/95)

576 Stering, Shirley. *My Name Is Seepeetza* (5–10). 1997, Douglas & McIntyre paper $7.95 (0-88899-

165-7). Told in diary form, this autobiographical novel about a sixth-grade Native American girl tells of her heartbreak at the terrible conditions at her school where she is persecuted because of her race. (Rev: BL 3/1/97)

577 Sullivan, Charles, ed. *Here Is My Kingdom: Hispanic-American Literature and Art for Young People* (7–12). 1994, Abrams $24.95 (0-8109-3422-1). A collection of Latino prose, poetry, painting, and photography, with profiles of leading figures from Cervantes to singer Gloria Estefan. (Rev: BL 7/94*)

578 Talbert, Marc. *Star of Luis* (5–9). 1999, Houghton $15.00 (0-395-91423-X). Racial prejudice is the theme of this story about a Hispanic American boy in New Mexico during World War II who discovers he is Jewish. (Rev: BL 3/1/99; SLJ 5/99; VOYA 6/99)

579 Tan, Amy. *The Kitchen God's Wife* (9–12). 1992, Ivy Books paper $7.99 (0-8041-0753-X). The mesmerizing story a Chinese emigré mother tells her daughter. (Rev: BL 4/15/91*; SLJ 12/91)

580 Tan, Amy. *The Moon Lady* (5–8). Illus. 1992, Macmillan LB $16.95 (0-02-788830-4). An adaptation of "The Moon Lady" from Tan's adult best-seller *The Joy Luck Club*, which speaks to our common nightmares and secret wishes. (Rev: BL 9/1/92; SLJ 9/92)

581 Taylor, Mildred D. *The Road to Memphis* (7–12). 1990, Dial paper $15.00 (0-8037-0340-6). Set in 1941, this is a continuation of the story of the Logans, a poor black southern family who were previously featured in *Roll of Thunder, Hear My Cry* and *Let the Circle Be Unbroken*. (Rev: BL 5/15/90; SLJ 1/90; VOYA 8/90)

582 Uchida, Yoshiko. *The Happiest Ending* (6–8). 1985, Macmillan $15.00 (0-689-50326-1). There is a clash of cultures in this story of Japanese American families and an arranged marriage. By the author of *The Best Bad Thing*. (Rev: BL 11/1/85; SLJ 11/85)

583 Uchida, Yoshiko. *A Jar of Dreams* (6–8). 1981, Macmillan $16.00 (0-689-50210-9). In California of Depression days, a young Japanese girl encounters prejudice.

584 Uchida, Yoshiko. *Journey Home* (7–9). Illus. 1978, Macmillan $16.00 (0-689-50126-9); paper $4.95 (0-689-71641-9). A Japanese American family return to their ordinary life after being relocated during World War II.

585 Ujaama, E. James. *Coming Up* (10–12). 1996, Ujaama paper $12.95 (0-910303-66-5). The difficult realities of becoming successful as an African American male in white-dominated America are explored in this novel of 2 friends, Hakim and Andre, and their problems. (Rev: VOYA 8/96)

586 Vanasse, Deb. *A Distant Enemy* (6–9). 1997, Dutton paper $16.99 (0-525-67549-3). Joseph, who is half-white and half-Yup'ik Eskimo, is so consumed with hatred for white intruders that he risks his life by running off into the Alaska tundra. (Rev: BL 1/1–15/97; BR 9–10/97; SLJ 1/97; VOYA 6/98)

587 Velasquez, Gloria. *Maya's Divided World* (7–12). 1995, Arte Publico $12.95 (1-55885-126-7). A Chicana who seemingly leads a charmed life discovers that her parents are divorcing and her world falls apart. (Rev: BL 3/1/95; SLJ 4/95)

588 Velie, Alan R., ed. *The Lightning Within: An Anthology of Contemporary American Indian Fiction* (9–12). 1991, Univ. of Nebraska Pr. $30.00 (0-8032-4659-5). A thoughtfully selected sampling of fiction by 7 noted modern Native American writers, among them Momaday, Erdrich, Dorris, Silko, Vizenor, and Ortiz. (Rev: BL 5/15/91; SLJ 9/91)

589 Voigt, Cynthia. *Come a Stranger* (6–9). 1986, Simon & Schuster LB $15.95 (0-689-31289-X); Fawcett paper $3.95 (0-449-70246-4). Mina Smiths, a young black girl introduced in *Dicey's Song,* has trouble achieving her identity as an individual and is helped by a young minister, Tamer Shipp (from *The Runner*). (Rev: BL 9/15/86; SLJ 10/86; VOYA 4/87)

590 Walters, Eric. *War of the Eagles* (6–9). 1998, Orca $14.00 (1-55143-118-1). In this novel set during World War II in Canada, Jed Blackburn, who lives on the coast of British Columbia with his mother and grandmother, both Tsimshian Indians, is shaken when his best friend's family is sent to a detention camp for Japanese Canadians and he experiences racism because of his native heritage. (Rev: BL 12/15/98; BR 5–6/99; SLJ 12/98)

591 Wartski, Maureen C. *Candle in the Wind* (9–12). 1995, Fawcett paper $4.50 (0-449-70442-4). Drawn from newspaper headlines, the shocking story of the murder of a Japanese American teen and the climate of racial hate that led to it. (Rev: BL 11/15/95; SLJ 3/96; VOYA 2/96)

592 Washington, Mary Helen, ed. *Memory of Kin: Stories about Family by Black Writers* (9–12). 1991, Doubleday paper $14.95 (0-385-24783-4). A wide-ranging collection of short stories and poetry dealing with the African American family experience. (Rev: BL 1/1/91; SLJ 7/91)

593 West, Dorothy. *The Wedding* (9–12). 1995, Doubleday $20.00 (0-385-47143-2). In an African American community on Martha's Vineyard, Massachusetts, Lute tries to win Shelby away from her white fiancé. (Rev: BL 12/1/94; SLJ 7/95)

594 Williams-Garcia, Rita. *Blue Tights* (9–12). 1996, Viking paper $3.99 (0-14-038045-0). A talented black teenager has difficulty being accepted in her integrated high school. (Rev: BL 12/15/87)

595 Williams-Garcia, Rita. *Fast Talk on a Slow Track* (9–12). 1991, Dutton $15.00 (0-525-67334-2). After graduating from high school as valedictorian, Denzel attends Princeton's summer session for minority students and fails for the first time in his life. (Rev: BL 4/1/91; SLJ 4/91*)

596 Winslow, Vicki. *Follow the Leader* (5–8). Illus. 1997, Delacorte $14.95 (0-385-32285-2). When schools in Winston, North Carolina, are desegregated in 1971, Amanda feels out of place when she finds that she is one of only a few white girls in her sixth-grade class. (Rev: BL 11/1/97; SLJ 12/97)

597 Woodson, Jacqueline. *The Dear One* (6–9). 1992, Dell paper $3.99 (0-440-21420-3). A pregnant African American teenager lives with the family of her mother's friend until the baby is born in this exploration of issues of women's sexuality. (Rev: BL 11/15/91)

598 Woodson, Jacqueline. *From the Notebooks of Melanin Sun May* (6–10). 1995, Scholastic $14.95 (0-590-45880-9). A 13-year-old black boy's mother announces that she loves a fellow student, a white woman. (Rev: BL 4/15/95; SLJ 8/95)

599 Woodson, Jacqueline. *Maizon at Blue Hill* (5–8). 1992, 1994, Dell paper $3.99 (0-440-40899-7). Seventh-grader Maizon reluctantly leaves her Brooklyn home, her best friend, and her grandmother to attend a private boarding school for girls, where she must confront issues of race, class, prejudice, and identity. (Rev: BL 7/92; SLJ 11/92)

600 Wright, Richard. *Native Son* (10–12). 1998, HarperCollins paper $10.00 (0-06-092980-4). The tragic life of a black youth named Bigger Thomas who was raised in a Chicago slum.

601 Wright, Richard. *Rite of Passage* (7–12). 1994, HarperCollins LB $13.89 (0-06-023420-2). This newly discovered novella, written in the 1940s, concerns a gifted 15-year-old who runs away from his loving Harlem home and survives on the streets with a violent gang. (Rev: BL 1/1/94; SLJ 2/94; VOYA 4/94)

602 Yep, Laurence, ed. *American Dragons: Twenty-Five Asian American Voices* (7–12). 1995, Harper-Collins paper $5.95 (0-06-440603-2). Autobiographical stories, poems, and essays about children whose parents come from China, Japan, Korea, and Tibet, struggling to find "an identity that isn't generic." (Rev: BL 5/15/93; SLJ 7/93; VOYA 10/93)

603 Yep, Laurence. *Child of the Owl* (6–9). 1977, HarperCollins LB $14.89 (0-06-026743-7). A young girl goes to live with her grandmother in San Francisco's Chinatown.

604 Yep, Laurence. *Dragonwings* (7–9). 1975, HarperCollins LB $15.89 (0-06-026738-0); paper $5.95 (0-06-440085-9). At the turn of the century, a young Chinese boy in San Francisco becomes an aviation pioneer. (Rev: BL 3/1/88)

605 Yep, Laurence. *The Star Fisher* (6–10). 1991, Morrow $16.00 (0-688-09365-5); 1992, Penguin paper $4.99 (0-14-036003-4). Drawing on his mother's childhood, Yep depicts a Chinese family's experiences when they arrive in West Virginia in 1927 to open a laundry. (Rev: BL 5/15/91; SLJ 5/91)

606 Yep, Laurence. *Thief of Hearts* (5–8). 1995, HarperCollins $15.89 (0-06-025342-8). Stacy learns of her mixed Chinese and American heritage when she, her mother, and great-grandmother travel to San Francisco's Chinatown. (Rev: BL 7/95; SLJ 8/95)

Family Life and Problems

607 Adler, C. S. *Ghost Brother* (6–8). 1990, Clarion $15.00 (0-395-52592-6). Visits from his dead brother help Wally adjust to his death and to the presence of Aunt Flo, who has come to take care of him. (Rev: BL 5/15/90; SLJ 5/90; VOYA 8/90)

608 Alcock, Vivien. *The Cuckoo Sister* (6–9). 1997, Houghton paper $4.95 (0-395-81651-3). A tough street waif appears at the Setons' door in London and claims to be the older daughter kidnapped many years before. (Rev: BL 8/86; SLJ 4/86; VOYA 8/86)

609 Alvarez, Julia. *Yo!* (10–12). 1997, Algonquin $29.95 (1-56512-157-0). The 16 stories in this collection feature the family and friends of Yolanda Garcia, whose roots are in the Dominican Republic. (Rev: BL 9/15/96; SLJ 4/97)

610 Anderson, Janet S. *The Monkey Tree* (6–9). 1998, Dutton $15.99 (0-525-46032-2). Susanna's life seems to be coming apart, her grandmother has just died, the family has taken in reclusive Uncle Louie, her best friend has abandoned her, and her art teacher no longer thinks her work is good. (Rev: BL 11/15/98; SLJ 11/98; VOYA 6/99)

611 Avi. *Sometimes I Think I Hear My Name* (6–9). 1995, Avon paper $4.50 (0-380-72424-3). A young boy disobeys his guardians to visit New York and find his parents.

612 Bauer, Joan. *Backwater* (7–10). 1999, Putnam $16.99 (0-399-23141-2). When 16-year-old Ivy Breedlove begins working on her family history, the trail leads to the New York State Adirondacks and eccentric, talented Aunt Jo. (Rev: BL 5/15/99; SLJ 6/99; VOYA 8/99)

613 Bauer, Joan. *Rules of the Road* (6–10). 1998, Putnam $16.99 (0-399-23140-4). Jenna Boller is the confident, smart, and moral heroine of this novel that deals with the effects of alcoholism on a family and a girl's growing friendship with a wealthy, elderly woman. (Rev: BL 2/1/98; BR 1–2/99; SLJ 3/98*; VOYA 6/98)

614   Bawden, Nina. *The Outside Child* (6–8). 1994, Puffin paper $3.99 (0-14-036858-2). Jane discovers that her absent father remarried years ago and has a family she would like to meet. (Rev: BL 9/1/89; BR 3–4/90; SLJ 10/89; VOYA 12/89)

615   Bechard, Margaret. *If It Doesn't Kill You* (9–12). 1999, Viking $15.99 (0-670-88547-9). Ben, a fine high school football player, is unhappy to be compared to his father, also a star athlete, because Ben has discovered his father is gay. (Rev: BL 7/99; SLJ 7/99)

616   Bechard, Margaret. *My Mom Married the Principal* (5–8). 1998, Viking $14.99 (0-670-87394-2). For Jonah the eighth grade is the pits, and having his stepfather as principal doesn't help. (Rev: BL 3/1/98; SLJ 3/98; VOYA 2/98)

617   Berne, Suzanne. *A Crime in the Neighborhood* (10–12). 1997, Algonquin $28.95 (1-56512-165-1). A hurt and confused girl who can't accept her father's desertion begins to analyze her family and neighborhood using the same methods as Sherlock Holmes. (Rev: BL 4/15/97; SLJ 12/97)

618   Berry, James. *A Thief in the Village and Other Stories* (7–12). 1988, Penguin paper $4.99 (0-14-034357-1). Nine stories about a teenager in Jamaica and everyday life on this Caribbean island. (Rev: BL 4/15/88; BR 9–10/88)

619   Birdseye, Tom. *Tucker* (5–8). 1990, Holiday House $15.95 (0-8234-0813-2). A story set in rural Kentucky of a young boy reunited with his younger sister after 7 years of separation caused by divorce. (Rev: BL 7/90; SLJ 6/90)

620   Bledsoe, Jerry. *The Angel Doll* (10–12). 1997, St. Martin's $13.95 (0-312-17104-8). This novel tells how 10-year-old Whitey and his friends work together to grant the wish of Whitey's 4-year-old sister, a polio victim, to receive for Christmas a doll like the one in "The Littlest Angel." (Rev: BL 11/1/97; SLJ 2/98)

621   Block, Francesca L. *The Hanged Man* (10–12). 1994, HarperCollins LB $15.89 (0-06-024537-9). Against a backdrop of Hollywood excess, alienated Laura struggles to cope with her dead father's acts of incest while her mother lives in denial. (Rev: BL 9/15/94; SLJ 9/94; VOYA 12/94)

622   Block, Francesca L. *Witch Baby* (7–12). 1992, HarperCollins paper $4.95 (0-06-447065-2). This sequel to *Weetzie Bat* focuses on the foundling Witch Baby as she searches for her parents. (Rev: BL 8/91; SLJ 9/91*)

623   Blume, Judy. *It's Not the End of the World* (6–8). 1972, Bradbury LB $17.00 (0-02-711050-8); Dell paper $4.99 (0-440-44158-7). Karen cannot believe that her parents are heading for a divorce.

624   Bond, Nancy. *Truth to Tell* (6–8). 1994, Macmillan paper $17.95 (0-689-50601-5). A 14-year-old girl finds herself on her way to New Zealand with her mother and not really understanding the reason for the relocation. (Rev: BL 4/15/94; SLJ 6/94; VOYA 8/94)

625   Bonosky, Phillip. *A Bird in Her Hair and Other Stories* (9–12). 1987, International Pubs. paper $5.95 (0-7178-0661-8). A collection of short stories about the struggles of working people in Pennsylvania from the 1930s into the 1950s. (Rev: BL 2/15/88)

626   Boswell, Robert. *Mystery Ride* (9–12). 1993, Knopf $22.00 (0-679-41292-1). Angela, unable to control her defiant daughter Dulcie, 15, drives her to Iowa, where Dulcie is expected to spend the summer with Dulcie's father, Angela's compassionate ex-husband. (Rev: BL 12/15/92*)

627   Boyd, Candy Dawson. *Chevrolet Saturdays* (5–10). 1993, Macmillan LB $16.00 (0-02-711765-0). After his parents divorce, Joey's mother marries Mr. Johnson, but Joey rejects and alienates his kindly stepfather. When Joey makes amends, new family ties are formed. (Rev: BL 5/15/93; SLJ 5/93)

628   Bradbury, Ray. *Dandelion Wine* (9–12). 1975, Knopf $24.95 (0-394-49605-1); Bantam paper $6.50 (0-553-27753-7). A tender novel about one summer in the life of a 12-year-old boy growing up in a small Illinois town during 1928. A reissue.

629   Bridgers, Sue Ellen. *Home Before Dark* (7–10). 1998, Replica Books $29.95 (0-7351-0053-5). A migrant worker and his family settle down in a permanent home.

630   Bridgers, Sue Ellen. *Notes for Another Life* (7–12). 1981, Knopf LB $13.99 (0-394-94889-0). A brother and sister cope with a frequently absent mother and a mentally ill father. (Rev: BL 9/1/85; SLJ 10/85; VOYA 4/86)

631   Brooks, Bruce. *Midnight Hour Encores* (7–10). 1986, HarperCollins paper $4.95 (0-06-447021-0). Cello-playing Sib and her father Taxi take a transcontinental trip to meet Sib's mother, who left after her birth. (Rev: BL 9/15/86; SLJ 9/86; VOYA 12/86)

632   Bunting, Eve. *A Sudden Silence* (7–12). 1988, Harcourt $14.95 (0-15-282058-2). Jesse sets out to find the hit-and-run driver who killed his brother. (Rev: BL 4/15/88; SLJ 5/88)

633   Bunting, Eve. *Surrogate Sister* (7–10). 1984, HarperCollins LB $13.89 (0-397-32099-X). A 16-year-old girl copes with a pregnant mother who has offered to be a surrogate mother for a childless couple.

634   Bunting, Eve. *Will You Be My Posslq?* (9–12). 1987, Harcourt $12.95 (0-15-297399-0). Without her parents' approval freshman Kyle asks her friend Jamie to become her posslq (person of opposite sex sharing living quarters). (Rev: BL 10/1/87; SLJ 10/87; VOYA 4/88)

635 Burch, Robert. *Ida Early Comes over the Mountain* (5–8). 1980, Avon paper $2.50 (0-380-57091-2). The 4 Sutton kids find a new and most unusual housekeeper in Ida.

636 Byalick, Marcia. *It's a Matter of Trust* (7–9). 1995, Browndeer $11.00 (0-15-276660-X); paper $5.00 (0-15-200240-5). Erika's father confesses to a white-collar crime, and this novel traces the effects of this confession on the family, particularly on 16-year-old Erika and her relations with boyfriend Greg. (Rev: BR 1–2/96; SLJ 12/95; VOYA 2/96)

637 Byars, Betsy. *The Glory Girl* (6–8). 1985, Puffin paper $4.99 (0-14-031785-6). Anna, part of a family of gospel singers, teams up with an uncle fresh from prison to help in a family crisis.

638 Cadnum, Michael. *Taking It* (9–12). 1995, Viking paper $15.99 (0-670-86130-8). Anna shoplifts as a way to test her limits amid her parents' divorce and her feelings of alienation from family and friends. But it eventually catches up to her. (Rev: BL 7/95*; SLJ 8/95; VOYA 2/96)

639 Cadnum, Michael. *Zero at the Bone* (8–12). 1996, Viking paper $15.99 (0-670-86725-X). Anita, Cray's independent older sister, mysteriously disappears and, then, several months later, a body is found that meets her general description. (Rev: BL 8/96*; BR 1–2/97; SLJ 7/96*; VOYA 2/97)

640 Calvert, Patricia. *Glennis, Before and After* (6–8). 1996, Simon & Schuster $16.00 (0-689-80641-8). When her father is sent to prison for fraud, 12-year-old Glennis is sent to live with her eccentric, much-divorced Aunt Wanda. (Rev: BL 9/1/96; BR 5–6/97; SLJ 9/96)

641 Campbell, Bebe Moore. *Singing in the Comeback Choir* (10–12). 1998, Putnam $24.95 (0-399-14298-3); Berkley paper $7.50 (0-425-16662-7). This is the story of 2 strong black women, Maxine, a television producer with marital problems, and her grandmother, Lindy, a former blues singer, who has just suffered a minor stroke. (Rev: SLJ 4/99)

642 Caseley, Judith. *Losing Louisa* (8–12). 1999, Farrar paper $17.00 (0-374-34665-8). Lacey Levine, 16, who is living with her immature, profane mother, discovers that her older unmarried sister is pregnant. (Rev: BL 3/1/99; SLJ 3/99; VOYA 6/99)

643 Casey, Maude. *Over the Water* (7–12). 1994, Holt $15.95 (0-8050-3276-2). A young girl's rite of passage from dissension with her controlling mother to understanding her mother as a person. (Rev: BL 5/15/94; SLJ 6/94*; VOYA 8/94)

644 Christian, Mary Blount. *Growin' Pains* (6–8). 1985, Penguin paper $3.95 (0-317-63785-1). With the help of a disabled neighbor, Ginny Ruth contin-

ues to develop her writing talent in spite of her mother's objections. (Rev: BL 2/1/86; BR 5–6/86)

645 Christiansen, C. B. *A Small Pleasure* (7–10). 1988, Macmillan $13.95 (0-689-31369-1). A young high school girl hides her grief over her father's fatal cancer by becoming the most popular girl in school. (Rev: BL 4/1/88; BR 9–10/88; SLJ 3/88; VOYA 6/88)

646 Cleary, Beverly. *Sister of the Bride* (7–9). 1963, Morrow LB $16.93 (0-688-31742-1); Avon paper $4.99 (0-380-72807-9). A young girl becomes too involved with the plans for her sister's wedding.

647 Cleaver, Vera. *Sweetly Sings the Donkey* (6–9). Illus. 1985, HarperCollins LB $12.89 (0-397-32157-0). Fourteen-year-old Lily Snow and her family hope that their inheritance in Florida will help them financially but this is not to be. (Rev: BL 10/1/85)

648 Cleaver, Vera, and Bill Cleaver. *Dust of the Earth* (7–9). 1975, HarperCollins $13.95 (0-397-31650-X). Fern and her family face problems when they move to a farm in South Dakota. (Rev: BL 3/1/89)

649 Cleaver, Vera, and Bill Cleaver. *Queen of Hearts* (7–9). 1978, HarperCollins $14.00 (0-397-31771-9). Wilma must take care of her grandmother whom she really dislikes.

650 Cleaver, Vera, and Bill Cleaver. *Where the Lilies Bloom* (6–10). Illus. 1969, HarperCollins $15.95 (0-397-31111-7). When her father dies, Mary Call must take care of her 2 siblings and keep the family together. A sequel is: *Trial Valley*. (Rev: BL 2/1/89)

651 Clements, Bruce. *Anywhere Else but Here* (7–9). 1989, Farrar paper $3.50 (0-374-40420-8). Mollie's father faces poverty until he discovers the value in a dollhouse.

652 Close, Jessie. *The Warping of Al* (9–12). 1990, HarperCollins $15.95 (0-06-021280-2). Al tries to cope with a domineering father and a subservient mother. (Rev: BL 1/1/91; SLJ 9/90)

653 Cole, Brock. *The Facts Speak for Themselves* (9–12). 1997, Front Street $15.95 (1-886910-14-6). A ground-breaking, sexually explicit story about Linda and how the experiences in her life lead to murder. (Rev: BL 10/1/97; SLJ 10/97*; VOYA 12/97)

654 Collier, James L. *Outside Looking In* (6–8). 1990, Avon paper $2.95 (0-380-70961-9). Fergie and his sister hate the nomadic life their parents lead and long to settle down. (Rev: BL 4/1/87; BR 9–10/87; SLJ 5/87; VOYA 10/87)

655 Colman, Hila. *Diary of a Frantic Kid Sister* (6–8). 1975, Archway paper $2.95 (0-671-61926-8). In diary format, Sarah tells of the frustrations of growing up in the shadow of a glamorous older sister.

656 Colman, Hila. *Rich and Famous Like My Mom* (6–9). 1988, Crown $10.95 (0-517-56836-5). Cassandra is growing up in the shadow of her mother, a world-famous rock star. (Rev: BL 6/15/88)

657 Coman, Carolyn. *Bee and Jacky* (9–12). 1998, Front Street $14.95 (1-886910-33-2). This is a controversial novel about the emotional consequences of a incestuous relationship between a 17-year-old boy and his younger sister. (Rev: BL 10/1/98; SLJ 11/98; VOYA 12/98)

658 Coman, Carolyn. *What Jamie Saw* (5–8). 1995, Front Street $13.95 (1-886910-02-2). A tale about a young boy with an abusive father from whom he, his mother, and baby sister flee. (Rev: BL 12/15/95*; SLJ 12/95*)

659 Conly, Jane L. *Crazy Lady!* (5–8). 1993, HarperCollins LB $13.89 (0-06-021360-4). In a poor city neighborhood, Vernon, failing seventh grade, befriends Maxine—who hollers and screams on the street when she's drunk—and helps care for her disabled teenage son. (Rev: BL 5/15/93*; SLJ 4/93*)

660 Conly, Jane L. *When No One Was Watching* (5–8). 1995, Holt $16.95 (0-8050-3934-1). When 11-year-old Earl and his 2 younger siblings are left in the care of inattentive Aunt Lulu by their traveling father and must fend for themselves, Earl unwittingly becomes an accomplice when Lulu's son uses him to help steal bicycles and rob the homeless. (Rev: BL 5/15/98; SLJ 7/98)

661 Conrad, Pam. *Holding Me Here* (7–9). 1986, HarperCollins LB $12.89 (0-06-021339-6). Robin attempts to help a divorced woman who is hiding from her abusive former husband and fails tragically. (Rev: BL 3/15/86; BR 11–12/86; SLJ 3/86; VOYA 6/86)

662 Conrad, Pam. *My Daniel* (6–9). 1989, HarperCollins LB $15.89 (0-06-021314-0). A grandmother's trip to a science museum unlocks memories of her own childhood. (Rev: BL 4/15/89; BR 11–12/89; SLJ 4/89; VOYA 6/89)

663 Conroy, Pat. *The Great Santini* (10–12). 1987, Bantam paper $7.99 (0-553-26892-9). This novel about family discourse centers on a Marine captain who treats his family as he does his troops. (Rev: BL 2/15/91)

664 Cook, Karin. *What Girls Learn: A Novel* (10–12). 1997, Pantheon $23.00 (0-679-44828-4). In this emotional novel, Tilden, an adolescent girl, and her slightly younger sister move with their mother to suburban Long Island, where Tilden has social problems and her mother discovers she is dying of cancer. (Rev: BL 2/15/97; BR 9–10/97; SLJ 7/97)

665 Cooney, Caroline B. *Tune in Anytime* (7–10). 1999, Delacorte $8.95 (0-385-32649-1). When her father files for divorce to marry his older daughter's college roommate and her mother is too self-involved to do anything it, Sophie's life seems to fly out of control. (Rev: SLJ 9/99; VOYA 12/99)

666 Cooney, Caroline B. *The Voice on the Radio* (7–10). 1996, Delacorte $15.95 (0-385-32213-5). In this sequel to *The Face on the Milk Carton* and *Whatever Happened to Janie?*, Janie realizes that her betrayer is actually her boyfriend, Reeve. (Rev: BL 10/1/96; BR 3–4/97; SLJ 9/96*; VOYA 12/96)

667 Cooney, Caroline B. *Whatever Happened to Janie?* (6–10). 1993, Delacorte $15.95 (0-385-31035-8); 1994, Dell paper $3.99 (0-440-21924-8). Janie, 15, after discovering she's a missing child on a milk carton, returns to her birth family, which has been searching for her since her kidnapping at age 3. Sequel to *The Face on the Milk Carton*. (Rev: BL 6/1–15/93; SLJ 6/93; VOYA 8/93)

668 Cooper, Ilene. *Buddy Love: Now on Video* (5–8). 1995, HarperCollins LB $13.89 (0-06-024664-2). A boy gets a camcorder and begins to see his family, friends, and eventually himself through a new lens. (Rev: BL 9/15/95; SLJ 10/95; VOYA 4/96)

669 Corcoran, Barbara. *Family Secrets* (5–8). 1992, Atheneum LB $13.95 (0-689-31744-1). A teenager contemplates the advantages and disadvantages of family after discovering she was adopted. (Rev: BL 3/1/92; SLJ 2/92)

670 Corcoran, Barbara. *I Am the Universe* (6–8). 1993, Harcourt paper $14.00 (0-15-300366-9). With an indifferent father at home and her mother seriously ill in the hospital, Katherine and her older brother take care of the house. (Rev: BL 10/1/86; SLJ 10/86; VOYA 12/86)

671 Corcoran, Barbara. *The Potato Kid* (6–8). 1993, Avon paper $3.50 (0-380-71213-X). The Ellis family decides to help a 10-year-old child from a poor Maine family and then the problems begin. (Rev: BL 11/15/89; SLJ 10/89; VOYA 2/90)

672 Creech, Sharon. *Walk Two Moons* (7–9). 1994, HarperCollins LB $15.89 (0-06-023337-0). The story of Sal, 13, who goes to Idaho with her grandparents to be with her mother, who has actually been killed in a bus accident. (Rev: BL 11/15/94; SLJ 10/94*; VOYA 2/95)

673 Cross, Gillian. *Chartbreaker* (8–12). 1987, Holiday House $15.95 (0-8234-0647-4). Janis, a lead singer with a British rock group, tells her story. (Rev: BL 3/1/87; SLJ 4/87; VOYA 8/87)

674 Cummings, Priscilla. *Autumn Journey* (4–8). 1997, Cobblehill paper $14.99 (0-525-65238-8). Tensions in the family mount when Will's father loses his job and the family has to move to Grampa's farm in Pennsylvania. (Rev: SLJ 10/97)

675 Danziger, Paula. *The Divorce Express* (6–9). 1998, Putnam paper $3.99 (0-698-11685-2). A 14-year-old girl divides time between her divorced parents.

676 Danziger, Paula. *It's an Aardvark-Eat-Turtle World* (6–9). 1996, Bantam paper $3.99 (0-440-41399-0). When Rosie's father and the mother of her best friend move in together, complications begin. (Rev: BL 3/1/85; BR 9–10/85; SLJ 4/85; VOYA 6/85)

677 Danziger, Paula. *The Pistachio Prescription* (6–9). 1999, Putnam paper $3.99 (0-698-11690-9). Cassie, 13 years old, faces many family and personal problems including a compulsive need for pistachio nuts.

678 Deaver, Julie Reece. *Chicago Blues* (6–10). 1995, HarperCollins $15.95 (0-06-024675-8). Two sisters are forced to make it on their own because of an alcoholic mother and experience struggle, success, and eventual forgiveness. (Rev: BL 9/1/95; SLJ 8/95; VOYA 12/95)

679 Deedy, Carmen A. *The Last Dance* (7–10). Illus. 1995, Peachtree $16.95 (1-56145-109-6). A picture book for young adults that tells of the abiding love through the years of husband and wife Ninny and Bessie. (Rev: BL 1/1–15/96; SLJ 1/96)

680 Deem, James M. *3 NBs of Julian Drew* (7–12). 1994, Houghton $15.95 (0-395-69453-1). Julian, 15, is emotionally and physically abused by his father and his demented stepmother. He finds strength by writing to his deceased mother in coded notebooks. (Rev: BL 10/15/94; SLJ 10/94*; VOYA 12/94)

681 Delinsky, Barbara. *Coast Road* (10–12). 1998, Simon & Schuster $24.00 (0-684-84576-8). When Jack McGill's ex-wife lies close to death after an auto accident, he and his 2 teenage daughters piece together the history of his failed marriage. (Rev: BL 5/1/98; SLJ 12/98)

682 Derby, Pat. *Grams, Her Boyfriend, My Family and Me* (7–10). 1994, Farrar $16.00 (0-374-38131-3). A laid-back teenager finds himself becoming involved in family politics when his mother returns to work and his grandmother comes to live in their tiny house. (Rev: BL 3/15/94; SLJ 11/94*; VOYA 4/94)

683 Dewey, Jennifer O. *Navajo Summer* (5–8). Illus. 1998, Boyds Mills $14.95 (1-56397-248-4). When family life becomes intolerable to 12-year-old Jamie, she runs away to spend time with the Wilsons, a close-knit Navajo family she met when horse-trading with her father. (Rev: BL 10/1/98; SLJ 11/98)

684 Doherty, Berlie. *The Snake-Stone* (6–10). 1996, Orchard LB $16.99 (0-531-08862-6). Fifteen-year-

old James tries to come to terms with his childhood adoption by setting out to find his biological parents. (Rev: BL 2/15/96; BR 11–12/96; SLJ 6/96*; VOYA 6/96)

685 Doody, Margaret Anne, ed. *The Annotated Anne of Green Gables* (7–12). 1997, Oxford $44.95 (0-19-510428-5). The novel is accompanied by a biography of Lucy Maud Montgomery and notes and annotations explaining references to the places, people, and settings in Prince Edward island that figure in the story. (Rev: SLJ 3/98; VOYA 6/98)

686 Dorris, Michael. *The Window* (6–9). 1997, Hyperion $16.95 (0-7868-0301-0). When her mother is placed in an alcohol rehab center, 11-year-old Rayona Taylor, half-black and half-Native American, must visit her father's relatives in Louisville. (Rev: BL 9/15/97; BR 3–4/98; SLJ 11/97)

687 Duffey, Betsy. *Coaster* (5–8). 1994, Viking paper $13.99 (0-670-85480-8). Hart, 12, barely sees his father since his parents' divorce and desperately hopes he will show up for their annual roller-coaster trip. (Rev: BL 8/94; SLJ 9/94; VOYA 4/95)

688 Farmer, Penelope. *Penelope* (5–8). 1996, Simon & Schuster paper $16.00 (0-689-80121-1). Flora, who is being raised by her aunt's family in London, believes that she lived a previous life as Penelope, an 18th-century lord's daughter. (Rev: BL 4/1/96; SLJ 5/96; VOYA 8/96)

689 Ferris, Jean. *Relative Strangers* (6–10). 1993, Farrar $16.00 (0-374-36243-2). The child of separated parents, Berkeley must learn to accept her father as less than the idealized fantasy she imagined when he takes her to Europe with his new family. (Rev: BL 10/1/93; VOYA 12/93)

690 Feuer, Elizabeth. *Lost Summer* (5–8). 1995, Farrar $16.00 (0-374-31020-3). A 12-year-old girl is shipped off to camp one summer as her parents reconstruct their lives following divorce. (Rev: BL 5/15/95; SLJ 5/95)

691 Fine, Anne. *The Book of the Banshee* (6–9). 1992, Little, Brown $13.95 (0-316-28315-0). English teenager Will Flowers's younger sister, Estelle, has become a banshee, and he decides his family life is like an account of World War I he is reading. (Rev: BL 12/1/91*)

692 Fleischman, Paul. *Rear-View Mirrors* (7–10). 1986, HarperCollins $12.95 (0-06-021866-2). After her father's death, Olivia relives through memory a summer when she and her estranged father reconciled. (Rev: BL 3/1/86; BR 11–12/86; SLJ 5/86; VOYA 8/86)

693 Foggo, Cheryl. *One Thing That's True* (5–8). 1998, Kids Can $14.95 (1-55074-411-9). Roxanne is heartbroken when her older brother runs away after learning that he is adopted. (Rev: BL 2/15/98; BR 11–12/98; SLJ 4/98)

694 Forbes, Kathryn. *Mama's Bank Account* (7–10). 1968, Harcourt paper $6.95 (0-15-656377-0). The story, told in vignettes, of a loving Norwegian family and of Mama's mythical bank account.

695 Fox, Paula. *The Eagle Kite* (6–10). 1995, Orchard LB $16.99 (0-531-08742-5). Liam goes through a tangle of denial, anger, shame, grief, and empathy after learning that his father is dying of AIDS. His mother says he got it from a blood transfusion, but Liam remembers seeing his father embrace a young man 2 years before. (Rev: BL 2/1/95*; SLJ 4/95*; VOYA 5/95)

696 Fox, Paula. *The Moonlight Man* (8–12). 1986, Bradbury LB $14.95 (0-02-735480-6). During a stay together in a house in Nova Scotia, teenager Catherine learns more about her adored alcoholic father than she wants to. (Rev: BL 4/15/86; SLJ 4/86; VOYA 8/86)

697 Fox, Paula. *The Village by the Sea* (6–8). 1988, Orchard $16.95 (0-531-05788-7). A 10-year-old girl is sent to live with an aunt whom she grows to despise. (Rev: BL 9/1/88; VOYA 10/88)

698 Fox, Paula. *Western Wind* (6–9). 1993, Orchard LB $17.99 (0-531-08652-6). Elizabeth is sent to live for a month with her beloved Gran on an island off Maine, but she's not told of Gran's serious heart condition. (Rev: BL 10/15/93; SLJ 12/93*; VOYA 12/93)

699 Franklin, Kristine L. *Dove Song* (5–8). 1999, Candlewick $16.99 (0-7636-0409-7). When their father in declared missing in action during the Vietnam War and their mother sinks into a deep depression, Bobbie and her older brother must fend for themselves. (Rev: BL 10/15/99; SLJ 9/99)

700 Franklin, Kristine L. *Eclipse* (6–9). 1995, Candlewick $14.99 (1-56402-544-6). A young girl feels confused and powerless when her father becomes ill and her family seems to fall apart. (Rev: BL 3/15/95; SLJ 4/95)

701 Fraustino, Lisa R., ed. *Dirty Laundry: Stories about Family Secrets* (9–12). 1998, Viking $16.99 (0-670-87911-8). A collection of 11 original stories by YA writers exploring various family relationships and secrets. (Rev: BL 5/15/98; SLJ 7/98; VOYA 12/98)

702 Fredriksson, Marianne. *Hanna's Daughters: A Novel of Three Generations* (10–12). Trans. from Swedish by Joan Tate. 1998, Ballantine $24.00 (0-345-42664-9). In this multigenerational novel set in Sweden, Anna recounts the difficult lives of her mother, Johanna, and grandmother, Hanna, and then tells about her own life. (Rev: BL 7/98; SLJ 3/99)

703 Freeman, Suzanne. *The Cuckoo's Child* (5–8). 1996, Greenwillow $15.00 (0-688-14290-7). In 1962, Mia and her 2 older half-sisters are sent from Lebanon by their parents to spend a safe summer with Aunt Kit in Ionia, Tennessee. (Rev: BL 3/15/96*; BR 9–10/96; SLJ 4/96*)

704 Friesen, Gayle. *Janey's Girl* (6–9). 1998, Kids Can $14.95 (1-55074-461-5). When Claire and her mother visit her mother's hometown in rural British Columbia, the young girl meets her father for the first time and begins to find out truths about her family's past. (Rev: SLJ 11/98)

705 Fuqua, Jonathon Scott. *The Reappearance of Sam Webber* (9–12). 1999, Bancroft $23.95 (1-890862-02-9). Confused and lonely, 11-year-old Sam can't adjust to the disappearance of his father and, when his mother is forced to move to a poor neighborhood in Baltimore, Sam faces new problems, including the school bully. (Rev: BL 3/1/99; SLJ 7/99)

706 Gaarder, Jostein. *The Solitaire Mystery* (10–12). Trans. from Norwegian by Sarah Jane Hails. Illus. 1996, Farrar $22.00 (0-374-26651-4). During a journey with his father to find his mother who disappeared years before, 12-year-old Hans Thomas is entertained by reading about the fantastic adventures of Baker Hans who traveled to a land where playing cards came to life. (Rev: BL 7/96; BR 3–4/97; SLJ 9/96; VOYA 12/96)

707 Garden, Nancy. *Lark in the Morning* (7–10). 1991, Farrar $14.95 (0-374-34338-1). Gillie tries to keep 2 secrets from her parents: that she has discovered 2 abused runaways are living on the family's property and that she is gay. (Rev: BL 7/91; SLJ 6/91)

708 Garland, Sherry. *Rainmaker's Dream* (6–9). 1997, Harcourt paper $6.00 (0-15-200652-4). After her family falls apart, 13-year-old Caroline runs away to a Wild West show where she discovers a secret about her mother's identity. (Rev: BL 4/1/97; SLJ 6/97)

709 Gates, Doris. *Blue Willow* (5–8). 1940, Penguin paper $4.99 (0-14-030924-1). An easily read novel about a poor girl and the china plate that belonged to her mother.

710 Giff, Patricia Reilly. *The Gift of the Pirate Queen* (7–9). Illus. 1983, Dell paper $3.99 (0-440-43046-1). Grace's problems, which include taking care of a father and a diabetic sister, are reduced with the arrival of an Irish cousin.

711 Gottlieb, Eli. *The Boy Who Went Away* (10–12). 1997, St. Martin's $21.95 (0-312-15070-9). An autobiographical novel set in New Jersey in 1967 about a teenage boy growing up in a family with a mentally ill older brother. (Rev: BL 12/15/96; SLJ 5/97)

712 Grant, Cynthia D. *Mary Wolf* (7–12). 1995, Atheneum $16.78 (0-689-80007-X). A tale of a homeless family in which the only person who is logical and reasonable is the 16-year-old daughter. (Rev: BL 10/1/95; SLJ 10/95; VOYA 12/95)

713 Grant, Cynthia D. *Shadow Man* (7–12). 1992, Atheneum $13.95 (0-689-31772-7). Chapters are narrated by various inhabitants of a California town where Gabriel, 18, is found dead in a car accident after leaving a party alone and drunk. (Rev: BL 11/1/92; SLJ 10/92)

714 Greene, Constance C. *Nora: Maybe a Ghost Story* (6–8). 1993, Harcourt $10.95 (0-15-277696-6); paper $4.95 (0-15-276895-5). When Nora and Patsy's father announces his intention to marry after 3 years of widowhood, they have to deal with resentment and their mother's ghostly presence. (Rev: BL 10/1/93; VOYA 12/93)

715 Griffin, Adele. *Dive* (5–8). 1999, Hyperion LB $15.49 (0-7868-2389-5). The story of 2 stepbrothers and their troubled relationship. (Rev: BL 9/15/99; VOYA 12/99)

716 Griffin, Adele. *Other Shepards* (5–8). 1998, Disney $14.95 (0-7868-0423-8). The 2 Shepard children live under the specter of the death of their 3 older siblings before they were born, but then Annie arrives in the household and gives them a new lease on life. (Rev: BL 8/98; SLJ 9/98; VOYA 10/98)

717 Griffin, Adele. *Split Just Right* (5–8). 1997, Hyperion LB $15.49 (0-7868-2288-0); Disney paper $5.99 (0-7868-1295-8). Even though Danny's father has been gone as long as she can remember, she still wonders about him. (Rev: BL 6/1–15/97; SLJ 6/97)

718 Griffin, Peni R. *Vikki Vanishes* (6–9). 1995, Macmillan paper $15.00 (0-689-80028-2). A long-absent dad shows up and enchants and steals away his 16-year-old daughter. (Rev: BL 5/15/95; SLJ 9/95)

719 Grunwald, Lisa. *New Year's Eve* (10–12). 1997, Crown $24.00 (0-517-70491-9). Using observances of New Year's Eve from 1985 through 1991 as a focus, this novel tells of a family's adjustment to the death of a 4-year-old son and how the family members gradually build for the future. (Rev: BL 11/1/96; SLJ 7/97)

720 Guest, Judith. *Errands* (10–12). 1997, Ballantine $25.00 (0-345-40904-3). When her husband of 17 years dies of cancer, Annie Browner must find ways to support herself and her 3 children. (Rev: BL 10/15/96; SLJ 7/97; VOYA 8/97)

721 Guest, Judith. *Ordinary People* (10–12). 1982, Viking paper $8.95 (0-14-006517-2). The accidental death of one of 2 sons brings a family to crisis and disintegration. (Rev: BL 6/1/88)

722 Haas, Dan. *You Can Call Me Worm* (6–9). 1997, Houghton $15.00 (0-395-85783-X). Will, also known as Worm, and his brother are determined to visit their emotionally unstable father whom they are forbidden to see. (Rev: BL 10/15/97; BR 3–4/98; SLJ 11/97; VOYA 2/98)

723 Haddix, Margaret P. *Don't You Dare Read This, Mrs. Dunphrey* (7–10). 1996, Simon & Schuster paper $16.99 (0-689-80097-5). Tish keeps a journal for her sophomore English class in which she chronicles her many family problems culminating in the abandonment of herself and little brother by her parents. (Rev: BL 10/15/96; SLJ 10/96; VOYA 12/96)

724 Hahn, Mary D. *As Ever, Gordy* (5–8). 1998, Houghton $15.00 (0-395-83627-1). The life of 13-year-old Gordy becomes a series of problems and he seems destined to reform school when he goes to live with his older brother's family. A sequel to *Stepping on the Cracks* and *Following My Own Footsteps*. (Rev: BL 5/1/98; BR 11–12/98; SLJ 7/98; VOYA 4/99)

725 Hall, Barbara. *Dixie Storms* (7–12). 1990, Harcourt $15.95 (0-15-223825-5). Dutch's troubled relationships within her family worsen when cousin Norma comes to stay. (Rev: BL 5/1/90; SLJ 9/90)

726 Hall, Lynn. *Flying Changes* (7–12). 1991, Harcourt $13.95 (0-15-228790-6). An awkward Kansas teenager must give up her romantic dreams after her father is paralyzed and her mother, who abandoned her years before, returns home. (Rev: BL 6/15/91*)

727 Hamilton, Virginia. *Junius Over Far* (9–12). 1985, HarperCollins $12.95 (0-06-022194-1). Fearful that grandfather is lonely as he approaches death on a Caribbean island, 14-year-old Junius and his father go to visit him. (Rev: BL 5/15/85; BR 11–12/85; SLJ 8/85; VOYA 6/85)

728 Hamilton, Virginia. *M.C. Higgins, the Great* (6–10). 1974, Macmillan LB $17.00 (0-02-742480-4); paper $4.99 (0-02-043490-1). A young black boy growing up in Appalachia uses the strength of his family's past to ensure its future. Newbery Medal 1975.

729 Hamilton, Virginia. *Second Cousins* (5–8). 1998, Scholastic $14.95 (0-590-47368-9). In this sequel to *Cousins*, 12-year-old Cammy learns a family secret during a family reunion in her small Ohio town. (Rev: BL 8/98; SLJ 11/98; VOYA 2/99)

730 Hassler, Jon. *Grand Opening* (9–12). 1987, Ballantine paper $6.99 (0-345-35016-2). The Foster family moves to a small, unfriendly town to open up a grocery store. (Rev: BR 11–12/87; SLJ 2/88)

731 Hathorn, Libby. *Thunderwith* (7–10). 1991, Little, Brown $15.95 (0-316-35034-6). This story of an unhappy 15-year-old girl and a beautiful dingolike dog she finds is set in the Australian rain forest. (Rev: BL 9/1/91; SLJ 5/91*)

732 Hausman, Gerald. *Doctor Moledinky's Castle: A Hometown Tale* (5–8). 1995, Simon & Schuster paper $15.00 (0-689-80019-3). Twelve-year-old Andy and his best friend, Pauly, 11, spend the summer of 1957 getting involved in adventures and getting to know the different personalities in their hometown, Berkeley Bend, New Jersey. (Rev: BL 12/1/95; SLJ 10/95; VOYA 2/96)

733 Haynes, David. *Right by My Side* (9–12). 1993, New Rivers paper $12.95 (0-89823-147-7). African American teen Marshall Field Finney describes a year of his life—the year his mother left him and his father ran away to Las Vegas to find himself. (Rev: BL 2/15/93*; SLJ 12/93)

734 Hermes, Patricia. *Cheat the Moon: A Novel* (5–8). Illus. 1998, Little, Brown $15.95 (0-316-35929-7). After her mother's death, 12-year-old Gabby takes care of herself and her younger brother, with occasional help from her alcoholic father. (Rev: BL 6/1–15/98; BR 11–12/98; SLJ 6/98; VOYA 8/98)

735 Hernandez, Irene B. *The Secret of Two Brothers* (7–10). 1995, Arte Publico $14.95 (1-55885-141-0); paper $9.95 (1-55885-142-9). An action-packed story about 2 Mexican American boys who meet many challenges. Especially appealing to those whose first language is Spanish or for reluctant readers. (Rev: BL 10/1/95; SLJ 11/95)

736 Hickman, Janet. *Jericho* (5–8). 1994, Greenwillow $15.00 (0-688-13398-3). Angela, 12, resents having to care for her elderly, increasingly forgetful grandmother, Arminda. As Angela learns of Arminda's life, she begins to connect it to her own. (Rev: BL 9/1/94; SLJ 9/94)

737 High, Linda O. *Maizie* (5–8). 1995, Holiday House $14.95 (0-8234-1161-3). The mother of tough, resilient Maizie has left, and Maizie must care for her sister and her father, who drinks too much. (Rev: BL 4/15/95; SLJ 4/95)

738 Hinton, S. E. *Taming the Star Runner* (7–12). 1989, Bantam paper $4.99 (0-440-20479-8). A tough delinquent is sent to his uncle's ranch to be straightened out and there he falls in love with Casey, who is trying to tame a wild horse named Star Runner. (Rev: BL 10/15/88; BR 11–12/88; SLJ 10/88; VOYA 12/88)

739 Hobbs, Valerie. *Carolina Crow Girl* (5–8). 1999, Farrar paper $16.00 (0-374-31153-6). Carolina, who lives in a school bus with her mother and baby sister, longs for a home like other sixth graders have, but when she gets it, she realizes that there are more important things in life. (Rev: BL 2/15/99; SLJ 4/99)

740 Holcomb, Jerry K. *The Chinquapin Tree* (6–9). 1998, Marshall Cavendish $14.95 (0-7614-5028-9). When they learn that they might be returned to their abusive mother, 3 youngsters decide to run away from their loving foster home. (Rev: BL 5/1/98; BR 1–2/99; SLJ 5/98)

741 Holt, Kimberly Willis. *My Louisiana Sky* (6–9). 1998, Holt $15.95 (0-8050-5251-8). When Tiger Ann's caring grandmother dies, the young girl is tempted to leave her retarded parents and relocate to Baton Rouge to live with an aunt. (Rev: BL 4/15/98; BR 11–12/98; SLJ 7/98; VOYA 8/98)

742 Honeycutt, Natalie. *Twilight in Grace Falls* (5–9). 1997, Orchard LB $17.99 (0-531-33007-9). A moving novel about the closing of a lumber mill that brings unemployment to 11-year-old Dasie Jenson's father. (Rev: BL 3/15/97; BR 11–12/97; SLJ 5/97; VOYA 8/97)

743 Horrocks, Anita. *What They Don't Know* (7–9). 1999, Stoddart paper $8.95 (0-7737-6001-6). After Hannah discovers a family secret that involves her identity, she heads down a path of self-destruction that her older sister tries to stop. (Rev: BL 11/1/99; SLJ 8/99; VOYA 10/99)

744 Hughes, Dean. *Team Picture* (6–8). 1996, Simon & Schuster $16.00 (0-689-31924-X). In this sequel to *Family Pose* (1989), young David, a devoted baseball player, must confront his foster parent, Paul, because of his alcohol abuse. (Rev: BL 11/15/96*; SLJ 11/96*)

745 Iida, Deborah. *Middle Son* (10–12). 1996, Algonquin $29.95 (1-56512-119-8). The death of an older brother haunts Spencer in this novel about a Japanese American family in Hawaii. (Rev: BL 3/1/98; SLJ 1/97)

746 Jaffe, Sherril. *Ground Rules: What I Learned My Daughter's Fifteenth Year* (10–12). 1997, Kodansha $20.00 (1-56836-172-6). Told from a mother's point of view, this novel tells of the clash between the mother and her 15-year-old daughter, who becomes increasingly unhappy, uncooperative, and defiant. (Rev: SLJ 8/97)

747 Johnson, Angela. *Heaven* (6–10). 1998, Simon & Schuster paper $16.00 (0-689-82229-4). Marley, a 14-year-old African American girl, is devastated when she learns that she is adopted and that the couple she has regarded as her mother and father are really her aunt and uncle. Coretta Scott King Award, 1999. (Rev: BL 9/15/98; BR 5–6/99; SLJ 10/98; VOYA 2/99)

748 Johnson, Angela. *Songs of Faith* (5–8). 1998, Orchard LB $16.99 (0-531-33023-0). Doreen is a child of divorce who is particularly upset at seeing her younger brother's problems adjusting after their father moves away. (Rev: BL 2/15/98; SLJ 3/98; VOYA 6/98)

749 Johnson, R. M. *The Harris Men* (10–12). 1999, Simon & Schuster $22.50 (0-684-84470-2). This novel traces the fate of 3 African American boys after their father deserts them and the father's attempts to contact them after 20 years. (Rev: SLJ 9/99)

750 Johnston, Julie. *The Only Outcast* (6–10). 1998, Tundra $14.95 (0-88776-441-X). Based on fact, this is the story of the summer of 1904 when Fred Dickinson spent the summer with his grandparents in Ontario and found romance and a mystery. (Rev: BL 10/1/98; BR 1–2/99; SLJ 1/99; VOYA 2/99)

751 Joosse, Barbara M. *Pieces of the Picture* (6–8). 1989, HarperCollins LB $12.89 (0-397-32343-3). After her father's death, Emily and her mother move to try to earn a livelihood running an inn. (Rev: BL 6/1/89; BR 11–12/89)

752 Karas, Phyllis. *Cry Baby* (5–9). 1996, Avon paper $4.50 (0-380-78513-7). Sam Sloan, 14, the youngest of 4 daughters, is horrified to learn that her 47-year-old mother is pregnant, begins failing tests at school, and secretly dates the boyfriend of her best friend, who is suffering from a severe eating disorder. (Rev: VOYA 4/97)

753 Kehret, Peg. *I'm Not Who You Think I Am* (6–9). 1999, Dutton $15.99 (0-525-46153-1). Ginger is followed by a mentally unbalanced woman who claims to be her mother, while also facing problems involved with saving her favorite teacher's job. (Rev: BL 3/1/99; SLJ 4/99; VOYA 6/99)

754 Khashoggi, Soheir. *Mirage* (9–12). 1997, Forge paper $6.99 (0-614-20507-7). A novel with the plight of a Middle Eastern Islamic woman at its heart, from an author who is a product of a similar culture. (Rev: BL 12/1/95*)

755 Kimmel, Eric A. *One Good Tern Deserves Another* (6–9). 1994, Holiday House $14.95 (0-8234-1138-9). After his stepfather is killed, Peebee, 14, moves with his mother to Oregon. He falls for Lani, an avid bird watcher, and his mother falls for Lani's widowed father. (Rev: BL 11/1/94; SLJ 10/94; VOYA 4/95)

756 Kinsey-Warnock, Natalie. *As Long As There Are Mountains* (5–8). 1997, Dutton paper $14.99 (0-525-65236-1). When her father is injured, 13-year-old Iris wants to retain the family farm, but her older brother wants to sell it. (Rev: BL 8/97; BR 9–10/98; SLJ 8/97*; VOYA 4/98)

757 Klein, Norma. *Breaking Up* (7–10). 1981, Avon paper $2.25 (0-380-55830-0). While visiting her divorced father in California, Alison falls in love with her best friend's brother.

758 Klein, Norma. *Going Backwards* (9–12). 1986, Scholastic paper $12.95 (0-590-40328-1). A wrenching story of a boy and his grandmother, who is suf-

fering from Alzheimer's disease, that introduces the theme of mercy killing. (Rev: BL 10/15/86; SLJ 1/87; VOYA 2/87)

759 Klein, Norma. *It's OK If You Don't Love Me* (9–12). 1987, Fawcett paper $4.50 (0-449-70236-7). Young people must cope with their parents' marital crises.

760 Klein, Norma. *Mom, the Wolfman and Me* (6–8). 1976, Avon paper $3.50 (0-380-00791-6). Brett's mother is single but the Wolfman is becoming more than a steady boyfriend.

761 Klein, Robin. *The Sky in Silver Lace* (6–9). 1996, Viking $13.99 (0-670-86266-5). The four Melling sisters and their mother move to a large city in Australia to find better times. (Rev: BL 2/15/96; BR 9–10/96; SLJ 2/96)

762 Koertge, Ron. *Tiger, Tiger, Burning Bright* (6–10). 1994, Orchard LB $18.99 (0-531-08690-9). This story of a boy and his ailing grandfather is set in a small, economically depressed town in the desert hills of California. (Rev: BL 2/15/94; SLJ 3/94; VOYA 6/94)

763 Koller, Jackie F. *A Place to Call Home* (7–10). 1995, Atheneum $16.00 (0-689-80024-X). Biracial Anna, 15, is a strong character in search of love and roots following sexual abuse and rejection from her own family. (Rev: BL 10/15/95; SLJ 10/95; VOYA 2/96)

764 Konigsburg, E. L. *Father's Arcane Daughter* (7–9). 1976, Macmillan LB $15.00 (0-689-30524-9). After a 17-year absence Caroline appears—or is it Caroline?

765 Koss, Amy Goldman. *The Ashwater Experiment* (5–8). 1999, Dial $16.99 (0-8037-2391-1). After Hillary spends 9 months in Ashwater, California, she doesn't want to leave when her nomadic, hippie parents decide to move on. (Rev: BL 6/1–15/99; SLJ 8/99; VOYA 10/99)

766 Kotker, Zane. *Try to Remember* (10–12). 1997, Random $23.00 (0-679-44042-9). Told from 4 different viewpoints (a father, mother, and their 2 grown daughters), this novel explores the turmoil caused when a therapist, who has her own agenda, persuades the oldest daughter to falsely accuse her father of sexual abuse. (Rev: SLJ 2/98)

767 Lafaye, Alexandria. *Strawberry Hill* (5–8). 1999, Simon & Schuster $16.95 (0-684-82441-6). In this novel set in the 1970s, 12-year-old Raleia longs for a secure, old-fashioned life that her hippie parents don't provide. (Rev: BL 8/99)

768 Lafaye, Alexandria. *The Year of the Sawdust Man* (6–9). 1998, Simon & Schuster paper $16.00 (0-689-81513-1). Set in a small Louisiana town in 1933, this novel tells of 11-year-old Nissa and her confusion and unhappiness when her mother leaves and her father shows a growing attachment to another woman. (Rev: BL 6/1–15/98; SLJ 7/98)

769 Lantz, Francess. *Someone to Love* (7–10). 1997, Avon paper $14.00 (0-380-97477-0). Sara's secure family life changes when her parents decide to adopt the yet-unborn child of Iris, an unmarried teen. (Rev: BL 4/15/97; BR 9–10/97)

770 Lasky, Kathryn. *Memoirs of a Bookbat* (5–9). 1994, Harcourt $10.95 (0-15-215727-1). A free-thinking teen evaluates her conservative, religious parents as weird and affirms that her free-ranging reading makes her free. (Rev: BL 4/15/94; SLJ 7/94; VOYA 6/94)

771 Lattany, Kristin Hunter. *Kinfolks* (10–12). 1996, Ballantine $23.00 (0-345-40706-7). Two African American women, both single mothers, discover they have the same father and set out to find their kinfolk. (Rev: BL 10/15/96; SLJ 5/97)

772 Lelchuk, Alan. *On Home Ground* (7–10). Illus. 1987, Harcourt $9.95 (0-15-200560-9). Aaron seems to have nothing in common with his father, a Russian immigrant. (Rev: BL 1/1/88; SLJ 12/87; VOYA 4/88)

773 L'Engle, Madeleine. *Meet the Austins* (6–9). 1981, Dell paper $4.50 (0-440-95777-X). The Austin family—a tightly knit loving group with 4 children—is disrupted when a young orphan girl comes to live with them.

774 L'Engle, Madeleine. *The Moon by Night* (7–10). 1963, Farrar $16.00 (0-374-35049-3); Dell paper $4.99 (0-440-95776-1). In this novel about the Austins, the family takes a cross-country camping trip and Vicki finds she is attracted to the wealthy, irresponsible Zachery Gray.

775 Levinson, Marilyn. *No Boys Allowed* (5–8). 1993, Troll paper $13.95 (0-8167-3135-7). After her father leaves her family to marry his young law partner, Cassie must learn to trust men again. (Rev: BL 10/1/93; SLJ 11/93)

776 Levitin, Sonia. *The Singing Mountain* (7–12). 1998, Simon & Schuster $17.00 (0-689-80809-7). Family secrets are revealed when Carlie accompanies her aunt Vivian to Israel to convince Vivian's son to return to America. (Rev: BL 9/15/98; SLJ 11/98; VOYA 2/99)

777 Levitin, Sonia. *Yesterday's Child* (7–10). 1997, Simon & Schuster $17.00 (0-689-80810-0). After her parent's death, Laura discovers some amazing family secrets when she goes through her mother's things. (Rev: BL 6/1–15/97; SLJ 6/97)

778 Lewis, Beverly. *Whispers Down the Lane* (6–8). (Summerhill Secrets) 1995, Bethany House paper $5.99 (1-55661-476-4). Calling on her faith to help her, Merry Hanson decides to hide her friend Lissa who is being physically abused at home. (Rev: BL 9/1/95; SLJ 2/96)

779 Lowry, Lois. *Autumn Street* (7–9). 1980, Houghton $16.00 (0-395-27812-0); Dell paper $4.50 (0-440-40344-8). With her father away, Elizabeth with her mother and older sister move in with grandmother. (Rev: BL 12/15/89)

780 Lowry, Lois. *Find a Stranger, Say Goodbye* (7–10). 1978, Houghton $16.95 (0-395-26459-6). A college-bound girl decides to find her birth mother.

781 Lowry, Lois. *Rabble Starkey* (6–9). 1987, Houghton $14.95 (0-395-43607-9); Dell paper $4.50 (0-440-40056-2). The story of a friendship between 2 girls (Rabble and Veronica), their sixth-grade year, and their many experiences with family and friends. (Rev: BL 3/15/87; BR 9–10/87; SLJ 4/87; VOYA 4/87)

782 Lowry, Lois. *Us and Uncle Fraud* (6–9). 1984, Houghton $14.95 (0-395-36633-X). Uncle Claude visits his sister's family with her 4 children and an experience in human relations begins.

783 Lynch, Chris. *Shadow Boxer* (6–10). 1993, HarperCollins LB $14.89 (0-06-023028-2). Their father's death leaves 14-year-old George and his hyperactive younger brother in conflict that can only be resolved by dispelling their father's shadow. (Rev: BL 12/15/93; SLJ 9/93*; VOYA 12/93)

784 McKinney-Whetstone, Diane. *Tempest Rising* (10–12). 1998, Morrow $24.00 (0-688-14994-4); paper $12.00 (0-688-16640-7). After the death of their father and the mental collapse of their mother, 3 African American adolescent sisters are placed in a foster-home, where new relationships are built. (Rev: BL 2/15/98; SLJ 10/98)

785 MacKinnon, Bernie. *Song for a Shadow* (8–12). 1991, Houghton $18.00 (0-395-55419-5). This novel concerns 18-year-old Aaron's attempts to sort out his relationships with his parents—his father has always seemed too wrapped up in his career, and his mother is emotionally troubled. (Rev: BL 3/15/91; SLJ 4/91)

786 MacLachlan, Patricia. *All the Place to Love* (5–8). Illus. 1994, HarperCollins LB $16.89 (0-06-021099-0). A lyrical narrative about the childhood and youth of Eli, and how in time he tells his young sister about the people and places on their farm that he loves. (Rev: BL 6/1–15/94*; SLJ 6/94)

787 MacLachlan, Patricia. *Baby* (5–10). 1993, Delacorte $15.95 (0-385-31133-8). In this moving, beautifully written story, "Baby" refers to two youngsters: Larkin's brother (who died before the story begins) and Sophie, who's left in a basket on the driveway of Larkin's home. (Rev: BL 9/1/93; SLJ 11/93; VOYA 10/93)

788 McMurtry, Larry. *Terms of Endearment* (10–12). 1989, Simon & Schuster paper $8.95 (0-671-68208-

3). The complex relationship between mother and daughter, which involves adjustments to marriage, and a fatal illness form the basis of this novel.

789 McNamee, Graham. *Hate You* (9–12). 1999, Bantam Doubleday Dell $14.95 (0-385-32593-2). After Alice and her mother leave Alice's abusive father, Alice begins a new life and has a boyfriend, but then learns that her father is dying and wants to see her. (Rev: BL 2/1/99; SLJ 3/99; VOYA 4/99)

790 McPhee, Martha. *Bright Angel Time* (10–12). 1997, Random $23.00 (0-679-45008-4); Harcourt paper $12.00 (0-15-600586-7). A novel of loss and love as seen through the eyes of 8-year-old Kate who, after her father leaves the family, accompanies her mother, 2 older sisters, her mother's boyfriend, and his family as they travel through the Southwest in a camper. (Rev: BL 6/1–15/97; SLJ 6/98)

791 Manley, Frank. *The Cockfighter* (10–12). 1998, Coffee House Pr. $19.95 (1-56689-073-X). In this novel set in the rural South, the hatred that develops between a sensitive 13-year-boy and his crude, red-neck father who raises cocks for illegal cockfighting erupts in a bloody climax. (Rev: BL 3/15/98; SLJ 10/98)

792 Marino, Jan. *For the Love of Pete* (6–8). 1993, Avon paper $3.50 (0-380-72010-8). Phoebe is on her way from Georgia to Maine to find the father she's never met. (Rev: BL 6/1–15/93; SLJ 5/93*)

793 Marsden, John. *Letters from the Inside* (8–12). 1994, Houghton $14.95 (0-395-68985-6). Two teenage girls begin a correspondence, with their initial letters describing ideal fictitious lives. With time, they reveal that one has a violent brother and the other feels trapped within her family. (Rev: BL 10/15/94; SLJ 9/94*; VOYA 12/94)

794 Martin, Nora. *The Eagle's Shadow* (6–9). Illus. 1997, Scholastic $15.95 (0-590-36087-6). Twelve-year-old Clearie is sent to live with Tlingit relatives in Alaska and comes to accept the desertion by her mother. (Rev: BL 8/97; BR 11–12/97; SLJ 10/97; VOYA 4/98)

795 Mazer, Harry. *Who Is Eddie Leonard?* (7–10). 1995, Demco $9.34 (0-606-08379-0). When his grandmother dies, Eddie sees a missing-child poster that convinces him he's really the kidnapped Jason Diaz. But the Diazes aren't the perfect family he imagined. (Rev: BL 11/15/93; SLJ 11/93; VOYA 4/94)

796 Mazer, Norma Fox. *After the Rain* (7–10). 1987, Morrow $16.00 (0-688-06867-7); Avon paper $4.99 (0-380-75025-2). Rachel gradually develops a warm relationship with her terminally ill grandfather who is noted for his bad temper. (Rev: BL 5/1/87; BR 5–6/87; SLJ 5/87; VOYA 6/87)

797 Mazer, Norma Fox. *D, My Name Is Danita* (6–8). 1991, Scholastic $13.95 (0-590-43655-4). The latest in this light series presents an interesting premise: Girl meets boy who turns out to be her older half-brother. (Rev: BL 4/1/91; SLJ 3/91)

798 Mazer, Norma Fox. *Downtown* (7–10). 1984, Avon paper $4.50 (0-380-88534-4). Pete, 15, the son of anti-war demonstrators who are in hiding, faces problems when his mother reappears and wants to be part of his life.

799 Mazer, Norma Fox. *Missing Pieces* (7–10). 1995, Morrow $16.00 (0-688-13349-5). A 14-year-old seeks a missing part of her life by looking for a father who abandoned her. (Rev: BL 4/1/95; SLJ 4/95*; VOYA 5/95)

800 Mazer, Norma Fox. *Mrs. Fish, Ape, and Me, the Dump Queen* (7–9). 1981, Avon paper $3.50 (0-380-69153-1). Joyce has been hurt by supposed friends but somehow she trusts the school custodian, Mrs. Fish.

801 Mazer, Norma Fox. *Taking Terri Mueller* (7–10). 1983, Avon paper $4.50 (0-380-79004-1). Terri realizes that her beloved father has actually kidnapped her to keep her from her mother.

802 Metzger, Lois. *Missing Girls* (5–8). 1999, Viking $15.99 (0-670-87777-8). Thirteen-year-old Carrie doesn't seem to fit in anywhere until she meets the seemingly ideal family of her friend Mona, but this, too, is revealed to be less than perfect. (Rev: BL 2/1/99; BR 9–10/99; SLJ 4/99; VOYA 6/99)

803 Mickle, Shelley Fraser. *Replacing Dad* (9–12). 1993, Algonquin $25.95 (1-56512-017-5). A teenage boy and his mother relate their experiences and the emotional upheaval that followed the mother's divorce, told in alternating chapters. (Rev: BL 5/15/93)

804 Miles, Betty. *Just the Beginning* (6–8). 1976, Avon paper $2.50 (0-380-01913-2). An eighth-grader has a "perfect" older sister and a mother who has become a cleaning lady.

805 Miller, Dorothy R. *Home Wars* (5–8). 1997, Simon & Schuster $16.00 (0-689-81411-9). Halley has misgivings when her father brings home 3 rifles, one for himself and the others for her 2 brothers. (Rev: BL 9/1/97; SLJ 10/97)

806 Mitchard, Jacquelyn. *The Most Wanted* (10–12). 1998, Viking $24.95 (0-6708-7884-7). Various aspects of motherhood are explored in this novel about a 14-year-old girl who falls in love with and bears the child of a prison inmate who later escapes. (Rev: SLJ 2/99)

807 Montgomery, L. M. *Anne of Green Gables* (7–9). 1995, Holt $15.95 (0-8050-3126-X); Puffin paper $3.99 (0-14-036741-1). This is a reissue of the classic Canadian story of Anne and how she was gradually accepted in a foster home. Her story continued in *Anne of Avonlea, Anne of the Island, Anne of Windy Poplars, Anne's House of Dreams,* and *Anne of Ingleside.*

808 Montgomery, L. M. *Emily of New Moon* (7–9). 1986, Bantam paper $4.99 (0-553-23370-X). Beginning when Emily is only 11, this trilogy continues in *Emily Climbs* and *Emily's Quest* and tells about the making of a writer. These are reissues.

809 Mori, Kyoko. *One Bird* (8–12). 1996, Fawcett paper $4.50 (0-449-70453-X). A coming-of-age story set in Japan about 15-year-old girl Megumi, who loses her mother yet finds people who understand and love her. (Rev: BL 10/15/95; SLJ 11/95; VOYA 2/96)

810 Morrell, David. *Fireflies* (9–12). 1999, Warner paper $12.99 (0-446-67590-3). A "nonfiction novel" about the death of the author's 15-year-old son from bone cancer. (Rev: BL 9/1/88)

811 Mosher, Richard. *The Taxi Navigator* (5–8). 1996, Philomel $15.95 (0-399-23104-8). As his parents head for divorce, 9-year-old Kyle shares many adventures with his taxi-driving Uncle Hank. (Rev: BL 9/15/96; SLJ 1/97)

812 Myers, Anna. *Rosie's Tiger* (5–8). 1994, Walker $22.95 (0-8027-8305-8). When Rosie's brother returns from the Korean War, he brings a wife and son with him and Rosie becomes consumed by the tiger of jealousy. (Rev: BL 9/15/94; SLJ 11/94)

813 Myers, Walter Dean. *Somewhere in the Darkness* (7–12). 1992, Scholastic $15.95 (0-590-42411-4). A father and son get to know each other after the father is released from prison. (Rev: BL 2/1/92*; SLJ 4/92*)

814 Naylor, Phyllis Reynolds. *Ice* (6–8). 1995, Atheneum $16.00 (0-689-80005-3). A 13-year-old girl learns about herself and relationships in her search for her father and her isolation from her mother. (Rev: BL 8/95; SLJ 10/95; VOYA 12/95)

815 Naylor, Phyllis Reynolds. *Walker's Crossing* (6–12). 1999, Simon & Schuster $16.00 (0-689-82939-6). Shy Ryan Walker is beset with family problems—a sick father, a depressed mother, an older sister who wants to become Rodeo Queen, and a brother who has joined a militia group. (Rev: BL 9/15/99)

816 Nelson, Theresa. *Earthshine* (5–9). 1994, Orchard LB $17.99 (0-531-08717-4). "Slim" decides to live with her father and his lover, who is dying of AIDS. At a support group, she meets Isaiah, whose pregnant mother also has AIDS. (Rev: BL 9/1/94; SLJ 9/94*; VOYA 10/94)

817 Nolan, Han. *A Face in Every Window* (7–10). 1999, Harcourt $16.00 (0-15-201915-4). Fourteen-year-old JP finds his life is coming undone when his grandmother dies and he is left with his impractical mother and retarded father. (Rev: BL 11/1/99; SLJ 9/99; VOYA 12/99)

818 Nye, Jody Lynn. *Don't Forget Your Spacesuit, Dear* (10–12). 1996, Baen paper $5.99 (0-671-87732-1). The various roles of mothers are explored in this imaginative collection of 18 stories, whose subjects include mothers who are computers, animals, or aliens. (Rev: SLJ 7/97)

819 O'Connor, Barbara. *Beethoven in Paradise* (5–8). 1997, Farrar $15.00 (0-374-30666-4). Against his brutal father's wishes, Martin, who is growing up in a squalid trailer park, takes up music and begins playing a violin. (Rev: BL 4/15/97; BR 11–12/97; SLJ 4/97)

820 Oughton, Jerrie. *The War in Georgia* (7–12). 1997, Houghton $14.95 (0-395-81568-1); Bantam Doubleday Dell paper $4.50 (0-440-22752-6). During the last days of World War II in Atlanta, 13-year-old Shanta befriends a girl and her brain-injured brother and, through them, enters the nightmare world of child abuse. (Rev: BL 4/1/97; BR 9–10/97; SLJ 5/97)

821 Paterson, Katherine. *Come Sing, Jimmy Jo* (6–10). 1985, Dutton $15.99 (0-525-67167-6); Avon paper $3.99 (0-380-70052-2). When 11-year-old James joins his family of musicians as a performer, a new life begins. (Rev: BL 5/1/85; SLJ 4/85)

822 Patneaude, David. *Framed in Fire* (6–9). 1999, Albert Whitman LB $14.95 (0-8075-9098-3). Peter Larson, who lives with his mother and verbally abusive stepfather, discovers that his mother has lied to him about the death of his real father and sets out to find the truth. (Rev: SLJ 4/99)

823 Paulsen, Gary. *The Tent: A Parable in One Sitting* (6–10). 1995, Harcourt $14.00 (0-15-292879-0). A 14-year-old struggles to keep his values when his father fraudulently poses as an itinerant preacher. (Rev: BL 3/15/95; SLJ 5/95)

824 Paulsen, Gary. *The Winter Room* (6–8). 1989, Watts LB $16.99 (0-531-08439-6). A quiet novel about an 11-year-old boy growing up on a farm in Minnesota. (Rev: BL 11/1/89; BR 5–6/90; SLJ 10/89; VOYA 12/89)

825 Peck, Richard. *Father Figure* (7–10). 1996, Puffin paper $3.99 (0-14-037969-X). Jim and his younger brother are sent to live in Florida with a father they scarcely know.

826 Peck, Richard. *Strays Like Us* (5–8). 1998, Dial $15.99 (0-8037-2291-5). Molly, who is living temporarily with a great-aunt, and next door neighbor Will, who has been taken in by his grandparents, are 2 of the strays in this book about family relationships and secrets, and trying to fit into a new school environment. (Rev: BL 4/1/98; BR 1–2/99; SLJ 5/98; VOYA 6/98)

827 Peck, Robert Newton. *Arly* (5–8). 1989, Walker $25.95 (0-8027-6856-3). A teacher changes the life of a young boy in a migrant camp in Florida in 1927. (Rev: BL 7/89; BR 9–10/89; VOYA 8/89)

828 Peck, Robert Newton. *A Day No Pigs Would Die* (7–9). 1973, Knopf $24.00 (0-394-48235-2); Random paper $4.99 (0-679-85306-5). A Shaker farm boy in Vermont must give up his pet pig to help his family. (Rev: BL 3/1/89)

829 Pendergraft, Patricia. *Miracle at Clement's Pond* (6–8). 1987, Putnam paper $13.95 (0-399-21438-0). Three children think they are doing a good deed when they deposit a baby they have found on a spinster's porch. (Rev: BL 8/87; SLJ 8/87; VOYA 8/87)

830 Pevsner, Stella. *Would My Fortune Cookie Lie?* (5–8). 1996, Clarion $14.95 (0-395-73082-1). Thirteen-year-old Alexis, already upset by her father's desertion and a possible family move, becomes involved with a mysterious stranger and a devastating family secret. (Rev: BL 2/15/96; BR 9–10/96; SLJ 4/96)

831 Pfeffer, Susan Beth. *The Year Without Michael* (7–12). 1988, Demco $9.85 (0-606-03959-7). When Jody's brother Michael, a high school freshman, disappears, the solidarity of her family is shattered. (Rev: BL 10/1/87; BR 5–6/88; SLJ 11/87; VOYA 10/87)

832 Pohl, Peter, and Kinna Gieth. *I Miss You, I Miss You!* (9–12). Trans. from Swedish by Roger Greenwald. 1999, Farrar $17.00 (91-29-63935-2). A 13-year-old's life dramatically changes after her identical twin's death in a car crash. (Rev: SLJ 3/99; VOYA 6/99)

833 Porte, Barbara Ann. *Something Terrible Happened* (6–10). 1994, Orchard LB $17.99 (0-531-08719-0); 1996, Troll paper $4.50 (0-8167-3868-8). Part white, part West Indian, Gillian, 12, must adjust to living with her deceased father's "plain white" relatives when her mother contracts AIDS. (Rev: BL 9/15/94; SLJ 10/94; VOYA 10/94)

834 Powell, Randy. *Tribute to Another Dead Rock Star* (7–12). 1999, Farrar $17.00 (0-374-37748-0). Fifteen-year-old Gary returns to Seattle to speak at a concert honoring his deceased rock-star mother, who abused drugs and behaved irresponsibly, and must confront his mother's ex-boyfriend, the ex-boyfriend's new wife, and his mentally disabled stepbrother. (Rev: BL 3/1/99; SLJ 5/99; VOYA 6/99)

835 Pressler, Mirjam. *Halinka* (7–10). Trans. by Elizabeth D. Crawford. Illus. 1998, Holt $16.95 (0-8050-5861-3). The disturbing story of a 12-year-old Gypsy girl who lives with 6 other girls in a welfare home in Germany and of her many problems and her hope for a stable homelife. (Rev: BL 10/15/98; SLJ 1/99; VOYA 4/99)

836 Pringer, Nancy. *Toughing It* (7–10). 1994, Harcourt $10.95 (0-15-200008-9); paper $4.95 (0-15-200011-9). Tuff lives in a trailer with his alcoholic mother and her abusive boyfriend. When Tuff is murdered, Dillon, his younger brother, runs to the man who could be his father. (Rev: BL 9/1/94; SLJ 9/94; VOYA 8/94)

837 Provoost, Anne. *My Aunt Is a Pilot Whale* (6–9). Trans. by Ria Bleumer. 1995, Women's Press, Ltd. paper $8.95 (0-88961-202-1). A story of family relationships and friendship but also of incest. (Rev: BL 3/1/95)

838 Quarles, Heather. *A Door Near Here* (7–10). 1998, Doubleday $13.95 (0-385-32595-9). When her mother loses her job and retreats into alcoholism, 15-year-old Katherine must take care of herself and 3 younger siblings. (Rev: BL 9/1/98; VOYA 10/98)

839 Quindlen, Anna. *Black and Blue* (10–12). 1998, Random $23.00 (0-375-50051-0). Love between parent and child, the importance of honesty in relationships, and self-knowledge as an essential part of healing are among the themes in this story of a battered wife who flees an abusive marriage with her 10-year-old son, but lives in fear that her husband will track her down. (Rev: SLJ 4/98)

840 Quindlen, Anna. *Object Lessons* (9–12). 1992, Ivy Books paper $6.99 (0-8041-0946-X). Maggie, 12, learns important lessons in life during the summer of 1960 in her home in the Bronx. (Rev: BL 1/15/91; SLJ 9/91)

841 Quirk, Anne. *Dancing with Great-Aunt Cornelia* (5–8). 1997, HarperCollins LB $14.89 (0-06-027333-X). Connie discovers a family secret when she spends a few weeks with her super-rich great aunt Cornelia in Manhattan. (Rev: BL 6/1–15/97; BR 11–12/97; SLJ 5/97)

842 Reynolds, Marilyn. *Baby Help: True-to-Life Series from Hamilton High* (8–12). (Hamilton High) 1998, Morning Glory Pr. $15.95 (1-885356-26-9); paper $8.95 (1-885356-27-7). Partner-abuse is explored in this novel about a teenage mother who is living with a difficult boyfriend and his unsympathetic mother. (Rev: BL 2/1/98; SLJ 3/98; VOYA 6/98)

843 Reynolds, Marjorie. *The Starlite Drive-in* (10–12). 1997, Morrow $23.00 (0-688-15389-5). A 13-year-old girl growing up in rural Indiana during 1956 becomes alarmed when an attractive drifter begins paying attention to her emotionally unbalanced mother. (Rev: SLJ 3/98)

844 Roberts, Willo Davis. *What Are We Going to Do about David?* (5–8). 1993, Atheneum $16.00 (0-689-

31793-X). Because his parents are considering divorce, David, 11, is sent to live with his grandmother, an understanding woman who helps him gain self-reliance and confidence. (Rev: BL 3/15/93; SLJ 4/93)

845 Robinson, Lee. *Gateway* (6–9). 1996, Houghton $14.95 (0-395-72772-3). The divorce process as seen from the standpoint of daughter Mac, whose parents have separated and taken new lovers. (Rev: BL 5/15/96; SLJ 3/96; VOYA 8/96)

846 Rodowsky, Colby. *Hannah in Between* (5–8). 1994, Farrar $15.00 (0-374-32837-4). Hannah struggles with what to do when she discovers that her mother is a secret alcoholic. (Rev: BL 4/1/94; SLJ 5/94; VOYA 10/94)

847 Ross, Ramon R. *The Dancing Tree* (6–9). 1995, Simon & Schuster $14.00 (0-689-80072-X). When 12-year-old Zeenie's mother leaves home, the girl's grandmother tells her that in every generation of her family there is a lonely and incomplete life. (Rev: BL 9/1/95; SLJ 2/96)

848 Roybal, Laura. *Billy* (7–9). 1994, Houghton $14.95 (0-395-67649-5). A teenage New Mexico cowhand is forced to leave his biological father, who kidnapped him 6 years earlier, and return to his Iowa family. (Rev: BL 3/15/94; SLJ 5/94; VOYA 6/94)

849 Rubalcaba, Jill. *Saint Vitus' Dance* (8–12). 1996, Clarion $13.95 (0-395-72768-5). As her mother sinks further and further into madness caused by Huntington's chorea, Melanie wonders if she is destined for a similar fate. (Rev: BL 1/1–15/97; BR 3–4/97; SLJ 9/96; VOYA 6/97)

850 Ryan, Mary E. *Alias* (6–10). 1997, Simon & Schuster paper $4.99 (0-689-82264-2). Teenager Toby discovers that his mother's constant moves and change of identity are because she is wanted by the FBI for terrorist activities during the Vietnam War. (Rev: BL 4/15/97; BR 11–12/97; SLJ 7/97*; VOYA 8/97)

851 Rylant, Cynthia. *A Blue-Eyed Daisy* (6–8). 1985, Bradbury LB $15.00 (0-02-777960-2). There are 14 interrelated stories in this book about an 11-year-old girl growing up in West Virginia. (Rev: BL 6/15/85; SLJ 4/85)

852 Sachs, Marilyn. *Baby Sister* (7–10). 1986, Avon paper $3.50 (0-380-70358-0). Penny is torn between her admiration for her older sister and the realization that she is really selfish. (Rev: BL 2/15/86; BR 5–6/86; SLJ 8/86; VOYA 8/86)

853 Sachs, Marilyn. *Ghosts in the Family* (5–8). 1995, Dutton paper $15.99 (0-525-45421-7). After her mother's death, Gabriella discovers disturbing news about her family and her absent father. (Rev: BL 1/1–15/96; SLJ 12/95; VOYA 4/96)

854 Sachs, Marilyn. *Just Like a Friend* (6–9). 1990, Avon paper $2.95 (0-380-70964-3). The friendship between a mother and a daughter falls apart when father has a heart attack. (Rev: BL 10/15/89; BR 3–4/90; SLJ 12/89; VOYA 12/89)

855 Sachs, Marilyn. *The Truth about Mary Rose* (6–8). 1995, Puffin paper $3.99 (0-14-037083-8). The first Mary Rose died at age 11 saving lives in a fire, but her modern counterpart learns the truth about her.

856 Saroyan, William. *The Human Comedy* (7–12). 1973, Dell paper $5.99 (0-440-33933-2). Homer Macauley is growing up during World War II in America and becomes part of the everyday life that is the human comedy.

857 Sarsfield, Mairuth. *No Crystal Stair* (10–12). 1997, Stoddart $14.95 (1-896867-02-2). Set in a black community in Quebec during the 1940s, this is a story of a widow with 3 children and her fight to keep her family fed and together. (Rev: SLJ 10/97)

858 Savage, Deborah. *Summer Hawk* (7–10). 1999, Houghton $16.00 (0-395-91163-X). In this coming-of-age story, 15-year-old Taylor has trouble relating to her mother and father, shuns the company of Rail Bogart, the other smart kid in her school, and showers her attention and affection on a young hawk she rescues. (Rev: BL 3/1/99; SLJ 4/99; VOYA 4/99)

859 Scarbrough, George. *A Summer Ago* (10–12). 1986, St. Luke's $13.95 (0-918518-46-6). A gentle story about a teenage boy and summer spent in rural Tennessee in the early Depression years. (Rev: SLJ 2/87)

860 Schmidt, Gary D. *The Sin Eater* (6–9). 1996, Dutton paper $15.99 (0-525-67541-8). When his father commits suicide, young Cole, who is living on a farm with his grandparents in New Hampshire, must assume new responsibilities. (Rev: BL 11/1/96; BR 3–4/97; SLJ 1/97)

861 Schwartz, Steven. *Lives of the Fathers* (9–12). 1991, Univ. of Illinois Pr. $16.95 (0-252-01815-X). Ten short stories portray the powerful, often complicated relationships between fathers and sons. (Rev: BL 7/91*)

862 Sebestyen, Ouida. *Far from Home* (7–10). 1980, Little, Brown $15.95 (0-316-77932-6); Dell paper $2.50 (0-440-92640-8). An orphaned boy is taken in by a couple who run a boardinghouse and there he uncovers secrets about his family's past.

863 Shusterman, Neal. *What Daddy Did* (7–10). 1991, Little, Brown paper $15.95 (0-316-78906-2). A young boy recounts the story of how his father murdered his mother and how he ultimately comes to understand and forgive him. (Rev: BL 7/91; SLJ 6/91)

864   Smith, Anne Warren. *Sister in the Shadow* (7–10). 1986, Avon paper $2.75 (0-380-70378-5). In competition with her successful younger sister, Sharon becomes a live-in baby-sitter with unhappy results. (Rev: BL 5/1/86; SLJ 5/86; VOYA 8/86)

865   Stacey, Cherylyn. *How Do You Spell Abducted?* (4–8). 1996, Red Deer paper $7.95 (0-88995-148-9). When their divorced father abducts Deb, Paige, and Cory, the 3 youngsters must escape from his home in the U.S. and make their way back to their mother in Canada. (Rev: BR 3–4/97; SLJ 12/96)

866   Steinbeck, John. *The Pearl* (9–12). Illus. 1993, Viking paper $5.95 (0-14-017737-X). The lives of a poor Mexican pearl fisher and his family change dramatically after he uncovers a fabulous pearl.

867   Sweeney, Joyce. *The Spirit Window* (7–12). 1998, Delacorte $15.95 (0-385-32510-X). When 15-year-old Miranda journeys to Florida with her father, she falls in love with an older, part-Cherokee boy and becomes involved in environmental causes, both of which bring her into conflict with her parent. (Rev: BL 2/15/98; BR 11–12/98; SLJ 3/98; VOYA 4/98)

868   Sweeney, Joyce. *The Tiger Orchard* (9–12). 1995, Dell paper $3.99 (0-440-21927-2). Zack leaves home to find his father, which is the key to understanding himself and shapes his maturation. (Rev: BL 4/1/93; SLJ 5/93)

869   Talbert, Marc. *The Purple Heart* (5–8). 1992, HarperCollins $14.95 (0-06-020428-1); Avon paper $3.50 (0-380-71985-1). Luke's father has returned from Vietnam an anguished, brooding war hero, and Luke loses his father's Purple Heart, leading to confrontation and reconciliation. (Rev: BL 12/15/91*; SLJ 2/92)

870   Talbert, Marc. *A Sunburned Prayer* (5–8). 1995, 1997, Simon & Schuster paper $4.50 (0-689-81326-0). Eloy walks 17 miles under the New Mexico sun to ask God for a miracle to save his grandmother's life. (Rev: BL 8/95; SLJ 7/95)

871   Thesman, Jean. *The Last April Dancers* (7–10). 1987, Avon paper $2.75 (0-380-70614-8). Catherine tries to recover from the guilt caused by her father's suicide through friendship and love of a neighboring boy. (Rev: BL 9/15/87; SLJ 10/87; VOYA 10/87)

872   Thesman, Jean. *The Tree of Bells* (7–10). 1999, Houghton $15.00 (0-395-90510-9). In this sequel to *The Ornament Tree*, the strong Deveraux women and their boarding house in Seattle are again featured, with the focus on Claire, now 16 and anxious for independence. (Rev: BL 6/1–15/99; SLJ 7/99; VOYA 10/99)

873   Tomey, Ingrid. *The Queen of Dreamland* (6–9). 1996, Simon & Schuster $15.00 (0-689-80458-X). On her 14th birthday, Julie secretly discovers who her birth mother really is and begins living a double life by hiding this information from her step-parents. (Rev: BL 9/15/96; BR 5–6/97; SLJ 10/96; VOYA 4/97)

874   Townsend, John Rowe. *Downstream* (9–12). 1987, HarperCollins LB $12.89 (0-397-32189-9). A teenage English boy finds himself in competition with his father for the affections of an attractive divorcée. (Rev: BL 7/87; SLJ 8/87; VOYA 6/87)

875   Trevor, Penelope. *Listening for Small Sounds* (9–12). 1997, Allen & Unwin paper $11.95 (1-86448-145-5). Raw language and brutal situations are featured in this Australian novel about a girl growing up in a family with an alcoholic father who physically abuses her and her mother. (Rev: BL 11/1/97; SLJ 1/98)

876   Velasquez, Gloria. *Rina's Family Secret* (8–12). 1998, Arte Publico $16.95 (1-55885-236-0); paper $9.95 (1-55885-233-6). Puerto Rican teenager Rina cannot endure life with her alcoholic stepfather, and so moves in with her grandmother. (Rev: BL 8/98; SLJ 10/98)

877   Voigt, Cynthia. *Dicey's Song* (6–9). 1982, Macmillan $17.00 (0-689-30944-9). Homeless Dicey and his younger siblings arrive at their grandmother's home. Newbery Medal, 1983. The story of their journey is told in *Homecoming* (1981). (Rev: BL 12/15/89)

878   Voigt, Cynthia. *The Runner* (9–12). 1985, Macmillan LB $15.95 (0-689-31069-2). The story of Bullet Tillerman, a loner who escapes a terrible home situation through his love of running and later by enlisting and going to Vietnam. Some senior high students might wish to read other stories about the Tillermans including *Dicey's Song*. (Rev: BL 3/15/85; SLJ 5/85)

879   Voigt, Cynthia. *Seventeen Against the Dealer* (7–12). 1989, Macmillan $18.00 (0-689-31497-3). In this, the last of the Tillerman cycle, Dicey, now 21, decides to earn her living building boats. (Rev: BL 3/15/89; BR 9–10/89; SLJ 2/89; VOYA 4/89)

880   Voigt, Cynthia. *A Solitary Blue* (7–9). 1983, Macmillan $18.00 (0-689-31008-0). Jeff is invited to spend a summer with his divorced mother.

881   Voigt, Cynthia. *Sons from Afar* (6–10). 1987, Macmillan LB $15.95 (0-689-31349-7); Fawcett paper $4.50 (0-449-70293-6). In this part of the Tillerman family story sons James and Sammy set out to see a father they have never known. (Rev: BL 9/15/87; SLJ 9/87; VOYA 10/87)

882   Voigt, Cynthia. *Tree by Leaf* (6–8). 1988, Macmillan $15.95 (0-689-31403-5). Clothilde's father returns to Maine from World War I to find his family impoverished and himself a bitter, disfigured outcast. (Rev: BL 4/1/88; BR 9–10/88; SLJ 5/88; VOYA 8/88)

883 Wartski, Maureen C. *Dark Silence* (7–10). 1994, Ballantine paper $5.50 (0-449-70418-1). Teenager Randy must deal with her mother's recent death and the abuse of her neighbor, Delia. (Rev: BL 4/1/94; SLJ 7/94; VOYA 6/94)

884 Weissenberg, Fran. *The Streets Are Paved with Gold* (7–9). 1990, Harbinger paper $5.95 (0-943173-51-5). Debbie is from a poor immigrant Jewish family and she is ashamed to bring her friends home. (Rev: BL 8/90; SLJ 8/90)

885 White, Ellen E. *White House Autumn* (7–10). 1985, Avon paper $2.95 (0-380-89780-6). The daughter of the first female president of the United States feels her family is coming apart after an assassination attempt on her mother. (Rev: BL 11/1/85; SLJ 2/86; VOYA 4/86)

886 White, Ruth. *Belle Prater's Boy* (5–9). 1996, Farrar $16.00 (0-374-30668-0). Set in Appalachia in the 1950s, this moving, often humorous story tells about Gypsy and her unusual cousin Woodrow, who hides a secret involving his mother's disappearance. (Rev: BL 4/15/96; BR 9–10/96; SLJ 4/96*)

887 Wilde, Nicholas. *Down Came a Blackbird* (6–8). 1992, Holt $15.95 (0-8050-2001-2). James, 13, resorts to a dream world to deal with his anger and grief over his mother's neglect, his killing of a blackbird, and a life beyond his control. (Rev: BL 12/1/92; SLJ 2/93)

888 Wilhelm, Kate. *The Good Children* (10–12). 1998, St. Martin's $22.95 (0-312-17914-6); Fawcett paper $6.99 (0-449-00455-4). When their only remaining parent dies, the 4 McNair children decide to hide the fact to prevent possible separation and institutionalization. (Rev: BL 2/1/98; SLJ 9/98; VOYA 10/98)

889 Wolff, Virginia E. *Make Lemonade* (7–12). 1993, Holt $15.95 (0-8050-2228-7); 1994, Scholastic paper $4.99 (0-590-48141-X). Rooted in the community of poverty, this story offers a penetrating view of the conditions that foster ignorance, destroy self-esteem, and challenge strength. (Rev: BL 6/1–15/93*; SLJ 7/93*; VOYA 10/93)

890 Wolitzer, Hilma. *Wish You Were Here* (7–9). 1984, Farrar paper $3.45 (0-374-48412-0). Bernie decides to move out when his new stepfather moves in.

891 Wong, Norman. *Cultural Revolution* (10–12). 1994, One World paper $10.00 (0-345-39648-0). In this story of 2 generations of a Chinese family, the first part focuses on Wei's childhood and family relationships in China; the second follows Wei's marriage and move to Hawaii, where he fathers 2 children, one of whom is gay and whose struggles are the focus of this part of the book. (Rev: VOYA 4/96)

892 Wood, June R. *A Share of Freedom* (6–8). 1994, Putnam $15.95 (0-399-22767-9). Freedom, an intelligent, independent seventh-grader, has never met her father. Her mother's severe alcoholism lands Freedom and her brother in a foster home. (Rev: BL 9/1/94; SLJ 10/94*; VOYA 4/95)

893 Wood, June R. *When Pigs Fly* (5–8). 1995, Putnam $16.95 (0-399-22911-6). A 13-year-old girl learns to cope with many problems, one of which is a younger sister with Down's syndrome. (Rev: BL 12/1/95; SLJ 10/95; VOYA 12/95)

894 Woodbury, Mary. *Brad's Universe* (5–8). 1998, Orca paper $7.95 (1-55143-120-3). In this novel set in a small Canadian town, Brad, at 14, is looking forward to being reunited with his absent father, but through vague clues comes to realize that the man has been convicted of child molesting. (Rev: SLJ 2/99; VOYA 4/99)

895 Woodson, Jacqueline. *Lena* (6–9). 1999, Bantam Doubleday Dell $15.95 (0-385-32308-5). In this sequel to *I Hadn't Meant to Tell You This,* 13-year-old Lena and her young sister leave their abusive father after their mother's death and hit the road disguised as boys. (Rev: BL 2/1/99; SLJ 5/99; VOYA 2/99)

896 Wynne-Jones, Tim. *Stephen Fair: A Novel* (7–10). 1998, DK Publg. $15.95 (0-7894-2495-9). Long-hidden family secrets are revealed as 15-year-old Stephen Fair begins to experience nightmares that have deep meanings. (Rev: BL 6/1–15/98; BR 11–12/98; SLJ 5/98; VOYA 8/98)

897 Yep, Laurence. *Ribbons* (4–8). 1996, Putnam $15.95 (0-399-22906-X). Robin begins to sympathize with her Chinese grandmother after she learns the woman's secret. (Rev: BL 1/1–15/96; SLJ 2/96)

Physical and Emotional Problems

898 Abelove, Joan. *Saying It Out Loud* (7–12). 1999, DK Publg. $15.95 (0-7894-2609-9). A complex novel about a high school senior whose relations with her mother change and deepen when she learns that her mother is dying of a brain tumor. Her father has always been unhelpful and uncommunicative, and she begins finding others to look to for support. (Rev: BL 9/1/99; SLJ 9/99; VOYA 10/99)

899 Anderson, Rachel. *Black Water* (6–9). 1995, Holt $14.95 (0-8050-3847-7). A portrait of a disabled child in Victorian England's back streets. (Rev: BL 5/15/95; SLJ 7/95)

900 Anderson, Rachel. *The Bus People* (8–12). 1992, Holt $13.95 (0-8050-2297-X). Six stories that focus on the physically, emotionally, and mentally disabled passengers who ride Bertram's Bus to a special school daily. (Rev: BL 11/15/92; SLJ 1/93*)

901 Arrick, Fran. *Steffie Can't Come Out to Play* (7–10). 1978, Simon & Schuster $8.95 (0-87888-135-2). Steffie runs away to New York City and is dragged into the nightmare world of prostitution.

902 Banks, Sarah Harrell. *Under the Shadow of Wings* (5–9). 1997, Simon & Schuster $15.00 (0-689-81207-8). In this novel set in the South during World War II, Tattnall, age 11, has a special relationship with her older brain-damaged cousin. (Rev: BL 5/15/97; BR 11–12/97; SLJ 6/97)

903 Bennett, Cherie. *Life in the Fat Lane* (6–9). 1998, Delacorte $15.95 (0-385-32274-7). Lara has everything—looks, a boyfriend, elected queen of the prom—but her life falls apart when she begins gaining weight and soon weighs over 200 pounds. (Rev: BL 1/1–15/98; BR 9–10/98; SLJ 3/98; VOYA 8/98)

904 Blume, Judy. *Deenie* (6–8). 1973, Bradbury LB $16.00 (0-02-711020-6); Dell paper $4.99 (0-440-93259-9). Beautiful young Deenie, intent on a modeling career, finds out she has curvature of the spine and must wear a back brace.

905 Bradford, Barbara Taylor. *Her Own Rules* (10–12). 1996, HarperCollins $32.00 (0-06-017721-7). A successful business woman unravels the mystery of her past when she visits an ancient abbey in England and experiences feelings of sadness and loss. (Rev: SLJ 2/97)

906 Brancato, Robin F. *Winning* (7–9). 1977, Bantam paper $2.95 (0-553-26597-0). A boy must adjust to paralysis that was the result of a football accident. (Rev: BL 10/15/88)

907 Brooks, Bruce. *Vanishing* (5–8). 1999, HarperCollins LB $14.89 (0-06-028237-1). A challenging novel about a hospitalized girl, who gives up eating so she can't be sent home to her dysfunctional family, and the boy she meets who is in remission from a fatal disease. (Rev: BL 5/15/99; SLJ 6/99; VOYA 10/99)

908 Brown, Kay. *Willy's Summer Dream* (6–9). 1989, Harcourt $13.95 (0-15-200645-1). Willy lacks confidence because he is a slow learner. (Rev: BL 2/1/90; SLJ 12/89)

909 Buchanan, Dawna Lisa. *The Falcon's Wing* (6–9). 1992, Orchard LB $15.99 (0-531-08586-4). A teenage girl learns to understand and defend her retarded cousin. (Rev: BL 2/1/92; SLJ 4/92)

910 Bunting, Eve. *Face at the Edge of the World* (9–12). 1985, Ticknor paper $6.95 (0-89919-800-7). Jed tries to find out the whys behind the suicide of his friend Charlie, a gifted black student. (Rev: BL 8/85; BR 9–10/86; SLJ 12/85; VOYA 8/85)

911 Burgess, Melvin. *Smack* (10–12). 1998, Holt paper $16.95 (0-8050-5801-X). This novel, which won Britain's Carnegie Medal, is a harrowing, provocative story of teen heroin addiction in Bristol during the 1980s. (Rev: BL 4/15/98; SLJ 5/98)

912 Cadnum, Michael. *Edge* (8–12). 1997, Viking $15.99 (0-670-87335-7). Zachary, a confused high school dropout from a broken home, seeks revenge when his father is shot in the spine during a street robbery. (Rev: BL 6/1–15/97; SLJ 7/97; VOYA 12/97)

913 Calvert, Patricia. *Picking Up the Pieces* (5–9). 1993, Scribners $15.00 (0-684-19558-5). A story of adjustments: Megan, 14, is wheelchair-bound for life after an accident and Julia, an aging actress, is trying to adjust to her declining career. (Rev: BL 5/1/93; SLJ 6/93; VOYA 8/93)

914 Clauser, Suzanne. *A Girl Named Sooner* (9–12). 1976, Avon paper $2.95 (0-380-00216-7). A neglected girl is given a home by a veterinarian and his wife.

915 Cleaver, Vera, and Bill Cleaver. *Me Too* (7–9). 1973, HarperCollins $13.95 (0-397-31485-X); paper $2.95 (0-06-440161-8). Linda is convinced that she can make her slightly retarded sister normal.

916 Cole, Barbara. *Alex the Great* (8–12). 1989, Rosen LB $12.95 (0-8239-0941-7). The events leading up to Alex's drug overdose is told first by Alex and then by her friend, Deonna. (Rev: BR 9–10/89; VOYA 8/89)

917 Cormier, Robert. *The Bumblebee Flies Anyway* (7–12). 1983, Dell paper $4.99 (0-440-90871-X). A terminally ill boy and his gradual realization of his situation.

918 Cormier, Robert. *Heroes: A Novel* (7–12). 1998, Delacorte $15.95 (0-385-32590-8). In this powerful novel, Francis returns home disfigured after World War II to seek revenge and murder his childhood hero. (Rev: BL 6/1–15/98; SLJ 8/98; VOYA 8/98)

919 Covington, Dennis. *Lizard* (9–12). 1991, Dell paper $4.50 (0-440-21490-4). This work explores the themes of gaining worldly wisdom and resolving adolescent fears of being different—in this case, having a facial deformity and other birth defects. (Rev: BL 5/1/91*; SLJ 6/91)

920 Crutcher, Chris. *Chinese Handcuffs* (9–12). 1989, Greenwillow $14.00 (0-688-08345-5). A brutal novel about basketball, a young man trying to adjust to his brother's suicide, and a sexually abused girl. (Rev: BL 3/15/90; BR 9–10/89; SLJ 4/89; VOYA 6/89)

921 Crutcher, Chris. *Staying Fat for Sarah Byrnes* (7–12). 1993, Greenwillow $16.00 (0-688-11552-7). Overweight Eric's only friend is Sarah, whose face was severely burned as a child. Their attempt to escape her unbalanced father leads to an almost deadly climax. (Rev: BL 3/15/93; SLJ 3/93*; VOYA 8/93)

922 Davis, Deborah. *My Brother Has AIDS* (6–9). 1994, Atheneum $15.00 (0-689-31922-3). In this realistic, accurate portrait of the caretaking families that love people with AIDS, Lacy, 13, is unprepared for the announcement that her beloved older brother is homosexual and dying of AIDS. (Rev: BL 11/15/94; SLJ 1/95; VOYA 5/95)

923 Dessen, Sarah. *That Summer* (7–12). 1996, Orchard LB $17.99 (0-531-08888-X). Haven is 15 and 5 feet 11, and to make matters worse, she has to be bridesmaid at her picture-perfect sister's wedding. (Rev: BL 10/15/96*; BR 3–4/97; SLJ 10/96; VOYA 12/96)

924 Diezeno, Patricia. *Why Me? The Story of Jenny* (7–10). 1976, Avon paper $3.50 (0-380-00563-8). A young rape victim doesn't know how to cope.

925 Draper, Sharon M. *Forged by Fire* (7–10). 1997, Simon & Schuster $16.00 (0-689-80699-X). Nine-year-old African American Gerald Nickelby must leave the comfort of his aunt's home to live with a neglectful mother, her daughter Angel, and husband Jordan, who is secretly sexually abusing young Angel. A companion volume to *Tears of a Tiger.* Coretta Scott King Award, 1998. (Rev: BL 2/15/97; SLJ 3/97; VOYA 6/97)

926 Draper, Sharon M. *Tears of a Tiger* (7–10). 1994, Atheneum $16.00 (0-689-31878-2). A star basketball player is killed in an accident after he and his friends drink and drive. The driver, who survives, is depressed and ultimately commits suicide. (Rev: BL 11/1/94; SLJ 2/95)

927 Durant, Penny R. *When Heroes Die* (6–9). 1992, Atheneum $15.00 (0-689-31764-6). Gary, 12, has to face the fact that his uncle-hero is homosexual and has contracted AIDS. (Rev: BL 10/15/92; SLJ 11/92)

928 Ethridge, Kenneth E. *Toothpick* (7–10). 1985, Troll paper $2.50 (0-8167-1316-2). A friendship between Jamie, an outsider who is unsure of himself, and Janice, a terminally ill girl, gives him the confidence he needs. (Rev: BL 11/15/85; SLJ 12/85; VOYA 4/86)

929 Farnes, Catherine. *Snow* (5–9). 1999, Bob Jones Univ. Pr. $6.49 (1-57924-199-9). A thoughtful novel about an albino girl's problems being accepted even among students who profess to have Christian charity. (Rev: BL 7/99)

930 Ferris, Jean. *Invincible Summer* (9–12). 1987, Avon paper $3.50 (0-380-70619-9). The story of a friendship and later a love shared by 2 courageous teenagers, both suffering from leukemia. (Rev: SLJ 8/87)

931 Fleischman, Paul. *Mind's Eye* (8–12). 1999, Holt $15.95 (0-8050-6314-5). The story of the relationship that develops among 3 people in a contemporary nursing home: Courtney, a 16-year-old girl paralyzed from an accident; May, who suffers from Alzheimer's disease; and Elva, a former high school English teacher, who tries to bring Courtney out of her bouts of sullenness and self-pity. (Rev: BL 9/1/99; SLJ 8/99; VOYA 12/99)

932 Fox, Paula. *Radiance Descending* (5–8). 1997, DK Publg. $14.95 (0-7894-2467-3). Paul learns the true meaning of love when he gradually accepts his younger brother who has Down's syndrome. (Rev: SLJ 9/97; VOYA 2/98)

933 Fox, Paula. *The Stone-Faced Boy* (6–8). 1968, Bradbury LB $13.95 (0-02-735570-5). In his family Gus gets the reputation of being stone-faced because he cannot express emotion.

934 Frank, Lucy. *I Am an Artichoke* (6–9). 1995, Holiday House $14.95 (0-8234-1150-8). Sarah, 15, spends a summer as a mother's helper for Emily, who is 12 and anorexic and whose mother alternates between denial and obsession. (Rev: BL 2/1/95; SLJ 3/95)

935 Fraustino, Lisa Rowe. *Ash* (9–12). 1995, Orchard LB $17.99 (0-531-08739-5). A 15-year-old recalls, in diary form, his older brother's slide into schizophrenia. (Rev: BL 4/1/95; SLJ 4/95; VOYA 5/95)

936 Froehlich, Margaret W. *Hide Crawford Quick* (7–9). 1983, Houghton $9.95 (0-395-33884-0). A family's first boy is born with a physical handicap.

937 Gantos, Jack. *Joey Pigza Swallowed the Key* (5–8). 1998, Farrar $16.00 (0-374-33664-4). Joey, who suffers from attention deficit disorder, causes so much trouble that he is sent to a special education center, where he learns to cope with his problem. (Rev: BL 12/15/98; SLJ 12/98*; VOYA 2/99)

938 Gleitzman, Morris. *Blabber Mouth* (6–8). 1995, Harcourt $11.00 (0-15-200369-X); paper $5.00 (0-15-200370-3). A mute girl is anything but silent as she talks with her hands and inside her head. (Rev: BL 5/1/95; SLJ 6/95)

939 Gould, Marilyn. *The Twelfth of June* (5–8). 1994, Allied Crafts $12.95 (0-9632305-4-9). Janis, who suffers from cerebral palsy, is suffering the first pangs of adolescence and is still fighting the battle to be treated like other girls her age, in this sequel to *Golden Daffodils* (1982). (Rev: SLJ 11/86; VOYA 12/86)

940 Grant, Cynthia D. *The White Horse* (9–12). 1998, Simon & Schuster $16.00 (0-689-82127-1). A brutally graphic story of a girl hooked on heroin, her life, emotional abuse, and decisions she must make when she discovers that she is pregnant. (Rev: BL 10/15/98; SLJ 12/98; VOYA 12/98)

941 Greenberg, Joanne. *I Never Promised You a Rose Garden* (10–12). 1989, NAL paper $5.99 (0-451-16031-2). A 16-year-old Jewish girl sinks into schizophrenia and receives help in an asylum.

942 Greene, Shep. *The Boy Who Drank Too Much* (7–9). 1979, Dell paper $4.50 (0-440-90493-5). At one time Buff's main concern was sports, now it's alcohol.

943 Grima, Tony, ed. *Not the Only One: Lesbian and Gay Fiction for Teens* (10–12). 1995, Alyson Pubs. paper $7.95 (1-55583-275-X). This collection of lesbian/gay fiction deals with young-adult characters, including works by Leslea Newman, Laurel Winter, Emily Ormand, and Raymond Luczak. (Rev: BL 7/95; VOYA 4/96)

944 Guy, Rosa. *My Love, My Love, or the Peasant Girl* (9–12). 1995, Holt paper $9.95 (0-8050-1659-7). This, a modern retelling of the Little Mermaid story, uses a Caribbean Island as its setting and tells of the tragic love of a poor peasant girl for a rich mulatto. (Rev: BL 9/15/85; SLJ 1/86; VOYA 4/86)

945 Hall, Liza F. *Perk! The Story of a Teenager with Bulimia* (6–9). 1997, Gurze paper $10.95 (0-936077-27-1). The story of Priscilla, who binges on food then vomits, her disapproving parents, and her crush on an unsuitable boy. (Rev: BL 9/15/97; SLJ 4/98; VOYA 4/98)

946 Hamilton, Virginia. *The Planet of Junior Brown* (7–9). 1971, Macmillan LB $18.00 (0-02-742510-X); paper $4.50 (0-02-043540-1). A 300-pound misfit is taken care of by his friends.

947 Harrison, Stuart. *The Snow Falcon* (10–12). 1999, St. Martin's $23.95 (0-312-20166-4). Michael Somers returns to his hometown from psychiatric treatment hoping to reshape his life and encounters a boy who has become mute because of trauma and a snow falcon that has been wounded by a hunter. (Rev: BL 1/1–15/99; SLJ 5/99)

948 Helfman, Elizabeth. *On Being Sarah* (7–9). Illus. 1992, Albert Whitman LB $13.95 (0-8075-6068-5). Based on the life of a real person, this is the story of Sarah, 12, who has cerebral palsy, cannot vocalize, and is confined to a wheelchair, and communicates through Blissymbols. (Rev: BL 12/15/92; SLJ 1/93)

949 Hesse, Karen. *The Music of Dolphins* (6–9). 1996, Scholastic $19.99 (0-590-89797-7). An intriguing novel about a young girl who has been raised by dolphins and, after being returned to the world of humans, longs for her life in the sea. (Rev: BL 10/15/96; BR 11–12/96; SLJ 11/96*; VOYA 2/97)

950 Hesser, Terry S. *Kissing Doorknobs* (6–12). 1998, Delacorte $15.95 (0-385-32329-8). The funny, moving story of a girl afflicted with obsessive-compulsive disorder who even worries about her excessive worrying, and how she eventually gets help. (Rev: BL 6/1–15/98; BR 1–2/99; SLJ 6/98; VOYA 12/98)

951 Hoban, Julia. *Acting Normal* (9–12). 1998, HarperCollins $14.95 (0-06-023519-5). Stephanie confronts the memory of childhood abuse when she visits a therapist to determine the reasons for her recent nervous breakdown. (Rev: BL 4/15/98; SLJ 5/98; VOYA 12/98)

952 Holt, Kimberly Willis. *When Zachary Beaver Came to Town* (6–9). 1999, Holt $16.95 (0-8050-6116-9). In this first-person narrative, 13-year-old Toby describes his growing compassion for a 600-pound teenager named Zachery Beaver. (Rev: BL 9/15/99; VOYA 12/99)

953 Howe, James. *The Watcher* (8–12). 1997, Simon & Schuster $15.00 (0-689-80186-6). The lives of 3 troubled teens converge in a horrific climax in this novel of child abuse. (Rev: BL 6/1–15/97; BR 11–12/97; SLJ 5/97; VOYA 8/97)

954 Hughes, Monica. *Hunter in the Dark* (7–10). 1983, Avon paper $2.95 (0-380-67702-4). In spite of his leukemia, Mike goes on a secret hunting trip into a Canadian wilderness. (Rev: BL 11/1/88)

955 Hurwin, Davida Wills. *A Time for Dancing* (7–12). 1995, Little, Brown $15.95 (0-316-38351-1). A powerful story of 2 friends, one of whom is diagnosed with lymphoma. Their friendship becomes a story of saying good-bye and death. (Rev: BL 11/1/95*; SLJ 10/95; VOYA 12/95)

956 Johnson, Angela. *Humming Whispers* (8–12). 1995, Orchard LB $16.99 (0-531-08748-4). Sophy, 14, reveals the impact of her 24-year-old sister Nicole's schizophrenia on the lives of those who love her. (Rev: BL 2/15/95; SLJ 4/95; VOYA 5/95)

957 Kata, Elizabeth. *A Patch of Blue* (10–12). 1983, Amereon $18.95 (0-89190-119-1); Warner paper $5.99 (0-446-31485-4). A blind girl finds love with a man who also has a number of personal problems.

958 Keith, Lois. *A Different Life* (9–12). (Livewire) 1998, Women's Press, Ltd. paper $11.95 (0-7043-4946-9). In this moving novel, 15-year-old Libby adjusts to a crippling disease with the help of a handicapped social worker, a school chum named Jesse, and her own fortitude. (Rev: SLJ 7/98)

959 Keyes, Daniel. *Flowers for Algernon* (10–12). 1966, Harcourt $18.95 (0-15-131510-8). When the I.Q. of a mentally handicapped man is changed by an operation, he faces serious problems. (Rev: BL 10/15/88)

960 Klass, Sheila S. *Rhino* (7–10). 1993, Scholastic $13.95 (0-590-44250-3). Fourteen-year-old Annie suffers from a nose that is a family trait and looks too big for her face. (Rev: BL 1/15/94; SLJ 11/93; VOYA 12/93)

961 Klein, Norma. *Family Secrets* (10–12). 1987, Fawcett paper $3.99 (0-449-70195-6). Two seniors in high school become lovers and then discover that the mother of one is going to marry the father of the other. (Rev: BL 10/1/85; BR 5–6/86; SLJ 12/85)

962 Klein, Norma. *Sunshine* (9–12). 1976, Avon paper $3.99 (0-380-00049-0). This is the moving account of a gallant woman who died of cancer at age 20.

963 Koller, Jackie F. *The Falcon* (7–12). 1998, Simon & Schuster $16.00 (0-689-81294-9). In fulfilling a school journalism assignment, Luke explores his inner feelings and finds an emotional demon that has haunted him for years. (Rev: BL 4/15/98; BR 1–2/99; SLJ 5/98; VOYA 2/99)

964 Lachtman, Ofelia Dumas. *Leticia's Secret* (5–8). 1997, Arte Publico $14.95 (1-55885-205-5); paper $7.95 (1-55885-209-3). Rosario, from a Mexican American family, shares many adventures with her cousin, the pretty Leticia, and is devastated to learn that she has a fatal disease. (Rev: SLJ 1/98)

965 Laird, Elizabeth. *Secret Friends* (5–8). 1999, Putnam $14.99 (0-399-23334-2). Lucy tells the story of her ill-fated friendship with the class outsider who has been nicknamed Earwig because of her protruding ears. (Rev: BL 1/1–15/99; BR 9–10/99; SLJ 3/99)

966 Lantz, Francess. *Fade Far Away: A Novel* (8–12). 1998, Avon paper $14.00 (0-380-97553-X). Fifteen-year-old Sienna realizes that her world-famous sculptor father is a fallible human being when she gets close to him after he is stricken with an inoperable brain tumor. (Rev: SLJ 7/98; VOYA 8/98)

967 Larson, Rodger. *What I Know Now* (9–12). 1997, Holt $15.95 (0-8050-4869-3). At 14, Dave becomes deeply attached to Gene Tole, the family gardener, because he represents all the virtues and integrity that Dave admires—then, suddenly, Dave discovers that Gene is gay. (Rev: BL 5/1/97; SLJ 5/97; VOYA 6/97)

968 Lee, Joanna, and T. S. Cook. *Mary Jane Harper Cried Last Night* (7–10). 1978, NAL paper $2.95 (0-451-13980-1). Mary Jane is the silent victim of her mother's physical abuse.

969 LeMieux, A. C. *Dare To Be, M.E.!* (5–8). Illus. 1997, Avon paper $14.00 (0-380-97496-7). In this sequel to *Fruit Flies, Fish, and Fortune Cookies* (1994), Mary Ellen helps her friend Justine cope with bulimia. (Rev: BL 6/1–15/97; SLJ 7/97)

970 Levenkron, Steven. *The Best Little Girl in the World* (10–12). 1989, Warner paper $6.99 (0-446-35865-7). Francessa's desire to be perfect leads her into the world of an anorexic.

971 Levoy, Myron. *Alan and Naomi* (7–9). 1977, HarperCollins paper $4.95 (0-06-440209-6). Alan tries to reach Naomi, whose mind has been warped by memories of the Holocaust. (Rev: BL 10/1/97)

972 Lipsyte, Robert. *One Fat Summer* (7–12). 1991, HarperCollins paper $4.95 (0-06-447073-3). Bobby Marks is 14, fat, and unhappy in this first novel of 3 that traces Bobby's career through his first year of college. (Rev: BL 1/1–15/98)

973 McCracken, Elizabeth. *The Giant's House* (10–12). 1996, Dial $19.95 (0-385-31433-7). This novel, set on Cape Cod, traces the friendship and love shared by Peggy Cort, a librarian, and a youngster, James Sweatt, who grows to over 8 feet by the age of 19. (Rev: BL 5/15/96; SLJ 11/96)

974 McDaniel, Lurlene. *Saving Jessica* (7–10). 1996, Bantam paper $4.99 (0-553-56721-7). When Jessica is stricken with kidney failure, her boyfriend, Jeremy, volunteers to donate one of his but his parents, fearful that he will die, refuse permission. (Rev: VOYA 4/96)

975 McDaniel, Lurlene. *Too Young to Die* (7–9). 1989, Bantam paper $4.99 (0-553-28008-2). Melissa discovers that she has leukemia and must learn to cope with this tragedy. Also use: *Goodbye Doesn't Mean Forever* (1989). (Rev: SLJ 8/89; VOYA 12/89)

976 Maclean, John. *Mac* (8–12). 1987, Avon paper $2.95 (0-380-70700-4). A high school sophomore's life falls apart after he is sexually assaulted by a doctor during a physical exam. (Rev: BL 10/1/87; SLJ 11/87)

977 Magorian, Michelle. *Good Night, Mr. Tom* (7–9). 1981, HarperCollins LB $15.89 (0-06-024079-2); paper $4.95 (0-06-440174-X). A quiet recluse takes in an abused 8-year-old who has been evacuated from World War II London.

978 Marsden, John. *Checkers* (7–12). 1998, Houghton $15.00 (0-395-85754-6). A harrowing story, set in Australia, about a teenager who suffers a nervous breakdown after her prominent father is accused of unethical business practices, and of the love she and her dog, Checkers, share. (Rev: BL 10/15/98; BR 5–6/99; SLJ 9/98; VOYA 12/98)

979 Mathis, Sharon. *Teacup Full of Roses* (7–12). 1987, Puffin paper $4.99 (0-14-032328-7). For mature teens, a novel about the devastating effects of drugs on a black family.

980 Mazer, Harry. *The Wild Kid* (4–8). 1998, Simon & Schuster paper $15.00 (0-689-80751-1). Sammy, a young boy with Down's syndrome, gets into all sorts of difficulties but finally makes a friend of a wild kid named Kevin who understands him and his problems. (Rev: BL 8/98; SLJ 10/98; VOYA 2/99)

981 Mazer, Norma Fox. *Silver* (6–9). 1988, Morrow $16.00 (0-688-06865-0). Sarabeth moves to a posh school and finds that her best friend there is being sexually abused. (Rev: BL 11/1/88; BR 11–12/88; SLJ 11/88; VOYA 2/89)

982 Metzger, Lois. *Barry's Sister* (6–9). 1992, Atheneum $15.95 (0-689-31521-X). The story of a child with cerebral palsy and its impact on the family. (Rev: BL 4/15/92; SLJ 6/92)

983 Metzger, Lois. *Ellen's Case* (7–12). 1995, Atheneum $16.00 (0-689-31934-7). In this sequel to *Barry's Sister,* Ellen—now 16 and more understanding of her brother's cerebral palsy—is involved in an intense malpractice trial. (Rev: BL 8/95; SLJ 10/95; VOYA 12/95)

984 Mikaelsen, Ben. *Petey* (6–9). 1998, Disney $15.95 (0-7868-0426-2). This is a touching story of an eighth grade student, Trevor Ladd, and his friendship with Petey, an elderly man crippled from cerebral palsy, who was misdiagnosed as "an idiot" at the age of 2 and spent 68 years in an asylum, where he developed close relationships with his caretakers. (Rev: BL 11/1/98; SLJ 11/98; VOYA 2/99)

985 Miklowitz, Gloria D. *Past Forgiving* (8–10). 1995, Simon & Schuster paper $16.00 (0-671-88442-5). A teenage girl caught in an abusive relationship with her boyfriend. (Rev: BL 5/1/95; SLJ 6/95)

986 Moon, Pat. *The Spying Game* (5–8). 1999, Putnam $16.99 (0-399-23354-7). Twelve-year-old Joe Harris is so filled with anger at the death of his father that he begins stalking the driver of the car that killed him. (Rev: SLJ 8/99; VOYA 10/99)

987 Mowry, Jess. *Babylon Boyz* (9–12). 1997, Simon & Schuster paper $16.00 (0-689-80839-9). In this novel for mature readers, three alienated boys— one homosexual, another with a severe heart condition, and the third fat—try to escape their squalid inner-city neighborhood called Babylon in Oakland, California. (Rev: BL 2/15/97; SLJ 9/97*; VOYA 6/97)

988 Myers, Walter Dean. *Sweet Illusions* (10–12). 1987, Teachers & Writers paper $8.95 (0-915924-15-3). Stories about teenage pregnancy from both male and female points of view. (Rev: BL 6/15/87; VOYA 8/87)

989 Naylor, Phyllis Reynolds. *The Keeper* (6–10). 1986, Macmillan $16.00 (0-689-31204-0). Nick and his mother agonize over whether or not to have Nick's mentally ill father institutionalized. (Rev: BL 4/1/86; SLJ 5/86; VOYA 2/87)

990 Neufeld, John. *Lisa, Bright and Dark* (7–9). 1969, Phillips $27.25 (0-87599-153-X); NAL paper $2.95 (0-451-16093-2). Her friend notices that Lisa is gradually sinking into mental illness but her parents seem indifferent.

991 Oneal, Zibby. *The Language of Goldfish* (7–10). 1990, Puffin paper $4.99 (0-14-034540-X). Carrie appears to be slowly sinking into mental illness and seems unable to help herself.

992 Orr, Wendy. *Peeling the Onion* (8–12). 1997, Holiday House $16.95 (0-8234-1289-X); Bantam Doubleday Dell paper $4.50 (0-440-22773-9). An automobile accident leaves Anna with a broken back, debilitating pain, physical and mental handicaps, and questions about what to do with her life. (Rev: BL 4/1/97; SLJ 5/97*; VOYA 10/97)

993 Park, Barbara. *Beanpole* (7–9). 1983, Avon paper $2.95 (0-380-69840-4). On her 13th birthday Lillian, who is extra tall for her age, makes 3 wishes and they seem to be coming true.

994 Paulsen, Gary. *The Monument* (6–9). 1991, Delacorte $15.00 (0-385-30518-4). A 13-year-old girl's friendship with an artist who is hired to create a monument in her small town transforms her into dedicating herself to art. (Rev: BL 9/15/91; SLJ 10/91*)

995 Peck, Richard. *Remembering the Good Times* (7–10). 1986, Delacorte $12.95 (0-385-29396-8); Bantam paper $4.99 (0-440-97339-2). A strong friendship between 2 boys and a girl is destroyed when one of them commits suicide. (Rev: BL 3/1/85; BR 9–10/85)

996 Platt, Kin. *The Ape Inside Me* (6–8). 1979, HarperCollins LB $11.89 (0-397-31863-4). Eddie and Debbie work together to try and curb their terrible tempers.

997 Reid, P. Carey. *Swimming in the Starry River* (9–12). 1994, Hyperion $19.95 (0-7868-6005-7). In this chronicle of courage, frustration, and compassion, a father forges a powerful bond with his young child who has a debilitating disease. (Rev: BL 5/15/94)

998 Rosen, Lillian. *Just Like Everybody Else* (7–9). 1981, Harcourt $12.95 (0-15-241652-8). Jenny finds the courage to accept her deafness, which was caused by a bus accident.

999 Rubin, Susan G. *Emily Good As Gold* (6–8). 1993, Harcourt $10.95 (0-15-276632-4). Emily's parents see their developmentally disabled child as never being able to grow up, but Emily begins to do so on her own, especially sexually. (Rev: BL 11/1/93; SLJ 10/93)

1000 Ruckman, Ivy. *The Hunger Scream* (7–10). 1983, Walker $22.95 (0-8027-6514-9). Lily starves herself to become a popular member of the in-crowd.

1001 Samuels, Gertrude. *Run, Shelley, Run!* (9–12). 1975, NAL paper $2.50 (0-451-13987-9). Shelley, a rebellious young girl, plans on escaping from the state training school where the courts have sent her.

1002 Scoppettone, Sandra. *Long Time between Kisses* (7–10). 1982, HarperCollins $12.95 (0-06-025229-4). A 16-year-old brings together a victim of multiple sclerosis and his fiancée.

1003 Scott, Virginia M. *Belonging* (9–12). 1986, Kendall Green paper $2.95 (0-930323-33-5). A 15-year-old girl must adjust to deafness caused by an attack of meningitis. (Rev: VOYA 4/88)

1004 Seago, Kate. *Matthew Unstrung* (7–12). 1998, Dial $16.99 (0-8037-2230-3). Set in 1910, this novel portrays the descent into madness of a sensitive, teenage seminarian and his institutionalization after a nervous breakdown. (Rev: BL 5/1/98; SLJ 3/98; VOYA 2/98)

1005 Seidler, Tor. *The Silent Spillbills* (5–8). 1998, HarperCollins LB $14.89 (0-06-205181-4). Katrina faces problems trying to overcome her stuttering and stand up to her tyrannical grandfather to help save from extinction a rare bird known as the silent spillbill. (Rev: BL 12/15/98; SLJ 4/99)

1006 Shyer, Marlene Fanta. *Welcome Home, Jellybean* (6–8). 1996, Peter Smith $18.50 (0-8446-6884-2); Simon & Schuster paper $4.99 (0-689-71213-8). A 12-year-old boy tells about the return home of his older retarded sister.

1007 Sirof, Harriet. *Because She's My Friend* (7–10). 1993, Atheneum $16.00 (0-689-31844-8). Two girls of opposite temperament become friends when strong-willed Valerie's right leg is paralyzed after an accident and she meets well-behaved Terri. (Rev: BL 9/15/93; SLJ 10/93; VOYA 12/93)

1008 Snyder, Anne. *Goodbye, Paper Doll* (10–12). 1980, NAL paper $2.95 (0-451-15943-8). Seventeen-year-old Rosemary must overcome anorexia nervosa as well as a multitude of other personal problems.

1009 Snyder, Anne. *My Name Is Davy: I'm an Alcoholic* (7–10). 1978, NAL paper $3.50 (0-451-14976-9). Davy has become so dependent on alcohol that he steals to feed his habit.

1010 Springer, Nancy. *Colt* (5–9). 1994, Puffin paper $3.99 (0-14-036480-3). Colt, in a wheelchair with spina bifida, enjoys a physical therapy program of horseback riding. (Rev: BL 11/1/91)

1011 Sultan, Faye, and Teresa Kennedy. *Over the Line* (10–12). 1997, Doubleday $21.95 (0-385-48525-5). Portia McTeague, a forensic psychologist, investigates the case of Jimmy the Weird, a mentally handicapped young man who has committed 2 murders, to make a decision concerning a plea of insanity. (Rev: BL 11/15/97; SLJ 8/98)

1012 Tashjian, Janet. *Multiple Choice* (5–9). 1999, Holt $16.95 (0-8050-6086-3). Fourteen-year-old Monica realizes she needs outside help when her attempts to cope with her obsessive drive for perfection spin out of control with almost tragic consequences. (Rev: BL 6/1–15/99; SLJ 9/99; VOYA 10/99)

1013 Tashjian, Janet. *Tru Confessions* (7–10). 1997, Holt $15.95 (0-8050-5254-2). Young Tru, an amateur filmmaker, begins a documentary about her handicapped twin brother, Eddie, in this novel made up of Tru's diary entries, Internet conversations, and Eddie's computer graphics. (Rev: BL 1/1–15/98; SLJ 12/97; VOYA 12/97)

1014 Terris, Susan. *Nell's Quilt* (9–12). 1996, Farrar paper $4.95 (0-374-45497-3). In turn-of-the-century Amherst, a young girl cracks under the strain of having to marry a man she does not like. (Rev: BL 11/1/87; SLJ 11/87)

1015 Thomas, Joyce C. *Marked by Fire* (8–12). 1982, Avon paper $4.50 (0-380-79327-X). After she is raped, a Southern black girl seems to lose her beautiful singing voice. A sequel is *Bright Shadow* (1984). (Rev: BL 7/88)

1016 Voigt, Cynthia. *Izzy, Willy-Nilly* (7–12). 1986, Macmillan $17.00 (0-689-31202-4). A 15-year-old girl's life changes dramatically when she has a leg amputated. (Rev: BL 5/1/86; SLJ 4/86; VOYA 12/86)

1017 Walter, Virginia. *Making Up Megaboy* (6–9). Illus. 1998, DK Publg. $16.95 (0-7894-2488-6). After Robbie, age 13, shoots and kills the elderly proprietor of a liquor store, everyone is baffled as to the reason why. (Rev: BL 2/15/98; BR 11–12/98; SLJ 4/98; VOYA 8/98)

1018 Warner, Sally. *Sort of Forever* (5–8). 1998, Knopf LB $17.99 (0-679-98648-0); Random paper $4.99 (0-375-80207-X). Cady has always relied on the strength of her friend Nana, but now Nana has leukemia and it appears it will be fatal. (Rev: BL 6/1–15/98; SLJ 7/98)

1019 Werlin, Nancy. *Are You Alone on Purpose?* (5–8). 1994, Houghton $16.00 (0-395-67350-X). Opposites attract when Alison, 13, hesitantly falls in love with the unruly Harry, who has an accident that confines him to a wheelchair. (Rev: BL 8/94; SLJ 9/94; VOYA 10/94)

1020 Wersba, Barbara. *Fat: A Love Story* (8–12). 1987, HarperCollins $11.95 (0-06-026400-4). Rita Formica, fat and unhappy, falls for rich, attractive Robert. (Rev: BL 6/1/87; SLJ 8/87; VOYA 6/87)

1021 White, Ruth. *Weeping Willow* (7–10). 1992, Farrar paper $3.95 (0-374-48280-2). This uplifting novel conveying hill country life is about a girl who overcomes abuse to make her own way. (Rev: BL 6/15/92; SLJ 7/92)

1022 Williams, Karen L. *A Real Christmas This Year* (5–8). 1995, Clarion $13.95 (0-395-70115-5). Megan worries that she won't have a happy Christmas because her brother Kevin suffers from physical and emotional problems that exhaust their mother and strain their finances. Eventually, she gets the Christmas she wants—and some unexpected lessons about life. (Rev: BL 9/15/95; VOYA 12/95)

1023 Wolff, Virginia E. *Probably Still Nick Swansen* (7–12). 1988, Holt $14.95 (0-8050-0701-6). Nick, a 16-year-old victim of slight brain dysfunction, tells his story of rejection and separation. (Rev: BL 11/15/88; BR 5–6/89; SLJ 12/88; VOYA 6/89)

1024 Wood, June R. *The Man Who Loved Clowns* (5–8). 1992, Putnam $16.99 (0-399-21888-2). Delrita's views of living and dying, appreciating and surrendering, are transformed after the death of her parents in an auto accident and the death of her uncle from Down's syndrome. (Rev: BL 11/15/92; SLJ 9/92*)

1025 Woodruff, Joan L. *The Shiloh Renewal* (7–10). 1998, Black Heron $22.95 (0-930773-50-0). Sandy, who has been mentally and physically injured since an automobile accident, tries to regain basic skills, recover from the brain trauma, and straighten out her life in this novel that takes place on a small farm near the Shiloh National Park in Tennessee. (Rev: VOYA 12/98)

Personal Problems and Growing into Maturity

1026 Adler, C. S. *Not Just a Summer Crush* (5–8). 1998, Houghton $15.00 (0-395-88532-9). When 12-year-old Hana Riley meets her former teacher during the family's summer vacation on Cape Cod, an innocent friendship develops to which Hana's parents object. (Rev: BL 11/15/98; BR 5–6/99; SLJ 11/98)

1027 Aker, Don. *Stranger at Bay* (6–9). 1998, Stoddart paper $4.95 (0-7736-7468-3). Set in a town on the Bay of Fundy in Canada, this novel tells about Randy Forsythe's adjustment to a new home and stepmother while coping with a gang of bullies who want him to steal drugs from his father, who is a pharmaceutical salesman. (Rev: SLJ 7/98)

1028 Anderson, Laurie Halse. *Speak* (8–12). 1999, Farrar $16.00 (0-374-37152-0). A victim of rape, high school freshman Mellinda Sordino finds that her attacker is again threatening her. (Rev: BL 9/15/99; SLJ 10/99; VOYA 12/99)

1029 Anderson, Mary. *Tune in Tomorrow* (7–9). 1985, Avon paper $2.50 (0-380-69870-6). Jo is fixat-

ed on 2 soap opera characters whom she later meets in real life.

1030 Angell, Judie. *The Buffalo Nickel Blues Band* (7–10). 1991, Simon & Schuster paper $3.95 (0-689-71448-3). Some friends form a band and are sent on the road.

1031 *Annie's Baby: The Diary of Anonymous, a Pregnant Teenager* (6–10). 1998, Demco $10.34 (0-606-13145-0); Avon paper $4.99 (0-380-79141-2). In diary format, this is the story of 14-year-old Annie, her love for an abusive rich boyfriend, and her rape and subsequent pregnancy. (Rev: SLJ 7/98; VOYA 6/98)

1032 Antle, Nancy. *Lost in the War* (6–10). 1998, Dial $15.99 (0-8037-2299-0). Lisa's father was killed during the Vietnam War and her mother was a nurse during the conflict, so her family is haunted by memories of a war that many people in their lives opposed. (Rev: BL 8/98; SLJ 8/98; VOYA 8/98)

1033 Ashley, Bernard. *All My Men* (7–9). 1978, Phillips $25.95 (0-87599-228-5). In this English story, Paul pays a heavy price to be part of the "in" crowd.

1034 Ashley, Bernard. *Terry on the Fence* (6–8). Illus. 1977, Phillips $25.95 (0-87599-222-6). Unhappy at home, Terry unwillingly becomes a member of a street gang.

1035 Avi. *Blue Heron* (5–8). 1992, Bradbury LB $15.00 (0-02-707751-9). A young girl with a troubled family life finds comfort in nature and a beautiful bird. (Rev: BL 1/15/92*; SLJ 4/92)

1036 Avi. *Nothing but the Truth: A Documentary Novel* (7–10). 1991, Orchard LB $17.99 (0-531-08559-7). A boy's expulsion from school is reported in a biased, inflammatory newspaper story and takes on patriotic and political overtones. (Rev: BL 9/15/91*; SLJ 9/91*)

1037 Avi. *A Place Called Ugly* (6–9). 1995, Avon paper $4.99 (0-380-72423-5). A 14-year-old boy protests the tearing down of a beach cottage to build a hotel.

1038 Avi. *What Do Fish Have to Do with Anything?* (5–8). Illus. 1997, Candlewick $17.99 (0-7636-0329-5); paper $4.99 (0-7636-0412-7). Seven excellent stories about youngsters facing the first pangs of adolescence. (Rev: BL 11/15/97; SLJ 12/97*; VOYA 4/98)

1039 Baker, Jennifer. *Most Likely to Deceive* (6–10). (Class Secrets) 1995, Pocket Books paper $3.99 (0-671-51033-9). Newcomer Suzanne Willis discovers that even the most popular teens in the school have problems. (Rev: SLJ 2/96)

1040 Barnes, Joyce Annette. *Promise Me the Moon* (5–8). 1997, Dial paper $14.99 (0-8037-1798-9).

Annie faces many problems in eighth grade, including being labeled an egghead, in this sequel to *The Baby Grand, the Moon in July, and Me* (1994). (Rev: BL 11/15/96; BR 11–12/97; SLJ 2/97; VOYA 10/97)

1041 Bauer, Marion Dane. *Like Mother, Like Daughter* (6–9). 1985, Clarion $12.70 (0-89919-356-0). Rejecting her mother as a role model, Leslie turns to Ms. Perl, her journalism teacher. (Rev: BR 9–10/86; SLJ 1/86; VOYA 12/85)

1042 Bawden, Nina. *The Peppermint Pig* (6–8). 1975, HarperCollins LB $13.89 (0-397-31618-6). A brother and sister save a pig that they soon regard as a pet but they find something terrible is going to happen to it.

1043 Bertrand, Diane Gonzales. *Trino's Choice* (6–9). 1999, Arte Publico $16.95 (1-55885-279-4); paper $9.95 (1-55885-268-9). A Latino boy growing up in a Texas trailer park succumbs to the offer of a hood who offers him chance at quick cash, but in time it leads to tragedy. (Rev: BL 6/1–15/99)

1044 Betancourt, Jeanne. *Kate's Turn* (5–8). 1992, Scholastic $13.95 (0-590-43103-X). This story of the young ballerina Kate, who decides the price of fame is too high, shows the grueling, often painful life of a dancer. (Rev: BL 1/1/92; SLJ 2/92)

1045 Block, Francesca L. *Baby Be-Bop* (8–12). 1995, HarperCollins LB $13.89 (0-06-024880-7). Dirk is gay and struggles with self-loathing, among a number of debilitating emotions and experiences, until his grandmother shares her wisdom about loving and living. (Rev: BL 10/1/95*; SLJ 9/95)

1046 Block, Francesca L. *Cherokee Bat and the Goat Guys* (9–12). 1993, HarperCollins paper $4.95 (0-06-447095-4). In Block's third punk fairy tale, the youths form a rock band, which finds success until corruption sets in, when wise Coyote puts them right and heals them. (Rev: BL 8/92; SLJ 9/92)

1047 Block, Francesca L. *Violet & Claire* (10–12). 1999, HarperCollins LB $14.89 (0-06-0277750-5). For mature readers, this is the story of the friendship between 2 teenage girls, one of whom gains success as a screenwriter and the other who falls in love with her unfaithful poetry instructor. (Rev: BL 9/1/99; SLJ 9/99)

1048 Block, Francesca L. *Weetzie Bat* (9–12). 1989, HarperCollins $14.95 (0-06-020534-2). Four teenagers into punk culture—2 gay and a straight couple—set up housekeeping but the realities of life spoil their demi-Eden. A controversial book that received mixed reviews. (Rev: BL 3/15/89; BR 3–4/90; SLJ 4/89; VOYA 10/89)

1049 Bloor, Edward. *Tangerine* (7–10). 1997, Harcourt $17.00 (0-15-201246-X); Scholastic paper $4.99 (0-590-43277-X). Although he wears thick glasses, Paul is able to see clearly the people around

him, their problems and their mistakes, as he adjusts to his new home in Tangerine County, Florida. (Rev: BL 5/15/97; SLJ 4/97; VOYA 8/97)

1050 Blume, Judy. *Forever . . .* (9–12). 1975, Bradbury LB $16.00 (0-02-711030-3). A girl's awakening sexuality is explored in this novel that contains frank language and explicit scenes. (Rev: BL 10/15/88)

1051 Blume, Judy. *Here's to You, Rachel Robinson* (6–8). 1993, 1994, Dell paper $4.50 (0-440-40946-2). This sequel to *Just As Long As We're Together* is full of multidimensional characters. (Rev: BL 9/1/93; SLJ 11/93; VOYA 12/93)

1052 Blume, Judy. *Just as Long as We're Together* (6–8). 1987, Dell paper $4.99 (0-440-40075-9). A student entering junior high faces problems involving weight, friendships, and a family that is disintegrating. (Rev: BL 8/87; BR 1–2/88; VOYA 2/88)

1053 Blume, Judy. *Summer Sisters* (10–12). 1998, Delacorte $21.95 (0-385-32405-7). An entertaining adult novel about the friendship of 2 girls and their experiences, worries, and emotions as teenagers growing into maturity during 6 summers that they spend together. (Rev: BL 3/15/98; SLJ 6/98)

1054 Blume, Judy. *Then Again, Maybe I Won't* (6–8). 1971, Dell paper $4.50 (0-440-48659-9). Thirteen-year-old Tony faces many problems when his family relocates to suburban Long Island.

1055 Blume, Judy. *Tiger Eyes* (7–10). 1981, Dell paper $4.99 (0-440-98469-6). The painful adjustment a girl must make to her father's death. (Rev: BL 7/88)

1056 Bohlmeijer, Arno. *Something Very Sorry* (5–8). 1996, Houghton $15.00 (0-395-74679-5). A terrible automobile accident in which Rose and her family are involved brings death into the family and changes her life forever. (Rev: BL 4/1/96; SLJ 7/96*)

1057 Bond, Nancy. *The Love of Friends* (9–12). 1997, Simon & Schuster paper $17.00 (0-689-81365-1). On a trip to remote parts of Scotland, Charlotte, Oliver, and an American friend discover a great deal about themselves, their families, and their friendship. (Rev: BL 11/15/97; BR 3–4/98; SLJ 10/97; VOYA 12/97)

1058 Borntrager, Mary Christner. *Rebecca* (7–12). 1989, Herald Pr. paper $7.95 (0-8361-3500-8). A coming-of-age novel about an Amish girl and her attraction to a Mennonite young man. (Rev: SLJ 11/89)

1059 Bottner, Barbara. *Nothing in Common* (7–10). 1986, HarperCollins $12.95 (0-06-020604-7). When Mrs. Gregori dies both her daughter and Melissa Warren, a teenager in the household where Mrs. Gregori worked, enter a period of grief. (Rev: VOYA 2/87)

1060 Brancato, Robin F. *Come Alive at 505* (7–10). 1980, Knopf LB $8.00 (0-394-94294-9). A teenage would-be disc jockey faces maturation problems.

1061 Brancato, Robin F. *Facing Up* (9–12). 1984, Knopf LB $9.99 (0-394-95488-2). The friendship between Jep and Dave is strained by the attentions of Jep's girlfriend.

1062 Branscum, Robbie. *Johnny May Grows Up* (6–8). Illus. 1987, HarperCollins $11.95 (0-06-020606-3). Johnny May, a spunky mountain girl, has no money to continue her schooling after 8th grade. (Rev: BL 10/1/87; BR 3–4/88; SLJ 12/87)

1063 Bridgers, Sue Ellen. *All We Know of Heaven* (10–12). 1996, Banks Channel $22.00 (0-9635967-4-8). For mature readers, this a shocking story, with finely drawn characters, about a love that eventually leads to betrayal, madness, and death. (Rev: BL 10/1/96; SLJ 1/97)

1064 Bridgers, Sue Ellen. *Keeping Christina* (7–10). 1998, Replica Books LB $29.95 (0-7351-0042-X). Annie takes sad newcomer Christina under her wing, but she turns out to be a liar and troublemaker, which creates conflicts with Annie's family, friends, and boyfriend. (Rev: BL 7/93; SLJ 7/93)

1065 Bridgers, Sue Ellen. *Permanent Connections* (8–12). 1998, Replica Books LB $29.95 (0-7351-0043-8). When Rob's behavior gets out of control, the teenager is sent to his uncle's farm to cool off. (Rev: BL 2/15/87; BR 9–10/87; SLJ 3/87; VOYA 4/87)

1066 Brooks, Bruce. *Asylum for Nightface* (8–12). 1996, HarperCollins LB $13.89 (0-06-027061-6). When Zim's parents undergo a religious conversion, they decide that he should become a poster boy and spokesperson for their new sect. (Rev: BL 6/1–15/96; BR 9–10/96; SLJ 6/96)

1067 Brooks, Bruce. *What Hearts* (8–12). 1995, Demco $11.30 (0-606-08362-6). Four long stories about the boy Asa, especially his relationship with his emotionally fragile mother and his hostile competition with his stepfather. (Rev: BL 9/1/92*; SLJ 11/92)

1068 Brooks, Martha. *Bone Dance* (9–12). 1997, Orchard LB $17.99 (0-531-33021-4). When Alex drives out to see the property her dead father has left her, she meets and becomes involved with Lonnie, stepson of the land's former owner. (Rev: BL 10/1/97; SLJ 11/97; VOYA 12/97)

1069 Brooks, Martha. *Traveling On into the Light* (7–12). 1994, Orchard LB $16.99 (0-531-08713-1). Stories about runaways, suicide, and desertion, featuring romantic, sensitive, and smart teenage outsiders. (Rev: BL 8/94; SLJ 8/94*; VOYA 10/94)

1070 Brown, Larry. *Joe* (9–12). 1991, Algonquin $29.95 (0-945575-61-0). Hard-drinking Joe helps turn the life of a neglected teenager around. (Rev: BL 8/91*)

1071 Bunin, Sherry. *Dear Great American Writers School* (9–12). 1995, Houghton $15.00 (0-395-71645-4). A sensitive, bittersweet story of a young aspiring writer who is drawn into a magazine's scheme to train young writers. (Rev: BL 11/15/95; SLJ 10/95; VOYA 12/95)

1072 Bunting, Eve. *Blackwater* (5–8). 1999, HarperCollins $15.95 (0-06-027838-2). When 13-year-old Brodie reads a note he receives, he realizes that someone knows the truth about his part in the drowning accident of his two friends, Pauline and Otis. (Rev: SLJ 8/99)

1073 Bunting, Eve. *If I Asked You, Would You Stay?* (8–10). 1984, HarperCollins LB $12.89 (0-397-32066-3). Two lonely people find comfort in love for each other.

1074 Bunting, Eve. *Jumping the Nail* (7–12). 1991, Harcourt $15.95 (0-15-241357-X). A dependent, unstable girl becomes unhinged when she is persuaded by her danger-seeking boyfriend to jump off a cliff with him. (Rev: BL 11/1/91; SLJ 12/91)

1075 Burch, Robert. *Queenie Peavy* (6–8). 1987, Penguin paper $4.99 (0-14-032305-8). Queenie, whose father is in prison, is growing up a defiant, disobedient girl in rural Georgia.

1076 Cadnum, Michael. *Breaking the Fall* (8–12). 1992, Viking paper $15.00 (0-670-84687-2). To help him forget that his parents are separating and he isn't playing baseball anymore, Stanley and Jared start housebreaking, taking token items to mark their daring. (Rev: BL 11/15/92; SLJ 9/92)

1077 Cadnum, Michael. *Rundown* (9–12). 1999, Viking $15.99 (0-670-88377-8). In this fast-paced suspense novel, wealthy teenager Jennifer Thayer reports an attempted rape that did not occur in order to gain attention. (Rev: BL 6/1–15/99; SLJ 8/99; VOYA 10/99)

1078 Callan, Jamie. *Over the Hill at Fourteen* (7–9). 1982, NAL paper $1.95 (0-451-13090-1). A successful young model is torn with fears about the future.

1079 Calvert, Patricia. *The Stone Pony* (7–9). 1983, NAL paper $2.99 (0-451-13729-9). In this touching novel, Jo Beth must adjust to the death of her older sister.

1080 Cannon, A. E. *The Shadow Brothers* (7–12). 1992, Dell paper $3.99 (0-440-21167-0). Two foster brothers, one an American Indian, gradually grow apart under the strain of outside pressures. (Rev: BL 5/1/90; BR 5–6/90; SLJ 6/90)

1081 Capote, Truman. *The Thanksgiving Visitor* (10–12). 1968, Random $27.71 (0-394-44824-3). In this tender reminiscence, a young boy learns the meaning of compassion from his spinster cousin. Also use: *A Christmas Memory* (1966).

1082   Cart, Michael. *My Father's Scar* (7–12). 1996, Simon & Schuster paper $16.00 (0-689-80749-X). Andy Logan, a college freshman, is about to have his first gay relationship and recalls growing up a lonely boy in a homophobic community. (Rev: BL 4/1/96; BR 3–4/97; SLJ 5/96; VOYA 8/96)

1083   Carter, Alden R. *Dogwolf* (7–10). 1994, Scholastic $13.95 (0-590-46741-7). In this coming-of-age novel, Pete realizes that a dogwolf that he's set free must be found and killed before it kills a human. (Rev: BL 1/1/95; SLJ 4/95; VOYA 2/95)

1084   Casanova, Mary. *Riot* (5–8). 1996, Hyperion LB $13.89 (0-7868-2204-X). Young Bryan is caught up in his father's conflict concerning the hiring of nonunion workers at his workplace. (Rev: BL 11/1/96; BR 3–4/97; SLJ 10/96)

1085   Chambers, Aidan. *NIK: Now I Know* (10–12). 1988, HarperCollins $13.95 (0-06-021208-X). Nik questions his religious beliefs but by a tortuous route recovers his faith. (Rev: BL 7/88; BR 5–6/89; SLJ 8/88; VOYA 10/88)

1086   Chambers, Veronica. *Marisol and Magdalena: The Sound of Our Sisterhood* (6–9). 1998, Hyperion LB $14.89 (0-7868-2385-8). Two Hispanic American girls who are dear friends are separated when one is sent to Panama to spend a year with her grandmother and meet her father, whom she has never known. (Rev: BL 10/1/98; SLJ 12/98)

1087   Chan, Gillian. *Glory Days and Other Stories* (7–10). 1997, Kids Can $14.95 (1-55074-381-3). Five stories about young people at Elmwood High School, each of whom faces problems because of decisions that have been made. (Rev: BL 1/1–15/98; SLJ 10/97)

1088   Chan, Gillian. *Golden Girl and Other Stories* (7–10). 1997, Kids Can $14.95 (1-55074-385-6). Short stories about different students in a high school, with details on their pleasures, pains, and concerns. (Rev: BL 9/15/97; SLJ 11/97)

1089   Chbosky, Stephen. *The Perks of Being a Wallflower* (9–12). 1999, MTV paper $12.00 (0-671-02734-4). In letter format, outsider Charlie writes about his freshman year in high school, his new, insightful, bohemian friends, his defiance of conformity, and his evolution into a man of action. (Rev: BL 2/15/99; SLJ 6/99; VOYA 12/99)

1090   Chedid, Andree. *The Multiple Child* (10–12). 1995, Mercury House paper $12.95 (1-56279-079-X). In this novel, a lonely 10-year-old boy who has lost an arm in a car bombing in Lebanon is sent by his grandfather to live with relatives in Paris. (Rev: BL 9/1/95; SLJ 7/96)

1091   Childress, Alice. *Those Other People* (9–12). 1989, Putnam $14.95 (0-399-21510-7). A 17-year-old gay boy is blackmailed along with a black boy into silence over the attempted rape they have witnessed. (Rev: BL 1/1/89; SLJ 2/89; VOYA 4/89)

1092   Choi, Sook N. *Gathering of Pearls* (7–10). 1994, Houghton $13.95 (0-395-67437-9). Sookan Bak leaves Korea in 1954 to attend a New York women's college, where she struggles to fit in. Second sequel to *The Year of Impossible Goodbyes*. (Rev: BL 9/1/94; SLJ 10/94; VOYA 10/94)

1093   Cleaver, Vera, and Bill Cleaver. *Ellen Grae* (6–8). 1967, HarperCollins $12.89 (0-397-30938-4). Ellen Grae, an imaginative girl, finds it impossible to assimilate the story of the death of her friend Ira's parents. Included in this volume is the sequel: *Lady Ellen Grae*.

1094   Cleaver, Vera, and Bill Cleaver. *Grover* (7–9). 1987, HarperCollins $13.95 (0-397-31118-4). The death of his beloved mother seems more than Grover can handle. A reissue.

1095   Cleaver, Vera, and Bill Cleaver. *Hazel Rye* (6–9). 1983, HarperCollins LB $13.89 (0-397-31952-5); paper $3.95 (0-06-440156-1). Eleven-year-old Hazel rents the Poole family a small house in a citrus grove.

1096   Cohen, Leah H. *Heat Lightning* (10–12). 1997, Avon paper $22.00 (0-380-97468-1). Mole, 11, and her older sister, Tilly, become involved with a family that moves into their small Maine community for the summer, leading to unusual confrontations and sexual tensions. (Rev: BL 6/1–15/97; SLJ 6/98)

1097   Cohen, Miriam. *Robert and Dawn Marie 4Ever* (6–9). 1986, HarperCollins $11.95 (0-06-021396-5). Robert, a street waif, finds a new home and forms a friendship with Dawn Marie, a young girl whose mother disapproves of Robert. (Rev: BL 11/1/86; SLJ 12/86; VOYA 12/86)

1098   Cole, Brock. *The Goats* (6–9). 1987, Farrar $15.00 (0-374-32678-9); paper $4.95 (0-374-42575-2). Two misfits at summer camp find inner strength and self-knowledge when they are cruelly marooned on an island by fellow campers. (Rev: BL 11/15/87; SLJ 11/87; VOYA 4/88)

1099   Cole, Sheila. *What Kind of Love?* (8–10). 1995, Lothrop $15.00 (0-688-12848-3). A 15-year-old becomes pregnant and deals with hard decisions. (Rev: BL 3/15/95; SLJ 5/95)

1100   Collins, Pat L. *Signs and Wonders* (8–10). 1999, Houghton $15.00 (0-395-97119-5). Through letters to her grandmother, her father, and an imaginary guardian angel, a young girl in boarding school reveals her feelings of unhappiness, loneliness, and betrayal—and her belief that she has been chosen to bear the prophet of the next millennium. (Rev: BL 10/1/99; SLJ 10/99; VOYA 10/99)

1101 Coman, Carolyn. *Tell Me Everything* (6–9). 1993, Farrar $15.00 (0-374-37390-6). When Roz Jacoby's mother dies rescuing Nate from a mountain, Roz seeks him out and tries to find freedom from her pain through forgiveness and God. (Rev: BL 9/15/93*; SLJ 11/93*; VOYA 12/93)

1102 Conford, Ellen. *Crush* (7–12). 1998, Harper-Collins $14.95 (0-06-025414-9). In this collection of interrelated short stories, high school students face problems such as peer pressure, self-esteem, respect, alienation, greed, and heartbreak. (Rev: BL 1/1–15/98; SLJ 1/98; VOYA 6/98)

1103 Conford, Ellen. *You Never Can Tell* (7–9). 1984, Little, Brown $14.95 (0-316-15267-6). Katie's soap opera heartthrob enters her high school.

1104 Conly, Jane L. *Trout Summer* (6–8). 1995, Holt $15.95 (0-8050-3933-3). During a summer spent in a rustic cabin with her mother and brother, 13-year-old Shana meets a crotchety neighbor and adjusts to her grandfather's death and father's desertion. (Rev: BL 1/1–15/96; BR 9–10/96; SLJ 12/95; VOYA 2/96)

1105 Cooney, Caroline B. *Driver's Ed* (7–12). 1994, Delacorte $16.95 (0-385-32087-6). Remy and Morgan are driving around town on an escapade ripping off street signs when they accidentally cause the death of an innocent pedestrian. (Rev: BL 6/1–15/94*; SLJ 8/94; VOYA 10/94)

1106 Cooney, Caroline B. *Summer Nights* (7–12). 1992, Scholastic paper $3.25 (0-590-45786-1). At a farewell party, 5 high school girls look back on their school years and their friendship. (Rev: SLJ 1/89)

1107 Cooney, Caroline B. *What Child Is This? A Christmas Story* (6–10). 1997, Delacorte $14.95 (0-385-32317-4). In a New England community, 3 teenagers and a child try to find what Christmas is all about. (Rev: BL 9/1/97; SLJ 10/97; VOYA 12/97)

1108 Cooper, Ilene. *My Co-Star, My Enemy* (6–9). (Hollywood Wars) 1993, Penguin paper $3.25 (0-14-036156-1). Shy Alison, 15, accompanies a friend to an audition and ends up starring in a TV show, but her onscreen stepsister resents almost everything about her. (Rev: BL 5/1/93; SLJ 6/93)

1109 Cooper, Ilene. *Star-Spangled Summer* (5–8). (Holiday Five) 1996, Viking paper $14.99 (0-670-85655-X). Five sixth-grade girls struggle to make sure that their plans for summer camp are not spoiled. (Rev: BL 4/15/96; SLJ 5/96)

1110 Corcoran, Barbara. *You Put Up with Me, I'll Put Up with You* (6–8). 1989, Avon paper $2.50 (0-380-70558-3). A somewhat self-centered girl moves with her mother to a new community and has problems adjusting. (Rev: BL 3/15/87; BR 11–12/87; SLJ 3/87; VOYA 4/87)

1111 Cormier, Robert. *Beyond the Chocolate War* (9–12). 1985, Dell paper $4.99 (0-440-90580-X). The misuse of power at Trinity High by Brother Leon and the secret society of Vigils is again explored in this sequel to *The Chocolate War* (1974). (Rev: BL 3/15/85; BR 9–10/85; SLJ 4/85)

1112 Cormier, Robert. *The Chocolate War* (7–12). 1993, Dell paper $3.99 (0-440-90032-8). A chocolate sale in a boys' private school creates power struggles. Followed by: *Beyond the Chocolate War.*

1113 Cormier, Robert. *Eight Plus One* (9–12). 1980, Pantheon LB $7.99 (0-394-94595-6). These 9 stories involve such problems of growing up as coping with one's first love experience and a boy trying to grow a mustache.

1114 Cormier, Robert. *Frenchtown Summer* (6–10). 1999, Delacorte $16.95 (0-385-32704-8). A verse novel about a boy growing up in a small town in Massachusetts after World War I, the father he can't seem to reach, and the first pangs of adolescence. (Rev: BL 9/15/99; SLJ 9/99; VOYA 12/99)

1115 Cormier, Robert. *I Am the Cheese* (7–12). 1977, Pantheon $20.00 (0-394-83462-3). A multi-level novel about a boy's life after his parents are forced to go underground. (Rev: BL 6/1/88)

1116 Cormier, Robert. *Tunes for Bears to Dance To* (6–12). 1992, 1994, Dell paper $4.50 (0-440-21903-5). In a stark morality tale set in a Massachusetts town after World War II, Henry, 11, is tempted, corrupted, and redeemed. (Rev: BL 6/15/92; SLJ 9/92)

1117 Cormier, Robert. *We All Fall Down* (8–12). 1991, Dell paper $5.50 (0-440-21556-0). Random violence committed by 4 high school seniors is observed by the Avenger, who also witnesses the budding love affair of one of the victims of the attack. (Rev: BL 9/15/91*; SLJ 9/91*)

1118 Coryell, Susan. *Eaglebait* (6–9). 1989, Harcourt $14.95 (0-15-200442-4). An unpopular teenage nerd thinks he has found a friend in a new science teacher. (Rev: BL 11/1/89; SLJ 6/90)

1119 Cossi, Olga. *The Magic Box* (7–9). 1990, Pelican $12.95 (0-88289-748-9). Mara cannot seem to give up smoking until her mother, a former smoker, develops throat cancer. (Rev: BL 10/15/90; SLJ 8/90; VOYA 8/90)

1120 Cottonwood, Joe. *Babcock* (7–10). 1996, Scholastic $15.95 (0-590-22221-X). A teenager named Babcock recounts with humor and insight several months of his life in a town in the California Bay area, including everyday school experiences, falling in love, playing softball, and coping with an unexpected visit by an unwanted uncle. (Rev: BR 11–12/96; VOYA 6/97)

1121 Cottonwood, Joe. *Danny Ain't* (6–10). 1992, Scholastic $13.95 (0-590-45067-0). His mother is dead and his father is in a veterans hospital, but Danny manages to endure poverty alone and forge a value system. (Rev: BL 9/1/92; SLJ 10/92)

1122 Cox, Elizabeth. *Night Talk* (10–12). 1997, Graywolf $23.95 (1-55597-267-5). This story tells of the 40-year friendship, beginning in 1949, between an African American woman and her white female employer in Georgia and of a similar bond between their two daughters. (Rev: BL 10/15/97; SLJ 2/98)

1123 Creech, Sharon. *Bloomability* (5–8). 1998, HarperCollins LB $15.89 (0-06-026994-4). In this amusing first-person narrative, middle-schooler Dinnie adjusts to her "second life" at a school in Switzerland as she makes friends from around the world and gains a sense of her own self-worth. (Rev: BL 9/15/98; SLJ 10/98; VOYA 2/99)

1124 Creech, Sharon. *Chasing Redbird* (6–9). 1997, HarperCollins LB $15.89 (0-06-026988-X). Thirteen-year-old Zinny's journey to self-discovery involves planting zinnias on an overgrown trail, untangling a family secret, and determining the intentions of a local boy who seems to be paying attention to her. (Rev: BL 3/15/97; BR 9–10/97; SLJ 4/97*)

1125 Cronin, A. J. *The Citadel* (10–12). 1983, Little, Brown $16.95 (0-316-16158-6). An idealistic doctor finds he must battle with the establishment.

1126 Cronin, A. J. *The Keys of the Kingdom* (10–12). 1984, Little, Brown $16.45 (0-316-16189-6). An inspiring story about a young priest and his missionary work.

1127 Cross, Gillian. *A Map of Nowhere* (8–12). 1989, Holiday House $13.95 (0-8234-0741-1). Nick feels that he is being exploited by his brother's street gang but he likes the sense of status and importance from being accepted by an older group. (Rev: BL 3/1/89; SLJ 6/89; VOYA 8/89)

1128 Cross, Gillian. *Tightrope* (7–12). 1999, Holiday House $16.95 (0-8234-1512-0). To take her mind off the hours she spends caring for her invalid mother, Ashley begins to hang out with a local street gang. (Rev: BL 9/15/99; SLJ 10/99)

1129 Crutcher, Chris. *Athletic Shorts: 6 Short Stories* (8–12). 1991, Greenwillow $16.00 (0-688-10816-4). These short stories focus on themes important to teens, such as sports, father-son friction, insecurity, and friendship. (Rev: BL 10/15/91; SLJ 9/91*)

1130 Danziger, Paula. *Can You Sue Your Parents for Malpractice?* (6–9). 1998, Putnam paper $3.99 (0-698-11688-7). Lauren, 14 years old, faces a variety of problems both at home and at school.

1131 Danziger, Paula. *The Cat Ate My Gymsuit* (6–9). 1998, Demco paper $9.09 (0-606-13091-8). Marcy hates gym but finds in her school a support-

ive teacher. A sequel is *There's a Bat in Bunk Five* (1980).

1132 Danziger, Paula. *Remember Me to Harold Square* (6–9). Illus. 1999, Putnam paper $3.99 (0-698-11694-1). Kendra gets to know attractive Frank when they participate in scavenger hunts in New York City. (Rev: BL 10/1/87; BR 11–12/87; SLJ 11/87; VOYA 12/87)

1133 Danziger, Paula, and Ann M. Martin. *P. S. Longer Letter Later* (5–8). 1998, Scholastic $15.95 (0-590-21310-5). Through letters to each other, flamboyant Tara*Starr, who lives in Ohio, and her friend Elizabeth, in the East, share secrets and stories about their families, growing up, and adjustments they have to make. (Rev: BL 6/1–15/98; BR 9–10/98; SLJ 5/98; VOYA 8/98)

1134 Davis, Donald. *Thirteen Miles from Suncrest* (9–12). 1994, August House $22.95 (0-87483-379-5). The youngest child of a farm family comes of age in quaint Close Creek, North Carolina. This journal chronicles his life from 1910 to 1913. (Rev: BL 9/15/94; SLJ 1/95)

1135 Demsky, Andy. *Dark Refuge: A Story of Cults and Their Seductive Appeal* (9–12). 1995, Pacific paper $7.97 (0-8163-1241-9). A coming-of-age story in which young Anita is inadvertently abused by her mother and then falls into the hands of a "prophet" of a cult. (Rev: BL 11/1/95*)

1136 Derby, Pat. *Visiting Miss Pierce* (6–8). 1986, Farrar paper $3.50 (0-374-48156-3). A high school freshman finds new meaning in his life when he visits a senile woman in a nursing home. (Rev: BL 8/86; BR 11–12/86; SLJ 8/86)

1137 Dessen, Sarah. *Keeping the Moon* (6–10). 1999, Viking $15.99 (0-670-88549-5). Colie, a 15-year-old girl with little self-esteem, spends a summer with an eccentric aunt and finds a kind of salvation in a friendship with 2 waitresses and the love of a shy teenage artist. (Rev: BL 9/1/99; SLJ 9/99; VOYA 12/99)

1138 Dessen, Sarah. *Someone Like You* (7–12). 1998, Viking $15.99 (0-670-87778-6). Young Halley discovers that her best friend Scarlett is pregnant and Scarlett's boyfriend has been killed in an accident. (Rev: BL 5/15/98; SLJ 6/98; VOYA 8/98)

1139 De Vries, Anke. *Bruises* (6–10). Trans. by Stacey Knecht. 1996, Front Street $15.95 (1-886910-03-0); Dell paper $4.50 (0-440-22694-5). This novel, set in Holland, tells of the friendship between a sympathetic boy, Michael, and Judith, a disturbed, abused young girl. (Rev: BL 4/1/96; SLJ 6/96; VOYA 6/96)

1140 Dines, Carol. *Talk to Me: Stories & a Novella* (8–12). 1997, Bantam Doubleday Dell $15.95 (0-385-32271-2). Teenage problems like romance, family relations, jobs, and school troubles are the subjects of these 6 stories and a novella. (Rev: BL 7/97; BR 9–10/97; SLJ 7/97; VOYA 8/97)

1141 Doherty, Berlie. *Dear Nobody* (7–12). 1992, 1994, Morrow paper $4.95 (0-688-12764-9). This complex novel explores the consequences of a teenager's pregnancy and the resulting tensions with her boyfriend. (Rev: BL 10/1/92*; SLJ 10/92*)

1142 Dragonwagon, Crescent, and Paul Zindel. *To Take a Dare* (9–12). 1982, HarperCollins $12.95 (0-06-026858-1). After 3 years of wandering, Chrysta must find herself.

1143 Draper, Sharon M. *Romiette and Julio* (6–10). 1999, Simon & Schuster $16.00 (0-689-82180-8). An updated version of Romeo and Juliet set in contemporary Cincinnati involving a Hispanic American boy, an African American girl, street gangs, and, in this case, a happy ending. (Rev: BL 9/15/99; SLJ 9/99; VOYA 12/99)

1144 Duncan, Lois. *Trapped! Cages of the Mind & Body* (7–12). 1998, Simon & Schuster $16.00 (0-689-81335-X). Limitations caused by the mind and/or the body are explored in 13 stories, each by a different YA writer. (Rev: BL 7/98; SLJ 6/98; VOYA 8/98)

1145 Ellis, Sarah. *Pick-up Sticks* (5–8). 1992, Macmillan LB $15.00 (0-689-50550-7). A disgruntled teen learns a lesson in life after being sent to live with relatives. (Rev: BL 1/15/92; SLJ 3/92*)

1146 Evans, Douglas. *So What Do You Do?* (5–8). 1997, Front Street $14.95 (1-886910-20-0). Two middle-schoolers help their beloved former teacher who has become a homeless drunk. (Rev: BL 11/1/97; BR 3–4/98; SLJ 1/98; VOYA 2/98)

1147 Eyerly, Jeannette. *Someone to Love Me* (7–10). 1987, HarperCollins LB $11.89 (0-397-32206-2). An unpopular high school girl is seduced by the school's glamor boy and decides, when she finds she is pregnant, to keep the child. (Rev: BL 2/1/87; BR 9–10/87; SLJ 4/87; VOYA 4/87)

1148 Facklam, Margery. *The Trouble with Mothers* (6–8). 1991, Avon paper $2.95 (0-380-71139-7). Troy is incensed when the town censors target his mother's historical novel. (Rev: BL 3/1/89; SLJ 5/89; VOYA 6/89)

1149 Farish, Terry. *Talking in Animal* (7–9). 1996, Greenwillow $15.00 (0-688-14671-6). Siobhan lives partly in a fantasy world that revolves around training her beloved dog, Tree, to win competitions, but she moves toward reality when Tree becomes more and more sick and must be put down. (Rev: BR 11–12/96; SLJ 11/96; VOYA 4/97)

1150 Farr, Judith. *I Never Came to You in White* (10–12). 1996, Houghton $21.95 (0-395-78840-4). Using imaginary letters from Emily Dickinson to

and from friends, this novel probes the spirit, challenges, attitudes, pranks, and poems of the celebrated writer. (Rev: SLJ 1/97)

1151 Farrell, Mame. *Marrying Malcolm Murgatroyd* (5–8). 1995, Farrar $14.00 (0-374-34838-3). Hannah defends the class nerd because he has been kind to her handicapped younger brother. (Rev: BL 11/1/95; SLJ 11/95; VOYA 2/96)

1152 Ferris, Jean. *Bad* (7–10). 1998, Farrar $16.00 (0-374-30479-3). Dallas gains self knowledge when she is sent to a women's correctional center for 6 months and meets gang members, drug dealers, a 14-year-old prostitute, and other unfortunates. (Rev: BL 10/1/98; SLJ 12/98; VOYA 2/99)

1153 Ferris, Jean. *Signs of Life* (6–10). 1995, Farrar $14.00 (0-374-36909-7). Hannah and her parents must come to grips with their grief over her twin's death while on vacation at the painted caves in Lascaux, France. (Rev: BL 7/95; SLJ 4/95)

1154 Ferry, Charles. *A Fresh Start* (7–10). 1996, Proctor paper $8.95 (1-882792-18-1). This novel explores the problems of troubled teens in a summer-school program for young alcoholics. (Rev: SLJ 5/96; VOYA 10/96)

1155 Filichia, Peter. *What's in a Name?* (7–12). 1988, Avon paper $2.75 (0-380-75536-X). Rose is so unhappy with her foreign-sounding last name that she decides to change it. (Rev: BL 3/1/89; VOYA 4/89)

1156 Fine, Anne. *The Tulip Touch* (4–9). 1997, Little, Brown $15.95 (0-316-28325-8). Natalie forms a dangerous friendship with Tulip, a girl going completely out of control. (Rev: BL 9/15/97; SLJ 9/97*)

1157 Fitch, Janet. *Kicks* (8–12). 1995, Clarion $14.00 (0-395-69624-0). When Laurie's domineering parents make her think her friend's life is ideal, she becomes involved in seamy adventures that can only end in disaster. (Rev: BL 8/95; SLJ 6/95)

1158 Fitzhugh, Louise. *Harriet the Spy* (6–8). 1964, HarperCollins LB $15.89 (0-06-021911-4); Dell paper $4.85 (0-06-440331-9). The story of a girl whose passion for honesty gets her into trouble. Followed by *The Long Secret*.

1159 Flake, Sharon G. *A Freak Like Me* (5–9). 1999, Hyperion paper $15.49 (0-7868-1307-5). In her inner-city middle school, Maleeka Madison is picked on by classmates because she is poorly dressed, darker than the others, and gets good grades. (Rev: BL 9/1/98; SLJ 11/98)

1160 Fleischman, Paul. *Whirligig* (7–10). 1998, Holt $16.95 (0-8050-5582-7). As penance for killing a teenager in an automobile accident, Brent must fashion 4 whirligigs and place them in the 4 corners of the United States. (Rev: BL 4/1/98; SLJ 4/98; VOYA 6/98)

1161 Fletcher, Ralph. *Flying Solo* (5–8). 1998, Clarion $15.00 (0-395-87323-1). This novel answers the question, "What would a sixth grade class do if their substitute teacher fails to appear and they are left alone for a whole day?" (Rev: BL 8/98; SLJ 10/98)

1162 Fletcher, Ralph J. *Spider Boy* (5–8). 1997, Houghton $15.00 (0-395-77606-6). Bobby—nicknamed Spider Boy because he knows so much about spiders—has trouble adjusting to his new life in the town of New Paltz, New York. (Rev: BL 6/1–15/97; SLJ 7/97)

1163 Fox, Paula. *Monkey Island* (5–10). 1991, Orchard LB $16.99 (0-531-08562-7). A homeless, abandoned 11-year-old boy in New York City contracts pneumonia and is cared for by a homeless African American teenager and retired teacher, who share their place in the park with him. (Rev: BL 9/1/91*; SLJ 8/91)

1164 Fox, Paula. *One-Eyed Cat* (6–9). 1984, Bradbury $14.95 (0-02-735540-3); Dell paper $5.50 (0-440-46641-5). A boy growing up in upstate New York during the 1930s confronts his own guilt when he secretly disobeys his father. (Rev: BL 6/1/88)

1165 Fox, Paula. *A Place Apart* (7–9). 1980, NAL paper $2.25 (0-451-14338-8). In a small town where she and her mother have moved after her father's death, Victoria meets the unusual Hugh Todd.

1166 Frank, Lucy. *Oy, Joy!* (7–10). 1999, DK Publg. $16.95 (0-7894-2538-6). Joy, a high school freshman in New York City, has trouble living up to her name when she loses her bedroom to an ailing uncle and her best friend deserts her. (Rev: SLJ 9/99; VOYA 10/99)

1167 Freeman, Martha. *The Year My Parents Ruined My Life* (6–9). 1997, Holiday House $15.95 (0-8234-1324-1). Twelve-year-old Kate has many problems adjusting to her new home in a small Pennsylvania town and longs to return to the suburbs of Los Angeles, her friends, and dreamy boyfriend. (Rev: BL 12/1/97; SLJ 12/97)

1168 Friel, Maeve. *Charlie's Story* (8–10). 1997, Peachtree $14.95 (0-56145-167-3). Charlie, who was abandoned by her mother as a child, now lives with her father in Ireland and, at age 14, is facing a group of bullies at school who accuse her of a theft and cause a terrible field hockey incident. (Rev: BL 1/1–15/98; VOYA 2/98)

1169 Gabhart, Ann. *Bridge to Courage* (6–8). 1993, Avon paper $3.50 (0-380-76051-7). Luke is afraid of bridges and walks away from the initiation rites of the elite Truelanders, who then shun him. Luke finally learns self-confidence in this deftly plotted tale. (Rev: BL 5/15/93; VOYA 10/93)

1170 Gallo, Donald R., ed. *No Easy Answers: Short Stories about Teenagers Making Tough Choices* (6–12). 1997, Delacorte $16.95 (0-385-32290-9). A collection of short stories by some of today's best writers for young adults, including Ron Koertze and Gloria Miklowitz, about teenagers who face moral and ethical dilemmas. (Rev: BL 11/15/97; BR 5–6/98; SLJ 12/97; VOYA 10/97)

1171 Gallo, Donald R., ed. *Sixteen: Short Stories by Outstanding Writers for Young Adults* (9–12). 1984, Dell paper $5.50 (0-440-97757-6). This anthology of original short stories covers such subjects as friendship, love, and families.

1172 Gantos, Jack. *Jack's Black Book* (6–8). 1997, Farrar $16.00 (0-374-33662-8). In this third semiautobiographical novel, Jack is living in Florida with his family, tries to build a coffin for his dead dog, hopes to improve his writing skills, and is sent to a vocational training school. (Rev: BL 10/15/97; BR 3–4/98; SLJ 10/97)

1173 Garden, Nancy. *Good Moon Rising* (9–12). 1996, Farrar $16.00 (0-374-32746-7). While coaching a new junior in the school play, Jan, a senior, finds that she is falling in love, and soon gay baiting in the school begins. (Rev: BL 10/1/96; BR 3–4/97; SLJ 10/96; VOYA 12/96)

1174 Garden, Nancy. *The Year They Burned the Books* (7–12). 1999, Farrar $17.00 (0-374-38667-6). High school senior Jamie Crawford's problems as editor of the school newspaper under attack by a right-wing group are compounded when she realizes that she is a lesbian and falling in love with Tessa, a new girl in school. (Rev: BL 8/99; SLJ 9/99; VOYA 12/99)

1175 Garland, Sherry. *Letters from the Mountain* (6–10). 1996, Harcourt $12.00 (0-15-200661-3); paper $6.00 (0-15-200659-1). Tyler is unhappy spending the summer with elderly relatives and, through a series of letters to his mother and friends, he vents his anger and also tells of his gradual adjustment. (Rev: BL 10/1/96; BR 3–4/97; SLJ 11/96; VOYA 4/97)

1176 Gelb, Alan. *Real Life: My Best Friend Died* (7–12). 1995, Pocket Books paper $3.50 (0-671-87273-7). A high school senior, living a happy, normal life, finds his world exploding when he feels responsible for his friend's death. (Rev: BL 4/1/95; SLJ 6/95; VOYA 5/95)

1177 Gifaldi, David. *Rearranging and Other Stories* (6–10). 1998, Simon & Schuster $16.00 (0-689-81750-9). In these 9 short stories, young teens face problems related to adolescence and reaching maturity. (Rev: BL 4/15/98; BR 1–2/99; SLJ 6/98; VOYA 8/98)

1178 Gilbert, Barbara Snow. *Broken Chords* (8–12). 1998, Front Street $15.95 (1-886910-23-5). As she prepares for the piano competition that could lead to a place at Juillard, Clara has doubts about a lifetime of sacrifice that a career in music would require. (Rev: BL 12/15/98; SLJ 12/98; VOYA 2/99)

1179 Gilbert, Barbara Snow. *Stone Water* (5–9). 1996, Front Street $15.95 (1-886910-11-1). Fourteen-year-old Grant must decide if he will honor his ailing grandfather's wish to help him commit suicide. (Rev: BL 12/15/96; SLJ 12/96*; VOYA 4/97)

1180 Godden, Rumer. *An Episode of Sparrows* (7–10). 1993, Pan Books paper $16.95 (0-330-32779-8). In postwar London 2 waifs try to grow a secret garden. (Rev: SLJ 6/89)

1181 Goldman-Rubin, Susan. *Emily in Love* (6–9). 1997, Harcourt $14.00 (0-15-200961-2). Developmentally disabled Emily of *Emily Good as Gold* (o.p.), deludes herself and deceives those around her in her pursuit of a boyfriend. (Rev: BL 5/15/97; SLJ 5/97; VOYA 6/97)

1182 Gordon, Amy. *When JFK Was My Father* (6–9). 1999, Houghton $15.00 (0-395-91364-0). Georgia daydreams at her new boarding school that JFK is her real father, but she must face reality when her boyfriend appears and wants her to run away with him. (Rev: BL 6/1–15/99; SLJ 4/99; VOYA 6/99)

1183 Grattan-Dominguez, Alejandro. *Breaking Even* (9–12). 1997, Arte Publico paper $11.95 (1-55885-213-1). This coming-of-age story set in the 1950s tells how 18-year-old Valentin Cooper, a Mexican American, leaves his family and pregnant girlfriend in their small West Texas town on a quest to find his father. (Rev: SLJ 4/98)

1184 Gray, Keith. *Creepers* (7–10). 1997, Putnam $15.95 (0-399-23186-2). Creeping is the sport of running the length of a neighborhood through backyards, and 2 teenagers engage in a particularly difficult creep in this suspenseful British novel. (Rev: BL 2/1/98)

1185 Greenberg, Jan. *Exercises of the Heart* (7–10). 1986, Farrar $14.00 (0-374-32237-6). Roxie has problems with her partially disabled mother and a friend, Glo, who refuses to accept responsibility for her actions. (Rev: BL 9/15/86; BR 11–12/86; SLJ 11/86; VOYA 12/86)

1186 Greenberg, Jan. *Just the Two of Us* (6–8). 1988, Farrar $14.00 (0-374-36198-3). Holly tries every way possible not to move from New York City with her mother. (Rev: BL 1/15/89; BR 3–4/89; SLJ 12/88)

1187 Greene, Constance C. *Monday I Love You* (7–10). 1988, HarperCollins $11.95 (0-06-022183-6). An overdeveloped bust is just one of the problems faced by 15-year-old Grace. (Rev: BL 7/88; VOYA 8/88)

1188 Greene, Constance C. *Your Old Pal, Al* (6–8). 1999, Viking paper $3.99 (0-14-036849-3). Al has

problems with her father, a boy she recently met, and her best friend. Part of a series.

1189 Grimes, Martha. *Hotel Paradise* (10–12). 1996, Knopf $24.00 (0-679-44187-5). Set in a small town, this is the story of a lonely and disaffected 12-year-old girl who becomes obsessed first with the death of another ignored young girl in the past and then with a murder that has occurred in the present. (Rev: SLJ 10/96)

1190 Grove, Vicki. *The Crystal Garden* (5–8). 1995, Putnam $15.95 (0-399-21813-0). A girl learns to evaluate her choices in friends and fun in order to survive. (Rev: BL 9/1/95; SLJ 5/95)

1191 Grove, Vicki. *Reaching Dustin* (5–8). 1998, Putnam $16.99 (0-399-23008-4). As part of a sixth grade assignment, Carly must get to know Dustin Groat, the class outcast, and as she learns more about him and his family, she realizes that her attitudes toward him in the past have helped create his problems. (Rev: BL 5/1/98; BR 11–12/98; SLJ 5/98)

1192 Haas, Jessie. *Skipping School* (7–10). 1992, Greenwillow $14.00 (0-688-10179-8). A realistic, ultimately upbeat portrait of a boy's reluctant coming-of-age and of a family's eventual acceptance of death. (Rev: BL 11/15/92; SLJ 11/92)

1193 Haddix, Margaret P. *Just Ella* (7–12). 1999, Simon & Schuster paper $17.00 (0-689-82186-7). The story of Cinderella after the ball, when she finds out that castle life with Prince Charming isn't all it's cut out to be, meets a social activist tutor, and rethinks her priorities in life. (Rev: BL 9/1/99; SLJ 9/99; VOYA 12/99)

1194 Hahn, Mary D. *Daphne's Book* (6–8). 1983, Clarion $15.00 (0-89919-183-5). A seventh-grader conscious of her social position is paired for an assignment with an outsider.

1195 Hahn, Mary D. *Following My Own Footsteps* (5–8). 1996, Clarion $15.00 (0-395-76477-7). Living with a grandmother to escape a drunken, abusive father, Gordy has problems adjusting and becomes friends with the boy next door, who has polio and is wheelchair bound. (Rev: BL 9/15/96*; SLJ 11/96)

1196 Haines, J. D. *Vision Quest: Journey to Manhood* (6–9). 1999, Arrowsmith paper $11.95 (0-9653119-0-2). A 13-year-old boy is mentored by his Native American grandfather when he and his mother move from gang-ridden Chicago to the wilderness of Oklahoma. (Rev: BL 9/1/99)

1197 Hall, Lynn. *Where Have All the Tigers Gone?* (7–12). 1989, Macmillan LB $13.95 (0-684-19003-6). A 50-year-old woman at her class reunion recalls her school years. (Rev: BL 4/15/89; BR 9–10/89; SLJ 5/89; VOYA 8/89)

1198 Halvorson, Marilyn. *Cowboys Don't Cry* (6–8). 1986, Dell paper $3.25 (0-440-91303-9). While drunk, Shane's father was involved in an accident in which his wife was killed and Shane cannot forgive him for the death of his mother. (Rev: SLJ 9/85; VOYA 6/85)

1199 Hamilton, Morse. *Yellow Blue Bus Means I Love You* (8–10). 1994, Greenwillow $14.00 (0-688-12800-9). A teenage Russian immigrant attends a prep school, where he falls passionately in love with an American girl. (Rev: BL 9/1/94; SLJ 6/94; VOYA 10/94)

1200 Hamilton, Virginia. *A Little Love* (7–10). 1985, Berkley paper $2.50 (0-425-08424-8). An overweight girl leaves home with her boyfriend to find her father who left her years before.

1201 Hamilton, Virginia. *A White Romance* (8–12). 1987, Harcourt paper $3.95 (0-15-295888-6). A formerly all-black high school becomes integrated and social values and relationships change. (Rev: SLJ 1/88; VOYA 2/88)

1202 Hautman, Pete. *Stone Cold* (7–12). 1998, Simon & Schuster paper $16.00 (0-689-81759-2). In this entertaining first-person narrative, Fenn becomes adept at gambling and soon finds that he is a gambling addict. (Rev: BL 9/15/98; BR 5–6/99; SLJ 9/98; VOYA 2/99)

1203 Hawks, Robert. *The Twenty-Six Minutes* (6–10). 1988, Square One paper $4.95 (0-938961-03-9). Two teenage misfits join an anti-nuclear protest group. (Rev: SLJ 11/88; VOYA 4/89)

1204 Haynes, David. *Business as Usual* (5–8). Illus. 1997, Milkweed paper $6.95 (1-57131-608-6). When an economics teacher assigns his sixth grade class to form their own companies and compete to see who can make the most profits, unforeseen rivalries and problems arise between a racially mixed group of boys known as the West 7th Wildcats and another group. (Rev: BL 10/15/97; SLJ 3/98)

1205 Hazelgrove, William Elliot. *Ripples* (9–12). 1992, Pantonne Pr. paper $6.95 (0-9630052-9-4). Branton, age 18, feels betrayed when his best friend steals his summer love. (Rev: BL 3/15/92)

1206 Head, Ann. *Mr. and Mrs. Bo Jo Jones* (7–12). 1973, NAL paper $2.75 (0-451-15734-6). The perennial favorite of 2 teenagers madly in love but unprepared for the responsibilities of parenthood.

1207 Heide, Florence Parry. *Growing Anyway Up* (6–8). 1976, HarperCollins $12.95 (0-397-31657-7). Florence is shy when confronted with new situations but an aunt helps her conquer her fears.

1208 Hendry, Diana. *Double Vision* (7–9). 1993, Candlewick $14.95 (1-56402-125-4). In 1950s England, Eliza, 15, must deal with first love, insecurity, betrayal, and her friend's pregnancy. (Rev: BL 3/1/93*)

1209 Herman, John. *Deep Waters* (7–12). 1998, Putnam $17.99 (0-399-23235-4). At a summer camp, 13-year-old Andy falls under the spell of conniving Julian and soon becomes involved in a murder. (Rev: BL 9/15/98; BR 9–10/99; SLJ 10/98; VOYA 4/99)

1210 Hermes, Patricia. *You Shouldn't Have to Say Goodbye* (7–9). 1982, Harcourt $11.95 (0-15-299944-2). A moving novel about a girl who must cope with her mother's death from cancer.

1211 Heynen, Jim. *Being Youngest* (7–12). 1997, Holt $15.95 (0-8050-5486-3). Two Iowa farm kids, Henry and Gretchen, become friends when they realize that being the youngest in their respective families brings a certain number of problems. (Rev: BL 10/15/97; BR 5–6/98; SLJ 11/97; VOYA 4/98)

1212 High, Linda O. *The Summer of the Great Divide* (5–8). 1996, Holiday House $15.95 (0-8234-1228-8). With the political events of 1969 as a backdrop, 13-year-old Wheezie sorts herself out at her relatives' farm. (Rev: BL 6/1–15/96; BR 11–12/96; SLJ 4/96)

1213 Hill, Ernest. *A Life for a Life* (10–12). 1998, Simon & Schuster $23.00 (0-684-82278-4). Young D-Ray flees after he kills a young clerk while robbing a convenience store to get money to rescue his brother from drug dealers, becomes involved in a life of crime, and eventually ends up in juvenile prison, where he must learn to forgive himself. (Rev: BL 6/1–15/98; SLJ 4/99)

1214 Hobbs, Valerie. *Get It While It's Hot; or Not* (9–12). 1996, Orchard LB $17.99 (0-531-08890-1). The pregnancy of her best friend forces Megan to rethink her relationships, particularly with boyfriend Joe, in a novel that also explores themes involving friendship, freedom of the press, and mother-daughter relations. (Rev: BL 10/15/96; SLJ 10/96; VOYA 12/96)

1215 Hobbs, Will. *Changes in Latitudes* (9–12). 1988, Macmillan $16.00 (0-689-31385-3). Teenager Travis supports his young brother's crusade to help endangered sea turtles. (Rev: BL 5/15/88; BR 9–10/88; SLJ 3/88; VOYA 6/88)

1216 Holeman, Linda. *Mercy's Birds* (6–10). 1998, Tundra paper $5.95 (0-88776-463-0). Fifteen-year-old Mercy lives a life of loneliness and hurt as she cares for a depressed mother and an alcoholic aunt while working after school in a flower shop. (Rev: BL 12/15/98; SLJ 3/99; VOYA 12/98)

1217 Holland, Isabelle. *The Man Without a Face* (7–10). 1972, HarperCollins paper $4.50 (0-06-447028-8). Charles's close relations with his reclusive tutor lead to a physical experience.

1218 Holmes, Barbara W. *Letters to Julia* (7–12). 1997, HarperCollins LB $14.89 (0-06-027342-9). Through letters to a book editor, Liz, a budding writer, displays parts of her novel-in-progress and opens up about her problems with parents who are divorced. (Rev: BL 7/97; BR 1–2/98; SLJ 6/97; VOYA 8/97)

1219 Hopper, Nancy J. *The Seven 1/2 Sins of Stacey Kendall* (7–9). 1982, Dell paper $2.25 (0-440-47736-0). Stacey finds out the true meaning of beauty when she goes into the ear-piercing business.

1220 Hossack, Sylvie. *Green Mango Magic* (5–9). 1998, Avon paper $14.00 (0-380-97613-7). Maile, a young girl growing up in Kauai, Hawaii, absorbs the culture and hopes that "Ho-oponopono," an island magic of old Hawaii, might help her adjust to the death of her mother and the absence of her father and set her life straight. (Rev: BL 5/99; SLJ 2/99; VOYA 8/99)

1221 Howe, Norma. *God, the Universe, and Hot Fudge Sundaes* (7–10). 1986, Avon paper $2.50 (0-380-70074-3). A 16-year-old girl would like to share her mother's born-again faith but can't.

1222 Hrdlitschka, Shelley. *Beans on Toast* (6–8). 1998, Orca paper $6.95 (1-55143-116-5). Thirteen-year-old Madison is having trouble accepting her parents' divorce and fitting in at summer Band Camp. (Rev: SLJ 2/99; VOYA 6/99)

1223 Hrdlitschka, Shelley. *Disconnected* (7–12). 1999, Orca paper $6.95 (1-55143-105-X). The lives of Tanner, a hockey-playing teen who has recurring dreams of trying to escape an underwater attacker, and Alex, a boy escaping his father's abuse, connect in a most unusual way. (Rev: BL 4/1/99; SLJ 6/99; VOYA 6/99)

1224 Hughes, Dean. *Family Pose* (6–8). 1989, Macmillan LB $14.95 (0-689-31396-9). An 11-year-old runaway finds a home in a Seattle hotel where the employees shelter him. (Rev: BL 4/1/89; BR 9–10/89; SLJ 4/89; VOYA 8/89)

1225 Hurwitz, Johanna. *Even Stephen* (5–9). Illus. 1996, Morrow $15.00 (0-688-14197-8). Allison's older brother, Stephen, who excels in both sports and school work, is considered both confident and independent until his basketball coach dies and he sinks into a deep depression. (Rev: BL 4/1/96; BR 9–10/96; SLJ 3/96)

1226 Huser, Glen. *Touch of the Clown* (7–10). 1999, Groundwood $15.95 (0-88899-343-9). Neglected sisters Barbara and Livvy discover a new life with the eccentric Cosmo, who runs a teen clown workshop. (Rev: VOYA 10/99)

1227 Ingold, Jeanette. *Pictures, 1918* (6–9). 1998, Harcourt $16.00 (0-15-201802-3). In this novel set in the final days of World War I, 16-year-old Asa faces many personal problems but finds release when she becomes an apprentice to the local portrait photographer. (Rev: VOYA 2/99)

1228 *Into the Widening World: International Coming-of-Age Stories* (9–12). 1995, Persea paper $12.95 (0-89255-204-2). The innocence and daring of youth are elegantly captured in this anthology of brilliant voices from 22 countries. (Rev: BL 1/1/95; SLJ 8/95; VOYA 5/95)

1229 Irwin, Hadley. *The Lilith Summer* (6–8). 1979, Feminist Pr. $8.95 (0-912670-52-5). Ellen is taking care of a 77-year-old woman for the summer and learns a lot from the experience.

1230 Jackson, Sheneska. *Caught Up in the Rapture* (10–12). 1996, Simon & Schuster $21.00 (0-634-81487-0). Street life in South Central Los Angeles is the subject of this novel about Jazmine Deems, who wants to be a singer, and her gangsta-rapper boyfriend known as the X-Man. (Rev: SLJ 8/96)

1231 Jenkins, A. M. *Breaking Boxes* (8–12). 1997, Delacorte $15.95 (0-385-32513-4). Charlie and Brandon form a friendship at high school, but when word gets out that Charlie's brother is gay, Brandon rejects both his friend and his family. (Rev: BL 9/1/97; BR 1–2/98; SLJ 10/97; VOYA 12/97)

1232 Johnson, Angela. *Gone from Home: Short Takes* (7–12). 1998, DK Publg. $15.95 (0-7894-2499-1). A collection of 12 short vignettes about lonely people who don't have roots and their problems finding a place that can be called home. (Rev: BL 8/98; SLJ 12/98*; VOYA 2/99)

1233 Johnston, Julie. *Adam and Eve and Pinch-Me* (7–9). 1994, 1995, Penguin .paper $4.99 (0-14-037588-0). A neglected child learns the meaning of love in this coming-of-age story. (Rev: BL 5/15/94*; SLJ 7/94; VOYA 8/94)

1234 Johnston, Norma. *The Time of the Cranes* (7–10). 1990, Macmillan LB $14.95 (0-02-747713-4). A girl filled with self-doubt about her abilities receives an unexpected inheritance. (Rev: BL 4/1/90; SLJ 5/90; VOYA 6/88)

1235 Jukes, Mavis. *Expecting the Unexpected: Human Interactions with Mrs. Gladys Furley, R.N.* (6–8). 1996, Delacorte $15.95 (0-385-32242-9). Twelve-year-old River is learning a lot about sex and family living in her human interactions class with Mrs. Flurey. Soon, she is beginning to apply this new knowledge to her own life, with mixed results. (Rev: BL 10/1/96; SLJ 9/96; VOYA 12/96)

1236 Kaplow, Robert. *Alessandra in Between* (8–12). 1992, HarperCollins LB $13.89 (0-06-023298-6). A young heroine has a lot on her mind, including her grandfather's deteriorating health, her friendships, and an unrequited love. (Rev: BL 9/15/92; SLJ 9/92)

1237 Kassem, Lou. *Secret Wishes* (6–8). 1989, Avon paper $2.95 (0-380-75544-0). A girl summons up her resources to try to lose weight to be a cheerleader. (Rev: BL 4/15/89; SLJ 4/89)

1238 Katz, Welwyn W. *Out of the Dark* (5–8). 1996, Simon & Schuster $16.00 (0-689-80947-6). A young boy escapes the painful present by imagining himself as a Viking shipbuilder. (Rev: BL 10/15/96; SLJ 9/96; VOYA 12/96)

1239 Kaye, Marilyn. *The Atonement of Mindy Wise* (6–9). 1991, Harcourt $15.95 (0-15-200402-5). A Jewish girl reviews a year's worth of sins on Yom Kippur and realizes she isn't as bad as she thought. (Rev: BL 6/15/91)

1240 Kaye, Marilyn. *Cassie* (6–9). 1987, Harcourt paper $4.95 (0-15-200422-X). A shoplifting incident forces Cassie to examine her values. A companion volume is *Lydia*, about Cassie's older sister. (Rev: SLJ 12/87)

1241 Keillor, Garrison, and Jenny L. Nilsson. *The Sandy Bottom Orchestra* (5–8). 1996, Hyperion LB $14.89 (0-7868-2145-0). Rachel, age 14, faces problems in growing up, including the ending of a treasured friendship. (Rev: BL 1/1–15/97; BR 3–4/97; SLJ 1/97)

1242 Kellogg, Marjorie. *Tell Me That You Love Me, Junie Moon.* 2nd ed. (10–12). 1993, Farrar paper $3.95 (0-374-47510-5). After they have been released from the hospital, 3 misfits decide to live together.

1243 Kennedy, Pagan. *The Exes* (10–12). 1998, Simon & Schuster $23.00 (0-684-83481-2). Four bright, creative young people—3 men and one woman—form a band called the Exes because they were all romantically involved with each other at one time and set out in a broken-down van in search of success. (Rev: BL 7/98; SLJ 3/99)

1244 Kerr, M. E. *Dinky Hocker Shoots Smack!* (7–9). 1989, HarperCollins paper $4.95 (0-06-447006-7). Overweight and underloved Dinky finds a unique way to gain her parents' attention.

1245 Kerr, M. E. *Gentlehands* (7–12). 1990, HarperCollins paper $4.95 (0-06-447067-9). Buddy Boyle wonders if the grandfather he has recently grown to love is really a Nazi war criminal in this novel set on the eastern tip of Long Island.

1246 Kerr, M. E. *"Hello," I Lied* (9–12). 1997, HarperCollins LB $15.89 (0-06-027530-8). Lang is gay and has a loving relationship with Alex, but he is torn about coming out to his friends and about feelings he has for a young woman. (Rev: BL 4/15/97; BR 11–12/97; SLJ 6/97; VOYA 6/97)

1247 Kerr, M. E. *I Stay Near You* (7–10). 1997, Harcourt paper $6.00 (0-15-201420-9). These 3 stories of love and self-acceptance span 3 generations in a small town. (Rev: BL 4/15/85; BR 1–2/86; SLJ 4/85; VOYA 6/85)

1248 Kerr, M. E. *Linger* (7–12). 1995, HarperCollins paper $4.95 (0-06-447102-0). In a story filled with wit and sadness, Kerr tells of kids entan-gled in love, war, and work. (Rev: BL 6/1–15/93; SLJ 7/93; VOYA 8/93)

1249 Kerr, M. E. *The Son of Someone Famous* (7–10). 1991, HarperCollins paper $3.95 (0-06-447069-5). In chapters alternately written by each, 2 teenagers in rural Vermont write about their friendship and their problems.

1250 Kerr, M. E. *What I Really Think of You* (7–10). 1982, HarperCollins $13.00 (0-06-023188-2); paper $3.50 (0-06-447062-8). The meeting of 2 teenagers who represent 2 kinds of religion—the evangelical mission and the TV pulpit. (Rev: BL 9/1/95)

1251 Ketchum, Liza. *Blue Coyote* (7–12). 1997, Simon & Schuster $16.00 (0-689-80790-2). High school junior Alex Beekman denies that he is gay, but, in time, he realizes the truth about himself. (Rev: BL 6/1–15/97; BR 9–10/97; SLJ 5/97; VOYA 8/97)

1252 Kincaid, Jamaica. *Annie John* (9–12). 1985, NAL paper $6.95 (0-452-26016-7). A beautifully detailed novel about a girl's childhood and adolescence on the Caribbean island of Antigua. (Rev: BL 4/1/85; SLJ 9/85)

1253 Kindl, Patrice. *The Woman in the Wall* (7–10). 1997, Houghton $14.95 (0-395-83014-1). A dreamlike story about a girl who emerges into the world after living alone for most of her 14 years in secret rooms in the family house. (Rev: BL 3/15/97; BR 9–10/97; SLJ 4/97; VOYA 8/97)

1254 Klass, Sheila S. *Next Stop: Nowhere* (6–10). 1995, Scholastic $14.95 (0-590-46686-0). Exiled to Vermont to live with her eccentric father, Beth must deal with separation from her close friend and from her new romantic interest, Josef, who's moved to Israel. (Rev: BL 1/15/95; SLJ 4/95; VOYA 2/95)

1255 Klass, Sheila S. *The Uncivil War* (6–9). 1997, Holiday House $15.95 (0-8234-1329-2). An engaging novel about a sixth-grade girl who wants to get control of her life, which includes dealing with a life-long weight problem and the pending birth of a sibling. (Rev: BL 2/15/98; SLJ 4/98)

1256 Knowles, John. *Peace Breaks Out* (10–12). 1997, Bantam paper $5.99 (0-553-27574-7). During the 1945–46 school year a former student who is suffering from wartime trauma returns to his private prep school as a teacher. A sequel to *A Separate Peace.*

1257 Knowles, John. *A Separate Peace* (10–12). 1987, Macmillan $40.00 (0-02-564850-0); Bantam paper $5.99 (0-553-28041-4). Life during a World War II year in a private boys' school and a student rivalry that ends in tragedy.

1258 Koertge, Ron. *The Arizona Kid* (8–12). 1989, Avon paper $3.99 (0-380-70776-4). Teenage Billy discovers that his uncle Wes is gay. (Rev: BL 5/1/88; BR 9–10/88; SLJ 6/88; VOYA 10/88)

1259 Koertge, Ron. *Confess-O-Rama* (7–9). 1996, Orchard LB $17.99 (0-531-08865-0). Beset with problems about his mother and his new school, Tony unburdens himself on Confess-O-Rama, a telephone hot line, only to discover he has told all to the school's weirdo, who has made Tony her new project. (Rev: BL 10/1/96; BR 3–4/97; SLJ 9/96*; VOYA 12/96)

1260 Koertge, Ron. *The Harmony Arms* (7–9). 1992, 1994, Avon paper $3.99 (0-380-72188-0). Gabriel and his father have gone to Los Angeles to break into the movies. By summer's end, Gabriel has embarked on his first romance and confronted death for the first time. (Rev: BL 10/15/92; SLJ 8/92*)

1261 Koller, Jackie F. *The Last Voyage of the Misty Day* (6–9). 1992, Atheneum $14.00 (0-689-31731-X). The story of a young girl and her friendship with an ailing neighbor. (Rev: BL 5/1/92; SLJ 6/92)

1262 Konigsburg, E. L. *Jennifer, Hecate, Macbeth, William McKinley, and Me, Elizabeth* (6–8). 1967, Macmillan $16.00 (0-689-30007-7); Dell paper $4.50 (0-440-44162-5). Elizabeth finds a new friend in Jennifer, an unusual girl who is interested in witchcraft.

1263 Konigsburg, E. L. *T-Backs, T-Shirts, Coat, and Suit* (5–8). 1993, Atheneum $14.00 (0-689-31855-3). Conformity and freedom of expression are looked at in this story of a girl and her ex-hippy stepaunt. (Rev: BL 11/1/93; SLJ 10/93*; VOYA 12/93)

1264 Konigsburg, E. L. *Throwing Shadows* (7–10). 1988, Macmillan paper $4.50 (0-02-044140-1). Five short stories about teenagers learning about themselves and their emotions.

1265 Krantz, Hazel. *Walks in Beauty* (6–9). 1997, Northland LB $12.95 (0-87358-667-0); paper $6.95 (0-87358-671-9). The story of a 15-year-old Navajo girl and how she copes with such adolescent woes as popularity, boyfriends, prom dates, and family problems. (Rev: BL 8/97; BR 11–12/97; SLJ 10/97)

1266 Kropp, Paul. *Moonkid and Liberty* (6–9). 1990, Little, Brown $13.95 (0-316-50485-8). The teenage son and daughter of 2 hippies try to sort out their lives and plan for their future. (Rev: BL 6/15/90; SLJ 4/90; VOYA 6/90)

1267 Kropp, Paul. *Moonkid and Prometheus* (6–8). 1998, Stoddart paper $5.95 (0-7736-7465-9). In this sequel to *Moonkid and Liberty*, Moonkid takes on the job of tutoring a black student, Prometheus, in reading and Pro in turn teaches Moonkid techniques in basketball. (Rev: BL 6/1–15/98; SLJ 10/98)

1268 Krumgold, Joseph. *Onion John* (6–8). 1959, HarperCollins LB $15.89 (0-690-04698-7); paper $4.95 (0-06-440144-8). In this Newbery Medal winner, Andy is torn between 2 relationships—one with his father and the other with an old immigrant.

1269 Kurland, Morton L. *Our Sacred Honor* (7–12). 1987, Rosen LB $12.95 (0-8239-0692-2). A story from 2 points of view about a pregnant teenage girl, her boyfriend, and their decision for abortion. (Rev: SLJ 6/87)

1270 Lamott, Anne. *Crooked Little Heart* (10–12). 1997, Pantheon $24.00 (0-679-43521-2). Using the world of tennis as a backdrop, this is the story of 2 adolescent friends and doubles partners, one of whom has problems adjusting to the problems of puberty. (Rev: BL 4/1/97; SLJ 7/97)

1271 Larimer, Tamela. *Buck* (7–10). 1986, Avon paper $2.50 (0-380-75172-0). The friendship between runaway Buck and Rich is threatened when Buck becomes friendly with Rich's girlfriend. (Rev: BL 4/87; SLJ 6/87; VOYA 4/87)

1272 Lawson, Julie. *Turns on a Dime* (5–8). 1999, Stoddart paper $6.95 (0-7737-5942-5). In this sequel to *Goldstone* (1998), set in British Columbia, 11-year-old Jo faces many new situations, including finding a boyfriend, discovering that she is adopted, and learning that her beloved babysitter is pregnant. (Rev: SLJ 6/99)

1273 Layton, George. *The Swap* (5–8). 1997, Putnam $16.95 (0-399-23148-X). A series of stories narrated by an 11-year-old working-class boy in the north of England, who is troubled by bullying and growing up without a father. (Rev: BL 10/1/97; BR 1–2/98; SLJ 9/97)

1274 Lehrman, Robert. *Juggling* (10–12). 1982, HarperCollins $11.50 (0-06-023818-6). An explicit novel about a teenager—his love for soccer and his first sexual encounters. (Rev: BL 3/87)

1275 L'Engle, Madeleine. *A House Like a Lotus* (7–12). 1984, Farrar $17.00 (0-374-33385-8); Dell paper $4.99 (0-440-93685-3). Polly O'Keefe, of previous L'Engle novels, is now 17 and encounters both lesbianism and a heterosexual romance in this probing novel.

1276 L'Engle, Madeleine. *A Ring of Endless Light* (7–10). 1980, Dell paper $5.50 (0-440-97232-9). The Austin family are again central characters in this novel in which Vicki must adjust to her grandfather's death while exploring her telepathic powers with dolphins.

1277 Lester, Alison. *The Quicksand Pony* (5–8). 1998, Houghton $15.00 (0-395-93749-3). In this novel set in Australia, 17-year-old Joycie fakes a drowning and seeks a new life in the bush with her infant son, but 2 young girls stumble on the truth 9 years later. (Rev: BL 12/15/98; SLJ 10/98; VOYA 2/99)

1278 Lester, Jim. *Fallout* (7–10). 1996, Dell paper $3.99 (0-440-22683-X). A fast-paced novel told in a confessional format about the problems faced by

Kenny Francis, self-styled "terminal goofball," when he transfers to a fancy prep school. (Rev: BL 1/1–15/96; BR 5–6/96; SLJ 2/96; VOYA 2/96)

1279 Letts, Billie. *The Honk and Holler Opening Soon* (10–12). 1998, Warner $22.00 (0-446-52158-2). A story of love, hope, and humanity revolving around Caney Paxton, a crippled Vietnam veteran, and a cast of memorable characters he attracts at his restaurant in rural Oklahoma. (Rev: BL 5/1/98; SLJ 1/99)

1280 Leverich, Kathleen. *The New You* (6–8). 1998, Greenwillow $15.00 (0-688-16076-X). Insecure in her new surroundings after a move to the city with her father and new stepmother, 13-year-old Abbie decides it's time to create a new identity. (Rev: BL 11/1/98; SLJ 11/98)

1281 Levy, Elizabeth. *Cheater, Cheater* (5–8). 1994, Scholastic paper $3.50 (0-590-45866-3). Lucy Lovello has been labeled a cheater and even her teachers don't trust her,. When she finds her best friend cheating, she faces a moral dilemma. (Rev: BL 10/1/93; SLJ 10/93; VOYA 12/93)

1282 Levy, Marilyn. *Is That Really Me in the Mirror?* (7–10). 1991, Ballantine paper $3.95 (0-449-70343-6). Joanne is envious of her beautiful, popular older sister until an automobile accident and plastic surgery transform Joanne into a very pretty stranger. (Rev: BL 11/1/91)

1283 Lewis, Beverly. *Catch a Falling Star* (5–8). (Summerhill Secrets) 1995, Bethany House paper $5.99 (1-55661-478-0). An Amish boy faces excommunication when he begins paying too much attention to a non-Amish girl. (Rev: BL 3/15/96)

1284 Lewis, Beverly. *Night of the Fireflies* (5–8). (Summerhill Secrets) 1995, Bethany House paper $4.99 (1-55661-479-9). In this sequel to *Catch a Falling Star* (1995), Levi, an Amish boy, tries to save his young sister, who has been struck by a car. (Rev: BL 3/15/96)

1285 Lewis, Linda. *Is There Life After Boys?* (6–9). 1990, Archway paper $2.95 (0-671-69559-2). When Linda transfers to an all-girl school she finds the social change unbearable. (Rev: SLJ 2/88)

1286 Littke, Lael. *Loydene in Love* (8–10). 1986, Harcourt $13.95 (0-15-249888-5). A high school junior from a small town gets a different view of life when she visits Los Angeles for the summer. (Rev: BL 2/15/87; SLJ 3/87)

1287 Littke, Lael. *Shanny on Her Own* (6–9). 1985, Harcourt $12.95 (0-15-273531-3). Shanny is sent to live with an aunt in rural Idaho to counteract her developing punkiness. (Rev: BL 1/1/86; SLJ 12/85; VOYA 4/86)

1288 Loughery, John, ed. *First Sightings: Stories of American Youth* (9–12). 1993, Persea $29.95 (0-

89255-186-0); paper $11.95 (0-89255-187-9). An anthology of 20 dramatic stories about children and teens by John Updike, Philip Roth, Alice Walker, Joyce Carol Oates, and others. (Rev: BL 4/15/93)

1289 Lowry, Lois. *A Summer to Die* (7–10). Illus. 1977, Houghton $16.00 (0-395-25338-1). Meg is confused and dismayed by her older sister's death. (Rev: BL 7/88)

1290 Lowry, Lois. *Taking Care of Terrific* (7–9). 1983, Houghton $16.00 (0-395-34070-5); Dell paper $4.50 (0-440-48494-4). A baby-sitting job leads to all sorts of hectic adventures for 14-year-old Enid.

1291 Lynch, Chris. *Blood Relations* (8–12). 1996, HarperCollins LB $13.89 (0-06-025399-1); paper $4.50 (0-06-447122-5). The beginning of a violent, disturbing trilogy about 15-year-old Mick, his working-class Irish family, his drug-ridden neighborhood, and the Latino classmates to whom he turns for help. Followed by *Dog Eat Dog* (1996) and *Mick* (1996). (Rev: BL 4/1/96; SLJ 3/96; VOYA 8/96)

1292 Lynch, Chris. *Extreme Elvin* (8–10). 1999, HarperCollins LB $15.89 (0-06-028210-X). Elvin of *Slot Machine* is back, and this time he has discovered girls and a whole new set of relationships. (Rev: BL 2/1/99; SLJ 2/99; VOYA 10/99)

1293 Lynch, Chris. *Slot Machine* (8–10). 1995, HarperCollins LB $14.89 (0-06-023585-3). Elvin is a 13-year-old boy, overweight, and expected to perform with exuberance everything forced upon him. (Rev: BL 9/1/95*; SLJ 10/95; VOYA 12/95)

1294 Lyon, George E. *With a Hammer for My Heart* (10–12). 1997, DK Publg. $21.95 (0-7894-2460-6). The story of 15-year-old Lawanda, her life and family in Pine Mountain, and the friendship she develops with an older alcoholic veteran and its tragic consequences. (Rev: BL 9/1/97; BR 3–4/98; SLJ 10/97)

1295 McCall, Edith. *Better Than a Brother* (6–9). 1988, Walker $14.85 (0-8027-6783-4). Hughie turns to her friend Jerry for help when she loses her new gold locket. (Rev: BR 9–10/88; SLJ 5/88)

1296 McCants, William D. *Much Ado about Prom Night* (9–12). 1995, Harcourt $11.00 (0-15-200083-6); paper $5.00 (0-15-200081-X). Becca's ordeals form the basis for a witty novel joining the angst of high school with sly points about love and sex, politics, and peer pressure. (Rev: BL 7/95; SLJ 6/95)

1297 McColley, Kevin. *Sun Dance* (9–12). 1995, Simon & Schuster $16.00 (0-689-80008-8). Randy, his older brother, Mike, and 2 friends travel across the country in an old Firebird intent on carrying out a harebrained plan to blow up a nuclear reactor. (Rev: BL 1/1–15/96*; BR 5–6/96; SLJ 11/95; VOYA 12/95)

1298 McDaniel, Lurlene. *The Girl Death Left Behind* (6–9). 1999, Bantam paper $4.50 (0-553-57091-9).

A touching story of a girl's adjustment to the sudden death of her parents and starting a new life living with relatives. (Rev: SLJ 3/99; VOYA 4/99)

1299 McDaniel, Lurlene. *I'll Be Seeing You* (6–9). 1996, Bantam paper $4.99 (0-553-56718-7). Carley's face has been disfigured by the removal of a tumor and she tries to keep this secret from a blind boy with whom she has fallen in love. (Rev: BL 7/96; SLJ 12/96)

1300 McDaniel, Lurlene. *Starry, Starry Night* (6–10). 1998, Bantam $8.95 (0-553-57130-3). Three Christmas season stories about different heroines, each with a problem. One finally adjusts to her mother's pregnancy and then is devastated when the baby is born with severe brain damage; another discovers that a cancer patient has a crush on her; the third has difficulty with her boyfriend and must regain her perspective. (Rev: SLJ 10/98; VOYA 12/98)

1301 MacDonald, Caroline. *Speaking to Miranda* (7–10). 1992, HarperCollins LB $13.89 (0-06-021103-2). Set in Australia and New Zealand, Ruby, 18, leaves her boyfriend, travels with her father, and gradually decides to explore the mysteries of her life: Who was her mother? Who is her family? Who is she? (Rev: BL 12/15/92*; SLJ 10/92)

1302 McDonald, Joyce. *Swallowing Stones* (7–10). 1997, Delacorte $15.95 (0-385-32309-3). When Michael accidentally kills a man with his rifle, he and his friend decide to hide the gun and feign ignorance. (Rev: BL 10/15/97; BR 11–12/97; SLJ 9/97; VOYA 12/97)

1303 McElfresh, Lynn E. *Can You Feel the Thunder?* (4–8). 1999, Simon & Schuster $16.00 (0-689-82324-X). Mic, a seventh grader, has trouble adjusting to his blind and deaf older sister and also finds that if he doesn't master mathematical fractions, he won't be allowed to play baseball at school. (Rev: BL 6/1–15/99; SLJ 7/99; VOYA 8/99)

1304 McGuigan, Mary A. *Where You Belong* (5–9). 1997, Simon & Schuster $16.00 (0-689-81250-7). In 1963 in the Bronx, a lonely white girl growing up in poverty forms a friendship with a black girl. (Rev: BL 6/1–15/97; BR 11–12/97; SLJ 7/97; VOYA 8/97)

1305 McInerney, Jay. *The Last of the Savages* (10–12). 1996, Knopf $24.00 (0-679-42845-3). The story of the lasting friendship between Patrick, who becomes a successful New York lawyer, and Will, who is involved in rock and soul music and a lifestyle that includes drink and drugs. (Rev: SLJ 9/96)

1306 McKenna, Colleen O'Shaughnessy. *The Brightest Light* (6–10). 1992, Scholastic $13.95 (0-590-45347-5). A young girl discovers the secret behind her hometown's strange behavior during one long, hot summer. (Rev: BL 9/15/92; SLJ 12/92)

1307 MacLachlan, Patricia. *Unclaimed Treasures* (6–8). 1984, HarperCollins paper $4.95 (0-06-440189-8). Wila and her twin brother plus friend Horace spend an unusual and productive summer.

1308 McNaughton, Janet. *To Dance at the Palais Royale* (7–10). 1999, Stoddart paper $5.95 (0-7736-7473-X). The story of the loneliness and growing maturity of Aggie Maxwell who leaves her home in Scotland at age 17 to become a domestic servant with her sister in Toronto. (Rev: SLJ 5/99; VOYA 10/99)

1309 McVeity, Jen. *On Different Shores* (6–10). 1998, Orchard LB $17.99 (0-531-33115-6). The problems of a teenage Australian girl surface when the guerrilla environmental group to which she belongs is caught and a crisis develops over a beached whale. (Rev: BL 11/15/98; BR 5–6/99; SLJ 3/99; VOYA 10/98)

1310 Maguire, Gregory. *Oasis* (7–10). 1996, Clarion $14.95 (0-395-67019-5). This story of grief and guilt involves 13-year-old Hand, his adjustment to his father's sudden death, and his mother's efforts to save the motel her husband had managed. (Rev: BL 9/15/96; BR 3–4/97; SLJ 11/96; VOYA 2/97)

1311 Mahon, K. L. *Just One Tear* (5–10). 1994, Lothrop $14.00 (0-688-13519-6). The diary of a 14-year-old girl tells the story of a 13-year-old boy whose father is shot in front of him and tells how the boy deals with his grief. (Rev: BL 5/15/94; SLJ 5/94; VOYA 10/94)

1312 Mahy, Margaret. *The Catalogue of the Universe* (8–12). 1987, Scholastic paper $2.75 (0-590-42318-5). Through their friendship Angela, who longs to meet her absent father, and Tycho, who believes he is physically ugly, find tenderness and compassion. (Rev: BL 3/15/86; SLJ 4/86; VOYA 12/86)

1313 Mahy, Margaret. *The Other Side of Silence* (7–10). 1995, Viking $14.99 (0-670-86455-2). A gothic story with a menacing tone about a young woman's quest for individuality and personal power. (Rev: BL 10/1/95*; SLJ 10/95; VOYA 4/96)

1314 Makris, Kathryn. *A Different Way* (7–10). 1989, Avon paper $2.95 (0-380-75728-1). A newcomer in a Texas high school wonders if acceptance by the in crowd is worth the effort. (Rev: BL 10/15/89)

1315 Marino, Jan. *Searching for Atticus* (7–10). 1997, Simon & Schuster paper $16.00 (0-689-80066-5). During a stay at an aunt's home with her exhausted father, a Vietnam War veteran, 15-year-old Tessa falls in love with handsome but dangerous Caleb. (Rev: BL 11/15/97; BR 3–4/98; SLJ 10/97; VOYA 12/97)

1316 Martin, Ann M. *The Slam Book* (6–9). 1987, Holiday House $12.95 (0-08234-0666-0). Revealing the contents of a notebook in which students write freely about each other leads to broken friendships and a suicide. (Rev: SLJ 12/87; VOYA 2/88)

1317 Mason, Bobbie Ann. *In Country* (9–12). 1986, HarperCollins paper $13.00 (0-06-091350-9). This understated novel deals with a teenage girl and her gradual acceptance of the death of her father in the Vietnam War. (Rev: BL 8/85; SLJ 2/86)

1318 Matthews, Phoebe. *Switchstance* (7–10). 1989, Avon paper $2.95 (0-380-75729-X). After her parents' divorce, Elvy moves in with her grandmother and forms friendships with 2 very different boys. (Rev: VOYA 2/90)

1319 Maynard, Meredy. *Blue True Dream of Sky* (7–10). 1997, Polestar Book Publishers paper $7.95 (1-896095-23-2). Nickie, a 14-year-old albino girl, faces new problems when her brother sinks into a coma after a car crash, and she begins a crusade to save a stand of trees near her Pacific Northwest home. (Rev: BR 1–2/98; VOYA 10/97)

1320 Mazer, Anne, ed. *America Street: A Multicultural Anthology of Stories* (5–8). 1993, Persea $14.95 (0-89255-190-9); paper $4.95 (0-89255-191-7). Fourteen short stories about growing up in America's diverse society by Robert Cormier, Langston Hughes, Grace Paley, Gary Soto, and others. (Rev: BL 9/1/93; SLJ 11/93; VOYA 12/93)

1321 Mazer, Anne, ed. *Working Days: Stories about Teenagers & Work* (6–12). 1997, Persea $18.95 (0-89255-223-9); paper $7.95 (0-89255-224-7). An anthology of 15 varied, multicultural short stories about teenagers at their jobs. (Rev: BL 7/97; SLJ 9/97; VOYA 12/97)

1322 Mazer, Harry. *The Girl of His Dreams* (9–12). 1987, Avon paper $2.95 (0-380-70599-0). Willis Pierce is now 18 and into running while also being intent on his new girlfriend Sophie. Pierce was first introduced in Mazer's *The War on Villa Street*. (Rev: BL 9/15/87; BR 3–4/88; SLJ 1/88; VOYA 12/87)

1323 Mazer, Harry. *Hey, Kid! Does She Love Me?* (7–12). 1986, Avon paper $2.50 (0-380-70025-5). Stage-struck Jeff falls in love with a woman who was once an aspiring actress in this romance that contains some sexually explicit language.

1324 Mazer, Harry. *I Love You, Stupid!* (9–12). 1983, Avon paper $3.50 (0-380-61432-4). In this sequel to *The Dollar Man*, 17-year-old Marcus and friend Wendy experiment with sex and find love. (Rev: BL 6/87)

1325 Mazer, Norma Fox. *Out of Control* (7–12). 1993, Morrow $16.00 (0-688-10208-5); 1994, Avon paper $4.99 (0-380-71347-0). This novel deals directly and realistically with the complexities of sexual harassment. (Rev: BL 6/1–15/93; VOYA 8/93)

1326 Mazer, Norma Fox. *Someone to Love* (7–12). 1985, Dell paper $3.25 (0-440-98062-3). A lonely college student moves in with her boyfriend, a dropout.

1327 Mazer, Norma Fox. *When She Was Good* (10–12). 1997, Scholastic $21.99 (0-590-13506-6). When her sister dies unexpectedly, Em feels a complicated mixture of liberation and loss. (Rev: BL 9/1/97; BR 1–2/98; SLJ 9/97*; VOYA 10/97)

1328 Meyer, Carolyn. *Drummers of Jericho* (6–9). 1995, Harcourt $11.00 (0-15-200441-6); paper $5.00 (0-15-200190-5). Jewish Pazit Trujillo goes to live with her father in the small town of Jericho, but trouble breaks out when she objects to Christian symbols at school. (Rev: BL 6/1–15/95; SLJ 9/95; VOYA 5/95)

1329 Miklowitz, Gloria D. *Anything to Win* (7–12). 1989, Demco $9.09 (0-606-04608-9). A high school football player takes steroids in order to get a chance at a college scholarship. (Rev: BL 7/89; BR 11–12/89; SLJ 11/89; VOYA 10/89)

1330 Miles, Betty. *The Real Me* (6–8). 1975, Avon paper $2.75 (0-380-00347-3). Barbara rebels against all the restrictions placed on her life because she is a girl.

1331 Miles, Betty. *The Trouble with Thirteen* (6–9). 1979, Knopf LB $12.99 (0-394-93930-1); paper $2.95 (0-394-82043-6). Divorce and death, among other changes, make 2 friends realize that they are growing up.

1332 Miller-Lachmann, Lyn. *Hiding Places* (8–12). 1987, Square One paper $4.95 (0-938961-00-4). Mark runs away from his suburban home and ends up in a shelter in New York City. (Rev: SLJ 5/87)

1333 Moeyaert, Bart. *Bare Hands* (9–12). Trans. by Davi Colmer. 1998, Front Street $14.95 (1-886910-32-4). A provocative novel about a boy's confused feelings when his actions provoke a neighboring farmer, who is courting the boy's single mother, into killing the boy's dog. (Rev: BL 12/15/98; SLJ 2/99; VOYA 6/99)

1334 Moiles, Steven. *The Summer of My First Pediddle* (7–9). 1995, Royal Fireworks paper $5.00 (0-88092-122-6). Set in a small Illinois town during 1953, this is 14-year-old Brad Thatcher's story of how he weathered 2 firsts in his life—first love and his first encounter with prejudice after his father is investigated during the McCarthy hearings. (Rev: BR 1–2/96; VOYA 2/96)

1335 Moore, Martha. *Under the Mermaid Angel* (5–8). 1995, Delacorte $14.95 (0-385-32160-0). A 13-year-old girl meets a glamorous 30-year-old woman, Roxanne, the archetypal stranger who brings excitement and lessons about life and then leaves town. (Rev: BL 8/95; SLJ 10/95; VOYA 12/95)

1336 Morgenstern, Susie. *Secret Letters from 0 to 10* (5–8). Illus. 1998, Viking $15.99 (0-670-88007-8). Ten-year-old Ernest has lived a monotonous, sheltered existence until he meets classmate Victoria, and then his life turns around. (Rev: SLJ 10/98; VOYA 8/99)

1337 Mori, Kyoko. *Shizuko's Daughter* (9–12). 1993, Holt $15.95 (0-8050-2557-X). After an adolescence in protective, self-imposed isolation, Yuki leaves home in Kobe, Japan, to study art in Nagasaki. (Rev: BL 2/1/93; SLJ 6/93; VOYA 10/93)

1338 Morris, Winifred. *Liar* (7–10). 1996, Walker $23.95 (0-8027-8461-5). Fourteen-year-old Alex starts life over on his grandparents' farm in Oregon, but there are many obstacles, including school bullies, a hostile principal, and an unloving grandfather. (Rev: BL 12/1/96; SLJ 1/97; VOYA 12/96)

1339 Mosier, Elizabeth. *My Life as a Girl* (8–12). 1999, Random LB $18.99 (0-679-99035-6). Jamie wants to become a new person when she enters Bryn Mawr as a freshman, but her precollege summer boyfriend reminds her that she must come to terms with persistent family problems, including a father who has driven the family into financial ruin. (Rev: BL 4/1/99; SLJ 6/99)

1340 Myers, Anna. *Ethan Between Us* (7–10). 1998, Walker $25.95 (0-8027-8670-7). The lives of 2 close friends growing up in a small Oklahoma town are changed and their friendship shattered when they become involved with a handsome, troubled young man to whom both are attracted. (Rev: BL 8/98; BR 1–2/99; SLJ 10/98)

1341 Myers, Walter Dean. *Crystal* (9–12). 1990, Bantam paper $5.95 (0-440-80157-5). A beautiful young black model finds success hard to handle. (Rev: BL 6/1/87; BR 9–10/87; SLJ 6/87; VOYA 4/88)

1342 Myers, Walter Dean. *Won't Know Till I Get There* (7–10). 1982, Penguin paper $4.99 (0-14-032612-X). A young subway graffiti artist is sentenced to help out in a senior citizens' home.

1343 Namioka, Lensey. *Ties That Bind, Ties That Break* (7–10). 1999, Delacorte $15.95 (0-385-32666-1). In this novel set in early 20th-century China, a period of dramatic and political changes, Ailin rebels against traditions that represses women, and after a lonely and difficult journey to America, eventually achieves self-fulfillment. (Rev: BL 5/15/99; SLJ 7/99)

1344 Naylor, Phyllis Reynolds. *Alice in April* (5–8). 1993, Atheneum $15.00 (0-689-31805-7); Dell paper $4.50 (0-440-91032-3). Alice is back, this time

caught between her desire to be a perfect housekeeper and her fascination with her developing body. (Rev: BL 3/1/93; SLJ 6/93)

1345 Neenan, Colin. *In Your Dreams* (9–12). 1995, Harcourt $11.00 (0-15-200885-3). In this humorous, first-person narrative, 15-year-old Hale O'Reilly reveals several problems, including adjusting to his parents' divorce, his secret love for his older brother's girlfriend, to whom he has been writing Cyrano de Bergerac-type letters for his brother, and the fact that his younger sister's punk girlfriend likes him. (Rev: SLJ 5/95; VOYA 2/96)

1346 Neenan, Colin. *Live a Little* (8–12). 1996, Harcourt $12.00 (0-15-201242-7); paper $6.00 (0-15-202143-5). Hale's last days in high school are plagued with disappointments and he experiences bouts of self-pity when he discovers that good friend Zoe is pregnant. (Rev: BL 9/1/96; BR 3–4/97; SLJ 3/97; VOYA 12/96)

1347 Nelson, Theresa. *The Beggar's Ride* (6–8). 1992, Orchard LB $17.99 (0-531-08496-5). A compelling chronicle of a runaway's time on the tawdry boardwalks of Atlantic City. (Rev: BL 11/1/92; SLJ 11/92*)

1348 Nelson, Vaunda M. *Possibles* (4–8). 1995, Putnam $15.95 (0-399-22823-3). Twelve-year-old Sheppy comes to accept the death of her father through caring for an unusual 36-year-old woman who has broken her leg. (Rev: BL 2/1/96; SLJ 10/95; VOYA 12/95)

1349 Neufeld, John. *Boys Lie* (7–10). 1999, DK Publg. $16.95 (0-7894-2624-2). After a sexual attack by boys in a swimming pool in New York City, Gina moves with her mother to California, but ugly gossip and rumors follow her. (Rev: BL 2/15/99; SLJ 3/99; VOYA 10/99)

1350 Neville, Emily C. *It's Like This, Cat* (7–9). Illus. 1963, HarperCollins LB $15.89 (0-06-024391-0); paper $4.95 (0-06-440073-5). A New York City 14-year-old boy has more in common with his cat than his father. Newbery Medal, 1964.

1351 Nixon, Joan Lowery. *Maggie Forevermore* (5–8). 1987, Harcourt $13.95 (0-15-250345-5). In this sequel to *Maggie, Too* and *And Maggie Makes Three* (both o.p.), 13-year-old Maggie resents spending Christmas with her father and his new wife in California. (Rev: BL 3/87; SLJ 3/87)

1352 Nolan, Han. *Dancing on the Edge* (7–10). 1997, Harcourt $16.00 (0-15-201648-1). Beset by a series of personal and family crises, Miracle slowly descends into madness. (Rev: BL 10/1/97; SLJ 9/97*; VOYA 2/98)

1353 Nolan, Han. *Send Me Down a Miracle* (6–9). 1996, Harcourt $13.00 (0-15-200979-5); paper $6.00 (0-15-200978-7). Fourteen-year-old Charity is caught in the middle when her preacher father objects violently when Charity's friend, artist Adrienne Dabney, claims to have had a vision of Jesus. (Rev: BL 3/15/96*; SLJ 4/96*; VOYA 6/96)

1354 O'Dell, Scott. *Kathleen, Please Come Home* (7–10). 1978, Houghton $12.95 (0-395-26453-7). Kathleen's mother is pleading for the return of her runaway daughter.

1355 Oke, Janette. *Nana's Gift: Some Things in This World Are Very Expensive, but Others Are Priceless* (7–12). 1996, Bethany House $12.99 (1-55661-898-0). A sentimental story about great-grandmother Lizzie and Beth, her soul mate, who injures her spine in a car accident shortly before her wedding but is able to show strength because of the love of her fiancé and Nana and the many important lessons about love and sacrifice she learned from her Nana. (Rev: VOYA 6/97)

1356 Oke, Janette. *A Quiet Strength* (7–9). (Prairie Legacy) 1999, Bethany House paper $10.99 (0-7642-2156-6). The problems and joys of the first days of marriage for Virginia Simpson and her beau from former days. (Rev: BL 9/15/99)

1357 Okimoto, Jean D. *The Eclipse of Moonbeam Dawson* (7–10). 1997, Tor $17.95 (0-312-86244-X). Fifteen-year-old Moonbeam Dawson rebels against his mother's unconventional ways and takes a job and an apartment at posh Stere Island Lodge, where he changes his name and tries to change his values. (Rev: SLJ 11/97; VOYA 4/98)

1358 O'Leary, Patsy Baker. *With Wings as Eagles* (7–10). 1997, Houghton $15.00 (0-395-70557-6). Set in rural North Carolina in 1938, this novel tells about young Bubba's becoming reacquainted with a father newly released from prison, his family's struggle with poverty, and Bubba's friendship with a black boy. (Rev: BL 10/15/97; BR 5–6/98; SLJ 12/97*)

1359 Paterson, Katherine. *Jacob Have I Loved* (7–10). 1980, HarperCollins LB $14.89 (0-690-04079-2); Avon paper $2.95 (0-380-56499-8). Louise resents her twin sister's beauty and accomplishments in this novel set in the Chesapeake Bay area. Newbery Medal, 1981. (Rev: BL 6/1/88)

1360 Paulsen, Gary. *Alida's Song* (6–10). 1999, Delacorte paper $15.95 (0-385-32586-X). A 14-year-old boy discovers a new life when he leaves his alcoholic parents and accepts an invitation from his grandmother to spend time on her quiet northern Minnesota farm. (Rev: BL 6/1–15/99; BR 9–10/99; SLJ 7/99)

1361 Paulsen, Gary. *The Boy Who Owned the School* (6–9). 1990, Orchard $15.95 (0-531-05865-4). Jacob's main object in life is to be as invisible as possible and to avoid trouble. (Rev: BL 4/1/90; SLJ 4/90; VOYA 6/90)

1362 Paulsen, Gary. *The Car* (6–9). 1994, Harcourt $15.00 (0-15-292878-2). The cross-country adventures of Terry, 14, and Waylon, a 45-year-old Vietnam vet who sometimes suffers flashback memories and becomes violent. (Rev: BL 4/1/94; SLJ 5/94; VOYA 6/94)

1363 Paulsen, Gary. *The Crossing* (8–10). 1987, Dell paper $4.99 (0-440-20582-4). An alcoholic American soldier and a homeless street waif become friends in a Mexican border town. (Rev: BL 10/15/87; BR 1–2/88; SLJ 11/87; VOYA 10/87)

1364 Paulsen, Gary. *Dancing Carl* (7–9). 1987, Puffin paper $3.95 (0-685-19101-X). A young boy recalls his friendship with Carl, a troubled man who is an expert ice skater.

1365 Paulsen, Gary. *The Island* (7–10). 1988, Orchard $17.95 (0-531-05749-6). A 15-year-old boy finds peace and a meaning to life when he explores his own private island. (Rev: BL 3/15/88; BR 9–10/88; SLJ 5/88; VOYA 6/88)

1366 Paulsen, Gary. *Popcorn Days and Buttermilk Nights* (8–12). 1989, Penguin paper $4.99 (0-14-034204-4). Carley finds adventure after he is sent to his Uncle David's farm in Minnesota to sort himself out.

1367 Paulsen, Gary. *Sisters/Hermanas* (8–10). Trans. by Gloria de Aragón Andújar. 1993, Harcourt $10.95 (0-15-275323-0); paper $6.00 (0-15-275324-9). The bilingual story of 2 girls, age 14, in a Texas town, one an illegal Mexican immigrant prostitute, the other a superficial blond cheerleader. (Rev: BL 1/1/94; SLJ 1/94; VOYA 12/93)

1368 Paulsen, Gary. *Tracker* (7–9). 1984, Bradbury paper $3.95 (0-317-62280-3). John's encounters with nature help him accept the approaching death of his grandfather.

1369 Pearson, Gayle. *The Secret Box* (5–8). 1997, Simon & Schuster $15.00 (0-689-81379-1). Five short stories set in Oakland, California, about the pangs of growing up. (Rev: BL 8/97; BR 3–4/98; SLJ 6/97)

1370 Peck, Richard. *Are You in the House Alone?* (7–10). 1977, Bantam paper $4.99 (0-440-90227-4). Gail is raped by a classmate while she is on a babysitting assignment. (Rev: BL 2/15/88)

1371 Peck, Richard. *Bed & Breakfast* (10–12). 1998, Viking paper $23.95 (0-670-87368-3). A novel about the lasting friendship between Lesley, Julia, and Margo that culminates in a reunion where the 3 are dramatically changed after a stay at an elegant bed-and-breakfast in London run by the mysterious Mrs. Smith-Porter. (Rev: BL 6/1–15/98; SLJ 8/98)

1372 Pennebaker, Ruth. *Conditions of Love* (8–10). 1999, Holt $16.95 (0-8050-6104-5). In this first-person narrative, 14-year-old Sarah tells of her problems adjusting to her her father's death and getting along with her mother, plus difficulties at her school where she is considered an outsider. (Rev: BL 5/15/99; SLJ 5/99; VOYA 6/99)

1373 Pennebaker, Ruth. *Don't Think Twice* (9–12). 1996, Holt $15.95 (0-8050-4407-8). Anne, an intelligent, caustic 18-year-old girl "in trouble," narrates this story about a group of girls in a home for pregnant teens in rural Texas. (Rev: BL 5/1/96; BR 1–2/97; SLJ 5/96*; VOYA 8/96)

1374 Peters, Julie A. *How Do You Spell G-E-E-K?* (4–8). 1996, Little, Brown $12.95 (0-316-70266-8). Kim feels left out when her best friend, Ann, befriends Luriene, a new student. (Rev: BL 9/15/96; BR 5–6/97; SLJ 10/96)

1375 Peterseil, Tehila. *The Safe Place* (5–8). 1996, Pitspopany $16.95 (0-943706-71-8); paper $12.95 (0-943706-72-6). This touching story of an Israeli girl with a learning disability shows the impact a single understanding teacher can have. (Rev: SLJ 12/96)

1376 Pevsner, Stella. *Call Me Heller, That's My Name* (7–9). 1973, Clarion $7.95 (0-395-28874-6). Hildegard, alias Heller, finally calms down and admits she is a girl.

1377 Pevsner, Stella. *Cute Is a Four-Letter Word* (7–9). 1980, Archway paper $2.75 (0-671-68845-6). The best-laid plans of Clara go awry.

1378 Pfeffer, Susan Beth. *Kid Power* (6–9). Illus. 1988, Scholastic paper $3.99 (0-590-42607-9). A group of youngsters join together to do jobs for money.

1379 Philbrick, Rodman. *The Fire Pony* (5–8). 1996, Scholastic $14.95 (0-590-55251-1). Rescued from a foster home by his half-brother Joe, Roy hopes that life will be better on the ranch where Joe finds work. (Rev: BL 5/1/96; SLJ 9/96; VOYA 10/96)

1380 Philbrick, Rodman. *Freak the Mighty* (7–10). 1993, Scholastic $15.95 (0-590-47412-X). When Maxwell Kane, the son of Killer Kane, becomes friends with Kevin, a new boy with a birth defect, he gains a new interest in school and learning. (Rev: BL 12/15/93; SLJ 12/93*; VOYA 4/94)

1381 Pinkney, Andrea D. *Raven in a Dove House* (6–10). 1998, Harcourt $16.00 (0-15-201461-6). In this story about African American families, 12-year-old Nell is staying with her aunt in upstate New York when her cousin, Foley, is accused of shooting his friend, Slade. (Rev: BL 2/15/98; SLJ 5/98; VOYA 10/98)

1382 Platt, Kin. *Crocker* (7–10). 1983, Harper-Collins $11.95 (0-397-32025-6). Dorothy is attracted to a new boy in school.

1383 Platt, Randall B. *The Cornerstone* (8–12). 1998, Catbird Pr. $21.95 (0-945774-40-0). Using flashbacks, this novel tells about the growth of a tough 15-year-old charity case at summer camp on a scholarship in 1944, where he meets a Navy man on medical leave who changes his life. (Rev: VOYA 2/99)

1384 Porter, David. *Vienna Passage* (9–12). 1995, Crossway paper $10.99 (0-89107-824-X). A deeply religious young Englishman matures to an understanding of the evils of anti-Semitism and the fulfillment of a life with the love of a woman, art, and music. (Rev: BL 9/1/95*)

1385 Potok, Chaim. *My Name Is Asher Lev* (9–12). 1972, Knopf $25.00 (0-394-46137-1); Fawcett paper $6.99 (0-449-20714-5). This novel traces the conflict that a sensitive Jewish boy experiences with his strict Orthodox beliefs.

1386 Potok, Chaim. *Zebra & Other Stories* (7–12). Illus. 1998, Random LB $19.99 (0-679-95440-6). An anthology of 6 stories about experiences that youngsters have that help them along the road to maturity. (Rev: BL 7/98; SLJ 9/98; VOYA 10/98)

1387 Rapp, Adam. *The Buffalo Tree* (9–12). 1997, Front Street $15.95 (1-886910-19-7). Sura, who has adjusted to his confined world in a juvenile detention center, learns about himself through sessions with a counselor. (Rev: BL 9/1/97; SLJ 6/97*; VOYA 8/97)

1388 Rapp, Adam. *Missing the Piano* (9–12). 1994, Viking $14.99 (0-670-95340-2). In his new military academy, Mike discovers racism and intimidation in this story about values, basketball, and friendship. (Rev: BL 6/1–15/94; SLJ 6/94)

1389 Reed, Don C. *The Kraken* (6–10). 1997, Boyds Mills paper $7.95 (1-56397-693-5). In Newfoundland in the late 1800s, a boy struggles to survive against the impersonal rich and the harsh environment. (Rev: BL 3/15/95; SLJ 2/95)

1390 Reynolds, Marilyn. *Beyond Dreams* (9–12). 1995, Morning Glory Pr. $15.95 (1-885356-01-3); paper $8.95 (1-885356-00-5). Using alternate male and female voices, Reynolds presents short stories of teens in crisis. (Rev: BL 11/15/95; SLJ 9/95; VOYA 2/96)

1391 Reynolds, Marilyn. *But What About Me?* (9–12). (True-to-Life) 1996, Morning Glory Pr. $15.95 (1-885356-11-0); paper $8.95 (1-885356-10-2). Eighteen-year-old Erica is trying to remain true to herself while her boyfriend is spiraling down a path to self-destruction in this story of the trials of true love. (Rev: BR 3–4/97; SLJ 10/96; VOYA 2/97)

1392 Reynolds, Marilyn. *Detour for Emmy* (8–12). 1993, Morning Glory Pr. paper $8.95 (0-930934-76-8). Emmy is a good student and a hunk's girlfriend, but her home life includes a deserter father and an alcoholic mother. Emmy's pregnancy causes more hardship when she keeps the baby. (Rev: BL 10/1/93; SLJ 7/93; VOYA 12/93)

1393 Reynolds, Marilyn. *If You Loved Me: True-to-Life Series from Hamilton High* (8–12). 1999, Morning Glory Pr. $15.95 (1-885356-54-4); paper $8.95 (1-885356-55-2). Seventeen-year-old Lauren, born to a drug-addicted mother now deceased, vows to abstain from drugs and sex, but the latter is particularly difficult because of an insistent boyfriend. (Rev: BL 9/1/99)

1394 Reynolds, Marilyn. *Telling: True-to-Life Series from Hamilton High* (7–10). 1996, Morning Glory Pr. paper $8.95 (1-885356-03-X). Twelve-year-old Cassie is confused and embarrassed when her adult neighbor makes sexual advances towards her. (Rev: BL 4/1/96; SLJ 5/96; VOYA 6/96)

1395 Reynolds, Marilyn. *Too Soon for Jeff* (8–12). 1994, Morning Glory Pr. $15.95 (0-930934-90-3); paper $8.95 (0-930934-91-1). Jeff's hopes of going to college on a debate scholarship are put in jeopardy when his girlfriend happily announces she's pregnant. Jeff reluctantly prepares for fatherhood. (Rev: BL 9/15/94; SLJ 9/94; VOYA 12/94)

1396 Rhue, Morton. *The Wave* (7–10). 1981, Dell paper $4.99 (0-440-99371-7). A high school experiment to test social interaction backfires when an elitist group is formed.

1397 Roberts, Laura P. *Get a Life* (7–10). (Clearwater Crossing) 1998, Bantam Doubleday Dell paper $3.99 (0-553-57118-4). A group of teenagers, each with a problem or a family secret not to be shared, come together as volunteers planning a high school charity carnival. (Rev: BR 9–10/98; SLJ 11/98)

1398 Rodowsky, Colby. *Remembering Mog* (7–12). 1996, Farrar $15.00 (0-374-34663-1); Avon paper $3.99 (0-380-72922-9). With the death of her older sister and mentor, Annie must face the future alone and make her own decisions. (Rev: BL 2/1/96; BR 9–10/96; SLJ 3/96*; VOYA 6/96)

1399 Rodowsky, Colby. *Sydney, Invincible* (7–10). 1995, Farrar $14.00 (0-374-37365-5). In this sequel to *Sydney, Herself,* a girl yearns to write and struggles with the idea of responsible journalism. (Rev: BL 4/15/95)

1400 Roos, Stephen. *Confessions of a Wayward Preppie* (7–10). 1986, Dell paper $2.75 (0-440-91586-4). Through an unusual bequest, Cary is able to attend a classy prep school but there his troubles begin. (Rev: BL 6/1/86; BR 9–10/86; SLJ 5/86; VOYA 8/86)

1401 Rosen, Roger, and Patra M. Sevastiades, eds. *Coming of Age: The Art of Growing Up* (9–12). 1994, Rosen LB $16.95 (0-8239-1805-X); paper $8.95 (0-8239-1806-8). This multicultural anthology of short fiction and essays confronts traditional—and more complex—coming-of-age issues. (Rev: BL 1/1/95; SLJ 1/95)

1402 Rosenberg, Liz. *Heart & Soul* (8–12). 1996, Harcourt $11.00 (0-15-200942-6); paper $5.00 (0-15-201270-2). It is only when Willie helps a troubled Jewish classmate that she is able to straighten out her own problems. (Rev: BL 6/1–15/96; VOYA 8/96)

1403 Rottman, S. L. *Hero* (5–8). 1997, Peachtree $14.95 (1-56145-159-2). When his home life becomes unbearable, Sean is sent to Carbondale Ranch, where his sense of self-worth gradually grows. (Rev: BL 12/1/97; SLJ 12/97; VOYA 12/97)

1404 Rottman, S. L. *Rough Waters* (7–12). 1998, Peachtree $14.95 (1-56145-172-X). After the deaths of their parents, teenage brothers Gregg and Scott move to Colorado to live with an uncle who runs a white-water rafting business. (Rev: BL 5/1/98; BR 11–12/98; SLJ 8/98; VOYA 8/98)

1405 Ryan, Mary E. *The Trouble with Perfect* (5–8). 1995, Simon & Schuster $15.00 (0-689-80276-5). Through coping with problems with honesty, cheating, failure, and the value of competition plus a father who drinks too much, Kyle learns to understand himself and others. (Rev: BL 10/1/95; SLJ 11/95; VOYA 2/96)

1406 Ryden, Hope. *Wild Horse Summer* (5–8). Illus. 1997, Clarion $15.00 (0-395-77519-1). During a summer on her relatives' Wyoming ranch, Alison overcomes anxieties and fears. (Rev: BL 8/97; SLJ 9/97)

1407 Rylant, Cynthia. *A Fine White Dust* (6–8). 1986, Bradbury LB $16.00 (0-02-777240-3). A 13-year-old boy falls under the spell of a traveling preacher with tragic results. (Rev: BL 9/1/86; BR 3–4/87; SLJ 9/86)

1408 Sachar, Louis. *Holes* (6–9). 1998, Farrar $16.00 (0-374-33265-7). After being wrongfully accused of stealing a baseball star's sneakers, Stanley spends 6 months in a detention center where he and his fellow inmates dig holes in a dry lake bed to fulfill the wishes of the sicko warden. Newbery Medal, 1999. (Rev: BL 6/1–15/98; BR 5–6/99; SLJ 9/98; VOYA 12/98)

1409 Sachs, Marilyn. *Almost Fifteen* (6–8). 1988, Avon paper $2.95 (0-380-70357-2). A lightweight story of a practical girl, her boyfriends, and her impractical parents. (Rev: BL 6/15/87; SLJ 5/87)

1410 Sachs, Marilyn. *Class Pictures* (7–9). 1980, Avon paper $2.95 (0-380-61408-1). The friendship from kindergarten through high school between 2 girls is recalled through old class pictures.

1411 Sachs, Marilyn. *Fourteen* (7–9). 1983, Avon paper $2.95 (0-380-69842-0). First love comes to Rebecca by way of a new neighbor.

1412 Sachs, Marilyn. *Peter and Veronica* (7–9). 1995, Puffin paper $4.99 (0-14-037082-X). Peter's friendship with non-Jewish Veronica faces a crisis over his bar mitzvah.

1413 Sachs, Marilyn. *Surprise Party* (5–8). 1998, NAL $15.99 (0-525-45962-6). Gen tries to win over an enemy by enlisting her help in plans for her parents' 25th wedding anniversary, and she and her brother develop a secret relationship with their grandmother, with whom their parents had a falling out years ago. (Rev: BL 6/1–15/98; SLJ 5/98)

1414 Salinger, J. D. *The Catcher in the Rye* (7–12). 1951, Little, Brown $25.00 (0-316-76953-3); Bantam paper $3.95 (0-553-25025-6). For mature readers, the saga of Holden Caulfield and his 3 days in New York City. (Rev: BL 10/1/88)

1415 Salisbury, Graham. *Jungle Dogs* (5–8). 1998, Doubleday $15.95 (0-385-32187-2). In this novel set in a poor Hawaiian village, young, bespeckled Boy must face his fears and confront the dogs that terrorize him on his paper route. (Rev: BL 9/1/98; SLJ 10/98; VOYA 10/98)

1416 Savage, Deborah. *Under a Different Sky* (7–9). 1997, Houghton $16.00 (0-395-77395-4). Two troubled teenagers—Ben, a born horseman, and Lara, a newcomer in the area—find friendship in this novel set in a poor rural Pennsylvania community. (Rev: BL 3/15/97; BR 9–10/97; SLJ 5/97*; VOYA 6/97)

1417 Schaeffer, Frank. *Portofino* (9–12). 1992, Macmillan $15.00 (0-02-607051-0). An insecure adolescent remembers vacations during the 1960s with his eccentric "born-again" family. (Rev: BL 9/15/92)

1418 Scoppettone, Sandra. *Trying Hard to Hear You* (7–10). 1996, Alyson Pubs. paper $9.95 (1-55583-367-5). Two boys who are lovers face the problems of acceptance by their friends.

1419 Sebestyen, Ouida. *Out of Nowhere* (6–9). 1994, Orchard LB $17.99 (0-531-08689-5). The story of the bonding into a sort of family of a quirky group of characters, among them Harley, 13, who's left home; his dog Ishmael; Bill, a junk collector; and May, the "queen of clean." (Rev: BL 4/1/94; SLJ 3/94; VOYA 4/94)

1420 Sefton, Catherine. *Island of the Strangers* (7–9). 1985, Harcourt $12.95 (0-15-239100-2). City kids from Belfast clash with town toughs in this novel set on an island off Northern Ireland. (Rev: BL 1/1/86; SLJ 1/86)

1421 Seymour, Tres. *The Revelation of Saint Bruce* (7–12). 1998, Orchard $16.95 (0-531-30109-5). Because of his honesty, Bruce is responsible for the expulsion of several friends from school. (Rev: BL 10/15/98; BR 5–6/99; SLJ 9/98; VOYA 2/99)

1422 Shoup, Barbara. *Stranded in Harmony* (7–10). 1997, Hyperion LB $17.89 (0-7868-2284-8). Lucas, an 18-year-old popular senior in high school, is discontented until he meets and becomes friendly with an older woman. (Rev: BL 7/97; BR 11–12/97; SLJ 6/97*)

1423 Silvey, Anita, ed. *Help Wanted: Short Stories about Young People Working* (6–12). 1997, Little, Brown $15.95 (0-316-79148-2). A collection of 12 short stories by such writers as Michael Dorris, Norma Fox Mazer, and Gary Soto that deal with teenagers at work. (Rev: BL 11/1/97; BR 3–4/98; SLJ 11/97; VOYA 12/97)

1424 Sinclair, April. *Coffee Will Make You Black* (9–12). 1994, Hyperion $19.95 (1-56282-796-0). Set in late 1960s Chicago, 11-year-old "Stevie" Stevenson's growth from child to woman parallels the growth of African American pride and equality. (Rev: BL 12/15/93)

1425 Singer, Marilyn. *The Course of True Love Never Did Run Smooth* (10–12). 1983, HarperCollins $12.95 (0-06-025753-9). A gay couple "come out" during a school production of *A Midsummer Night's Dream*. (Rev: BL 6/87)

1426 Singer, Marilyn, ed. *Stay True: Short Stories for Strong Girls* (7–12). 1998, Scholastic $16.95 (0-590-36031-0). There are 11 new short stories in this collection that explores the problems girls face growing up and how they discover inner strength. (Rev: BL 4/1/98; BR 11–12/98; SLJ 5/98; VOYA 4/98)

1427 Skinner, David. *The Wrecker* (6–9). 1995, Simon & Schuster paper $14.00 (0-671-79771-9). A bully, a genius, and a newcomer (the narrator) are part of a story with elements as compelling as those of Robert Cormier or Stephen King. (Rev: BL 8/95*; VOYA 5/95)

1428 Slepian, Jan. *The Broccoli Tapes* (6–8). 1989, Putnam $14.95 (0-399-21712-6). Sara and her older brother Sam spend time in Hawaii in this novel that explores family relationships. (Rev: BL 4/15/89; SLJ 4/89; VOYA 6/89)

1429 Smith, Betty. *Joy in the Morning* (9–12). 1963, HarperCollins paper $6.50 (0-06-080368-1). Two young people face a number of problems when their families disown them after finding out about their marriage.

1430 Smith, Doris Buchanan. *Return to Bitter Creek* (6–8). 1986, Penguin paper $4.99 (0-14-032223-X). In spite of grandma's hostility, Lacey and her mother journey back home to North Carolina to rejoin mother's lover David. (Rev: BL 7/86; SLJ 9/86)

1431 Snyder, Zilpha Keatley. *The Runaways* (4–8). 1999, Delacorte $15.95 (0-385-32599-1). Twelve-year-old Dani O'Donnell, angry at her mother for moving them to a desert town where she feels lost, makes plans to run away. (Rev: BL 1/1–15/99; BR 9–10/99; SLJ 3/99)

1432 Sonenklar, Carol. *My Own Worst Enemy* (5–8). 1999, Holiday House $15.95 (0-8234-1456-6). In this first-person narrative, Eve Belkin finds there is a price to pay when she outdoes herself to be popular in her new school. (Rev: BL 5/15/99; SLJ 8/99; VOYA 10/99)

1433 Soto, Gary. *Baseball in April and Other Stories* (5–9). 1990, Harcourt $16.00 (0-15-205720-X). A group of stories about young Hispanics growing up in Southern California. (Rev: BL 3/1/90; SLJ 6/90; VOYA 8/90)

1434 Soto, Gary. *Buried Onions* (8–12). 1997, Harcourt $17.00 (0-15-201333-4). A junior college dropout, 19-year-old Eddie is trying to support himself in this story set in the barrio of Fresno, California. (Rev: BL 11/15/97; SLJ 1/98; VOYA 10/97)

1435 Southgate, Martha. *Another Way to Dance* (6–8). 1996, Delacorte $15.95 (0-385-32191-0). A young black girl is thrilled to spend a summer at the School of American Ballet in New York City but encounters unforeseen problems. (Rev: BL 12/1/96; BR 11–12/96; SLJ 12/96; VOYA 10/96)

1436 Spark, Muriel. *The Prime of Miss Jean Brodie* (9–12). 1984, NAL paper $6.95 (0-452-26179-1). The story of an unusual teacher in a private girls' school in Edinburgh and of the changes she detects in her students.

1437 Spinelli, Jerry. *Crash* (5–8). 1996, Knopf LB $17.99 (0-679-97957-3). Crash Coogan changes his bullying ways after his grandfather suffers a stroke, and even accepts the friendship of Penn Webb whom he has tormented for years. (Rev: SLJ 6/96*)

1438 Spinelli, Jerry. *Jason and Marceline* (7–10). 1994, Little, Brown paper $5.95 (0-316-80702-8). Jason, now in the ninth grade, sorts out his feelings toward girls in general and Marceline in particular. Preceded by *Space Station Seventh Grade*. (Rev: BL 1/1/87; SLJ 2/87)

1439 Spinelli, Jerry. *Space Station Seventh Grade* (6–8). 1991, Little, Brown paper $5.95 (0-316-80804-0). Jason has many adventures, mostly hilarious, during his seventh grade year.

1440 Springer, Nancy. *Secret Star* (7–10). 1997, Putnam $15.95 (0-399-23028-9). Fourteen-year-old Tess Mathis, strong but dirt-poor, can't remember anything before age 10, but when a scar-faced stranger comes to town, she must confront her past. (Rev: BL 4/1/97; BR 5–6/97; SLJ 5/97; VOYA 12/97)

1441 Stanley, Diane. *A Time Apart* (6–9). 1999, Morrow $16.00 (0-688-16997-X). A 13-year-old girl discovers she has inner strengths when she spends a summer with her father on an archaeological project to replicate an Iron Age village in England. (Rev: BL 6/1–15/99; SLJ 9/99)

1442 Staples, Suzanne F. *Dangerous Skies* (7–10). 1996, Farrar $16.00 (0-374-31694-5). An interracial friendship, sexual abuse, and family secrets are themes in this novel about a white boy and a black girl growing up in the eastern shore of Virginia. (Rev: BL 9/1/96*; BR 1–2/97; SLJ 10/96; VOYA 12/96)

1443 Stevens, Diane. *Liza's Blue Moon* (6–8). 1995, Greenwillow $15.00 (0-688-13542-0). A coming-of-age story where a young girl feels she has been left behind by all that matters in life. (Rev: BL 4/1/95; SLJ 4/95)

1444 Stevens, Diane. *Liza's Star Wish* (6–10). 1997, Greenwillow $15.00 (0-688-15310-0). In this sequel to *Liza's Blue Moon*, Liza and her mother spend time in Rockport one summer, and Liza deals with vast changes in her life, including family relationships and friendships. (Rev: BL 9/15/97; SLJ 10/97)

1445 Stinson, Susan. *Fat Girl Dances with Rocks* (9–12). 1994, Spinsters Ink paper $10.95 (1-883523-02-8). Char, 17 and overweight, struggles with her identity, the meaning of beauty, and her confusion when her best friend, Felice, kisses her on the lips. (Rev: BL 9/1/94; VOYA 5/95)

1446 Strasser, Todd. *How I Changed My Life* (7–12). 1995, Simon & Schuster $16.00 (0-671-88415-8). Introverted Bo, the theater department stage manager, works on her self-image and weight problem when handsome football captain Kyle joins a production. (Rev: BL 5/1/95; SLJ 5/95)

1447 Swarthout, Glendon. *Bless the Beasts and Children* (7–12). 1995, Pocket Books paper $6.50 (0-671-52151-9). At summer camp a group of misfits prove they have the right stuff. (Rev: BL 9/1/97)

1448 Tamar, Erika. *The Things I Did Last Summer* (7–9). 1994, Harcourt $10.95 (0-15-282490-1); paper $3.95 (0-15-200020-8). A teenager spending the summer on Long Island with his pregnant stepmother loses his virginity when he meets a deceptive older woman. (Rev: BL 3/15/94; SLJ 4/94; VOYA 6/94)

1449 Taylor, William. *The Blue Lawn* (9–12). 1999, Alyson Pubs. paper $9.95 (1-55583-493-0). In this novel set in New Zealand, two teenage boys, one quiet and introspective, the other wild and adventurous, are drawn together in a friendship that in time turns sexual. (Rev: SLJ 7/99)

1450 Testa, Maria. *Dancing Pink Flamingos and Other Stories* (8–12). 1995, Lerner $19.95 (0-8225-0738-2). Unsentimental short stories about young women who must face the difficult realities of life and rediscover the positive directions they must go. (Rev: BL 10/1/95; SLJ 9/95)

1451 Thesman, Jean. *Cattail Moon* (6–9). 1994, Houghton $16.00 (0-395-67409-3); 1995, Avon paper $4.50 (0-380-72504-5). Julia, 14, is at odds with her mother, who wants to transform her from a classical musician into a cheerleader. (Rev: BL 4/1/94; SLJ 5/94; VOYA 8/94)

1452 Thesman, Jean. *Couldn't I Start Over?* (7–10). 1989, Avon paper $2.95 (0-380-75717-6). Growing up in a caring family situation, teenager Shiloh still faces many problems in her coming of age. (Rev: BL 11/15/89; VOYA 2/90)

1453 Thesman, Jean. *The Rain Catchers* (7–12). 1991, Houghton $15.00 (0-395-55333-4). Grayling learns the importance of storytelling in keeping the past alive, understanding others and herself, and surviving difficult times. (Rev: BL 4/15/91*; SLJ 3/91)

1454 Thesman, Jean. *Summerspell* (7–10). 1995, Simon & Schuster $15.00 (0-671-50130-5). A web of lies and secrets are behind a girl's escape from sexual harassment to a cabin where life had been safe and happy in the past. (Rev: BL 5/1/95; SLJ 6/95)

1455 Thomas, Joyce C. *Bright Shadow* (10–12). 1983, Avon paper $4.99 (0-380-84509-1). A 20-year-old black college student's encounter with love is marred when she becomes involved in a murder.

1456 Thomas, Joyce C. *When the Nightingale Sings* (6–8). 1992, 1994, HarperCollins paper $3.95 (0-06-440524-9). Marigold's only joy in her stepfamily is singing, which leads her to audition for a Baptist church choir, where she discovers self-worth, her family, and happiness. (Rev: BL 1/1/93; SLJ 2/93)

1457 Thomas, Rob. *Rats Saw God* (8–12). 1996, Simon & Schuster paper $4.50 (0-689-80777-5). At the suggestion of his counselor, high school senior Steve York explores his life, his problems, and how things went wrong when he moved from Texas to California. (Rev: BL 6/1–15/96; BR 1–2/97; SLJ 6/96*; VOYA 6/96)

1458 Thomas, Rob. *Satellite Down* (9–12). 1998, Simon & Schuster $16.00 (0-689-80957-3). Seventeen-year-old Patrick Sheridan faces adult situations and decisions when he is chosen to leave his small Texas town to become a student journalist for a satellite television station, first in Los Angeles and later in Belfast. (Rev: BL 5/15/98; SLJ 6/98; VOYA 6/98)

1459 Thompson, Julian. *Facing It* (7–9). 1989, Avon paper $2.95 (0-380-84491-5). An accident ruins the baseball chances of the star at Camp Raycroft. A reissue.

1460 Thompson, Julian. *Philo Fortune's Awesome Journey to His Comfort Zone* (8–12). 1995, Hyperion $16.95 (0-7868-0067-4). A story of a youth who

discovers the possibilities of the man he might become. (Rev: BL 5/1/95; SLJ 5/95; VOYA 2/96)

1461 Todd, Pamela. *Pig and the Shrink* (5–8). 1999, Delacorte $14.95 (0-385-32657-2). After Tucker's science project is rejected, he substitutes a study on childhood and obesity with overweight "Pig" Pighetti, also from the seventh grade, as his subject. (Rev: BL 10/1/99; SLJ 9/99)

1462 Tolan, Stephanie S. *Plague Year* (8–12). 1991, Fawcett paper $4.50 (0-449-70403-3). Nonconformist Bran, whose father is a mass murderer, faces problems of acceptance at his new high school. (Rev: BL 4/1/90; SLJ 6/90)

1463 Tomey, Ingrid. *Nobody Else Has to Know* (8–10). 1999, Delacorte $15.95 (0-385-32624-6). Fifteen-year-old Webb, a high school track star, feels increasing guilt after he hits a young girl while driving without a license and his grandfather takes the blame. (Rev: SLJ 9/99)

1464 Tomey, Ingrid. *Savage Carrot* (7–9). 1993, Scribners $14.95 (0-684-19633-6). When the death of Carrot's father robs her of her hero, she withdraws from everyone except her developmentally disabled uncle. (Rev: BL 3/1/94; SLJ 2/94; VOYA 4/94)

1465 Toten, Teresa. *The Onlyhouse* (5–8). 1996, Red Deer paper $7.95 (0-88995-137-3). Eleven-year-old Lucija, whose family was originally from Croatia, relocates to a new house in suburban Toronto after several years in a dense downtown neighborhood with a large immigrant population, and must adjust to a new school, peer pressures, and bullies. (Rev: SLJ 7/96)

1466 Trembath, Don. *The Tuesday Cafe* (6–9). 1996, Orca paper $6.95 (1-55143-074-6). Harper Winslow, a disaffected, wealthy teenager, learns about life and grows up when he is forced to join a local writing group called "The Tuesday Cafe." (Rev: BL 8/97; SLJ 9/96; VOYA 2/97)

1467 Vail, Rachel. *Do-Over* (5–9). 1992, 1994, Avon paper $3.99 (0-380-72180-5). The story of 13-year-old Whitman Levy's first crush, first kiss, first heartbreak, and first real boy-girl relationship, as well as assorted family problems. (Rev: BL 8/92*; SLJ 9/92)

1468 Vail, Rachel. *Ever After* (5–9). 1994, Orchard LB $16.99 (0-531-08688-7); 1995, Avon paper $3.99 (0-380-72465-0). Describes a 14-year-old starting high school and her concerns about dieting, friendship, family, and the future. (Rev: BL 3/1/94; SLJ 5/94*; VOYA 6/94)

1469 Vande Velde, Vivian. *Curses, Inc.: And Other Stories* (6–10). 1997, Harcourt $16.00 (0-15-201452-7). In the title story in this collection of tales with surprise endings, Bill Essler thinks he has found the perfect way to get even with his girlfriend, who humiliated him, by utilizing a web site, Curses, Inc. (Rev: SLJ 6/97*; VOYA 6/97)

1470 Velasquez, Gloria. *Tommy Stands Alone* (7–10). 1995, Arte Publico $14.95 (1-55885-146-1); paper $9.95 (1-55885-147-X). An engaging story about a Latino gay teen who is humiliated and rejected but finds understanding from a Chicano therapist. (Rev: BL 10/15/95; SLJ 11/95; VOYA 12/95)

1471 Verdelle, A. J. *The Good Negress* (9–12). 1995, Algonquin $29.95 (1-56512-085-X). Neesey, 13, returns to Detroit from her grandmother's in the South and rages internally over family obligations and a desire for white people's education. (Rev: BL 2/15/95; SLJ 10/95)

1472 Voigt, Cynthia. *Tell Me If the Lovers Are Losers* (7–10). 1982, Macmillan LB $17.00 (0-689-30911-2). Three college roommates clash until they find a common interest in volleyball. (Rev: BL 3/87)

1473 Walker, Paul R. *The Method* (8–12). 1990, Harcourt $14.95 (0-15-200528-5). A candid novel about a 15-year-old boy, his acting aspirations, and his sexual problems. (Rev: BL 8/90; SLJ 6/90)

1474 Wallace, Bill. *Aloha Summer* (7–9). 1997, Holiday House paper $15.95 (0-8234-1306-3). Fourteen-year-old John Priddle moves with his family to Hawaii in 1925 and finds less than the island paradise he expected. However, his friendship with a Hawaiian classmate brings new meaning to his life. (Rev: BL 10/1/97; SLJ 10/97; VOYA 12/97)

1475 Warlick, Ashley. *The Distance from the Heart of Things* (10–12). 1996, Houghton $21.95 (0-395-74177-7). Mavis Black returns to her small town in South Carolina after college and sees life from a different perspective. (Rev: BL 3/1/96; SLJ 8/96)

1476 Warner, Sally. *Some Friend* (5–8). 1996, Knopf $15.00 (0-679-87620-0). Case faces a difficult choice when a friend, who has run away from a foster home, asks for help. (Rev: BL 6/1–15/96; SLJ 5/96)

1477 Wartski, Maureen C. *My Name Is Nobody* (7–10). 1988, Walker $24.95 (0-8027-6770-2). A victim of child abuse survives a suicide attempt and is given a second chance by a tough ex-cop. (Rev: BL 2/1/88; BR 9–10/88; SLJ 3/88; VOYA 4/88)

1478 Weiss, M. Jerry, and Helen S. Weiss, eds. *From One Experience to Another: Stories about Turning Points* (6–12). 1997, Tor $18.95 (0-312-86253-9). In 15 original stories, well-known young adult writers tell about incidents that were important turning points in their lives. (Rev: BL 2/1/98; BR 5–6/98; SLJ 11/97; VOYA 12/97)

1479 Wersba, Barbara. *Beautiful Losers* (9–12). 1988, HarperCollins $11.95 (0-06-026363-6). The concluding volume in the trilogy about teenaged Rita Formica and her love for Arnold, who is twice her

age. Also use: *Love Is the Crooked Thing* (1987). (Rev: BL 3/15/88; SLJ 3/88)

1480 Wersba, Barbara. *Whistle Me Home* (9–12). 1997, Holt $14.95 (0-8050-4850-2). The story of 17-year-old Noli, her former boyfriend, TJ, their relationship, and how it ended when she discovered he was gay. (Rev: BL 4/1/97; SLJ 6/97; VOYA 8/97)

1481 Wersba, Barbara. *Wonderful Me* (9–12). 1989, HarperCollins $12.95 (0-06-026361-X). Seventeen-year-old Heidi Rosenbloom spends the summer making money dog walking and coping with the worshipful attention of a mentally unstable English teacher. A sequel to *Just Be Gorgeous* (1988). (Rev: BL 5/1/89; BR 11–12/89; SLJ 4/89; VOYA 6/89)

1482 Whitney, P. L. *This Is Graceanne's Book* (10–12). 1999, St. Martin's $22.95 (0-312-20597-X). Nine-year-old Charlie narrates this story about his older sister, 11-year-old Graceanne, the beatings she gets from her abusive mother, and the black girl next door who becomes her friend. (Rev: BL 5/99; SLJ 9/99)

1483 Wieler, Diana. *Drive* (10–12). 1999, Douglas & McIntyre $15.95 (0-88899-347-1). Jens Friesen and his younger brother Daniel, both talented musicians, set out on a road trip in Canada, playing gigs in small towns to raise much-needed money, in this mature novel for older teens. (Rev: BL 5/1/99; SLJ 4/99; VOYA 8/99)

1484 Wieler, Diana. *Ran Van: The Defender* (7–12). 1997, Douglas & McIntyre $16.95 (0-88899-270-X). Orphaned Rhan Van, who lives with his grandmother in a city apartment, begins hanging out in bad company and soon finds he is vandalizing school and private property. (Rev: BL 2/1/98; SLJ 3/98)

1485 Williams, Carol L. *If I Forget, You Remember* (5–8). 1998, Delacorte $15.95 (0-385-32534-7). Self-centered seventh-grader Elyse gradually puts her life in perspective when her grandmother, who has Alzheimer's disease, moves in. (Rev: BL 4/15/98; BR 9–10/98; SLJ 3/98; VOYA 10/98)

1486 Williams, Carol L. *The True Colors of Caitlynne Jackson* (6–10). 1997, Delacorte $14.95 (0-385-32249-6). Left on her own by an unstable mother, Caitlynne learns to be strong and resourceful while caring for her younger half-sister. (Rev: BL 3/1/97; BR 5–6/97; SLJ 2/97*)

1487 Williams-Garcia, Rita. *Like Sisters on the Homefront* (8–10). 1995, Lodestar paper $15.99 (0-525-67465-9). After 14-year-old Gayle Ann has an abortion to end her second pregnancy, her mother sends her down South to be rehabilitated by her God-fearing brother, a minister, whose family leads a very structured life and where Gayle Ann must follow rules and help care for her aged but strong-minded grandmother. (Rev: BL 9/1/95*; BR 1–2/96; SLJ 10/95; VOYA 4/96)

1488 Wilson, Budge. *Sharla* (7–10). 1998, Stoddart paper $4.95 (0-7736-7467-5). A run-in with a polar bear, adjusting to a new school, trying to make friends, and getting used to severe weather are some of the problems 15-year-old Sharla faces when she moves with her family from Ottawa to Churchill, a small community in northern Manitoba. (Rev: SLJ 8/98)

1489 Wimsley, Jim. *Dream Boy* (10–12). 1995, Algonquin $29.95 (1-56512-106-6). Nathan—bookish and slight and sexually abused by his father—moves to a farm, where he meets and falls in love with Roy, the outgoing, popular boy next door. (Rev: BL 9/15/95; SLJ 3/96; VOYA 2/96)

1490 Winton, Tim. *Lockie Leonard, Human Torpedo* (6–8). 1992, Little, Brown $13.95 (0-316-94753-9). Set in Australia, the story of a 14-year-old surfer and his confusion as he begins a more intimate relationship with his girlfriend. (Rev: BL 12/15/91; SLJ 12/91)

1491 Withrow, Sarah. *Bat Summer* (5–8). 1999, Groundwood $15.95 (0-88899-351-X). In this story that reveals the complexities underlying young people's seemingly simple lives, Terence makes new friends while his only friend is away at summer camp, and his friendship with one of them, Lucy, who identifies closely with bats, is strained when she runs away and he is torn between whether to hide her or get her back home. (Rev: BL 7/99; SLJ 9/99; VOYA 8/99)

1492 Wittlinger, Ellen. *Hard Love* (8–12). 1999, Simon & Schuster paper $17.00 (0-689-82134-4). Two outsiders, John, a high school junior and fan of "zines," and Marison, a self-proclaimed virgin lesbian, form an unusual relationship in this well-crafted novel that explores many teenage problems. (Rev: BL 10/1/99; SLJ 7/99; VOYA 8/99)

1493 Wojciechowska, Maia. *Shadow of a Bull* (6–8). 1973, Macmillan $16.00 (0-689-30042-5). Manolo, the son of a famous bullfighter, discovers there are many kinds of courage. Newbery Medal, 1965.

1494 Wolff, Virginia E. *The Mozart Season* (9–12). 1991, Holt $15.95 (0-8050-1571-X). Violinist and softball player Allegra Shapiro learns about life through sports analogies when she becomes a finalist in a large youth music contest. (Rev: BL 6/1/91; SLJ 7/91)

1495 Wood, June R. *Turtle on a Fence Post* (5–8). 1997, Putnam $16.95 (0-399-23184-6). After the deaths of her parents and an uncle, Delrita, now living with an aunt and her husband, is so emotionally upset that it seems she will never love anyone again. A sequel to *The Man Who Loved Clowns*. (Rev: BL 11/15/97; SLJ 9/97)

1496 Woodson, Jacqueline. *The House You Pass on the Way* (6–9). Illus. 1997, Delacorte $14.95 (0-385-32189-9). A young girl from an interracial marriage feels left out and becomes a loner until she falls in love with a girl cousin who comes to visit. (Rev: BL 8/97; BR 3–4/98; SLJ 10/97; VOYA 10/97)

1497 Wright, Betty R. *The Summer of Mrs. MacGregor* (6–8). 1986, Holiday House $15.95 (0-8234-0628-8). Meeting an exotic teenager who calls herself Mrs. Lillina MacGregor helps Linda solve her problem of jealousy toward her older sister. (Rev: BL 11/1/86; SLJ 11/86; VOYA 4/87)

1498 Yang, Margaret. *Locked Out* (6–9). 1996, Tudor $17.95 (0-936389-40-0). Gina is outraged and goaded into activism when she learns that the principal of her school, in an effort to curb smoking, has closed all the bathrooms except those close to his office. (Rev: SLJ 5/96)

1499 Young, Ronder T. *Moving Mama to Town* (5–8). 1997, Orchard LB $18.99 (0-531-33025-7). Although his father is a gambler and a failure, Fred never loses faith in him in this story of a boy who must help support his family although he's only 13. (Rev: BL 6/1–15/97; BR 9–10/97; SLJ 6/97)

1500 Zach, Cheryl. *Dear Diary: Runaway* (7–12). 1995, Berkley paper $4.50 (0-425-15047-X). In diary form, young, pregnant Cassie tells how she and her lover, Seth, become runaways seeking a place that will give them shelter and security. (Rev: BL 1/1–15/96)

1501 Zalben, Jane Breskin. *Unfinished Dreams* (6–9). 1996, Simon & Schuster paper $16.00 (0-689-80033-9). Jason, a sixth grader and aspiring violinist, discovers that his beloved school principal has AIDS. (Rev: BL 6/1–15/96; BR 1–2/97; SLJ 6/96; VOYA 8/96)

1502 Zalben, Jane Breskin. *Water from the Moon* (8–10). 1987, Farrar $15.00 (0-374-38238-7). Nicky Berstein, a high school sophomore, tries too hard to make friends and is hurt in the process. (Rev: BL 5/15/87; SLJ 5/87; VOYA 8/87)

1503 Zindel, Bonnie, and Paul Zindel. *A Star for the Latecomer* (7–10). 1980, HarperCollins $12.95 (0-06-026847-6). When her mother dies, Brooke is freed of the need to pursue a dancing career.

1504 Zindel, Paul. *The Amazing and Death-Defying Diary of Eugene Dingman* (9–12). 1987, HarperCollins LB $14.89 (0-06-026863-8); Bantam paper $4.50 (0-553-27768-5). An unhappy teenager is sent to a resort hotel to work as a busboy. (Rev: BL 10/15/87; BR 3–4/88; SLJ 10/87; VOYA 10/87)

1505 Zindel, Paul. *A Begonia for Miss Applebaum* (7–12). 1990, Bantam paper $4.99 (0-553-28765-6). Two unconventional teens take under their wings a favorite teacher who is dying of cancer. (Rev: BL 3/15/89; BR 11–12/89; SLJ 4/89)

1506 Zindel, Paul. *Confessions of a Teenage Baboon* (7–9). 1984, Bantam paper $4.50 (0-553-27190-3). Chris has difficulty adjusting to his mother's employer, a somewhat bitter loner.

1507 Zindel, Paul. *David and Della* (7–12). 1995, Bantam paper $4.50 (0-553-56727-6). High school playwright David hires Della—who pretends to be blind and to have studied under Lee Strasberg—to be his coach until he overcomes writer's block. (Rev: BL 12/1/93; SLJ 12/93; VOYA 2/94)

1508 Zindel, Paul. *I Never Loved Your Mind* (8–12). 1970, Bantam paper $4.50 (0-553-27323-X). Two dropouts working in a hospital together suffer the pangs of love and loss.

1509 Zindel, Paul. *My Darling, My Hamburger* (8–12). 1969, Bantam paper $4.50 (0-553-27324-8). Two young couples each in love face life's complications including one girl's abortion.

1510 Zindel, Paul. *Pardon Me, You're Stepping on My Eyeball* (10–12). 1983, Bantam paper $4.50 (0-553-26690-X). Marsh Mallow and Edna Shinglebox form a friendship to help solve problems caused by the adults around them. Also use: *Harry and Hortense at Hormone High* (1984).

1511 Zindel, Paul. *The Pigman* (10–12). 1984, Bantam paper $5.50 (0-553-26599-7). Two teenagers must face the responsibility of causing the death of an old man they befriend. A sequel is *The Pigman's Legacy* (1984). (Rev: BL 10/15/88)

1512 Zolotow, Charlotte, ed. *Early Sorrow: Ten Stories of Youth* (8–12). 1986, HarperCollins $12.95 (0-06-026936-7). This excellent collection of 12 adult stories about growing up is a companion piece to *An Overpraised Season* (o.p.), another anthology about adolescence. (Rev: BL 10/1/86; BR 3–4/87; SLJ 1/87; VOYA 2/87)

World Affairs and Contemporary Problems

1513 Abelove, Joan. *Go and Come Back* (8–10). 1998, DK Publg. $16.95 (0-7894-2476-2). The story of 2 female anthropologists studying a primitive Peruvian Indian village, written from the perspective of Alicia, one of the village teenagers. (Rev: BL 3/1/98; BR 1–2/99; SLJ 3/98*; VOYA 10/98)

1514 Anderson, Mary. *The Unsinkable Molly Malone* (7–10). 1991, Harcourt $16.95 (0-15-213801-3). Molly, 16, sells her collages outside New York's Metropolitan Museum, starts an art class for kids on welfare, and learns that her boyfriend is rich. (Rev: BL 11/15/91; SLJ 12/91)

1515 Castaneda, Omar S. *Among the Volcanoes* (7–10). 1996, Bantam paper $4.50 (0-440-91118-4). Set in a remote Guatemalan village, this story is about a Mayan woodcutter's daughter, Isabel, who is caught between her respect for the old ways and her yearning for something more. (Rev: BL 5/15/91; SLJ 3/91)

1516 Covington, Dennis. *Lasso the Moon* (7–10). 1996, Bantam $20.00 (0-385-30991-0). After April and her divorced doctor father move to Saint Simons Island, April takes a liking to Fernando, an illegal alien from El Salvador being treated by her father. (Rev: BL 1/15/95; SLJ 3/95; VOYA 4/95)

1517 Davis, Jenny. *Checking on the Moon* (6–9). 1991, Orchard $17.99 (0-531-08560-0). A 13-year-old, forced to spend the summer in a run-down Pittsburgh neighborhood with a grandmother she has never met, discovers community activism and her own abilities. (Rev: BL 9/15/91; SLJ 10/91*)

1518 Doyle, Brian. *Easy Avenue* (6–9). 1998, Douglas & McIntyre $14.95 (0-88899-338-2). The luck of Hulbert, who is used to a life of poverty and deprivation, mysteriously changes, and his homelife and relationships begin to erode and he finds that he is becoming a snob. (Rev: BL 12/1/98; SLJ 11/98; VOYA 6/99)

1519 Fox, Paula. *Lily and the Lost Boy* (6–9). 1987, Watts LB $16.99 (0-531-08320-9). Using the tiny island of Thasos in Greece as a setting the author tells a story of the maturation of a 12-year-old American girl and her older brother. (Rev: BL 7/87; BR 1–2/88; VOYA 2/88)

1520 Gillison, Samantha. *The Undiscovered Country* (10–12). 1998, Grove Atlantic $23.00 (0-8021-1627-2). An American couple and their daughter journey into the rain forests of New Guinea to do medical research and find that their lives, values, and relationships change. (Rev: BL 6/1–15/98; SLJ 3/99)

1521 Golio, Janet, and Mike Golio. *A Present from the Past* (6–8). 1995, Portunus paper $8.95 (0-9641330-9). In this blend of fact and fiction, Sarah and her friend become concerned about their environment after they discover some petroglyphs. (Rev: BL 1/1–15/96)

1522 Gordimer, Nadine. *My Son's Story* (10–12). 1990, Farrar $19.95 (0-374-21751-3). The story of the love between a dedicated black teacher and Hannah, a white activist, set in South Africa. (Rev: BL 9/15/90)

1523 Gordimer, Nadine. *Selected Stories* (10–12). 1983, Penguin paper $14.95 (0-14-006737-X). The men of the stories in this collection reflect the racial situation in South Africa.

1524 Hall, Lynn. *If Winter Comes* (7–10). 1986, Macmillan $16.00 (0-684-18575-X). Two teenagers spend what they believe to be their last weekend on earth because of the imminent threat of a nuclear war. (Rev: BL 6/1/86; SLJ 9/86; VOYA 8/86)

1525 Hentoff, Nat. *The Day They Came to Arrest the Book* (7–10). 1983, Dell paper $4.99 (0-440-91814-6). Some students at Geoge Mason High think Huckleberry Finn is a racist book.

1526 Hesse, Karen. *Phoenix Rising* (6–8). 1994, Holt $15.95 (0-8050-3108-1). A 13-year-old and her grandmother on a Vermont farm hope to avoid radiation contamination from a nuclear plant. They are visited by Boston evacuees, one of them a boy with whom the girl falls in love. (Rev: BL 5/15/94; SLJ 6/94*; VOYA 8/94)

1527 Ho, Minfong. *Rice without Rain* (7–12). 1990, Lothrop $16.00 (0-688-06355-1). Jinda, a 17-year-old girl, experiences personal tragedy and the awakening of love in this novel set during revolutionary times in Thailand during the 1970s. (Rev: BL 7/90; SLJ 9/90)

1528 Hobbet, Anastasia. *Pleasure of Believing* (10–12). 1997, Soho Pr. $24.00 (1-56947-085-5). When Muirie retreats to her aunt and uncle's ranch in Wyoming, she finds that her aunt is in conflict with her neighbors because she has converted the ranch into a bird hospital. (Rev: BL 2/15/97; SLJ 7/97)

1529 Hoffman, Nancy, and Florence Howe, eds. *Women Working: An Anthology of Stories and Poems* (10–12). Illus. 1979, Feminist Pr. paper $13.95 (0-912670-57-6). This collection of stories and poems explores the world of work as experienced by women.

1530 Howe, Norma. *The Adventures of Blue Avenger* (8–10). 1999, Holt $16.95 (0-8050-6062-6). When David Schumaker decides on his 16th birthday to change his name to Blue Avenger, he suddenly finds that he his accomplishing tasks that only a superhero could. (Rev: BL 3/15/99; SLJ 4/99; VOYA 6/99)

1531 Jicai, Feng. *Let One Hundred Flowers Bloom* (7–10). Trans. by Christopher Smith. 1996, Viking paper $13.99 (0-670-85805-6). A bleak story about a talented artisan in contemporary China whose life is destroyed when he is accused of counterrevolutionary behavior. (Rev: BL 4/15/96; SLJ 6/96)

1532 Kemal, Yasher. *Memed, My Hawk* (10–12). 1993, HarperCollins paper $12.00 (0-00-217112-0). This tragic story, set in southern Turkey, takes place in an area where feudal conditions still exist.

1533 Koestler, Arthur. *Darkness at Noon* (10–12). Trans. by Daphne Hardy. 1984, Bantam paper $6.99 (0-553-26595-4). In this 1940 novel, life in a Soviet political prison is depicted as seen through the experiences of one inmate.

1534 Levitin, Sonia. *The Return* (6–10). 1987, Macmillan $16.00 (0-689-31309-8); Fawcett paper $4.50 (0-449-70280-4). Seen from the viewpoint of a teenage girl, this is the story of a group of African Jews who journey from Ethiopia to the Sudan to escape persecution. (Rev: BL 4/15/87; BR 11–12/87; SLJ 5/87; VOYA 6/87)

1535 McDaniel, Lurlene. *Baby Alicia Is Dying* (8–10). 1993, Bantam paper $4.99 (0-553-29605-1). In an attempt to feel needed, Desi volunteers to care for HIV-positive babies and discovers a deep commitment in herself. (Rev: BL 10/1/93; SLJ 7/93; VOYA 8/93)

1536 Mazer, Norma Fox, and Harry Mazer. *Bright Days, Stupid Nights* (7–10). 1993, Bantam paper $3.50 (0-553-56253-3). Charts the course of 4 youths who are brought together for a summer newspaper internship. (Rev: BL 6/15/92; SLJ 7/92)

1537 Mead, Alice. *Adem's Cross* (7–10). 1996, Farrar $15.00 (0-374-30057-7). A novel about Adem and his Albanian family living in Kosovo under Serbian oppression. (Rev: BL 11/15/96; BR 3–4/97; SLJ 11/96; VOYA 12/96)

1538 Michener, James A. *Legacy* (10–12). 1987, Fawcett paper $6.99 (0-449-21641-1). A contemporary novel about an army officer involved with the Contras in Nicaragua. (Rev: BL 8/87)

1539 Miles, Betty. *Maudie and Me and the Dirty Book* (5–8). 1980, Knopf paper $3.99 (0-394-82595-0). Kate causes a community furor when she presents a picture book to first-graders about a dog having pups.

1540 Myers, Bill. *The Society* (7–9). (Forbidden Doors) 1994, Tyndale paper $5.99 (0-8423-5922-2). Scott and Becka have left Brazil and begun the year at their new U.S. school when they discover that a local bookshop is the hub of a Ouija board cult. (Rev: BL 1/15/95)

1541 Neufeld, John. *A Small Civil War* (7–10). 1996, Simon & Schuster $16.00 (0-689-80770-8). A revised edition of the 1981 novel about 13-year-old Georgia and her fight against censorship when *The Grapes of Wrath* is challenged in her high school. (Rev: BL 10/15/96; BR 5–6/97; SLJ 11/96; VOYA 2/97)

1542 Neville, Emily C. *The China Year* (5–8). 1991, HarperCollins $15.95 (0-06-024383-X). Henri, 14, has left his New York City home, school, and friends to go to Peking University for a year with his father. (Rev: BL 5/1/91; SLJ 5/91)

1543 O'Connor, Edwin. *The Last Hurrah* (10–12). 1956, Little, Brown paper $14.00 (0-316-62659-7). An old-style politician who has been mayor of a large American city for about 40 years finds that his power is being challenged.

1544 Paton, Alan. *Cry, the Beloved Country* (10–12). 1948, Macmillan $35.00 (0-684-15559-1). A black minister tries to save his son, accused of murder, in this touching novel set in South Africa.

1545 Paulsen, Gary. *The Rifle* (7–9). 1995, Harcourt $16.00 (0-15-292880-4). An exploration of the history of a flintlock rifle, from its use in the Revolutionary War into the 20th century, where it ends up killing a teen in a freak accident. (Rev: BL 9/15/95; SLJ 10/95; VOYA 2/96)

1546 Paulsen, Gary. *Sentries* (8–12). 1986, Bradbury LB $17.00 (0-02-770100-X); Penguin paper $3.95 (0-317-62279-X). The stories of 4 different young people are told. However, before their stories can be resolved, they are all wiped out by a super-bomb. (Rev: BL 5/1/86; SLJ 8/86; VOYA 8/86)

1547 Peck, Richard. *The Last Safe Place on Earth* (7–10). 1996, Bantam paper $4.50 (0-440-22007-6). Todd has a crush on Laura, who baby-sits for his sister, but he discovers that she's a fundamentalist Christian who brainwashes and terrifies the child by telling her about witches and devils. (Rev: BL 1/15/95; SLJ 4/95; VOYA 2/95)

1548 Qualey, Marsha. *Hometown* (7–10). 1995, Houghton $14.95 (0-395-72666-2). A new resident in a small Minnesota town takes flak when the Persian Gulf War breaks out and he learns that his father escaped to Canada during the Vietnam War. (Rev: BL 10/1/95; SLJ 12/95; VOYA 12/95)

1549 Rand, Ayn. *Atlas Shrugged* (10–12). 1957, Random $35.00 (0-394-41576-0); NAL paper $6.95 (0-451-15748-6). In an age where everyone looks to the state for guidance and protection, one man wants to go it alone.

1550 Rand, Ayn. *The Fountainhead* (10–12). 1943, Macmillan $45.00 (0-02-600910-2); NAL paper $5.99 (0-451-15823-7). The story of the careers of 2 very different men in the world of New York architecture.

1551 Rochman, Hazel, ed. *Somehow Tenderness Survives: Stories of Southern Africa* (8–12). 1988, HarperCollins $12.95 (0-06-025022-4); paper $4.95 (0-06-447063-6). Ten stories by such writers as Nadine Gordimer about growing up in South Africa. (Rev: BL 8/88; BR 5–6/89; SLJ 12/88; VOYA 12/88)

1552 Ruby, Lois. *Skin Deep* (8–12). 1994, Scholastic $14.95 (0-590-47699-8). Dan, the frustrated new kid in town, falls in love with popular senior Laurel, but he destroys their relationship when he joins a neo-Nazi skinhead group. (Rev: BL 11/15/94*; SLJ 3/95; VOYA 12/94)

1553 Scott, Paul. *Staying On* (10–12). 1979, Avon paper $3.50 (0-380-46045-9). Mr. and Mrs. Smalley decide to stay on in India after the country gains independence.

1554 Solzhenitsyn, Alexander. *One Day in the Life of Ivan Denisovich* (10–12). 1984, Bantam paper $4.99 (0-553-24777-8). A harrowing short novel about life in a Stalinist labor camp in Siberia.

1555 Staples, Suzanne F. *Shabanu: Daughter of the Wind* (7–10). 1989, Knopf LB $18.99 (0-394-94815-7). The story of a young girl coming-of-age in a family living in a desert region of Pakistan. (Rev: BL 10/1/89; SLJ 11/89; VOYA 4/90)

1556 Steinbeck, John. *Tortilla Flat* (10–12). 1962, Penguin paper $6.95 (0-14-004240-7). The life of some poor but carefree friends in Monterey, California, during the 1930s.

1557 Styron, William. *Sophie's Choice* (10–12). 1979, Random $29.95 (0-394-46109-6). In a Jewish boarding house in Brooklyn, Sophie, a survivor of Auschwitz, meets 2 men who will change her life.

1558 Taylor, Theodore. *The Bomb* (7–10). 1995, Harcourt $15.00 (0-15-200867-5). In this tale—based on Taylor's memory of a visit to Bikini Atoll as it was being prepared for testing of the atomic bomb—a 14-year-old boy suspects that the Americans are less than honest about their plans. Scott O'Dell Historical Fiction Award, 1996. (Rev: BL 10/1/95*; SLJ 12/95; VOYA 4/96)

1559 Temple, Frances. *Grab Hands and Run* (6–12). 1993, Orchard LB $16.99 (0-531-08630-5). Jacinto opposes the oppressive government of El Salvador. When he disappears, his wife, Paloma, and their son, 12-year-old Felipe, try to escape to freedom in Canada. (Rev: BL 5/1/93*; SLJ 4/93*)

1560 Trice, Dawn Turner. *Only Twice I've Wished for Heaven* (10–12). 1996, Crown $23.00 (0-517-70428-5). Prejudice, child abuse, friendship, pride, and poverty are some of the themes in this powerful novel about a wealthy African American community pitted against the poor, slum-infested community next door. (Rev: BL 11/15/96; SLJ 6/97)

1561 Yolen, Jane. *Children of the Wolf* (6–8). 1993, Puffin paper $4.99 (0-14-036477-3). Based on fact, this is the story of a Christian minister in India who finds 2 children who have been reared in the wild.

Fantasy

1562 Aamodt, Donald. *A Name to Conjure With* (9–12). 1989, Avon paper $3.50 (0-380-75137-2). A reluctant participant embarks on a quest with a bumbling sorcerer. (Rev: BL 8/89; VOYA 10/89)

1563 Abbey, Lynn. *Unicorn & Dragon* (10–12). Illus. 1988, Avon paper $3.50 (0-380-75567-X). A fantasy set in eleventh-century England that pits Druid magic against Norman sorcery. (Rev: SLJ 6/87)

1564 Adams, Richard. *The Plague Dogs* (10–12). 1986, Fawcett paper $5.95 (0-449-21182-7). For better readers, this is a novel about 2 dogs that flee from a research center.

1565 Adams, Richard. *Tales from Watership Down* (9–12). 1996, Knopf $23.00 (0-679-45125-0). Familiar animal characters from the author's *Watership Down* reappear in these delightful stories for animal fantasy fans. (Rev: BR 5–6/97; SLJ 1/97)

1566 Adams, Richard. *Watership Down* (7–12). 1974, Macmillan $40.00 (0-02-700030-3); Avon paper $6.99 (0-380-00293-0). In this fantasy a group of male rabbits set out to find a new home.

1567 Alcock, Vivien. *The Red-Eared Ghosts* (5–8). 1997, Houghton $15.95 (0-395-81660-2). Mary Frewin travels through time to solve a mystery involving her great-great-grandmother. (Rev: BL 3/1/97; BR 11–12/97; SLJ 4/97; VOYA 10/97)

1568 Alexander, Lloyd. *The Arkadians* (6–9). 1995, Dutton paper $16.99 (0-525-45415-2). A focus on the goddess culture and its role in history and myth. Lucian and Fronto are forced to flee a castle and hunt for the goddess who can help them. (Rev: BL 5/1/95; SLJ 5/95; VOYA 12/95)

1569 Alexander, Lloyd. *The First Two Lives of Lukas-Kasha* (6–9). 1998, Puffin paper $4.99 (0-14-130057-4). Lukas-Kasha, because of a showman's tricks, finds himself king of the land of Abadan.

1570 Alexander, Lloyd. *The Foundling and Other Tales of Prydain* (6–8). 1999, Holt $17.95 (0-8050-6130-4). Six stories of Alexander's enchanted land of Prydain.

1571 Alexander, Lloyd. *The Iron Ring* (6–9). 1997, NAL paper $16.99 (0-525-45597-3). When he loses in a dice game, Tamar must fulfill a promise to journey to the kingdom of King Jaya in this fantasy based on Indian mythology. (Rev: BL 5/15/97; BR 11–12/97; SLJ 5/97*; VOYA 10/97)

1572 Alexander, Lloyd. *The Remarkable Journey of Prince Jen* (6–9). 1991, 1993, Dell paper $4.99 (0-440-40890-3). Prince Jen searches for the legendary court of T'ien-kuo, finds a flute girl, faces death at the hands of a bandit, and learns how to be a man and a ruler. (Rev: BL 12/1/91*; SLJ 12/91*)

1573 Alexander, Lloyd. *The Wizard in the Tree* (5–8). Illus. 1988, Demco $10.34 (0-606-13070-5). Mallory finds a wizard in a tree and must help him when he is accused of murder.

1574 Almond, David. *Skellig* (5–8). 1999, Delacorte $15.95 (0-385-32653-X). Michael discovers a ragged man in his garage existing on dead flies in this book that becomes part fantasy, part mystery, and part family story. (Rev: BL 2/1/99; SLJ 2/99)

1575 Anthony, Mark. *Beyond the Pale* (9–12). 1998, Bantam paper $14.95 (0-553-37955-0). Two strangers find themselves in the land of Eldh, a medieval-like fantasy world, where they each discover their hidden magical powers. (Rev: VOYA 4/99)

1576 Anthony, Piers. *Being a Green Mother* (10–12). 1987, Ballantine paper $5.95 (0-345-32223-1). In this concluding part of the 5-book series Incarnations of Immortality, Orb falls in love with a man who might be Satan. (Rev: BL 10/15/87; VOYA 6/88)

1577 Anthony, Piers. *Demons Don't Dream* (9–12). (Xanth Saga) 1994, Tor paper $5.99 (0-8125-3483-2). An interactive video game transports a 16-year-old boy to the infamous land of Xanth. (Rev: BL 12/15/92; VOYA 8/93)

1578 Anthony, Piers. *Faun & Games* (9–12). 1997, St. Martin's $23.95 (0-312-86162-1). In this Xanth novel, Forrst Faun consults Good Magician Humfrey to find a suitable creature to adopt his neighboring tree. (Rev: BL 9/1/97; VOYA 4/98)

1579 Anthony, Piers. *Geis of the Gargoyle* (9–12). (Xanth Saga) 1995, Tor $22.95 (0-312-85391-2). An environmentally conscious gargoyle searches for a spell to purify a polluted river. (Rev: BL 1/1/95)

1580 Anthony, Piers. *Golem in the Gears* (10–12). 1986, Ballantine paper $6.99 (0-345-31886-2). In this ninth Xanth novel, Grundy the Golem sets out to find the lost dragon of Princess Ivy. (Rev: BL 2/15/86; SLJ 5/86; VOYA 6/86)

1581 Anthony, Piers. *Roc and a Hard Place* (9–12). (Xanth Saga) 1995, Tor $23.95 (0-312-85392-0). Demoness Metria must find a jury to acquit Roxanne Roc of bizarre crimes. (Rev: BL 9/1/95; VOYA 4/96)

1582 Anthony, Piers. *A Spell for Chameleon* (10–12). 1987, Ballantine paper $6.99 (0-345-34753-6). This is the introductory Xanth novel where the reader first meets the young hero Bink and his quest to find magical powers. Two others in this extensive series are: *Castle Roogna* and *The Source of Magic* (both 1987).

1583 Anthony, Piers. *Wielding a Red Sword* (10–12). 1987, Ballantine paper $6.99 (0-345-32221-5). In the fourth book of the Incarnations of Immortality series, Mym is forced to do Satan's work and finds it impossible to stop. For better readers. (Rev: BL 9/1/86)

1584 Anthony, Piers. *With a Tangled Skein* (10–12). 1985, Ballantine paper $6.99 (0-345-31885-4). In this volume in the Incarnations of Immortality series, Niobe sets out to avenge her lover's death. An earlier volume was *On a Pale Horse* (1986).

1585 Anthony, Piers. *Zombie Lover* (9–12). 1998, Tor $23.95 (0-312-86690-9). In this Xanth novel, 15-year-old Breanna doesn't want to marry the Zombie Xeth and sets out with friends to find another bride for him, learning valuable lessons about prejudice, love, and growing up along the way. (Rev: BL 9/15/98; VOYA 4/99)

1586 Anthony, Piers, and Mercedes Lackey. *If I Pay Thee Not in Gold* (9–12). 1993, Simon & Schuster $20.00 (0-671-72175-5). Xylina must retrieve a powerful shard of crystal from a distant, dangerous land. (Rev: BL 4/15/93; VOYA 12/93)

1587 Ashley, Mike, ed. *The Chronicles of the Holy Grail* (10–12). 1996, Carroll & Graf paper $12.95 (0-7867-0363-6). A collection of 12 stories that deal with the quest for the Holy Grail. (Rev: VOYA 4/97)

1588 Ashley, Mike, ed. *The Merlin Chronicles* (10–12). 1995, Carroll & Graf paper $12.95 (0-7867-0275-3). A collection of Arthurian stories by fantasy authors like Jane Yolan, Marion Zimmer Bradley, and Tanith Lee. (Rev: VOYA 6/96)

1589 Asprin, Robert. *Myth Conception* (10–12). 1986, Ace paper $5.99 (0-441-55521-7). An apprentice magician and his friends are pitted against an army of invaders.

1590 Avi. *Bright Shadow* (5–8). 1994, Simon & Schuster paper $4.50 (0-689-71783-0). At the death of the great wizard, Morenna finds she possesses the last 5 wishes in the world. (Rev: SLJ 12/85)

1591 Avi. *City of Light, City of Dark: A Comic-Book Novel* (6–9). Illus. 1995, Orchard paper $7.95 (0-531-07058-1). In black-and-white comic book format, Sarah and her friend Carlos must save her father from the evil Underton and pay tribute to the Kurbs before Manhattan freezes. (Rev: BL 9/15/93; VOYA 2/94)

1592 Avi. *The Man Who Was Poe* (7–10). 1991, Avon paper $4.99 (0-380-71192-3). When Edmund goes out to search for his missing mother and sister, he encounters Edgar Allan Poe in disguise as his detective Auguste Dupin. (Rev: BL 10/1/89; BR 5–6/90; SLJ 9/89; VOYA 2/90)

1593 Bach, Richard. *Jonathan Livingston Seagull* (10–12). 1970, Macmillan $20.00 (0-02-504540-7); Avon paper $5.99 (0-380-01286-3). Because of his unusual love of flying, Jonathan is treated as an outsider.

1594 Ball, Margaret. *No Earthly Sunne* (9–12). 1994, Baen paper $5.99 (0-671-87633-3). A new version of the classic fantasy concerning the rescue of a mortal from the land of faerie. (Rev: BL 12/15/94; VOYA 5/95)

1595 Ball, Margaret. *The Shadow Gate* (9–12). 1991, Baen paper $5.99 (0-671-72032-5). A young secretary is drawn into a magical world where she is hailed as a long-exiled queen. (Rev: BL 1/1/91; SLJ 9/91)

1596 Banks, Lynne Reid. *Angela and Diabola* (5–8). 1997, Avon paper $14.00 (0-380-97562-9). A wicked

romp that chronicles the lives of twins, the angelic Angela and the truly horrible and destructive Diabola. (Rev: BR 9–10/97; SLJ 7/97)

1597 Banks, Lynne Reid. *The Key to the Indian* (4–8). 1998, Avon paper $16.00 (0-380-97717-6). In this fifth installment of the Indian in the Cupboard series, Omri and Dad use the magical cupboard to help Little Bear deal with problems caused by a European settlement. Others in this series are also recommended. (Rev: BL 11/15/98; SLJ 12/98)

1598 Banks, Lynne Reid. *Melusine* (8–12). 1997, Avon paper $4.50 (0-380-79135-8). While staying with his family in an old French chateau, Roger discovers Melusine, a supernatural creature that is half woman and half snake. (Rev: BL 10/1/89; SLJ 11/89; VOYA 2/90)

1599 Banks, Lynne Reid. *The Mystery of the Cupboard* (5–8). Illus. 1993, Morrow LB $15.93 (0-688-12635-9). The fourth book in the "cupboard" series deals with a diary describing a magic cupboard and a box containing plastic Indian figures that come to life and explain the cupboard's secrets. (Rev: BL 4/1/93; SLJ 6/93; VOYA 10/93)

1600 Barron, T. A. *The Ancient One* (6–9). 1992, Putnam $18.99 (0-399-21899-8); 1994, Tor paper $5.99 (0-8125-3654-1). A fight to save a stand of Oregon redwoods occupies Kate, 13, in this time-travel fantasy. (Rev: BL 9/1/92; SLJ 11/92)

1601 Barron, T. A. *The Fires of Merlin* (7–10). Illus. (Lost Years of Merlin) 1998, Putnam $19.99 (0-399-23020-3). A complex sequel to *The Seven Songs of Merlin*, in which young Merlin once again faces the threat of the dragon Valdearg, who is preparing to conquer the land of Fincayra. (Rev: BL 9/1/98; BR 5–6/99; SLJ 3/99; VOYA 2/99)

1602 Barron, T. A. *The Lost Years of Merlin* (7–10). 1996, Putnam paper $19.99 (0-399-23018-1). The author has created a magical land populated by remarkable creatures in this first book of a trilogy about the early years of the magician, Merlin. (Rev: BL 9/1/96; BR 3–4/97; SLJ 9/96; VOYA 10/96)

1603 Barron, T. A. *The Merlin Effect* (6–9). 1994, Putnam $17.95 (0-399-22689-3). Kate, 13, accompanies her father, a King Arthur expert, to a remote lagoon where they search a sunken ship for the magical horn of Merlin. Sequel to *Heartlight* (1990) and *The Ancient One* (1992). (Rev: BL 11/1/94; SLJ 11/94; VOYA 12/94)

1604 Barron, T. A. *The Seven Songs of Merlin* (7–10). 1997, Putnam $19.95 (0-399-23019-X). In this sequel to *The Lost Years of Merlin*, Emrys, who will become Merlin, must travel to the Otherworld to save his mother who has been poisoned. (Rev: BL 9/1/97; SLJ 9/97)

1605 Base, Graeme. *The Discovery of Dragons* (5–8). Illus. 1996, Abrams $16.95 (0-8109-3237-7). A humorous account of the 3 pioneers in dragon research. (Rev: BL 11/15/96; SLJ 11/96)

1606 Beagle, Peter S. *A Fine and Private Place* (10–12). 1992, NAL paper $14.95 (0-451-45096-5). An unusual fantasy about an old man, a graveyard, and the ghosts he befriends there.

1607 Beagle, Peter S. *The Folk of the Air* (10–12). 1988, Ballantine paper $4.50 (0-345-34699-8). For better readers, a story of how role-playing at being medieval characters leads to unleashing a power involving black magic. (Rev: BL 11/1/86)

1608 Beagle, Peter S. *Giant Bones* (10–12). 1997, Roc paper $14.95 (0-451-45651-3). A fine collection of 6 novellas, including one in which a magician is forced by a wicked queen to teach her his secrets so she can take over the world. (Rev: BL 7/97; VOYA 10/97)

1609 Beagle, Peter S. *The Last Unicorn* (9–12). 1991, NAL paper $13.95 (0-451-45052-3). A beautiful unicorn sets off to find others of her species.

1610 Bear, Greg. *Dinosaur Summer* (8–12). 1998, Warner $23.00 (0-446-52098-5). Photographer Anthony Belzoni and his teenage son Peter join an expedition to return a group of circus dinosaurs back to their natural habitat, atop an isolated mesa in South America. (Rev: VOYA 8/98)

1611 Bedard, Michael. *A Darker Magic* (6–8). 1987, Avon paper $2.95 (0-380-70611-3). An intricate fantasy about the strange effects of a magic show run by Professor Mephisto. (Rev: BL 9/1/87; SLJ 9/87)

1612 Belden, Wilanne Schneider. *Mind-Hold* (6–9). 1987, Harcourt $14.95 (0-15-254280-9). After a violent earthquake, Carson and his sister, who has the gift of ESP, move into the desert hoping to find new friends. (Rev: BL 2/15/87; SLJ 3/87)

1613 Bell, Clare E. *Ratha's Challenge* (6–12). 1994, Macmillan paper $16.95 (0-689-50586-8). When a tribe of prehistoric cats faces challenges to survival, their leader, Ratha, hopes to domesticate the tusked face-tails to ensure a steady food supply. (Rev: BL 1/1/95; SLJ 1/95; VOYA 5/95)

1614 Bemmann, Hans. *The Stone and the Flute* (10–12). Trans. by Anthea Bell. 1987, Penguin paper $14.95 (0-14-007445-7). A lengthy book about young Listener and his quest for self-fulfillment. (Rev: BL 3/1/87)

1615 Benet, Stephen Vincent. *The Devil and Daniel Webster* (10–12). 1990, Creative Ed. LB $13.95 (0-88682-295-5). This classic short novel is a variation on the Faust legend, this time set in New Hampshire.

1616 Bennett, Cherie. *Love Never Dies* (7–10). (Teen Angels) 1996, Avon paper $3.99 (0-380-78248-0). In this fantasy, a teen angel is sent back to earth to help a rock star bent on self-destruction. (Rev: VOYA 6/96)

1617 Benson, Ann. *The Plague Tales* (10–12). 1997, Delacorte $23.95 (0-385-31651-8). Two parallel tales are told, one about bubonic plague fighters in 14th-century England and the other concerning a deadly epidemic in 2005. (Rev: BL 4/15/97; SLJ 10/97)

1618 Berry, Liz. *The China Garden* (8–12). 1996, Farrar $18.00 (0-374-31248-6). Mysterious occurrences involving villagers who appear to know Clare and a handsome young man on a motorcycle happen when she accompanies her mother to an estate named Ravensmere. (Rev: BL 3/15/96; BR 9–10/96; SLJ 5/96; VOYA 6/96)

1619 Billingsley, Franny. *The Folk Keeper* (5–8). 1999, Simon & Schuster $16.00 (0-689-82876-4). In this fantasy, Corinna, whose job is to keep the ravenous Folk who live underground at bay, is called to the estate of a dying lord in the Northern Isles to be the Folk Keeper and join his household. (Rev: BL 9/1/99; SLJ 10/99; VOYA 12/99)

1620 Billingsley, Franny. *Well Wished* (5–8). 1997, Simon & Schuster $16.00 (0-689-81210-8). An intriguing fantasy that involves a lonely girl and a wishing well that grants each person a single wish. (Rev: BL 6/1–15/97; SLJ 5/97)

1621 Bisson, Terry. *Talking Man* (10–12). 1987, Avon paper $2.95 (0-380-75141-0). For better readers, this is a fantasy involving godlike creatures and their relations with humans. (Rev: BL 10/1/86)

1622 Block, Francesca L. *I Was a Teenage Fairy* (8–12). 1998, HarperCollins $14.89 (0-06-027748-3). Barbie Marks, at 16 a successful model, sorts herself out with the help of a fairy named Mab, after her father leaves and she is molested by a photographer. (Rev: BL 10/15/98; SLJ 12/98*; VOYA 10/98)

1623 Block, Francesca L. *Missing Angel Juan* (8–12). (Weetzie Bat Saga) 1993, HarperCollins $14.89 (0-06-023007-X). Witch Baby, aided by her grandfather's ghost, roams New York City looking for Angel Juan, who's left her behind to play music on the city streets. (Rev: BL 10/15/93; SLJ 10/93*; VOYA 12/93)

1624 Bond, Nancy. *A String in the Harp* (6–8). 1978, Penguin paper $5.99 (0-14-032376-7). In Wales the Morgan children find a magic harp-tuning key that takes them back in time. (Rev: BL 1/1/90)

1625 Botkin, Gleb. *Lost Tales: Stories for the Tsar's Children* (7–12). Trans. from Russian by Masha Tolstoya Sarandinaki. Illus. 1996, Villard $35.00 (0-679-45142-0). This book contains 3 fantasies about a heroic bear who works to restore a monarch to his throne. They were written by the personal physician to Tsar Nicholas II and illustrated by his son to amuse the royal children held captive during the Russian Revolution. (Rev: SLJ 7/97)

1626 Bradbury, Ray. *A Graveyard for Lunatics* (10–12). 1990, Knopf $24.50 (0-394-57877-5). The real and the imaginary, the past and the present, all mingle in this fantasy set in a Hollywood back lot. (Rev: SLJ 12/90)

1627 Bradbury, Ray. *The Halloween Tree* (7–12). 1972, Knopf $19.95 (0-394-82409-1). Nine boys discover the true meaning—and horror—of the holiday, Halloween.

1628 Bradbury, Ray. *The Illustrated Man* (7–12). 1990, Bantam paper $6.50 (0-553-27449-X). A tattooed man tells a story for each of his tattoos.

1629 Bradbury, Ray. *Something Wicked This Way Comes* (9–12). 1983, Bantam paper $5.50 (0-553-28032-5). This tale tells what happens after "The Pandemonium Shadow Show" plays in a small town.

1630 Bradbury, Ray. *The Toynbee Convector* (10–12). 1988, Knopf $17.95 (0-394-54703-9). A new collection of short stories that cover such areas as fantasy, horror, and science fiction. (Rev: BL 5/1/88; BR 1–2/89)

1631 Bradley, Marion Zimmer. *City of Sorcery* (10–12). 1984, D A W Books paper $6.99 (0-88677-332-6). This novel in the Darkover series traces the quest of Magdalen Loone.

1632 Bradley, Marion Zimmer. *The Firebrand* (10–12). 1991, Pocket Books paper $6.99 (0-671-74406-2). A retelling of this fantasy of events concerned with the Trojan War by the author of *Mists of Avalon.* (Rev: BL 9/15/87)

1633 Bradley, Marion Zimmer. *Ghostlight* (10–12). 1995, Tor $22.95 (0-312-85881-7). In this contemporary fantasy, parapsychologist Truth Jourdemayne researches the life of her father, the leader of an occult group, and visits a 19th-century estate, Shadow's Gate, where she makes discoveries about her family, the death of her mother during an occult ritual nearly 30 years ago, and ghosts of the past, while trying to elude evil spirits of the present. (Rev: BL 9/1/95; VOYA 4/96)

1634 Bradley, Marion Zimmer. *The Gratitude of Kings* (9–12). 1997, NAL paper $14.95 (0-451-45641-6). When magician/minstrel Lythande sees the bride-to-be of Lord Tashgan, she senses that magic is afoot. (Rev: VOYA 4/98)

1635 Bradley, Marion Zimmer. *Hawkmistress!* (10–12). 1982, D A W Books paper $5.99 (0-88677-239-7). A Darkover novel about Romilly, a girl who has special abilities to communicate with hawks and horses.

1636 Bradley, Marion Zimmer. *Sword of Chaos* (10–12). 1982, D A W Books paper $3.50 (0-88677-172-2). This anthology of Darkover stories contains short fantasies by Zimmer and other writers using her locale.

1637 Bradley, Marion Zimmer, and Rachel E. Holmen, eds. *Sword and Sorceress XIV* (9–12). 1997, D A W Books paper $5.99 (0-88677-741-0). This edition of this annual collection of fantasy stories contains a variety of locales and mostly female-centered themes. (Rev: VOYA 2/98)

1638 Bradshaw, Gillian. *The Land of Gold* (5–8). 1992, Greenwillow $14.00 (0-688-10576-9). In this sequel to *The Dragon and the Thief* (o.p.), a clever Egyptian thief and his sidekicks save a princess from being sacrificed and help her reclaim her throne. (Rev: BL 9/15/92; SLJ 10/92)

1639 Britain, Kristin. *Green Rider* (10–12). 1998, D A W Books $23.95 (0-88677-824-7). An adventure-filled fantasy about a young girl who must overcome incredible obstacles to deliver a message to the king. (Rev: VOYA 12/98)

1640 Brooks, Terry. *The Druid of Shannara* (10–12). 1991, Ballantine $19.95 (0-345-36298-5). In this, the second of the Heritage of Shannara series, the evil Shadowen continue to control the Four Lands. (Rev: BL 12/1/90; SLJ 7/91)

1641 Brooks, Terry. *The Elf Queen of Shannara* (9–12). (Heritage of Shannara) 1993, Ballantine paper $6.99 (0-345-37558-0). Wren and her friend Garth must survive the perils of the jungle to find the Elves and then persuade them to return to the environmentally endangered Westlands. (Rev: BL 12/15/91)

1642 Brooks, Terry. *First King Shannara* (9–12). 1996, Del Rey $23.50 (0-345-39652-9). The Druid Bremen seeks helps from followers who know the Druid Magic Arts to counter the threat of the evil Brona, the Warlock Lord, and his plans to conquer the Four Lands with his knowledge of Druid Magic. (Rev: VOYA 10/96)

1643 Brooks, Terry. *A Knight of the Word* (10–12). 1998, Ballantine $25.95 (0-345-37963-2). Nest, of *Running with the Demon,* must warn her friend John Ross that the evil force known as the Void is after him in this novel set in contemporary Seattle. (Rev: BL 5/15/98; VOYA 12/98)

1644 Brooks, Terry. *Running with the Demon* (10–12). 1997, Ballantine $25.95 (0-345-37962-4). Nest, a 14-year-old girl who has a six-inch-tall friend and magical abilities, finds herself in the middle of a power struggle between Knight of the Word John Ross and the spirit of evil, who has taken the form of a human demon. (Rev: VOYA 4/98)

1645 Brooks, Terry. *The Scions of Shannara* (10–12). 1990, Ballantine $23.00 (0-345-35695-0). In this, the first of a new trilogy, The Heritage of Shannara, the forces of good battle a race using evil magic. (Rev: BL 1/1/90; SLJ 9/90)

1646 Brooks, Terry. *The Talismans of Shannara* (9–12). (Heritage of Shannara) 1993, Ballantine paper $6.99 (0-345-38674-4). With their quests fulfilled, Par, Walker Bob, and Wren are drawn back together to face the Shadowen in the final book of the Shannara saga. (Rev: BL 1/1/93)

1647 Brooks, Terry. *The Tangle Box* (9–12). 1995, Ballantine paper $6.99 (0-345-38700-7). This humorous fantasy concerns Ben Holiday, sovereign of the magic kingdom of Landover, and some exiled sorcerers seeking revenge upon the fairy folk. (Rev: BL 3/15/94; VOYA 8/94)

1648 Brooks, Terry. *The Wishsong of Shannara* (9–12). 1988, Ballantine paper $6.99 (0-345-35636-5). In the concluding volume of the Shannara saga, a young girl finds she holds the power of the wishsong, a weapon that the Four Lands can use against their enemies. Preceded by *The Sword of Shannara* and *The Elfstones of Shannara*. (Rev: BL 4/1/85; SLJ 8/85; VOYA 12/85)

1649 Brown, Joseph F. *Dark Things* (6–9). 1995, Royal Fireworks paper $7.99 (0-88092-110-2). A fantasy that spans 130 years, from the Civil War to the present, about a boy who never grows old and the magical powers he possesses. (Rev: VOYA 4/96)

1650 Brown, Mary. *Pigs Don't Fly* (9–12). 1994, Baen paper $6.99 (0-671-87601-5). With her unknown father's magic ring, the daughter of a village whore sets out to seek her fortune, accompanied by an assortment of animal characters and a blind, amnesiac knight. (Rev: BL 3/1/94; VOYA 10/94)

1651 Brown, Mary. *The Unlikely Ones* (10–12). 1986, Baen paper $4.99 (0-671-65361-X). Seven unlikely companions, including a hornless unicorn, are forced to go on a quest because of a witch's curse. (Rev: BL 10/1/86)

1652 Buffie, Margaret. *Angels Turn Their Backs* (7–9). 1998, Kids Can $14.95 (1-55074-415-1). When 15-year-old Addy moves with her mother to Winnipeg, she suffers panic attacks at the thought of going to a new school and trying to make new friends, but she gets help from a helpful ghost who speaks through a parrot. (Rev: SLJ 11/98; VOYA 4/99)

1653 Buffie, Margaret. *The Haunting of Frances Rain* (7–10). 1989, Scholastic paper $12.95 (0-590-42834-9). Through a pair of magic spectacles, Lizzie is able to see events that occurred more than 50 years ago. (Rev: BL 10/1/89; SLJ 9/89)

1654 Bull, Emma. *Finder* (9–12). 1994, Tor $21.95 (0-312-85418-8). Set in Borderland, just outside the Elflands, this is the story of a cop who exploits a finder's talents to track down a killer sorcerer. (Rev: BL 2/15/94; SLJ 6/95; VOYA 6/94)

1655 Butts, Nancy. *Cheshire Moon* (5–8). 1996, Front Street $14.95 (1-886910-08-1). A 12-year-old hearing-impaired girl is able to contact the ghost of her best friend who was killed in a canoeing accident. (Rev: BL 10/15/96; SLJ 11/96; VOYA 4/97)

1656 Calhoun, Dia. *Firegold* (7–12). 1999, Winslow $15.95 (1-890817-10-4). A fantasy in which a 13-year-old boy is persecuted in his village because of his different looks and behavior and is forced to travel to the Red Mountains, home of fierce barbarians. (Rev: BL 5/15/99; BR 9–10/99; SLJ 6/99; VOYA 8/99)

1657 Callander, Don. *Geomancer* (9–12). 1994, Berkley paper $5.50 (0-441-28036-6). Captured apprentice Douglas Brightgale races to crack the spell of an ancient geomancer and to pass his firemaster examination in time for his wedding. (Rev: BL 1/1/94; VOYA 6/94)

1658 Card, Orson Scott. *Seventh Son* (10–12). 1993, Tor paper $5.99 (0-8125-3305-4). In this the first volume of the Tales of Alvin Maker series, the author has created another world using early nineteenth-century America as a model. (Rev: BL 5/1/87; SLJ 12/87; VOYA 12/87)

1659 Chalker, Jack L. *Midnight at the Well of Souls* (10–12). 1985, Ballantine paper $5.99 (0-345-32445-5). This story about Nathan Brazil is the first part of the Saga of the Well World. Other volumes are: *Exiles at the Well of Souls*, *Quest for the Well of Souls*, *The Return of Nathan Brazil*, and *Twilight at the Well of Souls*.

1660 Charnas, Suzy McKee. *The Kingdom of Kevin Malone* (7–10). 1993, Harcourt $16.95 (0-15-200756-3). This novel melds the world of the teenage problem novel with that of fantasy in a story that pokes gentle fun at the conventions of fantasy fiction. (Rev: BL 6/1–15/93; SLJ 1/94; VOYA 8/93)

1661 Cherryh, C. J. *Exile's Gate* (10–12). 1988, NAL paper $5.50 (0-88677-254-0). In this fourth installment of the adventures of Morgaine, she and her liegeman continue their quest to close the disrupting Gates. The preceding volume was: *Fires of Azeroth* (1979). (Rev: BL 11/1/87; VOYA 6/88)

1662 Cherryh, C. J., and Mercedes Lackey. *Reap the Whirlwind* (9–12). 1989, Baen paper $4.99 (0-671-69846-X). In this fantasy, a horde of barbarians threaten the power of the Order of the Sword of Knowledge. (Rev: VOYA 4/90)

1663 Chetwin, Grace. *The Crystal Stair: From Tales of Gom in the Legends of Ulm* (6–8). 1988, Macmillan LB $14.95 (0-02-718311-4). Young Gom sets out to find a wizard who will teach him magic in this sequel to *The Riddle and the Rune*. (Rev: BL 4/1/88; SLJ 6/88)

1664 Christensen, James C., and Renwick St. James. *Voyage of the Basset* (10–12). Illus. 1996, Workman $29.95 (1-885183-58-5). In 1850, a professor of myths and legends and his daughters are transported to the ancient land of myths, where they have a series of adventures and meet such mythical characters as a manticore, Oberon and Titania, harpies, a sphinx, minotaur, mermaids, trolls, gryphon, Medusa, unicorn, and a dragon. (Rev: SLJ 1/97)

1665 Clayton, Jo. *Drum Warning* (9–12). 1996, Tor $23.95 (0-312-86177-X). In this exciting fantasy 2 worlds touch magically, allowing magical energies and some inhabitants to cross over, and when the mages of each seek to conquer the other, 2 organizations and 2 youngsters from the 2 worlds band together to oppose these forces of chaos and save their worlds from destruction. (Rev: VOYA 4/97)

1666 Cochran, Molly, and Warren Murphy. *The Broken Sword* (10–12). 1997, Tor $24.95 (0-312-86283-0). Merlin and King Arthur are reincarnated in the 20th century as an old man and a teenager whose mission is to rescue the Holy Grail from a gang of villains. (Rev: SLJ 8/97)

1667 Coelho, Paulo. *The Alchemist* (9–12). 1993, Harper San Francisco $18.00 (0-06-250217-4). Parable about a boy who must learn to listen to his heart before he can find his treasure. (Rev: BL 5/1/93; SLJ 7/93)

1668 Conrad, Pam. *Zoe Rising* (5–8). 1996, Harper-Collins LB $14.89 (0-06-027218-X). Traumatized into an out-of-body state, 14-year-old Zoe returns to her island home where she lives with her grandparents and finds she has the power to control their experiences. (Rev: BR 1–2/97; SLJ 11/96; VOYA 12/96)

1669 Cooney, Caroline B. *Prisoner of Time* (6–10). 1998, Delacorte $15.95 (0-385-32244-5). In this conclusion to Cooney's Time Travel trilogy, there is again a contrast between the life-styles of today and those of 100 years ago as a girl is rescued from an unsuitable marriage. (Rev: BL 6/1–15/98; SLJ 5/98; VOYA 6/98)

1670 Cooper, Louise. *Inferno* (9–12). 1989, Tor paper $3.95 (0-8125-0246-9). In this sequel to *Nemesis* (1989), Indigo must kill the demon she freed from the Tower of Regrets. (Rev: VOYA 4/90)

1671 Cooper, Susan. *Over Sea, Under Stone* (6–9). Illus. 1966, Harcourt $17.00 (0-15-259034-X); paper $3.95 (0-02-042785-9). Three contemporary children enter the world of King Arthur in this the first volume of The Dark Is Rising series. Followed by:

The Dark Is Rising (1973); *Greenwitch* (1985); *The Grey King* (1975); and *Silver on the Tree* (1977).

1672 Cooper, Susan. *Seaward* (6–9). 1983, Macmillan LB $16.00 (0-689-50275-3); paper $3.95 (0-02-042190-7). Two youngsters embark on a fantastic voyage to find their parents.

1673 Coville, Bruce. *A Glory of Unicorns* (5–8). Illus. 1998, Scholastic $16.95 (0-590-95943-3). A collection of stories by fantasy authors, including the editor and his wife, that deal with unicorns. (Rev: BL 6/1–15/98; BR 5–6/98; SLJ 5/98; VOYA 8/98)

1674 Crispin, A. C. *The Paradise Snare* (9–12). 1997, Bantam paper $5.99 (0-553-57415-9). This is the first novel in a trilogy about the con man of *Star Wars* fame, Han Solo. The others are: *The Hunt Gambit* (1997) and *Rebel Dawn* (1997). (Rev: VOYA 12/98)

1675 Crispin, A. C. *Voices of Chaos* (8–12). 1998, Ace paper $5.99 (0-441-00516-0). In this story of romance, political intrigue, and coming of age, the students and teachers at Starbridge Academy are introduced to a race of feline beings—expressive, intelligent, ambitious, and skillful at deception and manipulation—when Prince Khyriz and Shiksara, a girl from the merchant class, come to study. (Rev: BL 3/1/98; VOYA 6/98)

1676 Crompton, Anne E. *Merlin's Harp* (9–12). 1995, Donald I. Fine paper $5.99 (0-451-45583-5). The Arthurian story is retold from the standpoint of a woman, Niviene, Merlin's apprentice and daughter of the Lady of the Lake. (Rev: VOYA 6/97)

1677 Cross, Gillian. *Pictures in the Dark* (5–8). 1996, Holiday House $16.95 (0-8234-1267-9). A boy whose life is miserable uses supernatural means to escape the pressures including, at one point, becoming an otter. (Rev: BL 1/1–15/97; BR 3–4/97)

1678 Curry, Jane L. *Dark Shade* (6–10). 1998, Simon & Schuster paper $16.00 (0-689-81812-2). Maggie Gilmour and her silent, withdrawn friend, Kip, travel in time to 1758 and the time of the French and Indian Wars. (Rev: BL 4/1/98; BR 1–2/99; SLJ 5/98; VOYA 8/98)

1679 Curry, Jane L. *Moon Window* (5–8). 1996, Simon & Schuster $16.00 (0-689-80945-X). Joellen travels back in time and meets several of her ancestors. (Rev: BL 10/15/96; SLJ 12/96)

1680 Dahl, Roald. *Two Fables* (10–12). Illus. 1987, Farrar $12.95 (0-374-28018-5). Two parables for adults involving princesses and magic kingdoms. (Rev: BL 9/1/87)

1681 Dalkey, Kara. *The Heavenward Path* (7–12). 1998, Harcourt $17.00 (0-15-201652-X). In this sequel to *Little Sister*, 16-year-old Mitsuko escapes from an arranged marriage by flying away on the wings of her friend Goranu. (Rev: BL 6/1–15/98; SLJ 5/98; VOYA 6/98)

1682 Dalkey, Kara. *Little Sister* (7–10). 1996, Harcourt $17.00 (0-15-201392-X). In this historical fantasy, a Japanese girl from a noble family, who is a helper for her newly married oldest sister, travels into a hell-like land and back. (Rev: BL 10/1/96; BR 3–4/97; SLJ 12/96; VOYA 2/97)

1683 Datlow, Ellen, and Terri Windling, eds. *Black Thorn, White Rose* (9–12). 1994, Avon $22.00 (0-688-13713-X). Variations of famous European folktales involving dwarves, witches, elves, and trolls, including a retelling of "Rumpelstiltskin." (Rev: BL 8/94; VOYA 4/95)

1684 Davies, Valentine. *Miracle on 34th Street* (6–9). Illus. 1984, Harcourt $16.95 (0-15-254526-3). Kris Kringle, living in an old folks home, plays Santa at Macy's in this 1947 fantasy.

1685 Dean, J. David. *Ravennetus* (9–12). 1996, Pandea $21.95 (0-9646604-4-X). In this medieval fantasy, young Nelsyn is sent out into the world by 2 villains to find the secret power that will allow them to dominate the world. (Rev: BL 3/15/96)

1686 Deem, James M. *The Very Real Ghost Book of Christina Rose* (7–9). 1996, Houghton $15.00 (0-395-76128-X). In this book that combines detection, the paranormal, and humor, 12-year-old Christina deals with her mother's death by immersing herself in the study of paranormal activities and wearing only dark, depressing colors. (Rev: BL 5/1/96; SLJ 5/96; VOYA 10/96)

1687 DeFelice, Cynthia. *The Strange Night Writing of Jessamine Colter* (6–9). 1988, Macmillan paper $13.95 (0-02-726451-3). A short tender novel about a woman who has the gift of seeing into the future. (Rev: BL 10/1/88; SLJ 11/88; VOYA 4/89)

1688 Deitz, Tom. *Fireshaper's Doom* (9–12). 1987, Avon paper $3.95 (0-380-75329-4). Because he accidentally caused the death of a faerie boy, Sullivan faces the wrath of the boy's mother in this sequel to *Windmaster's Bane*. (Rev: BL 11/15/87)

1689 Deitz, Tom. *Windmaster's Bane* (10–12). 1986, Avon paper $4.99 (0-380-75029-5). A man with second sight finds himself back in the time of legendary struggles involving the Celts. (Rev: BL 11/15/86)

1690 Del Rey, Lester, and Risa Kessler, eds. *Once upon a Time: A Treasury of Modern Fairy Tales* (9–12). 1991, Ballantine $25.00 (0-345-36263-2). Ten original fairy tales for adults by Asimov, Cherryh, Hambly, McCaffrey, and others. (Rev: BL 11/15/91; SLJ 8/92)

1691 De Lint, Charles. *Trader* (10–12). 1997, Tor $24.95 (0-312-85847-7). Max Trader awakens to find that he has inexplicably traded bodies with a

womanizing loser named Johnny Devlin. (Rev: BL 1/1–15/97; VOYA 8/97)

1692 DeVos, Elisabeth. *The Seraphim Rising* (10–12). 1997, Roc paper $5.99 (0-451-45655-6). An action-packed quest by 2 young men to prove or disprove the claim that a new messiah has arrived on earth. (Rev: VOYA 2/98)

1693 Dickinson, Peter. *The Lion-Tamer's Daughter & Other Stories* (6–9). 1997, Bantam Doubleday Dell $15.95 (0-385-32327-1). Four fantastic stories that deal with transformations, other worlds, and duplicate identities. (Rev: BL 4/1/97; SLJ 3/97*; VOYA 4/97)

1694 Dickson, Gordon R. *The Dragon & the Gnarly King* (9–12). 1997, St. Martin's $24.95 (0-312-86157-5). Living in a time-warp medieval setting, Jim Ekert, a 20th-century college professor, matches wit and skills with the Gnarly King in a fight for the return of his kidnapped son. (Rev: BL 8/97; VOYA 4/98)

1695 Dickson, Gordon R. *The Dragon, the Earl, and the Troll* (9–12). 1994, Berkley paper $21.95 (0-441-00098-3). The latest in the series about Dragon Knight, a 20th-century American transported into an analogue of medieval England. (Rev: BL 12/1/94; VOYA 4/95)

1696 Doherty, Berlie. *Daughter of the Sea* (6–9). Illus. 1997, DK Publg. $14.95 (0-7894-2469-X). A fantasy about a lonely couple who raise a baby found in the water, although they know she is from the selkie, seal people who shed their skins and walk on land. (Rev: BL 10/1/97; BR 3–4/98; SLJ 9/97; VOYA 4/98)

1697 Donaldson, Stephen R. *Lord Foul's Bane* (10–12). 1987, Ballantine paper $6.99 (0-345-34865-6). Thomas Covenant, a leper, finds himself in a magical world in this first volume of the Chronicles of Thomas Covenant the Unbeliever series. Others are *The Illearth War* and *The Power That Preserves*.

1698 Donoghue, Emma. *Kissing the Witch: Old Tales in New Skins* (10–12). (Joanna Cotler Bks.) 1997, HarperCollins $14.89 (0-06-027576-6). Such familiar tales as *Beauty and the Beast*, *Rumpelstiltskin*, and *Cinderella* are retold from a lesbian, feminist point of view. (Rev: BL 6/1–15/97; BR 1–2/98; SLJ 6/97; VOYA 8/97)

1699 Doyle, Debra, and James D. MacDonald. *The Knight's Wyrd* (6–9). 1992, Harcourt $16.95 (0-15-200764-4). On the eve of his knighting, young Will learns his wyrd (fate) from his father's wizard, which sets off a series of adventures. (Rev: BL 11/15/92; SLJ 11/92)

1700 Duane, Diane. *The Book of Night with Moon* (9–12). 1997, Warner paper $12.99 (0-446-67302-1).

An Evil has invaded the underground culture of the magical world beneath Grand Central Station, and 4 cats are dispatched to send the Evil back to the Darkness. (Rev: VOYA 4/98)

1701 Duane, Diane. *A Wizard Abroad* (6–9). (Wizardry) 1997, Harcourt $15.00 (0-15-201209-5). The fourth book in the Wizardry series concerns 14-year-old Nita and her struggle against the Fomori, monster people who are trying to destroy the ancient symbols of power in Ireland. (Rev: BL 10/1/97; SLJ 9/97)

1702 Duel, John. *Wide Awake in Dreamland* (5–8). Illus. 1992, Stargaze Publg. $15.95 (0-9630923-0-8). An evil warlock threatens to steal a 9-year-old's imagination unless the young boy can find a friendly wizard first. (Rev: BL 3/1/92; SLJ 5/92)

1703 Duncan, David. *The Stricken Field* (9–12). (Handful of Men) 1993, Ballantine $19.00 (0-345-37898-9). In the third book of the series, the magic-wielding King Rap and his comrades must fight the evil dwarf Zinixo and his legions of sorcerers. (Rev: BL 8/93; VOYA 2/94)

1704 Eddings, David. *Guardians of the West* (10–12). 1987, Ballantine paper $6.99 (0-345-35266-1). The beginning volume of a saga about King Garion. In this installment he sets out to save his son from an evil force. (Rev: BL 3/1/87)

1705 Ende, Michael. *The Neverending Story* (7–12). Trans. by Ralph Manheim. 1984, Penguin paper $11.95 (0-14-007431-7). An overweight boy with many problems enters the magic world of Fantastica in this charming fantasy.

1706 Farjeon, Eleanor. *The Glass Slipper* (6–9). 1986, HarperCollins LB $11.89 (0-397-32181-3). A romantic retelling in prose of the Cinderella story. (Rev: BL 10/15/86)

1707 Fitch, Marina. *The Seventh Heart* (9–12). 1997, Ace paper $5.99 (0-441-00451-2). The 4 elements of the universe, Earth, Wind, Fresh Water, and Sea Water, rebel against humanity's abuses in this exciting fantasy. (Rev: VOYA 12/97)

1708 Fletcher, Susan. *Dragon's Milk* (5–9). 1989, Macmillan LB $15.95 (0-689-31579-1). To save her brother, Kaeldra embarks on a quest to find dragon's milk. (Rev: BL 11/1/89; BR 3–4/90; SLJ 11/89; VOYA 12/89)

1709 Fletcher, Susan. *Sign of the Dove* (7–10). 1996, Atheneum $17.00 (0-689-80460-1). Lyf, her foster sister, Kaeldra, and Kaeldra's husband are dedicated to saving dragon hatchlings from the Krags in this allegory in which Lyf finds herself alone in a world of wild dragons. (Rev: BL 5/1/96; BR 1–2/97; SLJ 5/96; VOYA 8/96)

1710 Foster, Alan Dean. *Spellsinger* (10–12). 1983, Warner paper $5.50 (0-446-35647-6). A young graduate student named Jonathan Meriweather is summoned to another world to lead a struggle for freedom. Others in this series are: *The Day of the Dissonance* (Phantasia, 1984), and *The Moment of the Magician* (Phantasia, 1986).

1711 Friedman, C. S. *Crown of Shadows* (9–12). 1995, NAL paper $21.95 (0-88677-664-3). Racing against time to prevent the enslavement of their world, warrior priest Damien Vryce and immortal sorcerer Gerald Tarrant find themselves trapped between justice and retribution. (Rev: BL 9/15/95; VOYA 2/96)

1712 Fromental, Jean-Luc. *Broadway Chicken* (5–8). Trans. by Suzi Baker. Illus. 1995, Hyperion LB $14.89 (0-7868-2048-9). A tale of success and failure with, yes, a dancing chicken as the protagonist. (Rev: BL 12/15/95; SLJ 2/96)

1713 Fry, Stephen. *Making History* (10–12). 1998, Random $24.00 (0-679-45955-3). In this humorous yet thought-provoking fantasy written by a British comedian, a graduate student at Cambridge is able to stop the birth of Hitler through time travel, creating a contemporary world that is entirely different and unexpected. (Rev: BL 2/1/98; SLJ 8/98)

1714 Furlong, Monica. *Juniper* (7–12). 1992, Demco $10.34 (0-606-01569-8). A rich coming-of-age novel about Ninnoc, the only child of King Mark of Cornwall, as Christianity is beginning to overcome the ancient Celtic religion of the Mother Goddess. (Rev: BL 2/15/91; SLJ 5/91)

1715 Gaiman, Neil. *Stardust* (10–12). 1999, Avon paper $22.00 (0-380-97728-1). A fantasy fairy tale about a young man, an evil witch, and the sons of a lord, all seeking the star, a young woman living in the land of Faerie. (Rev: BL 11/1/98; SLJ 2/99)

1716 Galloway, Priscilla. *The Snake Dreamer's Story* (6–10). 1998, Delacorte $14.95 (0-385-32264-X). While trying to cure a sleep disorder at a clinic on an exotic Greek island, Dusa finds she is being used to resurrect the spirit of the ancient Gorgon, Medusa. (Rev: BL 6/1–15/98; BR 11–12/98; SLJ 7/98; VOYA 12/98)

1717 Garden, Nancy. *The Door Between* (6–8). 1987, Farrar $15.00 (0-374-31833-6). In this the third of a series, Melissa enters the Otherworld to confront an evil hermit. The first 2 were: *Fours Crossing* (1981) and *Watersmeet* (1983). (Rev: BL 11/1/87; SLJ 12/87)

1718 Gardner, John. *Grendel* (10–12). 1971, Knopf $15.95 (0-394-47143-1). A retelling of the Beowulf legend, from the standpoint of the monster Grendel.

1719 Gilman, Laura Anne, and Keith R. A. DeCandido, eds. *Otherwere: Stories of Transformation* (9–12). 1996, Ace paper $5.99 (0-441-00363-X). Fifteen stories whose plots focus on some sort of transformation—animals, creatures, or people. (Rev: VOYA 4/97)

1720 Gilmore, Kate. *Enter Three Witches* (6–10). 1990, Houghton $13.95 (0-395-50213-6). Bren's mother and grandmother are witches causing problems for the boy's social life. (Rev: BL 3/15/90; SLJ 3/90; VOYA 4/90)

1721 Goldman, William, retel. *The Princess Bride: S. Morgenstern's Classic Tale of True Love and High Adventure* (9–12). 1982, Ballantine paper $6.99 (0-345-34803-6). A hilarious fast-paced fantasy with a hero named Westley and a heroine named Buttercup.

1722 Goodkind, Terry. *Wizard's First Rule* (9–12). 1994, Tor $27.95 (0-312-85705-5). With the sword of Truth, young Richard Cypher goes on a quest, encountering wizards, dragons, and other evils with a modern touch of ambiguity. (Rev: BL 9/1/94; VOYA 2/95)

1723 Gordon, Lawrence. *User Friendly* (7–10). (Ghost Chronicles) 1999, Karmichael paper $11.95 (0-9653966-0-6). Frank, a teenage ghost in limbo, contacts Eddie through the computer to get help to free himself and his friend, a runaway slave, from the purgatory in which they are living. (Rev: BL 1/1–15/99; SLJ 1/99)

1724 Greenberg, Martin H., ed. *Elf Fantastic* (8–12). 1997, D A W Books paper $5.99 (0-88677-736-4). Each of the 19 short stories about elves in this collection offers a fresh insight into humankind. (Rev: VOYA 10/97)

1725 Greenberg, Martin H., ed. *Wizard Fantastic* (9–12). 1997, D A W Books paper $5.99 (0-88677-756-9). This is a collection of 21 original stories about wizards, many of them by well-known writers. (Rev: VOYA 10/98)

1726 Griffin, Peni R. *Switching Well* (5–9). 1993, Macmillan $16.00 (0-689-50581-7); 1994, Penguin paper $4.99 (0-14-036910-4). Ada lives in 1891 San Antonio; Amber lives there in 1991. Each wishes she lived in the other's time, and their wishes are granted. Predictably, they soon wish they were back in familiar surroundings. (Rev: BL 6/1–15/93*; SLJ 6/93*; VOYA 8/93)

1727 Grove, Vicki. *Rimwalkers* (6–10). 1993, Putnam $14.95 (0-399-22430-0). On an Illinois farm for the summer, Tory develops self-esteem as she unravels a mystery involving the apparition of a small boy. (Rev: BL 10/15/93; SLJ 10/93; VOYA 12/93)

1728 Hambly, Barbara. *The Time of the Dark* (10–12). 1984, Ballantine paper $5.99 (0-345-31965-6). In this first part of the Darweth trilogy, a wizard and a prince flee the powers of the Dark. Followed by: *The Walls of Air* and *The Armies of Daylight* (both 1983).

1729 Hamilton, Virginia. *Justice and Her Brothers* (7–10). 1998, Scholastic paper $4.99 (0-590-36214-3). Four children with supernatural powers move in time in this complex novel. Sequels are *Dustland* and *The Gathering*.

1730 Hansen, Brooks. *Caesar's Antlers* (5–8). Illus. 1997, Farrar $16.00 (0-374-31024-6). In this animal fantasy, Caesar, the reindeer, and his friend Bette, the sparrow, and her 2 offspring set out to contact some human friends to get help for the winter. (Rev: BL 10/1/97; BR 3–4/98; SLJ 11/97)

1731 Hartwell, David G. *Visions of Wonder* (9–12). 1996, St. Martin's $35.00 (0-312-86224-5); paper $24.95 (0-312-85287-8). An interesting anthology of 1990s science fiction and fantasy, plus several essays on various aspects of the genre. (Rev: VOYA 6/97)

1732 Hautman, Pete. *Mr. Was* (8–12). 1996, Simon & Schuster $16.00 (0-689-81068-7). In this complex fantasy, Jack escapes his father's drunken rage by entering a door in his grandfather's house that takes him back to 1941. (Rev: BL 9/15/96; SLJ 10/96; VOYA 12/96)

1733 Helprin, Mark. *The Veil of Snows* (4–8). Illus. 1997, Viking paper $24.00 (0-670-87491-4). This fantasy is also a political fable in which a reactionary queen tries to turn back the clock. (Rev: BL 11/15/97; SLJ 11/97)

1734 Highwater, Jamake. *Rama: A Legend* (5–9). 1997, Replica Books LB $24.95 (10-7351-0001-2). When he's wrongfully banished from his father's kingdom and his wife, Sita, is kidnapped, valiant Prince Rama charges back to avenge the evil that's befallen his world. (Rev: BL 11/15/94; SLJ 12/94; VOYA 2/95)

1735 Hilton, James. *Lost Horizon* (9–12). 1983, Buccaneer LB $28.95 (0-89966-450-4). This fantasy is about Shangri-la, a land where time stands still.

1736 Hindle, Lee J. *Dragon Fall* (9–12). 1984, Avon paper $2.95 (0-380-88468-2). The monsters Gabe creates for a toy company come alive and try to kill him.

1737 Hite, Sid. *Answer My Prayer* (7–10). 1995, Holt $15.95 (0-8050-3406-4). A girl meets a fortune-teller who forecasts a strange future that includes a sleeping stranger. (Rev: BL 5/1/95*)

1738 Hite, Sid. *The Distance of Hope* (6–8). 1998, Holt $16.95 (0-8050-5054-X). Young prince Yeshe embarks on a perilous journey to find the White Bean Lama who will help him save his diminishing eyesight. (Rev: BL 3/15/98; SLJ 5/98; VOYA 6/98)

1739 Hite, Sid. *Dither Farm* (6–10). 1992, Holt $15.95 (0-8050-1871-9). An 11-year-old orphan is taken in by a farm family and discovers joys and miracles. (Rev: BL 5/15/92*; SLJ 5/92)

1740 Hoban, Russell. *The Trokeville Way* (5–8). 1996, Knopf $17.00 (0-679-88148-4). A magical jigsaw puzzle leads Nick into a strange new universe. (Rev: BL 11/15/96; SLJ 12/96)

1741 Hobbs, Will. *Kokopelli's Flute* (6–9). 1995, Atheneum $16.00 (0-689-31974-6). A teen finds a bone flute at an ancient Anasazi cliff dwelling that grave robbers have plundered. Strange events occur each night when the boy plays this ancient flute. (Rev: BL 10/1/95; SLJ 10/95; VOYA 2/96)

1742 Holch, Gregory. *The Things with Wings* (5–8). 1998, Scholastic $15.95 (0-590-93501-1). In this mystery fantasy, Newton and his classmate Vanessa learn about the Emerald Rainbow butterflies, become involved in the disappearance of a friend, and discover the magic of flying. (Rev: BL 8/98; SLJ 5/98; VOYA 6/98)

1743 Holman, Felice. *Real* (8–12). 1997, Simon & Schuster $16.00 (0-689-80772-4). While still trying to accept the death of his mother, young Colly, who is spending time in the desert with his father, is befriended by some Native Americans and meets Sparrow, a Cahuilla Indian who, with his grandmother, is trapped in time. (Rev: BL 10/1/97; SLJ 11/97; VOYA 2/98)

1744 Holt, Tom. *Who's Afraid of Beowulf?* (9–12). 1991, Ace paper $5.50 (0-441-88591-8). In this time-warp story, a present-day archaeologist and some ancient Vikings combat an evil wizard. (Rev: BL 1/15/89; VOYA 6/89)

1745 Hoobler, Dorothy, and Thomas Hoobler. *The Ghost in the Tokaido Inn* (6–12). 1999, Putnam $17.99 (0-399-23330-X). Set in 18th-century Japan, this is the story of 14-year-old Seikei, his dreams of becoming a samurai, and what happened after he saw a legendary ghost stealing a valuable jewel. (Rev: BL 6/1–15/99; SLJ 6/99; VOYA 10/99)

1746 Hood, David. *Wizard's Heir* (8–12). 1995, Ace paper $4.99 (0-441-00231-5). In this humorous fantasy, Liam insists he is not a wizard, but things keep happening that convince his neighbors otherwise. (Rev: VOYA 2/96)

1747 Huff, Tanya. *Summon the Keeper* (9–12). 1998, D A W Books paper $5.99 (0-88677-784-4). When she takes over the management of the Elysian Fields guesthouse, Claire discovers the Keeper upstairs asleep, which suggests there is a hole in the fabric of the universe. (Rev: VOYA 10/98)

1748 Hughes, Monica, ed. *What If . . . ? Amazing Stories Selected by Monica Hughes* (7–12). 1998, McClelland & Stewart Tundra Books paper $6.95 (0-88776-458-4). A thoughtful collection of 14 science fiction and fantasy stories that provide unusual answers to the question "What if?" in various situations. (Rev: BL 2/15/99; SLJ 6/99; VOYA 6/99)

1749 Hunter, Mollie. *The Mermaid Summer* (5–8). 1988, HarperCollins LB $14.89 (0-06-022628-5). Two children challenge the power of a mermaid who threatens to destroy their village. (Rev: BL 6/1/88; BR 1–2/89; SLJ 6/88)

1750 Hunter, Mollie. *A Stranger Came Ashore* (7–9). 1977, HarperCollins paper $4.95 (0-06-440082-4). In this fantasy set in the Shetland Islands, a bull seal takes human form and comes ashore.

1751 Ibbotson, Eva. *Which Witch?* (5–9). Illus. 1999, Dutton $15.99 (0-525-46164-7). Arriman the Awful agrees to marry to insure an heir to the throne of darkness, so all the witches of the Toldcaster coven are invited to a contest to win his hand by performing the blackest magic possible. (Rev: BL 8/99; SLJ 8/99)

1752 Ingold, Jeanette. *The Window* (7–10). 1996, Harcourt $13.00 (0-15-201265-6); paper $6.00 (0-15-201264-8). While staying with relatives in Texas, a newly blinded girl time travels to discover secrets about her family. (Rev: BL 11/1/96; BR 3–4/97; SLJ 12/96; VOYA 12/96)

1753 Jacques, Brian. *The Long Patrol* (5–8). Illus. 1998, Putnam $21.99 (0-399-23165-X). In this tenth Redwall adventure, the villainous Rapscallions decide to attack the peaceful Abbey of Redwall. (Rev: BL 12/15/97; BR 3–4/98; SLJ 1/98)

1754 Jacques, Brian. *Marlfox* (5–8). 1999, Putnam $22.99 (0-399-23307-5). While Redwall Abbey is under siege, 4 youngsters search for the tapestry depicting Martin the Warrior to return it to the abbey in this eleventh book of the Redwall saga. (Rev: BL 12/15/98; BR 9–10/99; SLJ 4/99; VOYA 2/99)

1755 Jacques, Brian. *Mattimeo* (5–8). 1990, Putnam $22.99 (0-399-21741-X). The evil fox kidnaps the animal children of Redwall Abbey in this continuation of *Mossflower* (1988) and *Redwall* (1987). (Rev: BL 4/15/90; SLJ 9/90; VOYA 8/90)

1756 Jacques, Brian. *Outcast of Redwall* (4–8). Illus. 1996, Philomel $22.99 (0-399-22914-0). This episode in the Redwall saga involves the badger Sunflash, his buddy Skarlath the kestrel, and their enemy the ferret Swartt Sixclaw. (Rev: BL 3/1/96; BR 3–4/96; SLJ 5/96; VOYA 10/96)

1757 Jacques, Brian. *The Pearls of Lutra* (5–8). 1997, Putnam $21.99 (0-399-22946-9). The evil marten Mad Eyes threatens the peaceful Redwall Abbey in this book, the ninth in the series. (Rev: BL 2/15/97; SLJ 3/97*; VOYA 6/97)

1758 James, Mary. *Frankenlouse* (5–8). 1994, Scholastic $13.95 (0-590-46528-7). Nick, 14, is enrolled at Blister Military Academy, which is run by his father. He escapes into his own comic book creations featuring an insect named Frankenlouse. (Rev: BL 10/15/94; SLJ 11/94; VOYA 12/94)

1759 Jones, Diana Wynne. *The Crown of Dalemark* (6–9). (Dalemark Quartet) 1995, Greenwillow $17.00 (0-688-13363-0). Readers familiar with the first 3 books in this quartet will enjoy its conclusion about Noreth, a teen who believes she is destined to become queen, and Maewen, who is sent to impersonate her. New readers should start with book one. (Rev: BL 12/15/95; SLJ 8/96)

1760 Jones, Diana Wynne. *Dark Lord of Derkholm* (7–10). 1998, Greenwillow $16.00 (0-688-16004-2). A humorous, scary fantasy about the efforts of a band of inhabitants to stop the incursions of Mr. Chesney's Pilgrim Parties who have been wreaking havoc on their lands for 40 years. (Rev: BL 9/1/98; BR 5–6/99; SLJ 10/98; VOYA 2/99)

1761 Jones, Diana Wynne. *Dogsbody* (7–10). 1990, Random paper $3.50 (0-394-82031-2). The Dogstar, Sirius, is sent to Earth in the form of a dog to fulfill a dangerous mission. (Rev: BR 11–12/88; VOYA 2/89)

1762 Jones, Diana Wynne. *Howl's Moving Castle* (7–12). 1986, Greenwillow $16.00 (0-688-06233-4). A fearful young girl is changed into an old woman and in that disguise moves into the castle of Wizard Howl. (Rev: BL 6/1/86; SLJ 8/86; VOYA 8/86)

1763 Jones, Diana Wynne. *The Lives of Christopher Chant* (5–9). 1998, Morrow paper $5.95 (0-688-16365-3). At night Christopher can leave his body and travel from London to other worlds. (Rev: BR 5–6/88; SLJ 5/88; VOYA 6/88)

1764 Jones, Diana Wynne. *The Time of the Ghost* (6–9). 1996, Greenwillow $15.00 (0-668-14598-1). Sally, the ghost of one of 4 sisters whose parents run a school for boys, tries to undo a bargain she made with an evil goddess when she was young. (Rev: BL 8/96; SLJ 11/96; VOYA 4/97)

1765 Jordan, Robert. *A Crown of Swords* (8–12). (Wheel of Time) 1996, Tor $27.95 (0-312-85767-5). In this seventh book of this series, Rand and his army of Aiel warriors prepare to do battle with the Dark One. (Rev: VOYA 2/97)

1766 Jordan, Robert. *Eye of the World* (10–12). 1990, Tor paper $6.99 (0-8125-1181-6). In this novel, the first of a series, a group of ordinary people flee from evil magic. (Rev: BL 10/1/89; VOYA 6/90)

1767 Jordan, Robert. *Lord of Chaos* (9–12). (Wheel of Time Saga) 1994, Tor $25.95 (0-312-85428-5). Rand al'Thor teaches magic to men while being pursued by the hostile Aes Sedai. Mat Cauthon is advised by dead generals and Nynaeve learns to restore magic. (Rev: BL 10/15/94; VOYA 5/95)

1768 Jordan, Robert. *The Shadow Rising* (9–12). (Wheel of Time Saga) 1992, Tor $27.95 (0-312-

85431-5). The fourth volume in the saga is ambitious, rich, and detailed. (Rev: BL 10/1/92*)

1769 Kelleher, Victor. *Brother Night* (7–9). 1991, Walker $25.95 (0-8027-8100-4). Rabon, 15, was raised by a foster father in a small town and ends up on a quest to the city with his dark, ugly twin, both learning about their heritage along the way. (Rev: BL 6/15/91; SLJ 5/91)

1770 Kellogg, Marjorie. *The Book of Water* (9–12). 1997, D A W Books paper $5.99 (0-88677-688-0). In this book set in 2013 in a land facing ecological disaster, Erde, the heroine from the first book in this series, and D'Nock, an egocentric, foul-mouthed adventurer, act as human guides for their dragons, Earth and Water, and the four of them face many challenges. (Rev: VOYA 6/98)

1771 Kemp, Kenny. *I Hated Heaven: A Novel of Life after Death* (10–12). 1998, Alta Films $12.00 (1-8924-4210-8). After his death, Tom Waring finds that Heaven will not allow him to fulfill his dying wish to return to earth once to tell his wife that heaven really exists. (Rev: BL 8/98; SLJ 12/98)

1772 Kerner, Elizabeth. *Song in the Silence: The Tale of Lanen Kaelar* (9–12). 1996, Tor $23.95 (0-312-85780-2). After her father's death, Lanen gets her wish to travel to the Dragon Isle to speak to the Greater Kindred, the Dragons. (Rev: BL 2/15/97; VOYA 6/97)

1773 Kerr, Katherine. *Darkspell* (10–12). 1994, Bantam paper $6.99 (0-553-56888-4). Three companions combat a group of evil sorcerers in this sequel to *Daggerspell*. (Rev: BL 9/1/87)

1774 Kerr, Peg. *Emerald House Rising* (10–12). 1997, Warner paper $5.99 (0-446-60393-7). While struggling to master the skills of wizardry, Jena finds herself drawn to a mysterious nobleman named Morgan. (Rev: VOYA 8/97)

1775 Kimmel, Elizabeth C. *The Ghost of the Stone Circle* (5–8). 1998, Scholastic $15.95 (0-590-21308-3). Fourteen-year-old Cristyn, who is spending the summer in Wales with her historian father, discovers a ghost in the house her father has rented. (Rev: BL 4/15/98; SLJ 4/98; VOYA 8/98)

1776 Kindl, Patrice. *Owl in Love* (5–9). 1993, Houghton $15.00 (0-395-66162-5). Owl, a shapeshifter, is an ordinary high school girl by day, and she falls in love with her science teacher. (Rev: BL 9/1/93; VOYA 12/93)

1777 King, Gabriel. *The Golden Cat* (10–12). 1999, Del Rey $24.50 (0-345-42304-6). In this sequel to *The Wild Road*, a group of talking cats seek allies in the animal kingdom to counter renewed threats from the evil scientist known as the Alchemist. (Rev: BL 5/15/99; SLJ 8/99)

1778 King, Gabriel. *The Wild Road* (10–12). 1998, Ballantine $24.95 (0-345-42302-X). In this fantasy, an evil sorcerer tortures cats who can talk in order to harness the power of the Wild Road, a dimension that contains the memories of all animals that have gone before. (Rev: SLJ 2/99; VOYA 6/98)

1779 King, Stephen. *The Drawing of the Three* (10–12). Illus. 1989, NAL paper $16.95 (0-452-26214-3). Roland lives out the predictions of tarot cards dealt him by the man in black in the first volume in King's The Dark Tower fantasy series, *The Gunslinger* (1988). (Rev: BL 12/15/88)

1780 King, Stephen. *The Eyes of the Dragon* (9–12). 1987, NAL paper $7.99 (0-451-16658-2). In this tale of potions and evil magic, a king dies mysteriously and his older son is unjustly accused. (Rev: BL 11/1/86; BR 9–10/87; SLJ 6/87; VOYA 8/87)

1781 King, Stephen. *The Gunslinger* (10–12). Illus. 1988, NAL paper $10.95 (0-452-26134-1). A young marksman and a boy stalk a man in black in this, volume one of The Dark Tower series. (Rev: BL 7/88)

1782 King, Stephen. *The Waste Lands* (9–12). (Dark Tower) 1992, NAL paper $17.95 (0-452-26740-4). This third installment tells of Roland of Mid-World and 3 New Yorkers who proceed ever nearer the Dark Tower, where the source of the planet's cultural degradation lies. (Rev: BL 10/15/91*; SLJ 8/92)

1783 King-Smith, Richard. *Godhanger* (7–10). 1999, Crown LB $18.99 (0-517-80036-5). Skymaster, a Christlike bird, comes to Godhanger Wood to help save the animals from a merciless gamekeeper. (Rev: BL 3/1/99; SLJ 2/99)

1784 Kipling, Rudyard. *Kipling's Fantasy* (9–12). Ed. by John Brunner. 1992, Tor $17.95 (0-312-85354-8). Atmospheric tales of myth and horror, with rich language and image. (Rev: BL 10/15/92; SLJ 6/93)

1785 Kirwan-Vogel, Anna. *The Jewel of Life* (6–8). Illus. 1991, Harcourt $15.95 (0-15-200750-4). Young orphan Duffy travels to other worlds, brings back a precious cockatrice feather, and creates the Philosopher's Stone. (Rev: BL 6/15/91; SLJ 6/91)

1786 Koller, Jackie F. *If I Had One Wish* . . . (6–8). 1991, Little, Brown $14.95 (0-316-50150-6). When eighth-grader Alec is granted his wish that his little brother had never been born, he learns a lesson about charity, kindness, and old-fashioned family values. (Rev: BL 11/1/91; SLJ 11/91)

1787 Konigsburg, E. L. *Up from Jericho Tel* (6–9). 1986, Macmillan $17.00 (0-689-31194-X). The ghost of a dead actress named Tallulah makes Jeanmarie and friend Malcolm invisible to accomplish the search for a necklace. (Rev: BL 5/1/86; SLJ 5/86; VOYA 12/86)

1788 Konwicki, Tadeusz. *The Anthropos-Specter-Beast* (7–9). Trans. by George and Audrey Korwin-Rodziszewski. 1977, S. G. Phillips $25.95 (0-87599-218-8). Peter is transported to a remote place by the talking dog Sebastian.

1789 Kotzwinkle, William. *The Bear Went Over the Mountain* (10–12). 1996, Doubleday $22.50 (0-385-48428-3). A satirical fantasy in which a humanlike bear named Hal Jam finds a manuscript under a tree and heads to New York to have it published. (Rev: SLJ 12/96)

1790 Kretzer-Malvehy, Terry. *Passage to Little Bighorn* (6–12). 1999, Northland paper $6.95 (0-87358-713-8). In this fantasy, Dakota Miles, a half-Lakota, half-Caucasian 15-year-old boy, time travels to the Battle of Little Bighorn. (Rev: BL 5/15/99; SLJ 6/99; VOYA 10/99)

1791 Kurtz, Katherine. *Camber of Culdi* (10–12). 1987, Ballantine paper $4.95 (0-345-34767-6). In this first volume of the Legends of Camber of Culdi series the Deryni, a race with unusual mental powers, revolt against their cruel masters. Others in the series are *Saint Camber* and *Camber the Heretic* (both 1987).

1792 Kurtz, Katherine, and Deborah T. Harris. *The Adept* (9–12). 1991, Berkley paper $5.99 (0-441-00343-5). Strange events in museums, ruined abbeys, and Loch Ness lead Adam Sinclair, a Scottish psychiatrist, to the discovery that evil magic is being revived. (Rev: BL 3/1/91; SLJ 9/91)

1793 Kurtz, Katherine, and Deborah T. Harris. *The Adept, No. 3: The Templar Treasure* (9–12). 1993, Berkley paper $6.50 (0-441-00345-1). Psychiatrist Adam Sinclair and companions call upon the powers of King Solomon and the Knights Templar to prevent a crazed academic from freeing the powers of evil. (Rev: BL 6/1–15/93; VOYA 10/93)

1794 Lackey, Mercedes. *The Eagle and the Nightingales* (9–12). (Bardic Voices) 1995, Baen $22.00 (0-671-87636-8). One of the nightingales is a gypsy bard, who is up to her eyebrows in intrigues both mundane and magical at the Kingsford Faire. (Rev: BL 12/15/94; VOYA 5/95)

1795 Lackey, Mercedes. *Fiddler Fair* (9–12). 1998, Simon & Schuster paper $5.99 (0-671-87866-2). A collection of 12 fantastic stories that deal with such topics as televangelists, animals rights zealots, and old-fashioned men. (Rev: VOYA 10/98)

1796 Lackey, Mercedes. *The Fire Rose* (10–12). 1995, Baen $22.00 (0-671-87687-2). A fantasy retelling of *Beauty and the Beast,* set in San Francisco in 1905 at the time of the earthquake, in which a rich man who was partially transformed into a wolf by a magical spell is helped by an orphaned young woman. (Rev: VOYA 4/96)

1797 Lackey, Mercedes. *Firebird* (10–12). 1996, Tor $24.95 (0-312-85812-4). A retelling of the medieval Russian folktale in which an unhappy young son of a boyar makes contact with a magical bird, gains the power to speak with animals, and overcomes the evil Katschei. (Rev: BL 1/1–15/97; SLJ 5/97; VOYA 6/97)

1798 Lackey, Mercedes. *Winds of Fate* (9–12). (Mage Winds) 1991, NAL $18.95 (0-88677-489-6). Princess Elspeth, heir to Valdemar's throne, rides in search of a mage to save the realm from the magical machinations of Ancar of Hardom. (Rev: BL 8/91; SLJ 5/92)

1799 Lackey, Mercedes, and Larry Dixon. *The Silver Gryphon* (10–12). (The Mage Wars) 1996, D A W Books $21.95 (0-88677-684-8). In this third book of the series, Silverblade, a human, and Tadrith, a gryphon, are sent on a danger-filled mission to guard a remote outpost far from their peaceful city, White Gryphon. (Rev: SLJ 8/96; VOYA 8/96)

1800 Lally, Soinbhe. *A Hive for the Honeybee* (8–12). Illus. 1999, Scholastic $16.95 (0-590-51038-X). An allegory about life and work that takes place in a bee hive with such characters as Alfred, the bee poet, and Mo, a radical drone. (Rev: BL 2/1/99; SLJ 5/99; VOYA 4/99)

1801 Larson, Gary. *There's a Hair in My Dirt! A Worm's Story* (10–12). Illus. 1998, HarperCollins $15.95 (0-06-019104-X). An offbeat, macabre fantasy told by an earthworm to his son who is disgusted when he finds a human hair in his dirt and with his position in life as "the lowest of the low." (Rev: SLJ 12/98)

1802 Laumer, Keith, ed. *Dangerous Vegetables* (9–12). 1998, Baen paper $5.99 (0-671-57781-6). A collection of fantastic stories, all dealing with plant life, by such well-known authors as Bradbury, Saberhagen, and John Christopher. (Rev: VOYA 6/99)

1803 Lawhead, Stephen R. *Merlin* (10–12). 1990, Avon paper $6.99 (0-380-70889-2). The story of how Merlin prepared the world for the arrival of Arthur. (Rev: VOYA 4/89)

1804 Layefsky, Virginia. *Impossible Things* (5–8). 1998, Marshall Cavendish $14.95 (0-7614-5038-6). Twelve-year-old Brady has a number of impossible things he would like to believe, including that he can somehow find his mother who was killed in an accident and that the dragonlike creature that has hatched in his secret hiding place really exists. (Rev: SLJ 11/98)

1805 Lee, Tanith. *Black Unicorn* (7–10). Illus. 1993, Tor paper $3.99 (0-8125-2459-4). The 16-year-old daughter of a sorceress reconstructs a unicorn from a cache of golden bones that impels her to run away from her desert home to a seaside city. (Rev: BL 10/15/91; SLJ 11/91)

1806 Lee, Tanith. *Gold Unicorn* (7–10). 1994, Atheneum $15.95 (0-689-31814-6). This sequel to *Black Unicorn* continues the adventures of Tanaquil, 16, runaway daughter of an odd sorceress, after she is captured by Empress Veriam, who turns out to be her half-sister. (Rev: BL 1/15/95; SLJ 2/95; VOYA 4/95)

1807 Lee, Tanith. *Red Unicorn* (7–10). 1997, St. Martin's $20.95 (0-312-86265-2). This continuation of the fantasies *Black Unicorn* and *Gold Unicorn* tells of Tanaquil's encounters with her double, Princess Tanakil, who lives in an alternate world. (Rev: BL 6/1–15/97; VOYA 12/97)

1808 Le Guin, Ursula K. *Tehanu: The Last Book of Earthsea* (7–10). 1990, Macmillan $15.95 (0-689-31595-3). In the fourth and last of the Earthsea books, Tenar is summoned by a dying mage or wise one to teach a child the spells and magic that give the power to lead. (Rev: BL 3/1/90; SLJ 4/90; VOYA 6/90)

1809 Le Guin, Ursula K. *The Wind's Twelve Quarters* (10–12). 1995, HarperCollins paper $4.99 (0-06-105605-7). This collection includes 17 stories by Le Guin, the winner of both Hugo and Nebula awards.

1810 Le Guin, Ursula K. *A Wizard of Earthsea* (8–12). Illus. 1968, Parnassus $13.95 (0-395-27653-5). An apprentice wizard accidentally unleashes an evil power onto the land of Earthsea. Followed by *The Tombs of Atuan* and *The Farthest Shore*.

1811 L'Engle, Madeleine. *An Acceptable Time* (8–12). 1989, Farrar $18.00 (0-374-30027-5). Polly O'Keefe time travels (like her parents did years before in the Time trilogy) but this time to visit a civilization of Druids that lived 3,000 years ago. (Rev: BL 1/1/90; BR 5–6/90; SLJ 1/90; VOYA 4/90)

1812 Levin, Betty. *The Banished* (5–8). 1999, Greenwillow $16.00 (0-688-16602-4). An engaging prequel to *The Ice Bear*, in which Siri must make a dangerous sea journey to deliver an ice bear to her people's king. (Rev: BL 8/99; SLJ 10/99)

1813 Levine, Gail C. *Ella Enchanted* (5–8). 1997, HarperCollins LB $15.89 (0-06-027511-1); paper $5.95 (0-06-440705-5). A superb, cleverly plotted retelling of the Cinderella story. (Rev: BL 4/15/97; BR 1–2/98; SLJ 4/97*; VOYA 8/97)

1814 Levitin, Sonia. *The Cure* (6–9). 1999, Harcourt $16.00 (0-15-201827-1). In the 25th century, Gemm, because he is unconventional, is sent to 14th-century Strasbourg, where, as a Jew, he experiences terrible anti-Semitism as part of his cure. (Rev: BL 6/1–15/99; BR 9–10/99; SLJ 5/99; VOYA 6/99)

1815 Levy, Robert. *Clan of the Shape-Changers* (6–9). 1994, Houghton $13.95 (0-395-66612-0). The hair-raising adventures of Susan, 16, and young Jeffrey, who are shape-changers being pursued by the evil shaman Ometerer. (Rev: BL 4/1/94; SLJ 5/94; VOYA 6/94)

1816 Levy, Robert. *Escape from Exile* (6–8). 1993, Houghton $16.00 (0-395-64379-1). Daniel, 13, is struck by lightning and transported to Lithia, where his new telepathic powers help him cope with a bitter civil war. (Rev: BL 3/15/93; SLJ 5/93; VOYA 8/93)

1817 Lewis, C. S. *The Lion, the Witch and the Wardrobe* (5–8). Illus. 1988, Macmillan LB $22.95 (0-02-758200-0). Four children enter the kingdom of Narnia through the back of an old wardrobe. The other 6 volumes in this series are *Prince Caspian*, *The Voyage of the Dawn Treader*, *The Silver Chair* (1986), *The Horse and His Boy*, *The Magician's Nephew*, and *The Last Battle.*

1818 Lindbergh, Anne. *Three Lives to Live* (6–8). 1995, Pocket Books paper $3.50 (0-671-86732-6). A teenager discovers that her laundry chute is a conduit through time and that she, her grandmother, and her little sister are all the same person. (Rev: BL 4/15/92; SLJ 6/92)

1819 Lipsyte, Robert. *The Chemo Kid* (9–12). 1992, HarperCollins $14.00 (0-06-020284-X). A high school junior gains superhuman strength after undergoing cancer treatments. (Rev: BL 3/1/92; SLJ 3/92)

1820 Lisle, Holly. *In the Rift: Glenraven II* (9–12). (Glenraven) 1998, Simon & Schuster $21.00 (0-671-87870-0). Kate focuses her magical powers to help a group of wanderers return home to their parallel world of Glenraven. (Rev: VOYA 10/98)

1821 Lowry, Lois. *The Giver* (6–9). 1993, Houghton $14.95 (0-395-64566-2); 1994, Dell paper $5.99 (0-440-21907-8). A dystopian fantasy in which Jonas receives his life assignment as Receiver of Memory and learns that a land with no war, poverty, fear, or hardship is also one where "misfits" are killed. Newbery Medal, 1994. (Rev: BL 4/15/93*; SLJ 5/93*; VOYA 8/93)

1822 Lyon, George E. *Here and Then* (6–8). 1994, Orchard $15.95 (0-531-06866-8). Abby, 13, becomes connected across time to Eliza, a nurse she portrays in a Civil War reenactment, and goes back in time to help her. (Rev: BL 10/1/94; SLJ 10/94; VOYA 10/94)

1823 Macaulay, David. *Baaa* (7–12). Illus. 1985, Houghton $13.95 (0-395-38948-8); paper $5.95 (0-395-39588-7). An allegory about the world after humans have left and intelligent sheep take control. (Rev: BL 9/1/85; BR 3–4/86; SLJ 10/85)

1824 McCaffrey, Anne. *Acorna's Quest* (9–12). 1998, HarperCollins $23.00 (0-06-105297-3). In this sequel to *Acorna: The Unicorn Girl* (1997), the humanoid Acorna leaves with her friend Calum to

search for the survival pod she came from and her home world. (Rev: VOYA 10/98)

1825 McCaffrey, Anne. *All the Weyrs of Pern* (9–12). (Pern) 1992, Tor paper $6.99 (0-345-36893-2). In this sequel to *Dragonsdawn,* human settlers of Pern rediscover their original landing site and revitalize a long-lost artificial intelligence system. (Rev: BL 10/1/91*)

1826 McCaffrey, Anne. *Damia's Children* (9–12). 1993, 1994, Berkley paper $6.99 (0-441-00007-X). The saga of a telepathic/telekinetic family and alien contact, with teenage main characters. (Rev: BL 12/1/92; SLJ 11/93)

1827 McCaffrey, Anne. *Dragonflight* (6–12). Adapted by Brynne Stephens. Illus. (Dragonriders of Pern) 1991, Eclipse Books $4.95 (1-56060-074-8). Book one of a 3-part graphic novel based on *Dragonflight* from the Dragonriders of Pern series. (Rev: BL 9/1/91)

1828 McCaffrey, Anne. *Dragonseye* (10–12). (Dragonriders of Pern) 1997, Ballantine $24.00 (0-345-38821-6). In this Dragonriders of Pern story, most of the riders want to prepare for the approach of the Red Star and the dreaded Thread, but Lord Holder, their abusive leader, refuses to take any action. (Rev: BL 12/15/96; SLJ 7/97)

1829 McCaffrey, Anne. *The Girl Who Heard Dragons* (9–12). 1995, Tor $3.99 (0-8125-1099-2). Fifteen short fiction pieces that demonstrate the range and scope of the author's work. (Rev: BL 3/15/94; VOYA 10/94)

1830 McCaffrey, Anne. *If Wishes Were Horses* (7–12). 1998, NAL $13.95 (0-451-45642-4). When Tirza turns 16 and earns her own magic crystal, she wishes for a horse for her twin brother—with unexpected results. (Rev: VOYA 2/99)

1831 McCaffrey, Anne. *The MasterHarper of Pern* (10–12). 1998, Ballantine $25.00 (0-345-38823-2). In this Pern novel (set prior to *Dragonflight*), the reader is told the story of the beloved harper Robinton—of rejection by his father during his childhood, the loss of his wife and best friend, and his career before he becomes Masterharper of Pern. (Rev: BL 10/15/97; SLJ 8/98; VOYA 8/98)

1832 McCaffrey, Anne. *Nerilka's Story: A Pern Adventure* (9–12). 1986, Ballantine paper $5.99 (0-345-33949-5). A young girl leaves her Hold to help nurse the sick stricken with a terrible plague. (Rev: BL 3/1/86; SLJ 5/86)

1833 McCaffrey, Anne. *No One Noticed the Cat* (5–8). 1996, Roc paper $13.95 (0-451-45578-9). Niffy, an extraordinary cat, protects her young master, Prince Jamas, when he is threatened by the wicked King Egdril. (Rev: VOYA 4/97)

1834 McCaffrey, Anne. *The Renegades of Pern* (9–12). 1989, Ballantine paper $19.95 (0-345-34096-5). The adult Dragonriders series and the juvenile Harper Hall books are brought together by mixing their characters in this fantasy that takes place in the southern part of Pern. (Rev: BL 9/15/89; VOYA 4/90)

1835 McKenzie, Ellen Kindt. *A Bowl of Mischief* (5–8). 1992, Holt $14.95 (0-8050-2090-X). The clever mischief of young Ranjii, combined with visions, dreams, portents, and luck, leads to the freeing of the ruler Superus and his people. (Rev: BL 11/15/92; SLJ 11/92)

1836 McKenzie, Ellen Kindt. *The Golden Band of Eddris* (6–9). 1998, Holt $16.95 (0-8050-4389-6). A brother and sister combat the forces of evil that are terrorizing the land of Adnor in this complex fantasy. (Rev: BL 2/15/98; SLJ 3/98; VOYA 4/98)

1837 McKiernan, Dennis L. *Caverns of Socrates* (9–12). 1995, Penguin $24.95 (0-451-45455-3); paper $14.95 (0-451-45476-6). Role-playing meets virtual reality, and both meet a mad computer. (Rev: BL 12/15/95; VOYA 4/96)

1838 McKillip, Patricia A. *The Changeling Sea* (7–9). 1989, Ballantine paper $4.99 (0-345-36040-0). An unhappy young girl causes a giant monster to rise from the sea. (Rev: BL 9/15/88; BR 1–2/89; SLJ 11/88; VOYA 12/88)

1839 McKillip, Patricia A. *The Cygnet and the Firebird* (9–12). 1993, Berkley paper $17.95 (0-441-12628-6). *The Sorceress and the Cygnet*'s (1991) sequel shows cousins Nyx Ro and Meguet Vervaine encountering a sorcerer in search of an ancient key, a firebird with amnesia, and a city of dragons. (Rev: BL 9/15/93; SLJ 5/94; VOYA 12/93)

1840 McKillip, Patricia A. *Winter Rose* (10–12). 1996, Ace paper $19.95 (0-441-00334-6). Rois must cross the threshold between worlds to save her sister and rescue Corbet, whom both she and her sister love, from a curse that is keeping him a prisoner of winter. (Rev: BL 7/96; VOYA 2/97)

1841 McKinley, Robin. *Beauty: A Retelling of the Story of Beauty and the Beast* (9–12). 1978, HarperCollins $15.95 (0-06-024149-7). From the standpoint of Beauty, this is the story of her quest in the forest where she encounters Beast. (Rev: BL 6/1/88)

1842 McKinley, Robin. *The Blue Sword* (7–10). 1982, Greenwillow $16.00 (0-688-00938-7). The king of Damar kidnaps a girl to help in his war against the Northerners. A prequel to *The Hero and the Crown*. Newbery Medal 1985. (Rev: BL 12/15/89)

1843 McKinley, Robin. *The Door in the Hedge* (7–9). 1981, Greenwillow $15.00 (0-688-00312-5). Four tales, 2 of which originated in the folklore of the Grimm Brothers.

1844 McKinley, Robin. *A Knot in the Grain and Other Stories* (9–12). 1994, Greenwillow $14.00 (0-688-09201-2). Four love stories set in Damar, a world mixing the real and the magical, featuring magicians, witches, and healers. (Rev: BL 8/94; SLJ 5/94; VOYA 10/94)

1845 McKinley, Robin. *Rose Daughter* (6–12). Illus. 1997, Greenwillow $16.00 (0-688-15439-5). As in her award-winning *Beauty*, the author returns to the Beauty and Beast fairy tale in this outstanding reworking of the traditional story. (Rev: BL 8/97; BR 11–12/97; SLJ 9/97; VOYA 2/98) [398.2]

1846 McKinley, Robin. *The Stone Fey* (6–10). Illus. 1998, Harcourt $17.00 (0-15-200017-8). A fantasy in which young Maddy temporarily falls in love with a stone fey while her fiancé is away earning money for their future together. (Rev: BL 11/1/98; SLJ 1/99)

1847 Mahy, Margaret. *The Changeover: A Supernatural Romance* (8–12). 1984, Macmillan $16.00 (0-689-50303-2). To save her brother from an evil force, Laura must use the powers of witchcraft.

1848 Marsden, John. *Tomorrow, When the War Began* (9–12). 1995, Houghton $15.00 (0-395-70673-4). A girl and her friends return from a camping trip in the bush to find that Australia has been invaded and their families taken prisoner. (Rev: BL 4/15/95; SLJ 6/95)

1849 Marston, Ann. *Kingmaker's Sword* (10–12). 1996, HarperCollins paper $5.99 (0-06-105629-4). In this first book of the Rune Blade trilogy, a boy raised as a slave realizes that he is destined to be the bearer of one of the Ceale Rune Blades and form a ruling dynasty. Followed by *The Western King* and *Broken Blade*. (Rev: VOYA 8/97)

1850 Massie, Elizabeth. *Maryland: The Night the Harbor Lights Went Out* (5–8). 1995, Z-Fave paper $3.50 (0-8217-5059-3). In this time travel story, 2 teenage girls, one an African American slave trying to escape from Baltimore in 1849, and the other, a contemporary white eighth-grader on a field trip to the Baltimore aquarium, exchange places. (Rev: VOYA 2/96)

1851 Matas, Carol, and Perry Nodelman. *More Minds* (6–8). 1996, Simon & Schuster paper $16.00 (0-689-80388-5). Rebellious Princess Lenora and her clairvoyant fiancé, Coren, set out to find the giant that is terrorizing the land. (Rev: SLJ 10/96; VOYA 6/97)

1852 Matas, Carol, and Perry Nodelman. *Of Two Minds* (5–8). 1995, Simon & Schuster paper $16.00 (0-689-80138-6). Two youths, trapped in a strange land and stripped of their power of ESP, must work together to triumph over evil. (Rev: SLJ 10/95; VOYA 4/96)

1853 Matas, Carol, and Perry Nodelman. *Out of Their Minds* (5–8). Illus. 1998, Simon & Schuster $16.00 (0-689-81946-3). In this fantasy (the third in the Minds series), Princess Lenora and Prince Coren journey to Andilla to marry but find that some force is upsetting The Balance. Could it be the evil Hevak again trying to gain power? (Rev: SLJ 9/98; VOYA 2/99)

1854 Melling, Orla. *The Druid's Tune* (6–10). 1993, O'Brien Pr. paper $9.95 (0-86278-285-6). Peter, a Druid lost in the 20th century, involves 2 teenagers in a time-travel spell that sends them back to Ireland's Iron Age. (Rev: BL 2/15/93)

1855 Michaels, Melisa C. *Far Harbor* (9–12). 1989, Tor paper $2.99 (0-8125-4581-8). A fantasy romance in which a clumsy, lanky girl meets the prince of her dreams. (Rev: VOYA 12/89)

1856 Modesitt, L. E., Jr. *The Soprano Sorceress* (9–12). 1997, Tor $25.95 (0-312-86022-6). Anna is transported in time to the land of Erde, where she can use her beautiful voice to create magic. (Rev: BL 2/1/97; VOYA 10/97)

1857 Morpurgo, Michael. *Little Foxes* (6–9). 1987, David & Charles $15.95 (0-7182-3972-5). Two orphans—a boy and a fox—are helped by a swan in this magical story. (Rev: BR 1–2/88; SLJ 9/87)

1858 Morpurgo, Michael. *The War of Jenkins' Ear* (6–9). 1995, Putnam $16.95 (0-399-22735-0). Set in England at a prep school, Toby meets a boy who is different from the rest, taking the role of peacemaker. Could this unusual boy be Jesus disguised as a British schoolboy? (Rev: BL 9/1/95; SLJ 9/95; VOYA 12/95)

1859 Murphy, Shirley Rousseau. *Cat Raise the Dead* (9–12). 1997, HarperCollins paper $5.99 (0-06-105602-2). Two intrepid cats, Joe Grey and Dulcie, investigate some burglaries and several disappearances at an old folks home in their seaside village in California. (Rev: VOYA 2/98)

1860 Murphy, Shirley Rousseau. *The Catswold Portal* (9–12). 1993, NAL paper $6.99 (0-451-45275-5). Feline fantasy set on 1957 Earth, as well as in the Netherworld, ties an evil queen and a human artist together. (Rev: BL 4/15/92*; SLJ 8/92)

1861 Myers, Walter Dean. *The Legend of Tarik* (6–9). 1991, Scholastic paper $3.50 (0-590-44426-3). Tarik, a black teenager in Africa of years ago, acquires a magic sword.

1862 Napoli, Donna Jo. *Zel* (7–12). 1996, Dutton $15.99 (0-525-4561-0). Set in fifteenth-century Switzerland, this is a brilliant reworking of the *Rapunzel* fairy tale told from 3 different points of view. (Rev: BL 9/1/96; BR 9–10/97)

1863 Napoli, Donna Jo, and Richard Tchen. *Spinners* (8–12). 1999, Dutton $15.99 (0-525-46065-9).

Fifteen-year-old Saskia is saved by the mysterious spinner Rumpelstiltskin, whose secret is that he is the girl's father. (Rev: BL 9/1/99; SLJ 9/99; VOYA 12/99)

1864 Naylor, Phyllis Reynolds. *Sang Spell* (6–9). 1998, Simon & Schuster $16.00 (0-689-82007-0). Recently orphaned, Josh wanders into a magical village inhabited by descendants of colonists who settled in North America before Jamestown. (Rev: BL 9/15/98; SLJ 10/98; VOYA 2/99)

1865 Niles, Douglas. *A Breach in the Watershed* (10–12). 1995, Ace paper $13.00 (0-441-00208-0). The beginning of a fantasy series in which the land of Watershed is threatened by the power of the Sleepstealer and his minions. Followed by *Darkenheight* (1996). (Rev: VOYA 6/97)

1866 Nimmo, Jenny. *Griffin's Castle* (5–8). 1997, Orchard LB $17.99 (0-531-33006-0). When Dinah and her young mother, Rosalie, move into the run-down mansion owned by Rosalie's boyfriend, Dinah brings to life several carved animals for protection. (Rev: SLJ 6/97; VOYA 8/97)

1867 Niven, Larry, ed. *The Magic Goes Away* (10–12). 1985, Ace paper $4.99 (0-441-51554-1). The first novel in a trilogy about a land where magic is used for both good and evil. It is followed by: *The Magic May Return*.

1868 Nodelman, Perry. *A Completely Different Place* (5–8). 1997, Simon & Schuster paper $16.00 (0-689-80836-4). Johnny awakes from a nightmare to find that he has shrunk in size and is in the land of the green-skinned Strangers. (Rev: BL 7/97; SLJ 6/97; VOYA 8/97)

1869 Nodelman, Perry. *The Same Place but Different* (5–9). 1995, Simon & Schuster paper $15.00 (0-671-89839-6). A teen visits the land of Strangers, evil fairies, to rescue his sister. In this reversal of expectations, good fairies and benevolent creatures become sinister and terrifying. (Rev: BL 10/1/95)

1870 Norton, Andre. *Gryphon's Eyrie* (10–12). Illus. 1992, Tor paper $3.99 (0-8125-3169-8). In this installment of the Witch World series, 2 young lovers tell, in alternating chapters, of their war against the Dark.

1871 Norton, Andre. *The Monster's Legacy* (7–10). 1996, Simon & Schuster $17.00 (0-689-80731-7). In this novel, part of the *Dragonflight* series, a young apprentice embroiderer and her 2 friends flee invaders and escape to a land inhabited by Loden, a monster who preys on humans. (Rev: BL 4/1/96; SLJ 6/96; VOYA 8/96)

1872 Norton, Andre. *Moon Mirror* (10–12). 1989, Tor paper $4.99 (0-8125-0303-1). Nine short fantasies about such subjects as ESP, witches, magic, and quests. (Rev: BL 1/1/89; VOYA 6/89)

1873 Norton, Andre, and Martin H. Greenberg, eds. *Catfantastic IV* (9–12). 1996, D A W Books paper $5.99 (0-88677-711-9). This is the fourth collection of original stories about cats in fantastic situations. (Rev: VOYA 12/96)

1874 Norton, Andre, and Lyn McConchie. *Ciara's Song: A Chronicle of Witch World* (9–12). 1998, Warner paper $6.50 (0-446-60644-8). After her family, which has a witch ancestry, is murdered by a mob, Ciara is raised by the powerful Tarnoor, and under his protection she discovers her magical healing powers and dangers that they hold for her. (Rev: BL 6/1–15/98; VOYA 12/98)

1875 Norton, Andre, and Lyn McConchie. *The Key of the Keplian* (9–12). 1995, Warner paper $5.50 (0-446-60220-5). A part-Native American, part-Celtic girl passes into Witch World, where she must develop her own magic to survive in the realm. (Rev: BL 7/95; VOYA 2/96)

1876 Nye, Jody Lynn. *Magic Touch* (8–12). 1996, Warner paper $5.99 (0-446-60210-8). In this fantasy, Ray, a young black man, helps save members of the fairy godpersons union who have been captured by a wicked genie seeking to capture their magic. (Rev: VOYA 6/96)

1877 O'Donohoe, Nick. *Under the Healing Sign* (9–12). 1995, Berkley paper $4.99 (0-441-00180-7). In this sequel to *The Magic and the Healing* (o.p.), the community fights an amoral villain, which brings back veterinarian B. J. Vaugh. (Rev: BL 3/15/95; VOYA 5/95)

1878 Ogiwara, Noriko. *Dragon Sword and Wild Child* (7–10). Trans. by Cathy Hirano. 1993, Farrar $17.00 (0-374-30466-1). Drawing on Japanese mythology, this story centers on Saya, who learns that she is the reincarnation of the Water Maiden, dedicated to the Goddess of Darkness. (Rev: BL 8/93; VOYA 8/93)

1879 Oppel, Kenneth. *Silverwing* (5–9). 1997, Simon & Schuster paper $16.00 (0-689-81529-8). The existence of the bat colony is threatened when a newborn Silverwing bat challenges a stronger bat to commit a forbidden act, to look at the sun. (Rev: SLJ 10/97; VOYA 4/98)

1880 Orgel, Doris. *The Princess and the God* (7–10). 1996, Orchard LB $16.99 (0-531-08866-9); Bantam paper $4.50 (0-440-22691-0). A handsome retelling of the Cupid and Psyche myth in novel format, in which the power of pure love is shown conquering overwhelming obstacles. (Rev: BL 2/1/96; BR 9–10/96; SLJ 4/96)

1881 Orwell, George. *Animal Farm* (9–12). Illus. 1983, NAL paper $5.95 (0-451-52634-1). A fantasy of world politics in which farm animals revolt to form a society in which everyone is meant to be equal.

1882 Osborne, Mary P. *Haunted Waters* (7–10). 1994, Candlewick $14.95 (1-56402-119-X). Lord Huldbrand travels through a demon-haunted peninsula and falls in love with the sea-loving Undine, but the demon follows them. (Rev: BL 11/1/94; SLJ 12/94; VOYA 2/95)

1883 O'Shea, Pat. *The Hounds of the Morrigan* (6–8). 1986, Holiday House $15.95 (0-8234-0595-8). The forces of good and evil in Irish mythology battle over 2 children who are on a quest for a magic pebble. (Rev: BL 4/1/86; SLJ 3/86)

1884 Pattou, E. *Fire Arrow* (7–10). 1998, Harcourt $18.00 (0-15-201635-X); paper $0.00 (0-15-202264-3). In this sequel to *Hero's Song,* Brie sets out to avenge the death of her father by confronting his torturer. (Rev: BL 5/15/98; SLJ 7/98; VOYA 10/98)

1885 Pattou, Edith. *Hero's Song* (7–10). 1991, Harcourt $16.95 (0-15-233807-1). This fantasy-quest novel, infused with Irish myth and folklore, concerns a youth's search for his beloved sister, a wicked queen, and a clash between good and evil. (Rev: BL 10/15/91; SLJ 1/92)

1886 Paxson, Diana. *The Book of the Spear* (10–12). 1999, Avon paper $10.00 (0-380-80546-4). In this, the second part of a reworking of the Arthurian legend, Oesc, a Saxon warrior, uses his magic spear to combat the powers of Arthur's sword. (Rev: SLJ 8/99)

1887 Peck, Richard. *Voices after Midnight* (6–9). 1990, Dell paper $4.50 (0-440-40378-2). A 14-year-old boy and his family move to a brownstone in Manhattan and soon become involved with events and people of 100 years ago. (Rev: BL 10/1/89; BR 11–12/89; SLJ 9/89; VOYA 2/90)

1888 Pierce, Tamora. *Briar's Book* (6–9). (Circle of Magic) 1999, Scholastic $15.95 (0-590-55359-3). In this fantasy, Brier, former street urchin and petty thief, and his teacher, Rosethorn, search for the cause of a deadly plague that is sweeping through their land. (Rev: BL 2/15/99; SLJ 3/99; VOYA 6/99)

1889 Pierce, Tamora. *Daja's Book* (5–9). (Circle of Magic) 1998, Scholastic $15.95 (0-590-55358-5). Daja Kisubo, a mage-in-training, creates a living vine out of metal that nomadic traders seek to own. (Rev: BL 12/1/98; SLJ 12/98; VOYA 2/99)

1890 Pierce, Tamora. *The Realms of the Gods* (6–10). (The Immortals) 1996, Simon & Schuster $17.00 (0-689-31990-8). In this fourth volume of The Immortals series, Daine and the mage Numair triumph over evil Stormwing and Uusoae, the Queen of Chaos. (Rev: BL 10/15/96; SLJ 11/96; VOYA 4/97)

1891 Pierce, Tamora. *Sandry's Book* (6–9). (Circle of Magic) 1997, Scholastic $15.95 (0-590-55356-9).

Four misfits are brought to Winding Circle Temple to learn new magical crafts in this first volume of a fantasy series. (Rev: BL 9/1/97; BR 11–12/97; SLJ 9/97; VOYA 12/97)

1892 Pierce, Tamora. *Tris's Book* (6–9). (Circle of Magic) 1998, Scholastic $21.99 (0-590-55357-7). Tris, a young mage, must control her talents and her temper to save her friends from marauding pirates in this sequel to *Sandry's Book*. (Rev: BL 8/98; SLJ 4/98; VOYA 8/98)

1893 Pierce, Tamora. *Wild Magic: The Immortals* (6–10). 1992, Atheneum $17.00 (0-689-31761-1). An exciting tale in which teenager Daine gradually accepts the fact that she possesses wild magic. (Rev: BL 10/15/92; SLJ 11/92)

1894 Pierce, Tamora. *Wolf-Speaker* (7–9). 1994, Atheneum $16.00 (0-689-31833-2). A girl who speaks the language of animals works to help humans and animals move beyond species prejudice to prevent an ecological disaster. (Rev: BL 3/15/94; SLJ 5/94; VOYA 8/94)

1895 Pope, Elizabeth Marie. *The Perilous Gard* (9–12). 1992, Puffin paper $5.99 (0-14-034912-X). Kate wants to save Christopher who has given himself as a sacrifice to the Fairy folk. Also use *The Sherwood Ring* (Peter Smith, 1990).

1896 Porte, Barbara Ann. *Hearsay: Tales from the Middle Kingdom* (5–8). Illus. 1998, Greenwillow $15.00 (0-688-15381-X). Each of these 15 entertaining fantasies contains elements of Chinese folklore and culture. (Rev: BR 11–12/98; SLJ 6/98)

1897 Pratchett, Terry. *Jingo: A Novel of Discworld* (10–12). 1998, HarperCollins $24.00 (0-06-105047-4). In this clever, unpredictable Discworld novel, the cities of Ankh-Morpork and Al-Khali quarrel over which has the right to annex the newly found island of Leshp. (Rev: BL 6/1–15/98; SLJ 8/98; VOYA 12/98)

1898 Price, Susan. *Ghost Dance: The Czar's Black Angel* (7–9). 1994, Farrar $16.00 (0-374-32537-5). A young shaman apprentice, Shingebiss, is moved by the plight of the Northmen, who are worried about their land being destroyed by the czar's orders. (Rev: BL 11/15/94; SLJ 12/94)

1899 Price, Susan. *Ghost Song* (6–9). 1992, Farrar $15.00 (0-374-32544-8). A fantasy set in the far North, where the heroes must battle cold, darkness, and powerful beings from other worlds. (Rev: BL 9/15/92*; SLJ 1/93)

1900 Prince, Maggie. *The House on Hound Hill* (6–10). 1998, Houghton $15.00 (0-395-90702-0). When Emily and her family move to a historic house in London, she is gradually drawn into time traveling to the 17th century and a London beset with the

bubonic plague. (Rev: BL 11/15/98; SLJ 9/98; VOYA 2/99)

1901 Pullman, Philip. *The Golden Compass* (7–12). 1996, Knopf $20.00 (0-679-87924-2); Ballantine paper $5.99 (0-345-41335-0). In this first book of a fantasy trilogy, young Lyre and her alter ego, a protective animal named Pantalaimon, escape from the child-stealing Gobblers and join a group heading north to rescue a band of missing children. (Rev: BL 3/1/96*; BR 9–10/96; SLJ 4/96)

1902 Pullman, Philip. *The Subtle Knife* (7–12). 1997, Random $20.00 (0-679-87925-0); Ballantine paper $5.99 (0-345-41336-9). In this second volume of the Dark Materials trilogy, Will and Lyra travel from world to world searching for the mysterious Dust and Will's long-lost father. (Rev: BL 7/97; SLJ 10/97)

1903 Pullman, Philip. *The Tin Princess* (9–12). 1994, Knopf $16.00 (0-679-84757-X). In the tiny Germanic kingdom of Razkavia, Adelaide, the unlikely Cockney queen, and her companion/translator, Becky Winter, are involved in political intrigue and romance. (Rev: BL 2/15/94; SLJ 4/94; VOYA 8/94)

1904 Purtill, Richard. *Enchantment at Delphi* (6–9). 1986, Harcourt $14.95 (0-15-200447-5). On a trip to Delphi, Alice finds herself transported back in time to the days of Apollo and other Greek gods. (Rev: SLJ 11/86)

1905 Rabkin, Eric S., ed. *Fantastic Worlds: Myths, Tales and Stories* (10–12). 1979, Oxford paper $16.95 (0-19-502541-5). A classic collection of fantasy and some science fiction from the ancient Greeks to the present.

1906 Rawn, Melanie. *The Mageborn Traitor* (10–12). 1997, D A W Books paper $23.95 (0-88677-730-5). On Lenfell, Cailet who dreams of creating her own mage academy, finds her plans thwarted by her sister, who is allied with the evil Malerrisi. (Rev: VOYA 10/97)

1907 Rawn, Melanie, et al. *The Golden Key* (10–12). 1996, D A W Books paper $24.95 (0-88677-691-0). A tour-de-force in which 3 authors have each written a third of this saga about the Limners, master painters whose masterpieces come to life. (Rev: VOYA 2/97)

1908 Reichet, Mickey Zucker, and Jennifer Wingert. *Spirit Fox* (9–12). 1998, D A W Books $23.95 (0-88677-806-9). Kiarda is born at the moment that an orphaned fox is killed, and in later life, the animal's spirit gradually turns her into a fox. (Rev: VOYA 6/99)

1909 Reiss, Kathryn. *Pale Phoenix* (7–10). 1994, Harcourt $10.95 (0-15-200030-5); paper $3.95 (0-15-200031-3). Miranda Browne's parents take in an orphan girl who can disappear at will and who was the victim of a tragedy in a past life in Puritan Massachusetts. (Rev: BL 3/15/94; SLJ 5/94; VOYA 6/94)

1910 Reiss, Kathryn. *Paperquake: A Puzzle* (5–8). 1998, Harcourt $17.00 (0-15-201183-8). In this novel set in contemporary San Francisco, Violet receives a message from a girl who lived during the 1906 earthquake warning her of a disaster soon to come. (Rev: BL 5/15/98; SLJ 6/98; VOYA 6/98)

1911 Reiss, Kathryn. *Time Windows* (6–9). 1991, Harcourt $17.00 (0-15-288205-7). Miranda, age 13, finds a dollhouse in the attic that replicates the details of her new home. When she looks inside, she witnesses disturbing past events. (Rev: BL 11/1/91; SLJ 10/91)

1912 Roberson, Jennifer. *Sword-Born: A Novel of Tiger & Del* (10–12). (Sword Dancer Saga) 1998, D A W Books $24.95 (0-88677-776-3). Two homeless wanderers, Tiger, a former slave of unknown origin, and his companion, Delila, travel to Skandi seeking Tiger's heritage and are captured by pirates in this novel that explores relationships and various types of power and control. (Rev: SLJ 8/98; VOYA 8/98)

1913 Roberts, Laura P. *Ghost of a Chance* (6–9). 1997, Delacorte $14.95 (0-385-32508-8). Melissa must deal with her feelings about her parents' divorce and jealousy of her best friend Chloe when they both fall in love with James, a ghost. (Rev: BR 3–4/98; SLJ 10/97)

1914 Rodowsky, Colby. *Keeping Time* (7–9). 1983, Farrar $11.95 (0-374-34061-7). Drew is mysteriously transported to Elizabethan London where he forms new friendships.

1915 Rogers, Mark E. *Samurai Cat Goes to the Movies* (9–12). 1994, Tor paper $10.95 (0-312-85744-6). Japanese feline Miowara and his nephew, Shiro, take on Hollywood and satirize assorted film classics. (Rev: BL 9/15/94; VOYA 4/95)

1916 Rowling, J. K. *Harry Potter and the Chamber of Secrets* (4–8). 1999, Scholastic $17.95 (0-439-06486-4). In this highly celebrated sequel to *Harry Potter and the Sorcerer's Stone,* Harry Potter spends a second, very eventful year at Hogwarts School for Witchcraft and Wizardry. (Rev: BL 5/15/99; BR 9–10/99; SLJ 7/99; VOYA 10/99)

1917 Rowling, J. K. *Harry Potter and the Prisoner of Azkaban* (4–8). Illus. 1999, Scholastic $19.95 (0-439-13625-0). In this Harry Potter adventure, a murderer has escaped from prison and is after our young hero. (Rev: BL 9/1/99)

1918 Rowling, J. K. *Harry Potter and the Sorcerer's Stone* (5–8). Illus. 1998, Scholastic $16.95 (0-590-35340-3). In this humorous and suspenseful story, 11-year-old Harry Potter attends the Hogwarts School of Witchcraft and Wizardry, where he dis-

covers that he is a wizard just as his parents had been and that someone at the school is trying to steal a valuable stone with the power to make people immortal. (Rev: BL 9/15/98; SLJ 10/98; VOYA 12/98)

1919 Rubinstein, Gillian. *Foxspell* (7–9). Illus. 1996, Simon & Schuster $16.00 (0-689-80602-7). In this fantasy, a troubled boy is tempted by a fox spirit to receive peace and immortality if he will assume a fox shape forever. (Rev: BL 10/15/96; SLJ 9/96; VOYA 12/96)

1920 Rubinstein, Gillian. *Under the Cat's Eye: A Tale of Morph & Mystery* (6–9). 1998, Simon & Schuster $16.00 (0-689-81800-9). Jai realizes that there's something strange about his new boarding school, particularly after discovering that 2 of the hired help are shapechangers, in this story that includes mistaken identity, time travel, mystery, fantasy, and animals. (Rev: BL 8/98; SLJ 10/98; VOYA 10/98)

1921 Russell, Barbara T. *Blue Lightning* (4–8). 1997, Viking $14.99 (0-670-87023-4). Calvin dies but returns to life, only to find that the ghost of another boy, Rory, who "died" at the same time, has followed him and won't leave him alone. (Rev: BL 2/15/97; SLJ 2/97)

1922 Russell, Barbara T. *The Taker's Stone* (7–12). 1999, DK Publg. $16.95 (1-7894-2568-8). When 14-year-old Fischer steals some glowing red gemstones from a man at a campsite, he unleashes the terrible evil of Belial, some catastrophic weather, and the beginning of the end of the world. (Rev: VOYA 10/99)

1923 Russell, P. Craig. *Fairy Tales of Oscar Wilde, Vol. 3: The Birthday of the Infanta* (5–8). Illus. 1998, N B M Publg. $15.95 (1-56163-213-9). In this comic book-graphics book, Wilde's fairy tale about the misshapen dwarf who dies of a broken heart over his love for a princess is retold. (Rev: BL 4/1/99)

1924 Rylant, Cynthia. *The Islander* (5–8). 1998, DK Publg. $14.95 (0-7894-2490-8). Growing up on a lonely island off the coast of British Columbia with his grandfather, Daniel encounters a mermaid and, through her, learns about his family. (Rev: BL 2/1/98; SLJ 3/98; VOYA 8/98)

1925 Saint-Exupery, Antoine de. *The Little Prince* (5–9). Trans. by Katherine Woods. 1943, Harcourt $16.00 (0-15-246503-0); paper $11.00 (0-15-646511-6). An airplane pilot crashes in a desert and encounters a little prince who seeks harmony for his planet.

1926 Salsitz, Rhondi V. *The Twilight Gate* (6–10). Illus. 1993, Walker $25.95 (0-8027-8213-2). Distressed by the upheaval disrupting their lives, teen George and his younger sisters seek protection through magic and instead upset the balance between light and darkness. (Rev: BL 4/15/93; SLJ 5/93; VOYA 8/93)

1927 Salvatore, R. A. *The Dragon's Dagger* (9–12). 1994, Berkley paper $6.50 (0-441-00078-9). Gary Leger, the reluctant hero of Faerie, must return to battle Robert the Dragon and the wicked witch with his magic talking lance. (Rev: BL 8/94; VOYA 12/94)

1928 Salvatore, R. A. *The Woods Out Back* (9–12). 1993, Berkley paper $6.50 (0-441-90872-1). A young factory worker's imaginative daydreams become reality when a leprechaun transports him to the fairy realm to take part in a quest. (Rev: BL 10/15/93; VOYA 2/94)

1929 Sargent, Pamela. *Climb the Wind: A Novel of Another America* (9–12). 1998, HarperCollins $25.00 (0-06-105029-6). An alternate history that poses the question, What would have happened if Native American tribes in the West had united and used modern warfare methods to stop white expansionism in the years following the Civil War? (Rev: VOYA 4/99)

1930 Scarboro, Elizabeth. *The Godmother's Apprentice* (9–12). 1995, Ace paper $19.95 (0-441-00252-8). In this fantasy, 14-year-old Sno Quantrill faces unexpected adventures and meets fantastic creatures when she flies to Ireland to become the apprentice of Dame Felicity Fortune. (Rev: BL 12/15/95; VOYA 6/96)

1931 Schimel, Lawrence. *Camelot Fantastic* (8–12). 1998, D A W Books paper $5.99 (0-88677-790-9). A collection of original novelettes written by well-known authors of fantasy, science fiction, and mystery, that present a different perspective on characters and incidents associated with King Arthur's Camelot. (Rev: VOYA 12/98)

1932 Schultz, Mark. *Dinosaur Shaman: Nine Tales from the Xenozoic Age* (9–12). 1990, Kitchen Sink $29.95 (0-87816-117-1). These stories are set in the Xenozoic Age—a future time when humans and prehistoric beasts coexist—and describe the further adventures of Jack Tennrec and Hannah Dundee. (Rev: BL 9/1/91)

1933 Sheffield, Charles. *The Ganymede Club* (9–12). 1995, Tor $23.95 (0-312-85662-8). Two teenagers foil the fiendish plots of the Ganymede Club, a small group of people who have discovered the means to immortality. (Rev: VOYA 6/96)

1934 Sherman, Josepha. *Windleaf* (7–12). 1993, Walker $22.95 (0-8027-8259-0). Count Thierry falls in love with half-faerie Glinfinial, only to have her father, the Faerie Lord, steal her away. (Rev: BL 11/1/93*; SLJ 12/93; VOYA 2/94)

1935 Shetterly, Will. *Elsewhere* (8–12). 1991, Harcourt $16.95 (0-15-200731-8). Set in Bordertown,

between the real world and Faerie world, home to runaway elves and humans, this is a fantasy of integration, survival, and coming of age. (Rev: BL 10/15/91; SLJ 11/91)

1936 Shetterly, Will. *Nevernever* (8–12). 1993, Harcourt $16.95 (0-15-257022-5); Tor paper $4.99 (0-8125-5151-6). This sequel to *Elsewhere* (1991) shows Wolfboy trying to protect Florida, the heir of Faerie, from gangs of Elves out to get her, while one of his friends is framed for murder. (Rev: BL 9/15/93; SLJ 10/93; VOYA 12/93)

1937 Shinn, Sharon. *The Shape-Changer's Wife* (9–12). 1995, Ace paper $4.99 (0-441-00261-7). Apprentice wizard Aubrey falls in love with his master's wife but wonders if she is really only one of his master's shape changes. (Rev: VOYA 2/96)

1938 Shusterman, Neal. *Downsiders* (8–12). 1999, Simon & Schuster paper $16.00 (0-689-80375-3). A fantasy about the people who live in the Downside, the subterranean world beneath New York City, and a teenage boy who ventures Topside to get medicine for his sick sister, leading to a dangerous chain of events. (Rev: SLJ 7/99; VOYA 8/99)

1939 Silverberg, Robert, ed. *Legends: New Short Novels* (9–12). 1998, Tor $27.95 (0-312-86787-5). A collection of 11 fantasy novellas by such writers as Anne McCaffrey, Robert Silverberg, Tad Williams, and Ursula Le Guin. (Rev: BL 8/98; VOYA 4/99)

1940 Silverberg, Robert, ed. *SFFWA Fantasy Hall of Fame* (10–12). 1998, HarperCollins paper $14.00 (0-06-105215-9). This is a collection of short fantasy fiction written between 1939 and 1990 by such authors as James Blish, Poul Anderson, and Anthony Boucher. (Rev: VOYA 8/98)

1941 Singer, Isaac Bashevis. *The Topsy-Turvy Emperor of China* (4–8). Illus. 1996, Farrar $16.00 (0-374-37681-6). A new edition of the tale of a wicked emperor who inflicts his twisted values on his subjects. (Rev: SLJ 6/96)

1942 Singer, Marilyn. *Deal with a Ghost* (7–9). 1996, Holt $15.95 (0-8050-4797-2). Overly confident 15-year-old Deal meets her match when she is dumped on a grandmother she scarcely knows, encounters a ghost, and becomes involved with a boy who sees through her game. (Rev: BL 6/1–15/97; SLJ 6/97; VOYA 10/98)

1943 Sirof, Harriet. *Bring Back Yesterday* (6–9). 1996, Simon & Schuster $15.00 (0-689-80638-8). While grieving the deaths of her parents, Lisa goes to live with her aunt and there is transported to Elizabethan England by her imaginary friend, Rooji. (Rev: BL 10/15/96; SLJ 10/96; VOYA 12/96)

1944 Sleator, William. *The Boxes* (5–8). 1998, Dutton $15.99 (0-525-46012-8). Uncle Marco gives Anne two boxes. The first contains a crablike crea-

ture that reproduces and builds a palace in her base-
ment with its offspring, and the second, a device that
can slow down time. (Rev: BL 6/1–15/98; SLJ 6/98;
VOYA 12/98)

1945 Sleator, William. *Rewind* (5–8). 1999, Dutton
$15.99 (0-525-46130-2). Peter realizes how his
behavior affects other people when, after he is killed
in a car accident, he is given a chance to relive parts
of his life and avoid his death. (Rev: BL 10/15/99;
SLJ 8/99; VOYA 10/99)

1946 Small, David. *Fenwick's Suit* (4–8). Illus.
1996, Farrar $15.00 (0-374-32298-8). In this picture
book, Fenwick discovers that his new suit has a life
of its own. (Rev: BL 9/15/96; SLJ 9/96)

1947 Smith, Sherwood. *Court Duel* (5–8). 1998,
Harcourt $17.00 (0-15-201609-0). In this fantasy,
Meliara has problems at court when she can't distin-
guish friends from enemies. A sequel to *Crown Duel.*
(Rev: BL 3/1/98; SLJ 4/98; VOYA 8/98)

1948 Smith, Sherwood. *Crown Duel* (5–8). 1997,
Harcourt $17.00 (0-15-201608-2). A fast moving tale
of young Meliara and her brother, Bran, who rise
against wicked King Galdran to protect their lands.
(Rev: BL 4/15/97; SLJ 8/97; VOYA 6/97)

1949 Smith, Sherwood. *Wren's Quest* (5–9). 1993,
Harcourt $16.95 (0-15-200976-0). Wren takes time
out from magician school to search for clues to her
parentage. Sequel to *Wren to the Rescue.* (Rev: BL
4/1/93*; SLJ 6/93)

1950 Smith, Sherwood. *Wren's War* (5–8). 1995,
Harcourt $17.00 (0-15-200977-9). In this sequel to
Wren to the Rescue and *Wren's Quest,* Princess Ter-
essa struggles to control herself and her destiny
when she finds her parents murdered. (Rev: BL
3/1/95*; SLJ 5/95)

1951 Sneve, Virginia Driving Hawk. *The Trickster
and the Troll* (4–8). 1997, Univ. of Nebraska Pr.
$22.00 (0-8032-4261-1). In this fantasy, 2 folktale
characters, the Sioux trickster Iktomi and a troll who
has followed a Norwegian family to this country,
develop a friendship as they see the country grow
and change. (Rev: BL 9/15/97; BR 1–2/98; SLJ
12/97)

1952 Sobol, Donald J. *"My Name Is Amelia"* (5–8).
1994, Atheneum $14.00 (0-689-31970-3). Lisa, 16,
is thrown overboard while sailing in the Bahamas
and ends up on an island where an evil scientist has
assembled history's most gifted statesmen and
inventors. (Rev: BL 1/1/95; SLJ 1/95; VOYA 2/95)

1953 Spencer, William Browning. *Zod Wallop*
(9–12). 1995, St. Martin's $21.95 (0-312-13629-3).
In this thought-provoking, paradoxical fantasy, Raymond suspects that the dark, disturbing events in a
children's book written by a friend are becoming part
of his real life. (Rev: BL 10/15/95; VOYA 2/96)

1954 Spicer, Dorothy. *The Humming Top* (6–8).
1968, Phillips $25.95 (0-87599-147-5). An orphan
finds she is able to predict future events.

1955 Springer, Nancy. *Red Wizard* (6–8). 1990,
Macmillan $13.95 (0-689-31485-X). Ryan is called
into another world by an inept wizard and must find
the secret of the Deep Magic of colors before he can
return. (Rev: SLJ 7/90; VOYA 4/90)

1956 Stearns, Michael, ed. *A Wizard's Dozen: Stories of the Fantastic* (7–12). 1993, Harcourt $16.95
(0-15-200965-5). This collection of 13 strange and
magical tales includes works by Vivian Vande Velde,
Patricia Wrede, and Bruce Coville. (Rev: BL
12/15/93; SLJ 12/93; VOYA 4/94)

1957 Stevenson, Laura C. *The Island and the Ring*
(7–10). 1991, Houghton $16.95 (0-395-56401-8).
Princess Tania's kingdom and family are destroyed
by Ascanet, who plans to conquer the world, and she
realizes her destiny is to drive him away. (Rev: BL
12/1/91; SLJ 9/91)

1958 Stevenson, Robert Louis. *The Bottle Imp*
(6–8). Illus. 1996, Clarion $16.95 (0-395-72101-6).
This fantasy tells about the various people who have
owned a magic bottle that contains an imp able to
grant their wishes. (Rev: BL 2/15/96; SLJ 5/96)

1959 Stevermer, Caroline. *River Rats* (7–10). 1992,
Harcourt $17.00 (0-15-200895-0). This action-
packed story begins in the years following a nuclear
disaster when 6 orphans, living on an old paddle
wheeler, are threatened by a fugitive with a menac-
ing past. (Rev: BL 4/1/92; SLJ 8/92)

1960 Stewart, Mary. *Mary Stewart's Merlin Trilogy*
(9–12). Illus. 1980, Morrow $19.95 (0-688-00347-
8). This fictionalized account of the story of King
Arthur consists of three novels: *The Crystal Cave,
The Hollow Hills,* and *The Last Enchantment.* On the
same subject use the author's *The Wicked Day*
(1984).

1961 Strasser, Todd. *Help! I'm Trapped in Obedi-
ence School* (5–8). 1995, Scholastic paper $4.50 (0-
590-54209-5). Andy, trapped in a dog's body, must
adjust to eating dog food and engaging in other typical canine activities. (Rev: BL 2/1/96; SLJ 2/96)

1962 Strasser, Todd. *Hey Dad, Get a Life!* (5–8).
1996, Holiday House $15.95 (0-8234-1278-4).
Twelve-year-old Kelly and her younger sister use the
ghost of their dead father to accomplish their everyday chores and finally let their mother know about
their secret helper. (Rev: BL 2/15/97; SLJ 3/97)

1963 Strauss, Victoria. *Guardian of the Hills* (7–10).
1995, Morrow $15.00 (0-688-06998-3). Pamela,
who is part Quapaw Indian, experiences cultural
conflict when her grandfather organizes an excava-
tion of the sacred burial grounds to learn more of

their spiritual heritage. (Rev: BL 10/15/95*; SLJ 10/95)

1964 Strickland, Brad. *The Bell, the Book, and the Spellbinder* (5–8). 1997, Dial $14.99 (0-8037-1831-4). Fergie seems to fall under a strange spell when he opens a library book written by a sorcerer who has been kidnapping boys and taking possession of their bodies for the past 300 years. (Rev: BL 9/1/97; SLJ 8/97)

1965 Strickland, Brad. *The Wrath of the Grinning Ghost* (5–8). 1999, Dial $16.99 (0-8037-2222-2). The forces of good and evil clash as Johnny and his friend Professor Childermass journey to the realm of a magical falcon to destroy a force that is trying to destroy the world. (Rev: BL 9/15/99; SLJ 10/99)

1966 Strieber, Whitley. *The Wild* (9–12). 1991, Tor paper $5.95 (0-8125-1277-4). Bob Duke stares at a wolf one day at a zoo, and its gaze seems to invade his soul. Soon Bob is transformed into a wolf and must flee the police. (Rev: BL 5/1/91*)

1967 Sutcliff, Rosemary. *Chess-Dream in a Garden* (6–9). Illus. 1993, Candlewick $16.95 (1-56402-192-0). A picture book for older readers that is an unusual combination of chess, fantasy, and fable. (Rev: BL 9/1/93; SLJ 11/93)

1968 Sweeney, Joyce. *Shadow* (7–10). 1995, Bantam $20.95 (0-385-30988-0). Sarah's cat, Shadow, has mysteriously returned from the dead. Sarah and Cissy, the psychic housemaid, try to figure out why. (Rev: BL 7/94; SLJ 9/94; VOYA 10/94)

1969 Tarr, Judith. *His Majesty's Elephant* (6–9). 1993, Harcourt $16.95 (0-15-200737-7). Set in the court of Charlemagne, this fantasy tells of a teenage princess who joins forces with a witch and an enchanted elephant to save her father. (Rev: BL 1/1/94; VOYA 2/94)

1970 Thesman, Jean. *The Other Ones* (7–9). 1999, Viking $15.99 (0-670-88594-0). Bridget must decide if she should try to be a normal human or, because she possesses supernatural powers, remain part of the Other Ones. (Rev: BL 5/99; SLJ 6/99; VOYA 8/99)

1971 Thompson, Julian. *Herb Seasoning* (9–12). 1990, Scholastic paper $12.95 (0-590-43023-8). Herbie, a teenager at loose ends, uses a counseling service to travel through time to find his destiny. (Rev: BL 5/15/90; SLJ 3/90)

1972 Thompson, Kate. *Midnight's Choice* (6–9). 1999, Hyperion LB $15.49 (0-7868-2329-1). In this sequel to *Switchers,* 15-year-old Tess must choose whether to remain human or assume a permanent animal form and, if the latter, whether to become immortal as a phoenix, the embodiment of good, or as a vampire, the embodiment of evil. (Rev: SLJ 7/99)

1973 Tolkien, J. R. R. *The Hobbit; Or, There and Back Again* (5–10). Adapted by Charles Dixon and Sean Deming. Illus. 1990, Eclipse Books paper $12.95 (0-345-36858-4). The classic story of Bilbo Baggins and his companions is introduced to reluctant readers in this full-color graphic novel. (Rev: BL 9/1/91)

1974 Tolkien, J. R. R. *The Hobbit: Or, There and Back Again* (7–12). Illus. 1938, Houghton $14.95 (0-395-07122-4); Ballantine paper $6.99 (0-345-33968-1). In this fantasy, a prelude to The Lord of the Rings, the reader meets Bilbo Baggins, a hobbit, in a land filled with dwarfs, elves, goblins, and dragons.

1975 Tolkien, J. R. R. *The Lord of the Rings* (9–12). 1967, Houghton $14.95 each (Vol. 1: 0-395-08254-4; Vol. 2: 0-395-08255-2; Vol. 3: 0-395-08256-0); Ballantine paper $6.99 each (Vol. 1: 0-345-33970-3; Vol. 2: 0-345-33971-1; Vol. 3: 0-345-33973-8). This combined volume includes all three books of the trilogy first published in 1954 and 1955. They are: *The Fellowship of the Ring, The Two Towers,* and *The Return of the King.*

1976 Tolkien, J. R. R. *Roverandom* (4–9). 1998, Houghton $17.00 (0-395-89871-4); paper $12.00 (0-395-95799-0). This fantasy deals with a dog named Roverandom who has the misfortune of insulting a wizard and having to pay the consequences. (Rev: BL 7/98; SLJ 6/98; VOYA 10/98)

1977 Tolkien, J. R. R. *The Silmarillion* (9–12). 1977, Ballantine paper $5.95 (0-345-32581-8). These modern legends deal with such subjects as the creation of the world.

1978 Tolkien, J. R. R. *Unfinished Tales of N'umenor and Middle-Earth* (10–12). Illus. 1980, Houghton paper $16.00 (0-395-32441-6). A collection of short pieces involving the legendary creatures found in some of the author's other works.

1979 Townsend, John Rowe. *The Fortunate Isles* (7–12). 1989, HarperCollins LB $13.89 (0-397-32366-2). Eleni and her friend Andreas seek the living god in this novel set in a mythical land. (Rev: BL 10/15/89; SLJ 10/89)

1980 Trondheim, Lewis. *Harum Scarum* (10–12). Trans. from French by Kim Thompson. Illus. 1998, Fantagraphics paper $10.95 (1-56097-288-2). A graphic novel about McConey, who looks like a well-dressed pink rabbit, his friends, and magic powers that can turn a city's population (all animals) into self-destructing monsters. Also use for the same audience: *The Hoodoodad* (1998). (Rev: SLJ 2/99)

1981 Turner, Ann. *Rosemary's Witch* (5–8). 1991, HarperCollins paper $3.95 (0-06-440494-3). Rosemary discovers that her new home is haunted by the spirit of a girl named Mathilda, who's become a witch because of her pain and anger. (Rev: BL 4/1/91; SLJ 5/91*)

1982 Turner, Megan W. *The Thief* (5–8). 1996, Greenwillow $15.00 (0-688-14627-9). To escape life imprisonment, Gen must steal a legendary stone in this first-person fantasy set in olden days. (Rev: BL 1/1–15/97; BR 11–12/96; SLJ 10/96; VOYA 6/97)

1983 Vande Velde, Vivian. *Changeling Prince* (9–12). 1997, HarperCollins paper $5.99 (0-06-105705-3). Weiland, who was changed from a cub to a human child, is never sure when the capricious sorceress Daria will change him back again. (Rev: VOYA 6/98)

1984 Vande Velde, Vivian. *A Coming Evil* (5–9). 1998, Houghton $16.00 (0-395-90012-3). Through encounters with the ghost of a 14th-century knight at her aunt's home in Nazi-occupied France, Lizette gains the courage to help her aunt hide several Jewish and Gypsy children. (Rev: BL 10/1/98; SLJ 11/98; VOYA 10/98)

1985 Vande Velde, Vivian. *Conjurer Princess* (9–12). 1997, HarperCollins paper $4.99 (0-06-105704-5). Sixteen-year-old Lylene sets out to rescue her older sister, who has been abducted by a warlord on her wedding day. (Rev: VOYA 2/98)

1986 Vande Velde, Vivian. *Dragon's Bait* (7–10). 1992, Harcourt $17.00 (0-15-200726-1). A young girl accused of being a witch and sentenced to be killed by a dragon becomes friends with a shapechanger who promises to help her take revenge. (Rev: BL 9/15/92; SLJ 9/92)

1987 Vande Velde, Vivian. *There's a Dead Person Following My Sister Around* (6–9). 1999, Harcourt $16.00 (0-15-202100-0). The appearance of the ghosts of an African American mother and child before his 5-year-old sister in contemporary Rochester, New York, leads 12-year-old Ted into an investigation that eventually uncovers his great-great-grandmother's role in the Underground Railroad. (Rev: BL 9/1/99; SLJ 9/99; VOYA 12/99)

1988 Vick, Helen H. *Tag Against Time* (6–9). 1996, Harbinger $15.95 (1-57140-006-0); paper $9.95 (1-57140-007-9). In this third volume about Tag, our hero thinks it is time to leave the 1200s and the Hopi culture he has grown to love and return to the present. (Rev: SLJ 10/96; VOYA 2/97)

1989 Vick, Helen H. *Walker's Journey Home* (7–10). 1995, Harbinger $14.95 (1-57140-000-1); paper $9.95 (1-57140-001-X). Walker leads the Sinagua Indians through treacherous challenges from both old enemies and new, and learns that greed and jealousy have been destructive forces throughout history. Sequel to *Walker of Time* (1993). (Rev: BL 8/95)

1990 Vinge, Joan D. *The Snow Queen* (10–12). 1989, Warner paper $6.99 (0-445-20529-6). When spring comes, the Snow Queen does not want to give up her throne.

1991 Voigt, Cynthia. *Building Blocks* (7–10). 1985, Fawcett paper $3.99 (0-449-70130-1). A boy travels back in time to witness his father's childhood.

1992 Voigt, Cynthia. *Elske* (7–12). (The Kingdom) 1999, Simon & Schuster $18.00 (0-689-82472-6). In the fourth and final volume of this fantasy, 12-year-old Elske accompanies Beriel, an exiled noblewoman, on her quest to recover her kingdom's throne. (Rev: BL 9/1/99; SLJ 10/99; VOYA 10/99)

1993 Voigt, Cynthia. *The Wings of a Falcon* (7–12). 1993, Scholastic $14.95 (0-590-46712-3). An epic tale of heroism and cowardice, love and loss, loyalty and betrayal. (Rev: SLJ 10/93*; VOYA 12/93)

1994 Walsh, Jill Paton. *A Chance Child* (7–9). 1978, Avon paper $1.95 (0-380-48561-3). In this English novel, a young boy who has been a prisoner all his life suddenly travels back in time. (Rev: BL 5/1/89)

1995 Walsh, Jill Paton. *Torch* (6–10). 1988, Farrar $15.00 (0-374-37684-0). Dio and Cal carry a magical torch on a quest that exposes them to forces of good and evil. (Rev: BL 4/15/88; SLJ 5/88)

1996 Wangerin, Walter, Jr. *The Book of the Dun Cow* (7–10). 1978, HarperCollins $12.95 (0-06-026346-6). A farmyard fable with talking animals that retells the story of Chanticleer the Rooster.

1997 Wangerin, Walter, Jr. *The Crying for a Vision* (6–10). 1994, Simon & Schuster $16.00 (0-671-79911-8). An epic account of a boy's sacrifice to save a Native American nation from the aftermath of a near-apocalyptic war. (Rev: BL 12/15/94; SLJ 1/95; VOYA 4/95)

1998 Watt-Evans, Lawrence. *With a Single Spell* (9–12). 1987, Ballantine paper $4.95 (0-345-32616-4). In this humorous fantasy a wizard's apprentice decides to make it on his own. (Rev: BL 3/1/87)

1999 Weis, Margaret, and Tracy Hickman, eds. *Treasures of Fantasy* (10–12). 1997, HarperCollins paper $14.00 (0-06-105327-9). A collection of fantasy short stories by some of the best contemporary writers in the field. (Rev: VOYA 12/97)

2000 Westall, Robert. *The Promise* (6–10). 1991, Scholastic $13.95 (0-590-43760-7). Bob's friendship with beautiful, sickly Valerie becomes romantic; when she dies, only Bob knows that her spirit still lingers among the living. (Rev: BL 3/1/91; SLJ 3/91)

2001 White, T. H. *The Book of Merlyn: The Unpublished Conclusion to "The Once and Future King"* (9–12). 1988, Univ. of Texas Pr. paper $13.95 (0-292-70769-X). An antiwar postscript to White's retelling of the Arthurian legend.

2002 White, T. H. *The Once and Future King* (10–12). 1958, Putnam $25.95 (0-399-10597-2). Beginning with *The Sword in the Stone* (1939), this omnibus includes all four of T. H. White's novels about the life and career of King Arthur. It was this version that became the basis for the musical Camelot.

2003 White, T. H. *The Sword in the Stone* (7–12). 1993, Putnam $22.95 (0-399-22502-1); Dell paper $5.50 (0-440-98445-9). In this, the first part of *The Once and Future King,* the career of Wart is traced until he becomes King Arthur.

2004 Whitmore, Arvella. *Trapped between the Lash and the Gun: A Boy's Journey* (5–8). 1999, Dial $16.99 (0-8037-2384-9). Jordan, age 12, travels back to the days of slavery and the Underground Railroad, experiences that give him a sense of history and family. (Rev: BL 11/15/98; BR 9–10/99; SLJ 1/99; VOYA 4/99)

2005 Wilde, Oscar. *The Canterville Ghost* (7–12). Illus. 1996, North-South $16.95 (1-55858-624-5); paper $6.95 (1-55858-611-3). An American family buys an English manor house and causes problems for the resident ghost in this classic fantasy from Oscar Wilde. (Rev: BL 12/15/96; SLJ 1/97)

2006 Williams, Tad. *To Green Angel Tower* (9–12). 1993, NAL $25.00 (0-88677-521-3). The concluding volume of the epic Memory, Sorrow and Thorn trilogy about the exploits of Simon, the scullery boy turned knight. (Rev: BL 2/1/93; SLJ 11/93)

2007 Windling, Terri. *The Wood Wife* (10–12). 1996, Tor $22.95 (0-312-85988-0). After Maggie moves to a cabin in the Arizona desert, she encounters spirits, both human and animal, that inhabited the area. (Rev: SLJ 7/97; VOYA 2/97)

2008 Wood, Beverly, and Chris Wood. *Dog Star* (5–8). 1998, Orca paper $6.95 (0-896095-37-2). On a cruise to Alaska with his family, 13-year-old Jeff Beacon encounters a magical pet bull terrier who transports him back in time to the Juneau of 1932. (Rev: BR 1–2/99; VOYA 8/98)

2009 Wrede, Patricia C. *Book of Enchantments* (5–8). 1996, Harcourt $17.00 (0-15-201255-9). A collection of the author's stories in various settings, each dealing with an enchantment. (Rev: BL 5/15/96; SLJ 6/96; VOYA 8/96)

2010 Wrede, Patricia C. *Magician's Ward* (9–12). 1997, Tor $22.95 (0-312-85369-6). Teenager Kim, who is living with magician Mairelon in his London townhouse as his ward and apprentice, discovers that some wizards have disappeared and Mairelon's powers are mysteriously stolen. (Rev: BL 11/1/97; VOYA 4/98)

2011 Wrede, Patricia C. *Searching for Dragons* (6–12). (Enchanted Forest Chronicles) 1991, Harcourt $16.95 (0-15-200898-5). Cimorene goes on a quest with Mendanbar, king of the forest, to find the dragon king Kazul by borrowing a faulty magic carpet from a giant. (Rev: BL 10/1/91; SLJ 12/91)

2012 Wrede, Patricia C. *Talking to Dragons* (6–10). (Enchanted Forest Chronicles) 1993, Harcourt $16.95 (0-15-284247-0). The fourth book in the series opens 16 years after *Calling on Dragons* with King Menenbar still imprisoned in his castle by a wizard's spells. (Rev: BL 8/93; VOYA 12/93)

2013 Wynne-Jones, Diana. *Fantasy Stories* (5–8). 1994, Kingfisher paper $6.95 (1-85697-982-2). Fantasies and folktales, primarily excerpts from classics by 18 authors. (Rev: BL 3/1/95; SLJ 11/94)

2014 Wynne-Jones, Tim. *Some of the Kinder Planets* (5–8). 1995, Orchard LB $16.99 (0-531-08751-4). Nine stories about ordinary boys and girls in offbeat situations. (Rev: BL 3/1/95*; SLJ 4/95)

2015 Yarbro, Chelsea Q. *Beyond the Waterlilies* (6–10). Illus. 1997, Simon & Schuster $17.00 (0-689-80732-5). Geena Howe has a unique talent—entering paintings, and has an amazing adventure when she enters a huge Monet painting of water lilies in a castle moat. (Rev: BL 6/1–15/97; SLJ 6/97)

2016 Yep, Laurence. *Dragon Cauldron* (6–10). 1991, 1994, HarperCollins paper $4.95 (0-06-440398-X). Monkey narrates this sequel to *Dragon Steel,* continuing the quest of a band of humans and wizards and Shimmer, a dragon princess, to fulfill Shimmer's task of repairing the damaged cauldron. (Rev: BL 5/15/91; SLJ 6/91)

2017 Yep, Laurence. *Dragon Steel* (6–8). 1985, HarperCollins $12.95 (0-06-026748-8). The dragon princess Shimmer tries to save her clan who are forced to work in an undersea volcano in this sequel to *Dragon of the Lost Sea.* (Rev: BL 5/15/85; SLJ 9/85; VOYA 8/85)

2018 Yep, Laurence. *Dragon War* (6–10). 1992, HarperCollins paper $4.95 (0-06-440525-7). In this sequel to *Dragon Cauldron,* the heroes use shape-changing magic and the help of a Dragon King to save the day. (Rev: BL 4/15/92; SLJ 6/92)

2019 Yolen, Jane. *Briar Rose* (9–12). 1992, Tor $17.95 (0-312-85135-9). A young girl seeks to carry out a promise to her dying grandmother and discovers her roots in Poland and the Holocaust. (Rev: BL 9/15/92; SLJ 4/93*)

2020 Yolen, Jane. *The Devil's Arithmetic* (7–12). 1988, Viking $15.99 (0-670-81027-4). At Passover service the prophet Elijah takes 12-year-old Hannah back to 1942 and the Holocaust concentration camps. (Rev: BL 9/1/88; BR 1–2/89; SLJ 11/88)

2021 Yolen, Jane. *Hobby: The Young Merlin Trilogy Book Two* (5–8). Illus. (Young Merlin Trilogy) 1996, Harcourt $15.00 (0-15-200815-2). The story of the youth of Merlin when he sets out alone into the medieval world, is held captive by a villain named Fowler, and eventually joins a traveling magic show, where he is known as Hobby and where the performers take advantage of his ability to look into the future. Book one is *The Passager* (1996) (Rev: BL 1/1–15/97; SLJ 9/96)

2022 Yolen, Jane. *Merlin* (5–8). 1997, Harcourt $15.00 (0-15-200814-4); Scholastic paper $3.50 (0-590-37119-3). In this last of the Young Merlin trilogy, 12-year-old Hawk-Hobby (Merlin) is rescued from imprisonment by wild folk through the intervention of a young boy who will latter become King Arthur. (Rev: BL 4/15/97; SLJ 5/97)

2023 Yolen, Jane. *The One-Armed Queen* (8–10). 1998, Tor $23.95 (0-312-85243-6). Scillia, the adopted daughter of Queen Jenna, is being groomed to rule when her younger brother decides that he should become king. (Rev: VOYA 4/99)

2024 Yolen, Jane. *A Sending of Dragons* (7–12). 1987, Harcourt paper $6.00 (0-15-200864-0). In this concluding volume of the Pit Dragon trilogy, hero and heroine, Jakkin and Akki, are captured by primitive people who live underground. Previous volumes are *Dragon's Blood* and *Heart's Blood*. (Rev: BL 11/1/87; BR 11–12/87; SLJ 1/88)

2025 Yolen, Jane. *Sister Light, Sister Dark* (10–12). 1995, Tor $3.95 (0-8125-0249-3). The first of a series about an orphaned girl brought up by the Sisterhood. (Rev: BL 10/1/88; SLJ 12/88; VOYA 4/89)

2026 Yolen, Jane. *The Transfigured Hart: Nan* (5–8). 1997, Harcourt paper $5.00 (0-15-201195-1). Richard, a lonely 12-year-old orphan who lives with his aunt and uncle, and outgoing, popular Heather, 13, become friends as they make plans to find and capture a mysterious animal they see in the Five Mile Wood. (Rev: VOYA 4/98)

2027 Yolen, Jane. *Twelve Impossible Things Before Breakfast: Stories by Jane Yolen* (6–9). 1997, Harcourt $17.00 (0-15-201524-8). Twelve fantastic short stories on a variety of topics, including a variation on Peter Pan, are included in this collection by this prolific author. (Rev: BL 11/1/97; SLJ 12/97; VOYA 12/97)

2028 Yolen, Jane. *The Wild Hunt* (6–12). 1995, Harcourt $17.00 (0-15-200211-1). The myth of the Wild Hunt is combined with other European legends when Jerold and Gerund become pawns in a game between the Horned King Winter and his wife. (Rev: BL 6/1–15/95; SLJ 6/95; VOYA 12/95)

2029 Yolen, Jane, et al., eds. *Dragons & Dreams* (6–10). 1986, HarperCollins $12.95 (0-06-026792-5). A collection of 10 fantasy and some science fiction stories that can be a fine introduction to these genres. (Rev: BR 11–12/86; SLJ 5/86; VOYA 6/86)

2030 Zelazny, Roger. *Blood of Amber* (9–12). 1986, Avon paper $4.99 (0-380-89636-2). Merle Corey, hero of *Trumps of Doom* (1985), escapes from prison

with the help of a woman who has many shapes. This is the seventh Amber novel. (Rev: BL 9/15/86; VOYA 2/87)

2031 Zelazny, Roger. *Trumps of Doom* (9–12). 1986, Avon paper $5.99 (0-380-89635-4). In this sixth Amber book, Merlin fights against mysterious foes from the worlds of Amber and Chaos. (Rev: BL 5/15/85)

2032 Zuroy, Michael. *Second Death* (9–12). 1992, Walker $30.95 (0-8027-1181-2). A Special Intelligence Squad must track down the creator of a violent, zombielike killer. (Rev: BL 2/15/92; SLJ 11/92)

Historical Fiction and Foreign Lands

Prehistory

2033 Auel, Jean M. *The Mammoth Hunters* (10–12). 1985, Crown $19.95 (0-517-55627-8). This is the third and final story set in prehistoric times about the amazing woman Ayla and her ability to survive endless hardships. The first 2 were *The Clan of the Cave Bear* (1980) and *The Valley of Horses* (1982). (Rev: BL 11/1/85)

2034 Auel, Jean M. *The Plains of Passage* (10–12). 1990, Crown $24.95 (0-517-58049-7). A sexually explicit novel for mature readers that is part of the Earth's Children series. This installment tells of Ayla and her mate Jondalar and their journey back to Jondalar's people. (Rev: BL 9/1/90; SLJ 4/91)

2035 Brennan, J. H. *Shiva Accused: An Adventure of the Ice Age* (6–9). 1991, HarperCollins LB $13.89 (0-06-020742-6). In this sequel to *Shiva* (o.p.), a prehistoric orphan girl is accused of murder by a rival tribe. (Rev: BL 8/91; SLJ 11/91)

2036 Brennan, J. H. *Shiva's Challenge: An Adventure of the Ice Age* (6–9). 1992, HarperCollins LB $16.89 (0-06-020826-0). In the third entry in the series, Cro-Magnon Shiva is spirited away by the shamanistic Crones to test her powers and see if she can survive the ordeals that will maker her a Crone, too. (Rev: BL 12/15/92)

2037 Cowley, Marjorie. *Anooka's Answer* (5–8). 1998, Clarion $16.00 (0-395-88530-2). Set in France during Paleolithic times, this sequel to *Dar and the Spear Thrower* tells how 13-year-old Anooka sets out to find her mother. (Rev: BL 11/15/98; BR 5–6/99; SLJ 12/98)

2038 Denzel, Justin. *Return to the Painted Cave* (5–8). 1997, Putnam $16.95 (0-399-23117-X). In this adventure story set in the Stone Age, Tao, a 14-year-old boy, faces the mad shaman Zugor in a deadly power struggle. (Rev: BL 11/1/97; BR 1–2/98; SLJ 11/97)

2039 Dickinson, Peter. *A Bone from a Dry Sea* (7–10). 1993, 1995, Dell paper $4.99 (0-440-21928-0). The protagonists are Li, a girl in a tribe of "sea apes" living 4 million years ago, and Vinny, the teenage daughter of a modern-day paleontologist. (Rev: BL 2/1/93; SLJ 4/93*)

2040 Dickinson, Peter. *Noli's Story* (4–8). (The Kin) 1998, Grosset $14.99 (0-399-23328-8); paper $3.99 (0-448-41710-3). In this tale set in prehistoric time, Noli and Suth and 4 younger children search for a new home after they are separated from their Moon-hawk Kin by a volcanic eruption. (Rev: SLJ 1/99)

2041 Dickinson, Peter. *Peter Dickinson's The Kin: Po's Story* (7–10). 1998, Grosset $14.99 (0-399-23349-0); paper $3.99 (0-448-41711-1). In prehistoric times, Po sets out to find water for his people and instead finds a different tribe of people. (Rev: VOYA 10/99)

2042 Jordan, Sherryl. *Wolf-Woman* (6–9). 1994, Houghton $13.95 (0-395-70932-6). Tanith, 16, must choose among the familiar but unhappy world of her clan, a warrior of a nearby tribe, and the lure of the wolf pack. (Rev: BL 11/15/94; SLJ 10/94; VOYA 12/94)

Ancient and Medieval History

GENERAL AND MISCELLANEOUS

2043 Carter, Dorothy Sharp. *His Majesty, Queen Hatshepsut* (6–9). 1987, HarperCollins LB $15.89 (0-397-32179-1). A fictionalized biography of Queen Hatshepsut, daughter of Thutmose I and the only female pharaoh of Egypt. (Rev: BR 3–4/88; SLJ 10/87; VOYA 12/87)

2044 Fletcher, Susan. *Shadow Spinner* (7–10). 1998, Simon & Schuster $17.00 (0-689-81852-1). The story of Shahrazad and how she collected her tales that kept her and her harem companions alive for 1,001 nights. (Rev: BL 6/1–15/98; BR 1–2/99; SLJ 6/98; VOYA 4/99)

2045 Gormley, Beatrice. *Miriam* (6–8). 1999, Eerdmans paper $6.00 (0-8028-5156-8). The story of how Moses's older sister, Miriam, was able to save her young brother's life and how she grew to enjoy living in the pharaoh's palace after she became a servant there. (Rev: BL 4/1/99; SLJ 5/99)

2046 Hunt, Angela E. *Brothers* (10–12). 1997, Bethany House paper $10.99 (1-55661-608-2). An exciting retelling of the Bible story of Joseph, a leader in Egypt, who is visited by his 10 brothers when they come to buy grain for the starving in Israel. (Rev: SLJ 1/98)

2047 Hunt, Angela E. *Dreamers* (10–12). 1996, Bethany House paper $10.99 (1-55661-607-4). This retelling of the Bible story about Joseph, who is able to interpret dreams, tells how a capricious Joseph, sold by his jealous brothers into slavery in Egypt, went from being a servant to becoming an administrator favored by the pharaoh in a royal court permeated by intrigue. (Rev: SLJ 8/96; VOYA 8/96)

2048 Levitin, Sonia. *Escape from Egypt* (8–10). 1996, Puffin paper $4.99 (0-14-037537-6). Historical fiction related to the biblical tale of the Exodus told from the point of view of 2 teens. (Rev: BL 5/1/94*; SLJ 4/94; VOYA 4/94)

2049 Miklowitz, Gloria D. *Masada: The Last Fortress* (7–10). 1998, Eerdmans $16.00 (0-8028-5165-7). This novel tells of the fall of Masada as seen through the eyes of a young Jewish man and a Roman commander. (Rev: BL 10/1/98; SLJ 12/98; VOYA 2/99)

2050 Napoli, Donna Jo. *Song of the Magdalene* (9–12). 1996, Scholastic $21.99 (0-590-93705-7). In biblical times Miriam, who suffers from seizures, is helped by a crippled young man who becomes her lover. After experiencing many difficulties, Miriam makes sense of her life when she meets the healer Joshua. (Rev: BL 10/1/96; BR 1–2/97; SLJ 11/96; VOYA 2/97)

2051 Pfitsch, Patricia C. *The Deeper Song* (8–10). 1998, Simon & Schuster $16.00 (0-689-81183-7). In this story, set at the time of King Solomon, a high-spirited girl named Judith decides to write down the oral traditions of the Jewish people, thus creating a book that will become a cornerstone of Judaism. (Rev: BL 10/1/98; SLJ 11/98; VOYA 8/99)

2052 Speare, Elizabeth George. *The Bronze Bow* (7–10). 1961, Houghton paper $6.95 (0-395-13719-5). The Newbery Award winner about a boy growing up in Roman-occupied Galilee at the time of Jesus. (Rev: BL 9/1/95)

2053 Tarr, Judith. *Lord of the Two Lands* (9–12). 1994, Tor paper $4.99 (0-8125-2078-5). Unveils the destiny of Alexander the Great, who is supported and guided by the Egyptian priestess Meriamon, daughter of a pharaoh. (Rev: BL 2/15/93; VOYA 8/93)

GREECE AND ROME

2054 Borchardt, Alice. *The Silver Wolf* (10–12). 1998, Ballantine $24.95 (0-345-42360-7). The splendor and decadence of ancient Rome are explored in this novel about a teenage female were-wolf, Regeane, who must hide her natural wolfish instincts to save her life. (Rev: VOYA 12/98)

2055 Bradshaw, Gillian. *The Beacon at Alexandria* (9–12). 1986, Houghton $17.95 (0-395-41159-9). In the Roman Empire in the fourth century, a young girl disguises herself as a man to enter the medical school at Alexandria. (Rev: BL 9/1/86)

2056 Bradshaw, Gillian. *Island of Ghosts* (10–12). 1998, St. Martin's $22.95 (0-312-86439-6). In a tale of adventure, treachery, and romance, this novel traces the career of Ariantes, a Sarmatian mercenary, who leads an army of 8,000 against the forces that are threatening Roman authority in the far reaches of the empire. (Rev: BL 8/98; SLJ 3/99)

2057 Davis, Lindsey. *Three Hands in the Fountain* (10–12). 1999, Mysterious $23.00 (0-892-96691-2). In this mystery set in 1st-century Rome, Marcus Didius Falco investigates the appearance of body parts in the water supply. (Rev: BL 4/15/99; SLJ 9/99)

2058 McLaren, Clemence. *Inside the Walls of Troy* (7–10). 1996, Simon & Schuster $16.00 (0-689-31820-0). The story of the Trojan War and the fall of Troy as told by Helen, the lover of Paris, and by Cassandra, who foresees the tragedy to come. (Rev: BL 10/15/96; BR 5–6/97; SLJ 10/96; VOYA 2/97)

2059 Napoli, Donna Jo. *Sirena* (7–12). 1998, Scholastic $15.95 (0-590-38388-4). Using the Trojan War and Greek mythology as a background, this is the story of the mermaid Sirena and her love for Philoctetes, the man destined to kill Paris, the lover of Helen. (Rev: BL 9/15/98; BR 11–12/98; SLJ 10/98; VOYA 12/98)

2060 Renault, Mary. *The King Must Die* (10–12). 1958, Random paper $11.00 (0-394-75104-3). A historical adventure story based on the legend of Theseus. Followed by *The Bull from the Sea* (1962). Also use: *The Mask of Apollo* (1988).

2061 Schneider, Mical. *Between the Dragon and the Eagle* (5–8). 1997, Carolrhoda LB $21.27 (0-87614-649-3). A historical novel that follows a piece of silk from China, past the Great Wall, up the Pamir Mountain, through deserts, into Egypt, and finally into Ancient Rome. (Rev: BL 2/1/97; SLJ 4/97)

2062 Sutcliff, Rosemary. *The Eagle of the Ninth* (7–12). 1993, Farrar paper $5.95 (0-374-41930-2). A reissue of the historical novel about the Roman legion that went to battle and disappeared. (Rev: BR 1–2/87)

2063 Tarr, Judith. *Throne of Isis* (9–12). 1995, Tor $5.99 (0-8125-2079-3). A carefully researched story about Antony and Cleopatra. (Rev: BL 4/15/94; VOYA 8/94)

MIDDLE AGES

2064 Alder, Elizabeth. *The King's Shadow* (7–12). 1995, Farrar $17.00 (0-374-34182-6). Set in medieval Britain, mute Evyn is sold into slavery, but as Earl Harold of Wessex's squire and eventual fos-

ter son, he chronicles the king's life and becomes a storyteller. (Rev: BL 7/95; SLJ 7/95)

2065 Avi. *Midnight Magic* (5–8). 1999, Scholastic $15.95 (0-590-36035-3). An action-filled adventure story set in the Middles Age involving young Fabrizio and his master, the magician Mangus. (Rev: BL 9/15/99; SLJ 10/99; VOYA 12/99)

2066 Barrett, Tracy. *Anna of Byzantium* (6–10). 1999, Delacorte $14.95 (0-385-32626-2). A novel about Anna Comnena, an 11th-century princess who was cheated out of her right to inherit the throne of Byzantium by her brother, John. (Rev: BL 4/1/99; SLJ 7/99; VOYA 10/99)

2067 Blacklock, Dyan. *Pankration: The Ultimate Game* (5–8). 1999, Albert Whitman LB $15.95 (0-8075-6323-4). This story set in ancient Greece follows the adventures of a boy who escapes from slavery and a sea captain in training for the Olympic event, the Pankration, a combination of wrestling and bare-fisted boxing. (Rev: SLJ 4/99)

2068 Bradford, Karleen. *There Will Be Wolves* (7–10). 1996, Dutton paper $15.99 (0-525-67539-6). In this novel set in the Middle Ages, Ursula, who is accused of witchcraft, must join a crusade that is leaving Cologne to go to Jerusalem. (Rev: BL 8/96; BR 9–10/97; SLJ 8/96; VOYA 4/97)

2069 Chaikin, Linda. *Swords and Scimitars* (9–12). (Golden Pavilions) 1996, Bethany House paper $9.99 (1-55661-881-6). This historical adventure with Christian undertones tells the exciting story of 2 young people and events involving the First Crusade at the end of the 11th century. Followed by *Golden Palaces* (1996). (Rev: VOYA 10/97)

2070 Coulter, Catherine. *Lord of Falcon Ridge* (9–12). 1995, Berkley paper $6.99 (0-515-11584-3). In this conclusion to the trilogy, set in Britain in A.D. 922, Cleve and Chessa meet and fall in love as he transports her to her intended husband and she's pursued by a kidnapper. (Rev: BL 1/15/95; SLJ 9/95)

2071 Cushman, Karen. *Catherine, Called Birdy* (6–9). 1994, Clarion $14.95 (0-395-68186-3). Life in the last decade of the 12th century as seen through the eyes of a teenage girl. (Rev: BL 4/15/94; SLJ 6/94*; VOYA 6/94)

2072 Cushman, Karen. *The Midwife's Apprentice* (7–12). 1995, Clarion $10.95 (0-395-69229-6). A homeless young woman in medieval England becomes strong as she picks herself up and learns from a midwife to be brave. Newbery Medal, 1996. (Rev: BL 3/15/95*; SLJ 5/95)

2073 Dana, Barbara. *Young Joan* (6–10). 1991, HarperCollins $17.95 (0-06-021422-8); paper $5.95 (0-06-440661-X). A fictional account of Joan of Arc that questions how a simple French farm girl hears, assimilates, and acts upon a message from God. (Rev: BL 5/15/91*; SLJ 5/91)

2074 Doyle, Arthur Conan. *The White Company* (9–12). 1988, Morrow $22.00 (0-688-07817-6). This rich historical novel set in the dying days of the age of chivalry tells how lowly Alleyne achieved knighthood. (Rev: SLJ 2/88)

2075 Jordan, Sherryl. *The Raging Quiet* (8–12). 1999, Simon & Schuster paper $17.00 (0-689-82140-9). In this novel set in the Middle Ages, 16-year-old Marnie is shunned when she befriends the local madman, whom she discovers is only deaf, not mad. (Rev: BL 5/1/99; SLJ 5/99; VOYA 8/99)

2076 Medeiros, Teresa. *Fairest of Them All* (10–12). 1995, Bantam paper $5.99 (0-553-56333-5). When the fair Holly de Chaste discovers that her father has offered her as the prize in a tournament of knights, she decides to disguise her beauty to foil the wedding plans. (Rev: SLJ 3/96)

2077 Morressy, John. *The Juggler* (7–10). 1996, Holt $16.95 (0-8050-4217-2); paper $5.95 (0-06-447174-8). In this adventure story set in the Middle Ages, a young man regrets the bargain he has made with the devil to become the world's greatest juggler in exchange for his soul. (Rev: BR 11–12/96; SLJ 6/96)

2078 Morris, Gerald. *The Squire, His Knight, & His Lady* (5–9). 1999, Houghton $15.00 (0-395-91211-3). This is a retelling, from the perspective a knight's squire, of the classic story of Sir Gawain and the Green Knight. (Rev: BL 5/1/99; SLJ 5/99; VOYA 8/99)

2079 Morris, Gerald. *The Squire's Tale* (5–9). 1998, Houghton $15.00 (0-395-86959-5). The peaceful existence of 14-year-old Terence is shattered when he becomes the squire of Sir Gawain and becomes involved in a series of quests. (Rev: BL 4/15/98; BR 11–12/98; SLJ 7/98; VOYA 8/98)

2080 O'Dell, Scott. *The Road to Damietta* (7–10). 1987, Fawcett paper $4.50 (0-449-70233-2). A novel set in 13th-century Italy and involving St. Francis of Assisi. (Rev: SLJ 12/85; VOYA 2/86)

2081 Pargeter, Edith. *The Heaven Tree Trilogy* (9–12). 1993, Warner $24.95 (0-446-51708-9). *The Heaven Tree* (1960), *The Green Branch* (1962), and *The Scarlet Seed* (1963) make up this trilogy about a medieval British family of artisans and their power-hungry benefactors. (Rev: BL 10/1/93*)

2082 Penman, Sharon Kay. *Cruel as the Grave: A Medieval Mystery* (10–12). 1998, Holt $22.00 (0-8050-5608-4). Justin de Quincy, a medieval private eye, investigates the murder of the daughter of a poor peddler and negotiates with Prince John, who is plotting to gain the English throne while his brother,

Richard Lionheart, is held hostage in Austria. (Rev: BL 10/15/98; SLJ 3/99)

2083 Penman, Sharon Kay. *The Reckoning* (9–12). 1991, Holt $24.95 (0-8050-1014-9). A battle over the Welsh throne in the 13th century leads to vows of revenge and acts of heroism. (Rev: BL 8/91; SLJ 7/92)

2084 Rosen, Sidney, and Dorothy S. Rosen. *The Magician's Apprentice* (5–8). 1994, Carolrhoda LB $21.27 (0-87614-809-7). An orphan in a French abbey in the Middle Ages is accused of having a heretical document in his possession and is sent to spy on Roger Bacon, the English scientist. (Rev: BL 5/1/94; SLJ 6/94)

2085 Skurzynski, Gloria. *Spider's Voice* (8–12). 1999, Simon & Schuster $16.95 (0-689-82149-2). A retelling of the classic love story set in 12th-century France between the young teacher Abelard and his pupil, the beautiful Eloise. (Rev: BL 2/15/99; SLJ 3/99; VOYA 4/99)

2086 Springer, Nancy. *I Am Mordred: A Tale from Camelot* (7–12). 1998, Putnam $16.99 (0-399-23143-9). Told in the first person, this is the story of Mordred, bastard son of King Arthur, who is destined to kill his father. (Rev: BL 4/15/98; BR 1–2/99; SLJ 5/98; VOYA 4/98)

2087 Temple, Frances. *The Ramsay Scallop* (7–10). 1994, Orchard LB $19.99 (0-531-08686-0). In 1299, 14-year-old Elenor and her betrothed nobleman are sent on a chaste pilgrimage to Spain and hear the stories of their fellow travelers. (Rev: BL 3/15/94*; SLJ 5/94; VOYA 4/94)

2088 Tomlinson, Theresa. *The Forestwife* (8–12). 1995, Orchard LB $15.99 (0-531-08750-6). A Robin Hood legend with Marian as the benevolent Green Lady of the forest. (Rev: BL 3/1/95*; SLJ 3/95; VOYA 5/95)

2089 Voigt, Cynthia. *Jackaroo* (8–10). 1985, Macmillan $20.00 (0-689-31123-0). In this novel set in the Middle Ages, a 16-year-old girl assumes the identity of a Robin Hood-like character named Jackaroo. (Rev: BL 9/15/85; SLJ 12/85)

Africa

2090 Dickinson, Peter. *AK* (7–10). 1992, 1994, Dell paper $3.99 (0-440-21897-7). A young soldier survives a bloody civil war in an African country but must use his gun again after his father is kidnapped during a military coup. (Rev: BL 4/15/92; SLJ 7/92)

2091 Drew, Eileen. *The Ivory Crocodile* (10–12). 1996, Coffee House Pr. $21.95 (1-56689-042-X). A novel about a young American woman who grew up in Africa and later returns to teach English in an isolated bush post, but finds she cannot escape her white skin and her Western heritage. (Rev: BL 5/1/96; SLJ 3/97)

2092 Farmer, Nancy. *A Girl Named Disaster* (6–10). 1996, Orchard $19.95 (0-531-09539-8). Set in modern-day Africa, this is the story, with fantasy undertones, of Nhamo, who flees from her home in Mozambique to escape a planned marriage and settles with her father's family in Zimbabwe. (Rev: BL 9/1/96; SLJ 10/96*; VOYA 12/96)

2093 Gordimer, Nadine. *Crimes of Conscience* (9–12). (African Writers) 1991, Heinemann paper $8.95 (0-435-90668-2). The themes of these dark, beautiful stories by the great South African writer are betrayal and its opposite: the unexpected good people find in themselves. (Rev: BL 5/1/91)

2094 Kurtz, Jane. *The Storyteller's Beads* (5–8). Illus. 1998, Harcourt $15.00 (0-15-201074-2). Two Ethiopian refugees, one a girl from a traditional Ethiopian culture and the other a blind Jewish girl, overcome generations of prejudice against Jews when they face common danger as they flee war and famine during the 1980s. (Rev: BL 5/1/98; SLJ 7/98; VOYA 10/98)

2095 Matthee, Dalene. *Fiela's Child* (9–12). 1992, Univ. of Chicago Pr. paper $13.95 (0-226-51083-2). A white boy in South Africa, who has been raised by a black family, is suddenly at age 12 claimed by a white family as its own. (Rev: BL 5/1/86)

2096 Naidoo, Beverley. *No Turning Back* (5–9). 1997, HarperCollins LB $14.89 (0-06-027506-5). Jaabu, a homeless African boy, looks for shelter in contemporary Johannesburg. (Rev: BL 12/15/96*; BR 9–10/97; SLJ 2/97; VOYA 10/97)

2097 Quintana, Anton. *The Baboon King* (8–12). Trans. by John Nieuwenhuizen. 1999, Walker $16.95 (0-8027-8711-8). After being exiled by his East African tribe after accidentally killing a tribesman, arrogant Morengru joins a troop of baboons, becomes their leader, and develops a sense of humanity. (Rev: SLJ 6/99; VOYA 10/99)

2098 Rupert, Janet E. *The African Mask* (6–9). 1994, Clarion $15.00 (0-395-67295-3). Layo and her grandmother compete with another clan to make a death mask in this story of a Yoruba girl living 900 years ago in Africa. (Rev: BL 7/94; SLJ 9/94)

2099 Temple, Frances. *The Beduins' Gazelle* (7–10). 1996, Orchard LB $16.99 (0-531-08869-3). In this 14th century adventure, a companion piece to *The Ramsay Scallop*, young scholar Etienne becomes involved in the lives of 2 lovers when he goes to Fez to study at the university. (Rev: BL 2/15/96; BR 9–10/96; SLJ 4/96*; VOYA 12/96)

2100 Zemser, Amy B. *Beyond the Mango Tree* (6–12). 1998, Greenwillow $15.00 (0-688-16005-0). Trapped in her home by a domineering mother, Sari-

na, a 12-year-old white American girl living in Liberia, befriends a gentle African boy named Boima. (Rev: BL 11/1/98; SLJ 10/98; VOYA 4/99)

Asia and the Pacific

2101 Ballard, John H. *A Novel to End World Hunger, with an Introduction by Mother Teresa & The Gandhi Foundation* (9–12). Illus. 1998, World Citizens $16.95 (0-932279-06-6); paper $14.95 (0-932279-05-8). Teenager MacBurnie King discovers a whole new world when she and her father begin working in a mission in India and encounter disease, hunger, caste injustice, and monsoon rains. (Rev: SLJ 6/98; VOYA 8/98)

2102 Binstock, R. C. *Tree of Heaven* (9–12). 1995, Soho Pr. $22.00 (1-56947-038-3). Two lovers try to escape doom during the Japanese invasion of China in the 1930s. (Rev: BL 8/95; SLJ 10/95)

2103 Bosse, Malcolm. *Deep Dream of the Rain Forest* (6–10). 1993, Farrar $15.00 (0-374-31757-7). Orphaned Harry Windsor goes to Borneo to be with his uncle, where he's forced to join a native warrior's dreamquest. (Rev: BL 10/1/93; SLJ 10/93*; VOYA 12/93)

2104 Bosse, Malcolm. *The Examination* (8–12). 1994, Farrar $17.00 (0-374-32234-1). During the Ming Dynasty, 2 very different Chinese brothers try to understand one another as they travel to Beijing, where one brother hopes to pass a government examination. (Rev: BL 11/1/94*; SLJ 12/94; VOYA 12/94)

2105 Bosse, Malcolm. *Tusk and Stone* (6–10). 1995, Front Street $15.95 (1-886910-01-4). Set in 7th-century India, this story tells about a young Brahman who is separated from his sister and sold to the military as a slave, goes on to gain recognition and fame for his skills and bravery as a warrior, and ultimately discovers his true talents and nature as a sculptor and stone carver. (Rev: BL 12/1/95; VOYA 2/96)

2106 Choi, Sook N. *Echoes of the White Giraffe* (7–10). 1993, Houghton $14.95 (0-395-64721-5). Sookan, 15, struggles for independence within the restrictions of life in a refugee camp during the Korean War. (Rev: BL 4/1/93; SLJ 5/93; VOYA 8/93)

2107 Choi, Sook N. *Year of Impossible Goodbyes* (6–10). 1991, Houghton $16.00 (0-395-57419-6). An autobiographical novel of 2 children in North Korea following World War II who become separated from their mother while attempting to cross the border into South Korea. (Rev: BL 9/15/91; SLJ 10/91*)

2108 Disher, Garry. *The Bamboo Flute* (5–8). 1993, Ticknor $12.00 (0-395-66595-7). In this brief, quiet novel of self-discovery, an Australian boy, age 12, brings music back into the life of his impoverished family. (Rev: BL 9/1/93)

2109 Ganesan, Indira. *Inheritance* (10–12). 1998, Knopf $22.00 (0-679-43442-9). During a summer on an island off the coast of India at the home of her grandmother, 15-year-old Sonil meets her mother, who sent her to live with aunts when she was a baby, and tries to unravel family secrets while engaging in a passionate relationship with an American man twice her age. (Rev: BL 1/1–15/98; SLJ 7/98)

2110 Garland, Sherry. *Song of the Buffalo Boy* (7–10). 1992, Harcourt $15.95 (0-15-277107-7); paper $6.00 (0-15-200098-4). An Amerasian teenager wants to escape the prejudice of a Vietnam village and tries to find her father. (Rev: BL 4/1/92; SLJ 6/92)

2111 Gee, Maurice. *The Champion* (6–10). 1993, Simon & Schuster paper $16.00 (0-671-86561-7). Rex, 12, must overcome his own racism and recognize a true hero when an African American war veteran is sent to recuperate in Rex's New Zealand home. (Rev: BL 10/1/93*; SLJ 10/93; VOYA 2/94)

2112 Gunesekera, Romesh. *Reef* (9–12). 1995, New Pr. $20.00 (1-56584-219-7). This coming-of-age story tells of defiance and growth during the Marxist rebellion in Sri Lanka in 1962. (Rev: BL 1/15/95; SLJ 4/95)

2113 Haugaard, Erik C. *The Boy and the Samurai* (6–9). 1991, Houghton $16.00 (0-395-56398-4). Despite his prejudice against samurai, Saru concocts a plot to rescue a samurai's imprisoned wife. (Rev: BL 5/1/91*; SLJ 4/91)

2114 Haugaard, Erik C. *The Revenge of the Forty-Seven Samurai* (7–12). 1995, Houghton $14.95 (0-395-70809-5). In a true story set in feudal Japan, a young servant is a witness to destiny when his master meets an unjust death. (Rev: BL 5/15/95; SLJ 4/95)

2115 Ho, Minfong. *The Clay Marble* (5–9). 1991, Farrar $14.95 (0-374-31340-7). After fleeing from her Cambodian home in the early 1980s, 12-year-old Dara is separated from her family during an attack on a refugee camp on the Thailand border. (Rev: BL 11/15/91; SLJ 10/91)

2116 Kim, Helen. *The Long Season of Rain* (10–12). 1996, Holt $15.95 (0-8050-4758-1). Set in Seoul, Korea, in 1969, this novel tells of the inequalities that women suffer in marriage and of one girl's struggle to help her mother. (Rev: BL 11/1/96; BR 9–10/97; SLJ 12/96*; VOYA 2/97)

2117 Kimmel, Eric A. *Sword of the Samurai: Adventure Stories from Japan* (4–8). 1999, Harcourt $15.00 (0-15-201985-5). A collection of 11 tales about the medieval Japanese warriors, their exploits, and their strict traditions. (Rev: SLJ 6/99)

2118 Lewis, Elizabeth Foreman. *Young Fu of the Upper Yangtze* (5–8). 1973, Holt $18.95 (0-8050-0549-8). In this Newbery Medal winner set in pre-World War II China, a young boy and his mother move from the countryside to Chung King.

2119 Lord, Bette Bao. *The Middle Heart* (9–12). 1996, Knopf $25.00 (0-394-53432-8). A tale of the horrible realities of modern China in which 3 youth forge an unlikely alliance that survives 5 decades, with China's cultural revolution and the Tiananmen Square uprising as the background. (Rev: BL 12/15/95*; SLJ 7/96)

2120 McCullough, Colleen. *The Thorn Birds* (10–12). 1998, Random $10.99 (0-517-20165-8); Avon paper $6.99 (0-380-01817-9). A family saga covering 1915 through 1969 in the lives of the Clearys of Australia.

2121 McFerrin, Linda Watanabe. *Namako: Sea Cucumber* (10–12). 1998, Coffee House Pr. paper $14.95 (1-56689-075-6). Ellen, who is part Scottish and part Japanese, suffers culture shock when her parents uproot her from her comfortable American suburban existence and move to a Japanese countryside. (Rev: BL 7/98; SLJ 1/99)

2122 Marchetta, Melina. *Looking for Alibrandi* (8–10). 1999, Orchard LB $17.99 (0-531-33142-3). In this novel set in Sydney, Australia, teenage Josie Alibrandi is torn between her family's cultural ties to Italy and her Australian environment. (Rev: BL 2/15/99; BR 9–10/99; SLJ 7/99; VOYA 6/99)

2123 Namioka, Lensey. *Den of the White Fox* (6–10). 1997, Harcourt $14.00 (0-15-201282-6); paper $6.00 (0-15-201283-4). Set in medieval Japan, this sequel to *The Coming of the Bear* (1992) continues the adventures of 2 ronin (unemployed samurai). In this tale, they try to solve the mystery of an elusive white fox. (Rev: BL 6/1–15/97; SLJ 6/97; VOYA 8/97)

2124 Paterson, Katherine. *Rebels of the Heavenly Kingdom* (7–9). 1983, Dutton $14.99 (0-525-66911-6); Avon paper $2.95 (0-380-68304-0). In 19th-century China a 15-year-old boy and a young girl engage in activities to overthrow the Manchu government.

2125 Robson, Lucia St. Clair. *The Tokaido Road: A Novel of Feudal Japan* (9–12). 1992, Ballantine paper $5.99 (0-345-35639-X). This picaresque romance is based on an actual feud and steeped in the customs and culture of 18th-century Japan. (Rev: BL 4/1/91*)

2126 Soto, Gary. *Pacific Crossing* (6–9). 1992, Harcourt paper $8.00 (0-15-259188-5). As part of a summer exchange program, Lincoln Mendoza adapts to life on a Japanese farm, practices a martial art, embraces Japanese customs, and shares his own. (Rev: BL 11/1/92; SLJ 11/92)

2127 Staples, Suzanne F. *Haveli: A Young Woman's Courageous Struggle for Freedom in Present-Day Pakistan* (9–12). 1993, Knopf $18.00 (0-679-84157-1); 1995, Random paper $4.99 (0-679-86569-1). This novel, a sequel to *Shabanu,* presents the issue of a woman's role in traditional Pakistani society, intrigue, tough women characters, and fluid writing. (Rev: BL 6/1–15/93*; VOYA 12/93)

2128 Watkins, Yoko K. *My Brother, My Sister, and I* (6–10). 1994, Bradbury paper $16.95 (0-02-792526-9). Tells of a once-secure middle-class child who is now homeless, hungry, and in danger. A sequel to the fictionalized autobiography *So Far from the Bamboo Grove* (1986). (Rev: BL 5/1/94; SLJ 9/94; VOYA 8/94)

2129 Wilson, Diane Lee. *I Rode a Horse of Milk White Jade* (6–10). 1998, Orchard $17.95 (0-531-30024-2). This adventure story set in medieval China tells the story of Oyuna and her adventures delivering a package to the court of the great Kublai Khan. (Rev: BL 4/1/98; BR 1–2/99; SLJ 6/98; VOYA 8/98)

2130 Wu, Priscilla. *The Abacus Contest: Stories from Taiwan and China* (5–8). Illus. 1996, Fulcrum $15.95 (1-55591-243-5). Six simple short stories explore life in a city on Taiwan. (Rev: BL 7/96; SLJ 6/96)

2131 Yep, Laurence. *Mountain Light* (8–12). 1997, HarperCollins $5.95 (0-06-440667-9). Yep continues to explore life in nineteenth-century China through the experience of a girl, Cassia, her father and friends, and their struggle against the Manchus in this sequel to *The Serpent's Children.* (Rev: BL 9/15/85; SLJ 1/87; VOYA 12/85)

2132 Yumoto, Kazumi. *The Friends* (5–8). 1996, Farrar $15.00 (0-374-32460-3). Three Japanese boys who are intrigued with death begin surveillance on an old man they think is about to die and find friendship instead. (Rev: BL 10/15/96; SLJ 12/96; VOYA 4/97)

2133 Yumoto, Kazumi. *The Spring Tone* (8–10). Trans. by Cathy Hirano. Illus. 1999, Farrar $16.00 (0-374-37153-9). A Japanese novel about 2 youngsters from a dysfunctional family, Tonomi and Tetsu, as they befriend a woman who feeds stray cats at the local dump. (Rev: BL 5/15/99; SLJ 5/99; VOYA 8/99)

Europe and the Middle East

2134 Austen-Leigh, Joan. *Later Days at Highbury* (10–12). 1996, St. Martin's $19.95 (0-312-14642-6). Written by a descendent of Jane Austen, this novel uses the same locale and similar characters in this epistolary novel of manners. (Rev: SLJ 3/97)

2135 Banks, Lynne Reid. *Broken Bridge* (7–12). 1995, Morrow $15.00 (0-688-13595-1). In this sequel to *One More River,* (1992) a woman's daughter sees her cousin killed by an Arab terrorist while living on a kibbutz, posing some tough moral questions. (Rev: BL 3/15/95; SLJ 4/95; VOYA 5/95)

2136 Bawden, Nina. *The Real Plato Jones* (5–8). 1993, Clarion $13.95 (0-395-66972-3). British teen Plato Jones and his mother return to Greece for his grandfather's funeral, where Plato discovers that his grandfather may have been a coward and traitor while serving in the Greek Resistance. (Rev: BL 10/15/93; SLJ 11/93*)

2137 Blackwood, Gary L. *Shakespeare Stealer* (5–8). 1998, NAL paper $15.99 (0-525-45863-8). A 14-year-old apprentice at the Globe Theater is sent by a rival theater company to steal Shakespeare's plays. (Rev: BL 6/1–15/98; SLJ 6/98; VOYA 8/98)

2138 Branford, Henrietta. *Fire, Bed, and Bone* (5–9). 1998, Candlewick $16.99 (0-7636-0338-4). An outstanding historical novel narrated by a loyal old hunting dog about the peasant revolt led by Wat Tyler and the preacher John Ball in late-14th-century England. (Rev: BL 3/15/98; BR 9–10/98; SLJ 5/98; VOYA 10/98)

2139 Brown, Molly. *Invitation to a Funeral* (10–12). 1998, St. Martin's $22.95 (0-312-18598-7). Set in London during 1676 and the reign of King Charles II, this adventure-mystery involves Aphra Behn, a young playwright, who becomes involved in the deaths of 2 brothers who helped her many years before. (Rev: BL 5/15/98; SLJ 11/98)

2140 Cadnum, Michael. *In a Dark Wood* (7–10). 1998, Orchard LB $18.99 (0-531-33071-0). The story of Robin Hood as seen through the eyes of the sheriff of Nottingham and his young squire, Hugh. (Rev: BL 3/1/98; BR 11–12/98; SLJ 4/98; VOYA 8/98)

2141 Chisholm, P. F. *A Surfeit of Guns* (10–12). 1997, Walker $31.95 (0-8027-3304-2). An adventure yarn set in 1592, based on real-life Englishman Sir Robert Carey, whose efforts to trace stolen arms leads him to the court of James VI at Dumfries, Scotland. (Rev: BL 5/1/97; SLJ 1/98)

2142 Conlon-McKenna, Marita. *Fields of Home* (7–10). Illus. 1997, Holiday House paper $15.95 (0-8234-1295-4). In this sequel to *Under the Hawthorn Tree* (1990) and *Wildflower Girl* (1992), the Irish O'Driscoll family saga continues as Michael and Eily try to make progress in spite of the hard times in Ireland. (Rev: BL 4/15/97; BR 9–10/97; SLJ 6/97)

2143 Crichton, Michael. *The Great Train Robbery* (10–12). 1975, Knopf $25.00 (0-394-49401-6); Ballantine paper $7.99 (0-345-39092-X). This is an entertaining re-creation of a robbery that shocked Victorian England.

2144 Crompton, Anne E. *Gawain and Lady Green: A Novel* (10–12). 1997, Penguin paper $20.95 (1-55611-507-5). Using both Sir Gawain and Lady Green as narrators, the Camelot of King Arthur is recreated with its code of honor and ideals of chivalry. (Rev: SLJ 9/97)

2145 Curtis, Chara M. *No One Walks on My Father's Moon* (4–8). Illus. 1996, Voyage LB $16.95 (0-9649454-1-X). A Turkish boy is accused of blasphemy when he states that a man has walked on the moon. (Rev: BL 11/15/96)

2146 Deane, Seamus. *Reading in the Dark* (10–12). 1997, Knopf $23.00 (0-394-57440-0). This fictional memoir of a boy growing up after World War II in Donegal is filled with pathos, hardship, mystery, and humor. (Rev: BL 4/1/97; BR 11–12/97; SLJ 7/97)

2147 Degens, T. *Freya on the Wall* (6–9). 1997, Harcourt $19.00 (0-15-200210-3). After the Berlin Wall collapses, an American girl learns details about her distant cousin's childhood in East Germany under the Communists. (Rev: SLJ 6/97; VOYA 6/97)

2148 de Trevino, Elizabeth Borton. *I, Juan de Pareja* (7–9). 1987, Farrar paper $4.95 (0-374-43525-1). The story of the slave who became an inspiration for his master, the Spanish painter Velazquez. Newbery Medal, 1966. A reissue.

2149 Dickinson, Peter. *Shadow of a Hero* (7–12). 1995, Doubleday $20.95 (0-385-30976-7). Letta's grandfather fights for the freedom of Varina, her family's Eastern European homeland. Living in England, she becomes interested in Varina's struggle. (Rev: BL 9/15/94*; SLJ 11/94; VOYA 10/94)

2150 Dukthas, Ann. *In the Time of the Poisoned Queen* (10–12). 1998, St. Martin's $22.95 (0-312-18030-6). With lots of action and a fast-moving plot, this historical novel investigates the poisoning of Queen Mary, the Bloody Mary of history, in 1558, weaving in historic facts, figures, and occurrences. (Rev: SLJ 10/98)

2151 Du Maurier, Daphne. *Jamaica Inn* (9–12). 1977, Avon paper $4.95 (0-380-00072-5). A suspenseful yarn set on the coast of England during the days of pirates. Also use *Frenchman's Creek* (1971) and *Mary Anne* (1971).

2152 Du Maurier, Daphne. *My Cousin Rachel* (9–12). 1952, Bentley LB $20.00 (0-8376-0413-3). A rich historical novel about a young man who is beginning to believe his new wife is a murderer.

2153 Dunlop, Eileen. *Tales of St. Patrick* (6–9). 1996, Holiday House $15.95 (0-8234-1218-0). Using original sources when possible, the author has fashioned a fictionalized biography of St. Patrick that focuses on his return to Ireland as a bishop and his efforts to convert the Irish. (Rev: BL 4/15/96; VOYA 8/96)

2154 Forester, C. S. *Mr. Midshipman Hornblower* (10–12). 1984, Little, Brown paper $13.00 (0-316-28912-4). This is one of a series of adventure stories about a courageous British seaman as he climbs the ranks. Some others are: *Admiral Hornblower in the West Indies*, *Lieutenant Hornblower*, and *Lord Hornblower*.

2155 Garden, Nancy. *Dove and Sword* (10–12). 1995, Farrar $17.00 (0-374-34476-0). The story of Gabrielle, a French peasant girl who disguises herself as a boy and follows Joan of Arc into battle. (Rev: BL 12/15/95; BR 3–4/96; SLJ 11/95; VOYA 2/96)

2156 Gerstein, Mordicai. *Victor* (7–12). 1998, Farrar $17.00 (0-374-38142-9). Based on fact, this is the story of a dedicated teacher of the deaf who tried to tame the famous wild boy of Aveyron who had lived like a savage and was caught by villagers during the time of the French Revolution. (Rev: BL 10/1/98; SLJ 10/98; VOYA 2/99)

2157 Giardino, Vittorio. *A Jew in Communist Prague: Rebellion* (10–12). Trans. from French by Joe Johnson. Illus. 1998, NBM paper $11.95 (1-56163-209-0). A novel in which the story and emotions are conveyed through text and drawings. This is the third in a series of novels about the hardships suffered by Jonas in Russian-occupied Prague. The others are *Loss of Innocence* and *Adolescence*. (Rev: BL 7/98; SLJ 2/99)

2158 Goodman, Joan E. *The Winter Hare* (4–8). Illus. 1996, Houghton $15.95 (0-395-78569-3). In twelfth-century England, Will becomes a page to the wicked Earl Aubrey. (Rev: BL 11/15/96; BR 9–10/97; SLJ 11/96; VOYA 2/97)

2159 Herr, Ethel. *The Dove and the Rose* (6–9). (Seekers) 1996, Bethany House paper $9.99 (1-55661-746-1). A moving story of 2 young people who are in love and the religious conflicts during the Dutch Reformation of the 16th century that keep them apart. (Rev: BL 6/1–15/96)

2160 Hilton, James. *Good-bye Mr. Chips* (9–12). 1962, Little, Brown $17.95 (0-316-36420-7). A loving tribute, in novel form, to a tough but excellent teacher in an English private school. First published in 1934.

2161 Holub, Joseph. *The Robber and Me* (5–8). Trans. from German by Elizabeth D. Crawford. 1997, Holt $16.95 (0-8050-5591-1). On his way to live with his uncle, an orphan is helped by a mysterious stranger and he must later make a decision about whether to stand up to his uncle and the town authorities to clear the name of this man in this novel set in 19th-century Germany. (Rev: SLJ 12/97*)

2162 Hunter, Mollie. *The King's Swift Rider* (7–12). 1998, HarperCollins $16.95 (0-06-027186-8). A fast-paced historical novel about a young Scot, Martin

Crawford, who became Robert the Bruce's page, confidante, and spy. (Rev: BL 9/15/98; SLJ 12/98)

2163 Hunter, Mollie. *You Never Knew Her As I Did!* (7–10). Illus. 1981, HarperCollins $13.95 (0-06-022678-1). A historical novel about a plan to help the imprisoned Mary, Queen of Scots, to escape from prison.

2164 Kelly, Eric P. *The Trumpeter of Krakow* (6–9). Illus. 1966, Macmillan LB $17.00 (0-02-750140-X). The celebration of a brave act and the story of a valuable jewel and its guardian in this story set in old Poland. Newbery Medal, 1929.

2165 Konigsburg, E. L. *A Proud Taste for Scarlet and Miniver* (7–9). Illus. 1973, Macmillan $17.00 (0-689-30111-1). Eleanor of Aquitaine tells her story in heaven while awaiting her second husband, Henry II.

2166 Konigsburg, E. L. *Second Mrs. Giaconda* (7–9). 1978, Macmillan paper $5.95 (0-689-70450-X). Leonardo da Vinci's valet narrates this story that tells the truth about Mona Lisa and her smile. (Rev: BL 3/1/90)

2167 Lasky, Kathryn. *The Night Journey* (7–9). Illus. 1986, Penguin paper $4.99 (0-14-032048-2). The escape of a group of Russian Jews from Tsarist cruelty told in a series of flashbacks from the present. (Rev: BL 1/1/90)

2168 Lawrence, Iain. *The Smugglers* (5–9). 1999, Delacorte $15.95 (0-385-32663-7). In this continuation of *The Wreckers,* 16-year-old John Spencer faces more sea adventures in 19th-century England aboard the Dragon, where he faces powerful enemies and must bring the ship safely to port. (Rev: BL 4/1/99; SLJ 6/99)

2169 Lawrence, Iain. *The Wreckers* (5–8). 1998, Delacorte $15.95 (0-385-32535-5); Bantam Double-day Dell paper $4.99 (0-440-41545-4). In this historical novel, young John Spencer narrowly escapes with his life after the ship on which he is traveling with his father, the owner, is wrecked off the Cornish coast, lured to its destruction by a gang seeking to plunder its cargo. (Rev: BL 6/1–15/98; BR 11–12/98; SLJ 6/98; VOYA 2/99)

2170 Llewellyn, Richard. *How Green Was My Valley* (9–12). 1983, Amereon LB $30.95 (0-88411-936-X). The enduring saga of a Welsh mining town and of the Morgan family who live and work there.

2171 Llywelyn, Morgan. *1916* (10–12). 1998, St. Martin's $24.95 (0-312-86101-X). Fifteen-year-old Llwelyn becomes a courier for the rebels in this epic novel set in Ireland at the time of the Easter Rebellion in 1916. (Rev: SLJ 8/98)

2172 McCaffrey, Anne. *Black Horses for the King* (5–8). 1996, Harcourt $17.00 (0-15-227322-0). In this historical novel set in 5th-century Roman Britain, young Galwyn is hired by Lord Artos (later King Arthur) to help find and transport giant Libyan horses from continental Europe to Britain, where Galwyn trains them for the wars against the Saxons. (Rev: BL 6/1–15/96; SLJ 6/96; VOYA 12/96)

2173 McCaughrean, Geraldine. *El Cid* (5–9). Illus. 1997, Oxford paper $19.95 (0-19-274169-1). A retelling of the epic poem of Spain's national hero. (Rev: VOYA 6/90)

2174 McCaughrean, Geraldine. *The Pirate's Son* (7–10). 1998, Scholastic $16.95 (0-590-20344-4). In 1717 England, Nathan and his little sister, Maud, are taken aboard a pirate ship and sail to Madagascar in this terrific adventure story. (Rev: BL 8/98; BR 11–12/98; SLJ 11/98; VOYA 2/99)

2175 Magorian, Michelle. *Back Home* (7–9). 1992, HarperCollins paper $5.95 (0-06-440411-0). A young English girl who returns to Britain after World War II wants to go back to her second home in the United States.

2176 Matas, Carol. *The Garden* (8–12). 1997, Simon & Schuster paper $15.00 (0-689-80349-4). This novel, a continuation of *After the War,* follows Ruth Mendelson to a kibbutz in Palestine and describes the tensions she and other kibbutzniks face as the United Nations prepares to vote on a plan to partition Palestine into Jewish and Arab lands. (Rev: BL 4/1/97; BR 11–12/97; SLJ 5/97)

2177 Matas, Carol. *Sworn Enemies* (7–10). 1994, Dell paper $3.99 (0-440-21900-0). In czarist Russia, the enemies are Aaron, a young Jewish scholar, and Zev, hired to kidnap fellow Jews to fulfill military quotas. (Rev: BL 2/1/93; SLJ 2/93)

2178 Meyer, Carolyn. *Mary, Bloody Mary* (6–9). 1999, Harcourt $16.00 (0-15-201906-5). A historical novel that traces the life of England's Queen Mary I from age 10 to 20. (Rev: BL 9/15/99; SLJ 10/99)

2179 Mooney, Bel. *The Voices of Silence* (5–9). 1997, Bantam Doubleday Dell $14.95 (0-385-32326-3). In Communist Romania, 13-year-old Flora and her family are living under very harsh conditions when she overhears a conversation about plans by her father to run for freedom. (Rev: BL 4/1/97; BR 5–6/97; SLJ 3/97*)

2180 Morpurgo, Michael. *Joan of Arc* (6–8). Illus. 1999, Harcourt $23.00 (0-15-201736-4). Beginning in the present, this novel goes back in time and shows Joan of Arc as a real person who experiences both confidence in her divine mission and doubts as she faces a cruel death. (Rev: SLJ 5/99)

2181 Newth, Mette. *The Dark Light* (8–12). Trans. by Faith Ingwersen. 1998, Farrar $17.00 (0-374-31701-1). Set in early-19th-century Norway, this novel tells of Tora, afflicted with leprosy, and her harrowing stay at a hospital surrounded by the horror of the disease. (Rev: BL 6/1–15/98; SLJ 6/98; VOYA 2/99)

2182 Orczy, Emmuska. *The Scarlet Pimpernel* (10–12). 1984, Buccaneer LB $21.95 (0-89966-508-X). An English fop is actually a leader of a group that helps aristocrats flee the French Revolution in this novel first published in 1905. Others in the series are: *The Triumph of the Scarlet Pimpernel, The Way of the Scarlet Pimpernel,* and *The Adventures of the Scarlet Pimpernel.*

2183 Orlev, Uri. *The Lady with the Hat* (7–10). Trans. by Hillel Halkin. 1995, Houghton $14.95 (0-395-69957-6). Yulek, a concentration camp survivor, encounters anti-Semitism on her return to Poland, while another Jewish girl, hidden from the Nazis, wants to be a nun. (Rev: BL 3/15/95; SLJ 5/95)

2184 Pelgrom, Els. *The Acorn Eaters* (7–10). Trans. by Johanna H. Prins and Johanna W. Prins. 1997, Farrar $16.00 (0-374-30029-1). In this semifictional memoir that spans 8 years, a boy grows up in Granada in the aftermath of the Spanish Civil War. (Rev: BL 9/15/97; BR 5–6/98; SLJ 11/97)

2185 Peyton, K. M. *Snowfall* (8–12). 1998, Houghton $16.00 (0-395-89598-7). Set in Victorian times, this novel tells of a young girl brought up in a vicarage and her escape into a world where she falls in love with 3 exciting men. (Rev: BL 9/15/98; SLJ 9/98; VOYA 4/99)

2186 Posell, Elsa. *Homecoming* (6–8). 1987, Harcourt $14.95 (0-15-235160-4). After the Russian Revolution, a Jewish family faces incredible hardships until they are able to escape to America. (Rev: BL 12/1/87; SLJ 12/87; VOYA 4/88)

2187 Pullman, Philip. *The Ruby in the Smoke* (8–10). 1987, Knopf paper $4.99 (0-394-89589-4). Sally Lockhart, alone in Dickensian London, encounters murder, opium dens, and romance in her search for her inheritance. Continued in *Shadow in the North* (1988) and *The Tiger in the Well.* (Rev: BL 3/1/87; BR 11–12/87; SLJ 4/87; VOYA 10/87)

2188 Pyle, Howard. *Men of Iron* (7–9). 1965, Airmont paper $3.95 (0-8049-0093-0). The days of chivalry are re-created in this tale that takes place during the reign of King Henry IV. A reissue.

2189 Rutherford, Edward. *London* (10–12). 1997, Crown $25.95 (0-517-59181-2). A lengthy novel that traces London's history from trading post to the hub of an empire, told through the everyday lives of families that lived through these ages. (Rev: BL 5/15/97; SLJ 12/97)

2190 Schmidt, Gary D. *Anson's Way* (5–9). 1999, Houghton $15.00 (0-395-91529-5). During the reign of George II, Anson Stapyton begins his proud career in the British army as part of the forces occupying Ireland, then becomes disillusioned as he develops a

growing respect and concern for the Irish. (Rev: BL 4/1/99; SLJ 4/99; VOYA 8/99)

2191 Schur, Maxine R. *The Circlemaker* (6–10). 1994, Dial paper $14.99 (0-8037-1354-1). A 12-year-old Jewish boy in a Ukrainian shtetl escapes 25 years of forced conscription in the czar's army in 1852. (Rev: BL 1/15/94; SLJ 2/94)

2192 Schur, Maxine R. *Sacred Shadows* (7–10). 1997, Dial paper $15.99 (0-8037-2295-8). Growing up in post-World War I Germany, young Lena Katz witnesses the growing anti-Semitism and decides that she will leave for Palestine. (Rev: BL 9/15/97; BR 3–4/98; SLJ 12/97; VOYA 12/97)

2193 Shimony, Abner. *Tibaldo and the Hole in the Calendar* (10–12). Illus. 1997, Springer-Verlag $21.00 (0-387-94935-6). Using both real and fictitious characters, this novel describes events in 1582 when the Gregorian calendar was adopted and the problem this causes for 11-year-old Tibaldo, who will lose his birthday as a result. (Rev: SLJ 3/98)

2194 Siegel, Deborah Spector. *The Cross by Day, the Mezuzzah by Night* (6–8). 1999, Jewish Publication Soc. $14.95 (0-8276-0597-8). In this gripping first-person narrative set in Spain in 1492 during the Inquisition, Ruth discovers that her family is secretly Jewish and that they must flee or face torture or burning at the stake. (Rev: BL 8/99)

2195 Singer, Isaac Bashevis. *Stories for Children* (7–9). 1984, Farrar $22.95 (0-374-37266-7); paper $14.00 (0-374-46489-8). This collection includes 36 stories most of which are fantasies about Jewish life in old Europe.

2196 Skurzynski, Gloria. *Manwolf* (7–9). 1981, Clarion $10.95 (0-395-30079-7). A diseased boy is accused of being a werewolf in 14th-century Poland.

2197 Stone, Irving. *Lust for Life: The Novel of Vincent van Gogh* (10–12). Illus. 1954, NAL paper $14.95 (0-452-26249-6). A lengthy fictionalized biography of the Dutch painter, Vincent van Gogh.

2198 Sutcliff, Rosemary. *Bonnie Dundee* (10–12). 1990, Peter Smith $21.50 (0-8446-6363-8). An adventure story set in Scotland during the war between King James and William and featuring a 17-year-old hero.

2199 Sutcliff, Rosemary. *Flame-Colored Taffeta* (6–9). 1986, Farrar paper $4.95 (0-374-42341-5). Damaris and her friends help a wounded smuggler in this story set in 18th-century England. (Rev: BL 11/15/86; SLJ 2/87; VOYA 2/87)

2200 Sutcliff, Rosemary. *The Shining Company* (7–12). 1990, Farrar $14.95 (0-374-36807-4). A novel set in early Britain about a young man who with his friends confronts the enemy Saxons. (Rev: BL 6/15/90; SLJ 7/90)

2201 Sutcliff, Rosemary. *Sword Song* (9–12). 1998, Farrar $18.00 (0-374-37363-9). A posthumously published novel about a Viking swordsman who, after being banished from his homeland as a boy, becomes a mercenary on a ship sailing from Dublin along the coast of Scotland. (Rev: BL 11/1/98; BR 5–6/99; SLJ 9/98; VOYA 2/99)

2202 Szablya, Helen M., and Peggy K. Anderson. *The Fall of the Red Star* (7–9). 1996, Boyds Mills $15.95 (1-56397-419-3). A novel, partially based on fact, about a 14-year-old Hungarian boy who becomes a freedom fighter during the rebellion against the Soviets in 1956. (Rev: BL 2/1/96; SLJ 2/96; VOYA 6/96)

2203 Veryan, Patricia. *The Riddle of Alabaster Royal* (10–12). 1997, St. Martin's $23.95 (0-312-17121-8). Set in Regency England, this witty mystery novel involves Captain Jack Vesper and lovely Consuela Jones, who believes that her father was murdered on Vesper's estate. (Rev: SLJ 4/98)

2204 Von Canon, Claudia. *The Moonclock* (7–9). 1979, Houghton $6.95 (0-395-27810-4). Through a series of letters 2 couples relive their adventures during the Turkish invasion of Austria in the seventeenth century.

2205 Walsh, Jill Paton. *Grace* (9–12). 1992, Farrar $16.00 (0-374-32758-0); paper $5.95 (0-374-42792-5). A novel based on the life of Grace Darling, the young English woman who became a hero when she rowed out from a lighthouse in 1838 to save shipwreck survivors. (Rev: BL 6/15/92; SLJ 7/92*)

2206 Westall, Robert. *Gulf* (6–9). 1996, Scholastic $14.95 (0-590-22218-X). A savage tale of a psychic child witnessing the terrors of the Gulf War through the eyes of Latif, a 13-year-old Iraqi soldier. (Rev: SLJ 1/96; VOYA 4/96)

2207 Wheeler, Thomas Gerald. *All Men Tall* (7–9). 1969, Phillips $25.95 (0-87599-157-2). An adventurous tale set in England during the Middle Ages about a 15-year-old boy's search for security.

2208 Wheeler, Thomas Gerald. *A Fanfare for the Stalwart* (7–9). 1967, Phillips $25.95 (0-87599-139-4). An injured Frenchman is left behind when Napoleon retreats from Russia.

2209 Whyte, Jack. *Saxon Shore* (10–12). 1998, St. Martin's $26.95 (0-312-86596-1). In this book, the third of a series about King Arthur, Merlin adopts Arthur to assure his safety until Arthur becomes king, and in a series of adventures rallies forces to support him. (Rev: BL 6/1–15/98; SLJ 4/99)

2210 Woolley, Persia. *Queen of the Summer Stars* (10–12). 1991, Pocket Books paper $6.50 (0-671-62202-1). In this part of the retelling of the Arthurian legend, Arthur marries Guinevere, who now

begins to have strong feelings for Lancelot. (Rev: BL 5/1/90; SLJ 9/90)

Latin America and Canada

2211 Alvarez, Julia. *In the Time of the Butterflies* (9–12). 1994, Algonquin $29.95 (1-56512-038-8). Follows the real-life struggles of the Mirabel sisters from girlhood to womanhood as they struggle under, and ultimately resist, the Trujillo dictatorship in the Dominican Republic. (Rev: BL 7/94)

2212 Atwood, Margaret. *Alias Grace* (10–12). 1996, Doubleday $24.95 (0-385-47571-3). Set in Canada, this complex novel, based on a true case, is about Grace Marks, who in 1843, at the age of 16, was convicted of being an accomplice in the murder of her employer and his housekeeper. (Rev: BL 9/15/96; SLJ 6/97)

2213 Belpré, Pura. *Firefly Summer* (5–8). 1996, Piñata Books $14.95 (1-55885-174-7); paper $9.95 (1-55885-180-1). This gentle novel depicts family and community life in rural Puerto Rico at the turn of the century as experienced by young Teresa Rodrigo, who has just completed seventh grade. (Rev: BR 3–4/97; SLJ 2/97; VOYA 4/97)

2214 Clark, Ann Nolan. *Secret of the Andes* (6–8). 1970, Penguin paper $4.99 (0-14-030926-8). A young Inca boy searches for his birthright and his identity. Newbery Medal, 1953.

2215 Danticat, Edwidge. *The Farming of Bones* (10–12). 1998, Soho Pr. $23.00 (1-56947-126-6). An emotion-charged historical novel about the people of Haiti and the Dominican Republic in which Amabelle, an aging Haitian woman, recalls the the terrible massacre of 1937 and what happened to her and the man she loved. (Rev: BL 8/98; SLJ 11/98)

2216 de la Garza, Beatriz. *Pillars of Gold and Silver* (9–12). 1997, Arte Publico paper $9.95 (1-55885-206-9). After her father is killed in the Korean War, young Blanca Estela and her mother move from California to Mexico in this story of a girl trying to fit into a new culture and make new friends. (Rev: BL 2/1/98; BR 5–6/98; SLJ 7/98)

2217 de Trevino, Elizabeth Borton. *Leona Alone: A Love Story* (7–10). 1994, Farrar $15.00 (0-374-34382-9). Set in Mexico in the early 19th century, this historical novel, based on real characters, tells how young Leona Vicario became involved in the struggle to free Mexico from the Spaniards and of her love for a brilliant young lawyer. (Rev: BL 6/1–15/94; SLJ 9/94; VOYA 10/94)

2218 Dorris, Michael. *Morning Girl* (5–9). 1992, Hyperion $12.95 (1-56282-284-5). The lovely and surprising coming-of-age story of Morning Girl and Star Boy, Arawak Indians on the eve of Columbus's exploration of the West Indies. (Rev: BL 8/92*; SLJ 10/92)

2219 Durbin, William. *The Broken Blade* (5–8). 1997, Delacorte $14.95 (0-385-32224-0). To help his family, 13-year-old Pierre becomes a *voyageur,* a fur trader working out of old Quebec. (Rev: BL 3/1/97; BR 5–6/97; SLJ 2/97; VOYA 4/97)

2220 Eboch, Chris. *The Well of Sacrifice* (5–8). Illus. 1999, Houghton $16.00 (0-395-90374-2). In this novel set during Mayan times, Eveningstar Macaw sets out to avenge the death of her older brother, Smoke Shell. (Rev: BL 4/1/99; SLJ 5/99)

2221 Gantos, Jack. *Jack's New Power: Stories from a Caribbean Year* (5–8). 1995, Farrar $16.00 (0-374-33657-1). In this follow-up to *Heads or Tails,* 8 stories, some laugh-out-loud funny, tell more from Jack's journal when his family moves to the Caribbean. (Rev: BL 12/1/95; SLJ 11/95)

2222 Haworth-Attard, Barbara. *Home Child* (5–8). 1996, Roussan paper $6.95 (1-896184-18-9). Set in Canada during the early 1900s, this is the story of 13-year-old Arthur Fellowes, a London orphan who is treated like an outcast when he joins the Wilson family as a home child, that is, a cheap farm laborer. (Rev: VOYA 8/97)

2223 Holeman, Linda. *Promise Song* (5–8). 1997, Tundra paper $6.95 (0-88776-387-1). In 1900, Rosetta, an English orphan who has been sent to Canada, becomes an indentured servant. (Rev: BL 6/1–15/97; SLJ 10/97)

2224 Houston, James. *Running West* (10–12). Illus. 1992, Kensington paper $4.99 (0-8217-3505-5). Both a love story and an adventure novel, this is the story of a man indentured to the Hudson Bay Company, a Dene Indian woman, and a journey into the wilderness for furs and gold. (Rev: SLJ 11/90)

2225 Jenkins, Lyll Becerra de. *So Loud a Silence* (7–10). 1996, Dutton paper $16.99 (0-525-67538-8). In contemporary Colombia, 17-year-old Juan leaves the city slums to find peace at his grandmother's mountain home, but instead becomes involved in the civil war conflict and the violence of the army and the guerrillas. (Rev: BL 9/15/96; BR 3–4/97; SLJ 12/96; VOYA 2/97)

2226 Lawson, Julie. *Goldstone* (5–8). 1998, Stoddart paper $8.95 (0-7737-5891-7). Karin, a 13-year-old Swedish Canadian girl, and her family live in a mountainous town in British Columbia in 1910 when heavy winter snows bring avalanches that cause death and destruction. (Rev: BL 7/97; SLJ 5/98)

2227 Limón, Graciela. *Song of the Hummingbird* (6–10). 1996, Arte Publico paper $12.95 (1-55885-091-0). The conquest of the Aztec Empire by Cortes is told through the experiences of Huizitzilin (Hum-

mingbird), a descendent of Mexican kings. (Rev: VOYA 8/97)

2228 Merino, Jose Maria. *Beyond the Ancient Cities* (7–10). Trans. by Helen Lane. 1994, Farrar $16.00 (0-374-34307-1). The perils and adventures of Miguel and his godfather among Mayan, Incan, and Spanish cultures as they travel from Mexico to Panama. (Rev: BL 4/1/94; SLJ 5/94; VOYA 10/94)

2229 Merino, Jose Maria. *The Gold of Dreams* (6–9). Trans. by Helen Lane. 1992, Farrar paper $4.95 (0-374-42584-1). A young explorer hunts for a golden treasure and discovers his real family instead. (Rev: BL 1/15/92; SLJ 2/92)

2230 O'Dell, Scott. *The Captive* (7–9). 1979, Houghton $16.00 (0-395-27811-2). During a voyage in the 1500s, a young Jesuit seminarian discovers that the crew of his ship plans to enslave a colony of Mayans. A sequel is *The Feathered Serpent.*

2231 O'Dell, Scott. *The King's Fifth* (7–10). 1966, Houghton $17.00 (0-395-06963-7). In a story told in flashbacks, Esteban explains why he is in jail in the Mexico of the Conquistadors. Also use: *The Hawk That Dare Not Hunt by Day.*

2232 O'Dell, Scott. *My Name Is Not Angelica* (6–8). 1989, Houghton $18.00 (0-395-51061-9). A novel about an African girl and her lover who are taken as slaves to the Danish Virgin Islands. (Rev: BR 3–4/90; SLJ 10/89; VOYA 12/89)

2233 Slaughter, Charles H. *The Dirty War* (6–9). 1994, Walker $24.95 (0-8027-8312-0). Arte, 14, lives in Buenos Aires, Argentina. When his father is taken prisoner by the government, his grandmother stages public protests. (Rev: BL 11/1/94; SLJ 12/94; VOYA 2/95)

2234 Talbert, Marc. *Heart of a Jaguar* (7–10). 1995, Simon & Schuster paper $16.00 (0-689-80282-X). A death-inducing drought takes its toll in the heart of a Mayan village. (Rev: BL 9/15/95; SLJ 11/95; VOYA 12/95)

2235 Temple, Frances. *Taste of Salt: A Story of Modern Haiti* (7–12). 1992, Orchard LB $17.99 (0-531-08609-7). A first novel simply told in the voices of 2 Haitian teenagers who find political commitment and love. (Rev: BL 8/92; SLJ 9/92*)

United States

NATIVE AMERICANS

2236 Ackerman, Ned. *Spirit Horse* (5–8). 1998, Scholastic $15.95 (0-590-39650-1). Set in Blackfoot territory in the 1700s, this novel traces the adventures of young Running Crane, his struggle for survival alone in the wilderness, and his taming of the magnificent wild horse named Spirit Horse. (Rev: BL 6/1–15/98; BR 5–6/98; SLJ 4/98)

2237 Benchley, Nathaniel. *Only Earth and Sky Last Forever* (6–9). 1972, HarperCollins paper $4.95 (0-06-440049-2). The Battle of Little Big Horn is a pivotal event in this novel of an Indian boy's journey to manhood.

2238 Borland, Hal. *When the Legends Die* (9–12). 1963, Bantam paper $5.99 (0-553-25738-2). At the death of his parents, a young Native American boy must enter the world of the white man. (Rev: BL 11/1/87)

2239 Bruchac, Joseph. *Turtle Meat and Other Stories* (9–12). 1992, Holy Cow! Pr. paper $12.95 (0-930100-49-2). Abenaki writer Bruchac presents mythic, historical, and contemporary stories with wit and a fine sense of character. (Rev: BL 11/15/92; SLJ 12/92)

2240 Burks, Brian. *Runs with Horses* (5–9). 1995, Harcourt $12.00 (0-15-200264-2); paper $5.00 (0-15-200994-9). An adventure story set in 1886 in which 16-year-old Runs with Horses completes his Apache warrior training by performing feats of endurance, survival, and daring, and partly as a result of information he gathers during raids, his tribe realizes that they can no longer continue to resist the white man. (Rev: BL 11/1/95; BR 1–2/96; SLJ 11/95; VOYA 2/96)

2241 Burks, Brian. *Walks Alone* (6–9). 1998, Harcourt $16.00 (0-15-201612-0). An accurate, heartbreaking account of the decimation of the Apache Indians circa 1879 by the U.S. Army, as experienced by a 15-year-old Indian girl, Walks Alone. (Rev: BL 5/1/98; SLJ 4/98; VOYA 4/99)

2242 Conley, Robert. *War Woman: A Novel of the Real People* (10–12). 1997, St. Martin's $25.95 (0-312-17058-0). This fast-moving novel tells about first encounters between Cherokees and Europeans from the viewpoint of War Woman, a Native American woman of extraordinary skills and abilities. (Rev: SLJ 5/98)

2243 Dorris, Michael. *Sees Behind Trees* (4–8). 1996, Hyperion LB $14.89 (0-7868-2215-5). Set in the 15th century, this story about Native Americans features a young man with an unusual talent who journeys with a village elder to find the land of water. (Rev: BR 3–4/97; SLJ 10/96*)

2244 Doughty, Wayne Dyre. *Crimson Moccasins* (7–9). 1980, HarperCollins paper $2.95 (0-06-440015-8). During the Revolutionary War a white boy is raised as the son of an Indian chief.

2245 Duey, Kathleen. *Celou Sudden Shout: Idaho, 1826* (4–8). 1998, Simon & Schuster paper $3.99 (0-689-81622-7). After a band of Crow Indians kidnaps her mother and brothers, 12-year-old Celou follows the raiding party hoping to plan a rescue. (Rev: SLJ 6/98)

2246 Ellison, Suzanne Pierson. *The Last Warrior* (7–12). 1997, Northland LB $12.95 (0-87358-678-6). A historical novel about a young Apache man who is forced to live in a white man's world and, as his long-held beliefs are challenged, finds himself caught between 2 cultures. (Rev: BL 12/1/97; SLJ 12/97; VOYA 4/98)

2247 Erdrich, Louise. *Golden Woodpecker* (4–8). 1999, Hyperion LB $15.49 (0-7868-2241-4). Filled with details about Ojibwa life, this is the story of an 8-year-old Indian girl living on an island in Lake Superior who, in 1847, witnesses the white people settling her people's land. (Rev: BL 4/1/99)

2248 Finley, Mary Peace. *Soaring Eagle* (5–9). 1993, Simon & Schuster paper $16.00 (0-671-75598-6). In this coming-of-age story, Julio searches for his heritage among mid-19th-century Cheyenne Indians. (Rev: BL 8/93; VOYA 2/94)

2249 Gall, Grant. *Apache: The Long Ride Home* (7–10). 1988, Sunstone paper $9.95 (0-86534-105-2). Pedro was only 9 when Apache raiders kidnapped him and renamed him Cuchillo. (Rev: BL 9/15/87; BR 9–10/88)

2250 Gregory, Kristiana. *The Legend of Jimmy Spoon* (6–8). 1990, Harcourt $15.95 (0-15-200506-4). The story of a 12-year-old white boy who is adopted by the Shoshoni in 1855. (Rev: BL 7/90)

2251 Harvey, Karen, ed. *American Indian Voices* (7–12). (Writers of America) 1995, Millbrook LB $23.90 (1-56294-382-0). Thirty selections giving insights into the cultures and experiences of American Indians. (Rev: BL 5/15/95; SLJ 5/95)

2252 Highwater, Jamake. *Legend Days* (7–10). 1984, HarperCollins $12.95 (0-06-022303-0). This beginning story about a young Indian girl begins a moving Ghost Horse trilogy about 3 generations of Native Americans and their fate in a white man's world. Followed by: *The Ceremony of Innocence* and *I Wear the Morning Star*.

2253 La Farge, Oliver. *Laughing Boy* (9–12). 1981, Buccaneer LB $24.95 (0-89966-367-2); NAL paper $3.50 (0-451-52244-3). A touching novel first published in 1929 about 2 young Navahos and the love they feel for each other.

2254 Lederer, Paul Joseph. *Cheyenne Dreams* (9–12). 1985, NAL paper $3.50 (0-451-13651-9). The story of a young Indian orphan and her adoption by a tribe of Cheyenne. Part of the Indian Heritage series. (Rev: VOYA 2/86)

2255 Levin, Beatrice. *John Hawk: A Seminole Saga* (6–10). 1995, Roberts Rinehart paper $9.95 (1-57098-000-4). John Hawk, a runaway son of a plantation master and a slave, becomes a leader of the Seminoles in Florida and leads the remnants of his tribe to Oklahoma. (Rev: SLJ 6/95; VOYA 8/97)

2256 Matcheck, Diane. *The Sacrifice* (7–9). 1998, Farrar $16.00 (0-374-36378-1). Taken prisoner by the Pawnee, a young Indian girl makes her escape and returns to her tribe in this adventurous survival story. (Rev: BL 6/1–15/98; BR 11–12/98; SLJ 10/98; VOYA 2/99)

2257 Medawar, Mardi O. *Witch of the Palo Duro: A Tay-Bodal Mystery* (10–12). 1997, St. Martin's $21.95 (0-312-17065-3). Set in the Wild West of 1866, this murder mystery involves Kiowa Indians, the ghosts of their forefathers, and the sudden death of the wife of their chief. (Rev: BL 9/15/97; SLJ 4/98)

2258 O'Dell, Scott. *Sing Down the Moon* (7–10). 1970, Houghton $17.00 (0-395-10919-1). A young Navaho girl sees her culture destroyed by Spanish slavers and white soldiers. (Rev: BL 11/1/87)

2259 O'Dell, Scott, and Elizabeth Hall. *Thunder Rolling in the Mountains* (5–9). 1992, Houghton $17.00 (0-395-59966-0); 1993, Dell paper $5.50 (0-440-40879-2). From the viewpoint of Chief Joseph's daughter, this historical novel concerns the forced removal of the Nez Perce from their homeland in 1877. (Rev: BL 6/15/92*; SLJ 8/92)

2260 Oke, Janette. *Drums of Change* (9–12). 1996, Bethany House paper $8.99 (1-55661-812-3). Two Blackfoot youngsters are taken from the tribe to attend a boarding school where the chief's son, Silver Fox, adopts the white man's religion, but the girl, Running Fawn, longs for the old ways of her tribe. (Rev: VOYA 10/96)

2261 Sandoz, Mari. *The Horsecatcher* (7–9). 1957, Univ. of Nebraska Pr. paper $7.95 (0-8032-9160-4). A Cheyenne youth gains stature with his tribe and gains the name of Horsecatcher. (Rev: BL 11/1/87)

2262 Speare, Elizabeth George. *The Sign of the Beaver* (6–9). 1983, Houghton $16.00 (0-395-33890-5); Dell paper $5.50 (0-440-47900-2). After the French and Indian wars, a young boy is raised by Indians. (Rev: BL 3/1/88)

2263 Wood, Nancy. *Thunderwoman* (9–12). Illus. 1998, Viking $19.95 (0-525-45498-5). Enhanced by beautiful illustrations by Richard Erdoes, and weaving in legend, mysticism, and myth, this novel traces the tragic history of the Pueblos and other Indian peoples in the Western Hemisphere after 10,000 years of peace, beginning with Spanish conquests in the 1500s and up to atom bomb testing in New Mexico. (Rev: BL 2/15/99; SLJ 5/99)

DISCOVERY AND EXPLORATION

2264 Durbin, William. *Wintering* (5–8). 1999, Bantam Doubleday Dell $14.95 (0-385-32598-3). In this companion volume to *The Broken Blade*, young Pierre LaPage again lives the exciting life of a voyageur and spends a winter in the Great Lakes area transporting furs. (Rev: BL 2/15/99; BR 9–10/99; SLJ 2/99)

2265 Garland, Sherry. *Indio* (7–10). 1995, Harcourt $11.00 (0-15-238631-9); paper $6.00 (0-15-200021-6). Ipa-ta-chi's life is destroyed when Spanish conquistadors enslave her. When her brother is injured and her sister raped in the silver mines, Ipa attempts to escape but is charged with murder. (Rev: BL 6/1–15/95; SLJ 6/95)

2266 Karwoski, Gail L. *Seaman: The Dog Who Explored the West with Lewis & Clark* (4–8). 1999, Peachtree paper $8.95 (1-56145-190-8). This historical novel dramatizes the story of Seaman, the Newfoundland dog that accompanied Lewis and Clark on their expedition. (Rev: BL 8/99; BR 9–10/99; SLJ 10/99)

COLONIAL PERIOD AND FRENCH AND INDIAN WARS

2267 Avi. *Night Journeys* (6–9). 1994, Morrow paper $4.95 (0-688-13628-1). In the Pennsylvania of 1767, a 12-year-old orphan boy joins a hunt for escaped bondsmen. Another novel set at the same time by this author is *Encounter at Easton* (1994).

2268 Clapp, Patricia. *Constance: A Story of Early Plymouth* (7–9). 1987, Morrow paper $5.95 (0-688-10976-4). An imaginary diary kept by a young Pilgrim girl who sailed on the Mayflower.

2269 Collier, James L., and Christopher Collier. *The Bloody Country* (7–10). 1985, Macmillan $12.95 (0-590-07411-3); Scholastic paper $4.50 (0-590-43126-9). A pioneer story about a family that settles in the 1750s in what is now Wilkes-Barre, Pennsylvania. Also use another fine historical novel by these authors: *The Winter Hero* (1985).

2270 Coombs, Karen M. *Sarah on Her Own* (6–10). 1996, Avon paper $3.99 (0-380-78275-8). Through the eyes of a sensitive English teenager who voyaged to America in 1620, the reader relives the harsh realities and joys of life in an early Virginia settlement. (Rev: SLJ 9/96)

2271 Durrant, Lynda. *The Beaded Moccasins: The Story of Mary Campbell* (5–9). 1998, Clarion $15.00 (0-395-85398-2). Told in the first person, this is a fictionalized account of the true story of 12-year-old Mary Campbell who was captured by the Delaware Indians in 1759. (Rev: BL 3/15/98; SLJ 6/98; VOYA 12/98)

2272 Durrant, Lynda. *Echohawk* (5–9). 1996, Clarion $14.95 (0-395-74430-X). Raised by Mohican Indians after the death of his family in 1738, Jonathan Starr, renamed Echohawk, is eventually sent to a white teacher to learn English and becomes reacquainted with his true heritage. (Rev: BL 9/1/96; BR 3–4/97; SLJ 9/96)

2273 Durrant, Lynda. *Turtle Clan Journey* (5–9). 1999, Clarion $15.00 (0-395-90369-6). In this sequel to *Echohawk* set in 1747, Jonathan, whose Mohawk name is Echohawk, is forced to leave the Indians who have raised him and is sent to live in Albany with an aunt he doesn't know. (Rev: BL 5/1/99; SLJ 6/99)

2274 Fleischman, Paul. *Saturnalia* (6–9). 1990, HarperCollins LB $14.89 (0-06-021913-0). The harshness of Colonial life is seen through the eyes of a young Indian boy who is a printer's apprentice. (Rev: BL 5/1/90; SLJ 5/90; VOYA 6/90)

2275 Goodman, Joan E. *Hope's Crossing* (5–8). 1998, Houghton $15.00 (0-395-86195-0). Kidnapped by British loyalists during the Revolution, Hope must try to escape and find her way home. (Rev: BL 6/1–15/98; SLJ 5/98; VOYA 8/98)

2276 Greene, Jacqueline D. *Out of Many Waters* (6–8). 1988, Walker $16.95 (0-8027-6811-3). A historical novel that begins in Brazil and ends with a group of Jewish settlers who, after landing in New Amsterdam, began the first synagogue in America. (Rev: BL 1/15/89; BR 1–2/89; SLJ 10/88; VOYA 12/88)

2277 Gregory, Kristiana. *Jenny of the Tetons* (6–9). 1989, Harcourt $13.95 (0-15-200480-7). An orphaned girl is brought by a trapper into his house to help care for his children in this story based on fact. (Rev: BL 7/89; SLJ 6/89; VOYA 6/90)

2278 Grote, JoAnn A. *Queen Anne's War* (5–8). (The American Adventure) 1998, Chelsea LB $15.95 (0-7910-5045-9). During Queen Anne's War in 1710, Will Smith's family becomes involved in the attempt to drive the French out of New England, but 11-year-old Will is preoccupied with a jealous classmate. (Rev: SLJ 1/99)

2279 Harrah, Madge. *My Brother, My Enemy* (6–8). 1997, Simon & Schuster paper $16.00 (0-689-80968-9). Using details of Bacon's Rebellion as a backdrop, this is an exciting historical novel, set in 17th-century Virginia, about a teenage boy who is awaiting death by hanging. (Rev: BL 5/1/97; BR 11–12/97; SLJ 7/97; VOYA 10/97)

2280 Jacobs, Paul S. *James Printer: A Novel of King Philip's War* (5–8). 1997, Scholastic $15.95 (0-590-16381-7). Though he has been raised as an Englishman in colonial Cambridge, Massachusetts, an Indian boy feels he must choose sides when the English and Indians go to war. (Rev: BL 4/15/97; SLJ 6/97; VOYA 6/98)

2281 Johnston, Mary. *To Have and to Hold* (9–12). 1976, Lightyear LB $18.95 (0-89968-149-2). In this historical novel first published in 1900, a young girl escapes an intolerable situation by fleeing to Virginia with a cargo of brides.

2282 Keehn, Sally M. *I Am Regina* (8–10). 1991, Putnam $15.95 (0-399-21797-5). In this novel based on a true story, a white girl who is kidnapped by Indians at the age of 10 becomes so assimilated into the tribe's culture that she can't remember anything about her early years when she is rescued 9 years later. (Rev: BL 7/91; SLJ 6/91)

2283 Keehn, Sally M. *Moon of Two Dark Horses* (6–9). 1995, Putnam $16.95 (0-399-22783-0). A friendship sensitively drawn between a Native American boy and a white settler. (Rev: BL 11/15/95*; SLJ 11/95; VOYA 12/95)

2284 Kilian, Michael. *Major Washington* (10–12). 1998, St. Martin's $25.95 (0-312-18131-0). A novel that fictionalizes the life of George Washington during the period from 1753–1755, when he made 3 journeys into the Allegheny wilderness to spy on the French. (Rev: BL 1/1–15/98; SLJ 1/99)

2285 Kirkpatrick, Katherine. *Trouble's Daughter: The Story of Susanna Hutchinson, Indian Captive* (5–8). 1998, Doubleday $14.95 (0-385-32600-9). Based on fact, this outstanding historical novel recounts Susanna Hutchinson's life after she is kidnapped by Lenape Indians who massacre her family on Long Island in 1663. (Rev: BL 8/98; SLJ 9/98; VOYA 4/99)

2286 Koller, Jackie F. *The Primrose Way* (7–10). 1992, Harcourt $17.95 (0-15-256745-3). A historical romance in which Rebekah, 16, falls in love with Mishannock, a Pawtucket holy man. (Rev: BL 10/15/92; SLJ 9/92)

2287 Laird, Marnie. *Water Rat* (7–9). Illus. 1998, Winslow $15.95 (1-890817-08-2). An action-filled adventure story set in Colonial times about Matt, a 14-year-old orphan, and his struggle to survive and prove his worth. (Rev: SLJ 1/99; VOYA 2/99)

2288 Lasky, Kathryn. *Beyond the Burning Time* (7–12). 1994, Scholastic $14.95 (0-590-47331-X). In this docunovel that captures the ignorance, violence, and hysteria of the Salem witch trials, Mary, 12, tries to save her mother, accused of witchcraft. (Rev: BL 10/15/94; SLJ 1/95; VOYA 12/94)

2289 O'Dell, Scott. *The Serpent Never Sleeps: A Novel of Jamestown and Pocahontas* (6–9). Illus. 1987, Houghton $17.00 (0-395-44242-7); Fawcett paper $4.50 (0-449-70328-2). A young English girl becomes part of a settlement at Jamestown and there meets Pocahontas. (Rev: BL 11/1/87; BR 9–10/88; SLJ 9/87; VOYA 10/87)

2290 Rinaldi, Ann. *A Break with Charity: A Story about the Salem Witch Trials* (7–10). 1992, Harcourt $17.00 (0-15-200353-3). This blend of history and fiction brings to life the dark period in American history of the Salem witch trials. (Rev: BL 10/1/92; SLJ 9/92)

2291 Rinaldi, Ann. *Hang a Thousand Trees with Ribbons* (7–12). 1996, Harcourt $12.00 (0-15-200876-4); paper $6.00 (0-15-200877-2). A well-researched novel about the life of Phillis Wheatley, who was bought by the Wheatleys in 1761 and who later became America's first black poet. (Rev: BL 9/1/96; BR 3–4/97; SLJ 11/96; VOYA 12/96)

2292 Rinaldi, Ann. *A Stitch in Time* (7–10). (Quilt Trilogy) 1994, Scholastic $13.95 (0-590-46055-2). This historical novel set in 18th-century Salem, Massachusetts, concerns the tribulations of a 16-year-old girl and her family. (Rev: BL 3/1/94; SLJ 5/94; VOYA 4/94)

2293 Speare, Elizabeth George. *Calico Captive* (6–9). 1957, Houghton $17.00 (0-395-07112-7); Dell paper $4.99 (0-440-41156-4). In Colonial America, the Johnson family are captured by Indians and forced on a long trek.

2294 Speare, Elizabeth George. *The Witch of Blackbird Pond* (6–9). 1958, Houghton $16.00 (0-395-07114-3); Dell paper $5.50 (0-440-99577-9). Kit Tyler's wild ways lead to problems in witch conscious Colonial Connecticut. Newbery Medal, 1959. (Rev: BL 7/88)

2295 Stainer, M. L. *The Lyon's Cub* (5–9). Illus. 1998, Chicken Soup Pr. LB $9.95 (0-9646904-5-4); paper $6.95 (0-9646904-6-2). This novel, a continuation of *The Lyon's Roar* (1997), tells what happened to the settlers of the Lost Colony of Roanoke and their life with peaceful Native American tribes. Continued in *The Lyon's Pride* (1998). (Rev: SLJ 8/98)

2296 Wisler, G. Clifton. *This New Land* (6–9). 1987, Walker LB $28.90 (0-8027-6727-3). A well-researched novel about a Pilgrim boy's adventures on the Mayflower and in the Plymouth Rock colony. (Rev: BL 3/15/88; BR 5–6/88; SLJ 11/87)

2297 Wyeth, Sharon D. *Once on This River* (6–10). 1997, Knopf $16.00 (0-679-88350-9). Set in an African American community in colonial New York in 1760, this novel tells about a young black girl who discovers that her mother gave her away so that she could grow up free. (Rev: BL 12/15/97; BR 5–6/98; SLJ 4/98)

2298 Youmans, Marly. *Catherwood* (10–12). 1996, Farrar $20.00 (0-374-11972-4). While returning home from visiting friends in a neighboring community in 17th-century New York Colony, Catherwood and her infant daughter become lost and spend seven months in the wilderness in this gripping survival story. (Rev: BL 5/15/96; SLJ 11/96)

REVOLUTIONARY PERIOD (1775–1809)

2299 Anderson, Joan. *1787* (7–10). 1987, Harcourt $14.95 (0-15-200582-X). The story of a teenager who became James Madison's aide during the 1787 Constitutional Convention in Philadelphia. (Rev: BL 5/87; VOYA 12/87)

2300 Avi. *The Fighting Ground* (6–9). 1984, HarperCollins LB $14.89 (0-397-32074-4); paper $4.95 (0-06-440185-5). One eventful day in the life of a 13-year-old boy during the Revolutionary War. (Rev: BL 4/87)

2301 Collier, James L., and Christopher Collier. *My Brother Sam Is Dead* (7–10). 1974, Macmillan LB $17.00 (0-02-722980-7). A young boy tells of the tragic events leading up to his brother's death in the Revolutionary War. (Rev: BL 4/87)

2302 Denenberg, Barry. *The Journal of William Thomas Emerson: A Revolutionary War Patriot* (4–8). (My Name Is America) 1998, Scholastic $10.95 (0-590-31350-9). This novel set in Boston on the eve of the Revolution tells about an orphan boy who gets involved in intrigue while working in a tavern. (Rev: BL 11/1/98; SLJ 5/99)

2303 Fast, Howard. *April Morning* (9–12). 1961, Bantam paper $5.99 (0-553-27322-1). A short novel about the first days of the American Revolution as experienced by a 15-year-old boy.

2304 Fast, Howard. *The Immigrants* (7–12). 1998, Harcourt paper $12.00 (0-15-600512-3). During the early stages of the Revolutionary War, 15-year-old Adam Cooper becomes a man.

2305 Fleischman, Paul. *Path of the Pale Horse* (7–9). 1992, HarperCollins paper $3.95 (0-06-440442-0). Dr. Peale and his apprentice help fight a yellow fever epidemic in 1793 Philadelphia.

2306 Forbes, Esther. *Johnny Tremain* (7–9). Illus. 1943, Houghton $15.00 (0-395-06766-9); Dell paper $5.99 (0-440-94250-0). Paul Revere's apprentice during the early days of the Revolution. Newbery Medal, 1944. (Rev: BL 1/1/90)

2307 Gaeddert, Louann. *Breaking Free* (5–8). 1994, Atheneum paper $16.00 (0-689-31883-9). In upstate New York circa 1800, 12-year-old Richard, an orphan, works on his uncle's farm and secretly teaches a young slave to read and then helps her to escape with her father to Canada. (Rev: BL 4/1/94; SLJ 5/94; VOYA 8/94)

2308 Gregory, Kristiana. *The Winter of Red Snow: The Revolutionary War Diary of Abigail Jane Stewart* (5–8). (Dear America) 1996, Scholastic $10.95 (0-590-22653-3). In this novel, the hardships faced by the Revolutionary Army at Valley Forge in 1777–1778 are seen through the eyes of a young girl whose family lived close to the encampment. (Rev: SLJ 9/96; VOYA 10/96)

2309 O'Dell, Scott. *Sarah Bishop* (7–10). 1980, Houghton $16.00 (0-395-29185-2); Scholastic paper $4.99 (0-590-44651-7). Sarah, 15 years old, tries to ignore the Revolution in her country home in Westchester, New York. (Rev: BL 3/1/88)

2310   Reit, Seymour. *Guns for General Washington: A Story of the American Revolution* (6–8). 1992, Harcourt paper $6.00 (0-15-232695-2). The true account of Colonel Henry Knox's attempt to bring cannons and artillery to the Continental Army during the blockade of 1775-1776. (Rev: BL 1/1/91; SLJ 1/91)

2311   Rinaldi, Ann. *Cast Two Shadows* (6–9). 1998, Harcourt $16.00 (0-15-200881-0). Set during the American Revolution, this novel describes Caroline Whitaker's changing perspectives on the war with Britain as a result of her experiences, including the hanging of her 14-year-old friend Kit, the imprisonment of her father, and the takeover of her house by the British. (Rev: BL 9/15/98; SLJ 9/98; VOYA 10/98)

2312   Rinaldi, Ann. *The Fifth of March: A Story of the Boston Massacre* (7–12). 1993, Harcourt $13.00 (0-15-200343-6); paper $6.00 (0-15-227517-7). In 1770, 14-year-old Rachel, an indentured servant in the household of John Adams, becomes caught up in political turmoil when she befriends a young British soldier. (Rev: BL 1/15/94*; SLJ 1/94; VOYA 2/94)

2313   Rinaldi, Ann. *Finishing Becca: The Story of Peggy Shippen and Benedict Arnold* (7–10). 1994, Harcourt $11.00 (0-15-200880-2). Historical fiction based on the author's contention that it was Peggy Shippen Arnold, wife of Benedict, who was responsible for her husband's betrayal of the American Revolution. (Rev: BL 11/15/94; SLJ 12/94; VOYA 2/95)

2314   Rinaldi, Ann. *A Ride into Morning: The Story of Temple Wick* (7–10). 1991, Harcourt $15.95 (0-15-200573-0). The story of a woman who hid her horse in her house to keep it from rebellious soldiers during the Revolutionary War. (Rev: BL 8/91; SLJ 5/91)

2315   Rinaldi, Ann. *The Secret of Sarah Revere* (7–10). 1995, Harcourt $12.00 (0-15-200393-2); paper $5.00 (0-15-200392-4). The daughter of Paul Revere recalls the events of the past 2 years against a background of historically significant events. (Rev: BL 11/15/95; SLJ 11/95; VOYA 12/95)

2316   Rinaldi, Ann. *Wolf by the Ears* (8–12). 1991, Scholastic $13.95 (0-590-43413-6). Harriet Hemings—the alleged daughter of Thomas Jefferson and his slave mistress—faces moral dilemmas in regard to freedom, equal rights, and her future. (Rev: BL 2/1/91; SLJ 4/91)

2317   Rosenburg, John. *First in War: George Washington in the American Revolution* (7–10). Illus. 1998, Millbrook LB $23.40 (0-7613-0311-1). This second part of the fictionalized biography of George Washington covers his career from 1775, when he was elected commander-in-chief, to the end of 1783,

when he resigned from his military duties. (Rev: SLJ 7/98; VOYA 4/99)

2318   Shaik, Fatima. *Melitte* (6–9). 1997, Dial $15.99 (0-8037-2106-4). A horrifying look at slavery as experienced by a young girl, Melitte, in late-18th-century Louisiana. (Rev: BL 10/15/97; BR 3–4/98; SLJ 10/97; VOYA 2/98)

2319   Sterman, Betsy. *Saratoga Secret* (5–8). 1998, Dial $16.00 (0-8037-2332-6). In the Upper Hudson River Valley during 1777, young Amity must warn the Continentals of an impending attack by General Burgoyne. (Rev: BL 11/1/98; SLJ 10/98)

2320   Walter, Mildred P. *Second Daughter: The Story of a Slave Girl* (6–10). 1996, Scholastic $15.95 (0-590-48282-3). A fictional account of the dramatic incident in Massachusetts during 1781 when a slave woman, Mum Bett, took her owner to court and won her freedom. (Rev: BL 2/15/96; BR 5–6/96; SLJ 2/96; VOYA 8/96)

NINETEENTH CENTURY TO THE CIVIL WAR (1809–1861)

2321   Armstrong, Jennifer. *Steal Away* (7–10). 1993, Scholastic paper $3.99 (0-590-46921-5). Two unhappy 13-year-old girls—one a slave, the other a white orphan—disguise themselves as boys and run away. (Rev: BL 2/1/92)

2322   Auch, Mary Jane. *Journey to Nowhere* (4–8). 1997, Holt $16.95 (0-8050-4922-3). In 1815, 11-year-old Mem and her family relocate from Connecticut to the wilderness of Genesee County in western New York. (Rev: BL 4/15/97; SLJ 5/97)

2323   Avi. *Beyond the Western Sea: Book Two: Lord Kirkle's Money* (6–9). 1996, Orchard LB $19.99 (0-531-08870-7). In this sequel to *Beyond the Western Sea: The Escape from Home* (1996), Patrick and Maura O'Connell and their 2 friends arrive in America, end up in the mill town of Lowell, Massachusetts, and encounter the villains that pursued them in the first book. (Rev: SLJ 10/96; VOYA 12/96)

2324   Avi. *Beyond the Western Sea: The Escape from Home* (6–10). 1996, Orchard LB $19.99 (0-531-08863-4). Three immigrant youngsters—2 poor Irish peasants and the third, an English stowaway—face dangers and hardships on their journey to America in this suspenseful adventure novel set in the 1850s. (Rev: BL 2/1/96*; BR 9–10/96; SLJ 6/96; VOYA 6/96)

2325   Avi. *The True Confessions of Charlotte Doyle* (6–9). 1990, Watts LB $17.99 (0-531-08493-0). An adventure story set in the 1850s about a 13-year-old girl and her voyage to America on a ship with a murderous crew. (Rev: BL 9/1/90; SLJ 9/90)

2326   Ayres, Katherine. *North by Night: A Story of the Underground Railroad* (6–10). 1998, Delacorte

$15.95 (0-385-32564-9). Told in diary form, this is the story of 16-year-old Lucinda and her role in helping slaves escape via the Underground Railroad. (Rev: BL 10/1/98; SLJ 10/98; VOYA 2/99)

2327 Benton, Amanda. *Silent Stranger* (5–9). 1997, Avon paper $14.00 (0-380-97486-X). During the War of 1812, Jessica finds a wounded stranger in the family barn who cannot or will not talk about his past. (Rev: BL 10/15/97; SLJ 12/97)

2328 Blos, Joan W. *A Gathering of Days: A New England Girl's Journal, 1830–32* (6–9). 1979, Macmillan $15.00 (0-684-16340-3). In the 1830s, a young teenager faces adjusting to a new stepmother. Newbery Medal, 1980.

2329 Bryant, Louella. *The Black Bonnet* (8–12). 1996, New England Pr. paper $12.95 (1-881535-22-3). An exciting story of 2 young escaped slaves, Charity and her older sister, Bea, and their last stop on the Underground Railroad in Burlington, Vermont, which they find is crawling with slave hunters. (Rev: BL 2/1/97; SLJ 2/97)

2330 Bryant, Louella. *Father by Blood* (6–9). 1999, New England Pr. paper $12.95 (1-881535-33-9). The story of John Brown and his raid on Harper's Ferry as seen through the eyes of his daughter Annie. (Rev: SLJ 9/99)

2331 Carbone, Elisa. *Stealing Freedom* (7–10). 1998, Knopf $17.00 (0-679-89307-5). Based on fact, this historical novel tells of a young teenage slave in Maryland and her escape to Canada via the Underground Railway in the 1850s. (Rev: BL 1/1–15/99; SLJ 2/99)

2332 Charbonneau, Eileen. *Honor to the Hills* (8–10). 1996, Tor $18.95 (0-312-86094-3). Returning to her home in the Catskill Mountains in 1851, 15-year-old Lily Woods finds that her family is involved in the Underground Railroad. (Rev: VOYA 6/96)

2333 Charbonneau, Eileen. *In the Time of the Wolves* (6–9). 1994, Tor paper $3.99 (0-8125-3361-5). In this story set in New York State 170 years ago, twin Josh struggles for his identity within his family and copes with prejudice against his Dutch/English/French/Native American heritage. (Rev: BL 12/1/94; VOYA 4/95)

2334 Chase-Riboud, Barbara. *The President's Daughter* (9–12). 1995, Ballantine paper $12.00 (0-345-38970-0). Harriet—daughter of Thomas Jefferson and his mistress and slave, Sally Hemings—passes as white and starts a new life as a free woman. Sequel to *Sally Hemings*. (Rev: BL 9/1/94)

2335 Cooper, J. California. *Family* (9–12). 1991, Doubleday $21.00 (0-385-41171-5). An African American slave commits suicide but returns as a spirit to watch her children mature and experience freedom after the Civil War. (Rev: BL 1/15/91; SLJ 8/91)

2336 DeFelice, Cynthia. *The Apprenticeship of Lucas Whitaker* (5–8). 1996, Farrar $15.00 (0-374-34669-0). In the mid-1800s, orphan Lucas becomes an apprentice to the local dentist/barber/undertaker. (Rev: BL 10/1/96; BR 3–4/97; SLJ 8/96*)

2337 Denenberg, Barry. *So Far from Home: The Diary of Mary Driscoll, an Irish Mill Girl* (4–8). (Dear America) 1997, Scholastic $10.95 (0-590-92667-5). Using a diary format, this novel tells the story of Mary Driscoll's journey to the United States from Ireland and her ordeals as a worker in a Massachusetts textile mill in the 1800s. (Rev: BL 12/15/97; SLJ 10/97)

2338 Ferris, Jean. *Into the Wind* (9–12). (American Dreams) 1996, Avon paper $3.99 (0-380-78198-0). In this romantic historical novel set in 1814, 17-year-old Rosie sets sail on a ship engaged to fight the British Navy. (Rev: SLJ 9/96)

2339 Fox, Paula. *The Slave Dancer* (6–9). Illus. 1973, Bradbury $16.95 (0-02-735560-8); Dell paper $5.50 (0-440-96132-7). A young fifer is kidnapped and forced to play his instrument to exercise slaves on a slave ship. Newbery Medal, 1974.

2340 Houston, Gloria. *Bright Freedom's Song: A Story of the Underground Railroad* (5–8). 1998, Harcourt $16.00 (0-15-201812-3). This novel focuses on the daily routine of the Camerons, a family involved in the Underground Railroad, and, in particular, of daughter Bright from age 6 to 15 as she grows to understand slavery and becomes committed to what her family is doing. (Rev: BL 11/1/98; BR 5–6/99; SLJ 12/98; VOYA 2/99)

2341 Joslyn, Mauriel Phillips. *Shenandoah Autumn: Courage under Fire* (6–10). 1999, White Mane $8.95 (1-57249-137-X). During the Civil War, young Mattie and her mother, though afraid of the Union troops around their Virginia home, save a wounded Confederate soldier and return him to his companions. (Rev: BL 5/1/99)

2342 Karr, Kathleen. *Gideon and the Mummy Professor* (5–8). 1993, Farrar $16.00 (0-374-32563-4). After Gideon, 12, finds a golden scarab in the mummy of the vaudeville act he shares with his father, they are pursued by various scoundrels in this 1855 New Orleans adventure. (Rev: BL 7/93; SLJ 6/93)

2343 Karr, Kathleen. *The Great Turkey Walk* (6–8). 1998, Farrar $16.00 (0-374-32773-4). In 1860, 15-year-old Simon decides to make his fortune by walking 1,000 turkeys from Missouri to Denver, where meat is scarce. (Rev: BL 6/1–15/98; BR 1–2/99; SLJ 3/98*)

2344 Landis, Jill Marie. *Just Once* (10–12). 1997, Jove paper $6.50 (0-515-12062-6). This romance set in the Louisiana woods of 1816 deals with adventurous Jemma and her woodsman guide, Hunter. (Rev: SLJ 4/98)

2345 Lasky, Kathryn. *True North* (6–8). 1996, Scholastic $14.95 (0-590-20523-4). Lucy, a 14-year-old girl living in Boston in 1858, and an escaped slave named Afrika travel north to Canada via the Underground Railroad. (Rev: BL 11/15/96; BR 3–4/97; SLJ 12/96; VOYA 4/97)

2346 Lyons, Mary E. *Letters from a Slave Girl: The Story of Harriet Jacobs* (7–12). 1992, Scribners $16.00 (0-684-19446-5). Based on Jacobs's autobiography, these "letters," written to lost relatives and friends, provide a look at what slavery meant for a young female in the mid-1800s. (Rev: BL 10/1/92; SLJ 12/92*)

2347 Lyons, Mary E. *The Poison Place* (6–8). Illus. 1997, Simon & Schuster $16.00 (0-689-81146-2). While taking his daughter on a tour of Philadelphia's Peale Museum, freed slave Moses Williams tells how his family and the Peales were entwined in family intrigue. (Rev: BL 12/1/97; BR 3–4/98; SLJ 11/97; VOYA 12/97)

2348 McCaughrean, Geraldine, adapt. *Moby Dick* (5–8). Illus. 1997, Oxford $33.95 (0-19-274156-X). A shortened version of this classic tale that does not sacrifice the quality or mood of the original. (Rev: SLJ 5/97*)

2349 McKissack, Patricia, and Fredrick McKissack. *Let My People Go* (5–8). Illus. 1998, Simon & Schuster $20.00 (0-689-80856-9). This novel mingles Bible stories and the hardships endured by slaves as told by Price Jefferson, a former slave who at the time of this novel is a free black abolitionist living in South Carolina. (Rev: BL 10/1/98; SLJ 11/98)

2350 Monfredo, Miriam G. *The Stalking Horse* (10–12). 1997, Berkley paper $21.95 (0-425-15783-0). In this fifth in a series of historical novels, Bronwyn Llyr and her friend try to foil a plan to assassinate President Lincoln. (Rev: BL 3/15/98; SLJ 8/98)

2351 Oates, Stephen B. *The Fires of Jubilee: Nat Turner's Fierce Rebellion* (10–12). 1982, NAL paper $3.95 (0-451-62308-8). A fictionalized account of the slave rebellion led by Nat Turner in 1831 in Southampton County, Virginia.

2352 Paterson, Katherine. *Jip, His Story* (5–9). 1996, Dutton paper $15.99 (0-525-67543-4). Jip, a foundling boy in Vermont of the 1850s, wonders about his origins, particularly after he finds he is being watching by a mysterious stranger. Scott O'Dell Historical Fiction Award, 1998. (Rev: BL 9/1/96*; BR 3–4/97; SLJ 10/96*; VOYA 4/97)

2353 Paterson, Katherine. *Lyddie* (9–12). 1991, Dutton $15.99 (0-525-67338-5). The life and hard times of a young girl growing up in the mid-19th century. (Rev: BL 1/1/91*; SLJ 2/91*)

2354 Patrick, Denise Lewis. *The Adventures of Midnight Son* (5–8). 1997, Holt $15.95 (0-8050-4714-X). Fleeing slavery on a horse given to him by his parents, Midnight rides to Mexico and freedom. (Rev: BL 12/15/97; BR 3–4/98; SLJ 12/97)

2355 Paulsen, Gary. *Nightjohn* (6–12). 1993, Delacorte $15.95 (0-385-30838-8). Told in the voice of Sarny, 12, Paulsen exposes the myths that African American slaves were content, well cared for, ignorant, and childlike, and that brave, resourceful slaves easily escaped. (Rev: BL 12/15/92)

2356 Pella, Judith, and Tracie Peterson. *Distant Dreams* (10–12). 1997, Bethany House paper $10.99 (1-55661-862-X). This novel set in 1830 during Andrew Jackson's presidency tells of a 15-year-old girl who becomes fascinated with locomotives and railroads in spite of the scorn of her mother and sister. (Rev: SLJ 9/97)

2357 Pesci, David. *Amistad* (10–12). 1997, Marlowe $22.95 (1-56924-748-X). The author of this fine historical novel fills in gaps and creates fascinating characters in this retelling of the slave revolt aboard the Spanish ship *Amistad*, led by Singbe-Pleh, later known as Joseph Cinque. (Rev: BL 5/15/97; SLJ 2/98)

2358 Rees, Douglas. *Lightning Time* (6–9). 1997, DK Publg. $15.95 (0-7894-2458-4). In Concord in 1857, young Theodore is so impressed with the words and deeds of John Brown that he runs away from home to join him and later takes part in the events at Harper's Ferry. (Rev: BL 1/1–15/98; BR 3–4/98; SLJ 12/97; VOYA 4/98)

2359 Rinaldi, Ann. *The Blue Door* (5–8). 1996, Scholastic $15.95 (0-590-46051-X). In this third volume of the Quilt trilogy—following *A Stitch in Time* (1994) and *Broken Days*—Amanda is forced to take a mill job in Lowell, Massachusetts, because of an identity misunderstanding. (Rev: BL 11/1/96; BR 3–4/97; VOYA 2/97)

2360 Rinaldi, Ann. *Broken Days* (6–10). 1995, Scholastic $14.95 (0-590-460053-6). When her cousin steals the piece of quilt that will establish her identity, Walking Breeze, who has come to live with her white family in Massachusetts at the age of 14 after being raised by Shawnees, is demoted to servant status and must work in the family's cotton mills in this story that takes place during the War of 1812. The second part of the Quilt Trilogy. (Rev: VOYA 4/96)

2361 Rinaldi, Ann. *Mine Eyes Have Seen* (8–12). 1998, Scholastic $16.95 (0-590-54318-0). The story of the raid at Harper's Ferry is retold through the eyes of John Brown's daughter Annie. (Rev: BL 2/15/98; BR 11–12/98; SLJ 2/98; VOYA 4/98)

2362 Rosenburg, John. *William Parker: Rebel Without Rights* (4–8). 1996, Millbrook LB $21.90 (1-56294-139-9). A fast-moving novel based on a little-known event involving a group of former slaves, led by William Parker, who fought back when their Maryland slave owner attempted to reclaim his human "property." (Rev: BL 2/15/96; BR 5–6/96; SLJ 5/96)

2363 Rossner, Judith. *Emmeline* (10–12). 1998, Doubleday paper $14.95 (0-385-33344-7). Based on fact, this is the story of a girl who was a mill girl in Lowell, Massachusetts, during the 1830s.

2364 Ruby, Lois. *Steal Away Home* (7–10). 1994, Macmillan paper $16.00 (0-02-777883-5). Dana, 12, finds a skeleton in a secret room of her Kansas home that turns out to be the remains of Lizbet, a conductor on the Underground Railroad in this story that moves from the present day to the 1850s. (Rev: BL 1/1/95; SLJ 2/95; VOYA 4/95)

2365 Smucker, Barbara. *Runaway to Freedom: A Story of the Underground Railway* (6–9). Illus. 1979, HarperCollins paper $4.95 (0-06-440106-5). Two young slave girls try for freedom via the Underground Railway.

2366 Stolz, Mary. *Cezanne Pinto: A Memoir* (6–10). 1994, Knopf $16.00 (0-679-84917-3). This fictionalized memoir of a runaway slave who became a soldier, cowboy, and teacher includes quotations and stories of the great figures of the time. (Rev: BL 1/15/94; SLJ 12/93; VOYA 6/94)

2367 Stone, Irving. *The President's Lady* (10–12). 1996, Rutledge Hill paper $14.95 (1-55853-431-8). The story of the great love between Andrew Jackson and his wife, Rachel.

2368 Wall, Bill. *The Cove of Cork* (5–9). 1999, Irish American paper $7.95 (0-85635-225-0). In this novel, the third in a trilogy revolving around the War of 1812, an Irish lad, the first mate of the American schooner *Shenandoah*, sees action in a battle against a British vessel and eventually wins the hand of the granddaughter of a shipbuilding magnate. (Rev: SLJ 7/99)

2369 Wanttaja, Ronald. *The Key to Honor* (5–9). 1996, Royal Fireworks paper $7.00 (0-88092-270-2). During the War of 1812, midshipman Nate Lawton has doubts about his courage in battle and worries about his father, who has been taken prisoner by the British. (Rev: VOYA 8/96)

2370 Whelan, Gloria. *Farewell to the Island* (5–8). 1998, HarperCollins $14.95 (0-06-027751-3). In this sequel to *Once on This Island,* Mary leaves her Michigan home after the War of 1812 and travels to England where she falls in love with Lord Lindsay. (Rev: BL 12/1/98; SLJ 1/99)

2371 Whelan, Gloria. *Once on This Island* (5–8). 1995, HarperCollins $15.95 (0-06-026248-6). Mary and her older brother and sister are left to tend the family farm on Mackinac Island when their father goes off to fight after the British capture the island in the War of 1812. (Rev: BL 10/1/95; BR 3–4/96; SLJ 11/95; VOYA 2/96)

2372 Wisler, G. Clifton. *Caleb's Choice* (5–8). 1996, Dutton paper $14.99 (0-525-67526-4). In northern Texas, during 1858, 13-year-old Caleb helps 2 escaped slaves. (Rev: BL 8/96; BR 11–12/96; SLJ 8/96)

THE CIVIL WAR (1861–1865)

2373 Armstrong, Jennifer. *The Dreams of Mairhe Mehan* (7–12). 1996, Knopf $18.00 (0-679-88152-2). A grim, challenging novel that takes place in Civil War Washington and involves a poor immigrant Irish serving maid and her family. (Rev: BL 1/1–15/97; BR 1–2/97; SLJ 10/96)

2374 Bartoletti, Susan C. *No Man's Land* (5–9). 1999, Scholastic $15.95 (0-590-38371-X). The story of a young boy's life as a Confederate soldier after he lies about his age and joins the Okefenokee Rifles in 1861. (Rev: BL 4/1/99; SLJ 6/99; VOYA 12/99)

2375 Bass, Cynthia. *Sherman's March* (9–12). 1994, Villard $21.00 (0-679-43033-4). A fast-paced fictionalized account of Sherman's infamous march to the sea. (Rev: SLJ 12/94)

2376 Beatty, Patricia. *Charley Skedaddle* (6–8). 1987, Troll paper $4.95 (0-8167-1317-0). A young deserter from the Union army finds out the true meaning of courage in the Virginia mountains. (Rev: BL 11/15/87; BR 11–12/87; SLJ 11/87; VOYA 12/87)

2377 Beatty, Patricia. *Jayhawker* (6–9). 1995, Morrow paper $4.95 (0-688-14422-5). The story of 12-year-old Elijah, son of a Kansas abolitionist, who becomes a spy and infiltrates Charles Quantrill's infamous Bushwhacker network. (Rev: BL 9/1/91*; SLJ 9/91*)

2378 Brown, Dee Alexander. *The Way to Bright Star* (10–12). 1998, Forge $24.95 (0-312-86612-7). An adventure story, set in the American frontier during the Civil War, about Ben Butterfield, his friends, and the dangers they confront on a wagon train traveling through war-torn territory. (Rev: BL 5/1/98; SLJ 3/99)

2379 Clapp, Patricia. *The Tamarack Tree: A Novel of the Siege of Vicksburg* (7–10). 1986, Lothrop $16.00 (0-688-02852-7). The siege of Vicksburg as seen through the eyes of a 17-year-old English girl who is trapped inside the city. (Rev: BL 11/15/86; BR 1–2/87; SLJ 10/86; VOYA 2/87)

2380 Collier, James L., and Christopher Collier. *With Every Drop of Blood: A Novel of the Civil War* (6–10). 1994, Dell paper $4.99 (0-440-21983-3). A Civil War docunovel about Johnny, a young Confederate soldier, and Cush, a black Union soldier who captures him. Together, the two experience the horrors of war and bigotry. (Rev: BL 7/94; SLJ 8/94; VOYA 12/94)

2381 Coyle, Harold. *Look Away* (10–12). 1995, Simon & Schuster $24.00 (0-684-80392-5). An unscrupulous, politically ambitious father takes advantage of his two sons in a way that they find themselves on opposite sides in this suspenseful Civil War novel. (Rev: BL 4/15/95; SLJ 5/96)

2382 Duey, Kathleen. *Amelina Carrett: Bayou Grand Coeur, Louisiana, 1863* (5–8). 1999, Simon & Schuster $3.99 (0-689-82402-5). Set in Cajun country during the Civil War, this novel tells of Amelina and the wounded Yankee soldier she finds in the woods. (Rev: SLJ 9/99)

2383 Ellison, Suzanne Pierson. *The Best of Enemies* (7–12). 1998, Northland $12.95 (0-87358-714-6); paper $8.95 (0-87358-717-0). During the Civil War, the son of a wealthy Hispanic rancher, a Texas soldier, and an honorable Navajo girl find themselves stranded in the desert. (Rev: BL 2/1/99; BR 5–6/99; SLJ 5/99; VOYA 4/99)

2384 Ernst, Kathleen. *The Bravest Girl in Sharpsburg* (6–9). 1998, White Mane paper $8.95 (1-57249-083-7). Told from the viewpoint of 3 girls in Maryland during the Civil War, this is the story of friendships that are tested when the the girls support different sides and what happens when the Confederate Army marches through their town, thrusting the community into the middle of the war. (Rev: SLJ 9/98)

2385 Ernst, Kathleen. *The Night Riders of Harpers Ferry* (6–8). Illus. 1996, White Mane paper $7.95 (1-57249-013-6). Told from the standpoint of 17-year-old Solomon, this is a story of romance, divided families, and dangerous secrets, set on the border between North and South during the Civil War. (Rev: BL 1/1–15/97; SLJ 5/97)

2386 Fleischman, Paul. *Bull Run* (6–12). 1993, HarperCollins LB $14.89 (0-06-021447-3). Spotlights the diary entries of 16 fictional characters, 8 each from the South and the North, throughout the battle. (Rev: BL 1/15/93*; SLJ 3/93*)

2387 Forman, James D. *Becca's Story* (5–8). 1992, Scribners LB $15.00 (0-684-19332-9). Forman uses his ancestors' Civil War-era letters and diaries to weave the story of Becca, who is courted by 2 young men who go off to fight in the Union Army. (Rev: BL 12/1/92; SLJ 11/92*)

2388 Frazier, Charles. *Cold Mountain* (10–12). 1997, Atlantic Monthly $24.00 (0-87113-679-1). In this best-selling novel set during Civil War times, a soldier deserts and treks through the wilderness to Cold Mountain, where 2 women, Ruby and Ada, are trying to eke out a living. (Rev: BL 6/1–15/97; SLJ 11/97)

2389 Gibbons, Kaye. *On the Occasion of My Last Afternoon* (10–12). 1998, Putnam $22.95 (0-399-14299-1); Avon paper $12.50 (0-380-73214-9). This novel, set before and during the Civil War, tells of the childhood of a Southern belle, her marriage to a Northern doctor, and her transformation from a self-absorbed child to a loving, mature wife and mother. (Rev: BL 5/15/98; SLJ 9/98)

2390 Gindlesperger, James. *Escape from Libby Prison* (10–12). 1996, Burd Street $24.95 (0-942597-97-5). Fictional characters and figures from history are interwoven in this novel about the escape of 109 Union officers from the gruesome hell known as Libby Prison during the Civil War. (Rev: SLJ 2/97)

2391 Greenberg, Martin H., and Charles G. Waugh, eds. *Civil War Women II: Stories by Women About Women* (7–10). 1997, August House paper $9.95 (0-87483-487-2). A collection of short stories by such female writers as Louisa May Alcott and Edith Wharton that deal with women's lives during the Civil War. (Rev: SLJ 8/97)

2392 Hansen, Joyce. *Out from This Place* (6–9). 1992, Avon paper $4.50 (0-380-71409-4). In this volume, Easter, the companion of Obi, a slave who joined the Northern Army during the Civil War in *Which Way Freedom*, tells her story and how she spent much of the war with other former slaves in the Carolina Sea Islands. (Rev: BL 1/15/89; BR 1–2/89; SLJ 12/88; VOYA 2/89)

2393 Hill, Pamela S. *A Voice from the Border* (6–8). 1998, Holiday House $16.95 (0-8234-1356-X). Set in Missouri, a border state during the Civil War, this novel introduces 15-year-old Reeves, whose family owns slaves and whose house is commandeered by Union forces after Reeves' father dies in battle. (Rev: SLJ 9/98)

2394 Johnson, Nancy. *My Brother's Keeper: A Civil War Story* (6–10). 1997, Down East $14.95 (0-89272-414-5). Two orphaned brothers from upstate New York, ages 15 and 13, join the Union Army, one as a soldier, the other as a drummer boy, and soon find themselves surrounded by the blood and tragedy of battle in this story based on the experiences of the author's great-great-uncles. (Rev: BR 5–6/98; SLJ 1/98)

2395 Jones, Madison. *Nashville 1864: The Dying of the Light* (10–12). 1997, Sanders $17.95 (1-879941-35-X). This novel, set during the Civil War, tells of

12-year-old Steven who, with his slave, Dink, sets out to locate his father who is fighting on the Confederate side. (Rev: SLJ 1/98)

2396 Keith, Harold. *Rifles for Watie* (7–10). 1957, HarperCollins paper $5.95 (0-06-447030-X). Jeff, a Union soldier, learns about the realities of war when he becomes a spy. Newbery Award, 1958.

2397 Lasky, Kathryn. *Alice Rose & Sam* (6–9). 1998, Hyperion LB $16.49 (0-7868-2277-5); paper $5.99 (0-7868-1222-2). Growing up in Nevada during the Civil War, Alice Rose forms a friendship with young Samuel Clemens, and together they solve the mystery of a murdered drunk and uncover a Confederate plot. (Rev: SLJ 5/98)

2398 Love, D. Anne. *Three Against the Tide* (5–8). 1998, Holiday House $15.95 (0-8234-1400-0). In this Civil War novel, a 12-year-old Confederate girl must take care of herself and 2 younger brothers when her father goes to war. (Rev: BL 12/1/98; SLJ 1/99)

2399 Meriwether, Louise. *Fragments of the Ark* (9–12). 1995, Pocket Books paper $10.00 (0-671-79948-7). Based on a true account, this historical novel is about a group of slaves who escaped to join Union forces and the bigotry they faced from their "rescuers." (Rev: BL 2/15/94; SLJ 11/94)

2400 Mitchell, Margaret. *Gone with the Wind* (9–12). 1936, Avon paper $6.50 (0-380-00109-8). The magnificent Civil War novel about Scarlett O'Hara and her family at Tara.

2401 Mrazek, Robert J. *Stonewall's Gold* (10–12). 1999, St. Martin's $22.95 (0-312-20024-2). During the last year of the Civil War, 15-year-old Jamie kills a man who attempts to rape his mother and comes into possession of a treasure map that will lead him into adventure and danger. (Rev: BL 12/15/98; SLJ 4/99)

2402 Murphy, Jim. *The Journal of James Edmond Pease: A Civil War Union Soldier* (7–12). 1998, Scholastic $10.95 (0-590-43814-X). A young misfit in the Union Army records his company's activities in a journal that also tells about his gradual maturation. (Rev: BL 11/15/98; SLJ 7/99)

2403 Nixon, Joan Lowery. *A Dangerous Promise* (6–8). 1996, Delacorte $15.95 (0-385-32073-6). Mike Kelly, 12, and his friend Todd Blakely run away to help the Union forces in the Civil War and experience the terrors of war. (Rev: BL 9/1/94; SLJ 11/94; VOYA 10/94)

2404 Nixon, Joan Lowery. *Keeping Secrets* (5–8). (Orphan Train) 1996, Demco $9.85 (0-606-08789-3). Set in Missouri during the Civil War, Peg, 11, unwittingly becomes involved with a Union spy. (Rev: BL 3/1/95; SLJ 3/95; VOYA 4/95)

2405 Paulsen, Gary. *Sarny: A Life Remembered* (6–12). 1997, Delacorte $15.95 (0-385-32195-3). In this sequel to *Nightjohn,* the slave Sarny sets out during the Civil War to find her son and daughter, who were sold and are now impossible to locate. (Rev: BL 10/1/97; BR 11–12/97; SLJ 9/97; VOYA 2/98)

2406 Paulsen, Gary. *Soldier's Heart* (5–8). 1998, Doubleday $15.95 (0-385-32498-7). A powerful novel that re-creates the agony of the Civil War, based on the real-life experiences of a Union soldier who was only 15 when he went to war. (Rev: BL 6/1–15/98; SLJ 9/98; VOYA 10/98)

2407 Pinkney, Andrea D. *Silent Thunder: A Civil War Story* (5–8). 1999, Hyperion LB $16.49 (0-7868-2388-7). The brutal oppression of slavery is revealed in this story told by 2 black children living on a Virginia plantation during the Civil War. (Rev: BL 9/1/99)

2408 Reeder, Carolyn. *Across the Lines* (5–9). 1997, Simon & Schuster $16.00 (0-689-81133-0). Edward and his slave friend, Simon, are separated when Yankees capture their Virginia plantation in this Civil War novel. (Rev: BL 4/1/97; BR 11–12/97; SLJ 6/97; VOYA 8/97)

2409 Reeder, Carolyn. *Captain Kate* (6–8). 1999, Avon paper $15.00 (0-380-97628-5). This is an unusual Civil War story about 12-year-old Kate, her stepbrother Seth, and their dangerous trip down the C&O Canal on the family's coal boat. (Rev: BL 1/1–15/99; SLJ 1/99)

2410 Reeder, Carolyn. *Shades of Gray* (6–8). 1989, Macmillan LB $15.00 (0-02-775810-9). Immediately after the Civil War young Will must live with an uncle whom he considers a coward because he would not fight in the war. (Rev: BL 3/15/90; VOYA 2/90)

2411 Rinaldi, Ann. *In My Father's House* (7–10). 1993, Scholastic $14.95 (0-590-44730-0). A coming-of-age novel set during the Civil War about 7-year-old Oscie. (Rev: BL 2/15/93)

2412 Sappey, Maureen Stack. *Letters from Vinnie* (7–10). 1999, Front Street $16.95 (1-886910-31-6). A novel that mixes fact and fiction to tell the story of the tiny woman who sculpted the large statue of Abraham Lincoln found in the Capitol Building in Washington. (Rev: BL 9/15/99)

2413 Shaara, Jeff. *Gods and Generals* (10–12). 1996, Ballantine $25.00 (0-345-40492-0). This clever novel of the Civil War is told from the viewpoint of 4 important generals, Lee, Jackson, Hancock, and Chamberlain. (Rev: SLJ 8/97)

2414 Stone, Irving. *Love Is Eternal* (10–12). 1994, Buccaneer LB $27.95 (1-56849-556-0). A lengthy, rewarding novel about Lincoln's marriage to Mary Todd.

2415 Travis, Lucille. *Captured by a Spy* (6–10). 1995, Baker paper $5.99 (0-8010-8915-8). A story of mercy and compassion during the Civil War, when 2 Northern boys, one white and one African American, are taken to Canada by blockade runners and placed in the hands of an infamous, exiled Confederate sympathizer. (Rev: BL 9/15/95)

2416 Walker, Margaret. *Jubilee* (9–12). 1983, Bantam paper $6.99 (0-553-27383-3). A novel often compared with *Gone with the Wind,* about blacks and poor whites living in the South before, during, and after the Civil War. (Rev: BL 2/15/98)

2417 West, Jessamyn. *The Friendly Persuasion* (9–12). 1982, Buccaneer LB $27.95 (0-89966-395-8). The pacifist views of the Quaker Birdwell family cause problems during the Civil War.

2418 Williams, Jeanne. *The Confederate Fiddle* (6–9). 1997, Hendrick-Long $16.95 (1-885777-04-3). On his wagon train taking cotton to Mexico in 1862, 17-year-old Vin Clayburn is torn between fulfilling his duty to his family or joining his brother fighting on the Southern side in the Civil War. (Rev: BL 3/15/98)

2419 Wisler, G. Clifton. *The Drummer Boy of Vicksburg* (5–8). 1997, Lodestar paper $15.99 (0-525-67537-X). The story of a drummer boy in the Union Army during the Civil War. (Rev: BL 12/1/96; BR 9–10/97; SLJ 3/97)

2420 Wisler, G. Clifton. *Mustang Flats* (5–8). 1997, Dutton paper $14.99 (0-525-67544-2). Abby wants to help his family when his father returns from the Civil War a broken, bitter man. (Rev: BL 8/97; BR 1–2/98; SLJ 7/97)

2421 Wisler, G. Clifton. *Red Cap* (6–8). 1991, 1994, Penguin paper $3.99 (0-14-036936-8). An adolescent boy lies about his age to join the Union Army and ends up as a prisoner of war in the infamous Andersonville camp. (Rev: BL 8/91; SLJ 8/91)

2422 Wisler, G. Clifton. *Thunder on the Tennessee* (7–10). 1995, Puffin paper $4.99 (0-14-037612-7). A 16-year-old Southern boy learns the value of courage and honor during the Civil War.

WESTERN EXPANSION AND PIONEER LIFE

2423 Aldrich, Bess Streeter. *A Lantern in Her Hand* (9–12). 1983, Amereon LB $21.95 (0-88411-260-8). This novel, originally published in 1928, tells about a young bride and her husband who are homesteaders in Nebraska in 1865. A sequel is *A White Bird Flying.*

2424 Alter, Judith MacBain. *Luke and the Van Zandt County War* (6–9). Illus. 1984, Texas Christian Univ. Pr. $10.95 (0-912646-88-8). Set in Texas after the Civil War, this novel centers on Theo, her doctor-father, and Luke, her father's apprentice.

2425 Altsheler, Joseph A. *Kentucky Frontiersman: The Adventures of Henry Ware, Hunter and Border Fighter* (6–10). Illus. 1988, Voyageur $16.95 (0-929146-01-8). A reissue of a fine frontier adventure story featuring young Henry Ware who is captured by an Indian hunting party. (Rev: BR 3–4/89; SLJ 3/89)

2426 Applegate, Stan. *The Devil's Highway* (5–8). Illus. 1998, Peachtree paper $8.95 (1-56145-184-3). Set along the Natchez Trail in the early 1800s, this adventure novel introduces 14-year-old Zeb, on a quest for his missing grandfather, and Hannah, a half-Choctaw girl who has escaped kidnappers and is trying to find her tribe and family. (Rev: SLJ 2/99)

2427 Arnold, Elliott. *Blood Brother* (10–12). 1979, Univ. of Nebraska Pr. paper $13.95 (0-8032-5901-8). This novel depicts the struggle between white settlers and the Apaches, led by Cochise.

2428 Auch, Mary Jane. *Frozen Summer* (4–8). 1998, Holt $15.95 (0-8050-4923-1). In this sequel to *Journey to Nowhere,* set in 1816 in upstate New York, 12-year-old Mem struggles to hold her family together in spite of her mother's bouts of severe depression. (Rev: BL 1/1–15/99; BR 5–6/99; SLJ 12/98; VOYA 8/99)

2429 Avi. *The Barn* (5–8). 1994, Orchard LB $15.99 (0-531-08711-5). In this story set in 1850s Oregon, Ben and his siblings must run their farm alone after their father becomes paralyzed, and Ben decides they must fulfill their father's dream and build a barn. (Rev: BL 9/1/94*; SLJ 10/94)

2430 Benchley, Nathaniel. *Gone and Back* (7–9). 1971, HarperCollins paper $1.95 (0-06-440016-6). Obed's family moves West to take advantage of the Homestead Act and he soon finds he must assume new family responsibilities.

2431 Benner, J. A. *Uncle Comanche* (5–8). 1996, Texas Christian Univ. Pr. paper $12.95 (0-87565-152-6). Based on fact, this is the story of the adventures of 12-year-old Sul Ross, who runs away from home in pre-Civil War Texas and is pursued by a family friend nicknamed Uncle Comanche. (Rev: VOYA 10/96)

2432 Blair, Clifford. *The Guns of Sacred Heart* (9–12). 1991, Walker $28.95 (0-8027-4123-1). Outlaws trying to free their leader, who is a prisoner at a remote mission school, are fought off by a marshal, a cowboy, and the school's staff and students. (Rev: BL 11/1/91; SLJ 5/92)

2433 Bonner, Cindy. *Lily* (9–12). 1992, Algonquin $26.95 (0-945575-95-5). An old-fashioned Western romance in which an innocent girl falls in love with a worldly guy from an outlaw family. (Rev: BL 9/1/92*; SLJ 12/92)

2434 Bowers, Terrell L. *Ride Against the Wind* (7–10). 1996, Walker $21.95 (0-8027-4156-8). Set in Eden, Kansas, in the late 1800s, this sequel to *The Secret of Snake Canyon* (1993) involves Jerrod Danmyer and his attachment to Marion Gates, daughter of his family's sworn enemies. (Rev: BL 12/15/96; VOYA 8/97)

2435 Brewer, James D. *No Justice* (10–12). 1996, Walker $21.95 (0-8057-3283-6). Set along the Mississippi River during Reconstruction, this adult novel features an unlikely trio—a woman who makes a living entertaining gentlemen on riverboats, a former Union soldier, and a wounded Southern soldier—who join forces to solve a murder mystery. (Rev: SLJ 12/96)

2436 Burks, Brian. *Soldier Boy* (6–9). 1997, Harcourt $12.00 (0-15-201218-4); paper $6.00 (0-15-201219-2). To escape a crooked boxing ring in 1870s Chicago, Johnny joins the army to fight Indians and eventually finds himself at Little Big Horn with Custer. (Rev: BL 5/15/97; SLJ 5/97; VOYA 8/97)

2437 Calvert, Patricia. *Bigger* (5–8). 1994, Scribners paper $16.00 (0-684-19685-9). Accompanied by an abused stray dog named Bigger, Tyler, 12, sets out on an 800-mile trip from Missouri to the Rio Grande to find his father after the Civil War. (Rev: BL 4/1/94; SLJ 4/94; VOYA 4/94)

2438 Calvert, Patricia. *The Snowbird* (7–9). 1982, NAL paper $1.95 (0-451-13353-6). Two orphans—one 14 and the other 8—are sent to the Dakota territory of 1883 to live with their uncle.

2439 Calvert, Patricia. *Sooner* (5–9). 1998, Simon & Schuster $16.00 (0-689-81114-4). After the Civil War, Tyler's father leaves the family to seek his fortune in Mexico, and 13-year-old Tyler must assume adult responsibilities in this sequel to *Bigger*. (Rev: BL 6/1–15/98; BR 1–2/99; SLJ 6/98)

2440 Charbonneau, Eileen. *Rachel LeMoyne* (10–12). (Women of the West) 1998, Forge $22.95 (0-312-86448-5). An adventure story, based on fact, about a mixed-blood Choctaw student who goes to Ireland to help famine victims, marries, and returns to America with her Irish husband to cross the frontier to settle in Oregon. (Rev: BL 5/15/98; SLJ 2/99; VOYA 12/98)

2441 Clark, Walter Van Tilburg. *The Ox-Bow Incident* (10–12). 1989, NAL paper $5.95 (0-451-52525-6). Mob vengeance and a lynching are the focus of this novel about justice in the Old West.

2442 Clements, Bruce. *I Tell a Lie Every So Often* (7–9). 1974, Farrar paper $3.50 (0-374-43539-1). Set on the Mississippi River during 1848, this is the story of 2 brothers, one of whom is known for stretching the truth.

2443 Conrad, Pam. *Prairie Songs* (6–9). Illus. 1985, HarperCollins $15.89 (0-06-021337-X); paper $4.95 (0-06-440206-1). On the wide Nebraska prairie young Louisa forms a friendship with a doctor's wife whose hold on reality is slipping away. (Rev: BL 9/1/85; SLJ 10/85; VOYA 12/85)

2444 Coville, Bruce. *Fortune's Journey* (5–8). 1995, Troll $13.95 (0-8167-3650-2). A teen romance in which a 16-year-old girl leads a troupe of actors west along the Oregon Trail in a Conestoga wagon. (Rev: BL 10/15/95; SLJ 11/95; VOYA 2/96)

2445 Curtis, Jack. *Pepper Tree Rider* (9–12). 1994, Walker $30.95 (0-8027-4137-1). A subtle Western where a fast gun isn't always the answer; from the pen of the screenplay writer of *Gunsmoke*. (Rev: BL 5/1/94; SLJ 10/94)

2446 Cushman, Karen. *The Ballad of Lucy Whipple* (5–8). 1996, Clarion $15.00 (0-395-72806-1). Lucy hates being stuck in the California wilderness with an overbearing mother who runs a boarding house. (Rev: BL 8/96*; SLJ 8/96*; VOYA 12/96)

2447 DeAndrea William L. *Written in Fire* (9–12). 1995, Walker $28.95 (0-8027-3270-4). A mystery story set in the Wyoming Territory in the 1800s featuring Quinn Booker, a pulp fiction novelist who investigates the near-fatal shooting of his friend Lobo Blacke. (Rev: BL 1/1–15/96; VOYA 2/96)

2448 DeFelice, Cynthia. *Weasel* (7–9). 1990, Macmillan paper $15.00 (0-02-726457-2). Set in rural Ohio in 1839, this is the story of a boy's initiation into the cruel realities of life and death. (Rev: BL 5/15/90; SLJ 5/90; VOYA 6/90)

2449 Donahue, Marilyn Cram. *The Valley in Between* (6–9). 1987, Walker LB $29.90 (0-8027-6733-8). In a story that spans a 4-year period, a young girl comes of age in California of the 1850s. (Rev: BL 11/1/87; BR 5–6/88; SLJ 11/87; VOYA 12/87)

2450 Eckert, Allan W. *Return to Hawk's Hill: A Novel* (6–10). Illus. 1998, Little, Brown $15.45 (0-316-21593-7). In this sequel to *Incident at Hawk's Hill*, young Ben, who is able to communicate with animals, escapes danger and is rescued by friendly Metis Indians. (Rev: BL 6/1–15/98; SLJ 6/98; VOYA 6/98)

2451 Eickhoff, Randy Lee, and Leonard Lewis. *Bowie* (10–12). 1998, Forge $23.95 (0-312-86619-4). A fictionalized biography of the adventurer James Bowie, gambler, slave runner, land speculator, and brawler, who died at the Alamo, told from various perspectives by a variety of "witnesses" to the events of his life. (Rev: SLJ 4/99)

2452 Estleman, Loren D. *Billy Gashade* (10–12). 1997, Forge $23.95 (0-312-85997-X). An exciting historical novel about a young boy who is an accomplished pianist and his adventures in the Wild West of "Wild Bill" Hickok and Billy the Kid. (Rev: BL 5/1/97; SLJ 3/98)

2453 Estleman, Loren D. *Journey of the Dead* (10–12). 1998, St. Martin's $21.95 (0-312-85999-6). A western for mature readers about Pat Garrett, Billy the Kid's killer, and how he is haunted by the ghost of the dead outlaw. (Rev: SLJ 10/98)

2454 Ferber, Edna. *Cimarron* (9–12). 1998, Amereon $28.95 (0-88411-548-8). The story of the fortunes of Yancey Cravat and his wife Sabra set against the days of the land rush of 1889 in Oklahoma. Also use: *Saratoga Trunk* (1986).

2455 Fleischman, Paul. *The Borning Room* (5–10). 1991, HarperCollins paper $4.95 (0-06-447099-7). Georgina remembers her life's "turnings," most of which occurred in the room set aside for giving birth and dying in her grandfather's house in 19th-century rural Ohio. (Rev: BL 10/1/91*; SLJ 9/91*)

2456 Garland, Sherry. *A Line in the Sand: The Alamo Diary of Lucinda Lawrence* (5–8). (Dear America) 1998, Scholastic $10.95 (0-590-39466-5). Early Texas farm life during the exciting events of the Texas Revolution of 1835 and 1836 come to life through the diary of 13-year-old Lucinda Lawrence. (Rev: BL 3/1/99; SLJ 1/99)

2457 Gloss, Molly. *The Jump-Off Creek* (9–12). 1989, Houghton $16.45 (0-395-51086-4). A realistic portrait of the struggles of a lone homesteader and her problems. (Rev: BL 9/1/89)

2458 Gregory, Kristiana. *The Great Railroad Race: The Transcontinental Railroad Diary of Libby West* (4–8). (Dear America) 1999, Scholastic $10.95 (0-590-10991-X). The story of the building of the transcontinental railroad as seen through the eyes of a 14-year-old girl whose father is a reporter following the progress of the massive undertaking. (Rev: BL 4/1/99; SLJ 8/99; VOYA 10/99)

2459 Gregory, Kristiana. *Jimmy Spoon and the Pony Express* (6–8). 1997, Scholastic paper $3.99 (0-590-46578-3). Jimmy answers an ad for Pony Express riders, but he's haunted by his previous life with the Shoshoni (see *The Legend of Jimmy Spoon,* Harcourt, 1991), especially the beautiful Nahanee. (Rev: BL 11/15/94; SLJ 11/94; VOYA 4/95)

2460 Grey, Zane. *The Last Trail* (10–12). Illus. 1996, Univ. of Nebraska Pr. paper $12.00 (0-8032-7063-1). Originally published in 1909, this western tells of Helen Sheppard who, with her father, relocates to the Ohio Valley, where she encounters dangers from hostile Indians and romance with a borderman. (Rev: SLJ 8/96)

2461 Grey, Zane. *Riders of the Purple Sage* (9–12). 1990, Viking paper $9.95 (0-14-018440-6). This is probably the best known of Grey's westerns, a number of which are available in paperback. This one takes place in the wilderness of Utah in 1871.

2462 Hahn, Mary D. *The Gentleman Outlaw and Me-Eli: A Story of the Old West* (5–8). 1996, Clarion $15.00 (0-395-73083-X). On her trip west to find her father, Eliza, disguised as a boy, encounters a young would-be con artist in this historical story set in the Ol' West. (Rev: BL 4/1/96; BR 11–12/96; SLJ 5/96; VOYA 6/96)

2463 Heitzmann, Kristen. *Honor's Pledge* (8–12). 1997, Bethany House paper $10.99 (0-7642-2031-4). Set in frontier America after the Civil War, this romance is about how, after a terrible storm, a kidnapping, encounters with local Comanches, and several deaths, Abbie finally gets the man she loves. (Rev: BL 5/1/98; VOYA 12/98)

2464 Hickman, Janet. *Susannah* (5–8). 1998, Greenwillow $15.00 (0-688-14854-9). Set in the Ohio frontier, this novel explores the world of a sensitive girl who, after her mother's death, lives with her father in a Shaker community surrounded by hostile, unsympathetic settlers. (Rev: BL 10/15/98; SLJ 10/98)

2465 Hill, Pamela S. *Ghost Horses* (6–9). 1996, Holiday House $15.95 (0-8234-1229-6). In this novel set in the late 19th century, Tabitha rebels at her preacher father's old-fashioned ideas and, disguised as a boy, joins an expedition digging for dinosaur bones in the American West. (Rev: BL 4/15/96; BR 11–12/96; SLJ 3/96)

2466 Holland, Cecilia. *The Bear Flag* (9–12). 1992, Kensington paper $5.99 (1-55817-635-7). A widow survives life on the American frontier in this novel about the race for settlement of California. (Rev: SLJ 8/90)

2467 Holland, Isabelle. *The Promised Land* (5–8). 1996, Scholastic $15.95 (0-590-47176-7). Orphaned Maggie and Annie, who have been happily living with the Russell family on the Kansas frontier for 3 years, are visited by an uncle who wants them to come home with him to Catholicism and their Irish heritage in New York City. A sequel to *The Journey Home.* (Rev: BL 4/15/96; SLJ 8/96; VOYA 6/96)

2468 Holmas, Stig. *Apache Pass* (6–8). Trans. from Norwegian by Anne Born. Illus. (Chiricahua Apache) 1996, Harbinger $15.95 (1-57140-010-9); paper $9.95 (1-57140-011-7). The kidnapping of a white boy by Indians leads to confrontations and killings in this novel set in what is now New Mexico. (Rev: SLJ 1/97; VOYA 4/97)

2469 Jones, J. Sydney. *Frankie* (5–8). 1997, Lodestar paper $16.99 (0-525-67574-4). At the time of the coal miners' strike in Ludlow, Colorado, a strange girl shows up in this novel that uses historical figures like Mother Jones as characters. (Rev: BR 3–4/98; SLJ 11/97)

2470 Karr, Kathleen. *Oh, Those Harper Girls!* (6–9). 1992, Farrar $16.00 (0-374-35609-2). Faced with the foreclosure of their Texas ranch, 6 sisters are determined to help their unlucky father save their homestead. (Rev: BL 4/15/92)

2471 Karr, Kathleen. *Oregon Sweet Oregon* (5–8). (Petticoat Party) 1997, HarperCollins LB $14.89 (0-06-027234-1); paper $4.95 (0-06-440497-8). This novel, set in Oregon City, Oregon, from 1846 through 1848, recounts the adventures of 13-year-old Phoebe Brown and her family when they stake a land claim along the Willamette River. (Rev: BL 7/97; SLJ 7/98)

2472 Lasky, Kathryn. *Beyond the Divide* (7–9). 1983, Macmillan LB $17.00 (0-02-751670-9). A young girl and her father join the rush for gold in 1849. (Rev: BL 2/15/88)

2473 Laxalt, Robert. *Dust Devils* (6–10). 1997, Univ. of Nevada Pr. paper $16.00 (0-87417-300-0). A Native American teenager named Ira sets out to retrieve his prize-winning horse that has been stolen by a rustler named Hawkeye. (Rev: BL 10/15/97; VOYA 12/98)

2474 Loveday, John. *Goodbye, Buffalo Sky* (5–8). 1997, Simon & Schuster $16.00 (0-689-81370-8). Two girls are kidnapped by a vengeful Sioux warrior in this exciting adventure set in the Great Plains during the 1870s. (Rev: BL 1/1–15/98; BR 3–4/98; SLJ 11/97)

2475 Luger, Harriett M. *The Last Stronghold: A Story of the Modoc Indian War, 1872–1873* (5–8). 1995, Linnet paper $16.50 (0-208-02403-4). The Modoc Indian War of 1872–73 is re-created in this story involving 3 young people: Charka, a Modoc youth, Ned, a frontier boy, and Yankel, a Russian Jew who has been tricked into joining the army. (Rev: VOYA 6/96)

2476 McClain, Margaret S. *Bellboy: A Mule Train Journey* (6–10). Illus. 1989, New Mexico $17.95 (0-9622468-1-6). Set in California in the 1870s, this is the story of a 12-year-old boy and his first job on a mule train. (Rev: BL 3/1/90; SLJ 3/90)

2477 McDonald, Brix. *Riding on the Wind* (5–10). 1998, Avenue paper $5.95 (0-9661306-0-X). Talented, stubborn 15-year-old Carrie Sutton, growing up in Wyoming in 1860, becomes a Pony Express rider and gets involved with a sinister Confederate agent. (Rev: SLJ 1/99)

2478 McKissack, Patricia. *Run Away Home* (5–8). 1997, Scholastic $14.95 (0-590-46751-4). In 1888 rural Alabama, a young African American girl helps shelter a fugitive Apache boy. (Rev: BL 10/1/97; SLJ 11/97)

2479 Mazzio, Joann. *Leaving Eldorado* (6–9). 1993, Houghton $14.95 (0-395-64381-3). The adventures of Maude, 14, in 1896 New Mexico Territory. (Rev: BL 3/15/93; SLJ 5/93)

2480 Meyer, Carolyn. *Where the Broken Heart Still Beats: The Story of Cynthia Ann Parker* (7–12). 1992, Harcourt $16.95 (0-15-200639-7); paper $7.00 (0-15-295602-6). A fictional retelling of the abduction of Cynthia Parker, who was stolen by Comanches as a child and lived with them for 24 years, first as a slave, then as a chief's wife. (Rev: BL 12/1/92; SLJ 9/92)

2481 Moore, Robin. *The Bread Sister of Sinking Creek* (7–10). 1990, HarperCollins LB $14.89 (0-397-32419-7). An orphaned 14-year-old girl becomes a servant in Pennsylvania during pioneer days. (Rev: BL 7/90; SLJ 4/90; VOYA 8/90)

2482 Murphy, Jim. *West to a Land of Plenty: The Diary of Teresa Angelino Viscardi, New York to Idaho Territory, 1883* (4–8). (Dear America) 1998, Scholastic $10.95 (0-590-73888-7). Written in diary format, this historical novel tells about Italian American Teresa Viscardi and her family as they travel west to relocate in the Idaho Territory. (Rev: BR 9–10/98; SLJ 4/98)

2483 Myers, Walter Dean. *The Journal of Joshua Loper: A Black Cowboy* (5–8). 1999, Scholastic $10.95 (0-590-02691-7). In this fictionalized biography, set in 1871, 16-year-old Joshua Loper learns that age, race, and background are unimportant when you are on a cattle drive on the Chisholm Trail driving a herd of 2,200 cattle. (Rev: BL 2/15/99; SLJ 4/99)

2484 Nesbitt, John D. *Twin Rivers* (9–12). 1995, Walker $28.95 (0-8027-4152-5). This western, set in the Wyoming countryside, involves Clay Westbrook, a wrangler who must fight a challenge to the claim he has filed for 160 acres of land, and the Mexican girl he loves. (Rev: BL 1/1–15/96; VOYA 6/96)

2485 Nixon, Joan Lowery. *Circle of Love* (5–8). (Orphan Train Adventures) 1997, Delacorte $15.95 (0-385-32280-1). Confused by the reluctance of her boyfriend, a wounded Civil War veteran, to commit to marriage, Frances agrees to chaperone 30 orphaned children on the train ride to New York, where they are to meet their relatives or adoptive families. (Rev: BL 4/1/97; BR 5–6/97; SLJ 5/97)

2486 Nixon, Joan Lowery. *In the Face of Danger* (5–8). 1996, Bantam paper $4.50 (0-440-22705-4). Megan fears she will bring bad luck to her adoptive family in this story set in the prairies of Kansas. This is the third part of the Orphan Train Quartet. (Rev: BR 11–12/88; SLJ 12/88; VOYA 12/88)

2487 O'Dell, Scott. *Carlota* (7–9). 1977, Houghton $15.95 (0-395-25487-6); Dell paper $4.50 (0-440-90928-7). After the Mexican-American War some Californians continue to battle the U.S. Army.

2488 O'Dell, Scott. *Streams to the River, River to the Sea: A Novel of Sacagawea* (5–9). 1986, Houghton $16.00 (0-395-40430-4); Fawcett paper $4.50 (0-449-70244-8). A novelized life of Sacagawea that supplies details about the Lewis and Clark expedition. (Rev: BL 3/15/86; BR 9–10/86; SLJ 5/86; VOYA 6/86)

2489 Paine, Lauran. *Riders of the Trojan Horse* (9–12). 1991, Walker $30.95 (0-8027-4116-9). A brave stagecoach driver pursues thieves who have stolen his stagecoach and kidnapped the sheriff. (Rev: BL 7/91; SLJ 10/91)

2490 Patrick, Denise Lewis. *The Longest Ride* (6–9). 1999, Holt $16.95 (0-8050-4715-8). In this sequel to *The Adventures of Midnight Son,* escaped Texas slave Midnight Sun becomes lost during a long cattle drive, is rescued by some Arapahos, and is eventually reunited with his family. (Rev: BL 6/1–15/99)

2491 Paulsen, Gary. *Call Me Francis Tucket* (5–8). 1995, Delacorte $14.00 (0-385-32116-3). In this sequel to *Mr. Tucket,* 15-year-old Francis continues his journey westward, becomes separated from his wagon train headed for Oregon and must survive the wilderness. (Rev: BL 7/95; SLJ 6/95; VOYA 5/95)

2492 Paulsen, Gary. *Mr. Tucket* (6–9). 1994, Delacorte $15.95 (0-385-31169-9). A 14-year-old boy strays from his family's wagon on the Oregon Trail and ends up with the Pawnees. A trapper helps him escape and teaches him much about life and survival. (Rev: BL 5/1/94; VOYA 4/94)

2493 Portis, Charles. *True Grit* (7–12). 1995, NAL paper $5.50 (0-451-18545-5). A 14-year-old girl in the old West sets out to avenge her father's death.

2494 Richter, Conrad. *The Light in the Forest* (7–9). 1953, Knopf $23.00 (0-394-43314-9). At age 15, a white boy returns to his family after living many years with Indians. (Rev: BL 11/1/87)

2495 Riefe, Barbara. *Westward Hearts: The Amelia Dale Archer Story* (10–12). 1998, Forge $22.95 (0-312-86077-3). In the 1850s, Dr. Amelia Archer and her 4 granddaughters face hardships and danger as they travel by wagon trail west to Los Angeles, where she believes women have a chance to be recognized on their own merit. (Rev: SLJ 2/99)

2496 Rinaldi, Ann. *The Second Bend in the River* (5–9). 1997, Scholastic $15.95 (0-590-74258-2). Seven-year-old Rebecca begins a long-lasting friendship with the Shawnee chief Tecumseh in Ohio in 1798 that eventually leads to a marriage proposal. (Rev: BL 2/15/97; BR 5–6/97; SLJ 6/97)

2497 Roberts, Willo Davis. *Jo and the Bandit* (6–8). 1992, Atheneum $15.00 (0-689-31745-X). Orphans Jo and her brother are sent to live with their uncle in 1860s Texas. When the stagecoach is robbed, Jo hides the son of the gang leader and helps him escape. (Rev: BL 6/1/92; SLJ 7/92)

2498 Ruckman, Ivy. *Cassie of Blue Hill* (5–8). 1998, Bantam Doubleday Dell $14.95 (0-385-32514-2). In turn-of-the-century Nebraska, the peace and quiet of the Tucker family and 11-year-old Cassie are shattered with the arrival of Evan, a cousin who has a mind of his own. (Rev: BL 8/98; SLJ 10/98)

2499 Sauerwein, Leigh. *The Way Home* (7–12). Illus. 1994, Farrar $15.00 (0-374-38247-6). Short stories set in the American West about the struggles of frontier life, several involving relationships between whites and Native Americans. (Rev: BL 3/15/94; SLJ 4/94; VOYA 6/94)

2500 Schaefer, Jack. *Shane* (9–12). Illus. 1954, Houghton $18.00 (0-395-07090-2). A stranger enters the Starret household and helps them fight an oppressive land baron.

2501 Snelling, Lauraine. *An Untamed Land* (9–12). (Red River of the North) 1996, Bethany House paper $9.99 (1-55661-576-0). This novel re-creates the experiences of the 2 Bjorklund brothers of Norway as they struggle to farm in the Dakota prairies, as told by the wife of the elder brother. (Rev: VOYA 8/96)

2502 Turner, Nancy E. *These Is My Words: The Diary of Sarah Agnes Prine, 1881–1902* (10–12). 1998, HarperCollins $23.00 (0-06-039225-8). A heartwarming and heartbreaking story, based on the author's family memoirs, about Sarah, who settles on a ranch in Tucson in the 1880s as an illiterate 17-year-old with her family and develops into an educated, determined, devoted wife and mother as she and her family encounter many hardships. (Rev: BL 2/15/98; SLJ 6/98)

2503 Vick, Helen H. *Charlotte* (6–8). (Courage of the Stone) 1999, Roberts Rinehart $15.95 (1-57098-278-3); paper $9.95 (1-57098-282-1). After her parents are killed by Apache warriors in frontier Arizona Territory, 13-year-old Charlotte learns the ways of survival from an elderly Native American woman. (Rev: SLJ 7/99)

2504 Wallace, Bill. *Buffalo Gal* (6–8). 1992, Holiday House $15.95 (0-8234-0943-0). Amanda's plans for an elegant 16th birthday party evaporate when her mother drags her to the wilds of Texas to search for buffalo with cowboys. (Rev: BL 6/15/92; SLJ 5/92)

2505 Watson, Jude. *Impetuous: Mattie's Story* (9–12). (Brides of Wildcat County) 1996, Simon & Schuster paper $3.99 (0-614-15784-6). In this title in the Brides of Wildcat County series, tomboy Mattie comes to Last Chance, a California mining town, as a mail order bride but decides she wants to be independent upon discovering that she can do anything a man can do. (Rev: VOYA 6/96)

2506 Wheeler, Richard S. *Second Lives: A Novel of the Gilded Age* (10–12). 1997, Forge $24.95 (0-312-86330-0). A novel about ordinary people, their aspirations, failures, and fulfillments, in Denver during the late 1880s. (Rev: SLJ 4/98)

2507 Wilder, Laura Ingalls. *The Long Winter* (5–8). Illus. 1953, HarperCollins LB $15.89 (0-06-026461-6). Number 6 in the Little House books. In this one the Ingalls face a terrible winter with only seed grain for food.

2508 Wister, Owen. *The Virginian* (10–12). 1988, Viking paper $10.95 (0-14-039065-0). The classic novel of the American West first published in 1902 and containing the phrase "When you call me that, smile."

2509 Yep, Laurence. *Dragon's Gate* (6–9). 1993, HarperCollins $14.95 (0-06-022971-3). The adventures of a privileged Chinese teenager who travels to California in 1865 to join his father and uncle working on the transcontinental railroad. (Rev: BL 1/1/94; SLJ 1/94; VOYA 12/93)

RECONSTRUCTION TO WORLD WAR I (1865–1914)

2510 Alcott, Louisa May. *The Inheritance* (10–12). 1997, Dutton $18.00 (0-525-45756-9). This recently discovered novel was written by Alcott when she was only 17 and tells a rags-to-riches story of an orphan named Edith Adelon. (Rev: BL 2/15/97; SLJ 4/97)

2511 Armstrong, Jennifer. *Mary Mehan Awake* (6–10). 1997, Knopf $18.00 (0-679-88276-6). After the Civil War, Mary escapes the trauma the war caused by relocating from Washington, D.C., to upstate New York, where she meets a deaf war veteran, Henry Till. A sequel to *The Dreams of Mairhe Mehan*. (Rev: BL 12/1/97; BR 3–4/98; SLJ 1/98)

2512 Burns, Olive Ann. *Cold Sassy Tree* (9–12). 1984, Ticknor $26.00 (0-89919-309-9). Fourteen-year-old Will has a crush on his grandfather's young bride in this novel set in turn-of-the-century Georgia. (Rev: BL 6/87)

2513 Carroll, Lenore. *One Hundred Girls' Mother* (10–12). 1998, Forge $24.95 (0-312-85994-5). An inspiring story, based on fact, about a mission director in San Francisco's Chinatown at the turn of the century and her efforts to save Chinese girls sold into slavery or prostitution. (Rev: BL 8/98; SLJ 11/98)

2514 Collier, James L. *My Crooked Family* (6–8). 1991, Simon & Schuster paper $15.00 (0-671-74224-8). Roger, 14, living in the slums in the early

1900s, steals to feed himself and becomes involved with a gang that killed his father. (Rev: BL 12/1/91; SLJ 10/91)

2515 Cross, Gillian. *The Great American Elephant Chase* (5–8). 1993, Holiday House $15.95 (0-8234-1016-1). In 1881, Tad, 15, and young friend Cissie attempt to get to Nebraska with her showman father's elephant, pursued by 2 unsavory characters who claim they have bought the elephant. (Rev: BL 3/15/93*; SLJ 5/93*; VOYA 10/93)

2516 Cutler, Jane. *The Song of the Molimo* (5–8). Illus. 1998, Farrar $16.00 (0-374-37141-5). During the St. Louis World's Fair of 1904, 12-year-old Harry, who is spending the summer with his aunt and uncle and anthropologist cousin, becomes friends with Pygmy Ota Benga, who is part of one of the displays, one of several in which people are exhibits. (Rev: BL 10/15/98; SLJ 11/98; VOYA 6/99)

2517 Duey, Kathleen. *Alexia Ellery Finsdale: San Francisco, 1905* (6–8). 1997, Simon & Schuster paper $4.50 (0-689-81620-0). Set in San Francisco in 1905, this historical novel tells of motherless Alexia, her unscrupulous father, and the tough decisions she is forced to make because of his bad behavior. (Rev: SLJ 4/98)

2518 Duffy, James. *Radical Red* (5–8). 1993, Scribners $16.95 (0-684-19533-X). This shows the plight of women in 1894 through 12-year-old Connor O'Shea, who, along with her mother, is abused at home and is drawn into a suffrage demonstration. (Rev: BL 12/1/93; SLJ 1/94; VOYA 2/94)

2519 Eidson, Tom. *All God's Children* (10–12). 1997, Dutton $23.95 (0-525-94235-1). A story of uplifting courage about a widowed Quaker woman raising 4 young sons in 1891 Kansas who faces the wrath of local rednecks when she takes a black fugitive and a family of poor Japanese immigrants into her home. (Rev: SLJ 1/98)

2520 Ferber, Edna. *Show Boat* (9–12). 1994, NAL paper $5.95 (0-451-52600-7). The favorite novel about life on a Mississippi show boat and the romance between Magnolia and Gaylord Ravenal. Also use: *So Big* and *Ice Palace*.

2521 Forrester, Sandra. *My Home Is over Jordan* (7–10). 1997, Dutton paper $15.99 (0-525-67568-X). In this sequel to *Sound the Jubilee*, the Civil War is over and Maddie and her family try to start life over in North Carolina, but some whites resent their intrusion. (Rev: BL 10/1/97; SLJ 12/97)

2522 Fuller, Jamie. *The Diary of Emily Dickinson* (9–12). 1993, Mercury House $18.00 (1-56279-048-X). This fictionalized diary combines Dickinson's poetry with made-up entries about her life, unrequited loves, relationship with her father, faith, and love of writing. (Rev: BL 9/15/93*)

2523 Gibbons, Kaye. *Charms for the Easy Life* (9–12). 1993, Putnam $19.95 (0-399-13791-2). Appealing characters and carefully selected period details make this intergenerational novel a delight. (Rev: BL 1/15/93; SLJ 9/93*)

2524 Haas, Jessie. *Westminster West* (6–9). 1997, Greenwillow $15.00 (0-688-14883-2). This novel, set in 1884 Vermont, features 2 very different sisters and their struggle for position and control within their farming family. (Rev: BL 4/15/97; BR 9–10/97; SLJ 5/97)

2525 Hansen, Joyce. *I Thought My Soul Would Rise and Fly: The Diary of Patsy, a Freed Girl* (4–8). (Dear America) 1997, Scholastic $10.95 (0-590-84913-1). Newly freed after the Civil War, Patsy is still living on the plantation and doesn't know what to do with her life in this novel in diary form. (Rev: BL 12/15/97; SLJ 11/97)

2526 Houston, Gloria. *Littlejim's Dreams* (5–8). Illus. 1997, Harcourt $16.00 (0-15-201509-4). Littlejim wants to become a writer, but his father thinks he should be a farmer and logger like himself, in this novel set in 1920 Appalachia. A sequel to *Littlejim* (1990). (Rev: SLJ 7/97)

2527 Hurmence, Belinda. *Tancy* (7–12). 1984, Houghton $12.70 (0-89919-228-9). After being freed from slavery at the end of the Civil War, 18-year-old Tancy sets out to find her real mother. (Rev: BL 3/1/88)

2528 Jackson, Dave, and Neta Jackson. *Danger on the Flying Trapeze* (6–8). 1995, Bethany House paper $5.99 (1-55661-469-1). A 14-year-old joins the circus with his family to escape a dreary life. The boy hears the great evangelist D. L. Moody and learns something about the meaning of courage and faith. (Rev: BL 9/1/95; SLJ 12/95)

2529 Klass, Sheila S. *A Shooting Star: A Novel about Annie Oakley* (4–8). 1996, Holiday House $15.95 (0-8234-1279-2). A fictionalized biography of the woman who rose from poverty to become a famous show business sharpshooter. (Rev: BL 12/15/96; SLJ 5/97)

2530 Lafaye, Alexandria. *Edith Shay* (6–10). 1998, Viking $15.99 (0-670-87598-8). The story of a girl who decides to leave her 1860s Wisconsin settlement and find a new life for herself in Chicago. (Rev: BL 10/15/98; BR 5–6/99; SLJ 10/98; VOYA 4/99)

2531 Lasky, Kathryn. *Dreams in the Golden Country: The Diary of Zipporah Feldman, a Jewish Immigrant Girl* (4–8). 1998, Scholastic paper $10.95 (0-590-02973-8). Twelve-year-old Zipporah Feldman, a Jewish immigrant from Russia, keeps a diary about her life with her family on the Lower East Side around 1910. (Rev: SLJ 5/98)

2532 Lewin, Michael Z. *Cutting Loose* (9–12). 1999, Holt $23.95 (0-8050-6225-4). A complex, mature, historical novel about the early days of baseball, a girl who disguises herself as a man to play ball, and a murder that takes her to England and involvement with another girl who also spends part of her life as a man. (Rev: BL 9/15/99)

2533 McEachin, James. *Tell Me a Tale* (10–12). 1996, Lyford Bks. $18.95 (0-89141-584-X). Set in a small town in North Carolina at the beginning of Reconstruction, a young slave named Moses tells of his family's past to 4 old-timers who have stopped to listen to the youngster's tale. (Rev: SLJ 9/96)

2534 Marshall, Catherine. *Christy* (8–12). 1976, Avon paper $6.99 (0-380-00141-1). This story set in Appalachia in 1912 tells about a spunky young girl who goes there to teach. (Rev: BL 5/1/89)

2535 Morris, Lynn, and Gilbert Morris. *Toward the Sunrising* (10–12). 1996, Bethany House paper $10.99 (1-55661-425-X). A complex novel about a feisty Yankee woman doctor, Cheney Duvall, and her struggles in Charleston, South Carolina, during Reconstruction. (Rev: SLJ 8/96; VOYA 10/96)

2536 Myers, Anna. *Fire in the Hills* (6–10). 1996, Walker $23.95 (0-8027-8421-6). In rural Oklahoma during World War I, 16-year-old Hallie takes care of her younger siblings after her mother's death and also tries to help a German family fight the prejudice of their neighbors. (Rev: BL 4/15/96*; BR 9–10/96; SLJ 4/96; VOYA 6/96)

2537 Neufeld, John. *Gaps in Stone Walls* (6–8). 1996, Simon & Schuster $16.00 (0-689-80102-5). In this historical novel set on Martha's Vineyard in 1880, 12-year-old Merry, a deaf girl, is one of 4 people accused of murdering the villainous Ned Nickerson. (Rev: BL 4/1/96; BR 11–12/96; SLJ 5/96; VOYA 6/96)

2538 Nixon, Joan Lowery. *Land of Dreams* (6–9). (Ellis Island) 1994, Dell paper $3.99 (0-440-21935-3). A Swedish immigrant in rural Minnesota who longs to move to the city of Minneapolis learns the importance of community support when fire strikes her home. (Rev: BL 2/15/94; SLJ 2/94)

2539 Nixon, Joan Lowery. *Land of Hope* (6–9). (Ellis Island) 1993, Dell paper $4.50 (0-440-21597-8). Rebekah, 15, and her family escape persecution in Russia in the early 1900s and flee to New York City to join Uncle Avir, where life is harsh but hopeful. (Rev: BL 12/15/92; SLJ 10/92)

2540 Nixon, Joan Lowery. *Land of Promise* (6–9). (Ellis Island) 1993, 1994, Dell paper $3.99 (0-440-21904-3). This novel focuses on Irish Rosie, one of 3 immigrant girls who arrive in the United States in the early 1900s, and her adjustment to life in Chicago. (Rev: BL 12/1/93; VOYA 10/93)

2541 Paterson, Katherine. *Preacher's Boy* (5–8). 1999, Clarion $15.00 (0-395-83897-5). In small-town Vermont in 1899, a time of new ideas and technological change, Robbie, the restless, imaginative, questioning son of a preacher, causes unforeseen trouble when he plans his own kidnapping for profit. (Rev: BL 8/99; SLJ 8/99)

2542 Perez, N. A. *Breaker* (6–9). 1988, Houghton $16.00 (0-395-45537-5). A teenage boy enters the mines in 1902 Pennsylvania when his father is killed in an accident. (Rev: BL 7/88; BR 11–12/88; SLJ 8/88; VOYA 10/88)

2543 Perez, N. A. *One Special Year* (7–10). 1985, Houghton $13.95 (0-395-36693-3). Family life in a small upper New York State town in 1900 is vividly portrayed in this sensitive novel about a girl reaching maturity. (Rev: BL 6/15/85; BR 9–10/85; SLJ 8/85)

2544 Raphael, Marie. *Streets of Gold* (7–9). 1998, TreeHouse paper $7.95 (1-883088-05-4). After fleeing Poland and conscription in the Russian czar's army, Stefan and his sister Marisia begin a new life in America on the Lower East Side of New York City at the turn of the century. (Rev: SLJ 12/98)

2545 Rinaldi, Ann. *Acquaintance with Darkness* (7–10). 1997, Harcourt $16.00 (0-15-201294-X). A coming-of-age historical novel about a 14-year-old girl living in Washington, D.C., who becomes involved in political intrigue after the assassination of Lincoln. (Rev: BL 9/15/97; SLJ 10/97; VOYA 2/98)

2546 Rinaldi, Ann. *The Coffin Quilt: The Feud between the Hatfields and the McCoys* (6–10). 1999, Harcourt $16.00 (0-15-202015-2). The infamous Hatfield-McCoy feud is flamed into violence when a McCoy daughter elopes with a Hatfield in this novel set in the late 1800s in West Virginia/Kentucky. (Rev: BL 9/1/99; VOYA 10/99)

2547 Schnur, Steven. *Beyond Providence* (6–9). 1996, Harcourt $12.00 (0-15-200982-5); paper $6.00 (0-15-200981-7). In this historical novel set in Rhode Island, 12-year-old Nathan tells about life on his family farm, the tense relations between his father and older brother, and 2 relatives, Kitty and Zeke, who come to live with them. (Rev: BL 4/1/96; SLJ 4/96; VOYA 6/96)

2548 Sherman, Eileen B. *Independence Avenue* (5–9). 1990, Jewish Publication Soc. $14.95 (0-8276-0367-3). This story of Russian Jews who immigrate to Texas in 1907 has a resourceful, engaging hero, an unusual setting, and plenty of action. (Rev: BL 2/15/91; SLJ 1/91)

2549 Shivers, Louise. *A Whistling Woman* (9–12). 1993, Longstreet $15.00 (1-56352-085-0). Set in North Carolina after the Civil War, this novel examines the relationship between a mother and daughter. (Rev: BL 8/93*)

2550 Smith, Betty. *A Tree Grows in Brooklyn* (9–12). 1943, Buccaneer LB $41.95 (0-89966-303-6). The touching story of Francie Nolan growing up in a poor section of Williamsburg in Brooklyn during the early 1900s.

2551 Stephens, C. A. *Stories from Old Squire's Farm* (10–12). 1995, Rutledge Hill $18.95 (1-55853-334-6). Written over 100 years ago, these 36 stories revolve around 6 cousins orphaned by the Civil War and their everyday life on Old Squire's farm in Maine. (Rev: SLJ 4/96)

2552 Stone, Bruce. *Autumn of the Royal Tar* (5–8). 1995, HarperCollins $13.95 (0-06-021492-9). Young Nora's life changes suddenly when a ship carrying passengers and circus animals burns and capsizes close to her island home off the coast of Maine. (Rev: BL 1/1–15/96; BR 3–4/96; SLJ 2/96; VOYA 4/96)

2553 Walker, Jim. *The Rail Kings* (9–12). 1995, Bethany House paper $8.99 (1-55661-430-6). Undercover Wells Fargo agent Zac Cobb finds himself drawn into the no-holds-barred rivalry between 2 big railroad companies in the late 1800s, and must deal with kidnap attempts, nonstop fighting, and the love of the daughter of the president of one of the companies. (Rev: VOYA 4/96)

2554 White, Ellen E. *Voyage on the Great Titanic: The Diary of Margaret Ann Brady* (4–8). (Dear America) 1998, Scholastic paper $10.95 (0-590-96273-6). A moving, powerful novel about a young girl who earns her passage to America to be with her brother by serving as a companion to a wealthy woman aboard the *Titanic*. (Rev: BL 10/15/98; SLJ 12/98)

BETWEEN THE WARS AND THE GREAT DEPRESSION (1919–1948)

2555 Blackwood, Gary L. *Moonshine* (5–8). 1999, Marshall Cavendish $14.95 (0-7614-5056-4). In Depression days in rural Missouri, young Thad helps his mother, who has been deserted by his father, by delivering moonshine from the local illegal still. (Rev: BL 9/1/99; SLJ 10/99)

2556 Burandt, Harriet, and Shelley Dale. *Tales from the Homeplace: Adventures of a Texas Farm Girl* (4–8). 1997, Holt $15.95 (0-8050-5075-2). A family story that takes place on a Texas cotton farm during the Depression and features a spunky heroine, 12-year-old Irene, and her 6 brothers and sisters. (Rev: SLJ 4/97*; VOYA 12/97)

2557 Collier, James L. *The Jazz Kid* (6–9). Illus. 1994, Holt $15.95 (0-8050-2821-8). Twelve-year-old Paulie becomes involved in the world of jazz of the roaring 20s and runs away from home to pursue his career. (Rev: BL 6/1–15/94; SLJ 6/94; VOYA 8/94)

2558 Corbin, William. *Me and the End of the World* (5–8). 1991, Simon & Schuster paper $15.00 (0-671-74223-X). When fringe religious leaders announce the world will end on May 1, 1928, Tim believes he has only a few months to live and assigns himself important challenges. (Rev: BL 11/1/91; SLJ 9/91)

2559 Craven, Margaret. *Walk Gently This Good Earth* (9–12). 1995, Buccaneer LB $21.95 (1-56849-646-X). The saga of an American family surviving the Depression and World War II.

2560 Crew, Linda. *Fire on the Wind* (6–9). 1995, Delacorte $14.95 (0-385-32185-6). A 13-year-old girl's maturation through her experiences as a "log camp kid" in Depression-era Oregon. (Rev: BL 8/95; SLJ 11/95)

2561 Edwards, Pat. *Nelda* (6–8). 1987, Houghton $12.70 (0-395-43021-6). In this novel set in Depression days, young Nelda has high hopes for the future though her present situation as part of a migrant worker's family is bleak. (Rev: BL 4/15/87; BR 9–10/87; SLJ 5/87; VOYA 8/87)

2562 Fisher, Leonard E. *The Jetty Chronicles* (5–9). Illus. 1997, Marshall Cavendish LB $15.95 (0-7614-5017-3). A series of vignettes based on fact about the unusual people the author met while growing up in Sea Gate, New York, at a time when the United States was drifting into World War II. (Rev: BL 10/15/97; BR 3–4/98; SLJ 12/97; VOYA 2/98)

2563 Green, Connie Jordan. *Emmy* (5–8). 1992, Macmillan $13.95 (0-689-50556-6). A story of perseverance and survival in a 1924 Kentucky mining town revolving around Emmy, 11; her brother, Gene, 14; their depressed father; and their mother, who is forced to take in boarders to make ends meet. (Rev: BL 12/1/92; SLJ 12/92)

2564 Hesse, Karen. *Letters from Rifka* (5–8). 1992, Holt $14.95 (0-8050-1964-2); 1993, Penguin paper $4.99 (0-14-036391-2). In letters to Russia, Rifka, 12, recounts her journey to the United States in 1919, from the dangerous escape over the border, across Europe and the sea, to America. (Rev: BL 7/92; SLJ 8/92*)

2565 Hesse, Karen. *A Time of Angels* (5–8). 1995, Hyperion LB $16.49 (0-7868-2072-1). As influenza sweeps her city killing thousands, Hannah tries to escape its ravages by moving to Vermont, where an old farmer helps her. (Rev: BL 12/1/95; SLJ 12/95)

2566 Hill, Donna. *Surfman!* (6–9). 1998, Clarion $15.00 (0-395-86614-6). A headstrong, spoiled 16-year-old gains maturity while in training with a squad whose job is rescuing sailors and passengers from foundering ships in this novel set on Cape Cod during the 1870s. (Rev: BL 6/1–15/98; SLJ 6/98)

2567 Hunt, Irene. *No Promises in the Wind* (7–9). 1987, Berkley paper $4.99 (0-425-09969-5). During the Great Depression, Josh must assume responsibilities far beyond his years. A reissue.

2568 Kendall, Jane. *Miranda Goes to Hollywood: Adventures in the Land of Palm Trees, Cowboys, and Moving Pictures* (5–8). 1999, Harcourt $16.00 (0-15-202059-4). The early history of movies is intertwined with this story about attempts by 12-year-old Miranda, who travels to Hollywood with her aunt, and 16-year-old Bobby Gilmer to break into Hollywood's emerging silent film industry. A sequel to *Miranda and the Movies*. (Rev: BL 4/1/99; SLJ 6/99)

2569 Levine, Gail C. *Dave at Night* (5–9). 1999, HarperCollins LB $15.89 (0-06-028154-5). Set in New York City in 1926, this novel is about an orphan who escapes from the hellish Hebrew Home for Boys and, through a chance encounter, meets amazing characters of the Harlem Renaissance. (Rev: BL 6/1–15/99; SLJ 9/99)

2570 Little, Jean. *His Banner over Me* (6–9). 1995, Viking paper $13.99 (0-670-85664-9). A child of missionaries moves from Taiwan to Canada, where her parents leave her for many years to grow up on her own and a terminally ill woman changes her life dramatically. (Rev: BL 11/15/95; SLJ 12/95)

2571 Marshall, Catherine. *Julie* (9–12). 1985, Avon paper $6.99 (0-380-69891-9). During the Depression, Julie and her family move to a small town in Pennsylvania where she finds fulfillment working on her father's newspaper.

2572 Mills, Claudia. *What about Annie?* (6–8). 1985, Walker $9.95 (0-8027-6573-4). A harrowing story of a family in Baltimore living through the Depression as seen through the eyes of a young teenage girl. (Rev: BL 9/1/85)

2573 O'Sullivan, Mark. *Wash-Basin Street Blues* (7–10). 1996, Wolfhound paper $9.95 (0-86327-467-6). In 1920s New York City, 16-year-old Nora is reunited with her 2 younger brothers but the reunion causes unforeseen problems. A sequel to *Melody for Nora*. (Rev: BL 6/1–15/96)

2574 Pfitsch, Patricia C. *Keeper of the Light* (5–8). 1997, Simon & Schuster paper $16.00 (0-689-81492-5). Set in 1872, this is the story of Faith, who after keeping the lighthouse light on the shores of Lake Superior burning after her father's death, is replaced by an inexperienced keeper and moved from the island home where she grew up. (Rev: BL 11/1/97; BR 9–10/98; SLJ 5/98; VOYA 2/98)

2575 Porter, Tracey. *Treasures in the Dust* (4–8). 1997, HarperCollins LB $14.89 (0-06-027564-2). With alternating points of view, 2 girls from poor families in the Oklahoma Dust Bowl tell their stories. (Rev: BL 8/97; SLJ 12/97*; VOYA 10/98)

2576 Rabe, Berniece. *Hiding Mr. McMulty* (5–8). 1997, Harcourt $18.00 (0-15-201330-X). This novel, set in southeast Missouri in 1937, tells of race and class conflicts as experienced by 11-year-old Rass. (Rev: BL 10/15/97; SLJ 12/97; VOYA 2/98)

2577 Reeder, Carolyn. *Moonshiner's Son* (7–10). 1993, Macmillan LB $14.95 (0-02-775805-2). It's Prohibition, and Tom, 12, is learning the art of moonshining from his father—until he becomes friendly with the new preacher's daughter. (Rev: BL 6/1–15/93; SLJ 5/93; VOYA 8/93)

2578 Robinet, Harriette G. *Mississippi Chariot* (6–10). 1994, Atheneum $14.95 (0-689-31960-6). Life in the 1930s Mississippi Delta is vividly evoked in this story of Shortning Bread, 12, whose father has been wrongfully convicted of a crime and sentenced to a chain gang. (Rev: BL 11/15/94; SLJ 12/94; VOYA 5/95)

2579 Rostkowski, Margaret I. *After the Dancing Days* (6–9). 1986, HarperCollins LB $14.89 (0-06-025078-X); paper $4.95 (0-06-440248-7). Annie encounters the realities of war when she helps care for wounded soldiers after World War I. (Rev: BL 10/15/86; SLJ 12/86; VOYA 4/87)

2580 Singer, Isaac Bashevis. *The Certificate* (9–12). Trans. by Leonard Wolf. 1992, Farrar $22.00 (0-374-12029-3). A shy, 19-year-old aspiring writer enters into a "fictive marriage" with an aristocratic woman who loves another man. (Rev: BL 10/15/92)

2581 Snyder, Zilpha Keatley. *Gib Rides Home* (5–8). 1998, Delacorte $15.95 (0-385-32267-4). Set in post-World War I America, this is the story of an orphan boy and how he conquers hardships and deprivations. (Rev: BL 1/1–15/98; BR 9–10/98; SLJ 1/98*)

2582 Steinbeck, John. *Of Mice and Men* (10–12). 1992, Demco $12.30 (0-606-00200-6). The friendship between two migrant workers—one a schemer and the other mentally deficient—is the subject of this short novel.

2583 Stolz, Mary. *Ivy Larkin* (7–9). 1986, Harcourt $13.95 (0-15-239366-8). During the Depression in New York City, 15-year-old Ivy's father loses his job and the family moves to the Lower East Side. (Rev: BL 11/1/86; SLJ 12/86)

2584 Thesman, Jean. *The Ornament Tree* (7–10). 1996, Houghton $15.95 (0-395-74278-1). Fourteen-year-old Bonnie moves into a boardinghouse run by her female relatives in Seattle in 1914, and through the years she adjusts to these strong-willed ladies and meets several interesting guests. (Rev: BL 5/1/96; BR 1–2/97; SLJ 3/96; VOYA 8/96)

2585 Thesman, Jean. *The Storyteller's Daughter* (6–9). 1997, Houghton $16.00 (0-395-80978-9). During the Depression in Seattle, Quinn believes that her father is smuggling liquor from Canada to help supplement the dwindling family income. (Rev: BL 11/1/97; BR 5–6/98; SLJ 9/97; VOYA 2/98)

WORLD WAR II AND THE HOLOCAUST

2586 Almagor, Gila. *Under the Domim Tree* (6–9). 1995, Simon & Schuster $15.00 (0-671-89020-4). An autobiographical novel about young Holocaust survivors in an agricultural youth village in Israel in 1953. (Rev: BL 5/1/95; SLJ 6/95)

2587 Anderson, Rachel. *Paper Faces* (6–12). 1993, Holt $14.95 (0-8050-2527-8). Dot has lived in poverty in World War II London with her mother. The end of the war brings change—including her father's return—that she dreads. (Rev: BL 11/1/93*; SLJ 12/93; VOYA 12/93)

2588 Atlan, Lilane. *The Passersby* (9–12). Trans. by Rochelle Owens. Illus. 1993, Holt $13.95 (0-8050-3054-9). This prose poem depicts No, an anorexic teenager, who is searching for an ideal, purpose, and friends while confronted with the reality of her adopted brother's experiences in Auschwitz. (Rev: BL 12/1/93; SLJ 12/93; VOYA 2/94)

2589 Atlema, Martha. *A Time to Choose* (8–12). 1995, Orca paper $6.95 (1-55143-045-2). While growing up in Holland under the Nazi occupation, 16-year-old Johannes tries to separate himself from his father, who is considered a collaborator. (Rev: VOYA 10/97)

2590 Baer, Edith. *Walk the Dark Streets* (7–12). 1998, Farrar $18.00 (0-374-38229-8). This novel, based on fact, tells of the growing anti-Semitism in Germany from 1933 to 1940 as experienced by a Jewish girl who manages to escape to the United States at the beginning of World War II. (Rev: BL 11/1/98; SLJ 11/98; VOYA 12/98)

2591 Bawden, Nina. *Carrie's War* (6–9). Illus. 1973, HarperCollins LB $14.89 (0-397-31450-7). Carrie relives her days during World War II when she and her brothers were evacuated to Wales. (Rev: BL 3/1/88)

2592 Benchley, Nathaniel. *Bright Candles* (6–9). 1974, HarperCollins $13.95 (0-06-020461-3). The Danish underground during World War II. (Rev: BL 7/88)

2593 Bergman, Tamar. *Along the Tracks* (6–9). Trans. by Michael Swirsky. 1991, Houghton $16.00 (0-395-55328-8). The story of an 8-year-old Jewish boy who is separated from his parents during World War II and wanders through Russia for 4 years searching for them. (Rev: BL 9/15/91; SLJ 12/91)

2594 Booth, Martin. *War Dog* (6–8). 1997, Simon & Schuster paper $15.00 (0-689-81380-5). Such events as Dunkirk and the London blitz are incorporated into this tale of World War II England and Jet, a dog that is trained for combat duty. (Rev: BL 11/1/97; BR 3–4/98; SLJ 10/97; VOYA 2/98)

2595 Boulle, Pierre. *The Bridge over the River Kwai* (9–12). Trans. by Xan Fielding. 1954, Amereon $23.75 (0-89190-571-5). The thoughtful story of life in a Japanese prisoner-of-war camp that pits a British officer against his captors.

2596 Buckvar, Felice. *Dangerous Dream* (6–9). 1998, Royal Fireworks paper $6.99 (0-88092-277-X). In postwar Germany, 13-year-old Hella, a concentration camp survivor, mistakenly believes that a new arrival in the infirmary is her father. (Rev: SLJ 4/99; VOYA 8/99)

2597 Bunting, Eve. *Spying on Miss Miller* (6–8). 1995, Clarion $15.00 (0-395-69172-9). During World War II in Belfast, Jessie, 13, believes her half-German teacher is a spy. (Rev: BL 3/15/95*; SLJ 5/95)

2598 Carter, Peter. *The Hunted* (8–12). 1994, Farrar $17.00 (0-374-33520-6). In 1943, Vito Salvani travels from Italy to his home in France with a small Jewish boy, pursued by the Milici (Italy's Gestapo). (Rev: BL 4/1/94; SLJ 6/94; VOYA 10/94)

2599 Cooper, Susan. *Dawn of Fear* (7–9). 1970, Harcourt $14.95 (0-15-266201-4); Aladdin paper $4.99 (0-689-71327-4). Three boys in a London suburb become friends amid the violence of World War II. (Rev: BL 4/87)

2600 DeJong, Meindert. *The House of Sixty Fathers* (6–9). 1956, HarperCollins LB $15.89 (0-06-021481-3). In war-torn China, a young boy searches for his family as the Japanese invade his country.

2601 Douglas, Kirk. *The Broken Mirror* (5–10). 1997, Simon & Schuster paper $13.00 (0-689-81493-3). This short novel by the famous actor depicts the despair and loss of faith that occurs to a Jewish child who has lost all his loved ones in the Holocaust. (Rev: BL 10/1/97; SLJ 9/97; VOYA 2/98)

2602 Drucker, Malka, and Michael Halperin. *Jacob's Rescue: A Holocaust Story* (6–10). 1993, 1994, Dell paper $4.50 (0-440-40965-9). The fictionalized true story of 2 Jewish children saved from the Holocaust in Poland by "righteous Gentiles." (Rev: BL 2/15/93; SLJ 5/93)

2603 Dubis, Michael. *The Hangman* (10–12). 1998, Erica House paper $10.95 (0-9659308-6-6). The disturbing story of the Holocaust as experienced by Erik Byrnes, an SS officer whose assignment was to liquidate a ghetto outside of Vienna. (Rev: BL 12/15/98)

2604 Ferry, Charles. *Raspberry One* (7–10). 1983, Houghton $13.95 (0-395-34069-1). Friendship found on a Navy bomber during World War II. (Rev: BL 7/88)

2605 Fox, Robert Barlow. *To Be a Warrior* (6–9). 1997, Sunstone paper $12.95 (0-86534-253-9). A Navajo boy joins the marines after Pearl Harbor and becomes one of the celebrated "code talkers." (Rev: BL 9/1/97; BR 5–6/98)

2606 Frank, Anne. *Anne Frank's Tales from the Secret Annex* (8–12). 1994, Bantam paper $4.50 (0-553-56983-X). This is a collection of all of Anne Frank's writings—apart from the diary, that is—stories, sketches, and fairy tales. [839.3]

2607 Giff, Patricia Reilly. *Lily's Crossing* (5–8). 1997, Delacorte $15.95 (0-385-32142-2). During World War II, motherless Lily loses her father when he is sent to fight in France but becomes friendly with Albert, an orphaned Hungarian refugee. (Rev: BL 2/1/97; SLJ 2/97)

2608 Gille, Elizabeth. *Shadows of a Childhood: A Novel of War & Friendship* (9–12). Trans. by Linda Coverdale. 1998, New Pr. $23.00 (1-56584-388-6). Based on fact, this novel traces the complex story of a Jewish girl in France who survived World War II as a Gentile and her subsequent search for truth and her own identity. (Rev: BL 1/1–15/98; VOYA 12/98)

2609 Hahn, Mary D. *Stepping on the Cracks* (5–8). 1991, Clarion $14.95 (0-395-58507-4). A sixth-grade girl in a small town experiences moral conflict when she must decide whether to help a pacifist deserter during World War II. (Rev: BL 10/15/91*; SLJ 12/91*)

2610 Harrison, Barbara. *Theo* (5–9). 1999, Clarion $15.00 (0-395-19959-3). Set in World War II Greece, this is the story of orphan Theo, whose brother and then his friend are killed by the Nazis, and his heroic role in the Resistance. (Rev: SLJ 9/99)

2611 Hartling, Peter. *Crutches* (6–9). 1988, Lothrop $12.95 (0-688-07991-1). A young war refugee makes friends with a one-legged man in postwar Vienna. (Rev: BL 2/1/89; SLJ 11/88; VOYA 2/89)

2612 Heggen, Thomas. *Mister Roberts* (10–12). 1983, Buccaneer LB $16.95 (0-89966-445-8). The waste of war is one of the themes of this richly comic but also touching story of life on a supply ship during World War II.

2613 Heneghan, James. *Wish Me Luck* (5–8). 1997, Farrar $16.00 (0-374-38453-3); Bantam Doubleday Dell paper $4.50 (0-440-22764-X). When Jamie is evacuated to Canada from England during World War II, the ship he is on is sunk by a German U-boat. (Rev: BL 6/1–15/97; BR 9–10/97; SLJ 6/97)

2614 Hertenstein, Jane. *Beyond Paradise* (6–10). 1999, Morrow $16.00 (0-688-16381-5). This historical novel recounts the horrors of life in Japanese internment camps in the Pacific during World War II as seen through the eyes of a missionary's daughter. (Rev: BL 8/99; SLJ 9/99)

2615 Howard, Ellen. *A Different Kind of Courage* (7–12). 1996, Simon & Schuster $15.00 (0-689-80774-0). A complex novel about 2 youngsters from different parts of France and their perilous journey in 1940 to reach safety in the United States. (Rev: BL 9/15/96; SLJ 11/96)

2616 Huth, Angela. *Land Girls* (10–12). 1996, St. Martin's $23.95 (0-312-14296-X). This story, set in England during World War II, tells of 3 girls who become friends when they meet as Land Girls—volunteer workers who took the place of farm hands fighting in the war—on a small farm owned by the Lawrences. (Rev: SLJ 10/96)

2617 Keneally, Thomas. *Schindler's List* (10–12). 1993, Simon & Schuster paper $12.00 (0-671-88031-4). A mature novel that is a fictionalized treatment of the life of the German industrialist who saved the lives of many Jews during World War II.

2618 Kertesz, Imre. *Fateless* (9–12). Trans. by Christopher C. Wilson. 1992, Northwestern Univ. Pr. $58.95 (0-8101-1024-5); paper $14.95 (0-8101-1049-0). A Holocaust survival tale told from the viewpoint of a Hungarian Jewish teenager. (Rev: BL 9/15/92)

2619 Laird, Christa. *But Can the Phoenix Sing?* (7–10). 1995, Greenwillow $16.00 (0-688-13612-5). A Holocaust survivor story in which a young boy learns that cruelty and tenderness can reside at the same time in one person. (Rev: BL 11/15/95; SLJ 10/95)

2620 Laird, Christa. *Shadow of the Wall* (6–10). 1990, Greenwillow $12.95 (0-688-09336-1). The harrowing story of a teenage Jewish boy living in the Warsaw Ghetto during World War II. (Rev: BL 5/15/90; SLJ 7/90; VOYA 8/90)

2621 Levitin, Sonia. *Annie's Promise* (6–10). 1993, Atheneum $15.00 (0-689-31752-2); paper $3.99 (0-689-80440-7). Set near the end of World War II, this sequel to *Silver Days* focuses on 13-year-old Annie's break from her overprotective Jewish immigrant parents. (Rev: BL 2/1/93; SLJ 4/93)

2622 Levitin, Sonia. *Silver Days* (7–9). 1992, Simon & Schuster paper $3.95 (0-689-71570-6). The Platt family moves to California as World War II breaks out and adjustments to the New World must be made. This is a sequel to *Journey to America*. (Rev: BL 4/1/89; BR 9–10/89; SLJ 5/89; VOYA 6/89)

2623 Manley, Joan B. *She Flew No Flags* (7–10). 1995, Houghton $16.00 (0-395-71130-4). A strongly autobiographical World War II novel about a 10-year-old's voyage from India to her new home in the United States and the people she meets on the ship. (Rev: BL 3/15/95; SLJ 4/95; VOYA 5/95)

2624 Matas, Carol. *After the War* (5–9). 1996, Simon & Schuster paper $16.00 (0-689-80350-8). A harrowing docunovel about 15-year-old Ruth, who after being liberated from Buchenwald in 1945, leads a group of children across Europe to eventual safety in Palestine. (Rev: BL 4/1/96*; BR 1–2/97; SLJ 5/96; VOYA 8/96)

2625 Matas, Carol. *Daniel's Story* (6–9). 1994, Scholastic paper $4.99 (0-590-46588-0). In this companion to an exhibit at the U.S. Holocaust Memorial Museum, Daniel symbolizes the millions of young people who suffered or died under Hitler's regime. (Rev: BL 5/15/93)

2626 Matas, Carol. *Greater Than Angels* (7–10). 1998, Simon & Schuster paper $16.00 (0-689-81353-8). Although told in a somewhat confused manner, this is a gripping account of one of the Jewish children hidden from the Nazis in the French village of Le Chambon. (Rev: BL 4/15/98; BR 1–2/99; SLJ 6/98; VOYA 10/98)

2627 Matas, Carol. *In My Enemies House* (7–10). 1999, Simon & Schuster paper $16.00 (0-689-81354-6). Marisa, 15, Jewish but Aryan-looking, assumes a new identity during World War II after her family and friends are killed by the Nazis in Poland. (Rev: BL 2/1/99; SLJ 3/99; VOYA 4/99)

2628 Mazer, Harry. *The Last Mission* (7–10). 1981, Dell paper $4.50 (0-440-94797-9). An underage Jewish American boy joins the Air Corps and is taken prisoner by the Germans. (Rev: BL 5/1/88)

2629 Mazer, Norma Fox. *Good Night, Maman* (5–9). 1999, Harcourt $16.00 (0-15-201468-3). A first-person account of a young Jewish girl's experiences in Europe during the Holocaust and later in a refugee camp in Oswego, New York. (Rev: BL 8/99)

2630 Michaels, Anne. *Fugitive Pieces* (10–12). 1997, Knopf $25.00 (0-679-45439-X). A novel about a survivor of the Holocaust, his memories of a peaceful past, and his life after he was smuggled out of Poland to Greece. (Rev: BL 2/15/97; SLJ 6/97)

2631 Michener, James A. *South Pacific* (5–9). Illus. 1992, Harcourt $16.95 (0-15-200618-4). A retelling, for young people of Michener's stories on which the musical *South Pacific* was based. (Rev: BL 9/1/92; SLJ 11/92)

2632 Monsarrat, Nicholas. *The Cruel Sea* (9–12). 1988, Naval Institute Pr. $32.95 (0-87021-055-6). A novel that explores in human terms the war at sea during World War II as seen through the eyes of the men of 2 British ships.

2633 Morpurgo, Michael. *Waiting for Anya* (5–8). 1991, Viking paper $14.99 (0-670-83735-0). In this story set in occupied France, 12-year-old Jo helps a group of Jewish children hide from the Germans and then escape over the mountains to Spain. (Rev: BL 5/15/91; SLJ 4/91*)

140

2634 Myers, Walter Dean. *The Journal of Scott Pendleton Collins: A World War II Soldier* (5–9). Illus. (My Name Is America) 1999, Scholastic $10.95 (0-439-05013-8). Through a series of letters, readers get to know 17-year-old Collins, an American soldier who participates in the D-Day invasion of Europe. (Rev: BL 6/1–15/99; SLJ 7/99)

2635 Napoli, Donna Jo. *Stones in Water* (5–8). 1997, Dutton paper $15.99 (0-525-45842-5). The exciting story of 2 Italian boys, one of whom is Jewish, who are transported to work camps by the Nazis during World War II, and the survival adventure of one of them after he escapes and tries to make his way to the Italian partisans. (Rev: BL 10/1/97; BR 3–4/98; SLJ 11/97*; VOYA 2/98)

2636 Nolan, Han. *If I Should Die Before I Wake* (7–10). 1994, Harcourt $18.00 (0-15-238040-X). Teenager Hilary, who hangs out with neo-Nazis, is in a hospital after an accident. Next to her is a Holocaust survivor, Chana, and before Hilary regains consciousness, she slips into Chana's memory and travels back in time to Auschwitz. (Rev: BL 4/1/94; SLJ 4/94; VOYA 6/94)

2637 Orgel, Doris. *The Devil in Vienna* (7–10). 1978, Penguin paper $5.99 (0-14-032500-X). Two friends, one Jewish and the other the daughter of a Nazi, growing up in German-occupied Austria.

2638 Orlev, Uri. *The Island on Bird Street* (7–9). Trans. by Hillel Halkin. 1984, Houghton $16.00 (0-395-33887-5). An 11-year-old boy tries to survive in an empty Polish ghetto during World War II. (Rev: BL 11/1/88)

2639 Orlev, Uri. *The Man from the Other Side* (6–10). Trans. by Hillel Halkin. 1991, Houghton $14.95 (0-395-53808-4). The story of a teenager in Nazi-occupied Warsaw who helps desperate Jews despite his dislike of them. (Rev: BL 6/15/91*; SLJ 9/91*)

2640 Pausewang, Gudrun. *The Final Journey* (8–12). Trans. by Patricia Crampton. 1996, Viking $15.99 (0-670-86456-0). The story of an 11-year-old Jewish girl and her horrifying train ride in a crowded freight car to a Nazi death camp. (Rev: BL 10/1/96; BR 3–4/97; VOYA 4/97)

2641 Propp, Vera W. *When the Soldiers Were Gone* (4–9). 1999, Putnam $14.99 (0-399-23325-3). The heartrending story of a young Jewish boy who, after World War II, must return to his own people and leave behind the loving farm family who had protected him and saved his life. (Rev: BL 1/1–15/99*; SLJ 2/99)

2642 Ray, Karen. *To Cross a Line* (7–10). 1994, Orchard LB $16.99 (0-531-08681-X). The story of a 17-year-old Jewish boy who is pursued by the Gestapo and encounters barriers in his desperate attempts to escape Nazi Germany. (Rev: BL 2/15/94; SLJ 6/94; VOYA 6/94)

2643 Reuter, Bjarne. *The Boys from St. Petri* (7–10). Trans. by Anthea Bell. 1994, Dutton $15.99 (0-525-45121-8). Danish teenager Lars and his friends fight the Nazi occupation of their hometown during World War II and plan to blow up a train. (Rev: BL 2/1/94; SLJ 2/94; VOYA 4/94)

2644 Richter, Hans Peter. *Friedrich* (7–9). Trans. by Edite Kroll. 1987, Penguin paper $4.99 (0-14-032205-1). The story of a Jewish boy and his family caught in the horror of the rise of the Nazi party and the Holocaust. (Rev: BL 4/1/90)

2645 Rinaldi, Ann. *Keep Smiling Through* (5–8). 1996, Harcourt $12.00 (0-15-200768-7); paper $6.00 (0-15-201072-6). Life on the home front in New Jersey as seen through the eyes of Kate, a lonely 10-year-old. (Rev: BL 7/96; SLJ 6/96; VOYA 8/96)

2646 Rochman, Hazel, and Darlene Z. McCampbell, eds. *Bearing Witness: Stories of the Holocaust* (7–12). 1995, Orchard LB $16.99 (0-531-08788-3). This anthology of 24 works revolving around the Holocaust includes memoirs, poetry, short stories, a film script, a letter, and a comic strip. (Rev: BL 6/1–15/95; SLJ 9/95; VOYA 12/95)

2647 Rylant, Cynthia. *I Had Seen Castles* (6–12). 1993, Harcourt $10.95 (0-15-238003-5). A strong message about the physical and emotional costs of war—in this story, the toll of World War II on John, a Canadian adolescent. (Rev: BL 9/1/93; VOYA 2/94)

2648 Salisbury, Graham. *Under the Blood-Red Sun* (5–9). 1994, Delacorte $15.95 (0-385-32099-X). Tomi, born in Hawaii of Japanese parents, struggles during World War II, facing suspicion and hatred from classmates. His father is sent to a U.S. prison camp. (Rev: BL 10/15/94*; SLJ 10/94; VOYA 10/94)

2649 Tamar, Erika. *Good-bye, Glamour Girl* (7–10). 1984, HarperCollins LB $12.89 (0-397-32088-4). Liesl and her family flee from Hitler's Europe and Liesl must now become Americanized. (Rev: BL 1/1/85)

2650 Thesman, Jean. *Molly Donnelly* (6–9). 1993, Houghton $13.95 (0-395-64348-1); 1994, Avon paper $4.50 (0-380-72252-6). The saga of a young girl's growing up in Seattle during World War II and coping with not only the changes wrought by war but typical adolescent concerns. (Rev: BL 4/1/93; SLJ 5/93; VOYA 8/93)

2651 Uris, Leon. *Mila 18* (10–12). 1961, Bantam paper $7.99 (0-553-24160-5). A dramatic story involving the Warsaw Ghetto freedom fighters during World War II.

2652 Van Dijk, Lutz. *Damned Strong Love: The True Story of Willi G. and Stefan K.* (8–12). Trans. by Elizabeth D. Crawford. 1995, Holt $15.95 (0-8050-3770-5). Nazi persecution of homosexuals, based on the life of Stefan K., a Polish teenager. (Rev: BL 5/15/95; SLJ 8/95)

2653 Van Steenwyk, Elizabeth. *A Traitor among Us* (6–9). 1998, Eerdmans $15.00 (0-8028-5150-9). Set in Nazi-occupied Holland in 1944, this thriller describes the resistance activities of 13-year-old Pieter including his hiding of a wounded American soldier. (Rev: BL 8/98; SLJ 8/98)

2654 Voigt, Cynthia. *David and Jonathan* (8–12). 1992, Scholastic paper $14.95 (0-590-45165-0). A Holocaust survivor darkens the life of his American cousin with gruesome stories of the prison camps. (Rev: BL 3/1/92; SLJ 3/92)

2655 Vos, Ida. *Dancing on the Bridge at Avignon* (5–8). Trans. by Terese Edelstein and Inez Smidt. 1995, Houghton $14.95 (0-395-72039-7). A translation from the Dutch of wartime experiences of Jews in the Netherlands and one particular Jewish girl, Rosa. (Rev: BL 10/15/95; SLJ 10/95; VOYA 2/96)

2656 Walsh, Jill Paton. *Fireweed* (7–10). 1988, Farrar paper $3.50 (0-374-42316-4). A reissue of the novel about the friendship between a 15-year-old boy and a younger girl during the London blitz.

2657 Watts, Irene. *Good-Bye Marianne: A Story of Growing up in Nazi Germany* (5–8). 1998, Tundra paper $7.95 (0-88776-445-2). This autobiographical novel tells about the cruel living conditions inflicted on Jews in Germany that led one family to send their daughter to Britain in the Kindertransport of 1938. (Rev: BL 8/98; SLJ 8/98)

2658 Westall, Robert. *The Kingdom by the Sea* (6–9). 1991, Farrar $15.00 (0-374-34205-9). A World War II survival adventure about a 12-year-old boy who is on his own on the northern English coast after his family home is bombed. (Rev: BL 11/1/91; SLJ 11/91)

2659 Westall, Robert. *The Machine Gunners* (6–9). 1997, Morrow paper $4.95 (0-688-15498-0). A reissue of the prize-winning English novel about a boy during World War II who finds a downed German plane with a machine gun intact. (Rev: VOYA 8/90)

2660 Westall, Robert. *Time of Fire* (6–9). 1997, Scholastic $15.95 (0-590-47746-3). World War II becomes real for young Sonny in Manchester, England, when his mother is killed in a bombing raid and his father dies in the armed forces. (Rev: BL 8/97; BR 11–12/97; SLJ 7/97; VOYA 6/98)

2661 Williams, Laura E. *Behind the Bedroom Wall* (5–8). Illus. 1996, Milkweed $15.95 (1-57131-607-8); paper $6.95 (1-57131-606-X). Korinna, a young Nazi, discovers that her parents are hiding a Jewish

couple in wartime Germany. (Rev: BL 8/96; BR 1–2/97; SLJ 9/96)

2662 Winter, Kathryn. *Katarina* (7–12). 1998, Farrar $17.00 (0-374-33984-8). A gripping autobiographical novel about a Jewish orphan in hiding in Slovakia during World War II. (Rev: BL 3/1/98; BR 11–12/98; SLJ 7/98)

2663 Wouk, Herman. *The Caine Mutiny* (10–12). 1992, Little, Brown paper $14.00 (0-316-95510-8). The story of the men aboard the mine sweeper Caine and of her psychotic captain named Queeg.

2664 Wouk, Herman. *The Winds of War* (10–12). 1992, Little, Brown paper $6.99 (0-316-95516-7). This novel traces the effects of the beginning of World War II on the family of Commander Pug Henry. A sequel is *War and Remembrance.*

KOREAN, VIETNAM, AND OTHER WARS

2665 Karlin, Wayne, and Le Minh Khue, eds. *The Other Side of Heaven: Post-War Fiction by Vietnamese and American Writers* (10–12). 1995, Curbstone paper $17.95 (1-880684-31-4). A collection of short stories, many about the effects of the Vietnam War, written by Vietnamese and American writers. (Rev: BL 9/1/95; BR 3–4/96; SLJ 4/96)

2666 Michener, James A. *The Bridges at Toko-Ri* (9–12). 1953, Random $16.95 (0-394-41780-1); Fawcett paper $5.95 (0-449-20651-3). The story of a young navy pilot and his bombing missions over Korea during the early 1950s. (Rev: BL 10/1/88)

2667 Myers, Walter Dean. *Fallen Angels* (9–12). 1988, Scholastic $14.95 (0-590-40942-5). A 17-year-old black boy and his brutal but enabling experiences in the Vietnam War. (Rev: BL 4/15/88; BR 9–10/88; SLJ 6/88; VOYA 8/88)

2668 Porcelli, Joe. *The Photograph* (10–12). 1996, Wyrick & Co. $22.95 (0-941711-30-7). This autobiographical novel traces Joe's early years in Korea, his school years and military training in Charleston, South Carolina, his second rotation in Vietnam, during which he commanded an elite company of volunteers, and his lifelong search for his older brother, who disappeared after their parents were killed in the early days of Korea's civil war. (Rev: SLJ 11/96)

2669 Potok, Chaim. *I Am the Clay* (9–12). 1994, Fawcett paper $5.99 (0-44922138-5). An injured orphan boy touches the hearts of a crusty Korean refugee and his more compassionate wife. (Rev: BL 4/1/92; SLJ 12/92)

2670 Qualey, Marsha. *Come in from the Cold* (9–12). 1994, Houghton $16.00 (0-395-68986-4). In 1969, Maud, whose sister is killed while protesting the Vietnam War, and Jeff, whose brother dies fighting in it, are drawn together by mutual grief and hope. (Rev: BL 9/15/94; SLJ 12/94; VOYA 10/94)

2671 Rostkowski, Margaret I. *The Best of Friends* (7–12). 1989, HarperCollins $12.95 (0-06-025104-2). How the Vietnam War affects 3 teenaged Utah friends as each tells a part of the story. (Rev: BL 9/1/89; SLJ 9/89; VOYA 12/89)

2672 White, Ellen E. *The Road Home* (8–12). 1995, Scholastic $15.95 (0-590-46737-9). This story re-creates a Vietnam War medical base in claustrophobic and horrific detail, and features army nurse Rebecca Phillips, from the Echo Company book series. (Rev: BL 1/15/95; SLJ 4/95; VOYA 4/95)

Horror Stories and the Supernatural

2673 Aiken, Joan. *A Fit of Shivers: Tales for Late at Night* (7–10). 1995, Bantam paper $4.50 (0-440-41120-3). Vengeful ghosts, eerie dreams, and haunted houses abound in these 10 tales. (Rev: BL 9/1/92)

2674 Aiken, Joan. *A Foot in the Grave* (6–10). Illus. 1992, Demco $9.09 (0-606-06383-8). A series of ghost stories illustrated by surrealistic paintings. (Rev: BL 3/15/92; SLJ 5/92)

2675 *Alfred Hitchcock's Supernatural Tales of Terror and Suspense* (7–10). Illus. 1973, Random paper $4.99 (0-394-85622-8). Horrifying tales by such masters as Patricia Highsmith and Raymond Chandler.

2676 Ambrose, David. *Superstition* (10–12). 1998, Warner $24.00 (0-446-52344-5). In a deadly experiment, 8 people create the ghost of a fictitious person that, in time, seems to be responsible for the deaths of some of the participants. (Rev: SLJ 1/99)

2677 Anderson, M. T. *Thirsty* (7–12). 1997, Candlewick $17.99 (0-7636-0048-2). In addition to all kinds of family problems, Chris discovers that he is turning into a vampire. (Rev: BR 9–10/97; SLJ 3/97)

2678 Andrews, V. C. *Flowers in the Attic* (10–12). 1990, Pocket Books paper $7.50 (0-671-72941-1). This horror story about youngsters being held prisoners in an attic is long on horror but short on quality. Continued in *Petals on the Wind; If There Be Thorns;* and *Seeds of Yesterday.*

2679 Anthony, Piers. *Shade of the Tree* (10–12). 1987, Tor paper $3.95 (0-8125-3103-5). The horror mounts slowly as a New York man and his 2 children move into a deserted estate in Florida. (Rev: BL 3/15/86; VOYA 8/86)

2680 Asimov, Isaac, et al., eds. *Devils* (9–12). 1987, NAL paper $3.50 (0-451-14867-3). A devilish collection of stories drawn from such sources as folklore and tales of horror.

2681 Asimov, Isaac, et al., eds. *Tales of the Occult* (9–12). 1989, Prometheus paper $21.95 (0-87975-531-8). A collection of 22 stories that explore such subjects as telepathy and reincarnation. (Rev: BL 4/1/89)

2682 Asimov, Isaac, et al., eds. *Young Witches & Warlocks* (6–9). 1987, HarperCollins $12.95 (0-06-020183-5). A collection of 10 stories, most of them scary, about witches. (Rev: BL 7/87; SLJ 1/88)

2683 Atwater-Rhodes, Amelia. *In the Forests of the Night* (7–12). 1999, Delacorte $8.95 (0-385-32674-2). In this story written by a 13-year-old author, Risika, a 300-year-old vampire, takes revenge against Aubrey, another vampire and her age-old enemy, when Aubrey threatens to harm Risika's only friend, Tora, a Bengal tiger in a zoo. (Rev: BL 6/1–15/99; SLJ 7/99; VOYA 8/99)

2684 Avi. *Devil's Race* (7–9). 1984, Avon paper $3.50 (0-380-70406-4). John Proud is in constant battle with a demon who has the same name and was hanged in 1854.

2685 Bawden, Nina. *Devil by the Sea* (6–8). 1976, HarperCollins $12.95 (0-397-31683-6). Is the strange old man Hilary sees at the beach really the devil?

2686 Bedard, Michael. *Painted Devil* (7–10). 1994, Atheneum $15.95 (0-689-31827-8). A girl helping to renovate an old puppet theater discovers that the vicious-looking devil puppet has evil powers. (Rev: BL 3/1/94; SLJ 4/94; VOYA 6/94)

2687 Brown, Roberta Simpson. *The Queen of the Cold-Blooded Tales* (6–9). 1993, August House $19.95 (0-87483-332-9). A collection of 23 contemporary horror stories. (Rev: BL 9/1/93; VOYA 4/94)

2688 Buffie, Margaret. *The Dark Garden* (6–10). 1997, Kids Can $14.95 (1-55074-288-4). Thea, who suffers from amnesia after an accident, begins hearing voices, one of which belongs to a young woman who died tragically years before. (Rev: BL 10/15/97; BR 1–2/98; SLJ 10/97)

2689 Buffie, Margaret. *Someone Else's Ghost* (8–12). 1995, Scholastic $14.95 (0-590-46922-3). A girl's brother dies and haunts the family both literally and figuratively, for the family's new home seems to have a presence. (Rev: BL 3/1/95; SLJ 3/95; VOYA 4/95)

2690 Butler, Charles. *The Darkling* (6–9). 1998, Simon & Schuster paper $16.00 (0-689-81796-7). Soon after Petra visits Mr. Century, a mysterious hermit, she finds that she is being taken over by the spirit of the old man's dead love, Euridice. (Rev: BL 4/1/98; BR 1–2/99; SLJ 5/98)

2691 Card, Orson Scott. *Homebody: A Novel* (10–12). 1998, HarperCollins $24.00 (0-06-017655-5). A supernatural novel about a man who unleashes spirits from the past when he begins restoring a faded Southern mansion. (Rev: SLJ 8/98; VOYA 8/98)

2692 Cargill, Linda. *The Surfer* (6–9). 1995, Scholastic paper $3.99 (0-590-22215-5). After Nick meets Marina, a strange but beautiful surfer, he realizes that she is an immortal who has plotted against male members of his family for generations. (Rev: SLJ 1/96)

2693 Cerf, Bennett, ed. *Famous Ghost Stories* (10–12). 1956, Amereon LB $24.95 (0-88411-146-6). This is a superior anthology of truly scary stories.

2694 Cervantes, Esther DeMichael, and Alex Cervantes. *Barrio Ghosts* (7–12). Illus. 1988, New Readers $14.25 (0-88336-315-1). Five fantastic stories feature young people in the East Los Angeles barrio. (Rev: BL 5/15/89)

2695 Cohen, Daniel. *Phantom Animals* (6–9). 1993, Pocket Books paper $2.99 (0-671-75930-2). Short selections featuring ghostly dogs, scary kangaroos, menacing birds, and phantom cats. (Rev: BL 8/91; SLJ 7/91)

2696 Conrad, Pam. *Stonewords: A Ghost Story* (6–9). 1990, HarperCollins LB $10.00 (0-06-021316-7). Through the years Zoe makes friends with a girl who visits from time to time but who is actually a ghost. (Rev: VOYA 6/90)

2697 Cook, Robin. *Coma* (10–12). 1977, NAL paper $7.99 (0-451-15953-5). A young medical student uncovers a plot to kill patients.

2698 Cooney, Caroline B. *Night School* (7–10). 1995, Scholastic paper $3.50 (0-590-47878-8). Four California teens enroll in a mysterious night school course and encounter an evil instructor and their own worst character defects. (Rev: BL 5/1/95)

2699 Coville, Bruce. *The Ghost Wore Gray* (5–8). 1988, Bantam paper $3.99 (0-553-15610-1). Nina and friend Chris investigate a haunted inn in the Catskill Mountains. (Rev: BL 9/15/88; SLJ 9/88)

2700 Coville, Bruce. *Oddly Enough* (6–9). 1994, Harcourt $15.95 (0-15-200093-3). Nine short horror stories involving blood drinking, elves, unicorns, ghosts, werewolves, and executioners. (Rev: BL 10/1/94; SLJ 12/94; VOYA 2/95)

2701 Cray, Jordan. *Gemini 7* (6–10). 1997, Simon & Schuster paper $3.99 (0-689-81432-1). In this horror story, Jonah Lanier begins to realize that his new friend, Nicole, might be responsible for the mysterious disasters that are befalling his family and other friends. (Rev: SLJ 1/98)

2702 Cross, Gillian. *The Dark Behind the Curtain* (7–9). Illus. 1984, Oxford $12.95 (0-19-271457-0). Colin sees his friend Marshall turn into the character he is portraying in the school play—the demon barber Sweeney Todd.

2703 Cross, Gillian. *Roscoe's Leap* (7–9). 1987, Holiday House $15.95 (0-8234-0669-5). For Stephen his family's mansion, Roscoe's Leap, holds secrets that make him relive a previous existence during the French Revolution. (Rev: BL 11/15/87; SLJ 11/87; VOYA 4/88)

2704 Cuddon, J. A., ed. *The Penguin Book of Ghost Stories* (9–12). 1985, Penguin paper $13.95 (0-14-006800-7). A collection of 33 spine tinglers by English, American, and European authors. (Rev: BL 7/85)

2705 Datlow, Ellen, ed. *The Year's Best Fantasy & Horror: Tenth Annual Collection* (9–12). 1997, St. Martin's paper $17.95 (0-312-15701-0). A collection of horror and fantasy stories, some gripping, others stomach churning. (Rev: BL 9/1/97; VOYA 6/98)

2706 Dean, Jan. *Finders* (6–9). 1995, Macmillan paper $15.00 (0-689-50612-0). Helen Draper, 16, inherits her grandfather's gift of "finding" people and things, but when kelpie Nicholas Morgan asks her to find a special stone, her life is in jeopardy. (Rev: BL 5/1/95)

2707 Dimartino, Nick. *Seattle Ghost Story* (10–12). Illus. 1998, Rosebriar paper $12.95 (0-9653918-2-5). A horror story in which Billy Beck accidentally unleashes a deadly ghost that brings havoc to his quiet neighborhood. (Rev: SLJ 1/99)

2708 Doyle, Arthur Conan. *The Best Supernatural Tales of Arthur Conan Doyle* (10–12). 1979, Dover paper $8.95 (0-486-23725-7). A group of 15 ghost stories by this master of suspense.

2709 Du Maurier, Daphne. *Echoes from the Macabre: Selected Stories* (9–12). 1977, Aeonian $25.95 (0-88411-543-7). Nine stories of suspense including the classic "The Birds."

2710 Duncan, Lois. *Gallows Hill* (6–9). 1997, Bantam Doubleday Dell $15.95 (0-385-32331-X); paper $4.99 (0-440-22725-9). Sarah is alarmed when her harmless future telling turns out to be true and she begins dreaming of the Salem Witch Trials. (Rev: BL 4/15/97; BR 5–6/97; SLJ 5/97; VOYA 4/97)

2711 Duncan, Lois. *Locked in Time* (7–10). 1985, Dell paper $4.99 (0-440-94942-4). Nore's father marries into a family that somehow never seems to age. (Rev: BL 7/85; BR 9–10/85; SLJ 11/85)

2712 Duncan, Lois, ed. *Night Terrors: Stories of Shadow and Substance* (6–12). 1996, Simon & Schuster paper $16.00 (0-689-80346-X). An anthology of 11 horror-supernatural stories by such popular writers as Joan Aiken, Chris Lynch, and Norma Fox Mazer. (Rev: BL 5/15/96; BR 1–2/97; SLJ 6/96; VOYA 8/96)

2713 Duncan, Lois. *Stranger with My Face* (7–10). 1984, Dell paper $4.99 (0-440-98356-8). A girl encounters her evil twin who wishes to take her place.

2714 Duncan, Lois. *Summer of Fear* (7–10). 1976, Dell paper $4.99 (0-440-98324-X). An orphaned cousin who comes to live with Rachel's family is really a witch.

2715 Dunlop, Eileen. *Clementina* (6–9). 1987, Holiday House $12.95 (0-8234-0642-3). A British novel in which the young heroine, Daisy, finds that an acquaintance is reliving events that occurred centuries ago and ended in a violent death. (Rev: BL 4/15/87; SLJ 5/87; VOYA 8/87)

2716 Dunlop, Eileen. *The House on the Hill* (6–9). 1987, Troll paper $3.50 (0-8167-1323-5). In this British mystery, Philip and his cousin Sarah investigate a mysterious light that shines from an empty room. (Rev: BL 10/15/87; SLJ 11/87)

2717 Durant, Alan, ed. *Vampire and Werewolf Stories* (5–10). (Kingfischer Story Library) 1998, Kingfisher paper $6.95 (0-7534-5152-2). Eighteen stories, many written originally for an adult audience, are included in this classic gothic horror anthology about vampires and werewolves. (Rev: BL 1/1–15/99)

2718 Edgerton, Leslie H., ed. *Monday's Meal* (10–12). 1997, Univ. of North Texas Pr. paper $14.95 (1-57441-026-1). A collection of 21 unique, often gruesome, horror stories, many of which are set in the French Quarter of New Orleans. (Rev: SLJ 1/98)

2719 Ellis, Sarah. *Back of Beyond Stories* (6–10). 1997, Simon & Schuster $15.00 (0-689-81484-4). Each of the 12 stories in this collection by the author begin with real world problems but soon slip into the realm of the supernatural. (Rev: BL 1/1–15/98; SLJ 11/97*; VOYA 12/97)

2720 Forrest, Elizabeth. *Killjoy* (10–12). 1996, D A W Books paper $5.99 (0-88677-695-3). A horror thriller about 3 outsiders who are being pursued because one of them has in his possession a mysterious power that can create zombies. (Rev: VOYA 8/96)

2721 Furlong, Monica. *Wise Child* (6–8). 1987, Demco $10.34 (0-606-04425-6). Set in ancient Scotland, this is a story of a young girl torn between the good and evil aspects of witchcraft. (Rev: BL 12/1/87; SLJ 9/87)

2722 Gabhart, Ann. *Wish Come True* (7–10). 1988, Avon paper $2.50 (0-380-75653-6). Lyssie receives as a gift a mirror that grants her wishes. (Rev: VOYA 6/89)

2723 Gifaldi, David. *Yours Till Forever* (7–10). 1989, HarperCollins LB $13.89 (0-397-32356-5). In this easily read novel, a high school senior sees disturbing similarities between his friends and his dead parents. (Rev: BL 10/1/89; SLJ 11/89; VOYA 2/90)

2724 Gorog, Judith. *Please Do Not Touch* (6–12). 1995, Scholastic paper $3.50 (0-590-46683-6). The reader enters a different fantasy for each of the 11 horror stories. (Rev: BL 9/1/93; VOYA 12/93)

2725 Gorog, Judith. *When Nobody's Home* (6–12). 1996, Scholastic $15.95 (0-590-46862-6). A collection of 15 terrifying (supposedly true) tales on the theme of baby-sitting. (Rev: BL 5/1/96; BR 9–10/96; SLJ 4/96; VOYA 12/96)

2726 Greenberg, Martin H. *Miskatonic University* (10–12). 1996, D A W Books paper $5.99 (0-88677-722-4). These horror stories, not for the faint of heart, involve a university where spell casting and prophesy are taught and strange events occur in its underground tunnels and cellars. (Rev: VOYA 6/97)

2727 Greenberg, Martin H., et al., eds. *Great Writers & Kids Write Spooky Stories* (5–8). Illus. 1995, Random $17.00 (0-679-87662-6). An anthology of 13 original horror stories by prominent authors who were commissioned to write the stories for this collection in collaboration with their children or grandchildren. (Rev: SLJ 2/96)

2728 Hahn, Mary D. *Look for Me by Moonlight* (7–10). 1995, Clarion $14.95 (0-395-69843-X). A 16-year-old girl seeking friendship meets a boy whose attention has dangerous strings attached. (Rev: BL 3/15/95; SLJ 5/95)

2729 Hambly, Barbara. *Traveling with the Dead* (9–12). 1995, Ballantine $22.00 (0-345-38102-5). In this sequel to *Those Who Hunt the Night* (1988), a retired British intelligence officer discovers an Austrian spymaster who can command the services of the undead as well as the living. (Rev: BL 9/15/95; SLJ 6/96; VOYA 4/96)

2730 Hambly, Barbara, and Martin H. Greenberg, eds. *Sisters of the Night* (9–12). 1995, Warner paper $17.99 (0-446-67143-6). Fourteen original stories by such masters as Jane Yolan, Tanith Lee, and Larry Niven explore the world of the female vampire. (Rev: VOYA 4/96)

2731 Hamilton, Virginia. *Sweet Whispers, Brother Rush* (7–10). 1982, Putnam $17.95 (0-399-20894-1). A 14-year-old girl, who cares for her older retarded brother, meets a charming ghost who reveals secrets of her past.

2732 Hartwell, David G., ed. *The Screaming Skull and Other Great American Ghost Stories* (10–12). 1995, Tor $4.99 (0-812-55178-8). A collection of 12 high-quality ghost stories by such writers as Edgar Allan Poe, F. Marion Crawford, Mark Twain, Nathaniel Hawthorne, Willa Cather, and Edith Wharton. (Rev: VOYA 4/96)

2733 Hawes, Louise. *Rosey in the Present Tense* (8–12). 1999, Walker $15.95 (0-8027-8685-5). After the death of his girlfriend, Rosey, 17-year-old Franklin can't stop living in the past until the ghost of Rosey and his family and friends help him accept his loss and begin to think of the present. (Rev: BL 4/1/99; BR 9–10/99; SLJ 5/99; VOYA 10/99)

2734 Hill, Mary, ed. *Creepy Classics: Hair-Raising Horror from the Masters of the Macabre* (6–10). 1994, Random paper $4.99 (0-679-86692-2). Gothic horror stories, poems, and novel excerpts by masters of the genre, including selections from Poe and an excerpt from Shelley's *Frankenstein*. (Rev: BL 10/15/94; SLJ 11/94)

2735 Hodges, Margaret. *Hauntings: Ghosts and Ghouls from Around the World* (5–8). Illus. 1991, Little, Brown $16.95 (0-316-36796-6). A diverse collection of 16 familiar and lesser-known tales about the supernatural. (Rev: BL 11/15/91; SLJ 11/91)

2736 Hotze, Sollace. *Acquainted with the Night* (8–12). 1992, Clarion $13.95 (0-395-61576-3). A novel that combines a tantalizing mystery/ghost story (based on a true story) with an exploration of the relationship between Molly, 17, and her older cousin Caleb, who is recovering from the Vietnam War and his father's suicide. (Rev: BL 12/1/92*; SLJ 11/92)

2737 Hughes, Dean. *Nutty's Ghost* (6–8). 1993, Atheneum $13.95 (0-689-31743-3). Nutty lands the lead in a terrible movie, and the ghost of a Shakespearean actor uses Nutty to gain revenge on the movie's director. (Rev: BL 2/15/93; SLJ 5/93)

2738 Jackson, Shirley. *The Haunting of Hill House* (9–12). 1984, Penguin paper $11.95 (0-14-007108-3). Four people decide to stay in Hill House to see if it is really haunted.

2739 Jackson, Shirley. *The Lottery* (8–12). 1949, Farrar paper $13.00 (0-374-51681-2). Macabre stories by this master that include the classic about a village and its horrifying annual tradition. (Rev: BL 9/1/97)

2740 Jennings, Paul. *Uncovered! Weird, Weird Stories* (5–8). 1996, Viking paper $14.99 (0-670-86856-6). A collection of spooky stories, each of which changes an everyday occurrence into a thing of horror. (Rev: BL 4/15/96; SLJ 4/96)

2741 Jennings, Paul. *Undone! More Mad Endings* (5–8). 1995, Viking paper $14.99 (0-670-86005-0). In this collection of 8 stories, the Australian author steps into fantastical realms without ever losing touch with firm ground. (Rev: BL 1/1/95; SLJ 1/95)

2742 Kelleher, Victor. *Del-Del* (7–12). Illus. 1992, Walker $27.95 (0-8027-8154-3). A family believes its son is possessed by an evil alien. (Rev: BL 3/1/92; SLJ 6/92)

2743 King, Stephen. *Carrie* (10–12). 1974, Doubleday $29.95 (0-385-08695-4); NAL paper $4.95 (0-451-15071-6). Carrie, a teenager with telekenetic powers, takes horrible revenge on her tormentors.

2744 King, Stephen. *Christine* (9–12). 1983, Viking $4.99 (0-670-22026-4); NAL paper $7.99 (0-451-16044-4). Arnie buys an old Plymouth that has mystical powers to possess and destroy.

2745 King, Stephen. *Cujo* (10–12). 1981, NAL paper $7.99 (0-451-16135-1). This is a horror story about a huge Saint Bernard that runs amok.

2746 King, Stephen. *The Dead Zone* (9–12). 1979, NAL paper $7.99 (0-451-15575-0). A number of men named John Smith find themselves in the strange area known as The Dead Zone.

2747 King, Stephen. *Firestarter* (9–12). 1980, NAL paper $7.99 (0-451-16780-5). A child is born with the incredible power to start fires.

2748 King, Stephen. *Night Shift* (10–12). 1978, Doubleday $30.00 (0-385-12991-2); paper $5.95 (0-451-16045-2). Vampires and demons inhabit these horror stories by a master of the macabre. (Rev: BL 10/15/88)

2749 King, Stephen. *Nightmares and Dreamscapes* (9–12). 1993, Viking paper $27.50 (0-670-85108-6). A collection of short stories, including pastiches of Doyle and Chandler, a vampire story, and a sports story. (Rev: BL 7/93*)

2750 King, Stephen. *Pet Sematary* (10–12). 1983, Doubleday $30.00 (0-385-18244-9); NAL paper $4.95 (0-451-15775-3). The frightening horror story about a family that moves next to an ancient Indian burial ground.

2751 King, Stephen. *The Shining* (10–12). 1977, Doubleday $27.50 (0-385-12167-9); NAL paper $7.99 (0-451-16091-6). The Torrances take over a deserted hotel that is haunted by the spirits of the dead.

2752 Klause, Annette Curtis. *The Silver Kiss* (8–12). 1992, Bantam paper $4.50 (0-440-21346-0). A teenage girl, beset with personal problems, meets a silver-haired boy who is a vampire in this suspenseful, sometimes gory, novel. (Rev: BL 10/15/90; SLJ 9/90)

2753 Klaveness, Jan O'Donnell. *The Griffin Legacy* (7–9). 1985, Dell paper $3.25 (0-440-43165-4). Two ghosts are laid to rest when the secret of the Griffin legacy is revealed.

2754 Klein, Robin. *Tearaways* (6–10). 1991, Viking paper $12.95 (0-670-83212-X). This short-story collection combines shivery horror with laughter. (Rev: BL 6/15/91; SLJ 6/91)

2755 Koontz, Dean. *Phantoms* (10–12). 1983, Berkley paper $7.99 (0-425-10145-2). A quiet town in California is gradually being consumed by a beast from the past in this horror story.

2756 Koontz, Dean. *Strangers* (10–12). 1986, Berkley paper $7.99 (0-425-11992-0). In this somewhat complex novel 8 unrelated characters share the same terrible fears and anxieties. (Rev: BL 3/1/86; VOYA 8/86)

2757 Kurtz, Katherine, and Deborah T. Harris. *The Lodge of the Lynx* (9–12). (Adept) 1992, Berkley paper $6.99 (0-441-00344-3). Black magic and the occult are investigated by a would-be detective and his assistant. (Rev: BL 5/15/92; SLJ 9/92)

2758 Levin, Ira. *Rosemary's Baby* (10–12). 1997, NAL paper $6.99 (0-451-19400-4). Rosemary is pregnant and under the increased influence of witchcraft.

2759 Levy, Elizabeth. *The Drowned* (9–12). 1995, Hyperion $16.95 (0-7868-0135-2). A supernatural thriller with a demented mother who ritually drowns a teenager and a drowned victim who returns to life. (Rev: BL 12/1/95; SLJ 12/95)

2760 Littke, Lael. *Haunted Sister* (7–10). 1998, Holt $16.95 (0-8050-5729-3). After a near-death experience, Janine becomes involved with the ghost of her dead twin sister, who in time inhabits Janine's spirit and body. (Rev: BL 10/1/98; SLJ 10/98; VOYA 2/99)

2761 Lovecraft, H. P. *The Case of Charles Dexter Ward* (10–12). 1987, Ballantine paper $0.05 (0-345-35490-7). Charles discovers he has inherited the powers of witchcraft. Also use: *At the Mountains of Madness and Other Tales of Terror* (1985).

2762 Lovecraft, H. P. *The Horror in the Museum* (9–12). 1996, Carroll & Graf paper $4.95 (0-7867-0387-3). A collection of Lovecraft's collaborations with other authors. (Rev: VOYA 6/97)

2763 Lumley, Brian. *The Source* (9–12). 1998, Tor $26.95 (0-312-86764-6); paper $6.99 (0-8125-2127-7). In this, the third volume of the Necroscope series, scientists find in the Ural mountains the entrance to a world where vampires and other horrible creatures live. (Rev: VOYA 2/90)

2764 Lutzen, Hanna. *Vlad the Undead* (9–12). 1998, Groundwood $15.95 (0-88899-341-2). A haunting novel, told in a series of manuscripts, letters, and diary entries, that deals with the Dracula legend and Lucia, a Danish medical student who becomes the Romanian Vlad Dracula. (Rev: SLJ 3/99)

2765 MacDonald, Caroline. *Hostilities: Nine Bizarre Stories* (7–10). 1994, Scholastic $13.95 (0-590-46063-3). A collection of 9 tales with strange, unsettling themes and Australian locales. (Rev: BL 1/15/94; SLJ 3/94; VOYA 10/94)

2766 McDonald, Collin. *The Chilling Hour: Tales of the Real and Unreal* (6–8). 1992, Dutton paper $14.99 (0-525-65101-2). Eight scary stories with unexpected twists. (Rev: BL 12/1/92; SLJ 8/92)

2767 McKean, Thomas. *Into the Candlelit Room and Other Strange Tales* (6–9). 1999, Putnam $17.99 (0-399-23359-8). A collection of offbeat stories, some in the form of letters and diary entries, about 5 young people and their encounters with the "dark side." (Rev: BL 7/99; SLJ 9/99; VOYA 10/99)

2768 McKissack, Patricia. *The Dark-Thirty: Southern Tales of the Supernatural* (5–8). Illus. 1992, Knopf LB $17.99 (0-679-91863-9). Ten original stories rooted in African American history and the oral-storytelling tradition on such subjects as slavery, belief in "the sight," and the Montgomery bus boycott. (Rev: BL 12/15/92; SLJ 12/92*)

2769 McNally, Clare. *Stage Fright* (9–12). 1993, Tor paper $5.99 (0-812-54839-6). Years after her lover and best friend were murdered, Hayley Seagel discovers that their ghosts have returned to help her and her friends fight a malevolent ghost. (Rev: VOYA 2/96)

2770 McNeil, W. K., ed. *Ghost Stories from the American South* (9–12). Illus. 1985, August House paper $9.95 (0-935304-84-3). A collection of blood-curdlers from locales ranging from Virginia to Texas. (Rev: SLJ 12/85)

2771 Mahy, Margaret, and Susan Cooper. *Don't Read This! And Other Tales of the Unnatural* (7–10). 1998, Front Street $15.95 (1-886910-22-7). Great stories of ghosts and the supernatural are included in this international collection that represents some of the top writers of scary fiction at work today. (Rev: BL 4/1/99; BR 9–10/99; SLJ 7/99; VOYA 6/99)

2772 Martin, Valerie. *Mary Reilly* (9–12). 1996, Pocket Books paper $5.99 (0-671-52113-6). A retelling of Stevenson's classic horror story from the standpoint of Dr. Jekyll's maid. (Rev: BL 12/1/89)

2773 Mayne, William, ed. *Supernatural Stories: A Hair-raising Collection* (7–9). Illus. 1996, Kingfisher $10.95 (0-7534-5026-7). A collection of literate, supernatural stories by such authors as Kipling, Capote, Mark Twain, and Saki. (Rev: SLJ 4/97)

2774 Mazer, Anne. *A Sliver of Glass: And Other Uncommon Tales* (5–8). 1996, Hyperion LB $13.89 (0-7868-2165-5). Eleven intriguing stories of horror and mystery. (Rev: SLJ 2/97)

2775 Michaels, Barbara. *Other Worlds* (10–12). 1999, HarperCollins $23.00 (0-06-019235-6). A group of experts on the occult, among them Sir Arthur Conan Doyle and Harry Houdini, listen to 2 famous folktales about poltergeists and hauntings and then venture their ideas concerning what really happened and why. (Rev: SLJ 7/99)

2776 Morgan, Jill. *Blood Brothers* (5–8). 1996, HarperCollins paper $4.50 (0-06-440562-1). A fast-paced adventure in which identical twins are turned into vampires. (Rev: BL 12/1/96; SLJ 1/97)

2777 Morpurgo, Michael, ed. *Ghostly Haunts* (6–9). 1997, Trafalgar paper $16.95 (1-85793-833-6). Some of Britain's best writers for young people, including Dick King-Smith and Joan Aiken, have contributed to this collection of supernatural stories. (Rev: BL 3/15/97)

2778 Moser, Barry, ed. *Great Ghost Stories* (7–12). Illus. 1998, Morrow $22.00 (0-688-14587-6). A collection of 13 ghost stories, some by established authors, others less-well known, but all effective particularly because of the eerie illustrations by the editor. (Rev: BL 11/15/98; SLJ 10/98; VOYA 2/99)

2779 Murphy, Jim. *Night Terrors* (6–9). 1993, Scholastic $13.95 (0-590-45341-6). Five gruesome horror stories dealing with vampires, mummies, cannibals, and other creatures. (Rev: BL 10/1/93; VOYA 12/93)

2780 Nixon, Joan Lowery. *The Haunting* (6–10). 1998, Doubleday $15.95 (0-385-32247-X). Anne is determined to rid Graymoss, an old mansion, of ghosts so that her mother can convert it into a home for unwanted children. (Rev: BL 7/98; SLJ 8/98; VOYA 12/98)

2781 Nixon, Joan Lowery. *Whispers from the Dead* (7–12). 1991, Bantam paper $4.50 (0-440-20809-2). After being saved from drowning, Sarah is able to communicate with dead spirits. (Rev: BL 9/15/89; BR 11–12/89; SLJ 9/89; VOYA 12/89)

2782 Norton, Andre, and Phyllis Miller. *House of Shadows* (7–9). 1984, Tor paper $2.95 (0-8125-4743-8). Three children encounter ghosts in their great aunt's home.

2783 Patneaude, David. *Dark Starry Morning: Stories of This World and Beyond* (5–8). 1995, Albert Whitman LB $13.95 (0-8075-1474-8). Six tales about beneficial encounters with the unknown and the world beyond. (Rev: BL 9/1/95; SLJ 9/95)

2784 Pierce, Meredith Ann. *The Darkangel* (10–12). 1998, Harcourt paper $6.00 (0-15-201768-2). In this vampire story, Airiel tries to rescue the fiend's brides.

2785 Pike, Christopher. *Bury Me Deep* (6–10). 1991, Pocket Books paper $3.99 (0-671-69057-4). A scuba-diving vacation in Hawaii turns into an adventure involving murder, ghosts, and underwater thrills. (Rev: BL 9/1/91)

2786 Pike, Christopher. *Scavenger Hunt* (9–12). 1990, Pocket Books paper $3.99 (0-671-73686-8). Two groups of teenagers on a scavenger hunt encounter horror that leads to a terrifying climax.

Also use: *Remember Me* (1989). (Rev: BL 9/1/89; VOYA 2/90)

2787 Pines, T., ed. *Thirteen: 13 Tales of Horror by 13 Masters of Horror* (8–12). 1991, Scholastic paper $4.99 (0-590-45256-8). Popular horror writers' stories of revenge, lust, and betrayal. (Rev: BL 3/1/92)

2788 Preussler, Otfried. *The Satanic Mill* (7–10). 1985, Peter Smith $19.50 (0-8446-6196-1). A 14-year-old boy is apprenticed to a mysterious master in this tale of black magic. A reissue. (Rev: BL 6/1–15/98)

2789 Price, Susan, ed. *Horror Stories* (6–12). 1995, Kingfisher $6.95 (1-85697-592-4). Two dozen Halloween read-alouds from such writers as Joan Aiken, Stephen King, Edgar Allan Poe, and John Steinbeck. (Rev: BL 10/15/95)

2790 Pullman, Philip. *Clockwork, or All Wound Up* (5–8). Illus. 1998, Scholastic $14.95 (0-590-12999-6); paper $4.99 (0-590-12998-8). In this complex novel of a story within a story, the lives of a novelist, an apprentice clockmaker, and Dr. Kalenius, a brilliant clockmaster, become entwined with supernatural results. (Rev: BL 9/15/98; BR 1–2/99; SLJ 10/98; VOYA 12/98)

2791 Rice, Anne. *Interview with the Vampire* (10–12). 1986, Ballantine paper $7.99 (0-345-33766-2). A 200-year-old vampire reveals every horrifying detail of his life. Rice has written other horror novels involving vampires.

2792 Rice, Bebe F. *The Year the Wolves Came* (5–8). 1994, Dutton paper $14.99 (0-525-45209-5). In Canada in 1906, wolves have returned to a village to menace the homesteaders and kill livestock as they look for their leader. (Rev: BL 1/15/95; SLJ 12/94)

2793 Roach, Marilynne K. *Encounters with the Invisible World* (6–9). 1977, HarperCollins $12.95 (0-690-01277-2). Spooky stories about witches, demons, spells, and ghosts in New England.

2794 Roberts, Nora. *River's End* (10–12). 1999, Putnam $23.95 (0-399-14470-6). When she was only 4, Olivia saw a monster with her father's face kill her mother, and now, years later, the vision resurfaces when a young writer contacts her about a book he is writing about the murder at the request of her imprisoned father. (Rev: BL 1/1–15/99; SLJ 9/99)

2795 Roos, Stephen. *My Favorite Ghost* (6–8). 1988, Macmillan LB $13.95 (0-689-31301-2). Derek persuades his friends to give him money to free a ghost from the spirit world. (Rev: BL 4/15/88; BR 9–10/88)

2796 Ryan, Alan, ed. *Haunting Women* (9–12). 1988, Avon paper $3.95 (0-380-89881-0). Fourteen horror stories written by such women as Shirley Jackson and Ruth Rendell. (Rev: BL 11/15/88; VOYA 2/89)

2797 Saberhagen, Fred. *A Sharpness on the Neck* (10–12). 1996, Tor $23.95 (0-312-85799-3). In this novel that switches between the French Revolution and today, contemporary newlyweds in the western United States are kidnapped by Vlad Dracula to protect them from Vlad's evil brother, Radu Dracula. (Rev: BL 11/15/97; VOYA 4/97)

2798 Saul, John. *Comes the Blind Fury* (9–12). 1990, Dell paper $6.99 (0-440-11475-6). An antique doll actually contains the evil spirit of a dead girl. Also use: *Cry for the Strangers* (1986), *Suffer the Children,* and *When the Wind Blows.*

2799 Shepard, Leslie, ed. *The Dracula Book of Great Horror Stories* (10–12). 1977, Citadel $10.00 (0-8065-0565-6). Thirteen old-fashioned but still chilling horror stories.

2800 Shusterman, Neal. *Mindtwisters: Stories to Shred Your Head* (6–9). 1997, Tor paper $3.99 (0-812-55199-0). These 8 short stories deal with such bizarre and supernatural occurrences as a boy who can make people disappear and a store that sells "what might have been." (Rev: SLJ 11/97; VOYA 10/97)

2801 Shusterman, Neal. *Scorpion Shards* (8–12). 1996, Tor paper $4.99 (0-8125-2465-9). A horror story in which 6 misfits and outsiders must face and exorcise the monsters that dwell within them. (Rev: BL 2/1/96; SLJ 3/96; VOYA 4/96)

2802 Slade, Arthur G. *Draugr* (6–9). Illus. (Northern Frights) 1998, Orca paper $6.95 (1-55143-094-0). Three youngsters who are spending the summer with their grandfather in Manitoba become involved with a supernatural creature, Kar, who is a draugr, or undead man. (Rev: SLJ 10/98)

2803 Slade, Arthur G. *The Haunting of Drang Island* (5–8). Illus. 1999, Orca paper $6.95 (1-55143-111-4). On a island off the coast of British Columbia, 15-year-old Michael meets Fiona, a girl his age who is there alone, and together they encounter ghosts, sea serpents, and spirits in this story that evokes ancient Norse mythology. (Rev: BL 4/1/99; SLJ 8/99)

2804 Sleator, William. *The Beasties* (6–9). 1997, NAL paper $15.99 (0-525-45598-1). Fifteen-year-old Doug and his 10-year-old sister, Colette, encounter the beasties, forest-dwelling ghouls who remove the arms and legs of their victims. (Rev: BL 10/1/97; BR 5–6/98; SLJ 12/97; VOYA 4/98)

2805 Sleator, William. *Dangerous Wishes* (5–9). 1995, Dutton paper $14.99 (0-525-45283-4). In this sequel to *The Spirit House,* Dominic Kamen travels to Thailand, where he seeks to return a jade carving to escape a vengeful spirit. (Rev: BL 8/95; SLJ 11/95; VOYA 4/96)

2806 Sleator, William. *The Spirit House* (6–9). 1993, Puffin paper $3.99 (0-14-036483-8). A Thai exchange student living with an American family reveals sinister mystical powers when one of his hosts builds a traditional spirit house as a gift for him. (Rev: BL 10/1/91; SLJ 12/91)

2807 Smith, L. J. *Night World: Secret Vampire* (9–12). 1996, Pocket Books paper $3.99 (0-671-55133-7). Faced with certain death from cancer, teenage Poppy accepts an invitation from a friend to become a vampire. (Rev: BL 8/96; VOYA 8/96)

2808 Springer, Nancy. *Sky Rider* (5–8). 1999, Avon paper $15.00 (0-380-97604-8). In this contemporary supernatural mystery, Dusty's beloved horse Tazz is cured by a visitor who turns out to be the angry ghost of a teenage boy recently killed on her father's property. (Rev: SLJ 8/99)

2809 Spruill, Steven. *Daughter of Darkness* (10–12). 1997, Doubleday $22.95 (0-385-48432-1). A haunting novel about hemophages, humans with a genetic defect that requires them to feed on human blood to survive. (Rev: BL 5/15/97; SLJ 12/97)

2810 Starkey, Dinah, ed. *Ghosts and Bogles* (5–10). Illus. 1987, David & Charles $17.95 (0-434-96440-9). A collection of 16 British ghost stories, each nicely presented with illustrations. (Rev: SLJ 9/87)

2811 Stearns, Michael, ed. *A Nightmare's Dozen: Stories from the Dark* (6–9). Illus. 1996, Harcourt $17.00 (0-15-201247-8). A collection of original, bizarre, nightmarish stories by such YA authors as Bruce Coville and Jane Yolen. (Rev: BL 1/1–15/97; SLJ 12/96)

2812 Strickland, Brad, and John Bellairs. *The Specter from the Magician's Museum* (5–8). 1998, Dial $15.99 (0-8037-2202-8). When Rose Rita accidentally cuts her finger on an enchanted scroll, she and friend Lewis begin a series of supernatural adventures. This is part of a series of supernatural adventures by John Bellairs that has been continued by Brad Strickland. (Rev: BR 5–6/99; SLJ 11/98; VOYA 6/99)

2813 Tolan, Stephanie S. *The Face in the Mirror* (6–9). 1998, Morrow $15.00 (0-688-15394-1). When Jared relocates to live with his father, a theater director, he isn't prepared for the malicious pranks of his stepbrother or the encounters with George Marsden, a sympathetic ghost. (Rev: BL 9/1/98; SLJ 11/98; VOYA 4/99)

2814 Tolan, Stephanie S. *Who's There?* (5–8). 1994, Morrow $15.00 (0-688-04611-8). Drew, 14, and her younger brother, who has been mute since their parents died, are living with their father's family and she becomes convinced their house is haunted. (Rev: BL 9/1/94; SLJ 10/94)

2815 Tunnell, Michael O. *School Spirits* (5–8). 1997, Holiday House LB $15.95 (0-8234-1310-1). Three students at creepy Craven Hill School, including the son of the new principal, discover a ghost and solve a decades-old murder mystery involving an 8-year-old boy. (Rev: BL 2/15/98; BR 11–12/98; SLJ 3/98; VOYA 8/98)

2816 Ury, Allen B. *Scary Stories for When You're Home Alone* (5–8). 1996, Lowell House paper $5.95 (1-56565-382-3). A collection of 10 truly scary stories that deal with paranormal and supernatural phenomena, including extraterrestrials, time warps, fetish dolls, and Ouija boards. (Rev: SLJ 7/96)

2817 Vande Velde, Vivian. *Companions of the Night* (7–10). 1995, Harcourt $17.00 (0-15-200221-9). A 16-year-old finds herself caught in a life-and-death chase after she helps an injured young man who may be a vampire. (Rev: BL 4/1/95; SLJ 5/95)

2818 Vande Velde, Vivian. *Never Trust a Dead Man* (7–12). 1999, Harcourt $17.00 (0-15-201899-9). A witch helps Selwyn escape the death penalty for a murder he didn't commit and, with the help of the ghost of the dead man, he solves the mystery. (Rev: BL 4/1/99; BR 9–10/99; SLJ 5/99; VOYA 8/99)

2819 Westall, Robert. *Ghost Abbey* (6–9). 1990, Scholastic paper $3.25 (0-590-41693-6). Maggi realizes that the abbey her father is restoring seems to have a life of its own. (Rev: SLJ 3/89; VOYA 6/89)

2820 Westall, Robert. *Shades of Darkness: More of the Ghostly Best Stories of Robert Westall* (7–12). 1994, Farrar $22.50 (0-374-36758-2). Eleven eerie tales, not the guts-and-gore variety of supernatural fiction but haunting and insightful stories. (Rev: BL 4/15/94; SLJ 5/94; VOYA 8/94)

2821 Westall, Robert. *The Stones of Muncaster Cathedral* (8–12). 1993, Farrar $11.00 (0-374-37263-2). Joe is repairing a cathedral tower, and when his partner and 2 boys die in mysterious falls, Joe, a police officer, and a chaplain uncover and destroy the evil that has possessed the tower for centuries. (Rev: BL 5/1/93; SLJ 6/93)

2822 Westwood, Chris. *Calling All Monsters* (7–12). 1993, HarperCollins LB $14.89 (0-06-022462-2). Joanne is a huge fan of a horror writer, so when she starts seeing nightmare creatures from his books, she recognizes them. (Rev: BL 6/1–15/93; SLJ 7/93; VOYA 12/93)

2823 Westwood, Chris. *He Came from the Shadows* (5–8). 1991, HarperCollins LB $14.89 (0-06-021659-X). In a cautionary tale about the dangers of wishing for too much, odd things start to happen after a stranger comes to town. (Rev: BL 4/1/91; SLJ 6/91)

2824 Windsor, Patricia. *The Blooding* (9–12). 1996, Scholastic $15.95 (0-590-43309-1). A horror story that involves a young American girl in England, the death of woman in whose house she is living, and the

menace of werewolves. (Rev: BR 1–2/97; SLJ 12/96; VOYA 4/97)

2825 Yashinsky, Dan, ed. *Ghostwise: A Book of Midnight Stories* (7–12). 1997, August House paper $11.95 (0-87483-499-6). A collection of 35 short but chilling stories of the supernatural and ghosts. (Rev: VOYA 2/98)

2826 Yolen, Jane. *Here There Be Ghosts* (6–9). Illus. 1998, Harcourt $19.00 (0-15-201566-3). A collection of not very scary stories about ghosts and their activities. (Rev: BL 11/1/98; SLJ 11/98; VOYA 12/98)

2827 Yolen, Jane, and Martin H. Greenberg, eds. *Werewolves: A Collection of Original Stories* (6–9). 1988, HarperCollins $13.95 (0-06-026798-4). Fifteen mostly scary stories about all kinds of werewolves. (Rev: BL 7/88; BR 1–2/88; SLJ 9/88; VOYA 8/88)

2828 Young, Richard, and Judy Dockery Young. *Ozark Ghost Stories* (6–12). 1995, August House paper $12.95 (0-87483-410-4). Spooky Ozark stories are the focus of this horror anthology, including old favorites and less well known jokes and tales. (Rev: BL 6/1–15/95)

2829 Young, Richard, and Judy Dockery Young. *The Scary Story Reader* (6–9). 1993, August House $19.00 (0-87483-271-3). Forty-one scary urban legends are presented, including traditional tales of horror as well as less well known stories from Alaska and Hawaii. (Rev: BL 11/15/93; SLJ 5/94)

2830 Zindel, Paul. *The Doom Stone* (6–10). 1995, HarperCollins LB $14.89 (0-06-024727-4). A slimy, truly evil creature stalks the moors and inhabits the mind of the protagonist's aunt. (Rev: BL 12/15/95; SLJ 12/95; VOYA 4/96)

2831 Zindel, Paul. *Loch* (7–10). 1994, HarperCollins LB $14.89 (0-06-024543-3). Lovable, though human-eating, creatures trapped in a Vermont lake become prey for a ruthless man. (Rev: BL 11/15/94; SLJ 1/95; VOYA 4/95)

Humor

2832 Alford, Jan. *I Can't Believe I Have to Do This* (5–8). 1997, Putnam $16.95 (0-399-23130-7). When Dean turns 12, his mother gives him a diary, and the entries he makes are funny, terse, and authentic. (Rev: BL 10/15/97; BR 1–2/98; SLJ 9/97)

2833 Avi. *Punch with Judy* (6–8). Illus. 1993, Bradbury LB $14.95 (0-02-707755-1). The orphan boy Punch encounters tragedy and comedy in his attempt to keep a medicine show alive with the help of the owner's daughter. (Rev: BL 3/15/93; SLJ 6/93; VOYA 8/93)

2834 Avi. *Romeo and Juliet: Together (and Alive) at Last!* (6–8). 1987, Watts LB $16.99 (0-531-08321-7); Avon paper $4.50 (0-380-70525-7). Ed Sitrow decides to help true love along by casting his friends as Romeo and Juliet in a school play. Sitrow is also the "genius" behind the soccer escapades in *S.O.R. Losers.* (Rev: BL 8/87; SLJ 10/87)

2835 Bawden, Nina. *Granny the Pag* (5–8). 1996, Clarion $15.00 (0-395-77604-X). Catriona, left by her parents with her grandmother and embarrassed by her grandmother's eccentric ways, such as riding a motorcycle and wearing a leather jacket, grows to love her and hires a lawyer when her parents want her back. (Rev: BR 11–12/96; SLJ 4/96; VOYA 6/96)

2836 Byars, Betsy. *Bingo Brown, Gypsy Lover* (6–8). 1990, Viking paper $12.95 (0-670-83322-3). In this installment of the Bingo Brown saga, our hero finds himself in love. (Rev: BL 5/1/90; SLJ 6/90)

2837 Byars, Betsy. *Bingo Brown's Guide to Romance* (5–8). 1992, Viking paper $14.00 (0-670-84491-8). Romance, confusion, and comedy occur when Bingo Brown meets his true love in the produce section of the grocery store. (Rev: BL 4/1/92; SLJ 4/92)

2838 Carkeet, David. *Quiver River* (7–10). 1991, HarperCollins LB $14.89 (0-06-022454-1). Two 16-year-old boys spending the summer working at a California campground find their relationship changing when one has his first sexual experience with a college girl. (Rev: BL 10/15/91)

2839 Clarke, J. *Al Capsella and the Watchdogs* (7–10). 1991, Holt $14.95 (0-8050-1598-1). Al Capsella, 15, and his Australian high school friends spend much of their time bemoaning the tactics their parents use to be involved in all phases of their lives. (Rev: BL 8/91; SLJ 8/91)

2840 Clarke, J. *The Heroic Life of Al Capsella* (7–10). 1990, Holt $14.95 (0-8050-1310-5). In this humorous Australian novel, all of young Al's attempts to find stature with his peers seem thwarted. (Rev: BL 3/15/90; SLJ 7/90)

2841 Conford, Ellen. *The Alfred G. Graebner Memorial High School Handbook of Rules and Regulations* (6–9). 1976, Little, Brown $14.95 (0-316-15293-5). The trials and tribulations of student life in a typical high school. (Rev: BL 7/88)

2842 Conford, Ellen. *Dear Lovey Hart: I Am Desperate* (6–9). 1975, Little, Brown $14.95 (0-316-15306-0). Carrie's power as a lonely hearts columnist on the school paper causes her unexpected problems. Followed by *We Interrupt This Semester for an Important Bulletin.* (Rev: BL 10/15/87)

2843 Conford, Ellen. *Seven Days to Be a Brand-New Me* (6–9). 1990, Scholastic paper $3.50 (0-590-43824-7). Maddy knows she will become a teenage vamp after following Dr. Dudley's program.

2844 Conford, Ellen. *Why Me?* (6–9). 1985, Little, Brown $14.95 (0-316-15326-5). G.G. Graffman has a crush on Hobie who only has eyes for Darlene who is ga-ga over Warren. (Rev: BL 10/15/85; BR 5–6/86; SLJ 11/85; VOYA 2/86)

2845 Creech, Sharon. *Absolutely Normal Chaos* (5–8). 1995, HarperCollins LB $14.89 (0-06-026992-8). Mary Lou, 13, keeps a journal during summer vacation, chronicling the roller-coaster process of adolescence—evolving friendships, her first kiss, and the gradual appreciation of people different from her. (Rev: BL 10/1/95; SLJ 11/95)

2846 Dahl, Roald. *The Umbrella Man & Other Stories* (8–12). 1998, Viking $16.99 (0-670-87854-5). A collection of 13 stories originally written for adults that display Dahl's wit and penchant for irony. (Rev: BL 5/15/98; BR 5–6/99; SLJ 8/98; VOYA 8/98)

2847 Danziger, Paula. *This Place Has No Atmosphere* (6–9). 1989, Bantam paper $3.99 (0-440-40205-0). In this humorous story set in 2057, Aurora and her family move to the moon. (Rev: BL 10/15/86; BR 3–4/87; SLJ 11/86; VOYA 2/87)

2848 Davis, Donald. *Barking at a Fox-Fur Coat* (9–12). 1991, August House $19.95 (0-87483-141-5); paper $12.95 (0-87483-140-7). Seventeen original tales based on the author's childhood and family experiences in rural North Carolina, each highlighting a set of human foibles and ending with an ironic twist. (Rev: BL 10/15/91; SLJ 4/92)

2849 Ferris, Jean. *Love Among the Walnuts* (7–10). 1998, Harcourt $16.00 (0-15-201590-6). A good-natured, hilarious spoof in which young Sandy and his rich family are forced to move to a loony bin to escape the schemes of relatives intent on stealing their money. (Rev: SLJ 8/98; VOYA 2/99)

2850 Fleischman, Paul. *A Fate Totally Worse Than Death* (7–12). Illus. 1995, Candlewick $15.99 (1-56402-627-2). An offbeat mix of horror story and satire about self-centered rich girls who want to teach a beautiful exchange student a lesson. (Rev: BL 10/15/95; SLJ 10/95; VOYA 4/96)

2851 Gleitzman, Morris. *Worry Warts* (6–8). 1993, Harcourt $12.95 (0-15-299666-4). In this sequel to *Misery Guts,* Keith tries—and fails—to save his parents' marriage by going off to Australian opal fields to make money. (Rev: BL 7/93; SLJ 5/93)

2852 Hardman, Ric L. *Sunshine Rider: The First Vegetarian Western* (9–12). 1998, Delacorte $15.95 (0-385-32543-6). This humorous adventure story about 17-year-old Wylie Jackson, who becomes a vegetarian after he is instructed to shoot a calf while on a cattle drive and then decides to become a doctor, is part western, part cookbook, and part picaresque novel. (Rev: BL 2/15/98; BR 9–10/98; SLJ 2/98; VOYA 4/98)

2853 Hayes, Daniel. *Eye of the Beholder* (5–8). 1992, Godine $14.95 (0-87923-881-X). Tyler and Lymie are in trouble again when they sculpt some rocks and throw them in the river to be found as "lost treasures" of a sculptor who once lived in the town. (Rev: BL 2/1/93; SLJ 12/92)

2854 Hayes, Daniel. *Flyers* (8–12). Illus. 1996, Simon & Schuster paper $16.00 (0-689-80372-9). A funny and clever novel that involves 15-year-old Gabe, the movie he and his friends are making, and a series of odd events that change their lives. (Rev: BL 9/15/96; SLJ 11/96; VOYA 2/97)

2855 Hite, Sid. *Those Darn Dithers* (5–8). 1996, Holt $15.95 (0-8050-3838-8). A humorous novel about the dithering Dithers with adventures involving Porcellina the dancing pig and an eccentric who drifts out to sea on a rubber raft. (Rev: BL 12/15/96; BR 9–10/97; SLJ 12/96; VOYA 10/97)

2856 Horvath, Polly. *When the Circus Came to Town* (5–8). 1996, Farrar $15.00 (0-374-38308-1). Ivy witnesses a division in town opinion when a circus troupe decides to relocate there. (Rev: BL 11/15/96; SLJ 12/96*)

2857 Howe, James. *The New Nick Kramer or My Life as a Baby-Sitter* (5–9). 1995, Hyperion LB $13.89 (0-7868-2053-5). Nick and rival Mitch make an unusual bet on who will win the affections of newcomer Jennifer. (Rev: SLJ 1/96)

2858 Kalman, Maira. *Max in Hollywood, Baby* (6–9). 1992, Viking paper $16.99 (0-670-84479-9). Max the dog has gone Hollywood; everybody's favorite poet pooch just couldn't resist the call of the Big Screen. The ongoing saga of Max the dog—in words, pictures, and typography. (Rev: BL 12/1/92*; SLJ 11/92)

2859 Kalman, Maira. *Swami on Rye: Max in India* (5–9). 1995, Viking $16.00 (0-670-85646-0). Max the dog is whisked away by a swami to India, where Kalman ridicules adult affectations and silliness in their search for meaning in life. (Rev: BL 10/15/95; SLJ 11/95)

2860 Kaufman, Bel. *Up the Down Staircase* (10–12). 1991, Demco $18.85 (0-606-12559-0). A humorous, often poignant story of a young schoolteacher in a New York high school.

2861 Keller, Beverly. *The Amazon Papers* (7–10). 1996, Harcourt $12.00 (0-15-201345-8); paper $5.00 (0-15-201346-6). Iris's life is transformed, not necessarily for the better, when she falls for a handsome, pizza-delivering, high school dropout named Foster

Prizer. (Rev: BL 1/1–15/97; BR 3–4/97; SLJ 10/96; VOYA 12/96)

2862 Kendall, Jane. *Miranda and the Movies* (6–9). Illus. 1989, Crown LB $14.99 (0-517-57357-1). Miranda and her world suddenly come alive when a movie company moves next door. (Rev: BL 10/1/89; BR 3–4/90; SLJ 10/89)

2863 Kiesel, Stanley. *The War between the Pitiful Teachers and the Splendid Kids* (7–9). 1980, Avon paper $3.50 (0-380-57802-6). A humorous fantasy about a group of schoolchildren who decide to wage war on their teachers.

2864 Klise, Kate. *Letters from Camp* (5–8). 1999, Avon paper $15.00 (0-380-97539-4). A humorous mystery about 3 sets of quarreling siblings who are sent to Camp Happy Harmony to learn to get along, told entirely through letters, memos, journal entries, telegrams, receipts, lists, and drawings. (Rev: BL 7/99; SLJ 6/99)

2865 Koertge, Ron. *Where the Kissing Never Stops* (10–12). 1993, Avon paper $3.99 (0-380-71796-4). A candid, sometimes bawdy story about a 17-year-old boy, his love life, and his mother who is a stripper. (Rev: BL 11/1/86; SLJ 12/86; VOYA 12/86)

2866 Korman, Gordon. *Don't Care High* (7–10). 1986, Scholastic paper $2.50 (0-590-40251-X). A new student in a high school where apathy is so rife it's nicknamed Don't Care High decides to infuse some school spirit into the student body. (Rev: BL 10/15/85)

2867 Lantz, Francess. *Stepsister from the Planet Weird* (5–8). 1997, Random LB $11.99 (0-679-97330-3); paper $3.99 (0-679-87330-9). Megan and her almost-stepsister Ariel, an alien from outer space, conspire to prevent Megan's mother and Ariel's alien father from marrying. (Rev: SLJ 2/98)

2868 Letts, Billie. *Where the Heart Is* (10–12). 1995, Warner $17.95 (0-446-51972-3). An unusual, humorous novel about a pregnant teenager who finds herself stranded outside a Wal-Mart in Sequoyah, Oklahoma, and is adopted and helped by an unlikely group of local inhabitants. (Rev: BL 9/1/95; SLJ 4/96)

2869 Littke, Lael. *Trish for President* (6–10). 1984, Harcourt $13.95 (0-15-290512-X). Trish's political campaign for junior class president turns out to be a model of inefficiency. (Rev: BL 1/1/85)

2870 Lowry, Lois. *Anastasia at This Address* (5–9). 1991, Houghton $15.00 (0-395-56263-5); 1992, Dell paper $4.50 (0-440-40652-8). This irrepressible heroine is in top form when she decides that she's ready for romance and answers a personal ad, with typically hilarious results. (Rev: BL 4/1/91; SLJ 8/91)

2871 Lowry, Lois. *The One Hundredth Thing about Caroline* (7–9). 1983, Houghton $16.00 (0-395-34829-3); Dell paper $4.50 (0-440-46625-3). Caroline thinks that her mother's new boyfriend looks and acts like a savage dinosaur. (Rev: BL 5/15/89)

2872 Lowry, Lois. *Your Move, J.P.!* (6–8). 1990, Houghton $15.00 (0-395-53639-1). J. P. Tate, a seventh-grader, is hopelessly in love with Angela. (Rev: BL 3/1/90; SLJ 5/90; VOYA 4/90)

2873 Lubar, David. *Hidden Talents* (6–9). 1999, Tor $16.95 (0-312-86646-1). This humorous novel involves Martin Anderson, who has been expelled from three schools, the Boy Scouts, and Little League, and the group of misfits he befriends at his new alternative school—all of whom possess psychic powers. (Rev: BL 9/15/99; VOYA 10/99)

2874 Lynch, Chris. *Political Timber* (7–10). 1996, HarperCollins LB $14.89 (0-06-027361-5). In this political satire, Mayor Foley, now in prison on several counts of racketeering, coaches his 18-year-old grandson to win the mayoralty election and become his successor. (Rev: BL 10/15/96; BR 3–4/97; SLJ 1/97; VOYA 2/97)

2875 Lynch, Chris. *Scratch and the Sniffs* (5–8). 1997, HarperCollins LB $13.89 (0-06-027416-6). The members of the He-Man Women Haters Club, under the leadership of wheelchair-bound Wolf, decide to form their own rock band. (Rev: BL 4/15/97; SLJ 8/97)

2876 McCauley, Stephen. *The Object of My Affection* (10–12). 1998, Pocket Books paper $6.99 (0-671-02066-8). In this sunny novel a gay teacher decides to help his roommate who is expecting a baby. (Rev: BL 3/1/87)

2877 McFann, Jane. *Deathtrap and Dinosaur* (7–12). 1989, Avon paper $2.75 (0-380-75624-2). An unlikely pair join forces to force the departure of a disliked history teacher. (Rev: SLJ 10/89; VOYA 10/89)

2878 Mackay, Claire, sel. *Laughs* (5–8). 1997, Tundra paper $6.95 (0-88776-393-6). An anthology of humorous stories (and some poems) by several well-known Canadian writers. (Rev: SLJ 9/97)

2879 McKay, Hilary. *The Exiles in Love* (5–8). Illus. 1998, Simon & Schuster paper $16.00 (0-689-81752-5). The 4 Conroy sisters of the "Exiles" books are growing up and falling in love, particularly with a charming French boy who takes them on a holiday in France. (Rev: BL 5/1/98; SLJ 5/98)

2880 McKean, Thomas. *My Evil Twin* (5–8). 1997, Avon paper $14.00 (0-380-97445-2). Because of duplicate records sent to his new school, Jellimiah is considered 2 people, and he goes along with this deception, becoming alternately sloppy, wise-cracking Jelly and courteous, reserved John. (Rev: BR 5–6/98; SLJ 2/98; VOYA 4/98)

2881 McManus, Patrick F. *Never Cry "Arp!" and Other Great Adventures* (6–9). 1996, Holt $16.95 (0-8050-4662-3). Based on fact, the 12 stories in this collection deal humorously with the problems of growing up in the mountains of Idaho. (Rev: BL 8/96; BR 11–12/96; SLJ 7/96)

2882 Manes, Stephen. *Comedy High* (7–10). 1992, Scholastic $13.95 (0-590-44436-0). A comic story of a new high school designed to graduate jocks, performers, gambling experts, and hotel workers. (Rev: BL 12/1/92; SLJ 11/92)

2883 Many, Paul. *These Are the Rules* (7–10). 1997, Walker $23.95 (0-8027-8619-7); Knopf paper $4.99 (0-679-88978-7). In this hilarious first-person narrative, Colm tries to figure out the rules of dating, driving, girls, and getting some direction in his life. (Rev: BL 5/1/97; SLJ 5/97)

2884 Merrill, Jean. *The Pushcart War* (6–12). Illus. 1987, Bantam paper $4.99 (0-440-47147-8). Mack's truck runs down Morris's pushcart and starts a war that is humorous and also reveals many human foibles. (Rev: BL 4/87)

2885 Mulford, Philippa Greene. *Making Room for Katherine* (5–9). 1994, Macmillan paper $14.95 (0-02-767652-8). A 16-year-old is recovering from her father's death when a 13-year-old cousin arrives from Paris to visit for the summer. (Rev: BL 4/15/94; SLJ 5/94; VOYA 8/94)

2886 Naylor, Phyllis Reynolds. *Alice in Lace* (6–8). 1996, Simon & Schuster $15.00 (0-689-80358-3). Alice, in her usual bumbling, endearing way, confronts society's greatest problems when her health class does a unit on "Critical Choices." (Rev: BL 3/1/96; BR 1–2/96; SLJ 4/96; VOYA 8/96)

2887 Naylor, Phyllis Reynolds. *Alice in Rapture, Sort Of* (6–8). 1989, Macmillan $16.00 (0-689-31466-3); Dell paper $3.99 (0-440-40462-2). Our young heroine, now in seventh grade, wonders how to behave with her boyfriend, Patrick, in this sequel to *The Agonies of Alice*. (Rev: BL 3/1/89; SLJ 4/89)

2888 Naylor, Phyllis Reynolds. *Alice on the Outside* (6–9). 1999, Simon & Schuster $15.00 (0-689-80359-1). In this eleventh book about Alice, our young heroine continues her adolescent exploration of the problems of growing up, particularly adjusting to the opposite sex. (Rev: BL 5/1/99; SLJ 7/99; VOYA 12/99)

2889 Naylor, Phyllis Reynolds. *All but Alice* (5–8). 1992, Atheneum $15.00 (0-689-31773-5). A nerd suddenly becomes popular in seventh grade, but she may have to risk her new status for a friendship. (Rev: BL 3/1/92; SLJ 5/92*)

2890 Naylor, Phyllis Reynolds. *Outrageously Alice* (6–8). 1997, Simon & Schuster $15.00 (0-689-80354-0); paper $3.99 (0-689-80596-9). Alice, now 13 and in the eighth grade, is confused about boys and how to act with them. (Rev: BL 5/15/97; BR 11–12/97; SLJ 6/97; VOYA 10/97)

2891 Naylor, Phyllis Reynolds. *Reluctantly Alice* (5–8). 1991, Atheneum $15.00 (0-689-31681-X). A klutzy seventh-grader copes with class bullies and her desire to mature. (Rev: BL 2/1/91; SLJ 3/91*)

2892 Nodelman, Perry. *Behaving Bradley* (8–10). 1998, Simon & Schuster $16.00 (0-689-81466-6). In this screwball comedy, junior Bradley Gold represents student interests when his high school prepares a code of conduct. (Rev: BL 6/1–15/98; SLJ 6/98; VOYA 8/98)

2893 Park, Barbara. *Buddies* (6–8). 1985, Avon paper $2.95 (0-380-69992-3). Dinah's dreams of being popular at camp are dashed in this humorous novel because she is forever being accompanied by Fern, the camp nerd. (Rev: BL 4/15/85)

2894 Paulsen, Gary. *Harris and Me: A Summer Remembered* (6–12). 1993, Harcourt $13.95 (0-15-292877-4). The 11-year-old narrator is dumped on his aunt and uncle's farm for the summer by his alcoholic parents, but through his exploits with his cousin Harris, it becomes his home. (Rev: BL 12/1/93*; SLJ 1/94; VOYA 2/94)

2895 Paulsen, Gary. *The Schernoff Discoveries* (4–8). 1997, Delacorte $15.95 (0-385-32194-5). A humorous novel about the misadventures of 2 friends, both self-confessed geeks. (Rev: BL 6/1–15/97; BR 9–10/97; SLJ 7/97; VOYA 10/97)

2896 Peck, Richard. *A Long Way from Chicago* (6–10). 1998, Dial $15.99 (0-8037-2290-7). Seven stories are included in this book, each representing a different summer from 1929 to 1935 that Joey spent visiting in Illinois with his lying, cheating, conniving, and thoroughly charming grandmother. (Rev: BL 9/1/98; SLJ 10/98; VOYA 12/98)

2897 Peck, Robert Newton. *Soup* (6–8). 1974, Knopf LB $15.99 (0-394-92700-1); Dell paper $4.50 (0-440-48186-4). The humorous story of the friendship between 2 boys growing up in a small town some years ago. The first of several engaging books about Soup and his friend. (Rev: BL 5/1/89)

2898 Pinkwater, Daniel M. *The Education of Robert Nifkin* (10–12). 1998, Farrar $16.00 (0-374-31969-3). In this humorous novel, a nerd growing up in 1950s Chicago becomes involved with some weird people and events. (Rev: BL 6/1–15/98; SLJ 7/98; VOYA 8/98)

2899 Pinkwater, Jill. *Buffalo Brenda* (7–9). 1992, Simon & Schuster paper $3.95 (0-689-71586-2). Brenda Tuna and her friend India Ink decide to rev-

olutionize their high school. (Rev: BL 7/89; BR 11–12/89; SLJ 12/89; VOYA 8/89)

2900 Ragz, M. M. *French Fries up Your Nose* (5–8). 1994, Pocket Books paper $2.99 (0-671-88410-7). When the class clown runs for student council president, he struggles to maintain his irresponsible image while developing serious, election-winning habits. (Rev: BL 3/15/94)

2901 Riggs, Bob. *My Best Defense* (6–10). 1996, Ward Hill paper $5.95 (1-886747-01-6). Sarcasm is the best defense of the narrator in this humorous story of a family and the unusual characters they attract. (Rev: SLJ 8/96; VOYA 10/96)

2902 Rodgers, Mary. *Freaky Friday* (6–9). 1972, HarperCollins LB $15.89 (0-06-025049-6); paper $4.95 (0-06-440046-8). Annabel switches with her mother for one hilarious day. Followed by: *A Billion for Boris* and *Summer Switch*. (Rev: BL 4/15/89)

2903 Ross, Leonard Q. *The Education of H*Y*M*A*N K*A*P*L*A*N* (9–12). 1968, Harcourt paper $9.00 (0-15-627811-1). A series of hilarious stories about an immigrant Jew and his battle with the English language at night school.

2904 Ryan, Mary C. *Who Says I Can't?* (7–10). 1988, Little, Brown $12.95 (0-316-76374-8). Tessa decides to get revenge on a boy who shows too much ardor in his romancing. (Rev: SLJ 11/88)

2905 Smith, Edwin R. *Blue Star Highway, Vol. 1: A Tale of Redemption from North Florida* (7–12). 1997, Mile Marker Twelve Publg. paper $9.95 (0-9659054-0-3). In this humorous novel, 14-year-old Marty Crane tells of the events in his life leading up to being sentenced to a detention home in 1962. (Rev: BL 2/15/99)

2906 Somtow, S. P. *The Vampire's Beautiful Daughter* (7–10). Illus. 1997, Simon & Schuster $17.00 (0-689-31968-1). Johnny meets Rebecca Teppish, a fascinating girl who is part vampire. (Rev: BL 9/1/97; SLJ 10/97)

2907 Soto, Gary. *Summer on Wheels* (5–8). 1995, Scholastic $13.95 (0-590-48365-X). In a sequel to *Crazy Weekend,* Hector and Mando take an 8-day bike ride from their East Los Angeles barrio to Santa Monica, moving from relative to relative. (Rev: BL 1/15/95; SLJ 4/95; VOYA 4/95)

2908 Spinelli, Jerry. *The Library Card* (4–8). 1997, Scholastic $15.95 (0-590-46731-X). Four humorous, poignant stories about how books changed the lives of several youngsters. (Rev: BL 2/1/97; BR 3–4/97; SLJ 3/97; VOYA 10/97)

2909 Strasser, Todd. *Girl Gives Birth to Own Prom Date* (7–10). 1996, Simon & Schuster paper $16.00 (0-689-80482-2). Telling their stories in alternating chapters, friends Nichole and Brad discuss the frantic high school social scene and the oncoming senior prom. (Rev: BL 10/1/96; SLJ 9/96; VOYA 4/97)

2910 Taha, Karen T. *Marshmallow Muscles, Banana Brainstorms* (6–8). 1988, Harcourt $13.95 (0-15-200525-0). A puny youngster tries a regime of body development through the help of his dream girl. (Rev: BL 1/1/89)

2911 Thomas, Rob. *Slave Day* (9–12). 1997, Simon & Schuster paper $16.00 (0-689-80206-4). A clever, funny school story for mature readers about African American students who object to a fund-raising event called Slave Day where student body leaders and several teachers allow themselves to be "slaves" for a good cause. (Rev: BR 3–4/98; SLJ 4/97*)

2912 Thompson, Julian. *Simon Pure* (10–12). 1987, Scholastic paper $3.50 (0-590-41823-8). Simon has some unusual but always hilarious adventures when he enters Riddle University. (Rev: BL 4/15/87; SLJ 3/87; VOYA 4/87)

2913 Townsend, Sue. *Adrian Mole: The Lost Years* (9–12). 1994, Soho Pr. $22.00 (1-56947-014-6). In this sequel to *The Secret Diary of Adrian Mole*, Adrian chronicles his struggle with the raging hormones of adolescence and his search for a suitable career. (Rev: BL 8/94; SLJ 1/95)

2914 Townsend, Sue. *The Secret Diary of Adrian Mole, Age Thirteen and Three Quarters* (9–12). 1984, Avon paper $4.99 (0-380-86876-8). The trials and tribulations of a young English boy as revealed through his hilarious diary entries. (Rev: BL 1/1–15/97)

2915 Trembath, Don. *A Fly Named Alfred* (7–10). 1997, Orca paper $6.95 (1-55143-083-5). In this sequel to *The Tuesday Cafe*, Harper Winslow gets into more trouble when he write an anonymous column in the school newspaper that enrages the school bully. (Rev: BL 8/97; SLJ 9/96)

2916 Voigt, Cynthia. *Bad, Badder, Baddest* (5–8). 1997, Scholastic $16.95 (0-590-60136-9). A hilarious mix of funny situations and outrageous dialogue is featured in this novel about 2 sixth-grade outsiders who deserve their reputation for being bad. (Rev: BL 11/1/97; SLJ 11/97)

2917 Welter, John. *I Want to Buy a Vowel: A Novel of Illegal Alienation* (10–12). 1996, Algonquin $29.95 (1-56512-118-X). A humorous novel about an illegal alien who speaks only lines from TV commercials, two young sisters, and the teenage son of the local preacher, and how their lives intersect in their small Texas town. (Rev: SLJ 5/97)

2918 Wersba, Barbara. *You'll Never Guess the End* (7–12). 1992, HarperCollins $14.00 (0-06-020448-6). A send-up of the New York City literary scene, rich dilettantes, and Scientology. (Rev: BL 11/15/92; SLJ 9/92)

2919 Weyn, Suzanne. *The Makeover Club* (7–9). 1986, Avon paper $2.50 (0-380-75007-4). Three girls decide they are going to be glamorous by forming the Makeover Club. (Rev: SLJ 1/87; VOYA 12/86)

2920 Wibberley, Leonard. *The Mouse That Roared* (7–12). 1992, Buccaneer LB $27.95 (0-89966-887-9). To get foreign aid the tiny Duchy of Grand Fenwick declares war on the United States.

2921 Winton, Tim. *Lockie Leonard, Scumbuster* (6–8). 1999, Simon & Schuster $16.00 (0-684-82247-2). A humorous Australian novel about the efforts of Lockie Leonard and his friend, Egg Eggleston, to clean up the waters of a polluted bay. (Rev: BL 6/1–15/99)

Mysteries, Thrillers, and Spy Stories

2922 Adamson, Lydia. *A Cat on Stage Left: An Alice Nestleton Mystery* (10–12). 1998, NAL $19.95 (0-525-94419-2). Told with humor and lots of dialogue, this mystery involves Alice, professional cat sitter and amateur sleuth, and the murder of Mary, one of Alice's wealthy clients. (Rev: SLJ 9/98)

2923 Aiken, Joan. *The Teeth of the Gale* (7–9). 1988, HarperCollins $14.95 (0-06-020044-8). Eighteen-year-old Felix tries to rescue 3 children who have been kidnapped. A sequel to *Go Saddle the Sea* and *Bridle the Wind*. (Rev: BL 9/15/88; BR 5–6/89; SLJ 11/88; VOYA 12/88)

2924 Albert, Susan Wittig. *Chile Death* (10–12). (China Bayles Mystery) 1998, Prime Crime $21.95 (0-425-16539-6). China Bayles and her fiancé, Mike, a disabled former police officer, investigate the mysterious sudden death of a judge at a chili cook-off and the mistreatment of several older residents at Mike's nursing home, and the two investigations become linked. (Rev: BL 10/15/98; SLJ 1/99)

2925 Alcock, Vivien. *The Mysterious Mr. Ross* (6–8). 1987, Delacorte $14.95 (0-385-29581-2). Felicity saves a man from drowning and finds herself in the middle of the mystery surrounding him. (Rev: BL 11/1/87; BR 11–12/87; SLJ 10/87; VOYA 12/87)

2926 Alcock, Vivien. *Stranger at the Window* (5–8). 1998, Houghton paper $16.00 (0-395-81661-0). After 11-year-old Lesley discovers that her neighbor's children are hiding an illegal immigrant child in the attic of their home in London, England, she eagerly enters the conspiracy. (Rev: BL 5/15/98; SLJ 6/98)

2927 Aubert, Rosemary. *Free Reign: A Suspense Novel* (10–12). 1997, Bridge Works Pub. $21.95 (1-

882593-18-9). A recluse rejoins society and experiences romance and extreme danger while investigating the meaning of a ringed hand placed in his garden. (Rev: BL 4/15/97; SLJ 10/97)

2928 Avi. *Wolf Rider: A Tale of Terror* (7–12). 1986, Macmillan paper $17.00 (0-02-707760-8). In this thrilling mystery, a 15-year-old boy tries to learn the identity of a telephone caller who claims he is a murderer. (Rev: BL 11/15/86; BR 5–6/87; SLJ 12/86)

2929 Babbitt, Natalie. *Goody Hall* (6–8). 1971, Sunburst paper $4.95 (0-374-42767-4). A student and his new tutor investigate the mysterious death of the boy's father.

2930 Barnard, Robert. *A Fatal Attachment* (9–12). 1992, Scribners $20.00 (0-684-19412-0). By taking control of her nephews' lives, Lydia alienated her sister and brother-in-law from their adolescent sons. Twenty years later, history seems to be repeating itself. (Rev: BL 8/92; SLJ 2/93)

2931 Barr, Nevada. *Blind Descent* (10–12). 1998, Putnam $22.95 (0-399-14371-8). Anna Pigeon investigates dirty dealings and the murder of a fellow park ranger in the depths of Lechugilla Cavern, forcing herself to overcome claustrophobia and near terror as she works her way through the total blackness underground. (Rev: BL 2/15/98; SLJ 7/98)

2932 Barr, Nevada. *Endangered Species* (10–12). 1997, Putnam $22.95 (0-399-14246-0). Park ranger Anna Pigeon investigates the wreckage of an airplane on Cumberland Island, Georgia, and suspects foul play. (Rev: BL 2/15/97; SLJ 11/97)

2933 Barron, Stephanie. *Jane & the Wandering Eye* (10–12). 1998, Bantam paper $5.99 (0-553-57817-0). Jane Austen turns sleuth when a theater manager is murdered in Bath and a portrait of an eye is found on the body. (Rev: SLJ 7/98)

2934 Baum, Thomas. *Out of Body* (10–12). 1997, St. Martin's $22.95 (0-312-15620-0). A gripping mystery story about a man accused of murder who finds that he can have out-of-body experiences and witness events in other locations. (Rev: BL 4/15/97; SLJ 10/97)

2935 Beaton, M. C. *Death of a Perfect Wife* (9–12). 1990, Ivy Books paper $4.99 (0-8041-0593-6). A delightful mystery about some unusual characters who get involved in a murder in a quiet Scottish village. (Rev: BL 11/15/89)

2936 Beaton, M. C. *Death of an Addict* (10–12). 1999, Mysterious $22.00 (0-89296-675-0). Set in the highlands of Scotland, Constable Hamish Macbeth goes undercover and solves the mysterious death of a young man, supposedly from a drug overdose, and uncovers a drug ring. (Rev: BL 4/15/99; SLJ 9/99)

2937 Beatty, Patricia. *The Coach That Never Came* (6–8). 1985, Morrow $14.00 (0-688-05477-3).

While doing research on Colorado history, Paul unravels the mystery of a missing stagecoach that contained payroll. (Rev: BL 12/15/85; SLJ 11/85)

2938 Beechey, Alan. *An Embarrassment of Corpses* (10–12). 1997, Thomas Dunne Books $22.95 (0-312-16936-1). A witty mystery set in London about serial murders investigated by a police detective and his nephew, a writer of children's books. (Rev: SLJ 5/98)

2939 Benjamin, Carol Lea. *The Dog Who Knew Too Much* (10–12). 1997, Walker $29.95 (0-8027-3312-3). With the help of her pit bull Dashiell, private investigator Rachel Alexander investigates the death of a young woman in Greenwich Village. (Rev: BL 9/1/97; VOYA 12/97)

2940 Benjamin, Carol Lea. *This Dog for Hire* (10–12). 1996, Walker $30.95 (0-8027-3292-5). Private investigator Rachel Alexander and her pit bull, Dashiell, are hired to track down a hit-and-run driver who killed a young New York artist. (Rev: SLJ 4/97; VOYA 2/97)

2941 Bennett, Jay. *Coverup* (8–10). 1992, Fawcett paper $4.50 (0-449-70409-2). Realizing his friend has killed a pedestrian on a deserted road after a party, Brad returns to the accident scene and meets a girl searching for her homeless father. (Rev: BL 11/1/91)

2942 Bennett, Jay. *The Dark Corridor* (7–12). 1990, Fawcett paper $4.50 (0-449-70337-1). Kerry believes that his girlfriend's death was not suicide but murder. (Rev: BR 3–4/89; SLJ 11/88; VOYA 2/89)

2943 Bennett, Jay. *The Haunted One* (7–12). 1987, Fawcett paper $3.99 (0-449-70314-2). Paul Barrett, an 18-year-old lifeguard, is haunted by the memory of the girl he loved, who drowned before his eyes. (Rev: BR 3–4/88; SLJ 11/87)

2944 Bennett, Jay. *Sing Me a Death Song* (7–12). 1991, Fawcett paper $4.50 (0-449-70369-X). Eighteen-year-old Jason wonders if his accused mother is really a murderer. (Rev: SLJ 4/90; VOYA 8/90)

2945 Bennett, Jay. *The Skeleton Man* (7–12). 1988, Fawcett paper $4.50 (0-449-70284-7). Ray receives money from his uncle just before his death—but the gambling syndicate claims it as theirs. (Rev: BL 11/1/86; BR 1–2/87; SLJ 10/86; VOYA 4/87)

2946 Benoit, Margaret. *Who Killed Olive Soufflé?* (7–10). (Crime Files) 1997, McGraw-Hill paper $5.95 (0-07-006275-7). Trapped in a country lodge by a snowstorm and surrounded by possible suspects, detective Angel Cardoni must find the murderer of the famous chef Olive Souffle. (Rev: SLJ 11/97)

2947 Berenson, Laurien. *Watchdog* (10–12). 1998, Kensington $20.00 (1-57566-350-3). Mel Travis puts her detective skills to work when her brother is wrongfully accused of murdering his financial backer. (Rev: BL 8/98; SLJ 3/99)

2948 Bernhardt, William. *Naked Justice* (10–12). 1997, Ballantine $22.00 (0-345-38685-X). The public believes that Tulsa's black mayor, Wallace Barrett, murdered his wife and daughters, but are they correct? (Rev: BL 1/1–15/97; SLJ 6/97)

2949 Black, Veronica. *A Vow of Adoration* (10–12). 1997, St. Martin's $20.95 (0-312-18205-8). An English adventure mystery involving Sister Joan, her convent, and a murder on the Cornish moors. (Rev: SLJ 6/98)

2950 Bowen, Rhys, and J. Bowen. *Evans Above* (10–12). 1997, St. Martin's $21.95 (0-312-16828-4). A well-crafted mystery about a young constable in a Welsh village who sets out to solve the mystery of the murders of 3 alpine hikers. (Rev: SLJ 5/98)

2951 Brandon, Jay. *Rules of Evidence* (9–12). 1992, Pocket Books paper $6.50 (0-671-79389-6). A loner cop accused of murder hires an African American lawyer to defend him. (Rev: BL 1/1/92*)

2952 Braun, Lilian Jackson. *The Cat Who Lived High* (9–12). 1991, Jove paper $6.99 (0-515-10566-X). Qwill and his famous Siamese cat Koko discover that the penthouse in which they are living was the scene of a murder-suicide. (Rev: BL 8/90)

2953 Braun, Lilian Jackson. *The Cat Who Sang for the Birds* (10–12). 1998, Putnam $22.95 (0-399-14333-5); Jove paper $6.99 (0-515-12463-X). in this part of a mystery series involving the sleuthing team of Jim Qwilleran and his cats, Koko the cat uses his talents to predict future events and helps Jim solve the mystery of the death of his elderly neighbor and the disappearance of a young artist. (Rev: BL 11/1/97; SLJ 8/98)

2954 Braun, Lilian Jackson. *The Cat Who Sniffed Glue* (10–12). 1989, Jove paper $6.99 (0-515-09954-6). The return of the 2 Siamese cats whose series of mysteries starring them includes *The Cat Who Knew Shakespeare* (1988). (Rev: BL 9/15/88)

2955 Braun, Lilian Jackson. *The Cat Who Talked to Ghosts* (10–12). 1990, Jove paper $6.99 (0-515-10265-2). The tenth mystery about the reluctant sleuth Jim "Qwill" Qwilleran and his Siamese cat, Koko. (Rev: BL 1/1/90)

2956 Brewer, James D. *No Escape* (9–12). 1998, Walker $32.95 (0-8027-3318-2). Luke Williamson, Masey Baldridge, and Salina Tyner of the Big River Detective Agency are hired by the mayor of Memphis, Tennessee, to investigate embezzlement and the murders of fever victims at the beginning of the 1873 Yellow Fever epidemic. (Rev: VOYA 10/98)

2957 Brewer, James D. *No Remorse: A Masey Baldridge/Luke Williamson Mystery* (10–12). 1997, Walker $32.95 (0-8027-3302-6). Set after the end of the Civil War, this novel features riverboat captain/detective Luke Williamson and detective agency partners Masey Baldridge and Salina Tyner, who take on a case in which the widow of Williamson's competitor engages him to clear her son of his father's murder. (Rev: BL 8/97; VOYA 4/98)

2958 Brown, Rita Mae, and Sneaky Pie Brown. *Murder on the Prowl* (10–12). Illus. 1998, Bantam $23.95 (0-553-09970-1). When obituaries begin appearing before the deaths have occurred, Harry Haristeen and her talking pets begin an investigation. (Rev: BL 2/1/98; SLJ 12/98)

2959 Bunting, Eve. *The Haunting of Safe Keep* (7–10). 1985, HarperCollins LB $12.89 (0-397-32113-9). In this romantic mystery, 2 college friends work out their family problems while investigating strange occurrences where they work. (Rev: BL 4/15/85; BR 11–12/85; SLJ 5/85; VOYA 8/85)

2960 Burke, Jan. *Hocus* (10–12). 1997, Simon & Schuster $22.00 (0-684-80344-5). When her police hero husband is kidnapped by a group out to avenge murders that occurred years ago, sleuth/reporter Irene Kelly must unravel the complicated, long-ago murder case and find the real killer in order to save him. (Rev: BL 5/1/97; SLJ 11/97)

2961 Busch, Frederick. *Girls* (10–12). 1997, Harmony $23.00 (0-517-70455-2). Jack, a disturbed Vietnam veteran who feels grief and guilt over the accidental death over his baby daughter, sets out to find the murderer of an adolescent girl who has been killed in a neighboring town in western New York state. (Rev: BL 1/1–15/97; SLJ 7/97)

2962 Cargill, Linda. *Pool Party* (7–10). 1996, Scholastic paper $3.99 (0-590-58111-2). Sharon's beach party at a resort with a reputation for being haunted ends in murder. (Rev: SLJ 1/97)

2963 Carlon, Patricia. *The Souvenir* (10–12). 1996, Soho Pr. $20.00 (1-56947-048-0). The story of 2 girls who are hitchhiking in Australia, a murder, and a conspiracy of lies. (Rev: BL 1/1–15/96; SLJ 4/96)

2964 Case, John. *The Genesis Code* (10–12). 1997, Fawcett $24.95 (0-449-91101-2). In this suspense novel that shifts from Italy to the United States, Joe Lassiter sets out to find the murderer of his sister and her son, and finds that the leads take him to a fertility clinic in Italy that has links to similar murders. (Rev: SLJ 10/97)

2965 Christie, Agatha. *Curtain* (9–12). 1975, Amereon $22.95 (0-88411-386-8). Hercule Poirot returns to the country manor of Styles, the site of his first case (The Mysterious Affair at Styles), to solve another murder. This is one of many suitable titles by Christie.

2966 Christie, Agatha. *Death on the Nile* (9–12). 1992, HarperCollins paper $5.99 (0-06-100369-7).

Everyone on board the steamer sailing along the Nile envies Linnet Doyle—until she is murdered. One of many recommended mysteries involving Hercule Poirot.

2967 Christie, Agatha. *Evil under the Sun* (9–12). 1991, Berkley paper $5.99 (0-425-12960-8). M. Poirot solves the mystery of the murder of beautiful Arlena Marshall. One of many suitable Poirot mysteries.

2968 Christie, Agatha. *The Harlequin Tea Set and Other Stories* (10–12). 1997, Putnam $21.95 (0-399-14287-8). A collection of 9 mystery stories never before published in the United States. (Rev: BL 3/15/97; SLJ 11/97)

2969 Christie, Agatha. *Miss Marple: The Complete Short Stories* (9–12). 1985, Berkley paper $12.95 (0-425-09486-3). Miss Marple, the sleuth of St. Mary Mead, shines in this collection of 20 stories. (Rev: BL 12/15/85)

2970 Christie, Agatha. *The Murder at the Vicarage* (9–12). 1984, Berkley paper $5.99 (0-425-09453-7). The first Miss Marple mystery by this prolific author, who has about 100 mysteries in print.

2971 Christie, Agatha. *The Murder of Roger Ackroyd* (9–12). 1985, Pocket Books paper $3.50 (0-671-49856-8). One of the earlier Hercule Poirot mysteries (first published in 1926), this one involves the murder of a retired businessman.

2972 Christie, Agatha. *Murder on the Orient Express* (9–12). 1991, HarperCollins paper $5.99 (0-06-100274-7). M. Poirot in one of his most famous cases, where each of the suspects appears to have a valid motive for murder.

2973 Christie, Agatha. *Sleeping Murder* (9–12). 1992, Demco $11.34 (0-606-12521-3); HarperCollins paper $5.99 (0-06-100380-8). Christie's famous female sleuth, Miss Marple, solves the mystery of a murder that occurred 18 years earlier. One of many recommended titles involving this unusual sleuth.

2974 Christie, Agatha. *Ten Little Indians* (9–12). 1984, Samuel French paper $5.50 (0-573-61639-6). One of the earliest (1939) and best of this prolific writer's mysteries.

2975 Christie, Agatha. *Witness for the Prosecution* (10–12). 1987, Berkley paper $5.99 (0-425-06809-9). One of the most famous mystery tales by this very popular writer.

2976 Ciencin, Scott. *Faceless* (6–10). (The Lurker Files) 1996, Random paper $6.99 (0-679-88235-9). An online/offline complicated thriller involving university students, a chat room, cyber-identities, and e-mail threats from "Dethboy" who claims to be responsible for the disappearance and possible death of one of the students. (Rev: SLJ 4/97)

2977 Ciencin, Scott. *Know Fear* (7–9). 1996, Random paper $6.99 (0-679-88236-7). This second book in the Lurker Files series is another horror/suspense novel set at Wintervale University. To understand the plot and characters access to a computer is necessary. (Rev: SLJ 5/97)

2978 Clancy, Tom. *Without Remorse* (10–12). 1993, Putnam $24.95 (0-399-13825-0). Vietnam vet John Kelly's revenge against the murderers of his 20-year-old girlfriend is an integral part of this complex thriller. (Rev: BL 6/1–15/93; SLJ 11/93)

2979 Clark, Carol Higgins. *Iced* (9–12). 1996, Warner paper $5.99 (0-446-60198-5). Los Angeles PI Regan Reilly, vacationing in Colorado, stumbles across a series of art thefts. (Rev: BL 5/15/95; SLJ 1/96)

2980 Clark, Mary Higgins. *All Around the Town* (9–12). 1993, Pocket Books paper $7.99 (0-671-79348-9). A traumatized college student is defended against murder charges by her level-headed attorney sister. (Rev: BL 4/15/92)

2981 Clark, Mary Higgins. *The Cradle Will Fall* (9–12). 1991, Pocket Books paper $7.99 (0-671-74119-5). A young lawyer uncovers a conspiracy at a local hospital in this thriller.

2982 Clark, Mary Higgins. *A Cry in the Night* (9–12). 1993, Pocket Books paper $7.99 (0-671-88666-5). Jenny finds that the home of her new husband contains a terrible secret.

2983 Clark, Mary Higgins. *I'll Be Seeing You* (9–12). 1994, Pocket Books paper $7.99 (0-671-88858-7). The puzzling death of the heroine's father, unethical procedures at a fertility clinic, dual identities, and hidden motives. (Rev: BL 4/15/93; SLJ 11/93)

2984 Clark, Mary Higgins, ed. *The International Association of Crime Writers Presents Bad Behavior* (8–12). 1995, Harcourt $20.00 (0-15-200179-4). Features many stories with young characters and less overt violence than adult fare. Includes works by Sara Paretsky, P. D. James, Lawrence Block, and Liza Cody. (Rev: BL 7/95)

2985 Clark, Mary Higgins. *Let Me Call You Sweetheart* (9–12). 1995, Simon & Schuster $7.50 (0-684-80396-8). Prosecutor Kerry McGrath scours the world of gem thieves, child stalkers, the Irish Mafia, and more to solve the murder of the beautiful Suzanne Reardon. (Rev: BL 4/1/95; SLJ 9/95)

2986 Clark, Mary Higgins. *Silent Night* (9–12). 1995, Simon & Schuster $16.00 (0-684-81545-1). Following a thief who has stolen his mother's wallet, 7-year-old Brian is kidnapped by an escaped convict who needs a hostage. (Rev: SLJ 2/96)

2987 Clark, Mary Higgins. *Stillwatch* (9–12). 1997, Pocket Books paper $7.99 (0-671-52820-3). A TV documentary producer finds mystery and danger when she begins investigating a vice presidential candidate in Washington.

2988 Clark, Mary Higgins. *A Stranger Is Watching* (9–12). 1991, Simon & Schuster $17.00 (0-671-74549-2); Pocket Books paper $7.99 (0-671-74120-9). Steve Peterson's son and girlfriend are kidnapped by a psychopath in this taut thriller.

2989 Clark, Mary Higgins. *Weep No More, My Lady* (9–12). 1993, Dell paper $6.99 (0-440-20098-9). At a fashionable California spa, Elizabeth encounters the man she thinks murdered her sister in this taut mystery. (Rev: BL 5/1/87)

2990 Clark, Mary Higgins. *Where Are the Children?* (9–12). 1992, Pocket Books paper $7.99 (0-671-74118-7). The son and daughter of Nancy Eldredge, a Cape Cod housewife, disappear and the police believe that she has murdered them.

2991 Clark, Mary Higgins. *While My Pretty One Sleeps* (9–12). 1990, Pocket Books paper $7.99 (0-671-67368-8). While investigating a murder, our heroine becomes convinced that someone has been hired to kill her. (Rev: BL 4/1/89; VOYA 4/89)

2992 Coel, Margaret. *The Story Teller* (10–12). 1998, Prime Crime $21.95 (0-425-16538-8). Native American lawyer Vicky Holden's quest for an historic Arapaho ledger book leads to a trail of murder and deception. (Rev: BL 9/15/98; SLJ 5/99)

2993 Conant, Susan. *Animal Appetite* (10–12). 1997, Doubleday $21.95 (0-385-47725-2). Holly Winter, a writer challenged to write about something other than her usual topic, dogs, researches a local 17th-century heroine who turned out to have been a murderer and ends up investigating a murder that took place 18 years earlier—which involved a dog. (Rev: SLJ 12/97)

2994 Cooper, Ilene. *I'll See You in My Dreams* (6–9). 1997, Viking $15.99 (0-670-86322-X). Karen, whose dreams foretell the future, dreams about a tragedy that involves a new boy in school and his young brother. (Rev: BL 6/1–15/97; BR 1–2/98; SLJ 8/97)

2995 Cormier, Robert. *In the Middle of the Night* (10–12). 1995, Delacorte $15.95 (0-385-32158-9). In this exploration of the dark underside of human emotions, a 16-year-old is drawn into a telephone game that drags him close to disaster. (Rev: BL 4/1/95; SLJ 5/95; VOYA 5/95)

2996 Cormier, Robert. *Tenderness* (10–12). 1997, Delacorte $16.95 (0-385-32286-0). For mature high school readers, this is a glimpse into the mind of a teenage serial killer who is about to be released from a detention center for murdering his mother and stepfather. (Rev: BL 2/1/97; BR 9–10/97; SLJ 3/97*; VOYA 4/97)

2997 Cornwell, Patricia. *All That Remains* (10–12). 1992, Scribners $20.00 (0-684-19395-7). A whodunit about the baffling serial murders of 5 college-age couples. (Rev: BL 6/1/92; SLJ 12/92)

2998 Cornwell, Patricia. *Cruel and Unusual* (10–12). 1993, Scribners $21.00 (0-684-19530-5). An edge-of-your-seat thriller with plenty of action, a gripping plot, and a mind-boggling climax. (Rev: BL 4/15/93; SLJ 11/93)

2999 Cornwell, Patricia. *From Potter's Field* (10–12). 1995, Scribners $23.50 (0-684-19598-4); 1996, Berkley paper $7.99 (0-425-15409-2). The Central Park (New York) murder of a young, homeless woman on Christmas sends medical examiner Scarpetta, her friend Captain Marino, and her niece on a chase that ends in the subway. (Rev: BL 5/1/95*)

3000 Cray, Jordan. *Dead Man's Hand* (5–9). (danger.com) 1998, Simon & Schuster paper $3.99 (0-689-82383-5). In this light read, Nick Annunciato and his stepsister, Annie Hanley, use their brains and a computer to solve a murder and escape a biological-weapons smuggling ring. Also use from the same series and author, *Shiver* (1998). (Rev: SLJ 2/99)

3001 Cresswell, Helen, ed. *Mystery Stories: An Intriguing Collection* (8–12). Illus. 1996, Kingfisher paper $10.95 (0-7534-5025-9). A collection of 19 mystery stories from such writers as Sir Arthur Conan Doyle, Agatha Christie, Ray Bradbury, and Emily Brontë. (Rev: SLJ 2/97)

3002 Crew, Gary. *Angel's Gate* (8–12). 1995, Simon & Schuster paper $16.00 (0-689-80166-1). A murder mystery/coming-of-age story about a dead man's children who have escaped to live in the wild and a 13-year-old girl who draws them back to civilization. (Rev: BL 10/1/95; SLJ 10/95; VOYA 4/96)

3003 Crew, Gary. *No Such Country* (6–9). 1994, Simon & Schuster paper $15.00 (0-671-79760-3). A mystery with elements of fantasy about an Australian fishing village with a secret. The text is strong on adolescent self-questioning and aboriginal history. (Rev: BL 5/1/94; SLJ 7/94)

3004 Crider, Bill. *Murder Takes a Break* (9–12). 1997, Walker $29.95 (0-8027-3308-5). Tru Smith, a detective who hates to leave his home and computer, investigates the disappearance of a college student. (Rev: BL 10/15/97; VOYA 12/97)

3005 Cross, Amanda. *The Collected Stories of Amanda Cross* (10–12). 1997, Ballantine $19.95 (0-345-40817-9). In this collection of mystery stories, the reader is invited to solve each case from a complete set of clues. (Rev: BL 12/15/96; SLJ 5/97)

3006 Cross, Gillian. *On the Edge* (6–9). 1985, Holiday House $15.95 (0-8234-0559-1). In rural England, Jinny discovers that a young kidnapping victim is being held in a nearby cottage. (Rev: BL 9/1/85; SLJ 8/85)

3007 Cullen, Robert. *Dispatch from a Cold Country* (10–12). 1996, Fawcett $21.00 (0-449-91258-2). Deputy foreign news editor Colin Burke takes a leave from his job and goes to Russia to investigate the brutal murder there of Jennifer Morelli, a young reporter, who had discovered important information for a news story but was killed before she could reveal it. (Rev: SLJ 3/97)

3008 Davidson, Nicole. *Dying to Dance* (8–12). 1996, Avon paper $3.99 (0-380-78152-2). Carrie, a competitor on the ballroom-dance circuit, is suspected of murdering her arch rival. (Rev: SLJ 7/96)

3009 Davis, Lindsey. *The Iron Hand of Mars* (10–12). 1993, Ballantine paper $5.99 (0-345-38024-X). Roman history and the detective story meet: Marcus Didius Falco, a private eye in 70 A.D., becomes involved with a rebel chief, a priestess, a legion, and a missing legate. (Rev: BL 9/15/93; SLJ 3/94)

3010 Dawson, Janet. *Nobody's Child* (10–12). 1995, Fawcett $21.00 (0-449-90976-X). In this baffling mystery, private investigator Jeri Howard is hired by a woman to find out if a recently discovered body is that of her missing teenage daughter. (Rev: BL 10/1/95; SLJ 4/96)

3011 Day, Dianne. *The Bohemian Murders: A Fremont Jones Mystery* (10–12). 1997, Doubleday $21.95 (0-385-47923-9). While working as a lighthouse keeper on the California coast in 1907, Fremont Jones discovers the body of a murdered woman and decides she must find the culprit. (Rev: BL 7/97; SLJ 12/97)

3012 Day, Marele. *The Disappearances of Madalena Grimaldi* (10–12). 1996, Walker $29.95 (0-8027-3277-1). Claudia, a 30+ Australian detective, is hired to find a missing teenage girl, while at the same time trying to solve the 30-year-old mystery of her own missing father. (Rev: SLJ 11/96)

3013 DeFelice, Cynthia. *The Light on Hogback Hill* (5–8). 1993, Macmillan paper $15.00 (0-02-726453-X). When 11-year-olds Hadley and Josh discover that the Witch Woman of Hogback Hill is really a shy, deformed woman, they help her find the courage to return to town. (Rev: BL 11/1/93; SLJ 11/93)

3014 Delaney, Mark. *Of Heroes and Villains* (7–10). 1999, Peachtree paper $5.95 (1-56145-178-9). Using the world of comic books as a backdrop, this mystery features 4 teen sleuths known as the Misfits and the puzzle of a stolen motion picture film starring comic book hero Hyperman. (Rev: BL 7/99)

3015 Dexter, Catherine. *I Dream of Murder* (6–9). 1997, Morrow $15.00 (0-688-13182-4). Jere encounters the man he saw commit a murder when Jere was only 4 years old. (Rev: BL 6/1–15/97; BR 5–6/97; SLJ 5/97)

3016 Draanen, Wendelin Van. *Sammy Keyes & the Skeleton Man* (5–8). 1998, Random LB $16.99 (0-679-98850-5); Knopf paper $4.99 (0-375-80054-9). Sammy, a youthful sleuth, is challenged when she tries to solve the mystery of a man dressed in a skeleton costume who has set fire to the murky Bush House. (Rev: BL 9/1/98; BR 11–12/98; SLJ 9/98)

3017 Du Maurier, Daphne. *Rebecca* (9–12). 1938, Doubleday $20.00 (0-385-04380-5); Avon paper $5.99 (0-380-00917-X). In this gothic romance, a timid girl marries a wealthy widower whose wife died mysteriously. Two other exciting novels by Du Maurier are *Hungry Hill* and *The Scapegoat*. (Rev: BL 6/1/88)

3018 Dunant, Sarah. *Fatlands* (9–12). 1994, Penzler Books paper $21.00 (1-883402-82-4). Investigator Hannah Wolfe baby-sits for a famous scientist's daughter. When a bomb kills the child, Hannah believes it was meant for the scientist so she hunts for the killers. (Rev: BL 11/1/94*)

3019 Duncan, Lois. *Daughters of Eve* (7–10). 1979, Dell paper $4.99 (0-440-91864-2). A group of girls come under the evil influence of the faculty sponsor of their club.

3020 Duncan, Lois. *Don't Look Behind You* (7–12). 1990, Bantam paper $4.99 (0-440-20729-0). April and her family are on the run trying to escape from a hired hit man. (Rev: BL 5/15/89; SLJ 7/89; VOYA 8/89)

3021 Duncan, Lois. *Down a Dark Hall* (7–10). 1974, Little, Brown paper $4.99 (0-440-91805-7). From the moment of arrival, Kit feels uneasy at her new boarding school.

3022 Duncan, Lois. *A Gift of Magic* (6–9). Illus. 1990, Pocket Books paper $3.99 (0-671-72649-8). Twelve-year-old Kirby comes to terms with her gift of ESP.

3023 Duncan, Lois. *I Know What You Did Last Summer* (7–10). 1990, Pocket Books paper $3.99 (0-671-73589-6). Four teenagers try to hide a hit-and-run accident in which they were involved.

3024 Duncan, Lois. *Killing Mr. Griffin* (7–10). 1978, Dell paper $4.99 (0-440-94515-1). A kidnapping plot involving a disliked English teacher leads to murder. (Rev: BL 10/15/88)

3025 Duncan, Lois. *The Third Eye* (7–10). 1984, Little, Brown $15.95 (0-316-19553-7); Dell paper $4.99 (0-440-98720-2). Karen learns that she has mental powers that enable her to locate missing children. (Rev: BL 7/87)

3026 Duncan, Lois. *The Twisted Window* (7–10). 1987, Dell paper $4.99 (0-440-20184-5). Tracy

160

grows to regret the fact that she has helped a young man kidnap his 2-year-old half-sister. (Rev: BL 9/1/87; BR 1–2/88; SLJ 9/87; VOYA 11/87)

3027 Dunlop, Eileen. *Green Willow* (6–8). 1993, Holiday House $14.95 (0-8234-1021-8). When her sister dies, Kit Crawford and her mother move to an apartment, where Kit discovers an old Japanese man, a ghost, and a new friend. (Rev: BL 12/1/93; SLJ 1/94; VOYA 4/94)

3028 Dunning, John. *The Bookman's Wake* (9–12). 1995, Scribners $21.00 (0-684-80003-9). Ex-cop-turned-book dealer Cliff Janeway tracks down a priceless edition of a book and encounters intrigue and murder. (Rev: BL 4/1/95*)

3029 Edwards, Grace F. *A Toast Before Dying* (9–12). 1998, Doubleday $21.95 (0-385-48524-7). During a sizzling hot summer in Harlem, former cop Mali Anderson has to keep her wits about her in life-compromising situations as she races to clear the name of a murder suspect. (Rev: VOYA 12/98)

3030 Epstein, Carole. *Perilous Relations: A Barbara Simons Mystery* (9–12). 1997, Walker $29.95 (0-8027-3309-3). Barbara Simmons, who loves poking her nose into other people's business, has her hands full when she tries to solve the mystery surrounding the death of her former boss. (Rev: VOYA 4/98)

3031 Evanovich, Janet. *One for the Money* (9–12). 1994, Scribners $20.00 (0-684-19639-5). An out-of-work discount-lingerie buyer becomes a bounty hunter to earn money and is hired to find a wanted cop from her past. (Rev: BL 9/1/94*)

3032 Evarts, Hal G. *Jay-Jay and the Peking Monster* (7–9). 1984, Peter Smith $15.75 (0-8446-6166-X). Two teenagers discover the bones of a prehistoric man and then the criminals move in.

3033 Feder, Harriet K. *Mystery of the Kaifeng Scroll* (6–9). 1995, Lerner LB $13.13 (0-8225-0739-0). In this sequel to *Mystery in Miami Beach*, Vivi Hartman, 15, must use her wits and knowledge of the Torah to save her mother from Palestinian terrorists. (Rev: BL 6/1–15/95)

3034 Ferguson, Alane. *Overkill* (7–10). 1992, Bradbury LB $14.95 (0-02-734523-8); 1994, Avon paper $3.99 (0-380-72167-8). Lacey is seeing a therapist about nightmares in which she stabs her friend Celeste; when Celeste is found dead, Lacey is falsely arrested for the crime. (Rev: BL 1/1/93; SLJ 1/93)

3035 Ferguson, Alane. *Show Me the Evidence* (7–12). 1989, Avon paper $3.99 (0-380-70962-7). In this mystery story, a 17-year-old girl is fearful that her best friend might be involved in the mysterious deaths of several children. (Rev: BL 4/1/89; BR 1–2/90; SLJ 3/89; VOYA 6/89)

3036 Ford, G. M. *Cast in Stone* (10–12). 1996, Walker $32.95 (0-8027-3267-4). Marge contacts hard-boiled Leo Waterman, a former flame and now a private investigator, to examine the mysterious circumstances surrounding the death of her son and his fiancée. (Rev: BL 4/1/96; SLJ 1/97)

3037 Francis, Dick. *Bolt* (10–12). 1988, Fawcett paper $5.95 (0-449-21239-4). Steeplechase jockey Kit Fielding becomes involved in a plot to sell guns to terrorists. (Rev: BL 12/1/86)

3038 Francis, Dick. *Break In* (10–12). 1987, Fawcett paper $5.99 (0-449-20755-2). A jockey and family are the targets of some unfounded slurs in a gossip column in this mystery. Also use *Enquiry*. (Rev: BL 1/15/86; VOYA 6/86)

3039 Francis, Dick. *Come to Grief* (9–12). 1999, Pocket Books paper $9.98 (0-671-04422-2). Ex-jockey-turned-sleuth Sid Halley searches for the culprit who has committed senseless acts of mutilation on prized race horses and discovers it is his old pal and rival. (Rev: BL 8/95*)

3040 Francis, Dick. *The Edge* (10–12). 1990, Fawcett paper $6.99 (0-449-21719-1). In a mixture of horse racing and railroads, this murder mystery takes place on a transcontinental train in Canada. (Rev: BL 11/15/88)

3041 Francis, Dick. *To the Hilt* (10–12). 1996, Putnam $24.95 (0-399-14185-5). A young painter living in Scotland returns to London and investigates the disappearance of his stepfather's financial advisor and a considerable amount of cash. (Rev: SLJ 1/97)

3042 Francis, Dick. *Whip Hand* (10–12). 1999, Penguin paper $6.99 (0-515-12504-0). An ex-jockey turned private investigator is hired to probe into the causes of several mysterious events at a racetrack. Also use: *Proof* and *Risk*.

3043 Francis, Dick. *Wild Horses* (9–12). 1995, Jove paper $5.99 (0-515-11789-7). A filmmaker's latest movie is based upon a real-life horse-racing tragedy involving a hanging death ruled a suicide. As the film producer uncovers new secrets, he suspects murder. (Rev: BL 8/94; SLJ 1/95)

3044 Friedman, Kinky. *God Bless John Wayne* (10–12). 1995, Simon & Schuster $22.00 (0-684-81051-4). A fast-paced mystery about detective Kinky Friedman, who is hired to find the birth mother of his friend Ratso (a.k.a. Larry Sloman) and confronts a number of obstacles in solving the case, among them Ratso's failure to fill him in on everything (including the death of a previous investigator). (Rev: BL 9/1/95; SLJ 4/96)

3045 Gaines, Ernest J. *A Lesson Before Dying* (9–12). (Borzoi Reader) 1993, Knopf $25.00 (0-679-41477-0); Random paper $12.00 (0-679-74166-6). In the 1940s in rural Louisiana, an uneducated African American man is sentenced to die for a crime he was incapable of committing. (Rev: SLJ 7/93*; VOYA 10/93)

3046 Gardner, John. *Maestro* (9–12). 1993, Penzler Books $23.00 (1-883402-24-7). A multigenerational epic spanning 10 decades that focuses on a world-famous orchestra conductor who becomes a spy. (Rev: BL 9/1/93*)

3047 Gavin, Thomas. *Breathing Water* (9–12). 1994, Arcade $21.95 (1-55970-232-X). The mystery of a young boy's identity confuses the citizens of Rising Sun and causes tragedy to the boy. (Rev: SLJ 7/94)

3048 Gee, Maurice. *The Fat Man* (8–10). 1997, Simon & Schuster $16.00 (0-689-81182-9). At first, this small New Zealand town welcomes back Herbert, a mysterious fat man who supposedly made good in America, but soon everyone becomes suspicious of his motives. (Rev: BL 12/15/97; BR 5–6/98; SLJ 11/97*; VOYA 12/97)

3049 Gee, Maurice. *The Fire-Raiser* (6–12). 1992, Houghton $14.95 (0-395-62428-2). A thriller set in New Zealand during World War I dramatizes the secret fury of a pyromaniac and relates it to the mob violence let loose in the community by jingoism and war. (Rev: BL 10/15/92*; SLJ 9/92)

3050 Gibbs, Tony. *Shadow Queen* (9–12). 1992, Mysterious paper $4.99 (0-446-40108-0). The security of the House of Windsor is threatened by a girl possessed by the spirit of her ancestor, Mary, Queen of Scots, and her possession of letters supposedly written by her. (Rev: BL 12/15/91*)

3051 Giberga, Jane Sughure. *Friends to Die For* (9–12). 1997, Dial $15.99 (0-8037-2094-7). In the world of wealthy New York teens, Crissy does not realize that she has invited a murderer to her party. (Rev: BR 1–2/98; VOYA 12/97)

3052 Giff, Patricia Reilly. *Have You Seen Hyacinth Macaw?* (6–9). 1982, Dell paper $4.50 (0-440-43450-5). Two junior detectives sort out some confusing clues in their search for Hyacinth Macaw.

3053 Goldberg, Leonard S. *Deadly Exposure* (10–12). 1998, NAL $23.95 (0-525-94427-3). Forensic pathologist Joanna Blalock joins a scientific expedition off the coast of Alaska and encounters murder, a deadly bacterium, a pending epidemic, an earthquake, a shipwreck, and icebergs. (Rev: BL 9/15/98; SLJ 4/99)

3054 Goulart, Ron. *Groucho Marx: Master Detective* (10–12). 1998, Thomas Dunne Books $22.95 (0-312-18106-X). Set in Hollywood during 1937, this murder mystery involving the death of a starlet features Groucho Marx and detective Frank Denby, who is hired by the comedian to solve the crime. (Rev: SLJ 7/98)

3055 Grace, C. L. *The Merchant of Death* (9–12). 1995, St. Martin's $19.95 (0-312-13124-0). In this mystery set in medieval Britain, healer Kathryn Swinbrooke and soldier Colum Murtagh must find a tax collector's murderer to recover the royal taxes stolen from him. (Rev: BL 6/1–15/95; SLJ 11/95)

3056 Grafton, Sue. *"G" Is for Gumshoe* (10–12). 1990, Holt $25.00 (0-8050-0461-0). In this installment of the alphabet murders, Kinsey Millhone is involved in a missing persons case and a hired killer is out to get her. (Rev: BL 3/15/90; SLJ 9/90)

3057 Grafton, Sue. *"M" Is for Malice* (10–12). 1996, Holt $25.00 (0-8050-3637-7). After detective Kinsey finds Guy Malek, missing heir to a huge fortune, the man is murdered in this part of Grafton's alphabet mystery series. (Rev: BL 9/15/96; SLJ 3/97)

3058 Green, Timothy. *Twilight Boy* (7–10). 1998, Northland LB $12.95 (0-87358-670-0); paper $6.95 (0-87358-640-9). Navajo folkways form the background of this gripping mystery about a boy who is haunted by the memory of his dead brother and an evil that is preying on his Navajo community. (Rev: BL 4/15/98; VOYA 8/98)

3059 Grisham, John. *The Client* (9–12). 1993, Doubleday $23.50 (0-385-42471-X). Mark Sway, 11, witnesses a Mafia lawyer's suicide, which puts him in danger from Barry the Blade and a politically ambitious U.S. attorney. (Rev: BL 2/1/93*; SLJ 7/93; VOYA 8/93)

3060 Grisham, John. *The Pelican Brief* (9–12). 1992, Doubleday $24.95 (0-385-42198-2). A law student runs for her life after discovering who murdered 2 supreme court justices. (Rev: BL 1/15/92)

3061 Guy, Rosa. *The Disappearance* (7–10). 1979, Delacorte paper $3.99 (0-440-92064-7). A 16-year-old black boy is accused of a kidnapping. Follow by *New Guys Around the Block* and *And I Heard a Bird Sing*.

3062 Hahn, Mary D. *The Dead Man in Indian Creek* (6–8). 1990, Clarion $15.00 (0-395-52397-4). On a harmless camping trip, Matt and friend Parker find a body floating in Indian Creek. (Rev: BL 2/15/90; SLJ 4/90)

3063 Hall, Lynn. *A Killing Freeze* (6–10). 1990, Avon paper $2.95 (0-380-75491-6). A loner endangers her own life to find a murderer. (Rev: BL 8/88; BR 1–2/89; SLJ 9/88; VOYA 12/88)

3064 Hall, Lynn. *Ride a Dark Horse* (7–10). 1987, Avon paper $2.95 (0-380-75370-7). A teenage girl is fired from her job on a horse-breeding farm because she is getting too close to solving a mystery. (Rev: BL 9/15/87; BR 11–12/87; SLJ 12/87; VOYA 10/87)

3065 Hamilton, Virginia. *The House of Dies Drear* (6–9). Illus. 1968, Macmillan $17.00 (0-02-742500-2); paper $4.50 (0-02-043520-7). The Smalls move to a new house that was formerly the home of a murdered abolitionist. A sequel is *The Mystery of Drear House* (1987). (Rev: BL 10/15/87)

3066 Hardwick, Michael. *The Revenge of the Hound: The New Sherlock Holmes Novel* (9–12). Illus. 1987, Windsor paper $3.95 (1-55817-166-5). A collection of short stories that faithfully re-create the characters and the suspense of the original Sherlock Holmes stories. (Rev: BR 5–6/88; SLJ 4/88; VOYA 6/88)

3067 Harris, Lee. *The Labor Day Murder* (9–12). 1998, Fawcett paper $5.99 (0-449-15017-8). A murder is committed on Fire Island over Labor Day, and vacationers Christine Bennett and husband Jack begin an investigation. (Rev: SLJ 12/98)

3068 Hastings, Beverly. *Watcher in the Dark* (7–10). 1986, Berkley paper $3.99 (0-425-10131-2). Erin does not count on kidnapping attempts when she babysits 4-year-old Abby. (Rev: BL 6/15/86; SLJ 10/86)

3069 Hathaway, Robin. *The Doctor Digs a Grave* (10–12). 1998, St. Martin's $22.95 (0-312-18568-5). This mystery involves a sleuth cardiologist, Dr. Andrew Fenimore, the forgotten customs of the Lenape Indians, and the death of a young girl, whose body is found buried in an upright position facing east. (Rev: SLJ 10/98)

3070 Hayes, Daniel. *The Trouble with Lemons* (5–8). 1991, Godine $16.95 (0-87923-825-9). Tyler, 14, has all kinds of problems—allergies, asthma, and nightmares—and then he finds a dead body. (Rev: BL 5/1/91; SLJ 6/91)

3071 Haynes, Betsy. *Deadly Deception* (7–10). 1994, 1995, Dell paper $3.99 (0-440-21947-7). A 17-year-old gets involved in the murder of a favorite school counselor. (Rev: BL 5/15/94; SLJ 6/94)

3072 Henry, Sue. *Death Takes Passage* (10–12). 1997, Avon paper $22.00 (0-380-97469-X). An Alaska state trooper and his girlfriend investigate a series of severe crimes including murder aboard a ship during a reenactment of a historic moment from the Klondike Gold Rush. (Rev: BL 7/97; SLJ 12/97)

3073 Hess, Joan. *The Maggody Militia* (10–12). 1997, Dutton paper $21.95 (0-525-94236-X). This humorous mystery set in a small Arkansas town involves the murder of a visiting survivalist. (Rev: BL 2/15/97; SLJ 9/97)

3074 Higgins, Jack. *The Eagle Has Flown* (9–12). 1990, Pocket Books paper $6.99 (0-671-72737-7). The sequel to *The Eagle Has Landed,* in which Devlin is asked by the Germans to parachute into England to free the formerly believed-dead Steiner. (Rev: BL 3/1/91)

3075 Higgins, Jack. *The President's Daughter* (10–12). 1997, Putnam $23.95 (0-399-14239-8). Three dedicated sleuths try to locate a daughter the president had while he was stationed in Vietnam and who now has been kidnapped by a group of villains. (Rev: BL 3/15/97; SLJ 11/97)

3076 Hill, Reginald. *Killing the Lawyers* (10–12). 1997, St. Martin's $23.95 (0-312-16877-2). Joe Sixsmith, a black English private investigator, tries to clear his own name as a murder suspect while solving the mystery of threats to the life of a popular young athlete. (Rev: SLJ 3/98)

3077 Hill, William. *The Vampire Hunters* (7–12). 1998, Otter Creek $19.95 (1-890611-05-0); paper $12.95 (1-890611-02-6). A gang called the Graveyard Armadillos are convinced that Marcus Chandler is a vampire, and 15-year-old Scooter Keyshaw is determined to find the truth. (Rev: BL 10/15/98; SLJ 2/99)

3078 Hillerman, Tony. *The First Eagle* (10–12). 1998, HarperCollins $25.00 (0-06-017581-8). Jim Chee of the Navajo Tribal Police and Joe Leaphorn, now a private detective, join forces once again to investigate a murder and the disappearance of a noted biologist. (Rev: BL 7/97; SLJ 1/99)

3079 Hillerman, Tony. *The Joe Leaphorn Mysteries: Dance Hall of the Dead, Listening Woman* (9–12). 1994, Random $9.99 (0-517-12584-6). Three novels all featuring the Navaho police lieutenant Joe Leaphorn in western settings. (Rev: BL 10/15/89)

3080 Hillerman, Tony, ed. *The Mysterious West* (9–12). 1995, HarperCollins paper $6.50 (0-06-109262-2). This is a collection of 20 mystery and suspense stories with Western themes that feature humor, action, and murder. (Rev: BL 10/1/94; SLJ 3/95)

3081 Hillerman, Tony. *People of Darkness* (10–12). 1991, HarperCollins paper $6.50 (0-06-109915-5). Set in the Southwest, this mystery features Navajo police detective Jim Chee and gives rich background information about the culture of these Native Americans. Others in this series are *Listening Woman, The Blessing Way, Dance Hall of the Dead*, and *The Fly on the Wall*.

3082 Hillerman, Tony. *Talking God* (10–12). 1991, HarperCollins paper $6.99 (0-06-109918-X). The 2 Navaho police officers, Jim Chee and Joe Leaphorn, featured together in the author's earlier *A Thief of Time* and *Skinwalkers*, once more solve a puzzling, complex murder mystery set in New Mexico. (Rev: BL 5/1/89; SLJ 11/89; VOYA 10/89)

3083 Hoff, B. J. *Winds of Graystone Manor* (9–12). 1995, Bethany House paper $9.99 (1-55661-435-7). In this gothic novel set in Staten Island after the Civil War, the first in a trilogy, Roman St. Clare, exhausted by his search for the murderer of his pregnant wife, is drawn unwillingly into involvement with murder, kidnapping, grave robberies, and mutilations by the guests and employees at Graystone Manor, the rooming house in which he is staying. (Rev: BL 9/1/95; VOYA 4/96)

3084 Hoffman, William. *Tidewater Blood* (10–12). 1998, Algonquin $31.95 (1-56512-187-2). Charley LeBlanc, the black sheep of a wealthy plantation family in Virginia, is wrongfully accused of killing his mother and father and sets out to find the real murderer. (Rev: BL 2/1/98; SLJ 10/98)

3085 Holt, Victoria. *The Captive* (9–12). 1990, Fawcett paper $3.50 (0-449-21817-1). A romantic mystery involving a young heroine trapped on a desert island with a murderer. (Rev: BL 8/89; VOYA 2/90)

3086 Howe, James. *Dew Drop Dead* (6–8). 1990, Macmillan $16.00 (0-689-31425-6). A group of boys discover a corpse, but by the time the police arrive it has disappeared. (Rev: BL 3/1/90; SLJ 4/90)

3087 Howe, James. *Stage Fright* (6–8). 1991, Avon paper $3.99 (0-380-71331-4). Thirteen-year-old Sebastian Barth, the detective of *What Eric Knew*, tackles the problem of who is trying to kill a famous movie actress. (Rev: BL 5/1/86; VOYA 2/87)

3088 Jackson, Shirley. *We Have Always Lived in the Castle* (9–12). 1962, Amereon LB $22.95 (0-89190-623-1); Penguin paper $9.95 (0-14-007107-5). Two sisters have become recluses after the arsenic poisoning of 4 members of their family.

3089 James, Bill. *Take* (9–12). 1994, Countryman $20.00 (0-88150-294-4). A small-time crook gets involved in a plan to steal a payroll, but the caper turns out to be much more than expected. (Rev: BL 5/15/94*)

3090 James, P. D. *A Certain Justice* (10–12). 1997, Knopf $25.00 (0-375-40109-1). A challenging adult English mystery concerning detective Adam Dalgleish and his investigation of the murder of a brilliant barrister. (Rev: BL 10/15/97; SLJ 4/98)

3091 James, P. D. *Original Sin* (9–12). 1995, Knopf $24.00 (0-679-43889-0). Set in the modern publishing world, where traditions may crumble but such timeless emotions as grief, rage, love—and murder—prevail. (Rev: BL 1/1/95*)

3092 Johnston, Norma. *The Dragon's Eye* (7–10). 1990, Four Winds LB $14.95 (0-02-747701-0). The life of high school junior Jenny begins to unravel when nasty, cryptic messages start appearing at school. (Rev: BL 1/15/91; SLJ 12/90)

3093 Jorgensen, Christine T. *Curl Up and Die* (10–12). 1997, Walker $32.95 (0-8027-3288-7). Stella Stargazer, writer of an astrology lovelorn column, tries to help a friend with romantic problems and finds herself involved in a case of blackmail and murder. (Rev: BL 12/15/96; SLJ 6/97)

3094 Jorgensen, Christine T. *Death of a Dustbunny: A Stella the Stargazer Mystery* (8–12). 1998, Walker $22.95 (0-8027-3315-8). An uncomplicated mystery in which sleuth Stella the Stargazer, who writes a combination astrology and advice to the lovelorn column for a local newspaper, investigates the disappearance of her friend Elena Ruiz, an employee of the Dustbunnies housekeeping and nanny agency. (Rev: VOYA 8/98)

3095 Kaminsky, Stuart. *The Dog Who Bit a Policeman* (10–12). 1998, Mysterious $22.00 (0-89296-667-X). A story of murder, corruption, and mayhem in contemporary Moscow that features Inspector Porfiry Rostnikov and an investigation of an illegal dogfight ring. (Rev: BL 6/1–15/98; SLJ 3/99)

3096 Kaminsky, Stuart. *Lieberman's Day* (9–12). 1994, Holt $19.95 (0-8050-2575-8). Two Chicago police officers deal with murder, brutality, drugs, and difficult moral issues in this action-filled novel. (Rev: BL 2/15/94*)

3097 Karas, Phyllis. *For Lucky's Sake* (5–8). 1997, Avon paper $3.99 (0-380-78647-8). In this mystery with an animal rights theme, Benjy investigates a mysterious fire in which 2 greyhounds rescued from a research lab are killed. (Rev: BL 10/1/97)

3098 Karas, Phyllis. *The Hate Crime* (7–10). 1995, Avon paper $3.99 (0-380-78214-6). A docu-novel/whodunit about a teen who scrawls the names of 7 concentration camps on a Jewish temple. (Rev: BL 12/1/95; VOYA 2/96)

3099 Karr, Kathleen. *In the Kaiser's Clutch* (6–9). 1995, Farrar $16.00 (0-374-33638-5). While making an anti-German film during World War I, twins Fitzhugh and Nelly Dalton become the target of an unknown villain who plans to ruin their movie. (Rev: SLJ 1/96)

3100 Kehret, Peg. *Deadly Stranger* (6–8). 1997, Troll paper $3.95 (0-8167-1308-1). Two 12-year-old girls are being stalked by a mentally deranged man. (Rev: BL 6/1/87)

3101 Kelly, Mary Anne. *Foxglove* (9–12). 1994, St. Martin's paper $4.50 (0-312-95202-3). After moving to a new home with her son and police officer husband, a woman becomes involved in the mystery of the death of an old friend. (Rev: BL 12/1/92*)

3102 Kemelman, Harry. *The Day the Rabbi Resigned* (9–12). 1993, Fawcett paper $5.99 (0-449-21908-9). A rabbi joins forces with the police to discover the truth behind the death of a prominent professor. (Rev: BL 3/1/92; SLJ 9/92)

3103 Kerr, M. E. *Fell* (8–12). 1987, HarperCollins paper $4.95 (0-06-447031-8). In a bizarre identity switch a teenager from a middle-class background enters a posh prep school. Followed by *Fell Back* and *Fell Down*. (Rev: BL 6/1/87; SLJ 8/87; VOYA 10/87)

3104 Kerr, M. E. *Fell Down* (7–12). 1991, Harper-Collins $15.00 (0-06-021763-4). Fell has dropped out of prep school but is haunted by the death of his best friend there, so he returns, to find kidnapping, murder, and obsession. (Rev: BL 9/15/91*; SLJ 10/91)

3105 King, Laurie R. *The Beekeeper's Apprentice; or, On the Segregation of the Queen* (9–12). 1994, St. Martin's $22.95 (0-312-10423-5). Sherlock Holmes and a brilliant 15-year-old girl become a detective duo and match wits with great criminal minds in England during World War I. (Rev: BL 2/1/94*; SLJ 7/94)

3106 King, Laurie R. *A Darker Place* (10–12). 1999, Bantam $23.95 (0-553-10711-9). Ann Waverly, a theology professor, occasional FBI agent, and former cult member, is called in to conduct an undercover investigation of a cult group with international ties and becomes unable to emotionally detach herself from the assignment, placing herself in danger. (Rev: BL 1/1–15/99; SLJ 7/99)

3107 King, Laurie R. *A Monstrous Regiment of Women* (10–12). 1995, St. Martin's $22.95 (0-312-13565-3). Sherlock Holmes's apprentice, Mary Russell, solves a case involving the strange deaths of several wealthy young women in Oxford. (Rev: BL 9/1/95; SLJ 2/96)

3108 King, Laurie R. *The Moor* (10–12). 1998, St. Martin's $23.95 (0-312-16934-5). Mr. and Mrs. Sherlock Holmes visit the site of *The Hound of the Baskervilles* to solve an eerie murder. (Rev: BL 1/1–15/98; SLJ 4/98; VOYA 10/98)

3109 King, Stephen. *The Green Mile* (10–12). 1996, Signet paper $18.94 (0-451-93302-8). This 6-part series involves, among others, a sadistic prison guard, Percy Wetmore, a seemingly simple-minded criminal, John Coffey, and a mouse named Mr. Jingles. (Rev: VOYA 12/96)

3110 Koontz, Dean. *Fear Nothing* (10–12). 1998, Bantam paper $7.99 (0-553-57975-4). A well-plotted thriller about a nocturnal person whose investigation of his father's death uncovers a sinister conspiracy involving experiments with animal intelligence. (Rev: SLJ 6/98; VOYA 6/98)

3111 Krich, Rochelle M. *Fertile Ground: A Mystery* (10–12). 1998, Avon paper $22.00 (0-380-97378-2). Dr. Lisa Brockman uncovers a web of greed, fraud, and coverups following the murder of an egg donor at a renowned fertility clinic and the disappearance of its director, while at the same time struggling with her feelings about the religious practices of the Orthodox Jewish parents who adopted her. (Rev: BL 1/1–15/98; SLJ 6/98)

3112 Kuraoka, Hannah. *Missing!* (6–8). 1995, Avon paper $3.99 (0-380-77374-0). A mystery set in Seattle involving Kelly Donovan, a high school student,

a teen mother who attends Kelly's school, and a demented child kidnapper. (Rev: SLJ 1/96)

3113 Langton, Jane. *Face on the Wall* (10–12). 1998, Viking paper $21.95 (0-670-87674-7). In this mystery, illustrator Annie Swann's life becomes a nightmare after she is blamed for the death of her tenant's Down's syndrome child. (Rev: SLJ 9/98)

3114 Lanier, Virginia. *Blind Bloodhound Justice* (10–12). 1998, HarperCollins $24.00 (0-06-017547-8). A cleverly crafted mystery novel that involves Jo Beth Sidden and her trusty bloodhounds in an investigation of 2 kidnappings and murders that occurred 30 years apart. (Rev: SLJ 1/99)

3115 Laurie, Hugh. *The Gun Seller* (10–12). 1997, Soho Pr. $24.00 (1-56947-087-1). A British spoof on spy thrillers that moves at an exciting pace and involves not only Brits but CIA personnel, international arms dealers, and terrorists. (Rev: BL 4/15/97; SLJ 6/97)

3116 Le Carre, John. *The Tailor of Panama* (10–12). 1996, Knopf $25.00 (0-679-45446-2). This humorous satire on spies features an unwilling espionage agent in Panama who invents news when he has nothing to report. (Rev: SLJ 2/97)

3117 Lehane, Dennis. *A Drink Before the War* (9–12). 1994, Harcourt $22.95 (0-15-100093-X). Patrick and Angelo are hired by 2 state senators to locate a black cleaning woman who filched several sensitive documents. (Rev: BL 11/15/94*)

3118 Lehane, Dennis. *Sacred* (10–12). 1997, Morrow $23.00 (0-688-14381-4). An intricate mystery story that involves detectives Patick Kenzie and Angie Gennaro on the trail of a missing heiress. (Rev: BL 6/1–15/97; SLJ 1/98)

3119 L'Engle, Madeleine. *Dragon in the Waters* (7–9). 1982, Dell paper $4.99 (0-440-91719-0). On board an ocean liner, 13-year-old Simon encounters murder and a mystery surrounding a stolen portrait.

3120 L'Engle, Madeleine. *Troubling a Star* (7–10). 1994, Farrar $17.00 (0-374-37783-9). Vicki Austin, 16, travels to Antarctica and meets a Baltic prince looking for romance, and the two try to solve a mystery involving nuclear waste. (Rev: BL 8/94; SLJ 10/94; VOYA 12/94)

3121 Levitin, Sonia. *Evil Encounter* (8–10). 1996, Simon & Schuster paper $17.00 (0-689-80216-1). Michelle must find the killer when her mother is wrongfully accused of murdering the charismatic leader of a therapy group to which they belong. (Rev: BL 5/1/96; BR 1–2/97; SLJ 5/96; VOYA 6/96)

3122 Levitin, Sonia. *Incident at Loring Groves* (7–12). 1988, Dial $14.95 (0-8037-0455-0); Fawcett paper $4.50 (0-449-70347-9). High school students find the body of a murdered classmate and decide to remain silent about it. (Rev: BL 9/1/88; BR 11–12/88; SLJ 6/88; VOYA 12/88)

3123 Levy, Harry. *Chain of Custody* (10–12). 1999, Fawcett paper $6.99 (0-449-00449-X). A cardiologist and now practicing attorney is wrongfully accused of his estranged wife's murder in this mystery that also features the hero's angry and confused teenage son. (Rev: SLJ 9/98)

3124 Lewin, Michael Z. *Underdog* (9–12). 1993, Mysterious $18.95 (0-89296-440-5). When homeless Jan Moro uncovers a police sting to catch thug Billy Cigar, his own entrepreneurial plan, which depends on Cigar's partnership, is endangered. (Rev: BL 10/1/93*)

3125 Lott, Bret. *The Hunt Club: A Novel* (10–12). 1999, HarperCollins paper $5.99 (0-06-101390-0). In this murder mystery, 15-year-old Huger Dillard, his mother, and blind uncle are kidnapped and must fight for their lives. (Rev: SLJ 11/98)

3126 Lucashenko, Melissa. *Killing Darcy* (8–10). 1998, Univ. of Queensland Pr. paper $12.95 (0-7022-3041-3). In this complex supernatural murder mystery set in New South Wales, 16-year-old Filomena uncovers a family murder, discovers a camera that can take pictures of the past, and she and her brother are helped by a gay Aboriginal boy to solve the mystery. (Rev: SLJ 2/99)

3127 McCrumb, Sharyn. *The Hangman's Beautiful Daughter* (9–12). (Ballad) 1992, Scribners $19.00 (0-684-19407-4). A minister's wife unravels the mystery of a family's murder-suicide in Appalachia. (Rev: BL 3/15/92*)

3128 McCrumb, Sharyn. *She Walks These Hills* (9–12). (Ballad) 1994, Scribners $21.00 (0-684-19556-9). A radio talk show host, a graduate student, and a police dispatcher travel the haunted foothills of the Appalachian Trail, each searching for clues to troubled pasts. (Rev: BL 8/94; SLJ 3/95)

3129 McGarrity, Michael. *Tularosa* (10–12). 1996, Norton $25.00 (0-393-03922-6). A private eye named Kevin Kerney travels to Tularosa, New Mexico, to investigate the strange disappearance of his godson, a soldier at the White Sands Missile Range. (Rev: BL 3/15/96; SLJ 1/97)

3130 MacGregor, Rob. *Hawk Moon* (7–10). 1996, Simon & Schuster paper $16.00 (0-689-80171-8). Sixteen-year-old Will Lansa, having returned to Aspen, Colorado, to learn more about his Hopi heritage, finds himself at the center of an investigation of the murder of his girlfriend. (Rev: SLJ 11/96*; VOYA 2/97)

3131 McMullan, Kate. *Under the Mummy's Spell* (5–8). 1992, Farrar $16.00 (0-374-38033-3). A novel that weaves together the tales of Peter, a present-day 12-year-old New Yorker, and Nephia, an Egyptian princess who lived 3,000 years ago. (Rev: BL 7/92; SLJ 7/92)

3132 McQuillan, Karin. *The Cheetah Chase* (9–12). 1994, Ballantine $20.00 (0-345-38183-1). When safari specialist Jazz Jasper witnesses her friend Nick being stung to death by a scorpion, she teams up with Inspector Ormondi to investigate the suspicious death, and uncovers murder. (Rev: BL 8/94; SLJ 12/94)

3133 Martin, Les. *Humbug* (5–8). (X-Files) 1996, HarperCollins paper $3.95 (0-06-440627-X). Even for veteran FBI agents Fox Mulder and Dana Scully, the murder of "The Alligator Man" is bizarre. (Rev: SLJ 6/96)

3134 Michaels, Barbara. *Shattered Silk* (10–12). 1998, HarperCollins paper $6.50 (0-06-104473-3). When Karen sets up a boutique in Georgetown, she receives mysterious threats on her life. (Rev: BL 8/86; SLJ 2/87)

3135 Michaels, Barbara. *Stitches in Time* (9–12). 1998, HarperCollins paper $6.99 (0-06-104474-1). This novel weaves an incredible mystery based on a haunted quilt. (Rev: BL 5/1/95; SLJ 11/95)

3136 Miles, Keith. *Murder in Perspective: An Architectural Mystery* (10–12). 1997, Walker $29.95 (0-8027-3298-4). A solid mystery with a sympathetic hero who has been wrongfully accused of murder and a glimpse at the world of architecture through appearances by Frank Lloyd Wright. (Rev: BL 2/15/97; VOYA 6/97)

3137 Mitchell, Sara. *Trial of the Innocent* (10–12). (Shadow Catchers) 1995, Bethany House paper $9.99 (1-55661-497-7). In this romantic mystery set in Virginia in 1891, Eve suspects her new brother-in-law of crimes. (Rev: SLJ 5/96)

3138 Moody, Bill. *The Sound of the Trumpet* (10–12). 1997, Walker $32.95 (0-8027-3291-7). A murder mystery with a jazz backdrop that involves the death of a secretive man who collects jazz tapes. (Rev: BL 2/15/97; VOYA 4/97)

3139 Moore, Ruth Nulton. *Mystery of the Missing Stallions* (7–9). Illus. 1984, Herald Pr. paper $6.99 (0-8361-3376-5). Fourteen-year-old twins solve the mystery of the missing stallions. Part of a series about Sara and Sam.

3140 Mowry, Jess. *Ghost Train* (6–9). 1996, Holt $14.95 (0-8050-4440-X). Remi, a 13-year-old immigrant from Haiti, who is interested in the supernatural, sees a ghost train and witnesses an unsolved murder that occurred 50 years ago. (Rev: BR 9–10/97; SLJ 12/96*; VOYA 2/97)

3141 Murphy, Shirley Rousseau. *Cat in the Dark* (10–12). 1999, HarperCollins $22.00 (0-06-105096-2). In this mystery-fantasy, Joe Grey and Dulcie, 2 cats that are able to speak, read, and act like detectives, come across an investment scam and 3 deaths. (Rev: BL 12/15/98; SLJ 5/99)

3142 Murphy, T. M. *The Secrets of Cranberry Beach* (5–8). (A Belltown Mystery) 1996, Silver Burdett paper $4.95 (0-382-39303-1). After an encounter with the murderer that almost costs him his life, amateur detective 16-year-old Orville Jacques solves a baffling crime. (Rev: SLJ 1/97)

3143 Murray, Susan, and Robert Davies. *Mayhem on Maui* (6–8). (K. C. Flanagan, Girl Detective) 1999, Robert Davies Multimedia paper $5.99 (1-55207-022-0). While vacationing in Maui, K. C. Flanagan and her older brother investigate a series of mysterious fires that appear to be the work of the Japanese mafia. (Rev: SLJ 7/99)

3144 Murray, Susan, and Robert Davies. *Panic in Puerto Vallarta* (7–9). (K. C. Flanagan, Girl Detective) 1998, Robert Davies Multimedia paper $8.99 (1-55207-015-8). After witnessing a murder in Puerto Vallarta, young K. C. Flanagan finds that the killers are out to get her. (Rev: SLJ 12/98)

3145 Nevins, Francis M., and Martin H. Greenberg, eds. *Hitchcock in Prime Time* (10–12). 1985, Avon paper $9.00 (0-380-89673-7). This is a collection of 20 stories that formed the basis of some of Hitchcock's best television shows.

3146 Newman, Robert. *The Case of the Baker Street Irregular: A Sherlock Holmes Story* (6–8). 1984, Macmillan paper $4.95 (0-689-70766-5). Andrew becomes a Baker Street urchin who occasionally helps Sherlock Holmes or Scotland Yard inspector Peter Wyatt solve crimes. Others in this series are: *The Case of the Threatened King* and *The Case of the Vanishing Corpse.*

3147 Nixon, Joan Lowery. *A Candidate for Murder* (6–12). 1991, 1992, Dell paper $4.50 (0-440-21212-X). While Cary's father enters the political limelight, his daughter gets embroiled in a series of strange events. (Rev: BL 3/1/91)

3148 Nixon, Joan Lowery. *The Dark and Deadly Pool* (7–12). 1989, Bantam paper $4.50 (0-440-20348-1). Mary Elizabeth becomes aware of strange happenings at the health club where she works. (Rev: BL 11/1/87; BR 11–12/87; SLJ 2/88; VOYA 12/87)

3149 Nixon, Joan Lowery. *The Ghosts of Now* (7–10). 1984, Dell paper $4.50 (0-440-93115-0). Angie investigates a hit-and-run accident that has left her brother in a coma.

3150 Nixon, Joan Lowery. *The Island of Dangerous Dreams* (7–12). 1989, Dell paper $4.50 (0-440-20258-2). Seventeen-year-old Andrea helps in the investigation of the murder of a judge in the Bahamas. (Rev: VOYA 8/89)

3151 Nixon, Joan Lowery. *The Kidnapping of Christina Lattimore* (7–9). 1979, Dell paper $4.50

(0-440-94520-8). Christina faces rumors that she engineered her own kidnapping.

3152 Nixon, Joan Lowery. *Murdered, My Sweet* (6–9). 1997, Delacorte $15.95 (0-385-32245-3). The son of a millionaire is murdered and young Jenny and her mystery-writer mother try to solve the case. (Rev: BL 9/1/97; BR 1–2/98; SLJ 9/97; VOYA 2/98)

3153 Nixon, Joan Lowery. *The Name of the Game Was Murder* (6–8). 1994, Dell paper $4.50 (0-440-21916-7). Teenager Samantha must work with her uncle's houseguests to find a damning manuscript and uncover the murderer of its author. (Rev: BL 3/1/93)

3154 Nixon, Joan Lowery. *The Other Side of Dark* (7–10). 1986, Dell paper $4.50 (0-440-96638-8). After waking from a 4-year coma, Stacy is now the target of the man who wounded her and killed her mother. (Rev: BL 9/15/86; BR 3–4/87; SLJ 9/86; VOYA 12/86)

3155 Nixon, Joan Lowery. *The Seance* (7–10). 1981, Dell paper $4.50 (0-440-97937-4). An innocent séance leads to a double murder in this fast-paced mystery.

3156 Nixon, Joan Lowery. *Search for the Shadowman* (5–8). 1996, Delacorte $15.95 (0-385-32203-8). Using computer research, Andy tries to clear the name of a long-dead relative accused of treachery. (Rev: BL 10/1/96; BR 11–12/96; SLJ 11/96; VOYA 12/96)

3157 Nixon, Joan Lowery. *Shadowmaker* (7–9). 1995, Dell paper $4.50 (0-440-21942-6). When Katie's mother, an investigative journalist, probes evidence of toxic-waste dumping, Katie discovers that events at her school are related. (Rev: BL 3/1/94; SLJ 5/94; VOYA 8/94)

3158 Nixon, Joan Lowery. *The Specter* (7–10). 1993, Dell paper $3.99 (0-440-97740-1). Seventeen-year-old Dina protects a child who believes she is going to be murdered.

3159 Nixon, Joan Lowery. *Spirit Seeker* (6–9). 1995, Delacorte paper $15.95 (0-385-32062-0). Holly Campbell is pitted against her police detective father in a race to exonerate her boyfriend of a charge of double murder. (Rev: BL 9/15/95; SLJ 9/95; VOYA 2/96)

3160 Nixon, Joan Lowery. *The Stalker* (9–12). 1985, Dell paper $4.50 (0-440-97753-3). In Corpus Christi, Jennifer sets out to prove the innocence of her friend, who has been accused of murder. (Rev: BR 9–10/85; SLJ 5/85; VOYA 6/85)

3161 Nixon, Joan Lowery. *The Weekend Was Murder!* (6–10). 1992, 1994, Dell paper $3.99 (0-440-21901-9). A teen sleuth and her boyfriend attend a murder mystery enactment weekend and discover a real murder. (Rev: BL 2/15/92; SLJ 3/92)

3162 Nixon, Joan Lowery. *Who Are You?* (6–10). 1999, Bantam Doubleday Dell $15.95 (0-385-32566-5). Teenager Kristi Evans sets out to solve the mystery of a murdered art collector and find out why he had been keeping a file on her. (Rev: BL 4/15/99; SLJ 6/99; VOYA 10/99)

3163 Norman, Hilary. *The Pact* (10–12). 1997, Dutton paper $24.95 (0-525-94256-4). Three friends who were orphaned as a result of a helicopter crash find that someone is trying to harm them in this mystery that involves flashbacks to the Holocaust. (Rev: BL 6/1–15/97; SLJ 12/97)

3164 North, Suzanne. *Seeing Is Deceiving* (10–12). 1996, McClelland & Stewart Tundra Books $25.99 (0-7710-6805-0). TV camerawoman Phoebe Fairfax gets involved in a murder when she is sent to cover a psychic fair. (Rev: SLJ 4/97)

3165 Olson, Arielle North, and Howard Schwartz, eds. *Ask the Bones: Scary Stories from around the World* (5–9). 1999, Viking $15.99 (0-670-87581-3). A collection of 22 scary stories about subjects ranging from ghosts to witches and voodoo spells, accompanied by scary illustrations. (Rev: BL 5/1/99; BR 9–10/99; SLJ 4/99)

3166 Osborne, Charles, adapt. *Black Coffee: A Hercule Poirot Novel* (10–12). 1998, St. Martin's $22.95 (0-312-19241-X). Before Hercule Poirot can fulfill his obligation to visit Sir Claud, the man is murdered in this clever adaptation of Christie's play *Black Coffee*. (Rev: BL 8/98; SLJ 12/98)

3167 Page, Katherine H. *Christie & Company* (6–8). 1996, Avon paper $14.00 (0-380-97393-6). At her new boarding school in Massachusetts, Christie sets out to find out who is sending her insulting messages and who is stealing valuables from her dorm. (Rev: BL 12/1/96; SLJ 3/97)

3168 Page, Katherine H. *Christie & Company Downeast* (5–8). 1997, Avon paper $14.00 (0-380-97396-0). Three girls spend a month at an inn on Maine's Little Bittern Island and become involved in a puzzling mystery. (Rev: BL 5/1/97; SLJ 7/97)

3169 Page, Katherine H. *Christie & Company in the Year of the Dragon* (5–8). 1997, Avon paper $14.00 (0-380-97397-9). In this fast-paced mystery, 3 teenage amateur sleuths try to help a recent immigrant from China foil criminals who are threatening to have her and her family deported. (Rev: SLJ 5/98)

3170 Paretsky, Sara. *Guardian Angel* (9–12). 1993, Dell paper $6.99 (0-440-21399-1). Intrepid female private eye V. I. Warshawski is involved with greedy Yuppies offloading risky bonds on Chicago seniors. (Rev: BL 12/1/91; SLJ 9/92)

3171 Patneaude, David. *Someone Was Watching* (6–9). 1993, Albert Whitman LB $14.95 (0-8075-7531-3). David, 13, must determine whether his baby sister drowned at a picnic or was kidnapped and embarks on a cross-country chase of possible kidnappers. (Rev: BL 7/93; SLJ 7/93)

3172 Pearce, Philippa. *Who's Afraid? And Other Strange Stories* (6–9). 1987, Greenwillow $11.95 (0-688-06895-2). Eleven stories that explore the disturbing dark side of life. (Rev: BL 4/87; BR 5–6/87; SLJ 5/87)

3173 Peck, Richard. *Through a Brief Darkness* (7–9). 1997, Penguin paper $3.99 (0-14-038557-6). Karen must discover the truth about her father and hopes to find out when she visits relatives in England.

3174 Penman, Sharon Kay. *The Queen's Man: A Medieval Mystery* (10–12). 1996, Holt $20.00 (0-8050-3885-X). An intriguing mystery set in England during the time of Eleanor of Aquitaine and Richard Lionheart. (Rev: BL 11/1/96; SLJ 3/97)

3175 Perry, Anne. *Brunswick Gardens* (10–12). 1998, Fawcett $25.00 (0-449-90845-3); paper $6.99 (0-449-00318-3). A murder mystery set in Victorian England in which Inspector Pitt investigates the death of a woman noted as an agitator for woman's rights. (Rev: SLJ 11/98)

3176 Perutz, Leo. *Master of the Day of Judgment* (9–12). 1994, Arcade $19.95 (1-55970-171-4). In 1909 Vienna, Baron von Yosch is accused of killing an actor whose wife was once his lover and discovers a terrifying secret when he investigates. (Rev: BL 10/15/94*)

3177 Peters, Elizabeth. *The Ape Who Guards the Balance* (10–12). 1998, Avon paper $24.00 (0-380-97657-9). A complex murder mystery set in 1907 that involves grisly murder and archaeological sites in Egypt. (Rev: BL 6/1–15/98; SLJ 2/99)

3178 Peters, Ellis. *The Holy Thief* (9–12). 1993, Mysterious $17.95 (0-89296-524-X). In this mystery set in medieval times, thievery and murder intrude upon Brother Cadfael's well-ordered monastery life. (Rev: BL 3/1/93; SLJ 7/93)

3179 Petersen, P. J. *Liars* (6–9). 1992, Simon & Schuster $15.00 (0-671-75035-6). When Sam, 14, discovers that he can tell when someone is lying, his ability makes him suspicious of almost everyone, even his father. (Rev: BL 6/1/92; SLJ 4/92*)

3180 Pike, Christopher. *Chain Letter* (9–12). 1986, Avon paper $3.99 (0-380-89968-X). Six teenagers must perform acts of repentance in connection with the hit-and-run death of a man. (Rev: VOYA 8/86)

3181 Pike, Christopher. *Gimme a Kiss* (7–12). 1991, Pocket Books paper $4.50 (0-671-63682-5). A girl fakes her own death in a wild plot to get revenge. (Rev: BL 10/15/88; VOYA 4/89)

3182 Pike, Christopher. *Last Act* (7–10). 1991, Pocket Books paper $3.99 (0-671-73683-3). The blanks in Melanie's stage pistol turn out to be real. Is she really guilty of murder? (Rev: BL 6/15/88; SLJ 11/88; VOYA 8/88)

3183 Pike, Christopher. *Slumber Party* (7–10). 1985, Scholastic paper $3.50 (0-590-43014-9). Six teenage girls stranded in a winter vacation home experience mysterious occurrences that bring terror into their lives. (Rev: SLJ 12/86)

3184 Pike, Christopher. *Spellbound* (10–12). 1990, Pocket Books paper $4.50 (0-671-73681-7). Cindy is determined to find out who murdered one of the cheerleaders at her high school. (Rev: VOYA 8/88)

3185 Powers, Martha. *Sunflower* (10–12). 1998, Simon & Schuster $22.00 (0-684-83767-6). A gripping mystery story in which Sheila Brady, a police detective, investigates a series of murders in her small Wisconsin town of young girls who are killed and then raped. (Rev: SLJ 1/99)

3186 Preston, Douglas, and Lincoln Child. *Reliquary* (10–12). 1997, Tom Doherty Assoc. $24.95 (0-312-86095-1). Margo Green of the Natural History Museum joins several investigators as their search for a brutal murderer leads them to investigate the mole people who live underground in New York City. (Rev: BL 3/15/97; SLJ 9/97)

3187 Preston, Richard. *The Cobra Event* (10–12). 1997, Random $25.95 (0-679-45714-3). A frightening thriller about a mad scientist who releases a deadly virus in New York City. (Rev: BL 11/15/97; SLJ 3/98)

3188 Pronzini, Bill. *A Wasteland of Strangers* (10–12). 1997, Walker $29.95 (0-8027-3301-8). A swiftly plotted mystery in which scar-faced John Faith is wrongfully accused of murder and is sheltered by 3 women during an escape attempt. (Rev: BL 6/1–15/97; VOYA 2/98)

3189 Prowell, Sandra West. *The Killing of Monday Brown* (9–12). 1994, Walker $19.95 (0-8027-3184-8). Private eye Phoebe Siegel investigates a missing dealer in Native American artifacts. (Rev: BL 5/15/94*)

3190 Prowell, Sandra West. *When Wallflowers Die* (10–12). 1996, Walker $32.95 (0-8027-3254-2). An exciting mystery in which Phoebe Siegal, a gutsy PI, finds her life is in danger when she begins an investigation of a murder that occurred years before. (Rev: BL 7/96; SLJ 2/97)

3191 Pullman, Philip. *Count Karlstein* (6–9). 1998, Random LB $18.99 (0-679-99255-3). Fun and suspense mingle in this melodrama about efforts to prevent wicked Count Karlstein from sacrificing his young nieces to the Demon Huntsman. (Rev: BL 8/98; SLJ 9/98)

3192 Pullman, Philip, ed. *Detective Stories* (7–12). Illus. 1998, Larousse Kingfisher Chambers $12.95 (0-7534-5157-3); paper $6.95 (0-7534-5146-8). A collection of mystery and detective stories by such authors as Agatha Christie, Ellery Queen, Conan Doyle, Damon Runyan, and Dorothy Sayers. (Rev: BL 5/15/98; SLJ 9/98)

3193 Qualey, Marsha. *Close to a Killer* (9–12). 1999, Bantam Doubleday Dell $15.95 (0-385-32597-5). Barrie finds herself in the middle of a puzzling mystery when her mother's beauty salon is linked to 2 murders. (Rev: BL 2/1/99; SLJ 3/99; VOYA 4/99)

3194 Qualey, Marsha. *Thin Ice* (7–12). 1997, Delacorte $14.95 (0-385-32298-4). Arden Munro's brother appears to have been drowned after a snowmobile accident but no body has been found, and the girl believes he has simply escaped his dull life by running away. (Rev: BL 11/1/97; SLJ 11/97; VOYA 10/97)

3195 Quick, Amanda. *I Thee Wed* (10–12). 1999, Bantam $23.95 (0-553-10084-X). An amusing murder mystery and love story, set in Regency English society, involving a young financier, Edison, and his new fiancée, Emma, originally hired by Edison to help him investigate a stolen ancient manuscript. (Rev: BL 2/1/99; SLJ 7/99)

3196 Raskin, Ellen. *The Westing Game* (6–9). 1978, Dutton $15.99 (0-525-42320-6); Avon paper $3.50 (0-380-67991-4). Sixteen possible heirs try to decipher an enigmatic will. Newbery Award, 1979.

3197 Read Magazine. *Read If You Dare: Twelve Twisted Tales* (6–9). 1997, Millbrook LB $22.40 (0-7613-0046-5). Twelve scary tales that explore fate and irony by masters that range from Chaucer to Stephen King. (Rev: BL 12/15/97; SLJ 11/97; VOYA 6/98)

3198 Reaver, Chap. *A Little Bit Dead* (8–12). 1992, Delacorte $15.00 (0-385-30801-9); 1994, Dell paper $3.99 (0-440-21910-8). When Reece saves an Indian boy from lynching by U.S. marshals, lawmen claim that Reece murdered one of the marshals and he must clear himself. (Rev: BL 9/1/92; SLJ 9/92)

3199 Rendell, Ruth. *Heartstones* (10–12). Illus. 1987, Ballantine paper $4.95 (0-345-34800-1). In this short but powerful mystery an anorexic girl believes she is guilty of murder. (Rev: BL 6/1/87; SLJ 11/87)

3200 Rendell, Ruth. *The Keys to the Street* (10–12). 1996, Crown $24.00 (0-517-70685-7). A mystery story and a romance set in London about a mousy woman, who falls in love and inherits a massive fortune, and a series of murders of homeless men. (Rev: SLJ 3/97)

3201 Robb, Candace. *The Riddle of St. Leonard's: An Owen Archer Mystery* (10–12). 1997, St. Martin's $21.95 (0-312-16983-3). In England during 1369, Owen Archer is pressed into service for Sir Richard to investigate murders at St. Leonard's Hospital during a resurgence of the plague. (Rev: BL 9/15/97; SLJ 12/97)

3202 Roberts, Les. *The Lake Effect* (9–12). 1994, St. Martin's $21.95 (0-312-11537-7). Private-eye Milan Jacovich returns a favor for a mobster and helps run Barbara Corn's mayoral campaign. When the competing candidate's wife is murdered, Jacovich investigates. (Rev: BL 11/1/94*)

3203 Roberts, Willo Davis. *Nightmare* (7–10). 1989, Macmillan $16.00 (0-689-31551-1). After a series of unusual occurrences where 17-year-old Nick is the victim, he finds he is being followed. (Rev: BL 9/15/89; BR 3–4/90; SLJ 9/89; VOYA 12/89)

3204 Roberts, Willo Davis. *Pawns* (5–8). 1998, Simon & Schuster $16.00 (0-689-81668-5). Pregnant Dori claims to be the wife of Mamie's dead son, but Teddi, whom Mamie has raised, thinks that Dori is lying and sets out to prove that she is right. (Rev: BL 11/15/98; BR 5–6/99; SLJ 11/98; VOYA 4/99)

3205 Roberts, Willo Davis. *Twisted Summer* (6–8). 1996, Simon & Schuster $16.00 (0-689-80459-8). In this mystery set in rural Michigan, Cici helps 17-year-old Jake to clear his brother of a murder charge. (Rev: BL 3/15/96; BR 1–2/97; SLJ 4/96; VOYA 6/96)

3206 Roberts, Willo Davis. *The View from the Cherry Tree* (7–9). 1994, Simon & Schuster paper $4.50 (0-689-71784-9). A boy who witnesses a murder becomes targeted as the next victim.

3207 Robinson, Lynda S. *Eater of Souls* (10–12). 1997, Walker $29.95 (0-8027-3294-1). An engrossing mystery in which Lord Meren, King Tutankhamun's guru, tries to solve the mystery of Queen Nefertiti's death and becomes involved with a serial killer. (Rev: BL 4/15/97; SLJ 8/97; VOYA 4/98)

3208 Robinson, Lynda S. *Murder at the Feast of Rejoicing* (10–12). 1996, Walker $30.95 (0-8027-3274-7). An unusual murder mystery takes place on the Egyptian Nile at the time of Tutankhamun in this third book in the highly praised series featuring Lord Meren, confidant to the young pharaoh. (Rev: BL 1/1–15/96; SLJ 5/96)

3209 Robinson, Peter. *In a Dry Season* (10–12). 1999, Avon paper $24.00 (0-380-97581-5). Detective Chief Inspector Alan Banks is brought in to investigate the 50-year-old murder of a young woman during World War II discovered when a skeleton is found in the ruins of a deserted village in England. (Rev: SLJ 9/99)

3210 Roosevelt, Elliott. *Murder and the First Lady* (10–12). 1985, Avon paper $4.99 (0-380-69937-0). A mystery in which Eleanor Roosevelt serves as supersleuth.

3211 Roosevelt, Elliott. *Murder at the Palace* (10–12). 1989, Avon paper $4.99 (0-380-70405-6). Eleanor Roosevelt again stars in this, the fifth of this series. The locale is Buckingham Palace during World War II. (Rev: BL 2/15/88)

3212 Roosevelt, Elliott. *Murder in the Oval Office* (10–12). 1990, Avon paper $4.99 (0-380-70528-1). First Lady Eleanor Roosevelt solves the murder of a congressman. (Rev: BL 12/15/88)

3213 Roosevelt, Elliott. *The White House Pantry Murder* (10–12). 1987, Avon paper $4.50 (0-380-70404-8). This is the fourth mystery involving Eleanor Roosevelt as sleuth. In this one a body is found in a large White House refrigerator. (Rev: BL 12/15/86)

3214 Ross, Ramon R. *Harper and Moon* (6–8). 1993, Atheneum $15.00 (0-689-31803-0). Set in 1942, the story of Harper and Moon deals with child abuse, animal abuse, suspected murder, and a suicide attempt. (Rev: BL 5/15/93; SLJ 9/93*)

3215 Rushford, Patricia H. *Abandoned* (6–9). (Jennie McGrady Mystery) 1999, Bethany House paper $4.99 (0-7642-2120-5). In this twelfth Jennie McGrady mystery, teen detective Jennie is involved in murders of pro-life advocates while also trying to help a girl who has recently learned she was adopted after being abandoned in a dumpster. (Rev: BL 7/99)

3216 Rushford, Patricia H. *Betrayed* (6–10). (Jennie McGrady Mystery) 1996, Bethany House paper $4.99 (1-55661-560-4). Jennie encounters a long list of suspects when she tries to find the murderer of her uncle on a dude ranch in Montana. (Rev: BL 6/1–15/96; SLJ 6/96; VOYA 12/96)

3217 Rushford, Patricia H. *Dying to Win* (6–10). (Jennie McGrady Mystery) 1995, Bethany House paper $4.99 (1-55661-559-0). A suspenseful Jennie McGrady mystery about the disappearance of a rebellious schoolchum known as the "Rainbow Girl." (Rev: BL 1/1–15/96; SLJ 2/96; VOYA 6/96)

3218 Rushford, Patricia H. *Without a Trace: Nick Is Missing and Now They Are After Her . . .* (6–9). (Jennie McGrady Mystery) 1995, Bethany House paper $4.99 (1-55661-558-2). In the fifth book in the series, Jennie practices her sleuthing skills when her young brother and one of his friends disappear. (Rev: BL 9/1/95; SLJ 9/95; VOYA 2/96)

3219 Ryan, Mary E. *Alias* (6–10). 1997, Simon & Schuster $16.00 (0-689-80789-9). Fifteen-year-old Toby Chase decides to secretly find out why he and his mother are constantly moving. (Rev: BL 4/15/97; SLJ 7/97)

3220 Saul, John. *Black Lightning* (9–12). 1995, Ballantine $23.00 (0-449-90864-X). Two years after the execution of serial killer Richard Kraven, reporter Anne Jeffer finds her husband has changed and the murders have begun again. (Rev: BL 6/1–15/95; SLJ 12/95)

3221 Saul, John. *The Presence* (10–12). 1997, Fawcett $25.00 (0-449-91055-5). An action-packed thriller that involves an archaeologist, her 16-year-old son, and the discovery that deadly medical experiments are being performed in a seemingly harmless high-tech laboratory. (Rev: SLJ 4/98)

3222 Sayers, Dorothy L., and Jill Paton-Walsh. *Thrones, Dominations* (10–12). 1998, St. Martin's $23.95 (0-312-18196-5). This murder mystery featuring the famous Lord Peter Wimsey and his wife, Harriet Vane, was completed after Sayers's death. (Rev: SLJ 7/98)

3223 Scott, Holden. *Skeptic* (10–12). 1999, St. Martin's $24.95 (0-312-19334-3). In this medical thriller, a graduate student in physician Mike Ballantine's lab discovers that ghosts exist and that the memories of dead people are incorporated into the brains of the living—and there are villains who will stop at nothing, including murder, to get hold of the research. (Rev: SLJ 7/99)

3224 Scott, Willard. *Murder under Blue Skies: A Stanley Waters Mystery* (10–12). 1998, NAL $23.95 (0-525-94324-2). When one of his guests at his bed-and-breakfast is murdered, Stanley Waters finds that the chief investigator is his high-school sweetheart. (Rev: BL 1/1–15/98; SLJ 9/98)

3225 Sebestyen, Ouida. *The Girl in the Box* (9–12). 1988, Little, Brown $12.95 (0-316-77935-0). A high school girl is kidnapped by a masked man and kept prisoner in a damp, dark room. (Rev: BL 11/1/88; BR 1–2/89; SLJ 10/88; VOYA 2/89)

3226 Seil, William. *Sherlock Holmes and the Titanic Tragedy: A Case to Remember* (10–12). 1996, Breese Books, Ltd. paper $14.95 (0-947533-35-4). Holmes and Watson are aboard the *Titanic* guarding a young secret agent who is transporting important submarine plans for the U. S. Navy. (Rev: SLJ 4/97)

3227 Shaw, Diana. *Lessons in Fear* (6–9). 1987, Little, Brown $12.95 (0-316-78341-2). An unpopular teacher has a series of mysterious accidents and one of her students, Carter Colborn, decides she must investigate them. (Rev: BL 4/15/88; BR 9–10/87; SLJ 10/87)

3228 Siciliano, Sam. *The Angel of the Opera: Sherlock Holmes Meets the Phantom of the Opera* (9–12). 1994, Penzler Books $21.95 (1-883402-46-8). Sherlock Holmes's cousin is the narrator in this mystery that takes place at the Paris Opera house. (Rev: BL 5/15/94; SLJ 12/94)

3229 Skurzynski, Gloria, and Alane Ferguson. *Wolf Stalker* (5–8). (National Parks Mystery) 1997, National Geographic $15.00 (0-7922-7034-7). Three youngsters solve the mystery of who is killing the wolves of Yellowstone Park. (Rev: BR 3–4/98; SLJ 1/98)

3230 Smith, April. *North of Montana* (9–12). 1994, Knopf $23.00 (0-679-43197-7). FBI agent Ana, hungry for a career-making case, investigates movie star Jayne Mason's claim that her doctor has hooked her on painkillers. (Rev: BL 9/15/94*; SLJ 5/95)

3231 Stabenow, Dana. *A Cold-Blooded Business* (9–12). 1994, Berkley paper $17.95 (0-425-14173-X). Aleut private eye Kate Shugak travels north of the Arctic Circle to investigate a rise in cocaine use among Alaskan oil field workers. Also use: *Play with Fire* (1995). (Rev: BL 3/1/94*; SLJ 9/94)

3232 Steiber, Ellen. *The X-Files #4: Squeeze* (7–9). 1996, HarperCollins paper $4.50 (0-06-440621-0). In this novelization of a screenplay from the The X-Files television series, FBI agents Dana Scully and Fox Mulder investigate 3 murders that took place in rooms locked from the inside and find a 10-inch long fingerprint. Also use *Shapes* (1996). (Rev: VOYA 4/97)

3233 Steiner, Barbara. *Dreamstalker* (8–12). 1992, Avon paper $3.50 (0-380-76611-6). A girl wonders if she's psychic when her terrifying nightmares start coming true. (Rev: BL 3/15/92)

3234 Steiner, Barbara. *Spring Break* (7–10). 1996, Scholastic paper $3.99 (0-590-54419-5). Five high schoolers rent a haunted house where they contend with odd appearances and disappearances, arson, and a skeleton. (Rev: SLJ 12/96)

3235 Stewart, Mary. *Thornyhold* (9–12). 1989, Fawcett paper $6.99 (0-449-21712-4). Geillis discovers that a magic spell controls the people in her cousin's house. (Rev: BL 10/1/88)

3236 Stine, R. L. *The Overnight* (7–10). 1991, Pocket Books paper $3.99 (0-671-74650-2). While on an overnight camping trip, one of the 6 campers accidentally kills a stranger she meets in the woods. Also use: *The New Girl* (1991). (Rev: BL 12/15/89)

3237 Stine, R. L. *The Wrong Number* (5–9). 1990, Pocket Books paper $3.99 (0-671-69411-1). While making a crank telephone call, a teenager hears a murder being committed. (Rev: SLJ 6/90)

3238 Sumner, M. C. *Night Terrors* (7–10). 1997, Pocket Books paper $3.99 (0-671-00241-4). When her father disappears from his top-secret research facility and her friend begins having terrifying nightmares, Kathleen decides to investigate. (Rev: SLJ 8/97)

3239 Sykes, Shelley. *For Mike* (7–10). 1998, Delacorte $15.95 (0-385-32337-9). Mystery, suspense, and romance are combined in this novel in which Jeff and a girlfriend try to solve the mystery of the disappearance of Jeff's best friend, Mike. (Rev: BL 4/1/98; BR 9–10/98; SLJ 5/98; VOYA 4/98)

3240 Terris, Susan. *Octopus Pie* (6–8). 1983, Farrar $11.95 (0-374-35571-1). The friendship between Kristin and Mari becomes stronger when they must find out who kidnapped their pet octopus.

3241 Thesman, Jean. *Rachel Chance* (6–9). 1990, Houghton $15.00 (0-395-50934-3). Rachel's young brother has been kidnapped, but no one seems to be taking any action. (Rev: BL 5/1/90; SLJ 4/90)

3242 Thompson, Julian. *The Fling* (7–10). 1994, Holt $15.95 (0-8050-2881-1). A story on paper becomes the story in reality in this book about a mysterious woman living in a mansion with other enigmatic characters. (Rev: BL 5/1/94; SLJ 6/94; VOYA 8/94)

3243 Thurlo, Aimée, and David Thurlo. *Death Walker* (10–12). 1996, Tom Doherty Assoc. $23.95 (0-312-85651-2). Ellen Clah, a police investigator on the Navajo Reservation, sets out to find the killer of several of the tribal cultural leaders. (Rev: SLJ 3/97)

3244 Thurlo, Aimée, and David Thurlo. *Enemy Way* (10–12). 1998, Forge $23.95 (0-312-85520-6). The geography on the Southwest figures prominently in this mystery involving Ella Clah of the Navaho police force, gang warfare, a murder, and skinwalkers, or Navajo witches. (Rev: BL 9/15/98; SLJ 1/99)

3245 Truman, Margaret. *Murder at the FBI* (10–12). 1986, Fawcett paper $5.99 (0-449-20618-1). In this, the sixth of her murder mysteries set in Washington, Truman poses the question, "Who murdered FBI special agent George L. Pritchard?" (Rev: BL 5/15/85)

3246 Truman, Margaret. *Murder at the Kennedy Center* (10–12). 1989, Random $17.95 (0-394-57602-0). A fund-raiser at Kennedy Center seems to be a success until the body of a murdered girl is found. (Rev: BL 6/1/89)

3247 Truman, Margaret. *Murder in the White House* (10–12). 1988, Warner paper $5.99 (0-446-31488-9). In this thriller, the secretary of state is murdered in private quarters in the White House. This is one of many recommended mysteries set in Washington, D.C., that include *Murder in the Supreme Court* and *Murder in the Smithsonian.*

3248 Truman, Margaret. *Murder on Capitol Hill* (10–12). 1989, Warren paper $5.99 (0-446-31518-4). A prominent senator is murdered at his own testimonial dinner in this mystery which is part of a series that includes *Murder on Embassy Row.*

3249 Van Draanen, Wendelin. *Sammy Keyes and the Runaway Elf* (5–8). 1999, Knopf LB $16.99 (0-679-98854-8). Young Sammy Keyes, a seventh-grade

sleuth, is on the trail of the dognappers who snatched Marique, the famous calendar cover dog. (Rev: BL 9/1/99; SLJ 9/99)

3250 Van Draanen, Wendelin. *Sammy Keyes and the Sisters of Mercy* (5–8). 1999, Knopf LB $16.99 (0-679-98852-1). Wise-cracking seventh grader Sammy Keyes tackles another mystery when a treasured papal cross is stolen and she notices a mysterious girl at the church's soup kitchen. (Rev: BL 4/1/99; SLJ 7/99)

3251 Van Thal, Herbert, ed. *The Mammoth Book of Great Detective Stories* (9–12). 1989, Carroll & Graf paper $9.95 (0-88184-530-2). A total of 26 classic stories by such writers as Sayers, Simenon, Chandler, and Chesterton. (Rev: BL 9/15/89)

3252 Vine, Barbara. *No Night Is Too Long* (9–12). 1995, Crown $23.00 (0-517-79964-2). A man who thinks he has gotten away with murder begins receiving mysterious letters in this tale of psychological suspense. (Rev: BL 12/1/94*)

3253 Vivelo, Jackie. *Chills in the Night: Tales That Will Haunt You* (5–9). 1997, DK Publg. $14.95 (0-7894-2463-0). Everyday experiences become strange and fearsome in this collection of 8 bizarre, sometimes scary, stories. (Rev: BL 1/1–15/98; SLJ 1/98)

3254 Voigt, Cynthia. *The Callender Papers* (9–12). 1983, Fawcett paper $4.50 (0-449-70184-0). A part-time position sorting out some archival papers leads to uncovering unsolved family mysteries.

3255 Voigt, Cynthia. *The Vandemark Mummy* (6–9). 1991, Atheneum $15.95 (0-689-31476-0). This story involves a break-in at a museum of Egyptian antiquities and 2 teenage siblings who attempt to solve the mystery. (Rev: BL 9/1/91; SLJ 9/91)

3256 Walsh, Jill Paton. *Unleaving* (7–10). 1990, Farrar paper $3.50 (0-374-48068-0). In this English novel, a young female university student ponders whether a cliff tragedy was really a murder.

3257 Werlin, Nancy. *The Killer's Cousin* (7–12). 1998, Bantam $15.95 (0-385-32560-6). A tautly plotted thriller about a boy who tries to escape the guilt related to the accidental death of his girlfriend by moving in with relatives, but instead uncovers some horrifying family secrets. (Rev: BL 9/1/98; BR 5–6/99; SLJ 11/98; VOYA 10/98)

3258 Wesley, Valerie W. *Easier to Kill* (10–12). 1998, Putnam $23.95 (0-399-14445-5). African American detective Tamara Hayle is hired by a radio personality to find the identity of the person sending her threatening letters and to solve the mystery of the stabbing death of her stylist. (Rev: SLJ 2/99)

3259 West, Tracy. *The Butterflies of Freedom* (6–9). 1988, Crosswinds paper $2.25 (0-373-98023-X). An easily read mystery involving a missing deed to valuable property. (Rev: VOYA 8/88)

3260 Whitney, Phyllis A. *Daughter of the Stars* (9–12). 1994, Crown $20.00 (0-517-59929-5). Lacy discovers the family that has been her mother's secret for years. She ventures to Harper's Ferry to help them and learns of her father's unsolved murder. (Rev: BL 9/15/94; SLJ 3/95)

3261 Whitney, Phyllis A. *Dream of Orchids* (9–12). 1987, Fawcett paper $5.99 (0-449-20743-9). While visiting on the Florida Keys, Laurel becomes involved in murder. (Rev: SLJ 5/85)

3262 Whitney, Phyllis A. *Emerald* (9–12). 1983, Fawcett paper $5.99 (0-449-20099-X). When Carol and her son relocate to Palm Springs, she confronts a terrible mystery. This is one of many recommended romantic mysteries by this author that include *Golden Unicorns, Seven Tears for Apollo,* and *Stone Bull.*

3263 Whitney, Phyllis A. *Feather on the Moon* (9–12). 1989, Fawcett paper $5.99 (0-449-21625-X). Jennifer Blake travels to Victoria, British Columbia, in search of her daughter, kidnapped 4 years before. (Rev: BL 2/1/88)

3264 Whitney, Phyllis A. *Rainbow in the Mist* (9–12). 1990, Fawcett paper $5.95 (0-449-21742-6). Christy has the psychic gift of locating dead bodies—a talent that leads her to a murder mystery. (Rev: BL 11/15/88)

3265 Whitney, Phyllis A. *Rainsong* (9–12). 1984, Fawcett paper $5.99 (0-449-20510-X). Some question whether rock singer Ricky Sands's death was a suicide.

3266 Whitney, Phyllis A. *The Singing Stones* (9–12). 1991, Fawcett paper $5.95 (0-449-21897-X). A therapist is brought in to help the disturbed daughter of her first husband in this tale of mystery and romance. (Rev: BL 12/15/89; SLJ 8/90; VOYA 6/90)

3267 Woods, Paula L., ed. *Spooks, Spies, and Private Eyes: Black Mystery, Crime, and Suspense Fiction* (9–12). 1995, Doubleday $22.95 (0-385-48082-2). Short mysteries by such African American writers as Richard Wright (*The Man Who Killed a Shadow*) and George Schuyler (*The Shoemaker Murder*). (Rev: BL 11/15/95)

3268 Woods, Stuart. *Orchid Beach* (10–12). 1998, HarperCollins $25.00 (0-06-019181-3). Holly Barker, newly appointed assistant police chief in Orchid Beach, Florida, discovers her boss and his friend have been murdered. (Rev: BL 9/1/98; SLJ 3/99)

3269 Yep, Laurence. *The Case of the Firecrackers* (5–8). 1999, HarperCollins $14.95 (0-06-024449-6). Lily and her aunt are on the trail of the murderer who killed the star of the television show in which they were extras. (Rev: BL 9/15/99; SLJ 9/99)

3270 Zindel, Paul. *The Undertaker's Gone Bananas* (7–9). 1984, Bantam paper $4.50 (0-553-27189-X). Bobby and Lauri are convinced that their new neighbor is a murderer.

Romances

3271 Adler, C. S. *The Lump in the Middle* (6–10). 1991, Avon paper $3.50 (0-380-71176-1). When Kelsey's father loses his job, Kelsey and her family move to Cape Cod but there she meets Gabe. (Rev: BR 1–2/90; VOYA 2/90)

3272 Alcott, Louisa May. *A Long Fatal Love Chase* (9–12). 1996, Dell paper $6.99 (0-440-22301-6). Written in 1866, this racy tale about Rosamond is melodramatic but intriguing, dramatizing the plight of women in oppressive times. (Rev: BL 9/15/95; SLJ 2/96)

3273 Allenbaugh, Kay, ed. *Chocolate for a Lover's Heart: Soul-Soothing Stories That Celebrate the Power of Love* (10–12). (Chocolate) 1999, Simon & Schuster paper $11.00 (0-684-86298-0). This collection of 49 stories tells how love conquers all and shines through in spite of misunderstandings, unfaithfulness, illness, or death. (Rev: SLJ 7/99)

3274 Applegate, Katherine. *July's Promise* (7–10). 1995, Archway paper $3.99 (0-671-51031-2). Sixteen-year-old Summer finds romance and adventure when she visits her hostile cousin on Crab Claw Key in Florida. Preceded by *June Dreams* and followed by *August Magic.* (Rev: VOYA 2/96)

3275 Applegate, Katherine. *Sharing Sam* (7–10). 1995, Bantam paper $3.99 (0-553-56660-1). A sacrificial love story where a girl's best friend is dying of a brain tumor and boyfriend Sam is shared. (Rev: BL 3/15/95; SLJ 2/95)

3276 Applegate, Katherine, et al. *See You in September* (7–9). 1995, Avon paper $3.99 (0-380-78088-7). Four chaste and charming short stories by 4 popular YA "romance" authors. (Rev: BL 1/1–15/96; SLJ 3/96)

3277 Bat-Ami, Miriam. *Two Suns in the Sky* (8–12). 1999, Front Street Cricket Books $15.95 (0-8126-2900-0). A docunovel set in upstate New York during 1944 about the love between a Catholic teenage girl and a Jewish Holocaust survivor from Yugoslavia who is living in a refugee camp. (Rev: BL 4/15/99; SLJ 7/99; VOYA 10/99)

3278 Bauer, Joan. *Thwonk* (7–10). 1996, Bantam paper $4.50 (0-440-21980-9). "Thwonk" is the sound of Cupid's bow when A. J.'s wish that hunky Peter become hers alone comes true. Unfortunately,

Peter's adoration is more than she bargained for. (Rev: BL 1/1/95; SLJ 1/95)

3279 Bedford, Martyn. *The Houdini Girl* (10–12). 1999, Pantheon $24.00 (0-375-40527-5). When the wife of professional magician Red Brandon dies after only 1 year of marriage, the young man travels across Europe to collect information about her past and the reasons for her death. (Rev: SLJ 7/99)

3280 Bennett, Cherie, and Jeff Gottesfeld. *Trash* (6–9). 1997, Berkley paper $3.99 (0-425-15851-9). Romance, intrigue, and action combine in this light novel about an 18-year-old girl who has been selected to be a summer intern at "Trash," a New York-based TV talk show. (Rev: SLJ 10/97)

3281 Bennett, Jay. *I Never Said I Love You* (9–12). 1984, Avon paper $2.50 (0-380-86900-4). A boy must choose between fulfilling his father's wishes and the girl he loves.

3282 Bernardo, Anilu. *Loves Me, Loves Me Not* (7–10). 1998, Arte Publico $16.95 (1-55885-258-1). A teen romance that involves Cuban American Maggie, a basketball player named Zach, newcomer Justin, and Maggie's friend, Susie. (Rev: BL 1/1–15/99)

3283 Bertrand, Diane Gonzales. *Lessons of the Game* (7–10). 1998, Arte Publico paper $9.95 (1-55885-245-X). Student teacher Kaylene Morales is attracted to the freshman football coach but wonders if romance and her school assignments will mix. (Rev: BL 1/1–15/99; VOYA 10/99)

3284 Binchy, Maeve. *The Glass Lake* (9–12). 1995, Delacorte $23.95 (0-385-31354-3). Helen is presumed to have drowned in an Irish lake, but she's fled to London with her lover. Years later, she tries to reestablish contact with her teenage daughter, Kit. (Rev: BL 1/1/95; SLJ 8/95)

3285 Blake, Michael. *Airman Mortensen* (9–12). 1991, Seven Wolves Publg. $20.00 (0-9627387-7-8). The poignant summer romance between an 18-year-old airman awaiting court martial and the base commander's daughter is described in this story of the loss of innocence. (Rev: BL 10/1/91; SLJ 11/91)

3286 Brooks, Martha. *Two Moons in August* (7–12). 1992, Little, Brown $15.95 (0-316-10979-7). A midsummer romance in the 1950s between a newcomer to a small Canadian community and a 16-year-old girl who is mourning her mother's death. (Rev: BL 11/15/91*; SLJ 3/92*)

3287 Cann, Kate. *Diving In* (7–9). 1997, Women's Press, Ltd. paper $7.95 (0-7043-4937-X). A British romantic novel about Collette's love for Art and her problem deciding if she should have sex with him. (Rev: SLJ 10/97)

3288 Carr, Philippa. *The Changeling* (9–12). 1990, Fawcett paper $4.95 (0-449-14697-9). A historical romance involving 2 babies being switched at birth. (Rev: BL 3/1/89)

3289 Cleary, Beverly. *Fifteen* (7–9). 1956, Morrow LB $15.93 (0-688-31285-3); Avon paper $4.99 (0-380-72804-4). A young adolescent discovers that having a boyfriend isn't the answer to all her social problems.

3290 Cleary, Beverly. *Jean and Johnny* (7–9). 1959, Morrow $15.95 (0-688-21740-0). Jean is shy and uncertain of herself around handsome Johnny.

3291 Cleary, Beverly. *The Luckiest Girl* (7–9). 1958, Morrow LB $16.93 (0-688-31741-3); Avon paper $4.99 (0-380-72806-0). New social opportunities arise when a young girl spends her senior year at a school in California.

3292 Crew, Linda. *Long Time Passing* (7–10). 1997, Delacorte $15.95 (0-385-32496-0). Set in a small Oregon town during the 1960s, this novel tells of the budding romance between high school sophomore Kathy Shay and the outspoken James Holderread. (Rev: BR 3–4/98; SLJ 10/97; VOYA 4/98)

3293 Daly, Maureen. *First a Dream* (7–10). 1990, Scholastic paper $12.95 (0-590-40846-1). The love that Retta and Dallas feel for each other is tested during a summer when they are separated in this sequel to *Acts of Love* (1986). (Rev: BL 4/1/90; SLJ 4/90; VOYA 4/90)

3294 Daly, Maureen. *Seventeenth Summer* (6–8). 1981, Harmony LB $19.95 (0-89967-029-6); Archway paper $4.50 (0-671-61931-4). Angie experiences an idyllic summer after she meets Jack in this classic 1942 novel.

3295 Danziger, Paula. *Thames Doesn't Rhyme with James* (7–10). 1994, Putnam $15.95 (0-399-22526-9). Kendra and her family take a joint vacation to London with the Lees and their son Frank, Kendra's boyfriend. (Rev: BL 12/1/94; SLJ 1/95; VOYA 4/95)

3296 Davis, Leila. *Lover Boy* (7–12). 1989, Avon paper $2.95 (0-380-75722-2). Ryan finds that his racy reputation is keeping him from the girl he really loves. (Rev: SLJ 10/89; VOYA 8/89)

3297 Delinsky, Barbara. *Three Wishes* (10–12). 1997, Simon & Schuster $23.00 (0-684-84507-5). A near-fatal accident brings Bree and Tom together in a love that transcends time and death. (Rev: SLJ 1/98)

3298 Dokey, Cameron. *Hindenburg, 1937* (7–10). 1999, Archway paper $4.99 (0-671-03601-7). On board the *Hindenburg* on its last voyage to America in 1937, Anna, a German girl fleeing from her Nazi officer brother who is pressuring her to accept an arranged marriage, is torn between 2 suitors who suspect each other of being a spy. (Rev: VOYA 10/99)

3299 DuJardin, Rosamond. *Boy Trouble* (7–9). 1988, HarperCollins LB $12.89 (0-397-32263-1). A harmless romance first published in the 1960s and now back in print. (Rev: SLJ 2/88)

3300 Ellis, Jana. *Better Than the Truth* (7–10). 1989, Troll paper $2.50 (0-8167-1362-6). Lori's lab partner Frank begins spreading vicious rumors about her. Also use *Junior Weekend* and *Never Stop Smiling* (both 1988). (Rev: SLJ 4/89)

3301 Ephron, Amy. *A Cup of Tea* (10–12). 1997, Morrow $20.00 (0-688-14997-9). When Rosemary Fell invited a penniless young woman into her house, she did not anticipate that her fiancé would fall in love with her. (Rev: BL 8/97; SLJ 11/97)

3302 Fiedler, Lisa. *Lucky Me* (6–10). 1998, Clarion $15.00 (0-395-89131-0). In this sequel to *Curtis Piperfield's Biggest Fan,* Cecily Caruthers wants to be more adventurous sexually and this leads to a series of humorous situations. (Rev: BL 11/15/98; BR 5–6/99; SLJ 3/99; VOYA 6/99)

3303 Filichia, Peter. *Not Just Another Pretty Face* (7–10). 1988, Avon paper $2.50 (0-380-75244-1). A high school story where the course of true love does not run smoothly for Bill Richards. (Rev: BL 3/1/88; SLJ 5/88)

3304 Frank, Lucy. *Will You Be My Brussels Sprout?* (7–10). 1996, Holiday House $15.95 (0-8234-1220-2). In this continuation of *I Am an Artichoke,* Emily, now 16, studies the cello at a New York music conservatory and falls in love for the first time. (Rev: BL 4/15/96; SLJ 4/96; VOYA 10/96)

3305 Garwood, Julie. *A Girl Named Summer* (7–9). 1998, Pocket Books paper $4.50 (0-671-02342-X). To impress her new boyfriend, Summer tells lies that eventually catch up with her. (Rev: BL 1/1–15/99; SLJ 4/99)

3306 Geras, Adèle. *Pictures of the Night* (7–12). 1993, Harcourt $16.95 (0-15-261588-1). A modern version of *Snow White,* with the heroine an 18-year-old singer in London and Paris. (Rev: BL 3/1/93; SLJ 6/93)

3307 Geras, Adèle. *The Tower Room* (7–12). 1992, Harcourt $15.95 (0-15-289627-9). The fairy tale *Rapunzel* is updated and set in an English girls' boarding school in the 1960s. (Rev: BL 2/15/92; SLJ 5/92)

3308 Gerber, Merrill Joan. *Handsome as Anything* (8–12). 1990, Scholastic $13.95 (0-590-43019-X). Rachel is attracted to 3 different boys and in making her choice learns a lot about herself. (Rev: BL 9/15/90; SLJ 12/90)

3309 Gregory, Diana. *Two's a Crowd* (7–10). 1985, Bantam paper $3.50 (0-553-24992-4). Peggy finds that her business rival in a catering business is a handsome young man. (Rev: BL 10/15/85; SLJ 9/85)

3310 Hahn, Mary D. *The Wind Blows Backward* (8–12). 1993, Clarion $13.95 (0-395-62975-6); 1994, Avon paper $4.50 (0-380-77530-1). Spencer's downward emotional spiral and Lauren's deep commitment evoke a fantasy love gone awry. (Rev: BL 5/1/93; SLJ 5/93)

3311 Hart, Bruce, and Carole Hart. *Waiting Games* (7–10). 1981, Avon paper $3.50 (0-380-79012-2). Jessie and Michael are in love and must make difficult decisions about sex.

3312 Hart, Bruce, and Carole Hart. *Sooner or Later* (8–12). 1978, Avon paper $2.95 (0-380-42978-0). In order to fool her 17-year-old boyfriend into thinking she is older than 13, Jessie begins an intricate pattern of lies.

3313 Haynes, Betsy. *The Great Dad Disaster* (6–8). 1994, Bantam paper $3.50 (0-553-48-169-X). When two girlfriends begin to date boys, one finds her father too strict and the other, too lenient. (Rev: BL 6/1–15/94)

3314 Hilton, James. *Random Harvest* (10–12). 1982, Buccaneer LB $29.95 (0-89966-414-8). A highly romantic novel set in World War I days about an amnesia victim who has forgotten his first true love.

3315 Hite, Sid. *Cecil in Space* (7–10). 1999, Holt $15.95 (0-8050-5055-8). At 17, Cecil begins to takes life seriously when he falls in love with the richest, sexiest girl in town. (Rev: BL 4/15/99; SLJ 5/99; VOYA 6/99)

3316 Hoh, Diane. *Titanic, the Long Night* (7–12). 1998, Scholastic paper $4.99 (0-590-33123-X). In this novel set on the ill-fated *Titanic* in 1912, wealthy first-class passenger Elizabeth Farr meets Max Whittaker, a wealthy but rebellious artist, while in a parallel plot in third class, Irish rogue Paddy Kelleher and talented singer Katie Hanrahan fall in love. (Rev: BR 1–2/99; VOYA 2/99)

3317 Holt, Victoria. *Daughter of Deceit* (9–12). 1992, Fawcett paper $5.99 (0-449-22058-3). The daughter of a recently deceased London actress must call off her wedding when it is revealed that her fiancé is probably her half-brother. (Rev: BL 9/1/91; SLJ 4/92)

3318 Holt, Victoria. *Secret for a Nightingale* (10–12). 1987, Fawcett paper $3.50 (0-449-21296-3). In this Gothic romance set in the 19th century, a young woman seeks revenge for the death of her son. (Rev: BL 8/86)

3319 Holt, Victoria. *The Silk Vendetta* (9–12). 1989, Fawcett paper $5.99 (0-449-21548-2). A suspenseful romance that uses the historic trade of silk weaving as its subject. (Rev: BL 8/87)

3320 Jones, Jill. *Emily's Secret* (10–12). 1995, St. Martin's paper $4.99 (0-312-95576-6). This historical novel combines a modern-day romance with the life of Emily Brontë as seen through the eyes of one of her descendants. (Rev: BL 8/95; SLJ 4/96)

3321 Kaplow, Robert. *Alessandra in Love* (8–10). 1989, HarperCollins LB $12.89 (0-397-32282-8). Alessandra's boyfriend turns out to be a self-centered disappointment. (Rev: BL 4/15/89; SLJ 4/89; VOYA 8/89)

3322 Kay, Susan. *Phantom* (9–12). 1992, Dell paper $6.99 (0-440-21169-7). Fans of *Phantom of the Opera* will recognize Erik, whose character is well drawn in his dual roles of adored hero and hated villain. (Rev: BL 2/15/91; SLJ 9/91)

3323 King, Tabitha. *One on One* (9–12). 1994, NAL paper $5.99 (0-451-17981-1). A coming-of-age story featuring the fierce, unexpected attraction between 2 mismatched high school basketball stars: Deannie, female, who's a pierced, tattooed skinhead, and Sam, a virgin who's an Adonis with a ponytail. (Rev: BL 2/1/93; SLJ 7/93)

3324 Kirby, Susan. *Blue Moon* (7–9). 1997, Berkley paper $4.50 (0-425-15414-9). Dee hopes that her friendship with Michael will turn to romance, but the young man is preoccupied with caring for his grandfather, who has Alzheimer's disease. (Rev: SLJ 1/98)

3325 Klass, David. *Screen Test* (7–9). 1997, Scholastic $16.95 (0-590-48592-X). Sixteen-year-old Liz Weaton is whisked off to Hollywood, where she almost falls in love with her costar. (Rev: BL 12/1/97; BR 11–12/97; SLJ 10/97)

3326 Knudson, R. R. *Just Another Love Story* (7–10). 1983, Avon paper $2.50 (0-380-65532-2). Dusty takes up body building to help forget the girlfriend who has spurned him.

3327 Lachtman, Ofelia Dumas. *The Girl from Playa Bianca* (7–12). 1995, Arte Publico $14.95 (1-55885-148-8); paper $9.95 (1-55885-149-6). A gothic romance in which a Mexican teenager and her young brother travel to Los Angeles in search of their father. (Rev: BL 11/15/95; SLJ 10/95; VOYA 12/95)

3328 L'Engle, Madeleine. *And Both Were Young* (9–12). 1983, Dell paper $4.99 (0-440-90229-0). Flip feels like a misfit at her Swiss school until she meets Paul.

3329 L'Engle, Madeleine. *Camilla* (10–12). 1982, Dell paper $4.50 (0-440-91171-0). A sensitive young girl experiences first love and the breakup of her family.

3330 McCants, William D. *Anything Can Happen in High School (and It Usually Does)* (6–8). 1993, Harcourt $10.95 (0-15-276604-9); paper $3.95 (0-15-276605-7). In his attempts to win back his summer love, Janet, by starting a school club, T. J. Burant realizes her shallowness isn't for him. (Rev: BL 10/1/93; SLJ 10/93; VOYA 12/93)

3331 McDaniel, Lurlene. *Angels Watching Over Me* (8–10). 1996, Bantam paper $4.99 (0-553-56724-1). Romance, mystery, and personal problems mingle in this novel about a girl who has bone cancer, the boy she is attracted to in the hospital, and a mysterious nurse. (Rev: BR 11–12/96; SLJ 3/97)

3332 McDaniel, Lurlene. *Don't Die, My Love* (7–12). 1995, Bantam paper $4.99 (0-553-56715-2). A young couple, Julie and Luke, "engaged" since sixth grade, discover that Luke has Hodgkin's lymphoma. (Rev: BL 9/15/95; SLJ 10/95; VOYA 12/95)

3333 McFann, Jane. *Maybe by Then I'll Understand* (7–9). 1987, Avon paper $2.50 (0-380-75221-2). Cath and Tony become a pair but Tony demands more attention and loyalty than she can give. (Rev: BL 11/15/87; SLJ 1/88; VOYA 12/87)

3334 Magorian, Michelle. *Not a Swan* (9–12). 1992, HarperCollins LB $17.89 (0-06-024215-9). During World War II, Rose, 17, and her 2 older sisters are evacuated to the English countryside, where Rose falls in love with a veteran who supports her efforts to become a writer. (Rev: BL 8/92)

3335 Martin, Ann M. *Just a Summer Romance* (6–8). 1987, Holiday House $13.95 (0-8234-0649-0). While spending a summer on Fire Island, 14-year-old Melanie becomes attracted to Justin. (Rev: BL 4/1/87; SLJ 6/87; VOYA 10/87)

3336 Matthews, Phoebe. *The Boy on the Cover* (6–8). 1988, Avon paper $2.75 (0-380-75407-X). Cyndi falls in love with a boy whose picture is on the cover of a book she owns. (Rev: VOYA 2/89)

3337 Mauser, Pat Rhoads. *Love Is for the Dogs* (7–10). 1989, Avon paper $2.50 (0-380-75723-0). Janna realizes that Brian, the boy next door, can be very desirable. (Rev: BL 4/15/89; SLJ 4/89)

3338 Mekler, Eva. *Sunrise Shows Late* (10–12). 1997, Bridge Works Pub. $21.95 (1-882593-17-0). Manya, living in a displaced-persons camp in Germany after World War II, is attracted to 2 very different men and must make a choice. (Rev: BL 3/15/97; SLJ 7/97)

3339 Miller, Sandy. *Smart Girl* (7–10). 1982, NAL paper $2.25 (0-451-11887-1). Sandy finds that some of the boys resent that she is so intelligent.

3340 Mines, Jeanette. *Risking It* (7–9). 1988, Avon paper $2.75 (0-380-75401-0). Jeannie is attracted to Trent Justin who has joined her senior class. (Rev: BL 9/1/88; SLJ 1/89; VOYA 6/88)

3341 Napoli, Donna Jo. *Love in Venice* (7–9). 1998, Delacorte $15.95 (0-385-32531-2). Two young adults, one an American and the other an Italian, fall in love but clash about their beliefs concerning the future of Venice, where they both live. (Rev: BL 5/1/98; SLJ 6/98; VOYA 10/98)

3342 Pascal, Francine. *Can't Stay Away* (7–10). (Sweet Valley High Senior Year) 1999, Bantam paper $4.50 (0-553-49234-9). A better-than-average Sweet Valley High novel about new friendships and rivalries that result when the students of El Carro High have to finish the year at Sweet Valley because of an earthquake. (Rev: SLJ 2/99)

3343 Pascal, Francine, and Jamie Suzanne. *Get Real* (6–8). (Sweet Valley Jr. High) 1999, Bantam paper $4.50 (0-553-48603-9). A quick read about twins Jessica and Elizabeth Wakefield and the adjustments they must make when their middle school becomes a junior high, and they, as eighth graders, are no longer top dogs. (Rev: SLJ 2/99)

3344 Peterson, Tracie. *Controlling Interests* (10–12). 1998, Bethany House paper $8.99 (0-7642-2064-0). A love story that involves a modern, adult orphan, Denali Deveraux, who, though brilliant and successful, longs for the security and comfort of a family. (Rev: SLJ 2/99)

3345 Plain, Belva. *Eden Burning* (10–12). 1987, Dell paper $7.50 (0-440-12135-3). This is one of several recommended family sagas by the author of the popular *Evergreen* (1982) and *Random Winds*.

3346 Plummer, Louise. *The Unlikely Romance of Kate Bjorkman* (7–10). 1997, Bantam paper $4.50 (0-440-22704-6). A brainy teen foils a beautiful, evil temptress and gets the man of her dreams. (Rev: SLJ 10/95; VOYA 12/95)

3347 Powell, Randy. *Is Kissing a Girl Who Smokes Like Licking an Ashtray?* (7–12). 1992, Farrar paper $5.95 (0-374-43627-4). High school senior Biff has never had a girlfriend until he meets the wild, beautiful loner Heidi, who is as troubled and mouthy as he is shy and fumbling. (Rev: BL 6/1/92*; SLJ 6/92)

3348 Randle, Kristen D. *Breaking Rank* (7–12). 1999, Morrow $16.00 (0-688-16243-6). Told from alternating viewpoints, this is the story of 17-year-old Casey and her experiences after she has agreed to tutor the enigmatic rebel, Thomas, who belongs to a group of outsiders known as the Clan. (Rev: BL 5/1/99; SLJ 5/99; VOYA 12/99)

3349 Rees, Elizabeth M. *Moving as One* (6–10). (Heart Beats) 1998, Aladdin paper $3.99 (0-689-81948-X). When teenage ballerina Sophy's dance school merges with a school of Latin dance run by attractive Carlos Vargas, everyone wonders if ballet and salsa will mix. (Rev: BL 8/98; SLJ 11/98)

3350 Roberts, Nora. *Born in Ice* (10–12). 1995, Jove paper $7.50 (0-515-11675-0). A readable romance about an Irish innkeeper and an American mystery writer. (Rev: SLJ 3/96)

3351 Rodowsky, Colby. *Lucy Peale* (8–12). 1992, Farrar $15.00 (0-374-36381-1); 1994, paper $3.95 (0-374-44659-8). Lucy, a rape victim, is pregnant,

alone, and terrified when she meets Jake, and their friendship slowly evolves into love. (Rev: BL 7/92; SLJ 7/92)

3352 Rosenthal, Lucy, ed. *Great American Love Stories* (9–12). 1988, Little, Brown $24.95 (0-316-75734-9). A collection of 28 stories and short novels that show the varied and changing faces of love. (Rev: BL 7/88; BR 1–2/89)

3353 Rostkowski, Margaret I. *Moon Dancer* (7–10). 1995, Harcourt $11.00 (0-15-276638-3); paper $5.00 (0-15-200194-8). A 15-year-old accompanies others to view ancient canyon rock art of Native American women and feels connections to the archetypal images. (Rev: BL 5/1/95; SLJ 9/95)

3354 Ryan, Mary C. *Frankie's Run* (6–8). 1987, Little, Brown $12.95 (0-316-76370-5). In this teen novel, Mary Frances falls for the new boy in town but also organizes a run to aid her local library. (Rev: BL 8/87; BR 9–10/87; SLJ 5/87)

3355 Sachs, Marilyn. *Thunderbird* (7–10). Illus. 1985, Dutton $10.95 (0-525-44163-8). Two high school seniors meet and fall in love in the public library. (Rev: BL 4/15/85; SLJ 10/85)

3356 Sheldon, Dyan. *The Boy of My Dreams* (6–10). 1997, Candlewick $16.99 (0-7636-0004-0). Mike, short for Michelle, falls head over heels in love with sophisticated Bill and begins to neglect her true friends. (Rev: BL 11/1/97; BR 1–2/98; SLJ 10/97; VOYA 2/98)

3357 Sierra, Patricia. *One-Way Romance* (7–10). 1986, Avon paper $2.50 (0-380-75107-0). A talented girl who does well with carpentry and track seems to be losing out with her boyfriend. (Rev: BL 8/86; SLJ 11/86; VOYA 12/86)

3358 Sonnenmark, Laura. *The Lie* (6–10). 1992, Scholastic $13.95 (0-590-44740-8). A teenage girl goes to great lengths to get the attention of a handsome classmate. (Rev: BL 4/15/92; SLJ 4/92)

3359 Stacey, Cherylyn. *Gone to Maui* (7–9). 1996, Roussan paper $6.95 (1-896184-14-6). In this novel, teenage Becky accompanies her mother, who is leading a tour for seniors in Maui, and there finds romance. (Rev: VOYA 4/97)

3360 Stanek, Lou W. *Katy Did* (8–12). 1992, Avon paper $2.99 (0-380-76170-X). A shy country girl and popular city boy fall in love, with tragic consequences. (Rev: BL 3/15/92)

3361 Steel, Danielle. *The Promise* (10–12). 1978, Dell paper $6.99 (0-440-17079-6). A wealthy architect and a poor artist decide to marry in this romance. Other recommended titles by the author are: *Once in a Lifetime, Now and Forever, Palomino, The Ring*, and *Season of Passion*.

3362 Strasser, Todd. *How I Spent My Last Night on Earth* (7–10). 1998, Simon & Schuster paper $16.00 (0-689-81113-6). In this Time Zone High story, rumors spread that a giant asteroid is heading for Earth, and "Legs" Hanover finds romance with a handsome surfer classmate after being jilted by her boyfriend. (Rev: BL 11/1/98; BR 5–6/99; SLJ 11/98; VOYA 8/99)

3363 Sunshine, Tina. *An X-Rated Romance* (7–9). 1982, Avon paper $2.50 (0-380-79905-7). Two 13-year-old girls have a crush on their English teacher. A reissue.

3364 Thesman, Jean. *Jamie* (6–9). 1998, Avon paper $3.99 (0-380-78681-8). Jamie relies on help from her cousins, friends, and parents to end an unhealthy relationship with her boyfriend, Rick. First in a series about 3 cousins, Jamie, Meredith, and Teresa, who live in the Seattle area. (Rev: SLJ 9/98)

3365 Thesman, Jean. *Who Said Life Is Fair?* (7–9). 1987, Avon paper $3.50 (0-380-75088-0). Teddy is trying to cope with work on the school newspaper while keeping her love life in order. (Rev: BL 5/87; VOYA 8/87)

3366 Thomas, Abigail. *An Actual Life* (10–12). 1996, Algonquin $28.95 (1-56512-133-3). This novel tells of a young couple who married because of a pregnancy and of their eventual attractions to other possible partners. (Rev: BL 4/1/96; SLJ 3/97)

3367 Thompson, Julian. *Shepherd* (9–12). 1993, Holt $15.95 (0-8050-2106-X). When popular Mary Sutherland makes advances to Shep Catlett, he declares himself in love and tries to save her from her drinking. (Rev: BL 12/15/93; SLJ 11/93; VOYA 2/94)

3368 Trembath, Don. *A Beautiful Place on Yonge Street* (8–10). 1999, Orca paper $6.95 (1-55143-121-1). Budding writer Harper Winslow falls in love with Sunny Taylor when he attends a summer writing camp, and experiences all the angst that goes with it. (Rev: BL 3/1/99; SLJ 7/99; VOYA 6/99)

3369 Veryan, Patricia. *Lanterns* (10–12). 1996, St. Martin's $23.95 (0-312-14640-X). This historical romance set in Sussex, England, in 1818, tells of Marietta Warrington's struggles to keep the family together after her father's gambling debts drive them into poverty, and involves kidnapping, ancient treasure, sinister dealings, and true love. (Rev: BL 10/15/96; SLJ 3/97)

3370 Victor, Cynthia. *The Secret* (10–12). 1997, Dutton $23.95 (0-525-94034-0). When her husband suddenly leaves her and her 3 children, Miranda takes over his secret identity as a writer of trashy best-sellers. (Rev: BL 6/1–15/97; SLJ 3/98)

3371 Voigt, Cynthia. *Glass Mountain* (9–12). 1991, Harcourt $19.95 (0-15-135825-7). A wealthy New

Yorker posing as a butler falls in love with his employer's fiancée. (Rev: BL 11/1/91; SLJ 4/92)

3372 Watson, Jude. *Audacious: Ivy's Story* (7–9). (Brides of Wildcat County) 1995, Simon & Schuster paper $3.95 (0-689-80328-1). Leaving her Maine community because of family problems, Ivy begins teaching school in a California mining community but is tracked down by her former fiancé, who reveals a secret she doesn't want anyone to know. (Rev: SLJ 3/96)

3373 Watson, Jude. *Dangerous: Savannah's Story* (7–10). (Brides of Wildcat County) 1995, Simon & Schuster paper $3.95 (0-689-80326-5). Savannah leaves the East and heads to a gold-mining town in California, where she finds romance in the arms of the son of gold mine owner. (Rev: SLJ 2/96)

3374 Watson, Jude. *Scandalous: Eden's Story* (7–10). (Brides of Wildcat County) 1995, Simon & Schuster paper $3.95 (0-689-80327-3). Eden, who has a criminal background, arrives in Last Chance, a gold mining town in California, where her reputation as a card shark threatens her love for rich Josiah Bullock. (Rev: SLJ 2/96; VOYA 4/96)

3375 Weyn, Suzanne. *The Makeover Summer* (6–8). 1988, Avon paper $2.95 (0-380-75521-1). An exchange student who needs help joins three girls of the Makeover Club. (Rev: BL 2/15/89)

3376 Williams, Carol L. *My Angelica* (5–9). 1999, Delacorte $15.95 (0-385-32622-X). The relationship between Sage and her friend, George, deepens into a romance in spite of Sage's problems as an aspiring writer of romance novels. (Rev: BL 12/15/98; BR 9–10/99; SLJ 1/99; VOYA 8/99)

3377 Winfrey, Elizabeth. *More Than a Friend* (9–12). 1995, Bantam paper $4.50 (0-553-56666-0). Cain and Delia, two high school seniors who have been best friends for years, slowly realize that they love one another. (Rev: VOYA 6/96)

3378 Winfrey, Elizabeth. *My So-called Boyfriend* (6–10). (Love Stories) 1996, Bantam paper $3.99 (0-553-56668-7). After a fall that causes snobbish Tashi Pendleton to loose her memory, a boy she once embarrassed concocts a scheme to get even in this light romance. (Rev: SLJ 8/96)

3379 Wittlinger, Ellen. *Lombardo's Law* (7–10). 1993, Houghton $14.95 (0-395-65969-8); 1995, Morrow paper $4.95 (0-688-05294-0). The conventions of romance are thrown aside when sophomore Justine and eighth-grader Mike find themselves attracted to each other, despite obstacles. (Rev: BL 9/15/93; VOYA 12/93)

3380 Wittlinger, Ellen. *Noticing Paradise* (6–10). 1995, Houghton $14.95 (0-395-71646-2). Told in alternate first-person narratives, a story about 16-year-olds who fall in love while on an excursion to the Galapagos Islands. Includes much about endangered species. (Rev: BL 11/1/95; SLJ 10/95; VOYA 2/96)

3381 Woodson, Jacqueline. *If You Come Softly* (7–10). 1998, Putnam $15.99 (0-399-23112-9). The story of the love between a black boy and a white girl, their families, and the prejudice they encounter. (Rev: BL 10/1/98; SLJ 12/98; VOYA 12/98)

3382 Young, Karen R. *The Beetle & Me: A Love Story* (6–9). 1999, Morrow $15.00 (0-688-15922-2). While trying to sort out her love interests, 15-year-old Daisy Pandolfi tries to restore a 1957 purple Volkswagen Beetle to running order. (Rev: BL 4/15/99; SLJ 5/99; VOYA 10/99)

3383 Zalben, Jane Breskin. *Here's Looking at You, Kid* (9–12). 1984, Dell paper $2.50 (0-440-93573-3). A high school senior finds he is attracted to 2 girls.

Science Fiction

3384 Adams, Douglas. *The Hitchhiker's Guide to the Galaxy* (9–12). 1989, Crown $15.00 (0-517-54209-9); Pocket Books paper $5.99 (0-671-74606-5). An episodic science fiction novel that is made up of equal parts of adventure and humor. Others in the series are: *The Restaurant at the End of the Universe*, *Life, the Universe, and Everything*, and *So Long, Thanks for the Fish*. (Rev: BL 6/87)

3385 Adams, Douglas. *The Long Dark Tea-Time of the Soul* (9–12). 1988, Demco $12.09 (0-606-01764-X); Pocket Books paper $6.99 (0-671-74251-5). Dirk Gently, private detective and slob first introduced in *Dirk Gently's Holistic Detective Agency* returns in another hilarious series of misadventures. (Rev: BL 1/15/89)

3386 Adams, Douglas. *Mostly Harmless* (9–12). (Hitchhiker's Trilogy) 1992, Crown $20.00 (0-517-57740-2). The intergalactic adventures of Arthur Dent and Ford Prefect continue as the heroes are whipped between parallel universes that eventually collide. (Rev: BL 9/15/92)

3387 Adler, Bill, ed. *Time Machines* (9–12). 1997, Carroll & Graf $24.00 (0-7867-0493-4). A fine collection of 22 time travel stories by such authors as Poe, Kipling, Asimov, Bradbury, and Serling. (Rev: SLJ 6/98)

3388 Allen, Roger MacBride. *Isaac Asimov's Inferno* (9–12). 1994, Berkley paper $12.00 (0-441-00023-1). In this sequel to *Caliban* (o.p.), the Three Laws of Robotics are further explored when a murder takes place on a planet of Earth Settlers and Spacers. (Rev: BL 9/15/94; VOYA 4/95)

3389 Anderson, Kevin J., ed. *War of the Worlds: Global Dispatches* (7–12). 1996, Bantam $22.95 (0-553-10352-9). This tribute to H. G. Wells's *War of the Worlds* features stories of Martian invasions that are either take-offs on the writing styles of such famous authors as Conrad, London, Verne, and Kipling, or the experiences of famous individuals, such as Teddy Roosevelt and Pablo Picasso, during a Martian invasion. (Rev: VOYA 10/96)

3390 Anderson, Poul. *Cold Victory* (10–12). 1985, Tor paper $2.95 (0-8125-3057-8). Six stories about the Psychotechnic League. Some other books by this master are: *Conflict*, *Fire Time*, and *A Midsummer Tempest*.

3391 Anderson, Poul. *The Long Night* (10–12). 1999, Tor paper $3.95 (0-8125-1396-7). This is a collection of 5 novellas.

3392 Anthony, Piers. *For Love of Evil* (10–12). 1990, Avon paper $6.99 (0-380-75285-9). The penultimate volume (number 6) of the Incarnations of Immortality series. In this episode Satan is the protagonist. (Rev: BL 9/1/88)

3393 Anthony, Piers. *Man from Mundania* (9–12). 1989, Avon paper $5.99 (0-380-75289-1). A Xanth novel that completes the trilogy begun with *Vale of the Vole* and continued in *Heaven Cent*. (Rev: BL 9/89; VOYA 12/89)

3394 Anthony, Piers. *Race Against Time* (7–12). 1986, Tor paper $3.50 (0-8125-3101-9). John Smith and an African girl named Ala are different from others because they are racially pure.

3395 Anthony, Piers. *Split Infinity* (10–12). 1987, Ballantine paper $6.99 (0-345-35491-5). In this first part of the Apprentice Adept series, someone is trying to kill Stile on the planet Proton. Other titles are: *Blue Adept* and *Juxtaposition*.

3396 Anthony, Piers. *Total Recall* (9–12). 1990, Avon paper $4.50 (0-380-70874-4). A novelization of the movie about a secret agent on Mars searching for his past. Also use *But What of Earth?* (Tor, 1989). (Rev: BL 8/89)

3397 Applegate, K. A. *Animorphs #1: The Invasion* (5–8). 1996, Scholastic paper $4.99 (0-590-62977-8). Jake, an average suburban kid, is confronted one night by a creature from space who teaches him how to morph into the forms of other creatures. (Rev: VOYA 12/96)

3398 Archer, Chris. *Alien Blood* (6–8). (Mindwarp) 1997, Pocket Books paper $3.99 (0-671-01483-8). Using her supersonic hearing and sight, Ashley Rose is able to foil an alien killer. (Rev: SLJ 3/98)

3399 Archer, Chris. *Alien Terror* (6–8). (Mindwarp) 1997, Pocket Books paper $3.99 (0-671-01482-X). On his 13th birthday, Ethan finds he possesses superhuman strength and unearthly fighting skills. (Rev: SLJ 3/98)

3400 Asimov, Isaac. *The Best Science Fiction of Isaac Asimov* (9–12). 1988, NAL paper $4.95 (0-451-15196-8). A collection of 28 of the stories the author thinks are his best. (Rev: BL 8/86)

3401 Asimov, Isaac. *Caves of Steel* (10–12). 1991, Bantam paper $6.99 (0-553-29340-0). One of this prolific author's classics of science fiction. Also use: *Pebble in the Sky* (Robert Bentley, 1982) and *Naked Sun* (1991).

3402 Asimov, Isaac. *Forward the Foundation* (9–12). 1993, 1994, Bantam paper $6.99 (0-553-56507-9). The conclusion to Asimov's efforts to bind his various universes together into one vast future history. Part of the Foundation series. (Rev: BL 2/15/93; SLJ 3/94)

3403 Asimov, Isaac. *I, Robot* (10–12). 1991, Bantam paper $6.99 (0-553-29438-5). A collection about Dr. Susan Calvin and the product she produces at her factory, robots.

3404 Asimov, Isaac. *Nemesis* (9–12). 1990, Bantam paper $6.99 (0-553-28628-5). A space colony arrives at a planet only to find it is slated for destruction. (Rev: BL 8/89)

3405 Asimov, Isaac. *Prelude to Foundation* (10–12). 1989, Bantam paper $6.99 (0-553-27839-8). This novel links the Empire and Foundation series and supplies a chronology of novels in these 2 series as a guide to readers. (Rev: BL 4/1/88; VOYA 10/88)

3406 Asimov, Isaac. *Robots and Empire* (9–12). 1985, Ballantine paper $5.99 (0-345-32894-9). The heroine of the earlier *Robots at Dawn* travels through space with a friend and 2 robots to defeat a plot against Earth. (Rev: BL 8/85)

3407 Asimov, Isaac, and Roger MacBride Allen. *Utopia* (9–12). (Utopia) 1993, Berkley paper $9.95 (0-441-09079-6). A sheriff trails a rogue robot that has escaped from a lab. (Rev: BL 3/1/93; VOYA 8/93)

3408 Asimov, Isaac, et al., eds. *Computer Crimes and Capers* (9–12). 1983, Academy Chicago paper $10.00 (0-89733-087-0). A lively anthology of stories featuring computers as masters, servants, or—sometimes—arch criminals.

3409 Asimov, Isaac, et al., eds. *Young Extraterrestrials* (7–9). 1984, HarperCollins paper $7.95 (0-06-020167-3). Eleven stories by well-known authors about youngsters who are aliens from space.

3410 Asimov, Janet. *Norby and the Terrified Taxi* (4–8). 1997, Walker $23.95 (0-8027-8642-1). Norby, the bungling robot, is kidnapped, and while trying to find him, Jeff and his friends stumble on a plot by Garc the Great to take over the Federation. This is

one of a large series of Norby books suitable for middle school readers. (Rev: BL 1/1–15/98; SLJ 12/97)

3411 Asimov, Janet, and Isaac Asimov. *Norby and the Invaders* (5–8). 1985, Walker LB $10.85 (0-8027-6607-2). Jeff and his unusual robot Norby travel to a planet to help one of Norby's ancestors. Part of a series that includes *Norby's Other Secret*. (Rev: BL 3/1/86)

3412 Asimov, Janet, and Isaac Asimov. *Norby and Yobo's Great Adventure* (5–8). 1989, Walker LB $13.85 (0-8027-6894-6). Norby the robot time travels to help Admiral Yobo of Mars to trace his family roots. Part of a series that also includes *Norby Down to Earth*. (Rev: BL 10/15/89)

3413 Askounis, Christina. *The Dream of the Stone* (7–12). 1993, Farrar $17.00 (0-374-31877-8). Fifteen-year-old Sarah, an orphan, flees evil agents from CIPHER into an alternative universe. (Rev: BL 6/1–15/93; SLJ 6/93; VOYA 8/93)

3414 Asprin, Robert. *Phule's Company* (10–12). 1990, Berkley paper $8.99 (0-441-66251-X). The beginning of a new series about the adventures of Captain Willard Phule, an officer in the Space Legion. (Rev: BL 6/15/90)

3415 Babbitt, Lucy Cullyford. *Children of the Maker* (8–10). 1988, Farrar $15.00 (0-374-31245-1). The 2 young rulers of Melde find that theirs is not the only colony on their planet in this sequel to *The Oval Amulet*. (Rev: BL 2/1/89; BR 3–4/89; SLJ 2/89; VOYA 4/89)

3416 Ball, Margaret. *Lost in Translation* (8–12). 1995, Baen $5.99 (0-671-87638-0). American teenager Allie flies to France to attend a university but lands in a fantasy world filled with spells of every kind, where people communicate through voice-bubbles and a group of terrifying monsters control an important subterranean substance called landvirtue. (Rev: VOYA 4/96)

3417 Bawden, Nina. *Off the Road* (5–9). 1998, Clarion $16.00 (0-395-91321-7). In this science fiction novel set in a time when the elderly are exterminated, 11-year-old Tom follows his grandfather to the "savage jungle" Outside the Wall where the old man hopes to escape his fate and discovers a much different kind of society. (Rev: BL 9/15/98; BR 5–6/99; SLJ 11/98)

3418 Bear, Greg. *Moving Mars* (9–12). 1994, Tor paper $6.99 (0-8125-2480-2). A physicist on Mars links up with an artificial intelligence and a revolutionary woman determined to give her world a future. (Rev: BL 9/15/93; VOYA 4/94)

3419 Bear, Greg, ed. *New Legends* (10–12). 1995, Tor $22.95 (0-312-85930-9). A collection of original hard science fiction stories by writers that include

Poul Anderson, Gregory Benford, Ursula K. Le Guin, and Robert Silverberg. (Rev: VOYA 2/96)

3420 Belden, Wilanne Schneider. *Mind-Find* (6–9). 1988, Harcourt $14.95 (0-15-254270-1). A 13-year-old girl adjusts with difficulty to her amazing powers of ESP. (Rev: BL 2/15/88; SLJ 8/88)

3421 Blisson, Terry. *Pirates of the Universe* (10–12). 1996, Tor $22.95 (0-312-85412-9). Science fiction and a page-turning adventure yarn combine in this story of Gunter Glenn and his search for justice in a world gone mad. (Rev: BL 4/15/96; SLJ 10/96; VOYA 8/96)

3422 Boulle, Pierre. *Planet of the Apes* (7–12). 1964, NAL paper $2.50 (0-451-14324-8). Stranded on the planet Soror, Ulysse Merou discovers a civilization ruled by apes.

3423 Bova, Ben. *Orion Among the Stars* (9–12). (Orion the Hunter) 1995, Tor $22.95 (0-312-85637-7). Orion the Hunter realizes that he and his human clone soldiers are pawns of the gods, whose fighting among themselves has placed the very survival of the Galaxy at risk, and learns that his love, the goddess Anya, is on the opposite side. (Rev: VOYA 2/96)

3424 Bova, Ben. *Vengeance of Orion* (9–12). 1988, Tor paper $3.95 (0-8125-3161-2). In this novel, Orion time travels to the time of Troy and ancient Egypt. This is a sequel to *Orion*. (Rev: VOYA 6/88)

3425 Bradbury, Ray. *Farhenheit 451* (7–12). 1953, Ballantine paper $6.99 (0-345-34296-8). In this futuristic novel, book reading has become a crime.

3426 Bradbury, Ray. *The Martian Chronicles* (10–12). 1999, Simon & Schuster $24.95 (0-7838-8635-7). These interrelated short stories tell of the colonization of Mars.

3427 Bradbury, Ray. *The October Country* (7–12). 1999, Avon $16.00 (0-380-97387-1). Ordinary people are caught up in unreal situations in these 19 strange stories.

3428 Bradbury, Ray. *The Stories of Ray Bradbury* (8–12). 1980, Knopf $40.00 (0-394-51335-5). An imaginative group of stories that often bridge the gap between fantasy and science fiction.

3429 Bradley, Marion Zimmer. *Exile's Song: A Novel of Darkover* (10–12). 1996, D A W Books paper $21.95 (0-88677-705-4). After 20 years, Margaret returns to the planet of her childhood, Darkover, and confronts disturbing memories. (Rev: BL 6/1–15/96; VOYA 12/96)

3430 Brin, David. *Otherness* (9–12). 1994, Bantam paper $6.99 (0-553-29528-4). Short fiction, essays, and commentaries that strive to define the term *otherness*, including stories about extraterrestrial con-

tact and the limits of our perception of reality. (Rev: BL 8/94; VOYA 2/95)

3431 Brittain, Bill. *Shape-Changer* (5–8). 1995, HarperCollins paper $4.50 (0-06-440514-1). Three seventh-graders meet an extraterrestrial police officer from the planet Rodinam who is escorting a dangerous criminal to an asteroid. (Rev: BL 4/15/94; SLJ 6/94)

3432 Brooks, Terry. *Wizard at Large* (10–12). 1989, Ballantine paper $6.99 (0-345-36227-6). In this, the third book about the Magic Kingdom of Landover, High Lord Ben Holiday travels to Earth. Preceded by: *Magic Kingdom for Sale—Sold!* and *The Black Unicorn*. (Rev: BL 9/1/88; VOYA 4/89)

3433 Bujold, Lois M. *Cetaganda* (9–12). 1996, Baen $21.00 (0-671-87701-1). In this Vorkosigan saga (number 10), hero Miles and his handsome cousin Ivan encounter intrigue and romance when they are sent to the planet Cetagnada on a diplomatic mission. (Rev: BL 11/15/95; VOYA 6/96)

3434 Bujold, Lois M. *Komarr* (10–12). 1998, Pocket Books $22.00 (0-671-87877-8). Investigator Miles Vorkosigan's first case is to determine if the collision between a space freighter and a satellite was really an accident. (Rev: BL 5/15/98; VOYA 10/98)

3435 Bunting, Eve. *The Cloverdale Switch* (7–9). 1979, HarperCollins LB $12.89 (0-397-31867-7). John and Cindy encounter unusual changes in their world and find a mysterious black box.

3436 Burroughs, Edgar Rice. *At the Earth's Core* (7–12). 1990, Ballantine paper $3.95 (0-345-36668-9). David Innes travels 500 miles into the earth and finds a subterranean world. Sequels *Pellucidar* and *Tamar of Pellucidar* are also included in this volume.

3437 Burroughs, Edgar Rice. *A Princess of Mars* (9–12). 1985, Ballantine paper $4.99 (0-345-33138-9). This is the beginning of a series of "space operas" involving John Carter on Mars. Some others are: *Gods of Mars*, *Warlord of Mars*, and *The Chessmen of Mars*.

3438 Butler, Susan. *The Hermit Thrush Sings* (5–8). 1999, DK Publg. $16.95 (0-7894-2489-4). Leora, who is living in a future civilization in North America, must leave the safety of her walled village controlled by the Rulers and find rebels who are working to overthrow the government. (Rev: BL 2/15/99; SLJ 4/99; VOYA 12/99)

3439 Butts, Nancy. *The Door in the Lake* (5–8). 1997, Front Street $15.95 (1-886910-27-8). Twenty-seven months after being abducted by aliens, Joey returns home to find that everything has changed while he has remained the same. (Rev: BL 5/15/98; SLJ 6/98; VOYA 10/98)

3440 Card, Orson Scott. *Alvin Journeyman* (10–12). (Tales of Alvin Maker) 1995, Tor $23.95 (0-312-

85053-0). In this fourth installment of the series, Alvin Maker falls victim to the manipulations of The Unmaker, an ancient enemy. (Rev: SLJ 6/96; VOYA 4/96)

3441 Card, Orson Scott. *The Call of Earth* (9–12). (Homecoming Saga) 1994, Tor paper $6.99 (0-8125-3261-9). Teenagers are at the heart of this story featuring a sentient computer whose plans involve a return to Earth. (Rev: BL 11/15/92; VOYA 8/93)

3442 Card, Orson Scott. *Children of the Mind* (10–12). 1996, Tor $23.95 (0-312-85395-5). This novel is the last of the Ender saga and deals with the fate of humankind as well as the death of our hero. (Rev: SLJ 1/97; VOYA 2/97)

3443 Card, Orson Scott, ed. *Future on Ice* (9–12). 1998, Tor $24.95 (0-312-86694-1). A fine collection of 18 short stories by some of the most popular science fiction writers of the 1980s. (Rev: BL 9/15/98; SLJ 3/99; VOYA 4/99)

3444 Card, Orson Scott. *The Memory of Earth: Homecoming, Vol. 1* (9–12). (Homecoming Saga) 1993, Tor paper $5.99 (0-8125-3259-7). A science fiction saga set on the planet Harmony, where a computer rules the population. (Rev: BL 1/1/92)

3445 Card, Orson Scott. *Pastwatch: The Redemption of Christopher Columbus* (9–12). 1996, Tor $23.95 (0-312-85058-1). Time travelers from a ruined future Earth journey to the time of Columbus, hoping to reshape events. (Rev: BL 12/1/95; VOYA 4/96)

3446 Card, Orson Scott. *Speaker for the Dead* (10–12). 1986, Tor $21.95 (0-312-93738-5). Ender tries to prevent a war with a nonhuman intelligent race in this sequel to *Ender's Game*. (Rev: BL 12/15/85; VOYA 8/86)

3447 Cart, Michael, ed. *Tomorrowland: 10 Stories about the Future* (7–10). 1999, Scholastic $15.95 (0-590-37678-0). Ten writers, including Ron Koertge, Lois Lowry, and Katherine Paterson, have contributed original stories to this anthology that reflect their concepts of the future. (Rev: BL 8/99; SLJ 9/99; VOYA 12/99)

3448 Carter, Raphael. *The Fortunate Fall* (9–12). 1996, Tor $21.95 (0-312-86034-X). In a future world where 20th century pop culture is viewed as "classical civilization," schoolchildren study the Brady Bunch the way students today study Shakespeare, and past horrors are hidden through manipulation of people's thoughts and memories, young Maya uncovers a genocide that was committed 100 years before and defies the authorities by trying to tell others about it. (Rev: BL 7/96; VOYA 4/97)

3449 Carver, Jeffrey A. *A Neptune Crossing* (9–12). 1995, Tor $5.99 (0-8125-3515-4). While doing survey work on Neptune's moon Triton, loner John Bandicut becomes a reluctant accomplice to aliens'

efforts to save Earth. (Rev: BL 3/15/94; VOYA 12/94)

3450 Cherryh, C. J. *Finity's End* (9–12). 1997, Warner paper $22.00 (0-446-57072-1). Fletcher, who has spent his first 17 years on Pell as a "stationer," is suddenly claimed by the crew of *Finity's End*, a space vehicle where his deceased mother once lived, and taken aboard to be a member of their community. (Rev: BL 8/97; VOYA 12/97)

3451 Cherryh, C. J. *Inheritor* (10–12). 1996, D A W Books $21.95 (0-88677-689-9). In this third story about Bren, a human, and the alien culture of Atevi, Bren works to promote trust and understanding between the 2 very different cultures. (Rev: BL 4/15/96; VOYA 6/96)

3452 Cherryh, C. J. *The Pride of Chanur* (10–12). 1987, Phantasia $17.00 (0-932096-45-X); NAL paper $5.99 (0-88677-292-3). A human finds refuge on a spaceship operated by catlike beings. A sequel is *Chanur's Venture*.

3453 Christopher, John. *A Dusk of Demons* (6–9). 1994, Macmillan LB $14.95 (0-02-718425-0). In a primitive future society, Ben and Paddy set out to find their family, which disappeared after the Demons set fire to their home. (Rev: BL 6/1–15/94; SLJ 7/94; VOYA 12/94)

3454 Christopher, John. *When the Tripods Came* (6–9). 1990, Macmillan paper $4.99 (0-02-042575-9). In this prequel to the White Mountain trilogy, the author explains how the Tripods first came to Earth. (Rev: BL 7/88; BR 5–6/89; SLJ 8/88; VOYA 8/88)

3455 Christopher, John. *The White Mountains* (7–10). 1967, Simon & Schuster LB $16.00 (0-02-718360-2); Macmillan paper $3.95 (0-02-042711-5). The first of the Tripods trilogy, followed by: *The City of Gold and Lead* and *The Pool of Fire*. (Rev: BL 9/15/98)

3456 Ciencin, Scott. *Dinoverse* (5–8). 1999, Random $18.00 (0-679-88842-X). Bertram's science project really works and he and his 3 schoolmates are caught in a time warp in which Bertram and his friends become dinosaurs. (Rev: BL 4/1/99; SLJ 4/99)

3457 Clancy, Tom, and Steve Pieczenik. *Virtual Vandals* (7–12). (Net Force) 1999, Berkley paper $4.99 (0-425-16173-0). In 2025, after Matt Hunter and his computer friends attend an all-star virtual reality baseball game where a gang of terrorists shoot wildly at the stands, our hero and his chums set out to catch the culprits. Followed by *The Deadliest Game*. (Rev: BL 3/15/99)

3458 Clarke, Arthur C. *Childhood's End* (7–12). 1963, Harcourt $14.95 (0-15-117205-6); Ballantine paper $6.99 (0-345-34795-1). The overlords' arrival on Earth marks the beginning of the end for mankind.

3459 Clarke, Arthur C. *The City and the Stars* (10–12). 1957, NAL paper $3.50 (0-451-14822-3). This novel is now considered a science fiction classic. Also by the same author are *Reach for Tomorrow* (1975), *Island in the Sky* (1979), *The Deep Range* (1981), and *The Sentinel* (1986).

3460 Clarke, Arthur C. *Expedition to Earth* (7–10). 1998, Ballantine paper $10.00 (0-345-43073-5). Eleven stories about space exploration.

3461 Clarke, Arthur C. *The Hammer of God* (9–12). 1994, Bantam paper $6.99 (0-553-56871-X). The struggle to avoid an asteroid on a collision course with Earth. (Rev: BL 4/15/93; VOYA 12/93)

3462 Clarke, Arthur C. *Rendezvous with Rama* (10–12). 1990, Bantam paper $6.99 (0-553-28789-3). Bill Norton and his crew set out to investigate a strange missile that has entered the earth's atmosphere.

3463 Clarke, Arthur C. *2061: Odyssey Three* (9–12). 1988, Ballantine paper $6.99 (0-345-35879-1). Heywood Floyd takes part in the space mission of landing on Halley's Comet. (Rev: BL 11/1/87; BR 9–10/88)

3464 Clarke, Arthur C. *2010: Odyssey Two* (9–12). 1997, Ballantine paper $11.00 (0-345-41397-0). A team of scientists try to save the deserted spaceship Discovery.

3465 Clarke, Arthur C. *2001: A Space Odyssey* (9–12). 1968, NAL paper $3.95 (0-451-15580-7). This novel, based on the screenplay of the famous movie, introduces a most unusual computer named Hal.

3466 Clarke, Arthur C. *The Wind from the Sun: Stories from the Space Age* (9–12). 1972, NAL paper $1.95 (0-451-11475-2). Eighteen science fiction stories, many with surprise endings.

3467 Clarke, Arthur C., and Gentry Lee. *Rama Revealed* (9–12). (Rama) 1995, Bantam paper $6.99 (0-553-56947-3). The fourth book of the series focuses on the New Eden colony, which is ruled by Nakamura, a dictator who overthrew the governess and wages war on the octospiders. (Rev: BL 12/1/93; VOYA 6/94)

3468 Cooper, Clare. *Ashar of Qarius* (5–8). 1990, Harcourt $14.95 (0-15-200409-2). A teenage girl, 2 children, and their pets are left alone in a space dome and must find a way to survive. (Rev: BL 5/15/90; SLJ 7/90)

3469 Cormier, Robert. *Fade* (10–12). 1991, Bantam paper $4.99 (0-440-21091-7). A disturbing and sometimes terrifying novel about a 13-year-old who

can make himself disappear. (Rev: BL 9/1/88; BR 11–12/88; SLJ 10/88; VOYA 12/88)

3470 Coville, Bruce. *Aliens Stole My Body* (5–8). Illus. (Alien Adventures) 1998, Pocket Books $14.00 (0-671-02414-0). To safeguard Rod from BKR, the cruelest being in the universe, and protect the important weapons formula that Rod knows, the boy's brain is separated from his body and enters the body of a six-legged blue alien. (Rev: BL 11/1/98; SLJ 2/99)

3471 Crichton, Michael. *The Andromeda Strain* (9–12). 1969, Knopf $25.00 (0-394-41525-6). A mysterious capsule from space brings a threat of a deadly epidemic in this fast-paced novel.

3472 Crichton, Michael. *Jurassic Park* (9–12). 1990, Knopf $25.00 (0-394-58816-9). This thriller takes place in an amusement park on an island off Costa Rica where genetically engineered dinosaurs live. (Rev: BL 10/1/90; SLJ 3/91)

3473 Crichton, Michael. *Sphere* (9–12). 1987, Knopf $27.50 (0-394-56110-4); Ballantine paper $7.99 (0-345-35314-5). A group of scientists journey to the bottom of the sea to explore a sunken spaceship in this thriller from the author of *The Andromeda Strain* (1969). (Rev: BL 5/15/87; SLJ 11/87)

3474 Crichton, Michael. *The Terminal Man* (9–12). 1972, Knopf $23.00 (0-394-44768-9); Ballantine paper $7.99 (0-345-35462-1). A man who is slipping into insanity has a computer implanted into his brain.

3475 Cross, Gillian. *New World* (6–9). 1995, Holiday House $15.95 (0-8234-1166-4). Miriam and Stuart, both 14, have been chosen to test a new virtual reality game and have been sworn to secrecy about it, but scenes in it enact their most secret fears. (Rev: BL 2/1/95; SLJ 3/95; VOYA 12/95)

3476 David, Peter. *Babylon 5: In the Beginning* (7–10). 1998, Ballantine paper $5.99 (0-345-42452-2). This is a novelization of the first full-length movie in the TV science fiction series *Babylon 5*. (Rev: VOYA 8/98)

3477 Dedman, Stephen. *The Art of Arrow Cutting* (10–12). 1997, Tor $22.95 (0-312-86320-9). Mage, a young man who holds the power to perform miracles, is pursued by Tamenaga, a dead man who wants to possess this power. (Rev: VOYA 12/97)

3478 De Haven, Tom. *The Orphan's Tent* (7–10). 1996, Simon & Schuster $18.00 (0-689-31967-3). After Del, a young singer-songwriter, mysteriously disappears, her 2 friends, while trying to trace her, find themselves transported to another world. (Rev: SLJ 10/96; VOYA 12/96)

3479 Del Rey, Lester. *The Best of Lester del Rey* (7–10). 1978, Ballantine paper $5.99 (0-345-32933-3). Sixteen stories by this master of science fiction writing. Some full-length novels by del Rey are

Attack from Atlantis; Moon from Atlantis; Mysterious Planet; and *Rocket Jockey* (all 1982).

3480 Dicks, Terrance. *Doctor Who and the Genesis of the Daleks* (7–9). 1979, Amereon $18.95 (0-8488-0151-2). Based on the TV series, this is the story of an unusual Time Lord and his adventures in space.

3481 Dietz, William C. *Rebel Agent* (9–12). (Star Wars: Dark Forces) 1998, Putnam $24.95 (0-399-14396-3); Berkley paper $14.95 (0-425-16862-X). In this Star Wars novel, Kyle accepts the power of the Force, begins training as a Jedi Knight, falls in love, and completes a quest for secret information. (Rev: SLJ 10/98)

3482 Doyle, Debra, and James D. MacDonald. *Groogleman* (5–8). 1996, Harcourt $15.00 (0-15-200235-9). In this novel set in the future, 13-year-old Dan finds that he is immune to the plague that is devastating the countryside and sets out with friend Leesie to help tend the sick. (Rev: BR 3–4/97; SLJ 12/96; VOYA 6/97)

3483 Dozois, Gardner, ed. *The Year's Best Science Fiction: Eleventh Annual Collection* (9–12). 1994, St. Martin's paper $17.95 (0-312-11104-5). The annual collection of outstanding sci-fi short stories. (Rev: BL 7/94; VOYA 2/95)

3484 Dozois, Gardner, ed. *The Year's Best Science Fiction: Fifteenth Annual Collection* (9–12). 1998, St. Martin's paper $17.95 (0-312-19033-6). A worthwhile collection of 28 of the best science fiction stories. (Rev: BL 7/98; VOYA 12/98)

3485 Dozois, Gardner, and Sheil Williams, eds. *Isaac Asimov's Moons* (9–12). 1997, Ace paper $5.99 (0-441-00453-9). This is a collection of 7 well-crafted stories about lunar exploits with themes involving revenge, love, endurance, and survival. (Rev: VOYA 10/97)

3486 Duane, Diane. *Doctor's Orders* (9–12). 1990, Pocket Books paper $5.50 (0-671-66189-2). In this Star Trek novel, Kirk disappears and Dr. McCoy must take over the Enterprise. (Rev: BL 6/15/90; SLJ 12/90)

3487 Dvorkin, David. *The Captain's Honor* (9–12). 1991, Pocket Books paper $5.50 (0-671-74140-3). In this Star Trek novel, the Enterprise tries to help the planet Tenara after it is attacked by the M'dok. (Rev: VOYA 2/90)

3488 Dvorkin, David. *Timetrap* (9–12). 1988, Pocket Books paper $4.95 (0-671-64870-5). In this Star Trek novel, Captain Kirk travels 100 years into the future. (Rev: BL 6/15/88)

3489 Farmer, Nancy. *The Ear, the Eye and the Arm* (7–10). 1994, Orchard LB $19.99 (0-531-08679-8). In Zimbabwe, in 2194, the military ruler's son, 13, and his younger siblings leave their technologically overcontrolled home and embark on a series of perilous adventures. (Rev: BL 4/1/94; SLJ 6/94; VOYA 6/94)

3490 Farmer, Philip Jose. *Dayworld Breakup* (10–12). 1991, Tor paper $4.95 (0-8125-0889-0). The third volume about Dayworld, the land where overcrowding is so acute that people must spend half of their lives in suspended animation. Preceded by *Dayworld* (1984) and *Dayworld Rebel* (1987). (Rev: BL 5/1/90)

3491 Farmer, Philip Jose. *Gods of Riverworld* (10–12). 1998, Ballantine paper $12.95 (0-345-41971-5). In this, the fifth and last of the recommended Riverworld series, people who lived on Earth in the past are resurrected.

3492 Farmer, Philip Jose. *The Magic Labyrinth* (10–12). 1998, Ballantine paper $12.95 (0-345-41970-7). This is a volume in one of the major science creations, the Riverworld saga. Some others are: *The Gods of Riverworld* (1985), *The Dark Design* (1984), and *To Your Scattered Bodies Go* (1985).

3493 Feintuch, David. *Fisherman's Hope* (10–12). (Seafort Saga) 1996, Warner paper $6.50 (0-446-60099-7). In this science fiction novel, Seafort, in his mid-20s, is responsible for the training of 400 Navy cadets and stands up to inept authority. (Rev: VOYA 8/96)

3494 Feintuch, David. *Voices of Hope* (9–12). (Seafort Saga) 1996, Warner paper $6.50 (0-446-60333-3). Jared, the rebellious son of Seafort's close friend, runs away with plans to sell information about Seafort to a cyberspace news outlet, only to find himself in the middle of violent class conflict and a genocidal war. (Rev: BL 10/15/96; VOYA 10/96)

3495 Finch, Sheila. *Tiger in the Sky* (4–8). (Out of Time) 1999, Avon paper $4.99 (0-380-79971-5). Nan and Britisher Will time travel from 1579 to the edge of the solar system where furry creatures are disrupting scientific research in the 2300s. (Rev: BL 9/1/99)

3496 Forward, Robert L. *Dragon's Egg* (10–12). 1983, Ballantine paper $5.99 (0-345-31666-5). In this imaginative novel, life on a neutron star is depicted.

3497 Foster, Alan Dean. *The Deluge Drivers* (10–12). 1987, Ballantine paper $5.99 (0-345-33330-6). In this conclusion to the trilogy that began with *Icerigger* and *Mission to Moulokin* (both 1987), Ethan Fortune must foil a plot to disturb the ecological balance on his planet. (Rev: BL 5/15/87)

3498 Foster, Alan Dean. *The Hand of Dinotopia* (6–10). 1999, HarperCollins $22.95 (0-06-028005-0). In this adventure involving dinosaurs, our heroes journey through the Great Desert and Outer Island to find the key to a sea route that will link Dinotopia to the rest of the world. (Rev: BL 5/1/99; SLJ 4/99)

3499 Foster, Alan Dean. *Jed the Dead* (9–12). 1997, Ace paper $5.99 (0-441-00399-0). An unusual fantasy in which Ross Ed finds a dead alien in a cave and begins using it as a ventriloquist's dummy on a wild ride across the country. (Rev: VOYA 4/97)

3500 Foster, Alan Dean. *Quozl* (9–12). 1989, Berkley paper $5.99 (0-441-69454-3). An amusing science fiction novel about aliens who look like large rabbits and their visit to Earth. (Rev: BL 5/15/89; SLJ 8/89)

3501 Foster, Alan Dean. *Splinter of the Mind's Eye* (8–12). 1978, Ballantine paper $5.99 (0-345-32023-9). A novel about Luke Skywalker and Princess Leia of *Star Wars* fame and their battle against the Empire.

3502 Frakes, Jonathan. *The Abductors: Conspiracy* (8–10). 1996, St. Martin's $22.95 (0-312-86208-3). The world is secretly being attacked by the Klar, who plan on abducting humans and creating copies that can carry nuclear bombs into the world's major cities. (Rev: VOYA 6/97)

3503 Fuller, Kimberly. *Home* (7–10). 1997, Tor $16.95 (0-312-86152-4). When an attractive alien lands on her planet, Maran Thopel is attracted to him and to his mission to regain the planet for the people from whom it was taken. (Rev: BR 9–10/97; SLJ 7/97; VOYA 8/97)

3504 Gerrold, David. *Chess with a Dragon* (8–12). 1988, Avon paper $3.50 (0-380-70662-8). The entire human race becomes slaves of giant slugs and Yake must save them. (Rev: BL 6/15/87; BR 11–12/87; SLJ 9/87)

3505 Gier, Scott G. *Genellan: Planetfall* (10–12). 1995, Del Rey paper $5.99 (0-345-39509-3). Lieutenant Sharl Buccari faces problems when her spaceship lands in an unfamiliar world with winged natives hovering about. (Rev: VOYA 2/96)

3506 Gilmore, Kate. *The Exchange Student* (6–9). 1999, Houghton $15.00 (0-395-57511-7). Set in the year 2094, this novel describes the problems faced by a group of exchange students from the planet Chela who are studying on Earth. (Rev: BL 9/15/99; SLJ 10/99)

3507 Goldman, E. M. *The Night Room* (6–10). 1995, Viking paper $14.99 (0-670-85838-2). Seven high school juniors take part in an experiment with virtual reality: a simulation of their 10-year reunion. (Rev: BL 1/1/95; SLJ 5/94)

3508 Gould, Steven. *Wild Side* (10–12). 1996, Tor $22.95 (0-312-85473-0). In this riveting science fiction novel, 18-year-old Charlie discovers a gateway to a parallel earth that is a pollution-free, human-free

Eden, where animals extinct on earth still survive. (Rev: BL 3/15/96; VOYA 2/97)

3509 Greenberg, Martin H., ed. *Lord of the Fantastic: Stories in Honor of Roger Zelazny* (9–12). 1998, Avon paper $14.00 (0-380-78737-7). This collection of 20 original science fiction novels by well-known writers is a tribute to sci-fi great Roger Zelazny, who died at age 58 in 1995. (Rev: SLJ 3/99)

3510 Greeno, Gayle. *Mind Snare* (9–12). 1997, D A W Books paper $5.99 (0-88677-749-6). In this novel set in 2158, Rose, who wants revenge because of her husband's infidelity many years before, plots to kill both the woman he had an affair with and the teenage son who was the product of this union. (Rev: VOYA 12/97)

3511 Griffith, Helen V. *Journal of a Teenage Genius* (5–8). 1987, Troll paper $2.50 (0-8167-1325-1). In diary form, a young hero tells of his encounter with a time machine. (Rev: BR 11–12/87; SLJ 10/87; VOYA 12/87)

3512 Gutman, Dan. *Cyberkid* (4–8). 1998, Hyperion LB $14.49 (0-7868-2344-5). Yip, a computer savvy 12-year-old, and his sister, Paige, create a "virtual actor," or "vactor," who breaks out of cyberspace and reveals a serious flaw: his database does not include a conscience. (Rev: BL 6/1–15/98; SLJ 8/98)

3513 Haddix, Margaret P. *Among the Hidden* (5–8). 1998, Simon & Schuster paper $16.00 (0-689-81700-2). Set in the near future when couples are allowed to have only 2 children, this is the story of the third child, 12-year-old Luke, who must hide in the attic for survival. (Rev: BR 5–6/99; SLJ 9/98; VOYA 10/98)

3514 Haldeman, Joe. *Forever Peace* (10–12). 1997, Ace $21.95 (0-441-00406-7). In the world of 2043, Julilan Cross, a physicist and pacifist, must kill to prevent worldwide destruction. (Rev: BL 9/15/97; VOYA 2/98)

3515 Halperin, James L. *The First Immortal* (10–12). 1998, Del Rey $24.95 (0-345-42092-6). This family saga spans 200 years, from 1925 to 2125, with most of the same characters present throughout, or in different periods, because of cryogenics, the science of freezing people to be resurrected at a later time. (Rev: SLJ 12/98; VOYA 8/98)

3516 Hambly, Barbara. *Ishmael* (9–12). 1991, Pocket Books paper $5.50 (0-671-74355-4). In this Star Trek novel, Spock goes back in time to foil a plan to change history. (Rev: BL 7/85; VOYA 2/86)

3517 Hartwell, David G., ed. *Year's Best SF* (9–12). 1996, HarperCollins paper $6.50 (0-06-105641-3). In this edition of an annual collection, there are 14 well-constructed, thoughtful, and entertaining stories, many by well-known authors, representing a variety of SF subgenres including cyberpunk, time travel, alternative history, and hard science fiction. (Rev: VOYA 4/97)

3518 Heinlein, Robert A. *Between Planets* (7–10). 1984, Ballantine paper $5.99 (0-345-32099-9). Revolt on Venus against an interplanetary alliance causes painful decisions for Don.

3519 Heinlein, Robert A. *The Cat Who Walks through Walls* (10–12). 1985, Ace paper $7.50 (0-441-09499-6). Colonel Colin Campbell and his wife travel through time to get help solving a murder mystery. (Rev: BL 8/85)

3520 Heinlein, Robert A. *Citizen of the Galaxy* (6–8). 1987, Ballantine paper $5.99 (0-345-34244-5). First published in 1957, this science fiction classic tells about the adventures of a young boy rescued from slavery to fulfill an unusual mission. (Rev: BL 6/1/87)

3521 Heinlein, Robert A. *The Door into Summer* (9–12). 1986, Ballantine paper $5.99 (0-345-33012-9). An inventor has an opportunity to look into the future in this science fiction novel.

3522 Heinlein, Robert A. *Farmer in the Sky* (7–10). 1985, Ballantine paper $5.99 (0-345-32438-2). A family decides to leave Earth to find better resources on another planet. A reissue.

3523 Heinlein, Robert A. *Have Space Suit, Will Travel* (7–9). 1977, Ballantine paper $5.99 (0-345-32441-2). Kip Russell realizes his dream of visiting the moon in his own spacesuit.

3524 Heinlein, Robert A. *Red Planet* (7–10). 1981, Ballantine paper $5.99 (0-345-34039-6). A novel about the first space exploration of the planet Mars.

3525 Heinlein, Robert A. *Rocket Ship Galileo* (8–12). 1986, Ballantine paper $4.99 (0-345-33660-7). Four amateurs land on the moon. Also use: *Starship Troopers* (1987).

3526 Heinlein, Robert A. *The Rolling Stones* (7–10). 1985, Ballantine paper $5.99 (0-345-32451-X). The Stone family takes on the universe in this unusual science fiction adventure. A reissue.

3527 Heinlein, Robert A. *Space Cadet* (7–10). 1984, Ballantine paper $5.99 (0-345-35311-0). In the year 2075, several members of the Solar Patrol have fantastic adventures.

3528 Heinlein, Robert A. *The Star Beast* (7–10). 1977, Macmillan $15.00 (0-684-15329-7). A pet smuggled to Earth never seems to stop growing.

3529 Heinlein, Robert A. *Starman Jones* (7–10). 1985, Ballantine paper $5.99 (0-345-32811-6). Anxious for adventure, Max Jones stows away on an intergalactic spaceship. A reissue.

3530 Heinlein, Robert A. *Stranger in a Strange Land* (10–12). 1991, Ace paper $16.95 (0-441-78838-6). A young man from Mars comes to Earth and must learn our strange ways.

3531 Heintze, Ty. *Valley of the Eels* (5–8). 1993, Eakin $14.95 (0-89015-904-1). A dolphin leads 2 boys to an underwater station where friendly aliens are cultivating trees for replanting on their own planet. (Rev: BL 3/1/94)

3532 Herbert, Frank. *Dune* (10–12). 1984, Putnam $26.95 (0-399-12896-4). In this, the first of a series, the Atreides family is banished to planet Dune where the ferocious Fremen live. Others in the series are: *Children of Dune* (1985), *Dune Messiah* (1976), and *God Emperor of Dune* (1981).

3533 Hickman, Tracy. *The Immortals* (10–12). 1996, Roc $19.95 (0-451-45402-2). In this futuristic novel, a terrible plague is covering the United States and Michael Barris finds his son in an internment camp for infected, "pre-deceased" people and he becomes involved in the inmates' struggle for survival. (Rev: VOYA 10/96)

3534 Hill, William. *The Magic Bicycle* (5–8). 1998, Otter Creek paper $13.95 (1-890611-00-X). For helping an alien escape, Danny receives a magical bicycle that is capable of transporting him through time and space. (Rev: BL 1/1–15/98; SLJ 3/98)

3535 Hopkinson, Nalo. *Brown Girl in the Ring* (10–12). 1998, Warner paper $13.99 (0-446-67433-8). In this science fiction novel set in postmodern Toronto in the near future, Ti-Jeanne, living with her child and grandmother in urban squalor, must conquer her fears and find a way out of their dismal situation. (Rev: BL 5/15/98; SLJ 11/98; VOYA 8/98)

3536 Howarth, Lesley. *Maphead* (6–8). 1994, Candlewick $14.95 (1-56402-416-4). Maphead, living in a parallel universe, wants to meet his mortal mother, so he assumes human form, attends school, and befriends his mother's other son. (Rev: BL 10/1/94; SLJ 10/94; VOYA 2/95)

3537 Howarth, Lesley. *MapHead: The Return* (5–9). 1997, Candlewick $15.99 (0-7636-0344-9). In this sequel to *Maphead*, our 13-year-old hero from a parallel universe moves in with a family where his ability to control the minds of others causes trouble. (Rev: BR 3–4/98; SLJ 1/98; VOYA 4/98)

3538 Howarth, Lesley. *Weather Eye* (6–8). 1995, Candlewick $16.99 (1-56402-616-7). A 13-year-old with special powers monitors the weather in her small English town. (Rev: BL 9/15/95*; SLJ 11/95)

3539 Hughes, Monica. *Invitation to the Game* (7–10). 1991, Simon & Schuster paper $3.95 (0-671-86692-3). In 2154, a high school graduate and her friends face life on welfare in a highly robotic society and are invited to participate in a sinister government "game." (Rev: BL 9/15/91)

3540 Jablokov, Alexander. *The Breath of Suspension* (9–12). 1994, Arkham $20.95 (0-87054-167-6). Short stories with such themes as time-traveling detectives, a cyborg whale that explores Jupiter's atmosphere, and manmade alternate universes. (Rev: BL 8/94; VOYA 12/94)

3541 James, Roby. *Commencement* (9–12). 1996, Del Rey paper $5.99 (0-345-40038-0). Ronica finds herself on a low technology planet and without the power to control her mind, and she consents to work with the Lord of one of the tribes in exchange for getting back her lost mental functions. (Rev: VOYA 8/96)

3542 Jeter, K. W. *The Mandalorian Armor* (7–9). 1998, Bantam paper $5.99 (0-553-57885-5). This first installment in The Bounty Hunter Wars trilogy involves Boba Fett, the bounty hunter who captured Han Solo in *The Empire Strikes Back.* (Rev: VOYA 2/99)

3543 Jones, Diana Wynne. *Hexwood* (8–12). 1994, Greenwillow $16.00 (0-688-12488-7). A complex science fiction story about virtual realism, time manipulation, and a young girl who investigates the disappearance of guests at Hexwood Farm. (Rev: BL 6/1–15/94; SLJ 3/94; VOYA 10/94)

3544 Jones, Terry. *Douglas Adams' Starship Titanic* (10–12). 1997, Harmony Books $20.00 (0-609-60103-2). Inspired by an episode in one of Douglas Adams's novels, this is a comic science fiction novel loaded with absurdities about a group of inept characters who must bring a starship's computer brain back online while avoiding destruction by a bomb and an army of hostile shipbuilders. (Rev: BL 9/15/97; SLJ 5/98; VOYA 4/98)

3545 Kanaly, Michael. *Virus Clans: A Story of Evolution* (10–12). 1998, Ace paper $12.00 (0-441-00500-4). A science fiction thriller in which a young entomologist discovers that a group of viruses he has grown are communicating with each other. (Rev: BL 2/15/98; SLJ 9/98)

3546 Kaye, Marilyn. *Amy, Number Seven: How Many Are Out There?* (6–10). 1998, Bantam Doubleday Dell paper $4.50 (0-553-49238-1). When Amy finds that her personality is mysteriously changing, her mother is acting strangely, and she is developing extraordinary new abilities, she sets out to find the truth about her past. (Rev: BL 10/15/98; SLJ 10/98)

3547 Kaye, Marilyn. *Pursuing Amy* (6–8). (Replica) 1998, Bantam paper $3.99 (0-553-49239-X). Amy, Tasha's 12-year-old friend, is actually a clone from a genetic engineering project and now she not only has superhuman capabilities but also is being pursued by the evil forces that funded the project. (Rev: BL 1/1–15/99; SLJ 7/99)

3548 Key, Alexander. *The Forgotten Door* (7–9). 1986, Scholastic paper $3.99 (0-590-43130-7). An alien from another planet gets a hostile reception on Earth. A reissue.

3549 Kiesel, Stanley. *Skinny Malinky Leads the War for Kidness* (6–8). 1984, Avon paper $2.50 (0-380-69875-7). Skinny is about to be captured by a powerful mutant red ant.

3550 Kilworth, Garry. *The Electric Kid* (6–9). 1995, Orchard LB $15.99 (0-531-08786-7). Two homeless young people struggle for survival in a large city's oppressive underworld in this bleak novel set in the horrifying world of 2061. (Rev: BL 1/1–15/96; SLJ 10/95; VOYA 12/95)

3551 Klause, Annette Curtis. *Alien Secrets* (5–8). 1993, Delacorte $15.95 (0-385-30928-7). Modern variations on the best of 1950s–1960s science fiction by Heinlein, Norton, Bova, et al. (Rev: BL 6/1–15/93*; SLJ 9/93*; VOYA 8/93)

3552 Kress, Nancy. *Beggars and Choosers* (9–12). 1994, Tor $22.95 (0-312-85749-7). The future world is divided among 3 feuding groups: the superhuman Sleepless, the genetically altered ruling elite called "homo superior," and the poor masses. (Rev: BL 10/1/94; SLJ 5/95; VOYA 4/95)

3553 Kress, Nancy. *Beggars Ride* (10–12). 1996, Tor $23.95 (0-312-85817-5). The concluding volume in this thrilling science fiction trilogy about a genetically altered ruling elite that began with *Beggars in Spain* (1993) and *Beggars and Choosers.* (Rev: SLJ 7/97; VOYA 6/97)

3554 Kress, Nancy. *Yanked!* (4–8). (Out of Time) 1999, Avon paper $4.99 (0-380-79968-5). Two teens from the 1990s time travel to the mid-2300s to help some kids lost on an alien planet. (Rev: BL 9/1/99)

3555 Kritlow, William. *Backfire* (7–10). (Virtual Reality) 1995, Thomas Nelson paper $4.99 (0-7852-7925-3). Teens obtain access to a virtual reality machine and live out their fantasies until an evil programmer comes along. (Rev: BL 12/1/95)

3556 Kritlow, William. *The Deadly Maze* (7–10). (Virtual Reality) 1995, Thomas Nelson paper $5.99 (0-7852-7924-5). Teens don virtual reality suits and enter a strange computer-generated world where evil is pervasive. (Rev: BL 12/1/95)

3557 Kurtz, Katherine. *The Bishop's Heir* (10–12). 1987, Ballantine paper $5.99 (0-345-34761-7). This is the beginning of a trilogy in the Deryni series, The Histories of King Kelson.

3558 Lawrence, Louise. *Andra* (6–10). 1991, HarperCollins $14.95 (0-06-023685-X). This novel is set 2,000 years in the future, when humanity, having destroyed Earth's environment, lives in rigidly governed, sealed, underground cities. (Rev: BL 5/1/91; SLJ 5/91)

3559 Lawrence, Louise. *Dream-Weaver* (7–12). 1996, Clarion $15.00 (0-395-71812-0). The horror of psychic manipulation is explored in this science fiction thriller about a girl who, in her dream body, joins a space ship full of colonists bound for her planet. (Rev: BL 10/1/96*; SLJ 10/96; VOYA 2/97)

3560 Lawrence, Louise. *The Patchwork People* (7–10). 1994, Clarion $14.95 (0-395-67892-7). This brooding story takes place in a bleak Wales of the future, where natural resources are nearly depleted and jobs are scarce. (Rev: BL 12/15/94*; SLJ 11/94)

3561 Le Guin, Ursula K. *The Lathe of Heaven* (10–12). 1982, Bentley $14.00 (0-8376-0464-8); Avon paper $5.50 (0-380-01320-7). In this novel set in the 21st century, a young man finds that his dreams are premonitions of events to come.

3562 Le Guin, Ursula K. *The Left Hand of Darkness* (7–12). 1969, Ace paper $6.99 (0-441-47812-3). An envoy is sent to the ice-covered planet Gethen where people can be either male or female at will.

3563 Le Guin, Ursula K. *A Wizard of Earthsea* (7–12). 1984, Bantam paper $6.99 (0-553-26250-5). Beginning when Ged is a boy wizard, this is the first volume of the Earthsea trilogy. Followed by: *The Tombs of Atuan* and *Farthest Shore* (both 1984).

3564 Le Guin, Ursula K., and Brian Attebery, eds. *The Norton Book of Science Fiction, 1960–1990* (9–12). 1993, Norton $29.95 (0-393-03546-8). The last 3 decades of North American science fiction are represented in 60 stories that focus on themes rather than on author reputation. (Rev: BL 10/1/93)

3565 Lehmann, Christian. *Ultimate Game* (10–12). Trans. by William Rodarmor. 1999, Godine $15.95 (1-56792-107-8). In this gritty, disturbing young adult novel, three boys discover different violent realities when they purchase a new video game. (Rev: BL 8/99)

3566 Leiber, Fritz. *The Big Time* (10–12). 1976, Amereon LB $20.95 (0-88411-931-9). A young girl lives outside the confines of time on a space station.

3567 Leiber, Fritz. *The Dealings of Daniel Kesserich* (9–12). 1997, Tor $18.95 (0-312-85408-0). When George Kramer visits his friend John to comfort him after his wife's death, mysterious events begin to occur, including the disappearance of the wife's body. (Rev: BL 2/1/97; VOYA 8/97)

3568 Lem, Stanislaw. *Cyberiad: Fables for the Cybernetic Age* (10–12). 1985, Harcourt paper $11.00 (0-15-623550-1). Each of these 13 stories deals with computers. Also use: *Tales of Pirx the Pilot* (1990).

3569 L'Engle, Madeleine. *Many Waters* (7–10). 1986, Farrar $18.00 (0-374-34796-4); Dell paper $5.50 (0-440-40548-3). The Murry twins, from the author's Wrinkle in Time trilogy, time travel to the

Holy Land prior to the Great Flood. (Rev: BL 8/86; SLJ 11/86; VOYA 12/86)

3570 L'Engle, Madeleine. *A Wrinkle in Time* (6–9). 1962, Farrar $17.00 (0-374-38613-7); Dell paper $5.99 (0-440-49805-8). Meg and Charles Wallace Murry, with the help of Calvin O'Keefe, set out in space to find their scientist father. Newbery Award 1963. Followed by *A Wind in the Door* (1973) and *A Swiftly Tilting Planet* (1978).

3571 Lettow, Donna. *Highlander: Zealot* (9–12). 1997, Warner paper $5.99 (0-446-60457-7). In this tie-in to the television and movie series, Duncan MacLeod, an Immortal who was born in 1592 and who can die only if another Immortal beheads him, takes on the Israeli-Palestinian conflict. (Rev: VOYA 6/98)

3572 Lowenstein, Sallie. *Evan's Voice* (5–8). Illus. 1998, Lion Stone Books paper $15.00 (0-9658486-1-2). In this science fiction novel, Jake and his near catatonic younger brother, Evan, enter the Dead Zone in search of a storyteller who knows how civilization can escape destruction. (Rev: BL 3/1/99; VOYA 6/99)

3573 Lucas, George. *Star Wars* (7–9). 1995, Del Rey $16.00 (0-345-40077-1). This is an enjoyable novelization of Lucas's movie *Star Wars: From the Adventures of Luke Skywalker*. (Rev: VOYA 4/96)

3574 Lucas, George. *Star Wars: From the Adventures of Luke Skywalker* (8–12). 1977, Ballantine paper $5.99 (0-345-34146-5). The adventures of Luke Skywalker and friends against the evil Darth Vader.

3575 Lucas, George, and Chris Claremont. *Shadow Moon: First in the Chronicles of the Shadow War* (9–12). 1996, Bantam paper $5.99 (0-553-57285-7). Lucas of *Star Wars* fame and Claremont of Marvel Comics offer the first in a planned trilogy of sci-fi novels. (Rev: BL 10/1/95; VOYA 2/96)

3576 McCaffrey, Anne. *The Chronicles of Pern: First Fall* (9–12). 1994, Ballantine paper $5.99 (0-345-36899-1). Five original stories by the author of the popular Pern series offer a glimpse into the early history of the Dragonriders. (Rev: BL 9/1/93; VOYA 4/94)

3577 McCaffrey, Anne. *The Crystal Singer* (10–12). 1985, Ballantine paper $6.99 (0-345-32786-1). This novel involves a crystal singer from the Planet Ballybran and the young girl he influences. (Rev: BL 12/15/87)

3578 McCaffrey, Anne. *Dinosaur Planet Survivors* (9–12). 1984, Ballantine paper $5.99 (0-345-27246-3). After 43 years of suspended animation, the 2 central characters of the author's earlier *Dinosaur Planet* (1978) awake to find their beloved planet is again in danger. (Rev: BL 1/15/85)

3579 McCaffrey, Anne. *The Dolphins of Pern* (9–12). (Pern) 1995, Ballantine paper $6.99 (0-345-36895-9). Young Dragonrider T'lion rebuilds the world of Pern's ancient relationship with the "ship-fish," dolphins that came to Pern with its early human settlers. (Rev: BL 9/15/94; VOYA 2/95)

3580 McCaffrey, Anne. *Dragonflight* (9–12). 1981, Ballantine $8.95 (0-345-27749-X); paper $6.99 (0-345-33546-5). This is the first volume of the author's popular Dragonriders of Pern series. It is followed by *Dragonquest* and *White Dragon* (both 1986).

3581 McCaffrey, Anne. *Dragonsdawn* (9–12). 1989, Ballantine paper $6.99 (0-345-36286-1). A novel that takes place before the Dragonriders of Pern series. This describes how the planet Pern was colonized and the origins of the deadly Threadfall. (Rev: BL 9/1/88; VOYA 4/89)

3582 McCaffrey, Anne. *Dragonsong* (7–12). 1977, Bantam paper $6.99 (0-553-25852-4). The first volume of the Harper Hall trilogy begins the story of Menolly, her magic harp, and the dread Thread that falls from the sky. Followed by *Dragonsinger* (1977) and *Dragondrums* (1979).

3583 McCaffrey, Anne. *Killashandra* (9–12). 1985, Ultramarine $25.00 (0-89366-187-2); Ballantine paper $6.99 (0-345-31600-2). While visiting a neighboring planet, crystal singer Killashandra is kidnapped. (Rev: SLJ 2/86)

3584 McCaffrey, Anne. *Lyon's Pride* (9–12). 1995, Ace paper $6.99 (0-441-00141-6). An alliance between humans and aliens searches for creatures that destroy indigenous life forms on any planet they inhabit. (Rev: BL 1/1/94; SLJ 9/94; VOYA 10/94)

3585 McCaffrey, Anne. *Moreta: Dragonlady of Pern* (9–12). 1984, Ballantine paper $6.99 (0-345-29873-X). The dragonriders of Pern are in danger from a mutated strain of influenza. (Rev: BL 12/15/87)

3586 McDevitt, Jack. *The Engines of God* (9–12). 1994, Berkley $21.95 (0-441-00077-0). An interstellar archeologist races to uncover the secrets of planet Quragua's alien artifacts before it is settled by humans fleeing an environmentally destroyed Earth. (Rev: BL 9/15/94; VOYA 12/94)

3587 Mackel, Kathy. *A Can of Worms* (5–8). 1999, Avon paper $15.00 (0-380-97681-1). A humorous science fiction story about seventh-grader Mike Pillsbury, who receives several extraterrestrial responses to his intergalactic appeal to be rescued from this planet when things go wrong in his life, including from the imaginary evil creatures in the stories he makes up. (Rev: SLJ 6/99; VOYA 4/99)

3588 McKinney, Jack. *Invid Invasion* (9–12). 1987, Del Rey paper $5.99 (0-345-34143-0). Scott Bernard is battling the Invid Regis to regain Earth in this story continued in *Metamorphosis* and *Symphony of Light* (both 1987). (Rev: VOYA 4/88)

3589 Marley, Louise. *Receive the Gift* (10–12). 1997, Ace paper $5.99 (0-441-00486-5). When Oho plots to take over the planet Nevya, it takes an alliance of several unlikely individuals to stop him. (Rev: VOYA 2/98)

3590 Metz, Melinda. *The Outsider* (6–9). (Roswell High) 1998, Pocket Books paper $1.99 (0-671-02374-8). The first book about Max and Isabel, 2 teenagers attending a high school in New Mexico who are actually aliens trying to hide their real identities. (Rev: SLJ 3/99)

3591 Modesitt, L. E. *Chaos Balance* (10–12). 1997, St. Martin's $25.95 (0-312-86389-6); Tor paper $6.99 (0-8125-7130-4). A complex story, combining science fiction and fantasy, of the travels of Nylan and his companion, Ayrlyn, as they seek a new home and peace. This is eighth in a series of challenging novels. (Rev: BL 9/15/97; SLJ 7/98; VOYA 2/98)

3592 Modesitt, L. E., Jr. *The Death of Chaos* (10–12). 1995, Tor $24.95 (0-312-85721-7). In this fifth and final volume of the Recluse series, Lerris, a woodworker and earth wizard, combats the technology-based empire of Hamor. (Rev: BL 9/1/95; VOYA 2/96)

3593 Mohan, Kim, ed. *Amazing Stories: The Anthology* (9–12). 1995, Tor paper $13.95 (0-312-89048-6). Classic science fiction short stories. (Rev: BL 4/15/95)

3594 Moon, Elizabeth. *Remnant Population* (10–12). 1996, Baen $22.00 (0-671-87718-6). Ofelia hides when her people abandon their space colony in this novel about survival, self-esteem, and courage. (Rev: BL 4/15/96; SLJ 1/97; VOYA 10/96)

3595 Morrow, James, ed. *Nebula Awards 27: SFWA's Choices for the Best Science Fiction and Fantasy of the Year* (9–12). 1993, Harcourt $24.95 (0-15-164935-9). The best science fiction stories of 1991, including a series of tributes to Isaac Asimov. (Rev: BL 3/15/93; VOYA 10/93)

3596 Morrow, James, ed. *Nebula Awards 26: SFWA's Choices for the Best Science Fiction and Fantasy of the Year* (9–12). 1992, Harcourt paper $12.95 (0-15-665472-5). The best science fiction and fantasy stories of 1990. (Rev: BL 3/15/92)

3597 Morwood, Peter. *Star Trek: Rules of Engagement* (9–12). 1990, Pocket Books paper $4.99 (0-671-66129-9). Kirk and the *Enterprise* are sent to evacuate personnel from a politically dangerous planet. (Rev: BL 2/15/90; VOYA 6/90)

3598 Nelson, O. T. *The Girl Who Owned a City* (7–9). 1977, Dell paper $4.99 (0-440-92893-1). A mysterious virus kills off Earth's population except for children under the age of 13.

3599 Niven, Larry. *Ringworld* (10–12). 1981, Ballantine paper $5.99 (0-345-33392-6). In this prize-winning book, 4 unique characters are sent to explore a distant place called Ringworld. A sequel is *The Ringworld Engineers* (1985).

3600 Nix, Garth. *Shade's Children* (7–12). 1997, HarperCollins LB $15.89 (0-06-027325-9). In this science fiction novel, when a person reaches age 16, he or she is sent to the Meat Factory, where one's body parts are turned into hideous creatures. (Rev: BL 10/1/97; BR 3–4/98; SLJ 8/97; VOYA 6/98)

3601 Norton, Andre. *Key Out of Time* (7–12). 1978, Ultramarine $25.00 (0-89366-186-4). Two Time Agents recreate the conflict that destroyed life on the planet Hawaika.

3602 Norton, Andre, and Martin H. Greenberg, eds. *Catfantastic* (9–12). 1989, NAL paper $6.99 (0-88677-355-5). A collection of 13 stories about cat-beings with unusual powers. (Rev: BL 7/89; VOYA 2/90)

3603 O'Brien, Robert C. *Z for Zachariah* (7–10). 1975, Macmillan paper $4.99 (0-02-044650-0). After a nuclear holocaust, Ann believes she is the only surviving human—but is she? (Rev: BL 7/88)

3604 Oldham, June. *Found* (7–12). 1996, Orchard LB $17.99 (0-531-08893-6). In this novel set in the 21st century, Ren becomes lost in a bleak countryside, gets involved with 3 other misfits, and finds an abandoned baby. (Rev: BL 9/15/96; BR 3–4/97; SLJ 10/96; VOYA 2/97)

3605 Parker, Daniel. *April* (7–10). (Countdown) 1999, Simon & Schuster paper $3.99 (0-689-81822-X). In this fourth book in this complex series, teenagers find that they must take over the earth when a terrible plague kills everyone except those between 16 and 20 years of age. It is necessary to read all the books in sequence to follow the story. The others are: *January, February,* and *March* (1999). (Rev: SLJ 6/99)

3606 Paulsen, Gary. *The Transall Saga* (7–12). 1998, Delacorte $15.95 (0-385-32196-1). While on a hiking trip, young Mark is transported to a primitive world in this science fiction novel with a strong survival theme. (Rev: BL 5/15/98; BR 11–12/98; SLJ 5/98; VOYA 10/98)

3607 Peel, John. *The Zanti Misfits* (6–10). 1997, Tor paper $3.99 (0-8125-9063-5). This quick read, a product of *The Outer Limits* television show, tells how the planet Zanti sent to Earth a shipload of their worst criminals and how 3 teenagers wander into their landing area. Also use books 3 and 4: *The Choice* and *The Time Shifter* (both 1997). (Rev: VOYA 4/98)

3608 Pepper, Dennis, ed. *The Young Oxford Book of Aliens* (5–10). Illus. 1998, Oxford $35.50 (0-19-

278155-3). Classic and current authors are represented in this fine science fiction collection of stories about aliens. (Rev: BL 4/1/99)

3609 Pinkwater, Daniel M. *The Snarkout Boys & the Avocado of Death* (6–10). 1983, NAL paper $2.50 (0-451-15852-0). Two boys search for friend Rat's uncle, an unusual scientist, in this wacky adventure. A sequel is: *The Snarkout Boys & the Baconburg Horror* (1984).

3610 Pohl, Frederik. *Midas World* (10–12). 1984, Tor paper $2.95 (0-8125-4925-2). In this novel, the world's energy crisis is solved by using robots.

3611 Pohl, Frederik, and Jack Williamson. *Land's End* (9–12). 1989, Tor paper $4.95 (0-8125-0024-5). A meteor shower wakens an alien asleep on the ocean bottom. (Rev: BL 8/88; VOYA 2/89)

3612 Read Magazine, ed. *Read into the Millennium: Tales of the Future* (6–8). 1999, Millbrook LB $22.40 (0-7613-0962-4). This collection of 10 science fiction stories includes works by Robert Lipsyte, Kurt Vonnegut, and Lois Lowry, plus adaptations of Wells's *The Time Machine* and Shelley's *Frankenstein*. (Rev: BL 5/15/99; BR 9–10/99; SLJ 6/99)

3613 Resnick, Mike. *Kirinyaga: A Fable of Utopia* (10–12). 1998, Del Rey $25.00 (0-345-41701-1). Set in the 22nd century, Koriba, a well-educated man, tries to save his utopian planetoid society by reinstating the ancient customs and strict laws of his Kikuyu ancestors of Kenya, but in spite of the best intentions, it appears his efforts will fail. (Rev: BL 2/15/98; SLJ 3/99; VOYA 10/98)

3614 Rubinstein, Gillian. *Galax-Arena* (7–10). 1995, Simon & Schuster paper $15.00 (0-689-80136-X). A 13-year-old girl and 20 other children from Earth are removed to another planet and trained to perform dangerous acrobatic tricks. (Rev: BL 10/15/95*; SLJ 10/95)

3615 Sargent, Pamela. *Alien Child* (8–12). 1988, HarperCollins $13.95 (0-06-025202-2). A teenage girl raised in an alien world discovers there is another human living in her complex. (Rev: BL 2/1/88; BR 9–10/88; SLJ 4/88; VOYA 8/88)

3616 Sargent, Pamela, ed. *Nebula Awards 29: SFWA's Choices for the Best Science Fiction and Fantasy of the Year* (9–12). 1995, Harcourt paper $17.00 (0-15-600119-5). A collection of prize-winning science fiction and fantasy stories for the year 1993. (Rev: BL 4/15/95; SLJ 10/95)

3617 Sargent, Pamela, ed. *Women of Wonder: The Classic Years: Science Fiction by Women from the 1940s to the 1970s* (9–12). 1995, Harcourt paper $15.00 (0-15-600031-8). The first of 2 volumes updating the previous 3 out-of-print *Women of Wonder* titles. Includes 21 stories and a perceptive introductory overview of women in science fiction. (Rev: BL 8/95)

3618 Sargent, Pamela, ed. *Women of Wonder: The Contemporary Years: Science Fiction by Women from the 1970s to the 1990s* (9–12). 1995, Harcourt paper $15.00 (0-15-600033-4). The second of 2 volumes updating the out-of-print *Women of Wonder* titles includes 21 stories published between 1978 and 1993, with suggestions for further reading. (Rev: BL 8/95)

3619 Sawyer, Robert J. *Illegal Alien* (10–12). 1997, Ace paper $21.95 (0-441-00476-8). Science fiction and a legal thriller are combined in this novel in which a popular astronomer and TV personality is found horribly murdered after a disabled alien spacecraft lands on an aircraft carrier he's on in the middle of the ocean. (Rev: VOYA 8/98)

3620 Scrimger, Richard. *The Nose from Jupiter* (5–8). 1998, Tundra paper $7.95 (0-88776-428-2). Alan doesn't mind that Norbert, an alien from Jupiter, is living in his nose, but Norbert's outspoken remarks often get Alan into trouble. (Rev: BL 7/98; BR 11–12/98)

3621 Sheffield, Charles. *Cold As Ice* (9–12). 1993, Tor paper $4.99 (0-8125-1163-8). Nine sleeping infants, once nestled in pods and ejected from a doomed ship, have grown up to become the key to an extraordinary race. (Rev: BL 6/15/92*)

3622 Sheffield, Charles. *Godspeed* (9–12). 1994, Tor $4.99 (0-8125-1992-2). Teenager Jay Hara falls into a space voyage to find the Godspeed Drive, which would make interstellar travel possible and bring Jay's home planet out of isolation. (Rev: BL 11/15/93; VOYA 4/94)

3623 Sheffield, Charles. *Putting Up Roots: A Jupiter Novel* (9–12). 1997, Tor $21.95 (0-312-86241-5). Fourteen-year-old Josh and an autistic girl his age, Dawn, are sold into service to a company that has a farming franchise on the planet Solferino. (Rev: BL 8/97; VOYA 2/98)

3624 Shelley, Mary. *Frankenstein* (8–12). Illus. (Whole Story) 1998, Viking $25.99 (0-670-87800-6). Illustrations plus period prints and maps enhance this complete version of the early science fiction thriller. (Rev: BL 9/1/98; SLJ 10/98)

3625 Shusterman, Neal. *The Dark Side of Nowhere: A Novel* (6–9). 1996, Little, Brown $15.95 (0-316-78907-0). Jason, who has been living an ordinary life, discovers that his parents are aliens and that his friend has been transformed into an otherworldly being. (Rev: BL 4/1/97; BR 9–10/97; SLJ 7/97; VOYA 12/97)

3626 Silverberg, Robert. *Lord Valentine's Castle* (10–12). 1995, HarperCollins paper $6.50 (0-06-105487-9). A young amnesiac slowly realizes that he

is the real Lord Valentine, ruler of his planet. Sequels in this series are *Majipoor Chronicles* and *Valentine Pontifex* (both 1983).

3627 Silverberg, Robert, ed. *Robert Silverberg's Worlds of Wonder: Exploring the Craft of Science Fiction* (9–12). 1987, Warner $12.95 (0-446-39012-7). A collection of short science fiction plus a guide to science fiction writing. (Rev: BL 10/1/87; VOYA 2/88)

3628 Skurzynski, Gloria. *Virtual War* (6–9). Illus. 1997, Simon & Schuster paper $16.00 (0-689-81374-0). Fourteen-year-old Corgan and 2 other youngsters are chosen by the Council to represent the Western Hemisphere Federation in a virtual war. (Rev: BL 8/97; SLJ 7/97; VOYA 8/97)

3629 Sleator, William. *The Boy Who Reversed Himself* (8–12). 1998, Puffin paper $4.99 (0-14-038965-2). Laura travels into the fourth dimension with her gifted neighbor and literally everything in her life becomes upside down. (Rev: BL 10/15/86; BR 5–6/87; SLJ 11/86; VOYA 6/87)

3630 Sleator, William. *The Duplicate* (7–10). 1990, Bantam paper $3.99 (0-553-28634-X). A teenager discovers a machine that allows him the power to duplicate himself. (Rev: BL 5/15/88; SLJ 4/88; VOYA 12/88)

3631 Sleator, William. *House of Stairs* (7–10). 1991, Puffin paper $4.99 (0-14-034580-9). Five teenage orphans are kidnapped to become part of an experiment on aggression.

3632 Sleator, William. *Interstellar Pig* (7–10). 1996, Peter Smith $18.50 (0-8446-6898-2); Puffin paper $3.99 (0-14-037595-3). Barney plays a strange board game with strangers who are actually aliens from space.

3633 Sleator, William. *The Night the Heads Came* (6–9). 1996, Dutton $15.99 (0-525-45463-2). A thrilling science fiction adventure in which Leo has problems adjusting to normal life after being abducted by aliens. (Rev: BL 3/15/96; BR 9–10/96; SLJ 4/96)

3634 Sleator, William. *Singularity* (7–12). 1995, Puffin paper $4.99 (0-14-037598-8). Twin boys discover a playhouse on the property they have inherited that contains a mystery involving monsters from space and a new dimension in time. (Rev: BL 4/1/85; SLJ 8/85)

3635 Sleator, William. *Strange Attractors* (7–12). 1991, Puffin paper $4.99 (0-14-034582-5). Max travels through time by using a device several people would kill to possess. (Rev: BL 1/15/90; SLJ 12/89; VOYA 2/90)

3636 Slote, Alfred. *My Robot Buddy* (5–8). Illus. 1986, HarperCollins $12.95 (0-397-31641-0); paper $4.95 (0-06-440165-0). An easily read novel about

Danny and the robot that is created for him. (Rev: BL 11/1/87)

3637 Stabenow, Dana. *Red Planet Run* (9–12). 1995, Berkley paper $5.50 (0-441-00135-1). The feisty heroine, Star Svensdottir, and her twins experience a series of fast-paced adventures, beginning with trouble over the design of an asteroid being turned into a space habitat. (Rev: BL 1/1/95; VOYA 5/95)

3638 Stackpole, Michael A. *I, Jedi* (8–12). 1998, Bantam $23.95 (0-553-10820-4). In order to find his wife, Corran must take a quick course at the Jedi Academy founded by Luke Skywalker to be able to learn to use his hidden powers. (Rev: VOYA 12/98)

3639 Steele, Allen. *The Jericho Iteration* (9–12). 1994, Berkley paper $19.95 (0-441-00097-5). In 2012, a reporter uncovers the militaristic Emergency Relief Agency's scheme to use an antimissile satellite to stop civilian unrest and implement martial law. (Rev: BL 10/1/94; VOYA 12/94)

3640 Stemp, Jane. *Waterbound* (6–10). 1996, Dial paper $15.99 (0-8037-1994-9). Gem, who lives in the tightly controlled culture of the future, discovers another world where the misfits are kept. (Rev: BL 8/96; BR 3–4/97; SLJ 9/96; VOYA 8/97)

3641 Stewart, George R. *Earth Abides* (10–12). 1993, Buccaneer LB $29.95 (0-89969-370-3); Fawcett paper $6.99 (0-449-21301-3). A classic about a group of people who survive a catastrophe that almost destroys the Earth.

3642 Thompson, Julian. *Goofbang Value Daze* (9–12). 1989, Scholastic paper $12.95 (0-590-41946-3). In a high school of the future, the students are being unfairly dictated to by its administrators. (Rev: BL 3/1/89; SLJ 2/89; VOYA 6/89)

3643 Thompson, Kate. *Switchers* (5–8). 1998, Hyperion LB $15.49 (0-7868-2328-3); paper $5.99 (0-7868-1266-4). Two teens who are able to change shape and become any animal they wish, real or imaginary, set out to stop a group of mysterious ice creatures who are causing severe blizzards. (Rev: BL 3/15/98; SLJ 5/98)

3644 Thomson, Amy. *The Color of Distance* (10–12). 1995, Ace paper $13.00 (0-441-00244-7). Biologist/space explorer Juna, the lone human survivor on a strange, rain forest planet inhabited by the Tendu, intelligent, tree-dwelling amphibian creatures, must almost totally transform herself and assimilate into Tendu society. (Rev: VOYA 4/96)

3645 Tolan, Stephanie S. *Welcome to the Ark* (7–10). 1996, Morrow $15.00 (0-688-13724-5). Science fiction and adventure combine in the story of 4 young people who are able to act for good or evil through telecommunications. (Rev: BL 10/15/96; BR 11–12/96; SLJ 10/96; VOYA 4/97)

3646 Townsend, John Rowe. *The Creatures* (7–10). 1980, HarperCollins $12.95 (0-397-31864-2). Earth is dominated by creatures from another planet who believe in mind over emotion.

3647 Turtledove, Harry. *The Great War: American Front* (10–12). (The Great War) 1998, Del Rey $25.00 (0-345-40615-X). An alternative history novel set during the early 20th century, at the outbreak of World War I, in which Teddy Roosevelt allies his supporters with Germany and Woodrow Wilson joins with France and Great Britain, bringing a divided nation into trench warfare on United States soil. (Rev: SLJ 3/99; VOYA 12/98)

3648 Ure, Jean. *Plague* (7–12). 1991, Harcourt $16.95 (0-15-262429-5); 1993, Puffin paper $4.99 (0-14-036283-5). Three teenagers must band together to survive in a hostile, nearly deserted London after a catastrophe has killed almost everyone. (Rev: BL 11/15/91*; SLJ 10/91)

3649 Verne, Jules. *Around the Moon* (8–12). 1968, Airmont paper $1.50 (0-8049-0182-1). An early science fiction relic about a trip to the moon. Also use: *From the Earth to the Moon* (1984).

3650 Verne, Jules. *Master of the World* (9–12). n.d., Amereon $20.95 (0-89190-518-9). A scientist who has invented an amazing machine claims he is the master of the world.

3651 Vinge, Joan D. *Psion* (9–12). 1996, Warner paper $5.99 (0-446-60354-6). A 16-year-old boy named Cat finds the gift of telepathy a mixed blessing.

3652 Waugh, Charles G., and Martin H. Greenberg, eds. *Sci-Fi Private Eye* (9–12). 1997, Roc paper $5.99 (0-451-45582-4). Most of the 9 stories in this collection, by such writers as Donald Westlake, Robert Silverberg, and Philip K. Dick, are mysteries with a science fiction twist. (Rev: VOYA 10/97)

3653 Weber, David. *Honor Among Enemies* (9–12). 1996, Baen $21.00 (0-671-87723-2). Captain Honor Harrington is brought out of retirement by the Royal Manticoran Navy to lead a task force of interstellar vessels against evil pirates who are plundering merchant ships and ravaging their crews. (Rev: BL 6/1–15/96; VOYA 12/96)

3654 Weis, Margaret, ed. *A Magic-Lover's Treasury of the Fantastic* (9–12). 1998, Warner paper $13.99 (0-446-67284-X). Twenty stories of science fiction and fantasy by such well-known writers as Katherine Kurtz, Orson Scott Card, and Robert Silverberg. (Rev: VOYA 10/98)

3655 Wells, H. G. *First Men in the Moon* (7–12). 1993, Tuttle paper $3.95 (0-460-87304-0). The first men on the moon discover strange creatures living there.

3656 Wells, H. G. *The Food of the Gods* (10–12). 1978, Pendulum paper $2.95 (0-88301-314-2). This novel is set in a land where people do not stop growing.

3657 Wells, H. G. *In the Days of the Comet* (10–12). 1999, Troll paper $2.95 (0-89375-704-7). The world changes as a result of gases emitted by an approaching comet.

3658 Wells, H. G. *The Invisible Man* (8–12). 1987, Buccaneer LB $21.95 (0-89966-377-X); Bantam paper $4.95 (0-553-21353-9). Two editions of many available of the story of a scientist who finds a way to make himself invisible.

3659 Wells, H. G. *Island of Doctor Moreau* (9–12). 1983, Buccaneer LB $16.95 (0-89966-470-9); NAL paper $4.95 (0-451-52191-9). A shipwrecked sailor arrives at an island where strange experiments are taking place.

3660 Wells, H. G. *Time Machine* (7–12). 1984, Bantam paper $4.95 (0-553-21351-2). This is one of the earliest novels to use traveling through time as its subject.

3661 Wells, H. G. *The War of the Worlds* (7–12). 1988, Bantam paper $4.95 (0-553-21338-5). In this early science fiction novel, first published in 1898, strange creatures from Mars invade England.

3662 Westwood, Chris. *Virtual World* (6–9). 1997, Viking $15.99 (0-670-87546-5). When 14-year-old Jack North plays a pirated copy of a computer game called Silicon Sphere, he suddenly finds he has been transported to the world of virtual reality. (Rev: BL 9/1/97; BR 3–4/98; SLJ 1/98; VOYA 6/98)

3663 Wieler, Diana. *RanVan: A Worthy Opponent* (7–10). 1998, Douglas & McIntyre $16.95 (0-88899-271-8); paper $5.95 (0-88899-219-X). Though 15-year-old nerdy RanVan dreams of saving civilization like in the video games he plays, real life is different, until, when put to the test, he discovers hidden powers. Preceded by *RanVan: The Defender* and followed by *RanVan: Magic Nation* (1998). (Rev: BL 11/15/98; SLJ 3/98)

3664 Williamson, Jack. *The Black Sun* (9–12). 1997, Tor $23.95 (0-312-85937-6). Carlos Mondragon, who always dreamed of space travel, stows away on the last of the quantum-wave starships. (Rev: VOYA 8/97)

3665 Willis, Connie. *Impossible Things* (9–12). 1994, Bantam paper $6.50 (0-553-56436-6). In this second collection of her science fiction short stories, Willis presents 11 works, including award-winning "The Last of the Winnebagos," "Even the Queen," and "At the Rialto." (Rev: BL 12/15/93*; SLJ 3/95; VOYA 6/94)

3666 Wilson, F. Paul, and Matthew J. Costello. *Masque* (9–12). 1998, Warner $23.00 (0-446-51977-

4). A high-tech adventure set in 2058 in which Kaze Glom secret agent Tristan, who is a mime—a cloned human being who can be transformed into a genetic copy of any human or creature—is tricked into bringing back a virus that destroys the Kaze Glom's entire mime population. (Rev: VOYA 8/98)

3667 Wismer, Donald. *Starluck* (6–8). 1982, Ultramarine $20.00 (0-89366-255-0). A boy with unusual powers tries to overthrow a wicked emperor.

3668 Wulffson, Don L. *Future Fright: Tales of High-Tech Terror* (6–9). 1996, Lowell House paper $4.95 (1-56565-393-9). In this collection of 6 creepy tales, each of the protagonists falls victim to some technological mishap. (Rev: SLJ 3/97)

3669 Wyndham, John. *The Day of the Triffids* (10–12). 1985, Ballantine paper $5.99 (0-345-32817-5). A combined science fiction and horror story about some flesh-eating plants that cause havoc on Earth.

3670 Yolen, Jane, ed. *Xanadu* (9–12). 1994, Tor paper $4.99 (0-8125-2082-3). An anthology of sci-fi tales and poems, many with youthful protagonists and situations. Also use *Xanadu 2* and *Xanadu 3*. (Rev: BL 1/15/93; VOYA 8/93)

3671 Yolen, Jane, et al., eds. *Spaceships & Spells* (5–9). 1987, HarperCollins $12.95 (0-06-026796-8). A collection of 13 original tales, mostly of science fiction but also some fantasy. (Rev: BL 1/15/88; BR 3–4/88; SLJ 11/87)

3672 Zelazny, Roger. *A Dark Traveling* (9–12). 1987, Avon paper $3.50 (0-380-70567-2). A fast-moving plot about parallel worlds highlights this Hugo Award-winning novella. (Rev: BL 4/1/87; SLJ 8/87; VOYA 8/87)

3673 Zelazny, Roger. *Knight of Shadows* (10–12). 1990, Avon paper $5.99 (0-380-75501-7). This is the ninth book in the Amber series about a modern Merlin. (Rev: BL 10/15/89)

3674 Zelazny, Roger, ed. *Williamson Effect* (8–12). 1996, Tor $23.95 (0-312-85748-9). A collection of short stories by such SF writers as Andre Norton and Frederik Pohl that pay tribute to the "Grand Master" of science fiction, Jack Williamson, who conceived of and wrote about genetic engineering, anti-matter, and time travel. (Rev: BL 5/1/96; VOYA 10/96)

Sports

3675 Adler, C. S. *Winning* (5–8). 1999, Clarion $14.00 (0-395-65017-8). Vicky lacks the courage and self-confidence to challenge her tennis partner when she catches her cheating. (Rev: BL 10/1/99; SLJ 9/99)

3676 Altman, Millys N. *Racing in Her Blood* (7–12). 1980, HarperCollins LB $12.89 (0-397-31895-2). A junior novel about a young girl who wants to succeed in the world of automobile racing.

3677 Bauer, Joan. *Sticks* (5–8). 1996, Delacorte $15.95 (0-385-32165-1). Ten-year-old Mickey, who is recovering from his father's death, gets an old family friend to teach him pool tricks so that he will have a chance at the Pool Hall Youth Championship. (Rev: BL 5/1/96; SLJ 6/96)

3678 Bennett, James. *Blue Star Rapture* (7–12). 1998, Simon & Schuster paper $16.00 (0-689-81580-8). T. J., a basketball hopeful, goes to a basketball camp, where he meets a girl from a religious cult in this novel about sports, politicking, religion, and loyalty. (Rev: BL 4/15/98; BR 1–2/99; SLJ 6/98; VOYA 12/98)

3679 Brooks, Bruce. *Billy* (4–8). (Wolfbay Wings) 1998, Demco $9.60 (0-606-13927-3). A first-person narrative by Billy, the center of the Wolfbay Wings hockey team, who describes his problems with an overbearing, interfering father and his difficulty, as the youngest team member, in finding his place on the team. (Rev: SLJ 7/98)

3680 Brooks, Bruce. *Dooby* (5–8). (Wolfbay Wings) 1998, HarperCollins LB $14.89 (0-06-027898-6); paper $4.50 (0-06-440708-X). Dooby sulks when he is not made captain of his Peewee hockey team, but is completely humiliated to learn he has lost out to a girl. Also use in the same series *Reed* (1998). (Rev: SLJ 2/99)

3681 Brooks, Bruce. *The Moves Make the Man* (7–9). 1984, HarperCollins $15.00 (0-06-020679-9); paper $4.95 (0-06-447022-9). Jerome, the only black student in his high school and a star basketball player, forms an unusual friendship with Bix. (Rev: BL 3/87)

3682 Brooks, Bruce. *Prince* (5–8). (Wolfbay Wings) 1998, HarperCollins $14.89 (0-06-027542-1); paper $4.50 (0-06-440600-8). In this story of the Wolfbay Wings hockey team, Prince, their only black player, is being pressured by his middle-school coach to switch to basketball. (Rev: SLJ 6/98)

3683 Brooks, Bruce. *Shark* (5–8). (Wolfbay Wings) 1998, HarperCollins $14.89 (0-06-027570-7); paper $4.50 (0-06-440681-4). In spite of being fat, slow, and confused, Shark becomes a valuable player on the Wolfbay Wings hockey team. (Rev: SLJ 6/98)

3684 Cadnum, Michael. *Heat* (7–12). 1998, Viking $15.99 (0-670-87886-3). Bonnie, a competitive diver who has bashed her head on the bottom of the swimming pool, also faces a family problem when her father is accused of fraud. (Rev: BL 8/98; BR 1–2/99; SLJ 9/98; VOYA 12/98)

3685 Calvert, Patricia. *The Hour of the Wolf* (7–10). 1985, NAL paper $2.50 (0-451-13493-1). A boy enters a famous dogsled race in Alaska to honor his friend who committed suicide. (Rev: BL 11/1/88)

3686 Carter, Alden R. *Bull Catcher* (7–10). 1997, Scholastic $15.95 (0-590-50958-6). High school friends Bull and Jeff seem to live for baseball and plan their futures around the sport, but one of them begins to move in a different direction. (Rev: BL 4/15/97; BR 5–6/97; SLJ 5/97; VOYA 10/97)

3687 Cheripko, Jan. *Imitate the Tiger* (8–12). 1996, Boyds Mills $14.95 (1-56397-514-9). This novel deals with the problems of Chris Serbo, a fine high school football player who also has a severe alcohol problem. (Rev: SLJ 6/96; VOYA 8/96)

3688 Christopher, Matt. *Spike It!* (5–8). 1999, Little, Brown $15.95 (0-316-13451-1); paper $3.95 (0-316-13401-5). Jamie's new stepsister, Michaela, seems to be taking over her life, but at least she has her interest in volleyball to herself—at least, until Michaela joins the team. (Rev: SLJ 6/99)

3689 Cochran, Thomas. *Roughnecks* (8–12). 1997, Harcourt $15.00 (0-15-201433-0). Senior Travis Cody, the narrator, wonders if he will be able to redeem himself with his football teammates after being responsible for a crucial loss because of a missed block. (Rev: BL 9/15/97; SLJ 10/97; VOYA 12/97)

3690 Crutcher, Chris. *The Crazy Horse Electric Game* (7–12). 1987, Greenwillow $14.00 (0-688-06683-6); Dell paper $4.50 (0-440-20094-6). A motorboat accident ends the comfortable life and budding baseball career of a teenage boy. (Rev: BL 4/15/87; BR 9–10/87; SLJ 5/87; VOYA 6/87)

3691 Crutcher, Chris. *Ironman* (8–12). 1995, Greenwillow $16.00 (0-688-13503-X). A psychological/sports novel in which a 17-year-old carries an attitude that fuels the plot. (Rev: BL 3/1/95*; SLJ 3/95; VOYA 5/95)

3692 Crutcher, Chris. *Running Loose* (7–10). 1983, Greenwillow $17.95 (0-688-02002-X); Bantam paper $4.99 (0-440-97570-0). A senior in high school faces problems when he opposes the decisions of a football coach. (Rev: BL 3/87)

3693 Deuker, Carl. *Heart of a Champion* (8–10). 1993, 1994, Avon paper $4.50 (0-380-72269-0). Explores the ups and downs of the 5-year friendship between Seth and Jimmy, from their first meeting on a baseball field at age 12. (Rev: BL 6/1–15/93; SLJ 6/93)

3694 Deuker, Carl. *On the Devil's Court* (8–12). 1991, Avon paper $4.50 (0-380-70879-5). In this variation on the Faust legend, a senior high basketball star believes he has sold his soul to have a perfect season. (Rev: BL 12/15/88; BR 9–10/89; SLJ 1/89; VOYA 4/89)

3695 Deuker, Carl. *Painting the Black* (8–12). 1997, Houghton $14.95 (0-395-82848-1). Ryan's spot on the baseball team hinges on catching the pitches of Josh Daniels, a sharp new player who is adept in both baseball and football. (Rev: BL 6/1–15/97; BR 11–12/97; SLJ 5/97; VOYA 8/97)

3696 Drumtra, Stacy. *Face-off* (5–9). 1992, Avon paper $3.50 (0-380-76863-1). When T. J. transfers to his twin brother's school, their competition for friends, recognition, and hockey greatness turns bitter. (Rev: BL 4/1/93; VOYA 8/93)

3697 Dygard, Thomas J. *Backfield Package* (6–10). 1992, Morrow $14.00 (0-688-11471-7). Two high school football stars want to play together in college, but only one of them is offered a scholarship. (Rev: BL 9/15/92; SLJ 9/92)

3698 Dygard, Thomas J. *Game Plan* (6–9). 1993, Morrow $14.00 (0-688-12007-5); 1995, Penguin paper $4.99 (0-14-036970-8). Beano, a high school football student manager, must coach the team when the team's coach is injured in a car accident. (Rev: BL 9/1/93; SLJ 10/93; VOYA 2/94)

3699 Dygard, Thomas J. *Halfback Tough* (7–12). 1986, Penguin paper $4.99 (0-14-034113-7). Joe Atkins tries to leave his troubled past behind when he attends a new school and joins the school's football team. (Rev: BL 4/1/86; BR 9–10/86; SLJ 10/86; VOYA 6/86)

3700 Dygard, Thomas J. *Infield Hit* (6–9). 1995, Morrow $16.00 (0-688-14037-8). A boy struggles to make new friends by playing baseball. (Rev: BL 4/15/95; SLJ 3/95)

3701 Dygard, Thomas J. *Quarterback Walk-On* (7–9). 1982, Penguin paper $4.99 (0-14-034115-3). A fourth-string quarterback becomes an instant star.

3702 Dygard, Thomas J. *The Rebounder* (7–10). 1994, Morrow $16.00 (0-688-12821-1). Chris quits playing basketball after accidentally injuring an opponent. After transferring to a new school, he is guided back to the sport by a sensitive coach. (Rev: BL 9/1/94; SLJ 10/94)

3703 Dygard, Thomas J. *The Rookie Arrives* (7–12). 1989, Puffin paper $4.99 (0-14-034112-9). Ted Bell comes of age when he becomes a major-leaguer fresh from high school. (Rev: BL 3/1/88; BR 5–6/88; SLJ 3/88)

3704 Dygard, Thomas J. *Running Wild* (7–10). 1996, Morrow $15.00 (0-688-14853-0). When Pete is forced to attend football practices, he discovers that he really enjoys the game. (Rev: BL 8/96; SLJ 9/96)

3705 Dygard, Thomas J. *Second Stringer* (6–12). 1998, Morrow $15.00 (0-688-15981-8). A knee injury suffered by the quarterback gives second stringer Kevin Taylor the opportunity of a lifetime his senior year in high school. (Rev: BL 9/1/98; SLJ 12/98; VOYA 2/99)

3706 Dygard, Thomas J. *Tournament Upstart* (7–9). 1984, Penguin paper $4.99 (0-14-034114-5). A tiny high school produces a prize-winning basketball team.

3707 Farrell, Mame. *Bradley & the Billboard* (5–8). 1998, Farrar $16.00 (0-374-30949-3). Brad Wilson, a precocious kid who plays amazing baseball, finds a new life when he enters the modeling world. (Rev: BL 7/98; SLJ 5/98)

3708 Godfrey, Martyn. *Ice Hawk* (7–12). Illus. 1986, EMC paper $13.50 (0-8219-0235-0). An easy-to-read story about a young minor league hockey player who balks at unnecessary use of violence. (Rev: BL 2/1/87)

3709 Guy, David. *Football Dreams* (9–12). 1982, NAL paper $5.95 (0-451-15868-7). A story about the thoughts and actions of a freshman at Arnold Academy who wants to make the football team.

3710 Hoffius, Stephen. *Winners and Losers* (7–10). 1993, Simon & Schuster paper $16.00 (0-671-79194-X). When star runner Daryl collapses during a meet, the coach, his father, starts to ignore him and push Daryl's friend Curt to train harder. (Rev: BL 7/93; VOYA 2/94)

3711 Jarzyna, Dave. *Slump* (5–8). 1999, Delacorte $14.95 (0-385-32618-1). Everything seems to be going wrong with 13-year-old Mitchie Evers after he quits the soccer team due to a disagreement with the coach, but when life looks darkest, Mitchie decides to do something about it. (Rev: SLJ 8/99)

3712 Johnson, Scott. *Safe at Second* (5–8). 1999, Putnam $17.99 (0-399-23365-2). The story of the friendship between Paulie and Todd, their love of baseball, and what happens after Todd is hit during a game and loses an eye. (Rev: BL 6/1–15/99; SLJ 7/99; VOYA 8/99)

3713 Klass, David. *Danger Zone* (7–12). 1996, Scholastic $16.95 (0-590-48590-3). Jimmy Doyle, a young basketball star, tries to prove to himself as well as to his mostly African American teammates that he deserves a place on the American High School Dream Team. (Rev: BL 4/1/96; BR 5–6/96; SLJ 3/96; VOYA 4/96)

3714 Knudson, R. R. *Fox Running* (7–9). Illus. 1977, Avon paper $2.50 (0-380-00930-7). Kathy and an Apache Indian girl find friendship and inspiration in their mutual love of running.

3715 Konigsburg, E. L. *About the B'nai Bagels* (6–8). 1973, Dell paper $3.99 (0-440-40034-1). In this easily read story, Mark is uncomfortable at the thought of his mother's being the manager of his Little League baseball team. (Rev: BL 5/1/89)

3716 Korman, Gordon. *The Zucchini Warriors* (6–8). 1991, Scholastic paper $4.50 (0-590-44174-4). Hank, a former football player, promises to build Bruno and Boots's school a recreation hall if their team has a winning season. (Rev: BR 1–2/89; VOYA 10/88)

3717 Levy, Marilyn. *Run for Your Life* (7–9). 1996, Houghton $15.00 (0-395-74520-9). Thirteen-year-old Kisha tries to escape the Oakland projects and her parents' crumbling marriage by joining a track team that has been started by a new community center director. (Rev: BL 4/1/96; BR 9–10/96; SLJ 3/96; VOYA 6/96)

3718 Lynch, Chris. *Iceman* (8–12). 1994, Harper-Collins $15.00 (0-06-023340-0). An emotionally fragile teenager expresses his anger in violent hockey games and spends time at the local mortuary with a disturbed recluse who works there. (Rev: BL 2/1/94; SLJ 3/94; VOYA 4/94)

3719 McGinley, Jerry. *Joaquin Strikes Back* (6–9). 1998, Tudor $18.95 (0-936389-58-3). Joaquin forms a soccer team in his new school that eventually plays the team from his former school. (Rev: BL 3/15/98; SLJ 3/99)

3720 Maclean, John. *When the Mountain Sings* (6–9). 1992, Houghton $14.95 (0-395-59917-2). Sam, 13, pushes himself and achieves more than he believes he can as a competitive skier. (Rev: BL 11/15/92; SLJ 12/92)

3721 Murrow, Liza Ketchum. *Twelve Days in August* (8–12). 1993, Holiday House $14.95 (0-8234-1012-9). In the course of a school year, Todd, 16, must cope with a soccer team bully, homophobia, peer pressure, and girlfriend problems. (Rev: BL 3/1/93; VOYA 10/93)

3722 Myers, Walter Dean. *Hoops* (7–10). 1981, Dell paper $4.99 (0-440-93884-8). Lonnie plays basketball in spite of his coach, a has-been named Cal. Followed by *The Outside Shot* (1987).

3723 Neumann, Peter J. *Playing a Virginia Moon* (8–12). 1994, Houghton $14.95 (0-395-66562-0). A fiercely competitive high school senior is determined to win a cross-country championship and plans his race strategy as if for battle, using General Robert E. Lee as his model. (Rev: BL 3/15/94; SLJ 5/94; VOYA 6/94)

3724 Norman, Rick. *Cross Body Block* (8–10). 1996, Colonial Pr. paper $9.95 (1-56883-060-2). An anguished story about a middle-aged football coach and his personal family tragedies, including the brutal death of a son. (Rev: BR 9–10/96; VOYA 8/96)

3725 Platt, Kin. *Brogg's Brain* (6–9). 1981, Harper-Collins LB $11.89 (0-397-31946-0). Monty is a runner who is pushed by his father and his coach to win.

3726 Powell, Randy. *Dean Duffy* (8–12). 1995, Farrar $15.00 (0-374-31754-2). A Little League baseball great has problems with his pitching arm and sees his career collapse. (Rev: BL 4/15/95; SLJ 5/95)

3727 Powell, Randy. *The Whistling Toilets* (7–10). 1996, Farrar $17.00 (0-374-38381-2). When Stan tries to help his friend Ginny with her tennis game, he finds that something strange is troubling the rising young tennis star. (Rev: BL 9/15/96; BR 3–4/97; SLJ 10/96; VOYA 12/96)

3728 Quies, Werner. *Soccer Shots* (6–9). 1995, Frontier paper $10.95 (0-939116-37-5). A 16-year-old East German boy pursues his dream of becoming a professional soccer player in the West. (Rev: BL 12/1/95)

3729 Revoyr, Nina. *The Necessary Hunger* (10–12). 1997, Simon & Schuster $22.50 (0-684-83234-8). Nancy Takahiro, a senior in high school and a gifted basketball player, is attracted to another player, Raina Webber, in this novel that also explores the many layers of racial prejudice. (Rev: SLJ 12/97; VOYA 12/97)

3730 Ritter, John H. *Choosing up Sides* (5–9). 1998, Putnam $16.99 (0-399-23185-4). Jake is a great southpaw in baseball, but his father, a preacher, forbids him to use his left hand for pitching because he believes it is the instrument of Satan. (Rev: BL 5/1/98; SLJ 6/98; VOYA 12/98)

3731 Rogo, Thomas Paul. *A Surfrider's Odyssey* (5–8). Illus. 1999, Bess Pr. $19.95 (1-57306-082-8). This is the story of Earl, an all-American boy in the 1940s who teaches himself surfing and, in spite of a series of misadventures, proves himself a hero. (Rev: SLJ 8/99)

3732 Romain, Joseph. *The Mystery of the Wagner Whacker* (7–12). 1997, Warwick Publg. paper $8.95 (1-895629-94-2). Matt, a baseball enthusiast, is upset at moving to a small Canadian town where the sport is all but unknown, but an accidental travel in time to 1928 changes the situation. (Rev: BL 7/98; SLJ 7/98)

3733 Schulman, L. M., ed. *The Random House Book of Sports Stories* (7–12). 1990, Random LB $16.99 (0-394-92874-1). From a wide range of authors, past and present, comes a fine anthology of sports stories. (Rev: BL 12/1/90)

3734 Smith, Charles R., Jr. *Rimshots: Basketball Pix, Rolls, and Rhythms* (5–9). 1999, Dutton $15.99 (0-525-46099-3). In a series of poems and prose pieces, the author-photographer explores different facets of basketball and reveals a deep love of the game. (Rev: SLJ 2/99)

3735 Spinelli, Jerry. *There's a Girl in My Hammer-lock* (5–8). 1991, Simon & Schuster paper $14.00 (0-671-74684-7). This story of a girl who goes out for junior high wrestling, to the consternation of almost everyone but her mother, raises questions about gender roles and personal identity. (Rev: BL 10/15/91; SLJ 9/91*)

3736 Staudohar, Paul D., ed. *Baseball's Best Short Stories* (9–12). 1997, Chicago Review paper $16.95 (1-55652-319-X). Baseball stories from such renowned authors as Zane Grey, Robert Penn Warren, and James Thurber. (Rev: BL 11/15/95)

3737 Tunis, John R. *Keystone Kids* (6–9). 1990, Harcourt paper $3.95 (0-15-242388-5). A reissue of the classic 1943 baseball story about 2 exceptional brothers. Also use *Highpockets* (1948) and *World Series* (1941). (Rev: BL 4/1/90)

3738 Tunis, John R. *The Kid from Tomkinsville* (6–9). 1990, Harcourt paper $6.00 (0-15-242567-5). This novel, first published in 1940, introduces Roy Tucker and his remarkable pitching arm. It is continued in *The Kid Comes Back* (1946). Also use *Rookie of the Year* (1944). (Rev: BL 4/1/90)

3739 Wallace, Rich. *Shots on Goal* (7–10). 1997, Knopf LB $18.99 (0-679-98670-7). Set against the exciting world of high school soccer, this novel also deals with the friendship of two of the team's players and how trouble with girls is dividing them. (Rev: BL 9/15/97; BR 1–2/98; SLJ 11/97)

3740 Wallace, Rich. *Wrestling Sturbridge* (9–12). 1996, Knopf $17.00 (0-679-87803-3). Ben, a high school senior, faces a bleak future in his Pennsylvania hometown and decides to turn things around by trying out for the state's wrestling title. (Rev: BL 9/1/96*; BR 11–12/96; SLJ 10/96; VOYA 6/97)

3741 Weaver, Will. *Farm Team* (7–12). 1995, HarperCollins LB $14.89 (0-06-023589-6). Shy Billy Baggs, with many responsibilities for his age, finds success playing baseball. A sequel to *Striking Out*. (Rev: BL 9/1/95)

3742 Weaver, Will. *Hard Ball* (7–12). 1998, HarperCollins LB $15.89 (0-06-027122-1). Young, poor Billy Baggs discovers that his rival for the star position on the freshman baseball team is also his rival for the attention of the girl he is attracted to. (Rev: BL 1/1–15/98; SLJ 4/98; VOYA 6/98)

3743 Weaver, Will. *Striking Out* (8–12). 1993, 1995, HarperCollins paper $4.95 (0-06-447113-6). When Minnesota farmboy Billy Baggs picks up a stray baseball and fires it back to the pitcher, his baseball career begins, but his family isn't enthusiastic. (Rev: BL 11/1/93; SLJ 10/93; VOYA 12/93)

3744 Webster-Doyle, Terrence. *Breaking the Chains of the Ancient Warrior: Tests of Wisdom for Young Martial Artists* (5–8). Illus. 1995, Martial Arts for Peace paper $14.95 (0-942941-32-2). A collection of inspirational stories, karate parables, and tests that promote ethical behavior, with accompanying follow-up questions and a message for adult readers. (Rev: SLJ 1/96)

3745 Wells, Rosemary. *When No One Was Looking* (8–12). 1987, Fawcett paper $2.95 (0-449-70251-0). This story about tennis is also a mystery involving the death of the heroine's arch rival.

3746 Wolff, Virginia E. *Bat 6* (5–9). 1998, Scholastic $16.95 (0-590-89799-3). A Japanese American girl who has just spent 6 years in an internment camp meets a bitter girl whose father was killed in Pearl Harbor, and the two become rivals in baseball in this story narrated by the members of the opposing teams. (Rev: BL 5/1/98; SLJ 5/98; VOYA 6/98)

3747 Wunderli, Stephen. *The Heartbeat of Halftime* (6–9). 1996, Holt $14.95 (0-8050-4713-1). Wing tries to forget his father's declining health by becoming totally absorbed in football. (Rev: BL 10/1/96; BR 3–4/97; SLJ 11/96; VOYA 10/96)

Short Stories and General Anthologies

3748 Asher, Sandy, ed. *But That's Another Story: Famous Authors Introduce Popular Genres* (6–8). 1996, Walker $24.95 (0-8027-8424-0). Thirteen stories are included in this anthology, each representing a different genre, such as science fiction, fantasy, and adventure, with each written by a well-known YA author. (Rev: BL 6/1–15/96; BR 11–12/96; SLJ 7/96; VOYA 8/96)

3749 Bauer, Marion Dane, ed. *Am I Blue?* (8–12). 1995, HarperCollins paper $5.95 (0-06-440587-7). Sixteen short stories from well-known YA writers who have something meaningful to share about gay awareness and want to present positive, credible gay role models. (Rev: BL 5/1/94*; SLJ 6/94; VOYA 8/94)

3750 *Best-Loved Stories Told at the National Storytelling Festival* (9–12). 1991, National Storytelling Pr. paper $11.95 (1-879991-00-4). The 37 traditional stories collected here cover a wide range of ethnic backgrounds, genres, and colloquial voices. (Rev: BL 10/15/91)

3751 Blume, Judy, ed. *Places I Never Meant to Be: Original Stories by Censored Writers* (7–12). 1999, Simon & Schuster paper $16.95 (0-689-82034-8). A collection of original stories by 12 authors who have been both honored and censored, among them Walter Dean Myers, Norma Fox Mazer, Julius Lester, Katherine Paterson, Harry Mazer, David Klass, Chris Lynch, and Paul Zindel. Royalties from this book go to the National Coalition Against Censorship. (Rev: BL 6/1–15/99; SLJ 8/99; VOYA 12/99)

3752 Coville, Bruce. *Odder than Ever* (6–8). 1999, Harcourt $16.00 (0-15-201747-X). In this companion to *Oddly Enough,* the author has collected 9 of his short stories, each dealing with a thought-provoking theme or, sometimes, a light fantasy. (Rev: BL 5/15/99; BR 9–10/99; SLJ 6/99; VOYA 10/99)

3753 Crane, Milton, ed. *50 Great American Short Stories* (10–12). 1984, Bantam paper $5.99 (0-553-27294-2). This excellent anthology spans the entire history of American literature and represents the best of many authors.

3754 Eighth Grade Writers. *Eighth Grade: Stories of Friendship, Passage & Discovery* (6–12). Ed. by Christine Lord. 1996, Merlyn's Pen paper $9.95 (1-886427-08-9). This is a group of short stories collected by *Merlyn's Pen* magazine that were written by eighth graders. Also in this series are *Freshman: Fiction, Fantasy, and Humor by Ninth Grade Writers* and *Sophomores: Tales of Reality, Conflict, and the Road,* plus 8 other volumes (all 1996). Each is accompanied by an audiotape. (Rev: VOYA 6/98)

3755 Fleischman, Paul. *Graven Images: Three Stories* (7–9). Illus. 1982, HarperCollins paper $4.95 (0-06-440186-3). Three stories that explore various aspects of human nature.

3756 Gallo, Donald R., ed. *Time Capsule: Short Stories about Teenagers throughout the Twentieth Century* (9–12). 1999, Delacorte $16.95 (0-385-32675-0). Writers like Richard Peck and Bruce Brooks have contributed to this 10-story anthology with settings spanning the 20th century. (Rev: BL 9/15/99)

3757 Giovanni, Nikki, ed. *Grand Fathers: Reminiscences, Poems, Recipes, and Photos of the Keepers of Our Traditions* (6–12). Illus. 1999, Holt $18.95 (0-8050-5484-7). A collection of family stories and memoirs, some by famous writers but most by ordinary people, with memories about fathers that range from the inspirational to the sad and angry. (Rev: BL 6/1–15/99; SLJ 7/99; VOYA 10/99) [810.8]

3758 Golden, Lilly, ed. *A Literary Christmas: Great Contemporary Christmas Stories* (9–12). 1994, Grove Atlantic paper $15.00 (0-87113-583-3). Twenty-seven stories and novel excerpts from such authors as Annie Dillard, Raymond Carver, Leo Rosten, Tobias Wolf, and Ntozake Shange. (Rev: BL 10/15/92)

3759 Haynes, David, and Julie Landsman, eds. *Welcome to Your Life: Writings for the Heart of Young America* (7–12). 1999, Milkweed paper $15.95 (1-57131-017-7). Nearly 50 award-winning contributors each tell of a pivotal childhood experience, most with a focus on race and ethnicity, that affected the rest of his or her life. Subjects include gangs, bigotry, enemies, parents, and friends. (Rev: BL 5/1/99)

3760 Henry, O. *Forty-one Stories* (9–12). 1986, NAL paper $5.95 (0-451-52254-0). A collection by the master of the surprise ending that includes all of the favorites such as "Gift of the Magi."

3761 Henry, O. *The Gift of the Magi and Other Stories* (7–12). Illus. 1997, Morrow $22.00 (0-688-14581-7). A handsome edition of 14 of O. Henry's most famous stories. (Rev: BL 10/15/97)

3762 Hudson, Wade, and Cheryl W. Hudson, eds. *In Praise of Our Fathers & Our Mothers* (6–12). Illus. 1997, Just Us $29.95 (0-940975-59-9); paper $17.95 (0-940975-60-2). Nearly 50 well-known African American writers, among them Walter Dean Myers, Virginia Hamilton, and Brian Pinkney, recall their family life in this anthology of poetry, essays, paintings, and interviews. (Rev: BL 4/1/97; SLJ 6/97)

3763 Ketchin, Susan, and Neil Giordano, eds. *25 & Under: Fiction* (10–12). 1997, Norton $25.00 (0-393-04120-4). This is a collection of 15 stories that deal with such themes as sexuality, friendship, families, loneliness, addiction, and death, all written by authors age 25 or younger. (Rev: VOYA 6/98)

3764 Kulpa, Kathryn, ed. *Something Like a Hero* (6–10). 1995, Merlyn's Pen paper $9.75 (1-886427-03-8). A collection of 11 short stories from different genres reprinted from the national magazine of student writing, *Merlyn's Pen.* (Rev: VOYA 2/96)

3765 McEwen, Christian, ed. *Jo's Girls: Tomboy Tales of High Adventure, True Grit and Real Life* (10–12). 1997, Beacon paper $30.50 (0-8070-6211-1). A well-edited collection of fiction and memoirs about girls who assume the role of tomboy by such writers as Annie Dillard, Ursula Le Guin, Toni Morrison, Colette, and Willa Cather. (Rev: BL 6/1–15/97; SLJ 3/98)

3766 Mazer, Anne, ed. *A Walk in My World: International Short Stories about Youth* (9–12). 1998, Persea $17.95 (0-89255-237-9). Sixteen stories about young people from the pens of distinguished writers from around the world afford a powerful and lasting reading experience. (Rev: BL 1/1–15/99; BR 5–6/99; SLJ 6/99; VOYA 4/99)

3767 Mee, Susie, ed. *Downhome: An Anthology of Southern Women Writers* (10–12). 1995, Harcourt paper $17.00 (0-15-600121-7). Southern life is reflected in this collection of short stories spanning several decades by women authors ranging from Eudora Welty and Zora Neale Hurston to Ellen Gilchrist and Dorothy Allison. (Rev: BL 10/15/95; SLJ 2/96)

3768 *More Best-Loved Stories Told at the National Storytelling Festival* (9–12). 1992, National Storytelling Pr. $19.95 (1-879991-09-8); paper $11.95 (1-879991-08-X). Stories featuring familiar folklore, family anecdotes, and tales from many cultures, with a brief note on each storyteller. (Rev: BL 11/15/92)

3769 Murphy, Mark. *House of Java* (10–12). Illus. 1998, N B M Publg. paper $8.95 (1-56163-202-3). A collection of short stories about the frequenters of a Seattle coffee shop and its neighborhood. (Rev: SLJ 8/98)

3770 Paterson, Katherine, ed. *Angels and Other Strangers: Family Christmas Stories* (6–9). 1979, HarperCollins paper $4.95 (0-06-440283-5). A collection of 9 short stories that explore the true meaning of Christmas.

3771 Paterson, Katherine. *A Midnight Clear: Stories for the Christmas Season* (5–10). 1995, Dutton paper $16.00 (0-525-67529-9). Stories that reveal the spirit of Christmas in contemporary life and provide hope and light in a dark, uncertain world. (Rev: BL 9/15/95)

3772 Pawlak, Mark, et al., eds. *Bullseye: Stories and Poems by Outstanding High School Writers* (9–12). 1995, Hanging Loose Pr. paper $15.00 (1-882413-12-1). A collection of poems and short narratives written by 68 teenagers taken from the pages of the literary magazine *Hanging Loose*. (Rev: BL 2/1/96; SLJ 12/95)

3773 Pilling, Ann, ed. *Love Stories* (4–8). Illus. 1997, Kingfisher paper $6.95 (0-7534-5117-4). This collection of 20 stories, many by well-known authors, deals with all kinds of love: romantic, platonic, familial, and love of humankind. (Rev: BR 3–4/98; SLJ 12/97)

3774 Rosen, Roger, and Patra McSharry, eds. *Teenage Soldiers, Adult Wars* (9–12). (Icarus World Issues) 1991, Rosen LB $16.95 (0-8239-1304-X); paper $8.95 (0-8239-1305-8). Short stories and essays by teenage soldiers in troubled areas around the world—from Northern Ireland to the Middle East—who express their frontline views of military conflict. (Rev: BL 6/15/91; SLJ 4/91)

3775 Rosen, Roger, and Patra M. Sevastiades, eds. *On Heroes and the Heroic: In Search of Good Deeds* (7–12). (Icarus World Issues) 1993, Rosen LB $16.95 (0-8239-1384-8); paper $8.95 (0-8239-1385-

6). Nine fiction and nonfiction pieces explore the concepts of heroes and antiheroes. (Rev: BL 9/15/93; SLJ 1/94; VOYA 12/93)

3776 Salisbury, Graham. *Blue Skin of the Sea* (8–12). 1992, Delacorte $15.95 (0-385-30596-6). These 11 stories contain a strong sense of time and place, fully realized characters, stylish prose, and universal themes. (Rev: BL 6/15/92*; SLJ 6/92*)

3777 *Second Sight: Stories for a New Millennium* (7–12). 1999, Putnam $14.99 (0-399-23458-6). A collection of 8 stories that focus on the millennium by such writers as Avi, Natalie Babbitt, and Richard Peck. (Rev: BL 9/15/99)

3778 Sherman, Josepha, ed. *Orphans of the Night* (6–10). 1995, Walker $25.95 (0-8027-8368-6). Brings together 11 short stories and 2 poems about creatures from local folklore, most with teen protagonists. (Rev: BL 6/1–15/95; SLJ 6/95; VOYA 12/95)

3779 Thomas, Roy E. *Come Go with Me* (9–12). 1994, Farrar $16.00 (0-374-37089-3). Ninety-four stories taken from interviews in the Appalachians, Ozarks, and Ouachita Mountain regions. (Rev: BL 5/1/94; SLJ 7/94)

3780 Villasenor, Victor. *Walking Stars: Stories of Magic and Power* (7–12). 1994, Arte Publico $16.95 (1-55885-118-6). Short stories, based on fact, describing the everyday magic and family love found in the author's Mexican and Native American heritage. (Rev: BL 10/15/94; SLJ 11/94; VOYA 4/95)

3781 Warren, Robert Penn, and Albert Erskine, eds. *Short Story Masterpieces* (10–12). 1954, Dell paper $7.50 (0-440-37864-8). An international collection of 36 masterpieces of short fiction.

3782 Wynne-Jones, Tim. *Lord of the Fries* (6–10). 1999, DK Publg. $17.95 (0-7894-2623-4). A collection of 8 stories by the author about youngsters in a variety of dramatic situations. (Rev: BL 2/15/99; SLJ 4/99; VOYA 10/99)

Plays

General and Miscellaneous Collections

3783 Beard, Jocelyn A., ed. *The Best Men's Stage Monologues of 1993* (9–12). 1994, Smith & Kraus paper $8.95 (1-880399-43-1). Includes 52 monologues from 1993 plays. (Rev: BL 4/1/94; VOYA 8/94) [808.82]

3784 Beard, Jocelyn A., ed. *The Best Men's Stage Monologues of 1992* (9–12). 1993, Smith & Kraus paper $8.95 (1-880399-11-3). Monologues for men from outstanding 1992 theatrical works. (Rev: BL 6/1–15/93) [808.82]

3785 Beard, Jocelyn A., ed. *The Best Women's Stage Monologues of 1993* (9–12). 1994, Smith & Kraus paper $8.95 (1-880399-42-3). Includes 58 monologues from 1993 plays. (Rev: BL 4/1/94; VOYA 8/94) [808.82]

3786 Beard, Jocelyn A., ed. *The Best Women's Stage Monologues of 1992* (9–12). 1993, Smith & Kraus paper $8.95 (1-880399-10-5). Monologues for women from outstanding 1992 theatrical works. (Rev: BL 6/1–15/93) [808.82]

3787 Beard, Jocelyn A., ed. *Monologues from Classic Plays 468 B.C to 1960 A.D.* (9–12). 1993, Smith & Kraus paper $11.95 (1-880399-09-1). Monologues from early Greek, Roman, medieval, and Restoration plays and the modern works of Williams, Pinter, and Beckett. (Rev: BL 6/1–15/93) [808.82]

3788 Bland, Joellen, adapt. *Stage Plays from the Classics* (6–9). 1987, Plays paper $15.95 (0-8238-0281-7). Fifteen plays adapted from such classics as *Oliver Twist, Dracula,* and *The Purloined Letter.* (Rev: BR 1–2/88; SLJ 3/88) [812]

3789 Cerf, Bennett, and Van H. Cartmell, eds. *30 Famous One-Act Plays* (10–12). 1949, Modern Library $16.00 (0-394-60473-3). The playwrights range from Strindberg to Coward and Saroyan in the anthology that also includes biographical sketches. [808.82]

3790 Cerf, Bennett, and Van H. Cartmell, eds. *24 Favorite One-Act Plays* (10–12). 1958, Doubleday paper $14.95 (0-385-06617-1). An international collection of short plays—both comedies and tragedies—by such masters as Inge, Coward, and O'Neill. [808.82]

3791 Horvath, John, et al., eds. *Duo! The Best Scenes for the 90's* (9–12). 1995, Applause Theatre paper $14.95 (1-55783-030-4). Some 130 scenes for 2 actors from productions by established playwrights of the 1980s and 1990s. (Rev: BL 4/15/95) [808.82]

3792 Houghton, Norris, ed. *Romeo and Juliet and West Side Story* (10–12). 1965, Dell paper $5.99 (0-440-97483-6). This combined edition affords an interesting comparison between the two versions of the same story. [808.1]

3793 Kamerman, Sylvia, ed. *The Big Book of Large-Cast Plays: 27 One-Act Plays for Young Actors* (5–10). 1994, Plays $18.95 (0-8238-0302-3). Thirty short plays on varied subjects, arranged according to audience appeal. (Rev: BL 3/15/95) [812]

3794 Kamerman, Sylvia, ed. *Christmas Play Favorites for Young People* (6–10). 1983, Plays paper $13.95 (0-8238-0257-4). Eighteen one-act plays that could be used in both elementary and high schools. [812.08]

3795 Kehret, Peg. *Encore! More Winning Monologs for Young Actors* (9–12). 1988, Meriwether paper $14.95 (0-916260-54-2). A collection of 63 short pieces suitable for recitations or auditions. (Rev: SLJ 8/88) [808.85]

3796 Kraus, Eric, ed. *Monologues from Contemporary Literature, Vol. 1* (9–12). 1993, Smith & Kraus paper $8.95 (1-880399-04-0). Monologues from such literary sources as Paul Theroux's Chicago Loop. (Rev: BL 6/1–15/93) [808.82]

3797 Latrobe, Kathy Howard, and Mildred Knight Laughlin. *Readers Theatre for Young Adults: Scripts and Script Development* (7–12). 1989, Libraries Unlimited paper $20.00 (0-87287-743-4). A collection of short scripts based on literary classics plus tips on how to do one's own adaptations. (Rev: BL 1/1/90) [808.5]

3798 Nolan, Paul T. *Folk Tale Plays round the World* (9–12). 1982, Plays paper $13.95 (0-8238-0253-1). This collection contains short plays based on folktales from both the Western and Eastern worlds. [808.2]

3799 Ratliff, Gerald L., and Theodore O. Zapel, eds. *Playing Contemporary Scenes: 31 Famous Scenes & How to Play Them* (8–12). 1996, Meriwether paper $16.95 (1-56608-025-8). A selection of scenes by contemporary playwrights, arranged according to gender and age. (Rev: VOYA 6/97) [812]

3800 Shengold, Nina, ed. *The Actor's Book of Contemporary Stage Monologues* (9–12). Illus. 1987, Penguin paper $12.95 (0-14-009649-3). A splendid collection of monologues from both well-known and obscure scripts. (Rev: SLJ 1/88; VOYA 4/88) [659.1]

3801 Slaight, Craig, and Jack Sharrar, eds. *Great Monologues for Young Actors* (9–12). 1999, Smith & Kraus paper $14.95 (1-57525-106-X). Taken from the writing of contemporary playwrights as well as classical sources, this is a fine collection of monologues for older students. (Rev: SLJ 10/99; VOYA 10/99) [808.82]

3802 Slaight, Craig, and Jack Sharrar, eds. *Great Scenes and Monologues for Children* (5–8). (Young Actors) 1993, Smith & Kraus paper $11.95 (1-880399-15-6). Includes selections from children's novels and fairy tales, as well as adult drama and short stories. (Rev: BL 10/1/93; SLJ 11/93) [808.82]

3803 Slaight, Craig, and Jack Sharrar, eds. *Great Scenes for Young Actors from the Stage* (9–12). 1991, Smith & Kraus paper $11.95 (0-9622722-6-4). A collection of 45 scenes from contemporary and classic theater, graded according to ability level and including a brief synopsis of each play. (Rev: BL 11/1/91) [808.82]

3804 Slaight, Craig, and Jack Sharrar, eds. *Multicultural Monologues for Young Actors* (9–12). 1995, Smith & Kraus paper $11.95 (1-880399-47-4). Includes 20 poems, plays, and other fiction, arranged by gender. Monologues represent various cultures and dramatic literatures, both contemporary and classic. Some strong language and mature themes. (Rev: BL 8/95; SLJ 9/95) [808.82]

3805 Slaight, Craig, and Jack Sharrar, eds. *Multicultural Scenes for Young Actors* (9–12). 1995, Smith & Kraus paper $11.95 (1-880399-48-2). Contemporary and classic materials for groups and pairs from a variety of cultural and dramatic literatures. Some strong language and mature themes. (Rev: BL 8/95) [808.82]

3806 Slaight, Craig, and Jack Sharrar, eds. *Short Plays for Young Actors* (8–12). 1996, Smith & Kraus paper $16.95 (1-880399-74-1). An impressive collection of short plays in a variety of genres plus material on how to approach acting as a serious pursuit. (Rev: BL 9/15/96; BR 1–2/97) [812]

3807 Smith, Marissa, ed. *Showtime's Act One Festival: The One-Act Plays 1994* (10–12). 1995, Smith & Kraus paper $16.95 (1-800399-96-2). This is a collection of 13 prize-winning one-act plays, some of which deal with teen situations. (Rev: BL 11/15/95; VOYA 6/96) [812]

3808 Steffensen, James L., Jr., ed. *Great Scenes from the World Theater* (10–12). 1972, Avon paper $5.95 (0-380-00793-2). A collection of 180 scenes ranging from Euripides to Albee. [808.82]

3809 Stevens, Chambers. *Magnificent Monologues for Kids* (4–8). Ed. by Renee Rolle-Whatley. 1999, Sandcastle Publg. paper $13.95 (1-883995-08-6). After explaining the fundamentals of delivery, the book presents 51 monologues divided into 2 sections, one for girls and the other for boys. (Rev: BL 4/1/99; SLJ 8/99) [808.82]

3810 Swortzell, Lowell, ed. *Theatre for Young Audiences: Around the World in Twenty-One Plays* (6–12). 1996, Applause Theatre $29.95 (1-55783-263-3). A collection of 21 plays, with background information, including 8 traditional and 13 contemporary works by such authors as Langston Hughes, Ossie Davis, Gertrude Stein, and August Strindberg. (Rev: BL 6/1–15/97; SLJ 6/97) [808.82]

Geographical Regions

Europe

GREAT BRITAIN AND IRELAND

3811 Bolt, Robert. *A Man for All Seasons* (9–12). 1990, Vintage paper $9.00 (0-679-72822-8). The story in play form of the conflict between Sir Thomas More and Henry VIII. [822]

3812 Christie, Agatha. *The Mousetrap and Other Plays* (10–12). 1993, HarperCollins paper $7.50 (0-06-100374-3). Eight mystery thrillers, including *Witness for the Prosecution*. [822]

3813 Chute, Marchette. *An Introduction to Shakespeare* (7–12). 1959, NAL paper $3.00 (0-452-

00895-6). An introduction that retells the plots of Shakespeare's plays plus background information. [822.3]

3814 Coville, Bruce. *William Shakespeare's Macbeth* (4–8). Illus. 1997, Dial $16.99 (0-8037-1899-3); paper $16.89 (0-8037-1900-0). Using a picture book format, the story of Macbeth is retold with emphasis on the supernatural aspects. (Rev: BL 11/1/97; SLJ 12/97) [822.3]

3815 Early, Margaret, and William Shakespeare. *Romeo & Juliet* (4–8). Illus. 1998, Harry N. Abrams $18.95 (0-8109-3799-9). A retelling in prose of Shakespeare's tragedy, illustrated with paintings in the style of Italian Renaissance art. (Rev: BL 5/1/98; BR 11–12/98; SLJ 6/98) [822]

3816 Garfield, Leon. *Shakespeare Stories* (5–9). Illus. 1991, Houghton $26.00 (0-395-56397-6). A modern retelling of the stories of 12 of Shakespeare's most popular plays. (Rev: BL 1/1/86) [822.3]

3817 Lamb, Charles, and Mary Lamb. *Tales from Shakespeare* (7–9). Illus. 1993, Buccaneer LB $24.95 (1-56849-117-4); NAL paper $5.95 (0-451-52391-1). The famous retelling of 20 of Shakespeare's plays in a version first published in 1807. [822.3]

3818 Lipson, Greta Barclay, and Susan Solomon. *Romeo and Juliet: Plainspoken* (10–12). Illus. 1985, Good Apple paper $17.99 (0-86653-283-8). The book in which a modern-language version of *Romeo and Juliet* is given on one page and the Shakespeare version opposite. (Rev: SLJ 8/86) [822.3]

3819 Miles, Bernard. *Favorite Tales from Shakespeare* (7–10). Illus. 1993, Checkerboard $14.95 (1-56288-257-0). A modern retelling of Shakespeare's most famous plays. [822.3]

3820 Shakespeare, William. *The Complete Works of William Shakespeare* (9–12). Illus. 1990, Random $18.99 (0-517-05361-6). One of many editions available of the complete works of Shakespeare. [822.3]

3821 Shakespeare, William. *A Midsummer Night's Dream* (10–12). 1980, Oxford paper $8.95 (0-19-831926-6). One of many editions of this comedy about 2 pairs of lovers lost in an enchanted forest. [822.3]

3822 Shakespeare, William. *Romeo and Juliet* (10–12). 1989, NAL paper $2.75 (0-451-52136-6). One of many editions of this play currently available. [822.3]

3823 Wilde, Oscar. *The Importance of Being Earnest* (9–12). 1976, Avon paper $4.50 (0-380-01277-4). Mistaken identities is one of the dramatic ploys used in this comedy of manners. [822]

3824 Goldoni, Carlo. *Villeggiatura: A Trilogy Condensed* (9–12). Trans. by Robert Cornthwaite. (Young Actors) 1995, Smith & Kraus paper $14.95 (1-880399-72-5). A 3-act comedy of manners in 18th-century Italian court life, perfect for drama classes or theater groups. (Rev: BL 2/1/95; SLJ 4/95) [852]

3825 Winther, Barbara. *Plays from Hispanic Tales: One-Act, Royalty-Free Dramatizations for Young People, from Hispanic Stories and Folktales* (6–10). 1998, Plays paper $13.95 (0-8238-0307-4). A nicely balanced collection of 11 short plays based on folktales and legends from Spain, South and Central America, and the Caribbean. (Rev: BL 11/15/98; SLJ 9/98) [812]

United States

3826 Blinn, William. *Brian's Song* (9–12). 1983, Bantam paper $4.99 (0-553-26618-7). This edition is the screenplay of the television movie about the doomed football player Brian Piccolo. [808.1]

3827 Cassady, Marsh, ed. *Great Scenes from Minority Playwrights: Seventy-four Scenes of Cultural Diversity* (9–12). 1997, Meriwether paper $15.95 (1-56608-029-0). This work contains condensations of 9 modern plays representing 5 minority groups and exploring insights into the various cultures and aspects of prejudice. (Rev: BL 10/1/97; SLJ 11/97) [812]

3828 Dove, Rita. *The Darker Face of the Earth* (9–12). 1994, Story Line paper $10.95 (0-934257-74-4). This verse play, based on the story of Oedipus and placed within the context of slavery, is set on a plantation in antebellum South Carolina. (Rev: BL 2/15/94*) [812.54]

3829 Fairbanks, Stephanie S. *Spotlight: Solo Scenes for Student Actors* (7–12). 1996, Meriwether paper $12.95 (1-56608-020-7). This book contains 55 excellent 1-to-3-page monologues, some specifically for girls, others for boys, and others nonspecific. (Rev: BL 12/1/96; SLJ 5/97) [812]

3830 Gallo, Donald R., ed. *Center Stage: One-Act Plays for Teenage Readers and Actors* (7–12). 1990, HarperCollins $17.00 (0-06-022170-4); paper $7.95 (0-06-447078-4). A collection of 10 one-act plays especially written for this collection by such authors as Walter Dean Myers and Ouida Sebestyen. (Rev: BL 12/1/90; SLJ 9/90) [812]

3831 Gardner, Herb. *Conversations with My Father* (9–12). 1994, Pantheon $20.00 (0-679-42405-9); paper $11.00 (0-679-74766-4). This play—set in a New York City bar spanning the 1930s and 1940s—

depicts the relationship between a Jewish immigrant and his 2 sons. (Rev: BL 1/1/94) [812]

3832 Garner, Joan. *Stagings* (6–12). 1995, Teacher Ideas Pr. paper $27.00 (1-56308-343-4). A collection of royalty-free short plays suitable for teens, also including character and costume descriptions, set suggestions, staging options, and lesson plans. (Rev: BL 2/1/96; BR 3–4/96; VOYA 4/96) [812]

3833 Gibson, William. *The Miracle Worker: A Play for Television* (7–12). 1957, Knopf $20.00 (0-394-40630-3); Bantam paper $5.50 (0-553-24778-6). An expanded version of the television play about Annie Sullivan and Helen Keller. [812]

3834 Goldman, James. *A Lion in Winter* (10–12). 1983, Penguin paper $8.95 (0-14-048174-5). A rich historical play about Henry II, his wife Eleanor of Aquitaine, and their 3 sons. [812]

3835 Goodrich, Frances. *The Diary of Anne Frank* (7–12). Illus. 1958, Dramatists Play Service paper $5.25 (0-8222-0307-3). A translation into play format of the famous diary kept by the Jewish girl hiding from the Nazis. [812]

3836 Graham, Kristen, ed. *The Great Monologues from the Women's Project* (9–12). 1995, Smith & Kraus paper $7.95 (1-880399-35-0). Fifty-three monologues provide dramatic, funny, angry, and sexual performance opportunities. (Rev: BL 2/15/95) [808.82]

3837 *Great Scenes for Young Actors* (7–12). (Young Actors) 1997, Smith & Kraus paper $14.95 (1-57525-107-8). A variety of scenes representing different forms of drama are reprinted from such playwrights as Arthur Miller, George S. Kaufman, Horton Foote, and Paul Zindel. (Rev: BL 3/1/99; SLJ 6/99) [808.82]

3838 Halline, Allan G., ed. *Six Modern American Plays* (10–12). 1966, McGraw-Hill paper $7.75 (0-07-553660-9). The 6 plays in this collection are *The Glass Menagerie, Mister Roberts, Emperor Jones, The Man Who Came to Dinner, The Little Foxes,* and *Winterset.* [812]

3839 Hamlett, Christina. *Humorous Plays for Teen-Agers* (7–10). 1987, Plays paper $12.95 (0-8238-0276-0). Easily read one-act plays for beginners in acting. (Rev: BL 5/1/87; BR 5–6/87; SLJ 11/87) [812]

3840 Handman, Wynn, ed. *Modern American Scenes for Student Actors* (9–12). 1978, Bantam paper $4.95 (0-553-25844-3). A total of 50 scenes are included plus information on the plot of each play and its playwright. [812.08]

3841 Hansberry, Lorraine. *A Raisin in the Sun: A Drama in Three Acts* (7–12). Illus. 1987, NAL paper $8.95 (0-452-25942-8). The drama that involves a middle-class black family in Chicago. [812]

3842 Hellman, Lillian. *Six Plays by Lillian Hellman* (9–12). 1979, Random paper $15.00 (0-394-74112-9). This collection includes *Watch on the Rhine, The Little Foxes,* and *The Children's Hour.* [812]

3843 Henderson, Heather H. *The Flip Side: 64 Point-of-View Monologs for Teens* (10–12). 1998, Meriwether paper $12.95 (1-56608-045-2). This is a collection of original, short monologues written for this anthology. (Rev: VOYA 10/99) [808.82]

3844 Jennings, Coleman A., and Gretta Berghammer, eds. *Theatre for Youth: Twelve Plays with Mature Themes* (6–9). 1986, Univ. of Texas Pr. paper $19.95 (0-292-78085-0). A collection of short plays dealing with such topics as death, courage, sexuality, and moral standards. (Rev: BL 1/15/87) [812]

3845 Jones, Tom, and Harvey Schmidt. *The Fantasticks: The Thirtieth Anniversary Edition* (9–12). 1990, Applause Theatre $19.95 (1-55783-074-6). The text and lyrics of the long-running musical about young love and meddling fathers. [812]

3846 Kamerman, Sylvia, ed. *The Big Book of Holiday Plays* (6–9). 1990, Plays $16.95 (0-8238-0291-4). An assortment of one-act plays and adaptations, both dramas and comedies, related to 14 holidays. (Rev: BL 2/1/91; SLJ 1/91) [812]

3847 Kamerman, Sylvia, ed. *Great American Events on Stage: 15 Plays to Celebrate America's Past* (5–8). 1996, Plays paper $15.95 (0-8238-0305-8). A collection of short plays each of which revolves around a single incident or individual important in U.S. history. (Rev: BR 5–6/97; SLJ 5/97) [812]

3848 Kamerman, Sylvia, ed. *Plays of Black Americans: The Black Experience in America, Dramatized for Young People* (7–12). 1994, Plays paper $13.95 (0-8238-0301-5). Eleven dramas focus on the history of African Americans. (Rev: BL 5/15/95; SLJ 2/95) [812]

3849 Krell-Oishi, Mary. *Perspectives: Relevant Scenes for Teens* (9–12). 1997, Meriwether paper $12.95 (1-56608-030-4). Problems such as dating, teen pregnancy, family relationships, abortion, and homosexuality are explored in 23 original scenes for high school and college actors. (Rev: BL 10/1/97; SLJ 11/97) [812]

3850 Laurents, Arthur. *West Side Story: A Musical* (7–12). Illus. 1958, Random $13.95 (0-394-40788-1). This contemporary variation on the Romeo and Juliet story contains the script and lyrics by Stephen Sondheim. (Rev: BL 10/1/88) [812]

3851 Lawrence, Jerome, and Robert E. Lee. *Inherit the Wind* (9–12). 1969, Bantam paper $5.50 (0-553-26915-1). A dramatic re-creation of the evolution trial that pitted Darrow against Bryan. [812]

3852 Lawrence, Jerome, and Robert E. Lee. *The Night Thoreau Spent in Jail* (9–12). 1983, Bantam paper $5.99 (0-553-27838-X). A play based on the incident when Thoreau refused to pay taxes. [812]

3853 Lerner, Alan Jay. *Camelot* (7–12). 1961, Random $13.95 (0-394-40521-8). This musical tells of the tragic love of King Arthur and Guenevere. [812]

3854 Lerner, Alan Jay. *My Fair Lady* (7–12). 1978, NAL paper $2.95 (0-451-13890-2). This adaptation of Shaw's *Pygmalion* contains both the script and the lyrics by Lerner. [812]

3855 Levin, Ira. *Deathtrap* (9–12). 1979, Random $9.95 (0-394-50727-4). A suspenseful mystery with interesting plot twists that keep the reader guessing. [812]

3856 Luce, William. *The Belle of Amherst: A Play Based on the Life of Emily Dickinson* (9–12). 1978, Houghton paper $7.95 (0-395-26253-4). A one-woman play based on the life of Emily Dickinson. [812]

3857 McCullough, L. E. *Plays of America from American Folklore for Young Actors* (7–12). (Young Actors) 1996, Smith & Kraus paper $14.95 (1-57525-040-3). Ten original short plays based on folk traditions are included, along with suggestions for staging and costumes. (Rev: BL 8/96; SLJ 8/96) [812]

3858 Mason, Timothy. *The Children's Theatre Company of Minneapolis: 10 Plays for Young Audiences* (6–9). (Young Actors) 1997, Smith & Kraus paper $19.00 (1-57525-120-5). This is a collection of 10 plays, each about an hour long, adapted from such classics as Pinocchio, Aladdin, and Huckleberry Finn. (Rev: SLJ 8/98) [812]

3859 Miller, Arthur. *The Crucible* (10–12). 1987, Penguin paper $8.95 (0-14-048138-9). A powerful play that deals with the Salem witch trials of 1692. [812]

3860 Miller, Arthur. *Death of a Salesman* (10–12). 1949, Viking paper $7.95 (0-14-048134-6). The powerful drama of Willy Loman and his tragic end. (Rev: BL 2/15/91) [812]

3861 Nemiroff, Robert, ed. *Lorraine Hansberry: The Collected Last Plays* (10–12). 1983, NAL paper $8.95 (0-452-25414-0). This collection of 3 plays includes *Les Blancs, The Drinking Gourd,* and *What Use Are Flowers?* [812]

3862 Richards, Stanley, ed. *The Most Popular Plays of the American Theatre: Ten of Broadway's Longest-Running Plays* (9–12). Illus. 1979, Scarborough House $24.95 (0-8128-2682-5). The 10 hits include *Life with Father, Tobacco Road, Abie's Irish Rose,* and more recent plays like *Same Time, Next Year* and *Barefoot in the Park.* [812.08]

3863 Shaffer, Peter. *Amadeus* (9–12). 1981, Harper-Collins paper $11.00 (0-06-090783-5). A highly sub-

jective view in dramatic format of the relationship between Mozart and Salieri. [822]

3864 Simon, Neil. *Barefoot in the Park* (9–12). Illus. 1984, Random $11.95 (0-394-40515-3). A witty play about a young married couple coping in a New York apartment. [812]

3865 Simon, Neil. *Brighton Beach Memoirs* (7–12). 1984, Random $14.95 (0-394-53739-4); NAL paper $3.95 (0-451-14765-0). The first of 3 semiautobiographical plays about the growing pains of Brooklyn-born Eugene Jerome. The other 2 are: *Biloxi Blues* (1986) and *Broadway Bound* (1988). (Rev: BL 6/87) [812]

3866 Simon, Neil. *Broadway Bound* (9–12). 1987, Random $13.95 (0-394-56395-6). The concluding semiautobiographical play in the humorous but touching trilogy that included the also-recommended *Brighton Beach Memoirs* (1984) and *Biloxi Blues* (1986). (Rev: BL 3/1/88; SLJ 5/88) [812]

3867 Simon, Neil. *The Collected Plays of Neil Simon* (9–12). 1979, Random $29.95 (0-394-50770-3); NAL paper $12.95 (0-452-25871-5). This volume includes such plays as *The Sunshine Boys* and *California Suite.* Earlier plays are found in volume one, published by NAL. [812]

3868 Simon, Neil. *Lost in Yonkers* (9–12). 1992, Random $16.50 (0-679-40890-8). Prize-winning play about 2 brothers forced to live with their strict grandmother and ditzy aunt after their mother dies. (Rev: BL 3/15/92; SLJ 6/92) [812]

3869 Slaight, Craig, ed. *New Plays from A.C.T.'s Young Conservatory* (9–12). 1993, Smith & Kraus paper $14.95 (1-880399-25-3). Five contemporary plays written from the viewpoints of the young actors ages 13 to 22, who perform them. (Rev: BL 8/93; VOYA 8/93) [812]

3870 Slaight, Craig, ed. *New Plays from A.C.T.'s Young Conservatory, vol. II* (10–12). 1996, Smith & Kraus paper $14.95 (1-880399-73-3). Mature in subject matter and language, this is a collection of 4 thought-provoking new plays (including a heartbreaker by Paul Zindel) for today's teens. (Rev: SLJ 7/96; VOYA 12/96) [812]

3871 Smith, Marisa, ed. *Seattle Children's Theatre: Six Plays for Young Audiences* (9–12). 1996, Smith & Kraus $14.95 (1-57525-008-X). A collection of 6 plays commissioned and performed by the Seattle Children's Theatre that explore adolescence, its problems and concerns. (Rev: BL 6/1–15/97; BR 11–12/97; SLJ 6/97) [812]

3872 Smith, Ronn. *Nothing but the Truth* (7–10). 1997, Avon paper $4.99 (0-380-78715-6). This is a play version of Avi's novel about a ninth-grader whose suspension from school becomes a national issue. (Rev: VOYA 8/97) [812]

3873 Soto, Gary. *Novio Boy: A Play* (6–8). 1997, Harcourt paper $7.00 (0-15-201531-0). A lighthearted play about Rudy, a ninth-grade Hispanic American boy, and his date with an older girl. (Rev: BL 4/15/97; SLJ 6/97; VOYA 8/97) [812]

3874 Stein, Joseph, and Sheldon Harnick. *Fiddler on the Roof: Based on Sholem Aleichem's Stories* (9–12). 1990, Limelight paper $8.95 (0-87910-136-9). The script and lyrics of this musical set in pre-revolutionary Russia. [812]

3875 Vigil, Angel. *¡Teatro! Hispanic Plays for Young People* (4–8). Illus. 1996, Teacher Ideas Pr. paper $25.00 (1-56308-371-X). This collection contains 14 English-language scripts that integrate elements of the Hispanic traditions of the Southwest. (Rev: BL 3/1/97; BR 3–4/97; VOYA 6/97) [812]

3876 Wasserman, Dale. *Man of La Mancha* (7–12). Illus. 1966, Random paper $9.95 (0-394-40619-2). Based loosely on Cervantes' novel, this is the story of the adventures of Don Quixote and his servant Sancho Panza. [812]

3877 Wilder, Thornton. *Our Town* (10–12). 1998, HarperCollins paper $8.00 (0-06-092984-7). Life in the town of Grover's Corners in New Hampshire as portrayed in the prize-winning play. [812]

3878 Williams, Tennessee. *A Streetcar Named Desire* (10–12). 1980, New Directions paper $9.95 (0-8112-0765-X). The tragic story of Blanche, her sister Stella, and husband Stanley, set in New Orleans. [812]

3879 Wilson, August. *Fences* (10–12). 1986, NAL paper $6.95 (0-452-26048-5). The prize-winning play about a black family living in Pittsburgh in 1957 and ruled by a domineering father. (Rev: BL 9/1/86) [812]

3880 Wilson, August. *The Piano Lesson* (9–12). 1990, 1990, NAL paper $9.95 (0-452-26534-7). Pulitzer Prize–winning play about an African American family in Pittsburgh in the 1930s. (Rev: BL 1/1/91) [812.54]

3881 Zindel, Paul. *The Effect of Gamma Rays on Man-in-the-Moon Marigolds* (9–12). Illus. 1971, HarperCollins $18.00 (0-06-026829-8); Bantam paper $5.99 (0-553-28028-7). This play deals with a widow and her 2 daughters, one of whom finds fulfillment in a science project. (Rev: BL 10/15/88) [812]

Poetry

General and Miscellaneous Collections

3882 Agard, John, comp. *Life Doesn't Frighten Me at All* (7–12). Illus. 1990, Holt $14.95 (0-8050-1237-0). A collection of accessible contemporary poetry aimed specifically at today's young adults. (Rev: BL 6/1/90; SLJ 8/90) [821]

3883 Baker, Russell, ed. *The Norton Book of Light Verse* (10–12). 1986, Norton $29.95 (0-393-02366-4). An amusing collection that spans centuries and a large number of past and present writers. (Rev: BL 1/1/87) [821]

3884 Brewton, Sara, et al., eds. *My Tang's Tungled and Other Ridiculous Situations* (6–9). 1973, HarperCollins $12.95 (0-690-57223-9). A wonderful collection of humorous verse. [811]

3885 Ciardi, John, and Miller Williams. *How Does a Poem Mean?* (10–12). 1975, Houghton paper $27.16 (0-395-18605-6). By analyzing several poems, the authors explain the value and nature of poetry. [821.08]

3886 Dore, Anita, ed. *The Premier Book of Major Poets* (10–12). 1996, Fawcett paper $11.00 (0-449-91186-1). This is a collection of English and American poetry from the Middle Ages to the present. [808.1]

3887 Duffy, Carol Ann, ed. *I Wouldn't Thank You for a Valentine: Poems for Young Feminists* (6–12). Illus. 1994, Holt $14.95 (0-8050-2756-4). This anthology draws on poets from many cultures and includes works by Nikki Giovanni, Sharon Olds, and Mary Oliver. (Rev: BL 3/1/94*; SLJ 1/94; VOYA 4/94) [808.81]

3888 Duffy, Carol Ann, ed. *Stopping for Death: Poems of Death and Loss* (7–10). Illus. 1996, Holt $14.95 (0-8050-4717-4). An anthology of poems from around the world, including many contemporary poets like Auden, that deal with dying, death, and loss. (Rev: BL 8/96; SLJ 8/96; VOYA 10/96) [808.81]

3889 Felleman, Hazel, ed. *Poems That Live Forever* (9–12). 1965, Doubleday $18.95 (0-385-00358-7). A collection of familiar poems arranged under subjects like love, friendship, and home. [821.08]

3890 Foster, John, ed. *Let's Celebrate: Festival Poems* (8–12). Illus. 1997, Oxford paper $16.50 (0-19-276085-8). With many illustrations, this handsome volume includes poems on many of the world's holidays by 41 English-speaking poets. (Rev: VOYA 8/90) [808.81]

3891 Gilbert, Sandra M., et al., eds. *Mother Songs: Poems for, by, and about Mothers* (9–12). 1995, Norton $22.50 (0-393-03771-1). Poems by men and women for and about mothers. (Rev: BL 5/1/95) [811.008]

3892 Gordon, Ruth, ed. *Peeling the Onion* (8–12). 1993, HarperCollins $14.89 (0-06-021728-6). A collection of 66 poems by world famous contemporary poets each of which reveals multilayered meanings. (Rev: BL 6/1–15/93*; SLJ 7/93; VOYA 8/93) [808.81]

3893 Gordon, Ruth, ed. *Pierced by a Ray of Sun* (7–12). 1995, HarperCollins LB $15.89 (0-06-023614-0). A compilation of poems from across cultures and eras on topics from the timely to the timeless and emotions from hope to despair. (Rev: BL 5/1/95*; SLJ 6/95) [808.81]

3894 Gordon, Ruth, sel. *Under All Silences: Shades of Love* (8–12). 1987, HarperCollins $13.00 (0-06-022154-2). Sixty-six love poems, from Ancient

Egypt to modern days. (Rev: BL 9/15/87; BR 3–4/88; SLJ 10/87; VOYA 4/88) [808.1]

3895 Hall, Linda, ed. *An Anthology of Poetry by Women: Tracing the Tradition* (9–12). 1995, Cassell paper $15.95 (0-304-32434-5). Women's poetry from early times, organized by themes. (Rev: BL 3/1/95) [811]

3896 Harrison, Michael, and Christopher Stuart-Clark, comps. *One Hundred Years of Poetry for Children* (6–12). 1999, Oxford $24.95 (0-19-276190-0). An outstanding, thematically arranged collection of poetry written in the 20th century for youngsters as well as adult poems that are suitable for young people. (Rev: BL 9/1/99; SLJ 7/99) [808.1]

3897 Harrison, Michael, and Christopher Stuart-Clark, eds. *The Oxford Book of Christmas Poems* (7–12). Illus. 1999, Oxford paper $18.95 (0-19-276214-1). A total of 120 British and American poems are included. [808.81]

3898 Harrison, Michael, and Christopher Stuart-Clark, eds. *The Oxford Treasury of Time Poems* (6–10). 1999, Oxford $40.50 (0-19-276175-7). This anthology of classic poems contains about 100 selections on subjects associated with time, such as clocks, birthdays, partings, memories, and history. (Rev: BL 5/1/99) [821.008]

3899 Hollis, Jill, ed. *Love's Witness: Five Centuries of Love Poetry by Women* (9–12). 1993, Carroll & Graf paper $11.95 (0-7867-0030-0). This anthology of 5 centuries of love poetry by women reflects the similarities and differences of love through the ages. (Rev: BL 11/15/93) [821]

3900 Homer. *The Iliad* (10–12). 1989, Doubleday paper $8.95 (0-385-05941-8). One of many recommended editions of this great Greek epic about the Trojan War. [883]

3901 Homer. *The Odyssey* (10–12). 1996, Viking $49.95 (0-14-086430-X); Farrar paper $10.00 (0-374-52574-9). These 2 editions represent the many available of this epic poem about the wanderings of Ulysses on his way home from the Trojan War. [883]

3902 Janeczko, Paul B., ed. *Looking for Your Name: A Collection of Contemporary Poems* (9–12). 1993, Orchard LB $17.99 (0-531-08625-9). A wide variety of poems by men and women about soldiers' war memories, family violence, gay/lesbian lives, sports, love, AIDS, suicide, and other aspects of life. (Rev: BL 1/15/93*) [811]

3903 Janeczko, Paul B., sel. *The Place My Words Are Looking For: What Poets Say about and through Their Work* (5–9). 1990, Bradbury paper $16.00 (0-02-747671-5). A varied collection of poems by contemporaries who also comment on their poems. (Rev: SLJ 5/90; VOYA 6/90) [808.81]

3904 Janeczko, Paul B., ed. *Wherever Home Begins: 100 Contemporary Poems* (8–12). 1995, Orchard LB $16.99 (0-531-08781-6). One hundred poems that express various approaches to a sense of place. (Rev: BL 10/1/95; SLJ 11/95; VOYA 12/95) [811]

3905 Koch, Kenneth, and Kate Farrell. *Talking to the Sun: An Illustrated Anthology of Poems for Young People* (5–9). Illus. 1985, Holt $26.95 (0-8050-0144-1). A collection of poems on many subjects illustrated by reproductions from the Metropolitan Museum of Art. (Rev: BL 1/1/86; BR 9–10/86; SLJ 1/87) [808.81]

3906 Larrick, Nancy, ed. *Piping Down the Valleys Wild: Poetry for the Young of All Ages* (6–9). Illus. 1999, Bantam paper $5.99 (0-440-41582-9). A collection of favorite poems that deal with subjects related to the experience of young people. [808.81]

3907 Livingston, Myra Cohn, ed. *Call Down the Moon: Poems of Music* (6–12). 1995, Macmillan $16.00 (0-689-80416-4). A collection of poems by Tennyson, Whitman, and others, who use words to express how we create and listen to music. (Rev: BL 10/1/95; SLJ 11/95; VOYA 2/96) [821.008]

3908 Livingston, Myra Cohn, ed. *A Time to Talk: Poems of Friendship* (7–12). 1992, Macmillan paper $14.00 (0-689-50558-2). Poems from many times and places express how friends bring us joy and support; how they betray and leave us; how we miss them when they're gone; and other aspects of friendship. (Rev: BL 10/15/92; SLJ 11/92) [808.81]

3909 McCullough, Frances, ed. *Earth, Air, Fire, & Water*. Rev. ed. (9–12). 1989, HarperCollins $13.95 (0-06-024207-8). A collection of poems from many cultures that have been chosen for their specific appeal to young adults. (Rev: BL 5/15/89; SLJ 6/89; VOYA 8/89) [808.81]

3910 McCullough, Frances, ed. *Love Is Like a Lion's Tooth: An Anthology of Love Poems* (7–12). 1984, HarperCollins $12.95 (0-06-024138-1). A collection of love poems that span time from ancient days to the 20th century. [808.81]

3911 Nye, Naomi S., ed. *This Same Sky: A Collection of Poems from Around the World* (7–12). 1992, Four Winds paper $17.00 (0-02-768440-7). An extraordinary collection of 129 poems by contemporary poets from 68 countries, with an index by country. (Rev: BL 10/15/92*; SLJ 12/92) [808.81]

3912 Nye, Naomi S. *What Have You Lost?* (6–12). Illus. 1999, Greenwillow $19.00 (0-688-16184-7). A collection of 140 poems about loss—some losses that are trivial, others that are serious. (Rev: BL 4/1/99; BR 9–10/99; SLJ 4/99; VOYA 10/99) [811.008]

3913 Nye, Naomi Shihab, and Paul B. Janeczko, eds. *I Feel a Little Jumpy around You: A Book of Her*

Poems & His Poems Collected in Pairs (8–12). 1996, Simon & Schuster paper $18.00 (0-689-80518-7). This anthology of some 200 poems explores how the genders sometimes view things differently and sometimes the same. (Rev: BL 4/1/96; BR 3–4/97; SLJ 5/96*; VOYA 8/96) [808.81]

3914 Okutoro, Lydia Omolola, ed. *Quiet Storm: Voices of Young Black Poets* (8–12). 1999, Hyperion $16.99 (0-7868-0461-0). This anthology features poems written by black youth ages 13 to 21 from the United States, Canada, England, the West Indies, and several African countries. (Rev: BL 6/1–15/99; SLJ 7/99; VOYA 12/99) [811.008]

3915 Oliver, Mary. *A Poetry Handbook* (9–12). 1994, Harcourt paper $12.00 (0-15-672400-6). A handbook on the formal aspects and structure of poetry from a Pulitzer Prize–winning poet. (Rev: BL 7/94) [808.1]

3916 Opie, Iona, and Peter Opie, eds. *The Oxford Book of Children's Verses* (6–9). Illus. 1995, Oxford paper $26.50 (0-19-282349-3). Using a chronological arrangement, the editors have included 332 famous selections. [821.08]

3917 Philip, Neil, ed. *War and the Pity of War* (6–12). 1998, Clarion $20.00 (0-395-84982-9). An outstanding collection of poetry from different times and cultures that explores the cruelty, bravery, and tragedy of war. (Rev: BL 9/15/98; BR 5–6/99; SLJ 9/98; VOYA 2/99) [808.81]

3918 Prelutsky, Jack, ed. *The Random House Book of Poetry for Children* (6–9). Illus. 1983, Random LB $21.99 (0-394-95010-0). A selection of verse suitable for children that concentrates on light verse written recently. [821.08]

3919 Rosen, Michael, ed. *Classic Poetry: An Illustrated Collection* (6–8). 1998, Candlewick $21.99 (1-56402-890-9). A fine selection of poems by major writers. A brief biography is given of each, plus 1 or 2 poems and an illustration that evokes the poet's times or the mood of the poems. (Rev: BL 1/1–15/99; BR 5–6/99; SLJ 5/99) [821.008]

3920 Rosenberg, Liz, ed. *Earth-Shattering Poems* (7–12). 1997, Holt $15.95 (0-8050-4821-9). An anthology of poems from more than 40 poets that deal with life's serious moments and intense experiences. (Rev: BL 12/15/97; BR 9–10/98; SLJ 2/98; VOYA 2/98) [808.81]

3921 Rothenberg, Jerome, and Pierre Joris, eds. *Poems for the Millennium: The University of California Book of Modern & Postmodern Poetry, vol. 2* (10–12). 1998, Univ. of California Pr. $70.00 (0-520-20863-3); paper $24.95 (0-520-20864-1). An excellent international collection of poetry from post-World War II through the Cold War and its aftermath representing a wide range of well-known poets and movements. (Rev: SLJ 12/98) [808.8]

3922 Schiff, Hilda, ed. *Holocaust Poetry* (9–12). 1995, St. Martin's $20.00 (0-312-13086-4). An anthology of 85 poems provide a stark memoir of the Holocaust. (Rev: BL 5/15/95*) [808.81]

3923 Siegen-Smith, Nikki, comp. *Welcome to the World: A Celebration of Birth and Babies from Many Cultures* (10–12). 1996, Orchard $17.95 (0-531-36006-7). A collection of 20 international poems, each with a full-page photograph, that describe the pain and joy of childbirth and raising babies. (Rev: SLJ 10/96) [811]

3924 Stallworthy, Jon, ed. *The Oxford Book of War Poetry* (10–12). 1984, Oxford $30.00 (0-19-214125-2). This anthology covers war poetry from ancient times to Vietnam and contemporary Northern Ireland. [808.81]

3925 Sullivan, Charles, ed. *Imaginary Animals* (6–10). 1996, Abrams $22.95 (0-8109-3470-1). A collection of works by such writers as D. H. Lawrence, Ogden Nash, and William Butler Yeats, and by artists from Andy Warhol to Marc Chagall to Winslow Homer, featuring all kinds of delightful animals, imaginary and real, among them the Jabberwock, prancing centaurs, rearing dragons, the Loch Ness monster and Salvador Dali's photo of a lobster telephone. (Rev: SLJ 2/97) [811]

3926 Viorst, Judith. *If I Were in Charge of the World and Other Worries: Poems for Children and Their Parents* (5–8). Illus. 1984, Macmillan paper $4.95 (0-689-70770-3). This is a collection of easily read poems that is short and on topics familiar to children such as cats and spring fever. [811]

3927 Virgil. *The Aeneid of Virgil* (10–12). 1981, Bantam paper $4.95 (0-553-21041-6). One of several fine editions of the epic poem about the journey of Aeneas from Troy to Italy. [873]

3928 Willard, Nancy, ed. *Step Lightly: Poems for the Journey* (7–12). 1998, Harcourt paper $12.00 (0-15-202052-7). These works from the pens of about 40 poets represent the poems that the editor particularly loves. (Rev: BL 10/1/98; BR 5–6/99; SLJ 11/98; VOYA 4/99) [811:008]

3929 Wong, Janet S. *A Suitcase of Seaweed and Other Poems* (6–8). Illus. 1996, Simon & Schuster $15.00 (0-689-80788-0). A group of poems that celebrate the poet's 3 cultures, Korean, Chinese, and American. (Rev: BL 4/1/96; SLJ 9/96; VOYA 10/96) [811]

3930 Yolen, Jane, ed. *Mother Earth, Father Sky* (5–8). 1995, Boyds Mills $15.95 (1-56397-414-2). An anthology of 40 poems, chiefly from well-known English and American writers, that celebrate the wonders of nature. (Rev: BL 2/1/96; SLJ 3/96) [808.81]

3931 Yolen, Jane. *Sacred Places* (5–9). Illus. 1996, Harcourt $16.00 (0-15-269953-8). A worldwide collection of informational poems about the places sacred to various faiths. (Rev: BL 10/1/96; SLJ 3/96) [811]

Geographical Regions

Europe

GREAT BRITAIN AND IRELAND

3932 Barron, W. R., ed. *Sir Gawain and the Green Knight* (10–12). 1972, Viking paper $7.95 (0-14-044902-5). A fine edition of the medieval poem dealing with the testing of Gawain's courage. [821]

3933 Berry, James, ed. *Classic Poems to Read Aloud* (5–8). 1995, Kingfisher $16.95 (1-85697-987-3). Jamaican writer Berry has collected old favorites, mostly British, along with new voices usually excluded from the literary canon. (Rev: BL 5/1/95; SLJ 5/95) [808.81]

3934 Chaucer, Geoffrey. *The Canterbury Tales* (5–9). Adapted by Geraldine McCaughrean. Illus. 1985, Checkerboard $14.95 (1-56288-259-7). An adaptation for young readers of 13 tales that still keep the flavor and spirit of the original. (Rev: SLJ 2/86) [826]

3935 Coleridge, Samuel Taylor. *The Rime of the Ancient Mariner* (7–12). Illus. 1994, Random paper $8.99 (0-517-11849-1). Haunting interpretation of a 200-year-old poem that tells the story of a sailor locked in a living nightmare after he shoots an innocent albatross and watches all his shipmates die. (Rev: BL 3/15/92; SLJ 4/92) [821]

3936 Corrin, Sara, and Stephen Corrin. *The Pied Piper of Hamelin* (6–9). Illus. 1989, Harcourt $14.95 (0-15-261596-2). A fine edition of the Browning poem with stunning illustrations by Errol Le Cain. (Rev: BL 4/1/89) [398.2]

3937 Dahl, Roald. *Rhyme Stew* (7–10). Illus. 1999, Viking paper $3.99 (0-14-034365-2). Lots of silly poems and parodies charmingly illustrated by Quentin Blake. (Rev: BL 5/15/90; SLJ 9/90) [821]

3938 Eliot, T. S. *Old Possum's Book of Practical Cats* (9–12). 1982, Harcourt $15.00 (0-15-168656-4); paper $7.00 (0-15-668570-1). Many of the poems in this delightful collection were used in the musical *Cats*. [821]

3939 Gardner, Helen, ed. *The New Oxford Book of English Verse, 1250–1950* (10–12). 1972, Oxford $52.50 (0-19-812136-9). The first edition of this anthology appeared in 1900, and it has continued to maintain its high standards in all subsequent editions. [821.08]

3940 Heaney, Seamus. *The Spirit Level* (10–12). 1996, Farrar $18.00 (0-374-26779-0). A collection of poems by the Nobel Prize-winning Irish poet that deal with balances in life and the middle ground one often must settle for. (Rev: BL 5/1/96; SLJ 11/96) [821]

3941 Hughes, Ted. *Moon-Whales and Other Moon Poems* (7–9). Illus. 1976, Ultramarine $15.00 (0-670-48864-X). The respected English poet imagines all sorts of strange creatures that live on the moon. Also use his *Season Songs* (1976). [821]

3942 Kipling, Rudyard. *Gunga Din* (7–12). Illus. 1987, Harcourt $12.95 (0-15-200456-4). A splendid edition of this poem dealing with the Indian Mutiny of 1857 and the heroics of an abused water carrier. (Rev: BL 11/1/87; SLJ 12/87) [821]

3943 Livingston, Myra Cohn, comp. *Poems of Lewis Carroll* (7–9). Illus. 1986, HarperCollins LB $11.89 (0-690-04540-9). A complete collection of rhymes, poems, and riddles from the creator of Alice. (Rev: SLJ 8/86) [821]

3944 Millay, Edna St. Vincent. *Edna St. Vincent Millay's Poems Selected for Young People* (7–10). Illus. 1979, HarperCollins $14.00 (0-06-024218-3). A fine selection of the poet's work illustrated with woodcuts. [811]

3945 Opie, Iona, and Peter Opie. *I Saw Esau: The Schoolchild's Pocket Book* (7–12). Illus. 1992, Candlewick $19.95 (1-56402-046-0). Traces schoolyard folk rhymes to their roots. (Rev: BL 4/15/92*; SLJ 6/92) [821]

3946 Pollinger, Gina, ed. *Something Rich and Strange: A Treasury of Shakespeare's Verse* (7–12). Illus. 1995, Kingfisher $26.95 (1-85697-597-5). A thematic arrangement of Shakespeare's sonnets and poetry from his plays, with many bright pictures. (Rev: BL 11/1/95; SLJ 12/95) [822.3]

3947 Thomas, Dylan. *A Child's Christmas in Wales* (10–12). Illus. 1997, New Directions $10.95 (0-8112-1308-0); paper $6.00 (0-8112-1309-9). A poem that deals with the celebration of Christmas in a small Welsh town. [828]

3948 Woodring, Carl, and James Shapiro. *The Columbia Anthology of British Poetry* (10–12). 1995, Columbia Univ. Pr. $34.00 (0-231-10180-5). A collection of major British poetry from Beowulf to the present. (Rev: SLJ 5/96) [821]

United States

3949 Adoff, Arnold. *All the Colors of the Race: Poems* (6–8). Illus. 1987, Morrow $15.93 (0-688-00880-1). A collection of poems featuring a young girl with a black mother and a white father.

3950 Adoff, Arnold, ed. *I Am the Darker Brother: An Anthology of Modern Poems by Black Americans* (9–12). Illus. 1997, Simon & Schuster paper $4.99 (0-689-80869-0). This anthology of 64 poems by 29 black poets of the 20th century explores the black person's role in American life. (Rev: BL 2/15/97; SLJ 5/97) [811.08]

3951 Adoff, Arnold, ed. *My Black Me: A Beginning Book of Black Poetry* (7–10). 1974, Dutton $12.95 (0-525-35460-3). Fifty poems about black people and the joys and sorrows of being black. (Rev: BL 10/1/88) [811.08]

3952 Adoff, Arnold. *Slow Dance Heartbreak Blues* (7–10). 1995, Lothrop $15.00 (0-688-10569-6). Gritty, hip-hop poetry for modern, urban teens. (Rev: BL 12/15/95; SLJ 9/95; VOYA 6/96) [811]

3953 Angelou, Maya. *And Still I Rise* (10–12). 1978, Random $13.00 (0-394-50252-3). A highly personalized volume of poetry by the author of such companion books of poetry as *Just Give Me a Cool Drink of Water 'fore I Die* (1971), *Oh Pray My Wings Are Gonna Fit Me Well* (1975), and *Shaker, Why Don't You Sing?* (1983). [811]

3954 Angelou, Maya. *I Shall Not Be Moved* (10–12). 1990, Random $16.00 (0-394-58618-2). This slim volume is the author's fifth book of poetry and like the others conveys the richness, joy, and pain of being black. (Rev: BL 5/15/90; SLJ 9/90) [811]

3955 Baker, Paul. *Joker, Joker, Deuce* (9–12). 1994, Penguin paper $14.95 (0-14-058723-3). This hiphop poetry expresses the emotions of the youth of the inner city. (Rev: BL 2/15/94) [811]

3956 Begay, Shonto. *Navajo: Visions and Voices Across the Mesa* (7–12). 1995, Scholastic $17.95 (0-590-46153-2). Poetry that speaks to the ongoing struggle of living in a "dual society" and paintings firmly rooted in Navajo culture. (Rev: BL 4/1/95; SLJ 3/95) [811]

3957 Berry, James. *Rough Sketch Beginning* (4–8). Illus. 1996, Harcourt $18.00 (0-15-200112-3). A poem about the work of a landscape artist is accompanied by expressive drawings and a concluding painting of the outdoors. (Rev: BL 5/1/96; SLJ 5/96*) [821]

3958 Blum, Joshua, et al. *The United States of Poetry* (10–12). 1996, Abrams $29.95 (0-8109-3927-4). A collection of 80 poems from a variety of sources including famous poets, rappers, rockers, beats, and cowboys, all reflecting a fresh view of America in this handsomely illustrated book. (Rev: BL 5/15/96; SLJ 9/96) [811]

3959 Bouchard, David. *If Sarah Will Take Me* (4–8). Illus. 1997, Orca $16.95 (1-55143-081-9). With accompanying full-page paintings, this is the poetic reminiscence by the author, who is paralyzed from

the neck down, of his love of nature and his many inspiring experiences outdoors. (Rev: SLJ 8/97) [811]

3960 Burleigh, Robert. *Hoops* (4–8). Illus. 1997, Harcourt $16.00 (0-15-201450-0). A poem that expresses the joy, exhilaration, and excitement of basketball, as seen from the players' point of view. (Rev: BL 11/15/97; SLJ 11/97*) [811]

3961 Carlson, Lori M., ed. *Cool Salsa: Bilingual Poems on Growing Up Latino in the United States* (7–12). 1994, Holt $14.95 (0-8050-3135-9). An anthology of poetry that describes the experience of growing up with a dual heritage. (Rev: BL 11/1/94; SLJ 8/94*; VOYA 2/95) [811]

3962 Clinton, Catherine, ed. *I, Too, Sing America: Three Centuries of African American Poetry* (6–10). Illus. 1998, Houghton $20.00 (0-395-89599-5). This heavily illustrated volume of 36 poems by 25 authors traces the history of African American poetry, from Phillis Wheatley to Rita Dove. (Rev: BL 11/15/98; BR 5–6/99; SLJ 11/98; VOYA 8/99) [712.2]

3963 Daniels, Jim, ed. *Letters to America: Contemporary American Poetry on Race* (9–12). 1995, Wayne State Univ. Pr. paper $21.95 (0-8143-2542-4). Accessible, readable poems that speak to race and racism. (Rev: BL 11/15/95) [811]

3964 Dickinson, Emily. *The Complete Poems of Emily Dickinson* (10–12). 1960, Little, Brown $32.50 (0-316-18414-4); paper $18.00 (0-316-18413-6). This definitive edition contains 1,775 poems and fragments. [811]

3965 Dickinson, Emily. *I'm Nobody! Who Are You?* (6–9). Illus. 1978, Stemmer $21.95 (0-916144-21-6); paper $14.95 (0-916144-22-4). A well-illustrated edition of poems that young people can appreciate. [811]

3966 Dickinson, Emily. *Poems for Youth* (7–9). 1996, Little, Brown $15.95 (0-316-18435-7). A collection of poems by Emily Dickinson suitable for young readers. (Rev: BL 7/96; SLJ 9/96; VOYA 10/96) [811]

3967 Dove, Rita. *Mother Love* (9–12). 1995, Norton $17.95 (0-393-03808-4). Sonnets on the timeless tragedy of Demeter and Persephone. (Rev: BL 5/1/95*) [811]

3968 Dove, Rita. *Selected Poems* (9–12). 1993, Random paper $12.00 (0-679-75080-0). Three collections of poetry by the U.S. poet laureate are gathered here into one volume: *The Yellow House on the Corner; Museum;* and the Pulitzer Prize–winning *Thomas and Beulah*. Dove's images draw on African American history and family experiences to illuminate today's world. (Rev: BL 10/15/93) [811]

3969 Dunbar, Paul Laurence. *The Complete Poems of Paul Laurence Dunbar* (7–12). 1980, Dodd paper

$10.95 (0-396-07895-8). The definitive collection first published in 1913 of this black poet's work. [811]

3970 Fleischman, Paul. *I Am Phoenix: Poems for Two Voices* (4–9). Illus. 1985, HarperCollins paper $4.95 (0-06-446092-4). A group of love poems about birds that are designed to be read by 2 voices or groups of voices. (Rev: BL 12/1/85; BR 3–4/86) [811]

3971 Fletcher, Ralph. *Buried Alive: The Elements of Love* (5–8). 1996, Simon & Schuster $14.00 (0-689-80593-4). A series of free-verse poems that explore various aspects of love—puppy and otherwise. (Rev: BL 5/1/96; SLJ 5/96; VOYA 10/96) [811]

3972 Fletcher, Ralph. *Ordinary Things: Poems from a Walk in Early Spring* (5–9). Illus. 1997, Simon & Schuster $16.00 (0-689-81035-0). Thirty-three short poems that comment on objects in nature like birds' nests, leaves, birch trees, and snakeskins. (Rev: BL 4/15/97; BR 11–12/97; SLJ 5/97*; VOYA 12/97) [811]

3973 Fletcher, Ralph J. *Room Enough for Love: The Complete Poems of I Am Wings & Buried Alive* (7–12). 1998, Simon & Schuster paper $4.99 (0-689-81976-5). A collection of simple, gentle poems about various aspects of romantic love, taken from Fletcher's earlier books. (Rev: VOYA 8/98) [811]

3974 Frost, Robert. *A Swinger of Birches* (6–9). Illus. 1982, Stemmer $21.95 (0-916144-92-5); paper $14.95 (0-916144-93-3). A collection of Frost's poems suitable for young readers in a well-illustrated edition. [811]

3975 Frost, Robert. *You Come Too: Favorite Poems for Young Readers* (7–12). Illus. 1959, Holt $16.95 (0-8050-0299-5); paper $7.95 (0-8050-0316-9). A fine introduction to this poet's works through 50 of his more accessible poems. [811]

3976 Gardner, Joann, ed. *Runaway with Words: Poems from Florida's Youth Shelters* (6–12). 1996, Anhinga Pr. paper $14.95 (0-938078-47-X). Joy, anger, confusion, and fear are some of the emotions expressed in this collection of poems culled from writing workshops for teens in Florida's shelters. (Rev: BL 6/1–15/97) [811]

3977 Gillan, Maria M., and Jennifer Gillan, eds. *Unsettling America: An Anthology of Contemporary Multicultural Poetry* (9–12). 1994, Penguin paper $15.95 (0-14-023778-X). Features poets from various cultures and backgrounds, including Native American Joy Harjo, Hawaiian Garrett Hongo, and African American Rita Dove. (Rev: BL 10/1/94; SLJ 5/95) [811]

3978 Giovanni, Nikki. *Ego-Tripping and Other Poems for Young People* (9–12). Illus. 1994, Chicago Review $14.95 (1-55652-188-X). Ten poems have

been added to Giovanni's 1973 collection for a total of 23 poems celebrating ordinary folks and their struggles for liberation. (Rev: BL 4/15/94) [811]

3979 Giovanni, Nikki, ed. *Grand Mothers: Poems, Reminiscences, and Short Stories about the Keepers of Our Traditions* (7–12). 1994, Holt $15.95 (0-8050-2766-1). An anthology of 27 poems, memories, and stories about grandmothers, written in diverse styles and expressing a wide range of sentiments and experiences. (Rev: BL 9/15/94; SLJ 10/94; VOYA 12/94) [811]

3980 Giovanni, Nikki. *The Selected Poems of Nikki Giovanni (1968–1995)* (9–12). 1996, Morrow $22.00 (0-688-14047-5). A rich synthesis of Giovanni's work that reveals the evolution of her poetic voice. (Rev: BL 12/15/95) [811]

3981 Giovanni, Nikki, ed. *Shimmy Shimmy Shimmy like My Sister Kate: Looking at the Harlem Renaissance through Poems* (9–12). 1996, Holt $17.95 (0-8050-3494-3). A collection of African American poetry that covers both the Harlem Renaissance with writers like Langston Hughes as well as contemporaries including Ntozake Shange and LeRoi Jones. (Rev: BL 3/15/96; BR 11–12/96; SLJ 5/96*; VOYA 10/96) [811]

3982 Giovanni, Nikki. *Those Who Ride the Night Winds* (10–12). 1984, Morrow paper $9.00 (0-688-02653-2). Poems about love and about people who are special to the poet like Rosa Parks and John Lennon. [811]

3983 Glenn, Mel. *Jump Ball: A Basketball Season in Poems* (6–12). 1997, Dutton paper $15.99 (0-525-67554-X). In a series of poems, people involved in an inner city high school are introduced, including basketball players, parents, teachers, and friends. (Rev: BL 10/15/97; SLJ 11/97*; VOYA 12/97) [811]

3984 Glenn, Mel. *Who Killed Mr. Chippendale? A Mystery in Poems* (7–12). 1996, Dutton $14.99 (0-525-67530-2). Using free verse, the author explores the shooting death of a high school teacher from the point of view of several characters, including students in his class and investigating police officers. (Rev: BL 6/1–15/96; SLJ 7/96*; VOYA 12/96) [811]

3985 Grimes, Nikki. *A Dime a Dozen* (5–8). 1998, Dial $15.99 (0-8037-2227-3). Through a series of poems, the writer explores her childhood—its happy moments, its painful memories, including divorce, foster homes, and parents with drinking and gambling problems, and her search for herself as a teenager. (Rev: BL 12/1/98; SLJ 11/98; VOYA 4/99) [811]

3986 Grimes, Nikki. *Hopscotch Love: A Family Treasury of Love Poems* (4–8). Illus. 1999, Lothrop $14.95 (0-688-15667-3). This collection of poems celebrates all kinds of love as experienced by African Americans including sibling love, teenage crushes, parental love, and love of a husband and wife and a graying couple. (Rev: BL 2/15/99; SLJ 1/99) [811]

3987 Harmon, William, ed. *The Oxford Book of American Light Verse* (7–12). 1979, Oxford $63.95 (0-19-502509-1). In addition to poems like "A Visit from St. Nicholas," this anthology covers lyrics by Cole Porter and Stephen Sondheim. [811.08]

3988 Hearne, Betsy. *Polaroid and Other Poems of View* (7–12). Illus. 1991, Macmillan $13.95 (0-689-50530-2). A collection of short poems using the camera as a metaphor, drawing connections between word pictures created by the poet and those taken by a photographer. (Rev: BL 8/91) [811]

3989 Herrera, Juan F. *Laughing Out Loud, I Fly (A Caracajadas Yo Vuelo): Poems in English & Spanish* (6–10). Illus. 1998, HarperCollins $14.95 (0-06-027604-5). In this series of poems in both English and Spanish, the poet celebrates incidents in his childhood. (Rev: SLJ 5/98; VOYA 6/99) [811]

3990 Holbrook, Sara. *Walking on the Boundaries of Change: Poems of Transition* (8–12). 1998, Boyds Mills paper $8.95 (1-56397-737-0). In this collection of 53 poems, the author explores the problems of being a teen with amazing insight into concerns and decisions. (Rev: VOYA 2/99) [811]

3991 Hopkins, Lee Bennett, ed. *Hand in Hand* (5–8). 1994, Simon & Schuster $20.00 (0-671-73315-X). A browsable collection that includes selections from Frost, Longfellow, Whitman, Hughes, and Sandberg, among others. (Rev: BL 1/1/95; SLJ 12/94; VOYA 4/95) [811]

3992 Hopkins, Lee Bennett, sel. *Lives: Poems about Famous Americans* (4–8). Illus. 1999, HarperCollins LB $15.89 (0-06-027768-8). Poetry brings to life 16 important Americans, among them Paul Revere, Eleanor Roosevelt, Babe Ruth, and Langston Hughes. (Rev: SLJ 6/99) [811]

3993 Hopkins, Lee Bennett, ed. *Love & Kisses* (7–10). Illus. 1983, Houghton $8.95 (0-395-34554-5); paper $3.95 (0-395-34921-4). A selection of 25 American poems celebrating various aspects of love. [811.08]

3994 Hopkins, Lee Bennett, ed. *Rainbows Are Made* (6–9). 1982, Harcourt $17.95 (0-15-265480-1). Poems by Carl Sandburg that are suitable for young readers are included in this anthology. [811]

3995 Hughes, Langston. *The Dream Keeper and Other Poems* (6–12). Illus. 1994, Knopf LB $14.99 (0-679-94421-4). A classic poetry collection by the renowned African American, originally published in 1932, is presented in an updated, illustrated edition. (Rev: BL 3/15/94; VOYA 6/94) [811]

3996 Hughes, Langston, et al., eds. *The Collected Poems of Langston Hughes* (9–12). 1994, Knopf

$35.50 (0-679-42631-0). A large collection of the African American poet's work. Hughes speaks in jazzlike rhythms of the pain of everyday life, Harlem street life, prejudice, Southern violence, and love. (Rev: BL 10/1/94*) [811]

3997 Janeczko, Paul B., ed. *Poetspeak: In Their Work, about Their Work* (7–12). Illus. 1991, Simon & Schuster paper $9.95 (0-02-043850-8). The works of 60 modern American poets are represented plus comments by the poets themselves on their work. [811.08]

3998 Johnson, Angela. *The Other Side: Shorter Poems* (7–12). 1998, Orchard $15.95 (0-531-30114-1). A small collection of poems in which the author recalls growing up in Shorter, Alabama. (Rev: BL 11/15/98; BR 5–6/99; SLJ 9/98; VOYA 2/99) [811]

3999 Knudson, R. R., and May Swenson, eds. *American Sports Poems* (7–12). 1988, Watts LB $19.99 (0-531-08353-5). An excellent collection that concentrates on such popular sports as baseball, football, and swimming. (Rev: BL 8/88; BR 3–4/89; SLJ 11/88; VOYA 10/88) [811]

4000 Lawrence, Jacob. *Harriet and the Promised Land* (6–12). 1993, Simon & Schuster paper $18.00 (0-671-86673-7). The efforts of Harriet Tubman's to lead slaves to freedom in the North is retold in rhythmic text and narrative paintings. (Rev: BL 10/1/93*) [811]

4001 Levin, Jonathan, ed. *Walt Whitman: Poetry for Young People* (5–9). Illus. 1997, Sterling $14.95 (0-8069-9530-0). After a brief biographical sketch, this volume contains 26 poems and excerpts from longer poems, each introduced with an analysis and an appreciation. (Rev: SLJ 11/97) [811]

4002 Livingston, Myra Cohn. *Cricket Never Does: A Collection of Haiku and Tanka* (5–8). Illus. 1997, Simon & Schuster $15.00 (0-689-81123-3). Seasonal changes are explored in more than 60 short haiku and tanka. (Rev: BL 3/1/97; BR 11–12/97; SLJ 4/97) [811]

4003 Livingston, Myra Cohn, ed. *I Am Writing a Poem About . . . A Game of Poetry* (9–12). 1997, Simon & Schuster $16.00 (0-689-81156-X). These are the poems that resulted when students in the author's poetry-writing classes were asked to write poems using randomly selected words as inspirations. (Rev: BL 9/1/97; SLJ 10/97; VOYA 2/98) [811]

4004 Livingston, Myra Cohn, ed. *Lots of Limericks* (5–10). Illus. 1991, Macmillan $15.00 (0-689-50531-0). Arranged by subject, 210 absurd and amusing verses, many of them by anonymous writers. (Rev: BL 10/1/91; SLJ 1/92) [821]

4005 Loewen, Nancy, ed. *Walt Whitman* (7–12). 1994, Creative Ed. LB $18.95 (0-88682-608-X). A dozen selections from *Leaves of Grass* are juxtaposed with biographical vignettes and sepia photos. (Rev: SLJ 7/94*) [811]

4006 Longfellow, Henry Wadsworth. *Hiawatha* (7–12). Illus. 1983, Dial LB $13.89 (0-8037-0014-8). The epic narrative poem about the deeds of the famous Ojibway brave. (Rev: BL 1/1/88) [811]

4007 Lyne, Sandford, comp. *Ten-Second Rainshowers: Poems by Young People* (4–9). Illus. 1996, Simon & Schuster paper $16.00 (0-689-80113-0). Through poetry written in free verse, 130 young people ages 8 to 18 give brief, evocative glimpses of life. (Rev: SLJ 12/96; VOYA 12/96) [811]

4008 Major, Clarence, ed. *The Garden Thrives: Twentieth Century African-American Poetry* (10–12). 1996, HarperPerennial paper $20.00 (0-06-095121-4). An impressive anthology arranged chronologically that includes the work of Paul Lawrence Dunbar, Langston Hughes, Lucille Clifton, Nikki Giovanni, and Rita Dove. (Rev: SLJ 5/97) [811]

4009 Marius, Richard, and Keith Frome, eds. *The Columbia Book of Civil War Poetry* (9–12). 1994, Columbia Univ. Pr. $31.50 (0-231-10002-7). An anthology of Civil War poetry, including famous songs and verses that appeared in newspapers by unknown writers. (Rev: BL 9/15/94; SLJ 11/94) [811.008]

4010 Marquis, Don. *Archyology: The Long Lost Tales of Archy and Mehitable* (10–12). Illus. 1996, Univ. Press of New England Pr. $14.95 (0-874-51745-1). Light, humorous verse about Archy the cockroach and Mehitable the cat. (Rev: BL 4/1/96; SLJ 2/97) [811]

4011 Merriam, Eve. *The Inner City Mother Goose* (9–12). Illus. 1996, Simon & Schuster $16.00 (0-689-80677-9). A new edition (with a few additional poems) of this unflinchingly sour parody of Mother Goose that deals straightforwardly with topics like city violence, racism, and corruption. (Rev: BL 4/15/96; BR 1–2/97; SLJ 5/96*) [811]

4012 Moss, Jeff. *The Dad of the Dad of the Dad of Your Dad: Stories About Kids and Their Fathers* (4–8). Illus. 1997, Ballantine $18.00 (0-345-38591-8). Eight humorous poems trace the history of families, from a prehistoric father and his son to a futuristic dad and his brood. (Rev: SLJ 7/97) [811]

4013 Mullins, Tom, ed. *Running Lightly . . . .: Poems for Young People* (4–9). 1998, Mercier paper $12.95 (1-85342-193-9). A charming collection of old songs and ballads, nonsense rhymes, and lyrics. (Rev: BL 5/15/98; SLJ 7/98) [811]

4014 Myers, Walter Dean. *Angel to Angel* (4–8). Illus. 1998, HarperCollins LB $15.89 (0-06-027722-X). A photo/poetry montage with 10 distinctly styled

poems and photographs focusing on African American mothers and children, and reflecting the relationship between words and pictures. (Rev: BL 2/15/98; SLJ 6/98) [811]

4015 Nash, Ogden. *I Wouldn't Have Missed It: Selected Poems of Ogden Nash* (9–12). Illus. 1975, Little, Brown $33.00 (0-316-59830-5). A selection of over 400 poems chosen by the poet's daughter after his death. [811]

4016 Nash, Ogden. *The Pocket Book of Ogden Nash* (9–12). 1991, Buccaneer LB $18.95 (0-89966-867-4). A fine collection of this writer's wittiest and most endearing poems. [811]

4017 Poe, Edgar Allan. *Annabel Lee* (5–9). Illus. 1987, Tundra $19.95 (0-88776-200-X). A haunting rendition of the Poe poem with paintings by the French Canadian artist Gilles Tibo. (Rev: BL 10/15/87; SLJ 12/87) [811]

4018 Robb, Laura, sel. *Music and Drum: Voices of War and Peace, Hope and Dreams* (5–9). 1997, Philomel $16.95 (0-399-22024-0). An anthology of war poems that are strikingly illustrated with photos reflecting the power and emotions of the poems. (Rev: BL 4/1/97; SLJ 5/97) [808]

4019 Rosenberg, Liz, ed. *The Invisible Ladder: An Anthology of Contemporary American Poems for Young Readers* (6–10). 1996, Holt $17.95 (0-8050-3836-1). As well as an excellent anthology of modern American poetry, this volume provides commentary by the poets, photographs of them, and suggestions for using each of the poems. (Rev: BL 9/15/96; BR 9–10/97; SLJ 2/97; VOYA 2/97) [811]

4020 Rylant, Cynthia. *Soda Jerk* (7–12). Illus. 1990, Watts LB $14.95 (0-531-08464-7). A group of poems about the inhabitants of a small town written from the viewpoint of a teenage soda jerk. (Rev: BL 2/15/90; SLJ 4/90; VOYA 6/90) [811]

4021 Rylant, Cynthia. *Something Permanent* (7–12). Illus. 1994, Harcourt $18.00 (0-15-277090-9). Combines Rylant's poetry with Walker Evans's photos to evoke strong emotions of Southern life during the Depression. (Rev: BL 7/94*; SLJ 8/94; VOYA 12/94) [811]

4022 Rylant, Cynthia. *Waiting to Waltz: A Childhood* (7–9). Illus. 1984, Bradbury $16.00 (0-02-778000-7). In 30 poems, the author conveys the experience of growing up in a small Appalachian town. [808.81]

4023 Sandburg, Carl. *Early Moon* (6–9). Illus. 1930, Harcourt paper $7.00 (0-15-627326-8). About 70 poems for young people illustrated by James Daugherty. [811]

4024 Sandburg, Carl. *Grassroots* (4–8). Illus. 1998, Harcourt $18.00 (0-15-200082-8). This collection of 16 poems describing the seasons in America's Midwest is illustrated with watercolor landscapes. (Rev: BL 3/15/98; SLJ 6/98) [811]

4025 Schoonmaker, Frances, ed. *Henry Wadsworth Longfellow* (4–8). Illus. (Poetry for Young People) 1999, Sterling $14.95 (0-8069-9417-7). A generous, carefully-selected presentation of Longfellow's poetry illustrated by full-color paintings and accompanied by biographical notes. (Rev: SLJ 3/99) [811]

4026 Silverstein, Shel. *A Light in the Attic* (6–9). Illus. 1981, HarperCollins LB $16.89 (0-06-025674-5). Over 100 humorous poems that deal with children's interests and need for fun. Also use the author's earlier: *Where the Sidewalk Ends* (1974). [811]

4027 Smith, William J. *Here Is My Heart: Love Poems* (5–8). 1999, Little, Brown $12.95 (0-316-19765-3). This is a delightful collection of short love poems, including some by the compiler. (Rev: BL 1/1–15/99; SLJ 1/99) [821.008]

4028 Soto, Gary. *A Fire in My Hands: A Book of Poems* (6–10). Illus. 1992, Scholastic paper $3.99 (0-590-44579-0). An illustrated collection of 23 poems, accompanied by advice to young poets. (Rev: BL 4/1/92; SLJ 3/92) [811]

4029 Stafford, William. *Learning to Live in the World: Earth Poems* (8–12). 1994, Harcourt $17.00 (0-15-200208-1). Fifty nature poems that will appeal to teens. (Rev: BL 1/1/95; SLJ 12/94) [811]

4030 Steig, Jeanne. *Alpha Beta Chowder* (5–8). Illus. 1992, HarperCollins LB $14.89 (0-06-205007-9). A collection of nonsense verses celebrating the joy of words—their sound and meaning—with each verse playing with a letter of the alphabet. (Rev: BL 11/15/92; SLJ 12/92) [811]

4031 Strickland, Michael R., ed. *My Own Song: And Other Poems to Groove To* (6–12). Illus. 1997, Boyds Mills $14.95 (1-56397-686-2). A collection of poems about music and its relationship to such subjects as love, cities, and birds. (Rev: BL 10/15/97; SLJ 12/97) [811]

4032 Sullivan, Charles, ed. *Imaginary Gardens: American Poetry and Art for Young People* (6–10). Illus. 1989, Abrams $19.95 (0-8109-1130-2). A collection of well-known poems, from Ogden Nash to Walt Whitman, with accompanying illustrations that also represent a wide range of artists and styles. (Rev: BL 12/1/89; SLJ 2/89) [700]

4033 Turner, Ann. *Grass Songs: Poems* (7–12). Illus. 1993, Harcourt $16.95 (0-15-136788-4). Dramatic monologues in poetic form that express courage and despair, passion and loneliness, and the struggle to find a home in the wilderness. (Rev: BL 6/1–15/93; VOYA 8/93) [811]

4034 Turner, Ann. *Mississippi Mud: 3 Prairie Journals* (4–8). Illus. 1997, HarperCollins LB $15.89 (0-06-024433-X). The author has written a series of simple poems based on journals kept by the 3 older children of a family journeying west to settle in a new land in the 19th century. (Rev: BL 4/15/97; SLJ 6/97) [811]

4035 Turner, Ann W. *A Lion's Hunger: Poems of First Love* (8–12). Illus. 1999, Marshall Cavendish $15.95 (0-7614-5035-1). Written from a young woman's point of view, this is a collection of poems by the author chronicling the joys and sorrows of first love. (Rev: BL 3/1/99; BR 5–6/99; SLJ 1/99; VOYA 2/99) [811]

4036 Whipple, Laura, ed. *Celebrating America: A Collection of Poems and Images of the American Spirit* (5–10). 1994, Putnam $19.95 (0-399-22036-4). An anthology of poetry and art that reflects the wide range of American cultures, styles, and periods. (Rev: BL 9/1/94*; SLJ 9/94) [811.008]

4037 Whitman, Walt. *Voyages: Poems by Walt Whitman* (7–12). Illus. 1988, Harcourt $15.95 (0-15-294495-8). After an introductory biographical sketch, there are 53 representative poems selected by Lee Bennett Hopkins. (Rev: BL 11/15/88; BR 3–4/89; SLJ 12/88; VOYA 1/89) [811.3]

4038 Wong, Janet S. *The Rainbow Hand: Poems about Mothers & Children* (5–8). Illus. 1999, Simon & Schuster paper $15.00 (0-689-82148-4). This collection of 18 poems deals with maternal love, some from the mother's point of view and others from the child's. (Rev: BL 4/1/99; SLJ 4/99; VOYA 6/99) [811]

4039 Yolen, Jane, sel. *Once Upon Ice: And Other Frozen Poems* (4–8). 1997, Boyds Mills $17.95 (1-56397-408-8). A collection of 17 poems, each inspired by photographs of a different ice formation, which are also in the book. (Rev: BL 2/1/97; SLJ 3/97) [811]

Other Regions

4040 Berry, James R. *Everywhere Faces Everywhere* (6–10). Illus. 1997, Simon & Schuster $16.00 (0-689-80996-4). A collection of 46 of the author's poems that describe his childhood in Jamaica and his adult life in the United Kingdom. (Rev: BL 5/1/97; BR 11–12/97; SLJ 6/97; VOYA 10/97) [821]

4041 Chipasula, Stella, and Frank Chipasula, eds. *Heinemann Book of African Women's Poetry* (9–12). 1995, Heinemann paper $10.95 (0-435-90680-1). A wide range of poetic voices celebrating Africa's racial and cultural diversity. (Rev: BL 2/15/95*) [821]

4042 Field, Edward. *Magic Words* (5–9). Illus. 1998, Harcourt $17.00 (0-15-201498-5). This is a collection of free verse narratives based on Inuit creation myths and songs. (Rev: BL 10/15/98; SLJ 12/98) [811]

4043 Mado, Michio. *The Animals: Selected Poems* (5–10). Trans. by the Empress Michiko of Japan. Illus. 1992, Simon & Schuster $16.95 (0-689-50574-4). Twenty Japanese poems about animals, with English versions on facing pages. (Rev: BL 12/1/92; SLJ 2/93) [895.6]

4044 Nye, Naomi Shihab, ed. *The Space between Our Footsteps: Poems and Paintings from the Middle East* (8–12). Illus. 1998, Simon & Schuster paper $19.95 (0-689-81233-7). More than 100 poets and artists from 19 countries in the Middle East are featured in this handsome volume of verse that deals with families, friends, and everyday events. (Rev: BL 3/1/98; SLJ 5/98; VOYA 10/98) [808.81]

4045 Service, Robert W. *The Best of Robert Service* (9–12). 1989, Putnam $12.95 (0-399-55008-9). The poet of the Yukon is presented well in this collection of his most popular poems. [811]

4046 Service, Robert W. *The Cremation of Sam McGee* (5–9). Illus. 1987, Greenwillow $18.00 (0-688-06903-7). The famous gold rush poem amusingly illustrated by Ted Harrison. (Rev: BL 4/15/87; SLJ 3/87) [811]

4047 Service, Robert W. *The Shooting of Dan McGrew* (6–9). Illus. 1995, Godine paper $10.95 (1-56792-065-9). A bunch of the boys are still whooping it up in this nicely illustrated edition. (Rev: BL 1/1/89; SLJ 12/88) [811]

Folklore and Fairy Tales

4048 Ausubel, Nathan, ed. *A Treasury of Jewish Folklore, Stories, Traditions, Legends, Humor, Wisdom and Folk Songs of the Jewish People* (9–12). 1989, Crown $22.00 (0-517-50293-3). A treasury of Jewish wit and wisdom through the ages that also reveals a great deal about Jewish history and religion. (Rev: SLJ 6/90) [296]

4049 Caduto, Michael J. *Earth Tales from around the World* (5–8). Illus. 1997, Fulcrum paper $17.95 (1-55591-968-5). Arranged by topics that explore the earth and humankind's relationship to it, this collection of folktales from around the world explores the theme of respect for the natural world. (Rev: BL 4/1/98; SLJ 5/98; VOYA 4/98) [398.27]

4050 Climo, Shirley. *A Treasury of Mermaids: Mermaid Tales from around the World* (4–8). Illus. 1997, HarperCollins $16.95 (0-06-023876-3). A fine retelling of 8 folktales from around the world about mermaids and other enchanted sea creatures. (Rev: BL 11/15/97; SLJ 10/97) [398.21]

4051 Cole, Joanna, ed. *Best-Loved Folktales of the World* (7–12). Illus. 1982, Doubleday paper $17.00 (0-385-18949-4). A collection of 200 tales from around the globe arranged geographically. [398.2]

4052 Creeden, Sharon. *Fair Is Fair: World Folktales of Justice* (9–12). 1995, August House $19.95 (0-87483-400-7). Thirty folktales adapted from different times and places related to law and justice. (Rev: BL 5/15/95; SLJ 10/95) [398.2]

4053 Crossley-Holland, Kevin, ed. *The Young Oxford Book of Folk Tales* (5–8). 1999, Oxford $35.50 (0-19-278141-3). A delightful collection of folktales from around the world, with accompanying notes on their origins. (Rev: BL 5/15/99; SLJ 10/99) [398.2]

4054 De Caro, Frank, ed. *The Folktale Cat* (9–12). 1993, August House paper $14.95 (0-87483-303-5). An international collection of 51 classic and lesser-known feline folktales, with a discussion of the domestic cat's role in folklore. (Rev: BL 4/15/93; SLJ 11/93) [398.2]

4055 Doherty, Berlie. *Tales of Wonder & Magic* (5–8). Illus. 1998, Candlewick $21.99 (1-56402-891-7). An elegantly illustrated anthology of 9 traditional fairy tales plus one original one by Doherty. (Rev: BL 5/15/98; SLJ 7/98) [398.2]

4056 Dorson, Richard M., ed. *Folktales Told Around the World* (10–12). Illus. 1987, Univ. of Chicago Pr. paper $30.00 (0-226-15874-8). An international selection of folktales in authentic retellings and translations. [398.2]

4057 Ferguson, Gary. *Spirits of the Wild: The World's Great Nature Myths* (10–12). 1996, Clarkson N. Potter $21.00 (0-517-70369-6). A collection of 60 short myths and legends from around the world explaining how a variety of natural phenomena came to be. (Rev: BR 3–4/97; SLJ 1/97) [398.2]

4058 Forest, Heather. *Wisdom Tales from Around the World: Fifty Gems of Story and Wisdom from Such Diverse Traditions as Sufi, Zen, Taoist, Christian, Jewish, Buddhist, African, and Native American* (10–12). 1996, August House $27.95 (0-87483-478-3); paper $17.95 (0-87483-479-1). Gems of wisdom on the conduct of life are contained in this collection of folktales, proverbs, and parables from around the world. (Rev: BL 3/1/97; SLJ 4/97; VOYA 6/97) [398.2]

4059 Jaffe, Nina, and Steve Zeitlin. *The Cow of No Color: Riddle Stories & Justice Tales from Around the World* (5–8). Illus. 1995, St. Martin's $15.95 (0-

8050-3736-5). A collection of folk tales from around the world that deal with the theme of justice. (Rev: BL 11/1/98; SLJ 12/98) [398.2]

4060 Lester, Julius. *When the Beginning Began: Stories about God, the Creatures, and Us* (4–8). Illus. 1999, Harcourt $17.00 (0-15-201138-9). A collection of creation tales, some from the Book of Genesis and others from traditional Jewish legends. (Rev: BL 4/15/99; SLJ 5/99) [296.1]

4061 McCaughrean, Geraldine. *The Silver Treasure: Myths & Legends of the World* (6–8). Illus. 1997, Simon & Schuster paper $19.95 (0-689-81322-8). A collection of 23 myths and legends that includes such familiar ones as *Rip Van Winkle* and *The Tower of Babel* as well as many lesser-known ones. (Rev: BL 4/15/97; SLJ 4/97*; VOYA 8/97) [398.121]

4062 Mayer, Marianna. *Women Warriors: Myths and Legends of Heroic Women* (4–8). 1999, Morrow $18.00 (0-688-15522-7). A collection of 12 myths and legends about folk heroines from India, Africa, Japan, North America, and the British Isles. (Rev: BL 9/15/99; SLJ 9/99) [398.2]

4063 Opie, Iona, and Peter Opie, eds. *The Classic Fairy Tales* (9–12). Illus. 1987, Oxford paper $23.95 (0-19-520219-8). The definitive retelling of 24 of the most popular fairy tales of all time. [398.2]

4064 Phelps, Ethel Johnston. *The Maid of the North: Feminist Folk Tales from around the World* (7–9). 1982, Holt paper $9.95 (0-8050-0679-6). An international collection of folktales featuring many wily and clever heroines. [398]

4065 Sadeh, Pinhas, ed. *Jewish Folktales* (9–12). Illus. 1989, Doubleday paper $16.00 (0-385-19574-5). This collection is distinguished by the worldwide coverage represented in the tales included. (Rev: BL 11/1/89) [398.2]

4066 San Souci, Robert D. *Even More Short & Shivery: Thirty Spine-Tingling Stories* (5–8). Illus. 1997, Delacorte $14.95 (0-385-32252-6). A collection of 30 scary stories, mostly folktales from around the world, that are great for reading aloud or giving presentations before a group. (Rev: BL 7/97; SLJ 10/97) [398.25]

4067 San Souci, Robert D. *A Terrifying Taste of Short & Shivery: Thirty Creepy Tales* (5–9). Illus. 1998, Delacorte $14.95 (0-385-32635-1). Drawn from folktales and ghost stories from around the world, this is a fine collection of 30 short supernatural stories. (Rev: SLJ 11/98) [398.2]

4068 Sherman, Josepha. *Merlin's Kin: World Tales of the Heroic Magician* (5–8). 1998, August House $21.95 (0-87483-523-2); paper $11.95 (0-87483-519-4). A splendid international collection of folktales that feature magicians, sorcerers, shamans,

healers, and wizards. (Rev: BL 4/15/99; BR 1–2/99; SLJ 3/99; VOYA 12/98) [398.21]

4069 Sherman, Josepha. *Trickster Tales: Forty Folk Stories from Around the World* (6–10). Illus. 1996, August House $28.95 (0-87483-449-X). The tricksters in this collection of 40 folktales include Tyl Eulenspiegel of Germany, Anansi the spider from Africa, Coyote from North America, and Pedro de Urdemalas of Mexico. (Rev: SLJ 6/97) [398.2]

4070 Yolen, Jane, ed. *Favorite Folktales from around the World* (9–12). 1988, Pantheon paper $18.00 (0-394-75188-4). This collection of 160 tales represents such diverse stories as American Indian legends and others from the Brothers Grimm. (Rev: SLJ 12/86) [398]

4071 Young, Richard A., and Judy Dockery Young. *Stories from the Days of Christopher Columbus: A Multicultural Collection for Young Readers* (5–9). 1992, August House paper $8.95 (0-87483-198-9). Anthology of stories from the times of Christopher Columbus, translated from Spanish, Aztec, and other languages. (Rev: BL 9/15/92; SLJ 7/92) [398.2]

Geographical Regions

Africa

4072 Abrahams, Roger D., ed. *African Folktales: Traditional Stories of the Black World* (7–12). Illus. 1983, Pantheon paper $17.00 (0-394-72117-9). A collection of about 100 tales from south of the Sahara. [398.2]

4073 Berry, Jack. *West African Folktales* (9–12). Ed. by Richard Spears. 1991, Northwestern Univ. Pr. $29.00 (0-8101-0979-4); paper $14.95 (0-8101-0993-X). Vivid folktales imparting basic life lessons collected over 35 years by a linguist who specialized in the spoken art of Sierra Leone, Ghana, and Nigeria. (Rev: BL 10/15/91) [398.2]

4074 Courlander, Harold, ed. *Treasury of African Folklore* (10–12). Illus. 1995, Marlowe paper $15.95 (1-56924-816-8). A wide and varied selection of myths from various African tribes south of the Sahara. [398.2]

4075 Green, Roger L. *Tales of Ancient Egypt* (5–9). 1972, Penguin paper $4.99 (0-14-036716-0). A collection of folktales from ancient Egypt including one about the source of the Nile. [398]

4076 Kituku, Vincent Muli Wa, retel. *East African Folktales: From the Voice of Mukamba* (6–9). Illus. 1997, August House paper $9.95 (0-87483-489-9). This bilingual book contains 18 folktales in English and Kikamba, the language of the Kamba Community in Kenya. (Rev: SLJ 8/97) [398.2]

4077 Mama, Raouf, retel. *Why Goats Smell Bad and Other Stories from Benin* (4–8). Illus. 1998, Linnet LB $19.95 (0-208-02469-7). A delightful collection of 20 folktales from the Fon culture of Benin, handsomely illustrated with woodcuts. (Rev: BL 2/15/98; SLJ 4/98) [398.2]

Asia and the Middle East

4078 Alderson, Brian. *The Arabian Nights; or, Tales Told by Sheherazade During a Thousand Nights and One Night* (5–8). Illus. 1995, Morrow $20.00 (0-688-14219-2). The tales are written in a colloquial style, retaining more of the earthiness and vigor of the original than other versions. Border pictures like Persian miniatures and double-page spreads enhance the pages. (Rev: BL 10/15/95; SLJ 9/95) [398.22]

4079 *The Arabian Nights* (9–12). 1991, NAL paper $5.95 (0-451-52542-6). Sinbad and Aladdin are only 2 of the famous characters that come alive in these ancient tales. [398]

4080 Beck, Brenda E. F., et al., eds. *Folktales of India* (9–12). 1989, Univ. of Chicago Pr. paper $22.50 (0-226-04082-8). There are 99 tales in this collection and they represent a number of different cultures and districts. (Rev: BL 5/1/87) [398.2]

4081 Kendall, Carol, retel. *Haunting Tales from Japan* (6–9). Illus. 1985, Spencer Museum Publns. paper $6.00 (0-913689-22-X). A retelling of 6 Japanese folktales, some of which deal with murder and suicide. (Rev: SLJ 2/86) [398]

4082 Krishnaswami, Uma. *Shower of Gold: Girls and Women in the Stories of India* (6–10). 1999, Linnet LB $19.95 (0-208-02484-0). This book contains Hindu and Buddhist tales, folklore, fables, and legends from the Indian subcontinent, based on the lives of real women. (Rev: BL 3/15/99; SLJ 8/99) [891]

4083 Lang, Andrew. *The Arabian Nights Entertainments* (6–9). Illus. 1969, Dover paper $8.95 (0-486-22289-6). Aladdin and Sinbad are only 2 of the characters in these 26 tales taken from the 1001 nights collection. (Rev: BL 9/1/89) [398.2]

4084 Lewis, Naomi. *Stories from the Arabian Nights* (6–9). Illus. 1991, Random $9.99 (0-517-05480-9). A total of 30 stories are retold through the voice of Shahrazad, master storyteller. (Rev: BL 2/1/88; SLJ 2/88) [382.2]

4085 Livo, Norma J., and Dia Cha, eds. *Folk Stories of the Hmong: Peoples of Laos, Thailand, and Vietnam* (9–12). 1991, Libraries Unlimited LB $22.00 (0-87287-854-6). The unique culture and heritage of the Hmong people are celebrated in this collection of folktales. Includes an introduction to Hmong history. (Rev: BL 10/1/91) [398.2]

4086 McAlpine, Helen, and William McAlpine. *Japanese Tales & Legends* (8–12). Illus. 1989, Oxford paper $20.95 (0-19-274140-3). A standard work first published in 1958 that retells Japanese creation myths, epics, and fairy tales. (Rev: BR 3–4/90) [398]

4087 Mayer, Marianna. *Turandot* (6–8). Illus. 1995, Morrow $16.00 (0-688-09073-7). The Chinese tale of the princess who will consent to marry only the one man who can answer her 3 riddles. Beautifully illustrated. (Rev: BL 10/15/95; SLJ 10/95) [398.2]

4088 Meeker, Clare Hodgson. *A Tale of Two Rice Birds: A Folktale from Thailand* (5–8). Illus. 1994, Sasquatch $14.95 (1-57061-008-8). An enchanting folktale that dates back to the days of Siam. (Rev: BL 1/15/95; SLJ 11/94) [398.24]

4089 Quayle, Eric. *The Shining Princess and Other Japanese Legends* (6–8). Illus. 1989, Little, Brown $15.95 (0-316-72865-9). A collection of 10 legends vividly retold. (Rev: BL 12/15/89) [398.2]

4090 Riordan, James. *Tales from the Arabian Nights* (7–9). Illus. 1985, Checkerboard $14.95 (1-56288-258-9). Among the 10 stories retold are those involving Sinbad, Ali Baba, and Aladdin. (Rev: SLJ 3/86) [398.2]

4091 Roberts, Moss. *Chinese Fairy Tales and Fantasies* (10–12). 1980, Pantheon paper $16.00 (0-394-73994-9). Culled from 25 centuries of folklore, this is a collection of 100 tales. [398]

4092 Tyler, Royall, ed. *Japanese Tales* (9–12). 1989, Pantheon paper $18.00 (0-394-75656-8). Arranged by themes, this is a mammoth collection of folktales that concentrates on those originating in the 12th through the 14th centuries. (Rev: BL 5/1/87) [398.2]

4093 Yeoman, John, retel. *The Seven Voyages of Sinbad the Sailor* (5–8). Illus. 1997, Simon & Schuster $19.95 (0-689-81368-6). In these stories adapted from the *Arabian Nights,* Sinbad tells about his 7 amazing voyages that brought him horror, disaster, adventure, and, eventually, wealth. (Rev: BL 1/1–15/98; SLJ 12/97) [398]

4094 Yep, Laurence. *The Rainbow People* (7–10). Illus. 1989, HarperCollins $16.00 (0-06-026760-7); paper $4.95 (0-06-440441-2). The retelling of 20 Chinese folktales with illustrations by David Wiesner. (Rev: BL 4/1/89; BR 11–12/90; SLJ 5/89) [398.2]

Australia and the Pacific Islands

4095 Oodgeroo. *Dreamtime: Aboriginal Stories* (6–10). Illus. 1994, Lothrop $16.00 (0-688-13296-0). Traditional and autobiographical stories of Aboriginal culture and its roots. Also examines current

Aboriginal life alongside white civilization. (Rev: BL 10/1/94; SLJ 10/94) [398.2]

4096 Te Kanawa, Kiri. *Land of the Long White Cloud: Maori Myths, Tales and Legends* (7–12). Illus. 1997, Pavilion paper $16.95 (1-86205-075-9). A group of Maori magical folktales about sea gods, fairies and monsters, and fantastic voyages retold by the famous opera singer from New Zealand. (Rev: BL 9/1/97) [398.2]

Europe

4097 Afanasév, Aleksandr. *Russian Folk Tales* (9–12). 1976, Pantheon paper $18.00 (0-394-73090-9). This is a standard collection of these traditional Russian tales. [398]

4098 Andersen, Hans Christian. *Tales and Stories* (9–12). Illus. 1980, Univ. of Washington Pr. paper $18.95 (0-295-95936-3). These 27 stories are retold for an adult audience. [398.2]

4099 Asbjörnsen, Peter Christen, and Jörgen Moe. *Norwegian Folk Tales* (9–12). Trans. by Pat Shaw and Carl Norman. Illus. 1982, Pantheon paper $14.00 (0-394-71054-1). From an authoritative collection that first appeared in 1845, about 25 Norwegian folktales have been reprinted. [398]

4100 Burkert, Nancy Ekholm. *Valentine & Orson* (5–10). Illus. 1989, Farrar $16.95 (0-374-38078-3). A stunningly illustrated retelling in verse of the old folktale of twins separated at birth, one raised in wealth and the other in poverty. (Rev: BL 9/1/89; SLJ 11/89) [843]

4101 Calvino, Italo, retel. *Italian Folktales* (9–12). Trans. by George Martin. 1956, Harcourt $27.95 (0-15-145770-0); paper $24.00 (0-15-645489-0). A lively retelling of Italian folktales that include variations on such stories as "Snow White" and "Cinderella." (Rev: BL 12/15/89) [398]

4102 Colum, Padraic, ed. *A Treasury of Irish Folklore*. 2nd rev. ed. (9–12). 1985, Random $12.99 (0-517-42046-5). In addition to folktales this anthology includes jokes, anecdotes, and songs. [398.2]

4103 Creswick, Paul. *Robin Hood* (7–9). Illus. 1984, Macmillan $28.00 (0-684-18162-2). A fine retelling of the stories of Robin Hood with superb illustrations by N. C. Wyeth. [398.2]

4104 Crossley-Holland, Kevin, retel. *British Folk Tales: New Versions* (6–12). Illus. 1987, Watts $24.95 (0-531-05733-X). A total of 55 tales—some familiar, others lesser known—are retold. (Rev: BL 1/15/88; SLJ 1/88) [398.2]

4105 Day, David. *The Search for King Arthur* (10–12). 1995, Facts on File $24.95 (0-8160-3370-6). Complemented by 170 stunning color illustra-

tions, this work traces the evolution of King Arthur from the earliest records to the present. (Rev: BL 11/15/95; BR 5–6/96; SLJ 2/96) [942]

4106 Delamare, David. *Cinderella* (7–12). 1993, Simon & Schuster $15.00 (0-671-76944-8). The familiar story is set in a locale much like Venice and enhanced by Delamare's paintings, both realistic and surreal. (Rev: BL 9/15/93; SLJ 12/93) [398.2]

4107 Green, Roger L. *Adventures of Robin Hood* (5–9). 1994, Knopf $13.95 (0-679-43636-7); Puffin paper $3.99 (0-14-036700-4). The exploits of this folk hero of England are retold in this classic version. [398]

4108 Green, Roger L. *King Arthur and His Knights* (5–9). 1974, Penguin paper $2.95 (0-14-030073-2). The classic retelling of the deeds of this famous king and his knights. [398]

4109 Grimm Brothers. *The Complete Grimms' Fairy Tales* (10–12). 1974, Pantheon $17.00 (0-394-49415-6). This early collection of folktales by the Grimm brothers is still considered the authoritative one. [398]

4110 Jacobs, Joseph, ed. *Celtic Fairy Tales* (10–12). 1968, Dover paper $6.95 (0-486-21826-0). One of the great collectors of folktales presents these from Ireland. Also use: *More Celtic Fairy Tales* (1968), *Indian Fairy Tales* (1969), and *English Fairy Tales* (Penguin, 1990). [398]

4111 Kilgannon, Eily. *Folktales of the Yeats Country* (5–8). Illus. 1990, Mercier paper $10.95 (0-85342-861-1). Seventeen folktales that originate in County Sligo in Ireland. (Rev: BL 8/90; SLJ 2/91) [398.2]

4112 Leavy, Una. *Irish Fairy Tales and Legends* (4–8). Illus. 1997, Roberts Rinehart $18.95 (1-57098-177-9). An attractive book that contains 10 Irish legends, some going back 2,000 years. (Rev: BL 2/1/98; SLJ 2/98) [398.2]

4113 McKinley, Robin. *The Outlaws of Sherwood* (9–12). 1988, Greenwillow $17.00 (0-688-07178-3). A reworking of the Robin Hood story in which our hero becomes a moody, self-doubting, somewhat ordinary man. (Rev: BL 12/15/88; BR 5–6/89; SLJ 1/89; VOYA 4/89) [398.2]

4114 Markale, Jean. *King of the Celts: Arthurian Legends and Celtic Tradition* (9–12). Trans. by Christine Hauch. 1994, Inner Traditions paper $14.95 (0-89281-452-7). A survey of Arthurian lore in Celtic history that illustrates how the legends were misappropriated by propagandists of the courtly nobility. (Rev: BL 3/1/94) [942.01]

4115 Miles, Bernard. *Robin Hood: His Life and Legend* (7–9). Illus. 1979, Checkerboard $12.95 (1-56288-412-3). A collection of tales about this English folk hero and his merry

4116 Napoli, Donna Jo. *The Magic Circle* (6–12). 1993, Dutton paper $14.99 (0-525-45127-7). A "history" of the witch in *Hansel and Gretel*. (Rev: BL 7/93; VOYA 8/93) [398.2]

4117 Nye, Robert. *Beowulf: A New Telling* (7–9). 1982, Dell paper $4.99 (0-440-90560-5). A retelling in modern English of the monster Grendel and the hero Beowulf. [398.2]

4118 Paterson, Katherine. *Parzival: The Quest of the Grail Knight* (5–8). Illus. 1998, Dutton $15.99 (0-525-67579-5). A retelling of the epic poem about the quest for the Holy Grail and the sin that led the knight Parzival to wander the world looking for peace. (Rev: BL 3/1/98; BR 9–10/98; SLJ 2/98*; VOYA 6/98) [398.22]

4119 Phillips, Graham, and Martin Keatman. *King Arthur: The True Story* (9–12). 1994, Arrow paper $9.95 (0-09-929681-0). A scholarly examination of the Arthurian legend that attempts to document its roots and determine whether the king ever really existed. (Rev: BL 1/15/94) [942.01]

4120 Pyle, Howard. *Merry Adventures of Robin Hood* (10–12). 1986, NAL paper $4.95 (0-451-52284-2). One of many retellings of the stories about Robin Hood and his merry men. [398]

4121 Pyle, Howard. *The Merry Adventures of Robin Hood of Great Renown in Nottinghamshire* (7–9). Illus. n.d., Peter Smith $22.50 (0-8446-2765-8); Dover paper $8.95 (0-486-22043-5). The classic (first published in 1883) retelling of 22 of the most famous stories. [398.2]

4122 Pyle, Howard. *The Story of King Arthur and His Knights* (7–9). Illus. n.d., Peter Smith $23.00 (0-8446-2766-6); Dover paper $8.95 (0-486-21445-1). A retelling that has been in print since its first publication in 1903. [398.2]

4123 Pyle, Howard. *The Story of Sir Launcelot and His Companions* (7–9). Illus. 1991, Dover paper $9.95 (0-486-26701-6). The story of one of Arthur's famous knights with illustrations by Howard Pyle. [398.2]

4124 Pyle, Howard. *The Story of the Champions of the Round Table* (7–9). Illus. 1984, Macmillan LB $19.95 (0-684-18171-1). A reissue of the 1905 book about the feats of Launcelot, Tristram, and Percival. Also reissued is: *The Story of the Grail and the Passing of Arthur* (1984). [398.2]

4125 Riordan, James. *King Arthur* (5–8). Illus. 1998, Oxford $25.00 (0-19-274176-4). This is a straightforward retelling of the life of King Arthur from his boyhood with Merlin to his death in the final battle with Mordred. (Rev: SLJ 4/99; VOYA 12/98) [398.2]

4126 Singer, Isaac Bashevis. *The Golem* (7–9). Illus. 1996, Farrar paper $8.95 (0-374-42746-1). The 16th-century Jewish tale retold about the rabbi in old Prague who brought a statue to life to help his people. [398.2]

4127 Spariosu, Mihai I., and Dezso Benedek. *Ghosts, Vampires, and Werewolves: Eerie Tales from Transylvania* (6–10). 1994, Orchard LB $16.99 (0-531-08710-7). An anthology of horror tales by 2 authors who heard the stories as children living in the Transylvanian Alps. (Rev: BL 10/15/94; SLJ 10/94) [398.2]

4128 Sutcliff, Rosemary. *Dragon Slayer* (5–9). 1976, Penguin paper $4.99 (0-14-030254-9). A simple retelling of the story of Beowulf and his battle against Grendel. [398]

4129 Sutcliff, Rosemary. *The Light Beyond the Forest: The Quest for the Holy Grail* (7–9). Illus. 1994, Puffin paper $3.99 (0-14-037150-8). The first volume of the trilogy about the search for the Holy Grail by King Arthur and his knights. Continued in: *The Sword in the Circle* and *The Road to Camelann* (both 1981). [398.2]

4130 Tolkien, J. R. R. *Sir Gawain and the Green Knight* (10–12). 1979, Ballantine paper $5.99 (0-345-27760-0). A retelling of 3 tales from the age of chivalry. [398]

4131 Vande Velde, Vivian. *Tales from the Brothers Grimm and the Sisters Weird* (4–8). Illus. 1995, Harcourt $17.00 (0-15-200220-0). Using a role-reversal technique, the author examines the nature of good and evil in some of the standard tales from the Brothers Grimm. (Rev: SLJ 1/96) [398.2]

4132 Vivian, E. Charles. *The Adventures of Robin Hood* (6–9). n.d., Airmont paper $2.50 (0-8049-0067-1). The principal stories about Robin Hood and his men are retold in this inexpensive edition. [398]

4133 Warner, Elizabeth. *Heroes, Monsters and Other Worlds from Russian Mythology* (7–12). Illus. 1996, Bedrick LB $24.95 (0-87226-925-6). A collection of stories from Russian folklore organized into chapters dealing with such subjects as giants and midgets, serpents and dragons, and blacksmiths and ploughmen. (Rev: BL 5/15/96; SLJ 5/96; VOYA 8/96) [299]

4134 Wein, Elizabeth E. *The Winter Prince* (7–12). 1993, Atheneum $15.95 (0-689-31747-6). Renaming the main characters in Arthurian legend, Wein looks at the psyche of Medraut, son of King Artos, and his half-sister, Modgause, and Medraut's relationship with Artos's legitimate son, Lleu. (Rev: BL 11/15/93; SLJ 10/93; VOYA 12/93) [398.2]

North America

GENERAL AND MISCELLANEOUS

4135 Abrahams, Roger D., ed. *Afro-American Folktales: Stories from Black Traditions in the New World* (9–12). 1985, Pantheon paper $17.00 (0-394-72885-8). A rich collection of Afro-American folktales from South and Central America, the Caribbean, and southern United States. (Rev: BL 2/1/85; BR 11–12/85) [398.2]

4136 Kimmel, Eric A. *The Witch's Face: A Mexican Tale* (7–12). Illus. 1993, Holiday House LB $15.95 (0-8234-1038-2). Kimmel uses a picture book format for this Mexican tale of a man who rescues his love from becoming a witch, only to lose her to his own doubt. (Rev: BL 11/15/93; SLJ 2/94) [398.22]

4137 McManus, Kay. *Land of the Five Suns* (6–8). (Looking at Myths and Legends) 1997, NTC $17.95 (0-8442-4762-6). Classic Aztec myths, including creation stories and tales of Aztec gods, are retold in novelized format. (Rev: SLJ 4/98) [398.2]

4138 Turenne Des Pres, Francois. *Children of Yayoute: Folktales of Haiti* (6–9). 1994, Universe $19.95 (0-87663-791-8). Traditional folktales that depict Haitian history and customs. Includes paintings that illustrate island life. (Rev: BL 10/1/94; SLJ 1/95) [398.2]

4139 West, John O., ed. *Mexican-American Folklore* (9–12). Illus. 1988, August House paper $17.95 (0-87483-059-1). A collection of stories, proverbs, legends, and other forms of folklore reflecting the Mexican-American culture. (Rev: BL 11/15/88) [398]

NATIVE AMERICANS

4140 Bierhorst, John. *The Mythology of North America* (8–12). Illus. 1986, Morrow paper $13.00 (0-688-06666-6). A region-by-region examination of the folklore and mythology of the North American Indian. (Rev: BL 6/15/85; SLJ 8/85) [291.1]

4141 Bierhorst, John. *Native American Stories* (6–12). Illus. 1998, Morrow $16.00 (0-688-14837-9). A collection of 22 tales about "little people" from 14 Native American groups, including the Inuits, Aztecs, and Mayans. (Rev: BL 5/15/98; SLJ 9/98) [398.2 08997]

4142 Bierhorst, John. *The Way of the Earth: Native America and the Environment* (7–12). 1994, Morrow $15.00 (0-688-11560-8). Explores the mythologic and folkloric patterns of Native American belief systems. (Rev: BL 5/15/94; SLJ 5/94; VOYA 10/94) [179]

4143 Bierhorst, John. *The White Deer and Other Stories Told by the Lenape* (8–12). 1995, Morrow $15.00 (0-688-12900-5). This collection of Lenape/Delaware tribal stories is organized by type and includes a history of the tribe. (Rev: BL 6/1–15/95; SLJ 9/95) [398.2]

4144 Bruchac, Joseph. *Flying with the Eagle, Racing the Great Bear: Stories from Native North America* (5–8). 1993, Troll $13.95 (0-8167-3026-1). This collection includes 16 Native American rites-of-passage stories about young males, organized geographically with black-and-white illustrations. (Rev: BL 12/15/93) [398.2]

4145 Bruchac, Joseph. *Native American Animal Stories* (5–8). Illus. 1992, Fulcrum paper $12.95 (1-55591-127-7). Animal stories from various Native American tribes, for reading aloud and storytelling. (Rev: BL 9/1/92; SLJ 11/92) [398.2]

4146 Bruchac, Joseph, and Gayle Ross. *The Girl Who Married the Moon: Tales from Native North America* (9–12). 1994, Troll paper $5.95 (0-8167-3481-X). Sixteen stories from various North American native peoples that explore the roles of women in their cultures. (Rev: BL 10/1/94; SLJ 11/94) [398.2]

4147 Erdoes, Richard, and Alfonso Ortiz, eds. *American Indian Myths and Legends* (10–12). Illus. 1984, Pantheon paper $18.00 (0-394-74018-1). From the entire North American continent, here is a collection of 160 tales from native American folklore. [398.2]

4148 Goble, Paul. *The Legend of the White Buffalo Woman* (4–8). Illus. 1998, National Geographic $16.95 (0-7922-7074-6). In this picture book for older readers recounting a Lakata Indian tale, an earth woman and an eagle mate after a great flood to produce a new people. (Rev: BL 3/15/98; SLJ 5/98) [398.2]

4149 Highwater, Jamake. *Anpao: An American Indian Odyssey* (7–9). Illus. 1977, HarperCollins $14.00 (0-397-31750-6). A number of Indian tradition tales are interwoven into this story of a demigod, Anpao. [398.2]

4150 Lelooska, Chief. *Echoes of the Elders: The Stories and Paintings of Chief Lelooska* (8–12). Ed. by Christine Normandin. Illus. 1997, DK Publg. $24.95 (0-7894-2455-X). This is a fine retelling of 5 folktales from the Northwest Coast Indians, accompanied by the author's bold, colorful artwork. (Rev: BL 12/15/97; SLJ 11/97) [398.2]

4151 Lelooska, Chief. *Spirit of the Cedar People: More Stories and Paintings of Chief Lelooska* (6–12). Ed. by Christine Normandin. 1998, DK Publg. $24.95 (0-7894-2571-8). A handsome, oversize book with stunning illustrations that contains 5 tales from the Northwest Coast Indians, accompanied by a compact disk in which Chief Lelooska tells the tales with chants and drumming. (Rev: BL 12/1/98; SLJ 12/98) [398.2]

4152 Norman, Howard. *The Girl Who Dreamed Only Geese and Other Stories of the Far North*

(4–8). Illus. 1997, Harcourt $22.00 (0-15-230979-9). A fine collection of Inuit tales, enhanced by illustrations resembling stone carvings. (Rev: BL 9/15/97; SLJ 11/97*) [398.2]

4153 Pijoan, Teresa. *White Wolf Woman: Native American Transformation Myths* (7–12). 1992, August House paper $11.95 (0-87483-200-4). Drawn from a wide range of Indian tribes, a collection of 37 stories about animal and human transformations and connections. (Rev: BL 10/1/92) [398.2]

4154 Shenandoah, Joanne, and Douglas M. George-Kanentiio. *Skywoman: Legends of the Iroquois* (4–8). Illus. 1998, Clear Light $14.95 (0-940666-99-5). Good writing and effective artwork are combined in this retelling of nine traditional Iroquois tales, including a series of creation stories. (Rev: SLJ 2/99) [398.2]

4155 Van Etten, Teresa. *Ways of Indian Magic* (7–12). Illus. 1985, Sunstone paper $8.95 (0-86534-061-7). A fine retelling of 6 legends of the Pueblo Indians. (Rev: BR 3–4/86) [398.2]

4156 Van Etten, Teresa. *Ways of Indian Wisdom* (7–10). 1987, Sunstone paper $10.95 (0-86534-090-0). A collection of 20 Pueblo tales that reflect the Southeastern Indians' culture and customs. (Rev: BR 1–2/88) [398.2]

UNITED STATES

4157 Anaya, Rudolfo A. *My Land Sings: Stories from the Rio Grande* (5–9). 1999, Morrow $17.00 (0-688-15078-0). A magical collection of 10 stories, set mostly in New Mexico, that deal with Mexican and Native American folklore. (Rev: BL 8/99; SLJ 9/99) [398.2]

4158 Avila, Alfred. *Mexican Ghost Tales of the Southwest* (7–9). Ed. by Kat Avila. 1994, Arte Publico paper $9.95 (1-55885-107-0). A collection of Mexican tales of ghosts and the spirit world from the Southwest. (Rev: BL 10/1/94; SLJ 9/94; VOYA 4/95) [398.25]

4159 Blair, Walter. *Tall Tale America: A Legendary History of Our Humorous Heroes* (10–12). Illus. 1987, Univ. of Chicago Pr. paper $17.95 (0-226-05596-5). Mike Fink, Davy Crockett, Johnny Appleseed, and Pecos Bill are only 4 of the many tall-tale heroes the reader meets in this collection of folktales. [398.2]

4160 Botkin, B. A., ed. *A Treasury of American Folklore* (9–12). 1989, Crown $14.99 (0-517-67978-7). This collection, first published in 1944, cuts across racial and ethnic lines and represents various parts of our country. [398.2]

4161 Cohen, Daniel. *Southern Fried Rat & Other Gruesome Tales* (7–10). Illus. 1989, Avon paper $3.50 (0-380-70655-5). A collection of stories based

on tales about people living in urban areas today. [398.2]

4162 Cohn, Amy L., comp. *From Sea to Shining Sea: A Treasury of American Folklore and Folk Songs* (6–12). Illus. 1993, Scholastic $29.95 (0-590-42868-3). Contains 140-plus folk songs and stories, from traditional American Indian to more modern tellings. Illustrated by 15 Caldecott winners and honor artists. (Rev: BL 9/15/93*; SLJ 11/93*) [398.2]

4163 Hamilton, Virginia. *Her Stories: African American Folktales, Fairy Tales, and True Tales* (5–8). Illus. 1995, Scholastic $19.95 (0-590-47370-0). Nineteen tales about African American females retold in the wonderful style of Virginia Hamilton. (Rev: BL 11/1/95*; SLJ 11/95) [398.2]

4164 Hamilton, Virginia. *The People Could Fly: American Black Folk Tales* (5–9). Illus. 1985, Knopf LB $18.99 (0-394-96925-1). A retelling of 24 black folktales—some little known, others familiar like Tar Baby. (Rev: BL 7/85) [398.2]

4165 Lester, Julius. *Black Folktales* (9–12). Illus. 1991, Grove Atlantic paper $11.00 (0-8021-3242-1). A modern retelling with contemporary references to 12 African and Afro-American folktales. [398.2]

4166 Lester, Julius. *Further Tales of Uncle Remus* (4–9). Illus. 1990, Dial LB $14.89 (0-8037-0611-1). The third volume of Uncle Remus stories, wittily retold with illustrations by Jerry Pinkney. Preceded by *The Tales of Uncle Remus* (1987) and *More Tales of Uncle Remus* (1988). (Rev: BL 4/15/90) [398.2]

4167 Lester, Julius. *The Last Tales of Uncle Remus* (5–9). Illus. 1994, Dial paper $17.89 (0-8037-1304-5). This fourth volume in the Uncle Remus series draws together 39 African American tall tales, ghost stories, and trickster tales, with many illustrations. (Rev: BL 12/15/93*; SLJ 1/94) [398.2]

4168 MacDonald, Margaret Read. *Ghost Stories from the Pacific Northwest* (10–12). (American Folklore) 1995, August House $24.95 (0-87483-436-8). A collection of folktales and ghost stories from Oregon, Washington, and British Columbia that are ideal for telling around a campfire. (Rev: SLJ 3/96) [398.2]

4169 Philip, Neil, ed. *American Fairy Tales: From Rip Van Winkle to the Rootabaga Stories* (6–8). Illus. 1996, Hyperion LB $22.89 (0-7868-2171-X). A collection of 12 stories by such famous authors as Hawthorne, Sandburg, Alcott, and Baum. (Rev: BL 12/15/96; SLJ 11/96) [398.2]

4170 Reneaux, J. J. *Cajun Folktales* (6–8). 1992, August House $19.95 (0-87483-283-7); paper $11.95 (0-87483-282-9). An assortment of Cajun folktales divided into broad groups: animal tales, fairy tales, funny folk tales, and ghost stories. (Rev: BL 9/15/92) [398.2]

4171 Rhyne, Nancy. *More Tales of the South Carolina Low Country* (7–9). 1984, Blair paper $6.95 (0-89587-042-8). A collection of eerie and unusual folktales. [398.2]

4172 Rounds, Glen. *Ol' Paul, the Mighty Logger* (6–8). Illus. 1976, Holiday House $16.95 (0-8234-0269-X); paper $5.95 (0-8234-0713-6). The colorful saga of the great tall-tale hero of American folklore. [398.2]

4173 Schwartz, Alvin. *Scary Stories to Tell in the Dark* (6–9). Illus. 1981, HarperCollins LB $15.89 (0-397-31927-4). Stories about ghosts and witches that are mostly scary but often also humorous. Continued in: *More Scary Stories to Tell in the Dark* (1984). [398.2]

4174 Shepherd, Esther. *Paul Bunyan* (7–10). Illus. 1941, Harcourt $12.95 (0-15-259749-2); paper $6.95 (0-15-259755-7). The life of this lumberjack tall tale hero is well brought to life by the author and stunning illustrations by Rockwell Kent. [398.2]

4175 Smith, Jimmy Neil. *Homespun* (9–12). Illus. 1988, Crown $19.95 (0-517-56936-1). A wonderful collection of 22 favorite folktales from the country's top storytellers. (Rev: SLJ 3/89) [398.2]

South and Central America

4176 Aldana, Patricia, ed. *Jade and Iron: Latin American Tales from Two Cultures* (5–8). Trans. by Hugh Hazelton. Illus. 1996, Douglas & McIntyre $18.95 (0-88899-256-4). Fourteen folktales on a variety of subjects and from many regions in Latin America are retold in this large-format picture book. (Rev: BL 12/1/96) [398.2]

4177 Delacre, Lulu, retel. *Golden Tales: Myths, Legends, and Folktales from Latin America* (4–8). Illus. 1996, Scholastic $18.95 (0-590-48186-X). Twelve important Latin American folktales from before and after the time of Columbus are featured. (Rev: BL 12/15/96; SLJ 9/96) [398.2]

4178 Dorson, Mercedes, and Jeanne Wilmot. *Tales from the Rain Forest: Myths and Legends from the Amazonian Indians of Brazil* (5–8). Illus. 1997, Ecco $18.00 (0-88001-567-5). Ten entertaining folktales from the Amazonian Indians of Brazil. (Rev: BL 2/15/98) [398.2]

Mythology

General and Miscellaneous

4179 Asimov, Isaac. *Words from the Myths* (7–10). Illus. 1961, Houghton paper $2.50 (0-451-14097-4). In dictionary format explanations are given for words derived from mythology that have found their way into the English language. [292]

4180 Evslin, Bernard. *Pig's Ploughman* (7–12). Illus. 1990, Chelsea LB $19.95 (1-55546-256-1). In Celtic mythology, Pig's Ploughman is the huge hog who fights Finn McCool. (Rev: BL 8/90; SLJ 3/91) [398.2]

4181 Gifford, Douglas. *Warriors, Gods & Spirits from Central & South American Mythology* (7–12). Illus. 1993, NTC paper $14.95 (0-87226-915-9). Latin American mythology from Aztec tales to those reflecting Western influences. [299]

4182 Hamilton, Dorothy. *Mythology* (8–12). Illus. 1942, Little, Brown $27.95 (0-316-34114-2); NAL paper $5.95 (0-451-62702-4). An introduction to the mythology of Greece and Scandinavia plus a retelling of the principal myths. [292]

4183 Hamilton, Virginia. *In the Beginning: Creation Stories from around the World* (6–9). Illus. 1988, Harcourt $26.00 (0-15-238740-4). Twenty-five creation myths from around the world are retold with notes about the sources of each. (Rev: BL 9/15/88; SLJ 12/88; VOYA 6/89) [291.2]

4184 Harris, Geraldine. *Isis and Osiris* (6–8). (Looking at Myths and Legends) 1997, NTC $17.95 (0-8442-4763-4). In a novel format, this is the story of Isis, her marriage to her brother Osiris, and the murder of Osiris by his jealous brother Seth. (Rev: SLJ 4/98) [398.2]

4185 O'Neill, Cynthia, ed. *Goddesses, Heroes and Shamans: The Young People's Guide to World Mythology* (5–8). Illus. 1997, Kingfisher paper $25.95 (0-7534-5058-5). Organized geographically, this book introduces myths from around the world, discussing their purpose, significance, patterns and themes, and important characters. (Rev: BL 10/1/97) [291.1]

4186 Philip, Neil. *The Illustrated Book of Myths* (5–8). Illus. 1995, DK Publg. $19.95 (0-7894-0202-5). Ancient myths from both the Old and New Worlds have been collected under such headings as creation, destruction, and fertility. (Rev: BL 12/1/95; SLJ 12/95; VOYA 4/96) [291.1]

4187 Philip, Neil. *Mythology* (4–8). (Eyewitness) 1999, Knopf $19.00 (0-375-80135-9). A lavishly illustrated volume that covers such topics in world mythology and folklore as creation, the sun, floods, fertility, birth, tricksters, death, and mythical beasts. (Rev: SLJ 9/99) [398.2]

4188 Ross, Anne. *Druids, Gods and Heroes of Celtic Mythology* (6–10). Illus. 1994, Bedrick LB $24.95 (0-87226-918-3); paper $14.95 (0-87226-919-1). An oversized book that gives detailed information on Irish and Welsh Celtic mythology as well as material on King Arthur. (Rev: SLJ 2/87) [291.1]

4189 Van Over, Raymond, ed. *Sun Songs: Creation Myths from Around the World* (10–12). 1980, NAL paper $4.95 (0-452-00730-5). This work of general mythology discusses creation myths from all regions of the world. [291.1]

Classical

4190 Aesop. *Aesop's Fables* (7–12). 1988, Scholastic paper $4.50 (0-590-43880-8). This is one of many editions of the short moral tales from ancient Greece. [398.2]

4191 Aesop. *The Fables of Aesop* (9–12). Trans. by Patrick Gregory and Justina Gregory. Illus. 1975, Gambit $13.95 (0-87645-074-5); paper $8.95 (0-87645-116-4). This book, one of many available editions, covers 100 of the fables and deletes the moralizing conclusions. [398.2]

4192 Barber, Antonia. *Apollo & Daphne: Masterpieces of Mythology* (6–8). 1998, J. Paul Getty Trust Publns. $16.95 (0-89236-504-8). This book pairs 15 common Greek and Roman myths with paintings from around the world that illustrate the myths. (Rev: BL 10/15/98; SLJ 9/98) [753.7]

4193 Bulfinch, Thomas. *Bulfinch's Mythology: The Age of Fable; The Age of Chivalry; Legends of Charlemagne* (9–12). 1993, Modern Library $22.95 (0-679-60046-9); paper $16.95 (vol. 1); $3.95 (vol. 2); $4.95 (vol. 3) (Vol. 1: 0-375-75147-5; Vol. 2: 0-451-62252-9; Vol. 3: 0-451-62659-1). These 3 volumes comprise the classic overview of world mythology first published between 1855 and 1862. [291]

4194 Claybourne, Anna, and Kamini Khanduri, retels. *Greek Myths: Ulysses and the Trojan War* (5–10). Illus. 1999, EDC $24.95 (0-7460-3361-3). A chatty retelling of the adventures of Ulysses on his way home from Troy, with illustrations that resemble comic-book drawings of men and women. (Rev: SLJ 6/99) [398.2]

4195 Coolidge, Olivia. *Greek Myths* (6–8). Illus. 1949, Houghton $16.00 (0-395-06721-9). A simplified retelling of the major Greek myths arranged by topics such as "Great Heroes." [292]

4196 Craft, M. Charlotte, retel. *Cupid and Psyche* (5–8). Illus. 1996, Morrow LB $15.93 (0-688-13164-6). The Greek myth retold, with 40 full-page paintings. (Rev: SLJ 4/96) [398.2]

4197 Edmondson, Elizabeth. *The Trojan War* (5–8). Illus. (Great Battles and Sieges) 1992, Macmillan LB $17.95 (0-02-733273-X). A history of the Trojan War from the abduction of Helen to the long siege of Troy and the eventual destruction of the city by the Greeks. (Rev: BL 11/1/92; SLJ 1/93) [939]

4198 Evslin, Bernard. *The Adventures of Ulysses: The Odyssey of Homer* (8–12). 1989, Scholastic paper $4.99 (0-590-42599-4). A modern retelling of the adventures of Ulysses during the 10 years he wandered after the Trojan War. [292]

4199 Evslin, Bernard. *Anteus* (6–9). Illus. 1988, Chelsea LB $19.95 (1-55546-241-3). A retelling of the story of Hercules and his battle against the horrible giant Anteus. Also use by the same author: *Hecate* (1988). (Rev: BL 9/1/88) [292]

4200 Evslin, Bernard. *Cerberus* (6–12). Illus. 1987, Chelsea LB $19.95 (1-55546-243-X). The story of the 3-headed dog in Greek mythology that guards the gates of Hell. Also in this series: *The Dragons of Boeotia* and *Geryon* (both 1987). (Rev: BL 11/15/87; SLJ 1/88) [398.2]

4201 Evslin, Bernard. *The Chimaera* (6–10). Illus. 1987, Chelsea LB $19.95 (1-55546-244-8). This ugly, dangerous creature is composed of equal parts lion, goat, and reptile. Another in the series is *The Sirens* (1987). (Rev: BL 3/1/88) [398.2]

4202 Evslin, Bernard. *The Cyclopes* (6–12). Illus. 1987, Chelsea LB $19.95 (1-55546-236-7). The story of the ferocious one-eyed monster and how he was blinded by Ulysses. Others in this series about mythical monsters are: *Medusa; The Minotaur;* and *Procrustes* (all 1987). (Rev: BL 6/15/87; SLJ 8/87) [398.2]

4203 Evslin, Bernard. *The Furies* (7–12). Illus. 1989, Chelsea LB $19.95 (1-55546-249-9). In Greek mythology the Furies were 3 witches. This retelling also includes the story of Circe, the famous sorceress. (Rev: BL 12/15/89; SLJ 4/90) [398.21]

4204 Evslin, Bernard. *Heroes and Monsters of Greek Myth* (7–12). 1984, Scholastic paper $3.99 (0-590-43440-3). A simple retelling of the most famous of Greek myths. Also use: *The Greek Gods* (1988). [292]

4205 Evslin, Bernard. *Heroes, Gods and Monsters of Greek Myths* (8–12). Illus. 1984, Bantam paper $5.99 (0-553-25920-2). The most popular Greek myths are retold in modern language. [292]

4206 Evslin, Bernard. *Ladon* (7–12). Illus. 1990, Chelsea LB $19.95 (1-55546-254-5). A splendid retelling of the Greek myth about the sea serpent called up by Hera to fight Hercules. (Rev: BL 8/90) [398.24]

4207 Evslin, Bernard. *The Trojan War: The Iliad of Homer* (8–12). 1988, Scholastic paper $2.95 (0-590-41626-X). The story of the 10-year war between the Greeks and the Trojans is retold for the modern reader. [292]

4208 Fleischman, Paul. *Dateline: Troy* (6–9). Illus. 1996, Candlewick $15.99 (1-56402-469-5). The story of the Trojan War is juxtaposed with recent newspaper articles on each page that cover similar current events, e.g., Paris chooses the most beautiful woman alongside coverage of a Miss Universe contest. (Rev: BL 3/15/96; BR 9–10/96; SLJ 5/96; VOYA 12/96) [398.2]

4209 Galloway, Priscilla, retel. *Aleta and the Queen: A Tale of Ancient Greece* (5–8). Illus. 1995, Annick LB $29.95 (1-55037-400-1); paper $14.95 (1-55037-462-1). This story expands on and embellishes the story of Penelope and her wait for the return of Odysseus. (Rev: BL 1/1–15/96; SLJ 1/96) [398.2]

4210 Galloway, Priscilla. *Daedalus and the Minotaur* (5–9). Illus. (Tales of Ancient Lands) 1997, Annick LB $27.95 (1-55037-459-1); paper $14.95 (1-55037-458-3). The dramatic story of Daedalus and his adventures in Crete are retold, ending as he and his son, Icarus, launch themselves in flight. (Rev: BL 1/1–15/98; SLJ 2/98) [398.2]

4211 Gates, Doris. *A Fair Wind for Troy* (6–9). Illus. 1976, Penguin paper $4.99 (0-14-031718-X). A well-known telling of the events that led up to the Trojan War. [292]

4212 Grant, Michael. *Myths of the Greeks and Romans* (9–12). 1989, NAL paper $5.95 (0-317-02799-9). This collection of stories bridges the gap between these 2 similar mythologies. [292]

4213 Graves, Robert. *Greek Gods and Heroes* (6–8). 1973, Dell paper $4.99 (0-440-93221-1). Tales of 12 of the most important figures in Greek mythology in 27 short chapters. [292]

4214 Green, Roger L. *The Tale of Troy* (5–9). 1974, Puffin paper $3.95 (0-14-030120-8). A retelling of the story of the Trojan War and the events leading to it. [291.1]

4215 Green, Roger L. *Tales of the Greek Heroes* (5–9). 1974, Penguin paper $4.95 (0-14-030119-4). This volume includes stories about Prometheus, Dionysus, Perseus, and Heracles. [291.1]

4216 McBride-Smith, Barbara. *Greek Myths, Western Style: Toga Tales with an Attitude* (9–12). 1999, August House $14.95 (0-87483-524-0). These 16 Greek myths take on a new life when their locale is changed to wild and woolly Texas and their characters become contemporaries, e.g., Bacchus is a drunken womanizer. (Rev: SLJ 8/99) [398.2]

4217 Mikolaycak, Charles. *Orpheus* (9–12). 1992, Harcourt $19.95 (0-15-258804-3). A picture book version of the Orpheus myth that combines classical and romantic images that celebrate the human body. (Rev: BL 10/15/92; SLJ 9/92) [398.21]

4218 Nardo, Don. *Greek & Roman Mythology* (5–8). Illus. (World History) 1997, Lucent LB $17.96 (1-56006-308-4). In addition to retelling well-known myths and identifying important characters and moral lessons, the author explains what myths are and where they come from, their importance in early Greek and Roman cultures, and how that has changed. (Rev: SLJ 5/98) [398.2]

4219 Pickels, Dwayne E. *Roman Myths, Heroes, and Legends* (5–8). (Costume, Tradition, and Culture: Reflecting on the Past) 1998, Chelsea $16.95 (0-7910-5164-1). Using double-page spreads and old collectors cards as illustrations, this work retells the major Roman myths and introduces their important characters. (Rev: BL 3/15/99) [398.2]

4220 Strachan, Ian. *The Iliad* (5–8). Illus. 1997, Kingfisher $17.95 (0-7534-5107-7). This large, handsome volume gives an exciting account of the main events and people involved in the siege and fall of Troy. (Rev: BL 1/1–15/98; SLJ 11/97) [883]

4221 Sutcliff, Rosemary. *Black Ships Before Troy: The Story of the Iliad* (6–12). Illus. 1993, Delacorte $24.95 (0-385-31069-2). A re-creation of the classic epic, with a compelling vision and sensitivity to language, history, and heroics. (Rev: BL 10/15/93) [883]

4222 Sutcliff, Rosemary. *The Wanderings of Odysseus: The Story of the Odyssey* (5–8). Illus. 1996, Delacorte $24.95 (0-385-32205-4). An oversize volume that retells Homer's *Odyssey* and the adventures of Odysseus on his homeward journey from the Trojan War. (Rev: BL 9/1/96; SLJ 6/96*) [883]

4223 Switzer, Ellen. *Greek Myths: Gods, Heroes, and Monsters—Their Sources, Their Stories and Their Meanings* (7–12). Illus. 1988, Macmillan $18.00 (0-689-31253-9). A collection of myths that includes 13 stories about such characters as Perseus, Odysseus, and Medusa. (Rev: BL 4/1/88; BR 1–2/89; SLJ 4/88) [292]

4224 Usher, Kerry. *Heroes, Gods & Emperors from Roman Mythology* (8–12). Illus. 1992, NTC LB $24.95 (0-87226-909-4). The origins of Roman mythology are given plus a generous retelling of famous myths. [292]

Humor, Satire, and Memoirs

4225 Allen, Woody. *Without Feathers* (9–12). 1987, Ballantine paper $5.99 (0-345-33697-6). Sixteen humorous pieces plus 2 one-act plays are included in this collection. Also use: *Getting Even* (1971). [817]

4226 Ayres, Alex, ed. *The Wit & Wisdom of Mark Twain* (9–12). 1987, NAL paper $7.95 (0-452-00982-0). An alphabetically arranged collection of mostly humorous quotations by Mark Twain. (Rev: BL 8/87) [818]

4227 Barry, Dave. *Dave Barry in Cyberspace* (10–12). 1996, Crown $22.00 (0-517-59575-3). These short, amusing pieces are particularly suited to those who are not impressed with computers, enjoy a few laughs, and can absorb some sexual innuendos. (Rev: SLJ 2/97) [808.84]

4228 Bombeck, Erma. *At Wit's End* (9–12). 1986, Fawcett paper $5.99 (0-449-21184-3). A fine collection of pieces by one of America's favorite humorists. Also use: *Just Wait Till You Have Children of Your Own, If Life Is a Bowl of Cherries, What Am I Doing in the Pits?, The Grass Is Always Greener over the Septic Tank*, and *I Lost Everything in the Post-Natal Depression* (1986). [808.7]

4229 Bombeck, Erma. *Family: The Ties That Bind . . . and Gag!* (9–12). 1987, Fawcett paper $5.95 (0-449-21529-6). Bombeck writes humorously about family life and being a mother as she did in *Motherhood: The Second Oldest Profession* (1983). (Rev: BL 8/87) [306.85]

4230 Cosby, Bill. *Love and Marriage* (9–12). 1990, Bantam paper $6.50 (0-553-28467-3). The comedian remembers his first attempts at love affairs and his experiences in marriage. (Rev: BL 4/15/89) [306.7]

4231 Keillor, Garrison. *Leaving Home: A Collection of Lake Woebegon Stories* (9–12). 1990, Penguin paper $12.95 (0-14-013160-4). A collection of stories and anecdotes about Lake Woebegon culled from monologues given on American Public Radio network's *Prairie Home Companion*. (Rev: BR 1–2/88; SLJ 2/88; VOYA 4/88) [808.7]

4232 Kerr, Jean. *Please Don't Eat the Daisies* (9–12). 1994, Buccaneer LB $28.95 (0-56849-298-7). This is a humorous look at bringing up a family in suburbia. [808.7]

4233 Kostman, Joel. *Keys to the City: Tales of a New York City Locksmith* (10–12). 1997, DK Publg. $19.95 (0-7894-2461-4). This is a collection of 14 mostly humorous true stories about the author's experiences as a professional locksmith in New York. (Rev: BL 9/1/97; SLJ 9/97; VOYA 4/98) [808.84]

4234 Macaulay, David. *Motel of the Mysteries* (10–12). Illus. 1979, Houghton paper $13.00 (0-395-28425-2). A satire on archaeology and civilization that involves unearthing a motel in the year 4022. (Rev: BL 6/87) [817]

4235 Rooney, Andrew A. *A Few Minutes with Andy Rooney* (9–12). 1982, Warner paper $4.95 (0-446-34766-3). This is a collection of short humorous pieces by the writer who gained prominence on television's *"60 Minutes."* Also use *And More by Andy Rooney* (1983). [808.7]

4236 Rooney, Andrew A. *Not That You Asked . . .* (9–12). 1989, Random $15.95 (0-394-57837-6). A collection of short pieces on such topics as ladies' underwear and real estate deals. (Rev: BL 2/15/89) [814.54]

4237 Sherrin, Ned, ed. *The Oxford Dictionary of Humorous Quotations* (10–12). 1995, Oxford $45.00 (0-19-214244-5). This volume includes over 5,000 quotes that represent a wide selection of puns, insults, one liners, and other types of witty and humorous quotes. (Rev: SLJ 6/96) [808.87]

4238 Twain, Mark. *Life on the Mississippi* (10–12). 1983, Buccaneer LB $25.95 (0-89966-469-5). A nonfiction account of life on the Mississippi with many humorous passages. First published in 1874. [817]

4239 Twain, Mark. *Roughing It* (10–12). 1986, Buccaneer LB $25.95 (0-89966-524-1); Penguin paper $11.95 (0-14-039010-3). A humorous account first published in 1872 of a trip to California and Hawaii. [817]

4240 Baker, Russell, ed. *Russell Baker's Book of American Humor* (9–12). 1993, Norton $30.00 (0-393-03592-1). More than 100 humorous pieces divided into 12 categories, such as "Shameless Frivolity" and "This Sex Problem." (Rev: BL 11/1/93) [818.02]

4241 Fiffer, Sharon S., and Steve Fiffer, eds. *Home: American Writers Remember Rooms of Their Own* (10–12). Illus. 1995, Pantheon $22.00 (0-679-44206-5). In this collection of essays, 18 contemporary American writers remember rooms that were important to them in the past. For example, Jane Smiley sought peace and solitude in bathrooms. (Rev: BL 11/1/95; SLJ 6/96) [808.84]

4242 Halliburton, Warren J., ed. *Historic Speeches of African Americans* (7–12). (African American Experience) 1993, Watts LB $25.00 (0-531-11034-6). Chronologically organized speeches by such leaders as Sojourner Truth, Frederick Douglass, Marcus Garvey, James Baldwin, Angela Davis, and Jesse Jackson. (Rev: BL 4/15/93; SLJ 7/93) [815]

4243 Kingsolver, Barbara. *High Tide in Tucson* (10–12). 1995, HarperCollins $22.00 (0-06-017291-6). A collection of general essays about such diverse subjects as hermit crabs, weddings in Benin, and an obsolete Titan missile site, weaving in such themes as the joys of parenting; respect for all creatures, religions, and points of view; and the importance of the natural world in our lives. (Rev: SLJ 2/96) [808]

4244 Roberts, Cokie. *We Are Our Mothers' Daughters* (10–12). 1998, Morrow $19.95 (0-688-15198-1). This noted TV and radio news correspondent has written a series of personal essays on her relationship to her mother and family and the place of women and mothers in the world today. (Rev: SLJ 8/98) [808]

4245 Rosen, Roger, and Patra McSharry, eds. *East-West: The Landscape Within* (7–12). (World Issues) 1992, Rosen LB $16.95 (0-8239-1375-9); paper $8.95 (0-8239-1376-7). Short stories and nonfiction selections by diverse authors of varied nationalities on their culture's beliefs and values, among them the Dalai Lama, Joseph Campbell, Lydia Minatoya, and Aung Aung Taik. (Rev: BL 12/15/92; SLJ 2/93) [909]

4246 Sanders, Scott R. *Writing from the Center* (10–12). 1995, Indiana Univ. Pr. $25.00 (0-253-32941-8). In this collection of 12 inspiring and penetrating essays, the author examines technology, community, love and strife within families, and the search for spiritual ground as seen through the eyes of a midwesterner. (Rev: SLJ 2/96) [808]

Literary History and Criticism

General and Miscellaneous

4247 *Dear Author: Students Write about the Books That Changed Their Lives* (5–9). 1995, Conari Pr. paper $9.95 (1-57324-003-6). A collection of letters that resulted from a group of YAs writing to authors, both dead and alive, expressing, with wit and honesty, how their books have affected them. (Rev: BL 1/1–15/96; SLJ 11/95) [028.5]

4248 Kanigel, Robert. *Vintage Reading: From Plato to Bradbury, a Personal Tour of Some of the World's Best Books* (10–12). 1998, Bancroft paper $16.95 (0-9631246-7-6). In a series of essays, the author discusses his personal choices of the world's best books, among them *Pride and Prejudice* and *Native Son*. (Rev: BL 2/15/98; BR 9–10/98; SLJ 9/98) [807]

4249 Knox, Bernard, ed. *The Norton Book of Classical Literature* (9–12). 1993, Norton $29.95 (0-393-03426-7). More than 300 pieces of classical literature, primarily Greek but also some Roman. (Rev: BL 2/15/93) [880]

4250 Sullivan, Charles, ed. *Children of Promise: African-American Literature and Art for Young People* (7–12). 1991, Abrams $24.95 (0-8109-3170-2). An anthology of African American literature and art from the time of slavery through the 1980s. (Rev: BL 11/16/91; SLJ 1/92) [700]

Fiction

General and Miscellaneous

4251 Barlowe, Wayne Douglas, and Neil Duskis. *Barlowe's Guide to Fantasy* (7–12). Illus. 1996, HarperCollins paper $19.95 (0-06-100817-6). Using double-page spreads, this handsome book covers the history of fantasy literature from ancient times to the present by highlighting 50 examples, among them *Beowulf, Wind in the Willows,* and *Mists of Avalon.* (Rev: VOYA 10/97)

4252 Blom, Margaret Howard. *Charlotte Brontë* (10–12). 1977, Twayne $21.95 (0-8057-6673-1). A critical study of the life and works of the creator of *Jane Eyre.* [823.09]

4253 Bloom, Harold, ed. *Charlotte Brontë's Jane Eyre* (8–12). (Bloom's Notes) 1996, Chelsea LB $16.95 (0-7910-4063-1). In addition to a collection of critical essays on *Jane Eyre,* there is a biography of the author, a plot summary, and character sketches. (Rev: BL 1/1–15/97; SLJ 4/97) [823]

4254 Bloom, Harold, ed. *Fyodor Dostoevsky's Crime and Punishment* (10–12). (Bloom's Notes) 1996, Chelsea LB $17.95 (0-7910-4056-9). This introduction to Dostoyevsley's novel contains excerpts and scholarly essays about the work, discusses the author's life, summarizes the themes and the plot, and describes the characters. (Rev: SLJ 4/97) [891.7]

4255 Bloom, Harold, ed. *Lord of the Flies* (10–12). (Modern Critical Interpretations) 1998, Chelsea LB $34.95 (0-7910-4777-6). Sixteen critical essays written between 1961 and 1993 examine various aspects of this modern classic. (Rev: SLJ 2/99) [823]

4256 Clute, John. *Science Fiction: The Illustrated Encyclopedia* (10–12). 1995, DK Publg. $39.95 (0-7894-0185-1). Arranged chiefly by decade in each chapter, this history of science fiction covers visions of the future, themes in history, influential magazines, nonprint media, and other subjects, with sketches of over 100 writers, photographs, signatures, and chronological bibliographies of major works. (Rev: BL 5/15/98; BR 5–6/96; SLJ 1/96; VOYA 6/96) [813]

4257 Clute, John, and John Grant, eds. *The Encyclopedia of Fantasy* (10–12). 1997, St. Martin's $75.00 (0-312-15897-1). This comprehensive research on fantasy literature and media includes material on authors, awards, movies, TV shows, themes, and articles on the fantasy literature of various countries. (Rev: BL 9/1/97; SLJ 8/97) [813]

4258 Foster, Robert. *The Complete Guide to Middle-Earth: From The Hobbit to The Silmarillion* (10–12). 1985, Ballantine paper $6.99 (0-345-32436-6). An alphabetically arranged concordance to the writing of Tolkien. [808.3]

4259 Hallissy, Margaret. *A Companion to Chaucer's Canterbury Tales* (10–12). 1995, Greenwood $49.95 (0-313-29189-6). After an introduction to Chaucer's world and language, this companion supplies a guide to each of the tales and to the many colorful characters in them. (Rev: SLJ 6/96; VOYA 4/96) [823]

4260 Hornback, Bert G. *Great Expectations: A Novel of Friendship* (9–12). Illus. 1987, Twayne $23.95 (0-8057-7956-6). A critical analysis of this novel often studied in high school. (Rev: BL 5/15/87; SLJ 9/87) [823]

4261 Immell, Myra H., ed. *Readings on the Diary of a Young Girl* (10–12). (Literary Companions) 1998, Greenhaven LB $20.96 (1-56510-661-X). A collection of essays about the themes and historical background of Anne Frank's *Diary.* (Rev: BL 2/15/98; SLJ 4/98) [839.3]

4262 Johnson, Tamara, ed. *Readings on Fyodor Dostoyevsky* (10–12). (Literary Companions) 1997, Greenhaven paper $12.96 (1-56510-587-7). This collection contains essays that explore Dostoyevsky's themes, characters, plots, and settings, and others that deal with individual major works. (Rev: BL 3/15/98; SLJ 7/98) [891.7]

4263 Kappel, Lawrence, ed. *Readings on Great Expectations* (10–12). (Literary Companions) 1998, Greenhaven paper $17.45 (1-56510-820-5). This volume includes analysis and criticism of *Great Expectations,* as well as essays on Dickens's social criticism, characters, and use of humor and tragedy. (Rev: BL 9/15/98; BR 5–6/99) [823]

4264 Kelly, Richard. *Lewis Carroll* (9–12). 1990, Twayne $32.00 (0-8057-6988-9). This critical survey of Carroll's writings concentrates on the Alice books and *The Hunting of the Snark.* [828]

4265 Lefebure, Molly. *Thomas Hardy's World: The Life, Times and Works of the Great Novelist and Poet* (8–12). Illus. 1999, Carlton $24.95 (1-85868-245-2). This large-format book presents the life of Thomas Hardy, analysis of his works, including commentary from a feminist perspective, and articles on life in Hardy's Victorian England. (Rev: BL 9/1/99) [823.809]

4266 Mitchell, Hayley R., ed. *Readings on Wuthering Heights* (10–12). (Literary Companions) 1998, Greenhaven LB $20.96 (1-56510-833-7); paper $17.45 (1-56510-832-9). The essays in this book guide readers through the tempestuous love of Cathy and Heathcliff, with material on the complex structure and themes of Emily Brontë's only novel. (Rev: BL 1/1–15/99) [823]

4267 Nardo, Don, ed. *Readings on Homer* (10–12). (Literary Companions) 1997, Greenhaven LB $21.96 (1-56510-639-3); paper $17.45 (1-56510-638-5). Essays in this collection discuss the *Iliad* and *Odyssey,* their themes, characters, structure, and continuing popularity. (Rev: BL 10/15/97; SLJ 4/98) [883]

4268 Nardo, Don, ed. *Readings on The Canterbury Tales* (10–12). (Literary Companion) 1997, Greenhaven LB $21.96 (1-56510-586-9); paper $16.20 (1-56510-585-0). This is a collection of incisive essays by Chaucer scholars analyzing the themes, stories, and characters in *The Canterbury Tales.* (Rev: BL 12/15/96; SLJ 2/97) [821]

4269 Nardo, Don, ed. *A Tale of Two Cities* (10–12). (Literary Companions) 1997, Greenhaven LB $21.96 (1-56510-649-0); paper $22.00 (1-56510-648-2). This collection of critical essays on Dickens' novel of the French Revolution covers major themes, characters, and the social and historical background. (Rev: BL 6/1–15/97; SLJ 8/97; VOYA 12/97) [823]

4270 Nelson, Harland S. *Charles Dickens* (10–12). 1981, Twayne $32.00 (0-8057-6805-X). This account focuses on 5 novels, including *David Copperfield, Oliver Twist,* and *Great Expectations.* [823.09]

4271 O'Neill, Jane. *The World of the Brontës* (8–12). Illus. 1999, Carlton $24.95 (1-85868-341-6). This book describes the lives and works of Emily, Charlotte, and Anne Brontë and gives a good picture of 19th-century English society, quoting frequently from their diaries and letters as well as their novels. (Rev: BL 9/1/99) [823.809]

4272 O'Neill, Terry, ed. *Readings on All Quiet On the Western Front* (10–12). (Literary Companions) 1998, Greenhaven LB $20.96 (1-56510-825-6); paper $17.45 (1-56510-824-8). Essays in this anthology discuss this amazing novel that captures the terror, bitterness, and boredom experienced by a young German soldier during World War I. (Rev: BL 12/15/98) [833]

4273 O'Neill, Terry, ed. *Readings on Animal Farm* (10–12). (Literary Companions) 1998, Greenhaven LB $20.96 (1-56510-651-2). The plot, symbolism, characters, and structure of this highly respected fable are approached from different perspectives in this anthology of critical writings. (Rev: BL 3/15/98; SLJ 6/98) [823]

4274 Rainey, Richard. *The Monster Factory* (6–12). 1993, Macmillan LB $13.95 (0-02-775663-7). A discussion of 7 famous monster-story writers and their most-loved works. (Rev: BL 8/93; VOYA 10/93) [809.3]

4275 Reid, Suzanne Elizabeth. *Presenting Young Adult Science Fiction* (7–12). (Twayne's United States Authors) 1998, Twayne $28.00 (0-8057-1653-X). This comprehensive introduction to science fiction describes the history of the genre, profiles such classical masters as Asimov, Bradbury, Heinlein, and Le Guin, and presents members of the new generation, among them Orson Scott Card, Pamela Service, Piers Anthony, and Douglas Adams. (Rev: SLJ 6/99) [808.3]

4276 Riley, Dick, and Pam McAllister. *The Bedside, Bathtub & Armchair Companion to Sherlock Holmes* (10–12). 1999, Continuum $29.95 (0-8264-1140-1). Everything one would like to know about Sherlock Holmes, including a synopsis of all his adventures and a brief biography of his creator. (Rev: BL 1/1–15/99; SLJ 7/99) [823]

4277 Riley, Dick, and Pam McAllister, eds. *The New Bedside, Bathtub & Armchair Companion to Agatha Christie* (10–12). Illus. 1986, Ungar paper $15.95 (0-8044-6725-0). Many enthusiasts of Christie have contributed articles on her novels, their plots, and characters. [823.09]

4278 Saposnik, Irving S. *Robert Louis Stevenson* (10–12). 1974, Twayne $22.95 (0-8057-1517-7). Biographical information is given as well as an analysis of Stevenson's works in several genres. [828]

4279 *A Scholarly Look at Anne Frank* (10–12). (Modern Critical Interpretations) 1999, Chelsea LB $34.95 (0-7910-5192-7). A mature look at the Anne Frank legacy, including the various adaptations and versions of the diary. (Rev: VOYA 10/99) [839.3]

4280 Smyer, Richard I. *Animal Farm: Pastoralism & Politics* (9–12). 1988, Twayne $25.95 (0-8057-7980-9); paper $14.95 (0-8057-8030-0). A detailed analysis of this allegory that explains its structure and layers of meaning. (Rev: SLJ 8/88) [823.09]

4281 Swisher, Clarice, ed. *Lord of the Flies* (10–12). (Literary Companion) 1997, Greenhaven LB $21.96 (1-56510-629-6); paper $16.20 (1-56510-628-8). This dark novel of evil and human nature is examined in essays that explore its themes, symbolism, characters, and continued popularity. (Rev: BL 6/1–15/97; SLJ 7/97) [823]

4282 Swisher, Clarice, ed. *Readings on Charles Dickens* (10–12). (Literary Companions) 1997, Greenhaven LB $21.96 (1-56510-590-7). This volume includes essays on Dickens's many literary talents, such as character creation, plus articles on individual works like *A Christmas Carol* and *Oliver Twist*. (Rev: BL 12/15/97; SLJ 4/98) [823]

4283 Swisher, Clarice, ed. *Readings on Heart of Darkness* (9–12). 1999, Greenhaven LB $125.76 (1-56510-823-X); paper $77.76 (1-56510-822-1). A collection of critical essays on Conrad's masterpiece. (Rev: BL 9/15/99) [825.9]

4284 Swisher, Clarice, ed. *Readings on Jane Austen* (10–12). (Literary Companions) 1997, Greenhaven paper $16.20 (1-56510-577-X). In this anthology, essays on such specific works as *Pride and Prejudice* are complemented by general overviews of themes in Austen's novels and biographical material. (Rev: BL 1/1–15/97; SLJ 5/97) [823]

4285 Swisher, Clarice, ed. *Readings on Joseph Conrad* (10–12). (Literary Companions) 1998, Greenhaven LB $20.96 (1-56510-637-7). Themes, characters, and literary style are the subjects of some of the essays in this anthology on Conrad that also contains writings on individual works such as *Lord Jim*. (Rev: BL 2/15/98; SLJ 3/98) [823]

4286 Swisher, Clarice, ed. *Readings on Pride and Prejudice* (10–12). (Literary Companions) 1998, Greenhaven LB $20.96 (1-56510-861-2); paper $17.45 (1-56510-860-4). This collection of essays delves into the themes, characters, writing style, gentle satire, and lifestyles found in *Pride and Prejudice*, Jane Austen's most popular novel. (Rev: BL 12/15/98) [823]

4287 Teachman, Debra. *Understanding Pride & Prejudice: A Student Casebook to Issues, Sources & Historical Documents* (9–12). (Literature in Context) 1997, Greenwood $39.95 (0-313-30126-3). An engaging introduction to this classic novel, with material on characters, plot, themes, and information on the history, customs, attitudes, and culture of 18th-century England. (Rev: SLJ 9/98) [823]

4288 Thompson, Stephen P., ed. *Readings on Beowulf* (10–12). (Literary Companions) 1998, Greenhaven

LB $21.96 (1-56510-813-2); paper $17.45 (1-56510-812-4). The 18 essays reprinted in this book provide the historical and cultural background of this epic and an analysis of themes, characters, and style. (Rev: BL 7/98; SLJ 11/98) [829]

4289 Tolkien, J. R. R. *The Shaping of Middle-Earth* (9–12). Illus. 1986, Houghton $24.95 (0-395-42501-8). Background notes and information on the famous fantasy written by Tolkien and edited by his son. (Rev: BL 11/86; SLJ 3/87) [808.3]

4290 Wagoner, Mary S. *Agatha Christie* (9–12). 1986, Twayne $22.95 (0-8057-6936-6). An analysis of this mystery story writer's works with an accompanying brief biography. (Rev: BL 2/1/87) [823]

United States

4291 Bail, Paul. *John Saul: A Critical Companion* (10–12). (Critical Companions to Popular Contemporary Writers) 1996, Greenwood $29.95 (0-313-29575-1). This is an extensive analysis of the works of John Saul, a famous writer of horror stories whose works include *Suffer the Children* and *Black Lightning*. (Rev: SLJ 10/96) [813]

4292 Baym, Nina. *The Scarlet Letter: A Reading* (10–12). 1986, Twayne $29.00 (0-8057-7957-4); paper $13.95 (0-8057-8001-7). An analysis of this novel, often studied in high school, plus an introduction to the life of its author, Nathaniel Hawthorne. (Rev: BL 7/86; SLJ 5/87) [813]

4293 Bishop, Rudine Sims. *Presenting Walter Dean Myers* (9–12). 1990, Twayne $28.00 (0-8057-8214-1). A profile of the life and work of this black American writer with an analysis of each of his most important books. (Rev: BL 10/15/90) [813]

4294 Bloom, Harold, ed. *Ernest Hemingway's The Sun Also Rises* (10–12). (Bloom's Notes) 1996, Chelsea LB $17.95 (0-7910-4075-5). After a short biographical sketch and a thorough description of the novel, there are a number of critical essays that discuss various aspects of this classic. (Rev: SLJ 3/97) [813]

4295 Bloom, Harold, ed. *Eudora Welty* (9–12). 1999, Chelsea LB $18.95 (0-7910-5126-9). This critical study of 4 of Welty's most popular stories also contains some biographical material and an index to themes and ideas in her work. (Rev: SLJ 7/99) [8113]

4296 Bloom, Harold, ed. *Harper Lee's To Kill a Mockingbird* (9–12). (Modern Critical Interpretations) 1998, Chelsea LB $34.95 (0-7910-4779-2). An outstanding collection about *To Kill a Mockingbird*, including critical essays, initial reviews from the *Saturday Review* and *New York Herald Tribune*

Book Review, a catalog of attempts in Hanover County, Virginia, to censor the book in 1966, an exploration of the novel and the law, and an analysis of Horton Foote's screenplay for the 1962 film based on the novel. (Rev: VOYA 10/99) [813]

4297 Bloom, Harold, ed. *Invisible Man* (10–12). (Modern Critical Interpretations) 1998, Chelsea LB $34.95 (0-7910-4776-8). Reprints of 12 highly intellectual articles that deal with various aspects of Ralph Ellison's novel in a somewhat esoteric manner. (Rev: SLJ 3/99) [813]

4298 Bloom, Harold, ed. *Maya Angelou's I Know Why the Caged Bird Sings* (8–12). (Bloom's Notes) 1996, Chelsea LB $17.95 (0-7910-3666-9). A collection of critical essays on this work by Maya Angelou, plus a detailed analysis of the book and its characters, accompanied by material on the author's life. (Rev: BL 1/1–15/97; SLJ 3/97) [818]

4299 Buranelli, Vincent. *Edgar Allan Poe* (10–12). 1977, Twayne $28.95 (0-8057-7189-1); paper $4.95 (0-672-61502-9). This book analyzes the fiction as well as the poetry and nonfiction by Poe. [818]

4300 Burns, Landon C. *Pat Conroy: A Critical Companion* (10–12). (Critical Companions to Popular Contemporary Writers) 1996, Greenwood $29.95 (0-313-29419-4). Biographical material is combined with critical comments on the themes, plots, character development, and writing style in the works of Pat Conroy. (Rev: SLJ 10/96) [813]

4301 Cady, Edwin H. *Stephen Crane* (10–12). 1980, Twayne $32.00 (0-8057-7299-5). An analysis of the short-lived author's work and career. [813.09]

4302 Campbell, Patricia J. *Presenting Robert Cormier.* 2nd ed. (9–12). Illus. 1989, Twayne $20.95 (0-8057-8212-5). A profile of this author and his work through the novel *Fade.* (Rev: BL 9/15/89; BR 5–6/90; SLJ 12/89) [813.54]

4303 Carmean, Karen. *Ernest J. Gaines: A Critical Companion* (10–12). (Critical Companions to Popular Contemporary Writers) 1998, Greenwood $29.95 (0-313-30286-3). The author provides biographical information about Gaines followed by a literary analysis of several of his novels, including *The Autobiography of Miss Jane Pittman,* and a collection of short stories. Other books in this series cover Tom Clancy, James Herriot, Anne McCaffrey, Toni Morrison, Anne Tyler, and Leon Uris. (Rev: BR 1–2/99; VOYA 6/99) [813]

4304 Cart, Michael. *Presenting Robert Lipsyte* (8–12). 1995, Twayne $20.95 (0-8057-4151-8). A probing look at Lipsyte's life and work. (Rev: BL 6/1–15/95; BR 3–4/96; VOYA 6/96) [813]

4305 Clareson, Thomas D. *Frederik Pohl* (10–12). 1987, Starmont House LB $31.00 (0-930261-34-8); paper $21.00 (0-930261-33-X). An analysis of the

works and life of one of sci-fi's greatest writers. (Rev: BL 1/15/88) [813]

4306 Curry, Barbara K., and James Michael Brodie. *Sweet Words So Brave: The Story of African American Literature* (5–8). Illus. 1996, Zino $24.95 (1-55933-179-8). An outline of African American literature, from slave narratives to the great writers of today, such as Nikki Giovanni and Toni Morrison. (Rev: BL 2/15/97; SLJ 4/97) [810.9]

4307 Daly, Jay. *Presenting S. E. Hinton.* 2nd ed. (9–12). Illus. 1989, Twayne $20.95 (0-8057-8211-7). A biography of this popular author plus an analysis of her work including *Taming the Star Runner.* (Rev: BL 9/15/89; SLJ 3/90) [813.54]

4308 De Koster, Katie, ed. *Readings of Ernest Hemingway* (10–12). (Literary Companions) 1997, Greenhaven LB $19.95 (1-56510-463-5); paper $17.45 (1-56510-462-5). General essays about Hemingway and his work, along with essays on *The Sun Also Rises* and several other Hemingway novels. (Rev: BL 1/1–15/97; SLJ 4/97) [813]

4309 De Koster, Katie, ed. *Readings on F. Scott Fitzgerald* (10–12). (Literary Companions) 1997, Greenhaven LB $21.96 (1-56510-461-7); paper $20.25 (1-56510-460-9). Essays in this volume explore Fitzgerald's major novels, themes, characters, and the life-style of the 1920s that he depicted in his works. (Rev: BL 10/15/97; SLJ 12/97) [813]

4310 De Koster, Katie. *Readings on Mark Twain* (9–12). (Literary Companion to American Authors) 1996, Greenhaven LB $21.96 (1-56510-471-4). After a brief biography, there are 24 critical essays on Twain's writings, some general, others on specific works like *Huckleberry Finn.* (Rev: BL 5/15/96; SLJ 8/96) [818]

4311 De Koster, Katie, ed. *Readings on The Adventures of Huckleberry Finn* (10–12). (Literary Companions) 1998, Greenhaven LB $20.96 (1-56510-819-1); paper $20.96 (1-56510-818-3). This landmark work in the history of American literature is discussed in 15 essays on background material, characters, themes, plot, and the controversies surrounding it. (Rev: BL 7/98; SLJ 12/98) [813]

4312 De Koster, Katie, ed. *Readings on The Adventures of Tom Sawyer* (10–12). (Literary Companions) 1998, Greenhaven LB $20.96 (1-56510-845-0); paper $17.45 (1-56510-844-2). This anthology explores facets of Twain's masterpiece based partly on his Missouri childhood. (Rev: BL 11/15/98; BR 5–6/99) [813]

4313 De Koster, Katie, ed. *Readings on The Call of the Wild* (9–12). (Literary Companions) 1999, Greenhaven LB $20.96 (1-56510-831-0). A collection of articles that examines the allegorical elements in this adventure story as well as exploring its main themes and London's personal and political beliefs. (Rev: BL 9/15/99) [813]

4314 De Koster, Katie, ed. *Readings on The Great Gatsby* (10–12). (Literary Companions) 1997, Greenhaven paper $16.20 (1-56510-644-X). The novel that epitomizes the "lost generation" is discussed in this collection of essays that comment on its themes, symbols, structure, and characters. (Rev: BL 12/15/97; SLJ 1/98) [813]

4315 De Koster, Katie, ed. *Readings on Thornton Wilder* (10–12). (Literary Companions) 1998, Greenhaven LB $20.96 (1-56510-815-9); paper $17.45 (1-56510-814-0). General essays in this anthology discuss Wilder's style, themes, and characters, and others deal with specific works like *Our Town*. (Rev: BL 7/98; SLJ 8/98) [812]

4316 Doyle, Paul A. *Pearl S. Buck* (10–12). 1980, Twayne $22.95 (0-8057-7325-8). A critical study of this writer that covers topics like plots, themes, and writing style. [813.09]

4317 Engle, Steven. *Readings on the Catcher in the Rye* (7–12). (Literary Companions) 1998, Greenhaven LB $20.96 (1-56510-817-5); paper $16.20 (1-56510-816-7). A helpful collection about this coming-of-age classic that explores the novel's themes, imagery, issues, and the narrator, Holden Caulfield. (Rev: BL 8/98) [813.54]

4318 Felgar, Robert. *Understanding Richard Wright's Black Boy: A Student Casebook to Issues, Sources & Historical Documents* (8–12). (Literature in Context) 1998, Greenwood $39.95 (0-313-30221-9). This book analyzes *Black Boy* from various standpoints, including structure and themes, its position in relation to other important autobiographies, and its place in the cultural and social conditions of the time. (Rev: BR 1–2/99; SLJ 9/98) [818]

4319 Gallo, Donald R. *Presenting Richard Peck* (9–12). 1989, Twayne $20.95 (0-8057-8209-5). Part biography but chiefly an examination of Peck's works including those intended for an adult audience. (Rev: BL 11/1/89; BR 3–4/90; SLJ 12/89; VOYA 12/89) [818]

4320 Gibson, Donald B. *The Red Badge of Courage* (10–12). 1988, Twayne $25.95 (0-8057-7961-2); paper $18.00 (0-8057-8014-9). Part of an extensive series from Twayne that analyzes the great works of literature in depth. (Rev: SLJ 8/88) [813.09]

4321 Hipple, Ted. *Presenting Sue Ellen Bridgers* (9–12). 1990, Twayne $20.95 (0-8057-8213-3). A biography and analysis of the work of one of the major writers of young adult novels. (Rev: BL 6/1/90) [813]

4322 Huntley, E. D. *Amy Tan: A Critical Companion* (10–12). 1998, Greenwood $29.95 (0-313-30207-3). The life and works of Amy Tan, including discussion of the Asian American literary tradition, concerns about biculturalism that Tan shares with other Asian American writers, and the universality of Tan's work, plus a literary analysis of *The Joy Luck Club, The Kitchen God's Wife,* and *The Hundred Secret Senses.* (Rev: BR 1–2/99; VOYA 6/99) [813]

4323 Johnson, Claudia Durst. *Understanding Adventures of Huckleberry Finn: A Student Casebook to Issues, Sources, and Historic Documents* (10–12). (Literature in Context) 1996, Greenwood $35.00 (0-313-29327-9). This work not only analyzes the novel, but also discusses censorship, racism, the life of Mark Twain, and the complex social and political issues of the time. (Rev: SLJ 12/96) [813]

4324 Johnson, Claudia Durst. *Understanding The Red Badge of Courage* (9–12). (Literature in Context) 1998, Greenwood $39.95 (0-313-30122-0). This book describes the novel's Civil War setting and everyday life in the war camps and in the battlefield, analyzes the novel, with a chapter-by-chapter breakdown of the novel's plot and discussion of symbols and characters, and examines the concepts of desertion and cowardice and the book as an antiwar novel. (Rev: VOYA 4/99) [813]

4325 Johnson, Claudia Durst. *Understanding The Scarlet Letter* (10–12). 1995, Greenwood $35.00 (0-313-29328-7). In addition to a literary analysis of the novel, the author uses both historical and contemporary documents to provide a deeper understanding of the themes, including records on Hawthorne's family history, the transcript of Anne Hutchinson's trial, and articles on such contemporary issues as single motherhood, corrupt ministries, child custody, separation of church and state, and corporal punishment. (Rev: VOYA 2/96) [813]

4326 Johnson-Feelings, Dianne. *Presenting Laurence Yep* (8–12). 1995, Twayne $28.00 (0-8057-8201-X). A biocritical study that uses material from the Chinese American artist Laurence Yep's autobiography *The Lost Garden.* (Rev: BL 12/15/95) [813]

4327 Jones, Patrick. *What's So Scary about R. L. Stine?* (9–12). (Scarecrow Studies in Young Adult Literature) 1998, Scarecrow $32.50 (0-8108-3468-5). An appreciation and critique of R. L. Stine's popular horror stories for young people. (Rev: SLJ 7/99) [813]

4328 Jordan, Shirley M., ed. *Broken Silences: Interviews with Black and White Women Writers* (9–12). 1993, Rutgers Univ. Pr. $35.00 (0-8135-1932-2). Focuses on how African American and white women writers have depicted each other in their stories, with specific inquiries into each author's handling of race in her work. (Rev: BL 5/1/93) [810.9]

4329 Karson, Jill, ed. *Readings on A Separate Peace* (10–12). (Literary Companions) 1998, Greenhaven LB $20.96 (1-56510-827-2); paper $17.45 (1-56510-826-4). First published in 1960, this novel has remained a favorite of young adults. This collection of essays examines the themes, structure, characters, and locale of the novel. (Rev: BL 2/15/98) [813]

4330 Karson, Jill, ed. *Readings on Of Mice and Men* (10–12). (Literary Companions) 1997, Greenhaven paper $16.20 (1-56510-652-0). Essays analyze the story of the tragic relationship between George and Lennie, as well as the novel's themes, structure, symbols, and its adaptation to stage and screen. (Rev: BL 12/15/97; SLJ 2/98; VOYA 6/99) [813]

4331 Karson, Jill, ed. *Readings on The Pearl* (10–12). (Literary Companions) 1998, Greenhaven LB $26.20 (1-56510-855-8); paper $17.45 (1-56510-854-X). This anthology of writings on the novel about a poor peasant who finds a valuable pearl discusses its structure, symbolism, language, and characters. (Rev: BL 10/15/98; BR 5–6/99) [813]

4332 MacDonald, Gina. *James Clavell: A Critical Companion* (10–12). (Critical Companions to Popular Contemporary Writers) 1996, Greenwood $29.95 (0-313-29494-1). In addition to biographical information and general material on Clavell's writing, this book contains chapters on *King Rat, Shogun,* and other individual works. (Rev: SLJ 10/96) [813]

4333 MacRae, Cathi Dunn. *Presenting Young Adult Fantasy Fiction* (7–12). 1998, Twayne $28.00 (0-8057-8220-6). An excellent survey of current writers of fantasy plus in-depth interviews with Terry Brooks, Barbara Hambly, Jane Yolan, and Meredith Ann Pierce. (Rev: BL 1/1–15/99; VOYA 8/98) [813]

4334 Megna-Wallace, Joanne. *Understanding I Know Why the Caged Bird Sings: A Student Casebook to Issues, Sources, and Historical Documents* (9–12). (Literature in Context) 1998, Greenwood $39.95 (0-313-30229-4). Along with literary criticism, this book places *Caged Bird* in its historical context with material and original documents on race relations in the South, sexual abuse, the African America family, the African American church, and censorship. (Rev: SLJ 1/99; VOYA 8/99) [808.4]

4335 Morey, Eileen, ed. *Readings on The Scarlet Letter* (10–12). (Literary Companions) 1997, Greenhaven paper $16.20 (1-56510-756-X). This antholo- gy of critical essays about Hester Prynne's scarlet "A" includes contributors such as Henry James and Carl van Doren. (Rev: BL 12/15/97; SLJ 5/98) [813]

4336 Pelzer, Linda. *Mary Higgins Clark: A Critical Companion* (9–12). 1995, Greenwood $29.95 (0-313-29413-5). A guide to the life and work of this best selling author of popular mysteries. (Rev: VOYA 6/96) [813]

4337 Perret, Patti. *The Faces of Fantasy* (9–12). 1996, St. Martin's paper $22.95 (0-312-86216-4). A handsome, oversize book of revealing black-and-white photographic portraits of fantasy authors,

accompanied by brief reflections by the authors. (Rev: VOYA 6/97) [813]

4338 Perret, Patti. *The Faces of Science Fiction* (9–12). Illus. 1984, St. Martin's $35.00 (0-698-10348-X); paper $11.95 (0-685-10347-1). Photographs of 80 major science fiction and fantasy writers are given as well as comments on their work. (Rev: BL 2/15/85) [813]

4339 Reid, Suzanne. *Presenting Cynthia Voigt* (9–12). 1995, Twayne $28.00 (0-8057-8219-2). A biographical sketch of this popular author, followed by literary criticism in thematic chapters of 20 of Voigt's young adult novels. (Rev: BL 1/1/95; BR 3–4/96; VOYA 4/96) [813]

4340 Reino, Joseph. *Stephen King: The First Decade, Carrie to Pet Sematary* (9–12). Illus. 1988, Twayne $32.00 (0-8057-7512-9). An analysis of King's most important works published from 1973 to 1983. (Rev: BL 2/15/88) [813]

4341 Rovin, Jeff. *Aliens, Robots, and Spaceships* (7–12). Illus. 1995, Facts on File $35.00 (0-8160-3107-X). Alphabetically arranged entries on characters, creatures, and places in the world of science fiction, with over 100 black-and-white illustrations. (Rev: BR 1–2/96; SLJ 12/95; VOYA 4/96) [813]

4342 Russell, Sharon A. *Stephen King: A Critical Companion* (9–12). 1996, Greenwood $29.95 (0-313-29417-8). Following biographical information about Stephen King and background on the horror genre, the author examines the plots, character development, and themes of King's most important, most popular, and most recent works, in chronological order. (Rev: VOYA 6/97) [813]

4343 Salvner, Gary M. *Presenting Gary Paulsen* (9–12). (Young Adult Authors) 1996, Macmillan $28.00 (0-8057-4150-X). After 2 chapters on the eventful life of Gary Paulsen, the author of more than 100 books for people of all ages, this book analyzes the major themes and subjects of his young adult novels. (Rev: VOYA 8/98) [813]

4344 Sloane, David E. *The Adventures of Huckleberry Finn: American Comic Vision* (9–12). 1988, Twayne $29.00 (0-8057-7963-9); paper $18.00 (0-8057-8016-5). This paperback gives a detailed analysis of this novel—structure, themes, and characters. (Rev: BR 9–10/88; SLJ 8/88; VOYA 2/89) [813.09]

4345 Smith, Henry Nash, ed. *Mark Twain: A Collection of Critical Essays* (10–12). 1963, Prentice Hall $12.95 (0-13-933317-7). Many prominent writers and critics have contributed to this collection of essays, many of which deal with individual works by Twain. [813.09]

4346 Smith, Lucinda I. *Women Who Write, Vol. 2* (8–12). 1994, Messner $15.00 (0-671-87253-2).

Interviews and short biographies of contemporary women writers, including Margaret Atwood and Sue Grafton. Addresses the desire to write and provides tips for aspiring authors. (Rev: BL 10/15/94; SLJ 11/94; VOYA 12/94) [809.8]

4347 Stover, Leon. *Robert A. Heinlein* (9–12). 1987, Twayne $21.00 (0-8057-7509-9). An in-depth study of the science fiction of this acclaimed American writer. (Rev: BL 11/15/87) [813]

4348 Stover, Lois T. *Presenting Phyllis Reynolds Naylor* (9–12). 1997, Twayne $28.00 (0-8057-7805-5). In this scholarly work, the author presents a brief biography and an analysis of the Alice series, several novels, and other writings, showing how Naylor's life experiences are reflected in her major themes: how characters cope with family instability, how they develop a sense of self apart from family, and how they solve moral dilemmas. (Rev: SLJ 4/98; VOYA 10/98) [813]

4349 Swisher, Clarice, ed. *Readings on John Steinbeck* (9–12). (Literary Companion to American Authors) 1996, Greenhaven LB $21.96 (1-56510-469-2); paper $20.25 (1-56510-468-4). The 21 critical essays about Steinbeck and his work contained in this volume focus on his short novels and *The Grapes of Wrath*. (Rev: BL 5/15/96; SLJ 8/96) [813]

4350 Swisher, Clarice, ed. *Readings on Nathaniel Hawthorne* (9–12). (Literary Companion to American Authors) 1996, Greenhaven LB $21.96 (1-56510-459-5); paper $16.20 (1-56510-458-7). The 22 critical readings in this volume cover Hawthorne's principal stories and novels including 4 examinations of *The Scarlet Letter*. (Rev: BL 5/15/96; SLJ 8/96) [813]

4351 Swisher, Clarice, ed. *Readings on William Faulkner* (10–12). (Literary Companions) 1997, Greenhaven paper $17.45 (1-56510-640-7). Includes general essays on Faulkner's literary style, sense of structure, and characters as well as on individual works like *The Sound and the Fury* and such important short stories as *The Bear*. (Rev: BL 12/15/97; SLJ 2/98) [813]

4352 Szumski, Bonnie, ed. *Readings on Edgar Allan Poe* (10–12). (Literary Companions) 1997, Greenhaven LB $26.20 (0-56510-589-3). The first essays explore Poe's many accomplishments, among them the perfection of the short story form and creation of the detective story, followed by critiques of his most popular works. (Rev: BL 12/15/97) [813.09]

4353 Szumski, Bonnie, ed. *Readings on Herman Melville* (10–12). (Literary Companions) 1997, Greenhaven paper $32.75 (1-56510-583-4). Some essays in this anthology analyze themes in Melville's works, such as ancient mythology, the Civil War, and

religion, while others discuss specific works like *Billy Budd* and *Moby Dick*. (Rev: BL 1/1–15/97; SLJ 3/97) [813]

4354 Szumski, Bonnie, ed. *Readings on Stephen Crane* (9–12). (Literary Companion to American Authors) 1997, Greenhaven LB $20.96 (1-56510-643-1); paper $17.45 (1-56510-642-3). After a short biography of Crane, this collection of essays focuses on his themes, style, and major works, including *The Red Badge of Courage* and *The Open Boat*. (Rev: SLJ 4/98; VOYA 4/99) [813]

4355 Szumski, Bonnie, ed. *Readings on The Old Man and the Sea* (10–12). (Literary Companions) 1998, Greenhaven LB $20.96 (1-56510-843-4); paper $17.45 (1-56510-842-6). A collection of critical essays on the last of Ernest Hemingway's books published during his lifetime. (Rev: BL 10/15/98; BR 5–6/99) [813]

4356 Trembley, Elizabeth A. *Michael Crichton: A Critical Companion* (10–12). 1996, Greenwood LB $29.95 (0-313-29414-4). A carefully researched book that gives a biography of Crichton plus an analysis of 10 of his most popular books, beginning with *The Andromeda Strain*. (Rev: BR 9–10/96; VOYA 10/96) [813]

4357 Underwood, Tim, and Chuck Miller, eds. *Kingdom of Fear: The World of Stephen King* (10–12). 1987, NAL paper $3.95 (0-451-14962-9). For all Stephen King enthusiasts, here is a collection of essays about his writing and the films they inspired. (Rev: SLJ 1/87; VOYA 2/87) [809.3]

4358 Weidt, Maryann N. *Presenting Judy Blume* (9–12). Illus. 1989, Twayne $20.95 (0-8057-8208-7). A biography and a thorough analysis of Judy Blume's work with asides from both critics and Ms. Blume. (Rev: BL 11/1/89; VOYA 12/89) [813]

4359 Wiener, Gary, ed. *Readings on the Grapes of Wrath* (10–12). (Literary Companions) 1998, Greenhaven LB $220.96 (0-56510-955-4); paper $17.45 (1-56510-954-6). The saga of the Joad family is covered in this anthology that includes writings on the novel's creation, characters, themes, and structure, and an evaluation of its merits and flaws. (Rev: BL 9/15/98; BR 5–6/99) [813]

4360 Winter, Douglas E. *Stephen King: The Art of Darkness* (10–12). Illus. 1986, NAL paper $5.95 (0-451-14612-3). A study of the novels and novellas by this master of horror fiction. [813.09]

4361 Yunghans, Penelope. *Prize Winners: Ten Writers for Young Readers* (5–9). (World Writers) 1995, Morgan Reynolds LB $18.95 (1-883846-11-0). How some of the most popular writers of youth fiction came to pen their stories. (Rev: BL 12/15/95; SLJ 12/95; VOYA 2/96) [810.9]

Plays and Poetry

General and Miscellaneous

4362 Auslander, Joseph, and Frank Ernest Hill. *The Winged Horse: The Story of Poets and Their Poetry* (10–12). 1969, Haskell House LB $75.00 (0-8383-0328-5). This book first published in 1928 gives a history of world poetry from its beginning to the early 20th century. [809.1]

4363 Bloom, Harold, ed. *Anton Chekhov* (10–12). (Modern Critical Views) 1998, Chelsea LB $34.95 (0-7910-4783-0). A collection of literary criticism that discusses both the plays and short stories of Chekhov, with additional material on his life and personality. (Rev: SLJ 2/99) [891.7]

4364 Bloom, Harold, ed. *Sophocles' Oedipus Plays* (10–12). (Bloom's Notes) 1996, Chelsea LB $17.95 (0-7910-4070-4). A comprehensive collection of essays on Sophocles and his works are included plus notes on the plots, themes, and characters. (Rev: SLJ 4/97) [882]

4365 Bugeja, Michael J. *The Art and Craft of Poetry* (9–12). 1994, Writer's Digest $19.99 (0-89879-633-4). Describes various genres, elements, styles, and forms of poetry, and includes exercises and examples from master poets. (Rev: BL 3/15/94) [808.1]

4366 Deutsch, Babette. *Poetry Handbook: A Dictionary of Terms.* 4th ed. (7–12). 1981, Barnes & Noble paper $13.00 (0-06-463548-1). The standard introduction to the technical aspects of poetry through definitions of terms with examples. [808.1]

4367 Jerome, Judson. *The Poet's Handbook* (10–12). 1980, Writer's Digest paper $14.99 (0-89879-219-3). A handbook that covers such topics as meter, rhyme, rhythm, and the history of poetry. [808.1]

4368 Lyon, George E. *Where I'm From, Where Poems Come From* (9–12). 1999, Absey & Co. paper $13.95 (1-888842-12-1). Using her own poems and experiences as examples, the author presents a guide to the elements of poetry. (Rev: BL 9/1/99) [811]

4369 Mitchell, Hayley R., ed. *Readings on a Doll's House* (10–12). (Literary Companions) 1998, Greenhaven LB $16.20 (0-7377-0048-3). This drama by Ibsen is discussed in essays on its structure, characters, and the sociological implications of Nora's leaving. (Rev: BL 1/1–15/99) [839.8]

4370 Nardo, Don, ed. *Readings on Sophocles* (10–12). (Literary Companion) 1997, Greenhaven paper $16.20 (1-56510-581-8). Though Sophocles wrote over 100 plays, only 7 survive. This collection of critical essays discusses these 7 plays, with emphasis on the Oedipus trilogy, and the ancient Greek theater in general. (Rev: BL 12/15/96; SLJ 2/97) [882]

Shakespeare

4371 Birch, Beverley, retel. *Shakespeare's Stories: Comedies* (5–9). Illus. 1990, Bedrick paper $6.95 (0-87226-225-1). This is the first of 3 volumes that retell in attractive, straightforward prose the most popular of his plays. The others are: *Shakespeare's Stories: Histories* and *Shakespeare's Stories: Tragedies* (both 1988). (Rev: BL 2/15/89; BR 1–2/89; SLJ 2/89) [813]

4372 Bloom, Harold, ed. *William Shakespeare's A Midsummer Night's Dream* (10–12). (Bloom's Notes) 1996, Chelsea LB $17.95 (0-7910-4066-6). After a selection of critical excerpts, this book gives a biography of Shakespeare, a summary of the play, analysis of themes and characters, and a bibliography. (Rev: SLJ 4/97) [822.3]

4373 Derrick, Thomas. *Understanding Shakespeare's Julius Caesar* (8–12). Illus. (Literature in Context) 1998, Greenwood $39.95 (0-313-29638-3). An entertaining approach to *Julius Caesar* that brings to life the diverse worlds of history, theater, language, metaphor, plot, and source material, and even includes a chapter on pop culture treatments of the play. (Rev: VOYA 10/99) [822.3]

4374 Garfield, Leon. *Shakespeare Stories II* (6–10). Illus. 1995, Houghton $24.95 (0-395-70893-1). Plot synopses of *Julius Caesar* and 8 less familiar plays. (Rev: BL 4/1/95; SLJ 6/95) [823]

4375 Gurr, Andrew, and John Orrell. *Rebuilding Shakespeare's Globe* (9–12). 1989, Routledge $25.00 (0-685-26528-5). A history of the project in London to rebuild the Globe as it was originally, from its inception in the 1890s to the present. (Rev: BR 3–4/90) [822.3]

4376 Nardo, Don, ed. *Readings of Hamlet* (10–12). (Literary Companions) 1998, Greenhaven LB $21.96 (1-56510-837-X); paper $17.45 (1-56510-836-1). This collection of readings on *Hamlet* will help students understand the play's structure, themes, plot, and characters. (Rev: BL 11/15/98; VOYA 4/99) [822]

4377 Nardo, Don, ed. *Readings on Julius Caesar* (10–12). (Literary Companions) 1998, Greenhaven LB $20.96 (1-56510-853-1); paper $17.45 (1-56510-852-3). Contributors to this anthology on Shakespeare's tragedy examine major themes of the play, its characters, historical background, and Shakespeare's use of language. (Rev: BL 2/15/98) [822.3]

4378 Nardo, Don, ed. *Readings on Romeo and Juliet* (10–12). (Literary Companions) 1997, Greenhaven LB $21.96 (1-56510-647-4); paper $16.20 (1-56510-646-6). A collection of essays on Shakespeare's famous tragedy that discusses structure, characters, themes, staging considerations, plot, and ways of interpreting the play. (Rev: SLJ 12/97; VOYA 4/99) [822.3]

4379 Olster, Fredi, and Rick Hamilton. *A Midsummer Night's Dream: A Workbook for Students* (8–12). (Discovering Shakespeare) 1996, Smith & Kraus paper $19.95 (1-57525-042-X). The text of the play is presented in a double-page, 4-column format that provides stage directions, scene description, the original text, plus its version in the vernacular. Supplemental background material is also appended. (Rev: BL 1/1–15/97; SLJ 12/96; VOYA 2/97) [822.3]

4380 Olster, Fredi, and Rick Hamilton. *Romeo and Juliet: A Workbook for Students* (8–12). (Discovering Shakespeare) 1996, Smith & Kraus paper $19.95 (1-57525-044-6). This Shakespearean tragedy is presented in a 4-column format that gives the original text, stage directions, scene descriptions, and a reworking into modern English. (Rev: BL 1/1–15/97) [822.3]

4381 Olster, Fredi, and Rick Hamilton. *The Taming of the Shrew* (7–12). (Discovering Shakespeare) 1997, Smith & Kraus paper $14.95 (1-57525-046-2). This guide to Shakespeare's comedy uses a paraphrased text opposite the script with details on stage directions. (Rev: BL 2/15/97; BR 11–12/97; SLJ 6/97; VOYA 2/97) [822.3]

4382 Ross, Stewart. *Shakespeare and Macbeth: The Story Behind the Play* (5–8). Illus. 1994, Viking paper $16.99 (0-670-85629-0). An approach grounded in ordinary daily life, including Shakespeare's commercial considerations at the time. (Rev: BL 3/15/95; SLJ 1/95) [822.3]

4383 Swisher, Clarice, ed. *Readings on Macbeth* (10–12). (Literary Companions) 1998, Greenhaven LB $20.96 (1-56510-851-5); paper $17.45 (1-56510-850-7). Topics covered in this anthology include the motivations of Macbeth and his wife, the use of the themes of guilt, fear, and ambition, the production and directing of the drama, and its structure and language. (Rev: BL 11/15/98; BR 5–6/99; VOYA 4/99) [822]

4384 Swisher, Clarice, ed. *Readings on Shakespeare: The Comedies* (10–12). (Literary Companion) 1997, Greenhaven LB $19.95 (1-56510-574-7); paper $17.45 (1-56510-573-7). Well known writers and famous Shakespearian scholars are represented in this collection of critical essays on the Bard's lighter works. (Rev: BL 12/15/96; SLJ 4/97) [822.3]

4385 Swisher, Clarice, ed. *Readings on the Sonnets of William Shakespeare* (10–12). 1997, Greenhaven LB $20.96 (1-56510-572-9); paper $17.45 (1-56510-571-0). In this collection of critical essays, the form and content of Shakespeare's sonnets, as well as individual poems, are analyzed. (Rev: BL 12/15/96; SLJ 1/97) [821]

4386 Swisher, Clarice, ed. *Readings on the Tragedies of William Shakespeare* (10–12). (Literary Companion) 1996, Greenhaven LB $20.96 (1-56510-467-6); paper $17.45 (1-56510-466-8). A collection of critical essays on 6 of Shakespeare's popular tragedies, including *Romeo and Juliet* and *Macbeth*. (Rev: BL 11/15/96; SLJ 8/96) [822.3]

4387 Swisher, Clarice, ed. *Readings on William Shakespeare: The Histories* (10–12). (Literary Companions) 1998, Greenhaven LB $20.96 (1-56510-556-7); paper $17.45 (1-56510-555-9). Critical essays examine the historical background of these plays, with material on their language, characters, and structure. There are also companion volumes on Shakespeare's comedies, tragedies, and sonnets. (Rev: BL 7/98; SLJ 8/98) [822.3]

4388 Whalen, Richard F. *Shakespeare: Who Was He? The Oxford Challenge to the Bard of Avon*

(9–12). 1994, Praeger $19.95 (0-275-94850-1). Probes the authorship of the works of Shakespeare and presents evidence suggesting the plays were written by others. (Rev: BL 11/1/94) [822.3]

4389 Williams, Marcia. *Tales from Shakespeare: Seven Plays* (5–8). Illus. 1998, Candlewick $16.99 (0-7636-0441-0). Using a comic strip format, this oversize book describes what it would have been like to attend performances of such plays as *Hamlet*, *Macbeth*, and *A Midsummer Night's Dream* at the Globe Theatre. (Rev: BL 11/1/98; SLJ 10/98) [741.5 973]

United States

4390 Angelou, Maya, and Tom Feelings. *Now Sheba Sings the Song* (9–12). Illus. 1987, Dutton paper $9.95 (0-525-48374-8). Drawings of 25 black women from various backgrounds by Tom Feelings are accompanied by short poems by Maya Angelou. (Rev: BL 3/15/87; BR 11–12/87; SLJ 10/87; VOYA 10/87) [811]

4391 Bloom, Harold, ed. *The Crucible* (10–12). (Modern Critical Interpretations) 1998, Chelsea LB $34.95 (0-7910-4775-X). A collection of 13 critical essays on various aspects of *The Crucible,* including language, characters, feminist perspectives, and structure. (Rev: SLJ 2/99) [812]

4392 DeFusco, Andrea, ed. *Readings on Robert Frost* (9–12). (Literary Companion) 1999, Greenhaven LB $21.96 (1-56510-999-6). A collection of essays that explores the life of the "people's poet" and examines individual poems as well as his major themes and imagery. (Rev: BL 9/15/99) [811]

4393 Ferlazzo, Paul J. *Emily Dickinson* (10–12). 1976, Twayne $32.00 (0-8057-7180-8); Macmillan paper $4.95 (0-672-61511-8). This book analyzes such subjects in Dickinson's poetry as love, death, and nature. [811.09]

4394 Gerber, Philip. *Robert Frost* (10–12). 1982, Twayne $32.00 (0-8057-7348-7). This book concentrates on an analysis of Frost's work but also gives coverage of his life and career. [811.09]

4395 Johnson, Tamara, ed. *Emily Dickinson* (10–12). (Literary Companions) 1997, Greenhaven LB $21.96 (1-56510-635-0); paper $18.75 (1-56510-634-2). A collection of commentaries, many by well-known poets, on Emily Dickinson's life, her poetic themes, and her reclusive nature and how it affected her poetry, plus a line-by-line analysis of several poems. (Rev: BL 6/1–15/97; SLJ 8/97) [811]

4396 Moss, Leonard. *Arthur Miller* (10–12). 1980, Twayne $21.95 (0-8057-7311-8). A thorough review of the components of each of Miller's plays, their themes, and structure. [812.09]

4397 Siebold, Thomas, ed. *Readings on Arthur Miller* (10–12). (Literary Companions) 1996, Greenhaven LB $20.96 (1-56510-580-X); paper $22.00 (1-56510-579-6). This collection of critical essays covers general topics related to the playwright's work as well as individual plays like *Death of a Salesman*. (Rev: BL 2/15/97; SLJ 4/97) [812]

4398 Siebold, Thomas, ed. *Readings on Death of a Salesman* (10–12). (Literary Companions) 1998, Greenhaven LB $20.96 (1-56510-839-6); paper $17.45 (1-56510-838-8). This drama about Willy Loman's descent into insanity and suicide is covered in a series of essays that also discuss American materialism, the business world, and the meaning of success. (Rev: BL 1/1–15/99) [812]

4399 Siebold, Thomas, ed. *Readings on Eugene O'Neill* (10–12). (Literary Companions) 1997, Greenhaven paper $17.45 (1-56510-654-7). This book includes essays on the major plays of O'Neill like *Long Day's Journey into Night* as well as material on major themes and characters. (Rev: BL 12/15/97; SLJ 4/98) [813]

4400 Siebold, Thomas, ed. *Readings on The Crucible* (10–12). (Literary Companions) 1998, Greenhaven LB $20.96 (1-56510-849-3); paper $20.25 (1-56510-848-5). This collection of readings shows how Arthur Miller used historical events to explore themes such as evil, power, freedom, fear, hysteria, and guilt. (Rev: BL 10/15/98; BR 5–6/99; SLJ 3/99) [812]

4401 Siebold, Thomas, ed. *Readings on The Glass Menagerie* (10–12). (Literary Companions) 1998, Greenhaven LB $20.96 (1-56510-829-9); paper $16.20 (1-56510-828-0). Over 15 essays explore the play's themes, characters, structure, philosophy, and impact on the American theater. (Rev: BL 7/98; SLJ 8/98) [812]

4402 Wiener, Gary, ed. *Readings on Walt Whitman* (9–12). (Literary Companion) 1999, Greenhaven LB $27.46 (0-7377-0077-7). The articles in this collection explore Whitman's output as a poet, essayist, and journalist, plus discussing such topics as why he was not popular with his contemporaries. (Rev: BL 9/15/99) [811]

4403 Williams, Mary E., ed. *Maya Angelou* (10–12). (Literary Companions) 1997, Greenhaven LB $21.96 (1-56510-631-8); paper $16.20 (1-56510-630-X). A collection of critical essays that analyze the works of this noted poet, essayist, and writer of her autobiography. (Rev: BL 6/1–15/97; SLJ 9/97; VOYA 12/97) [818]

Language and Communication

Symbols, Words, and Languages

4404 Agee, Jon. *Sit on a Potato Pan, Otis! More Palindromes* (4–8). Illus. 1999, Farrar $14.41 (0-374-31808-5). A whimsical book illustrated with black-and-white cartoons that contains 60 humorous palindromes. (Rev: BL 3/1/99; SLJ 3/99) [418]

4405 Agee, Jon. *Who Ordered the Jumbo Shrimp? And Other Oxymorons* (5–10). Illus. 1998, Harper-Collins $12.95 (0-06-205159-8). An amusing collection of oxymorons like "permanent temp," and "Great Depression," cleverly illustrated with black-and-white cartoons. (Rev: SLJ 11/98) [412]

4406 Brook, Donna. *The Journey of English* (4–8). Illus. 1998, Lerner $17.00 (0-395-71211-4). This richly illustrated volume describes the history of English, its changing composition, its spread, and the cultures around the world that use it. (Rev: BL 5/15/98; SLJ 7/98) [420.9]

4407 Cox, Brenda S. *Who Talks Funny? A Book about Languages for Kids* (7–12). 1995, Linnet LB $25.00 (0-208-02378-X). Explores the importance of learning other languages, describes the development of languages and common elements, and provides interesting information, such as how to say the days of the week in 27 languages. (Rev: BL 7/95; SLJ 4/95) [400]

4408 Crampton, William. *Flag* (5–9). Illus. 1989, Knopf LB $16.99 (0-394-92255-7). Stunning photographs and text introduce the use and nature of flags with many accompanying examples. (Rev: BL 10/15/89) [929.9]

4409 Ehrlich, Eugene, comp. *Les Bons Mots* (10–12). 1997, Holt $24.00 (0-8050-4711-5). A delightful collection of French phrases and aphorisms, with their pronunciations and both literal and colloquial meanings. (Rev: BR 1–2/98; SLJ 1/98) [440]

4410 Fakih, Kimberly O. *Off the Clock: A Lexicon of Time Words and Expressions* (6–10). 1995, Ticknor $16.00 (0-395-66374-1). A look at how we talk about time in folklore, anthropology, myth, history, semantics, and physics. (Rev: BL 1/1/95; SLJ 3/95) [428.1]

4411 Fisher, Leonard E. *Alphabet Art: Thirteen ABC's from around the World* (7–9). Illus. 1978, Macmillan $16.95 (0-02-735230-7). From Arabic to Tibetan, 13 alphabets are introduced and depicted in full-page illustrations. [745.6]

4412 Flexner, Stuart, and Anne H. Soukhanov. *Speaking Freely: A Guided Tour of American English from Plymouth Rock to Silicon Valley* (10–12). 1997, Oxford $63.95 (0-19-510692-X). An informal look at the development of American English that includes a general history plus material on specific words and phrases. (Rev: BL 10/1/97; SLJ 2/98) [422]

4413 Gay, Kathlyn. *Getting Your Message Across* (6–12). 1993, Macmillan LB $18.95 (0-02-735815-1). Factors in communication are examined, such as body language, facial expression, ability to listen, and clothing. Also covers advertising. (Rev: BL 10/1/93; SLJ 11/93; VOYA 2/94) [302.2]

4414 *In Few Words/En Pocas Palabras: A Compendium of Latino Folk Wit & Wisdom* (6–12). Trans. by Jose A. Burciaga. 1996, Mercury House paper $14.95 (1-56279-093-5). This bilingual collection features popular sayings, proverbs, maxims, and adages that permeate Hispanic culture. (Rev: VOYA 6/97) [468.1]

4415 Jones, Charlotte F. *Eat Your Words: A Fascinating Look at the Language of Food* (4–8). Illus. 1999, Delacorte $16.95 (0-385-32575-4). Food and its effects on language are explored in this delightful book that covers topics like food named for people (peach melba), places (buffalo wings) and animals (horseradish), plus trivia about sayings, word etymologies, and silly laws all dealing with food. (Rev: BL 4/15/99; SLJ 7/99) [418]

4416 Kelly, Martin. *Parents Book of Baby Names* (9–12). 1985, Ballantine paper $5.99 (0-345-31428-X). This handbook consists of lists of boys' and girls' names and their derivations. (Rev: BL 10/1/85) [929.44]

4417 Kennedy, John. *Word Stems: A Dictionary* (10–12). 1996, Soho Pr. paper $12.00 (1-56947-051-0). This book supplies the word stems for common words used in English and gives definitions and language roots for each. (Rev: SLJ 5/97) [420]

4418 Modley, Rudolf. *Handbook of Pictorial Symbols: 3,250 Examples from International Sources* (9–12). Illus. 1976, Dover paper $10.95 (0-486-23357-X). All sorts of symbols are presented and explained in this source organized by subjects. [001.56]

4419 Muschell, David. *What in the Word? Origins of Words Dealing with People and Places* (9–12). 1996, McGuinn & McGuire Publg. paper $14.95 (1-881117-14-6). Explains the origins of real and imaginary person and place names. (Rev: BL 1/1/91) [422]

4420 Samoyault, Tiphaine. *Give Me a Sign! What Pictograms Tell Us Without Words* (4–8). Trans. by Esther Allen. Illus. 1997, Viking $13.99 (0-670-87466-3). This book explains road signs and travel signage, as well as other pictograms. (Rev: BL 10/15/97; SLJ 1/98) [302.23]

4421 Schwartz, Alvin, comp. *The Cat's Elbow, and Other Secret Languages* (7–9). Illus. 1982, Farrar $15.00 (0-374-31224-9). Thirteen different secret languages and codes are described and explained. [410]

4422 Schwartz, Alvin. *Chin Music: Tall Talk and Other Talk* (7–9). Illus. 1979, HarperCollins LB $12.89 (0-397-31870-7). A collection of folk words and their meanings. [410]

4423 Soukhanov, Anne H. *Watch Word: The Stories Behind the Words of Our Lives* (9–12). 1995, Holt $25.00 (0-8050-3564-8). The editor of American Heritage Dictionary discusses definitions, usage, and history of common words and looks at new words in our vernacular. (Rev: BL 6/1–15/95) [422]

4424 Swisher, Clarice. *The Beginning of Language* (6–9). Illus. 1989, Greenhaven LB $22.45 (0-89908-064-2). Many theories concerning how language originated are presented and evaluated. (Rev: SLJ 3/90) [400]

4425 Vinton, Ken. *Alphabet Antics: Hundreds of Activities to Challenge and Enrich Letter Learners of All Ages* (5–8). Illus. 1996, Free Spirit paper $19.95 (1-57542-008-2). For each letter of the alphabet, there is a history, how it appears in different alphabets, important words that begin with the letter, a quotation from someone whose name starts with it, and a number of interesting related projects. (Rev: SLJ 1/97) [411]

4426 Warburton, Lois. *The Beginning of Writing* (5–8). 1990, Lucent LB $17.96 (1-56006-113-8). Discusses communication strategies invented by prealphabetic societies. (Rev: BL 5/1/91; SLJ 5/91) [652]

4427 Young, Ed. *Voices of the Heart* (4–8). Illus. 1997, Scholastic $22.99 (0-590-50199-2). In this sumptuous picture book, the author lists and explains 26 Chinese characters, each of which expresses a different emotion. (Rev: BL 4/15/97; SLJ 6/97) [179]

Writing and the Media

General and Miscellaneous

4428 Ammer, Christine. *Cool Cats, Top Dogs, and Other Beastly Expressions* (9–12). Illus. 1999, Houghton paper $14.00 (0-395-95730-3). This entertaining book gives the meanings and origins of 1,200 English expressions involving animals, such as scapegoat and hot dog. (Rev: SLJ 8/99) [410]

4429 Bauer, Marion Dane. *Our Stories: A Fiction Workshop for Young Authors* (6–10). 1996, Clarion $14.95 (0-395-81598-3); paper $6.95 (0-395-81599-1). Using critiques of 30 selections by students, the author explores such writing techniques as character development, dialogue, and point of view. (Rev: BL 10/15/96; BR 3–4/97; SLJ 12/96; VOYA 12/96) [808.3]

4430 Hackwell, W. John. *Signs, Letters, Words: Archaeology Discovers Writing* (6–9). Illus. 1987, Macmillan LB $14.95 (0-684-18807-4). The story of the development of writing and how this has affected civilization. (Rev: BL 8/87; SLJ 1/88; VOYA 10/87) [652]

4431 Henderson, Kathy. *Market Guide for Young Writers.* 5th ed. (7–12). Illus. 1996, F & W Publns. paper $16.99 (0-89879-721-7). A guide for writers under age 18 on how to prepare manuscripts, where to sell them, and the kinds of material that are marketable. (Rev: BL 11/15/86) [070]

4432 Jean, Georges. *Writing: The Story of Alphabets and Scripts* (7–12). (Discoveries) 1992, Abrams paper $12.95 (0-8109-2893-0). Traces the beginnings of writing from the development of alphabets to printing and bookmaking, emphasizing the technological rather than intellectual aspects of the process. (Rev: BL 7/92) [652.1]

4433 Ogg, Oscar. *The 26 Letters.* Rev. ed. (10–12). Illus. 1971, HarperCollins $13.95 (0-690-84115-9).

This book traces the history of writing from the caveman on. [411]

4434 *Scrawl! Writing in Ancient Times* (5–8). (Buried Worlds) 1994, Lerner LB $23.93 (0-8225-3209-3). A history of writing worldwide, from prehistoric symbols to the invention of printing. Revised, updated edition of Ancient Scrolls. (Rev: BL 1/15/95) [411]

4435 Senn, Joyce. *The Young People's Book of Quotations* (5–10). 1999, Millbrook $37.90 (0-7613-0267-0). Beginning with "accomplishment" and ending with "zoos," this is a collection of 2,000 quotations of special interest to young people, arranged by topic. (Rev: BL 3/1/99; SLJ 4/99) [082]

4436 Van Allsburg, Chris. *The Mysteries of Harris Burdick* (7–9). Illus. 1984, Houghton $17.95 (0-395-35393-9). Fourteen drawings and captions invite the reader to write stories that explain them. (Rev: BL 9/86) [808]

Books and Publishing

4437 Brookfield, Karen. *Book* (5–9). (Eyewitness Books) 1993, Knopf LB $20.99 (0-679-94012-X). The evolution of writing is traced and the formats in which it has been recorded are covered. (Rev: BL 10/1/93) [002]

4438 Garcia, John. *The Success of Hispanic Magazine* (7–10). Illus. (Success) 1996, Walker LB $16.85 (0-8027-8310-4). A behind-the-scenes look at the magazine business, from starting out to marketing research, staffing, sales, circulation, and distribution. Traces an article from initial conception to final version and publication. (Rev: BL 5/15/96; SLJ 4/96) [051]

4439 Madama, John. *Desktop Publishing: The Art of Communication* (7–12). 1993, Lerner LB $21.27 (0-8225-2303-5). Introduces desktop publishing elements and terminology to beginning computer users, with advice on writing, editing, layout, type, illustration, and printing. (Rev: BL 5/15/93; SLJ 6/93) [686.2]

4440 Olmert, Michael. *The Smithsonian Book of Books* (9–12). 1992, Smithsonian $49.95 (0-89599-030-X). Celebrates the powerful link between readers and the printed page as it follows books from the days of scribes to moveable type to children's book illustration. (Rev: BL 9/1/92; SLJ 1/93*) [002]

4441 Toussaint, Pamela. *Great Books for African American Children* (6–12). 1999, NAL paper $12.95 (0-452-28044-3). This book lists 250 recommended books for African American children from preschool to young adults, each with a lengthy, informative annotation. (Rev: BL 2/15/99; SLJ 9/99) [810]

4442 Wilson, Elizabeth B. *Bibles and Bestiaries: A Guide to Illuminated Manuscripts* (6–9). 1994, Farrar $25.00 (0-374-30685-0). Describes how a book was made in the Middle Ages. (Rev: BL 1/1/95; SLJ 12/94*) [745.6]

Print and Other Media

4443 Cooper, Alison. *Media Power?* (6–8). Illus. (Viewpoints) 1997, Watts $22.50 (0-531-14452-6). Double-page spreads cover such topics as the use and misuse of the media by advertisers and governments, the effect of the media on recent trials, privacy issues, and the formation of public opinion. (Rev: BL 1/1–15/98) [302.23]

4444 Daniels, Les. *Marvel: Five Fabulous Decades of the World's Greatest Comics* (9–12). 1991, Abrams $49.50 (0-8109-3821-9). The story of the development of Marvel Comics is told through artwork, biographies, and profiles of the publishers' foremost heroes and villains. (Rev: BL 11/1/91) [741.5]

4445 Day, Nancy. *Sensational TV: Trash or Journalism?* (7–10). Illus. 1996, Enslow LB $19.95 (0-89490-733-6). A history of tabloid journalism both in print and on TV, plus a discussion of present-day controversies surrounding it. (Rev: BL 4/1/96; SLJ 4/96; VOYA 6/96) [791.45]

4446 Fleming, Thomas. *Behind the Headlines: The Story of American Newspapers* (6–10). 1989, Walker LB $29.90 (0-8027-6891-1). A lively history of American newspapers from the Revolution on and an indication of their continued importance today. (Rev: BL 1/1/90; BR 5–6/90; SLJ 1/90; VOYA 12/90) [071.3]

4447 Ritchie, Donald A. *American Journalists: Getting the Story* (8–12). Illus. 1998, Oxford $56.00 (0-

19-509907-9). Fifty-six biographical sketches of journalists, supplemented by photographs, reproductions, and brief items about other news media notables, provide a glimpse into the journalism profession from Benjamin Franklin's time to today. (Rev: BL 2/15/98; BR 5–6/98; SLJ 7/98; VOYA 10/98) [070]

4448 Senna, Carl. *The Black Press and the Struggle for Civil Rights* (7–12). (African American Experience) 1993, Watts LB $23.60 (0-531-11036-2). The history of African American publications and their role in the fight for freedom and civil rights is traced, from Freedom's Journal in 1827 to today. (Rev: BL 1/1/94; SLJ 1/94; VOYA 2/94) [071]

4449 Shepard, Richard. *The Paper's Papers: A Reporter's Journey Through the Archives of the New York Times* (10–12). 1996, Times Bks. $30.00 (0-8129-2453-3). An entertaining, anecdotal history of The New York Times that relies heavily on archival memos, letters, excerpts from articles, and cartoons. (Rev: SLJ 4/97) [070]

4450 Stay, Byron L., ed. *Mass Media* (8–12). 1999, Greenhaven LB $167.68 (0-7377-0055-6); paper $20.25 (0-7377-0054-8). How does television affect society? Is advertising harmful? How do the media influence politics? Should pornography on the Internet be regulated? Do TV content labels benefit children? These are some of the questions explored in this collection of writings about the mass media. (Rev: BL 4/15/99) [303.6]

4451 Wakin, Edward. *How TV Changed America's Mind* (7–12). 1996, Lothrop $15.00 (0-688-13482-3). This book chronicles the impact of television journalism on U.S. history over the past 50 years by analyzing how the major news stories of the time were reported. (Rev: SLJ 7/96) [070.1]

4452 Winchester, Simon. *The Professor and the Madman: A Tale of Murder, Insanity, and the Making of the Oxford English Dictionary* (10–12). 1998, HarperCollins $22.00 (0-06-017596-6). The story of the writing of the famous Oxford English Dictionary and the relationship between its editor, James Murray, and Dr. William Chester Minor, a major contributor and former Civil War doctor who was a patient in England's most famous insane asylum during their entire collaboration. (Rev: BL 8/98; SLJ 3/99) [410]

4453 Woodward, Fred. *Rolling Stone: The Complete Covers, 1967–1997* (9–12). Illus. 1998, Harry N. Abrams $39.95 (0-8109-3797-2). A collection of the 773 covers of Rolling Stone magazine from November 1967 (the first issue) through November 1997 (Mick Jagger holds the record with 19 covers), supplemented by magazine headlines and features reflecting the political and social issues of that period and commentary about how the magazine developed into a major publication of popular culture. (Rev: BL 5/15/98; SLJ 8/98) [050]

Philosophy and Religion

Philosophy

4454 Bender, David L., ed. *Constructing a Life Philosophy* (9–12). (Opposing Viewpoints) 1993, Greenhaven LB $26.20 (0-89908-198-3); paper $21.81 (0-89908-173-8). Essays related to developing a philosophy on the meaning of life by such diverse writers as Plato, Joseph Campbell, and Billy Graham. (Rev: BL 6/1–15/93) [140]

4455 Curry, Patrick, and Oscar Zarate. *Introducing Machiavelli* (10–12). Ed. by Richard Appignanesi. 1996, Totem paper $9.95 (1-874166-28-5). The life and political theories of this Italian philosopher are introduced through black-and-white comics and brief text. (Rev: SLJ 7/96) [100]

4456 Eichhoefer, Gerald W. *Enduring Issues in Philosophy* (10–12). (Enduring Issues) 1995, Greenhaven LB $27.45 (1-56510-252-5); paper $17.45 (1-56510-251-7). This book explores 6 controversies in philosophy such as: what can we know? what is ultimately real? does God exist? and what is morality? (Rev: BL 7/95; SLJ 8/95) [100]

4457 Fulghum, Robert. *All I Really Need to Know I Learned in Kindergarten: Uncommon Thoughts on Common Things* (10–12). 1988, Random $18.95 (0-394-57102-9). A collection of essays extolling the simple things in life. (Rev: BL 10/15/88) [128]

4458 Magee, Bryan. *The Story of Philosophy* (10–12). 1998, DK Publg. $29.95 (0-7894-3511-X). With an accessible text and excellent illustrations, this is a fine overview of philosophy in chronologically arranged chapters beginning with "The Greeks and Their World" and ending with "20th Century Philosophy." (Rev: BL 12/1/98; SLJ 3/99) [100]

4459 Weate, Jeremy. *A Young Person's Guide to Philosophy* (6–12). 1998, DK Publg. $16.95 (0-7894-3074-6). After a discussion of what constitutes philosophy, this well-illustrated volume tells about the life, times, and thoughts of 25 of the world's great thinkers. (Rev: BL 12/15/98; BR 5–6/99; SLJ 1/99) [100]

World Religions and Holidays

General and Miscellaneous

4460 Aaseng, Rolf E. *A Beginner's Guide to Study-ing the Bible* (9–12). 1991, Augsburg paper $10.99 (0-8066-2571-6). Outlines basic techniques and resources for enriching Bible study. (Rev: BL 4/1/92) [220.07]

4461 Andryszewski, Tricia. *Communities of the Faithful: American Religious Movements Outside the Mainstream* (6–10). 1997, Millbrook LB $22.40 (0-7613-0067-8). Seven religious orders—Old Order Amish, Shakers, Mormons, Catholic Workers, Nation of Islam, Lubavitcher Hasidim, and Quak-ers—are introduced, with material on their beliefs and contributions to American culture. (Rev: BR 5–6/98; SLJ 2/98) [200]

4462 Andryszewski, Tricia. *School Prayer: A Histo-ry of the Debate* (8–12). Illus. (Issues in Focus) 1997, Enslow LB $19.95 (0-89490-904-5). A thor-ough, balanced account that explores all sides of the controversy concerning school prayer, with material on the separation of church and state. (Rev: BL 10/1/97; SLJ 3/98; VOYA 2/98) [344.73]

4463 Armstrong, Carole. *Women of the Bible* (7–10). Illus. 1998, Simon & Schuster paper $18.00 (0-689-81728-2). With accompanying art, this book intro-duces the lives of 17 women from the Bible, includ-ing Rachel and Leah, Deborah, Delilah, Bathsheba, the Virgin Mary, and Salome. (Rev: BL 3/1/98; SLJ 3/98; VOYA 8/98) [220.9]

4464 Asimov, Isaac. *Asimov's Guide to the Bible* (7–12). 1981, Crown $16.99 (0-517-34582-X). This is a book-by-book guide to both the Old and New Testaments. [220.7]

4465 Asimov, Isaac. *Asimov's Guide to the Bible: The Old Testament* (10–12). 1976, Avon paper $10.95 (0-380-01032-1). A historical study of the Old Testament. Followed by: *Asimov's Guide to the Bible: The New Testament* (1982). [220]

4466 Bahree, Patricia. *Hinduism* (6–9). Illus. 1985, Batsford $19.95 (0-7134-3654-9). The basic beliefs and gods of Hinduism are discussed under 100 sub-jects arranged alphabetically. (Rev: BL 5/1/85) [294.5]

4467 Barr, Robert R. *What Is the Bible?* (9–12). 1984, HarperCollins $4.95 (0-86683-727-2). This is a popular introduction to the characters and stories in the Bible and their significance. [220]

4468 Bowker, John. *World Religions* (10–12). 1997, DK Publg. $34.95 (0-7894-1439-2). In this heavily illustrated volume, 2 or 3 pages are devoted to each of the world's important religions, with material on principles, symbols, events, people, buildings, works of art, and similarities to other religions. (Rev: BR 9–10/97; SLJ 12/97; VOYA 10/97) [200]

4469 Breuilly, Elizabeth, et al. *Religions of the World: The Illustrated Guide to Origins, Beliefs, Tra-ditions & Festivals* (7–12). Illus. 1997, Facts on File $29.95 (0-8160-3723-X). This well-illustrated work defines religion generally, discusses each of the world's major religions, points out similarities, and links each religion to current events and internation-al politics. (Rev: BL 10/1/97; SLJ 2/98) [291]

4470 Brunelli, Roberto. *A Family Treasury of Bible Stories: One for Each Week of the Year* (4–8). Illus. 1997, Abrams $24.95 (0-8109-1248-7). A collection of 52 short stories, one for each week, from the Old and New Testaments. (Rev: BL 10/1/97; SLJ 2/98) [220.9]

4471 Chaikin, Miriam. *Clouds of Glory: Legends and Stories about Bible Times* (4–8). Illus. 1998, Clarion $19.00 (0-395-74654-X). This is a hand-some retelling of the legends found in the book of

Genesis, with an emphasis on the angel world and Satan's fight with God over humans. (Rev: BL 4/1/98; SLJ 4/98) [296.1]

4472 Cooper, Ilene. *The Dead Sea Scrolls* (5–8). Illus. 1997, Morrow $15.00 (0-688-14300-8). This account tells about the discovery of the Dead Sea Scrolls, their contents and their archaeological importance. (Rev: BL 3/1/97; SLJ 6/97) [296.1]

4473 Dhanjal, Beryl. *Sikhism* (7–10). Illus. 1987, David & Charles $19.95 (0-7134-5202-1). In alphabetical order, the major tenets, doctrines, and personages of this religion are discussed. (Rev: SLJ 9/87) [294.6]

4474 Durrett, Deanne, ed. *Angels* (6–9). Illus. (Opposing Viewpoints Great Mysteries) 1996, Greenhaven LB $16.95 (1-56510-353-X). This collection of sources discusses the pros and cons of the existence of angels and their activities. (Rev: BL 4/15/96; SLJ 5/96) [291.2]

4475 Ellwood, Robert S., and Gregory D. Alles, eds. *The Encyclopedia of World Religions* (7–12). Illus. 1998, Facts on File $35.00 (0-8160-3504-0). Though basically intended as a reference book, this is a work interesting to browse through on religions, past and present, and general topics that figure in religious studies like the sun, moon, music, and science. (Rev: BL 9/1/98; SLJ 11/98) [200]

4476 France, Peter. *An Encyclopedia of Bible Animals* (9–12). Illus. 1986, Salem House $26.95 (0-7099-3737-7). An alphabetically arranged treatment of all the animals mentioned in the Bible with references to specific passages and illustrations. (Rev: BL 11/1/86) [220]

4477 Gaer, Joseph. *What the Great Religions Believe* (7–12). 1963, NAL paper $3.95 (0-451-14320-5). The principal beliefs of 11 world religions are explained and excerpts are given from various holy books. [291]

4478 Ganeri, Anita. *Out of the Ark: Stories from the World's Religions* (4–8). Illus. 1996, Harcourt $18.00 (0-15-200943-4). Traditional tales from 7 of the world's major religions are retold in this thematically arranged book. (Rev: SLJ 4/96) [200]

4479 Gellman, Marc, and Thomas Hartman. *How Do You Spell God? Answers to the Big Questions from Around the World* (5–8). Illus. 1995, Morrow $16.00 (0-688-13041-0). This survey of a variety of religions poses major questions about life, then presents answers according to the beliefs of Judaism, Islam, Christianity, Buddhism, and Hinduism. (Rev: BL 6/1–15/95; SLJ 5/95) [200]

4480 Gold, Susan D. *Religions of the Western Hemisphere* (5–8). Illus. (Comparing Continents) 1997, Twenty-First Century $21.40 (0-8050-5603-3). This work explores the history and influence of religions,

beliefs, and customs on life in the United States, Canada, and Latin America, with discussion of the roles of religious leaders in the government, economy, and everyday life. (Rev: BL 2/1/98; SLJ 3/98) [200]

4481 Hartz, Paula R. *Taoism* (6–9). Illus. (World Religions) 1993, Facts on File $26.95 (0-8160-2448-0). A clear, objective explanation of the Chinese religion Taoism, with details on its metamorphosis from mysticism to a more secular form. (Rev: BL 7/93) [299]

4482 Harvey, Michael. *Miracles* (9–12). (Great Mysteries) 1990, Greenhaven LB $22.45 (0-89908-084-7). Explores mostly Christian miracles, including healings and the appearance of religious images. (Rev: BL 1/1/91) [231.7]

4483 Hoobler, Thomas, and Dorothy Hoobler. *Confucianism* (6–9). (World Religions) 1993, Facts on File $26.95 (0-8160-2445-6). Describes how the teachings of Confucius evolved from a social order to a religion, permeating all phases of Chinese life for 2,000 years. (Rev: BL 3/1/93) [299]

4484 Kimmel, Eric A. *Be Not Far from Me: The Oldest Love Story: Legends from the Bible* (4–8). Illus. 1998, Simon & Schuster $25.00 (0-689-81088-1). This collection of stories about 19 men and one woman from the Old Testament adds incidents and details from ancient midrashic tradition that emphasize magic, and includes violence and cruelty. (Rev: BL 4/1/98; SLJ 6/98) [220]

4485 Krishnaswami, Uma. *The Broken Tusk: Stories of the Hindu God Ganesha* (4–8). Illus. 1996, Linnet $19.95 (0-208-02242-5). A collection of tales about the elephant-headed Hindu god Ganesha, the god of good beginnings. (Rev: SLJ 7/97) [294.5]

4486 Levinson, David. *Religion: A Cross-Cultural Encyclopedia* (10–12). 1996, ABC-CLIO LB $49.50 (0-87436-865-0). A browsable reference book that gives information of 16 religions as well as 41 allied subjects like ritual, taboo, and supernatural beings. (Rev: BL 3/1/97; BR 9–10/97; SLJ 8/97) [200]

4487 Lyden, John, ed. *Enduring Issues in Religion* (10–12). (Enduring issues) 1995, Greenhaven LB $27.45 (1-56510-260-6). Classic religious texts and the writings of modern theologians are used to explore topics involving the nature of religion, the meaning of life, and what lies beyond death. (Rev: BL 7/95) [200]

4488 McFarlane, Marilyn, retel. *Sacred Myths: Stories of World Religions* (6–10). 1996, Sibyl $26.95 (0-9638327-7-8). The author retells 35 stories from the world's main religions, using sources from Buddhist, Christian, Hindu, Islamic, Judaic, and Native American traditions as well as stories associated with Paganism, Goddess Religion, and other beliefs. (Rev: BL 10/1/96; SLJ 1/97) [200]

4489 MacMillan, Dianne M. *Diwali: Hindu Festival of Lights* (4–8). (Best Holiday Books) 1997, Enslow LB $18.95 (0-89490-817-0). This book on the Hindu Diwali festival discusses its significance and relationship to the history, culture, and people of India, and includes material on the food, crafts, instruments, and costumes of the festival. (Rev: SLJ 8/97) [294.5]

4490 Mark, Jan. *God's Story* (6–9). Illus. 1998, Candlewick $17.99 (0-7636-0376-7). A remarkably original work in which the author cleverly reworks familiar Old Testament tales about such characters as Adam and Eve, Noah, Abraham, Moses, and David. (Rev: BL 10/1/97; SLJ 1/98) [221.9]

4491 Morgan, Peggy. *Buddhism* (7–10). Illus. 1987, David & Charles $19.95 (0-7134-5203-X). In a dictionary format, the major points concerning this religion and its founder are described. (Rev: SLJ 9/87) [294.3]

4492 Pandell, Karen, and Barry Bryant. *Learning from the Dalai Lama: Secrets of the Wheel of Time* (5–8). 1995, Dutton paper $16.99 (0-525-45063-7). An excellent introduction to the essentials of Buddhism and the Kalachakra teaching, including instructions for creating a sand mandala and supplemented by photographs. (Rev: BL 1/1–15/96; SLJ 3/96) [294.3]

4493 Parrinder, Geoffrey, ed. *World Religions from Ancient History to the Present.* Rev. ed. (10–12). Illus. 1985, Facts on File paper $17.95 (0-8160-1289-X). The first 12 chapters describe ancient religions and the final 9 chapters discuss the most important modern religions. (Rev: BR 9–10/86) [200]

4494 Paterson, John, and Katherine Paterson. *Images of God: Views of the Invisible* (5–8). Illus. 1998, Houghton $20.00 (0-395-70734-X). After explaining the differences between the Hebrew and the Christian Bibles, the authors describe the images of God in these texts, as well as the portrayal of such elements as light, water, wind, fire, rocks, and clouds. (Rev: BL 5/1/98; BR 11–12/98; SLJ 4/98) [231]

4495 Potter, Charles Francis. *Is That in the Bible?* (9–12). 1985, Ballantine paper $4.99 (0-345-32109-X). An amazing collection of facts and trivia culled from the Bible. [220]

4496 Rohr, Janelle, ed. *Science & Religion: Opposing Viewpoints* (9–12). Illus. (Opposing Viewpoints) 1988, Greenhaven paper $16.20 (0-89908-406-0). The conflicts and areas of agreement between scientific truth and religious beliefs are explored from various viewpoints. (Rev: BL 5/1/88) [215]

4497 Schouweiler, Thomas. *The Devil* (6–9). (Opposing Viewpoints Great Mysteries) 1992, Greenhaven LB $18.96 (0-89908-091-X). Examines the question of the devil's existence and the begin-

nings of devil mythology, worship, and possession, looking at both sides and giving no definitive answers. (Rev: BL 5/1/93) [133.4]

4498 Seeger, Elizabeth. *Eastern Religions* (7–12). Illus. 1973, HarperCollins $14.95 (0-690-25342-7). A fine overview of such religions as Hinduism, Buddhism, Confucianism, and Taoism. [291]

4499 Simpson, Nancy. *Face-to-Face with Women of the Bible* (6–8). Illus. 1996, Chariot-Victor $15.99 (0-7814-0251-4). Both well-known and obscure women from the Bible are introduced in 2 or 3 pages per subject. (Rev: BL 10/15/96) [220.92]

4500 Singh, Nikky-Guninder Kaur. *Sikhism* (6–9). (World Religions) 1993, Facts on File $26.95 (0-8160-2446-4). Describes the development of Sikhism an outgrowth of Hinduism and discusses its traditions, customs, and beliefs. (Rev: BL 7/93) [294.6]

4501 Sita, Lisa. *Worlds of Belief: Religion and Spirituality* (5–8). (Our Human Family) 1995, Blackbirch LB $22.45 (1-56711-125-4). Using many illustrations, this book gives a global tour of the world's religions, with an emphasis on similarities rather than differences among people. (Rev: SLJ 1/96) [200]

4502 Tutu, Desmond, ed. *The African Prayer Book* (9–12). 1995, Doubleday $19.95 (0-385-47730-9). African prayers, poems, and litanies, both Christian and non-Christian. (Rev: BL 5/1/95) [242]

4503 Viswanathan, Ed. *Am I a Hindu?* (9–12). 1992, Halo Books paper $15.95 (1-879904-06-3). A comprehensive introduction to Hinduism written in "catechism" form, with questions and answers grouped according to topic. (Rev: BL 10/15/92) [294.5]

4504 Wangu, Madhu Bazaz. *Buddhism* (6–9). (World Religions) 1993, Facts on File $26.95 (0-8160-2442-1). Describes Buddha's life, the spread of Buddhism, and its existence today. (Rev: BL 3/1/93; SLJ 6/93) [294.3]

4505 Wangu, Madhu Bazaz. *Hinduism* (6–9). (World Religions) 1991, Facts on File $26.95 (0-8160-2447-2). A detailed, in-depth look at this major religion, with particular emphasis on how it is practiced in India. (Rev: BL 4/15/92; SLJ 3/92) [294.5]

4506 Ward, Hiley H. *My Friends' Beliefs: A Young Person's Guide to World Religions* (7–10). 1988, Walker $19.85 (0-8027-6793-1). An introduction to the history and beliefs of the world's great religions, plus interviews with young members. (Rev: VOYA 8/88) [200]

4507 Westwood, Jennifer. *Sacred Journeys: An Illustrated Guide to Pilgrimages Around the World* (10–12). 1997, Holt $35.00 (0-8050-4845-6). Representing all faiths, this heavily illustrated book describes various modern day religious pilgrimages, including the sites, routes, rules, dates, etc. (Rev: BR 9–10/97; SLJ 7/97) [200]

4508 Wilson, Colin. *The Atlas of Holy Places & Sacred Sites* (10–12). 1996, DK Publg. $29.95 (0-7894-1051-6). After a series of double-page spreads on sites like Stonehenge and Easter Island, there is a gazetteer with 16 maps and a listing of over 1,000 sacred places in this well-illustrated volume. (Rev: BL 10/15/96; BR 5–6/97; SLJ 7/97; VOYA 4/97) [200]

Christianity

4509 Beckett, Wendy. *Sister Wendy's Book of Saints* (10–12). 1998, DK Publg. $19.95 (0-7894-2398-7). Using artwork from the Italian State Libraries, Sister Wendy introduces the lives and works of 35 saints. (Rev: BR 11–12/98; SLJ 6/98; VOYA 10/98) [200]

4510 Bolick, Nancy O., and Sallie Randolph. *Shaker Inventions* (6–8). Illus. 1990, Walker LB $14.85 (0-8027-6934-9). This book describes the Shaker religion and explores the many contributions of the Shakers to American life, such as the clothespin and washing machine. (Rev: BL 8/90) [289]

4511 Bolick, Nancy O., and Sallie Randolph. *Shaker Villages* (6–8). Illus. 1993, Walker LB $26.90 (0-8027-8210-8). Offers insights into one of the world's longest-lived communal societies, its founder, its faith, its daily life, and its village organization. (Rev: BL 3/15/93; SLJ 6/93) [289]

4512 Brown, Stephen F. *Christianity* (6–9). (World Religions) 1991, Facts on File $26.95 (0-8160-2441-3). This account describes the origins of Christianity, its historical and contemporary impact, and its branches and beliefs. (Rev: BL 4/15/92; SLJ 1/92) [200]

4513 *The Easter Story: According to the Gospels of Matthew, Luke, and John from the King James Bible* (4–8). Illus. 1999, Holt $19.95 (0-8050-5052-3). Using passages from various books of the New Testament and stunning paintings, this is the story of Holy Week from the cleansing of the temple to Christ's appearance to the disciples after the Resurrection. (Rev: SLJ 3/99) [232.9]

4514 Kenna, Kathleen. *A People Apart* (5–8). Illus. 1995, Houghton $18.00 (0-395-67344-5). A thoughtful photoessay on the lives of the Mennonites by a woman who attended the church as a child. Interviews and the history of the group flesh out the text. (Rev: BL 11/1/95*; SLJ 12/95*) [289.7]

4515 Lincoln, Frances. *A Family Treasury of Prayers* (4–8). 1996, Simon & Schuster $16.00 (0-689-80956-5). An elegant book of Christian prayers

divided into groups: praise, forgiveness, and troubled times, and illustrated by works of the Old Masters (mostly Renaissance). (Rev: BL 10/1/96; SLJ 10/96; VOYA 6/97) [242]

4516 Lincoln, Frances. *Stories from The Old Testament: With Masterwork Paintings Inspired by the Stories* (5–8). 1996, Simon & Schuster $18.00 (0-689-80955-7). Scenes from the Old Testament (the Hebrew Bible) are told in the King James version and are illustrated with masterpieces of world art. (Rev: BL 10/1/96; SLJ 10/96; VOYA 6/97) [222]

4517 MacArthur, John F., Jr. *God with Us: The Miracle of Christmas* (9–12). Illus. 1989, Zondervan $12.99 (0-310-28690-5). A splendidly illustrated account of the events surrounding the birth of Christ and their significance. (Rev: VOYA 4/90) [263]

4518 Nardo, Don, ed. *The Rise of Christianity* (10–12). (Turning Points in World History) 1998, Greenhaven LB $21.96 (1-56510-963-5). This anthology of 19 essays by top scholars in the field of religion and history provides an overview of the birth, growth, and spread of Christianity, the problems faced by the early church, and Christianity's emergence as a world religion. (Rev: BL 1/1–15/99; BR 5–6/99) [270.1]

4519 Potter, Giselle. *Lucy's Eyes and Margaret's Dragon: The Lives of the Virgin Saints* (4–8). 1997, Chronicle $17.95 (0-8118-1515-3). This book contains brief descriptions of 13 virgin saints of the Catholic Church who performed good works and led exemplary lives, and endured cruelty and torture because of their devotion to Christianity. (Rev: SLJ 2/98) [282]

4520 Rollins, Charlemae Hill, ed. *Christmas Gif': An Anthology of Christmas Poems, Songs, and Stories* (5–10). Illus. 1993, Morrow $14.00 (0-688-11667-1). A reissue of this Christmas anthology of African American songs, stories, poems, spirituals, and recipes, newly illustrated by Ashley Bryan. (Rev: BL 7/93) [810.8]

4521 Schmidt, Gary D., retel. *The Blessing of the Lord: Stories from the Old and New Testaments* (5–8). Illus. 1997, Eerdmans $20.00 (0-8028-3789-1). Using 25 Old and New Testament stories as a focus, these insightful accounts describe how Biblical personalities react to such events as Daniel's struggle with the lions and Jesus causing nets to be filled with fish. (Rev: BL 11/1/97; SLJ 10/97) [222]

4522 Sprigg, June. *Simple Gifts: A Memoir of a Shaker Village* (10–12). Illus. 1998, Knopf $22.00 (0-679-45504-3). This is an account of the author's summer with small Shaker groups in Canterbury, New Hampshire, with good background material on the history, beliefs, and spiritual rewards of this sect. (Rev: BL 6/1–15/98; SLJ 12/98) [246]

4523 Stein, Stephen J. *The Shaker Experience in America: A History of the United Society of Believers* (9–12). 1992, Yale Univ. Pr. $55.00 (0-300-05139-5). A history of these seemingly radical religious people from the classic 18th-century Shaker period to their modern resurgence. (Rev: BL 5/1/92) [289]

4524 Stewart, Martha. *Martha Stewart's Christmas* (9–12). Illus. 1989, Random $25.00 (0-517-57416-0). A how-to book on making Christmas decorations and gifts. (Rev: BR 3–4/90) [293]

4525 Stoltzfus, Louise. *Amish Women: Lives and Stories* (9–12). 1994, Good Books $14.95 (1-56148-129-7). Amish women reveal their unique place in their religion as well as their hopes and aspirations. (Rev: BL 12/1/94; SLJ 6/95) [305.48]

4526 *Stories from the New Testament* (6–9). Illus. 1997, Simon & Schuster $18.00 (0-689-81297-3). Using language from the King James version of the Bible, 17 stories from the New Testament are presented, each with a famous masterpiece of art that depicts the crucial action. (Rev: BL 10/1/97; SLJ 10/97) [225.5]

4527 Teresa, Mother. *Words to Love By* (7–12). 1983, Ave Maria Pr. paper $9.95 (0-87793-261-1). A collection of the writing and meditations of the Nobel Prize–winning nun. [242]

4528 Wernecke, Herbert H. *Christmas Customs Around the World* (9–12). Illus. 1959, Westminster paper $13.95 (0-664-24258-8). Using a geographical arrangement, the author describes unusual Christmas traditions around the world. [394.2]

4529 Williams, Jean K. *The Amish* (6–9). Illus. 1996, Watts LB $22.00 (0-531-11275-6). This book tells about the Amish, their history, beliefs, social structure, and how their lifestyle differs from that of most other Americans. (Rev: BL 10/1/96; SLJ 1/97) [289.7]

4530 Williams, Jean K. *The Christian Scientists* (7–12). (The American Religious Experience) 1997, Watts LB $22.00 (0-531-11309-4). This serves as both a history and exploration of the Christian Science faith and a biography of founder Mary Baker Eddy, who believed that mind is spirit and that sin and disease should be conquered solely by prayer. (Rev: SLJ 8/97) [289.5]

4531 Williams, Jean K. *The Mormons* (6–9). Illus. 1996, Watts LB $22.00 (0-531-11276-4). How the Church of Jesus Christ of Latter-day Saints began is told, plus information on the beliefs and practices of its members. (Rev: BL 10/1/96; SLJ 1/97) [289.3]

4532 Williams, Jean K. *The Quakers* (6–12). Illus. (American Religious Experience) 1998, Watts LB $22.00 (0-531-11377-9). From the time they left England and came to this country in the 17th centu-

ry, this is the story of the Quakers, their beliefs and doctrines, and the role they have played in American history. (Rev: BL 10/1/98; SLJ 1/99) [289.6]

4533 Williams, Jean K. *The Shakers* (6–10). Illus. (American Religious Experience) 1997, Watts LB $22.00 (0-531-11342-6). The story of this religious sect, its origins in England, how members came to America in the late 1700s, its history here, and the group's emphasis on hard work, celibacy, orderliness, and simplicity. (Rev: BL 12/1/97; SLJ 2/98) [289]

Islam

4534 Child, John. *The Rise of Islam* (6–8). 1995, Bedrick $17.95 (0-87226-116-6). A historical approach to Islam's impact on world history. Discusses its beginnings and middle development but only briefly discusses Islam today. (Rev: BL 9/1/95; SLJ 8/95) [297]

4535 Dunn, John. *The Spread of Islam* (8–12). Illus. (World History) 1996, Lucent LB $17.96 (1-56006-285-1). This account begins with the life of Mohammed and then chronicles how his teachings spread around the world. (Rev: BL 7/96; BR 5–6/99; SLJ 7/96) [909]

4536 Gordon, Matthew S. *Islam* (6–9). (World Religions) 1991, Facts on File $26.95 (0-8160-2443-X). An overview of the history of Islam, its branches, the Koran, and Islam's place in the modern world. (Rev: BL 4/15/92; SLJ 1/92) [297]

4537 Lippman, Thomas W. *Understanding Islam: An Introduction to the Moslem World* (10–12). 1982, NAL paper $3.95 (0-451-62666-4). The life and works of Mohammed are introduced as well as a discussion of the beliefs and practices of Islam. [297]

4538 Robinson, Francis, ed. *The Cambridge Illustrated History of the Islamic World* (10–12). 1996, Cambridge Univ. Pr. $39.95 (0-521-43510-2). With outstanding illustrations, this work explores the history and practices of Islam and its economic and social ramifications. (Rev: SLJ 3/97) [297]

4539 Spencer, William. *Islam Fundamentalism in the Modern World* (7–10). 1995, Millbrook LB $22.40 (1-56294-435-5). Explains the tenets of Islam and the general nature of religious fundamentalism. (Rev: BL 4/15/95; SLJ 5/95) [320.5]

4540 Swisher, Clarice, ed. *The Spread of Islam* (9–12). (Turning Points in World History) 1998, Greenhaven LB $20.96 (1-56510-967-8); paper $17.45 (1-56510-966-X). This anthology traces the growth of Islam from Mohammed's teachings in the 7th century to the present, with chapters on Islamic art and thought, sects, and modern Islamic fundamentalism. (Rev: BL 10/15/98) [297.09]

4541 Tames, Richard. *Islam* (8–10). Illus. 1985, David & Charles $18.95 (0-7134-3655-7). A topically arranged overview of Islam that covers such topics as marriage, mosques, festivals, and beliefs. (Rev: BL 8/85; SLJ 1/86) [297]

4542 Wormser, Richard. *American Islam: Growing Up Muslim in America* (7–12). 1994, Walker $16.85 (0-8027-8344-9). A portrait of Muslim American youth and their faith. (Rev: BL 12/15/94; SLJ 3/95; VOYA 2/95) [297]

Judaism

4543 Burstein, Chaya M. *The Jewish Kids Catalog* (7–9). 1983, Jewish Publication Soc. paper $14.95 (0-8276-0215-4). All sorts of information is given on Jewish culture and history including holidays, folktales, and even some recipes. [296]

4544 Cardozo, Arlene. *Jewish Family Celebrations: Shabbat, Festivals and Traditional Ceremonies* (9–12). Illus. 1982, St. Martin's paper $11.95 (0-312-44232-7). This account explores the year from the standpoint of Jewish religious holidays and observances. [296.4]

4545 Chaikin, Miriam. *Menorahs, Mezuzas, and Other Jewish Symbols* (5–9). 1990, Clarion $17.00 (0-89919-856-2). A Jewish historian explores and explains some of the symbols of the faith. (Rev: BL 1/15/91; SLJ 1/91) [296.4]

4546 David, Jo, and Daniel B. Syme. *The Book of the Jewish Life* (5–8). Illus. 1997, U A H C Pr. paper $12.00 (0-8074-0628-7). This book explores common Jewish traditions in such subjects as birth and naming, religious schools, bar/bat mitzvahs, confirmation, marriage, and mourning. (Rev: SLJ 9/98) [296]

4547 Fisher, Leonard E. *To Bigotry No Sanction: The Story of the Oldest Synagogue in America* (5–8). Illus. 1998, Holiday House $16.95 (0-8234-1401-9). Beginning with the expulsion of the Jews from Spain in 1492, the author traces the history of Jews in America in general and the building of the Touro Synagogue, the oldest synagogue in America, in Newport, Rhode Island, in 1763, with the blessing of George Washington. (Rev: BL 2/1/99; SLJ 3/99) [296.097457]

4548 Goldin, Barbara D. *The Passover Journey: A Seder Companion* (5–8). Illus. 1994, Viking paper $15.99 (0-670-82421-6). This illustrated celebration of the Jewish holiday mixes biblical excerpts with rabbinic Passover stories and explains the origins

and symbolism of the Seder. (Rev: BL 3/1/94*; SLJ 2/94) [269.4]

4549 Jacobs, Louis. *The Jewish Religion: A Companion* (10–12). 1995, Oxford $72.50 (0-19-826463-1). Arranged alphabetically, this compendium of information covers a wide variety of topics about one of the world's oldest religions, Judaism. (Rev: SLJ 6/96) [296]

4550 Kimmel, Eric A., ed. *A Hanukkah Treasury* (5–8). 1998, Holt $19.95 (0-8050-5293-3). A diverse collection of Hanukkah stories, songs, poems, and activities, such as making a menorah, playing dreidel games, and cooking special foods associated with the holiday. (Rev: BL 12/1/98; SLJ 10/98) [296.4]

4551 Mack, Stanley. *The Story of the Jews: A 4,000 Year Adventure* (10–12). 1998, Random House $19.95 (0-375-50130-4). A facile presentation of the history and experiences of the Jewish people in relation to major social and political developments in world history. (Rev: SLJ 9/98; VOYA 6/99) [296]

4552 Morrison, Martha, and Stephen F. Brown. *Judaism* (6–9). Illus. (World Religions) 1991, Facts on File $26.95 (0-8160-2444-8). An illustrated study of the impact Judaism has had on civilization and a look at its evolution, branches, holidays, and traditions. (Rev: BL 4/15/92; SLJ 3/92) [296]

4553 Salkin, Jeffrey K. *For Kids—Putting God on Your Guest List: How to Claim the Spiritual Meaning of Your Bar or Bat Mitzvah* (6–8). 1998, Jewish Lights Publg. paper $14.95 (1-58023-015-6). Rabbi Salkin explains the religious and cultural significance of this rite of passage in the Jewish religion. (Rev: BL 3/1/99) [296.4]

4554 Scharfstein, Sol. *Understanding Jewish History I* (6–9). Illus. 1996, KTAV paper $15.95 (0-88125-545-9). Using many colorful illustrations, this work traces Jewish history from biblical times to the expulsion of the Jews from Spain in the 15th century. (Rev: BL 10/1/96; SLJ 1/97) [909]

4555 Trepp, Leo. *The Complete Book of Jewish Observance* (9–12). Illus. 1980, Simon & Schuster $25.50 (0-671-47197-5). Working from a weekly schedule to the important observances of a lifetime, Jewish rituals are explained. [296.4]

4556 Wood, Angela. *Being a Jew* (6–10). Illus. 1988, David & Charles $19.95 (0-7134-4668-4). This book deals with the history, religion, customs, and traditions of Jewish people around the world. (Rev: SLJ 8/88) [296]

4557 Wood, Angela. *Judaism* (5–8). 1995, Raintree Steck-Vaughn LB $24.26 (1-56847-376-1). An informative text on Judaism, with a glossary, bibliography, and map of where the religion flourishes. (Rev: BL 9/1/95; SLJ 11/95) [296]

Religious Cults

4558 Barghusen, Joan D. *Cults* (7–12). Illus. (Overview) 1997, Lucent LB $17.96 (1-56006-199-5). The author recounts the history of cults in America, attempts to demystify them through an examination of their beliefs, recruitment methods, funding, and various practices, and reviews the anticult movement, including the practice of deprogramming. (Rev: BL 5/1/98; SLJ 8/98) [291.0460973]

4559 Cohen, Daniel. *Cults* (7–10). 1994, Millbrook LB $22.40 (1-56294-324-3). This work describes cults throughout American history, including Pilgrims, Quakers, Moonies, and Satanists. Examines the recruiting methods they use. (Rev: BL 11/1/94; SLJ 2/95; VOYA 2/95) [291.9]

4560 Cole, Michael D. *The Siege at Waco: Deadly Inferno* (5–9). (American Disasters) 1999, Enslow $18.95 (0-7660-1218-2). The story of the disaster that ended the 51-day siege at Waco and resulted in the deaths of cult leader David Koresh and 73 of his followers. (Rev: BL 2/15/99) [976.4 284063]

4561 Gay, Kathlyn. *Communes and Cults* (7–12). 1997, Twenty-First Century LB $21.40 (0-8050-3803-5). After tracing the history of cults that rely on communal living, the author discusses contemporary cults, their similarities and differences, their appeal, and their problems. (Rev: BL 9/1/97; BR 11–12/97; SLJ 7/97; VOYA 10/97) [280]

4562 Singer, Margaret, and Janja Lalich. *Cults in Our Midst* (9–12). 1995, Jossey-Bass $25.00 (0-7879-0051-6). An analysis of the cult phenomenon. (Rev: BL 4/15/95) [291.9]

4563 Streissguth, Thomas. *Charismatic Cult Leaders* (7–12). 1995, Oliver Pr. LB $16.95 (1-881508-18-8). A balanced presentation of a potentially sensational topic. Includes biblical references where appropriate in the discussion of various cults and their leaders. (Rev: BL 8/95; SLJ 5/95) [291]

4564 Zeinert, Karen. *Cults* (7–12). Illus. (Issues in Focus) 1997, Enslow LB $19.95 (0-89490-900-2). Following a history of cults in America from the days of the Salem witches on, this book discusses all forms of present-day cults, from the more establishment (Jehovah's Witnesses and Mormonism) to the extremist (Branch Davidians and the Freemen of Montana). (Rev: BL 6/1–15/97; BR 11–12/97; VOYA 10/97) [291.9]

Society and the Individual

Government and Political Science

United Nations and Other International Organizations

4565 Burger, Leslie, and Debra L. Burger. *United Nations High Commissioner for Refugees: Making a Difference in Our World* (5–8). (International Cooperation) 1996, Lerner LB $22.60 (0-8225-2699-9). This volume describes the backgrounds and plight of refugees worldwide, outlines the history of modern international efforts to help them, and speculates about their future. (Rev: SLJ 1/97; VOYA 2/97) [362.87]

4566 Burger, Leslie, and Debra L. Rahm. *Red Cross Red Crescent: When Help Can't Wait* (5–8). (International Cooperation) 1996, Lerner $22.60 (0-8225-2698-0). The story of the Red Cross and the role it plays in helping people around the world today. (Rev: BL 1/1–15/97; SLJ 1/97; VOYA 4/97) [361.7]

4567 Jacobs, William J. *Search for Peace: The Story of the United Nations* (7–10). 1994, Scribners paper $14.95 (0-684-19652-2). Describes the formation of the United Nations and discusses the difficulties the organization has faced in its efforts to maintain peace. (Rev: BL 7/94; SLJ 8/94) [341.23]

4568 Janello, Amy, and Brennon Jones, eds. *A Global Affair: An Inside Look at the United Nations* (9–12). 1995, Jones & Janello $35.00 (0-9646322-0-9). A celebration in essay form of the political and humanitarian work of the United Nations. (Rev: BL 9/15/95) [341.23]

4569 *The United Nations* (8–12). (At Issue) 1996, Greenhaven paper $15.75 (1-56510-547-8). This book traces the history, composition, and functions of the United Nations in such areas as population control, pollution, hunger, and economic development. (Rev: BL 5/15/97; SLJ 7/97) [341.23]

4570 *A World in Our Hands: In Honor of the 50th Anniversary of the United Nations* (6–8). 1995, Ten Speed Pr. paper $15.95 (1-883672-31-7). The history and accomplishments of the United Nations are the focus of this collection of prose, poetry, and art by young people from around the world. (Rev: BL 2/1/96) [341.23]

4571 *Your United Nations: The Official Guidebook* (9–12). 1985, U.N. Publns. $11.95 (92-1-100315-6). A guide to the United Nations buildings that also describes its structure and routines. [341.23]

International Relations, Peace, and War

4572 Altman, Linda J. *Genocide: The Systematic Killing of a People* (7–12). (Issues in Focus) 1995, Enslow LB $19.95 (0-89490-664-X). Discusses the history of genocide and explores the Them-Us mentality and racist stereotypes that are still used today to execute genocidal policies. (Rev: BL 10/15/95; SLJ 11/95; VOYA 12/95) [364.15]

4573 Barber, Benjamin, and Patrick Watson. *The Struggle for Democracy* (9–12). Illus. 1989, Little, Brown $29.95 (0-316-08058-6). An examination of the nature of democracy and its problems from the ancient Greeks to the present. (Rev: BL 10/1/89) [321.8]

4574 Carter, Jimmy. *Talking Peace: A Vision for the Next Generation* (8–12). 1995, Puffin paper $5.99 (0-14-037440-X). Carter encourages youth to work for world peace by improving human rights, civil liberties, environmental protection, and aid for the poor. The 1995 revised edition updates events in some of the wartorn areas Carter discussed previously and includes a chapter about his peace missions to

Korea, Haiti, Bosnia, and Sudan. (Rev: BL 8/93; SLJ 10/93*) [327.1]

4575 Chalberg, John C., ed. *Isolationism* (9–12). (Opposing Viewpoints in American History) 1995, Greenhaven LB $26.20 (1-56510-223-1); paper $20.25 (1-56510-222-3). Excerpts from historical speeches, editorials, and essays espousing and opposing isolationist views. (Rev: BL 3/15/95; SLJ 5/95) [327.73]

4576 Cheney, Glenn. *Nuclear Proliferation: The Problems and Possibilities* (8–12). 1999, Watts $24.00 (0-531-11431-7). This account traces the history of nuclear weapons and radioactive materials, describes the treaties to control them, and discusses the current problems in controlling their use, the role of rogue nations, and illegal trade in radioactive materials. (Rev: BL 7/99; SLJ 6/99) [327.1]

4577 Cozic, Charles P., ed. *Nationalism and Ethnic Conflict* (10–12). (Current Controversies) 1994, Greenhaven LB $26.20 (1-56510-080-8); paper $16.20 (1-56510-079-4). This collection of articles probes questions related to nationalism involving ethnic violence, whether it is ever justified, the advisability of intervention, and how ethnic conflicts can be prevented. (Rev: BL 6/1–15/94; SLJ 3/94) [306.82]

4578 Gold, Susan D. *Arms Control* (6–9). Illus. (Pacts and Treaties) 1997, Twenty-First Century LB $21.40 (0-8050-4812-X). Beginning with the 1868 Declaration of St. Petersburg calling for a ban on the use of explosive projectiles, the author tells of the many subsequent attempts by world leaders to limit the sale and use of arms. (Rev: BL 9/1/97; SLJ 12/97) [327.1]

4579 Grant, R. G. *Genocide* (5–10). Illus. (Talking Points) 1999, Raintree Steck-Vaughn LB $27.11 (0-8172-5314-9). This book covers the Holocaust in World War II as well as more recent massacres in Cambodia, Rwanda, and Bosnia, and probes such controversies as who is guilty of genocide—the person who pulls the trigger or those who plan and organize it, and what about the bystander? (Rev: BL 9/1/99; BR 9–10/99) [304.6]

4580 Hamanaka, Sheila, ed. *On the Wings of Peace* (6–12). Illus. 1995, Clarion $21.95 (0-395-72619-0). Sixty authors and illustrators donated their talents to produce this mature picture book on war and its effects, particularly on children. (Rev: BL 1/1–15/96; SLJ 10/95) [080]

4581 Kronenwetter, Michael. *Covert Action* (9–12). 1991, Watts LB $24.00 (0-531-13018-5). An overview of the history and impact of covert activity by the U.S. government from Washington to Reagan, with material on modern-day operations in places like Afghanistan, Guatemala, and Iran. (Rev: BL 3/1/91; SLJ 5/91) [327.12]

4582 Landau, Elaine. *Big Brother Is Watching: Secret Police and Intelligence Services* (7–12). 1992, Walker LB $15.85 (0-8027-8161-6). Describes the activities and methods of intelligence and police services in several Western and former Eastern-bloc nations, including the KGB, the Mossad, the CIA, and Honduran death squads. (Rev: BL 6/1/92; SLJ 8/92) [363.2]

4583 Leone, Bruno, ed. *Internationalism: Opposing Viewpoints*. Rev. ed. (9–12). Illus. (Opposing Viewpoints) 1986, Greenhaven $26.20 (0-89908-383-8); paper $16.20 (0-89908-358-7). The original sources in this volume explore conflicting viewpoints on parochial versus global interests and how they can or cannot be reconciled. (Rev: BL 8/86; SLJ 10/86) [341.2]

4584 Leone, Bruno, ed. *Nationalism: Opposing Viewpoints*. Rev. ed. (9–12). Illus. 1986, Greenhaven LB $26.20 (0-89908-387-0); paper $16.20 (0-89908-362-5). A compendium of opinions on the beneficial and harmful aspects of nationalism. (Rev: BL 7/86; SLJ 10/86) [320]

4585 Loescher, Gil, and Ann D. Loescher. *The Global Refugee Crisis* (7–12). (Contemporary World Issues) 1995, ABC-CLIO LB $39.50 (0-87436-753-0). This volume introduces the problem of refugees and discusses how the United States and the international community have dealt with it. (Rev: BR 9–10/96; SLJ 1/96) [341.4]

4586 Ousseimi, Maria. *Caught in the Crossfire: Growing Up in a War Zone* (6–10). 1995, Walker LB $20.85 (0-8027-8364-3). Examines the effects of violence on children and how violence changes children's perception of the world. (Rev: BL 9/1/95; SLJ 9/95; VOYA 12/95) [305.23]

4587 Polesetsky, Matthew, ed. *The New World Order* (7–12). (Opposing Viewpoints) 1991, Greenhaven LB $26.20 (0-89908-183-5); paper $16.20 (0-89908-158-4). A collection of documents exploring what the next new world order might be and the part the United States could play in it. (Rev: BL 10/1/91; SLJ 12/91) [327.09]

4588 Roleff, Tamara L., ed. *War* (8–12). (Opposing Viewpoints) 1999, Greenhaven LB $21.96 (0-7377-0061-0); paper $17.45 (0-7377-0060-2). An anthology of varying viewpoints on topics related to the causes and prevention of war, international intervention, and the role of the U.S. as a peace broker. (Rev: BL 3/15/99) [341.6]

4589 Winters, Paul A., ed. *Interventionism* (7–12). (Current Controversies) 1995, Greenhaven LB $26.20 (1-56510-233-9). Various kinds of international intervention like military, trade, economic sanctions, and humanitarian aid are explored in this collection of documents. (Rev: BL 6/1–15/95) [341.5]

United States Government and Institutions

General and Miscellaneous

4590 Clucas, Richard A. *Encyclopedia of American Political Reform* (9–12). 1996, ABC-CLIO LB $60.00 (0-87436-855-3). From "Abscam" to "zero-based budgeting," this work identifies and gives background information on a variety of terms, places, and people connected with American political reform. (Rev: BR 5–6/97; SLJ 5/97) [336.73]

4591 Kronenwetter, Michael. *How Democratic Is the United States?* (7–12). (Democracy in Action) 1994, Watts LB $24.00 (0-531-11155-5). Presents the problems of politics and government in the United States and discusses proposals for change. (Rev: BL 11/15/94; SLJ 1/95) [324.6]

4592 Nardo, Don. *Democracy* (6–8). Illus. (Overview) 1994, Lucent LB $22.45 (1-56006-147-2). This book explains the basic principles of government by and for the people, its evolution through history, and its status in the world today. (Rev: BL 7/94) [321.8]

4593 Weizmann, Daniel. *Take a Stand!* (5–8). Illus. 1996, Price Stern Sloan $6.95 (0-8431-7997-X). This book introduces and describes American government and tells how young people can get involved through grassroots activities, letter writing, or volunteering, with an emphasis on environmental and human-care issues. (Rev: SLJ 12/96) [324]

The Constitution

4594 Banfield, Susan. *The Fifteenth Amendment: African-American Men's Right to Vote* (7–12). Illus. (Constitution) 1998, Enslow LB $19.95 (0-7660-1033-3). This is the stormy history of the constitutional amendment passed during Reconstruction that barred states from denying voting rights to black males. (Rev: BL 9/1/98) [324.6 2 08996073]

4595 Bartholomew, Paul C., and Joseph F. Menez. *Summaries of Leading Cases on the Constitution* (10–12). 1991, Littlefield Adams paper $21.95 (0-8226-3008-7). This volume summarizes the cases involving constitutional law that have come before the Supreme Court. [342]

4596 Bjornlund, Lydia. *The U.S. Constitution* (8–12). Illus. (Words That Changed History) 1999, Lucent LB $18.96 (1-56006-486-2). Topics covered in this volume include the need for the Constitution, factors considered in deciding on the structure of the government, important figures in its history, controversies and compromises, amendments, and an evaluation of its success. (Rev: BL 6/1–15/99; SLJ 8/99) [342.73]

4597 Collier, Christopher, and James L. Collier. *Creating the Constitution, 1787* (5–8). Illus. (Drama of American History) 1998, Marshall Cavendish LB $29.93 (0-7614-0776-6). This history of the U. S. Constitution describes the background and importance of the document and the compromises made to win ratification. (Rev: BL 2/15/99) [342.73 029]

4598 Dudley, William, ed. *The Bill of Rights* (9–12). (Opposing Viewpoints) 1994, Greenhaven LB $21.96 (1-56510-088-3). Differing views on various civil rights issues arising from contemporary interpretations of constitutional intent. (Rev: BL 3/1/94) [342.73]

4599 Dudley, William, ed. *The Creation of the Constitution* (9–12). (Opposing Viewpoints in American History) 1995, Greenhaven paper $20.25 (1-56510-220-7). An in-depth look at the controversies surrounding the creation and ratification of the U.S. Constitution. (Rev: BL 7/95; SLJ 1/95) [342.73]

4600 Farish, Leah. *The First Amendment: Freedom of Speech, Religion, and the Press* (6–9). Illus. 1998, Enslow LB $19.95 (0-89490-897-9). Using many actual cases as examples, the author explores the complexities of the First Amendment to the Constitution, which guarantees basic freedoms. (Rev: BL 3/15/98; BR 9–10/98; SLJ 6/98) [342.73]

4601 Feinberg, Barbara S. *Constitutional Amendments* (5–8). (Inside Government) 1996, Twenty-First Century LB $15.98 (0-8050-4619-4). After presenting a brief history of the Constitution, this work examines the Bill of Rights and then covers the remaining amendments in chapters arranged by topic. (Rev: SLJ 12/96) [342.73]

4602 Gay, Kathlyn. *Church and State: Government and Religion in the United States* (9–12). 1992, Millbrook LB $23.90 (1-56294-063-5). Explores the legal, political, and social questions surrounding the doctrine of separation of church and state, using actual court cases. (Rev: BL 9/1/92; SLJ 10/92) [322]

4603 Gerberg, Mort. *The U.S. Constitution for Everyone* (8–12). Illus. 1987, Putnam paper $6.95 (0-399-51305-1). The text of the Constitution and amendments is analyzed with many interesting asides and background information. (Rev: BL 5/1/87) [342.73]

4604 Hanson, Freya Ottem. *The Second Amendment: The Right to Own Guns* (6–8). (The Constitution) 1998, Enslow LB $19.95 (0-89490-925-8). Using historical background material, case studies, legal decisions, and statistics, the author presents a balanced account of the controversy surrounding the owning of arms and the demand for gun control. (Rev: BR 11–12/98; SLJ 12/98) [347]

4605 Judson, Karen. *The Constitution of the United States* (7–10). (American Government in Action)

1996, Enslow LB $19.95 (0-89490-586-4). This book focuses on the historical background of the constitutional convention and the issues that were debated, with less information on the constitution's actual content. (Rev: SLJ 5/96) [342.73]

4606 Leinwand, Gerald. *Do We Need a New Constitution?* (7–12). (Democracy in Action) 1994, Watts LB $24.00 (0-531-11127-X). Discusses whether or not the U.S. Constitution is adequate to cope with problems unforeseen by the nation's founders. (Rev: BL 9/15/94; SLJ 9/94; VOYA 12/94) [342.73]

4607 Leone, Bruno, ed. *Free Speech* (9–12). (Current Controversies) 1994, Greenhaven LB $17.95 (1-56510-078-6); paper $16.20 (1-56510-077-8). Places current censorship battles in a historical context. (Rev: BL 4/15/94; SLJ 6/94) [323.44]

4608 Lucas, Eileen. *The Eighteenth & Twenty-First Amendments: Alcohol, Prohibition, & Repeal* (7–12). Illus. (Constitution) 1998, Enslow LB $19.95 (0-89490-926-6). An account of the circumstances that led to the passage of Prohibition, its effects, and later repeal. (Rev: BL 9/1/98) [344.73 0541]

4609 Morin, Isobel V. *Our Changing Constitution: How and Why We Have Amended It* (9–12). Illus. 1998, Millbrook LB $22.90 (0-7613-0222-0). After historical background on the U.S. Constitution and the provisions for revising it, each of the amendments is discussed, including the historical events and constitutional and legal arguments surrounding each, how each was passed, and their impact. (Rev: VOYA 8/98) [347]

4610 Nardo, Don. *The Bill of Rights* (7–12). Illus. (Opposing Viewpoints Digests) 1997, Greenhaven paper $13.70 (1-56510-740-3). This volume explores controversies surrounding the Bill of Rights, among them what should and should not be included, and the new challenges to this document. (Rev: BL 3/1/98) [342.73]

4611 Pascoe, Elaine. *Freedom of Expression: The Right to Speak Out in America* (7–10). 1992, Millbrook LB $23.90 (1-56294-255-7). A concise presentation of the debate over flag burning, Nazi marches, "hate speech," and other free speech issues. (Rev: BL 11/15/92; SLJ 12/92) [342.73]

4612 Schleichert, Elizabeth. *The Thirteenth Amendment: Ending Slavery* (8–10). 1998, Enslow LB $19.95 (0-89490-923-1). The stormy history of this constitutional amendment that ended slavery and fundamentally changed American society. (Rev: BL 8/98; BR 11–12/98; SLJ 1/99) [342.73]

4613 Wetterer, Charles M. *The Fourth Amendment: Search and Seizure* (8–10). 1998, Enslow LB $19.95 (0-89490-924-X). Though enacted early in this country's history, this amendment on privacy has continued to have an important impact throughout the years. (Rev: BL 8/98) [342.73]

The Presidency

4614 Aaseng, Nathan. *You Are the President* (7–10). 1994, Oliver Pr. LB $18.95 (1-881508-10-2). Devotes one chapter each to a crisis faced by 8 presidents in this century, among them Theodore Roosevelt, Eisenhower, and Nixon. (Rev: BL 4/1/94; SLJ 7/94; VOYA 8/94) [973.9]

4615 Aaseng, Nathan. *You Are the President II: 1800–1899* (7–10). Illus. (Great Decisions) 1994, Oliver Pr. LB $18.95 (1-881508-15-3). This work discusses the powers of the presidency during the 19th century and the major decisions made by presidents during that time. (Rev: BL 11/15/94; SLJ 12/94) [973.5]

4616 Bernstein, Richard B., and Jerome Agel. *The Presidency* (8–12). Illus. 1989, Walker LB $13.85 (0-8027-6831-8). A basic history of this institution with some biographical information and a final section that explores the advisability of concentrating such power in one office. (Rev: BL 5/1/89; BR 3–4/89; SLJ 1/89; VOYA 4/89) [353.03]

4617 Black, Christine M. *The Pursuit of the Presidency: '92 and Beyond* (7–12). 1993, Oryx paper $29.00 (0-89774-845-X). Using the presidential campaign of 1992, the author examines the inner workings of a political campaign and how campaigns relate to actual governing. (Rev: BL 4/15/94) [324.973]

4618 Graff, Henry F., ed. *The Presidents: A Reference History*. 2nd. ed. (10–12). 1996, Scribners $173.75 (0-684-80471-9). Each president is introduced by a different presidential scholar and material is given on each administration. (Rev: SLJ 5/97) [353.03]

4619 Judson, Karen. *The Presidency of the United States* (7–10). (American Government in Action) 1996, Enslow LB $19.95 (0-89490-585-6). This introduction to the American presidency includes material on the roles of the president, the constitutional basis of the office, the operations of the White House, and the organization of the executive branch. (Rev: SLJ 5/96) [353.03]

4620 Lindop, Edmund. *Presidents by Accident* (7–12). 1991, Watts LB $24.00 (0-531-11059-1). This collective biography focuses on the 9 men who "accidentally" assumed the U.S. presidency, and presents an overview of the status of the vice-presidency. (Rev: BL 9/1/91; SLJ 11/91) [973]

4621 Morin, Isobel V. *Impeaching the President* (8–12). 1996, Millbrook LB $22.40 (1-56294-668-4). This book, written before the Clinton impeachment, explains what impeachment is, its processes, and its role in American history. (Rev: BR 9–10/96; SLJ 6/96; VOYA 10/96) [336.73]

4622 Nardo, Don. *The U.S. Presidency* (6–8). (Overview) 1995, Lucent LB $22.45 (1-56006-157-X). This book explores the events that shaped the presidency and the changing views of the president's role in legislative affairs, foreign policy, war, and the appointment process. (Rev: BL 7/95) [353.03]

4623 Nelson, W. Dale. *Who Speaks for the President? The White House Press Secretary from Cleveland to Clinton* (10–12). 1998, Syracuse Univ. Pr. $29.95 (0-8156-0514-5). In 1893, President Grover Cleveland appointed a confidential stenographer. This account traces the evolution of the White House press secretary to what is today, with information on the people, the powers, and the relationships connected with the position. (Rev: BL 6/1–15/98; SLJ 2/99) [324]

4624 Rubel, David. *Scholastic Encyclopedia of the Presidents and Their Times*. rev. ed. (4–9). 1997, Scholastic $17.95 (0-590-49366-3). This book examines the political and personal lives of the U.S. presidents, from Washington up to the beginning of Clinton's second term, and the U.S. and worldwide events, historical movements, and personalities that shaped their administrations. (Rev: BR 9–10/97; SLJ 5/97) [353.03]

Federal Government, Its Agencies, and Public Administration

4625 Aaseng, Nathan. *You Are the Senator* (7–10). Illus. (Great Decisions) 1997, Oliver Pr. LB $18.95 (1-881508-36-6). This book describes the duties and responsibilities of a U.S. senator and the nature of the decisions that senators make. (Rev: BL 4/15/97; BR 11–12/97; SLJ 8/97; VOYA 8/97) [328.73]

4626 Bernstein, Richard B., and Jerome Agel. *The Congress* (7–12). Illus. 1989, Walker LB $13.85 (0-8027-6833-4). An introduction to this branch of the government with material arranged chronologically. Some coverage is given to recent scandals and recent decline in prestige. (Rev: BL 5/1/89; SLJ 1/89; VOYA 4/89) [328.73]

4627 Dolan, Edward F., and Margaret M. Scariano. *Shaping U.S. Foreign Poicy: Profiles of Twelve Secretaries of State* (7–12). Illus. (Democracy in Action) 1996, Watts LB $22.00 (0-531-112640-0). This book tells about 5 secretaries of state who made major acquisitions of land, and 7 who dealt with the search for peace or with the Cold War. (Rev: BL 6/1–15/96; SLJ 7/96) [327.73]

4628 Duvall, Jill D. *Congressional Committees* (10–12). 1997, Watts LB $24.00 (0-531-11343-4). This work presents a vast amount of information on congressional committees, their types, functions, and their changing roles. (Rev: BR 5–6/98; SLJ 2/98) [336.73]

4629 Feinberg, Barbara S. *Next in Line: The American Vice Presidency* (7–12). Illus. (Democracy in Action) 1996, Watts LB $24.00 (0-531-11283-7). This account presents a careful historical and political analysis of the vice presidency, important individuals who held the office, and its possible future. (Rev: BL 11/15/96; SLJ 2/97) [353.03]

4630 Greenberg, Ellen. *The House and Senate Explained* (10–12). 1996, Norton $19.95 (0-393-03984-6); paper $12.00 (0-393-31496-0). A clear, well-organized guide to the organization, powers, and composition of the legislative branch of our government. (Rev: SLJ 4/97) [328.73]

4631 Lindop, Edmund. *Presidents versus Congress: Conflict and Compromise* (7–12). Illus. (Democracy in Action) 1994, Watts LB $24.00 (0-531-11165-2). The story of the highly charged relationship between the executive and legislative branches, the system of checks and balances, and ways to avoid gridlock. (Rev: BL 6/1–15/94; SLJ 7/94) [353.03]

4632 Nardo, Don. *The U.S. Congress* (6–8). Illus. (Overview) 1994, Lucent LB $22.45 (1-56006-155-3). A clearly written introduction to the composition, responsibilities, and problems of Congress. (Rev: BL 6/1–15/94) [328.73]

4633 Pollack, Jill S. *Women on the Hill: A History of Women in Congress* (7–12). Illus. (Women Then—Women Now) 1996, Watts LB $25.00 (0-531-11306-X). As well as explaining how Congress works, this book presents brief biographies of almost 40 women who have served in Congress, past and present. (Rev: BL 3/15/97; SLJ 1/97; VOYA 2/97) [328.73]

4634 Ritchie, Donald A. *The Young Oxford Companion to the Congress of the United States* (7–12). 1993, Oxford $62.50 (0-19-507777-6). Selected biographies of members of Congress and concise articles on events, documents, policies, and procedures are covered through 1992. (Rev: BL 3/15/94) [328.73]

4635 Sandak, Cass R. *Congressional Committees* (7–9). (Inside Government) 1995, Twenty-First Century LB $18.90 (0-8050-3425-0). An overview of how congressional committees came into existence and their role, including how they control legislation. (Rev: BL 12/15/95; SLJ 1/96) [336.73]

4636 Sandak, Cass R. *Lobbying* (7–9). (Inside Government) 1995, Twenty-First Century LB $18.90 (0-8050-3424-2). A look at how legislation is influenced, including a brief history of lobbies and descriptions of domestic and foreign public interest groups. (Rev: BL 12/15/95; SLJ 1/96) [328.73]

4637 Sandak, Cass R. *The National Debt* (5–8). (Inside Government) 1996, Twenty-First Century LB $18.90 (0-8050-3423-4). The origins and causes of the national debt are covered, with options for the future. (Rev: BL 5/15/96; BR 9–10/96; SLJ 8/96) [336.3]

State and Municipal Governments and Agencies

4638 Conway, W. Fred. *Firefighting Lore: Strange but True Stories from Firefighting History* (9–12). 1993, Fire Buff House paper $9.95 (0-925165-14-X). Written by a former fire chief, this history of firefighting in the United States provides short accounts of famous and lesser-known major fires. (Rev: BL 1/1/94) [363.378]

4639 Gorrell, Gena K. *Catching Fire: The Story of Firefighting* (7–10). 1999, Tundra paper $16.95 (0-88776-430-4). This is a history of firefighting, from the bucket brigades of yesterday to the sophisticated equipment of today, with related information on how fires burn, important fires in history, equipment, firefighting tactics, forms of arson, wildfires, and more. (Rev: BL 6/1–15/99; SLJ 6/99) [363.3]

4640 Levinson, Isabel Simone. *Gibbons v. Ogden: Controlling Trade between States* (8–10). (Landmark Supreme Court Cases) 1999, Enslow $19.95 (0-7660-1086-4). States' rights and autonomy were the subject of this important Supreme Court case that focused on trade between the states. (Rev: BL 8/99) [353]

4641 Ryan, Bernard. *Serving with Police, Fire, and EMS* (7–12). (Community Service for Teens) 1998, Ferguson LB $15.95 (0-89434-232-0). This work explains how teens can play an active and productive role in police, fire, and allied community agencies. (Rev: BL 9/15/98; BR 11–12/98; SLJ 2/99) [361.8]

Libraries and Other Educational Institutions

4642 Thomson, Peggy, and Barbara Moore. *The Nine-Ton Cat: Behind the Scenes at an Art Museum* (6–10). 1997, Houghton $21.95 (0-395-82655-1); paper $14.95 (0-395-82683-7). Using a day's activities at the National Gallery of Art in Washington as a framework, this book describes in photos and text the people and processes needed to make an art museum operate. (Rev: BL 3/15/97; SLJ 4/97) [069]

The Law and the Courts

4643 Aaseng, Nathan. *The O. J. Simpson Trial: What It Shows Us about Our Legal System* (6–9). 1996, Walker LB $16.85 (0-8027-8405-4). The author uses the Simpson trial to explain such aspects of the American judicial system as investigative techniques, the grand jury, defense, prosecution, the

media's role, and emerging technologies. (Rev: BL 5/1/96; SLJ 4/96) [345.73]

4644 Aaseng, Nathan. *You Are the Juror* (6–10). 1997, Oliver Pr. LB $18.95 (1-881508-40-4). The author recreates 8 famous criminal trials of the 20th century, including the Lindbergh kidnapping case, the Patty Hearst and O. J. Simpson trials, and the Ford Pinto case, and asks the reader to become a jury member and make a decision. (Rev: SLJ 1/98) [347.73]

4645 Aaseng, Nathan. *You Are the Supreme Court Justice* (7–10). Illus. (Great Decisions) 1994, Oliver Pr. LB $23.75 (1-881508-14-5). A description of how the Supreme Court works and the decisions and responsibilities involved in being a Justice. (Rev: BL 11/15/94; SLJ 12/94) [347.73]

4646 Anderson, Kelly C. *Police Brutality* (6–10). (Overview) 1995, Lucent $22.45 (1-56006-164-2). A discussion of the reasons for police behavior, the stress and danger of the job and the possible misuse of power. (Rev: BL 4/15/95; SLJ 3/95) [363.2]

4647 Bernstein, Richard B., and Jerome Agel. *The Supreme Court* (8–12). Illus. 1989, Walker LB $13.85 (0-8027-6835-0). An account that gives a history of the Supreme Court, details on landmark cases, and an outline of how it operates today. (Rev: BL 5/1/89; BR 3–4/89; SLJ 1/89; VOYA 4/89) [347]

4648 Biskup, Michael D., ed. *Criminal Justice* (9–12). (Opposing Viewpoints) 1993, Greenhaven LB $19.95 (0-89908-624-1); paper $16.20 (0-89908-623-3). A collection of articles that present opposing viewpoints on the criminal justice system. (Rev: BL 6/1–15/93) [364.098]

4649 Calabro, Marian. *Great Courtroom Lawyers: Fighting the Cases That Made History* (6–9). 1996, Facts on File $19.95 (0-8160-3323-4). This book provides profiles of 9 important lawyers, including Clarence Darrow, Thurgood Marshall, and William Kunstler, and presents highlights of such important cases as Roe v. Wade and the O. J. Simpson trial. (Rev: BL 10/15/96; VOYA 6/97) [349.73]

4650 Carrel, Annette. *It's the Law! A Young Person's Guide to Our Legal System* (8–12). 1994, Volcano Pr. paper $12.95 (1-884244-01-7). The book's goal is voter responsibility through understanding of the laws, how they developed, and how they can be changed. (Rev: BL 2/15/95; VOYA 12/95) [349.73]

4651 Chadwick, Bruce. *Infamous Trials* (6–9). Illus. (Crime, Justice, and Punishment) 1997, Chelsea LB $19.95 (0-7910-4293-6). This book highlights 8 cases in the history of American justice, from the Salem witchcraft trials to the Chicago Seven, including Benedict Arnold's court-martial, the Scopes "monkey trial," and the Scottsboro boys. (Rev: BL 9/1/97; BR 11–12/97; SLJ 10/97) [345.73]

4652 Ciment, James. *Law and Order* (6–9). (Life in America 100 Years Ago) 1995, Chelsea LB $19.95 (0-7910-2843-7). An examination of how the rule of law was established in the U.S. and how basic institutions involving the courts, law enforcement officials, and the legal profession evolved. (Rev: BL 2/1/96) [349.73]

4653 DeVillers, David. *Marbury v. Madison: Powers of the Supreme Court* (6–10). (Landmark Supreme Court Cases) 1998, Enslow LB $19.95 (0-89490-967-3). The steps, arguments, and personalities in this early court case that helped define the powers of the Supreme Court. (Rev: BL 2/15/98; SLJ 6/98) [3437]

4654 Dudley, Mark E. *Brown v. Board of Education (1954)* (6–10). Illus. (Supreme Court Decisions) 1994, Twenty-First Century LB $18.90 (0-8050-3657-1). Discusses the issues, the players, and the arguments involved in this important case that successfully challenged school segregation. (Rev: BL 12/15/94; SLJ 1/95) [344.73]

4655 Dudley, Mark E. *Engel v. Vitale (1962): Religion and the Schools* (5–9). (Supreme Court Decisions) 1995, Twenty-First Century LB $18.90 (0-8050-3916-3). The story of the Supreme Court case on school prayer that originated with two Jewish youngsters who objected to being forced to pray every morning in a New York City school. (Rev: BL 11/15/95; SLJ 1/96; VOYA 4/96) [347]

4656 Dudley, Mark E. *United States v. Nixon (1974)* (6–10). Illus. (Supreme Court Decisions) 1994, Twenty-First Century LB $18.90 (0-8050-3658-X). This landmark Supreme Court case concerning the definition of presidential powers is reported on in a step-by-step analysis of the arguments in the Watergate case. (Rev: BL 12/15/94; SLJ 2/95) [342.73]

4657 Ehrenfeld, Norbert, and Lawrence Treat. *You're the Jury: Solve Twelve Real-Life Court Cases along with the Juries Who Decided Them* (9–12). 1992, Holt paper $9.95 (0-8050-1951-0). Presents the testimony and evidence of 12 actual court cases, with analysis, pertinent questions, and the courtroom verdict. (Rev: BL 7/92; SLJ 9/92) [347.73]

4658 Galang, M. Evelina. *Her Wild American Self* (10–12). 1996, Coffee House Pr. paper $12.95 (1-56689-040-3). In a series of essays, the author tells of her life as a Filipino American woman, her cultural background, and her assimilation into American life. (Rev: SLJ 11/96) [304]

4659 Garza, Hedda. *Barred from the Bar: A History of Women and the Legal Profession* (10–12). (Women Then—Women Now) 1996, Watts LB $25.00 (0-531-11265-9). A well-researched history of how women won the right to practice law as well as rights in other fields, weaving in the stories of several remarkable women from the mid-19th century to the present whose determination has slowly rolled back legal and social obstacles to equality. An entire chapter highlights the double discrimination experienced by women of color. (Rev: BR 11–12/96; SLJ 7/96; VOYA 8/96) [346]

4660 Gold, Susan D. *Miranda v. Arizona (1966)* (6–10). (Supreme Court Decisions) 1995, Twenty-First Century LB $18.90 (0-8050-3915-5). This book describes the court case that defined the rights of suspects, with good historical background and a discussion of its impact through 1994. (Rev: BL 6/1–15/95; SLJ 8/95) [345.73]

4661 Grabowski, John. *The Death Penalty* (7–10). 1999, Lucent LB $17.96 (0-56006-371-8). Does the death penalty deter crime? Can the death penalty be meted out fairly and without bias? These and other questions are discussed in this overview of this controversial subject. (Rev: BL 8/99) [345]

4662 Haas, Carol. *Engel v. Vitale: Separation of Church and State* (6–10). 1994, Enslow LB $19.95 (0-89490-461-2). A discussion of the arguments presented by both sides in this landmark Supreme Court case concerning the separation of church and state as it applies to religion in public schools. (Rev: BL 11/15/94; VOYA 12/94) [344.73]

4663 Harrington, Mon. *Women Lawyers: Rewriting the Rules* (9–12). 1994, Knopf $24.00 (0-394-58025-7). Through interviews with female graduates of Harvard Law School, the author paints a disturbing picture of sexism in the legal profession and offers practical solutions. (Rev: BL 1/15/94*) [349.73]

4664 Harrison, Maureen, and Steve Gilbert, eds. *Landmark Decisions of the United States Supreme Court II* (9–12). 1992, Excellent Books paper $20.25 (0-9628014-2-9). Synopses of far-reaching Supreme Court rulings, including decisions on slavery, women's suffrage, Bible reading in public schools, book banning, and the death penalty. (Rev: BL 1/1/92) [347]

4665 Henson, Burt, and Ross R. Olney. *Furman v. Georgia: The Constitution and the Death Penalty* (7–10). (Historic Supreme Court Cases) 1996, Watts LB $25.00 (0-531-11285-3). In this 1972 case, the Supreme Court ruled that the imposition of the death penalty as then applied was unconstitutional. This account gives the legal background, a history of capital punishment, and pros and cons of the death penalty. (Rev: SLJ 4/97) [345]

4666 Herda, D. J. *Furman v. Georgia: The Death Penalty Case* (6–10). (Landmark Supreme Court Cases) 1994, Enslow LB $19.95 (0-89490-489-2). Summarizes the historical background of this case, the case itself, and the impact it has had. (Rev: BL 11/15/94; SLJ 11/94) [345.73]

4667 Herda, D. J. *New York Times v. United States: National Security and Censorship* (6–10). Illus.

(Landmark Supreme Court Cases) 1994, Enslow LB $19.95 (0-89490-490-6). This exciting, controversial Supreme Court case involved the Pentagon Papers and helped define freedom of the press when it conflicts with what may be considered national security. (Rev: BL 11/15/94; SLJ 1/95) [342.73]

4668 Herda, D. J. *Roe v. Wade: The Abortion Question* (6–10). Illus. (Landmark Supreme Court Cases) 1994, Enslow LB $19.95 (0-89490-459-0). This book describes the arguments on both sides of the abortion debate, how the justices of the Supreme Court reacted, their decision, and its consequences. (Rev: BL 6/1–15/94; SLJ 7/94; VOYA 8/94) [344.73]

4669 Hogrogian, John. *Miranda v. Arizona: The Rights of the Accused* (9–12). (Famous Trials) 1999, Lucent $22.45 (1-56006-471-4). This groundbreaking Supreme Court case changed criminal justice in the United States by defining the rights of accused criminals. (Rev: BL 9/15/99) [347]

4670 Horne, Gerald. *Powell vs. Alabama: The Scottsboro Boys & American Justice* (9–12). (Historic Supreme Court Cases) 1997, Watts LB $25.00 (0-531-11314-0). The right to effective counsel in court cases was established by this Supreme Court decision that came after the tragic miscarriage of justice involving the Scottsboro boys. (Rev: BL 4/15/97; SLJ 6/97) [345.73]

4671 Karson, Jill, ed. *Criminal Justice* (8–12). (Opposing Viewpoints) 1998, Greenhaven LB $21.96 (1-56510-795-0); paper $20.25 (1-56510-794-2). This anthology of opinions explores criminal justice topics, such as rights of the accused, reform, sentencing laws, and the relationship between the legal and law enforcement systems. (Rev: BL 6/1–15/98) [345]

4672 Kraft, Betsy H. *Sensational Trials of the 20th Century* (6–10). Illus. 1998, Scholastic $16.95 (0-590-37205-X). This book profiles 8 important American trials including Sacco and Vanzetti, the Rosenbergs, Scopes, Watergate, O. J. Simpson, and John Hinckley. (Rev: BL 3/1/99; SLJ 11/98; VOYA 6/99) [347.73]

4673 Kronenwetter, Michael. *The Supreme Court of the United States* (7–10). (American Government in Action) 1996, Enslow LB $19.95 (0-89490-536-8). After presenting an example of the power of the Supreme Court, the author describes the judicial system and a brief history of the court, discusses how it operates and the increasingly political nature of appointments and decisions, and details some of its most significant decisions. (Rev: SLJ 5/96) [347]

4674 Paddock, Lisa. *Facts About the Supreme Court of the United States* (8–12). 1996, H.W. Wilson $65.00 (0-8242-0896-X). A one-stop reference source for information about the Supreme Court,

from individual justices to the court's history and important cases. (Rev: VOYA 12/96) [347]

4675 Pascoe, Elaine. *America's Courts on Trial: Questioning Our Legal System* (6–9). Illus. (Issue and Debate) 1997, Millbrook LB $21.90 (0-7613-0104-6). A concise history of the origins, evolution, and current status of the American legal system, with explanations of such terms as jury trial, habeas corpus, and due process. (Rev: BL 3/15/98; BR 3–4/98; SLJ 3/98; VOYA 4/98) [347.73]

4676 Persico, Deborah A. *Mapp vs. Ohio: Evidence & Search Warrants* (6–10). Illus. (Landmark Supreme Court Cases) 1997, Enslow LB $19.95 (0-89490-857-X). A step-by-step account of the Supreme Court decision that established a citizen's rights concerning search warrants and the collection of evidence. (Rev: BL 4/15/97; SLJ 6/97) [345.73]

4677 Persico, Deborah A. *New Jersey v. T.L.O.: Drug Searches in Schools* (7–12). Illus. (Landmark Supreme Court Cases) 1998, Enslow LB $19.95 (0-89490-969-X). This Supreme Court case lasted 5 years and explored the rights of a student, identified as T.L.O., whose handbag was searched by a school administrator who found marijuana and articles that indicated the student was selling drugs. (Rev: BL 8/98; SLJ 8/98; VOYA 2/99) [345.73]

4678 Reichel, Philip, ed. *Criminal Justice* (10–12). (Perspectives) 1998, Greenhaven LB $29.96 (1-56510-901-5); paper $26.50 (1-56510-900-7). Essays explore aspects of the criminal justice system, including victims' rights, causes of crime, law enforcement, the courts, and criminal proceedings. (Rev: BL 7/98) [364]

4679 Riley, Gail B. *Miranda v. Arizona: Rights of the Accused* (6–10). Illus. 1994, Enslow LB $18.95 (0-89490-404-X). This account analyzes the Supreme Court case that defined the rights of an accused person based on what became known as Miranda rights. (Rev: BL 11/15/94) [345.73]

4680 Roleff, Tamara L., ed. *The Legal System* (8–12). (Opposing Viewpoints) 1996, Greenhaven LB $21.96 (1-56510-405-6); paper $16.20 (1-56510-404-8). This collection of original sources tackles such questions as: Does the legal system work? Does it need reforms? Is there too much litigation in this country? Is the criminal justice system fair? and How do the media affect the legal system? (Rev: BL 7/96) [347.73]

4681 Roleff, Tamara L., ed. *Police Brutality* (9–12). (Current Controversies) 1998, Greenhaven LB $21.96 (0-7377-0013-0); paper $20.25 (0-7377-0012-2). Topics debated in this anthology include the extent of police brutality, its causes, its effects on society, and how it can be reduced. (Rev: BL 2/1/99) [363.2 32]

4682 Stevens, Leonard A. *The Case of Roe v. Wade* (8–12). 1996, Putnam $16.99 (0-399-22812-8). Complete with fascinating details and numerous quotes, this account gives an objective account of this landmark court case and its ramifications. (Rev: BL 10/1/96*; BR 11–12/96; SLJ 1/97; VOYA 12/96) [344.73]

4683 Swisher, Carl Brent. *Historic Decisions of the Supreme Court*. 2nd ed. (10–12). 1979, Krieger paper $11.50 (0-88275-813-6). In chronological order, the decisions of the Supreme Court are introduced with appropriate background material. [342]

4684 Tompkins, Nancy. *Roe v. Wade: The Fight over Life and Liberty* (7–12). Illus. (Supreme Court Cases) 1996, Watts LB $25.00 (0-531-11286-1). This account of the landmark Supreme Court case focuses on the case itself and the controversy that the decision has caused. (Rev: BL 2/1/97; SLJ 2/97) [344.73]

4685 Trespacz, Karen L. *Ferrell v. Dallas I. S. D.* (6–10). (Landmark Supreme Court Cases) 1998, Enslow LB $19.95 (0-7660-1054-6). The dramatic story of the school district case that was adjudicated by the Supreme Court. (Rev: BL 8/98; BR 11–12/98; SLJ 1/99; VOYA 2/99) [347]

4686 Wice, Paul B. *Miranda v. Arizona* (7–12). (Historic Supreme Court Cases) 1996, Watts LB $25.00 (0-531-11250-0). A reconstruction of the important Supreme Court case in which a confession was judged invalid because the suspect had not been informed of his rights. (Rev: SLJ 9/96) [347]

4687 Williams, Mary E., ed. *The Jury System* (8–12). (At Issue) 1996, Greenhaven paper $15.75 (1-56510-539-7). This book presents various aspects of the jury system, controversies surrounding it, and possible changes that would affect its effectiveness. (Rev: BL 5/15/97; SLJ 7/97) [347]

Politics

GENERAL AND MISCELLANEOUS

4688 Archer, Jules. *Special Interests: How Lobbyists Influence Legislation* (7–12). Illus. 1997, Millbrook LB $23.90 (0-7613-0060-0). This timely account looks at special interest groups, why lobbyists have so much power, how lobbies were created, and the role they play in influencing policy. (Rev: BL 12/15/97; BR 3–4/98; SLJ 1/98; VOYA 2/98) [324]

4689 Cozic, Charles P., ed. *Politicians and Ethics* (7–12). (Current Controversies) 1996, Greenhaven LB $26.20 (1-56510-407-2). This collection of original sources covers various points of view concerning the behavior and ethics of politicians, the problems of scrutiny, and the degree that legal measures should be used. (Rev: BL 6/1–15/96) [172]

4690 Gay, Kathlyn. *Who's Running the Nation? How Corporate Power Threatens Democracy* (7–12). (Impact) 1998, Watts $24.00 (0-531-11489-9). In this analysis of business influence on government, the author explains in a fairly objective tone exactly how corporations use campaign contributions and lobbying to influence policies, and demonstrates how this disenfranchises ordinary citizens. (Rev: SLJ 3/99) [324.2]

4691 Kronenwetter, Michael. *Political Parties of the United States* (6–9). Illus. 1996, Enslow LB $19.95 (0-89490-537-6). A history of political parties and how they function plus how they influence every aspect of the country's political life. (Rev: BL 6/1–15/96; BR 9–10/96; SLJ 6/96) [324.273]

4692 Lindop, Edmund. *Political Parties* (5–8). (Inside Government) 1996, Twenty-First Century LB $18.90 (0-8050-4618-6). This work traces the origins of political parties and the role they play in presidential elections. (Rev: BL 9/15/96; SLJ 12/96) [324.273]

4693 Tipp, Stacey L., and Carol Wekesser, eds. *Politics in America* (5–8). (Opposing Viewpoints) 1992, Greenhaven LB $15.95 (0-89908-189-4); paper $16.20 (0-89908-164-9). Strongly differing viewpoints on politics are presented to foster critical thinking skills. (Rev: BL 5/1/92) [320.973]

4694 Winters, Paul A., ed. *The Media and Politics* (8–12). 1996, Greenhaven LB $11.95 (1-56510-383-6); paper $11.20 (1-56510-382-3). A collection of articles about the relationship between the media and politics and how messages can be influenced by the agendas of journalists, politicians, and special interest groups. (Rev: BL 3/15/96; SLJ 4/96; VOYA 8/96) [302.23]

ELECTIONS

4695 Archer, Jules. *Winners and Losers: How Elections Work in America* (7–10). Illus. 1984, Harcourt $14.95 (0-15-297945-X). The mechanics of the election process are described with emphasis on the need to participate. [324.6]

4696 Coil, Suzanne M. *Campaign Financing: Politics and the Power of Money* (7–12). 1994, Millbrook LB $23.90 (1-56294-220-4). Some shocking but well-supported facts about what it takes to run a campaign. (Rev: BL 4/15/94; SLJ 3/94; VOYA 8/94) [324.7]

4697 Cunningham, Liz. *Talking Politics: Choosing the President in the Television Age* (9–12). 1995, Praeger $19.95 (0-275-94187-6). Ten well-known media and political personalities discuss the relationship between presidential candidates and television broadcasters. (Rev: BL 4/15/95) [791.45]

4698 Majure, Janet. *Elections* (5–8). Illus. (Overview) 1996, Lucent LB $22.45 (1-56006-174-X). After a general history of elections, this account explains present-day procedures and practices. (Rev: BL 7/96; VOYA 10/96) [324.7]

4699 Melder, Keith. *Hail to the Candidate: Presidential Campaigns from Banners to Broadcasts* (9–12). 1992, Smithsonian paper $24.95 (1-56098-178-4). A look at the many components of a presidential campaign and how they help determine the course of history. (Rev: BL 5/1/92; SLJ 6/92) [324.973]

4700 Reische, Diana. *Electing a U.S. President* (7–12). 1992, Watts LB $24.00 (0-531-11043-5). A straightforward look at the presidential campaign process and the people involved in it. (Rev: BL 4/15/92; SLJ 8/92) [324.0973]

4701 Winters, Paul A., ed. *Voting Behavior* (8–12). (At Issue) 1996, Greenhaven LB $12.95 (1-56510-413-7); paper $11.20 (1-56510-412-9). Various opinions are represented on topics like citizen participation in a democracy, the role of public opinion polls and the media, and the significance of campaign politics. (Rev: BL 8/96; SLJ 8/96; VOYA 12/96) [324.973]

The Armed Forces

4702 Aaseng, Nathan. *You Are the General* (7–12). Illus. (Great Decisions) 1994, Oliver Pr. $14.95 (1-881-1508-11-0). This book deals with decisions that have to be made by members of the military, with many examples. (Rev: BL 6/1–15/94) [355]

4703 da Cruz, Daniel. *Boot: The Inside Story of How a Few Good Men Became Today's Marines* (10–12). Illus. 1987, St. Martin's paper $6.99 (0-312-90060-0). The story of a Marine boot camp platoon from induction to graduation. (Rev: BL 2/15/87) [359.9]

4704 Doherty, Kieran. *Congressional Medal of Honor Recipients* (6–9). Illus. 1998, Enslow LB $19.95 (0-7660-1026-0). This work profiles 11 winners of this prestigious medal, beginning with Jacob Parrott, who earned the first medal in 1863. (Rev: BL 3/15/98) [355.1]

4705 Ferrell, Nancy W. *The U.S. Coast Guard* (6–10). Illus. 1989, Lerner LB $23.93 (0-8225-1431-1). The account gives a history of the Coast Guard, explains its functions, and tells what life is like in it. (Rev: BL 5/1/89; SLJ 6/89) [355]

4706 Haskins, Jim. *African American Military Heroes* (7–12). (Black Stars) 1998, Wiley $19.95 (0-471-14577-7). Profiles of 33 black servicemen and servicewomen and their contributions, from the 1760s to the 1990s, are given in this book that stress-

es the struggle for equality. (Rev: BL 9/1/98; SLJ 11/98) [355.008996073]

4707 Kohlhagen, Gale Gibson, and Ellen Heinbach. *The United States Naval Academy: A Pictorial Celebration of 150 Years* (9–12). 1995, Abrams $49.95 (0-8109-3932-0). A pictorial retrospective of the United States Naval Academy. (Rev: BL 3/15/95) [359]

4708 Moran, Tom. *The U.S. Army* (5–8). (Armed Services) 1990, Lerner LB $23.93 (0-8225-1434-6). Overview of the U.S. Army's development from colonial militia to the 1989 action in Panama. (Rev: BL 1/1/91; SLJ 1/91) [335]

4709 Reef, Catherine. *Black Fighting Men: A Proud History* (4–8). Illus. (African-American Soldiers) 1994, Twenty-First Century LB $17.90 (0-8050-3106-5). A general overview of the contributions that African Americans have made in the armed services. (Rev: BL 9/15/94) [355]

4710 Robertshaw, Andrew. *A Soldier's Life: A Visual History of Soldiers Through the Ages* (4–8). 1997, Lodestar paper $16.99 (0-525-67550-7). Using color photos and interesting text, this book traces a soldier's uniform, food and supplies, and living conditions through the ages, from Roman soldiers in 50 A.D. to World War II. (Rev: BL 6/1–15/97; SLJ 6/97) [355.02]

4711 Sherrow, Victoria. *Women and the Military: An Encyclopedia* (8–12). 1996, ABC-CLIO LB $60.00 (0-87436-812-X). This alphabetically arranged work lists women in the military, places, organizations, social and legal issues, and battles. (Rev: BL 5/1/97; BR 9–10/97; SLJ 8/97) [355]

4712 Stewart, Robert. *The Brigade in Review: A Year at the U.S. Naval Academy* (9–12). 1993, Naval Institute Pr. $41.95 (1-55750-776-7). This illustrated volume covers the Annapolis year, from the introduction of the academy plebes to the senior midshipmen's graduation. (Rev: BL 2/1/94) [359]

4713 Stillwell, Paul, ed. *The Golden Thirteen: Recollections of the First Black Naval Officers* (9–12). 1993, Naval Institute Pr. $34.95 (1-55750-779-1). Oral histories of African Americans who faced prejudice and overcame limitations to become the first commissioned officers of their race in the U.S. Navy. (Rev: BL 1/15/93) [359]

4714 Stremlow, Mary V. *Coping with Sexism in the Military* (7–12). 1990, Rosen LB $17.95 (0-8239-1025-3). An analysis of the military from the perspective of the female recruit that reflects conditions in the late 1980s. (Rev: BL 2/15/91) [355]

4715 Waller, Douglas C. *The Commandos: The Inside Story of America's Secret Soldiers* (9–12). 1994, Simon & Schuster $22.50 (0-671-78717-9). This history of U.S. military special operations gives an account of the training of special forces and the SEALs and describes their activities in Panama and the Persian Gulf. (Rev: BL 1/1/94) [356]

4716 Wekesser, Carol, and Matthew Polesetsky, eds. *Women in the Military* (9–12). (Current Controversies) 1991, Greenhaven LB $26.20 (0-89908-579-2); paper $16.20 (0-89908-585-7). A look at the pros and cons of women serving in the armed forces. (Rev: BL 6/15/92; SLJ 3/92) [355.4]

4717 Worth, Richard. *Women in Combat: The Battle for Equality* (7–12). (Issues in Focus) 1999, Enslow $19.95 (0-7660-1103-8). A study of the changing role of women in the armed forces from the First World War to the Gulf War. (Rev: BL 5/1/99) [355]

Citizenship and Civil Rights

Civil and Human Rights

4718 Alderman, Ellen, and Caroline Kennedy. *The Right to Privacy* (10–12). 1995, Knopf $26.95 (0-679-41986-1). This adult look at the right to privacy features a rundown of court cases on such subjects as strip searches, right-to-die decisions, ownership of frozen embryos, televised death, searches in schools, and videotaping of sex acts without the subject's approval. (Rev: BL 10/1/95; BR 5–6/96; SLJ 5/96) [323.44]

4719 Allen, Zita. *Black Women Leaders of the Civil Rights Movement* (6–9). Illus. 1996, Watts LB $25.00 (0-531-11271-3). An overview of the civil rights movement from 1900 to 1964 that focuses on the many and varied contributions that black women made to the cause. (Rev: BL 2/15/97; SLJ 1/97) [323.3]

4720 Alonso, Karen. *Schenck v. United States: Restrictions on Free Speech* (7–10). (Landmark Supreme Court Cases) 1999, Enslow $19.95 (0-7660-1089-9). A re-creation of this landmark Supreme Court case that explored the limitations of free speech, including a follow-up on its consequences. (Rev: BL 8/99) [323.44]

4721 Arnest, Lauren Krohn. *Children, Young Adults, and the Law: A Dictionary* (8–12). 1998, ABC-CLIO LB $55.00 (0-87436-879-0). Using a dictionary arrangement, this volume contains about 200 articles on legal issues involving children and young adults, with entries on important court cases and decisions. (Rev: BL 10/15/98; SLJ 2/99; VOYA 6/99) [346.73]

4722 Bender, David, and Bruno Leone, eds. *Feminism* (7–12). (Opposing Viewpoints) 1995, Greenhaven LB $20.96 (1-56510-178-2); paper $22.00 (1-56510-179-0). Essays supporting different view-

points are presented. Topics include feminism's effects on women and society and its future and goals. (Rev: BL 7/95; SLJ 2/95) [305.42]

4723 Bradley, Catherine. *Freedom of Movement* (5–8). Illus. (What Do We Mean by Human Rights?) 1998, Watts $22.00 (0-531-14447-X). This lavishly illustrated book uses a series of double-page spreads to explore immigration, nationalism, refugees, and many seemingly unimportant personal experiences, all of which impact on one's freedom of movement. (Rev: BL 4/1/98; BR 11–12/98) [323]

4724 Brill, Marlene T. *Women for Peace* (6–10). (Women Then—Women Now) 1997, Watts LB $25.00 (0-531-11328-0). A chronicle of the involvement of women in peace movements from ancient Greece to the Vietnam War. (Rev: BL 5/15/97; SLJ 4/97; VOYA 12/97) [327.1]

4725 Bullard, Sara. *Free at Last: A History of the Civil Rights Movement and Those Who Died in the Struggle* (6–10). 1993, Oxford $40.00 (0-19-508381-4). Following an overview of the history of African Americans, an in-depth look at the civil rights movement is presented, with 40 biographies of civil rights martyrs. (Rev: BL 11/1/93; VOYA 8/93) [323.1]

4726 Carson, Clayborne, et al., eds. *The Eyes on the Prize Civil Rights Reader: Documents, Speeches, and Firsthand Accounts from the Black Freedom Struggle, 1954–1990* (9–12). 1991, Penguin paper $16.95 (0-14-015403-5). Contains much of the material that is basic to the U.S. civil rights movement, including speeches by Martin Luther King, Jr. and writings by Malcolm X. (Rev: BL 9/15/91) [973]

4727 Cary, Eve. *The Rights of Students* (6–12). (ACLU Handbooks for Young Americans) 1997, Penguin paper $8.99 (0-14-037784-0). Published with the cooperation of the American Civil Liberties Union, this book outlines the rights of young people at home, at school, and in the workplace. (Rev: BL 1/1–15/98) [344.73]

4728 *Civil Rights in America: 1500 to the Present* (9–12). 1998, Gale $125.35 (0-7876-0612-X). A well-researched book that explores historical and contemporary issues involved in civil rights, including the experiences of various ethnic, racial, cultural, and religious groups; rights that all Americans enjoy (voting and education); and major court decisions that have had an impact on civil rights. (Rev: BL 11/15/98; VOYA 2/99) [323.4]

4729 Dolan, Edward F. *Your Privacy: Protecting It in a Nosy World* (7–12). 1995, Dutton paper $14.99 (0-525-65187-X). A historical and practical look at one of our most important rights. (Rev: BL 1/1/95; SLJ 2/95) [323.44]

4730 Dudley, Mark E. *Gideon v. Wainwright (1963): Right to Counsel* (6–10). (Supreme Court Decisions) 1995, Twenty-First Century LB $18.90 (0-8050-3914-7). Reviews how the case was built, argued, and decided, and discusses its impact. (Rev: BL 6/1–15/95; SLJ 8/95) [347.3]

4731 Dudley, William, ed. *The Civil Rights Movement* (9–12). (Opposing Viewpoints) 1996, Greenhaven LB $21.96 (1-56510-369-6); paper $20.25 (1-56510-368-8). A collection of primary source documents that express a variety of views on the civil rights movement, including those of demonstrators, segregationists, movement leaders, Supreme Court justices, and journalists. (Rev: BL 6/1–15/96; SLJ 8/96) [323.1]

4732 Dunn, John M. *The Civil Rights Movement* (7–9). Illus. (World History) 1998, Lucent LB $17.96 (1-56006-310-6). After summarizing the civil rights struggle of African Americans, the author focuses on the civil rights movement of the 20th century, with boxed excerpts from writings and speeches. (Rev: BL 2/15/98; SLJ 3/98) [323.1]

4733 Edelman, Marian W. *Stand for Children* (5–8). Illus. 1998, Hyperion LB $16.49 (0-7868-2310-0). A picture book for older readers in which collages, photos, and excerpts from the author's speech at a children's rights rally are used to illuminate the rights of children and how they can be protected. (Rev: BL 7/98; SLJ 8/98) [305.23]

4734 Faherty, Sara. *Victims and Victims' Rights* (7–12). (Justice and Punishment) 1998, Chelsea LB $19.95 (0-7910-4308-8). A multifaceted overview of the victims' rights movement in the United States and its development over the past 25 years. (Rev: BL 3/15/99) [362.88]

4735 Farish, Leah. *Tinker vs. Des Moines: Student Protest* (6–10). Illus. (Landmark Supreme Court Cases) 1997, Enslow LB $19.95 (0-89490-859-6). This book traces step-by-step this case that was argued in the Supreme Court and that determined the

rights of students in schools and campuses. (Rev: BL 4/15/97; SLJ 5/97) [341.4]

4736 Finkelstein, Norman H. *Heeding the Call: Jewish Voices in the Civil Rights Struggle* (6–9). 1997, Jewish Publication Soc. paper $14.95 (0-8276-0590-9). Beginning with the 1600s when both Africans and Jews first came to first country, this book traces the bond between these groups as they fought for civil rights. (Rev: BL 2/15/98) [323.1]

4737 Fireside, Harvey. *New York Times v. Sullivan: Affirming Freedom of the Press* (6–10). (Landmark Supreme Court Cases) 1999, Enslow $19.95 (0-7660-1085-6). The limits to freedom of the press was the subject of this Supreme Court case that had far-reaching results in the world of journalism. (Rev: BL 8/99) [347.3]

4738 Fireside, Harvey. *Plessy vs. Ferguson: Separate but Equal?* (6–10). Illus. (Landmark Supreme Court Cases) 1997, Enslow LB $19.95 (0-89490-860-X). This book gives a step-by-step account of the hearings in the Supreme Court of this case that challenged the basic underpinnings of segregation laws. (Rev: BL 7/97; SLJ 10/97) [342.73]

4739 Fireside, Harvey, and Sarah B. Fuller. *Brown v. Board of Education: Equal Schooling for All* (6–10). (Landmark Supreme Court Cases) 1994, Enslow LB $19.95 (0-89490-469-8). Presents background information, the case itself, and the far-reaching impact it has had. (Rev: BL 11/15/94) [344.73]

4740 Frost-Knappman, Elizabeth, and Kathryn Cullen-DuPont. *Women's Rights on Trial: 101 Historic Trials from Anne Hutchinson to the Virginia Military Institute Cadets* (6–12). 1997, Gale $66.00 (0-7876-0384-8). The description of each of these landmark trials defining women's rights includes background information, partial transcripts, courtroom action, and the decision and its significance. (Rev: SLJ 5/97) [346]

4741 Fuller, Sarah B. *Hazelwood v. Kuhlmeier: Censorship in School Newspapers* (6–12). (Landmark Supreme Court Cases) 1998, Enslow $19.95 (0-89490-971-1). A court case resulted in 1963 when a school principal deleted 2 pages of text about teenage pregnancy from the school paper. This book tells about the case that was finally judged by the U.S. Supreme Court in 1987. (Rev: BL 3/15/99) [344.73]

4742 Galas, Judith C. *Gay Rights* (6–9). Illus. (Overview) 1996, Lucent LB $16.95 (1-56006-176-6). After a brief discussion of the nature of homosexuality, the author gives a history of the gay rights movement and the fight for equality in the family, workplace, and the military. (Rev: BL 3/1/96; SLJ 2/96; VOYA 8/96) [305.9]

4743 Gold, Susan D. *Human Rights* (6–9). Illus. (Pacts and Treaties) 1997, Twenty-First Century LB

$21.40 (0-8050-4811-1). This is a history of the fight for worldwide human rights that begins with the Geneva Convention of 1863 and ends with the present-day efforts by both political and private organizations. (Rev: BL 9/1/97; SLJ 7/97) [341.4]

4744 Gold, Susan D. *In Re Gault (1967): Juvenile Justice* (5–9). (Supreme Court Decisions) 1995, Twenty-First Century LB $18.90 (0-8050-3917-1). Inequalities in juvenile sentencing was the subject of this Supreme Court case that heard an appeal of a 6-year sentence to a reform school given to a juvenile for making an obscene phone call. (Rev: BL 11/15/95; SLJ 1/96; VOYA 4/96) [347]

4745 Gottfried, Ted. *Privacy: Individual Rights v. Social Needs* (8–12). 1994, Millbrook LB $23.90 (1-56294-403-7). Discusses debates on privacy in relation to law enforcement, surveillance, abortion, AIDS, and the media. (Rev: BL 9/15/94; SLJ 10/94; VOYA 2/95) [342.73]

4746 Guernsey, JoAnn B. *Affirmative Action: A Problem or a Remedy?* (7–10). Illus. (Pro/Con) 1998, Lerner LB $23.93 (0-8225-2614-X). An exploration of differing viewpoints on affirmative action, and whether it rights social wrongs or creates new ones. (Rev: BL 3/15/98; SLJ 6/98; VOYA 6/98) [331.13]

4747 Guernsey, JoAnn B. *Voices of Feminism: Past, Present, and Future* (7–10). Illus. (Frontline) 1996, Lerner LB $19.93 (0-8225-2626-3). After a 150-year history of feminism, this account covers the complicated issues and concerns surrounding this subject and discusses past and present leaders in the movement. (Rev: BL 9/15/96; SLJ 7/97; VOYA 4/97) [305.42]

4748 Haskins, Jim. *Separate but Not Equal: The Dream and the Struggle* (7–10). Illus. 1998, Scholastic $15.95 (0-590-45910-4). A history of the struggle of African Americans for equality in education beginning from the time of slavery, with coverage of key court cases and incidents and beliefs of such black leaders as W. E. B. Du Bois and Booker T. Washington. (Rev: BL 2/15/98; SLJ 2/98; VOYA 10/98) [379.2]

4749 Haughton, Emma. *Equality of the Sexes?* (6–8). Illus. (Viewpoints) 1997, Watts LB $22.50 (0-531-14443-7). Brief 2-page spreads introduce women's place in the workplace, at home, in marriage, and under the law, with sections on women in government, religion, sports, and the arts. (Rev: BL 1/1–15/98; SLJ 12/97) [305.3]

4750 Helmer, Diana Star. *Women Suffragists* (7–10). (American Profiles) 1998, Facts on File $19.95 (0-8160-3579-2). This is a fine introduction to 10 outspoken women in the struggle for women's rights including Sojourner Truth, Elizabeth Cady Stanton,

Victoria Woodhull, Carrie Chapman Catt, and Alice Paul. (Rev: BL 8/98; BR 11–12/98; SLJ 12/98) [346]

4751 Hempelman, Kathleen A. *Teen Legal Rights: A Guide for the '90s* (7–12). 1994, Greenwood $39.95 (0-313-28760-0). A guide to the legal rights and concerns of teenagers, including students' rights, sexual privacy, personal appearance, and juvenile court. (Rev: BL 9/15/94; VOYA 10/94) [346.7301]

4752 Hinding, Andrea, ed. *Feminism: Opposing Viewpoints* (9–12). Illus. (Opposing Viewpoints) 1986, Greenhaven paper $16.20 (0-89908-363-3). Women's rights are explored from various viewpoints as well as such topics as women in the workplace and women's role in marriage. (Rev: BL 6/15/86; SLJ 11/86) [305.4]

4753 Hirst, Mike. *Freedom of Belief* (4–8). Illus. (What Do We Mean by Human Rights?) 1997, Watts LB $22.50 (0-531-14435-6). An information-packed overview of religious and political freedom and the people who fought and sometimes died for it. (Rev: BL 1/1–15/98) [323.44]

4754 Hu, Evaleen. *A Level Playing Field: Sports and Race* (5–8). Illus. (Sports Issues) 1995, Lerner LB $21.50 (0-8225-3302-2). A frank, thorough examination of the problems involving race in sports and how different athletes have dealt with them. (Rev: BL 1/1–15/96; SLJ 9/95) [796]

4755 Jacobs, Thomas A. *What Are My Rights? 95 Questions and Answers about Teens and the Law* (7–12). 1997, Free Spirit paper $14.95 (1-57542-028-7). Using a question and answer format, this topically arranged manual describes in simple terms concerns related to teens' rights within the family, at school, and on the job. (Rev: BL 4/1/98; SLJ 4/98; VOYA 6/98) [346.7301]

4756 King, Casey. *Oh, Freedom! Kids Talk about the Civil Rights Movement with the People Who Made It Happen* (5–9). 1997, Knopf LB $19.99 (0-679-95856-8); Random paper $10.99 (0-679-89005-X). In 31 interviews, children ask family members, neighbors, and friends about the part they played in the civil rights movement. (Rev: BL 4/1/97; BR 11–12/97; SLJ 6/97*) [973]

4757 King, David C. *The Right to Speak Out* (4–8). (Land of the Free) 1997, Millbrook LB $19.90 (0-7613-0063-5). Background material on the freedom of speech is given, its use and abuse, and landmark courts cases that have defined it. (Rev: BL 5/15/97; SLJ 10/97) [351.81]

4758 King, Martin Luther, Jr. *I Have a Dream* (4–8). Illus. 1997, Scholastic $21.99 (0-590-20516-1). The full text of Dr. King's speech is reprinted, with illustrations by 15 award-winning African American artists. (Rev: BL 2/15/98; SLJ 11/97) [305.896]

4759 King, Martin Luther, Jr. *The Words of Martin Luther King, Jr.* (7–12). Illus. 1983, Newmarket Pr. $14.95 (0-937858-28-5). A selection from the writings and speeches of Dr. King that covers a great number of topics. [323.4]

4760 Kuklin, Susan. *Irrepressible Spirit* (7–12). 1996, Putnam $18.95 (0-399-22762-8); paper $9.95 (0-399-23045-9). This moving document profiles, through interviews, 11 activists from around the world and describes each one's struggle for civil rights and social justice. (Rev: BL 5/1/96*; BR 3–4/97; SLJ 4/96; VOYA 2/97) [323]

4761 Landau, Elaine. *Your Legal Rights: From Custody Battles to School Searches, the Headline-Making Cases That Affect Your Life* (6–10). 1995, Walker LB $14.85 (0-8027-8360-0). A review of advances in protection of the legal rights of children and teenagers. (Rev: BL 5/15/95; SLJ 8/95) [346.7301]

4762 Lucas, Eileen. *Civil Rights: The Long Struggle* (7–12). (Issues in Focus) 1996, Enslow LB $19.95 (0-89490-729-8). The controversies surrounding the civil rights movement are stressed in this book, which gives a good, current view on the subject. (Rev: BL 9/15/96; BR 5–6/97; SLJ 12/96) [323.1]

4763 McDonald, Laughlin, and John A. Powell. *The Rights of Racial Minorities* (6–10). (ACLU Handbooks for Young Americans) 1998, Penguin paper $9.99 (0-14-037785-9). This handbook traces how the rights of racial minorities have gained legal protection and provides information on current laws. (Rev: BL 5/15/98; SLJ 6/98) [323.4]

4764 McKissack, Patricia, and Fredrick McKissack. *The Civil Rights Movement in America from 1865 to the Present.* 2d ed. (5–10). 1991, Children's Pr. LB $45.80 (0-516-00579-0). This book traces the history of civil rights in the United States beginning after the Civil War. (Rev: BL 2/15/98) [323.1]

4765 Malaspina, Ann. *Children's Rights* (5–8). (Overview) 1998, Lucent LB $22.45 (1-56006-175-8). A study of how children's rights and adult rights have sometimes been in conflict, and how the rights of children are gradually being defined through the courts. (Rev: BL 8/98; SLJ 6/98) [323.4]

4766 Meyers, Madeleine, ed. *Forward into Light: The Struggle for Woman's Suffrage* (5–8). (Perspectives on History) 1994, Discovery Enterprises paper $5.95 (1-878668-25-0). The story of the long struggle for women's right to vote, including the roles of Elizabeth Cady Stanton, Susan B. Anthony, Sojourner Truth, and other leaders. (Rev: BL 8/94) [324.6]

4767 Monroe, Judy. *The Nineteenth Amendment: Women's Right to Vote* (6–8). Illus. 1998, Enslow LB $19.95 (0-89490-922-3). Beginning with the historic Seneca Falls meeting in 1848, this book highlights the events, movements, and people involved in the passage of the 19th Amendment giving women the right to vote. (Rev: BL 4/15/98; BR 9–10/98; SLJ 6/98; VOYA 4/98) [324-6]

4768 Moss, Kary L. *The Rights of Women and Girls* (6–10). (ACLU Handbooks for Young Americans) 1998, Penguin paper $9.99 (0-14-037782-4). This handbook traces how women achieved equality before the law and describes the situation today. (Rev: BL 5/15/98; SLJ 8/98) [342]

4769 Nash, Carol R. *The Fight for Women's Right to Vote in American History* (7–10). (In American History) 1998, Enslow LB $19.95 (0-89490-986-X). The struggle for women's right to vote is told concisely and clearly, with thumbnail sketches of the leading personalities involved. (Rev: BL 8/98; BR 1–2/99; SLJ 1/99) [324.6]

4770 Nunez, Sandra, and Trish Marx. *And Justice for All: The Legal Rights of Young People* (6–12). Illus. (ACLU Handbooks for Young Americans) 1997, Millbrook LB $23.90 (0-7613-0068-6). After a historical overview, this work outlines the rights of young people at home, school, and work, including information on legal rights in criminal situations. (Rev: BL 2/1/98; BR 3–4/98; SLJ 1/98; VOYA 4/98) [346.7301]

4771 O'Connor, Maureen. *Equal Rights* (5–8). Illus. (What Do We Mean by Human Rights?) 1998, Watts $22.00 (0-531-14448-8). An exploration of topics like racism, the Holocaust, and prejudice involving gender, disability, and sexual preferences through a series of double-page spreads containing photos, drawings, inserts, boxes, and screens. (Rev: BL 4/1/98; BR 11–12/98) [323]

4772 Oliver, Marilyn Tower. *Gay and Lesbian Rights: A Struggle* (7–12). 1998, Enslow LB $19.95 (0-89490-958-4). After recounting 2 incidents of gay bashing, the author reviews the history of gay rights from the ancient Greeks to today, with material on discrimination, law, health, and family issues. (Rev: BL 12/1/98; SLJ 2/99; VOYA 10/99) [305.9]

4773 Patterson, Charles. *The Civil Rights Movement* (6–12). (Social Reform Movement) 1995, Facts on File $19.95 (0-8160-2968-7). Chronicles the civil rights movement in the United States, including a time line, chapter notes, and a reading list. (Rev: BL 11/15/95; SLJ 11/95; VOYA 12/95) [323.1196]

4774 Payne, Charles M. *I've Got the Light of Freedom: The Organizing Tradition and the Mississippi Freedom Struggle* (9–12). 1995, Univ. of California Pr. $45.00 (0-520-08515-9). Community organizing for civil rights, the groundwork laid by the local NAACP, and its impact in the Mississippi Delta. (Rev: BL 4/15/95*) [323.0972]

4775 Peck, Rodney. *Working Together Against Human Rights Violations* (7–12). (Library of Social Activism) 1995, Rosen LB $16.95 (0-8239-1778-9).

Presents the struggles over a wide range of human rights issues. (Rev: BL 4/15/95; SLJ 4/95) [323]

4776 Price, Janet R., et al. *The Rights of Students: The Basic ACLU Guide to a Student's Rights* (9–12). 1988, Southern Illinois Univ. Pr. paper $11.95 (0-8093-1423-1). In a question-and-answer format, the civil rights of teenage students are explored. (Rev: BL 5/15/88) [344.73]

4777 Redman, Nina, and Lucille Whalen. *Human Rights: A Reference Handbook*. Second Ed. (9–12). (Contemporary World issues) 1998, ABC-CLIO $45.00 (1-57607-041-7). A one-volume compendium of facts about the historical, religious, philosophical, legal, and political foundations of human rights, the history of international human rights struggles, and material on such pressing concerns as global poverty, the use of land mines, prisons and torture, ethnic cleansing, racism, and the environment. (Rev: BL 3/1/99; VOYA 8/99) [341.4]

4778 Roleff, Tamara L., ed. *Civil Liberties* (8–12). (Opposing Viewpoints) 1998, Greenhaven LB $20.96 (1-56510-937-6); paper $20.25 (1-56510-936-8). This collection of essays explores potential restrictions on freedom of expression, the right to privacy, the separation of church and state, and freedom to use the Internet. (Rev: BL 8/98; SLJ 1/99; VOYA 6/99) [342]

4779 Roleff, Tamara L. *Gay Marriage* (9–12). (At Issue) 1997, Greenhaven LB $14.96 (1-56510-693-8); paper $13.96 (1-56510-692-X). Proponents of same-sex marriage believe that homosexuals deserve the same benefits as heterosexuals, but opponents maintain it will undermine the institution of marriage. These and other points of view are presented in this anthology. (Rev: BL 5/1/98; SLJ 7/98) [306.84]

4780 Shapiro, Joseph P. *No Pity: How the Disability Rights Movement Is Changing America* (9–12). 1993, Times Bks. $25.00 (0-8129-1964-5). A history of the struggle to overcome negative public perception of the disabled. Discusses the movement's diversity and its aggressive attack on myths and stereotypes through 1992. (Rev: BL 4/15/93) [323.3]

4781 Shein, Lori, ed. *Inequality: Opposing Viewpoints in Social Problems* (9–12). (Opposing Viewpoints) 1997, Greenhaven LB $30.96 (1-56510-737-3); paper $21.20 (1-56510-736-5). Leading policy makers, activists, and scientists debate the causes of and solutions to race, gender, age, and class inequality. (Rev: BL 2/15/98; SLJ 4/98) [305]

4782 Springer, Jane. *Listen to Us: The World's Working Children* (7–12). Illus. 1997, Douglas & McIntyre $24.95 (0-88899-291-2). This impressive photoessay looks at the exploitation of children around the world in industry, agriculture, the home,

the military, and on the street. (Rev: BL 1/1–15/98; SLJ 3/98) [331.3]

4783 Stalcup, Brenda, ed. *The Women's Rights Movement* (9–12). (Opposing Viewpoints) 1996, Greenhaven LB $21.96 (1-56510-367-X); paper $16.20 (1-56510-366-1). An extensive collection of documents covering the women's rights movement from Colonial times to the present, with emphasis on current controversies. (Rev: BL 6/1–15/96; SLJ 8/96) [973.917]

4784 Walker, Samuel. *Hate Speech: The History of an American Controversy* (9–12). 1994, Univ. of Nebraska Pr. paper $11.95 (0-8032-9751-3). The first comprehensive history of hate speech and its effects. (Rev: BL 4/15/94) [342.73]

4785 Walvin, James. *Slavery and the Slave Trade: A Short Illustrated History* (9–12). Illus. 1983, Univ. Press of Mississippi Pr. paper $16.95 (0-87805-181-3). A well-illustrated account that deals with slavery from ancient times through the 19th century. [326]

4786 Wawrose, Susan C. *Griswold v. Connecticut: Contraception and the Right of Privacy* (6–10). Illus. (Historic Supreme Court Cases) 1996, Watts LB $25.00 (0-531-11249-7). In this discussion of the case against Estelle Griswold of the Planned Parenthood League in Connecticut, who broke a state law prohibiting distribution of contraceptives, the author brings into focus many issues involving women's rights, sex, and personal privacy. (Rev: BL 7/96; SLJ 9/96; VOYA 10/96) [342.746]

4787 Weatherford, Doris. *A History of the American Suffragist Movement* (10–12). 1998, ABC-CLIO $50.00 (1-57607-065-4). Beginning in 1637, this account traces the long and difficult struggle for women's suffrage that ended with the passing of the 19th Amendment in 1920. (Rev: BR 1–2/99; SLJ 3/99) [324.6]

4788 Webb, Sheyann, and Rachel W. Nelson. *Selma, Lord, Selma: Girlhood Memories of the Civil-Rights Days* (7–12). Illus. 1980, Univ. of Alabama Pr. $17.95 (0-8173-0031-7). Recollections of 2 girls who, when only ages 8 and 9, participated in the Selma civil rights struggle. (Rev: BL 9/1/87) [323.4]

4789 Weiss, Ann E. *Who's to Know? Information, the Media, and Public Awareness* (6–9). 1990, Houghton $14.95 (0-395-49702-7). This book discusses the right to know, the importance of access to information and, on the other hand, the need for personal privacy. (Rev: BL 6/15/90; SLJ 5/90; VOYA 6/90) [363.2]

4790 Williams, Mary, ed. *Discrimination* (8–12). Illus. (Opposing Viewpoints) 1997, Greenhaven LB $20.96 (1-56510-657-1); paper $16.20 (1-56510-656-3). Essays express different points of view on various aspects of discrimination, such as its seriousness, frequency, causes, and cures. (Rev: BL 4/15/97; BR 1–2/98; SLJ 7/97; VOYA 12/97) [305.8]

4791 Williams, Mary, ed. *Human Rights* (9–12). (Opposing Viewpoints) 1998, Greenhaven LB $26.20 (1-56510-797-7); paper $20.25 (1-56510-796-9). The rights of women, refugees, child laborers, and political prisoners, the nature of human rights and whether human rights and freedom are culturally relative, and how human rights should be protected are among the issues debated in this anthology of articles and essays. (Rev: BL 5/15/98) [323]

4792 Wilson, Reginald. *Our Rights: Civil Liberties and the U.S.* (7–12). Illus. 1988, Walker $28.90 (0-8027-6751-6). A book that explains what civil rights are, how we have these freedoms, and how to protect them. (Rev: SLJ 8/88; VOYA 8/88) [323.4]

Immigration

4793 Andryszewski, Tricia. *Immigration: Newcomers and Their Impact on the U.S.* (7–9). 1995, Millbrook LB $23.90 (1-56294-499-1). A detailed study of immigration as it pertains to the United States. (Rev: BL 1/15/95; SLJ 5/95) [304.8]

4794 Ashabranner, Brent. *Our Beckoning Borders: Illegal Immigration to America* (6–10). Illus. 1996, Dutton paper $15.99 (0-525-65223-X). Individual case studies and good photographs are used to explain the problems of illegal immigration, border patrols, and the involvement of human rights groups. (Rev: BL 4/15/96; BR 11–12/96; SLJ 5/96) [304.8]

4795 Ashabranner, Brent. *Still a Nation of Immigrants* (7–12). 1993, Dutton paper $15.99 (0-525-65130-6). Looks at the present influx of immigrants and discusses why they come and what they bring with them. (Rev: BL 9/1/93; VOYA 2/94) [325.73]

4796 Barbour, William, ed. *Illegal Immigration* (9–12). (Current Controversies) 1994, Greenhaven LB $16.95 (1-56510-072-7); paper $16.20 (1-56510-071-9). An anthology of articles representing a variety of viewpoints regarding the seriousness of the problem of illegal immigration. (Rev: BL 4/15/94; SLJ 3/94) [353.0081]

4797 Brimelow, Peter. *Alien Nation: Common Sense about Immigration and the American Future* (9–12). 1995, Random $24.00 (0-679-43058-X). A British immigrant probes what he sees as the adverse impact of immigration in the United States and the consequences of current immigration policy. (Rev: BL 3/15/95) [304.8]

4798 Budhos, Marina. *Remix: Conversations with Immigrant Teenagers* (7–12). 1999, Holt $16.95 (0-8050-5113-9). This book contains interviews with 20 older teens from around the world who comment on their experiences as immigrants in the United States and the cultural differences they have encountered. (Rev: BL 9/15/99; VOYA 12/99) [341.4]

4799 Caroli, Betty Boyd. *Immigrants Who Returned Home* (6–10). Illus. 1990, Chelsea LB $19.95 (0-87754-864-1). An account of immigrants who found life in the United States less than expected and therefore returned home to their countries. (Rev: BL 4/15/90; SLJ 8/90) [304.8]

4800 Cole, Carolyn Kozo, and Kathy Kobayashi. *Shades of L.A.: Pictures from Ethnic Family Albums* (7–12). 1996, New Pr. paper $20.00 (1-56584-313-4). A collection of photographs of African American, Mexican American, Asian American, and Native American family life in Los Angeles' ethnic and racial neighborhoods prior to 1965. (Rev: BL 8/96; VOYA 2/97) [979.4]

4801 Cox, Vic. *The Challenge of Immigration* (7–12). (Multicultural Issues) 1995, Enslow LB $19.95 (0-89490-628-3). An introduction to the controversial issues concerning immigration. (Rev: BL 5/1/95; SLJ 5/95) [325.73]

4802 Cozic, Charles P., ed. *Illegal Immigration* (9–12). (Opposing Viewpoints) 1997, Greenhaven LB $20.96 (1-56510-514-1); paper $16.20 (1-56510-513-3). Treatment of illegal immigrants, their contributions to the United States, whether illegal immigrants harm the United States, and how the United States should respond to these issues are debated in this collection of essays that replaces the 1990 edition. (Rev: BL 1/1–15/97; BR 5–6/97; SLJ 1/97) [364.6]

4803 Emsden, Katharine, ed. *Coming to America: A New Life in a New Land* (5–8). (Perspectives on History) 1993, Discovery Enterprises paper $5.95 (1-878668-23-4). Diaries, journals, and letters of immigrants from many countries are used to provide insights into their lives. (Rev: BL 11/15/93) [325.73]

4804 Goldish, Meish. *Immigration: How Should It Be Controlled?* (6–9). Illus. (Issues of Our Time) 1994, Twenty-First Century LB $18.90 (0-8050-3182-0). An unbiased, clear look at current positions and solutions to the immigration problem, particularly as they apply to the United States. (Rev: BL 6/1–15/94; SLJ 7/94) [325.73]

4805 Greenberg, Judith E. *Newcomers to America: Stories of Today's Young Immigrants* (7–10). Illus. 1996, Watts LB $25.00 (0-531-11256-X). An overview of the new wave of immigration to this country, followed by excerpts from 14 interviews of recent immigrants who came here as teens. (Rev: BL 6/1–15/96; BR 11–12/96; SLJ 8/96; VOYA 2/97) · [304.8]

4806 Hauser, Pierre. *Illegal Aliens* (5–8). (Immigrant Experience) 1996, Chelsea LB $19.95 (0-7910-3363-5). A history of government policies that have encouraged or prohibited immigration is given, followed by a discussion of illegal immigrants, where they come from, why they came, and the government's policy toward them. (Rev: SLJ 2/97) [932]

4807 Kosof, Anna. *Living in Two Worlds: The Immigrant Children's Experience* (7–12). Illus. 1996, Twenty-First Century LB $21.40 (0-8050-4083-8). After a brief introduction on the history of immigration, this book describes the problems and the reception of present-day teenage immigrants, using many first-person accounts. (Rev: BL 10/1/96; BR 11–12/96; SLJ 10/96; VOYA 2/97) [305.23]

4808 Leinwand, Gerald. *American Immigration: Should the Open Door Be Closed?* (7–12). 1995, Watts LB $24.00 (0-531-13038-X). A historical perspective on the current immigration debate reveals the racism that still underlies the melting-pot argument. (Rev: BL 8/95; VOYA 12/95) [325.73]

4809 Levine, Herbert M. *Immigration* (7–12). Illus. (American Issues Debated) 1997, Raintree Steck-Vaughn LB $27.83 (0-8172-4353-4). Questions involving immigration and the economy, the rights of illegal immigrants, and English-only laws are covered from various points of view. (Rev: BL 11/15/97; BR 1–2/98) [304.873]

4810 Mills, Nicolaus, ed. *Arguing Immigration: The Debate over the Changing Face of America* (9–12). 1994, Simon & Schuster paper $12.00 (0-671-89558-3). Authors such as Toni Morrison discuss immigration, its costs, benefits, and cultural impact. (Rev: BL 9/1/94) [325.73]

4811 Morrow, Robert. *Immigration: Blessing or Burden?* (7–10). Illus. (Pro/Con) 1998, Lerner LB $23.93 (0-8225-2613-1). This book examines our changing attitudes toward immigration, how we regard immigration laws, and the controversy over multiculturalism vs. assimilation. (Rev: BL 3/15/98; SLJ 4/98) [304.8]

4812 Press, Petra. *A Multicultural Portrait of Immigration* (6–9). (Perspectives Series) 1996, Benchmark LB $28.50 (0-7614-0055-9). An easy-to-read look at the various ethnic groups that have immigrated to the U.S. since the 1600s. (Rev: BR 1–2/97; SLJ 8/96) [325.73]

4813 Reimers, David M. *A Land of Immigrants* (5–8). (Immigrant Experience) 1995, Chelsea LB $19.95 (0-7910-3361-9). An overview of immigration to the United States and Canada. (Rev: BL 10/15/95; SLJ 12/95) [304.8]

4814 Roleff, Tamara L., ed. *Immigration* (8–12). (Opposing Viewpoints) 1998, Greenhaven LB $20.96 (1-56510-799-3); paper $16.20 (1-56510-798-5). Questions concerning restrictions on immigration, the extent of the immigration problem, how to cope with illegal immigrants, and possible reforms in our policies are discussed in this anthology of differing opinions. (Rev: BL 6/1–15/98) [341.4]

4815 Sawyer, Kem K. *Refugees: Seeking a Safe Haven* (7–12). (Multicultural Issues) 1995, Enslow LB $19.95 (0-89490-663-1). This book describes the lives and problems of refugees admitted into this country, with material on why they left their homelands and their reception here. (Rev: BL 6/1–15/95; SLJ 8/95) [362.87]

4816 Stewart, Gail B. *Illegal Immigrants* (9–12). Illus. (The Other America) 1997, Lucent LB $17.96 (1-56006-339-4). Four illegal immigrants explain why they are here, describe lives filled with apprehension, work, and fear, and reflect on what they eventually hope to accomplish in America. (Rev: BL 6/1–15/97; BR 11–12/97; SLJ 8/97) [305.9]

4817 Strom, Yale. *Quilted Landscape: Conversations with Young Immigrants* (5–8). Illus. 1996, Simon & Schuster paper $18.00 (0-689-80074-6). Young immigrants from 15 countries tell about their homelands and the lives they now lead in the United States. (Rev: BL 10/15/96; SLJ 12/96) [305.8]

4818 Ungar, Sanford J. *Fresh Blood: The New American Immigrants* (9–12). 1995, Simon & Schuster $24.50 (0-684-80860-9). From the former host of National Public Radio's *All Things Considered* comes this look at the new immigrants—"the illegal aliens"—their relationship to their current communities, and their reception by earlier immigrants. (Rev: BL 10/15/95) [305.8]

4819 Yans-McLaughlin, Virginia, and Marjorie Lightman. *Ellis Island and the Peopling of America: The Official Guide* (10–12). 1997, New Press paper $19.95 (1-56584-364-9). This book chronicles the role of Ellis Island in U.S. history and reviews the waves of immigration to this country and past and present immigration policy, using reproductions of letters, visas, editorials and political cartoons, maps, charts and legal documents to bring the facts to life. (Rev: BL 8/97; SLJ 3/98; VOYA 4/98) [973]

Ethnic Groups and Prejudice

General and Miscellaneous

4820 Birdseye, Debbie H., and Tom Birdseye. *Under Our Skin: Kids Talk About Race* (4–8). 1997, Holiday House LB $15.95 (0-8234-1325-X). In separate chapters, 6 eighth-grade students in Oregon from different racial and ethnic backgrounds talk about race and what racism means to them. (Rev: SLJ 4/98) [572.973]

4821 *CityKids Speak on Prejudice* (7–12). 1995, Random paper $5.99 (0-679-86552-7). Identifies areas in which intolerance is common and cites unexpected examples of discrimination as seen through the eyes of young people. (Rev: BL 5/1/95) [303.3]

4822 Cozic, Charles P., ed. *Ethnic Conflict* (8–12). (At Issue) 1995, Greenhaven LB $18.70 (1-56510-298-3); paper $24.94 (1-56510-265-7). This anthology examines the deep conflicts related to ethnic hatred in this country and efforts to alleviate and resolve them. (Rev: BL 3/15/95) [305.8]

4823 Garg, Samidha, and Jan Hardy. *Racism* (6–10). Illus. (Global Issues) 1996, Raintree Steck-Vaughn LB $25.69 (0-8172-4548-0). This study of racism, supplementing statistics and facts with personal experiences, discusses prejudice, immigration, and citizenship, with separate chapters on Europe, South Africa, the United States, and Australia. (Rev: BL 2/1/97) [305.8]

4824 Garza, Hedda. *African Americans and Jewish Americans: A History of Struggle* (8–12). Illus. (African American Experience) 1995, Watts LB $24.00 (0-531-11217-9). An overview of the relationship between Jews and African Americans past and present, with material on how relations between these 2 groups have become strained because of current social developments. (Rev: BL 4/1/96) [973]

4825 Gaskins, Pearl Fuyo, ed. *What Are You? Voices of Mixed-Race Young People* (7–12). 1999, Holt $17.95 (0-8050-5968-7). In essays, interviews, and poetry, 45 mixed-race young people ages 14 to 26 talk about themselves and growing up. (Rev: BL 5/15/99; SLJ 7/99; VOYA 10/99) [973]

4826 Gay, Kathlyn. *I Am Who I Am: Speaking Out about Multiracial Identity* (7–12). 1995, Watts LB $25.00 (0-531-11214-4). A look at what it's like to grow up in a mixed-race environment, including cultural, historical, and political perspectives and opinions from experts. (Rev: BL 6/1–15/95; SLJ 8/95) [305.8]

4827 Gillam, Scott. *Discrimination: Prejudice in Action* (7–12). (Multicultural Issues) 1995, Enslow LB $18.95 (0-89490-643-7). This book shows how racial discrimination is still practiced in this country and discusses how it can be combated. (Rev: BL 6/1–15/95; SLJ 9/95) [303.3]

4828 Hooks, Bell. *Killing Rage: Ending Racism* (9–12). 1995, Holt $20.00 (0-8050-3782-9). Passionate essays about race and racism written from an African American and feminist point of view. (Rev: BL 9/15/95) [305.8]

4829 Hull, Mary. *Ethnic Violence* (5–8). Illus. (Overview) 1997, Lucent LB $17.96 (1-56006-184-7). The causes and types of violence caused by ethnic and racial conflict are surveyed, with many examples from the past and discussion of how this problem can be lessened. (Rev: BL 8/97; BR 1–2/98; SLJ 9/97) [305.8]

4830 Hurley, Jennifer A., ed. *Racism* (7–12). 1998, Greenhaven LB $20.96 (1-56510-809-4). How prevalent is racism in U.S. society? How does racism affect minorities? Is affirmative action effective? How can racism by combated? These are some of the questions explored in this collection of essays. (Rev: BL 8/98) [305.8]

4831 Jacobs, Bruce. *Race Manners: Navigating the Minefield between Black and White Americans* (10–12). 1999, Arcade $22.95 (1-55970-453-5). This book about interracial relations in America today discusses such topics as dating, everyday social life, stereotyping, and ethnic jokes. (Rev: BL 2/15/99; SLJ 5/99) [305.8]

4832 Katz, William L. *The Great Migrations: History of Multicultural America* (7–12). (History of Multicultural America) 1993, Raintree Steck-Vaughn LB $22.83 (0-8114-6278-1). Shows the impact that women and minorities have had in the formation and development of this country. (Rev: BL 6/1–15/93; VOYA 10/93) [973]

4833 Katz, William L. *Minorities Today* (7–9). (Multicultural America) 1993, Raintree Steck-Vaughn LB $25.68 (0-8114-6281-1). This book examines the conditions of minorities in the United States. (Rev: BL 10/1/93; VOYA 2/94) [305.8]

4834 Kranz, Rachel. *Straight Talk about Prejudice* (7–10). (Straight Talk About) 1992, Facts on File LB $19.95 (0-8160-2488-X). A look at prejudice and how it has affected various racial, ethnic, and religious groups in the United States. (Rev: BL 5/15/92; SLJ 7/92) [303.3]

4835 Kronenwetter, Michael. *Prejudice in America: Causes and Cures* (7–12). 1993, Watts LB $24.00 (0-531-11163-6). Focuses on race, religion, and ethnicity in an exploration of how prejudice is engendered by fear and fostered by stereotypes. (Rev: BL 2/15/94; VOYA 4/94) [303.3]

4836 Maharidge, Dale. *The Coming White Minority: California's Eruptions and the Nation's Future* (10–12). 1996, Random $25.00 (0-8129-2289-1). The changing profile of the American populace is explored through profiles of a Mexican American politician, a black sheriff, an Asian American student, and a white community activist. (Rev: BL 9/15/96; SLJ 7/97) [325.73]

4837 Milios, Rita. *Working Together Against Racism* (7–12). (Library of Social Activism) 1995, Rosen LB $16.95 (0-8239-1840-8). A history of civil rights in America and ways to protect citizens from racism. (Rev: BL 4/15/95; SLJ 4/95) [305.8]

4838 Nash, Gary B. *Forbidden Love: The Secret History of Mixed-Race America* (9–12). 1999, Holt $21.95 (0-8050-4953-3). This book, in many ways a history of racism in the United States, reviews the history of racially mixed people and the fight for tolerance from colonial times to the present. (Rev: BL 5/15/99; SLJ 7/99; VOYA 10/99) [305.868]

4839 Newman, Gerald, and Eleanor N. Layfield. *Racism: Divided by Color* (7–12). (Multicultural Issues) 1995, Enslow LB $18.95 (0-89490-641-0). A well-documented history of color barriers in America and efforts to eradicate them. (Rev: BL 9/15/95; SLJ 12/95; VOYA 2/96) [305.8]

4840 O'Hearn, Claudine Chiawei, ed. *Half and Half: Writers on Growing Up Biracial and Bicultural* (7–12). 1998, Pantheon paper $13.00 (0-375-70011-0). This work contains 18 personal essays by people who live and work in the U.S. but because they are biracial and bicultural aren't sure of where they belong. (Rev: BL 9/1/98) [306.84]

4841 Pascoe, Elaine. *Racial Prejudice: Why Can't We Overcome?* (7–12). (Impact) 1997, Watts LB $24.00 (0-531-11402-3). This title explores the causes and effects of racial prejudice through separate chapters on African Americans, Hispanic Americans, Asian Americans, and Native Americans. (Rev: BL 5/15/97) [305.8]

4842 Sheftel-Gomes, Nasoan. *Everything You Need to Know about Racism* (6–9). Illus. (Need to Know Library) 1998, Rosen LB $17.95 (0-8239-2057-7). This book provides a brief history of racism and discusses its many faces—both subtle and blatant—how to deal with it, and when to confront it in others and ourselves. (Rev: BL 11/1/98; SLJ 1/99) [305.8 00973]

4843 Szumski, Bonnie, ed. *Interracial America* (9–12). (Opposing Viewpoints) 1996, Greenhaven LB $21.96 (1-56510-393-9); paper $21.50 (1-56510-392-0). Recent articles representing various points of view are used to explore the current status of race relations in America. (Rev: BL 6/1–15/96; SLJ 7/96) [305.8]

4844 Tatum, Beverly. *Why Are All the Black Kids Sitting Together in the Cafeteria?* (10–12). 1997, HarperCollins $25.00 (0-465-09127-X). Beginning with racial segregation in an integrated school situation, this book explores race relations and the development of racial identity from many different viewpoints. (Rev: BL 9/1/97; SLJ 3/98) [305.8]

4845 Williams, Mary E. *Minorities* (9–12). (Current Controversies) 1998, Greenhaven LB $20.96 (1-56510-681-4); paper $16.20 (1-56510-680-6). This book discusses discrimination, the present status of race relations, policies that benefit minorities, the changing racial demographics, and other controver-

sial issues of concern to minorities. (Rev: BL 5/1/98) [305.8]

4846 Winters, Paul A., ed. *Race Relations* (9–12). (Opposing Viewpoints) 1996, Greenhaven paper $16.20 (1-56510-356-4). This collection of articles presents a wide range of viewpoints on the state of race relations, affirmative action, the justice system, Black, Asian, and Latino political powerbases, and how race relations can be improved. (Rev: BL 12/15/95; SLJ 1/96; VOYA 6/96) [303.3]

4847 Wright, David K. *A Multicultural Portrait of Life in the Cities* (7–12). (Perspectives) 1993, Marshall Cavendish LB $28.50 (1-85435-659-3). An upbeat discussion of 8 representative cities: New York, Los Angeles, Chicago, Detroit, San Francisco, New Orleans, Miami, and San Antonio. (Rev: BL 3/15/94; SLJ 3/94) [305.8]

African Americans

4848 *African American Quotations* (9–12). 1998, Oryx $65.00 (1-57356-118-5). Interesting to browse through, this compilation of 2,500 quotations from 500 individuals is arranged by such subjects as "Adolescence," "Black Pride," and "Women." (Rev: BR 1–2/99; SLJ 11/98) [080]

4849 Altman, Susan. *The Encyclopedia of African-American Heritage* (6–12). 1997, Facts on File $40.00 (0-8160-3289-0). An alphabetically arranged series of entries that covers African American history from the standpoint of famous people, places, culture, events, and politics. (Rev: BL 3/15/97; BR 1–2/99; SLJ 2/98; VOYA 6/97) [973]

4850 Asante, Molefi K., and Mark T. Mattson. *The African-American Atlas: Black History and Culture An Illustrated Reference* (9–12). 1998, Macmillan $147.75 (0-02-864984-2). This chronologically arranged atlas introduces African American history by interweaving text about the people and events that influenced the nation's development with maps, charts, reproductions, and photographs. (Rev: BL 4/15/99; SLJ 5/99) [973]

4851 Ball, Edward. *Slaves in the Family* (10–12). 1998, Farrar $30.00 (0-374-26582-8); Ballantine paper $15.95 (0-345-43105-7). A meticulously researched history of the author's family since their arrival in South Carolina in 1698, tracing their role as slave owners and slave traders, including the author's successful search for several of his distant African American cousins. (Rev: BL 2/15/98; SLJ 6/98) [973]

4852 Banks, William H., Jr. *The Black Muslims* (5–10). (African American Achievers) 1996, Chelsea LB $19.95 (0-7910-2593-4); paper $9.95 (0-7910-2594-2). The story of the founding of the Nation of

Islam, its leaders, the Million Man March, and the reign of Louis Farrakhan. (Rev: SLJ 5/97) [323]

4853 Baron, Deborah G., and Susan B. Gall, eds. *Asian American Chronology* (6–9). 1996, Gale $51.50 (0-8103-9692-0). A browsable compendium of facts about Asian Americans that begins with migrations across the Bering Sea millenniums ago and ends with Connie Chung being fired from CBS Evening News in 1995. (Rev: SLJ 2/97) [973]

4854 Bontemps, Arna. *100 Years of Negro Freedom* (7–12). 1961, Greenwood LB $59.50 (0-313-22218-5). The history of black Americans since the Civil War told primarily in terms of their leaders. [305.8]

4855 Branch, Muriel M. *Juneteenth: Freedom Day* (5–8). 1998, NAL paper $15.99 (0-525-65222-1). A photoessay that describes how this holiday that celebrates the end of slavery is celebrated today, with background on its origin and history. (Rev: BL 2/15/98; BR 9–10/98; SLJ 10/98) [394.2]

4856 Carrol, Rebecca. *Sugar in the Raw: Voices of Young Black Girls in America* (10–12). 1997, Crown paper $12.00 (0-517-88497-6). This is a collection of 15 monologues by black teenage women about their lives, attitudes, hopes, dreams, frustrations, and experiences. (Rev: BL 12/15/96; BR 5–6/97; SLJ 2/98) [305.8]

4857 Cole, Michael D. *The Los Angeles Riots: Rage in the City of Angels* (5–9). (American Disasters) 1999, Enslow $18.95 (0-7660-1219-0). This book describes the police beating of Rodney King in Los Angeles and the subsequent riots, the worst in U.S. history. (Rev: BL 2/1/99; SLJ 6/99) [979.4 94053]

4858 Collins, Charles M., and David Cohen, eds. *The African Americans* (9–12). 1993, Viking $45.00 (0-670-84982-0). In choosing African Americans past and present to honor here, the editors selected both famous and ordinary, everyday heroes. Includes photographs and commentary. (Rev: BL 12/15/93) [973]

4859 Cooper, Michael L. *Bound for the Promised Land* (5–9). 1995, Dutton paper $15.99 (0-525-67476-4). A short history of the African Americans who left the South for a better life in the North, and in the process changed the face of the nation. (Rev: BL 11/1/95; SLJ 12/95*; VOYA 4/96) [973]

4860 Cottman, Michael H. *The Wreck of the Henrietta Marie: An African American's Spiritual Journey to Uncover a Sunken Slave Ship's Past* (10–12). 1999, Harmony $23.00 (0-517-70328-9). The author traces the history of the slave ship *Henrietta Marie* that sank off the Florida keys almost 3 centuries ago by visiting sites associated with it, including researching its building and its crew in England, visits to the slave port in Senegal, talks with descendants of slaves in Jamaica, and dives undersea at the wreck site. (Rev: BL 2/15/99; SLJ 7/99) [973]

4861 Currie, Stephen. *Slavery* (7–12). (Opposing Viewpoints Digests) 1998, Greenhaven LB $17.96 (1-56510-881-7); paper $11.96 (1-56510-880-9). Diverse opinions are presented in this anthology on issues related to slavery and human rights, morality, justice, abolition, and resistance. (Rev: BL 4/15/99) [177]

4862 De Angelis, Therese. *Louis Farrakhan* (6–10). (Black Americans of Achievement) 1998, Chelsea LB $19.95 (0-7910-4688-5); paper $9.95 (0-7910-4689-3). This book provides information about Farrakhan and explains the evolution of his leadership, but it is more a history of the Nation of Islam movement, with coverage of the role of such African American leaders as Malcolm X, Elijah Muhammad, and Roy Wilkins. (Rev: SLJ 2/99) [305.8]

4863 Dornfeld, Margaret. *The Turning Tide: From the Desegregation of the Armed Forces to the Montgomery Bus Boycott* (7–10). (Milestones in Black American History) 1995, Chelsea LB $19.95 (0-7910-2255-2); paper $9.95 (0-7910-2681-7). This work surveys the period in African American history from 1948 through 1956 and includes Rosa Parks, Ralph Ellison, Charlie Parker, and Adam Clayton Powell, Jr. (Rev: BL 8/95) [973]

4864 Dudley, William, ed. *African Americans* (9–12). (Opposing Viewpoints: American History) 1997, Greenhaven LB $21.96 (1-56510-522-2); paper $16.20 (1-56510-521-4). This anthology of articles documents the history of African Americans from the days of slavery, with coverage of affirmative action, black nationalists, white supremacists, and civil rights movements. (Rev: BL 3/15/97; SLJ 3/97) [973]

4865 Ebony, eds. *Ebony Pictorial History of Black America* (7–12). Illus. 1971, Johnson Pub. $54.95 (set) (0-87485-049-5). The 3 volumes trace black history from slavery to today's fight for integration and equality. [305.8]

4866 Feelings, Tom. *The Middle Passage: White Ships Black Cargo* (10–12). 1995, Dial paper $45.00 (0-8037-1804-7). A powerful visual record and concise narrative of the slave trade that describes life in Africa and horrifying details of slave ships. (Rev: BL 10/15/95; SLJ 2/96) [973]

4867 Feelings, Tom. *Tommy Traveler in the World of Black History* (5–8). 1991, Black Butterfly $13.95 (0-86316-202-9). A history of African Americans seen through the eyes of a black boy who imagines himself participating in the important events. (Rev: BL 9/15/91; SLJ 2/92) [973]

4868 Frank, Andrew. *The Birth of Black America: The Age of Discovery and the Slave Trade* (6–8). (Milestones in Black American History) 1996, Chelsea LB $19.95 (0-7910-2257-9). This work covers the explosion of black slavery during the colonization of the Americas and the birth of African-American history and culture, and concludes with the end of the slave trade. (Rev: SLJ 10/96) [973.2]

4869 Franklin, John Hope. *From Slavery to Freedom: A History of Negro Americans.* 7th ed. (10–12). 1994, McGraw-Hill $34.75 (0-07-021907-9); paper $22.95 (0-685-02834-8). A history that begins with African origins and ends in the 1970s. [305.8]

4870 Freund, David M. P., and Marya Annette McQuirter. *Biographical Supplement and Index* (7–12). (Young Oxford History of African Americans) 1997, Oxford $35.50 (0-19-510258-4). In this, the last volume of the fine Young Oxford History of African Americans, there is an index to the 10-volume set plus brief biographies of key people mentioned in the set. (Rev: BL 9/1/97; BR 11–12/97; VOYA 12/97) [973]

4871 Gates, Henry Louis, Jr. *Thirteen Ways of Looking at a Black Man* (10–12). 1997, Random $22.00 (0-679-45713-5). The subject of being a black man in America is explored in a series of articles that deal with various aspects of this subject and uses, as examples, prominent personalities like Colin Powell, Louis Farrakhan, and Wynton Marsalis. (Rev: BL 2/15/97; SLJ 8/97) [973]

4872 Genovese, Eugene D. *Roll, Jordan, Roll: The World the Slaves Made* (10–12). 1976, Random paper $18.00 (0-394-71652-3). This is a history of slavery in America that concentrates on the daily life and traditions of slaves. [305.8]

4873 Greene, Meg. *Slave Young, Slave Long: The American Slave Experience* (5–8). Illus. (People's History) 1999, Lerner $22.60 (0-8225-1739-6). Using quotes from both victims and perpetrators, and illustrated by historical prints and photographs, this book presents the story of slavery in the United States. (Rev: BL 4/1/99; SLJ 10/99) [973.0496]

4874 Hacker, Andrew. *Two Nations: Black and White, Separate, Hostile, Unequal* (9–12). 1992, Scribners $24.95 (0-684-19148-2). This survey interprets research results on race relations in the United States. (Rev: BL 2/15/92) [305.8]

4875 Halberstam, David. *The Children* (10–12). 1998, Random $29.95 (0-679-41561-0); Fawcett paper $17.95 (0-449-00439-2). This prize-winning reporter profiles the 8 courageous students who launched the sit-ins in Nashville, Tennessee, in 1960, outlines the moral and political roots of the civil rights movement and the philosophical divisions that developed, assesses the impact of television coverage of the movement, and traces the 8 students' later lives and how their experiences affected them as adults. (Rev: BL 1/1–15/98; SLJ 11/98) [370.19]

4876 Hamilton, Virginia. *Many Thousand Gone: African Americans from Slavery to Freedom* (5–9). Illus. 1993, Random LB $18.99 (0-394-92873-3).

Combining history with personal slave narratives and biography, Hamilton tells of the famous—Douglass, Truth, Tubman—and the unknown—slaves, rebels, and conductors. (Rev: BL 12/1/92*; SLJ 5/93*) [973.7]

4877 Haskins, Jim. *The Day Martin Luther King, Jr., Was Shot: A Photo History of the Civil Rights Movement* (5–9). 1992, Scholastic paper $5.99 (0-590-43661-9). A photographic history of the African American struggle from the time of slavery to the early 1990s. (Rev: BL 2/1/92; SLJ 5/92) [323.4]

4878 Haskins, Jim, and Kathleen Benson. *Bound for America: The Forced Migration of Africans to the New World* (4–9). Illus. (From African Beginnings) 1999, Lothrop LB $17.93 (0-688-10259-X). Using strong oil-wash paintings and brief chapters, this work focuses on the horrible conditions aboard slave ships, on which thousands died. (Rev: BL 12/15/98; BR 5–6/99; SLJ 1/99*) [382]

4879 Hatt, Christine. *Slavery: From Africa to the Americas* (5–8). Illus. 1997, NTC $19.95 (0-87226-552-8). With the effective use of maps, illustrations, and reproductions of documents, this book presents a basic overview of the history of slavery in the United States. (Rev: SLJ 5/98) [973]

4880 Hauser, Pierre. *Great Ambitions: From the "Separate but Equal" Doctrine to the Birth of the NAACP (1896–1909)* (7–10). (Milestones in Black American History) 1995, Chelsea $19.95 (0-7910-2264-1); paper $8.95 (0-7910-2690-6). The history of African Americans at the end of the 19th and beginning of the 20th century, with coverage of such political and cultural pioneers as W. E. B. Du Bois, Charles Chesnutt, Paul Laurence Dunbar, and Scott Joplin. (Rev: BL 2/15/95) [323.1]

4881 Henry, Christopher. *Forever Free: From the Emancipation Proclamation to the Civil Rights Bill of 1875 (1863–1875)* (7–10). (Milestones in Black American History) 1995, Chelsea LB $19.95 (0-7910-2253-6); paper $9.95 (0-7910-2679-5). The history of African Americans during Reconstruction, covering the tearing down of racial barriers and the journey of blacks from political impotence to civil power. (Rev: BL 7/95; SLJ 10/95) [323.1]

4882 Hinds, Patricia Mignon, ed. *Essence: 25 Years Celebrating Black Women* (9–12). 1995, Abrams $35.00 (0-8109-3256-3). A celebration of one of the most important publications for African American women, with excellent photography and articles by poets, writers, and scholars. (Rev: BL 11/1/95) [305.48]

4883 Hine, Darlene Clark. *The Path to Equality: From the Scottsboro Case to the Breaking of Baseball's Color Barrier* (7–10). (Milestones in Black American History) 1995, Chelsea LB $19.95 (0-7910-2251-X); paper $9.95 (0-7910-2677-9). This section of African American history covers the Great Depression and World War II, and features the accomplishments of such people as Marion Anderson, Thurgood Marshall, A. Philip Randolph, and Jackie Robinson. (Rev: BL 8/95) [973]

4884 Hurmence, Belinda, ed. *Slavery Time When I Was Chillun* (8–12). Illus. 1997, Putnam $17.95 (0-399-23048-3); paper $8.95 (0-399-23194-3). A disturbing collection of 12 slave narratives that give firsthand accounts of brutality, family separation, and hard labor, as well as some of kindly masters and happy times. (Rev: BL 3/15/98) [975]

4885 Hutchinson, Earl Ofari. *Beyond O.J.: Race, Sex, and Class Lessons for America* (9–12). 1996, Middle Passage $19.95 (1-881032-12-4). A discussion about the implications of the Simpson case regarding race, class, and sex in America. (Rev: BL 12/15/95) [305.8]

4886 Johnson, Venice, ed. *Heart Full of Grace* (10–12). 1995, Simon & Schuster $21.00 (0-684-81428-5). An interesting collection of words of inspiration from African Americans, mostly from the 20th century. (Rev: BL 11/15/95; SLJ 5/96) [808.88]

4887 Johnson, Venice, ed. *Voices of the Dream: African-American Women Speak* (4–8). 1996, Chronicle $12.95 (0-8118-1113-1). A handsome anthology with quotes from such writers as Toni Morrison and Zora Neale Hurston, accompanied on the facing pages by paintings and drawings from equally celebrated African American women artists. (Rev: BL 2/15/96) [081]

4888 Karenga, Maulana. *Kwanzaa: A Celebration of Family, Community & Culture, Special Commemorative Edition* (6–12). Illus. 1997, Univ. of Sankore Pr. $25.00 (0-943412-21-8). This complete book on Kwanzaa explains its African and African American origins, devotes a chapter to each of its 7 principles, suggests activities, and gives answers to the most frequently asked questions about this holiday. (Rev: SLJ 10/98) [394.2]

4889 King, Martin Luther, Jr. *Strength to Love* (10–12). 1985, Fortress Pr. paper $16.00 (0-8006-1441-0). A collection of sermons against injustice and racism. [151]

4890 King, Martin Luther, Jr. *Why We Can't Wait* (7–12). 1988, NAL paper $4.95 (0-451-62675-3). A history of the black civil rights movement to the struggle in Birmingham, Alabama. [323.4]

4891 King, Wilma. *Toward the Promised Land: From Uncle Tom's Cabin to the Onset of the Civil War (1851–1861)* (7–10). (Milestones in Black American History) 1995, Chelsea paper $9.95 (0-7910-2691-4). This work examines the major trends and personalities in the struggle to end slavery before the Civil War, with material on Frederick Douglass, Sojourner Truth, Harriet Beecher Stowe,

and John Brown. (Rev: BL 7/95; SLJ 10/95; VOYA 12/95) [973]

4892 Kotlowitz, Alex. *The Other Side of the River: A Story of Two Towns, a Death, & America's Dilemma* (10–12). 1998, Doubleday $24.95 (0-385-47720-1). Race relations in 2 small neighboring lake towns in Michigan are explored in the author's investigation of the unsolved 1991 murder of a black teenager who dared to defy racial barriers. (Rev: BL 12/1/97; SLJ 6/98; VOYA 12/98) [305.8]

4893 Kranz, Rachel, and Philip Koslow. *The Biographical Dictionary of African Americans* (6–12). 1999, Facts on File $35.00 (0-8160-3903-8); paper $18.95 (0-8160-3904-6). Arranged chronologically from Colonial times on, this volume contains brief profiles of 230 African Americans ranging from our earliest times to entries for Queen Latifah and Tupac Shakur. (Rev: BL 4/15/99; SLJ 8/99) [973]

4894 Lester, Julius. *From Slave Ship to Freedom Road* (5–10). Illus. 1998, Dial $17.99 (0-8037-1893-4). This book combines art, history, and commentary to produce a graphically gripping history of slavery. (Rev: BL 2/15/98; SLJ 2/98*) [759.13]

4895 Lester, Julius. *To Be a Slave* (7–9). Illus. 1968, Dial $16.99 (0-8037-8955-6). A powerful account of what it means to be a slave drawn largely from actual documents. [326]

4896 Levine, Ellen. *Freedom's Children: Young Civil Rights Activists Tell Their Own Stories* (6–12). 1993, 1994, Avon paper $4.99 (0-380-72114-7). In this collection of oral histories, 30 African Americans who were part of the civil rights struggles in the 1950s–1960s South as children or teenagers recall what it was like. (Rev: BL 12/15/92*; SLJ 3/93*) [973]

4897 Lusane, Clarence. *No Easy Victories: Black Americans and the Vote* (8–12). Illus. (The African-American Experience) 1996, Watts LB $25.00 (0-531-11270-5). This history of African Americans' struggle for the right to vote begins with the Revolutionary War and continues through the Civil War, Reconstruction, the New Deal, and the Voting Rights Acts of 1965, and on to Jesse Jackson's bid for the Democratic nomination for president and the struggles of the early 1990s. (Rev: BL 2/15/97; SLJ 4/97) [323.1]

4898 Macht, Norman L., and Mary Hull. *The History of Slavery* (6–9). Illus. (World History) 1997, Lucent LB $17.96 (1-56006-302-5). This overview of slavery in the United States contains extensive quotes from original sources and a chronology. (Rev: BL 8/97; BR 11–12/97; SLJ 11/97) [306.3]

4899 McKissack, Patricia, and Fredrick McKissack. *Black Hands, White Sails: The Story of African-American Whalers* (6–10). Illus. 1999, Scholastic $15.95 (0-590-48313-7). This account of African

American involvement in the whaling industry from colonial times through the 19th century also tells how it figured in the abolitionist movement, the Underground Railroad, and the Northern side of the Civil War. (Rev: BL 9/1/99; BR 9–10/99) [639.2]

4900   Nash, Sunny. *Bigmama Didn't Shop at Woolworth's* (10–12). 1996, Texas A & M Univ. Pr. $19.95 (0-890-96716-4). A collection of vignettes by an African American woman who remembers growing up in the 1950s in a segregated neighborhood in Bryan, Texas, and the poverty, prejudice, and indignities of the time. (Rev: SLJ 12/96) [323.4]

4901   Okwu, Julian. *Face Forward: Young African American Men in a Critical Age* (10–12). 1997, Chronicle paper $19.95 (0-8118-1215-4). This is a photographic essay that describes the lives and work of 39 African American men who have defied traditional stereotypes and lead interesting, productive lives. (Rev: BL 6/1–15/97; SLJ 2/98; VOYA 10/97) [323.1]

4902   Parks, Rosa, and Gregory J. Reed. *Dear Mrs. Parks: A Dialogue with Today's Youth* (5–8). 1996, Lee & Low $16.95 (1-880000-45-8). This book contains a sampling of the thousands of letters sent to civil rights leader Rosa Parks and her replies. (Rev: BL 12/1/96; SLJ 12/96) [323]

4903   Patrick, Diane. *The New York Public Library Amazing African American History: A Book of Answers for Kids* (5–9). Illus. 1998, Wiley paper $12.95 (0-471-19217-1). Using a question-and-answer format, this book traces the history of African Americans from slavery to the present day. (Rev: BL 2/15/98; SLJ 4/98) [973]

4904   Potter, Joan, and Constance Claytor. *African-American Firsts* (9–12). 1994, Pinto Pr. paper $14.95 (0-9632476-1-1). Celebrates African American contributions to history and culture, from business and government to the theater and visual arts. (Rev: BL 1/15/94; SLJ 8/94) [973]

4905   Powledge, Fred. *We Shall Overcome: Heroes of the Civil Rights Movement* (7–10). 1993, Scribners $17.00 (0-684-19362-0). A history of the civil rights movement: why it began, the system of segregation that existed with the government's tacit approval, and the movement's milestones and heroes. (Rev: BL 6/1–15/93; VOYA 8/93) [323.1]

4906   Raboteau, Albert J. *African-American Religion* (9–12). (Religion in American Life) 1999, Oxford $22.00 (0-19-510680-6). The author explores religious freedom as a basic part of American history and society, traces the influence of black churches in America from Colonial times to the present, and examines the contributions of varied religious traditions to African American culture and identity, particularly in the struggle against racism. (Rev: BL 9/15/99; SLJ 8/99) [261.1]

4907   Rasmussen, R. Kent. *Farewell to Jim Crow: The Rise and Fall of Segregation in America* (8–12). (Library of African American History) 1997, Facts on File $19.95 (0-8160-3248-3). This is a history of segregation in the United States in such areas as housing, education, employment, transportation, and public accommodations, and efforts to end it. (Rev: BR 1–2/98; VOYA 2/98) [973]

4908   Reef, Catherine. *Africans in America: The Spread of People and Culture* (6–9). (Library of African American History) 1999, Facts on File $19.95 (0-8160-3772-8). The author traces the dispersion of African peoples and cultures in the New World as a result of the slave trade and their influence on the Americas. (Rev: BL 2/15/99; SLJ 6/99) [970.00496]

4909   Robeson, Paul, Jr. *Paul Robeson, Jr. Speaks to America* (9–12). 1993, Rutgers Univ. Pr. $25.00 (0-8135-1985-3). Essays precisely defining the issues at stake in "the struggle between the mosaic and the melting pot" and the nation's angry cultural wars. (Rev: BL 6/1–15/93) [305.8]

4910   Rogers, James T. *The Antislavery Movement* (7–12). (Social Reform Movements) 1994, Facts on File $19.95 (0-8160-2907-5). This work traces slavery and its repercussions from 1619 to the present and provides insights into the conflicting interests and positions. (Rev: BL 1/1/95; SLJ 12/94; VOYA 5/95) [973]

4911   Thomas, Hugh. *The Slave Trade: The Story of the Atlantic Slave Trade, 1440–1870* (10–12). Illus. 1997, Simon & Schuster $37.50 (0-684-81063-8). Every aspect of the slave trade is covered from the early 16th century to its abolition in the early 20th century, with particular attention to the economics and politics of slavery and its worldwide social acceptance and the widespread involvement of governments and people everywhere. (Rev: BL 10/1/97; SLJ 7/98) [326]

4912   Tillage, Leon W. *Leon's Story* (4–9). Illus. 1997, Farrar $14.00 (0-374-34379-9). An autobiographical account of growing up black and poor in the segregated South and of participating in the civil rights movement. (Rev: BL 10/1/97; BR 5–6/98; SLJ 12/97) [975.6]

4913   Ugwu-Oju, Dympna. *What Will My Mother Say: A Tribal African Girl Comes of Age in America* (9–12). 1995, Bonus $24.95 (1-56625-042-0). An African American mother born in Nigeria struggles with cultural conflicts while raising her American-born daughter. (Rev: BL 11/1/95) [306]

4914   Van Peebles, Mario, et al. *Panther: A Pictorial History of the Black Panthers and the Story Behind the Film* (8–12). 1995, Newmarket Pr. $29.95 (1-55704-233-0); paper $16.95 (1-55704-227-6). The first part of this heavily illustrated book recounts the beginnings of the Black Panther Party and its eventual collapse; the second half describes the making of the movie about the party. (Rev: VOYA 2/96) [973]

4915 Walter, Mildred P. *Mississippi Challenge* (7–12). 1992, Bradbury LB $18.95 (0-02-792301-0). An in-depth history of the civil rights struggle in Mississippi that tells how ordinary people worked to change the political system. (Rev: BL 11/1/92; SLJ 1/93) [305.896]

4916 Weber, Michael. *Causes & Consequences of the African-American Civil Rights Movements* (6–10). (Causes and Consequences) 1998, Raintree Steck-Vaughn $27.11 (0-8172-4058-6). The author traces the legal and social history of African Americans that led up to the historic 1963 March on Washington, recounts events of the 1950s and 1960s such as the integration of schools, the growing urban tensions, and the rise of the black power movement, and discusses the movement's lasting achievements and current problems. (Rev: SLJ 6/98) [973]

4917 Weisbrot, Robert. *Marching Toward Freedom* (7–12). (Milestones in Black American History) 1994, Chelsea paper $9.95 (0-7910-2682-5). This history covers African American affairs from the founding of the Southern Christian Leadership Conference to the assassination of Malcolm X (1957–1965), with material on Martin Luther King, Jr., James Farmer, Elijah Muhammad, and Malcolm X, among others. (Rev: BL 11/15/94; SLJ 9/94; VOYA 10/94) [973]

4918 Wepman, Dennis. *The Struggle for Freedom* (7–12). Illus. (Library of African American History) 1996, Facts on File $19.95 (0-8160-3270-X). This well-researched work, using many maps and primary sources, traces slavery from ancient Sumerian times and continues through the centuries, exploring the slave trade triangle involving Africa, American, and England, the role of public opinion, slave revolts, working conditions and treatment, the Underground Railroad, the Civil War, and the revolt of Caribbean slaves led by Toussaint L'Ouverture. (Rev: VOYA 10/96) [973]

4919 Whittemore, Katharine, and Gerald Marzorati. *Voices in Black and White: Writings on Race in America from Harper's Magazine* (9–12). 1992, Franklin Square Pr. LB $21.95 (1-879957-07-8); paper $14.95 (1-879957-06-X). This collection of articles on the American obsession with race includes writings by Mark Twain, William Faulkner, James Baldwin, Shelby Steele, and Jesse Jackson. (Rev: BL 11/15/92) [305.8]

4920 Woodson, Jacqueline, ed. *A Way out of No Way: Writings about Growing Up Black in America* (8–12). Illus. 1996, Holt $15.95 (0-8050-4570-8). A fine collection of prose and poetry, fiction and nonfiction, from some of the best African American

writers, among them James Baldwin, Paul Beatty, Jamaica Kincaid, and Langston Hughes, about growing up in America. (Rev: BL 2/15/97; BR 11–12/97; SLJ 7/97; VOYA 6/97) [808.898]

Asian Americans

4921 Auerbach, Susan. *Vietnamese Americans* (7–10). (American Voices) 1991, Rourke LB $18.95 (0-86593-136-4). Traces the history of Vietnamese Americans from their first struggles after arriving in the United States. (Rev: BL 2/15/92; SLJ 2/92) [973]

4922 Bandon, Alexandra. *Chinese Americans* (6–12). (Footsteps to America) 1994, Silver Burdett LB $14.95 (0-02-768149-1). A look at Chinese people in the United States, beginning with their first large immigration in the mid-19th century to the 1990s. (Rev: BL 10/15/94; SLJ 11/94; VOYA 2/95) [973]

4923 Bandon, Alexandra. *Filipino Americans* (6–10). (Footsteps to America) 1993, Macmillan LB $18.95 (0-02-768143-2). Examines why Filipino Americans left their homeland and their culture, politics, education, religion, and holidays in the United States. (Rev: BL 12/15/93; SLJ 12/93) [973]

4924 Brownstone, David M. *The Chinese-American Heritage* (7–12). Illus. 1988, Facts on File $16.95 (0-8160-1627-5). A lucid, honest account of why many Chinese migrated to the United States, their treatment here, and their gradual assimilation into American life and culture. (Rev: BL 3/1/89; BR 5–6/89; VOYA 6/89) [973]

4925 Chow, Claire S., ed. *Leaving Deep Water: The Lives of Asian American Women at the Crossroads of Two Cultures* (10–12). 1998, Dutton paper $24.95 (0-525-94075-8). In a series of personal narratives, Asian American women describe cultural conflicts, feelings of being different, sexism, and the generation gap. (Rev: BL 3/15/98; SLJ 1/99) [305.8]

4926 Dudley, William, ed. *Asian Americans* (7–12). (Opposing Viewpoints in American History) 1997, Greenhaven LB $21.96 (1-56510-524-9); paper $21.50 (1-56510-523-0). A collection of documents tracing attitudes and policies toward Asian immigrants and Asian American citizens from the 1850s to the present. (Rev: BL 12/15/96) [973]

4927 Hoobler, Dorothy, and Thomas Hoobler. *The Chinese American Family Album* (6–10). 1994, Oxford LB $25.00 (0-19-508130-7). The text is excerpted from letters, journals, oral histories, and newspaper accounts of Chinese Americans who describe life in China, their journey to North America, the difficulties they encountered, and the jobs they took. (Rev: BL 4/1/94; SLJ 5/94; VOYA 2/95) [973]

4928 Kassam, Nadya, ed. *Telling It Like It Is: Young Asian Women Talk* (7–12). 1998, Livewire paper $9.95 (0-7043-4941-8). These 22 short, informal essays reveal various attitudes toward sexism and racism as experienced by Hindu and Moslem girls whose families are from the Indian subcontinent but are now living in Britain. (Rev: BL 9/15/98; SLJ 8/98) [305.8914]

4929 Kessler, Lauren. *Stubborn Twig: Three Generations in the Life of a Japanese American Family* (9–12). 1993, Random $25.00 (0-679-41426-6). Kessler charts the history of a Japanese American family from 1908, when Masuo Yasui and his brothers settled in the Hood River Valley, through World War II and evacuation to internment camps, to the present day. (Rev: BL 11/15/93; SLJ 5/94) [973]

4930 Kim, Elaine H., and Eui-Young Yu. *East to America: Korean American Life Stories* (10–12). 1996, New Pr. $25.00 (1-56584-297-9). Using quotations from 38 interviews, this book presents a good cross-section of Korean American life in all strata of U.S. society. (Rev: SLJ 11/96) [305.895]

4931 Kitano, Harry. *The Japanese Americans* (5–8). (Land of Immigrants) 1995, Chelsea LB $19.95 (0-7910-3358-9); paper $9.95 (0-7910-3380-5). Provides extensive information on the history of Japanese Americans. (Rev: BL 10/15/95; VOYA 2/96) [305.895]

4932 Ng, Franklin. *The Taiwanese Americans* (10–12). (The New Americans) 1998, Greenwood $39.95 (0-313-29762-2). After an introduction to Taiwan, this book describes the immigration of Taiwanese to the United States principally after 1965, their reception here, and their present life and contributions. (Rev: SLJ 11/98) [973]

4933 Ragaza, Angelo. *Lives of Notable Asian Americans: Business, Politics, Science* (6–10). (Asian American Experience) 1995, Chelsea LB $18.95 (0-7910-2189-0). Asian Americans who have contributed in the business, political, and scientific arenas. (Rev: BL 8/95; VOYA 12/95) [973]

4934 Rolater, Fred S., and Jeannette Baker Rolater. *Japanese Americans* (7–10). (American Voices) 1991, Rourke LB $18.95 (0-86593-138-0). A history of Japanese immigration to this country, with material on their treatment here, their lifestyles, and their contributions. (Rev: BL 2/15/92) [973]

4935 St. Pierre, Stephanie. *Teenage Refugees from Cambodia Speak Out* (7–12). 1995, Rosen LB $16.95 (0-8239-1848-3). Grim stories of the escape from the "killing fields" and powerful testimony to the reality of refugee life. (Rev: BL 5/15/95; SLJ 5/95) [973]

4936 She, Colleen. *Teenage Refugees from China Speak Out* (7–12). (In Their Own Voices) 1995, Rosen LB $16.95 (0-8239-1847-5). Interviews with native Chinese teenagers who are now living in the United States. (Rev: BL 6/1–15/95; SLJ 5/95) [305.23]

4937 Stanley, Jerry. *I Am an American: A True Story of Japanese Internment* (5–10). 1994, Crown LB $17.99 (0-517-59787-X). A photoessay detailing the experiences of Japanese Americans during World War II. Focuses on war hysteria and the unjust use of internment camps. (Rev: BL 10/15/94*; SLJ 11/94*) [940.53]

4938 Takaki, Ronald. *Ethnic Islands: The Emergence of Urban Chinese America* (6–10). (Asian American Experience) 1994, Chelsea LB $19.95 (0-7910-2180-7). First-person accounts of the Chinese American experience in the 20th century. (Rev: BL 9/15/94; SLJ 9/94) [973]

4939 Takaki, Ronald. *From Exiles to Immigrants: The Refugees from Southeast Asia* (6–10). (Asian American Experience) 1995, Chelsea LB $19.95 (0-7910-2185-8). Personal histories of Southeast Asian refugees in the United States. (Rev: BL 8/95; VOYA 12/95) [978]

4940 Takaki, Ronald. *From the Land of Morning Calm: The Koreans in America* (6–10). (Asian American Experience) 1994, Chelsea LB $19.95 (0-7910-2181-5). Oral histories and local documents challenge stereotypes that plague Korean Americans. Photos and a chronology. (Rev: BL 9/1/94; SLJ 9/94; VOYA 12/94) [973]

4941 Takaki, Ronald. *In the Heart of Filipino America: Immigrants from the Pacific Isles* (6–10). (Asian American Experience) 1994, Chelsea LB $19.95 (0-7910-2187-4). A historic overview of Filipinos in the United States. (Rev: BL 12/15/94; VOYA 4/95) [973]

4942 Takaki, Ronald. *India in the West: South Asians in America* (6–10). (Asian American Experience) 1994, Chelsea LB $19.95 (0-7910-2186-6). This overview of the Asian Indian experience in the United States describes how, when, and why South Asians came to this country and the problems they have confronted. (Rev: BL 12/15/94; SLJ 3/95) [970]

4943 Takaki, Ronald. *Issei and Nisei: The Settling of Japanese America* (6–10). Adapted by Rebecca Steloff. Illus. (Asian American Experience) 1994, Chelsea LB $19.95 (0-7910-2179-3). A thorough, easy-to-read history of Japanese Americans from their first arrival in the late 1880s up until 1940. (Rev: BL 6/1–15/94; SLJ 6/94; VOYA 10/94) [973]

4944 Takaki, Ronald. *Journey to Gold Mountain: The Chinese in 19th-Century America* (6–10). Adapted by Rebecca Stefoff. Illus. (Asian American Experience) 1994, Chelsea LB $19.95 (0-7910-2177-7). The story of early Chinese American immigration, their reception, settlements, and role in the building of the railroads. (Rev: BL 6/1–15/94; SLJ 8/94) [973]

4945 Wapner, Kenneth. *Teenage Refugees from Vietnam Speak Out* (7–12). (In Their Own Voices) 1995, Rosen LB $16.95 (0-8239-1842-4). Interviews with native Vietnamese teenagers who are now living in the United States. (Rev: BL 6/1–15/95; SLJ 5/95) [305.23]

4946 Wilson, John. *Chinese Americans* (7–10). (American Voices) 1991, Rourke LB $18.95 (0-86593-135-6). A history of the immigration of Chinese to this country, with material on their customs, traditions, and contributions to U.S. culture. (Rev: BL 2/15/92) [973]

4947 Yamaguchi, Yoji. *A Student's Guide to Japanese American Genealogy* (8–12). 1996, Oryx $29.50 (0-89774-979-0). This book describes Japanese immigration to the United States and where they settled, followed by information on general genealogical research and on researching Japanese Americans' genealogies. (Rev: VOYA 8/96) [973]

Hispanic Americans

4948 Aliotta, Jerome J. *The Puerto Ricans* (5–8). (Land of Immigrants) 1995, Chelsea LB $19.95 (0-7910-3360-0). This account provides an extensive history of Puerto Ricans living in the United States, their struggles, traditions, and way of life. (Rev: BL 10/15/95) [305.868]

4949 Ashabranner, Brent. *Children of the Maya: A Guatemalan Indian Odyssey* (6–9). Illus. 1986, Dodd $14.95 (0-396-08786-8). The story of the Mayan Indians from Guatemala who are refugees in Florida. (Rev: BL 3/87; SLJ 8/86) [341.4]

4950 Bandon, Alexandra. *Mexican Americans* (6–10). (Footsteps to America) 1993, Macmillan LB $18.95 (0-02-768142-4). A look at Mexico and the culture of Mexican American immigrants in the United States, with first-person narratives of immigrant experiences. (Rev: BL 12/15/93; SLJ 12/93; VOYA 2/94) [305.868]

4951 Bernardo, Anilu. *Fitting In* (6–8). 1996, Arte Publico $14.95 (1-55885-176-3); paper $9.95 (1-55885-173-9). Five stories, each featuring an adolescent girl of Cuban background and a social concern about growing up Hispanic American. (Rev: BL 12/15/96; SLJ 11/96; VOYA 4/97)

4952 Carlson, Lori M., ed. *Barrio Streets Carnival Dreams: Three Generations of Latino Artisty* (9–12). 1996, Holt $15.95 (0-8050-4120-6). In this exploration of Hispanic cultural traditions, 3 generations of 20th-century American artists of Caribbean, Mexican, and South American ancestry describe their work, the difficulties of assimilation, and their desire to preserve Latino culture. (Rev: BR 1–2/97; SLJ 8/96; VOYA 12/96) [973]

4953 Cerar, K. Melissa. *Teenage Refugees from Nicaragua Speak Out* (7–12). (In Their Own Voices) 1995, Rosen LB $16.95 (0-8239-1849-1). The horror of the contra war, after the corrupt rule of the Somoza family was ended by the Sandinistas, is recalled by Nicaraguan teens who fled their country, leaving their families, to seek refuge in the United States. (Rev: BL 6/1–15/95) [973]

4954 Cockcroft, James D. *The Hispanic Struggle for Social Justice: The Hispanic Experience in the Americas* (8–12). (Hispanic Experience in the Americas) 1994, Watts LB $24.00 (0-531-11185-7). After a discussion of the diverse experiences of Mexican Americans, Puerto Ricans, and other Latinos in this country, the author examines their ethnic history and struggles around labor, immigration, civil rights, and women's rights issues. (Rev: BL 2/1/95) [305.868]

4955 Gonzalez-Pando, Miguel. *The Cuban Americans* (10–12). (The New Americans) 1998, Greenwood $39.95 (0-313-29824-6). Beginning with a history of Cuba including Castro's regime, this book tells why and how Cubans left their homeland, their reception here, and their current situation. (Rev: BR 11–12/98; SLJ 10/98; VOYA 12/98) [305.868]

4956 Lannert, Paula. *Mexican Americans* (7–10). (American Voices) 1991, Rourke LB $18.95 (0-86593-139-9). Traces the history of Mexican Americans, from the earliest migrations to the United States to the group's present status. (Rev: BL 2/15/92) [973]

4957 Marvis, Barbara. *Famous People of Hispanic Heritage, Vol. I* (5–10). Illus. (Multiracial Biography) 1995, Mitchell Lane LB $21.95 (1-883845-21-1); paper $12.95 (1-883845-20-3). This first volume of an 8-volume set contains biographies of 2 men and 2 women of Latino heritage who have gained fame in a variety of fields. (Rev: SLJ 1/96) [305]

4958 Novas, Himilce. *Everything You Need to Know about Latino History* (9–12). 1994, NAL paper $12.95 (0-452-27100-2). Surveys Latino culture, contributions, and history, including the Spanish-American War and the Mexican War. (Rev: BL 9/15/94) [973]

4959 Ochoa, George. *The New York Public Library Amazing Hispanic American History: A Book of Answers for Kids* (4–9). 1998, Wiley paper $12.95 (0-471-19204-X). Using a question-and-answer format, this work explores such topics as Hispanic American identity and history, cultural groups, accomplishments, and immigrant experiences. (Rev: BL 12/1/98; SLJ 11/98) [973]

4960 Ryskamp, George R., and Peggy Ryskamp. *A Student's Guide to Mexican American Genealogy* (6–10). (Oryx Family Tree) 1996, Oryx $29.50 (0-

89774-981-2). This book provides an interesting review of Mexican American history as well as an introduction to genealogy and a discussion of non-traditional families. (Rev: SLJ 2/97) [973]

4961 Sinnott, Susan. *Extraordinary Hispanic Americans* (5–10). (Extraordinary People) 1991, Children's Pr. LB $37.00 (0-516-00582-0). Biographies of Spanish-speaking people who made a significant impact on U.S. history from 1400 to the present. (Rev: BL 2/1/92) [973]

Indians and Other Native Americans

4962 Fixico, Donald L. *Urban Indians* (7–12). (Indians of North America) 1991, Chelsea LB $19.95 (1-55546-732-6). A challenge to current stereotypes about Native Americans and their role in modern society. (Rev: BL 7/91; SLJ 12/91) [307.76]

4963 Gravelle, Karen. *Soaring Spirits: Conversations with Native American Teens* (7–12). Illus. 1995, Watts LB $24.00 (0-531-11221-7). Seventeen young people from various tribes and reservations describe, through interviews, the problems and satisfactions of growing up Native American today. (Rev: BL 3/15/96) [305.23]

4964 Hoig, Stan. *People of the Sacred Arrows: The Southern Cheyenne Today* (6–8). 1992, Dutton $15.00 (0-525-65088-1). Portrayal of modern life of the southern Cheyenne. (Rev: BL 9/1/92; SLJ 11/92) [976.6]

4965 Roleff, Tamara L., ed. *Native American Rights* (9–12). (Current Controversies) 1997, Greenhaven LB $21.96 (1-56510-685-7); paper $16.20 (1-56510-684-9). This anthology presents a full range of opinions on 4 controversial issues: Native American culture, resources, sovereignty, and gaming. (Rev: SLJ 3/98) [307.76]

Jewish Americans

4966 Alepher, Joseph, ed. *Encyclopedia of Jewish History: Events and Eras of the Jewish People* (10–12). Illus. 1986, Facts on File $40.00 (0-8160-1220-2). In 100 entries, world Jewish history is detailed with accompanying maps, diagrams, and photographs. (Rev: BL 4/15/86) [909]

4967 Brooks, Philip. *Extraordinary Jewish Americans* (5–8). 1998, Children's Pr. LB $37.00 (1-516-20609-5); paper $16.95 (1-516-26350-1). A slim book that contains brief biographies of 60 notable Jews who have contributed to the United States culturally, commercially, and intellectually. (Rev: VOYA 6/99) [973]

4968 Leder, Jane. *A Russian Jewish Family* (5–8). (Journey Between Two Worlds) 1996, Lerner LB

$22.60 (0-8225-3401-0); paper $8.95 (0-8225-9744-6). This account compares the living conditions of a Jewish family in Russia and their new American home. (Rev: BL 11/1/96; SLJ 11/96) [977.3]

4969 Muggamin, Howard. *The Jewish Americans* (5–8). (Immigrant Experience) 1995, Chelsea LB $19.95 (0-7910-3365-1); paper $9.95 (0-7910-3387-2). An examination of Jewish Americans, their history of immigration and their reception in this country, and their achievements and contributions. (Rev: BL 11/15/95) [973]

4970 Schleifer, Jay. *A Student's Guide to Jewish American Genealogy* (7–12). (American Family Tree) 1996, Oryx $29.50 (0-89774-977-4). An in-depth survey of Jewish history serves as a framework for realistic genealogical information, with plenty of valuable sources cited. (Rev: SLJ 1/97) [973]

4971 Shamir, Ilana, and Shlomo Shavit, eds. *The Young Reader's Encyclopedia of Jewish History* (5–10). Illus. 1987, Viking paper $17.95 (0-670-81738-4). From a home for nomadic tribes to the present, here is a history of Israel and the Jewish people in many brief chapters. (Rev: BL 3/15/88; SLJ 2/88) [909]

4972 Suberman, Stella. *The Jew Store: A Family Memoir* (10–12). 1998, Algonquin $30.95 (1-56512-198-8). Russian immigrant Aaron Bronson moved his family from New York City and opened a store in a tiny Tennessee town in the 1920s. This is the story of the only Jewish family in town as recalled by the youngest member of the family. (Rev: BL 7/98; SLJ 11/98) [305.8]

Other Ethnic Groups

4973 Ashabranner, Brent. *To Seek a Better World: The Haitian Minority in America* (5–10). 1997, NAL paper $16.99 (0-525-65219-1). A photoessay that explores the world of Haitian Americans, their homeland, culture, and contributions to the United States. (Rev: BL 5/15/97; BR 9–10/97; SLJ 5/97) [973]

4974 Bandon, Alexandra. *West Indian Americans* (6–12). (Footsteps to America) 1994, Silver Burdett LB $18.95 (0-02-768148-3). This work describes immigration from the West Indies, its causes, who immigrated, where they settled, and their lives here. (Rev: BL 10/15/94; SLJ 12/94) [973]

4975 Brockman, Terra Castiglia. *A Student's Guide to Italian American Genealogy* (7–12). (American Family Tree) 1996, Oryx $29.50 (0-89774-973-1). This book, a guide to searching for Italian American ancestors, contains web sites, computer programs, addresses, and other sources of information. (Rev: SLJ 10/96) [929]

4976 Brownstone, David M. *The Irish-American Heritage* (7–12). Illus. 1989, Facts on File $16.95 (0-8160-1630-5). The story of the waves of Irish immigration and how these people became assimilated into American life. (Rev: BL 9/1/89; SLJ 6/90; VOYA 2/90) [973]

4977 Cook, Bernard A., and Rosemary Petralle Cook. *German Americans* (7–10). (American Voices) 1991, Rourke LB $18.95 (0-86593-140-2). A review of the waves of German immigration to the United States, the reasons, their reception, and their contributions. (Rev: BL 2/15/92) [973]

4978 Franck, Irene M. *The German-American Heritage* (7–12). Illus. 1988, Facts on File $19.95 (0-8160-1629-1). This book contains not only an account of the progress of Germans in this country but also a brief history of Germany. (Rev: BL 3/15/89; BR 5–6/89) [973]

4979 Galicich, Anne. *The German Americans* (5–8). Illus. (Immigrant Experience) 1996, Chelsea LB $19.95 (0-7910-3362-7). This account traces the history of German Americans, from their reasons for leaving Germany and their initial reception in the United States to their present status. (Rev: BL 7/96) [973]

4980 Halliburton, Warren J. *The West Indian-American Experience* (7–10). 1994, Millbrook LB $22.40 (1-56294-340-5). Tells the story of a Jamaican family's emigration to the United States in the 1980s, the history of the Caribbean, and immigration to the United States. (Rev: BL 4/1/94; SLJ 7/94) [973]

4981 Israel, Fred L. *The Amish* (5–8). Illus. (Immigrant Experience) 1996, Chelsea LB $19.95 (0-7910-3368-6). The story of this conservative division of the Mennonites, why they settled in the United States, and their contributions to the nation. (Rev: BL 7/96; SLJ 10/96) [305.6]

4982 Johnson, Anne E. *A Student's Guide to British American Genealogy* (7–12). (American Family Tree) 1995, Oryx $29.50 (0-89774-982-0). This book gives instructions on how to start a genealogical search, explains English, Scottish, and Welsh history and traditions, and describes names, nobility, clans, and the history of British immigration to America. (Rev: SLJ 4/96) [973]

4983 Katz, William L. *Black Indians: A Hidden Heritage* (7–10). 1986, Macmillan $17.00 (0-689-31196-6). A history of the group that represented a mixture of the Indian and black races and its role in opening up the West. (Rev: BL 6/15/86; SLJ 8/86) [970]

4984 McGill, Allyson. *The Swedish Americans* (5–8). (The Immigrant Experience) 1997, Chelsea $19.95 (0-7910-4551-X); paper $9.95 (0-7910-4552-8). An account that explains why Swedes have emigrated from their homeland, their reception in the

United States, and their contributions to the nation. (Rev: BL 10/15/97) [322.4]

4985 McKenna, Erin. *A Student's Guide to Irish American Genealogy* (7–12). Illus. 1996, Oryx $29.50 (0-89774-976-6). Along with giving practical tips on how to trace Irish ancestors, this book traces Irish history, immigration, Irish culture, and contributions. (Rev: BL 3/1/97; VOYA 4/97) [973]

4986 Naff, Alixa. *The Arab Americans* (6–10). (The Immigrant Experience) 1998, Chelsea LB $19.95 (0-7910-5051-3); paper $9.95 (0-7910-5053-X). After a brief description of Arab culture and homelands, this book describes the different cycles in Arab immigration to this country, the reception Arabs received, their new identities and contributions, and famous Arab Americans such as Ralph Nader and Donna Shalala. (Rev: SLJ 1/99) [305.8]

4987 O'Connor, Karen. *A Kurdish Family* (5–8). (Journey Between Two Worlds) 1996, Lerner LB $22.60 (0-8225-3402-9); paper $8.95 (0-8225-9743-8). This work describes the living conditions endured by a Kurdish family in their homeland and their new life in the United States. (Rev: BL 11/1/96; SLJ 11/96) [305.891]

4988 Paddock, Lisa, and Carl S. Rollyson. *A Student's Guide to Scandinavian American Genealogy* (7–12). (American Family Tree) 1996, Oryx $29.50 (0-89774-978-2). An introduction to the Scandinavian countries, people, and emigration to America, and information on how to research specific nationalities. (Rev: SLJ 10/96) [929]

4989 Sawyers, June S. *Famous Firsts of Scottish-Americans* (4–8). Illus. 1996, Pelican $13.95 (1-56554-122-7). Brief biographies of 30 Americans of Scottish descent, including Neil Armstrong, Alexander Calder, Herman Melville, and Patrick Henry. (Rev: BL 6/1–15/97) [920]

4990 Strazzabosco-Hayn, Gina. *Teenage Refugees from Iran Speak Out* (7–12). 1995, Rosen LB $16.95 (0-8239-1845-9). Iranian teens tell their grim stories as powerful testimony to the reality of refugee life. (Rev: BL 5/15/95; SLJ 5/95) [973]

4991 Tekavec, Valerie. *Teenage Refugees from Haiti Speak Out* (7–12). (In Their Own Voices) 1995, Rosen LB $16.95 (0-8239-1844-0). Interviews with native Haitian teenagers who are now living in the United States. (Rev: BL 6/1–15/95; SLJ 6/95) [305.23]

4992 Ueda, Reed, and Sandra Stotsky, eds. *Irish-American Answer Book* (6–10). 1999, Chelsea LB $17.95 (0-7910-4795-4); paper $9.95 (0-7910-4796-2). Using a question-and-answer format, this book examines the history, culture, politics, and religion of Irish Americans from the 1800s to the present. (Rev: VOYA 2/99) [973]

4993 Watts, J. F. *The Irish Americans* (5–8). (Immigrant Experience) 1995, Chelsea paper $8.95 (0-7910-3388-0). A lively, informative account of why the Irish came to America, the conditions they found here, and how they have fared. (Rev: BL 10/15/95) [973]

4994 Whitehead, Sandra. *Lebanese Americans* (5–8). (Cultures of America) 1996, Benchmark LB $28.50 (0-7614-0163-6). This work outlines the cultural traditions, food, family life, and customs of Lebanese Americans. (Rev: BR 9–10/96; SLJ 6/96) [973]

4995 Witkoski, Michael. *Italian Americans* (7–10). (American Voices) 1991, Rourke LB $18.95 (0-86593-137-2). The history of Italian Americans from the early explorers to the present day. (Rev: BL 2/15/92; SLJ 2/92) [973]

4996 Zamenova, Tatyana. *Teenage Refugees from Russia Speak Out* (7–12). (In Their Own Voices) 1995, Rosen LB $16.95 (0-8239-1846-7). Teenage Russian refugees describe their lives under socialism, leaving Russia, and adjusting to life in North America. (Rev: BL 6/1–15/95) [973]

Social Concerns and Problems

General and Miscellaneous

4997 Andryszewski, Tricia. *The Militia Movement in America: Before and After Oklahoma City* (7–12). Illus. 1997, Millbrook LB $22.40 (0-7613-0119-4). This work traces the roots of the anti-government militia movement in the United States from the late 1800s to the present, with coverage of events in Ruby Ridge, Idaho; Waco, Texas; Oklahoma City, Oklahoma; and elsewhere. (Rev: BL 2/15/97; BR 9–10/97; SLJ 3/97; VOYA 2/98) [320.4]

4998 Bekoff, Marc, and Carron A. Meaney, eds. *Encyclopedia of Animal Rights and Animal Welfare* (7–12). 1998, Greenwood $59.95 (0-313-29977-3). Signed entries explore different aspects of the animal rights issue, including such topics as hunting, genetic engineering, and laboratory use. (Rev: BL 9/15/98; SLJ 2/99; VOYA 2/99) [179]

4999 Bernards, Neal. *Gun Control* (6–9). (Overview) 1991, Lucent LB $22.45 (1-56006-127-8). Examines various approaches toward gun control, different interpretations of the Second Amendment, whether gun control reduces crime, and gun control in Canada, Japan, and Great Britain. (Rev: BL 8/92; SLJ 6/92) [363.3]

5000 Bowman-Kruhm, Mary, and Claudine G. Wirths. *Coping with Discrimination and Prejudice* (8–12). (Coping) 1998, Rosen $17.95 (0-8239-2782-2). This book deals with discrimination on the basis of race, gender, religion, and disabilities, examines both its obvious and subtle forms, and discusses how to recognize acts of discrimination and deal with them. (Rev: SLJ 2/99; VOYA 10/99) [305]

5001 Cann, Kate. *Living in the World* (5–9). Illus. (Life Education) 1997, Watts LB $19.00 (0-531-14430-5). This book uses cartoon drawings, photographs, anecdotes, and pointed questions to explore group and interpersonal interactions, including such issues as racism, prejudice, and social activism, and suggests ways of coping with peer pressure. (Rev: SLJ 1/98) [305.8]

5002 Chaiet, Donna, and Francine Russell. *The Safe Zone: A Kid's Guide to Personal Safety* (6–10). 1998, Morrow $15.00 (0-688-15307-0); paper $4.95 (0-688-15308-9). This book about violent crimes alerts youngsters to danger signs, gives advice on body language and self-esteem, and offers tips on how to avoid threatening situations. (Rev: BR 11–12/98; SLJ 4/98) [364.3]

5003 Cohen, Daniel. *Animal Rights: A Handbook for Young Adults* (6–9). 1993, Millbrook LB $22.40 (1-56294-219-0). Discusses the use of animals for medical experimentation, zoos, marine theme parks, rodeos, factory farming and hunting, puppy mills, and classroom dissection. (Rev: BL 7/93; VOYA 2/94) [179]

5004 Cox, Vic. *Guns, Violence, and Teens* (7–12). Illus. (Issues in Focus) 1997, Enslow LB $17.95 (0-89490-721-2). Topics covered in this book include the evolution of gun use in America, gun control, teenage violence, and the impact that guns have on teenagers. (Rev: BL 10/15/97; BR 11–12/97; SLJ 1/98; VOYA 2/98) [363.4]

5005 Cozic, Charles P., ed. *The Militia Movement* (8–12). (At Issue) 1996, Greenhaven LB $14.94 (1-56510-542-7); paper $15.75 (1-56510-541-9). A presentation of a broad spectrum of opinions on the militia movement, from those who say it is racist, extremist, and potentially violent to advocates who stress the Constitutional right to bear arms. (Rev: BL 3/1/97; SLJ 4/97) [322.4]

5006 Cozic, Charles P., and Paul A. Winters, eds. *Gambling* (7–12). (Current Controversies) 1995, Greenhaven LB $21.96 (1-56510-235-5); paper

$16.20 (1-56510-234-7). A collection of viewpoints on gambling, on why people become addicted, and on its social and economic effects. (Rev: BL 8/95; SLJ 10/95) [363.4]

5007 Davidson, Osha Gray. *Under Fire: The NRA and the Battle for Gun Control* (9–12). 1993, Holt $25.00 (0-8050-1904-9). Focuses on the history, agenda, influence, and status of the powerful National Rifle Association. (Rev: BL 4/1/93*) [363.3]

5008 Dolan, Edward F., and Margaret M. Scariano. *Guns in the United States* (7–12). 1994, Watts LB $24.00 (0-531-11189-X). Discusses rising gun violence in America, without taking sides in the gun-control debate, to encourage readers to investigate and take a knowledgeable stand on gun control. (Rev: BL 1/15/95; VOYA 5/95) [363.3]

5009 Ennew, Judith. *Exploitation of Children* (6–10). Illus. (Global Issues) 1996, Raintree Steck-Vaughn LB $24.26 (0-8172-4546-4). This book presents historical material, statistical data, case studies, and differing viewpoints on how children are exploited in many countries of the world. (Rev: BL 2/1/97; VOYA 6/97) [305.23]

5010 Fraser, Laura, et al. *The Animal Rights Handbook: Everyday Ways to Save Animal Lives* (10–12). 1990, Living Planet paper $4.95 (0-9626072-0-7). This guide to animals' rights includes sections on uses of animals, their treatment in various situations, important addresses, and suggestions for change. (Rev: BL 10/1/90; SLJ 4/91) [179.3]

5011 Freedman, Russell. *Kids at Work: Lewis Hine and the Crusade Against Child Labor* (5–9). Photos. 1994, Clarion $18.00 (0-395-58703-4). A profile of the investigative photographer and how he used his camera to expose the horrors of forced child labor in the United States during the early 20th century. His dramatic photos are included. (Rev: BL 8/94; SLJ 9/94*) [331.3]

5012 Frost, Helen, ed. *Why Darkness Seems So Light: Young People Speak Out About Violence* (9–12). 1998, Pecan Grove Pr. $10.00 (1-877603-58-9). This is a collection of 40 essays by high school students in Allen County, Indiana, who answer the question, "Have you ever been personally affected by violence?" (Rev: VOYA 4/99) [616.85]

5013 Gay, Kathlyn. *Child Labor: A Global Crisis* (6–10). 1998, Millbrook LB $21.40 (0-7613-0368-5). The horrors of child labor are revealed through personal accounts of children in the United States, India, Mexico, Burma, Pakistan, and many other countries, along with a description of efforts by international organizations to improve the conditions of child laborers and the complexity of enacting and enforcing child protection laws. (Rev: SLJ 4/99) [331.3]

5014 Gay, Kathlyn. *Militias: Armed and Dangerous* (7–12). Illus. (Issues in Focus) 1997, Enslow LB $19.95 (0-89490-902-9). A disturbing look at the militia movement in the U.S. and the attraction it holds for such malcontents as survivalists, neo-Nazis, white supremacists, Christian fanatics, and government haters. (Rev: BL 11/15/97; VOYA 2/98) [322.4]

5015 Gay, Kathlyn. *Neo-Nazis: A Growing Threat* (8–12). Illus. (In Focus) 1997, Enslow LB $19.95 (0-89490-901-0). After a discussion of 8 recent neo-Nazi-related crimes, the author describes the philosophy and goals of this movement, current groups, and how to fight hate crimes. (Rev: BL 9/1/97; BR 11–12/97; SLJ 10/97) [320.53]

5016 Haddock, Patricia. *Teens and Gambling: Who Wins?* (7–12). Illus. (Issues in Focus) 1996, Enslow LB $19.95 (0-89490-719-0). The controversial subject of gambling is introduced—its lure, addiction, and problems, particularly as related to teenagers. (Rev: BL 8/96; SLJ 8/96; VOYA 10/96) [363.4]

5017 Hamilton, Neil A. *Militias in America: A Reference Handbook* (9–12). (Contemporary World Issues) 1996, ABC-CLIO LB $45.00 (0-87436-859-6). The history of the militia movement in this country is covered, with material on their philosophies, organization, activities, and motivational focuses like alienation, paranoia, conspiracy theories, and disenchantment with the government. (Rev: BL 3/1/97; SLJ 3/97; VOYA 6/97) [302.3]

5018 Harnack, Andrew, ed. *Animal Rights* (8–12). (Opposing Viewpoints) 1996, Greenhaven LB $21.96 (1-56510-399-8); paper $17.96 (1-56510-398-X). Topics discussed in this well-balanced anthology cover such questions as: Do animals have rights? Should they be used in experiments? Should animals be used for food and other commodities? Is wildlife protection necessary? and What are the issues that need to be resolved in the animal rights movement? (Rev: SLJ 9/96; VOYA 10/96) [179]

5019 Hjelmeland, Andy. *Legalized Gambling: Solution or Illusion?* (8–12). (Pro/Con) 1998, Lerner $23.93 (0-8225-2615-8). After a brief history of gambling since ancient times, this book discusses current forms of legalized gambling including lotteries, the controversy over various forms of legalized gambling, and the operation of casinos—including tactics used by casinos to keep their customers gambling. (Rev: SLJ 12/98) [795]

5020 Hurley, Jennifer A. *Animal Rights* (7–12). (Opposing Viewpoints Digests) 1998, Greenhaven LB $17.96 (1-56510-869-8); paper $11.96 (1-56510-868-X). The rights of animals are defined and their place in experimentation and hunting and slaughter for human consumption explored in this book that presents different attitudes and opinions. (Rev: BL 4/15/99) [179]

5021 Hyde, Margaret O. *Gambling: Winners and Losers* (6–10). 1995, Millbrook LB $22.40 (1-56294-532-7). A timely subject gets rather dry treatment in this book that tells of the history, types, and psychology of gambling, with quotes from many case studies. (Rev: BL 12/15/95; BR 5–6/96; SLJ 3/96) [363.4]

5022 James, Barbara. *Animal Rights* (7–10). (Talking Points) 1999, Raintree Steck-Vaughn LB $27.11 (00-8172-5317-3). Various aspects of the animal rights controversy are explored in an objective, straightforward manner. (Rev: BL 8/99; BR 9–10/99) [179.3]

5023 Klee, Sheila. *Working Together Against School Violence* (6–10). (The Library of Social Activism) 1996, Rosen LB $16.95 (0-8239-2262-6). This guide introduces the increase in school violence and its causes in the context of violence in society, and shows students what they can do to reduce it in their schools. (Rev: SLJ 2/97) [371.5]

5024 Kopka, Deborah L. *School Violence* (7–12). (Contemporary World issues) 1997, ABC-CLIO LB $45.00 (0-87436-861-8). An overview of juvenile violence over the last 30 years, potential risk factors in youth violence, and efforts to curb school violence. (Rev: BR 3–4/98; SLJ 2/98) [371.5]

5025 Kreiner, Anna. *Everything You Need to Know about School Violence* (6–8). (Need to Know Library) 1996, Rosen LB $17.95 (0-8239-2054-2). Reasons for increased violence in schools are discussed, along with ways students can protect themselves and work for positive change. (Rev: SLJ 3/96) [364.3]

5026 Kronenwetter, Michael. *Encyclopedia of Modern American Social Issues* (7–12). 1997, ABC-CLIO LB $65.00 (0-87436-779-4). In alphabetically arranged articles, this book presents well-balanced information on such controversial issues as abortion, child abuse, drug testing, gun control, Head Start, same-sex marriage, Ebonics, and secondhand smoke. (Rev: BR 9–10/98; SLJ 5/98) [306]

5027 Kruschke, Earl R. *Gun Control: A Reference Handbook* (9–12). (Contemporary World Issues) 1995, ABC-CLIO LB $48.50 (0-87436-695-X). A culmination of 35 years of research, this handbook presents varied ways of viewing the problem of gun control, citing important historical cases and laws and including a philosophical chronology from Plato to the present. (Rev: BR 9–10/96; SLJ 5/96; VOYA 6/96) [172]

5028 Lang, Paul. *The English Language Debate: One Nation, One Language?* (7–12). Illus. 1995, Enslow LB $18.95 (0-89490-642-9). A well-documented account that explores such multicultural topics as the English-only movement, bilingual education, and other current political aspects of the

teaching, status, and use of English in this country. (Rev: BL 6/1–15/95) [306.4]

5029 Levine, Herbert M. *Animal Rights* (7–12). Illus. (American Issues Debated) 1997, Raintree Steck-Vaughn LB $28.55 (0-8172-4350-X). Should animals be banned from use in science? Should hunting be illegal? Should people be ashamed of wearing fur? These and other questions related to animals are explored from different points of view. (Rev: BL 11/15/97; BR 1–2/98; VOYA 2/98) [179]

5030 Levine, Herbert M. *Gun Control* (7–12). Illus. (American Issues Debated) 1997, Raintree Steck-Vaughn LB $27.83 (0-8172-4351-8). The debate on the effectiveness of gun control in reducing crime is presented, along with questions concerning handgun bans, waiting periods, and penalties for illegal gun use. (Rev: BL 11/15/97; BR 1–2/98) [363.3]

5031 Maguire, Stephen, and Bonnie Wren, eds. *Torn by the Issues: An Unbiased Review of the Watershed Issues in American Life* (9–12). 1994, Fithian paper $15.95 (1-56474-093-5). Presents opposing viewpoints surrounding the nation's most contentious social issues, among them abortion, AIDS, animal rights, global warming, homelessness, gun control, and welfare. (Rev: BL 7/94) [306]

5032 Meltzer, Milton. *Cheap Raw Material: How Our Youngest Workers Are Exploited and Abused* (9–12). 1994, Viking paper $15.99 (0-670-83128-X). Survey of the history of child labor that reveals the continuing exploitation of young people in the U.S. workplace. (Rev: BL 3/1/94*; SLJ 7/94) [331.3]

5033 Miller, Maryann. *Everything You Need to Know About Dealing with the Police* (8–12). (Need to Know) 1994, Rosen LB $17.95 (0-8239-1875-0). After an examination of situations where teens might be involved with police, this book discusses minors' rights and how to behave when dealing with the police. (Rev: BR 9–10/96; SLJ 12/95; VOYA 2/96) [363.2]

5034 Nisbet, Lee, ed. *The Gun Control Debate: You Decide* (10–12). 1990, Prometheus paper $18.95 (0-87975-618-7). From a variety of sources, this is a collection of 22 essays that explore various aspects of the gun control controversy. (Rev: BL 12/15/90) [363.3]

5035 Owen, Marna. *Animal Rights: Yes or No?* (6–10). 1993, Lerner LB $23.93 (0-8225-2603-4). A discussion of the various positions on animal rights. (Rev: BL 1/15/94; SLJ 3/94) [179]

5036 Parker, David L., et al. *Stolen Dreams: Portraits of Working Children* (6–12). Illus. 1997, Lerner LB $19.95 (0-8225-2960-2). This compelling photoessay deals with child labor around the world, particularly in the Far East. (Rev: BL 11/1/97; VOYA 2/98) [331.3]

5037 Patterson, Charles. *Animal Rights* (6–10). 1993, Enslow LB $19.95 (0-89490-468-X). A thorough examination of the topic, including a history of animal rights movements. (Rev: BL 10/15/93; SLJ 11/93; VOYA 2/94) [179]

5038 Pringle, Laurence. *The Animal Rights Controversy* (7–12). Illus. 1989, Harcourt $16.95 (0-15-203559-1). A book about the way animals are abused and misused that covers topics such as factory farming, experimentation, and zoos. (Rev: BL 1/15/90; SLJ 5/90; VOYA 4/90) [197]

5039 Ridgeway, James. *Blood in the Face: The Ku Klux Klan, Aryan Nations, Nazi Skinheads, and the Rise of a New White Culture* (9–12). 1991, Thunder's Mouth $29.95 (1-560250-02-X); paper $19.95 (1-56025-100-X). Analysis of the racist far right and its organized hatred. (Rev: BL 1/15/91) [305.8]

5040 Rochford, Dierdre. *Rights for Animals?* (4–8). (Viewpoints) 1997, Watts LB $22.50 (0-531-14414-3). A presentation of different viewpoints on the use of animals in cosmetic and drug testing, blood sports such as bull fighting, hunting, endangered animals, zoos, farming practices that support meat production, and protesters. (Rev: SLJ 5/97) [179.3]

5041 Saunders, Carol Silverman. *Straight Talk about Teenage Gambling* (7–12). (Straight Talk) 1999, Facts on File $24.95 (0-8160-3718-3). This book details the physical and emotional stakes involved with games of chance and what happens when teens become completely preoccupied with gambling. (Rev: BL 1/1–15/99; BR 9–10/99; SLJ 8/99) [362.2]

5042 Schleifer, Jay. *Everything You Need to Know about Weapons in School and at Home* (7–12). Illus. (Everything You Need to Know) 1994, Rosen LB $17.95 (0-8239-1531-X). This timely book discusses why young people carry guns, how schools are combating this, and how to settle quarrels reasonably with alternative methods of self-defense. (Rev: BL 4/15/94; SLJ 6/94; VOYA 8/94) [363.3]

5043 Schwartz, Ted. *Kids and Guns: The History, the Present, the Dangers, and the Remedies* (7–12). 1999, Watts $24.00 (0-531-11723-5). This book describes the issue of kids and guns, the scope of the problem, issues involved in gun ownership, teenage violence and the media, and how to create safe schools. (Rev: BL 7/99; SLJ 9/99) [303.6]

5044 Sherman, Aliza. *Working Together Against Violence Against Women* (6–10). (Library of Social Activism) 1996, Rosen LB $16.95 (0-8239-2258-8). This work introduces violence against women, including date rape, stranger rape, assault, and domestic violence, explores actions being taken by both government and private agencies, and offers advice on how teenagers can help themselves, a

friend, and their communities. (Rev: SLJ 2/97; VOYA 6/97) [303.6]

5045 Sherry, Clifford J. *Animal Rights* (7–12). (Contemporary World Issues) 1995, ABC-CLIO LB $39.50 (0-87436-733-6). A well-organized volume that introduces the philosophical basis for the animal rights movement, present day problems, and the pros and cons of using animals in research. (Rev: SLJ 1/96) [346]

5046 Stewart, Gail B. *Militias* (7–12). Illus. (Overview) 1997, Lucent LB $18.96 (1-56006-501-X). This book traces the historical development of the militia movement and discusses prominent contemporary militia groups, their purposes, the beliefs and attitudes of their members and leaders, their activities, and why they are flourishing. (Rev: BL 1/1–15/98) [322.4]

5047 Streissguth, Thomas. *Hatemongers and Demagogues* (6–9). 1995, Oliver Pr. LB $18.95 (1-881508-23-4). A survey of American leaders who have used hate and inflammatory language to incite violence, along with an examination of the conditions that led people to support these demagogues, from the individuals who provoked the Salem witch hunts to Louis Farrakhan. (Rev: BL 12/15/95; BR 9–10/96; SLJ 2/96; VOYA 6/96) [305.8]

5048 Sugarmann, Josh. *NRA: Money, Firepower and Fear* (9–12). 1991, National Press Books $19.95 (0-915765-88-8). An in-depth review of the National Rifle Association and the methods it's used to transform a constitutional right into the social nightmare of unregulated possession of weapons. (Rev: BL 12/1/91) [363.3]

5049 Thompson, Sharon E. *Hate Groups* (6–8). Illus. (Overview) 1994, Lucent LB $22.45 (1-56006-144-8). An in-depth look at hate groups in America, what motivates them, their targets, and ways to combat them. (Rev: BL 3/15/94; VOYA 8/94) [305.8]

5050 Warner, Rachel. *Refugees* (6–10). Illus. (Global Issues) 1996, Raintree Steck-Vaughn LB $24.26 (0-8172-4547-2). After a brief history of the refugee problems, current case studies are used to explore this issue and how it is being confronted in today's world. (Rev: BL 3/15/97) [362.87]

5051 Williams, Mary E., ed. *Child Labor and Sweatshops* (9–12). (At Issue) 1998, Greenhaven LB $20.96 (0-7377-0003-3); paper $12.45 (0-7377-0002-5). This anthology of 17 articles explores the international use of cheap labor, chiefly women and children, and how this terrible exploitation of the most vulnerable can be reduced and perhaps prevented. (Rev: BR 9–10/99; SLJ 6/99) [306]

5052 Williams, Mary E., ed. *Working Women* (8–12). (Opposing Viewpoints) 1997, Greenhaven LB $21.96 (1-56510-677-6). Differing viewpoints on the impact of women entering the work force, sexual harassment, discrimination, and women in the military are presented in this anthology of articles. (Rev: BL 11/15/97; VOYA 6/98) [5.4.1]

5053 Wiloch, Tom. *Everything You Need to Know about Protecting Yourself & Others from Abduction* (6–9). Illus. (Need to Know Library) 1998, Rosen LB $17.95 (0-8239-2553-6). This book describes the dangers of abduction and its frequency in America and provides safety tips for home, at school, while babysitting, jogging, and bicycling, and using the Internet. (Rev: BR 9–10/98; SLJ 9/98) [364]

5054 Winters, Paul A., ed. *America's Victims* (9–12). (Opposing Viewpoints) 1996, Greenhaven LB $20.96 (1-56510-401-3); paper $16.20 (1-56510-400-5). Current selections from books and periodicals explore various points of view on victimhood in America in relation to such areas as the criminal justice system, the civil rights movement, and drug therapy/ recovery programs. (Rev: BL 12/15/96; BR 1–2/97; SLJ 11/96; VOYA 2/97) [306]

Environmental Issues

General and Miscellaneous

5055 Aldis, Rodney. *Towns and Cities* (5–8). (Ecology Watch) 1992, Dillon LB $17.95 (0-87518-496-0). A discussion of urban life and environmental problems that it creates. (Rev: BL 12/15/92) [574.5]

5056 Allen, Judy, ed. *Anthology for the Earth* (4–8). 1998, Candlewick $21.99 (0-7636-0301-5). In this illustrated anthology of poetry and prose, the natural world and how human intervention has changed it are explored. (Rev: BR 9–10/98; SLJ 4/98; VOYA 2/99) [363.7]

5057 Amdur, Richard. *The Fragile Earth* (9–12). 1994, Chelsea LB $19.95 (0-7910-1572-6). A discussion, in understandable terms, of the origin of the universe and the interdependence of life. (Rev: BL 5/1/94; VOYA 6/94) [363.7]

5058 Andryszewski, Tricia. *The Environment and the Economy: Planting the Seeds for Tomorrow's Growth* (7–12). 1995, Millbrook LB $23.90 (1-56294-524-6). Traces the emergence of environment-versus-economy issues. (Rev: BL 12/1/95; SLJ 11/95) [363.7]

5059 Bilger, Burkhard. *Global Warming* (9–12). (Earth at Risk) 1991, Chelsea LB $19.95 (0-7910-1575-0). A well-researched book that explains the scientific, political, and social issues related to global warming. (Rev: BL 4/1/92; SLJ 3/92) [363.73]

5060 Breton, Mary Joy. *Women Pioneers for the Environment* (10–12). 1998, Northeastern Univ. Pr. $37.50 (1-55553-365-5). A collection of biographi-

cal profiles, each in a political and social context, of women who have led struggles to combat destruction of the environment over the last 300 years. (Rev: SLJ 5/99) [363.7]

5061 Brower, Michael, and Warren Leon. *The Consumer's Guide to Effective Environmental Choices: Practical Advice from the Union of Concerned Scientists* (9–12). 1999, Three Rivers paper $15.00 (0-609-80281-X). The authors present steps people can take to live more ecologically safe and aware lifestyles. (Rev: BL 4/1/99; SLJ 9/99) [363.7]

5062 Caldicott, Helen. *If You Love This Planet: A Plan to Heal the Earth* (9–12). 1992, Norton paper $12.95 (0-393-30835-9). Presents, as a medical metaphor, the diagnosis and tough cure for an ailing planet Earth. (Rev: BL 3/1/92*) [363.7]

5063 Chandler, Gary, and Kevin Graham. *Environmental Causes* (5–10). (Celebrity Activists) 1997, Twenty-First Century $20.40 (0-8050-5232-1). This book discusses how entertainers like Robert Redford, Sting, and Chevy Chase and other celebrities such as Al Gore, Ted Turner, and Jerry Greenfield support environmental causes. (Rev: BR 3–4/98; SLJ 1/98) [363.7]

5064 Chandler, Gary, and Kevin Graham. *Kids Who Make a Difference* (4–8). Illus. (Making a Better World) 1996, Twenty-First Century LB $23.90 (0-8050-4625-9). This book describes various community environmental projects in which young people have played a significant role. (Rev: BL 12/1/96; SLJ 4/97; VOYA 2/97) [363.7]

5065 Chandler, Gary, and Kevin Graham. *Protecting Our Air, Land, and Water* (4–8). Illus. (Making a Better World) 1996, Twenty-First Century LB $23.90 (0-8050-4624-0). This book focuses on successful efforts to protect our natural resources like purifying water, preserving wetlands, and reducing air pollution. (Rev: BL 12/15/96; SLJ 1/97; VOYA 2/97) [363.7]

5066 Collard, Sneed B. *Alien Invaders: The Continuing Threat of Exotic Species* (6–12). Illus. 1996, Watts LB $25.00 (0-531-11298-5). An account that explores the dangers of introducing nonindigenous or "exotics" into a new environment. (Rev: BL 11/1/96; BR 3–4/97; SLJ 1/97) [574.5824]

5067 Collins, Carol C., ed. *Our Food, Air and Water: How Safe Are They?* (9–12). Illus. 1985, Facts on File $29.95 (0-87196-967-X). A collection of editorials and cartoons that covers such environmental problems as water pollution and toxic wastes. (Rev: BL 3/15/85) [363.7]

5068 Cozic, Charles P., ed. *Global Resources* (8–12). 1997, Greenhaven LB $21.96 (1-56510-673-3); paper $16.20 (1-56510-672-5). In a series of articles expressing different points of view, this book discusses the extent of depletion of resources, types of energy sources, agricultural policies, and how global resources can be protected. (Rev: BL 10/15/97; SLJ 1/98) [363.7]

5069 Dashefsky, H. Steven. *Environmental Science: High-School Fair Experiments* (7–12). Illus. 1994, TAB paper $12.95 (0-8306-4586-1). Topics covered in this project book suitable for both junior and senior high school students include applied ecology, soil ecosystems, energy, aquatic ecosystems, and environmental problems. (Rev: BL 6/1–15/94) [574.5]

5070 Fisher, Marshall. *The Ozone Layer* (9–12). (Earth at Risk) 1991, Chelsea LB $19.95 (0-7910-1576-9). Covers the historical and scientific background and steps that have been taken to counteract the depletion of the ozone layer. (Rev: BL 2/1/92) [363.73]

5071 Fleisher, Paul. *Ecology A to Z* (6–10). 1994, Dillon LB $14.95 (0-87518-561-4). Defines words and phrases related to ecology and to our interaction with the environment. (Rev: BL 4/1/94; SLJ 5/94; VOYA 6/94) [363.7]

5072 Gardner, Robert. *Celebrating Earth Day: A Sourcebook of Activities and Experiments* (5–9). 1992, Millbrook LB $22.40 (1-56294-070-8). Discusses such global problems as solid waste, water conservation, overpopulation, and acid rain. Includes easy experiments. (Rev: BL 12/1/92; SLJ 11/92) [333.7]

5073 Gartner, Bob. *Working Together Against the Destruction of the Environment* (7–12). (Library of Social Activism) 1995, Rosen LB $21.00 (0-8239-1774-6). Describes efforts to protect the environment, such as recycling, emission laws, and sewage dump restrictions, and provides suggestions for how everyone can help. (Rev: BL 4/15/95) [363.7]

5074 Gay, Kathlyn. *Saving the Environment: Debating the Costs* (8–12). Illus. (Impact) 1996, Watts $22.50 (0531-11263-2). This book explores environmental issues in which there is a conflict between the health of the environment and cost to the economy, such as saving endangered species, and property rights vs. pollution. (Rev: BL 9/1/96; BR 11–12/96; SLJ 10/96; VOYA 10/96) [363.7]

5075 Gelbspan, Ross. *The Heat Is On* (10–12). 1997, Addison-Wesley $23.00 (0-201-13295-8). A sobering, adult look at the coming emergency of global warming caused by mass industrialization. (Rev: BL 5/15/97; SLJ 3/98) [574.5]

5076 Gonick, Larry, and Alice Outwater. *The Cartoon Guide to the Environment* (10–12). Illus. 1996, HarperPerennial paper $15.00 (0-06-273274-9). Using cartoons, this sobering account tells how humanity is gradually destroying the earth through heedless misuse of the environment. (Rev: SLJ 9/96) [320.5]

5077 Johnson, Rebecca L. *Investigating the Ozone Hole* (5–8). 1994, Lerner LB $23.95 (0-8225-1574-1). A discussion of the ozone hole above Antarctica and the continuing threat of further ozone depletion. (Rev: BL 3/1/94) [551.5]

5078 Kidd, J. S., and Renee A. Kidd. *Into Thin Air: The Problem of Atmospheric Pollution* (7–12). (Into Thin Air) 1998, Facts on File $19.95 (0-8160-3585-7). This book evaluates how scientists have studied atmospheric chemistry and explores controversial theories on the effects of pollution, acid rain, the greenhouse effect, global warming, and El Niño. (Rev: BL 12/1/98) [363.739]

5079 Krensky, Stephen. *Four Against the Odds: The Struggle to Save Our Environment* (5–8). 1992, Scholastic paper $3.50 (0-590-44743-2). Introduces the work of 4 people who fought to raise public awareness about important environmental issues: John Muir, Chico Mendes, Rachel Carson, and Lois Gibb. (Rev: BL 6/1/92; SLJ 10/92) [363.7]

5080 Lanier-Graham, Susan D. *The Ecology of War: Environmental Impacts of Weaponry and Warfare* (9–12). 1993, Walker $35.95 (0-8027-1262-2). Covers the effects of Agent Orange, Gulf War oil spills and fires, unexploded ammunition in the Pacific, and pollution around military bases. (Rev: BL 5/1/93) [363.73]

5081 Lear, Linda, ed. *Lost Woods: The Discovered Writing of Rachel Carson* (10–12). 1998, Beacon $38.50 (0-8070-8546-4). Previously uncollected or unpublished writings by the great conservationist, covering topics in biology, ecology, and wildlife and wilderness preservation. (Rev: BL 11/1/98; SLJ 3/99) [363.7]

5082 Markham, Adam. *The Environment* (6–8). Illus. 1988, Rourke LB $25.27 (0-86592-286-1). Such dangers to our environment as acid rain, the breakdown of the ozone layer, and the greenhouse effect are discussed. (Rev: BL 12/15/88; SLJ 5/89) [363.7]

5083 Netzley, Patricia. *Environmental Groups* (6–10). Illus. (Our Endangered Planet) 1997, Lucent LB $17.96 (1-56006-195-2). This objective source introduces conflicting attitudes toward protection of species, lobbying tactics, economic issues, and scientific findings related to environmental issues. (Rev: SLJ 9/98) [363.7]

5084 Netzley, Patricia. *Issues in the Environment* (7–10). (Contemporary Issues) 1997, Lucent LB $17.96 (1-56006-475-7). Proponents and detractors state their cases in this volume that explores methods used to protect the environment, their cost, their effectiveness, and the possible use of other, less drastic alternatives. (Rev: SLJ 4/98) [363.7]

5085 Petrikin, Jonathan S., ed. *Environmental Justice* (8–12). (At Issue) 1995, Greenhaven LB $19.95

(0-56510-264-9). A collection of essays exploring whether the wealthy and powerful are risking the health and living conditions of others while protecting their own resources. (Rev: BL 3/15/95) [363.7]

5086 Robbins, Ocean, and Sol Solomon. *Choices for Our Future* (7–12). 1994, Book Publg. paper $9.95 (1-57067-002-1). The founders of Youth for Environmental Sanity believe that young people can convince other young people to adopt more ecologically responsible life-styles. This book explains how we can all help. (Rev: BL 3/15/95) [363.7]

5087 Roleff, Tamara L., ed. *Global Warming* (8–12). (Opposing Viewpoints) 1997, Greenhaven LB $21.96 (1-56510-512-5); paper $17.45 (1-56510-511-7). An anthology of writings that explores the gravity of global warming, its possible effects, and measures that can be taken to combat it. (Rev: BL 12/15/96; BR 5–6/97) [363.73]

5088 Rosen, Roger, and Patra McSharry, eds. *Planet Earth: Egotists and Ecosystems* (9–12). 1991, Rosen LB $16.95 (0-8239-1334-1); paper $8.95 (0-8239-1335-X). Short stories, articles, and photoessays addressing environmental abuse. (Rev: BL 2/15/92; SLJ 4/92) [809]

5089 Rubin, Charles T. *The Green Crusade: Rethinking the Roots of Environmentalism* (9–12). 1998, Rowman & Littlefield paper $16.95 (0-8476-8817-8). A critical examination of utopianism in the environmental movement and the anticapitalist ethics of leading authors in the field. (Rev: BL 2/1/94) [363.7]

5090 Ryan, Bernard. *Protecting the Environment* (7–12). (Community Service for Teens) 1998, Ferguson LB $15.95 (0-89434-228-2). After a general introduction on volunteerism, the author describes how teens can become involved in existing conservation projects and begin their own. (Rev: BL 9/15/98; BR 11–12/98; SLJ 2/99; VOYA 8/99) [363.7]

5091 Sadler, A. E., ed. *The Environment* (8–12). (Opposing Viewpoints) 1996, Greenhaven LB $21.96 (1-56510-397-1); paper $16.20 (1-56510-396-3). This book presents different opinions concerning the extent of air and water pollution, the effects of conservation on the economy, how to prevent pollution, and to what extent should the environment be protected. (Rev: BL 7/96) [363.7]

5092 Scott, Michael. *Ecology* (5–8). Illus. (Young Oxford) 1996, Oxford LB $30.00 (0-19-521166-9). An attractive introduction to the world of ecology, adaptation, conservation, and species diversity. (Rev: BL 3/1/96; SLJ 3/96; VOYA 4/96) [574.5]

5093 Stefoff, Rebecca. *The American Environmental Movement* (7–10). 1995, Facts on File $19.95 (0-8160-3046-4). A study of efforts to preserve the environment from the 15th century to the present,

with discussion of prominent figures and events in the movement. (Rev: BL 9/1/95; SLJ 9/95) [363.7]

5094 Stouffer, Marty. *Marty Stouffer's Wild America* (8–12). 1988, Times Bks. $30.00 (0-8129-1610-7). A wildlife documentary maker discusses his career and the importance of conservation. (Rev: BR 3–4/89; VOYA 4/89) [320.5]

5095 Student Environmental Action Coalition. *The Student Environmental Action Guide* (9–12). 1991, EarthWorks Pr. paper $4.95 (1-879682-04-4). A short manual describing opportunities for recycling in the campus environment and including campus success stories that encourage collective student action. (Rev: BL 10/15/91) [363.7]

5096 Turner, Tom. *Sierra Club: 100 Years of Protecting Nature* (9–12). Photos. 1991, Abrams $49.50 (0-8109-3820-0). A commemoration of the Sierra Club's founding that provides a history of the organization, its mission, and its accomplishments. (Rev: BL 11/15/91) [333.9516]

5097 Wilcove, David S. *The Condor's Shadow: The Loss and Recovery of Wildlife in America* (9–12). 1999, W. H. Freeman paper $24.95 (0-7167-3115-0). This work discusses the contemporary dangers to wildlife in America, including habitat destruction, pollution, and the introduction of nonnative species. (Rev: SLJ 8/99) [363.7]

Pollution

5098 Blashfield, Jean F., and Wallace B. Black. *Oil Spills* (5–8). (Saving Planet Earth) 1991, Children's Pr. LB $30.50 (0-516-05508-9). A close look at this huge threat to the environment, with suggestions on how to get involved in solving the problem. (Rev: BL 3/1/92; SLJ 5/92) [363.73]

5099 Bullard, Robert D., ed. *Unequal Protection: Environmental Justice and Communities of Color* (9–12). 1994, Sierra Club $25.00 (0-87156-450-5). Academics, journalists, activists, and others provide details on environmental racism throughout the United States. (Rev: BL 5/1/94) [363.703]

5100 Collinson, Alan. *Pollution* (5–8). (Repairing the Damage) 1992, Macmillan LB $17.96 (0-02-722995-5). A historical overview of nuclear waste, river pollution, overpopulation, and other aspects of pollution. (Rev: BL 9/15/92) [363.73]

5101 Cozic, Charles P., ed. *Pollution* (9–12). (Current Controversies) 1994, Greenhaven LB $26.20 (1-56510-076-X); paper $17.45 (1-56510-075-1). A presentation of differing opinions on how serious pollution is, who is responsible, the effectiveness of recycling and what methods work best, and the role of the Environmental Protection Agency. (Rev: BL 4/15/94) [363.73]

5102 Dolan, Edward F. *Our Poisoned Waters* (7–12). Illus. 1997, Dutton paper $14.99 (0-525-65220-5). With extensive use of first-person accounts, this book tells of the impact that humans have had on the water supply and about attempts to conserve and clean our water. The last chapter tells how readers can help the cause. (Rev: BL 3/1/97; BR 11–12/97; SLJ 3/97; VOYA 10/97) [363.739]

5103 Gay, Kathlyn. *Air Pollution* (7–12). (Impact) 1991, Watts LB $24.00 (0-531-13002-9). An examination of the alarming ecological effects and health risks of atmospheric pollution and an outline of combative strategies. (Rev: BL 12/1/91) [363.73]

5104 Gutnik, Martin J. *Experiments That Explore Acid Rain* (5–8). Illus. (Investigate!) 1992, Millbrook LB $21.40 (1-56294-115-1). Simple experiments explore the nature of acid rain and suggest solutions for this problem. (Rev: BL 2/1/92; SLJ 5/92) [628.5]

5105 Lucas, Eileen. *Acid Rain* (5–8). (Saving Planet Earth) 1991, Children's Pr. LB $30.50 (0-516-05503-8). This thought-provoking study of the environmental problem known as acid rain discusses its causes, effects, and prevention. (Rev: BL 3/1/92) [363.73]

5106 Miller, Christina G., and Louise A. Berry. *Acid Rain: A Sourcebook for Young People* (6–8). Illus. 1986, Messner LB $12.95 (0-671-60177-6). An account that describes the origins of acid rain, its effects, and what can be done about it. (Rev: BL 2/15/87; SLJ 1/87) [363.7]

5107 Miller, Christina G., and Louise A. Berry. *Air Alert: Rescuing the Earth's Atmosphere* (5–9). Illus. 1996, Simon & Schuster $16.00 (0-689-31792-1). A clear overview of such atmospheric problems as acid rain, smog, the greenhouse effect, and depletion of the ozone layer. (Rev: BL 3/1/96; BR 1–2/97; SLJ 5/96; VOYA 12/96) [363.73]

5108 Nadis, Steve, et al. *Car Trouble* (9–12). (Guides to the Environment) 1993, Beacon paper $22.50 (0-8070-8523-5). A book that addresses the impact of automobile pollution on the earth's resources and examines ways to alleviate it. (Rev: BL 1/15/93) [363.73]

5109 Pringle, Laurence. *Oil Spills: Damage, Recovery, and Prevention* (5–8). 1993, Morrow LB $14.93 (0-688-09861-4). A discussion of damage caused by oil spills, cleanup, and prevention efforts, with a description of how petroleum forms, how it is removed from the ground, and its uses as background. (Rev: BL 9/15/93) [363.73]

5110 Rock, Maxine. *The Automobile and the Environment* (9–12). (Earth at Risk) 1992, Chelsea LB $19.95 (0-7910-1592-0). A description of the pollution and environmental problems caused by automo-

biles and how it is being addressed. (Rev: BL 12/1/92) [363.73]

5111 Tesar, Jenny. *The Waste Crisis* (5–9). (Our Fragile Planet) 1991, Facts on File $19.95 (0-8160-2491-X). Emphasizes the urgency of the problem and offers possibilities for solutions. (Rev: BL 11/15/91; SLJ 11/91) [363.72]

5112 Tyson, Peter. *Acid Rain* (9–12). (Earth at Risk) 1991, Chelsea LB $19.95 (0-7910-1577-7). An objective presentation of the nature, distribution, and dangers of acid rain and prospects for its reduction. (Rev: BL 4/1/92) [363.73]

Recycling

5113 Chandler, Gary, and Kevin Graham. *Recycling* (4–8). Illus. 1996, Twenty-First Century LB $20.40 (0-8050-4622-4). Reports on recycling programs and their beneficial results. (Rev: BL 12/1/96; SLJ 4/97) [363.72]

5114 Cozic, Charles P., ed. *Garbage & Waste* (7–12). (Current Controversies) 1997, Greenhaven LB $20.96 (1-56510-566-4); paper $20.25 (1-56510-565-6). An anthology of articles about the seriousness of the waste problem, the dangers of toxic waste, the usefulness of recycling, and the extent that government should interfere in this problem. (Rev: BL 7/97; SLJ 10/97) [363.72]

5115 Emory, Jerry. *Dirty, Rotten, Dead? A Worm's-eye View of Death, Decomposition . . . and Life* (5–8). Illus. 1996, Harcourt paper $15.00 (0-15-200695-8). Along with a number of experiments and ecological projects, this book discusses death and recycling in nature, including such topics as the parts of the human body that become waste (e.g. hair, nails, skin), digestion and human excretion, processing of sewage, water pollution, diseases of the immune system, and contemporary mortician practices. (Rev: SLJ 8/96) [628.4]

5116 Hall, Eleanor J. *Garbage* (5–8). Illus. (Overview) 1997, Lucent LB $22.45 (1-56006-188-X). A history of how waste disposal has been handled, and current ecological and environmental approaches, including recycling. (Rev: BL 8/97; BR 1–2/98) [363.72]

5117 McVicker, Dee. *Easy Recycling Handbook* (9–12). 1994, Grassroots paper $8.95 (0-9638428-5-4). An introduction to recycling methods and waste management, with advice on overcoming limitations posed by time and space. (Rev: BL 3/15/94) [363.7]

5118 Murphy, Pamela, et al. *The Garbage Primer: A Handbook for Citizens* (9–12). 1993, Lyons Pr. paper $12.95 (1-55821-250-7). This describes how society deals with garbage and what people need to know to dispose of it responsibly. Includes a disposal milestone timeline. (Rev: BL 11/15/93) [363.72]

5119 Stefoff, Rebecca. *Recycling* (9–12). (Earth at Risk) 1991, Chelsea LB $19.95 (0-7910-1573-4). A wide-ranging overview of the common types of materials recycled, specific recycling procedures, and challenges. (Rev: BL 6/15/91) [363.72]

Population Issues

General and Miscellaneous

5120 Allison, Anthony. *Hear These Voices: Youth at the Edge of the Millennium* (7–12). 1999, Dutton paper $22.99 (0-525-45353-9). Testimonies from troubled teenagers around the world, such as a 14-year-old Thai girl whose stepfather sold her into prostitution, comprise this harrowing anthology of case studies, accompanied by short, follow-up interviews with adults who have tried to help. (Rev: BL 1/1–15/99*; SLJ 2/99; VOYA 4/99) [305.235]

5121 Gallant, Roy A. *The Peopling of Planet Earth: Human Population Growth through the Ages* (7–12). Illus. 1990, Macmillan LB $15.95 (0-02-735772-4). A history of patterns of world population, the present conditions in relation to resources, and the different future we face. (Rev: BL 3/1/90; VOYA 4/90) [304.6]

5122 Hohm, Charles, and Lori Jones, eds. *Population* (7–12). (Opposing Viewpoints) 1995, Greenhaven paper $16.20 (1-56510-214-2). Different sides of major issues related to population are discussed by experts, who debate how serious the problem is and different methods of controlling it. (Rev: BL 7/95; SLJ 8/95) [304.6]

5123 Roberts, Sam. *Who Are We: A Portrait of America Based on the 1990 Census* (9–12). 1994, Times Bks. $18.00 (0-8129-2192-5). This analysis of the 1990 census results points out troubling changes in American society, such as increased polarization and economic discrimination. (Rev: BL 2/1/94) [304.6]

Aging and Death

5124 Cozic, Charles P., ed. *An Aging Population* (8–12). (Opposing Viewpoints) 1996, Greenhaven LB $21.96 (1-56510-395-5); paper $16.20 (1-56510-394-7). A collection of documents expressing various points of view on how the aged will affect America in the future, their entitlement programs, quality of life, health care, and society's acceptance of the elderly. (Rev: BL 7/96; BR 1–2/97; SLJ 8/96; VOYA 10/96) [305.26]

5125 Gignoux, Jane Hughes. *Some Folk Say: Stories of Life, Death, & Beyond* (6–12). Illus. 1998, Foulketale $29.95 (0-9667168-0-9). A collection of 38 literary selections on various aspects of death and how people adjust to it, taken from world folklore and such writers as Shakespeare and Walt Whitman. (Rev: BL 2/15/99) [398.27]

5126 Winters, Paul A., ed. *Death and Dying* (8–12). (Opposing Viewpoints) 1997, Greenhaven LB $21.96 (1-56510-671-7); paper $16.20 (1-56510-670-9). Topics dealt with in this anthology of articles include the treatment of terminally ill patients, the right to die, how to cope with death, and whether death is the end of life. (Rev: BL 10/15/97; SLJ 2/98) [179]

Crime, Gangs, and Prisons

5127 Aaseng, Nathan. *Treacherous Traitors* (5–9). (Profiles) 1997, Oliver Pr. LB $18.95 (1-881508-38-2). This book profiles 12 Americans who were tried for treason, including Benedict Arnold, John Brown, Alger Hiss, Julius and Ethel Rosenberg, and Aldrich Ames. (Rev: BR 1–2/98; SLJ 2/98) [355.3]

5128 Atkin, S. Beth. *Voices from the Streets: Young Former Gang Members Tell Their Stories* (8–12). Illus. 1996, Little, Brown $17.95 (0-316-05634-0). First-person accounts are used to tell the stories of several young people who have left gangs and how they are now rebuilding their lives. (Rev: BL 11/1/96; BR 3–4/97; SLJ 10/96*; VOYA 12/96) [364]

5129 Axelrod, Alan, and Charles Phillips. *Cops, Crooks, and Criminologists: An International Biographical Dictionary of Law Enforcement* (10–12). 1996, Facts on File $45.00 (0-81160-3016-2). In 600 descriptive entries, this volume features significant figures in the history of crime, criminology, and law enforcement throughout history. (Rev: SLJ 1/97) [364]

5130 Ballinger, Erich. *Detective Dictionary: A Handbook for Aspiring Sleuths* (5–8). 1994, Lerner LB $19.95 (0-8225-0721-8). Focuses on the elements of detective work, including deductive puzzles and instructions on creating a crime lab. (Rev: BL 9/15/94) [363.2]

5131 Barbour, Scott, and Karin L. Swisher, eds. *Violence* (9–12). Illus. (Opposing Viewpoints) 1996, Greenhaven paper $20.25 (1-56510-354-8). A presentation of different opinions on the causes of violence, policies aimed at reducing it, and various kinds of violence, such as teen and domestic violence. (Rev: BL 4/1/96; SLJ 3/96) [303.6]

5132 Bedau, Hugo Adam, ed. *The Death Penalty in America: Current Controversies*. rev. ed. (10–12). (Current Controversies) 1997, Oxford $40.00 (0-19-

510438-2). The 40 essays in this anthology explore various aspects of the death penalty, its effectiveness, its legality, and disparities in sentencing. (Rev: SLJ 10/97) [364.6]

5133 Bender, David, and Bruno Leone, eds. *Crime and Criminals* (9–12). (Opposing Viewpoints) 1995, Greenhaven paper $16.20 (1-56510-177-4). A presentation of opposing viewpoints on the causes and prevention of crime, gun control, and treatment of young offenders. (Rev: BL 4/1/95; VOYA 4/95) [364.973]

5134 Bode, Janet, and Stanley Mack. *Hard Time* (7–12). Illus. 1996, Delacorte $16.95 (0-385-32186-4). A series of horrifying and heartbreaking case histories about teens, including many who are in prison, who have been either the perpetrators or the victims of excessive violence. (Rev: BL 4/1/96; BR 9–10/96; SLJ 4/96*; VOYA 4/96) [364.3]

5135 Boostrom, Ron, ed. *Enduring Issues in Criminology* (9–12). (Opposing Viewpoints) 1995, Greenhaven LB $27.45 (1-56510-256-8); paper $17.45 (1-56510-255-X). A debate on criminology issues through presentation of a question and essays written in response supporting differing viewpoints. (Rev: BL 7/95) [364]

5136 Bosch, Carl. *Schools under Siege: Guns, Gangs, and Hidden Dangers* (7–12). Illus. (Issues in Focus) 1997, Enslow LB $17.95 (0-89490-908-8). This work surveys teenage crime, its history and causes, the juvenile justice system, pertinent Supreme Court decisions, and types of school violence. (Rev: BL 8/97; SLJ 9/97) [363.119371]

5137 Corwin, Miles. *The Killing Season: A Summer Inside an LAPD Homicide Division* (10–12). 1997, Simon & Schuster $22.50 (0-684-80235-X). A chronicle of 7 months in 1994 that the author spent with a supervising detective, Pete Razanskas, and his trainee partner, Marcella Winn, as they work together in Los Angeles' tough South Central area. (Rev: BL 5/1/97; SLJ 1/98) [363.2]

5138 Cozic, Charles P., ed. *America's Prisons* (8–12). Illus. (Opposing Viewpoints) 1997, Greenhaven LB $21.96 (1-56510-550-8); paper $17.45 (1-56510-549-4). A series of articles expressing differing opinions about the effectiveness of America's prisons, their purposes, and alternatives. (Rev: BL 4/15/97; BR 1–2/98) [365]

5139 Cozic, Charles P., ed. *Gangs* (8–12). (Opposing Viewpoints) 1995, Greenhaven LB $21.96 (1-56510-363-7); paper $16.20 (1-56510-362-9). A thought-provoking, alarming, and moving discussion of gangs and violence in the United States. (Rev: BL 12/15/95; VOYA 6/96) [364.1]

5140 D'Angelo, Laura. *Hate Crimes* (6–9). Illus. (Crime, Justice, & Punishment) 1997, Chelsea LB $15.95 (0-7910-4266-9). This book examines the nature and causes of hate crimes based on differences in race, ethnicity, religion, or sexual preference, and the individuals or groups responsible for them, with interesting case studies and psychological profiles. (Rev: BL 5/15/98) [364.1]

5141 Day, Nancy. *Violence in Schools: Learning in Fear* (7–12). Illus. (Issues in Focus) 1996, Enslow LB $19.95 (0-89490-734-4). Such forms of violence in schools as guns, sexual harassment, gay bashing, and gang fighting are discussed with material on their causes, effects, and the recent formation of student advocacy groups. (Rev: BL 6/1–15/96; SLJ 7/96) [371.5]

5142 Dulles, Allen. *Great True Spy Stories* (9–12). 1992, Book Sales $7.98 (0-89009-716-X). This is a collection of thrillers about spy capers that really happened.

5143 Fisher, David. *Hard Evidence: How Detectives Inside the FBI's Sci-Crime Lab Have Helped Solve America's Toughest Cases* (9–12). 1995, Simon & Schuster $23.00 (0-671-79369-1). An introduction to the FBI crime laboratory in Washington, D.C. (Rev: BL 3/1/95) [363.2]

5144 Gaines, Ann. *Prisons* (8–12). (Crime, Justice and Punishment) 1998, Chelsea LB $15.95 (0-7910-4315-0). A thought-provoking look inside America's prisons, with background material on the history and philosophy of incarceration and an examination of issues in penology. (Rev: VOYA 4/99) [365]

5145 Gardner, Robert. *Crime Lab 101: Experimenting with Crime Detection* (6–9). 1992, Walker LB $27.90 (0-8027-8159-4). Details how law enforcement agencies use science and technology to solve crimes, with 25 crime lab activities and 8 exercises. (Rev: BL 8/92; SLJ 10/92) [363.2]

5146 Goldentyer, Debra. *Street Violence* (4–8). (Preteen Pressures) 1998, Raintree Steck-Vaughn $24.26 (0-8172-5028-X). This book discusses types of street violence and how young people can protect themselves, as well as gang issues and alternatives to participation. (Rev: BL 5/15/98; SLJ 6/98) [364]

5147 Goodwin, William. *Teen Violence* (7–10). Illus. (Overview: Teen Issues) 1997, Lucent LB $17.96 (1-56006-511-7). A clear, in-depth discussion of the scope, causes, and prevention of teen violence; the relationships between the media, gangs, and violence; and the treatment of juvenile offenders in the justice system. (Rev: BL 5/15/98) [364.36]

5148 Gottfried, Ted. *Capital Punishment: The Death Penalty Debate* (6–12). Illus. (Issues in Focus) 1997, Enslow LB $19.95 (0-89490-899-5). The author presents strong arguments on all sides of the death penalty controversy, including material on its history, moral justification, purpose, legal procedures, and questions of race and geography. (Rev: BL 2/1/97; SLJ 7/97) [345.73]

5149 Greenberg, Keith E. *Out of the Gang* (5–8). 1992, Lerner LB $19.93 (0-8225-2553-4). Reveals what gang life is like and profiles a man who escaped gang life and a boy who has managed to stay out of it. (Rev: BL 6/15/92; SLJ 9/92) [364.1]

5150 Guernsey, JoAnn B. *Should We Have Capital Punishment?* (7–10). (Pro/Con) 1993, Lerner LB $19.95 (0-8225-2602-6). A presentation of both sides of the capital punishment debate, with graphic photos. (Rev: BL 7/93) [364.6]

5151 Guernsey, JoAnn B. *Youth Violence: An American Epidemic?* (7–10). (Frontline) 1996, Lerner LB $19.93 (0-8225-2627-1). Chapters in this book include discussions on violence at home and school, gangs and gang violence, and the influence of such factors as guns, drugs, alcohol. poverty, race, and discrimination. (Rev: SLJ 1/97; VOYA 2/97) [364.3]

5152 Hinojosa, Maria. *Crews: Gang Members Talk to Maria Hinojosa* (9–12). 1995, Harcourt $17.00 (0-15-292873-1); paper $9.00 (0-15-200283-9). A National Public Radio correspondent interviews New York City gang members after a subway stabbing. (Rev: BL 3/15/95; SLJ 4/95*; VOYA 5/95) [302.3]

5153 Hjelmeland, Andy. *Prisons: Inside the Big House* (4–8). Illus. (Pro/Con) 1996, Lerner LB $21.27 (0-8225-2607-7). Opposing viewpoints on the purposes of prisons, prison conditions, and alternate forms of rehabilitation are discussed in this book. (Rev: BL 8/96; SLJ 9/96) [365]

5154 Hutchinson, Earl Ofari. *The Mugging of Black America* (9–12). 1990, African American Images paper $8.95 (0-913543-21-7). An angry discourse on what defines African Americans as the perpetrators and victims of crime and as the casualties of the criminal justice system. Also offers guidelines for change. (Rev: BL 9/1/91) [305.8]

5155 Hyde, Margaret O. *Kids in and out of Trouble* (6–9). 1995, Dutton $13.99 (0-525-65149-7). A dark picture of the juvenile justice system and juvenile violence. (Rev: BL 5/15/95; SLJ 5/95; VOYA 12/95) [364.3]

5156 Jackson, Donna M. *The Bone Detectives: How Forensic Anthropologists Solve Crimes and Uncover Mysteries of the Dead* (5–9). 1996, Little, Brown $16.95 (0-316-82935-8). This work explores the role of forensic anthropologists in solving crimes, including murder. (Rev: BL 4/1/96; SLJ 5/96*; VOYA 8/96) [363.2]

5157 Jah, Yusuf, and Sister Shah'Keyah. *Uprising: Crips and Bloods Tell the Story of America's Youth in the Crossfire* (9–12). 1995, Scribners $22.50 (0-684-80460-3). Probing interviews with gang members, who talk about the worthwhile aspects of gang membership and how it can be channeled into peaceful, productive activities. (Rev: BL 11/1/95) [364.1]

5158 Johnson, Toni E. *Handcuff Blues: Helping Teens Stay Out of Trouble with the Law* (6–9). Illus. 1999, Goofy Foot paper $10.95 (1-885535-43-0). Twelve case histories about teens in trouble for drunk driving, vandalism, shoplifting, and drive-by shootings are given with background information, details of the crime, and finally the legal action taken and the outcome. (Rev: SLJ 8/99; VOYA 12/99) [364.3]

5159 Jones, Charlotte F. *Fingerprints & Talking Bones: How Real-Life Crimes Are Solved* (5–8). Illus. 1997, Delacorte $16.95 (0-385-32299-2). A clear, concise account of what forensic science means and how it has been applied in real cases. (Rev: BL 6/1–15/97; SLJ 8/97) [363.2]

5160 Kaminer, Wendy. *It's All the Rage: Crime and Culture* (9–12). 1995, Addison-Wesley $22.00 (0-201-62274-2). High-profile cases are used to stimulate discussion of the criminal justice system, cultural mores, and violence. (Rev: BL 4/1/95) [364.1]

5161 Kim, Henny H., ed. *Youth Violence* (7–12). 1998, Greenhaven LB $20.96 (1-56510-811-6). This book presents different opinions on the seriousness of youth violence, its causes, how it can be reduced, and punishments for young offenders. (Rev: BL 8/98) [302.3]

5162 Kinnear, Karen L. *Gangs: A Reference Handbook* (9–12). 1996, ABC-CLIO LB $45.00 (0-87436-821-9). This book presents an overview of gangs (why people join, racial and ethnic gangs, prevention, etc.) plus a chronology, biographical sketches, documents, and a wide list of sources. (Rev: BR 5–6/97; SLJ 2/97; VOYA 6/97) [302.3]

5163 Kirwin, Barbara. *The Mad, the Bad, and the Innocent: The Criminal Mind on Trial* (10–12). 1997, Little, Brown $23.95 (0-316-49499-2). The author, a New York forensic psychologist who has tested and testified for over 100 defendants who have used the insanity plea, reviews its recent history and criticizes both its misuse and the inadequate way in which the legal system deals with the criminally mentally ill. (Rev: BL 8/97; SLJ 1/98) [363.2]

5164 Landau, Elaine. *Stalking* (7–12). Illus. 1996, Watts LB $25.00 (0-531-11295-0). All kinds of stalking and stalkers, e.g., former husbands, ex-boyfriends, fans, and total strangers, are discussed, with examples from actual case studies. (Rev: BL 2/15/97; SLJ 2/97) [364.1]

5165 Margolis, Jeffrey A. *Teen Crime Wave: A Growing Problem* (7–12). Illus. (Issues in Focus) 1997, Enslow LB $17.95 (0-89490-910-X). The teenage crime phenomenon is examined, with material on frequency, causes, the juvenile justice system, Supreme Court decisions, and historical background. (Rev: BL 8/97; SLJ 9/97) [364.36]

5166 Melton, H. Keith. *The Ultimate Spy Book* (10–12). 1996, DK Publg. $29.95 (0-7894-0443-5). This book discusses motivations for spying, breaks down the different kinds of spies—couriers, double agents, defectors, saboteurs, moles, etc.—and provides a fascinating description of their equipment, techniques, communications, and weapons. (Rev: SLJ 7/96; VOYA 10/96) [327.12]

5167 Meltzer, Milton. *Crime in America* (6–10). 1990, Morrow $12.95 (0-688-08513-X). Survey of crime, law enforcement, and the justice system, including the strengths and weaknesses of the current judicial structure. (Rev: BL 1/1/91; SLJ 12/90) [364.973]

5168 Morris, Norval, and David J. Rothman, eds. *The Oxford History of the Prison: The Practice of Punishment in Western Society* (9–12). 1995, Oxford $79.95 (0-19-506153-5). A collection of 8 historical essays and 6 articles about prisons. (Rev: BL 12/15/95) [365]

5169 Newton, David E. *Teen Violence: Out of Control* (7–10). Illus. (Issues in Focus) 1995, Enslow LB $19.95 (0-89490-506-6). A well-researched account that covers all types of teen violence, the nature-nurture controversy, ways of preventing teen violence, and types of punishment currently being used. (Rev: BL 3/1/96; SLJ 6/96; VOYA 2/96) [364.3]

5170 Oliver, Marilyn Tower. *Gangs: Trouble in the Streets* (5–8). 1995, Enslow LB $19.95 (0-89490-492-2). Discusses the roots of gangs in the 19th century, aspects of modern gang life, and how a member (sometimes) quits a gang. (Rev: BL 8/95) [364.1]

5171 Oliver, Marilyn Tower. *Prisons: Today's Debate* (7–12). (Issues in Focus) 1997, Enslow LB $19.95 (0-89490-906-1). The debate concerning the effectiveness of America's prisons and their purposes is presented clearly, with all sides represented fairly. (Rev: BL 11/15/97; SLJ 12/97) [365]

5172 Owens, Lois Smith, and Vivian Verdell Gordon. *Think about Prisons and the Criminal Justice System* (6–10). (Think) 1991, Walker LB $28.90 (0-8027-8121-7); paper $14.95 (0-8027-7370-2). Basic information on incarceration, crime and its consequences, the criminal justice system, and the basis for laws. (Rev: BL 6/1/92; SLJ 2/92) [364.973]

5173 Platt, Richard. *Spy* (4–9). Illus. 1996, Knopf LB $20.99 (0-679-98122-5). All aspects of spying, including equipment and techniques, are described, along with profiles of famous spies. (Rev: BL 12/1/96; SLJ 6/97) [327.12]

5174 Rodriguez, Luis J. *Always Running: A Memoir of La Vida Loca Gang Days in L.A.* (9–12). 1993, Curbstone $19.95 (1-880684-06-3). Frank recollections about the author's membership in a barrio gang in the 1960s and 1970s personalize crime statistics. (Rev: BL 12/15/92*; SLJ 7/93) [364.1]

5175 Ross, Stewart. *Spies and Traitors* (5–8). (Fact or Fiction) 1995, Millbrook paper $24.90 (1-56294-648-X). A history of the people who have placed themselves above their country in the dangerous game of espionage and betrayal. (Rev: SLJ 3/96) [355.3]

5176 Ryan, Patrick J. *Organized Crime* (9–12). (Contemporary World Issues) 1995, ABC-CLIO LB $45.00 (0-87436-746-8). Covering 1850 to the present, this work gives a history of organized crime internationally, with material on various criminal organizations and their members. (Rev: BL 11/1/95; BR 9–10/96; SLJ 3/96) [364]

5177 Sadler, A. E., and Scott Barbour, eds. *Juvenile Crime* (6–12). (Opposing Viewpoints) 1997, Greenhaven LB $21.96 (1-56510-516-8); paper $17.45 (1-56510-515-X). Excerpts from books and articles probe different viewpoints on juvenile violence and crime—its causes, frequency, and punishments. (Rev: BL 2/1/97; BR 5–6/97; SLJ 4/97) [364.3]

5178 Salak, John. *Violent Crime: Is It out of Control?* (6–8). (Issues of Our Time) 1995, Twenty-First Century LB $18.90 (0-8050-4239-3). An honest presentation of why violent crimes are being committed more frequently and how young people are becoming increasingly involved in them. (Rev: BL 2/1/96; SLJ 2/96) [364.1]

5179 Schonebaum, Steve, ed. *Does Capital Punishment Deter Crime?* (8–12). (At Issue) 1998, Greenhaven LB $16.96 (1-56510-791-8); paper $12.45 (1-56510-091-3). This anthology presents arguments by those who maintain the death penalty deters crime and by others with statistics, studies, and other evidence that point to the opposite conclusion. (Rev: BL 6/1–15/98) [364.6]

5180 Schroeder, Andreas. *Fakes, Frauds, and Flimflammery: Even More of the World's Most Outrageous Scams* (9–12). 1999, McClelland & Stewart Tundra Books paper $15.95 (0-7710-79540). This entertaining work profiles the scams of 16 colorful swindlers, con artists, forgers, and extortionists. (Rev: SLJ 8/99) [364]

5181 Silverstein, Herma. *Kids Who Kill* (7–10). Illus. 1997, Twenty-First Century $21.40 (0-8050-4369-1). This volume examines the reasons for the escalation in the number of juvenile killers, who they are, why they kill, the environmental factors involved, and how the court system deals with underage criminals. (Rev: BL 12/15/97; SLJ 1/98; VOYA 2/98) [364.14]

5182 Silverstein, Herma. *Threads of Evidence: Using Forensic Science to Solve Crimes* (7–12). 1996, Twenty-First Century LB $21.40 (0-8050-4370-5). A discussion of the new forensic technology now available to criminologists, such as the use of DNA, blood splatters, fibers, and shell casings, and the role this science has played in solving famous cases. (Rev: BL 12/1/96; SLJ 2/97; VOYA 6/97) [363.2]

5183 Solomon, Louis. *The Ma and Pa Murders and Other Perfect Crimes* (7–9). 1976, HarperCollins $12.95 (0-397-31577-5). Here is an account of 6 unsolved crimes including the murders involving Lizzie Borden. [364]

5184 Sonder, Ben. *Gangs* (7–12). Illus. 1996, Marshall Cavendish LB $24.21 (0-7614-0021-4). A discussion of the origin of gangs, why people join them, their activities and rituals, and how to leave them safely. (Rev: BL 8/96; BR 11–12/96; SLJ 8/96) [364.3]

5185 Sparks, Beatrice, ed. *Almost Lost: The True Story of an Anonymous Teenager's Life on the Streets* (9–12). 1996, Avon paper $4.99 (0-380-78341-X). This is the story of runaway Sammy, who at 15 was a member of a street gang and who finally returned to his family and began the road to recovery. (Rev: SLJ 7/96; VOYA 10/96) [364.1]

5186 Steele, Philip. *Smuggling* (5–9). (Past and Present) 1993, Macmillan LB $16.95 (0-02-786884-2). A colorful history of smuggling through the ages. (Rev: BL 8/93) [364.1]

5187 Steins, Richard. *The Death Penalty: Is It Justice?* (6–9). (Issues of Our Time) 1993, Twenty-First Century LB $18.90 (0-8050-2571-5). Jumping off from Gary Gilmore's execution, this book looks at the death penalty through history and presents the current debate. (Rev: BL 11/1/93) [364.6]

5188 Stewart, Gail B. *The Death Penalty* (7–12). (Opposing Viewpoints Digests) 1998, Greenhaven LB $17.96 (1-56510-745-4); paper $20.25 (1-56510-744-6). Controversies surround the death penalty. Issues covered in this volume include whether it is just, effective, constitutional, and applied fairly. (Rev: BL 5/15/98; BR 9–10/98) [179]

5189 Stewart, Gail B. *Drug Trafficking* (6–8). 1990, Lucent LB $22.45 (1-56006-116-2). The author follows marijuana, cocaine, and heroin from the fields through the refinement process to their sale on the streets. (Rev: BL 4/15/91; SLJ 3/91) [363.4]

5190 Stewart, Gail B. *Gangs* (8–10). Illus. (The Other America) 1997, Lucent LB $17.96 (1-56006-340-8). Four gang members reveal in interviews why they joined a gang, what gang life is like, and problems trying to leave gangs. (Rev: BL 5/15/97; BR 11–12/97; SLJ 3/97; VOYA 4/98) [364.3]

5191 Stewart, Gail B. *Gangs* (7–12). 1998, Greenhaven LB $17.96 (1-56510-751-9); paper $17.12 (1-56510-750-0). Issues discussed in this volume include why gangs attract members, how to control them, and the seriousness of the problem. (Rev: BL 5/15/98; BR 9–10/98; SLJ 6/98) [364.1]

5192 Stewart, Gail B. *Teens in Prison* (8–10). Illus. (The Other America) 1996, Lucent LB $22.45 (1-56006-338-6). Four teens tell why they were sent to prison at such an early age and the life they found there. (Rev: BL 5/15/97; BR 11–12/97; SLJ 4/97; VOYA 8/97) [364.3]

5193 Streissguth, Thomas. *Hoaxers and Hustlers* (7–10). 1994, Oliver Pr. LB $18.95 (1-881508-13-7). Chronicles con artists and con games from the 1800s to the present, including pyramid schemes, the "Martian invasion" radio hoax, and Jim and Tammy Faye Bakker's real-estate scam. (Rev: BL 9/1/94; SLJ 7/94) [364.1]

5194 Thomas, Peggy. *Talking Bones: The Science of Forensic Anthropology* (6–9). (Science Sourcebooks) 1995, Facts on File $19.95 (0-8160-3114-2). This work provides an accessible introduction to the history and technology of forensic anthropology, with material on how forensic anthropologists are able to solve crimes through the analysis of human bones. (Rev: BL 10/15/95; BR 3–4/96; SLJ 1/96; VOYA 4/96) [613]

5195 Trapani, Margi. *Working Together Against Gang Violence* (4–8). (The Library of Social Activism) 1996, Rosen LB $16.95 (0-8239-2260-X). After a general discussion on gang behavior, the author gives pointers to help young people cope with the threat of gangs and suggestions for working with others against gang violence. (Rev: SLJ 2/97) [302.3]

5196 Volkman, Ernest. *Spies: The Secret Agents Who Changed the Course of History* (9–12). 1994, Wiley $24.95 (0-471-55714-5). Forty-five true spy stories featuring famous and less-familiar moles, defectors, and spy masters. (Rev: BL 1/15/94) [355.3]

5197 Wilker, Josh. *Classic Cons and Swindles* (6–9). Illus. (Crime, Justice, and Punishment) 1997, Chelsea LB $19.95 (0-7910-4251-0). This book explains such common con games and swindles as the pigeon drop and the bunco scam. (Rev: BL 9/1/97; BR 11–12/97; VOYA 12/97) [364.163]

5198 Wilkerson, David. *The Cross and the Switchblade* (9–12). 1987, Jove paper $4.99 (0-515-09025-5). A country minister works with the street gangs of New York City. [364.3]

5199 Williams, Stan, and Barbara C. Becnel. *Life in Prison* (6–12). Illus. 1998, Morrow $15.00 (0-688-15589-8). The author, a founder of the Crips gang in California, describes his life on death row, providing graphic, disturbing details of prison life and his reaction to imprisonment. (Rev: SLJ 9/98; VOYA 4/99) [364.6]

5200 Williams, Stanley, and Barbara C. Becnel. *Gangs and the Abuse of Power* (4–8). (Tookie Speaks Out Against Gang Violence) 1996, Rosen LB

303

$15.93 (0-8239-2346-0). A former active gang member in Los Angeles tells what his life was like as a member and how to avoid his mistakes. Also use in this series *Gangs and Wanting to Belong* (1996). (Rev: SLJ 1/97) [302.3]

5201 Williams, Stanley, and Barbara C. Becnel. *Gangs and Weapons* (4–8). (Tookie Speaks Out Against Gang Violence) 1996, Rosen LB $13.95 (0-8239-2342-8). The use of weapons in gangs to gain and maintain power and how they are obtained are 2 of the topics covered in this cautionary account written by a former gang member who was seriously wounded in a shootout. Also use *Gangs and Your Friends* (1996). (Rev: SLJ 1/97) [302.3]

5202 Williams, Stanley, and Barbara C. Becnel. *Gangs and Your Neighborhood* (4–8). (Tookie Speaks out Against Violence) 1996, Rosen LB $15.93 (0-8239-2347-9). How gangs grow in neighborhoods and how they change them are 2 of the topics covered in this book about the dangers of gangs and how to avoid joining one. (Rev: SLJ 1/97) [302.3]

5203 Winters, Paul A., ed. *Crime* (8–12). (Current Controversies) 1997, Greenhaven LB $21.96 (1-56510-687-3); paper $17.45 (1-56510-686-5). A collection of articles debating the causes of crime, methods of prevention, whether or not it is increasing, and juvenile crime. (Rev: BL 2/1/98) [364]

5204 Winters, Paul A., ed. *The Death Penalty* (9–12). (Opposing Viewpoints) 1997, Greenhaven LB $21.96 (1-56510-510-9); paper $17.45 (1-56510-509-5). Prominent lawyers and writers explore the morality and constitutionality of capital punishment in this new collection of documents that complements the 1991 edition. (Rev: BL 1/1–15/97; BR 5–6/97) [364.6]

5205 Winters, Paul A., ed. *Hate Crimes* (9–12). (Current Controversies) 1996, Greenhaven LB $20.96 (1-56510-373-4); paper $16.20 (1-56510-372-6). A collection of articles from 1992–1994 explore such questions as: Are hate crimes a serious problem? Should hate speech be limited? Are special penalties appropriate? and Are particular groups responsible for these crimes? (Rev: BL 2/1/96; SLJ 6/96) [364.1]

5206 Wolf, Robert V. *Capital Punishment* (6–9). (Crime, Justice, and Punishment) 1997, Chelsea $19.95 (0-7910-4311-8). This book reviews the history of capital punishment, explores the moral, philosophical, and legal issues involved, and presents case studies of several death-row inmates. (Rev: BR 1–2/98; SLJ 2/98) [364.6]

5207 Wormser, Richard. *Juveniles in Trouble* (8–12). 1994, Messner $15.00 (0-671-86775-X). Extensive use of first-person narratives of troubled youths, with hard-hitting facts on important choices kids in

trouble need to make. (Rev: BL 5/15/94; SLJ 6/94; VOYA 12/94) [364.3]

5208 Zeinert, Karen. *Victims of Teen Violence* (7–12). Illus. (Issues in Focus) 1996, Enslow LB $19.95 (0-89490-737-9). An exploration of teen violence that focuses of guns, gangs, sexual harassment, and gay bashing, and includes causes, consequences, victims, and solutions. (Rev: BL 6/1–15/96; SLJ 7/96; VOYA 8/96) [362.88]

Poverty, Homelessness, and Hunger

5209 Albeda, Randy, et al. *The War on the Poor: A Defense Manual* (10–12). Illus. 1996, New Pr. paper $10.95 (1-56581-262-6). This adult book presents alarming facts and statistics abut the status of the poor in the United States today. (Rev: VOYA 10/96) [339.4]

5210 Ayer, Eleanor. *Homeless Children* (5–8). Illus. (Overview) 1997, Lucent LB $17.96 (1-56006-177-4). The causes and consequences of homelessness are explored, with a focus on children and the ways the problem is being handled. (Rev: BL 3/15/97; BR 11–12/97) [362.7]

5211 Barbour, Scott, ed. *Hunger* (7–12). (Current Controversies) 1995, Greenhaven LB $21.96 (1-56510-239-8); paper $14.50 (1-56510-238-X). This compilation of articles, essays, and book excerpts written by journalists, scholars, and activists will challenge young people to evaluate the information and develop their own conclusions about world hunger, the extent of the problem, and how it can be reduced. (Rev: BL 8/95; SLJ 10/95) [363.8]

5212 Berck, Judith. *No Place to Be: Voices of Homeless Children* (7–12). 1992, Houghton $17.00 (0-395-53350-3). Honest testimony of homeless young people, with quotes from their writing, including poetry. (Rev: BL 4/1/92*; SLJ 6/92) [362.7]

5213 Cozic, Charles P., ed. *Welfare Reform* (8–12). (At Issue) 1997, Greenhaven LB $18.70 (1-56510-546-X); paper $15.57 (1-56510-545-1). This anthology of different opinions on welfare reform explores such alternatives as workfare, establishment of orphanages, and reliance on private charities. (Rev: BL 1/1–15/97; SLJ 6/97) [361.973]

5214 Cozic, Charles P., and Paul A. Winters, eds. *Welfare* (8–12). (Opposing Viewpoints) 1997, Greenhaven LB $21.96 (1-56510-520-6); paper $16.20 (1-56510-519-2). In this anthology of 35 essays, prominent politicians and writers debate questions about welfare, including its necessity, abuse, and reform. (Rev: BL 12/15/96; BR 5–6/97; SLJ 2/97) [362.5]

5215 Criswell, Sara D. *Homelessness* (7–12). Illus. (Overview) 1997, Lucent LB $17.96 (1-56006-180-

4). This book reviews the causes of homelessness, describes life on the streets and the lives of homeless children, and discusses the shelter system and possible ways to help the homeless. (Rev: BL 7/98; SLJ 1/99) [362.5 0973]

5216 Davis, Bertha. *Poverty in America: What We Do about It* (7–10). 1991, Watts LB $24.00 (0-531-13016-9). A discussion about a critical issue of poverty in easy-to-understand language. (Rev: BL 5/15/91; SLJ 6/91) [362.5]

5217 De Koster, Katie, ed. *Poverty* (7–12). (Opposing Viewpoints) 1994, Greenhaven paper $16.20 (1-56510-065-4). Differing viewpoints are presented on such questions as what causes poverty and why women and minorities suffer from higher rates of poverty than white males. (Rev: BL 1/1/94) [362.5]

5218 Egendorf, Laura K., ed. *Poverty* (8–12). (Opposing Viewpoints) 1998, Greenhaven LB $20.96 (1-56510-947-3); paper $17.45 (1-56510-946-5). The seriousness of poverty today, its causes, and how it can be alleviated are covered in this collection of differing opinions on the subject. (Rev: BL 8/98) [362.5]

5219 Erlbach, Arlene. *Everything You Need to Know If Your Family Is on Welfare* (6–10). (Need to Know) 1997, Rosen LB $15.95 (0-8239-2433-5). This book explains the welfare system and details recipients' rights as well as offering tips on how to cope with being on welfare and the social stigma often associated with it. (Rev: SLJ 4/98) [362.5]

5220 Flood, Nancy Bohac. *Working Together Against World Hunger* (7–12). (Library of Social Activism) 1995, Rosen LB $16.95 (0-8239-1773-8). This book gives a rundown on world hunger, the conditions that cause it, and ways of becoming active in fighting it. (Rev: BL 4/15/95) [363.8]

5221 Fyson, Nance Lui. *Feeding the World* (6–8). Illus. 1985, Batsford $19.95 (0-7134-4264-6). This account introduces the world's increasing food problems, gives material on staple crops, and discusses production and distribution. (Rev: BL 5/15/85) [338.19]

5222 Gottfried, Ted. *Homelessness: Whose Problem Is It?* (6–12). (Issue and Debate) 1999, Millbrook $21.90 (0-7613-0953-5). After reviewing the history of homelessness in the United States, opposing views are presented on the causes of homelessness today, the responsibility of government and the individual, and methods of countering it. (Rev: BL 4/1/99; BR 9–10/99; SLJ 9/99) [305.569]

5223 Heater, Derek. *Refugees* (6–10). Illus. 1989, Rourke LB $25.27 (0-86592-077-X). Through text, illustrations, and maps, the plight of the world's homeless is explored. (Rev: BL 5/1/89; SLJ 6/89) [325]

5224 Hombs, Mary Ellen. *Welfare Reform: A Reference Handbook* (9–12). (Contemporary World Issues) 1996, ABC-CLIO LB $48.50 (0-87436-844-8). The author traces the history of social welfare programs from their inception in the 1930s to current attitudes toward them, examines the effectiveness of state and federal programs, profiles people who have influenced social welfare programs, and furnishes information on forms of assistance, agencies, and resources. (Rev: SLJ 6/97) [353]

5225 Hubbard, Jim. *Lives Turned Upside Down: Homeless Children in Their Own Words and Photographs* (4–8). 1996, Simon & Schuster paper $17.00 (0-689-80649-3). This work includes the case studies of 4 youngsters from homeless families. (Rev: BL 11/15/96; SLJ 12/96) [362.7]

5226 Johnson, Joan J. *Children of Welfare* (6–10). Illus. 1995, Twenty-First Century LB $21.40 (0-8050-2985-0). This work explains the emergence of the welfare system, what it is today, its impact on young people, and the importance of recent changes in the system as of 1995. (Rev: BL 6/1–15/97; BR 11–12/97; SLJ 6/97) [362.71]

5227 LeVert, Marianne. *The Welfare System* (7–12). 1995, Millbrook LB $23.90 (1-56294-455-X). A look at issues in the great welfare debate. (Rev: BL 4/15/95; SLJ 4/95) [361.6]

5228 McCauslin, Mark. *Homelessness* (6–9). 1994, Macmillan paper $4.95 (0-382-24757-4). Surveys and analyzes the decline of affordable housing over the past few decades, along with other economic and employment factors that have led to homelessness. (Rev: BL 2/1/95; SLJ 3/95) [362.5]

5229 Nichelason, Margery G. *Homeless or Hopeless?* (5–8). Illus. (Pro/Con) 1994, Lerner LB $23.93 (0-8225-2606-9). After an explanation of the roots and causes of homelessness, clearly written statements debate who is responsible for homelessness and how it should be handled. (Rev: BL 6/1–15/94; SLJ 7/94) [362.5]

5230 Parker, Julie. *Everything You Need to Know About Living in a Shelter* (8–12). 1995, Rosen LB $17.95 (0-8239-1874-2). A straightforward account that describes life for teens living in shelters, plus material on what they can do to control at least some aspects of their lives. (Rev: SLJ 12/95; VOYA 2/96) [362.5]

5231 Roleff, Tamara L., ed. *The Homeless* (8–12). Illus. (Opposing Viewpoints) 1996, Greenhaven LB $21.96 (1-56510-361-0); paper $14.50 (1-56510-360-2). Is homelessness a serious problem? Who are the homeless? What causes homelessness? How can society and government help the homeless? These are some of the questions discussed in this collection of articles representing different opinions on this subject. (Rev: BL 3/15/96; BR 9–10/96; SLJ 2/96; VOYA 6/96) [362.5]

5232 Rozakis, Laurie. *Homelessness: Can We Solve the Problem?* (6–9). (Issues of Our Time) 1995, Twenty-First Century LB $18.90 (0-8050-3878-7). A well-rounded discussion that will encourage readers to form their own conclusions. (Rev: BL 7/95; SLJ 9/95) [362.5]

5233 Seymour-Jones, Carole. *Homelessness* (5–9). (Past and Present) 1993, Macmillan $12.95 (0-02-786882-6). A discussion of the causes of homelessness, the extent of the problem and who is affected, and ways to end it. (Rev: BL 8/93) [362.5]

5234 Stavsky, Lois, and I. E. Mozeson. *The Place I Call Home: Faces and Voices of Homeless Teens* (8–12). Illus. 1990, Shapolsky $14.95 (0-944007-81-3). A series of interviews with homeless teens that reveal lives of violence, poverty, and drugs. (Rev: BL 11/15/90; SLJ 2/91) [362.7]

5235 Stearman, Kaye. *Homelessness* (6–8). (Talking Points) 1999, Raintree Steck-Vaughn LB $27.11 (0-8172-5312-2). A worldwide view of homelessness, its causes, including eviction, natural disasters, and war, and ways it is being combated internationally. (Rev: BL 9/1/99; BR 9–10/99; SLJ 8/99) [362.5]

5236 Stewart, Gail B. *The Homeless* (6–10). (The Other America) 1996, Lucent LB $17.96 (1-56006-331-9). Four homeless people are interviewed about their daily lives and the circumstances that led to their homelessness. (Rev: BR 9–10/96; SLJ 7/96; VOYA 8/96) [362.5]

5237 Stewart, Gail B. *Mothers on Welfare* (8–12). Illus. (The Other America) 1997, Lucent LB $17.96 (1-56006-576-1). The author traces the evolution of America's welfare system from the Depression to today, including efforts to "end welfare as we know it" under the Clinton presidency, then focuses on interviews with 4 young mothers on welfare from different backgrounds, with different problems, and with different values, perspectives, and prospects. (Rev: SLJ 6/98; VOYA 10/98) [361]

5238 Switzer, Ellen. *Anyplace but Here: Young, Alone, and Homeless: What to Do* (7–12). 1992, Atheneum $14.95 (0-689-31694-1). A description of the dreary future that awaits most teen runaways, with interviews with members of 2 runaway "families." (Rev: BL 10/1/92; SLJ 11/92) [362.7]

5239 Worth, Richard. *Poverty* (5–8). Illus. (Overview) 1997, Lucent LB $22.45 (1-56006-192-8). A carefully researched title that gives a history of poverty in America, changing attitudes toward it, and current policies and practices. (Rev: BL 8/97; SLJ 9/97) [362.5]

Public Morals

5240 Carnes, Jim. *Us and Them: A History of Intolerance in America* (7–12). Illus. 1996, Oxford $40.00 (0-19-510378-5). Each chapter focuses on an episode of intolerance and prejudice in our history, such as the Cherokee Trail of Tears, the internment of Japanese Americans during World War II, recent race riots in New York City, and the murder of a gay man in Maine. (Rev: BL 6/1–15/96; BR 11–12/96) [305.8]

5241 Dudley, William, ed. *Media Violence* (8–12). (Opposing Viewpoints) 1998, Greenhaven LB $20.96 (1-56510-945-7); paper $16.20 (1-56510-944-9). This exploration of violence in television, motion pictures, song lyrics, and other media questions its extent, effects, and proposals to restrict it. (Rev: BL 8/89) [384]

5242 Edgar, Kathleen J. *Everything You Need to Know about Media Violence* (6–9). Illus. (Need to Know) 1998, Rosen LB $16.95 (0-8239-2568-4). The author believes that media violence encourages similar behavior in society, explores violence in film, television, radio, music, and the Internet, and discusses the ratings systems and media violence studies. (Rev: BR 9–10/98; SLJ 10/98) [302.2]

5243 Foerstel, Herbert N. *Banned in the Media: A Reference Guide to Censorship in the Press, Motion Pictures, Broadcasting & the Internet* (9–12). 1998, Greenwood $49.95 (0-313-30245-6). This work begins with a history of censorship in the media, continues with coverage of 28 media-related censorship cases from 1812 to 1997, and ends with 6 editorial statements from spokespeople like Daniel Schorr and Walter Cronkite. (Rev: BR 1–2/99; SLJ 11/98; VOYA 12/98) [363.3]

5244 Gold, John C. *Board of Education v. Pico (1982)* (6–10). Illus. (Supreme Court Decisions) 1994, Twenty-First Century LB $18.90 (0-8050-3660-1). A thorough analysis of the Supreme Court case that began in a Long Island school and involved censoring library materials. (Rev: BL 11/15/94; SLJ 1/95) [344.73]

5245 Gottfried, Ted. *Pornography: Debating the Issues* (9–12). Illus. (Issues in Focus) 1997, Enslow LB $19.95 (0-89490-907-X). This book supplies historical background on pornography, the complicated social and legal issues that surround it, and the possible connection between violence and sexual exploitation and obscene material. (Rev: BL 4/15/97; BR 11–12/97; SLJ 7/97) [363.4]

5246 Johnson, Joan J. *Teen Prostitution* (8–12). 1992, Watts LB $24.00 (0-531-11099-0). Explores what makes teenage boys and girls turn to prostitution and what keeps some turning tricks even after they have a chance to escape. (Rev: BL 12/1/92; SLJ 12/92) [306.74]

5247 King, David C. *Freedom of Assembly* (4–8). (Land of the Free) 1997, Millbrook LB $19.90 (0-7613-0064-3). This book covers this basic civil right with examples throughout U.S. history and landmark court cases that helped define its limits. (Rev: BL 5/15/97; SLJ 10/97) [342.73]

5248 Lang, Susan S., and Paul Lang. *Censorship* (8–12). 1993, Watts LB $23.60 (0-531-10999-2). Discusses a wide range of issues related to First Amendment rights, arguing for free exchange of ideas and speech even when the ideas expressed are distasteful. (Rev: BL 6/1–15/93; SLJ 7/93; VOYA 10/93) [363.3]

5249 Leinwand, Gerald. *Heroism in America* (7–12). Illus. (Democracy in Action) 1996, Watts LB $24.00 (0-531-11282-9). The author asserts that U.S. culture does not give recognition to modern-day heroes and discusses 14 "exemplars," such as Chief Joseph, Rosa Parks, and Cesar Chavez. (Rev: BL 2/1/97; SLJ 2/97) [973.92]

5250 Miller, J. Anthony. *Texas vs. Johnson: The Flag-Burning Case* (6–10). Illus. (Landmark Supreme Court Cases) 1997, Enslow LB $19.95 (0-89490-858-8). The limits of civil disobedience was the subject of this important Supreme Court case. (Rev: BL 7/97; BR 11–12/97) [342.73]

5251 Newton, David E. *Violence and the Media* (9–12). (Contemporary World Issues) 1996, ABC-CLIO LB $39.50 (0-87436-843-X). Following an overview of violence in movies, television, music, and video games, there are profiles of key people involved in the debate and excerpts from laws and regulations, court cases, policy statements, research reports, and opinions about TV violence. (Rev: BL 11/15/96; BR 11–12/97; SLJ 12/96) [303.6]

5252 Sherrow, Victoria. *Censorship in Schools* (6–9). Illus. (Issues in Focus) 1996, Enslow LB $19.95 (0-89490-728-X). After defining censorship, the author discusses when, how, and why it occurs in schools, with several citations of famous cases. (Rev: BL 1/1–15/97; BR 3–4/97; SLJ 12/96; VOYA 4/97) [025.213]

5253 Sherrow, Victoria. *Violence and the Media: The Question of Cause and Effect* (6–9). Illus. 1996, Millbrook LB $22.90 (1-56294-549-1). A thought-provoking book that examines the data on how violence in the media—television, movies, video games, and music—changes behavior. (Rev: BL 5/15/96; BR 9–10/96; SLJ 4/96) [303.6]

5254 Stay, Byron L., ed. *Censorship* (8–12). (Opposing Viewpoints) 1997, Greenhaven LB $21.99 (1-56510-508-7); paper $20.25 (1-56510-507-9). This new edition of the 1990 title presents arguments on such controversial areas of the censor-

ship battle as antipornography laws, campus speech codes, and use of the V-chip on the Internet. (Rev: BL 12/15/96; BR 5–6/97; VOYA 6/97) [363.3]

5255 Steffens, Bradley. *Censorship* (7–10). Illus. 1996, Lucent LB $22.45 (1-56006-166-9). A historical survey that presents the conflict between freedom and censorship, beginning with the Ten Commandments and the Bill of Rights and ending with today's controversy over rock lyrics. (Rev: BL 2/15/96; SLJ 3/96) [363.3]

5256 Steins, Richard. *Censorship: How Does It Conflict with Freedom?* (6–9). (Issues of Our Time) 1995, Twenty-First Century LB $18.90 (0-8050-3879-5). Current positions and trends are covered in this discussion of censorship and the First Amendment. (Rev: BL 7/95; SLJ 9/95) [363.3]

5257 Wekesser, Carol, ed. *Pornography* (8–12). (Opposing Viewpoints) 1997, Greenhaven LB $21.96 (1-56510-518-4); paper $20.25 (1-56510-517-6). What is pornography? Is it harmful? Should it be censored? Can it be controlled on the Internet? These are some of the questions explored in this collection of writings representing different points of view. (Rev: BL 12/15/96; BR 5–6/97; SLJ 2/97) [363.7]

5258 Wekesser, Carol, ed. *Violence in the Media* (7–12). (Current Controversies) 1995, Greenhaven LB $26.20 (1-56510-237-1); paper $20.25 (1-56510-236-3). Differing viewpoints on violence in the media, its possible harmful effects, and controversies over controlling it. (Rev: BL 8/95; SLJ 10/95) [303.6]

5259 Whitehead, Fred. *Culture Wars* (8–12). (Opposing Viewpoints) 1994, Greenhaven LB $17.95 (1-56510-101-4); paper $16.20 (1-56510-100-6). Includes essays by a variety of writers on such cultural topics as intellectual freedom, artistic quality, values, and public morality. (Rev: BL 5/1/94; SLJ 3/94; VOYA 4/94) [306]

5260 Williams, Mary, ed. *Culture Wars: Opposing Viewpoints* (9–12). Illus. (Opposing Viewpoints) 1998, Greenhaven LB $20.96 (1-56510-939-2); paper $16.20 (1-56510-938-4). This collection of essays discusses such topics as cultural values, popular culture, multiculturalism, and government regulation of cultural values. (Rev: BL 2/1/99) [306.0973]

5261 Zeinert, Karen. *Free Speech: From Newspapers to Music Lyrics* (7–10). 1995, Enslow LB $19.95 (0-89490-634-8). The censorship battle in the context of various mediums, from a historical perspective. (Rev: BL 4/1/95; SLJ 6/95) [323.44]

Sex Roles

5262 Bender, David, and Bruno Leone, eds. *Male/Female Roles* (9–12). (Opposing Viewpoints)

1995, Greenhaven LB $19.95 (1-56510-174-X); paper $14.50 (1-56510-175-8). A discussion of how sex roles are established, whether they have changed for the better, and predictions for the future. (Rev: BL 4/1/95; SLJ 2/95; VOYA 5/95) [305.3]

5263 Brooks, Bruce. *Boys Will Be* (6–12). 1993, Holt $14.95 (0-8050-2420-4). Geared to both boys and their parents, a discussion of common growing-up issues during the teen years, such as choice of friends, involvement in sports that may be dangerous, and reading matter. (Rev: BL 12/1/93; SLJ 12/93; VOYA 2/94) [305.23]

5264 Chipman, Dawn, et al. *Cool Women: The Reference* (6–9). 1998, Girl Pr. paper $19.95 (0-9659754-0-1). This work spotlights an eclectic variety of heroines, past and present, real and fictional, from around the world, ranging from athletes and spies to Amazons and comic book queens, chosen for their uniqueness, strength, tenacity, contributions, and ability to blaze new trails for women. (Rev: VOYA 2/99) [305.4]

5265 Hanmer, Trudy J. *The Gender Gap in Schools: Girls Losing Out* (7–12). Illus. (Issues in Focus) 1996, Enslow LB $19.95 (0-89490-718-2). Sex discrimination at the school level is introduced with an objective presentation of the many facets of this complex question. (Rev: BL 8/96; SLJ 6/96) [376]

5266 Stearman, Kaye, and Nikki van der Gaag. *Gender Issues* (6–10). Illus. (Global Issues) 1996, Raintree Steck-Vaughn LB $24.26 (0-8172-4545-6). Using historical background material, statistics, and case studies, the various issues involving gender roles and sex discrimination around the world are explored. (Rev: BL 3/15/97; VOYA 6/97) [305.3]

Social Action, Social Change, and Futurism

5267 Brooks, Susan M. *Any Girl Can Rule the World* (9–12). 1998, Fairview paper $12.95 (1-57749-068-1). Based on the principle that information and knowledge equals power, this book is a call to action for young women to get involved in social, political, and economic issues, and a guide on how to do so. (Rev: VOYA 4/99) [361.2]

5268 Carlson, Richard, and Bruce Goldman. *2020 Visions: Long View of a Changing World* (9–12). 1991, Stanford Alumni Association paper $12.95 (0-916318-44-3). Optimistic futurist speculation that concentrates on the long-term impact of such trends as an aging population, a restructured economy, and a divided society. (Rev: BL 11/1/91) [303.49]

5269 Erlbach, Arlene. *Worth the Risk: True Stories about Risk Takers, Plus How You Can Be One, Too*

(5–9). 1999, Free Spirit paper $12.95 (1-57542-051-1). These are 20 case studies of teenagers who took risks, from defying the dominant cliques in school to entering a burning house to save siblings. (Rev: BL 5/1/99; SLJ 8/99) [158]

5270 Gaillard, Frye. *If I Were a Carpenter: Twenty Years of Habitat for Humanity* (10–12). 1996, Blair $24.95 (0-89587-148-3). The story of the founding of Habitat for Humanity, its successes and failures in building houses for the poor, and the contributions of such people as Jimmy Carter. (Rev: BL 6/1–15/96; BR 11–12/96; SLJ 10/96) [361.7]

5271 *How We Made the World a Better Place: Kids and Teens Write on How They Changed Their Corner of the World* (5–8). 1998, Fairview paper $9.95 (1-57749-079-7). This is a collection of essays written by children and teens about how they have made the world a better place. The answers include working with the homeless, volunteering in an orphanage, and conducting environment projects. (Rev: VOYA 6/99) [361.2]

5272 Kronenwetter, Michael. *Protest!* (7–12). Illus. 1996, Twenty-First Century LB $21.40 (0-8050-4103-6). This book describes various forms of protest, from simple actions in everyday life to those related to political and social issues aimed at changing social conditions in the U.S. and around the world, providing a historical, sociological, and psychological context. (Rev: BL 1/1–15/97; SLJ 1/97; VOYA 6/97) [303.48]

5273 Kurian, George Thomas, and Graham T. T. Molitor, eds. *The 21st Century* (8–12). 1999, Macmillan $125.00 (0-02-864977-X). This book makes predictions for future developments in such areas as abortion, artificial intelligence, crime, extinction, household appliances, sexual behavior, and utopias. (Rev: BL 4/1/99; SLJ 8/99) [133.3]

5274 Lesko, Wendy Schaetzel. *Youth: The 26% Solution* (7–12). 1998, Information U. S. A. paper $14.95 (1-878346-47-4). A community action handbook for teens prepared by Project 2000 that provides basic, workable advice, based on the premise that the 26 percent of the population of the United States under the age of 18 can make a difference. (Rev: BL 11/1/98; VOYA 12/98) [361.8]

5275 Lewis, Barbara A. *The Kid's Guide to Social Action: How to Solve the Social Problems You Choose—and Turn Creative Thinking into Positive Action*. rev. ed. (4–8). 1998, Free Spirit paper $16.95 (1-57542-038-4). An inspirational guide that shows how young people can make a difference by becoming involved in social action, such as instigating a cleanup of toxic waste, lobbying, or youth rights campaigns. (Rev: SLJ 1/99) [361.6]

5276 Markley, Oliver W., and Walter R. McCuan, eds. *21st Century Earth* (7–12). (Opposing Viewpoints) 1996, Greenhaven LB $21.96 (1-56510-415-3); paper $16.20 (1-56510-414-5). An assortment of forecasts for the near future, including the effects of overpopulation and new technologies. (Rev: BL 4/1/96; SLJ 3/96) [303.49]

5277 Meltzer, Milton. *Who Cares? Millions Do . . . A Book about Altruism* (7–10). 1994, Walker LB $11.95 (0-8027-8325-2). Stories of people who help their fellow beings, both individually and through organizations. (Rev: BL 11/15/94; VOYA 2/95) [171]

5278 Ryan, Bernard. *Caring for Animals* (7–12). 1998, Ferguson LB $15.95 (0-89434-227-4). After a general introduction to volunteerism, this book outlines ways that teens can help care for unwanted and abandoned animals in their neighborhood. (Rev: BL 9/15/98; BR 11–12/98; SLJ 11/98; VOYA 8/99) [361.8]

5279 Ryan, Bernard. *Expanding Education and Literacy* (7–12). (Community Service for Teens) 1998, Ferguson LB $15.95 (0-89434-231-2). This book describes literacy and reading programs in the United States and how teens can participate in them. (Rev: BL 9/15/98; BR 11–12/98; SLJ 11/98) [361.3]

5280 Ryan, Bernard. *Helping the Ill, Poor and the Elderly* (7–12). (Community Service for Teens) 1998, Ferguson LB $15.95 (0-89434-229-0). This book outlines the many ways that teens can help the less fortunate in their communities both informally and working through service agencies. (Rev: BL 9/15/98; BR 11–12/98; SLJ 11/98) [361.8]

5281 Ryan, Bernard. *Promoting the Arts and Sciences* (7–12). (Community Service for Teens) 1998, Ferguson LB $15.95 (0-89434-234-7). This work tells how teens can become involved in local agencies that promote the arts and sciences and how their services can make a difference both to the community and themselves. (Rev: BL 9/15/98; BR 11–12/98; SLJ 2/99) [361.8]

5282 Ryan, Bernard, Jr. *Participating in Government: Opportunities to Volunteer* (7–12). (Community Service for Teens) 1998, Ferguson LB $15.95 (0-89434-230-4). This upbeat guide advises teens about how they can volunteer in the areas of government and politics and become involved in their community. Also use *Promoting the Arts and Sciences: Opportunities to Volunteer* (1998). (Rev: BR 11–12/98; SLJ 2/99) [302.14]

5283 Seo, Danny. *Generation React: Activism for Beginners* (7–12). 1997, Ballantine paper $10.95 (0-345-41242-7). This book gives step-by-step directions for starting an activist group, with material on fund raising, protesting and boycotting, lobbying, publicity, and related topics. (Rev: BL 10/1/97; VOYA 2/98) [303.4]

Social Customs and Holidays

5284 Barkin, Carol, and Elizabeth James. *The Holiday Handbook* (5–8). Illus. 1994, Clarion $17.00 (0-395-65011-9); paper $8.95 (0-395-67888-9). Both secular and religious holidays are included in this handbook arranged by the seasons. For each holiday, background information is given plus interesting sidelights and creative activities. (Rev: BL 6/1–15/94; SLJ 5/94) [394.2]

5285 Dover, Laura D. *The Big Book of Halloween: Creative & Creepy Projects for Revellers of All Ages* (9–12). Illus. 1998, Lark $19.95 (1-57990-063-1). A variety of Halloween projects from simple to complex are included in this volume, plus historical material about the holiday and Halloween trivia. (Rev: SLJ 10/98) [745.5]

5286 Dresser, Norine. *Multicultural Celebrations: Today's Rules of Etiquette for Life's Special Occasions* (9–12). 1999, Three Rivers paper $14.00 (0-609-80259-3). This book provides practical advice and social dos and don'ts for the customs, rituals, and holidays of various cultures around the world. (Rev: SLJ 9/99) [394.2]

5287 Harris, Jessica. *A Kwanzaa Keepsake: Celebrating the Holiday with New Traditions and Feasts* (9–12). 1995, Simon & Schuster $22.00 (0-684-80045-4). A collection of ethnic recipes for celebrating Kwanzaa, plus an explanation of the 7 principles that are the basis of the celebration. (Rev: BL 11/15/95; SLJ 5/96) [394.2]

5288 King, Elizabeth. *Quinceanera* (5–8). 1998, NAL paper $15.99 (0-525-45638-4). This photoessay traces the everyday life of 2 beautiful young Latin American women as they prepare for quinceanera, a coming-of-age ritual when girls turn 15. (Rev: BL 8/98; SLJ 12/98; VOYA 2/99) [395.2 4]

5289 MacMillan, Dianne M. *Thanksgiving Day* (4–8). (Best Holiday Books) 1997, Enslow LB $18.95 (0-89490-822-7). In spite of a dull format, this book gives solid information about Thanksgiving, its history, common traditions, and modern observances. (Rev: SLJ 8/97) [394.2]

5290 McSharry, Patra, and Roger Rosen, eds. *Coca-Cola Culture: Icons of Pop* (10–12). (Icarus World Issues) 1994, Rosen LB $16.95 (0-8239-1593-X); paper $8.95 (0-8239-1594-8). Essays and fiction on how America's commercial products have influenced the way other countries perceive us as well as how we see ourselves, using such examples as rock music in China, the TV series *Dallas* in Poland, and the changing portrayal of Native Americans. (Rev: BL 3/1/94) [306.4]

5291 Perl, Lila. *Piñatas and Paper Flowers: Holidays of the Americas in English and Spanish* (6–9).

Illus. 1983, HarperCollins paper $6.95 (0-89919-155-X). The origins and customs of 8 holidays celebrated in the Americas are outlined in a bilingual text. [394.2]

5292 Santino, Jack. *All Around the Year: Holidays and Celebrations in American Life* (9–12). 1994, Univ. of Illinois Pr. $24.95 (0-252-02049-9). The effect of holidays on American life. (Rev: BL 4/15/94) [394.269]

5293 Thompson, Sue Ellen. *Holiday Symbols: A Guide to the Legend & Lore Behind the People, Places, Foods, & Other Symbols Associated with Holidays & Holy Days, Feasts & Fasts, & Other Celebrations* (5–10). 1997, Omnigraphics $55.00 (0-7808-0072-9). This volume gives background material on 174 holidays and information about 750 symbols associated with them. (Rev: BL 3/15/98; BR 5–6/98; SLJ 5/98) [394.2]

5294 Wilkinson, Philip. *A Celebration of Customs & Rituals of the World* (5–8). Illus. 1996, Facts on File $40.00 (0-8160-3479-6). A discussion of customs and rituals connected with birth, death, marriage, and coming-of-age. (Rev: BL 4/1/96; VOYA 6/96) [394.2]

Terrorism

5295 Gaines, Ann. *Terrorism* (7–12). (Crime, Justice, and Punishment) 1998, Chelsea LB $19.95 (0-7910-4596-X). Beginning with the bombing of Pan Am flight 103 over Lockerbie, Scotland, in 1988, this thorough account discusses terrorism around the world and the groups that are responsible. (Rev: BL 12/15/98; SLJ 3/99) [364.1]

5296 Sadler, A. E., and Paul A. Winters, eds. *Urban Terrorism* (9–12). (Current Controversy) 1996, Greenhaven LB $20.96 (1-56510-411-0); paper $20.25 (1-56510-410-2). Twenty-eight essays explore topics related to urban terrorism: Should we fear it? Who is responsible for these attacks? Does media coverage encourage terrorism? and Do antiterrorist measures infringe on civil liberties? (Rev: BL 7/96; SLJ 9/96) [363.3]

5297 Sherrow, Victoria. *The World Trade Center Bombing: Terror in the Towers* (4–8). Illus. (American Disasters) 1998, Enslow $18.95 (0-7660-1056-2). The causes of the World Trade Center bombing and the people responsible are discussed, with illustrations of its effects and acts of heroism. (Rev: BL 1/1–15/99; BR 5–6/99; SLJ 3/99; VOYA 4/99) [363.2]

5298 Streissguth, Thomas. *International Terrorists* (6–10). Illus. (Profiles) 1993, Oliver Pr. LB $18.95 (1-881508-07-2). This book describes the causes of international terrorism, the responsible organizations, and famous incidents. (Rev: BL 10/15/93; SLJ 1/94; VOYA 2/94) [909.82]

Urban and Rural Life

5299 Barr, Roger. *Cities* (6–8). (Overview) 1995, Lucent LB $22.45 (1-56006-158-8). A historical as well as a contemporary look at cities. (Rev: BL 7/95; SLJ 4/95) [307.76]

5300 Kidder, Tracy. *Home Town* (10–12). 1999, Random $25.95 (0-679-45588-4). A profile of the town of Northampton, Massachusetts, as seen through the eyes of its citizens, particularly a young police officer whose job leads him to see different aspects of the town, from the plush Northampton of yuppies and Smith College professors to the projects and the seamier sides of life. (Rev: BL 3/1/99; SLJ 8/99) [307.7]

5301 Leuzzi, Linda. *Urban Life* (6–9). 1995, Chelsea LB $19.95 (0-7910-2841-0). A look at urban life in U.S. cities a century ago, from both a contemporary perspective and the viewpoint of someone living then. (Rev: BL 7/95; SLJ 9/95) [973]

5302 Trefil, James. *A Scientist in the City* (9–12). 1994, Doubleday $23.95 (0-385-24797-4). An examination of the technological wonder that is the urban ecosystem, viewed as a natural combination of inanimate structures and living organisms. (Rev: BL 1/1/94; SLJ 9/94) [307.76]

5303 Vergara, Camilo José. *The New American Ghetto* (9–12). 1995, Rutgers Univ. Pr. $49.95 (0-8135-2209-9). Chilean-born Vergara has photographed American ghettos since 1977 and has gathered his work here as a documentation of their geography and ecology. (Rev: BL 12/1/95*) [307.3]

Economics and Business

General and Miscellaneous

5304 Brenner, Joel Glenn. *The Emperors of Chocolate: Inside the Secret World of Hershey and Mars* (10–12). 1999, Random $25.95 (0-679-42190-4). Espionage, secrecy, paranoia, personality clashes, dreams, and failures are among the components of this story of the intense rivalry between the Mars and Hershey chocolate empires. (Rev: BL 12/1/98; SLJ 5/99) [338]

5305 Folbre, Nancy, and The Center for Popular Economics. *The New Field Guide to the U.S. Economy: A Compact and Irreverent Guide to Economic Life in America* (9–12). Illus. 1995, New Pr. paper $16.95 (1-56584-153-0). A compact introduction to the U.S. economy and the factors that affect it, presented in a humorous manner through easy-to-read graphs, illustrations, cartoons, and text divided into such chapters as workers, women, people of color, health, environment, and the global economy. (Rev: VOYA 12/96) [330.73]

5306 Heilbroner, Robert L., and Lester C. Thurow. *Economics Explained: Everything You Need to Know about How the Economy Works and Where It's Going* (9–12). 1994, Simon & Schuster paper $12.00 (0-671-88422-0). Two well-known economists present a primer on economics and provide an overview of the history of economic thought. (Rev: BL 1/15/94) [330]

5307 Karnes, Frances A., and Suzanne M. Bean. *Girls & Young Women Entrepreneurs: True Stories about Starting & Running a Business Plus How You Can Do It Yourself* (6–10). Illus. 1997, Free Spirit paper $12.95 (1-57542-022-8). This inspirational book introduces dozens of young women ages 9 to 25 who have started business ventures, and provides advice and information for young females who would also like to become entrepreneurs. (Rev: BR 9–10/98; SLJ 6/98) [338]

5308 Katz, Donald. *Just Do It! The Nike Spirit in the Corporate World* (9–12). 1994, Random $23.00 (0-679-43275-2). An examination of all aspects of Nike—its Oregon "campus," its Far East factories, its retailers, the symbiotic relationship between athletes and Nike, its company culture, its successes, and its failures. (Rev: BL 5/1/94; SLJ 11/94) [338.7]

5309 Oleksy, Walter. *Business and Industry* (6–12). Illus. (Information Revolution) 1996, Facts on File $19.95 (0-8160-3075-8). This book describes how companies use Powerbook computers, supercomputers, modems, and videophones to distribute information, increase productivity, and make better business decisions. (Rev: BL 2/15/96; BR 9–10/96; VOYA 6/96) [650]

5310 Roleff, Tamara L., ed. *Business Ethics* (9–12). (At Issue) 1996, Greenhaven LB $12.95 (1-56510-385-8); paper $11.20 (1-56510-384-X). Excerpts from articles and books explore controversies around inflated CEO salaries, corporate influence buying, and overseas business policies. (Rev: BL 3/15/96) [174]

5311 Savitt, William, and Paula Bottorf. *Global Development* (9–12). (Contemporary World Issues) 1995, ABC-CLIO LB $39.50 (0-87436-774-3). This survey of world economic development since World War II contains background information, history, biographical sketches, statistics, organizations, and other resources. (Rev: SLJ 6/96) [330]

5312 Strasser, J. B., and Laurie Becklund. *Swoosh: The Story of Nike and the Men Who Played There* (9–12). 1992, Harcourt $24.95 (0-15-187430-1). This biographical history of the Nike corporation and its key figures describes the company's rise to the top in the athletic-shoe business. (Rev: BL 12/1/91) [338.7]

5313 Waterman, Robert H. *What America Does Right: Learning from Companies That Put People First* (9–12). 1994, Norton $23.00 (0-393-03597-2). Examines the successful operations of companies that recognize, understand, and try to meet their employees' needs. (Rev: BL 2/15/94) [658.5]

Economic Systems and Institutions

General and Miscellaneous

5314 Aaseng, Nathan. *You Are the Corporate Executive* (7–10). Illus. (Great Decisions) 1997, Oliver Pr. LB $18.95 (1-881508-35-8). This book describes the work of a company's CEO and the nature and consequences of the decisions that CEOs have to make. (Rev: BL 6/1–15/97; BR 11–12/97; SLJ 6/97) [658.4]

5315 Godfrey, Neale S. *Neale S. Godfrey's Ultimate Kids' Money Book* (5–8). Illus. 1998, Simon & Schuster paper $18.00 (0-689-81717-7). An outstanding book that combines history, fables, games, and vocabulary to give young readers a history of money and economics. (Rev: BL 11/1/98; SLJ 2/99) [332.024]

5316 Leone, Bruno, ed. *Capitalism: Opposing Viewpoints*. Rev. ed. (9–12). Illus. (Opposing Viewpoints) 1986, Greenhaven paper $16.20 (0-89908-359-5). A collection of primary sources that explore the history of capitalism and its vices and virtues. (Rev: BL 8/86; SLJ 10/86) [330.12]

5317 Leone, Bruno, ed. *Communism: Opposing Viewpoints*. Rev. ed. (9–12). Illus. (Opposing Viewpoints) 1986, Greenhaven LB $26.20 (0-89908-385-4); paper $16.20 (0-89908-360-9). This collection of documents tries to explain the concepts involved in communism and to enumerate its successes and failures as seen from several viewpoints. (Rev: BL 8/86; SLJ 10/86) [335.43]

5318 O'Neill, Terry, and Karin L. Swisher, eds. *Economics in America* (7–10). (Opposing Viewpoints) 1992, Greenhaven paper $16.20 (0-89908-162-2). A look at the state of the U.S. economy, the budget deficit, taxation, the banking system, and the future of labor as of 1990. (Rev: BL 6/15/92) [338.973]

5319 Trahant, LeNora B. *The Success of the Navajo Arts and Crafts Enterprise* (7–10). Illus. (Success) 1996, Walker LB $16.85 (0-8027-8337-6). After a brief history of the Navajo Nation, the author describes how the arts and crafts of the Navajos have prospered under a manufacturing and marketing cooperative. (Rev: BL 5/15/96; SLJ 7/96) [381]

Consumerism

5320 Barach, Arnold B. *Famous American Trademarks* (9–12). Illus. 1971, Public Affairs Pr. paper $9.00 (0-8183-0165-1). The origins and history of about 100 trademarks are traced by text and pictures. [341.7]

5321 Klein, David, and Marymae E. Klein. *Getting Unscrewed and Staying That Way: The Sourcebook of Consumer Protection* (9–12). 1993, Holt $25.00 (0-8050-2590-1). Provides addresses and phone numbers for obtaining redress for consumer problems. (Rev: BL 7/93) [381.3]

5322 Milios, Rita. *Shopping Savvy* (9–12). (Lifeskills Library) 1992, Rosen LB $12.95 (0-8239-1455-0). Basic guidelines for shopping, budgeting, and prioritizing needs. (Rev: BL 2/15/93; SLJ 1/93) [640]

5323 Schmitt, Lois. *Smart Spending: A Consumer's Guide* (6–9). 1989, Macmillan $13.95 (0-684-19035-4). A thorough account that covers such topics as advertising promotions, consumer fraud, mail-order problems, budgets, warranties, and consumerism. (Rev: BL 5/1/89; BR 11–12/89; SLJ 7/89; VOYA 12/89) [640.73]

Employment and Jobs

5324 Atkin, S. Beth, ed. *Voices from the Fields: Children of Migrant Farmworkers Tell Their Stories* (7–12). 1993, Little, Brown $17.95 (0-316-05633-2). Oral histories from 9 children. Each interview demonstrates a strong sense of family devotion and provides a reminder that education is the key to escaping the fields. (Rev: BL 5/1/93*; VOYA 2/94) [305.23]

5325 Packard, Gwen K. *Coping When a Parent Goes Back to Work* (8–12). (Coping) 1995, Rosen LB $16.95 (0-8239-1698-7). Gives children whose parents return to work tips on adapting to the new situation. Includes real-life examples. (Rev: BL 7/95) [306.874]

Labor Unions and Labor Problems

5326 Bendor, David, and Bruno Leone, eds. *Work* (7–12). Illus. (Opposing Viewpoints) 1995, Greenhaven $21.96 (1-56510-219-3); paper $17.45 (1-56510-218-5). A collection of essays explores problems related to workers and society such as the education of the workforce, government intervention, and inequality in the workplace. (Rev: BL 7/95; SLJ 8/95) [331]

5327 Colman, Penny. *Strike! The Bitter Struggle of American Workers from Colonial Times to the Present* (6–9). 1995, Millbrook LB $23.40 (1-56294-459-2). An overview of 200 years of labor struggles and strikes, describing in poignant detail workers' courageous struggles for improved working conditions and fair wages, supplemented by colorful quotations and anecdotes, full-page photos, and reproductions drawn from newspaper accounts. (Rev: BL 11/95; SLJ 1/96) [331.88]

5328 Laughlin, Rosemary. *The Pullman Strike of 1894: American Labor Comes of Age* (7–12). 1999, Morgan Reynolds LB $18.95 (1-883846-28-5). An engrossing account of this bitter railroad strike, with good background material on the railroad industry, the planned city of Pullman, the depression of 1893, and the personalities involved, including Eugene Debs. (Rev: BL 7/99; SLJ 8/99) [331.892]

5329 McKissack, Patricia, and Fredrick McKissack. *A Long Hard Journey* (5–9). Illus. 1989, Walker LB $32.90 (0-8027-6885-7). A 150-year saga of the organization of porters into the first black American union, the Brotherhood of Sleeping Car Porters. (Rev: BL 9/15/89; SLJ 1/90; VOYA 12/89) [331]

5330 Meltzer, Milton. *Bread and Roses: The Struggle of American Labor* (9–12). 1990, NAL paper $3.95 (0-451-62396-7). A history of how labor organized in America. [331.88]

5331 Stanley, Jerry. *Big Annie of Calumet: A True Story of the Industrial Revolution* (5–10). Illus. 1996, Crown LB $19.99 (0-517-70098-0). The tragic story of the miners strike in Upper Michigan in 1913 and the part that "Big Annie" Clemenc played in this chapter of labor's early struggle to unionize and improve working conditions. (Rev: BL 6/1–15/96; BR 9–10/96; SLJ 7/96) [331.89]

Money and Trade

5332 Resnick, Abraham. *Money* (6–8). (Overview) 1995, Lucent LB $21.25 (1-56006-165-0). A history

of money from ancient times when barter was used to today, when the movement is toward a cashless society and the elimination of money. (Rev: BL 7/95) [332.4]

5333 *Sold! The Origins of Money and Trade* (5–8). (Buried Worlds) 1994, Runestone LB $23.93 (0-8225-3206-9). A beautifully illustrated account of early forms of money, how coins were made, and what they reveal to archaeologists about the people who used them. (Rev: BL 9/15/94; SLJ 9/94) [737.4]

Marketing and Advertising

5334 Day, Nancy. *Advertising: Information or Manipulation?* (6–12). (Issues in Focus) 1999, Enslow $19.95 (0-7660-1106-2). In addition to presenting an introduction to advertising, its history, and its impact on U.S. society, this book questions many advertising practices, provides information on advertising methods and targeting, and offers tips on how to evaluate advertising critically. (Rev: BL 7/99) [659.1]

5335 Dunn, John. *Advertising* (5–8). Illus. (Overview) 1996, Lucent LB $17.96 (1-56006-182-0). The world of advertising is introduced, with a look at its inner workings, types of advertising, the media, and considerations involving deception and misleading material. (Rev: BL 5/15/97; SLJ 7/97) [659.1]

5336 McMath, Robert. *What Were They Thinking? Marketing Lessons I've Learned from over 80,000 New Products, Innovations, and Idiocies.* (10–12). 1998, Times Books $23.00 (0-8129-2950-0). A browsable, easy-to-read book, arranged by subject, that explores the world of marketing, its pitfalls, and its practices. (Rev: SLJ 6/98) [380.1]

5337 Schulberg, Jay. *The Milk Mustache Book: A Behind-the-Scenes Look at America's Favorite Advertising Campaign* (9–12). 1998, Ballantine paper $18.00 (0-345-42729-7). For young readers interested in marketing and advertising, this is the story of the successful "Milk Mustache" campaign, its origins, stars, and aftermath. (Rev: SLJ 3/99) [659.1]

Guidance and Personal Development

Education and Schools

General and Miscellaneous

5338 Banfield, Susan. *The Bakke Case: Quotas in College Admissions* (6–10). (Landmark Supreme Court Cases) 1998, Enslow LB $19.95 (0-89490-968-1). The court case that challenged quotas in higher education to correct racial inequality is chronicled in this dramatic account that gives good background information. (Rev: BL 2/15/98; BR 9–10/98; SLJ 6/98) [378]

5339 Codell, Esmé Raji. *Educating Esmé: Diary of a Teacher's First Year* (9–12). 1999, Algonquin $28.95 (1-56512-225-9). The journal of a first-time teacher, her year with her fifth grade class, and her success teaching them reading and creative writing. (Rev: SLJ 7/99) [371.1]

5340 Cozic, Charles P., ed. *Education in America* (5–8). (Opposing Viewpoints) 1992, Greenhaven paper $16.20 (0-89908-163-0). A valuable collection of well-chosen, readable articles that bring most of today's major educational issues into focus. (Rev: BL 5/1/92; SLJ 7/92) [370]

5341 Hurwitz, Sue. *High Performance through Effective Scheduling* (8–12). Illus. (The Learning-A-Living Library) 1996, Rosen LB $16.95 (0-8239-2204-9). This book discusses the basic skill of scheduling time and how it helps students at school, in extracurricular activities, and on the job. (Rev: BL 8/96; BR 1–2/97; SLJ 12/96; VOYA 2/97) [640]

5342 Kane, Pearl Rock, ed. *The First Year of Teaching: Real-World Stories from America's Teachers* (9–12). 1991, Walker $27.95 (0-8027-1170-7); paper $18.95 (0-8027-7359-1). A collection of the best essays by educators asked to describe the trials and rewards of their first year as teachers. (Rev: BL 10/1/91) [371.1]

5343 Marx, Jeff. *How to WIN a High School Election: Advice and Ideas Collected from Over 1000 High School Seniors* (9–12). 1999, Independent Pubs. Group paper $12.95 (0-9667824-0-2). Using quotes from many students, this account identifies qualities most likely to lead to a school election victory, such as sincerity and the ability to talk (and listen) and make good speeches, and gives practical tips for successful strategies. (Rev: BL 9/1/99; SLJ 7/99) [371]

5344 Mernit, Susan. *Everything You Need to Know about Changing Schools* (7–10). (Need to Know Library) 1992, Rosen LB $17.95 (0-8239-1326-0). Tips on making new friends and getting along with teachers for students who move to a new school. (Rev: BL 4/15/92) [371.2]

5345 Pickering, Marianne. *Lessons for Life: Education and Learning* (5–8). (Our Human Family) 1995, Blackbirch LB $22.45 (1-56711-127-0). Using an international approach and many illustrations, this book describes educational practices around the world and shows that, regardless of the culture, there are great similarities. (Rev: SLJ 1/96) [370]

5346 Rubin, Louis D., Jr., ed. *An Apple for My Teacher: Twelve Authors Tell about Teachers Who Made the Difference* (9–12). Illus. 1987, Algonquin paper $16.95 (0-912697-57-1). In chapters of various lengths, 12 writers discuss their favorite teachers and what made them memorable. (Rev: SLJ 8/87) [371.1]

5347 Schneider, Meg. *Help! My Teacher Hates Me* (5–8). 1994, Workman paper $7.95 (1-56305-492-2). Helpful hints for developing a positive attitude in school. (Rev: BL 3/15/95) [371.8]

5348 Sherrow, Victoria. *Challenges in Education* (7–12). (Issues for the 90s) 1991, Messner LB $13.98 (0-671-70556-3). An overview of the major questions and concerns facing today's educators. (Rev: BL 11/1/91; SLJ 11/91) [370]

Development of Academic Skills

Study Skills

5349 Frank, Stanley D. *Remember Everything You Read: The Evelyn Wood Seven Day Speed Reading and Learning Program* (9–12). Illus. 1990, Times Bks. $23.00 (0-8129-1773-1). How to increase one's reading speed and still retain the content. (Rev: BL 4/15/90) [371.3]

5350 Fry, Ron. *How to Study*. 4th ed. (7–12). 1996, Career Pr. paper $9.99 (1-56414-229-9). Note taking, time management, reading skills, library research, and using online services are some of the topics covered in this guide to enhancing study skills. (Rev: SLJ 10/96) [371.3]

5351 Lorayne, Harry. *How to Develop a Super-Power Memory* (10–12). 1974, NAL paper $4.95 (0-451-16149-1). Tips and techniques for increasing your ability to remember. [371.3]

5352 McCutcheon, Randall J. *Get off My Brain: A Survival Guide for Lazy* Students (*Bored, Frustrated, & Otherwise Sick of School)* (9–12). Illus. 1998, Free Spirit paper $12.95 (1-57542-037-6). This candid, entertaining look at teenage academic life offers advice on how to do better in school, from test-taking strategies and analyzing one's learning skills to brown-nosing teachers and taking advantage of teachers' strengths and weaknesses. (Rev: VOYA 2/99) [371.3]

5353 Maddox, Harry. *How to Study* (10–12). 1983, Fawcett paper $4.50 (0-449-30011-0). Practical tips and strategies are outlined to make studying more effective. [378]

5354 Marks, Lillian S. *Touch Typing Made Simple*. Rev. ed. (8–12). Illus. 1985, Doubleday paper $12.95 (0-385-19426-9). A clear manual that gives information on specialized topics like types of letters, tabulations, and addressing envelopes. Part of a lengthy series. (Rev: BL 2/15/86) [652.3]

5355 Nathan, Amy. *Surviving Homework: Tips from Teens* (5–8). Illus. 1997, Millbrook LB $23.90 (1-56294-185-2). Using answers on questionnaires given to high school juniors and seniors, this book supplies many useful study tips and suggestions on how to organize one's time. (Rev: BL 6/1–15/97; BR 11–12/96; SLJ 7/97) [372.12]

5356 Schneider, Zola Dincin, and Phyllis B. Kalb. *Countdown to College: A Student's Guide to Getting the Most Out of High School* (9–12). 1989, College Entrance Examination Board paper $9.95 (0-87447-

335-7). A guide for high school students to such topics as time management, academic planning, and extracurricular activities. (Rev: BL 12/1/89; BR 3–4/90; VOYA 2/90) [373]

5357 Schumm, Jeanne Shay. *School Power: Strategies for Succeeding in School* (5–8). Illus. 1992, Free Spirit paper $13.95 (0-915793-42-3). Sensible suggestions for improving study skills: organization, note taking, improving reading, and writing reports. (Rev: BL 3/1/93) [371.3]

5358 Simpson, Carolyn. *High Performance through Organizing Information* (8–12). Illus. (Learning-a-Living Library) 1996, Rosen LB $16.95 (0-8239-2207-3). This book discusses the importance of an organized work environment, whether in school, at home, or on the job, and how to create one using filing systems, to-do lists, data sources, and other strategies. (Rev: BL 8/96; BR 1–2/97; SLJ 8/96; VOYA 2/97) [640]

Tests and Test Taking

5359 Fry, Ron. *"Ace" Any Test*. 3rd ed. (7–12). 1996, Career Pr. paper $6.99 (1-56414-230-2). This manual presents tips on time management, study techniques, test-taking, and how to reduce test anxiety. (Rev: SLJ 10/96) [371.3]

5360 Kern, Roy, and Richard Smith. *The Grade Booster Guide for Kids* (7–9). 1987, Hilton Thomas paper $7.95 (0-944162-00-2). This book covers the proper strategies and techniques to use for successful test-taking. (Rev: BR 5–6/88) [371.3]

Writing and Speaking Skills

5361 Amberg, Jay, and Mark Larson. *The Creative Writing Handbook* (9–12). 1992, Scott Foresman/GoodYear paper $7.95 (0-673-36013-X). A guide to putting effective words on a page. Does not cover marketing techniques. (Rev: BL 3/1/92) [808.02]

5362 Bauer, Marion Dane. *What's Your Story? A Young Person's Guide to Writing Fiction* (5–10). 1992, Clarion $14.95 (0-395-57781-0); paper $6.95 (0-395-57780-2). An award-winning writer gives advice to young authors, including suggestions for planning, writing, and revising. (Rev: BL 4/15/92; SLJ 6/92*) [808.3]

5363 Bauer, Marion Dane. *A Writer's Story from Life to Fiction* (5–8). 1995, Clarion $14.95 (0-395-72094-X); paper $6.95 (0-395-75053-9). An author for 20 years helps young writers find their writer's voice and discusses her own life. (Rev: BL 9/15/95; SLJ 10/95; VOYA 2/96) [813]

5364 Block, Francesca L., and Hillary Carlip. *Zine Scene: The Do-It-Yourself Guide to Zines* (8–12).

Illus. 1998, Girl Pr. paper $14.95 (0-9659754-3-6). This is a step-by-step guide to producing one's own magazine, from getting started and writing to layout, production, and marketing. (Rev: VOYA 8/99) [808]

5365 Brantley, C. L. *The Princeton Review Write Smart Junior* (6–8). Illus. 1995, Random paper $12.00 (0-679-76131-4). From writing haiku to keeping a journal, this entertaining manual explains how to write well. (Rev: VOYA 4/96) [808]

5366 Brown, Cynthia Stokes. *Like It Was: A Complete Guide to Writing Oral History* (9–12). 1988, Teachers & Writers paper $13.95 (0-915924-12-9). A handbook that tells the reader how to conduct an oral history project, from planning it to the final transcription of the interviews. (Rev: BL 2/1/89; SLJ 6/89) [907]

5367 Bruchac, Joseph. *Tell Me a Tale* (4–8). 1997, Harcourt $16.00 (0-15-201221-4). This introduction to storytelling for young readers explains how to find stories and how to evaluate and deliver them as well as providing a generous supply of suitable stories. (Rev: BL 3/15/97; SLJ 8/97) [808.5]

5368 Clark, Thomas. *Queries & Submissions* (10–12). 1995, Writer's Digest $15.99 (0-89879-660-1). A practical guide to aspiring writers of nonfiction magazine articles with tips on writing effective query letters to editors and how to write dynamically. (Rev: SLJ 1/96) [418]

5369 Detz, Joan. *You Mean I Have to Stand Up and Say Something?* (7–12). 1986, Macmillan LB $13.95 (0-689-31221-0). An entertaining guide to preparation of talks and overcoming the fear of facing an audience. (Rev: BL 2/87; SLJ 3/87) [808.5]

5370 Dragisic, Patricia. *How to Write a Letter* (7–12). (Speak Out, Write On!) 1998, Watts $25.00 (0-531-11391-4). A readable, practical guide to writing personal notes, business letters, resumes, applications, memos, e-mail, and other forms of written communication. (Rev: BL 11/15/98; SLJ 1/99) [808.6]

5371 Ehrlich, Amy, ed. *When I Was Your Age* (5–9). Illus. 1999, Candlewick $16.99 (0-7636-0407-0). Ten well-known writers for young people, like Norma Fox Mazer and Paul Fleischman, tell of their childhood experiences and how key incidents affected their writing. (Rev: BL 4/15/99; SLJ 7/99; VOYA 10/99) [810.9]

5372 Estepa, Andrea, and Philip Kay, eds. *Starting with "I": Personal Essays by Teenagers* (7–12). 1997, Persea paper $13.95 (0-89255-228-X). This is a collection of 35 brief essays written by teenagers about their families, neighborhoods, race, and culture. (Rev: BL 9/15/97; BR 1–2/98; SLJ 10/97; VOYA 10/97) [305.235]

5373 Everhart, Nancy. *How to Write a Term Paper* (7–12). 1995, Watts LB $25.00 (0-531-11200-4). This revised edition of *So You Have to Write a Term Paper* (1987) includes new information on electronic sources and data management by computer. (Rev: BL 6/1–15/95; SLJ 5/95) [808]

5374 Graham, Paula W. *Speaking of Journals; Children's Book Writers Talk about Their Diaries, Notebooks, and Sketchbooks* (5–8). 1999, Boyds Mills paper $14.95 (1-56397-741-9). This work contains interviews with 27 writers such as Jim Arnosky, Pam Conrad, and Jean George about keeping personal journals, how to do it, and the rewards. (Rev: BL 3/1/99; BR 9–10/99; SLJ 5/99) [818]

5375 Grant, Janet. *The Young Person's Guide to Becoming a Writer.* Rev. Ed. (5–8). 1995, Free Spirit paper $13.95 (0-915793-90-3). This comprehensive beginner's guide provides information young people interested in writing as a career should know, such as ways to explore writing, different writing genres in the publishing industry and how an individual might be drawn toward one or another, practical information about the writing industry, how to find a publisher, manuscript preparation, and marketing. (Rev: SLJ 12/95; VOYA 2/96) [808]

5376 Hamilton, Fran Santoro. *Hands-On English* (4–8). Illus. 1998, Portico paper $9.95 (0-9664867-0-6). A user-friendly volume that takes a visual approach to illustrate sentence patterns, such as using icons to represent the 8 parts of speech, with clear, interesting explanations. Also included are irregular verbs, using modifiers, spelling rules, punctuation and capitalization, homonyms, and how to make outlines. (Rev: SLJ 2/99; VOYA 4/99) [415]

5377 Hansen, Randall S., and Katharine Hansen. *Write Your Way to a Higher GPA: How to Dramatically Boost Your GPA Simply By Sharpening Your Writing Skills* (10–12). 1997, Ten Speed Pr. paper $11.95 (0-89815-903-2). A guide to virtually any type of writing that might be required in high school or college, as well as where to go for more help at school, in libraries, and online. (Rev: SLJ 1/98) [808]

5378 Harmon, Charles, ed. *Using the Internet, Online Services, and CD-ROMs for Writing Research and Term Papers* (7–12). (NetGuide) 2000, Neal-Schuman $35.00 (1-55570-374-7). This book shows all of the steps in writing a report, from selecting and narrowing a topic to collecting information electronically to preparing the final copy. (Rev: BL 4/15/96) [371.2]

5379 Heiligman, Deborah. *The New York Public Library Kid's Guide to Research* (5–8). Illus. 1998, Scholastic $14.95 (0-590-30715-0). A fine introduction to the principles of research, with material on such topics as note taking, evaluating sources, using nonprint materials, questionnaires and surveys, interviews, gathering information from 800 numbers and via the mail, and searching the Internet. (Rev: SLJ 2/99) [808.023]

5380 Henry, Thomas. *Better English Made Easy* (10–12). 1985, Warner paper $4.99 (0-446-31190-1). This manual covers such subjects as grammar, spelling, and speech. [420]

5381 James, Elizabeth, and Carol Barkin. *How to Write a Term Paper* (7–12). 1980, Lothrop paper $3.95 (0-688-45025-3). A practical step-by-step approach to good report writing that uses many examples. [808]

5382 Janeczko, Paul B. *How to Write Poetry* (4–8). (Scholastic Guides) 1999, Scholastic $12.95 (0-590-10077-7). Using many examples from famous and student writers, the author covers topics like writing free verse, composing rhyming verses, and revising a poem. (Rev: BL 3/15/99; SLJ 7/99; VOYA 8/99) [808.1]

5383 Janeczko, Paul B., comp. *Poetry from A to Z: A Guide for Young Writers* (4–8). 1994, Simon & Schuster LB $16.00 (0-02-747672-3). This book of 72 poems, alphabetized by topic, gives examples to get young writers started, and the 23 poets represented give advice on how to become a better poet. (Rev: BL 12/15/94; VOYA 5/95) [808.1]

5384 Kerr, M. E. *Blood on the Forehead: What I Know about Writing* (6–10). 1998, HarperCollins $21.95 (0-06-027996-6); paper $12.95 (0-06-446207-2). This writer shares where she gets ideas for her stories and books and describes the writing process, which is far from easy, as the title would suggest. (Rev: BL 4/1/98; SLJ 5/98; VOYA 6/99) [808.3]

5385 Kowit, Steve. *In the Palm of Your Hand: The Poet's Portable Workshop* (9–12). 1995, Tilbury paper $14.95 (0-88448-149-2). An informal discussion of the technical demands and creative sources of poetry. (Rev: BL 9/1/95) [808.1]

5386 Krementz, Jill. *The Writer's Desk* (10–12). Illus. 1996, Random $35.00 (0-679-45014-9). Fifty-seven prominent writers are captured in stunning photographs and written descriptions of their work habits and techniques. (Rev: SLJ 4/97) [808]

5387 Ledoux, Denis. *Turning Memories into Memoirs: A Handbook for Writing Lifestories* (9–12). 1993, Soleil Pr. paper $19.95 (0-9619373-2-7). A step-by-step handbook that encourages individuals to record their oral histories as a legacy for their families. (Rev: BL 3/15/93) [808.06]

5388 Lester, James D., Sr., and James D. Lester, Jr. *The Research Paper Handbook* (9–12). 1992, Scott Foresman/GoodYear paper $7.95 (0-673-36016-4). A manual with chapters covering topic selection, note taking, outlining, and bibliographies. (Rev: BL 2/15/92) [808.023]

5389 Lewis, Norman. *Thirty Days to Better English* (10–12). 1985, NAL paper $4.95 (0-451-15702-8). One of several fine English handbooks by this author. This one concentrates on grammar and usage. [425]

5390 Lewis, Norman, and Wilfred Funk. *Thirty Days to a More Powerful Vocabulary* (10–12). 1991, Pocket Books paper $5.99 (0-671-74349-X). This is a proven program for vocabulary building. [413]

5391 Mooney, Bill, and David Holt. *Storyteller's Guide: Share Advice for the Classroom, Boardroom, Showroom, Podium, Pulpit and Central Stage* (9–12). 1996, August House paper $23.95 (0-87483-482-1). Professional storytellers advise young people on every aspect of storytelling, from selecting the right stories to tell to setting up the location and the actual presentation. (Rev: BR 5–6/97; VOYA 6/97) [808.5]

5392 Ochoa, George, and Jeff Osier. *The Writer's Guide to Creating a Science Fiction Universe* (9–12). 1993, Writer's Digest $18.95 (0-89879-536-2). An overview of the sciences to help the sci-fi writer avoid scientific errors. (Rev: BL 3/1/93) [808.3]

5393 Otfinoski, Steven. *Speaking Up, Speaking Out: A Kid's Guide to Making Speeches, Oral Reports, and Conversation* (5–8). Illus. 1996, Millbrook LB $23.90 (1-56294-345-6). All kinds of public-speaking situations are introduced, with suggestions on how to be a success at each. (Rev: BL 1/1–15/97; SLJ 1/97) [808.5]

5394 Rosen, Lucy. *High Performance through Communicating Information* (8–12). Illus. (The Learning-A-Living Library) 1996, Rosen LB $16.95 (0-8239-2201-4). Such communication skills as writing and speaking are discussed with tips on how to improve them and apply them effectively. (Rev: BL 8/96; BR 1–2/97; SLJ 3/97; VOYA 2/97) [153.6]

5395 Ryan, Elizabeth A. *How to Build a Better Vocabulary* (5–9). 1991, Troll paper $3.95 (0-8167-2461-X). A traditional study of prefixes, suffixes, and roots, with sections on foreign words. (Rev: BL 4/1/92; SLJ 4/92) [372.6]

5396 Ryan, Elizabeth A. *How to Write Better Book Reports* (5–9). 1991, Troll LB $10.50 (0-8167-2458-X). Recommendations for brainstorming, outlining, rough drafts, and rewriting the perfect book report. (Rev: BL 4/1/92; SLJ 4/92) [372.6]

5397 Ryan, Margaret. *How to Give a Speech* (7–12). 1995, Watts LB $25.00 (0-531-11199-7). This revision of *So You Have to Give a Speech* (1987) includes new information on electronic sources and data management by computer. (Rev: BL 6/1–15/95; SLJ 6/95) [808.5]

5398 Ryan, Margaret. *How to Write a Poem* (7–12). Illus. 1996, Watts LB $25.00 (0-531-11252-7); paper $7.95 (0-531-15788-1). From the idea to the final product, this helpful guide covers the techniques of writing, along with imagery, form, meter, and other aspects of poetry, and provides tips on entering poetry contests and getting published. (Rev: BL 2/1/97; SLJ 1/97) [808.1]

5399 Safire, William, and Leonard Safir, eds. *Good Advice on Writing: Writers Past and Present on How to Write Well* (9–12). 1992, Simon & Schuster $22.00 (0-671-77005-5). Authors counsel would-be writers. (Rev: BL 9/15/92) [808]

5400 Seuling, Barbara. *Becoming a Writer* (4–8). 1995, Holt LB $16.98 (0-8050-4692-5). A well-organized how-to book that gives good advice to budding writers, including how to outline a book and define characters. (Rev: BL 6/1–15/97; SLJ 8/97; VOYA 10/97) [808]

5401 Shipman, Robert Oliver. *A Pun My Word: A Humorously Enlightened Path to English Usage* (9–12). 1991, Littlefield Adams paper $14.95 (0-8226-3011-7). Humorous examples help explain common problems in grammar and word usage. (Rev: BL 7/91) [428]

5402 Stevens, Carla. *A Book of Your Own: Keeping a Diary or Journal* (5–8). 1993, Clarion $14.95 (0-89919-256-4). Guidelines for keeping a journal and examples of diary entries from such familiar diarists as Anne Frank and Louisa May Alcott. (Rev: BL 1/15/94; SLJ 11/93; VOYA 2/94) [808]

5403 Sullivan, Helen, and Linda Sernoff. *Research Reports: A Guide for Middle and High School Students* (6–10). 1996, Millbrook LB $23.40 (1-56294-694-3). A well-organized, concise book on writing reports that covers each step from selecting a topic to compiling the final bibliography. (Rev: BR 3–4/97; SLJ 9/96) [372.6]

5404 Terban, Marvin. *Checking Your Grammar* (5–8). (Scholastic Guides) 1993, Scholastic $10.95 (0-590-49454-6). A guide to grammar that also covers sexist language, spelling, homonyms, and confusing words. (Rev: BL 10/1/93; SLJ 2/94) [428.2]

5405 Vassallo, Wanda. *Speaking with Confidence: A Guide for Public Speakers* (9–12). 1990, Betterway paper $9.95 (1-55870-147-8). For anyone fearful of facing an audience this is a guide that contains sound, workable advice. (Rev: BL 8/90; SLJ 7/90) [808.5]

5406 Wilber, Jessica. *Totally Private & Personal: Journaling Ideas for Girls and Young Women* (7–12). 1996, Free Spirit paper $9.95 (1-57542-005-8). The author, 14 years old when she wrote this book, offers advice for keeping a journal, including how, why, and what to put in it, with examples from her own journal. (Rev: VOYA 2/97) [808]

5407 Wooldridge, Susan Goldsmith. *Poemcrazy: Freeing Your Life with Words* (6–12). 1996, Clarkson N. Potter $22.00 (0-517-70370-X); paper $13.00 (0-609-80098-1). The author tries to show young people how to free their minds and spirits to write poetry and shares her own poetic experiences and inspirations as well as those of other poets. (Rev: VOYA 12/97) [811]

5408 Woolley, Persia. *How to Write and Sell Historical Fiction* (10–12). 1997, Writer's Digest $17.99 (0-89879-753-5). This offers pointers on writing historical fiction, techniques to master, and how to sell the final product to publishers and the reading public. (Rev: SLJ 9/97) [372.6]

5409 Writer's Digest. *The Writer's Digest Guide to Good Writing* (9–12). 1994, Writer's Digest $18.99 (0-89879-640-7). This retrospective anthology organized by decade contains essays providing advice and information for writers, by writers. (Rev: BL 3/15/94) [808.02]

5410 Young, Sue. *Writing with Style* (5–8). (Scholastic Guides) 1997, Scholastic paper $12.95 (0-590-50977-2). A guide for the novice writer, with chapters on planning, presenting, and publishing one's work. (Rev: BL 3/1/97; SLJ 5/97) [372.6]

Academic Guidance

General and Miscellaneous

5411 Grand, Gail L. *Student Science Opportunities* (7–12). 1994, Wiley paper $14.95 (0-471-31088-3). A guide to summer science programs offered throughout the United States as of 1993. (Rev: BL 5/1/94) [507]

5412 Lieberman, Susan A. *The Real High School Handbook: How to Survive, Thrive, and Prepare for What's Next* (8–12). 1997, Houghton paper $9.95 (0-395-79760-8). A book of tips about prospering in high school and making it enjoyable, with material on topics like grade points, testing, course selection, and getting into a college. (Rev: BL 10/15/97) [373.18]

5413 Llewellyn, Grace. *The Teenage Liberation Handbook: How to Quit School & Get a Real Life & Education* (9–12). 1998, Lowry House paper $19.00 (0-9629591-7-0). This book encourages thoughtful teens to construct their own educational design through independent learning and developing individual ways of satisfying one's intellectual curiosity. (Rev: VOYA 12/98) [371.4]

5414 Sherrow, Victoria. *Dropping Out* (7–12). Illus. (Life Issues) 1996, Marshall Cavendish LB $20.95 (0-7614-0018-4). The causes and consequences of dropping out of school are discussed with examples from actual case studies. (Rev: BL 8/96; BR 11–12/96; SLJ 7/96) [371.2]

5415 Unger, Harlow G. *But What If I Don't Want to Go to College? A Guide to Success Through Alternative Education* (10–12). 1991, Facts on File LB $22.95 (0-8160-2534-7). Discusses alternate forms of training, job descriptions, resume and cover-letter writing, job applications, and interviewing techniques. (Rev: BL 1/1/92; SLJ 5/92) [370.11]

Colleges and Universities

5416 Carroll, Joan. *The Black College Career Guide* (9–12). 1992, Zulema Enterprises paper $6.95 (1-881223-00-0). Presents information on 104 African American colleges: location, history, enrollment, curriculum, costs, financial aid, and scholarships as of 1991. (Rev: BL 2/15/93) [378.7]

5417 Cochrane, Kerry. *Researching Colleges on the World Wide Web* (10–12). Illus. 1997, Watts paper $16.00 (0-531-11294-2). This book shows how to use the Internet to get information on colleges and how to evaluate it. (Rev: BL 9/1/97; SLJ 1/98; VOYA 8/98) [378.73]

5418 Eberts, Marjorie, and Margaret Gisler. *How to Prepare for College* (9–12). 1990, VGM paper $9.95 (0-8442-6665-5). This account emphasizes such areas as the development of good study, speaking, and writing skills, plus how to define and reach goals. (Rev: BL 3/1/90; BR 5–6/90) [378]

5419 Funk, Gary. *A Balancing Act: Sports and Education* (5–8). Illus. (Sports Issues) 1995, Lerner LB $30.00 (0-8225-3301-4). A frank, thorough discussion of the many issues involved in sports and their place in educational institutions. (Rev: BL 1/1–15/96; SLJ 9/95) [796.04]

5420 Greenfeld, Barbara C., and Robert A. Weinstein. *The Kids' College Almanac: A First Look at College* (9–12). Illus. 1996, Gerson Publg. paper $16.95 (1-888584-00-9). This top-notch beginner's guide for those who are thinking of college begins with what a college education is about and continues with practical advice on how to learn about colleges and how to investigate topics like financial aid and extracurricular activities. (Rev: VOYA 4/97) [378.1]

5421 McGinty, Sarah Myers. *The College Application Essay* (9–12). Illus. 1997, College Board paper $12.95 (0-87447-575-9). A lucid, practical guide to writing effective college application essays, explaining each part of the essay in detail, showing students how to apply the writing skills they've developed during high school, and providing sample essays. (Rev: BL 10/15/97) [378.1]

5422 Pope, Loren. *Colleges That Change Lives: 40 Schools You Should Know about Even If You're Not a Straight A Student* (10–12). 1996, Penguin paper $11.95 (0-14-023951-0). This book highlights 40 colleges, mostly in the Northeast, South, and Midwest, that select students with a wide range of abilities, not necessarily the top academic achievers. (Rev: SLJ 11/96) [378]

5423 Robbins, Wendy H. *The Portable College Adviser: A Guide for High School Students* (9–12).

1996, Watts LB $25.00 (0-531-11257-8); paper $9.00 (0-531-15790-3). A manual that guides students through preparation for college, including course choices in high school, standardized test preparation, college applications and visits, plus financial aid information. (Rev: BL 7/96; BR 9–10/96; SLJ 8/96; VOYA 10/96) [378.1]

Scholarships and Financial Aid

5424 Minnis, Whitney. *How to Get an Athletic Scholarship: A Student-Athlete's Guide to Collegiate Athletics* (6–12). 1995, ASI paper $12.95 (0-9645153-0-X). Basic information on athletic scholarships and the recruitment process, plus tips on training and academic considerations. (Rev: BL 2/1/96) [796]

Careers and Occupational Guidance

General and Miscellaneous

5425 Baldwin, Louis. *Women of Strength* (9–12). 1996, McFarland paper $28.50 (0-7864-0250-4). This work contains short biographies of 106 women who have succeeded in traditionally male fields like the military, law, social reform, and religion. (Rev: VOYA 8/97) [331.7]

5426 Dwyer, Jack. *The Launch Manual: A Young Person's Introduction to the Principles of World Takeover* (10–12). 1998, Chairman paper $10.95 (0-9658366-5-7). This book describes the mind-set necessary to make sound career choices, including identifying one's strengths and weaknesses and setting goals. (Rev: SLJ 1/99) [650.14]

5427 Figler, Howard. *The Complete Job-Search Handbook: All the Skills You Need to Get Any Job and Have a Good Time Doing It* (9–12). 1995, Holt paper $14.95 (0-8050-0537-4). A practical, confidence-inspiring book that offers sound solutions to many job-hunting problems. (Rev: BL 5/15/88; BR 1–2/89; SLJ 11/88) [371.4]

5428 Jones, Lawrence K. *Job Skills for the 21st Century: A Guide for Students* (9–12). Illus. 1995, Oryx paper $40.75 (0-89774-956-1). This excellent manual on improving job skills and career guidance also shows how to assess one's skills, set realistic goals, and learn new skills. (Rev: BL 2/15/96) [331.7]

5429 Kaplan, Andrew. *Careers for Number Lovers* (9–12). Photos. 1991, Millbrook LB $20.90 (1-878841-21-1). Fourteen professionals profile their work, offering personal insights about the joy of working with numbers. (Rev: BL 3/1/91; SLJ 11/91) [510.23]

5430 Kenig, Graciela. *Best Careers for Bilingual Latinos: Market Your Fluency in Spanish to Get Ahead on the Job* (10–12). 1999, VGM paper $14.95 (0-8442-4541-0). This practical, well-researched handbook based on hundreds of interviews with Latino professionals discusses how to market bilingual skills and cope with workplace challenges such as ethnic stereotypes and office politics, and identifies the top fields for bilingual Latinos: health care, financial services, technology, sales and marketing, professional services, and international opportunities. (Rev: SLJ 8/99) [331.6]

5431 McFarland, Rhoda. *The World of Work: The Lifeskills Library* (9–12). (Lifeskills Library) 1993, Rosen LB $14.95 (0-8239-1467-4). Takes readers through the process of job hunting, with information on resumes, interviews, applications, general skills, and time management. (Rev: BL 6/1–15/93) [650.14]

5432 McGlothlin, Bruce. *High Performance Through Understanding Systems* (7–10). (Learning-a-Living) 1996, Rosen LB $16.95 (0-8239-2210-3). Aimed primarily at youths preparing to directly enter the world of work after graduation, this book explains systems ("any combination of elements that operate together and form a whole") in the family, at school, and at work, and tells how individuals can diagnose problems, predict outcomes, and improve the systems. (Rev: SLJ 3/97) [001.6]

5433 Mackall, Dandi. *Self Development Skills* (9–12). (Career Skills Library) 1997, Ferguson $14.95 (0-89434-214-2). This title explores behavior, desirable character traits, and habits to develop for the work place. Each of the other 7 titles in this series focuses on a skill that people looking for a job should be aware of. Three of these titles are: *Teamwork, Communication,* and *Leadership Skills* (all 1998). (Rev: VOYA 8/98) [650.14]

5434 Martin, Molly, ed. *Hard-Hatted Women: Life on the Job* (10–12). 1997, Seal Pr. paper $14.95 (1-878067-91-5). This book contains interviews with 26 women in carpentry, ironwork, mining, truck driving, and other blue collar work about their jobs, including their experiences with sexism and harassment. (Rev: VOYA 12/97) [331.7]

5435 Pedrvola, Cindy, and Debby Hobgood. *How to Get a Job If You Are a Teenager* (9–12). 1998, Alleyside Pr. paper $12.95 (0-57950-013-7). Using a question-and-answer format, this book covers all the necessary topics related to job hunting, from first thoughts about looking for a job, resumes, filling out an application, and preparing for an interview, to adjusting to the workplace, time management, and work etiquette. (Rev: BR 9–10/98; SLJ 7/98; VOYA 10/98) [650.14]

5436 Strazzabosco, Jeanne M. *High Performance through Dealing with Diversity* (8–12). Illus. (Learning-a-Living) 1996, Rosen LB $15.95 (0-8239-2202-2). Through applying attitudes of tolerance and positive feelings, this book prepares students to work with diverse populations in a multicultural workplace. (Rev: BL 8/96; BR 1–2/97) [650.1]

Careers

General and Miscellaneous

5437 Brenlove, Milovan S. *Vectors to Spare: The Life of an Air Traffic Controller* (9–12). 1993, Iowa State Univ. Pr. $29.95 (0-8138-0471-X). Conveys the flavor of the job of aerial cop, describing arrogant pilots, boom-lowering supervisors, career politics, and actual crashes and near misses. (Rev: BL 6/1–15/93) [629.136]

5438 Chmelynski, Carol Ann. *Opportunities in Restaurant Careers* (9–12). 1990, VGM $14.95 (0-8442-8662-1); paper $12.95 (0-8442-8664-8). From fast food to haute cuisine, here is a description of a variety of restaurant-related jobs from beginning level to owning one's own eatery. (Rev: BL 12/1/89; BR 5–6/90) [647]

5439 Curless, Maura. *Kids* (6–9). (Careers Without College) 1993, Peterson's Guides paper $7.95 (1-56079-251-5). Describes professions that deal with children, such as teacher aides, caregivers, and museum staff. (Rev: BL 10/1/93) [649]

5440 Dunlop, Reginald. *Come Fly with Me! Your Nineties Guide to Becoming a Flight Attendant* (9–12). 1993, Maxamillian paper $15.95 (0-9632749-9-6). Gives specifics on increasing the chances of employment in a competitive field. Provides a tutorial for presenting oneself in the best light. (Rev: BL 6/1–15/93) [387.7]

5441 Eberts, Marjorie, and Margaret Gisler. *Careers for Kids at Heart and Others Who Adore Children* (9–12). 1994, VGM $14.95 (0-8442-4110-5); paper

$9.95 (0-8442-4111-3). A career guide for those interested in working with children, focusing on jobs in child care, education, recreation, and health. (Rev: BL 8/94; VOYA 12/94) [362.7]

5442 Eberts, Marjorie, and Margaret Gisler. *Careers in Child Care* (9–12). 1994, VGM $17.95 (0-8442-4191-1); paper $13.95 (0-8442-4193-8). Profiles occupations relating to child care, including teaching, sports, recreation, welfare, the arts, and entertainment. (Rev: BL 8/94) [362.7]

5443 Fasulo, Michael, and Jane Kinney. *Careers for Environmental Types* (9–12). 1993, VGM $14.95 (0-8442-4102-4); paper $9.95 (0-8442-4103-2). Outlines the educational preparation necessary for environmental careers. (Rev: BL 5/15/93; VOYA 10/93) [363.7]

5444 Field, Shelly. *Careers As an Animal Rights Activist* (9–12). 1993, Rosen paper $9.95 (0-8239-1722-3). Concentrates on jobs within animal rights organizations, with lists of organizations and trade associations and a cruelty-free shopping guide. (Rev: BL 5/15/93; SLJ 6/93; VOYA 8/93) [179.4]

5445 Foote-Smith, Elizabeth. *Opportunities in Writing Careers* (9–12). 1988, VGM $14.95 (0-8442-6512-8); paper $11.95 (0-8442-6513-6). Working conditions are described plus necessary qualifications are given for a wide variety of jobs requiring writing skills. (Rev: BR 5–6/89; VOYA 4/89) [411]

5446 Frydenborg, Kay. *They Dreamed of Horses: Careers for Horse Lovers* (6–9). 1994, Walker LB $16.85 (0-8027-8284-1). Suggests career possibilities that involve working with horses, telling the stories of 13 women who love and work with them. (Rev: BL 7/94; SLJ 7/94; VOYA 8/94) [636.1]

5447 Hole, Dorothy. *The Air Force and You* (9–12). (Armed Forces) 1993, Macmillan LB $17.95 (0-89686-764-1). This is a concise, interesting guide to careers in the Air Force. (Rev: BL 3/15/94) [358.4]

5448 Hole, Dorothy. *The Army and You* (9–12). (Armed Forces Series) 1993, Silver Burdett $17.95 (0-89686-765-X). Not written as a recruitment text, this volume is an examination of the army as a career. (Rev: BL 3/15/94; SLJ 1/94) [355]

5449 Hole, Dorothy. *The Coast Guard and You* (9–12). (Armed Forces) 1993, Macmillan LB $17.95 (0-89686-766-8). A straightforward, factual description of life in the Coast Guard. (Rev: BL 3/15/94; SLJ 1/94) [359.9]

5450 Hole, Dorothy. *The Marines and You* (9–12). (Armed Forces) 1993, Macmillan LB $17.95 (0-89686-768-4). The United States Marines offer opportunities for recruits that are explored in this concise guide. (Rev: BL 3/15/94; SLJ 1/94) [359.9]

5451 Hole, Dorothy. *The Navy and You* (9–12). (Armed Forces) 1993, Macmillan LB $17.95 (0-

89686-767-6). Young people interested in a career in the U.S. Navy will find this concise guide offers practical, honest advice. (Rev: BL 3/15/94) [359]

5452 Hurwitz, Jane. *Choosing a Career in Animal Care* (4–8). 1996, Rosen LB $15.95 (0-8239-2268-5). Various careers in working with animals are described, along with the education qualifications, desirable character traits, and ways to break into the field. (Rev: SLJ 8/97) [636]

5453 Johnson, Neil. *All in a Day's Work: Twelve Americans Talk about Their Jobs* (7–10). Illus. 1989, Little, Brown $14.95 (0-316-46957-2). Twelve different occupations from musician and detective to farmer and factory worker are represented in these first-person accounts. (Rev: BL 5/1/90; SLJ 5/90) [311.7]

5454 Kirkwood, Tim. *The Flight Attendant Career Guide* (9–12). 1993, T K Enterprises paper $14.95 (0-9637301-4-2). Explores the career and life-style of a flight attendant, including information helpful for interviewing. (Rev: BL 10/1/93) [387.7]

5455 Krebs, Michelle. *Cars* (9–12). (Careers Without College) 1992, Peterson's Guides paper $7.95 (1-56079-221-3). Presents 5 kinds of jobs related to cars that may require further education but not a 4-year degree. (Rev: BL 2/15/93) [629.2]

5456 Lee, Barbara. *Working with Animals* (4–8). Illus. (Exploring Careers) 1996, Lerner LB $23.93 (0-8225-1759-0). Profiles of 12 careers involving animals such as veterinarians, animal shelter workers, and pet sitters. (Rev: BL 2/15/97) [591]

5457 Lee, Mary Price. *Opportunities in Animal and Pet Care Careers* (9–12). 1993, VGM $13.95 (0-8442-4079-6); paper $11.95 (0-8442-4081-8). All aspects of these careers are considered. (Rev: BL 3/15/94; VOYA 6/94) [636]

5458 Longshore, Shirley J. *Office* (10–12). Illus. (Careers without College) 1994, Peterson's Guides paper $7.95 (0-56079-353-8). This career guide gives details on various positions in the business office that do not require a college degree. (Rev: BL 9/15/94) [651.3]

5459 Mackall, Joseph. *Information Management* (9–12). Illus. 1998, Ferguson $14.95 (0-89434-215-0). This title shows teenagers how to collect, organize, and use information as it relates to practical situations on their jobs and careers. Others in this series are: *Organization, Problem-Solving,* and *Learning the Ropes* (all 1998). (Rev: VOYA 8/98) [350.14]

5460 Mason, Helen. *Great Careers for People Interested in Food* (6–10). (Career Connections) 1996, Gale $27.75 (0-7876-0860-2). All kinds of food-related careers are described in this book, along with career-path recommendations, training and experi-

ence requirements, and outlooks for the future. (Rev: BR 9–10/96; SLJ 9/96) [355.6]

5461 Mason, Helen. *Great Careers for People Who Like Being Outdoors* (9–12). (Career Connections) 1993, Gale $27.75 (0-8103-9390-5). Provides a list of outdoor occupations and a description of the work, profiles various people who hold these jobs, explains job requirements, preparation, and the hiring process, and gives an idea of future prospects. (Rev: BL 3/15/94; SLJ 12/93) [796.5023]

5462 Miller, Louise. *Careers for Animal Lovers and Other Zoological Types* (9–12). 1991, VGM paper $9.95 (0-8442-8125-5). Information on animal care employment, from pet-sitter to veterinarian. (Rev: BL 6/1/91) [636]

5463 Nelson, Corinna. *Working in the Environment* (6–8). (Exploring Careers) 1999, Lerner LB $23.93 (0-8225-1763-9). A recycling manager, a fisheries technician, and a nonprofit organization director are among the 12 people profiled in this title that describes the wide range of jobs related to the environment. (Rev: BL 7/99; SLJ 10/99) [363.7]

5464 Pasternak, Ceel, and Linda Thornburg. *Cool Careers for Girls with Animals* (7–12). 1999, Impact paper $12.95 (1-57023-105-2). Animal-related careers like veterinarian, pet-sitter, horse farmer, animal trainer, and bird handler are discussed, supplemented by interviews with women who work in each field. (Rev: SLJ 4/99; VOYA 8/99) [591]

5465 Pitz, Mary Elizabeth. *Careers in Government* (9–12). 1994, VGM $24.95 (0-8442-4194-6); paper $13.95 (0-8442-4195-4). A guide for those interested in employment in government. Explains the hiring processes for many nonelective occupations and federal jobs. (Rev: BL 8/94) [350]

5466 *Preparing for a Career in the Environment* (9–12). 1998, Ferguson $16.95 (0-89434-249-5). A variety of environmental careers are introduced, with material on aptitude, education, pay, advancement, and employment outlook. (Rev: SLJ 2/99) [331]

5467 Reeves, Diane L. *Career Ideas for Kids Who Like Talking* (5–9). Illus. 1998, Facts on File $18.95 (0-8160-3683-7); paper $12.95 (0-8160-3689-6). This is a guide to careers in communications, from hotel manager to publicist to broadcaster, with reports from people in the field, tests to check one's aptitude, and sources of information. (Rev: SLJ 10/98) [808]

5468 Reeves, Diane L. *Career Ideas for Kids Who Like Writing* (5–9). Illus. (Career Ideas for Kids Who Like) 1998, Facts on File $18.95 (0-8160-3685-3); paper $12.95 (0-8160-3691-8). A look at 15 careers related to writing, among them advertising copywriter, author, bookseller, editor, grant writer, journalist, librarian, literary agent, and publicist. (Rev: BR 5–6/99; SLJ 3/99) [808]

5469 Roberson, Virginia Lee. *Careers in the Graphic Arts* (9–12). 1988, Rosen $10.95 (0-8239-0803-8). Careers involving illustration, paste-up work, layout, art, and design are described with details on job opportunities, qualifications, and working conditions. (Rev: BL 12/15/88; BR 9–10/89; VOYA 6/89) [760]

5470 Ruhlman, Michael. *The Making of a Chef: Mastering Heat at the Culinary Institute of America* (10–12). 1997, Holt $27.50 (0-8050-4674-7). This is an engrossing account of the author's student days at the most prestigious cooking school in the United States, the Culinary Institute of America, with a description of its curriculum and what goes into becoming a master chef. (Rev: SLJ 5/98) [641.5]

5471 Shenk, Ellen. *Outdoor Careers: Exploring Occupations in Outdoor Fields* (9–12). 1992, Stackpole paper $16.95 (0-8117-2542-1). Provides job descriptions, profiles of men and women in various fields, resources, market information, government employment, etc. (Rev: BL 2/15/93; SLJ 5/93) [331.7]

5472 Shorto, Russell. *Careers for Animal Lovers* (9–12). (Choices) 1992, Millbrook LB $20.90 (1-56294-160-7). Includes career lists, an index of organizations, and interviews with a zookeeper, snake handler, veterinarian, and pet groomer. (Rev: BL 1/1/92; SLJ 2/92) [636]

5473 Stienstra, Tom, and Robin Schlueter. *Sunshine Jobs: Career Opportunities Working Outdoors* (9–12). 1997, Live Oak $16.95 (0-911781-15-3). This book uses a readable format to describe 103 jobs outdoors, from mountain climbing guide to operator of a canoe rental service. (Rev: VOYA 10/97) [976.5]

5474 VGM Career Horizons, eds. *VGM's Careers Encyclopedia.* 4th ed. (9–12). 1997, VGM $39.95 (0-8442-4525-9). A comprehensive report on 200 careers, arranged alphabetically. (Rev: BL 6/1/91) [331.7]

5475 Weiss, Ann E. *The Glass Ceiling: A Look at Women in the Workforce* (8–12). 1999, Twenty-First Century $22.40 (0-7613-1365-6). After a brief history of women's place in the world of work, this book focuses on recent changes and new opportunities (and dangers) for women in the work force. (Rev: BL 6/1–15/99; SLJ 9/99) [331.4]

5476 White, William C., and Donald N. Collins. *Opportunities in Agriculture Careers* (10–12). Illus. 1987, VGM $13.95 (0-8442-6554-3); paper $10.95 (0-8442-6555-1). A guide that covers standard careers plus related ones in transportation, research, and so on. (Rev: BL 6/1/88; BR 5–6/88) [630.203]

Arts, Entertainment, and Sports

5477 Bartlett, Gillian. *Great Careers for People Interested in Art & Design* (6–10). (Career Connections) 1996, Gale $27.75 (0-7876-0863-7). Using case studies of 6 people who have succeeded in careers related to art and design, this book discusses opportunities, career-path recommendations, qualifications, and the outlook for the future. (Rev: BR 9–10/96; SLJ 9/96) [746.9]

5478 Curless, Maura. *Fitness* (9–12). (Careers Without College) 1992, Peterson's Guides paper $7.95 (1-56079-223-X). Career opportunities in the fields of physical fitness and health care are explored in this practical guide. (Rev: BL 2/15/93) [613.7]

5479 Ferguson, J. G. *What Can I Do Now? Preparing for a Career in Journalism* (7–12). 1998, Ferguson $16.95 (0-89434-251-7). This book introduces careers in journalism and related fields, describes the preparation and aptitudes necessary, and suggests how teens can get involved in journalism while still in school. (Rev: SLJ 4/99) [070]

5480 Ferguson Publishing, eds. *Careers in Focus—Arts & Entertainment* (8–12). Illus. (Careers in Focus) 1998, Ferguson LB $13.95 (0-89434-245-2). This book describes over 20 careers in the performing arts, photography, film, and the fine arts, with a definition of each job title, the nature of the work, qualifications, how to research and enter the field, advancement opportunities, employment projections, pay, and working conditions. (Rev: SLJ 8/98; VOYA 6/99) [792]

5481 Ferguson Publishing, eds. *Careers in Focus—Sports* (8–12). (Careers in Focus) 1998, Ferguson LB $13.95 (0-89434-247-9). Over 20 careers related to sports, from golf-course superintendent to professional athlete to stadium vendor, are included in this volume, with information on qualifications, working conditions, salaries, opportunities, rewards, and methods of exploring and entering the field. (Rev: BR 9–10/98; SLJ 8/98) [796]

5482 Field, Sally. *Career Opportunities in the Music Industry.* rev. ed. (10–12). (Career Opportunities) 1995, Facts on File $45.00 (0-8160-3047-2). This volume offers realistic information on over 80 different jobs related to the music industry, including positions in the record business, radio and television, music retailing and wholesaling, education, publicity, and orchestras. (Rev: SLJ 6/96) [780]

5483 Greenspon, Jaq. *Careers for Film Buffs and Other Hollywood Types* (9–12). 1993, VGM $14.95 (0-8442-4100-8); paper $9.95 (0-8442-4101-6). An encyclopedia of job descriptions, covering such departments as production, camera and sound, special effects, grip and electric, makeup and costumes, and more. (Rev: BL 5/15/93) [791.43]

5484 Greenwald, Ted. *Music* (9–12). (Careers Without College) 1992, Peterson's Guides paper $7.95 (1-56079-219-1). Presents 5 types of occupations related to music that may require further education but not a 4-year degree. (Rev: BL 2/15/93) [780]

5485 Hopkins, Del, and Margaret Hopkins. *Careers As a Rock Musician* (9–12). 1993, Rosen LB $15.95 (0-8239-1518-2). Emphasizes that a clear understanding of the business side of the profession is vital for success. (Rev: BL 5/15/93; VOYA 10/93) [781.66]

5486 Isenberg, Marc, and Rick Rhoads. *The Real Athletes Guide: How to Succeed in Sports, School, and Life* (9–12). 1998, Athlete Network paper $19.95 (0-9666764-0-8). This overview examines scholarship opportunities in college athletics and tells how to choose the right college, handle the recruitment process, and prepare for a career. (Rev: BL 12/15/98; SLJ 3/99) [378.1]

5487 Jay, Annie, and Luanne Feik. *Stars in Your Eyes . . . Feet on the Ground: A Practical Guide for Teenage Actors (and Their Parents!)* (7–12). Illus. 1999, Theatre Directories paper $16.95 (0-933919-42-5). A young actress gives practical advice on how to break into show business, including information on publicity photos, auditions, managers, agents, publicity packages, resumes, and casting calls. (Rev: BL 6/1–15/99) [792.02]

5488 Kaplan, Andrew. *Careers for Artistic Types* (9–12). Photos. 1991, Millbrook LB $20.90 (1-878841-20-3). Presents an interesting assortment of artistic careers with information gathered directly from individuals in these occupations. (Rev: BL 3/1/91; SLJ 11/91) [702.3]

5489 Lantz, Francess. *Rock, Rap, and Rad: How to Be a Rock or Rap Star* (6–12). 1992, Avon paper $3.99 (0-380-76793-7). The author takes aspiring rock stars through the basic steps of choosing an instrument, finding other musicians and a place to play, lining up gigs, and on up to the top. (Rev: BL 7/93) [781.66]

5490 Lee, Barbara. *Working in Music* (4–8). Illus. (Exploring Careers) 1996, Lerner $23.93 (0-8225-1761-2). Such careers as composing, performing, music retailing, and violin making are covered in this book profiling 12 people who work in the music field. (Rev: BL 2/15/97; SLJ 2/97) [780]

5491 Lee, Barbara. *Working in Sports and Recreation* (7–12). Illus. (Exploring Careers) 1996, Lerner LB $23.93 (0-8225-1762-0). Twelve people whose careers involve various aspects of sports and recreation talk candidly about their professions. (Rev: BL 2/15/97) [796]

5492 Leshay, Jeff. *How to Launch Your Career in TV News* (9–12). 1993, VGM paper $14.95 (0-8442-4138-5). Describes how to get into a career in TV news, from the interviewing process on. Includes interviews with those in the business and information on college programs and scholarships. (Rev: BL 10/1/93) [070]

5493 Mayfield, Katherine. *Acting A to Z: The Young Person's Guide to a Stage or Screen Career* (6–12). Illus. 1998, Back Stage Books paper $16.95 (0-8230-8801-4). This slim, eye-catching paperback explores all facets of an acting career, from the general to the practical and the specific, including networking, casting, education, self-esteem, budgeting, resumes, and promotional photographs. (Rev: VOYA 6/99) [792]

5494 Mirault, Don. *Dancing . . . for a Living: Where the Jobs Are, What They Pay, What Choreographers Look For, What to Ask* (9–12). 1994, Rafter Publg. paper $15.95 (0-9637864-4-X). An experienced professional discusses employment opportunities and gives practical career suggestions for dancers. (Rev: BL 1/15/94) [792.8]

5495 Moss, Miriam. *Fashion Photographer* (6–9). 1991, Macmillan LB $17.95 (0-89686-608-4). Points out the prestige and perks, as well as the downside, of fashion photography. (Rev: BL 5/15/91; SLJ 7/91) [778.9]

5496 Pasternak, Ceel, and Linda Thornburg. *Cool Careers for Girls in Sports* (5–9). (Cool Careers for Girls in Sports) 1999, Impact $19.95 (1-57023-107-9); paper $12.95 (1-57023-104-4). This book explores careers in sports, such as golf professional, ski instructor, basketball official, sports broadcaster, and athletic director, through in-depth interviews with 10 women in these fields. (Rev: SLJ 7/99; VOYA 8/99) [796]

5497 Peterson, Linda. *Entertainment* (10–12). Illus. (Careers without College) 1994, Peterson's Guides paper $7.95 (0-56079-352-X). This career guide covers positions in the performing arts and broadcasting. (Rev: BL 9/15/94) [791]

5498 Powell, Stephanie. *Hit Me with Music: How to Start, Manage, Record, and Perform with Your Own Rock Band* (8–12). 1995, Millbrook LB $22.40 (1-56294-653-6). A good source for young rockers wanting to start their own band, with a bibliography and recommended reading. (Rev: BL 11/15/95; SLJ 2/96; VOYA 4/96) [781.66]

5499 Reeves, Diane L. *Career Ideas for Kids Who Like Art* (5–9). Illus. (Career Ideas for Kids Who Like) 1998, Facts on File $18.95 (0-8160-3681-0); paper $12.95 (0-8160-3687-X). A very useful book that describes in detail such jobs in the arts as actor, animator, chef, and photojournalist, with suggestions on how to test one's suitability for each area and reports from people working in the field. (Rev: SLJ 10/98; VOYA 8/98) [791]

5500 Reeves, Diane L., and Peter Kent. *Career Ideas for Kids Who Like Sports* (5–9). Illus. (Career

Ideas for Kids Who Like) 1998, Facts on File $18.95 (0-8160-3684-5); paper $12.95 (0-8160-3690-X). The 15 sports-related careers highlighted in this volume include coach, athlete, agent, recreational director, sportscaster, sportswriter, sports attorney, and sports equipment manufacturer. (Rev: BR 5–6/99; SLJ 6/99) [796]

5501 Rosenbaum, Jean, and Mary Prine. *Opportunities in Fitness Careers* (9–12). 1991, VGM $14.95 (0-8442-8185-9). Information on educational requirements and income expectations for one of today's fastest growing industries. (Rev: BL 6/1/91) [613.7]

5502 Salmon, Mark. *Opportunities in Visual Arts Careers* (9–12). 1992, VGM $14.95 (0-8442-4031-1); paper $11.95 (0-8442-4033-8). Discusses working for a company, freelance work, teaching art, and art therapy. (Rev: BL 2/15/93) [702.3]

5503 Steele, William Paul. *Stay Home and Star! A Step-by-Step Guide to Starting Your Regional Acting Career* (9–12). 1992, Heinemann paper $13.95 (0-435-08603-0). Practical advice about acting opportunities on the local level, emphasizing a businesslike approach and the basic requirements for success. (Rev: BL 2/1/92) [792]

5504 Weigant, Chris. *Careers as a Disc Jockey* (8–12). (Careers) 1997, Rosen LB $16.95 (0-8239-2528-5). This informative book gives many practical tips on how to get started and be successful in radio, with material on making demo tapes, applying for jobs and internships, and working oneself up. There are interviews with 8 DJs. Careers in management, sales, technical areas, talk shows, and others are included. (Rev: BR 3–4/98; SLJ 12/97; VOYA 2/98) [384.54]

5505 Williamson, Walter. *Early Stages: The Professional Theater and the Young Actor* (6–9). 1986, Walker LB $17.85 (0-8027-6630-7). Through examining the careers of several young actors, tips are given on how to enter show business. (Rev: BL 7/86; BR 11–12/86; SLJ 5/86) [792]

5506 Wilson, Lee. *Making It in the Music Business: A Business and Legal Guide for Songwriters and Performers* (9–12). 1995, NAL paper $12.95 (0-452-26848-6). A practical handbook of copyright law, trademarks, and other information, by a music attorney. (Rev: BL 4/1/95) [780]

Business

5507 Beckett, Kathleen. *Fashion* (9–12). (Careers Without College) 1992, Peterson's Guides paper $7.95 (1-56079-220-5). The world of fashion is explored in this career guide that explores occupations that do not require a college degree. (Rev: BL 2/15/93) [687]

5508 Dolber, Roslyn. *Opportunities in Fashion Careers*. 2nd ed. (9–12). 1992, VGM $13.95 (0-8442-4022-2); paper $10.95 (0-8442-4023-0). This career guide surveys the world of the fashion industry and highlights a variety of jobs involved. (Rev: BL 1/1/93) [687]

5509 Healy, Lisa, ed. *My First Year in Book Publishing: Real-World Stories from America's Book Publishing Professionals* (9–12). 1994, Walker $33.95 (0-8027-1294-0); paper $18.95 (0-8027-7425-3). A guide for those interested in book publishing, including testimony from agents, editors, publicists, and indexers describing their first year of work. (Rev: BL 9/1/94; VOYA 12/94) [070.5]

5510 Mogel, Leonard. *Making It in Advertising: An Insider's Guide to Career Opportunities* (9–12). 1993, Macmillan paper $10.00 (0-02-034552-6). Based on interviews with ad agency professionals, an introduction to advertising, describing available positions and the talents needed to succeed. (Rev: BL 4/15/93) [659.1]

5511 Moss, Miriam. *Fashion Model* (6–9). 1991, Macmillan LB $17.95 (0-89686-609-2). The prestige and perks as well as the downside of fashion modeling. (Rev: BL 5/15/91; SLJ 7/91) [659.1]

5512 Noronha, Shonan F. R. *Careers in Communications* (9–12). 1993, VGM $17.95 (0-8442-4182-2); paper $13.95 (0-8442-4183-0). Information on the fields of journalism, photography, film, radio, multimedia, television and video, advertising, and public relations. (Rev: BL 3/15/94) [384]

5513 Plawin, Paul. *Careers for Travel Buffs and Other Restless Types* (9–12). 1992, VGM $14.95 (0-8442-8109-3); paper $9.95 (0-8442-8127-1). Covers job descriptions, getting into the business, and future prospects of typical travel careers as well as positions that involve less traveling. (Rev: BL 6/1/92; SLJ 3/92) [331.7]

5514 Ring, Gertrude. *Careers in Finance* (9–12). 1993, VGM $17.95 (0-8442-4186-5); paper $13.95 (0-8442-4187-3). A basic guide to careers in the world of finance. (Rev: BL 5/15/93) [332]

5515 Rosenthal, Lawrence. *Exploring Careers in Accounting*. Rev. ed. (9–12). 1993, Rosen LB $16.95 (0-8239-1501-8). Covers types of jobs related to accounting and training that is required, with appendices of definitions, associations, accounting schools, and other information. (Rev: BL 5/15/93; SLJ 6/93) [657]

5516 Schiff, Kenny. *Opportunities in Desktop Publishing Careers* (9–12). 1993, VGM $14.95 (0-8442-4064-8); paper $11.95 (0-8442-4065-6). Notes the specialized areas where jobs are available and includes interviews with people employed in the field. (Rev: BL 5/15/93; VOYA 10/93) [686.2]

5517 Sharon, Donna, and Jo Anne Sommers. *Great Careers for People Interested in Travel & Tourism* (6–10). (Career Connections) 1996, Gale $21.00 (0-7876-0862-9). Tour director and travel agent are among the jobs discussed in this overview of careers related to travel and tourism, with information on qualifications, training, and opportunities. (Rev: BR 9–10/96; SLJ 9/96) [658]

5518 Steinberg, Margery. *Opportunities in Marketing Careers* (9–12). 1993, VGM $14.95 (0-8442-4076-1); paper $12.95 (0-8442-4078-8). Different types of marketing are introduced in this guide, with a rundown on the various occupations associated with each. (Rev: BL 3/15/94) [658.8]

Construction and Mechanical Trades

5519 Garvey, Lonny D. *Opportunities in the Machine Trades* (9–12). 1994, VGM $14.95 (0-8442-4123-7); paper $10.95 (0-8442-4124-5). The machine trades are introduced, with material on a variety of occupations in each. (Rev: BL 8/94) [671]

Education and Librarianship

5520 Edelfelt, Roy A., and Blythe Camenson. *Careers in Education* (9–12). 1992, VGM $17.95 (0-8442-4176-8); paper $13.95 (0-8442-4177-6). This career guide surveys the field of education and profiles various occupations associated with it. (Rev: BL 2/15/93) [370]

5521 Fine, Janet. *Opportunities in Teaching* (10–12). 1984, VGM $13.95 (0-8442-6504-7); paper $10.95 (0-8442-6250-1). Teaching careers at various levels are discussed and questions of suitability explored. [371.7]

Law, Police, and Other Society-Oriented Careers

5522 Davis, Mary L. *Working in Law and Justice* (6–8). (Exploring Careers) 1999, Lerner $23.93 (0-8225-1766-3). Twelve people are profiled representing various jobs and careers in law and related fields, among them a female deputy sheriff, a male law librarian, a bail bond agent, and a security firm owner. (Rev: BL 7/99; SLJ 10/99) [340]

5523 Males, Anne Marie, and Julie Czerneda. *Great Careers for People Fascinated by Government & the Law* (6–9). (Career Connections) 1996, Gale $21.00 (0-7876-0858-0). Six people whose jobs involve various aspects of the law and government are profiled, with information on related careers, opportunities, and education and training requirements. (Rev: BR 9–10/96; SLJ 11/96) [345]

5524 Munneke, Gary. *Opportunities in Law Careers* (9–12). 1993, VGM $14.95 (0-8442-4086-9); paper $10.95 (0-8442-4087-7). Various careers connected to the law are discussed, with information on training, opportunities, and aptitude. (Rev: BL 3/15/94; VOYA 6/94) [340]

5525 Paul, Caroline. *Fighting Fire* (9–12). 1998, St. Martin's $23.95 (0-312-18581-2); paper $6.99 (0-312-97000-5). A female firefighter, a former journalism student who applied for a firefighter position in order to write about the training and chose to make it her career instead, describes important moments, the courage, bravery, and physical and mental strength needed for the job, and difficulties she faced as a woman firefighter. (Rev: SLJ 10/98) [363]

5526 Selden, Annette, ed. *Handbook of Government and Public Service Careers* (9–12). 1993, VGM paper $17.95 (0-8442-4142-3). A reference book presenting basic information about 47 careers that are specific to government or can be found in a government context. (Rev: BL 3/15/94) [353.001]

5527 Wirths, Claudine G. *Choosing a Career in Law Enforcement* (6–10). (World of Work) 1996, Rosen LB $15.95 (0-8239-2274-X). Careers in law enforcement, such as police officer, security guard, and private investigator, are explored. (Rev: SLJ 3/97) [363]

Medicine and Health

5528 Duncan, Jane Caryl. *Careers in Veterinary Medicine* (8–12). Illus. 1994, Rosen LB $19.50 (0-8239-1678-2); paper $9.95 (0-8239-1719-3). A veterinarian gives an honest description of her profession and many practical tips. (Rev: BL 9/1/88; SLJ 10/88; VOYA 10/88) [636.089]

5529 Edwards, Lois. *Great Careers for People Interested in the Human Body* (9–12). (Career Connections) 1993, Gale $21.00 (0-8103-9386-7). Information from representatives of various medical fields, with activities and suggestions to stimulate further investigation. (Rev: BL 3/15/94; SLJ 12/93) [610.69]

5530 Ferguson Publishing, eds. *Careers in Focus— Medical Tech* (8–12). (Careers in Focus) 1998, Ferguson LB $13.95 (0-89434-246-0). Over 20 careers in medical technology are described, covering the nature of the job, educational requirements, rewards, salaries, working conditions, and how to get into the field. (Rev: BR 9–10/98; SLJ 8/98) [610]

5531 Frederickson, Keville. *Opportunities in Nursing Careers* (9–12). 1989, VGM paper $10.95 (0-8442-8636-2). This account describes various kinds of nursing careers, the training and personality necessary, and working conditions. (Rev: BR 3–4/90; VOYA 12/89) [610.73]

5532 Gordon, Susan, and Kristin Hohenadel. *Health Care* (9–12). (Careers Without College) 1992, Peterson's Guides paper $7.95 (1-56079-222-1). Presents 5 health-related occupations that may require further education but not a 4-year degree. (Rev: BL 2/15/93) [610]

5533 Kacen, Alex. *Opportunities in Paramedical Careers* (9–12). Illus. 1989, VGM $13.95 (0-8442-6506-3); paper $10.95 (0-8442-6507-1). A thorough rundown on the many jobs in the medical field involving technicians and assistants and how to prepare for entrance into these fields. (Rev: BR 5–6/89; VOYA 6/89) [610.69]

5534 Lee, Barbara. *Working in Health Care and Wellness* (4–8). Illus. (Exploring Careers) 1996, Lerner LB $23.93 (0-8225-1760-4). This book profiles 12 people who are in health care professions, and includes the pros and cons of each career. (Rev: BL 2/15/97) [610.69]

5535 *Preparing for a Career in Nursing* (9–12). (What Can I Do Now?) 1998, Ferguson $16.95 (0-89434-252-5). This book provides useful information about nursing careers, including a history of the profession, the aptitudes and skills necessary, education, certification, opportunities for advancement, pay, and working conditions. (Rev: SLJ 2/99) [610]

5536 Ramsdell, Melissa, ed. *My First Year As a Doctor: Real-World Stories from America's M.D.'s* (9–12). 1994, Walker $33.95 (0-8027-1290-8); paper $15.95 (0-8027-7418-0). A guide for those interested in becoming doctors, including testimony from professionals describing their first year of working in the field. (Rev: BL 9/1/94; VOYA 4/95) [610.69]

5537 Sacks, Terrence J. *Careers in Medicine* (9–12). (VGM Professional Careers) 1992, VGM $16.95 (0-8442-4178-4); paper $12.95 (0-8442-4179-2). Covers educational expenses, internships, and areas of specialty for physicians. Lists U.S. and Canadian medical schools, organizations, and specialty boards. (Rev: BL 2/15/93) [610.69]

5538 Schafer, R. C. *Opportunities in Chiropractic Health Care Careers* (9–12). 1986, VGM $14.95 (0-8442-6565-9); paper $12.95 (0-8442-6566-7). Schafer gives an overview of the field plus details on training and employment outlook. (Rev: BL 6/1/86; BR 9–10/86) [615.5]

5539 Selden, Annette, ed. *VGM's Handbook of Health Care Careers* (9–12). 1992, VGM paper $12.95 (0-8442-4148-2). A brief survey of a large number of jobs, with information on resumes, cover letters, and interviews. (Rev: BL 2/15/93) [610]

5540 Simpson, Carolyn, and Penelope Hall. *Careers in Medicine* (9–12). 1993, Rosen LB $16.95 (0-8239-1711-8). This description of various types of doctors and specialties includes schooling and

licensing procedures and a section on medical ethics. (Rev: BL 3/15/94; SLJ 1/94) [610.69]

5541 Snook, I. Donald. *Opportunities in Hospital Administration Careers* (9–12). 1988, VGM $14.95 (0-8442-6509-8); paper $11.95 (0-8442-6510-1). The types of careers involving hospital administration are described followed by detailed information on education and experience required, job hunting tips, and a typical day on the job. (Rev: BR 5–6/89; VOYA 6/89) [362.1]

5542 Snook, I. Donald, and Leo D'Ozraio. *Opportunities in Health and Medical Careers* (10–12). 1990, VGM $14.95 (0-8442-8573-0); paper $12.95 (0-8442-8574-9). This is a fine overview of the many positions available in this expanding field. (Rev: BL 12/15/90) [610]

Science and Engineering

5543 Basta, Nicholas. *Opportunities in Engineering Careers* (9–12). Illus. 1990, VGM $14.95 (0-8442-4591-7). After a general discussion of the field of engineering, this account gives specific information on its branches and the opportunities available. (Rev: BL 6/1/90) [620]

5544 Bortz, Alfred B. *To the Young Scientist: Reflections on Doing & Living Science* (6–12). (Venture) 1997, Watts LB $25.00 (0-531-11325-6). The author, 5 other men, and 6 women discuss their varied careers in science, why they chose them, and the rewards their professions have given them. (Rev: BL 6/1–15/97; SLJ 6/97; VOYA 4/98) [509]

5545 Easton, Thomas A. *Careers in Science* (10–12). 1989, VGM $14.95 (0-8442-6123-8); paper $9.95 (0-8442-6124-6). An overview of the jobs available in such areas as the life and physical sciences, mathematics, computers, and related social sciences. [500]

5546 Fulton, Michael T. *Exploring Careers in Cyberspace* (7–12). (Careers) 1997, Rosen paper $16.95 (0-8239-2633-8). A worthwhile source of information on how to prepare oneself to work in cyberspace, the types of jobs available, and the way to make a solid impression. (Rev: BL 6/1–15/98; BR 9–10/98; SLJ 7/98) [004.67 8 02373]

5547 Gable, Fred B. *Opportunities in Pharmacy Careers.* Rev.ed. (9–12). Illus. 1990, VGM $14.95 (0-8442-8591-9); paper $12.95 (0-8442-8592-7). A variety of pharmaceutical careers are explored with information on suitability, education necessary, and work conditions. (Rev: BL 9/15/90) [615.1]

5548 Grant, Lesley. *Great Careers for People Concerned about the Environment* (9–12). (Career Connections) 1993, Gale $27.75 (0-8103-9388-3). Profiles various professionals and their educational backgrounds, and includes science-oriented activities aimed at stimulating interest in various environmental fields. (Rev: BL 3/15/94) [363.7]

5549 Reeves, Diane L. *Career Ideas for Kids Who Like Science* (5–9). Illus. (Career Ideas for Kids Who Like) 1998, Facts on File $18.95 (0-8160-3680-2); paper $12.95 (0-8160-3686-1). An upbeat, breezy introduction to 15 careers in such scientific fields as archaeology, astronomy, chemistry, engineering, landscape architecture, pharmacy, and veterinary medicine. (Rev: SLJ 9/98) [500]

5550 Vincent, Victoria. *Great Careers for People Interested in the Past* (6–10). (Career Connections) 1996, Gale $27.75 (0-7876-0861-0). Careers in history, paleontology, and anthropology are among the many careers described in this occupational guide book that provides information on common and lesser-known jobs related to this field and how to get them. (Rev: SLJ 9/96) [930]

5551 *What Can I Do Now? Preparing for a Career in Engineering* (7–12). (What Can I Do Now?) 1998, Ferguson $16.95 (0-89434-248-7). Following a general introduction to engineering, the book describes jobs in the field, education and skill requirements, and salary ranges, and tells students what they can do now, emphasizing volunteer opportunities and internships. (Rev: SLJ 4/99) [620]

Technical and Industrial Careers

5552 Bone, Jan. *Opportunities in Cable Television*. 2nd ed. (9–12). 1992, VGM $14.95 (0-8442-4026-5); paper $10.95 (0-8442-4027-3). This career handbook describes a variety of jobs associated with cable television and gives specifics on working conditions, pay, and education requirements. (Rev: BL 1/1/93) [384.55]

5553 Czerneda, Julie, and Victoria Vincent. *Great Careers for People Interested in Communications Technology* (6–9). (Career Connections) 1996, Gale $21.00 (0-7876-0859-9). Using case studies of 6 people, this career book explores the many fields related to communications technology and the requisite job qualifications. (Rev: BR 9–10/96; SLJ 11/96) [621.38]

5554 Dudzinski, George A. *Opportunities in Tool and Die Careers* (9–12). 1993, VGM $14.95 (0-8442-4047-8); paper $11.95 (0-8442-4048-6). Profiles a variety of jobs associated with tool and die industries. (Rev: BL 5/15/93) [621.9]

5555 Eberts, Marjorie, and Margaret Gisler. *Careers for Computer Buffs and Other Technological Types* (9–12). 1998, VGM paper $14.95 (0-8442-4707-3). Industries that use computers are covered in this text,

developed around informative statements by individuals in the field. (Rev: BL 3/15/94) [004]

5556 Henderson, Harry. *Career Opportunities in Computers and Cyberspace* (7–12). 1999, Facts on File $29.95 (0-8160-773-6); paper $18.95 (0-8160-3774-4). A well-organized resource that covers nearly 200 professions and jobs in computer-related fields. (Rev: BL 6/1–15/99) [004]

5557 Munday, Marianne F. *Opportunities in Word Processing Careers* (9–12). 1991, VGM $14.95 (0-8442-8164-6); paper $11.95 (0-8442-8165-4). A comprehensive if somewhat dated guide to understanding word processing in today's business world and what the future holds for those interested in pursuing a career in the field. (Rev: BL 6/1/91) [652.5]

5558 Noronha, Shonan F. R. *Opportunities in Television and Video Careers* (9–12). 1993, VGM $19.95 (0-8442-4090-7); paper $16.95 (0-8442-4091-5). A variety of careers involving the television and video industries are profiled, with information on training, pay, and working conditions. (Rev: BL 3/15/94) [384.55]

5559 Pasternak, Ceel, and Linda Thornburg. *Cool Careers for Girls in Computers* (7–12). Illus. 1999, Impact paper $12.95 (1-57023-103-6). This career book for girls features interviews with 10 women in computer-related fields, including a software engineer, sales executive, online specialist, technology trainer, and network administrator. (Rev: VOYA 8/99) [004.6]

5560 Reeves, Diane L., and Peter Kent. *Career Ideas for Kids Who Like Computers* (5–9). Illus. (Career Ideas for Kids Who Like) 1998, Facts on File $18.95 (0-8160-3682-9); paper $12.95 (0-8160-3688-8). This book helps readers determine their interests and aptitudes and examines 15 computer-related careers, including a list of skills needed for each job, a description of the position, and a profile of someone in the profession. (Rev: BR 5–6/99; SLJ 6/99) [004.6]

5561 Richardson, Peter, and Bob Richardson. *Great Careers for People Interested in How Things Work* (9–12). (Career Connections) 1993, Gale $21.00 (0-8103-9389-1). Information about a variety of careers, traditional and nontraditional, involving technology. (Rev: BL 3/15/94; SLJ 1/94) [602.3]

5562 Richardson, Peter, and Bob Richardson. *Great Careers for People Interested in Math and Computers* (9–12). (Career Connections) 1993, Gale $21.00 (0-8103-9385-9). The theoretical side of the computer industry is highlighted in this rundown of behind-the-scenes jobs in the computer industry. (Rev: BL 3/15/94) [004.023]

5563 Rowh, Mark. *Opportunities in Electronics Careers* (9–12). 1992, VGM $14.95 (0-8442-8183-

2); paper $11.95 (0-8442-8184-0). An overview of the types of careers available in electronics, providing information on background and skills needed, along with future prospects. (Rev: BL 6/1/92) [621.281]

5564 Scharnberg, Ken. *Opportunities in Trucking Careers* (9–12). 1992, VGM $19.95 (0-8442-8181-6); paper $11.95 (0-8442-8182-4). A thorough discussion of how the complexities involved in scheduling and organizing driver, vehicle, client/customer, freight, and destination are handled, as well as salary structures. (Rev: BL 6/1/92) [388.3]

5565 Weintraub, Joseph. *Exploring Careers in the Computer Field*. Rev. ed. (9–12). 1993, Rosen paper $9.95 (0-8239-1723-1). Provides interviews with people who work in the field, discusses future trends, and lists colleges offering computer science majors and associations. (Rev: BL 5/15/93) [001.64]

5566 Williams, Linda. *Computers* (9–12). (Careers Without College) 1992, Peterson's Guides paper $7.95 (1-56079-224-8). A guide to a number of computer-related careers that do not require a college education in computer technology. (Rev: BL 2/15/93) [004]

Personal Finances

Money-Making Ideas

General and Miscellaneous

5567 Belliston, Larry, and Kurt Hanks. *Extra Cash for Kids* (9–12). 1989, Wolgemuth & Hyatt paper $9.95 (0-943497-70-1). A book that outlines about 100 ways young adults can make money. [650]

5568 Bernstein, Daryl. *Better Than a Lemonade Stand! Small Business Ideas for Kids* (5–8). Illus. 1992, Beyond Words paper $7.95 (0-941831-75-2). The author, a 15-year-old entrepreneur, provides ideas for starting 51 different small businesses and offers advice on start-up costs, billing, and customer relations. (Rev: BL 10/1/92; SLJ 1/93) [650.1]

5569 Byers, Patricia, et al. *The Kids Money Book: Great Money Making Ideas* (7–10). 1983, Liberty paper $4.95 (0-89709-041-1). A wide variety of jobs are introduced that can be part-time and money-producing. [658.1]

5570 Kravetz, Stacy. *Girl Boss: Running the Show Like the Big Chicks* (7–10). Illus. 1999, Girl Pr. paper $15.95 (0-9659754-2-8). This book gives practical advice and tips for teenage girls who want to start a business of their own. (Rev: VOYA 8/99) [658.1]

5571 Mariotti, Steve, and Tony Towle. *The Young Entrepreneur's Guide to Starting and Running a Business* (7–12). Illus. 1996, Times Bks. paper $15.00 (0-8129-2627-7). A thorough, practical guide to starting a business, from the fundamentals of setting up procedures to details on marketing, record keeping, and legal structure. (Rev: BL 2/15/96) [658.1]

5572 Otfinoski, Steven. *The Kid's Guide to Money: Earning It, Saving It, Spending It, Growing It, Sharing It* (4–8). Illus. 1996, Scholastic $12.95 (0-590-

53850-0); paper $4.95 (0-590-53853-5). This practical guide for kids on how to earn money and manage it responsibly includes budgeting, standard consumer advice, basic information about the stock market, credit cards, and sharing. (Rev: BL 4/1/96; SLJ 6/96; VOYA 6/96) [332.4]

5573 Pendleton, Scott. *The Ultimate Guide to Student Contests, Grades 7–12* (6–12). Illus. 1997, Walker paper $23.95 (0-8027-7512-8). This is a guide to various academically oriented contests open to young adults, arranged by subjects such as mathematics and foreign languages. (Rev: BL 8/97) [373.18]

Baby-sitting

5574 Kuch, K. D. *The Babysitter's Handbook* (5–10). Illus. (KidBacks) 1997, Random paper $5.99 (0-679-88369-X). This is a fact-filled manual on all aspects of baby-sitting including feeding and playing with babies, emergency measures, games and songs, and basic first aid. (Rev: SLJ 7/97) [649]

5575 Zakarin, Debra M. *The Ultimate Baby-Sitter's Handbook: So You Wanna Make Tons of Money?* (4–8). Illus. 1997, Price Stern Sloan paper $4.95 (0-8431-7936-8). A practical, easily read guide to baby-sitting and setting up a business. (Rev: BL 9/15/97; SLJ 12/97) [649]

Managing Money

5576 Guthrie, Donna, and Jan Stiles. *Real World Math: Money, Credit, & Other Numbers in Your Life* (6–9). Illus. 1998, Millbrook LB $24.40 (0-7613-0251-4). A practical and entertaining guide that shows how math is used in everyday situations like shopping, managing money, buying a car, or using credit wisely. (Rev: BL 6/1–15/98; BR 11–12/98; SLJ 6/98; VOYA 8/98) [332.024]

5577 Hurwitz, Jane. *High Performance through Effective Budgeting* (8–12). Illus. (The Learning-A-Living Library) 1996, Rosen LB $15.95 (0-8239-2203-0). Basic budgeting skills are presented for both personal and on-the-job application. (Rev: BL 8/96; BR 1–2/97; SLJ 10/96; VOYA 2/97) [332.024]

5578 Karlitz, Gail, and Debbie Honig. *Growing Money: A Complete Investing Guide for Kids* (4–8).

1999, Price Stern Sloan paper $6.99 (0-8431-7481-1). This work explains such terms as investing and compound interest, decodes the financial page of the newspaper, and gives advice to budding entrepreneurs. (Rev: SLJ 9/99) [658.1]

5579 Rendon, Marion, and Rachel Kranz. *Straight Talk about Money* (7–12). (Straight Talk About) 1992, Facts on File LB $24.95 (0-8160-2612-2). Provides a brief history and description of money and the U.S. economy, followed by suggestions young adults can use when earning and managing money. (Rev: BL 6/15/92) [332.4]

Health and the Human Body

General and Miscellaneous

5580 *The Complete Manual of Fitness and Well-Being* (9–12). Illus. 1988, Reader's Digest $34.95 (0-88850-154-4). In addition to exercise and diet, this account covers such topics as human growth, body parts, and health. (Rev: BL 5/1/88; SLJ 6/88) [613]

5581 Gutman, Bill. *Harmful to Your Health* (5–8). Illus. (Focus on Safety) 1996, Twenty-First Century LB $20.40 (0-8050-4144-3). This volume outlines the problems inherent in drugs, alcohol, AIDS, steroids, and sexual abuse, with material on how to be alert to their dangers. (Rev: BL 2/1/97; SLJ 2/97) [616.86]

5582 Isler, Charlotte, and Alwyn T. Cohall. *The Watts Teen Health Dictionary* (7–12). Illus. 1996, Watts LB $24.95 (0-513-11236-5); paper $16.00 (0-531-15792-X). This book in dictionary format contains articles on such subjects as STDs, contraceptives, medications, diseases, eating disorders, breast exams, and immunization. (Rev: BR 11–12/96; VOYA 10/96) [613]

5583 O'Neill, Terry. *Biomedical Ethics* (7–12). (Opposing Viewpoints Digests) 1998, Greenhaven LB $18.96 (1-56510-875-2); paper $11.96 (1-56510-874-4). This concise overview of biomedical ethics covers topics like cloning, organ transplants, and the questions associated with experiments and research. (Rev: BL 4/15/99; SLJ 6/99) [575.1]

5584 Roleff, Tamara L., ed. *Biomedical Ethics* (8–12). (Opposing Viewpoints) 1998, Greenhaven LB $20.96 (1-56510-793-4); paper $21.50 (1-56510-792-6). An anthology of opinions on the ethical considerations related to cloning, human transplants,

modern reproductive techniques, and genetic research. (Rev: BL 6/1–15/98) [573.2]

5585 Villarosa, Linda, ed. *Body and Soul: The Black Women's Guide to Physical Health and Emotional Well-Being* (9–12). 1994, HarperPerennial paper $20.00 (0-06-095085-4). Contributors to this straight-from-the-heart guide include black female scientists, academics, health care practitioners, and writers. (Rev: BL 11/15/94*) [613]

5586 Yount, Lisa. *Issues in Biomedical Ethics* (6–9). Illus. (Contemporary Issues) 1997, Lucent LB $17.96 (1-56006-476-5). This book discusses issues involving morals vs. scientific exploration, such as possible limits in cloning research, genetic engineering, the use of animals in research, and physician-assisted suicide. (Rev: BL 5/15/98; SLJ 8/98) [174.2]

Aging and Death

5587 Baird, Robert M., and Stuart E. Rosenbaum, eds. *Euthanasia: The Moral Issues* (10–12). 1989, Prometheus paper $16.95 (0-87975-555-5). In this collection of 19 essays, euthanasia is explained and the various legal and moral questions surrounding it are explored. (Rev: BL 3/1/90) [179.7]

5588 Colman, Penny. *Corpses, Coffins, and Crypts: A History of Burial* (7–12). Illus. 1997, Holt $17.95 (0-8050-5066-3). Customs associated with death and burial traditions in various cultures and times are covered in a text enlivened with many photographs. (Rev: BL 11/1/97; SLJ 12/97*) [393]

5589 Digiulio, Robert, and Rachel Kranz. *Straight Talk about Death and Dying* (7–12). (Straight Talk About) 1995, Facts on File $24.95 (0-8160-3078-2). Among the topics covered in this book about death and dying are Kubler-Ross's 5 psychological stages experienced by the dying and various aspects of mourning. (Rev: BL 9/15/95; SLJ 12/95) [155.9]

5590 Egendorf, Laura K., ed. *Assisted Suicide* (7–12). (Current Controversies) 1998, Greenhaven LB $20.96 (1-56510-807-8). An anthology of opinions on topics related to assisted suicide, including its morality, legal status, and individual rights. (Rev: BL 8/98; SLJ 1/99) [179]

5591 Fry, Virginia. *Part of Me Died, Too: Stories of Creative Survival among Bereaved Children and Teenagers* (5–8). 1995, Dutton $19.99 (0-525-45068-8). Each of the 11 true-life stories is followed by a selection of self-help activities to aid the bereaved. (Rev: BL 1/1/95; SLJ 2/95) [155.9]

5592 Gaffron, Norma. *Dealing with Death* (6–12). 1989, Lucent LB $22.45 (1-56006-108-1). This account tells how various religions regard death and ways of coping with it in our present culture. (Rev: SLJ 4/90) [128]

5593 Gay, Kathlyn. *The Right to Die: Public Controversy, Private Matter* (7–12). (Issue and Debate) 1993, Millbrook LB $23.90 (1-56294-325-1). Discusses euthanasia and assisted suicide in depth—from Greek times to the present—and includes actual recent cases. (Rev: BL 10/1/93) [179]

5594 Gravelle, Karen, and Charles Haskins. *Teenagers Face to Face with Bereavement* (7–12). 1989, Messner paper $5.95 (0-671-65856-5). An exploration of how to cope with death and grieving that uses the words of 17 young people who have been through this experience. (Rev: BL 5/15/89; VOYA 12/89) [155.9]

5595 Grollman, Earl A. *Straight Talk about Death for Teenagers: How to Cope with Losing Someone You Love* (7–12). 1993, Beacon paper $16.00 (0-8070-2501-1). Grollman validates the painful feelings teens experience following the death of a loved one, conveying a sense of the grief as well as getting on with life. (Rev: BL 4/1/93; SLJ 6/93; VOYA 8/93) [155.9]

5596 Grosshandler-Smith, Janet. *Coping When a Parent Dies* (7–12). (Coping) 1995, Rosen LB $17.95 (0-8239-1514-X). A high school guidance counselor offers a wide range of coping skills to meet the feelings and situations experienced when a parent dies. Glossary and a list for further reading. (Rev: BL 8/95; VOYA 12/95) [155.9]

5597 Hyde, Margaret O., and Lawrence E. Hyde. *Meeting Death* (5–8). 1989, Walker LB $28.90 (0-8027-6874-1). After a history of how various cultures regard death, the authors discuss this phenomenon, the concept of grieving, and how to face death. (Rev: BL 1/1/90; SLJ 11/89) [306.9]

5598 Landau, Elaine. *The Right to Die* (7–12). 1993, Watts LB $24.00 (0-531-13015-0). A balanced, in-depth examination of the controversial issue, including a chapter on the rights of adolescents to refuse medical treatment. (Rev: BL 1/15/94; SLJ 2/94; VOYA 2/94) [174]

5599 Leder, Jane. *Dead Serious: A Book for Teenagers about Teenage Suicide* (7–12). 1987, Avon paper $3.50 (0-380-70661-X). This book deals specifically with the symptoms of a suicidal situation and how to cope with the aftereffects of the suicide of a relative or friend. (Rev: SLJ 8/87; VOYA 6/87) [179]

5600 Leone, Daniel, ed. *Physician-Assisted Suicide* (8–12). (At Issue) 1997, Greenhaven $16.96 (1-56510-019-0); paper $17.25 (1-56510-018-2). Authors represented in this anthology debate whether doctors should be allowed to help terminally ill patients end their lives rather than suffer prolonged pain. (Rev: BL 5/15/98; SLJ 5/98) [179.7]

5601 O'Connor, Nancy. *Letting Go with Love: The Grieving Process* (9–12). 1985, La Mariposa $24.95 (0-9613714-1-2); paper $14.95 (0-9613714-0-4). How to cope with the death of a loved one is the subject of this self-help book. [128]

5602 Schleifer, Jay. *Everything You Need to Know When Someone You Know Has Been Killed* (6–12). Illus. (Need to Know Library) 1998, Rosen $16.95 (0-8239-2779-2). This book helps young people deal with sudden death, describes the grieving process, and gives advice concerning the painful issues associated with death. (Rev: BL 10/1/98) [155.9]

5603 Sprung, Barbara. *Death* (4–8). (Preteen Pressures) 1998, Raintree Steck-Vaughn $24.26 (0-8172-5029-8). This book supplies information on topics like terminal illness, sudden death, and suicide, as well as customs of remembrance and the grieving process. (Rev: BL 5/15/98) [304.6]

5604 Walker, Richard. *A Right to Die?* (4–8). (Viewpoints) 1997, Watts LB $22.50 (0-531-14413-5). This objective book discusses traditional views of death, describes the impact of modern medicine on life spans, and presents different points of view on suicide, euthanasia, life-support systems, doctors' duties and responsibilities in terminal situations, hospice programs, living wills, and funeral choices. (Rev: SLJ 5/97) [306.88]

5605 Weiss, Stefanie Iris. *Everything You Need to Know about Dealing with Losses* (7–12). (Need to Know Library) 1998, Rosen LB $16.95 (0-8239-2780-6). This book discusses many kinds of loss, among them parent, friend, pet, or home, and provides guidance through the grieving process and concrete suggestions for coping with loss. (Rev: SLJ 1/99) [304.6]

5606 Wekesser, Carol, ed. *Euthanasia* (7–12). (Opposing Viewpoints) 1995, Greenhaven LB $20.96 (1-56510-244-4); paper $15.00 (1-56510-243-6). The ethical aspects of euthanasia, whether or not it should be legalized, physician-assisted suicide, and who should make decisions in these matters are addressed from a variety of viewpoints. (Rev: BL 7/95; SLJ 9/95; VOYA 12/95) [179]

Alcohol, Drugs, and Smoking

5607 Algeo, Philippa. *Acid and Hallucinogens* (5–8). Illus. 1990, Watts LB $20.80 (0-531-10932-1). This book discusses the composition and effects of such drugs as LSD, mescaline, marijuana, and angel dust. (Rev: BL 8/90; SLJ 10/90) [615]

5608 Alvergue, Anne. *Ecstasy: The Danger of False Euphoria* (6–10). Illus. (Drug Prevention Library) 1997, Rosen LB $17.95 (0-8239-2506-4). A discussion of how the drug MDMA, known as ecstasy, affects the mind and body, outlining the dangers. (Rev: SLJ 5/98) [6.5.3]

5609 Anderson, M. A. *Tracey: A Mother's Journal of Teenage Addiction* (9–12). 1988, Black Heron paper $7.95 (0-930773-08-X). The harrowing story of one family's fight to save their 14-year-old daughter Tracey from drug addiction. (Rev: VOYA 2/89) [613.8]

5610 Avraham, Regina. *The Downside of Drugs* (8–12). Illus. 1988, Chelsea LB $19.95 (1-55546-232-4). This account covers the effects of such drugs as nicotine, alcohol, narcotics, stimulants, and hallucinogens. (Rev: SLJ 6/88) [613.8]

5611 Avraham, Regina. *Substance Abuse* (8–12). 1988, Chelsea LB $19.95 (1-55546-219-7). This account describes how drugs affect behavior and how addiction is treated. (Rev: BR 1–2/89; VOYA 4/89) [616.86]

5612 Ayer, Eleanor. *Teen Smoking* (6–12). 1998, Lucent LB $17.96 (1-56006-442-0). In spite of warnings, nearly 2 million teens smoke. This book traces the influences that make them start and gives advice on how to quit. (Rev: BL 1/1–15/99) [362.29]

5613 Banfield, Susan. *Inside Recovery: How the Twelve-Step Program Can Work for You* (7–10). (Drug Abuse Prevention Library) 1998, Rosen LB $17.95 (0-8239-2634-6). Using first-hand knowledge, the author describes the 12-step program and the many problems one can face going through this program, which has been a successful route for many on the road to recovery from addiction. (Rev: VOYA 2/99) [613.8]

5614 Barbour, Scott, ed. *Alcohol* (8–12). (Opposing Viewpoints) 1997, Greenhaven LB $26.20 (1-56510-675-X); paper $21.50 (1-56510-674-1). Excerpts from books and articles explore questions involving the degree of harm that alcohol causes, treatments for alcoholism, the responsibility of the alcohol industry, and how to reduce alcohol-related problems. (Rev: BL 10/15/97; SLJ 1/98; VOYA 6/98) [613.8]

5615 Beal, Eileen. *Ritalin: Its Use and Abuse* (7–10). (Drug Abuse Prevention) 1999, Rosen LB $17.95 (0-8239-2775-X). This book explores the drug Ritalin, widely used for attention deficit disorder, and presents the controversies surrounding it. (Rev: BL 5/15/99) [616.85]

5616 Benner, Janet. *Smoking Cigarettes: The Unfiltered Truth—Understanding Why and How to Quit* (9–12). 1987, Joelle paper $10.95 (0-942723-12-0). An account that describes the physical effects of smoking on the body and outlines various methods of quitting. (Rev: BL 12/15/87) [613.85]

5617 Berger, Gilda. *Alcoholism and the Family* (8–12). (Changing Family) 1993, Watts LB $25.00 (0-531-12548-3). This discussion of alcoholism, presented in question-and-answer format, focuses on its effects on the family and covers causes, prevention, treatment, and recovery. (Rev: BL 1/15/94; SLJ 12/93; VOYA 2/94) [362.29]

5618 Berger, Gilda, and Nancy Levitin. *Crack* (6–12). 1995, Watts LB $23.60 (0-531-11188-1). Emphasizes the dangers of crack to users, the cost to society, and crack's ability to claim innocent victims: crack babies. (Rev: BL 5/1/95) [362.29]

5619 Biggers, Jeff. *Transgenerational Addiction* (6–9). (Drug Abuse Prevention Library) 1998, Rosen LB $18.40 (0-8239-2757-1); Hazelden Information & Educational Services paper $6.95 (1-56838-247-2). This book deals with entire families that battle addiction to drugs and alcohol, and how each member must deal with the challenge individually. (Rev: BL 5/15/98) [362.29 13]

5620 Boyd, George A. *Drugs and Sex* (5–10). Illus. (Drug Abuse Prevention Library) 1994, Rosen LB $17.95 (0-8239-1538-7). A careful examination of the hazards of combining drugs and sex, including unsafe sex, pregnancy, AIDS, and other sexually transmitted diseases. (Rev: BL 6/1–15/94; SLJ 5/94) [613.9]

5621 Carroll, Marilyn. *Cocaine and Crack* (9–12). (Drug Library) 1994, Enslow LB $19.95 (0-89490-472-8). Everything you need to know about crack and cocaine. (Rev: BL 4/15/95; SLJ 4/95; VOYA 5/95) [616.86]

5622 Claypool, Jane. *Alcohol and You*. 3rd ed. (6–10). (Impact Books: Drugs and Alcohol) 1997, Watts $24.00 (0-531-11351-5). A readable new edition of a standard, well-respected work on alcohol and teenage drinking problems. (Rev: BR 5–6/98; SLJ 2/98) [613.8]

5623 Clayton, Lawrence. *Diet Pill Drug Dangers* (5–9). (Drug Dangers) 1999, Enslow $19.95 (0-7660-1158-5). With liberal use of case histories, this book explores the dangers of diet pill use, their effects on the human body, and prevention techniques. (Rev: SLJ 9/99) [362.29]

5624 Clayton, Lawrence. *Tranquilizers* (7–10). Illus. (Drug Library) 1997, Enslow LB $19.95 (0-89490-849-9). Information is presented about tranquilizers, their beneficial effects, and the potential consequences of abuse and addiction. (Rev: BL 3/15/97; SLJ 6/97) [615]

5625 Clayton, Lawrence. *Working Together Against Drug Addiction* (6–10). 1996, Rosen LB $16.95 (0-8239-2263-4). In addition to discussing drugs and addiction, this work takes an activist approach by providing ways for teens to locate drug and alcohol counselors and programs and ways they can become involved and make a difference. (Rev: SLJ 5/97) [362]

5626 Condon, Judith. *The Pressure to Take Drugs* (5–8). Illus. 1990, Watts LB $20.80 (0-531-10934-8). This book gives specific advice to young people on how to avoid drugs and how to respond when solicitations are made. (Rev: BL 8/90) [362.29]

5627 Connelly, Elizabeth Russell. *Through a Glass Darkly: The Psychological Effects of Marijuana and Hashish* (8–12). (Encyclopedia of Psychological Disorders) 1999, Chelsea $24.95 (0-7910-4897-7). After an overview of the history of marijuana and hashish, this volume surveys their medicinal and recreational use, effects of interaction with other drugs, potential disorders from their use, the dangers of addiction, and treatments available. (Rev: VOYA 8/99) [362.29]

5628 Croft, Jennifer. *Drugs & the Legalization Debate* (6–10). Illus. (Drug Abuse Prevention Library) 1997, Rosen LB $17.95 (0-8239-2509-9). A well-balanced presentation of the pros and cons of legalizing drugs, along with a discussion of drug abuse and penalties and a brief look at how other countries deal with the issue. (Rev: SLJ 5/98) [362.29]

5629 Croft, Jennifer. *PCP: High Risk on the Streets* (7–10). (Drug Abuse Prevention Library) 1998, Rosen LB $17.95 (0-8239-2774-1). This book provides readers with important information about phencyclidine, or angel dust, the behavior it produces, and its dangers. (Rev: BL 11/15/98; BR 1–2/99; SLJ 12/98) [362.29]

5630 Debenedette, Valerie. *Caffeine* (8–10). (Drug Library) 1996, Enslow LB $19.95 (0-89490-741-7). A well-documented, well-organized look at caffeine, where it is found, its effects, and its abuse. (Rev: BL 9/15/96; SLJ 9/96) [615]

5631 Galas, Judith C. *Drugs and Sports* (5–8). Illus. (Overview) 1997, Lucent LB $22.45 (1-56006-185-5). The kinds of illegal drugs that are taken by athletes and the reasons are discussed, with material on how their use can be detected. (Rev: BL 3/15/97; BR 11–12/97) [362.29]

5632 Gilbert, Richard J. *Caffeine: The Most Popular Stimulant* (8–12). Illus. 1986, Chelsea LB $19.95 (0-87754-756-4). Tea, coffee, and chocolate are covered in this account of what the author calls "the most popular drug in the world." (Rev: BL 7/86) [615]

5633 Glass, George. *Drugs and Fitting In* (6–9). Illus. (Drug Abuse Prevention Library) 1998, Rosen LB $17.95 (0-8239-2554-4). After a description of teen culture and its pressures to conform and be popular, this book presents alternatives and advice on how to remain drug-free. (Rev: BL 3/15/98; BR 9–10/98; VOYA 6/98) [362.29]

5634 Glass, George. *Narcotics: Dangerous Painkillers* (6–9). Illus. (Drug Abuse Prevention Library) 1998, Rosen $16.95 (0-8239-2719-9). This book explains the dangers of abusing prescribed painkilling drugs and their street derivatives, including death, and discusses issues related to addiction and treatment. (Rev: BL 5/15/98; SLJ 10/98) [616.86 32]

5635 Glowa, John R. *Inhalants: The Toxic Fumes* (9–12). Illus. 1986, Chelsea LB $19.95 (0-87754-758-0). The dangers of using such inhalants as shoe polish are described and places where help can be obtained are given. (Rev: BL 2/15/87) [616.86]

5636 *Go Ask Alice* (9–12). 1971, Avon paper $4.50 (0-380-00523-9). A harrowing account in diary form of a 15-year-old girl's drug addiction and its consequences. [613.8]

5637 Goldish, Meish. *Dangers of Herbal Stimulants* (6–10). Illus. (Drug Abuse Prevention Library) 1997, Rosen LB $17.95 (0-8239-2555-2). Teens are enticed to use herbal substances to get high, lose weight, or solve other emotional and physical problems. This book describes the products available, their potential dangers, and the laws that regulate their use. (Rev: SLJ 5/98; VOYA 2/99) [362.29]

5638 Grabish, Beatrice R. *Drugs and Your Brain* (6–10). Illus. (Drug Abuse Prevention Library) 1998, Rosen paper $6.95 (1-56838-214-6). This book describes how drugs affect the brain and the risks of permanent as well as short-term damage. (Rev: BL 4/15/98; BR 9–10/98; SLJ 6/98) [616.86]

5639 Grosshandler-Smith, Janet. *Working Together Against Drinking and Driving* (4–8). (The Library of Social Activism) 1996, Rosen LB $16.95 (0-8239-2259-6). With an emphasis on prevention, the author presents a general discussion on drinking and driving and its consequences, followed by pointers on how to avoid embarrassing situations and how to handle peer pressure about drinking. (Rev: SLJ 2/97) [613.8]

5640 Gwynne, Peter. *Who Uses Drugs?* (7–10). Illus. 1987, Chelsea LB $19.95 (1-55546-223-5). An overview of different kinds of drugs and who uses them. (Rev: BL 5/1/88) [362.2]

5641 Hanan, Jessica. *When Someone You Love Is Addicted* (5–9). (Drug Abuse Prevention Library) 1999, Rosen $17.95 (0-8239-2831-4). This work describes alcohol and drug addiction, when and when not to intervene, and where to go for help. (Rev: SLJ 7/99) [362.29]

5642 Harris, Jacqueline L. *Drugs and Disease* (5–8). (Bodies in Crisis) 1993, Twenty-First Century LB $14.95 (0-8050-2602-9). Case studies are included in this book about drug abuse. (Rev: BL 1/15/94) [616.86]

5643 Harris, Jonathan. *This Drinking Nation* (7–12). 1994, Four Winds paper $15.95 (0-02-742744-7). Discusses America's alcohol consumption from 1607 to the present, including information on the Prohibition period of 1920–1933. Also examines teenage drinking and alcoholism. (Rev: BL 7/94; SLJ 9/94; VOYA 10/94) [394.1]

5644 Harris, Neil. *Drugs and Crime* (6–10). Illus. 1989, Watts LB $20.80 (0-531-10800-7). This account traces the connection between addiction and crime from the city streets to international syndicates. (Rev: SLJ 4/90) [613.8]

5645 Haughton, Emma. *Alcohol* (7–10). (Talking Points) 1999, Raintree Steck-Vaughn LB $27.11 (0-8172-5318-1). A candid look at the use and abuse of alcohol and its physical and emotional effects. (Rev: BL 8/99; BR 9–10/99) [613.8]

5646 Haughton, Emma. *A Right to Smoke?* (4–8). (Viewpoints) 1997, Watts LB $22.50 (0-531-14412-7). Using double-page spreads, this book offers different viewpoints on who smokes, why they start, the physical dangers, second-hand smoke, the tobacco industry giants, taxes on cigarettes, advertising, and programs to discourage people from smoking. (Rev: BL 6/1–15/97; SLJ 5/97) [362.2]

5647 Hirschfelder, Arlene. *Kick Butts: A Kid's Action Guide* (5–8). 1998, Silver Burdett $19.95 (0-382-39632-4); paper $9.95 (0-382-39633-2). This book describes the history of smoking in the United States and its connection with various diseases, followed by examples of steps taken by young anti-smoking activists to create a smoke-free environment. The *Kids Action Guide* also suggests activities for kids to help others stop smoking and advice on how to quit. (Rev: BL 6/1–15/98; SLJ 7/98; VOYA 2/99) [613.85]

5648 Hoobler, Thomas, and Dorothy Hoobler. *Drugs & Crime* (7–12). Illus. 1987, Chelsea LB $19.95 (1-

55546-228-6). An account of how the drug traffic is fostered by layers of crime and corruption both international and local. (Rev: BL 3/15/88; SLJ 5/88) [364.2]

5649 Hyde, Margaret O. *Drug Wars* (7–12). 1990, Walker LB $12.85 (0-8027-6901-2). This account discusses the violence and despair that crack cocaine has brought to America and ways in which its production and distribution can be halted. (Rev: SLJ 6/90; VOYA 6/90) [616.86]

5650 Hyde, Margaret O. *Know about Drugs.* 4th ed. (5–8). 1995, Walker LB $27.90 (0-8027-8395-3). An introduction to drugs and their effects, including marijuana, alcohol, PCP, inhalants, crack/cocaine, heroin, and nicotine. (Rev: SLJ 3/96) [362.2]

5651 Jamiolkowski, Raymond M. *Drugs and Domestic Violence* (7–12). (Drug Abuse Prevention Library) 1996, Rosen LB $17.95 (0-8239-2062-3). This volume points out that domestic violence increases when drugs are used in the home and gives pointers to teens in these situations on how to stay safe. (Rev: SLJ 3/96) [362.2]

5652 Jones, Ralph. *Straight Talk: Answers to Questions Young People Ask about Alcohol* (7–9). 1989, TAB paper $4.95 (0-8306-9005-0). Fifty questions concerning alcohol and physical and psychological effects are answered in this short, straightforward book. (Rev: VOYA 12/89) [661]

5653 Keyishian, Elizabeth. *Everything You Need to Know about Smoking* (6–10). Illus. 1989, Rosen $24.50 (0-8239-1017-2). This book covers such topics as why people smoke, its effects, and how to quit. (Rev: SLJ 2/90) [613.8]

5654 Klein, Wendy. *Drugs and Denial* (7–10). (Drug Abuse Prevention Library) 1998, Rosen LB $17.95 (0-8239-2773-3). This book describes the signs of addiction and the stages of adolescent drug use, helps teens to admit it if they have a drug problem, and provides tips for teens to help people they know who may be in denial. (Rev: BL 11/15/98) [362.29]

5655 Knox, Jean McBee. *Drinking, Driving & Drugs* (7–10). Illus. 1988, Chelsea LB $19.95 (1-55546-231-6). An overview of this national problem that focuses on teenage offenders and victims. (Rev: BL 7/88; BR 1–2/89; SLJ 9/88) [363.1]

5656 Lamberg, Lynne. *Drugs & Sleep* (8–12). Illus. 1987, Chelsea LB $19.95 (1-55546-213-8). The nature of sleep is explored and the effects that drugs have on it are described. (Rev: BL 5/1/88; SLJ 4/88) [616.8]

5657 Landau, Elaine. *Hooked: Talking about Addictions* (6–10). 1995, Millbrook LB $21.90 (1-56294-469-X). Vignettes from real-life situations are used to explain the causes and effects of different types of addictions and to provide advice to young people in trouble with drugs. (Rev: BL 1/1/96; SLJ 1/96) [362.2]

5658 Landau, Elaine. *Teenage Drinking* (7–12). (Issues in Focus) 1994, Enslow LB $19.95 (0-89490-575-9). This book focuses on the causes and effects of teenage drinking and prevention measures that have worked. (Rev: BL 11/15/94; SLJ 11/94; VOYA 12/94) [362.29]

5659 Lang, Susan S., and Beth H. Marks. *Teens and Tobacco: A Fatal Attraction* (7–12). Illus. 1996, Twenty-First Century LB $17.98 (0-8050-3768-3). Along with quotes from teens who smoke, this book describes the attraction of smoking, advertising tactics, health costs, and current concerns of the tobacco industry. (Rev: BL 7/96; BR 9–10/96; SLJ 6/96; VOYA 8/96) [362.29]

5660 Lee, Mary Price, and Richard S. Lee. *Drugs and Codependency* (6–10). (Drug Abuse Prevention Library) 1995, Rosen LB $17.95 (0-8239-2065-8). This book explores the vulnerability of teens who live in a household where drugs are abused. (Rev: BL 9/15/95; SLJ 10/95) [616.869]

5661 Lee, Mary Price, and Richard S. Lee. *Drugs and the Media* (5–10). Illus. (Drug Abuse Prevention Library) 1994, Rosen LB $17.95 (0-8239-1537-9). This book shows that the media often unintentionally glamorize drug use and describes how teens can evaluate the media's mixed messages. (Rev: BL 6/1–15/94; SLJ 5/94) [070.4]

5662 Levine, Herbert M. *The Drug Problem* (7–12). Illus. (American Issues Debated) 1997, Raintree Steck-Vaughn $27.83 (0-8172-4354-2). The pros and cons of issues related to drugs are presented fairly, with discussion on the effectiveness of the war on drugs, decriminalizing drugs, and the possible discrimination against minorities in our drug policies. (Rev: BL 11/15/97; BR 1–2/98; VOYA 4/98) [362.2]

5663 Littell, Mary Ann. *Heroin Drug Dangers* (5–8). (Drug Dangers) 1999, Enslow $19.95 (0-7660-1156-9). Anecdotes, facts, and statistics are used effectively in this book that describes heroin and its effects. (Rev: BL 9/15/99) [362.29]

5664 Littell, Mary Ann. *LSD* (6–9). Illus. (The Drug Library) 1996, Enslow LB $19.95 (0-89490-739-5). A history of the drug, details on how it is made, its different forms, and the physical and psychological effects of its use. (Rev: BL 12/1/96; BR 3–4/97; SLJ 4/97) [362.29]

5665 Lukas, Scott E. *Steroids* (7–10). (Drug Library) 1994, Enslow LB $19.95 (0-89490-471-X). An exploration of the physical, psychological, and legal consequences of using steroids. (Rev: BL 1/1/95; SLJ 1/95; VOYA 4/95) [362.29]

5666 McGuire, Paula. *Alcohol* (4–8). Illus. (Preteen Pressures) 1998, Raintree Steck-Vaughn LB $24.26 (0-8172-5026-3). This volume provides preteens with facts about how alcohol affects the body, warning signs of alcoholism, fetal alcohol syndrome, and other dangers of the misuse of alcohol. (Rev: BL 4/15/98) [362.29]

5667 McLaughlin, Miriam S., and Sandra P. Hazouri. *Addiction: The "High" That Brings You Down* (7–12). (Teen Issues) 1997, Enslow LB $19.95 (0-89490-915-0). This honest, accurate book lists causes of addiction, characteristics, and the results of compulsive, uncontrolled behavior, with a focus on the roles played by various members and an emphasis on where teenage addicts can find help and support at school and in the community. (Rev: SLJ 8/97; VOYA 10/97) [362.29]

5668 McMillan, Daniel. *Teen Smoking: Understanding the Risk* (6–12). (Issues in Focus) 1998, Enslow LB $17.95 (0-89490-722-0). An interesting, informative account that discusses nicotine addiction, secondhand smoke, health hazards, smoking prevention, and treatments for people who want to stop. (Rev: VOYA 8/98) [362.2]

5669 Madsen, Christine. *Drinking and Driving* (6–10). Illus. 1989, Watts LB $20.80 (0-531-10799-X). The effects of alcohol are outlined in relation to driving. Material on how society is penalizing drunk drivers is also presented. (Rev: SLJ 4/90) [613.8]

5670 Marshall, Eliot. *Legalization: A Debate* (7–10). Illus. 1988, Chelsea LB $19.95 (1-55546-229-4). Using a trial format, this is a pro-and-con examination of the possible legalization of marijuana. (Rev: BL 6/15/88; SLJ 6/88) [344.73]

5671 Meer, Jeff. *Drugs & Sports* (7–12). Illus. 1987, Chelsea LB $19.95 (1-55546-226-X). An account that explains how various drugs affect an athlete's performance and how this abuse is being viewed by segments of the athletic world. (Rev: BL 11/1/87) [613]

5672 Miller, Maryann. *Drugs and Date Rape* (6–10). (Drug Abuse Prevention Library) 1995, Rosen LB $15.95 (0-8239-2064-X). This book shows how drugs can break down important inhibitors, possibly leading to date rape, and how to avoid becoming a victim. (Rev: BL 9/15/95; SLJ 10/95) [362.88]

5673 Miller, Maryann. *Drugs and Gun Violence* (6–10). (Drug Abuse Prevention Library) 1995, Rosen LB $17.95 (0-8239-2060-7). This book explores the connection between violent crimes and drug use with lessons that teens can use for survival. (Rev: BL 9/15/95; SLJ 10/95) [364.2]

5674 Miller, Maryann. *Drugs and Violent Crime* (6–10). (Drug Abuse Prevention Library) 1996, Rosen LB $17.95 (0-8239-2282-0). This book gives general information about drugs and their effects and explores the relationship between drug use and violent crime. (Rev: SLJ 3/97) [362.29]

5675 Mitchell, Hayley R. *Teen Alcoholism* (7–12). Illus. (Teen Issues) 1997, Lucent LB $22.45 (1-56006-514-1). This book defines alcoholism and explains its causes, prevention, symptoms, and recovery programs. (Rev: BL 2/1/98) [362.29]

5676 Monroe, Judy. *Antidepressants* (7–10). (The Drug Library) 1997, Enslow LB $19.95 (0-89490-848-0). Current information is given about these frequently abused drugs, actual case studies are cited, and discussion questions provided. (Rev: BL 5/15/97) [616.85]

5677 Monroe, Judy. *Inhalant Drug Dangers* (5–9). 1999, Enslow $18.95 (0-7660-1153-4). Inhalant drugs are introduced, using case histories to describe their effects, with material on treatment programs and prevention strategies. (Rev: BL 8/99; SLJ 9/99) [362.29]

5678 Monroe, Judy. *Nicotine* (7–10). (Drug Library) 1995, Enslow LB $19.95 (0-89490-505-8). This provides a concise, easy-to-use look at nicotine, where it is found, its effects, and how to avoid its use. (Rev: BL 7/95; SLJ 9/95) [613.85]

5679 Monroe, Judy. *Steroid Drug Dangers* (5–8). Illus. (Drug Dangers) 1999, Enslow $19.95 (0-7660-1154-2). Both legal and illegal steroids, their uses and their effects, are covered in this colorful, well-organized book. (Rev: BL 9/15/99) [362.29]

5680 Murdico, Suzanne J. *Drug Abuse* (4–8). (Pre-teen Pressures) 1998, Raintree Steck-Vaughn $24.97 (0-8172-5027-1). This work discusses drug abuse and how it affects everyone, with material on healthy alternatives and solutions to typical drug-related problems faced by many young people. (Rev: BL 5/15/98) [362.2]

5681 Myers, Arthur. *Drugs and Emotions* (6–10). (Drug Abuse Prevention Library) 1996, Rosen LB $17.95 (0-8239-2283-9). This book explains how teens may be attracted to drugs as a way of dealing with feelings of sadness, pain, confusion, and frustration, and how they can become hooked to both legal and illegal drugs. Much of the discussion deals with how to recognize that a problem exists and where to get help. (Rev: SLJ 3/97) [362.29]

5682 Myers, Arthur. *Drugs and Peer Pressure* (6–10). (Drug Abuse Prevention Library) 1995, Rosen LB $17.95 (0-8239-2066-6). An exploration of peer pressure as a major reason that teens begin to use drugs, with suggestions for resisting it. (Rev: BL 9/15/95; SLJ 10/95) [362.29]

5683 Newman, Gerald, and Eleanor N. Layfield. *PCP* (7–10). (Drug Library) 1997, Enslow LB $19.95 (0-89490-852-9). Case studies, discussion questions, and chapter notes are highlights of this informative book on PCP, a frequently abused drug. (Rev: BL 12/15/97; BR 3–4/98; SLJ 12/97) [362.2]

5684 Newton, David E. *Drug Testing: An Issue for School, Sports and Work* (6–12). Illus. (In Focus) 1999, Enslow $19.95 (0-89490-954-1). The question of civil rights vs. drug testing is explored in this volume that presents extreme positions and viewpoints in between. (Rev: BL 4/1/99; BR 5–6/99; SLJ 4/99) [658.3]

5685 Oliver, Marilyn Tower. *Drugs: Should They Be Legalized?* (7–12). 1996, Enslow LB $19.95 (0-89490-738-7). After a clear presentation of the facts, this account supplies strong arguments for each side of the drug legalization controversy. (Rev: BL 9/15/96; SLJ 3/97) [362.29]

5686 Packard, Helen C. *Prozac: The Controversial Cure* (6–9). Illus. (Drug Abuse Prevention Library) 1998, Rosen LB $16.95 (0-8239-2551-X). This book explores the controversy around this antidepressant, called the miracle drug of the 1990s, and gives teens sound advice concerning its use and misuse. (Rev: BL 5/15/98; SLJ 10/98) [616.85 27061]

5687 Pietrusza, David. *Smoking* (7–10). (Overview) 1997, Lucent LB $17.96 (1-56006-186-3). In addition to discussing why people smoke and the effects of smoking, this book covers topics like the rights of smokers and nonsmokers, lawsuits against tobacco companies, and how cigarette advertisements influence people. (Rev: BL 8/97; BR 11–12/97; SLJ 7/97; VOYA 8/97) [362.2]

5688 Pringle, Laurence. *Drinking: A Risky Business* (6–9). Illus. 1997, Morrow $16.00 (0-688-15044-6). A well-documented book about the toll that alcohol has taken on society over the years, its pervasiveness, and how alcohol peddling is a big business. (Rev: BL 12/15/97; BR 3–4/98; SLJ 1/98) [362.292]

5689 Pringle, Laurence. *Smoking: A Risky Business* (5–10). 1996, Morrow $16.00 (0-688-13039-9). After a history of tobacco, this book describes the dangers of smoking and the advertising strategies used to get people to smoke. (Rev: BL 12/1/96; SLJ 1/97; VOYA 4/97) [362.2]

5690 Robbins, Paul R. *Crack and Cocaine Drug Dangers* (5–9). (Drug Dangers) 1999, Enslow $19.95 (0-7660-1155-0). The use of cocaine, its effects, addiction, and consequences are introduced using case studies, good factual information, and statistics. (Rev: BL 9/15/99) [362.29]

5691 Robbins, Paul R. *Designer Drugs* (7–12). (Drug Library) 1995, Enslow LB $19.95 (0-89490-488-4). An exploration of the growing problem of drugs made by "kitchen chemists." (Rev: BL 5/1/95; SLJ 5/95) [362.29]

5692 Robbins, Paul R. *Hallucinogens* (7–10). Illus. (Drug Library) 1996, Enslow LB $19.95 (0-89490-

743-3). Drugs that cause auditory and visual hallucinations are described, along with their availability, dangerous effects, and current use. (Rev: BL 6/1–15/96; SLJ 7/96; VOYA 8/96) [362.29]

5693 Rogak, Lisa A. *Steroids: Dangerous Game* (6–9). 1992, Lerner LB $19.93 (0-8225-0048-5). Discusses what steroids are and why they are so dangerous physically and psychologically. Covers drug testing, use of steroids in sports, and tips for training without them. (Rev: BL 2/15/93; SLJ 12/92) [362.29]

5694 Roleff, Tamara L., and Mary Williams, eds. *Tobacco & Smoking* (8–12). (Opposing Viewpoints) 1998, Greenhaven LB $20.96 (1-56510-803-5); paper $20.25 (1-56510-802-7). This anthology presents different opinions on such topics as the health effects of smoking, the influence of tobacco advertising, government intervention, and possible controls on the tobacco industry. (Rev: BL 6/1–15/98) [613.8]

5695 Salak, John. *Drugs in Society: Are They Our Suicide Pill?* (6–9). (Issues of Our Time) 1993, Twenty-First Century LB $18.90 (0-8050-2572-3). Current opinions and treatments for drug addiction are discussed in this book that examines how common drugs of all types are used and abused in our society. (Rev: BL 1/15/94) [362.29]

5696 Sanders, Pete, and Steve Myers. *Drinking Alcohol* (4–8). Illus. (What Do You Know About) 1997, Millbrook LB $20.90 (0-7613-0573-4). An introduction to alcohol use and abuse, with material on how alcohol affects the body and behavior. (Rev: SLJ 10/97) [613.8]

5697 Santamaria, Peggy. *Drugs and Politics* (6–10). (Drug Abuse Prevention Library) 1994, Rosen LB $17.95 (0-8239-1703-7). A discussion of the influence of drugs in politics, such as in Colombia, where the government is involved with and intimidated by powerful drug interests. (Rev: BL 3/15/95; SLJ 3/95) [363.4]

5698 Schleichert, Elizabeth. *Marijuana* (7–10). Illus. (Drug Library) 1996, Enslow LB $19.95 (0-89490-740-9). This easy-to-read account discusses the history of marijuana use, its effects, availability, and controversies surrounding it, such as whether to legalize it. (Rev: BL 6/1–15/96; SLJ 7/96; VOYA 8/96) [362.29]

5699 Schleifer, Jay. *Methamphetamine: Speed Kills* (5–9). (Drug Abuse Prevention Library) 1999, Rosen LB $16.95 (0-8239-2512-9). Methamphetamine, or speed, is a dangerous drug to which many teens are becoming addicted. This book describes the drug, its effects, the crime and violence associated with it, and agencies and organizations where help is available. (Rev: SLJ 7/99) [362.29]

5700 Schnoll, Sidney. *Getting Help: Treatments for Drug Abuse* (7–12). Illus. 1986, Chelsea LB $19.95 (0-87754-775-0). This book concentrates on the many kinds of treatments available and the agencies involved in supplying this help. (Rev: BL 2/15/87) [362.2]

5701 Serry, Clifford. *Drugs and Eating Disorders* (5–10). Illus. (Drug Abuse Prevention Library) 1994, Rosen LB $17.75 (0-8239-1540-9). The book shows how diet pills and other weight-loss products can lead to drug abuse and, in some cases, addiction. (Rev: BL 6/1–15/94; SLJ 6/94) [616.85]

5702 Sherry, Clifford J. *Inhalants* (5–10). 1994, Rosen LB $14.95 (0-8239-1704-5). Definitions of inhalants are given, where they are found, and how they affect the body. (Rev: BL 2/15/95; SLJ 3/95) [362.29]

5703 Shuker, Nancy. *Everything You Need to Know about an Alcoholic Parent.* Rev. ed. (7–12). Illus. 1998, Rosen $17.95 (0-8239-2869-1). After a general discussion of alcoholism, Shuker explains how it changes human relationships and how young people can cope with it. (Rev: BL 1/15/90; BR 3–4/90; VOYA 4/90) [362.29]

5704 Silverstein, Alvin, and Virginia Silverstein. *Alcoholism* (7–10). 1975, HarperCollins LB $12.89 (0-397-31648-8). Alcohol use and abuse are introduced, plus alcoholism and the problems it causes. [613.8]

5705 Simpson, Carolyn. *Methadone* (5–9). (Drug Abuse Prevention Library) 1997, Rosen LB $15.95 (0-8239-2286-3). The dangers of heroin are discussed, followed by an objective discussion of the pros and cons of methadone, the legal drug used to combat heroin addiction. (Rev: SLJ 11/97) [362.29]

5706 Smith, C. Fraser. *Lenny, Lefty, and the Chancellor* (9–12). 1992, Bancroft paper $12.95 (0-9631246-0-9). When a college basketball star dies of a drug overdose, school officials attempt to avoid a scandal. (Rev: BL 3/15/92; SLJ 8/92) [796.323]

5707 Sonder, Ben. *Dangerous Legacy: The Babies of Drug-Taking Parents* (7–12). 1994, Watts LB $23.60 (0-531-11195-4). Discusses the effects drugs have on a developing fetus. (Rev: BL 12/1/94; SLJ 2/95; VOYA 4/95) [362.29]

5708 Steins, Richard. *Alcohol Abuse: Is This Danger on the Rise?* (6–9). (Issues of Our Time) 1995, Twenty-First Century LB $15.98 (0-8050-3882-5). Includes a definition of alcoholism, the disease's short- and long-term effects on a family, the physical effects on young drinkers, peer pressure, and drinking and driving. (Rev: BL 10/15/95; SLJ 2/96) [362.29]

5709 Stewart, Gail B., ed. *Drugs & Sports* (7–10). (Opposing Viewpoints Digests) 1998, Greenhaven LB $17.96 (1-56510-749-7); paper $13.70 (1-56510-748-9). Covering topics like the prevention and prevalence of drug use and abuse, and the legitimacy of drug testing, this volume explores drugs in both amateur and professional sports. (Rev: BL 8/98) [362.29]

5710 Strazzabosco-Hayn, Gina. *Drugs and Sleeping Disorders* (7–12). (Drug Abuse Prevention Library) 1996, Rosen LB $17.95 (0-8239-2144-1). This book describes sleep disorders and potential problems and dangers of using drugs for sleep. (Rev: SLJ 3/96) [362.2]

5711 Swisher, Karin L. *Drug Trafficking* (9–12). (Current Controversies) 1991, Greenhaven LB $19.95 (0-89908-576-8); paper $16.20 (0-89908-582-2). The pros and cons of waging a war on drugs, legalizing drugs, and campaigns to stem the flow of drugs into the United States. (Rev: BL 6/15/92; SLJ 5/92) [363.4]

5712 Swisher, Karin L., ed. *Legalizing Drugs* (8–12). (At Issue) 1996, Greenhaven LB $11.95 (1-56410-379-3); paper $11.20 (1-56510-378-5). Would legalizing drugs end the stalemate on the war on drugs or simply admit defeat? This issue is argued through a series of provocative articles that express different viewpoints. (Rev: BL 1/1–15/96) [364.1]

5713 Terkel, Susan N. *The Drug Laws: A Time for Change?* (9–12). Illus. 1997, Watts LB $25.00 (0-531-11316-7). A thorough discussion of current drug policies, with attention to arguments for and against legalizing drugs and how this controversy relates to moral, medical, health, economic, and social concerns. (Rev: BL 10/1/97) [364.1]

5714 Thompson, Stephen P., ed. *War on Drugs* (7–12). (Opposing Viewpoints) 1998, Greenhaven LB $21.96 (1-56510-805-1); paper $16.20 (1-56510-804-3). In this anthology of various opinions, questions are raised about the techniques used in the war against drugs, the nature of new strategies, and whether some drugs, particularly marijuana, should be legalized under certain conditions. (Rev: BL 7/98) [363.4]

5715 Torr, James D., ed. *Drug Abuse* (8–12). (Opposing Viewpoints) 1999, Greenhaven LB $27.45 (0-7377-0051-3); paper $20.25 (0-7377-0050-5). This collection of articles and essays debates such topics as how serious the nation's drug problem is, what programs are effective, the value of government policies, and the legalization of selected drugs. (Rev: BL 4/15/99) [362.29]

5716 Trapani, Margi. *Inside a Support Group: Help for Teenage Children of Alcoholics* (6–9). Illus. (Drug Abuse Prevention Library) 1997, Rosen LB $15.95 (0-8239-2508-0). Teens with alcoholic parents get helpful information from this inside look at Alateen, an organization designed to help teens cope with a loved one's addiction to alcohol. (Rev: BL 12/15/97; SLJ 1/98) [362.292]

5717 Washburne, Carolyn K. *Drug Abuse* (5–8). Illus. (Overview) 1996, Lucent LB $18.96 (1-56006-169-3). A carefully researched presentation of important background information on drug abuse and current practices and problems. (Rev: BL 1/1–15/96; VOYA 8/96) [362.29]

5718 Webb, Margot. *Drugs and Gangs* (7–12). (Drug Abuse Prevention Library) 1996, Rosen LB $17.95 (0-8239-2059-3). This book describes the connections between gangs and drugs, in both selling and using, and provides teens with tips on how to avoid these dangers. (Rev: SLJ 3/96; VOYA 6/96) [362.29]

5719 Weir, William. *In the Shadow of the Dope Fiend: America's War on Drugs* (9–12). 1995, Shoe String LB $35.00 (0-208-02384-4). A social history of drug use. (Rev: BL 4/1/95; VOYA 12/95) [363.4]

5720 Wekesser, Carol, ed. *Alcoholism* (9–12). (Current Controversies) 1994, Greenhaven LB $20.96 (1-56510-074-3); paper $16.20 (1-56510-073-5). An anthology that covers the question of whether alcoholism is a disease, the most effective treatments, the effect of alcohol advertisements, and help for the children of alcoholics. (Rev: BL 4/15/94; SLJ 3/94) [362.29]

5721 Wekesser, Carol, ed. *Chemical Dependency* (8–12). Illus. (Opposing Viewpoints) 1997, Greenhaven LB $21.96 (1-56510-552-4); paper $16.20 (1-56510-551-6). Such topics as the magnitude of chemical dependency, the causes, treatments, and the possible reforming of drug laws are discussed in this collection of articles. (Rev: BL 7/97; BR 1–2/98) [362.29]

5722 Wekesser, Carol, ed. *Smoking* (7–12). (Current Controversies) 1996, Greenhaven LB $20.96 (1-56510-534-6); paper $16.20 (1-56510-533-8). This collection of various opinions about smoking covers health risks, the amount of blame that tobacco companies should assume, measures to combat smoking, and the degree that the government can interfere. (Rev: BL 12/15/96; BR 11–12/97; SLJ 3/97) [362.29]

5723 Wilkinson, Beth. *Drugs and Depression* (6–12). Illus. (Drug Abuse Prevention Library) 1994, Rosen $17.95 (0-8239-3004-1). Some young people turn to drugs to deal with their depression. This book shows the dangers in this approach and offers positive ways of handling depression and places to get assistance. (Rev: BL 6/1–15/94) [616.86]

5724 Winters, Paul A., ed. *Teen Addiction* (7–12). (Current Controversies) 1997, Greenhaven LB $26.20 (1-56510-536-2). The causes, effects, prevention, and regulation of teenage drug, tobacco, and alcohol consumption are explored in a series of documents expressing different opinions. (Rev: BL 2/15/97; SLJ 3/97) [362.29]

5725 Woods, Geraldine. *Heroin* (7–10). (Drug Library) 1994, Enslow LB $19.95 (0-89490-473-6). A well-researched, clearly written, and carefully sourced book about heroin use and addiction. (Rev: BL 1/1/95; SLJ 1/95; VOYA 4/95) [362.29]

5726 Ziemer, Maryann. *Quaaludes* (7–10). Illus. (Drug Library) 1997, Enslow LB $19.95 (0-89490-847-2). The uses and effects of these frequently prescribed drugs are discussed, along with problems of misuse and addiction. (Rev: BL 3/15/97; SLJ 6/97) [613.8]

Diseases and Illnesses

5727 Altman, Linda J. *Plague & Pestilence: A History of Infectious Disease* (6–12). Illus. (Issues in Focus) 1998, Enslow LB $19.95 (0-89490-957-6). A history of plagues and epidemics in world history, from the Black Death and leprosy to AIDS and spinal meningitis. (Rev: BL 3/1/99; SLJ 1/99) [614.4]

5728 Benowitz, Steven I. *Cancer* (7–12). (Diseases and People) 1999, Enslow $19.95 (0-7660-1181-X). A discussion of the nature and treatment of various forms of cancer and possible cures in the future. (Rev: BL 9/15/99) [616.994]

5729 Beshore, George. *Sickle Cell Anemia* (7–12). 1994, Watts LB $25.00 (0-531-12510-6). An informative overview that includes a history of the disease, how it is transmitted from parent to child, and the importance of genetic testing. (Rev: BL 1/1/95; SLJ 1/95; VOYA 4/95) [616.1]

5730 Biddle, Wayne. *Field Guide to Germs* (9–12). 1995, Holt $22.50 (0-8050-3531-1). Historical information on the various bacteria and viruses that attack humans, presented in an informal, humorous way. (Rev: BL 8/95; SLJ 1/96) [616]

5731 Biskup, Michael D., and Karin L. Swisher, eds. *AIDS* (7–12). (Opposing Viewpoints) 1992, Greenhaven paper $16.20 (0-89908-165-7). The pros and cons of AIDS as a moral issue, effectiveness of testing and treatment, and prevention of the disease's spread. (Rev: BL 11/15/92) [362.1]

5732 Bode, Janet. *Food Fight: A Guide to Eating Disorders for Pre-Teens and Their Parents* (6–10). 1997, Simon & Schuster paper $16.00 (0-689-80272-2). Using interviews with young people who have experienced the anger and self-loathing associated with eating disorders, this book explains the nature and causes of these problems, and treatments. (Rev: BL 6/1–15/97; BR 11–12/97; SLJ 8/97; VOYA 8/97) [616.85]

5733 Brodman, Michael, et al. *Straight Talk about Sexually Transmitted Diseases* (7–12). (Straight Talk About) 1993, Facts on File $24.95 (0-8160-2864-8). Discusses the ways sexually transmitted diseases are contracted, symptoms, possible consequences, and treatment. (Rev: BL 3/15/94; SLJ 6/94) [616.95]

5734 Burby, Liza N. *Bulimia Nervosa: The Secret Cycle of Bingeing and Purging* (6–10). (Teen Health Library of Eating Disorder Prevention) 1998, Rosen LB $17.95 (0-8239-2762-8). Bulimia is an eating disorder characterized by bingeing and purging. This book describes various eating disorders, then focuses on bulimia, its causes, physical and psychological effects, the roles of peer pressure, media images, family relationships, and genetics, and treatment and recovery. (Rev: BR 5–6/99; SLJ 1/99) [616.85]

5735 Burkett, Elinor. *The Gravest Show on Earth: America in the Age of AIDS* (9–12). 1995, Houghton $22.95 (0-395-74537-3). There are 3 essential books on AIDS—Shilts's *And the Band Played On,* Fumento's *Myth of Heterosexual AIDS,* and this one, in which Burkett exposes the profiteering and exploitation of AIDS. (Rev: BL 10/1/95*) [362]

5736 Carson, Mary Kay. *Epilepsy* (7–12). (Diseases and People) 1998, Enslow LB $19.95 (0-7660-1049-X). This book describes the causes of epilepsy, gives a history of society's attitude toward epileptics, and describes current treatments and drugs used to control it. (Rev: BL 7/98; BR 1–2/99; SLJ 9/98; VOYA 2/99) [616.8]

5737 Check, William A. *AIDS* (8–12). Illus. (Encyclopedia of Health) 1999, Chelsea LB $24.95 (0-7910-4885-3). This updated and revised edition gives a history of the AIDS epidemic, the latest information on breakthrough HIV treatment methods, and advice on how to avoid contracting the disease. (Rev: BL 8/98; SLJ 9/98) [616.9]

5738 Check, William A. *Alzheimer's Disease* (9–12). Illus. 1989, Chelsea LB $19.95 (0-7910-0056-7). A succinct explanation of what Alzheimer's disease is, its possible causes, treatments, and the personal toll it takes on families. (Rev: BL 3/1/89; BR 9–10/89; SLJ 6/89; VOYA 8/89) [618.97]

5739 Chiu, Christina. *Eating Disorder Survivors Tell Their Stories* (7–12). (Teen Health Library of Eating Disorder Prevention) 1998, Rosen LB $17.95 (0-8239-2767-9); Hazelden Information & Educational Services paper $6.95 (1-56838-259-6). In candid interviews, survivors of eating disorders share their experiences, treatments, and roads to recovery, and offer advice to other teens who might need help. (Rev: BL 3/1/99; BR 5–6/99; SLJ 1/99; VOYA 4/99) [616.85]

5740 Cozic, Charles P., and Tamara L. Roleff, eds. *AIDS* (9–12). (Opposing Viewpoints) 1997, Greenhaven LB $21.96 (1-56510-667-9); paper $20.25 (1-

56510-666-0). The seriousness of the AIDS epidemic, policies on HIV testing, various AIDS treatments, mandatory testing and partner notification, and measures to prevent the spread of AIDS are among the topics debated in this anthology. (Rev: BL 2/15/98; VOYA 6/98) [616.97]

5741 Crisfield, Deborah. *Eating Disorders* (6–9). 1994, Macmillan paper $4.95 (0-382-24756-6). The psychological/behavioral disorders anorexia nervosa, bulimia, and overeating. (Rev: BL 3/1/95; SLJ 3/95) [616.85]

5742 Curran, Christine Perdan. *Sexually Transmitted Diseases* (7–12). 1998, Enslow LB $19.95 (0-7660-1050-3). This work discusses various kinds of sexually transmitted diseases, including those that are bacterial, like syphilis, those that are viral, like HIV, and those that are neither, like scabies and pubic lice. (Rev: BL 12/15/98; VOYA 2/99) [616.95]

5743 Daugirdas, John T. *S.T.D. Sexually Transmitted Diseases, Including HIV/AIDS*. 3rd ed. (8–12). 1992, MedText $14.95 (0-9629279-1-0). This overview simplifies the language and prunes unnecessary medical terminology. (Rev: BL 10/1/92; SLJ 11/92) [616.951]

5744 DiSpezio, Michael. *The Science, Spread, and Therapy of HIV Disease: Everything You Need to Know, but Had No Idea Who to Ask* (9–12). 1997, A T L Pr. $26.95 (1-882360-20-6); paper $13.95 (1-882360-19-2). This comprehensive book in a question-and-answer format addresses both general and specific topics and gives current information on HIV and AIDS. (Rev: BL 2/15/98; SLJ 5/98; VOYA 6/98) [616.97]

5745 Dominick, Andie. *Needles: A Memoir of Growing Up with Diabetes* (10–12). 1998, Scribners $22.00 (0-684-84232-7). The story of how diabetes affected the life of one family, as told by one of the victims. (Rev: BL 9/1/98; SLJ 5/99) [616]

5746 Dudley, William, ed. *Epidemics* (8–12). (Opposing Viewpoints) 1998, Greenhaven LB $20.96 (1-56510-941-4); paper $16.20 (1-56510-940-6). Topics covered in this anthology of different points of view include the threat of infectious diseases, the AIDS epidemic, vaccination programs, and the prevention of food-borne illnesses. (Rev: BL 11/15/98) [616.9]

5747 Edelson, Edward. *Allergies* (7–12). Illus. 1989, Chelsea LB $19.95 (0-7910-0055-9). Various types of allergies are described, including their effects and their treatments that have been found to help sufferers. (Rev: BL 9/1/89; BR 11–12/89; SLJ 12/89) [616.97]

5748 Edelson, Edward. *The Immune System* (7–10). Illus. 1989, Chelsea LB $19.95 (0-7910-0021-4). After a general discussion of cell structure and antibodies, Edelson introduces the immune system and

what happens when it fails to function. (Rev: BL 1/15/90) [616.07]

5749 Eisenpreis, Bettijane. *Coping: A Young Woman's Guide to Breast Cancer Prevention* (7–12). (Coping) 1996, Rosen LB $15.95 (0-8239-2436-X). The author, a breast cancer survivor, answers the often-unspoken anxieties evoked by a diagnosis of breast cancer, discussing the nature of breast cancer, treatments, and common-sense health tips for cancer prevention, as well as such issues as puberty, the role of fashion in breast perception, plastic surgery, and self-exams. (Rev: BR 5–6/97; SLJ 1/97) [616.99]

5750 Eisenpreis, Bettijane. *Coping with Scoliosis* (7–10). (Coping) 1999, Rosen LB $17.95 (0-8239-2557-9). The author explores the physical and emotional issues involved in the diagnosis and treatment of scoliosis, curvature of the spine, using scientific explanations and firsthand accounts. (Rev: SLJ 5/99) [616]

5751 Epstein, Rachel. *Eating Habits and Disorders* (7–12). Illus. 1990, Chelsea LB $19.95 (0-7910-0048-6). A little history on eating disorders is given, but the major focus of this book is on the kinds of eating disorders and their treatments. (Rev: BL 6/1/90; SLJ 8/90) [616.85]

5752 Erlanger, Ellen. *Eating Disorders: A Question and Answer Book about Anorexia Nervosa and Bulimia Nervosa* (6–8). Illus. 1988, Lerner LB $19.93 (0-8225-0038-8). Case studies are used to introduce the cases, symptoms, and treatment of these disorders. (Rev: BL 3/15/88; SLJ 4/88) [616.85]

5753 Farrell, Jeanette. *Invisible Enemies: Stories of Infectious Disease* (7–12). 1997, Farrar $17.00 (0-374-33637-7). This is a dramatic retelling of human reactions to such diseases as malaria, leprosy, tuberculosis, and AIDS, and of the medical breakthroughs associated with each. (Rev: BL 6/1–15/98; SLJ 7/98; VOYA 10/98) [616.9 09]

5754 Feldman, Douglas A., and Julia Wang Miller. *The AIDS Crisis: A Documentary History* (8–12). (Primary Documents in American History and Contemporary Issues) 1998, Greenwood LB $49.95 (0-31-28715-5). Beginning with the first medical report on AIDS in 1981, this is a fine collection of documents related to the disease and people involved with it. (Rev: BR 1–2/99; VOYA 2/99) [616]

5755 Ferber, Elizabeth. *Diabetes* (6–10). Illus. 1996, Millbrook LB $23.90 (1-56294-655-2). This book supplies information aimed at adolescents on the nature of diabetes, its diagnosis, treatment, and how young people with the disease and their families and friends cope with it. (Rev: BL 12/15/96; BR 3–4/97; SLJ 2/97) [616.4]

5756 Fine, Judylaine. *Afraid to Ask: A Book about Cancer* (7–12). 1986, Lothrop paper $6.95 (0-688-06196-6). In this straightforward account about the nature, causes, and treatment of cancer, the author tries to minimize the fear and emotion surrounding the topic. (Rev: BL 3/1/86; BR 5–6/86; VOYA 8/86) [616.99]

5757   Flynn, Tom, and Karen Lound. *AIDS: Examining the Crisis* (7–12). 1995, Lerner LB $19.93 (0-8225-2625-5). An informative explanation in clear language about HIV and AIDS. (Rev: BL 5/1/95; SLJ 6/95) [362.1]

5758   Ford, Michael T. *100 Questions and Answers about AIDS: A Guide for Young People* (8–12). 1992, Macmillan LB $14.95 (0-02-735424-5). Answers to common queries that clarify background, distinguish misinformation, and guide readers toward safer behaviors. (Rev: BL 8/92; SLJ 1/93*) [616.97]

5759   Ford, Michael T. *The Voices of AIDS* (8–12). 1995, Morrow $15.00 (0-688-05322-X). Dedicated to getting the word out about AIDS, told by 12 men and women. (Rev: BL 8/95*; SLJ 11/95) [362.1]

5760   Frankenberger, Elizabeth. *Food and Love: Dealing with Family Attitudes About Weight* (7–12). (Teen Health Library of Eating Disorder Prevention) 1998, Rosen LB $17.95 (0-8239-2760-1). This book explores the role the home plays in developing a healthy self-image and affecting a teenager's attitudes toward food. (Rev: BR 5–6/99; VOYA 4/99) [616.85]

5761   Friedlander, Mark P., and Terry M. Phillips. *The Immune System: Your Body's Disease-Fighting Army* (6–10). 1997, Lerner $23.93 (0-8225-2858-4). Topics included in this introduction to the immune system include the makeup of the immune system, how it reacts to invaders, vaccination, nutrition, allergies, disorders of the system, and medicines that help it. (Rev: BL 6/1–15/98) [616.07 9]

5762   Frissell, Susan, and Paula Harney. *Eating Disorders and Weight Control* (7–10). Illus. 1998, Enslow LB $19.95 (0-89490-919-3). This book covers anorexia, bulimia, binge eating disorders, and weight control issues with material on how to cope with them in a healthy, realistic manner. (Rev: BL 4/15/98; BR 5–6/98; SLJ 3/98) [616.85]

5763   Giblin, James Cross. *When Plague Strikes: The Black Death, Smallpox, AIDS* (6–12). 1995, Harper-Collins LB $14.89 (0-06-025864-0). A discussion, combining social history, science, and technology, of the great plagues in history. (Rev: BL 10/15/95; SLJ 10/95; VOYA 4/96) [614.4]

5764   Gravelle, Karen, and Bertram A. John. *Teenagers Face to Face with Cancer* (7–12). 1986, Messner paper $5.95 (0-671-65975-8). From the accounts of 16 young people ages 13 to 21, one discovers what it is like to live with cancer. (Rev: BL 1/15/87; SLJ 2/87) [618.92]

5765   Harmon, Dan. *Anorexia Nervosa: Starving for Attention* (8–12). (Encyclopedia of Psychological Disorders) 1999, Chelsea $24.95 (0-7910-4901-9). Citing many case studies, some of prominent people, this work defines anorexia nervosa, discusses its causes and the physical consequences, and covers the treatments available. (Rev: VOYA 8/99) [616.85]

5766   Harmon, Dan. *Life out of Focus: Alzheimer's Disease and Related Disorders* (7–12). 1999, Chelsea $24.95 (0-7910-4896-9). This title demonstrates the devastating effect of Alzheimer's disease on sufferers and their caregivers, and provides biological and psychological explanations of the symptoms as well as solid data and analysis on research and various treatments. (Rev: BL 8/99) [616.8]

5767   Harris, Jacqueline L. *Communicable Diseases* (5–8). (Bodies in Crisis) 1993, Twenty-First Century LB $18.90 (0-8050-2599-5). Information on how contagious diseases are transmitted, how the body responds, and what methods are available for treatment and prevention. (Rev: BL 1/15/94) [616.9]

5768   Harris, Jacqueline L. *Hereditary Diseases* (7–10). Illus. (Bodies in Crisis) 1993, Twenty-First Century $18.90 (0-8050-2603-7). A slim volume that discusses the diagnosis, effects, and treatment of hereditary diseases. (Rev: BL 1/15/94; SLJ 1/94) [616]

5769   Hornbacher, Marya. *Wasted: A Memoir of Anorexia & Bulimia* (10–12). 1997, HarperCollins $23.00 (0-06-018739-5). A candid, painful, but hopeful account of a girl who was bulimic as a fourth grader and anorexic at age 15 but whose fortitude and desire to live eventually saved her from death. (Rev: BL 1/1–15/98; SLJ 9/98) [618.92]

5770   Huegel, Kelly. *Young People and Chronic Illness: True Stories, Help, and Hope* (7–12). 1998, Free Spirit paper $14.95 (1-57542-041-4). After a series of case histories of people suffering from such chronic illnesses as diabetes and asthma, this book discusses topics like getting support, coping with hospital stays, and planning for the future. (Rev: BL 11/15/98; SLJ 10/98; VOYA 2/99) [618.92]

5771   Hyde, Margaret O., and Elizabeth Forsyth. *AIDS: What Does It Mean to You?* rev. ed. (6–10). 1995, Walker LB $27.90 (0-8027-8398-8). This book traces the process of infection and the progress of the disease in the body, along with material on its history, treatment, prevention, and worldwide statistics. (Rev: SLJ 3/96; VOYA 4/96) [616.97]

5772   Hyde, Margaret O., and Elizabeth Forsyth. *The Disease Book: A Kid's Guide* (5–8). Illus. 1997, Walker LB $17.85 (0-8027-8498-4). A simple, straightforward overview of the causes, symptoms, and treatments of more than 100 physical and mental diseases. (Rev: BL 9/15/97; BR 3–4/98; SLJ 11/97) [616]

5773 Johannsson, Phillip. *Heart Disease* (7–12). (Diseases and People) 1998, Enslow LB $19.95 (0-7660-1051-1). The causes and types of heart disease are described, along with an overview of current treatments and potential future advances. (Rev: BL 7/98) [616.1]

5774 Johnson, Earvin "Magic." *What You Can Do to Avoid AIDS* (9–12). 1992, Times Bks. paper $3.99 (0-8129-2063-5). Facts, answers to common questions, and interviews comprise this excellent guide to AIDS for teens. (Rev: BL 6/1/92) [616.97]

5775 Jussim, Daniel. *AIDS & HIV: Risky Business* (9–12). Illus. (Teen Issues) 1997, Enslow LB $19.95 (0-89490-917-7). A straightforward, carefully researched account that explains AIDS, how it is contracted, how to prevent its spread, and its consequences. (Rev: BL 6/1–15/97; SLJ 8/97; VOYA 6/97) [616.97]

5776 Karlen, Arno. *Man and Microbes* (10–12). 1995, Putnam $24.95 (0-87477-759-3). A history of communicable diseases, including material on plagues that have changed history. This work also has a fine chapter on the AIDS virus and other STDs, and how these diseases are transmitted. (Rev: BL 4/1/95; SLJ 1/96) [616]

5777 Kelly, Pat. *Coping with Diabetes* (8–12). (Coping) 1998, Rosen $17.95 (0-8239-2549-8). Various kinds of diabetes are described, along with material on diagnosis, emotional issues, effects on family and school life, diet, exercise, and types of treatment. (Rev: SLJ 7/98; VOYA 4/99) [616.4]

5778 Kittredge, Mary. *Teens with AIDS Speak Out* (8–12). 1992, Messner LB $8.95 (0-671-74543-3). Combines facts and interviews on AIDS, its history, transmission, treatment, and prevention, as well as safer-sex practices and discrimination against people with AIDS. (Rev: BL 6/1/92; SLJ 7/92) [362.1]

5779 Landau, Elaine. *Alzheimer's Disease* (7–12). Illus. (Venture-Health and the Human Body) 1996, Watts LB $25.00 (0-531-11268-3). Designed to help young people cope with having an Alzheimer's patient in the family, this book presents several case studies and discusses the cause, nature, and progression of the disease, various treatments, and what family members can do. (Rev: BL 10/15/96; SLJ 8/96) [362.1]

5780 Landau, Elaine. *Parkinson's Disease* (7–12). 1999, Watts $25.00 (0-531-11423-6). This account describes a history of this baffling disease, how it can be diagnosed, its characteristics, and today's treatments. (Rev: BL 7/99; SLJ 6/99) [616.8]

5781 Landau, Elaine. *Tourette's Syndrome* (6–12). (Venture Series.: Health & the Human Body) 1998, Watts LB $25.00 (0-531-11399-X). Tourette's syndrome is a neurological condition involving uncontrollable verbalization and involuntary tics. This

book explains its causes and treatments and gives profiles of many people, some of them famous, who are afflicted. (Rev: BL 7/98; BR 11–12/98; SLJ 7/98; VOYA 12/98) [616.8]

5782 Landau, Elaine. *Tuberculosis* (6–10). 1995, Watts LB $25.00 (0-531-12555-6). The author reviews the history and nature of tuberculosis and its treatments, and warns of the danger presented by the rise of new drug-resistant strains today. (Rev: BL 6/1–15/95; SLJ 8/95; VOYA 2/96) [616]

5783 Landau, Elaine. *Why Are They Starving Themselves? Understanding Anorexia Nervosa and Bulimia* (7–10). 1983, Messner paper $5.95 (0-671-49492-9). Case studies are used as a focal point for explaining these eating disorders. [616.8]

5784 Latta, Sara L. *Allergies* (6–10). (Diseases and People) 1998, Enslow LB $19.95 (0-7660-1048-1). Using a number of case studies, this book describes the nature of allergies, their symptoms, methods of detection, and treatments. (Rev: BL 7/98) [616.9]

5785 Latta, Sara L. *Food Poisoning and Foodborne Diseases* (7–12). (Diseases and People) 1999, Enslow $19.95 (0-7660-1183-6). Using case studies and questions and answers, this book describes the causes, effects, and treatments for food poisoning and related illnesses. (Rev: BL 9/15/99) [615.9]

5786 Leone, Daniel, ed. *The Spread of AIDS* (8–12). (At Issue) 1997, Greenhaven paper $17.00 (1-56510-537-0). This anthology of different opinions explores the successes and failures of various educational strategies, health care programs, and political policies designed to prevent the spread of AIDS. (Rev: BL 1/1–15/97; SLJ 4/97) [362.1]

5787 Levenkron, Steven. *Treating and Overcoming Anorexia Nervosa* (9–12). 1988, Warner paper $5.99 (0-446-34416-8). Symptoms, causes, stages of development, and therapies connected with anorexia nervosa and bulimia are covered. [616.8]

5788 LeVert, Marianne. *AIDS: A Handbook for the Future* (7–12). Illus. 1996, Millbrook LB $23.90 (1-56294-660-9). This book covers the basic facts about AIDS, its causes, prevention, present treatments, and current research. (Rev: BL 12/15/96; BR 3–4/97; SLJ 11/96; VOYA 6/97) [616.97]

5789 Little, Marjorie. *Diabetes* (7–12). (Encyclopedia of Health) 1990, Chelsea LB $19.95 (0-7910-0061-3). A clear, organized account that covers the history of diabetes, its causes, and present-day treatments. (Rev: BL 3/15/91) [616.4]

5790 McGuire, Paula. *AIDS* (4–8). (Preteen Pressures) 1998, Raintree Steck-Vaughn $24.26 (0-8172-5025-5). Straight facts and current statistics are given about AIDS, along with material on prevention and human interest stories about people with HIV/

AIDS, including Magic Johnson and the late Ryan White. (Rev: BL 5/15/98) [312]

5791 McHugh, Mary. *Special Siblings: Growing Up with Someone with a Disability* (7–12). 1999, Hyperion $23.95 (0-7868-6285-8). This book discusses a variety of physical and mental disabilities and how to cope with these handicaps when they affect a member of your family. (Rev: BL 2/15/99; VOYA 8/99) [616]

5792 McIvor, Kirsten. *Exposure: Victims of Radiation Speak Out* (9–12). 1992, Kodansha paper $12.00 (4-7700-2605-1). Reporters present data on radiation contamination in 15 countries, hoping their effort will help reduce the use of nuclear power for any purpose. (Rev: BL 9/15/92) [363.17]

5793 Majure, Janet. *AIDS* (7–10). 1998, Enslow LB $19.95 (0-7660-1182-8). This informative book describes AIDS, who gets it and how, symptoms, treatment, prevention, and prospects for the future, and touches on related social, economic, and legal issues. (Rev: VOYA 2/99) [616]

5794 Maloney, Michael, and Rachel Kranz. *Straight Talk about Eating Disorders* (7–12). 1991, Facts on File $24.95 (0-8160-2414-6). This subject is addressed in a matter-of-fact manner and includes recommendations for dealing with the problem. (Rev: BL 4/15/91; SLJ 10/91) [616.85]

5795 Manning, Karen. *AIDS: Can This Epidemic Be Stopped?* (6–8). (Issues of Our Time) 1995, Twenty-First Century LB $15.98 (0-8050-4240-7). A frank, unbiased look at AIDS, its causes, effects on society, and perspectives for the future. (Rev: BL 2/1/96; SLJ 2/96; VOYA 4/96) [616.97]

5796 Miller, Martha J. *Kidney Disorders* (7–12). (Encyclopedia of Health) 1992, Chelsea LB $19.95 (0-7910-0066-4). This book explains the function of the kidneys, how they can malfunction, and treatments that are available, including transplants. (Rev: BL 12/1/92) [616.6]

5797 Moe, Barbara. *Coping with Eating Disorders* (7–10). 1991, Rosen $12.95 (0-8239-2113-6). Actual case histories are used to explain the characteristics of bulimia, anorexia, and compulsive-eating patterns. Practical coping suggestions are also offered. (Rev: BL 7/91; SLJ 11/91) [616.85]

5798 Moe, Barbara. *Coping with PMS* (7–12). (Coping) 1998, Rosen $17.95 (0-8239-2716-4). Supplemented by personal accounts, this book explains how PMS can be a manageable problem, with material on physiology, diet, life-style, attitude, and the relationship between nutrition and PMS control (recipes are included). (Rev: BL 5/15/98; SLJ 5/98) [618.1 72]

5799 Moe, Barbara. *Inside Eating Disorder Support Groups* (6–10). (Teen Health Library of Eating Dis-

order Prevention) 1998, Rosen LB $17.95 (0-8239-2769-5). After a general discussion of eating disorders and available treatments, this book explains the dynamics of support groups and how they can help teens recover from eating disorders and come to terms with their problems. (Rev: BR 5–6/99; SLJ 1/99) [616.85]

5800 Morrison, Jaydene. *Coping with ADD/ADHD: Attention Deficit Disorder/Attention Deficit Hyperactivity Disorder* (7–12). (Coping) 1995, Rosen LB $17.95 (0-8239-2070-4). This book defines these disorders, which affect 3.5 million American youngsters, and provides information on treatment and counseling. (Rev: SLJ 5/96; VOYA 8/96) [371.9]

5801 Mulcahy, Robert. *Diseases: Finding the Cure* (7–9). 1996, Oliver Pr. LB $19.95 (1-881508-28-5). After a general introduction on disease fighting, single chapters explore the breakthroughs of such scientists as Edward Jenner, Louis Pasteur, Alexander Fleming, and Jonas Salk, with a special afterword on AIDS. (Rev: SLJ 10/96) [616]

5802 Murphy, Wendy. *Asthma* (7–12). (Millbrook Medical Library) 1998, Millbrook LB $23.90 (0-7613-0364-2). Beginning with the causes of asthma, this book describes what happens during an attack, how the disease is controlled, and various avenues of medical treatment. (Rev: BL 1/1–15/99; SLJ 1/99) [616.2]

5803 Nash, Carol R. *AIDS: Choices for Life* (7–12). Illus. (Issues in Focus) 1997, Enslow LB $19.95 (0-89490-903-7). This book offers information about AIDS and protease inhibitors, drug cocktails, the AIDS virus, current and future medical concerns, and prevention tactics, plus a history of the disease. (Rev: BL 12/1/97; SLJ 12/97; VOYA 6/98) [616.97]

5804 Nourse, Alan E. *The Virus Invaders* (8–10). 1992, Watts LB $25.00 (0-531-12511-4). Virology is explained in lay terms, including a history of viruses and the prognosis for treatment of killers like malaria and AIDS. (Rev: BL 9/15/92; SLJ 7/92) [616]

5805 O'Brien, Eileen. *Starving to Win: Athletes and Eating Disorders* (6–12). (The Teen Health Library of Eating Disorders Prevention) 1998, Rosen LB $17.95 (0-8239-2764-4). This book describes the pressures on athletes to gain or lose weight and the temptation, particularly in track, gymnastics, ballet, and wrestling, to resort to dangerous crash diets, fasts, or drugs. The author stresses that health is more important than weight. (Rev: BR 5–6/99; SLJ 2/99) [616.85]

5806 Ouriou, Katie. *Love Ya Like a Sister: A Story of Friendship* (8–12). Ed. by Julie Johnston. 1999, Tundra paper $7.95 (0-88776-454-1). After her death from leukemia when only 16 years old, Katie Ouriou's life and thoughts during her last months were reconstructed from journal entries and e-mail correspondence with her many friends. (Rev: SLJ 5/99; VOYA 6/99) [616.95]

5807 Packer, Kenneth L. *HIV Infection: The Facts You Need to Know* (9–12). Illus. (Venture Books) 1998, Watts LB $25.00 (0-531-11333-7). This book provides a clear, concise explanation of HIV and AIDS and teaches young readers to be responsible for their actions and to have compassion for those infected with the virus. (Rev: BL 4/15/98; BR 11–12/98; SLJ 4/98; VOYA 2/99) [616.97]

5808 Pipher, Mary. *Hunger Pains: The Modern Woman's Tragic Quest for Thinness* (7–12). 1997, Ballantine paper $10.00 (0-345-41393-8). This book explains eating disorders, probes into their basic causes, and offers suggestions for help, with separate chapters on bulimia, anorexia, obesity, and diets. (Rev: VOYA 8/97) [616.95]

5809 Potts, Eve, and Marion Morra. *Understanding Your Immune System* (9–12). 1986, Avon paper $3.95 (0-380-89728-8). Using a question-and-answer format, the authors explain the immune system, how it can be strengthened, and what happens when it malfunctions. (Rev: BL 6/1/86) [612]

5810 Powers, Mary C. *Arthritis* (7–12). (Encyclopedia of Health) 1992, Chelsea LB $19.95 (0-7910-0057-5). Illustrated with black-and-white pictures, this book describes the causes of arthritis, therapies, and treatments. (Rev: BL 10/1/92) [616.7]

5811 Radetsky, Peter. *The Invisible Invaders: The Story of the Emerging Age of Viruses* (9–12). 1991, Little, Brown $22.95 (0-316-73216-8). What is known about viruses and recent genetic discoveries based on viral research. (Rev: BL 1/1/91) [616.01]

5812 Robbins, Paul R. *Anorexia and Bulimia* (7–12). (Diseases and People) 1998, Enslow LB $19.95 (0-7660-1047-3). The history of anorexia, bulimia, and binge eating is given, with material on symptoms, possible causes, prevention, and treatment. (Rev: BL 1/1–15/99; SLJ 1/99) [616.85]

5813 Roth, Geneen. *Feeding the Hungry Heart: The Experience of Compulsive Eating* (10–12). 1983, NAL paper $5.95 (0-451-15825-3). This book explains how one can avoid eating binges by overcoming emotional problems. [615]

5814 Sacker, Ira M., and Marc A. Zimmer. *Dying to Be Thin* (9–12). 1987, Warner paper $14.99 (0-446-38417-8). This account tells about the onset, symptoms, dangers, and treatment of various eating disorders. (Rev: VOYA 12/87) [613.2]

5815 Shader, Laurel, and Jon Zonderman. *Mononucleosis and Other Infectious Diseases* (7–12). Illus. 1989, Chelsea LB $19.95 (0-7910-0069-9). Although many diseases like syphilis and smallpox are discussed, the emphasis is on mononucleosis, a disease

that often attacks teens. (Rev: BL 1/15/90; BR 11–12/89; SLJ 11/89) [616.9]

5816 Shein, Lori. *AIDS* (5–8). (Overview) 1998, Lucent LB $17.96 (1-56006-193-6). The story of the AIDS epidemic from the early 1980s on, methods used to treat and restrict the spread of the disease, and the controversies surrounding AIDS are covered in this concise overview. (Rev: BL 8/98) [616.97]

5817 Siegel, Dorothy, and David E. Newton. *Leukemia* (7–12). 1994, Watts LB $25.00 (0-531-12509-2). An introduction to leukemia, emphasizing the advances in research and the cure rate. (Rev: BL 2/15/95; SLJ 1/95; VOYA 4/95) [616.99]

5818 Silverstein, Alvin, et al. *Asthma* (7–12). Illus. (Diseases and People) 1997, Enslow LB $19.95 (0-89490-712-3). This book discusses the nature, causes, and treatment of asthma and possible cures. (Rev: BL 2/15/97; SLJ 4/97; VOYA 6/97) [616.2]

5819 Silverstein, Alvin, et al. *Chickenpox and Shingles* (6–10). (Diseases and People) 1998, Enslow LB $19.95 (0-89490-715-8). The nature and treatment of these 2 diseases are discussed, supplemented by case studies. (Rev: BL 7/98) [616]

5820 Silverstein, Alvin, et al. *Cystic Fibrosis* (7–12). 1994, Watts LB $24.00 (0-531-12552-1). Explains the often-fatal hereditary disease, how it is transmitted, and how it affects the body. Outlines current treatment and research. (Rev: BL 9/15/94; SLJ 8/94; VOYA 10/94) [616.37]

5821 Silverstein, Alvin, et al. *Diabetes* (7–12). Illus. (Diseases and People) 1994, Enslow LB $19.95 (0-89490-464-7). This book examines the causes and treatment of diabetes, with material on how to detect it and sources of possible cures. (Rev: BL 10/15/94; SLJ 12/94; VOYA 12/94) [616.4]

5822 Silverstein, Alvin, et al. *Mononucleosis* (7–10). (Diseases and People) 1994, Enslow LB $19.95 (0-89490-466-3). Examines this disease's history, causes, treatment, prevention, and societal response. (Rev: BL 1/15/95; SLJ 3/95) [616.9]

5823 Silverstein, Alvin, et al. *Sickle Cell Anemia* (7–12). Illus. 1997, Enslow LB $19.95 (0-89490-711-5). A clear, concise description of the causes, effects, and treatment of this condition, with information on why it attacks African Americans particularly. (Rev: BL 2/15/97; SLJ 2/97; VOYA 6/97) [616.1]

5824 Silverstein, Alvin, and Virginia Silverstein. *Allergies* (7–10). Illus. 1977, HarperCollins $13.00 (0-397-31758-1). The types of allergies—such as hay fever and asthma—as well as their causes, effects, and treatments are discussed. [616.97]

5825 Silverstein, Alvin, and Virginia Silverstein. *Measles and Rubella* (6–12). Illus. (Diseases and People) 1997, Enslow LB $19.95 (0-89490-714-X).

The authors examine the nature of measles and rubella, their treatment, and the possibility of a cure. (Rev: BL 3/1/98; SLJ 5/98) [616.9]

5826 Silverstein, Alvin, and Virginia Silverstein. *Runaway Sugar: All about Diabetes* (7–10). Illus. 1981, HarperCollins LB $12.89 (0-397-31929-0). Among other topics, this book discusses what causes diabetes and how it can be controlled. [616.4]

5827 Simpson, Carolyn. *Coping with Compulsive Eating* (7–12). 1997, Rosen LB $17.95 (0-8239-2516-1). This volume describes the various kinds of compulsive eating disorders, possible causes, and treatments available. (Rev: VOYA 2/98) [616.85]

5828 Simpson, Carolyn. *Coping with Sleep Disorders* (7–12). (Coping) 1995, Rosen LB $17.95 (0-8239-2068-2). This book discusses sleeping disorders from snoring to insomnia and offers a wide range of possible solutions. (Rev: SLJ 6/96; VOYA 8/96) [613.7]

5829 Simpson, Carolyn. *Everything You Need to Know about Asthma* (5–10). Illus. (Need to Know Library) 1998, Rosen LB $17.95 (0-8239-2567-6). This book contains vital background information about the causes and effects of asthma, symptoms, and treatments that teens should be aware of. (Rev: SLJ 10/98) [616.2]

5830 Smart, Paul. *Everything You Need to Know about Mononucleosis* (5–10). Illus. (Need to Know Library) 1998, Rosen LB $17.95 (0-8239-2550-1). A straightforward presentation about the "kissing disease," which is often undiagnosed or mistaken for the flu and which requires long periods of rest for recovery. (Rev: SLJ 10/98) [616.9]

5831 Smith, Erica. *Anorexia Nervosa: When Food Is the Enemy* (6–10). (Teen Health Library of Eating Disorder Prevention) 1998, Rosen LB $17.95 (0-8239-2766-0). The author describes anorexia nervosa and its symptoms and treatment, and discusses what to do if you suspect someone is suffering from the eating disorder. Society's attitudes toward weight and body image and the role of peer pressure, media images, family relationships, and genetics are examined, along with how to deal with these influences. (Rev: BR 5–6/99; SLJ 1/99) [616.85]

5832 Sonder, Ben. *Eating Disorders: When Food Turns Against You* (7–10). 1993, Watts LB $24.00 (0-531-11175-X). Discusses the psychology of eating disorders such as anorexia nervosa and bulimia, the effects of pop culture, research on weight and eating, and hazards of dieting. (Rev: BL 10/1/93; SLJ 6/93; VOYA 8/93) [616.85]

5833 Sparks, Beatrice, ed. *It Happened to Nancy* (7–12). 1994, Avon paper $4.99 (0-380-77315-5). In diary format, this is the story of 14-year-old Nancy who was raped by her boyfriend and infected with

the HIV virus. (Rev: BL 6/1–15/94; SLJ 6/94; VOYA 10/94) [362.196]

5834 Stewart, Gail B. *Diabetes* (5–8). (Overview) 1999, Lucent LB $18.96 (1-56006-527-3). This book reviews the history, causes, complications, and latest breakthroughs in treatment and prevention of diabetes, the seventh leading cause of death in the United States. (Rev: BL 8/1/99; SLJ 8/99) [616.4]

5835 Stone, Tanya L. *Medical Causes* (5–10). (Celebrity Activists) 1997, Twenty-First Century $20.40 (0-8050-5233-X). The contributions of such celebrity activists as Elizabeth Taylor, Elton John, Paul Newman, Jerry Lewis, and Linda Ellerbee to various medical causes are highlighted, with material on each of their causes. (Rev: BR 3–4/98; SLJ 1/98) [616]

5836 Storad, Conrad J. *Inside AIDS: HIV Attacks the Immune System* (8–12). 1998, Lerner LB $23.93 (0-8225-2857-6). An unusual book about the HIV virus that tells about the cellular structure of the body, its immune system, and how the virus tricks the host cells into replicating it. (Rev: BL 12/15/98; SLJ 1/99) [616.97]

5837 Trillin, Alice Stewart. *Dear Bruno* (9–12). Illus. 1996, New Pr. $12.00 (1-56584-057-7). Originally intended as a letter to a friend's son who had cancer, this work is filled with love, compassion, and humor in spite of the grim subject. (Rev: VOYA 10/96) [616.99]

5838 Turkington, Carol A., and Jeffrey S. Dover. *Skin Deep: An A-Z of Skin Disorders, Treatments & Health* (10–12). 1996, Facts on File $45.00 (0-8160-3071-5). Hundreds of topics related to skin are covered, including the causes, cures, treatments, and symptoms of a wide variety of disorders, with information on current surgeries such as life laser therapy and rhinoplasty. (Rev: BR 5–6/96; SLJ 6/96) [616.5]

5839 Veggeberg, Scott. *Lyme Disease* (7–12). 1998, Enslow LB $19.95 (0-7660-1052-X). The causes, prevention, and treatments of this disease passed on by wood ticks are discussed. (Rev: BL 7/98; SLJ 9/98) [616.7]

5840 Vollstadt, Elizabeth Weiss. *Teen Eating Disorders* (7–12). (Teen Issues) 1999, Lucent LB $22.45 (1-56006-516-8). This book defines the various kinds of teenage eating disorders and, using many anecdotes, describes their causes, effects, treatment, and prevention. (Rev: BL 7/99; SLJ 8/99) [616.85]

5841 Votava, Andrea. *Coping with Migraines & Other Headaches* (7–12). (Coping) 1997, Rosen $17.95 (0-8239-2566-8). The book gives the facts about the different kinds of headaches, what kinds of medications are available, and alternative pain treatments such as meditation, massage therapy, and biofeedback. (Rev: BL 5/1/98; SLJ 7/98) [616.8 491]

5842 Weeldreyer, Laura. *Body Blues: Weight and Depression* (6–12). (The Teen Health Library of Eating Disorder Prevention) 1998, Rosen LB $17.95 (0-8239-2761-X). This book uses case studies of 3 teenagers who are trying to come to terms with food and their bodies to explore the relationship between weight and depression, and encourages teenagers to learn to accept their bodies rather than aspiring to some media ideal. (Rev: BR 5–6/99; SLJ 2/99) [155.5]

5843 Woods, Samuel G. *Everything You Need to Know about Sexually Transmitted Disease* (7–12). Illus. (Need to Know) 1990, Rosen $12.95 (0-8239-1010-5). Various kinds of venereal diseases are introduced, with their symptoms and treatments. (Rev: SLJ 9/90; VOYA 8/90) [305.4]

5844 Yancey, Diane. *The Hunt for Hidden Killers: Ten Cases of Medical Mystery* (7–12). 1994, Millbrook LB $22.40 (1-56294-389-8). A chronicle of the determined efforts of health workers attempting to unravel such medical enigmas as AIDS and Lyme disease. (Rev: BL 3/15/94; SLJ 7/94) [614.4]

5845 Yount, Lisa. *Cancer* (6–8). (Overview) 1999, Lucent LB $22.45 (1-56006-363-7). This objective overview explains how cancer cells develop, types of cancer, causes, and past and present treatments, both traditional and alternative. (Rev: SLJ 7/99) [616.99]

5846 Zonderman, Jon, and Laurel Shader. *Environmental Diseases* (5–8). (Bodies in Crisis) 1993, Twenty-First Century LB $18.90 (0-8050-2600-2). Focuses on several present-day diseases, with illustrations and charts explaining such ailments as Lyme disease. (Rev: BL 7/94; SLJ 4/94) [616.9]

5847 Zonderman, Jon, and Laurel Shader. *Nutritional Diseases* (5–8). (Bodies in Crisis) 1993, Twenty-First Century LB $18.90 (0-8050-2601-0). Discusses causes and possible treatments for such nutritional diseases as obesity, anorexia, bulimia, and bingeing. (Rev: BL 7/94; SLJ 4/94) [616.3]

Doctors, Hospitals, and Medicine

5848 Bourdillon, Hilary. *Women As Healers: A History of Women and Medicine* (10–12). Illus. 1989, Cambridge Univ. Pr. paper $13.95 (0-521-31090-3). An account of the roles played by women in the history of western medicine. (Rev: BL 7/89) [610]

5849 Carter, Sharon, and Judy Monnig. *Coping with a Hospital Stay* (7–10). 1987, Rosen LB $17.95 (0-8239-0682-5). Tips for teenagers who are facing a stay in the hospital. (Rev: BL 3/15/88; SLJ 3/88) [362.1]

5850 Cosner, Shaaron. *War Nurses* (6–9). Illus. 1988, Walker $17.85 (0-8027-6828-8). A history of the important role nurses have played tending the wounded from our Civil War through the Vietnam conflict. (Rev: BL 12/1/88; BR 3–4/89; SLJ 12/88) [355.3]

5851 Facklam, Howard. *Alternative Medicine: Cures or Myths?* (6–9). 1996, Twenty-First Century LB $21.40 (0-8050-4169-9). A look at the controversies surrounding alternative medicine, such as acupuncture, homeopathy, hypnosis, and herbal medicine. (Rev: BL 12/15/96; SLJ 3/97*) [615.5]

5852 Fleming, Robert. *Rescuing a Neighborhood: The Bedford-Stuyvesant Volunteer Ambulance Corps* (5–8). 1995, Walker LB $15.85 (0-8027-8330-9). A chronicle of a volunteer emergency corps in Bedford-Stuyvesant, Brooklyn. (Rev: BL 5/1/95; SLJ 9/95) [362.1]

5853 Fradin, Dennis B. *"We Have Conquered Pain": The Discovery of Anesthesia* (5–8). Illus. 1996, Simon & Schuster paper $16.00 (0-689-50587-6). The convoluted story of who discovered anesthesia (four 19th-century American doctors claimed credit) is unraveled in this fascinating account. (Rev: BL 5/15/96; BR 1–2/97; SLJ 5/96; VOYA 8/96) [617.9]

5854 Glasser, Ronald. *The Light in the Skull: An Odyssey of Medical Discovery* (10–12). 1997, Faber $24.95 (0-571-19916-X). An attention-getting history of medical discoveries and present-day advances in such fields as genetics, the immune system, cancer, microbiology, and evolution, including fascinating tales of the people involved and the influence of politics on medical funding and priorities. (Rev: BL 4/15/97; SLJ 1/98) [610]

5855 Gordon, James S. *Holistic Medicine* (7–10). Illus. 1988, Chelsea LB $19.95 (0-7910-0085-0). A noncritical view of holistic medicine that is currently popular. (Rev: BR 11–12/88; SLJ 10/88; VOYA 4/88) [616]

5856 Kidd, J. S., and Renee A. Kidd. *Mother Nature's Pharmacy: Potent Medicines from Plants* (7–12). Illus. (Science and Society) 1998, Facts on File $19.95 (0-8160-3584-9). An interesting account of the long history of natural plant remedies, the individuals whose discoveries brought plant remedies to public attention, and the expanding role of the government in researching and sanctioning their use, along with information on recent advances. (Rev: BL 10/15/98; SLJ 1/99; VOYA 2/99) [615.32]

5857 Klass, Perri Elizabeth. *A Not Entirely Benign Procedure: Four Years as a Medical Student* (10–12). 1988, NAL paper $4.50 (0-451-15358-8). The process of becoming a doctor as described by a woman who spent 4 years at Harvard Medical School. (Rev: BL 4/1/87) [610.7]

5858 Kowalski, Kathiann M. *Alternative Medicine: Is It for You?* (7–9). Illus. (Issues in Focus) 1998, Enslow LB $19.95 (0-89490-955-X). After explaining the differences between traditional and alternative medicine, this book describes homeopathy, chiropractic medicine, medical practices from India and China, nutritional therapies, biofeedback, and healing based on prayer and meditation. (Rev: BL 10/1/98; BR 1–2/99; SLJ 12/98) [615.5]

5859 Levitin, Nancy. *America's Health Care Crisis: Who's Responsible?* (7–12). 1994, Watts LB $24.00 (0-531-11187-3). Examines major controversial health care issues, including costs and who should pay. (Rev: BL 4/15/95; SLJ 3/95) [338.4]

5860 Masoff, Joy. *Emergency!* (4–8). 1999, Scholastic $16.95 (0-590-97898-5). In a series of double-page spreads, this book explores various aspects of a medical emergency, from getting help to victims, with an explanation of what goes on in an emergency room, to giving advice on precautions youngsters can take to be prepared for an emergency. (Rev: BL 1/1–15/99; SLJ 8/99) [362.1]

5861 Miller, Brandon M. *Just What the Doctor Ordered: The History of American Medicine* (5–8). (People's History) 1997, Lerner LB $21.37 (0-8225-1737-X). A history of American medicine from early Indian ceremonies and remedies to today's use of laser surgery, placing medical developments in a historical context, such as the role disease played in the Revolutionary and Civil Wars. (Rev: SLJ 5/97*) [610.9]

5862 Murphy, Wendy, and Jack Murphy. *Nuclear Medicine* (7–12). (Encyclopedia of Health) 1993, Chelsea LB $19.95 (0-7910-0070-2). This work presents current information on the role played by nuclear research in health care, including radiation treatments. (Rev: BL 12/1/93) [616.07]

5863 Oleksy, Walter. *Science and Medicine* (6–12). (Information Revolution) 1995, Facts on File $19.95 (0-8160-3076-6). A summary of computer technology used in medicine and in science classrooms. (Rev: BL 11/15/95; SLJ 11/95) [502]

5864 Porter, Roy, ed. *Cambridge Illustrated History of Medicine* (10–12). 1996, Cambridge Univ. Pr. $39.95 (0-521-44211-7). Arranged thematically, this well-illustrated volume presents a concise history of medicine from ancient times to the present, placed in a context of other developments and events of the day. (Rev: BR 3–4/97; SLJ 5/97) [610.9]

5865 Powledge, Fred. *Pharmacy in the Forest* (5–8). 1998, Simon & Schuster $17.00 (0-689-80863-1). Writing from an environmental point of view, the author discusses medicinal plants, with examples of plants that have been useful in treating disease, and shows the reader how to identify potentially useful plants. (Rev: BL 8/98; BR 1–2/99; SLJ 6/98; VOYA 2/99) [610]

5866 Rattenbury, Jeanne. *Understanding Alternative Medicine* (7–10). Illus. 1999, Watts $25.00 (0-531-11413-9). An attractive book that supplies information on topics like osteopathy, chiropractic treatments, homeopathy, acupuncture, herbal medicine, and mind-body therapy. (Rev: BL 6/1–15/99; SLJ 7/99) [615]

5867 Sherrow, Victoria. *Bioethics and High-Tech Medicine* (7–12). 1996, Twenty-First Century LB $21.40 (0-8050-3832-9). The ethical problems evoked by recent biotechnology developments are discussed, including organ transplant priorities, confidentiality, cost, and who should make these decisions. (Rev: BL 8/96; BR 9–10/96; SLJ 6/96; VOYA 12/96) [174]

5868 Sherrow, Victoria. *The U.S. Health Care Crisis: The Fight over Access, Quality, and Cost* (7–12). 1994, Millbrook LB $23.90 (1-56294-364-2). Examines U.S. health care options, current and past controversies, and the possibility of universal coverage. (Rev: BL 10/15/94; SLJ 11/94; VOYA 2/95) [362.1]

5869 Stille, Darlene R. *Extraordinary Women of Medicine* (6–8). Illus. (Extraordinary People) 1997, Children's Pr. LB $37.00 (0-516-20307-X). A profile of 50 women who have reached prominence in medicine from the well-known, like the legendary Florence Nightingale, to many lesser-known, present-day achievers, spanning 2 centuries and organized according to groups or themes. (Rev: BL 10/1/97) [610]

5870 Storring, Rod. *A Doctor's Life: A Visual History of Doctors and Nurses through the Ages* (4–8). 1998, Dutton $17.99 (0-525-67577-9). Profiles of ordinary doctors and nurses are used to describe the development of medicine and medical beliefs from the ancient Romans to the present, with double-page spreads devoted to each practitioner and period. (Rev: BL 1/1–15/99; BR 5–6/99; SLJ 12/98) [610]

5871 Thomas, Peggy. *Medicines from Nature* (7–12). Illus. 1997, Twenty-First Century LB $21.40 (0-8050-4168-0). A detailed account of the search for various medicines derived from plants, sea creatures, and even insects. (Rev: BL 9/15/97; BR 11–12/97; SLJ 8/97) [615]

5872 Wekesser, Carol, ed. *Health Care in America* (7–12). Illus. (Opposing Viewpoints) 1994, Greenhaven LB $26.20 (1-56510-135-9); paper $20.25 (1-56510-134-0). This anthology covers topics related to the present status of health care in America, the role of doctors in the system, the place of alternative medicine, possible reforms, and costs. (Rev: BL 6/1–15/94; SLJ 6/94) [362.1]

5873 Winkler, Kathy. *Radiology* (4–8). (Inventors and Inventions) 1996, Benchmark LB $25.64 (0-

7614-0075-3). This work outlines the history of radiology, provides short profiles of leaders in the field, and describes the effects of too many x-rays on tissue, how x-rays are made, their use in diagnosis and treatment, and other medical imaging such as ultrasound and MRIs. (Rev: BL 7/96; SLJ 9/96) [616.07]

5874 Yalof, Ina. *Life and Death: The Story of a Hospital* (10–12). 1989, Random $18.95 (0-394-56215-1). Through interviews with 74 various workers at Columbia-Presbyterian Hospital, a profile of life in a big city hospital emerges. (Rev: BL 1/15/89; BR 9–10/89; SLJ 5/89) [362.1]

5875 Yount, Lisa. *Medical Technology* (6–12). (Milestones in Discovery & Invention) 1998, Facts on File $19.95 (0-8160-3568-7). An overview of medical inventors, including interesting accounts about the lives and work of such technologists as William Morton, Joseph Lister, Christian Barnard, and Norman Shumway. (Rev: BL 5/15/98; SLJ 6/98) [610.9]

Genetics

5876 Bryan, Jenny. *Genetic Engineering* (7–9). 1995, Thomson Learning LB $24.26 (1-56847-268-4). Recounts the advances of gene research, including a discussion of the ethical questions involved. (Rev: BL 8/95; SLJ 8/95) [575.1]

5877 Brynie, Faith H. *Genetics and Human Health: A Journey Within* (6–9). 1995, Millbrook LB $23.90 (1-56294-545-9). An introduction to genetics and health, including the history of genetics, current uses, and genetic diseases such as cystic fibrosis, Marfan's syndrome, and sickle-cell anemia. (Rev: BL 6/1–15/95; SLJ 5/95) [616]

5878 Cohen, Daniel. *Cloning* (7–10). 1998, Millbrook $22.90 (0-7613-0356-1). A balanced examination of the social and ethical concerns raised by the recent cloning of a sheep named Dolly, including the history and scientific background of this area of research and a discussion of genetic engineering. (Rev: SLJ 3/99) [575.1]

5879 Edelson, Edward. *Francis Crick and James Watson and the Building Blocks of Life* (9–12). Illus. 1998, Oxford $33.95 (0-19-511451-5). The exciting story of Watson and Crick and their scientific explorations leading up to the 1953 announcement of the discovery of the molecular structure of DNA. (Rev: BL 6/1–15/98; BR 11–12/98; SLJ 8/98) [572.8]

5880 Kidd, J. S., and Renee A. Kidd. *Life Lines: The Story of the New Genetics* (7–12). (Science and Society) 1999, Facts on File $19.95 (0-8160-3586-5). This work explores the history of genetic research, from Mendel's early experiments to recent debates about cloning and genetic engineering. (Rev: BL

12/1/98; BR 9–10/99; SLJ 7/99; VOYA 10/99) [576.5]

5881 Lee, Thomas F. *The Human Genome Project: Cracking the Genetic Code of Life* (9–12). 1991, Plenum $24.50 (0-306-43965-4). Provides background information on DNA and genes, examines the Human Genome Project, and discusses genetic diseases and their possible therapeutic treatment. (Rev: BL 9/15/91) [573.2]

5882 Marion, Robert. *Was George Washington Really the Father of Our Country? A Clinical Geneticist Looks at World History* (9–12). 1994, Addison-Wesley $22.95 (0-201-62255-6). An exploration of the impact of genetic abnormalities on world history, including Washington's sterility, Napoleon's growth hormone deficiency, and Lincoln's Marfan's syndrome. (Rev: BL 1/15/94) [909.08]

5883 Marshall, Elizabeth L. *The Human Genome Project: Cracking the Code within Us* (8–12). Illus. 1996, Watts LB $24.00 (0-531-11299-3). Concepts in genetic research are discussed along with a history of the international Human Genome Project, which is to be completed in 2005. (Rev: BL 12/1/96; SLJ 8/97) [547.87]

5884 Swisher, Clarice. *Genetic Engineering* (5–8). Illus. (Overview) 1996, Lucent LB $18.96 (1-56006-179-0). An introduction to DNA, how the genetic code can by altered, and some of the people behind these discoveries. (Rev: BL 7/96; SLJ 1/97; VOYA 12/96) [575.1]

5885 Tagliaferro, Linda. *Genetic Engineering: Progress or Peril?* (7–10). Illus. (Pro/Con) 1997, Lerner LB $21.27 (0-8225-2620-7). This book presents the complex issues in the controversy over the manipulation of genes, such as the possibility of finding cures for hereditary diseases on the one hand, and on the other, the possibility of abusing it to create a made-to-order human race. (Rev: BL 9/1/97; SLJ 8/97) [575.1]

5886 Thro, Ellen. *Genetic Engineering: Shaping the Material of Life* (7–12). 1993, Facts on File LB $19.95 (0-8160-2629-7). Many charts and drawings are used to enhance the author's explanations of DNA and cell structure as well as chromosomes and genes, the determinants of heredity. (Rev: BL 9/1/93) [660]

5887 Wade, Nicholas, ed. *The Science Times Book of Genetics* (10–12). 1999, Lyons Pr. $25.00 (1-55821-765-7). This resource contains some 40 articles on the history and structure of DNA, genetic research, and ethical concerns related in genetic engineering, all from the *New York Times*. (Rev: BL 1/1–15/99; SLJ 7/99) [575.1]

5888 Wilcox, Frank H. *DNA: The Thread of Life* (7–10). Illus. 1988, Lerner LB $23.95 (0-8225-1584-9). The basic DNA structure is explained and material is given on what it does and what its functions are. (Rev: SLJ 6/88) [574.87]

5889 Winters, Paul A. *Cloning* (8–12). (At Issue) 1997, Greenhaven LB $16.96 (1-56510-753-5); paper $17.25 (1-56510-752-7). The successful cloning of a sheep has ignited many ethical questions concerning its application to humans. This controversy is explored in this anthology of various points of view. (Rev: BL 5/15/98; SLJ 1/99; VOYA 8/98) [174.957]

5890 Yount, Lisa. *Genetics and Genetic Engineering: Milestones in Discovery and Invention* (6–12). Illus. (Milestones in Discovery and Invention) 1997, Facts on File $19.95 (0-8160-3566-0). A clear explanation of genetics and its key concepts, with materials on heredity, gene mapping, the structure of DNA, disease-causing genes, and gene therapy. (Rev: BL 12/1/97) [576.5]

Grooming, Personal Appearance, and Dress

5891 Altman, Douglas. *For Guys* (6–9). Illus. 1989, Rourke LB $19.93 (0-86625-284-3). This is a good grooming manual for boys that covers such topics as diet, exercise, clothes, and hygiene. (Rev: SLJ 6/89) [646.7]

5892 Banks, Tyra, and Vanessa T. Bush. *Tyra's Beauty Inside & Out* (10–12). 1998, HarperCollins paper $16.95 (0-06-095210-5). A successful model shares her beauty secrets for skin care, cosmetics, hair, exercise, and fashion. (Rev: SLJ 8/98; VOYA 10/98) [646]

5893 Coen, Patricia, and Joe Maxwell. *Beautiful Braids* (9–12). Illus. 1983, Crown paper $4.95 (0-517-55222-1). The techniques and types of hair braiding are introduced in text and pictures. [611]

5894 Dawson, Mildred L. *Beauty Lab: How Science Is Changing the Way We Look* (5–10). 1997, Silver Moon $13.95 (1-881889-84-X). This work on health and hygiene contains chapters on skin, eyes, teeth, fitness, and hair. (Rev: BR 5–6/97; SLJ 3/97) [613.7]

5895 Landau, Elaine. *The Beauty Trap* (8–12). 1994, Macmillan LB $18.95 (0-02-751389-0). An examination of society's obsession with an unrealistic standard of feminine beauty and the damage it causes. (Rev: BL 3/15/94; SLJ 3/94; VOYA 2/95) [155.6]

5896 Murray, Maggie Pexton. *Changing Styles in Fashion: Who, What, Why* (10–12). Illus. 1989, Fairchild $46.00 (0-87005-585-2). The world of high fashion past and present is introduced and several modern couturiers are highlighted. (Rev: BL 4/15/89) [746.92]

5897 Peiss, Kathy. *Hope in a Jar: The Making of America's Beauty Culture* (9–12). 1998, Holt $25.00 (0-8050-5550-9). This is a fascinating look at the history and use of cosmetics in America from colonial days to modern times. (Rev: BL 5/15/98; SLJ 12/98) [391]

5898 Quant, Mary. *Ultimate Makeup and Beauty* (10–12). 1996, DK Publg. $24.95 (0-7894-1056-7). An attractive, well-illustrated guide to makeup that uses examples from various ethnic groups as well as different facial shapes. (Rev: SLJ 2/97) [646]

5899 Reybold, Laura. *Everything You Need to Know about the Dangers of Tattooing and Body Piercing* (7–12). Illus. 1996, Rosen LB $16.95 (0-8239-2151-4). After a brief history of tattooing and body piercing, the author presents specific information about the risks and consequences involved and suggests alternatives, such as temporary tattoos. (Rev: BL 4/15/96; SLJ 5/96; VOYA 8/96) [617.9]

5900 Silverstein, Alvin, et al. *Overcoming Acne: The How and Why of Healthy Skin Care* (7–12). 1990, Morrow $16.00 (0-688-08344-7). This should be a popular book considering that 90 percent of adolescents suffer from some form of acne and that this account is thorough and well balanced. (Rev: BL 4/15/90; SLJ 6/90) [616.5]

5901 Wilkinson, Beth. *Coping with the Dangers of Tattooing, Body Piercing, and Branding* (9–12). (Coping) 1998, Rosen $17.95 (0-8239-2717-2). Tattooing, body piercing, and branding are discussed, including descriptions of the procedures, health risks, care following the procedures, and first-person experiences. The dangers and potential negative consequences are stressed. (Rev: BR 9–10/98; SLJ 4/98; VOYA 8/98) [391]

5902 Zeldis, Yona. *Coping with Beauty, Fitness, and Fashion: A Girl's Guide* (7–12). Illus. 1987, Rosen LB $17.95 (0-8239-0731-7). A practical guide covering such topics as makeup, exercise, dress, and skin care. (Rev: BL 7/87; BR 11–12/87; SLJ 9/87) [646.7]

The Human Body

General and Miscellaneous

5903 Bruun, Ruth Dowling, and Bertel Bruun. *The Human Body* (6–9). Illus. 1982, Random LB $15.99 (0-394-94424-0); paper $12.99 (0-394-84424-6). The first part of this book describes the parts of the body and the second part reviews its various systems. [612]

5904 Burnie, David. *The Concise Encyclopedia of the Human Body* (7–12). Illus. 1995, DK Publg. $19.95 (0-7894-0204-1). A small, thematically arranged book on the human body that is outstanding for its basic coverage and magnificent illustrations. (Rev: VOYA 2/96) [612]

5905 Day, Trevor. *The Random House Book of 1001 Questions and Answers about the Human Body* (5–8). 1994, Random paper $15.00 (0-679-85432-0). Using a question-and-answer format, this book introduces the parts of the body, its systems, and how they work. (Rev: BL 12/1/94; SLJ 7/94) [612]

5906 Ganeri, Anita. *Inside the Body* (4–8). Illus. (Lift the Flap) 1996, DK Publg. $16.95 (0-7894-0999-2). When the tabs are lifted, various organs and muscles are revealed underneath. (Rev: BL 12/15/96; SLJ 8/96) [612]

5907 *Incredible Voyage: Exploring the Human Body* (9–12). 1998, National Geographic $35.00 (0-7922-7148-3). Interesting text and outstanding photographs trace human growth, anatomy, and physiology through all stages of life, sick or healthy, with information on many of the innovative, developing breakthroughs that are in the news. (Rev: SLJ 2/99) [612]

5908 Llamas, Andreu. *Digestion and Reproduction* (8–12). Illus. (Human Body) 1998, Gareth Stevens LB $21.27 (0-8368-2111-4). Using double-page spreads and lavish illustrations, the digestive and reproductive systems are explained. (Rev: BL 12/15/98; SLJ 3/99) [612]

5909 Llamas, Andreu. *Respiration and Circulation* (8–12). Illus. (Human Body) 1998, Gareth Stevens LB $21.27 (0-8368-2110-6). Double-page spreads and lavish illustrations are used to introduce the human respiration and circulation systems. (Rev: BL 12/15/98; SLJ 3/99) [612.1]

5910 Miller, Jonathan. *The Human Body* (7–12). Illus. 1983, Viking paper $22.50 (0-670-38605-7). Based on the TV series of the same name, this is a fascinating pop-up book on body parts with accompanying text. [612]

5911 Nilsson, Lennart. *Behold Man: A Photographic Journey of Discovery inside the Body* (7–12). Illus. 1974, Little, Brown $29.95 (0-316-60751-7). An unusually illustrated book (many photographs represent magnifications of 45,000 times) on the body and its systems. [612]

5912 Orlock, Carol. *Inner Time: The Science of Body Clocks and What Makes Us Tick* (9–12). 1993, Birch Lane $18.95 (1-55972-194-4). A lively overview of the discoveries and science of biological clocks. (Rev: BL 8/93) [574.1882]

5913 Parker, Steve. *Human Body* (5–8). (Eyewitness Science) 1993, DK Publg. $15.95 (1-56458-325-2). A handsomely illustrated introduction to the human body, its parts, and their functions. (Rev: BL 11/15/93) [612]

5914 Parramon Editorial Team, ed. *The Human Body: Understanding and Taking Care of Your Body* (5–9). Illus. 1998, Barron's $19.95 (0-7641-5078-2). A well-illustrated book that gives a general introduction to the human body, with separate chapters on each system. (Rev: VOYA 4/99) [612]

5915 Platt, Richard. *Stephen Biesty's Incredible Body* (5–9). Illus. 1998, DK Publg. $19.95 (0-7894-3424-5). Using clever cutaway illustrations, foldout pages, and visual jokes, this book explores the human body, its structure, and how it works. (Rev: BL 12/1/98; SLJ 1/99) [611]

5916 Sneddon, Pamela Shires. *Body Image: A Reality Check* (6–10). (Issues in Focus) 1999, Enslow $19.95 (0-89490-960-6). This book discusses body image and actions, often destructive, people take to control it, like anorexia, bulimia, steroid use, cosmetic surgery, and body piercing. (Rev: BL 5/1/99; SLJ 7/99) [155.9]

5917 Stein, Sara Bonnett. *The Body Book* (6–9). 1992, Workman paper $11.95 (0-89480-805-2). Follows human development from conception to birth and discusses what shapes us and how our bodies work. (Rev: BL 11/1/92; SLJ 12/92) [612]

5918 Walker, Richard, ed. *The Eyewitness Visual Dictionary of Human Anatomy* (8–12). Illus. 1996, DK Publg. $18.95 (0-7894-0445-1). This visual work is divided into 2 parts. The first deals with the 10 systems of the body, and the second with the 9 regions, such as head and neck, trunk, and thorax, with illustrations presenting increasingly deeper views of each region and showing how the systems work in the context of other systems. (Rev: BR 3–4/97; SLJ 10/96; VOYA 10/96) [612]

5919 Whitfield, Philip, ed. *The Human Body Explained: A Guide to Understanding the Incredible Living Machine* (9–12). 1995, Holt $56.80 (0-8050-3752-7). A guide to the body, discussing the major organs in terms of day-to-day life and their function in the survival of the species. (Rev: BL 12/1/95) [612]

5920 Williams, Frances. *Human Body* (5–9). (Inside Guides) 1997, DK Publg. $15.95 (0-7894-1506-2). Three-dimensional models and many photographs are used along with an informative text to introduce the human body and each of its systems. (Rev: SLJ 8/97) [612]

Brain and Nervous System

5921 Aaseng, Nathan, and Jay Aaseng. *Head Injuries* (6–10). Illus. 1996, Watts LB $24.00 (0-531-11267-5). A book that deals with brain injuries, their effects, and the emotional and behavioral problems that they can cause. (Rev: BL 8/96; SLJ 7/96) [617.4]

5922   August, Paul Nordstrom. *Brain Function* (9–12). Illus. 1987, Chelsea LB $19.95 (0-55546-204-9). An introduction to the nervous system that gives details on the brain and how drugs affect it. (Rev: BL 2/15/88) [612]

5923   Barmeier, Jim. *The Brain* (5–9). Illus. (Overview) 1996, Lucent LB $17.96 (1-56006-107-3). Many kinds of graphics, including cartoons and photographs, illustrate this introduction to the brain, its functions, and how we have learned about it. (Rev: BL 3/15/96; SLJ 7/96) [612.8]

5924   Barrett, Susan L. *It's All in Your Head: A Guide to Understanding Your Brain and Boosting Your Brain Power* (6–10). Illus. 1992, Free Spirit paper $9.95 (0-915793-45-8). Covers subjects as diverse as brain anatomy, intelligence, biofeedback, creativity, ESP, and brain scans. (Rev: BL 2/15/93) [153]

5925   Berger, Melvin. *Exploring the Mind and Brain* (7–10). Illus. 1983, HarperCollins LB $12.89 (0-690-04252-3). A book about the functions—both normal and abnormal—of the brain. [612]

5926   Brynie, Faith H. *101 Questions Your Brain Has Asked about Itself* (6–10). 1998, Millbrook $23.90 (0-7613-0400-2). Basic questions about the brain's structure and functions are answered in a lively style, including such topics as drugs and the brain, mental illness, epilepsy, and memory. (Rev: SLJ 4/99) [612.8]

5927   Edelson, Edward. *Nutrition and the Brain* (10–12). Illus. 1987, Chelsea LB $19.95 (1-55546-210-3). An explanation of how behavior and emotion are influenced by food. (Rev: BL 2/1/88) [612]

5928   Edelson, Edward. *Sleep* (7–10). (Encyclopedia of Health) 1991, Chelsea LB $19.95 (0-7910-0092-3). This book discusses the uses of sleep, people's sleeping habits, and sleeping disorders. (Rev: BL 11/15/91) [612.8]

5929   Facklam, Margery, and Howard Facklam. *The Brain: Magnificent Mind Machine* (7–12). Illus. 1982, Harcourt $12.95 (0-15-211388-6). Brain research from early times to current work on biofeedback is emphasized in this account. [612]

5930   Greenfield, Susan A., ed. *The Human Mind Explained: An Owner's Guide to the Mysteries of the Mind* (10–12). 1996, Holt $40.00 (0-8050-4499-X). Using double-page spreads and clear, concise language, this book is a guide to the human brain's composition, areas, functions, processes, and disorders. (Rev: SLJ 5/97) [612]

5931   Llamas, Andreu. *The Nervous System* (8–12). Illus. (Human Body) 1998, Gareth Stevens LB $21.27 (0-8368-2113-0). The human nervous system is described with double-page spreads and lavish illustrations. (Rev: BL 12/15/98; SLJ 3/99) [612.8]

5932   Parker, Steve. *The Brain & the Nervous System* (5–8). (The Human Body) 1997, Raintree Steck-Vaughn LB $25.69 (0-8172-4802-1). Double-page spreads introduce parts of the brain and their functions, what brain waves are, the nature of sleep and dreams, and other aspects of the brain and the nervous system. (Rev: BL 6/1–15/97; SLJ 8/97) [612.8]

5933   Policoff, Stephen P. *The Dreamer's Companion: A Beginner's Guide to Understanding Dreams & Using Them Creatively* (8–12). Illus. 1997, Chicago Review paper $12.95 (1-55652-280-0). This book covers mastering the art of lucid dreaming, the causes of dreams, how to analyze them, and how to keep a dream journal. (Rev: BL 5/15/98; SLJ 6/98) [154.6 3]

5934   Powledge, Tabitha. *Your Brain: How You Got It and How It Works* (7–12). 1994, Scribners paper $14.95 (0-684-19659-X). An informative overview of brain composition, development, and function. (Rev: BL 12/1/94; SLJ 9/95) [612.8]

5935   Restak, Richard. *Brainscapes: An Introduction to What Neuroscience Has Learned about the Structure, Function, and Abilities of the Brain* (9–12). 1995, Hyperion $19.95 (0-7868-6113-4). A neurologist discusses major advances in knowledge about the brain. (Rev: BL 10/1/95) [612.8]

5936   Rowan, Pete. *Big Head! A Book about Your Brain & Head* (5–9). Illus. 1998, Random $20.00 (0-679-89018-1). Using double-page spreads, this is a useful introduction to the anatomy, functions, and physiology of the head and neck, including such topics as hearing, speaking, emotions, and balance. (Rev: BR 1–2/99; SLJ 9/98) [612.8]

5937   Sekuler, Robert, and Randolph Blake. *Star Trek on the Brain: Alien Minds, Human Minds* (10–12). 1998, W. H. Freeman paper $21.95 (0-7167-3279-3). Episodes and concepts found in *Star Trek* are used to explain the human mind in this up-to-date primer on neurology and the nervous system. (Rev: SLJ 11/98) [616]

5938   Silverstein, Alvin, and Virginia Silverstein. *Sleep and Dreams* (7–9). 1974, HarperCollins LB $12.89 (0-397-31325-X). Research into sleep is reviewed and a description of our sleep patterns, dreams, and what they mean is presented. [154.6]

Circulation System

5939   Ballard, Carol. *The Heart & Circulatory System* (5–8). Illus. (The Human Body) 1997, Raintree Steck-Vaughn LB $25.69 (0-8172-4800-5). Topics discussed in this nicely illustrated volume include how blood is made, how it is pumped through the body, and how the heart and circulation system work together. (Rev: BL 6/1–15/97; SLJ 8/97) [612.1]

5940 Silverstein, Alvin, and Virginia Silverstein. *Heart Disease: America's #1 Killer.* Rev. ed. (7–10). Illus. 1985, HarperCollins LB $12.89 (0-397-32084-1). After a description of heart diseases, the authors present material on current treatments and preventative measures. (Rev: BR 5–6/86; SLJ 1/86) [611]

5941 Silverstein, Alvin, and Virginia Silverstein. *Heartbeats: Your Body, Your Heart* (7–10). Illus. 1983, HarperCollins LB $13.89 (0-397-32038-8). Following a description of the heart and how it works, there are sections on heart disease and current research. [612]

Digestive and Excretory Systems

5942 Avraham, Regina. *The Digestive System* (6–12). Illus. 1989, Chelsea LB $19.95 (0-7910-0015-X). In a few photographs and diagrams plus text, the human digestive system is explored with a history of how we gradually accumulated knowledge about it. (Rev: BL 9/1/89; BR 11–12/89) [612]

5943 Ballard, Carol. *The Stomach & Digestive System* (5–8). Illus. (The Human Body) 1997, Raintree Steck-Vaughn LB $25.69 (0-8172-4801-3). Topics discussed in this well-illustrated book include the digestive organs, how they work together, how food is tasted, and where nutrients are stored. (Rev: BL 6/1–15/97; SLJ 8/97) [612.3]

5944 Parker, Steve. *Food and Digestion.* Rev. ed. (6–8). Illus. 1990, Watts LB $19.00 (0-531-14027-X). The process of digestion is analyzed and pointers on nutrition and good health are provided. (Rev: BL 5/15/90) [612.3]

5945 Silverstein, Alvin, et al. *The Digestive System* (5–8). Illus. (Human Body Systems) 1994, Twenty-First Century LB $20.40 (0-8050-2832-3). Beginning with food assimilation in plants and animals, this book focuses on the human digestive system. (Rev: BL 3/15/95; SLJ 3/95) [612.3]

5946 Silverstein, Alvin, et al. *The Excretory System* (5–8). Illus. (Human Body Systems) 1994, Twenty-First Century LB $20.40 (0-8050-2834-X). Waste elimination in nature is discussed, with emphasis on this function in the human body. (Rev: BL 3/15/95; SLJ 3/95) [612.4]

Musculoskeletal System

5947 Ballard, Carol. *The Skeleton and Muscular System* (5–8). (Human Body) 1997, Raintree Steck-Vaughn $25.69 (0-8172-4805-6). This well-organized book uses text and pictures to introduce types of muscles and how they work, joint diseases, bones, and skeletal diseases. (Rev: SLJ 2/98) [612]

5948 Feinberg, Brian. *The Musculoskeletal System* (7–12). (Encyclopedia of Health) 1993, Chelsea LB $19.95 (0-7910-0028-1). An introduction to the muscles and bones in the human body and how they work together to form a single system. (Rev: BL 12/1/93) [612.7]

5949 Llamas, Andreu. *Muscles and Bones* (8–12). (Human Body) 1998, Gareth Stevens LB $21.27 (0-8368-2112-2). The musculoskeletal system is introduced in a series of double-page spreads with lavish illustrations. (Rev: BL 12/15/98; SLJ 3/99) [612]

5950 Silverstein, Alvin, et al. *The Muscular System* (5–8). Illus. (Human Body Systems) 1994, Twenty-First Century LB $21.90 (0-8050-2836-6). Full-color diagrams, drawings, and photographs highlight this survey of the human muscular system. (Rev: BL 3/15/95; SLJ 5/95) [612.7]

5951 Silverstein, Alvin, et al. *The Skeletal System* (5–8). Illus. (Human Body Systems) 1994, Twenty-First Century LB $20.40 (0-8050-2837-4). The purpose and nature of the human skeleton, its maintenance and repair, and the composition of bones are 3 of the topics discussed. (Rev: BL 3/15/95; SLJ 5/95) [612.7]

TEETH

5952 Lee, Jordan. *Coping with Braces & Other Orthodontic Work* (4–9). Illus. (Coping) 1998, Rosen $17.95 (0-8239-2721-0). Although wearing braces is common among young teens, many feel embarrassed and uncomfortable. This book explains why braces and other orthodontic work may be needed, different kinds of braces and the orthodontic procedures involved, and suggests ways to cope socially while wearing them. (Rev: SLJ 11/98) [617]

5953 Rourke, A. *Teeth and Braces* (6–9). Illus. 1989, Rourke LB $19.93 (0-86625-282-7). Topics covered in this book include teeth structure, dental care, malocclusion, and gum problems. (Rev: SLJ 6/89) [617.6]

5954 Siegel, Dorothy. *Dental Health* (7–12). (Encyclopedia of Health) 1994, Chelsea LB $19.95 (0-7910-0014-1). An explanation of what teeth are made of, their uses, diseases, and how to take care of them. (Rev: BL 1/1/94) [617.6]

5955 Silverstein, Alvin, and Virginia Silverstein. *So You're Getting Braces: A Guide to Orthodontics* (6–9). 1978, HarperCollins LB $12.89 (0-397-31786-7). The dental specialization of orthodontics is explained as well as why braces are often needed. [617.6]

Respiratory System

5956 Kittredge, Mary. *The Respiratory System* (6–12). Illus. 1989, Chelsea LB $19.95 (0-7910-0026-5). Beginning with an explanation of how animals breathe, the author describes the human breathing system and ills connected with it. (Rev: BL 3/15/89; BR 11–12/89; VOYA 8/89) [612]

5957 Parker, Steve. *The Lungs & Respiratory System* (5–8). Illus. (The Human Body) 1997, Raintree Steck-Vaughn LB $25.69 (0-8172-4803-X). The mechanisms of respiration, how oxygen is transferred, and air pollution are some of the areas covered in a series of double-page spreads. (Rev: BL 6/1–15/97; SLJ 8/97) [612.2]

5958 Silverstein, Alvin, et al. *The Respiratory System* (5–8). Illus. (Human Body Systems) 1994, Twenty-First Century LB $20.40 (0-8050-2831-5). The purpose and process of breathing are discussed, with the text and illustrations focusing on the human respiratory system. (Rev: BL 3/15/95; SLJ 4/95) [612.2]

Senses

5959 Churchill, E. Richard. *Optical Illusion Tricks & Toys* (6–10). Illus. 1989, Sterling $12.95 (0-8069-6868-0). A collection of over 60 optical illusions and tricks that are both fun to perform and instructive in the principles of optics. (Rev: BL 7/89; SLJ 10/89) [152.1]

5960 Cobb, Vicki. *How to Really Fool Yourself: Illusions for All Your Senses* (7–9). Illus. 1999, Wiley paper $12.95 (0-471-31592-3). A book about perception, how illusions are created, and how they are present in everyday life. [152.1]

5961 Connelly, Elizabeth Russell. *A World Upside Down & Backwards* (9–12). (Encyclopedia of Psychological Disorders) 1998, Chelsea $22.95 (0-7910-4894-2). Using brief case studies, this book explores the realities of dyslexia and other learning disorders, with material on the neurological and genetic origins and treatments, as well as examples of how they affect the classroom, family life, and society. Case studies of famous people who have overcome their learning disorder are included. (Rev: BL 4/1/99; SLJ 6/99) [371.91]

5962 Martin, Paul D. *Messengers to the Brain: Our Fantastic Five Senses* (6–9). Illus. 1984, National Geographic LB $12.50 (0-87044-504-9). A well-illustrated introduction to the 5 senses and how they work. [612]

5963 Silverstein, Alvin, and Virginia Silverstein. *Glasses and Contact Lenses: Your Guide to Eyes, Eyewear, and Eye Care* (6–9). Illus. 1989, HarperCollins LB $14.89 (0-397-32185-6). A description of how the eye functions, disorders connected with it, and how glasses can help. (Rev: BL 6/15/89; BR 1–2/90; SLJ 6/89; VOYA 8/89) [617.7]

5964 Simon, Seymour. *The Optical Illusion Book* (7–9). Illus. 1984, Morrow LB $12.93 (0-688-03255-9); paper $6.95 (0-688-03254-0). How optical illusions are created and the part that the brain as well as the eye plays in their perception. [152.1]

Hygiene and Physical Fitness

5965 Ball, Jacqueline A. *Hygiene* (6–9). Illus. 1989, Rourke LB $19.93 (0-86625-285-1). This book is aimed at preteen and teenage girls and gives tips on care of nails, skin, hair, and so on. (Rev: SLJ 6/89) [613]

5966 Barbour, Scott, and Karin L. Swisher, eds. *Health and Fitness* (7–12). (Opposing Viewpoints) 1996, Greenhaven $21.96 (1-56510-403-X); paper $16.25 (1-56510-402-1). Using carefully selected articles, this book explores different attitudes and controversies concerning diet, physical fitness, and exercise. (Rev: BL 9/15/96; BR 1–2/97; SLJ 8/96; VOYA 10/96) [613]

5967 Brody, Jane. *Jane Brody's The New York Times Guide to Personal Health* (9–12). Illus. 1982, Random $19.95 (0-686-95972-8); Avon paper $15.00 (0-380-64121-6). A popular introduction to topics related to health and medicine with emphasis on everyday concerns, prevention, and treatments. [613]

5968 Bull, Deborah C., and Torje Eike. *Totally Fit* (10–12). 1998, DK Publg. paper $11.95 (0-7894-2990-X). Though written for adults, the guide to complete fitness through dieting, nutrition, and exercise will appeal to older teens. (Rev: BL 2/15/98; SLJ 7/98) [613]

5969 Christensen, Alice. *The American Yoga Association Beginners' Manual.* Rev. ed. (10–12). Illus. 1987, Simon & Schuster paper $16.00 (0-671-61935-7). A basic manual on the philosophy and practice of yoga with material on 75 postures. (Rev: BL 9/1/87) [613.7]

5970 Curran, Delores. *Traits of a Healthy Family* (10–12). 1984, Ballantine paper $5.99 (0-345-31750-5). This book reports on a study of 500 families and what keeps them healthy. [610]

5971 Dixon, Barbara M., and Josleen Wilson. *Good Health for African-Americans* (9–12). 1994, Crown $26.00 (0-517-59170-7). Nutritionist Dixon places African Americans' health challenges and solutions in historical context and offers advice on lifestyle improvement through a 24-week diet. (Rev: BL 2/15/94) [613]

5972 Feuerstein, Georg, and Stephan Bodian, eds. *Living Yoga: A Comprehensive Guide for Daily Life* (9–12). 1993, Putnam paper $16.95 (0-87477-729-1). Interviews, essays, and articles on yoga's practices and teachings. (Rev: BL 3/15/93) [181.45]

5973 Fitness Magazine, and Karen Andes, eds. *The Complete Book of Fitness: Mind, Body, Spirit* (9–12). 1999, Three Rivers paper $24.95 (0-609-80155-4). A highly readable, oversize book divided into 4 sections covering all aspects of fitness: strength training, cardiovascular training, diet and nutrition, and wellness. (Rev: SLJ 8/99) [613.7]

5974 Gallagher-Mundy, Chrissie. *The Essential Guide to Stretching* (10–12). 1997, Crown paper $17.00 (0-517-88775-4). A visually attractive guide to stretching: its purpose; warmups; detailed beginning, intermediate, and advanced routines; and stretches for specific personal needs and for particular sports. (Rev: SLJ 11/97) [613.7]

5975 Jenner, Bruce, and Bill Dobbins. *The Athletic Body: A Complete Fitness Guide for Teenagers—Sports, Strength, Health, Agility* (7–12). Illus. 1984, Simon & Schuster $17.95 (0-671-46549-X). A guide to physical fitness through sports, weight training, and good nutrition. [613.7]

5976 Kaminker, Laura. *Exercise Addiction: When Fitness Becomes an Obsession* (6–10). (Teen Health Library of Eating Disorder Prevention) 1998, Rosen $17.95 (0-8239-2759-8). Some teens become addicted to exercise and exercise too much for the wrong reasons. This book defines the problem, risks, and causes, describes the symptoms, and tells where to get help and support if needed. (Rev: BL 3/1/89; BR 5–6/99; SLJ 1/99) [613.7]

5977 Milan, Albert R. *Breast Self-Examination* (10–12). Illus. 1980, Workman paper $3.50 (0-89480-124-4). A well-illustrated manual on how to conduct a breast examination. [613]

5978 Rosas, Debbie, and Carlos Rosas. *Non-Impact Aerobics: Introducing the NIA Technique* (9–12). Illus. 1988, Avon paper $9.95 (0-380-70522-2). A stress-free exercise system is described in this account with many photographs. (Rev: SLJ 10/88) [613.7]

5979 Self Magazine. *Self's Better Body Book* (9–12). 1998, Clarkson Potter $24.95 (0-609-60319-1). An exercise book with illustrated, step-by-step instructions for young women who want stronger, healthier bodies, also stressing the importance of good nutrition. (Rev: SLJ 11/98) [613.7]

5980 Simon, Nissa. *Good Sports: Plain Talk about Health and Fitness for Teens* (7–10). Illus. 1990, HarperCollins LB $14.89 (0-690-04904-8). This book covers a variety of topics including nutrition, different kinds of exercise, and sports injuries. (Rev: BL 9/15/90) [613]

5981 Sivananda, Swami, and Swami Vishnu de Vananda. *Yoga Mind & Body* (10–12). 1996, DK Publg. $24.95 (0-7894-0447-8). Five main principles of yoga, based on "proper living and high thinking," are introduced through words and pictures, with a chapter devoted to each principle, the longest being on proper exercise. The chapter on vegetarianism contains 20 pages of recipes. (Rev: SLJ 7/96) [613.7]

5982 Stiefer, Sandy. *A Risky Prescription* (7–12). Illus. (Sports Issues) 1997, Lerner LB $23.93 (0-8225-3304-9). This book explores the relationship between sports and health, how some sports activities can lead to disabilities, and how performance-enhancing drugs can compromise or even ruin one's health. (Rev: BL 12/1/97; SLJ 3/98) [631.7]

Mental Disorders and Emotional Problems

5983 Adler, Joe Anne. *Stress: Just Chill Out!* (7–10). 1997, Enslow LB $17.95 (0-89490-918-5). This book identifies 3 types of stress frequently experienced by teenagers—life transition stress, enduring life stress, and chronic daily stress—with chapters on their causes and treatment. (Rev: SLJ 10/97) [152.4]

5984 Axelrod, Toby. *Working Together Against Teen Suicide* (6–10). (The Library of Social Activism) 1996, Rosen LB $16.95 (0-8239-2261-8). The author examines the reasons for teenage suicide, suggests ways teens can cope with problems, and explains how telephone hotlines, community agencies, and institutions work to combat teen suicide and how teenagers can help. (Rev: SLJ 5/97) [394]

5985 Barbour, William, ed. *Mental Illness* (7–12). (Opposing Viewpoints) 1995, Greenhaven LB $21.96 (1-56510-209-6); paper $20.25 (1-56510-208-8). Each thematic chapter contains opinion pieces and excerpts from scientific studies supporting various viewpoints on mental health issues. (Rev: BL 7/95; VOYA 5/95) [362.2]

5986 Barrett, Deirdre. *The Pregnant Man and Other Cases from a Hypnotherapist's Couch* (10–12). 1998, Times Bks. $23.00 (0-8129-2905-5). Using 7 case studies, the author, a hypnotist, shows how hypnotherapy can be helpful when used in conjunction with traditional psychotherapy, and explains why hypnosis will work for some and not others and how people are treated. (Rev: BL 8/98; SLJ 12/98) [154.7]

5987 Beal, Eileen. *Everything You Need to Know About ADD ADHD* (6–8). Illus. (Need to Know Library) 1998, Rosen $17.95 (0-8239-2748-2). In 6 short chapters, the author describes attention deficit disorder and attention deficit hyperactivity disorder, their symptoms, the pros and cons of behavior modification and medications, and how teens can manage these disorders and use them to tap into special talents. (Rev: SLJ 9/98; VOYA 8/99) [371.9]

5988 Beckelman, Laurie. *Stress* (6–9). Illus. (Hot Line) 1994, Silver Burdett $17.95 (0-89686-848-6). Through interviews with teenagers and quotes from professionals, the world of adolescent stress is explored, with tips on how to deal with it. (Rev: BL 2/15/94) [155.9]

5989 Bernstein, Jane. *Loving Rachel: A Family's Journey from Grief* (9–12). 1994, Coyne & Chenoweth paper $15.00 (0-941038-01-7). A mother's story of how she raised her second daughter who was born with learning disorders. (Rev: BL 5/1/88) [362.3]

5990 Clarke, Alicia. *Coping with Self-Mutilation: A Helping Book for Teens Who Hurt Themselves* (7–10). (Coping) 1999, Rosen LB $17.95 (0-8239-2559-5). This volume defines various forms of self-mutilation, such as cutting and burning, examines the causes and the physiological and psychological effects, and discusses available treatments and self-help measures. (Rev: SLJ 5/99) [362.2]

5991 Cobain, Bev. *When Nothing Matters Anymore: A Survival Guide for Depressed Teens* (7–12). 1998, Free Spirit paper $21.95 (1-57542-036-8). The author, a psychiatric nurse who works with teens, discusses the types, causes, and warning signs of depression, the dangers of addictions and eating disorders, and the relationship between depression and suicide, and provides information on treatment options and suggestions for developing good mental and physical health. (Rev: SLJ 3/99; VOYA 2/99) [155]

5992 Cohen, Susan, and Daniel Cohen. *Teenage Stress* (8–12). 1984, M. Evans $19.50 (0-87131-423-1). The nature of stress, how it can be avoided, and how it can be lessened are 3 topics of discussion. (Rev: BL 6/15/90) [155]

5993 Crook, Marion. *Teenagers Talk about Suicide* (7–12). 1988, NC Pr. paper $12.95 (1-55021-013-0). Interviews with 30 Canadian teenagers who have tried suicide are reprinted. (Rev: BR 9–10/88) [362.2]

5994 Dinner, Sherry H. *Nothing to Be Ashamed Of: Growing up with Mental Illness in Your Family* (5–10). 1989, Lothrop LB $12.93 (0-688-08482-6). A psychologist gives good advice to those who must live with a mentally ill person. (Rev: BL 6/1/89; BR 11–12/89; SLJ 4/89; VOYA 8/89) [616.89]

5995 Fisher, Gary L., and Rhoda Woods Cummings. *The Survival Guide for Kids with LD (Learning Differences)* (5–8). Illus. 1990, Free Spirit paper $9.95 (0-915793-18-0). A book that explains various kinds of learning disabilities and how to cope with them. (Rev: BL 7/90; SLJ 6/90) [371.9]

5996 Fynn, Anna. *Mister God, This Is Anna* (10–12). 1985, Ballantine paper $5.99 (0-345-32722-5). The haunting story of the life and death of a London waif. [155.4]

5997 Goldman, M. Nikki. *Teenage Suicide* (7–12). Illus. (Life Issues) 1996, Marshall Cavendish LB $24.21 (0-7614-0020-6). The causes, prevention, and telltale warning signs of teen suicide are discussed, along with surviving the suicide death of someone you know. (Rev: BL 8/96; BR 11–12/96; SLJ 8/96) [362.2]

5998 Grob, Gerald N. *The Mad among Us: A History of the Care of America's Mentally Ill* (9–12). 1994, Free Pr. $24.95 (0-02-912695-9). An overview of the changing attitudes toward and the treatment of mental illness, showing the 20th-century progression from an asylum-related to a private-office practice. (Rev: BL 2/1/94) [362.2]

5999 Gutkind, Lee. *Stuck in Time: The Tragedy of Childhood Mental Illness* (9–12). 1993, Holt $25.00 (0-8050-1469-1). An eye-opening view of a health care system ill-equipped to deal with the problems of mentally ill youth. (Rev: BL 7/93; SLJ 1/94) [616.89]

6000 Hales, Dianne. *Depression* (7–10). Illus. 1989, Chelsea LB $19.95 (0-7910-0046-X). Types of depression are outlined. Includes material on the causes, effects, and cures of depression. (Rev: BL 11/1/89; BR 11–12/89; SLJ 2/90; VOYA 2/90) [616.85]

6001 Hall, David E. *Living with Learning Disabilities: A Guide for Students* (5–8). 1993, Lerner LB $19.93 (0-8225-0036-1). A pediatrician provides background information on learning disabilities, as well as coping strategies. (Rev: BL 1/1/94; SLJ 4/94) [371.9]

6002 Hermes, Patricia. *A Time to Listen: Preventing Youth Suicide* (8–12). 1987, Harcourt $13.95 (0-15-288196-4). Through questions and answers plus many case studies, the author explores many aspects of suicidal behavior and its causes. (Rev: BL 4/1/88; SLJ 3/88; VOYA 6/88) [362.2]

6003 Hurley, Jennifer A., ed. *Mental Health* (7–12). (Current Controversies) 1999, Greenhaven LB $20.96 (1-56510-953-8); paper $17.45 (1-56510-952-X). This anthology explores such questions as what constitutes good mental health, what treatments should be used for mentally ill patients, and how should society and the legal system respond to mentally ill people. (Rev: BL 7/99) [616.89]

6004 Hyde, Margaret O., and Elizabeth Forsyth. *Know about Mental Illness* (5–8). Illus. 1996, Walker LB $15.85 (0-8027-8429-1). This book describes a variety of mental illnesses like anorexia, schizophrenia, and depression, tells about treatments and symptoms, and has a section on 15 myths about mental illness. (Rev: BL 9/1/96; SLJ 7/96) [616.89]

6005 Kingsley, Jason, and Mitchell Levitz. *Count Us In: Growing Up with Down Syndrome* (9–12). 1994, Harcourt $19.95 (0-15-150447-4). The 2 authors write about their own experiences of living with Down's syndrome, including its effects on their families, marriage, sex, employment, ambitions, and education. (Rev: BL 11/15/93; SLJ 6/94) [362.1]

6006 Klebanoff, Susan. *Ups & Downs: How to Beat the Blues & Teen Depression* (6–9). Illus. (Plugged In) 1998, Price Stern Sloan $13.89 (0-8431-7460-9); paper $4.99 (0-8431-7450-1). Written in an informal style, this is an informative, useful discussion of teen depression, its causes, and treatments. (Rev: BL 4/15/99; BR 9–10/99; SLJ 10/99; VOYA 8/99) [616.85]

6007 Kuklin, Susan. *After a Suicide: Young People Speak Up* (7–12). 1994, Putnam $16.95 (0-399-22605-2); paper $9.95 (0-399-22801-2). Focuses on failed suicide attempts. Also looks at friends and family members who suffer shock, guilt, and loss when suicide succeeds. (Rev: BL 10/15/94; SLJ 12/94; VOYA 2/95) [362.2]

6008 Lauren, Jill. *Succeeding with LD*: 20 True Stories about Real People with LD* (*Learning Differences)* (5–8). Ed. by Elizabeth Verdick. Illus. 1997, Free Spirit paper $14.95 (1-57542-012-0). Case studies of 20 people ages 10 to 61 who overcome various learning difficulties. (Rev: BL 6/1–15/97; SLJ 7/97; VOYA 8/97) [371.92]

6009 Lee, Jordan. *Coping with Anxiety and Panic Attacks* (7–10). (Coping) 1997, Rosen LB $17.95 (0-8239-2548-X). This book describes the different forms of anxiety and panic attacks, their causes, standard treatments, and treatments for very severe cases. (Rev: SLJ 12/97) [155.5]

6010 Lee, Mary Price, and Richard S. Lee. *Everything You Need to Know about Natural Disasters and Post-Traumatic Stress Disorder* (5–9). (Need to Know) 1996, Rosen LB $17.95 (0-8239-2053-4). This book explains how disasters like hurricanes, floods, and earthquakes can cause post-traumatic stress disorder and how to get help and counseling. (Rev: SLJ 6/96; VOYA 8/96) [155.5]

6011 Leigh, Vanora. *Mental Illness* (6–8). (Talking Points) 1999, Raintree Steck-Vaughn $27.11 (0-8172-5311-4). This book defines mental illness, gives examples, and discusses causes, treatments, and how to keep mental healthy. (Rev: BL 8/1/99; BR 9–10/99; SLJ 8/99) [362.2]

6012 Levine, Mel. *Keeping a Head in School: A Student's Book about Learning Abilities and Learning Disorders* (8–12). Illus. 1990, Educators Publg.

paper $30.75 (0-8388-2069-7). This account deals with all sorts of learning disorders, how they affect the learning process, and how they can be be treated. (Rev: BL 6/15/90) [371.9]

6013 Lundy, Allan. *Diagnosing and Treating Mental Illness* (7–12). Illus. 1990, Chelsea LB $19.95 (0-7910-0047-8). An account that explains various mental disorders and covers the work of Freud, among others. (Rev: BL 6/1/90; VOYA 8/90) [616.89]

6014 MacCracken, Mary. *Lovey: A Very Special Child* (8–12). 1977, NAL paper $3.50 (0-451-13364-1). The story of a remarkable teacher and how she was able to reach a troubled child. [618]

6015 Maloney, Michael, and Rachel Kranz. *Straight Talk about Anxiety and Depression* (7–12). 1991, Facts on File LB $16.95 (0-8160-2434-0). Discusses teenage emotional pressures, stress, and sexual concerns, identifies the causes of depression and anxiety, and suggests coping strategies and techniques. (Rev: BL 10/15/91; SLJ 3/92) [155.5]

6016 Martin, Russell. *Out of Silence: A Journey into Language* (9–12). 1994, Holt $22.50 (0-8050-1998-7). Documents the continuing odyssey of the author's nephew, who was diagnosed as autistic after receiving a routine childhood inoculation. (Rev: BL 3/15/94) [616.8]

6017 Monroe, Judy. *Phobias: Everything You Wanted to Know, But Were Afraid to Ask* (6–10). (Issues in Focus) 1996, Enslow LB $19.95 (0-89490-723-9). This book on phobias contains an "A to Z" list detailing each phobia as well as information on causes, treatments, and where to get help. (Rev: SLJ 6/96; VOYA 8/96) [616.85]

6018 Moragne, Wendy. *Attention Deficit Disorder* (6–9). (Medical Library) 1996, Millbrook LB $23.90 (1-56294-674-9). This book exposes the myths and misunderstandings associated with ADD, and includes personal narratives of young people with ADD who are productive and continue to pursue the activities they enjoy. (Rev: SLJ 2/97) [153.1]

6019 Moragne, Wendy. *Dyslexia* (7–9). Illus. (Millbrook Medical Library) 1997, Millbrook LB $23.90 (0-7613-0206-9). Nine young adults are profiled in this explanation of the causes, symptoms, and treatment of the disorder that causes problems in oral and written communication. (Rev: BL 5/1/97; BR 9–10/97; SLJ 3/97; VOYA 10/97) [616.85]

6020 Packard, Gwen K. *Coping with Stress* (7–12). (Coping) 1997, Rosen LB $17.95 (0-8239-2081-X). This book explains the nature and causes of stress, discusses various methods of dealing with it, such as positive thinking, staying healthy, and talking with friends, family, and/or counselors and support groups, and offers sound advice for handling pressures of puberty, family, school, and natural disasters. (Rev: SLJ 8/97; VOYA 10/97) [152.4]

6021 Pickover, Clifford A. *Strange Brains & Genius: The Secret Lives of Eccentric Scientists & Madmen* (10–12). Illus. 1998, Plenum $28.95 (0-306-45784-9). The author explores the mental disorders of a number of geniuses and talented people, such as Ted Kaczynski, the Unabomber; Francis Galton, world traveler, inventor, and racist; and Nikola Tesla, who was incapable of conversation with anyone wearing pearls. (Rev: SLJ 4/99) [362.2]

6022 Porterfield, Kay M. *Straight Talk About Post-Traumatic Stress Disorder* (10–12). 1995, Facts on File $24.95 (0-8160-3258-0). PTSD (post-traumatic stress disorder) is discussed, with material on its causes, consequences, and ways of dealing with it, and including several case histories. (Rev: VOYA 2/96) [362.2]

6023 Quinn, Patricia O. *Adolescents and ADD: Gaining the Advantage* (6–12). Illus. 1996, Magination paper $12.95 (0-945354-70-3). As well as citing many case studies, this book on teens and attention deficit disorder provides useful background information plus tips on how to adjust to this condition and how to create a lifestyle that accommodates it. (Rev: BL 1/1–15/96; SLJ 3/96; VOYA 8/96) [371.94]

6024 Roleff, Tamara L., ed. *Suicide* (8–12). (Opposing Viewpoints) 1997, Greenhaven LB $21.96 (1-56510-665-2); paper $17.45 (1-56510-664-4). Twenty-four articles express various points of view concerning the ethical and legal aspects of suicide, with special attention to the causes of teen suicide and how it can be prevented. (Rev: BL 11/1/97; BR 11–12/97; SLJ 1/98; VOYA 10/98) [362.28]

6025 Sebastian, Richard. *Compulsive Behavior* (7–12). (Encyclopedia of Health) 1993, Chelsea LB $19.95 (0-7910-0044-3). This book explores the origins of compulsive behavior, its consequences, and its treatment. (Rev: BL 1/1/93) [616.85]

6026 Sherrow, Victoria. *Mental Illness* (6–9). Illus. (Overview) 1996, Lucent LB $16.95 (1-56006-168-5). After a general review of what constitutes mental illness, the author focuses on the history of society's treatment of the mentally ill, followed by a discussion of current controversies and approaches to therapy. (Rev: BL 3/1/96; SLJ 2/96; VOYA 8/96) [362.2]

6027 Silverstein, Alvin. *Depression* (6–10). Illus. (Diseases and People) 1997, Enslow LB $19.95 (0-89490-713-1). Topics covered in this appealing examination of depression include types, symptoms, and treatments. An extensive bibliography includes Internet sites. (Rev: BL 2/1/98; SLJ 4/98) [616.85]

6028 Silverstein, Alvin, and Virginia Silverstein. *Epilepsy* (7–10). Illus. 1975, HarperCollins $12.95 (0-397-31615-1). Sweeping aside all the untruths associated with this problem, the authors describe the cause and effect of seizures and their treatment. [616.8]

6029 Simpson, Carolyn, and Dwain Simpson. *Coping with Post-Traumatic Stress Disorder* (7–10). (Coping) 1997, Rosen LB $17.95 (0-8239-2080-1). Post-traumatic stress disorder (PTSD) affects people who have experienced natural disasters, rape, war, or other traumatic events. This book explains the causes and primary signs of PTSD and how it affects family and friends, as well as the victim, and provides useful information on treatment. (Rev: SLJ 10/97) [362]

6030 Sprung, Barbara. *Stress* (4–8). Illus. (Preteen Pressures) 1998, Raintree Steck-Vaughn $24.26 (0-8172-5033-6). This book explores the various causes of stress, how the body reacts to it, peer pressure, and ways to manage stress. (Rev: BL 4/15/98; SLJ 6/98) [155.4]

6031 Stewart, Gail B. *Teen Dropouts* (7–12). (The Other America) 1998, Lucent LB $22.45 (1-56006-399-8). Four troubled teenagers—2 girls and 2 boys—tell their sad stories about how and why they have become alienated from the mainstream and have withdrawn from life. (Rev: BL 4/15/99; SLJ 4/99) [373.12]

6032 Stewart, Gail B. *Teens & Depression* (6–12). Illus. (Other America) 1997, Lucent LB $18.96 (1-56006-577-X). A discussion of possible causes of teenage clinical depression and how to recognize and treat it as early as possible, supplemented by case studies of 4 teens and their battles to overcome the condition. (Rev: BL 5/15/98; SLJ 6/98; VOYA 10/98) [616.85 27 00835]

6033 Weaver, Robyn M. *Depression* (9–12). (Overview) 1998, Lucent LB $17.96 (1-56006-437-4). The nature and causes of this incapacitating condition are covered, with discussion of various treatments and the stigma that is still often attached to it. (Rev: BL 1/1–15/99; BR 5–6/99) [616.85]

6034 Wolff, Lisa. *Teen Depression* (6–12). (Overview: Teen Issues) 1998, Lucent $17.96 (1-56006-519-2). The complexities of teen depression and its causes, symptoms, and treatment are discussed. (Rev: BL 1/1–15/99) [616.85]

6035 Woog, Adam. *Suicide* (5–8). Illus. (Overview) 1997, Lucent LB $17.96 (1-56006-187-1). An in-depth view of suicide, including causes, frequency, consequences, and detectable warning signs. (Rev: BL 3/15/97; SLJ 4/97) [362.2]

6036 Young, Patrick. *Mental Disturbances* (7–10). Illus. 1988, Chelsea LB $19.95 (1-55546-206-5). A discussion of various forms of mental illness such as phobias and bulimia that often affect teenagers. (Rev: BL 7/88) [616.89]

6037 Young, Patrick. *Schizophrenia* (9–12). Illus. 1988, Chelsea LB $19.95 (0-7910-0052-4). A look at the origins and treatment of this mysterious disease that sometimes emerges in the late teens. (Rev: BL 7/88; BR 9–10/88) [616.89]

Nutrition and Diet

6038 Craig, Jenny, and Brenda L. Wolfe. *Jenny Craig's What Have You Got to Lose? A Personalized Weight Management Program* (9–12). 1992, Villard $19.50 (0-679-40527-5). Guide to weight-management principles through a program of nutritious foods and regular exercise. (Rev: BL 3/1/92) [613.2]

6039 Drohan, Michele I. *Weight-Loss Programs: Weighing the Risks & Realities* (6–10). Illus. (Teen Health Library of Eating Disorder Prevention) 1998, Rosen LB $17.95 (0-8239-2770-9). This book explores weight-loss programs, sheds light on potential dangers, and discusses safe and sensible approaches to weight loss. (Rev: BL 3/1/99; SLJ 1/99) [616.85]

6040 Edelstein, Barbara. *The Woman Doctor's Diet for Teenage Girls* (9–12). 1987, Ballantine paper $5.99 (0-345-34601-7). A cautious approach is recommended in this guide to weight loss for teenage girls. [613.2]

6041 Gelinas, Paul J. *Coping with Weight Problems* (7–10). 1983, Rosen LB $17.95 (0-8239-0598-5). A guide to weight problems, their causes, and their solutions. [613.2]

6042 Haas, Robert. *Eat to Win: The Sports Nutrition Bible* (9–12). 1983, NAL paper $5.99 (0-451-15509-2). A sports diet program that gives a 28-day menu program and recipes. [613.2]

6043 *The Human Fuel Handbook: Nutrition for Peak Athletic Performance* (9–12). 1988, Health for Life paper $24.95 (0-944831-17-6). Written primarily for athletes, this is a no-nonsense guide to top performance through proper diet. (Rev: BL 3/1/89) [613.2]

6044 Kane, June Kozak. *Coping with Diet Fads* (7–12). 1990, Rosen LB $17.95 (0-8239-1005-9). An account that explores the wrong and right ways to diet and also furnishes useful advice. (Rev: BL 3/15/90; SLJ 10/90; VOYA 8/90) [613]

6045 Krizmanic, Judy. *A Teen's Guide to Going Vegetarian* (7–12). 1994, Viking $14.99 (0-670-85114-0); paper $8.99 (0-14-036589-3). Explains the health, ethical, and environmental benefits of switching to a vegetarian diet. Discusses nutrition and provides recipes. (Rev: BL 10/1/94; SLJ 2/95; VOYA 2/95) [613.2]

6046 Lamb, Lawrence E. *The Weighting Game: The Truth about Weight Control* (9–12). Illus. 1988, Lyle Stuart $15.95 (0-8184-0487-6). A practical account of what causes fat accumulation that stresses know-

ing your own body and learning to live with it. (Rev: BL 1/1/89) [613.2]

6047 Le Bow, Michael D. *Overweight Teenagers: Don't Bear the Burden Alone* (6–12). 1995, Plenum $23.95 (0-306-45047-X). By a sympathetic director of an obesity clinic; does not include food plans. (Rev: BL 12/1/95) [613.2]

6048 Lukes, Bonnie L. *How to Be a Reasonably Thin Teenage Girl* (6–9). Illus. 1986, Macmillan $15.00 (0-689-31269-5). A common sense guide that addresses the particular weight problems of young teenagers. (Rev: BL 1/1/87; SLJ 11/86; VOYA 4/87) [613.2]

6049 MacClancy, Jeremy. *Consuming Culture: Why You Eat What You Eat* (9–12). 1993, Holt $23.00 (0-8050-2578-2). A multicultural romp through the history of world cuisine, presenting little-known facts about food taboos, fads, nutritional illogic, food politics, even cannibalism. (Rev: BL 6/1–15/93) [394.1]

6050 Nardo, Don. *Vitamins and Minerals* (7–12). (Encyclopedia of Health) 1994, Chelsea LB $19.95 (0-7910-0032-X). A description of the vitamins and minerals needed by the human body and the importance of each. (Rev: BL 8/94; VOYA 6/94) [613.2]

6051 Navarra, Tova, and Myron A. Lipkowitz. *Encyclopedia of Vitamins, Minerals and Supplements* (10–12). 1996, Facts on File $35.00 (0-8160-3183-5). This reference work contains over 500 alphabetically arranged entries on vitamins, minerals, and food supplements, with information on their properties, benefits, proper dosage, and effects. (Rev: SLJ 11/96) [641.1]

6052 Parr, Jan. *The Young Vegetarian's Companion* (6–12). Illus. 1996, Watts LB $25.00 (0-531-11277-2). A guide to vegetarianism (with some horrifying descriptions of the meat industry) that stresses health and nutrition and provides a fine directory of further information sources such as films, online sites, and organizations. (Rev: BL 10/15/96; BR 3–4/97; SLJ 12/96; VOYA 6/97) [641.5]

6053 Peavy, Linda, and Ursula Smith. *Food, Nutrition, and You* (7–10). Illus. 1982, Macmillan LB $16.00 (0-684-17461-8). A discussion of digestion, food values, weight, and weight problems. [613.2]

6054 Pierson, Stephanie. *Vegetables Rock! A Complete Guide for Teenage Vegetarians* (7–12). 1999, Bantam paper $12.95 (0-553-37924-0). Animal rights and health issues are touched on in this book that describes philosophical and practical aspects of vegetarianism and provides a guide to good foods and balancing nutritional needs. (Rev: BL 3/1/99) [613.2]

6055 Polunin, Miriam. *Healing Foods: A Practical Guide to Key Foods for Good Health* (10–12). 1997, DK Publg. $24.95 (0-7894-1456-2). This is a rundown on the nutritional benefits of a variety of foods that also contains a great deal of food lore, recipes, and examples of 50 foods that promote good health. (Rev: BL 8/97; SLJ 9/97) [641.1]

6056 Reuben, David. *Everything You Always Wanted to Know about Nutrition* (9–12). 1979, Avon paper $4.50 (0-380-44370-8). Through a question-and-answer approach, basic information about foods and the food industry is given. [641.1]

6057 Salter, Charles A. *Food Risks and Controversies: Minimizing the Dangers in Your Diet* (6–10). (Teen Nutrition) 1993, Millbrook LB $22.40 (1-56294-259-X). A nutritionist/research scientist answers questions about the dangers in a teenager's diet. (Rev: BL 12/1/93; SLJ 11/93) [615.9]

6058 Salter, Charles A. *The Nutrition-Fitness Link: How Diet Can Help Your Body and Mind* (6–10). (Teen Nutrition) 1993, Millbrook LB $22.40 (1-56294-260-3). A professional nutritionist/researcher discusses the dos and don'ts of nutrition for athletes. (Rev: BL 12/1/93; SLJ 11/93; VOYA 2/94) [613.2]

6059 Salter, Charles A. *The Vegetarian Teen: A Teen Nutrition Book* (7–10). 1991, Millbrook LB $22.40 (1-56294-048-1). A positive introduction to vegetarianism that addresses the special concerns of teenagers and gives advice on achieving proper nutritional balance. (Rev: BL 10/1/91; SLJ 11/91) [613.2]

6060 Spence, Annette. *Nutrition* (7–9). Illus. 1989, Facts on File $18.95 (0-8160-1670-4). After general information on nutrition, this account gives details on the use of food to improve and maintain health. (Rev: VOYA 8/89) [641.1]

6061 Stare, Frederick J., et al. *Your Guide to Good Nutrition* (9–12). 1991, Prometheus paper $17.95 (0-87975-692-6). Professional, no-nonsense answers are given to basic questions about nutrition, weight control, dietary supplements, and the claims of the health food industry. (Rev: BL 10/1/91; SLJ 12/91) [613.2]

6062 Wann, Marilyn. *Fat! So? Because You Don't Have to Apologize for Your Size* (9–12). 1999, Ten Speed Pr. paper $12.95 (0-89815-995-4). This breezy title filled with facts and humorous anecdotes, aimed largely at oversize women, preaches good health through eating right, exercise, and not worrying about weight. (Rev: SLJ 8/99; VOYA 12/99) [641.1]

Physical Disabilities and Problems

6063 Cheney, Glenn. *Teens with Physical Disabilities: Real-Life Stories of Meeting the Challenges* (6–9). 1995, Enslow LB $19.95 (0-89490-625-9). Accounts of teens' daily lives as they struggle and

triumph over the challenges imposed by disabilities. Includes short biographies and photos. (Rev: BL 8/95; SLJ 8/95) [362.4]

6064 Costello, Elaine. *Signing: How to Speak with Your Hands* (7–9). Illus. 1995, Bantam paper $17.95 (0-553-37539-3). A simple explanation of and a guide to the use of sign language for the deaf. [001.56]

6065 Kent, Deborah, and Kathryn A. Quinlan. *Extraordinary People with Disabilities* (5–8). Illus. 1996, Children's Pr. LB $37.00 (0-516-20021-6). A variety of notable historical and contemporary people with disabilities introduce their conditions and describe the adjustments they have made to live with them. (Rev: BL 3/1/97; SLJ 3/97) [363.4]

6066 Landau, Elaine. *Living with Albinism* (5–8). Illus. (Living With) 1997, Watts $22.50 (0-531-20296-8). This book defines albinism, discusses its genetic causes and the accompanying problems related to vision and skin care, and tells how to live with this condition. (Rev: BL 11/15/98; SLJ 8/98) [616]

6067 Lutkenhoff, Marlene, and Sonya G. Oppenheimer, eds. *SPINAbilities: A Young Person's Guide to Spina Bifida* (8–12). Illus. 1997, Woodbine paper $16.95 (0-933149-86-7). A collection of essays on spina bifida—the nature of the disability, daily care concerns, and social adjustments. (Rev: BL 2/15/97; SLJ 4/97) [616.8]

6068 Stalcup, Brenda, ed. *The Disabled* (7–12). (Current Controversies) 1997, Greenhaven LB $26.20 (1-56510-530-3). This collection of documents explores such questions as the effectiveness of the Americans with Disabilities Act, the degree that the disabled should be helped, and the advisability of mainstreaming of children. (Rev: BL 2/15/97) [362.4]

Reproduction and Child Care

6069 Aitkens, Maggi. *Kerry, a Teenage Mother* (6–9). Photos. Illus. 1994, Lerner LB $19.93 (0-8225-2556-9). A day in the life of an 18-year-old mother on welfare who is trying to make a better life for herself and her daughter. (Rev: BL 12/15/94; SLJ 12/94) [362.83]

6070 Andryszewski, Tricia. *Abortion: Rights, Options, and Choices* (9–12). Illus. (Debate) 1996, Millbrook LB $23.90 (1-56294-573-4). This book discusses thoroughly Roe. v. Wade and its impact, the moral and medical aspects of abortion, and points of view of groups opposed to or supporting the right to abortion. (Rev: BL 4/15/96; BR 9–10/96; SLJ 5/96; VOYA 10/96) [344.73]

6071 Arnoldi, Katherine. *The Amazing True Story of a Teenage Single Mom* (9–12). 1998, Hyperion $16.00 (0-7868-6420-6). In this autobiography, an abused child and rape victim copes with becoming a single mother at 17. (Rev: BL 11/15/98; SLJ 1/99; VOYA 2/99) [306.874]

6072 Buckingham, Robert W., and Mary P. Derby. *"I'm Pregnant, Now What Do I Do?"* (10–12). Illus. 1997, Prometheus paper $13.95 (1-57392-117-3). After a brief discussion of the reproductive process, this candid, helpful book discusses the pros and cons of the 3 alternatives available to pregnant teens—adoption, abortion, or becoming a parent. (Rev: BL 2/15/97) [306.874]

6073 Caplan, Theresa. *The First Twelve Months of Life: Your Baby's Growth Month by Month* (9–12). 1993, Putnam paper $15.95 (0-399-51804-5). Organized month by month, this book charts the first year of infant development. (Rev: BL 7/93) [613.9]

6074 Coles, Robert. *The Youngest Parents* (8–12). Illus. 1997, Norton $27.50 (0-393-04082-8). The first two-thirds of this adult book consists of interviews by the author, a child psychiatrist, with teenagers who are or about to be parents, and the last part is a moving photoessay that includes many rural, underprivileged teen parents and their children as subjects. (Rev: BL 2/1/97; VOYA 6/98) [306.85]

6075 Cozic, Charles P., and Jonathan Petrikin, eds. *The Abortion Controversy* (7–12). (Current Controversies) 1995, Greenhaven LB $20.96 (1-56510-229-0); paper $16.20 (1-56510-228-2). The morality of abortion and access to it is argued from many points of view. (Rev: BL 3/15/95; SLJ 5/95) [363.4]

6076 Day, Nancy. *Abortion: Debating the Issue* (8–12). (Issues in Focus) 1995, Enslow LB $17.95 (0-89490-645-3). A balanced presentation of the subject, with black-and-white photos, glossary, and extensive notes. (Rev: BL 8/95; SLJ 12/95) [363.4]

6077 Edelson, Paula. *Straight Talk about Teenage Pregnancy* (7–12). (Straight Talk) 1998, Facts on File $24.95 (0-8160-3717-5). A frank, nonjudgmental discussion on such topics as abstinence, safe sex, abortion, adoption, and teen parenting, to help young people make wise decisions and take responsibility for their actions. (Rev: BL 3/1/99; BR 9–10/99; SLJ 2/99) [306.874]

6078 Flanagan, Geraldine Lux. *Beginning Life: The Marvelous Journey from Conception to Birth* (10–12). 1996, DK Publg. $19.95 (0-7894-0609-8). Using many color photographs and a clear text, this is the story of human life from conception to birth. (Rev: BR 1–2/97; SLJ 5/97; VOYA 2/97) [612]

6079 Fontanel, Beatrice, and Claire D'Harcourt. *Babies: History, Art, & Folklore* (10–12). 1998, Harry N. Abrams $39.95 (0-8109-1244-9). This is a lavishly illustrated history about all aspects of child rearing from ancient to modern times, from teething, hygiene, and nutrition to birth instruments, clothing, and toys, placed in a context of changing theories related to childbirth and child raising over the centuries. (Rev: SLJ 5/98) [305]

6080 Gay, Kathlyn. *Pregnancy: Private Decisions, Public Debates* (7–12). 1994, Watts LB $25.00 (0-531-11167-9). Discusses topics involving reproductive freedom, including the pro-choice/pro-life debate, reproductive technologies, population growth, and childbirth methods. (Rev: BL 8/94; SLJ 7/94; VOYA 10/94) [363.9]

6081 Gravelle, Karen, and Leslie Peterson. *Teenage Fathers* (7–12). 1992, Messner paper $5.95 (0-671-72851-2). Thirteen teenage boys describe their situations and feelings when they became fathers, with comments by the authors. (Rev: BL 10/15/92) [306.85]

6082 Hales, Dianne. *Pregnancy and Birth* (9–12). Illus. 1989, Chelsea LB $19.95 (0-7910-0040-0). A well-illustrated book that deals with fetal development and methods of childbirth. (Rev: BL 7/89; BR 11–12/89; SLJ 1/90; VOYA 12/89) [618.2]

6083 Hammerslough, Jane. *Everything You Need to Know about Teen Motherhood* (7–12). Illus. (Need to know) 1997, Rosen LB $17.95 (0-8239-2619-2). An account of the problems that young mothers face and how to cope with them. (Rev: SLJ 9/90; VOYA 8/90) [305.4]

6084 Hughes, Tracy. *Everything You Need to Know about Teen Pregnancy* (7–12). Illus. (Need to Know) 1988, Rosen $24.50 (0-8239-0810-0). A simple unbiased introduction to teen pregnancy and the options available. (Rev: SLJ 4/89) [612]

6085 Jakobson, Cathryn. *Think about Teenage Pregnancy* (7–12). Illus. 1993, Walker LB $29.90 (0-8027-8128-4); paper $14.95 (0-8027-7372-9). Problems of teenagers who are pregnant. All possible options are presented plus the social issues involved. (Rev: SLJ 8/88; VOYA 10/88) [612]

6086 Judges, Donald P. *Hard Choices, Lost Voices: How the Abortion Conflict Has Divided America, Distorted Constitutional Rights and Damaged the Courts* (9–12). 1993, Ivan R. Dee $25.00 (1-56663-016-9). A balanced overview of the controversy, concentrating on legal issues, the Supreme Court's role, and the judicial system's seeming ambivalence. (Rev: BL 5/15/93) [363.4]

6087 Kitzinger, Sheila. *The Complete Book of Pregnancy and Childbirth*. Rev. ed. (9–12). Illus. 1989, Knopf $22.50 (0-394-58011-7). A sensitive, thorough account of prenatal development and care and the birth experience. (Rev: BL 12/1/89) [618.2]

6088 Lang, Paul, and Susan S. Lang. *Teen Fathers* (7–12). 1995, Watts LB $25.00 (0-531-11216-0). A fact book not often seen concerning the dilemmas teen fathers face. (Rev: BL 9/1/95; SLJ 12/95) [306.85]

6089 Lerman, Evelyn. *Teen Moms: The Pain and the Promise* (10–12). Illus. 1997, Morning Glory Pr. $21.95 (1-885356-24-2); paper $14.95 (1-885356-25-0). Combining good background research and interviews with 50 teens, this resource explores teenage sex, teen pregnancy, and what motherhood means. (Rev: BR 3–4/98; SLJ 1/98) [618.2]

6090 Lindsay, Jeanne W. *Challenge of Toddlers: For Teen Parents—Parenting Your Child from One to Three* (8–12). Illus. (Teens Parenting) 1998, Morning Glory Pr. $18.95 (1-885356-38-2); paper $12.95 (1-885356-39-0). A practical, updated manual on how teens can raise children from ages 1 to 3, including information on developmental problems. (Rev: BL 10/15/98) [649]

6091 Lindsay, Jeanne W. *Pregnant? Adoption Is an Option: Making an Adoption Plan for a Child* (7–12). Illus. 1996, Morning Glory Pr. paper $11.95 (1-885356-08-0). Using quotes from many case studies, this book describes the steps in the adoption process and how to develop an adoption plan. (Rev: BL 12/1/96; SLJ 2/97; VOYA 4/97) [362.7]

6092 Lindsay, Jeanne W. *Teen Dads: Rights, Responsibilities and Joys* (7–12). Illus. 1993, Morning Glory Pr. $15.95 (0-930934-77-6); paper $9.95 (0-930934-78-4). Teenage fatherhood is explored with good quotations from case histories. (Rev: BL 10/15/93; SLJ 10/93; VOYA 2/94) [649.1]

6093 Lindsay, Jeanne W. *Your Baby's First Year: A Guide for Teenage Parents* (8–12). Illus. (Teens Parenting) 1998, Morning Glory Pr. $18.95 (1-885356-32-3); paper $12.95 (1-885356-33-1). This book discusses growth changes that occur in babies from birth to age one and how teenage parents can handle these changes and adjust to them. (Rev: BL 10/15/98; SLJ 2/99; VOYA 8/99) [649]

6094 Lindsay, Jeanne W., and Jean Brunelli. *Your Pregnancy & Newborn Journey: A Guide for Pregnant Teens* (8–12). Illus. 1998, Morning Glory Pr. $18.95 (1-885356-29-3); paper $12.95 (1-885356-30-7). This guide for teens explains the stages of pregnancy, what health care measures should be taken, the process of giving birth, and the special needs of some babies. (Rev: BL 10/15/98; SLJ 12/98; VOYA 8/99) [618.2]

6095 Lindsay, Jeanne W., and Sally McCullough. *Discipline from Birth to Three: How Teen Parents Can Prevent & Deal with Discipline Problems with Babies & Toddlers* (8–12). Illus. (Teens Parenting) 1998, Morning Glory Pr. $18.95 (1-885356-35-8); paper $12.95 (1-885356-36-6). This volume gives practical advice for teen parents on how to handle

behavioral problems with their children ages 1 to 3. (Rev: BL 10/15/98) [649.64]

6096 Lowenstein, Felicia. *The Abortion Battle: Looking at Both Sides* (7–12). Illus. (Issues in Focus) 1996, Enslow LB $19.95 (0-89490-724-7). After a presentation of the facts, the author analyzes arguments on both sides of the abortion controversy. Appended are a glossary, hot line numbers, and a reading list. (Rev: BL 7/96; BR 9–10/96; SLJ 9/96; VOYA 8/96) [363.4]

6097 Lunneborg, Patricia. *Abortion: A Positive Decision* (9–12). 1992, Bergin & Garvey $19.95 (0-89789-243-7). A look at the pro-choice side of this controversial issue, based on interviews with more than 100 women. (Rev: BL 2/15/92) [363.4]

6098 Marzollo, Jean. *Fathers and Babies: How Babies Grow and What They Need from You from Birth to 18 Months* (9–12). 1993, HarperCollins paper $13.00 (0-06-096908-3). This practical, illustrated guide describes normal chronological development and offers how-to information on such subjects as making simple toys. (Rev: BL 5/1/93) [306.874]

6099 Moe, Barbara. *A Question of Timing: Successful Men Talk about Having Children* (6–12). Illus. (The Teen Pregnancy Prevention Library) 1997, Rosen LB $16.95 (0-8239-2253-7). Men from a variety of backgrounds talk abut why they waited to have children and how they feel about that choice. (Rev: BL 6/1–15/97; BR 9–10/97; VOYA 10/97) [306.874]

6100 Nathanson, Laura Walther. *The Portable Pediatrician for Parents* (9–12). (Omnibus) 1994, HarperCollins paper $23.00 (0-06-273176-9). Details what to expect at every stage of infancy and toddlerhood and counsels on broader aspects of child rearing as well. (Rev: BL 2/1/94) [618.92]

6101 Richards, Arlene Kramer, and Irene Willis. *What to Do If You or Someone You Know Is Under 18 and Pregnant* (9–12). Illus. 1983, Lothrop paper $8.95 (0-688-01044-X). A practical guide that covers such topics as abortion, adoption, marriage, sex, and birth control. (Rev: BL 10/15/88) [362.7]

6102 Roleff, Tamara L., ed. *Abortion* (9–12). (Opposing Viewpoints) 1997, Greenhaven LB $21.96 (1-56510-506-0); paper $22.00 (1-56510-505-2). This replacement of the 1991 title contains an anthology of writings about abortion that covers morality, ethical concerns, and safety, and also considers justification and whether abortion rights should be restricted. (Rev: BL 1/1–15/97; BR 5–6/97; VOYA 10/97) [363.4]

6103 Romaine, Deborah S. *Roe v. Wade: Abortion and the Supreme Court* (9–12). (Famous Trials) 1998, Lucent LB $17.96 (1-56006-274-6). An account of the Supreme Court decision in 1973 that protected a woman's right to abortion. (Rev: BL 8/98; SLJ 9/98) [179]

6104 Sherman, Aliza. *Everything You Need to Know about Placing Your Baby for Adoption* (9–12). Illus. (Need to Know) 1997, Rosen LB $17.95 (0-8239-2266-9). This book provides good information on the practical and personal issues involved in deciding whether to place a child for adoption, methods of adoption, and organizations that can help. (Rev: BL 10/15/97; BR 1–2/98; SLJ 2/98) [362.7]

6105 Silverstein, Alvin, et al. *The Reproductive System* (5–8). Illus. (Human Body Systems) 1994, Twenty-First Century LB $16.95 (0-50-2838-2). Reproduction in the plant and animal worlds is introduced, focusing on the human system and body parts. (Rev: BL 3/15/95) [612.6]

6106 Silverstein, Herma. *Teenage and Pregnant: What You Can Do* (7–12). 1989, Messner paper $5.95 (0-671-65222-2). Options available to pregnant teens are discussed plus related material on such subjects as contraception and care for the expectant mother. (Rev: BL 3/15/89; BR 9–10/89; SLJ 1/89; VOYA 8/89) [306.7]

6107 Simpson, Carolyn. *Coping with an Unplanned Pregnancy* (9–12). (Coping) 1996, Rosen LB $17.95 (0-8239-2265-0). This book discusses options available to pregnant teenagers, adjustments that have to be made, and what happens if one decides to become a mother. (Rev: VOYA 8/90) [618.2]

6108 Stewart, Gail B. *Teen Fathers* (7–12). Illus. (Other America) 1998, Lucent LB $17.96 (1-56006-575-3). Using case studies and many photographs, this account reveals the various levels of responsibility assumed by teens when they become fathers. (Rev: BL 4/15/98; SLJ 6/98) [306.874]

6109 Stewart, Gail B. *Teen Mothers* (6–10). (The Other America) 1996, Lucent LB $17.96 (1-56006-332-7). Four teen moms in different situations, from living in a teen shelter to being at home with parents, describe the difficulties, frustrations, disruptions, and despair they have experienced as a result of teen parenthood. (Rev: BR 9–10/96; SLJ 7/96; VOYA 6/96) [649]

6110 Thompson, Stephen P., ed. *Teenage Pregnancy* (9–12). Illus. (Opposing Viewpoints) 1997, Greenhaven LB $20.96 (1-56510-562-1); paper $16.20 (1-56510-561-3). Various points of view are expressed in chapters that include: Is teenage pregnancy a serious problem? What factors contribute to teenage pregnancy? How can teenage pregnancy be prevented? and What new initiatives would reduce teenage pregnancy? (Rev: BL 6/1–15/97; BR 1–2/98; SLJ 6/97; VOYA 12/97) [304.6]

6111 Trapani, Margi. *Listen Up: Teenage Mothers Speak Out* (6–12). Illus. (The Teen Pregnancy Prevention Library) 1997, Rosen LB $16.95 (0-8239-

2254-5). Young women speak candidly about why they had children at an early age and the impact this has had on their lives. (Rev: BL 6/1–15/97; BR 9–10/97; SLJ 6/97; VOYA 10/97) [306.874]

6112 Trapani, Margi. *Reality Check: Teenage Fathers Speak Out* (7–10). 1997, Rosen LB $16.95 (0-8239-2255-3). Case studies of teenage fathers who did not plan on becoming parents are discussed in this book that does not shun the hardships of being a teenage parent. (Rev: BL 6/1–15/97; SLJ 6/97; VOYA 10/97) [306.85]

6113 Wekesser, Carol, ed. *Reproductive Technologies* (7–12). (Current Controversies) 1996, Greenhaven LB $26.20 (1-56510-377-7); paper $16.20 (1-56510-376-9). The fact that science has enabled infertile couples to have children has raised a number of ethical and legal concerns. These are explored in this collection of original sources. (Rev: BL 6/1–15/96; SLJ 3/96) [176]

6114 Wilks, Corinne Morgan, ed. *Dear Diary, I'm Pregnant: Teenagers Talk about Their Pregnancy* (7–12). Illus. 1997, Annick paper $9.95 (1-55037-440-0). Ten teenage girls talk about how they got pregnant, what they decided to do about it, and how the pregnancy has changed their lives. (Rev: BL 2/1/98; BR 11–12/97; SLJ 8/97; VOYA 12/97) [306.874]

Safety and First Aid

6115 Auerbach, Paul S. *Medicine for the Outdoors: A Guide to Emergency Medical Procedures and First Aid* (9–12). Illus. 1986, Little, Brown $24.95 (0-316-05928-5); paper $12.95 (0-316-05929-3). A first-aid manual for the outdoor person that stresses prevention and safety measures. (Rev: BL 1/15/86) [616.02]

6116 Children's Hospital at Yale-New Haven. *Now I Know Better: Kids Tell Kids about Safety* (5–9). 1996, Millbrook LB $21.90 (0-7613-0109-7); paper $7.95 (0-7613-0149-6). This book on safety features true accounts from young people whose lives have been changed by accidents. (Rev: BL 10/15/96; SLJ 2/97) [613.6]

6117 Goedecke, Christopher J., and Rosmarie Hausherr. *Smart Moves: A Kid's Guide to Self-Defense* (6–8). 1995, Simon & Schuster $16.00 (0-689-80294-3). A martial arts instructor offers this sourcebook of safety and survival strategies. (Rev: BL 9/15/95; SLJ 12/95; VOYA 2/96) [613.6]

6118 Grosser, Vicky, et al. *Take a Firm Stand: The Young Woman's Guide to Self-Defence* (9–12). 1993, Virago $11.95 (1-85381-390-7). Discusses reasons for knowing self-defense, presents case histories and pictorial demonstrations of escape techniques, and addresses the emotions following an attack. (Rev: BL 5/15/93) [613.66]

6119 Gutman, Bill. *Be Aware of Danger* (5–8). Illus. (Focus on Safety) 1996, Twenty-First Century LB $20.40 (0-8050-4142-7). Situations that could be dangerous to young people are highlighted, with preventive measures outlined. (Rev: BL 2/1/97; SLJ 2/97) [613.6]

6120 Gutman, Bill. *Hazards at Home* (4–8). (Focus on Safety) 1996, Twenty-First Century LB $20.40 (0-8050-4141-9). This book calls attention to sources of potential accidents in the home and stresses prevention, with information on first-aid procedures. (Rev: BR 11–12/96; SLJ 9/96) [363.1]

6121 Gutman, Bill. *Recreation Can Be Risky* (4–8). (Focus on Safety) 1996, Holt LB $20.40 (0-8050-4143-5). The author gives practical suggestions for enjoying such activities as baseball, biking, or hiking while also keeping safe through warm-up exercises, proper equipment, correct clothing, etc. (Rev: BL 7/96; BR 11–12/96; SLJ 9/96; VOYA 10/96) [790]

6122 Rosenberg, Stephen N. *The Johnson & Johnson First Aid Book* (9–12). Illus. 1985, Warner paper $16.95 (0-446-38252-3). A spiral-bound handy manual that covers most emergency situations with clear text and line drawings. (Rev: BL 7/85) [616.02]

Sex Education and Sexual Identity

6123 Akagi, Cynthia G. *Dear Michael: Sexuality Education for Boys Ages 11–17* (6–10). Illus. 1996, Gylantic $12.95 (1-880197-16-2). Written by a mother to her adolescent son, these letters effectively explore male puberty, the male's role in conception, concerns about dating, and the problems involved in sexual relationships. (Rev: BL 1/1–15/97; VOYA 6/97) [613.9]

6124 Ball, Jacqueline A. *Puberty* (6–9). Illus. 1989, Rourke LB $19.93 (0-86625-283-5). This account aimed at young girls covers such topics as maturation, social problems, and menstruation. (Rev: SLJ 6/89) [305.2]

6125 Basso, Michael J. *The Underground Guide to Teenage Sexuality* (7–12). 1997, Fairview paper $14.95 (1-57749-034-7). Using chiefly a question-and-answer format, this guide contains information on the basics of sexuality plus coverage of topics like contraception, sexually transmitted diseases, and homosexuality. (Rev: SLJ 8/97) [613.9]

6126 Bell, Ruth. *Changing Bodies, Changing Lives* (9–12). 1998, Times Bks. paper $23.00 (0-8129-2990-X). A new edition of this ground-breaking, nonjudgmental, explicit book on sex, physical and emotional health, and personal relationships. (Rev: BL 11/1/98) [613.9 07]

6127 Brimner, Larry Dane. *Being Different: Lambda Youths Speak Out* (9–12). (Lesbian and Gay Experience) 1996, Watts LB $24.00 (0-531-11222-5). The author's commentary links the narratives of 15 gay, lesbian, and bisexual young people who tell about their search for sexual identity, coming out, and the pain of being gay in high school, as well as their fears, relationships, hopes, and expectations. (Rev: SLJ 5/96) [305.38]

6128 Brimner, Larry Dane, ed. *Letters to Our Children: Lesbian and Gay Adults Speak to the New Generation* (8–12). Illus. 1997, Watts LB $24.00 (0-531-11322-1). This collection of essays from writers of an older generation offers hope, support, and advice for gay and lesbian youth who are facing problems with their sexuality. (Rev: BL 9/15/97; SLJ 11/97; VOYA 12/97) [305.9]

6129 Bull, David. *Cool and Celibate? Sex or No Sex* (8–12). 1998, Element Books paper $4.95 (1-901881-17-2). In this discussion of sex, the author argues against teens having sex until they are in stable married relationships. (Rev: SLJ 3/99) [362.29]

6130 Diamond, Shifra N. *Everything You Need to Know about Going to the Gynecologist* (7–12). (Need to Know Library) 1999, Rosen LB $17.95 (0-8239-2839-X). This book explains what a gynecologist does, when teenage girls should see one, and how to find one. There is helpful information on menstruation, breast self-examinations, treatments for common reproductive problems, contraception, myths, and what to expect from a pelvic examination. (Rev: SLJ 5/99; VOYA 8/99) [612]

6131 Dunbar, Robert E. *Homosexuality* (7–10). (Issues in Focus) 1995, Enslow LB $19.95 (0-89490-665-8). An objective introduction to homosexuality that contains some interesting first-person accounts. (Rev: BL 12/15/95; SLJ 6/96; VOYA 2/96) [305.9]

6132 Ford, Michael T. *Outspoken: Role Models from the Lesbian & Gay Community* (7–12). 1998, Morrow $16.00 (0-688-14896-4); paper $4.95 (0-688-14897-2). Six men and 5 women who represent the gay, lesbian, bisexual, and transgendered community tell about their lives, families, and how they have grown to accept their identity. (Rev: BL 5/1/98; BR 9–10/98; SLJ 6/98; VOYA 8/98) [305.9]

6133 Gravelle, Karen. *What's Going on Down There? Answers to Questions Boys Find Hard to Ask* (6–9). Illus. 1998, Walker $25.95 (0-8027-8671-5); paper $14.95 (0-8027-7540-3). Straightforward information for boys on topics like puberty, sex, birth control, and sexually transmitted diseases. (Rev: BL 11/1/98; BR 5–6/99; SLJ 12/98) [612.6 61]

6134 Gravelle, Karen, and Jennifer Gravelle. *The Period Book: Everything You Don't Want to Ask (But*

Need to Know) (6–10). Illus. 1996, Walker $23.95 (0-8027-8420-8); paper $13.95 (0-8027-7478-4). Presented in an appealing format, this chatty discussion of menstruation gives basic information, with cartoon-style illustrations. (Rev: BL 3/15/96; BR 9–10/96; SLJ 3/96; VOYA 6/96) [618]

6135 Gray, Mary L. *In Your Face: Stories from the Lives of Queer Youth* (9–12). 1999, Haworth LB $29.95 (0-7890-0076-8); paper $17.95 (1-56023-887-9). Boldly honest, verbatim narratives by 15 gay, lesbian, and bisexual teens who share their experiences awakening to their sexual identity, their coming out, their search for love, and their hopes for the future. (Rev: BL 6/1–15/99) [305.235]

6136 Gurian, Michael. *Understanding Guys: A Guide for Teenage Girls* (8–10). Illus. (Plugged In) 1999, Price Stern Sloan $13.89 (0-8431-7476-5); paper $4.99 (0-8431-7475-7). A practical, often humorous explanation of what boys go through physically, emotionally, and psychologically during puberty, with advice for girls on how to deal with them. (Rev: BR 9–10/99; SLJ 8/99) [612]

6137 Hoch, Dean, and Nancy Hoch. *The Sex Education Dictionary for Today's Teens & Pre-Teens* (7–12). Illus. 1990, Landmark paper $12.95 (0-9624209-0-5). A dictionary of 350 words related to sex, sexuality, and reproduction all given clear, concise definitions. (Rev: BL 8/90) [306.7]

6138 Hyde, Margaret O., and Elizabeth Forsyth. *Know about Gays and Lesbians* (7–12). 1994, Millbrook LB $22.40 (1-56294-298-0). This overview of homosexuality attacks stereotypes, surveys history, examines current controversies, reviews religious responses, and shows how pervasive homophobia still is. (Rev: BL 3/1/94; SLJ 4/94; VOYA 4/94) [305.9]

6139 Jukes, Mavis. *Growing Up: It's a Girl Thing: Straight Talk about First Bras, First Periods & Your Changing Body* (4–8). Illus. 1998, Random LB $16.99 (0-679-99027-5); Knopf paper $10.00 (0-679-89027-0). Essential information about the changes girls experience during puberty, with half the book devoted to what to expect and how to plan for their first period, presented in an easy, big-sister style. (Rev: BL 11/1/98; SLJ 11/98) [612]

6140 Jukes, Mavis. *It's a Girl Thing: How to Stay Healthy, Safe, and in Charge* (5–9). Illus. 1996, Knopf LB $16.99 (0-679-94325-0); paper $12.00 (0-679-87392-9). This guide to puberty for girls discusses such topics as menstruation, drinking and drugs, body changes, contraceptives, sexually transmitted diseases, and sexual abuse and harassment. (Rev: SLJ 6/96*) [612.6]

6141 Lauersen, Niels H., and Eileen Stukane. *You're in Charge: A Teenage Girl's Guide to Sex and Her Body* (8–12). 1993, Ballantine paper $12.00 (0-449-

90464-4). An ob/gyn discusses sexual maturation, including pubertal change, sexually transmitted diseases, orgasm, sexual intimacy, condoms, abortion, menstruation, and more. (Rev: BL 5/1/93) [613.9]

6142 Madaras, Lynda, and Area Madaras. *The What's Happening to My Body? Book for Girls* (7–12). Illus. 1988, Newmarket Pr. paper $11.95 (0-937858-98-6). A thorough introduction for girls to puberty that, in this new edition, includes material on such subjects as pregnancy and AIDS. (Rev: VOYA 6/89) [612]

6143 Madaras, Lynda, and Dane Saavedra. *The What's Happening to My Body? Book for Boys* (7–12). Illus. 1988, Newmarket Pr. paper $11.95 (0-937858-99-4). A new edition of this fine sex education manual that now includes material on such topics as sexually transmitted diseases and AIDS. (Rev: VOYA 6/89) [612]

6144 Mahoney, Ellen Voelckers. *Now You've Got Your Period* (6–9). Illus. 1988, Rosen $12.95 (0-8239-0792-9). In conversational tone, this book describes the process of menstruation and gives tips on how to ease cramps, how to use sanitary protection, and so on. (Rev: BL 7/88; SLJ 8/88; VOYA 10/88) [612]

6145 Marcus, Eric. *Is It a Choice? Answers to 300 of the Most Frequently Asked Questions about Gays and Lesbians* (9–12). 1993, Harper San Francisco paper $13.00 (0-06-250664-1). A comprehensive primer on homosexuality, answering questions about sex, relationships, discrimination, religion, coming out, AIDS, aging, and many other topics. (Rev: BL 5/1/93) [305.9]

6146 Marshall, Elizabeth L. *Conquering Infertility: Medical Challenges and Moral Dilemmas* (9–12). Illus. (The Changing Family) 1997, Watts $25.00 (0-531-11344-2). This book traces the history of modern reproductive medicine, discusses the causes of infertility, presents all of the options currently available to infertile couples, and comments on the controversies surrounding in vitro fertilization. (Rev: BL 12/1/97; BR 5–6/98; SLJ 9/97) [616.6]

6147 Marzollo, Jean. *Getting Your Period: A Book about Menstruation* (5–10). 1989, Dial $6.95 (0-8037-0356-2). A clear introduction to puberty in general and the menstrual cycle in particular. (Rev: BL 7/89; BR 1–2/90; SLJ 7/89; VOYA 8/89) [612]

6148 Mastoon, Adam. *The Shared Heart* (8–12). Illus. 1997, Morrow $24.50 (0-688-14931-6). Through photographs and personal essays, young gays, lesbians and bisexuals share their memories and the problems of coming out. (Rev: BL 11/15/97; BR 3–4/98; SLJ 2/98*) [305.235]

6149 Moe, Barbara. *Everything You Need to Know About PMS* (8–12). 1995, Rosen LB $17.95 (0-8239-1877-7). Symptoms of premenstrual syndrome are described, along with ways to cope with it. (Rev: SLJ 11/95; VOYA 2/96) [530.8]

6150 Montpetit, Charles, ed. *The First Time, vol. 1* (10–12). (True stories) 1996, Orca paper $6.95 (1-55143-037-1). For mature readers, this consists of 8 true stories of initial sexual experiences that run the gamut of young love, gay love, sexual abuse, tragic consequences, embarrassment, and bliss. Followed by a second volume that contains 8 more vignettes. (Rev: SLJ 8/96; VOYA 10/97) [306.7]

6151 Nardo, Don. *Teen Sexuality* (5–8). Illus. (Overview) 1997, Lucent LB $17.96 (1-56006-189-8). This book tries to tell teens what they need to know about sexuality and how they should learn about it. (Rev: BL 3/15/97; BR 11–12/97; SLJ 2/97) [362.29]

6152 O'Grady, Kathleen, and Paula Wansbrough, eds. *Sweet Secrets: Telling Stories of Menstruation* (6–10). 1997, Second Story Pr. paper $9.95 (0-929005-33-3). Following an interesting review of attitudes and rituals related to menstruation in various cultures throughout history, the main body of the book recounts 20 anecdotes about young teens and their first periods, interspersed with boxes providing information on topics like tampons, toxic shock syndrome, and breast examinations. (Rev: VOYA 6/98) [530.8]

6153 Parker, Steve. *The Reproductive System* (5–9). 1997, Raintree Steck-Vaughn LB $25.69 (0-8172-4806-4). A well-organized, straightforward description of the male and female anatomy, genes, fertility problems, contraception, STDs, and human development from conception to adolescence. (Rev: SLJ 2/98) [613.9]

6154 Pogany, Susan Browning. *Sex Smart: 501 Reasons to Hold Off on Sex* (8–12). 1998, Fairview paper $14.95 (1-57749-043-6). The author uses quotes from teenagers, "Dear Abby," and other sources to explore emotional issues involved in making sexual choices and to argue for abstinence. (Rev: VOYA 4/99) [613.9]

6155 Pollack, Rachel, and Cheryl Schwartz. *The Journey Out: A Guide for and about Lesbian, Gay, and Bisexual Teens* (7–12). 1995, Viking $14.99 (0-670-85845-5); Penguin paper $6.99 (0-14-037254-7). An approachable discussion with sections on terms commonly used, the varied character of the gay community, and special concerns of bisexuals; offers support and opportunities for activism. (Rev: BL 12/1/95; BR 9–10/96; SLJ 1/96*; VOYA 4/96) [305.23]

6156 Reed, Rita. *Growing up Gay: The Sorrows & Joys of Gay & Lesbian Adolescence* (10–12). 1997, Norton paper $19.95 (0-393-31659-9). This book concentrates on the lives of 2 teens, one gay and the other lesbian, and their experiences after they came out. (Rev: VOYA 6/98) [305.9]

6157 Roberts, Tara, ed. *Am I the Last Virgin? Ten African-American Reflections on Sex and Love* (10–12). 1997, Simon & Schuster $15.00 (0-689-80449-0); paper $3.99 (0-689-81254-X). A brutally frank collection of 10 essays about sex and sexuality for African American women in their late teens and up. For mature senior high readers. (Rev: BL 2/15/97; SLJ 2/97; VOYA 4/97) [306.7]

6158 Roleff, Tamara L. *Gay Rights* (9–12). (Current Controversies) 1997, Greenhaven LB $21.96 (1-56510-532-X); paper $16.20 (1-56510-531-1). This work discusses various points of view on such questions as homosexual marriage, gays in the military, legal protection, civil rights, child custody problems, and domestic partner benefits. (Rev: BL 4/1/97; SLJ 2/97) [306.76]

6159 Roleff, Tamara L., ed. *Sex Education* (7–12). (At Issue) 1999, Greenhaven LB $15.96 (0-7377-0009-2); paper $12.45 (0-7377-0008-4). A collection of essays and opinion on issues related to teaching about sex, including contraception, sexual abstinence, safe sex, sexual identity, and families with gay parents. (Rev: BL 5/15/99; BR 9–10/99) [613.9]

6160 Rue, Nancy N. *Everything You Need to Know about Getting Your Period* (6–9). (Need to Know Library) 1995, Rosen LB $15.95 (0-8239-1870-X). A straightforward discussion of the physiological changes that come with puberty. (Rev: BL 11/1/95; SLJ 1/96) [612.6]

6161 Shyer, Marlene Fanta, and Christopher Shyer. *Not Like Other Boys: Growing Up Gay: A Mother and Son Look Back* (10–12). 1996, Houghton $21.95 (0-395-70939-3). Told in alternating chapters by a mother and her son, Christopher, this is the story of Chris's life from age 5 until his early adult years, when he told his family that he was gay. (Rev: BL 1/1–15/96; SLJ 10/96) [616.85]

6162 Solin, Sabrina, and Paula Elbirt. *The Seventeen Guide to Sex and Your Body* (7–10). 1996, Simon & Schuster $17.00 (0-689-80796-1); paper $8.99 (0-689-80795-3). Using a question-and-answer format, this book by the authors of *Seventeen*'s column "Sex and Body" explores common concerns about sex and puberty. (Rev: BL 10/1/96; SLJ 11/96; VOYA 6/97) [613.9]

6163 Stalcup, Brenda, et al., eds. *Human Sexuality* (9–12). (Opposing Viewpoints) 1995, Greenhaven LB $21.96 (1-56510-246-0); paper $16.20 (1-56510-245-2). This anthology covers the purposes of sex, gender and sexual orientation, what is considered normal sexually, and society's changing attitudes on this subject. (Rev: BL 9/15/95) [306.7]

6164 Stewart, Gail B. *Gay & Lesbian Youth* (9–12). Illus. (Other America) 1996, Lucent LB $18.96 (1-56006-337-8). Through the painful stories of 4 gay young people, readers learn the value of friendship, tolerance, and understanding. (Rev: BL 3/1/97; SLJ 6/97; VOYA 8/97) [305.23]

6165 Stoppard, Miriam. *Sex Ed* (7–12). Illus. 1997, DK Publg. $14.95 (0-7894-2385-5); paper $9.95 (0-7894-1751-0). Using lots of cartoon art and a breezy style, this is a straightforward book on sex education that covers topics like sexual orientation, menstruation, intercourse, masturbation, and pregnancy. (Rev: BL 11/15/97; SLJ 2/98; VOYA 6/98) [613.9]

6166 Thomson, Ruth. *Have You Started Yet? All About Getting Your Period . . . Period!* (5–8). Illus. 1997, Price Stern Sloan $4.95 (0-8431-7950-3). This book for girls explains the changes that occur during puberty and provides information on menstruation and reproductive anatomy. (Rev: BL 11/1/97; SLJ 1/98) [612.6]

6167 Westheimer, Ruth. *Dr. Ruth Talks to Kids: Where You Came From, How Your Body Changes, and What Sex Is All About* (5–9). Illus. 1993, Macmillan LB $14.00 (0-02-792532-3). Discusses a wide range of common preteen and teen concerns: puberty, sex, contraception, birth, and AIDS. (Rev: BL 7/93; SLJ 6/93; VOYA 8/93) [306.7]

6168 White, Joe. *Pure Excitement: A Radical Righteous Approach to Sex, Love, and Dating* (7–12). 1996, Focus on the Family paper $8.99 (1-56179-483-X). Taking a conservative approach, this book, written by a minister and using many conversations with teens, proposes that premarital sex is harmful to young adults. (Rev: VOYA 8/97) [613.9]

6169 Williams, Mary E., ed. *Homosexuality* (8–12). (Opposing Viewpoints) 1999, Greenhaven LB $20.96 (0-7377-0053-X); paper $17.45 (0-7377-0052-1). The causes of homosexuality, discrimination against gays and lesbians, possible acceptance policies, and gay and lesbian families are some of the topics explored in this collection of different points of view. (Rev: BL 4/15/99) [305.9]

Sex Problems
(Abuse, Harassment, etc.)

6170 Bandon, Alexandra. *Date Rape* (6–9). 1994, Macmillan LB $13.95 (0-382-24755-8). A definition of the controversial subject, with information and profiles of both the victim and the attacker. (Rev: BL 3/1/95; SLJ 3/95) [362.88]

6171 Benedict, Helen. *Safe, Strong, and Streetwise* (8–12). 1987, Little, Brown paper $6.95 (0-87113-100-5). A rape-crisis specialist discusses sexual assault, its prevention and treatment. (Rev: BL 1/1/87; BR 1–2/87; SLJ 5/87; VOYA 2/87) [362.7]

6172 Black, Beryl. *Coping with Sexual Harassment* (9–12). (Coping) 1987, Rosen LB $17.95 (0-8239-0732-5). Advice for both homosexual and heterosexual males and females on how to handle sexual harassment at school and work. (Rev: BR 11–12/87; SLJ 9/87; VOYA 10/87) [305.4]

6173 Bode, Janet. *Voices of Rape* (9–12). 1998, Watts $25.00 (0-531-11518-6). This updated edition of the 1990 book contains first-person testimonies from victims, a rapist, and corrections officers, plus excerpts from current newspaper articles. (Rev: BL 11/1/98; SLJ 5/99; VOYA 8/99) [364.15 32 0973]

6174 Chaiet, Donna. *Staying Safe at School* (7–12). (Get Prepared Library) 1995, Rosen LB $16.95 (0-8239-1864-5). How to stay alert and protect oneself while at school, plus tips for girls on avoiding violent crimes on or near school campuses. (Rev: BL 11/15/95; BR 1–2/96; SLJ 2/96) [613.6]

6175 Chaiet, Donna. *Staying Safe at Work* (7–12). (Get Prepared Library) 1995, Rosen LB $16.95 (0-8239-1867-X). How to stay alert and protect oneself at work, with material for girls on how to create their own space and give clear messages to others. (Rev: BL 11/15/95; BR 1–2/96; SLJ 2/96; VOYA 4/96) [613.6]

6176 Chaiet, Donna. *Staying Safe on Dates* (7–12). (Get Prepared Library) 1995, Rosen LB $16.95 (0-8239-1862-9). Information for young women concerning verbal/physical abuse, invasion of boundaries, and acquaintance/date rape. (Rev: BR 1–2/96; SLJ 1/96; VOYA 4/96) [362.88]

6177 Chaiet, Donna. *Staying Safe on Public Transportation* (6–12). (Get Prepared Library) 1995, Rosen LB $16.95 (0-8239-1866-1). This book for young women traveling alone on buses, trains, or subways stresses the importance of awareness, verbal and physical self-defense, having a plan, and listening to one's instincts. (Rev: BL 11/15/95; BR 1–2/96; SLJ 2/96; VOYA 4/96) [363.1]

6178 Chaiet, Donna. *Staying Safe on the Streets* (7–12). (Get Prepared Library) 1995, Rosen LB $16.95 (0-8239-1865-3). Discusses situations young women should avoid outside the home and protection techniques. (Rev: SLJ 1/96) [613.6]

6179 Chaiet, Donna. *Staying Safe While Shopping* (7–12). (Get Prepared Library) 1995, Rosen LB $16.95 (0-8239-1869-6). This book tells girls how to stay alert and protect themselves while shopping. (Rev: BL 11/15/95; BR 1–2/96; SLJ 1/96) [364]

6180 Chaiet, Donna. *Staying Safe While Traveling* (6–12). (Get Prepared Library) 1995, Rosen LB $16.95 (0-8239-1868-8). In this book for girls traveling alone, the importance of awareness, how to use verbal and physical self-defense, and listening to one's instincts are stressed and examples are given for handling specific situations. (Rev: BL 11/15/95; BR 1–2/96; SLJ 2/96; VOYA 4/96) [363.1]

6181 Cooney, Judith. *Coping with Sexual Abuse* (9–12). (Coping) 1987, Rosen $17.95 (0-8239-0684-1). An explicit report that concentrates on the sexual abuse that occurs in the home and how to handle it. (Rev: BL 9/1/87; BR 11–12/87; SLJ 9/87; VOYA 10/87) [362.7]

6182 Cozic, Charles P., and Bruno Leone, eds. *Sexual Values* (9–12). (Opposing Viewpoints) 1995, Greenhaven LB $21.96 (1-56510-211-8); paper $14.50 (1-56510-210-X). Debates moral values, how homosexuals should be regarded by society, and sexual values for children. (Rev: BL 4/1/95; SLJ 2/95; VOYA 5/95) [306.7]

6183 Gay, Kathlyn. *Rights and Respect: What You Need to Know about Gender Bias and Sexual Harassment* (7–12). 1995, Millbrook LB $22.40 (1-56294-493-2). A good source for student research on gender bias and harassment in the workplace and in education. (Rev: BL 10/1/95; SLJ 11/95) [305.42]

6184 Gerdes, Louise, ed. *Sexual Harassment* (9–12). (Current Controversies) 1999, Greenhaven LB $21.96 (0-7377-0067-X); paper $16.20 (0-7377-0066-1). A presentation of a wide range of viewpoints on the depth of the problem of sexual harassment, its causes, how to define it legally, and how it can be reduced. (Rev: BL 9/1/99) [305.3]

6185 Guernsey, JoAnn B. *Sexual Harassment: A Question of Power* (7–12). (Frontline) 1995, Lerner LB $19.93 (0-8225-2608-5). The issue of harassment in the workplace, school, and everyday life is discussed. Includes historical background and male perspectives. (Rev: BL 7/95; SLJ 8/95) [305.42]

6186 Hicks, John. *Dating Violence: True Stories of Hurt and Hope* (7–12). Illus. 1996, Millbrook LB $23.90 (1-56294-654-4). Beginning with a case study of sexual and physical abuse, this book analyzes dating relationships in which there is violence and identifies destructive behavioral patterns. (Rev: BL 11/15/96; BR 1–2/97; SLJ 11/96; VOYA 6/97) [362.88]

6187 Hyde, Margaret O., and Elizabeth Forsyth. *The Sexual Abuse of Children and Adolescents* (7–12). Illus. 1997, Millbrook LB $22.40 (0-7613-0058-9). The causes and effects of sexual abuse of children and young adults are covered in this thorough account that also discusses topics like the history of sexual abuse, Megan's Law, and possible treatments for sex offenders. (Rev: BL 2/15/97; BR 11–12/97; SLJ 3/97; VOYA 8/97) [362.7]

6188 Kaminker, Laura. *Everything You Need to Know about Dealing with Sexual Assault* (7–12). (Need to Know Library) 1998, Rosen $17.95 (0-8239-2837-3). This book by a survivor of a sexual assault contains first-person narratives, a table that

separates myth from fact, a script that could be used for trying to help a friend who has been assaulted, and ways to play it safe. (Rev: SLJ 1/99) [362.888]

6189 Kinnear, Karen L. *Childhood Sexual Abuse* (9–12). (Contemporary World Issues) 1995, ABC-CLIO LB $39.50 (0-87436-691-7). This compendium of information includes material on the nature and frequency of child sexual abuse, federal laws, court decisions, and a directory of organizations and resource materials. (Rev: BR 9–10/96; SLJ 7/96) [305]

6190 Landau, Elaine. *Sexual Harassment* (8–12). 1993, Walker LB $30.90 (0-8027-8266-3). Attempts to establish a sense of what constitutes inappropriate behavior, still not agreed upon in the courts or in mainstream America. (Rev: BL 6/1–15/93) [305.42]

6191 La Valle, John. *Everything You Need to Know When You Are the Male Survivor of Rape or Sexual Assault* (7–12). (Need to Know Library) 1996, Rosen LB $15.95 (0-8239-2084-4). A book for young men that helps sort out the shame, trauma, humiliation, and anger surrounding male rape or sexual assault. (Rev: BL 1/1–15/96; BR 9–10/96; SLJ 3/96) [382.88]

6192 Layman, Nancy S. *Sexual Harassment in American Secondary Schools: A Legal Guide for Administrators, Teachers, and Students* (9–12). 1994, Contemporary Research paper $18.95 (0-935061-52-5). Provides definitions of sexual harassment, examines laws regarding it in secondary schools, and outlines how schools can both avoid and deal with it. (Rev: BL 8/94; VOYA 4/95) [344.73]

6193 Leone, Bruno, ed. *Rape on Campus* (8–12). (At Issue) 1995, Greenhaven LB $16.96 (1-56510-296-7); paper $11.20 (1-56510-263-0). This anthology of sources explores the rise in rape cases on campuses and the different definitions of rape. (Rev: BL 3/15/95; SLJ 5/95) [364.1]

6194 McFarland, Rhoda. *Working Together Against Sexual Harassment* (7–12). (Library of Social Activism) 1996, Rosen LB $16.95 (0-8239-1775-4). Following a review of the history of sexual harassment (of females) and recent scandals, the book emphasizes how teens can combat sexual harassment by responding politically, from fighting for official policies against it at school to organizing chapters of NOW or other organizations. (Rev: SLJ 4/97; VOYA 6/97) [344.73]

6195 McGowan, Keith. *Sexual Harassment* (9–12). (Overview) 1998, Lucent LB $22.45 (1-56006-507-9). The author explores the legal aspects of sexual harassment and how to define it in schools, on the job, and in the military, and discusses its effects. (Rev: BL 1/1–15/99; BR 5–6/99; SLJ 3/99) [305.3]

6196 Mufson, Susan, and Rachel Kranz. *Straight Talk about Date Rape* (7–12). (Straight Talk About) 1993, Facts on File $24.95 (0-8160-2863-X). Using examples and analogies, the authors define date rape, tell how it can be avoided, and give suggestions to help date rape victims. (Rev: BL 9/1/93) [362.88]

6197 Munson, Lulie, and Karen Riskin. *In Their Own Words: A Sexual Abuse Workbook for Teenage Girls* (7–12). 1997, Child Welfare League of America paper $10.95 (0-87868-596-0). This manual (for use in therapy situations) helps girls who have been sexually abused work through their problems and plan for the future. (Rev: VOYA 10/97) [382.88]

6198 Nash, Carol R. *Sexual Harassment: What Teens Should Know* (7–12). Illus. (Issues in Focus) 1996, Enslow LB $19.95 (0-89490-735-2). After a general introduction to sexual harassment and its many forms, this account focuses on teens, the ways in which they encounter it, and techniques to fight it. (Rev: BL 7/96; SLJ 10/96; VOYA 8/96) [370.19]

6199 Parrot, Andrea. *Coping with Date Rape & Acquaintance Rape* (9–12). (Coping) 1988, Rosen $22.95 (0-8239-0784-8). An examination of types of rape, date rape in particular, and its effects on victims of both sexes. (Rev: BL 10/15/88; SLJ 8/88; VOYA 8/88) [362.8]

6200 Reinert, Dale R. *Sexual Abuse and Incest* (7–12). (Teen Issues) 1997, Enslow LB $17.95 (0-89490-916-9). After a general explanation of what constitutes sexual abuse and incest, this work explains how to identify potential abusive situations, and what to do about them. (Rev: BL 12/1/97; SLJ 12/97; VOYA 6/98) [362.76]

6201 Robson, Ruthann. *Gay Men, Lesbians, and the Law* (9–12). Illus. (Contemporary Issues) 1996, Chelsea $24.95 (0-7910-2612-4); paper $16.95 (0-7910-2963-8). After a brief historical background, the author examines the myriad ways in which legal issues affect the everyday lives of gay men and lesbians. (Rev: BL 9/15/96; BR 11–12/96; SLJ 10/96; VOYA 2/97) [346.7301]

6202 Shaw, Victoria. *Coping with Sexual Harassment and Gender Bias* (7–10). (Coping) 1998, Rosen LB $17.95 (0-8239-2547-1). This book provides a basic understanding of gender bias, sexism, and sexual harassment, with an emphasis on gender stereotyping, discusses emotional and legal aspects of these problems, and includes a good section on coping strategies and proactive steps. (Rev: SLJ 5/99) [305.42]

6203 Shuker-Haines, Frances. *Everything You Need to Know about Date Rape* (7–12). Illus. 1995, Rosen LB $17.95 (0-8239-2223-5). The author explains how date rape occurs and what precautionary measures can be taken. (Rev: BL 1/15/90; VOYA 4/90) [362.88]

6204 Silver, Diane. *The New Civil War: The Lesbian and Gay Struggle for Civil Rights* (8–12). (The Lesbian and Gay Experience) 1997, Watts LB $24.00 (0-531-11290-X). As gay and lesbian groups are fighting for equality under the law, conservative and religious groups are opposing it. This book gives an unbiased account of both sides of this question. (Rev: BL 9/15/97; SLJ 11/97) [305.9]

6205 Warshaw, Robin. *I Never Called It Rape* (10–12). 1994, HarperCollins paper $13.00 (0-0609-2572-8). Case studies of women who have been raped by friends or acquaintances. (Rev: SLJ 3/89) [364.1]

6206 Wekesser, Carol, et al., eds. *Sexual Harassment* (9–12). (Current Controversies) 1992, Greenhaven LB $26.20 (1-56510-021-2); paper $16.20 (1-56510-020-4). Includes arguments about the causes and seriousness of the problem, what constitutes actionable behavior, and the best means to reduce harassment. (Rev: BL 4/15/93; SLJ 5/93) [331.4]

6207 Williams, Mary, ed. *Sexual Violence* (9–12). Illus. (Opposing Viewpoints) 1997, Greenhaven LB $21.96 (1-56510-560-5); paper $16.20 (1-56510-559-1). This anthology of articles explores the cause of sexual violence, its consequences, and prevention. (Rev: BL 7/97; BR 1–2/98; SLJ 7/97) [364.15]

6208 Williams, Mary E., ed. *Date Rape* (10–12). (At Issue) 1998, Greenhaven LB $16.96 (1-56510-699-7); paper $12.45 (1-56510-698-9). In this collection of articles, the controversy surrounding rape by an acquaintance is examined. (Rev: BL 4/15/98; SLJ 5/98) [362.883]

6209 Winkler, Kathleen. *Date Rape* (7–12). Illus. (Hot Issue) 1999, Enslow $19.95 (0-7660-1198-4). Personal stories and easily read data highlight this treatment of a growing problem. (Rev: BL 9/15/99) [362.883]

6210 Winters, Paul A. *Child Sexual Abuse* (9–12). (At Issue) 1997, Greenhaven LB $15.96 (1-56510-689-X); paper $17.25 (1-56510-688-1). A wide range of opinions and information are presented about the causes, effects, and perpetrators of sexual abuse of children. (Rev: BL 5/1/98; SLJ 5/98) [362.76 0973]

Human Development and Behavior

General and Miscellaneous

6211 Beckelman, Laurie. *Body Blues* (6–9). Illus. (Holt Line) 1994, Silver Burdett LB $17.95 (0-8968-842-7). This book is designed to help adolescents understand the changes that are occurring to their body and give reassurance through interviews with other teenagers experiencing the same changes. (Rev: BL 2/15/95) [155.5]

6212 Glover, David. *The Young Oxford Book of the Human Being: The Body, the Mind, and the Way We Live* (7–12). (Young Oxford Book) 1998, Oxford LB $30.00 (0-19-521374-2). Humankind is explored from 4 different perspectives: evolution, anatomy and physiology, psychology, and sociology. (Rev: BR 9–10/98; SLJ 4/98) [301]

6213 Hirsch, Karen D. *Mind Riot: Coming of Age in Comix* (8–12). 1997, Simon & Schuster paper $9.99 (0-689-80622-1). This is an anthology of comic strips dealing with adolescents—their identity, their sexuality, their feelings, their friendships, their families, with thumbnail sketches of the artists. (Rev: BL 6/1–15/97; SLJ 8/97) [741.5]

6214 Wirths, Claudine G., and Mary Bowman-Kruhm. *Coping with Confrontations and Encounters with the Police* (7–12). (Coping) 1997, Rosen LB $17.95 (0-8239-2431-9). This book gives teens essential and realistic information that will help them deal successfully with police encounters and minimize potential risks. (Rev: SLJ 4/98; VOYA 2/98) [364.3]

Psychology and Human Behavior

General and Miscellaneous

6215 Broude, Gwen J. *Growing Up: A Cross-Cultural Encyclopedia* (10–12). (Encyclopedia of the Human Experience) 1995, ABC-CLIO LB $55.00 (0-87436-767-0). This work on cultural anthropology contrasts nearly 100 practices involving pregnancy, childbirth, and child rearing in about 100 different cultures around the world. The material is presented in alphabetically arranged articles ranging from one to several pages. (Rev: BR 9–10/96; SLJ 8/96) [301]

6216 Carlson, Dale B., and Hannah Carlson. *Where's Your Head? Teenage Psychology* (8–12). Illus. 1998, Bick Publishing House paper $14.95 (1-884158-19-6). This book explores in readable format the basic elements of psychological thought concerning personality, influences on beliefs and behavior, the stages of adolescence, and mental illness. (Rev: VOYA 8/98) [150]

6217 Gartner, Bob. *High Performance through Teamwork* (9–12). (Learning-a-Living Library) 1996, Rosen LB $16.95 (0-8239-2209-X). This book shows teens how to work with others and gives advice on how to identify, discuss, and resolve problems as a group. (Rev: BL 9/15/96; BR 1–2/97; SLJ 8/96) [658.3]

6218 Salinger, Adrienne. *In My Room: Teenagers in Their Bedrooms* (8–12). 1995, Chronicle paper $16.95 (0-8118-0796-7). A thought-provoking photoessay that explores the thoughts and private domains—the bedrooms—of 40 teenagers, providing a revealing glimpse of the lives of teenagers in the 1990s. (Rev: VOYA 4/96) [612]

6219 Schmidt, Mark Ray, ed. *Human Nature* (7–12). (Opposing Viewpoints) 1999, Greenhaven LB $21.96 (0-7377-0073-4); paper $16.20 (0-7377-0072-6). Using diverse writings from renowned thinkers like Sartre, Fromm, Rousseau, Pascal, Solzhenitsyn, and Adler, this Opposing Viewpoints volume explores human nature and behavior, gender roles, socialization, the causes of human conflicts, and humanity's future. (Rev: BL 6/1–15/99) [128]

6220 *Teens Write Through It: Essays from Teens Who Have Triumphed Over Trouble* (9–12). 1998, Fairview paper $9.95 (1-57749-083-5). A collection of essays written by youngsters ages 12 through 19 about their struggles with anorexia, depression, drug abuse, divorce, sexual assault, death, and other problems. (Rev: VOYA 4/99) [305.2]

6221 Thompson, Marcia A., ed. *Who Cares What I Think? American Teens Talk about Their Lives and Their Country* (8–12). Illus. 1994, Close Up paper $13.00 (0-932765-49-1). Sixteen teenagers from different strata of society and geographical locations talk about racism, government, citizenship, and related topics. (Rev: BL 6/1–15/94; SLJ 6/94) [305.23]

6222 Wright, Lawrence. *Twins: Their Remarkable Double Lives & What They Tell Us about Who We Are* (10–12). 1997, Wiley $22.95 (0-471-25220-4). A fascinating book that summarizes 50 years of research on identical twins who were separated at birth yet are found to exhibit similar habits and personalities when reunited as adults. (Rev: BL 2/1/98; SLJ 9/98) [155.4]

Ethics and Moral Behavior

6223 Canfield, Jack, et al. *Chicken Soup for the Teenage Soul: 101 Stories of Life, Love and Learning* (7–12). 1997, Health Communications paper $19.50 (1-55874-463-0). An inspirational collection of writings, about one-third by teenagers, that discuss the problems of growing up and how others have faced them. (Rev: BL 10/1/97) [158.1]

6224 Canfield, Jack, and Mark V. Hansen. *Chicken Soup for the Teenage Soul II: 101 More Stories of Life, Love & Learning* (7–12). 1998, Health Communications $24.00 (1-55874-615-3); paper $12.95 (1-55874-616-1). A new collection of personal stories from teens that supply inspiration and guidance. (Rev: BL 11/1/98) [158.1]

6225 Kincher, Jonni. *The First Honest Book about Lies* (7–12). 1992, Free Spirit paper $12.95 (0-915793-43-1). Provides tools to extract "real" information from statistics, advertisements, etc., as well as techniques for arguing persuasively. (Rev: BL 3/1/93) [155.9]

6226 Kuklin, Susan. *Speaking Out: Teenagers Take on Sex, Race and Identity* (7–12). 1993, Putnam paper $8.95 (0-399-22532-3). Students give their views on prejudice, sex, race, and identity. (Rev: BL 8/93; SLJ 7/93) [305.2]

6227 Margulies, Alice. *Compassion* (8–12). Illus. 1990, Rosen LB $15.95 (0-8239-1108-X). A discussion of the different kinds of compassion and how each helps both the individual and society. (Rev: SLJ 6/90) [152.4]

6228 Nathan, Amy. *Conflict Resolution* (7–10). (Need to Know) 1996, Rosen LB $17.95 (0-8239-2058-5). This book discusses different kinds of conflicts, which the author emphasizes are inevitable in life, and ways to resolve them through words and mediation rather than violence. (Rev: SLJ 1/97; VOYA 6/97) [371.18]

6229 Teens at Risk. *Teens at Risk* (8–12). Ed. by Laura K. Egendorf and Jennifer A. Hurley. (Opposing Viewpoints) 1998, Greenhaven LB $26.25 (1-56510-949-X); paper $16.20 (1-56510-948-1). Questions explored in this anthology involve the factors that put teens at risk, teenage crime and violence, prevention of teenage pregnancy, and the roles of government and the media in teenage difficulties. (Rev: BL 9/15/98) [306]

6230 Tivnan, Edward. *The Moral Imagination Confronting the Ethical Issues of Our Day* (9–12). 1995, Simon & Schuster $24.00 (0-671-74708-8). Essays on such controversial topics as suicide, abortion, affirmative action, and capital punishment. (Rev: BL 3/15/95) [170]

6231 Weiss, Ann E. *Lies, Deception and Truth* (6–9). 1988, Houghton $13.95 (0-395-40486-X). The author tackles tough questions, such as should you lie to protect someone and when is it wise not to be perfectly honest, in this challenging account. (Rev: BL 1/15/89; BR 1–2/89; SLJ 5/89; VOYA 12/88) [177.3]

6232 Wekesser, Carol, ed. *Ethics* (7–12). (Current Controversies) 1995, Greenhaven LB $20.96 (1-56510-231-2); paper $16.20 (1-56510-230-4). Focuses on business, biomedical, and professional ethics, as well as such general issues as individual responsibility. (Rev: BL 3/15/95; SLJ 5/95) [174]

6233 Wilker, Josh. *Revenge & Retribution* (10–12). (Crime, Justice, and Punishment) 1998, Chelsea LB $48.00 (0-7910-4321-5). The author uses literature, photographs of classical sculptures, reproductions of etchings and paintings, and stills of modern films to illustrate that revenge and retribution have played a role in human relations throughout history. (Rev: BR 1–2/99; SLJ 12/98) [152.4]

Etiquette and Manners

6234 Hoving, Walter. *Tiffany's Table Manners for Teenagers* (7–12). Illus. 1989, Random $16.00 (0-394-82877-1). A practical guide to good table manners. (Rev: BR 9–10/89; SLJ 6/89) [395]

6235 Packer, Alex J. *How Rude! The Teenagers' Guide to Good Manners, Proper Behavior, and Not Grossing People Out* (6–12). Illus. 1997, Free Spirit paper $19.95 (1-57542-024-4). A candid, often humorous guide to good manners for teenagers that stresses common sense and covers unusual situations like in-line skating and computer hacking. (Rev: BL 2/1/98; SLJ 2/98; VOYA 6/98) [395.1]

6236 Post, Elizabeth L., and Joan M. Coles. *Emily Post's Teen Etiquette* (7–12). 1995, HarperCollins paper $12.50 (0-06-273337-0). Full of information on good manners and consideration for others. (Rev: BL 10/1/95; VOYA 12/95) [395]

6237 Robert, Henry M. *Robert's Rules of Order* (8–12). 1993, Revell paper $5.99 (0-8007-8610-6). The most authoritative guide to running meetings. [060.4]

6238 Stefoff, Rebecca. *Friendship and Love* (9–12). Illus. 1989, Chelsea LB $19.95 (0-7910-0039-7). Theories on how friendship and love develop are explained, and ways of coping with these 2 feelings are explored. (Rev: BL 4/1/89; BR 11–12/89; SLJ 6/89; VOYA 8/89) [177]

Intelligence and Thinking

6239 Galbraith, Judy, and Jim Delisle. *The Gifted Kids' Survival Guide: A Teen Handbook*. rev. ed. (7–12). Illus. 1996, Free Spirit paper $14.95 (1-57542-003-1). Topics included in this very useful discussion of gifted children include definitions of giftedness, IQ testing, perfectionism, goal setting, college choices, peers, and suicide among gifted and talented teens. (Rev: SLJ 2/97; VOYA 6/97) [371.95]

6240 Rue, Nancy N. *Everything You Need to Know about Peer Mediation* (7–12). Illus. (Need to Know) 1997, Rosen LB $16.95 (0-8239-2435-1). Through discussion and examples, the author explains the principles of peer mediation and tells how teens can create a peer mediation program. (Rev: BL 11/15/97; BR 1–2/98; SLJ 2/98) [303.6]

6241 Simpson, Carolyn. *High Performance through Negotiation* (8–12). (Learning-a-Living Library) 1996, Rosen LB $16.95 (0-8239-2206-5). This book discusses negotiation skills and how students can resolve conflicts in a variety of situations. (Rev: BL 9/15/96; BR 1–2/97; SLJ 10/96; VOYA 2/97) [158]

6242 Wartik, Nancy, and La Vonne Carlson-Finnerty. *Memory and Learning* (7–12). (Encyclopedia of Health) 1993, Chelsea LB $19.95 (0-7910-0022-2). Explores 2 operations of the brain and explains how they function and sometimes malfunction. (Rev: BL 3/15/93; VOYA 8/93) [153.1]

Personal Guidance

6243 Arnold, Caroline. *Coping with Natural Disasters* (7–10). Illus. 1988, Walker LB $28.90 (0-8027-6717-6). Various natural disasters like earthquakes, hurricanes, and blizzards are discussed, with information on how to react in these emergencies. (Rev: SLJ 6/88; VOYA 10/88) [904]

6244 Arredia, Joni. *Sex, Boys, & You: Be Your Own Best Girlfriend* (5–9). Illus. 1998, Perc Publg. paper $15.95 (0-9653203-2-4). A self-help book for younger teen girls with advice on how to accept oneself, when to say "no" to sex, how to assess one's strengths and weaknesses, and how to develop healthy relationships with boys. (Rev: BR 5–6/99; SLJ 10/98) [305.23]

6245 Benson, Peter L., et al. *What Kids Need to Succeed: Proven, Practical Ways to Raise Good Kids* (7–12). 1998, Free Spirit paper $5.99 (1-57542-030-9). This book contains 1,200 ideas for building "assets," such as commitment to learning, positive values, social skills, and positive identity, that have been found to be factors in leading a successful life. (Rev: VOYA 8/99) [305.23]

6246 Benson, Peter L., and Judy Galbraith. *What Teens Need to Succeed: Proven, Practical Ways to Shape Your Own Future* (7–12). Illus. 1998, Free Spirit paper $14.95 (1-57542-027-9). Based on surveys from 350,000 U.S. teens, this book discusses positive "external assets" (families, peers, spiritual support systems, schools) and "internal assets" (honesty, motivation, decision-making skills, resistance skills) that contribute to a successful life. (Rev: SLJ 4/99; VOYA 8/99) [305.23]

6247 Blume, Judy. *Letters to Judy: What Your Kids Wish They Could Tell You* (6–9). 1986, Pocket Books paper $4.50 (0-671-62696-5). This collection of letters and advisory comments covers all the problems encountered by young teens such as menstruation, drugs, popularity, and divorce. (Rev: BL 6/1/86; VOYA 8/86) [305.2]

6248 Bolden, Tonya, ed. *33 Things Every Girl Should Know: Stories, Songs, Poems & Smart Talk by 33 Extraordinary Women* (6–12). 1998, Crown LB $17.99 (0-517-70999-6); paper $13.00 (0-517-70936-8). A collection of highly readable pieces by well-known and successful women on the difficult transition from childhood to adulthood. (Rev: BL 5/15/98; BR 11–12/98; SLJ 5/98) [810.8]

6249 Bridgers, Jay. *Everything You Need to Know about Having an Addictive Personality* (7–12).

(Need to Know Library) 1998, Rosen $17.95 (0-8239-2777-6). The author examines the social, psychological, and biochemical aspects of an "addictive personality," explains why some people are more susceptible to addiction than others, and offers sound advice on how teens can cope with addiction. (Rev: SLJ 1/99) [157]

6250 Burke, Delta, and Alexis Lipsitz. *Delta Style* (10–12). 1998, St. Martin's $24.95 (0-312-15454-2); paper $13.99 (0-312-19855-8). The former star of *Designing Women* combines personal anecdotes and reminiscences with beauty tips for large women (like herself), while stressing that a large person has as much unique beauty as a small person and that while looking good is important, the key to happiness is feeling good from within. (Rev: BL 3/15/98; SLJ 9/98) [305.23]

6251 Carlson, Dale B., and Hannah Carlson. *Girls Are Equal Too: How to Survive—For Teenage Girls* (6–9). Illus. 1998, Bick Publishing House paper $14.95 (1-884158-18-8). This work tells girls that it is okay to be smart, successful, a leader, and feel good. (Rev: VOYA 10/98) [305.23]

6252 *CityKids Speak on Relationships* (7–12). 1995, Random paper $5.99 (0-679-86553-5). Quick bits on everything from meeting people and falling in love to sexual behavior and harassment. (Rev: BL 5/1/95) [302]

6253 Cohen, Susan, and Daniel Cohen. *Teenage Competition: A Survival Guide* (9–12). 1987, M. Evans $13.95 (0-87131-487-8). A discussion of the constructive and destructive aspects of competition and how teenagers can adjust to them. (Rev: BL 6/1/87; SLJ 8/87) [155.5]

6254 Daldry, Jeremy. *The Teenage Guy's Survival Guide: The Real Deal on Girls, Growing Up, and Other Guy Stuff* (6–9). 1999, Little, Brown $8.95 (0-316-17824-1). From pimples to pornography, this guide book for boys is humorous, frank, and truthful about such subjects as dating, masturbation, drugs, mood swings, and homosexuality. (Rev: BL 5/15/99; SLJ 7/99; VOYA 10/99) [305.235]

6255 Davis, Brangien. *What's Real, What's Ideal: Overcoming a Negative Body Image* (7–12). (Teen Health Library of Eating Disorder Prevention) 1998, Rosen LB $17.95 (0-8239-2771-7). Because teenager's bodies are changing so quickly, many become confused about an ideal figure. This book describes why teens develop negative body images and offers suggestions for overcoming self-defeating perceptions. (Rev: BR 5–6/99; VOYA 4/99) [305.23]

6256 Dee, Catherine. *The Girl's Guide to Life* (5–8). 1997, Little, Brown paper $14.95 (0-316-17952-3). Such female concerns as self-esteem, political awareness, cultural stereotypes, and sexual harassment are introduced through first-person narratives,

poetry, and advice. (Rev: BL 7/97; BR 3–4/98; VOYA 8/97) [305.42]

6257 Denson, Al. *I Gotta Know!* (9–12). 1999, Tyndale paper $9.99 (0-8423-3859-4). A Christian evangelist supplies spiritual responses to questions involving drugs and alcohol, peer pressure, rejection, fear of dying, sex, family problems, and other concerns. (Rev: BL 6/1–15/99) [248.8]

6258 Dentemaro, Christine, and Rachel Kranz. *Straight Talk about Student Life* (6–10). (Straight Talk About) 1993, Facts on File $24.95 (0-8160-2735-8). This book explores problems that students are likely to experience, including communication with teachers and other students, parental pressures, homework, and developing a healthy social life. (Rev: BL 9/1/93) [373.18]

6259 DeVenzio, Dick. *Smart Moves: How to Succeed in School, Sports, Career, and Life* (10–12). 1989, Prometheus paper $17.95 (0-87975-546-6). A compendium of practical advice on such topics as how to do well at school, make and keep friends, and succeed in career goals. (Rev: BR 3–4/90) [155.5]

6260 Eagan, Andrea B. *Why Am I So Miserable if These Are the Best Years of My Life?* (9–12). 1976, HarperCollins $12.95 (0-397-31655-0). An updated version of this fine handbook that answers many of the questions adolescents, particularly girls, ask. (Rev: VOYA 8/88) [155.5]

6261 Farro, Rita. *Life Is Not a Dress Size: Rita Farro's Guide to Attitude, Style, and a New You* (10–12). 1996, Chilton paper $16.95 (0-8019-8758-X). This is a practical handbook for large women, with advice on how to dress with style, how to maintain a positive attitude, and how to gain self-esteem and a proper self-image. (Rev: SLJ 5/97) [646]

6262 Fromon, David K. *Running Away* (7–12). Illus. (Life Issues) 1996, Marshall Cavendish LB $24.21 (0-7614-0019-2). After presenting several cases involving runaways, this book discusses the causes and consequences of running away and provides such helpful resources as the Runaway's hot line. (Rev: BL 8/96; BR 11–12/96; SLJ 7/96) [362.7]

6263 Gordon, Sol. *The Teenage Survival Book* (7–12). 1981, Times Bks. paper $20.00 (0-8129-0972-0). This book discusses the important concerns and worries of adolescents and gives sound practical advice. [155.5]

6264 Gray, Heather, and Samantha Phillips. *Real Girl/Real World: Tools for Finding Your True Self* (9–12). Illus. 1998, Seal Pr. paper $14.95 (1-58005-005-0). Body image, self-esteem, and sexuality are the focus of this personal guide for teen girls facing the problems of growing up. (Rev: BL 10/1/98; SLJ 3/99; VOYA 2/99) [305.235]

6265 Harlan, Judith. *Girl Talk: Staying Strong, Feeling Good, Sticking Together* (6–10). Illus. 1977, Walker $23.95 (0-8027-8640-5); paper $13.50 (0-8027-7524-1). A breezy, lighthearted guide to approaching everyday problems faced by adolescent girls, with practical tips on how to solve them. (Rev: BL 12/1/97; VOYA 2/98) [305.23]

6266 Ignoffo, Matthew. *Everything You Need to Know about Self-Confidence* (6–8). Illus. 1995, Rosen LB $15.95 (0-8239-2149-2). This book is a guide that outlines ways of breaking habits that contribute to low self-esteem and suggests strategies for developing self-confidence. (Rev: BL 3/1/96; SLJ 3/96) [158]

6267 Johnson, Julie Tallard. *Celebrate You! Building Your Self-Esteem* (7–10). 1991, Lerner LB $19.93 (0-8225-0046-9). An upbeat guide that encourages teenagers to take pride in themselves and explains how to do it. (Rev: BL 2/1/91; SLJ 5/91) [158]

6268 Johnson, Kevin. *Could Someone Wake Me Up before I Drool on the Desk? Conquering School and Finding Friends Who Count* (6–9). 1995, Bethany House paper $6.99 (1-55661-416-0). Between Bible verses, the author supplies homey, often humorous observations and advice for about 45 different problems and concerns facing teenagers. (Rev: BL 2/15/96; SLJ 1/96) [242]

6269 Johnson, Kevin. *Does Anybody Know What Planet My Parents Are From?* (6–9). 1996, Bethany House paper $6.99 (1-55661-415-2). Using a religious framework and a breezy style, the author offers young teens advice on how to get along at home and at school. (Rev: BL 10/1/96; VOYA 2/97) [248.8]

6270 Johnston, Andrea. *Girls Speak Out: Finding Your True Self* (6–9). 1997, Scholastic $17.95 (0-590-89795-0). Based on a self-esteem and consciousness-raising workshop in which young women are encouraged to speak out and express their true feelings. (Rev: BR 11–12/97; SLJ 2/97) [158]

6271 Keltner, Nancy, ed. *If You Print This, Please Don't Use My Name* (7–12). Illus. 1992, Terra Nova Pr. paper $8.95 (0-944176-03-8). Letters from a California advice column for teens on topics ranging from sexuality to school. (Rev: BL 1/1/92; SLJ 7/92) [305.23]

6272 Kimball, Gayle. *The Teen Trip: The Complete Resource Guide* (9–12). 1997, Equality Pr. paper $16.95 (0-938795-26-0). Comments by 1,500 teenagers via the Internet are the highlight of this book about the teen experience, from abortion and yeast infection to self-esteem and peer pressure. (Rev: SLJ 6/97) [305.23]

6273 Kreiner, Anna. *Creating Your Own Support System* (7–10). (Need to Know) 1996, Rosen LB $17.95 (0-8239-2215-4). An easy-to-read account that teaches how to create a support system of friends, neighbors, relatives, clergy members, and teachers, if support is not available at home. (Rev: SLJ 1/97) [305.23]

6274 Landau, Elaine. *Interracial Dating and Marriage* (7–12). 1993, Messner LB $13.98 (0-671-75258-8). Narratives from 10 young adults and 5 adults relate their experiences with and reactions to interracial relationships. (Rev: BL 11/1/93) [306.73]

6275 Lang, Denise V. *But Everyone Else Looks So Sure of Themselves: A Guide to Surviving the Teen Years* (7–9). 1991, Betterway paper $9.95 (1-55870-177-X). Self-help guide for teens covering such subjects as peer pressure, family relationships, school, and the opposite sex. (Rev: BL 8/91) [305.23]

6276 *Let's Talk About Me! A Girl's Personal, Private, and Portable Instruction Book for Life* (6–10). Illus. 1997, Archway paper $12.00 (0-671-01521-4). A self-help book that discusses problems girls experience growing up, best for use with individuals because of its many fill-in-the-blank quizzes and spaces for diary entries. (Rev: VOYA 2/98) [305.23]

6277 Lewis, Barbara A. *What Do You Stand For? A Kid's Guide to Building Character* (6–9). 1997, Free Spirit paper $18.95 (1-57542-029-5). This book explores the topic of character building through self-assessment, recommended readings, and activities that explore one's attitudes and reactions to real-life situations. (Rev: BR 11–12/98; VOYA 8/98) [305.23]

6278 Lindsay, Jeanne W. *Caring, Commitment and Change: How to Build a Relationship That Lasts* (7–12). (Teenage Couples) 1995, Morning Glory Pr. $15.95 (0-930934-92-X); paper $9.95 (0-930934-93-8). The personal issues involved in a marriage partnership. (Rev: BL 4/15/95; SLJ 3/95) [646.7]

6279 McCoy, Kathy, and Charles Wibbelsman. *Growing & Changing: A Handbook for Preteens* (6–8). Illus. 1987, Putnam paper $14.00 (0-399-51280-2). A guide to the physical, social, and emotional changes that occur during early adolescence. (Rev: BL 3/1/87; SLJ 4/87) [649]

6280 McCoy, Kathy, and Charles Wibbelsman. *Life Happens* (7–12). 1996, Berkley paper $11.00 (0-399-51987-4). In a concise, practical way, this book covers such teenage crisis-producing situations as death in the family, stress, alcoholism, teen pregnancy, homosexuality, and the breakup of relationships. (Rev: BL 2/1/96) [616.98]

6281 McCoy, Kathy, and Charles Wibbelsman. *The New Teenage Body Book*. Rev. ed. (7–12). Illus. 1992, Putnam paper $15.95 (0-399-51725-1). This revised edition provides information and advice concerning the use of drugs, alcohol, and cigarettes; how to handle peer pressure; contraceptive methods; and abortion. (Rev: BL 6/15/92; SLJ 5/92) [613]

6282 McCune, Bunny, and Deb Traunstein. *Girls to Women: Sharing Our Stories* (7–10). Illus. 1998, Celestial Arts paper $14.95 (0-89087-881-1). Arranged under thematic chapters that deal with self-esteem, friendships, menstruation, sexuality, and mother-daughter relations, this collection of essays, stories, and poems explore various aspects of being young and female. (Rev: SLJ 4/99) [305.23]

6283 McFarland, Rhoda. *Coping through Assertiveness* (9–12). 1986, Rosen $12.95 (0-8239-0680-9). The author explains the difference between assertiveness and aggressive behavior and, among other things, how to say "no." (Rev: BL 1/15/87; BR 1–2/87; SLJ 1/87) [158.1]

6284 Monson-Burton, Marianne, comp. *Girls Know Best 2: Tips On Life and Fun Stuff to Do!* (5–8). (Girls Power) 1998, Beyond Words paper $8.95 (1-885223-84-6). About 50 girls from ages 10 to 16 give advice and hundreds of tips on such subjects as coping with death, keeping friends, solving problems, starting businesses, and even how to have a great slumber party. (Rev: SLJ 1/99) [305.23]

6285 Noel, Carol. *Get It? Got It? Good! A Guide for Teenagers* (7–12). Illus. 1996, Serious Business paper $7.95 (0-9649479-0-0). A teenage self-help guide that discusses such topics as self-esteem, sex, health, relations with others, goals, and violence. (Rev: BL 6/1–15/96) [361.8]

6286 Parker, Julie. *Everything You Need to Know about Decision-Making* (7–12). (Need to Know) 1996, Rosen LB $17.95 (0-8239-2055-0). The author guides teens through the steps of weighing and assessing information in order to make intelligent choices concerning a wide range of conflicts and problems. (Rev: SLJ 5/96) [302.3]

6287 Parker, Julie. *High Performance through Leadership* (8–12). (Learning-a-Living Library) 1996, Rosen LB $16.95 (0-8239-2205-7). This book discusses the ability to lead and teach others and shows students how they can take the initiative in problem solving and decision making. (Rev: BL 9/15/96; BR 1–2/97; SLJ 12/96) [158]

6288 Pratt, Jane. *Beyond Beauty* (6–9). Illus. 1997, Crown paper $30.00 (0-609-80148-1). An oversize book of profiles of young woman from ages 14 to 19, some of them well known, who discuss their lives, interests, work, clothes, and attitudes toward beauty, by the founder of *Sassy* and *Jane* magazines. (Rev: BL 2/1/98; VOYA 4/98) [613]

6289 Roehm, Michelle, comp. *Girls Know Best: Advice for Girls from Girls on Just About Everything!* (5–9). 1997, Beyond Words paper $8.95 (1-885223-63-3). In 26 topically arranged chapters, girls ranging in age from 7 to 16 give advice on such matters as life's embarrassments, difficult parents, volunteerism, boys, depression, divorce, backyard camping, and saving the environment. (Rev: SLJ 12/97) [305.23]

6290 Sanders, Pete, and Steve Myers. *It's My Life* (5–9). Illus. (Life Education) 1997, Watts LB $19.00 (0-531-14429-1). This book of practical advice focuses on the emotional changes that accompany the onset of puberty and adolescence, including relationships with families and friends, lifestyle choices, peer pressure, drugs, and making decisions. (Rev: SLJ 1/98) [305.23]

6291 Santamaria, Peggy. *High Performance through Self-Management* (8–12). (Learning-a-Living Library) 1996, Rosen LB $16.95 (0-8239-2208-1). This volume shows students how to work with others and teaches them to identify, discuss, and resolve problems as a group. (Rev: BL 9/15/96; BR 1–2/97; SLJ 8/96) [640]

6292 Schleifer, Jay. *The Dangers of Hazing* (7–12). (Need to Know) 1996, Rosen LB $17.95 (0-8239-2217-0). The phenomenon of hazing in high schools and colleges is discussed, with material on how to avoid it, its dangers, and how to report incidents. (Rev: SLJ 1/97) [305.23]

6293 Schneider, Meg. *Popularity Has Its Ups and Downs* (6–8). 1992, Messner paper $5.95 (0-671-72849-0). Common-sense information is presented about popularity and why it may not be what it seems, along with a discussion of self-confidence and friendship. (Rev: BL 11/15/92) [158]

6294 Schwager, Tina, and Michele Schuerger. *The Right Moves: A Girl's Guide to Getting Fit and Feeling Good* (6–12). 1998, Free Spirit paper $14.95 (1-57542-035-X). Topics like self-esteem, diet, and exercise are covered in this upbeat guide for girls that promotes a positive, healthy lifestyle. (Rev: BL 1/1–15/99; BR 5–6/99; SLJ 1/99*; VOYA 8/99) [613.7]

6295 Shellenberger, Susie, and Greg Johnson. *Cars, Curfews, Parties, and Parents* (9–12). 1995, Bethany House paper $7.99 (1-55661-482-9). Written from an openly Christian viewpoint, this is a guide for teens that emphasizes communication with parents, compassion for others, and an attitude of seeking God's will. (Rev: VOYA 6/96) [305.23]

6296 Shellenberger, Susie, and Greg Johnson. *Lockers, Lunch Lines, Chemistry, and Cliques* (9–12). 1995, Bethany House paper $7.99 (1-55661-483-7). This personal guidance book covers topics like time management, organizational skills, building a relationship with God, and keeping healthy. (Rev: SLJ 11/95; VOYA 4/96) [305.23]

6297 Stoppard, Miriam. *Every Girl's Life Guide* (7–12). 1999, DK Publg. $7.95 (0-7894-3758-9). This book on personal guidance for girls includes topics related to health, sexuality, and physical development as well as advice on family relationships and how to cope with problems like divorce and death. (Rev: BL 3/15/99) [646.7]

6298 Taulbert, Clifton L. *Eight Habits of the Heart: The Timeless Values That Build Strong Communities* (6–10). 1997, Viking paper $16.95 (0-670-87545-7). The author recalls the 8 habits he found growing up in a small African American Mississippi Delta community that build strong lives and communities: a nurturing attitude, dependability, responsibility, friendship, brotherhood, high expectations, courage, and hope. (Rev: BR 5–6/98; SLJ 10/97) [305.23]

6299 Van Buren, Abigail. *The Best of Dear Abby* (10–12). 1989, Andrews & McMeel paper $9.95 (0-8362-6241-7). This is a collection of the best of the advice columns written by this popular counselor. [361.3]

6300 Walker, Cassandra. *Stories from My Life: Cassandra Walker Talks to Teens About Growing Up* (6–9). 1997, Free Spirit paper $6.95 (1-57542-016-3). This well-known speaker and columnist informally discusses topics like peer pressure, crushes, first dates, embarrassments, family, and feelings of inadequacy. (Rev: VOYA 10/97) [305.23]

6301 Wesson, Carolyn McLenahan. *Teen Troubles* (7–12). 1988, Walker $17.95 (0-8027-1011-5); paper $17.95 (0-8027-7310-9). A candid, sometimes humorous self-help book on teenage problems and how to face them. (Rev: VOYA 12/88) [155.5]

6302 Weston, Carol. *For Girls Only: Wise Words, Good Advice* (4–8). 1998, Avon paper $5.99 (0-380-79538-8). Arranged by broad topics like friendship, love, and family, this is a collection of quotations from people ranging from Aesop and Socrates to Oprah Winfrey and Madonna. (Rev: SLJ 7/98; VOYA 8/98) [305.23]

6303 White, Lee, and Mary Ditson. *The Teenage Human Body Operator's Manual* (6–10). Illus. 1999, Northwest Media paper $9.95 (1-892194-01-5). Using an appealing layout and cartoon illustrations, this is an overview of teenagers' physical and psychological needs, touching on hygiene, nutrition, disease, pregnancy and birth control, and mental health. (Rev: SLJ 11/98) [305.23]

6304 Zimbardo, Philip G. *Shyness* (10–12). 1990, Addison-Wesley paper $13.00 (0-201-55018-0). What causes shyness and how to relieve this anxiety are explored in this volume. [152.4]

Social Groups

Family and Family Problems

6305 Bloomfield, Harold H., and Leonard Felder. *Making Peace with Your Parents* (10–12). 1984, Bal-

lantine paper $5.95 (0-345-30904-9). For better readers, this is a manual on how to resolve differences between parents and teenagers. [306.9]

6306 Blue, Rose. *Staying Out of Trouble in a Troubled Family* (7–10). 1998, Twenty-First Century $21.40 (0-7613-0365-0). Using 8 case studies, this book features family problems that will be familiar to teens, analyses by professionals, and avenues for help. (Rev: BL 2/1/99; SLJ 6/99) [362.7]

6307 Bode, Janet. *Truce: Ending the Sibling War* (8–12). 1991, Watts LB $25.00 (0-531-10996-8). Case studies and interviews with teens, followed by professional analyses and potential solutions. (Rev: BL 3/15/91; SLJ 6/91) [155.44]

6308 Bolick, Nancy O'Keefe. *How to Survive Your Parents' Divorce* (7–12). (The Changing Family) 1994, Watts LB $24.00 (0-531-11054-0). Interviews with teens who have lived through the divorce of their parents, with analysis of their feelings and behaviors. (Rev: BL 1/1/95; SLJ 3/95; VOYA 4/95) [306.89]

6309 Brondino, Jeanne, et al. *Raising Each Other* (7–12). Illus. 1988, Hunter House paper $8.95 (0-89793-044-4). This book, written and illustrated by a high school class, is about parent-teen relationships, problems, and solutions. (Rev: SLJ 1/89; VOYA 4/89) [306.1]

6310 Carlish, Anne. *Divorce* (7–10). (Talking Points) 1999, Raintree Steck-Vaughn LB $27.11 (0-8172-5310-6). This book discusses the cause of divorce, the legal aspects, and the difficult adjustments that must be made. (Rev: BL 8/99; BR 9–10/99) [306.89]

6311 Check, William A. *Child Abuse* (7–12). Illus. 1989, Chelsea LB $19.95 (0-7910-0043-5). A thorough treatment that covers such topics as the nature of abusers, social and economic factors that promote abuse, and the kinds of abuse and treatment. (Rev: BL 11/15/89; SLJ 5/90; VOYA 2/90) [362.7]

6312 Cline, Ruth K. J. *Focus on Families* (9–12). 1990, ABC-CLIO LB $39.50 (0-87436-508-2). An account that outlines problems such as single parenting and abuse that often characterize the modern family. (Rev: SLJ 9/90) [306.8]

6313 Connors, Patricia. *Runaways: Coping at Home & on the Street* (7–12). (Coping) 1989, Rosen LB $16.95 (0-8239-1019-9). Using interviews and case studies the author describes why young people run away and what usually happens to them on the streets. (Rev: BR 3–4/90; VOYA 12/89) [362.7]

6314 Currie, Stephen. *Adoption* (5–8). Illus. (Overview) 1997, Lucent LB $22.45 (1-56006-183-9). This look at adoption explains what is involved, its problems, legal issues, and disclosure concerns. (Rev: BL 5/15/97; BR 11–12/97; SLJ 4/97) [362.7]

6315 Davies, Nancy M. *Foster Care* (6–12). 1994, Watts LB $25.00 (0-531-11081-8). Details foster-care laws and operational procedures and explores the varied feelings of children in foster homes, with suggestions for possible alternatives. (Rev: BL 8/94; SLJ 7/94; VOYA 10/94) [362.7]

6316 Desetta, Al, ed. *The Heart Knows Something Different: Teenage Voices from the Foster Care System* (9–12). 1996, Persea $24.95 (0-89255-215-8); paper $13.95 (0-89255-218-2). Divided into 4 parts, the 57 essays in this book, written by teens who were foster children, tell about individual situations leading to foster-care placement, living in foster homes, self-awareness, and hopes of the future. (Rev: BL 5/15/96; SLJ 6/96; VOYA 8/96) [362.7]

6317 Dolan, Edward F. *Child Abuse*. Rev. ed. (7–12). 1992, Watts LB $24.00 (0-531-11042-7). Information on programs to help families and children harmed by child abuse, controversy arising from child abuse laws, and other aspects. (Rev: BL 1/15/93; SLJ 1/93) [362.7]

6318 Douglas, Ann. *The Family Tree Detective: Cracking the Case of Your Family's Story* (4–8). Illus. 1999, Owl $19.95 (1-895688-88-4); paper $9.95 (1-895688-89-2). In 16 compact chapters, this book covers the basics of genealogical research, from background material on relatedness to specifics like gathering information, using appropriate organizations, providing forms for making a family tree, and recording family facts. (Rev: SLJ 6/99) [929]

6319 Dudevszky, Szabinka. *Close-Up* (6–8). Trans. by Wanda Boeke. 1999, Front Street $15.95 (1-886910-40-5). The stories of 15 teens from the Netherlands who left their homes and lived in foster homes, reform schools, alone, or with friends. (Rev: SLJ 9/99; VOYA 12/99) [306]

6320 DuPrau, Jeanne. *Adoption: The Facts, Feelings, and Issues of a Double Heritage* (7–12). 1990, Messner LB $18.95 (0-671-69328-X); paper $5.95 (0-671-69329-8). A book that deals primarily with the conflicts and emotional problems related to adoption and how to get help. (Rev: BL 3/15/90; SLJ 7/90; VOYA 6/90) [362.7]

6321 Falke, Joseph. *Everything You Need to Know about Living in a Foster Home* (6–10). (Need to Know Library) 1995, Rosen LB $17.95 (0-8239-1873-4). This book discusses types of foster care and ways of dealing with the sense of dislocation common among foster children as well as techniques for settling in. (Rev: BR 9–10/96; SLJ 1/96) [362.7]

6322 Gardner, Richard. *The Boys and Girls Book about Stepfamilies* (6–9). 1985, Creative Therapeutics paper $6.50 (0-933812-13-2). Written from a youngster's view, this is a frank discussion of the problems that can exist in stepfamilies. [306.8]

6323 Gerdes, Louise, ed. *Battered Women* (7–12). (Contemporary Issues Companion) 1998, Greenhaven LB $21.96 (1-56510-897-3). Personal narratives of battered women are used in this anthology that investigates patterns of domestic violence and examines legal and other measures that can be used to protect women. (Rev: BL 3/15/99; BR 9–10/99) [362.82]

6324 Ginott, Haim. *Between Parent and Teenager* (9–12). 1982, Avon paper $5.99 (0-380-00820-3). This is a guide to developing good relations between parents and teenagers, plus solid advice about handling the problems of adolescence. [306.9]

6325 Goldentyer, Debra. *Child Abuse* (4–8). (Preteen Pressures) 1998, Raintree Steck-Vaughn $24.26 (0-8172-5032-8). This work describes the types, causes, and effects of child abuse and supplies material about how to change an abusive situation. (Rev: BL 5/15/98) [362.7]

6326 Goldentyer, Debra. *Divorce* (4–8). (Preteen Pressures) 1998, Raintree Steck-Vaughn $24.26 (0-8172-5030-1). This work includes a discussion of the reasons for divorce, the legal aspects, what youngsters experience, remarriage, and relationships with new family members. (Rev: BL 5/15/98; SLJ 6/98) [306.8]

6327 Gravelle, Karen, and Susan Fischer. *Where Are My Birth Parents? A Guide for Teenage Adoptees* (7–12). 1993, Walker LB $29.90 (0-8027-8258-2). Includes firsthand experiences of young people who searched for their birth families with varied success. (Rev: BL 9/1/93; SLJ 7/93; VOYA 10/93) [362.7]

6328 Greenberg, Keith E. *Family Abuse: Why Do People Hurt Each Other?* (6–9). Illus. (Issues of Our Time) 1994, Twenty-First Century LB $18.90 (0-8050-3183-9). The causes and forms of family violence and abuse are traced, with coverage given to their effects and how they can be prevented or contained. (Rev: BL 6/1–15/94; SLJ 9/94) [362.82]

6329 Greenberg, Keith E. *Runaways* (6–10). 1995, Lerner LB $19.93 (0-8225-2557-7). Greenberg uses the personal approach, focusing on the lives of 2 runaways, to dispel the idea that runaways are "bad" kids. (Rev: BL 10/15/95; SLJ 12/95) [362.7]

6330 Harnack, Andrew. *Adoption* (7–12). (Opposing Viewpoints) 1995, Greenhaven LB $21.96 (1-56510-213-4); paper $20.25 (1-56510-212-6). Presents various perspectives on the hot-button issues related to adoption, with provocative articles from well-known advocates. (Rev: BL 10/15/95; VOYA 6/96) [362.7]

6331 Helmbold, F. Wilbur. *Tracing Your Ancestry* (9–12). 1978, Oxmoor House paper $9.95 (0-8487-0414-2). This is a step-by-step guide to researching one's family history. [929]

6332 Hong, Maria. *Family Abuse: A National Epidemic* (8–12). Illus. (Issues in Focus) 1997, Enslow LB $17.95 (0-89490-720-4). This book takes a long, thorough look at this national epidemic that includes spousal and child abuse as well as children terrorizing a family and abuse of elderly parents. (Rev: BL 12/1/97; SLJ 12/97; VOYA 6/98) [362.82]

6333 Hurley, Jennifer A., ed. *Child Abuse* (8–12). (Opposing Viewpoints) 1998, Greenhaven LB $20.96 (1-56510-935-X); paper $21.81 (1-56510-173-1). Questions explored in this anthology of opinions include: the causes of child abuse, false accusations, how the legal system should deal with child molesters, and how child abuse can be reduced. (Rev: BL 9/15/98) [362.7]

6334 Hyde, Margaret O. *Know about Abuse* (7–12). (Know About) 1992, Walker LB $14.85 (0-8027-8177-2). Provides facts on child abuse, reasons, symptoms, examples, and solutions, covering a wide range of abuse, from obvious to subtle. (Rev: BL 11/1/92; SLJ 9/92) [362.7]

6335 Hyde, Margaret O. *Missing and Murdered Children* (9–12). Illus. 1998, Watts $25.00 (0-531-11384-1). Using real-life stories, this book examines how children come to be missing (runaways, kidnappings, "thrownaways"), what happens to them, and how children can be protected, with material on location networks, agencies, and helplines. (Rev: BL 3/1/98; BR 11–12/98; SLJ 3/98) [362.76]

6336 Ito, Tom. *Child Abuse* (6–10). (Overview) 1995, Lucent LB $17.96 (1-56006-115-4). Researched carefully, with the author searching for change in individuals and society. (Rev: BL 4/15/95; SLJ 5/95; VOYA 5/95) [362.7]

6337 Kempe, C. Henry, and Ray E. Helfer, eds. *The Battered Child*. 4th ed. (10–12). Illus. 1987, National Center for the Prevention of Child Abuse $37.00 (0-318-14670-3). The causes, treatment, and prevention of child abuse are covered in this sympathetic account. [362.7]

6338 Kinstlinger-Bruhn, Charlotte. *Everything You Need to Know About Breaking the Cycle of Domestic Violence* (6–10). (Need to Know) 1997, Rosen LB $16.95 (0-8239-2434-3). This book discusses physical, emotional, and sexual abuse, focusing on dating relationships and parental violence against children, and provides information on warning signs of an abusive relationship, how to seek help, and self-protection. (Rev: SLJ 4/98) [364.3]

6339 Koffinke, Carol. *"Mom, You Don't Understand!": A Mother and Daughter Share Their Views* (9–12). 1993, Deaconess paper $8.95 (0-925190-66-7). A counselor and her daughter, 15, alternately share viewpoints on dating, privacy, and other issues, sometimes with painful honesty. (Rev: BL 6/1–15/93; VOYA 10/93) [306.874]

6340 Koh, Frances M. *Adopted from Asia: How It Feels to Grow Up in America* (5–8). 1993, East-West $16.95 (0-9606090-6-7). Interviews with 11 young people who were born in Korea and adopted by Americans. (Rev: BL 2/15/94) [306.874]

6341 Kosof, Anna. *Battered Women: Living with the Enemy* (7–12). 1995, Watts LB $25.00 (0-531-11203-9). Attempts to answer the fundamental question "Why don't you just leave?" and discusses the development of abusive relationships. (Rev: BL 4/15/95; SLJ 3/95) [362.82]

6342 La Valle, John. *Coping When a Parent Is in Jail* (8–12). (Coping) 1995, Rosen LB $17.95 (0-8239-1967-6). Discusses the effects of having a parent in jail on a child and tries to give an idea of what the parent's life in prison is like. (Rev: BL 7/95) [362.7]

6343 Levine, Beth. *Divorce: Young People Caught in the Middle* (7–12). 1995, Enslow LB $19.95 (0-89490-633-X). A straightforward, commonsense manual for teens dealing with divorce. (Rev: BL 3/15/95; SLJ 6/95) [306.89]

6344 Lindsay, Jeanne W. *Coping with Reality: Dealing with Money, In-Laws, Babies and Other Details of Daily Life* (7–12). (Teenage Couples) 1995, Morning Glory Pr. $15.95 (0-930934-87-3); paper $9.95 (0-930934-86-5). Counsel on the day-to-day aspects of being a part of a couple. (Rev: BL 4/15/95; SLJ 3/95) [306.81]

6345 Lindsay, Jeanne W. *Teenage Couples Expectations & Reality: Teen Views On Living Together, Roles, Work, Jealousy & Partner Abuse* (9–12). (Teenage Couples) 1996, Morning Glory Pr. $21.95 (0-930934-99-7); paper $14.95 (0-930934-98-9). This book addresses a number of problems teens face when they live together, such as partner abuse, parenting, sharing, and in-laws. (Rev: BR 3–4/97; SLJ 6/96; VOYA 8/96) [649]

6346 McCue, Margi L. *Domestic Violence* (7–12). (Contemporary World Issues) 1995, ABC-CLIO LB $39.50 (0-87436-762-X). This book concentrates on spousal abuse, reactions to the problem, important events, laws and legislation, statistics, and interviews with survivors of violence. (Rev: BR 9–10/96; SLJ 5/96) [362.82]

6347 Mufson, Susan, and Rachel Kranz. *Straight Talk about Child Abuse* (7–12). (Straight Talk About) 1991, Facts on File $24.95 (0-8160-2376-X). Beginning with a general discussion of child abuse, this book describes the common signs of physical, emotional, and sexual abuse, gives some case studies, and offers some solutions. (Rev: BL 4/1/91; SLJ 3/91) [362.7]

6348 Nash, Renea D. *Everything You Need to Know about Being a Biracial/Biethnic Teen* (6–10). (Need to Know Library) 1995, Rosen LB $17.95 (0-8239-1871-8). How to deal with prejudice and discrimination while celebrating a unique heritage is the basic purpose of this book that explores our multiracial society. (Rev: BL 11/15/95; SLJ 1/96) [306.8]

6349 Packer, Alex J. *Bringing Up Parents: The Teenager's Handbook* (8–12). Illus. 1993, Free Spirit paper $14.95 (0-915793-48-2). Discusses in detail the art of coping with parents: building trust, diffusing family power struggles, waging effective verbal battles, developing listening skills, and expressing feelings nonaggressively. (Rev: BL 5/1/93*; VOYA 8/93) [306.874]

6350 Perl, Lila. *The Great Ancestor Hunt: The Fun of Finding Out Who You Are* (5–9). Illus. 1989, Clarion $16.00 (0-89919-745-0). A how-to manual on tracing your family's roots with important information on immigration to this country. (Rev: BL 11/1/89; SLJ 12/89; VOYA 2/90) [929]

6351 Quindlen, Anna. *Siblings* (10–12). 1998, Penguin $24.95 (0-670-87882-0). A series of essays, with photographs, on the subject of life with brothers and sisters. (Rev: BL 11/1/98; SLJ 5/99) [306]

6352 Rench, Janice E. *Family Violence: How to Recognize and Survive It* (6–8). 1992, Lerner LB $18.95 (0-8225-0047-7). This book speaks directly to children, with explanations of what constitutes different kinds of abuse, who is at fault, what motivates abusers, and what to do if violence occurs. (Rev: BL 11/1/92; SLJ 9/92) [362.82]

6353 Rofes, Eric, ed. *The Kids' Book of Divorce: By, for and about Kids* (6–10). 1982, Random paper $10.00 (0-394-71018-5). Twenty youngsters from ages 11 to 14 who are children of divorce were asked to state their reactions and feelings. [306.8]

6354 Roleff, Tamara L., and Mary E. Williams, eds. *Marriage and Divorce* (8–12). (Current Controversies) 1997, Greenhaven LB $26.20 (1-56510-568-0); paper $16.20 (1-56510-567-2). An anthology of 32 articles presenting diverse viewpoints on premarital cohabitation, the effect of divorce on children, child custody, and same-sex marriage. (Rev: SLJ 10/97) [306.8]

6355 Rue, Nancy N. *Coping with an Illiterate Parent* (7–12). (Coping) 1990, Rosen LB $17.95 (0-8239-1070-9). The causes, problems, and treatment of illiteracy as seen from a teenager's point of view. (Rev: BL 3/1/90; SLJ 10/90) [306]

6356 Ryan, Elizabeth A. *Straight Talk about Parents* (7–12). 1989, Facts on File $24.95 (0-8160-1526-0). A self-help manual to help teens sort out their feelings about parents. (Rev: BL 8/89; BR 11–12/89; SLJ 9/89; VOYA 2/90) [306.8]

6357 Sadler, A. E., ed. *Family Violence* (7–12). (Current Controversies) 1996, Greenhaven LB $21.96 (1-56510-371-8); paper $16.25 (1-56510-370-X). An anthology of original sources that explores the

prevalence of family violence, its victims and perpetrators, and how this violence can be reduced. (Rev: BL 6/1–15/96; SLJ 4/96) [362.82]

6358 St. Pierre, Stephanie. *Everything You Need to Know When a Parent Is in Jail* (7–12). Illus. (Everything You Need to Know) 1994, Rosen $17.95 (0-823-9-1526-3). Using many real-life examples, this book gives advice to youngsters who suffer both emotional and financial crises after a parent is sent to prison. (Rev: BL 4/15/94) [362.7]

6359 St. Pierre, Stephanie. *Everything You Need to Know When a Parent Is Out of Work* (6–12). (Need to Know Library) 1991, Rosen $12.95 (0-8239-1217-5). Explains how parents can lose their jobs and the effects unemployment can have on a parent's behavior, family routines, and relationships. (Rev: BL 10/1/91) [331.137]

6360 Sander, Joelle. *Before Their Time: Four Generations of Teenage Mothers* (9–12). 1991, Harcourt $19.95 (0-15-111638-5). An oral history of 4 African American teenage mothers—great-grandmother, grandmother, mother, and daughter—that illustrates a repetitive cycle of poverty, violence, and neglect. (Rev: BL 11/1/91) [306.85]

6361 Sanders, Pete, and Steve Myers. *Divorce and Separation* (4–8). Illus. (What Do You Know About) 1997, Millbrook LB $20.90 (0-7613-0574-2). An introduction to separation and divorce, with an emphasis on tips to help youngsters adjust and cope. (Rev: SLJ 10/97) [306.8]

6362 Sandweiss, Ruth, and Rachel Sandweiss. *Twins* (9–12). Illus. 1998, Running Pr. $27.50 (0-7624-0404-3). The unique relationship between twins is explored in this collection of essays and photographs that focuses on 27 sets of twins, among them dancers, athletes, farmers, models, astronauts, identical and fraternal twins, old twins and new twins, twins who married twins, twins separated at birth, and even a set of twin girls who share an undivided torso. (Rev: BL 12/1/98; VOYA 4/99) [618.2]

6363 Shires-Sneddon, Pamela. *Brothers & Sisters: Born to Bicker?* (6–10). (Teen Issues) 1997, Enslow LB $17.95 (0-89490-914-2). This book explores a variety of sibling relationships, how social pressures affect them, and the damaging impact of drugs, alcohol, divorce, death, and abuse. (Rev: BL 4/15/97; BR 9–10/97; VOYA 10/97) [306.875]

6364 Shultz, Margaret A. *Teens with Single Parents: Why Me?* (6–12). (Teen Issues) 1997, Enslow LB $17.95 (0-89490-913-4). Using interviews with teens as a focus, this book examines the problems of living with a single parent and makes some suggestions for coping strategies. (Rev: BL 7/97; BR 11–12/97; SLJ 10/97) [306.5]

6365 Simpson, Carolyn. *Everything You Need to Know About Living with a Grandparent or Other*

Relatives (8–12). 1995, Rosen LB $15.95 (0-8239-1872-6). This book explores the various situations that may cause teenagers to move in with grandparents, how to adjust, ways to maintain privacy, and the different emotions involved on both sides. (Rev: BR 9–10/96; VOYA 2/96) [306]

6366 Stewart, Gail B. *Battered Women* (9–12). Illus. (The Other America) 1996, Lucent LB $17.96 (1-56006-341-6). Four battered women tell their stories and advise others on how to avoid becoming victims as they were. A section on how the reader can become involved in this social problem is included. (Rev: BL 6/1–15/97; BR 11–12/97; SLJ 8/97) [362.82]

6367 Stewart, Gail B. *Teen Runaways* (9–12). Illus. (Other America) 1996, Lucent LB $17.96 (1-56006-336-X). Four teenage runaways tell about life on the streets, why teens leave home, and ways to help them. (Rev: BL 3/1/97; BR 11–12/97; SLJ 6/97) [362.7]

6368 Swisher, Karin L., ed. *Domestic Violence* (8–12). (At Issue) 1996, Greenhaven LB $16.96 (1-56510-381-5); paper $11.20 (1-56510-380-7). An anthology of different viewpoints involving the incidence and seriousness of spousal abuse by both men and women. (Rev: BL 1/1–15/96) [362.82]

6369 Swisher, Karin L., ed. *Single-Parent Families* (8–12). (At Issue) 1997, Greenhaven LB $15.96 (1-56510-544-3); paper $15.57 (1-56510-543-5). An anthology that presents different viewpoints about the problems and rewards of single-parenting. (Rev: BL 1/1–15/97; SLJ 7/97) [306.85]

6370 Taylor, Paul, and Diane Taylor. *Coping with a Dysfunctional Family* (7–12). (Coping) 1990, Rosen $22.95 (0-8239-1180-2). Through case studies, this account explores family problems that stem from such conditions as abuse, drugs, and neglect. (Rev: BL 11/1/90) [362.82]

6371 Torr, James D., and Karin L. Swisher, eds. *Violence against Women* (9–12). (Current Controversies) 1998, Greenhaven LB $21.96 (0-7377-0015-7). This anthology covers the seriousness of domestic violence, its causes, legal considerations, and ways it can be reduced. (Rev: BL 3/15/99; BR 5–6/99) [362.88]

6372 Westheimer, Ruth, and Pierre A. Lehu. *Dr. Ruth Talks About Grandparents: Advice for Kids on Making the Most of a Special Relationship* (5–8). Illus. 1997, Farrar $15.00 (0-374-31873-5). Sound advice is given on how to get along with grandparents and how to make these relationships pleasant and communicative. (Rev: BL 8/97; SLJ 9/97) [306.874]

6373 Williams, Mary E., ed. *The Family* (8–12). (Opposing Viewpoints) 1997, Greenhaven LB $21.96 (1-56510-669-5); paper $20.25 (1-56510-668-7). An anthology of articles presenting different points of view on the status of the family, divorce, work-related topics, adoption, and the changing values in society that affect the family structure. (Rev: BL 10/15/97; SLJ 12/97) [306.8]

6374 Worth, Richard. *Single-Parent Families* (6–10). 1992, Watts LB $24.00 (0-531-11131-8). Examines the social changes that led to the rise of the single-parent family, the long-term effects of divorce, the difficulties facing single parents, and other aspects. (Rev: BL 12/1/92) [306.85]

Youth Groups

6375 Boy Scouts of America. *The Official Boy Scout Handbook.* 10th ed. (7–9). Illus. 1990, Boy Scouts of America $6.45 (0-8395-3229-6). Though basically an orientation to scouting, this guide also includes much valuable material on such topics as camping, first aid, and wildlife. [369.43]

6376 Maupin, Melissa. *The Ultimate Kids' Club Book* (5–8). Ed. by Rosemary Wallner. Illus. 1996, Free Spirit paper $11.95 (1-57542-007-4). This book shows youngsters how to form and run a club successfully, with tips on raising money and choosing activities. (Rev: VOYA 2/97) [367]

6377 Moore, David L. *Dark Sky, Dark Land: Stories of the Hmong Boy Scouts of Troop 100* (7–10). Illus. 1989, Tessera paper $14.95 (0-9623029-0-2). A collection of stories of hardship and bravery behind Boy Scout Troop 100 in Minneapolis composed of young refugees from war-torn Laos. (Rev: BL 9/15/90) [977.6]

The Arts and Entertainment

General and Miscellaneous

6378 Craven, Wayne. *American Art: History and Culture* (9–12). 1994, Abrams $65.00 (0-8109-1942-7). Places architecture, decorative arts, painting, photography, and sculpture within a cultural and historical context. (Rev: BL 3/15/94) [709.73]

6379 Halliwell, Sarah, ed. *The 18th Century: Artists, Writers, and Composers* (6–9). (Who and When?) 1997, Raintree Steck-Vaughn LB $28.55 (0-8172-4727-0). A discussion of the lives and works of several artists like Wateau, Hogarth, and David; composers like Vivaldi, Bach, and Haydn; and writers like Defoe, Swift, and Voltaire. (Rev: BL 12/15/97; SLJ 2/98) [700]

6380 Halliwell, Sarah, ed. *The 17th Century: Artists, Writers, and Composers* (6–9). (Who and When?) 1997, Raintree Steck-Vaughn LB $28.55 (0-8172-4726-2). This work profiles artists like Caravaggioi, Rubens, Velazquez, and Rembrandt and discusses works by such writers as Shakespeare, Donne, and Milton and the composer Monteverdi. (Rev: BL 12/15/97; SLJ 2/98) [700]

6381 Heide, Robert, and John Gilman. *Popular Art Deco: Depression Era Style and Design* (9–12). 1991, Abbeville $39.95 (1-55859-030-7). Explores art deco's origins and illustrates its influence on the futuristic, streamlined appearance of everything from toasters to skyscrapers. (Rev: BL 9/1/91) [709]

Architecture and Building

General and Miscellaneous

6382 Gardner, Robert. *Architecture* (6–9). Illus. (Yesterday's Science, Today's Technology) 1994, Twenty-First Century LB $20.40 (0-8050-2855-2). This book contains an explanation of architectural concepts and practices, with hands-on activities that would be good for science fair projects. (Rev: BL 3/15/95) [721]

6383 Young, Michael. *Architectural and Building Design: An Introduction* (9–12). Illus. 1987, David & Charles paper $29.95 (0-434-92448-2). An interesting introduction to all sorts of building styles, external factors in planning structures, and special problems designers face. (Rev: BL 4/15/88) [721]

History of Architecture

6384 Corbishley, Mike. *The World of Architectural Wonders* (5–8). Illus. (The World Of) 1997, Bedrick LB $19.95 (0-87226-279-0). The story of 14 architectural wonders worldwide, including Stonehenge, the pyramids of Egypt, Chartes Cathedral, the Taj Mahal, and Hoover Dam. (Rev: BL 6/1–15/97; SLJ 7/97) [720]

6385 Glenn, Patricia Brown. *Under Every Roof: A Kid's Style and Field Guide to the Architecture of American Houses* (5–8). 1993, Preservation $16.95 (0-89133-214-6). An introduction to the history and styles of architecture of American homes, with a look at over 70 houses. (Rev: BL 7/94; SLJ 6/94) [728]

6386 Lynch, Anne, ed. *Great Buildings* (5–8). (Nature Company Discoveries) 1996, Time-Life Books $16.00 (0-8094-9371-3). Some of the world's most impressive structures are introduced, including a Mayan pyramid, Notre Dame, St. Peter's, and the Baths of Caracalla. (Rev: SLJ 3/97) [720.9]

6387 Macaulay, David. *Building the Book Cathedral* (5–9). 1999, Houghton $29.95 (0-395-92147-3). The author retells the fascinating story behind the creation of the original *Cathedral* book 25 years ago and adds numerous changes as he leads a tour of the cathedral of Chutreaux., such as alterations in scale and page placement. (Rev: BL 11/15/99; SLJ 9/99) [726]

6388 Macaulay, David. *Castle* (9–12). Illus. 1977, Houghton $18.00 (0-395-25784-0). In excellent line drawings and text, the author describes the construction of a castle in Wales during the 13th century. (Rev: BL 10/15/87) [728.8]

6389 Macaulay, David. *Cathedral: The Story of Its Construction* (9–12). Illus. 1973, Houghton $18.00 (0-395-17513-5). The story of how an imaginary cathedral was built in France from its conception in 1252 to its completion in 1338. [726]

6390 Macaulay, David. *Great Moments in Architecture* (9–12). Illus. 1978, Houghton $22.95 (0-395-25500-7); paper $13.95 (0-395-26711-0). An amusing look at what might have been disasters in the history of world architecture. [720]

6391 Macaulay, David. *Mill* (7–12). Illus. 1983, Houghton $18.00 (0-395-34830-7). Four different Rhode Island textile mills of the 19th century are described in text and excellent drawings. [690]

6392 Macaulay, David. *Pyramid* (7–12). Illus. 1975, Houghton $18.00 (0-395-21407-6); paper $8.95 (0-395-32121-2). In beautiful line drawings, the author describes how an ancient Egyptian pyramid was constructed. [726]

Painting, Sculpture, and Photography

General and Miscellaneous

6393 Berkey, John. *Painted Space* (9–12). 1991, Friedlander paper $19.95 (0-9627154-1-7). A collection of a science fiction artist's creations, including historical works and movie posters. (Rev: BL 1/15/92) [759.13]

6394 Capek, Michael. *Murals: Cave, Cathedral, to Street* (5–8). Illus. 1996, Lerner LB $23.93 (0-8225-2065-6). A history of mural painting, from cave painting to such modern masters as Diego Rivera. (Rev: BL 6/1–15/96; SLJ 10/96; VOYA 10/96) [751.7]

6395 Cumming, Robert. *Annotated Art* (9–12). 1995, DK Publg. $24.95 (1-56458-848-3). Forty-five art masterpieces from the gothic, Renaissance, neoclassic, baroque, and romantic periods are reproduced in 2-page spreads, with history and technique notes on each. (Rev: BL 6/1–15/95; SLJ 8/95) [750]

6396 Davidson, Rosemary. *Take a Look: An Introduction to the Experience of Art* (5–9). 1994, Viking paper $18.99 (0-670-84478-0). This overview, with examples from many cultures, describes how art fits into everyday experience and how we use it to express ourselves. (Rev: BL 3/1/94; SLJ 2/94; VOYA 6/94) [701]

6397 Lewis, J. D. *Journeys in Art* (5–8). (Let's Investigate Art) 1996, Marshall Cavendish LB $22.14 (0-7614-0009-5). This book examines works of art that portray great journeys, from Greek mythology and the Vikings to pioneers of the West. (Rev: SLJ 1/97) [709]

6398 Somerville, Louisa. *Animals in Art* (5–8). (Let's Investigate Art) 1996, Marshall Cavendish LB $22.14 (0-7614-0012-5). Beginning with cave art, this book traces the history of the depiction of ani-mals in art, accompanied by many suggestions for art projects. (Rev: SLJ 1/97) [709]

6399 Yenawine, Philip. *Key Art Terms for Beginners* (9–12). 1995, Abrams $24.95 (0-8109-1225-2). This is an introduction to terms used in the art world, with more than 140 reproductions as examples. (Rev: BL 6/1–15/95) [703]

History of Art

6400 Beckett, Wendy. *The Duke and the Peasant: Life in the Middle Ages* (4–8). (Adventures in Art) 1997, Prestel $14.95 (3-7913-1813-6). The 12 calendar paintings from the Duc de Berry's *Books of Hours* are reproduced, with explanations of each and an introduction to the art of the Middle Ages. (Rev: BL 8/97; SLJ 10/97) [940.1]

6401 Beckett, Wendy, and Patricia Wright. *The Story of Painting* (9–12). 1994, DK Publg. $39.95 (1-56458-615-4). A look at artists, historical periods, styles, movements, aesthetics, and spirituality. (Rev: BL 11/1/94*; SLJ 5/95; VOYA 4/95) [759]

6402 Corrain, Lucia. *The Art of the Renaissance* (6–12). Illus. (Masters of Art) 1998, Bedrick LB $22.50 (0-87226-526-9). An oversize volume packed with lots of small, full-color pictures and information-packed text introducing Renaissance artists and their times. (Rev: BL 3/1/98; SLJ 2/98) [709]

6403 Corrain, Lucia. *Giotto and Medieval Art* (6–12). (Masters of Art) 1995, Bedrick LB $22.50 (0-87226-315-0). A beautifully illustrated book that explores the art of Giotto and other masters of the Middle Ages. (Rev: BL 11/15/95) [759.5]

6404 De la Croix, Horst, and Richard G. Tansey. *Gardner's Art Through the Ages.* 10th ed. (7–12).

Illus. 1995, Harcourt paper $64.00 (0-15-501618-0). A standard adult history of art that has often been revised since its first publication in 1926. [709]

6405 Gombrich, E. H. *The Story of Art*. Rev. ed. (9–12). 1995, Chronicle $49.95 (0-7148-3355-X); paper $29.95 (0-7148-3247-2). A revision of a comprehensive standard art book, with 443 color illustrations. (Rev: BL 10/1/95) [709]

6406 Govignon, Brigitte, ed. *The Beginner's Guide to Art* (8–12). Trans. from French by John Goodman. 1998, Abrams $24.95 (0-8109-4002-7). Using a broad subject approach (architecture, sculpture, painting), this is a comprehensive guide to world art and artists, with generous use of color illustrations. (Rev: SLJ 3/99) [709]

6407 Guerrilla Girls Staff. *The Guerrilla Girls' Bedside Companion to the History of Western Art* (10–12). Illus. 1998, Viking paper $18.95 (0-14-025997-X). An introductory overview of traditional art history is followed by chapters highlighting the work of female artists during each time period, with reproductions of "mistresspieces" that have been overlooked by traditional male critics. The Guerrilla Girls are a group of anonymous artists and art professionals who seek to expose racism, sexism, and homophobia in the art world. (Rev: SLJ 9/98) [709]

6408 Halliwell, Sarah, ed. *Impressionism and Post-impressionism: Artists, Writers, and Composers* (6–9). Illus. (Who and When?) 1998, Raintree Steck-Vaughn LB $28.55 (0-8172-4730-0). Clear reproductions and a concise text introduce such artists as Pissarro, Monet, Renoir, Gauguin, and van Gogh as well as writers like Zola and the composer Debussy. (Rev: BL 12/15/97) [700]

6409 Harris, Nathaniel. *Renaissance Art* (6–10). (Art and Artists) 1994, Thomson Learning LB $24.26 (1-56847-217-X). A general overview of this rich period in art history, with illustrations of paintings, sculpture, and architecture. (Rev: BL 11/15/94; SLJ 10/94) [709]

6410 Heslewood, Juliet. *The History of Western Painting: A Young Person's Guide* (5–9). Illus. 1995, Raintree Steck-Vaughn LB $25.68 (0-8172-4000-4). Beginning with cave paintings, this large-format book gives a cursory overview of Western painting, with several pages devoted to contemporary artists and movements. (Rev: BL 1/1–15/96; SLJ 12/95) [759]

6411 Heslewood, Juliet. *The History of Western Sculpture* (5–9). Illus. 1995, Raintree Steck-Vaughn LB $25.68 (0-8172-4001-2). This oversize, heavily illustrated book traces the history of Western sculpture from the ancient Greeks to contemporary masters. (Rev: BL 1/1–15/96; SLJ 12/95) [730]

6412 Isaacson, Philip M. *A Short Walk Around the Pyramids and Through the World of Art* (5–8). 1993, Knopf LB $20.99 (0-679-91523-0). Art is shown in its broadest sense as a part of the everyday world, using examples of sculpture, architecture, photography, and painting. (Rev: BL 9/15/93; SLJ 8/93*) [700]

6413 Janson, H. W. *History of Art*. 3rd ed. (8–12). Illus. 1986, Abrams $49.50 (0-8109-1094-2). This standard history of art contains a time-line integrating important events in art history with those in other fields. (Rev: BL 5/1/86) [709]

6414 Janson, H. W., and Anthony F. Janson. *History of Art for Young People*. 5th ed. (7–12). Illus. 1997, Abrams $49.50 (0-8109-4150-3). A much-expanded, thoroughly revised edition of the standard history of art for young people that now includes the 1990s. (Rev: BL 2/1/97; BR 9–10/97) [709]

6415 Knapp, Ruthie, and Janice Lehmberg. *Impressionist Art* (5–9). 1999, Davis paper $8.95 (0-87192-385-8). This pocket-size guide supplies an overview of this movement in art and brief introductions to major Impressionist artists, including Sisley and Monet. (Rev: BL 1/1–15/99) [709.03]

6416 Lauber, Patricia. *Painters of the Caves* (4–8). 1998, National Geographic $17.95 (0-7922-7095-9). This lavishly illustrated book describes the paintings in the Chauvet cave in southeastern France and the life of the Neanderthal people who produced them. (Rev: BL 5/1/98; SLJ 3/98*) [759.01 12 094482]

6417 *Louvre* (10–12). Trans. from French by Susan Mackervoy, Anthony Roberts and Simon Dalgleish. 1995, Knopf paper $25.00 (0-679-76452-6). This small volume provides a quick tour of the art and architecture of the world-famous museum and art galley. (Rev: SLJ 1/96) [708]

6418 Newhall, Beaumont. *The History of Photography: From 1839 to the Present Day*. Rev. ed. (10–12). Illus. 1982, Bulfinch paper $32.95 (0-87070-381-1). A history of photography that gives many prints representing the best from the past and present. [770.9]

6419 Opie, Mary-Jane. *Sculpture* (7–12). (Eyewitness Art) 1994, DK Publg. $16.95 (1-56458-613-8). A handsome book filled with color illustrations introducing the world of sculpture, its history, and its various forms and materials. (Rev: BL 12/1/94; SLJ 6/95; VOYA 5/95) [730]

6420 Powell, Jillian. *Ancient Art* (6–10). (Art and Artists) 1994, Thomson Learning LB $24.21 (1-56847-216-1). This book covers the ancient civilizations and their contributions to the history of art. (Rev: BL 11/15/94; SLJ 10/94) [709]

6421 Richardson, Joy. *Looking at Pictures: An Introduction to Art for Young People* (5–8). Illus. 1997, Harry N. Abrams $19.95 (0-8109-4252-6). With separate sections on such themes as portraits, landscapes, and techniques, including color and light, this is an approachable guide to art appreciation for middle school students. (Rev: BL 4/15/97; SLJ 6/97*) [750]

6422 Roalf, Peggy. *Cats* (6–12). (Looking at Paintings) 1992, Hyperion paper $6.95 (1-56282-091-5). Pictures of cats, from Egyptian wall paintings to the Cheshire cat in *Alice in Wonderland* and more. (Rev: BL 5/15/92; SLJ 7/92) [758.3]

6423 Roalf, Peggy. *Families* (6–12). (Looking at Paintings) 1992, Hyperion paper $6.95 (1-56282-087-7). Pictures of families from various time periods. (Rev: BL 5/15/92; SLJ 7/92) [757]

6424 Romei, Francesca. *The Story of Sculpture* (6–12). (Masters of Art) 1995, Bedrick LB $22.50 (0-87226-316-9). Using outstanding illustrations, this book covers a world history of sculpture with many examples of various styles and materials. (Rev: BL 11/15/95) [730]

6425 Roukes, Nicholas. *Humor in Art: A Celebration of Visual Wit* (10–12). 1997, Davis $32.50 (0-87912-304-1). With numerous black-and-white and color illustrations and a lively text, this book explores humor in art, with examples from artists both past and present. (Rev: SLJ 12/97) [701]

6426 Sills, Leslie. *Visions: Stories about Women Artists* (5–8). 1993, Albert Whitman LB $18.95 (0-8075-8491-6). Melds information about the personal histories of women artists—such as Mary Cassatt, Betye Saar, Mary Frank—with insight into their art. (Rev: BL 4/1/93; SLJ 5/93*) [709]

6427 Steffens, Bradley. *Photography: Preserving the Past* (6–10). (Encyclopedia of Discovery and Invention) 1991, Lucent LB $23.70 (1-56006-212-6). A history of photography that describes its impact on the modern world and profiles men and women involved in it. (Rev: BL 4/15/92) [770]

6428 Wakin, Edward, and Daniel Wakin. *Photos That Made U.S. History, Vol. 1: From the Civil War Era to the Atomic Age* (6–9). 1993, Walker LB $13.85 (0-8027-8231-0). Photos that altered the perceptions of people and governments during times of military and social crisis. Also use: *Photos That Made U.S. History, Vol. 2: From the Cold War to the Space Age* (1993). (Rev: BL 5/1/94; SLJ 2/94) [973.9]

6429 Welton, Jude. *Impressionism* (9–12). (Eyewitness Art) 1993, DK Publg. $16.95 (1-56458-173-X). Brief text copiously illustrated with reproductions of artworks, details of paintings, photos of artists' mate-

rials, equipment, maps, and artist portraits. (Rev: BL 5/1/93) [759.09]

Regions

Africa

6430 Thompson, Robert Farris. *Face of the Gods: Art and Altars of Africa and the African Americas* (9–12). 1994, Prestel $85.00 (3-7913-1281-2). A survey of the sacred art of Africa and its influence on the art and worship practices of African Americans. (Rev: BL 2/15/94) [726.5]

Asia and the Middle East

6431 Finley, Carol. *Art of Japan: Wood Block Color Prints* (6–9). (Art Around the World) 1998, Lerner $23.93 (0-8225-2077-X). This richly illustrated book describes the 18th- and 19th-century wood block prints made in Japan, with background material on Japanese history and culture. (Rev: BL 4/1/99) [769.952]

6432 Knapp, Ruthie, and Janice Lehmberg. *Egyptian Art* (5–9). 1999, Davis paper $8.95 (0-87192-384-X). This pocket-size art appreciation book discusses mummies, sculpture, hieroglyphs, and other artifacts from Egyptian art. (Rev: BL 1/1–15/99) [709.32]

Europe

6433 Muhlberger, Richard. *What Makes a Raphael a Raphael?* (5–10). (What Makes a . . .) 1993, Viking paper $9.95 (0-670-85204-X). An in-depth look at the paintings of Raphael and distinguishing features. (Rev: BL 1/15/94; SLJ 12/93) [759.5]

6434 Muhlberger, Richard. *What Makes a Rembrandt a Rembrandt?* (5–10). (What Makes a . . .) 1993, Viking paper $9.95 (0-670-85199-X). The basic characteristics of this great Dutch master's work are pinpointed through a series of reproductions. (Rev: BL 1/15/94) [759.9492]

6435 Muhlberger, Richard. *What Makes a Van Gogh a Van Gogh?* (5–10). (What Makes a . . .) 1993, Viking $11.99 (0-670-85198-1). Reproductions are used to illustrate van Gogh's distinctive style, accompanied by information on his life. (Rev: BL 1/15/94) [759.9492]

6436 Salvi, Francesco. *The Impressionists: The Origins of Modern Painting* (6–12). (Masters of Art) 1995, Bedrick LB $22.50 (0-87226-314-2). An overview of Paris during the Impressionist period that includes many large, handsome reproductions. (Rev: BL 4/1/95; VOYA 5/95) [759.05]

North America

UNITED STATES

6437 Adams, Ansel. *Ansel Adams: Our National Parks* (9–12). 1992, Little, Brown paper $19.95 (0-8212-1910-3). A collection of photographs, essays, and letters. (Rev: BL 5/15/92) [770]

6438 Adams, Ansel. *The Portfolios of Ansel Adams* (9–12). Illus. 1977, Bulfinch $45.00 (0-8212-0723-7). A collection of 85 examples of this master photographer's work in black and white. [779]

6439 Cummings, Pat. *Talking with Artists* (4–8). (Talking with Artists) 1999, Clarion $20.00 (0-395-89132-9). In this third volume of the series, 13 artists are introduced, with examples of their art going back to their childhood. Among the artists are Jane Dyer, Peter Catalanotto, Anna Rich, Peter Sis, and Paul O. Zelinsky. (Rev: BL 3/15/99; SLJ 4/99) [741.6]

6440 Finch, Christopher. *The Art of Walt Disney: From Mickey Mouse to the Magic Kingdoms* (7–12). Illus. 1973, Crown $4.99 (0-517-66474-7). The life and career of Walt Disney are covered, but the main attraction in this book is a collection of almost 800 illustrations from his work. [791.43]

6441 Greenberg, Jan, and Sandra Jordan. *The American Eye: Eleven Artists of the Twentieth Century* (6–12). 1995, Delacorte $22.50 (0-385-32173-2). The art of these 11 artists is analyzed without jargon or pretension. A list of museums displaying their art-

work is included. (Rev: BL 9/1/95*; SLJ 11/95) [709]

6442 Hainey, Michael. *Blue* (5–10). Illus. 1997, Addison-Wesley paper $12.99 (0-201-87396-6). Collages, cartoons, and funky art are used with a clever text to illustrate uses of the color blue in our culture. (Rev: BL 2/1/98) [535.6]

6443 Horwitz, Elinor Lander. *Contemporary American Folk Artists* (7–9). Illus. 1975, HarperCollins paper $3.95 (0-397-31627-5). An explanation of what folk art is plus samples of the products of many artists. [709]

6444 Kloss, William. *Treasures from the National Museum of American Art* (9–12). Illus. 1986, Smithsonian $45.00 (0-87474-594-2). This book highlights 81 color paintings (and others in black and white) and gives a good introduction to the most important artists in the history of American art. (Rev: BL 6/1/86) [709]

6445 Knapp, Ruthie, and Janice Lehmberg. *American Art* (5–9). (Off the Wall Museum Guide for Kids) 1999, Davis paper $8.95 (0-87192-386-6). An informal pocket-size art appreciation book that features portraits from several centuries of American art, plus various artifacts and furniture. (Rev: BL 1/1–15/99) [709.73]

6446 Salinger, Margaretta. *Masterpieces of American Painting in the Metropolitan Museum of Art* (9–12). Illus. 1986, Random House $50.00 (0-394-55491-4). Historical and descriptive notes are given for reproductions of 100 paintings from the Met's collection that effectively trace a history of American art. (Rev: BL 2/1/87) [759.13]

Music

General and Miscellaneous

6447 Ardley, Neil. *A Young Person's Guide to Music* (5–8). 1995, DK Publg. $24.95 (0-7894-0313-7). This volume, accompanied by a CD, supplies a concise history of music and focuses on classical music and the instruments that create it. (Rev: BL 12/15/95; SLJ 1/96) [780]

6448 Igus, Toyomi. *I See the Rhythm* (5–8). Illus. 1998, Children's Book Pr. $15.95 (0-89239-151-0). Using a timeline to set the social context, this title traces African American contributions to such musical forms as the blues, big band, jazz, bebop, gospel, and rock. Coretta Scott King Award, 1999. (Rev: BL 2/15/98; SLJ 6/98) [780]

6449 Jones, K. Maurice. *Say It Loud: The Story of Rap Music* (7–12). Illus. 1994, Millbrook LB $27.40 (1-56294-386-3). Rap's history, its cultural roots, present practitioners, and controversies surrounding it are covered, along with hip-hop slang, examples of lyrics, and a generous use of illustrations. (Rev: BL 6/1–15/94; SLJ 5/94; VOYA 8/94) [782.42]

6450 Marsalis, Wynton. *Marsalis on Music* (9–12). 1995, Norton $29.95 (0-393-03881-5). A manual that uses examples from jazz greats to teach the fundamentals of jazz and the elements of improvisation. Includes a CD. (Rev: BL 10/1/95) [780]

6451 Turnbull, Walter. *Lift Every Voice: Expecting the Most and Getting the Best from All God's Children* (9–12). 1995, Hyperion $19.95 (0-7868-6164-9). The director of the Boys Choir of Harlem describes his beliefs and successes in sharing the joys of music with African American children. (Rev: BL 12/1/95) [780.7]

History of Music

6452 Davis, Francis. *The History of the Blues: The Roots, the Music, the People—From Charley Patton to Robert Cray* (9–12). 1995, Hyperion $24.95 (0-7868-6052-9). Using a first-person perspective, Davis explores the history, evolution, and marketing of contemporary blues artists and their music. (Rev: BL 1/15/95*) [781.643]

6453 Floyd, Samuel A. *The Power of Black Music* (9–12). 1995, Oxford $56.00 (0-19-508235-4). Traces African American music from Africa to the United States and explores the influence and contribution of African American musicians. (Rev: BL 4/1/95) [780]

6454 Gaar, Gillian. *She's a Rebel: The History of Women in Rock and Roll* (9–12). 1992, Seal Pr. paper $16.95 (1-878067-08-7). The contributions of female songwriters, singers, and other female musicians are traced through 4 decades of popular music. (Rev: BL 10/1/92) [781.66]

6455 Gourse, Leslie. *Blowing on the Changes: The Art of the Jazz Horn Players* (8–12). (The Art of Jazz) 1997, Watts $25.00 (0-531-11357-4). This book explores the influence on jazz of great artists of the trumpet, saxophone, trombone, clarinet, and other wind instruments. (Rev: BR 5–6/98; SLJ 11/97) [784]

6456 Medearis, Angela Shelf, and Michael R. Medearis. *Music* (5–9). (African-American Arts) 1997, Twenty-First Century LB $16.98 (0-8050-4482-5). The course of African American music from slave chants to jazz, blues, gospel, and later rock, soul music, and rap is traced in this informative history. (Rev: SLJ 7/97) [780]

6457 Ventura, Piero. *Great Composers* (5–9). Illus. 1989, Putnam $25.95 (0-399-21746-0). From ancient times to the Beatles, this is a multicultural treatment of the topic with most emphasis on Western composers. (Rev: BL 1/15/90; SLJ 4/90) [780]

Jazz and Popular Music (Country, Rap, Rock, etc.)

6458 Aquila, Richard. *That Old Time Rock & Roll: A Chronicle of an Era, 1954–1963* (8–12). 1989, Schirmer $25.00 (0-02-870082-1). A history complete with important biographies from the first decade of rock. (Rev: BL 9/15/89) [784.5]

6459 Awmiller, Craig. *This House on Fire: The Story of the Blues* (8–12). Illus. 1996, Watts LB $24.00 (0-531-11253-5). A history of the blues from its origins in slave songs and spirituals to its influence on the pop music of today, with profiles of such blues greats as Ma Rainey and Robert Johnson. (Rev: BL 6/1–15/96*; BR 11–12/96; VOYA 2/97) [781.643]

6460 Carlin, Richard. *Jazz* (9–12). (World of Music) 1991, Facts on File $19.95 (0-8160-2229-1). A history of this distinctly American music form, highlighting jazz greats and others who contributed to its development. (Rev: BL 9/15/91; SLJ 6/91) [781.65]

6461 Carr, Ian Digby Fairweather, and Brian Priestly, ed. *Jazz: The Rough Guide* (10–12). 1995, Penguin paper $24.95 (1-85828-137-7). There are profiles of nearly 2,000 jazz musicians and groups from the 20th century, plus a list of recommended recordings and a glossary of terms. (Rev: SLJ 8/96) [781]

6462 Christgau, Robert. *Christgau's Record Guide: Rock Albums of the '80's* (9–12). 1990, Pantheon paper $17.95 (0-679-73015-X). This is a guide to the rock albums of the 1980s with quotes from over 3,000 reviews. (Rev: BL 10/1/90; SLJ 6/91) [016.78]

6463 Collier, James L. *Jazz: An American Saga* (7–10). 1997, Holt $16.95 (0-8050-4121-4). A concise history of this uniquely American art form, from its African and European roots to the present day, and including the influences of various musicians on its development. (Rev: SLJ 1/98; VOYA 4/98) [781.65]

6464 Dawidoff, Nicholas. *In the Country of Country: People and Places in American Music* (10–12). 1997, Pantheon $25.00 (0-679-41567-X). Using a geographical approach, this work consists of a series of biographical essays about country and western music stars, among them Buck Owens, Patsy Cline, Chet Atkins, and Johnny Cash. (Rev: BL 2/15/97; SLJ 2/98) [780]

6465 Ellison, Curtis W. *Country Music Culture: From Hard Times to Heaven* (9–12). 1995, Univ. Press of Mississippi Pr. $40.00 (0-87805-721-8); paper $14.95 (0-87805-722-6). An account of the country music industry and its performers. (Rev: BL 2/15/95) [781.642]

6466 Elmer, Howard. *Blues: Its Birth and Growth* (6–9). Illus. (Library of African American Arts and Culture) 1999, Rosen $17.95 (0-8239-1853-X). This book traces the blues back to the song traditions of Africa and shows how it was influenced by the African American experience. The careers of such pioneers as Robert Johnson, Bessie Smith, and Muddy Waters are highlighted. (Rev: BR 9–10/99; SLJ 8/99; VOYA 8/99) [781.66]

6467 Gourse, Leslie. *Deep Down in Music: The Art of the Great Jazz Bassists* (7–10). (The Art of Jazz) 1998, Watts LB $25.00 (0-531-11410-4). By tracing the work of the great innovators on the bass fiddle, this book explores the development of jazz bass techniques and how these low sounds supply the foundation of the music. (Rev: BR 11–12/98; SLJ 7/98; VOYA 10/99) [781.65]

6468 Gourse, Leslie. *Striders to Beboppers and Beyond: The Art of Jazz Piano* (7–10). 1997, Watts LB $25.00 (0-531-11320-5). In this history of jazz pianists, the author profiles 23 great performers, including Jelly Roll Morton, Mary Lou Williams, Thelonius Monk, and Bud Powell. (Rev: SLJ 7/97) [786.4]

6469 *The Grateful Dead* (7–9). Illus. (Pop Culture Legends) 1997, Chelsea $19.95 (0-7910-3250-7); paper $8.95 (0-7910-4454-8). A colorful portrait of this band that has become a rock and roll legend and of its many dedicated fans, who are known as Deadheads. (Rev: BL 7/97; BR 9–10/97; SLJ 7/97) [782.42]

6470 Gregory, Hugh. *A Century of Pop: A Hundred Years of Music That Changed the World* (9–12). 1998, A Capella paper $29.95 (1-55652-338-6). Using a magazine format with plenty of illustrations, this book gives a decade-by-decade history of popular music in the United States during the 20th century. (Rev: SLJ 3/99) [781]

6471 Guterman, Jimmy, and Owen O'Donnell. *The Worst Rock and Roll Records of All Time: A Fan's Guide to the Stuff You Love to Hate* (9–12). 1991, Citadel paper $14.95 (0-8065-1231-8). An opinionated guide to 50 "atrocious" rock-and-roll songs. (Rev: BL 6/1/91) [781.66]

6472 Jancik, Wayne, and Ted Lathrop. *Cult Rockers* (10–12). 1995, Fireside paper $14.00 (0-684-81112-X). Profiles are given of 150 of the most popular, outrageous, and intriguing rock musicians around. (Rev: SLJ 7/96) [782]

6473 Leikin, Molly-Ann. *How to Write a Hit Song* (10–12). Illus. 1995, Hal Leonard paper $9.95 (0-88188-881-8). Practical advice on writing lyrics, composing, collaborating, and publishing songs. (Rev: VOYA 2/96) [784]

6474 Liggett, Mark, and Cathy Liggett. *The Complete Handbook of Songwriting: An Insider's Guide to Making It in the Music Industry* (9–12). 1985, NAL paper $9.95 (0-452-25687-9). This manual not only outlines the techniques of songwriting but also covers such areas as royalties, contracts, and even setting up one's own music publishing firm. (Rev: BL 8/85) [784]

6475 Morse, Tim. *Classic Rock Stories: The Stories behind the Greatest Songs of All Time* (10–12). 1998, Griffin paper $12.95 (0-312-18067-5). A history of rock during the 1960s and 1970s, with insights into hit songs and the artists who recorded them, among them Paul McCartney, Mick Jagger, Rod Stewart, Elton John, and Alice Cooper, plus an update on where they are today. (Rev: SLJ 1/99) [781.66]

6476 O'Dair, Barbara. *The Rolling Stone Book of Women in Rock: Trouble Girls* (10–12). 1997, Random paper $25.00 (0-679-76874-2). Fifty-six well-written essays by 44 women discuss the role of women in popular music, including rock and roll, jazz, gospel, rhythm and blues, and country; solo artists and girl groups of the 1950s and 1960s; rock in the 1960s and 1970s; pop singers and punksters of the 1970s; and more. (Rev: SLJ 6/98) [780]

6477 Reisfeld, Randi. *This Is the Sound: The Best of Alternative Rock* (7–9). Illus. 1996, Simon & Schuster paper $7.99 (0-689-80670-1). Although it is now somewhat dated, this is a rundown on the hottest alternative rock bands as of 1996. (Rev: BL 6/1–15/96; SLJ 7/96; VOYA 12/96) [791.66]

6478 Robertson, Brian. *Little Blues Book* (10–12). Illus. 1996, Algonquin paper $15.95 (1-56512-137-6). A history of the blues and blues singers covering the past 70 years, with numerous quotes from the artists and their songs. (Rev: SLJ 6/97) [782]

6479 Rose, Tricia. *Black Noise: Rap Music and Black Culture in Contemporary America* (9–12). 1994, Wesleyan Univ. Pr. paper $16.95 (0-8195-6275-0). An analysis of various facets of rap, including a discussion of hip-hop and the neglected recognition of women's role in rap. (Rev: BL 4/15/94) [782.42]

6480 Scherman, Tony, and Mark Rowland, eds. *The Jazz Musician* (9–12). 1994, St. Martin's paper $12.95 (0-312-09500-7). Profiles of jazz greats in which the legendary musicians recall important points in their lives. (Rev: BL 2/1/94) [781.65]

6481 Shirley, David. *The History of Rock & Roll* (6–9). 1997, Watts LB $25.00 (0-531-11332-9). A history of rock and roll that includes trends, stories, scandals, and personalities as well as coverage of such genres as rockabilly, folk rock, and glam rock. (Rev: BL 4/15/97; SLJ 6/97; VOYA 10/97) [781.66]

6482 Stroff, Stephen M. *Discovering Great Jazz: A New Listener's Guide to the Sounds and Styles of the Top Musicians and Their Recordings on CDs, LPs, and Cassettes* (9–12). 1991, Newmarket Pr. $19.95 (1-55704-103-2). A description of the stylistic developments in the history of jazz, with recommendations for the best recorded performances from each period up to the 1990s. (Rev: BL 10/1/91) [781.65]

6483 Talevski, Nick. *The Unofficial Encyclopedia of the Rock & Roll Hall of Fame* (8–12). 1998, Greenwood LB $45.00 (0-313-30032-1). This book provides background on the Rock and Roll Hall of Fame in Cleveland and covers, in alphabetical order, the first 150 inductees, with interesting personal as well as professional information, anecdotes, comments, and insights. (Rev: VOYA 2/99) [781.66]

6484 Woog, Adam. *The History of Rock and Roll* (6–9). (World History) 1999, Lucent LB $53.88 (1-56006-498-6). The history of rock from its origins in blues, country, and gospel music to its present forms in rap, hip-hop, and grunge. (Rev: BL 9/15/99) [781.66]

Opera and Musicals

6485 Brener, Milton. *Opera Offstage: Passion and Politics Behind the Great Operas* (10–12). 1996, Walker $38.95 (0-8027-1313-0). For each of the 26 operas discussed, a full plot summary is provided, along with material on musical forms used in the opera and its sources, which may include history, mythology, literature, politics, even the everyday experiences of the composer. (Rev: SLJ 7/97) [782.1]

6486 Englander, Roger. *Opera: What's All the Screaming About?* (7–12). Illus. 1983, Walker $19.95 (0-8027-6491-6). After a general introduction to the history and conventions of opera, 50 popular operas are introduced. (Rev: BL 9/1/87) [782.1]

6487 Freeman, John W. *The Metropolitan Opera Stories of the Great Operas* (9–12). Illus. 1984, Norton $29.95 (0-393-01888-1). Plots are given for 150 great operas with accompanying biographical material on their composers. [782.1]

6488 Gatti, Anne, retel. *The Magic Flute* (4–8). Illus. 1997, Chronicle $16.95 (0-8118-1003-8). This is an elegant retelling of Mozart's opera, with an accompanying CD of excerpts. (Rev: SLJ 1/98*) [782.1]

6489 Lerner, Alan Jay. *The Musical Theatre: A Celebration* (9–12). Illus. 1989, Da Capo paper $16.95 (0-306-80364-X). An anecdotal history of the American musical from its beginning to its maturity after World War II. (Rev: BL 11/15/86) [782.81]

6490 Novak, Elaine A., and Deborah Novak. *Staging Musical Theatre: A Complete Guide for Directors, Choreographers & Producers* (10–12). 1996, Betterway paper $19.99 (1-55870-407-8). A practical, readable guide to staging musicals, from auditions to printing the programs. (Rev: SLJ 2/97) [792]

6491 Perry, George. *The Complete Phantom of the Opera* (9–12). Illus. 1987, Holt $35.00 (0-8050-0657-5). A lavish volume that includes the original novel, the history of the musical, and the complete script. (Rev: BL 1/15/88; BR 5–6/88; SLJ 3/88; VOYA 6/88) [782.81]

6492 Sondheim, Stephen, and James Lapine. *Into the Woods* (9–12). 1989, Theatre Communications paper $10.95 (0-930452-93-3). The text and lyrics of the prize-winning musical about fairy tale characters and what happens to their "happily ever after." (Rev: BL 9/1/89) [782.81]

6493 Sullivan, Arthur. *I Have a Song to Sing, O! An Introduction to the Songs of Gilbert and Sullivan* (5–8). Ed. by John Langstaff. Illus. 1994, Macmillan $17.95 (0-689-50591-4). An introduction to the lives and accomplishments of Gilbert and Sullivan as well as a songbook of some of their greatest gems. (Rev: BL 12/1/94; SLJ 10/94) [781]

6494 Townshend, Pete, and Des McAnuff. *The Who's Tommy: The Musical* (9–12). 1993, Pantheon $40.00 (0-679-43066-0). This behind-the-scenes look at the rock opera by The Who includes production stills, anecdotes by cast and production members, and a CD. (Rev: BL 12/15/93) [782.1]

Orchestra and Musical Instruments

6495 Ardley, Neil. *Music* (5–9). Illus. 1989, Knopf LB $20.99 (0-394-92259-X). A profusely illustrated account that concentrates on musical instruments and their history. (Rev: BL 7/89; BR 11–12/89; SLJ 8/89) [781.91]

6496 Dearling, Robert, ed. *The Illustrated Encyclopedia of Musical Instruments* (8–12). 1996, Schirmer $96.50 (0-02-864667-3). In addition to material on the history, development, and characteristics of each musical instrument, this oversize, well-illustrated book gives a history of music-making, plus coverage of composers and performers. (Rev: BL 1/1–15/97; SLJ 5/97) [784.19]

6497 Evans, Roger. *How to Play Guitar: A New Book for Everyone Interested in Guitar* (8–12). Illus. 1980, St. Martin's paper $9.95 (0-312-36609-0). An easily followed basic guidebook on how to play the guitar with information on such topics as buying equipment and reading music. [787.6]

6498 Gruhn, George, and Walter Carter. *Acoustic Guitars and Other Fretted Instruments: A Photographic History* (9–12). 1993, Miller Freeman/GPI Books $49.95 (0-87930-240-2). Presents a history of U.S. fretted instruments from their beginnings to the present day, including photos of celebrity guitars. (Rev: BL 6/1–15/93) [787.87]

6499 Monath, Norman. *How to Play Popular Piano in Ten Easy Lessons* (10–12). 1984, Simon & Schuster paper $12.00 (0-671-53067-4). A useful guide that requires a great deal of work on the part of the reader. [786.2]

6500 Roth, Arlen. *Arlen Roth's Complete Acoustic Guitar* (9–12). Illus. 1985, Schirmer paper $18.95 (0-02-872150-0). Various styles like folk and rock are discussed and essential information on how to play each is given. (Rev: BL 4/1/86) [787.6]

6501 Steinberg, Michael. *The Symphony: A Concert Guide* (9–12). 1995, Oxford $30.00 (0-19-506177-2). Essays based on program notes Steinberg wrote for the Boston and San Francisco orchestras spanning 20 years. (Rev: BL 11/1/95) [784.2]

6502 Wollitz, Kenneth. *The Recorder Book* (9–12). 1982, Knopf paper $17.00 (0-394-74999-5). From beginning player to expert, this book covers all levels of recorder playing. [781.91]

Songs and Folk Songs

6503 Axelrod, Alan. *Songs of the Wild West* (5–9). 1991, Simon & Schuster paper $19.95 (0-671-74775-4). A collection of 45 songs from the Old West, with an overview of the Western expansionist movement and brief essays linking the music with art and history. (Rev: BL 12/15/91; SLJ 1/92) [784.7]

6504 Berger, Melvin. *The Story of Folk Music* (7–9). 1976, S. G. Phillips LB $28.95 (0-87599-215-3). The story of the origins and characteristics of folk music with many examples. [781.7]

6505 Blood-Patterson, Peter, ed. *Rise Up Singing* (8–12). Illus. 1988, Sing Out LB $39.95 (0-9626704-8-0); paper $17.95 (0-9626704-9-9). Words, chords, and some background material on 1,200 songs, some folk, others pop. (Rev: BL 12/15/88; BR 3–4/89) [784.5]

6506 Boy Scouts of America. *Boy Scout Songbook* (7–10). 1970, Boy Scouts of America paper $1.85 (0-

8395-3224-5). Using popular melodies as a basis, this book contains the words to more than 100 scouting songs. [784]

6507 Downes, Belinda. *Silent Night: A Christmas Carol Sampler* (7–12). 1995, Knopf $18.00 (0-679-86959-X). This 32-page collection of Christmas carols is illustrated with a full-page embroidered tapestry facing each carol. Words and piano music are provided. (Rev: BL 9/15/95*) [782.281]

6508 *The First Noel: Christmas Carols to Play & Sing* (4–8). 1998, DK Publg. $12.95 (0-7894-3483-0). In picture-book format, the words and simple arrangements are given for 13 Christmas carols. (Rev: BL 11/1/98) [782.28 1723 0268]

6509 Sandburg, Carl. *The American Songbag* (7–12). Illus. 1970, Harcourt paper $22.00 (0-15-605650-X). A fine collection of all kinds of American folksongs with music and background notes from Mr. Sandburg. [784.7]

6510 Seeger, Pete. *The Incompleat Folksinger* (9–12). 1992, Univ. of Nebraska Pr. paper $16.95 (0-8032-9216-3). This is a handbook on folksongs and folk music in the United States. Also use: *American Favorite Ballads* (1981). [781.7]

6511 Silverman, Jerry. *Just Listen to This Song I'm Singing: African-American History through Song* (6–10). Illus. 1996, Millbrook LB $30.90 (1-56294-673-0). American history from 1860 to the 1960s is reflected in 13 songs, including "Go Down, Moses," "Casey Jones," and "We Shall Overcome." (Rev: BL 4/15/96; SLJ 6/96*; VOYA 2/97) [782.42162]

6512 Silverman, Jerry. *Songs and Stories from the American Revolution* (6–10). 1994, Millbrook LB $27.90 (1-56294-429-0). The author, a noted folk singer, describes the origins of the songs of the Revolution, places them geographically, and supplies simple musical notations for each. (Rev: BL 12/1/94; SLJ 2/95) [782.42]

399

Theater, Dance, and Other Performing Arts

Dance (Ballet, Modern, etc.)

6513 Balanchine, George, and Francis Mason. *101 Stories of the Great Ballets* (7–12). 1975, Doubleday paper $14.00 (0-385-03398-2). Both the classics and newer ballets are introduced plus general background material such as a brief history of ballet. [792.8]

6514 Ganeri, Anita. *The Young Person's Guide to the Ballet: With Music from the Nutcracker, Swan Lake, & the Sleeping Beauty* (5–8). 1998, Harcourt $25.00 (0-15-201184-6). Complete with a CD of familiar ballet music, this is a basic introduction to ballet, including its history, choreography, behind the scenes activities such as sewing costumes and making sets, and great ballet dancers, famous choreographers, composers, and ballet companies. (Rev: BL 11/1/98; SLJ 9/98; VOYA 2/99) [792.84]

6515 Grau, Andrea. *Dance* (4–9). (Eyewitness) 1998, Knopf LB $20.00 (0-679-99316-9). A well-illustrated introduction to the world of dance around the world, including ballet. (Rev: BL 8/98; SLJ 1/99) [792]

6516 Haskins, Jim. *Black Dance in America: A History Through Its People* (7–12). 1990, HarperCollins LB $14.89 (0-690-04659-6). Beginning with the dances brought from Africa by the slaves, this history moves to the present with the contributions of such people as Gregory Hines and Alvin Ailey. (Rev: BL 8/90; SLJ 6/90; VOYA 6/90) [792.8]

6517 Heth, Charlotte, ed. *Native American Dance: Ceremonies and Social Traditions* (9–12). 1993, Starwood Publg. paper $29.95 (1-56373-021-9). Celebrates Indian dance ceremonies and social traditions, past and present, throughout the Americas. Color photos. (Rev: BL 4/1/93*) [394.3]

6518 Horosko, Marian, ed. *Martha Graham: The Evolution of Her Dance Theory and Training, 1926–1991* (9–12). 1992, Chicago Review $29.95

(1-55652-142-1). Recollections by dancers and actors that provide insight into the development of Graham's training theories and methods. (Rev: BL 12/15/91) [792.8]

6519 Medearis, Angela Shelf, and Michael R. Medearis. *Dance* (5–9). (African-American Arts) 1997, Twenty-First Century $20.40 (0-8050-4481-7). This book traces the African American influences on dance in such areas as jazz dancing, vaudeville, disco, rock, and hip-hop. Profiles are given of such stars as Katherine Dunham, Bill "Bojangles" Robinson, and Alvin Ailey. (Rev: SLJ 7/97) [794]

Motion Pictures

6520 Adamson, Joe. *The Bugs Bunny Golden Jubilee: 50 Years of America's Favorite Rabbit* (9–12). Illus. 1990, Holt $35.00 (0-8050-1190-0). An oversize book that is a profusely illustrated tribute to the life and times of this fabulous rabbit. (Rev: BL 2/15/90; SLJ 12/90) [741.5]

6521 *Amistad: "Give us Free": A Celebration of the Film by Steven Spielberg* (9–12). Illus. 1998, Newmarket Pr. paper $27.50 (1-55704-351-5). After reviewing the *Amistad* insurrection, this book focuses on the casting, producing, and shooting of the film. (Rev: SLJ 12/98) [791.43]

6522 Beck, Jerry. *"I Tawt I Taw a Puddy Tat": Fifty Years of Sylvester and Tweety* (9–12). 1991, Holt $35.00 (0-8050-1644-9). A tribute to Sylvester and Tweety on their 50th birthdays. Includes over 300 color-frame enlargements, cels, storyboards, and animation drawings. (Rev: BL 1/1/92) [741.5]

6523 Brackett, Leigh, and Lawrence Kasdan. *The Empire Strikes Back: The Illustrated Screenplay* (8–12). 1998, Ballantine paper $12.00 (0-345-42070-5). The shooting script for the second of the original *Star Wars* trilogy, with action direction and drawings of action scenes, preceded by an introduction that includes background and thoughts about the movie trilogy from the perspectives of people who were involved with the first release of the films. (Rev: SLJ 12/98) [791.43]

6524 Cavelos, Jeanne. *The Science of Star Wars* (9–12). 1999, St. Martin's $22.95 (0-312-20958-4). An astrophysicist and mathematician examines the actual science in the *Star Wars* films and finds that in the two decades since the debut of *Star Wars: A New Hope,* George Lucas's fictional universe has come much closer to reality. (Rev: SLJ 7/99) [791.43]

6525 Cowie, Peter, ed. *World Cinema: Diary of a Day* (9–12). 1995, Overlook $29.95 (0-87951-573-2). An overview of filmmaking, with input from directors, producers, technicians, and performers. (Rev: BL 3/15/95) [791.43]

6526 Ebert, Roger, and Gene Siskel. *The Future of the Movies* (9–12). 1991, Andrews & McMeel paper $9.95 (0-8362-6216-6). Interviews and discussions of cinema craft with 3 influential American filmmakers: Martin Scorsese, Steven Spielberg, and George Lucas. (Rev: BL 9/1/91) [791.43]

6527 Finch, Christopher. *The Art of the Lion King* (9–12). 1994, Hyperion $50.00 (0-7868-6028-6). Describes the making of the Disney film, including hundreds of production stills, sketches, animation drawings, and background paintings. (Rev: BL 9/1/94) [741.5]

6528 Flynn, John L. *The Films of Arnold Schwarzenegger* (9–12). 1993, Citadel paper $17.95 (0-8065-1423-X). Schwarzenegger's films, from *Hercules in New York* to his most recent, are given a critical look, with behind-the-scenes glimpses of the actor. (Rev: BL 11/1/93) [791.43]

6529 Hemming, Roy. *The Melody Lingers On: The Great Songwriters and Their Movie Musicals* (9–12). 1999, Newmarket Pr. paper $24.95 (1-55704-380-9). A look at the great Hollywood musicals that featured songs and lyrics of 10 great writers, including Berlin, Gershwin, Kern, Porter, and Rogers. (Rev: SLJ 8/99) [791.43]

6530 Hitzeroth, Deborah, and Sharon Heerboth. *Movies: The World on Film* (6–8). (Encyclopedia of Discovery and Invention) 1991, Lucent LB $18.96 (1-56006-210-X). This introduction to the world of cinema covers the history of moviemaking and the influence of films on society. (Rev: BL 12/1/91; SLJ 4/92) [791.43]

6531 Holden, Anthony. *Behind the Oscar: The Secret History of the Academy Awards* (9–12). 1994, NAL paper $16.95 (0-452-27131-2). Facts and statistics about the Oscar and the Academy Awards show, as well as backstage gossip. (Rev: BL 3/15/93; SLJ 2/94) [791.43]

6532 *James Cameron's Titanic* (6–12). Illus. 1997, HarperCollins $50.00 (0-06-757516-1); paper $20.00 (0-00-649060-3). A behind the scenes look at the creation of this blockbuster movie, with material and pictures on subjects like set design, costuming, and digital imaging. (Rev: VOYA 8/98) [791.43]

6533 Jenkins, Robert. *The Biology of Star Trek* (9–12). 1998, HarperCollins $22.00 (0-06-019154-6). The authors, both medical researchers, use incidents and characters from *Star Trek* to speculate on such possible fascinating science developments as interspecies mating, gene manipulation, and increased use of the senses. (Rev: BL 5/15/98; VOYA 10/98) [791.43]

6534 Johnson, Shane. *Technical Star Wars Journal* (7–12). Illus. 1995, Del Rey $35.00 (0-345-40182-4). An intriguing look at the ships, droids, armor, and appliances that were developed for and featured in the original *Star Wars* trilogy. (Rev: VOYA 4/96) [791.43]

6535 Jones, K. Maurice. *Spike Lee and the African American Filmmakers: A Choice of Colors* (7–12). Illus. 1996, Millbrook LB $27.90 (1-56294-518-1). The role of African American filmmakers during the 20th century is covered, with information on directors, actors, and screenwriters, including Spike Lee, Gordon Parks, Robert Townsend, Terry McMillan, and Denzel Washington. (Rev: BL 1/1–15/97; BR 9–10/97; SLJ 2/97; VOYA 6/97) [791.43]

6536 Kasdan, Lawrence, and George Lucas. *Return of the Jedi: The Illustrated Screenplay* (8–12). 1998, Ballantine paper $12.00 (0-345-42079-9). The third of the original *Star Wars* trilogy is featured, with the screenplay, background information, and drawings of action scenes from the film. (Rev: SLJ 12/98) [791.43]

6537 Kerr, Walter. *The Silent Clowns* (10–12). Illus. 1975, Da Capo paper $19.95 (0-306-80387-9). A series of sketches about the great comedians who flourished during the days of silent film. [791.43]

6538 Koenig, David. *Mouse Under Glass: Secrets of Disney Animation & Theme Parks* (10–12). 1997, Bonaventure Pr. $23.95 (0-9640605-0-7). This is a chronological overview of Disney's 30 films, from "Snow White" through "The Hunchback of Notre Dame," giving background information (but no pictures) about each. (Rev: BL 1/1–15/97; SLJ 11/97) [791.43]

6539 Margulies, Edward, and Stephen Rebello. *Bad Movies We Love* (9–12). 1993, NAL paper $12.00 (0-452-27005-7). A compendium of movies so bad that they are entertaining. (Rev: BL 7/93) [791.43]

6540 Mast, Gerald. *A Short History of the Movies.* 6th ed. (8–12). Illus. 1992, Macmillan $35.00 (0-02-580510-X). A lavishly illustrated history that deals with both the creative and technical aspects of movie history. (Rev: BL 1/15/87) [791.43]

6541 Merritt, Russell, and J. B. Kaufman. *Walt in Wonderland: The Silent Films of Walt Disney* (9–12). 1994, Johns Hopkins Univ. Pr. $39.95 (0-8018-4907-1). Profiles Disney films of the 1920s, showing how they laid the foundation for later animation techniques and conventions. (Rev: BL 9/1/94) [791.43]

6542 Nowell-Smith, Geoffrey, ed. *The Oxford History of World Cinema* (10–12). 1996, Oxford $79.95 (0-19-811257-2). This is a fine resource on world cinema that highlights major figures and their contributions. (Rev: SLJ 4/97) [791.43]

6543 Platt, Richard. *Film* (5–9). (Eyewitness Books) 1992, Knopf LB $20.99 (0-679-91679-2). A discussion of the development of motion pictures and the use of film in other media. (Rev: BL 6/1/92) [791.43]

6544 Reynolds, David West. *Star Wars: Incredible Cross-Sections* (4–8). 1998, DK Publg. $19.95 (1-7894-3480-6). This large-format book includes cross-sections of the TIE fighter, the X-wing fighter, the AT-AT, the Millennium Falcon, Jabba's sail barge, and the Death Star. (Rev: BL 12/15/98) [791.43]

6545 Reynolds, David West. *Star Wars: The Visual Dictionary* (4–8). 1998, DK Publg. $19.95 (0-7894-3481-4). Using a large-format dictionary approach, the people, creatures, and droids of the Star Wars saga are presented, with large photos of the characters and many stills from the movies. (Rev: BL 12/15/98; SLJ 2/99) [791.43]

6546 Reynolds, David West. *Star Wars Episode I: The Visual Dictionary* (4–8). 1999, DK Publg. $19.95 (0-7894-4701-0). In this large-format book, a follow-up to *Star Wars: The Visual Dictionary,* the author, an archaeologist reports on creatures and events in *Episode I,* explaining the galaxy's history, technology, anthropology, and politics, with movie stills and posed photos. (Rev: BL 8/99) [791.43]

6547 Sansweet, Stephen J. *Star Wars Encyclopedia* (9–12). 1998, Ballantine $49.95 (0-345-40227-8). Made for browsing, this is an exhaustive, alphabetically arranged collection of data about *Star Wars*—characters, memorabilia, weapons, movies, books, toys, and planets. (Rev: SLJ 12/98) [791.43]

6548 Sauter, Michael. *The Worst Movies of All Time; or, What Were They Thinking?* (9–12). 1995, Citadel paper $14.95 (0-8065-1577-5). A delight in chronicling bad movies motivates this book, with a look at some behind-the-scenes craziness. (Rev: BL 11/15/95) [791.43]

6549 Schroeder, Russell. *Mickey Mouse: My Life in Pictures* (4–8). 1997, Disney LB $14.89 (0-7868-5059-0). After his meeting with Walt Disney, Mickey tells of his career decade by decade, using very brief text and numerous captioned illustrations of cartoon shorts, comic strips, TV programs, and feature films in which he appeared. (Rev: SLJ 2/98) [791.43]

6550 Schultz, Ron. *Looking Inside Cartoon Animation* (5–8). Illus. (X-Ray Vision) 1992, John Muir paper $6.95 (1-56261-066-X). Breaks down the animator's art to its scientific underpinnings and then to the roles of key people in the process. (Rev: BL 1/15/93; SLJ 2/93) [741.5]

6551 Shipman, David. *A Pictorial History of Science Fiction Films* (8–12). Illus. 1986, Salem House $17.95 (0-600-38520-5). From the French 19th-century efforts to today's works by Lucas and Spielberg, this is a heavily illustrated account of science fiction and fantasy movies. (Rev: BL 2/15/86) [791.435]

6552 Smith, Marisa, and Amy Schewel, eds. *The Actor's Book of Movie Monologues* (9–12). 1986, Penguin paper $12.95 (0-14-009475-X). A collection of 80 monologues starting with *M* and ending with *The Breakfast Club.* (Rev: BL 11/1/86) [791.43]

6553 Solomon, Charles. *The Disney That Never Was: The Stories and Art from Five Decades of Unproduced Animation* (9–12). 1995, Hyperion $40.00 (0-7868-6037-5). The Disney projects that were abandoned, accompanied by many illustrations, concept art, and animation drawings. (Rev: BL 12/1/95) [741.5]

6554 Thomas, Bob. *Disney's Art of Animation: From Mickey Mouse to Beauty and the Beast* (9–12). 1991, Hyperion $39.95 (1-56282-997-1). An update of the 1958 book, written with the cooperation of the Disney studio, chronicling the history of Disney animation using art from studio archives. (Rev: BL 11/1/91; SLJ 3/92) [741.5]

6555 Wallace, Daniel. *Star Wars: The Essential Guide to Planets and Moons* (6–12). Illus. 1998, Del Rey paper $18.95 (0-345-42068-3). This volume provides fascinating information on 110 different planets and moons in the Star Wars universe, arranged alphabetically from Abregado-rae, a popular stop for smugglers, to Zhar, a gas-filled giant, covering each world's inhabitants, climate, language, points of interest, and history. (Rev: VOYA 6/99) [791.45]

6556 Winfrey, Oprah. *Journey to Beloved* (10–12). 1998, Hyperion $40.00 (0-7868-6458-3). This is the diary Oprah Winfrey kept during the filming of Toni Morrison's *Beloved,* in which she writes about her fears and insecurities as an actress, the emotions she felt in dealing with the subject matter, and the pull of outside events. (Rev: SLJ 2/99) [791.43]

6557 Wright, Bruce Lanier. *Yesterday's Tomorrows: The Golden Age of Science Fiction Movie Posters, 1950–1964* (9–12). 1993, Taylor $29.95 (0-87833-818-7); paper $19.95 (0-87833-824-1). Nearly 100 color posters for vintage sci-fi movies, accompanied by mini-essays on each film and a guide for collectors. (Rev: BL 5/1/93) [791.43]

Radio, Television, and Video

6558 Borgenicht, David. *Sesame Street Unpaved: Scripts, Stories, Secrets, and Songs* (9–12). 1998, Hyperion $24.95 (0-7868-6460-5). The author reveals the behind-the-scenes secrets of the successful 30-year-old public television program in this book, which includes many illustrations and stories about the characters and activities that have made *Sesame Street* a cultural icon. (Rev: SLJ 3/99) [791.45]

6559 Cader, Michael, ed. *Saturday Night Live: The First Twenty Years* (9–12). 1994, Houghton $25.00 (0-395-70895-8). Celebrates the 20th anniversary of the TV show *Saturday Night Live,* with photos and descriptions of many sketches. (Rev: BL 9/1/94; SLJ 3/95) [791.4572]

6560 Catalano, Grace. *Meet the Stars of Dawson's Creek* (6–10). 1998, Bantam Doubleday Dell paper $4.99 (0-440-22821-2). This book describes how the *Dawson's Creek* television show was developed, profiles its stars and creator/producer, and summarizes the first 6 episodes. (Rev: VOYA 12/98) [791.45]

6561 Cavelos, Jeanne. *The Science of The X-Files* (8–12). 1998, Berkley paper $12.95 (0-425-16711-9). Combining pop culture and hard science, this book analyzes specific episodes of the *X-Files* from a scientific perspective. (Rev: VOYA 4/99) [791.45]

6562 Johnson, Hillary, and Nancy Rommelmann. *The Real Real World* (9–12). Illus. 1995, Pocket Books paper $16.00 (0-671-54525-6). This book chronicles the first 4 seasons of MTV's popular *Real World* program, with lots of pictures and an episode-by-episode synopsis. (Rev: VOYA 6/96) [791.45]

6563 Killick, Jane. *Babylon 5: The Coming of Shadows* (7–12). 1998, Ballantine paper $11.00 (0-345-42448-4). This is the second of a 5-volume guide to this popular television series. (Rev: VOYA 12/98) [791.45]

6564 Kraus, Lawrence M. *The Physics of Star Trek* (7–12). Illus. 1996, HarperPerennial paper $12.00 (0-06-097710-8). Warp, transporter beams, antimatter, and other scientific concepts popularized in *Star Trek* are examined, with speculations on their possible application in the future. (Rev: VOYA 8/97) [791.45]

6565 Lackman, Ron. *Same Time . . . Same Station: An A to Z Guide to Radio from Jack Benny to Howard Stern* (10–12). 1996, Facts on File $45.00 (0-8160-2862-1). A history of radio as a source of both news and entertainment, covering hundreds of old radio shows and their stars. (Rev: SLJ 4/96) [791.44]

6566 Okuda, Michael, and Denise Okuda. *Star Trek Chronology: The History of the Future* (10–12). 1996, Pocket Books paper $25.00 (0-671-53610-9). Using over 1,000 color photos and exhaustive coverage, this is a guide to all 4 of the *Star Trek* TV series as well as the motion pictures. (Rev: SLJ 5/97) [791.45]

6567 Owen, Rob. *Gen X TV: The Brady Bunch to Melrose Place* (10–12). 1997, Syracuse Univ. Pr. $29.95 (0-8156-0443-2). A history of popular television programs that shows not only how Gen Xers influenced network programming, but also how television affected their lives. (Rev: SLJ 2/98) [384.55]

6568 Perry, George. *Life of Python* (10–12). 1984, Little, Brown paper $12.95 (0-316-70015-0). A thorough rundown on the Monty Python gang and their television programs. [384.55]

6569 Ritchie, Michael. *Please Stand By: A Prehistory of Television* (9–12). 1994, Overlook $23.95 (0-87951-546-5). The story of television before 1948, chronicling the technological struggles and advances during the medium's infancy. (Rev: BL 9/15/94; SLJ 5/95) [791.45]

6570 Solow, Herbert F., and Robert H. Justman. *Inside Star Trek: The Real Story* (10–12). 1996, Pocket Books $30.00 (0-671-89628-8). A behind-the-scenes look at the phenomenal original *Star Trek* TV series that reveals how it was conceived, the obstacles to production such as personality conflicts, production difficulties, battles with NBC executives, etc., and reasons for its success. (Rev: SLJ 6/97) [791.45]

6571 Wallner, Rosemary. *Fresh Prince of Bel Air* (7–10). 1992. ABDO, $12.95 (1-56239-140-2) The story behind the TV series, now in reruns, that made a star of Will Smith.

Recordings

6572 Early, Gerald. *One Nation under a Groove: Motown and American Culture* (9–12). 1995, Ecco $17.00 (0-88001-379-6). The history of the African American record company Motown and how it brought rhythm and blues into the mainstream. (Rev: BL 6/1–15/95) [306.4]

Theater and Other Dramatic Forms

6573 Alberts, David. *Talking about Mime: An Illustrated Guide* (9–12). 1994, Heinemann paper $14.95

(0-435-08641-3). Instructions for learning mime fundamentals and performance, including specific exercises and a short history of the art. (Rev: BL 11/1/94) [792.3]

6574 Alter, Judith. *Beauty Pageants: Tiaras, Roses, and Runways* (4–8). Illus. 1997, Watts LB $22.50 (0-531-20253-4). After introducing various kinds of pageants, this book describes in detail the Miss America pageant, its history, and organization. (Rev: BL 12/1/97; SLJ 9/97) [791.6]

6575 Brown, John Russell, ed. *The Oxford Illustrated History of Theatre* (9–12). 1995, Oxford $35.00 (0-19-212997-X). A well-written general history of the theater, in the form of connected essays, that avoids the usual Eurocentric approach. (Rev: BL 11/1/95; SLJ 3/96) [792]

6576 Caruso, Sandra, and Susan Kosoff. *The Young Actor's Book of Improvisation: Dramatic Situations from Shakespeare to Spielberg: Ages 12–16* (6–12). 1998, Heinemann paper $22.95 (0-325-00049-2). This work supplies hundreds of situations suitable for improvisation culled from all forms of literature, plays, and movie scripts, arranged by themes such as confrontation and relationships. (Rev: BL 9/15/98; SLJ 1/99) [793]

6577 Cassady, Marsh. *The Theatre and You: A Beginning* (9–12). 1992, Meriwether paper $15.95 (0-916260-83-6). A comprehensive introduction to theater as a performing art and craft, outlining 5 broad areas of study: theaters and stages, directing, design, acting, and theater history. (Rev: BL 11/1/92) [792]

6578 Currie, Stephen. *Life in a Wild West Show* (6–10). (The Way People Lived) 1998, Lucent LB $17.96 (1-56006-352-1). Personal struggles, individual jobs, and daily routines are stressed in this account of traveling shows that depicted life on the wild American frontier. (Rev: BL 11/15/98) [791.8]

6579 Cushman, Kathleen, and Montana Miller. *Circus Dreams* (6–12). Illus. 1990, Little, Brown $15.95 (0-316-16561-1). A look at the professional college for circus artists in France, following the experiences of one of its students. (Rev: BL 1/15/91; SLJ 1/91) [791.3]

6580 Frantz, Donald. *Beauty and the Beast: A Celebration of the Broadway Musical* (9–12). 1995, Hyperion $35.00 (0-7868-6179-7). Production photos from the stage production, plus behind-the-scenes information. (Rev: BL 12/15/95) [782.1]

6581 Granfield, Linda. *Circus: An Album* (4–8). Illus. 1998, DK Publg. $19.95 (0-7894-2453-3). Following a review of the intriguing history of the circus from ancient times to the present, this title describes famous people connected with the circus and explores such issues as circus family life, con-

troversies over animal abuse and freak shows, and the future of the circus. (Rev: BL 3/1/98; SLJ 3/98*; VOYA 10/98) [791.3]

6582 Grote, David. *Staging the Musical: Planning, Rehearsing, and Marketing the Amateur Production* (10–12). 1986, Simon & Schuster $10.95 (0-13-840182-9). An excellent guide for anyone involved in amateur theatrics with tips on such topics as scenery, costumes, and sound. (Rev: BL 4/15/86) [782.81]

6583 Halpern, Charna, et al. *Truth in Comedy: The Manual for Improvisation* (9–12). 1994, Meriwether paper $16.95 (1-56608-003-7). A thorough manual of comedic improvisation by 3 improv gurus. (Rev: BL 4/15/94) [792]

6584 Kipnis, Claude. *The Mime Book* (7–12). Illus. 1988, Meriwether paper $14.95 (0-916260-55-0). One of the world's greatest mimes explains what it is and how it is done. [792.3]

6585 Lee, Robert L. *Everything about Theatre! The Guidebook of Theatre Fundamentals* (7–12). Illus. 1996, Meriwether paper $16.95 (1-56608-019-3). This excellent introduction to the backstage world includes material ranging from theater history to stagecraft, acting, and play production. (Rev: BL 12/1/96; SLJ 2/97) [792]

6586 Nardo, Don. *Greek and Roman Theater* (8–12). Illus. (World History) 1995, Lucent LB $17.96 (1-56006-249-5). This overview not only supplies details on the importance of the theater in ancient times, but also tells of the construction and parts of the theater, practices associated with it, and famous playwrights. (Rev: BL 2/15/95; SLJ 2/95) [792]

6587 Schindler, George. *Ventriloquism: Magic with Your Voice* (8–12). Illus. 1986, McKay paper $6.95 (0-679-14127-8). This book not only explains how to throw one's voice but also gives material on stage techniques, kinds of puppet figures, and writing routines. [793.8]

6588 Stolzenberg, Mark. *Be a Clown!* (7–12). Illus. 1989, Sterling paper $10.95 (0-8069-5804-9). A how-to manual that describes how to create a clown character and supplies a number of routines. (Rev: BL 1/1/90) [791.3]

6589 Straub, Cindie, and Matthew Straub. *Mime: Basics for Beginners* (7–12). Illus. 1984, Plays paper $13.95 (0-8238-0263-9). The fundamentals of traditional mime are explained in text, line drawings, and photographs. (Rev: BL 2/1/85) [792.3]

6590 Trussler, Simon. *The Cambridge Illustrated History of British Theatre* (9–12). 1994, Cambridge Univ. Pr. $39.95 (0-521-41913-1). A historical overview of British theater. (Rev: BL 3/1/95) [792]

Biography, Memoirs, Etc.

General and Miscellaneous

6591 Fannon, Cecilia. *Leaders* (5–8). (Women Today) 1991, Rourke LB $17.95 (0-86593-118-6). Integrates thumbnail biographies with general chapters on women achievers in politics, business, medicine, sports, and the arts. (Rev: BL 11/1/91; SLJ 2/92) [920]

6592 Felder, Deborah G. *The 100 Most Influential Women of All Time: A Ranking Past and Present* (9–12). 1995, Citadel $24.95 (0-8065-1726-3). Part of the series that includes *The Black 100* and *The Jewish 100*. (Rev: BL 12/1/95) [920]

6593 Masters, Anthony. *Heroic Stories* (5–8). 1994, Kingfisher paper $6.95 (1-85697-983-0). Attempts to isolate the qualities that prepared the 23 individuals profiled in these biographies. (Rev: BL 3/1/95) [920]

6594 Salisbury, Harrison E. *Heroes of My Time* (9–12). 1993, Walker $30.95 (0-8027-1217-7). The *New York Times* journalist emeritus profiles both famous and unknown people who strove to reform the world through deeds, not words. (Rev: BL 4/15/93; VOYA 12/93) [920]

Adventurers and Explorers

Collective

6595 Foss, Joe, and Matthew Brennan. *Top Guns: America's Fighter Aces Tell Their Stories* (9–12). 1992, Pocket Books paper $5.99 (0-671-68318-7). Twenty-seven aviators who served in various conflicts from World War II to Vietnam give stirring accounts of combat. (Rev: BL 5/15/91) [920]

6596 Lomask, Milton. *Great Lives: Exploration* (6–9). Illus. 1989, Macmillan $25.00 (0-684-18511-3). An account of 25 world explorers from the ancient Greeks to the Polar expeditions of the 20th century. (Rev: BL 3/15/89; SLJ 1/89) [910]

6597 Murphy, Claire R., and Jane G. Haigh. *Gold Rush Women* (7–12). Illus. 1997, Alaska Northwest paper $16.95 (0-88240-484-9). This is a collective biography of several women in the late 19th century who went to the Yukon and Alaska where they panned for gold, ran boarding houses, and worked as dance hall girls and prostitutes. (Rev: BL 8/97; BR 1–2/98; SLJ 11/97*) [920]

6598 Schraff, Anne. *American Heroes of Exploration and Flight* (6–9). (Collective Biographies) 1996, Enslow LB $19.95 (0-89490-619-4). Ten brief biographies of people who made important contributions to flight and exploration, including Matthew Henson, Robert Peary, Amelia Earhart, and Sally Ride. (Rev: BL 4/15/96; BR 9–10/96; SLJ 5/96; VOYA 6/96) [920]

6599 Stefoff, Rebecca. *Scientific Explorers: Travels in Search of Knowledge* (6–9). (Extraordinary Explorers) 1993, Oxford $41.95 (0-19-507689-3). This is a collective biography of travelers and explorers like Humbolt and Darwin whose undertakings produced significant knowledge. (Rev: BL 6/1–15/93) [920]

6600 Stefoff, Rebecca. *Vasco da Gama and the Portuguese Explorers* (6–9). (World Explorers) 1993, Chelsea LB $19.95 (0-7910-1303-0). An account of how different Portuguese explorers beginning with Vasco da Gama were able to visit unknown territories, particularly in the New World. (Rev: BL 3/15/93) [920]

6601 Stefoff, Rebecca. *Women of the World: Women Travelers and Explorers* (6–9). (Extraordinary Explorers) 1993, Oxford $44.95 (0-19-507687-7). Focuses on little-known women of the 19th and 20th centuries whose explorations challenged notions of propriety and possibility. (Rev: BL 6/1–15/93) [920]

6602 Weatherly, Myra. *Women Pirates: Eight Stories of Adventure* (6–9). Illus. 1998, Morgan Reynolds LB $20.95 (1-883846-24-2). Eight females who sailed, plundered, and fought as pirates in the 17th and 18th centuries are highlighted, most of them from the United Kingdom and the American colonies, but also including one who was a Viking and another from China. (Rev: SLJ 7/98; VOYA 10/98) [920]

6603 Yount, Lisa. *Women Aviators* (6–9). 1995, Facts on File $19.95 (0-8160-3062-6). Profiles of 11 prominent female aviators. (Rev: BL 4/1/95) [920]

Individual

ADAMS, HARRIET CHALMERS

6604 Anema, Durlynn. *Harriet Chalmers Adams: Adventurer and Explorer* (6–12). Illus. 1997, Morgan Reynolds LB $18.95 (1-883846-18-8). This book tells of the unconventional life of Harriet Chalmers Adams, a writer, lecturer, and humanitarian who explored primitive areas in South America, the Caribbean, and the Far East to find proof that

Native Americans originally came from Asia, was the first woman correspondent allowed to travel to the front during World War I, and founded a society for women geographers. (Rev: BL 3/1/97; BR 11–12/97; SLJ 4/97; VOYA 10/97) [921]

BROWN, TOM, JR.

6605 Brown, Tom, Jr. *The Way of the Scout* (10–12). 1995, Berkley paper $12.95 (0-425-14779-7). This autobiographical account of the adolescence and young adulthood of a forest scout who now runs a wilderness survival school combines a message of spirituality, love of beauty, and environmentalism with breathtaking adventures. (Rev: SLJ 7/96) [921]

BYRD, ADMIRAL

6606 Burleigh, Robert. *Black Whiteness: Admiral Byrd Alone in the Antarctic* (4–9). Illus. 1998, Simon & Schuster $16.00 (0-689-81299-X). An outstanding picture biography, with generous quotes from Byrd's diary, that tells of his great endurance and his lonely vigil in a small underground structure in the Antarctic. (Rev: BL 1/1–15/98; SLJ 3/98) [921]

CAHILL, TIM

6607 Cahill, Tim. *A Wolverine Is Eating My Leg* (9–12). 1989, Random paper $13.00 (0-679-72026-X). A fascinating travel writer tells about his adventures around the world in this continuation of *Jaguars Ripped My Flesh* (1987). (Rev: BL 2/15/89) [921]

CARTER, JENNIFER

6608 Carter, Jennifer, and Joel Hirschhorn. *Titanic Adventure* (9–12). 1999, New Horizon Pr. $26.95 (0-88282-170-9). The autobiography of this courageous woman who was a skydiver, balloonist, river rafter, hang glider and, eventually, a deep sea diver who became the leader of a French American expedition to film a documentary on salvaging artifacts from the *Titanic*. (Rev: BL 9/1/98; SLJ 7/99) [921]

CID, EL

6609 Kislow, Philip. *El Cid* (5–9). (Hispanics of Achievement) 1993, Chelsea LB $19.95 (0-7910-1239-5). The story of the great Spanish hero and conqueror. (Rev: BL 9/15/93) [921]

CLEMENS, ARABELLA

6610 Greenberg, Judith E., and Helen C. McKeever, eds. *A Pioneer Woman's Memoir* (6–9). (In Their Own Words) 1995, Watts LB $13.93 (0-531-11211-X). From a memoir written by the author in her 80s, this book chronicles a trek by covered wagon to Ore-

gon. Black-and-white illustrations. (Rev: BL 9/1/95; SLJ 10/95; VOYA 2/96) [921]

COCHRAN, JACQUELINE

6611 Smith, Elizabeth Simpson. *Coming Out Right: The Story of Jacqueline Cochran, the First Woman Aviator to Break the Sound Barrier* (6–8). 1991, Walker LB $15.85 (0-8027-6989-6). Cochran's accomplishments, honors, and awards are presented in detail. (Rev: BL 4/15/91; SLJ 5/91) [921]

COLEMAN, BESSIE

6612 Hart, Philip S. *Up In the Air: The Story of Bessie Coleman* (5–8). 1996, Carolrhoda LB $23.93 (0-87614-949-2). Forced by restrictions in the United States to get her training in France in the 1920s, Coleman became the first African American female airplane pilot. (Rev: BL 8/96; SLJ 8/96) [921]

COLUMBUS, CHRISTOPHER

6613 Jones, Mary Ellen, ed. *Christopher Columbus and His Legacy* (9–12). (Opposing Viewpoints) 1992, Greenhaven paper $16.20 (0-89908-171-1). Offers differing perspectives from writers of various ethnic and national backgrounds on Columbus and his impact on the New World. (Rev: BL 1/15/93) [921]

6614 Yue, Charlotte, and David Yue. *Christopher Columbus: How He Did It* (5–8). Illus. 1992, Houghton $14.95 (0-395-52100-9). Includes basic history but concentrates more on the knowledge and technology that made his explorations possible. Includes maps, charts, diagrams. (Rev: BL 6/15/92*; SLJ 7/92) [921]

CORTES, HERNANDO

6615 Lilley, Stephen R. *Hernando Cortes* (4–8). Illus. (The Importance Of) 1996, Lucent LB $17.96 (1-56006-066-2). A biography of this Spanish conquistador and the effects of his invasion on the history of the New World. (Rev: BL 3/15/96; SLJ 1/96) [921]

6616 Marks, Richard. *Cortes: The Great Adventurer and the Fate of Aztec Mexico* (9–12). 1993, Knopf $27.50 (0-679-40609-3). A presentation of the life of Cortes and his conquest of the Aztecs in which Cortes is portrayed as neither a hero nor a murderer. (Rev: BL 9/15/93*) [921]

D'ABOVILLE, GERARD

6617 D'Aboville, Gerard. *Alone: The Man Who Braved the Vast Pacific—and Won* (9–12). 1993, Arcade $21.95 (1-55970-218-4). Journal entries describe d'Aboville's solo crossing of the Pacific in a 26-foot rowboat. (Rev: BL 7/93) [920]

DE SOTO, HERNANDO

6618 Duncan, David Ewing. *Hernando de Soto: A Savage Quest in the Americas* (9–12). 1996, Crown $40.00 (0-517-58222-8). A carefully researched and documented text on a controversial conquistador. (Rev: BL 12/15/95) [921]

DRAKE, SIR FRANCIS

6619 Duncan, Alice Smith. *Sir Francis Drake and the Struggle for an Ocean Empire* (6–9). (World Explorers) 1993, Chelsea LB $19.95 (0-7910-1302-2). The story of the intrepid Elizabethan explorer and adventurer who helped establish England's claims in the New World. (Rev: BL 3/15/93) [921]

6620 Marrin, Albert. *The Sea King: Sir Francis Drake and His Times* (6–10). 1995, Atheneum $20.00 (0-689-31887-1). This biography includes Drake's trip around the world, his life as a privateer, and his role in defeating the Spanish Armada. (Rev: BL 7/95; SLJ 9/95) [921]

EARHART, AMELIA

6621 Earhart, Amelia. *The Fun of It: Random Records of My Own Flying and of Women in Aviation* (7–12). 1990, Omnigraphics $42.00 (1-55888-980-9); n.d., Academy Chicago paper $12.00 (0-915864-55-X). Autobiographical in part, this account is also a tribute to other women aviation pioneers. First published in 1932. [921]

6622 Goldstein, Donald M., and Katherine V. Dillon. *Amelia* (10–12). 1997, Brassey's $24.95 (1-57488-134-5). A well-written adult biography of Amelia Earhart that depicts a woman not just interested in aviation but also in women's rights. (Rev: SLJ 3/98) [921]

6623 Leder, Jane. *Amelia Earhart* (6–9). Illus. 1990, Greenhaven LB $16.95 (0-89908-070-7). A thorough biography and good coverage of theories about Earhart's disappearance. (Rev: BL 3/1/90; SLJ 5/90) [921]

6624 Parr, Jan. *Amelia Earhart: First Lady of Flight* (5–8). Illus. (Book Report Biographies) 1997, Watts $22.00 (0-531-11407-4). A short, useful biography that tells about the public and private life of this adventurer who broke many records and helped open up the world of flight to women. (Rev: BL 11/15/97; SLJ 11/97) [921]

6625 Sloate, Susan. *Amelia Earhart: Challenging the Skies* (5–8). Illus. 1990, Fawcett paper $4.99 (0-449-90396-6). The aviator's life story is told along with an examination of all the theories concerning her disappearance. (Rev: SLJ 6/90) [921]

6626 Szabo, Corinne. *Sky Pioneer: A Photobiography of Amelia Earhart* (4–8). Illus. 1997, National Geographic $16.00 (0-7922-3737-4). A lavishly illustrated biography of Amelia Earhart that concentrates more on her accomplishments than her disappearance. (Rev: BL 2/15/97; SLJ 4/97) [921]

6627 Ware, Susan. *Still Missing: Amelia Earhart and the Search for Modern Feminism* (9–12). 1993, Norton $22.00 (0-393-03551-4). Portrays Earhart as an inspiration to the women's movement of the 1920s and 1930s in analyzing her accomplishments. (Rev: BL 11/15/93) [629.13]

FLIPPER, HENRY O.

6628 Harris, Theodore, ed. *Black Frontiersman: The Memoirs of Henry O. Flipper* (10–12). 1997, Texas Christian Univ. Pr. $22.95 (0-87565-171-2). This is a biography of Henry Flipper, the first black West Point graduate, who was court-martialed and dismissed from the army on trumped-up charges and left detailed accounts of his life as an army officer, mining engineer, surveyor, and Senate aide in the post-Civil War American Southwest and the Depression Era. (Rev: SLJ 2/98; VOYA 6/98) [921]

6629 Pfeifer, Kathryn B. *Henry O. Flipper* (5–8). (African American Soldiers) 1993, Twenty-First Century LB $17.90 (0-8050-2351-8). Chronicles the life of the first African American to graduate from West Point. (Rev: BL 2/15/94) [921]

GRAHAM, ROBIN LEE

6630 Graham, Robin Lee, and Derek Gill. *Dove* (7–12). Illus. 1991, HarperCollins paper $13.00 (0-06-092047-5). A 5-year solo voyage around the world and a tender romance with a girl the author met in Fiji. [921]

HENSON, MATTHEW

6631 Gilman, Michael. *Matthew Henson* (6–10). Illus. 1988, Chelsea LB $19.95 (1-55546-590-0). The life story of the black explorer who accompanied Peary on expeditions in search of the North Pole. (Rev: BL 6/15/88; SLJ 4/88) [921]

HILLARY, EDMUND

6632 Stewart, Whitney. *Sir Edmund Hillary: To Everest and Beyond* (5–8). (Newsmakers) 1996, Lerner LB $25.26 (0-8225-4927-1). The life of the famous beekeeper turned mountain climber and adventurer is presented, recounting his mountain climbing experiences and his current efforts to conserve the Himalayan Mountain Region and help the Sherpa people. (Rev: SLJ 9/96) [921]

KILEY, DEBORAH SCALING

6633 Kiley, Deborah Scaling, and Meg Noonan. *Albatross: The True Story of a Woman's Survival at Sea* (9–12). 1994, Houghton $19.95 (0-395-65573-0). What happened when Kiley and 4 companion sailors were shipwrecked off the coast of North Carolina on a routine yacht delivery. (Rev: BL 4/1/94) [921]

LEWIS AND CLARK

6634 Ambrose, Stephen E. *Undaunted Courage: Meriwether Lewis, Thomas Jefferson, and the Opening of the American West* (10–12). 1996, Simon & Schuster $27.50 (0-684-81107-3). Though primarily a biography of Meriwether Lewis, this book also provides fascinating sketches of Thomas Jefferson, William Clark, Sacagawea, and other contemporaries. (Rev: BL 1/1–15/96; SLJ 6/96) [921]

6635 Edwards, Judith. *Lewis & Clark's Journey of Discovery in American History* (6–10). (In American History) 1998, Enslow $19.95 (0-7660-1127-5). This story of the overland expedition to find the Pacific Ocean begins with Lewis and Clark getting their commission from Jefferson and ends with their return home 2 years later. (Rev: BL 2/15/99) [921]

6636 National Geographic Society, eds. *Lewis & Clark* (10–12). 1998, National Geographic $35.00 (0-7922-7084-3). The author and his family retraced the route taken by Lewis and Clark that opened up the American West. The book is equally about the explorers' expedition and the author's thoughts about their impact on the land and the people. This volume is superbly illustrated with full-color photos and reproductions of paintings by the 2 explorers. (Rev: BL 9/15/98; SLJ 4/99) [917.3]

6637 Streissguth, Thomas. *Lewis and Clark: Explorers of the Northwest* (5–8). (Historical American Biographies) 1998, Enslow LB $19.95 (0-7600-1016-3). The story of the 2 intrepid explorers who made their way to the Pacific Ocean on an overland expedition that took from 1804 to 1806. (Rev: BL 8/98) [921]

LINDBERGH, CHARLES A.

6638 Davies, R. E. *Charles Lindbergh: An Airman, His Aircraft, & His Great Flights* (9–12). Illus. 1997, Paladwr Pr. $30.00 (1-888962-04-6). Using many illustrations, including full paintings of his aircraft, this biography of Lindbergh is a gripping, human document. (Rev: VOYA 6/98) [921]

6639 Denenberg, Barry. *An American Hero: The True Story of Charles A. Lindbergh* (8–12). Illus. 1996, Scholastic $16.95 (0-590-46923-1). Beginning with Lindbergh's transatlantic flight, this fascinating biography then recounts the story of his early years followed by details about his multifaceted life. (Rev:

BL 3/15/96*; BR 9–10/96; SLJ 7/96; VOYA 6/96) [921]

6640 Giblin, James Cross. *Charles A. Lindbergh: A Human Hero* (6–12). Illus. 1997, Clarion $20.00 (0-395-63389-3). A book about the public and private life of one of America's heroes that deals with his pro-Nazi sympathies and anti-Semitism, the adoration he received for his transatlantic flight, and pity the public felt for the kidnapping and murder of his child. (Rev: BL 9/15/97; SLJ 11/97*; VOYA 6/98) [921]

LIVINGSTONE, DAVID

6641 Wellman, Sam. *David Livingstone: Missionary and Explorer* (9–12). (Heroes of the Faith) 1998, Chelsea LB $17.95 (0-7910-5038-6). A detailed biography of David Livingstone, a Scottish missionary and doctor who explored central Africa while attempting to spread Christianity. (Rev: BL 10/1/98) [921]

MAGELLAN, FERDINAND

6642 Joyner, Tim. *Magellan* (9–12). 1992, International Marine paper $16.95 (0-87742-263-X). Details the ventures of the 16th-century explorer best known for being the first to sail around the world. (Rev: BL 3/1/92) [921]

6643 Stefoff, Rebecca. *Ferdinand Magellan and the Discovery of the World Ocean* (7–12). Illus. 1990, Chelsea LB $19.95 (0-7910-1291-3). Using many quotes from original sources, this is an engrossing account of the explorer and his voyage. (Rev: BL 6/15/90) [921]

MARKHAM, BERYL

6644 Gourley, Catherine. *Beryl Markam: Never Look Back* (6–10). 1997, Conari Pr. paper $6.95 (1-57324-073-7). An engaging biography of the unconventional woman who was the first person to fly solo from east to west across the Atlantic Ocean. (Rev: BL 3/15/97; BR 9–10/97) [921]

6645 Trzebinski, Errol. *The Lives of Beryl Markham* (10-12), 1995, Norton, pap. $12.00 (0-393-31252-6). A deft and intimate portrait of the aviator who made a pioneering transatlantic flight.

MORGAN, SIR HENRY

6646 Marrin, Albert. *Terror of the Spanish Main: Sir Henry Morgan and His Buccaneers* (7–12). 1999, Dutton $19.99 (0-525-45942-1). The story of Henry Morgan, a murderous cutthroat who, in the name of the English flag, wreaked havoc on Spanish colonies, using Jamaica as his home base. (Rev: BL 1/1–15/99; SLJ 1/99*; VOYA 8/99) [921]

O'GRADY, SCOTT

6647 O'Grady, Scott. *Basher Five-Two* (6–10). 1997, Doubleday $16.95 (0-385-32300-X). The true story of the fighter pilot who miraculously survived for 6 days in the enemy territory of the Bosnian Serbs. (Rev: BL 7/97; BR 11–12/97; SLJ 7/97) [921]

PEARY, ROBERT

6648 Dwyer, Christopher. *Robert Peary and the Quest for the North Pole* (6–9). (World Explorers) 1992, Chelsea LB $19.95 (0-7910-1316-2). The exciting story of Peary's expeditions to reach the South Pole and of the courage and endurance displayed. (Rev: BL 2/1/93) [921]

PFETZER, MARK

6649 Pfetzer, Mark, and Jack Galvin. *Within Reach: My Everest Story* (7–12). 1998, Dutton $16.95 (0-525-46089-6). The autobiography of the youngest person to climb Mount Everest, with material on how he became interested in mountain climbing. (Rev: BL 11/15/98; SLJ 11/98; VOYA 2/99) [921]

POLO, MARCO

6650 Polo, Marco. *The Travels of Marco Polo* (10–12). 1958, Penguin paper $13.95 (0-14-044057-7). One of many editions of this account kept by Marco Polo of his travels in Asia in the 13th century. [915]

PONCE DE LEÓN, JUAN

6651 Dolan, Sean. *Juan Ponce de León* (5–9). (Hispanics of Achievement) 1995, Chelsea LB $19.95 (0-7910-2023-1). The story of the Spanish explorer who after accompanying Columbus on his second voyage set out on his own and eventually became the discoverer of Florida. (Rev: BL 10/15/95) [921]

POWELL, JOHN WESLEY

6652 Bruns, Roger. *John Wesley Powell: Explorer of the Grand Canyon* (5–8). (Historical American Biographies) 1997, Enslow LB $19.95 (0-89490-783-2). This biography tells about Powell's youth, education, and Civil War days, as well as his many expeditions and research activities. (Rev: SLJ 10/97) [921]

RIDE, SALLY

6653 Camp, Carole Ann. *Sally Ride: First American Woman in Space* (6–10). Illus. (People to Know) 1997, Enslow LB $19.95 (0-89490-829-4). A lively account of Sally Ride's work as an astronaut and astrophysicist, with material on her training, shuttle flight, and life in microgravity. (Rev: BL 1/1–15/98; SLJ 12/97) [921]

6654 Hurwitz, Jane, and Sue Hurwitz. *Sally Ride: Shooting for the Stars* (5–8). 1989, Ballantine paper $5.99 (0-449-90394-X). An interestingly written account in paperback format of the female space pioneer. (Rev: BL 12/15/89; BR 3–4/90; SLJ 2/90; VOYA 2/90) [921]

6655 Kramer, Barbara. *Sally Ride: A Space Biography* (4–8). Illus. (Countdown to Space) 1998, Enslow LB $18.95 (0-89490-975-4). A brief, well-written biography of Sally Ride that describes her training, experience, and space flights. (Rev: BR 9–10/98; SLJ 5/98) [921]

SACAGAWEA

6656 Waldo, Donna Lee. *Sacajawea* (10–12). 1979, Avon paper $8.50 (0-380-84293-9). A lengthy account of the Indian girl who accompanied the Lewis and Clark Expedition. [921]

6657 White, Alana J. *Sacagawea: Westward with Lewis and Clark* (4–8). (Native American Biographies) 1997, Enslow LB $19.95 (0-89490-867-7). A well-written account of this gallant woman's life, accompanied by a reading list, chapter notes, and a chronology. (Rev: BL 4/15/97; SLJ 8/97; VOYA 8/97) [921]

SERRA, JUNÍPERO

6658 Dolan, Sean. *Junípero Serra* (5–9). (Hispanics of Achievement) 1991, Chelsea LB $19.95 (0-7910-1255-7). The story of the devoted Spanish Franciscan missionary who was responsible for founding the famous missions on the coast of California. (Rev: BL 11/1/91; SLJ 2/92) [921]

6659 Genet, Donna. *Father Junipero Serra* (6–9). Illus. (Hispanic Biographies) 1996, Enslow LB $19.95 (0-89490-762-X). This book divides its contents equally between a biography of Father Junípero Serra and the story of the founding, history, and significance of the California missions. (Rev: BL 10/15/96; SLJ 9/96) [979.4]

Artists, Composers, Entertainers, and Writers

Collective

6660 Aronson, Virginia. *Literature* (6–9). (Female Firsts in Their Fields) 1999, Chelsea $16.95 (0-7910-5146-3). Biographies of pioneering women authors Phillis Wheatley, Edith Wharton, Pearl Buck, Toni Morrison, Alice Walker, and Judy Blume. (Rev: BL 5/15/99) [920]

6661 Bearden, Romare, and Harry Henderson. *A History of African-American Artists: From 1792 to the Present* (9–12). 1993, Pantheon $65.00 (0-394-57016-2). The lives and careers of 36 African American artists born before 1925 are part of this comprehensive history of African American art. Includes more than 300 black-and-white and color prints. (Rev: BL 10/15/93*) [920]

6662 Bloom, Harold, ed. *American Women Fiction Writers 1900–1960*, vol. 2 (9–12). (Women Writers of English and Their Works) 1997, Chelsea $29.95 (0-7910-4481-5); paper $16.95 (0-7910-4497-1). This volume, the second in a set of 3, gives biographies and criticism for 11 women authors, including Zora Neale Hurston, Shirley Jackson, and Carson McCullers. (Rev: BR 3–4/98; SLJ 1/98) [920]

6663 Bloom, Harold, ed. *British Women Fiction Writers, 1900–1960*, vol. 1 (9–12). (Women Writers of English and Their Works) 1997, Chelsea $29.95 (0-7910-4483-1); paper $14.95 (0-7910-4499-8). This volume is the first of a 2-volume set and highlights the life and work of 14 writers, among them Agatha Christie, Daphne du Maurier, Rumer Godden, Storm Jameson, Margaret Kennedy, and Mary Lavin. (Rev: BR 3–4/98; SLJ 1/98) [920]

6664 Bloom, Harold, ed. *British Women Fiction Writers of the 19th Century* (9–12). Illus. (Women Writers of English and Their Works) 1998, Chelsea

LB $29.95 (0-7910-4482-3); paper $16.95 (0-7910-4498-X). This volume supplies biographical and critical information on 10 women writers, including Jane Austen, the 3 Brontë sisters, George Eliot, and Mary Shelley. (Rev: SLJ 10/98) [920]

6665 Bloom, Harold, ed. *Native American Women Writers* (10–12). Illus. 1998, Chelsea $29.95 (0-7910-4479-3); paper $16.95 (0-7910-4495-5). This collective biography contains biographical material and literary criticism on such Native American poets and novelists as Paula Gunn Allen, Louise Erdrich, Joy Harjo, E. Pauline Johnson, and Mourning Dove. (Rev: SLJ 9/98) [920]

6666 Bredeson, Carmen. *American Writers of the 20th Century* (5–8). Illus. 1996, Enslow LB $19.95 (0-89490-704-2). Brief profiles of 10 important contemporary writers, such as Toni Morrison, Maya Angelou, and F. Scott Fitzgerald, include personal hardships they experienced and details about how they became writers. (Rev: BL 6/1–15/96; BR 9–10/96; SLJ 9/96) [920]

6667 Cahill, Susan, ed. *Writing Women's Lives: An Anthology of Autobiographical Narratives by Twentieth-Century American Women Writers* (9–12). 1994, HarperPerennial paper $18.00 (0-06-096998-9). A collection of autobiographical narratives by 20th-century women writers, including Jane Addams and Edith Wharton. (Rev: BL 4/15/94) [920]

6668 Chiu, Christina. *Lives of Notable Asian Americans: Literature and Education* (6–10). Illus. (The Asian American Experience) 1995, Chelsea LB $19.95 (0-7910-2182-3). Brief biographies of important Asian American writers and educators. (Rev: BL 1/1–15/96; BR 9–10/96) [920]

6669 Cumming, Robert. *Great Artists* (9–12). Illus. 1998, DK Publg. $24.95 (0-7894-2391-X). Arranged in chronological order, this volume gives facts on 50 great artists plus reproductions of their most famous

413

works and a discussion of their techniques and impact. (Rev: SLJ 7/98; VOYA 12/98) [920]

6670 Datnow, Claire. *American Science Fiction & Fantasy Writers* (5–8). (Collective Biographies) 1999, Enslow $19.95 (0-7660-1090-2). This book profiles 10 great science fiction and fantasy writers: Heinlein, Asimov, Pohl, Bradbury, Herbert, Anderson, Norton, L'Engle, Le Guin, and Butler. (Rev: BL 4/15/99; VOYA 6/99) [920]

6671 Davidson, Sue. *Getting the Real Story: Nellie Bly and Ida B. Wells* (6–10). 1992, Seal Pr. paper $8.95 (1-878067-16-8). A dual biography of 2 women who broke down barriers in journalism and how their different races shaped their individual stories. (Rev: BL 3/1/92; SLJ 7/92) [920]

6672 Ehrlich, Amy, ed. *When I Was Your Age* (5–8). 1996, Candlewick $15.99 (1-56402-306-0). Ten well-known writers, such as Avi, Susan Cooper, and Nicholasa Mohr, recall incidents from their childhood. (Rev: BL 4/15/96; BR 9–10/96; SLJ 8/96; VOYA 10/96) [920]

6673 Faber, Doris, and Harold Faber. *Great Lives: American Literature* (5–9). 1995, Simon & Schuster paper $24.00 (0-684-19448-1). Ten-page biographies of 30 noted U.S. writers, from Poe and Twain to Hemingway. (Rev: BL 9/1/95; SLJ 6/95; VOYA 12/95) [920]

6674 Gaines, Ann. *Entertainment and Performing Arts* (6–9). (Female Firsts in Their Fields) 1999, Chelsea $16.95 (0-7910-5145-5). Emphasizing their importance as role models, this book discusses the lives of 6 pioneering women in the fields of the performing arts and entertainment. (Rev: BL 5/15/99) [920]

6675 Glenn, Patricia Brown. *Discover America's Favorite Architects* (6–9). Illus. 1996, Preservation paper $19.95 (0-471-14354-5). The lives and careers of 10 major American architects, including Thomas Jefferson, Frederick Law Olmsted, Louis Henri Sullivan, Frank Lloyd Wright, Julia Morgan, Philip Johnson, and I. M. Pei. (Rev: SLJ 1/97) [921]

6676 Glubok, Shirley. *Painting* (5–8). 1993, Scribners $24.95 (0-684-19052-4). Profiles 23 American and European painters, including Michelangelo, Picasso, Rembrandt, and Georgia O'Keeffe. Includes a 16-page color insert. (Rev: BL 7/94; SLJ 7/94) [920]

6677 Gourse, Leslie. *Swingers and Crooners: The Art of Jazz Singing* (6–10). 1997, Watts LB $25.00 (0-531-11321-3). Through the biographies of such great singers as Ella Fitzgerald, Louis Armstrong, Bing Crosby, and Harry Connick, Jr., the history of jazz is covered, from its roots in gospel and blues, through the big band and bebop eras, to the singers of today. (Rev: SLJ 6/97) [920]

6678 Gowing, Lawrence. *Biographical Dictionary of Artists* (9–12). 1995, Facts on File $50.00 (0-8160-3252-1). Biographical sketches summarize the individual styles and important works of 1,340 artists. (Rev: BL 1/1–15/96; SLJ 1/96) [920]

6679 Hill, Anne E. *Broadcasting and Journalism* (6–9). (Female Firsts in Their Fields) 1999, Chelsea $16.95 (0-7910-5139-0). The biographies of 6 pioneering women in the mass media and how their work became an inspiration for other women. (Rev: BL 5/15/99) [920]

6680 Hipple, Ted. *Writers for Young Adults* (7–12). 1997, Macmillan $308.50 (0-684-80474-3). This resource presents biographical and critical essays on 129 classic and contemporary writers for young adults, from Joan Aiken to Paul Zindel. (Rev: BL 10/15/97; SLJ 8/98) [920]

6681 Hirschfelder, Arlene. *Artists and Craftspeople* (8–12). Illus. (American Indian Lives) 1994, Facts on File $19.95 (0-8160-2960-1). This book profiles 18 Native Americans like Nampeyo, Maria Martinez, and Oscar Howe, who are famous in history or contemporary times for their contributions to craftwork and art. (Rev: BL 11/15/94; SLJ 11/94; VOYA 4/95) [920]

6682 Horitz, Margot F. *A Female Focus: Great Women Photographers* (7–12). Illus. (Women Then—Women Now) 1996, Watts LB $25.00 (0-531-11302-7). This collective biography highlights the lives of several dozen female photographers from the beginning, when women helped their photographer-husbands, to contributions by photographers like Margaret Bourke-White, Dorothea Lange, and contemporaries Jeanne Moutoussany-Ashe and Annie Leibovitz. (Rev: BL 3/15/97; SLJ 2/97; VOYA 8/97) [920]

6683 Jackson, Nancy. *Photographers: History & Culture Through the Camera* (7–12). Illus. (American Profiles) 1997, Facts on File $19.95 (0-8160-3358-7). The life stories of 8 famous photographers, including Mathew Brady, Alfred Stieglitz, Edward Steichen, Dorothea Lange, and Gordon Parks, are included in this collective biography. (Rev: BL 5/1/97; SLJ 7/97) [920]

6684 Knapp, Ron. *American Legends of Rock* (6–9). Illus. 1996, Enslow LB $19.95 (0-89490-709-3). Brief biographies of such personalities as Chuck Berry, Elvis Presley, Buddy Holly, and Jimi Hendrix. (Rev: BL 11/15/96; SLJ 12/96; VOYA 2/97) [920]

6685 Krull, Kathleen. *Lives of the Musicians: Good Times, Bad Times (And What the Neighbors Thought)* (5–8). Illus. 1993, Harcourt $20.00 (0-15-248010-2). Biographies of 16 musical giants, from Vivaldi, Mozart, and Beethoven to Gershwin, Joplin, and Woody Guthrie. (Rev: BL 4/1/93*; SLJ 5/93*) [920]

6686 Mandell, Sherri Lederman. *Writers of the Holocaust* (9–12). Illus. (Global Profiles) 1999,

Facts on File LB $19.95 (0-8160-3729-9). This work profiles 10 Jewish writers who lived in Europe during the Holocaust, including Elie Wiesel, Jerzy Kosinski, Ida Fink, and Anne Frank. (Rev: BL 2/1/99; SLJ 7/99) [920]

6687 Mazer, Anne, ed. *Going Where I'm Coming From: Memoirs of American Youth* (8–12). 1995, Persea $15.95 (0-89255-205-0); paper $7.95 (0-89255-206-9). Writers from different cultures talk about growing up and the incidents in their lives that helped to establish their identities. (Rev: BL 1/15/95; VOYA 5/95) [818]

6688 Mour, Stanley L. *American Jazz Musicians* (6–9). (Collective Biographies) 1998, Enslow LB $19.00 (0-7660-1027-9). Ten greats of jazz are profiled chronologically, including Scott Joplin, Louis Armstrong, Duke Ellington, Charlie Parker, Miles Davis, and John Coltrane. (Rev: SLJ 1/99) [920]

6689 Nichols, Janet. *Women Music Makers: An Introduction to Women Composers* (6–12). 1992, Walker LB $19.85 (0-8027-8169-1). A glimpse into the personal lives and careers of 10 diverse female composers. (Rev: BL 9/15/92; SLJ 10/92) [920]

6690 Price-Groff, Claire. *Extraordinary Women Journalists* (7–10). (Extraordinary People) 1997, Children's Pr. LB $37.00 (0-516-20474-2). Over 50 well-known and lesser-known female reporters, publishers, humorists, columnists, photographers, and television journalists from colonial times to the present are profiled, including Nellie Bly, Hedda Hopper, Ann Landers, Abigail Van Buren, and Barbara Walters. (Rev: BR 5–6/98; SLJ 3/98; VOYA 4/98) [920]

6691 Rennert, Richard, ed. *Female Writers* (6–9). (Profiles of Great Black Americans) 1994, Chelsea LB $15.95 (0-7910-2063-0); paper $5.95 (0-7910-2064-9). Biographical overviews of such writers as Alice Walker, Maya Angelou, and Toni Morrison. (Rev: BL 2/15/94; SLJ 3/94) [920]

6692 Rennert, Richard, ed. *Jazz Stars* (6–9). (Profiles of Great Black Americans) 1993, Chelsea LB $16.95 (0-7910-2059-2); paper $5.95 (0-7910-2060-6). Profiles of 8 jazz greats: Louis Armstrong, Count Basie, Charlie Parker, Ella Fitzgerald, Billie Holiday, Duke Ellington, Dizzy Gillespie, and John Coltrane. (Rev: BL 1/1/94; SLJ 12/93) [781.65]

6693 Rennert, Richard, ed. *Male Writers* (6–9). (Profiles of Great Black Americans) 1994, Chelsea LB $13.95 (0-7910-2061-4); paper $5.95 (0-7910-2062-2). Biographical overviews of such writers as James Baldwin, Alex Haley, and Richard Wright. (Rev: BL 2/15/94) [920]

6694 Rennert, Richard, ed. *Performing Artists* (6–9). Illus. (Profiles of Great Black Americans) 1994, Chelsea paper $6.95 (0-7910-2070-3). Alvin Ailey, Marian Anderson, Josephine Baker, Bill Cosby, Katerine Dunham, Lena Horne, Sidney Poitier, and

Paul Robeson are the performing artists included in this collective biography. (Rev: BL 6/1–15/94) [920]

6695 Shirley, Lynn M. *Latin American Writers* (8–12). Illus. (Global Profiles) 1996, Facts on File $19.95 (0-8160-3202-5). This work profiles the life and works of 8 prominent contemporary Latin American authors including Borges, Marquez, Amado, Fuentes, Vargas Llosa, and Isabel Allende. (Rev: BL 3/15/97) [920]

6696 Strickland, Michael R. *African-American Poets* (5–10). Illus. (Collective Biographies) 1996, Enslow LB $19.95 (0-89490-774-3). The lives and works of 10 prominent African American poets from Phillis Wheatley to Rita Dove are covered, with quotes from their works and a single full-length poem from each. (Rev: BL 2/15/97; SLJ 1/97) [920]

6697 Stux, Erica. *Eight Who Made a Difference: Pioneer Women in the Arts* (7–10). 1999, Avisson LB $0.00 (1-888105-37-2). This volume profiles 8 famous women in the arts: Marian Anderson, Mary Cassatt, Nadia Boulanger, Margaret Bourke-White, Julia Morgan, Louise Nevelson, Beverly Sills, and Maria Tallchief. (Rev: BL 2/15/99; SLJ 5/99; VOYA 10/99) [920]

6698 Sullivan, George. *Black Artists in Photography, 1840–1940* (5–8). Illus. 1996, Dutton paper $16.99 (0-525-65208-6). This volume features 7 important African American photographers who worked between 1840 and 1940. (Rev: BL 10/15/96; BR 3–4/97; SLJ 10/96) [920]

6699 Terkel, Studs, and Milly Hawk Daniel. *Giants of Jazz.* 2nd ed. (7–10). 1992, HarperCollins LB $16.89 (0-690-04917-X). Thirteen subjects are highlighted including Benny Goodman, Louis Armstrong, Bessie Smith, and Dizzy Gillespie. [920]

6700 Verde, Tom. *Twentieth-Century Writers, 1950–1990* (9–12). Illus. (American Profiles) 1996, Facts on File $19.95 (0-8160-2967-9). This book presents biographies and critical analyses of the works of Eudora Welty, Saul Bellow, J. D. Salinger, Jack Kerouac, Kurt Vonnegut, James Baldwin, Flannery O'Connor, and James Updike. (Rev: BL 5/1/96; BR 11–12/96; VOYA 4/96) [920]

6701 Weitzman, David. *Great Lives: Theater* (8–12). Illus. 1996, Simon & Schuster $24.00 (0-689-80579-9). This collective biography gives thumbnail sketches of 26 people (mostly dead) who have contributed to the theater as actors, producers, or playwrights, including Edwin Booth, Sarah Bernhardt, and P. T. Barnum. (Rev: BL 2/1/97; BR 5–6/97; SLJ 11/96; VOYA 12/96) [920]

6702 Whitelaw, Nancy. *They Wrote Their Own Headlines: American Women Journalists* (6–10). 1994, Morgan Reynolds LB $17.95 (1-883846-06-4). Biographies of 7 women journalists such as advice columnist Ann Landers and war correspondent Marguerite Higgins, examining the drive that brought success in a male-dominated field. (Rev: BL 7/94; SLJ 6/94; VOYA 8/94) [920]

6703 Wolf, Sylvia. *Focus: Five Women Photographers* (5–8). 1994, Albert Whitman LB $18.95 (0-8075-2531-6). Examines the methods, perspectives, and attitudes toward their art of 5 women photographers. (Rev: BL 10/15/94*; SLJ 11/94) [770]

Artists and Architects

AUDUBON, JOHN JAMES

6704 Kastner, Joseph. *John James Audubon* (7–12). (First Impressions) 1992, Abrams $19.95 (0-8109-1918-4). Smooth, professional writing and fine art reproductions make for a fine account of Audubon's adventurous life. (Rev: BL 10/15/92; SLJ 12/92) [921]

BEARDEN, ROMARE

6705 Brown, Kevin. *Romare Bearden* (7–10). (Black Americans of Achievement) 1995, Chelsea LB $19.95 (0-7910-1119-4). The story of the Harlem-raised African American painter who tries to portray the everyday experiences of African Americans. (Rev: BL 3/15/95; SLJ 3/95) [921]

BOSCH, HIERONYMUS

6706 Schwartz, Gary. *Hieronymus Bosch* (9–12). Illus. (First Impressions) 1997, Abrams $19.95 (0-8109-3138-9). An introduction to the life and paintings of the 15th-century Dutch painter Hieronymus Bosch, with many full-color reproductions of his bizarre, surreal paintings. (Rev: BL 12/15/97; BR 5–6/98) [921]

BOURKE-WHITE, MARGARET

6707 Ayer, Eleanor. *Margaret Bourke-White: Photographing the World* (6–10). (People in Focus) 1992, Dillon LB $18.95 (0-87518-513-4). A lively account of the photographer's craft and technique, her long association with *Life* magazine, and the subjects she recorded, from the Depression and Buchenwald concentration camp to Gandhi. (Rev: BL 12/1/92; SLJ 11/92) [921]

6708 Daffron, Carolyn. *Margaret Bourke-White* (7–12). Illus. 1988, Chelsea LB $19.95 (1-55546-644-3). The life story of this famous photographer in an account well illustrated with the artist's work. (Rev: BL 5/1/88; BR 5–6/88; SLJ 8/88) [921]

6709 Welch, Catherine A. *Margaret Bourke-White: Racing with a Dream* (4–8). Illus. 1998, Carolrhoda $23.93 (1-57505-049-8). A readable biography,

accompanied by small photos, of the life and work of this great photographer whose subjects included people during the Depression, skyscrapers, survivors of Buchenwald, and gold miners in South Africa. (Rev: BL 10/1/98; SLJ 7/98) [921]

BRADY, MATHEW

6710 Sullivan, George. *Mathew Brady: His Life and Photographs* (6–10). 1994, Dutton $15.99 (0-525-65186-1). A biography of the photographer known for capturing the Civil War on film; includes reproductions of Brady's photos. (Rev: BL 7/94; SLJ 12/94; VOYA 12/94) [921]

BRAQUE, GEORGES

6711 Wilkin, Karen. *Georges Braque* (9–12). (Modern Masters) 1992, Abbeville $14.95 (0-89659-944-2); paper $29.95 (0-89659-947-7). Examines the life, works, and style of the cocreator of Cubism. (Rev: BL 3/15/92) [921]

CALDER, ALEXANDER

6712 Lemaire, Gerard-Georges, ed. *Calder* (10–12). Trans. by Sophie Hawkes. Illus. 1998, Harry N. Abrams $11.98 (0-8109-4668-8). A colorful book that presents an overview of Calder's life and work, supplemented by full-color plates to introduce his major periods and styles. (Rev: SLJ 11/98) [921]

6713 Lipman, Jean, and Margaret Aspinwall. *Alexander Calder and His Magical Mobiles* (7–9). Illus. 1981, Hudson Hills $19.95 (0-933920-17-2). A biography of the noted sculptor with many interesting incidents from his childhood. [921]

CARLE, ERIC

6714 Carle, Eric. *Flora and Tiger: 19 Very Short Stories from My Life* (4–8). Illus. 1997, Putnam $17.99 (0-399-23203-6). This autobiographical account presents vignettes from the artist's childhood in Germany to his life in the United States, where he has lived since 1952. (Rev: BL 12/15/97; SLJ 2/98) [921]

CASSATT, MARY

6715 Cain, Michael. *Mary Cassatt* (7–10). Illus. 1989, Chelsea LB $19.95 (1-55546-647-8). A well-illustrated account of the evolution of the American artist who broke with tradition and worked with the Impressionists. (Rev: BL 5/15/89; BR 9–10/89; SLJ 6/89; VOYA 8/89) [921]

6716 Mathews, Nancy Mowll. *Mary Cassatt: A Life* (9–12). (Rizzoli Art) 1994, Villard $28.00 (0-394-58497-X); 1993, Rizzoli paper $7.95 (0-8478-1611-7). This biography of the renowned American Impressionist painter details her life as a single woman in the Parisian artistic community. (Rev: BL 3/1/94*) [921]

6717 Plain, Nancy. *Mary Cassatt: An Artist's Life* (6–9). 1994, Silver Burdett LB $13.95 (0-87518-597-5). Includes clear explanations of artistic techniques and discusses Cassatt's relationships with other Impressionists. (Rev: BL 1/15/95; SLJ 2/95) [921]

6718 Streissguth, Thomas. *Mary Cassatt* (4–8). (Trailblazers) 1999, Lerner $23.93 (1-57505-291-1). Full-color illustrations enhance this biography of the American painter, who was associated with the Impressionists and spent most of her adult life in France. (Rev: BL 5/1/99; SLJ 9/99) [921]

CEZANNE, PAUL

6719 Sellier, Marie. *Cézanne from A to Z* (4–8). Trans. from French by Claudia Zoe Bedrick. 1996, Bedrick LB $14.95 (0-87226-476-9). An imaginative, well-executed account of the life and works of Cézanne, enhanced by reproductions of many of his paintings. (Rev: SLJ 5/96) [921]

CHAGALL, MARC

6720 Kagan, Andrew. *Marc Chagall* (9–12). Illus. 1989, Abbeville $32.95 (0-89659-932-9); paper $14.95 (0-89659-935-3). The life and work of this Russian Jewish painter whose faith and fantastic imagination dominated his work. (Rev: BL 12/15/89) [921]

6721 Pozzi, Gianni. *Chagall* (6–12). Illus. (Masters of Art) 1998, Bedrick LB $22.50 (0-87226-527-7). The life and times of Chagall, along with his painting techniques, methods, and materials, are covered in text and full-color illustrations in this oversize book. (Rev: BL 3/1/98; SLJ 12/97) [709]

CHANG, WAH MING

6722 Riley, Gail B. *Wah Ming Chang: Artist and Master of Special Effects* (4–8). Illus. (Multicultural Junior Biographies) 1995, Enslow LB $18.95 (0-89490-639-9). A thorough, well-documented biography of this Chinese American who has gained prominence in the field of special effects. (Rev: BL 2/15/96; SLJ 2/96) [921]

CHONG, GORDON H.

6723 *The Success of Gordon H. Chong and Associates: An Architecture Success Story* (7–10). Illus. (Success) 1996, Walker $23.95 (0-8027-8307-4). The amazing rise of the contemporary American architect, with examples of his work. (Rev: BL 5/15/96; SLJ 9/96) [921]

CLOSE, CHUCK

6724 Greenberg, Jan, and Sandra Jordan. *Chuck Close, Up Close* (7–12). 1998, DK Publg. $19.95 (0-7894-2486-X). This is the inspiring story of the artist Chuck Close, who, in spite of a spinal collapse that left him paralyzed and in a wheelchair, continued to paint with a brush strapped to his hand. (Rev: BL 3/15/98; SLJ 3/98; VOYA 8/98) [921]

COROT, JEAN CAMILLE

6725 Larroche, Caroline. *Corot from A to Z* (5–8). Trans. from French by Claudia Zoe Bedrick. (Artists from A to Z) 1996, Bedrick LB $14.95 (0-87226-477-7). Although the text is somewhat confusing, the strength of this account of Corot's life and work is the full-color reproductions of his work. (Rev: SLJ 1/97) [921]

CURTIS, EDWARD S.

6726 Lawlor, Laurie. *Shadow Catcher: The Life and Work of Edward S. Curtis* (6–12). 1994, Walker LB $20.85 (0-8027-8289-2). The personal and professional highlights of the life of this little known, largely unappreciated photojournalist who was determined to preserve the lore of Native Americans. (Rev: BL 12/1/94; SLJ 2/95; VOYA 12/94) [921]

DA VINCI, LEONARDO

6727 Herbert, Janis. *Leonardo DaVinci for Kids: His Life & Times* (4–8). Illus. 1998, Chicago Review paper $16.95 (1-55652-298-3). This biography of Leonardo da Vinci contains background information on history, art techniques, science, and philosophy. (Rev: BL 3/1/99; SLJ 4/99) [921]

DAY, TOM

6728 Lyons, Mary E. *Master of Mahogany: Tom Day, Free Black Cabinetmaker* (5–8). 1994, Scribners paper $15.95 (0-684-19675-1). Chronicles the life of an 18th-century African American cabinetmaker, using quotations from Day's diary and photos of his work. (Rev: BL 10/1/94; SLJ 10/94*) [921]

DEGAS, EDGAR

6729 Meyer, Susan E. *Edgar Degas* (7–12). 1994, Abrams $19.95 (0-8109-3220-2). The life and work of this French painter are examined in this well-illustrated volume that contains reproductions of both his paintings and sculpture. (Rev: BL 1/1/95; SLJ 10/94) [921]

DISNEY, WALT

6730 Greene, Katherine, and Richard Greene. *The Man Behind the Magic: The Story of Walt Disney*

(6–9). 1991, Viking paper $18.99 (0-670-82259-0). This biography concentrates on the personal characteristics of Disney and life at the Disney studio, clearly differentiating the man from his creations. (Rev: BL 10/1/91; SLJ 10/91) [921]

EVANS, MINNIE

6731 Lyons, Mary E. *Painting Dreams: Minnie Evans, Visionary Artist* (4–8). 1996, Houghton $14.95 (0-395-72032-X). The life story of this deeply religious, visionary African American folk artist born in 1892, whose family and friends considered her mentally unstable and who was discovered by a photographer in the 1960s. (Rev: BL 7/96; SLJ 7/96) [921]

FOREMAN, MICHAEL

6732 Foreman, Michael. *After the War Was Over* (4–8). Illus. 1996, Arcade $18.95 (1-55970-329-6). In this sequel to the memoir *War Game* (1990), the British artist describes growing up after World War II in a small English fishing village. (Rev: BL 5/15/96) [921]

GAUGUIN, PAUL

6733 Greenfeld, Howard. *Paul Gauguin* (7–12). (First Impressions) 1993, Abrams $19.95 (0-8109-3376-4). An examination of the life and work of this sometime-friend of van Gogh who journeyed to the South Seas in search of artistic inspiration and freedom. (Rev: BL 12/1/93; SLJ 1/94) [921]

GORMAN, R. C.

6734 Hermann, Spring. *R. C. Gorman: Navajo Artist* (4–8). Illus. (Multicultural Junior Biographies) 1995, Enslow LB $19.95 (0-89490-638-0). The story of the contemporary Native American artist, who reflects his heritage in his work. (Rev: BL 2/15/96; SLJ 3/96) [921]

HOMER, WINSLOW

6735 Beneduce, Ann Keay. *A Weekend with Winslow Homer* (4–9). Illus. (Weekend with the Artists) 1993, Rizzoli $19.95 (0-8478-1622-2). An introduction to the famous New England painter of landscapes and the sea, including samples of his work. (Rev: BL 12/15/93; SLJ 11/93) [921]

HOUSTON, JAMES

6736 Houston, James. *Fire into Ice: Adventures in Glass Making* (5–9). Illus. 1998, Tundra $18.99 (0-88776-459-2). The author, who lived with the Inuits and wrote about them, tells about how he left the Arctic in the early 1960s and became a glassmaker for Steuben glass, where his drawings and the art he

learned in the North became translated into a new medium. (Rev: BL 4/15/99; SLJ 1/99) [921]

HUNTER, CLEMENTINE

6737 Lyons, Mary E. *Talking with Tebe; Clementine Hunter, Memory Artist* (7–12). 1998, Houghton $16.00 (0-395-72031-1). This richly illustrated book, which quotes extensively from taped interviews and is as much about social history as about painting, tells the story of the first illiterate, self-taught African American folk artist to receive national attention for her work. (Rev: BL 8/98; BR 5–6/99; SLJ 9/98) [921]

KAHLO, FRIDA

6738 Cruz, Barbara C. *Frida Kahlo: Portrait of a Mexican Painter* (6–9). Illus. (Hispanic Biographies) 1996, Enslow LB $19.95 (0-89490-765-4). A biography of one of Mexico's greatest artists that includes material on her relationship with artist Diego Rivera. (Rev: BL 11/1/96; BR 1–2/97; SLJ 10/96) [921]

6739 Garza, Hedda. *Frida Kahlo* (5–9). (Hispanics of Achievement) 1994, Chelsea LB $19.95 (0-7910-1698-6); paper $7.95 (0-7910-1699-4). Known once only as the wife of Diego Rivera, this painter, who lived most of her life in Mexico, is now considered a great female artist. (Rev: BL 3/1/94) [921]

KANE, BOB

6740 Kane, Bob, and Tom Andrae. *Batman & Me* (9–12). Illus. 1989, Eclipse Books $40.00 (1-56060-016-0); paper $14.95 (1-56060-017-9). An autobiography of the creator of Batman, Robin, and other characters in the comics plus lots of illustrations. (Rev: BL 4/15/90) [921]

LANGE, DOROTHEA

6741 Partridge, Elizabeth. *Restless Spirit: The Life & Work of Dorothea Lange* (6–12). 1998, Viking $19.99 (0-670-87888-X). Using over 60 photographs, this photoessay tells of the personal and professional life of photographer Lange, her many problems, and her artistic accomplishments, particularly during the Depression and World War II. (Rev: BL 10/15/98; SLJ 10/98; VOYA 8/99) [921]

LAWRENCE, JACOB

6742 Duggleby, John, and Jacob Lawrence. *Story Painter: The Life of Jacob Lawrence* (5–8). 1998, Chronicle $16.95 (0-8118-2082-3). The life of the great African American artist and his role in the Harlem Renaissance are covered in this work that contains 50 full-page color reproductions. (Rev: BL 10/15/98; SLJ 12/98) [921]

LEONARDO DA VINCI

6743 McLanathan, Richard. *Leonardo da Vinci* (7–12). 1990, Abrams $19.95 (0-8109-1256-2). A readable, inviting introduction to the master painter, inventor, and scientist. (Rev: BL 12/15/90; SLJ 2/91*) [921]

6744 Romei, Francesca. *Leonardo da Vinci: Artist, Inventor and Scientist of the Renaissance* (6–12). Illus. (Masters of Art) 1995, Bedrick LB $22.50 (0-87226-313-4). Historical and artistic overview of Leonardo, his life, art, inventions, and other accomplishments. (Rev: BL 4/1/95; SLJ 2/95) [921]

LEWIN, TED

6745 Lewin, Ted. *I Was a Teenage Professional Wrestler* (7–12). 1993, 1994, Hyperion paper $6.95 (0-7868-1009-2). Memoir of a children's book author/illustrator about his wrestling career in the 1950s, showing the human side of the sport. (Rev: BL 6/1–15/93*; SLJ 7/93*; VOYA 10/93) [921]

6746 Lewin, Ted. *Touch and Go: Travels of a Children's Book Illustrator* (6–9). Illus. 1999, Lothrop $15.00 (0-688-14109-9). The noted picture book illustrator tells about his unusual experiences around the world in search of subjects for his books. (Rev: BL 4/15/99; SLJ 7/99) [921]

LEWIS, EDMONIA

6747 Wolfe, Rinna. *Edmonia Lewis: Wildfire in Marble* (6–10). Illus. (People in Focus) 1998, Silver Burdett LB $18.95 (0-382-39713-4); paper $7.95 (0-382-39714-2). An excellent documentary about the life and work of a woman with African/Chippewa Indian roots who overcame racism to get a college education, went to Europe to develop her talent, and became the first American woman of African/Chippewa heritage to achieve international acclaim as a sculptor. (Rev: SLJ 8/98; VOYA 8/98) [921]

MARTINEZ, MARIA

6748 Morris, Juddi. *Tending the Fire: The Story of Maria Martinez* (5–8). 1997, Northland paper $6.95 (0-87358-654-9). The life story of New Mexico's most famous potter, who was born in an Indian pueblo in 1887. (Rev: BL 12/1/97; BR 11–12/97; SLJ 12/97) [921]

MATISSE, HENRI

6749 Kostenevich, Albert, and Lory Frankel. *Henri Matisse* (9–12). Illus. (First Impressions Introductions to Art) 1997, Abrams $19.95 (0-8109-4296-8). A handsome introduction to the life and work of Matisse, with material on his artistic experimentation and evolving techniques. (Rev: BL 2/1/98; BR 5–6/98) [921]

6750 Roddari, Florian. *A Weekend with Matisse* (4–9). Illus. (A Weekend with Matisse) 1994, Rizzoli $19.95 (0-8478-1792-X). This is a fine introduction to the life and work of Matisse, with accompanying illustrations that show his major works and styles. (Rev: BL 9/15/94) [921]

MICHELANGELO BUONARROTI

6751 Di Cagno, Gabriella. *Michelangelo* (6–12). Illus. (Masters of Art) 1996, Bedrick LB $22.50 (0-87226-319-3). The life, times, and accomplishments of Michelangelo are covered through use of outstanding reproductions, brief text, and many illustrations. (Rev: BL 11/15/96; SLJ 12/96; VOYA 4/97) [921]

6752 McLanathan, Richard. *Michelangelo* (7–12). (First Impressions) 1993, Abrams $19.95 (0-8109-3634-8). A handsomely illustrated volume that surveys the life, times, and art of this Italian master. (Rev: BL 6/1–15/93) [700921]

MIRÓ, JOAN

6753 Higdon, Elizabeth. *Joan Miró* (7–12). (Rizzoli Art) 1993, Rizzoli paper $7.95 (0-8478-1667-2). A lavishly illustrated biography of this influential, innovative 20th-century Spanish painter. (Rev: BL 1/15/94) [921]

MONET, CAUDE

6754 Waldron, Ann. *Claude Monet* (7–12). (First Impressions) 1991, Abrams $19.95 (0-8109-3620-8). This illustrated biographical study of the pioneering Impressionist painter explores his fascination with nature and his experimentation with the effects of light. (Rev: BL 11/15/91; SLJ 1/92) [921]

MORGAN, JULIA

6755 James, Cary. *Julia Morgan: Architect* (7–10). Illus. 1990, Chelsea LB $19.95 (1-55546-669-9). The story of the outstanding female architect who now has over 700 projects to her credit. (Rev: SLJ 8/90) [921]

MOSES, GRANDMA

6756 Biracree, Tom. *Grandma Moses* (7–10). Illus. 1989, Chelsea LB $19.95 (1-55546-670-2). This primitive artist's life and works are discussed, and insets are provided of some of her paintings. (Rev: BL 12/1/89; BR 3–4/90; SLJ 1/90; VOYA 2/90) [921]

NAST, THOMAS

6757 Shirley, David. *Thomas Nast: Cartoonist and Illustrator* (6–10). (Book Report Biographies) 1998,

Watts $22.00 (0-531-11372-8). A biography of the famous 19th-century cartoonist who created the images of Uncle Sam, the Republican elephant, and the Democratic donkey, and whose cartoons covered such events as the Civil War, Reconstruction, the Boss Tweed Ring, and various presidential elections. (Rev: BR 11–12/98; SLJ 4/98) [921]

O'KEEFFE, GEORGIA

6758 Berry, Michael. *Georgia O'Keeffe: Painter* (7–12). Illus. 1988, Chelsea LB $19.95 (1-55546-673-7). Illustrated chiefly in black and white, this is the story of the artist who reached maturity painting subjects in the southwestern states. (Rev: BL 9/15/88; BR 5–6/89; SLJ 9/88; VOYA 2/89) [921]

6759 Gherman, Beverly. *Georgia O'Keeffe: The Wideness and Wonder of Her World* (7–9). Illus. 1986, Macmillan LB $13.95 (0-689-31164-8). This biography emphasizes the total commitment this artist felt toward her work. (Rev: BL 4/1/86; SLJ 5/86) [921]

OROZCO, JOSE

6760 Cruz, Barbara C. *Jose Clemente Orozco: Mexican Artist* (7–12). (Hispanic Biographies) 1998, Enslow LB $19.95 (0-7660-1041-4). The story of the great artist Orozco, as well as an introduction to the mural painters of Mexico and how they used designs from Aztec and Mayan art. (Rev: BL 1/1–15/99; SLJ 3/99) [921]

PARKS, GORDON

6761 Parks, Gordon. *Half Past Autumn: A Retrospective* (7–12). 1997, Bulfinch $65.00 (0-8212-2298-8); paper $40.00 (0-8212-2503-0). Using nearly 300 photos, this great photographer recounts and reflects on his life and struggles. (Rev: BL 8/97; VOYA 12/98) [921]

PEALE, CHARLES WILLSON

6762 Giblin, James Cross. *The Mystery of the Mammoth Bones* (4–8). 1999, HarperCollins $15.95 (0-06-027493-X). Paleontologist Charles Willson Peale's study of mastodon (mammoth) fossil bones is told in the context of the cultural and intellectual history of the time. (Rev: BL 1/1–15/99*; SLJ 4/99) [921]

6763 Wilson, Janet. *The Ingenious Mr. Peale: Painter, Patriot and Man of Science* (5–8). Illus. 1996, Simon & Schuster $16.00 (0-689-31884-7). A profile of the famous portrait painter of the Colonial period, with details about his varied interests. (Rev: BL 5/15/96; BR 1–2/97; SLJ 6/96*; VOYA 8/96) [921]

PICASSO, PABLO

6764 Beardsley, John. *Pablo Picasso* (7–12). (First Impressions) 1991, Abrams $19.95 (0-8109-3713-1). Succinctly describes Picasso's bohemian lifestyle and analyzes his ever-changing styles, methods, and subjects. (Rev: BL 11/15/91; SLJ 1/92) [921]

6765 Loria, Stefano. *Picasso* (6–12). Illus. (Masters of Art) 1996, Bedrick LB $22.50 (0-87226-318-5). A stunning combination of text and excellent reproductions bring this Spanish artist's life and work into focus. (Rev: BL 5/15/96) [921]

6766 Selfridge, John W. *Pablo Picasso* (5–9). (Hispanics of Achievement) 1993, Chelsea LB $19.95 (0-7910-1777-X). A brief outline of this Spanish artist's life and work, with some examples of his enormous output. (Rev: BL 3/1/94) [9212]

REMBRANDT VAN RIJN

6767 Bonafoux, Pascal. *A Weekend with Rembrandt* (5–9). (A Weekend With) 1992, Rizzoli $19.95 (0-8478-1441-6). This book introduces the artist on a personal level and also gives details on his life and work. (Rev: BL 8/92) [921]

6768 Pescio, Claudio. *Rembrandt and Seventeenth-Century Holland* (6–12). Illus. (Masters of Art) 1996, Bedrick LB $22.50 (0-87226-317-7). This excellent art book traces the flowering of Dutch art through text and reproductions by focusing on Rembrandt, his work, and his followers. (Rev: BL 5/15/96; SLJ 3/96*; VOYA 6/96) [921]

6769 Schwartz, Gary. *Rembrandt* (7–12). (First Impressions) 1992, Abrams $19.95 (0-8109-3760-3). This jargon-free, accessible biography presents Rembrandt with all his flaws and quirks. (Rev: BL 5/1/92; SLJ 6/92*) [921]

6770 Silver, Larry. *Rembrandt* (9–12). (Rizzoli Art) 1993, Rizzoli paper $7.95 (0-8478-1519-6). This handsome, oversize book consists mainly of reproductions but also provides material on the artist's life and times. (Rev: BL 4/1/93; SLJ 1/93) [921]

RENOIR, AUGUSTE

6771 Rayfield, Susan. *Pierre-Auguste Renoir* (7–12). (First Impressions) 1998, Abrams $19.95 (0-8109-3795-6). A stunning book that focuses on Renoir's development as an Impressionist painter, with detailed discussions about individual pictures, full-color, full-page reproductions, and 2 double-page foldouts. (Rev: BL 12/1/98) [921]

RIVERA, DIEGO

6772 Braun, Barbara. *A Weekend with Diego Rivera* (4–9). Illus. (Weekend with) 1994, Rizzoli $19.95 (0-8478-1749-0). A well-researched introduction to the life and work of this Mexican artist, best known as a muralist. (Rev: BL 9/15/94; SLJ 5/94) [921]

6773 Cockcroft, James D. *Diego Rivera* (5–9). (Hispanics of Achievement) 1991, Chelsea LB $19.95 (0-7910-1252-2). The life of this Mexican artist and activist, with several illustrations. (Rev: BL 11/1/91; SLJ 1/92) [921]

6774 Goldstein, Ernest. *The Journey of Diego Rivera* (7–10). Illus. 1996, Lerner LB $23.93 (0-8225-2066-4). Though short on biographical material, this profusely illustrated volume is a fine introduction to Rivera's art and its connections to the history of Mexico. (Rev: BL 4/15/96; SLJ 1/96; VOYA 10/96) [921]

6775 Gonzales, Doreen. *Diego Rivera: His Art, His Life* (6–9). Illus. (Hispanic Americans) 1996, Enslow LB $19.95 (0-89490-764-6). The story of the great Mexican painter and muralist and his relationship with Frida Kahlo. (Rev: BL 11/1/96; BR 1–2/97; SLJ 10/96) [921]

ROCKWELL, NORMAN

6776 Durrett, Deanne. *Norman Rockwell* (4–8). Illus. (The Importance Of) 1997, Lucent LB $17.96 (1-56006-080-8). An introduction to the life and work of this beloved New England artist whose paintings glorified everyday American life. (Rev: BL 1/1–15/97; BR 9–10/97; SLJ 3/97) [921]

SIMMONS, PHILIP

6777 Lyons, Mary E. *Catching the Fire: Philip Simmons, Blacksmith* (4–8). 1997, Houghton $16.00 (0-395-72033-8). A biography of the contemporary African American craftsman and artist from Charleston, South Carolina, with extensive quotes from personal interviews. (Rev: BL 9/1/97; SLJ 9/97) [921]

UNGERER, TOMI

6778 Ungerer, Tomi. *Tomi: A Childhood under the Nazis* (6–10). 1998, Roberts Rinehart $29.95 (1-57098-163-9). Using many memorabilia of the time, this is the illustrator's story of his life during World War II after the Germans entered his Alsace town in 1940 when he was 8 years old. (Rev: BL 12/15/98; SLJ 3/99) [921]

VAN GOGH, VINCENT

6779 Bonafoux, Pascal. *Van Gogh: The Passionate Eye* (7–12). (Discoveries) 1992, Abrams paper $12.95 (0-8109-2828-0). An overview of the life and work of this disturbed Dutch painter. (Rev: BL 7/92) [021]

6780 Crispino, Enrica. *Van Gogh* (6–12). Illus. (Masters of Art) 1996, Bedrick LB $22.50 (0-87226-

525-0). The story of van Gogh's life and art is covered in a concise text, excellent reproductions, and engrossing diagrams. (Rev: BL 11/15/96; SLJ 12/96; VOYA 4/97) [921]

6781 Tyson, Peter. *Vincent van Gogh: Artist* (8–12). Illus. (Great Achievers: Lives of the Physically Challenged) 1996, Chelsea LB $19.95 (0-7910-2422-9). This mature biography discusses van Gogh's life and work and his contributions to Impressionism, achieved despite the deterioration of his mental health. (Rev: BL 5/1/96; SLJ 8/96) [921]

WANG YANI

6782 Zhensun, Zheng, and Alice Low. *A Young Painter: The Life and Paintings of Wang Yani—China's Extraordinary Young Artist* (5–8). 1991, Scholastic $17.95 (0-590-44906-0). The story of a self-taught prodigy whose paintings are highly regarded in China. Includes many examples of her unique work, based on the traditional Chinese style. (Rev: BL 10/1/91*; SLJ 8/91) [921]

WARHOL, ANDY

6783 Faerna, Jose M., ed. *Warhol* (10–12). Illus. 1997, Harry N. Abrams $11.98 (0-8109-4655-6). This tribute to the artist Andy Warhol contains an essay about the times in which he lived, a biography, and a section of full-color reproductions of his work. (Rev: BL 11/15/97; SLJ 5/98) [921]

WHISTLER, JAMES MCNEILL

6784 Berman, Avis. *James McNeill Whistler* (7–12). (First Impressions) 1993, Abrams $19.95 (0-8109-3968-1). A failure at West Point and in the Coast Guard, Whistler later pursued a career in art in Paris, where he gained worldwide renown. This well-illustrated account traces his life and work. (Rev: BL 12/1/93) [921]

WOOD, GRANT

6785 Duggleby, John. *Artist in Overalls: The Life of Grant Wood* (4–8). 1996, Chronicle $15.95 (0-8118-1242-1). The life of this American artist tells of his difficult struggle with poverty and his great attachment to the Midwest. (Rev: BL 4/15/96; SLJ 5/96) [921]

WOOD, MICHELE

6786 Igus, Toyomi. *Going Back Home: An Artist Returns to the South* (4–8). Illus. 1996, Children's Book Pr. $15.95 (0-89239-137-5). The author recreates the family history and life of the African American illustrator Michele Wood. (Rev: BL 9/15/96; SLJ 7/97) [921]

WRIGHT, FRANK LLOYD

6787 Boulton, Alexander O. *Frank Lloyd Wright, Architect: An Illustrated Biography* (8–12). 1993, Rizzoli $24.95 (0-8478-1683-4). Examines both Wright's architecture and his private life in detail. Photos and other illustrations. (Rev: BL 12/15/93; SLJ 11/93) [921]

6788 Davis, Frances A. *Frank Lloyd Wright: Maverick Architect* (5–9). Illus. 1996, Lerner LB $25.26 (0-8225-4953-0). A well-documented life of this influential 20th-century architect, with many black-and-white photos of his most important buildings. (Rev: BL 1/1–15/97; SLJ 1/97) [921]

6789 Rubin, Susan G. *Frank Lloyd Wright* (9–12). (First Impressions) 1994, Abrams $19.95 (0-8109-3974-6). A handsomely illustrated look at the architect's life and work. (Rev: BL 1/1/95; SLJ 1/95) [921]

WYETH, ANDREW

6790 Meryman, Richard. *Andrew Wyeth* (6–12). (First Impressions) 1991, Abrams $19.95 (0-8109-3956-8). Insights into the artist's childhood show how various events influenced his life in this introduction to the work of this contemporary American master. (Rev: BL 8/91) [921]

ZHANG, SONG NAN

6791 Zhang, Song Nan. *A Little Tiger in the Chinese Night: An Autobiography in Art* (5–8). 1993, Tundra $19.95 (0-88776-320-0). A Canadian immigrant artist tells the story of a life buffeted by changing Chinese policies, regimes, and conditions since World War II. (Rev: BL 1/1/94*; SLJ 5/94) [921]

Authors

ALCOTT, LOUISA MAY

6792 Burke, Kathleen. *Louisa May Alcott* (6–10). Illus. 1988, Chelsea LB $19.95 (1-55546-637-0). A portrait of this remarkable strong woman who assumed unusual family responsibilities while pursuing a writing career. (Rev: BL 3/1/88) [921]

ALVAREZ, JULIA

6793 Alvarez, Julia. *Something to Declare* (10–12). 1998, Algonquin $32.95 (1-56512-193-7). In 24 autobiographical essays, the author presents her Dominican childhood, her family's immigration to the United States, her college years, writing, marriages, and return trips to her homeland. (Rev: BL 8/98; SLJ 4/99) [921]

ANGELOU, MAYA

6794 Angelou, Maya. *All God's Children Need Traveling Shoes* (10–12). 1986, Random $19.95 (0-394-52143-9). In this fifth volume of Angelou's autobiography she tells of her 4 years in Ghana and a visit from Malcolm X. In order of publication and coverage the first 4 are: *I Know Why the Caged Bird Sings* (1970), *Gather Together in My Name* (1974), *Singin' and Swingin' and Gettin' Merry Like Christmas* (1976), and *The Heart of a Woman* (1981). (Rev: BL 2/1/86; SLJ 8/86; VOYA 8/86) [921]

6795 Cuffie, Terrasita A. *Maya Angelou* (4–8). (The Importance Of) 1999, Lucent LB $22.45 (1-56006-532-X). A biography that traces Maya Angelou's life from a childhood in the rural South, through overcoming poverty and bigotry, to gaining fame as a writer. (Rev: BL 9/15/99) [921]

6796 Kite, L. Patricia. *Maya Angelou* (6–9). (A and E Biography) 1999, Lerner $25.26 (0-8225-4944-1). Beginning in 1993, when Maya Angelou read her poetry at President Clinton's inauguration, this biography flashes back to her birth in 1928 and continues through 1996, covering personal aspects of her life and honors she has received, and including brief descriptions of her poetry and other writing. (Rev: SLJ 7/99) [921]

6797 Lisandrelli, Elaine S. *Maya Angelou: More than a Poet* (7–12). Illus. (African American Biographies) 1996, Enslow LB $19.95 (0-89490-684-4). A biography of the famous African American writer that includes her work as a dancer, singer, actress, and spokesperson for African American causes. (Rev: BL 9/1/96; BR 9–10/96; SLJ 6/96; VOYA 10/96) [921]

6798 Pettit, Jayne. *Maya Angelou: Journey of the Heart* (5–8). (Rainbow Biography) 1996, Lodestar paper $14.99 (0-525-67518-3). Drawing on Angelou's autobiographical writing, the author has created a moving portrait of this celebrated African American woman. (Rev: BL 2/15/96; SLJ 4/96) [921]

6799 Shapiro, Miles. *Maya Angelou* (7–10). Illus. (Black Americans of Achievement) 1994, Chelsea LB $19.95 (0-7910-1862-8). A chronological narrative of the life of this amazing African American writer that tells of her hardships and triumphs. (Rev: BL 6/1–15/94; SLJ 6/94) [921]

ASIMOV, ISAAC

6800 Boerst, William J. *Isaac Asimov: Writer of the Future* (5–9). 1998, Morgan Reynolds LB $18.95 (1-883846-32-3). An engaging biography of the amazingly prolific author and scientist who, as a youngster, was considered a misfit. (Rev: BL 12/1/98; BR 9–10/99; SLJ 1/99) [921]

6801 Judson, Karen. *Isaac Asimov: Master of Science Fiction* (5–9). 1998, Enslow $19.95 (0-7660-1031-7). A biography of Asimov that includes two chapters particularly helpful to researchers: his importance as a writer of science fiction, and his work in other genres. (Rev: BL 12/1/98; SLJ 2/99) [921]

AUSTEN, JANE

6802 Le Faye, Deirdre. *Jane Austen* (9–12). (British Library Writer's Lives) 1999, Oxford $36.95 (0-19-521440-4). An entertaining biography of this writer who lived a short, quiet life. The work is illustrated with plenty of photos and sketches of places and people. (Rev: BL 3/15/99; BR 9–10/99; VOYA 6/99) [921]

AVI

6803 Markham, Lois. *Avi* (5–8). 1996, Learning Works paper $6.95 (0-88160-280-9). This biography of the gifted writer recounts his triumph over dysgraphia, a learning disability that makes writing difficult, and explores his creative process and the major themes of his work. (Rev: BL 4/1/96; SLJ 8/96) [921]

6804 Mercier, Cathryn M., and Susan P. Bloom. *Presenting Avi* (6–10). (Twayne's United States Authors) 1997, Macmillan $24.95 (0-8057-4569-6). This biography of the noted writer of books for children and young adults is divided into chapters based on a role he has assumed as a writer, including storyteller, stylist, magician, and historian, and explores his many beliefs about the significance of literature. (Rev: SLJ 6/98) [921]

BALDWIN, JAMES

6805 Gottfried, Ted. *James Baldwin: Voice from Harlem* (7–12). (Impact Biographies) 1997, Watts LB $24.00 (0-531-11318-3); paper $9.95 (0-531-15863-2). This biography, enlivened with many photographs, discusses Baldwin's childhood, beliefs, gay identity, and principal works. (Rev: BL 5/15/97; SLJ 7/97; VOYA 10/97) [921]

6806 Kenan, Randall. *James Baldwin* (9–12). (Lives of Notable Gay Men and Lesbians) 1994, Chelsea LB $19.95 (0-7910-2301-X). Chronicles the pain and poverty of Baldwin's early adult years in Paris and gives a sense of his life as a black homosexual in a white world. (Rev: BL 3/1/94; SLJ 6/94; VOYA 6/94) [921]

6807 Rosset, Lisa. *James Baldwin* (8–10). Illus. 1989, Chelsea $19.95 (1-55546-572-2). A biography of this important black writer plus a discussion of his work. (Rev: BL 6/15/89; BR 9–10/89; SLJ 8/89; VOYA 10/89) [921]

6808 Tackach, James. *James Baldwin* (4–8). Illus. (The Importance Of) 1997, Lucent LB $17.96 (1-56006-070-0). This account covers both the life and accomplishments of this great 20th-century African American writer. (Rev: BL 1/1–15/97; SLJ 2/97) [921]

BARRIE, J. M.

6809 Aller, Susan Bivin. *J. M. Barrie: The Magic Behind Peter Pan* (6–8). 1994, Lerner LB $25.26 (0-8225-4918-2). This biography of the author reveals Barrie's similarities to his character Peter Pan and also gives details of his failed marriages. (Rev: BL 11/1/94; SLJ 12/94) [921]

BAWDEN, NINA

6810 Bawden, Nina. *In My Own Time: Almost an Autobiography* (8–12). 1995, Clarion $25.95 (0-395-74429-6). Bawden, the British author of numerous well-loved children's stories, writes of her own life. (Rev: BL 12/1/95) [921]

BORGES, JORGE LUÍS

6811 Lennon, Adrian. *Jorge Luís Borges* (5–9). (Hispanics of Achievement) 1991, Chelsea LB $19.95 (0-7910-1236-0). A simple account that describes the life and work of one of South America's great contemporary writers. (Rev: BL 3/15/92; SLJ 7/92) [921]

BRAGG, RICK

6812 Bragg, Rick. *All Over but the Shoutin'* (10–12). 1997, Pantheon $25.00 (0-679-44258-8). A memoir of the talented journalist who grew up in poverty in Alabama and grew to become a Pulitzer Prize–winning feature writer for the *New York Times*. (Rev: BL 9/15/97; SLJ 4/98) [921]

BRAY, ROSEMARY

6813 Bray, Rosemary L. *Unafraid of the Dark: A Memoir* (10–12). 1998, Random $24.00 (0-679-42555-1); Doubleday paper $14.00 (0-385-49475-0). The author recounts growing up in Chicago on welfare, the development of her interest in the civil rights movement while in high school, the winning of a scholarship to Yale, and her eventual appointment as an editor at the *New York Times Book Review*, concluding with a strong statement, based on her childhood, against the 1996 welfare-reform bill. (Rev: BL 1/1–15/98; SLJ 6/98) [921]

BRESLIN, ROSEMARY

6814 Breslin, Rosemary. *Not Exactly What I Had in Mind: An Incurable Love Story* (10–12). 1997, Villard $23.00 (0-679-45217-6). This painful yet humorous and heartwarming autobiography of the daughter of writer Jimmy Breslin tells of her rebellious teens and early 20s, her incurable blood disease, and the great love that came into her life and later became her husband. (Rev: BL 12/1/96; SLJ 9/97) [921]

BRONTË, CHARLOTTE

6815 Ross, Stewart. *Charlotte Brontë and Jane Eyre* (5–8). Illus. 1997, Viking $16.99 (0-670-87486-8). A picture book biography of Charlotte Brontë that focuses on the writing of *Jane Eyre* and provides a detailed plot summary. (Rev: BL 1/1–15/98; SLJ 1/98) [921]

6816 Sellars, Jane. *Charlotte Brontë* (8–12). Illus. 1998, Oxford $35.50 (0-19-521439-0). A handsomely illustrated biography of Charlotte Brontë by the director of the Brontë Museum in Haworth, Yorkshire, England. (Rev: BL 3/15/98; SLJ 5/98; VOYA 4/98) [921]

BRONTË FAMILY

6817 Bentley, Phyllis. *The Brontës and Their World* (9–12). Illus. 1986, Thames & Hudson paper $12.95 (0-500-26016-8). A richly illustrated biography of the 3 Brontë sisters and their wayward brother. [921]

6818 Guzzetti, Paula. *A Family Called Brontë* (6–9). 1994, Dillon LB $18.95 (0-87518-592-4). An account of the Brontë family written specifically for teenagers. (Rev: BL 5/15/94; SLJ 8/94; VOYA 8/94) [921]

6819 Martin, Christopher. *The Brontës* (7–12). Illus. 1989, Rourke LB $25.27 (0-86592-299-3). The life and works of the 3 Brontë sisters—Charlotte, Emily, and Anne—are highlighted as well as details of the society in which they lived. (Rev: BL 3/1/89) [921]

BROWN, CLAUDE

6820 Brown, Claude. *Manchild in the Promised Land* (9–12). 1965, NAL paper $4.95 (0-451-15741-9). A realistic picture of growing up in Harlem in the 1950s. [921]

BRUCHAC, JOSEPH

6821 Bruchac, Joseph. *Bowman's Store: A Journey to Myself* (9–12). Illus. 1997, Dial $17.99 (0-8037-1997-3). The prolific Native American author writes about his childhood, his racial heritage, and his maternal grandfather, who raised him and gave him support and encouragement. (Rev: BL 9/1/97; SLJ 12/97; VOYA 2/98) [921]

BUCK, PEARL

6822 La Farge, Ann. *Pearl Buck* (7–10). Illus. 1988, Chelsea LB $19.95 (1-55546-645-1). The life of the

writer who introduced pre-Revolutionary China to millions of American readers. (Rev: BL 8/88) [921]

BURNETT, FRANCES HODGSON

6823 Carpenter, Angelica S. *Frances Hodgson Burnett: Beyond the Secret Garden* (5–8). 1990, Lerner LB $25.26 (0-8225-4905-0). A glimpse into the private life of the woman who wrote *The Secret Garden*. (Rev: BL 1/15/91; SLJ 3/91*) [921]

CAMUS, ALBERT

6824 Bronner, Stephen Eric. *Albert Camus: The Thinker, the Artist, the Man* (9–12). (Impact Biographies) 1996, Watts LB $24.00 (0-531-11305-1). A clear examination of the Nobel Prize winner's personal life, thoughts, and writing. (Rev: SLJ 2/97) [921]

CATHER, WILLA

6825 Keene, Ann T. *Willa Cather* (7–12). 1994, Messner LB $15.00 (0-671-86760-1). A biography examining the writer's childhood, college years, jobs as editor and teacher, travels, and friends, as well as her reputed lesbianism. (Rev: BL 10/1/94; SLJ 11/94; VOYA 4/95) [813]

6826 O'Brien, Sharon. *Willa Cather* (7–12). (Lives of Notable Gay Men and Lesbians) 1994, Chelsea LB $19.95 (0-7910-2302-8); paper $9.95 (0-7910-2877-1). This biography of the author focuses on her reputed lesbianism and shows how Cather created a nurturing network of women friends and lovers. (Rev: BL 11/1/94; SLJ 11/94; VOYA 2/95) [921]

CERVANTES, MIGUEL DE

6827 Goldberg, Jake. *Miguel de Cervantes* (5–9). (Hispanics of Achievement) 1993, Chelsea LB $19.95 (0-7910-1238-7). The story of the Spanish writer whose life rivaled that of his adventurous hero, Don Quixote. (Rev: BL 9/15/93) [921]

CHESNUTT, CHARLES

6828 Thompson, Cliff. *Charles Chesnutt* (7–10). (Black Americans of Achievement) 1992, Chelsea LB $19.95 (1-55546-578-1). The life of this pioneering African American writer who explored themes related to slavery and the Reconstruction period in his fiction. (Rev: BL 12/1/92) [921]

CHRISTIE, AGATHA

6829 Dommermuth-Costa, Carol. *Agatha Christie: Writer of Mystery* (5–9). (Biographies Series) 1997, Lerner LB $25.26 (0-8225-4954-9). A biography of the "First Lady of Crime," with material on her personal life, including her 2 marriages. (Rev: SLJ 8/97; VOYA 4/98)

CISNEROS, SANDRA

6830 Mirriam-Goldberg, Caryn. *Sandra Cisneros: Latina Writer and Activist* (5–8). Illus. (Hispanic Biographies) 1998, Enslow LB $19.95 (0-7760-1045-7). A biography, enlivened with many quotes, of the woman who received Cs and Ds in school and later became a first-rate author and leading Hispanic American activist. (Rev: BL 1/1–15/99; VOYA 10/99) [921]

CLEARY, BEVERLY

6831 Cleary, Beverly. *A Girl from Yamhill: A Memoir* (6–12). Illus. 1988, Morrow $19.95 (0-688-07800-1). Details the early life in the Northwest of one of the greats of children's literature. (Rev: BL 6/1/88; BR 5–6/88; SLJ 5/88; VOYA 6/88) [921]

6832 Cleary, Beverly. *My Own Two Feet* (7–12). 1995, Morrow $16.00 (0-688-14267-2). In the second part of Cleary's candid autobiography, she departs for college. Although most appreciated by adults who grew up with her books, it also has a place on youth shelves. (Rev: BL 8/95*; SLJ 9/95) [921]

COURLANDER, HAROLD

6833 Jaffe, Nina. *A Voice for the People: The Life and Work of Harold Courlander* (7–10). Illus. 1997, Holt $16.95 (0-8050-3444-7). A biography of the famous collector of folk tales from minority groups who was also a noted writer and storyteller. (Rev: BL 11/1/97; SLJ 12/97) [921]

CRUTCHER, CHRIS

6834 Davis, Terry. *Presenting Chris Crutcher* (6–10). 1997, Macmillan $28.00 (0-8057-8223-0). A warm biography of this important young adult author, who combines sports stories with important themes like tolerance and the meaning of friendship. (Rev: SLJ 6/98; VOYA 6/98) [921]

DAHL, ROALD

6835 Dahl, Roald. *Boy: Tales of Childhood* (7–12). Illus. 1984, Farrar $16.00 (0-374-37374-4); Penguin paper $5.99 (0-14-031890-9). The famous author's autobiography—sometimes humorous, sometimes touching—of growing up in Wales in a Norwegian family. (Rev: BL 6/87) [921]

6836 Dahl, Roald. *Going Solo* (9–12). Illus. 1986, Farrar $14.95 (0-374-16503-3); Penguin paper $9.95 (0-14-010306-6). This book recounts the author's World War II activities in Africa and the Royal Air Force. For an older audience than his earlier autobi-

ographical *Boy* (1985). (Rev: BL 9/1/86; VOYA 2/87) [921]

DANZIGER, PAULA

6837 Krull, Kathleen. *Presenting Paula Danziger* (6–12). (United States Authors) 1995, Twayne $28.00 (0-8057-4153-4). Examines writer Danziger's personal problems, humorous teaching experiences, and group discussions of her books in 6 thematic chapters. (Rev: BL 9/1/95; VOYA 2/96) [921]

DICKENS, CHARLES

6838 Ayer, Eleanor. *Charles Dickens* (4–8). (The Importance of) 1998, Lucent LB $17.96 (1-56006-525-7). This biography of Dickens concentrates on his work and its significance. (Rev: BL 5/15/98; SLJ 7/98; VOYA 6/99) [921]

DICKINSON, EMILY

6839 Dommermuth-Costa, Carol. *Emily Dickinson: Singular Poet* (6–9). 1998, Lerner LB $25.26 (0-8225-4958-1). Extensive quotes from poems and letters add interesting details to this biography of Emily Dickinson. (Rev: BL 12/15/98; BR 1–2/99; SLJ 11/98) [921]

6840 Olsen, Victoria. *Emily Dickinson* (7–12). Illus. 1990, Chelsea LB $19.95 (1-55546-649-4). An illustrated biography that describes the life of Emily Dickinson as well as her work. (Rev: BL 7/90) [921]

6841 Steffens, Bradley. *Emily Dickinson* (5–10). Illus. (The Importance Of) 1997, Lucent LB $18.96 (1-56006-089-1). A comprehensive look at Emily Dickinson's personal history, psychological influences, religious explorations, and creative process. (Rev: SLJ 6/98; VOYA 6/99) [921]

DOYLE, SIR ARTHUR CONAN

6842 Adams, Cynthia. *The Mysterious Case of Sir Arthur Conan Doyle* (5–8). Illus. (World Writers) 1999, Morgan Reynolds LB $18.95 (1-883846-34-X). This book traces the life of Sir Arthur Conan Doyle from his Scottish boyhood and failed medical practice to success as a writer and creator of Sherlock Holmes. (Rev: BL 3/1/99; BR 9–10/99; SLJ 9/99; VOYA 10/99) [921]

6843 Symons, Julian. *Conan Doyle: Portrait of an Artist* (9–12). Illus. 1987, Mysterious $9.95 (0-89296-926-1). A biography that points out the similarities between Doyle and his creation, Sherlock Holmes. (Rev: BL 11/1/87) [921]

DUNBAR, PAUL LAURENCE

6844 Gentry, Tony. *Paul Laurence Dunbar* (7–12). Illus. 1988, Chelsea LB $19.95 (1-55546-583-8). A richly illustrated biography of one of the chief poets of the Harlem Renaissance of the 1920s. (Rev: BL 2/15/89; BR 1–289; SLJ 3/89; VOYA 2/89) [921]

EDMONDS, WALTER D.

6845 Edmonds, Walter D. *Tales My Father Never Told* (9–12). 1995, Syracuse Univ. Pr. $29.95 (0-8156-0307-X). An author's memoir of his privileged New York upbringing with a demanding father and loving mother. (Rev: BL 3/15/95) [921]

ELLISON, RALPH

6846 Bishop, Jack. *Ralph Ellison* (9–12). Illus. 1987, Chelsea LB $19.95 (1-55546-585-4). A biography of the writer of the acclaimed novel *Invisible Man* and his struggle for acceptance in both black and white cultures. (Rev: BL 2/15/88; SLJ 6/88) [921]

FLEISCHMAN, SID

6847 Fleischman, Sid. *The Abracadabra Kid: A Writer's Life* (6–12). Illus. 1996, Greenwillow $16.00 (0-688-14859-X). The exciting autobiography of the famous author who was also a magician, gold miner, and World War II sailor. (Rev: BL 9/1/96*; BR 9–10/96; SLJ 8/96*; VOYA 4/97) [921]

FRITZ, JEAN

6848 Fritz, Jean. *China Homecoming* (8–12). Illus. 1985, Putnam $16.95 (0-399-21182-9). This autobiographical account describes the return of this author to China, where she spent her childhood. (Rev: SLJ 8/85) [921]

6849 Fritz, Jean. *Homesick, My Own Story* (9–12). 1982, Putnam $15.99 (0-399-20933-6); Dell paper $4.99 (0-440-43683-4). This popular author writes about her early life in China. (Rev: BL 2/1/89) [921]

FROST, ROBERT

6850 Meyers, Jeffrey. *Robert Frost: A Biography* (10–12). 1996, Houghton $30.00 (0-395-72809-6). A detailed biography of this beloved American poet, focusing on his development as a poet and including explanations of many of his works and links to the Bible, classics, and other great poets. (Rev: BL 4/1/96; SLJ 9/96) [921]

GUY, ROSA

6851 Norris, Jerrie. *Presenting Rosa Guy* (9–12). 1988, Twayne $20.95 (0-8057-8207-9). A critical biography of the West Indian-born writer who has recreated Harlem life so vividly in her books for young adults. (Rev: BR 5–6/89; SLJ 12/88; VOYA 12/88) [921]

HALEY, ALEX

6852 Shirley, David. *Alex Haley* (7–10). (Black Americans of Achievement) 1993, Chelsea LB $19.95 (0-7910-1979-9); paper $9.95 (0-7910-1980-2). The story of the African American writer who gave us the family saga *Roots*. (Rev: BL 2/15/94) [921]

HANSBERRY, LORRAINE

6853 Hansberry, Lorraine. *To Be Young, Gifted and Black* (9–12). 1970, NAL paper $6.99 (0-451-15952-7). An autobiographical collection of reminiscences, letters, and quotes from Hansberry's plays. [921]

6854 McKissack, Patricia, and Fredrick McKissack. *Young, Black, and Determined: A Biography of Lorraine Hansberry* (8–12). Illus. 1997, Holiday House paper $18.95 (0-8234-1300-4). This story of the late black playwright who skyrocketed to fame in 1959 when she was only 28 for the play *A Raisin in the Sun* that opened on Broadway and won the Drama Critics Award. (Rev: BL 2/15/98; SLJ 4/98; VOYA 8/98) [921]

6855 Scheader, Catherine. *Lorraine Hansberry: Playright and Voice of Justice* (7–10). Illus. (African-American Biographies) 1998, Enslow LB $19.95 (0-89490-945-2). Raised on Chicago's South Side, Lorraine Hansberry, writer and civil rights activist, used this setting for her prize-winning play *Raisin in the Sun*. (Rev: BL 9/1/98; SLJ 11/98) [921]

6856 Sinnott, Susan. *Lorraine Hansberry: Award-Winning Playwright & Civil Rights Activist* (7–12). 1998, Conari Pr. paper $6.95 (1-57324-093-1). This story of the great African American playwright who grew up with a passion for theater and politics conveys a sense of the politics from the 1930s to the 1960s and the pressures of fame on an artist. (Rev: BL 2/15/99) [921]

6857 Tripp, Janet. *Lorraine Hansberry* (4–8). (The Importance Of) 1997, Lucent LB $17.96 (1-56006-081-6). This short biography tells of the short but brilliant life of this important black playwright who wrote *Raisin in the Sun*. (Rev: BL 10/15/97; SLJ 1/98) [921]

HAWTHORNE, NATHANIEL

6858 Whitelaw, Nancy. *Nathaniel Hawthorne: American Storyteller* (7–9). (World Writers) 1996, Morgan Reynolds LB $18.95 (1-883846-16-1). In spite of a rather confusing presentation, this book contains valuable information about this author, with frequent quotes from his works. (Rev: BR 9–10/96; SLJ 3/97) [921]

HELLMAN, LILLIAN

6859   Turk, Ruth. *Lillian Hellman: Rebel Playwright* (7–10). 1995, Lerner LB $21.50 (0-8225-4921-2). This biography looks at the playwright's critical work and life during the turmoil of the 1960s and the years of the House Un-American Activities Committee. (Rev: BL 6/1–15/95; SLJ 8/95) [921]

HEMINGWAY, ERNEST

6860   McDaniel, Melissa. *Ernest Hemingway: The Writer Who Suffered from Depression* (8–12). (Great Achievers: Lives of the Physically Challenged) 1996, Chelsea LB $19.95 (0-7910-2420-2). This personal and literary biography emphasizes the way Hemingway contributed to and changed American literature, using many excerpts from his works as well as quotes from reviewers and critics, while also discussing his problems with alcohol and battles with the emotional problems that eventually led to his suicide. (Rev: BR 5–6/97; SLJ 3/97) [921]

6861   Sandison, David. *Ernest Hemingway: An Illustrated Biography* (9–12). 1999, Chicago Review $24.95 (1-55652-399-4). A visually attractive, insightful biography organized into 8 chronological chapters, combining biography, history, literature, and photography to show an amazingly talented yet tormented man. (Rev: SLJ 8/99) [921]

6862   Tessitore, John. *The Hunt and the Feast: A Life of Ernest Hemingway* (7–12). Illus. (Impact Biographies) 1996, Watts LB $24.00 (0-531-11289-6). An excellent introduction to the life and works of the writer considered to be one of America's great 20th-century masters. (Rev: BL 1/1–15/97; BR 3–4/97; SLJ 1/97) [921]

6863   Yannuzzi, Della A. *Ernest Hemingway: Writer and Adventurer* (6–10). (People to Know) 1998, Enslow LB $19.95 (0-89490-979-7). An engrossing biography of the tempestuous writer whose life and loves were as exciting as his novels. (Rev: BL 11/15/98; SLJ 4/99) [921]

HENRY, MARGUERITE

6864   Collins, David R. *Write a Book for Me: The Story of Marguerite Henry* (7–10). Illus. (World Writers) 1999, Morgan Reynolds LB $18.95 (1-883846-39-0). A short, simple biography of the writer of such memorable books for young people as *King of the Wind*. (Rev: SLJ 9/99; VOYA 10/99) [921]

HOOKS, BELL

6865   Hooks, Bell. *Bone Black, Memories of Girlhood* (10–12). 1996, Holt $20.00 (0-8050-4145-1). Using 61 short vignettes, the author describes growing up in a southern town as an African American

rebel in a large family, and how she became the writer she is today. (Rev: BL 9/15/96; SLJ 3/97) [921]

HUGHES, LANGSTON

6866   Hill, Christine M. *Langston Hughes: Poet of the Harlem Renaissance* (6–10). (African American Biographies) 1997, Enslow LB $19.95 (0-89490-815-4). An easy-to-read, accurate look at the poet's life and times, with good quality black-and-white photographs. (Rev: BR 3–4/98; SLJ 1/98) [921]

6867   Meltzer, Milton. *Langston Hughes: A Biography* (7–10). 1968, HarperCollins $14.95 (0-690-48525-5). A rounded biography of the great black writer and poet who spoke with great pride of his race. [921]

6868   Meltzer, Milton. *Langston Hughes: An Illustrated Edition* (6–12). Illus. 1997, Millbrook LB $39.40 (0-7613-0205-0); paper $20.95 (0-7613-0327-8). This is a new, large, well-illustrated edition of the highly respected 1968 biography of Langston Hughes. (Rev: BL 8/97; BR 3–4/98; SLJ 11/97; VOYA 2/98) [920]

6869   Osofsky, Audrey. *Free to Dream: The Making of a Poet, Langston Hughes* (6–10). Illus. 1996, Lothrop $16.00 (0-688-10605-6). An attractive biography that covers the writer's life and works as well as general information on the Harlem Renaissance. (Rev: BL 4/1/96; BR 9–10/96; SLJ 7/96) [921]

6870   Rummel, Jack. *Langston Hughes* (8–10). Illus. 1988, Chelsea LB $19.95 (1-55546-595-1). A highly readable biography of the black poet and fiction writer that is well illustrated and contains excerpts from his writings. Part of the Black Americans of Achievement series. (Rev: BL 12/1/87; BR 1–2/89; VOYA 10/88) [921]

HURSTON, ZORA NEALE

6871   Calvert, Roz. *Zora Neale* (5–8). 1993, Chelsea LB $16.95 (0-7910-1766-4). A biography of Hurston, the rediscovered author of the Harlem Renaissance. (Rev: BL 5/1/93; SLJ 6/93) [921]

6872   Lyons, Mary E. *Sorrow's Kitchen: The Life and Folklore of Zora Neale Hurston* (7–12). 1990, Scribners $15.00 (0-684-19198-9). A brief biography of the African American novelist whose use of dialect sometimes brought criticism from other writers and who until recently was largely forgotten. (Rev: BL 12/15/90; SLJ 1/91*) [921]

6873   Porter, A. P. *Jump at de Sun: The Story of Zora Neale Hurston* (7–12). 1992, Carolrhoda LB $26.93 (0-87614-667-1); paper $6.95 (0-87614-546-2). A brief, easy-to-read biography that places Hurston within the context of the racism of her era. (Rev: BL 12/15/92; SLJ 1/93*) [921]

6874 Witcover, Paul. *Zora Neale Hurston* (9–12). Illus. 1990, Chelsea LB $19.95 (0-7910-1129-1). A biography of this black American who was a folklorist, author, and anthropologist during the Harlem renaissance. (Rev: BL 12/15/90; SLJ 3/91) [921]

6875 Yannuzzi, Della A. *Zora Neale Hurston: Southern Storyteller* (7–12). Illus. (African American Biographies) 1996, Enslow LB $19.95 (0-89490-685-2). The story of the Harlem Renaissance author who died penniless but left a priceless legacy in her writings. (Rev: BL 9/1/96; BR 9–10/96; SLJ 6/96) [921]

JEWETT, SARAH ORNE

6876 Silverthorne, Elizabeth. *Sarah Orne Jewett: A Writer's Life* (9–12). 1993, Overlook $22.95 (0-87951-484-1). A sympathetic biography of the American realist/regionalist author that draws on unpublished letters and diaries. (Rev: BL 3/15/93) [921]

JOHNSON, JAMES WELDON

6877 Tolbert-Rouchaleau, Jane. *James Weldon Johnson* (9–12). Illus. 1988, Chelsea LB $19.95 (1-55546-596-X). The biography of the black writer who was also involved with the NAACP and the struggle for equality. (Rev: BL 6/1/88) [921]

KERR, M. E.

6878 Nilsen, Alleen P. *Presenting M. E. Kerr.* rev. ed. (8–12). (Twayne's United States Authors) 1997, Twayne $22.95 (0-8057-9248-1). A biography of this popular young adult writer that also discusses her works, with a detailed analysis of her 5 most popular books. (Rev: SLJ 4/98; VOYA 4/98) [810]

KING, STEPHEN

6879 Keyishian, Amy, and Marjorie Keyishian. *Stephen King* (7–12). (Pop Culture Legends) 1995, Chelsea LB $19.95 (0-7910-2340-0); paper $8.95 (0-7910-2365-6). Gives insight into the life of one of the world's most successful writers, covering King's childhood poverty and abandonment by his father, support by his mother, and influences on his work of such giants as C. S. Lewis, H. G. Wells, and Bram Stoker. (Rev: BL 12/15/95; BR 11–12/96; SLJ 1/96) [921]

KLEIN, NORMA

6880 Phy, Allene Stuart. *Presenting Norma Klein* (9–12). Illus. 1988, Twayne $20.95 (0-8057-8205-2). A biography and critical analysis of the writer, Norma Klein, who broke many taboos regarding young adult literature. (Rev: BL 7/88; SLJ 10/88) [921]

KOONTZ, DEAN

6881 Greenberg, Martin H., ed. *The Dean Koontz Companion* (9–12). 1994, Berkley paper $13.00 (0-425-14135-7). An interview with the prolific author of horror fiction, commentary on his works, and short tongue-in-cheek pieces by Koontz himself. (Rev: BL 1/1/94; SLJ 5/94; VOYA 8/94) [814.54]

L'ENGLE, MADELEINE

6882 Gonzales, Doreen. *Madeleine L'Engle: Author of "A Wrinkle in Time"* (5–8). (People in Focus) 1991, Dillon LB $13.95 (0-87518-485-5). A short biography of the beloved writer of such juvenile favorites as *Wrinkle in Time* and the many books about the Austin family. (Rev: BL 2/15/92; SLJ 3/92) [921]

LASKY, KATHRYN

6883 Brown, Joanne. *Presenting Kathryn Lasky* (9–12). (Twayne's United States Authors) 1998, Twayne $28.00 (0-8057-1677-7). An objective, lively biography of this popular young adult author that illuminates how her experiences have influenced her writing, plus a critical analysis of her books. (Rev: SLJ 6/99) [921]

LEWIS, C. S.

6884 Coren, Michael. *The Man Who Created Narnia: The Story of C. S. Lewis* (6–9). Illus. 1996, Eerdmans $22.00 (0-8028-3822-7). The life story of the creator of the Narnia series, with insight into its inspiration and creation. (Rev: BL 10/1/96; BR 5–6/97) [921]

6885 Gormley, Beatrice. *C. S. Lewis: Christian and Storyteller* (6–9). Illus. 1997, Eerdmans paper $8.00 (0-8028-5069-3). This biography of the author of the Narnia saga tells about his problems as a child after his mother's death and his gradual journey from atheism to Christianity. (Rev: BL 3/15/98; SLJ 6/98; VOYA 6/98) [921]

LONDON, JACK

6886 Dyer, Daniel. *Jack London: A Biography* (7–10). Illus. 1997, Scholastic $17.95 (0-590-22216-3). The hard life and early death of author Jack London, an adventurous, passionate lover of life. (Rev: BL 9/15/97; BR 3–4/98; SLJ 9/97; VOYA 10/98) [921]

LONGFELLOW, HENRY WADSWORTH

6887 Lukes, Bonnie L. *Henry Wadsworth Longfellow: America's Beloved Poet* (6–12). (World Writers) 1998, Morgan Reynolds $18.95 (1-883846-31-5). This biography introduces Longfellow's poetry and describes his life, his personal problems, and his friendships with such writers as Washington Irving, Charles Dickens, and Nathaniel Hawthorne. (Rev: BL 9/15/98; BR 11–12/98; SLJ 10/98) [921]

LOWRY, LOIS

6888 Lowry, Lois. *Looking Back: A Photographic Memoir* (4–8). Illus. 1998, Houghton $16.00 (0-395-89543-X). A collection of photos from the author's past provide biographical information as well as insights into her work. (Rev: BL 11/1/98; BR 5–6/99; SLJ 9/98; VOYA 4/99) [921]

6889 Markham, Lois. *Lois Lowry* (5–8). (Meet the Author) 1995, Learning Works paper $6.95 (0-88160-278-7). This biography of the Newbery Award–winning author tells how she became a writer and about personal experiences that are reflected in her books. (Rev: SLJ 1/96) [921]

MCCALL, BRUCE

6890 McCall, Bruce. *Thin Ice: Coming of Age in Canada* (10–12). 1997, Random $24.00 (0-679-44847-0). A memoir by a Canadian humorist about his life growing up with an abusive father, an alcoholic mother, and four brothers, who, like him, sought escape in the arts. (Rev: BL 6/1–15/97; BR 1–2/98; SLJ 10/97) [921]

MERTON, THOMAS

6891 Bryant, Jennifer. *Thomas Merton: Poet, Prophet, Priest* (7–12). Illus. 1997, Eerdmans $15.00 (0-8028-5109-6). The life story of this remarkable monk who was a highly successful writer, a civil rights activist, and a student of comparative religion. (Rev: BL 6/1–15/97) [921]

MILLAY, EDNA ST. VINCENT

6892 Daffron, Carolyn. *Edna St. Vincent Millay* (7–12). Illus. 1989, Chelsea LB $19.95 (1-55546-668-0). The life and career of this noted poet with examples of her work. (Rev: BL 12/1/89; BR 3–4/90; SLJ 3/90) [921]

MONTGOMERY, L. M.

6893 Andronik, Catherine M. *Kindred Spirit: A Biography of L. M. Montgomery, Creator of Anne of Green Gables* (6–9). 1993, Atheneum $16.00 (0-689-31671-2). Montgomery's biography uses her journals to portray her childhood with her grandparents on Prince Edward Island, her literary career and friendships, and her midlife marriage to a minister. (Rev: BL 11/1/93; SLJ 11/93; VOYA 12/93) [921]

MORRISON, TONI

6894 Century, Douglas. *Toni Morrison* (8–12). (Black Americans of Achievement) 1994, Chelsea LB $19.95 (0-7910-1877-6). A biography of the Nobel Prize–winning African American author, examining her life and the major themes of her novels. (Rev: BL 9/1/94; SLJ 7/94; VOYA 8/94) [921]

6895 Kramer, Barbara. *Toni Morrison: Nobel Prize-Winning Author* (7–12). (African-American Biographies) 1996, Enslow LB $19.95 (0-89490-688-7). Using many quotes and first-person comments, this biography recreates the life and important works of this African American Nobel Prize winner. (Rev: BL 9/15/96; BR 1–2/97; SLJ 11/96; VOYA 6/97) [921]

NERUDA, PABLO

6896 Goodnough, David. *Pablo Neruda: Nobel Prize-Winning Poet* (6–12). Illus. 1998, Enslow LB $19.95 (0-7660-1042-2). A brief, interesting biography of the great Chilean poet that includes good background material on the rise and fall of the dictator Allende. (Rev: BL 8/98; SLJ 9/98; VOYA 10/98) [921]

6897 Roman, Joseph. *Pablo Neruda* (7–12). (Hispanics of Achievement) 1992, Chelsea LB $19.95 (0-7910-1248-4). Traces the great Chilean poet's life from his early years through his career as a diplomat and acclaimed writer. (Rev: BL 6/1/92; SLJ 9/92) [921]

O'CONNOR, FLANNERY

6898 Balee, Susan. *Flannery O'Connor: Literary Prophet of the South* (8–12). 1994, Chelsea LB $19.95 (0-7910-2418-0). A brief biography of this acclaimed writer whose stories were set in the old, sometimes decadent, South. (Rev: BL 1/1/95; SLJ 1/95; VOYA 2/95) [921]

PATERSON, KATHERINE

6899 Cary, Alice. *Katherine Paterson* (5–8). (Meet the Author) 1997, Learning Works paper $6.95 (0-88160-281-7). A biography of the 2-time Newbery winner, with quotes from interviews and autobiographical essays. (Rev: BL 5/1/97; SLJ 7/97) [921]

PAULSEN, GARY

6900 Paulsen, Gary. *Eastern Sun, Winter Moon: An Autobiographical Odyssey* (9–12). 1993, Harcourt $22.95 (0-15-127260-3). The vivid, sometimes horrifying, story of Paulsen's incredible childhood, much of it spent in the Philippines. (Rev: BL 1/15/93) [921]

6901 Peters, Stephanie True. *Gary Paulsen* (4–8). Illus. 1999, Learning Works paper $6.95 (0-88160-

324-4). A biography of this popular author that tells of his love of adventure and the outdoors, his struggle with alcoholism, and his continuing health problems. (Rev: BL 6/1–15/99; SLJ 6/99) [921]

PECK, RICHARD

6902 Peck, Richard. *Anonymously Yours* (6–9). 1992, Messner LB $14.98 (0-671-74161-6). An account of how the author became a writer, filled with commentary, quips, and advice for aspiring writers. (Rev: BL 4/15/92; SLJ 5/92) [921]

POE, EDGAR ALLAN

6903 Anderson, Madelyn Klein. *Edgar Allan Poe: A Mystery* (7–12). 1993, Watts LB $24.00 (0-531-13012-6). Photos, letters, reviews, and Poe's writings contribute to this view of him as brilliant and gifted, yet opinionated, arrogant, and impractical. (Rev: BL 10/1/93; VOYA 10/93) [921]

RODRIGUEZ, LUIS

6904 Schwartz, Michael. *Luis Rodriguez* (4–8). Illus. (Contemporary Hispanic Americans) 1997, Raintree Steck-Vaughn LB $24.26 (0-8172-3990-1). The life of this contemporary Hispanic American who went from gang leader and drug addict to writer, journalist, publisher, speaker, and youth activist. (Rev: BL 4/15/97; SLJ 6/97) [921]

SEBESTYEN, OUIDA

6905 Monseau, Virginia R. *Presenting Ouida Sebestyen* (6–12). (United States Authors) 1995, Twayne $20.95 (0-8057-8224-9). Sebestyen's unorthodox writing habits enliven this text, with biographical information and detailed analysis of 6 novels. (Rev: BL 9/1/95) [921]

SHAKESPEARE, WILLIAM

6906 Thrasher, Thomas. *The Importance of William Shakespeare* (4–8). (The Importance of) 1998, Lucent LB $18.96 (1-56006-374-2). This work discusses Shakespeare and the contribution his work has made to world culture. (Rev: BL 12/15/98; VOYA 6/99) [921]

SHELLEY, MARY

6907 Miller, Calvin C. *Spirit like a Storm: The Story of Mary Shelley* (7–10). Illus. 1996, Morgan Reynolds LB $18.95 (1-883846-13-7). The life story of the fascinating, talented creator of *Frankenstein,* who was also the wife of poet Percy Bysshe Shelley. (Rev: BL 2/15/96; BR 1–2/97; SLJ 3/96; VOYA 6/96) [921]

6908 Nichols, Joan Kane. *Mary Shelley: Frankenstein's Creator, First Science Fiction Writer* (10–12). (Barnard Biography) 1998, Conari Pr. paper $6.95 (1-57324-087-7). A compelling biography of the spirited rebel and talented author who was the creator of *Frankenstein* and the wife of the poet Shelley. (Rev: SLJ 2/99) [921]

SINGER, ISAAC BASHEVIS

6909 Singer, Isaac Bashevis. *A Day of Pleasure: Stories of a Boy Growing Up in Warsaw* (6–8). Illus. 1969, Farrar paper $7.95 (0-374-41696-6). Autobiographical anecdotes of Singer's growing up Jewish in Poland; includes photographs of the time. [921]

SPINELLI, JERRY

6910 Spinelli, Jerry. *Knots in My Yo-Yo String: The Autobiography of a Kid* (5–8). 1998, Knopf LB $16.99 (0-679-98791-6); paper $9.99 (0-679-88791-1). The author recalls his childhood in Norristown, Pennsylvania, and how his experiences there influenced his later writing. (Rev: BL 5/1/98; SLJ 6/98; VOYA 12/98) [921]

STEINBECK, JOHN

6911 Parini, Jay. *John Steinbeck* (10–12). 1995, Holt $30.00 (0-8050-1673-2). A finely wrought portrait of Steinbeck's youth, friendships, marriages, travels, and the creation of each book, play, and film. (Rev: BL 1/15/95*) [921]

6912 Reef, Catherine. *John Steinbeck* (7–12). Illus. 1996, Clarion $17.95 (0-395-71278-5). A handsome photobiography that not only covers salient aspects of Steinbeck's life but also explores the themes and locales of his work. (Rev: BL 5/1/96; BR 9–10/96; SLJ 3/96; VOYA 8/96) [921]

STEVENSON, ROBERT LOUIS

6913 Carpenter, Angelica S., and Jean Shirley. *Robert Louis Stevenson: Finding Treasure Island* (5–8). Illus. 1997, Lerner LB $25.26 (0-8225-4955-7). A lively biography of this great writer who was a disappointment to his family because he did not become a minister. (Rev: BL 11/15/97; SLJ 12/97) [921]

6914 Gherman, Beverly. *Robert Louis Stevenson: Teller of Tales* (5–8). Illus. 1996, Simon & Schuster $16.00 (0-689-31985-1). The story of the author of *Treasure Island* who, though always in poor health, lived a full, adventurous life. (Rev: BL 10/1/96; BR 5–6/97; SLJ 2/97) [921]

STOKER, BRAM

6915 Whitelaw, Nancy. *Bram Stoker: Author of Dracula* (6–10). Illus. 1998, Morgan Reynolds LB

$16.75 (1-883846-30-7). A well-documented biography of the writer who was fascinated with horror even as a child and eventually wrote the classic vampire tale *Dracula*. (Rev: BL 10/1/98; SLJ 6/98; VOYA 10/99) [921]

STOWE, HARRIET BEECHER

6916 Coil, Suzanne M. *Harriet Beecher Stowe* (7–12). 1993, Watts LB $24.00 (0-531-13006-1). An admiring biography of the celebrated author that documents the writing of *Uncle Tom's Cabin* and includes excerpts from her letters and works. (Rev: BL 1/15/94; SLJ 1/94; VOYA 4/94) [921]

6917 Fritz, Jean. *Harriet Beecher Stowe and the Beecher Preachers* (5–9). 1994, Putnam $15.99 (0-399-22666-4). A biography of the writer of *Uncle Tom's Cabin,* examining Stowe's role as an outspoken woman author in the mid-19th century. (Rev: BL 8/94; SLJ 9/94; VOYA 8/94) [921]

6918 Hedrick, Joan D. *Harriet Beecher Stowe: A Life* (9–12). 1994, Oxford $56.00 (0-19-506639-1). This biography of the influential author of *Uncle Tom's Cabin* relates her complex personal story while capturing the spirit of antebellum United States. (Rev: BL 1/15/94*) [921]

6919 Jakoubek, Robert E. *Harriet Beecher Stowe: Author and Abolitionist* (6–9). Illus. 1989, Chelsea LB $19.95 (1-55546-680-X). This account is valuable not only as a biography of this famous writer but also as an insight into the horrors of slavery. (Rev: SLJ 6/89) [921]

TAN, AMY

6920 Kramer, Barbara. *Amy Tan: Author of the Joy Luck Club* (6–12). Illus. 1996, Enslow LB $19.95 (0-89490-699-2). The story of the Chinese American writer who at first denied her immigrant background and later grew to accept and celebrate it in her fiction. (Rev: BL 6/1–15/96; SLJ 10/96; VOYA 10/96) [921]

TOLKIEN, J. R. R.

6921 Collins, David R. *J. R. R. Tolkien: Master of Fantasy* (6–9). Illus. 1992, Lerner LB $25.26 (0-8225-4906-9). A biography of this professor and author of fantasy fiction. (Rev: BL 5/15/92; SLJ 7/92) [921]

6922 Hammond, Wayne G., and Christina Scull. *J. R. R. Tolkien: Artist and Illustrator* (10–12). 1996, Houghton $40.00 (0-395-74816-X). In addition to covering the life, ideas, and writings of this imaginative author, this book includes reproductions of over 200 of Tolkien's paintings, drawings, and sketches. (Rev: BL 1/1–15/96; SLJ 7/96) [921]

TWAIN, MARK

6923 Cox, Clinton. *Mark Twain: America's Humorist, Dreamer, Prophet* (5–9). 1995, Scholastic $14.95 (0-590-45642-3). A biography that includes a discussion of Twain's views on race and how they changed. (Rev: BL 9/15/95; SLJ 9/95; VOYA 12/95) [921]

6924 Lyttle, Richard B. *Mark Twain: The Man and His Adventures* (7–12). 1994, Atheneum $15.95 (0-689-31712-3). A sturdy biography that concentrates on the adventurous life Twain lead during his formative years. (Rev: BL 12/1/94; SLJ 1/95; VOYA 2/95) [921]

6925 Meltzer, Milton. *Mark Twain: A Writer's Life* (7–12). Illus. 1985, Watts LB $28.00 (0-531-10072-3). A fine portrait of this writer that uses many quotes from Twain himself to reveal specific points like his genius for comedy. (Rev: BL 10/1/85; SLJ 12/85) [921]

6926 Neider, Charles, ed. *The Autobiography of Mark Twain* (10–12). Illus. 1990, HarperCollins paper $14.00 (0-06-092025-4). This is a well-edited version of the mass of material left by Twain to serve as his autobiography. [921]

6927 Press, Skip. *Mark Twain* (5–8). 1994, Lucent LB $17.96 (1-56006-043-3). The private, public, and literary aspects of Twain's life. (Rev: BL 5/15/94; SLJ 4/94) [921]

6928 Rasmussen, R. Kent. *Mark Twain from A to Z: The Essential Reference to His Life and Writings* (9–12). (Literary A to Z) 1995, Facts on File $45.00 (0-8160-2845-1). This award-winning comprehensive study of Twain's life and times contains nearly 1,300 entries that cover all important aspects of his life and works. (Rev: BR 3–4/96; SLJ 3/96) [921]

6929 Ross, Stewart. *Mark Twain and Huckleberry Finn* (5–8). Illus. 1999, Viking $16.99 (0-670-88181-3). This account of Mark Twain's life in picture book format also contains material on the novel *Huckleberry Finn,* with coverage on the sources of the characters and true incidents that have been incorporated into the plot. (Rev: BL 3/1/99; SLJ 5/99) [921]

WALTON, JENNY

6930 Walton, Jenny. *Jenny Walton's Packing for a Woman's Journey* (10–12). 1998, Crown $20.00 (0-517-70662-8). This work consists of a series of upbeat stories about families and friends involved with the author during her growing-up years in the Midwest. (Rev: SLJ 7/98) [921]

WATSON, LYALL

6931 Watson, Lyall. *Warriors, Warthogs, and Wisdom: Growing Up in Africa* (4–8). Illus. 1997, Kingfisher $26.95 (0-7534-5066-6). This well-known nature writer describes his childhood in the South African bush and how, at an early age, he learned to live off the land with his Zulu friend. (Rev: BL 10/1/97; BR 11–12/97; SLJ 8/97) [921]

WELLS, H. G.

6932 Martin, Christopher. *H. G. Wells* (7–12). Illus. 1989, Rourke LB $25.27 (0-86592-297-7). The life of the English writer who rose from poverty to be a well-known author in many genres including science fiction. (Rev: BL 3/1/89) [921]

WERSBA, BARBARA

6933 Poe, Elizabeth Ann. *Presenting Barbara Wersba* (8–12). (United States Authors) 1998, Macmillan $24.95 (0-8057-4154-2). An excellent introduction to the life and works of this groundbreaking young adult novelist. (Rev: BL 9/1/98; SLJ 9/98; VOYA 12/98) [921]

WHARTON, EDITH

6934 Turk, Ruth. *Edith Wharton: Beyond the Age of Innocence* (7–10). Illus. 1997, Tudor $18.95 (0-936389-45-1). A touching portrait of the unusual American novelist, including her struggles with an unsupportive family and her eventual literary and personal success. (Rev: BL 2/1/98; SLJ 10/97) [921]

6935 Worth, Richard. *Edith Wharton* (10–12). 1994, Messner $15.00 (0-671-86615-X). A discussion of Wharton's life and an examination of her works. (Rev: BL 5/15/94; SLJ 11/94; VOYA 4/95) [921]

WHEATLEY, PHILLIS

6936 Jensen, Marilyn. *Phyllis Wheatley* (9–12). 1987, Sayre LB $21.95 (0-87460-326-9). The story of a slave in Boston who became the first black poet in Colonial America and gained sufficient fame to be invited to England to meet the king. (Rev: BR 11–12/87; SLJ 12/87) [921]

6937 Richmond, Merle. *Phillis Wheatley* (7–10). Illus. 1988, Chelsea LB $19.95 (1-55546-683-4). A heavily illustrated account of this poet who triumphed over slavery. (Rev: BL 2/15/88; SLJ 4/88) [921]

WHITE, E. B.

6938 Gherman, Beverly. *E. B. White: Some Writer!* (5–9). 1992, Atheneum $16.00 (0-689-31672-0). A look at the life of the author of *Charlotte's Web* reveals a man who loved words and craved solitude. (Rev: BL 4/15/92; SLJ 7/92) [921]

6939 Tingum, Janice. *E. B. White: The Elements of a Writer* (7–10). 1995, Lerner LB $25.26 (0-8225-4922-0). This quiet biography of the author of the

much-beloved *Charlotte's Web* and other books discusses the underside of White's success: his shyness and depression. (Rev: BL 11/1/95) [921]

WHITMAN, WALT

6940 Reef, Catherine. *Walt Whitman* (7–12). 1995, Clarion $16.95 (0-395-68705-5). A biography of the 19th-century poet who sang of America and the self. (Rev: BL 5/1/95; SLJ 5/95) [921]

WILDE, OSCAR

6941 Nunokawa, Jeff. *Oscar Wilde* (10–12). (Notable Biographies) 1994, Chelsea LB $19.95 (0-7910-2311-7); paper $9.95 (0-7910-2884-4). A well-researched biography of the witty English playwright and author who was imprisoned under Dickensian conditions because of a homosexual scandal and died 3 years after his release at the age of 46. (Rev: BL 11/15/94; SLJ 11/94; VOYA 2/95) [921]

WILDER, LAURA INGALLS

6942 Wadsworth, Ginger. *Laura Ingalls Wilder: Storyteller of the Prairie* (5–8). (Biography Series) 1997, Lerner LB $25.26 (0-8225-4950-6). A solid, readable biography of this author that clarifies the chronology in the Little House books. (Rev: BL 3/1/97; SLJ 4/97) [921]

6943 Zochert, Donald. *Laura: The Life of Laura Ingalls Wilder* (9–12). 1976, Avon paper $5.99 (0-380-01636-2). An honest, sympathetic biography of and tribute to the author of the Little House books. [921]

WINNEMUCCA, SARAH

6944 Scordato, Ellen. *Sarah Winnemucca: Northern Paiute Writer and Diplomat* (9–12). (North American Indians of Achievement) 1992, Chelsea LB $19.95 (0-7910-1710-9). The story of this extraordinary Native American woman and her diverse achievements. (Rev: BL 11/1/92; SLJ 1/93) [921]

WOODSON, CARTER G.

6945 Durden, Robert F. *Carter G. Woodson: Father of African-American History* (6–10). (African-American Biographies) 1998, Enslow LB $19.95 (0-89490-946-0). This balanced, documented account focuses on the successes and failures of this historian, pioneering writer, and publisher, who devoted his life to the study of African American history and culture. (Rev: BR 11–12/98; SLJ 1/99) [921]

WRIGHT, RICHARD

6946 Urban, Joan. *Richard Wright* (7–10). Illus. 1989, Chelsea LB $19.95 (1-55546-618-4). A well-illustrated biography that also tells a little about the author's work. (Rev: BL 6/15/89; BR 9–10/89; SLJ 8/89) [921]

ZINDEL, PAUL

6947 Forman, Jack Jacob. *Presenting Paul Zindel* (9–12). Illus. 1988, Twayne $20.95 (0-8057-8206-0). An analysis of both the life and works of this popular author whose trailblazing books have influenced the course of young adult literature. (Rev: BL 7/88; SLJ 9/88; VOYA 10/88) [921]

Composers

BACH, JOHANN SEBASTIAN

6948 Bettmann, Otto L. *Johann Sebastian Bach As His World Knew Him* (9–12). 1995, Birch Lane $22.50 (1-55972-279-7). A biography of the great musician and personal essays on Bach's life. (Rev: BL 3/15/95) [921]

BEETHOVEN, LUDWIG VAN

6949 Balcavage, Dynise. *Ludwig Van Beethoven: Composer* (4–8). (Great Achievers: Lives of the Physically Challenged) 1997, Chelsea LB $19.95 (0-7910-2082-7). This is an information-rich account of the composer's public and private life, with good coverage of his compositions. (Rev: SLJ 7/97) [921]

BERNSTEIN, LEONARD

6950 Hurwitz, Johanna. *Leonard Bernstein: A Passion for Music* (5–8). Illus. 1993, Jewish Publication Soc. $12.95 (0-8276-0501-3). This biography acquaints readers with Bernstein as conductor, composer, pianist, and teacher and shows how his Jewish heritage was a powerful motivating influence. (Rev: BL 2/15/94; SLJ 12/93) [921]

GUTHRIE, WOODY

6951 Guthrie, Woody. *Bound for Glory* (10–12). Illus. 1943, Peter Smith $23.50 (0-8446-6178-3); NAL paper $13.95 (0-452-26445-6). The saga of the man who grew up in poverty in the Oklahoma dust bowl and in time became one of America's most famous troubadours. [921]

6952 Yates, Janelle. *Woody Guthrie: American Balladeer* (6–10). 1995, Ward Hill LB $14.95 (0-9623380-0-1); paper $10.95 (0-9623380-5-2). Describes Guthrie's creative life and provides important historical information, including the many tragedies suffered by his family and his friendly relationship with labor, members of the Communist

Party, and other musicians. (Rev: BL 2/1/95; SLJ 3/95) [921]

JONES, QUINCY

6953 Kavanaugh, Lee H. *Quincy Jones: Musician, Composer, Producer* (5–8). 1998, Enslow LB $19.95 (0-89490-814-6). This biography describes Quincy Jones's 50-year career in music and how he overcame poverty, racism, and health problems to become a musical director, composer, producer, arranger, and driving force behind many award-winning recordings. (Rev: VOYA 8/98) [921]

JOPLIN, SCOTT

6954 Curtis, Susan. *Dancing to a Black Man's Tune: A Life of Scott Joplin* (9–12). 1994, Univ. of Missouri Pr. $29.95 (0-8262-0949-1). Curtis traces the life of Joplin, best known for his piano rag "The Entertainer," from his Texas origins through his success as a performer and composer to his troubled stay in Harlem and the failure of his opera, *Treemonisha.* (Rev: BL 5/1/94) [780]

6955 Preston, Katherine. *Scott Joplin: Composer* (7–10). Illus. 1988, Chelsea LB $19.95 (1-55546-598-6). The story of the talented musician, composer, and performer and the legacy of ragtime music he has left us. (Rev: BL 2/1/88; SLJ 5/88) [921]

MOZART, WOLFGANG AMADEUS

6956 Switzer, Ellen. *The Magic of Mozart: Mozart, The Magic Flute, and the Salzburg Marionettes* (5–9). 1995, Atheneum $19.95 (0-689-31851-0). A book in 3 parts: Mozart's life, a child-friendly libretto of the opera *The Magic Flute,* and photos of the Salzburg Marionette Theater, which specializes in Mozart operas. (Rev: BL 11/15/95; SLJ 9/95; VOYA 2/96) [921]

SCHUBERT, FRANZ

6957 Thompson, Wendy. *Franz Schubert* (6–9). (Composer's World) 1991, Viking paper $17.95 (0-670-84172-2). An introduction to the life, times, and music of Franz Schubert. (Rev: BL 1/1/92) [921]

WEBBER, ANDREW LLOYD

6958 Walsh, Michael. *Andrew Lloyd Webber* (9–12). Illus. 1989, Abrams $49.50 (0-8109-1275-9). An oversized volume that deals with the British musical phenomenon and composer of the music for such hits as *Cats* and *Phantom of the Opera.* (Rev: BL 1/1/90) [921]

Performers
(Actors, Musicians, etc.)

ABDUL, PAULA

6959 Zannos, Susan. *Paula Abdul* (4–8). (Real-Life Reader Biography) 1999, Mitchell Lane LB $15.95 (1-883845-74-2). A brief biography of this choreographer and recording artist that recounts her many problems, including a struggle with bulimia and a series of failed marriages. (Rev: BL 6/1–15/99) [921]

AEROSMITH

6960 Huxley, Martin. *Aerosmith: The Fall and the Rise of Rock's Greatest Band* (9–12). 1995, St. Martin's paper $12.95 (0-312-11737-X). Picks up the Aerosmith story after their youth and looks at the elements of the rock group's rise to fame and fortune. (Rev: BL 3/1/95) [921]

ALLEN, TIM

6961 Wukovits, John. *Tim Allen* (6–9). Illus. (Overcoming Adversity) 1998, Chelsea paper $8.95 (0-7910-4697-4). A sympathetic portrait of the show business star who once went to jail for selling cocaine and rebounded to gain success on TV's *Home Improvement*. (Rev: SLJ 11/98) [921]

ALLEN, WOODY

6962 Brode, Douglas. *Woody Allen* (9–12). Illus. 1987, Carol paper $14.95 (0-8065-1067-6). Biographical details on this writer and comedian are given plus critical comment on his films through the mid-1980s. [921]

ALONSO, ALICIA

6963 Arnold, Sandra M. *Alicia Alonso: First Lady of the Ballet* (6–10). 1993, Walker LB $15.85 (0-8027-8243-4). Overcoming the lack of dance schools in her native Cuba and going blind in her 20s, Alicia Alonso became a prima ballerina and went on to teach, study, and perform in Cuba. (Rev: BL 12/15/93; SLJ 11/93; VOYA 2/94) [921]

ANDERSON, MARIAN

6964 Tedards, Anne. *Marian Anderson* (6–10). Illus. 1987, Chelsea LB $19.95 (1-55546-638-9). The life story of the great singer-artist who helped destroy many color barriers. (Rev: BL 2/1/88; SLJ 4/88) [921]

ARMSTRONG, LOUIS

6965 Collier, James L. *Louis Armstrong: An American Genius* (10–12). Illus. 1983, Oxford paper $22.50 (0-19-503727-8). A thoroughly researched biography of this jazz great who was also a popular entertainer. [921]

6966 Old, Wendie C. *Louis Armstrong: King of Jazz* (5–9). (African-American Biographies) 1998, Enslow LB $19.95 (0-89490-997-5). A biography of the legendary jazz trumpeter know as Satchmo who lived from 1900 to 1971. (Rev: BL 11/15/98; SLJ 11/98) [921]

6967 Tanenhaus, Sam. *Louis Armstrong* (7–10). Illus. 1989, Chelsea LB $19.95 (1-55546-571-4). The story of the black musician who rose from poverty in New Orleans to the heights of the jazz world. (Rev: BL 3/15/89) [921]

BALANCHINE, GEORGE

6968 Kristy, Davida. *George Balanchine: American Ballet Master* (6–9). Illus. 1996, Lerner LB $25.26 (0-8225-4951-4). A biography of the Russian-born choreographer who changed forever the ballet world through his work and the New York City Ballet he founded. (Rev: BL 9/1/96; SLJ 8/96) [921]

BARR, ROSEANNE

6969 Gaines, Ann. *Roseanne: Entertainer* (5–8). (Overcoming Adversity) 1999, Chelsea LB $19.95 (0-7910-4706-7); paper $8.95 (0-7910-4707-5). The story of how this overweight housewife made difficult decisions and many sacrifices to achieve her goal of becoming successful not just in show business, but in the difficult field of comedy, and later as a TV personality. (Rev: VOYA 8/98) [921]

BASIE, COUNT

6970 Kliment, Bud. *Count Basie* (7–10). (Black Americans of Achievement) 1992, Chelsea LB $19.95 (0-7910-1118-6). The story of this trailblazing band leader and his contributions to jazz and popular music. (Rev: BL 9/15/92) [781.65]

BEATLES (MUSICAL GROUP)

6971 DeWitt, Howard A. *The Beatles: Untold Tales* (9–12). Illus. 1985, Horizon paper $14.95 (0-938840-03-7). Based on over 50 interviews, this is a fine behind-the-scenes look at the lads from Liverpool. (Rev: SLJ 1/86) [921]

6972 Martin, Marvin. *The Beatles: The Music Was Never the Same* (7–9). Illus. (Impact Biographies) 1996, Watts LB $24.00 (0-531-11307-8). In spite of a rather plodding style, this is an attractive biography of the Mersey four, with emphasis on how they changed the course of pop music. (Rev: BL 2/1/97; SLJ 3/97) [921]

6973 Norman, Philip. *Shout! The Beatles in Their Generation* (9–12). 1983, Warner paper $4.95 (0-446-32255-5). A candid, honest portrayal of the rock group from Liverpool and of each of its 4 members. [920]

6974 Woog, Adam. *The Beatles* (4–8). (The Importance Of) 1997, Lucent LB $17.96 (1-56006-088-3). A work that outlines the lives and careers of these 4 Liverpool natives and their many achievements. (Rev: BL 10/15/97; SLJ 12/97) [921]

BEIDERBECKE, BIX

6975 Collins, David R. *Bix Beiderbecke: Jazz Age Genius* (7–12). Illus. (Notable Americans) 1998, Morgan Reynolds LB $18.95 (1-883846-36-6). This biography chronicles the rise and fall of the amazing jazz cornet player Bix Beiderbecke, who died of alcoholism at age 28. (Rev: BL 7/98; SLJ 1/99) [921]

BLADES, RUBÉN

6976 Cruz, Barbara C. *Ruben Blades: Salsa Singer and Social Activist* (5–9). (Hispanic Biographies) 1997, Enslow LB $19.95 (0-89490-893-6). The inspiring story of the Panama-born musician and his involvement in social activism and politics. (Rev: BR 5–6/98; SLJ 1/98; VOYA 2/98) [921]

6977 Marton, Betty A. *Rubén Blades* (5–9). (Hispanics of Achievement) 1992, Chelsea LB $19.95 (0-7910-1235-2). The story of this Panamanian salsa singer who is also a poet and activist. (Rev: BL 10/1/92; SLJ 11/92) [921]

BRANDY (PERFORMER)

6978 Nerz, A. Ryan. *Brandy* (5–8). Illus. (Scene) 1999, Aladdin paper $6.99 (0-689-82545-5). A fanzine treatment of this star's life and career. Also use *Jennifer Love Hewitt* (1999). (Rev: VOYA 6/99) [921]

BURKE, CHRIS

6979 Geraghty, Helen M. *Chris Burke* (5–9). (Great Achievers: Lives of the Physically Challenged) 1994, Chelsea LB $19.95 (0-7910-2081-9). This biography of the star of TV's *Life Goes On* looks at Burke's family life and career success despite Down's syndrome. (Rev: BL 10/15/94) [921]

BURNETT, CAROL

6980 Burnett, Carol. *One More Time* (9–12). Illus. 1987, Avon paper $4.95 (0-380-70449-8). Written in letter form to her daughters, the famous performer

talks about her life and rise to fame. (Rev: BR 3–4/87; SLJ 2/87) [921]

CAREY, MARIAH

6981 Cole, Melanie. *Mariah Carey* (5–10). (A Real-Life Reader Biography) 1997, Mitchell Lane LB $15.95 (1-883845-51-3). For hi-lo collections, this biography of the popular singer tells of her difficulties in reaching the top and of her career since then. (Rev: BL 6/1–15/98; SLJ 2/98) [921]

6982 Nickson, Chris. *Mariah Carey: Her Story* (8–10). 1995, St. Martin's paper $9.95 (0-312-13121-6). Traces Carey's rise to stardom, while avoiding depravity, excess, and mania. (Rev: BL 6/1–15/95) [921]

CARREY, JIM

6983 Wukovits, John. *Jim Carrey* (7–10). (People in the News) 1999, Lucent LB $107.76 (1-56006-561-3). From his boyhood in Canada to stardom in such movies as *The Truman Show* this biography reveals Carrey's efforts to become a multidimensional actor. (Rev: BL 8/99) [921]

CASALS, PABLO

6984 Garza, Hedda. *Pablo Casals* (5–9). (Hispanics of Achievement) 1993, Chelsea LB $19.95 (0-7910-1237-9). The story of the legendary Spanish cellist and his exile from his homeland during Franco's regime. (Rev: BL 4/1/93; SLJ 7/93; VOYA 8/93) [921]

CHAPLIN, CHARLIE

6985 Schroeder, Alan. *Charlie Chaplin: The Beauty of Silence* (7–12). (Impact Biographies) 1997, Watts LB $24.00 (0-531-11317-5); paper $9.95 (0-531-15864-0). This biography recreates a history of Hollywood in its golden days, while capturing the life and work of this comic artist who was able through his art and technique to explore the relationship between tragedy and humor in his films. (Rev: BL 6/1–15/97; SLJ 6/97) [921]

CHARLES, RAY

6986 Ritz, David. *Ray Charles: Voice of Soul* (6–10). 1994, Chelsea LB $19.95 (0-7910-2080-0); paper $8.95 (0-7910-2093-2). The story of Ray Charles Robinson, who overcame the hardships of poverty, racism, drug addiction, and blindness to become one of America's most influential musicians. (Rev: BL 11/15/94) [921]

6987 Turk, Ruth. *Ray Charles: Soul Man* (5–8). (Newsmakers) 1996, Lerner LB $25.26 (0-8225-4928-X). A candid biography of the great blind entertainer that includes compelling details about his childhood. (Rev: SLJ 8/96) [921]

CLAPTON, ERIC

6988 Coleman, Ray. *Clapton!* (9–12). 1988, Warner paper $14.95 (0-446-38630-8). A biography of the famous rock guitarist from late adolescence to the mid-1980s. (Rev: SLJ 1/87) [921]

6989 Schumacher, Michael. *Crossroads: The Life and Music of Eric Clapton* (9–12). 1995, Hyperion $24.95 (0-7868-6074-X). A biography of British rock star Eric Clapton. (Rev: BL 4/1/95) [787.87]

COSBY, BILL

6990 Schuman, Michael A. *Bill Cosby: Actor and Comedian* (6–12). (People to Know) 1995, Enslow LB $17.95 (0-89490-548-1). Describes the life and career of one of the most successful comedians in modern times. (Rev: BL 9/15/95; SLJ 2/96; VOYA 2/96) [921]

6991 Smith, Ronald L. *Cosby: The Life of a Comedy Legend.* rev. ed. (10–12). 1997, Prometheus $25.95 (1-57392-126-2). A serious, adult look at Cosby's life, from his early childhood through his climb to fame. The book ends with the tragic death of his son, Ennis. (Rev: BL 2/1/97; SLJ 11/97) [921]

CRONKITE, WALTER

6992 Cronkite, Walter. *A Reporter's Life* (10–12). 1996, Knopf $26.95 (0-394-57879-1). A memoir by one of America's most respected journalists, with material on the important stories he covered, including World War II, the Vietnam War, and the Apollo space program. (Rev: BL 11/1/96; SLJ 7/97) [921]

CRUISE, TOM

6993 Powell, Phelan. *Tom Cruise* (6–9). (Overcoming Adversity) 1999, Chelsea LB $19.95 (0-7910-4940-X); paper $9.95 (0-7910-4941-8). The story of this famous actor, his struggle with dyslexia and his parents' divorce, and his eventual fame in film. (Rev: BL 5/15/99) [921]

DAMON, MATT

6994 Busch, Kristen. *Golden Boy* (6–12). 1998, Ballantine paper $5.99 (0-345-42816-1). This is a well-researched, fun read about Matt Damon, the young star who was co-author and star of *Good Will Hunting* and star of *Saving Private Ryan*. (Rev: VOYA 12/98) [921]

6995 Diamond, Maxine, with Harriet Hemmings. *Matt Damon: A Biography* (6–12). 1998, Pocket Books paper $4.50 (0-671-02649-6). A fast read that gives a well-researched look at this likable, multital-ented young movie star, with plenty of off-screen gossip. (Rev: VOYA 12/98) [921]

6996 Scott, Kieran. *Matt Damon* (5–8). Illus. (Scene) 1999, Aladdin paper $6.99 (0-689-82405-X). A fan magazine treatment of this popular young actor's life and career, with many color photographs. Also use *James van der Beek* (1999). (Rev: VOYA 6/99) [921]

DAVIS, MILES

6997 Crisp, George. *Miles Davis* (9–12). (Impact Biographies) 1997, Watts LB $24.00 (0-531-11319-1). The amazing life of this jazz great who was a trumpeter, bandleader, and composer, as well as a great influence on the course of jazz history. (Rev: BL 5/15/97; SLJ 7/97) [921]

6998 Frankl, Ron. *Miles Davis* (7–10). (Black Americans of Achievement) 1995, Chelsea LB $19.95 (0-7910-2156-4). The story of the famous African American trumpeter and his contributions to jazz. (Rev: BL 11/15/95) [921]

DICAPRIO, LEONARDO

6999 Catalano, Grace. *Leonardo DiCaprio: Modern-Day Romeo* (5–9). 1997, Dell paper $4.99 (0-440-22701-1). A pre-*Titanic* look at the teen heartthrob, with details on his career. (Rev: VOYA 10/97) [921]

7000 Stauffer, Stacey. *Leonardo DiCaprio* (5–8). Illus. (Galaxy of Superstars) 1999, Chelsea $16.95 (0-7910-5151-X). The rise of this young superstar is chronicled with material on his movies, particularly *Titanic*. (Rev: BL 4/15/99; BR 9–10/99; SLJ 5/99) [921]

7001 Thompson, Douglas. *Leonardo DiCaprio* (6–12). 1998, Berkley paper $11.95 (0-425-16752-6). Sixty color photographs highlight this tribute to the young actor's life through *Titanic* and *Man in the Iron Mask*. (Rev: BR 11–12/98; VOYA 10/98) [921]

DOMINGO, PLÁCIDO

7002 Stefoff, Rebecca. *Plácido Domingo* (5–9). (Hispanics of Achievement) 1992, Chelsea LB $19.95 (0-7910-1563-7). The story of the amazing Spanish-born tenor and his sensational international career, with some information on his private life. (Rev: BL 12/1/92; SLJ 1/93) [921]

DYLAN, BOB

7003 Richardson, Susan. *Bob Dylan* (7–12). (Pop Culture Legends) 1995, Chelsea LB $19.95 (0-7910-2335-4); paper $9.95 (0-7910-2360-5). The life of this creative icon who influenced both country and pop music. (Rev: BL 8/95) [921]

EDWARDS, HONEYBOY

7004 Edwards, David H. *The World Don't Owe Me Nothing: The Life & Times of Delta Bluesman Honeyboy Edwards* (10–12). Illus. 1997, Chicago Review $24.00 (1-55652-275-4). The biography of a black traveling country-blues musician that chronicles the brutality he suffered because of his class and color and recounts his experiences with gambling, romance, and classic blues artists over 65-plus years. (Rev: SLJ 5/98) [921]

ELLINGTON, DUKE

7005 Dance, Stanley. *The World of Duke Ellington* (10–12). Illus. 1970, Da Capo paper $12.95 (0-306-80136-1). Based on a series of interviews, this is a portrait of Duke Ellington, the people around him, and the world of jazz. [921]

7006 Frankl, Ron. *Duke Ellington: Bandleader and Composer* (6–10). Illus. 1988, Chelsea LB $19.95 (1-55546-584-6). The story of the evolution of a great composer and of his life in music. (Rev: BR 1–2/89; SLJ 8/88) [921]

7007 Old, Wendie C. *Duke Ellington: Giant of Jazz* (7–12). (African-American Biographies) 1996, Enslow LB $19.95 (0-89490-691-7). An attractive biography of this giant of jazz who was a brilliant composer and arranger as well as an outstanding performer. (Rev: BL 9/15/96) [921]

ESTEFAN, GLORIA

7008 Gonzales, Doreen. *Gloria Estefan: Singer & Entertainer* (5–9). (Hispanic Biographies) 1998, Enslow LB $19.95 (0-89490-890-1). This story of the singer who started with the Miami Sound Machine and then branched out as a soloist also reveals her devotion to her family and many social causes. (Rev: BR 9–10/98; SLJ 10/98; VOYA 10/98) [921]

7009 Rodriguez, Janel. *Gloria Estefan* (4–8). Illus. (Contemporary Hispanic Americans) 1995, Raintree Steck-Vaughn LB $24.26 (0-8172-3982-0). A fine biography of this Cuban American entertainer who, at the height of her career, overcame severe medical problems and remained a star singer. (Rev: BL 3/15/96; SLJ 1/96) [921]

7010 Stefoff, Rebecca. *Gloria Estefan* (5–9). (Hispanics of Achievement) 1991, Chelsea LB $19.95 (0-7910-1244-1). An account that traces the singer from her birth in Cuba through her career success with the Miami Sound Machine. (Rev: BL 8/91; SLJ 12/91) [782.42164]

FONDA, JANE

7011 Shorto, Russell. *Jane Fonda: Political Activism* (6–12). (New Directions) 1991, Millbrook LB $21.90 (1-56294-045-7). The life of actress, activist, and entrepreneur Fonda portrays her strong beliefs and deep involvement in controversial political and environmental issues, set against the backdrop of tumultuous times. (Rev: BL 10/1/91; SLJ 10/91) [921]

FRANKLIN, ARETHA

7012 Gourse, Leslie. *Aretha Franklin, Lady Soul* (7–10). 1995, Watts LB $24.00 (0-531-13037-1). A biography of the now-legendary singer that recalls the problems in her life, including the disappearance of her mother when she was 6, as well as her many concert triumphs. (Rev: SLJ 10/95; VOYA 2/96) [921]

7013 Sheafer, Silvia A. *Aretha Franklin: Motown Superstar* (6–10). (African American Biographies) 1996, Enslow LB $19.95 (0-89490-686-0). The life story of one of America's most popular singers is told, accompanied by a discography, chronology, and index. (Rev: BL 12/15/96; SLJ 9/96) [921]

GALAN, NELY

7014 *Nely Galan* (4–8). Illus. (Contemporary Hispanic Americans) 1997, Raintree Steck-Vaughn LB $24.26 (0-8172-3991-X). The life of this contemporary Hispanic American who, as a Hollywood producer, is responsible for developing TV and video projects for other Hispanic Americans. (Rev: BL 4/15/97) [921]

GILLESPIE, DIZZY

7015 Gourse, Leslie. *Dizzy Gillespie and the Birth of Bebop* (6–10). 1994, Atheneum $14.95 (0-689-31869-3). Bebop became a national music trend due in part to the influence of this trumpet-playing jazz legend. (Rev: BL 1/1/95; SLJ 3/95) [921]

GOLDBERG, WHOOPI

7016 Blue, Rose, and Corinne J. Naden. *Whoopi Goldberg* (7–10). (Black Americans of Achievement) 1995, Chelsea LB $19.95 (0-7910-2152-1); paper $8.95 (0-7910-2153-X). A biography that tells how in spite of great odds, this unusual comedian and actress rose to the top. (Rev: BL 3/15/95) [921]

7017 Gaines, Ann. *Whoopi Goldberg* (6–9). (Overcoming Adversity) 1999, Chelsea LB $19.95 (0-7910-4938-8); paper $9.95 (0-7910-4939-6). The story of Whoopi Goldberg, her struggle with dyslexia, and how she dropped out of school at the age of 13 and turned to a life of drugs and sex before finding acting and a new life. (Rev: BL 5/15/99) [921]

7018 Katz, Sandor. *Whoopi Goldberg: Performer with a Heart* (5–8). (Junior Black Americans of Achievement) 1996, Chelsea $15.95 (0-7910-2396-

6). A look at Whoopi Goldberg's life and career, focusing on how she feels about her profession and the causes she believes in. (Rev: BL 10/15/96; SLJ 1/97) [921]

GRAHAM, MARTHA

7019 Freedman, Russell. *Martha Graham: A Dancer's Life* (4–8). 1998, Clarion $18.00 (0-395-74655-8). Martha Graham's amazing talents, her driving force, and her complex personality are well depicted in this handsomely illustrated biography. (Rev: BL 4/1/98; SLJ 5/98; VOYA 8/98) [921]

7020 Newman, Gerald, and Eleanor N. Layfield. *Martha Graham: Founder of Modern Dance* (6–9). (Book Report Biographies) 1998, Watts $22.00 (0-531-11442-2). Using many quotes from Martha Graham, this is a serviceable introduction to the life of this great dancer and choreographer. (Rev: BL 1/1–15/99) [921]

7021 Pratt, Paula B. *Martha Graham* (5–8). (The Importance Of) 1995, Lucent LB $22.45 (1-56006-056-5). A description of the life of this dance giant and her lasting impact on the world of dance. (Rev: BL 1/15/95; SLJ 1/95) [921]

7022 Probosz, Kathilyn S. *Martha Graham* (6–10). (People in Focus) 1995, Silver Burdett paper $7.95 (0-382-24961-5). With high-quality photos, the book tells about Graham's life and her contributions to dance. (Rev: BL 8/95; SLJ 10/95) [921]

HANSON (MUSICAL GROUP)

7023 Matthews, Jill. *Hanson: Mmmbop to the Top* (5–9). 1997, Pocket Books paper $3.99 (0-671-01913-9). Hard work is emphasized, along with lots of material on each of the 3 brothers who became the popular band, Hanson. (Rev: VOYA 10/98) [921]

7024 Powell, Phelan. *Hanson* (5–8). (Galaxy of Superstars) 1999, Chelsea $16.95 (0-7910-5148-X); paper $9.95 (0-7910-5325-3). An attractive volume that contains biographies of the 3-brother singing group that hails from Tulsa, Oklahoma. (Rev: BL 4/15/99; BR 9–10/99) [921]

HELGOFF, DAVID

7025 Helfgott, Gillian, and Alissa Tanskaya. *Love You to Bits and Pieces: Life with David Helfgott* (10–12). 1997, Penguin paper $11.95 (0-14-026644-5). The story, by his wife, of the brilliant Australian pianist David Helgott, who was institutionalized for 12 years after suffering a complete mental breakdown and whose life inspired the movie *Shine*. (Rev: SLJ 6/97) [921]

HENDRIX, JIMI

7026 Piccoli, Sean. *Jimi Hendrix* (6–9). 1996, Chelsea LB $19.95 (0-7910-2042-8); paper $14.93 (0-7910-2284-6). An objective account of Hendrix's phenomenal music career and the unfortunate circumstances surrounding his death. (Rev: SLJ 11/96) [921]

7027 Stockdale, Tom. *Jimi Hendrix* (7–9). Illus. (They Died Too Young) 1999, Chelsea LB $15.95 (0-7910-4632-X). Early musical influences, career-related events, and the effects of drugs and alcohol are covered in this biography of the entertainer and singer whose career highlights included a tour in 1968 and a performance at Woodstock. (Rev: SLJ 7/98) [921]

HENSON, JIM

7028 Finch, Christopher. *Jim Henson: The Works* (9–12). 1993, Random $40.00 (0-679-41203-4). Traces the career of the creator of the Muppets from local television in the 1950s through the triumph of *Sesame Street* and his experimental work. (Rev: BL 1/15/94) [921]

HOLIDAY, BILLIE

7029 Kliment, Bud. *Billie Holiday* (8–12). Illus. 1990, Chelsea LB $19.95 (1-55546-592-7). A stirring biography of one of the great ladies of song whose life ended tragically. (Rev: BL 2/15/90; SLJ 5/90; VOYA 5/90) [921]

7030 Nicholson, Stuart. *Billie Holiday* (9–12). 1995, Northeastern Univ. Pr. $42.50 (1-55553-248-9). A careful, factual account of the singer's tumultuous life. (Rev: BL 10/15/95) [782.42165]

HOUDINI, HARRY

7031 Brandon, Ruth. *The Life and Many Deaths of Harry Houdini* (9–12). 1994, Random $25.00 (0-679-42437-7). A biography of the escape artist, revealing his perfectionism, his obsession with death, and many of the secrets to his daring feats. (Rev: BL 9/15/94*; SLJ 5/95) [912]

7032 Woog, Adam. *Harry Houdini* (5–8). (The Importance Of) 1995, Lucent LB $22.45 (1-56006-053-0). Houdini's life story, demonstrating his lasting importance in the history of magic. (Rev: BL 1/15/95; SLJ 1/95) [793.8]

HOUSTON, WHITNEY

7033 Cox, Ted. *Whitney Houston: Singer Actress* (5–8). Illus. (Black Americans of Achievement) 1997, Chelsea LB $19.95 (0-7910-4455-6); paper $9.95 (0-7910-4456-4). A readable biography that tells of Whitney Houston growing up in New Jersey, the major influences in her life, her rise to fame, marriage, and philanthropic endeavors. (Rev: BL 8/98) [921]

HOWARD, RON

7034 Kramer, Barbara. *Ron Howard: Child Star & Hollywood Director* (7–10). (People to Know) 1998, Enslow $18.95 (0-89490-981-9). Using many photos of Howard at work, this book traces his career from sitcoms like *Happy Days* to becoming the director of such fine films as *Apollo 13*. (Rev: BL 2/15/99; SLJ 3/99) [921]

IGLESIAS, JULIO

7035 Martino, Elizabeth. *Julio Iglesias* (5–9). (Hispanics of Achievement) 1994, Chelsea LB $19.95 (0-7910-2017-7). The life story of this singer, who is a favorite on both sides of the Atlantic. (Rev: BL 9/15/94) [921]

JACKSON, MAHALIA

7036 Gourse, Leslie. *Mahalia Jackson: Queen of Gospel Song* (6–10). Illus. (Impact Biographies) 1996, Watts LB $24.00 (0-531-11228-4). Although she could have been a famous blues singer, Mahalia Jackson devoted her life to religious music and became the "Queen of Gospel Soul." (Rev: BL 8/96; BR 11–12/96; SLJ 8/96) [921]

JACKSON, MICHAEL

7037 Nicholson, Lois. *Michael Jackson* (5–8). (Black Americans of Achievement) 1994, Chelsea LB $19.95 (0-7910-1929-2); paper $9.95 (0-7910-1930-6). A biography of the pop star that examines his loneliness, his family ties, and the allegations against him of sexual abuse. (Rev: BL 10/15/94; SLJ 10/94) [921]

7038 Taraborelli, J. Randy. *Michael Jackson: The Magic and the Madness* (9–12). 1991, Birch Lane $21.95 (1-55972-064-6). An adult biography that probes into the public and personal life of this talented, controversial entertainer. (Rev: BL 4/15/91) [921]

JEWEL (PERFORMER)

7039 Kemp, Kristen. *Jewel: Pieces of a Dream* (6–10). 1998, Simon & Schuster paper $4.99 (0-671-02455-8). A somewhat sanitized version of the life of the phenomenal Jewel, musician and songwriter, that tells about her rugged childhood in Alaska; overcoming dyslexia; yodeling in bars with her folk-singing parents; a year in an exclusive boarding school; living out of a VW van while singing in coffee shops; and the release of her first successful CD. (Rev: SLJ 4/99) [921]

JOHN, ELTON

7040 Crimp, Susan, and Patricia Burstein. *The Many Lives of Elton John* (10–12). 1992, Birch Lane $19.95 (1-55972-111-1). An intimate glimpse into the singer's life, for mature readers. (Rev: BL 4/15/92) [Y]

7041 Norman, Philip. *Elton John* (9–12). 1992, Crown $22.50 (0-517-58762-9). An exhaustive biography of the legendary pop/rock musician by a celebrated rock journalist. (Rev: BL 12/15/91) [921]

JONES, JAMES EARL

7042 Hasday, Judy. *James Earl Jones: Actor* (7–10). Illus. (Overcoming Adversity) 1999, Chelsea LB $19.95 (0-7910-4702-4). A story of the great African American actor, noted for his deep, resonant voice, who conquered stuttering and muteness as a child. (Rev: SLJ 8/98; VOYA 8/98) [921]

JULIA, RAUL

7043 Perez, Frank, and Ann Weil. *Raul Julia* (4–8). Illus. (Contemporary Hispanic Americans) 1995, Raintree Steck-Vaughn LB $24.26 (0-8172-3984-7). The story of the brilliant stage and film actor who gained fame in *The Addams Family* and appearances on *Sesame Street*. This biography was written before his untimely death. (Rev: BL 3/15/96; SLJ 1/96) [921]

7044 Stefoff, Rebecca. *Raul Julia* (6–9). (Hispanics of Achievement) 1994, Chelsea LB $19.95 (0-7910-1556-4). A biography of the late Puerto Rican actor, describing his theater and film work, his involvement with the Hunger Project, and his battle against ethnic stereotyping. (Rev: BL 10/1/94; SLJ 8/94) [792]

LANG, K. D.

7045 Martinac, Paula. *k.d. lang* (9–12). (Lives of Notable Gay Men and Lesbians) 1996, Chelsea LB $19.95 (0-7910-2872-0); paper $9.95 (0-7910-2899-2). A highly readable biography of this successful Canadian country/jazz/rock singer's life that traces her rise to stardom, with emphasis on her creative genius, her down-to-earth personality, and her many facets as an individual, rather than her sexuality. (Rev: SLJ 11/96; VOYA 4/97) [921]

LATIFAH, QUEEN

7046 Latifah, Queen, and Karen Hunter. *Ladies First: Revelations of a Strong Woman* (10–12). 1999, Morrow $22.00 (0-688-15623-1). An honest, candid book by this actress and rapper who tells about her life, strength, faith in God, and problems as well as giving advice about drugs, sex, and men. (Rev: BL 1/1–15/99; SLJ 5/99) [921]

LEE, SPIKE

7047 Hardy, James Earl. *Spike Lee* (7–10). (Black Americans of Achievement) 1995, Chelsea LB $19.95 (0-7910-1875-X); paper $9.95 (0-7910-1904-7). The story of the African American film producer and director who has fought for the right to express his ideas in a tough motion picture world. (Rev: BL 11/15/95; SLJ 12/95) [921]

7048 Haskins, Jim. *Spike Lee: By Any Means Necessary* (6–10). Illus. 1997, Walker LB $16.85 (0-8027-8496-8). Compiling previously published biographical material, the author has produced an interesting profile of this important African American film maker, including a behind-the-cameras view of each of Lee's 10 films to see what it takes to make a movie. (Rev: BL 5/1/97; SLJ 6/97; VOYA 10/97) [921]

7049 McDaniel, Melissa. *Spike Lee: On His Own Terms* (6–9). (Book Report Biographies) 1999, Watts $6.95 (0-531-15935-3). The story of Spike Lee's devotion to making quality films is traced from his childhood in New York City, through film school, to becoming an independent filmmaker. (Rev: BL 2/15/99; SLJ 12/98) [921]

LENNON, JOHN

7050 Conord, Bruce W. *John Lennon* (7–12). (Pop Culture Legends) 1993, Chelsea LB $19.95 (0-7910-1739-7); paper $9.95 (0-7910-1740-0). Looks at Lennon's childhood in Liverpool, his career with the Beatles, and his life after their breakup. (Rev: BL 12/15/93; SLJ 11/93) [921]

7051 Wiener, Jon. *Come Together: John Lennon in His Time* (9–12). 1990, Univ. of Illinois Pr. $18.95 (0-252-06131-4). This biography of John Lennon gives many insights into the 1960s and the important issues of that time. [921]

7052 Wright, David K. *John Lennon: The Beatles and Beyond* (6–10). (People to Know) 1996, Enslow LB $19.95 (0-89490-702-6). This biography of the legendary founder of one of the most popular music groups of all time explores Lennon's background and his development as a songwriter and as a political activist, as well as recounting the history of the Beatles. (Rev: BL 10/15/96; SLJ 12/96; VOYA 2/97) [921]

LETTERMAN, DAVID

7053 Lefkowitz, Frances. *David Letterman* (7–9). (Pop Culture Legends) 1996, Chelsea LB $19.95 (0-7910-3252-3); paper $9.95 (0-7910-3253-1). This show business biography traces Letterman's career and the evolution of his style, with an emphasis on entertainers who influenced him. (Rev: SLJ 12/96) [921]

LUCAS, GEORGE

7054 Rau, Dana Meachen, and Christopher Rau. *George Lucas: Creator of Star Wars* (5–8). (Book Report Biographies) 1999, Watts $22.00 (0-531-11457-0). A story of the popular filmmaker's life and accomplishments, illustrated with black-and-white photographs. (Rev: SLJ 7/99) [921]

MCKAY, JIM

7055 McPhee, Jim. *The Real McKay: My Wide World of Sports* (10–12). 1998, NAL $24.95 (0-525-94418-4). The autobiography of the famous sportscaster, in which he shares his personal views and memories of the many notable events and people he covered, such as successful golfers and the many Olympic Games, including the tragedy in Munich in 1972. (Rev: SLJ 9/98) [921]

MADONNA

7056 Claro, Nicole. *Madonna* (7–10). (Pop Culture Legends) 1994, Chelsea LB $18.95 (0-7910-2330-3); paper $7.95 (0-7910-2355-9). Examines the pop diva's childhood, the early death of her mother, her rise to stardom, her love affairs, and her controversial personality. (Rev: BL 10/15/94; SLJ 11/94; VOYA 12/94) [021]

MARLEY, BOB

7057 Boot, Adrian, and Chris Slaewicz. *Bob Marley: Songs of Freedom* (9–12). 1995, Viking paper $34.95 (0-670-85784-X). A review of the life and career of Jamaican Bob Marley. (Rev: BL 4/15/95) [921]

7058 Dolan, Sean. *Bob Marley* (6–9). (Black Americans of Achievement) 1996, Chelsea LB $19.95 (0-7910-2041-X); paper $9.95 (0-7910-3255-8). The life story of the Jamaican entertainer, with historical background about his island home. (Rev: SLJ 11/96) [921]

7059 Taylor, Don. *Marley and Me: The Real Bob Marley* (9–12). 1995, Barricade Books paper $14.95 (1-56980-044-8). Marley's business manager sheds light on the complexities of this charismatic reggae musician's life. (Rev: BL 9/1/95) [921]

MARSALIS, WYNTON

7060 Marsalis, Wynton. *Sweet Swing Blues on the Road* (9–12). 1994, Norton $29.95 (0-393-03514-X). Jazz musician and composer Marsalis takes the reader with him and his band on their travels around the world. (Rev: BL 12/15/94) [788.9]

MARX, GROUCHO

7061 Tyson, Peter. *Groucho Marx* (7–12). Illus. (Pop Culture Legends) 1995, Chelsea $18.95 (07910-2341-9). The story of Groucho Marx, from his childhood on the Lower East Side of Manhattan to stardom with his brothers and, lastly, to fame as a quiz show host. (Rev: BL 7/95) [921]

MONROE, MARILYN

7062 Krohn, Katherine E. *Marilyn Monroe: Norma Jeane's Dream* (6–9). (Newsmakers Biographies) 1997, Lerner LB $25.26 (0-8225-4930-1). A well-illustrated biography that gives a good overview of the actress's life without probing into the mystery surrounding her death. (Rev: SLJ 7/97) [921]

7063 Lefkowitz, Frances. *Marilyn Monroe* (7–12). (Pop Culture Legends) 1995, Chelsea LB $19.95 (0-7910-2342-7); paper $9.95 (0-7910-2367-2). The story of the Hollywood star who, despite immense popularity, lived a tragic life. (Rev: BL 8/95) [921]

7064 Woog, Adam. *Marilyn Monroe* (6–10). (Mysterious Deaths) 1996, Lucent LB $22.45 (1-56006-265-7). After a brief overview of the star's life and career, this account describes her last night alive, and the many theories surrounding her death. (Rev: SLJ 3/97; VOYA 8/97) [921]

MORENO, RITA

7065 Suntree, Susan. *Rita Moreno* (5–9). (Hispanics of Achievement) 1992, Chelsea LB $19.95 (0-7910-1247-6). A biography of the Peurto Rican entertainer and her successes on stage and screen. (Rev: BL 2/1/93) [921]

MORRISON, JIM

7066 Lewis, Jon E. *Jim Morrison* (7–9). Illus. (They Died Too Young) 1997, Chelsea LB $15.95 (0-7910-4631-1). The great talent of this rock legend is highlighted in this biography that does not minimize the effects of drugs and alcohol. (Rev: SLJ 7/98) [921]

MURPHY, EDDIE

7067 Wilburn, Deborah A. *Eddie Murphy* (7–10). (Black Americans of Achievement) 1993, Chelsea LB $19.95 (0-7910-1879-2); paper $7.95 (0-7910-1908-X). A nicely illustrated introduction to the life of this talented actor/comedian. (Rev: BL 1/1/94; SLJ 1/94) [921]

NIMOY, LEONARD

7068 Nimoy, Leonard. *I Am Spock* (9–12). 1995, Hyperion $24.95 (0-7868-6182-7). This entertaining memoir of Nimoy's years with *Star Trek* follows his book, *I Am Not Spock,* by 20 years. (Rev: BL 9/15/95) [921]

O'DONNELL, ROSIE

7069 Kallen, Stuart A. *Rosie O'Donnell* (4–8). (People in the News) 1999, Lucent LB $23.70 (1-56006-546-X). A well-researched biography of this popular television star that gives forthright information in an accessible format. (Rev: BL 8/99) [921]

7070 Krohn, Katherine E. *Rosie O'Donnell* (4–8). (A and E Biography) 1998, Lerner $25.26 (0-8225-4939-5). A breezy biography of the stand-up comedian who became a movie star, talk show host, and pop idol with glimpses into her personal life and her fulfilling experience of adopting 2 children. (Rev: SLJ 2/99) [921]

OAKLEY, ANNIE

7071 Flynn, Jean. *Annie Oakley: Legendary Sharpshooter* (5–8). (Historical American Biographies) 1998, Enslow LB $18.95 (0-7600-1012-0). Using a concise text, fact boxes, and a chronology, this is the story of the star attraction of Buffalo Bill's Wild West Show. (Rev: BL 8/98) [921]

7072 Riley, Glenda. *The Life and Legacy of Annie Oakley* (9–12). 1994, Univ. of Oklahoma Pr. $24.95 (0-8061-2656-6). A biography of the sharpshooter of Buffalo Bill Cody's Wild West Show, describing her personal and professional accomplishments in historical, cultural, and sociological contexts. (Rev: BL 10/1/94) [921]

7073 Sayers, Isabelle S. *Annie Oakley and Buffalo Bill's Wild West* (9–12). Illus. 1981, Dover paper $6.95 (0-486-24120-3). Through a number of old photographs, the life of this sharp-shooter is re-created. [921]

7074 Wukovits, John. *Annie Oakley* (4–8). (Legends of the West) 1997, Chelsea LB $16.95 (0-7910-3906-4). A personalized account of the life of the famous sharpshooter and her career with Buffalo Bill's Wide West Show. (Rev: SLJ 10/97) [921]

OLMOS, EDWARD JAMES

7075 *Edward James Olmos* (4–8). Illus. (Contemporary Hispanic Americans) 1997, Raintree Steck-Vaughn LB $24.26 (0-8172-3989-8). Along with a time line and glossary, this book traces the life of this contemporary human rights activist and actor. (Rev: BL 4/15/97) [921]

PARKER, CHARLIE

7076 Frankl, Ron. *Charlie Parker* (7–10). (Black Americans of Achievement) 1992, Chelsea LB $19.95 (0-7910-1134-8). The story of the "Bird," his alto sax, and his contributions to jazz, particularly bebop. (Rev: BL 2/1/93) [921]

PAVAROTTI, LUCIANO

7077 Pavarotti, Luciano, and William Wright. *Pavarotti: My World* (9–12). 1995, Crown $25.00 (0-517-70027-1). The great tenor Pavarotti writes of his career and life, including his happiest and saddest moments. (Rev: BL 9/1/95) [921]

PITT, BRAD

7078 Dempsey, Amy. *Brad Pitt* (6–8). Illus. (Superstars of Film) 1999, Chelsea LB $15.95 (0-7910-4649-4). An easy-to-read biography about the teen idol and the hard work and seized opportunities that made him a star. (Rev: SLJ 10/98) [921]

PRESLEY, ELVIS

7079 Daily, Robert. *Elvis Presley: The King of Rock 'n' Roll* (6–9). (Impact Biographies) 1996, Watts LB $24.00 (0-531-11288-8). An objective account that takes Elvis from a 2-room shack in Tupelo, Mississippi, to the splendor of Graceland. (Rev: BL 4/1/97; SLJ 2/97) [921]

7080 Gentry, Tony. *Elvis Presley* (7–12). (Pop Culture Legends) 1994, Chelsea LB $19.95 (0-7910-2329-X); paper $8.95 (0-7910-2354-0). The life of the "King" is re-created in this nicely illustrated biography. (Rev: BL 9/15/94) [921]

7081 Kricun, Morrie E., and Virginia M. Kricun. *Elvis 1956 Reflections* (9–12). 1992, Morgin Pr. $49.95 (0-9630976-0-1). Follows Presley in 1956, an important year in his life and career. (Rev: BL 9/15/92) [782.42166]

7082 Woog, Adam. *Elvis Presley* (4–8). Illus. (The Importance Of) 1997, Lucent LB $16.95 (1-56006-084-0). The life of this famous rocker and his lasting influence on popular music are covered in this biography. (Rev: BL 1/1–15/97; BR 9–10/97; SLJ 1/97) [921]

QUINN, ANTHONY

7083 Amdur, Melissa. *Anthony Quinn* (5–9). (Hispanics of Achievement) 1993, Chelsea LB $19.95 (0-7910-1251-4). The story of this famous movie star who was born in Chihuahua, Mexico, in 1915 and has appeared in over 100 films. (Rev: BL 9/15/93) [921]

REEVE, CHRISTOPHER

7084 Finn, Margaret L. *Christopher Reeve: Actor & Activist* (6–10). 1997, Chelsea LB $19.95 (0-7910-4446-7); paper $8.95 (0-7910-4447-5). The story of the gallant film actor, his tragic accident, and the

causes he champions. (Rev: BR 5–6/98; VOYA 2/98) [921]

7085 Howard, Megan. *Christopher Reeve* (6–9). 1999, Lerner $25.26 (0-8225-4945-X). This is an inspiring portrait of the film star, his career, and the emotional and physical hardships he faced following his crippling horse-riding accident. Despite limitations and initial depression, Reeve has learned to focus on what he can do, rather than on what he can't. (Rev: BL 8/99) [921]

RIMES, LEANN

7086 Catalano, Grace. *LeAnn Rimes: Teen Country Queen* (5–8). 1997, Dell paper $4.99 (0-440-22737-2). In fanzine-like prose, this is an introduction to country music's hot young star. (Rev: VOYA 10/97) [921]

7087 Sgammato, Jo. *Dream Come True: The LeAnn Rimes Story* (5–8). 1997, Ballantine paper $4.99 (0-345-41650-3). Still in her teens, LeAnn Rimes is a country music phenomenon whose life is described here, with details on the country music circuit. (Rev: VOYA 10/97) [921]

7088 Zymet, Cathy Alter. *LeAnn Rimes* (5–8). (Galaxy of Superstars) 1999, Chelsea $16.95 (0-7910-5152-8); paper $9.95 (0-7910-5327-X). This book covers the rise to stardom and career of the country western singer who hails from Jackson, Mississippi. (Rev: BL 4/15/99; BR 9–10/99) [921]

ROBESON, PAUL

7089 Ehrlich, Scott. *Paul Robeson: Singer and Actor* (7–10). Illus. 1988, Chelsea LB $19.95 (1-55546-608-7). A biography of this talented actor, singer, and athlete whose career suffered for his civil rights activities and Communist affiliations. (Rev: BL 2/1/88; SLJ 5/88) [921]

7090 Larsen, Rebecca. *Paul Robeson: Hero before His Time* (7–12). Illus. 1989, Watts LB $24.00 (0-531-10779-5). The life of this controversial singer, actor, and civil rights pioneer. (Rev: BL 10/15/89; BR 3–4/90; SLJ 12/89; VOYA 2/90) [921]

7091 Robeson, Susan. *The Whole World in His Hands* (9–12). Illus. 1981, Citadel $17.95 (0-8065-0754-3); paper $14.95 (0-8065-0977-5). An album of photographs with captions from Paul Robeson's own words that describe his life, career, and persecutions. (Rev: BL 10/15/88) [921]

7092 Stewart, Jeffrey C., ed. *Paul Robeson: Artist and Citizen* (10–12). 1998, Rutgers Univ. Pr. $40.00 (0-8135-2510-1); paper $22.00 (0-8135-2511-X). A well-organized, skillfully designed collection of essays that offers a deep look at the famous African American performing artist, film actor, college athlete, political and civil rights activist, and government target, bringing out the complexity of Robeson's life and his many contributions. (Rev: BL 2/15/98; SLJ 2/99) [921]

7093 Wright, David K. *Paul Robeson: Actor, Singer, Political Activist* (5–9). (African American Biographies) 1998, Enslow LB $19.95 (0-89490-944-4). This book details Robeson's personal and professional life and the hardships he faced because of his race and beliefs. (Rev: BL 11/15/98; SLJ 11/98) [921]

RODRIGUEZ, ROBERT

7094 Marvis, Barbara. *Robert Rodriguez* (5–10). (A Real-Life Reader Biography) 1997, Mitchell Lane LB $15.95 (1-883845-48-3). This simple, attractive biography of the successful movie maker focuses on his problems growing up in a large family and clinging to his career dreams. (Rev: BL 6/1–15/98; SLJ 2/98) [921]

ROGERS, WILL

7095 Sonneborn, Liz. *Will Rogers: Cherokee Entertainer* (9–12). (North American Indians of Achievement) 1993, Chelsea LB $19.95 (0-7910-1719-2). A simple biography of the famous vaudeville star who later became popular in Hollywood and died tragically in an airplane crash. (Rev: BL 12/1/93; SLJ 1/94) [921]

RONSTADT, LINDA

7096 Amdur, Melissa. *Linda Ronstadt* (5–9). (Hispanics of Achievement) 1993, Chelsea LB $19.95 (0-7910-1781-8). This biography of the Mexican American singer tells of her roots and pride in her Hispanic heritage. (Rev: BL 9/15/93; SLJ 10/93) [921]

SCHUMANN, CLARA

7097 Reich, Susanna. *Clara Schumann: Piano Virtuoso* (5–8). Illus. 1999, Houghton $18.00 (0-395-89119-1). A well-researched biography of the remarkable musician, composer, wife, and mother, Clara Schumann, including her marriage to composer Robert Schumann and her crusade on behalf of his music after his death. (Rev: BL 8/99; SLJ 4/99) [921]

SCHWARZENEGGER, ARNOLD

7098 Bial, Daniel. *Arnold Schwarzenegger: Man of Action* (6–8). (Book Report Biographies) 1998, Watts $22.00 (0-531-11485-6). A workmanlike biography that recounts the basic facts of Schwarzenegger's life, with numerous quotes from his autobiography. (Rev: SLJ 1/99) [921]

7099 Doherty, Craig A., and Katherine M. Doherty. *Arnold Schwarzenegger: Larger Than Life* (6–10). 1993, Walker LB $15.85 (0-8027-8238-8). This biography portrays Schwarzenegger as an "American hero," outlining his life and applauding his physical fitness and business sense. (Rev: BL 12/1/93; SLJ 2/94; VOYA 4/94) [921]

SELENA

7100 Marvis, Barbara. *Selena* (5–10). (A Real-Life Reader Biography) 1997, Mitchell Lane LB $15.95 (1-883845-47-5). A simple, attractive biography of the singer, her supportive family, and her tragic death. (Rev: BL 6/1–15/98; SLJ 2/98) [921]

SIMON AND GARFUNKEL (MUSICAL GROUP)

7101 Morella, Joseph, and Patricia Barey. *Simon and Garfunkel: Old Friends* (9–12). 1991, Birch Lane $19.95 (1-55972-089-1). A dual biography of the famous folk-rock singer/songwriter pair, covering their Queens boyhoods, rise to fame in the 1960s, breakup at the decade's end, and subsequent separate careers. (Rev: BL 10/1/91) [921]

SMITH, WILL

7102 Berenson, Jan. *Will Power! A Biography of Will Smith, Star of Independence Day and Men in Black* (5–8). 1997, Pocket Books paper $3.99 (0-671-88784-X). An intimate look at the life of the rapper and TV and movie star Will Smith, who was known as the class clown because of his goofy antics. (Rev: VOYA 10/97) [921]

7103 Rodriguez, K. S. *Will Smith: From Fresh Prince to King of Cool* (6–10). 1998, HarperCollins paper $3.99 (0-06-107319-9). An appealing, easily read biography of this impressive TV/movie star and rap artist. (Rev: VOYA 4/99) [921]

7104 Stauffer, Stacey. *Will Smith* (6–10). (Black Americans of Achievement) 1998, Chelsea LB $19.95 (0-7910-4914-0); paper $9.95 (0-7910-4915-9). A serious biography of this popular star, beginning with *Independence Day* coverage, then moving back to Smith's childhood. (Rev: VOYA 8/99) [921]

7105 Stern, Dave. *Will Smith* (6–10). Illus. 1999, Aladdin paper $6.99 (0-689-82407-6). An oversize paperback with many color photos that give a fan-magazine treatment to this star's life and career. (Rev: VOYA 8/99) [921]

SPICE GIRLS (MUSICAL GROUP)

7106 Shore, Nancy. *Spice Girls* (5–8). (Galaxy of Superstars) 1999, Chelsea $16.95 (0-7910-5149-8); paper $9.95 (0-7910-5328-8). Biographies of the popular singing group that first took Britain by storm, and then the world. (Rev: BL 4/15/99; BR 9–10/99; SLJ 5/99) [921]

SPIELBERG, STEVEN

7107 Ferber, Elizabeth. *Steven Spielberg* (7–12). Illus. (Pop Culture Legends) 1996, Chelsea LB $19.95 (0-7910-3256-6); paper $9.95 (0-7910-3257-4). An account of America's popular filmmaker that includes material on *Jaws*, *E. T.*, *Jurassic Park*, and ends with *Schindler's List*. (Rev: BL 11/15/96; SLJ 1/97) [921]

SPRINGSTEEN, BRUCE

7108 Frankl, Ron. *Bruce Springsteen* (7–10). Illus. (Pop Culture Legends) 1994, Chelsea paper $9.95 (0-7910-2352-4). The compelling story of the famous rocker who has never forgotten his working-class roots. (Rev: BL 6/1–15/94) [921]

SUMMER, DONNA

7109 Haskins, Jim, and J. M. Stifle. *Donna Summer: An Unauthorized Biography* (7–12). Illus. 1983, Little, Brown $14.95 (0-316-35003-6). From a bit part in Hair to complete stardom, this account of Donna Summer's life ends in the early 1980s. [921]

TEMPTATIONS (MUSICAL GROUP)

7110 Cox, Ted. *The Temptations* (6–10). (African American Achievers) 1997, Chelsea LB $19.95 (0-7910-2587-X); paper $9.95 (0-7910-2588-8). A chronicle of the rise and fall of this musical group, with profiles of each of the members and insights into the influence of Motown records on the careers of many African American musicians in the 1960s. (Rev: SLJ 1/98) [921]

THREE STOOGES

7111 Scordato, Mark, and Ellen Scordato. *The Three Stooges* (7–12). (Pop Culture Legends) 1995, Chelsea LB $19.95 (0-7910-2344-3); paper $9.95 (0-7910-2369-9). A look at the 6 men who comprised the Three Stooges at various times. Includes black-and-white photos, a filmography, and a chronology. (Rev: BL 6/1–15/95) [921]

VALENS, RITCHIE

7112 Mendheim, Beverly. *Ritchie Valens: The First Latino Rocker* (8–12). Illus. 1987, Bilingual Pr. paper $15.00 (0-916950-79-4). The story of the popular Latino rocker who died in a plane crash in 1959. (Rev: BL 12/15/87) [921]

VON TRAPP FAMILY

7113 Von Trapp, Maria. *Story of the Von Trapp Family Singers* (9–12). 1987, Doubleday paper $11.95 (0-385-02896-2). The story of the Von Trapp family, their step-mother Maria, and their escape from the Nazis. [921]

WALLENDA, DELILAH

7114 Wallenda, Delilah, and Nan De Vicentis-Hayes. *The Last of the Wallendas* (9–12). 1993, New Horizon Pr. $22.95 (0-88282-116-4). Master high-wire artist Karl Wallenda's granddaughter describes the fading charisma and finances of the circus in the United States from a personal perspective and presents her version of family squabbles. (Rev: BL 4/15/93) [921]

WALTERS, BARBARA

7115 Remstein, Henna. *Barbara Walters* (5–8). 1998, Chelsea LB $19.95 (0-7910-4716-4); paper $9.95 (0-7910-4717-2). The life story of Barbara Walters, who broke many barriers for women in the communications field and has become an icon in the field of journalism. (Rev: VOYA 4/99) [921]

WASHINGTON, DENZEL

7116 Hill, Anne E. *Denzel Washington* (7–10). (Black Americans of Achievement) 1998, Chelsea LB $19.95 (0-7910-4692-3); paper $9.95 (0-7910-4693-1). A complimentary biography of this versatile, attractive actor who quickly rose to the top of the acting profession. (Rev: SLJ 3/99) [921]

WILLIAMS, VANESSA

7117 Boulais, Sue. *Vanessa Williams* (4–8). (Real-Life Reader Biography) 1999, Mitchell Lane LB $15.95 (1-883845-75-0). The life story of the African American who lost her title of Miss America in 1983 but rebounded with a brilliant career in show business. (Rev: BL 6/1–15/99) [921]

WINFREY, OPRAH

7118 Nicholson, Lois. *Oprah Winfrey: Talking with America* (5–8). (Junior Black Americans of Achievement) 1997, Chelsea LB $16.95 (0-7910-2390-7); paper $6.95 (0-7910-4460-2). A biography that skims the life of this personality, with material on her difficult childhood, sexual abuse, college experiences, early career, weight problems, and success on television. (Rev: SLJ 8/97) [921]

7119 Wooten, Sara McIntosh. *Oprah Winfrey: Talk Show Legend* (6–10). Illus. (African-American Biographies) 1999, Enslow $19.95 (0-7660-1207-7). The story of the amazing television personality who rose from a background of poverty, loneliness, and sexual abuse to become world-famous. (Rev: BL 9/15/99; VOYA 12/99) [921]

YOUNG, NEIL

7120 Heatley, Michael. *Neil Young: His Life and Music* (9–12). 1995, Hamlyn $29.95 (0-600-58541-7). A pictorial tribute to the godfather of grunge. (Rev: BL 2/15/95) [921]

7121 Rolling Stone, eds. *Neil Young: The Rolling Stone Files* (9–12). 1994, Hyperion paper $12.95 (0-7868-8043-0). Traces Young's musical career from his stint with Crosby, Stills, and Nash to the present. (Rev: BL 8/94) [921]

Miscellaneous Artists

BARNUM, P. T.

7122 Andronik, Catherine M. *Prince of Humbugs: A Life of P. T. Barnum* (6–9). 1994, Atheneum $15.95 (0-689-31796-4). The master of hockum and old-fashioned show business is revealed in this interesting biography. (Rev: BL 12/15/94; SLJ 2/95; VOYA 5/95) [921]

7123 Barnum, P. T. *Barnum's Own Story* (7–12). Illus. 1962, Peter Smith $19.25 (0-8446-4001-8). The autobiography of the showman who could fool people like no one else. [921]

7124 Barnum, P. T. *Struggles and Triumphs* (10–12). 1971, Ayer $53.95 (0-405-01651-4). An abridgment of the autobiography of one of America's first and greatest showmen. [921]

7125 Fleming, Alice. *P. T. Barnum: The World's Greatest Showman* (5–8). 1993, Walker LB $15.85 (0-8027-8235-3). This biography of the circus owner describes his childhood and various successful entrepreneurial ventures. (Rev: BL 1/15/94; SLJ 12/93; VOYA 2/94) [921]

7126 Kunhardt, Philip B., et al. *P. T. Barnum: America's Greatest Showman* (9–12). 1995, Knopf $45.00 (0-679-43574-3). The story of the master of showmanship and the greatest purveyor of freaks and wonders under the big top. (Rev: BL 9/1/95) [921]

7127 Tompert, Ann. *The Greatest Showman on Earth: A Biography of P.T. Barnum* (5–8). Illus. 1987, Dillon LB $18.95 (0-87518-370-0). An entertaining profile of the flamboyant showman and a discussion of his many money-making schemes. (Rev: BL 2/15/88; SLJ 3/88) [921]

STONE, OLIVER

7128 Riordan, James. *Stone: The Controversies, Excesses and Exploits of a Radical Filmmaker* (9–12). 1995, Hyperion $24.95 (0-7868-6026-X). The first biography written about Oliver Stone shows a complex personality who sought out the kinds of risks in life that he directs and writes about on screen. (Rev: BL 10/15/95) [9212]

Contemporary and Historical Americans

Collective

7129 Allen, Paula Gunn, and Patricia C. Smith. *As Long As the Rivers Flow: The Stories of Nine Native Americans* (5–8). Illus. 1996, Scholastic $15.95 (0-590-47869-9). Nine notable Native Americans are profiled, including both well-known individuals, like Geronimo and Jim Thorpe, and lesser-knowns, such as Weetammo and Louis Erdrich. (Rev: BL 12/1/96; BR 1–2/97; SLJ 1/97; VOYA 4/97) [920]

7130 Alter, Judith. *Extraordinary Women of the American West* (6–10). 1999, Children's Pr. $37.00 (0-516-20974-4). Profiles of 50 women, from the 18th century to modern times, representing a variety of races, careers, and contributions. (Rev: BL 8/99; SLJ 9/99) [920]

7131 Altman, Susan. *Extraordinary Black Americans: From Colonial to Contemporary Times* (5–9). Illus. 1989, Children's Pr. LB $37.00 (0-516-00581-2). A collection of 85 short biographies of important black Americans from a wide variety of fields. (Rev: BL 6/15/89) [920]

7132 Blassingame, Wyatt. *The Look-It-Up Book of Presidents* (6–9). Illus. 1990, Random LB $14.99 (0-679-90353-4); paper $8.99 (0-679-80358-0). The author devotes 2 to 6 pages on each president and covers all the salient facts about each. (Rev: SLJ 5/90) [920]

7133 Bolden, Tonya. *And Not Afraid to Dare: The Stories of Ten African American Women* (6–9). Illus. 1998, Scholastic $16.95 (0-590-48080-4). The compelling biographies of 10 African American women, including Ida B. Wells, Mary McLeod Bethune, and Toni Morrison. (Rev: BL 2/15/98; BR 11–12/98; SLJ 3/98; VOYA 6/98) [920]

7134 Bontemps, Arna, ed. *Great Slave Narratives* (10–12). 1969, Beacon paper $31.50 (0-8070-5473-9). This is a collection of autobiographical writings by slaves. [920]

7135 Burleigh, Robert. *Who Said That? Famous Americans Speak* (5–8). Illus. 1997, Holt $15.95 (0-8050-4394-2). Brief, insightful profiles of 33 famous personalities are presented, from Benjamin Franklin to Sojourner Truth to Marilyn Monroe to Louis Armstrong, using quotes from each. (Rev: BL 3/1/97; SLJ 5/97) [920]

7136 Calvert, Patricia. *Great Lives: The American Frontier* (4–8). Illus. 1997, Simon & Schuster $25.00 (0-689-80640-X). A large book that contains profiles of 27 individuals who played significant roles in the opening up of the West. (Rev: BL 2/15/98; BR 5–6/98; SLJ 1/98) [920]

7137 Diamonstein, Barbaralee. *Singular Voices: Conversations with Americans Who Make a Difference* (10–12). 1997, Abrams $19.95 (0-8109-2698-9). This volume consists of 17 interviews with noted contemporary contributors to American life, among them writers Edward Albee and William Styron and public figures Jimmy Carter and Gloria Steinem. (Rev: SLJ 12/97) [920]

7138 Emert, Phyllis R. *Top Lawyers and Their Famous Cases* (6–10). (Profiles) 1996, Oliver Pr. LB $18.95 (1-881508-31-5). Profiles of 8 notable lawyers and their outstanding legal cases, from colonial days to the present, including Alexander Hamilton, Morris Dees, Abraham Lincoln, Robert H. Jackson, Joseph Welsh, and Bella Lockwood. (Rev: BR 1–2/97; SLJ 11/96; VOYA 6/97) [920]

7139 Faber, Doris, and Harold Faber. *Great Lives: American Government* (6–9). Illus. 1988, Macmillan $23.00 (0-684-18521-0). Arranged chronologically, there are many thumbnail sketches of famous American statesmen from Washington to Nixon. (Rev: BL 2/1/88; SLJ 1/89) [920]

7140 Fireside, Bryna J. *Is There a Woman in the House . . . or Senate?* (6–10). 1994, Albert Whitman LB $14.95 (0-8075-3662-8). An examination of the careers of 10 women who have served in Congress. (Rev: BL 5/15/94; SLJ 3/94) [920]

7141 Franklin, John Hope, and August Meier, eds. *Black Leaders of the Twentieth Century* (7–12). Illus. 1982, Univ. of Illinois Pr. $29.95 (0-252-00870-7); paper $14.95 (0-252-00939-8). A total of 15 black Americans including W. E. B. Du Bois, Marcus Garvey, and Whitney Young, Jr., are highlighted. A companion volume is: *Black Leaders of the Nineteenth Century*. [920]

7142 Freedman, Russell. *Indian Chiefs* (6–9). Illus. 1987, Holiday House LB $19.95 (0-8234-0625-3). Brief biographies of 6 Indian chiefs including Red Cloud, Sitting Bull, and Joseph of the Nez Perce. (Rev: BL 5/1/87; SLJ 5/87; VOYA 8/87) [920]

7143 Furbee, Mary R. *Women of the American Revolution* (7–9). (History Makers) 1999, Lucent LB $22.45 (1-56006-489-7). Profiles of 6 women—Abigail Smith Adams, Peggy Shippen Arnold, Esther DeBerdt Reed, Deborah Sampson, Mercy Otis Warren, and Phillis Wheatley—who played very different roles during the American Revolution, with material on the general role of women during the Revolution and an overview of events leading up to it. (Rev: SLJ 9/99) [920]

7144 Gould, Lewis L., ed. *American First Ladies: Their Lives and Their Legacy* (10–12). 1996, Garland $75.00 (0-8153-1479-5). From Martha Washington to Hillary Clinton, this biographical resource shows the impact first ladies have had on U.S. history, discussing habits, traits, friends, health, and quotations about each. (Rev: BR 1–2/97; SLJ 8/96; VOYA 12/96) [920]

7145 Hacker, Carlotta. *Great African Americans in History* (5–8). (Outstanding African Americans) 1997, Crabtree LB $21.28 (0-86505-805-9); paper $8.95 (0-86505-819-9). There are profiles of 13 great African Americans in American history, including Frederick Douglass, Harriet Tubman, W. E. B. Du Bois, Mary McLeod Bethune, and George Washington Carver. (Rev: BL 9/15/97; SLJ 1/98) [920]

7146 Haley, Alex. *Roots* (9–12). 1976, Doubleday $25.00 (0-385-03787-2); paper $7.99 (0-440-17464-3). A thoroughly researched history of a black American's family from Africa to slavery in the United States, ending with the author's own generation. (Rev: BL 9/86) [920]

7147 Hancock, Sibyl. *Famous Firsts of Black Americans* (7–12). Illus. 1983, Pelican $11.95 (0-88289-240-1). Biographies of 20 famous black Americans

who have contributed in a unique way to our culture. [920]

7148 Hansen, Joyce. *Women of Hope: African Americans Who Made a Difference* (6–12). 1998, Scholastic $22.99 (0-590-93973-4). A large-size volume that celebrates the lives and accomplishments of 13 great black female leaders from various walks of life, including civil rights activists like Fannie Lou Hamer and writers like Maya Angelou. (Rev: BL 12/1/98; SLJ 10/98; VOYA 4/99) [920]

7149 Haskins, Jim. *One More River to Cross: The Stories of Twelve Black Americans* (5–8). 1992, Scholastic $13.95 (0-590-42896-9). Biographies of 12 African Americans who defied the odds to rise to the top of their fields. (Rev: BL 2/1/92; SLJ 4/92) [920]

7150 Jacobs, William J. *Great Lives: Human Rights* (5–8). Illus. 1990, Simon & Schuster $24.00 (0-684-19036-2). Jacobs profiles 30 American leaders who worked for human rights that span time from the colonist Roger Smith to Martin Luther King, Jr. (Rev: BL 7/90; SLJ 9/90) [921]

7151 Jones, Veda Boyd. *Government and Politics* (6–9). (Female Firsts in Their Fields) 1999, Chelsea $16.95 (0-7910-5140-4). Using black-and-white illustrations and clear, concise prose, this book profiles 6 women who were pioneers in American politics and government. (Rev: BL 5/15/99; VOYA 8/99) [920]

7152 Keenan, Sheila. *Scholastic Encyclopedia of Women in United States History* (4–9). 1996, Scholastic $17.95 (0-590-22792-0). Over 200 brief biographies of American women representing a variety of professions and accomplishments, organized into 6 chapters chronologically arranged. (Rev: BR 3–4/97; SLJ 2/97) [920]

7153 Kennedy, John F. *Profiles in Courage*. Memorial Ed. (7–12). 1964, Perennial Lib. paper $7.00 (0-06-080698-2). Sketches of several famous Americans who took unpopular stands during their lives. (Rev: BL 4/87) [920]

7154 Krull, Kathleen. *Lives of the Presidents* (4–8). 1998, Harcourt $20.00 (0-15-200808-X). An entertaining collective biography that stresses the human side of U.S. presidents, with interesting, insightful tidbits and details that bring the presidents to life. (Rev: BL 8/98; SLJ 9/98) [920]

7155 Lamb, Brian, comp. *Booknotes: Life Stories: Notable Biographies on the People Who Shaped America* (10–12). 1999, Times Bks. $27.50 (0-8129-3081-9). This is a collection of light, conversational interviews with biographers for C-SPAN's *Booknotes*, who provide insightful, colorful, and well-rounded portraits of their famous subjects, from George Washington and Abraham Lincoln to Newt

Gingrich and Bill Clinton. (Rev: BL 3/1/99; SLJ 7/99) [920]

7156 Lee, George. *Interesting People: Black American History Makers* (7–12). Illus. 1989, McFarland LB $15.95 (0-89950-403-5). Short biographies of over 200 famous black Americans both past and present are included in this volume. (Rev: BR 9–10/89) [920]

7157 Lilley, Stephen R. *Fighters Against American Slavery* (9–12). Illus. (History Makers) 1998, Lucent LB $17.96 (1-56006-036-0). Moral convictions and personal experience were the motivating forces that inspired abolitionists to act. This book highlights such heroes as Nat Turner, William Lloyd Garrison, Frederick Douglass, and Harriet Tubman. (Rev: BL 2/15/99; SLJ 6/99) [920]

7158 Lindop, Edmund. *Richard M. Nixon, Jimmy Carter, Ronald Reagan* (5–8). (Presidents Who Dared) 1996, Twenty-First Century LB $18.90 (0-8050-3405-6). This account traces salient events in each of these presidents' terms, for example: Nixon and Watergate and relations with China; Carter and ending the war between Egypt and Israel; and Reagan and his arms agreement with the Soviet Union. (Rev: SLJ 6/96) [920]

7159 Lindop, Edmund. *Woodrow Wilson, Franklin D. Roosevelt, Harry S. Truman* (5–9). 1995, Twenty-First Century LB $18.90 (0-8050-3403-X). This volume provides brief overviews of the lives and accomplishments of Wilson, FDR, and Truman, with a look at daring decisions each made during his presidency. (Rev: BL 1/1–15/96; BR 3–4/96; SLJ 11/95; VOYA 6/96) [920]

7160 Lindop, Laurie. *Champions of Equality* (7–10). Illus. (Dynamic Modern Women) 1997, Twenty-First Century LB $21.40 (0-8050-4165-6). This collective biography includes 10 contemporary women who are feminist leaders, a head of the NAACP, and a children's rights activist. Some names are Margarethe Cammermeyer, Marian Wright Edelman, Wilma Mankiller, and Eleanor Holmes Norton. (Rev: BL 9/1/97; BR 1–2/98; SLJ 9/97) [303.48]

7161 Lindop, Laurie. *Political Leaders* (6–12). Illus. (Dynamic Modern Women) 1996, Twenty-First Century LB $21.40 (0-8050-4164-8). Elizabeth Dole, Dianne Feinstein, Geraldine Ferraro, Ruth Bader Ginsburg, and Barbara Jordan are 5 of the 10 prominent women in politics profiled in this book, with details on the childhood, influences, education, and political career of each. (Rev: BL 1/1–15/97; SLJ 1/97; VOYA 2/97) [320]

7162 Litwack, Leon F., and August Meier, eds. *Black Leaders of the Nineteenth Century* (10–12). Illus. 1988, Univ. of Illinois Pr. $29.95 (0-252-01506-1). Seventeen biographical sketches about

such famous black Americans as Nat Turner and Harriet Tubman. (Rev: BL 4/1/88) [920]

7163 McElroy, Richard L. *American Presidents* (9–12). 1984, Daring Pr. paper $5.95 (0-938936-18-2). A pleasant collection of trivia and facts about American presidents. [920]

7164 Marvis, Barbara. *Famous People of Hispanic Heritage, v. 4* (5–9). Illus. 1996, Mitchell Lane LB $21.95 (1-883845-30-0); paper $12.95 (1-883845-29-7). The lives of 2 Hispanic men and 2 women who have succeeded in their careers are presented in an easy-to-read style. Other volumes in this series by the same author are available. (Rev: BL 12/15/96; SLJ 1/97; VOYA 2/97) [920]

7165 Mayo, Edith P., ed. *The Smithsonian Book of the First Ladies: Their Lives, Times, and Issues* (6–10). Illus. 1996, Holt $25.95 (0-8050-1751-8). From Martha Washington to Hillary Rodham Clinton, this book examines the lives and accomplishments of each First Lady with a 3- to 4-page biography and pictures. (Rev: BL 6/1–15/96; BR 1–2/97; SLJ 6/96; VOYA 8/96) [920]

7166 Morey, Janet Nomura, and Wendy Dunn. *Famous Hispanic Americans* (7–10). Illus. 1996, Dutton $15.99 (0-525-65190-X). Fourteen men and women of Hispanic heritage from science, sports, the arts, and other professions are featured in this collective biography. (Rev: BL 2/15/96; BR 9–10/96; SLJ 2/96; VOYA 8/96) [920]

7167 Morin, Isobel V. *Women of the U.S. Congress* (6–10). 1994, Oliver Pr. LB $18.95 (1-881508-12-9). Lists all the women who have served in Congress as of 1994 and provides political biographies of 7 of them, citing their accomplishments and their different backgrounds and views. (Rev: BL 7/94; SLJ 5/94; VOYA 6/94) [920]

7168 Morin, Isobel V. *Women Who Reformed Politics* (7–12). 1994, Oliver Pr. LB $18.95 (1-881508-16-1). Describes the political activism of 8 American women, including Abby Foster's abolition fight, Carrie Catt's suffrage battle, and Gloria Steinem's feminist crusade. (Rev: BL 10/15/94; SLJ 11/94; VOYA 2/95) [920]

7169 Pascoe, Elaine. *First Facts about the Presidents* (4–8). 1996, Blackbirch LB $25.45 (1-56711-167-X). Divided into 4 historical periods, this book covers the major historical events of the time, introduces each of the presidents, and briefly describes their presidencies. (Rev: SLJ 5/96) [920]

7170 Peters, Margaret. *The Ebony Book of Black Achievement* (10–12). Illus. 1974, Johnson Pub. $10.95 (0-87485-040-1). This volume contains brief biographies of 26 black American men and women who have achieved in a number of fields. [920]

7171 Potter, Joan, and Constance Claytor. *African Americans Who Were First* (4–8). Illus. 1997, Dutton paper $15.99 (0-525-65246-9). A brief introduction to 65 African Americans who earned "firsts" in a variety of fields. (Rev: BL 9/1/97; BR 3–4/98; SLJ 9/97) [920]

7172 Rennert, Richard, ed. *Book of Firsts: Leaders of America* (6–9). Illus. (Profiles of Great Black Americans) 1994, Chelsea paper $6.95 (0-7910-2066-5). This collective biography profiles the lives and works of 9 African American leaders, including Ralph Bunche, Shirley Chisholm, William H. Hastie, Colin Powell, and L. Douglas Wilder. (Rev: BL 6/1–15/94) [920]

7173 Satter, James. *Journalists Who Made History* (7–12). Illus. (Profiles) 1998, Oliver Pr. LB $18.95 (1-881508-39-0). Ten journalists famous for their fearless reporting are profiled, including Horace Greeley, Ida Tarbell, Carl Bernstein and Bob Woodward, William Randolph Hearst, and Edward R. Murrow. (Rev: BL 10/15/98; SLJ 11/98) [920]

7174 Smith, Gene. *Lee and Grant: A Dual Biography* (9–12). 1984, NAL paper $10.95 (0-452-00773-9). A double biography of the 2 opposing generals and their fateful clash. [921]

7175 Straub, Deborah G., ed. *Hispanic American Voices* (6–12). 1997, Gale $39.00 (0-8103-9827-3). Profiles of 16 Hispanic Americans, most of whom are civil and human rights leaders, politicians, attorneys, or civil rights activists. (Rev: BR 9–10/97; SLJ 11/97) [920]

7176 Streissguth, Thomas. *Legendary Labor Leaders* (7–12). Illus. (Profiles) 1998, Oliver Pr. LB $18.95 (1-881508-44-7). The eight labor leaders profiled in this collective biography are Samuel Gompers, Cesar Chavez, A. Philip Randolph, Jimmy Hoffa, Eugene Debs, William Haywood, Mother Jones, and John L. Lewis. (Rev: BL 10/15/98; SLJ 1/99) [920]

7177 Taylor, Kimberly H. *Black Abolitionists and Freedom Fighters* (6–10). 1996, Oliver Pr. LB $18.95 (1-881508-30-7). Profiles are given for 8 African Americans who fought to end slavery, some well-known like Nat Turner and Harriet Tubman, others less known, such as Ridhard Allen and Mary Terrell. (Rev: BR 1–2/97; SLJ 10/96) [920]

7178 Taylor, Kimberly H. *Black Civil Rights Champions* (6–12). Illus. 1995, Oliver Pr. LB $14.95 (1-881508-22-6). In separate chapters, 7 civil rights leaders, including W. E. B. Du Bois, James Farmer, Ella Baker, and Malcolm X, are profiled, with an 8th final chapter that gives thumbnail sketches of many more. (Rev: BL 1/1–15/96; BR 1–2/97; SLJ 3/96; VOYA 6/96) [920]

7179 Thro, Ellen. *Twentieth-Century Women Politicians* (7–12). (American Profiles) 1998, Facts on File $19.95 (0-8160-3758-2). Beginning in the mid-20th century, this work features 10 women who were elected to important public offices, including Margaret Chase Smith, Geraldine Ferraro, Dianne Feinstein, Christine Todd Whitman, and Ann Richards. (Rev: BL 12/15/98) [920]

7180 Unger, Harlow G. *Teachers and Educators* (7–10). Illus. (American Profiles) 1994, Facts on File $19.95 (0-8160-2990-3). This book profiles 8 great American educators of the past including John Dewey, Horace Mann, Emma Willard, Booker T. Washington, and Henry Barnard. (Rev: BL 7/95; VOYA 5/95) [920]

Civil and Human Rights Leaders

ABERNATHY, RALPH

7181 Reef, Catherine. *Ralph David Abernathy* (6–10). (People in Focus) 1995, Silver Burdett $18.95 (0-87518-653-X); paper $7.95 (0-382-24965-8). A just-the-facts approach, relating the events of the civil rights worker's life. (Rev: BL 8/95; SLJ 10/95) [921]

ANTHONY, SUSAN B.

7182 Kendall, Martha E. *Susan B. Anthony: Voice for Women's Voting Rights* (6–8). (Historical American Biographies) 1997, Enslow LB $19.95 (0-89490-780-8). A biography of this amazing women who campaigned for women's right to vote, hold political office, divorce, and own property, and for an end to slavery. (Rev: SLJ 8/97) [921]

7183 Sherr, Lynn. *Failure Is Impossible: Susan B. Anthony in Her Own Words* (9–12). 1995, Times Bks. $23.00 (0-8129-2430-4). One woman's passionate belief in equal rights for all people, as expressed in her own speeches, correspondence, and diary entries. (Rev: BL 2/1/95; SLJ 3/96) [921]

7184 Weisberg, Barbara. *Susan B. Anthony* (6–10). Illus. 1988, Chelsea LB $19.95 (1-55546-639-7). The biography of the woman who led the early suffragette movement. (Rev: BL 12/1/88) [921]

BETHUNE, MARY MCLEOD

7185 Halasa, Malu. *Mary McLeod Bethune* (6–10). Illus. 1988, Chelsea LB $19.95 (1-55546-574-9). A stirring biography of the black woman who fought for the right to a quality education for her people. (Rev: BL 3/15/89) [921]

BRADWELL, MYRA

7186 Wheaton, Elizabeth. *Myra Bradwell: First Woman Lawyer* (7–10). Illus. 1997, Morgan Reynolds LB $18.95 (1-883846-17-X). Denied admission to the bar because she was married, this 19th-century activist became an abolitionist, feminist, and defender of the underprivileged. (Rev: BL 3/1/97; BR 9–10/97; SLJ 4/97) [921]

BROWN, JOHN

7187 Cox, Clinton. *Fiery Vision: The Life and Death of John Brown* (7–10). Illus. 1997, Scholastic $15.95 (0-590-47574-6). A well-researched, detailed account of the life of the abolitionist who was hanged for the raid at Harper's Ferry. (Rev: BL 2/15/97; SLJ 6/97; VOYA 10/98) [921]

7188 Everett, Gwen. *John Brown: One Man Against Slavery* (5–9). Illus. 1993, Rizzoli $15.95 (0-8478-1702-4). The raid on Harper's Ferry is described from the viewpoint of abolitionist John Brown's daughter at 16. (Rev: BL 6/1–15/93*) [921]

7189 Scott, John A. *John Brown of Harper's Ferry* (7–12). Illus. 1988, Facts on File $19.95 (0-8160-1347-0). A biography of the headstrong abolitionist that focuses on the Harper's Ferry raid. (Rev: BL 2/1/88; BR 11–12/88; SLJ 5/88; VOYA 8/88) [921]

7190 Tackach, James. *The Trial of John Brown* (7–10). Illus. (Famous Trials) 1998, Lucent $17.96 (1-56006-468-4). A biography of John Brown that explains his hatred of slavery and how his upbringing and religious beliefs contributed to his radical actions, while also providing a broad history lesson on the late 1800s in America. (Rev: SLJ 8/98) [921]

BURNS, ANTHONY

7191 Hamilton, Virginia. *Anthony Burns: The Defeat and Triumph of a Fugitive Slave* (7–12). 1988, Knopf LB $14.99 (0-394-98185-5). Burns, who lived only 28 years, rebelled against his slave status with repercussions felt around the country. (Rev: BL 6/1/88; BR 11–12/88; SLJ 6/88; VOYA 10/88) [921]

CHAVEZ, CESAR

7192 Gonzales, Doreen. *Cesar Chavez: Leader for Migrant Farm Workers* (6–10). Illus. (Hispanic Biographies) 1996, Enslow LB $19.95 (0-89490-760-3). This biography concentrates on Chavez's struggle to organize California farmworkers, his belief in nonviolence, and his inspirational leadership. (Rev: BL 10/1/96; SLJ 6/96) [921]

CUFFE, PAUL

7193 Diamond, Arthur. *Paul Cuffe* (7–10). Illus. 1989, Chelsea LB $19.95 (1-55546-579-X). The story of the freed American slave who in 1810 proposed the founding of an African colony for black Americans. (Rev: BL 11/15/89; BR 11–12/89; SLJ 1/90; VOYA 12/89) [921]

DOUGLASS, FREDERICK

7194 Douglass, Frederick. *Escape from Slavery: The Boyhood of Frederick Douglass in His Own Words* (5–10). Illus. 1994, Knopf $15.00 (0-679-84652-2); paper $6.99 (0-679-84651-4). This shortened version of the famous abolitionist's 1845 autobiography dramatizes the abomination of slavery and the struggle of a man to break free. (Rev: BL 2/15/94*; SLJ 2/94) [921]

7195 Douglass, Frederick. *The Life and Times of Frederick Douglass* (10–12). 1962, Macmillan paper $14.95 (0-02-002350-2). The autobiography of the former slave who became an advisor to Presidents. (Rev: BL 1/15/90) [921]

7196 Douglass, Frederick. *Narrative of the Life of Frederick Douglass, an American Slave* (10–12). 1982, Penguin paper $8.95 (0-14-039012-X). An autobiography that tells of the life of this former slave and abolitionist. [921]

7197 Meltzer, Milton, ed. *Frederick Douglass: In His Own Words* (8–12). Illus. 1995, Harcourt $22.00 (0-15-229492-9). An introduction to the articles and speeches of the great 19th-century abolitionist leader, arranged chronologically. (Rev: BL 12/15/94; SLJ 2/95) [305.8]

7198 Miller, Douglas T. *Frederick Douglass and the Fight for Freedom* (7–12). Illus. 1988, Facts on File $19.95 (0-8160-1617-8). An engrossing biography of the self-taught former slave who led the abolitionist movement. (Rev: BL 11/1/88; BR 1–2/89; SLJ 10/88; VOYA 2/89) [921]

7199 Russell, Sharmen Apt. *Frederick Douglass* (6–10). Illus. 1988, Chelsea LB $19.95 (1-55546-580-3). This biography of the civil rights leader supplies detail in both his private and public life. (Rev: BL 2/1/88; SLJ 6/88) [921]

DU BOIS, W. E. B.

7200 Du Bois, W. E. B. *The Autobiography of W. E. B. Du Bois* (10–12). Illus. 1976, Kraus $20.00 (0-527-25262-X). Written when he was over 90, this is both an autobiography of a distinguished black American and a history of the civil rights movement. [921]

7201 Marable, Manning. *W. E. B. Du Bois: Black Radical Democrat* (10–12). Illus. 1986, Twayne $28.95 (0-8057-7750-4). A compact biography of the great black intellectual, humanitarian, and civil rights leader. (Rev: BL 11/1/86) [921]

7202 Moss, Nathaniel. *W. E. B. Du Bois: Civil Rights Leader* (5–8). (Junior World Biography) 1996, Chelsea LB $15.95 (0-7910-2382-6). A brief, somewhat superficial overview of this great pioneer in the civil rights movement and his accomplishments. (Rev: SLJ 7/96) [921]

7203 Stafford, Mark. *W. E. B. Du Bois* (6–9). Illus. 1989, Chelsea LB $19.95 (1-55546-582-X). A fine profile of the man who was not only an important writer but also a prominent opponent of racism. (Rev: BL 12/15/89; BR 1–2/90; SLJ 5/90) [921]

EDELMAN, MARIAN WRIGHT

7204 Siegel, Beatrice. *Marian Wright Edelman: The Making of a Crusader* (6–9). 1995, Simon & Schuster paper $15.00 (0-02-782629-5). This biography of children's advocate and civil rights activist Edelman portrays her segregated childhood, activist teenage years, and current passion for children's issues. (Rev: BL 6/1–15/95; VOYA 12/95) [921]

FARRAKHAN, LOUIS

7205 Haskins, Jim. *Louis Farrakhan and the Nation of Islam* (7–12). Illus. 1996, Walker LB $16.85 (0-8027-8423-2). Beginning with a history of black nationalism and the Nation of Islam, this biography places the life of Farrakhan within the movement for black solidarity. (Rev: BL 10/1/96; BR 1–2/97; SLJ 1/97) [921]

FREEMAN, ELIZABETH

7206 Wilds, Mary. *MumBet: The Life and Times of Elizabeth Freeman: The True Story of a Slave Who Won Her Freedom* (7–12). Illus. 1999, Avisson LB $27.71 (1-888105-40-2). The story of MumBet (Elizabeth Freeman), a black slave who sued for her freedom in Massachusetts in 1781 after hearing a reading of the Declaration of Independence and won, helping to set the legal precedents that ended slavery in New England. (Rev: BL 6/1–15/99; SLJ 6/99) [921]

GARVEY, MARCUS

7207 Lawler, Mary. *Marcus Garvey* (7–10). Illus. 1987, Chelsea LB $19.95 (1-55546-587-0). The story of the black leader who preached black separation and founded the Universal Negro Improvement Association. Part of an extensive series on black Americans. (Rev: BL 12/1/87; BR 1–2/89; VOYA 10/88) [921]

GRIMKE, ANGELINA

7208 Todras, Ellen H. *Angelina Grimke: Voice of Abolition* (9–12). Illus. 1999, Linnet LB $25.00 (0-208-02485-9). A handsome biography of the woman, born in Charleston in 1805, who became an outspoken foe of slavery and left the South for New England to work for the abolition of slavery and for women's rights. (Rev: BL 6/1–15/99; SLJ 5/99; VOYA 12/99) [921]

HAYDEN, LEWIS

7209 Strangis, Joel. *Lewis Hayden & the War Against Slavery* (7–12). 1998, Shoe String LB $23.50 (0-208-02430-1); paper $23.50 (0-208-02435-2). The dramatic story of the former slave who became an active abolitionist and a stationmaster on the Underground Railroad. (Rev: BL 2/15/99; BR 9–10/99; SLJ 5/99; VOYA 10/99) [921]

HUERTA, DOLORES

7210 Perez, Frank. *Dolores Huerta* (4–8). Illus. (Contemporary Hispanic Americans) 1995, Raintree Steck-Vaughn LB $22.83 (0-8172-3981-2). The accomplishments of Dolores Huerta, a Hispanic American who cofounded the United Farm Workers, are described in this informative biography. (Rev: BL 3/15/96) [921]

JACOBS, HARRIET

7211 Fleischner, Jennifer. *I Was Born a Slave: The Story of Harriet Jacobs* (4–8). Illus. 1997, Millbrook LB $24.90 (0-7613-0111-9). The turbulent life of Harriet Jacobs, who was born into slavery and lived for many years as a fugitive before winning her freedom and becoming an abolitionist. (Rev: BL 9/15/97; BR 1–2/98; SLJ 1/98) [921]

KING, CORETTA SCOTT

7212 King, Coretta Scott. *My Life with Martin Luther King, Jr.* Rev. ed. (9–12). 1993, Holt $17.95 (0-8050-2445-X). A revised, shortened edition of King's memoir of her life with her husband, Martin Luther King, Jr., with black-and-white photos. (Rev: BL 2/15/93; SLJ 2/93) [323]

7213 Rhodes, Lisa R. *Coretta Scott King—Humanitarian* (5–8). Illus. (Black Americans of Achievement) 1999, Chelsea LB $19.95 (0-7910-4690-7); paper $9.95 (0-7910-4691-5). This story of Coretta Scott King tells about her childhood, education, marriage, her work in the civil rights movement, and her work since her husband's assassination. (Rev: BL 8/98; SLJ 8/98) [323.092 B]

7214 Schraff, Anne. *Coretta Scott King: Striving for Civil Rights* (7–12). (African-American Biographies) 1997, Enslow LB $19.95 (0-89490-811-1). The life story of the gallant woman who has, with her family, continued the struggle for civil rights begun by her husband. (Rev: BL 6/1–15/97) [921]

KING, MARTIN LUTHER, JR.

7215 Darby, Jean. *Martin Luther King, Jr.* (6–8). Illus. 1990, Lerner LB $25.26 (0-8225-4902-6). An account that gives details of both King's life and the racial strife of the 1960s. (Rev: BL 7/90; SLJ 11/90) [921]

7216 Haskins, Jim. *I Have a Dream: The Life and Words of Martin Luther King, Jr.* (6–12). 1993, Millbrook LB $27.40 (1-56294-087-2). Describes King's early life, family, and education, and the impact of the civil rights movement and beliefs that he espoused. (Rev: BL 2/15/93; SLJ 6/93*) [921]

7217 Jakoubek, Robert E. *Martin Luther King, Jr.* (6–9). Illus. 1989, Chelsea LB $19.95 (1-55546-597-8). A stirring biography that also gives a good history of the nonviolent civil rights movement. (Rev: BL 12/15/89; BR 1–2/90; SLJ 3/90; VOYA 2/90) [921]

7218 Patterson, Lillie. *Martin Luther King, Jr. and the Freedom Movement* (7–12). Illus. 1989, Facts on File $19.95 (0-8160-1605-4). A biography of the civil rights leader and the movement he led. (Rev: BL 7/89; BR 11–12/89; SLJ 9/89; VOYA 12/89) [921]

7219 Schulke, Flip. *He Had a Dream: Martin Luther King, Jr., and the Civil Rights Movement* (9–12). 1995, Norton $39.95 (0-393-03729-0); paper $19.95 (0-393-31264-X). A photoessay documenting the life of Dr. Martin Luther King, Jr. (Rev: BL 3/1/95) [921]

7220 Schulke, Flip, and Penelope McPhee. *King Remembered* (9–12). Illus. 1986, Norton $22.95 (0-393-02256-0); paper $12.00 (0-671-62018-5). A heavily illustrated biography that stresses King's work in civil rights. (Rev: BL 1/1/86) [921]

7221 Schuman, Michael A. *Martin Luther King, Jr.: Leader for Civil Rights* (5–8). (African-American Biographies) 1996, Enslow LB $19.95 (0-89490-687-9). A straightforward biography that covers the important events in King's life. (Rev: SLJ 12/96) [921]

7222 Wukovits, John. *The Importance of Martin Luther King Jr.* (7–9). Illus. (The Importance Of) 1999, Lucent LB $22.45 (1-56006-483-8). Using quotes from tapes, letters, diaries, and other primary sources, this volume traces Martin Luther King's life and career, with extensive background on the historical and cultural forces that shaped his life, a history of the civil rights movement, and an assessment of King and his influence on race relations in the 20th century. (Rev: VOYA 8/99) [921]

LEWIS, JOHN

7223 Lewis, John. *Walking with the Wind: A Memoir of the Movement* (10–12). 1998, Simon & Schuster $25.50 (0-684-81065-4). The autobiography of the pioneer civil rights leader who was active in the civil rights movement almost from the beginning, including the lunch-counter sit-ins in 1960 and the march on Washington in 1963. (Rev: SLJ 12/98) [921]

MALCOLM X

7224 Brown, Kevin. *Malcolm X: His Life and Legacy* (7–12). 1995, Millbrook LB $27.40 (1-56294-500-9). This biography of Malcolm X covers his politics, the Nation of Islam's history, the 1960s struggle for civil rights, and Malcolm's status as a 1990s hero. (Rev: BL 6/1–15/95; SLJ 6/95; VOYA 12/95) [921]

7225 Collins, David R. *Malcolm X: Black Rage* (5–9). 1992, Dillon LB $12.95 (0-87518-498-7). A short biography of the influential African American activist, tracing the early events that led to his belief that whites were the enemy. (Rev: BL 10/15/92; SLJ 1/93) [921]

7226 Diamond, Arthur. *Malcolm X: A Voice for Black America* (6–12). Illus. (People to Know) 1994, Enslow $18.95 (0-89490-453-3). A sympathetic but unbiased account of the man, once a convict, who became an important black leader. (Rev: BL 6/1–15/94) [921]

7227 Gallen, David. *Malcolm X: As They Knew Him* (9–12). 1992, Carroll & Graf $21.95 (0-88184-851-4); paper $11.95 (0-88184-850-6). Interviews with and about Malcolm X, essays analyzing his political role, and personal reminiscences by a wide range of people—from Maya Angelou and Alex Haley to James Baldwin. (Rev: BL 5/15/92) [320.5]

7228 Malcolm X, and Alex Haley. *The Autobiography of Malcolm X* (7–12). 1999, Ballantine $20.00 (0-345-91536-4); paper $12.00 (0-345-91503-8). The story of the man who turned from Harlem drug pusher into a charismatic leader of his people. [921]

7229 Myers, Walter Dean. *Malcolm X: By Any Means Necessary* (6–12). 1993, Scholastic $13.95 (0-590-46484-1). An eloquent tribute to the brilliant, radical African American leader, quoting extensively from *Autobiography of Malcolm X*. (Rev: BL 11/15/92; SLJ 2/93) [921]

7230 Perry, Bruce. *Malcolm: A Life of the Man Who Changed Black America* (9–12). 1991, Station Hill $24.95 (0-88268-103-6). This biography shows various sides of the African American leader. (Rev: BL 6/15/91; SLJ 3/92) [921]

7231 Rummel, Jack. *Malcolm X* (6–9). Illus. 1989, Chelsea LB $19.95 (1-55546-600-1). A heavily illustrated portrait of the black leader and his movement for civil rights for his people. (Rev: BL 5/15/89; BR 9–10/89; SLJ 6/89; VOYA 8/89) [921]

7232 Sagan, Miriam. *Malcolm X* (7–9). Illus. (Mysterious Deaths) 1997, Lucent LB $17.96 (1-56006-264-9). After a brief biography of Malcolm X, this book focuses on the circumstances of his death and his rivalry with Louis Farrakhan, who was thought by many to be responsible for Malcolm's death, and his family's subsequent relationship with Farrakhan. (Rev: BL 2/15/97; SLJ 3/97; VOYA 8/97) [921]

MOTT, LUCRETIA

7233 Bryant, Jennifer. *Lucretia Mott: A Guiding Light* (7–12). Illus. 1995, Eerdmans paper $8.00 (0-8028-5098-7). The story of the famous fighter against injustice who was one of the initiators of the women's rights movement and played a major role in organizing the movement's first convention. (Rev: BL 5/1/96; BR 9–10/96; SLJ 6/96; VOYA 10/96) [305.42]

PARKER, JOHN P.

7234 Sprague, Stuart Seely, ed. *His Promised Land: The Autobiography of John P. Parker, Former Slave and Conductor on the Underground Railroad* (10–12). 1997, Norton $20.00 (0-393-03941-2). The recently discovered action-packed autobiography of John Parker, beginning with his life as a slave in chains when he was 8 years old and continuing to his amazing work with the Underground Railroad in Ripley, Ohio. (Rev: BL 10/15/96; SLJ 5/97) [921]

PARKS, ROSA

7235 Hull, Mary. *Rosa Parks* (7–10). Illus. (Black Americans of Achievement) 1994, Chelsea LB $19.95 (0-7910-1881-4). The story of the seemingly ordinary black woman who had the courage to fight bus segregation in Montgomery, Alabama. (Rev: BL 6/1–15/94; SLJ 8/94; VOYA 8/94) [921]

7236 Parks, Rosa, and Jim Haskins. *Rosa Parks: My Story* (6–10). 1992, Dial $17.99 (0-8037-0673-1). This autobiography of the civil rights hero becomes an oral history of the movement, including her recollections of Martin Luther King, Jr., Roy Wilkins, and others. (Rev: BL 12/15/91; SLJ 2/92) [921]

7237 Siegel, Beatrice. *The Year They Walked: Rosa Parks and the Montgomery Bus Boycott* (6–8). 1992, Four Winds $16.00 (0-02-782631-7). The story behind the historic bus boycott and the committed work of African Americans and whites who made it a success. (Rev: BL 2/15/92; SLJ 8/92) [921]

RANDOLPH, A. PHILIP

7238 Hanley, Sally. *A. Philip Randolph: Labor Leader* (6–9). Illus. 1989, Chelsea LB $19.95 (1-55546-607-9). The story of the black labor leader who founded the Brotherhood of Sleeping Car Porters. (Rev: BL 10/1/88; BR 1–2/89; VOYA 2/89) [921]

RUSTIN, BAYARD

7239 Haskins, Jim. *Bayard Rustin: Behind the Scenes of the Civil Rights Movement* (5–8). Illus.

1997, Hyperion LB $15.49 (0-7868-2140-X). The life of the great civil rights leader and 50 years in the struggle for equality are presented in this exciting biography. (Rev: BL 2/15/97; BR 9–10/97; SLJ 4/97; VOYA 2/98) [921]

STANTON, ELIZABETH CADY

7240 Cullen-DuPont, Kathryn. *Elizabeth Cady Stanton and Women's Liberty* (6–10). 1992, Facts on File LB $19.95 (0-8160-2413-8). Presents a humanistic picture of one of the founders of the women's rights movement and provides an intimate portrait of Stanton as wife, mother, and activist. (Rev: BL 10/1/92; SLJ 7/92) [921]

STEINEM, GLORIA

7241 Daffron, Carolyn. *Gloria Steinem* (7–12). Illus. 1988, Chelsea LB $19.95 (1-55546-679-6). The story of the influential woman who founded *Ms.* magazine and who is also a leader in the feminist movement. (Rev: BL 11/1/87; BR 11–12/88; VOYA 2/89) [921]

7242 Hoff, Mark. *Gloria Steinem: The Women's Movement* (6–12). (New Directions) 1991, Millbrook LB $21.90 (1-878841-19-X). A biography of the famous feminist. (Rev: BL 2/1/91) [921]

7243 Lazo, Caroline. *Gloria Steinem* (6–9). (Newsmakers Biographies) 1997, Lerner LB $25.26 (0-8225-4934-4). An well-illustrated biography of the feminist activist, writer, and lecturer who has made many contributions to the women's rights movement in the last 35 years. (Rev: BL 7/97; SLJ 7/98) [921]

TRUTH, SOJOURNER

7244 Krass, Peter. *Sojourner Truth* (7–12). Illus. 1988, Chelsea LB $19.95 (1-55546-611-7). The life of a woman who began as a slave and ended as a respected abolitionist and feminist. (Rev: BL 10/1/88) [921]

7245 McKissack, Patricia, and Fredrick McKissack. *Sojourner Truth: Ain't I a Woman?* (5–8). 1992, Scholastic $13.95 (0-590-44690-8). Drawing on the 1850 autobiography *Narrative of Sojourner Truth: A Northern Slave,* the authors integrate her personal story with a history of slavery, resistance, and abolitionism. (Rev: BL 11/15/92; SLJ 2/93) [921]

TUBMAN, HARRIET

7246 Bradford, Sarah. *Harriet Tubman, the Moses of Her People* (7–12). Illus. 1961, Peter Smith $9.00 (0-8446-1717-2). A biography first published in 1869 of this former slave who brought hundreds of slaves north to freedom. [921]

7247 Carlson, Judy. *Harriet Tubman: Call to Freedom* (5–8). 1989, Ballantine paper $4.99 (0-449-90376-1). A biography that is a lively account of the early fighter against slavery. (Rev: BL 12/15/89; BR 3–4/90; SLJ 2/90) [921]

TURNER, NAT

7248 Bisson, Terry. *Nat Turner: Slave Revolt Leader* (7–10). Illus. 1988, Chelsea LB $19.95 (1-55546-613-3). A biography of the courageous black man who led one of the nation's most important slave revolts. (Rev: BL 8/88; BR 1–2/89; SLJ 2/89; VOYA 2/89) [921]

VESEY, DENMARK

7249 Edwards, Lillie J. *Denmark Vesey: Slave Revolt Leader* (6–9). Illus. 1990, Chelsea LB $19.95 (1-55546-614-1). The story of the slave who bought his freedom and was later hanged for plotting a slave rebellion. (Rev: BL 7/90; SLJ 7/90) [921]

WASHINGTON, BOOKER T.

7250 Schroeder, Alan. *Booker T. Washington* (7–10). (Black Americans of Achievement) 1992, Chelsea LB $19.95 (1-55546-616-8). The story of the famous African American educator, leader, and founder of the Tuskegee Institute. (Rev: BL 9/15/92) [921]

7251 Washington, Booker T. *Up from Slavery: An Autobiography by Booker T. Washington* (7–12). Illus. 1963, Airmont paper $5.49 (0-8049-0157-0). The story of the slave who later organized the Tuskegee Institute. [921]

ZITKALA-SA (RED BIRD)

7252 Rappaport, Doreen. *The Flight of Red Bird: The Life of Zitkala-Sa* (7–10). 1997, NewStar Media paper $15.99 (0-8037-1438-6). The remarkable story of Zitkala-Sa (Red Bird), who was born to a Sioux mother and a white father in 1876 and devoted her life to advocating the rights of Native Americans. (Rev: BL 7/97; SLJ 7/97; VOYA 10/98) [921]

Presidents and Their Families

ADAMS, ABIGAIL

7253 Bober, Natalie S. *Abigail Adams: Witness to a Revolution* (6–12). 1995, Atheneum $18.00 (0-689-31760-3). A portrait of a woman and the age she lived in. (Rev: BL 4/15/95*; SLJ 6/95) [921]

7254 Osborne, Angela. *Abigail Adams* (6–10). Illus. 1988, Chelsea LB $19.95 (1-55546-635-4). The biography of the early feminist who was a strong influence on husband John and a fine recorder of

American history. (Rev: BL 12/1/88; BR 5–6/89; SLJ 1/89) [921]

ADAMS, JOHN

7255 Stefoff, Rebecca. *John Adams: 2nd President of the United States* (7–9). 1988, Garrett LB $21.27 (0-944483-10-0). Both the life and the times of our second president are well re-created in this account. (Rev: SLJ 9/88) [921]

BUSH, GEORGE

7256 Pemberton, William E. *George Bush* (6–12). (World Leaders) 1993, Rourke LB $25.27 (0-86625-478-1). A biography of the former vice-president and president of the United States and an assessment of his accomplishments in office. (Rev: BL 12/1/93) [921]

CARTER, JIMMY

7257 Carter, Jimmy. *Living Faith* (10–12). 1996, Times Bks. $23.00 (0-8129-2736-2). In this first-person account, the former president tells about his beliefs and how he tries to practice them in everyday life. (Rev: BL 9/15/96; SLJ 4/97) [921]

7258 Lazo, Caroline. *Jimmy Carter: On the Road to Peace* (7–9). (People in Focus) 1996, Silver Burdett LB $13.95 (0-382-39262-0); paper $7.95 (0-382-39263-9). Jimmy Carter's own written words are often used in this biography that covers both his political career and his post-presidential humanitarian efforts. (Rev: BL 8/96; SLJ 8/96) [921]

CLEVELAND, GROVER

7259 Collins, David R. *Grover Cleveland: 22nd and 24th President of the United States* (7–9). Illus. 1988, Garrett LB $21.27 (0-944483-01-1). A fine introduction to this president, his career, and interesting sidelights to his life that make this account interesting. (Rev: SLJ 9/88) [921]

CLINTON, BILL

7260 Cole, Michael D. *Bill Clinton: United States President* (6–9). 1994, Enslow LB $19.95 (0-89490-437-X). Surveys Clinton's life and accomplishments prior to his presidential election, emphasizing his tenure as governor of Arkansas. (Rev: BL 7/94; SLJ 7/94) [921]

7261 Cwiklik, Robert. *Bill Clinton: President of the 90's*. rev. ed. (4–8). (Gateway Biographies) 1997, Millbrook LB $20.90 (0-7613-0129-1); paper $8.95 (0-7613-0146-1). A readable biography that concentrates on Clinton's career as governor of Arkansas and his early years as president. (Rev: BL 9/15/97; SLJ 7/97) [921]

7262 Gallen, David. *Bill Clinton: As They Know Him: An Oral Biography* (9–12). 1994, Richard Gallen $21.95 (0-9636477-2-5). Interviews with people who have known the president provide anecdotes and observations about his childhood, governorship, and candidacy. (Rev: BL 3/15/94; SLJ 8/94) [921]

7263 Kelly, Michael. *Bill Clinton* (6–10). (Overcoming Adversity) 1998, Chelsea LB $19.95 (0-7910-4700-8). This book describes Bill Clinton's difficult childhood, including his abusive, alcoholic stepfather, but focuses on his political career, emphasizing the important role Hillary Rodham Clinton has played in his success, with a good balance between coverage of Clinton's achievements and problems, including the scandals. (Rev: SLJ 2/99) [921]

7264 Landau, Elaine. *Bill Clinton and His Presidency* (4–8). (First Books: Biographies) 1997, Watts LB $22.00 (0-531-20295-X). This biography traces the life and career of Bill Clinton through his first term as president. (Rev: BL 9/15/97; SLJ 9/97) [921]

7265 Maraniss, David. *First in His Class: The Biography of Bill Clinton* (9–12). 1995, Simon & Schuster $25.00 (0-671-87109-9). An adult biography of Bill Clinton that ends before the scandals of his second term. (Rev: BL 1/15/95) [921]

CLINTON, HILLARY RODHAM

7266 Boyd, Aaron. *First Lady: The Story of Hillary Rodham Clinton* (5–8). 1994, Morgan Reynolds LB $17.95 (1-883846-02-1). A companion of sorts to *Bill Clinton: President from Arkansas*. Focuses on the first lady's accomplishments and her role during her husband's first administration. (Rev: BL 4/15/94; SLJ 3/94; VOYA 12/94) [921]

7267 Kozar, Richard. *Hillary Rodham Clinton* (6–9). (Women of Achievement) 1998, Chelsea LB $19.95 (0-7910-4712-1). Updated through July 1997, this biography emphasizes the many ways in which Hillary Rodham Clinton has redefined the role of First Lady while she has been in the White House. (Rev: BR 1–2/99; SLJ 10/98; VOYA 4/99) [921]

EISENHOWER, DWIGHT D.

7268 Darby, Jean. *Dwight D. Eisenhower: A Man Called Ike* (6–9). Illus. 1989, Lerner LB $25.26 (0-8225-4900-X). An easily read account of the highlights in the life of this general and president. (Rev: BL 11/15/89; SLJ 9/89) [921]

7269 Ellis, Rafaela. *Dwight D. Eisenhower: 34th President of the United States* (6–8). Illus. 1989, Garrett LB $21.27 (0-944483-13-5). A clearly written biography of the soldier-statesman who became our thirty-fourth president. (Rev: BR 9–10/89; SLJ 8/89) [921]

7270 Sandberg, Peter Lars. *Dwight D. Eisenhower* (7–12). Illus. 1986, Chelsea LB $19.95 (0-87754-521-9). A brief biography of the president and war leader that emphasizes the human side of this historical figure. (Rev: SLJ 11/86) [921]

GRANT, ULYSSES S.

7271 Falkof, Lucille. *Ulysses S. Grant: 18th President of the United States* (6–9). Illus. 1988, Garrett LB $21.27 (0-944483-02-X). The career of the soldier statesman is re-created with information about the background events of his time. (Rev: SLJ 10/88) [921]

7272 Marrin, Albert. *Unconditional Surrender: U. S. Grant and the Civil War* (6–12). 1994, Atheneum $21.00 (0-689-31837-5). Part history, part biography, this is a fine study of Grant and his pivotal role in the Civil War. (Rev: BL 4/1/94*; SLJ 7/94*; VOYA 6/94) [921]

HOOVER, HERBERT

7273 Hilton, Suzanne. *The World of Young Herbert Hoover* (4–8). Illus. 1987, Walker LB $25.90 (0-8027-6709-5). This brief biography takes Hoover through his college years and gives some indication of events to follow. (Rev: SLJ 1/88) [921]

HOOVER, LOU

7274 Colbert, Nancy A. *Lou Hoover: The Duty to Serve* (5–8). Illus. 1997, Morgan Reynolds LB $18.95 (1-883846-22-6). The wife of an unpopular president, Lou Hoover was also a most interesting person, who, among other accomplishments, was the first woman to get a degree in geology in this country, the translator, with her husband, of a 16th-century Latin mining text; an advocate of physical education for women, and was fluent in seven languages, including Chinese. (Rev: BL 2/15/98; SLJ 3/98) [973.91]

JACKSON, ANDREW

7275 Meltzer, Milton. *Andrew Jackson and His America* (8–12). 1993, Watts LB $29.00 (0-531-11157-1). Presents a multifaceted picture of Jackson and his role in such historic operations as the Indian removal and in the abolitionist movement. (Rev: BL 1/15/94*; SLJ 1/94; VOYA 2/94) [921]

7276 Stefoff, Rebecca. *Andrew Jackson: 7th President of the United States* (7–9). Illus. 1988, Garrett LB $21.27 (0-944483-08-9). An interesting account of this president's life plus good background material on the period in which he lived. (Rev: SLJ 9/88) [921]

JEFFERSON, THOMAS

7277 Ellis, Joseph J. *American Sphinx: The Character of Thomas Jefferson* (10–12). 1997, Knopf $29.95 (0-679-44490-4). This well-written study of Jefferson shows the human side of this great historical figure—a man who made mistakes, a man with debts, a man with family problems. (Rev: BL 1/1–15/97; SLJ 9/97) [921]

7278 Ferris, Jeri. *Thomas Jefferson: Father of Liberty* (5–8). 1998, Lerner $23.93 (1-57505-009-9). This readable biography covers both the public side of Jefferson's life and the private, with details on his personality and his family. (Rev: BL 3/1/99; SLJ 12/98) [921]

7279 Meltzer, Milton. *Thomas Jefferson: The Revolutionary Aristocrat* (6–10). 1991, Watts LB $28.00 (0-531-11069-9). A presentation of the major events of Jefferson's life and a discussion of some troubling inconsistencies, such as his ownership of slaves. (Rev: BL 12/15/91*; SLJ 12/91*) [921]

7280 Miller, Douglas T. *Thomas Jefferson and the Creation of America* (8–12). (Makers of America) 1997, Facts on File $19.95 (0-8160-3393-5). This biography presents Jefferson as a complex character who personified ideals of equality and liberty yet lived a life of many contradictions and conflicts. (Rev: BL 11/15/97; BR 3–4/98) [921]

7281 Morris, Jeffrey. *The Jefferson Way* (5–8). (Great Presidential Decisions) 1994, Lerner LB $23.93 (0-8225-2926-2). Provides basic background information but focuses on Jefferson's term as president. (Rev: BL 12/15/94; SLJ 12/94) [921]

7282 Old, Wendie C. *Thomas Jefferson* (5–8). (United States Presidents) 1997, Enslow LB $19.95 (0-89490-837-5). An account of the life and career of the multifaceted Jefferson. (Rev: BL 2/1/98; SLJ 3/98) [921]

7283 Severance, John B. *Thomas Jefferson; Architect of Democracy* (7–12). 1998, Clarion $18.00 (0-395-84513-0). A thoughtful, well-rounded biography that focuses on Jefferson's accomplishments and his beliefs, with many quotes from his writings. (Rev: BL 9/1/98; BR 5–6/99; SLJ 12/98; VOYA 4/99) [921]

JOHNSON, LYNDON B.

7284 Eskow, Dennis. *Lyndon Baines Johnson* (8–12). (Impact Biographies) 1993, Watts LB $24.00 (0-531-13019-3). Well-chosen episodes and anecdotes illustrate the life of this Texas-born president. (Rev: BL 9/1/93; VOYA 10/93) [921]

7285 Falkof, Lucille. *Lyndon B. Johnson: 36th President of the United States* (6–8). Illus. 1989, Garrett LB $21.27 (0-944483-20-8). An informative biography that covers both the public and private life of this president. (Rev: BL 5/1/89; BR 9–10/89; SLJ 8/89) [921]

7286 Kaye, Tony. *Lyndon B. Johnson* (6–10). Illus. 1987, Chelsea LB $19.95 (0-87754-536-7). A biography of the president associated with Great Society legislation and the Vietnam War. (Rev: BL 1/15/88; SLJ 4/88) [921]

7287 Schuman, Michael A. *Lyndon B. Johnson* (6–10). (United States Presidents) 1998, Enslow $19.95 (0-89490-938-X). This biography focuses on Johnson's public career, his presidential administration, and his legacy. (Rev: SLJ 3/99) [921]

KENNEDY, JOHN F.

7288 Falkof, Lucille. *John F. Kennedy: 35th President of the United States* (6–9). Illus. 1988, Garrett LB $21.27 (0-944483-03-8). As well as the life and career of this president, the author gives good background material on the issues and general events of the times. (Rev: SLJ 10/88) [921]

7289 Lowe, Jacques. *JFK Remembered* (9–12). 1993, Random $37.50 (0-679-42399-0). The photos Lowe took as Kennedy's personal photographer are presented as full-page black-and-white spreads with identifying text. (Rev: BL 12/1/93) [921]

7290 Manchester, William. *One Brief Shining Moment: Remembering Kennedy* (9–12). Illus. 1988, Little, Brown paper $16.95 (0-316-54511-2). A remembrance of Kennedy in 200 photographs and quotes from friends and associates. [921]

7291 Netzley, Patricia. *The Assassination of President John F. Kennedy* (7–12). (American Events) 1994, Macmillan LB $18.95 (0-02-768127-0). An account of the events leading up to the assassination, the event itself, and the consequences. (Rev: BL 7/94) [921]

7292 Randall, Marta. *John F. Kennedy* (6–10). Illus. 1987, Chelsea LB $19.95 (0-87754-586-3). A biography of this beloved president that includes coverage of domestic and international crises. (Rev: BL 1/15/88; BR 9–10/88; VOYA 10/88) [921]

7293 Selfridge, John W. *John F. Kennedy: Courage in Crisis* (5–8). 1989, Ballantine paper $4.99 (0-449-90399-0). A simple biography of the late president that tells about his youth as well as his presidency. (Rev: BL 12/15/89; BR 3–4/90; SLJ 2/90) [921]

7294 Uschan, Michael V. *John F. Kennedy* (6–10). Illus. 1998, Lucent LB $22.45 (1-56006-482-X). An objective account that uses quotes from many original sources, chronicling fairly and honestly Kennedy's rise to power, his triumphs, and his faults. (Rev: SLJ 4/99; VOYA 8/99) [921]

7295 Waggoner, Jeffrey. *The Assassination of President Kennedy* (7–10). Illus. 1989, Greenhaven LB

$22.45 (0-89908-068-5). The evidence supporting various theories on the death of President Kennedy is presented in this readable account. (Rev: BL 3/1/90; SLJ 5/90) [921]

LINCOLN, ABRAHAM

7296 Bracken, Thomas. *Abraham Lincoln: U. S. President* (7–9). Illus. (Overcoming Adversity) 1999, Chelsea paper $9.95 (0-7910-4705-9). A biography of Lincoln that stresses the many obstacles he overcame, including lack of formal education, financial difficulties, and bouts of depression. (Rev: SLJ 10/98) [921]

7297 Donald, David Herbert. *Lincoln* (9–12). 1995, Simon & Schuster $35.00 (0-684-80846-3). A psychological portrait of the man from humble roots who slowly but determinedly found his niche as an attorney, then as a politician, and finally as president. (Rev: BL 8/95*) [921]

7298 Freedman, Russell. *Lincoln: A Photobiography* (5–10). Illus. 1987, Clarion $17.00 (0-89919-380-3). This title beautifully re-creates the life of this great American in text and pictures. Newbery Medal, 1988. (Rev: BL 12/15/87; SLJ 12/87) [921]

7299 Ito, Tom. *Abraham Lincoln* (7–9). Illus. (Mysterious Deaths) 1996, Lucent LB $22.45 (1-56006-259-2). This book reviews Lincoln's life and accomplishments, then focuses on his assassination and the aftermath. (Rev: BL 2/15/97; SLJ 5/97) [921]

7300 Kunhardt, Philip B., et al. *Lincoln* (9–12). 1992, Knopf $50.00 (0-679-40862-2). With many rare photos, this illustrated biography of Lincoln deserves a spot in high school collections. (Rev: BL 9/1/92; SLJ 7/93; VOYA 8/93) [921]

7301 Marrin, Albert. *Commander in Chief Abraham Lincoln and the Civil War* (7–12). Illus. 1997, Dutton paper $25.00 (0-525-45822-0). This is not only a stirring biography of Lincoln but also a history of the Civil War, with profiles of people involved in the fight against slavery, such as John Brown. (Rev: BL 12/15/97; BR 5–6/98; SLJ 2/98*; VOYA 4/98) [921]

7302 Meltzer, Milton, ed. *Lincoln in His Own Words* (6–9). Illus. 1993, Harcourt $22.95 (0-15-245437-3). A collection of excerpts of Lincoln's statements, with facts about his life. (Rev: BL 9/1/93; VOYA 12/93) [921]

7303 Oates, Stephen B. *With Malice Toward None: The Life of Abraham Lincoln* (10–12). 1978, NAL paper $4.95 (0-451-62314-2). This account probes into the personal life of Lincoln as well as his public career. [921]

7304 O'Neal, Michael. *The Assassination of Abraham Lincoln* (6–10). (Great Mysteries) 1991, Greenhaven LB $18.96 (0-89908-092-8). Outlines known facts about Lincoln's assassination and poses ques-

tions about the mysteries that remain unsolved. (Rev: BL 3/1/92; SLJ 4/92) [921]

7305 Reck, W. Emerson. *A. Lincoln: His Last 24 Hours* (9–12). Illus. 1987, McFarland LB $27.50 (0-89950-216-4). A vivid hour-by-hour recreation of the last day of Lincoln's life. (Rev: BL 8/87; BR 11–12/87; SLJ 11/87; VOYA 12/87) [921]

7306 Sandburg, Carl. *Abe Lincoln Grows Up* (6–9). 1975, Harcourt paper $7.00 (0-15-602615-5). From the pen of one of America's great poets, this is an account of the boyhood of his great hero. [921]

7307 Sloate, Susan. *Abraham Lincoln: The Freedom President* (5–8). 1989, Ballantine paper $3.95 (0-449-90375-3). An accessible account of the president who led his country through division back to unity. (Rev: BL 12/15/89; BR 3–4/90) [921]

7308 Stefoff, Rebecca. *Abraham Lincoln: 16th President of the United States* (6–8). Illus. 1989, Garrett LB $21.27 (0-944483-14-3). A serviceable biography that gives information about Lincoln's personality and his family life. (Rev: SLJ 8/89) [921]

MADISON, DOLLEY

7309 Pflueger, Lynda. *Dolley Madison: Courageous First Lady* (5–8). (Historical American Biographies) 1999, Enslow $19.95 (0-7660-1092-9). The interesting biography of the woman who defined the role of First Lady and who was known for her political acumen and diplomatic and social skills as well as her patriotism and her ability to inspire others. (Rev: BR 5–6/99; SLJ 1/99) [921]

MADISON, JAMES

7310 Fritz, Jean. *The Great Little Madison* (5–8). Illus. 1989, Putnam $15.95 (0-399-21768-1). With wit and imagination the author captures the life of our fourth president. (Rev: BL 10/1/89; BR 3–4/90; SLJ 11/89; VOYA 12/89) [921]

7311 Malone, Mary. *James Madison* (7–9). (United States Presidents) 1997, Enslow LB $19.95 (0-89490-834-0). This objective biography emphasizes Madison's intellectual and public-service contributions, with details on his role in drafting the Constitution and his 2 terms as president. (Rev: BL 9/15/97; SLJ 9/97) [921]

MONROE, JAMES

7312 Wetzel, Charles. *James Monroe* (6–10). Illus. 1989, Chelsea LB $19.95 (1-55546-817-9). The life of the Revolutionary War hero, his presidency, and the foreign policy named after him. (Rev: BL 7/89; BR 9–10/89) [921]

NIXON, RICHARD M.

7313 Barron, Rachel. *Richard Nixon: American Politician* (7–12). Illus. (Notable Americans) 1998, Morgan Reynolds $18.95 (1-883846-33-1). An objective biography of this contradictory figure who became the century's most controversial president. (Rev: BL 8/98; SLJ 12/98; VOYA 10/98) [921]

7314 Larsen, Rebecca. *Richard Nixon: Rise and Fall of a President* (6–9). 1991, Watts LB $24.00 (0-531-10997-6). A balanced look at the life and career of the 37th president of the United States. (Rev: BL 8/91; SLJ 8/91) [921]

7315 Randolph, Sallie. *Richard M. Nixon, President* (6–9). Illus. 1989, Walker LB $27.90 (0-8027-6849-0). A straightforward account using many original sources that doesn't skirt the controversial issues. (Rev: BL 1/15/90; SLJ 12/90; VOYA 2/90) [921]

7316 Ripley, C. Peter. *Richard Nixon* (6–10). Illus. 1987, Chelsea LB $19.95 (0-87754-585-5). Beginning with his 1974 resignation, Nixon's life is retraced and an assessment of his career is given. (Rev: BL 12/1/87; BR 5–6/88; SLJ 12/87) [921]

7317 Schuman, Michael A. *Richard M. Nixon* (6–9). (United States Presidents) 1998, Enslow LB $19.95 (0-89490-937-1). Opening with one of the highlights of Nixon's career, his trip to China in 1972, this objective account then recounts Nixon's life chronologically, personal and public, including the final years of his life and the continuing reassessments of his career in the years since his death. (Rev: SLJ 12/98) [921]

REAGAN, RONALD

7318 Sullivan, George. *Ronald Reagan.* Rev. ed. (5–8). 1991, Messner $14.98 (0-671-74537-9). The former president's life through his second term in the White House. (Rev: BL 1/15/92) [921]

ROOSEVELT, ELEANOR

7319 Freedman, Russell. *Eleanor Roosevelt: A Life of Discovery* (5–9). 1993, Clarion $17.95 (0-89919-862-7). This admiring photobiography captures Roosevelt's public role and personal sadness. (Rev: BL 7/93*; SLJ 8/93*; VOYA 2/94) [921]

7320 Gottfried, Ted. *Eleanor Roosevelt: First Lady of the Twentieth Century* (5–8). Illus. (Book Report Biographies) 1997, Watts $21.50 (0-531-11406-6). A short, useful biography that traces Eleanor Roosevelt's life and lasting accomplishments. (Rev: BL 11/15/97; SLJ 12/97) [921]

7321 Morey, Eileen. *Eleanor Roosevelt* (4–8). (The Importance Of) 1997, Lucent LB $17.96 (1-56006-086-7). The career of this famous First Lady and her many achievements fighting for world peace are highlighted in this biography. (Rev: BL 10/15/97; SLJ 12/97) [921]

7322 Spangenburg, Raymond, and Diane Moser. *Eleanor Roosevelt: A Passion to Improve* (8–12). (Makers of America) 1996, Facts on File $19.95 (0-8160-3371-4). A superior introduction to the life and significant achievements of Eleanor Roosevelt and her lifetime struggle for social equality for all people. (Rev: BL 1/1–15/97) [921]

7323 Toor, Rachel. *Eleanor Roosevelt* (6–10). Illus. 1989, Chelsea LB $19.95 (1-55546-674-5). An affectionate portrait of a first lady who was also a great humanitarian and internationalist. (Rev: BL 4/1/89; BR 5–6/89; SLJ 5/89; VOYA 8/89) [921]

7324 Westervelt, Virginia. *Here Comes Eleanor: A New Life of Eleanor Roosevelt for Young People* (6–8). Illus. 1998, Avisson paper $16.00 (1-888105-33-X). This work focuses on the many facets of Eleanor Roosevelt's public life and her many contributions to humankind as the representative of the people's voice. (Rev: BL 2/15/99; SLJ 7/99; VOYA 10/99) [921]

ROOSEVELT, FRANKLIN D.

7325 Devaney, John. *Franklin Delano Roosevelt, President* (6–10). Illus. 1987, Walker $19.95 (0-8027-6713-3). An account that details Roosevelt's personality as well as his career. (Rev: SLJ 1/88; VOYA 12/87) [921]

7326 Greenblatt, Miriam. *Franklin D. Roosevelt: 32nd President of the United States* (6–8). Illus. 1989, Garrett LB $21.27 (0-944483-06-2). A clearly written, objective biography of Roosevelt that also includes information about his family life. (Rev: SLJ 8/89) [921]

7327 Morris, Jeffrey. *The FDR Way* (5–8). Illus. (Great Presidential Decisions) 1996, Lerner LB $23.93 (0-8225-2929-7). A straightforward, incisive analysis of far-reaching, often painful decisions that FDR made, and an assessment of their consequences. (Rev: BL 3/15/96) [921]

7328 Nardo, Don. *Franklin D. Roosevelt: U.S. President* (7–10). (Great Achievers: Lives of the Physically Challenged) 1995, Chelsea LB $19.95 (0-7910-2406-7). This biography of Roosevelt stresses the physical challenges he faced and his strong personality that allowed him to achieve great success. (Rev: BR 3–4/96; SLJ 1/96) [921]

7329 Schuman, Michael A. *Franklin D. Roosevelt: The Four-Term President* (5–8). (People to Know) 1996, Enslow LB $19.95 (0-89490-696-8). A thoughtful, serious biography of this great president, his important decisions, and his significance in history. (Rev: SLJ 8/96) [921]

ROOSEVELT, THEODORE

7330 Fritz, Jean. *Bully for You, Teddy Roosevelt!* (5–8). Illus. 1991, Putnam $15.99 (0-399-21769-X). The story of the adventurous 26th president who was also founder of the Bull Moose Party in national politics. (Rev: BL 4/15/91; SLJ 7/91*) [921]

7331 Meltzer, Milton. *Theodore Roosevelt and His America* (7–12). 1994, Watts LB $29.00 (0-531-11192-X). Conveys a sense of the complexities and contradictions in the president who led the United States during the tumultuous first years of the 20th century. (Rev: BL 2/1/95; VOYA 5/95) [921]

7332 Schuman, Michael A. *Theodore Roosevelt* (5–8). (United States Presidents) 1997, Enslow LB $19.95 (0-89490-836-7). An objective biography of the life of this active president whose life spanned both the Civil War and World War I, with good background information. (Rev: BL 2/1/98; SLJ 2/98) [921]

7333 Stefoff, Rebecca. *Theodore Roosevelt: 26th President of the United States* (7–9). 1988, Garrett LB $21.27 (0-944483-09-7). The adventurous life of this president is re-created as well as his pioneering work in conservation. (Rev: SLJ 9/88) [921]

7334 Whitelaw, Nancy. *Theodore Roosevelt Takes Charge* (6–9). 1992, Albert Whitman $14.95 (0-8075-7849-5). A clear, credible biography of a larger-than-life American hero who was full of contradictions. (Rev: BL 6/1/92*; SLJ 7/92*) [921]

TRUMAN, HARRY S.

7335 Feinberg, Barbara S. *Harry S Truman* (7–12). 1994, Watts LB $24.00 (0-531-13036-3). Examines Truman's life and presidential administration, analyzing the events of his 2 terms and his struggles and triumphs. (Rev: BL 9/1/94; SLJ 9/94) [921]

7336 Fleming, Thomas. *Harry S Truman, President* (6–12). 1993, Walker LB $15.85 (0-8027-8269-8). The author of this uncritical biography of the former president had access to family photos and documents. (Rev: BL 1/1/94; SLJ 12/93; VOYA 2/94) [921]

7337 Greenberg, Morrie. *The Buck Stops Here: A Biography of Harry Truman* (5–9). Illus. 1989, Dillon LB $13.95 (0-87518-394-8). A competent retelling of the major events in Truman's life and of his importance as a U.S. president. (Rev: SLJ 4/89) [921]

7338 McCullough, David. *Truman* (9–12). 1992, Simon & Schuster $32.00 (0-671-45654-7). A landmark biography of the 33rd president and his times. (Rev: BL 4/15/92*) [921]

WASHINGTON, GEORGE

7339 Bruns, Roger. *George Washington* (6–10). Illus. 1986, Chelsea LB $19.95 (0-87754-584-7). A solid, readable biography of our first president. (Rev: BL 3/1/87; SLJ 5/87) [921]

7340 Falkof, Lucille. *George Washington: 1st President of the United States* (6–8). Illus. 1989, Garrett LB $21.27 (0-944483-19-4). An objective, readable portrait of the life and times of our first president. (Rev: BR 9–10/89; SLJ 8/89) [921]

7341 Foster, Genevieve, and Joanna Foster. *George Washington's World.* rev. ed. (5–8). 1997, Beautiful Feet paper $15.95 (0-9643803-4-X). An expanded version of the book (now over 50 years old) that tells about George Washington and world events during his lifetime. (Rev: SLJ 3/98) [921]

7342 Hilton, Suzanne. *The World of Young George Washington* (5–8). 1987, Walker $12.95 (0-8027-6657-9). Washington as a youth plus detailed information on life in pre-Revolutionary America. (Rev: BR 5–6/87; SLJ 4/87) [921]

7343 Old, Wendie C. *George Washington* (5–8). Illus. (United States Presidents) 1997, Enslow LB $19.95 (0-89490-832-4). Washington's personal life and political career are dealt with equally in this thoughtful biography. (Rev: BL 9/15/97; SLJ 12/97) [921]

7344 Rosenburg, John. *First in Peace: George Washington, the Constitution, and the Presidency* (7–10). 1998, Millbrook LB $22.40 (0-7613-0422-3). The last of the trilogy about Washington, this installment describes the emergence of the new nation and the role played by our first president. (Rev: SLJ 1/99) [921]

7345 Rosenburg, John. *Young George Washington: The Making of a Hero* (6–8). Illus. 1997, Millbrook LB $22.40 (0-7613-0043-0). Lively storytelling combined with excerpts from Washington's early journals result in an exciting, realistic portrait of the first president as a teenager through age 27. (Rev: BL 2/15/97; SLJ 4/97; VOYA 8/97) [973.3]

7346 Smith, Richard Norton. *Patriarch: George Washington and the New American Nation* (9–12). 1993, Houghton $24.95 (0-395-52442-3). A detailed account of Washington's presidency, leavened with quotations and anecdotes. (Rev: BL 12/1/92) [921]

WASHINGTON, MARTHA

7347 McPherson, Stephanie S. *Martha Washington: First Lady* (7–9). (Historical American Biographies) 1998, Enslow $19.95 (0-7660-1017-1). An affectionate portrait of the first First Lady, who was not well educated but put the skills she learned to good use running a household and living in polite society. (Rev: BL 1/1–15/99; SLJ 1/99) [921]

WILSON, WOODROW

7348 Collins, David R. *Woodrow Wilson: 28th President of the United States* (6–8). Illus. 1989, Garrett LB $21.27 (0-944483-18-6). An objective account of the life of the president who brought us through World War I. (Rev: SLJ 8/89) [921]

7349 Randolph, Sallie. *Woodrow Wilson, President* (5–9). (Presidential Biography) 1992, Walker LB $15.85 (0-8027-8144-6). Offers a concise overview of Wilson's tragic personal and political struggles, his achievements, and his place in history. (Rev: BL 12/15/91; SLJ 3/92) [921]

7350 Rogers, James T. *Woodrow Wilson: Visionary for Peace* (7–10). Illus. (Makers of America) 1997, Facts on File $19.95 (0-8160-3396-X). A thoughtful, in-depth biography the idealistic American president who overcame obstacles throughout his life and whose dream of an international League of Nations was shattered when the United States declined to join. (Rev: BL 5/15/97) [921]

Other Government and Public Figures

ADAMS, SAMUEL

7351 Fradin, Dennis B. *Samuel Adams: The Father of American Independence* (5–9). Illus. 1998, Houghton $18.00 (0-395-82510-5). A biography of the amazing Sam Adams, whom Jefferson called "the Man of the Revolution." (Rev: BL 7/98; BR 11–12/98; SLJ 7/98; VOYA 2/99) [921]

ADDAMS, JANE

7352 Hovde, Jane. *Jane Addams* (8–12). Illus. 1989, Facts on File $19.95 (0-8160-1547-3). The life and work of this early feminist and social worker. (Rev: BL 9/15/89; BR 11–12/89; VOYA 12/89) [921]

7353 Kittredge, Mary. *Jane Addams* (6–10). Illus. 1988, Chelsea LB $19.95 (1-55546-636-2). Jane Addams helped immigrants by founding the first settlement house, Hull House, in Chicago. (Rev: BL 6/15/88; BR 11–12/88; SLJ 1/89) [921]

7354 McPherson, Stephanie S. *Peace and Bread: The Story of Jane Addams* (5–8). 1993, Carolrhoda LB $23.93 (0-87614-792-9). An introduction to Jane Addams's work among the poor of Chicago and her leadership in international organizations on behalf of world peace. (Rev: BL 1/15/94; SLJ 2/94) [921]

7355 Wheeler, Leslie A. *Jane Addams* (7–12). (Pioneers in Change) 1990, Silver Burdett LB $13.98 (0-382-09962-1); paper $6.95 (0-382-09968-0). A biography of an outspoken social activist in turn-of-the-century Chicago. (Rev: BL 1/15/91) [921]

ALBRIGHT, MADELEINE

7356 Burgan, Michael. *Madeleine Albright* (8–10). 1998, Millbrook $24.90 (0-7613-0367-7). The life of the first woman U.S. secretary of state and highest-ranking woman ever in the federal government that tells of her European childhood, her arrival as a refugee in this country, and her experiences as a student, journalist, activist, teacher, mother, ambassador, and, finally, secretary of state. (Rev: SLJ 6/99) [921]

7357 Byman, Jeremy. *Madam Secretary: The Story of Madeleine Albright* (6–10). Illus. (Notable Americans) 1997, Morgan Reynolds LB $18.95 (1-883846-23-4). The emphasis in this biography is Albright's public life, first as advisor to various political figures, then as ambassador to the United Nations, and finally as secretary of state. (Rev: BL 12/15/97; SLJ 4/98; VOYA 6/98) [921]

7358 Hasday, Judy. *Madeleine Albright* (8–12). (Women of Achievement) 1998, Chelsea LB $19.95 (0-7910-4708-3); paper $9.95 (0-7910-4709-1). A well-rounded biography of Madeleine Albright, her career in American public service, and her childhood in Eastern Europe. (Rev: SLJ 3/99) [921]

ARNOLD, BENEDICT

7359 Fritz, Jean. *Traitor: The Case of Benedict Arnold* (7–9). Illus. 1981, Putnam $16.95 (0-399-20834-8). A biography that tries to probe the many reasons for Arnold's motives. [921]

7360 King, David C. *Benedict Arnold and the American Revolution* (5–9). (Notorious Americans and Their Times) 1998, Blackbirch LB $19.45 (1-56711-221-8). This is a biography of America's most infamous traitor who also was one of the nation's most talented military officers. (Rev: BL 12/15/98; SLJ 12/98) [921]

BARTON, CLARA

7361 Hamilton, Leni. *Clara Barton* (5–10). Illus. 1987, Chelsea LB $19.95 (1-55546-641-9). The story of the Civil War nurse and how she prepared for the founding of the American Red Cross. (Rev: BL 11/1/87) [921]

7362 Whitelaw, Nancy. *Clara Barton: Civil War Nurse* (5–9). (Historical American Biographies) 1997, Enslow LB $19.95 (0-89490-778-6). Using material from her diaries and published books, this biography relates Barton's life story and amazing accomplishments. (Rev: BL 3/15/98; SLJ 2/98) [921]

BLACK HAWK

7363 Bonvillain, Nancy. *Black Hawk: Sac Rebel* (9–12). (North American Indians of Achievement)

1994, Chelsea LB $19.95 (0-7910-1711-7). The story of the Sac Indian leader who fought on the side of the British in the War of 1812 and led his people in the Black Hawk War of 1832 in an unsuccessful attempt to protect their land. (Rev: BL 7/94) [921]

BOONE, DANIEL

7364 Faragher, John Mack. *Daniel Boone: The Life and Legend of an American Pioneer* (7–12). 1992, Holt $27.50 (0-8050-1603-1); paper $15.95 (0-8050-3007-7). A biography of the complex frontier pioneer/politician/maverick. (Rev: BL 11/1/92*; SLJ 5/93*) [921]

7365 Lawlor, Laurie. *Daniel Boone* (5–9). Illus. 1988, Whitman LB $13.95 (0-8075-1462-4). A sound, well-researched biography that tries to separate myth from truth concerning this solitary frontiersman. (Rev: BL 2/15/89; SLJ 12/88) [921]

BOOTH, JOHN WILKES

7366 Otfinoski, Steven. *John Wilkes Booth and the Civil War* (5–9). (Notorious Americans and Their Times) 1998, Blackbirch LB $19.45 (1-56711-222-6). Born into a theatrical family, John Wilkes Booth turned political over the slavery issue and plotted to kill President Lincoln. This is the story of his colorful life and death. (Rev: BL 12/15/98; SLJ 12/98) [921]

BRADFORD, WILLIAM

7367 Schmidt, Gary. *William Bradford: Plymouth's Faithful Pilgrim* (5–8). 1999, Eerdmans $18.00 (0-8028-5151-7); paper $8.00 (0-8028-5148-8). The story of the famous Pilgrim who helped found the Plymouth colony and who led it for many years. (Rev: BL 7/99; SLJ 6/99; VOYA 12/99) [921]

BRADLEY, BILL

7368 Bradley, Bill. *Time Present, Time Past* (9–12). 1996, Knopf $26.00 (0-679-44488-2). An impressive job of writing his memoirs. (Rev: BL 12/15/95*) [921]

7369 Jaspersohn, William. *Senator: A Profile of Bill Bradley in the U.S. Senate* (6–10). 1992, Harcourt $19.95 (0-15-272880-5). An in-depth photoessay about Congress in general and Senator Bradley of New Jersey in particular, showing how his sports career led to the Senate. (Rev: BL 7/92; SLJ 10/92) [921]

BRANDEIS, LOUIS

7370 Freedman, Suzanne. *Louis Brandeis* (4–9). Illus. (Justices of the Supreme Court) 1996, Enslow LB $19.95 (0-89490-678-X). A biography of the great justice who advocated many public causes and

was known as the "people's attorney." (Rev: BL 8/96; SLJ 11/96) [921]

BUNCHE, RALPH

7371 Schraff, Anne. *Ralph Bunche: Winner of the Nobel Peace Prize* (6–9). (African-American Biographies) 1999, Enslow $19.95 (0-7660-1203-4). A biography of this African American statesman from his childhood to a professorship at Howard University, his later government service and diplomatic life, and his work as a United Nations mediator, which brought peace between Israel and its Arab neighbors and earned Bunche the Nobel Peace Prize, making him the first African American to receive this honor. (Rev: SLJ 8/99) [921]

CAMPBELL, BEN NIGHTHORSE

7372 Henry, Christopher. *Ben Nighthorse Campbell: Cheyenne Chief and U.S. Senator* (5–8). Illus. (North American Indians of Achievement) 1994, Chelsea $19.95 (0-7919-2046-0). The story of the Cheyenne leader who gained prominence not only among his own people but also in the U.S. Congress. (Rev: BL 6/1–15/93) [921]

CHIEF JOSEPH

7373 Yates, Diana. *Chief Joseph: Thunder Rolling from the Mountains* (7–12). 1992, Ward Hill LB $14.95 (0-9623380-9-5); paper $10.95 (0-9623380-8-7). A sensitive distillation of the life and times of Chief Joseph of the Nez Perce. (Rev: BL 12/15/92; SLJ 12/92) [921]

COCHISE

7374 Schwarz, Melissa. *Cochise: Apache Chief* (9–12). (North American Indians of Achievement) 1992, Chelsea LB $19.95 (0-7910-1706-0). The story of the Apache chief who became involved in the struggle against the attempts of white Americans to subdue the Indian peoples of the Southwest during the 1860s. (Rev: BL 10/1/92; SLJ 12/92) [921]

CRAZY HORSE

7375 Freedman, Russell. *The Life and Death of Crazy Horse* (6–12). Illus. 1996, Holiday House $21.95 (0-8234-1219-9). This biography of Crazy Horse tells an uncompromising story of bloody wars, terrible grief, tragedy, and the Sioux's losing battle to preserve their independence and their land. (Rev: BL 6/1–15/96*; BR 11–12/96; SLJ 6/96*; VOYA 10/96) [921]

7376 Goldman, Martin S. *Crazy Horse: War Chief of the Oglala Sioux* (6–12). (American Indian Experience) 1996, Watts LB $24.00 (0-531-11258-6). This carefully researched biography recounts the life of this fascinating leader and of the decline of the Sioux. (Rev: SLJ 9/96) [921]

7377 St. George, Judith. *Crazy Horse* (7–10). 1994, Putnam $17.95 (0-399-22667-2). An account of the legendary Lakota leader who struggled to save his people's culture and way of life from destruction by white soldiers and settlers. (Rev: BL 10/1/94; SLJ 11/94; VOYA 2/95) [921]

DAVIS, BENJAMIN, JR.

7378 Reef, Catherine. *Benjamin Davis, Jr.* (5–8). (African American Soldiers) 1992, Twenty-First Century LB $14.95 (0-8050-2137-X). The story of the African American air force general and how he served his country in several wars beginning with World War II. (Rev: BL 12/15/92) [921]

DAVIS, JEFFERSON

7379 Burch, Joann J. *Jefferson Davis: President of Confederacy* (5–8). (Historical American Biographies) 1998, Enslow LB $19.95 (0-7660-1064-3). A biography of the man who served as president of the Confederacy from 1861 to 1865, told with a lively text plus photos, maps, fact boxes, and a chronology. (Rev: BL 10/15/98; SLJ 1/99) [921]

7380 King, Perry Scott. *Jefferson Davis* (7–10). Illus. 1990, Chelsea LB $19.95 (1-55546-806-3). With many illustrations, King recreates the life and times of the president of the Confederacy. (Rev: BL 8/90; SLJ 8/90) [921]

DAY, DOROTHY

7381 Kent, Deborah. *Dorothy Day: Friend to the Forgotten* (7–12). Illus. 1996, Eerdmans $15.00 (0-8028-5117-7); paper $8.00 (0-8028-5100-2). The biography of the great friend of the poor and helpless whose own life's drama involved an abortion, a short-lived marriage, imprisonment, political involvement, and questioning of her deep religious beliefs. (Rev: BL 6/1–15/96; BR 1–2/97; SLJ 8/96) [921]

EARP, WYATT

7382 Green, Carl R., and William R. Sanford. *Wyatt Earp* (5–8). (Outlaws and Lawmen of the Wild West) 1992, Enslow LB $15.95 (0-89490-367-5). An account of the life of this legendary lawman in which the violence of the times is realistically conveyed. (Rev: BL 10/1/92) [921]

FRANKLIN, BENJAMIN

7383 Cousins, Margaret. *Ben Franklin of Old Philadelphia* (6–8). 1963, Random paper $5.99 (0-394-84928-0). The story of this father of America who was a master in many fields. [921]

7384 Foster, Leila M. *Benjamin Franklin: Founding Father and Inventor* (5–8). (Historical American Biographies) 1997, Enslow LB $19.95 (0-89490-784-0). An admiring biography that describes Franklin's many talents as a printer, businessman, scientist, statesman, and inventor. (Rev: SLJ 11/97) [921]

7385 Franklin, Benjamin. *The Autobiography of Benjamin Franklin* (10–12). 1986, Norton paper $14.75 (0-393-95294-0). Written between 1771 and 1788, this is more than an account of Revolutionary times; it is also an exploration of the mind of a man of varied and deep interests. [921]

7386 Looby, Chris. *Benjamin Franklin* (6–10). Illus. 1990, Chelsea LB $19.95 (1-55546-808-X). A well-illustrated account of the life of this complex man that also introduces many of his contemporaries. (Rev: BL 8/90; SLJ 7/90; VOYA 8/90) [921]

GERONIMO

7387 Barrett, S. M., ed. *Geronimo: His Own Story* (10–12). 1983, Irvington paper $15.95 (0-8290-0658-3). The memoirs of the Apache warrior Geronimo with valuable background information about his people and their culture. [921]

7388 Hermann, Spring. *Geronimo: Apache Freedom Fighter* (6–9). (Native American Biographies) 1997, Enslow LB $19.95 (0-89490-864-2). This is a fine, well-rounded portrait of the man who became an Apache leader, fought at Little Bighorn, and died a prosperous man at age 85. (Rev: BL 4/15/97; SLJ 6/97) [921]

GINSBURG, RUTH BADER

7389 Ayer, Eleanor. *Ruth Bader Ginsburg: Fire and Steel on the Supreme Court* (5–8). 1995, Dillon LB $13.95 (0-87518-651-3); paper $7.95 (0-382-24721-3). A biography of the second woman to be named to the Supreme Court. (Rev: BL 5/15/95; SLJ 4/95; VOYA 5/95) [921]

GOODE, W. WILSON

7390 Goode, W. Wilson, and Joann Stevens. *In Goode Faith: Philadelphia's First Black Mayor Tells His Story* (9–12). 1992, Judson $15.00 (0-8170-1186-2). Philadelphia's first African American mayor recounts his early life and candidly describes his turbulent political career. (Rev: BL 10/1/92) [974.8]

HAMILTON, ALEXANDER

7391 Whitelaw, Nancy. *More Perfect Union: The Story of Alexander Hamilton* (5–8). (Notable Americans) 1997, Morgan Reynolds LB $18.95 (1-883846-20-X). This stirring biography traces Hamilton's life from his birth in Nevis in the British West Indies to his death in a duel with Aaron Burr, with interesting material on his role as Washington's aide during the Revolutionary War and his term as the new nation's first secretary of the treasury. (Rev: SLJ 10/97) [921]

HOLLIDAY, DOC

7392 Green, Carl R., and William R. Sanford. *Doc Holliday* (5–8). (Outlaws and Lawmen of the Wild West) 1995, Enslow LB $15.95 (0-89490-589-9). The life and exploits of this colorful western hero are reproduced with the help of photos and maps. (Rev: BL 6/1–15/95) [921]

HOUSTON, SAM

7393 Fritz, Jean. *Make Way for Sam Houston* (6–9). Illus. 1986, Putnam paper $7.95 (0-399-21304-X). An authentic portrait of this colorful figure who served the state of Texas faithfully. (Rev: BL 6/1/86; VOYA 6/86) [921]

JACKSON, STONEWALL

7394 Fritz, Jean. *Stonewall* (7–10). Illus. 1979, Putnam $15.95 (0-399-20698-1). The great Confederate general portrayed realistically as the complex man he was. [921]

7395 Pflueger, Lynda. *Stonewall Jackson: Confederate General* (5–8). Illus. (Historical American Biographies) 1997, Enslow LB $19.95 (0-89490-781-6). This sympathetic biography of Jackson, who favored neither slavery nor secession but became a Confederate general in the Civil War, provides good material on his personal life and beliefs, quoting generously from firsthand sources. (Rev: BL 10/1/97) [921]

JAMES, DANIEL "CHAPPIE"

7396 Super, Neil. *Daniel "Chappie" James* (5–8). 1992, Twenty-First Century LB $17.90 (0-8050-2138-8). A well-written, inspiring account of an African American boy who grew up in the 1920s and 1930s dreaming of flying. Despite segregation and racism, he achieved his dream and became a 4-star general. (Rev: BL 12/15/92; SLJ 11/92) [921]

JONES, MOTHER

7397 Horton, Madelyn. *The Importance of Mother Jones* (4–8). Illus. (The Importance Of) 1996, Lucent LB $16.95 (1-56006-057-3). The story of the activist who led a protest march against child labor to President Theodore Roosevelt's home in Oyster Bay, New York, in 1903. (Rev: BL 5/15/96; SLJ 7/96) [921]

7398 Josephson, Judith P. *Mother Jones: Fierce Fighter for Workers' Rights* (6–10). Illus. 1997, Lerner LB $25.26 (0-8225-4924-7). The story of this early labor leader in coal country is also a history of the struggle against long work hours, unsafe working

conditions, poor wages, and child labor. (Rev: BL 2/1/97; SLJ 4/97*) [921]

JORDAN, BARBARA

7399 Blue, Rose, and Corinne J. Naden. *Barbara Jordan* (7–10). (Black Americans of Achievement) 1992, Chelsea LB $19.95 (0-7910-1131-3). The colorful life of this former congresswoman and educator is re-created in this illustrated biography. (Rev: BL 9/15/92; SLJ 11/92) [921]

7400 Jeffrey, Laura S. *Barbara Jordan: Congresswoman, Lawyer, Educator* (7–12). Illus. (African-American Biographies) 1997, Enslow LB $19.95 (0-89490-692-5). This biography covers both the personal and professional life of this amazing woman who overcame great obstacles to fulfill a multi-faceted career. (Rev: BL 5/15/97; SLJ 3/97) [921]

7401 Rhodes, Lisa R. *Barbara Jordan: Voice of Democracy* (5–8). (Book Report Biographies) 1998, Watts $22.00 (0-531-11450-3). An effective, well-organized biography of this politician and teacher that begins with her role in the Watergate investigation. (Rev: SLJ 2/99) [921]

JOSEPH (NEZ PERCE INDIAN LEADER)

7402 Taylor, Marian W. *Chief Joseph: Nez Perce Leader* (9–12). Illus. (North American Indians of Achievement) 1993, Chelsea LB $19.95 (0-7910-1708-7). The biography of the Nez Perce Indian leader who led a skillful but ultimately unsuccessful retreat from U.S. forces in 1877. (Rev: BL 10/15/93; SLJ 10/93) [921]

KENNEDY, ROBERT F.

7403 Mills, Judie. *Robert Kennedy* (8–12). Illus. 1998, Millbrook LB $34.90 (1-56294-250-6). A useful, informative biography that tells of Robert Kennedy's life and career and places them in the context of other historical events. (Rev: BL 8/98; SLJ 9/98) [921]

7404 Terris, Daniel, and Barbara Harrison. *Ripple of Hope* (5–8). 1997, Dutton paper $16.99 (0-525-67506-X). An insightful story of the Kennedy brother who was not as social or as smart as his older brothers but later found his own path, developing a deep social conscience and dedication to his country's and the world's poor. (Rev: BL 6/1–15/97; BR 1–2/98; SLJ 8/97) [921]

LEE, ROBERT E.

7405 Brown, Warren. *Robert E. Lee* (6–10). (World Leaders—Past and Present) 1991, Chelsea LB $19.95 (1-55546-814-4). Using many illustrations and maps, this volume re-creates the life of the Confederate Civil War general. (Rev: BL 11/15/91) [921]

7406 Kerby, Mona. *Robert E. Lee: Southern Hero of the Civil War* (5–8). Illus. 1997, Enslow LB $19.95 (0-89490-782-4). This thorough, sympathetic biography of Lee points out that he did not approve of slavery or the South's secession from the Union. (Rev: BL 10/1/97; SLJ 9/97) [973.7]

7407 Marrin, Albert. *Virginia's General: Robert E. Lee and the Civil War* (6–12). 1994, Atheneum $22.00 (0-689-31838-3). Details Lee's childhood, education, marriage, and career, and then concentrates on the Civil War years. Quotations from Lee, his generals, and his soldiers offer insights into the times. (Rev: BL 12/15/94; SLJ 12/94; VOYA 4/95) [921]

7408 Thomas, Emory M. *Robert E. Lee* (9–12). 1995, Norton $30.00 (0-393-03730-4). A large, well-researched biography of Civil War general Robert E. Lee. (Rev: BL 4/1/95*) [921]

LONG, HUEY

7409 La Vert, Suzanne. *Huey Long: The Kingfish of Louisiana* (8–12). (Makers of America) 1995, Facts on File $19.95 (0-8160-2880-X). Looks at the motivations and political life of Huey Long, "Kingfish of Louisiana," including his assassination and the inner workings of the government. (Rev: BL 6/1–15/95) [921]

MACARTHUR, DOUGLAS

7410 Darby, Jean. *Douglas MacArthur* (6–9). Illus. 1989, Lerner LB $25.26 (0-8225-4901-8). The career of the controversial general who led the war in the Pacific is outlined in this volume. (Rev: SLJ 9/89) [921]

7411 Feinberg, Barbara S. *Douglas MacArthur: American Hero* (5–10). (Book Report Biographies) 1999, Watts $22.00 (0-531-11562-3). In an easy-to-read style and many accompanying black-and-white photographs, the life of this controversial general is re-created in this brief biography. (Rev: SLJ 7/99) [921]

7412 Finkelstein, Norman H. *The Emperor General: A Biography of Douglas MacArthur* (5–9). Illus. 1989, Dillon LB $18.95 (0-87518-396-4). The high points in the life of General MacArthur are covered in this attractive biography. (Rev: SLJ 4/89) [921]

7413 Fox, Mary V. *Douglas MacArthur* (4–8). (The Importance Of) 1999, Lucent LB $53.88 (1-56006-545-1). The story of one of the nation's most prominent generals who was also a controversial figure because of his unorthodox actions. (Rev: BL 9/15/99) [921]

7414 Scott, Robert A. *Douglas MacArthur and the Century of War* (7–12). (Makers of America) 1997, Facts on File $19.95 (0-8160-3098-7). From the bat-

tlefields of World War I to his opposition to the Vietnam War, this biography follows the life of one of the most famous generals in American history. (Rev: BL 11/15/97; BR 3–4/98) [9211]

MCCARTHY, JOSEPH

7415 Cohen, Daniel. *Joseph McCarthy: The Misuse of Political Power* (7–12). Illus. 1996, Millbrook LB $23.90 (1-56294-917-9). The dramatic story of the U.S. senator who used the threat of communism to gain power and ruin innocent lives. (Rev: BL 10/1/96; BR 1–2/97; SLJ 10/96) [921]

7416 Sherrow, Victoria. *Joseph McCarthy and the Cold War* (5–9). (Notorious Americans and Their Times) 1998, Blackbirch LB $19.45 (1-56711-219-6). The story of McCarthy, probably the most powerful senator of the 1950s, of his cunning, and how he destroyed the lives of hundreds of Americans. (Rev: BL 12/15/98; SLJ 1/99) [973.921]

MANKILLER, WILMA

7417 Schwarz, Melissa. *Wilma Mankiller: Principal Chief of the Cherokees* (9–12). (North American Indians of Achievement) 1994, Chelsea LB $19.95 (0-7910-1715-X). The biography of this Cherokee leader, born in 1945, who became an activist in the 1960s and participated in the symbolic occupation of Alcatraz Island by Native Americans in 1969. (Rev: BL 10/15/94; VOYA 2/95) [921]

MARSHALL, GEORGE C.

7418 Saunders, Alan. *George C. Marshall* (10–12). (Makers of America) 1995, Facts on File $19.95 (0-8160-2666-1). This work examines the colorful career of the man who was an army general, secretary of state, and secretary of defense. (Rev: BL 11/15/95; BR 9–10/96; SLJ 2/96) [921]

MARSHALL, THURGOOD

7419 Aldred, Lisa. *Thurgood Marshall* (7–10). Illus. 1990, Chelsea LB $19.95 (1-55546-601-X). The story of the first black American to serve as a justice on the Supreme Court. (Rev: BL 7/90; SLJ 10/90) [921]

7420 Davis, Michael D., and Hunter R. Clark. *Thurgood Marshall: Warrior at the Bar, Rebel on the Bench* (9–12). 1992, Birch Lane $22.00 (1-55972-133-2). Reviews the career of the first African American Supreme Court justice, who spearheaded great legal victories for desegregation and civil rights. (Rev: BL 11/1/92) [921]

7421 Haskins, Jim. *Thurgood Marshall: A Life for Justice* (6–9). 1992, Holt $14.95 (0-8050-2095-0). Readable, inspiring biography of the first African American Supreme Court justice, who devoted his life to fighting segregation and racism through the legal system. (Rev: BL 7/92*; SLJ 8/92) [921]

7422 Herda, D. J. *Thurgood Marshall: Civil Rights Champion* (6–10). Illus. (Justices of the Supreme Court) 1995, Enslow LB $18.95 (0-89490-557-0). The story of the first African American Supreme Court justice and his lifelong fight to champion the rights of the oppressed. (Rev: BL 3/15/96) [921]

7423 Marshall, Thurgood. *Thurgood Marshall* (4–8). Illus. (The Importance Of) 1997, Lucent LB $22.45 (1-56006-061-1). This book traces the career of this Supreme Court justice, highlighting Marshall's lasting contributions to his country and his race. (Rev: BL 6/1–15/97; SLJ 9/97) [921]

7424 Whitelaw, Nancy. *Mr. Civil Rights: The Story of Thurgood Marshall* (7–12). (Notable Americans) 1995, Morgan Reynolds LB $17.95 (1-883846-10-2). Demonstrates Marshall's deep involvement with and commitment to the civil rights movement. (Rev: BL 9/1/95) [921]

MURROW, EDWARD R.

7425 Finkelstein, Norman H. *With Heroic Truth: The Life of Edward R. Murrow* (6–9). 1997, Houghton $17.95 (0-395-67891-9). A well-written biography of this pioneer in broadcasting, enhanced by interviews with his wife and son, that describes personal acts of courage, his unique, straightforward broadcasts from London during World War II, and his principled exposé of Sen. Joe McCarthy. (Rev: BL 6/1–15/97; BR 9–10/97; SLJ 7/97) [921]

NADER, RALPH

7426 Celsi, Teresa. *Ralph Nader: The Consumer Revolution* (6–12). (New Directions) 1991, Millbrook LB $21.90 (1-56294-044-9). The story of the consumer advocate who has taken on some of the largest corporations in America and won. (Rev: BL 10/1/91; SLJ 10/91) [921]

O'CONNOR, SANDRA DAY

7427 Herda, D. J. *Sandra Day O'Connor: Independent Thinker* (6–10). Illus. (Justices of the Supreme Court) 1995, Enslow LB $17.95 (0-89480-558-9). The story of the first female Supreme Court justice, including her personal life and her most import decisions since becoming a Supreme Court member in 1981. (Rev: BL 2/15/96) [921]

PAINE, THOMAS

7428 Meltzer, Milton. *Tom Paine: Voice of Revolution* (9–12). Illus. 1996, Watts LB $29.00 (0-531-11291-8). A well-researched biography of this English-born American patriot known best for his influential revolutionary writings, notably *Common*

Sense and *The Rights of Man*. (Rev: BL 12/15/96; BR 3–4/97; SLJ 12/96; VOYA 2/97) [921]

7429 Vail, John. *Thomas Paine* (6–10). Illus. 1990, Chelsea LB $19.95 (1-55546-819-5). The story of the outspoken radical whose writings influenced the development of the American Revolution. (Rev: BL 8/90; SLJ 6/90; VOYA 8/90) [921]

PATTON, GEORGE

7430 Peifer, Charles, Jr. *Soldier of Destiny: A Biography of George Patton* (5–9). Illus. 1989, Dillon LB $13.95 (0-87518-395-6). The story of this colorful war hero and his importance in history. (Rev: BL 3/1/89; SLJ 4/89; VOYA 8/89) [921]

PENN, WILLIAM

7431 Doherty, Kieran. *William Penn: Quaker Colonist* (6–10). 1998, Millbrook LB $22.40 (0-7613-0355-3). A sympathetic biography that tells of Penn's turbulent youth in England, Ireland, and France, his character, and his accomplishments in what became Pennsylvania. (Rev: BL 11/15/98; SLJ 1/99) [921]

PHILIP, KING (WAMPANOAG CHIEF)

7432 Roman, Joseph. *King Philip: Wampanoag Rebel* (9–12). (North American Indians of Achievement) 1991, Chelsea LB $19.95 (0-7910-1704-4). The story of the Wampanoog chief known as King Philip, New England's devastating war with the Indians, and King Philip's eventual death at the hands of an angry dissident. (Rev: BL 3/1/92) [921]

PINKERTON, ALLAN

7433 Green, Carl R., and William R. Sanford. *Allan Pinkerton* (5–8). (Outlaws and Lawmen of the Wild West) 1995, Enslow LB $15.95 (0-89490-590-2). The story of the Scottish immigrant who organized Pinkerton's National Detective Agency, whose specialty was antiunion actions. (Rev: BL 11/15/95) [363.2]

POCAHONTAS

7434 Holler, Anne. *Pocahontas: Powhatan Peacemaker* (9–12). (North American Indians of Achievement) 1992, Chelsea $19.95 (0-7910-1705-2). A colorful re-creation of the life of this legendary Native American woman, how she saved Captain John Smith's life, and her death in England before she could return home. (Rev: BL 2/1/93) [921]

POWELL, COLIN

7435 Blue, Rose, and Corinne J. Naden. *Colin Powell: Straight to the Top*. rev. ed. (4–8). (Gateway Biographies) 1997, Millbrook LB $20.90 (0-7613-

0256-5); paper $8.95 (0-7613-0242-5). A balanced biography of Colin Powell that focuses on his adult life and his stint as chairman of the Joint Chiefs of Staff. (Rev: BL 9/15/97; SLJ 1/98) [921]

7436 Brown, Warren. *Colin Powell* (7–10). (Black Americans of Achievement) 1992, Chelsea LB $19.95 (0-7910-1647-1). A nicely illustrated account of the African American general who distinguished himself during the Persian Gulf War. (Rev: BL 8/92) [921]

7437 Finlayson, Reggie. *Colin Powell: People's Hero* (5–8). (Achievers Biographies) 1997, Lerner LB $21.27 (0-8225-2891-6). This is a simple, well-presented biography of Colin Powell from his birth in Harlem through his distinguished military career. (Rev: SLJ 4/97; VOYA 6/97) [921]

7438 Hughes, Libby. *Colin Powell: A Man of Quality* (7–9). (People in Focus) 1996, Silver Burdett LB $18.95 (0-382-39260-4); paper $7.95 (0-382-39261-2). Documentary materials and Powell's own words are used extensively in this account that gives good coverage of his youth and education as well as his military career. (Rev: SLJ 8/96) [921]

7439 Powell, Colin. *My American Journey* (10–12). 1995, Random $25.95 (0-679-43296-5). The autobiography of the American hero who grew up in the South Bronx and later became chairman of the Joint Chiefs of Staff. (Rev: BR 5–6/96; SLJ 2/96) [921]

7440 Reef, Catherine. *Colin Powell* (5–8). (African American Soldiers) 1992, Twenty-First Century LB $17.90 (0-8050-2136-1). A well-organized biography of this important army general, with emphasis on his role in the Persian Gulf War and after. (Rev: BL 12/15/92) [921]

7441 Schraff, Anne. *Colin Powell: Soldier & Patriot* (7–12). Illus. (African-American Biographies) 1997, Enslow LB $19.95 (0-89490-810-3). The biography of the career soldier who lead our forces in war and peace, and became an inspiration to all America. (Rev: BL 5/15/97; SLJ 3/97; VOYA 6/97) [921]

RICHARDS, ANN

7442 Siegel, Dorothy. *Ann Richards: Politician, Feminist, Survivor* (6–9). (People to Know) 1996, Enslow LB $19.95 (0-89490-497-3). The life and struggles of this amazing politician are described in 10 short chapters, illustrated with black-and-white photos. (Rev: SLJ 10/96) [921]

SCHWARZKOPF, NORMAN

7443 Hughes, Libby. *Norman Schwarzkopf: Hero with a Heart* (6–10). (People in Focus) 1992, Dillon LB $18.95 (0-87518-521-5). The story of the leader of the Persian Gulf War's Operation Desert Storm in

1991 and how he emerged a popular hero. (Rev: BL 1/15/93; SLJ 2/93) [921]

SEQUOYAH

7444 Shumate, Jane. *Sequoyah: Inventor of the Cherokee Alphabet* (9–12). (North American Indians of Achievement) 1994, Chelsea LB $19.95 (0-7910-1720-6). Using characters from the Greek and Roman alphabets, Sequoyah devised a Cherokee syllabary so that his language could be written and set in type. (Rev: BL 1/1/94) [921]

SHAW, ROBERT GOULD

7445 Burchard, Peter. *"We'll Stand by the Union": Robert Gould Shaw and the Black 54th Massachusetts Regiment* (8–12). 1993, Facts on File $19.95 (0-8160-2609-2). The life and times of the Union army commander charged with training and leading Massachusetts first black regiment. (Rev: BL 2/15/94; VOYA 6/94) [921]

SHERMAN, WILLIAM T.

7446 Whitelaw, Nancy. *William Tecumseh Sherman: Defender and Destroyer* (5–8). 1996, Morgan Reynolds LB $18.95 (1-883846-12-9). Both the personal and public life of this Civil War general, who brought destruction to the South, is retold, using many quotes and photographs. (Rev: BL 3/15/96; BR 11–12/96; SLJ 6/96; VOYA 10/96) [921]

SITTING BULL

7447 Bernotas, Bob. *Sitting Bull: Chief of the Sioux* (9–12). (North American Indians of Achievement) 1991, Chelsea LB $19.95 (0-7910-1703-6). Chronicles the life of the Native American leader. (Rev: BL 3/1/92; SLJ 6/92) [978]

7448 St. George, Judith. *To See with the Heart: The Life of Sitting Bull* (6–9). 1996, Putnam $17.95 (0-399-22930-2). In this biography, Sitting Bull is portrayed not only as a courageous warrior who had difficulty establishing his position in the tribe, but also as a holy man respected by all. (Rev: BL 3/1/96; BR 11–12/96; SLJ 7/96; VOYA 12/96) [921]

7449 Schleichert, Elizabeth. *Sitting Bull: Sioux Leader* (6–9). (Native American Biographies) 1997, Enslow LB $19.95 (0-89490-868-5). A well-documented account of this important Sioux leader, including his reasons for participating in Buffalo Bill's Wild West Show. (Rev: BL 4/15/97; SLJ 6/97) [921]

7450 Utley, Robert M. *The Lance and the Shield: The Life and Times of Sitting Bull* (9–12). 1993, Holt $25.00 (0-8050-1274-5). Presents a realistic picture of the culture of Sitting Bull's people and re-creates the actions he took that earned him the deep respect and loyalty of his people. (Rev: BL 4/15/93) [921]

STUART, JEB

7451 Pflueger, Lynda. *Jeb Stuart: Confederate Cavalry General* (5–8). (Historical American Biographies) 1998, Enslow LB $19.95 (0-7660-1013-9). The life of the brilliant general who figured at the battles at Bull Run, Antietam, and Fredericksburg, but who committed a tactical error at Gettysburg. (Rev: BL 8/98; SLJ 8/98) [921]

TECUMSEH (SHAWNEE CHIEF)

7452 Cwiklik, Robert. *Tecumseh: Shawnee Rebel* (9–12). (North American Indians of Achievement) 1993, Chelsea LB $19.95 (0-7910-1721-4). The story of the Shawnee chief and military leader who tried to form a pan-tribal confederacy to resist white American expansion onto Indian lands in the early 1800s. (Rev: BL 4/1/93; SLJ 7/93) [921]

7453 Immell, Myra H., and William H. Immell. *Tecumseh* (4–8). Illus. (The Importance Of) 1997, Lucent LB $17.95 (1-56006-087-5). The story of the great Shawnee Indian leader who tried to unify American Indians against white domination and was killed in the War of 1812. (Rev: BL 5/15/97; SLJ 8/97) [921]

7454 Stefoff, Rebecca. *Tecumseh & the Shawnee Confederacy* (6–10). Illus. (Library of American Indian History) 1998, Facts on File $19.95 (0-8160-3648-9). Through an examination of the life of Tecumseh, the charismatic leader of the Shawnee Confederation, this volume presents the Shawnee culture and an illuminating history of the Indian wars in the Ohio River Valley. (Rev: SLJ 7/98) [921]

THOMAS, CLARENCE

7455 Macht, Norman L. *Clarence Thomas* (6–9). 1995, Chelsea LB $19.95 (0-7910-1883-0); paper $9.95 (0-7910-1912-8). Details Thomas's life, culminating in his controversial appointment to the Supreme Court, with frank coverage of the congressional hearings. (Rev: BL 8/95; SLJ 9/95) [347.73]

THURMOND, STROM

7456 Cohodas, Nadine. *Strom Thurmond and the Politics of Southern Change* (9–12). 1993, Simon & Schuster $27.50 (0-671-68935-5). Biography of a pivotal figure in the emergence of the new South. (Rev: BL 12/1/92) [921]

WARREN, EARL

7457 Herda, D. J. *Earl Warren: Chief Justice for Social Change* (6–10). Illus. (Justices of the Supreme Court) 1995, Enslow LB $18.95 (0-89490-556-2).

The story of the chief justice who led the Supreme Court during a period of great change, and who headed the commission that investigated President Kennedy's death. (Rev: BL 3/15/96; SLJ 3/96) [921]

WOODHULL, VICTORIA

7458 Gabriel, Mary. *Notorious Victoria: The Life of Victoria Woodhull Uncensored* (10–12). 1998, Algonquin $39.95 (1-56512-132-5). The biography of the amazing 19th-century suffragette who at one time earned her keep as a clairvoyant and later established a brokerage firm and a newspaper, ran for president of the United States, espoused the ideals of both communism and free love, and was finally hounded out of the country. (Rev: BL 1/1–15/98; BR 3–4/98; SLJ 3/98; VOYA 6/98) [921]

7459 McLean, Jacqueline. *Victoria Woodhull: First Woman Presidential Candidate* (7–12). 1999, Morgan Reynolds LB $18.95 (1-883846-47-1). The fascinating story of Victoria Woodhull, an ardent suffragist and feminist who was nominated by the Equal Rights Party in 1872 as its presidential candidate. (Rev: BL 8/99; SLJ 10/99; VOYA 12/99) [921]

Miscellaneous Persons

ALEXANDER, SALLY HOBART

7460 Alexander, Sally H. *Taking Hold: My Journey into Blindness* (6–12). 1994, Macmillan paper $14.95 (0-02-700402-3). A true story of a third-grade teacher who lost her sight but found independence. (Rev: BL 1/15/95; SLJ 4/95; VOYA 4/95) [921]

BERG, MOE

7461 Andryszewski, Tricia. *The Amazing Life of Moe Berg: Catcher, Scholar, Spy* (6–9). Illus. 1996, Millbrook LB $22.40 (1-56294-610-2). This amazing man, the son of Jewish immigrants, played in baseball's major leagues and was also a lawyer, a linguist and, most important, a spy who spent War World II collecting information from European scientists about atomic weapons. (Rev: BL 4/1/96; BR 9–10/96; SLJ 3/96; VOYA 10/96) [921]

BLY, NELLIE

7462 Kroeger, Brooke. *Nellie Bly: Daredevil, Reporter, Feminist* (9–12). 1994, Times Bks. $27.50 (0-8129-1973-4). A comprehensive biography of the pioneering 19th-century investigative reporter that highlights her fearlessness and instinct for drama. (Rev: BL 2/1/94*) [921]

7463 Marks, Jason. *Around the World in 72 Days: The Race Between Pulitzer's Nellie Bly and Cosmopolitan's Elizabeth Bisland* (9–12). 1993, Gemittarius Pr. paper $12.95 (0-9633696-2-8). An account of the 1889 publicity stunt by rival publishers sending 2 female reporters on a race to beat the fictional record of Jules Verne's Phileas Fogg. (Rev: BL 4/15/93) [921]

7464 Peck, Ira, and Nellie Bly. *Nellie Bly's Book: Around the World in 72 Days* (6–8). 1998, Twenty-First Century $26.90 (0-7613-0971-3). An abridged version of the account written by the famous muckraking journalist about her trip around the world in which she beat Phileas Fogg's record by 6 days. (Rev: BL 2/15/99; SLJ 4/99) [921]

BONNEY, WILLIAM

7465 Cline, Don. *Alias Billy the Kid, the Man Behind the Legend* (8–12). Illus. 1986, Sunstone paper $12.95 (0-86534-080-3). The real story of Billy the Kid, clearing up many misconceptions. (Rev: BR 11–12/86) [921]

BOWDITCH, NATHANIEL

7466 Latham, Jean Lee. *Carry On, Mr. Bowditch* (7–9). 1955, Houghton $16.00 (0-395-06881-9). The story of the man who influenced American maritime history through his work on navigation. Newbery Medal, 1956. [921]

BRAGG, JANET HARMON

7467 Bragg, Janet Harmon. *Soaring above Setbacks: Autobiography of Janet Harmon Bragg as told to Marjorie M. Kriz* (10–12). 1996, Smithsonian $19.95 (1-56098-458-9). An inspiring autobiography of the African American woman who excelled in the health field, became the first black woman to earn a commercial pilot's license, and then as a social worker was so helpful to Ethiopian students in the United States that she was invited to visit Ethiopia as a guest of the king. (Rev: SLJ 9/96) [921]

BROWN, JESSE LEROY

7468 Taylor, Theodore. *The Flight of Jesse Leroy Brown* (10–12). 1998, Avon paper $23.00 (0-380-97689-7). This is the inspiring story of Jesse Brown, born to poor Southern sharecroppers, who went on to become the first black man to fly a navy fighter. He was killed during the Korean War but continues to be a symbol of courage and dignity. (Rev: BL 10/15/98; SLJ 4/99) [921]

CALAMITY JANE

7469 Faber, Doris. *Calamity Jane: Her Life and Her Legend* (5–9). 1992, Houghton $16.00 (0-395-56396-8). The author carefully distinguishes what is certain, what is possible, and what is blatantly untrue

in the legend of Calamity Jane and her later show business career. (Rev: BL 8/92; SLJ 10/92) [921]

CANTWELL, MARY

7470 Cantwell, Mary. *Manhattan, When I Was Young* (10–12). 1995, Houghton $21.95 (0-395-74441-5). An interesting autobiography of a fashion-magazine writer who came to New York in the 1950s fresh from college, lived in Greenwich Village, and found a new, exciting life. (Rev: BL 8/95; SLJ 1/96) [921]

CAPONE, AL

7471 Bergreen, Laurence. *Capone: The Man and the Era* (9–12). 1994, Simon & Schuster $30.00 (0-671-74456-9). Examines the career of Chicago gangster Al Capone, recounting his actions during the 1920s as well as his boyhood poverty and final years in prison. (Rev: BL 10/15/94) [921]

7472 King, David C. *Al Capone and the Roaring Twenties* (5–9). (Notorious Americans and Their Times) 1998, Blackbirch LB $19.45 (1-56711-218-8). The story of the 1920s mobster who was reared in an atmosphere of violence and corruption and raised organized crime to a new height as he terrorized the city of Chicago. (Rev: BL 12/15/98; SLJ 12/98) [921]

CARSON, KIT

7473 Quaife, Milo Milton, ed. *Kit Carson's Autobiography* (10–12). 1966, Univ. of Nebraska Pr. paper $9.00 (0-8032-5031-2). This autobiography dictated in the years 1856–57 gives fascinating details of the life of this famous hunter, trapper, and Indian fighter. [921]

CASSIDY, BUTCH

7474 Green, Carl R., and William R. Sanford. *Butch Cassidy* (5–8). (Outlaws and Lawmen of the Wild West) 1995, Enslow LB $15.95 (0-89490-587-2). The Wild West is re-created in this brief account of the life of this colorful outlaw, whose death remains a mystery. (Rev: BL 6/1–15/95) [921]

7475 Netzley, Patricia. *Butch Cassidy* (7–9). Illus. 1997, Lucent LB $22.45 (1-56006-266-5). The career of Butch Cassidy as an outlaw is touched on with a focus on his last years and the theories about his death, possibly in Latin America. (Rev: BL 2/15/97; BR 9–10/97; SLJ 4/97) [921]

CHAPMAN, JOHN

7476 Lawlor, Laurie. *The Real Johnny Appleseed* (4–8). Illus. 1995, Albert Whitman LB $13.95 (0-8075-6909-7). A well-researched biography of John Chapman, a.k.a. Johnny Appleseed, discounting the myths and highlighting his business acumen, his fondness for children and books, and his friendship with several American Indian tribes. (Rev: BL 9/1/95; SLJ 1/96) [921]

CODY, BUFFALO BILL

7477 Spies, Karen B. *Buffalo Bill Cody: Western Legend* (5–8). (Historical American Biographies) 1998, Enslow LB $19.95 (0-7660-1015-5). An in-depth look at this legendary frontiersman and the Wild West show he founded. (Rev: BL 3/15/98; SLJ 5/98) [921]

DALTON GANG

7478 Green, Carl R., and William R. Sanford. *The Dalton Gang* (5–8). (Outlaws and Lawmen of the Wild West) 1995, Enslow LB $15.95 (0-89490-588-0). The story of the gang of outlaws that terrorized frontier America. (Rev: BL 11/15/95) [921]

DAVIS, DONALD

7479 Davis, Donald. *See Rock City* (10–12). 1996, August House $22.95 (0-87483-448-1); paper $12.95 (0-87483-456-2). Beginning when he enters kindergarten in 1948 until he is a sophomore in college, this is the gentle, family-oriented autobiography of Donald Davis and his life in rural North Carolina. (Rev: BR 11–12/96; SLJ 9/96) [921]

ESCALANTE, JAIME

7480 Byers, Ann. *Jaime Escalante: Sensational Teacher* (6–10). Illus. (Hispanic Biographies) 1996, Enslow LB $19.95 (0-89490-763-8). A profile of the unique, inspiring teacher whose career became the basis of the film *Stand and Deliver*. (Rev: BL 10/1/96; SLJ 9/96; VOYA 12/96) [910]

EVANS, DALE

7481 Rogers, Dale Evans. *Angel Unaware* (10–12). 1991, Buccaneer LB $10.95 (0-89966-811-9); Revell paper $8.99 (0-8007-5434-4). Dale Evans tells about herself and her daughter's brief life in this moving autobiography. [921]

FORTUNE, AMOS

7482 Yates, Elizabeth. *Amos Fortune, Free Man* (6–9). Illus. 1950, Dutton paper $15.99 (0-525-25570-2). Based on fact, this tells of the courageous slave who not only bought his own freedom but also that of several others. Newbery Medal, 1951. [921]

FRAUNCES, PHOEBE

7483 Griffin, Judith Berry. *Phoebe the Spy* (7–9). 1989, Scholastic paper $3.99 (0-590-42432-7). The story of the 13-year-old black girl who saved George

Washington's life from an assassination attempt. [921]

GALLAGHER, HUGH

7484 Gallagher, Hugh Gregory. *Black Bird Fly Away: Disabled in an Able-Bodied World* (10–12). 1998, Vandamere $21.95 (0-918339-44-8). The autobiography of Hugh Gallagher, who, after becoming crippled by polio in college, became a disabled rights activist, lobbied for the Architectural Barriers Act of 1968, and became known as the grandfather of the Americans with Disabilities Act. The work weaves in his reaction to his paralysis and the evolution of his own feelings about himself as a paraplegic and as a human being. (Rev: BL 5/15/98; SLJ 1/99) [921]

GRAHAM, KATHARINE

7485 Whitelaw, Nancy. *Let's Go! Let's Publish! Katharine Graham and the Washington Post* (7–10). 1998, Morgan Reynolds LB $18.95 (1-883846-37-4). The life story of the famous female editor of the *Washington Post,* who lead it through such turbulent times as the Pentagon Papers and Watergate. (Rev: BL 1/1–15/99; SLJ 5/99) [921]

HUNTER-GAULT, CHARLAYNE

7486 Hunter-Gault, Charlayne. *In My Place* (9–12). 1992, Farrar $19.00 (0-374-17563-2). The renowned journalist writes about her early encounter with history as one of the first 2 African American students at the University of Georgia. (Rev: BL 11/1/92; SLJ 5/93) [921]

JAMES, JESSE

7487 Bruns, Roger. *Jesse James: Legendary Outlaw* (5–8). (Historical American Biographies) 1998, Enslow LB $19.95 (0-7660-1055-4). Using fact boxes, maps, a chronology, and chapter notes as well as an interesting text and black-and-white photographs, this book gives a fine biography of Jesse James and his exploits. (Rev: BL 10/15/98; SLJ 8/98) [921]

7488 Green, Carl R., and William R. Sanford. *Jesse James* (5–8). (Outlaws and Lawmen of the Wild West) 1992, Enslow LB $15.95 (0-89490-365-9). Portrays the legendary gunman as both outlaw and hero. (Rev: BL 3/1/92; SLJ 5/92) [921]

7489 Stiles, T. J. *Jesse James* (6–8). 1993, Chelsea LB $19.95 (0-7910-1737-0). This biography relates the details of the life and lore surrounding the notorious outlaw. (Rev: BL 2/1/94; SLJ 11/93) [921]

7490 Wukovits, John. *Jesse James* (5–8). (Legends of the West) 1996, Chelsea $16.95 (0-7910-3876-9). An action-packed biography that tries to probe the complex nature of this infamous bandit. (Rev: BR 5–6/97; SLJ 4/97) [921]

JENNINGS, CEDRIC

7491 Suskind, Ron. *A Hope in the Unseen: An American Odyssey from the Inner City to the Ivy League* (9–12). 1998, Broadway Books $25.00 (0-7679-0125-8). The true story of a poor inner-city African American boy and the determination, fortitude, and courage that allowed him to finish high school and gain admission to Brown University. (Rev: BL 3/1/98; SLJ 10/98) [921]

KELLER, HELEN

7492 Nicholson, Lois. *Helen Keller: Humanitarian* (7–10). (Great Achievers: Lives of the Physically Challenged) 1995, Chelsea LB $19.95 (0-7910-2086-X). The strong personality traits of Helen Keller that allowed her to rise above her physical handicaps are stressed in this biography of a remarkable woman. (Rev: BR 3–4/96; SLJ 1/96) [921]

7493 Wepman, Dennis. *Helen Keller* (6–10). Illus. 1987, Chelsea LB $19.95 (1-55546-662-1). The inspiring story of this handicapped woman and her struggle to help people like herself. (Rev: BL 8/87; SLJ 9/87) [921]

KOVIC, RON

7494 Moss, Nathaniel. *Ron Kovic: Antiwar Activist* (7–12). (Great Achievers: Lives of the Physically Challenged) 1994, Chelsea LB $19.95 (0-7910-2076-2). A biography of the disabled Vietnam veteran, antiwar activist, and author. (Rev: BL 1/15/94) [921]

KUUSISTO, STEPHEN

7495 Kuusisto, Stephen. *Planet of the Blind* (10–12). 1997, Doubleday $22.95 (0-385-31615-1); Dell paper $11.95 (0-385-33327-7). The biography of a young man who coped with legal blindness and bouts of obesity and anorexia before he reached out for help, accepted his disability, and learned to trust a seeing eye dog. (Rev: BL 11/15/97; SLJ 5/98) [921]

LINDBERGH, REEVE

7496 Lindbergh, Reeve. *Under a Wing: A Memoir* (10–12). 1998, Simon & Schuster $23.00 (0-684-80770-X). The story of the Lindbergh family from the standpoint of daughter Reeve, whose vivid descriptions of events range from taking flying lessons with her father to the effects of the kidnapping on her parents and the rest of the family. (Rev: SLJ 3/99) [921]

NEWTON, JOHN

7497 Granfield, Linda. *Amazing Grace: The Story of the Hymn* (4–8). Illus. 1997, Tundra $15.95 (0-88776-389-8). The life story of John Newton, a sea captain in the slave trade who later rejected slavery, became a minister, and wrote several hymns, including "Amazing Grace." (Rev: SLJ 8/97) [921]

OCHS, ADOLPH S.

7498 Faber, Doris. *Printer's Devil to Publisher: Adolph S. Ochs of The New York Times* (10–12). 1996, Black Dome Pr. paper $8.95 (1-883789-09-5). A rags-to-riches story about the trailblazing journalist and how he ran *The New York Times*, with a behind-the-scenes look at the newspaper's role in covering stories as the sinking of the *Titanic*. (Rev: SLJ 10/96) [921]

OSCEOLA

7499 Bland, Celia. *Osceola, Seminole Rebel* (5–8). Illus. (North American Indians of Achievement) 1994, Chelsea LB $19.95 (0-7910-1716-8). The story of the Seminole leader who resisted the removal of his people from Florida in the 1830s and died under mysterious circumstances in 1838. (Rev: BL 6/1–15/94; VOYA 4/94) [921]

PARKER, QUANAH

7500 Wilson, Claire. *Quanah Parker: Comanche Chief* (9–12). (North American Indians of Achievement) 1991, Chelsea LB $19.95 (0-7910-1702-8). Biography of the Comanche leader who fought white confiscation and settlement of his lands. (Rev: BL 3/1/92; SLJ 3/92) [921]

PAYNE, LUCILLE M. W.

7501 Rice, Dorothy M., and Lucille Payne. *The Seventeenth Child* (7–12). 1998, Linnet LB $18.50 (0-208-02414-X). A biography of an African American woman growing up in rural Virginia during the 1930s and 40s, as recorded and edited by her daughter. (Rev: SLJ 1/99; VOYA 6/99) [921]

RAY, JAMES EARL

7502 Posner, Gerald. *Killing the Dream: James Earl Ray and the Assassination of Martin Luther King, Jr.* (10–12). 1998, Random $25.00 (0-375-50082-0). The author examines in detail all of the conflicting stories about the killing of Martin Luther King, with a particular focus on the life of James Earl Ray. (Rev: BL 5/1/98; SLJ 3/99) [921]

SANTIAGO, ESMERALDA

7503 Santiago, Esmeralda. *When I Was Puerto Rican* (9–12). 1993, Addison-Wesley $20.00 (0-201-58117-5). The author recalls the hardships and joys of her life with humor and poignancy, from her childhood in Puerto Rico to her move to a very different life in Brooklyn, and, finally, her admission to the High School of Performing Arts. (Rev: BL 10/1/93; SLJ 2/94) [921]

SHREVE, HENRY MILLER

7504 McCall, Edith. *Mississippi Steamboatman: The Story of Henry Miller Shreve* (5–8). Illus. 1986, Walker $11.95 (0-8027-6597-1). The story of Henry Shreve, whose freight and passenger boats helped open up the Midwest. (Rev: BR 5–6/86; SLJ 3/86; VOYA 4/86) [921]

TATE, SONSYREA

7505 Tate, Sonsyrea. *Little X: Growing Up in the Nation of Islam* (7–12). 1997, Harper San Francisco $22.00 (0-06-251134-3). An autobiography of a girl who was reared and educated in the Nation of Islam community in Washington, DC, but later left to become an Orthodox Muslim. (Rev: BL 1/1–15/97; VOYA 10/97) [921]

WALKER, MAGGIE

7506 Branch, Muriel M., and Dorothy M. Rice. *Pennies to Dollars: The Story of Maggie Lena Walker* (5–8). 1997, Linnet LB $17.95 (0-208-02453-0); paper $13.95 (0-208-02455-7). Maggie Walker, the daughter of a former slave, helped African Americans through her financial schemes, including the founding of the Penny Savings Bank, the oldest, continuously operated black bank in the United States. (Rev: BL 11/1/97; SLJ 10/97) [921]

Science, Medicine, Industry, and Business

Collective

7507 Aaseng, Nathan. *Black Inventors* (6–12). Illus. (American Profiles) 1997, Facts on File $19.95 (0-8160-3407-9). This work profiles 10 African American inventors, including Lewis Temple, Elijah McCoy and Sarah Breedlove Walker, and tells how they were denied recognition for their achievements and overcame social and economic obstacles to achieve success. (Rev: BL 2/15/98; BR 1–2/98) [920]

7508 Altman, Linda J. *Women Inventors* (6–8). Illus. (American Profiles) 1997, Facts on File $19.95 (0-8160-3385-4). Relying heavily on primary sources, this book profiles 9 women inventors, including Carrie Everson, Madam C. J. Walker, Bette Graham, and Ruth Handler. (Rev: BL 5/1/97; BR 9–10/97) [920]

7509 Anderson, Margaret J., and Karen F. Stephenson. *Scientists of the Ancient World* (6–9). (Collective Biographies) 1999, Enslow $19.95 (0-7660-1111-9). Ten early scientists are profiled, including Pythagoras, Hippocrates, Aristotle, Archimedes, Pliny, Galen, and Al-Khwarizmi. (Rev: BL 12/1/98) [920]

7510 Archer, Jules. *To Save the Earth: The American Environmental Movement* (6–10). 1998, Viking $17.99 (0-670-87121-4). This work contains profiles of four important American environmentalists: John Muir, David McTaggart, Rachel Carson, and David Foreman. (Rev: BL 9/15/98; SLJ 12/98; VOYA 2/99) [920]

7511 Buchanan, Doug. *Air and Space* (6–9). (Female Firsts in Their Fields) 1999, Chelsea $16.95 (0-7910-5141-2). The biographies of 6 women who were pioneers in air and space technology. (Rev: BL 5/15/99) [920]

7512 Byrnes, Patricia. *Environmental Pioneers* (6–10). 1998, Oliver Pr. LB $18.95 (1-881508-45-5). This collective biography of early environmentalists includes profiles of John Muir, David Brower, Rachel Carson, Jay Darling, Rosalie Edge, Aldo Leopold, Olaus and Margaret Murie, and Gaylord Nelson. (Rev: BL 9/15/98; BR 1–2/99; SLJ 11/98) [920]

7513 Camp, Carole Ann. *American Astronomers: Searchers and Wonderers* (6–9). (Collective Biographies) 1996, Enslow LB $19.95 (0-89490-631-3). This volume presents brief profiles of 10 memorable astronomers, 5 men and 5 women, including Maria Mitchell and Carl Sagan. (Rev: BR 9–10/96; SLJ 5/96) [920]

7514 Cooney, Miriam P. *Celebrating Women in Mathematics and Science* (6–10). 1996, National Council of Teachers of Math paper $26.75 (0-87353-425-5). Covering ancient times to the present, this collective biography celebrates the struggles and triumphs of women in the fields of mathematics and sciences. (Rev: SLJ 10/96) [920]

7515 Curtis, Robert H. *Great Lives: Medicine* (5–8). (Great Lives) 1992, Scribners $24.00 (0-684-19321-3). Biographies of doctors and other medical professionals who made major contributions and discoveries throughout history. (Rev: BL 12/15/92; SLJ 6/93) [920]

7516 Dash, Joan. *The Triumph of Discovery: Four Nobel Women* (7–12). 1991, Messner paper $8.95 (0-671-69333-6). This collective biography highlights the work of 4 women who won the Nobel Prize in science, including Rita Levi-Montalcini, Maria Goeppert Mayer, and Barbara McClintock. (Rev: BL 3/15/91) [920]

7517 DeAngelis, Gina. *Science & Medicine* (6–9). (Female Firsts in Their Fields) 1999, Chelsea $16.95 (0-7910-5143-9). Biographies of 6 pioneer women in science and medicine—Elizabeth Blackwell, Clara Barton, Marie Curie, Margaret Mead, Rachel Carson, and Antonia Novello. (Rev: BL 5/15/99; SLJ 9/99; VOYA 8/99) [920]

7518 Fox, Karen. *The Chain Reaction: Pioneers of Nuclear Science* (6–12). (Lives of Science) 1998, Watts $25.00 (0-531-11425-2). The world of nuclear science is introduced through profiles of 7 men and women who have studied the atom, including Curie, Rutherford, Fermi, Lawrence, Oppenheimer, Goeppert-Mayer, and Sakharov. (Rev: BL 1/1–15/99; SLJ 2/99) [539.7]

7519 Haskins, Jim. *African American Entrepreneurs* (6–12). Illus. (Black Stars) 1998, Wiley $19.95 (0-471-14576-9). This is a collective biography of over 30 African Americans who have made their mark on the business community. (Rev: BL 2/15/98; BR 11–12/98; SLJ 7/98) [920]

7520 Haskins, Jim. *Outward Dreams: Black Inventors and Their Inventions* (7–12). 1991, Walker LB $14.85 (0-8027-6994-2). Examines the lives and inventions of black men and women who, only after the Civil War, were given recognition for their contributions. (Rev: BL 5/15/91) [920]

7521 Henderson, Harry. *Modern Mathematicians* (7–12). Illus. 1995, Facts on File LB $19.95 (0-8160-3235-1). Profiles of the lives and accomplishments of 9 men and 4 women, among them George Boole, Alan Turing, and Sophia Kovalevsky, who have contributed to the development of modern mathematics. (Rev: BL 1/1–15/96; BR 5–6/96; SLJ 2/96; VOYA 2/96) [920]

7522 Jeffrey, Laura S. *American Inventors of the 20th Century* (6–9). Illus. (Collective Biographies) 1996, Enslow LB $19.95 (0-89490-632-1). Ten short biographies of famous modern inventors such as Philo Farnsworth (television) and William Lear (Learjet) are presented in this easily read book. (Rev: BL 7/96; BR 9–10/96; SLJ 5/96) [920]

7523 Karnes, Frances A., and Suzanne M. Bean. *Girls and Young Women Inventing: Twenty True Stories about Inventors Plus How You Can Be One Yourself* (6–8). 1995, Free Spirit paper $12.95 (0-915793-89-X). Profiles of 20 young female inventors and their inventions plus material that demonstrates the importance of ingenuity, perseverance, imagination, and hard work. (Rev: BL 2/1/96; SLJ 12/95; VOYA 2/96) [920]

7524 Leuzzi, Linda. *To the Young Environmentalist: Lives Dedicated to Preserving the Natural World* (6–10). Illus. (To the Young . . .) 1997, Watts LB $25.00 (0-531-11359-0). This work profiles 8 individuals who have dedicated their lives to preserving the natural world. (Rev: BL 12/1/97; VOYA 6/98) [920]

7525 Lindop, Laurie. *Scientists and Doctors* (6–10). (Dynamic Women) 1997, Twenty-First Century LB $21.40 (0-8050-4166-4). This book contains biographies of women who have excelled in such areas as archaeology, physics, astronautics, and genetics, including Mildred Dresselhaus, Mae Jemison, Susan Love, Helen Taussig, and Rosalyn Yalow. (Rev: SLJ 9/97) [920]

7526 Lomask, Milton. *Great Lives: Invention and Technology* (5–8). (Invention and Technology) 1991, Scribners $23.00 (0-684-19106-7). Profiles of great names in invention and technology around the world. (Rev: BL 11/1/91; SLJ 1/92) [920]

7527 Lutz, Norma Jean. *Business and Industry* (6–9). (Female Firsts in Their Fields) 1999, Chelsea $16.95 (0-7910-5142-0). Six trail-blazing females in the business world are profiled, including their activism for women's rights. (Rev: BL 5/15/99; SLJ 9/99; VOYA 8/99) [920]

7528 Mulcahy, Robert. *Medical Technology: Inventing the Instruments* (5–8). 1997, Oliver Pr. LB $19.95 (1-881508-34-X). Seven short biographies are included of scientists who were responsible for such inventions as the X ray, stethoscope, thermometer, and electrocardiograph. (Rev: BR 11–12/97; SLJ 7/97) [920]

7529 Oleksy, Walter. *Hispanic-American Scientists* (7–10). Illus. (American Profiles) 1998, Facts on File $19.95 (0-8160-3704-3). Ten Hispanic American scientists are profiled, including Pedro Sanchez, Henry Diaz, Adriana Ocampo, and Francisco Dallmeier. (Rev: BL 3/1/99; BR 5–6/99; SLJ 2/99) [920]

7530 Pile, Robert B. *Top Entrepreneurs and Their Business* (6–12). 1993, Oliver Pr. LB $18.95 (1-881508-04-8). The rags-to-riches stories of 9 entrepreneurs, among them L. L. Bean, Walt Disney, and Sam Walton. With photos. (Rev: BL 11/15/93; SLJ 1/94) [920]

7531 Pile, Robert B. *Women Business Leaders* (6–12). Illus. (Profiles) 1995, Oliver Pr. LB $18.95 (1-881508-24-2). Profiles of 8 women, most of them not well known (except for Mary Kay Ash of the cosmetics firm), who have the "creativity, strength, and determination to run thriving businesses." (Rev: BL 1/1–15/96; SLJ 5/96; VOYA 4/96) [910]

7532 Polking, Kirk. *Oceanographers and Explorers of the Sea* (6–9). 1999, Enslow $19.95 (0-7660-1113-5). Biographies of 10 scientists and adventurers who have devoted their lives to the oceans, marine life, and ocean-related pursuits, including Maurice Ewing, who mapped the ocean floor, and Robert Ballard, discoverer of the *Titanic*. (Rev: BL 8/99; SLJ 9/99) [920]

7533 Rennert, Richard, ed. *Pioneers of Discovery* (6–9). Illus. (Profiles of Great Black Americans) 1994, Chelsea paper $6.95 (0-7910-2068-1). Eight

African American leaders in science and technology profiled here, among them Benjamin Banneker, James Beckwourth, George Washington Carver, Charles Drew, and Matthew Henson. (Rev: BL 6/1–15/94) [920]

7534 Shell, Barry. *Great Canadian Scientists* (5–8). Illus. 1998, Polestar Book Publishers paper $14.95 (1-896095-36-4). In profiles that average 5 or 6 pages, 19 important contemporary Canadian scientists and their work are introduced; an additional section gives short profiles of over 100 more. (Rev: SLJ 9/98) [920]

7535 Stille, Darlene R. *Extraordinary Women Scientists* (5–8). 1995, Children's Pr. LB $37.00 (0-516-00585-5). A profile of 49 women scientists and their achievements, with a historical overview of women in science. (Rev: BL 10/1/95; SLJ 12/95) [920]

7536 Sullivan, Otha R. *African American Inventors* (5–8). Ed. by Jim Haskins. Illus. (Black Stars) 1998, Wiley $22.95 (0-471-14804-0). Two- and 3-page spreads are used to highlight the work of African American inventors, some well-known, such as Benjamin Banneker and Madame C. J. Walker, and others less familiar, such as John Moon, who developed floppy disks, and Dr. Charles Drew, whose research laid the basis for blood donation. (Rev: BL 7/98; BR 11–12/98; SLJ 6/98) [920]

7537 Veglahn, Nancy. *Women Scientists* (7–10). (American Profiles) 1991, Facts on File LB $19.95 (0-8160-2482-0). This book profiles 11 women scientists of the 19th and 20th centuries, such as Alice Eastwood, Alice Hamilton, Margaret Mead, Barbara McClintock, and Rachel Carson. (Rev: BL 11/15/91; SLJ 3/92) [920]

7538 Yount, Lisa. *Asian-American Scientists* (6–10). (American Profiles) 1998, Facts on File $19.95 (0-8160-3756-6). This work features 12 Asian American scientists who have contributed to major scientific advances in the past century, among them Flossie Wong-Staal, Subrahmanyan Chandrasekhar, Tsutomo Shimomura, and David Da-i Ho. (Rev: BL 12/15/98; BR 5–6/99; SLJ 7/99) [920]

7539 Yount, Lisa. *Black Scientists* (7–12). (American Profiles) 1991, Facts on File LB $19.95 (0-8160-2549-5). Descriptions of the professional achievements of 8 black scientists and what led each to his/her particular field. (Rev: BL 11/15/91; SLJ 1/92) [920]

7540 Yount, Lisa. *Twentieth-Century Women Scientists* (7–12). Illus. 1995, Facts on File $19.95 (0-8160-3173-8). For each of the 11 women highlighted, there are details on the obstacles they faced, as well as information on their contributions and diverse backgrounds. (Rev: BL 4/15/96; SLJ 2/96; VOYA 4/96) [920]

Individual

BANNEKER, BENJAMIN

7541 Conley, Kevin. *Benjamin Banneker* (5–9). Illus. 1989, Chelsea LB $19.95 (1-55546-573-0). Banneker was a remarkable 18th-century black man who excelled in mathematics and science. (Rev: BL 1/1/90; SLJ 5/90; VOYA 4/90) [921]

7542 Litwin, Laura Baskes. *Benjamin Banneker: Astronomer and Mathematician* (6–10). Illus. (African-American Biographies) 1999, Enslow $19.95 (0-7660-1208-5). The story of the self-taught African American scientist who lived during the days of slavery and was responsible for some brilliant scientific inventions. (Rev: BL 9/15/99) [921]

BELL, ALEXANDER GRAHAM

7543 Pasachoff, Naomi. *Alexander Graham Bell: Making Connections* (6–9). (Oxford Portraits in Science) 1996, Oxford $33.95 (0-19-509908-7). A fine biography that focuses on Bell's work as a teacher of the deaf and his career as an inventor. (Rev: BR 11–12/96; SLJ 2/97*) [921]

BLACKWELL, ELIZABETH

7544 Brown, Jordan. *Elizabeth Blackwell* (7–10). Illus. 1989, Chelsea LB $19.95 (1-55546-642-7). The life story of the first woman doctor who also organized a nursing service during the Civil War and helped provide educational opportunities for other young women. (Rev: BL 5/15/89) [921]

7545 Kline, Nancy. *Elizabeth Blackwell: A Doctor's Triumph* (5–9). (Barnard Biography) 1997, Conari Pr. paper $6.95 (1-57324-057-5). The story of the first woman doctor in America, with generous excerpts from her journal and letters. (Rev: BL 2/15/97; BR 9–10/97; SLJ 6/97; VOYA 12/97) [921]

BROWN, HELEN GURLEY

7546 Falkof, Lucille. *Helen Gurley Brown: The Queen of Cosmopolitan* (5–8). (Wizards of Business) 1992, Garrett LB $17.26 (1-56074-013-2). An interesting, accessible, and inspiring biography of the magazine magnate. (Rev: BL 6/15/92; SLJ 7/92) [921]

BURROUGHS, JOHN

7547 Wadsworth, Ginger. *John Burroughs: The Sage of Slabsides* (5–8). Illus. 1997, Clarion $16.95 (0-395-77830-1). A biography of the American naturalist and essayist who lived in a cabin in the Catskill Mountains and wrote about his observations. (Rev: BL 3/15/97; BR 9–10/97; SLJ 5/97) [508.73]

CARNEGIE, ANDREW

7548 Meltzer, Milton. *The Many Lives of Andrew Carnegie* (7–10). Illus. 1997, Watts LB $29.00 (0-531-11427-9). The amazing life of this complex, successful businessman and philanthropist who sought to project himself as a generous industrial leader but used unscrupulous business tactics and treated his workers ruthlessly. (Rev: BL 10/1/97; BR 5–6/98; SLJ 10/97; VOYA 10/98) [921]

CARSON, RACHEL

7549 Jezer, Marty. *Rachel Carson* (6–9). 1988, Chelsea LB $19.95 (1-55546-646-X). The biography of the scientist who was one of the first to warn us of our environmental problems. (Rev: BL 9/1/88; BR 11–12/88; VOYA 2/89) [921]

7550 Wheeler, Leslie A. *Rachel Carson* (7–12). (Pioneers in Change) 1991, Silver Burdett LB $17.95 (0-382-24167-3); paper $6.95 (0-382-24174-6). A portrait of the pioneer conservationist whose exposé on the lasting damage caused by widespread use of pesticides had a major impact. (Rev: BL 2/1/92) [921]

CARVER, GEORGE WASHINGTON

7551 Adair, Gene. *George Washington Carver* (7–10). Illus. 1989, Chelsea LB $19.95 (1-55546-577-3). The story of the first black scientist to gain national prominence and of his efforts to help poor black farmers. (Rev: BL 11/15/89; BR 11–12/89; SLJ 1/90; VOYA 2/90) [921]

CURIE, MARIE

7552 Pasachoff, Naomi. *Marie Curie and the Science of Radioactivity* (7–12). Illus. (Portraits in Science) 1996, Oxford $33.95 (0-19-509214-7). Combining details of her scientific research with information on her personal life, this is a fascinating biography of Madame Curie. (Rev: BL 9/1/96; SLJ 8/96) [921]

7553 Pflaum, Rosalynd. *Marie Curie and Her Daughter Irene* (7–10). 1993, Lerner LB $25.26 (0-8225-4915-8). A detailed account of Marie Curie's discovery of radium, polonium, and natural radiation and Irene Curie's discovery of artificial radiation. (Rev: BL 8/93; SLJ 6/93) [921]

DARWIN, CHARLES

7554 Bowlby, John. *Charles Darwin: A Biography* (9–12). 1991, Norton paper $14.95 (0-393-30930-4). The story of the dedicated scientist, his many voyages to gather data, and the development of his theory of evolution. (Rev: BL 3/1/91) [921]

7555 Evans, J. Edward. *Charles Darwin: Revolutionary Biologist* (6–9). (Lerner Biographies) 1993, Lerner LB $25.26 (0-8225-4914-X). An account of Darwin's life that includes interesting anecdotes, such as the fact that he dropped out of medical school and that his father thought he would never amount to anything. (Rev: BL 12/1/93; SLJ 11/93) [921]

DREW, CHARLES

7556 Mahone-Lonesome, Robyn. *Charles Drew* (6–10). Illus. 1990, Chelsea LB $19.95 (1-55546-581-1). The biography of the black American scientist who did pioneer work in blood preservation and the establishment of blood banks. (Rev: BL 2/15/90; BR 5–6/90) [921]

EASTMAN, GEORGE

7557 Holmes, Burnham. *George Eastman* (7–12). (Pioneers in Change) 1992, Silver Burdett LB $17.95 (0-382-24170-3); paper $6.95 (0-382-24176-2). The story of the great inventor of photographic equipment, founder of Eastman Kodak Company, and renowned philanthropist. (Rev: BL 9/15/92) [921]

EDISON, THOMAS ALVA

7558 Adair, Gene. *Thomas Alva Edison: Inventing the Electric Age* (7–10). Illus. 1996, Oxford $33.95 (0-19-508799-2). A biography of this astounding genius who not only invented the light bulb, but also was involved with improving the telegraph, inventing the phonograph, and developing early motion pictures. (Rev: BL 6/1–15/96; SLJ 6/96; VOYA 8/96) [921]

7559 Anderson, Kelly C. *Thomas Edison* (5–8). (The Importance Of) 1994, Lucent LB $17.96 (1-56006-041-7). The biography of the most famous inventor in U.S. history, known best for his inventions of the telegraph, telephone, electric light, and motion pictures. (Rev: BL 8/94) [921]

7560 Baldwin, Neil. *Edison: Inventing the Century* (9–12). 1995, Hyperion $27.95 (0-7868-6041-3). A biography of the great inventor known as the wizard of Menlo Park, the New Jersey city where he lived. (Rev: BL 2/15/95) [921]

7561 Dolan, Ellen M. *Thomas Alva Edison: Inventor* (5–8). (Historical American Biographies) 1998, Enslow LB $19.95 (0-7600-1014-7). The story of the amazing inventor and his inventions is told with clarity and simplicity. (Rev: BL 8/98) [921]

EINSTEIN, ALBERT

7562 Goldberg, Jake. *Albert Einstein: The Rebel behind Relativity* (8–12). Illus. (Impact Biographies) 1996, Watts LB $24.00 (0-531-11251-9). Important aspects of Einstein's background, family, and accomplishments are recounted with a lucid explanation of his major theories. (Rev: BL 9/1/96; SLJ 12/96) [921]

7563 MacDonald, Fiona. *The World in the Time of Albert Einstein: 1879–1955* (6–9). (The World in the Time of . . .) 1998, Dillon LB $23.00 (0-382-39739-8). An overview of Einstein's life and accomplishments and an examination of the political, scientific, religious, and creative climate of the time. (Rev: SLJ 3/99) [921]

7564 Severance, John B. *Einstein: Visionary Scientist* (7–12). Illus. 1999, Clarion $15.00 (0-395-93100-2). This book covers Einstein's academic theories as well as his private life and his life as a celebrity. (Rev: BL 9/1/99; SLJ 9/99) [921]

FARADAY, MICHAEL

7565 Ludwig, Charles. *Michael Faraday: Father of Electronics* (9–12). 1988, Herald Pr. $9.99 (0-8361-3479-6). This is the story of the scientist who worked on such inventions as the dynamo, the generator, and the transformer. [921]

FERMI, ENRICO

7566 Cooper, Dan. *Enrico Fermi: And the Revolutions of Modern Physics* (8–12). (Oxford Portraits in Science) 1999, Oxford $32.00 (0-19-511762-X). A readable biography of the Italian scientist, who immigrated to the United States in 1939 and worked on the first atomic bomb. Some of the coverage on quantum and nuclear physics is challenging. (Rev: SLJ 6/99) [921]

FLEMING, ALEXANDER

7567 Gottfried, Ted. *Alexander Fleming: Discoverer of Penicillin* (6–10). Illus. (Book Report Biographies) 1997, Watts $22.00 (0-531-11370-1). In 1928, bacteriologist Alexander Fleming discovered a blue mold growing on a culture dish in his lab in London. This discovery lead to the development of the first antibiotic, penicillin, and a Nobel Prize. (Rev: BL 12/1/97; SLJ 2/98) [921]

FOSSEY, DIAN

7568 Mowat, Farley. *Woman in the Mists: The Story of Dian Fossey and the Mountain Gorillas of Africa* (10–12). Illus. 1987, Warner paper $19.99 (0-446-38720-7). A naturalist and writer has created a stirring life of the zoologist whose study of gorillas was trailblazing. (Rev: BL 9/1/87; SLJ 2/88; VOYA 4/88) [921]

FREUD, SIGMUND

7569 Muckenhoupt, Margaret. *Sigmund Freud: Explorer of the Unconscious* (10–12). Illus. (Oxford

Portraits in Science) 1997, Oxford $32.00 (0-19-509933-8). A detailed biography of the father of psychoanalysis that contains material on Freud's theories concerning dreams, the Oedipus complex, sexuality, and the unconscious. (Rev: BL 12/1/97; SLJ 1/98) [921]

GALILEO

7570 MacLachlan, James. *Galileo Galilei: First Physicist* (6–10). (Oxford Portraits in Science) 1997, Oxford $33.95 (0-19-509342-9). A fine portrait of this mathematician/physicist and his accomplishments, and a good introduction to the Renaissance world. (Rev: SLJ 3/98) [921]

GATES, BILL

7571 Boyd, Aaron. *Smart Money: The Story of Bill Gates* (6–10). 1995, Morgan Reynolds LB $17.95 (1-883846-09-9). A biography of Microsoft's billionaire mogul Bill Gates. (Rev: BL 4/1/95; SLJ 4/95; VOYA 2/96) [921]

7572 Dickinson, Joan D. *Bill Gates: Billionaire Computer Genius* (5–8). (People to Know) 1997, Enslow LB $19.95 (0-89490-824-3). This biography of the computer genius traces his life from his birth in 1955, showing how his personal drive made him into the richest man in America. (Rev: BL 10/15/97; BR 1–2/98; SLJ 12/97; VOYA 2/98) [921]

7573 Woog, Adam. *Bill Gates* (7–9). Illus. 1998, Lucent LB $22.45 (1-56006-256-8). A biography of the controversial cofounder and CEO of Microsoft, who has become not only the most important person in the computer industry, but also the richest man in America. (Rev: SLJ 4/99) [921]

GOODALL, JANE

7574 Meachum, Virginia. *Jane Goodall: Protector of Chimpanzees* (6–10). Illus. (People to Know) 1997, Enslow LB $19.95 (0-89490-827-8). The story of the great naturalist who fulfilled her childhood dream and made groundbreaking observations of chimpanzee behavior. (Rev: BL 1/1–15/98) [921]

7575 Pratt, Paula B. *Jane Goodall* (4–8). Illus. (The Importance Of) 1997, Lucent LB $17.96 (1-56006-082-4). The story of the great naturalist who studied and protected the primates of Africa. (Rev: BL 1/1–15/97; BR 9–10/97; SLJ 2/97) [921]

GROVE, ANDREW

7576 Byman, Jeremy. *Andrew Grove and the Intel Corporation* (6–12). 1999, Morgan Reynolds LB $18.95 (1-883846-38-2). A biography of the computer giant from his hiding with his mother from the Nazis in Budapest to the story of Intel, the corporation that he cofounded and that changed computer history. (Rev: BL 3/15/99; SLJ 5/99) [338.7]

HANKINS, ANTHONY M.

7577 Hankins, Anthony M., and Debbie Markley. *Fabric of Dreams: Designing My Own Success* (10–12). 1998, NAL $27.95 (0-525-94329-3). An easy-to-read, inspiring autobiography of the enterprising African American fashion designer, the obstacles he overcame, and the founding of his multimillion-dollar business while he was still in his 20s. (Rev: BL 2/15/98; SLJ 10/98) [921]

HARRIOT, THOMAS

7578 Staiger, Ralph C. *Thomas Harriot: Science Pioneer* (6–10). 1998, Clarion $19.00 (0-395-67296-1). The biography of the Elizabethan scientist who made contributions to navigation, optics, and astronomy and who accompanied Sir Walter Raleigh to Roanoke Island in 1585, where he studied the flora, fauna, and the native people. (Rev: BL 12/1/98; BR 5–6/99; SLJ 5/99; VOYA 2/99) [921]

HAWKING, STEPHEN

7579 Ferguson, Kitty. *Stephen Hawking: Quest for a Theory of the Universe* (9–12). 1991, Watts LB $24.00 (0-531-11067-2). This biography of the physicist, in addition to recounting his life story, uses everyday examples to help make his complex cosmological concepts more understandable. (Rev: BL 9/1/91*; SLJ 4/92) [921]

7580 Henderson, Harry. *Stephen Hawking* (5–8). (The Importance Of) 1995, Lucent LB $22.45 (1-56006-050-6). A biography of one of the few scientists who has examined not just individual theories or principles of physics but the universe as a whole. (Rev: BL 1/15/95) [921]

HERRIOT, JAMES

7581 Herriot, James. *All Creatures Great and Small* (8–12). 1972, St. Martin's $17.95 (0-312-01960-2); Bantam paper $7.50 (0-553-26812-0). The first volume of Herriot's memories of being a veterinarian in Yorkshire, England, during the 1930s. Continued in *All Things Bright and Beautiful* (1974), *All Things Wise and Wonderful* (1977), and *The Lord God Made Them All* (1981). [921]

7582 Herriot, James. *Every Living Thing* (9–12). 1992, St. Martin's $22.95 (0-312-08188-X). Veterinarian Herriot continues his delightful recollections of his work among the animals and people of the Yorkshire Dales in the 1950s. (Rev: BL 8/92; SLJ 12/92) [921]

HUBBLE, EDWIN

7583 Christianson, Gale E. *Edwin Hubble: Mariner of the Nebulae* (9–12). 1995, Farrar $27.50 (0-374-14660-8). An exploration of Hubble's contributions, his personal successes, and the activities and views that sometimes annoyed others inside and outside the scientific community. (Rev: BL 8/95*) [921]

7584 Datnow, Claire. *Edwin Hubble: Discoverer of Galaxies* (4–8). Illus. (Great Minds of Science) 1997, Enslow LB $19.95 (0-89490-934-7). Explanations of rather complicated discoveries are clearly written in this biography of the great astronomer noted for redefining our understanding of galaxies and the universe, and after whom the Hubble Space Telescope is named. (Rev: BL 12/1/97; SLJ 3/98; VOYA 12/97) [921]

7585 Fox, Mary V. *Edwin Hubble: American Astronomer* (6–10). Illus. (Book Report Biographies) 1997, Watts $22.00 (0-531-11371-X). The biography of the astronomer who changed our way of looking at our world when, in 1924, he presented us with a universe in which our Milky Way is only one of a great number of other galaxies. (Rev: BL 12/1/97; SLJ 11/97) [520]

JONES, CAROLINE

7586 Fleming, Robert. *The Success of Caroline Jones Advertising, Inc.* (7–10). Illus. (Success) 1996, Walker LB $16.85 (0-8027-8354-6). A biography of the amazing career of Caroline Jones and her rapid rise in the world of advertising. (Rev: BL 1/1–15/96; SLJ 4/96) [921]

KOOP, C. EVERETT

7587 Bianchi, Anne. *C. Everett Koop: The Health of the Nation* (6–12). 1992, Millbrook LB $21.90 (1-56294-103-8). The story of the long, difficult road to becoming surgeon general of the United States, a position Koop held for 8 controversial years. (Rev: BL 9/1/92; SLJ 9/92) [921]

LATIMER, LEWIS

7588 Norman, Winifred Latimer, and Lily Patterson. *Lewis Latimer* (7–10). (Black Americans of Achievement) 1993, Chelsea LB $19.95 (0-7910-1977-2). Follows Lattimer's career from Civil War veteran to executive at the Edison Company, where he helped Thomas Edison improve the light bulb and supervised the installation of electrical systems in several cities. (Rev: BL 11/15/93) [921]

LEAKEY, LOUIS AND MARY

7589 Morell, Virginia. *Ancestral Passions: The Leakey Family and the Quest for Humankind's Beginnings* (9–12). 1995, Simon & Schuster $30.00

(0-684-80192-2). The story of the Leakey family—Louis, Mary, and their son, Richard—and their paleoanthropologic work in the field of human evolution. (Rev: BL 7/95*) [921]

7590 Poynter, Margaret. *The Leakeys: Uncovering the Origins of Humankind* (5–8). Illus. (Great Minds of Science) 1997, Enslow LB $19.95 (0-89490-788-3). The story of the famous husband and wife team, Louis and Mary Leakey, and how they expanded our knowledge of evolution and anthropology. (Rev: BL 12/1/97; SLJ 12/97) [921]

LEEUWENHOEK, ANTONI VAN

7591 Yount, Lisa. *Antoni van Leeuwenhoek: First to See Microscopic Life* (4–8). (Great Minds of Science) 1996, Enslow LB $19.95 (0-89490-680-1). A brief biography of the Dutch maker of microscopes, who was also the first to examine closely bacteria and blood cells. (Rev: BL 10/15/96; SLJ 12/96) [921]

LINNAEUS, CARL

7592 Anderson, Margaret J. *Carl Linnaeus: Father of Classification* (4–8). (Great Minds of Science) 1997, Enslow LB $19.95 (0-89490-786-7). This biography discusses the personal life of Linnaeus, including his explorations in Lapland, but the focus is on the development of his important biological classification system. (Rev: BL 12/1/97; SLJ 9/97) [921]

LOVELACE, ADA BYRON

7593 Wade, Mary D. *Ada Byron Lovelace: The Lady and the Computer* (5–8). 1995, Silver Burdett LB $13.95 (0-87518-598-3); paper $7.95 (0-382-24717-5). The story of Ada Byron Lovelace, who explained Babbage's analytical engine, including a computer program and ideas for its use that even its inventor never imagined. (Rev: BL 5/1/95) [921]

MCCLINTOCK, BARBARA

7594 Fine, Edith Hope. *Barbara McClintock: Nobel Prize Geneticist* (6–8). (People to Know) 1998, Enslow $19.95 (0-89490-983-5). This biography of the famous female geneticist whose work on maize earned her a Nobel Prize, gives interesting details on her youth and the many honors she received later in life. (Rev: BL 1/1–15/99; SLJ 3/99) [921]

MCNAIR, RONALD E.

7595 Naden, Corinne J. *Ronald McNair* (5–8). 1990, Chelsea LB $19.95 (0-7910-1133-X). An inspirational biography of the second African American astronaut, a victim of the *Challenger* disaster. (Rev: BL 4/1/91; SLJ 3/91) [921]

MEAD, MARGARET

7596 Mark, Joan. *Margaret Mead: Coming of Age in America* (6–10). Ed. by Owen Gingerich. Illus. (Oxford Portraits in Science) 1999, Oxford $33.95 (0-19-511679-8). An introduction to the life and work of the pioneering anthropologist and her research with people of the South Seas, particularly in Samoa. (Rev: BL 4/1/99; SLJ 3/99) [921]

7597 Ziesk, Edra. *Margaret Mead* (6–10). Illus. 1989, Chelsea LB $19.95 (1-55546-667-2). Beginning with her work in Samoa and moving backward and forward this account emphasizes the anthropologist's professional career. (Rev: BL 2/15/90; SLJ 9/90; VOYA 8/90) [921]

MENDEL, GREGOR

7598 Edelson, Edward. *Gregor Mendel: And the Roots of Genetics* (7–10). (Oxford Portraits in Science) 1999, Oxford $33.95 (0-19-512226-7). This work describes Mendel's life and his work on plant heredity and the study of genetics in the context of the social, scientific, and political events of his time. (Rev: SLJ 7/99) [921]

7599 Klare, Roger. *Gregor Mendel: Father of Genetics* (5–8). (Great Men of Science) 1997, Enslow LB $19.95 (0-89490-789-1). The science of genetics is introduced through the life of Mendel and his experiments with peas. (Rev: BL 12/1/97; SLJ 12/97; VOYA 12/97) [921]

MITCHELL, MARIA

7600 Gormley, Beatrice. *Maria Mitchell: The Soul of an Astronomer* (6–9). 1995, Eerdmans paper $8.00 (0-8028-5099-5). An authentic, interesting biography of the 19th-century female astronomer, with details on her accomplishments and an accompanying 16-page centerfold of photographs. (Rev: BL 9/1/95; BR 9–10/96; SLJ 1/96) [921]

MOSS, CYNTHIA

7601 Pringle, Laurence. *Elephant Woman: Cynthia Moss Explores the World of Elephants* (4–8). 1997, Simon & Schuster $16.00 (0-689-80142-4). A biography of the conservationist who studied elephants for 25 years at the Amboseli National Park in Kenya. The book contains information on how elephants live, why they are endangered, and how they can be saved, and conveys a sense of how researchers live and conduct their research. (Rev: BL 11/15/97; SLJ 12/97*) [921]

MUIR, JOHN

7602 Ito, Tom. *The Importance of John Muir* (4–8). Illus. (The Importance Of) 1996, Lucent LB $22.45 (1-56006-054-9). A short biography of the great naturalist and traveler who pioneered the U.S. conservation movement. (Rev: BL 5/15/96) [921]

7603 Wadsworth, Ginger. *John Muir: Wilderness Protector* (6–12). 1992, Lerner LB $23.93 (0-8225-4912-3). Original photos and Muir's letters, journals, and writings provide an overview of the conservationist's personal life, achievements, and contributions to the environmental movement. (Rev: BL 8/92) [921]

NEWTON, ISAAC

7604 Christianson, Gale E. *Isaac Newton and the Scientific Revolution* (8–12). Illus. (Oxford Portraits in Science) 1996, Oxford $29.95 (0-19-509224-4). A challenging biography which gives the scientist's life history plus detailed explanations on theories of gravity, relativity, and calculus. (Rev: BL 12/1/96; SLJ 1/97; VOYA 2/97) [530]

OPPENHEIMER, ROBERT

7605 Rummel, Jack. *Robert Oppenheimer: Dark Prince* (7–12). 1992, Facts on File LB $19.95 (0-8160-2598-3). A straightforward biography of the physicist credited with developing the atomic bomb. (Rev: BL 9/15/92; SLJ 9/92) [921]

PASTEUR, LOUIS

7606 Smith, Linda W. *Louis Pasteur: Disease Fighter* (4–8). Illus. (Great Minds of Science) 1997, Enslow LB $19.95 (0-89490-790-5). The story of the "father of microbiology," who discovered pasteurization while working on a wine problem for Napoleon. (Rev: BL 12/1/97; SLJ 12/97) [921]

PAULING, LINUS

7607 Hager, Tom. *Linus Pauling and the Chemistry of Life* (9–12). Illus. (Portraits in Science) 1998, Oxford $33.95 (0-19-510853-1). A profile of the multitalented giant who won the Nobel Prize in chemistry as well as the Nobel Peace Prize for his participation in the antiwar and disarmament movements. (Rev: BL 5/15/98; SLJ 8/98) [921]

PLOTKIN, MARK

7608 Pascoe, Elaine, adapt. *Mysteries of the Rain Forest: 20th Century Medicine Man* (4–8). (The New Explorers) 1997, Blackbirch LB $17.95 (1-56711-229-3). This biography describes the life and findings of Mark Plotkin, an ethnobotanist, who has worked for years in the rain forests of the Amazon with Indians who use plants to treat diseases and injuries. (Rev: SLJ 2/98) [921]

PULITZER, JOSEPH

7609 Pfaff, Daniel W. *Joseph Pulitzer II and the Post-Dispatch: A Newspaperman's Life* (9–12). 1991, Pennsylvania State Univ. Pr. $45.00 (0-271-00748-6). This biography of the son of the newspaper empire's founder shows him to be an astute, principled journalist who helped establish the reputation of the St. Louis newspaper. (Rev: BL 9/15/91) [921]

7610 Whitelaw, Nancy. *Joseph Pulitzer and the New York World* (7–10). Illus. (Makers of the Media) 1999, Morgan Reynolds LB $18.95 (1-883846-44-7). The life story of the founder of "tabloid journalism," who revolutionized the newspaper industry by combining sensational news, visuals, and reports on political corruption to both attract readers and encourage social change, and after whom the Pulitzer Prize is named. (Rev: BL 6/1–15/99; SLJ 9/99) [921]

ROWLAND, MARY CANAGA

7611 Rowland, Mary Canaga. *As Long As Life: The Memoirs of a Frontier Woman Doctor* (9–12). 1994, Storm Peak paper $11.95 (0-9641357-0-1). The memoirs of an early 19th-century doctor who braved the wilderness to treat wounds, pull teeth, and deliver babies. (Rev: BL 11/1/94) [610]

SALK, JONAS

7612 Sherrow, Victoria. *Jonas Salk* (7–12). 1993, Facts on File $17.95 (0-8160-2805-2). Begins with a history of polio, moves on to Salk's education, research, and development of the polio vaccine, and ends with the Salk Institute's work on cancer and AIDS. (Rev: BL 9/15/93) [921]

SCHOEN, ALLEN M.

7613 Schoen, Allen M., and Pam Proctor. *Love, Miracles, and Animal Healing: A Veterinarian's Journey from Physical Medicine to Spiritual Understanding* (9–12). 1995, Simon & Schuster $21.50 (0-684-80207-4). A memoir of a veterinarian who gained new understanding and insights as he treated injured, ill, and abused animals over the years. (Rev: BL 4/15/95) [921]

STEWART, MARTHA

7614 Meachum, Virginia. *Martha Stewart: Successful Businesswoman* (6–10). (People to Know) 1998, Enslow $19.95 (0-89490-984-3). A well-documented biography of the Martha Kostyra Stewart, the human dynamo who has achieved notoriety as a model, master chef, expert homemaker, entertainer, author, and TV celebrity. (Rev: SLJ 1/99) [921]

STRAUSS, LEVI

7615 Henry, Sondra, and Emily Taitz. *Everyone Wears His Name: A Biography of Levi Strauss* (5–9). Illus. 1990, Dillon $13.95 (0-87518-375-1). The story of the German Jew and his family who made millions making riveted denim pants. (Rev: BL 4/1/90; SLJ 7/90) [921]

7616 Van Steenwyk, Elizabeth. *Levi Strauss: The Blue Jeans Man* (5–9). 1988, Walker LB $14.85 (0-8027-6796-6). A biography of the Bavarian immigrant, Levi Strauss, who became the blue jeans king of the western world. (Rev: BL 6/15/88; SLJ 10/88; VOYA 8/88) [921]

TESLA, NIKOLA

7617 Dommermuth-Costa, Carol. *Nikola Tesla: A Spark of Genius* (5–9). 1994, Lerner LB $25.26 (0-8225-4920-4). Traces the life and career of this pioneer in the field of electricity. (Rev: BL 12/15/94; SLJ 2/95) [921]

TURNER, TED

7618 Byman, Jeremy. *Ted Turner: Cable Television Tycoon* (7–10). Illus. 1998, Morgan Reynolds LB $18.95 (1-883846-25-0). Known as the "mouth of the south," Ted Turner, a born rebel, introduced CNN in 1980 and hasn't stopped expanding his cable empire since. This is a biography of this media mogul. (Rev: BL 4/1/98; BR 1–2/99; SLJ 8/98) [921]

WALKER, MADAM C. J.

7619 Bundles, A'Lelia Perry. *Madam C. J. Walker* (5–10). (Black Americans of Achievement) 1993, Chelsea LB $19.95 (1-55546-615-X); paper $9.95 (0-7910-0251-9). This biography, written by Walker's great-great-granddaughter, tells of the developer of a line of hair-care products whose entrepreneurial ability made her into the "foremost colored businesswoman in America." (Rev: BL 3/1/94) [921]

WOZNIAK, STEPHEN

7620 Kendall, Martha E. *Steve Wozniak: Inventor of the Apple Computer* (6–9). 1995, Walker $15.85 (0-8027-8342-2). A biography of the eccentric genius who revolutionized personal computing. (Rev: BL 3/1/95; SLJ 3/95) [921]

WRIGHT, WILBUR AND ORVILLE

7621 Freedman, Russell. *The Wright Brothers: How They Invented the Airplane* (6–10). 1991, Holiday House $19.95 (0-8234-0875-2). Chronicles the achievements of 2 brothers who built the first flying machine in an Ohio bicycle shop and ultimately saw their dream come true. (Rev: BL 6/15/91*; SLJ 6/91*) [921]

7622 Reynolds, Quentin. *The Wright Brothers* (6–8). 1963, Random paper $5.99 (0-394-84700-8). An easily read account of the 2 young men and their dream of flight. [921]

7623 Taylor, Richard L. *The First Flight: The Story of the Wright Brothers* (5–8). Illus. 1990, Watts LB $21.00 (0-531-10891-0). The story of the famous brothers and the drive and determination that finally led them to Kitty Hawk. (Rev: BL 4/15/90; SLJ 9/90) [921]

Sports Figures

Collective

7624 Aaseng, Nathan. *Athletes* (7–12). (American Indian Lives) 1995, Facts on File $19.95 (0-8160-3019-7). A collective biography that highlights the lives of 11 Native American athletes, including Jim Thorpe, Kitty O'Neil, Sonny Sixkiller, Billy Mills, and Henry Boucha. (Rev: BL 4/1/95) [920]

7625 Aaseng, Nathan. *True Champions* (6–9). 1993, Walker $22.95 (0-8027-8246-9). Tales of legendary athletes who have demonstrated heroism and self-sacrifice off the field. (Rev: BL 8/93; SLJ 6/93) [921]

7626 Bayne, Bijan C. *Sky Kings: Black Pioneers of Professional Basketball* (6–9). Illus. (The African-American Experience) 1997, Watts LB $25.00 (0-531-11308-6). This book tells the stories of Chuck Cooper, Nat Clifton, and Earl Lloyd, the 3 black players who integrated basketball in 1950. (Rev: BL 12/15/97; SLJ 12/97) [920]

7627 Crisfield, Deborah. *Louisville Slugger Book of Great Hitters* (4–8). 1998, Wiley paper $12.95 (0-471-19772-6). This book contains profiles of 100 sluggers, both the past and present, including some from the Negro Leagues, with plenty of accompanying black-and-white portraits and action shots. (Rev: SLJ 4/98) [920]

7628 Dolin, Nick, et al. *Basketball Stars* (4–8). Illus. 1997, Black Dog & Leventhal $24.98 (1-884822-61-4). This oversize book contains 50 double-page profiles with statistics of today's star basketball players. (Rev: BL 8/97) [920]

7629 Gaines, Ann. *Sports and Activities* (6–9). (Female Firsts in Their Fields) 1999, Chelsea $16.95 (0-7910-5144-7). A collection of 6 biographies of outstanding female trail blazers in athletics, focusing on how each achieved firsts for their sex. (Rev: BL 5/15/99) [920]

7630 Gutman, Bill. *Teammates: Michael Jordan & Scottie Pippen* (7–10). 1998, Millbrook LB $19.90 (0-7613-0420-7). The life stories of these two NBA stars are told, with emphasis on how the personal and professional development of each and their dedication to basketball influenced their roles as teammates. (Rev: SLJ 1/99; VOYA 4/99) [920]

7631 Hurley, Bob, and Phil Pepe. *Divided Loyalties: The Diary of a Basketball Father* (9–12). 1993, Zebra $19.95 (0-8217-4391-0). Bob Hurley's diary is the basis of this look at his work as basketball coach at an inner-city Catholic school and as father to 2 basketball stars. (Rev: BL 12/1/93) [796.323]

7632 Jacobs, William J. *They Shaped the Game* (6–9). 1994, Scribners $15.95 (0-684-19734-0). Profiles the lives of baseball greats Ty Cobb, Babe Ruth, and Jackie Robinson. (Rev: BL 1/15/95; SLJ 2/95) [920]

7633 Kaufman, Alan S., and James C. Kaufman. *The Worst Baseball Pitchers of All Time: Bad Luck, Bad Arms, Bad Teams, and Just Plain Bad* (9–12). 1993, McFarland paper $23.95 (0-89950-824-3). Honors pitchers since 1876 who "made a habit of losing." Includes statistics, anecdotes, and player profiles. (Rev: BL 4/1/93; VOYA 8/93) [796.357]

7634 Lindop, Laurie. *Athletes* (6–12). Illus. (Dynamic Modern Women) 1996, Twenty-First Century LB $21.40 (0-8050-4167-2). Biographies of 10 famous female athletes, including Bonnie Blair, Julie Krone, Nancy Lopez, Monica Seles, Lynette Woodard, and Kristi Yamaguchi, with details on their childhoods, education, and important influences in their lives. (Rev: BL 1/1–15/97; SLJ 2/97) [920]

7635 Molzahn, Arlene Bourgeois. *Top 10 American Women Sprinters* (4–8). (Sports Top 10) 1998,

Enslow LB $18.95 (0-7660-1011-2). An easily read survey of the lives and accomplishments of 10 important women runners in track and field. (Rev: SLJ 1/99) [920]

7636 Pare, Michael A. *Sports Stars: Series 3* (4–9). 1997, Gale $51.46 (0-7876-1749-0). Like the others in this series, this volume introduces biographical material on athletes from a variety of sports. (Rev: BL 9/1/97; SLJ 2/98) [920]

7637 Pare, Michael A. *Sports Stars Series: Series 4* (7–12). (Sports Stars) 1998, Visible Ink Pr. $39.00 (0-7876-2784-4). Thirty minibiographies are included in this book that introduces some of today's important athletes like Mark McGwire, Marion Jones, Dominik Hasek, and Martina Hingis. (Rev: BL 9/15/98; VOYA 2/99) [920]

7638 Pare, Michael A., ed. *Sports Stars Series 2* (5–10). 1996, Gale $55.00 (0-7876-0867-X). This second series of "Sports Stars" is in 2 volumes and contains biographical sketches of 60 leading professional and amateur figures from many different sports. (Rev: BL 9/1/97; BR 1–2/97; SLJ 2/97) [920]

7639 Rappoport, Ken. *Guts and Glory: Making It in the NBA* (5–9). 1997, Walker LB $16.85 (0-8027-8431-3). All of the 10 basketball players profiled in this book, men like Muggsy Bogues, Reggie Miller, Hakeem Olajuwon, and Isiah Thomas, had to overcome immense difficulties to get to the top. (Rev: BL 8/97; BR 11–12/97; SLJ 7/97) [920]

7640 Savage, Jeff. *Top 10 Professional Football Coaches* (6–9). (Sports Top 10) 1998, Enslow LB $18.95 (0-7660-1006-6). Using 2-page entries, this book profiles 10 top football coaches, with statistics and a picture. (Rev: SLJ 9/98; VOYA 12/98) [920]

7641 Schnakenberg, Robert. *Teammates: John Stockton & Karl Malone* (5–8). Illus. 1998, Millbrook LB $20.90 (0-7613-0300-6). Despite very different backgrounds, these 2 leading players on the Utah Jazz basketball team have become close personal friends. This is their story and rise to fame. (Rev: BL 8/98; SLJ 5/98) [920]

7642 Schulman, Arlene. *The Prizefighters: An Intimate Look at Champions and Contenders* (9–12). 1994, Lyons Pr. $27.95 (1-55821-309-0). Interviews with various figures in the world of boxing, including cornermen, trainers, and fighters, with photos. (Rev: BL 10/1/94) [920]

7643 Sehnert, Chris W. *Top 10 Sluggers* (5–8). Illus. (Top 10 Champions) 1997, ABDO LB $23.54 (1-56239-797-4). An overview of the careers of such notable hitters as Babe Ruth, Hank Aaron, and Roberto Clemente. (Rev: BL 1/1–15/98) [920]

7644 Spiros, Dean. *Top 10 Hockey Goalies* (6–9). (Sports Top 10) 1998, Enslow LB $18.95 (0-7660-1010-4). This book profiles 10 top hockey goalies

like Patrick Roy with brief biographical sketches and career statistics. (Rev: VOYA 12/98) [920]

7645 Teitelbaum, Michael. *Grand Slam Stars: Martina Hingis and Venus Williams* (6–10). 1998, HarperCollins paper $4.50 (0-06-107100-5). An easy read that contains biographies of the 2 most prominent teen sensations in the tennis world, Martina Hingis and Venus Williams. (Rev: VOYA 4/99) [920]

Automobile Racing

ANDRETTI, MARIO

7646 Prentzas, G. S. *Mario Andretti* (6–9). (Car Racing Legends) 1996, Chelsea LB $7.95 (0-7910-3176-4). This biography of the racing hero reveals Andretti's drive and endurance in his rise to the top. (Rev: SLJ 8/96) [921]

Baseball

AARON, HENRY

7647 Rennert, Richard. *Henry Aaron* (7–10). (Black Americans of Achievement) 1993, Chelsea LB $19.95 (0-7910-1859-8). The story of the African American baseball great who broke Babe Ruth's batting record in 1974. (Rev: BL 5/1/93) [921]

ABBOTT, JIM

7648 Savage, Jeff. *Sports Great Jim Abbott* (5–8). (Sports Greats) 1993, Enslow LB $15.95 (0-89490-395-0). The amazing career of the one-handed pitcher who came up with the California Angels and threw a no-hitter for the New York Yankees. (Rev: BL 3/1/93) [921]

AGUIRRE, HANK

7649 Copley, Robert E. *The Tall Mexican: The Life of Hank Aguirre, All-Star Pitcher, Businessman, Humanitarian* (6–12). 1998, Arte Publico $16.95 (1-55885-225-5). The story of this inspiring hero who overcame poverty to become a baseball star and entrepreneur and whose Mexican Industries provided work for minorities throughout Mexico. (Rev: BL 1/1–15/99; BR 5–6/99; SLJ 3/99; VOYA 4/99) [921]

ALOMAR, ROBERTO

7650 Macht, Norman L. *Roberto Alomar* (6–10). (Latinos in Baseball) 1999, Mitchell Lane LB $18.95 (1-883845-84-X). Using text, pictures, and career statistics, this book tells about the life of the Hispanic American baseball star Roberto Alomar. (Rev: BL 4/15/99; SLJ 5/99) [921]

ALOU, MOISES

7651 Muskat, Carrie. *Moises Alou* (6–10). Illus. (Latinos in Baseball) 1999, Mitchell Lane LB $18.95 (1-883845-86-6). This is the story of the baseball giant who came from a sports-minded family, and who faced a number of personal tragedies on his way to the the top. (Rev: BL 4/15/99) [921]

BERRA, YOGI

7652 Berra, Yogi, and Tom Horton. *Yogi: It Ain't Over . . .* (9–12). Illus. 1990, HarperCollins paper $5.99 (0-06-100012-4). A somewhat confusing memoir by this baseball great plus tributes from his friends. (Rev: BL 4/15/89) [921]

BONDS, BARRY

7653 Savage, Jeff. *Barry Bonds: Mr. Excitement* (4–8). (Sports Achievers) 1996, Lerner LB $21.27 (0-8225-2889-4); paper $5.95 (0-8225-9748-9). The story of this fantastic baseball player who has won the Most Valuable Player Award 3 times and who grew up in the shadow of a famous father. (Rev: BL 4/15/97; SLJ 2/97) [921]

BONILLA, BOBBY

7654 Rappoport, Ken. *Bobby Bonilla* (5–9). 1993, Walker LB $15.85 (0-8027-8256-6). A biography of the young New York Mets baseball player who rose from poverty in the South Bronx to superstardom and multimillionaire status. (Rev: BL 5/15/93; SLJ 5/93; VOYA 8/93) [921]

DIMAGGIO, JOE

7655 Johnson, Dick, and Glenn Stout. *DiMaggio: An Illustrated Life* (10–12). 1995, Walker $39.95 (0-8027-1311-4). Written before his death, this is a stirring biography of a baseball giant, with material on his life off the field and his impact on the game. (Rev: SLJ 6/96) [921]

DOBY, LARRY

7656 Moore, Joseph Thomas. *Pride against Prejudice: The Biography of Larry Doby* (9–12). 1988, Greenwood $55.00 (0-313-25995-X). The story of the first black player in the American League following Jackie Robinson's debut in the National League. (Rev: BL 3/15/88) [921]

GEHRIG, LOU

7657 Robinson, Ray. *Iron Horse: Lou Gehrig in His Time* (9–12). Illus. 1990, Norton $22.50 (0-393-

02857-7). A stirring life story of the quiet, dignified baseball great who inspired millions by his courage. (Rev: BL 7/90; SLJ 1/91) [921]

GIBSON, JOSH

7658 Holway, John B. *Josh Gibson* (7–10). (Black Americans of Achievement) 1995, Chelsea LB $19.95 (0-7910-1872-5). The inspiring story of this African American baseball hero. (Rev: BL 8/95) [921]

HERSHISER, OREL

7659 Knapp, Ron. *Sports Great Orel Hershiser* (5–8). (Sports Greats) 1993, Enslow LB $15.95 (0-89490-389-6). An easily read sports biography that re-creates the great moments in this baseball star's career up to 1993. (Rev: BL 4/1/93) [921]

KIDD, JASON

7660 Torres, John A. *Sports Great Jason Kidd* (5–8). (Sports Great) 1998, Enslow LB $16.95 (0-7660-1001-5). An action-filled biography of this basketball star complete with statistics and black-and-white photographs of Kidd in action. (Rev: BL 7/98) [921]

MCGWIRE, MARK

7661 Hall, Jonathan. *Mark McGwire: A Biography* (6–10). 1998, Archway paper $4.99 (0-671-03273-9). This biography covers the batter's childhood, his progress through minor leagues, and earlier major league experiences, then focuses on the sensational 1998 season. (Rev: VOYA 4/99) [921]

7662 Thornley, Stew. *Mark McGwire: Star Home Run Hitter* (4–8). (Sports Reports) 1999, Enslow $19.95 (0-7660-1329-4). A look at the life and accomplishments of this exciting baseball player. (Rev: SLJ 7/99; VOYA 8/99) [921]

MADDUX, GREG

7663 Thornley, Stew. *Sports Great Greg Maddux* (5–8). Illus. (Sports Great) 1997, Enslow LB $16.95 (0-89490-873-1). The life of this great player with the Chicago Cubs and Atlanta Braves is traced, with career statistics and many action photos. (Rev: BL 2/15/97; VOYA 6/97) [921]

MANTLE, MICKEY

7664 Falkner, David. *The Last Hero: The Life of Mickey Mantle* (9–12). 1996, Simon & Schuster $24.00 (0-684-81424-2). Not meant to be a definitive biography, but rather, focuses on Mantle's influence as a ballplayer and as a person. (Rev: BL 12/15/95) [921]

MARTINEZ, PEDRO

7665 Gallagher, Jim. *Pedro Martinez* (6–10). (Latinos in Baseball) 1999, Mitchell Lane LB $18.95 (1-883845-85-8). The life history and career highlights of Pedro Martinez, one of the many Hispanic Americans to become baseball stars. (Rev: BL 4/15/99) [921]

MATHEWS, EDDIE

7666 Mathews, Eddie, and Bob Buege. *Eddie Mathews and the National Pastime* (9–12). 1994, Douglas American Sports $22.95 (1-882134-41-9). Hall of Famer Mathews chronicles his life and baseball career, including anecdotes about Hank Aaron and Bob Uecker. (Rev: BL 9/15/94) [921]

MATHEWSON, CHRISTY

7667 Robinson, Ray. *Matty: American Hero: The Life and Career of Christy Mathewson* (9–12). 1994, Oxford paper $12.95 (0-19-509263-5). Tracks the pitching feats of the New York Giants' pitching hero of 1900–1916. (Rev: BL 7/93) [921]

MUSIAL, STAN

7668 Lansche, Jerry. *Stan the Man Musial: Born to Be a Ballplayer* (9–12). 1994, Taylor $19.95 (0-87833-846-2). A biography that sticks to baseball and avoids the fluffy, swell-guy approach. (Rev: BL 5/15/94) [921]

PAIGE, SATCHEL

7669 Shirley, David. *Satchel Paige* (7–10). (Black Americans of Achievement) 1993, Chelsea LB $19.95 (0-7910-1880-6). The story of the baseball Hall of Famer who was the first African American to pitch in the American League. (Rev: BL 5/1/93) [921]

RIPKEN, CAL, JR.

7670 Macnow, Glen. *Sports Great Cal Ripken, Jr.* (5–8). (Sports Greats) 1993, Enslow LB $16.95 (0-89490-387-X). The story of the baseball giant who gained fame as the star shortstop for the Baltimore Orioles. (Rev: BL 4/1/93) [921]

ROBINSON, JACKIE

7671 Scott, Richard. *Jackie Robinson* (5–10). Illus. 1987, Chelsea LB $19.95 (1-55546-609-5). A well-researched biography giving good material on Robinson's life outside of baseball. (Rev: BL 9/1/87; SLJ 9/87) [921]

7672 Weidhorn, Manfred. *Jackie Robinson* (6–12). 1993, Atheneum LB $15.95 (0-689-31644-5). This biography of the African American legend who inte-

grated baseball in 1947 focuses on the personal qualities of the boy, the man, and the athlete. (Rev: BL 3/15/94; SLJ 2/94; VOYA 4/94) [921]

RYAN, NOLAN

7673 Lace, William W. *Sports Great Nolan Ryan* (5–8). (Sports Greats) 1993, Enslow LB $16.95 (0-89490-394-2). The amazing story of this baseball phenomenon who became the baseball strike-out king. (Rev: BL 6/1–15/93) [921]

SOSA, SAMMY

7674 Gutman, Bill. *Sammy Sosa: A Biography* (6–10). 1998, Archway paper $4.99 (0-671-03274-7). The life story of this sensational slugger, in both English and Spanish, with about half the book devoted to the exciting 1998 season. (Rev: VOYA 4/99) [921]

7675 Muskat, Carrie. *Sammy Sosa* (6–10). Illus. (Latinos in Baseball) 1999, Mitchell Lane LB $18.95 (1-883845-92-0). This account of Sosa's life tells of his beginning as a poor shoeshine boy in the Dominican Republic and his rise in baseball to his record-setting home run at age 29. (Rev: BL 4/15/99; SLJ 5/99) [921]

THOMAS, FRANK

7676 Thornley, Stew. *Frank Thomas: Baseball's Big Hurt* (4–8). (Sports Achievers) 1997, Lerner $21.27 (0-8225-3651-X); paper $5.95 (0-8225-9759-4). In addition to being a big-time hitter in baseball, this star—nicknamed "the Big Hurt"—devotes much of his spare time to the fight against leukemia. (Rev: BL 1/1–15/98) [921]

WILLIAMS, TED

7677 Linn, Ed. *Hitter: The Life and Turmoil of Ted Williams* (9–12). 1993, Harcourt $23.95 (0-15-193100-3). Examines the baseball career of the legendary Boston Red Sox slugger, considered by many to be the greatest of all time. (Rev: BL 4/15/93) [921]

Basketball

ABDUL-JABBAR, KAREEM

7678 Abdul-Jabbar, Kareem, and Mignon McCarthy. *Kareem* (9–12). Illus. 1990, Random $18.95 (0-394-55927-4). A memoir of the great basketball player in the form of a diary of his last playing year. This forms a complementary volume to the player's earlier autobiography *Giant Steps* (1985). (Rev: BL 2/1/90; SLJ 8/90) [921]

BARKLEY, CHARLES

7679 Macnow, Glen. *Sports Great Charles Barkley* (5–8). (Sports Greats) 1992, Enslow LB $16.95 (0-89490-386-1). A short biography of this basketball star, with career statistics and action photographs. (Rev: BL 10/15/92) [921]

BOGUES, TYRONE "MUGGSY"

7680 Bogues, Tyrone "Muggsy," and David Levine. *In the Land of the Giants* (9–12). 1994, Little, Brown $19.95 (0-316-10173-7). The autobiography of the Charlotte Hornets' "Muggsy" Bogues, the shortest basketball player in the NBA, tells of his poverty-stricken youth and convict father. (Rev: BL 11/1/94; SLJ 5/95) [921]

BROWN, DALE

7681 Brown, Dale, and Don Yaeger. *Tiger in a Lion's Den: Adventures in LSU Basketball* (9–12). 1994, Hyperion $22.95 (0-7868-6044-8). Autobiography of the controversial Louisiana coach Brown, who once coached Shaquille O'Neal. (Rev: BL 10/15/94) [921]

HARDAWAY, ANFERNEE

7682 Rekela, George R. *Sports Great Anfernee Hardaway* (5–8). Illus. (Sports Great) 1996, Enslow LB $16.95 (0-89490-758-1). Career statistics and many black-and-white photos enliven the biography of this famous basketball star. (Rev: BL 3/15/96) [921]

HILL, GRANT

7683 Gutman, Bill. *Grant Hill: A Biography* (6–10). 1997, Archway paper $3.99 (0-671-88738-6). This covers the life and career of the Detroit Pistons basketball star who is outstanding not only as an athlete but also as a modest, well-liked man. (Rev: VOYA 8/97) [921]

7684 Rappoport, Ken. *Grant Hill* (6–9). Illus. 1996, Walker LB $16.85 (0-8027-8456-9). The story of the basketball star, from the AAU National Basketball Championship at age 13 through high school, where he played on the varsity team as a freshman, and his college years playing at Duke, to the Detroit Pistons, where he was the NBA Rookie of the Year. (Rev: BL 1/1–15/97; BR 3–4/97; SLJ 1/97; VOYA 8/97) [796.323]

7685 Savage, Jeff. *Grant Hill: Humble Hotshot* (4–8). (Sports Achievers) 1996, Lerner LB $21.27 (0-8225-2893-2); paper $5.95 (0-8225-9751-9). A brief biography of this humble basketball star who was a mainstay both at Duke University and with the Detroit Pistons. (Rev: BL 4/15/97; SLJ 6/97; VOYA 8/97) [921]

HOWARD, JUWAN

7686 Safage, Jeff. *Sports Great Juwan Howard* (5–8). (Sports Great) 1998, Enslow $16.95 (0-7660-1065-1). The basketball star of the Washington Wizards is profiled in this lively account, supplemented by many black-and-white photos. (Rev: BL 2/15/98; VOYA 6/99) [921]

7687 Sirak, Ron. *Juwan Howard* (5–8). 1998, Chelsea LB $7.95 (0-7910-4575-7). A biography of one of the great basketball players of the 1990s, with good material on his early years and the influence of his grandmother. (Rev: BR 11–12/98; VOYA 6/99) [921]

JOHNSON, MAGIC

7688 Dolan, Sean. *Magic Johnson* (7–10). 1993, Chelsea LB $19.95 (0-7910-1975-6); paper $8.95 (0-7910-1976-4). The story to 1992 of the Los Angeles Lakers star and his battle after testing HIV-positive. (Rev: BL 9/15/93) [921]

7689 Haskins, Jim. *Sports Great Magic Johnson.* Rev. ed. (5–8). 1992, Enslow LB $16.95 (0-89490-348-9). Revision of an earlier edition to include a discussion of the basketball star's HIV status, his 1991 retirement from the Lakers, and his role in the fight against AIDS. (Rev: BL 10/15/92) [921]

JORDAN, MICHAEL

7690 Dolan, Sean. *Michael Jordan* (7–10). (Black Americans of Achievement) 1993, Chelsea LB $19.95 (0-7910-2150-5); paper $9.95 (0-7910-2151-3). The life of this basketball legend to 1992 and how his determination and family support helped him rise to the top. (Rev: BL 3/1/94; VOYA 6/94) [921]

7691 Lovitt, Chip. *Michael Jordan* (6–10). 1998, Scholastic paper $4.50 (0-590-59644-6). This quick read, an update of the 1993 edition, traces Jordan's remarkable career from a young age to the end of the Chicago Bulls' 1998 season. (Rev: VOYA 4/99) [921]

MILLER, REGGIE

7692 Thornley, Stew. *Sports Great Reggie Miller* (5–8). (Sports Great) 1996, Enslow LB $16.95 (0-89490-874-X). The life of this basketball star is traced, with special emphasis on key games. (Rev: BL 9/15/96) [921]

MOURNING, ALONZO

7693 Fortunato, Frank. *Sports Great Alonzo Mourning* (5–8). Illus. (Sports Great) 1997, Enslow LB $16.95 (0-89490-875-8). An easily read biography of this amazing basketball star. (Rev: BL 2/15/97; VOYA 6/97) [921]

NUNEZ, TOMMY

7694 Marvis, Barbara. *Tommy Nunez, NBA Referee: Taking My Best Shot* (6–10). Illus. 1996, Mitchell Lane paper $10.95 (1-883845-28-9). The story of the youngster who grew up in the poverty of Phoenix's barrio to become the first (and so far the only) Mexican American referee in the NBA. (Rev: BL 5/15/96; SLJ 3/96; VOYA 6/96) [921]

O'NEAL, SHAQUILLE

7695 Sullivan, Michael J. *Sports Great Shaquille O'Neal* (5–8). (Sports Great) 1998, Enslow LB $16.95 (0-89490-594-5). This well-known basketball star is profiled in this easily read biography that also contains career statistics. (Rev: BL 2/15/98) [921]

PIPPEN, SCOTTIE

7696 Bjarkman, Peter C. *Sports Great Scottie Pippen* (5–8). (Sports Great) 1996, Enslow LB $16.95 (0-89490-755-7). Action photos, career statistics, and an account of important games are highlights of this basketball biography. (Rev: BL 9/15/96) [921]

RICHMOND, MITCH

7697 Grody, Carl W. *Sports Great Mitch Richmond* (5–8). (Sports Great) 1998, Enslow LB $16.95 (0-7600-1070-8). Using many black-and-white photos and a lively text, this book re-creates the life of this basketball great. (Rev: BL 2/15/99) [921]

RIVERS, DOC

7698 Rivers, Glenn, and Bruce Brooks. *Those Who Love the Game: Glenn "Doc" Rivers on Life in the NBA and Elsewhere* (7–12). 1994, Holt $15.95 (0-8050-2822-6). A sports autobiography that avoids the pitfalls of similar stories, which tend to be self-serving and too much play-by-play. (Rev: BL 4/15/94; SLJ 4/94; VOYA 6/94) [921]

ROBINSON, DAVID

7699 Aaseng, Nathan. *Sports Great David Robinson* (5–8). (Sports Greats) 1992, Enslow LB $16.95 (0-89490-373-X). A brief somewhat dated biography of this basketball star who was named Rookie of the Year in 1990 while with the San Antonio Spurs. (Rev: BL 10/15/92) [921]

7700 Green, Carl R., and Roxanne Ford. *David Robinson* (5–8). (Sports Headlines) 1994, Macmillan LB $17.95 (0-89686-839-7). A biography of the basketball player to 1993 that uses press quotations and photos to highlight important events in his career. (Rev: BL 10/1/94) [921]

RODMAN, DENNIS

7701 Frank, Steven. *Dennis Rodman* (4–8). (Basketball Legends) 1997, Chelsea LB $7.95 (0-7910-4388-6). A biography of the bad boy of basketball and his sensational career with the Chicago Bulls. (Rev: SLJ 4/98) [921]

7702 Thornley, Stew. *Sports Great Dennis Rodman* (5–8). Illus. (Sports Great) 1996, Enslow LB $16.95 (0-89490-759-X). The life of this controversial basketball star is told in a brisk text with many black-and-white photographs. (Rev: BL 3/15/96) [921]

STOCKTON, JOHN

7703 Aaseng, Nathan. *Sports Great John Stockton* (5–8). Illus. (Sports Great) 1995, Enslow LB $16.95 (0-89490-598-8). A short biography of the basketball great John Stockton, with sports action and lively photographs. (Rev: BL 9/15/95) [921]

WILKINS, DOMINIQUE

7704 Bjarkman, Peter C. *Sports Great Dominique Wilkins* (5–8). (Sports Great) 1996, Enslow LB $16.95 (0-89490-754-9). The story of this basketball star, with profiles of his most exciting games and career statistics. (Rev: BL 9/15/96) [921]

Boxing

ALI, MUHAMMAD

7705 Conklin, Thomas. *Muhammad Ali: The Fight for Respect* (6–12). (New Directions) 1992, Millbrook LB $21.90 (1-56294-112-7). This well-researched account of a man whose fame transcends the boxing arena takes a close look at Ali's conversion to the Black Muslim faith and his refusal to be inducted into the armed forces because of his religious beliefs. (Rev: BL 2/15/92; SLJ 4/92) [921]

7706 Hauser, Thomas. *Muhammad Ali: His Life and Times* (9–12). 1992, Simon & Schuster paper $16.00 (0-671-77971-0). This biography traces Muhammad Ali's contributions to boxing and to the betterment of his people through 1990. (Rev: BL 5/15/91) [921]

7707 Random House, eds. *Muhammed Ali* (6–10). 1997, Random $20.00 (0-517-20080-5). Using plenty of sidebars, quotations from his poetry, and photographs, this excellent biography, based on A&E cable TV's *Biography* show, traces the boxer's life from his days as a scrawny kid named Cassius Clay, Jr. to his becoming "the greatest," ending with the 1996 lighting of the Olympic torch in Atlanta, Georgia. (Rev: VOYA 8/98) [921]

7708 Rummel, Jack. *Muhammad Ali* (6–10). Illus. 1988, Chelsea LB $19.95 (1-55546-569-2). A biography that emphasizes the boxer's professional career rather than his personal life. (Rev: BL 6/15/88) [921]

7709 Schulman, Arlene. *Muhammad Ali: Champion* (6–9). (Newsmakers) 1996, Lerner LB $25.26 (0-8225-4925-5). An accurate account of Ali's youth, his career, his Muslim beliefs, and his civil rights activities. (Rev: SLJ 6/96) [921]

7710 Tessitore, John. *Muhammad Ali: The World's Champion* (7–12). (Impact Biographies) 1998, Watts $24.00 (0-531-11437-6). Crowned heavyweight champion of the world 3 times, Muhammad Ali also stands out as a courageous humanitarian, a champion of peace and civil rights, and a role model for all people. (Rev: BL 11/15/98; SLJ 12/98) [921]

DE LA HOYA, OSCAR

7711 Torres, John A. *Sports Great Oscar De La Hoya* (5–8). (Sports Great) 1998, Enslow $16.95 (0-7660-1066-X). The rise of this boxing sensation is told in this brief biography, with action photos and career statistics. (Rev: BL 2/15/98) [921]

HAWKINS, DWIGHT

7712 Hawkins, Dwight, and Morrie Greenberg. *Survival in the Square* (7–10). Illus. 1989, Brooke-Richards paper $5.95 (0-9622652-0-9). A story of a black American who overcame a physical handicap and became a boxing champion. (Rev: BL 11/15/89; VOYA 12/89) [921]

LOUIS, JOE

7713 Jakoubek, Robert E. *Joe Louis* (6–9). Illus. 1990, Chelsea LB $19.95 (1-55546-599-4). Both the professional career of Joe Louis and his often unfortunate personal life are handled in this account. (Rev: BL 5/1/90) [921]

7714 *Joe Louis* (4–8). Illus. (The Importance Of) 1997, Lucent LB $12.50 (1-56006-085-9). The story of the boxing champion, his triumphs, the racist obstacles he had to overcome, exploitation, and how he became a symbol of courage to his people. (Rev: BL 5/15/97) [921]

Football

AIKMAN, TROY

7715 Macnow, Glen. *Sports Great Troy Aikman* (5–8). (Sports Greats) 1995, Enslow LB $15.95 (0-89490-593-7). With good action photos and sports statistics, this is the life story of football great Troy Aikman. (Rev: BL 9/15/95) [921]

BETTIS, JEROME

7716 Majewski, Stephen. *Sports Great Jerome Bettis* (5–8). Illus. (Sports Greats) 1997, Enslow LB $16.95 (0-89490-872-3). The great football hero Jerome Bettis and his amazing career are highlighted in this easily read biography. (Rev: BL 2/15/97; VOYA 6/97) [921]

FAVRE, BRETT

7717 Gutman, Bill. *Brett Favre* (4–8). 1998, Pocket Books paper $3.99 (0-671-02077-3). The story of the quarterback of the Green Bay Packers, with many insider details of his life, play-by-play descriptions and game strategies, and early problems, among them a serious automobile injury and his comeback from addiction to a prescribed painkiller. (Rev: BL 12/1/98) [921]

7718 Savage, Jeff. *Sports Great Brett Favre* (5–8). (Sports Greats) 1998, Enslow LB $16.95 (0-7660-1000-7). An exciting biography of the star quarterback of the Green Bay Packers. (Rev: BL 3/15/98) [921]

KELLY, JIM

7719 Harrington, Denis J. *Sports Great Jim Kelly* (5–8). Illus. (Sports Greats) 1996, Enslow LB $16.95 (0-89490-670-4). A short, action-filled biography of this former star quarterback, complete with career statistics. (Rev: BL 3/15/96) [921]

PRIETO, JORGE

7720 Prieto, Jorge. *The Quarterback Who Almost Wasn't* (7–10). 1994, Arte Publico paper $9.95 (1-55885-109-7). The autobiography of a Mexican physician who struggled with poverty, racism, and political exile before he received a scholarship to play football at Notre Dame. (Rev: BL 8/94) [921]

RICE, JERRY

7721 Dickey, Glenn. *Sports Great Jerry Rice* (5–8). (Sports Greats) 1993, Enslow LB $16.95 (0-89490-419-1). A brief biography to 1992 of the football player who gained fame with the San Francisco 49ers. (Rev: BL 9/15/93) [921]

SANDERS, BARRY

7722 Knapp, Ron. *Sports Great Barry Sanders* (5–8). (Sports Greats) 1998, Enslow LB $16.95 (0-7660-1067-8). The life and career of this great football player are re-created in this book that contains sports statistics and action photographs. (Rev: BL 2/15/99) [921]

SEAU, JUNIOR

7723 Morgan, Terri. *Junior Seau: High Voltage Linebacker* (4–8). Illus. (Sports Achievers) 1996, Lerner $18.95 (0-8225-2896-7); paper $5.95 (0-8225-9746-2). A biography of this famous football player, complete with career statistics and action photos. (Rev: BL 12/15/96) [921]

SMITH, EMMITT

7724 Grabowski, John. *Sports Great Emmitt Smith* (5–8). (Sports Great) 1998, Enslow LB $16.95 (0-7660-1002-3). A high-interest biography of this football great that contains career statistics, action photographs, and exciting game action. (Rev: BL 7/98) [921]

7725 Thornley, Stew. *Emmitt Smith: Relentless Rusher* (4–8). (Sports Achievers) 1996, Lerner LB $19.95 (0-8225-2897-5). The professional life of one of the Dallas Cowboys is highlighted, supplemented by career statistics and action photos. (Rev: BL 4/15/97; SLJ 8/97) [921]

WILLIAMS, AENEAS

7726 Williams, Aeneas. *It Takes Respect* (9–12). 1998, Multnomah paper $11.99 (1-57673-453-6). This autobiography of the top defensive player of the Phoenix Cardinals tells of his professional career and devotion to Christ and his teachings. (Rev: VOYA 4/99) [921]

YOUNG, STEVE

7727 Morgan, Terri, and Shmuel Thaler. *Steve Young: Complete Quarterback* (5–8). (Sports Achievers) 1995, Lerner LB $19.93 (0-8225-2886-X); paper $5.95 (0-8225-9716-0). A profile of the San Francisco 49ers quarterback, with material on other aspects of his professional career, his character, and outside interests. (Rev: BL 11/15/95) [921]

Gymnastics

MILLER, SHANNON

7728 Miller, Claudia. *Shannon Miller: My Child, My Hero* (9–12). 1999, Oklahoma Univ. Pr. $19.95 (0-8061-3110-1). Told by her mother, this is the story of Shannon Miller, who overcame enormous odds, including painful injuries, to become a world champion gymnast and gold medal winner. (Rev: VOYA 10/99) [921]

7729 Miller, Shannon, and Nancy A. Richardson. *Winning Every Day: Gold Medal Advice for a Happy, Healthy Life!* (5–9). 1998, Bantam paper $12.95 (0-553-09776-8). The 1996 Olympic Gold Medal gymnast tells about her life and training and how she copes with stress, with generous amounts of sound advice on good sportsmanship and how to stay fit and healthy. (Rev: BL 6/1–15/98; SLJ 7/98) [921]

MOCEANU, DOMINIQUE

7730 Durrett, Deanne. *Dominique Moceanu* (5–8). (People in the News) 1999, Lucent LB $22.45 (1-56006-099-9). Drawing heavily on Moceanu's autobiography, this is the life story of the phenomenal gymnast, with behind-the-scenes glimpses of competitions, training, scoring, and routines. (Rev: SLJ 8/99) [921]

Ice Skating and Hockey

BLAIR, BONNIE

7731 Breitenbucher, Cathy. *Bonnie Blair: Golden Streak* (5–8). (Sports Achievers) 1994, Lerner LB $21.27 (0-8225-2883-5). Profiles the winner of more medals than any other U.S. athlete in Winter Olympics history. (Rev: BL 1/1/95; SLJ 1/95) [921]

BOITANO, BRIAN

7732 Boitano, Brian, and Suzanne Harper. *Boitano's Edge: Inside the Real World of Figure Skating* (4–8). Illus. 1997, Simon & Schuster paper $25.00 (0-689-81915-3). In this autobiography, Boitano tells about his life, the 1988 Olympics, his training programs, touring, and his preparation for competitions. (Rev: BL 2/15/98; SLJ 4/98; VOYA 4/98) [921]

FORREST, ALBERT

7733 McFarlane, Brian. *The Youngest Goalie* (6–9). 1997, Warwick Publg. paper $8.95 (1-895629-95-0). This is an exciting, fictionalized biography of Albert Forrest, who was born in 1887 and became the youngest goalie to play in a Stanley Cup final. (Rev: VOYA 2/99) [921]

GORDEEVA, EKATERINA

7734 Hill, Anne E. *Ekaterina Gordeeva* (6–9). (Overcoming Adversity) 1999, Chelsea LB $19.95 (0-7910-4948-5); paper $9.95 (0-7910-4949-3). The story of the amazing Russian ice skater, her Olympic triumphs, and her adjustment to the sudden death of her husband and partner, who was also a gold medal winner. (Rev: BL 5/15/99) [921]

7735 Shea, Pegi D. *Ekatarina Gordeeva* (4–8). Illus. 1999, Chelsea LB $7.95 (0-7910-5027-0). A biography of this popular skater's life before and after the death of her husband, Sergei Grinkov, including how she has dealt with her grief and continued with her life. (Rev: SLJ 4/99) [921]

GRETZKY, WAYNE

7736 Rappoport, Ken. *Sports Great Wayne Gretzky* (5–8). Illus. (Sports Great) 1996, Enslow LB $16.95 (0-89490-757-3). A brief biography of this hockey phenomenon, illustrated with black-and-white action photos. (Rev: BL 3/15/96) [921]

HAMILTON, SCOTT

7737 Brennan, Kristine. *Scott Hamilton* (6–9). (Overcoming Adversity) 1999, Chelsea LB $19.95 (0-7910-4944-2); paper $9.95 (0-7910-4945-0). A biography of the 4-time winner of the men's world figure skating championship between 1981 and 1984, and his gallant battle against cancer. (Rev: BL 5/15/99) [921]

KWAN, MICHELLE

7738 Epstein, Edward Z. *Born to Skate* (6–12). 1997, Ballantine paper $5.99 (0-345-42136-1). This book describes the career of figure skater Michelle Kwan from her first steps on ice at age 5 to her world championship in 1996 and disappointments in 1997. (This book was written before her 1998 Olympic triumphs.) (Rev: VOYA 4/98) [921]

7739 James, Laura. *Michelle Kwan: Heart of a Champion* (4–8). Illus. 1997, Scholastic $14.95 (0-590-76340-7). A highly personal account of this figure-skating champion, who describes how in 1997 she succeeded in placing second at the World Championships only one month after two falls cost her the position of U.S. women's champion, and who expresses emotions that reveal a maturity beyond her years. (Rev: BL 11/15/97; SLJ 11/97) [921]

LINDROS, ERIC

7740 Rappoport, Ken. *Sports Great Eric Lindros* (5–8). (Sports Greats) 1997, Enslow LB $16.95 (0-89490-871-5). A biography of the famous hockey star that includes career statistics and action photos. (Rev: BL 10/15/97) [921]

LIPINSKI, TARA

7741 Lipinski, Tara. *Tara Lipinski: Triumph on Ice* (4–8). 1997, Bantam $15.95 (0-553-09775-X). An autobiography of this famous ice skater that emphasizes the sacrifices and physical demands that are involved in a career in sports. (Rev: BL 1/1–15/98; SLJ 4/98) [921]

WITT, KATARINA

7742 Kelly, Evelyn B. *Katarina Witt* (6–9). (Female Figure Skating Legends) 1999, Chelsea LB $7.95 (0-7910-5026-2). This is the story of figure skating champion Katarina Witt, from her childhood in East Germany under Communist rule to her many Olympic competitions. (Rev: BL 3/1/99; VOYA 6/99) [921]

Tennis

AGASSI, ANDRE

7743 Knapp, Ron. *Andre Agassi: Star Tennis Player* (5–8). (Sports Reports) 1997, Enslow LB $19.95 (0-89490-798-0). An in-depth look at the life and career of this tennis star, with details of his childhood and his father's influence. (Rev: BL 8/97; SLJ 8/97) [921]

7744 Savage, Jeff. *Andre Agassi: Reaching the Top—Again* (4–8). (Sports Achievers) 1997, Lerner LB $14.96 (0-8225-2890-0). A short, easily read biography of this volatile tennis star. (Rev: BL 1/1–15/98) [921]

ASHE, ARTHUR

7745 Collins, David R. *Arthur Ashe: Against the Wind* (6–9). (People in Focus) 1994, Dillon LB $13.95 (0-87518-647-5). A portrait of the inspiring African American sports champion, humanitarian, and civil rights activist. (Rev: BL 2/1/95; SLJ 3/95; VOYA 5/95) [921]

7746 Martin, Marvin. *Arthur Ashe: Of Tennis & the Human Spirit* (6–12). 1999, Watts $24.00 (0-531-11432-5). In spite of incredible obstacles, Arthur Ashe achieved great heights in the tennis world, including becoming the first black world champion, and became admired as much for his humanitarian efforts and his dignified struggle against racism as for his tennis achievements. (Rev: BL 7/99; SLJ 6/99) [921]

7747 Wright, David K. *Arthur Ashe: Breaking the Color Barrier in Tennis* (7–12). Illus. (African-American Biographies) 1996, Enslow LB $19.95 (0-89490-689-5). The life story of this revered tennis star, his professional career, and gallant struggle against AIDS. (Rev: BL 12/15/96; SLJ 10/96) [921]

CHANG, MICHAEL

7748 Ditchfield, Christin. *Sports Great Michael Chang* (5–8). (Sports Greats) 1999, Enslow $16.95 (0-7660-1223-9). A biography of this tennis phenomenon, with career statistics and plenty of action photographs. (Rev: BL 3/15/99) [921]

GIBSON, ALTHEA

7749 Biracree, Tom. *Althea Gibson* (7–12). Illus. 1989, Chelsea LB $19.95 (1-55546-654-0). The rags-to-riches story of the black athlete who was once the best woman tennis player in the world. (Rev: BL 2/15/90; BR 3–4/90; SLJ 2/90; VOYA 2/90) [921]

NAVRATILOVA, MARTINA

7750 Blue, Adrianne. *Martina: The Lives and Times of Martina Navratilova* (9–12). 1995, Birch Lane $19.95 (1-55972-300-9). A biography of Navratilova, focusing on her career and touching on aspects of her personal life. (Rev: BL 9/15/95) [921]

SAMPRAS, PETE

7751 Miller, Calvin C. *Pete Sampras* (6–10). Illus. 1998, Morgan Reynolds LB $17.95 (1-883846-26-9). A candid biography of this usually quiet and staid tennis professional, with details on his phenomenal career. (Rev: BL 4/1/98; BR 1–2/99) [921]

7752 Sherrow, Victoria. *Sports Great Pete Sampras* (5–8). Illus. (Sports Great) 1996, Enslow LB $16.95 (0-89490-756-5). The life story of this charismatic tennis star is told in brief text and many photographs, accompanied by career statistics. (Rev: BL 3/15/96) [921]

SELES, MONICA

7753 Murdico, Suzanne J. *Monica Seles* (5–8). Illus. (Overcoming the Odds) 1998, Raintree Steck-Vaughn $24.26 (0-8172-4128-0). The story of the great tennis player and the courtside stabbing that resulted in a trauma difficult to overcome. (Rev: VOYA 8/98) [921]

WILLIAMS, VENUS

7754 Aronson, Virginia. *Venus Williams* (5–8). Illus. (Galaxy of Superstars) 1999, Chelsea $16.95 (0-7910-5153-6). This story of the wonder girl of tennis describes her childhood in a black ghetto in California and her rise to fame in spite of many obstacles. (Rev: BL 4/15/99; BR 9–10/99; SLJ 5/99) [921]

ZAHARIAS, BABE DIDRIKSON

7755 Cayleff, Susan E. *Babe: The Life and Legend of Babe Didrikson Zaharias* (9–12). 1996, Univ. of Illinois Pr. $14.95 (0-252-06593-X). Looks at Babe Didrikson Zaharias, pro golfer and Olympic gold medalist, examining how she lived her life, her public persona, and her lesbianism. (Rev: BL 6/1–15/95) [921]

7756 Freedman, Russell. *Babe Didrikson Zaharias: The Making of a Champion* (6–12). 1999, Clarion $18.00 (0-395-63367-2). Known to most for her tennis career, this entertaining biography points out that Babe Didrikson Zaharias was also an Olympic athlete, track star, golfer, entrepreneur, and leader of a woman's amateur basketball team. (Rev: BL 7/99; SLJ 7/99) [921]

7757 Lynn, Elizabeth A. *Babe Didrikson Zaharias* (6–10). Illus. 1988, Chelsea LB $19.95 (1-55546-684-2). The story of the all-around athlete best known for her accomplishments in golf. (Rev: BL 12/1/88; BR 5–6/89) [921]

Track and Field

GRIFFITH JOYNER, FLORENCE

7758 Koral, April. *Florence Griffith Joyner: Track and Field Star* (5–8). (First Book) 1992, Watts LB $22.00 (0-531-20061-2). A biography of the winner of 4 Olympic track medals that emphasizes her hard work and determination. (Rev: BL 10/1/92; SLJ 8/92) [921]

JOYNER-KERSEE, JACQUELINE

7759 Green, Carl R. *Jackie Joyner-Kersee* (5–8). (Sports Headlines) 1994, Macmillan LB $17.95 (0-89686-838-9). A biography of the track star that uses press quotations and photos to highlight important events in her career. (Rev: BL 10/1/94) [921]

7760 Harrington, Geri. *Jackie Joyner-Kersee: Champion Athlete* (6–10). 1995, Chelsea LB $19.95 (0-7910-2085-1). Describes Joyner-Kersee's 4 Olympic championships, despite asthma attacks. (Rev: BL 10/1/95) [921]

LEWIS, CARL

7761 Klots, Steve. *Carl Lewis* (7–10). (Black Americans of Achievement) 1994, Chelsea LB $19.95 (0-7910-2164-5). Describes the childhood, college career, and Olympic performances of this athlete, including his attempts at the long-jump record. (Rev: BL 3/15/95) [921]

O'BRIEN, DAN

7762 Gutman, Bill. *Dan O'Brien* (5–8). (Overcoming the Odds) 1998, Raintree Steck-Vaughn $24.26 (0-8172-4129-9). A biography of this great decathlete that describes his struggles to overcome attention-deficit hyperactivity disorder as well as various injuries and trauma as a result of failure. (Rev: VOYA 8/98) [921]

OWENS, JESSE

7763 Baker, William J. *Jesse Owens: An American Life* (10–12). Illus. 1986, Free Pr. paper $18.95 (0-02-901760-2). The story of the black American track star whose career involved triumph at Hitler's Olympics. [921]

7764 Gentry, Tony. *Jesse Owens: Champion Athlete* (6–9). Illus. 1990, Chelsea LB $19.95 (1-55546-603-6). The story of the black American track star who upset Hitler's master race theory at the Olympics. (Rev: SLJ 7/90; VOYA 8/90) [921]

7765 Josephson, Judith P. *Jesse Owens: Track and Field Legend* (6–10). (African American Biographies) 1997, Enslow LB $19.95 (0-89490-812-X). The life of this track star is retold with details about the prejudice he faced throughout his personal and professional life and his performance at the 1936 Berlin Olympics, where he won 4 gold medals, defying Adolf Hitler's view of Aryans as the "Master Race." (Rev: SLJ 1/98) [921]

7766 Nuwer, Hank. *The Legend of Jesse Owens* (7–12). 1998, Watts LB $24.00 (0-531-11356-6). In spite of pervasive racism and a frail constitution, Jesse Owens grew up to become the gold medal hero of the 1936 Olympics. This is his inspiring story. (Rev: BL 1/1–15/99; SLJ 1/99) [921]

RUDOLPH, WILMA

7767 Biracree, Tom. *Wilma Rudolph* (7–12). Illus. 1987, Chelsea LB $19.95 (1-55546-675-3). The inspiring story of the black athlete who conquered polio and won 3 Olympic gold medals in track in a single year. (Rev: BL 8/88) [921]

THORPE, JIM

7768 Bernotas, Bob. *Jim Thorpe: Sac and Fox Athlete* (9–12). (North American Indians of Achievement) 1992, Chelsea LB $19.95 (0-7910-1722-2). The story of this great all-around athlete who was stripped of his Olympic medals. (Rev: BL 11/1/92) [921]

7769 Wheeler, Robert W. *Jim Thorpe: World's Greatest Athlete* (9–12). 1981, Univ. of Oklahoma Pr. paper $14.95 (0-8061-1745-1). This biography traces the amazing career of the American Indian athlete who won both the decathlon and the pentathlon in 1912. [921]

Miscellaneous Sports

PELE

7770 Arnold, Caroline. *Pele: The King of Soccer* (5–8). (First Book) 1992, Watts LB $22.00 (0-531-20077-9). Traces Pele's soccer career from early promise to international superstardom. (Rev: BL 10/1/92) [921]

REECE, GABRIELLE

7771 Reece, Gabrielle, and Karen Karbo. *Big Girl in the Middle* (9–12). 1997, Crown $24.00 (0-517-70835-3). In this autobiography, Reece, a professional volleyball player as well as a television personality and fashion model, discusses how her contrasting careers reflect the different aspects of her personality and outlines her personal philosophies of Christian spirituality and self-esteem as well as her work ethic as an athlete and a model. (Rev: VOYA 4/98) [921]

STARK, PETER

7772 Stark, Peter. *Driving to Greenland* (9–12). 1994, Lyons Pr. $22.95 (1-55821-320-1). The author describes his adventures on skis, dogsled, and luge on mountains in Greenland and Iceland. (Rev: BL 9/1/94) [796.93]

TREVINO, LEE

7773 Gilbert, Thomas. *Lee Trevino* (5–9). (Hispanics of Achievement) 1991, Chelsea LB $19.95 (0-7910-1256-5). The story of one of golf's all-time greats to 1990. (Rev: BL 3/15/92) [796.352]

WOODS, TIGER

7774 Boyd, Aaron. *Tiger Woods* (9–12). 1997, Morgan Reynolds LB $17.95 (1-883846-19-6). This introduction to the life and golf training of this superstar contains many interesting anecdotes and includes his triumph at the first Masters. (Rev: BL 5/1/97; SLJ 8/97; VOYA 10/97) [921]

7775 Rosaforte, Tim. *Tiger Woods: The Makings of a Champion* (10–12). 1997, St. Martin's $21.95 (0-312-15672-3). This book tells of Tiger Woods's childhood and teen years and his rapid rise to the top of the golf world, ending prior to his winning the 1997 Masters tournament. (Rev: SLJ 9/97; VOYA 10/97) [921]

7776 Teague, Allison L. *Prince of the Fairway: The Tiger Woods Story* (8–12). 1997, Avisson LB $18.50 (1-888105-22-4). Written for young adults, this biography probes into Woods's childhood and the cultural values of his family as well as describing his golf training and career. (Rev: SLJ 10/97; VOYA 10/97) [921]

World Figures

Collective

7777 Brill, Marlene T. *Extraordinary Young People* (7–12). (Extraordinary Young People) 1996, Children's Pr. LB $37.00 (0-516-00587-1). This chronologically arranged collective biography profiles 50 famous people who made a mark in the world while still young, including such names as Genghis Khan, Joan of Arc, Mozart, Rachel Carson, Callas, Pele, Tiger Woods, and Midori. Also included are fascinating essays on youths who made a mark but are now little-known or forgotten. (Rev: SLJ 10/96) [920]

7778 Goldman, Elizabeth. *Believers: Spiritual Leaders of the World* (7–9). Illus. 1996, Oxford $49.95 (0-19-508240-0). This oversize book contains profiles of 40 religious leaders, from the well known, such as Moses and Jesus, to the obscure, such as Hildegard of Bingen and Isaac Luria. (Rev: BL 4/15/96) [920]

7779 Gulotta, Charles. *Extraordinary Women in Politics* (6–9). (Extraordinary People) 1998, Children's Pr. LB $37.00 (0-516-20610-9). From Cleopatra, Queen Victoria, and Catherine the Great to Margaret Thatcher, Bella Abzug, Sandra Day O'Connor, and Hillary Rodham Clinton, this book profiles 55 women who have had a powerful influence in the world's political arena. (Rev: BL 1/1–15/99; SLJ 1/99) [920]

7780 Hazell, Rebecca. *Heroines: Great Women through the Ages* (5–8). Illus. 1996, Abbeville $19.95 (0-7892-0210-7). This is a collective biography of 12 great women spanning the period from ancient Greece to modern times, including Sacagawea, Madame Sun Yat-Sen, Frido Kahlo, Joan of Arc, Harriet Tubman, and Marie Curie. (Rev: SLJ 12/96) [920]

7781 Lucas, Eileen. *Contemporary Human Rights Activists* (6–9). Illus. (Global Profiles) 1997, Facts on File $19.95 (0-8160-3298-X). A collection of 10 short biographies of post-World War II human rights leaders such as Desmond Tutu and Mother Theresa, with an introduction defining the concept of basic human rights and brief history of the modern human rights movement. (Rev: BL 8/97; BR 9–10/97) [323]

7782 Meltzer, Milton. *Ten Queens: Portraits of Women of Power* (5–8). Illus. 1998, Dutton $25.00 (0-525-45643-0). In this handsome book enhanced by reproductions of many paintings, 10 queens are profiled, including Esther, Cleopatra, Eleanor of Aquitaine, Isabella of Spain, Elizabeth I, and Catherine the Great. (Rev: BL 4/15/98; BR 1–2/99; SLJ 6/98; VOYA 4/99) [920]

7783 Nardo, Don. *Women Leaders of Nations* (6–10). Illus. (History Makers) 1999, Lucent LB $17.96 (1-56006-397.1). An overview of women in government, followed by chapters on several female leaders of nations, among them Cleopatra and Margaret Thatcher, and a chapter on other women leaders, including Amazon warriors and Queen Boudicca. (Rev: BL 6/1–15/99) [920]

7784 Pasachoff, Naomi. *Links in the Chain: Shapers of the Jewish Tradition* (9–12). (Oxford Profiles) 1998, Oxford $56.00 (0-19-509939-7). From Maimonides to Yitzhak Rabin, this collective biography supplies material on 40 shapers of Judaism and the Jewish state of Israel. (Rev: BL 1/1–15/98; BR 5–6/98; SLJ 4/98) [920]

7785 Price-Groff, Claire. *Twentieth-Century Women Political Leaders* (7–10). (Global Profiles) 1998, Facts on File LB $19.95 (0-8160-3672-1). This book contains profiles of 12 women political leaders in the second half of the 20th century: Golda Meir, Indira Gandhi, Eva Peron, Margaret Thatcher, Corazon Aquino, Winnie Mandela, Barbara Jordan, Violeta

Chamorro, Wilma Mankiller, Gro Harlem Brundtland, Aung San Suu Kyi, and Benazir Bhutto. (Rev: BR 1–2/99; SLJ 1/99) [920]

7786 Rasmussen, R. Kent. *Modern African Political Leaders* (7–12). Illus. (Global Profiles) 1998, Facts on File $19.95 (0-8160-3277-7). This book focuses on how personal incidents inspired the political actions of 8 African leaders of the 20th century who played major roles in the political changes throughout the continent, including Haile Selassie, Gamal Abdel Nasser, Kwame Nkrumah, Robert Mugabe, and Nelson Mandela. (Rev: BL 8/98; BR 11–12/98; SLJ 9/98) [920]

7787 Salsitz, Norman, and Amalie Petranker Salsitz. *Against All Odds: A Tale of Two Survivors* (9–12). 1991, Holocaust Publns. $24.95 (0-89604-148-4); paper $12.95 (0-89604-149-2). In these recollections of the Holocaust by 2 Polish Jews who married after the war, similar tales of Nazi brutality, false identities, close escapes, and great endurance are told. (Rev: BL 9/15/91) [940.53]

7788 Taitz, Emily, and Sondra Henry. *Remarkable Jewish Women* (7–12). Illus. 1996, Jewish Publication Soc. $29.95 (0-8276-0573-0). Thumbnail sketches of resourceful Jewish women throughout history, beginning with Ruth and Esther in the Bible to present-day notables. (Rev: BL 12/1/96; SLJ 6/97) [920]

7789 Traub, Carol G. *Philanthropists and Their Legacies* (7–12). Illus. (Profiles) 1997, Oliver Pr. LB $18.95 (1-881508-42-0). Profiles—warts and all—of 9 of the world's greatest benefactors, including Alfred Nobel, Andrew Carnegie, Cecil Rhodes, George Eastman, Will Kellogg, and John and Catherine MacArthur. (Rev: BL 2/15/98; BR 1–2/98; SLJ 2/98) [361.7]

7790 Wakin, Edward. *Contemporary Political Leaders of the Middle East* (6–12). Illus. (Global Profiles) 1996, Facts on File $19.95 (0-8160-3154-1). Profiles of 8 Israeli and Arab leaders who have shaped events in the Middle East, including Saddam Hussein, Mubarek, Quadaffi, Rabin, and Peres. (Rev: BL 4/15/96; SLJ 3/96; VOYA 4/96) [956.05]

7791 Welden, Amelie. *Girls Who Rocked the World: Heroines from Sacagawea to Sheryl Swoopes* (5–8). Illus. 1998, Beyond Words paper $8.95 (1-885223-68-4). This collective biography contains short profiles of 33 women who achieved extraordinary things before age 20, arranged chronologically, starting with Cleopatra and ending with tennis star Marina Hingis. (Rev: BL 7/97; SLJ 7/98) [920]

Africa

ADAMSON, JOY

7792 Neimark, Anne E. *Wild Heart: The Story of Joy Adamson, Author of Born Free* (6–10). 1999, Harcourt $17.00 (0-15-201368-7). This biography of the author of *Born Free* tells about her childhood in Austria, her later work with wild animals in Kenya (including raising the lion cub Elsa), and her pioneer work in conservation. (Rev: BL 3/15/99; SLJ 6/99; VOYA 10/99) [921]

CLEOPATRA

7793 Brooks, Polly Schoyer. *Cleopatra: Goddess of Egypt, Enemy of Rome* (7–10). 1995, HarperCollins LB $16.89 (0-06-023608-6). As much an account of the Roman struggle for power as a biography of the Egyptian queen, an intelligent and capable leader. (Rev: BL 11/1/95; SLJ 12/95; VOYA 4/96) [921]

7794 Hoobler, Dorothy, and Thomas Hoobler. *Cleopatra* (6–10). Illus. 1986, Chelsea LB $19.95 (0-87754-589-8). Through recounting the story of this amazing queen, the author tells about life in ancient Egypt. (Rev: BL 2/1/87; SLJ 2/87) [921]

7795 Nardo, Don. *Cleopatra* (8–12). (The Importance Of) 1994, Lucent LB $22.45 (1-56006-023-9). This illustrated biography discusses the life of the legendary queen in relation to the politics and power struggles of ancient Egypt and Rome. (Rev: BL 1/15/94; SLJ 3/94) [921]

MANDELA, NELSON

7796 Finlayson, Reggie. *Nelson Mandela* (5–8). (A and E Biography) 1998, Lerner $25.26 (0-8225-4936-0). An overview that concentrates on Mandela's childhood, his training as a lawyer, and his rise through the ranks of the African National Congress, with only brief coverage of his imprisonment, release, and presidency. (Rev: SLJ 2/99) [921]

7797 Hoobler, Dorothy, and Thomas Hoobler. *Mandela: The Man, the Struggle, the Triumph* (6–12). 1992, Watts LB $23.60 (0-531-11141-5). A review of the struggle against apartheid in South Africa from 1987 to 1992, which encompassed the repeal of the apartheid laws and the release of Nelson Mandela and other political prisoners from prison. (Rev: BL 5/15/92; SLJ 12/92) [921]

7798 Hughes, Libby. *Nelson Mandela: Voice of Freedom* (6–10). (People in Focus) 1992, Dillon LB $18.95 (0-87518-484-7). Integrates Mandela's political struggle against apartheid with his personal story. Extensive bibliography, photos. (Rev: BL 12/1/92; SLJ 1/93) [921]

Asia and the Middle East

ARAFAT, YASIR

7799 Ferber, Elizabeth. *Yasir Arafat: The Battle for Peace in Palestine* (7–12). 1995, Millbrook LB $23.90 (1-56294-585-8). A balanced presentation of Arafat's political career. (Rev: BL 10/1/95; SLJ 12/95) [921]

7800 Rubinstein, Danny. *The Mystery of Arafat* (9–12). 1995, Steerforth $18.00 (1-883642-10-8). An Israeli journalist writes this biography of the PLO leader and considers his place in history. (Rev: BL 5/15/95) [921]

CONFUCIUS

7801 Wilker, Josh. *Confucius: Philosopher and Teacher* (5–8). (Book Report Biographies) 1999, Watts $22.00 (0-531-11436-8). A serviceable biography of the great Chinese philosopher and religious leader, with ample quotations from his works. (Rev: SLJ 7/99) [921]

DALAI LAMA

7802 Perez, Louis G. *The Dalai Lama* (6–12). (World Leaders) 1993, Rourke LB $25.27 (0-86625-480-3). Tells of the Dali Lama's lonely childhood, nonviolent struggle for his people, years in exile, his impact and life through 1992. (Rev: BL 12/1/93) [921]

7803 Stewart, Whitney. *The 14th Dalai Lama: Spiritual Leader of Tibet* (5–8). (Newsmakers) 1996, Lerner LB $25.26 (0-8225-4926-3). The story of the 14th Dalai Lama from his childhood of rigorous Buddhist education to his present life in exile. (Rev: SLJ 6/96; VOYA 10/96) [921]

FARMAN FARMAIAN, SATTAREH

7804 Farman Farmaian, Sattareh, and Dona Munker. *Daughter of Persia: A Woman's Journey from Her Father's Harem Through the Islamic Revolution* (9–12). 1992, Crown $22.00 (0-517-58697-5). The daughter of a prominent Iranian recalls her privileged life in Tehran, her U.S. education, and her social reform work, which outraged Khomeini. (Rev: BL 1/1/92*) [921]

GANDHI, MAHATMA

7805 Fischer, Louis. *Gandhi* (10–12). 1982, NAL paper $5.99 (0-451-62742-3). An admiring biography of the man who led India through nonviolent revolt to freedom. [921]

7806 Severance, John B. *Gandhi, Great Soul* (6–9). Illus. 1997, Clarion $15.95 (0-395-77179-X). The life and times of Gandhi are covered in this attractive, informative book, which explains Gandhi's philosophy of peaceful resistance and describes the evolution of his beliefs. (Rev: BL 2/15/97; BR 9–10/97; SLJ 4/97*) [921]

GENGHIS KHAN

7807 Humphrey, Judy. *Genghis Khan* (6–10). Illus. 1987, Chelsea LB $19.95 (0-87754-527-8). The story of the fierce warrior who shaped the Mongolian empire in the twelfth century. (Rev: BL 11/15/87; SLJ 12/87) [921]

HERZL, THEODOR

7808 Finkelstein, Norman H. *Theodor Herzl: Architect of a Nation* (7–12). 1991, Lerner LB $25.26 (0-8225-4913-1). The story of the respected playwright/journalist who dedicated himself to helping the Jewish people obtain their own country. (Rev: BL 4/15/92; SLJ 7/92) [921]

HIROHITO (EMPEROR OF JAPAN)

7809 Hoyt, Edwin. *Hirohito: The Emperor and the Man* (9–12). 1992, Praeger $49.95 (0-275-94069-1). This biography presents the Japanese leader as a man of peace and goodwill. (Rev: BL 3/15/92) [921]

HUSSEIN, SADDAM

7810 Claypool, Jane. *Saddam Hussein* (6–12). (World Leaders) 1993, Rourke LB $25.27 (0-86625-477-3). Describes Hussein's violent childhood, his rise to power, his impact and his life to 1992. (Rev: BL 12/1/93; SLJ 1/94) [921]

7811 Stefoff, Rebecca. *Saddam Hussein: Absolute Ruler of Iraq* (7–12). 1995, Millbrook LB $15.90 (1-56294-475-4). A complex history of the Middle East is the backdrop for this biography of Hussein. (Rev: BL 3/15/95; SLJ 2/95) [921]

JIANG, JI-LI

7812 Jiang, Ji-li. *Red Scarf Girl: A Memoir of the Cultural Revolution* (6–10). 1997, HarperCollins $15.95 (0-06-027585-5). An engrossing memoir of a Chinese girl, her family, and how their lives became a nightmare during Chairman Mao's Cultural Revolution of the late 1960s. (Rev: BL 10/1/97; BR 3–4/98; SLJ 12/97; VOYA 6/98) [921]

KOLLEK, TEDDY

7813 Rabinovich, Abraham. *Teddy Kollek: Builder of Jerusalem* (5–8). Illus. 1996, Jewish Publication Soc. $14.95 (0-8276-0559-5); paper $9.95 (0-8276-0561-7). The story of the former mayor of Jerusalem, who supervised the city's unification after the Six

Days War in 1967. (Rev: BL 5/15/96; BR 9–10/96) [921]

KORDI, GOHAR

7814 Kordi, Gohar. *An Iranian Odyssey* (9–12). 1993, Serpent's Tail paper $13.95 (1-85242-213-0). A memoir of a blind Iranian-born woman, who without financial or emotional support from her parents graduated from Teheran University in 1970. (Rev: BL 1/15/93) [921]

MASIH, IQBAL

7815 Kuklin, Susan. *Iqbal Masih & the Crusaders Against Child Slavery* (6–12). Illus. 1998, Holt $16.95 (0-8050-5459-6). The story of the Pakistani boy who after escaping slavery devoted his young life to a crusade against child labor abuse until he was murdered at age 12. (Rev: BL 11/1/98; SLJ 11/98; VOYA 4/99) [331.3 4 092 B]

MEIR, GOLDA

7816 Hitzeroth, Deborah. *Golda Meir* (5–8). Illus. (The Importance Of) 1997, Lucent LB $17.96 (1-56006-090-5). Sidebars, quotes from original sources, and photos contribute to this biography of the woman who grew up in Czarist Russia, lived for a time in Milwaukee, moved to Palestine to raise a family, and became Israel's most famous female political leader. (Rev: SLJ 8/98) [921]

MIN, ANCHEE

7817 Min, Anchee. *Red Azalea* (9–12). 1999, Berkley paper $13.00 (0-425-16687-2). The hardships of Min's youth in Shanghai as a child of Mao's Cultural Revolution—a harsh portrait of China in the 1960s and 1970s. (Rev: BL 2/1/94) [921]

RABIN, YITZHAK

7818 Kort, Michael G. *Yitzhak Rabin: Israel's Soldier Statesman* (9–12). Illus. 1996, Millbrook LB $23.90 (0-7613-0100-3); paper $8.95 (0-7613-0135-6). The story of the slain Israeli leader and his struggle for peace are told against the backdrop of Middle East conflicts. (Rev: BL 1/1–15/97; BR 3–4/97; SLJ 2/97; VOYA 6/97) [956.9405]

SASAKI, SADAKO

7819 Nasu, Masamoto. *Children of the Paper Crane: The Story of Sadako Sasaki and Her Struggle with the A-Bomb Disease* (9–12). Trans. by Elizabeth W. Baldwin and others. 1991, M.E. Sharpe $50.95 (0-87332-715-2). A personal account of the legacy of the Hiroshima bombing that describes the devastating decline of one child and the effects on her family and all Japan. (Rev: BL 12/15/91) [921]

SUU KYI, AUNG SAN

7820 Ling, Bettina. *Aung San Suu Kyi: Standing Up for Democracy in Burma* (6–9). (Women Changing the World) 1999, Feminist Pr. $19.95 (1-55861-196-7). A biography of the woman who has fought for democracy in Burma, spent many years under house arrest, and was awarded the Nobel Peace Prize in 1991. (Rev: BL 3/15/99) [921]

7821 Parenteau, John. *Prisoner for Peace: Aung San Suu Kyi and Burma's Struggle for Democracy* (7–10). 1994, Morgan Reynolds LB $18.95 (1-883846-05-6). Chronicles Burma's struggle to be a democratic nation, focusing on the Nobel Prize winner's political activism and her arrest because of it. (Rev: BL 11/1/94; SLJ 9/94; VOYA 4/95) [921]

7822 Stewart, Whitney. *Aung San Suu Kyi: Fearless Voice of Burma* (6–9). 1997, Lerner LB $25.26 (0-8225-4931-X). A thorough, well-documented biography of the Nobel Peace Prize winner and fearless Burmese leader in the struggle for democracy. (Rev: BL 4/1/97; SLJ 5/97; VOYA 12/97) [921]

TAJ AL-SALTANA

7823 al-Saltana, Taj. *Crowning Anguish: Memoirs of a Persian Princess from the Harem to Modernity, 1884-1914* (9–12). Ed. by Abbas Amanat. Trans. by Anna Vanzan and Amin Neshati. 1993, Mage Publishers $29.95 (0-934211-35-3); paper $14.95 (0-934211-36-1). An Iranian princess's memoirs of her life in a sheik's palace that questions the traditions of this changing society. (Rev: BL 9/15/93) [921]

TAMERLANE

7824 Wepman, Dennis. *Tamerlane* (6–10). Illus. 1987, Chelsea LB $19.95 (0-87754-442-5). The story of the barbaric Mongol chieftain who lived in the fourteenth century and was responsible for the death of millions. (Rev: BL 7/87; SLJ 8/87) [921]

TERESA, MOTHER

7825 Rice, Tanya. *Mother Teresa* (5–8). Illus. (The Life and Times Of) 1999, Chelsea LB $15.95 (0-7910-4637-0). A straightforward account of the life of Mother Teresa, from her birth in Albania to devout Catholic parents and her religious calling as a child, to her work in India and her commitment to helping the poor, to the winning of the Nobel Peace Prize, and her death. (Rev: SLJ 8/98) [921]

WIESENTHAL, SIMON

7826 Jeffrey, Laura S. *Simon Wiesenthal: Tracking Down Nazi Criminals* (6–9). (People to Know) 1997, Enslow LB $19.95 (0-89490-830-8). The story of the great investigator of Holocaust crimes who was responsible for bringing to justice such infamous war criminals as Adolph Eichmann. (Rev: BR 5–6/98; SLJ 3/98) [921]

ZEDONG, MAO

7827 Stefoff, Rebecca. *Mao Zedong: Founder of the People's Republic of China* (7–12). Illus. 1996, Millbrook LB $22.40 (1-56294-531-9). A well-documented biography of this important Chinese politician that covers childhood influences, contributions to the development of the Republic of China, and his lasting impact on world history. (Rev: BL 5/1/96; BR 9–10/96; SLJ 6/96) [921]

Australia and the Pacific Islands

KA'IULANI, PRINCESS

7828 Linnea, Sharon. *Princess Ka'iulani: Hope of a Nation, Heart of a People* (5–8). 1999, Eerdmans $18.00 (0-8028-5145-2). The story of the Hawaiian princess who tried to prevent the annexation of her country by the United States and of her untimely death at age 22. (Rev: BL 7/99; SLJ 6/99; VOYA 10/99) [921]

Europe

ALEXANDER THE GREAT

7829 Stewart, Gail B. *Alexander the Great* (5–8). (The Importance Of) 1994, Lucent LB $17.96 (1-56006-047-6). The story of the great conqueror from Macedonia and of his lasting impact on Western civilization. (Rev: BL 8/94) [921]

ATATURK, KEMAL

7830 Tachau, Frank. *Kemal Ataturk* (6–10). Illus. 1987, Chelsea LB $19.95 (0-87754-507-3). A biography of the man who transformed Turkey and brought it into the twentieth century. (Rev: BL 1/1/88; SLJ 3/88) [921]

BERLAND-HYATT, FELICIA

7831 Berland-Hyatt, Felicia. *Close Calls: Memoirs of a Survivor* (9–12). 1991, Holocaust Publns. paper $13.95 (0-89604-138-7). A survivor's account of the Holocaust. (Rev: BL 1/15/92) [921]

BRAILLE, LOUIS

7832 Freedman, Russell. *Out of Darkness: The Story of Louis Braille* (4–8). Illus. 1997, Clarion $16.95 (0-395-77516-7). The story of the blind Frenchman who, more than 170 years ago, invented a system of reading using raised dots. (Rev: BL 3/1/97; BR 9–10/97; SLJ 3/97*) [686.2]

CAESAR, AUGUSTUS

7833 Walworth, Nancy Zinsser. *Augustus Caesar* (6–10). Illus. 1988, Chelsea LB $19.95 (1-55546-804-7). The story of Julius Caesar's adopted son who later avenged his death and led the Empire through a peaceful era. (Rev: BL 12/1/88; BR 5–6/89; SLJ 2/89; VOYA 2/89) [921]

CAESAR, JULIUS

7834 Bruns, Roger. *Julius Caesar* (6–10). Illus. 1987, Chelsea LB $19.95 (0-87754-514-6). Using many sources, the author creates an accurate picture of the rise and fall of this Roman leader. (Rev: BL 11/15/87; BR 9–10/88; SLJ 12/87; VOYA 10/88) [921]

7835 Green, Robert. *Julius Caesar* (5–8). (First Books: Ancient Biographies) 1996, Watts LB $22.50 (0-531-20241-0). This book describes Julius Caesar's role in creating the powerful Roman Empire, his early ambitions, his rise to power, his brilliant military career, and his violent death. (Rev: SLJ 2/97) [921]

7836 Nardo, Don. *Julius Caesar* (4–8). Illus. (The Importance Of) 1997, Lucent LB $16.95 (1-56006-083-2). An introductory biography that stresses the lasting importance of this great leader who expanded the Roman Empire. (Rev: BL 1/1–15/97; BR 9–10/97; SLJ 3/97) [921]

CALVIN, JOHN

7837 Stepanek, Sally. *John Calvin* (6–10). Illus. 1986, Chelsea LB $17.95 (0-87754-515-4). A well-researched biography of the sixteenth-century leader of the Protestant Reformation. (Rev: BL 3/1/87; SLJ 3/87) [921]

CARY, ELIZABETH

7838 Brackett, Ginger Roberts. *Elizabeth Cary: Writer of Conscience* (7–10). Illus. 1996, Morgan Reynolds LB $18.95 (1-883846-15-3). The story of the 17th-century Englishwoman and brilliant writer who defied society by becoming a Roman Catholic in heavily Protestant England. (Rev: BL 10/1/96; SLJ 10/96; VOYA 6/97) [921]

CHARLEMAGNE

7839 Biel, Timothy L. *Charlemagne* (4–8). Illus. (The Importance Of) 1997, Lucent LB $17.96 (1-56006-074-3). The story of the king of the Franks, his empire, and his lasting importance in European history. (Rev: BL 6/1–15/97; SLJ 9/97) [921]

7840 Westwood, Jennifer. *Stories of Charlemagne* (7–9). 1976, Phillips $25.95 (0-87599-213-7). A biography of the famous emperor of the Holy Roman Empire who was one of the most influential men of the Middle Ages. [921]

CHURCHILL, WINSTON

7841 Rose, Norman. *Churchill: The Unruly Giant* (9–12). 1995, Free Pr. $26.00 (0-02-874009-2). Charts Churchill's career and paints an image of the ambition, determination, and pugnacity that won him both respect and resentment. (Rev: BL 7/95) [921]

7842 Severance, John B. *Winston Churchill: Soldier, Statesman, Artist* (5–8). Illus. 1996, Clarion $17.95 (0-395-69853-7). A well-organized, clearly written account of the life and works of Britain's great statesman. (Rev: BL 4/15/96; SLJ 4/96*; VOYA 6/96) [941.084]

CLEMENCEAU, GEORGES

7843 Gottfried, Ted. *Georges Clemenceau* (6–10). Illus. 1987, Chelsea LB $19.95 (0-87754-518-9). A biography of the French political leader who served his country with distinction during World War I. (Rev: BL 11/15/87; SLJ 3/88) [921]

DAMAN, HORTENSE

7844 Bles, Mark. *Child at War: The True Story of a Young Belgian Resistance Fighter* (9–12). 1991, Mercury House $20.95 (1-56279-004-8). An exciting behind-the-front story of a teenager's fight for freedom in Belgium during World War II. (Rev: BL 3/1/91; SLJ 2/92) [921]

DE GAULLE, CHARLES

7845 Whitelaw, Nancy. *Charles de Gaulle: "I Am France"* (5–8). 1991, Dillon LB $13.95 (0-87518-486-3). Details the life and accomplishments of France's controversial leader. (Rev: BL 2/15/92) [921]

DIANA, PRINCESS OF WALES

7846 Brennan, Kristine. *Diana, Princess of Wales* (5–8). (Women of Achievement) 1998, Chelsea LB $19.95 (0-7910-4714-8); paper $9.95 (0-7910-4715-6). This book covers the facts about Diana's life, disappointing marriage, struggle for happiness, and untimely death. (Rev: VOYA 4/99) [921]

7847 Whitelaw, Nancy. *Lady Diana Spencer: Princess of Wales* (7–10). Illus. 1998, Morgan Reynolds LB $20.95 (1-883846-35-8). A quick read that gives details about Diana's privileged but troubled background and the many problems she faced as a member of the royal family. (Rev: BL 8/98; BR 1–2/99; SLJ 6/98; VOYA 10/98) [921]

EICHENGREEN, LUCILLE

7848 Eichengreen, Lucille. *From Ashes to Life: My Memories of the Holocaust* (9–12). 1994, Mercury House paper $17.95 (1-56279-052-8). A young girl's harrowing experiences in the Nazi death camps end with liberation, followed by survivor guilt and search for meaning. (Rev: SLJ 10/94) [921]

ELIZABETH I, QUEEN OF ENGLAND

7849 Thomas, Jane Resh. *Behind the Mask: The Life of Queen Elizabeth I* (5–8). 1998, Clarion $19.00 (0-395-69120-6). A behind-the-scenes look at Gloriana that discusses her childhood, how she overcame opposition to become queen, and her subsequent manipulation of people, the court, and foreigners to attain greatness. (Rev: BL 12/15/98; BR 5–6/99; SLJ 12/98*; VOYA 4/99) [921]

7850 Weir, Alison. *The Life of Elizabeth I* (9–12). 1998, Ballantine $27.50 (0-345-40533-1). A fully rounded portrait of the complex queen who surmounted intrigues, jealousies, plots, disease, and the betrayal of a loved one to lead her kingdom in its transformation from a debt-ridden country of little influence into a major European power. She gave her name to an age and influenced the course of British and European history for centuries. (Rev: BL 7/98; SLJ 4/99) [921]

ELIZABETH II, QUEEN OF GREAT BRITAIN

7851 Auerbach, Susan. *Queen Elizabeth II* (6–12). (World Leaders) 1993, Rourke LB $25.27 (0-86625-481-1). Queen Elizabeth's childhood during World War II, how she came to the throne, and the major events in her reign up to 1993. (Rev: BL 12/1/93) [921]

FABERGÉ, CARL

7852 von Habsburg-Lothringen, Geza. *Carl Fabergé* (6–10). 1994, Abrams $19.95 (0-8109-3324-1). The history of the creations of the Russian artisan known for the priceless Fabergé eggs, with color photos. (Rev: BL 7/94; SLJ 6/94) [921]

FILIPOVIC, ZLATA

7853 Filipovic, Zlata. *Zlata's Diary* (9–12). 1995, Demco $14.30 (0-606-08416-9). The personal journal of talented 11-year-old Sarajevan girl whose world was shattered by the chaos and terror of war. (Rev: BL 3/1/94; SLJ 7/94; VOYA 8/94) [921]

FRANK, ANNE

7854 Frank, Anne. *The Diary of a Young Girl* (7–12). Trans. by B. M. Mooyaart. Illus. 1967, Doubleday $25.95 (0-385-04019-9). The world-famous diary of the young Jewish girl kept while she was being hidden with her family from the Nazis. (Rev: BL 2/15/88) [921]

7855   Frank, Anne. *The Diary of a Young Girl: The Definitive Edition* (7–12). Trans. by Susan Massotty. 1995, Doubleday $25.00 (0-385-47378-8). This edition contains all of the writings of Anne Frank, including some short passages in the diary that had been formerly suppressed. (Rev: BL 4/15/95) [921]

7856   Frank, Anne. *The Diary of Anne Frank: The Critical Edition* (7–12). Illus. 1989, Doubleday $55.00 (0-385-24023-6). The most complete version of the diary to appear in English plus a history of the volume. (Rev: BL 5/15/89) [921]

7857   Gold, Alison L. *Memories of Anne Frank: Reflections of a Childhood Friend* (4–8). Illus. 1997, Scholastic $16.95 (0-590-90722-0). Anne Frank's story as told through recollections of her best friend in Amsterdam, Hannah Goslar, a survivor of the Holocaust. (Rev: BL 9/1/97; BR 11–12/97; SLJ 11/97) [921]

7858   Lindwer, Willy. *The Last Seven Months of Anne Frank* (8–12). 1992, Doubleday paper $12.95 (0-385-42360-8). Moving testimony from 6 women interned in a concentration camp with Anne Frank tells of the tragic conclusion of the young diarist's life. (Rev: BL 3/15/91) [921]

7859   Muller, Melissa. *Anne Frank: A Biography* (9–12). Trans. by Robert Kimber. 1998, Holt $23.00 (0-8050-5996-2); paper $14.00 (0-8050-5997-0). In this supplement to Anne Frank's diary, the author includes new information about the Frank family, possible betrayers of their hiding place, and their imprisonment in Westerbrok and Auschwitz, as well as insights into the character, personality, and quality of life of Anne's parents, relatives, and friends. (Rev: SLJ 4/99) [921]

7860   Wukovits, John. *Anne Frank* (6–10). (The Importance Of) 1998, Lucent LB $17.96 (1-56006-353-X). This biographical account also supplies good background material on Nazism, the death camps, the writing of the diary, and the controversy surrounding it. (Rev: BL 1/1–15/99; VOYA 8/99) [940.53]

FREEMAN, JOSEPH

7861   Freeman, Joseph. *Job: The Story of a Holocaust Survivor* (9–12). 1995, Paragon House paper $9.95 (1-55778-738-7). A survivor tells what he witnessed in the Polish ghetto and at Auschwitz. (Rev: BL 9/15/95) [921]

GARIBALDI, GIUSEPPI

7862   Viola, Herman J., and Susan P. Viola. *Giuseppi Garibaldi* (6–10). Illus. 1987, Chelsea LB $19.95 (0-87754-526-X). Garibaldi was a hero, patriot, and the man who led the movement to unify his country, Italy. (Rev: BL 11/15/87; SLJ 3/88) [921]

HAMMARSKJOLD, DAG

7863   Sheldon, Richard N. *Dag Hammarskjold* (6–10). Illus. 1987, Chelsea LB $19.95 (0-87754-529-4). The life story of the Swedish man who served as the secretary general of the United Nations for 8 years. (Rev: BL 9/1/87; SLJ 10/87) [921]

HANNIBAL

7864   Green, Robert. *Hannibal* (5–8). (First Books: Ancient Biographies) 1996, Watts LB $22.50 (0-531-20240-2). An engrossing account of the military genius who trekked through the Alps with elephants and threatened to topple the might of the Roman Empire. (Rev: SLJ 2/97) [921]

HENRY VIII, KING OF ENGLAND

7865   Dwyer, Frank. *Henry VIII* (7–12). Illus. 1988, Chelsea LB $19.95 (0-87754-530-8). This is a fact-crammed biography with a great deal of English history given for background. (Rev: BL 1/15/88; SLJ 3/88) [921]

HINDENBURG, PAUL VON

7866   Berman, Russell A. *Paul von Hindenburg* (6–10). Illus. 1987, Chelsea LB $19.95 (0-87754-532-4). The story of the German military and political leader who became famous during World War I. (Rev: BL 8/87; SLJ 11/87) [921]

HITLER, ADOLF

7867   Ayer, Eleanor. *Adolf Hitler* (4–8). (Importance Of) 1996, Lucent LB $17.96 (1-56006-072-7). This study of Hitler's rise includes analyses of the dictator's mental state, leadership qualities, and personality traits. (Rev: BL 3/15/95; SLJ 1/96) [921]

7868   Fuchs, Thomas. *The Hitler Fact Book* (10–12). Illus. 1990, Fountain paper $14.95 (0-9623202-9-3). This book gives all sorts of trivia about the dictator and the high German officials around him. (Rev: BL 3/1/90; SLJ 6/90) [921]

7869   Harris, Nathaniel. *Hitler* (8–12). Illus. 1989, David & Charles $19.95 (0-7134-5961-1). This biography surveys the life and times of Hitler and his impact on history. (Rev: SLJ 12/89) [921]

7870   Heyes, Eileen. *Adolf Hitler* (6–12). 1994, Millbrook LB $23.90 (1-56294-343-X). Analyzes the dictator's life and motivations and examines Hitler's childhood, the Nazi party, and the Holocaust. (Rev: BL 10/15/94; SLJ 11/94; VOYA 5/95) [921]

JAMES I, KING OF ENGLAND

7871 Dwyer, Frank. *James I* (6–10). Illus. 1988, Chelsea LB $19.95 (1-55546-811-X). The story of the first Stuart king of both England and Scotland. (Rev: BL 6/15/88) [921]

JOAN OF ARC

7872 Stanley, Diane. *Joan of Arc* (4–8). Illus. 1998, Morrow LB $15.93 (0-688-14330-X). Using glorious illustrations, this picture book for older readers gives a detailed history of the life and times of Joan of Arc. (Rev: BL 8/98; SLJ 9/98) [921]

JOHN PAUL II, POPE

7873 Sullivan, George. *Pope John Paul II: The People's Pope* (7–9). Illus. 1984, Walker $11.95 (0-8027-6523-8). A very readable biography of this beloved pope and his activities for world peace. [921]

LAFAYETTE, MARQUIS DE

7874 Fritz, Jean. *Why Not, Lafayette?* (5–8). Illus. 1999, Putnam $16.99 (0-399-23411-X). Using plenty of quotes, interesting anecdotes, and sly humor, this is a fine biography of General Lafayette. (Rev: BL 9/15/99) [921]

LENIN, VLADIMIR ILICH

7875 Haney, John. *Vladimir Ilich Lenin* (6–10). Illus. 1988, Chelsea LB $19.95 (0-87754-570-7). A biography of the man who led the Russia Revolution and established the U.S.S.R. (Rev: BL 4/1/88) [921]

7876 Rawcliffe, Michael. *Lenin* (7–10). Illus. 1989, David & Charles $19.95 (0-7134-5611-6). Besides supplying a biography of this Russian leader, this book evaluates Lenin's significance in history. (Rev: SLJ 5/89) [921]

LLOYD GEORGE, DAVID

7877 Shearman, Deidre. *David Lloyd George* (7–12). Illus. 1987, Chelsea LB $19.95 (0-87754-581-2). The biography of the Welsh statesman who was British prime minister during World War I. (Rev: BL 1/15/88) [921]

MARY STUART, QUEEN OF SCOTLAND

7878 Random House, eds. *Mary Stuart's Scotland* (9–12). Illus. 1995, Random $18.99 (0-517-14205-8). An accurate account of this tragic queen's life with beautiful photographs of her homeland, Scotland. (Rev: SLJ 4/88) [921]

7879 Stepanek, Sally. *Mary, Queen of Scots* (6–10). Illus. 1987, Chelsea LB $19.95 (0-87754-540-5).

The tragic story of this ill-fated queen, in prose and many pictures. (Rev: BL 6/1/87; SLJ 12/87) [921]

MUSSOLINI, BENITO

7880 Hartenian, Larry. *Benito Mussolini* (6–10). Illus. 1988, Chelsea LB $19.95 (0-87754-572-3). A fascinating biography of the Italian Fascist leader who brought his country to defeat in World War II. (Rev: BL 6/1/88) [921]

7881 Hoyt, Edwin. *Mussolini's Empire: The Rise and Fall of the Fascist Vision* (9–12). 1994, Wiley $24.95 (0-471-59151-3). Examines the career and personal life of Mussolini and provides psychological insight into the Italian dictator's character. (Rev: BL 2/15/94) [921]

NAPOLEON I, EMPEROR OF THE FRENCH

7882 Carroll, Bob. *Napoleon Bonaparte* (5–8). 1994, Lucent LB $17.96 (1-56006-021-2). A discussion of Napoleon's life, plus background on the French Revolution. (Rev: BL 5/15/94; SLJ 4/94) [921]

PADEREWSKI, IGNACE

7883 Lisandrelli, Elaine S. *Ignacy Jan Paderewski: Polish Pianist and Patriot* (6–9). 1998, Morgan Reynolds LB $18.95 (1-883846-29-3). An engaging biography of the great pianist, world diplomat, and lover of his native land Poland, which he helped regain a world position between the two World Wars. (Rev: BL 1/1–15/99; SLJ 5/99) [921]

PULASKI, CASIMIR

7884 Collins, David R. *Casimir Pulaski: Soldier on Horsback* (4–8). Illus. 1995, Pelican $14.95 (1-56554-082-4). A smoothly written biography of the Polish patriot who, though he could scarcely speak English, became an important figure helping the colonists during the Revolutionary War. (Rev: BL 2/15/96) [921]

ROMANOV, ANASTASIA

7885 Brewster, Hugh. *Anastasia's Album* (5–8). Illus. 1996, Hyperion $17.95 (0-7868-0292-8). The story of the youngest daughter of the last of the Romanov czars and of her family. (Rev: BL 10/1/96*; SLJ 12/96*) [921]

7886 Lovell, James Blair. *Anastasia: The Lost Princess* (9–12). 1991, Regnery Gateway $24.95 (0-89526-536-2). The story of the woman who claims to be the only surviving daughter of the last czar of Russia. (Rev: BL 8/91) [921]

SCHINDLER, OSKAR

7887 Fensch, Thomas, ed. *Oskar Schindler and His List: The Man, the Book, the Film, the Holocaust and Its Survivors* (9–12). 1995, Paul S. Eriksson $24.95 (0-8397-6472-3). Articles, essays, and interviews related to the development of the book and the film *Schindler's List*. (Rev: BL 9/15/95) [921]

7888 Roberts, Jack L. *Oskar Schindler* (4–8). Illus. (The Importance Of) 1996, Lucent LB $16.95 (1-56006-079-4). The inspiring story of one man's fight to save Jews from the Nazi death camps during World War II. (Rev: BL 3/15/96; SLJ 1/96) [921]

TITO, JOSIP BROZ

7889 Schiffman, Ruth. *Josip Broz Tito* (6–10). Illus. 1987, Chelsea LB $19.95 (0-87754-443-3). The story of this unusual Yugoslavian leader and of the unique Communist regime he founded. (Rev: BL 6/15/87; SLJ 8/87) [921]

VAN BEEK, CATO BONTJES

7890 Friedman, Ina R. *Flying Against the Wind: The Story of a Young Woman Who Defied the Nazis* (6–10). 1995, Lodgepole Pr. paper $11.95 (1-886721-00-9). The story of Cato Bontjes van Beek, who grew up in a progressive German household and was executed by the Nazis with her boyfriend for joining an underground movement. (Rev: BL 7/95; VOYA 4/96) [921]

VICTORIA, QUEEN

7891 Chiflet, Jean-Loup, and Alain Beaulet. *Victoria and Her Times* (6–10). Trans. from French by George Wen. (W5) 1996, Holt $19.95 (0-8050-5084-1). This oversized volume contains double-page spreads that describe various aspects of the life and times of Queen Victoria. (Rev: SLJ 3/97) [921]

7892 Erickson, Carolly. *Her Little Majesty: The Life of Queen Victoria* (10–12). 1997, Simon & Schuster $22.50 (0-684-80765-3). This is an entertaining biography of the stubborn, hot-tempered, but romantic queen who gave her name to an age, describing her unhappy childhood and difficult teen years, and her amazing inner resources, which saw her through crisis after crisis during the major changes of the 19th century. (Rev: SLJ 8/97) [921]

WALESA, LECH

7893 Kaye, Tony. *Lech Walesa* (7–10). Illus. 1989, Chelsea LB $19.95 (1-55546-856-X). Numerous illustrations complement this account of the much-admired Polish leader who helped bring his government to its knees. (Rev: BL 10/1/89; BR 11–12/89; SLJ 10/89; VOYA 12/89) [921]

YELTSIN, BORIS

7894 Miller, Calvin C. *Boris Yeltsin: First President of Russia* (6–9). 1994, Morgan Reynolds LB $18.95 (1-883846-08-0). The biography of the controversial Russian leader up to 1993. (Rev: BL 12/1/94; SLJ 4/95; VOYA 2/95) [921]

7895 Otfinoski, Steven. *Boris Yeltsin and the Rebirth of Russia* (7–12). 1995, Millbrook LB $22.40 (1-56294-478-9). Yeltsin's political career and the rise of the Russian Republic. (Rev: BL 4/1/95; SLJ 3/95) [921]

South and Central America and Canada

BOLIVAR, SIMON

7896 Goodnough, David. *Simon Bolivar: South American Liberator* (7–12). (Hispanic Biographies) 1998, Enslow LB $19.95 (0-7660-1044-9). The inspiring story of the young military leader who led the fight to free several South American countries from the oppression of the Spaniards. (Rev: BL 1/1–15/99; VOYA 10/99) [921]

CASTRO, FIDEL

7897 Bentley, Judith. *Fidel Castro of Cuba* (7–12). (In Focus Biographies) 1991, Messner LB $13.98 (0-671-70198-3); paper $7.95 (0-671-70199-1). Relates the Cuban leader's personal story to a detailed history of his country, its problems and achievements, and the changing international scene up to 1991. (Rev: BL 11/1/91) [921]

DUVALIER, FRANÇOIS AND JEAN-CLAUDE

7898 Condit, Erin. *The Duvaliers* (6–9). Illus. 1989, Chelsea LB $16.95 (1-55546-832-2). A history of modern Haiti is given as well as the life stories of these 2 dictators. (Rev: BL 8/89; VOYA 12/89) [921]

GUEVARA, CHE

7899 Neimark, Anne E. *Che! Latin America's Legendary Guerrilla Leader* (7–10). Illus. 1989, HarperCollins LB $13.00 (0-397-32309-3). A portrait of the Latin American revolutionary who tried to help the oppressed and poor of the nations in Spanish America. (Rev: BL 5/15/89; SLJ 5/89) [921]

L'OUVERTURE, TOUSSAINT

7900 Myers, Walter Dean. *Toussaint L'Ouverture: The Fight for Haiti's Freedom* (4–8). 1996, Simon & Schuster paper $16.00 (0-689-80126-2). Powerful paintings by Jacob Lawrence highlight this story of the black leader who fought to free Haiti. (Rev: BL 9/1/96; SLJ 11/96) [921]

MALINCHE (AZTEC)

7901 Duran, Gloria. *Malinche: Slave Princess of Cortez* (8–10). 1993, Linnet LB $19.50 (0-208-02343-7). The story of Cortes's Aztec mistress and interpreter, whom Cortes declared the greatest help, after God, in his conquest. (Rev: BL 6/1–15/93; SLJ 7/93) [921]

MARTI, JOSE

7902 Goodnough, David. *Jose Marti: Cuban Patriot and Poet* (6–10). Illus. (Hispanic Biographies) 1996, Enslow LB $19.95 (0-89490-761-1). This biography of the Cuban revolutionary who fought against Spanish rule also contains samples of his poetry in both Spanish and English. (Rev: BL 9/1/96; BR 9–10/96; SLJ 6/96) [921]

MUÑOZ MARÍN, LUIS

7903 Bernier-Grand, Carmen T. *Poet and Politician of Puerto Rico: Don Luis Muñoz Marín* (5–8). 1995, Orchard LB $16.99 (0-531-08737-9). A biography of

Munoz Marín and a history of the island. (Rev: BL 5/15/95; SLJ 4/95) [921]

TUM, RIGOBERTA MENCHU

7904 Schulze, Julie. *Rigoberta Menchú Túm: Champion of Human Rights* (8–12). Illus. (Contemporary Profile and Policy) 1998, John Gordon Burke $20.00 (0-934272-42-5); paper $12.95 (0-934272-43-3). This biography combines the life story of Nobel Peace Prize-winner Rigoberta Menchu Tum with the story of the struggle of the Mayan people for equality in Guatemala and throughout Central America. (Rev: BL 4/1/98) [921]

VILLA, PANCHO

7905 Carroll, Bob. *Pancho Villa* (4–8). Illus. (The Importance Of) 1996, Lucent LB $16.95 (1-56006-069-7). The story of this colorful fighter against tyranny and his importance in Mexican history. (Rev: BL 3/15/96; SLJ 2/96) [921]

7906 O'Brien, Steven. *Pancho Villa* (5–9). (Hispanics of Achievement) 1994, Chelsea LB $19.95 (0-7910-1257-3). The life and accomplishments of this Mexican freedom fighter. (Rev: BL 9/15/94; VOYA 8/94) [921]

Miscellaneous Interesting Lives

Collective

7907 Gonzales, Doreen. *AIDS: Ten Stories of Courage* (6–10). Illus. (Collective Biographies) 1996, Enslow LB $19.95 (0-89490-766-2). This is a collection of 10 biographies of people like Ryan White and Magic Johnson who have helped people understand AIDS and its effects. (Rev: BL 4/15/96; SLJ 5/96; VOYA 6/96) [920]

7908 Hazell, Rebecca. *Heroes: Great Men Through the Ages* (5–8). Illus. 1997, Abbeville $19.95 (0-7892-0289-1). A collection of 12 biographies, from Socrates to Martin Luther King, Jr., and including Shakespeare, Mohandas Gandhi, Leonardo da Vinci, and Jorge Louis Borges. (Rev: SLJ 6/97) [920]

7909 Rose, Phyllis, ed. *The Norton Book of Women's Lives* (9–12). 1993, Norton $30.00 (0-393-03532-8). This culturally and socially diverse anthology presents biographies of 61 20th-century women, among them Virginia Woolf, Anais Nin, and Kate Simon. (Rev: BL 9/15/93) [920.72]

Individual

ALICEA, GIL C.

7910 Alicea, Gil C., and Carmine De Sena. *The Air Down Here: True Tales from a South Bronx Boyhood* (7–12). 1995, Chronicle $14.95 (0-8118-1048-8). An autobiographical account, in 115 short essays, of Puerto Rican Gil Alicea's experiences growing up in the Bronx. (Rev: BL 10/15/95; SLJ 3/96) [921]

BITTON-JACKSON, LIVIA

7911 Bitton-Jackson, Livia. *My Bridges of Hope: Searching for Life and Love after Auschwitz* (8–12).

1999, Simon & Schuster paper $17.00 (0-689-82026-7). The true story of the author's life after her Holocaust experiences until she and her mother are able to emigrate illegally to the U. S. in 1951. (Rev: BL 5/1/99; SLJ 5/99; VOYA 6/99) [921]

BOYLE, FATHER GREG

7912 Fremon, Celeste. *Father Greg and the Home-boys: The Extraordinary Journey of Father Greg Boyle and His Work with the Latino Gangs of East L.A.* (9–12). 1995, Hyperion $24.95 (0-7868-6089-8). This look at the intervention work of Father Greg Boyle with inner-city gangbangers features 10 of their autobiographies. (Rev: BL 6/1–15/95) [921]

BRAITHWAITE, E. R.

7913 Braithwaite, E. R. *To Sir, with Love* (9–12). 1990, Jove paper $4.99 (0-515-10519-8). The inspiring story of a young black teacher from British Guiana and his class in a school in London's slums. [921]

BROOKS, GERALDINE

7914 Brooks, Geraldine. *Foreign Correspondence: A Pen Pal's Journey from Down Under to All Over* (10–12). Illus. 1997, Doubleday $22.95 (0-385-48269-8). As a youngster growing up in Australia, Geraldine Brooks had many pen pals from around the world; as an adult, she rediscovered their letters and set out to find out what happened to them. (Rev: BL 11/1/97; SLJ 6/98) [921]

BURCH, JENNINGS MICHAEL

7915 Burch, Jennings Michael. *They Cage the Animals at Night* (9–12). 1984, NAL paper $5.99 (0-451-15941-1). The story of a youth from a broken home and of the many shelters and foster homes where he spent his childhood while his mother tried to cope with her mounting responsibilities. [921]

CARY, LORENE

7916 Cary, Lorene. *Black Ice* (9–12). 1991, Knopf $25.00 (0-394-57465-6). Cary was a 15-year-old black student from Philadelphia who won a scholarship to an elite prep school in New England. She describes her transition to an unfamiliar life and the racism over which she triumphed. (Rev: BL 2/15/91*; SLJ 8/91) [921]

DEFERRARI, GABRIELLA

7917 De Ferrari, Gabriella. *Gringa Latina: A Woman of Two Worlds* (10–12). 1995, Houghton $19.95 (0-395-70934-2). An autobiographical account told in short vignettes of the American art curator's youth in a village in Peru, where her father was a successful businessman. (Rev: SLJ 1/96) [921]

DE LA RENTA, OSCAR

7918 Carrillo, Louis. *Oscar de la Renta* (4–8). Illus. (Contemporary Hispanic Americans) 1995, Raintree Steck-Vaughn LB $24.26 (0-8172-3980-4). This account focuses on the professional life of the renowned Hispanic American fashion designer who was born in the Dominican Republic. (Rev: BL 3/15/96; SLJ 1/96) [921]

DRUCKER, OLGA LEVY

7919 Drucker, Olga Levy. *Kindertransport* (6–12). 1992, Holt $14.95 (0-8050-1711-9). The author's 6 years in England as an evacuee from Nazi Germany and her eventual reunion with her parents in the United States after the war. (Rev: BL 11/1/92; SLJ 11/92) [921]

EQUIANO, OLAUDAH

7920 Cameron, Ann. *The Kidnapped Prince: The Life of Olaudah Equiano* (5–8). 1995, Knopf $16.00 (0-679-85619-6). This gripping story of an 11-year-old boy who spent 11 years as a slave in England was a best-seller when it was first published in 1789. (Rev: BL 1/1/95; SLJ 2/95) [921]

FORBES, SARAH BONETTA

7921 Myers, Walter Dean. *African Princess: The Life of Sarah Bonetta Forbes* (5–8). Illus. 1999, Scholastic $15.95 (0-590-48669-1). The intriguing biography of the African princess who, at age 7, was brought to England in 1850 and became the ward of Queen Victoria. (Rev: BL 4/1/99; SLJ 1/99) [921]

GLASBERG, RUTH

7922 Gold, Ruth G. *Ruth's Journey: A Survivor's Memoir* (10–12). 1996, Univ. of Florida Pr. $34.95 (0-8130-1400-X). When World War II came to Europe, Ruth Glasberg was 11 years old. This is the story of how she survived the concentration camp of Transnistria and finally found freedom in Palestine as the sole survivor of her family. (Rev: SLJ 8/96) [921]

HAIZLIP, SHIRLEY TAYLOR

7923 Haizlip, Shirley Taylor. *The Sweeter the Juice: A Family Memoir in Black and White* (9–12). 1994, Simon & Schuster $21.50 (0-671-79235-0). The author, a woman of African American, white, and Native American heritage, tells how race shattered the lives of her relatives and how she's tried to pick up the pieces. (Rev: BL 12/1/93*) [929.2]

HANNAM, CHARLES

7924 Hannam, Charles. *A Boy in That Situation: An Autobiography* (9–12). 1978, HarperCollins $12.95 (0-06-022218-2). The story of an unattractive Jewish boy growing up as the Nazis come to power. [921]

HAUTZIG, ESTHER

7925 Hautzig, Esther. *The Endless Steppe: Growing Up in Siberia* (7–12). 1968, HarperCollins paper $4.95 (0-06-447027-X). The autobiography of the Polish girl who with her family was exiled to Siberia during World War II. [921]

HOBBES, ANNE

7926 Hobbes, Anne, and Robert Specht. *Tisha: The Story of a Young Teacher in the Alaska Wilderness* (9–12). 1984, Bantam paper $5.99 (0-553-26596-2). This is the heartwarming biography of a young schoolteacher who at age 19 began working in the tiny Alaska town of Chicken. [921]

JOHNSON, ISAAC

7927 Marston, Hope I. *Isaac Johnson: From Slave to Stonecutter* (5–8). 1995, Dutton paper $14.99 (0-525-65165-9). Based on Johnson's 1901 autobiography, *Slavery Days in Old Kentucky,* Marston brings the story of Isaac Johnson to life. (Rev: BL 9/15/95; SLJ 9/95) [921]

KHERDIAN, VERON

7928 Kherdian, David. *The Road from Home: The Story of an Armenian Girl* (7–10). 1979, Greenwillow LB $15.93 (0-688-84205-4). A portrait of the youth of the author's mother, an Armenian girl who

503

suffered many hardships and finally arrived in America as a mail-order bride. [921]

KLECKLEY, ELIZABETH

7929   Rutberg, Becky. *Mary Lincoln's Dressmaker: Elizabeth Kleckley's Remarkable Rise from Slave to White House Confidante* (6–10). 1995, Walker $23.95 (0-8027-8224-8). The story of a slave, a fine seamstress, who was freed and became Mary Todd Lincoln's dressmaker. (Rev: BL 10/15/95; SLJ 12/95; VOYA 12/95) [921]

LEONOWENS, ANNA

7930   Landon, Margaret. *Anna and the King of Siam* (7–12). Illus. 1944, HarperCollins $16.95 (0-381-98136-3). The career of the indomitable schoolteacher whose life became the basis of a play, a musical, and 2 movies. [921]

LUND, ERIC

7931   Lund, Doris. *Eric* (9–12). 1974, HarperCollins $16.95 (0-397-01046-X). The tragic story of a gifted young man and his fatal bout with leukemia, as told by his mother. [921]

MOODY, ANNE

7932   Moody, Anne. *Coming of Age in Mississippi* (10–12). 1970, Dell paper $6.99 (0-440-31488-7). The story of a black girl growing up in the desperate poverty of rural Mississippi. [921]

NORLING, DONNA SCOTT

7933   Norling, Donna Scott. *Patty's Journey* (10–12). 1996, Univ. of Minnesota Pr. $17.95 (0-8166-2866-1). A thought-provoking true story of a girl growing up during the Depression who at the age of 4 was taken from her family by the state after her father was imprisoned for robbing a store, of her unhappy experiences in foster homes, eventual adoption, marriage, and search for her lost sister and brother. (Rev: SLJ 3/97) [921]

NYE, NAOMI SHIHAB

7934   Nye, Naomi S. *Never in a Hurry: Essays on People and Places* (10–12). 1996, Univ. of South Carolina Pr. paper $16.95 (1-57003-082-0). This collection of autobiographical essays on a variety of subjects reflects the people and places encountered by the author, a Palestinian American married to a Swedish American who has lived most of her life in San Antonio, Texas. (Rev: BL 8/96; SLJ 11/96) [921]

OATMAN, OLIVE

7935   Rau, Margaret. *The Ordeal of Olive Oatman: A True Story of the American West* (6–8). Illus. 1997, Morgan Reynolds LB $18.95 (1-883846-21-8). The biography of Olive Oatman, who was captured by Apaches while her family was crossing the Arizona desert and lived with them for 6 years. (Rev: BL 9/1/97; BR 11–12/98; SLJ 2/98; VOYA 12/97) [921]

PATTON, LARRY

7936   Kastner, Janet. *More Than an Average Guy* (9–12). Illus. 1989, Life Enrichment Pubs. paper $8.95 (0-938736-25-6). An inspiring story of a boy who was born with cerebral palsy and of the family that loved him. (Rev: BL 5/15/89) [921]

PRICE, MICHELLE

7937   Phillips, Carolyn E. *Michelle* (9–12). Illus. 1989, NAL paper $2.50 (0-451-14929-7). This is the inspiring story of a young girl's fight against bone cancer and how she never gave up, even after her leg was amputated. [921]

QUINTANILLA, GUADALUPE

7938   Wade, Mary D. *Guadalupe Quintanilla: Leader of the Hispanic Community* (4–8). Illus. (Multicultural Junior Biographies) 1995, Enslow LB $19.95 (0-89490-637-2). The story of the woman, once considered mentally retarded, who now teaches Spanish to non-Spanish-speaking police officers and others in the community to help them communicate with Hispanics. (Rev: BL 3/1/96; SLJ 2/96) [921]

REICHL, RUTH

7939   Reichl, Ruth. *Tender at the Bone: Growing up at the Table* (10–12). 1997, Random $23.00 (0-679-44987-6); Broadway Books paper $13.00 (0-7679-0338-2). This entertaining autobiography by the woman who reviewed restaurants for *The New York Times* for many years tells how she became interested in food, describes some of her kitchen disasters, and gives a few mouth-watering recipes. (Rev: BL 2/15/98; SLJ 6/98) [921]

REISS, JOHANNA

7940   Reiss, Johanna. *The Upstairs Room* (7–10). 1972, HarperCollins $15.95 (0-690-85127-8); paper $4.95 (0-06-447043-1). The author's story of the years spent hiding from the Nazis in occupied Holland. Followed by: *The Journey Back* (1976). (Rev: BL 3/1/88) [921]

RICHTER, HANS PETER

7941 Richter, Hans Peter. *I Was There* (7–9). Trans. by Edite Kroll. 1987, Penguin paper $4.99 (0-14-032206-X). The author tells of his youth in Nazi Germany as a member of Hitler Youth and later in the army. [921]

SHERBURNE, ANDREW

7942 Sherburne, Andrew. *The Memoirs of Andrew Sherburne: Patriot and Privateer of the American Revolution* (5–8). Ed. by Karen Zeinert. Illus. 1993, Linnet LB $17.50 (0-208-02354-2). This excerpt from Sherburne's autobiography of the war years tells of his early life at sea and his capture and imprisonment by the British. (Rev: BL 5/15/93; SLJ 7/93) [921]

SIEGAL, ARANKA

7943 Siegal, Aranka. *Upon the Head of the Goat: A Childhood in Hungary* (7–10). 1981, Farrar $16.00 (0-374-38059-7). A childhood in Hungary during Hitler's rise to power. (Rev: BL 12/15/89) [921]

SONE, MONICA

7944 Sone, Monica. *Nisei Daughter* (9–12). 1987, Univ. of Washington Pr. paper $14.95 (0-295-95688-7). From a happy childhood in Seattle to a World War II relocation center as seen through the eyes of a Japanese American girl. [921]

TOLL, NELLY S.

7945 Toll, Nelly S. *Behind the Secret Window: A Memoir of a Hidden Childhood* (6–9). 1993, Dial paper $17.99 (0-8037-1362-2). The harrowing account of the experiences of a Jewish family during World War II, based on a diary the author began at age 8. (Rev: BL 3/15/93) [921]

UCHIDA, YOSHIKO

7946 Uchida, Yoshiko. *Desert Exile: The Uprooting of a Japanese American Family* (10–12). 1982, Univ. of Washington Pr. paper $14.95 (0-295-96190-2). The story of a Japanese American family from California and their internment during World War II. [921]

WHITESTONE, HEATHER

7947 Whitestone, Heather, and Angela E. Hunt. *Listening with My Heart* (10–12). 1997, Doubleday $19.95 (0-385-48675-8). The life story of the first Miss America with a disability (she has been deaf since the age of 18 months), with details on her year as the reigning Miss America. (Rev: BL 6/1–15/97; SLJ 11/97) [921]

WOLLSTONECRAFT, MARY

7948 Miller, Calvin C. *Mary Wollstonecraft and the Rights of Women* (7–12). Illus. 1999, Morgan Reynolds LB $18.95 (1-883846-41-2). This is a biography of the passionate English fighter for women's rights who was motivated by the grinding poverty, discrimination, and lack of opportunity suffered by women in the late 18th and early 19th centuries. (Rev: BL 5/1/99; BR 9–10/99; SLJ 5/99; VOYA 12/99) [921]

History and Geography

General History and Geography

Miscellaneous Works

7949 Burger, Leslie, and Debra L. Rahm. *Sister Cities in a World of Difference* (4–8). Illus. 1996, Lerner LB $22.60 (0-8225-2697-2). The pairing of cities internationally is covered with material on the results, mostly positive. (Rev: BL 9/1/96; SLJ 9/96; VOYA 4/97) [303.48]

7950 *The Dorling Kindersley Visual Encyclopedia* (7–12). Illus. 1995, DK Publg. $44.95 (1-56458-985-4). Divided into 11 major subject areas including universe and space, Earth, living world, arts and media, sports, and science and technology, this general encyclopedia with over 50,000 facts and illustrated with over 15,000 photos and artwork, is fun to browse through. (Rev: VOYA 4/96) [030]

7951 Masters, Anthony. *Survival* (7–10). Illus. 1997, Sterling paper $8.95 (0-8069-9657-9). An entertaining collection of true stories about survival, such as the Baileys' 117-day ordeal adrift in the Pacific and Terry Waite's 1,763 days in solitary confinement in Beirut. (Rev: SLJ 12/97) [904]

7952 Matthews, Rupert. *Explorer* (5–9). (Eyewitness Books) 1991, Knopf LB $20.99 (0-679-91460-9). The world of exploration is introduced with highlights from the careers of the most famous. (Rev: BL 12/1/91) [910]

Atlases, Maps, and Mapmaking

7953 Bramwell, Martyn. *How Maps Are Made* (5–8). (Maps and Mapmakers) 1998, Lerner LB $22.60 (0-8225-2920-3). The difficulties in representing the globe on a flat surface are explored, with details on how maps are made both by hand and by computers and on the use of aerial photography in map making. Also use *Mapping Our World* (1998). (Rev: BL 3/15/99; SLJ 2/99) [526]

7954 Bramwell, Martyn. *Mapping Our World* (4–8). Illus. (Maps and Mapmakers) 1998, Lerner $23.54 (0-8225-2924-6). This work shows how different kinds of maps can be used to illustrate topography, geology, climate, vegetation, population, geography, minerals, trade, pollution, and habitat—the "physical world," the "human world," and the world's resources and the environment. (Rev: SLJ 2/99) [912]

7955 Bramwell, Martyn. *Maps in Everyday Life* (5–8). 1998, Lerner LB $22.60 (0-8225-2923-8). This book explains how different maps are used for different purposes, e.g., tourist maps and climate maps. Also use *Mapping the Seas and Airways* (1998). (Rev: BL 3/15/99) [912]

7956 Jouris, David. *All over the Map: An Extraordinary Atlas of the United States* (8–10). 1994, Ten Speed Pr. paper $11.95 (0-89815-649-1). A U.S. atlas that explores the history of the names of towns and cities, including such places as Peculiar, Ding Dong, Vendor, and Joy. (Rev: BL 7/94) [910]

7957 Pratt, Paula B. *Maps: Plotting Places on the Globe* (6–10). (Encyclopedia of Discovery and Invention) 1995, Lucent LB $23.70 (1-56006-255-X). Traces the evolution of mapmaking/cartography from ancient times to the present. (Rev: BL 4/15/95; SLJ 3/95) [912]

7958 Smith, A. G. *Where Am I? The Story of Maps and Navigation* (4–8). Illus. 1997, Stoddart paper $13.95 (0-7737-5836-4). Important discoveries and innovations in the history of map making are explained. (Rev: BL 9/1/97) [910]

7959 Whitfield, Peter. *The Image of the World: 20 Centuries of World Maps* (9–12). 1994, Pomegranate $35.00 (0-87654-080-9). Covers the important names in the history of world cartography. Includes 70 maps from the Middle Ages, the age of discovery, and modern times. (Rev: BL 11/15/94*) [912]

Paleontology

7960 Aaseng, Nathan. *American Dinosaur Hunters* (6–9). Illus. 1996, Enslow LB $19.95 (0-89490-710-7). A history of paleontology, the story of major discoveries, and brief biographies of such scientists as Edward Hitchcock and Roy Chapman Andrews. (Rev: BL 11/15/96; BR 1–2/97; SLJ 12/96) [560]

7961 Arduini, Paolo, and Giorgio Teruzzi. *Simon & Schuster's Guide to Fossils* (9–12). Illus. 1987, Simon & Schuster paper $14.00 (0-671-63132-2). In addition to a detailed description of the science of paleontology, this account, through photos and text, identifies particular fossils and gives hints on how to collect them. (Rev: BL 5/1/87) [560.9]

7962 Benton, Mike. *How Do We Know Dinosaurs Existed?* (5–8). (How Do We Know) 1995, Raintree Steck-Vaughn LB $24.26 (0-8114-3878-3). Dinosaurs' diets, movement, color, thinking abilities, and breeding are introduced in double-page chapters. (Rev: SLJ 1/96) [567.99]

7963 Brett-Surman, Michael, and Thomas Holtz. *The World of Dinosaurs: A North American Selection* (7–12). Illus. 1998, Greenwich Workshop $29.95 (0-86713-046-6). Using the 15 dinosaur stamps that he designed for the U. S. Postal Service, the author introduces the world of the dinosaur and provides background material for each of the stamps. (Rev: BL 6/1–15/98; SLJ 9/98) [567.9]

7964 Christian, Spencer, and Antonia Felix. *Is There a Dinosaur in Your Backyard? The World's Most Fascinating Fossils, Rocks, & Minerals* (5–8). (Spencer Christian's World of Wonders) 1998, Wiley paper $12.95 (0-471-19616-9). In addition to discussing dinosaurs, this fascinating book introduces earth science, with interesting details about rocks, minerals, and fossils. (Rev: BL 9/1/98; SLJ 10/98) [552]

7965 Clinton, Susan. *Reading Between the Bones: The Pioneers of Dinosaur Paleontology* (6–10). (Lives in Science) 1997, Watts LB $25.00 (0-531-11324-8). The lives and work of 8 major scientists involved in dinosaur paleontology are profiled in this

carefully documented book. (Rev: BL 5/1/97; SLJ 6/97; VOYA 12/97) [560]

7966 Crump, Donald J., ed. *Giants from the Past: The Age of Mammals* (7–10). Illus. 1983, National Geographic LB $12.50 (0-87044-429-8). A description of the first animals, like the mastodon, and how they evolved during the Ice Age. [569]

7967 Currie, Philip, and Kevin Padian, eds. *Encyclopedia of Dinosaurs* (8–12). Illus. 1997, Academic Pr. $99.95 (0-12-226810-5). An adult reference book, written by scientists, with interesting, alphabetically arranged articles on dinosaurs, digs, and sites. (Rev: BL 11/1/97; SLJ 5/98) [567.9]

7968 Currie, Philip J., and Colleayn O. Mastin. *The Newest and Coolest Dinosaurs* (4–8). Illus. 1998, Grasshopper $18.95 (1-895910-41-2). Using double-page spreads, this useful volume introduces 15 of the most recent finds in the world of dinosaurs. (Rev: SLJ 1/99) [560]

7969 Dingus, Lowell, and Luis Chiappe. *The Tiniest Giants: Discovering Dinosaur Eggs* (5–8). Illus. 1999, Doubleday $17.95 (0-385-32642-4). This is an account of the discovery of a huge dinosaur nest area in Patagonia and the eggs that contained fossilized remains of sauropod embryos. (Rev: BL 6/1–15/99; SLJ 6/99) [567.9]

7970 Dixon, Dougal. *Dougal Dixon's Dinosaurs* (4–8). Illus. 1998, Boyds Mills $19.95 (1-56397-722-2). This updated revision of the 1993 volume remains a good basic resource on dinosaurs. (Rev: SLJ 6/98) [567.9]

7971 Facklam, Margery. *Tracking Dinosaurs in the Gobi* (5–8). Illus. 1997, Twenty-First Century $21.40 (0-8050-5165-1). The story of the paleontologist Roy Chapman Andrews and his amazing dinosaur finds in the Gobi Desert beginning in the 1920s. (Rev: BL 2/1/98; SLJ 2/98*) [567.9]

7972 Farlow, James O. *On the Tracks of Dinosaurs* (5–8). Illus. 1991, Watts LB $24.00 (0-531-10991-7). Explains how fossil tracks are formed, how scientists study and name them, and what they reveal about dinosaur behavior. (Rev: BL 5/1/91; SLJ 7/91) [567.9]

7973 Halls, Kelly M. *Dino-Trekking: The Ultimate Dinosaur Lover's Travel Guide* (4–8). Illus. 1996, Wiley paper $14.95 (0-471-11498-7). This dinosaur directory describes sites, museums, and theme parks in the United States and Canada that focus on dinosaurs. (Rev: SLJ 3/96) [567.9]

7974 Krueger, Richard. *The Dinosaurs* (5–8). Illus. (Prehistoric North America) 1996, Millbrook LB $21.90 (1-56294-548-3). With plenty of color illustrations, this chatty overview tells about North American dinosaurs. (Rev: BL 5/15/96; SLJ 4/96) [567.9]

7975 Lambert, David. *A Field Guide to Dinosaurs* (7–12). Illus. 1983, Avon paper $9.95 (0-380-83519-3). A well-illustrated guide to over 340 different dinosaurs arranged by family groups. [567.9]

7976 Lambert, David. *The Ultimate Dinosaur Book* (9–12). 1993, DK Publg. $29.95 (1-56458-304-X). A handsomely illustrated survey of dinosaur anatomy and behavior, excavation and museum restoration techniques, and 55 types of dinosaur. (Rev: BL 10/15/93; SLJ 3/94) [567.9]

7977 Lessem, Don. *Dinosaur Worlds: New Dinosaurs, New Discoveries* (5–8). Illus. 1996, Boyds Mills $19.95 (1-56397-597-1). Dinosaur digs worldwide are visited in this review of what we know about these amazing creatures. (Rev: BL 11/15/96; BR 5–6/97; SLJ 12/96*) [567.9]

7978 Llamas, Andreu. *The Era of the Dinosaurs* (4–8). Illus. (Development of the Earth) 1996, Chelsea LB $15.95 (0-7910-3452-6). Various kinds of dinosaurs are introduced, with an emphasis on their evolution and on how geology and climate affected to their development. (Rev: SLJ 7/96) [567.9]

7979 Llamas, Andreu. *The First Amphibians* (4–8). Illus. (Development of the Earth) 1996, Chelsea LB $15.95 (0-7910-3453-4). Using many color illustrations, this book begins with the earliest land vertebrates and gives clear explanations of their adaptations over time. (Rev: SLJ 7/96) [567.9]

7980 McGowan, Christopher. *T-Rex to Go* (7–12). Illus. 1999, HarperPerennial paper $14.00 (0-06-095281-4). Along with a great deal of information about dinosaurs, particularly Tyrannosaurus Rex, this fascinating book explains in great detail how to make a model of the dinosaur using chicken bones and simple tools. (Rev: VOYA 10/99) [567.9]

7981 Mannetti, William. *Dinosaurs in Your Backyard* (7–9). Illus. 1982, Macmillan $15.00 (0-689-30906-6). A description of the characteristics of dinosaur behavior and why they died out. [567.9]

7982 Massare, Judy A. *Prehistoric Marine Reptiles* (5–8). 1991, Watts LB $24.00 (0-531-11022-2). A survey of sea life during the Mesozoic era, supplemented by many photos, drawings, and maps. (Rev: BL 2/15/92; SLJ 2/92) [567.9]

7983 Nardo, Don. *Dinosaurs: Unearthing the Secrets of Ancient Beasts* (6–10). (Encyclopedia of Discovery and Invention) 1995, Lucent LB $23.70 (1-56006-253-3). Describes dinosaurs and their habitats and highlights the dedicated men and women who have made significant discoveries about them. (Rev: BL 4/15/95) [567.9]

7984 Norman, David, and Angela Milner. *Dinosaur* (5–9). Illus. 1989, Knopf LB $20.99 (0-394-92253-0). Superb illustrations highlight this introduction to prehistoric life. (Rev: BL 10/15/89) [567.9]

7985 Parker, Steve. *The Practical Paleontologist* (9–12). 1991, Simon & Schuster paper $15.00 (0-671-69307-7). An overview of paleontology and how these specialists do their jobs. (Rev: BL 6/15/91) [560]

7986 Psihoyos, Louie, and John Knoebber. *Hunting Dinosaurs* (10–12). 1995, Random paper $23.00 (0-679-76420-8). Important figures in modern paleontology and their findings are introduced, featuring spectacular color photography. (Rev: SLJ 4/96; VOYA 4/96) [567.9]

7987 Stein, Wendy. *Dinosaurs* (6–10). (Great Mysteries) 1994, Greenhaven $18.96 (1-56510-096-4). An introduction to dinosaurs and an examination of the various theories about their extinction. (Rev: BL 4/15/94) [567.9]

7988 Thompson, Ida. *The Audubon Society Field Guide to North American Fossils* (7–12). Illus. 1982, Knopf $18.50 (0-394-52412-8). An illustrated guide to the identification of North American fossils plus some background information on their formation. [560]

7989 Thompson, Sharon E. *Death Trap: The Story of the La Brea Tar Pits* (5–8). 1995, Lerner LB $23.95 (0-8225-2851-7). The author describes the 40,000-year making of the La Brea Tar Pits in downtown Los Angeles, with color photos. (Rev: BL 6/1–15/95; SLJ 5/95) [560]

7990 Wilford, John Noble. *The Riddle of the Dinosaur* (10–12). 1986, Random paper $13.00 (0-394-74392-X). This fascinating account traces a history of paleontology in relation to dinosaurs and discusses current theories concerning their extinction. (Rev: BL 1/15/86; BR 9–10/86; SLJ 8/86; VOYA 6/86) [567.9]

7991 Zallinger, Peter. *Dinosaurs and Other Archosaurs* (6–10). Illus. 1986, Random paper $12.99 (0-394-84421-1). A colorful, chatty introduction to the world of the dinosaur. (Rev: VOYA 12/86) [565.9]

Anthropology and Evolution

7992 Angela, Alberto, and Piero Angela. *The Extraordinary Story of Human Origins* (9–12). Trans. by Gabriele Tonne. 1993, Prometheus $29.95 (0-87975-803-1). A comprehensive presentation of the still-growing body of knowledge of human evolution, including interesting speculations and conflicting claims. (Rev: BL 6/1–15/93) [573.2]

7993 Arnold, Caroline. *Stone Age Farmers Beside the Sea: Scotland's Prehistoric Village of Skara Brae* (5–8). 1997, Clarion $15.95 (0-395-77601-5). Using straightforward text and many photos, this book tells the story of the Stone Age village of Skara Brae, dating to about 3000 B.C., that was unearthed in the Orkney Islands in 1850. (Rev: BL 4/15/97; SLJ 7/97) [930]

7994 Buell, Janet. *Bog Bodies* (5–8). Illus. (Time Travelers) 1997, Twenty-First Century $20.40 (0-8050-5164-3). An account of the discovery of Lindow Man, a Celtic man preserved by an English bog, with details on his life and on how scientists use carbon dating, X-rays, and other forensic techniques. (Rev: BL 2/1/98; SLJ 3/98) [599.9]

7995 Buell, Janet. *Ice Maiden of the Andes* (5–8). Illus. (Time Travelers) 1997, Twenty-First Century $20.40 (0-8050-5185-6). The story of the discovery of the frozen body of a young Inca girl who died 500 years ago and of how forensic methods like DNA testing have revealed insights into Inca society, its religion, and gender roles. (Rev: BL 2/1/98; SLJ 3/98) [985]

7996 Facchini, Fiorenzo. *Humans: Origins and Evolution* (4–8). Illus. (Beginnings) 1995, Raintree Steck-Vaughn LB $24.26 (0-8114-3336-6). Theories and facts explaining human evolution are presented in a straightforward way, with extensive artwork and diagrams. (Rev: BL 4/15/95; SLJ 6/95) [573.2]

7997 Garassino, Alessandro. *Life, Origins and Evolution* (5–8). (Beginnings: Origins and Evolution) 1995, Raintree Steck-Vaughn LB $24.26 (0-8114-3335-8). Using informative visuals, the author presents theories concerning the beginnings of life in the world. (Rev: BL 5/1/95) [575]

7998 Lewin, Roger. *Thread of Life: The Smithsonian Looks at Evolution* (9–12). Illus. 1982, Smithsonian $35.00 (0-89599-010-5). A panoramic look at evolution with more than 300 color plates on animals, plants, and fossils. [575]

7999 Lindsay, William. *Prehistoric Life* (5–9). (Eyewitness Books) 1994, Knopf LB $20.99 (0-679-96001-5). Prolific and colorful photos and illustrations of fossils, prehistoric plants, animals, and dinosaurs. (Rev: BL 10/15/94) [560]

8000 MacDonald, Fiona, and Alison Roberts. *The Stone Age News* (5–8). 1998, Candlewick $16.99 (0-7636-0451-8). Using a newspaper format, this clever title introduces life during the Stone Age through society pages, religious news, real estate ads, and humor columns, such as "A Cave of One's Own," which suggests ways to make a cave a comfortable living space. (Rev: BL 5/15/98; SLJ 6/98) [560]

8001 Merriman, Nick. *Early Humans* (5–9). Illus. 1989, Knopf LB $20.99 (0-394-92257-3). An account of prehistoric life in text and lavish pictures. (Rev: BL 7/89; BR 11–12/89) [930.1]

8002 National Geographic Society, eds. *Primitive Worlds: People Lost in Time* (9–12). Illus. 1973, National Geographic $8.95 (0-87044-127-2). The societies of several primitive peoples in Africa, New Guinea, and Central America are described. [306]

8003 Netzley, Patricia. *The Stone Age* (6–10). Illus. 1997, Lucent LB $17.96 (1-56006-316-5). This book describes the major epochs in the evolution of humans and the development of stone-tool technology. (Rev: BL 5/15/98; SLJ 6/98) [930.12]

8004 Pickering, Robert. *The People* (5–8). Illus. (Prehistoric North America) 1996, Millbrook LB $21.90 (1-56294-550-5). An account of the development of the prehistoric North American tribes that may have crossed the land bridge from Asia to the Americas. (Rev: SLJ 4/96) [973.01]

8005 Silverstein, Alvin, and Virginia Silverstein. *Evolution* (6–9). (Science Concepts) 1998, Twenty-First Century LB $23.40 (0-7613-3003-8). This work explains the concept of evolution, provides background information on the development of this theory, and explains current thinking and applications. (Rev: SLJ 1/99) [575]

8006 Stefoff, Rebecca. *Charles Darwin and the Evolution Revolution* (9–12). Illus. 1996, Oxford $33.95 (0-19-508996-0). A well-illustrated account that describes Darwin's theories and their scientific, social, and political effects, with sidebars that give related information. (Rev: BL 7/96; SLJ 9/96) [575]

8007 Stein, Sara Bonnett. *The Evolution Book* (6–8). Illus. 1986, Workman paper $12.95 (0-89480-927-X). A history of evolution that covers time from 4,000 million years ago to the present. (Rev: BL 2/15/87; BR 5–6/87; SLJ 3/87; VOYA 4/87) [508]

8008 Thorndike, Jonathan L. *Epperson v. Arkansas: The Evolution-Creationism Debate* (6–10). (Landmark Supreme Court Cases) 1999, Enslow $19.95 (0-7660-1084-8). This book examines the issues involved in this case of evolution versus creationism, traces the case from lower courts to the Supreme Court, and discusses the present-day impact of the court's decision. (Rev: BL 3/15/99) [116]

8009 Unwin, David. *Prehistoric Life* (5–8). (Mysteries of . . .) 1996, Millbrook LB $22.90 (0-7613-0535-1). In addition to discussing dinosaurs, this book gives a history of the evolution of both animals and humans. (Rev: SLJ 1/97) [575]

8010 Westrup, Hugh. *The Mammals* (5–8). Illus. (Prehistoric North America) 1996, Millbrook LB $21.90 (1-56294-546-7). The woolly mammoth and saber-toothed tiger are 2 of the prehistoric mammals described in words and pictures. (Rev: BL 5/15/96; SLJ 4/96) [569]

8011 Wilkinson, Philip, and Jacqueline Dineen. *The Early Inventions* (5–8). Illus. 1995, Chelsea LB $19.95 (0-7910-2766-X). A look at the invention of early tools and processes, mostly for human survival purposes—eating and staying warm. (Rev: BR 5–6/96; SLJ 11/95; VOYA 2/96) [930]

Archaeology

8012 Avi-Yonah, Michael. *Dig This! How Archaeologists Uncover Our Past* (5–8). (Buried Worlds) 1993, Lerner LB $23.93 (0-8225-3200-X). A history of the discipline of archaeology, an examination of excavating methods, and a look at several ancient civilizations. (Rev: BL 1/15/94; SLJ 2/94) [930.1]

8013 Buell, Janet. *Ancient Horsemen of Siberia* (6–9). (Time Travelers) 1998, Millbrook LB $23.40 (0-7613-3005-4). This account describes the excavation of a 2,500-year-old burial site in the Altai Mountains in southern Siberia and recounts how the Russian archeologists were able to re-create the life of these primitive peoples through an examination of their artifacts. (Rev: SLJ 10/98) [930]

8014 Buell, Janet. *Greenland Mummies* (5–8). (Time Travelers) 1998, Twenty-First Century LB $23.40 (0-7613-3004-6). By examining mummified human corpses found in Greenland, archaeologists have been able to reconstruct the life and culture of Inuits who lived 500 years ago. (Rev: SLJ 10/98) [930]

8015 Clapp, Nicholas. *The Road to Ubar: Finding the Atlantis of the Sands* (9–12). 1998, Houghton $24.00 (0-395-87596-X). An engrossing book about how cultural myths, historical chronicles and maps, and scientific analysis of satellite images were all applied in the recent discovery of the fabled lost city of Ubar in Oman that was supposedly destroyed by God because of its sin of greed. (Rev: BL 2/1/98; SLJ 12/98) [930]

8016 Deem, James M. *Bodies from the Bog* (5–8). 1998, Houghton $16.00 (0-395-85784-8). A riveting book about the various humans from past European cultures who were mummified in bogs and discovered centuries later, with striking color and black-and-white photographs. (Rev: BL 5/15/98; SLJ 4/98) [569.9]

8017 Echo-Hawk, Roger C., and Walter R. Echo-Hawk. *Battlefields and Burial Grounds: The Indian Struggle to Protect Ancestral Graves in the United States* (7–10). 1994, Lerner LB $22.60 (0-8225-2663-8); paper $8.95 (0-8225-9722-5). A solid discussion of the conflict over Indian graves that have been plundered in the name of scientific research. (Rev: BL 5/15/94; SLJ 7/94*) [393]

8018 Forte, Maurizio, and Alberto Siliotti. *Virtual Archaeology: Re-Creating Ancient Worlds* (10–12). Trans. from Italian by Judith Toms and Robin Skeates. 1997, Abrams $49.50 (0-8109-3943-6). A beautiful book that covers archaeological sites in Africa, the Near East, Europe, Asia, and the Americas. (Rev: BL 4/15/97; SLJ 1/98) [930]

8019 Jameson, W. C. *Buried Treasures of the Atlantic Coast: Legends of Sunken Pirate Treasures, Mysterious Caches, and Jinxed Ships—From Maine to Florida* (4–8). (Buried Treasure) 1997, August House paper $11.95 (0-87483-484-8). This recounts how particular treasures were acquired, buried, or misplaced, along with accounts of failed modern attempts to find and retrieve them. (Rev: BR 5–6/99; SLJ 10/97) [910.4]

8020 Kent, Peter. *A Slice Through a City* (4–8). Illus. 1996, Millbrook LB $23.90 (0-7613-0039-2). This introduction to archaeology presents cutaway illustrations of a European city from the Stone Age to the present. (Rev: SLJ 3/97) [930]

8021 La Pierre, Yvette. *Native American Rock Art: Messages from the Past* (5–8). 1994, Thomasson-Grant $16.95 (1-56566-064-1). Discusses the mediums used to make these pictures and speculates on their significance to their creators. (Rev: BL 12/1/94; SLJ 11/94) [709]

8022 McGowen, Tom. *Adventures in Archaeology* (4–8). (Scientific American Sourcebooks) 1997, Twenty-First Century $25.90 (0-8050-4688-7). This is a history of archaeology through 1995, with coverage of important sites and finds around the world. (Rev: BR 3–4/98; SLJ 5/98; VOYA 6/98) [930]

8023 McIntosh, Jane. *The Practical Archaeologist* (8–12). 1986, Facts on File $26.95 (0-8160-1400-0); paper $15.95 (0-8160-1814-6). A discussion of how an archaeologist operates with particular emphasis on how sites are found and excavated. (Rev: BR 1–2/89; VOYA 10/88) [930.1]

8024 National Geographic Society, eds. *Splendors of the Past: Lost Cities of the Ancient World* (9–12). Illus. 1981, National Geographic $19.00 (0-87044-358-5). A lavishly illustrated volume that deals with such historical sites as Pompeii, Angkor, and those associated with the Hittite Empire. [930]

8025 O'Neal, Michael. *Pyramids* (6–9). (Great Mysteries: Opposing Viewpoints) 1995, Greenhaven LB $16.95 (1-56510-216-9). Different perspectives on the purpose and meaning of pyramids and the mysteries surrounding them. (Rev: BL 4/15/95; SLJ 3/95) [726]

8026 Perring, Stefania, and Dominic Perring. *Then and Now* (9–12). 1991, Macmillan $29.95 (0-02-599461-1). Two archaeologists fabricate reconstructions of 20 famous ruins using illustrated transparent overlays and photos, accompanied by text describing the civilizations that produced the ruins. (Rev: BL 12/15/91) [930]

8027 Scheller, William. *Amazing Archaeologists and Their Finds* (6–10). 1994, Oliver Pr. LB $18.95 (1-881508-17-X). This work presents the discoveries of 8 archaeologists, including the walls of Troy, the tomb of King Tut, Jericho, and Incan ruins. (Rev: BL 11/1/94; SLJ 2/95; VOYA 2/95) [930.1]

8028 Stefoff, Rebecca. *Finding the Lost Cities* (7–12). Illus. 1997, Oxford $48.00 (0-19-509249-X). Archaeological finds from around the world, including Troy, Crete, New Mexico, and Cambodia, are introduced in text and over 100 photographs. (Rev: BL 3/1/97; BR 1–2/98; SLJ 7/97*) [930.1]

8029 Stiebing, William H. *Uncovering the Past: A History of Archaeology* (9–12). 1993, Prometheus $29.95 (0-87975-764-7). Surveys the history of archaeology and documents the discoveries of numerous explorers. (Rev: BL 3/1/93) [930.1]

World History and Geography

General

8030 Aaseng, Nathan. *You Are the General II: 1800–1899* (6–9). (Great Decisions) 1995, Oliver Pr. LB $18.95 (1-881508-25-0). In this account of famous battles like Waterloo, Gettysburg, and Little Bighorn, the reader is asked to become a field marshal and interact with history. (Rev: SLJ 2/96) [900]

8031 Asimov, Isaac. *Asimov's Chronology of the World* (9–12). 1991, HarperCollins $40.00 (0-06-270036-7). This is a broadly based log of events in world history, concentrating on dates, leaders, generals, and wars. (Rev: BL 9/1/91) [902]

8032 Asimov, Isaac. *Words on the Map* (7–9). Illus. 1962, Houghton $9.95 (0-395-06569-0). An introduction to 1,500 place names and how they originated. [910.3]

8033 Bell, Neill. *The Book of Where; or, How to Be Naturally Geographic* (7–9). Illus. 1982, Little, Brown paper $12.95 (0-316-08831-5). Starting with one's own home environment and moving outward, this is an introduction to concepts in geography. [910]

8034 Chisholm, Jane. *The Usborne Book of World History Dates: The Key Events in History* (4–8). 1998, EDC paper $22.95 (0-7460-2318-9). Time lines and double-page spreads with brief topical essays are used to cover the major events in world history. (Rev: SLJ 5/99) [909]

8035 Cohen, Daniel. *Great Conspiracies and Elaborate Coverups* (7–10). 1997, Millbrook LB $22.40 (0-7613-0010-4). This work covers many of history's great conspiracy theories, including the Lincoln and Kennedy assassination plots, Jack the Ripper murder theories, Joseph McCarthy's Cold War rantings, and UFOs. (Rev: BR 3–4/98; SLJ 3/98) [909]

8036 Cowley, Robert, and Geoffrey Parker, eds. *The Reader's Companion to Military History* (10–12). 1996, Houghton $45.00 (0-395-66969-3). This well-illustrated, solidly researched book contains writings by military historians on many aspects of world military history, including wars and major battles, military philosophers and their theories, combat leaders, military technological advances, and strategies. (Rev: BL 2/1/97; SLJ 4/97) [355.1]

8037 Demko, George J., et al. *Why in the World: Geography for Everyone* (9–12). 1992, Doubleday paper $14.95 (0-385-26629-4). A study of the influences geography has had on physical, political, human, and historical matters. (Rev: BL 4/15/92) [910]

8038 Findling, John E., and Frank W. Thackeray, eds. *Events That Changed America in the Twentieth Century* (9–12). (Events That Changed America) 1996, Greenwood $39.95 (0-313-29080-6). This book covers important events in the 20th century, from World War I to the collapse of the Soviet Union, among them the Russian Revolution, the Great Depression, the rise of fascism, World War II, the Cold War, the Civil Rights Movement, and the Chinese Revolution. (Rev: SLJ 2/97; VOYA 12/96) [909.82]

8039 Gardner, Robert. *Where on Earth Am I?* (8–12). Illus. 1996, Watts LB $25.00 (0-531-11297-7). Topics related to geography and geology, like the Earth's shape and motion, maps, and distance and direction, are explored in 45 projects and activities. (Rev: BL 2/15/97; SLJ 2/97) [526]

8040 Gold, Susan D. *Governments of the Western Hemisphere* (5–8). Illus. (Comparing Continents) 1997, Twenty-First Century $21.40 (0-8050-5602-5). This book examines the struggles for independence in the United States, Canada, Mexico, Central America, and South America and the different directions taken by each once independence was achieved, highlighting the diversity across the nations in each area. (Rev: BL 2/1/98; SLJ 3/98) [320.3]

8041 Hoopes, James. *Oral History: An Introduction for Students* (10–12). 1979, Univ. of North Carolina Pr. paper $12.95 (0-8078-1344-3). This work explains the methodologies used in oral history collections and gives tips on how to put them into practice. [907]

8042 James, Naomi. *Courage at Sea: Tales of Heroic Voyages* (10–12). 1988, Salem House $24.95 (0-88162-320-2). Beginning with Magellan's trip, there are 15 harrowing sea voyages reported on in this book. (Rev: VOYA 12/88) [910]

8043 Kallen, Stuart A. *Life among the Pirates* (6–10). (The Way People Live) 1998, Lucent $23.45 (1-56006-393-9). The lives and exploits of pirates through the ages are covered in this account, with the use of many primary source quotations. (Rev: BL 11/15/98; SLJ 3/99) [910.45]

8044 Lauber, Patricia. *Tales Mummies Tell* (6–8). Illus. 1985, HarperCollins LB $17.89 (0-690-04389-9). A fascinating account of all we can learn about civilizations that used mummification to preserve bodies by examining the mummies themselves. (Rev: BL 6/15/85) [930]

8045 MacDonald, John. *Great Battlefields of the World* (9–12). Illus. 1985, Macmillan paper $25.95 (0-02-044464-8). This account describes 30 significant battles in world history from ancient times to present times. [904]

8046 McLynn, Frank. *Famous Trials: Cases That Made History* (10–12). 1995, Reader's Digest $27.95 (0-89577-655-1). Using many attractive illustrations, this work includes descriptions and the long-range ramifications of the trials of Socrates, Jesus, Thomas More, Danton, Dreyfus, Galileo, John Brown, Tojo, Scopes, and Nelson Mandela, and other famous people throughout history. (Rev: SLJ 5/96) [909]

8047 Marley, David F. *Wars of the Americas: A Chronology of Armed Conflict in the New World, 1492 to the Present* (9–12). 1998, ABC-CLIO LB $99.00 (0-87436-837-5). This annotated chronology covers every major war and most minor ones fought in North, South, and Central America from the arrival of Columbus to March 1998. (Rev: BL 1/1–15/99; BR 5–6/99; SLJ 2/99; VOYA 4/99) [909]

8048 Millard, Anne. *A Street Through Time* (4–8). Illus. 1998, DK Publg. $16.95 (0-7894-3426-1). Western European history is traced in this oversize book that contains 14 views of the same riverside location at various times in history, including the Stone Age, Viking times, the Roman period, the Middle Ages, and modern times. (Rev: BL 1/1–15/99; SLJ 12/98) [936]

8049 Noland, David. *Travels Along the Edge* (10–12). 1997, Vintage paper $14.00 (0-679-76344-9). A world traveler describes 40 different adventure trips around the world with tips and detailed advice. (Rev: BL 9/1/97; SLJ 2/98) [910.2]

8050 Perry, James M. *Arrogant Armies: Great Military Disasters and the Generals Behind Them* (10–12). 1996, Wiley $27.95 (0-471-11976-8). This collection of failed military missions over the past two and a half centuries, such as Braddock's campaign during the French and Indian Wars and Gordon's loss of Khartum in the Sudan, underlines the waste and horror of war. (Rev: SLJ 11/96) [900]

8051 *Photographs: Then and Now* (10–12). 1998, National Geographic $50.00 (0-7922-7202-1). The world's peoples, places, and cultures are presented in this collection of outstanding photographs from the *National Geographic* that span the period from 1888 to the present. (Rev: SLJ 3/99) [910]

8052 Platt, Richard. *Disaster! Catastrophes That Shook the World* (5–9). Illus. 1995, DK Publg. $15.95 (0-7894-2034-1). Using 2-page spreads, this oversize, well-illustrated book introduces disasters as Vesuvius, the Black Death, the *Hindenburg,* the *Titanic,* the Dust Bowl, and other catastrophes from 79 A.D. to 1974, with explanations of what caused the catastrophe, how people survived, and what life was like afterward. (Rev: VOYA 4/98) [910]

8053 Platt, Richard. *In the Beginning . . . The Nearly Complete History of Almost Everything* (5–8). Illus. 1995, DK Publg. $19.95 (0-7894-0206-8). An overview of the origins of life on Earth, followed by survey of human inventions and achievements (mostly of the Western world), from machines, communication and transportation devices, and bridges to weapons and modern skyscrapers, in one visually attractive survey volume. (Rev: BL 12/1/95; SLJ 1/96; VOYA 4/96) [909]

8054 Platt, Richard. *Pirate* (5–9). (Eyewitness Books) 1995, Knopf $19.00 (0-679-87255-8). Full-color photographs illustrate this book on piracy from the time of ancient Greece to the 19th century. (Rev: BL 8/95; SLJ 8/95) [364.1]

8055 Poole, Robert M., ed. *Nature's Wonderlands: National Parks of the World* (9–12). Illus. 1990, National Geographic $29.95 (0-87044-766-1). A photo-text tour of the national parks of the world with fuller coverage of those that are most important. (Rev: BL 5/1/90) [363.7]

8056 Russell, Jeffrey B. *A History of Witchcraft: Sorcerers, Heretics and Pagans* (9–12). Illus. 1983, Peter Smith $23.50 (0-8446-6052-3). A history of witchcraft that concentrates on Western Europe, Africa, and the United States. [133.4]

8057 Sobel, Dava. *Longitude: The True Story of a Lone Genius Who Solved the Greatest Scientific*

Problem of His Time (10–12). 1995, Walker $27.95 (0-8027-1312-2). The story of mariners' centuries-long search for ways of determining longitude that tells not only of the scientific advances but of the perseverance, pettiness, politics, and interesting anecdotes involved. (Rev: BL 9/1/95; SLJ 2/96) [527]

8058 Stearns, Peter N., and John H. Hinshaw. *The ABC-CLIO World History Companion to the Industrial Revolution* (8–12). 1996, ABC-CLIO $65.00 (0-87436-824-3). A good, alphabetically arranged reference book that discusses the wide-ranging impact of the Industrial Revolution on all aspects of life. (Rev: BR 3–4/97; SLJ 5/97) [909]

8059 Stefoff, Rebecca. *Accidental Explorers: Surprises and Side Trips in the History of Discovery* (6–9). (Extraordinary Explorers) 1993, Oxford $41.95 (0-19-507685-0). Focuses on swashbuckling adventurers and explorers who looked for things that weren't there or found things they weren't looking for. (Rev: BL 6/1–15/93) [910]

8060 Strouthes, Daniel P. *Law and Politics: A Cross-Cultural Encyclopedia* (10–12). (Encyclopedias of the Human Experience) 1995, ABC-CLIO LB $49.50 (0-87436-777-8). Using an alphabetical arrangement, this title explores how law and politics exist and function in different cultures. (Rev: BR 9–10/96; SLJ 6/96) [341]

Ancient History

General and Miscellaneous

8061 Avi-Yonah, Michael. *Piece by Piece! Mosaics of the Ancient World* (5–8). Illus. (Buried Worlds) 1993, Lerner LB $23.93 (0-8225-3204-2). This book shows how and where mosaics were made in the ancient world and how, through the wonders of archaeology, they are still being uncovered today. (Rev: BL 1/15/94; SLJ 3/94) [738.5]

8062 Brewer, Paul. *Warfare in the Ancient World* (7–10). (History of Warfare) 1999, Raintree Steck-Vaughn $27.12 (0-8172-5442-0). This account describes important wars and battles in the ancient world, from Egypt through the Roman Empire. (Rev: SLJ 3/99) [930]

8063 Caselli, Giovanni. *The First Civilizations* (6–8). Illus. 1985, Bedrick $18.95 (0-911745-59-9). This account traces the early history of man, from the first toolmakers to the civilizations of Egypt and Greece, through the objects that were made and used. (Rev: BL 11/15/85; BR 3–4/86; SLJ 1/87) [930]

8064 Connolly, Peter, and Hazel Dodge. *The Ancient City: Life in Classical Athens & Rome* (9–12). Illus. 1998, Oxford LB $52.95 (0-19-521409-9). The daily life, history, and architecture of Athens and Rome

are extensively covered, with extraordinary full-page color drawings detailing the design, construction, and use of such landmark constructions as the Parthenon and the Roman Colosseum. (Rev: BL 5/1/98; BR 1–2/99; SLJ 7/98; VOYA 2/99) [930]

8065 Corbishley, Mike. *How Do We Know Where People Came From?* (5–8). (How Do We Know) 1995, Raintree Steck-Vaughn LB $22.80 (0-8114-3880-5). Using double-page spreads, this book covers early cultures and touches on such subjects as early writing, Stonehenge, the Great Wall of China, the Easter Island statues, and the pyramids. (Rev: SLJ 1/96) [930]

8066 *Dazzling! Jewelry of the Ancient World* (5–8). Illus. (Buried Worlds) 1995, Lerner LB $23.93 (0-8225-3203-4). Pictures and descriptions of baubles, beads, necklaces, crowns, and other jewels worn by both men and women that have been uncovered at ancient world archaeological sites. (Rev: BL 7/95; SLJ 4/95) [739.27]

8067 De Angelis, Therese. *Wonders of the Ancient World* (5–8). (Costume, Tradition, and Culture: Reflecting on the Past) 1998, Chelsea $16.95 (0-7910-5170-6). Using double-page spreads, 25 important ancient structures from the Great Pyramids to Stonehenge and the statues of Easter Island are introduced. (Rev: BL 3/15/99) [930]

8068 Gaines, Ann. *Herodotus and the Explorers of the Classical Age* (6–9). Illus. (World Explorers) 1993, Chelsea LB $19.95 (0-7910-1293-X). A description of the exploration of the Mediterranean Sea region by adventurers of the ancient world, including the "father of history," Herodotus. (Rev: BL 12/15/93; SLJ 11/93) [909]

8069 Gonen, Rivka. *Fired Up! Making Pottery in Ancient Times* (5–8). Illus. (Buried Worlds) 1993, Lerner LB $23.93 (0-8225-3202-6). This book explains how pottery was made in ancient times, showing examples from different cultures, and tells how archaeologists are uncovering more and more examples. (Rev: BL 1/15/94; SLJ 4/94) [738.3]

8070 Leon, Vicki. *Outrageous Women of Ancient Times* (5–8). Illus. 1997, Wiley paper $12.95 (0-471-17006-2). Fifteen unusual women from ancient civilizations in Asia, Europe, and Africa are profiled, among them warriors, philosophers, empresses, artists, and professional poisoners, and including Cleopatra and Sappho. (Rev: BL 11/1/97; SLJ 12/97) [930]

8071 Malam, John. *Mesopotamia and the Fertile Crescent: 10,000 to 539 B.C.* (5–8). (Looking Back) 1999, Raintree Steck-Vaughn LB $25.69 (0-8172-5434-X). The story of the ancient civilizations that grew up in the rich area around the Tigris and Euphrates Rivers. (Rev: BL 5/15/99; SLJ 7/99) [930]

8072 Martell, Hazel M. *The Kingfisher Book of the Ancient World: From the Ice Age to the Fall of Rome* (4–8). Illus. 1995, Kingfisher $22.95 (1-85697-565-7). An attractive book that describes the ancient civilizations in 11 geographical regions, including the Mediterranean, Fertile Crescent, Middle and Far East, America, Africa, and Oceania. (Rev: BL 2/1/96; BR 5–6/96; SLJ 1/96) [930]

8073 Nardo, Don. *Greek and Roman Sport* (5–9). (World History) 1999, Lucent LB $22.45 (1-56006-436-6). A detailed look at sports in the ancient world, covering the Greek Olympics and other games, including some that were brutal, and what the Romans considered sport—gladiatorial games and massive animal hunts in the arenas. (Rev: BL 7/99; SLJ 8/99) [930]

8074 Wood, Tim. *Ancient Wonders* (4–8). (See Through History) 1997, Viking $17.99 (0-670-87468-X). This book introduces famous structures of the ancient world, and describes their construction and eventual fate. (Rev: BL 10/15/97; SLJ 1/98) [930]

Egypt and Mesopotamia

8075 Brier, Bob. *The Murder of Tutankhamen: A True Story* (10–12). 1998, Berkley paper $24.95 (0-399-14383-1). Reading like a contemporary whodunit, this is a reconstruction of Tutankhamen's life and death, arguing plausibly that he was murdered by his grand vizier. (Rev: SLJ 10/98) [932]

8076 Chapman, Gillian. *The Egyptians* (4–8). (Crafts from the Past) 1997, Heinemann $24.22 (1-57572-556-8). A variety of craft projects related to the ancient Egyptians are introduced and placed within their cultural context. (Rev: SLJ 4/98) [932]

8077 Charley, Catherine. *Tombs and Treasures* (4–8). Illus. (See Through History) 1995, Viking paper $15.99 (0-670-85899-4). An overview of ancient burial practices and the wealth often interred with the body, as in the cases of King Tut and other Egyptian pharaohs. (Rev: BL 1/1–15/96; SLJ 1/96) [393.1]

8078 Crosher, Judith. *Technology in the Time of Ancient Egypt* (4–8). (Technology in the Time of) 1998, Raintree Steck-Vaughn $25.69 (0-8172-4875-7). Using double-page spreads, Egyptian technology is discussed, focusing on such topics as metalwork, foods, building, and transportation. (Rev: SLJ 3/99) [932]

8079 David, Rosalie. *Handbook to Life in Ancient Egypt* (10–12). 1998, Facts on File $45.00 (0-8160-3312-9). Using topically arranged chapters, this overview presents a rounded picture of civilization of Egypt from its earliest times through the Roman period. (Rev: SLJ 1/99) [932]

8080 Harris, Geraldine. *Ancient Egypt* (5–8). Illus. 1990, Facts on File $17.95 (0-8160-1971-1). This account of Egyptian history is enlivened by excellent maps, photographs, and drawings. (Rev: SLJ 8/90) [932]

8081 Haynes, Joyce. *Egyptian Dynasties* (6–9). (First Books—African Civilizations) 1999, Watts LB $22.50 (0-531-20280-1). A history of the great ancient kingdoms of Egypt and their rulers. (Rev: BL 9/15/99; SLJ 8/99) [962]

8082 Haywood, John. *The Encyclopedia of Ancient Civilizations of the Near East & the Mediterranean* (8–12). Illus. 1997, M.E. Sharpe $95.00 (1-56324-799-2). Divided into 3 parts—ancient Near East and Egypt, the Greek world, and the Roman world—this adult narrative presents basic history and, through the use of sidebars, provides material on important places, cultural advances, scientific progress, religious practices, and military advances. (Rev: SLJ 8/98) [909]

8083 Katan, Norma Jean, and Barbara Mintz. *Hieroglyphs: The Writings of Ancient Egypt* (7–9). Illus. 1981, Macmillan $16.00 (0-689-50176-5). An explanation of hieroglyphics is given—how they originated and how the Rosetta Stone helped solve their mystery. [493]

8084 McNeese, Tim. *The Pyramids of Giza* (6–8). (Building History) 1997, Lucent LB $22.45 (1-56006-426-9). Although crammed with too much detail, this volume gives interesting information on what is known, and theorized, about how these massive monuments to the dead were built. (Rev: BR 1–2/98; SLJ 8/97) [932]

8085 McNeill, Sarah. *Ancient Egyptian People* (4–8). Illus. (People and Places) 1997, Millbrook LB $21.90 (0-7613-0056-2). This basic introduction to the people of ancient Egypt and how they lived consists of several attractive double-page spreads and a brief text. (Rev: BL 2/15/97; SLJ 3/97) [932]

8086 McNeill, Sarah. *Ancient Egyptian Places* (4–8). Illus. (People and Places) 1997, Millbrook LB $21.90 (0-7613-0057-0). Some of the great constructions of ancient Egypt are pictured in a series of elegant double-page spreads with a simple text. (Rev: BL 2/15/97; SLJ 3/97) [932]

8087 Malam, John. *Ancient Egypt* (5–8). Illus. (Remains to Be Seen) 1998, Evans Brothers $19.95 (0-237-51839-2). In double-page spreads with the generous use of illustrations and sidebars, this book presents a good overview of ancient Egypt's culture and history. (Rev: SLJ 9/98) [932]

8088 Marston, Elsa. *The Ancient Egyptians* (5–8). (Cultures of the Past) 1995, Benchmark LB $28.50 (0-7614-0073-7). With photographs of artifacts, monuments, and historical scenes, this book tells of ancient Egyptian history and culture, the rise and fall of the dynasties, and the people's religious beliefs and practices. (Rev: BR 9–10/96; SLJ 6/96) [932]

8089 Payne, Elizabeth. *The Pharaohs of Ancient Egypt* (6–8). 1981, Random paper $5.99 (0-394-84699-0). Through the story of the chief rulers of Egypt, a basic history and cultural overview of ancient Egypt are given. [932]

8090 Putnam, James. *Mummy* (5–9). Photos by Peter Hayman. (Eyewitness Books) 1993, Knopf LB $20.99 (0-679-93881-8). The process of mummification is discussed, with emphasis on the mummies of ancient Egypt. (Rev: BL 8/93) [393]

8091 Quie, Sarah. *The Myths and Civilization of the Ancient Egyptians* (4–8). Illus. (Myths and Civilization) 1999, Bedrick $16.95 (0-87226-282-0). Using the popular myths of the ancient Egyptians as a beginning, this book introduces the culture, history, and artifacts of this historical period. (Rev: SLJ 3/99) [932]

8092 Roberts, Russell. *Rulers of Ancient Egypt* (7–10). (History Makers) 1999, Lucent LB $17.96 (1-56006-438-2). The author uses both primary and secondary sources to describe the contributions and personalities of Hatshepsut, Akhenaten, Tutankhamon, Ramses II, and Cleopatra and to provide further insight into this period's culture and power structure. (Rev: SLJ 8/99) [932]

8093 Service, Pamela F. *Ancient Mesopotamia* (6–9). (Cultures of the Past) 1998, Marshall Cavendish LB $19.95 (0-7614-0301-9). This book explores the cultures of ancient Mesopotamia, their sacred tales and legends, their histories, and their legacy. (Rev: BL 12/15/98; BR 5–6/99; SLJ 4/99) [935]

8094 Shuter, Jane. *Egypt* (5–10). (Ancient World) 1998, Raintree Steck-Vaughn $27.12 (0-8172-5058-1). Ancient Egypt's mysterious hieroglyphics, treasure-filled tombs, puzzling pyramid construction, and embalming techniques, as well as its history, politics, ideas, religion, art, architecture, science, and everyday life are covered in this introductory volume. (Rev: BL 1/1–15/99; SLJ 3/99) [932]

8095 Smith, Brenda. *Egypt of the Pharaohs* (6–9). (World History) 1996, Lucent LB $16.95 (1-56006-241-X). This book explores ancient Egypt through periods of ascent and decline, its culture and contributions, and how the pharaohs helped shape the nation. (Rev: BL 2/15/96; SLJ 4/96) [932]

8096 Smith, Carter. *The Pyramid Builders* (5–8). (Turning Points in World History) 1991, Silver Burdett LB $14.95 (0-382-24131-2); paper $7.95 (0-382-24137-1). A testimonial to a brilliant culture at its peak. (Rev: BL 3/15/92) [932]

8097 Steedman, Scott. *The Egyptian News: The Greatest Newspaper in Civilization* (4–8). 1997, Candlewick $15.99 (1-56402-873-9). Using a mod-

ern newspaper format, this book a sense of daily life in ancient Egypt as well as topics like the pyramids, mummies, and pharaohs. (Rev: SLJ 9/97) [932]

8098 Stetter, Cornelius. *The Secret Medicine of the Pharaohs: Ancient Egyptian Healing* (9–12). 1993, Quintessence paper $19.95 (0-86715-265-6). Uses Egyptian papyri to reconstruct ancient Egyptian medicine and explain it in a modern scientific context. Many color illustrations. (Rev: BL 9/15/93) [610]

8099 Tiano, Oliver. *Ramses II and Egypt* (6–10). (W5) 1996, Holt $19.95 (0-8050-4659-3). Using all sorts of gimmicky illustrations and diagrams, this work presents basic facts about ancient Egypt, its culture, and its people. (Rev: SLJ 12/96) [932]

8100 Weeks, John. *The Pyramids* (7–12). Illus. 1977, Cambridge Univ. Pr. paper $12.95 (0-521-07240-9). An introduction to the construction of the pyramids of ancient Egypt. [726]

8101 *What Life Was Like on the Banks of the Nile, Egypt 3050–30 BC* (8–12). Illus. 1996, Time-Life Books $19.95 (0-8094-9378-0). An illustrated account that concentrates on everyday life in ancient Egypt, with information on several important kings. (Rev: BL 11/1/96; BR 1–2/97; SLJ 12/96) [932]

8102 Woods, Geraldine. *Science in Ancient Egypt* (4–8). (Science of the Past) 1998, Watts $25.00 (0-531-20341-7); paper $8.95 (0-531-15915-9). This book offers an intriguing look at the accomplishments of ancient Egyptians in the fields of architecture, astronomy, mathematics, medicine, and general science. (Rev: BL 6/1–15/98; BR 11–12/98; SLJ 6/98) [932]

Greece

8103 Adkins, Larry. *Handbook to Life in Ancient Greece* (10–12). 1997, Facts on File $45.00 (0-8160-3111-8). This excellent resource covers, in broad subject areas, 3,000 years of Greek history, from the Minoan civilization of Crete to the defeat of the Greeks by the Romans in 30 B.C. (Rev: BL 8/97; BR 1–2/98; SLJ 1/98) [938]

8104 Archibald, Zofia. *Discovering the World of the Ancient Greeks* (9–12). 1991, Facts on File $29.95 (0-8160-2614-9). A recounting of classical Greek history (ca. 6500–2900 B.C. to A.D. 550), through archaeological discoveries. (Rev: BL 1/1/92; SLJ 3/92) [938]

8105 Asimov, Isaac. *The Greeks: A Great Adventure* (7–10). Illus. 1965, Houghton $16.95 (0-395-06574-7). The history of ancient Greece from 200 B.C. to the fall of Constantinople. [938]

8106 *At the Dawn of Democracy: Classical Athens, 525–332 BC* (7–12). Illus. 1997, Time-Life Books

$19.95 (0-7835-5453-2). Using lavish color illustrations, this book re-creates the world of ancient Athens with coverage of daily life, sports, laws, politics, art, and religion. (Rev: BL 2/1/98; SLJ 5/98) [938]

8107 Baker, Rosalie F., and Charles F. Baker. *Ancient Greeks* (9–12). Illus. 1997, Oxford $51.95 (0-19-509940-0). Using the time span of 700 to 200 B.C., this work profiles the lives and accomplishments of 37 prominent men and women of ancient Greece. (Rev: BL 8/97; BR 3–4/98; SLJ 9/97) [938]

8108 Green, Peter. *Ancient Greece* (10–12). Illus. 1979, Thames & Hudson paper $16.95 (0-500-27161-5). In 200 illustrations and ample text, the history of Greece is traced to the death of Alexander the Great in 323 B.C. [938]

8109 Hodge, Susie. *Ancient Greek Art* (4–8). (Art in History) 1998, Heinemann $19.92 (1-57572-551-7). A solid introduction to ancient Greek art, covering painting, mosaics, pottery, architecture, and sculpture. (Rev: SLJ 5/98) [938]

8110 Hull, Robert. *Greece* (5–10). (The Ancient World) 1998, Raintree Steck-Vaughn $27.12 (0-8172-5055-7). This brief introduction to ancient Greece tells about its religion and mythology, its great philosophers, important historical events, and its contribution to world culture. (Rev: BL 1/1–15/99) [938]

8111 Levi, Peter. *Atlas of the Greek World* (10–12). Illus. 1981, Facts on File $45.00 (0-87196-448-1). Through maps and other kinds of illustrations, the history of ancient Greece is traced along with discussion of its lasting influence. [938]

8112 Martell, Hazel M. *The Myths and Civilization of the Ancient Greeks* (4–8). Illus. (Myths and Civilization) 1999, Bedrick $16.95 (0-87226-283-9). A handsome volume that combines Greek myths and legends with information about ancient Greek artifacts, culture, and history. (Rev: SLJ 3/99) [938]

8113 Nardo, Don. *Ancient Greece* (8–12). (World History) 1994, Lucent LB $17.96 (1-56006-229-0). Describes the lives and times of such ancient Greeks as Alexander the Great, Pericles, and Alcibiades. (Rev: BL 12/15/93; SLJ 1/94) [938]

8114 Nardo, Don. *The Battle of Marathon* (6–10). Illus. 1996, Lucent LB $20.96 (1-56006-412-9). A colorful, well-illustrated account that describes the causes, events, and aftermath of the battle in which the ancient Greeks repelled the Persian invasion. (Rev: BL 4/15/96; BR 9–10/96; SLJ 1/96) [938]

8115 Nardo, Don. *Life in Ancient Greece* (6–10). Illus. (The Way People Live) 1996, Lucent LB $18.96 (1-56006-327-0). Daily routines and everyday life are emphasized in this glimpse of ancient Greece from the perspective of citizens and slaves. (Rev: BL 1/1–15/96; BR 9–10/96) [938]

8116 Nardo, Don. *The Parthenon of Ancient Greece* (6–10). 1998, Lucent LB $18.96 (1-56006-431-5). The how and why of the construction of the Parthenon, its legacy as a symbol of classical Greek society and artistry, and its influence on Roman, American, and European architecture. (Rev: BL 12/15/98; BR 5–6/99; SLJ 3/99) [726]

8117 Nardo, Don. *Scientists of Ancient Greece* (7–12). Illus. 1998, Lucent LB $18.96 (1-56006-362-9). An introduction to the development of scientific thought in ancient Greece precedes chapters on the scientific theories and work of Democritus, Plato, Aristotle, Theophrastus, Archimedes, Ptolemy, and Galen. (Rev: BR 5–6/99; SLJ 4/99) [938]

8118 Nardo, Don. *The Trial of Socrates* (9–12). Illus. (Famous Trials) 1996, Lucent LB $17.96 (1-56006-267-3). This book describes the legal and ethical issues involved in the trial of Socrates and introduces the Greek city-state and the teachings of this great philosopher. (Rev: BL 6/1–15/97; BR 11–12/97; SLJ 6/97) [940.54]

8119 Pearson, Anne. *Ancient Greece* (5–9). (Eyewitness Books) 1992, Knopf LB $20.99 (0-679-91682-2). This attractively laid out book covers the history, religion, people and customs, occupations, recreation, and warfare of ancient Greeks. (Rev: BL 11/1/92; SLJ 12/92) [938]

8120 Robinson, C. E. *Everyday Life in Ancient Greece* (7–12). Illus. n.d., AMS $45.00 (0-404-14592-2). The classic account, first published in 1933, of how people lived during various periods in ancient Greek history. [938]

8121 Sacks, David. *Encyclopedia of the Ancient Greek World* (10–12). 1995, Facts on File $45.00 (0-8160-2323-9). An alphabetically arranged, browsable compendium of ancient Greek history, warfare, society, the arts, literature, mythology, science, clothing, religion and geography. (Rev: BR 3–4/96; SLJ 4/96; VOYA 4/96) [938]

8122 Schomp, Virginia. *The Ancient Greeks* (5–8). (Cultures of the Past) 1995, Benchmark LB $28.50 (0-7614-0070-2). Using quotes from period literature and many photographs and drawings, this volume examines the history of ancient Greece, its culture, and the importance of the numerous Greek gods and goddesses. (Rev: BR 9–10/96; SLJ 6/96) [938]

8123 Tournikiotis, Panayotis, ed. *The Parthenon and Its Impact in Modern Times* (10–12). 1996, Abrams $75.00 (0-8109-6314-0). The Parthenon's construction, its impact on Western democracy, architecture, and philosophy, and other perspectives on this structure are discussed in 11 original essays by noted Greek scholars and writers, enhanced by pictures. (Rev: SLJ 7/97) [938]

8124 Woodford, Susan. *The Parthenon* (7–12). Illus. 1983, Cambridge Univ. Pr. paper $12.95 (0-521-

22629-5). A history of the famous temple in Athens and of the religion of ancient Greece. [938]

Middle East

8125 Harik, Ramsay M., and Elsa Marston. *Women in the Middle East: Tradition and Change* (7–12). Illus. 1996, Watts LB $25.00 (0-531-11304-3). The public and private lives of a wide diversity of Arab and Muslim women chiefly from Lebanon, Egypt, and Tunisia. (Rev: BL 12/1/96; SLJ 1/97; VOYA 4/97) [305.42]

8126 Jenkins, Earnestine. *A Glorious Past: Ancient Egypt, Ethiopia and Nubia* (7–10). (Milestones in Black History) 1995, Chelsea LB $19.95 (0-7910-2258-7); paper $9.95 (0-7910-2684-1). A social and political survey of ancient Egypt, Nubia, the civilization to the south, and Ethiopia. (Rev: BL 4/15/95; SLJ 4/95) [932]

8127 Mann, Kenny. *The Ancient Hebrews* (6–9). (Cultures of the Past) 1998, Marshall Cavendish LB $28.50 (0-7614-0302-7). A fine introduction to the history of the ancient Jews, their culture, religion, and legacy. (Rev: BL 12/15/98; BR 5–6/99; SLJ 4/99) [909]

8128 Nardo, Don. *The Assyrian Empire* (6–9). Illus. (World History) 1998, Lucent LB $17.96 (1-56006-313-0). This account tells of the ancient civilization of the Near East and its preoccupation with warfare and military strength. (Rev: BL 6/1–15/98; SLJ 8/98) [935.03]

8129 Nardo, Don. *The Persian Empire* (6–9). (World History) 1997, Lucent LB $17.96 (1-56006-320-3). This comprehensive history of the Persian Empire describes the culture and life-style of the people as well as such events as the attempted conquest of Greece. (Rev: BL 12/15/97; SLJ 2/98) [935]

8130 Palmer, Alan. *The Decline and Fall of the Ottoman Empire* (9–12). 1994, M. Evans $22.50 (0-87131-754-0). Traces the long decline of the Ottoman Empire from 1683 to 1922 and explores the impact of its legacy on contemporary Middle Eastern society. (Rev: BL 2/1/94) [958.1]

8131 Zeinert, Karen. *The Persian Empire* (7–10). (Cultures of the Past) 1996, Benchmark LB $28.50 (0-7614-0089-3). A brief history of the Persian Empire, with material on the kings Cyrus, Darius, and Xerxes, is followed by chapters on daily life, culture, religion, and lasting contributions the empire made to human achievement. (Rev: SLJ 3/97) [935]

Rome

8132 Baker, Rosalie F., and Charles F. Baker. *Ancient Romans: Expanding the Classical Tradition* (9–12). Illus. (Oxford Profiles) 1998, Oxford $56.00

(0-19-510884-1). Divided into 5 time periods spanning 400 B.C.E. to 350 A.D., this work recounts the history of Rome's rise to power through the profiles of 39 notable Romans, including Virgil, Ovid, Julius Caesar, Constantine, Livia, and Spartacus. (Rev: BL 5/1/98; SLJ 8/98) [937]

8133 Cornell, Tim, and John Matthews. *Atlas of the Roman World* (10–12). Illus. 1982, Facts on File $45.00 (0-87196-652-2). In addition to many maps, there is an extensive text that traces the history of the Roman Empire to A.D. 565. [937]

8134 Davis, William Stearns. *A Day in Old Rome: A Picture of Roman Life* (9–12). Illus. 1959, Biblo & Tannen paper $10.00 (0-8196-0106-3). This account of the daily life, habits, and customs of ancient Romans first appeared in 1925. A companion volume is *A Day in Old Athens* (1959). [937]

8135 Hinds, Kathryn. *The Ancient Romans* (7–10). (Cultures of the Past) 1996, Benchmark LB $28.50 (0-7614-0090-7). A well-illustrated volume that tells about the Roman Empire, the architectural feats of the Romans, their religion and entertainments, and their lasting contributions to world civilization. (Rev: SLJ 3/97) [937]

8136 Hodge, Susie. *Ancient Roman Art* (4–8). (Art in History) 1998, Heinemann $19.92 (1-57572-552-5). A well-illustrated introduction to the architecture, painting, sculpture, pottery, and mosaics of ancient Rome,. (Rev: SLJ 5/98) [937]

8137 Langguth, A. J. *A Noise of War: Caesar, Pompey, Octavian and the Struggle for Rome* (9–12). 1994, Simon & Schuster $25.00 (0-671-70829-5). A history of the Roman Empire during its glory days that focuses on Caesar and Cicero and their political intrigues and alliances. (Rev: BL 3/15/94) [937]

8138 Langley, Andrew, and Philip de Souza. *The Roman News: The Greatest Newspaper in Civilization* (5–8). 1996, Candlewick $15.99 (0-7636-0055-5). Using the format of a tabloid newspaper, this book highlights the history of ancient Rome. (Rev: BL 10/1/96; SLJ 1/97) [937]

8139 Macaulay, David. *City: A Story of Roman Planning and Construction* (7–12). Illus. 1974, Houghton $18.00 (0-395-19492-X); paper $8.95 (0-395-34922-2). In text and detailed drawing, the artist explores an imaginary Roman city over approximately 125 years. [711]

8140 Nardo, Don. *The Age of Augustus* (6–9). Illus. (World History) 1996, Lucent LB $17.96 (1-56006-306-8). The history of the great Roman Caesar, who was responsible for reorganizing the empire, instituting political and fiscal reforms, and nurturing the arts. (Rev: BL 1/1–15/97; BR 11–12/97; SLJ 2/97) [937]

8141 Nardo, Don. *The Battle of Zama* (6–10). Illus. 1996, Lucent LB $26.20 (1-56006-420-X). An exciting account of the 202 B.C. battle in North Africa in which Hannibal's forces were defeated by the Romans during the second Punic War. (Rev: BL 4/15/96; BR 9–10/96; SLJ 4/96) [937]

8142 Nardo, Don. *Caesar's Conquest of Gaul* (7–10). (World History) 1996, Lucent LB $22.45 (1-56006-301-7). This is the story of how Caesar's conquest of Gaul destroyed one culture and created a new one that was to influence the development of modern Europe. (Rev: BL 2/15/96; SLJ 2/96) [937]

8143 Nardo, Don. *The Collapse of the Roman Republic* (6–10). (World History) 1997, Lucent LB $17.96 (1-56006-456-0). The story of how internal strife and corruption caused the end of the Roman Republic. (Rev: SLJ 3/98) [937]

8144 Nardo, Don. *The Decline & Fall of the Roman Empire* (6–9). Illus. (World History) 1998, Lucent LB $18.96 (1-56006-314-9). This book describes the gradual decline of the Roman Empire, which culminated in A.D. 476 when the last emperor was deposed by the superior forces of the Goths. (Rev: BL 6/1–15/98; SLJ 8/98) [937.06]

8145 Nardo, Don. *The Fall of the Roman Empire* (7–12). Illus. (Opposing Viewpoints Digests) 1997, Greenhaven LB $22.45 (1-56510-739-X); paper $13.70 (1-56510-738-1). Theories about why Rome fell are presented in a pro and con format. (Rev: BL 3/1/98) [937]

8146 Nardo, Don. *Life in Ancient Rome* (6–10). Illus. (Way People Live) 1997, Lucent LB $18.96 (1-56006-335-1). Daily routines and personal problems and struggles are the focus of this book that describes everyday social, family, and religious life in ancient Rome. (Rev: BL 3/15/97; SLJ 6/97) [937]

8147 Nardo, Don. *Life of a Roman Slave* (6–10). (Way People Live) 1998, Lucent LB $18.96 (1-56006-388-2). Roman slaves were important in households, industry, the arts, and entertainment. This book reports on their living conditions and the few we know of who fought for their freedom. (Rev: BL 7/98) [937]

8148 Nardo, Don. *The Punic Wars* (8–12). Illus. (World History) 1996, Lucent LB $22.45 (1-56006-417-X). A description of the 3 wars between Rome and Carthage, Hannibal and other leaders, and the significance of Rome's victory. (Rev: BL 2/15/96; SLJ 2/96) [937]

8149 Nardo, Don. *The Roman Colosseum* (6–10). Illus. (Building History) 1997, Lucent LB $17.96 (1-56006-429-3). The story behind the building of the Colosseum, and how both foreign architectural principles and Roman skill combined to produce an amazing feat of engineering. (Rev: BL 10/1/97; SLJ 2/98) [725]

8150 Nardo, Don. *The Roman Empire* (8–12). (World History) 1994, Lucent LB $18.96 (1-56006-231-2). Covers the Roman Empire from the Augustan Age to its fall, with descriptions of everyday life and quotes from people of the time. (Rev: BL 12/15/93; SLJ 1/94) [937]

8151 Nardo, Don. *Rulers of Ancient Rome* (7–12). Illus. (History Makers) 1998, Lucent LB $18.96 (1-56006-356-4). Following a brief history of Rome, the author discusses 8 military and political figures, including their backgrounds, successes, and weaknesses, among them Quintus Fabius Maximus, Caesar, Augustus, Nero, Constantine, and Justinian. (Rev: BR 5–6/99; SLJ 4/99) [937]

8152 Ochoa, George. *The Assassination of Julius Caesar* (5–8). (Turning Points in World History) 1991, Silver Burdett LB $14.95 (0-382-24130-4); paper $7.95 (0-382-24136-3). A study of the circumstances surrounding the murder of the Roman leader and its historical impact. (Rev: BL 3/15/92) [937]

8153 Ridd, Stephen, ed. *Julius Caesar in Gaul and Britain* (5–8). Illus. (History Eyewitness) 1995, Raintree Steck-Vaughn LB $24.26 (0-8114-8283-9). An edited version of Caesar's fascinating accounts of the Gallic Wars, with pictures and maps. (Rev: BL 4/15/95; SLJ 5/95) [937.05]

8154 Scarre, Chris. *Chronicle of the Roman Emperors: The Reign-by-Reign Record of the Rulers of Imperial Rome* (9–12). 1995, Thames & Hudson $29.95 (0-500-05077-5). The story of emperors from Augustus to Romulus Augustulus is told through surviving annals of classical historians, with photos of ruins from their reigns. (Rev: BL 10/15/95) [937]

8155 Sheehan, Sean, and Pat Levy. *Rome* (5–10). (The Ancient World) 1998, Raintree Steck-Vaughn $27.12 (0-8172-5057-3). A brief history of Rome and the Roman Empire, including its culture, buildings, amusements, and emperors. (Rev: BL 1/1–15/99; SLJ 3/99) [937]

8156 Snedden, Robert. *Technology in the Time of Ancient Rome* (4–8). (Technology in the Time of . . .) 1998, Raintree Steck-Vaughn $25.69 (0-8172-4876-5). Weaving, food production, construction, transportation, and metalwork are covered in this discussion of Roman technology and the tools they used. (Rev: SLJ 3/99) [937]

8157 Time-Life Books, eds. *When Rome Ruled the World: The Roman Empire, 100 B.C.–A.D. 200* (8–12). (What Life Was Like) 1997, Time-Life Books $19.95 (0-7835-5452-4). A wordy introduction to everyday life during the Roman Empire that is noteworthy for its excellent illustrations of art and artifacts. (Rev: SLJ 3/98) [937]

8158 Watkins, Richard. *Gladiator* (6–9). Illus. 1997, Houghton $17.00 (0-395-82656-X). In 12 brief chapters, 700 years of Roman gladiator sports are described, including equipment, animals used, contests, and the architecture and construction of the great amphitheaters. (Rev: BL 11/1/97; BR 9–10/98; SLJ 10/97*) [937]

Middle Ages Through the Renaissance (500–1700)

8159 *The Age of Exploration* (5–8). Illus. 1989, Marshall Cavendish $14.95 (0-86307-997-0). With lavish illustrations, this account details the careers of Marco Polo, Columbus, and Cortes. (Rev: SLJ 7/90) [910.92]

8160 Aston, Margaret. *Panorama of the Renaissance* (10–12). 1996, Abrams $45.00 (0-8109-3704-2). An illustrated tour for better readers through the Renaissance, including the period's art, architecture, religion, rulers, finances, philosophy, literature, and social life. (Rev: SLJ 2/97) [940.2]

8161 Barter, James. *Artists of the Renaissance* (6–10). Illus. (History Makers) 1999, Lucent LB $22.45 (1-56006-439-0). Following an overview of the Renaissance, including explanations of humanism and classicism, the book focuses on several great artists, among them Giotto, Leonardo da Vinci, and Michelangelo. (Rev: BL 6/1–15/99; SLJ 7/99) [709]

8162 Biel, Timothy L. *The Age of Feudalism* (8–12). (World History) 1994, Lucent LB $14.95 (1-56006-232-0). Using primary sources and quotations, the author traces the history of feudalism from its beginnings with Germanic tribes to its development in the Middle Ages. (Rev: BL 1/1/94) [321]

8163 Brewer, Paul. *Warfare in the Renaissance World* (7–10). (History of Warfare) 1999, Raintree Steck-Vaughn $27.12 (0-8172-5444-7). Using diagrams and other illustrations, this is an account of the wars and battles fought during the Renaissance period. (Rev: SLJ 3/99) [940.2]

8164 *Castle at War: The Story of a Siege* (4–8). 1998, DK Publg. paper $14.95 (0-7894-3418-0). A fictional siege on the medieval castle, detailing the preparations, the long weeks of the siege itself, and the slow recovery, is used to illustrate life in the Middle Ages. (Rev: SLJ 4/99) [940]

8165 Cooper, Tracy E. *Renaissance* (10–12). (Abbeville Stylebooks) 1995, Abbeville $12.95 (0-7892-0023-6). This handy, well-illustrated guide gives an overview of the Age of Exploration and then focuses on Renaissance architecture and design, with material on various kinds of buildings and furnishings. (Rev: SLJ 4/96) [940.2]

8166 Corbishley, Mike. *The Middle Ages* (6–9). Illus. 1990, Facts on File $17.95 (0-8160-1973-8).

An overview of medieval Europe is given, covering history and culture with some material on stained glassmaking. (Rev: SLJ 9/90) [909]

8167 Corrick, James A. *The Byzantine Empire* (6–9). (World History) 1996, Lucent LB $17.96 (1-56006-307-6). In a clear, concise style, this book tells how the Byzantine Empire survived the fall of Rome, existed for a thousand years, and was responsible for preserving the culture of the ancient world until its fall due to corruption, civil war, and foreign attacks. (Rev: BR 11–12/97; SLJ 4/97) [949.5]

8168 Corrick, James A. *The Early Middle Ages* (8–12). Illus. (World History) 1995, Lucent LB $17.96 (1-56006-246-0). This account tells how Europe recovered and regrouped its power structure into a feudal economy after the barbarian invasions destroyed the Roman Empire. (Rev: BL 2/15/95) [940.1]

8169 Corrick, James A. *The Renaissance* (6–9). (World History) 1998, Lucent LB $17.96 (1-56006-311-4). An exploration of the time of the rebirth of knowledge and culture in Europe that brought innovations in the arts, economics, religion, and the status of nations. (Rev: BL 5/15/98; SLJ 7/98) [940.2]

8170 Corzine, Phyllis. *The Black Death* (6–9). Illus. (World History) 1996, Lucent LB $17.96 (1-56006-299-1). The story of the plague that devastated Europe during the 14th century, destroying about three quarters of its population in a period of 30 years. (Rev: BL 1/1–15/97; BR 11–12/97; SLJ 2/97) [614.5]

8171 Emerson, Kathy Lynn. *The Writer's Guide to Everyday Life in Renaissance England, from 1485–1649* (10–12). 1996, Writer's Digest $18.99 (0-89879-752-7). This complete guide to the Renaissance covers everyday life, government and war, and society, with subtopics such as food and drink, clothing, crime, witchcraft, entertainment, and marriage. (Rev: SLJ 2/97) [940.2]

8172 Flowers, Sarah. *The Reformation* (8–12). (World History) 1996, Lucent LB $17.96 (1-56006-243-6). Examines the Reformation, including background information, causes and effects, and important figures. (Rev: BL 2/15/96; SLJ 3/96) [940]

8173 Gies, Joseph, and Frances Gies. *Life in a Medieval Castle* (10–12). Illus. 1979, HarperCollins paper $13.50 (0-06-090674-X). A Welsh castle is used as a model in this exploration of the feudal system and description of everyday life. [940.1]

8174 Gravett, Christopher. *Castle* (5–9). (Eyewitness Books) 1994, Knopf LB $20.99 (0-679-96000-7). A look at the evolution of the castle, its functions, parts, and construction. (Rev: BL 10/15/94) [623]

8175 Gravett, Christopher. *The World of the Medieval Knight* (5–10). Illus. 1997, Bedrick LB $19.95 (0-

87226-277-4). Various aspects of knighthood—from armor and jousting to castle life and the Crusades—are presented in this richly illustrated book. (Rev: BL 1/1–15/97; SLJ 3/97) [940.1]

8176 Halliwell, Sarah, ed. *The Renaissance: Artists and Writers* (6–9). Illus. (Who and When?) 1998, Raintree Steck-Vaughn LB $28.55 (0-8172-4725-4). This account covers the artistic life of the Renaissance and includes profiles of 13 artists and writers, including Giotto, Botticelli, Bosch, Dante, Chaucer, and Cervantes. (Rev: BL 12/15/97; SLJ 1/98) [700]

8177 Hanawalt, Barbara. *Growing Up in Medieval London: The Experience of Childhood in History* (9–12). 1993, Oxford $56.00 (0-19-508405-5). Court records lend immediacy to the lives of London's children in the Middle Ages. (Rev: SLJ 12/94) [940]

8178 Hanawalt, Barbara. *The Middle Ages: An Illustrated History* (8–12). Illus. 1999, Oxford $47.95 (0-19-510359-9). A carefully researched account of the Roman Empire and its gradual fall, the rise of the church, its use of power, and feudal society, including such topics as castles, the Crusades, the Black Death, the rise of guilds and universities, and the growth of the middle class. (Rev: BL 3/1/99; SLJ 4/99) [909.07]

8179 Harpur, James. *Revelations: The Medieval World* (10–12). 1995, Holt $35.00 (0-8050-4140-0). With extensive use of illustrations, this is a handsome description of life in the Middle Ages, divided into four sections: knights, nobles and castles; urban decline and the prosperity that resulted from increased commerce in the 11th century; the many cathedrals and churches; and the endemic warfare. (Rev: BR 5–6/96; SLJ 2/96) [940.1]

8180 Hicks, Peter. *How Castles Were Built* (6–8). (The Age of Castles) 1998, Raintree Steck-Vaughn $25.69 (0-8172-5121-9). This account describes castle design and construction, the purposes castles served, and an overview of castles around the world and their fates. (Rev: SLJ 2/99) [941]

8181 Hinds, Kathryn. *The Celts of Northern Europe* (7–10). (Cultures of the Past) 1996, Benchmark LB $28.50 (0-7614-0092-3). This book gives a history of the Celts, their religion, social structure, art, folklore, and how they helped keep Christianity alive in Ireland. (Rev: SLJ 3/97) [940.1]

8182 Howarth, Sarah. *The Middle Ages* (5–8). (See Through History) 1993, Viking paper $14.99 (0-670-85098-5). Describes the day-to-day lives of people in the Middle Ages, including family, clothing, food, and status. (Rev: BL 12/15/93; SLJ 2/94) [940.1]

8183 Hunt, Jonathan. *Bestiary: An Illuminated Alphabet of Medieval Beasts* (4–8). Illus. 1998, Simon & Schuster $17.00 (0-689-81246-9). A total of 26 wondrous, mostly scary, beasts from medieval times, among them the griffin, phoenix, sphinx, and ziphius,

are pictured and described in this eye-catching volume. (Rev: BL 9/1/98; SLJ 9/98) [940]

8184 Jones, Madeline. *Knights and Castles* (6–9). (How It Was) 1991, Batsford $19.95 (0-7134-6352-X). A re-creation of castles and knights and the time in which they existed. (Rev: BL 1/15/92; SLJ 3/92) [941]

8185 Jordan, William Chester. *Great Famine* (10–12). 1996, Princeton Univ. Pr. $42.50 (0-691-01134-6). From 1315 through 1322, Europe was in the grip of a terrible famine caused by heavy rains, harsh winters, animal disease, class warfare, and other factors. This account describes the Great Famine and its effects. (Rev: SLJ 2/97) [940.1]

8186 Lace, William W. *Defeat of the Spanish Armada* (6–10). (Battles) 1996, Lucent LB $24.94 (1-56006-458-7). The story of the war between England and Spain during the time of Elizabeth I, and how the defeat of Spain established England as a major sea power. (Rev: BL 4/15/97; BR 11–12/97; SLJ 6/97) [947]

8187 Langley, Andrew. *Medieval Life* (4–9). Illus. (Eyewitness Books) 1996, Knopf LB $20.99 (0-679-98077-6). This book goes behind the scenes of life in a castle during the Middle Ages, explaining and illustrating the castle's parts and how people lived within its walls. (Rev: BL 6/1–15/96; SLJ 7/96) [940.1]

8188 Langley, Andrew. *Renaissance* (4–8). (Eyewitness) 1999, Knopf LB $20.99 (0-375-90136-1). A well-illustrated book on the Renaissance, including the rise of city-states, trade, art, architecture, the church, daily life, and dress. (Rev: SLJ 9/99) [940]

8189 Leon, Vicki. *Outrageous Women of the Middle Ages* (5–10). 1998, Wiley paper $12.95 (0-471-17004-6). Using a witty writing style and modern comparisons, this fascinating book profiles a diverse group of amazing women who lived from the 6th through the 14th centuries in Europe, Asia, and Africa. (Rev: SLJ 8/98) [940.1]

8190 MacDonald, Fiona. *The World in the Time of Charlemagne: AD 700–900* (6–9). (The World in the Time of . . .) 1998, Dillon $23.00 (0-382-39737-1). After background material on Charlemagne's life and achievements, this book describes important developments in the arts, science, and religion during the 200-year period influenced by his reign. (Rev: SLJ 3/99) [921]

8191 Marshall, Chris. *Warfare in the Medieval World* (7–10). (History of Warfare) 1999, Raintree Steck-Vaughn $27.12 (0-8172-5443-9). The Hundred Years' War is one of the wars highlighted in this book that focuses on individual battles and is illustrated with many full-color maps and reproductions. (Rev: SLJ 3/99) [940.1]

8192 Martell, Hazel M. *The Celts* (5–8). (See Through History) 1996, Viking paper $19.99 (0-670-86558-3). A visually attractive, fact-filled book that uses not only text but full-color drawings and photographs of museum objects and archaeological findings to show the daily life of the Celts. (Rev: SLJ 3/96) [364]

8193 Matthew, Donald. *Atlas of Medieval Europe* (10–12). Illus. 1983, Facts on File $45.00 (0-87196-133-4). This collection of maps plus many pictures illustrate the political, social, and cultural history of Europe from the decline of the Roman Empire to the discovery of the New World. [911]

8194 Nardo, Don. *Life on a Medieval Pilgrimage* (6–9). Illus. (The Way People Live) 1996, Lucent LB $17.96 (1-56006-325-4). The daily lives of pilgrims in the Middle Ages is reconstructed, with material on their goals, travel conditions, and religious practices. (Rev: BL 3/15/96; BR 9–10/96) [248.4]

8195 Nardo, Don. *The Medieval Castle* (6–10). Illus. (Building History) 1997, Lucent LB $17.96 (1-56006-430-7). This study presents a history of the medieval European castle, including its structure, design, usage, and construction. (Rev: SLJ 5/98) [940.1]

8196 Nicolle, David. *Medieval Knights* (4–8). (See Through History) 1997, Viking $19.99 (0-670-87463-9). An introduction to knights—their functions, weapons, quests, training, and accomplishments. (Rev: BL 10/15/97; SLJ 1/98) [940]

8197 Norwich, Julius J. *A Short History of Byzantium* (10–12). 1997, Knopf $40.00 (0-679-45088-2). An exciting, detailed history of the intrigues, betrayals, rulers, and conquests that made up the 1,000-year history of the Byzantium Empire. (Rev: SLJ 2/98) [949.5]

8198 Osman, Karen. *The Italian Renaissance* (8–12). Illus. (World History) 1996, Lucent LB $16.95 (1-56006-237-1). A history of the great families and city states that emerged in Italy after the Dark Ages and how their prosperity brought a flowering of culture. (Rev: BL 2/15/96; SLJ 3/96) [945]

8199 Pernoud, Regine. *A Day with a Noblewoman* (5–8). Trans. by Dominique Clift. Illus. (A Day With) 1997, Runestone LB $22.60 (0-8225-1916-X). After a brief introduction to the Middle Ages, this book describes a busy day in the life of Blanche, the countess of Champagne, a French widow in the 13th century. (Rev: BL 1/1–15/98; SLJ 2/98) [940.1]

8200 Platt, Richard. *Castle* (5–10). Illus. (Stephen Biesty's Cross-Sections) 1994, DK Publg. $16.95 (1-56458-467-4). Describes through text and illustrations a 14th-century European castle, its construction and defenses, and the medieval trades, jousts, and feasts within. (Rev: BL 11/1/94; SLJ 10/94; VOYA 2/95) [940.1]

8201 Reid, Struan. *Cultures and Civilizations* (5–9). Illus. (The Silk and Spice Routes) 1994, Silver Burdett LB $19.95 (0-02-726315-0). The many historic cultures that thrived along the ancient trade route to the East are introduced a handsome, oversize book with stunning illustrations. (Rev: BL 12/15/94) [909]

8202 Rice, Earle, Jr. *Life during the Middle Ages* (6–10). (Way People Live) 1998, Lucent LB $17.96 (1-56006-386-6). An account of how serfs, lords, and clergy lived under feudalism in the Middle Ages, enduring warfare, famine, disease. (Rev: BL 7/98; SLJ 8/98) [941]

8203 Rice, Earle, Jr. *Life during the Crusades* (8–10). Illus. (The Way People Lived) 1998, Lucent LB $22.45 (1-56006-379-3). The period of the Crusades (1096–1272) is introduced, with material on feudal life, knighthood, reasons for the Crusades, Muslim culture, and key events of each of the Crusades. (Rev: BL 3/15/98; SLJ 5/98) [909.07]

8204 Riley-Smith, Jonathan, ed. *The Oxford Illustrated History of the Crusades* (9–12). 1995, Oxford $72.50 (0-19-820435-3). A history of the Crusades and their odd stories of conquest and compassion. (Rev: BL 11/1/95) [909.7]

8205 Stewart, Gail B. *Life during the Spanish Inquisition* (6–12). Illus. (Way People Live) 1997, Lucent LB $17.96 (1-56006-346-7). Using quotations from a wide variety of sources, this book examines graphically the beginning of the Spanish Inquisition during the reign of Ferdinand and Isabella, detailing its objectives and the nature of the punishments. (Rev: BL 1/1–15/98; SLJ 3/98; VOYA 12/99) [272]

8206 Thompson, Stephen P., ed. *The Reformation* (9–12). (Turning Points in World History) 1998, Greenhaven LB $21.96 (1-56510-961-9); paper $17.45 (1-56510-960-0). Beginning in the early 1500s, this book recounts the history of the movement to reform the Catholic Church, with emphasis on the work of Luther, Zwingli, and Calvin. (Rev: BL 5/15/99) [909.5]

8207 Time-Life Books, eds. *What Life Was Like in the Age of Chivalry: Medieval Europe A.D. 800–1500* (10–12). (What Life Was Like) 1997, Time-Life Books $34.95 (0-7835-5451-6). Divided into 4 main section on the clergy, knights, peasants and rural landowners, and town dwellers, this handsome volume describes life in the Middle Ages through descriptions of important figures like Charlemagne, Heloise and Abelard, Joan of Arc, and Thomas Becket. (Rev: SLJ 1/98) [940]

8208 Williams, Brian. *Forts and Castles* (5–8). (See Through History) 1995, Viking paper $16.99 (0-670-85898-6). This lavishly illustrated book is a general introduction to the construction, parts, and uses of forts and castles. (Rev: BL 10/15/95) [728.81]

8209 Wood, Tim. *The Renaissance* (5–8). (See Through History) 1993, Viking paper $19.99 (0-670-85149-3). Looks at the day-to-day lives of people during the Renaissance, including Far East trade, Italian city-states, women at court, art, and technology. (Rev: BL 12/15/93; SLJ 2/94) [940.2]

8210 *The World in 1492* (5–9). Illus. 1992, Holt $19.95 (0-8050-1674-0). Six writers among them, Jean Fritz, Margaret Mahy, and Jamake Highwater, contemplate life in the late 15th century. (Rev: BL 11/1/92; SLJ 11/92*) [940]

Eighteenth Through Nineteenth Centuries (1700–1900)

8211 Bachrach, Deborah. *The Charge of the Light Brigade* (6–10). Illus. (Battles) 1996, Lucent LB $24.94 (1-56006-455-2). An account of the "death charge of the 600" at Balaclava on Sept. 20, 1854, during the Crimean War. (Rev: BL 4/15/97; BR 11–12/97; SLJ 6/97) [947]

8212 Bachrach, Deborah. *The Crimean War* (8–12). Illus. (World History) 1997, Lucent LB $17.96 (1-56006-315-7). An easy-to-read account of the causes, main events, and consequences of the Crimean War, the first war to be extensively covered by the press, fought from 1853 to 1856 and involving Great Britain, France, Russia, Sardinia, and Turkey. (Rev: SLJ 6/98) [947]

8213 Corrick, James A. *The Industrial Revolution* (7–10). Illus. (World History) 1998, Lucent LB $17.96 (1-56006-318-1). Using over 20 original documents, this work examines the changes in technology and working conditions brought about by the Industrial Revolution in England, Europe, and America, and explores its far-reaching social impact spanning the 18th, 19th, and 20th centuries. (Rev: BL 9/1/98) [909.81]

8214 Dunn, John M. *The Enlightenment* (6–9). (World History) 1998, Lucent LB $17.96 (1-56006-242-8). The emergence from the Dark Ages of Western Europe in the 18th century and the rediscovery of ancient scholarship. (Rev: BL 12/15/98; BR 5–6/99) [940.2]

8215 Henderson, Harry. *The Age of Napoleon* (6–9). (World History) 1998, Lucent LB $17.96 (1-56006-319-X). Under Napoleon, France took center stage in early 19th-century Europe. This book tells about the events, ideas, and significance of this dictator's career. (Rev: BL 12/15/98; BR 5–6/99) [944.05]

8216 Killingray, David. *The Transatlantic Slave Trade* (7–12). Illus. 1987, Batsford $19.95 (0-7134-5469-5). This book gives detailed coverage on the causes, history, and end of the international slave trade and how it has affected demographics today. (Rev: SLJ 1/88) [380.1]

8217 Pietrusza, David. *The Battle of Waterloo* (6–10). Illus. (Great Battles in History) 1996, Lucent LB $19.95 (1-56006-423-4). The story of the last battle of the Napoleonic Wars is told with a generous use of graphics, including a time line and maps. (Rev: BL 4/15/96; BR 9–10/96; SLJ 4/96) [940.2]

8218 Sommerville, Donald. *Revolutionary and Napoleonic Wars* (8–10). (History of Warfare) 1998, Raintree Steck-Vaughn LB $27.12 (0-8172-5446-3). This well-illustrated book looks at the wars fought from the late-18th through mid-19th centuries, focusing primarily on the Americans and the French and their wars of independence and subsequent battles with other enemies. (Rev: SLJ 1/99) [909]

8219 Spencer, Lloyd. *Introducing the Enlightenment* (10–12). Illus. 1997, Totem paper $10.95 (1-874166-56-0). A serious but interesting introduction to 18th-century Europe that discusses individuals, events, accomplishments, and concepts of the Age of Enlightenment. (Rev: SLJ 1/98) [909]

8220 Thackeray, Frank W., and John E. Findling, eds. *Events That Changed the World in the Eighteenth Century* (9–12). 1998, Greenwood $39.95 (0-313-29077-6). Topics included in this resource include the reforms of Peter the Great, the War of the Spanish Succession, the Seven Years' War, the Enlightenment, the Agricultural Revolution, the American Revolution, the Atlantic slave trade, the French Revolution, and the Industrial Revolution. (Rev: BR 9–10/98; SLJ 2/99) [909.7]

8221 Westwell, Ian. *Warfare in the 18th Century* (8–10). (History of Warfare) 1998, Raintree Steck-Vaughn LB $27.12 (0-8172-5445-5). This account covers wars fought in Europe from the Great Northern War in 1700 to the death of Catherine the Great in 1796, including wars fought with Native Americans and over the fate of India. (Rev: SLJ 1/99) [909]

8222 Wilkinson, Philip, and Jacqueline Dineen. *The Industrial Revolution* (6–9). Illus. 1995, Chelsea LB $19.95 (0-7910-2767-8). This simple account shows how harnessing energy and the development of industry during the 19th century and afterward changed the way people lived and created a new social structure. (Rev: BR 5–6/96; VOYA 2/96) [909.8]

Twentieth Century

General and Miscellaneous

8223 Adams, Simon. *Visual Timeline of the 20th Century* (5–8). Illus. 1996, DK Publg. $15.95 (0-7894-0997-6). Important events of the 20th century are described in chronological order, using many photographs and other visuals. (Rev: BL 12/1/96; SLJ 1/97; VOYA 6/97) [909.8]

8224 Adams, Simon, et al. *Junior Chronicle of the 20th Century: Month-by-Month History of Our Amazing Century* (5–8). 1997, DK Publg. $39.95 (0-7894-2033-3). Using many photographs, tables, and other illustrations, this book allots double-page spreads to most years of the 20th century, including major world events, innovations, and entertainment happenings, interspersed with scientific advances, fashion, music, and various trends and novelties. (Rev: BL 10/1/97; BR 3–4/98; SLJ 1/98) [909.8]

8225 Clare, John D. *Growing Up in the People's Century* (6–12). 1998, BBC Books $23.95 (0-563-40410-8). Wonderful for browsers, this book uses double-page spreads with pictures and quotes to present a quick view of events of historical or cultural significance in the 20th century. (Rev: BL 1/1–15/99) [909.82]

8226 Hodgson, Godfrey. *People's Century: The Ordinary Men & Women Who Made the Twentieth Century* (9–12). 1998, Times Books $60.00 (0-8129-2843-1). A British publication that presents a broad chronological view of the 20th century, with many sidebars, quotes from individuals who lived through particular events, and thousands of photographs. (Rev: SLJ 9/98) [909.82]

8227 *National Geographic Eyewitness to the 20th Century* (9–12). 1998, National Geographic $40.00 (0-7922-7049-5). A record of the 20th century as recorded in *National Geographic* magazine, arranged by decades, each with a 6-page introduction followed by outstanding illustrations. (Rev: SLJ 3/99) [909]

8228 Ross, Stewart. *Oxford Children's Book of the 20th Century: A Concise Guide to a Century of Contrast and Change* (4–9). 1999, Oxford $18.95 (0-19-521488-9). Using double-page spreads, this book focuses on the people, places, and events of the 20th century, with interesting text, photos, maps, and time lines. (Rev: SLJ 7/99) [909.82]

8229 Tambini, Michael. *The Look of the Century* (7–12). 1996, DK Publg. $39.95 (0-7894-0950-X). A beautiful, oversize book that uses photos to trace life in the 20th century, useful more for browsing than research. (Rev: VOYA 4/97) [909.82]

8230 Time-Life Books, eds. *Events That Shaped the Century* (7–12). 1998, Time-Life Books $19.95 (0-7835-5502-4). Using outstanding photographs, this volume describes 125 events since 1900 that transformed America and affected all aspects of American life. (Rev: BR 11–12/98; SLJ 9/98) [909.82]

World War I

8231 Bosco, Peter. *World War I* (7–12). (America at War) 1991, Facts on File $19.95 (0-8160-2460-X). Highlights the major battles and personalities of World War I and discusses events leading to a declaration of war and the changes following the peace. (Rev: BL 10/15/91; SLJ 8/91) [940.3]

8232 Cooper, Michael L. *Hell Fighters: African American Soldiers in World War I* (5–9). Illus. 1997, Dutton paper $16.99 (0-525-67534-5). The story of the heroic African American World War I infantry regiment that became known as the "Hell Fighters." (Rev: BL 2/15/97; BR 3–4/98; SLJ 2/97*) [940.4]

8233 Dolan, Edward F. *America in World War I* (5–8). Illus. 1996, Millbrook LB $27.40 (1-56294-522-X). A large-format book that introduces background material on World War I and specific information on the role that the United States played in it. (Rev: BL 6/1–15/96; SLJ 5/96) [940.3]

8234 Dudley, William, ed. *World War I* (6–12). Illus. (Opposing Viewpoints: American History) 1997, Greenhaven LB $21.96 (1-56510-703-9); paper $16.20 (1-56510-702-0). The disagreements, debates, and international problems related to the First World War, including U.S. war preparedness, neutrality, and the League of Nations, are covered in this collection of viewpoints. (Rev: BL 5/15/98) [940.3]

8235 Gay, Kathlyn, and Martin Gay. *World War I* (5–8). 1995, Twenty-First Century LB $18.90 (0-8050-2848-X). Combines personal eyewitness accounts with general background information. (Rev: BL 12/15/95; SLJ 2/96) [940.3]

8236 Jantzen, Steven. *Hooray for Peace, Hurrah for War: The United States during World War I* (9–12). 1990, Facts on File $19.95 (0-8160-2453-7). A brief, readable account of American policy during World War I through to the rejection of the League of Nations. (Rev: SLJ 5/91) [940.3]

8237 Rice, Earle, Jr. *The Battle of Belleau Wood* (6–10). Illus. (Great Battles in History) 1996, Lucent LB $19.95 (1056006-424-2). This account of the victory over the Germans in June 1918 by chiefly American troops is retold with a generous use of illustrations, maps, and a timeline. (Rev: BL 4/15/96; BR 9–10/96) [940.4]

8238 Ross, Stewart. *Causes & Consequences of World War I* (7–10). (Causes and Consequences) 1998, Raintree Steck-Vaughn $27.11 (0-8172-4057-8). This volume analyzes the factors that led to World War I and the conflict's short-term and long-term effects, accompanied by contemporary illustrations. (Rev: BL 8/98; SLJ 6/98) [940.3 11]

8239 Stokesbury, James L. *A Short History of World War I* (9–12). 1981, Morrow paper $14.00 (0-688-00129-7). A brief but penetrating history of World War I that gives both political and military perspectives. [940.3]

8240 Uschan, Michael V. *A Multicultural Portrait of World War I* (7–10). (Perspectives) 1996, Benchmark

LB $28.50 (0-7614-0054-0). A readable examination of the origins and conduct of World War I, the participation by America's "melting pot" population, and the post-Armistice results that have spawned some of today's world problems. Also includes material about discrimination against German-Americans and the migration by African Americans from the South to the cities and wartime factories of the North. (Rev: BR 1–2/97; SLJ 6/96) [940.53]

World War II and the Holocaust

8241 Aaseng, Nathan. *Navajo Code Talkers* (6–9). 1992, Walker LB $16.85 (0-8027-8183-7). Describes how Navajos were recruited during World War II to create an unbreakable code that allowed the marines to transmit information quickly, accurately, and safely. (Rev: BL 12/1/92; SLJ 12/92) [940.54]

8242 Aaseng, Nathan. *Paris* (6–12). (Cities at War) 1992, Macmillan LB $14.95 (0-02-700010-9). Remembrances from people who experienced World War II in Paris. (Rev: BL 10/15/92) [944]

8243 Adelson, Alan, ed. *The Diary of Dawid Sierakowiak* (10–12). Trans. from Polish by Kamil Turowski. 1996, Oxford $56.00 (0-19-510450-1). These are the journals keep by a young Jewish boy in the Lodz ghetto from 1939 when he was 15 until his death from tuberculosis in 1943. (Rev: BL 8/96; SLJ 6/97) [940.54]

8244 Adler, David A. *We Remember the Holocaust* (6–9). Illus. 1989, Holt $18.95 (0-8050-0434-3). Through actual accounts, Adler re-creates the horror of the Holocaust. (Rev: BL 12/15/89; BR 3–4/90; SLJ 12/89) [940.53]

8245 Altman, Linda J. *Forever Outsiders: Jews and History from Ancient Times to August 1935* (6–12). Illus. (Holocaust) 1997, Blackbirch LB $19.45 (1-56711-200-5). An authoritative look at anti-Semitism throughout history ending with Hitler's rise to power and the beginnings of his Final Solution. (Rev: BL 10/15/97; BR 1–2/98; SLJ 2/98) [940.53]

8246 Altman, Linda J. *The Holocaust Ghettos* (8–12). (The Holocaust Series) 1998, Enslow LB $19.95 (0-89490-994-0). This volume explains the role that ghettos played in the Nazis' scheme to isolate and control the Jews in preparation for relocation to death camps. (Rev: BR 9–10/98; SLJ 7/98; VOYA 8/98) [940.54]

8247 Altshuler, David A. *Hitler's War Against the Jews: A Young Reader's Version of the War Against the Jews, 1933–1945, by Lucy S. Dawidowicz* (7–10). Illus. 1995, Behrman paper $14.95 (0-87441-298-6). The tragic story of Hitler's Final Solution and its aftermath. [940.54]

8248 Ambrose, Stephen E. *D-Day: June 6, 1944: The Climactic Battle of World War II* (9–12). 1994, Simon & Schuster $29.50 (0-671-67334-3). Long, detailed, immediate, and readable, this history is for teens who can't get enough of World War II drama. (Rev: BL 4/1/94) [940.54]

8249 Ambrose, Stephen E. *The Victors: Eisenhower and His Boys: The Men of World War II* (10–12). 1998, Simon & Schuster $28.00 (0-684-85628-X). Through hundreds of interviews and the examination of countless documents, the author has created a rounded portrait of Eisenhower in World War II, his relationship with his "boys," and a chronicle of American participation in the European theater. (Rev: SLJ 5/99) [940.54]

8250 Anflick, Charles. *Resistance: Teen Partisans and Resisters Who Fought Nazi Tyranny* (5–9). (Teen Witnesses to the Holocaust) 1998, Rosen LB $17.95 (0-8239-2847-0). This volume celebrates the teenagers who fought against the Nazis in ghettos, concentration camps, and inside Germany and the lands the Nazis conquered. (Rev: BL 4/15/99; BR 9–10/99; VOYA 8/99) [940.54]

8251 Axelrod, Toby. *In the Camps: Teens Who Survived the Nazi Concentration Camps* (5–9). (Teen Witnesses to the Holocaust) 1999, Rosen LB $18.50 (0-823-9-2844-6). These are the stories of teenagers who survived the death camps, their despair and sadness, and the hope they maintained despite the horror around them. (Rev: BL 7/99) [940.54]

8252 Axelrod, Toby. *Rescuers Defying the Nazis: Non-Jewish Teens Who Rescued Jews* (5–8). (Teen Witnesses to the Holocaust) 1999, Rosen $26.95 (0-8239-2848-9). This book relates the inspiring stories of teenage gentiles in Poland, Denmark, and Germany who risked their lives to help rescue Jews from the Holocaust. (Rev: BL 7/99; SLJ 8/99) [940.54]

8253 Ayer, Eleanor. *Berlin* (6–12). (Cities at War) 1992, Macmillan LB $18.00 (0-02-707800-0). Photoessay on the lives of ordinary people in Berlin during World War II, with eyewitness quotes. (Rev: BL 6/15/92; SLJ 9/92) [940.53]

8254 Ayer, Eleanor. *A Firestorm Unleashed: January 1942 to June 1943* (6–12). Illus. (Holocaust) 1997, Blackbirch LB $19.45 (1-56711-204-8). Historical narratives and personal accounts are blended in this story of the Holocaust that covers the year and a half that saw the beginning of American participation in the war. (Rev: BL 10/15/97; BR 1–2/98; SLJ 2/98) [940.53]

8255 Ayer, Eleanor. *In the Ghettos: Teens Who Survived the Ghettos of the Holocaust* (5–8). (Teens Witnesses to the Holocaust) 1999, Rosen $17.95 (0-8239-2845-4). This book relates the harrowing stories of courageous teenagers who survived life in the ghettos of Lodz, Theresienstadt, and Warsaw. (Rev: BL 7/99; SLJ 8/99) [940.54]

8256 Ayer, Eleanor. *Inferno: June 1943 to May 1945* (6–12). Illus. (Holocaust) 1997, Blackbirch LB $19.45 (1-56711-205-6). During the 2-year period covered in this part of the series Holocaust, Hitler and the Nazis fully implement their plans to destroy European Jews and the death camps reach their peak of activity. (Rev: BL 10/15/97; BR 1–2/98; SLJ 2/98) [940.53]

8257 Ayer, Eleanor. *The Survivors* (10–12). (The Holocaust Library) 1997, Lucent LB $17.96 (1-56006-096-4). This is the story of the hundreds of thousands of Jews who survived the death camps, and the saga of those who created a new homeland in the state of Israel. (Rev: BL 3/15/98; SLJ 7/98; VOYA 12/98) [940.54]

8258 Ayer, Eleanor, et al. *Parallel Journeys* (7–12). 1995, Atheneum $16.00 (0-689-31830-8). Personal narratives in alternating chapters of a Jewish woman and a former ardent member of the Hitler Youth, who grew up a few miles from each other. (Rev: BL 5/15/95*; SLJ 6/95) [943.086]

8259 Bachrach, Deborah. *The Resistance* (10–12). (Holocaust Library) 1997, Lucent LB $17.96 (1-56006-092-1). This account traces the history of the rare individuals and groups who opposed the Nazi tyranny to try to save lives and end Hitler's reign. (Rev: BL 12/15/97; SLJ 2/98) [940.54]

8260 Bachrach, Susan D. *Tell Them We Remember: The Story of the Holocaust* (5–9). 1994, Little, Brown $21.95 (0-316-69264-6). A photohistory focusing on the young who struggled through the brutality of the Holocaust following the destruction of their world of family and friends. (Rev: BL 7/94*; SLJ 11/94; VOYA 12/94) [940.54]

8261 Bar-on, Dan. *Legacy of Silence: Encounters with Children of the Third Reich* (9–12). 1989, Harvard Univ. Pr. $37.00 (0-674-52185-4). Interviews with 13 German men and women who were children during World War II telling of the roles their parents played in the Holocaust. (Rev: BL 9/15/89) [940.531]

8262 Berenbaum, Michael. *The World Must Know: A History of the Holocaust as Told in the United States Holocaust Memorial Museum* (9–12). 1993, Little, Brown paper $23.00 (0-316-09134-0). Includes moving photos of the Warsaw ghetto selected from the Holocaust Memorial Museum in Washington, D.C. (Rev: BL 3/1/93) [940.53]

8263 Besson, Jean-Louis. *October 45: Childhood Memories of the War* (4–8). Trans. from French by Carol Volk. Illus. 1995, Harcourt $22.00 (0-15-200955-8). This is the autobiographical account of a boy growing up with his family during World War II in France and enduring the occupation of the Nazis. (Rev: BL 12/15/95; SLJ 1/96) [940.54]

8264 Bitton-Jackson, Livia. *I Have Lived a Thousand Years: Growing Up in the Holocaust* (7–12). 1997, Simon & Schuster $17.00 (0-689-81022-9). Abridged from the author's adult book, this is the story of a 13-year-old Hungarian Jewish girl and how she survived Auschwitz. (Rev: BL 3/15/97; BR 9–10/97; SLJ 5/97; VOYA 6/97) [940.54]

8265 Bliven, Bruce, Jr. *Story of D-Day, June 6, 1944* (6–8). 1963, Random LB $8.99 (0-394-90362-5). An accurate but simple hour-by-hour account of the Allied invasion of Normandy. [940.53]

8266 Block, Gay, and Malka Drucker. *Rescuers: Portraits of Moral Courage in the Holocaust* (9–12). 1992, Holmes & Meier $49.95 (0-8419-1322-6); paper $29.95 (0-8419-1323-4). Profiles of 49 people who risked their lives to hide and protect Jews during the Holocaust. (Rev: BL 3/15/92) [940.53]

8267 Boas, Jacob. *We Are Witnesses: The Diaries of Five Teenagers Who Died in the Holocaust* (7–12). 1995, Holt $15.95 (0-8050-3702-0). Boas, born in 1943 in a Nazi camp, tells about being a Holocaust survivor and of the deaths of 5 other young inmates. (Rev: BL 5/15/95*) [940.53]

8268 Boisclaire, Yvonne. *In the Shadow of the Rising Sun* (10–12). 1997, Clearwood Publishers paper $14.95 (0-9649997-3-0). The horrifying, true story of U.S. Army Sergeant Robert Davis and how he and some colleagues survived the inhuman treatment in World War II Japanese prison camps in the Pacific. (Rev: VOYA 12/97) [940.54]

8269 Boyington, Gregory. *Baa Baa Black Sheep* (10–12). 1989, TAB $22.95 (0-8306-4008-8). This book deals with the men and exploits of the daring Flying Tigers during World War II. [940.54]

8270 Brager, Bruce L. *The Trial of Adolf Eichmann: The Holocaust on Trial* (8–12). (Famous Trials) 1999, Lucent LB $22.45 (1-56006-469-2). The story of the search for the infamous war criminal and of his trial in Israel in 1961, during which the horror of the Holocaust was relived. (Rev: BL 5/1/99; SLJ 8/99) [364.15]

8271 Brash, Sarah, ed. *World War II* (7–12). Illus. (The American Story) 1997, Time-Life Books $19.95 (0-7835-6253-5). The causes, events, and outcomes of World War II are covered in this well-illustrated account that emphasizes American participation. (Rev: BL 5/15/97) [940.53]

8272 Brickhill, Paul. *The Great Escape* (9–12). Illus. 1986, Fawcett paper $5.99 (0-449-21068-5). The exciting story of the digging of 3 tunnels in a German prisoner-of-war camp during World War II that were used to help 100 men escape. [940.54]

8273 Byers, Ann. *The Holocaust Camps* (8–12). (The Holocaust Remembered) 1998, Enslow LB $18.95 (0-89490-955-9). This work traces the evolution of political prison camps to labor camps and eventually to death camps during the Nazi regime. (Rev: BR 9–10/98; VOYA 8/98) [940.54]

8274 Churchill, Winston S. *The Great Battles and Leaders of the Second World War: An Illustrated History* (9–12). 1995, Houghton $40.00 (0-395-75516-6). A picture album with text excerpted from Churchill's classic 6-volume work *The Second World War.* (Rev: BL 12/1/95) [940.53]

8275 Cooper, Michael L. *African American Soldier* (6–8). 1998, NAL paper $16.99 (0-525-67562-0). An examination of the conditions under which African Americans served during World War II and of the twin wars that they fought—one against fascism abroad and the other against prejudice, discrimination, and lack of economic opportunity at home. (Rev: SLJ 10/98) [940.54]

8276 Cretzmeyer, Stacy. *Your Name Is Renée: Ruth Kapp Hartz's Story as a Hidden Child in Nazi-Occupied France* (5–8). 1999, Oxford $28.95 (0-19-513259-9). A detailed account of the German Jewish Kapp family's survival in Nazi-occupied France, where Ruth was sent to an orphanage run by Catholic nuns and told to forget her family and faith. (Rev: BL 6/1–15/99; SLJ 8/99; VOYA 10/99) [940.54]

8277 Daniels, Roger. *Prisoners Without Trial: Japanese Americans in World War II* (9–12). 1993, Hill & Wang paper $9.00 (0-8090-1553-6). A history of the racist internment of Japanese Americans in World War II. (Rev: BL 7/93; SLJ 6/94) [9.6.8.2.10]

8278 David, Kati. *A Child's War: Fifteen Children Tell Their Story* (9–12). 1989, Four Walls Eight Windows $17.95 (0-941423-24-7). Fifteen people representing a wide range of perspectives tell of their childhoods when they were between the ages of 5 and 10 during World War II. (Rev: BL 5/1/89) [940.53]

8279 Del Calzo, Rick. *The Triumphant Spirit: Portraits & Stories of Holocaust Survivors, Their Messages of Hope and Compassion* (10–12). 1997, Triumphant Spirit $45.00 (0-9655260-0-3); paper $29.95 (0-9655260-1-1). Black-and-white photographs intertwined with narratives of more than 90 Holocaust survivors. (Rev: BL 3/15/97; SLJ 10/97) [940.54]

8280 Devaney, John. *America Fights the Tide: 1942* (6–10). 1991, Walker $27.95 (0-8027-6997-7). Using a diary format and anecdotal accounts, this volume focuses on the United States' entry into World War II in both the European and the Pacific theaters. (Rev: BL 10/15/91; SLJ 10/91) [940.54]

8281 Devaney, John. *America Goes to War: 1941* (5–8). 1991, Walker LB $17.85 (0-8027-6980-2). An illustrated, datelined, day-by-day account that covers personal and public events of the first year of World War II. (Rev: BL 10/1/91; SLJ 8/91) [940.53]

8282 Devaney, John. *America on the Attack: 1943* (6–10). (Walker's World War II) 1992, Walker LB $33.90 (0-8027-8195-0). This well-illustrated account describes America's active participation in World War II once the war effort got underway. (Rev: BL 12/1/92) [940.53]

8283 Devaney, John. *America Storms the Beaches: 1944* (6–10). (World War II) 1993, Walker LB $18.85 (0-8027-8245-0). The story of D-day and the other invasions of Europe by the Allies in 1944 that spelled the beginning of the end of Nazi Germany. (Rev: BL 12/15/93; SLJ 12/93; VOYA 2/94) [940.54]

8284 Dudley, William, ed. *World War II* (7–12). (Opposing Viewpoints in American History) 1996, Greenhaven LB $21.96 (1-56510-528-1); paper $20.25 (1-56510-527-3). A thought-provoking anthology of different viewpoints on various aspects of World War II, representative of that time, including whether the United States should enter the war, the use of the atomic bomb, women's roles, and the internment of Japanese Americans but not German Americans or Italian Americans. (Rev: SLJ 3/97) [940.54]

8285 Durrett, Deanne. *Unsung Heroes of World War II: The Story of the Navajo Code Talkers* (7–12). Illus. (Library of American Indian History) 1998, Facts on File $19.95 (0-8160-3603-9). The story of the gallant Native American servicemen who developed a unique, unbreakable code based on the Navajos' complex, inflection-sensitive language, and transmitted and translated more than 800 messages in 48 hours without error during the battle of Iwo Jima. (Rev: BL 11/1/98; SLJ 1/99) [940.54 8673]

8286 Dvorson, Alexa. *The Hitler Youth: Marching toward Madness* (5–9). Illus. (Teen Witnesses to the Holocaust) 1999, Rosen LB $17.95 (0-8239-2783-0). This volume describes how hundreds of thousands of German boys and girls joined the Hitler Youth, why they were seduced into obeying the Nazis, and how their dreams were eventually shattered. (Rev: BL 4/15/99; BR 9–10/99) [943.086]

8287 Edvardson, Cordelia. *Burned Child Seeks the Fire: A Memoir* (10–12). Trans. from German by Joel Agee. 1997, Beacon $28.95 (0-8070-7094-7). The memoir of a girl who was raised as a Catholic but because she is discovered to be part Jewish, is sent to Auschwitz, where she miraculously survived. (Rev: BL 7/97; SLJ 12/97) [940.54]

8288 Fisch, Robert O. *Light from the Yellow Star: A Lesson of Love from the Holocaust* (7–12). Illus. 1996, Univ. of Minnesota Pr. $14.95 (1-885116-00-4); paper $9.95 (0-9644896-0-0). A biographical account that uses the author's abstract paintings to tell about his childhood in Budapest and his Holocaust death camp experiences. (Rev: BL 4/15/96) [940.53]

8289 Fox, Anne L., and Eva Abraham-Podietz. *Ten Thousand Children: True Stories Told by Children Who Escaped the Holocaust on the Kindertransport* (5–8). 1998, Behrman paper $12.95 (0-87441-648-5). Between December 1938 and September 1939, 10,000 Jewish children left Germany via the Kindertransport. This describes the massive rescue operation and its aftermath as told by 21 survivors. (Rev: BL 1/1–15/99) [940.53]

8290 Freeman, Charles. *The Rise of the Nazis* (7–12). (New Perspectives) 1998, Raintree Steck-Vaughn $27.11 (0-8172-5015-8). The differing views on Hitler and the Nazi Party as expressed by German politicians, leaders, and ordinary citizens. (Rev: BL 3/15/98; BR 1–2/99; SLJ 7/98) [940.54]

8291 Fremon, David K. *The Holocaust Heroes* (6–10). (Holocaust Remembered) 1998, Enslow LB $19.95 (0-7660-1046-5). This account of the Holocaust focuses on Resistance fighters, such as the people of the Warsaw Ghetto, and people like Raoul Wallenberg and the Danish nation who took risks to help Jews escape. (Rev: BL 9/15/98; BR 1–2/99; SLJ 12/98) [940.5318]

8292 Gay, Kathlyn, and Martin Gay. *World War II* (5–8). (Voices for the Past) 1995, Twenty-First Century LB $18.90 (0-8050-2849-8). The causes, events, and consequences of this major conflict are presented, along with personal accounts by ordinary people who were there. (Rev: BL 12/15/95; SLJ 2/96) [940.53]

8293 Geier, Arnold. *Heroes of the Holocaust: Extraordinary Accounts of Triumph* (10–12). 1998, Berkley paper $14.00 (0-425-16029-7). A moving collection of accounts by 28 survivors of the Holocaust who survived because of the unselfish acts of others. (Rev: SLJ 7/98) [940.54]

8294 Giddens, Sandra. *Escape: Teens Who Escaped the Holocaust to Freedom* (5–9). (Teen Witnesses to the Holocaust) 1999, Rosen $17.95 (0-8239-2843-8). This volume focuses on the ordeals of 4 Jewish teens who were able to elude and escape the Nazis during the Holocaust. (Rev: BL 4/15/99; BR 9–10/99; VOYA 8/99) [940.54]

8295 Gies, Miep, and Alison L. Gold. *Anne Frank Remembered: The Story of Miep Gies, Who Helped to Hide the Frank Family* (8–12). Illus. 1987, Simon & Schuster paper $13.00 (0-671-66234-1). The story of the woman who helped the Frank family during World War II and of the Resistance movement in the Netherlands. (Rev: BL 4/1/87; SLJ 11/87; VOYA 12/87) [940.53]

8296 Gilbert, Martin. *The Day the War Ended: May 8, 1945—Victory in Europe* (9–12). 1995, Holt $30.00 (0-8050-3926-0). In commemoration of the 50th anniversary of the end of World War II. Chronicles events leading up to and following the war in Europe. (Rev: BL 4/15/95) [940.54]

8297 Goldstein, Donald M., and Katherine V. Dillon. *Rain of Ruin: A Photographic History of Hiroshima and Nagasaki* (9–12). 1995, Brassey's $31.95 (1-57488-033-0). More than 400 black-and-white photos accompanied by text that generally supports the bombing of Hiroshima and Nagasaki. (Rev: BL 8/95) [940.54]

8298 Grant, R. G. *Hiroshima and Nagasaki* (7–12). Illus. (New Perspectives) 1998, Raintree Steck-Vaughn $27.12 (0-8172-5013-1). This account of the dropping of atomic bombs on Japan examines the different viewpoints of the scientists, politicians, and air crews involved, and the people who survived it. (Rev: BL 3/15/98; BR 1–2/99) [940.54]

8299 Grant, R. G. *The Holocaust* (7–12). (New Perspectives) 1998, Raintree Steck-Vaughn $27.11 (0-8172-5016-6). The story of the Holocaust, one of history's darkest moments, as shaped by the German perpetrators, witnessed by onlookers, and recalled by survivors. (Rev: BL 3/15/98; BR 1–2/99; SLJ 7/98) [940.54]

8300 Greenfeld, Howard. *The Hidden Children* (5–10). 1993, Ticknor $15.95 (0-395-66074-2). This account of what it was like to be a Jewish child hiding from the Nazis in World War II includes painful personal narratives of survivors. (Rev: BL 1/1/94*; SLJ 5/94*; VOYA 6/94) [940.53]

8301 Gruhzit-Hoyt, Olga. *They Also Served: American Women in World War II* (9–12). 1995, Birch Lane $19.95 (1-55972-280-0). Short profiles of women who served in World War II. (Rev: BL 5/1/95) [940.54]

8302 Handler, Andrew, and Susan V. Meschel, eds. *Young People Speak: Surviving the Holocaust in Hungary* (7–12). 1993, Watts LB $24.00 (0-531-11044-3). Memoirs of 11 Holocaust survivors who were children in Hungary during the Nazi occupation at the end of World War II. (Rev: BL 6/1–15/93; SLJ 7/93; VOYA 10/93) [940.53]

8303 Hanmer, Trudy J. *Leningrad* (6–12). (Cities at War) 1992, Macmillan $18.00 (0-02-742615-7). The story of the city of Leningrad during World War II and the terrible siege that destroyed a large percentage of the city and its inhabitants. (Rev: BL 10/15/92) [947]

8304 Hargrove, Hondon. *Buffalo Soldiers in Italy: Black Americans in World War II* (8–12). 1985, McFarland LB $35.00 (0-89950-116-8). A history of the last all-black U.S. army division and its record during World War II. (Rev: BR 9–10/85) [940.53]

8305 Harris, Jacqueline L. *The Tuskegee Airmen: Black Heroes of World War II* (6–9). Illus. 1996, Dillon $22.00 (0-382-39215-9); paper $7.95 (0-382-39217-5). The story of how black fliers in the service fought prejudice and eventually formed the extraordinary all-black Fighter Squadron during World War II. (Rev: BL 9/1/96; SLJ 9/96) [940.54]

8306 Hastings, Max. *Overlord: D-Day and the Battle for Normandy* (10–12). 1985, Simon & Schuster paper $13.00 (0-671-55435-2). A history of the events surrounding the Allied landings in Normandy during World War II. [940.53]

8307 Hastings, Max. *Victory in Europe: D-Day to V-E Day* (9–12). Illus. 1985, Little, Brown $25.00 (0-316-81334-6). Stills from a film by George Stevens are used to illustrate this account of the war in Europe after the Normandy invasions. (Rev: BL 6/15/85) [940.542]

8308 Heyes, Eileen. *Children of the Swastika: The Hitler Youth* (7–12). 1993, Millbrook LB $22.40 (1-56294-237-9). A study of the Hitler Youth's structure, purpose, impact on the war effort, and effects on the youth. (Rev: BL 2/15/93) [324.243]

8309 Hillesum, Etty. *Etty Hillesum: An Interrupted Life and Letters from Westerbork* (10–12). Trans. from Dutch by Arnold J. Pomerans. 1996, Holt $27.50 (0-8050-4894-4). This inspiring book contains the diaries and letters of a Jewish woman who died in her mid-20s in the Holocaust. (Rev: SLJ 4/97) [940.54]

8310 Hills, C. A. R. *The Second World War* (7–12). Illus. 1986, David & Charles $19.95 (0-7134-4531-9). A brief but comprehensive history of World War II as seen through the eyes of its leaders. (Rev: SLJ 11/86) [940.53]

8311 Holliday, Laurel. *Children in the Holocaust and World War II* (9–12). 1995, Pocket Books $20.00 (0-671-52054-7). Excerpts from 23 World War II diaries provide glimpses into the lives and thoughts of teenagers. (Rev: SLJ 9/95) [940.53]

8312 Hoyt, Edwin. *McCampbell's Heroes* (9–12). 1984, Avon paper $3.95 (0-380-68841-7). The story of the U.S. Navy's carrier fighters and their role in the Pacific area during World War II. Also use *Blue Skies and Blood: The Battle of the Coral Sea* (1989). [940.53]

8313 Ippisch, Hanneke. *Sky: A True Story of Resistance During World War II* (6–10). Illus. 1996, Simon & Schuster paper $17.00 (0-689-80508-X). An autobiographical account by the author who, as a teenage girl in 1943, joined the Dutch underground resistance movement and, after participating in many dangerous missions against the Nazis, was caught by the Germans and sent to prison. (Rev: BL 4/15/96; BR 1–2/97; SLJ 6/96; VOYA 8/96) [940.53]

8314 Isserman, Maurice. *World War II* (7–12). (America at War) 1991, Facts on File $19.95 (0-8160-2374-3). The major battles and personalities of World War II, events leading to war, and discussion of changes following the conflict. (Rev: BL 10/15/91; SLJ 8/92) [940.53]

8315 Jones, Catherine. *Navajo Code Talkers: Native American Heroes* (6–10). 1998, Tudor $13.95 (0-936389-51-6); paper $22.01 (0-936389-52-4). This is the story of the Navajo Code Talkers of the Marine Corps who, during World War II in the Pacific, used their secret language to communicate using a code that neither the Japanese or Americans could decipher. (Rev: SLJ 4/98) [940.54]

8316 Kimmett, Larry, and Margaret Regis. *The Attack on Pearl Harbor: An Illustrated History* (9–12). 1991, Navigator Publg. paper $15.95 (1-879932-00-8). An overview of the infamous attack, pieced together by numerous photos and maps of various targets. (Rev: BL 1/15/92) [940.54]

8317 Kodama, Tatsuharu. *Shin's Tricycle* (5–8). Trans. by Kazuko Hokumen-Jones. Illus. 1995, Walker LB $16.85 (0-8027-8376-7). The title stems from the tricycle the author's son wanted so badly and finally was able to acquire in spite of the wartime shortage of metal. The atom bomb exploded while his son was riding the tricycle. (Rev: BL 9/1/95*; SLJ 12/95) [940.54]

8318 Kopf, Hedda Rosner. *Understanding Anne Frank's The Diary of a Young Girl: A Student Casebook to Issues, Sources, and Historical Documents* (7–12). 1997, Greenwood $39.95 (0-313-29607-3). In addition to examining Anne Frank's diary as literature, this collection of materials supplies great amounts of background information on the Holocaust, anti-Semitism, the Frank family, and World War II. (Rev: SLJ 3/98) [940.54]

8319 Kronenwetter, Michael. *London* (6–12). (Cities at War) 1992, Macmillan $14.95 (0-02-751050-6). Photoessay on the lives of ordinary people in London during World War II, with eyewitness quotes. (Rev: BL 6/15/92; SLJ 9/92) [942.1084]

8320 Kustanowitz, Esther. *The Hidden Children of the Holocaust: Teens Who Hid from the Nazis* (5–8). 1999, Rosen $26.95 (0-8239-2562-5). Many first-person narratives are used in this account of teenage Jews who hid in homes, barns, and in the woods, and others who disguised themselves as non-Jews to escape the Nazis. (Rev: BL 7/99; SLJ 8/99) [940.54]

8321 Lace, William W. *The Death Camps* (10–12). (The Holocaust Library) 1997, Lucent LB $17.96 (1-56006-094-8). The story of the concentration camps that were specifically designed to murder Jews and other "undesirables" that were sent there. (Rev: BL 3/15/98; SLJ 5/98) [940.54]

8322 Lace, William W. *The Nazis* (10–12). Illus. (The Holocaust Library) 1997, Lucent LB $17.96 (1-56006-091-3). One of a planned 7-volume Holocaust Library series, this volume traces the Nazi movement and its relationship to the Holocaust and the killings based solely on racial hatred. (Rev: BL 10/1/97; SLJ 2/98) [943.086]

8323 Landau, Elaine. *The Warsaw Ghetto Uprising* (7–10). 1992, Macmillan LB $19.00 (0-02-751392-0). Recounts the horrors of the month-long battles between Nazis and Jews in 1943 Poland. (Rev: BL 2/15/93) [940.53]

8324 Landau, Elaine. *We Survived the Holocaust* (7–10). 1991, Watts LB $24.00 (0-531-11115-6). A series of personal accounts of survivors who were children during World War II that presents a picture of ethnic and religious persecution and courageous endurance. (Rev: BL 9/15/91; SLJ 10/91) [940.53]

8325 Lawson, Don. *The French Resistance* (7–10). 1984, Messner LB $8.00 (0-671-50832-6). The story of the many gallant French men and women who defied death to oppose the German forces that occupied their country. [940.53]

8326 Leapman, Michael. *Witnesses to War: Eight True-Life Stories of Nazi Persecution* (8–12). Illus. 1998, Viking $16.99 (0-670-87386-1). Eight case histories of children who suffered at the hands of the Nazis, some by being selected for "Germanization" and others who survived death camps and Nazi massacres. (Rev: BL 10/1/98; SLJ 11/98; VOYA 12/98) [940.53]

8327 Lee, Loyd E. *World War II* (9–12). (Guides to Historic Events of the Twentieth Century) 1999, Greenwood $39.95 (0-313-29998-6). This information-packed book covers the war from the rise of Hitler to its end in 1945, with additional material on its continuing significance and influence on international relations and a section containing 17 original-source documents. (Rev: BL 5/99; SLJ 7/99; VOYA 10/99) [940.54]

8328 Lewin, Rhoda G., ed. *Witness to the Holocaust: An Oral History* (9–12). 1990, Twayne $20.95 (0-8057-9100-0). In over 50 interviews, the stories of survivors of death camps, survivors who did not go to death camps, and American liberators are told. (Rev: BR 5–6/90; SLJ 8/90; VOYA 6/90) [940.53]

8329 Lifton, Betty Jean. *A Place Called Hiroshima* (9–12). Illus. 1985, Kodansha $24.95 (0-87011-649-5). In this album of text and photos, the author tells what has happened to Hiroshima and the survivors of the atomic attack 40 years after. (Rev: BL 10/1/85; SLJ 11/85) [940.54]

8330 Lobel, Anita. *No Pretty Pictures: A Child of War* (6–12). 1998, Greenwillow $16.00 (0-688-15935-4). The author, today a successful illustrator, tells the gripping story of her childhood during World War II in Poland—five years in hiding beginning at the age of 5, then her capture and transport, with her younger brother disguised as a girl, to a concentration camp. (Rev: BL 8/98; SLJ 9/98; VOYA 2/99) [940.53 18 092 B]

8331 Lord, Walter. *Day of Infamy* (8–12). Illus. 1998, NTC paper $12.99 (1-85326-670-1). An hour-by-hour re-creation of the attack on Pearl Harbor with extensive background information. [940.54]

8332 McGowen, Tom. *Germany's Lightning War: Panzer Divisions of World War II* (5–8). (Military Might) 1999, Twenty-First Century LB $23.90 (0-7613-1511-X). This book begins with a discussion of tank warfare in World War I, then focuses on their use by the Germans during World War II in the panzer units. (Rev: SLJ 9/99) [940.54]

8333 McGowen, Tom. *Sink the Bismarck: Germany's Super-Battleship of World War II* (5–8). 1999, Twenty-First Century LB $23.90 (0-7613-1510-1). The story of Britain's attempts to find and sink the German battleship *Bismarck* during World War II, and of their final success. (Rev: SLJ 9/99) [940.54]

8334 McKissack, Patricia, and Fredrick McKissack. *Red-Tail Angels: The Story of the Tuskegee Airmen of World War II* (6–8). Illus. 1995, Walker LB $20.85 (0-8027-8293-0). A carefully researched account of the formation and training of the 332nd Fighter Group of black military aviators and their exploits during World War II in the North African and European theaters of war. (Rev: BL 2/15/96*; SLJ 2/96; VOYA 4/96) [940.54]

8335 Maddox, Robert James. *Weapons for Victory: The Hiroshima Decision Fifty Years Later* (9–12). 1995, Univ. of Missouri Pr. $19.95 (0-8262-1037-6). The author argues that President Truman dropped the bomb to end the war, contrary to arguments made by revisionist historians. (Rev: BL 8/95) [940.54]

8336 Maruki, Toshi. *Hiroshima No Pika* (7–10). Illus. 1982, Lothrop $16.00 (0-688-01297-3). One family's experiences during the day the bomb dropped on Hiroshima told in text and moving illustrations by the author. (Rev: BL 3/87) [940.54]

8337 Marx, Trish. *Echoes of World War II* (5–8). 1994, Lerner LB $19.95 (0-8225-4898-4). The stories of 6 children from various backgrounds whose lives were drastically altered by the war. Maps and documents help depict the agonies of each. (Rev: BL 9/15/94; SLJ 5/94) [940.53]

8338 Meltzer, Milton. *Never to Forget: The Jews of the Holocaust* (8–12). 1976, HarperCollins LB $15.89 (0-06-024175-6). A history of the murder of 6 million Jews and of anti-Semitism. [940.54]

8339 Meltzer, Milton. *Rescue: The Story of How Gentiles Saved Jews in the Holocaust* (6–9). 1988, HarperCollins LB $16.89 (0-06-024210-8); paper $7.95 (0-06-446117-3). The uplifting story of those courageous few who helped save Jews from Nazi death camps. (Rev: BL 10/1/88; BR 1–2/89; SLJ 8/88; VOYA 8/88) [940.53]

8340 Meyers, Odette. *Doors to Madame Marie* (10–12). 1997, Univ. of Washington Pr. $24.95 (0-

295-97576-8). A deeply moving memoir of a Jewish girl in wartime France who was sent to live in the countryside, pretending to be Catholic for safety's sake, and returns to visit years later. (Rev: SLJ 12/97) [940.54]

8341 Miller, Nathan. *War at Sea: A Naval History of World War II* (9–12). 1995, Scribners $32.50 (0-684-80380-1). Miller, the author of 4 previous volumes of popular naval history, presents this history of naval power in an informal style. (Rev: BL 9/1/95) [940.54]

8342 Milman, Barbara. *Light in the Shadows* (5–9). Illus. 1997, Jonathan David paper $14.95 (0-8246-0401-6). Illustrated with powerful woodcut prints, this book tells the story of 5 Holocaust survivors. (Rev: BL 11/15/97) [940.53]

8343 Mitcham, Samuel W., Jr. *Rommel's Greatest Victory: The Desert Fox and the Fall of Tobruk, Spring 1942* (10–12). 1998, Presidio Pr. $27.95 (0-89141-656-0). A readable narrative, combined with firsthand accounts, about the amazing successes of General Erwin Rommel's efforts in World War II to drive the British out of the Sahara and back to Egypt, allowing the Germans to keep their toehold in Africa for another year and preventing the Allies from using the troops on another front. (Rev: SLJ 2/99) [940.54]

8344 Newman, Amy. *The Nuremburg Laws* (7–12). Illus. (Words That Changed History) 1998, Lucent LB $22.45 (1-56006-354-8). An overview of the Holocaust, including the roots and growth of Nazism and the war against the Jews, and a discussion of contemporary ethnic violence, laws that promote bigotry, and the power of words. (Rev: BL 4/15/99; SLJ 9/99) [342.43]

8345 Newton, David E. *Tokyo* (6–12). (Cities at War) 1992, Macmillan LB $14.95 (0-02-768235-8). Remembrances from people who experienced World War II in Tokyo. (Rev: BL 10/15/92; SLJ 1/93) [952]

8346 Nicholson, Dorinda M. *Pearl Harbor Child: A Child's View of Pearl Harbor—from Attack to Peace* (5–8). 1998, Woodson House paper $9.95 (1-892858-00-2). This photoessay describes a child's experience during the Japanese bombing, the temporary evacuation, and everyday life growing up in Hawaii during World War II. (Rev: BL 1/1–15/99) [996.9]

8347 Nieuwsma, Milton J., ed. *Kinderlager: An Oral History of Young Holocaust Survivors* (9–12). Illus. 1998, Holiday House $18.95 (0-8234-1358-6). This book contains the memoirs of three Jewish American women who, as children growing up in Poland, were sent to the children's section of the Auschwitz death camp. (Rev: BL 11/1/98; SLJ 12/98; VOYA 12/98) [940.53 18 0922438]

8348 Nir, Yehuda. *The Lost Childhood* (9–12). 1989, Harcourt $19.95 (0-15-158862-7). How 3 Polish Jews—a mother and 2 children—managed by their wits to elude their Nazi pursuers. (Rev: BL 9/1/89) [940.53]

8349 Oleksy, Walter. *Military Leaders of World War II* (7–10). (American Profiles) 1994, Facts on File $19.95 (0-8160-3008-1). Profiles of 10 American World War II leaders, including Claire Lee Chennault, Douglas MacArthur, Chester Nimitz, Jacqueline Cochran, Curtis LeMay, and George Patton. (Rev: BL 1/1/95; SLJ 3/95; VOYA 5/95) [940.54]

8350 O'Neill, William L. *World War II: A Student Companion* (9–12). (Oxford Student Companion to American History) 1999, Oxford $64.00 (0-19-510800-0). An alphabetically arranged series of articles covering all aspects of World War II, illustrated with photos, maps, and reproductions. (Rev: BL 7/99; BR 9–10/99; SLJ 7/99) [940.54]

8351 Opdyke, Irene Gut, and Jennifer Armstrong. *In My Hands: Memories of a Holocaust Rescuer* (9–12). 1999, Knopf LB $19.99 (0-679-99181-6). A first-person narrative of a Polish teenager recounting her experiences during the war, including rape by Russian soldiers and her increasing involvement in rescuing Jews, including passing information, smuggling Jews from a work camp into the forest, and hiding 10 Jewish men and women in the basement of the Nazi major for whom she worked. (Rev: BL 6/1–15/99; SLJ 6/99; VOYA 10/99) [940.53]

8352 Perl, Lila, and Marion B. Lazan. *Four Perfect Pebbles: A Holocaust Story* (5–9). Illus. 1996, Greenwillow $15.00 (0-688-14294-X). A memoir of the horror and incredible tribulations suffered by the author's family in the detention camps and later death camps during the Holocaust. (Rev: BL 4/1/96; BR 9–10/96; SLJ 5/96) [940.53]

8353 Pettit, Jayne. *A Time to Fight Back: True Stories of Wartime Resistance* (5–8). 1996, Houghton $14.95 (0-395-76504-8). Eight true stories about courageous acts involving young people during World War II. (Rev: BL 4/1/96; BR 11–12/96; SLJ 4/96; VOYA 6/96) [940.53]

8354 Pfeifer, Kathryn B. *The 761st Tank Battalion* (5–8). (African American Soldiers) 1994, Twenty-First Century LB $17.90 (0-8050-3057-3). The history of an outfit of African American soldiers who served with distinction during World War II but were marginalized by racism. (Rev: BL 9/1/94; SLJ 11/94) [940.54]

8355 Prange, Gordon W., et al. *December 7, 1941: The Day the Japanese Attacked Pearl Harbor* (9–12). 1987, Warner paper $21.99 (0-446-38997-8). A re-creation of the attack on Pearl Harbor with much material from eyewitness sources. (Rev: BL 10/15/87) [940.54]

8356 Prefer, Lathan N. *Patton's Ghost Corps: Cracking the Siegfried Line* (10–12). Illus. 1998, Presidio Pr. $24.95 (0-89141-646-3). This is the account of a little-known World War II campaign during 1945 in which General George S. Patton led an attack on the German Siegfried Line during blinding snow storms. (Rev: SLJ 7/98) [940.54]

8357 Rabinovici, Schoschana. *Thanks to My Mother* (8–12). Trans. from German by James Skofield. 1998, Dial $17.99 (0-8037-2235-4). A harrowing memoir on how the Holocaust destroyed this Lithuanian author's large, extended Jewish family, and how she and her mother were able to survive. (Rev: BR 11–12/98; SLJ 4/98; VOYA 4/98) [940.54]

8358 Reader's Digest, eds. *The World at Arms: The Reader's Digest Illustrated History of World War II* (9–12). Illus. 1989, Reader's Digest $29.95 (0-89577-333-3). An attractively organized and well-illustrated history of World War II. (Rev: BL 9/1/89; BR 1–2/90) [940.53]

8359 Rice, Earle, Jr. *The Attack on Pearl Harbor* (6–10). Illus. (Battles of World War II) 1997, Lucent LB $21.96 (1-56006-421-8). This dramatic recreation of the Japanese sneak attack on Pearl Harbor contains many eyewitness accounts. (Rev: BL 12/15/96; BR 11–12/97; SLJ 2/97) [940.54]

8360 Rice, Earle, Jr. *The Battle of Britain* (6–10). Illus. (Great Battles in History) 1996, Lucent LB $19.95 (1-56006-414-3). This account of the air battle in the skies over Britain during 1940 quotes many primary sources and uses extensive illustrations. (Rev: BL 4/15/96; BR 9–10/96) [940.54]

8361 Rice, Earle, Jr. *The Battle of Midway* (7–10). (Battles) 1996, Lucent LB $21.96 (1-56006-415-3). This exciting narrative tells of the defeat of the Japanese navy at the Battle of Midway and how this marked the beginning of the end of the war against Japan. (Rev: BL 4/15/96; BR 9–10/96; SLJ 2/96) [940.54]

8362 Rice, Earle, Jr. *The Final Solution* (10–12). Illus. (Holocaust Library) 1997, Lucent LB $18.96 (1-56006-095-6). This volume in the series tells of Hitler's plan to annihilate the Jews of Europe and how it was devised and implemented. (Rev: BL 10/1/97; SLJ 9/97) [940.53]

8363 Rice, Earle, Jr. *Nazi War Criminals* (10–12). Illus. (Holocaust Library) 1997, Lucent LB $18.96 (1-56006-097-2). This book profiles 6 of the most vicious perpetrators of the Holocaust: Heinrich Himmler, Julius Streicher, Reinhard Heydrich, Adolf Eichmann, Rudolf Hess, and Josef Mengele. (Rev: BL 10/1/97; SLJ 2/98) [341.6]

8364 Rice, Earle, Jr. *The Nuremberg Trials* (6–10). Illus. (Famous Trials) 1996, Lucent LB $17.96 (1-56006-269-X). Beginning with an account of the Nazi atrocities during World War II, this book describes the trials of the war criminals during 1945–46, the background of the accused, and their

fate. (Rev: BL 3/15/97; BR 11–12/97; SLJ 3/97) [341.6]

8365 Rogasky, Barbara. *Smoke and Ashes: The Story of the Holocaust* (6–12). Illus. 1988, Holiday House $19.95 (0-8234-0697-0). The incredible story of the Holocaust from the first rumblings of anti-Semitism in Nazi Germany to the liberation of the death camps. (Rev: BL 6/15/88; SLJ 6/88; VOYA 12/88) [940.53]

8366 Rogers, James T. *The Secret War* (8–12). (World Espionage) 1991, Facts on File LB $16.95 (0-8160-2395-6). A well-supported thesis stating that the British and Americans were more successful at espionage, counterespionage, and detection than either the Germans or the Japanese. (Rev: BL 3/1/92; SLJ 5/92) [940.54]

8367 Rosenberg, Maxine R. *Hiding to Survive: Stories of Jewish Children Rescued from the Holocaust* (5–10). Illus. 1994, Clarion $16.00 (0-395-65014-3). This book contains 14 first-person accounts by survivors of the Holocaust who, as children, were hidden from the Nazis during World War II. (Rev: BL 6/1–15/94; SLJ 10/94; VOYA 10/94) [940.53]

8368 Ross, Bill D. *Iwo Jima: Legacy of Valor* (9–12). Illus. 1985, Random paper $15.00 (0-394-74288-5). A day-by-day account of the 1945 battle in the Pacific against the Japanese by the Marine Corps. [940.54]

8369 Ross, Stewart. *World War II* (7–12). (Causes and Consequences) 1995, Raintree Steck-Vaughn LB $27.11 (0-8172-4050-0). This book identifies the factors that led to the outbreak of World War II and discusses its outcome, using eyewitness documents. (Rev: BL 12/15/95) [940.53]

8370 Roubickova, Eva M. *We're Alive and Life Goes On: A Theresienstadt Diary* (8–12). Trans. by Zaia Alexander. 1997, Holt $16.95 (0-8050-5352-2). This is a translation of a diary kept by a young Jewish woman during her 4 years in a Nazi concentration camp. (Rev: BL 11/1/97; BR 5–6/98; SLJ 2/98) [940.53]

8371 Sherrow, Victoria. *Amsterdam* (6–12). (Cities at War) 1992, Macmillan LB $14.95 (0-02-782465-9). Photoessay on the lives of ordinary people in Amsterdam during World War II, with quotes by eyewitnesses. (Rev: BL 6/15/92; SLJ 9/92) [940.53]

8372 Sherrow, Victoria. *The Blaze Engulfs: January 1939 to December 1941* (6–12). Illus. (Holocaust) 1997, Blackbirch LB $19.45 (1-56711-202-1). This account, book 3 of the Holocaust series, describes the first 2 years of World War II, when Hitler's racial programs were being put into place. (Rev: BL 10/15/97; BR 1–2/98; SLJ 2/98) [940.53]

8373 Sherrow, Victoria. *Hiroshima* (6–12). 1994, Silver Burdett LB $18.95 (0-02-782467-5). Chronicles the birth of the atomic age, concluding with graphic descriptions of the World War II bombing of Hiroshima. (Rev: BL 10/1/94; SLJ 11/94) [940.54]

8374 Sherrow, Victoria. *The Righteous Gentiles* (10–12). (The Holocaust Library) 1997, Lucent LB $17.96 (1-56006-093-X). The uplifting story of gentiles who braved death to help the Jews and others escape the Holocaust. (Rev: BL 3/15/98; SLJ 7/98) [940.54]

8375 Sherrow, Victoria. *Smoke to Flame: September 1935 to December 1938* (6–12). Illus. (Holocaust) 1997, Blackbirch LB $19.45 (1-56711-201-3). This volume covers the growing anti-Semitism of Hitler's first years in power until the beginning of World War II, by which time his war against "undesirables" was gaining momentum. (Rev: BL 10/15/97; SLJ 2/98) [940.53]

8376 Shohei, Ooka. *Taken Captive* (10–12). Trans. by Wayne P. Lammers. 1996, Wiley $27.95 (0-471-14285-9). The story of a Japanese soldier who was drafted into the army in 1944 and spent most of the remaining part of the war as a prisoner of the Americans. (Rev: BL 5/15/96; SLJ 2/97) [940.54]

8377 Shulman, William L., ed. *Resource Guide: A Comprehensive Listing of Media for Further Study* (6–12). Illus. 1997, Blackbirch LB $19.45 (1-56711-208-0). This eighth and last volume of the Holocaust series is a guide to other sources on the subject including CD-ROMS, books, videos, museums, and other resource centers. (Rev: BL 10/15/97; BR 1–2/98; SLJ 2/98) [940.53]

8378 Shulman, William L., ed. *Voices and Visions: A Collection of Primary Sources* (6–12). Illus. (Holocaust) 1997, Blackbirch LB $19.45 (1-56711-207-2). This seventh book of the Holocaust series contains primary sources, including eyewitness accounts, of the Holocaust and its many targets. (Rev: BL 10/15/97; BR 1–2/98; SLJ 2/98) [940.53]

8379 Shuter, Jane, ed. *Christabel Bielenberg and Nazi Germany* (5–8). Illus. (History Eyewitness) 1996, Raintree Steck-Vaughn LB $24.26 (0-8114-8285-5). Using a first-person narrative as a framework, this account traces the growth, flowering, and defeat of Nazism in Germany. (Rev: BL 5/15/96; SLJ 6/96) [943.086]

8380 Spiegelman, Art. *Maus: A Survivor's Tale II: And Here My Troubles Began* (9–12). 1991, Pantheon $23.00 (0-394-55655-0). Using a unique comic-strip-as-graphic-art format, the story of Vladek Spiegelman's passage through the Nazi Holocaust is told in his own words. (Rev: BL 10/15/91) [940.53]

8381 Stalcup, Ann. *On the Home Front: Growing up in Wartime England* (6–10). Illus. 1998, Shoe String LB $19.50 (0-208-02482-4). A vivid first-person account about growing up in a small English town in Shropshire during World War II. (Rev: BL 10/15/98; BR 11–12/98; SLJ 7/98) [940.54]

8382 Steidl, Franz. *Lost Battalions: Going for Broke in the Vosges Autumn 1944* (10–12). 1997, Presidio Pr. $21.95 (0-89141-622-6). The story of the famous 1944 World War II battle in which Japanese American soldiers distinguished themselves for bravery. (Rev: SLJ 9/97) [940.54]

8383 Steins, Richard. *The Allies Against the Axis: World War II (1940–1950)* (5–8). (First Person America) 1994, Twenty-First Century LB $18.90 (0-8050-2586-3). An introduction to World War II that includes excerpts from primary sources. (Rev: BL 5/15/94; SLJ 12/94) [940.53]

8384 Stewart, Gail B. *Hitler's Reich* (8–12). (World History) 1994, Lucent LB $17.96 (1-56006-235-5). An in-depth examination of Adolf Hitler, top-ranking accomplices, and the structure of Nazi Germany. (Rev: BL 12/15/93; SLJ 1/94) [943.086]

8385 Stewart, Gail B. *Life in the Warsaw Ghetto* (6–12). (The Way People Live) 1995, Lucent LB $16.95 (1-56006-075-1). An in-depth history of the Warsaw ghetto told by witnesses. (Rev: BL 3/15/95*; SLJ 4/95) [943.8]

8386 Stokesbury, James L. *A Short History of World War II* (9–12). 1980, Morrow paper $13.50 (0-688-08587-3). A concise history of the war with coverage of its causes and immediate aftermath. [940.53]

8387 Strahinich, Helen. *The Holocaust: Understanding and Remembering* (6–10). Illus. (Issues in Focus) 1996, Enslow LB $19.95 (0-89490-725-5). A fully documented account that covers such topics as the roots of anti-Semitism, the rise of Nazism, ghetto life, the roundups, death camps, liberation, and the Nuremberg trials. (Rev: BL 9/15/96; SLJ 10/96; VOYA 10/96) [940.53]

8388 Sullivan, George. *Strange but True Stories of World War II* (7–12). Illus. 1983, Walker $22.95 (0-8027-6489-4). Eleven true stories of bizarre incidents during World War II. [940.53]

8389 Taylor, Theodore. *Battle in the English Channel* (7–10). Illus. 1983, Avon paper $3.50 (0-380-85225-X). The retelling of the exciting World War II incident when Hitler tried to free 3 of his battleships from French waters. [940.54]

8390 Taylor, Theodore. *The Battle Off Midway Island* (7–10). Illus. 1981, Avon paper $3.95 (0-380-78790-3). The story of the brilliant victory of U.S. forces at Midway is excitingly retold. [940.54]

8391 Taylor, Theodore. *H.M.S. Hood vs. Bismarck: The Battleship Battle* (7–10). Illus. 1982, Avon paper $3.95 (0-380-81174-X). The subject of this book is the sinking of the battleship *Bismarck* by the English navy. [940.54]

8392 Ten Boom, Corrie, and John Sherrill. *The Hiding Place* (9–12). 1984, Bantam paper $6.99 (0-553-25669-6). The account of a Dutch girl growing up in Nazi-occupied Holland and her family who helped hide Jewish people. [940.54]

8393 Tito, Tina E. *Liberation: Teens in the Concentration Camps & the Teen Soldiers Who Liberated Them* (5–9). (Teen Witnesses to the Holocaust) 1998, Rosen $17.95 (0-8239-2846-2). A harrowing volume in which 2 teenage survivors of Nazi camps and 2 American soldiers who were also teenagers during World War II tell their respective stories. (Rev: BL 4/15/99; BR 9–10/99; VOYA 8/99) [940.53]

8394 Tregaskis, Richard. *Guadalcanal Diary* (6–9). Illus. 1993, Buccaneer LB $25.95 (1-56849-231-6). This is a simplified version of the adult book that tells of the Marine landing at Guadalcanal in 1942. [940.54]

8395 Tunnell, Michael O., and George W. Chilcoat. *The Children of Topaz: The Story of a Japanese-American Internment Camp Based on a Classroom Diary* (6–10). Illus. 1996, Holiday House $16.95 (0-8234-1239-3). This book consists of 20 excerpts from a classroom diary kept by a third grade Japanese American schoolteacher during her confinement in a desert relocation camp during 1943. (Rev: BL 7/96; SLJ 8/96*; VOYA 12/96) [769.8]

8396 Verhoeven, Rian, and Ruud van der Rol. *Anne Frank: Beyond the Diary: A Photographic Remembrance* (6–12). Trans. by Tony Langham and Plym Peters. 1993, Viking paper $17.00 (0-670-84932-4). Includes photos of people who knew Anne and of the places she lived and hid in, with excerpts from her diary. (Rev: BL 10/1/93*; SLJ 12/93*) [940.53]

8397 Wassiljewa, Tatjana. *Hostage to War: A True Story* (6–10). 1997, Scholastic $15.95 (0-590-13446-9). The World War II diary of a young Russian girl who endured hunger, cold, disease, brutality during the German occupation of Leningrad and then spent years in forced labor camps and factories in Germany. (Rev: BL 4/15/97; SLJ 6/97; VOYA 12/98) [940..54]

8398 Winston, Keith. *Letters from a World War II G.I.* (8–12). Ed. by Judith E. Greenberg and Helen Carey McKeever. 1995, Watts LB $25.00 (0-531-11212-8). A collection of letters home speaking of the hardships of life as a soldier. (Rev: BL 9/15/95; SLJ 9/95; VOYA 12/95) [940.54]

8399 Wright, Mike. *What They Didn't Teach You about World War II* (9–12). Illus. 1998, Presidio Pr. $24.95 (0-89141-649-8). Little-known facts about World War II are presented on such topics as sub-

marines, the home front, prisoners of war, spying, rationing, unusual weapons, and actors, comedians, and professional athletes who served. (Rev: SLJ 7/98) [940.54]

8400 Yamazaki, James N., and Louis B. Fleming. *Children of the Atomic Bomb: An American Physician's Memoir of Nagasaki, Hiroshima, and the Marshall Islands* (9–12). 1995, Duke Univ. Pr. $18.95 (0-8223-1658-7). Yamazaki, a pediatrician and a Nisei, writes this poignant memoir of his journey to Japan for the first time to gather firsthand accounts of the attack on Nagasaki. (Rev: BL 8/95) [618.92]

8401 Yeatts, Tabatha. *The Holocaust Survivors* (6–10). (Holocaust Remembered) 1998, Enslow LB $19.95 (0-89490-993-2). This work concentrates on the liberation of the Nazi death camps, the capture of war criminals, the Nuremberg trials, the founding of Israel, and the lives of individual survivors. (Rev: BL 9/15/98; BR 1–2/99; SLJ 12/98) [940.5318]

8402 Zeinert, Karen. *Those Incredible Women of World War II* (6–9). 1994, Millbrook LB $24.90 (1-56294-434-7). An illustrated account of the contributions made by women during World War II. (Rev: BL 1/15/95; SLJ 2/95) [940.54]

Modern World History (1945–)

8403 Ayer, Eleanor, and Stephen D. Chicoine. *From the Ashes: May 1945 and After* (6–12). Illus. (Holocaust) 1997, Blackbirch LB $19.45 (1-56711-206-4). This account of the Holocaust covers the end of the war, its aftermath, the war crimes trials, and the stories of death camp survivors. (Rev: BL 10/15/97; BR 1–2/98; SLJ 2/98) [940.53]

8404 Fisher, Trevor. *The 1960s* (8–12). Illus. 1989, David & Charles $19.95 (0-7134-5603-5). Under a broad subject arrangement, the major news stories and trends of the 1960s are chronicled. (Rev: SLJ 5/89) [973.92]

8405 Kort, Michael G. *The Cold War* (7–12). 1994, Millbrook LB $23.90 (1-56294-353-7). A suspenseful account of battle-by-battle events of the Cold War, interweaving what we knew then with what we had learned by 1994. (Rev: BL 4/15/94; SLJ 3/94; VOYA 6/94) [909.82]

8406 Parker, Thomas. *Day by Day: The Sixties* (9–12). Illus. 1983, Facts on File $125.00 (0-87196-648-4). Using a day-by-day chronology, this book, like others in the series, traces the events of a decade, in this case the 1960s. [909.82]

Geographical Regions

Africa

General and Miscellaneous

8407   Ayo, Yvonne. *Africa* (5–8). (Eyewitness Books) 1995, Knopf LB $20.99 (0-679-97334-6). This introduces the continent of Africa, with its amazing diversity of people, places, wildlife, and cultures. (Rev: BL 12/15/95; SLJ 1/96) [960]

8408   Baroin, Catherine. *Tubu: The Teda and the Daza* (7–12). Illus. (Heritage Library of African Peoples) 1997, Rosen LB $15.95 (0-8239-2000-3). This book contains a history and details of the present-day culture and politics of these peoples of Chad, Libya, Niger, and the Sudan. (Rev: BL 4/15/97) [967.43]

8409   Bessire, Aimee, and Mark Bessire. *Sukuma* (5–8). (Heritage Library of African Peoples) 1997, Rosen LB $16.95 (0-8239-1992-7). Describes the history, culture, leaders, customs, and present situation of the Sukuma people of Tanzania. (Rev: BL 9/15/97; VOYA 12/97) [967.6]

8410   Buettner, Dan. *Africatrek: A Journey by Bicycle Through Africa* (5–9). Illus. 1997, Lerner LB $23.93 (0-8225-2951-3). The thrilling story of a 262-day, 11,855-mile bicycle journey through 14 African countries, from Tunisia to the southern most tip of Africa, by the author and a group of white and black bicyclists, organized to set a record and to prove that blacks and whites could work as a team. (Rev: BL 9/15/97; SLJ 8/97; VOYA 4/98) [916.04]

8411   Davidson, Basil. *The African Slave Trade*. Rev. ed. (10–12). Illus. 1988, Little, Brown paper $15.95 (0-316-17438-6). This account gives details on the four centuries of the African slave trade, during which millions of people were cruelly forced to leave their homes. (Rev: BL 9/86) [967]

8412   Davidson, Basil. *The Lost Cities of Africa*. Rev. ed. (10–12). Illus. 1988, Little, Brown paper $16.95 (0-316-17431-9). This volume attempts to reconstruct the history and culture of Africa below the Sahara before the arrival of Europeans. [960]

8413   Davidson, Basil. *The Search for Africa: History, Culture, Politics* (9–12). 1993, Times Bks. $25.00 (0-8129-2278-6). Twenty wide-ranging essays that introduce major issues of African history, culture, politics, and economics. (Rev: BL 2/15/94) [967]

8414   Dostert, Pierre Etienne. *Africa* (9–12). Illus. 1996, Stryker-Post paper $11.50 (0-943448-96-4). This annual publication supplies background information on the history, economy, and culture of each of the countries in Africa. [960]

8415   Jones, Constance. *A Short History of Africa: 1500–1900* (8–12). 1993, Facts on File $17.95 (0-8160-2774-9). Jones describes the Islamic cultures of North Africa, the city-states and kingdoms of East Africa, the rich traditions of West Africa, and the roots of apartheid in South Africa. (Rev: BL 3/1/93; SLJ 10/93) [960]

8416   Martell, Hazel M. *Exploring Africa* (4–8). Illus. (Voyages of Discovery) 1998, Bedrick $18.95 (0-87226-490-4). A cursory introduction, using double-page spreads, maps, and illustrations, to the history and geography of Africa, including an overview of early trade, European exploration and colonization, and African independence movements. (Rev: SLJ 4/98) [960]

8417   Minks, Louise. *Traditional Africa* (6–10). (World History) 1996, Lucent LB $17.96 (1-56006-239-8). This book traces African history south of the Sahara before colonialism and tells of the great African kingdoms and societies, their governments, literature, religion, and art. (Rev: SLJ 5/96) [960]

8418 Murray, Jocelyn, ed. *Cultural Atlas of Africa* (9–12). Illus. 1981, Facts on File $45.00 (0-87196-558-5). With hundreds of maps and illustrations plus text, such topics as language, religion, culture, and education are covered for each country. (Rev: BL 9/86) [960]

8419 Reader, John. *Africa: A Biography of the Continent* (10–12). 1998, Knopf $45.00 (0-679-40979-3). A massive survey of the history of Africa and its people, from its earliest inhabitants to the present day, with extensive notes and lists of sources. (Rev: SLJ 1/99) [960]

8420 Rowell, Trevor. *The Scramble for Africa* (9–12). Illus. 1987, David & Charles $19.95 (0-7134-5200-5). The breakup of the continent of Africa by imperialists is documented by the key people involved. (Rev: SLJ 2/88) [960]

8421 Segal, Ronald. *The Black Diaspora* (9–12). 1995, Farrar $27.50 (0-374-11396-3). The first white South African to join the African National Congress and a political exile in Britain, Segal brings a rich personal background to this history of the black experience outside Africa over 5 centuries. (Rev: BL 8/95*) [970.004]

8422 Sheehan, Sean. *Great African Kingdoms* (5–10). (The Ancient World) 1998, Raintree Steck-Vaughn $27.12 (0-8172-5124-3). Coverage of the great African kingdoms includes the spectacular palace of Great Zimbabwe, the majestic sculptures of Benin, and the struggle for survival of the Zulu empire. (Rev: BL 1/1–15/99) [960]

8423 Shillington, Kevin. *Causes & Consequences of Independence in Africa* (6–9). (Causes and Consequences) 1998, Raintree Steck-Vaughn $27.11 (0-8172-4060-8). A concise overview of African history before, during, and after colonialism. (Rev: BL 7/98; SLJ 6/98) [960.3 2]

8424 Wekesser, Carol, and Christina Pierce. *Africa* (7–12). (Opposing Viewpoints) 1992, Greenhaven paper $16.20 (0-89908-161-4). The history and present conditions of Africa, from politics to social issues, are discussed in a essays from varying perspectives. (Rev: BL 5/15/92; SLJ 7/92) [960]

8425 Wepman, Dennis. *Africa: The Struggle for Independence* (7–10). 1993, Facts on File $19.95 (0-8160-2820-6). Focuses on the arbitrary division of the African continent by European countries and the struggles in different regions against colonial rule. (Rev: BL 2/15/94; VOYA 6/94) [960]

Central and Eastern Africa

8426 Barnes, Virginia Lee, and Janice Boddy, retels. *Aman* (10–12). 1995, Vintage paper $14.00 (0-679-76209-4). The candid story of a Somalian woman up

to the age of 19 and the sexual and social taboos of tribal society in her country. (Rev: BR 3–4/96; SLJ 2/96) [967]

8427 Blauer, Ettagale. *Uganda* (5–8). (Enchantment of the World) 1997, Children's Pr. LB $32.00 (0-516-20306-1). This introduction to Uganda covers topics geography, climate, plants and animals, history, religion, culture, and daily life. (Rev: BL 7/97) [967.61]

8428 Burnham, Philip. *Gbaya* (7–12). Illus. (Heritage Library of African Peoples) 1997, Rosen LB $16.95 (0-8239-1995-1). These African people who live in Cameroon, Central African Republic, Congo, and Zaire, are introduced through illustrations and simple text. (Rev: BL 4/15/97) [967]

8429 Creed, Alexander. *Uganda* (6–12). (Major World Nations) 1998, Chelsea LB $19.95 (0-7910-4770-9). This book presents background material on the history and geography of Uganda and good current information on the country's economic, cultural, and social conditions. (Rev: BL 9/15/98; BR 1–2/99) [967.61]

8430 Fox, Mary V. *Somalia* (5–8). Illus. (Enchantment of the World) 1996, Children's Pr. LB $32.00 (0-516-20019-4). An introduction to the land and people of this Muslim republic, which occupies the eastern horn of Africa. (Rev: BL 1/1–15/97) [967.73]

8431 Freeman, Charles. *Crisis in Rwanda* (7–12). (New Perspectives) 1998, Raintree Steck-Vaughn $27.12 (0-8172-5020-4). This book tells of the genocide of the Tutsi, the movements of Hutu refugees, and the actions of the international community from the viewpoints of survivors, aid workers, politicians, historians, and journalists. (Rev: BL 12/15/98; SLJ 2/99) [967.57]

8432 Gaertner, Ursula. *Elmolo* (7–10). (Heritage Library of African Peoples) 1995, Rosen LB $16.95 (0-8239-1764-9). Looks at the customs, daily life, and values of the Elmolo tribe in Kenya. (Rev: BL 7/95; SLJ 5/95) [967.62]

8433 Holtzman, Jon. *Samburu* (7–10). (Heritage Library of African Peoples) 1995, Rosen LB $16.95 (0-8239-1759-2). Discusses in great detail the culture and lifestyle of the Samburu people of Kenya. (Rev: BL 7/95; SLJ 5/95) [967]

8434 Hussein, Ikram. *Teenage Refugees from Somalia Speak Out* (7–12). (Teenage Refugees Speak Out) 1997, Rosen LB $16.95 (0-8239-2444-0). Teenage refugees from Somalia recount the violent anarchy and acute famine in their country and their journey from Africa to the United States. (Rev: BL 12/15/97; SLJ 12/97) [967]

8435 Ifemesia, Chieka. *Turkana* (7–10). Illus. (Heritage Library of African Peoples) 1996, Rosen LB $22.25 (0-8239-1761-4). Using a simple text and color photographs, this account describes the past and present of the Turkana people, who now live in Ethiopia, Kenya, Sudan, and Uganda. (Rev: BL 2/15/95) [960]

8436 Kabira, Wanjiku M. *Agikuyu* (7–10). (Heritage Library of African Peoples) 1995, Rosen LB $16.95 (0-8239-1762-2). Presents social and cultural aspects of the Agikuyu community of Kenya in ways that make them accessible to Western readers. (Rev: BL 7/95; SLJ 6/95) [967]

8437 Kurtz, Jane. *Ethiopia: The Roof of Africa* (5–9). (Discovering Our Heritage) 1991, Dillon LB $14.95 (0-87518-483-9). Conveys a lively sense of Ethiopian life through concrete descriptions. (Rev: BL 2/1/92; SLJ 5/92) [963]

8438 Njoku, Onwuka N. *Mbundu* (7–12). Illus. 1997, Rosen LB $16.95 (0-8239-2004-6). An introduction to the history and contemporary culture of this people of Angola. (Rev: BL 4/15/97) [967.3]

8439 Ojo, Onukaba A. *Mbuti* (7–10). Illus. (Heritage Library of African Peoples) 1996, Rosen LB $16.95 (0-8239-1998-6). The Mbuti people of Zaire are introduced with details on their environment, history, customs, and present situation. (Rev: BL 2/15/96; SLJ 7/96) [305.896]

8440 Okeke, Chika. *Kongo* (7–12). Illus. (Heritage Library of African Peoples) 1997, Rosen LB $15.95 (0-8239-2001-1). The Kongo people of Angola, Congo, and Zaire in central Africa are featured with material on their land, kingdoms, political life, and culture. (Rev: BL 4/15/97) [967]

8441 Peffer, John. *States of Ethiopia* (6–9). (First Books—African Civilizations) 1998, Watts $22.50 (0-531-20278-X). This is the history of this kingdom that converted to Christianity in the 4th century and then became Muslim in the 7th century, and of the turmoil this produced over the centuries. (Rev: BL 1/1–15/99) [963]

8442 *Peoples of Central Africa* (8–12). (Peoples of Africa) 1997, Facts on File $19.95 (0-8160-3486-9). A description of the history, culture, and present status of 17 African peoples who live in and around the present-day countries of Angola, Congo, and Zaire. (Rev: BR 11–12/97; SLJ 2/98) [967]

8443 *Peoples of East Africa* (6–12). (Peoples of Africa) 1997, Facts on File $19.95 (0-8160-3484-2). This book gives a concise overview of 15 ethnic groups of eastern Africa, with details on history, language, way of life, society, religion, and culture. Included are Falasha, Ganda, Hutus and Tutsis, Maasai, Nyoro, Somalis, and Swahili. (Rev: BR 11–12/97; SLJ 10/97) [967]

8444 Roberts, Mary N., and Allen F. Roberts. *Luba* (6–10). (Heritage Library of African Peoples) 1997, Rosen LB $16.95 (0-8239-2002-X). The Luba peo-

ple of Zaire are introduced with material on their history, present conditions, and cultural resources. (Rev: BL 9/15/97) [967]

8445 Russman, Edna R. *Nubian Kingdoms* (6–9). (First Books—African Civilizations) 1999, Watts $22.50 (0-531-20283-6). The story of the ancient civilization that grew up south of Egypt and of its greatness and later decline. (Rev: BL 9/15/99; SLJ 8/99) [967]

8446 Schnapper, LaDena. *Teenage Refugees from Ethiopia Speak Out* (5–10). (Teenage Refugees Speak Out) 1997, Rosen LB $16.95 (0-8239-2438-6). Ethiopian teens now living in America tell of the violence, famine, and civil war that drove them from their country and of their reception in America. (Rev: SLJ 2/98) [963]

8447 Twagilimana, Aimable. *Hutu and Tutsi* (5–9). (The Heritage Library of African Peoples) 1997, Rosen LB $15.95 (0-8239-1999-4). A large section of this book is devoted to the current struggle between the Hutu and Tutsi people of central Africa, along with chapters on art and religion. (Rev: BR 9–10/98; SLJ 3/98) [967]

8448 Twagilimana, Aimable. *Teenage Refugees from Rwanda Speak Out* (5–10). (Teenage Refugees Speak Out) 1997, Rosen LB $16.95 (0-8239-2443-2). Teenage refugees from Rwanda describe the warfare between Tutsi and Hutu peoples and the terrible living conditions that forced them to leave their country and discuss the challenges and difficulties they have experienced in the United States. (Rev: SLJ 2/98) [967]

8449 Walgren, Judy. *The Lost Boys of Nature; A School for Southern Sudan's Young Refugees* (7–10). 1998, Houghton $16.00 (0-395-70558-4). A photoessay that explores the plight of refugees in Africa by focusing on the boys in one school in southern Sudan. (Rev: BL 8/98) [305.23]

8450 Wangari, Estgher. *Ameru* (7–10). Illus. (The Heritage Library of African Peoples) 1995, Rosen $16.95 (0-8239-1766-5). An introduction to the history, traditions, and culture of the Ameru people of Kenya. (Rev: BL 9/15/95; SLJ 11/95) [967.6]

8451 Wilson, Thomas H. *City-States of the Swahili Coast* (6–9). (First Books—African Civilizations) 1998, Watts $22.50 (0-531-20281-X). The history of the separate kingdoms that grew up along the eastern coast of Africa from present-day Somalia to Mozambique. (Rev: BL 1/1–15/99) [963]

8452 Zeleza, Tiyambe. *Akamba* (7–10). Illus. (The Heritage Library of African Peoples) 1995, Rosen LB $16.95 (0-8239-1768-1). The history, traditions, and fight for freedom of the Akamba people of Kenya are covered in this book with many color illustrations. (Rev: BL 7/95; SLJ 6/95) [960]

8453 Zeleza, Tiyambe. *Mijikenda* (7–10). (Heritage Library of African Peoples) 1995, Rosen LB $15.95 (0-8239-1767-3). Combines history and anthropology to provide a portrait of the Mijikenda people. (Rev: BL 9/15/95; SLJ 11/95) [967]

North Africa

8454 Azuonye, Chukwuma. *Dogon* (7–10). Illus. (Heritage Library of African Peoples) 1995, Rosen LB $16.95 (0-8239-1976-5). Provides information on the history, culture, and lifestyles of the Dogan people of Mali. (Rev: BL 2/15/96) [966.23]

8455 Diamond, Arthur. *Egypt: Gift of the Nile* (5–9). (Discovering Our Heritage) 1992, Dillon $14.95 (0-87518-511-8). An introduction to Egypt that includes history, culture, folktales, maps, recipes, and a discussion of Egyptian immigrants in the United States. (Rev: BL 8/92; SLJ 11/92) [962]

8456 *Libya in Pictures* (5–8). Illus. (Visual Geography) 1996, Lerner LB $21.27 (0-8225-1907-0). An introduction to this North African country's geography, history, and people, with many illustrations including maps and charts. (Rev: BL 11/15/96) [961.2]

8457 *Peoples of North Africa* (8–12). (Peoples of Africa) 1997, Facts on File $21.95 (0-8160-3483-4). This book describes the history and cultures of North African peoples, including Arabs, Baggara, Beja, Berbers, Copts, Dinka, Muba, Nuer, Shilluk, and Tuareg. (Rev: BR 11–12/97; SLJ 2/98) [961]

8458 Raskin, Lawrie, and Debora Pearson. *52 Days by Camel: My Sahara Adventure* (4–8). Illus. 1998, Annick LB $24.95 (1-55037-519-9); paper $14.95 (1-55037-518-0). An engaging account of a trip from Fez in Morocco to Timbuktu by bus, jeep, train, truck, and camel, with details on places, people, and adventures, plus pertinent trivia. (Rev: BL 6/1–15/98; SLJ 7/98) [964]

8459 Schlesinger, Arthur M., Jr., and Fred L. Israel, eds. *Mysteries of the Sahara: Chronicles from National Geographic* (9–12). (Cultural and Geographical Exploration) 1999, Chelsea LB $19.95 (0-7910-5097-1). This article and its photographs originally appeared in a 1914 issue of *National Geographic* magazine and describes the then-current conditions in Morocco, Algeria, Tunisia, and Libya. (Rev: SLJ 6/99) [961]

South Africa

8460 Bessire, Mark. *Great Zimbabwe* (6–9). (First Books—African Civilizations) 1999, Watts $22.50 (0-531-20285-2). The story of the rise and fall of the civilization that flourished in the southern part of Africa. (Rev: BL 9/15/99) [968]

8461 Biesele, Megan, and Kxao Royal. *San* (7–10). (Heritage Library of African Peoples) 1997, Rosen LB $15.95 (0-8239-1997-8). The San people of Botswana, Namibia, and South Africa are featured in this account that tells of their rich tradition and their struggle for freedom. (Rev: BL 9/15/97) [960]

8462 Blauer, Ettagale, and Jason Lauré. *South Africa* (5–10). Illus. (Enchantment of the World) 1998, Children's Pr. $32.00 (0-516-20606-0). An basic introduction to the land and people of South Africa, with good coverage of modern political movements and the importance of Nelson Mandela. (Rev: SLJ 11/98) [968]

8463 Blauer, Ettagale, and Jason Lauré. *Swaziland* (5–8). Illus. (Enchantment of the World) 1996, Children's Pr. LB $32.00 (0-516-20020-8). This landlocked kingdom north of South Africa is introduced with material on its physical features, history, and economy. (Rev: BL 1/1–15/97) [968.87]

8464 Bolaane, Maitseo, and Part T. Mgadla. *Batswana* (6–10). (The Heritage Library of African Peoples) 1997, Rosen LB $15.95 (0-8239-2008-9). This work discusses the history, culture, and present status of the Batswana people of Botswana and South Africa. (Rev: BL 1/1–15/98) [968]

8465 Bradley, Catherine. *The End of Apartheid* (7–12). 1995, Raintree Steck-Vaughn LB $25.69 (0-8172-4055-1). This crucial world development is set in a historical and political context and is laid out like a long magazine article, with maps and photos. (Rev: BL 12/15/95; SLJ 1/96) [305.8]

8466 Brandenburg, Jim. *Sand and Fog: Adventures in Southern Africa* (5–9). 1994, Walker LB $17.85 (0-8027-8233-7). A full-color photoessay about the Namibian desert in southwest Africa by a photographer on assignment for National Geographic. (Rev: BL 3/1/94*; SLJ 5/94) [968.81]

8467 Canesso, Claudia. *South Africa* (6–10). (Major World Nations) 1998, Chelsea LB $19.95 (0-7910-4766-0). An accurate, informative, and unbiased account of the social, political, and economic conditions in South Africa today, supplemented by illustrations and maps. (Rev: BL 9/15/98; BR 1–2/99; SLJ 6/99) [968.06]

8468 Cunningham, Carol, and Joel Berger. *Horn of Darkness* (10–12). 1997, Oxford $36.95 (0-19-511113-3). Black rhinos and life in the Namibian desert are featured in the account of how the authors, 2 field biologists, tried to help in the crusade to save the black rhino from extinction. (Rev: SLJ 8/97) [968]

8469 Flint, David. *South Africa* (4–8). Illus. (Modern Industrial World) 1996, Raintree Steck-Vaughn $24.26 (0-8172-4554-5). The present economic status of South Africa is studied through personal narratives and case studies. (Rev: BL 2/15/97; SLJ 8/97) [968]

8470 Green, Rebecca L. *Merina* (7–12). Illus. (Heritage Library of African Peoples) 1997, Rosen LB $16.95 (0-8239-1991-9). The history and culture of the Merina people of Madagascar are covered in text and many illustrations. (Rev: BL 4/15/97; VOYA 6/97) [969.1]

8471 Hays, David, and Daniel Hays. *My Old Man and the Sea* (10–12). 1995, Algonquin $19.95 (1-56512-102-3). An exciting account of a father and grown son (plus their cat, Tiger), and their perilous voyage around Cape Horn in a 25-foot boat. (Rev: BL 6/1/95; SLJ 2/96) [968]

8472 Inserra, Rose, and Susan Powell. *The Kalahari* (5–8). (Ends of the Earth) 1997, Heinemann $25.45 (0-431-06932-8). An introduction to the history, animal and vegetable life, and future of this desert region of southern Botswana, eastern Namibia, and western South Africa. (Rev: SLJ 11/97) [968]

8473 Kaschula, Russel. *Xhosa* (5–9). (The Heritage Library of African Peoples) 1997, Rosen LB $15.95 (0-8239-2013-5). The Xhosa people of South Africa are introduced with stunning photos and material on their past as well as present culture. (Rev: BL 1/1–15/98) [968]

8474 Klopper, Sandra. *The Zulu Kingdom* (6–9). (First Books—African Civilizations) 1999, Watts $22.50 (0-531-20286-0). This book traces the growth of the Zulu empire in the south of Africa and how it was destroyed chiefly by Europeans. (Rev: BL 9/15/99) [968]

8475 Lauré, Jason. *Botswana* (5–8). (Enchantment of the World) 1993, Children's Pr. LB $32.00 (0-516-02616-X). A sympathetic portrait of this independent African nation. (Rev: BL 11/1/93; SLJ 4/94) [968.83]

8476 Lauré, Jason. *Namibia* (5–8). (Enchantment of the World) 1993, Children's Pr. LB $32.00 (0-516-02615-1). A description of the land and people of Namibia, which was once administered by South Africa and gained full independence in 1990. (Rev: BL 8/93) [968.81]

8477 Mann, Kenny. *Monomotapa, Zulu, Basuto: Southern Africa* (8–12). (African Kingdoms of the Past) 1996, Silver Burdett LB $15.95 (0-87518-659-9); paper $7.95 (0-382-39300-7). The history of 3 south African kingdoms using striking layouts, plenty of color, and clear writing. (Rev: SLJ 2/97; VOYA 2/97) [968]

8478 Nagle, Garrett. *South Africa* (6–12). (Country Studies) 1999, Heinemann $27.07 (1-57572-896-6). An excellent overview of South Africa, with particularly good coverage on current conditions and problems. (Rev: BL 8/99) [968]

8479 Ngwane, Zolani. *Zulu* (5–8). (Heritage Library of African Peoples) 1997, Rosen LB $15.95 (0-8239-2014-3). This work introduces the history and culture of the Zulus of South Africa. (Rev: BL 9/15/97; VOYA 12/97) [968]

8480 *No More Strangers Now: Young Voices from a New South Africa* (6–12). 1998, DK Publg. $19.95 (0-7894-2524-6). A photoessay in which 12 South African teens discuss their lives under apartheid and after. (Rev: BL 9/15/98; BR 5–6/99; SLJ 12/98*; VOYA 2/99) [968]

8481 Nwaezeigwe, Nwankwo T. *Ngoni* (7–12). Illus. (Heritage Library of African Peoples) 1997, Rosen LB $16.95 (0-8239-2006-2). This book describes the history, traditions, and struggle for freedom of this African group in Malawi. (Rev: BL 4/15/97) [968.97]

8482 Oluikpe, Benson O. *Swazi* (7–12). Illus. (Heritage Library of African Peoples) 1997, Rosen LB $15.95 (0-8239-2012-7). This book describes the history, traditions, and struggles for freedom of the Swazi people in Swaziland and South Africa. (Rev: BL 4/15/97; SLJ 12/97) [968]

8483 *Peoples of Southern Africa* (6–12). (Peoples of Africa) 1997, Facts on File $19.95 (0-8160-3487-7). The history, geography, culture, religion, and social life of 17 different South African peoples are highlighted, including Afrikaners, Cape Coloreds, Cape Malays, Indian South Africans, Ndebele, Swazi, Tswana, Venda, and Zulu. (Rev: BR 11–12/97; SLJ 10/97) [968]

8484 Pratt, Paula B. *The End of Apartheid in South Africa* (6–8). (Overview) 1995, Lucent LB $17.96 (1-56006-170-7). Describes the collapse of the apartheid regime in South Africa and the challenges facing a changing society. (Rev: BL 7/95) [323.1]

8485 Schneider, Elizabeth Ann. *Ndebele* (7–12). Illus. 1997, Rosen LB $16.95 (0-8239-2009-7). Topics covered about the Ndebele people of South Africa include environment, history, religion, social organization, politics, and customs. (Rev: BL 4/15/97) [968]

8486 Smith, Chris. *Conflict in Southern Africa* (6–12). (Conflicts) 1993, Macmillan LB $18.95 (0-02-785956-8). An overview of the politics of southern Africa: Angola, Mozambique, Zambia, Namibia, and South Africa. (Rev: BL 7/93; SLJ 12/93) [968]

8487 Stein, R. Conrad. *Cape Town* (5–8). (Cities of the World) 1998, Children's Pr. $26.00 (0-516-20781-4). A photoessay that shows this modern, multicultural, multiracial South African capital with its rich diversity of people at work, at school, and at play. (Rev: BL 12/15/98) [968.7]

8488 Udechukwu, Ada. *Herero* (7–10). (Heritage Library of African Peoples) 1996, Rosen LB $16.95

(0-8239-2003-8). This book introduces the 3 Herero subgroups that share a similar language and culture in today's Botswana, Angola, and Namibia, with an emphasis on their political history. (Rev: BL 3/15/96; SLJ 6/96) [968]

8489 Van Wyk, Gary N. *Basotho* (6–10). (Heritage Library of African Peoples) 1996, Rosen LB $15.95 (0-8239-2005-4). This work traces the history of the Basotho peoples of Lesotho and South Africa from ancient times to the present, with basic information on their geography, social life, religion, education, and the arts. (Rev: BL 11/15/96; SLJ 3/97) [968]

8490 *Zimbabwe* (5–9). Illus. (Major World Nations) 1999, Chelsea LB $19.95 (0-7910-4753-9). A good introduction to Zimbabwe's history, geography, government, people, pastimes, economy, and culture. (Rev: SLJ 8/98) [968]

West Africa

8491 Adeeb, Hassan, and Bonnetta Adeeb. *Nigeria: One Nation, Many Cultures* (4–8). (Exploring Cultures of the World) 1995, Benchmark LB $27.07 (0-7614-0190-3). Opening with the folktale of Sarki the Snake of Nigeria, this overview continues with an introduction to Nigeria's people, history, culture, and problems. (Rev: SLJ 6/96) [966.9]

8492 Anda, Michael O. *Yoruba* (7–10). (Heritage Library of African Peoples) 1996, Rosen LB $15.95 (0-8239-1988-9). This work describes one of the largest sub-Sahara ethnic groups, whose influence, because of the slave trade, spread to the New World, especially Brazil. (Rev: SLJ 6/96) [966.9]

8493 Azuonye, Chukwuma. *Edo: The Bini People of the Benin Kingdom* (7–10). Illus. (Heritage Library of African Peoples) 1996, Rosen LB $16.95 (0-8239-1985-4). A review of the history, culture, society, and the struggle for freedom of the Bini people, whose empire was part of present day Nigeria. (Rev: BL 3/15/96) [966.9]

8494 Beaton, Margaret. *Senegal* (5–8). (Enchantment of the World) 1997, Children's Pr. LB $32.00 (0-516-20304-5). An introduction to this West African nation, its people, and its cities, including the capital, Dakar. (Rev: BL 7/97) [916.63]

8495 Chambers, Catherine. *West African States: 15th Century to the Colonial Era* (5–8). (Looking Back) 1999, Raintree Steck-Vaughn $25.69 (0-8172-5427-7). A brief overview of the history and culture of the great empires of West Africa and how they disappeared with the arrival of the Europeans. (Rev: BL 5/15/99) [966.2]

8496 Conrad, David. *The Songhay Empire* (6–9). (First Books—African Civilizations) 1998, Watts LB $22.00 (0-531-20284-4). This African empire founded in Mali in western Africa around 700 A.D. by Berbers reached the height of its power about 1500. (Rev: BL 1/1–15/99) [966.7]

8497 *Ghana* (5–9). Illus. (Major World Nations) 1999, Chelsea LB $19.95 (0-7910-4739-3). Basic facts about Ghana's history, geography, politics, government, economy, natural resources, education, and people. (Rev: SLJ 8/98) [966.7]

8498 Greene, Rebecca L. *The Empire of Ghana* (6–9). (First Books—African Civilizations) 1998, Watts $22.50 (0-531-20276-3). This book describes the medieval African kingdom that grew up in what is now eastern Senegal, southwest Mali, and southern Mauritania, and how it flourished because it was on the trans-Sahara caravan routes. (Rev: BL 1/1–15/99) [966.7]

8499 Heale, Jay. *Democratic Republic of the Congo* (5–9). (Cultures of the World) 1998, Marshall Cavendish $24.95 (0-7614-0874-6). A history of this nation that has been stricken with civil wars and political instability, with descriptions of its history, economy, government, people, and culture. (Rev: SLJ 6/99) [967]

8500 Jordan, Manuel. *The Kongo Kingdom* (6–9). (First Books—African Civilizations) 1999, Watts LB $22.00 (0—531-20282-8). The story of the ancient African civilization that grew up around the banks of the Congo River. (Rev: BL 9/15/99) [966]

8501 Koslow, Philip. *Asante: The Gold Coast* (6–9). Illus. (Kingdoms of Africa) 1996, Chelsea LB $18.95 (0-7910-3139-X); paper $8.95 (0-7910-3140-3). The history of the mighty West African people who acquired great wealth from their gold mines and who were known worldwide for their artwork. (Rev: BL 6/1–15/96; BR 11–12/96) [966.7018]

8502 Koslow, Philip. *Benin: Lords of the River* (6–9). Illus. (Kingdoms of Africa) 1995, Chelsea paper $8.95 (0-7910-3134-9). A history of the people who lived around the Benin River, their conflicts with Europeans, and their lasting imperial grandeur. (Rev: BL 6/1–15/96) [966.9]

8503 Koslow, Philip. *Dahomey: The Warrior Kings* (5–8). (The Kingdoms of Africa) 1996, Chelsea LB $18.95 (0-7910-3137-3); paper $8.95 (0-7910-3138-1). A history of the West African kingdom that flourished in the 17th and 18th centuries and how the slave trade affected it. (Rev: BR 11–12/96; SLJ 12/96) [966]

8504 Koslow, Philip. *Lords of the Savanna: The Bambara, Fulani, Igbo, Mossi, and Nupe* (7–10). (The Kingdoms of Africa) 1997, Chelsea LB $15.95 (0-7910-3141-1); paper $8.95 (0-7910-3142-X). A strong narrative style and attractive illustrations are used to present the history and culture of these West African peoples of present-day Nigeria, Cameroon, and Burkina Faso. (Rev: SLJ 1/98) [966]

8505 Koslow, Philip. *Songhay: The Empire Builders* (6–9). Illus. (The Kingdoms of Africa) 1995, Chelsea LB $18.95 (0-7910-3128-4); paper $9.95 (0-7910-2943-3). This account concentrates on the 10th through 15th centuries, and tells about the great Songhay empire in West Africa that flourished under King Sunni Ali and later King Askia Muhammad, and produced such thriving cities as Timbuktu. (Rev: BL 2/15/96) [966.2]

8506 Koslow, Philip. *Yorubaland: The Flowering of Genius* (6–9). Illus. (The Kingdoms of Africa) 1995, Chelsea LB $18.95 (0-7910-3131-4); paper $7.95 (0-7910-3132-2). This account traces the 1,500-year history of the Yorubaland civilization in West Africa that dates back to the 4th century B.C. and produced an early sophisticated system of government. (Rev: BL 2/15/96; BR 11–12/96; SLJ 2/96) [960]

8507 Kummer, Patricia K. *Cote d'Ivoire* (5–8). (Enchantment of the World) 1996, Children's Pr. LB $32.00 (0-516-02641-0). An introduction to the small French-speaking African republic, Ivory Coast, which gained its freedom in 1960 and is now known as Cote d'Ivoire. (Rev: BL 7/96) [966.68]

8508 Mack-Williams, Kibibi V. *Mossi* (7–10). Illus. (Heritage Library of African Peoples) 1996, Rosen LB $16.95 (0-8239-1984-6). This account covers such topics as the land of the Mossi people of West Africa, their kingdoms, political life and customs, religion, colonization and independence. (Rev: BL 3/15/96) [966.25]

8509 Malaquais, Dominique. *The Kingdom of Benin* (6–9). (First Books—African Civilizations) 1998, Watts $22.50 (0-531-20279-8). Benin, formerly Dahomey was the center of a thriving kingdom known particularly for its arts before European intervention. (Rev: BL 1/1–15/99) [966.9]

8510 Mann, Kenny. *Ghana, Mali, Songhay: The Western Sudan* (4–8). (African Kingdoms of the Past) 1996, Silver Burdett $19.95 (0-87518-656-4); paper $7.95 (0-382-39176-4). An eloquently written book about the once powerful empires of Ghana, Mali, and Songhay, with information on the beginnings of Islam Africa and how the slave trade gradually took over. (Rev: SLJ 9/96) [960]

8511 Mann, Kenny. *Kongo Ndongo: West Central Africa* (8–12). (African Kingdoms of the Past) 1996, Silver Burdett $15.95 (0-87518-658-0); paper $7.95 (0-382-39298-1). A visually attractive book that outlines the history of this west African kingdom and utilizes many excellent sources. (Rev: SLJ 2/97; VOYA 2/97) [966]

8512 Mann, Kenny. *Oyo, Benin, Ashanti: The Guinea Coast* (6–10). (African Kingdoms of the Past) 1996, Silver Burdett $19.95 (0-87518-657-2); paper $7.95 (0-382-39177-2). Through legends and history, the author re-creates the story of these three West Africa kingdoms and their culture. (Rev: SLJ 6/96) [960]

8513 Millar, Heather. *The Kingdom of Benin in West Africa* (6–8). (Cultures of the Past) 1996, Benchmark LB $28.50 (0-7614-0088-5). This book describes the kingdom of Benin, the most remarkable of West Africa's empires of 500 years ago, with information on its gods, art, culture and way of life. (Rev: SLJ 3/97) [966]

8514 Ndukwe, Pat I. *Fulani* (7–10). Illus. (Heritage Library of African Peoples) 1995.64p, Rosen LB $16.95 (0-8239-1982-X). A description of the history, surroundings, politics, customs, and current conditions of the Fulani people, who live in Cameroon, Mali, and Nigeria. (Rev: BL 2/15/96; SLJ 7/96) [966]

8515 Nnoromele, Salome C. *Life among the Ibo Women of Nigeria* (9–12). Illus. (The Way People Live) 1997, Lucent LB $17.96 (1-56006-344-0). Before European contact, Ibo women were equal in power with men in the economy, politics, and the family, but English influences changed this. Today these women are caught between 2 cultures. (Rev: BL 9/1/98; SLJ 10/98) [966.9]

8516 Ogbaa, Kalu. *Igbo* (7–10). (Heritage Library of African Peoples) 1995, Rosen LB $15.95 (0-8239-1977-3). Explains the beliefs and worldview of the lgbo people of Nigeria and how they are reflected in their daily lives. (Rev: BL 9/15/95; SLJ 11/95) [966.9]

8517 *Peoples of West Africa* (6–12). (Peoples of West Africa) 1997, Facts on File $19.95 (0-8160-3485-0). Extensive background material is provided on the history, geography, languages, art, music, religion, and society of 13 West African peoples, including Asante, Bambara, Dogon, Fon, Hausa, Moors, Mossi, and Yoruba. (Rev: BL 8/97; BR 11–12/97; SLJ 10/97) [966]

8518 Sallah, Tijan M. *Wolof* (7–12). (Heritage Library of African Peoples) 1996, Rosen LB $16.95 (0-8239-1987-0). Using maps, many color illustrations, and text, this book introduces the Wolof people of Senegal and their history, social and political life, customs, religious beliefs, and relations with other peoples in their region. (Rev: SLJ 7/96) [966.3]

8519 Tenquist, Alasdair. *Nigeria* (5–8). Illus. (Economically Developing Countries) 1996, Raintree Steck-Vaughn LB $24.26 (0-8172-4527-8). This introduction to Nigeria emphasizes present-day government and economic conditions. (Rev: BL 3/1/97; SLJ 9/97) [330.9669]

8520 Thompson, Carol. *The Empire of Mali* (6–9). 1998, Watts $22.50 (0-531-20277-1). This book chronicles the rise of the great Mali Empire that flourished in western Africa from the 13th to the 16th century and describes its universities, legal system, and remarkable architecture, art, and crafts. (Rev: BL 1/1–15/99) [966.2]

8521 Zimmermann, Robert. *The Gambia* (5–8). Illus. (Enchantment of the World) 1994, Children's Pr. LB $32.00 (0-516-02625-9). This tiny West African country is introduced in text and color photos that cover all major topics related to this new nation. (Rev: BL 12/15/94; SLJ 4/95) [966.51]

Asia

General and Miscellaneous

8522 Franck, Irene M., and David M. Brownstone. *Across Asia by Land* (6–10). (Travel and Trade Routes) 1991, Facts on File $17.95 (0-8160-1874-X). Specific trade and travel routes tell historical tales from ancient times to the present. (Rev: BL 1/15/91; SLJ 6/91) [380.1]

8523 Pascoe, Elaine. *The Pacific Rim: East Asia at the Dawn of a New Century* (7–12). 1999, Twenty-First Century $24.90 (0-7613-3015-1). Brief historical information and current economic figures are given for Japan, China, Taiwan, the Koreas, Indonesia, Singapore, Malaysia, and the Philippines. (Rev: BL 7/99; SLJ 9/99) [950.4]

8524 Sayre, April P. *Asia* (5–8). (Seven Continents) 1999, Twenty-First Century LB $23.40 (0-7613-1368-0). This book provides a detailed overview of the people, land, geology, oceans, climate, soil, vegetation, and animals of Asia. (Rev: BL 8/99) [915]

8525 Schmidt, Jeremy. *Himalayan Passage: Seven Months in the High Country of Tibet, Nepal, China, India and Pakistan* (9–12). 1991, Mountaineers Books $22.95 (0-89886-262-0). The adventure-filled travels of 4 experienced mountaineers—on foot, by mountain bike, and in overcrowded buses and trucks—from Tibet to Sikkim. (Rev: BL 9/15/91) [915.49]

China

8526 Cozic, Charles P., ed. *U.S. Policy toward China* (8–12). (At Issue) 1996, Greenhaven LB $14.25 (1-56510-389-0); paper $11.20 (1-56510-388-2). Differences between China and the U.S. on such issues as human rights and copyright policies are explored from various points of view in this collection of articles. (Rev: BL 1/1–15/96; SLJ 5/96) [327.73]

8527 Ebrey, Patricia Buckley. *The Cambridge Illustrated History of China* (10–12). 1996, Cambridge Univ. Pr. $39.95 (0-521-43519-0). Over 5,000 years of Chinese civilization are covered, with a focus on cultural and social issues that affected people's lives. (Rev: SLJ 5/97) [951]

8528 Fairbank, John King. *The Great Chinese Revolution: 1800–1985* (10–12). 1986, HarperCollins $15.00 (0-06-039076-X). This account covers 185 years of Chinese history from the late imperial period to the mid-1980s. [951]

8529 Fritz, Jean. *China's Long March: 6,000 Miles of Danger* (6–9). Illus. 1988, Putnam $16.99 (0-399-21512-3). A description of the legend-making 6,000-mile march of the Chinese Communists during the 1930s. (Rev: BL 3/1/88; SLJ 5/88) [951.04]

8530 Goh, Sui Noi. *China* (4–8). (Countries of the World) 1998, Gareth Stevens LB $19.93 (0-8368-2124-6). An overview of the country's history, government, economy, geography, people, and the arts, followed by a "Closer Look" section that examines contemporary issues such as the role of women, secret societies, Tibet, Tiananman Square, and a final section on relations with North America. (Rev: SLJ 6/99) [951]

8531 Green, Robert. *China* (6–10). (Modern Nations of the World) 1999, Lucent LB $18.96 (1-56006-440-4). A well-organized overview of China and its emergence as a powerful political and economic power. (Rev: SLJ 8/99) [051]

8532 *Hong Kong* (5–8). Illus. (Cultures of the World) 1997, Marshall Cavendish LB $35.64 (0-7614-0692-1). Included in this introduction to Hong Kong are its geography, history, government, economy, people, religions, language, arts, festivals, and food. (Rev: SLJ 6/98) [951]

8533 Israel, Fred L., and Arthur M. Schlesinger, Jr., eds. *Peking* (6–10). Illus. (The World 100 Years Ago) 1999, Chelsea LB $29.95 (0-7910-4666-4). This is an edited version of travel essays by Burton Holmes, a popular traveler-lecturer during the first half of the 20th century, about the sights he saw in Peking on a tour that started in Nagasaki, continued through the city of Taku, and culminated in Peking. (Rev: SLJ 7/98) [951]

8534 *Journey into China* (9–12). Illus. 1982, Natl. Geographic Soc. LB $23.00 (0-87044-461-1). A region-by-region description by several travelers of their journeys in China. [915.1]

8535 Kort, Michael G. *China under Communism* (9–12). 1995, Millbrook LB $26.40 (1-56294-450-9). This detailed history of the Communist movement in China offers opportunities for discussion from both historical and cultural perspectives. (Rev: BL 1/1/95; SLJ 3/95) [951.05]

8536 Lord, Bette Bao. *Legacies: A Chinese Mosaic* (9–12). 1990, Knopf $19.95 (0-394-58325-6). Through interviews with members of Chinese families, the author re-creates Chinese social history from 1949 to 1989. (Rev: SLJ 7/90) [951]

8537 McNeese, Tim. *The Great Wall of China* (6–10). Illus. (Building History) 1997, Lucent LB $17.96 (1-56006-428-5). This book tells the fascinating history of the building of this mammoth construction that rivals any other on earth in its form, scope, and size. (Rev: BL 12/1/97; BR 1–2/98; SLJ 8/97) [931]

8538 Mann, Elizabeth. *The Great Wall: The Story of Thousands of Miles of Earth and Stone* (4–8). Illus. (Wonders of the World) 1997, Mikaya $18.95 (0-9650493-2-9). The story behind the building of this massive structure, which began as far back as 200 B.C. and involves historical battles for land and power between the Chinese and the nomadic Mongols. (Rev: BL 1/1–15/98; SLJ 12/97) [951]

8539 Millar, Heather. *China's Tang Dynasty* (6–10). (Cultures of the Past) 1996, Benchmark LB $28.50 (0-7614-0074-5). The story of the Chinese dynasty that existed from 618 to 907 and was noted for its great wealth and encouragement of the arts and literature. (Rev: BR 9–10/96; SLJ 6/96) [951]

8540 Murowchick, Robert E. *China: Ancient Culture, Modern Land* (9–12). (Cradles of Civilization) 1994, Univ. of Oklahoma Pr. $34.95 (0-8061-2683-3). Follows the development of Chinese cultural history from ancient times to the present, tracing the evolution of religion, philosophy, government, land, and language. (Rev: BL 10/1/94) [951]

8541 Pietrusza, David. *The Chinese Cultural Revolution* (6–9). Illus. (World History) 1996, Lucent LB $17.96 (1-56006-305-X). This book traces the rise of Mao Tse-tung, his failed 1958 Great Leap Forward, and his great political changes in the 1960s that have helped determine China's present economic and social conditions. (Rev: BL 1/1–15/97; BR 11–12/97; SLJ 2/97) [951.05]

8542 Salisbury, Harrison E. *Tiananmen Diary: Thirteen Days in June* (9–12). 1989, Little, Brown $18.95 (0-316-80904-7); paper $10.95 (0-316-80905-5). An eyewitness account by a master correspondent of the crackdown on student protests in China. (Rev: BL 9/15/89) [951.058]

8543 Starr, John B. *Understanding China: A Guide to China's Economy, History, and Political Structure* (10–12). 1997, Hill & Wang $25.00 (0-8090-9488-6). A series of articles that provide a fine introduction to China by covering such topics as culture, the Communist party, urban and rural problems, population control, foreign relations, human rights, and background history. (Rev: BL 9/1/97; SLJ 4/98) [951]

8544 Williams, Brian. *Ancient China* (6–9). (See Through History) 1996, Viking $19.99 (0-670-87157-5). Detailed illustrations and some overlays provide a glimpse at ancient China's farming, reli-

gion, clothing, architecture, and daily life. (Rev: SLJ 3/97) [951]

India, Pakistan, and Bangladesh

8545 Brace, Steve. *India* (7–10). (Country Studies) 1999, Heinemann $24.22 (1-57572-893-1). An excellent introduction to India that gives current information on such subjects as population, environment, problems, and economy. (Rev: BL 8/99) [954]

8546 Collins, Larry, and Dominique Lapierre. *Freedom at Midnight* (10–12). Illus. 1976, Avon paper $5.95 (0-380-00693-6). This covers the fateful final days of the British regime in India and the bloody riots during partition, and ends with the assassination of Gandhi in January 1948. [954.04]

8547 Cumming, David. *The Ganges Delta and Its People* (5–8). (People and Places) 1994, Thomson Learning LB $24.26 (1-56847-168-8). A description of the land and the people who live around the mouth of the Ganges River. (Rev: BL 10/15/94) [954]

8548 Hinds, Kathryn. *India's Gupta Dynasty* (6–10). (Cultures of the Past) 1995, Benchmark LB $28.50 (0-7614-0071-0). This historical introduction to the Gupta dynasty's religion, art, education, and customs, emphasizes the influence of Buddhism and Hinduism on various aspects of ancient Indian society and examines the role of women. (Rev: BR 9–10/96; SLJ 6/96) [954]

8549 Lauré, Jason. *Bangladesh* (5–8). (Enchantment of the World) 1992, Children's Pr. LB $32.00 (0-516-02609-7). This look at Bangladesh discusses geological, historical, meteorological, and engineering aspects of the country. (Rev: BL 12/15/92) [954.9]

8550 Mehta, Gita. *Snakes and Ladders: Glimpses of Modern India* (10–12). 1997, Nan A. Talese $22.95 (0-385-47495-4). In these 35 essays, the author discusses the paths of endeavor and conflict that India has experienced since gaining independence 50 years ago. (Rev: BL 5/1/97; SLJ 10/97) [954]

8551 Moorcroft, Christine. *The Taj Mahal* (5–8). (Great Buildings) 1998, Raintree Steck-Vaughn $25.69 (0-8172-4920-6). A beautifully illustrated book that describes the history of the Taj Mahal, its design, its construction, and its importance in architecture. (Rev: BL 2/1/98; SLJ 7/98) [954]

8552 Rothfarb, Ed. *In the Land of Taj Mahal: The World of the Fabulous Mughals* (9–12). 1998, Holt $21.95 (0-8050-5299-2). This is the story of the great Mughal Empire of the 16th and 17th centuries and its many contributions to art, architecture, and literature. (Rev: BL 5/1/98; SLJ 6/98) [954.02 5]

8553 Stewart, Melissa. *Science in Ancient India* (4–8). (Science of the Past) 1999, Watts $25.00 (0-

531-11626-3). Extending back in history to India's ancient cultures, this book describes the country's scientific progress in such areas as medicine, mathematics, astronomy, and physics. (Rev: SLJ 6/99) [954]

8554 Viswanath, R. *Teenage Refugees and Immigrants from India Speak Out* (7–12). (Teenage Refugees Speak Out) 1997, Rosen LB $16.95 (0-8239-2440-8). A description of the ethnic and religious conflicts and economic conditions that have caused the displacement of tens of thousands of Indians, plus the stories of those who came to the United States, told in first-person teenage accounts. (Rev: BL 12/15/97; SLJ 4/98) [954]

8555 Weston, Mark. *The Land and People of Pakistan* (6–9). (Land and People Of) 1992, HarperCollins LB $17.89 (0-06-022790-7). Pakistan's geography, ethnicity, and history as well as an exploration of political, social, economic, and cultural life. (Rev: BL 8/92; SLJ 12/92*) [954.91]

8556 Whyte, Mariam. *Bangladesh* (5–9). (Cultures of the World) 1998, Marshall Cavendish LB $24.95 (0-7614-0869-X). A sympathetic look at the history and geography of Bangladesh, with details on the country's rich background and current problems. (Rev: SLJ 6/99) [954.9]

Japan

8557 Avikian, Monique. *The Meiji Restoration and the Rise of Modern Japan* (5–8). (Turning Points in World History) 1991, Silver Burdett LB $14.95 (0-382-24132-0); paper $7.95 (0-382-24139-8). This account examines the major factors that resulted in the establishment of a new social order in Japan. (Rev: BL 3/15/92) [952.03]

8558 Dunn, Charles. *Everyday Life in Traditional Japan* (10–12). Illus. 1977, Tuttle paper $12.95 (0-8048-1384-1). A description of Japanese life during the reign of the Tokugawa shoguns, a period roughly from 1600 to 1850. [952]

8559 Hall, Eleanor J. *Life among the Samurai* (6–10). (The Way People Live) 1998, Lucent LB $17.96 (1-56006-390-4). A history of the feudal period in Japanese history that focuses on the warrior class and their exploits. (Rev: BL 11/15/98) [952]

8560 Hamanaka, Sheila, and Ayano Ohmi. *In Search of the Spirit: The Living National Treasures of Japan* (4–8). Illus. 1999, Morrow LB $15.93 (0-688-14608-2). In the 1950s, the Japanese government, concerned that ancient traditions were dying out, created a National Living Treasures program to honor elders practicing age-old crafts and performing arts and to give them grants to continue their work and to train apprentices. This book features 6 such elders: a sword maker, a puppet master, a yuzen

dyer who decorates silk kimonos, a bamboo weaver, a Noh actor, and a potter. (Rev: BL 3/1/99; SLJ 5/99) [952]

8561 Nardo, Don. *Modern Japan* (8–12). Illus. (World History) 1995, Lucent LB $17.96 (1-56006-281-9). This work includes a history of Japan since its opening up to the West in the mid-19th century, with details on its economic and political life since World War II. (Rev: BL 2/15/95) [952.02]

8562 Pilbeam, Mavis. *Japan Under the Shoguns, 1185–1868* (5–8). (Looking Back) 1999, Raintree Steck-Vaughn $25.69 (0-8172-5431-5). A detailed overview of the shogun society of Japan from 1185 to 1868, supplemented by color photographs and reproductions of original art. (Rev: BL 5/15/99) [452]

8563 Roberson, John R. *Japan Meets the World: The Birth of a Super Power* (7–12). 1998, Millbrook $24.90 (0-7613-0407-X). Beginning with the Shogans of the 16th century, this book traces Japanese history through various stages of progress, its development into an economic superpower, and its current economic crisis and social stresses. (Rev: BL 1/1–15/99; SLJ 2/99) [952]

8564 Ross, Stewart. *The Rise of Japan and the Pacific Rim* (7–12). (Causes and Consequences) 1995, Raintree Steck-Vaughn LB $25.69 (0-8172-4054-3). A thorough, unbiased account of the remarkable history of Japan since World War II, with well-documented details on the political, social, and economic conditions that made it possible, and also including material on the economic rise of other Pacific Rim nations. (Rev: BL 12/15/95; BR 3–4/96; SLJ 2/96) [952]

8565 Say, Allen. *Tea with Milk* (4–8). 1999, Houghton $17.00 (0-395-90495-1). The picture book story of the author's mother, who was forced by her father to leave her home in California and return the the family's original home in Japan. (Rev: BL 3/15/99*; SLJ 5/99) [952]

8566 Shelley, Rex. *Japan* (5–10). 1990, Marshall Cavendish LB $24.95 (1-85435-297-0). An introduction to Japan that covers all the basic information concerning people, history, culture, geography, and economics. (Rev: BL 2/15/91; SLJ 6/91) [952]

8567 Stefoff, Rebecca. *Japan* (6–10). (Major World Nations) 1998, Chelsea LB $19.95 (0-7910-4761-X). With emphasis on the present social, economic, and cultural conditions, this is a readable, informative introduction to Japan. (Rev: BL 9/15/98; BR 1–2/99) [952.04]

8568 Whyte, Harlinah. *Japan* (4–8). (Countries of the World) 1998, Gareth Stevens LB $25.26 (0-8368-2126-2). After a section that presents standard introductory information about Japan, this account describes unusual aspects of Japanese culture like sumo wrestling, sushi, and etiquette. (Rev: SLJ 6/99) [952]

8569 Zurlo, Tony. *Japan: Superpower of the Pacific* (5–9). (Discovering Our Heritage) 1991, Dillon LB $19.95 (0-87518-480-4). A book that highlights aspects of Japan's history and culture as well as its economic growth and living conditions to 1990. (Rev: BL 2/1/92; SLJ 4/92) [952]

Other Asian Countries

8570 Ansary, Mir T. *Afghanistan: Fighting for Freedom* (5–9). (Discovering Our Heritage) 1991, Dillon LB $14.95 (0-87518-482-0). A history of the troubled country of Afghanistan, covering its geography, people, and cultural divisions. (Rev: BL 2/1/92; SLJ 3/92) [958.1]

8571 Brill, Marlene T. *Mongolia* (5–8). (Enchantment of the World) 1992, Children's Pr. LB $32.00 (0-516-02605-4). An introduction to Mongolia's history, people, language, culture, daily life, geography, climate, plants, and animals. (Rev: BL 6/1/92) [951.7]

8572 *Cambodia in Pictures* (5–8). Illus. (Visual Geography) 1996, Lerner LB $21.27 (0-8225-1905-4). Cambodia is introduced with accurate text and many effective photos, maps, and charts. (Rev: BL 11/15/96) [959.6]

8573 Cole, Wendy M. *Vietnam* (6–10). Illus. (Major World Nations) 1999, Chelsea LB $19.95 (0-7910-4751-2). A revised edition of the author's 1989 introduction to Vietnam, with chapters on history, geography, people, culture, cities and villages, government and social services, resources and economy, and transportation and communications. (Rev: SLJ 5/98) [959.7]

8574 Cromie, Alice. *Taiwan* (5–8). Illus. (Enchantment of the World) 1994, Children's Pr. LB $32.00 (0-516-02627-5). This Asian nation is introduced in an attractive format, with many color photographs, covering such topics as history, government, people, and its economy. (Rev: BL 12/15/94) [951.24]

8575 Foster, Leila M. *Afghanistan* (5–8). Illus. (Enchantment of the World) 1996, Children's Pr. LB $32.00 (0-516-20017-8). This introduction to the troubled land of Afghanistan torn by civil war emphasizes its geography, peoples, culture, and history to the mid-1990s. (Rev: BL 1/1–15/97) [958.1]

8576 Goodman, Jim. *Thailand* (5–9). (Cultures of the World) 1991, Marshall Cavendish LB $24.95 (1-85435-402-7). Thailand's history, land, and culture. (Rev: BL 3/15/92) [959.3]

8577 Hansen, Ole Steen. *Vietnam* (5–8). Illus. (Economically Developing Countries) 1996, Raintree Steck-Vaughn LB $24.26 (0-8172-4526-X). This

introduction to Vietnam includes background information on its history and culture, but places emphasis on recent developments and its emerging economy. (Rev: BL 3/1/97) [959.7]

8578 Heinrichs, Ann. *Nepal* (5–8). Illus. (Enchantment of the World) 1996, Children's Pr. LB $32.00 (0-516-02642-9). Using color photos on each page, this attractive book introduces the history, geography, and people of Nepal. (Rev: BL 7/96) [954.96]

8579 Heinrichs, Ann. *Tibet* (5–8). Illus. (Enchantment of the World) 1996, Children's Pr. LB $32.00 (0-516-20155-7). An introduction to the history, people, and geography of this country, now occupied by China. (Rev: BL 1/1–15/97) [951]

8580 Jung, Sung-Hoon. *South Korea* (5–8). (Economically Developing Countries) 1997, Raintree Steck-Vaughn LB $24.26 (0-8172-4530-8). This overview of current economic conditions in South Korea describes the country's success with electronic exports and provides case studies of family-run companies. (Rev: BL 5/15/97) [951.95]

8581 Kamm, Henry. *Dragon Ascending: Vietnam and the Vietnamese* (10–12). 1996, Arcade $24.95 (1-55970-306-7). This is a detailed, accurate, personal account of Vietnam, written by a Pulitzer Prize-winning journalist. (Rev: BL 1/1–15/96; SLJ 10/96) [959.7]

8582 Kendra, Judith. *Tibetans* (5–8). (Threatened Cultures) 1994, Thomson Learning LB $24.26 (1-56847-152-1). Discusses Tibetan culture and religion, with emphasis on the denial by China of Tibetans' rights. Follows the daily lives of 2 Tibetan children, one living in the country, one in the city. (Rev: BL 7/94) [951]

8583 *Laos in Pictures* (5–8). Illus. (Visual Geography) 1996, Lerner LB $21.27 (0-8225-1906-2). The past and present of Laos are introduced using simple text and many illustrations, including maps and charts. (Rev: BL 11/15/96) [959.4]

8584 McNair, Sylvia. *Indonesia* (5–8). (Enchantment of the World) 1993, Children's Pr. LB $32.00 (0-516-02618-6). An objective look at Indonesia's history, geography, economy, and culture, with abundant photographs. (Rev: BL 11/1/93) [959.8]

8585 Rowell, Jonathan. *Malaysia* (5–8). (Economically Developing Countries) 1997, Raintree Steck-Vaughn LB $24.26 (0-8172-4531-6). The growth and development of Malaysia are traced, with material on its ventures with new technology. (Rev: BL 5/15/97) [330.95]

8586 Sis, Peter. *Tibet: Through the Red Box* (7–12). Illus. 1998, Farrar $25.00 (0-374-37552-6). Using a journal kept by the author's filmmaker father when he journeyed to Tibet long ago, old tales, and pictures of landscapes and intriguing illustrations inspired by the Tibetan wheel of life, the author writes about the past and present of this land, its culture, and its religion. (Rev: BL 9/15/98; BR 5–6/99; SLJ 10/98) [954.96]

8587 *Vietnam—in Pictures* (5–8). 1994, Lerner LB $21.27 (0-8225-1909-7). Clear, readable, and up-to-date description that students will find useful for reports. (Rev: BL 11/1/94) [915.97]

8588 Wright, David K. *Brunei* (5–8). (Enchantment of the World) 1991, Children's Pr. LB $32.00 (0-516-02602-X). This small country that is part of what was once Borneo is now largely dependent on oil and gas resources. (Rev: BL 2/1/92) [959.55]

8589 Zimmermann, Robert. *Sri Lanka* (5–8). (Enchantment of the World) 1992, Children's Pr. LB $32.00 (0-516-02606-2). Good basic information on this island formerly called Ceylon, followed by coverage up to 1992 of the civil strife that is dividing the island. (Rev: BL 6/1/92) [954.93]

8590 Zwier, Lawrence J. *Sri Lanka: War Torn Island* (8–12). Illus. (World in Conflict) 1998, Lerner LB $22.60 (0-8225-3550-5). The author describes the war and political struggle in Sri Lanka, with good historical information and material on the present standoff. (Rev: BL 4/15/98) [305.8]

Australia and the Pacific Islands

8591 Ansell, Rod, and Rachel Percy. *To Fight the Wild* (9–12). Illus. 1986, Harcourt $12.95 (0-15-289068-8). An amazing survival story about a 22-year-old man isolated in a remote part of the Australian bush country. (Rev: BL 6/15/86; SLJ 9/86) [613.6]

8592 Bligh, William. *Mutiny on Board HMS Bounty* (10–12). 1989, NAL paper $3.50 (0-451-52293-1). The story of the famous mutiny is told from the standpoint of Captain Bligh. [904]

8593 Crump, Donald J., ed. *Amazing Animals of Australia* (6–9). Illus. 1984, National Geographic LB $12.50 (0-87044-520-0). A colorful introduction to such animals as the kangaroo and platypus. [591.9]

8594 Flannery, Tim. *Throwim Way Leg: Tree-Kangaroos, Possums and Penis Gourds: On the Track of Unknown Mammals in Wildest New Guinea* (9–12). 1999, Atlantic Monthly $25.00 (0-87113-731-3). The adventures of an explorer and scientist during his many trips to the outreaches of New Guinea. (Rev: BL 12/15/98; SLJ 9/99) [996]

8595 Fox, Mary V. *New Zealand* (5–8). (Enchantment of the World) 1991, Children's Pr. LB $32.00 (0-516-02728-X). A good basic introduction to these

Pacific islands, the land, people, history, and culture. (Rev: BL 10/1/91) [993]

8596 Haney, David. *Captain James Cook and the Explorers of the Pacific* (6–9). (World Explorers) 1991, Chelsea LB $19.95 (0-7910-1310-3). The story of how the islands of the Pacific Ocean were discovered and explored by such men as the intrepid Captain Cook. (Rev: BL 4/1/92) [910]

8597 Heyerdahl, Thor. *Easter Island: The Mystery Solved* (10–12). Illus. 1989, Random $24.95 (0-394-57906-2). The engrossing story of the explorer and his attempt to explain the existence of the huge monuments on Easter Island. (Rev: VOYA 6/90) [996]

8598 Jones, Phillip. *Boomerang* (10–12). Illus. 1997, Ten Speed Pr. paper $14.95 (0-89815-943-1). A history of the development and use of the boomerang, which has been part of many cultures for more than 10,000 years, focusing on the Aboriginal culture of Australia. (Rev: SLJ 6/98) [994]

8599 Lowe, David, and Andrea Shimmen. *Australia* (4–8). Illus. (Modern Industrial World) 1996, Raintree Steck-Vaughn LB $24.26 (0-8172-4553-7). Australia's economic status, living standards, educational system, and industry are covered. (Rev: BL 2/15/97) [919.4]

8600 McGuinn, Taro. *East Timor: Island in Turmoil* (7–10). (World in Conflict) 1998, Lerner LB $25.26 (0-8225-3555-6). The country of East Timor, an island east of Indonesia, is introduced, with material on its internal ethnic and political conflicts. (Rev: BL 10/15/98; BR 1–2/99; SLJ 10/98) [959.8 6]

Europe

General and Miscellaneous

8601 *Cyprus—in Pictures* (5–8). (Visual Geography) 1992, Lerner LB $21.27 (0-8225-1910-0). The divided island of Cyprus is introduced, with good background and information on the standoff between Greece and Turkey up to 1992. (Rev: BL 2/1/93) [956.45]

8602 Dornberg, John. *Central and Eastern Europe* (10–12). (International Government and Politics) 1995, Oryx paper $45.00 (0-89774-942-1). A former bureau chief and correspondent for *Newsweek* magazine discusses the people, ethnic groups, economics, and internal affairs of the 12 countries of Central and Eastern Europe, beginning with the end of the Cold War in 1990. (Rev: SLJ 5/96) [914]

8603 Dornberg, John. *Western Europe* (9–12). (International Government and Politics) 1996, Oryx paper $45.00 (0-89774-943-X). After a general introduction of Western Europe and the formation of the

European Union, the author discusses controversial issues such as nationalism, the economy, crime, pollution, and immigration, followed by profiles of the individual countries involved. (Rev: SLJ 9/96) [940]

8604 Fox, Mary V. *Cyprus* (5–8). (Enchantment of the World) 1993, Children's Pr. LB $32.00 (0-516-02617-8). The history, geography, economy, and culture of Cyprus, with abundant and well-chosen photos and illustrations. (Rev: BL 11/1/93) [956.93]

Eastern Europe and the Balkans

8605 Balakian, Peter. *Black Dog of Fate* (10–12). 1997, Basic $24.00 (0-465-00704-X). While growing up in suburban New Jersey, the author, a poet, investigates his family's past and unearths incredible stories of atrocities during the Armenian genocide at the hands of the Turks. (Rev: SLJ 11/97) [961]

8606 Black, Eric. *Bosnia: Fractured Region* (9–12). (World in Conflict) 1999, Lerner LB $25.26 (0-8225-3553-X). In this book about the war in Bosnia, the author presents a clear, detailed, history of Yugoslavia and its neighbors, a careful account of the armed conflicts among Serbs, Croats, and Muslims, and a measured assessment of the future of the region. (Rev: BL 8/99*; SLJ 5/99) [949.6]

8607 Burke, Patrick. *Eastern Europe: Bulgaria, Czech Republic, Hungary, Poland, Romania, Slovakia* (5–8). (Country Fact Files) 1997, Raintree Steck-Vaughn LB $24.26 (0-8172-4628-2). In chapters 2 to 4 pages long, the impact of geography on the landscape, daily life, natural resources, transportation, and other aspects of life is examined for these 6 countries. (Rev: SLJ 8/97) [947]

8608 *Czech Republic—in Pictures* (5–8). (Visual Geography) 1995, Lerner LB $21.27 (0-8225-1879-1). This small republic is introduced with stunning photographs and concise text. (Rev: BL 8/95) [943.7]

8609 Fireside, Harvey, and Bryna J. Fireside. *Young People From Bosnia Talk about War* (6–9). Illus. (Issues in Focus) 1996, Enslow LB $19.95 (0-89490-730-1). Several students from Bosnia who have been brought to this country to study by the Bosnian Student Project tell about the effects of the war on them, their families, and their country. (Rev: BL 10/15/96; BR 1–2/97; SLJ 10/96; VOYA 2/97) [949.702]

8610 Harbor, Bernard. *Conflict in Eastern Europe* (6–12). (Conflicts) 1993, Macmillan LB $18.95 (0-02-742626-2). An overview of events that led to the demise of the Soviet empire in Eastern Europe and what transpired subsequently, up to 1993. (Rev: BL 10/1/93; SLJ 12/93) [947]

8611 Harris, Nathaniel. *The War in Former Yugoslavia* (7–12). Illus. (New Perspectives) 1998, Rain-

tree Steck-Vaughn $27.11 (0-8172-5014-X). Different perspectives on this war are expressed through the viewpoints of political leaders, ordinary citizens, soldiers, militiamen, foreign diplomats, rescue workers, and news reporters. (Rev: BL 3/15/98; BR 1–2/99) [940.54]

8612 Horrell, Sarah. *The History of Emigration from Eastern Europe* (4–8). (Origins) 1998, Watts LB $21.00 (0-531-14449-6). In 7 short chapters, the author presents an overview of emigration from Eastern European countries to Western Europe, North America, and Palestine (later Israel) from the 17th century to the present. (Rev: SLJ 9/98) [940]

8613 *Hungary—in Pictures* (5–8). (Visual Geography) 1993, Lerner LB $21.27 (0-8225-1883-X). Pictures and concise text introduce the land, history, and people of Hungary. (Rev: BL 12/1/93; SLJ 12/93) [943.9]

8614 Otfinoski, Steven. *Bulgaria* (6–10). (Nations In Transition) 1998, Facts on File $19.95 (0-8160-3705-1). This book reviews the history, politics, people, and culture of Bulgaria, now undergoing transition as a result of the fall of communism in Eastern Europe, plus material on relationships with Gypsies and other minorities. (Rev: BL 3/1/99; BR 5–6/99; SLJ 6/99) [949.903]

8615 Otfinoski, Steven. *Poland* (6–10). (Nations in Transition) 1995, Facts on File $19.95 (0-8160-3063-4). This work explains Poland's past and covers its present situation, with chapters on religion, economy, culture, and daily life. (Rev: BR 9–10/96; VOYA 8/96) [943]

8616 Rady, Martyn. *Collapse of Communism in Eastern Europe* (7–12). (Causes and Consequences) 1995, Raintree Steck-Vaughn LB $25.69 (0-8172-4052-7). This clear, accurate account of the reasons for the fall of the Soviet empire and the problems that have arisen as a result. (Rev: BL 12/15/95) [940]

8617 Reger, James P. *The Rebuilding of Bosnia* (6–8). Illus. (Overview) 1997, Lucent LB $17.96 (1-56006-190-1). After a discussion of the ethnic and religious strife in the Balkans for 1,500 years, this book focuses on the recent war in Bosnia and the uneasy peace following 1995's Dayton Accords. (Rev: BL 9/1/97; SLJ 8/97) [949.703]

8618 Ricchiardi, Sherry. *Bosnia: The Struggle for Peace* (5–8). Illus. 1996, Millbrook LB $23.40 (0-7613-0031-7). An account that gives background information but concentrates on recent (through 1995) events in Bosnia. (Rev: BL 7/96; SLJ 7/96) [949.702]

8619 Rohr, Janelle, ed. *Eastern Europe* (7–12). (Opposing Viewpoints) 1990, Greenhaven LB $15.95 (0-89908-480-X); paper $16.20 (0-89908-455-9). Articles and speeches from 1989-1990 by statesmen debating communism, economic policies, the role of a united Germany, and European unification. (Rev: BL 2/1/91) [947]

8620 Rollyson, Carl S. *Teenage Refugees from Eastern Europe Speak Out* (7–12). (Teenage Refugees Speak Out) 1997, Rosen LB $16.95 (0-8239-2437-8). Young refugees from Slovakia, Bulgaria, Hungary, Romania, Poland, Yugoslavia, and the former East Germany tell about conditions in their homelands and their receptions in the United States. (Rev: BL 12/15/97) [947]

8621 *Romania—in Pictures* (5–8). (Visual Geography) 1993, Lerner LB $21.27 (0-8225-1894-5). The land of Romania is introduced with good pictures and concise text. (Rev: BL 9/1/93) [949.8]

8622 Sanborne, Mark. *Romania* (9–12). 1996, Facts on File $19.95 (0-8160-3089-8). The first half of this book describes the history of Romania, and the second deals with current political and economic conditions and problems. (Rev: VOYA 10/96) [949.8]

8623 Sioras, Efstathia. *Czech Republic* (7–10). (Cultures of the World) 1998, Marshall Cavendish LB $35.64 (0-7614-0870-3). An attractive volume that covers the standard topics: geography, history, government, economy, leisure, festivals, and food, and includes full-color photographs, colorful sidebars, maps, charts, and recipes. (Rev: SLJ 6/99) [943.7]

8624 *Slovakia—in Pictures* (5–8). (Visual Geography) 1995, Lerner LB $21.27 (0-8225-1912-7). The newly formed country of Slovakia is introduced through pictures and concise text. (Rev: BL 11/15/95) [943.7305]

8625 Yancey, Diane. *Life in War-Torn Bosnia* (6–9). Illus. (The Way People Live) 1996, Lucent $16.95 (1-56006-326-2). Though now a few years old, this account gives valuable background material on the Balkans, tracing their history and problems from the Middle Ages. (Rev: BL 3/15/96; BR 9–10/96; SLJ 4/96) [949.7]

France

8626 Banfield, Susan. *The Rights of Man, the Reign of Terror: The Story of the French Revolution* (9–12). 1989, HarperCollins LB $14.00 (0-397-32354-9). A dramatically told account of the causes, events, and aftermath of the French Revolution. (Rev: BL 1/1/89; SLJ 4/90; VOYA 12/89) [944]

8627 Barter, James. *The Palace of Versailles* (6–10). (Building History) 1998, Lucent $18.96 (1-56006-433-1). An informative account of the building of the palace for King Louis XIV of France, which took 40 years and represents a pinnacle of opulence and grandeur. (Rev: BL 12/15/98; BR 5–6/99; SLJ 2/99) [944]

8628 Benedict, Kitty C. *The Fall of the Bastille* (5–8). (Turning Points in World History) 1991, Silver Burdett LB $14.95 (0-382-24129-0); paper $7.95 (0-382-24135-5). A study of the event that symbolized a tremendous change in French society. (Rev: BL 3/15/92) [944.04]

8629 Cobb, Richard, and Colin Jones, eds. *Voices of the French Revolution* (10–12). Illus. 1988, Salem House $29.95 (0-88162-338-5). Using eyewitness accounts plus additional material, this is an introduction to the major events and people involved in the French Revolution. (Rev: BL 10/15/88; VOYA 4/89) [944.04219]

8630 Corzine, Phyllis. *The French Revolution* (8–12). (World History) 1995, Lucent LB $17.96 (1-56006-248-7). Using many quotes, this history of the French Revolution shows how it began with idealism and ended in a bloody power struggle. (Rev: BL 2/15/95; SLJ 2/95) [944.04]

8631 Libby, Megan M. *Postcards from France* (8–12). 1998, HarperCollins paper $3.99 (0-06-101170-3). A compilation of 12 columns written for a local newspaper, this book tells of the experiences of Megan Libby, a high school student from Connecticut during her junior year in France. (Rev: BL 4/15/97) [944]

8632 Nardo, Don, ed. *The French Revolution* (9–12). (Turning Points in World History) 1998, Greenhaven LB $21.96 (1-56510-934-1); paper $17.45 (1-56510-933-3). The 19 essays in this anthology explore the historical background leading up to the French Revolution, the social upheaval it created, and its lasting impact on France and the world. (Rev: SLJ 11/98) [944]

8633 Nardo, Don. *The Trial of Joan of Arc* (7–10). (Famous Trials) 1997, Lucent LB $17.96 (1-56006-466-8). A scholarly discussion and analysis Joan of Arc's trial and execution, with a brief introductory biography. (Rev: SLJ 10/97) [944]

8634 Powell, Jillian. *A History of France through Art* (5–8). Illus. (History through Art) 1996, Thomson Learning LB $24.26 (1-56847-441-5). The basic history of France is covered in 21 double-page spreads, each dealing with an important event or subject and each containing works of art and informative background text. (Rev: BL 3/1/96; SLJ 2/96) [944]

8635 Shuter, Jane, ed. *Helen Williams and the French Revolution* (5–8). Illus. (History Eyewitness) 1996, Raintree Steck-Vaughn LB $24.26 (0-8114-8287-1). History comes alive through this first-person account of events in the French Revolution and the many authentic illustrations. (Rev: BL 5/15/96; SLJ 6/96) [944.04]

Germany and Switzerland

8636 Ayer, Eleanor. *Germany* (6–9). (Modern Nations of the World) 1998, Lucent LB $17.96 (1-56006-355-6). A fine introduction to Germany's history, geography, and culture that does not gloss over the atrocities of the Nazi regime and the problems of reunification. (Rev: BL 12/1/98) [943]

8637 Bornstein, Jerry. *The Wall Came Tumbling Down: The Berlin Wall and the Fall of Communism* (10–12). Illus. 1990, Arch Cape $12.99 (0-517-03306-2). A concise history with photographs of the events that led to the opening of the Berlin Wall on November 9, 1989. (Rev: BL 7/90) [335.43]

8638 Epler, Doris M. *The Berlin Wall: How It Rose and Why It Fell* (7–10). 1992, Millbrook LB $22.40 (1-56294-114-3). The history of the Berlin Wall from the rise of the Nazi regime between the world wars to the 1990 beginning of German reunification. (Rev: BL 12/1/91; SLJ 3/92) [943.1]

8639 Fulbrook, Mary. *A Concise History of Germany* (9–12). 1991, Cambridge Univ. Pr. $54.95 (0-521-36283-0); paper $18.95 (0-521-36836-7). Covers Germany from the medieval period and examines the political, social, and cultural context that led to reunification. (Rev: BL 2/15/91) [943]

8640 *Germany—in Pictures* (5–8). (Visual Geography) 1994, Lerner LB $21.27 (0-8225-1873-2). An introduction to united Germany, with some background material and numerous useful illustrations. (Rev: BL 1/15/95) [943]

8641 Grant, R. G. *The Berlin Wall* (7–12). (New Perspectives) 1998, Raintree Steck-Vaughn $27.12 (0-8172-5017-4). This presentation of various perspectives on the Berlin Wall, its uses, and its destruction in 1989, is also an overview of the history of the Cold War in Europe and the collapse of communism there. (Rev: BL 1/1–15/99) [943.1]

8642 Hargrove, Jim. *Germany* (5–8). (Enchantment of the World) 1991, Children's Pr. LB $32.00 (0-516-02601-1). An introduction to Germany that includes history, geography, government, economy, people, culture, daily life, and more. (Rev: BL 2/1/92) [943]

8643 Kitchen, Martin. *The Cambridge Illustrated History of Germany* (10–12). 1996, Cambridge Univ. Pr. $39.95 (0-521-45341-0). A lavishly illustrated history of Germany that covers 2,000 years of history, from the days of Julius Caesar to reunification in the 1990s. (Rev: BL 10/1/96; SLJ 3/97) [943]

8644 Mirable, Lisa. *The Berlin Wall* (5–8). (Turning Points in World History) 1991, Silver Burdett LB $14.95 (0-382-24133-9); paper $8.95 (0-382-24140-1). Discusses the political, economic, and religious

factors that led to a new social order in Germany. (Rev: BL 3/15/92) [943.1]

8645 Nardo, Don, ed. *The Rise of Nazi Germany* (7–12). (Turning Points in World History) 1999, Greenhaven LB $20.96 (1-56510-965-1); paper $17.45 (1-56510-964-3). This anthology of writings examines the emergence of fascism and National Socialism in Germany, the personality of Hitler, his use of propaganda, and his political maneuvering to seize control in 1933. (Rev: BL 6/1–15/99; SLJ 5/99) [943.086]

8646 Pollard, Michael. *The Rhine* (5–8). (Great Rivers) 1997, Benchmark LB $22.79 (0-7614-0500-3). After explaining how the Rhine was formed, this attractive book describes its history, importance, tributaries, tourism, and present-day role. (Rev: SLJ 3/98) [943]

8647 Spencer, William. *Germany Then and Now* (8–12). 1994, Watts LB $24.00 (0-531-11137-7). A history of Germany and its people, addressing such current issues as neo-Nazism and the problems created by uniting capitalist and socialist societies under a capitalist system. (Rev: BL 8/94; SLJ 8/94; VOYA 10/94) [943]

8648 *Switzerland in Pictures* (5–8). (Visual Geography) 1996, Lerner LB $21.27 (0-8225-1895-3). With a generous number of color pictures, this account traces the history and geography of Switzerland, with emphasis on the present and its people. (Rev: BL 9/15/96; SLJ 8/98) [949.4]

8649 Symynkywicz, Jeffrey B. *Germany: United Again* (6–9). (The Fall of Communism) 1995, Silver Burdett LB $18.95 (0-87518-634-3); paper $7.95 (0-382-39190-X). This account of German history from Kaiser Wilhelm to the present focuses on the fall of the Berlin Wall and the reunification of Germany. (Rev: SLJ 7/96) [943]

8650 Tames, Richard. *Nazi Germany* (9–12). Illus. 1986, Batsford $19.95 (0-7134-3538-0). This is a history of the Nazi period in Germany as seen through a series of portraits of people who lived through it. (Rev: SLJ 4/86) [943.08]

Great Britain and Ireland

8651 Ashby, Ruth. *Elizabethan England* (6–9). (Cultures of the Past) 1998, Marshall Cavendish LB $28.50 (0-7614-0269-1). This volume not only tells about the cultural and political events during the reign of Elizabeth I, but also places them within a broader historical context. (Rev: BL 12/15/98; BR 5–6/99; SLJ 2/99) [941]

8652 Atkins, Sinclair. *From Stone Age to Conquest* (7–10). Illus. 1986, Hulton paper $14.95 (0-7175-1305-X). A well-illustrated account of British history from prehistoric times to the Norman Conquest. (Rev: SLJ 4/86) [941.01]

8653 Black, Eric. *Northern Ireland: Troubled Land* (8–12). Illus. (World in Conflict) 1998, Lerner LB $25.26 (0-8225-3552-1). An information-packed, illustrated account of the historical background of the conflict in Northern Ireland and current developments. (Rev: BL 4/15/98) [941.6]

8654 Bland, Celia. *The Mechanical Age: The Industrial Revolution in England* (7–12). 1995, Facts on File $19.95 (0-8160-3139-8). Examines the technological and social advances of the Industrial Revolution in England, with detailed notes and an extensive bibliography. (Rev: BL 10/15/95; SLJ 11/95) [338.094]

8655 Corbishley, Mike, et al. *The Young Oxford History of Britain & Ireland, No. 9* (5–8). Illus. 1997, Oxford $53.95 (0-19-910035-7). This is a handsome overview of the history of Britain and Ireland from prehistoric times when Britain and Ireland were part of the European land mass to the end of the 20th century. (Rev: BL 5/15/97; SLJ 7/97; VOYA 10/98) [941]

8656 Corey, Melinda, and George Ochoa, eds. *The Encyclopedia of the Victorian World: A Reader's Companion to the People, Places, Events, and Everyday Life of the Victorian Era* (9–12). 1996, Holt $50.00 (0-8050-2622-3). A readable, fun reference tool that brings Victorian times to life with details on people, books, terms, discoveries, clothing, events, and slang. (Rev: BL 9/15/96; SLJ 5/96) [942]

8657 Flint, David. *Great Britain* (5–8). Illus. (Modern Industrial World) 1996, Raintree Steck-Vaughn LB $24.26 (0-8172-4555-3). Modern Great Britain is the focus of this volume, which concentrates on the economy and industrial development. (Rev: BL 2/15/96; SLJ 8/97) [330.941]

8658 Hodges, Michael. *Ireland* (9–12). 1988, David & Charles $20.75 (0-7134-5542-X). A history of Ireland that concentrates on the gaining of freedom and Irish-English relationships. (Rev: BR 9–10/89) [941.7]

8659 Holliday, Laurel, ed. *Children of "The Troubles": Our Lives in the Crossfire of Northern Ireland* (10–12). (Children in Conflict) 1997, Pocket Books $22.00 (0-671-53736-9). Children of Northern Ireland tell their stories of the internal conflict in their country through prose pieces, remembrances, and some poetry. (Rev: SLJ 7/97; VOYA 10/97) [941]

8660 Lace, William W. *Elizabethan England* (8–12). (World History) 1995, Lucent LB $17.96 (1-56006-278-9). Elements of the period are discussed, including biographical details about one of history's most able, successful, and influential queens. (Rev: BL 2/15/95; SLJ 3/95) [942.05]

8661 Lace, William W. *England* (7–10). (Modern Nations of the World) 1997, Lucent LB $17.96 (1-56006-194-4). A compact introduction to the past and present of England, arranged in 6 theme-based chapters, with good illustrations and interesting sidebars. (Rev: SLJ 9/97) [941]

8662 Lace, William W. *The Little Princes in the Tower* (7–9). Illus. (Mysterious Deaths) 1997, Lucent LB $22.45 (1-56006-262-2). The unsolved murders of Edward V and his brother in the Tower of London and the possible involvement of Richard III are explored in this book. (Rev: BL 2/15/96; BR 9–10/97; SLJ 3/97) [942.04]

8663 Lister, Maree, and Marti Sevier. *England* (5–8). (Countries of the World) 1998, Gareth Stevens LB $19.93 (0-8368-2125-4). In addition to basic information on the geography, history, economy, culture, and people of England, this book has a special section that describes characteristics that make this country unique, including particular places, people, and traditions. (Rev: BL 12/15/98; SLJ 2/99) [941]

8664 McCourt, Frank. *Angela's Ashes* (10–12). 1996, Scribners $23.00 (0-684-87435-0). The harrowing, true story of growing up in extreme poverty in Limerick, Ireland, by a writer whose humor and humanity outshine the terrible conditions he describes. (Rev: SLJ 6/97) [941.5]

8665 Mitchell, Graham. *The Napoleonic Wars* (5–9). Illus. 1990, Batsford $19.95 (0-7134-5729-5). This British import tells about the war chiefly from the British point of view and uses many quotes from original sources. (Rev: BR 3–4/90; SLJ 3/90) [944.05]

8666 Morrill, John, ed. *The Oxford Illustrated History of Tudor & Stuart Britain* (10–12). 1996, Oxford $72.50 (0-19-820325-X). Essays on various aspects of life in 16th- and 17th-century Great Britain, arranged by such topics as education, theater, and religion, followed by a detailed survey of the major events of the two centuries to give the essays a historical context. (Rev: BL 11/1/96; SLJ 7/97) [941]

8667 *Northern Ireland—in Pictures* (5–8). (Visual Geography) 1991, Lerner LB $21.27 (0-8225-1898-8). This beautiful but troubled land is introduced in text and pictures. (Rev: BL 2/15/92) [941.6]

8668 Ross, Stewart. *Elizabethan Life* (6–9). (How It Was) 1991, Batsford $19.95 (0-7134-6356-2). Laws, journals, and other historical sources from the period help re-create a vivid picture of Elizabethan life. (Rev: BL 1/15/92) [941]

8669 Sancha, Sheila. *The Luttrell Village: Country Life in the Middle Ages* (7–10). Illus. 1983, HarperCollins LB $13.89 (0-690-04324-4). Life and activities in an English village of 1328 are revealed in words and excellent drawings by the author. [942.03]

8670 Sauvain, Philip. *Hastings* (5–8). Illus. (Great Battles and Sieges) 1992, Macmillan $21.00 (0-02-781079-8). A description of the 1066 victory of Duke William of Normandy on the south coast of England that initiated Norman rule of Britain. (Rev: BL 10/1/92; SLJ 2/93) [941]

8671 Swisher, Clarice. *The Glorious Revolution* (8–12). Illus. (World History) 1996, Lucent LB $22.45 (1-56006-296-7). This account tells of the events in English history during 1688–89 when James II was deposed and William III and Mary came to the throne. (Rev: BL 2/15/96) [941.06]

8672 Yancey, Diane. *Life in Charles Dickens's England* (6–10). (The Way People Live) 1998, Lucent LB $17.96 (1-56006-098-0). From terrible squalor and grinding poverty to great wealth and comfort, the spectrum of British society, rural and urban, is explored during the days of Charles Dickens. (Rev: BL 10/15/98; SLJ 1/99; VOYA 12/99) [942]

8673 Yancey, Diane. *Life in the Elizabethan Theater* (6–10). Illus. (Way People Live) 1997, Lucent LB $18.96 (1-56006-343-2). An explanation of the design of the Elizabethan theater and of the roles of various people connected with it, such as actors, playwrights, and the audience. (Rev: BL 3/15/97; SLJ 4/97) [792]

Greece

8674 *Greece—in Pictures* (5–8). (Visual Geography) 1992, Lerner LB $19.95 (0-8225-1882-1). The beautiful land of Greece and its islands are introduced in text and many pictures. (Rev: BL 10/1/92) [949.5]

Italy

8675 Foster, Leila M. *Italy* (5–9). (Modern Nations of the World) 1998, Lucent LB $18.96 (1-56006-481-1). This title gives an overview of Italy, its history, geography, and culture through interesting text, photos, sidebars, and a chronology. (Rev: SLJ 5/99) [945]

8676 Hibbert, Christopher. *Rome: The Biography of a City* (10–12). Illus. 1985, Penguin paper $26.95 (0-14-007078-8). An illustrated history of the Eternal City from pre-Roman Etruscan times to World War II. (Rev: BL 6/15/85) [945]

8677 *Italy* (10–12). (Eyewitness Travel) 1996, DK Publg. paper $29.95 (0-7894-0425-7). A guide to Italy that includes much helpful information found in standard travel guides, but with extensive use of photographs, pictures, cutaway drawings, and maps. This book is part of an extensive recommended series. (Rev: SLJ 9/96) [945]

8678 Macaulay, David. *Rome Antics* (5–8). Illus. 1997, Houghton $18.00 (0-395-82279-3). The reader gets a pigeon-eye view of vistas and buildings as the bird flies over Rome. (Rev: BL 9/15/97; SLJ 11/97*) [945]

8679 Martin, Fred. *Italy* (5–8). (Country Studies) 1999, Heinemann $27.07 (1-57572-894-X). Using double-page spreads filled with charts, graphs, drawings, maps, and photographs, this book provides basic material about Italy with a focus on contemporary issues. (Rev: BL 8/99; SLJ 8/99) [945]

Russia and Other Former Soviet Republics

8680 *Armenia* (5–8). (Then and Now) 1992, Lerner LB $23.93 (0-8225-2806-1). The story up to 1991 of the former Soviet republic that faced many internal problems after it gained independence. (Rev: BL 2/1/93) [956.6]

8681 *Azerbaijan* (5–8). (Then and Now) 1993, Lerner LB $23.93 (0-8225-2810-X). This book introduces the small republic of Azerbaijan, once the Soviet Union's most important oil producing area. (Rev: BL 2/15/93) [947]

8682 Batalden, Stephen K., and Sandra L. Batalden. *The Newly Independent States of Eurasia: Handbook of Former Soviet Republics*. 2nd. ed. (7–12). 1997, Oryx paper $46.75 (0-89774-940-5). Arranged by geographical region, this volume examines each of the newly formed republics created from the former USSR, with details on their past, their culture, and key problems facing each today. (Rev: SLJ 11/97) [947]

8683 *Belarus* (5–8). (Then and Now) 1993, Lerner LB $23.93 (0-8225-2811-8). An introduction to the history and status as of 1993 of the former Soviet republic of Belarus, or Belorussia, which borders on the Ukraine. (Rev: BL 5/15/93) [947]

8684 Bradley, John. *Russia: Building Democracy* (6–8). (Topics in the News) 1995, Raintree Steck-Vaughn LB $22.83 (0-8172-4177-9). Russian history from the 9th century to modern times. (Rev: BL 2/15/96; SLJ 3/96) [947]

8685 Clark, Mary Jane Behrends. *The Commonwealth of Independent States* (6–8). (Headliners) 1992, Millbrook LB $23.40 (1-56294-081-3). Summarizes events in the formation of the CIS, created from 15 republics after the 1991 breakup of the Soviet Union. (Rev: BL 2/15/93; SLJ 1/93) [947.085]

8686 Cumming, David. *Russia* (5–8). 1994, Thomson Learning LB $24.26 (1-56847-240-4). A general introduction, emphasizing conditions during the first few years after the fall of the Soviet Union rather than cultural traditions and history. (Rev: BL 1/15/95; SLJ 3/95) [330.947]

8687 Duffy, James P., and Vincent L. Ricci. *Czars: Russia's Rulers for Over One Thousand Years* (10–12). 1995, Facts on File $35.00 (0-8160-2873-7). The history of the rulers of the Russian Empire from the Viking Rurik to the death of Nicholas II in 1918, 1,000 years later. (Rev: SLJ 6/96) [947.07]

8688 *Estonia* (5–8). 1992, Lerner LB $23.93 (0-8225-2803-7). Following an introduction about the fall of communism, the book provides an overview of the land and its peoples. (Rev: BL 2/1/93; SLJ 12/92) [914.7]

8689 Fader, Kim B. *Russia* (9–12). Illus. (Modern Nations of the World) 1997, Lucent LB $17.96 (1-56006-521-4). This history of Russia, with good use of maps and sidebars, covers the period from the Scythians in 800–200 B.C., the collapse of the Soviet Union, and the Russian Federation in 1997, including recent information on the transition and foreign policy. (Rev: SLJ 5/98) [947]

8690 *Georgia: Then and Now* (5–8). Illus. (Then and Now) 1994, Lerner LB $23.93 (0-8225-2807-X). This former Soviet Republic is introduced, including its geography, ethnic makeup, history, economy, and future challenges. (Rev: BL 2/1/94; SLJ 3/94) [947]

8691 Harbor, Bernard. *The Breakup of the Soviet Union* (6–12). (Conflicts) 1993, Macmillan LB $22.00 (0-02-742625-4). An overview of the conflicts and changes in the region. (Rev: BL 7/93; SLJ 12/93) [947.08]

8692 Israel, Fred L., and Arthur M. Schlesinger, Jr., eds. *Moscow* (6–10). Illus. (The World 100 Years Ago) 1999, Chelsea LB $29.95 (0-7910-4658-3). This book describes what Burton Holmes, a traveler-lecturer during the first half of the 20th century, saw when he visited Moscow around the beginning of the century, including a trip to the Kremlin, a visit to the public baths, and a breakfast with Leo Tolstoy. (Rev: SLJ 7/98) [947]

8693 Kagda, Sakina. *Lithuania* (7–10). (Cultures of the World) 1997, Marshall Cavendish LB $35.64 (0-7614-0681-6). An introduction to Lithuania, with material on geography, history, government, culture, daily life, and festivals. (Rev: BL 8/97; SLJ 10/97) [947]

8694 *Kazakhstan* (5–8). (Then and Now) 1993, Lerner LB $23.93 (0-8225-2815-0). This account traces the history of the second largest republic in the former USSR and gives information on its status as of 1993. (Rev: BL 9/1/93) [958]

8695 Kort, Michael G. *The Handbook of the Former Soviet Union* (7–12). Illus. 1997, Millbrook LB $34.90 (0-7613-0016-3). An expert in Russian history gives an overview of the former Soviet Union, the problems each state faces today and the important

personalities involved. (Rev: BL 2/1/98; BR 5–6/98; SLJ 1/98; VOYA 6/98) [947]

8696 Kort, Michael G. *Russia*. Rev. ed. (7–12). (Nations in Transition) 1998, Facts on File $19.95 (0-8160-3776-0). This book explains the rapid changes in Russia's economy, politics, social conditions, and daily life in recent years and reviews the country's complex history and its impact on today. (Rev: BL 3/15/99; SLJ 4/99) [947.085]

8697 *Latvia* (5–8). 1992, Lerner LB $23.93 (0-8225-2802-9). Following an introduction about the fall of communism, provides an overview of the land and its peoples. (Rev: BL 2/1/93; SLJ 12/92) [947]

8698 *Lithuania* (5–8). (Then and Now) 1992, Lerner LB $23.93 (0-8225-2804-5). This Baltic Sea republic is described, including its history, people, and conditions in the period immediately following its independence in 1990. (Rev: BL 2/1/93) [947]

8699 Loory, Stuart H., and Ann Imse. *CNN Reports: Seven Days That Shook the World: The Collapse of Soviet Communism* (9–12). 1992, Turner $29.95 (1-878685-11-2); paper $19.95 (1-878685-12-0). The fall of communism told largely through photos. (Rev: BL 1/1/92) [947.085]

8700 Lustig, Michael M. *Ukraine* (7–12). (Nations in Transition) 1999, Facts on File $19.95 (0-8160-3757-4). A slim volume that traces the history of the Ukraine and its people, with emphasis on today—its faltering economy, corruption in government, Crimean independence, and other current problems. (Rev: BL 4/15/99; SLJ 6/99) [947.7]

8701 *Moldova* (5–8). (Then and Now) 1992, Lerner LB $23.93 (0-8225-2809-6). The history of this small, landlocked republic, parts of which at one time or another have belonged to the Ottoman Turks, Romania, Russia, and the USSR, and which is now independent. (Rev: BL 2/1/93) [947]

8702 Murrell, Kathleen B. *Russia* (4–8). Illus. (Eyewitness) 1998, Random LB $20.99 (0-679-99118-2). Using double-page spreads with many color illustrations, this is a fine overview of Russia from the earliest times to the present. (Rev: BL 7/98; SLJ 8/98) [947]

8703 Pavlenkov, Victor, and Peter Pappas, eds. *Russia: Yesterday, Today, Tomorrow: Voice of the Young Generation* (8–12). Illus. 1997, FC-Izdat paper $12.95 (0-9637035-5-2). This is a collection of essays written by Russian high school students who reflect on the past, present, and future of their country. (Rev: BL 2/15/97) [947.08]

8704 Pipes, Richard. *A Concise History of the Russian Revolution* (9–12). 1995, Knopf $30.00 (0-679-42277-3). A skillfully researched history and analysis of Russia's revolution and the events that preceded and followed it. (Rev: BL 10/1/95*) [947.084]

8705 *Russia* (5–8). (Then and Now) 1992, Lerner LB $23.93 (0-8225-2805-3). A brief history of Russia with emphasis on its status in the period immediately following the fall of the USSR in 1991. (Rev: BL 2/1/93; SLJ 12/92) [947]

8706 Sallnow, John, and Tatyana Saiko. *Russia* (5–8). (Country Fact Files) 1997, Raintree Steck-Vaughn LB $24.26 (0-8172-4625-8). The impact of geography on different aspects of life in Russia, including natural resources, daily life, the landscape, and transportation, is explored. (Rev: SLJ 8/97) [947]

8707 Sherrow, Victoria. *Life during the Russian Revolution* (6–10). (Way People Live) 1998, Lucent LB $22.45 (1-56006-389-0). The story of the oppressed poor and the aristocrats in Russia from 1905 through 1917 and how the old political, economic, and governmental system collapsed. (Rev: BL 7/98; SLJ 8/98) [947]

8708 Smith, Brenda. *The Collapse of the Soviet Union* (6–8). (Overview) 1994, Lucent LB $14.95 (1-56006-142-1). Details of the Cold War, the Gorbachev years, and the breakup of the USSR are preceded by a brief summary of Karl Marx's ideas, the Bolshevik Revolution of 1917, and Soviet leadership through the decades. (Rev: BL 3/15/94; SLJ 3/94) [947]

8709 Spilling, Michael. *Estonia* (7–10). (Cultures of the World) 1999, Marshall Cavendish LB $35.64 (0-7614-0951-3). An overview of this Baltic land that covers basic information and contemporary life and culture. (Rev: SLJ 7/99) [947]

8710 Spilling, Michael. *Georgia* (6–10). (Cultures of the World) 1997, Marshall Cavendish LB $35.64 (0-7614-0691-3). A detailed introduction to the former Soviet republic of Georgia, its geography, history, government, and culture. (Rev: SLJ 2/98) [947]

8711 Strickler, Jim. *Russia of the Tsars* (6–12). (World History) 1997, Lucent LB $22.45 (1-56006-3-295-9). This history of Russia's ruling dynasty gives special material on Peter the Great, and Catherine as well as the events and tsars immediately preceding the Russian Revolution. (Rev: BL 12/15/97) [947]

8712 *Tajikistan* (5–8). Illus. (Then and Now) 1993, Lerner LB $23.93 (0-8225-2816-9). An introduction to the land and people of this remote former Soviet republic located north of Afghanistan. (Rev: BL 10/15/93; SLJ 11/93) [958.6]

8713 *Ukraine* (5–8). (Then and Now) 1992, Lerner LB $22.95 (0-8225-2808-8). The history of this Black Sea republic and its status in the period imme-

diately following its independence in 1991. (Rev: BL 2/1/93) [947]

8714 *Uzbekistan* (5–8). (Then and Now) 1993, Lerner LB $23.93 (0-8225-2812-6). This book gives a history of this Muslim republic, its economic situation, and prospects for the future as of 1993. (Rev: BL 5/15/93) [958.7]

8715 Vadrot, Claude-Maria, and Victoria Ivleva. *Russia Today: From Holy Russia to Perestroika* (9–12). Trans. by Harry Swalef. 1991, Atomium $31.95 (1-56182-004-0). A French photographer and Soviet photographer capture the essence of Russian life just before the fall of socialism. (Rev: BL 7/91) [947.08]

8716 Vail, John. *"Peace, Land, Bread?" A History of the Russian Revolution* (7–12). Illus. (World History Library) 1996, Facts on File LB $19.95 (0-8160-2818-4). This volume, illustrated with photos and maps, covers the period in Russian history from the revolt against the czar to the rise of Joseph Stalin. (Rev: BL 2/15/96; BR 9–10/96; SLJ 2/96; VOYA 4/96) [947.084]

8717 Winters, Paul A., ed. *The Collapse of the Soviet Union* (10–12). 1998, Greenhaven LB $20.96 (1-56510-997-X); paper $20.25 (1-56510-996-1). A collection of 21 brief essays, most by U.S. writers, chronicles the disintegration of the Soviet empire from the reforms of the 1980s to the dramatic events of 1991, with projections for the future of the newly independent states. (Rev: BL 11/15/98; BR 5–6/99; SLJ 12/98) [947.085]

Scandinavia, Iceland, and Greenland

8718 Carlsson, Bo Kage. *Sweden* (5–8). (Modern Industrial World) 1995, Thomson Learning LB $24.26 (1-56847-436-9). Provides general background and information on current economic conditions. (Rev: BL 12/15/95) [949.4]

8719 *Finland—in Pictures* (5–8). (Visual Geography) 1991, Lerner LB $21.27 (0-8225-1881-3). Using both text and plenty of color pictures, this book provides basic information about this Baltic land bordered by Russia, Norway, and Sweden, as well as the Baltic Sea, the Gulf of Finland, and the Gulf of Bothnia. (Rev: BL 12/15/91) [948.97]

8720 Janeway, Elizabeth. *The Vikings* (6–8). 1981, Random paper $4.99 (0-394-84885-3). The exploits, explorations, and contributions of the Vikings are given. [936]

8721 Lasky, Kathryn. *Surtsey: The Newest Place on Earth* (5–9). Photos. 1992, Hyperion LB $15.89 (1-56282-301-9). Conveys the dramatic beginnings of the island of Surtsey, which sprang up off the coast of Iceland in 1963. Many full-page photos. (Rev: BL 1/1/93*; SLJ 2/93*) [508.4912]

8722 Streissguth, Thomas. *Life among the Vikings* (7–10). (The Way People Live) 1998, Lucent LB $125.72 (1-56006-392-0). Using a topical approach, this book covers Vikings' everyday life, warfare, ships, farming, language, art, and poetry. (Rev: SLJ 6/99) [948]

8723 Wilcox, Jonathan. *Iceland* (5–9). (Cultures of the World) 1996, Marshall Cavendish LB $35.64 (0-7614-0279-9). The history, geography, people, and culture of this remote island republic are introduced, with many color photos. (Rev: SLJ 7/96) [949.12]

8724 Wright, Rachel. *The Viking News* (5–8). 1998, Candlewick $15.99 (0-7636-0450-X). Life in Viking times, presented in a clever newspaper format. (Rev: BL 5/15/98; BR 1–2/99; SLJ 6/98) [948.022]

Spain and Portugal

8725 Champion, Neil. *Portugal* (5–8). (Modern Industrial World) 1995, Thomson Learning LB $24.26 (1-56847-435-0). A colorful history of Portugal that emphasizes present day economic and social conditions. (Rev: BL 12/15/95) [946.904]

8726 Finkelstein, Norman H. *The Other 1492: Jewish Settlement in the New World* (6–9). Illus. 1989, Macmillan LB $13.95 (0-684-18913-5). The story of Spanish Jews and their expulsion in 1492 at the hands of the all-powerful Inquisition. (Rev: BL 11/1/89; SLJ 1/90; VOYA 2/90) [946]

8727 McDowall, David. *The Spanish Armada* (8–12). Illus. 1988, David & Charles $19.95 (0-7134-5671-X). A British import that tells about the events surrounding this Spanish fleet and also supplies many short biographies of the people involved. (Rev: BR 11–12/88; SLJ 3/89) [946]

8728 Millar, Heather. *Spain in the Age of Exploration* (6–9). 1998, Marshall Cavendish LB $28.50 (0-7614-0303-5). This book focuses on Spain's age of exploration, with material on the Inquisition and the Reformation, Spanish culture, and Spain's legacy in the New World. (Rev: BL 12/15/98; BR 5–6/99; SLJ 2/99) [946]

8729 Paris, Erna. *The End of Days: A Story of Tolerance, Tyranny, and the Expulsion of the Jews from Spain* (10–12). 1995, Prometheus $29.95 (1-57392-017-7). Spanish history from 1300 through 1500, including the early harmonious relationships and flourishing culture, the development of divisions within the Catholic Church, the forced conversions of Jews, and the Inquisition and eventual expulsion of the Jews and the Moors from Spain by the Catholic Church. (Rev: SLJ 11/96) [946]

8730 *Portugal—in Pictures* (5–8). (Visual Geography) 1991, Lerner LB $21.27 (0-8225-1886-4). The land and people of Portugal are introduced with good basic material and many color photographs. (Rev: BL 12/15/91) [946.9]

8731 Shubert, Adrian. *The Land and People of Spain* (6–9). (Land and People of) 1992, HarperCollins LB $17.89 (0-06-020218-1). A comprehensive, detailed history of Spain. (Rev: BL 8/92) [946]

8732 *Spain—in Pictures* (5–8). (Visual Geography) 1995, Lerner LB $21.27 (0-8225-1887-2). Using many color pictures and concise text, this attractive book provides basic background material on Spain. (Rev: BL 11/15/95) [914.6]

Middle East

General and Miscellaneous

8733 Cipkowski, Peter. *Understanding the Crisis in the Persian Gulf* (7–12). 1992, Wiley paper $12.95 (0-471-54816-2). Covers the political history of the region, discusses the events that resulted in U.S. intervention, and provides information on immediate postwar Iraq. (Rev: BL 9/15/92) [956.704]

8734 Dudley, William, ed. *The Middle East* (7–10). (Opposing Viewpoints) 1992, Greenhaven paper $16.20 (0-89908-160-6). Articles and essays examine the background causes of the Middle East conflicts. (Rev: BL 6/15/92; SLJ 7/92) [320.956]

8735 Due, Andrea. *The Atlas of the Bible Lands: History, Daily Life and Traditions* (4–9). Illus. 1999, Bedrick $19.95 (0-87226-559-5). This atlas presents an encyclopedic amount of information on the history and culture of the Middle East from prehistory to modern times, with maps supplemented by clearly written text and extensive artwork. (Rev: BR 9–10/99; SLJ 3/99) [956]

8736 King, John. *Conflict in the Middle East* (6–12). (Conflicts) 1993, Macmillan LB $13.95 (0-02-785955-X). This book gives good background information and history on the origins of the current problems in the Middle East. (Rev: BL 10/1/93; SLJ 12/93) [956.04]

Egypt

8737 Heinrichs, Ann. *Egypt* (5–8). (Enchantment of the World) 1997, Children's Pr. LB $32.00 (0-516-20470-X). This book covers the history of Egypt from the pharaohs through the country's present-day leadership in the Middle East, with information about modern Egypt's geography, economy, agriculture, religious groups, and education, as well as government, national holidays, and wildlife. (Rev: BL 2/1/98; SLJ 5/98) [962]

8738 Loveridge, Emma. *Egypt* (5–8). (Country Fact Files) 1997, Raintree Steck-Vaughn LB $24.26 (0-8172-4626-6). This book gives standard basic information about Egypt, including its climate, landscape, trade, industry, and daily life. (Rev: SLJ 9/97) [962]

Israel and Palestine

8739 Altman, Linda J. *The Creation of Israel* (6–9). (World History) 1998, Lucent $17.96 (1-56006-288-6). Founded as a home for the Jews fleeing war and persecution, this is the story of this nation that is now over 50 years old. (Rev: BL 6/1–15/98) [956.94]

8740 Altman, Linda J. *Life on an Israeli Kibbutz* (6–9). Illus. (The Way People Live) 1996, Lucent LB $17.96 (1-56006-328-9). After a history of the kibbutz, the author describes the problems and rewards in this type of communal living, and its possible future. (Rev: BL 3/15/96; BR 9–10/96; SLJ 4/96) [307.77]

8741 Baralt, Luis A. *Turkey* (5–8). Illus. (Enchantment of the World) 1997, Children's Pr. LB $30.00 (0-516-20305-3). A visually attractive book that covers such topics as Turkey's population, natural resources, historic landmarks, and people. (Rev: BL 8/97) [915.61]

8742 Blumberg, Arnold. *The History of Israel* (9–12). (Histories of the Modern Nations) 1998, Greenwood $35.00 (0-313-30224-3). Following a brief survey of Israel's early history, the author stresses events of the last 30 years. (Rev: BR 5–6/99; VOYA 6/99) [956.94]

8743 Corzine, Phyllis. *The Palestinian-Israeli Accord* (6–10). (Overview) 1996, Lucent LB $22.45 (1-56006-181-2). This work explores the historical roots of the Israeli-Palestinian conflict, discusses the foundation of Israel and its need for land, and traces the rise of Yasir Arafat. (Rev: BR 11–12/97; SLJ 5/97) [956.94]

8744 Finkelstein, Norman H. *Friends Indeed: The Special Relationship of Israel and the United States* (7–12). 1998, Millbrook LB $22.90 (0-7613-0114-3). This book explores the close, often rocky, relationship between Israel and the U.S. through 10 administrations and several wars. (Rev: BL 8/98; BR 9–10/98; SLJ 6/98) [327.73]

8745 Gorkin, Michael, and Rafiqa Othman. *Three Mothers, Three Daughters* (10–12). 1996, Univ. of California Pr. $24.95 (0-520-20329-1). Interviews with 3 Palestinian Moslem women from 3 different environments—one from East Jerusalem, one from a small village, and the other from a refugee camp on the West Bank. (Rev: SLJ 12/96) [956]

8746 Marshood, Nabil. *Palestinian Teenage Refugees and Immigrants Speak Out* (7–12). (Teenage Refugees Speak Out) 1997, Rosen LB $17.95 (00-8239-2442-4). The exodus of Palestinians, many to the United States, and their reasons for leaving their homes are recounted through the stories of several teenage immigrants. (Rev: BL 12/15/97) [956.04]

8747 Mozeson, I. E., and Lois Stavsky. *Jerusalem Mosaic: Young Voices from the Holy City* (6–12). 1994, Four Winds paper $15.95 (0-02-767651-X). Thirty-six lively monologues based on interviews with teenagers living in Jerusalem in the early 1990s—Jew and Arab, Muslim and Christian. (Rev: BL 12/1/94; SLJ 1/95) [305.23]

8748 Ross, Stewart. *The Arab-Israeli Conflict* (7–12). (Causes and Consequences) 1995, Raintree Steck-Vaughn LB $27.11 (0-8172-4051-9). This conflict is presented in a historical context, using a magazine format, maps, and photos, and lays the basis for understanding the current continuing hostility. (Rev: BL 12/15/95; BR 3–4/96; SLJ 2/96) [956.94]

8749 Schroeter, Daniel J. *Israel: An Illustrated History* (10–12). 1998, Oxford $40.00 (0-19-510885-X). From prebiblical times to the present, this is a history of Israel that uses historic photos, archival documents, and many art reproductions. (Rev: BL 1/1–15/99; VOYA 6/99) [956.94]

8750 Sha'Ban, Mervet A., and Galit Fink. *If You Could Be My Friend: Letters of Mervet Akram Sha'Ban & Galit Fink* (6–9). Trans. by Beatrice Khadige. Illus. 1998, Orchard LB $16.99 (0-531-33113-X). Two teenage girls—one an Israeli and the other a Palestinian—share their feelings and fears in a series of letters they exchanged from 1988 to 1991. (Rev: BL 10/15/98; SLJ 11/98; VOYA 12/98) [956.9405 4]

8751 Silverman, Maida. *Israel: The Founding of a Modern Nation* (6–9). Illus. 1998, Dial LB $15.89 (0-8037-2136-6). This history of the Jewish people covers 3,000 years, from Biblical times to the birth of the Jewish state in 1948. (Rev: BR 1–2/99; SLJ 6/98) [956.94]

8752 Stefoff, Rebecca. *West Bank/Gaza Strip* (7–12). (Major World Nations) 1999, Chelsea LB $19.95 (0-7910-4771-7). This work describes the long, confrontational history of this area, with information on its people, economics, geography, and the outlook for the future. (Rev: SLJ 6/99) [956.94]

8753 Tubb, Jonathan N. *Bible Lands* (5–9). (Eyewitness Books) 1991, Knopf LB $20.99 (0-679-91457-9). A history of the Middle Eastern lands that figured in the Bible and a description of their status at the beginning of the 1990s. (Rev: BL 12/1/91) [220.9]

Other Mideast Countries

8754 Augustin, Rebecca. *Qatar* (5–8). (Enchantment of the World) 1997, Children's Pr. LB $32.00 (0-516-20303-7). An introduction to the small oil-producing country on the Persian Gulf that describes its history under British rule and how the people now live. (Rev: BL 7/97) [953.63]

8755 Foster, Leila M. *Iraq* (4–9). 1997, Children's Pr. $32.00 (0-516-20584-6). This book describes the land of Iraq, its history starting with Mesopotamia, the role of Islam, and daily life of normal Iraqi citizens, and comments on Saddam Hussein. (Rev: SLJ 4/99) [956]

8756 Foster, Leila M. *Jordan* (5–8). (Enchantment of the World) 1991, Children's Pr. LB $32.00 (0-516-02603-8). The story of this ancient land that borders on Israel, including its land, people, culture, and economic conditions at the beginning of the 1990s. (Rev: BL 2/1/92) [956.95]

8757 Foster, Leila M. *Kuwait* (5–10). Illus. (Enchantment of the World) 1998, Children's Pr. $32.00 (0-516-20604-4). A brief introduction to the land and people of Kuwait, with about one-fifth of the text devoted to the Gulf War. (Rev: SLJ 11/98) [956]

8758 Foster, Leila M. *Lebanon* (5–8). (Enchantment of the World) 1992, Children's Pr. LB $32.00 (0-516-02612-7). A detailed look at Lebanon, from ancient history to civil unrest in the early 1990s. (Rev: BL 12/1/92; SLJ 10/92) [956.92]

8759 Foster, Leila M. *Saudi Arabia* (5–8). (Enchantment of the World) 1993, Children's Pr. LB $32.00 (0-516-02611-9). The huge, oil-rich middle eastern kingdom of Saudi Arabia is presented, with material on its current economic conditions, desire for isolation from the West, and social and religious beliefs. (Rev: BL 8/93) [953.8]

8760 Fox, Mary V. *Bahrain* (5–8). (Enchantment of the World) 1992, Children's Pr. LB $32.00 (0-516-02608-9). An in-depth introduction to Bahrain, including geological, meteorological, historical, and engineering aspects. (Rev: BL 12/15/92; SLJ 1/93) [953.65]

8761 Fox, Mary V. *Iran* (5–8). (Enchantment of the World) 1991, Children's Pr. LB $32.00 (0-516-02727-1). The story of the land once known as Persia is told with emphasis on modern history, government, and economic and social conditions until 1990. (Rev: BL 10/1/91) [955]

8762 Hiro, Dilip. *The Longest War: The Iran-Iraq Military Conflict* (9–12). 1991, Routledge paper $20.99 (0-415-90407-2). A detailed account of the 1980–1988 war between Iran and Iraq. (Rev: BL 2/1/91) [955.05]

8763 Meiselas, Susan, and A. Whitley. *Kurdistan: In the Shadow of History* (10–12). Illus. 1997, Random $100.00 (0-679-42389-3). This photodocumentary presents the long, agonizing history of the Kurdish people and their refugee status since the Gulf War, serving as both a personal testimony of survivors and a historical record. (Rev: SLJ 5/98) [955]

8764 Sheehan, Sean. *Lebanon* (5–10). (Cultures of the World) 1996, Marshall Cavendish LB $35.64 (0-7614-0283-7). A lively, well-written introduction to this war-ravaged country with details on history, economy, culture, religion and foods, including a recipe for a typical dish. (Rev: SLJ 6/97) [569.2]

8765 South, Coleman. *Jordan* (5–10). (Cultures of the World) 1996, Marshall Cavendish LB $35.64 (0-7614-0287-X). Everyday life in Jordan is the focus of this book that also covers history, religion, culture, geography festivals, and foods (a single recipe is included). (Rev: SLJ 6/97) [569.5]

8766 *Yemen—in Pictures* (5–8). (Visual Geography) 1993, Lerner LB $21.27 (0-8225-1911-9). In introduction to this Muslim republic on the Gulf of Aden, with material on its past and current economic and social conditions. (Rev: BL 12/1/93) [953.3]

North and South America (excluding the United States)

General History and Geography

8767 Barden, Renardo. *The Discovery of America* (6–9). Illus. 1990, Greenhaven LB $22.45 (0-89908-071-5). The exploits of the Vikings as well as exploits in Irish, Welsh, and African legends are retold in this search for the first discoverers of the New World. (Rev: BL 3/1/90; SLJ 5/90) [970.1]

8768 Murphy, Jim. *Gone a-Whaling: The Lure of the Sea and the Hunt for the Great Whale* (7–12). Illus. 1998, Clarion $18.00 (0-395-69847-2). Diary entries are used to describe American whale hunting and life aboard whaling vessels from the 19th century to the present. (Rev: BL 3/15/98; BR 11–12/98; SLJ 5/98; VOYA 12/98) [306.3]

8769 O'Neill, Thomas. *Lakes, Peaks, and Prairies: Discovering the United States-Canadian Border* (7–12). Illus. 1984, National Geographic LB $12.95 (0-87044-483-2). A trip across the continent that reveals much about the diversity of these regions. [973]

8770 Wood, Geraldine. *Science of the Early Americas* (4–8). (Science of the Past) 1999, Watts $25.00 (0-531-11524-0). This look at the science of the Aztecs, Incas, Mayans and various North American tribes covers the earliest times to the present. (Rev: SLJ 6/99) [970]

North America

CANADA

8771 Barlas, Robert, and Norman Tompsett. *Canada* (5–8). (Countries of the World) 1998, Gareth Stevens LB $19.93 (0-8368-2123-8). Using maps, illustrations, concise text, and a quick facts section, this book gives basic information about Canada, with particular attention to education and politics. (Rev: SLJ 2/99) [971]

8772 Coulter, Tony. *Jacques Cartier, Samuel de Champlain, and the Explorers of Canada* (5–8). Illus. (World Explorers) 1993, Chelsea LB $19.95 (0-7910-1298-0). This book about the early exploration of Canada includes material on Cartier, Champlain, Cabot, and Hudson, among others. (Rev: BL 1/1/93) [971]

8773 *Destination Vancouver* (6–9). Illus. (Port Cities of North America) 1998, Lerner LB $23.93 (0-8225-2787-1). A small volume that is full of information about Vancouver, its history, economy, and details about materials and goods that are shipped in and out of this port city. (Rev: SLJ 8/98) [971]

8774 Grabowski, John. *Canada* (5–8). Illus. (Overview Series: Modern Nations of the World) 1997, Lucent LB $17.96 (1-56006-520-6). A solid introduction to Canada and its people with coverage of major cities, industry, art and culture, and government, and the separatist movement in Quebec. (Rev: BL 6/1–15/98; SLJ 8/98) [971]

8775 Murphy, Claire R., and Jane G. Haigh. *Children of the Gold Rush* (6–9). 1999, Roberts Rinehart paper $14.95 (1-57098-257-0). The story of the Yukon Gold Rush of 1878–1898 from the perspectives of the children involved, using diary excerpts, advertisements of the day, archival photographs, maps, and illustrations. (Rev: SLJ 9/99) [971]

8776 Schultz, J. W. *Sinopah, the Indian Boy* (5–9). 1985, Confluence paper $7.95 (0-8253-0320-6). The story of the Blackfeet Nation and of a boy who reached manhood in it. (Rev: BR 5–6/85) [970.004]

8777 Thompson, Alexa. *Nova Scotia* (4–8). (Hello Canada) 1995, Lerner LB $19.93 (0-8225-2759-6). Nova Scotia's history, geography, and the economy are covered, with material on the various peoples and cultures. (Rev: SLJ 3/96) [971.6]

8778 Yates, Sarah. *Alberta* (4–8). (Hello Canada) 1995, Lerner LB $19.93 (0-8225-2763-4). A colorful, slim volume that crams many facts about this western Canadian province's culture, history, geography, and resources into a few attractive pages. (Rev: BL 12/15/95; SLJ 3/96) [971.23]

CENTRAL AMERICA

8779 Brill, Marlene T., and Harry R. Targ. *Guatemala* (5–8). (Enchantment of the World) 1993, Children's Pr. LB $32.00 (0-516-02614-3). An introduction to the war-torn Central American country of Guatemala through 1992. (Rev: BL 8/93) [972.81]

8780 Gaines, Ann. *The Panama Canal in American History* (4–8). (In American History) 1999, Enslow $19.95 (0-7660-1216-6). This is a carefully researched history of the building of the Panama Canal, including a review of events before U.S. involvement, how the United States established the country of Panama and gained control of the canal zone, details of the many difficulties encountered, and a description of how the canal locks operate. (Rev: BL 3/1/99; SLJ 8/99) [972.87]

8781 Galvin, Irene F. *The Ancient Maya* (6–8). (Cultures of the Past) 1996, Benchmark LB $28.50 (0-7614-0091-5). This overview of Maya history and culture describes Mayan art, poetry, religion, language, and way of life. (Rev: SLJ 3/97) [972]

8782 Gold, Susan D. *The Panama Canal Transfer: Controversy at the Crossroads* (7–10). 1999, Raintree Steck-Vaughn $26.95 (0-8172-5762-4). The first half of this book describes the building of the canal and the second half traces the process of returning the Canal Zone to Panama, including the 1978 treaty providing for the return, the positions of both countries, and the ill will and controversy that developed. (Rev: SLJ 8/99) [972.8]

8783 Hadden, Gerry. *Teenage Refugees from Guatemala Speak Out* (7–12). (Teenage Refugees Speak Out) 1997, Rosen LB $16.95 (0-8239-2439-4). Teens from Guatemala who now live in America tell of the violent military campaigns that destroyed villages and lives in their homeland. (Rev: BL 10/15/97; SLJ 1/98) [972.8]

8784 Lindop, Edmund. *Panama and the United States: Divided by the Canal* (5–8). Illus. 1997, Twenty-First Century LB $21.40 (0-8050-4768-9). A history of United States-Panama relations, from the building of the canal to the present. (Rev: BL 8/97; BR 11–12/97; SLJ 7/97) [327.7307287]

8785 McNeese, Tim. *The Panama Canal* (5–8). Illus. 1997, Lucent LB $17.95 (1-56006-425-0). A description of the building of the Panama Canal that also supplies valuable insights into the economic and social conditions of the times. (Rev: BL 8/97; BR 1–2/98; SLJ 7/97) [386]

8786 Morrison, Marion. *Belize* (5–8). Illus. (Enchantment of the World) 1996, Children's Pr. LB $32.00 (0-516-02639-9). An introduction to the small Central American nation formerly known as British Honduras. (Rev: BL 7/96) [972.82]

8787 *Route of the Mayas* (9–12). Illus. 1995, Knopf paper $25.00 (0-679-75569-1). Though designed as a travel guide, with standard information on history, food, and clothing, this book is a valuable reference source on Mayan culture, with such information as recipes and explanations of the symbolism of Mayan clothing. (Rev: VOYA 4/96) [972.81]

8788 Schlesinger, Arthur M., Jr., and Fred L. Israel, eds. *Building the Panama Canal: Chronicles from National Geographic* (9–12). (Cultural and Geographical Exploration) 1999, Chelsea LB $19.95 (0-7910-5102-1). In this reprint of 4 articles and pictures from *National Geographic* magazine originally published between 1904 and 1914, the reader gets an insider's look at the construction of the Panama Canal. Two of the articles were written by George Goethals, the project's chief engineer. (Rev: SLJ 8/99) [972.8]

8789 Sharer, Robert J. *Daily Life in Maya Civilization* (8–12). (Daily Life Through History) 1996, Greenwood $45.00 (0-313-29342-2). The latest research is included in this thorough study of Maya civilization from its beginnings to the Spanish conquest. (Rev: BR 5–6/97; SLJ 2/97) [972.81]

8790 Sheehan, Sean. *Guatemala* (6–10). (Cultures of the World) 1998, Marshall Cavendish LB $35.64 (0-7614-0812-6). A solid introduction to Guatemala's geography, politics, and culture. (Rev: SLJ 2/99) [972.8]

8791 Vazquez, Ana Maria B. *Panama* (5–8). (Enchantment of the World) 1991, Children's Pr. LB $32.00 (0-516-02604-6). An introduction to Panama that includes information on the canal and the country's history, government, economy, people, and daily life. (Rev: BL 2/1/92) [972.87]

MEXICO

8792 Ancona, George. *Charro* (4–8). 1999, Harcourt $18.00 (0-15-201047-5); paper $9.00 (0-15-201046-7). A handsome photoessay that focuses on Mexican cowboys, called Charros, and la charreada, a rodeolike competition where they display their skills. (Rev: BL 5/15/99; SLJ 6/99) [972]

8793 Baquedano, Elizabeth. *Aztec, Inca and Maya* (5–9). (Eyewitness Books) 1993, Knopf LB $20.99 (0-679-93883-4). A compare-and-contrast introduction to these ancient civilizations. (Rev: BL 10/1/93) [972]

8794 Berdan, Frances F. *The Aztecs* (7–10). Illus. 1988, Chelsea LB $19.95 (1-55546-692-3). An illustrated account of the rise and fall of this ancient Mexican civilization. (Rev: BL 3/1/89) [972]

8795 Burr, Claudia, et al. *Broken Shields* (4–8). Illus. 1997, Douglas & McIntyre $15.95 (0-88899-303-X); paper $6.95 (0-88899-304-8). The story of

the betrayal of Montezuma at the hands of the Spanish conqueror Cortes from firsthand eyewitness accounts. (Rev: BL 12/1/97; SLJ 1/98) [972]

8796 Chapman, Gillian. *The Aztecs* (4–8). (Crafts from the Past) 1997, Heinemann $22.79 (1-57572-555-X). A craft book with instructions for a variety of Aztec ornaments and artifacts, including textiles and statues. (Rev: SLJ 4/98) [745]

8797 Diaz del Castillo, Bernal. *Cortez and the Conquest of Mexico by the Spaniards in 1521* (9–12). Illus. 1988, Linnet LB $22.50 (0-208-02221-X). In abridged form, this is the actual diary of a man who accompanied Cortes on his conquest of Mexico. (Rev: VOYA 2/89) [972]

8798 Frost, Mary Pierce, and Susan Keegan. *The Mexican Revolution* (6–9). Illus. (World History) 1996, Lucent LB $17.96 (1-56006-292-4). The history of Mexico from the fall of Porfirio Diaz in 1911 through the end of Lazaro Cardenas' term in 1940, with discussion of reasons for political unrest, how leaders after 1940 have tried to correct the poverty and corruption in the country, and the frequent U.S. interventions to protect America's financial interests. (Rev: BL 1/1–15/97; BR 11–12/97; SLJ 1/97) [972.08]

8799 Goodwin, William. *Mexico* (8–10). Illus. (Modern Nations of the World) 1998, Lucent LB $17.96 (1-56006-351-3). A thorough and clear account of Mexico's past and turbulent present, with material on its rich and complex cultural heritage. (Rev: BL 2/1/99) [972]

8800 Hadden, Gerry. *Teenage Refugees from Mexico Speak Out* (7–12). (Teenage Refugees Speak Out) 1997, Rosen LB $16.95 (0-8239-2441-6). Teens who have left Mexico and come to the United States to escape economic conditions and political instability tell about their experiences. (Rev: BL 10/15/97; SLJ 1/98) [972]

8801 Harris, Zoe, and Suzanne Williams. *Piñatas and Smiling Skeletons* (4–8). Illus. 1998, Pacific View LB $19.95 (1-881896-19-6). This book describes 6 Mexican holidays, including their history and rituals. The holidays are the Feast of the Virgin of Guadalupe, Christmas, Carnaval, Corpus Christi, Independence Day, and the Day of the Dead. (Rev: BL 3/15/99; BR 5–6/99; SLJ 3/99) [394.26972]

8802 Helly, Mathilde, and Rémi Courgeon. *Montezuma and the Aztecs* (7–10). 1996, Holt $19.95 (0-8050-5060-4). Although the presentation is somewhat disorganized, this account describes the Aztecs, their culture, political structure, everyday life, and human sacrifices, as well as European invaders, and the ruler Montezuma. (Rev: BR 1–2/98; SLJ 3/97) [972]

8803 Hull, Robert. *Aztecs* (5–10). (The Ancient World) 1998, Raintree Steck-Vaughn $27.12 (0-

8172-5056-5). This history of the Aztecs and their culture tells about their great pyramids, feathered headdresses, evil gods, human sacrifices, and the coming of the Spanish. (Rev: BL 1/1–15/99) [972]

8804 Jermyn, Leslie. *Mexico* (5–8). (Countries of the World) 1998, Gareth Stevens LB $19.93 (0-8368-2127-0). Good basic information about Mexico, particularly in the areas of education and politics, is presented through clear text, full-page illustrations, maps, and a quick facts section. (Rev: SLJ 2/99) [972]

8805 Kent, Deborah. *Mexico: Rich in Spirit and Tradition* (4–8). (Exploring Cultures of the World) 1995, Benchmark LB $27.07 (0-7614-0187-3). This book begins with a Mexican folktale, then gives an overview of the country's people, culture, history, and problems. (Rev: SLJ 6/96) [972]

8806 Lewington, Anna. *Mexico* (5–8). Illus. (Economically Developing Countries) 1996, Raintree Steck-Vaughn LB $24.26 (0-8172-4528-6). A fine general profile of Mexico that includes jobs, industries, and other economic indicators. (Rev: BL 3/15/97; SLJ 2/97) [330.972]

8807 Libura, Krystyna, et al. *What the Aztecs Told Me* (4–8). Illus. 1997, Douglas & McIntyre $15.95 (0-88899-305-6); paper $6.95 (0-88899-306-4). Based on an original 12-volume work written in the 16th century, this book describes the Aztec people from observation and eyewitness accounts. (Rev: BL 12/1/97; SLJ 12/97) [972]

8808 Lilley, Stephen R. *The Conquest of Mexico* (6–9). Illus. (World History) 1997, Lucent LB $17.96 (1-56006-298-3). The story of the Spanish invasion and subjugation of the native Mexicans, told with the extensive use of eyewitness accounts. (Rev: BL 1/1–15/97; BR 11–12/97; SLJ 3/97) [972]

8809 Marquez, Heron. *Destination Veracruz* (5–8). (Port Cities of North America) 1998, Lerner LB $23.93 (0-8225-2791-X). A description of this port city on the Gulf of Mexico that reviews its history, everyday life, the effects of development on the environment, and the city's economy, including the impact of NAFTA and a discussion of international trade, economic systems, and free trade. (Rev: SLJ 3/99) [972]

8810 Marrin, Albert. *Aztecs and Spaniards: Cortes and the Conquest of Mexico* (7–10). Illus. 1986, Macmillan $15.95 (0-689-31176-1). The story of the decline and fall of the Aztec civilization and the Spanish conquistadors who caused it. (Rev: BL 4/15/86; SLJ 8/86; VOYA 2/87) [972.01]

8811 *The Mexican War of Independence* (7–10). (World History) 1996, Lucent LB $17.96 (1-56006-297-5). An account of Mexico's long struggle for independence from Spain, with interesting sidebars on race and class, Indian genocide, and other con-

current revolutions. (Rev: BR 11–12/97; SLJ 2/97) [972]

8812 Ochoa, George. *The Fall of Mexico City* (6–9). Illus. 1989, Silver Burdett LB $17.95 (0-382-09836-6); paper $7.95 (0-382-09853-6). An account of the American occupation of Mexico City during 1847 and 1848. (Rev: BL 11/1/89; BR 1–2/90; SLJ 12/89) [973]

8813 Pascoe, Elaine. *Mexico and the United States: Cooperation and Conflict* (7–12). Illus. 1996, Twenty-First Century LB $21.40 (0-8050-4180-X). After a history of the stormy relations between Mexico and the U.S., the author discusses current problems, such as drug trafficking, oil, the peso, and immigration. (Rev: BL 12/1/96; BR 3–4/97; SLJ 1/97) [303.48]

8814 Rosenblum, Morris. *Heroes of Mexico* (5–8). 1972, Fleet $9.50 (0-8303-0082-1). A collected group of profiles of people important in the history of Mexico. (Rev: BL 6/87) [972]

8815 Rummel, Jack. *Mexico* (6–12). (Major World Nations) 1998, Chelsea LB $19.95 (0-7910-4763-6). A well-illustrated account that emphasizes current economic, political, and cultural conditions, supplemented by good background information. (Rev: BL 9/15/98; BR 1–2/99; SLJ 12/98) [917.2]

8816 Schlesinger, Arthur M., Jr., and Fred L. Israel, eds. *Ancient Civilizations of the Aztecs and Maya: Chronicles from National Geographic* (9–12). 1999, Chelsea LB $19.95 (0-7910-5103-X). A collection of *National Geographic* magazine articles written by scholars, adventurers, and explorers in the early 20th century on the then-latest findings about the ancient Aztec and Mayan cultures, with an introduction that makes corrections and updates information. (Rev: SLJ 8/99) [972]

8817 Steele, Philip. *The Aztec News: The Greatest Newspaper in Civilization* (4–8). 1997, Candlewick $15.99 (0-7636-0115-2). Using a newspaper format, the author brings the past to life through short "articles," "columns," "eyewitness accounts," witty "ads," and pictures covering important historic events as well as the daily life and social milieu of the world of the Aztecs. (Rev: SLJ 9/97) [972]

8818 Stefoff, Rebecca. *Independence and Revolution in Mexico, 1810–1940* (7–12). 1993, Facts on File $19.95 (0-8160-2841-9). The history of Mexico's 130-year struggle for independence is explored, highlighting notable events and people. (Rev: BL 12/1/93) [972]

8819 Stein, R. Conrad. *The Aztec Empire* (5–8). (Cultures of the Past) 1995, Benchmark LB $28.50 (0-7614-0072-9). The Aztecs' history, beliefs, and lifestyles are examined in this book, with quotes from original sources and many color photographs of artifacts, monuments, and historical sites. (Rev: BR 9–10/96; SLJ 6/96) [972]

8820 Stein, R. Conrad. *The Mexican Revolution, 1910–1920* (7–9). 1994, Macmillan LB $14.95 (0-02-786950-4). An examination of significant political, emotional, economic, and ideological issues of the period, with profiles of the main leaders. (Rev: BL 3/1/94; SLJ 8/94; VOYA 8/94) [972.08]

PUERTO RICO, CUBA, AND OTHER CARIBBEAN ISLANDS

8821 Anthony, Suzanne. *West Indies* (6–12). (Major World Nations) 1998, Chelsea LB $19.95 (0-7910-4772-5). An introduction to the people, geography, history, and economy of the West Indies, with a focus on current conditions. (Rev: BL 9/15/98; BR 1–2/99) [975.9]

8822 Fernandez, Ronald M., et al. *Puerto Rico Past and Present: An Encyclopedia* (8–12). 1998, Greenwood $59.95 (0-313-29822-X). A browsable book that contains biographies of famous Puerto Ricans as well as political terms and groups, buildings, important court decisions, and other information on the island's cultural and historical developments. (Rev: BL 7/97; VOYA 10/98) [972.95]

8823 Harlan, Judith. *Puerto Rico: Deciding Its Future* (7–10). Illus. 1996, Twenty-First Century LB $21.40 (0-8050-4372-1). The statehood-commonwealth-independence question is presented with clarity, simplicity, and objectivity. (Rev: BL 1/1–15/97; SLJ 7/97) [972.95]

8824 Marquez, Heron. *Destination San Juan* (5–8). (Port Cities of North America) 1998, Lerner LB $23.93 (0-8225-2792-8). The author provides some background material on San Juan and Puerto Rico, but concentrates on the economic aspects of this port city, the shipping and commerce involved, dredging activities, and NAFTA. (Rev: SLJ 3/99) [972.95]

8825 Regler, Margaret, and Rhoda Hoff. *Uneasy Neighbors: Cuba & the United States* (9–12). (International Affairs) 1997, Watts LB $24.00 (0-531-11326-4). A compilation of primary source materials documenting Cuban-American relations from 1492 to the present. (Rev: BL 6/1–15/97; SLJ 7/97) [327.729]

8826 Tuck, Jay, and Norma C. Vergara. *Heroes of Puerto Rico* (5–8). 1969, Fleet $9.50 (0-8303-0070-8). A series of profiles of famous Puerto Ricans. (Rev: BL 6/87) [972.9]

South America

8827 Bender, Evelyn. *Brazil* (6–12). (Major World Nations) 1998, Chelsea LB $19.95 (0-7910-4758-X). Current economic and social conditions in Brazil are emphasized, supplemented by background material on history and geography. (Rev: BL 9/15/98; BR 1–2/99) [981]

8828 Bernhard, Brendan. *Pizarro, Orellana, and the Exploration of the Amazon* (6–9). (World Explorers) 1991, Chelsea LB $19.95 (0-7910-1305-7). An account of the hardships, dangers, and rewards faced by the early explorers of the Amazon. (Rev: BL 9/15/91; SLJ 12/91) [981]

8829 Brill, Marlene T. *Guyana* (5–8). Illus. (Enchantment of the World) 1994, Children's Pr. LB $32.00 (0-516-02626-7). With color photos on each page, this account introduces Guyana's geography, history, peoples, culture, and resources. (Rev: BL 12/15/94) [988.1]

8830 Hemming, John. *The Conquest of the Incas* (10–12). Illus. 1973, Harcourt paper $22.00 (0-15-622300-7). The story of the fall of the Inca Empire as caused by the Spanish conquest led by Pizarro and others. [985]

8831 Jermyn, Leslie. *Uruguay* (7–10). (Cultures of the World) 1998, Marshall Cavendish LB $24.95 (0-7614-0873-8). An attractive book that covers all the basic topics related to Uruguay, plus material on leisure activities, festivals, and food. (Rev: SLJ 6/99) [980]

8832 Kane, Joe. *Running the Amazon* (9–12). Illus. 1989, Knopf $19.95 (0-394-55331-4). The story of the expedition that tried to be the first to traverse the Amazon from its source to its mouth. (Rev: BR 11–12/90; SLJ 2/90; VOYA 2/90) [981]

8833 Kane, Joe. *Savages* (9–12). 1995, Knopf $25.00 (0-679-41191-7). An environmentalist recounts recent journeys to Amazonia, where he investigated the issues and parties involved in the destruction of the rain forest. (Rev: BL 9/15/95*) [333.3]

8834 Lepthien, Emilie U. *Peru* (5–8). (Enchantment of the World) 1992, Children's Pr. LB $32.00 (0-516-02610-0). An illustrated discussion of Peru's history, economy, and politics through 1990. (Rev: BL 2/1/93; SLJ 2/93) [985]

8835 Litteral, Linda L. *Boobies, Iguanas, and Other Critters: Nature's Story in the Galapagos* (6–10). 1994, American Kestrel $23.00 (1-883966-01-9). After a historical overview of the Galapagos Islands, this richly illustrated book covers the islands' animals, plants, and geology. (Rev: BL 6/1–15/94; SLJ 9/94) [508.866]

8836 McIntyre, Loren. *Exploring South America* (9–12). Illus. 1990, Crown $40.00 (0-517-56134-4). A photographic journey exploring the wonders of the vast, varied continent of South America. (Rev: BL 7/90) [918]

8837 McIntyre, Loren. *The Incredible Incas and Their Timeless Land* (10–12). Illus. 1975, National Geographic LB $12.00 (0-87044-182-5). An examination of the Incas, their history and culture, and the destruction of their empire by the Spaniards. [985]

8838 Martell, Hazel M. *Civilizations of Peru, before 1535* (5–8). (Looking Back) 1999, Raintree Steck-Vaughn $25.69 (0-8172-5428-5). This book explores the huge region covered by the Inca Empire, looking at various peoples that inhabited parts of Ecuador, Bolivia, Argentina, and Chile, as well as Peru, and focusing on the Inca civilization and its science, technology, religion, and everyday life. (Rev: BL 5/15/99; SLJ 7/99) [985]

8839 Morrison, Marion. *Paraguay* (5–8). (Enchantment of the World) 1993, Children's Pr. LB $32.00 (0-516-02619-4). An introduction to Paraguay's history, geography, economy, and culture. (Rev: BL 11/1/93; SLJ 3/94) [989.2]

8840 Morrison, Marion. *Uruguay* (5–8). (Enchantment of the World) 1992, Children's Pr. LB $32.00 (0-516-02607-0). An introduction to Paraguay's people, history, climate, geography, and government. (Rev: BL 6/1/92) [989.5]

8841 Parker, Edward. *Peru* (5–8). Illus. 1996, Raintree Steck-Vaughn LB $24.26 (0-8172-4525-1). After a general introduction to Peru, this account discusses such current economic indicators as the job market, industry, and agriculture. (Rev: BL 3/15/97; SLJ 2/97) [985]

8842 Pateman, Robert. *Bolivia* (5–8). (Cultures of the World) 1995, Marshall Cavendish LB $35.64 (0-7614-0178-4). The people of Bolivia, how they live, and their traditions, are some the topics covered in this general introduction. (Rev: SLJ 4/96) [984]

8843 Peck, Robert McCracken. *Headhunters and Hummingbirds: An Expedition into Ecuador* (7–10). Illus. 1987, Walker LB $14.85 (0-8027-6646-3). An account of an ill-fated scientific expedition into the land of the Jívaro Indians in Ecuador. (Rev: SLJ 6/87; VOYA 8/87) [986]

8844 Reinhard, Johan. *Discovering the Inca Ice Maiden: My Adventures on Ampato* (5–8). Illus. 1998, National Geographic $17.95 (0-7922-7142-4). In this oversize book with many photographs, the anthropologist who discovered the Inca girl buried in the Andes for over 500 years reconstructs her life and death. (Rev: BL 5/15/98; SLJ 5/98) [985]

8845 Robinson, Roger. *Brazil* (5–8). (Country Studies) 1999, Heinemann $18.95 (1-57572-892-3). Using colorful charts, graphs, drawings, maps, and photographs in double-page spreads, this book provides basic information about Brazil, with emphasis on regional contrasts and contemporary issues, such as population changes and the growth of agribusiness. (Rev: BL 8/1/99; SLJ 8/99) [981]

8846 Sayer, Chloe. *The Incas* (5–10). (Ancient World) 1998, Raintree Steck-Vaughn $27.12 (0-8172-5125-1). An in-depth look at Incan life, from their beautiful gold ornaments to their unique form of record keeping and their impressive citadels and forts. (Rev: BL 1/1–15/99) [985]

8847 Wood, Tim. *The Incas* (6–9). (See Through History) 1996, Viking $16.99 (0-670-87037-4). A beautifully illustrated history of the Incas, their empire, and the eventual conquest by the Spaniards. (Rev: SLJ 3/97) [985.37]

Polar Regions

8848 Aldis, Rodney. *Polar Lands* (5–8). (Ecology Watch) 1992, Dillon LB $13.95 (0-87518-494-4). The lands around both the North and South Poles are introduced, with discussion of their similarities and differences. (Rev: BL 11/1/92) [574.5]

8849 Armstrong, Jennifer. *Shipwreck at the Bottom of the World: The Extraordinary True Story of the Shackleton and the Endurance Expedition* (7–12). 1999, Crown LB $19.99 (0-517-80014-4). A gripping account of Sir Ernest Shackleton's trans-Antarctic expedition, during which he and his team were trapped for 19 months in the frozen Antarctic wasteland, enduring extreme cold, dangerous ice, and a perilous 800-mile open-boat journey—all without losing a single man. (Rev: BL 12/1/98; SLJ 4/99) [919.8]

8850 Billings, Henry. *Antarctica* (5–8). Illus. (Enchantment of the World) 1994, Children's Pr. LB $32.00 (0-516-02624-0). This book covers the history and geography of the Antarctic region, with material on plant and animal life and color photographs on each page. (Rev: BL 12/15/94) [998.9]

8851 Burch, Ernest S., and Werner Forman. *The Eskimos* (9–12). Illus. 1988, Univ. of Oklahoma Pr. $29.95 (0-8061-2126-2). Color photographs highlight this account of the history, livelihood, and culture of the Eskimo. (Rev: BL 9/1/88) [306]

8852 Green, Jen. *Exploring the Polar Regions* (4–8). Illus. (Voyages of Discovery) 1998, Bedrick $18.95 (0-87226-489-0). After a brief introduction to these 2 regions, this book uses double-page spreads to give details on their geography, exploration, and present status. (Rev: SLJ 4/98) [978.8]

8853 Johnson, Rebecca L. *Braving the Frozen Frontier: Women Working in Antarctica* (4–8). (Discovery) 1997, Lerner LB $23.95 (0-8225-2855-X). This book focuses on scientific and support work done of women in the Antarctic, from piloting helicopters and operating snowplows, to tagging seals, measuring glaciers, and tracking neutrinos. (Rev: BL 2/15/97; SLJ 3/97*) [998.9]

8854 Kimmel, Elizabeth C. *Ice Story: Shackelton's Lost Expedition* (4–8). Illus. 1999, Houghton $18.00 (0-395-91524-4). This is a thrilling re-creation of the failed 1914 attempt by Sir Ernest Shackleton and his 27-man team to cross the continent of Antarctica. (Rev: BL 4/1/99; SLJ 4/99) [979.8]

8855 Lynch, Wayne. *A Is for Arctic: Natural Wonders of a Polar World* (10–12). 1996, Firefly paper $24.95 (1-55209-048-5). Using an alphabetical arrangement, the author presents one or two fascinating facts about a variety of phenomenon and creatures found in the Arctic, including the aurora borealis, blizzards, ducks, lemmings, mosquitoes, spiders, and wolves. (Rev: BR 3–4/97; SLJ 6/97) [979.8]

8856 Sayre, April P. *Antarctica* (5–8). (Seven Continents) 1998, Twenty-First Century LB $23.40 (0-7613-3227-8). A well-written introduction to the Antarctic environment, including its geology, plants, animals, and research facilities. (Rev: BL 2/1/99; SLJ 4/99) [919.8 9]

8857 Schlesinger, Arthur M., Jr. *Robert E. Peary and the Rush to the North Pole: Chronicles from National Geographic* (9–12). 1999, Chelsea LB $19.95 (0-7910-5099-8). Twenty-three original articles and archival photographs published by *National Geographic* magazine in 1899–1920 highlighting the Peary expeditions in the Arctic and including a report by one of his competitors. (Rev: SLJ 7/99) [979.8]

8858 Schlesinger, Arthur M., Jr. *Race for the South Pole: The Antarctic Challenge: Chronicles from National Geographic* (9–12). 1999, Chelsea LB $19.95 (0-7910-5100-5). This is a collection of 27 articles and and original archival photographs that appeared in *National Geographic* magazine in 1899–1912 covering the race to the South Pole, including the expeditions led by Robert Scott, Ernest Shackleton, and the eventual winner, Roald Amundsen. (Rev: SLJ 7/99) [979.8]

8859 Senungetuk, Vivian, and Paul Tiulana. *A Place for Winter: Paul Tiulana's Story* (7–12). Illus. 1988, CIRI Foundation $17.95 (0-938227-02-5). The story of a King Island Eskimo boy, his childhood, and his people. (Rev: BL 5/15/88) [917.98]

8860 Shepherd, Donna Walsh. *Tundra* (4–8). (First Book: Science) 1996, Watts LB $22.50 (0-531-20249-6). The climate, life forms, and people of the Arctic tundra are introduced. (Rev: BL 2/1/97; SLJ 4/97) [551.4]

8861 Steger, Will, and Jon Bowermaster. *Over the Top of the World: Explorer Will Steger's Trek Across the Arctic* (4–8). 1997, Scholastic $17.95 (0-590-84860-7). This work describes the grueling, dangerous adventures involved in a present-day journey across the Arctic Ocean. (Rev: BL 4/15/97; SLJ 4/97*) [919.804]

8862 Taylor, Barbara. *Arctic and Antarctic* (5–9). (Eyewitness Books) 1995, Knopf $19.00 (0-679-87257-4). Spectacular photos and diagrams explain

ice formations, tundra, and plant, sea, and wildlife of each region. (Rev: BL 8/95; SLJ 9/95) [508.311]

8863 Tessendorf, K. C. *Over the Edge: Flying with the Arctic Heroes* (4–8). 1998, Simon & Schuster $17.00 (0-689-31804-9). The story of the many fearless pilots who have attempted, some successfully, some not, to fly by plane or balloon across the the North Pole's edge—the rim of the Arctic's million square miles of ice whose constantly shifting position and surface make it impossible to cross by ship or sled. (Rev: BL 12/15/98; SLJ 12/98) [910]

8864 Vaughan, Norman D., and Cecil Murphey. *With Byrd at the Bottom of the World* (10–12). 1990, Stackpole $22.95 (0-8117-1904-9). A re-creation of the Byrd expedition to the South Pole by the man who tended the dogs during this stressful trek. (Rev: BL 10/1/90) [919]

8865 Wallace, Mary. *The Inuksuk Book* (4–8). Illus. 1999, Owl $19.95 (1-895688-90-6); paper $12.95 (1-895688-91-4). Arctic life is introduced through an explanation of inuksuks (stone constructions, sometimes in the shape of human beings, that can act in place of people) and their role in Inuit culture. (Rev: BL 9/1/99; SLJ 6/99) [979.8]

8866 Yue, Charlotte, and David Yue. *The Igloo* (6–8). Illus. 1988, Houghton $16.00 (0-395-44613-9). This account describes the geography of the Arctic and the life led by the native Inuit. (Rev: BL 9/1/88; BR 9–10/89; SLJ 12/88) [970.004]

United States

General History and Geography

8867 Adams, John Winthrop, ed. *Stars and Stripes Forever: The History of Our Flag* (9–12). 1992, Smithmark $9.98 (0-8317-6658-1). A general history of the U.S. flag with a focus on colonial times. (Rev: BL 9/15/92) [929.9]

8868 Agel, Jerome. *Words That Make America Great* (10–12). 1996, Random $30.00 (0-679-44959-0). This useful anthology contains 130 documents that are vital to American history, divided into 15 sections and spanning the years 1570 to 1996. (Rev: BL 3/15/97; BR 5–6/97; SLJ 7/97; VOYA 6/97) [973]

8869 Andryszewski, Tricia. *Step by Step along the Appalachian Trail* (4–8). 1998, Twenty-First Century $23.90 (0-7613-0273-5). A state-by-state tour of the Appalachian Trail, with material on the terrain, elevations, landmarks, and sites along the way. (Rev: BL 3/1/99; SLJ 4/99) [973]

8870 Baxandall, Rosalyn, and Linda Gordon, eds. *America's Working Women: A Documentary History*

1600 to the Present (9–12). 1995, Norton paper $14.95 (0-393-31262-3). Chronologically arranged overview of the changing roles and contributions of women. (Rev: BL 3/15/95*) [331.4]

8871 Boorstin, Daniel J., ed. *An American Primer* (7–12). 1968, NAL paper $19.95 (0-452-00922-7). Eighty-three documents vital to our history are reproduced plus accompanying background articles. [973]

8872 Brokaw, Tom. *The Greatest Generation* (10–12). 1998, Random $24.95 (0-375-50202-5); paper $24.95 (0-375-70569-4). The TV anchorman describes the Americans who came of age during the Great Depression and World War II and created today's America, with stories told by a cross-section men and woman around the country and divided into 8 topics: Ordinary People; Homefront; Heroes; Women in Uniform and Out; Shame; Love, Marriage, and Commitment; Famous People; and the Arena. (Rev: BL 1/1–15/99; SLJ 4/99) [973.9]

8873 Colbert, David, ed. *Eyewitness to America: 500 Years of America in the Words of Those Who Saw It Happen* (10–12). 1997, Random $30.00 (0-679-44224-3). Using diaries, letters, interviews, memoirs, and other primary sources chronologically arranged, this book contains 300 firsthand observations of 500 years of events, developments, and innovations that have changed America. (Rev: SLJ 8/97) [973]

8874 Crump, Donald J., ed. *Exploring America's Scenic Highways* (9–12). Illus. 1985, National Geographic $12.95 (0-87044-479-4). A celebration of America's colorful highways in words and pictures. [917.3]

8875 Davis, Kenneth C. *Don't Know Much about History: Everything You Need to Know about American History but Never Learned* (9–12). 1990, Crown $24.95 (0-517-57706-2). Basic facts about American history are given and myths and misconceptions exposed. (Rev: BL 6/15/90; SLJ 10/90) [973]

8876 Dudley, William, ed. *The Industrial Revolution* (9–12). (Opposing Viewpoints: American History) 1998, Greenhaven LB $21.96 (1-56510-707-1); paper $16.20 (1-56510-706-3). The views of industrialists, labor organizers, and social critics are represented in this anthology that traces the evolution of the United States from agricultural colonies to industrial giant. (Rev: BL 7/98) [973]

8877 Dudley, William, ed. *Opposing Viewpoints in American History, v. 1: From Colonial Times to Reconstruction* (8–12). Illus. (Opposing Viewpoints) 1996, Greenhaven LB $31.96 (1-56510-348-3); paper $21.20 (1-56510-347-5). Alternative primary source opinions are given for such issues in early American history as Native American rights, accep-

tance of the Bill of Rights, and slavery. (Rev: BL 3/15/96) [973]

8878 Dudley, William, ed. *Opposing Viewpoints in American History, v. 2: From Reconstruction to the Present* (8–12). Illus. (Opposing Viewpoints) 1996, Greenhaven LB $30.95 (1-56510-350-5); paper $21.20 (1-56510-349-1). Conflicting opinions from primary sources are presented on such topics as women's rights, U.S. participation in World War I, the dropping of the atomic bomb, the New Deal, and the Cold War. (Rev: BL 3/15/96) [973]

8879 Ehlert, Willis J. *America's Heritage: Capitols of the United States* (6–12). 1993, State House Publg. paper $10.95 (0-9634908-3-4). Provides data on state capitals and capitol buildings, descriptions of architectural details, brief state histories, state symbols, and an extensive bibliography. (Rev: BL 4/15/93) [725]

8880 English, June A., and Thomas D. Jones. *Scholastic Encyclopedia of the United States at War* (5–8). 1998, Scholastic $18.95 (0-590-59959-3). A heavily illustrated volume that traces America's wars from the Revolution to the Gulf War, with each chapter including a time line, a map, and a discussion of causes, battles, new technologies, and the aftermath. (Rev: BL 10/15/98; SLJ 2/99) [973]

8881 Evans, Harold. *The American Century* (10–12). 1998, Knopf $50.00 (0-679-41070-8). Using over 1,000 excellent illustrations, this lively narrative traces the political history of the United States from 1889 to 1989, with the author's main thesis being that the United States dominated the world scene during these years because of its founding ideas on political and economic freedom. (Rev: BL 8/98; SLJ 2/99) [973]

8882 Faragher, John Mack, ed. *The American Heritage Encyclopedia of American History* (9–12). 1998, Holt $45.00 (0-8050-4438-8). With over 2,750 alphabetically arranged articles and numerous maps, pictures, drawings, and cartoons, this is a browsable, appealing overview of American history. (Rev: BL 11/15/98; SLJ 5/99) [973]

8883 Findling, John E., and Frank W. Thackeray, eds. *Events That Changed America in the Eighteenth Century* (7–12). 1998, Greenwood $39.95 (0-313-29082-2). Using an essay format, this overview of the 18th century covers the French and Indian War, the Stamp Act, the Boston Tea Party, the American Revolution, and the Constitutional Convention. (Rev: BR 1–2/99; SLJ 5/99) [973.3]

8884 Fodor's Travel Publications Staff. *The Complete Guide to America's National Parks, 1998–99* (9–12). 1998, Fodor's Travel Publns. paper $18.00 (0-679-03515-X). This is the official guide to America's national parks as prepared by the National Park Foundation. [719]

8885 Gay, Kathlyn, and Martin Gay. *After the Shooting Stops: The Aftermath of War* (7–12). 1998, Millbrook LB $21.40 (0-7613-3006-2). Using America's wars as a focus, this account describes the historic political, economic, and social changes that occurred in the aftermath, and as a result, of war. (Rev: BL 8/98; SLJ 9/98) [355.00973]

8886 Glackens, Ira. *Did Molly Pitcher Say That? The Men and Women Who Made American History* (9–12). Illus. 1989, Writers & Readers $18.95 (0-86316-097-2); paper $12.95 (0-86316-094-8). An informal view of American history with several amusing and fascinating sidelights. (Rev: BL 9/15/89) [973]

8887 Gross, Ernie. *The American Years: A Chronology of United States History* (6–12). 1998, Scribners $118.75 (0-684-80590-1). A chronology of events, developments, and trends from 1776 to 1997, in the following categories: international, national, transportation, religion, entertainment, education, arts/music, sports, business/industry/inventions, science/medicine, and literature/journalism. (Rev: BL 7/99; BR 9–10/99; SLJ 8/99) [973]

8888 Haban, Rita D. *How Proudly They Wave: Flags of the Fifty States* (4–9). Illus. 1989, Lerner LB $23.95 (0-8225-1799-X). Each of the state flags is pictured, and historical background is also given. (Rev: BL 12/15/89; SLJ 3/90) [929.9]

8889 Heffner, Richard D. *A Documentary History of the United States* (9–12). 1952, NAL paper $7.99 (0-451-62413-0). A basic collection of documents related to important events in American history. [973]

8890 Heinemann, Sue. *The New York Public Library Amazing Women in History* (6–10). Illus. 1998, Wiley paper $12.95 (0-471-19216-3). Using a question-and-answer format, this work supplies hundreds of facts about women in American history, arranged by topics that include activism, sports, recreation, and racial and ethnic groups. (Rev: BL 4/15/98; BR 11–12/98; SLJ 8/98) [973]

8891 Holsinger, M. Paul, ed. *War and American Popular Culture: A Historical Encyclopedia* (9–12). 1999, Greenwood LB $89.50 (0-313-29908-0). Arranged by war periods from Colonial days to the present, articles examine how wars have changed U.S. popular culture in the areas of songs, poetry, novels, television, movies, toys, and controversial war memorials. (Rev: BL 4/15/99; SLJ 8/99) [973]

8892 Howarth, W., et al. *America's Wild Woodlands* (9–12). Illus. 1985, National Geographic LB $12.95 (0-87044-547-2). From the flowering trees of the East to the West's sequoias, this is a description of the wonders of America's forests. [917.3]

8893 *Images of America: A Panorama of History in Photographs* (9–12). Illus. 1989, Smithsonian $47.50 (0-89599-023-7). A history of the United States as seen through the eyes of our great photographers. (Rev: BL 9/15/89) [973]

8894 Israel, Fred L. *Student's Atlas of American Presidential Elections 1789 to 1996* (7–12). 1997, Congressional Quarterly $53.25 (1-56802-377-4). Each of the 53 presidential elections in U.S. history are described on a page or two, accompanied by maps to illustrate election results. (Rev: BL 11/15/97; SLJ 11/97) [973]

8895 Jaffe, Steven H. *Who Were the Founding Fathers? Two Hundred Years of Reinventing American History* (7–12). Illus. 1996, Holt $16.95 (0-8050-3102-2). An exploration of our nation's founding fathers and how their ideas have been interpreted and reinterpreted by groups as diverse as suffragettes, the Ku Klux Klan, McCarthyites, and the yippies to promote their programs and theories. An excellent source for material on the Revolution, the Constitution, and issues associated with civil rights, immigration, citizenship, and slavery. (Rev: BL 12/1/96*; BR 3–4/97; SLJ 1/97*; VOYA 4/97) [973.3]

8896 Jennings, Peter, and Todd Brewster. *The Century* (10–12). Illus. 1998, Doubleday $60.00 (0-385-48327-9). A profusely illustrated, easy-to-read survey of the 20th century that focuses on how events affected American life. (Rev: SLJ 4/99) [973.9]

8897 Jones, Rebecca C. *The President Has Been Shot! True Stories of the Attacks on Ten U.S. Presidents* (7–9). 1996, Dutton paper $15.99 (0-525-45333-4). Detailed accounts are given of the attacks, some fatal, on 10 U.S. presidents. (Rev: BL 7/96; SLJ 9/96) [973]

8898 Katz, William L. *Exploration to the War of 1812, 1492–1814* (7–10). (History of Multicultural America) 1993, Raintree Steck-Vaughn LB $27.11 (0-8114-6275-7). Discusses America from before European colonization through the formation of the new nation, exploration of new territory, and the War of 1812. Includes the role and treatment of Native Americans, women, slaves, and free blacks. (Rev: BL 6/1–15/93) [973]

8899 King, David C. *First Facts about U.S. History* (4–8). Illus. (First Facts) 1996, Blackbirch LB $25.45 (1-56711-168-8). A brief chronological survey of major events in U.S. history. (Rev: BL 7/96; SLJ 7/96) [973]

8900 Lunardini, Christine. *What Every American Should Know about Women's History* (9–12). (What Every American Should Know) 1994, Bob Adams $16.00 (1-55850-417-6). Deals with significant contributions made by U.S. women from the early 17th century to the present. (Rev: BL 12/1/94) [973]

8901 McCormick, Anita Louise. *The Industrial Revolution in American History* (5–8). Illus. (In American History) 1998, Enslow LB $19.95 (0-89490-

985-1). A description of the causes of the Industrial Revolution and the changes that it brought to the United States up to 1946. (Rev: BL 9/1/98; BR 11–12/98) [338.0973]

8902 Mills, Kay. *From Pocahontas to Power Suits: Everything You Need to Know about Women's History in America* (9–12). 1995, NAL paper $11.95 (0-452-27152-5). A celebration of women in America's history, from civil rights and women in the workplace to education, arts, and sports. (Rev: BL 3/15/95) [305.4]

8903 Moser, Diane, and Raymond Spangenburg. *Political & Social Movements* (7–12). Illus. (American Historic Places) 1998, Facts on File $19.95 (0-8160-3404-4). Important political, philosophical, and social movements that changed America are traced using as a backdrop the places where they originated or took place, such as Valley Forge, Ellis Island, Ford's Theater, Clara Barton's house, and Wounded Knee, from the Revolution through the civil rights era. (Rev: BL 5/15/98; SLJ 8/98) [973]

8904 National Geographic Society, eds. *Preserving America's Past* (9–12). Illus. 1983, National Geographic LB $12.95 (0-87044-420-4). This volume highlights attempts to preserve America's past by restoring buildings, relearning crafts, and similar activities. [973]

8905 *Patriotism in America* (6–9). (Democracy in Action) 1997, Watts LB $24.00 (0-531-11310-8). This book emphasizes the aspects of U.S. life and history of which the nation can be proud and explores patriotic signs, symbols, and observances, but also includes references to less positive events in which the nation did not live up to its ideals. (Rev: BL 5/15/97; SLJ 9/97; VOYA 10/97) [320.5]

8906 Phillips, Louis. *Ask Me Anything about the Presidents* (5–8). Illus. 1992, Avon paper $4.50 (0-380-76426-1). A collection of curious facts and anecdotes about U.S. presidents, presented in question-and-answer form. (Rev: BL 4/15/92) [973]

8907 Pollard, Michael. *The Mississippi* (5–8). (Great Rivers) 1997, Benchmark LB $22.79 (0-7614-0502-X). Along with describing the Mississippi in modern times, the author tells of its geological formation, how is was used by Native Americans, its exploration, and its importance in American history. (Rev: SLJ 3/98) [973]

8908 Reader's Digest, eds. *America's Historic Places: An Illustrated Guide to Our Country's Past* (9–12). Illus. 1988, Reader's Digest $29.95 (0-89577-265-5). A guided tour in words and pictures to 500 places important in our past. (Rev: BL 5/15/88) [917.3]

8909 Reader's Digest, eds. *Reader's Digest Strange Stories, Amazing Facts of America's Past* (9–12). Illus. 1989, Reader's Digest $32.95 (0-89577-307-4). A collection of unusual facts and anecdotes about

the famous and infamous in American history with a chronological index by month and year. (Rev: BL 11/1/89) [973]

8910 Sedeen, Margaret. *Star-Spangled Banner: Our Nation and Its Flag* (9–12). 1993, National Geographic $37.50 (0-87044-944-3). Legends—such as the tale of Betsy Ross—are sorted from fact in this history of the U.S. flag, from Francis Scott Key to the modern controversy about flag desecration. Color photos. (Rev: BL 10/15/93) [929.9]

8911 Sheafer, Silvia A. *Women in America's Wars* (6–12). Illus. 1996, Enslow LB $19.95 (0-89490-553-8). From the American Revolution to the Persian Gulf War, this account profiles 10 women and the amazingly diversified roles they played in this nation's wars. (Rev: BL 4/15/96; BR 9–10/96; SLJ 5/96; VOYA 6/96) [355]

8912 Stienecker, David L. *First Facts about the States* (4–8). (First Facts) 1996, Blackbirch LB $25.45 (1-56711-166-1). Using a double-page spread for each state, this account gives basic information on such topics as state symbols, mottos, history, geography, and landmarks. (Rev: SLJ 7/96) [973]

8913 Sullivan, George. *The Day the Women Got the Vote: A Photo History of the Women's Rights Movement* (5–9). Illus. 1994, Scholastic paper $6.95 (0-590-47560-6). The history of the struggle for women's rights is covered in a series of 24 short photoessays. (Rev: BL 6/1–15/94; SLJ 7/94) [324.34]

8914 Sullivan, Mark, and Dan Rather, ed. *Our Times* (10–12). 1996, Scribners $40.00 (0-684-81573-7). This is a history of the United States from the 1890s to the late 1920s that conveys what the average person of the day thought of such topics as flight, automobiles, Teddy Roosevelt, World War I, jazz, unions, and Woodrow Wilson, using primary source documents, including archival visuals, political cartoons, direct quotes, and social, political, and economic commentary written by journalist Sullivan 60 years ago. (Rev: BL 12/15/95; SLJ 8/96) [973.9]

8915 *United States in Pictures* (5–8). Illus. (Visual Geography) 1995, Lerner LB $21.27 (0-8225-1896-1). A general introduction to the United States, with generous use of photos, maps, and charts. (Rev: BL 7/95) [973]

8916 Van Zandt, Eleanor. *A History of the United States through Art* (5–8). Illus. (History through Art) 1996, Thomson Learning LB $5.00 (1-56847-443-1). Important events and subjects in the history of the United States are covered in 21 double-page spreads that feature text and famous artwork. (Rev: BL 3/1/96; SLJ 2/96) [973]

8917 Vesilind, Priit. *National Geographic on Assignment U.S.A.* (10–12). 1997, National Geographic $50.00 (0-7922-7010-X). This masterpiece of photojournalism chronicles life in the United States as it explores both the geography of the country and the diversity of its people and their activities. (Rev: SLJ 5/98) [917.3]

8918 Wormser, Richard. *American Childhoods: Three Centuries of Youth at Risk* (7–12). Illus. 1996, Walker LB $17.85 (0-8027-8427-5). A graphic, realistic picture of childhood and growing up in America from the repressive Puritans to the present day with chapters on work, crime, disease, education, sex, and related topics. (Rev: BL 9/15/96; BR 11–12/96; SLJ 9/96; VOYA 12/96) [305.23]

8919 Wormser, Richard. *Hoboes: Wandering in America, 1870–1940* (6–12). Illus. 1994, Walker $27.95 (0-8027-8279-5). This account covers the history, rules, literature, songs, and customs of those who rode the rails from the end of the Civil War to the outbreak of World War II. (Rev: BL 6/1–15/94; SLJ 7/94) [305.5]

Historical Periods

INDIANS AND OTHER NATIVE AMERICANS

8920 Acatoz, Sylvio. *Pueblos: Prehistoric Indian Cultures of the Southwest* (9–12). Trans. by Barbara Fritzemeier. 1990, Facts on File $45.00 (0-8160-2437-5). An illustrated study of early Indian culture in the American Southwest. (Rev: BL 4/15/91) [979]

8921 Ashabranner, Brent. *A Strange and Distant Shore: Indians of the Great Plains in Exile* (6–9). 1996, Cobblehill paper $16.99 (0-525-65201-9). This is the story of 72 Plains Indians from different tribes who were imprisoned in St. Augustine, Florida, between 1875 and 1878 and of the art they produced. (Rev: BL 7/96; BR 3–4/97; SLJ 9/96) [973.8]

8922 Ayer, Eleanor. *The Anasazi* (6–9). 1993, Walker LB $14.95 (0-8027-8185-3). An in-depth look at the Anasazi Indians of the Southwest, who came to this country about 2,000 years ago. (Rev: BL 3/1/93; SLJ 11/93) [979]

8923 Baird, W. David. *The Quapaws* (6–10). Illus. 1989, Chelsea LB $19.95 (1-55546-728-8). A history of this Indian tribe that originally lived where the Arkansas and Mississippi rivers meet that also contains information on culture, population, and present status. (Rev: VOYA 8/89) [970.004]

8924 Baughman, Michael. *Mohawk Blood* (9–12). 1995, Lyons Pr. $19.95 (1-55821-376-7). Past and present struggles with Indian tradition and nonnative ways, from the grandson of the great Mohawk war chief Joseph Brant. (Rev: BL 3/1/95) [973]

8925 Bond, Fred G. *Flatboating on the Yellowstone, 1877* (7–12). 1998, Ward Hill $19.95 (1-886747-03-2). A first-person account of the relocation in 1877 of Chief Joseph and other Nez Perce Indians from Ore-

gon to Oklahoma by raft down the Yellowstone and Missouri Rivers, written by their pilot, who documented the trip for the New York Public Library in 1925. (Rev: BL 12/15/98) [973]

8926 Bonvillain, Nancy. *The Huron* (6–9). Illus. 1989, Chelsea LB $19.95 (1-55546-708-3). A study of the history of this tribe and its treatment by the invading white man. (Rev: BL 11/15/89; SLJ 3/90; VOYA 2/90) [971.3]

8927 Bonvillain, Nancy. *The Inuit* (6–9). (Indians of North America) 1995, Chelsea paper $9.95 (0-7910-0380-9). A history of the present residents of the tundra and arctic regions of North America, with material on their daily life, beliefs, culture, and origins. (Rev: BL 10/15/95) [971]

8928 Bonvillain, Nancy. *Native American Medicine* (6–9). (Indians of North America) 1997, Chelsea LB $19.95 (0-7910-4041-0). This volume follows the course of Native American medical practices, healing rituals, and treatments through history and offers an interesting account of America's first doctors. (Rev: BL 11/15/97; BR 1–2/98) [973]

8929 Bonvillain, Nancy. *Native American Religion* (6–10). (Indians of North America) 1995, Chelsea LB $19.95 (0-7910-2652-3); paper $9.95 (0-7910-3479-8). Explanations of native spiritual life, emphasizing the natural world and the earth. Also discusses holistic approaches toward illness and well-being. (Rev: BL 3/1/96; SLJ 2/96) [973]

8930 Bonvillain, Nancy. *The Sac and Fox* (6–9). (Indians of North America) 1995, Chelsea $19.95 (0-7910-1684-6). The tragic story of these Native American peoples whose fight to maintain their lands eventually led to the Black Hawk War and their resettlement in the Midwest. (Rev: BL 7/95) [977.1]

8931 Bonvillain, Nancy. *The Santee Sioux* (6–9). (Indians of North America) 1996, Chelsea LB $19.95 (0-7910-1685-4); paper $9.95 (0-7910-482-8). This account of the Native American tribe that lived on the Great Plains covers their way of life, history, and culture, as well as current issues and conflicts. (Rev: BL 12/15/96) [973]

8932 Bonvillain, Nancy. *The Teton Sioux* (6–9). (Indians of North America) 1994, Chelsea LB $19.95 (0-7910-1688-9). This account tells of the largest group on the Sioux confederacy, the Teton Dakotas, and their part in the history of their people, including the battle at Wounded Knee. (Rev: BL 10/15/94; VOYA 2/95) [977]

8933 Bonvillain, Nancy. *The Zuni* (6–9). (Indians of North America) 1995, Chelsea LB $19.95 (0-7910-1689-7). The history of the Zuni Indians of western New Mexico, including their crafts such as basket weaving and turquoise jewelry. (Rev: BL 10/15/95) [973]

8934 Brown, Dee. *Bury My Heart at Wounded Knee: An Indian History of the American West* (10–12). 1971, Holt $27.50 (0-8050-1045-9). The story of the white man's conquest of the Old West told from the Indians' point of view. [970.004]

8935 Bruchac, Joseph. *Lasting Echoes: An Oral History of Native American People* (7–12). Illus. 1997, Harcourt $16.00 (0-15-201327-X). Beginning with the welcoming speeches that Indian leaders delivered to the first Europeans, this work traces the history of Native Americans through their own words. (Rev: BL 12/15/97; SLJ 3/98; VOYA 10/98) [973]

8936 Bruchac, Joseph. *The Native American Sweat Lodge: History and Legends* (9–12). 1993, Crossing Pr. paper $12.95 (0-89594-636-X). Bruchac celebrates the importance of the sweat lodge (lodges or huts heated by steam from water poured on hot stones) in this overview of its history, meaning, and use to American Indians and other cultures. Includes 25 traditional Native American poems and stories. (Rev: BL 10/15/93) [391]

8937 Calloway, Colin G. *The Abenaki* (6–10). Illus. 1989, Chelsea LB $19.95 (1-55546-687-7). In addition to a history of this tribe, the author tells about its members' lifestyles and beliefs. (Rev: SLJ 11/89; VOYA 12/89) [970]

8938 Calloway, Colin G. *Indians of the Northeast* (6–10). (First Americans) 1991, Facts on File LB $23.95 (0-8160-2389-1). Focuses on the major tribes of the region. Coverage includes the French and Indian Wars and the government's policy toward Native Americans today. (Rev: BL 1/15/92) [974]

8939 Clifton, James A. *The Potawatomi* (6–9). Illus. 1987, Chelsea LB $19.95 (1-55546-725-3). A history of this tribe that lived in the Upper Great Lakes with material on their present-day lifestyle. (Rev: BL 11/1/87; SLJ 1/88) [970]

8940 Coe, Michael D., et al. *Atlas of Ancient America* (10–12). Illus. 1986, Facts on File $45.00 (0-8160-1199-0). A colorful collection of maps and other illustrations plus a comprehensive text explore the various Indian groups and their homelands. (Rev: BL 1/1/87; SLJ 3/87) [970]

8941 Cory, Steven. *Pueblo Indian* (5–8). Illus. (American Pastfinder) 1996, Lerner LB $21.95 (0-8225-2976-9). Color illustrations and maps accompany this account of the Pueblo Indians and the incredible cities they built. (Rev: BL 7/96) [973]

8942 Curtis, Edward. *Native Nations: First Americans as Seen by Edward S. Curtis* (9–12). 1993, Little, Brown $75.00 (0-8212-2052-7). One hundred plates and excerpts of Curtis's work documenting the tribes of North America illustrate this smaller version of the original book. (Rev: BL 11/15/93) [306]

8943 Denny, Sidney G., and Ernest L. Schusky. *The Ancient Splendor of Prehistoric Cahokia* (4–8). 1997, Ozark paper $3.95 (1-56763-272-6). Using the findings at the Cahokia Mounds in southern Illinois as a beginning, the author re-creates the life and culture of these prehistoric American Indians. (Rev: BL 5/1/97) [977.3]

8944 Dial, Adolph L. *The Lumbee* (6–9). (Indians of North America) 1993, Chelsea LB $19.95 (1-55546-713-X). A comprehensive and honest account of life and culture of these Native Americans who live in southeastern United States. (Rev: BL 4/15/94) [973]

8945 Dobyns, Henry F. *The Pima-Maricopa* (6–10). Illus. 1989, Chelsea LB $19.95 (1-55546-724-5). The history, culture, and present status of these Indian tribes with several illustrations. Part of an extensive Indians of North America series. (Rev: BL 8/89; BR 1–2/90; SLJ 1/90) [979]

8946 Dramer, Kim. *The Chipewyan* (6–9). Illus. 1995, Chelsea $19.95 (1-55546-139-5). An introduction to the life and culture of the nomadic Native American group that roamed northern Canada around the Churchill River. (Rev: BL 3/15/96) [971]

8947 Dramer, Kim. *Native Americans and Black Americans* (7–10). Illus. (Indians of North America) 1997, Chelsea LB $19.95 (0-7910-2653-1). This work gives a historic overview of the relationship between these 2 groups through slavery, the Civil War, land battles, segregation, and various political movements, as well as a basic history of each group's struggle for civil rights. (Rev: BL 8/97; SLJ 9/97) [303.48]

8948 Dudley, William, ed. *Native Americans* (9–12). Illus. (Opposing Viewpoints American History) 1998, Greenhaven LB $21.96 (1-56510-705-5); paper $16.20 (1-56510-704-7). The complex relationship between Native Americans and European settlers is discussed in this collection of documents, beginning with Powhatan's dealings with John Smith and ending with the recent American Indian Movement. (Rev: BL 4/1/98) [973]

8949 Durrett, Deanne. *Healers* (8–12). (American Indian Lives) 1997, Facts on File $17.95 (0-8160-3460-0). This work profiles 12 Native American healers, ranging from the traditional medicine man to modern physicians and nurses. (Rev: VOYA 8/97) [973]

8950 Engels, Mary Tate, ed. *Tales from Wide Ruins: Jean and Bill Cousins, Traders* (10–12). 1996, Texas Tech Univ. Pr. $29.95 (0-89672-368-2). The Cousinses were traders with Native Americans during the 1930s and 1940s. This book presents the stories they heard or experiences they had involving the past life of Native Americans and other ethnic groups living in the desert of the Southwest. (Rev: SLJ 12/96) [979]

8951 Faulk, Odie B., and Laura E. Faulk. *The Modoc* (7–10). Illus. 1988, Chelsea LB $19.95 (1-55546-716-4). The history of the Indian tribes now close to extinction whose home was in Oregon and Northern California. (Rev: BL 6/1/88) [970.004]

8952 Feest, Christian F. *The Powhatan Tribes* (7–10). Illus. 1990, Chelsea LB $19.95 (1-55546-726-1). A description of the Indian federation of groups that came into being in the 16th century. (Rev: BL 2/1/90) [973]

8953 Ferrell, Nancy W. *The Battle of the Little Bighorn* (5–9). (In American History) 1996, Enslow LB $19.95 (0-89490-768-9). A detailed account of the Battle of Little Bighorn from various points of view on both sides, along with a review of the conflicts between the U.S. government and Native Americans, the different cultures of various tribes, key figures such as Crazy Horse and Sitting Bull, and the aftermath of the battle. (Rev: BR 1–2/97; SLJ 12/96) [973.8]

8954 Franklin, Robert J. *The Paiute* (6–9). Illus. 1990, Chelsea LB $19.95 (1-55546-723-7). In this detailed account, both the past and the present of this Indian tribe are discussed in detail. (Rev: BL 6/15/90) [970.004]

8955 Freedman, Russell. *An Indian Winter* (6–9). 1992, Holiday House $21.95 (0-8234-0930-9); paper $12.95 (0-8234-1158-3). A German naturalist/explorer and a Swiss artist recorded in words and pictures their 1832 observations of Mandan and Hidatsa Indian tribes in North Dakota. (Rev: BL 6/1/92*; SLJ 6/92*) [917.804]

8956 Fronval, George, and Daniel Dubois. *Indian Signs and Signals* (9–12). Trans. by E. W. Egan. Illus. 1985, Crown $12.99 (0-517-46612-0). In thorough text and many illustrations, this book describes the sign language of the Plains Indian. [001.56]

8957 Garbarino, Merwyn S. *The Seminole* (6–10). Illus. 1989, Chelsea LB $19.95 (1-55546-729-6). Both the past and the present of the Seminole are covered with the inclusion of some folktales, biographical sketches, and many illustrations. (Rev: BL 12/1/88; SLJ 5/89; VOYA 4/89) [970.004]

8958 Gleason, Katherine. *Native American Literature* (6–9). (Junior Library of American Indians) 1996, Chelsea LB $16.95 (0-7910-2477-6). This is an excellent introduction to the long history of Native American oral and written literature that begins with chants, myths, and prayers and ends with such famous contemporary writers as Louise Erdrich and Michael Dorris. (Rev: SLJ 3/97) [973]

8959 Goetzmann, William H. *The First Americans: Photographs from the Library of Congress* (9–12). 1991, Starwood Publg. $34.95 (0-912347-96-1). This collection of turn-of-the-century commercial photos of Native Americans illustrates the "senti-mental notions about the vanishing American" popular at the time. (Rev: BL 11/15/91) [973.0497]

8960 Gold, Susan D. *Indian Treaties* (5–8). Illus. (Pacts and Treaties) 1997, Twenty-First Century LB $21.40 (0-8050-4813-8). This book gives a history of the treaties signed by Native Americans through which they gradually lost their homes and lives from the 1600s to 1871, when Congress decreed that Indians could no longer issue treaties. (Rev: BL 5/15/97; BR 9–10/97; SLJ 6/97) [323.1]

8961 Golston, Sydele E. *Changing Woman of the Apache: Women's Lives in Past and Present* (8–12). Illus. (American Indian Experience) 1996, Watts LB $24.00 (0-531-11255-1). This volume provides general information about the Apache culture and explores the lives of Apache women, both past and present. (Rev: BL 7/96; SLJ 11/96; VOYA 12/96) [305.48]

8962 Graymont, Barbara. *The Iroquois* (6–10). Illus. 1988, Chelsea LB $19.95 (1-55546-709-1). The story of the history and the culture of the Iroquois from about 1450 when the tribal union took place to the present day. (Rev: BL 12/1/88; SLJ 5/89; VOYA 4/89) [970.004]

8963 Green, Rayna. *Women in American Indian Society* (7–12). 1992, Chelsea LB $19.95 (1-55546-734-2). Discusses the strong role of native women before Europeans came to the United States and their changing role as Native Americans were stripped of their land and forced to assimilate into white culture. (Rev: BL 9/1/92; SLJ 8/92*) [305.48]

8964 Grumet, Robert S. *The Lenapes* (6–9). Illus. 1989, Chelsea LB $19.95 (1-55546-712-1). This tribe of the Delaware Indians is highlighted in this account that concentrates on the history, culture, and present status of this group. (Rev: BL 11/15/89; VOYA 2/90) [975.1]

8965 Hirschfelder, Arlene, and Beverly R. Singer. *Rising Voices: Writings of Young Native Americans* (5–8). 1992, Scribners $14.00 (0-684-19207-1). A variety of young Native Americans write about identity, family, homelands, rituals, education, and other subjects. (Rev: BL 7/92; SLJ 12/92*) [810.8]

8966 Hoig, Stan. *The Cheyenne* (7–10). Illus. 1989, Chelsea LB $19.95 (1-55546-696-6). In addition to a history of this Indian tribe, the book gives an account of its present-day conditions. (Rev: BL 3/1/89; VOYA 6/89) [973]

8967 Hoig, Stan. *Night of the Cruel Moon: Cherokee Removal and the Trail of Tears* (7–10). Illus. (Library of American Indian History) 1996, Facts on File $19.95 (0-8160-3307-2). Using original sources and first-person narratives, this well-documented account describes the tragic Cherokee Trail of Tears and the complexities of the situation. (Rev: BL 7/96) [976.6]

8968 Hoxie, Frederick E. *The Crow* (6–9). Illus. 1989, Chelsea LB $19.95 (1-55546-704-0). This Great Plains tribe is discussed in terms of their history, lifestyle, and relations with the white man. (Rev: BL 11/15/89; VOYA 4/90) [971.3]

8969 Hoyt-Goldsmith, Diane. *Potlatch: A Tsimshian Celebration* (4–8). 1997, Holiday House LB $16.95 (0-8234-1290-3). A 13-year-old boy explains the meaning of potlatch for the Tsimshian tribe in Alaska and describes the many rituals and activities it involves. (Rev: BL 5/1/97; SLJ 6/97) [394.2]

8970 Hubbard-Brown, Janet. *The Shawnee* (6–9). (Indians of North America) 1995, Chelsea paper $9.95 (0-7910-3475-5). The history of the Native American tribe that resisted white expansion, sided with the British in the American Revolution and again in the War of 1812, and who were led by Tecumseh, the warrior who sought to unite all northwestern Indians to fight for their land. (Rev: BL 7/95) [973]

8971 Iverson, Peter. *The Navajos* (6–9). Illus. 1990, Chelsea LB $19.95 (1-55546-719-9). An introduction to the history and culture of the Navajos and their relationship with the federal government. (Rev: BL 6/15/90; VOYA 8/90) [970.004]

8972 Johansen, Bruce E., and Donald A. Grinde, Jr. *Encyclopedia of Native American Biography: Six Hundred Life Stories of Important People from Powhatan to Wilma Mankiller* (9–12). 1997, Holt $50.00 (0-8050-3270-3). Though intended for an adult audience, this is an easily read collective biographical work listing hundreds of Native and non-Native Americans who played significant roles in Native American history and culture. (Rev: BL 5/1/97; BR 9–10/97; SLJ 2/98) [973]

8973 Jones, Constance. *The European Conquest of North America* (7–12). 1995, Facts on File $19.95 (0-8160-3041-3). A detailed account of Native American cultures and the methods used by European conquerors to subdue them. (Rev: BL 5/1/95) [970.01]

8974 Josephy, Alvin M. *500 Nations: An Illustrated History of North American Indians* (9–12). 1994, Knopf $50.00 (0-679-42930-1). This companion to the television documentary gives a chronological overview of the history of North American Indians from ancient legends to the present. (Rev: BL 10/15/94; SLJ 6/95) [970.004]

8975 Josephy, Alvin M. *The Indian Heritage of America* (10–12). Illus. 1991, Houghton paper $15.00 (0-395-57320-3). This is a fine survey of the cultures and history of the Native Americans of North, Central, and South America. [970.004]

8976 Katz, Jane B., ed. *We Rode the Wind: Recollections of Native American Life*. Rev. ed. (6–10). 1995, Lerner LB $22.60 (0-8225-3154-2). A collec-

tion of the autobiographical writings of 8 notable Native Americans, among them Charles Eastman and Black Elk, who grew up on the Great Plains. (Rev: BL 2/1/96; SLJ 12/95) [978]

8977 Kelly, Lawrence C. *Federal Indian Policy* (7–10). Illus. 1989, Chelsea LB $19.95 (1-55546-706-7). A historical account of the often shameful treatment American Indians received from the federal government. (Rev: BL 2/1/90; SLJ 4/90; VOYA 4/90) [323.1]

8978 Klots, Steve. *Native Americans and Christianity* (7–10). Illus. (Indians of North America) 1997, Chelsea paper $9.95 (0-7910-4463-7). The story of how early explorers and settlers tried to convert Native Americans to Christianity, the forms that this religion took, and the many ways Native Americans practice their religion today. (Rev: BL 8/97; SLJ 9/97) [277]

8979 Krehbiel, Randy. *Little Bighorn* (4–8). (Battlefields Across America) 1997, Twenty-First Century $23.40 (0-8050-5236-4). A review of the historical background and events leading up to the Little Bighorn, followed by a description of the battle itself and the site as it is today. (Rev: SLJ 1/98) [973.8]

8980 Lacey, Theresa Jensen. *The Blackfeet* (6–9). (Indians of North America) 1995, Chelsea LB $19.95 (0-7910-1681-1). The story of the nomadic Native Americans of the northern Great Plains and their history of struggles with the European settlers. (Rev: BL 7/95) [970.004]

8981 Lassieur, Allison. *Before the Storm: American Indians before the Europeans* (7–12). (Library of American Indian History) 1998, Facts on File $19.95 (0-8160-3651-9). This unique study reports on the flourishing civilizations of 7 "precontact Native American" peoples before contact with the European invaders. (Rev: BL 11/15/98; BR 1–2/99; SLJ 9/98) [970]

8982 Lavender, David. *Mother Earth, Father Sky: The Pueblo Indians of the American Southwest* (5–8). Illus. 1998, Holiday House $16.95 (0-8234-1365-9). After an introduction to the geographical area of the Southwest known as Four Corners, where Arizona, New Mexico, Colorado, and Utah meet, this book traces the history and culture of the Pueblo Indians who live there. (Rev: BL 9/1/98; BR 5–6/99; SLJ 11/98) [978.01]

8983 Liptak, Karen. *Indians of the Southwest* (6–10). (First Americans) 1991, Facts on File $18.95 (0-8160-2385-9). Describes the first Indian inhabitants of the area and highlights their social, political, and religious life before and after contact with Europeans. (Rev: BL 1/15/92) [979]

8984 Littlechild, George. *This Land Is My Land* (6–9). 1993, Children's Book Pr. $16.95 (0-89239-119-7). Littlechild draws on his Plains Cree background in this presentation of 17 of his full-color paintings that focus on Native American history. (Rev: BL 11/1/93; SLJ 1/94) [971]

8985 McCormick, Anita Louise. *Native Americans and the Reservation in American History* (7–10). Illus. (American History) 1996, Enslow LB $19.95 (0-89490-769-7). An overview of the relationship between whites and Native Americans that covers hundreds of years of history and discusses the cruelty of forced marches and life on the reservations. (Rev: BL 1/1–15/97; BR 3–4/97; SLJ 2/97) [973]

8986 McCutchen, David. *The Red Record: The Wallam Olum of the Lenni Lenape* (9–12). 1993, Avery paper $14.95 (0-89529-525-3). A translation/interpretation of the Wallam Olum, an ancient history of the Lenni Lenape (Delaware) Indians. (Rev: BL 2/15/93*; VOYA 10/93) [973]

8987 McKee, Jesse O. *The Choctaw* (6–9). Illus. 1989, Chelsea LB $19.95 (1-55546-699-0). The story of this southern Indian tribe, their legends, and way of life as well as their status today. (Rev: BL 7/89; VOYA 10/89) [973]

8988 Margolin, Malcolm, and Yolanda Montijo, eds. *Native Ways: California Indian Stories and Memories* (5–8). Illus. 1996, Heyday paper $7.95 (0-930588-73-8). Reminiscences and stories reflect California Indian culture, both past and present. (Rev: BL 7/96) [979.4]

8989 Marrin, Albert. *Plains Warrior: Chief Quanah Parker and the Comanches* (6–10). Illus. 1996, Simon & Schuster $18.00 (0-689-80081-9). The story of the great Comanche leader and his clashes with U.S. policy toward Native Americans makes for fine historical writing enlivened with many photographs. (Rev: BL 6/1–15/96*; BR 3–4/97; SLJ 6/96; VOYA 8/96) [973]

8990 Mayfield, Thomas Jefferson. *Adopted by Indians: A True Story* (5–8). Ed. by Malcolm Margolin. Illus. 1997, Heyday paper $10.95 (0-930588-93-2). This is an adaption of the memoirs of a white man who lived with the Choinumne Indians in California for 10 years, beginning in 1850 when he was 8. (Rev: BL 3/1/98) [979.4]

8991 Melody, Michael E. *The Apache* (7–10). Illus. 1988, Chelsea LB $19.95 (1-55546-689-3). Both past and present history of this tribe are given along with coverage on culture and social conditions. (Rev: BL 3/1/89) [973]

8992 Merrell, James H. *The Catawbas* (6–10). 1989, Chelsea LB $19.95 (1-55546-694-X). The history and culture of this tribe that lived on the Atlantic side of the Appalachians are given plus its members' conversion to Mormonism and lifestyles today. (Rev: VOYA 8/89) [970.004]

8993 Meyers, Madeleine, ed. *The Cherokee Nation: Life Before the Tears* (4–8). Illus. (Perspectives on History) 1994, Discovery Enterprises paper $5.95 (1-878668-26-9). A history of the Cherokees that emphasizes the leadership of Sequoyah and the life of the tribe before their forced displacement. (Rev: BL 8/94) [973.3]

8994 Miller, Lee, ed. *From the Heart: Voices of the American Indian* (9–12). 1995, Knopf $24.00 (0-679-43549-2). An anthology of 4 centuries of Northern Hemisphere Native American speeches, excerpts, and quotes. (Rev: BL 5/15/95) [973]

8995 Monroe, Jean Guard, and Ray A. Williamson. *First Houses: Native American Homes and Sacred Structures* (6–9). 1993, Houghton $16.00 (0-395-51081-3). A description in words and pictures of the dwellings of early Native Americans. (Rev: BL 10/15/93; VOYA 2/94) [299]

8996 Murdoch, David. *North American Indian* (4–9). Illus. (Eyewitness Books) 1995, Knopf $19.00 (0-679-86169-6). Full-color illustrations and a brisk text are used to introduce the history, culture, and present status of the North American Indians. (Rev: BL 8/95; SLJ 9/95) [970.004]

8997 Nardo, Don, ed. *North American Indian Wars* (9–12). (Turning Points in History) 1999, Greenhaven LB $21.96 (1-56510-959-7); paper $16.20 (1-56510-958-9). This anthology of essays covers the major themes and conflicts of the wars that ended in the defeat and devastation of America's Native American population. (Rev: BL 9/1/99) [973]

8998 *Native Americans* (5–8). (Nature Company Discoveries) 1995, Time-Life Books LB $16.00 (0-7835-4759-5). An overview of the history and culture of Native American Indians that compares, for example, modes of transportation and ways of life among the different cultures. Among the large foldouts is an 8-pager depicting a buffalo hunt. (Rev: BL 1/1–15/96; SLJ 1/96) [970.004]

8999 Nies, Judith. *Native American History: A Chronology of a Culture's Vast Achievements and Their Links to World Events* (6–12). 1997, Ballantine paper $13.95 (0-345-39350-3). This chronology of Native North American history and culture from 28,000 B.C. through 1996, using a split-page format to juxtapose simultaneous political, social, religious, and military developments occurring in North America and in other parts of the world. (Rev: SLJ 5/97) [970.003]

9000 Ortiz, Alfonso. *The Pueblo* (6–9). (Indians of North America) 1994, Chelsea LB $9.95 (1-55546-727-X); paper $9.95 (0-7910-0396-5). The story of the Native Americans who are descended from the Anasazi people and whose first contact with the West came with Coronado's expedition of 1540. (Rev: BL 1/1/94; VOYA 4/94) [979]

9001 Ourada, Patricia K. *The Menominee* (6–9). Illus. 1990, Chelsea LB $19.95 (1-55546-715-6). Many photographs are used to amplify this detailed description of the history and lifestyle of this Indian tribe. (Rev: BL 6/15/90) [970.004]

9002 Perdue, Theda. *The Cherokee* (7–10). Illus. 1988, Chelsea LB $19.95 (1-55546-695-8). An overview of the history of this tribe is given plus a glimpse of the federal regulations that now govern its existence. (Rev: BL 3/1/89) [973]

9003 Pevar, Stephen L. *The Rights of American Indians and Their Tribes* (6–12). (ACLU Handbooks for Young Americans) 1997, Penguin paper $8.99 (0-14-037783-2). After a brief history of federal Indian policy and definitions of terms, this book uses a question-and-answer format to explain the present-day rights of Native Americans. (Rev: BL 1/1–15/98; SLJ 3/98) [342.73]

9004 Philip, Neil, ed. *In a Sacred Manner I Live: Native American Wisdom* (4–9). Illus. 1997, Ticknor $20.00 (0-395-84981-0). More than 30 Native American leaders, such as Geronimo and Cochise, are quoted on topics related to the conduct of life and their beliefs. (Rev: BL 7/97; BR 5–6/98; SLJ 12/97) [970]

9005 Porter, Frank W. *The Coast Salish Peoples* (6–9). Illus. 1989, Chelsea LB $19.95 (1-55546-701-6). The home territory of this tribe is highlighted plus information on how these Indians lived and their fate at the hands of the white man. (Rev: BL 11/15/89) [970.004]

9006 Red Shirt, Delphine. *Bead on an Anthill: A Lakota Childhood* (10–12). 1998, Univ. of Nebraska Pr. $25.00 (0-8032-3908-4); paper $9.95 (0-8032-8976-6). The story of a Lakota Indian woman, her childhood in the 1960s and 1970s growing up on a reservation in South Dakota, and her remembrances of the culture and traditions of her people. (Rev: SLJ 11/98) [909]

9007 Rice, Earle, Jr. *Life Among the Great Plains Indians* (6–9). (The Way People Live) 1997, Lucent LB $17.96 (1-56006-347-5). This book focuses on the history and culture of the Plains Indians, depicting architecture, family life, philosophy and ethics, governance, religion and medical practice, decorative arts and leisure activities, and warfare, with material on the impact on the loss of the buffalo and the tragedy at Wounded Knee. (Rev: SLJ 4/98) [973]

9008 Roberts, David. *In Search of the Old Ones: Exploring the Anasazi World of the Southwest* (10–12). 1996, Simon & Schuster $24.00 (0-684-81078-6). This account takes the reader back 1,000 years to explore the life and culture of the "ancient ones," the Anasazi, the people of the Southwest who disappeared. (Rev: BL 3/1/96; SLJ 7/96) [973]

9009 Robinson, Charles M. *A Good Year to Die: The Story of the Great Sioux War* (9–12). 1995, Random $27.50 (0-679-43025-3). A balanced narrative about the Great Sioux War (1876), where Custer, Crazy Horse, and George Crook were major figures. (Rev: BL 9/1/95) [973.8]

9010 Rollings, Willard H. *The Comanche* (6–9). Illus. 1989, Chelsea LB $19.95 (1-55546-702-4). With a text supplemented by actual accounts and a number of illustrations, this book tells of the history and culture of this important tribe. Part of an extensive Indians of North American series. (Rev: BL 11/15/89; BR 1–2/90; VOYA 12/89) [973]

9011 Ruoff, A. La Vonne Brown. *Literatures of the American Indian* (7–12). Illus. 1991, Chelsea LB $19.95 (1-55546-688-5). Ritual dramas, pictographs, songs, speeches, myths, legends, autobiographies, poems, and stories describe the Native American cultural heritage. (Rev: BL 3/1/91) [973]

9012 Sandoz, Mari. *The Battle of the Little Bighorn* (10–12). 1966, Amereon $20.95 (0-89190-879-X). The story of this battle in the war against the Sioux and of the ambitions of General Custer. [973.8]

9013 Sandoz, Mari. *Cheyenne Autumn* (10–12). Illus. 1976, Avon paper $4.95 (0-380-01094-1). The heartbreaking saga of the Cheyenne Indian trek in 1878 back to their home in Yellowstone. [970.004]

9014 Schuster, Helen H. *The Yakima* (6–9). Illus. 1990, Chelsea LB $19.95 (1-55546-735-0). The history, culture, religion, and present condition of this northwestern tribe are discussed in detail in this account. (Rev: BL 6/15/90) [970.004]

9015 Seymour, Tryntje Van Ness. *The Gift of Changing Woman* (5–8). 1993, Holt $16.95 (0-8050-2577-4). A description of the Apache initiation rite for young women in picture-book format, illustrated by Apache artists. (Rev: BL 11/15/93; SLJ 3/94) [299]

9016 Sherrow, Victoria. *Cherokee Nation v. Georgia: Native American Rights* (6–10). (Landmark Supreme Court Cases) 1997, Enslow LB $19.95 (0-89490-856-1). This book re-creates vividly the important case of 1831 when the Supreme Court ruled that the Cherokee tribe was a "domestic, dependent nation" and not liable to regulation by the state of Georgia. (Rev: BL 10/15/97) [973]

9017 Shuter, Jane, ed. *Francis Parkman and the Plains Indians* (5–8). (History Eyewitness) 1995, Raintree Steck-Vaughn LB $24.26 (0-8114-8280-4). An eyewitness account taken from Parkman's writings that gives details on the social customs, family life, and hunting practices of the Plains Indians. (Rev: BL 4/15/95) [978]

9018 Simmons, William S. *The Narragansett* (6–10). Illus. 1989, Chelsea LB $19.95 (1-55546-718-0). An interesting profile of this northeastern Indian tribe that supplies details about its history and culture. (Rev: SLJ 11/89; VOYA 8/89) [970]

9019 Snow, Dean R. *The Archaeology of North America* (6–12). Illus. 1989, Chelsea LB $19.95 (1-55546-691-5). A comprehensive and somewhat difficult history of the first inhabitants of North America through the conquest of their land by the white man. (Rev: BL 5/1/89; SLJ 7/89; VOYA 8/89) [973]

9020 Spangenburg, Raymond, and Diane Moser. *The American Indian Experience* (7–10). Illus. (American Historic Places) 1997, Facts on File $18.95 (0-8160-3403-6). In pictures and text, this work explores over 10 sites associated with Native American history, including Mesa Verde National Historic Park, Ocmulgee National Monument, Nez Perce National Historical Park, Little Bighorn Battlefield, and Alcatraz Island. (Rev: BL 2/1/98; BR 5–6/98; SLJ 4/98; VOYA 8/98) [973]

9021 Steele, Philip. *Little Bighorn* (5–8). Illus. (Great Battles and Sieges) 1992, Macmillan $17.95 (0-02-786885-0). A description of the battle in which Cheyenne and Sioux Indians defeated General Custer and the U.S. Army in 1876. (Rev: BL 10/1/92; SLJ 2/93) [973.8]

9022 Streissguth, Thomas. *Wounded Knee, 1890: The End of the Plains Indian Wars* (7–12). Illus. (Library of American Indian History) 1998, Facts on File $19.95 (0-8160-3600-4). Using primary sources from soldiers, pioneers, missionaries, reporters, and Lakota Indians, this is the story of the events of 1890 that led to the devastation of an entire race. (Rev: BL 10/1/98; BR 1–2/99) [973.8]

9023 Tanner, Helen Hornbeck. *The Ojibwa* (6–9). (Indians of North America) 1991, Chelsea LB $19.95 (1-55546-721-0). An introduction to the Ojibwa or Chippewa people, who lived around the Great Lakes and today are one of the most populous Native American groups. (Rev: BL 1/1/92; SLJ 3/92) [970.004]

9024 Thompson, William N. *Native American Issues: A Reference Handbook* (9–12). 1996, ABC-CLIO $39.50 (0-87436-828-6). This is a fascinating reference book that provides an overview of major issues concerning Native Americans in the United States and Canada, summaries of such critical issues as land claims and sacred sites, religious freedom, gaming on reservations, political jurisdiction, and water rights, and discussions of Native sovereignty and court cases and legislation. (Rev: BR 5–6/97; SLJ 8/97) [909]

9025 Trafzer, Clifford E. *The Chinook* (6–9). Illus. 1990, Chelsea LB $19.95 (1-55546-698-2). A detailed account about this northwestern tribe, how they lived, and their conditions today. (Rev: BL 6/15/90) [970.004]

9026 Trafzer, Clifford E. *The Nez Perce* (6–9). (Indians of North America) 1992, Chelsea LB $19.95 (1-55546-720-2). The moving story of this Native American group, their tribulations caused by white land grabbers, and the brief war they fought under Chief Joseph. (Rev: BL 10/1/92) [973]

9027 Viola, Herman J. *It Is a Good Day to Die: Indian Eyewitnesses Tell the Story of the Battle of Little Big Horn* (5–8). 1998, Random LB $19.99 (0-517-70913-9). This book features eyewitness accounts of Native Americans who were involved in Custer's stunning defeat at Little Bighorn, which ultimately led to the surrender of the Plains Indians to the U.S. cavalry and the removal of the vast majority of them to reservations. (Rev: BL 9/1/98; SLJ 7/98) [973.8 2]

9028 Viola, Herman J. *North American Indians* (5–9). Illus. 1996, Crown $25.00 (0-517-59017-4). Using the standard cultural areas of North America as divisions, this book describes such Native American tribes as the Cherokee, Zuni, Chumash, Iroquois, Haida, Sioux, and Inuit. (Rev: BR 5–6/97; SLJ 3/97) [973]

9029 Waldman, Carl. *Atlas of the North American Indian* (9–12). Illus. 1985, Facts on File $35.00 (0-87196-850-9). Maps and accompanying essays give an excellent introduction to the history, culture, and present-day status of the American Indian. (Rev: BL 1/15/86) [970]

9030 Walens, Stanley. *The Kwakiutl* (6–9). (Indians of North America) 1992, Chelsea LB $19.95 (1-55546-711-3). An introduction to the Kwakiutl Indians, who are native to the Pacific Northwest, where they developed a rich culture and folklore. (Rev: BL 10/1/92) [970.004]

9031 Weinstein-Farson, Laurie. *The Wampanoag* (7–9). Illus. 1988, Chelsea LB $19.95 (1-55546-733-4). A detailed account of the history and fate of the Indian tribe that first greeted the Pilgrims. (Rev: BL 12/1/88; VOYA 4/89) [973]

9032 Welch, James, and Paul Stekler. *Killing Custer: The Battle of the Little Big Horn and the Fate of the Plains Indians* (9–12). 1994, Norton $25.00 (0-393-03657-X). Examines Custer's death at Little Bighorn and the Great Sioux War from a Native American perspective. (Rev: BL 11/1/94) [973.8]

9033 Westridge Young Writers Workshop. *Kids Explore the Heritage of Western Native Americans* (6–9). 1995, John Muir paper $9.95 (1-56261-189-5). A unique book that describes the life of a family member of each of 6 native Americans tribes (Creek, Arapaho, Navajo, Hopi, Yakama, and Sioux), with descriptions of customs, traditions, and history. (Rev: SLJ 4/96) [973]

9034 Williams, Jeanne. *Trails of Tears: American Indians Driven from Their Lands* (9–12). 1992, Hendrick-Long $15.95 (0-937460-76-1). Details the U.S. government's forced removal of Comanche, Cheyenne, Apache, Navajo, and Cherokee Indians from their native lands. (Rev: BL 6/1/92) [973]

9035 Wilson, Terry P. *The Osage* (7–9). Illus. 1988, Chelsea LB $19.95 (1-55546-722-9). The history, culture, and present status of the Indian tribe are given in this detailed account. (Rev: BL 12/1/88) [973]

9036 Wolfson, Evelyn. *From the Earth to Beyond the Sky: Native American Medicine* (5–8). 1993, Houghton $16.00 (0-395-55009-2). This look at Native American medicine describes how some common plants are used and the practices, training, roles, sacred objects, and ceremonies of medicine men. (Rev: BL 12/15/93; SLJ 12/93) [615.8]

9037 Wood, Nancy. *Sacred Fire* (7–12). Illus. 1998, Bantam Doubleday Dell $25.00 (0-385-32515-0). This meditation on the world of the Pueblo Indians, their beliefs about nature, and the drastic change in their lives after the Spanish invasion in 1540, is illustrated with breathtakingly beautiful paintings by Frank Howell. (Rev: BL 7/98; SLJ 10/98) [973]

9038 Wood, Nancy, ed. *The Serpent's Tongue: Prose, Poetry, and Art of the New Mexico Pueblos* (7–12). Illus. 1997, Dutton $35.00 (0-525-45514-0). A stirring collection of writings by and about the Pueblo people and art reproductions that span 500 years of history and spiritual life. (Rev: BL 12/1/97; BR 5–6/98; SLJ 12/97*; VOYA 6/98) [978.9004]

9039 Woodhead, Edward, ed. *The Woman's Way* (9–12). 1995, Time-Life Books $19.95 (0-8094-9729-8). Explains the traditional duties and customs of North American Indian women throughout history, with biographical sketches of several well-known Native-American women. (Rev: BL 9/1/95; SLJ 11/95) [305.48]

9040 Wunder, John R. *The Kiowa* (6–9). Illus. 1989, Chelsea LB $19.95 (1-55546-710-5). The story of the nomadic hunters of the plains, the Kiowa, and the effects of the white man's invasion of their land. (Rev: BL 7/89; VOYA 10/89) [973]

DISCOVERY AND EXPLORATION

9041 Faber, Harold. *The Discoverers of America* (6–12). 1992, Scribners $17.95 (0-684-19217-9). Discusses the exploration of North and South America, focusing on the period from Columbus to Lewis and Clark. (Rev: BL 5/15/92; SLJ 6/92) [970.01]

9042 Haskins, Jim. *Against All Opposition: Black Explorers in America* (5–9). 1992, Walker LB $14.85 (0-8027-8138-1). A collective biography of African and African American explorers. (Rev: BL 2/15/92; SLJ 6/92) [910]

9043 Meltzer, Milton. *Columbus and the World around Him* (7–10). 1990, Watts LB $29.00 (0-531-10899-6). A handsome addition to the literature about Columbus that also deals with the culture and attitudes of the Spanish at the time. (Rev: BL 4/15/90; SLJ 7/90) [970.01]

9044 Schouweiler, Thomas. *The Lost Colony of Roanoke* (6–10). (Great Mysteries) 1991, Greenhaven LB $13.95 (0-89908-093-6). Outlines what is known about the colony that disappeared and poses questions about its unsolved mysteries. (Rev: BL 3/1/92) [975.6]

9045 Straub, Deborah G., ed. *Native North American Voices* (6–12). 1997, Gale $39.00 (0-8103-9819-2). This is a collection of important speeches delivered by 20 Native Americans, beginning with one by Joseph Brant in 1794 and ending with the 1944 speech of Ada Deer of the Bureau of Indian Affairs. (Rev: BR 9–10/97; SLJ 11/97) [973]

COLONIAL PERIOD AND FRENCH AND INDIAN WARS

9046 Collier, Christopher, and James L. Collier. *Clash of Cultures, Prehistory–1638* (5–8). Illus. (Drama of American History) 1998, Marshall Cavendish LB $28.50 (0-7614-0436-8). This well-illustrated examination of the cultures on both sides of the Atlantic—Native American and European—in the years before and during the formation of the colonies. (Rev: BL 4/15/98; BR 11–12/98) [970.00497]

9047 Collier, Christopher, and James L. Collier. *The French and Indian War* (5–8). Illus. (Drama of American History) 1998, Marshall Cavendish LB $29.93 (0-7614-0439-2). Pertinent events during the war on both sides of the Atlantic are described in this nicely illustrated volume that gives a broad perspective to the conflict. (Rev: BL 4/15/98; BR 11–12/98) [973.2]

9048 Collier, Christopher, and James L. Collier. *The Paradox of Jamestown: 1585–1700* (5–8). Illus. (Drama of American History) 1998, Marshall Cavendish LB $28.50 (0-7614-0437-6). In this account, the paradox of Jamestown's history is that it gave democratic freedom through its elected legislature while introducing the first African slaves into the colonies. (Rev: BL 4/15/98; BR 11–12/98) [975.5]

9049 Daugherty, James. *Landing of the Pilgrims* (6–8). 1987, Random paper $5.99 (0-394-84697-4). A history of the first 3 years of the colony at Plymouth. [974.4]

9050 Dean, Ruth, and Melissa Thomson. *Life in the American Colonies* (4–8). (The Way People Live) 1999, Lucent LB $22.45 (1-56006-376-9). A description of life in the American colonies that covers immigrants, slaves, cities, farms, the frontier, home, crafts, professions, science, technology, and encounters with Native American culture. (Rev: BL 5/1/99; SLJ 7/99) [973.2]

9051 Doherty, Kieran. *Puritans, Pilgrims, and Merchants: Founders of the Northeastern Colonies* (4–8). 1999, Oliver Pr. LB $21.95 (1-881508-50-1). This book combines the history of the northeastern colonies with biographies of colonists who founded and led them, including William Bradford, John Winthrop, Peter Stuyvesant, Roger Williams, Thomas Hooker, Anne Hutchinson, John Wheelwright, and William Penn. (Rev: BL 8/99) [974]

9052 Doherty, Kieran. *Soldiers, Cavaliers, and Planters: Settlers of the Southeastern Colonies* (4–8). 1999, Oliver Pr. LB $27.44 (1-881508-51-X). This book focuses on the early southern colonies and their founders and leaders, among them Captain John Smith, Sir Walter Raleigh, and Pedro Menendez de Aviles. (Rev: BL 8/99; SLJ 10/99) [975]

9053 Hale, Anna W. *The Mayflower People: Triumphs and Tragedies* (5–8). Illus. 1995, Harbinger $15.95 (1-57140-002-8); paper $9.95 (1-57140-003-6). A human account of the Pilgrims that begins with their departure from Southampton, England, in 1620 and ends two years later in the New World with the death of of the Indian Squanto. (Rev: BL 1/1–15/96) [974.4]

9054 Hansen, Chadwick. *Witchcraft at Salem* (9–12). Illus. 1969, Braziller $12.95 (0-8076-0492-5); paper $11.95 (0-8076-1137-9). A readable, well-researched account of the Salem witch hunt and of colonial life in New England. [133.4]

9055 Hansen, Joyce, and Gary McGowan. *Breaking Ground, Breaking Silence: The Story of New York's African Burial Ground* (8–12). 1998, Holt $17.95 (0-8050-5012-4). The graphic story of the finding, in 1991, of the mid-18th-century African Burial Ground in Manhattan and what it reveals about the lives of slaves in New York. (Rev: BL 5/15/98; SLJ 5/98; VOYA 8/98) [305.5]

9056 Hawke, David Freeman. *Everyday Life in Early America* (9–12). Illus. 1988, HarperCollins paper $13.00 (0-06-091251-0). A detailed account of what life was like for the average colonists in America. (Rev: BL 12/1/87; SLJ 12/88) [973.2]

9057 Hill, Frances. *A Delusion of Satan: The Full Story of the Salem Witch Trials* (9–12). 1995, Doubleday $23.95 (0-385-47255-2). A careful, analytical examination of the Salem witch hunts, in which a group of young girls accused innocent women of practicing witchcraft. (Rev: BL 11/1/95*) [133.4]

9058 Howarth, Sarah. *Colonial People* (5–8). 1994, Millbrook LB $21.90 (1-56294-512-2). Provides portraits of the work and lifestyles of selected individuals in the colonial era. (Rev: BL 5/15/95; SLJ 3/95) [973.2]

9059 Howarth, Sarah. *Colonial Places* (5–8). 1994, Millbrook LB $21.90 (1-56294-513-0). Describes several sites around which life in early America revolved. (Rev: BL 5/15/95; SLJ 3/95) [973.2]

9060 Jackson, Shirley. *The Witchcraft of Salem Village* (6–9). Illus. 1956, Random LB $9.99 (0-394-90369-2). The causes and incidents involved in the Salem witchcraft trials of the 17th century. [133.4]

9061 January, Brendan. *Science in Colonial America* (4–8). (Science of the Past) 1999, Watts $25.00 (0-531-11525-9). This account of science in the colonies touches on such topics as Cotton Mather's work in inoculation, studies in natural history by Thomas Jefferson and John and William Bartram, and Ben Franklin's discoveries with electricity. (Rev: SLJ 6/99) [973.2]

9062 Kallen, Stuart A. *The Salem Witch Trials* (6–9). (World History) 1999, Lucent LB $23.70 (1-56006-544-3). This book re-creates the world of 17th-century Massachusetts and tells the story of the mass hysteria that produced hatred and death. (Rev: BL 9/15/99; SLJ 9/99) [973.3]

9063 Lizon, Karen H. *Colonial American Holidays and Entertainment* (5–8). (Colonial America) 1993, Watts LB $22.00 (0-531-12546-7). This book looks at the holidays celebrated during colonial times, including by slaves, Native Americans, and indentured servants. (Rev: BL 1/1/94; SLJ 12/93) [394.2]

9064 Loeper, John J. *Going to School in 1776* (7–9). Illus. 1973, Macmillan $16.00 (0-689-30089-1). A description of what schools were like during the late Colonial period. [370.9]

9065 Marrin, Albert. *Struggle for a Continent: The French and Indian Wars, 1690–1760* (6–9). Illus. 1987, Macmillan LB $15.95 (0-689-31313-6). A vivid re-creation of the events and personalities of these wars and how they helped lead to the Revolution. (Rev: BL 1/15/88; SLJ 12/87; VOYA 10/87) [973.2]

9066 Nardo, Don. *Braving the New World, 1619–1784: From the Arrival of the Enslaved Africans to the End of the American Revolution* (7–10). (Milestones in Black History) 1995, Chelsea LB $19.95 (0-7910-2259-5); paper $7.95 (0-7910-2685-X). How and why the slave trade became established in North America and the legacy of the slave culture. (Rev: BL 4/15/95) [973.2]

9067 O'Neill, Laurie A. *The Boston Tea Party* (4–8). (Spotlight on American History) 1996, Millbrook LB $21.90 (0-7613-0006-6). The causes and effects of the Boston Tea Party are discussed, along with material on the Battles of Lexington and Concord. (Rev: BL 1/1–15/97; SLJ 3/97) [973.3]

9068 Perl, Lila. *Slumps, Grunts, and Snickerdoodles: What Colonial America Ate and Why* (7–9).

Illus. 1975, Clarion $16.00 (0-395-28923-8). A description of what was eaten in the various colonies plus 13 recipes from the period. [641.5]

9069 Rice, Earle, Jr. *The Salem Witch Trials* (7–10). (Famous Trials) 1996, Lucent LB $18.96 (1-56006-272-X). This account of the Salem trials discusses dozens of the people involved in the proceedings and provides a social, political, and legal context. (Rev: BR 11–12/97; SLJ 6/97; VOYA 8/97) [973.2]

9070 Roach, Marilynne K. *In the Days of the Salem Witchcraft Trials* (4–8). Illus. 1996, Houghton $15.00 (0-395-69704-2). The Salem witch trials are discussed in the context of how people lived in this period and what they believed. (Rev: BL 5/15/96; SLJ 7/96) [973.3]

9071 Smith, Carter, ed. *The Arts and Sciences: A Sourcebook on Colonial America* (5–8). (American Albums from the Collections of the Library of Congress) 1991, Millbrook LB $25.90 (1-56294-037-6). This visual sourcebook chronicles the history of the arts and sciences in colonial America. (Rev: BL 1/1/92) [973.2]

9072 Smith, Carter, ed. *Daily Life: A Sourcebook on Colonial America* (5–8). (American Albums from the Collections of the Library of Congress) 1991, Millbrook LB $25.90 (1-56294-038-4). Authentic prints and other illustrations are used to introduce the everyday life of different kinds of colonial people. (Rev: BL 1/1/92) [973.2]

9073 Stevens, Bernardine S. *Colonial American Craftspeople* (5–8). (Colonial America) 1993, Watts LB $23.00 (0-531-12536-X). A description of colonial trades and the apprenticeship system, illustrated with period engravings and paintings. (Rev: BL 1/1/94; SLJ 2/94) [680]

9074 Stiles, T. J. *In Their Own Words: The Colonizers* (10–12). (In Their Own Words) 1998, Putnam $16.00 (0-399-52390-1). A collection of fascinating narratives by ordinary people as well as more prominent figures in French and British colonies from Canada to South Carolina, starting with Champlain's views on Quebec in 1608 and ending in 1760, with Bougainville's account of the French surrender to the British. (Rev: BL 3/1/98; SLJ 11/98) [973.2]

9075 Terkel, Susan N. *Colonial American Medicine* (5–8). (Colonial America) 1993, Watts LB $23.00 (0-531-12539-4). An account of traditional medicine that discusses the various illnesses colonists faced and the risks they faced even after seeking help from medical practitioners. (Rev: BL 1/1/94; SLJ 11/93) [632.1]

9076 Warner, John F. *Colonial American Home Life* (5–8). (Colonial America) 1993, Watts LB $23.00 (0-531-12541-6). Covers colonial clothing, food, work, education, housing, amusements, and methods

of communication. (Rev: BL 1/1/94; SLJ 2/94; VOYA 4/94) [973.2]

9077 Washburne, Carolyn K. *A Multicultural Portrait of Colonial Life* (7–12). (Perspectives) 1993, Marshall Cavendish LB $28.50 (1-85435-657-7). A picture of everyday colonial life as experienced by different strata of society, including women, Native Americans, and slaves. (Rev: BL 3/15/94; SLJ 4/94) [973.2]

9078 Wilson, Lori L. *The Salem Witch Trials: How History Is Invented* (6–12). Illus. (How History Is Invented) 1997, Lerner LB $23.93 (0-8225-4889-5). The story of the famous trial of 100 people in Massachusetts during 1692, and the hysteria and falsehoods that led to 20 people being put to death. (Rev: BL 9/1/97; SLJ 8/97*) [133.4]

9079 Wood, Peter H. *Strange New Land: African Americans 1617–1776* (7–12). Illus. (Young Oxford History of African Americans) 1996, Oxford LB $21.00 (0-19-508700-3). A well-organized description of slavery during the Colonial Period through the beginning of the Revolution. A chronology and illustrations add to the book's usefulness. (Rev: BL 2/15/96; SLJ 3/96) [973]

REVOLUTIONARY PERIOD AND THE YOUNG NATION (1775–1809)

9080 Allison, Robert J., ed. *American Eras: The Revolutionary Era (1754–1783)* (7–12). 1998, Gale $107.57 (0-7876-1480-7). A good reference source that opens with an overview of world events during the Revolutionary period, followed by chapters on specific topics such as the arts; business and the economy; law and justice; lifestyles, social trends, and fashions; religion; and sports and recreation. (Rev: SLJ 2/99) [973.3]

9081 Bennett, William J., ed. *The Country's Founders: A Book of Advice for Young People* (7–12). 1998, Simon & Schuster $17.00 (0-689-82106-9). The guiding principles of the founders of our country are revealed in this collection of writings by Washington, Jefferson, Adams, and others. (Rev: BL 8/98; SLJ 10/98) [973.099]

9082 Bliven, Bruce, Jr. *The American Revolution, 1760–1783* (6–9). Illus. 1958, Random LB $9.99 (0-394-90383-8); paper $5.99 (0-394-84696-6). A concise account of the causes, battles, and results of the Revolution. [973.3]

9083 Blumberg, Rhoda. *What's the Deal? Jefferson, Napoleon & the Louisiana Purchase* (5–9). Illus. 1998, National Geographic $18.95 (0-7922-7013-4). This excellent blend of scholarship and fine writing tells the dramatic history of the Louisiana territory, with an intriguing section on what might have happened if Napoleon had refused to sell it. (Rev: BL 11/1/98; SLJ 10/98) [973.4]

9084 Brenner, Barbara. *If You Were There in 1776* (5–8). 1994, Bradbury paper $17.00 (0-02-712322-7). The year 1776 in the American colonies, beginning with a world context and moving on to a description of the diverse populations of the colonies and their everyday life. (Rev: BL 5/15/94; SLJ 6/94) [973.3]

9085 Collier, Christopher, and James L. Collier. *The American Revolution: 1763–1783* (5–8). (Drama of American History) 1998, Marshall Cavendish LB $28.50 (0-7614-0440-6). Using period illustrations, this is a basic history of the Revolution, with material on how the colonialists felt, major battles, and major figures. (Rev: BL 4/15/98; BR 11–12/98) [973.3]

9086 Collier, Christopher, and James L. Collier. *Building a New Nation, 1789–1801* (5–8). Illus. (Drama of American History) 1998, Marshall Cavendish LB $28.50 (0-7614-0777-4). An account of how the Federalists began to use the Constitution as a blueprint for guiding the young nation. (Rev: BL 2/15/99) [973.4]

9087 Collier, Christopher, and James L. Collier. *Pilgrims and Puritans: 1620–1676* (5–8). Illus. (Drama of American History) 1998, Marshall Cavendish LB $28.50 (0-7614-0438-4). This volume describes the routes that the Pilgrims and Puritans used to come to America, their beliefs and practices, and how American life continues to be influenced by them today. (Rev: BL 4/15/98; BR 11–12/98) [974.4]

9088 Cox, Clinton. *Come All You Brave Soldiers: Blacks in the Revolutionary War* (6–10). 1999, Scholastic $21.99 (0-590-47576-2). Beginning with the Boston Massacre and ending with the Battle of Yorktown, this is a survey of the participation and contributions of African Americans in the American Revolution. (Rev: BL 2/15/99; SLJ 2/99; VOYA 6/99) [973.3]

9089 Davis, Burke. *Black Heroes of the American Revolution* (7–9). Illus. 1976, Harcourt $14.95 (0-15-208560-2). A book that highlights the contributions of a group of black patriots who fought for freedom. [973.3]

9090 De Pauw, Linda Grant. *Founding Mothers: Women in America in the Revolutionary Era* (7–10). Illus. 1975, Houghton $18.00 (0-395-21896-9). The role of women during the Revolutionary War period. [305.4]

9091 Dolan, Edward F. *The American Revolution: How We Fought the War of Independence* (6–9). 1995, Millbrook LB $27.40 (1-56294-521-1). This heavily illustrated, clearly written, battle-by-battle history of the Revolution looks at the causes, places, campaigns, and people, as well as the bloodiest battles. (Rev: BL 12/15/95; BR 5–6/96; SLJ 1/96) [973.3]

9092 Dudley, William, ed. *The American Revolution* (10–12). (Opposing Viewpoints in American History) 1992, Greenhaven LB $17.95 (1-56510-011-5); paper $15.00 (1-56510-010-7). Provides scholarly material representing a wide range of viewpoints, with a long annotated bibliography. (Rev: BL 4/15/93) [973.3]

9093 Ferrie, Richard. *The World Turned Upside Down: George Washington and the Battle of Yorktown* (5–9). Illus. 1999, Holiday House $18.95 (0-8234-1402-7). A lavishly illustrated account of the battle that was the turning point in the Revolution, with details on strategies, personalities, and period warfare. (Rev: BL 9/1/99; SLJ 10/99) [973.3]

9094 Gay, Kathlyn, and Martin Gay. *Revolutionary War* (5–8). (Voices from the Past) 1995, Twenty-First Century LB $18.90 (0-8050-2844-7). Eyewitness accounts are used extensively in this book that covers the causes, key events, and results of the Revolutionary War. (Rev: BL 12/15/95; SLJ 3/96) [973.3]

9095 Greenberg, Judith E., and Helen C. McKeever. *Journal of a Revolutionary War Woman* (6–10). Illus. (In Their Own Words) 1996, Watts LB $25.00 (0-531-11259-4). An intimate view of the American Revolution through the eyes of the wife of an officer in the Continental Army. (Rev: BL 9/1/96; BR 11–12/96; SLJ 8/96; VOYA 2/97) [973.3]

9096 Hull, Mary. *The Boston Tea Party in American History* (6–10). (In American History) 1999, Enslow $19.95 (0-7660-1139-9). The events leading up to this act of defiance that sparked the American Revolution are covered, in addition to the event itself, creating a sense that all eyes were on Boston as it dared to defy the crown in their struggle against British taxation. (Rev: BL 2/15/99) [973.3 115]

9097 Karapalides, Harry J. *Dates of the American Revolution: Who, What, and Where in the War for Independence* (7–12). 1998, Burd Street paper $19.95 (1-57249-106-X). A chronological record tracing the American Revolution from 1760, when King George II inherited the British throne, to 1799, with George Washington's death, with an emphasis on military action and commanders. (Rev: SLJ 2/99) [973.3]

9098 King, David. *Lexington and Concord* (4–8). (Battlefields Across America) 1997, Twenty-First Century $23.40 (0-8050-5225-9). A detailed account of the people and events leading up to these opening battles in the Revolutionary War, and the lasting consequences. (Rev: SLJ 1/98) [973.3]

9099 King, David C. *Saratoga* (5–8). Illus. (Battlefields Across America) 1998, Twenty-First Century LB $23.40 (0-7613-3011-9). The significance of the battle at Saratoga in 1777, in which General Burgoyne's British army was defeated, and where and how the history of this battle is preserved today. (Rev: SLJ 8/98) [973.3]

9100 Lancaster, Bruce, and J. H. Plumb. *The American Heritage Book of the Revolution* (9–12). 1985, Dell paper $15.00 (0-8281-0281-3). A concise, readable account of the causes, events, and consequences of the American Revolution. [973.3]

9101 Lukes, Bonnie L. *The American Revolution* (8–12). Illus. (World History) 1996, Lucent LB $17.96 (1-56006-287-8). This overview of the Revolution, with emphasis on key events and personalities, is enhanced by quotes from many sources and a chronology. (Rev: BL 4/15/96; SLJ 7/96) [973.3]

9102 Lukes, Bonnie L. *The Boston Massacre* (6–9). Illus. (Famous Trials) 1998, Lucent LB $18.96 (1-56006-467-6). This book explores the dramatic trial of the British soldiers who fired on rioting protesters in Boston, killing 6 outright and fatally wounding 2 others. (Rev: BL 4/15/98; SLJ 7/98) [973.3]

9103 Marrin, Albert. *The War for Independence: The Story of the American Revolution* (6–9). 1988, Macmillan $19.00 (0-689-31390-X). The great 8-year war that brought America's independence is well re-created along with the colorful characters involved in it. (Rev: BL 7/88; BR 11–12/88; SLJ 6/88; VOYA 6/88) [973.3]

9104 Minks, Louise, and Benton Minks. *The Revolutionary War* (7–12). (America at War) 1992, Facts on File $19.95 (0-8160-2508-8). A colorful account of the causes, main battles, and outcomes of the Revolutionary War. (Rev: BL 2/1/93) [973.3]

9105 Mitchell, Joseph B. *Decisive Battles of the American Revolution* (9–12). 1985, Fawcett paper $5.99 (0-449-30031-5). A re-creation of all the important battles in the Revolution from Lexington to Yorktown. [973.3]

9106 Murphy, Jim. *A Young Patriot: The American Revolution as Experienced by One Boy* (5–8). Illus. 1996, Clarion $16.00 (0-395-60523-7). The American Revolution as seen through the eyes of a 15-year-old volunteer. (Rev: BL 6/1–15/96*; SLJ 6/96*) [973.3]

9107 Nardo, Don. *The American Revolution* (7–12). (Opposing Viewpoints Digests) 1998, Greenhaven LB $17.96 (1-56510-755-1); paper $17.25 (1-56510-754-3). Quoting from dozens of primary and secondary sources, this book explores issues related to the Revolution, such as prewar disputes, patriotic vs. loyalist views, wartime concerns, and modern attitudes. (Rev: BL 5/15/98; SLJ 6/98) [973.3]

9108 Nardo, Don. *The Declaration of Independence: A Model for Individual Rights* (9–12). (Words That Changed History) 1998, Lucent LB $18.96 (1-56006-368-8). Using many primary and secondary source quotations, this is the history of the document

that continues to serve America 200 years after its signing. (Rev: BL 1/1–15/99; BR 5–6/99) [973.3]

9109 *The Revolutionaries* (7–12). Illus. (American Story) 1996, Time-Life Books $19.95 (0-7835-6250-0). Illustrations and personal narratives enhance this detailed chronological account of the drive for independence and the military high points of the American Revolution. (Rev: BL 12/15/96; BR 3–4/97; SLJ 1/97) [973.3]

9110 Smith, Carter, ed. *The Founding Presidents: A Sourcebook on the U.S. Presidency* (5–8). (American Albums) 1993, Millbrook LB $25.90 (1-56294-357-X). Using the collection of the Library of Congress, this is a visual sourcebook of the presidents who served immediately after the Revolution. (Rev: BL 12/1/93) [973]

9111 Smith, Carter, ed. *The Revolutionary War: A Sourcebook on Colonial America* (5–8). (American Albums from the Collections of the Library of Congress) 1991, Millbrook LB $25.90 (1-56294-039-2). This volume illustrates the major events leading up to the Revolution and the battles and personalities involved. (Rev: BL 1/1/92) [973.38]

9112 Steins, Richard. *A Nation Is Born: Rebellion and Independence in America (1700–1820)* (5–8). (First Person America) 1993, Twenty-First Century LB $18.90 (0-8050-2582-0). A look at the American Revolution, using extracts from diaries, letters, and journals of individuals from that period. (Rev: BL 2/1/94; SLJ 2/94) [973.3]

9113 Wilbur, Keith C. *Revolutionary Medicine, 1700–1800* (4–8). Illus. (Illustrated Living History) 1996, Chelsea $19.95 (0-7910-4532-3). In a large-book format, this account gives a great deal of information, some gruesome, some funny, but always informative, about medicine in 18th-century America. (Rev: BL 6/1–15/97; SLJ 7/97) [973.3]

9114 Wilbur, Keith C. *The Revolutionary Soldier, 1775–1783* (4–8). (Illustrated Living History) 1996, Chelsea LB $19.95 (0-7910-4533-1). Topics covered in this book about the Continental Army include clothing, weapons, camp life, food, hospitals, and leisure activities. (Rev: BL 6/1–15/97; SLJ 7/97) [973.3]

9115 Zall, P. M. *Becoming American: Young People in the American Revolution* (8–12). 1993, Linnet LB $25.00 (0-208-02355-0). Letters, journal entries, and testimonies by young people describing their lives, events, and social conditions in the years immediately before, during, and immediately after the Revolution. (Rev: BL 5/1/93; VOYA 8/93) [973.3]

9116 Zeinert, Karen. *Those Remarkable Women of the American Revolution* (5–8). Illus. 1996, Millbrook LB $27.40 (1-56294-657-9). A fascinating account of the conditions and status of women in Colonial America and their important contributions to the American Revolution, from fighting and spying to fund raising. (Rev: BL 12/1/96; SLJ 3/97; VOYA 4/97) [973.3]

9117   Zell, Fran. *A Multicultural Portrait of the American Revolution* (7–10). (Perspectives) 1996, Benchmark LB $28.50 (0-7614-0051-6). This account of the Revolutionary War points out the irony that while white European males were fighting for "life, liberty, and pursuit of happiness," African Americans were in slavery, and women and poor male European settlers had very few political rights, and notes the legacy of ideals left by the Revolution. (Rev: BR 1–2/97; SLJ 6/96) [973.3]

NINETEENTH CENTURY TO THE CIVIL WAR (1809–1861)

9118   Baker, Lindsay, and Julie P. Baker, eds. *Till Freedom Cried Out: Memories of Texas Slave Life* (10–12). Illus. 1997, Texas A & M Univ. Pr. $29.95 (0-89096-736-9). Part of the Oklahoma Slave Narrative Project established as part of the WPA, this is a collection of narratives by 32 slaves who were born in Texas and relocated to Oklahoma. (Rev: SLJ 12/97) [973.6]

9119   Baldwin, Robert F. *New England Whaler* (5–8). Illus. (American Pastfinder) 1996, Lerner LB $21.50 (0-8225-2978-5). Life on a 19th-century whaling ship is detailed, with many maps and color photos. (Rev: BL 7/96; SLJ 6/96) [638.2]

9120   Bentley, Judith. *"Dear Friend": Thomas Garrett & William Still, Collaborators on the Underground Railroad* (5–9). Illus. 1997, Dutton paper $15.99 (0-525-65156-X). This account of the "eastern line" of the network that helped bring slaves from the South to the North and freedom focuses on the courageous collaboration of Thomas Garrett, a white Quaker, and William Still, a free black. (Rev: BL 2/15/97; SLJ 6/97; VOYA 12/97) [973.7]

9121   Berlin, Ira, and Marc Favreau, eds. *Remembering Slavery: African Americans Talk about Their Personal Experiences of Slavery & Emancipation* (10–12). Illus. 1998, New Pr. $49.95 (1-56584-425-4). This book and cassette set recaptures the narratives of former slaves as they were first recorded in the 1930s as part of the Federal Writers' Project. These personal recollections convey the harshness, sadism, and brutality of slavery as well as the resilience, survival skills, sense of family, and community among the slaves. (Rev: BL 8/98; SLJ 4/99) [973]

9122   Bial, Raymond. *The Strength of These Arms: Life in the Slave Quarters* (5–8). 1997, Houghton $15.00 (0-395-77394-6). This photoessay re-creates daily life in the slave quarters on large plantations, contrasts it with the luxurious lifestyles of the slave holders, and documents how slaves tried to preserve

their heritage, dignity, and hope. (Rev: BL 9/15/97; SLJ 11/97) [975]

9123   Bredeson, Carmen. *The Battle of the Alamo: The Fight for Texas Territory* (5–8). (Spotlight on American History) 1996, Millbrook LB $21.90 (0-7613-0019-8). A well-organized account of the causes, events, and campaigns of the war in which much of California, Texas, and the Southwest became part of the United States. (Rev: SLJ 4/97) [973.6]

9124   Chalfant, William Y. *Dangerous Passage: The Santa Fe Trail and the Mexican War* (9–12). 1994, Univ. of Oklahoma Pr. $32.95 (0-8061-2613-2). A detailed account of the Santa Fe Trail during the Mexican War. (Rev: BL 2/1/94) [978]

9125   Collier, C., and J. L. Collier. *Andrew Jackson's America, 1824–1850* (5–8). Illus. (Drama of American History) 1998, Marshall Cavendish LB $28.50 (0-7614-0779-0). The account traces American history over an eventful 26 years that encompass great change, from the Industrial Revolution to the Trail of Tears. (Rev: BL 2/15/99) [973.5 6]

9126   Collier, C., and J. L. Collier. *Hispanic America, Texas & the Mexican War, 1835–1850* (5–8). Illus. 1998, Marshall Cavendish LB $28.50 (0-7614-0780-4). The account covers the history of Europeans in the Southwest, the Hispanic culture in the region, the doctrine of Manifest Destiny, the Mexican War, and the settling of California. (Rev: BL 2/15/99; SLJ 4/99) [979.02]

9127   Collier, C., and J. L. Collier. *The Jeffersonian Republicans, 1800–1823* (5–8). Illus. (Drama of American History) 1998, Marshall Cavendish LB $28.50 (0-7614-0778-2). This lively account describes 23 eventful years in our history that include the Louisiana Purchase, the Lewis and Clark expedition, and the War of 1812. (Rev: BL 2/15/99; SLJ 4/99) [973.4 6]

9128   Fleischner, Jennifer. *The Dred Scott Case: Testing the Right to Live Free* (5–8). (Spotlight on American History) 1997, Millbrook LB $21.90 (0-7613-0005-8). An account of the life of the slave Dred Scott and the historic court case of 1857 against his owner, John Sanford. (Rev: BL 5/1/97; SLJ 4/97) [342.73]

9129   Freedman, Florence. *Two Tickets to Freedom: The True Story of Ellen & William Craft, Fugitive Slaves* (5–9). 1989, Bedrick $12.95 (0-87226-330-4); paper $5.95 (0-87226-221-9). The story of 2 courageous married slaves and their flight to Canada and freedom. (Rev: BR 3–4/90) [973.5]

9130   Gay, Kathlyn, and Martin Gay. *War of 1812* (5–8). (Voices of the Past) 1995, Twenty-First Century LB $18.90 (0-8050-2846-3). Excerpts from letters, memoirs, and official reports highlight this well-illustrated history of the War of 1812 and its consequences. (Rev: BL 12/15/95; SLJ 3/96) [973.5]

9131 Gold, Susan D. *Land Pacts* (5–8). Illus. (Pacts and Treaties) 1995, Twenty-First Century LB $21.40 (0-8050-4810-3). The story of how the United States tripled its land holding through the Louisiana Purchase, the Guadalupe-Hidalgo Treaty, and the Alaska Purchase. (Rev: BL 5/15/97; BR 9–10/97; SLJ 6/97) [973.5]

9132 Gorrell, Gena K. *North Star to Freedom: The Story of the Underground Railroad* (5–10). Illus. 1997, Delacorte $17.95 (0-385-32319-0). A handsome, readable account that captures the danger and excitement connected to the Underground Railroad and the heroism and dedication of abolitionists in Canada as well as in the United States who helped slaves escape from the South. (Rev: BL 2/15/97; BR 9–10/97; SLJ 1/97*) [973.7]

9133 Greenblatt, Miriam. *The War of 1812* (7–12). Illus. (America at War) 1994, Facts on File $19.95 (0-8160-2879-6). A lively account of how our young nation tried to rid itself of foreign influences, tracing the causes of the war and describing the battles fought on land and sea. (Rev: BL 11/15/94; SLJ 12/94) [973.5]

9134 Hansen, Ellen, ed. *The Underground Railroad: Life on the Road to Freedom* (4–8). Illus. (Perspectives on History) 1993, Discovery Enterprises paper $5.95 (1-878668-27-7). The story of the Underground Railroad, its origins and accomplishments, and the people—white and black—who were responsible for its operation. (Rev: BL 8/94) [973.7]

9135 Herda, D. J. *The Dred Scott Case: Slavery and Citizenship* (6–10). Illus. (Landmark Supreme Court Cases) 1994, Enslow LB $19.95 (0-89490-460-4). An examination of the pre-Civil War case in which a slave was denied his freedom, and its consequences. (Rev: BL 6/1–15/94) [342.73]

9136 January, Brendan. *The Dred Scott Decision* (5–8). Illus. (Cornerstones of Freedom) 1998, Children's Pr. LB $20.00 (0-516-20833-0); paper $5.95 (0-516-26457-5). Using many photographs and reproductions, this book explores the landmark 1857 Supreme Court decision on slavery that helped lead the United States into civil war. (Rev: BR 11–12/98; SLJ 8/98) [973.7]

9137 Jurmain, Suzanne. *Freedom's Sons: The True Story of the Amistad Mutiny* (5–8). Illus. 1998, Lothrop $15.00 (0-688-11072-X). Told with true storytelling skill, this fascinating chapter in American history is re-created brilliantly, with a special focus on the nobility of Cinque and his men. (Rev: BL 2/15/98; SLJ 4/98) [326]

9138 Katz, William L. *Breaking the Chains: African-American Slave Resistance* (9–12). Illus. 1990, Simon & Schuster $16.00 (0-689-31493-0). A revealing account of American black slavery that

focuses on the many uprisings and rebellions. (Rev: BL 12/1/90; SLJ 11/90) [305.6]

9139 King, David C. *New Orleans* (5–8). Illus. (Battlefields Across America) 1998, Twenty-First Century LB $23.40 (0-7613-3010-0). The story of the famous 1815 battle in New Orleans in which the British were decisively defeated, including the background of the War of 1812, the role of Andrew Jackson, and the significance of this defeat to the British. (Rev: SLJ 8/98) [973.6]

9140 Langdon, William Chauncey. *Everyday Things in American Life, 1776–1876* (7–12). Illus. 1941, Macmillan $45.00 (0-684-17416-2). This illustrated account covers such topics as clothing, machinery, canals, bridges, and turnpikes. [973]

9141 Lord, Walter. *A Time to Stand* (9–12). 1978, Univ. of Nebraska Pr. paper $10.95 (0-8032-7902-7). A gripping account of the siege and fall of the Alamo. [973.6]

9142 Lukes, Bonnie L. *The Dred Scott Decision* (9–12). Illus. (Famous Trials) 1996, Lucent LB $17.96 (1-56006-270-3). The story of the slave Dred Scott and the historic 1857 court case against his owner, John Sanford. (Rev: BL 6/1–15/97; BR 11–12/97; SLJ 4/97) [342.73]

9143 McKissack, Patricia, and Fredrick McKissack. *Rebels against Slavery: American Slave Revolts* (5–8). Illus. 1996, Scholastic $14.95 (0-590-45735-7). A fascinating account of the men and women who led revolts against slavery, including Toussaint L'Ouverture, Cinque, Harriet Tubman, and Nat Turner. (Rev: BL 2/15/96; BR 3–4/96; SLJ 3/96; VOYA 4/96) [970]

9144 Mancall, Peter C., ed. *American Eras: Westward Expansion (1800–1860)* (8–12). 1999, Gale $98.67 (0-7876-1483-1). The period of growth and change in America from the early 19th century up to the Civil War is examined. (Rev: SLJ 8/99) [973.6]

9145 Myers, Walter Dean. *Amistad: A Long Road to Freedom* (5–9). Illus. 1998, Dutton paper $16.99 (0-525-45970-7). The fascinating story of the 1839 mutiny and its consequences, told with a skillful narrative that emphasizes the courage, strength, and dignity of the mutineers. (Rev: BL 2/15/98; SLJ 5/98; VOYA 6/98) [326]

9146 Nardo, Don. *The Mexican-American War* (6–9). (World History) 1999, Lucent LB $22.45 (1-56006-495-1). The author reviews the events leading up to this war involving Texas, Colorado, and California, the major battles, the large antiwar movement in the United States, and the bitterness that still exists among some Mexicans. (Rev: BL 9/15/99; SLJ 9/99) [973.6]

9147 Paulson, Timothy J. *Days of Sorrow, Years of Glory, 1831–1850: From the Nat Turner Revolt to* *the Fugitive Slave Law* (5–9). (Milestones in Black American History) 1994, Chelsea LB $19.95 (0-7910-2263-3); paper $14.93 (0-7910-2552-7). An examination of the Underground Railroad, slave resistance, the Seminole Wars, and the abolition movement. (Rev: BL 11/1/94; SLJ 4/95; VOYA 12/94) [973]

9148 Sawyer, Kem K. *The Underground Railroad in American History* (7–10). Illus. (In American History) 1997, Enslow LB $19.95 (0-89490-885-5). A description of the formation of the Underground Railroad, its functions, key people connected with it, and its importance in American history. (Rev: BL 7/97; BR 9–10/97) [973.7]

9149 Shuter, Jane, ed. *Charles Ball and American Slavery* (5–8). Illus. (History Eyewitness) 1995, Raintree Steck-Vaughn LB $24.26 (0-8114-8281-2). This autobiographical account in simplified language brings the horrors of slavery to life. (Rev: BL 4/15/95; SLJ 5/95) [973]

9150 Sigerman, Harriet. *An Unfinished Battle: American Women 1848–1865* (8–12). Illus. (The Young Oxford History of Women in the United States) 1994, Oxford $32.00 (0-19-508110-2). This volume explores the social and political conditions of women during the years prior to the Civil War and their contributions to and participation in the war. (Rev: BL 12/15/94; SLJ 1/95) [305.4]

9151 Sisson, Mary Barr. *The Gathering Storm: From the Framing of the Constitution to Walker's Appeal, 1787–1829* (7–10). Illus. (Milestones in Black American History) 1996, Chelsea LB $19.95 (0-7910-2252-8); paper $9.95 (0-7910-2678-7). The story of slavery in the early days of the Republic with emphasis on civil disobedience, militant action, and important figures of the period. (Rev: BL 10/15/96; BR 1–2/97; SLJ 2/97) [973]

9152 Sorrels, Roy. *The Alamo in American History* (6–8). Illus. (In American History) 1996, Enslow LB $19.95 (0-89490-770-0). This book gives an account of the events leading up to the battle plus detailed coverage of the siege of the Alamo and its significance in American history. (Rev: BL 3/1/97; BR 3–4/97) [976.4]

9153 Stein, R. Conrad. *John Brown's Raid on Harpers Ferry in American History* (7–10). (In American History) 1999, Enslow LB $19.95 (0-7660-1123-2). This account gives an in-depth look at this important moment in American history and its effects on the events to come. (Rev: BL 9/15/99) [973.6]

9154 Wallace, Anthony F. C. *The Long, Bitter Trail: Andrew Jackson and the Indians* (9–12). 1993, Hill & Wang paper $8.00 (0-8090-1552-8). The story of the forced removal of the Cherokees over the Trail of Tears to the Oklahoma Territory in the 1830s. (Rev: BL 7/93; SLJ 12/93) [323.1]

9155 White, Deborah Gray. *Let My People Go: African Americans, 1804–1860* (7–12). Illus. (Young Oxford History of African Americans) 1996, Oxford $35.50 (0-19-508769-0). The story of slavery in the United States during the 19th century, attempts to end it, efforts to rescue slaves, and events leading up to the Civil War. (Rev: BL 5/15/96; SLJ 6/96; VOYA 8/96) [973]

9156 Young, Mary, and Gerald Horne. *Testaments of Courage: Selections from Men's Slave Narratives* (7–12). (African-American Slave Narratives) 1995, Watts LB $25.00 (0-531-11205-5). Chilling and illuminating excerpts from the writings of slaves, beginning with one from 1831. (Rev: BR 1–2/96; SLJ 2/96) [973.6]

9157 Zeinert, Karen. *The Amistad Slave Revolt & American Abolition* (7–10). Illus. 1997, Shoe String LB $19.95 (0-208-02438-7); paper $10.95 (0-208-02439-5). The dramatic story of Cinque and 52 other slaves onboard the Spanish ship *Amistad* in 1839 and of their historic mutiny and subsequent trial. (Rev: BL 7/97; SLJ 6/97) [326]

CIVIL WAR (1861–1865)

9158 Anders, Curt. *Hearts in Conflict: A One-Volume History of the Civil War* (9–12). 1994, Birch Lane $29.95 (1-55972-184-7). A quick-reading journey through the battles and leaders of the Civil War. (Rev: BL 4/15/94) [973.7]

9159 Bailey, Ronald H. *Battle for Atlanta: Sherman Moves East* (9–12). Illus. 1985, Time-Life Books $29.95 (0-8094-4773-8). In pictures and text, this account tells of the Atlanta Campaign of 1864. Others in this Time-Life series on the Civil War include: *The Assassination* (1987), *The Coastal War*, and *Confederate Ordeal* (both 1984). [973.7]

9160 Bailey, Ronald H. *The Bloodiest Day: The Battle of Antietam* (7–12). Illus. 1984, Silver Burdett LB $25.93 (0-8094-4741-X). The story of Lee's defeat in the battle that caused terrible losses on both sides. [973.7]

9161 Bailey, Ronald H. *Forward to Richmond* (9–12). Illus. 1983, Silver Burdett LB $25.93 (0-8094-4721-5). A lavishly illustrated volume that deals with the Peninsula campaign of 1862. Some others in the Time-Life series on the Civil War are: *Decoying the Yanks* (1984), *The Fight for Chattanooga* (1985), and *Pursuit to Appomattox* (1989). [973.7]

9162 Batty, Peter, and Peter Parish. *The Divided Union: The Story of the Great American War 1861–1865* (9–12). Illus. 1987, Salem House $24.95 (0-88162-234-6). A fine popular history of the Civil

War notable both for its clarity and excellent illustrations. (Rev: SLJ 3/88) [973.7]

9163 Beller, Susan P. *Cadets at War: The True Story of Teenage Heroism at the Battle of New Market* (5–8). 1991, Betterway $9.95 (1-55870-196-6). Virginia Military Institute cadets, called to fight at the Battle of New Market in 1864, left a significant impact on the school and its traditions. (Rev: BL 8/91; SLJ 6/91) [973.7]

9164 Beller, Susan P. *Never Were Men So Brave: The Irish Brigade during the Civil War* (7–12). Illus. 1998, Simon & Schuster paper $15.00 (0-689-81406-2). This account focuses on the battles, leaders, and strategies of the Irish Brigade and its eventual fate during the Civil War. (Rev: BL 2/15/98; SLJ 2/98) [973.7041]

9165 Beller, Susan P. *To Hold This Ground: A Desperate Battle at Gettysburg* (8–12). 1995, Simon & Schuster paper $15.00 (0-689-50621-X). After a brief history of the Civil War to July 2, 1863, the author combines narrative and primary sources to recount the Battle of Gettysburg, with alternate chapters focusing on each regiment involved, telling their histories, giving brief biographies of their commanders, and describing the battle as opportunities were taken and lost. (Rev: BR 3–4/96; SLJ 12/95; VOYA 4/96) [973.7]

9166 Biel, Timothy L. *Life in the North during the Civil War* (6–10). Illus. (Way People Live) 1997, Lucent LB $17.96 (1-56006-334-3). This book tells how civilians in the North lived during the Civil War, far from the battles but nevertheless deeply affected by the war's terrible toll. (Rev: BL 3/15/97; SLJ 5/97) [973.7]

9167 *The Blockade: Runners and Raiders* (9–12). Illus. 1983, Silver Burdett LB $25.93 (0-8094-4709-6). With many authentic illustrations, this volume tells of the naval events of the Civil War. Some others in this Time-Life series on the Civil War are: *War on the Mississippi* (1985), *War on the Frontier* (1986), and *The Shenandoah in Flames* (1987). [973.7]

9168 Boritt, Gabor S., ed. *Why the Civil War Came* (9–12). 1995, Oxford $48.00 (0-19-507941-8). A breakdown of political developments in the 1850s on either side of the Mason-Dixon Line. (Rev: BL 10/15/95) [973.7]

9169 Bowman, John S., ed. *The Civil War Almanac* (9–12). Illus. 1986, Newspaper Enterprise Assn. paper $14.95 (0-345-35434-6). This book consists chiefly of a detailed chronology of the war plus 133 biographical sketches of key figures. [973.7]

9170 Buell, Thomas B. *The Warrior Generals: Combat Leadership in the Civil War* (10–12). 1997, Crown $35.00 (0-517-59571-0). An insightful examination of the successes and failures of of 3 Union

generals—Grant, Thomas, and Barlow—and 3 Confederate generals—Lee, Hood, and Gordon. (Rev: SLJ 7/97) [973.7]

9171 Burchard, Peter. *Lincoln and Slavery* (6–10). 1999, Simon & Schuster $17.00 (0-689-81570-0). This book discusses the predominance of slavery as a political and moral issue in 19th-century America and traces the evolution of Lincoln's ideas on slavery and how he put his beliefs into practice. (Rev: SLJ 7/99; VOYA 8/99) [973.7]

9172 Burgess, Lauren Cook, ed. *An Uncommon Soldier* (9–12). 1994, Minerva Center $25.00 (0-9634895-1-8). Letters of a New York farmer's daughter who disguised herself as a man to enlist in the Union Army in 1862—only the second such published account. (Rev: BL 5/15/94) [973.7]

9173 Catton, Bruce. *The Civil War* (7–12). Illus. 1985, Houghton paper $16.00 (0-8281-0305-4). A well-illustrated book that deals with the major events and personalities of the war. [973.7]

9174 Catton, Bruce. *Reflections on the Civil War* (10–12). Illus. 1984, Berkley paper $6.99 (0-425-10495-8). The well-known Civil War historian reflects on the causes and consequences of this war. [973.7]

9175 *Chancellorsville* (7–12). Illus. (Voices of the Civil War) 1996, Time-Life Books $24.95 (0-7853-4708-0). This handsome book tells of this key Civil War battle principally through regimental histories, letters, diaries, and memoirs. (Rev: BL 1/1–15/97) [973.7]

9176 Chang, Ina. *A Separate Battle: Women and the Civil War* (5–9). 1991, Dutton $17.99 (0-525-67365-2). The role women played in the Civil War and how it affected them. Includes profiles of Harriet Beecher Stowe, Harriet Tubman, and Clara Barton. (Rev: BL 1/15/92; SLJ 2/92*) [973.7]

9177 Clark, Champ. *Gettysburg: The Confederate High Tide* (9–12). Illus. 1985, Silver Burdett LB $25.93 (0-8094-4757-6). This volume in the Time-Life series vividly re-creates in words and pictures the horror and glory of this important battle. The final volume in this series is *The Nation Reunited* (1987). [973.7]

9178 Corrick, James A. *The Battle of Gettysburg* (6–10). Illus. (Great Battles in History) 1996, Lucent LB $20.96 (1-56006-451-X). This account of the decisive battle of the Civil War contains useful maps and time lines plus generous use of primary sources. (Rev: BL 4/15/96; SLJ 7/96) [973.7]

9179 Damon, Duane. *When This Cruel War Is Over* (5–8). Illus. 1996, Lerner LB $22.60 (0-8225-1731-0). The human side of the Civil War is stressed in this account that takes the reader behind the scenes at the battlefields and describes the conditions on the home front. (Rev: BL 8/96; SLJ 8/96*) [973.7]

9180 Davis, Burke. *The Civil War: Strange and Fascinating Facts* (9–12). Illus. 1982, Crown $7.99 (0-517-37151-0). An unusual compendium of little-known facts about the Civil War. [973.7]

9181 Davis, Burke. *Sherman's March* (9–12). Illus. 1980, Random $21.95 (0-394-50739-8); paper $14.00 (0-394-75763-7). This volume deals with the destructive march of Sherman and his men through Georgia and the Carolinas. [973.7]

9182 Davis, William C. *Brother against Brother: The War Begins* (9–12). Illus. 1983, Silver Burdett LB $25.93 (0-8094-4701-0). This is the first volume in the Time-Life series on the Civil War (see other entries in this section). It traces the events leading up to the outbreak of war. [973.7]

9183 Davis, William C. *Death in the Trenches: Grant at Petersburg* (9–12). Illus. 1986, Silver Burdett LB $25.93 (0-8094-4777-0). This volume of the Time-Life series deals with the Union Army's siege of Petersburg, Virginia. [973.7]

9184 Davis, William C. *First Blood: Fort Sumter to Bull Run* (9–12). Illus. 1983, Silver Burdett LB $25.93 (0-8094-4705-3). A survey in pictures and text of such early battles of the Civil War as Bull Run and Fort Sumter. Part of the Time-Life series. [973.7]

9185 Dolan, Edward F. *The American Civil War: A House Divided* (5–8). Illus. 1997, Millbrook LB $28.90 (0-7613-0255-7). A chronologically arranged, well-organized account of the Civil War, beginning with the shots fired at Fort Sumter. (Rev: BL 3/1/98; SLJ 3/98) [973.7]

9186 Farwell, Byron. *Ball's Bluff* (9–12). Illus. 1990, EPM paper $12.95 (0-939009-36-6). A gripping account of the small Civil War battle of Ball's Bluff and its aftermath. (Rev: SLJ 9/90) [973.7]

9187 Faust, Drew Gilpin. *Mothers of Invention: Women of the Slaveholding South in the American Civil War* (10–12). 1996, Univ. of North Carolina Pr. $34.95 (0-8078-2255-8). Using letters, journals, and other original sources, this account tells how upper-class Southern women coped during the Civil War, "reinventing" themselves and assuming new roles while their fathers, husbands, brothers, and sons were off fighting. (Rev: BL 3/1/96; SLJ 11/96) [973.7]

9188 *First Manassas* (7–12). (Voices of the Civil War) 1997, Time-Life Books $24.95 (0-7835-4712-9). The story of the first Battle of Bull Run fought close to the town of Manassas in north Virginia, told with extensive use of personal narratives. (Rev: BL 10/15/97) [973.7]

9189 Fleming, Thomas. *Band of Brothers: West Point in the Civil War* (6–9). Illus. 1988, Walker LB $27.90 (0-8027-6741-9). The influence in the Civil War of such men as Grant and Lee, all of whom were graduates of West Point. (Rev: BL 2/1/88) [973.7]

9190 Furgurson, Ernest B. *Ashes of Glory: Richmond at War* (10–12). 1996, Knopf $30.00 (0-679-42232-3). A unique work that looks at the Civil War as experienced by the people of Richmond, Virginia, including politicians, soldiers, workers, women, slaves, and Union prisoners of war. (Rev: SLJ 5/97) [973.7]

9191 Furgurson, Ernest B. *Chancellorsville 1863: The Souls of the Brave* (9–12). 1992, Knopf $25.00 (0-394-58301-9). A recounting of the many legendary episodes in the Chancellorsville campaign during the Civil War, supplemented by 15 maps. (Rev: BL 11/1/92*) [973.7]

9192 Gallagher, Gary, ed. *The Wilderness Campaign* (10–12). 1997, Univ. of North Carolina Pr. $29.95 (0-8078-2334-1). Eight essays by noted Civil War scholars examine various aspects of this battle in 1864 that launched a campaign that ended 11 months later with the surrender by General Robert E. Lee at Appomatox. (Rev: SLJ 3/98) [973.7]

9193 Gallman, J. Matthew. *The North Fights the Civil War: The Home Front* (9–12). 1994, Ivan R. Dee $22.50 (1-56663-049-5). The effects of the Civil War on the home front in the North, including its impact on women, African Americans, and immigrants. (Rev: BL 4/1/94) [973.7]

9194 Garrison, Webb. *A Treasury of Civil War Tales* (9–12). Illus. 1988, Rutledge Hill $14.95 (0-934395-95-0). A collection of 57 stories dealing with the Civil War from the first outcries against slavery to Reconstruction. (Rev: BL 10/15/88) [973.7]

9195 Gay, Kathlyn, and Martin Gay. *Civil War* (5–8). (Voices from the Past) 1995, Twenty-First Century LB $18.90 (0-8050-2845-5). An overview of the Civil War, including excerpts from letters, diaries, and newspaper accounts. (Rev: BL 12/15/95; SLJ 2/96) [973.7]

9196 *Gettysburg* (8–12). (Voices of the Civil War) 1995, Time-Life Books $29.95 (0-7835-4700-5). The Battle of Gettysburg, with illustrations showing the human dimension of the battle. (Rev: BL 5/15/95) [973.7]

9197 Golay, Michael. *The Civil War* (7–12). (America at War) 1992, Facts on File LB $19.95 (0-8160-2514-2). A comprehensive chronicle of the war, from the issues that gave rise to it to Lee's surrender at Appomattox. (Rev: BL 10/15/92) [973.7]

9198 Goolrick, William K. *Rebels Resurgent: Fredericksburg to Chancellorsville* (9–12). Illus. 1985, Silver Burdett LB $25.93 (0-8094-4749-5). In this volume in the Time-Life series, the early southern victories of 1862 and 1863 are reconstructed. [973.7]

9199 Gragg, Rod. *The Civil War Quiz and Fact Book* (9–12). 1985, HarperCollins paper $14.00 (0-06-091226-X). Fascinating questions and answers involving little-known facts about the Civil War. (Rev: BL 4/15/85) [973.7]

9200 Guernsey, Alfred H., and Henry M. Alden. *Harper's Pictorial History of the Civil War* (10–12). 1996, Random $39.99 (0-517-18334-X). This is a facsimile edition of the original work published in 1869, with thorough discussion of military, political, and social issues, accompanied by many maps, portraits, and black-and-white illustrations. (Rev: SLJ 12/96) [973.7]

9201 Haskins, Jim. *Black, Blue, & Gray: African Americans in the Civil War* (5–8). Illus. 1998, Simon & Schuster paper $16.00 (0-689-80655-8). A concise and rewarding picture of the role of African Americans before, during, and after the Civil War. (Rev: BL 2/15/98; SLJ 3/98*; VOYA 10/98) [973.7]

9202 Haskins, Jim. *The Day Fort Sumter Was Fired On: A Photo History of the Civil War* (5–8). 1995, Scholastic paper $6.95 (0-590-46397-7). A history of the Civil War told through reproductions of original photos, engravings, posters, and records, and including the role of African Americans and women. (Rev: BL 7/95) [973.7]

9203 Haythornthwaite, Philip. *Uniforms of the American Civil War in Color* (9–12). Illus. 1990, Sterling paper $14.95 (0-8069-5846-4). In vivid color, this book presents over 150 Confederate and Union army uniforms. (Rev: SLJ 11/85) [973.7]

9204 Hoehling, A. A. *Damn the Torpedoes! Naval Incidents of the Civil War* (10–12). Illus. 1989, John F. Blair $12.95 (0-89587-073-8). The author re-creates the ships and the naval battles of the Civil War from a variety of sources. (Rev: BL 12/15/89) [973.7]

9205 Horwitz, Tony. *Confederates in the Attic: Dispatches from the Unfinished Civil War* (10–12). 1998, Pantheon $27.50 (0-679-43978-1); Knopf paper $14.00 (0-679-75833-X). This is an exploration by a Pulitzer Prize-winning reporter on why the Civil War continues to fascinate Americans. The author gathered material for a year throughout the Old South, where he visited battlefields and interviewed hundreds of people. (Rev: BL 2/1/98; SLJ 7/98) [973.7]

9206 Hughes, Christopher. *Antietam* (5–8). (Battlefields Across America) 1998, Millbrook LB $23.40 (0-7613-3009-7). This book describes the battle at Antietam in detail, discusses its impact on the outcome of the war and on the future of the United States, profiles the major people involved, and provides information on where the history of this battle is preserved. (Rev: SLJ 8/98) [973.7]

9207 Jackson, Donald Dale. *Twenty Million Yankees: The Northern Home Front* (9–12). Illus. 1985, Silver Burdett LB $25.93 (0-8094-4753-3). This volume in the Time-Life series deals with life in the North during the Civil War. [973.7]

9208 Jaynes, Gregory. *The Killing Ground: Wilderness to Cold Harbor* (9–12). Illus. 1986, Silver Burdett LB $25.93 (0-8094-4769-X). The story of the bloody battles in Virginia early in 1864 are retold in this volume in the Time-Life series. [973.7]

9209 Johnson, Neil. *The Battle of Gettysburg* (5–9). Illus. 1989, Macmillan LB $16.00 (0-02-747831-9). An account of the battle that uses photographs of the 1988 reenactment to add graphic details. (Rev: BL 10/15/89; SLJ 12/89) [973.7]

9210 Kantor, MacKinlay. *Gettysburg* (6–9). Illus. 1952, Random paper $5.99 (0-394-89181-3). The story of the crucial battle of the Civil War that could have meant a total victory for the Confederacy. [973.7]

9211 Katcher, Philip. *The Civil War Source Book* (9–12). 1992, Facts on File $35.00 (0-8160-2823-0). This resource that can be read from cover to cover provides comprehensive coverage of events, issues, and details of the Civil War. (Rev: SLJ 1/93*) [973.7]

9212 Kelly, Orr, and Mary D. Kelly. *Dream's End: Two Iowa Brothers in the Civil War* (10–12). 1998, Kodansha $25.00 (1-56836-226-9). A genealogist uses creative historical research to re-create the world and events experienced by 2 young Iowa brothers who died in the Civil War. (Rev: BL 9/15/98; SLJ 4/99) [973.7]

9213 Korn, Jerry. *The Fight for Chattanooga: Chickamauga to Missionary Ridge* (9–12). Illus. 1985, Silver Burdett LB $25.93 (0-8094-4817-3). In this volume in the Time-Life Civil War series, 4 battles—Chickamauga, Chattanooga, Lookout Mountain, and Missionary Ridge—are highlighted. [973.7]

9214 Lawliss, Chuck. *The Civil War: A Traveler's Guide and Sourcebook* (9–12). 1991, Crown paper $20.00 (0-517-57767-4). A comprehensive guide to places, events, and personages of the Civil War. (Rev: BL 4/15/91; SLJ 4/92) [917.304]

9215 *Lee Takes Command: From Seven Days to Second Bull Run* (7–12). Illus. 1984, Silver Burdett LB $25.93 (0-8094-4805-X). A graphic account complemented with many illustrations of Lee's campaign during 1862. [973.7]

9216 Logue, Larry M. *To Appomattox and Beyond: The Civil War Soldier in War and Peace* (9–12). 1995, Ivan R. Dee $22.50 (1-56663-093-2). Traces Civil War soldiers from the time they enlisted to their discharge and their lives after the war. (Rev: BL 10/15/95) [973.7]

9217 McPherson, James M. *For Cause and Comrades: Why Men Fought in the Civil War* (10–12). 1997, Oxford $40.00 (0-19-509023-3). To show what motivated the soldiers on both sides in the Civil War, the famed historian uses quotes from over 25,000 letters and 249 diaries. (Rev: BL 2/1/97; SLJ 10/97) [973.7]

9218 McPherson, James M. *Images of the Civil War: The Paintings of Mort Kunstler* (9–12). 1992, Gramercy Books $24.99 (0-517-07356-0). An album of 70 full-color paintings covering a wide range of Civil War subjects, accompanied by a brief description of the war by McPherson, a renowned historian. (Rev: BL 11/1/92; SLJ 5/93) [973.7]

9219 Malone, John. *The Civil War Quiz Book* (9–12). 1992, Morrow paper $10.00 (0-688-11269-2). A year-by-year roundup of Civil War facts. (Rev: BL 2/15/92) [973.7]

9220 Murphy, Jim. *The Boys' War: Confederate and Union Soldiers Talk about the Civil War* (6–12). (Icarus World Issues) 1990, Clarion $18.00 (0-89919-893-7). Diaries, journals, and letters of young soldiers on both sides of the Civil War are used to describe their military role, early impressions of the war, life in the camps and field, and return home. (Rev: BL 12/1/90; SLJ 1/91*) [973.7]

9221 Murphy, Jim. *The Long Road to Gettysburg* (6–9). 1992, Clarion $15.95 (0-395-55965-0). An account of the Civil War from both the Union and Confederate perspectives. (Rev: BL 5/15/92*; SLJ 6/92*) [973.7]

9222 Nevin, David. *The Road to Shiloh: Early Battles in the West* (9–12). Illus. 1983, Silver Burdett LB $25.93 (0-8094-4717-7). This volume of the Time-Life series deals with the early battle in Kentucky and the Battle of Shiloh in 1862. [973.7]

9223 Nevin, David. *Sherman's March: Atlanta to the Sea* (9–12). Illus. 1986, Silver Burdett LB $25.93 (0-8094-4813-0). A reconstruction of the destructive march through Georgia and the Carolinas by Sherman. Part of the Time-Life Civil War series. [973.7]

9224 Piggins, Carol Ann. *A Multicultural Portrait of the Civil War* (7–12). (Perspectives) 1993, Marshall Cavendish LB $28.50 (1-85435-660-7). Concentrates on the events leading up to the Civil War, the crucial issue of slavery, and the continuing legacy of racism. (Rev: BL 3/15/94; SLJ 4/94) [973]

9225 Ray, Delia. *Behind the Blue and Gray: The Soldier's Life in the Civil War* (5–10). (Young Readers' History of the Civil War) 1991, Dutton paper $15.95 (0-525-67333-4). This sequel to *A Nation Torn* uses personal accounts to describe the life of the common soldier on both sides of the Civil War. (Rev: BL 9/1/91; SLJ 8/91*) [973.7]

9226 Reger, James P. *The Battle of Antietam* (6–10). Illus. (Battles) 1996, Lucent LB $19.95 (1-56006-454-4). The story of the bloody 1862 Civil War battle that cost both sides dearly but stopped the northern invasion of General Lee. (Rev: BL 1/1–15/97; SLJ 7/97) [973.7]

9227 Reger, James P. *Life in the South during the Civil War* (6–10). Illus. (Way People Live) 1997, Lucent LB $17.96 (1-56006-333-5). A behind-the-battlefront look at life in the cities and on the plantations of the South during the Civil War and how the war affected people's everyday lives. (Rev: BL 3/15/97; SLJ 3/97) [975]

9228 Ripple, Ezra Hoyt. *Dancing Along the Deadline: The Andersonville Memoir of a Prisoner of the Confederacy* (10–12). Ed. by Mark A. Snell. Illus. 1996, Presidio Pr. $19.95 (0-89141-577-7). This slim volume contains the memoirs of a Union soldier who was captured in July 1864 and spent time in Confederate prisons, including the infamous Andersonville. (Rev: SLJ 5/97) [973.7]

9229 Robertson, James I., Jr. *Civil War! America Becomes One Nation* (6–10). 1992, Knopf LB $16.99 (0-394-92996-9). A basic history of the Civil War, with each chapter devoted to one calendar year of the conflict. (Rev: BL 4/1/92; SLJ 5/92) [973.7]

9230 Robertson, James I., Jr. *Tenting Tonight: The Soldier's Life* (7–12). Illus. 1984, Silver Burdett LB $25.93 (0-8094-4737-1). The daily life of the common soldiers both Union and Confederate. Part of the Time-Life Books series on the Civil War. [973.7]

9231 *Second Manassas* (8–12). Illus. (Voices of the Civil War) 1995, Time-Life Books $29.95 (0-7835-4701-3). The gripping story of the important Civil War battle, the Second Battle of Bull Run, in 1862, re-created with extensive use of original documents. (Rev: BL 7/95) [973.7]

9232 Shea, William L., and Earl J. Hess. *Pea Ridge: Civil War Campaign in the West* (9–12). 1992, Univ. of North Carolina Pr. $34.95 (0-8078-2042-3). A comprehensive study of the 1862 Arkansas conflict that was the largest Civil War battle fought west of the Mississippi. (Rev: BL 11/1/92) [973.7]

9233 *Shiloh* (7–12). Illus. (Voices of the Civil War) 1996, Time-Life Books $29.95 (0-7835-4707-2). The horror and gallantry associated with the Battle of Shiloh come alive through this account rich in excerpts from military histories, letters, diary entries, and memoirs. (Rev: BL 1/1–15/97; BR 3–4/97) [973.7]

9234 Smith, Carter, ed. *Behind the Lines: A Sourcebook on the Civil War* (5–8). (American Albums from the Collections of the Library of Congress) 1993, Millbrook LB $25.90 (1-56294-265-4). An illustrated sourcebook about life behind the battle lines during the Civil War. (Rev: BL 3/1/93) [973.7]

9235 Smith, Carter, ed. *The First Battles: A Source-book on the Civil War* (5–8). (American Albums from the Collections of the Library of Congress) 1993, Millbrook LB $25.90 (1-56294-262-X). Using engravings, prints, photographs, and excerpts from books and other documents, this sourcebook presents a concise history of the early days of the Civil War. (Rev: BL 3/1/93) [973.7]

9236 Smith, Carter, ed. *One Nation Again: A Sourcebook on the Civil War* (5–8). (American Albums from the Collections of the Library of Congress) 1993, Millbrook LB $25.90 (1-56294-266-2). This heavily illustrated sourcebook chronicles the peace at Appomattox and the period immediately following. (Rev: BL 3/1/93) [973.8]

9237 Smith, Carter, ed. *Prelude to War: A Source-book on the Civil War* (5–8). (American Albums from the Collections of the Library of Congress) 1993, Millbrook LB $25.90 (1-56294-261-1). This volume illustrates the major political, social, and military events that led up to the Civil War. (Rev: BL 3/1/93) [973.7]

9238 Smith, Carter, ed. *Presidents of a Divided Nation: A Sourcebook on the U.S. Presidency* (5–8). (American Albums from the Collections of the Library of Congress) 1993, Millbrook LB $18.90 (1-56294-360-X). A visual sourcebook about the presidents during the Civil War and immediately after, from the Library of Congress collection on U.S. presidents. Also use *Presidents of a Growing Country*. (Rev: BL 12/1/93) [973.8]

9239 Smith, Carter, ed. *The Road to Appomattox: A Sourcebook on the Civil War* (5–8). (American Albums from the Collections of the Library of Congress) 1993, Millbrook LB $25.90 (1-56294-264-6). The last battles of the Civil War are covered in this album that uses period illustrations and excerpts from first-person accounts. (Rev: BL 3/1/93) [973.7]

9240 Somerlott, Robert. *The Lincoln Assassination in American History* (7–10). 1998, Enslow LB $18.95 (0-89490-866-3). A description of this important moment in American history, with details on the people involved and a report on the aftermath of Lincoln's death. (Rev: BL 7/98; BR 9–10/98) [973.7]

9241 Spaulding, Lily May, and John Spaulding, eds. *Civil War Recipes: Recipes from the Pages of Godey's Lady's Book* (9–12). 1999, Univ. Press of Kentucky Pr. $19.95 (0-8131-2082-9). Recipes for common, everyday meals drawn from 19th-century women's magazines, to which the authors have added interesting historical information such as Confederate and Union army rations, cooking utensils, and food substitutions frequently used by Southern cooks. (Rev: SLJ 7/99) [973.7]

9242 *Spies, Scouts, and Raiders: Irregular Operations* (9–12). Illus. 1985, Silver Burdett LB $25.93

(0-8094-4713-4). This pictorial volume, part of the Time-Life series, presents some of the unusual military operations of the Civil War. [973.7]

9243 Steins, Richard. *The Nation Divides: The Civil War (1820–1880)* (5–8). (First Person America) 1993, Twenty-First Century LB $18.90 (0-8050-2583-9). A look at the Civil War, using extracts from diaries, letters, and journals of individuals who lived through it. (Rev: BL 2/1/94) [973.7]

9244 Stiles, T. J., ed. *In Their Own Words: Civil War Commanders* (9–12). 1995, Putnam paper $15.00 (0-399-51909-2). Writings by Civil War commanders from both the North and South. (Rev: BL 3/15/95; SLJ 8/95) [973.7]

9245 Street, James, Jr. *The Struggle for Tennessee: Tupelo to Stones River* (9–12). Illus. 1985, Silver Burdett LB $25.93 (0-8094-4761-4). This part of the Time-Life series deals with the important areas of Tennessee and Kentucky during the Civil War. [973.7]

9246 Sullivan, George. *Portraits of War: Civil War Photographers and Their Work* (5–9). 1998, Twenty-First Century LB $24.40 (0-7613-3019-4). Having already written a book about Civil War photographer Matthew Brady, the author now focuses on other Civil War photographers, with many examples of their work. (Rev: BL 11/15/98) [973.7]

9247 Tackach, James. *The Emancipation Proclamation: Abolishing Slavery in the South* (8–12). Illus. (Words That Changed History) 1999, Lucent LB $23.70 (1-56006-370-X). This is the story of the short proclamation that changed U.S. history, with material on slavery, Abraham Lincoln, the Civil War, and the document's historical legacy. (Rev: BL 6/1–15/99; SLJ 8/99) [973.7]

9248 Time-Life Books, ed. *Charleston* (7–12). (Voices of the Civil War) 1997, Time-Life Books $24.95 (0-7835-4709-9). The story of the siege of Charleston and its fall to Union forces in February 1865, with quotes from original sources. (Rev: BL 5/15/97) [973.7]

9249 Time-Life Books, eds., ed. *Chickamauga* (7–12). (Voices of the Civil War) 1997, Time-Life Books $24.95 (0-7835-4710-2). Using many original sources, this is the story of the 1863 battle in northern Georgia after which the Union Army fell back to Chattanooga. (Rev: BL 7/97) [973.7]

9250 *Vicksburg* (7–12). Illus. (Voices of the Civil War) 1997, Time-Life Books $24.95 (0-7835-4713-7). The story of the siege of Vicksburg in 1863 and the Union victory that cut the Confederacy in two. (Rev: BL 1/1–15/97) [973.7]

9251 *War between Brothers* (7–12). Illus. 1996, Time-Life Books $19.95 (0-7835-6251-9). A discussion of the Civil War, including secession of the

Confederate states, key Civil War battles, and the assassination of Abraham Lincoln, using vivid text, first-person narratives, and numerous illustrations. (Rev: BL 12/15/96; BR 3–4/97) [973.7]

9252 Ward, Geoffrey, et al. *The Civil War: An Illustrated History* (9–12). Illus. 1990, Knopf $75.00 (0-394-56285-2). A handsome, readable account that was prepared for the television series on the Civil War that aired in 1990. (Rev: BL 8/90; SLJ 3/91) [973.7]

9253 Woodhead, Henry, et al. *Atlanta* (10–12). (Voices of the Civil War) 1996, Time-Life Books $29.95 (0-7835-4702-1). The history of Atlanta during the Civil War is retold with extensive use of diaries, memoirs, and letters, as well as outstanding illustrations. (Rev: BR 1–2/97; SLJ 3/97) [973.7]

9254 Woodhead, Henry, et al. *Soldier Life* (10–12). 1996, Time-Life Books $29.95 (0-7835-4703-X). The human side of being a soldier on both the Confederate and Union sides during the Civil War is explored in this account that uses primary sources extensively plus many illustrations and maps. (Rev: BR 1–2/97; SLJ 3/97) [973.3]

9255 Zeinert, Karen. *The Lincoln Murder Plot* (6–12). 1999, Shoe String LB $22.50 (0-208-02451-4). A detailed, well-documented retelling of the first assassination of a U.S. president and its world-shaking results. (Rev: BL 3/1/99; BR 9–10/99; SLJ 5/99; VOYA 4/99) [973.7]

WESTWARD EXPANSION AND PIONEER LIFE

9256 Altman, Linda J. *The California Gold Rush in American History* (4–8). (In American History) 1997, Enslow LB $19.95 (0-89490-878-2). After a brief history of the California gold rush, this book covers such topics as frontier injustice, racial discrimination, and the place of women in the American West. (Rev: BR 1–2/98; SLJ 3/98) [979.4]

9257 Barr, Roger. *The American Frontier* (6–9). (World History) 1996, Lucent LB $17.96 (1-56006-282-7). Using many primary source quotes, this book focuses on westward expansion and issues like manifest destiny and the treatment of Native Americans by the settlers. (Rev: SLJ 4/96) [978]

9258 Bentley, Judith. *Brides, Midwives, and Widows* (6–9). (Settling the West) 1995, Twenty-First Century LB $20.40 (0-8050-2994-X). The story of the women who helped settle the West, using diaries and other primary sources. (Rev: BL 8/95; SLJ 9/95) [978]

9259 Bentley, Judith. *Explorers, Trappers, and Guides* (6–9). (Settling the West) 1995, Twenty-First Century LB $20.40 (0-8050-2995-8). Unusually well-told stories about lesser-known explorers taken from first-person accounts. (Rev: BL 8/95; SLJ 11/95) [979.5]

9260 Blackwood, Gary L. *Life on the Oregon Trail* (5–8). (The Way People Live) 1999, Lucent LB $23.70 (1-56006-540-0). A thorough account of life on the Oregon Trail for pioneers making the journey from Missouri to the Pacific Ocean in the mid-1800s. (Rev: SLJ 8/99) [978]

9261 Brown, Dee. *The American West* (9–12). 1994, Scribners $25.00 (0-02-517421-5). Diaries, letters, and newspaper articles are used to describe conflicts and culture in the American West, including Indian wars, settlers' town life, and the gold rush. (Rev: BL 10/15/94*) [978]

9262 Brown, Dee. *Wondrous Times on the Frontier* (9–12). 1991, August House $23.95 (0-87483-137-7). A series of humorous stories from the American West, including bawdy and outrageous tales of American Indian and Mexican confrontations with pioneer settlers. (Rev: BL 10/15/91) [978]

9263 Bryan, Howard. *Robbers, Rogues and Ruffians: True Tales of the Wild West* (9–12). 1991, Clear Light $22.95 (0-940666-04-9). Includes accounts about lesser-known New Mexico Territory desperadoes and pioneers based on period newspaper stories and interviews. (Rev: BL 12/1/91) [978.9]

9264 Calabro, Marian. *The Perilous Journey of the Donner Party* (5–8). Illus. 1999, Houghton $20.00 (0-395-86610-3). The story of the ill-fated Donner Party and their horrifying end on their way to California, as seen through the eyes of 12-year-old Virginia Reed. (Rev: BL 4/1/99; SLJ 5/99) [979.4]

9265 Dary, David. *Cowboy Culture* (10–12). 1989, Avon paper $14.95 (0-7006-0390-5). A 500-year history of the American cowboy. [973]

9266 Dary, David. *Seeking Pleasure in the Old West* (10–12). 1995, Knopf $30.00 (0-394-56178-3). Using diaries, recollections, and period newspapers, the author re-creates everyday life in the old West and tells of the interesting and creative ways ordinary people entertained themselves, shattering the stereotypical portrayals of cowboys, gun fights, and bawdy houses. (Rev: BL 12/1/95; SLJ 7/96) [978]

9267 DeAngelis, Gina. *The Black Cowboys* (4–8). Illus. (Legends of the West) 1997, Chelsea LB $19.95 (0-7910-2589-6); paper $7.95 (0-7910-2590-X). This book details the contributions of African Americans such as Jim Beckwourth and Edward Rose to the exploration and settlement of the American West. (Rev: BL 2/15/98) [978]

9268 DeAngelis, Gina. *The Wild West* (5–8). (Costumes, Tradition, and Culture: Reflecting on the Past) 1998, Chelsea $16.95 (0-7910-5169-2). Using illustrations from collectors cards issued in the early 20th century, this book provides a grab bag of information about topics related to pioneer life in the West. (Rev: BL 3/15/99) [973]

9269 Duncan, Dayton. *People of the West* (5–10). Illus. 1996, Little, Brown $26.95 (0-316-19627-4). Individual people—both famous and less well known—tell in their own words about the opening up of the West. Based on the PBS series. (Rev: BL 8/96; SLJ 10/96) [978]

9270 Duncan, Dayton. *The West: An Illustrated History for Children* (5–10). Illus. 1996, Little, Brown $19.95 (0-316-19628-2). A brief history of the opening up of the West, based on the PBS series. (Rev: BL 8/96; SLJ 10/96) [978]

9271 Freedman, Russell. *Buffalo Hunt* (7–10). 1988, Holiday House LB $21.95 (0-8234-0702-0). A history of how the buffalo were hunted from the times of the Indians to the slaughter by whites that brought on the near extinction of this animal. (Rev: BL 10/1/88; SLJ 10/88) [973]

9272 Freedman, Russell. *Children of the Wild West* (6–9). Illus. 1983, Clarion $18.00 (0-89919-143-6). A look at the life of the children of pioneers. (Rev: BL 1/1/90) [978]

9273 Harris, Edward D. *John Charles Fremont and the Great Western Reconnaissance* (6–9). Illus. 1990, Chelsea LB $19.95 (0-7910-1312-X). An account of the exploration of the West that concentrates on the 5 major journeys taken by Fremont. (Rev: BL 9/15/90) [973.6]

9274 Harvey, Brett. *Farmers and Ranchers* (6–9). Illus. (Settling the West) 1995, Twenty-First Century LB $20.40 (0-8050-2999-0). Westward migration and homesteading are covered in this history that uses first-person accounts and the experiences of people of various backgrounds. (Rev: BL 8/95; SLJ 11/95) [978.02]

9275 Herb, Angela. *Beyond the Mississippi: Early Westward Expansion of the United States* (7–12). Illus. (Young Readers' History of the West) 1996, Dutton paper $16.99 (0-525-67503-5). This large-size, heavily illustrated history of westward expansion covers such subjects as traders and trappers, missionaries, the treatment of Native Americans, homesteaders, the Mexican War, the gold rush, and the Oregon Trail. (Rev: BL 10/15/96; SLJ 11/96; VOYA 2/97) [978]

9276 Hevly, Nancy. *Preachers and Teachers* (6–9). Illus. (Settling the West) 1995, Twenty-First Century LB $20.40 (0-8050-2996-6). The bringing of religion and education to the Western pioneers is the subject of this book that relies heavily of first-person accounts. (Rev: BL 8/95; SLJ 11/95) [278]

9277 Hilton, Suzanne. *Miners, Merchants, and Maids* (6–9). Illus. (Settling the West) 1995, Twenty-First Century LB $20.40 (0-8050-2998-2). Three

kinds of employment that helped open up the West are discussed, with quotes from many primary sources representing people of different backgrounds. (Rev: BL 8/95; SLJ 11/95) [978]

9278 Ito, Tom. *The California Gold Rush* (6–9). Illus. (World History) 1997, Lucent LB $18.96 (1-56006-293-2). A well-illustrated overview of the gold rush with many quotes from primary and secondary sources. (Rev: BL 1/1–15/97; BR 11–12/97; SLJ 3/97) [979.4]

9279 Kallen, Stuart A. *Life on the American Frontier* (6–10). (The Way People Live) 1998, Lucent LB $17.96 (1-56006-366-1). Primary source quotations, photographs, and a lively narrative re-create everyday life on the American frontier. (Rev: BL 10/15/98; SLJ 1/99; VOYA 12/99) [978]

9280 Katz, William L. *Black People Who Made the Old West* (7–10). Illus. 1992, Africa World Pr. $35.00 (0-86543-363-1); paper $14.95 (0-86543-364-X). Short sketches of 35 black Americans who contributed to the opening up of the West. [920]

9281 Katz, William L. *Black Pioneers: An Untold Story* (7–12). 1999, Simon & Schuster $17.00 (0-689-81410-0). The account describes the stories of the many determined black Americans who defied prejudice, slavery, and severe legal restrictions such as the Northwest Territory's "Black Laws" to make a new life for themselves in the frontier of pre-Civil War days. (Rev: BL 7/99; SLJ 9/99; VOYA 8/99) [977]

9282 Katz, William L. *Black Women of the Old West* (6–9). 1995, Atheneum $18.00 (0-689-31944-4). The role black women played in the settlement of the West—a topic virtually ignored in history books. (Rev: BL 12/15/95; SLJ 12/95; VOYA 4/96) [978]

9283 Katz, William L. *The Civil War to the Last Frontier: 1850–1880s* (7–9). (History of Multicultural America) 1993, Raintree Steck-Vaughn LB $27.11 (0-8114-6277-3). A history of the United States during this period, from a multicultural approach. (Rev: BL 9/1/93; VOYA 8/93) [973.5]

9284 Katz, William L. *The Westward Movement and Abolitionism, 1815–1850* (7–10). (History of Multicultural America) 1993, Raintree Steck-Vaughn LB $27.11 (0-8114-6276-5). Focuses on the concept of Manifest Destiny and its impact on Native Americans, the rise of resistance to slavery, and efforts of early feminists. (Rev: BL 6/1–15/93) [973.5]

9285 Ketchum, Liza. *The Gold Rush* (5–10). Illus. 1996, Little, Brown paper $12.95 (0-316-49047-4). An overview of the gold rush in California and its effects on the development of the West. Based on the PBS series. (Rev: BL 8/96; BR 5–6/97; SLJ 10/96) [979.4]

9286 Lavender, David. *The Great West* (9–12). Illus. 1985, Houghton paper $8.95 (0-8281-0481-6). This richly illustrated volume covers the history of the West and its development from 1763 through the beginning of the 20th century. [978]

9287 Lavender, David. *Snowbound: The Tragic Story of the Donner Party* (6–10). Illus. 1996, Holiday House $18.95 (0-8234-1231-8). With extensive use of primary documents and excellent illustrations, this account vividly reconstructs the hardships and horror of the Donner party's attempt to cross the Rockies. (Rev: BL 6/1–15/96; SLJ 7/96; VOYA 8/96) [978]

9288 Luchetti, Cathy. *Home on the Range: A Culinary History of the American West* (9–12). 1993, Random paper $25.00 (0-679-74484-3). A complete picture of the role food preparation and meals played in 19th-century daily life on the frontier, with photos, diary extracts, and recipes. (Rev: BL 7/93; SLJ 12/93) [394.1]

9289 Marrin, Albert. *Cowboys, Indians, and Gunfighters: The Story of the Cattle Kingdom* (6–10). 1993, Atheneum $22.95 (0-689-31774-3). An exciting account of the Old West, including Comanche vengeance, buffalo hunts, and frontier lawlessness. (Rev: BL 8/93; VOYA 10/93) [978]

9290 Matthews, Leonard J. *Cowboys* (6–9). Illus. 1988, Rourke LB $18.00 (0-86625-363-7). A glimpse of the old Wild West and the men who rode the ranges. Also use in the same series: *Gunfighters* (1989). (Rev: SLJ 6/89) [975.5]

9291 Matthews, Leonard J. *Indians* (6–9). Illus. 1988, Rourke LB $23.93 (0-86625-364-5). An overview of how Indians lived during the days of the Wild West. (Rev: SLJ 6/89) [970.004]

9292 Matthews, Leonard J. *Pioneers* (6–9). Illus. 1988, Rourke LB $18.00 (0-86625-362-9). A tribute to the homesteaders who risked their lives to find a new home in the West. Also use in the same series: *Railroaders and Soldiers* (both 1989). (Rev: SLJ 6/89) [973.5]

9293 Morris, Juddi. *The Harvey Girls: The Women Who Civilized the West* (6–9). Illus. 1994, Walker $24.95 (0-8027-8302-3). The story of the waitresses at Fred Harvey's restaurants along the Santa Fe railroad, and how they left their homes in the East in search of adventure and independence. (Rev: BL 6/1–15/94; SLJ 7/94) [979]

9294 Murdoch, David. *Cowboy* (5–9). (Eyewitness Books) 1993, Knopf LB $20.99 (0-679-94014-6). An illustrated history of cowboys in the American West and around the world. (Rev: BL 10/1/93) [978]

9295 Murphy, Virginia R. *Across the Plains in the Donner Party* (6–10). Ed. by Karen Zeinert. 1996, Linnet LB $19.50 (0-208-02404-2). As well as being a condensation of the memoirs of a teenage survivor of the Donner party, this account gives good background information and excerpts from other original sources. (Rev: BL 6/1–15/96; BR 1–2/97; SLJ 8/96; VOYA 8/96) [979.4]

9296 Parkman, Francis. *The Oregon Trail* (10–12). Illus. 1950, NAL paper $4.95 (0-451-52513-2). The authentic narrative written by Parkman about his adventures traveling west in 1846. [978]

9297 Pelta, Kathy. *Cattle Trails: "Get Along Little Dogies"* (5–8). (American Trails) 1997, Raintree Steck-Vaughn LB $27.83 (0-8172-4073-X). A discussion of the cattle drives that were part of the history of the American West from 1850 to 1890. (Rev: SLJ 12/97) [978]

9298 Pelta, Kathy. *The Royal Roads: Spanish Trails in North America* (5–8). (American Trails) 1997, Raintree Steck-Vaughn LB $27.83 (0-8172-4074-8). The story of the Spanish trails in Florida, California, New Mexico, and Texas, and the people who traveled them looking for spiritual or material gain. (Rev: SLJ 12/97) [970.01]

9299 Perl, Lila. *Hunter's Stew and Hangtown Fry: What Pioneer America Ate and Why* (7–12). Illus. 1979, Houghton $16.95 (0-395-28922-X). A history of many different American ethnic groups and their foods, and how these changed and developed in America. [973.5]

9300 Peters, Arthur K. *Seven Trails West* (10–12). 1996, Abbeville $39.95 (1-55859-782-4). This well-researched work traces the expansion of the American continent from 1804 to 1869 through the development of 7 important trails, including the Santa Fe Trail, the Oregon-California Trail, the Pony Express, the Transcontinental Telegraph, and the Transcontinental Railroad, and the trail taken by Lewis and Clark's expedition. (Rev: BL 6/1–15/96; SLJ 12/96) [978]

9301 Platt, Rutherford. *Adventures in the Wilderness* (6–10). Illus. 1963, Troll $14.95 (0-8167-1516-5). The story of the settling of the West is told in this account noted for its many fine illustrations. [973.5]

9302 Press, Petra. *A Multicultural Portrait of the Move West* (7–12). (Perspectives) 1993, Marshall Cavendish LB $28.50 (1-85435-658-5). Told from the viewpoint of the people who lived there, this history challenges popular stereotypes of brave white explorers and cowboys "opening up" an "unsettled" Western frontier. (Rev: BL 4/1/94; SLJ 4/94) [978]

9303 Reinfeld, Fred. *Pony Express* (7–12). Illus. 1973, Univ. of Nebraska Pr. paper $7.00 (0-8032-5786-4). A history of the communication system that linked the East and West and the courageous riders who manned it. [383]

9304 Richards, Colin. *Sheriff Pat Garrett's Last Days* (8–12). Illus. 1986, Sunstone paper $8.95 (0-86534-079-X). A history of the Wild West drawn into focus by the death of the man who shot Billy the Kid. (Rev: BR 11–12/86) [978]

9305 Rothschild, Mary Logan, and Pamela Claire Hronek. *Doing What the Day Brought: An Oral History of Arizona Women* (9–12). 1992, Univ. of Arizona Pr. $43.50 (0-8165-1032-6); paper $18.95 (0-8165-1276-0). The role and lives of pioneer women in Arizona. (Rev: BL 2/1/92) [305.4]

9306 Savage, William W. *The Cowboy Hero: His Image in American History and Culture* (10–12). Illus. 1987, Univ. of Oklahoma Pr. paper $15.95 (0-8061-1920-9). A history of the American cowboy with material on how he has been portrayed in the media. [973]

9307 Schlissel, Lillian. *Black Frontiers: A History of African American Heroes of the Old West* (5–8). 1995, Simon & Schuster $18.00 (0-689-80285-4). Almost a dozen men and women, including cowboy Nat Love, rodeo rider Bill Pickett, and real estate tycoon Biddy Mason, are introduced in this informative account of the Old West. (Rev: BL 1/1–15/96; SLJ 12/95; VOYA 4/96) [978]

9308 Schlissel, Lillian, et al. *Far from Home: Families of the Westward Journey* (9–12). Illus. 1989, Schocken $19.95 (0-8052-4052-7). From a number of different sources, the authors have pieced together the stories of 4 families, their journeys west, and their lives as pioneers. (Rev: BL 4/1/89) [978]

9309 Sherrow, Victoria. *Life during the Gold Rush* (6–10). (The Way People Live) 1998, Lucent LB $17.96 (1-56006-382-3). The story of the quarter million prospectors who flocked to California to find gold in 1848—of the few who became rich and the many who ended up penniless. (Rev: BL 8/98; SLJ 12/98) [979.4]

9310 Shuter, Jane, ed. *Sarah Royce and the American West* (5–8). Illus. (History Eyewitness) 1996, Raintree Steck-Vaughn LB $24.26 (0-8114-8286-3). The ordeals and achievements of American pioneers of the West are chronicled in this first-person account, accompanied by many splendid illustrations. (Rev: BL 5/15/96; SLJ 6/96) [978]

9311 Sigerman, Harriet. *Land of Many Hands: Women in the American West* (7–12). 1998, Oxford $39.95 (0-19-509942-7). A well-researched account that uses many original documents to tell the story of women's role in the opening up of the West, their struggles and triumphs, and how different ethnic groups were treated. (Rev: BL 2/15/98; BR 5–6/98; SLJ 4/98; VOYA 4/98) [978]

9312 Stanley, Jerry. *Frontier Merchants: Lionel and Barron Jacobs and the Jewish Pioneers Who Settled the West* (5–10). 1998, Crown LB $20.99 (0-517-

80020-9). This fascinating biography of the Jacobs brothers, who set up a successful business venture in Tucson in 1867, illustrates business development in pioneer communities and the role of Jewish immigrants in building the economic foundation of the West. (Rev: BR 5–6/99; SLJ 3/99) [973.8]

9313 Stefoff, Rebecca. *Children of the Westward Trail* (6–9). 1996, Millbrook LB $23.40 (1-56294-582-3). The true story of the Gay family and the father Martin Gay who took his family in 1851 from Springfield, Missouri, to resettle in the Willamette Valley of Oregon. (Rev: BL 5/15/96; SLJ 7/96) [978]

9314 Stefoff, Rebecca. *The Oregon Trail in American History* (6–10). Illus. (In American History) 1997, Enslow LB $19.95 (0-89490-771-9). The story of the Oregon Trail and the everyday life of the settlers who traveled it are re-created, with a guide to the trail as it exists today. (Rev: BL 2/1/98; SLJ 2/98) [978]

9315 Stefoff, Rebecca. *Women Pioneers* (6–12). (American Profiles) 1995, Facts on File $19.95 (0-8160-3134-7). Nine profiles of pioneer women noted for their courage, ingenuity, and triumphs are presented in this readable account that gives details of life on the American frontier. (Rev: BL 1/1/96; SLJ 2/96; VOYA 4/96) [973.8]

9316 Stewart, Gail B. *Cowboys in the Old West* (6–9). (The Way People Live) 1995, Lucent LB $22.45 (1-56006-077-8). A description of the life of the cowboy from 1865 to 1890. (Rev: BL 5/1/95; SLJ 5/95) [978]

9317 Stovall, TaRessa. *The Buffalo Soldiers* (6–10). Illus. (African American Achievers) 1997, Chelsea LB $19.95 (0-7910-2595-0); paper $9.95 (0-7910-2596-9). The story of the stirring achievements of the black U..S. Army regiments that distinguished themselves during numerous campaigns and played a vital role in the settlement of the American West. (Rev: BL 12/1/97) [978]

9318 Stratton, Joanne L. *Pioneer Women: Voices from the Kansas Frontier* (10–12). Illus. 1981, Simon & Schuster paper $12.95 (0-671-44748-3). This book is based on first-person accounts of almost 800 pioneer women who lived in Kansas between 1854 and 1890. [978.1]

9319 van der Linde, Laurel. *The Pony Express* (5–8). 1993, Macmillan LB $20.00 (0-02-759056-9). A history of the Pony Express, including its beginnings, routes, riders, ponies, dangers, problems and successes, and the reasons for its demise. (Rev: BL 9/1/93; SLJ 7/93) [383]

9320 Van Steenwyk, Elizabeth. *Frontier Fever: The Silly, Superstitious—and Sometimes Sensible—Medicine of the Pioneers* (5–8). 1995, Walker LB $16.85 (0-8027-8403-8). An exploration of medical practices by settlers and pioneers from colonial times to the 20th century. Includes contrasts with the very different practices and traditions of Native Americans. (Rev: BL 7/95; SLJ 12/95; VOYA 12/95) [610]

9321 Walker, Paul R. *Great Figures of the Wild West* (7–10). (American Profiles) 1992, Facts on File LB $19.95 (0-8160-2576-2). A vivid picture of the history of the American West, with profiles of such people as Jesse James, Sitting Bull, Wyatt Earp, Geronimo, Judge Roy Bean, and Belle Starr. (Rev: BL 9/1/92; SLJ 8/92) [978]

9322 Walker, Paul R. *Trail of the Wild West* (10–12). 1997, National Geographic $30.00 (0-79227-021-5). An easily read introduction to the history of the American West, including the California gold rush, cattle drives, the Oregon Trail, and notorious outlaws, in National Geographic format with wonderful photographs. (Rev: SLJ 2/98) [973.8]

9323 Wexler, Sanford. *Westward Expansion* (9–12). (Facts on File's Eyewitness History) 1991, Facts on File $50.00 (0-8160-2407-3). The territorial growth of the United States from 1754 to 1897 is described through diaries, letters, and official documents. (Rev: BL 7/91; SLJ 12/91) [973]

9324 Winslow, Mimi. *Loggers and Railroad Workers* (6–9). Illus. (Settling the West) 1995, Twenty-First Century LB $20.40 (0-8050-2997-4). First-person accounts from various workers in logging and on the railroad are woven together to give a report on these fledgling industries in the old West. (Rev: BL 7/95; SLJ 9/95) [338.7]

RECONSTRUCTION TO WORLD WAR I (1865–1917)

9325 Bartoletti, Susan C. *Growing Up in Coal Country* (5–8). Illus. 1996, Houghton $16.95 (0-395-77847-6). The life of child laborers in the coal mines of Pennsylvania 100 years ago is covered in this brilliant photo-essay. (Rev: BL 12/1/96*; BR 11–12/97; SLJ 2/97*) [331.3]

9326 Brown, Gene. *The Struggle to Grow: Expansionism and Industrialization (1880–1913)* (5–8). (First Person America) 1994, Twenty-First Century LB $18.90 (0-8050-2584-7). First-person accounts are used to describe settlement of the frontier, immigration, industry, and political reform during the period 1880–1913. (Rev: BL 2/1/94; SLJ 3/94) [973.8]

9327 Cohen, Daniel. *The Alaska Purchase* (4–8). (Spotlight on American History) 1996, Millbrook LB $21.90 (1-56294-528-9). The story of the purchase of Alaska from Russia in 1867 and how it changed the course of American history. (Rev: BL 3/15/96; SLJ 5/96) [979.8]

9328 Currie, Stephen. *We Have Marched Together: The Working Children's Crusade* (7–12). (People's History) Set), Lerner LB $22.60 (0-8225-1733-7).

The focus of this book is on child labor in the United States and the protest march from Philadelphia to New York led by Mother Jones in 1903. (Rev: BL 5/1/97; SLJ 7/97) [331.3]

9329 Fry, Annette R. *The Orphan Trains* (7–12). (American Events) 1994, Macmillan LB $14.95 (0-02-735721-X). Interviews, letters, and photos chronicle how slum children were sent on "orphan trains" to live in the West and how the move affected them. (Rev: BL 7/94; SLJ 1/95) [362.7]

9330 Gan, Geraldine. *Communication* (6–9). (Life in America 100 Years Ago) 1997, Chelsea LB $19.95 (0-7910-2845-3). This book explores how mail, books, newspapers, magazines, telegraphs, and telephones were all becoming a part of the American communications system at the turn of the century. (Rev: BL 10/15/97; SLJ 9/97) [973.8]

9331 Gay, Kathlyn, and Martin Gay. *Spanish-American War* (5–8). (Voices from the Past) 1995, Twenty-First Century LB $18.90 (0-8050-2847-1). This account of the Spanish-American War uses excerpts from letters, memoirs, and official reports to cover the causes, battles, and results of the war. (Rev: BL 12/15/95; SLJ 3/96) [973.8]

9332 Geary, Rick. *A Treasury of Victorian Murder: The Borden Tragedy* (10–12). 1997, NBM paper $8.95 (1-56163-189-2). Using a documentary comic book format, this is an exciting factual presentation of the Borden murders in Fall River, Massachusetts, as adapted from the memoirs of someone who was in Fall River at the time of the crime. (Rev: BL 12/1/97; SLJ 3/98) [973.8]

9333 Gourley, Catherine. *Good Girl Work: Factories, Sweatshops, and How Women Changed Their Role in the American Workforce* (7–10). 1999, Millbrook $22.40 (0-7613-0951-9). This history of the exploitation of female children at work in industry around the turn of the century includes dramatic, in-depth personal testimonies and first-person accounts from letters, diaries, memoirs, and newspaper interviews. (Rev: BL 5/1/99; BR 9–10/99; SLJ 8/99) [331.3]

9334 Hakim, Joy. *Reconstruction and Reform* (4–8). Illus. (History of US) 1994, Oxford $23.95 (0-19-507757-1). Using original sources and outstanding illustrations, this is a history of the Reconstruction period when the United States tried to recover from the destruction of the Civil War. (Rev: BL 10/15/94; SLJ 1/95; VOYA 4/95) [973.8]

9335 Havens, John C. *Government & Politics* (6–9). Illus. (Life in America 100 Years Ago) 1997, Chelsea LB $19.95 (0-7910-2847-X). This book focuses on the influences on politics at the turn of the century, such as the end of the Civil War, the rise of big business and the growing power of industry, and government scandals. (Rev: BL 6/1–15/97) [973]

9336 *Industry & Business* (6–9). Illus. (Life in America 100 Years Ago) 1996, Chelsea LB $19.95 (0-7910-2846-1). A look at the 20th-century Industrial Revolution that transformed the United States from a rural to an urban nation and set it on a course toward becoming a world power. (Rev: BL 6/1–15/97) [338.0973]

9337 Isserman, Maurice. *Journey to Freedom* (7–12). Illus. (Library of African American History) 1997, Facts on File $19.95 (0-8160-3413-3). This account tells of the African American men and women who traveled north at the beginning of the 20th century filled with hope and looking for freedom, dignity, and economic opportunity, and of the impact it had on the nation's politics and culture. (Rev: BL 2/15/98; BR 3–4/98) [975]

9338 Leuzzi, Linda. *Education* (6–9). (Life in America 100 Years Ago) 1998, Chelsea LB $19.95 (0-7910-2849-6). With fascinating examples and detailed descriptions, this book discusses the foundations and practices in turn-of-the-century schools and classrooms. (Rev: BL 3/15/98; BR 11–12/98) [973.8]

9339 Loeper, John J. *Going to School in 1876* (7–9). Illus. 1984, Macmillan $16.00 (0-689-31015-3). The students, their schools and teachers, and the curriculum are described in this interesting account. [370.9]

9340 Maurer, Richard. *The Wild Colorado: The True Adventures of Fred Dellenbaugh, Age 17, on the Second Powell Expedition into the Grand Canyon* (5–9). 1999, Crown LB $19.99 (0-517-70946-5). The is a firsthand account, with authentic photographs, of Major John Wesley Powell's 16-month journey down the Colorado River in the 1870s as recorded by a teenage crew member. (Rev: SLJ 8/99) [973.8]

9341 Mettger, Zak. *Reconstruction: America after the Civil War* (5–8). (Young Readers' History of the Civil War) 1994, Dutton $16.99 (0-525-67490-X). Describes the political, economic, and social upheaval during Reconstruction and the fight for the civil rights of the former slaves. (Rev: BL 10/1/94; SLJ 2/95) [973.8]

9342 Sherrow, Victoria. *The Triangle Factory Fire* (5–8). (Spotlight on American History) 1995, Millbrook LB $21.90 (1-56294-572-6). The story of the deadly factory fire that exposed the shameful labor exploitation in this country and led to needed reforms. (Rev: BR 1–2/96; SLJ 3/96) [363.37]

9343 Smith, Carter, ed. *Presidents in a Time of Change: A Sourcebook on the U.S. Presidency* (5–8). (American Albums from the Collections of the Library of Congress) 1993, Millbrook LB $25.90 (1-56294-362-6). A visual sourcebook about U.S. presidents during the late 19th century, from the collections of the Library of Congress. (Rev: BL 12/1/93; SLJ 4/94; VOYA 4/94) [973]

9344 Smith, Carter, ed. *Presidents of a Young Republic: A Sourcebook on the U.S. Presidency* (5–8). (American Albums from the Collections of the Library of Congress) 1993, Millbrook LB $25.90 (1-56294-359-6). The presidents who guided the young republic after the American Revolution are profiled in this illustrated history from the collections of the Library of Congress. (Rev: BL 12/1/93) [973.5]

9345 Smith, John David. *Black Voices from Reconstruction, 1865–1877* (8–12). Illus. 1996, Millbrook LB $27.40 (1-56294-583-1). Using original narratives and documents, this is the story of black people, their turmoil, and their disappointments during Reconstruction. (Rev: BL 11/1/96; BR 1–2/97; SLJ 2/97) [973]

9346 Smith, Karen M. *New Paths to Power: American Women 1890–1920* (8–12). (Young Oxford History of Women in the United States) 1994, Oxford $32.00 (0-19-508111-0). A history of women from the end of the 19th century to 1920, the year U.S. women finally won the right to vote. (Rev: BL 12/15/94; SLJ 1/95) [305.4]

9347 Stalcup, Brenda, ed. *Reconstruction* (8–12). Illus. (Opposing Viewpoints: American History) 1995, Greenhaven LB $21.96 (1-56510-227-4). An anthology of writings that present various points of view on the period of social transformation and controversy from 1865 through 1877 that is known as Reconstruction. (Rev: BL 3/15/95; SLJ 5/95) [973.8]

9348 Stein, R. Conrad. *The Transcontinental Railroad in American History* (6–10). Illus. (In American History) 1997, Enslow LB $19.95 (0-89490-882-0). This is a lively account of the building of the transcontinental railroad and the people involved, including the essential role of Chinese Americans. (Rev: BL 2/1/98; SLJ 1/98) [385]

9349 Stewart, Gail B. *1900s* (5–9). Illus. 1990, Crestwood LB $16.95 (0-89686-471-5). Both the serious history and the trivia associated with this decade are presented in chronological order. Also use *1910s* (1990). (Rev: SLJ 6/90) [973.9]

9350 Uschan, Michael V. *The 1910s* (7–10). Illus. 1998, Lucent LB $18.96 (1-56006-551-6). This volume presents an overview of the 1910s and everyday life, highlighting the Progressive movement, workers' rights, silent films, vaudeville, and other social developments, as well as the U.S. role in world affairs and later in World War I and the postwar period. (Rev: SLJ 4/99) [973.9]

9351 Wilder, Laura Ingalls. *West from Home: Letters of Laura Ingalls Wilder, San Francisco 1915* (7–9). 1974, HarperCollins $15.95 (0-06-024110-1); paper $4.95 (0-06-440081-6). The author describes her trip from Missouri to San Francisco in 1915. [973.9]

9352 Woog, Adam. *The 1900's* (7–10). Illus. 1998, Lucent LB $22.45 (1-56006-550-8). This overview of the 1900s includes material on the economy, working and living conditions, politics, important events and personalities, and the growing influences of advertising, movies, and mass transportation. (Rev: SLJ 4/99) [973.9]

BETWEEN THE WARS AND THE GREAT DEPRESSION (1918–1941)

9353 Allen, Frederick L. *Only Yesterday* (10–12). 1957, HarperCollins paper $8.00 (0-06-080004-6). A popularly written informal history of American life and politics in the decade before the Crash. [973.91]

9354 Allen, Frederick L. *Since Yesterday: The Nineteen-Thirties in America* (10–12). 1986, HarperCollins paper $14.00 (0-06-091322-3). From the stock market crash to the outbreak of war in Europe, this is a social history of America in the thirties. [973.91]

9355 Altman, Linda J. *The Decade That Roared: America During Prohibition* (7–10). 1997, Twenty-First Century $21.40 (0-8050-4133-8). The excitement and significance of the roaring twenties are conveyed, with vivid depictions of bootleggers, flagpole sitters, mobsters, revivalist preachers, and speakeasy queens, as well as laborers, blues and jazz musicians, participants in the "Scopes monkey trial," and even conservative rural dwellers. (Rev: BR 3–4/98; SLJ 1/98) [973.9]

9356 Brown, Gene. *Conflict in Europe and the Great Depression: World War I (1914–1940)* (5–8). (First Person America) 1994, Twenty-First Century LB $18.90 (0-8050-2585-5). The period 1914-1940 is re-created through excerpts from original source material as well as texts describing events and social conditions. (Rev: BL 5/15/94; SLJ 11/94) [973.9]

9357 Burg, David F. *The Great Depression: An Eyewitness History* (9–12). 1996, Facts on File $50.00 (0-8160-3095-2). Different primary sources are used to help the reader understand what it was like to live during the Great Depression. (Rev: BL 12/15/95; VOYA 4/96) [973.91]

9358 Candaele, Kerry. *Bound for Glory: From the Great Migration to the Harlem Renaissance, 1910–1930* (7–10). Illus. (Milestones in Black American History) 1996, Chelsea LB $19.95 (0-7910-2261-7); paper $9.95 (0-7910-2687-6). This account covers the mass movement of African Americans from the rural South to the northern cities in the early 20th-century and their achievements in the arts, politics, business, and sports, with emphasis on the origins of the Harlem Renaissance. (Rev: BL 10/15/96; BR 1–2/97; SLJ 2/97) [973]

9359 Carter, Ron. *The Youngest Drover* (5–9). 1995, Harbour $19.95 (0-9643672-1-1); paper $14.95 (0-9643672-0-3). In 1923, when he was 15, the author's father participated in an exciting cattle drive from Alberta to Montana. (Rev: BL 1/1–15/96) [978]

9360 Chambers, Veronica. *The Harlem Renaissance* (7–12). Illus. (African-American Achievers) 1997, Chelsea LB $19.95 (0-7910-2597-7); paper $9.95 (0-7910-2598-5). This history discusses the emergence of Harlem as a cultural center in the 1920s in the context of the social and political forces of the time, weaving in accounts of such greats as Langston Hughes, Countee Cullen, Zora Neale Hurston, and others who were part of this artistic and intellectual movement. (Rev: BL 2/15/98; BR 3–4/98; SLJ 4/98) [700]

9361 Cryan-Hicks, Kathryn, ed. *Pride and Promise: The Harlem Renaisssance* (4–8). Illus. (Perspectives on History) 1994, Discovery Enterprises paper $5.95 (1-878668-30-7). The key people in the arts that inspired the Harlem Renaissance are identified and their work discussed in this work that covers Harlem before the World Wars. (Rev: BL 8/94) [305.896]

9362 Davies, Nancy M. *The Stock Market Crash of 1929* (7–12). (American Events) 1994, Macmillan LB $14.95 (0-02-726221-9). The causes and effects of the devastating stock market crash of 1929 are traced, with a discussion of safeguards that were put in place. (Rev: BL 7/94) [338.5]

9363 Dudley, William, ed. *The Great Depression: Opposing Viewpoints* (7–12). Illus. (Opposing Viewpoints Digests) 1994, Greenhaven LB $17.95 (1-56510-084-0). This account uses dozens of quotations from primary and secondary sources to explore various facets of the Great Depression, including its causes, its effects, and the New Deal. (Rev: BL 2/1/94) [973.9]

9364 Farrell, Jacqueline. *The Great Depression* (8–12). Illus. (World History) 1996, Lucent LB $17.96 (1-56006-276-2). Using numerous quotes from eyewitnesses and many photographs, this is a vivid re-creation of the causes, highlights, and consequences of the stock market crash and what happened during the ensuing Depression. (Rev: BL 2/15/96; SLJ 2/96) [973.917]

9365 Fremon, David K. *The Great Depression in American History* (7–10). (In American History) 1997, Enslow LB $19.95 (0-89490-881-2). The Great Depression, its causes, its effects, and how it was ended, told with a lively text and many black-and-white photographs. (Rev: BL 5/15/97; BR 9–10/97) [338.5]

9366 Harris, Nathaniel. *The Great Depression* (7–12). Illus. 1988, David & Charles $19.95 (0-7134-5658-2). This account describes the 1930s not only in the United States but also in Britain and Europe. (Rev: SLJ 1/89) [973.91]

9367 Haskins, Jim. *The Harlem Renaissance* (6–10). Illus. 1996, Millbrook LB $30.90 (1-56294-565-3). This book offers a guided tour of the Harlem Renaissance from 1916 through 1940 and an introduction to the artists and writers involved. (Rev: BL 9/1/96; BR 11–12/96; SLJ 9/96; VOYA 12/96) [700]

9368 Herald, Jacqueline. *Fashions of a Decade: The 1920s* (7–12). (Fashions of a Decade) 1991, Facts on File $19.95 (0-8160-2465-0). An illustrated overview of fashions and trends of the 1920s as they reflected the development of modern life after World War I. (Rev: BL 12/15/91; SLJ 2/92) [391]

9369 Hintz, Martin. *Farewell, John Barleycorn: Prohibition in the United States* (6–10). Illus. (People's History) 1996, Lerner LB $22.60 (0-8225-1734-5). A well-organized, readable account that traces the history of alcohol use in the United States, covers the 18th Amendment and its effects, and ends with repeal of Prohibition. (Rev: BL 8/96; SLJ 10/96) [363.4]

9370 Jacques, Geoffrey. *Free within Ourselves: The Harlem Renaissance* (7–10). Illus. (The African-American Experience) 1996, Watts LB $25.00 (0-531-11272-1). The important black artists from the late 1920s including writers, painters, musicians, actors, and sculptors, are profiled in this history of the Harlem Renaissance. (Rev: BL 2/15/97; SLJ 1/97) [700]

9371 Katz, William L. *The New Freedom to the New Deal: 1913–1939* (7–9). (History of Multicultural America) 1993, Raintree Steck-Vaughn LB $24.26 (0-8114-6279-X). This title in the series presents covers the U.S. from World War I through the beginning of World War II from a multicultural perspective. (Rev: BL 9/1/93) [973.91]

9372 Lawson, Don. *FDR's New Deal* (7–9). 1979, HarperCollins $12.95 (0-690-03953-0). The story of how President Roosevelt's policies helped this country out of the Great Depression. [973.91]

9373 Meltzer, Milton. *Brother, Can You Spare a Dime? The Great Depression, 1929–1933* (7–12). (Library of American History) 1991, Facts on File $19.95 (0-8160-2372-7). Through firsthand accounts of workers, farmers, sharecroppers, veterans, and professionals, the author re-creates how this economic catastrophe affected millions of ordinary people. (Rev: BL 5/15/91; SLJ 10/91) [330.973]

9374 Nardo, Don. *The Great Depression* (7–12). Illus. (Opposing Viewpoints Digest) 1997, Greenhaven LB $18.96 (1-56510-743-8); paper $13.70 (1-56510-742-X). This volume presents various viewpoints on why the Depression occurred, the role of the government, and the pros and cons surrounding the New Deal as they were argued at the time and then as modern historians see it. (Rev: BL 3/1/98; SLJ 4/98; VOYA 2/99) [973.917]

9375 Nardo, Don. *The Scopes Trial* (6–10). Illus. (Famous Trials) 1996, Lucent LB $17.96 (1-56006-268-1). The story of the "Great Monkey Trial" of 1925 that revolved around a schoolteacher named Scopes and the teaching of evolution in schools, and involved a confrontation between two great orators, attorneys Clarence Darrow and William Jennings Bryan. (Rev: BL 5/1/97; BR 11–12/97; SLJ 4/97) [345.73]

9376 Nishi, Dennis. *Life During the Great Depression* (6–10). Illus. (Way People Live) 1997, Lucent LB $22.45 (1-56006-381-5). During the Great Depression, one in 5 Americans was unemployed. This is the story, drawing from documents as well as extensively from first-person accounts of how people lived, their morale, what they wore, how they sought to escape through movies, music, and sports, expressions of ethnic/gender stereotypes and inequalities, and other human aspects of those times. (Rev: BL 8/98; SLJ 7/98; VOYA 2/99) [973.91 6]

9377 Pietrusza, David. *The Roaring '20s* (7–10). Illus. (World History) 1997, Lucent LB $18.96 (1-56006-309-2). Prohibition, the Teapot Dome scandal, jazz, the economy and the stock market, the automobile, the speak-easy, and the Scopes Trial are among the topics covered in this history of the prosperous 1920s, when America became an urban society and headed for the Great Depression. (Rev: SLJ 7/98) [973.9]

9378 Ross, Stewart. *Causes & Consequences of the Great Depression* (7–10). (Causes and Consequences) 1998, Raintree Steck-Vaughn $27.11 (0-8172-4059-4). An analysis of the shortsightedness and limited understanding of larger economic principles that led to the Great Depression, a description of the general desperation it caused, and an assessment of both direct and indirect consequences, from World War II to the growth of international cooperation, with extensive use of illustrations including cartoons, posters, photos, and statistical charts as well as quotations from historians, documents, and world leaders. (Rev: BL 8/98; SLJ 6/98; VOYA 2/99) [338.5 42]

9379 Shannon, David, ed. *The Great Depression* (10–12). 1977, Peter Smith $20.00 (0-8446-2925-1). A look at how the Great Depression changed the lives of individuals. [330-973]

9380 Sherrow, Victoria. *Hardship & Hope—America & the Great Depression* (7–12). 1995, Twenty-First Century LB $21.40 (0-8050-4178-8). A succinct chronological narrative of the Great Depression in America that uses extensive first-person accounts, including some by young people. (Rev: BL 6/1–15/97; SLJ 8/97) [338.5]

9381 Smith, Carter, ed. *Presidents of a World Power: A Sourcebook on the U.S. Presidency* (5–8). (American Albums) 1993, Millbrook LB $25.90 (1-

56294-361-8). An illustrated review of the presidents who presided over the United States as a world power during the 20th century. (Rev: BL 12/1/93) [973.91]

9382 Sonnenfeld, Kelly. *Memories of Clason Point* (6–12). 1998, Dutton $16.99 (0-525-45961-8). This candid memoir by a daughter in a Jewish immigrant family living in the Bronx during the Great Depression recalls the material and emotional hardships it brought to her family and neighbors. (Rev: BL 2/1/98; SLJ 3/98; VOYA 4/98) [974.7]

9383 Stanley, Jerry. *Children of the Dust Bowl: The True Story of the School at Weedpatch Camp* (5–8). 1992, Crown LB $15.99 (0-517-58782-3). Records the enormity of the Dust Bowl, the migrants' desperate flight, and the story of the Weedpatch School and the "Okie" children who built it. (Rev: BL 9/1/92*; SLJ 11/92*) [371.96]

9384 Stewart, Gail B. *The New Deal* (6–9). 1993, Macmillan LB $14.95 (0-02-788369-8). Explains the causes of the Great Depression and how President Roosevelt tried to turn the economy and national morale around through the New Deal. (Rev: BL 11/15/93; VOYA 2/94) [973.917]

9385 Stewart, Gail B. *1920s* (5–9). Illus. 1990, Crestwood LB $11.95 (0-89686-473-1). A chronological description of the Great War and its aftermath plus material on the trivia associated with this period. Also use *1930s* (1990). (Rev: SLJ 6/90) [973.9]

9386 Stimpson, Eddie, Jr. *My Remembers: A Black Sharecropper's Recollections of the Depression* (10–12). 1996, Univ. of North Texas Pr. $19.95 (0-929398-98-X). The story of a black family and their life of poverty and hardship in rural Texas during and after the Great Depression. (Rev: SLJ 8/96) [973.9]

9387 Terkel, Studs. *Hard Times: An Oral History of the Great Depression* (9–12). 1970, Pantheon paper $15.00 (0-394-74691-0). This collection of first-person accounts re-creates graphically the ordeal of America during the 1930s. [973.91]

9388 Warren, Andrea. *Orphan Train Rider: One Boy's True Story* (4–8). 1996, Houghton $16.00 (0-395-69822-7). Between 1854 and 1930, more than 200,000 orphaned and abandoned children from cities on the East Coast were "placed out" to new homes and families in midwestern and western states. This is an account of one of them. (Rev: BL 7/96; SLJ 8/96*) [362.7]

9389 Watkins, T. H. *The Great Depression: America in the 1930s* (9–12). 1993, Little, Brown $24.95 (0-316-92453-9). Explores the impact of the Great Depression in the 1930s and its continuing effect today, with over 100 black-and-white photos. (Rev: BL 11/15/93; SLJ 6/94) [973.917]

9390 Woog, Adam. *Roosevelt & the New Deal* (7–10). Illus. (World History) 1997, Lucent LB $17.96 (1-56006-324-6). Through double-page spreads, sidebars, and political cartoons, photographs, reproductions, and first-person accounts, this book discusses Roosevelt's efforts to end the Great Depression through the New Deal, its impact on the nation, and what it did and did not accomplish. (Rev: SLJ 8/98) [973.9]

9391 Wormser, Richard. *Growing Up in the Great Depression* (6–12). 1994, Atheneum $15.95 (0-689-31711-5). Letters, photos, and interviews examine children's lives during the Great Depression. Includes accounts of job loss, child labor, and the struggles of African Americans. (Rev: BL 10/15/94; SLJ 12/94; VOYA 2/95) [973.91]

WORLD WAR II TO THE PRESENT (1945–)

9392 Alonso, Karen. *Korematsu v. United States: Japanese-American Internment Camps* (7–12). Illus. (Landmark Supreme Court Cases) 1998, Enslow LB $19.95 (0-89490-966-5). The book tells of the Japanese American internments during World War II and focuses on Fred Korematsu's case challenging the government's right to remove him from his home and imprison him simply because he was a Japanese American. (Rev: BL 5/1/98; BR 9–10/98; SLJ 8/98; VOYA 2/99) [323.1]

9393 Andryszewski, Tricia. *The March on Washington, 1963: Gathering to Be Heard* (5–10). Illus. (Spotlight on American History) 1996, Millbrook LB $21.90 (0-7613-0009-0). A full, gripping description of the civil rights march on Washington, in historic context, culminating in Dr. King's "I Have a Dream" speech. (Rev: BL 2/15/97; SLJ 3/97) [323.1]

9394 Archer, Jules. *The Incredible Sixties: The Stormy Years That Changed America* (7–12). 1986, Harcourt $17.95 (0-15-238298-4). A topically arranged overview of the events, trends, and significance of the 1960s and how they have shaped our future. (Rev: BL 5/15/86; SLJ 9/86; VOYA 4/87) [973.922]

9395 Armor, John, and Peter Wright. *Manzanar* (10–12). Illus. 1988, Times Bks. $27.00 (0-8129-1727-8). A description of the internment camp used to house Japanese Americans during World War II illustrated with touching photographs by Ansel Adams. (Rev: BL 11/1/88; BR 5–6/89; SLJ 5/89; VOYA 6/89) [940.5472]

9396 Baker, Patricia. *Fashions of a Decade: The 1950s* (7–12). (Fashions of a Decade) 1991, Facts on File $19.95 (0-8160-2468-5). An illustrated overview of fashions of the 1950s, set in a context of the political, economic, and social developments of the time. (Rev: BL 12/15/91; SLJ 2/92) [391]

9397 Baker, Patricia. *Fashions of a Decade: The 1940s* (7–12). Illus. (Fashions of a Decade) 1992, Facts on File $21.95 (0-8160-2467-7). Each book in the Fashions of a Decade series connects political and social history with particular modes of dress. Part of an 8-volume set that covers fashion from the 1920s through the 1990s. (Rev: BL 4/1/92) [391]

9398 Brimner, Larry Dane. *Voices from the Camps: Internment of Japanese Americans during World War II* (7–12). Illus. 1994, Watts LB $17.70 (0-531-111179-2). The shameful treatment of Japanese Americans in California during the second World War is re-created through interviews with survivors and their children. (Rev: BL 6/1–15/94) [940.53]

9399 Brown, Gene. *The 1992 Election* (5–8). Illus. (Headliners) 1993, Millbrook $23.40 (1-56294-080-5). The dramatic story of the presidential election that first brought Bill Clinton into national power and prominence. (Rev: BL 4/1/93) [973.9]

9400 Burby, Liza N. *The Watts Riot* (6–9). Illus. (World History) 1997, Lucent LB $17.96 (1-56006-300-9). Using many primary and secondary source quotations, this account describes the uprising in the black ghetto of Watts in Los Angeles and its impact on the rest of America. (Rev: BL 8/97; BR 11–12/97; SLJ 11/97) [979.4]

9401 Colman, Penny. *Rosie the Riveter* (6–12). 1995, Crown LB $20.99 (0-517-59791-8). An overview of the new role women played in the wartime workplace. (Rev: BL 4/15/95; SLJ 5/95) [331.4]

9402 Dolan, Sean. *Pursuing the Dream: From the Selma-Montgomery March to the Formation of PUSH (1965–1971)* (7–10). Illus. (Milestones in Black American History) 1995, Chelsea LB $18.95 (0-7910-2254-4); paper $7.95 (0-7910-2680-9). This chronicle of the civil rights movement of the 1960s tells of the demonstrations and confrontations plus background information on participation of blacks in sports and the arts. (Rev: BL 7/95) [323.1]

9403 Dudley, William, ed. *The 1960s* (9–12). Illus. (Opposing Viewpoints) 1996, Greenhaven LB $21.96 (1-56510-526-5); paper $16.20 (1-56510-525-7). A collection of opinions ranging from the conservative to liberal to radical about issues of the 1960s, including the Vietnam War, minority rights, and the counterculture. (Rev: BL 4/15/97; SLJ 7/97) [973.923]

9404 Dudley, William, and Bonnie Szumski, eds. *America's Future: Opposing Viewpoints* (9–12). Illus. (Opposing Viewpoints) 1990, Greenhaven LB $26.20 (0-89908-448-6); paper $16.20 (0-89908-423-0). A collection of different point of views on the present situation in America and where we are headed. (Rev: BL 7/90; SLJ 8/90) [324.2]

9405 Finkelstein, Norman H. *Thirteen Days/Ninety Miles: The Cuban Missile Crisis* (8–12). 1994, Messner LB $18.95 (0-671-86622-2). Declassified

materials, letters, and memoirs describe the tension-filled Cuban missile crisis, documenting the actions and ideologies of Kennedy and Khrushchev and revealing how narrowly nuclear war was averted. (Rev: BL 7/94*; SLJ 6/94) [973.992]

9406 Finkelstein, Norman H. *The Way Things Never Were: The Truth about the "Good Old Days."* (5–8). 1999, Simon & Schuster $17.00 (0-689-81412-7). The 1950s and 1960s are revisited in this social history that describes a time when the Cold War caused jitters, automobiles were unsafe, present-day vaccines weren't around, our diet was poor, and old age was not as enjoyable as today. (Rev: BL 9/1/99; SLJ 7/99) [973.92]

9407 Fremon, David K. *Japanese-American Internment in American History* (7–10). Illus. (In American History) 1996, Enslow LB $19.95 (0-89490-767-0). Drawing on a wide range of personal narratives, the author recreates the shameful period during World War II when Japanese Americans were forcibly evacuated to internment camps. (Rev: BL 1/1–15/97; BR 3–4/97; SLJ 6/97; VOYA 12/96) [940.53]

9408 Fremon, David K. *The Watergate Scandal in American History* (7–10). (In American History) 1997, Enslow LB $19.95 (0-89490-883-9). A clear, logically arranged, and objective account of the famous political scandal that ended the Nixon presidency. (Rev: BL 4/15/98; SLJ 5/98) [973.9]

9409 Fyson, Nance Lui. *The 1940s* (6–9). Illus. 1990, Batsford $19.95 (0-7134-5628-0). The story of World War II and its aftermath are covered plus development in such areas as sports, the arts, science, and invention. (Rev: SLJ 7/90) [973.9]

9410 Goodwin, Doris Kearns. *No Ordinary Time: Franklin and Eleanor Roosevelt: The Homefront in World War II* (9–12). 1994, Simon & Schuster $29.50 (0-671-64240-5). Details the inner workings of the White House during World War II, including FDR's and Eleanor's home front activities. (Rev: BL 8/94*) [973.917]

9411 Gow, Catherine H. *The Cuban Missile Crisis* (6–9). Illus. (World History) 1997, Lucent LB $16.95 (1-56006-289-4). The story of the most serious crisis in the Cold War, when war between the United States and the Soviet Union in 1962 was threatened, with key players being President Kennedy and Premier Nikita Khrushchev. (Rev: BL 8/97; BR 11–12/97; SLJ 8/97) [973.922]

9412 Hampton, Wilborn. *Kennedy Assassinated! The World Mourns* (5–8). Illus. 1997, Candlewick $17.99 (1-56402-811-9). A gripping first-person account of John Kennedy's assassination by a veteran newspaper reporter who was in Dallas working for UPI the day it happened. (Rev: BL 9/15/97; BR 3–4/98; SLJ 10/97) [364.1]

9413 Harding, Vincent, et al. *We Changed the World: African Americans, 1945–1970* (7–12). Illus. (Young Oxford History of African Americans) 1997, Oxford $35.50 (0-19-508796-8). This volume covers African American history immediately after World War II and traces the beginnings of the modern civil rights movement. (Rev: BL 9/1/97; BR 11–12/97) [973]

9414 Haskins, Jim. *Power to the People: The Rise and Fall of the Black Panther Party* (7–12). Illus. 1997, Simon & Schuster paper $16.00 (0-689-80085-1). A somewhat plodding account of this radical 1960s political organization whose leaders included Huey Newton and Bobby Seale. (Rev: BL 3/15/97; SLJ 3/97; VOYA 8/97) [322.4]

9415 Hendler, Herb. *Year by Year in the Rock Era* (7–12). 1983, Greenwood LB $38.95 (0-313-23456-6). A year-by-year chronicle of social events matched with information about artists, hits, and so on, of the rock era from 1954 through 1981. [973.92]

9416 Herda, D. J. *United States v. Nixon: Watergate and the President* (6–10). Illus. (Landmark Supreme Court Cases) 1996, Enslow LB $19.95 (0-89490-753-0). The Watergate scandal is reviewed with special emphasis on the legal aspects of this case that brought down the presidency of Richard Nixon. (Rev: BL 8/96; SLJ 7/96) [342.73]

9417 Houston, Jeanne W., and James D. Houston. *Farewell to Manzanar* (9–12). 1983, Bantam paper $5.99 (0-553-27258-6). The story of the 3 years during World War II that Jeanne Houston, a Japanese American, and her family spent at Manzanar, an internment camp. [940.54]

9418 Hull, Mary. *Struggle and Love, 1972–1997* (7–10). Illus. (Milestones in Black American History) 1996, Chelsea LB $19.95 (0-7910-2262-5); paper $9.95 (0-7910-2688-4). This book covers the past quarter of a century in African American history, highlighting the lives and careers of people like Jesse Jackson, Colin Powell, and Michael Jordan. (Rev: BL 3/15/97; SLJ 6/97) [973]

9419 Hunt, Conover. *JFK for a New Generation* (10–12). 1996, Southern Methodist Univ. Pr. $34.95 (0-87074-415-1); paper $19.95 (0-87074-395-3). This book is not a biography, but rather a commentary on how the myth of JFK was created and developed, and includes a minute-by-minute re-creation of the events that led up to his assassination and the events immediately following, and an assessment of subsequent theories surrounding it. (Rev: SLJ 1/97) [973.9]

9420 Javna, John, and Gordon Javna. *60s!* (9–12). Illus. 1983, St. Martin's paper $17.95 (0-312-01725-1). A portfolio of pictures with text about the popular culture of the 1960s. [973.92]

9421 Kallen, Stuart A. *The 1950s* (5–8). (Cultural History of the United States) 1998, Lucent LB $18.96 (1-56006-555-9). Readable text and many photos are used to survey the contrasting political and cultural trends, events, and movements of the 1950s in the United States and examine what life was like for teenagers at that time. (Rev: BL 1/1–15/99; SLJ 3/99) [973.921]

9422 Katz, William L. *The Great Society to the Reagan Era: 1964–1990* (7–9). (History of Multicultural America) 1993, Raintree Steck-Vaughn LB $27.11 (0-8114-6282-X). A history of race relations in the United States that covers the struggles, gains, and setbacks from the mid-1960s to 1990, spanning the Johnson, Nixon, Carter, and Reagan administrations. (Rev: BL 9/1/93) [973.92]

9423 Katz, William L. *World War II to the New Frontier: 1940–1963* (7–9). (History of Multicultural America) 1993, Raintree Steck-Vaughn LB $24.26 (0-8114-6280-3). From the beginning of World War II through the Kennedy Era, this is a history of race relations and the struggle for civil rights in this country. (Rev: BL 9/1/93) [305.8]

9424 Kronenwetter, Michael. *America in the 1960s* (6–9). Illus. (World History) 1997, Lucent LB $17.96 (1-56006-294-0). A re-creation of this tumultuous decade rocked by the antiwar and civil rights movements and a vast reassessment of social values by individuals and the nation as a whole. (Rev: BL 6/1–15/98; SLJ 8/98) [973.923]

9425 Landsman, Susan. *Who Shot JFK?* (6–8). (History Mystery) 1992, Avon paper $3.50 (0-380-77063-6). Takes on the controversial subject of JFK's assassination and examines the maze of theories, charges, and countercharges. (Rev: BL 4/1/93) [364.1]

9426 Lemann, Nicholas. *The Promised Land: The Great Black Migration and How It Changed America* (9–12). 1991, Knopf $24.95 (0-394-56004-3). Focusing on individual experiences, the author traces the movement of blacks from the rural South to the promise of a new life in the urban North during and after World War I. (Rev: BL 3/1/91*) [973.9]

9427 Levine, Ellen. *A Fence Away from Freedom: Japanese Americans and World War II* (7–12). 1995, Putnam $18.95 (0-399-22638-9). Many voices tell of their bitter experiences as Japanese Americans forced into internment camps during World War II. (Rev: BL 10/1/95; SLJ 12/95; VOYA 2/96) [940.53]

9428 Meltzer, Milton, ed. *The American Promise: Voices of a Changing Nation* (8–12). Illus. 1990, Bantam $15.95 (0-553-07020-7). In a series of excerpts from books, speeches, and interviews, the major movements affecting American life since World War II are outlined. (Rev: BL 12/15/90; SLJ 2/91) [973.92]

9429 Morris, Jeffrey. *The Reagan Way* (6–9). (Great Presidential Decisions) 1996, Lerner LB $23.93 (0-8225-2931-9). By examining Reagan's major presidential decisions, the author presents an even-handed look at Reagan's strengths and weaknesses. (Rev: SLJ 2/96) [973.9]

9430 Okihiro, Gary Y. *Whispered Silences: Japanese Americans and World War II* (10–12). 1996, Univ. of Washington Pr. $60.00 (0-295-97497-4); paper $29.95 (0-295-97498-2). A brief history of Japanese immigration to the United States precedes this account of the relocation of 110,000 Japanese Americans to 10 concentration camps in California, Washington, Oregon, and Arizona during World War II, and the racial enmity experienced by Japanese Americans. (Rev: SLJ 11/96) [973.9]

9431 O'Neil, Doris C., ed. *Life: The '60s* (9–12). Illus. 1989, Little, Brown $35.00 (0-8212-1752-6). An illustrated introduction to the 1960s through 250 photographs and connecting text. (Rev: BL 12/15/89) [973.92]

9432 *The Rock & Roll Generation: Teen Life in the '50s* (7–12). Illus. (Our American Century) 1998, Time-Life Books $29.95 (0-7835-5501-6). Outstanding photographs and short, simple text document important developments in the 1950s, including the birth of rock music; the beat generation; television; the Cold War; Korean War; McCarthyism; and the beginnings of the civil rights movement, and provides insights into teen life, such as what they did for fun; their favorite songs and television shows; and their goals. (Rev: BR 9–10/98; SLJ 9/98) [973.9]

9433 Sandak, Cass R. *The United States* (4–8). Illus. (Modern Industrial World) 1996, Raintree Steck-Vaughn LB $24.26 (0-8172-4556-1). This work examines the present economic and industrial situation in the United States, with additional information on education, living standards, and related subjects. (Rev: BL 2/15/97; SLJ 8/97) [973]

9434 Schwartz, Richard A. *Cold War Culture: Media & the Arts, 1945–1990* (10–12). 1997, Facts on File $40.00 (0-8160-3104-5). This reference book is also a browsable history of American culture during the years 1945 to 1990, with chapters on art, cartoons, consumer goods, dance, film, games, television, and theater. (Rev: BL 3/1/98; BR 5–6/98; SLJ 6/98) [973.9]

9435 Steins, Richard. *The Postwar Years: The Cold War and the Atomic Age (1950–1959)* (5–8). (First Person America) 1994, Twenty-First Century LB $18.90 (0-8050-2587-1). An introduction to the Cold War that includes primary sources. (Rev: BL 5/15/94) [973.92]

9436 Tackach, James. *Brown v. Board of Education* (7–10). Illus. (Landmark Supreme Court Cases)

1997, Lucent LB $17.96 (1-56006-273-8). Placed in a historic context, the landmark court case that destroyed the "separate but equal" decree, changed the legal landscape, and laid the groundwork for the civil rights movement, including a discussion of the rise of the NAACP and the work of young Thurgood Marshall. (Rev: BL 10/15/97; SLJ 1/98) [344.73]

9437 *Turbulent Years: The 60s* (9–12). (Our American Century) 1998, Time-Life Books $19.99 (0-7835-5503-2). Using photos from *Time* and *Life* magazines, this is a chronicle of the 1960s, including coverage of the Vietnam War, the civil rights movement, the space race, the counterculture, music, sports, and the arts. (Rev: BR 1–2/99; SLJ 5/99) [973.9]

9438 Uschan, Michael V. *The 1940s* (5–10). (Cultural History of the United States through the Decades) 1998, Lucent LB $18.96 (1-56510-554-0). Life at home and abroad during World War II dominate this book, which also discusses the Great Depression, the New Deal, events leading up to U.S. participation in the war, the beginnings of the Cold War, the growth of suburban living, and the rise of television, with sidebars on such topics as the Holocaust, the influences of radio, movies, and comics, 1940s slang, and the first computers. (Rev: SLJ 1/99) [973.9]

9439 Warren, James A. *Cold War: The American Crusade against World Communism, 1945–1991* (7–12). Illus. 1996, Lothrop $16.00 (0-688-10596-3). A meticulously researched account that covers the events, strategies, and personalities involved in the nation's 50-year effort to contain and subvert communism around the world. (Rev: BL 1/1–15/97; BR 11–12/96; SLJ 10/96*; VOYA 4/97) [327.73047]

9440 Weatherford, Doris. *American Women and World War II* (10–12). Illus. 1990, Facts on File $29.95 (0-8160-2038-8). A detailed social history of the contributions made by American women during World War II. (Rev: BL 9/1/90) [940.54]

9441 Woodward, Bob, and Carl Bernstein. *The Final Days* (10–12). 1994, Simon & Schuster paper $14.00 (0-671-89440-4). This book chronicles the last 2 months of the Nixon presidency from the dismissal of John Dean to the resignation of Nixon. [973.924]

9442 Yancey, Diane. *Life in a Japanese American Internment Camp* (6–12). Illus. (Way People Live) 1997, Lucent LB $18.96 (1-56006-345-9). Black-and-white photographs and excerpts from personal narratives are used to describe the shameful upheaval in the lives of Japanese Americans during World War II and daily life in an internment camp. (Rev: BL 1/1–15/98) [940.53]

9443 Zeinert, Karen. *McCarthy and the Fear of Communism* (7–10). (In American History) 1998, Enslow $19.95 (0-89490-987-8). The story of the reign of terror inflicted on America by the senator from Wisconsin during the 1950s and its aftermath. (Rev: BL 8/98; SLJ 12/98) [973.9]

KOREAN, VIETNAM, AND GULF WARS

9444 Barr, Roger. *The Vietnam War* (9–12). (America's Wars) 1991, Lucent LB $20.96 (1-56006-410-2). A view of U.S. military involvement in Southeast Asia. (Rev: BL 5/15/92; SLJ 6/92) [959.704]

9445 Boettcher, Thomas D. *Vietnam: The Valor and the Sorrow* (9–12). Illus. 1985, Little, Brown paper $21.95 (0-316-10081-1). An excellent popular history of the Vietnam War with many black-and-white photographs. (Rev: BL 7/85) [959.73]

9446 Brown, Gene. *The Nation in Turmoil: Civil Rights and the Vietnam War (1960–1973)* (5–8). (First Person America) 1994, Twenty-First Century LB $18.90 (0-8050-2588-X). An overview of the civil rights movement and the Vietnam War, highlighting excerpts from letters, diaries, and speeches. (Rev: BL 5/15/94) [973.92]

9447 Capps, Walter, ed. *The Vietnam Reader* (9–12). 1991, Routledge $45.00 (0-415-90126-X); paper $22.99 (0-415-90127-8). Essays by 36 writers, many of them veterans, on war experiences and the continuing effects of the Vietnam War. (Rev: BL 10/1/91) [959.704]

9448 Caraccilo, Dominic J. *The Ready Brigade of the 82nd Airborne in Desert Storm: A Combat Memoir by the Headquarters Company Commander* (9–12). 1993, McFarland paper $19.95 (0-89950-829-4). A memoir describing the company's 8 months in the desert during the Persian Gulf War moving, supplying, and setting up troops and equipment. (Rev: BL 6/1–15/93; VOYA 10/93) [956.704]

9449 Denenberg, Barry. *Voices from Vietnam* (7–12). 1995, Scholastic $16.95 (0-590-44267-8). Personal narratives of the Vietnam War from the late 1940s to 1975. (Rev: BL 2/15/95*; SLJ 3/95) [959.704]

9450 Dolan, Edward. *America in the Korean War* (7–12). 1998, Millbrook LB $28.90 (0-7613-0361-8). This study of the Korean War focuses on the battles, strategies, technological limitations, and personalities involved. (Rev: BL 1/1–15/99; SLJ 3/99) [951.904]

9451 Dudley, William, ed. *The Vietnam War* (9–12). (Opposing Viewpoints in American History) 1997, Greenhaven LB $21.96 (1-56510-701-2); paper $16.20 (1-56510-700-4). Presidents, antiwar activists, and soldiers are among those who debate the causes and consequences of America's involvement in Vietnam in this collection of documents. (Rev: BL 10/15/97; SLJ 11/97) [959.704]

9452 Dudley, William, and Stacey L. Tipp, eds. *Iraq* (9–12). (Current Controversies) 1991, Greenhaven LB $26.20 (0-89908-575-X); paper $16.20 (0-

89908-581-4). A study of the Persian Gulf War that examines military lessons of the war, media coverage, and other controversial aspects. (Rev: BL 6/15/92; SLJ 5/92) [956.704]

9453 Edwards, Richard. *The Korean War* (6–9). Illus. 1988, Rourke LB $23.93 (0-86592-036-2). A brief, objective, nicely illustrated account of the war and its aftermath. (Rev: SLJ 2/89) [951.9]

9454 Edwards, Richard. *The Vietnam War* (7–10). Illus. 1987, Rourke LB $23.93 (0-86592-031-1). An overview that covers both the war in Asia and the reaction in the United States. (Rev: SLJ 8/87) [959.704]

9455 Esper, George. *The Eyewitness History of the Vietnam War: 1961–1975* (9–12). Illus. 1986, Ballantine paper $20.00 (0-345-34294-1). This book contains a simple text and hundreds of photographs, both of which trace a basic history of the war. [959.704]

9456 Freedman, Suzanne. *Clay v. United States: Muhammad Ali Objects to War* (6–10). (Landmark Supreme Court Cases) 1997, Enslow LB $19.95 (0-89490-855-3). A thorough examination of Muhammad Ali's court case involving the Vietnam War. (Rev: BL 10/15/97; SLJ 12/97) [959.704]

9457 Friedman, Norman. *Desert Victory: The War for Kuwait* (9–12). 1991, Naval Institute Pr. $42.50 (1-55750-254-4). This book published by the Naval Institute concludes that U.S. strategy in the Persian Gulf War was largely successful but that U.S. intelligence failed to accurately gauge the strength and morale of Iraqi forces. (Rev: BL 10/15/91) [956.704]

9458 Gay, Kathlyn, and Martin Gay. *Korean War* (6–8). Illus. (Voices from the Past) 1996, Twenty-First Century LB $18.90 (0-8050-4100-1). A discussion of the often forgotten Korean War—its causes, its battles, and the people involved. (Rev: BL 11/15/96; SLJ 12/96; VOYA 4/97) [951.904]

9459 Gay, Kathlyn, and Martin Gay. *Persian Gulf War* (6–8). Illus. (Voices from the Past) 1996, Twenty-First Century LB $18.90 (0-8050-4102-8). This objective account of the Persian Gulf War contains many quotes from reporters, soldiers, military leaders, and ordinary people on every aspect of the war. (Rev: BL 11/15/96; SLJ 2/97; VOYA 6/97) [956.7044]

9460 Gay, Kathlyn, and Martin Gay. *Vietnam War* (6–8). Illus. (Voices from the Past) 1996, Twenty-First Century LB $18.90 (0-8050-4101-X). An objective overview of the Vietnam War, illustrated with black-and-white photographs. (Rev: BL 11/15/96; SLJ 12/96; VOYA 2/97) [959.704]

9461 Hastings, Max. *The Korean War* (9–12). Illus. 1988, Simon & Schuster paper $15.00 (0-671-66834-X). A readable, objective account of the war both in Korea and on the home front. (Rev: BL 10/15/87) [951.8]

9462 Hodgins, Michael C. *Reluctant Warrior* (10–12). 1996, Ballantine $24.00 (0-449-91059-8). This account of the final days of the Vietnam War tells what life was like for the common American soldier in the jungles and rice fields of Vietnam. (Rev: BL 1/1–15/97; SLJ 8/97) [959.704]

9463 Isserman, Maurice. *The Korean War* (7–12). (America at War) 1992, Facts on File LB $19.95 (0-8160-2688-2). A thorough re-creation of the Korean War, the first armed conflict of the Cold War. (Rev: BL 11/1/92) [951.904]

9464 Isserman, Maurice. *The Vietnam War: America at War* (7–12). (America at War) 1992, Facts on File $17.95 (0-8160-2375-1). A riveting account of the Vietnam War from its roots after World War II to U.S. withdrawal in 1975, and a review of the lessons learned. (Rev: BL 3/1/92) [959.7]

9465 King, John. *The Gulf War* (7–10). 1991, Dillon $18.95 (0-87518-514-2). A factual account of the Iraqi invasion of Kuwait, wartime operations, and the aftermath. (Rev: BL 3/1/92; SLJ 4/92) [956.704]

9466 Kovic, Ron. *Born on the Fourth of July* (10–12). 1990, Pocket Books paper $6.99 (0-671-73914-X). The biography of a young marine who was physically and emotionally ruined by the Vietnam War. [959.704]

9467 McCloud, Bill. *What Should We Tell Our Children about Vietnam?* (7–12). 1989, Univ. of Oklahoma Pr. $19.95 (0-8061-2229-3). Over 120 individuals including President Bush and Garry Trudeau tell what they think young people should know about the war. (Rev: BL 9/15/89) [959.704]

9468 MacLear, Michael. *The Ten Thousand Day War: Vietnam 1945–1975* (10–12). 1982, Avon paper $10.95 (0-380-60970-3). This account integrates 4 points of view on the conflict—French and American as well as those of North and South Vietnam. [959.704]

9469 Marrin, Albert. *America and Vietnam: The Elephant and the Tiger* (9–12). 1992, Viking paper $16.00 (0-670-84063-7). A historical review of Vietnam's fight for independence and the repercussions of U.S. involvement. (Rev: BL 3/1/92; SLJ 6/92*) [959.704]

9470 Noble, Dennis L. *Forgotten Warriors: Combat Art from Vietnam* (9–12). 1992, Praeger $37.95 (0-275-93868-9). Reproductions of drawings and paintings by combat artists illustrate letters, oral and official military histories, and excerpts from novels about the U.S. role in the Vietnam War. (Rev: BL 10/1/92) [959.704]

9471 Paschall, Rod. *Witness to War: Korea* (9–12). 1995, Putnam paper $12.00 (0-399-51934-3). First-hand accounts from soldiers and strategists who fought in the Korean War. (Rev: BL 5/1/95) [951.904]

9472 Prochnau, William. *Once Upon a Distant War: Young War Correspondents and the Early Vietnam Battles* (10–12). 1995, Times Bks. $27.50 (0-8129-2633-1). This is the story of a group of young U.S. journalists who were sent to cover the beginnings of what would become the lengthy Vietnam War, how they reported on what they saw, and the development of the "credibility gap" between what was reported and what the government said. (Rev: BL 11/1/95; SLJ 8/96) [959.704]

9473 Rice, Earle, Jr. *The Inchon Invasion* (6–10). Illus. (Great Battles in History) 1996, Lucent LB $26.20 (1-56006-418-8). The invasion of this Korean city on Sept. 15, 1950 during the Korean War is highlighted in this well-illustrated account that contains many quotes from primary and secondary sources. (Rev: BL 4/15/96) [951.904]

9474 Rice, Earle, Jr. *The Tet Offensive* (6–10). Illus. (Battles) 1996, Lucent LB $20.96 (1-56006-422-6). The story of the bloody Vietnam War battle and its consequences, with some general background coverage of the war. (Rev: BL 1/1–15/97; BR 11–12/97; SLJ 8/97) [959.704]

9475 Santoli, Al. *Everything We Had* (10–12). 1982, Ballantine paper $6.99 (0-345-32279-7). Interviews with 33 veterans of the Vietnam War on the war and its impact on their lives. (Rev: BL 9/15/89) [959.704]

9476 Sifry, Micah L., and Christopher Cerf, eds. *The Gulf War Reader: History, Documents, Opinions* (9–12). 1991, Times Bks. paper $17.00 (0-8129-1947-5). Writings by columnists, politicians, and political advisers on the 1990 events in Kuwait and Iraq. (Rev: BL 9/1/91) [956.704]

9477 Taylor, Thomas. *Lightning in the Storm: The 101st Air Assault Division in the Gulf War* (9–12). 1994, Hippocrene $29.50 (0-7818-0268-7). A mix of the anecdotal and the analytical describes the division's contributions in the Persian Gulf War. (Rev: BL 4/15/94) [956.704]

9478 Van Devanter, Lynda, and Joan A. Furey, eds. *Visions of War, Dreams of Peace: Writings of Women in the Vietnam War* (9–12). 1991, Warner paper $9.95 (0-446-39251-0). Recollections of women who served in the Vietnam War. (Rev: BL 5/15/91) [811]

9479 *A War Remembered* (9–12). Illus. 1986, Silver Burdett $16.95 (0-939526-20-4). This is one volume of an extensive 25-volume set from Time-Life Books that chronicles in text and many pictures the Vietnam War. [959.704]

9480 Willenson, Kim, et al. *The Bad War: An Oral History of the Vietnam War* (10–12). 1988, NAL paper $8.95 (0-452-26063-9). This book is the result of a series of interviews conducted by *Newsweek* reporters with both Vietnamese and Americans involved in this war. (Rev: SLJ 12/87) [959.704]

9481 Wills, Charles A. *The Tet Offensive* (6–9). Illus. 1989, Silver Burdett LB $17.95 (0-382-09849-8); paper $7.95 (0-382-09855-2). The story of the 1968 campaign in Vietnam plus general material about the war and the Memorial in Washington, D.C. (Rev: BL 11/1/89; BR 1–2/90) [959.704]

9482 Wormser, Richard. *Three Faces of Vietnam* (9–12). 1993, Watts LB $23.60 (0-531-11142-3). Examines the tragedy of the Vietnam War from a human perspective, narrating the personal histories of those who fought, those who protested, and Vietnamese civilians. (Rev: BL 2/15/94; SLJ 1/94; VOYA 2/94) [959.704]

9483 Wright, David. *Vietnam War* (7–12). (Causes and Consequences) 1995, Raintree Steck-Vaughn LB $25.69 (0-8172-4053-5). A review of the colonial background of Vietnam and the causes of the war, U.S. involvement, and the outcome of the war. (Rev: BL 12/15/95) [959.704]

9484 Wright, David K. *A Multicultural Portrait of the Vietnam War* (7–10). (Perspectives) 1996, Benchmark LB $28.50 (0-7614-0052-4). This account of the Vietnam War describes the various racial groups involved in the conflict, at home and overseas, and how the effects of this war are still being felt. (Rev: BR 1–2/97; SLJ 6/96) [959.704]

9485 Wright, David K. *War in Vietnam* (5–10). 1998, Children's Pr. $20.60 (0-516-02287-3). This is the first volume of an excellent 4-volume set. The other volumes are: *War in Vietnam, Book II: A Wider War; War in Vietnam, Book III: Vietnamization;* and *War in Vietnam, Book IV: Fall of Vietnam* (all 1989, available only as a set). (Rev: BL 6/1/89; SLJ 6/89) [959.704]

9486 Yetiv, Steve A. *The Persian Gulf Crisis* (10–12). (Guides to Historic Events of the Twentieth Century) 1997, Greenwood $39.95 (0-313-29943-9). This thorough examination of the Gulf War describes causes, personalities, events, and consequences. (Rev: BL 1/1–15/98; BR 3–4/98; SLJ 3/98) [956.7]

Regions

MIDWEST

9487 Bashfield, Jean F. *Wisconsin* (5–8). (American the Beautiful) 1998, Children's Pr. $32.00 (0-516-20640-0). This book supplies important facts about Wisconsin and material on famous people, dates, places, and the economy. (Rev: BL 1/1–15/99; SLJ 4/99) [977.5]

9488 Brill, Marlene T. *Illinois* (4–8). Illus. (Celebrate the States) 1996, Marshall Cavendish LB $24.95 (0-7614-0113-X). Six fact-filled chapters cover Illinois' geography, wildlife, history, economy, famous people, and tourist attractions. (Rev: BL 2/1/97; SLJ 2/97) [917.73]

9489 Brill, Marlene T. *Indiana* (4–8). Illus. (Celebrate the States) 1997, Marshall Cavendish LB $24.95 (0-7614-0147-4). An introduction to this Midwest state's agriculture, industries, famous natives, history, and geography. (Rev: BL 7/97; SLJ 8/97) [977.2]

9490 Jameson, W. C. *Buried Treasures of the Great Plains* (5–8). (Buried Treasure) 1997, August House paper $11.95 (0-87483-486-4). After a general introduction to the Great Plains, this work presents 3 to 7 legends per state about buried treasure in Kansas, Nebraska, North and South Dakota, Oklahoma, and Texas. (Rev: BR 5–6/99; SLJ 7/97) [977]

9491 Lamb, Nancy, and Children of Oklahoma City. *One April Morning: Children Remember the Oklahoma City Bombing* (5–8). Illus. 1996, Lothrop LB $15.93 (0-688-14724-0). Interviews with 50 children who were indirectly involved in the 1995 Oklahoma City bombing of the Federal Building are the basis of this book that deals with trauma, therapy, and healing. (Rev: SLJ 7/96) [976.6]

9492 Murphy, Jim. *The Great Fire* (5–9). 1995, Scholastic $16.95 (0-590-47267-4). This narrative of the great Chicago fire combines documents, personal accounts, illustrations, photos, and street maps to give an in-depth view of the disaster. (Rev: BL 6/1–15/95; SLJ 7/95) [977.3]

9493 Reedy, Jerry. *Oklahoma* (5–8). (America the Beautiful) 1998, Children's Pr. LB $32.00 (0-516-20639-7). Basic material on Oklahoma, plus a special reference section that includes key statistics, important dates, famous people, and maps. (Rev: BL 1/1–15/99; SLJ 2/99) [976.6]

9494 Rydjord, John. *Indian Place-Names* (9–12). 1982, Univ. of Oklahoma Pr. paper $19.95 (0-8061-1763-X). This book, organized by tribes and linguistic families, tells the stories behind Kansas place names originated by American Indians. [910]

9495 Santella, Andrew. *Illinois* (5–8). (America the Beautiful) 1998, Children's Pr. $32.00 (0-516-20633-8). The history of Illinois, plus its geography, people, culture, principal cities, and important landmarks. (Rev: BL 1/1–15/99) [977.3]

9496 Sherrow, Victoria. *The Oklahoma City Bombing: Terror in the Heartland* (4–8). 1998, Enslow $18.95 (0-7660-1061-9). The events leading up to this disaster are detailed, plus material on the bombing, the rescue operations, the aftermath for survivors, and the trials of Timothy McVeigh and Terry Nichols. (Rev: BL 1/1–15/99; BR 5–6/99; SLJ 3/99) [364.16]

MOUNTAIN AND PLAINS STATES

9497 Ayer, Eleanor. *Colorado* (4–8). Illus. (Celebrate the States) 1997, Marshall Cavendish LB $24.95 (0-7614-0148-2). An introduction to the Mountain State, with information on its history, geography, and people. (Rev: BL 7/97; SLJ 8/97) [978.8]

9498 Bass, Rick. *The Lost Grizzlies: A Search for Survivors in the Wilderness of Colorado* (10–12). Illus. 1995, Houghton $22.95 (0-395-71759-0). This is the story of the adventures of a small group of men who set out on several expeditions in the early 1990s to see if grizzly bears lived in the San Juan Mountains of southern Colorado. (Rev: BL 11/1/95; SLJ 7/96) [978.8]

9499 Bauer, Erwin A. *Yellowstone* (9–12). 1993, Voyageur $29.95 (0-89658-177-2). An accessible text and beautiful color photos of the flora and fauna of the nation's first national park. (Rev: BL 3/15/93) [917.87]

9500 Lourie, Peter. *In the Path of Lewis and Clark: Traveling the Missouri* (6–9). Illus. 1996, Silver Burdett LB $19.95 (0-382-39307-4); paper $14.95 (0-382-39308-2). A day-by-day account of the 1,700-mile trip on the Missouri River that the author took in 1995 with William Least Heat-Moon, mostly by motorboat, during Moon's cross-country trip, with relevant bits of history and river lore and numerous color photographs. (Rev: BL 2/15/97; SLJ 4/97) [917.804]

9501 Melford, Michael. *Big Sky Country: A View of Paradise* (10–12). 1996, Rizzoli $50.00 (0-8478-1964-7). This is a stunning pictorial survey of the natural beauty of Montana, North Dakota, Wyoming, and Idaho. (Rev: SLJ 5/97) [978.8]

9502 Minor, Wendell. *Grand Canyon: Exploring a Natural Wonder* (4–8). Illus. 1998, Scholastic $16.95 (0-590-47968-7). In watercolors and lyrical text, the author presents a grand portrait of the Grand Canyon. (Rev: BL 9/15/98; BR 1–2/99; SLJ 8/98) [978.8]

NORTHEASTERN AND MID-ATLANTIC STATES

9503 Arnosky, Jim. *Nearer Nature* (6–12). Illus. 1996, Lothrop $18.00 (0-688-12213-2). In 26 short chapters and using his own pencil sketches, the author introduces the animals and the beauty of life found on a wooded sheep farm in rural Vermont. (Rev: BL 8/96; SLJ 11/96; VOYA 4/97) [508.743]

9504 Ashabranner, Brent. *Their Names to Live: What the Vietnam Veterans Memorial Means to America* (5–8). 1998, Twenty-First Century $23.40 (0-7613-3235-9). The history of the Vietnam Veterans Memorial, its opening in 1982, and the powerful role it has played in the hearts and minds of the American people. (Rev: SLJ 3/99) [975.3]

9505 Bigler, Philip. *Washington in Focus: The Photo History of the Nation's Capital* (9–12). Illus. 1988, Vandamere paper $8.95 (0-918339-07-3). A history in pictures and text of Washington, D.C., from its beginnings to the Metro and the Vietnam Memorial. (Rev: BL 12/15/88) [975.3]

9506 Burchard, Sue. *The Statue of Liberty: Birth to Rebirth* (7–9). Illus. 1985, Harcourt $13.95 (0-15-279969-9). After a tour of present-day Liberty Island the author describes the history behind the statue. (Rev: BL 12/1/85; SLJ 12/85) [941.7]

9507 Conaway, James. *The Smithsonian: 150 Years of Adventure, Discovery, and Wonder* (9–12). 1995, Knopf $60.00 (0-679-44175-1). Provides historical background and a multitude of photos, with sidebars about many of the museum's scientific expeditions. (Rev: BL 11/1/95) [069]

9508 Elish, Dan. *Vermont* (4–8). Illus. (Celebrate the States) 1997, Marshall Cavendish LB $24.95 (0-7614-0146-6). An introduction to this New England state, including famous sights, history, and how the people live. (Rev: BL 7/97; SLJ 8/97) [974.3]

9509 Elish, Dan. *Washington, D.C.* (5–8). (Celebrate the States) 1998, Benchmark LB $2.95 (0-7614-0423-6). This work is a general introduction to the nation's capital, with sections on its history, government, economics, neighborhoods, ethnic composition, problems, and landmarks. (Rev: SLJ 1/99) [975.3]

9510 Fisher, Leonard E. *Niagara Falls: Nature's Wonder* (7–9). Illus. 1996, Holiday House $16.95 (0-8234-1240-7). Beginning with the European discovery of the Falls in 1678, the author focuses on this natural wonder as a cultural and historical institution. (Rev: BL 9/1/96; SLJ 10/96) [971.3]

9511 Fradin, Dennis B. *The Connecticut Colony* (5–9). Illus. 1990, Children's Pr. LB $32.00 (0-516-00393-3). A history of Connecticut from its first settlements to its statehood. (Rev: BL 8/90) [974.6]

9512 Garrett, Wendell, ed. *Our Changing White House* (9–12). 1995, Northeastern Univ. Pr. $45.00 (1-55553-222-5). Ten authoritative essays chart the White House's evolution, physically and politically, through the last 2 centuries, with photos, facts, and anecdotes. (Rev: BL 7/95*) [975.3]

9513 Goldstein, Ernest. *The Statue Abraham Lincoln* (5–8). 1997, Lerner LB $22.60 (0-8225-2067-2). This book provides a detailed description of the Lincoln Memorial and an introduction to the life and accomplishments of its sculptor, Daniel Chester French. (Rev: SLJ 5/98) [975.3]

9514 Jameson, W. C. *Buried Treasures of New England: Legends of Hidden Riches, Forgotten War*

Loots, and Lost Ship Treasures (4–8). (Buried Treasure) 1997, August House paper $11.95 (0-87483-485-6). This account describes how these treasures were amassed and lost, and furnishes maps to indicate their general location. (Rev: BR 5–6/99; SLJ 10/97) [910.4]

9515 Katz, William L. *Black Legacy: A History of New York's African Americans* (6–10). Illus. 1997, Simon & Schuster $19.00 (0-689-31913-4). A history of New York City's African American community is chronicled, beginning with New Amsterdam and continuing through the Revolution and Civil War to the Harlem Renaissance, and ending with the mayoralty of David Dinkins in the early 1990s. (Rev: BL 2/15/97; BR 1–2/98; SLJ 10/97*; VOYA 6/97) [974.7]

9516 Lourie, Peter. *Erie Canal: Canoeing America's Great Waterway* (5–8). Illus. 1997, Boyds Mills $17.95 (1-56397-669-2). This colorful book about a journey along the Erie Canal also supplies historical facts about its construction and uses. (Rev: BL 7/97; SLJ 9/97) [974.7]

9517 McNair, Sylvia. *Massachusetts* (5–8). (America the Beautiful) 1998, Children's Pr. $32.00 (0-516-20635-4). With a special reference section and a fine use of graphics, this book introduces the Bay State's history, geography, and important people. (Rev: BL 1/1–15/99) [974.4]

9518 McNeese, Tim. *The New York Subway System* (6–10). Illus. (Building History) 1997, Lucent LB $22.45 (1-56006-427-7). The story of the building of the 722 miles of tunnels that compose the subway system of New York City, the longest underground system in the world. (Rev: BL 12/1/97; BR 1–2/98; SLJ 11/97) [388.4]

9519 Myers, Walter Dean. *Harlem* (6–12). Illus. 1997, Scholastic $16.95 (0-590-54340-7). This book is an impressionistic appreciation of Harlem and its culture as seen through the eyes of author Walter Dean Myers and his artist son, Christopher. (Rev: BL 2/15/97; SLJ 2/97; VOYA 10/97) [811]

9520 Quiri, Patricia R. *The White House* (4–8). (First Books) 1996, Watts LB $22.00 (0-531-20221-6). A well-illustrated history of the White House, with a description of the exterior design and the rooms inside, interesting items such as the introduction of running water, and information about the families that have lived there. (Rev: BL 6/1–15/96; SLJ 8/96) [975.3]

9521 Schomp, Virginia. *New York* (4–8). Illus. (Celebrate the States) 1996, Marshall Cavendish LB $22.95 (0-7614-0108-1). The Empire State is introduced with information on history, geography, people, landmarks, and distinguished New Yorkers. (Rev: BL 2/15/97) [917.47]

9522 Stein, R. Conrad. *New Jersey* (5–8). 1998, Children's Pr. LB $32.00 (0-516-20637-0). Full-color graphics and a clear text highlight this introduction to New Jersey's history geography, economy, people, and culture. (Rev: BL 1/1–15/99) [974.9]

9523 Tagliaferro, Linda. *Destination New York* (4–8). (Port Cities of North America) 1998, Lerner $23.93 (0-8225-2793-6). Written with a focus on New York's economic life and its handling of goods moving in and out of the port, this book also gives information on the city's history, geography, and daily life. (Rev: SLJ 1/99) [974.7]

9524 *Washington, D.C. A Smithsonian Book of the Nation's Capital* (9–12). 1992, Smithsonian $39.95 (0-89599-032-6). Photoessays by historians, journalists, and scholars on the city's history, its trappings as a capital, its artworks and documents, and its buildings, parks, and streets. (Rev: BL 11/1/92) [975.3]

9525 Weinberg, Jeshajahu, and Rina Elieli Weinberg. *The Holocaust Museum in Washington* (9–12). 1995, Rizzoli $45.00 (0-8478-1906-X). Insights given into the design, plan, and construction of the museum and its exhibits. (Rev: BL 1/1–15/96; SLJ 3/96) [975.3]

9526 Wills, Charles A. *A Historical Album of Pennsylvania* (4–8). (Historical Albums) 1996, Millbrook LB $23.40 (1-56294-595-5); paper $6.95 (1-56294-853-9). Beginning with its Native American origins and settlement by Europeans and the Quakers, this book traces the history of Pennsylvania from the First Continental Congress and the ratification of the United States Constitution, through the Battle of Gettysburg and President Lincoln's famous Gettysburg Address, and up to today. (Rev: SLJ 7/96) [974.8]

PACIFIC STATES

9527 Altman, Linda J. *California* (4–8). Illus. (Celebrate the States) 1996, Marshall Cavendish LB $24.95 (0-7614-0111-3). A richly illustrated book that contains material on California's geography, history, economic life, contemporary challenges, society, contributions, and landmarks. (Rev: BL 2/1/97; SLJ 2/97) [979.4]

9528 Andryszewski, Tricia. *Step by Step along the Pacific Crest Trail* (4–8). 1998, Twenty-First Century $23.90 (0-7613-0274-3). After a short history of the Pacific Crest Trail, this account gives a south to north tour of the trail describing terrain, landmarks, elevations, and sites. (Rev: BL 3/1/99; SLJ 4/99) [979]

9529 Brown, Tricia. *Iditarod Country: Exploring the Route of the Last Great Race* (6–10). Ed. by Christine Ummel. Illus. 1998, Epicenter Pr. $16.95 (0-

945397-66-6). The author describes Alaska's people, places, and the spirit of the Last Great Race, the Iditarod, and presents an interesting perspective on Alaska's history, geography, remoteness, native culture, and bush lifestyle. (Rev: SLJ 7/98) [979.8]

9530 Bruder, Gerry. *Heroes of the Horizon: Flying Adventures of Alaska's Legendary Bush Pilots* (9–12). 1991, Alaska Northwest paper $14.95 (0-88240-363-X). The escapades of the last generation of frontier pilots to fly open planes to uncharted Alaskan settlements are told through interviews. (Rev: BL 10/1/91) [629.13]

9531 Corral, Kimberly. *A Child's Glacier Bay* (4–8). Illus. 1998, Graphic Arts Center $15.95 (0-88240-503-9). A photoessay chronicling a 3-week kayak trip by the Corral family in the marine park of Glacier Bay in Alaska, told from the 13-year-old daughter's perspective. (Rev: BL 7/98; SLJ 8/98) [978.652]

9532 Ferrell, Nancy W. *Destination Valdez* (6–9). Illus. (Port Cities of North America) 1997, Lerner LB $23.93 (0-8225-2790-1). A fact-filled book that describes the history, economy, and people of the port city of Valdez in Alaska, including an examination of the effect of the billion dollar oil shipping industry on a tiny, remote town in Alaska. (Rev: SLJ 8/98) [979]

9533 Fraser, Mary Ann. *A Mission for the People: The Story of La Purisima* (4–8). 1998, Holt $15.95 (0-8050-5050-7). Using softly colored illustrations and double-page spreads, the author/artist tells the history of the Chumash people of the Santa Barbara region of California and of the Spanish mission La Purisima. (Rev: BL 5/1/98; SLJ 4/98) [979.4 0049757

9534 Goldberg, Jake. *Hawaii* (5–8). (Celebrate the States) 1998, Benchmark LB $35.64 (0-7614-0203-9). Hawaii is introduced in text and photos that cover history, geography, landmarks, economy, government, and its people, including a section on music and dance. (Rev: SLJ 1/99) [996.9]

9535 Heinrichs, Ann. *California* (5–8). (America the Beautiful) 1998, Children's Pr. $32.00 (0-516-20631-1). A fine introduction to California's history, geography, government, economy, arts, and recreation. (Rev: BL 1/1–15/99; SLJ 2/99) [979.4]

9536 Jones, Charlotte F. *Yukon Gold: The Story of the Klondike Gold Rush* (4–8). 1999, Holiday House $18.95 (0-8234-1403-5). A story of the Alaska-Yukon gold rush from 1896 on that captures the excitement, adventure, and, for some, disappointment of the times. (Rev: SLJ 5/99; VOYA 12/99) [979.8]

9537 Krakauer, Jon. *Into the Wild* (9–12). 1996, Villard $22.00 (0-679-42850-X). A true story expanded from Krakauer's article about a young man who starved to death in Denali National Park in Alaska. (Rev: BL 12/1/95*) [917.9]

9538 Levi, Steven C. *Cowboys of the Sky: The Story of Alaska's Bush Pilots* (5–9). Illus. 1996, Walker LB $18.85 (0-8027-8332-5). The exciting life of the people who deliver medical supplies, mail, and passengers to remote areas in Alaska is vividly re-created. (Rev: BL 6/1–15/96; BR 9–10/96; SLJ 7/96; VOYA 8/96) [629.13]

9539 McConnaughey, Bayard, and Evelyn McConnaughey. *Pacific Coast* (9–12). Illus. 1985, Knopf paper $19.95 (0-394-73130-1). A nature guide to the ecology of the Pacific states with emphasis on the bird life. (Rev: SLJ 9/85) [979]

9540 Maharidge, Dale. *Yosemite: A Landscape of Life* (9–12). 1990, Yosemite paper $14.95 (0-939666-56-1). An insightful look at the inner workings of the national park. (Rev: BL 1/15/91) [979.4]

9541 Meyer, Carolyn. *In a Different Light: Growing Up in a Yup'ik Eskimo Village in Alaska* (6–9). Illus. 1996, Simon & Schuster $17.00 (0-689-80146-7). The author revisits a Yupik Eskimo village in Alaska after an 18-year absence and details how life has changed as the residents adopt modern ways of life and gradually forget their traditional arts and customs. (Rev: BL 5/1/96; BR 1–2/97; SLJ 6/96; VOYA 8/96) [979.8]

9542 Oliver, Marilyn Tower. *Alcatraz Prison in American History* (4–8). (In American History) 1998, Enslow LB $19.95 (0-89490-990-8). After years as first a settlement and then a fort and a lighthouse, the "Rock" became a military and federal prison. This is its history, including famous prisoners, escape attempts, and its evolution into a top tourist attraction. (Rev: SLJ 1/99) [979.4]

9543 Ryan, Alan, ed. *The Reader's Companion to Alaska* (10–12). 1997, Harcourt paper $16.00 (0-15-600368-6). A compilation of writings, many them first-person accounts, about impressions of Alaska, arranged geographically. (Rev: SLJ 1/98) [979.8]

9544 Senungetuk, Vivian. *Wise Words of Paul Tiulana: An Inupiat Alaskan's Life* (5–8). 1998, Watts $22.50 (0-531-11448-1). The story of Paul Tiulana's life and the culture of the natives who have lived for centuries on a tiny island in the Bering Sea between Siberia and Alaska. (Rev: BL 1/1–15/99; SLJ 2/99) [979.8]

9545 Sherrow, Victoria. *The Exxon Valdez Tragic Oil Spill* (4–8). (American Disasters) 1998, Enslow $18.95 (0-7660-1058-9). The story of the causes and effects of the terrible oil spill that has left lasting damage to parts of the Alaska coast and its wildlife. (Rev: BL 1/1–15/99; BR 5–6/99; SLJ 3/99; VOYA 4/99) [979.8]

9546 Sherrow, Victoria. *San Francisco Earthquake, 1989: Death and Destruction* (4–8). (American Disasters) 1998, Enslow $18.95 (0-7660-1060-0). The story of this San Francisco disaster with accounts of rescue efforts and the rebuilding of the city. (Rev: BL 1/1–15/99; SLJ 6/99) [363.34]

9547 Stefoff, Rebecca. *Oregon* (4–8). Illus. 1997, Marshall Cavendish LB $24.95 (0-7614-0145-8). Life in this Pacific state is covered, along with its history, famous sights, cities, and industries. (Rev: BL 7/97; SLJ 7/97) [917.95]

9548 Takaki, Ronald. *Raising Cane: The World of Plantation Hawaii* (6–10). Adapted by Rebecca Stefoff. Illus. (Asian American Experience) 1994, Chelsea LB $19.95 (0-7910-2178-5). A fascinating look at the part that Asian immigrants played in the development of the economy of Hawaii. (Rev: BL 6/1–15/94; SLJ 7/94) [996.9]

9549 Turnbull, Andy, and Debora Pearson. *By Truck to the North: My Arctic Adventure* (4–8). 1998, Annick LB $24.95 (1-55037-551-2); paper $14.95 (1-55037-550-4). An exciting account of an overland trip by truck from Vancouver, British Columbia, to the Arctic villages of Inuvik and Tuktoyaktuk. (Rev: BL 1/1–15/99; SLJ 1/99) [979.8]

9550 Wills, Charles A. *A Historical Album of Oregon* (4–8). (Historical Albums) 1995, Millbrook LB $23.40 (1-56294-594-7); paper $6.95 (1-56294-855-5). A good, broad overview of Oregon's history and current political and economic situation, places to see, and other information, with many illustrations. (Rev: BL 12/15/95; SLJ 1/96) [979.5]

SOUTH

9551 Ayers, Harvard, and Jenny Hager, eds. *An Appalachian Tragedy: Air Pollution and Tree Death in the Eastern Forests of North America* (10–12). 1998, Sierra Club $45.00 (0-87156-976-0). Forest ecology is highlighted in this beautifully illustrated account of the effects of 40 years of pollution on the Appalachian Mountains. (Rev: SLJ 12/98) [976.1]

9552 Barrett, Tracy. *Virginia* (4–8). Illus. (Celebrate the States) 1996, Marshall Cavendish LB $24.95 (0-7614-0110-5). An introduction to Virginia, including its history, culture, famous sites, and important Virginians. (Rev: BL 2/15/97; SLJ 6/97) [975.5]

9553 Bial, Raymond. *Mist Over the Mountains: Appalachia and Its People* (4–8). 1997, Houghton $14.95 (0-395-73569-6). The people and culture of Appalachia are introduced, including history, agriculture, and folk arts. (Rev: BL 3/1/97; SLJ 5/97) [976.1]

9554 Branch, Muriel M. *The Water Brought Us: The Story of the Gullah-Speaking People* (5–9). 1995, Dutton paper $16.99 (0-525-65185-3). About the Gullah people who live on the sea islands off the coast of South Carolina and Georgia and who are descendants of slaves. (Rev: BL 9/15/95; SLJ 10/95) [975.8]

9555 Bresee, Clyde. *How Grand a Flame: A Chronicle of a Plantation Family, 1813–1947* (9–12). 1991, Algonquin $33.95 (0-945575-55-6). An illustrated reconstruction of family life on a South Carolina cotton plantation based on original documents and personal remembrances. (Rev: BL 10/1/91) [975.7]

9556 Chang, Perry. *Florida* (5–8). (Celebrate the States) 1998, Benchmark LB $24.95 (0-7614-0420-1). A fine introduction to the history, geography, people, landmarks, and government of Florida, with material on the cultural diversity of its people. (Rev: SLJ 1/99) [975.9]

9557 Cocke, William. *A Historical Album of Virginia* (4–8). (Historical Albums) 1995, Millbrook LB $23.40 (1-56294-596-3); paper $6.95 (1-56294-856-3). A broad overview of Virginia's history, using many period prints and paintings, with equal space to past and current events, and including general information on the state. (Rev: SLJ 1/96) [975.5]

9558 Heinrichs, Ann. *Florida* (4–8). (America the Beautiful) 1998, Children's Pr. LB $32.00 (0-516-20632-X). This book provides background on the history, geography, and economy of Florida and describes the recent influx of people there, its major cities, and endangered wildlife. (Rev: SLJ 1/99) [975.9]

9559 Hintz, Martin. *Louisiana* (5–8). 1998, Children's Pr. $32.00 (0-516-20634-6). With a good use of graphics and clear writing, this book provides a wealth of information about Louisiana, past and present. (Rev: BL 1/1–15/99; SLJ 2/99) [975.6]

9560 Hintz, Martin, and Stephen Hintz. *North Carolina* (5–8). (America the Beautiful) 1998, Children's Pr. LB $32.00 (0-516-20638-9). A revised edition of this work on North Carolina's history, geography, natural resources, industry, people, and landmarks. (Rev: BL 1/1–15/99; SLJ 4/99) [975.6]

9561 LeVert, Suzanne. *Louisiana* (4–8). Illus. (Celebrate the States) 1997, Marshall Cavendish LB $24.95 (0-7614-0112-1). The unique aspects of life in this southern state are stressed in this introduction that also covers standard background material. (Rev: BL 7/97; SLJ 7/97) [976.3]

9562 Wills, Charles A. *A Historical Album of Alabama* (4–8). (Historical Albums) 1995, Millbrook LB $23.40 (1-56294-591-2); paper $6.95 (1-56294-854-7). Using many period prints and engravings, the author traces the history of Alabama from prehistoric days to today, including the impact of the shift away from cotton as a main crop, the civil rights movement, and the importance of football in the state. (Rev: BL 12/15/95; SLJ 1/96) [976.1]

SOUTHWEST

9563 Bredeson, Carmen. *Texas* (4–8). Illus. (Celebrate the States) 1996, Marshall Cavendish LB $24.95 (0-7614-0109-1). Basic information about Texas is presented in an attractive format with many color photos, maps, and diagrams. (Rev: BL 2/15/97; SLJ 6/97) [976.4]

9564 Fishbein, Seymour L. *Yellowstone Country: The Enduring Wonder* (9–12). Illus. 1989, National Geographic LB $12.00 (0-87044-718-1). A profile of the world's oldest national park with particularly good coverage on its flora and fauna. (Rev: BL 11/1/89; SLJ 1/90) [917.87]

9565 Lavender, David. *The Southwest* (10–12). 1984, Univ. of New Mexico Pr. paper $17.95 (0-8263-0736-1). The history of the entire Southwest is given, with emphasis on New Mexico and Arizona. [979.1]

9566 McCarry, Charles. *The Great Southwest* (7–12). Illus. 1980, National Geographic LB $12.00 (0-

87044-288-0). In pictures and text, descriptions are given of such states as New Mexico, Colorado, and Arizona. [979.1]

9567 Marrin, Albert. *Empires Lost & Won* (6–10). Illus. 1997, Simon & Schuster $19.00 (0-689-80414-8). Beginning with the destruction of Pueblo Indian cities and ending with the war between the U.S. and Mexico, this book provides a fascinating history of the 300-year struggle for control of the Southwest. (Rev: BL 7/97; BR 9–10/97; SLJ 6/97*; VOYA 6/97) [979]

9568 Turner, Robyn Montana. *Texas Traditions: The Culture of the Lone Star State* (4–8). Illus. 1996, Little, Brown $19.95 (0-316-85675-4); paper $12.95 (0-316-85639-8). This work examines the cultural, geographical, historical, and social influences of various ethnic groups that have changed Texas and contributed to its uniqueness. (Rev: BL 7/96; SLJ 4/97) [976.4]

Physical and Applied Sciences

General and Miscellaneous

9569 Aaseng, Nathan. *Yearbooks in Science: 1940–1949* (5–8). Illus. (Yearbooks in Science) 1995, Twenty-First Century LB $20.40 (0-8050-3434-X). An important decade in scientific discovery is chronicled, with emphasis on the impact of these advances on society. (Rev: BL 1/1–15/96; SLJ 5/96) [609]

9570 Ash, Russell. *Incredible Comparisons* (4–9). Illus. 1996, DK Publg. $19.95 (0-7894-1009-5). Such concepts in nature as speed, size, and weight are discussed in this fascinating book of comparisons. (Rev: BL 12/1/96*; SLJ 3/97) [031.02]

9571 Bruno, Leonard C. *Science & Technology Breakthroughs: From the Wheel to the World Wide Web* (5–8). 1997, Gale $63.00 (0-7876-1927-2). This expanded version contains over 1,200 paragraph-long entries in 12 chronologically arranged chapters: agriculture and everyday life; astronomy; biology; chemistry; communications; computers; earth sciences; energy, power systems, and weaponry; mathematics; medicine; physics; and transportation. (Rev: BL 3/1/98; BR 5–6/98; SLJ 5/98) [509]

9572 Bruno, Leonard C. *Science & Technology Firsts* (6–12). 1997, Gale $85.76 (0-7876-0256-6). More than 4,000 entries chronicle famous "firsts," arranged by branches of science and technology such as agriculture, astronomy, biology, chemistry, communications, and computers. (Rev: BL 8/97; BR 5–6/97; SLJ 5/97) [500]

9573 Butterfield, Moira. *Richard Orr's Nature Cross-Sections* (5–8). Illus. 1995, DK Publg. $17.95 (0-7894-0147-9). In a series of double-page spreads, 12 ecosystems are introduced, including a rain forest, a beehive, Arctic life, a beaver lodge, and a termite city. (Rev: BL 12/1/95; SLJ 1/96) [574.5]

9574 Calder, Nigel, and John Newell, eds. *On the Frontiers of Science* (9–12). Illus. 1989, Facts on File $35.00 (0-8160-2205-4). A compilation of writings by contemporary scientists about current work being accomplished in many different branches of science. (Rev: BR 5–6/90) [500]

9575 Corben, Bert. *The Struggle to Understand: A History of Human Wonder and Discovery* (9–12). 1992, Prometheus $34.95 (0-87975-683-7). How controversial science concepts evolved through history despite opposition. (Rev: BL 2/1/92) [509]

9576 Crump, Donald J., ed. *On the Brink of Tomorrow: Frontiers of Science* (7–9). Illus. 1982, National Geographic $12.95 (0-87044-414-X). With many color illustrations, this account covers recent advances in such areas as physics, astronomy, and medicine. [500]

9577 *The DK Science Encyclopedia*. rev. ed. (4–8). 1998, DK Publg. $39.95 (0-7894-2190-9). Using 1- or 2-page articles and a profusion of illustrations, this topically arranged, slightly updated version of the 1993 edition gives an overview of the field of science, emphasizing its interconnectedness with technology, under such headings weather, ecology, and reactions. (Rev: BL 12/1/98; SLJ 2/99; VOYA 4/99) [500]

9578 Francis, Raymond L. *The Illustrated Almanac of Science, Technology, & Invention: Day by Day Facts, Figures, & the Fanciful* (6–12). Illus. 1997, Plenum $28.95 (0-306-45633-8). For each day of the year, this almanac cites scientific events that occurred on that date, birth dates of famous scientists, discoveries, interesting technological achievements, or just quirky scientific happenings that made worldwide or even only local headlines. (Rev: BL 12/1/97; SLJ 5/98) [509]

9579 Gutfreund, Geraldine M. *Yearbooks in Science: 1970–1979* (5–8). Illus. (Yearbooks in Science) 1995, Twenty-First Century LB $20.40 (0-8050-3437-4). A decade of new scientific concepts and inventions is discussed, with profiles of the scientists behind them. (Rev: BL 1/1–15/96; SLJ 5/96) [609]

9580 Henderson, Harry, and Lisa Yount. *Twentieth Century Science* (6–9). (World History) 1997, Lucent LB $18.96 (1-56006-304-1). This history of 20th-century science describes advances in all branches of science, including details about the birth of quantum physics, genetics, molecular biology, and computer science. (Rev: BR 11–12/97; SLJ 9/97) [509]

9581 Horn, Bob, and W. P. Chips. *Dimension-5: Everything You Didn't Know You Didn't Know* (9–12). 1992, Fithian paper $9.95 (1-56474-007-2). Thought-provoking essays, both humorous and serious, on scientific, religious, and philosophical issues. (Rev: BL 2/15/92) [500]

9582 Jespersen, James, and Jane Fitz-Randolph. *Mummies, Dinosaurs, Moon Rocks: How We Know How Old Things Are* (6–8). Illus. 1996, Simon & Schuster $16.00 (0-689-31848-0). An investigation of the various ways that scientists are able to determine the age of natural and man-made materials. (Rev: BL 10/1/96; SLJ 9/96) [930.1]

9583 Kurtis, Bill. *New Explorers* (10–12). 1995, WTTW Chicago paper $28.95 (0-9647457-0-4). The frontiers of today's scientific research are divided into four categories—medical advances, great mysteries, amazing creatures, and fragile earth. Topics range from superconductors, endangered species, and care of newborn babies to the history of dinosaurs, pollution, and rain forests. (Rev: SLJ 4/96) [500]

9584 Kuttner, Paul. *Science's Trickiest Questions: 402 Questions That Will Stump, Amuse, and Surprise* (9–12). 1994, Holt paper $10.95 (0-8050-2873-0). Clear, concise answers to unusual questions in science provide entertaining reading. (Rev: BL 4/1/94) [502]

9585 McGowen, Tom. *The Beginnings of Science* (5–8). 1998, Twenty-First Century LB $25.90 (0-7613-3016-X). Beginning with primitive people and their use of magic, fire, counting, writing, and astronomy, this book traces the history of science through Greece and the Middle Ages, up to the 16th century. (Rev: BL 12/1/98) [509]

9586 McGowen, Tom. *Yearbooks in Science: 1900–1919* (5–8). 1995, Twenty-First Century LB $20.40 (0-8050-3431-5). An overview of human achievements in science and technology during the first 20 years of the 20th century, how they helped humanity, and the men and women involved. (Rev: BL 12/1/95; SLJ 1/96) [609]

9587 McGowen, Tom. *Yearbooks in Science: 1960–1969* (5–8). Illus. (Yearbooks in Science) 1996, Twenty-First Century LB $20.40 (0-8050-3436-6). Developments in the history of science and

technology during the 1960s are covered in an exciting step-by-step approach. (Rev: BL 1/1–15/96; SLJ 5/96) [609]

9588 Nardo, Don. *Greek & Roman Science* (5–8). Illus. (World History) 1997, Lucent LB $17.96 (1-56006-317-3). This is a history of the contributions made by the Greeks and Romans to modern scientific thought, including the beginnings of writing, math, medicine, astronomy, biology, medicine, mechanics, and the atom. (Rev: SLJ 5/98) [509]

9589 National Geographic Society, eds. *Inside Out: The Best of National Geographic Diagrams & Cutaways* (6–12). 1998, National Geographic $25.00 (0-7922-7371-0). Sixty outstanding paintings from the past 75 years of the *National Geographic* cover such topics as a prairie dog town, Spacelab, and Chernobyl's ruined core. (Rev: BL 10/15/98; SLJ 10/98) [686.2252]

9590 Newton, David E. *Yearbooks in Science: 1920–1929* (7–12). (Yearbooks in Science) 1995, Twenty-First Century LB $20.40 (0-8050-3432-3). The history of scientific advances in the 1920s, with chapters on various fields that explain the breakthroughs, how they helped humanity, and the scientists involved. (Rev: BL 12/1/95; SLJ 1/96) [609]

9591 Paul, Richard. *A Handbook to the Universe: Explorations of Matter, Energy, Space, and Time for Beginning Scientific Thinkers* (9–12). 1993, Chicago Review paper $14.95 (1-55652-172-3). A straightforward presentation of the principles of physics and astronomy that puts scientists and their work in a historic context. (Rev: BL 1/1/94) [500.2]

9592 Roberts, Royston M. *Serendipity: Accidental Discoveries in Science* (9–12). Illus. 1989, Wiley paper $16.95 (0-471-60203-5). An entertaining collection of anecdotes concerning the unusual circumstances surrounding some scientific discoveries. (Rev: BR 1–2/90; SLJ 11/89) [500]

9593 Silverstein, Alvin, et al. *Clocks and Rhythms* (5–8). Illus. 1999, Twenty-First Century LB $23.40 (0-7613-3224-3). This book focuses on natural rhythms of humans, animals, and the environment, including daily or circadian rhythms, monthly cycles, and seasonal patterns. (Rev: BL 9/1/99; SLJ 10/99) [571.7]

9594 Silverstein, Herma. *Yearbooks in Science: 1990 and Beyond* (5–8). Illus. (Yearbooks in Science) 1995, Twenty-First Century LB $20.40 (0-8050-3439-0). The final volume in this series not only traces recent developments in science and technology but also presents the challenges of the future. (Rev: BL 1/1–15/96) [609]

9595 Spangenburg, Raymond. *The History of Science from 1895 to 1994* (7–12). 1994, Facts on File $19.95 (0-8160-2742-0). Surveys scientific progress, discussing atomic energy, relativity, space exploration, genetics, and the achievements of various scientists spanning 100 years. (Rev: BL 9/1/94; VOYA 10/94) [509]

9596 Spangenburg, Raymond, and Diane Moser. *The History of Science in the Eighteenth Century* (9–12). (On the Shoulders of Giants) 1993, Facts on File $19.95 (0-8160-2740-4). This work covers science in the Age of Enlightenment and the Industrial Revolution, and the work of such scientists as Cavendish, Avogado, Franklin, Volta, and Hutton. (Rev: BL 11/1/93) [509]

9597 Spangenburg, Raymond, and Diane Moser. *Science and Invention* (6–12). Illus. (American Historic Places) 1997, Facts on File $19.95 (0-8160-3402-8). Illustrated profiles of eight sites around the country connected with great scientists and inventions, including the homes of Joseph Priestly, Luther Burbank, George Washington Carver, and Rachel Carson as well as Thomas Edison's lab, the Lick Observatory, and the Wright Brothers National Monument. (Rev: BL 12/1/97; BR 5–6/98) [609.73]

9598 Suplee, Curt. *Everyday Science Explained* (10–12). 1996, National Geographic $35.00 (0-7922-3410-3). The wonders of chemistry, physics, and biology, including the human body, are presented in an entertaining yet instructive way with many useful illustrations. (Rev: BL 12/1/96; BR 3–4/97; SLJ 5/97) [500]

9599 Taylor, Charles, and Stephen Pople. *The Oxford Children's Book of Science* (5–8). Illus. 1996, Oxford $30.00 (0-19-521165-0). A wide vari-

ety of science topics—from gravity and cells to the human body and DNA—are presented in this large-format, well-illustrated book. (Rev: BL 10/1/96; SLJ 8/96) [503]

9600 *Ultimate Visual Dictionary of Science* (6–10). Illus. 1998, DK Publg. $29.95 (0-7894-3512-8). Though not in dictionary form (as the title suggests), this is a heavily illustrated introduction that presents basic information about physics, chemistry, anatomy, medical science, ecology, earth science, astronomy, electronics, mathematics, and computers. (Rev: BL 12/1/98; SLJ 11/98; VOYA 4/99) [500]

9601 Wollard, Kathy. *How Come?* (5–9). 1993, Workman paper $12.95 (1-56305-324-1). Provides answers to some common and not-so-common questions about ordinary things. (Rev: BL 5/1/94) [500]

9602 Zimmerman, Barry E., and David J. Zimmerman. *Why Nothing Can Travel Faster Than Light... and Other Explorations in Nature's Curiosity Shop* (9–12). 1993, Contemporary paper $14.95 (0-8092-3821-7). Designed to appeal to "scientific illiterates," this book covers the basics of scientific thought, from Newton to quantum mechanics. (Rev: BL 9/15/93) [500]

9603 Zotti, Ed. *Know It All! Everything They Should Have Told You in School but Didn't* (9–12). 1993, Ballantine paper $9.00 (0-345-36232-2). Zotti provides no-nonsense, sometimes amusing, answers to questions about animals, weather, space, time, and many other subjects. (Rev: BL 7/93) [031]

Experiments and Projects

9604 Adams, Richard, and Robert Gardner. *Ideas for Science Projects* (9–12). Illus. (Projects for Young Scientists) 1997, Watts $25.00 (0-531-11347-7). A revised edition of the Robert Gardner book that presents more than 100 science projects in astronomy, chemistry, physics, mechanics, psychology, botany, and zoology. (Rev: BL 12/1/97; SLJ 12/97) [507]

9605 Adams, Richard, and Robert Gardner. *More Ideas for Science Projects*. rev. ed. (9–12). (Experimental Science) 1998, Watts $25.00 (0-531-11380-9). Using material from many scientific disciplines, including computer science, this revision of the 1989 title offers over 100 suggestions for projects, most with detailed instructions. (Rev: SLJ 1/99) [507]

9606 Bochinski, Julianne Blair. *The Complete Handbook of Science Fair Projects* (7–12). 1996, Wiley $29.95 (0-471-12378-1); paper $14.95 (0-471-12377-3). This revision of the 1991 edition contains 50 experiments (10 of them new) plus material on the international rules for science fairs. (Rev: BL 2/1/96; BR 5–6/96; SLJ 4/96) [507.9]

9607 Brown, Bob. *More Science for You: 112 Illustrated Experiments* (6–8). Illus. 1988, TAB paper $7.95 (0-8306-3125-9). A collection of simple experiments involving such topics as heat, sound, weight, and tricks. (Rev: VOYA 4/89) [507]

9608 Brown, Robert J. *333 Science Tricks and Experiments* (7–12). Illus. 1984, McGraw-Hill $15.95 (0-8306-0825-7); paper $9.95 (0-8306-1825-2). Basic scientific principles are demonstrated in experiments and projects. (Rev: BL 4/1/89) [507]

9609 Carrow, Robert. *Put a Fan in Your Hat! Inventions, Contraptions, & Gadgets Kids Can Build* (6–9). Illus. 1996, McGraw-Hill paper $14.95 (0-07-011658-X). An interesting collection of 12 projects like creating a power source, building an electric motor, and producing a drive train are explained with clear instructions and many diagrams. (Rev: BL 4/15/97; SLJ 5/97) [608]

9610 Cobb, Vicki. *Science Experiments You Can Eat* (7–9). Illus. 1994, HarperCollins LB $14.89 (0-06-023551-9); paper $5.95 (0-06-446002-9). Recipes for soups, ice cream dishes, gelatin, and other ordinary dishes are used to explain scientific phenomena. Continued in: *More Science Experiments You Can Eat* (1979). [507]

9611 Cobb, Vicki. *The Secret Life of Cosmetics: A Science Experiment Book* (6–8). Illus. 1985, HarperCollins LB $14.89 (0-397-32122-8). An examination of the history and composition of cosmetics and a number of experiments to perform using these materials. (Rev: BL 3/15/86; SLJ 1/86) [668]

9612 Cobb, Vicki. *The Secret Life of Hardware: A Science Experiment Book* (7–9). Illus. 1982, HarperCollins LB $13.89 (0-397-32000-0). A book of science activities and experiments that involve a hammer, saw, soaps, paints, and other commonly found items. [670]

9613 Cobb, Vicki, and Kathy Darling. *You Gotta Try This! Absolutely Irresistible Science* (4–8). Illus. 1999, Morrow $15.00 (0-688-15740-8). An easy, enjoyable book of 50 experiments, that gives clear directions, lists of materials, and an explanation of the concepts involved. Some require adult assistance. (Rev: BL 8/99; SLJ 8/99) [507]

9614 Dashefsky, H. Steven. *Zoology: 49 Science Fair Projects* (8–12). 1994, TAB paper $11.95 (0-07-015683-2). A step-by-step description of interesting science fair projects from various branches of science. (Rev: BL 1/15/95; SLJ 3/95) [591]

9615 Duensing, Edward. *Talking to Fireflies, Shrinking the Moon: Nature Activities for All Ages*

(5–9). Illus. 1997, Fulcrum paper $15.95 (1-55591-310-5). Over 40 nature activities are included in this volume, including how to hypnotize a frog, weave a daisy chain, and whistle for woodchucks. (Rev: VOYA 10/97) [507]

9616 Friedhoffer, Robert. *Science Lab in a Supermarket* (5–9). (Physical Science Labs) 1998, Watts $24.00 (0-531-11335-3). Common items found in a supermarket like milk, fruits, cereal, meat, and soap are used as ingredients in a series of experiments and projects that explore the nature of everyday things. (Rev: BL 12/1/98; SLJ 12/98) [540]

9617 Gardner, Robert. *Kitchen Chemistry: Science Experiments to Do at Home* (7–9). Illus. 1982, Messner paper $4.95 (0-671-67576-1). Simple gadgets and materials found in the kitchen are used in a series of entertaining and instructive experiments. [542]

9618 Gardner, Robert. *Science Projects about Kitchen Chemistry* (6–9). (Science Projects) 1999, Enslow $19.95 (0-89490-953-3). A book of clearly outlined experiments that range widely in difficulty and revolve around the kitchen and its contents. (Rev: SLJ 7/99) [507]

9619 Herbert, Don. *Mr. Wizard's Supermarket Science* (7–9). Illus. 1980, Random paper $10.00 (0-394-83800-9). Magic tricks and experiments performed using common household objects. [507]

9620 Hussey, Lois J., and Catherine Pessino. *Collecting for the City Naturalist* (7–9). Illus. 1975, HarperCollins $12.95 (0-690-00317-X). Science activities that can be carried out in an urban environment, such as collecting spider webs, are outlined. [500.7]

9621 Iritz, Maxine Haren. *Blue-Ribbon Science Fair Projects* (7–12). 1991, McGraw Hill $9.95 (0-07-157629-0). A variety of science fair projects for the novice are presented, with charts, graphs, photos, and a chapter on choosing a topic. (Rev: BL 9/15/91) [507.8]

9622 Iritz, Maxine Haren. *Science Fair: Developing a Successful and Fun Project* (8–12). Illus. 1987, TAB $16.95 (0-8306-0936-9); paper $9.95 (0-8306-2936-X). A thorough step-by-step introduction to doing a science project. (Rev: BL 4/15/88) [507]

9623 Newton, David E. *Making and Using Scientific Equipment* (9–12). (Experimental Science) 1993, Watts LB $25.00 (0-531-11176-8). An explanation of the workings of several pieces of scientific equipment and how to make and use them properly. (Rev: BL 9/1/93; VOYA 2/94) [681]

9624 Newton, David E. *Science/Technology/Society Projects for Young Scientists* (9–12). (Projects for Young Scientists) 1991, Watts LB $25.00 (0-531-

11047-8). An examination of science and technology issues that relate to everyday life, with suggestions for projects on such topics as population, nutrition, and environmental pollution. (Rev: BL 12/15/91; SLJ 3/92) [507.8]

9625 Nye, Bill. *Bill Nye the Science Guy's Big Blast of Science* (5–8). 1993, Addison-Wesley paper $15.00 (0-201-60864-2). Science information presented in an entertaining manner, covering such subjects as electricity, weather, space, matter, heat, light, fundamental forces, and scientific method. (Rev: BL 2/15/94) [507.8]

9626 Rainis, Kenneth G. *Exploring with a Magnifying Glass* (7–12). 1991, Watts LB $25.00 (0-531-12508-4). An introduction to how magnification works and a series of projects exploring photos, plants, minerals, fabrics, and more. (Rev: BL 1/15/92; SLJ 4/92) [507.8]

9627 Richards, Roy. *101 Science Tricks: Fun Experiments with Everyday Materials* (5–8). Illus. 1992, Sterling $16.95 (0-8069-8388-4). Fun, easy-to-perform science and math activities, with notes for parents and teachers. (Rev: BL 2/1/92; SLJ 1/92) [507.8]

9628 *Science Fairs: Ideas and Activities* (4–8). 1998, World Book $15.00 (0-7166-4498-3); paper $11.00 (0-7166-4497-5). Using many diagrams and logical step-by-step explanations, this work gives offers science projects in such areas as space, earth science, geology, botany, and machines. (Rev: SLJ 1/99) [507]

9629 Smith, Norman F. *How to Do Successful Science Projects.* Rev. ed. (5–8). Illus. 1990, Messner paper $5.95 (0-671-70686-1). This guide gives many fine tips and concentrates on the applications of the scientific method. (Rev: BL 7/90) [507.8]

9630 Sobey, Edwin J. C. *Wrapper Rockets and Trombone Straws: Science at Every Meal* (5–8). Illus. 1996, McGraw-Hill paper $14.95 (0-07-021745-9). Using simple items found in restaurants such as glasses, straws, and napkins, a number of simple tricks and experiments are introduced. (Rev: BL 3/1/97; SLJ 6/97) [500]

9631 Tocci, Salvatore. *How to Do a Science Fair Project* (9–12). Illus. (Experimental Science) 1997, Watts $25.00 (0-531-11346-9). This update of a popular title provides step-by-step suggestions for choosing, researching, planning, constructing, displaying, and presenting a science fair project. (Rev: BL 12/1/97; SLJ 12/97) [507]

9632 VanCleave, Janice. *Janice VanCleave's A+ Projects in Chemistry: Winning Experiments for Science Fairs and Extra Credit* (6–10). 1993, Wiley $27.95 (0-471-58631-5); paper $12.95 (0-471-58630-7). Thirty experiments that investigate such topics as calories, acids, and electrolytes, among others. (Rev: BL 12/1/95; SLJ 4/94) [930]

9633 Vecchione, Glen. *100 First Prize Make It Yourself Science Fair Projects* (4–8). Illus. 1998, Sterling $21.95 (0-8069-0703-7). The projects outlined in this good resource for project ideas range from the simple to complex and cover a wide range of branches of science. (Rev: SLJ 4/99) [507]

9634 Voth, Danna. *Kidsource: Science Fair Handbook* (5–8). Illus. 1998, Lowell House paper $9.95 (1-56565-514-1). This source provides excellent advice on selecting, preparing, and presenting science projects, with material on choosing workable topics, equipment needed, safety, measuring devices, and record keeping. (Rev: BL 2/15/99; SLJ 5/99) [507]

Astronomy and Space Science

General and Miscellaneous

9635 Asimov, Isaac. *Isaac Asimov's Guide to Earth and Space* (9–12). 1991, Random $19.50 (0-679-40437-6). Explains the workings of supernovas, comets, stars, planets, galaxies, and other cosmic phenomena. (Rev: BL 10/15/91) [520]

9636 Berry, Richard. *Discover the Stars* (9–12). Illus. 1987, Crown paper $12.95 (0-517-56529-3). A beginner's guide to exploring stars, planets, and the moon with hints on how to use a telescope. (Rev: SLJ 4/88; VOYA 4/88) [523]

9637 Burnham, Robert, et al. *Advanced Skywatching* (10–12). (Nature Company Guides) 1997, Time-Life Books $29.95 (0-7835-4941-5). This book supplies a wealth of material for dedicated amateur astronomers, including 20 maps of various regions of the sky. (Rev: BR 3–4/98; SLJ 3/98) [523]

9638 Dauber, Philip M., and Richard A. Muller. *The Three Big Bangs: Comet Crashes, Exploding Stars, and the Creation of the Universe* (9–12). 1996, Addison-Wesley $25.00 (0-201-40752-3). A description of the 3 main events that brought life to planet Earth. (Rev: BL 12/1/95) [523.1]

9639 Dickinson, Terence. *NightWatch: A Practical Guide to Viewing the Universe*. Rev. ed. (6–12). Illus. 1998, Firefly $45.00 (1-55209-300-X); paper $29.95 (1-55209-302-6). Exciting text and charts, tables, and full-color photos make this is an excellent handbook for amateur astronomers, with information on the sky, heavenly bodies, kinds of equipment, and how to photograph the universe. (Rev: SLJ 2/99) [523]

9640 Dickinson, Terence, and Alan Dyer. *The Backyard Astronomer's Guide* (9–12). 1991, Camden House $39.95 (0-921820-11-9). Provides detailed reviews of optical equipment and discusses techniques of observation and astrophotography. (Rev: BL 11/1/91) [520]

9641 Eicher, David. *The Universe from Your Backyard* (10–12). 1988, Kalmbach $29.95 (0-913135-13-5). Directions are given on how to find almost 700 celestial bodies in this anthology taken from the pages of *Astronomy* magazine. (Rev: BR 5–6/89) [523]

9642 Ford, Harry. *The Young Astronomer* (4–8). Illus. 1998, DK Publg. $15.95 (0-7894-2061-9). Using many fine illustrations and a series of interesting projects, this volume provides a basic introduction to astronomy and tells young people how to explore the worlds found in the sky. (Rev: BL 4/15/98) [520]

9643 Graham-Smith, Francis, and Bernard Lovell. *Pathways to the Universe* (9–12). Illus. 1989, Cambridge Univ. Pr. $38.95 (0-521-32004-6). A readable, well-organized introduction to astronomy that can be used both for reference and for recreational reading. (Rev: BL 4/15/89; BR 9–10/89) [523]

9644 Gustafson, John. *Planets, Moons and Meteors: The Young Stargazer's Guide to the Galaxy* (5–8). 1992, Messner LB $12.95 (0-671-72534-3); paper $6.95 (0-671-72535-1). This guidebook tells how and when to observe the solar system and provides basic information about the planets. (Rev: BL 11/1/92) [523]

9645 Halpern, Paul. *The Structure of the Universe* (10–12). 1997, Holt paper $10.95 (0-8050-4029-3). This history of astronomy ends with the current thinking on the organization of the universe and its future. (Rev: SLJ 8/97) [523]

9646 McAleer, Neil. *The Cosmic Mind-Boggling Book* (9–12). 1982, Warner paper $11.95 (0-446-

39046-1). A fascinating collection of unusual facts about the planets, stars, and universe. [523]

9647 Mitton, Jacqueline, and Stephen P. Maran. *Gems of Hubble* (10–12). 1996, Cambridge Univ. Pr. paper $13.95 (0-521-57100-6). Spectacular color photos accompany this history of telescopes and detailed coverage on the Hubble Space Telescope and what it has seen. (Rev: SLJ 7/97) [522]

9648 Mitton, Simon, and Jacqueline Mitton. *Astronomy* (5–8). Illus. (Young Oxford Books) 1996, Oxford LB $30.00 (0-19-521168-5). A well-written, lavishly illustrated introduction to astronomy, with large fact boxes to add depth and asides. (Rev: BL 3/15/96; SLJ 6/96) [520]

9649 Moche, Dinah L. *Astronomy Today* (7–10). Illus. 1982, Random LB $15.99 (0-394-94423-2); paper $12.99 (0-394-84423-8). A history is given of our discoveries in astronomy plus material on space exploration and our ideas of the universe today. [523]

9650 Moore, Patrick. *The New Atlas of the Universe* (7–12). Illus. 1984, Crown $29.99 (0-517-55500-X). A detailed series of maps that introduce our solar system and the universe beyond. [523]

9651 Newton, David E. *Black Holes & Supernovae* (4–8). Illus. (Secrets of Space) 1995, Twenty-First Century LB $20.40 (0-8050-4477-9). A richly illustrated volume that explores theories and facts about black holes and supernovas. (Rev: BL 7/97; SLJ 6/97) [523.8]

9652 North, John. *The Norton History of Astronomy and Cosmology* (9–12). (Norton History of Science) 1994, Norton $35.00 (0-393-03656-1); paper $18.95 (0-393-31193-7). Examines the sciences of astronomy and cosmology from ancient Egypt to the present and their evolution beyond myth and superstition. (Rev: BL 8/94) [520]

9653 Rasmussen, Richard Michael. *Mysteries of Space* (6–10). (Great Mysteries) 1994, Greenhaven LB $22.45 (1-56510-097-2). This introduction to astronomy explores some of the great unanswered questions about the universe. (Rev: BL 4/15/94) [520]

9654 Ronan, Colin A. *The Skywatcher's Handbook* (8–12). Illus. 1989, Crown paper $16.00 (0-517-57326-1). An excellent handbook that describes and explains a wide range of phenomena that occur in both the day and night skies. (Rev: BR 3–4/90; VOYA 2/90) [523]

9655 Sagan, Carl. *Cosmos* (9–12). Illus. 1980, Random paper $7.99 (0-345-33135-4). A chronological account of how and what we have learned about our universe. [520]

9656 Savage, Marshall T. *The Millennial Project: Colonizing the Galaxy—in 8 Easy Steps* (9–12). 1993, Empyrean LB $24.95 (0-9633914-8-8); paper $18.95 (0-9633914-9-6). An 8-step program, from colonies in the sea through orbiting colonies. (Rev: BL 1/15/93*) [629.47]

9657 Schaaf, Fred. *Seeing the Sky: 100 Projects, Activities & Explorations in Astronomy* (9–12). Illus. 1990, Wiley paper $18.95 (0-471-51067-X). In addition to many activities, from the simple to the complex, this informative work gives background facts about sky phenomena. (Rev: BL 10/15/90) [523]

9658 *Seeing Stars: The McDonald Observatory & Its Astronomers* (6–10). 1997, Sunbelt Media $15.95 (1-57168-117-5). This is a history of the famous observatory operated by the University of Texas in Austin, with material on the equipment used and the day-to-day operation. (Rev: SLJ 5/98) [523]

9659 Snow, Theodore P. *The Cosmic Cycle* (9–12). Illus. 1985, Darwin $14.95 (0-87850-041-3). A fine introduction to astronomy complete with 34 excellent color plates. (Rev: SLJ 3/86) [523]

9660 Steele, Philip. *Astronomy* (5–8). (Pocket Facts) 1991, Macmillan LB $10.95 (0-89686-586-X). An understandable introduction to astronomy, with photos. (Rev: BL 3/15/92) [520]

9661 Tyson, Nell De Grasse. *Universe Down to Earth* (9–12). 1994, Columbia Univ. Pr. $33.00 (0-231-07560-X). Translates the fundamental meaning of various scientific models of the cosmos into language comprehensible to the general reader. (Rev: BL 5/1/94) [523.1]

9662 *The Visual Dictionary of the Earth* (5–9). 1993, DK Publg. $18.95 (1-56458-335-X). Double-page, illustrated spreads describe the heavenly bodies in Earth's universe, telescopes, and space and lunar exploration equipment. (Rev: BL 12/15/93; SLJ 2/94) [550]

9663 Whitfield, Peter. *The Mapping of the Heavens* (9–12). 1995, Pomegranate $35.00 (0-87654-475-8). This album of historical maps moves from Babylonian representations of the zodiac to the mid-19th century and on to scientifically accurate modern maps. (Rev: BL 12/15/95) [525]

9664 Whitney, Charles A. *Whitney's Star Finder: A Field Guide to the Heavens*. Rev. ed. (9–12). Illus. 1985, Random paper $16.95 (0-679-72582-2). A simple guide to stars for use by the amateur without complex equipment. (Rev: BL 1/1/86; SLJ 4/86) [523]

Astronautics and Space Exploration

9665 Apt, Jay, and Michael Helfert. *Orbit: NASA Astronauts Photograph the Earth* (10–12). 1996, National Geographic $40.00 (0-7922-3714-5). Fascinating details on space travel are included in this book that contains outstanding photographs of Earth from outer space. (Rev: BL 1/1–15/97; SLJ 6/97) [523]

9666 Asimov, Isaac, and Frank White. *Think about Space: Where Have We Been and Where Are We Going?* (7–10). Illus. 1989, Walker LB $21.90 (0-8027-6766-4); paper $8.95 (0-8027-6767-2). A history of space exploration and a discussion of possible future developments. (Rev: BL 10/1/89; BR 5–6/90; SLJ 11/89) [500.5]

9667 Caes, Charles J. *Studies in Starlight: Understanding Our Universe* (10–12). Illus. 1988, TAB paper $12.95 (0-8306-2946-7). A brief history of astronomy plus a discussion of the present status of astrophysics. (Rev: BL 5/15/88) [523.01]

9668 Campbell, Ann-Jeanette. *The New York Public Library Amazing Space: A Book of Answers for Kids* (5–8). Illus. 1997, Wiley paper $12.95 (0-471-14498-3). This question-and-answer book introduces space exploration, the solar system, individual planets, galaxies, and related phenomena. (Rev: SLJ 7/97) [523]

9669 Clay, Rebecca. *Space & Travel Exploration* (4–8). Illus. (Secrets of Space) 1995, Twenty-First Century LB $20.40 (0-8050-4474-4). A history of modern space exploration, covering manned flights, space stations, space probes, and telescopes. (Rev: BL 7/97; SLJ 1/98) [629.5]

9670 Craig, Roy. *UFOs: An Insider's View of the Official Quest for Evidence* (9–12). 1995, Univ. of North Texas Pr. paper $19.95 (0-929398-94-7). The controversial investigation of UFOs in the late 1960s is reviewed by a chemist and field investigator who was there. (Rev: BL 10/1/95) [001.9]

9671 Dolan, Terrance. *Probing Deep Space* (6–9). (World Explorers) 1993, Chelsea LB $19.95 (0-7910-1326-X). A chronicle of how we have learned about outer space and the challenges that remain. (Rev: BL 10/1/93; VOYA 2/94) [520]

9672 Engelbert, Phillis. *Astronomy & Space: From the Big Bang to the Big Crunch* (4–8). 1997, Gale $84.00 (0-7876-0942-0). Some 300 entries about space exploration are arranged alphabetically on such topics as the physical laws and features of the universe, the history of astronomy, prominent astronauts, observatories, and the greenhouse effect. (Rev: BL 5/1/97; BR 5–6/97; SLJ 5/97) [523]

9673 Greeley, Ronald, and Raymond Batson. *The NASA Atlas of the Solar System* (6–12). 1996, Cambridge Univ. Pr. $159.95 (0-521-56127-2). This atlas contains full-color photos, photomontages, and maps of every solid celestial body visited by NASA spacecraft (a total of 30) in the past 40 years. (Rev: BL 8/97; BR 9–10/97; SLJ 8/97) [523]

9674 Harris, Alan, and Paul Weissman. *The Great Voyager Adventure: A Guided Tour Through the*

Solar System (5–8). 1990, Messner LB $16.95 (0-671-72538-6). Two scientists introduce novices to the missions, paths, and discoveries of the Voyager spacecraft. (Rev: BL 2/1/91; SLJ 2/91) [523.4]

9675 Hepplewhite, Peter. *Unexplained: Alien Encounters* (5–8). Illus. (The Unexplained) 1998, Sterling $14.95 (0-8069-3869-2). This book describes 5 unexplained incidents supposedly involving alien encounters and supplies several theories that might account for them. (Rev: SLJ 10/98) [001.9]

9676 Kennedy, Gregory P. *Apollo to the Moon* (6–9). (World Explorers) 1992, Chelsea LB $19.95 (0-7910-1322-7). A chronicle of the Apollo moon landing expedition and descriptions of the astronauts involved. (Rev: BL 9/1/92; SLJ 7/92) [629.45]

9677 Kettelkamp, Larry. *ETs and UFOs: Are They Real?* (5–8). Illus. 1996, Morrow $16.00 (0-688-12868-8). This account tries to sort out the truth from the massive amount of material on extraterrestrials and unidentified flying objects. (Rev: BL 12/15/96; SLJ 1/97) [001.9]

9678 Lovell, Jim, and Jeffrey Kluger. *Lost Moon: The Perilous Voyage of Apollo 13* (9–12). 1994, Houghton $22.95 (0-395-67029-2). Astronaut Lovell chronicles his harrowing, nearly fatal, failed mission to the moon, describing his crew's ingenuity in returning safely to Earth. (Rev: BL 9/15/94) [629.4]

9679 McCormick, Anita Louise. *Space Exploration* (6–8). (Overview) 1994, Lucent LB $22.45 (1-56006-149-9). A review of accomplishments in space exploration and an examination of questions about the future, including what the goals should be and who should decide. (Rev: BL 7/94) [919.9]

9680 McKay, David W., and Bruce G. Smith. *Space Science Projects for Young Scientists* (7–12). Illus. 1986, Watts LB $24.00 (0-531-10244-0). A series of clearly explained projects that involve possible space environments and forces such as gravity. (Rev: BL 12/15/86; BR 1–2/87; SLJ 12/86) [500.5]

9681 Markle, Sandra. *Pioneering Space* (5–8). 1992, Atheneum LB $14.95 (0-689-31748-4). Presents basic information about space travel and spacecraft operation and speculates about how people will live in space. (Rev: BL 9/1/92; SLJ 2/93) [629.4]

9682 Marsh, Carole. *Unidentified Flying Objects and Extraterrestrial Life* (5–8). (Secrets of Space) 1996, Twenty-First Century LB $20.40 (0-8050-4472-8). This book touches on a wide range of topics associated with UFOs, including a history of famous sightings, but the emphasis is on major SETI (Search for Extra Terrestrial Intelligence) projects undertaken to detect alien radio signals. The author concludes that there is no definitive proof of the existence of intelligent life outside Earth. (Rev: BL 12/1/96; SLJ 12/96) [001.9]

9683 Millspaugh, Ben. *Aviation and Space Science Projects* (7–12). 1991, TAB $16.95 (0-8306-2157-1); paper $10.95 (0-8306-2156-3). A series of experiments for young people who want to learn more about aviation and spaceflight. (Rev: BL 1/15/92; SLJ 6/92) [507]

9684 Nardo, Don. *Flying Saucers* (6–9). Illus. (Opposing Viewpoints Great Mysteries) 1996, Greenhaven LB $17.96 (1-56510-351-3). The pros and cons concerning flying saucers are detailed in this "Opposing Viewpoints" title. (Rev: BL 4/15/96) [001.9]

9685 Neal, Valerie, et al. *Spaceflight: A Smithsonian Guide* (9–12). (Smithsonian Guide) 1995, Macmillan $38.00 (0-02-860007-X). The history of space flight beginning with Sputnik, with photos of missions, launches, landings, and designs. (Rev: BL 6/1–15/95) [629.4]

9686 Nerys, Dee. *Fortune-Telling by Playing Cards* (9–12). 1982, Sterling paper $10.95 (0-85030-266-8). How to see into the future through a deck of playing cards. [133.3]

9687 Ordway, Frederick I., III, and Randy Liebermann, eds. *Blueprint for Space: Science Fiction to Science Fact* (9–12). 1992, Smithsonian $60.00 (1-56098-072-9); paper $24.95 (1-56098-073-7). More than 20 contemporary writers spin tales of space travel from the imaginings of ancient people to real-life, present-day missions. (Rev: BL 2/1/92; SLJ 11/92) [629.4]

9688 Pogue, William R. *How Do You Go to the Bathroom in Space?* (7–12). 1991, Tor paper $7.99 (0-8125-1728-8). In a question-and-answer format, the author, who spent 84 days in space, discusses the practical aspects of space travel. (Rev: VOYA 12/85) [629.47]

9689 Randles, Jenny. *UFOs and How to See Them* (9–12). 1993, Sterling paper $14.95 (0-8069-0297-3). This illustrated field guide includes a history of the UFO mystery, identification of objects often mistaken for UFOs, and advice on organizing a skywatch. (Rev: BL 4/15/93) [001.942]

9690 Ride, Sally, and Susan Okie. *To Space and Back* (8–12). Illus. 1986, Lothrop $19.00 (0-688-06159-1); paper $12.95 (0-688-09112-1). A photo-journey that begins 4 hours before launch and ends after landing. (Rev: BL 11/86; BR 11–12/86; SLJ 11/86; VOYA 12/86) [629]

9691 Riva, Peter, and Barbara Hitchcock, comps. *Sightseeing: A Space Panorama* (8–12). Illus. 1985, Knopf $24.95 (0-394-54243-6). A spectacular view of space as pictured in 84 captioned photographs from NASA's archives. (Rev: SLJ 5/86) [629.4]

9692 Sagan, Carl. *Pale Blue Dot: A Vision of the Human Future in Space* (9–12). 1994, Random $35.00 (0-679-43841-6). Examines space exploration and humans' evolutionary urge to explore frontiers and search for their place in the universe. (Rev: BL 10/15/94*) [629]

9693 Scott, Elaine. *Close Encounters: Exploring the Universe with the Hubble Telescope* (5–8). 1998, Hyperion LB $17.49 (0-7868-2120-5). A brief history of astronomy and telescopes as well as an explanation of the amazing astronomical finds that have been made with the Hubble telescope. (Rev: BL 5/15/98; SLJ 5/98) [523]

9694 Spangenburg, Raymond, and Diane Moser. *Opening the Space Frontier* (8–12). Illus. 1989, Facts on File $22.95 (0-8160-1848-0). A history of space exploration from the fiction of Jules Verne to the realities of today. (Rev: BR 5–6/90; SLJ 4/90; VOYA 4/90) [500.5]

9695 Steele, Philip. *Space Travel* (5–8). (Pocket Facts) 1991, Macmillan LB $3.95 (0-89686-585-1). An introduction to space flight, packed with facts and photos. (Rev: BL 3/15/92) [629.4]

9696 Stott, Carole. *Space Exploration* (4–8). (Eyewitness Books) 1997, Knopf LB $20.99 (0-679-98563-8). An overview of the history of space exploration, including the various missions and their findings. (Rev: BL 11/15/97; SLJ 1/98) [523]

9697 Strieber, Whitley. *Confirmation: The Hard Evidence of Aliens among Us* (10–12). Illus. 1998, St. Martin's $23.95 (0-312-18557-X). This book presents the "hard" evidence concerning aliens that should be investigated seriously by scientists, including material on UFO sightings, close encounters, and implants that appear to have been placed in people's bodies. (Rev: BL 3/15/98; SLJ 11/98) [001.9]

9698 Vogt, Gregory L. *Viking and the Mars Landing* (6–10). 1991, Millbrook LB $22.40 (1-878841-32-7). This book focuses on the U.S. space program, detailing specific missions and accomplishments since the space age began with details on the Mars landing. (Rev: BL 3/1/91) [629.4354]

9699 Wilson, Colin. *UFOs and Aliens* (5–8). Illus. 1997, DK Publg. $14.95 (0-7894-2166-6). Double-page spreads focus on occurrences that suggest visits by aliens, including stories of abduction and UFO sightings, and a few headline-making hoaxes. (Rev: BL 2/1/98; SLJ 2/98) [001.942]

Comets, Meteors, and Asteroids

9700 Asimov, Isaac. *How Did We Find Out about Comets?* (6–9). Illus. 1975, Walker LB $20.90 (0-8027-6204-2). After introducing comets, this volume outlines our knowledge and attitudes about comets from ancient times to today. [523.6]

9701 Bortz, Fred. *Martian Fossils on Earth? The Story of Meteorite ALH 84001* (5–9). 1997, Millbrook LB $21.40 (0-7613-0270-0). The story of the meteorite discovered in Antarctica that hints that life might have once existed on Mars, and the massive scientific investigation it has caused. (Rev: BL 1/1–15/98; SLJ 3/98) [523.5]

9702 Gallant, Roy A. *The Day the Sky Split Apart: Investigating a Cosmic Mystery* (7–12). 1995, Atheneum $16.00 (0-689-80323-0). An examination of the Tunguska meteorite that exploded over Siberia in 1908 and subsequent research on this "cosmic mystery." (Rev: BL 12/1/95; SLJ 11/95; VOYA 4/96) [523.5]

9703 Hutchinson, Robert, and Andrew Graham, eds. *Meteorites* (9–12). 1994, Sterling paper $12.95 (0-8069-0489-5). Questions and answers about natural objects that fall from space, with illustrations. (Rev: BL 1/1/94; SLJ 5/94) [523.5]

9704 Sagan, Carl, and Ann Druyan. *Comet* (9–12). Illus. 1985, Random $27.50 (0-394-54908-2). A richly illustrated book about all kinds of comets, but Halley's in particular. (Rev: BL 10/1/85; BR 11–12/86; VOYA 8/86) [523.6]

9705 Yeomans, Donald. *Comets: A Chronological History of Observation, Science, Myth, and Folklore* (9–12). 1991, Wiley $35.00 (0-471-61011-9). Examines the origins of comets and current scientific theories surrounding them through 1990. (Rev: BL 2/1/91) [523.6]

Earth and the Moon

9706 Alessandrello, Anna. *The Earth: Origins and Evolution* (4–8). Illus. (Beginnings) 1995, Raintree Steck-Vaughn LB $24.26 (0-8114-3331-5). An oversize book that discusses with lavish illustrations the theories on the formation of the earth, its structure and composition, and ways in which it is changing. (Rev: BL 4/15/95; SLJ 6/95) [550]

9707 Erickson, John. *A History of Life on Earth: Understanding Our Planet's Past* (10–12). (The Changing Earth) 1995, Facts on File $26.95 (0-8160-3131-2). A chronological study of life on this planet that spans billions of years, describing Earth's origins and its geological and biological history. (Rev: SLJ 5/96; VOYA 2/96) [575]

9708 Erickson, Jon. *Exploring Earth from Space* (8–12). Illus. 1989, TAB paper $15.95 (0-8306-3242-5). Beginning with the history of space exploration, this account also covers how we on Earth

profit from the use of space. (Rev: BR 1–2/90) [500.5]

9709 Gallant, Roy A., and Christopher J. Schuberth. *Earth: The Making of a Planet* (7–10). Illus. 1998, Marshall Cavendish LB $14.95 (0-7614-5012-2). Beginning with the big bang, this book describes the creation of Earth, with material on landforms, seas, the moon, rocks and minerals, and the ocean floor, and speculates about Earth's future. (Rev: BL 7/98; BR 11–12/98; SLJ 7/98) [550]

9710 Hockey, Thomas A. *The Book of the Moon* (10–12). Illus. 1986, Prentice Hall $19.95 (0-13-079971-8). Although mainly about the moon, this book also furnishes information on space exploration and astronomy. (Rev: BL 10/15/86) [523.3]

9711 Johnson, Kirk R., and Richard K. Stucky. *Prehistoric Journey* (10–12). 1995, Roberts Rinehart paper $19.95 (1-57098-145-4). A chronology of the evolution of life on Earth from its creation 4.6 billion years ago to the present. (Rev: BR 5–6/96; SLJ 5/96; VOYA 8/97) [575]

Stars

9712 Clay, Rebecca. *Stars and Galaxies* (4–8). (Secrets of Space) 1997, Twenty-First Century LB $22.40 (0-8050-4476-0). This book describes galaxies and their composition and the birth and death of stars. (Rev: BL 9/15/97; SLJ 6/97) [523.8]

9713 Gustafson, John. *Stars, Clusters and Galaxies: The Young Stargazer's Guide to the Galaxy* (5–8). (Young Stargazer's Guide to the Galaxy) 1993, Simon & Schuster LB $18.95 (0-671-72536-X); paper $6.95 (0-671-72537-8). Introduces stars, binary stars, star clusters, nebulae, and galaxies, and provides tips for viewing the night sky through binoculars and telescopes. (Rev: BL 7/93; SLJ 6/93; VOYA 10/93) [523.8]

9714 Menzel, Donald H., and Jay M. Pasachoff. *A Field Guide to the Stars and Planets*. 2nd ed. (7–12). Illus. 1983, Houghton $19.95 (0-395-34641-X); paper $14.95 (0-395-34835-8). Photographs, sky maps, charts, and timetables are features of this volume in the Peterson Field Guide series. [523]

9715 VanCleave, Janice. *Janice VanCleave's Constellations for Every Kid: Easy Activities That Make Learning Science Fun* (8–12). Illus. 1997, Wiley $29.95 (0-471-15981-6); paper $12.95 (0-471-15979-4). An excellent guide to the heavens, with each chapter presenting a different constellation with concise facts, new concepts, simple activities, and solutions to problems. (Rev: BL 12/1/97; SLJ 10/97) [523.8]

Sun and the Solar System

9716 Adams, Florence. *Catch a Sunbeam: A Book of Solar Study and Experiments* (7–9). Illus. 1978, Harcourt $10.95 (0-15-215197-4). With simple materials, 16 experiments using solar energy are described. [621.47]

9717 Cattermole, Peter. *Mars: The Story of the Red Planet* (9–12). 1992, Chapman & Hall paper $59.95 (0-412-44140-3). A detailed, technical look at the scientific study of Mars, filled with photos, graphs, and charts. (Rev: BL 10/1/92) [523.43]

9718 Cooper, Henry S. F. *The Evening Star: Venus Observed* (9–12). 1993, Farrar $22.00 (0-374-15000-1). An account of the 1989 Magellan spacecraft launched to gather data on Venus. (Rev: BL 7/93) [523.4]

9719 Dickinson, Terence. *Other Worlds: A Beginner's Guide to Planets and Moons* (5–9). Illus. 1995, Firefly LB $19.95 (1-895565-71-5); paper $9.95 (1-895565-70-7). An entertaining, well-illustrated introduction to the solar system, the planets, important moons, comets, brown dwarfs, and the search for evidence of other planetary systems. (Rev: BL 11/15/95; SLJ 1/96) [523.4]

9720 Evans, Barry. *The Wrong Way Comet and Other Mysteries of Our Solar System: Essays* (9–12). 1992, TAB $22.95 (0-8306-2679-4); paper $14.95 (0-8306-2670-0). An introduction to mysteries of the solar system in a series of informal essays. (Rev: BL 3/15/92) [523.2]

9721 Fradin, Dennis B. *The Planet Hunters: The Search for Other Worlds* (5–8). Illus. 1997, Simon & Schuster paper $19.95 (0-689-81323-6). This well-researched book traces the search for other worlds from the time of early civilization and the discovery of each of the planets, including the difficulty scientists had convincing the world that the Earth is also a planet. (Rev: BL 12/1/97; BR 3–4/98; SLJ 1/98) [523.4]

9722 Gallant, Roy A. *When the Sun Dies* (6–10). 1998, Marshall Cavendish LB $14.95 (0-7614-5036-X). After discussing the history and structure of the solar system, the author gives a blow-by-blow account of the Sun's last 9 billion years and his projections for its likely ending about a billion years from now. (Rev: SLJ 1/99; VOYA 6/99) [523.2]

9723 Lauber, Patricia. *Journey to the Planets* (5–8). 1990, Crown LB $16.99 (0-517-58125-6). Information and insights into the solar system, including facts gathered after the Voyager fly-by of Neptune in 1989. (Rev: BL 1/1/91) [523.4]

9724 Raeburn, Paul. *Mars: Uncovering the Secrets of the Red Planet* (9–12). 1998, National Geographic $40.00 (0-7922-7373-7). With magnificent illustrations ranging from superpanoramas to technical drawings, this book describes the findings of the Mars Pathfinder expedition and the work of the rover named Sojourner. (Rev: BL 8/98; SLJ 4/99) [523.2]

9725 Ripley, S. Dillon. *Fire of Life: The Smithsonian Book of the Sun* (10–12). Illus. 1981, Norton $24.95 (0-393-80006-7). This book describes what we know about the Sun and its effects on the environments of planets including the Earth. [523.7]

9726 Spangenburg, Raymond, and Diane Moser. *Exploring the Reaches of the Solar System* (7–10). Illus. 1990, Facts on File $22.95 (0-8160-1850-2). This is a fine summary of what the space probes have told us about the solar system. For historical information use *Opening the Space Frontier* (1989). (Rev: BL 4/15/90; SLJ 12/90) [639]

9727 Vogt, Gregory L. *The Solar System: Facts and Exploration* (5–8). 1995, Twenty-First Century LB $22.40 (0-8050-3249-5). A readable guide to the planets and moons and other bodies in the solar system. Includes images from the Hubble telescope and explanations of terms. (Rev: BL 12/1/95; SLJ 11/95; VOYA 4/96) [523.2]

9728 Wunsch, Susi Trautmann. *The Adventures of Sojourner: The Mission to Mars that Thrilled the World* (5–9). 1998, Mikaya LB $22.95 (0-9650493-5-3); paper $9.95 (0-9650493-6-1). The exciting story of the Mars Pathfinder mission and the success of the Sojourner rover. (Rev: SLJ 2/99) [523]

Universe

9729 Couper, Heather, and Nigel Henbest. *Big Bang* (5–8). Illus. 1997, DK Publg. $16.95 (0-7894-1484-8). This work explains, in double-page spreads, the Big Bang theory and it implications for the future. (Rev: BL 6/1–15/97; SLJ 8/97) [523.1]

9730 Couper, Heather, and Nigel Henbest. *Black Holes* (6–9). Illus. 1996, DK Publg. $16.95 (0-7894-0451-6). Complicated scientific principles related to black holes and other fascinating phenomena are explained simply and with many illustrations on double-page spreads. (Rev: BL 8/96; BR 11–12/96; SLJ 7/96; VOYA 4/97) [523.8]

9731 Jacobs, Francine. *Cosmic Countdown: What Astronomers Have Learned about the Life of the Universe* (7–9). Illus. 1983, M. Evans $9.95 (0-87131-404-5). The Big Bang theory, the life of stars, and radio astronomy are 3 topics covered here. [523.1]

9732 Kallen, Stuart A. *Exploring the Origins of the Universe* (4–8). (Secrets of Space) 1997, Twenty-

First Century LB $20.40 (0-8050-4478-7). This account explains in simple terms the major theories about how the universe was created, including creation stories and the Big Bang theory. (Rev: BL 9/15/97; SLJ 6/97) [523]

9733 Miotto, Enrico. *The Universe: Origins and Evolution* (5–8). (Beginnings) 1995, Raintree Steck-Vaughn LB $22.80 (0-8114-3334-X). This basic outline of the history of the universe begins with the Big Bang theory and finishes with the "Big Crunch" that may end time. (Rev: BL 4/15/95) [523.1]

9734 Rosen, Joe. *The Capricious Cosmos: Universe Beyond Law* (9–12). 1992, Macmillan $19.95 (0-02-604931-7). An discussion of the nature of science and metaphysics and the impact of modern science on humankind. (Rev: BL 2/15/92) [523.1]

9735 Ruiz, Andres L. *The Origin of the Universe* (4–9). (Sequences of Earth and Space) 1997, Sterling $12.95 (0-8069-9744-3). In simple, concise language, this work discusses various theories concerning the origin of the universe, including the Big Bang theory. (Rev: BL 12/15/97) [523]

Biological Sciences

General and Miscellaneous

9736 Amos, William H., and Stephen H. Amos. *Atlantic & Gulf Coasts* (9–12). Illus. 1985, Knopf paper $19.95 (0-394-73109-3). This volume describes the habitat thoroughly and then identifies the species that live there. (Rev: BL 7/85; SLJ 9/85) [574.5]

9737 Berrill, Michael, and Deborah Berrill. *A Sierra Club Naturalist's Guide to the North Atlantic Coast: Cape Cod to Newfoundland* (10–12). Illus. 1981, Sierra Club paper $16.00 (0-87156-243-X). As well as the general geology and climate of this region, there is extensive coverage on the marine habitats for animal and plant life that these coastlines contain. [574.9]

9738 Bowler, Peter J. *The Norton History of the Environmental Sciences* (9–12). 1993, Norton $35.00 (0-393-03535-2); paper $17.95 (0-393-31042-6). Historical highlights and development of the environmental sciences. (Rev: BL 7/93) [363.7]

9739 Brooks, Bruce. *The Red Wasteland* (6–10). 1995, Holt $15.95 (0-8050-4495-7). A fine anthology of essays, stories, poems, and book excerpts by some of the best nature writers, who raise themes and questions about crucial issues related to the environment. (Rev: BL 8/98; BR 1–2/99; SLJ 6/98; VOYA 8/98) [808]

9740 *DK Nature Encyclopedia* (5–8). 1998, DK Publg. $29.95 (0-7894-3411-3). A browsable reference book that covers topics like classification of living things, ecology, the origins and evolution of life, specific animal and plant groups, and the inner workings of plants and animals, all in a series of beautifully illustrated double-page spreads. (Rev: BL 12/1/98; SLJ 2/99) [574]

9741 Duensing, Edward, and A. B. Millmoss. *Backyard and Beyond: A Guide for Discovering the Outdoors* (9–12). 1992, Fulcrum paper $19.95 (1-55591-071-8). Descriptions of various animals, plants, and insects, with tips on how to observe and track them. (Rev: BL 3/15/92) [508.2]

9742 Hoagland, Mahlon, and Bert Dodson. *The Way Life Works* (9–12). 1995, Times Bks. $35.00 (0-8129-2020-1). A collaboration between Hoagland, a molecular biologist, and Dodson, an artist, emphasizing the unity of life rather than its differences. (Rev: BL 12/1/95) [574]

9743 Latourrette, Joe. *The National Wildlife Federation's Wildlife Watcher's Handbook: A Guide to Observing Animals in the Wild* (10–12). Illus. 1997, Holt paper $12.95 (0-8050-4685-2). A practical, informative handbook on how to observe wildlife effectively in habitat regions in the United States and Canada. (Rev: SLJ 4/98) [591]

9744 Lawlor, Elizabeth P. *Discover Nature at Sundown: Things to Know and Things to Do* (9–12). 1995, Stackpole paper $14.95 (0-8117-2527-8). Sensory awareness for nature lovers to track and observe creatures at night. (Rev: BL 2/15/95) [591.5]

9745 Murray, John A., ed. *American Nature Writing* (9–12). 1994, Sierra Club paper $12.00 (0-87156-479-3). The first of an annual anthology of writings (including poetry) about nature. There are also volumes for 1995, 1996, 1997, 1998, and 1999. (Rev: BL 4/15/94) [810]

9746 Murray, John A., ed. *Nature's New Voices* (9–12). 1992, Fulcrum paper $15.95 (1-55591-117-X). Personal literary observations on natural history by a contemporary generation of nature essayists. (Rev: BL 10/1/92) [508.73]

9747 Patent, Dorothy Hinshaw. *Biodiversity* (6–10). Illus. 1996, Clarion $18.00 (0-395-68704-7). This book discusses broad topics like habitats, ecosystems, and important species to show the connections between everything in nature. (Rev: BL 12/1/96; SLJ 12/96*) [333.95]

9748 Peck, Robert McCracken. *Land of the Eagle: A Natural History of North America* (9–12). 1991, BBC Books $30.00 (0-671-75596-X). A descriptive celebration of the North American terrain and animal and plant life as experienced by its native peoples and European settlers. (Rev: BL 11/15/91; SLJ 4/92) [508.7]

9749 Quinn, John R. *Wildlife Survivors: The Flora and Fauna of Tomorrow* (9–12). 1994, TAB $21.95 (0-8306-4346-X); paper $12.95 (0-8306-4345-1). A serious study that explores the concept that plants and animals will continue to survive despite the encroachment of human civilization. (Rev: BL 3/1/94) [574.5]

9750 Raham, R. Gary. *Dinosaurs in the Garden: An Evolutionary Guide to Backyard Biology* (6–10). Illus. 1988, Plexus $22.95 (0-937548-10-3). The author uses common creatures to explain how they fit into the scheme of nature and overall patterns of evolution. (Rev: BL 12/1/88) [575]

9751 Silverstein, Alvin, and Virginia Silverstein. *Food Chains* (6–9). (Science Concepts) 1998, Twenty-First Century LB $23.40 (0-7613-3002-X). A clearly written account that explains the concept of food chains, with background information and many examples, and reviews the most current information. (Rev: SLJ 1/99) [574.5]

9752 Silverstein, Alvin, and Virginia Silverstein. *Symbiosis* (5–9). (Science Concepts) 1998, Twenty-First Century $23.40 (0-7613-3001-1). The concept of cooperation in nature to produce mutual benefits is explored, with explanations of various forms of symbiotic partnerships, such as mutualism, commensalism, and parasitism, and discussion of the symbiotic relationships that humans have with animals, plants, fungi, and microorganisms. (Rev: SLJ 2/99) [574.5]

9753 Squire, Ann. *101 Questions and Answers About Backyard Wildlife* (5–8). Illus. 1996, Walker LB $16.85 (0-8027-8458-5). Using a question-and-answer format, this work provides fascinating information about common insects, birds, mammals, and reptiles. (Rev: SLJ 1/97; VOYA 8/97) [574]

9754 VanCleave, Janice. *Janice VanCleave's A+ Projects in Biology: Winning Experiments for Science Fairs and Extra Credit* (6–10). 1993, Wiley paper $12.95 (0-471-58628-5). Offers a variety of experiments in botany, zoology, and the human body. (Rev: BL 1/15/94; SLJ 11/93) [574]

9755 Walker, Richard. *The Visual Dictionary of the Skeleton* (5–10). (Eyewitness Visual Dictionaries) 1995, DK Publg. $18.95 (0-7894-0135-5). This handsomely illustrated dictionary is divided into two parts: skeleton varieties (human, animal, fish, insect, and plant), and bone structure and function. (Rev: SLJ 1/96; VOYA 6/96) [611]

Botany

General and Miscellaneous

9756 Bonnet, Robert L., and G. Daniel Keen. *Botany: 49 Science Fair Projects* (6–10). Illus. 1989, TAB $16.95 (0-8306-9277-0). Well-explained projects involving such phenomena as photosynthesis, hydroponics, fungi, and germination. (Rev: BL 1/15/90; BR 1–2/90; VOYA 2/90) [581]

9757 Ross, Bill. *Straight from the Bear's Mouth: The Story of Photosynthesis* (6–9). 1995, Atheneum $16.00 (0-689-31726-3). Young people at a science camp are asked to develop hypotheses and test them, in the process gaining knowledge about chemistry, physics, and botany. (Rev: BL 12/1/95; SLJ 12/95) [581.1]

9758 Silverstein, Alvin, and Virginia Silverstein. *Photosynthesis* (5–9). (Science Concepts) 1998, Twenty-First Century $23.40 (0-7613-3000-3). This book explains the process of photosynthesis, describes the history of discoveries leading to understanding photosynthesis, and discusses the relationship of photosynthesis to acid rain, the greenhouse effect, and scientific knowledge as a whole. (Rev: SLJ 2/99) [581.1]

Foods, Farms, and Ranches

GENERAL AND MISCELLANEOUS

9759 Busenberg, Bonnie. *Vanilla, Chocolate and Strawberry: The Story of Your Favorite Flavors* (6–9). Illus. (Discovery!) 1994, Lerner LB $23.95 (0-8225-1573-3). With the generous use of maps, diagrams, and photographs, this is the breezy overview of 3 popular flavors, how they are produced, and how they are used. (Rev: BL 6/1–15/94) [664.5]

9760 Chandler, Gary, and Kevin Graham. *Natural Foods and Products* (4–8). Illus. (Making a Better World) 1996, Twenty-First Century LB $20.40 (0-8050-4623-2). This title discusses genetically engineered foods and eco-friendly products and companies, with examples of new processes that are in harmony with nature. (Rev: BL 12/15/96; SLJ 1/97) [333.76]

9761 Halley, Ned. *Farm* (4–9). Illus. (Eyewitness Books) 1996, Knopf LB $20.99 (0-679-98078-4). This book takes a behind-the-scenes look at a farm, explaining with many illustrations its inner workings and the problems and rewards involved in managing one. (Rev: BL 6/1–15/96; SLJ 7/96) [630]

9762 Hughes, Meredith Sayles. *Glorious Grasses: The Grains* (5–8). (Plants We Eat) 1999, Lerner LB $23.93 (0-8225-2831-2). A description of the history, cultivation, processing, and dietary importance of wheat, rice, corn, millet, barley, oats, and rye. (Rev: BL 7/99; SLJ 8/99) [633.1]

9763 Igoe, Robert S. *Dictionary of Food Ingredients* (10–12). 1989, Van Nostrand paper $39.95 (0-442-31927-4). A dictionary of the approximately 1,000 food ingredients approved by the Food and Drug Administration. [664]

9764 Johnson, Sylvia A. *Potatoes, Tomatoes, Corn, & Beans: How the Foods in America Changed the World* (6–10). Illus. 1997, Simon & Schuster $16.00 (0-689-80141-6). The story of common foods that originated in America is told in this blend of history, botany, culinary arts, and geography. (Rev: BL 4/15/97; BR 11–12/97; SLJ 5/97; VOYA 12/97) [641.6]

9765 Marshall, Elizabeth L. *High-Tech Harvest: A Look at Genetically Engineered Foods* (6–9). 1999, Watts $24.00 (0-531-11434-1). A thorough discussion of gene manipulation and its results when applied to food production, such as cloning Dolly the sheep and producing the Flavr Savr tomato. (Rev: BL 5/15/99; SLJ 7/99) [641.3]

9766 Meltzer, Milton. *Food* (4–8). 1998, Millbrook $23.90 (0-7613-0354-5). A general history of food and interesting anecdotes about particular foods are presented in brief chapters like, "How Conquistadors Brought Chocolate to the World," and "How Pizza Came to America." (Rev: BL 1/1–15/99; SLJ 1/99) [641.3]

9767 Mott, Lawrie, and Karen Snyder. *Pesticide Alert: A Guide to Pesticides in Fruit and Vegetables* (10–12). Illus. 1988, Sierra Club paper $6.95 (0-87156-726-1). A guide to all the pesticides that are used in farming today, their effects, and how to remove them from fruits and vegetables. (Rev: BL 5/1/88; SLJ 7/89) [668]

9768 Paladino, Catherine. *One Good Apple: Growing Our Food for the Sake of the Earth* (4–8). 1999, Houghton $15.00 (0-395-85009-6). This photoessay describes the range and effects of the use of pesticides in this country, the government's response, and alternatives offered by organic farming, Community Supported Agriculture, and seed-saving organizations. (Rev: BL 4/1/99; SLJ 4/99) [630]

9769 Patent, Dorothy Hinshaw. *The Vanishing Feast: How Dwindling Genetic Diversity Threatens the World's Food Supply* (6–10). 1994, Harcourt $17.95 (0-15-292867-7). Explains the importance of maintaining plant and animal diversity and describes experiments with genetic engineering and factory farming. (Rev: BL 10/1/94; SLJ 12/94; VOYA 4/95) [338.1]

9770 Tesar, Jenny. *Food and Water: Threats, Shortages and Solutions* (5–9). (Our Fragile Planet) 1992, Facts on File LB $19.95 (0-8160-2495-2). A discussion of the world's water and food supplies, threats to them, and possible solutions. (Rev: BL 6/1/92) [333.91]

9771 VanCleave, Janice. *Janice VanCleave's Food and Nutrition for Every Kid: Easy Activities That Make Learning Science Fun* (4–8). Illus. (Science for Every Kid) 1999, Wiley $27.95 (0-471-17666-4); paper $12.95 (0-471-17665-6). Each of the 25 chapters in this book contains information about food, including food groups, the relationship between energy and food, how to read nutrition labels, and vitamins and minerals, plus dozens of easily performed projects that demonstrate these facts and concepts. (Rev: SLJ 8/99) [641.3]

9772 Wardlaw, Lee. *Bubblemania* (4–8). 1997, Simon & Schuster paper $4.99 (0-689-81719-3). A thorough history of chewing gum is given, plus descriptions of how gum in made, marketed, and distributed. (Rev: BL 10/1/97; SLJ 1/98) [641.3]

9773 Zubrowski, Bernie. *Soda Science: Designing and Testing Soft Drinks* (5–8). Illus. 1997, Morrow LB $14.93 (0-688-13917-5). More than 50 experiments explore the properties of soft drinks and give directions for producing and bottling one's own product. (Rev: BL 8/97; SLJ 10/97) [641.8]

VEGETABLES

9774 Hughes, Meredith Sayles. *Cool as a Cucumber, Hot as a Pepper* (5–8). (Foods We Eat) 1999, Lerner LB $23.93 (0-8225-2832-0). This lively book on vegetables gives botanical information, details on growing and harvesting, the history of many of these plants, and a number of mouth-watering recipes. (Rev: BL 7/99; SLJ 8/99) [635]

9775 Hughes, Meredith Sayles. *Stinky and Stringy: Stem & Bulb Vegetables* (5–8). (Plants We Eat) 1999, Lerner LB $23.93 (0-8225-2833-9). Stem and bulb vegetables onions and garlic are introduced with interesting historical information, details about their cultivation, harvesting and marketing, and a few tempting recipes. (Rev: BL 7/99; SLJ 8/99) [641.3]

9776 Phillips, Roger, and Martyn Rix. *The Random House Book of Vegetables* (9–12). (Random House Garden) 1994, Random paper $25.00 (0-679-75024-X). Reviews the vegetable families and the history of vegetables, and offers advice on cultivation, fertilization, and pest control. (Rev: BL 2/15/94) [635]

Forestry and Trees

9777 Beil, Karen Magnuson. *Fire in Their Eyes: Wildfires and the People Who Fight Them* (5–8). 1999, Harcourt paper $10.00 (0-15-201042-4). Dramatic pictures and text show the life, work, and training of firefighters, with additional material on the role of fire in nature. (Rev: SLJ 7/99) [581.5]

9778 Brockman, C. Frank. *Trees of North America* (7–12). Illus. 1998, Demco $19.05 (0-606-12005-X). This handy guide identifies 594 different trees that grow north of Mexico. [582.16]

9779 Burnie, David. *Tree* (6–8). Illus. 1988, Knopf LB $20.99 (0-394-99617-8). In a series of short, lushly illustrated chapters such topics as bark, leaves, cones, and tree diseases are introduced. (Rev: SLJ 12/88) [582.12]

9780 Cassie, Brian. *National Audubon Society First Field Guide: Trees* (4–8). 1999, Scholastic $17.95 (0-590-05472-4); paper $11.95 (0-590-05490-2). After a general, illustrated introduction to the characteristics and types of North American trees, this field guide then categorizes the trees according to the shape of their leaves. (Rev: SLJ 7/99) [582.16]

9781 Challand, Helen J. *Vanishing Forests* (5–8). (Saving Planet Earth) 1991, Children's Pr. LB $30.50 (0-516-05505-4). Interactive study of an alarming environmental problem. (Rev: BL 3/1/92; SLJ 3/92) [333.75]

9782 Forsyth, Adrian. *How Monkeys Make Chocolate: Foods and Medicines from the Rainforests* (5–8). 1995, Firefly $16.95 (1-895688-45-0); paper $9.95 (1-895688-32-9). A conservation biologist presents a narrative with a sense of wonder for the interdependence of plants, animals, and humans. (Rev: BL 12/1/95; SLJ 1/96) [581.6]

9783 Gallant, Roy A. *Earth's Vanishing Forests* (6–10). 1991, Macmillan LB $14.95 (0-02-735774-0). A carefully researched examination of the reasons for the destruction of the planet's forests and the implications of their loss. (Rev: BL 10/1/91; SLJ 5/92) [333.75]

9784 Gardner, Robert, and David Webster. *Science Project Ideas about Trees* (5–8). Illus. 1997, Enslow LB $18.95 (0-89490-846-4). The parts of trees and their functions are described, with activities involving leaves, seeds, flowers, roots, and twigs. (Rev: BL 12/1/97; BR 5–6/98; SLJ 2/98) [582.16]

9785 Little, Elbert L. *The Audubon Society Field Guide to North American Trees: Eastern Region* (7–12). Illus. 1980, Knopf $19.00 (0-394-50760-6). This volume describes through text and pictures of leaves, needles, and so on, the trees found east of the Rocky Mountains. [582.16]

9786 Little, Elbert L. *The Audubon Society Field Guide to North American Trees: Western Region* (7–12). Illus. 1980, Knopf $19.00 (0-394-50761-4). Trees east of the Rockies are identified and pictured in photos and drawings. [582.16]

9787 Patent, Dorothy Hinshaw. *Fire: Friend or Foe* (4–8). 1998, Clarion $16.00 (0-395-73081-3). Using a concise text and excellent photographs, the author describes the causes of forest fires, their effect on the land, and the equipment and practices used by firefighters, and discusses the growing belief that fire is part of the natural cycle of renewal and scientific evidence refuting the concept that fire is deadly to all wildlife. (Rev: BL 11/15/98; SLJ 12/98) [577.2]

9788 Petrides, George A. *A Field Guide to Trees and Shrubs* (7–12). Illus. 1972, Houghton paper $16.95 (0-395-17579-8). A total of 646 varieties found in northern United States and southern Canada are described and illustrated. [582.1]

Plants and Flowers

9789 Angier, Bradford. *Field Guide to Medicinal Wild Plants* (10–12). Illus. 1978, Stackpole paper $18.95 (0-8117-2076-4). With many color illustrations the author introduces more than 100 wild medicinal plants, many of them originally used by primitive tribes. [581.6]

9790 Arnold, Katya, and Sam Swope. *Katya's Book of Mushrooms* (5–8). Illus. 1997, Holt $16.95 (0-8050-4136-2). A field manual on edible and poisonous mushrooms, how to find and identify them, and the folklore surrounding them. (Rev: BL 4/1/97; SLJ 4/97) [589.2]

9791 Buckles, Mary Parker. *The Flowers Around Us: A Photographic Essay on their Reproductive Structures* (10–12). Illus. 1985, Univ. of Missouri Pr. $29.95 (0-8262-0402-3). Through photographs and text, the author shows the reproductive parts of various flowers and how they function in the production of seeds. (Rev: BL 12/1/85) [582]

9792 Burnie, David. *Plant* (5–9). Illus. 1989, Knopf LB $20.99 (0-394-92252-2). Extraordinary photographs and clear text are used to introduce the plant world. (Rev: BL 10/15/89) [581]

9793 Busch, Phyllis B. *Wildflowers and the Stories behind Their Names* (7–9). Illus. 1977, Macmillan $10.00 (0-684-14820-X). In this compact volume, 60 wildflowers are identified and pictured. [582.13]

9794 Dowden, Anne O. *The Clover & the Bee: A Book of Pollination* (5–10). Illus. 1990, HarperCollins LB $17.89 (0-690-04679-0). An account that introduces the parts of flowers, the need for pollination, and how it is accomplished. (Rev: BL 5/15/90; SLJ 7/90; VOYA 6/90) [582]

9795 Dowden, Anne O. *From Flower to Fruit* (6–9). Illus. 1984, HarperCollins $14.95 (0-690-04402-X). A description of seeds, how they are scattered, and how fruit is produced. [582]

9796 Garassino, Alessandro. *Plants: Origins and Evolution* (5–8). (Beginnings) 1995, Raintree Steck-Vaughn LB $24.26 (0-8114-3332-3). This treatment of plant evolution includes good factual data and discussion of several important concepts. (Rev: BL 4/15/95) [581.3]

9797 Gardner, Robert. *Science Projects about Plants* (5–8). (Science Projects) 1999, Enslow $19.95 (0-89490-952-5). This book contains a series of fascinating experiments and projects involving seeds, leaves, roots, stems, flowers, and whole plants. (Rev: BL 2/15/99; BR 5–6/99; SLJ 5/99) [580.78]

9798 Hood, Susan, and National Audubon Society, eds. *Wildflowers* (5–8). Illus. 1998, Scholastic $24.99 (0-590-05464-3). Fifty common wildflowers are pictured and described, along with information on what equipment to use and what to look for to observe and study wildflowers (leaves, blooms, habitat, height, range). (Rev: BL 8/98; SLJ 8/98) [583]

9799 Hudler, George W. *Magical Mushrooms, Mischievous Molds* (9–12). 1998, Princeton Univ. Pr. $29.95 (0-691-02873-7). This is a fact-filled, enjoyable history of how fungi have changed history and our lives, from the potato blight in Ireland that caused starvation and mass immigration to the United States to "sick building syndrome," penicillin, athlete's foot, and mushrooms in a salad. (Rev: SLJ 5/99) [589.2]

9800 Johnson, Sylvia A. *Roses Red, Violets Blue: Why Flowers Have Colors* (5–8). Illus. 1991, Lerner LB $23.95 (0-8225-1594-6). An examination of the role of color in the life of plants and its function in reproduction and communication. Includes photos and drawings. (Rev: BL 12/1/91; SLJ 1/92*) [582.13]

9801 Kowalchik, Claire, and William H. Hylton, eds. *Rodale's Illustrated Encyclopedia of Herbs* (9–12). Illus. 1987, Rodale $26.95 (0-87857-699-1). In addition to an alphabetically arranged description of each herb, this lavishly illustrated volume contains background historical material, plus coverage of such subjects as medicinal uses, cooking, and gardening. (Rev: BL 10/15/87) [635]

9802 Lincoff, Gary. *The Audubon Society Field Guide to North American Mushrooms* (7–12). Illus. 1981, Knopf $19.00 (0-394-51992-2). Over 700 species are introduced and pictured in color photographs. [589.2]

9803 Niehaus, Theodore F. *A Field Guide to Pacific States Wildflowers* (7–12). Illus. 1976, Houghton paper $18.00 (0-395-31662-6). About 1,500 wild-flowers from the Pacific states are highlighted in this volume of the Peterson Field Guide series. [582.13]

9804 Niering, William A., and Nancy C. Olmstead. *The Audubon Society Field Guide to North American Wildflowers: Eastern Region* (7–12). Illus. 1979, Knopf $19.00 (0-394-50432-1). From the Rockies to the Atlantic this guide identifies, describes, and pictures the most common wildflowers. [582.13]

9805 Overbeck, Cynthia. *Carnivorous Plants* (7–9). Illus. 1982, Lerner LB $22.60 (0-8225-1470-2). An explanation of how these plants evolved plus examples in text and pictures. [581.5]

9806 Pope, Joyce. *Practical Plants* (5–8). (Plant Life) 1990, Facts on File $15.95 (0-8160-2424-3). Outlines uses of plants, ranging from providing oxygen to supplying humans with food, medicine, and fiber. (Rev: BL 6/15/91; SLJ 8/91) [581.6]

9807 Reader's Digest, eds. *Magic and Medicine of Plants* (9–12). Illus. 1986, Random $28.00 (0-89577-221-3). Information about medicinal plants that covers fields like pharmacolognosy, myth, botany, and folklore. (Rev: BL 12/86; SLJ 5/87) [581.6]

9808 Reading, Susan. *Plants of the Tropics* (5–8). (Plant Life) 1990, Facts on File $15.95 (0-8160-2423-5). A tour of the rain forest, with descriptions of plants, their means of survival, and their partnership with animals. (Rev: BL 6/15/91; SLJ 8/91) [581.909]

9809 Richardson, P. Mick. *Flowering Plants: Magic in Bloom* (9–12). Illus. 1986, Chelsea LB $19.95 (0-87754-757-2). The story of plant-derived hallucinogenic substances is given plus information on their effects and their role in world folklore and religion. (Rev: BL 4/15/87) [398]

9810 Silverstein, Alvin, and Virginia Silverstein. *Plants* (7–10). (Kingdoms of Life) 1996, Twenty-First Century LB $21.40 (0-8050-3519-2). The classification system of plants is explained, from simple plants through ferns and on to flowering plants. (Rev: BL 6/1–15/96; SLJ 7/96) [581]

9811 Spellenberg, Richard. *The Audubon Society Field Guide to North American Wildflowers: Western Region* (7–12). Illus. 1979, Knopf $19.00 (0-394-50431-3). From California to Alaska this is a guide to more than 600 western wildflowers. [582.13]

9812 Taylor, Barbara. *Incredible Plants* (5–9). (Inside Guides) 1997, DK Publg. $15.95 (0-7894-1505-4). Using impressive reproductions of 3-dimensional models, this work introduces the parts of plants and their functions, reproduction in flowering, and nonflowering plants, defense, animal traps, cacti, succulents, and other topics related to plants. (Rev: SLJ 8/97) [580]

Zoology

General and Miscellaneous

9813 Aaseng, Nathan. *Invertebrates* (5–9). 1993, Watts LB $25.00 (0-531-12550-5). A discussion of the 95 percent of the world's population made up of invertebrates. (Rev: BL 3/15/94; SLJ 3/94) [592]

9814 Bix, Cynthia O., and Diana Landau. *Animal Athletes: Olympians of the Wild World* (5–8). Illus. 1996, Andrews & McMeel $15.95 (0-8362-2522-8). This book describes 15 of the biggest, strongest, and fastest animals, with details on their athletic abilities and physical characteristics, their behavior, and, where appropriate, conservation programs. (Rev: BL 12/1/96; SLJ 2/97) [591]

9815 Dashefsky, H. Steven. *Zoology: High School Science Fair Experiments* (7–12). 1995, TAB paper $12.95 (0-07-015687-5). Twenty zoology experiments are presented in the categories of people-related, biocides, animal lives, and animals and the environment. (Rev: BL 6/1–15/95) [591]

9816 Day, Nancy. *Animal Experimentation: Cruelty or Science?* (7–12). (Issues in Focus) 1994, Enslow LB $19.95 (0-89490-578-3). A balanced discussion of experiments that use animals, presenting alternatives to the practice, which some argue is cruel. (Rev: BL 11/1/94; SLJ 4/95; VOYA 2/95) [179]

9817 Fridell, Ron. *Amphibians in Danger: A Worldwide Warning* (7–12). Illus. 1999, Watts $25.00 (0-531-11737-5). A wealth of knowledge and lore is presented in this book about the history, place, and role of frogs, toads, and salamanders, along with material on their alarming current death rate and how scientists devise and conduct research. (Rev: BL 6/1–15/99; SLJ 8/99) [597.8]

9818 Hecht, Jeff. *Vanishing Life: The Mystery of Mass Extinctions* (7–12). 1993, Scribners paper $15.95 (0-684-19331-0). A study of mass extinctions throughout history and an examination of how geological evidence supports or discredits current theories. (Rev: BL 1/15/94; SLJ 2/94; VOYA 2/94) [575]

9819 Hiller, Ilo. *Introducing Mammals to Young Naturalists* (5–9). Illus. 1990, Texas A & M Univ. Pr. $9.00 (0-89096-427-0). An introduction to a number of mammals; most, like the squirrels, are common while others, like the armadillo, are more exotic. (Rev: BL 7/90) [599]

9820 McElroy, Susan Chernak. *Animals as Guides for the Soul: Stories of Life-Changing Encounters* (10–12). 1998, Ballantine $23.95 (0-345-42403-4). An exploration of the relationship between animals and humans, using personal anecdotes and stories from readers on such topics as the death of pets, witnessing cruelty to animals, the ethics of using animals in service to humans, and lessons animals can teach, and a discussion of changes in beliefs about the psychology, intelligence, and emotional nature of animals. (Rev: BL 11/1/98; SLJ 3/99) [591]

9821 Parker, Steve. *Natural World* (6–12). 1994, DK Publg. $29.95 (1-56458-719-3). A heavily illustrated introduction to biology, with extensive material on animals in our world. (Rev: BL 12/1/94; SLJ 1/95; VOYA 5/95) [591]

9822 Roop, Connie, and Peter Roop. *Walk on the Wild Side!* (4–8). Illus. 1997, Millbrook LB $21.40 (0-7613-0021-X). This book provides short introductions to 14 animals and their habitats, complete with jokes, riddles, and humorous illustrations. (Rev: SLJ 6/97) [591]

9823 Russo, Monica. *Watching Nature* (6–10). 1998, Sterling $21.95 (0-8069-9515-7). A basic manual for anyone interested in nature watching, with material on how to recognize animals by markings and habits, and how to decipher clues of wildlife activity in the area. (Rev: BL 12/1/98; SLJ 12/98) [508]

9824 Sayre, April P. *Put on Some Antlers and Walk Like a Moose: How Scientists Find, Follow, and Study Wild Animals* (5–8). 1997, Twenty-First Century $20.40 (0-8050-5182-1). This book outlines the many techniques used by scientists to study animals and animal behavior. (Rev: BL 12/1/97; SLJ 2/98*; VOYA 2/98) [590]

9825 *The Simon & Schuster Encyclopedia of Animals: A Visual Who's Who of the World's Creatures* (7–12). 1998, Simon & Schuster $50.00 (0-684-85237-3). Arranged by broad taxonomic classification, about 2,000 animals are introduced through pictures and information on their appearance, adaptations, habits, and habitats. (Rev: BL 10/15/98; SLJ 2/99) [591]

9826 Stewart, Melissa. *Life without Light* (5–8). 1999, Watts $25.00 (0-531-11529-1). This book explores the world of nature that exists without sun, including creatures discovered during research on hydrothermal vents, caves, aquifers, and rocks. (Rev: BL 7/99; SLJ 8/99) [577]

Amphibians and Reptiles

GENERAL AND MISCELLANEOUS

9827 Allen, Missy, and Michel Peissel. *Dangerous Reptilian Creatures* (9–12). (Encyclopedia of Danger) 1993, Chelsea LB $19.95 (0-7910-1789-3). Covers 25 deadly snakes from around the world. (Rev: BL 9/1/93) [597.9]

9828 Behler, John L. *National Audubon Society First Field Guide: Reptiles* (4–8). 1999, Scholastic $17.95 (0-590-05467-8); paper $11.95 (0-590-05487-2). This richly illustrated manual discusses common characteristics of North American reptiles, then presents individual species under 4 groups: crocodiles, turtles, lizards, and snakes. (Rev: SLJ 7/99) [597.9]

9829 Behler, John L., and F. W. King. *The Audubon Society Field Guide to North American Reptiles and Amphibians* (9–12). Illus. 1979, Knopf $19.00 (0-394-50824-6). This comprehensive account covers reptiles and amphibians found in continental United States, Canada, and Hawaii. [597.6]

9830 Clarke, Barry. *Amphibian* (5–9). Photos. (Eyewitness Books) 1993, Knopf LB $20.99 (0-679-93879-6). Stunning photographs and text introduce the world of amphibians. (Rev: BL 8/93) [597.6]

9831 Conant, Roger. *A Field Guide to Reptiles and Amphibians of Eastern and Central North America.* 2nd ed. (9–12). Illus. 1975, Houghton $17.95 (0-395-19979-4); paper $13.95 (0-395-19977-8). Using both photographs and hundreds of maps, 574 species and subspecies are identified and described. A companion volume is *A Field Guide to Western Reptiles and Amphibians* (1985). [597.6]

9832 Gibbons, Whit. *Their Blood Runs Cold: Adventures with Reptiles and Amphibians* (7–12). Illus. 1983, Univ. of Alabama Pr. paper $14.95 (0-8173-0133-X). An informal guide, geographically arranged, to snakes, crocodiles, turtles, salamanders, and toads. [597.6]

9833 Halliday, Tim, and Kraig Adler, eds. *The Encyclopedia of Reptiles and Amphibians* (9–12). Illus. 1986, Facts on File $29.95 (0-8160-1359-4). A lavishly illustrated book that gives both general information and specific details on each species. (Rev: BL 6/1/86) [597.6]

9834 Pipe, Jim. *The Giant Book of Snakes and Slithery Creatures* (4–8). Illus. 1998, Millbrook $17.95 (0-7613-0729-X). This richly illustrated, oversize volume contains details about snakes, lizards, and amphibians. (Rev: BL 8/98; SLJ 12/98) [597.9]

9835 Stebbins, Robert C. *A Field Guide to Western Reptiles and Amphibians.* Rev. ed. (9–12). Illus. 1985, Houghton $24.95 (0-395-38254-8); paper $18.00 (0-395-38253-X). A fine field guide that identifies species, gives a picture of each, and describes both habits and habitats. (Rev: BL 8/85) [597.6]

ALLIGATORS AND CROCODILES

9836 Ross, Charles A., ed. *Crocodiles and Alligators* (9–12). Illus. 1989, Facts on File $35.00 (0-8160-2174-0). A richly illustrated volume that tells about the origins, structure, habitats, and behavior of these amphibians. (Rev: BL 11/1/89) [597.98]

FROGS AND TOADS

9837 Mattison, Chris. *Frogs & Toads of the World* (8–12). Illus. 1987, Facts on File $29.95 (0-8160-1602-X). An overview of these amphibians under such topics as physiology, feeding, and reproduction. (Rev: BL 4/15/88; BR 3–4/88; VOYA 10/88) [597.8]

9838 White, William. *All about the Frog* (5–8). (Sterling Color Nature) 1992, Sterling $14.95 (0-8069-8274-8). A brief history of the frog and a discussion of its anatomy, reproduction, food, adaptations, and likely future. (Rev: BL 7/92; SLJ 9/92) [597.8]

SNAKES AND LIZARDS

9839 Greene, Harry W. *Snakes: The Evolution of Mystery in Nature* (10–12). 1997, Univ. of California Pr. $45.00 (0-520-20014-4). With unusual photographs and a lucid text, this is a tribute to snakes, their beauty, unique characteristics, history, and place in the environment. (Rev: BL 5/1/97; SLJ 12/97) [597.96]

9840 Mattison, Chris. *The Encyclopedia of Snakes* (10–12). 1995, Facts on File $35.00 (0-8160-3072-3). This book can be used for both browsing and research, because it offers interesting facts about all aspects of reptile life in an attractive text, with many colorful photographs. (Rev: BL 8/95; SLJ 2/96) [597.96]

9841 Mattison, Chris. *Snakes of the World* (9–12). Illus. 1986, Facts on File $29.95 (0-8160-1082-X). A richly illustrated account that covers diet, defense behavior, and the mythology of the snake. (Rev: BL 5/15/86) [597]

9842 Montgomery, Sy. *The Snake Scientist* (5–8). (Scientists in the Field) 1999, Houghton $16.00 (0-395-87169-7). This account captures the excitement of scientific discovery by focusing on a zoologist and young students who are studying the red-sided garter snake in Canada. (Rev: BL 2/15/99; SLJ 5/99) [597.96]

9843 Roever, J. M. *Snake Secrets* (6–9). 1979, Walker LB $11.85 (0-8027-6333-2). An in-depth look at snakes, their behavior, and how people react to them. [597.96]

9844 Rubio, Manny. *Rattlesnake: Portrait of a Predator* (9–12). Illus. 1998, Smithsonian $49.95 (1-56098-808-8). With 250 color photos and detailed text, this book describes the origin, habitats, physiology, and anatomy of the rattlesnake and chronicles a history of people's different relationships with it, from commercial exploitation to snake-handling religious sects. (Rev: BL 12/1/98; SLJ 4/99) [597.96]

9845 Simon, Seymour. *Poisonous Snakes* (6–9). Illus. 1981, Macmillan $11.95 (0-590-07513-6). An explanation of venom and fangs is given and an introduction to the world's most famous poisonous snakes. [597.9]

TORTOISES AND TURTLES

9846 Alderton, David. *Turtles & Tortoises of the World* (9–12). Illus. 1988, Facts on File $29.95 (0-8160-1733-6). This thorough introduction covers such topics as structure, anatomy, reproduction, and origin and distribution. (Rev: BR 5–6/89) [598.92]

9847 Ripple, Jeff. *Sea Turtles* (10–12). (World Life Library) 1996, Voyageur paper $16.95 (0-89658-315-5). Using over 50 color photographs, this book introduces the sea turtle and its distribution, behavior, anatomy, history, and characteristics, plus information on current conservation techniques and future trends. (Rev: SLJ 5/97) [597.92]

Animal Behavior

GENERAL AND MISCELLANEOUS

9848 Brooks, Bruce. *Predator!* (5–8). (Knowing Nature) 1991, Farrar $13.95 (0-374-36111-8). Examines the food chain, with explanations of how and why animals hunt and protect themselves. (Rev: BL 1/1/92; SLJ 2/92*) [591.53]

9849 Crump, Donald J., ed. *How Animals Behave: A New Look at Wildlife* (6–9). Illus. 1984, National Geographic LB $12.50 (0-87044-505-7). A general, colorful introduction to why and how animals perform such functions as courting, living together, and caring for their young. [591.5]

9850 Gardner, Robert, and David Webster. *Science Project Ideas about Animal Behavior* (5–8). Illus. (Science Project Ideas) 1997, Enslow LB $18.95 (0-89490-842-1). A workmanlike compilation of projects involving animal behavior, such as the language of honeybees, with full background information and clear instructions. (Rev: BR 5–6/98; SLJ 2/98) [591]

9851 Griffin, Donald R. *Animal Thinking* (10–12). 1984, Harvard Univ. Pr. paper $15.95 (0-674-03713-8). From the lowliest of creatures to communication between chimps, this is a thorough description of what we know about animal intelligence. [591.5]

9852 Halliday, Tim, ed. *Animal Behavior* (9–12). 1994, Univ. of Oklahoma Pr. $19.95 (0-8061-2647-7). A basic book on how animals are born, live, and die. Contains its share of cuddly creatures but does not shy away from portraying (with photos) their place in the food chain. (Rev: BL 5/1/94) [591.51]

9853 Kohl, Judith, and Herbert Kohl. *Pack, Band, and Colony: The World of Social Animals* (7–9). Illus. 1983, Farrar $13.95 (0-374-35694-7). Termites and wolves are 2 of the social animals described here. [591.5]

9854 Nichol, John. *Bites and Stings: The World of Venomous Animals* (9–12). Illus. 1989, Facts on File $21.50 (0-8160-2233-X). A guide to the animal life like wasps and jellyfish that can cause bodily harm if disturbed plus information on how to handle such injuries. (Rev: BL 7/89; BR 5–6/90) [591.6]

9855 Parker, Steve. *Mammal* (5–9). Illus. 1989, Knopf LB $20.99 (0-394-92258-1). In text and full-color photographs, animal evolution is explained and a variety of mammals are introduced. (Rev: BL 9/15/89; BR 11–12/89) [599]

9856 Settel, Joanne. *Exploding Ants: Amazing Facts about How Animals Adapt* (4–8). 1999, Simon & Schuster $16.00 (0-689-81739-8). Lurid details of animal life, such as predatory fireflies, regurgitating birds, and bloodsuckers, are presented in this attention-getting collection of biological facts. (Rev: BL 4/15/99; SLJ 4/99) [591]

COMMUNICATION

9857 Bailey, Gerald. *Talking to Animals: How Animals Really Communicate!* (4–8). Illus. 1999, Element Books paper $4.95 (1-901881-97-0). After introducing the topic of animal communication, using his dog as an example, the author discusses how wolves, cats, horses, dolphins, whales, manatees, chimpanzees, and gorillas communicate and express feelings and how this knowledge can be applied to make people better pet owners. (Rev: SLJ 7/99) [591.59]

9858 Brooks, Bruce. *Making Sense: Animal Perception and Communication* (5–8). (Knowing Nature) 1993, Farrar $17.00 (0-374-34742-5). A look at each of the senses and how they affect the behavior of animals. (Rev: BL 12/1/93; SLJ 1/94) [591.1]

9859 Morton, Eugene S., and Jake Page. *Animal Talk: Science and the Voices of Nature* (9–12). 1992, Random $22.00 (0-394-58337-X). Analysis of the origins and nature of animal communication. (Rev: BL 4/15/92) [591.59]

HOMES

9860 Brooks, Bruce. *Nature by Design* (5–8). (Knowing Nature) 1991, Farrar $13.95 (0-374-30334-7). A study of animal "architecture" and intelligence, with a glossary. (Rev: BL 1/1/92; SLJ 2/92*) [591.56]

REPRODUCTION AND BABIES

9861 Allport, Susan. *A Natural History of Parenting: From Emperor Penguins to Reluctant Ewes, a Naturalist Looks at Parenting in the Animal World and Ours* (10–12). 1997, Harmony $23.00 (0-517-70799-3). A fascinating look at birth and parenting in a wide variety of bird, fish, and mammals. (Rev: BL 2/1/97; SLJ 1/98) [591.3]

TRACKS

9862 Murie, Olaus J. *A Field Guide to Animal Tracks.* 2nd ed. (7–12). Illus. 1974, Houghton $24.95 (0-395-19978-6); paper $16.95 (0-395-18323-5). This important volume in the Peterson Field Guide series first appeared in 1954 and now has become a classic in the area of identifying animal tracks and droppings. [591.5]

Animal Species

GENERAL AND MISCELLANEOUS

9863 Aaseng, Nathan. *Nature's Poisonous Creatures* (5–9). (Scientific American Sourcebooks) 1997, Twenty-First Century $25.90 (0-8050-4690-9); Holt paper $8.00 (0-8050-4689-5). After a general introduction to animal poisons, why they are produced, and their composition, this book devotes separate chapters to such venom-bearing vertebrates and invertebrates as sea wasps, blue-ringed octopi, African killer bees, and marine toads. (Rev: BL 2/1/98; SLJ 8/98) [591.6]

9864 Ackerman, Diane. *Bats: Shadows in the Night* (5–8). 1997, Crown LB $19.99 (0-517-70920-1). The author reports on her bat-watching experiences in the Big Bend National Park in Texas from a unique perspective. (Rev: SLJ 10/97*) [599.4]

9865 Alden, Peter. *Peterson First Guide to Mammals of North America* (8–12). Illus. 1987, Houghton paper $4.95 (0-395-42767-3). An uncluttered basic guide to mammal identification with many illustrations and useful background material. (Rev: BL 5/15/87) [599]

9866 Anderson, Sydney, ed. *Simon and Schuster's Guide to Mammals* (9–12). Illus. 1984, Simon & Schuster paper $17.00 (0-671-42805-5). This guide, originally published in Italy, introduces the orders of mammals and highlights 426 species. [599]

9867 Bramwell, Martyn, and Steve Parker. *Mammals: The Small Plant-Eaters* (6–10). Illus. 1989, Facts on File $19.95 (0-8160-1958-4). An introduction to each animal is given in text and outstanding illustrations. (Rev: VOYA 12/89) [559]

9868 Burt, William Henry. *A Field Guide to the Mammals.* 3rd ed. (7–12). Illus. 1976, Houghton $24.95 (0-395-24082-4); paper $16.95 (0-395-24084-0). An identification guide to 380 species of mammals found in North America. [599]

9869 Fenton, M. Brock. *Just Bats* (7–12). Illus. 1983, Univ. of Toronto Pr. paper $15.95 (0-8020-6464-7). An introduction to this frequently misunderstood and very useful flying rodent. [599.4]

9870 Fleisher, Paul. *Life Cycles of a Dozen Diverse Creatures* (4–8). Illus. 1996, Millbrook LB $24.90 (0-7613-0000-7). The life cycles of 12 animals—including the oyster, honeybee, penguin, butterfly, and sea horse—are covered, with many brilliant illustrations. (Rev: BL 12/1/96*; SLJ 1/97) [591.3]

9871 Hare, Tony. *Animal Fact-File: Head-to-Tail Profiles of More Than 90 Mammals* (4–8). 1999, Facts on File $35.00 (0-8160-3921-6); paper $18.95 (0-8160-4016-8). Arranged alphabetically from aardvarks to wombats, this book provides basic introductions to over 90 mammals. (Rev: SLJ 9/99) [599]

9872 Hodgson, Barbara. *The Rat: A Perverse Miscellany* (10–12). 1997, Ten Speed Pr. paper $15.95 (0-89815-926-1). Everything you've wanted to know about rats, including their role throughout history, how different people view them, and how they spread around the world. (Rev: BL 8/97; SLJ 3/98) [599.32]

9873 Jarrow, Gail, and Paul Sherman. *The Naked Mole-Rat Mystery: Scientific Sleuths at Work* (6–8). Illus. (Discovery!) 1996, Lerner LB $23.95 (0-8225-2853-3). This is a thorough exploration of what we know, and how we found out about, the naked mole-rat, which is a mammal but has a reptilian body temperature and lives in colonies like social insects. (Rev: BL 9/1/96; SLJ 8/96) [599.32]

9874 MacDonald, David, ed. *The Encyclopedia of Mammals* (7–12). Illus. 1984, Facts on File $80.00 (0-87196-871-1). Almost 200 animal species are compiled in this volume on living mammals, which is illustrated with both photographs and drawings. [599]

9875 National Audubon Society, eds. *Mammals* (4–8). 1998, Scholastic $17.95 (0-590-05471-6); paper $10.95 (0-590-05489-9). An attractive guide to mammals, with maps showing habitats, a picture of each animal, and basic descriptive text. (Rev: SLJ 4/99) [599]

9876 North, Sterling. *Rascal: A Memoir of a Better Era* (7–12). Illus. 1963, Dutton paper $14.99 (0-525-18839-8). Remembrances of growing up in Wisconsin in 1918 and of the joys and problems of owning a pet raccoon. (Rev: BL 9/1/89) [599.74]

9877 Ryden, Hope. *Lily Pond: Four Years with a Family of Beavers* (10–12). Illus. 1997, Lyons Pr. paper $16.95 (1-55821-455-0). A fascinating account of beaver-watching over a 4-year period. (Rev: BL 11/15/89) [599.32]

9878 Tuttle, Merlin D. *America's Neighborhood Bats* (9–12). Illus. 1988, Univ. of Texas Pr. $19.95 (0-292-70403-8); paper $9.95 (0-292-70406-2). A brief account filled with amazing photographs that helps clarify misunderstandings about this very useful animal. (Rev: BL 3/1/89) [599.4]

9879 Whitaker, John O., Jr. *The Audubon Society Field Guide to North American Mammals* (7–12). Illus. 1980, Knopf $19.00 (0-394-50762-2). This excellent guide contains almost 200 pages of color photographs. [599]

APE FAMILY

9880 Goodall, Jane. *In the Shadow of Man*. Rev. ed. (8–12). 1988, Houghton paper $16.00 (0-395-33145-5). The story of a scientist's observations of chimpanzees at the Gombe Stream Chimpanzee Reserve in Tanzania. (Rev: BR 11–12/88) [599.8]

9881 Lasky, Kathryn. *Shadows in the Dawn: The Lemurs of Madagascar* (4–8). Illus. 1997, Harcourt $18.00 (0-15-200258-8); paper $9.00 (0-15-200281-2). An attractive photoessay about the origins and characteristics of the lemurs of Madagascar and the research of Malagasy students working in the field with primatologist Alison Jolly, who has studied the animals for 30 years, making new discoveries and dispelling myths about them. (Rev: SLJ 7/98) [599.8]

9882 Lewin, Ted, and Betsy Lewin. *Gorilla Walk* (4–8). 1999, Lothrop LB $15.93 (0-688-16510-9). A beautifully illustrated book about the Lewins' trip to Uganda to study mountain gorillas. (Rev: BL 8/99; SLJ 9/99) [599.8]

9883 Montgomery, Sy. *Walking with the Great Apes: Jane Goodall, Dian Fossey, Biruté Galdikas* (9–12). 1991, Houghton $19.45 (0-395-51597-1). Descriptions of the painstaking research by several scientists in their quest for knowledge about the behavior and habits of the great apes. (Rev: BL 3/15/91*) [599.88]

9884 Redmond, Ian. *Gorilla* (5–8). (Eyewitness Books) 1995, Knopf LB $20.99 (0-679-97332-X). Good layout, interesting photographs, and fascinating facts introduce the life, personality, and environment of the gorilla in a book that is best for browsing. (Rev: BL 12/15/95; SLJ 1/96) [599.8]

9885 Strum, Shirley C. *Almost Human: A Journey into the World of Baboons* (9–12). Illus. 1987, Random $22.50 (0-394-54724-1). A description of the life and habits of the Pumphouse Gang, a group of baboons living in Kenya. (Rev: BL 11/15/87) [599.8]

BEARS

9886 Calabro, Marian. *Operation Grizzly Bear* (5–8). Illus. 1989, Macmillan $13.95 (0-02-716241-9). An account by 2 naturalists on a 12-year study of silvertip bears in Yellowstone Park. (Rev: BL 3/15/90; VOYA 4/90) [599.74]

9887 Craighead, Frank C., Jr. *Track of the Grizzly* (10–12). Illus. 1979, Sierra Club paper $16.00 (0-87156-322-3). This introduction to the grizzly bear is a result of the 13-year study in Yellowstone National Park. [599.74]

9888 Ford, Barbara. *Black Bear: The Spirit of the Wilderness* (7–9). Illus. 1981, Houghton $8.95 (0-395-30444-X). A description of the behavior and habitats of this wilderness animal. [599.74]

9889 Lawter, William Clifford. *Smokey Bear 20252: A Biography* (9–12). 1994, Lindsay Smith $26.95 (0-9640017-0-5). Outlines the history of Smokey Bear (a real bear, rescued from a forest fire and sent to the National Zoo), the famous poster, and the uniforms worn by the nation's forest service. (Rev: BL 5/1/94) [363.377]

9890 Rosing, Norbert. *The World of the Polar Bear* (10–12). Trans. from German by Tecklenborg Erlag. 1996, Firefly $40.00 (1-55209-068-X). Over half of this book is photographs illustrating the behavior and habits of the polar bear and the flora and fauna of the Arctic. (Rev: SLJ 5/97) [599.74]

9891 Schullery, Paul, ed. *Mark of the Bear* (10–12). 1996, Sierra Club $30.00 (0-87156-903-5). Ten naturalists describe their encounters with bears, with over half the book devoted to full-page, full-color photographs. (Rev: BL 12/1/96; SLJ 1/97) [599.74]

9892 Turbak, Gary. *Grizzly Bears* (6–10). (World Life Library) 1997, Voyageur paper $14.95 (0-89658-334-1). High-quality photos and concise, readable text are used to introduce the grizzly bear's life cycle, origin, habits, anatomy, and future. (Rev: SLJ 10/97) [599.74]

CATS (LIONS, TIGERS, ETC.)

9893 Adamson, Joy. *Born Free: A Lioness of Two Worlds* (7–12). 1987, Pantheon $11.95 (0-679-56141-2). First published in 1960, this is an account of a young lioness growing up in captivity in Kenya. [599.74]

9894 Bolgiano, Chris. *Mountain Lion: An Unnatural History of Pumas and People* (9–12). 1995, Stackpole $19.95 (0-8117-1044-0). Details the mythological history and the impact of the mountain lion, from its use in Native American tales to its uses in modern advertising. (Rev: BL 8/95) [599.74]

9895 Levine, Stuart P. *The Tiger* (7–10). (Overview: Endangered Animals and Habitats) 1998, Lucent LB $17.96 (1-56006-465-X). This work describes the habits and habitats of the tiger and current efforts to protect it from extinction. (Rev: BL 10/15/98) [599.74]

9896 Lumpkin, Susan. *Small Cats* (5–8). (Great Creatures of the World) 1993, Facts on File $17.95 (0-8160-2848-6). This book covers cats that weigh in at 66 pounds or less, among them ocelots, lynxes, caracals, and jaguarundis. (Rev: BL 2/15/93) [599.74]

9897 National Geographic Society, eds. *The Year of the Tiger* (9–12). 1998, National Geographic $40.00 (0-7922-7377-X). Using over 100 stunning photographs, this photoessay gives an unprecedented view of the habits, play, and social life of tigers in the wild, with over half the book devoted to the tigers of the Bandhavgarh National Park in India, as well as in captivity. (Rev: SLJ 4/99) [599.74]

9898 Siedensticker, John. *Tigers* (10–12). (World Life Library) 1996, Voyageur paper $19.95 (0-89658-295-7). The distribution, anatomy, behavior, history, and endangered status of the tiger are discussed in this book that contains over 50 stunning color photos. (Rev: SLJ 5/97) [599.74]

9899 Thompson, Sharon E. *Built for Speed: The Extraordinary, Enigmatic Cheetah* (5–8). 1997, Lerner LB $19.93 (0-8225-2854-1). The habits, structure, and lifestyles of this endangered animal are introduced, with use of full-color photographs. (Rev: BL 6/1–15/98) [599.75 9]

COYOTES, FOXES, AND WOLVES

9900 Busch, Robert. *The Wolf Almanac* (9–12). 1995, Lyons Pr. $27.95 (1-55821-351-1). An introduction to wolves, with 100 illustrations. (Rev: BL 5/1/95) [599.74]

9901 Busch, Robert, ed. *Wolf Songs: The Classic Collection of Writing about Wolves* (9–12). 1994, Sierra Club $15.00 (0-87156-411-4). Personal essays about the misunderstood wolf, each arguing that wolves have the right to free existence in nature. (Rev: BL 10/15/94; SLJ 6/95; VOYA 4/95) [599.74]

9902 Hampton, Bruce. *The Great American Wolf* (10–12). 1997, Holt $35.00 (0-8050-3716-0). The author presents information about an organized campaign from the 1890s to eliminate wolves in this country and material on the wolves' habits, habitats, social organization, and food, plus a chapter on Native American wolf lore. (Rev: SLJ 9/97) [599.74]

9903 Lawrence, R. D. *In Praise of Wolves* (10–12). 1986, Ballantine paper $5.99 (0-345-34916-4). A book that resulted from the author's many years studying the habits and behavior of wolves. (Rev: VOYA 6/86) [599.74]

9904 Lawrence, R. D. *Secret Go the Wolves* (9–12). 1985, Ballantine paper $5.99 (0-345-33200-8). The story of how Lawrence and his wife raised a pair of wolf pups. [599.7]

9905 Leslie, Robert Franklin. *In the Shadow of a Rainbow* (10–12). 1986, Norton paper $9.95 (0-393-30392-6). The story of an unusual friendship between man and wolf. [599.74]

9906 Lopez, Barry. *Of Wolves and Men* (9–12). 1978, Macmillan paper $18.00 (0-684-16322-5). An account that contrasts the wolf of folklore with the true nature of this caring social creature. [599.74]

9907 Mech, L. David. *The Way of the Wolf* (9–12). 1991, Voyageur $29.95 (0-89658-163-2). Discusses wolves' place in the natural order and their similarity to domesticated dogs, dispels the myth that they attack people, and makes a case for their preservation. (Rev: BL 10/1/91) [599.75]

9908 Savage, Candace. *The World of the Wolf* (10–12). 1996, Sierra Club $27.50 (0-87156-899-3). Large color photographs and a simple text introduce the wolf, its habits and behavior, how and where it lives, and its relationship with humankind. (Rev: SLJ 3/97) [599.74]

9909 Smith, Roland. *Journey of the Red Wolf* (4–8). Illus. 1996, Dutton $16.99 (0-525-65162-4). The story of the endangered red wolf, how the last 17 were taken into captivity, and attempts to preserve the species. (Rev: BL 5/1/96; SLJ 5/96) [599.74]

9910 Swinburne, Stephen R. *Once a Wolf: How Wildlife Biologists Brought Back the Gray Wolf* (5–8). Illus. 1999, Houghton $16.00 (0-395-89827-7). This work chronicles the 25-year struggle to reintroduce the gray wolf to Yellowstone Park. (Rev: BL 3/1/99; SLJ 5/99) [333.95]

DEER FAMILY

9911 Cox, Daniel, and John Ozoga. *Whitetail Country* (8–12). Illus. 1988, Willow Creek Pr. $39.00 (0-932558-43-7). Wonderful photographs complement this account of the life and living habits of the deer. (Rev: BR 3–4/89) [599.73]

ELEPHANTS

9912 Caras, Roger A. *A Most Dangerous Journey: The Life of an African Elephant* (5–8). 1995, Dial paper $15.99 (0-8037-1880-2). Based on a composite picture of an elephant culled from Caras's observations in Africa, with critical comments about poachers and corrupt officials in search of ivory. (Rev: BL 10/15/95; SLJ 10/95; VOYA 4/96) [599.4]

9913 Chadwick, Douglas H. *The Fate of the Elephant* (9–12). 1992, Sierra Club $25.00 (0-87156-635-4). A revealing report on the impending extinction of the elephant. (Rev: BL 9/15/92; SLJ 5/93) [599.6]

9914 Di Silvestro, Roger L. *The African Elephant: Twilight in Eden* (9–12). 1991, Wiley $34.95 (0-471-53207-X). The social behavior of earth's largest land mammal, now endangered because of the ivory trade, and its association with humans from prehistory to the present day. (Rev: BL 10/15/91) [333.95]

9915 Levine, Stuart P. *The Elephant* (7–10). Illus. (Overview: Endangered Animals and Habitats) 1997, Lucent LB $17.96 (1-56006-522-2). After a general introduction to the elephant and its characteristics, evolution, and habitats, the author describes how it has become endangered and current attempts at conservation. (Rev: BL 5/1/98) [599.67]

9916 Redmond, Ian. *Elephant* (5–9). Photos. (Eyewitness Books) 1993, Knopf $19.00 (0-679-83880-5). A description of the elephant using text and pictures, with material on habits, habitats, and the reasons for its current endangered status. (Rev: BL 8/93) [599]

MARSUPIALS

9917 Phillips, Ken. *Koalas: Australia's Ancient Ones* (9–12). 1994, Prentice Hall $27.50 (0-671-79777-8). A study of Australia's beloved marsupial that chronicles koala rescues and describes the growth of the Koala Hospital. (Rev: BL 10/1/94) [599.2]

PANDAS

9918 Presnall, Judith J. *The Giant Panda* (7–10). Illus. (Overview: Endangered Animals and Habitats) 1998, Lucent LB $22.45 (1-56006-522-6). A discussion of the giant panda's evolution, habitats, life span, and breeding habits, how it became endangered, and attempts to conserve this dwindling population. (Rev: BL 5/1/98) [599.789]

9919 Schaller, George B. *The Last Panda* (9–12). 1993, Univ. of Chicago Pr. $24.95 (0-226-73628-8). A noted field biologist recounts his experiences researching the giant panda in the wilds of China. (Rev: BL 3/15/93) [599.74]

Birds

GENERAL AND MISCELLANEOUS

9920 Adler, Bill. *Impeccable Birdfeeding: How to Discourage Scuffling, Hull-Dropping, Seed-Throwing, Unmentionable Nuisances and Vulgar Chatter at Your Birdfeeder* (9–12). 1992, Chicago Review paper $9.95 (1-55652-157-X). Discusses birdbaths, birdfeeders, and birdhouses, and rates food and bird species on the basis of mess potential. (Rev: BL 10/1/92) [598]

9921 Bailey, Jill, and Steve Parker. *Birds: The Plant- and Seed-Eaters* (5–9). Illus. 1989, Facts on File $17.95 (0-8160-1964-9). Stunning photography and a well-organized text highlight this description of many of our common birds. (Rev: BL 1/15/90; BR 5–6/90) [598.2]

9922 *Book of North American Birds* (9–12). 1990, Random $32.95 (0-89577-351-1). About 600 U.S. and Canadian birds are pictured in color paintings and described in a lucid text. (Rev: BL 9/1/90) [598]

9923 Buff, Sheila. *The Birdfeeder's Handbook: An Orvis Guide* (9–12). 1991, Lyons Pr. paper $10.95 (1-55821-123-3). This manual offers basic information on birdfeeding, birdhouses, and avian behavior, including feeder manners, territories, courtship, breeding, and migration. (Rev: BL 9/1/91) [598]

9924 Bull, John, et al. *Birds of North America, Eastern Region: A Quick Identification Guide to Common Birds* (9–12). Illus. 1985, Macmillan paper $21.95 (0-02-079660-9). A picture guide to 253 species of birds found in the eastern part of Canada and the United States. Also use: *Birds of North America, Western Region* (1989). (Rev: BL 8/85) [598]

9925 Cronin, Edward W. *Getting Started in Bird Watching* (10–12). Illus. 1986, Houghton paper $9.95 (0-395-34397-6). Handy tips and checklists for 9 different regions of the United States highlight this beginner's manual. (Rev: BL 6/1/86) [598]

9926 Ehrlich, Paul R., et al. *The Birder's Handbook: A Field Guide to the Natural History of North American Birds* (9–12). Illus. 1988, Simon & Schuster paper $18.00 (0-671-65989-8). An extremely comprehensive guide to the 646 birds native to North America. (Rev: BL 10/1/88) [598.297]

9927 Farrand, John. *How to Identify Birds* (10–12). Illus. 1987, McGraw-Hill paper $17.95 (0-07-019975-2). A noted bird watcher tells how to identify birds by such characteristics as size, habitat, and voice. For more specific information see the author's *Eastern Birds* and *Western Birds* (both 1987). (Rev: BL 11/15/87) [598]

9928 Llamas, Andreu. *Birds Conquer the Sky* (4–8). Illus. (Development of the Earth) 1996, Chelsea LB $15.95 (0-7910-3455-0). A science book that explains prehistoric land birds as well as those that fly, along with explanations of the roles of feathers and bones in the evolution of flight. (Rev: SLJ 7/96) [598]

9929 Perrins, Christopher M., and Alex L. A. Middleton, eds. *The Encyclopedia of Birds* (9–12). Illus. 1985, Facts on File $45.00 (0-8160-1150-8). This expensive fully illustrated volume gives excellent information on all kinds of birds arranged by their general size. (Rev: BL 8/85) [598]

9930 Peterson, Roger Tory. *A Field Guide to the Birds.* 4th rev. ed. (7–12). Illus. 1980, Houghton $24.95 (0-395-26621-1); paper $18.00 (0-395-26619-X). An exhaustive guide to the birds found east of the Rockies. [598]

9931 Peterson, Roger Tory. *A Field Guide to Western Birds.* 3rd ed. (9–12). Illus. 1990, Houghton $26.00 (0-395-51749-4); paper $17.95 (0-395-51424-X). This book covers the birds found in the Rockies and West plus a section on the Hawaiian Islands. [598]

9932 Sayre, April P. *Endangered Birds of North America* (4–8). (Scientific American Sourcebooks) 1997, Twenty-First Century $25.90 (0-8050-4549-X). After giving some general facts about birds, the author focuses on five specific birds to demonstrate the difficulties endangered species face. (Rev: BL 12/1/97; BR 3–4/98; SLJ 1/98; VOYA 6/98) [333.95]

9933 Stokes, Donald. *A Guide to the Behavior of Common Birds* (7–12). Illus. 1979, Little, Brown $16.95 (0-316-81722-8); paper $15.00 (0-316-81725-2). The first of 3 volumes, each of which describes the behavior of 25 different birds. Volume 2 is: *A Guide to Bird Behavior: In the Wild and at Your Feeder* (1985); volume 3 is: *A Guide to Bird Behavior* (1989). [598]

9934 Stokes, Donald, and Lillian Stokes. *The Bird Feeder Book: An Easy Guide to Attracting, Identifying, and Understanding Your Feeder Birds* (8–12). Illus. 1987, Little, Brown paper $12.95 (0-316-81733-3). A manual that describes, with color photographs, 72 backyard birds, plus tips on how to attract and feed them. (Rev: BL 2/1/88) [598]

9935 Stokes, Donald, and Lillian Stokes. *The Complete Birdhouse Book: The Easy Guide to Attracting Nesting Birds* (9–12). Illus. 1990, Little, Brown paper $13.00 (0-316-81714-7). Plans for various birdhouses are given plus instructions on how to build them. (Rev: BL 9/15/90) [598]

9936 Taylor, Kenny. *Puffins* (6–9). (World Life Library) 1999, Voyageur paper $16.95 (0-89658-419-4). This lavishly illustrated book explores the world of puffins—their history, physical characteristics, behavior, and environmental problems. (Rev: BL 8/99) [598]

9937 Thurston, Harry. *The World of the Shorebirds* (10–12). 1996, Sierra Club $27.50 (0-87156-901-9). A variety of shorebirds are introduced in text and large color photographs, with details on their lives, habits, behavior, and relations with people. (Rev: SLJ 3/97) [598]

9938 Toops, Connie. *Hummingbirds: Jewels in Flight* (9–12). 1992, Voyageur $29.95 (0-89658-161-6). The author recounts her trips to observe hummingbirds in the Southwest and along the Gulf Coast and provides information on plants that attract them. (Rev: BL 11/1/92) [598.8]

9939 Weidensaul, Scott, and National Audubon Society, eds. *National Audubon Society First Field Guide: Birds* (4–8). Illus. 1998, Scholastic $1.95 (0-590-05446-5). After a general introduction to ornithology, this guide describes and pictures several species of birds, including markings, eating, mating and nesting habits, migration, and endangered status. (Rev: BL 8/98; SLJ 10/98) [598]

BEHAVIOR

9940 Dunning, Joan. *Secrets of the Nest: The Family of North American Birds* (9–12). 1994, Houghton $27.50 (0-395-62035-X). The author uses pen-and-ink drawings to illustrate the nesting behavior of robins, hummingbirds, ducks, egrets, the California condor, and other birds. (Rev: BL 3/15/94) [598.256]

9941 Johnson, Sylvia A. *Inside an Egg* (7–9). Illus. 1982, Lerner LB $22.60 (0-8225-1472-9); paper $5.95 (0-8225-9522-2). An excellently illustrated account tracing the growth of a chicken in an egg until it is hatched. [598]

9942 Short, Lester L. *The Lives of Birds: The Birds of the World and Their Behavior* (9–12). (American Museum of Natural History: Animal Behavior) 1993, Holt $25.00 (0-8050-1952-9). Describes how birds find mates, stake out territories, reproduce, navigate over long distances, what they eat, and why they sing. (Rev: BL 6/1–15/93) [598.2]

DUCKS AND GEESE

9943 Kerrod, Robin. *Birds: The Waterbirds* (5–9). Illus. 1989, Facts on File $17.95 (0-8160-1962-2). Ducks and geese are only 2 of the species described and pictured in this attractive volume. (Rev: BL 1/15/90; BR 5–6/90) [598.29]

9944 Lorenz, Konrad, et al. *Here I Am—Where Are You? The Behavior of the Greylag Goose* (9–12). Trans. by Robert D. Martin. 1991, Harcourt $26.95 (0-15-140056-3). Offers intimate observations of the social behavior of the greylag goose and covers decades of scientific inquiry by a pioneering expert on ducks and geese. (Rev: BL 10/15/91) [598]

EAGLES, HAWKS, AND OTHER BIRDS OF PREY

9945 Arnold, Caroline. *Hawk Highway in the Sky: Watching Raptor Migration* (4–8). 1997, Harcourt $18.00 (0-15-200868-3). This volume describes the HawkWatch International observation site in the Goshute Mountains of Nevada, where scientists and volunteers catch, measure, and trace flight patterns of hawks, eagles, and falcons. (Rev: BL 6/1–15/97; SLJ 6/97) [598.9]

9946 Bailey, Jill. *Birds of Prey* (5–8). Illus. 1988, Facts on File $13.95 (0-8160-1655-0). In brief, lavishly illustrated chapters, various characteristics of birds of prey are explored and the most important types are described. (Rev: SLJ 1/89) [598]

9947 Barghusen, Joan D. *The Bald Eagle* (7–10). (Overview: Endangered Animals and Habitats) 1998, Lucent LB $17.96 (1-56006-254-1). An introduction to the structure, habits, and habitats of the bald eagle and a description of the methods employed to save it. (Rev: BL 10/15/98) [598.9]

9948 Bramwell, Martyn. *Birds: The Aerial Hunters* (5–9). Illus. 1989, Facts on File $17.95 (0-8160-1963-0). Eagles, hawks, and condors are only 3 of the many predators described and pictured in lavish photographs. (Rev: BL 1/15/90; BR 5–6/90) [598.91]

9949 Clark, William S. *A Field Guide to Hawks: North America* (9–12). Illus. 1987, Houghton $24.95 (0-395-36001-3); paper $16.95 (0-395-44112-9). An extensively illustrated guide to 39 species of hawks. (Rev: BL 10/1/87) [598]

9950 Grambo, Rebecca L. *Eagles* (5–8). (World Life Library) 1999, Voyageur paper $16.95 (0-89658-363-5). This beautifully illustrated book describes the legends and lore surrounding eagles, their physical characteristics, behavior, habitats, and different species. (Rev: BL 8/99) [598.9]

9951 Houle, Marcy. *The Prairie Keepers: Secrets of the Grasslands* (9–12). 1995, Addison-Wesley $20.00 (0-201-60843-X). A memoir of a field biologist's 6-month study of hawks in an Oregon prairie. (Rev: BL 4/1/95*) [598.9]

9952 Savage, Candace. *Peregrine Falcons* (9–12). 1992, Sierra Club $30.00 (0-87156-504-8). A detailed discussion of the tragic effects of pesticide pollution on peregrine falcons. (Rev: BL 11/1/92; SLJ 7/93) [598.9]

9953 Winn, Marie. *Red-Tails in Love: A Wildlife Drama in Central Park* (10–12). 1998, Pantheon $24.00 (0-679-43997-8); paper $13.00 (0-679-75846-1). A true-life adventure involving a group of bird watchers in Central Park and the mating of a pair of red-tail hawks on the 12th-floor facade of a nearby apartment building. (Rev: BL 2/1/98; SLJ 8/98) [598.9]

OWLS

9954 Mowat, Farley. *Owls in the Family* (7–9). 1989, Tundra paper $6.99 (0-7710-6693-7). Two seemingly harmless owls turn a household upside down when they are adopted as pets. [598]

9955 Sutton, Patricia, and Clay Sutton. *How to Spot an Owl* (9–12). 1994, Chapters Publg. paper $14.95 (1-881527-36-0). A good starter book on owling in 2 sections: "An Introduction to Owling" and "The Owls of North America." (Rev: BL 4/15/94) [598.9]

PENGUINS

9956 Chester, Jonathan. *The World of the Penguin* (10–12). 1996, Sierra Club $27.50 (0-87156-900-0). Readable text and colorful illustrations introduce the penguin's habits, behavior, social life, and methods of survival. (Rev: BL 12/1/96; SLJ 3/97) [598.4]

9957 Kaehler, Wolfgang. *Penguins* (9–12). Illus. 1989, Chronicle $22.95 (0-87701-649-6); paper

$12.95 (0-87701-637-2). An inviting glimpse into the varieties of penguins and how and where they live. (Rev: BL 11/1/89) [598.4]

9958 Love, John. *Penguins* (9–12). (World Life Library) 1997, Voyageur paper $16.95 (0-89658-339-2). This book uses color photographs to introduce penguins, their anatomy, habits, food, mating rituals, and social life. (Rev: SLJ 1/98) [598]

9959 Peterson, Roger Tory. *Penguins* (10–12). Illus. 1998, Houghton paper $20.00 (0-395-89897-8). A richly illustrated narrative about the 16 different kinds of penguins and how they live. [598]

Environmental Protection and Endangered Species

9960 Adams, Douglas, and Mark Carwardine. *Last Chance to See* (10–12). Illus. 1992, Ballantine paper $10.00 (0-345-37198-4). The noted science fiction writer examines the plight of many of the earth's endangered species. (Rev: BL 12/1/90) [591.52]

9961 Cohen, Daniel. *The Modern Ark: Saving Endangered Species* (5–9). 1995, Putnam $15.95 (0-399-22442-4). An account of modern efforts to save such species as the red wolf, California condor, panda, and cheetah. (Rev: BL 12/1/95; BR 3–4/96; SLJ 2/96) [333.95]

9962 De Koster, Katie. *Endangered Species* (8–12). Illus. (Opposing Viewpoints) 1998, Greenhaven LB $17.96 (1-56510-747-0); paper $11.96 (1-56510-746-2). In some 30 excerpts from such personalities as Al Gore and Edward O. Wilson, this book presents various points of view on issues related to saving endangered species, including the economics of environment protection, ethical questions, and priorities. (Rev: SLJ 11/98) [591.52]

9963 Ehrlich, Paul R., and Anne H. Ehrlich. *Extinction* (10–12). 1981, Random $16.95 (0-394-51312-6). A book that explores questions of how and why species become extinct and how each disappearance affects the earth. [560]

9964 Ehrlich, Paul R., et al. *Birds in Jeopardy: The Imperiled and Extinct Birds of the United States and Canada, Including Hawaii and Puerto Rico* (9–12). 1992, Stanford Univ. Pr. paper $22.95 (0-8047-1981-0). Lists the endangered and extinct birds of North America, with information on nesting, food, and breeding. (Rev: BL 2/1/92) [333.95]

9965 Erickson, Jon. *Dying Planet: The Extinction of Species* (9–12). 1991, TAB paper $11.95 (0-8306-3615-3). A look at causes of extinction throughout the ages. (Rev: BL 6/1/91) [575]

9966 Gardner, Robert. *Science Projects about the Environment and Ecology* (6–9). (Science Experiments) 1999, Enslow $19.95 (0-89490-951-7). This well-organized, clearly presented book offers a wide range of experiments involving conservation, ecology, and the environment, supplemented by charts, tables, and drawings. (Rev: SLJ 7/99) [363]

9967 McClung, Robert M. *Last of the Wild: Vanished & Vanishing Giants of the Animal World* (8–12). Illus. 1997, Shoe String LB $27.50 (0-208-02452-2). Moving from continent to continent, this account gives historical and geographical background material on 60 animal species that have already disappeared or are currently in extreme danger of extinction. (Rev: BL 7/97; SLJ 11/97; VOYA 10/97) [591.51]

9968 McClung, Robert M. *Lost Wild America: The Story of Our Extinct and Vanishing Wildlife*. Rev. ed. (5–8). Illus. 1993, Shoe String LB $29.50 (0-208-02359-3). A history of American wildlife management from pioneer days to the present, with information on extinct and endangered species. (Rev: BL 1/1/94; SLJ 2/94; VOYA 2/94) [591.5]

9969 Mallory, Kenneth. *A Home by the Sea: Protecting Coastal Wildlife* (5–8). Illus. (New England Aquarium) 1998, Harcourt $18.00 (0-15-200043-7); paper $9.00 (0-15-201802-6). A description of the many successful efforts to protect coastal wildlife in New Zealand in spite of commercial, residential, and recreational development. (Rev: BL 9/1/98; BR 1–2/99; SLJ 9/98) [333.95 416 0993]

9970 Mann, Charles C., and Mark L. Plummer. *Noah's Choice: The Future of Endangered Species* (9–12). 1995, Knopf $29.95 (0-679-42002-9). A detailed overview of the biological, economic, and political considerations influencing the Endangered Species Act. (Rev: BL 2/15/95) [574.4]

9971 Nirgiotis, Nicholas, and Theodore Nirgiotis. *No More Dodos: How Zoos Help Endangered Wildlife* (5–8). Illus. 1996, Lerner $23.95 (0-8225-2856-8). An introduction to the activities and projects of many organizations that are trying to protect and preserve endangered wildlife worldwide. (Rev: BL 2/15/97; SLJ 2/97) [639.9]

9972 Sherrow, Victoria. *Endangered Mammals of North America* (5–8). (Scientific American Sourcebooks) 1995, Twenty-First Century LB $22.40 (0-8050-3253-3). A general introduction to why species become endangered, followed by a discussion of specific endangered mammals, such as the bowhead whale and the red wolf, their physical features, behavior, the history of their decline, and efforts to save them. (Rev: BL 12/1/95; SLJ 1/96; VOYA 4/96) [599]

9973 Silverstein, Alvin, et al. *Saving Endangered Animals* (6–8). (Better Earth) 1993, Enslow LB $19.95 (0-89490-402-7). Practical information about saving threatened animal species and reintroducing

them into their native environments. (Rev: BL 5/1/93; SLJ 5/93) [333.95]

9974 Simon, Noel. *Nature in Danger: Threatened Habitats and Species* (10–12). 1995, Oxford $45.00 (0-19-521152-9); paper $8.95 (0-685-20135-X). This thorough resource covers ecosystems and biomes in geographic regions around the world, including their flora and fauna, physical features, the role humans play there, ecological problems, and possible solutions. (Rev: BL 11/1/95; SLJ 6/96; VOYA 4/96) [363.7]

9975 Stalcup, Brenda, ed. *Endangered Species* (8–12). Illus. (Opposing Viewpoints) 1996, Greenhaven LB $21.96 (1-56510-365-3). Different point of views are expressed on such questions as: is extinction a serious problem? can endangered species be preserved? and, should endangered species take priority over jobs, development, and property rights? (Rev: BL 3/15/96) [574.5]

9976 Stefoff, Rebecca. *Extinction* (9–12). 1991, Chelsea LB $19.95 (0-7910-1578-5). A history of vanished species and how humans have, in some cases, accelerated the process of extinction. (Rev: BL 2/1/92; SLJ 11/91) [333.95]

9977 Tesar, Jenny. *Endangered Habitats* (5–9). (Our Fragile Planet) 1992, Facts on File LB $19.95 (0-8160-2493-6). A succinct overview of food chains and ecosystems, and an account of environmental problems, extinction, and endangered species. (Rev: BL 6/1/92; SLJ 9/92) [333.95]

9978 Tudge, Colin. *Last Animals at the Zoo: How Mass Extinction Can Be Stopped* (9–12). 1992, Island Pr. $30.00 (1-55963-158-9). Explains what zoos have accomplished in the area of conservation breeding. (Rev: BL 3/1/92) [639.9]

Farms and Ranches

GENERAL AND MISCELLANEOUS

9979 Goldberg, Jake. *The Disappearing American Farm* (8–12). Illus. 1996, Watts LB $24.00 (0-531-11261-6). After a brief history of farming and the economic aspects of U.S. farm policy, the author discusses the impact of technology and agricultural research on the farm industry, government intervention, and a number of other difficult issues facing farmers and the nation today. (Rev: BL 6/1–15/96; BR 11–12/96; SLJ 6/96; VOYA 10/96) [338.1]

9980 Haynes, Cynthia. *Raising Turkeys, Ducks, Geese, Pigeons, and Guineas* (10–12). Illus. 1987, TAB $24.95 (0-8306-0803-6). A general guide to the breeding and raising of a variety of poultry species. (Rev: BL 4/1/88) [636.5]

Insects and Arachnids

GENERAL AND MISCELLANEOUS

9981 Blum, Mark. *Bugs in 3-D* (10–12). Illus. 1998, Chronicle $18.95 (0-8118-1945-0). A stunning 3-D view of insects that uses special photographic plates and a built-in stereoscope attached to the cover of the book. (Rev: SLJ 4/99) [595.7]

9982 Borror, Donald J., and Richard E. White. *A Field Guide to the Insects of America North of Mexico* (9–12). Illus. 1970, Houghton paper $17.00 (0-395-18523-8). In addition to an identification manual, this book explains how to observe insects and how to collect and preserve them. [595.7]

9983 Buchmann, Stephen L., and Gary Paul Nabhan. *The Forgotten Pollinators* (10–12). Illus. 1996, Island Pr. $25.00 (1-55963-352-2). An exploration of how the poisoning of pollinators by herbicides and pesticides threatens the plants that the planet depends upon for survival, and recommendations for how to prevent this. (Rev: BL 7/96; SLJ 4/97) [595.7]

9984 Conniff, Richard. *Spineless Wonders: Strange Tales from the Invertebrate World* (10–12). Illus. 1996, Holt $25.00 (0-8050-4218-0). The fascinating world of invertebrates is introduced with material on such species as flies, leeches, fire ants, giant squids, dragonflies, beetles, worms, mosquitoes, and moths. (Rev: BL 11/1/96; SLJ 4/97) [592]

9985 Evans, Arthur V., and Charles L. Bellamy. *An Inordinate Fondness for Beetles* (10–12). 1996, Holt $40.00 (0-8050-3751-9). Amazing photographs and a lucid test are used to explore the world of beetles, their anatomy, history, habits, and uses. (Rev: BL 3/15/97; BR 9–10/97; SLJ 7/97) [595.76]

9986 Evans, Howard Ensign. *The Pleasures of Entomology: Portraits of Insects and the People Who Study Them* (10–12). Illus. 1985, Smithsonian paper $16.95 (0-87474-421-0). An enjoyable personal look at the study of insects plus information on many species and their habits. (Rev: BL 8/85) [595.7]

9987 Johnson, Sylvia A. *Ladybugs* (6–9). Illus. 1983, Lerner LB $22.60 (0-8225-1481-8). Lavish illustrations are used to give the life story and contributions of the ladybug. [595.7]

9988 Milne, Lorus, and Margery Milne. *The Audubon Society Field Guide to North American Insects and Spiders* (7–12). Illus. 1980, Knopf $19.00 (0-394-50763-0). An extensive use of color photographs makes this a fine guide for identifying insects. [595.7]

9989 O'Toole, Christopher, ed. *The Encyclopedia of Insects* (9–12). Illus. 1986, Facts on File $29.95 (0-8160-1358-6). A large format book with stunning illustrations that gives general information and detailed facts about individual species. (Rev: BL 6/1/86; BR 11–12/86) [595.7]

9990 Pipe, Jim. *The Giant Book of Bugs and Creepy Crawlies* (4–8). Illus. 1998, Millbrook $17.95 (0-7613-0648-X). Exotic and common insects and spiders are presented in this oversize book with eye-catching pictures and fascinating text. (Rev: BL 8/98) [595.7]

9991 Preston-Mafham, Rod, and Ken Preston-Mafham. *Butterflies of the World* (8–12). Illus. 1988, Facts on File $29.95 (0-8160-1601-1). An attractively illustrated book that introduces butterflies and moths and gives facts about their evolution, structure, types, and life cycles. (Rev: BR 3–4/89) [595.78]

9992 Pyle, Robert Michael. *The Audubon Society Field Guide to North American Butterflies* (7–12). Illus. 1981, Knopf $19.00 (0-394-51914-0). An introduction to over 600 species of butterflies in about 1,000 color photographs and text. [595.7]

9993 Wangberg, James K. *Do Bees Sneeze? And Other Questions Kids Ask About Insects* (7–10). Illus. 1997, Fulcrum paper $17.95 (1-55591-963-4). Full, interesting answers to over 200 questions about insects on such subjects as physical characteristics, anatomical features, locomotion, behavior, habitat, and human health and safety. (Rev: BL 1/1–15/98; SLJ 4/98) [595.7]

9994 Whalley, Paul. *Butterfly & Moth* (6–8). Illus. 1988, Knopf LB $20.99 (0-394-99618-6). Short chapters are used to describe the characteristics of moths and butterflies, the various species, and their life cycles. (Rev: BL 12/1/88; SLJ 12/88) [595.7]

9995 White, Richard E. *A Field Guide to the Beetles of North America* (9–12). Illus. 1983, Houghton $21.95 (0-395-31808-4); paper $18.00 (0-395-33953-7). An identification guide that also covers such topics as the habits and structure of beetles and how to collect them. [595.7]

9996 Wilsdon, Christina, and National Audubon Society, eds. *National Audubon Society First Field Guide: Insects* (4–8). Illus. 1998, Scholastic $17.95 (0-590-05447-3). Following a general introduction to entomology, specific insects are pictured and information is given on such topics as their eating, mating and social habits, physical structure, habitats, and identification markings. (Rev: SLJ 10/98) [595]

9997 Wootton, Anthony. *Insects of the World* (9–12). Illus. 1984, Facts on File $29.95 (0-87196-991-2). This nicely illustrated volume describes how insects evolved, their characteristics, and how to identify them. [595.7]

Marine and Freshwater Life

GENERAL AND MISCELLANEOUS

9998 *America's Seashore Wonderlands* (9–12). Illus. 1985, National Geographic $12.95 (0-87044-543-X). Beginning with the northwest coast and ending with New England, this is an illustrated tour of our seashores. (Rev: BL 5/1/86) [574.5]

9999 Arthur, Alex. *Shell* (5–9). Illus. 1989, Knopf LB $18.99 (0-394-92256-5). Through a series of stunning 2-page photographs, various kinds of animals with shells—like mollusks and turtles—are pictured and described in the text. (Rev: BL 9/15/89; BR 11–12/89) [594]

10000 Banister, Keith, and Andrew Campbell, eds. *The Encyclopedia of Aquatic Life* (9–12). Illus. 1986, Facts on File $45.00 (0-8160-1257-1). Thousands of species are covered in text and illustrations under 3 headings: fish, aquatic invertebrates, and aquatic mammals. (Rev: BL 2/1/86) [591.92]

10001 Boschung, Herbert T., Jr., et al. *The Audubon Society Field Guide to North American Fishes, Whales, and Dolphins* (7–12). Illus. 1983, Knopf $19.00 (0-394-53405-0). About 600 marine and freshwater fish and aquatic mammals are identified and described. [597]

10002 Cerullo, Mary. *The Octopus: Phantom of the Sea* (4–8). Illus. 1997, Dutton paper $16.99 (0-525-65199-3). Using sharp color photographs and concise text, this book introduces the octopus, with material on anatomy, feeding, mating, and defense mechanisms, with information on such relatives as the squid, cuttlefish, and chambered nautilus. (Rev: BL 2/1/97; SLJ 7/98) [594]

10003 Douglass, Jackie Leatherby. *Peterson First Guide to Shells of North America* (7–12). Illus. 1989, Houghton paper $4.95 (0-395-48297-6). This is an abridged edition of the complete field guide that is more accessible and less forbidding than the parent volume. (Rev: BL 6/1/89) [594]

10004 Ellis, Richard. *Monsters of the Sea* (9–12). 1994, Knopf $35.00 (0-679-40639-5). Examines whales, octopuses, giant squid, sharks, and manatees, once believed to be sea serpents, leviathans, and mermaids. (Rev: BL 11/1/94*) [591.92]

10005 Goodman, Susan E. *Ultimate Field Trip 3: Wading into Marine Biology* (5–8). (Ultimate Field Trip) 1999, Simon & Schuster $17.00 (0-689-81963-3). A description of a field trip by Boston middle school students to the Bay of Fundy, an area of extreme tides, with material on their reactions, the plants and animals that live there, and the tide pools the youngsters explored. (Rev: BL 4/15/99; SLJ 6/99) [574.92]

10006 Kovacs, Deborah, and Kate Madin. *Beneath Blue Waters: Meetings with Remarkable Deep-Sea Creatures* (5–8). Illus. 1996, Viking $16.99 (0-670-85653-3). Text and color photos are used in this remarkable exploration of marine life one mile below the ocean's surface. (Rev: BL 12/1/96*; SLJ 1/97) [591.92]

10007 Meinkoth, Norman A. *The Audubon Society Field Guide to North American Seashore Creatures* (7–12). Illus. 1981, Knopf $19.00 (0-394-51993-0). This is a guide to such invertebrates as sponges, corals, urchins, and anemones. [592]

10008 Morris, Percy A. *A Field Guide to Pacific Coast Shells, Including Shells of Hawaii and the Gulf of California.* 2nd rev. ed. (7–12). Illus. 1966, Houghton $21.95 (0-395-08029-0); paper $15.95 (0-395-18322-7). A total of 945 species are described and illustrated in this Peterson Field Guide. A companion volume is: *A Field Guide to Shells of the Atlantic and Gulf Coasts and the West Indies* (1973). [594]

10009 Parker, Steve. *Seashore* (5–9). Illus. 1989, Knopf LB $18.99 (0-394-92254-9). Text and stunning color photographs are used to supply much information about seashores and the life they support. (Rev: BL 10/15/89) [591.909]

10010 Rehder, Harold A. *The Audubon Society Field Guide to North American Seashells* (7–12). Illus. 1981, Knopf $19.00 (0-394-51913-2). Seven hundred of the most common seashells from our coasts are pictured in color photographs and described in the text. [594]

10011 Taylor, Leighton. *Creeps from the Deep* (4–8). Illus. 1997, Chronicle $13.95 (0-8118-1297-9). In startling color photos and fascinating text, this title examines the strange creatures that live in the deepest regions of the ocean. (Rev: BL 12/15/97; SLJ 4/98) [578.77]

CORALS AND JELLYFISH

10012 Cerullo, Mary. *Coral Reef: A City That Never Sleeps* (5–8). Illus. 1996, Dutton $17.99 (0-525-65193-4). Exceptional photographs highlight this account of coral reefs and the life they support. (Rev: BL 3/1/96; SLJ 1/96*) [574.9]

10013 Johnson, Rebecca L. *The Great Barrier Reef: A Living Laboratory* (5–8). 1992, Lerner LB $23.93 (0-8225-1596-2). A look at the world's largest coral reef, off the coast of Australia. (Rev: BL 5/15/92; SLJ 7/92) [574.9943]

10014 Johnson, Sylvia A. *Coral Reefs* (7–9). Illus. 1984, Lerner LB $22.60 (0-8225-1451-6). Through many illustrations and concise text, the reader is introduced to coral reefs and the life they help support. [574.92]

10015 Sammon, Rick. *Rhythm of the Reef: A Day in the Life of the Coral Reef* (10–12). 1995, Voyageur $14.95 (0-89658-311-2). Both browsers and researchers will enjoy this colorfully illustrated journey under the seas to witness the beauty and diversity of life on coral reefs. (Rev: SLJ 6/96) [593.6]

FISHES

10016 Eschmeyer, William N., and Earl S. Herald. *A Field Guide to Pacific Coast Fishes of North America: Fish the Gulf of Alaska to Baja California* (7–12). Illus. 1983, Houghton $21.95 (0-395-26873-7); paper $17.95 (0-395-33188-9). In this volume in the Peterson Field Guide series, about 500 fish are described and illustrated. [597]

10017 Filisky, Michael. *Peterson First Guide to Fishes of North America* (7–12). Illus. 1989, Houghton paper $4.95 (0-395-50219-5). This is a concise version of the parent Peterson guide that gives basic material on common fish but with less detail. (Rev: BL 6/1/89) [597]

10018 Parker, Steve. *Fish* (5–9). Illus. 1990, Knopf LB $20.99 (0-679-90439-5). A general introduction to fish, their physiology, and the main fish groups. (Rev: BL 7/90; SLJ 9/90) [597]

10019 Robins, C. Richard, and G. Carleton Ray. *A Field Guide to Atlantic Coast Fishes of North America* (9–12). Illus. 1986, Houghton paper $17.95 (0-395-39198-9). An excellent field guide that describes almost 1,100 species of fish that are found between the Arctic and the Caribbean. (Rev: BL 6/1/86) [597]

SHARKS

10020 Cerullo, Mary. *Sharks: Challengers of the Deep* (5–9). 1993, Dutton $15.99 (0-525-65100-4). Packed with information and photos on sharks' physical characteristics, behavior, ecology, and survival. (Rev: BL 1/15/93; SLJ 2/93*) [597]

10021 Coupe, Sheena M. *Sharks* (5–8). Illus. 1990, Facts on File $17.95 (0-8160-2270-4). An oversized book that contains a well-organized text and many illustrations. (Rev: BL 4/1/90; SLJ 7/90) [597]

10022 Dingerkus, Guido. *The Shark Watchers' Guide* (7–12). Illus. 1989, Messner paper $5.95 (0-671-68815-4). As well as materials on 30 different varieties of sharks this book tells about shark anatomy, habits, and evolution and gives tips on how to handle a shark attack. (Rev: BL 11/15/85; SLJ 12/85) [597]

10023 Gourley, Catherine. *Sharks! True Stories and Legends* (4–8). 1996, Millbrook LB $27.40 (0-7613-0001-5). Both fact and fiction about sharks are mixed in this informal, readable book. (Rev: BL 10/15/96; SLJ 12/96) [597]

10024 MacQuitty, Miranda. *Shark* (5–9). (Eyewitness Books) 1992, Knopf LB $20.99 (0-679-91683-0). A guide to the various species of sharks, their habits, and habitats accompanied by excellent photographs. (Rev: BL 11/1/92) [597]

10025 Reader's Digest, eds. *Sharks: Silent Hunters of the Deep* (8–12). Illus. 1987, Reader's Digest $19.95 (0-86438-014-3). This handsomely illustrated account describes the ways of sharks, gives material on famous encounters, and identifies all 344 species. (Rev: BL 5/15/87; BR 11–12/87; SLJ 1/88; VOYA 8/87) [597]

10026 Springer, Victor G., and Joy P. Gold. *Sharks in Question: The Smithsonian Answer Book* (9–12). Illus. 1989, Smithsonian paper $24.95 (0-87474-877-1). Using a question-and-answer format plus stunning photographs, the authors tell all and explode myths about this sea creature. (Rev: BL 6/1/89; SLJ 8/89) [597]

10027 Stafford-Deitsch, Jeremy. *Shark: A Photographer's Story* (10–12). Illus. 1987, Sierra Club paper $25.00 (0-87156-733-4). After a discussion of shark anatomy and behavior, the author takes you on a well-illustrated global exploration of their haunts. (Rev: BL 11/15/87; BR 3–4/88; VOYA 2/89) [597]

10028 Steel, Rodney. *Sharks of the World* (9–12). Illus. 1985, Facts on File $29.95 (0-8160-1086-2). Straightforward information is given on sharks plus intriguing photographs. (Rev: BL 2/1/86) [597]

10029 Stevens, John D., ed. *Sharks* (9–12). Illus. 1987, Facts on File $35.00 (0-8160-1800-6). An oversize book with stunning photographs on each page and 17 chapters each written by a shark specialist. (Rev: BL 9/15/87) [591]

WHALES, DOLPHINS, AND OTHER SEA MAMMALS

10030 Bonner, Nigel. *Whales of the World* (9–12). Illus. 1989, Facts on File $29.95 (0-8160-1734-4). A description of various kinds of whales and behavioral patterns, plus a discussion of the possible extinction that many species now face. (Rev: BL 10/1/89; BR 1–2/90) [599.5]

10031 Calambokidis, John, and Gretchen Steiger. *Blue Whales* (9–12). (World life Library) 1997, Voyageur paper $16.95 (0-89658-338-4). An oversize book with color photos and text that explores the evolution, anatomy, and habits of the blue whale and the impact of whaling on their numbers. (Rev: SLJ 1/98) [599.5]

10032 Clapham, Phil. *Humpback Whales* (10–12). (World Life Library) 1996, Voyageur paper $16.95 (0-89658-296-5). Over 50 full-color photographs enhance this introduction to the anatomy, behavior, characteristics, history, and present status of the humpback whale. (Rev: BR 5–6/97; SLJ 5/97) [599.5]

10033 Dow, Lesley. *Whales* (5–8). 1990, Facts on File $17.95 (0-8160-2271-2). A fine introduction to this endangered animal—its species and living habits—as well as information on legends concerning the whale. (Rev: BL 4/1/90) [599.5]

10034 Ellis, Richard. *The Book of Whales* (9–12). Illus. 1980, Knopf paper $35.00 (0-394-73371-1). A beautifully illustrated book that describes how whales evolved, various species, and their behavior. [599.5]

10035 Ellis, Richard. *Dolphins and Porpoises* (10–12). Illus. 1989, Random paper $35.00 (0-679-72286-6). A detailed account of each of the 43 different species and of the characteristics of each. (Rev: BR 11–12/89; VOYA 2/90) [599.5]

10036 Gardner, Robert. *The Whale Watchers' Guide* (9–12). 1984, Messner paper $5.95 (0-671-49807-X). This guide to an increasingly popular pastime helps one identify 26 different species of whales. [599.5]

10037 Gourley, Catherine. *Hunting Neptune's Giants: True Stories of American Whaling* (5–8). 1995, Millbrook LB $27.40 (1-56294-534-3). A look at the whaling industry's history through diaries and books by men and women involved in this once important industry. (Rev: BL 11/1/95*; SLJ 12/95) [639.3]

10038 Haley, Delphine, ed. *Marine Mammals of Eastern North Pacific and Arctic Waters*. 2nd ed. (10–12). Illus. 1986, Pacific Search paper $22.95 (0-931397-11-1). Separate articles written by 21 experts are given on each animal. Good illustrations. (Rev: BL 10/1/86) [599.09]

10039 Hand, Douglas. *Gone Whaling: A Search for Orcas in the Northwest Waters* (9–12). 1994, Simon & Schuster $19.50 (0-671-76840-9). The orca, a gentle beast undeservedly known as the "killer whale," is examined in its natural habitat and in captivity. (Rev: BL 7/94) [599.5]

10040 Harrison, Richard, and M. M. Bryden, eds. *Whales, Dolphins and Porpoises* (9–12). Illus. 1988, Facts on File $30.00 (0-8160-1977-0). A handsome oversize volume with lucid text and copious illustrations. (Rev: BL 1/1/89; BR 3–4/89) [599.5]

10041 Hoyt, Erich. *Meeting the Whales: The Equinox Guide to Giants of the Deep* (5–10). Illus. 1991, Camden House paper $9.95 (0-921820-23-2). This guide to 19 whale species describes their origins and habits. Includes a discussion on whale watching and photography. (Rev: BL 8/91) [599.5]

10042 Kelsey, Elin. *Finding Out about Whales* (4–8). Illus. (Science Explorers) 1998, Owl $19.95 (1-895688-79-5); paper $9.95 (1-895688-80-9). This

book discusses how information is gathered about whales and introduces 5 different species: blue, humpback, beluga, gray, and killer. (Rev: BL 3/1/99; SLJ 3/99) [595.5]

10043 Knudtson, Peter. *Orca: Visions of the Killer Whale* (10–12). 1996, Sierra Club $27.00 (0-87156-906-X). Chapters discuss the history, anatomy, habits, and habitats of orca, the killer whale, but the high point of this volume is its stunning photographs. (Rev: BL 12/1/96; SLJ 6/97) [599.5]

10044 Leatherwood, Stephen, and Randall R. Reeves. *The Sierra Club Handbook of Whales and Dolphins* (9–12). Illus. 1983, Sierra Club paper $18.00 (0-87156-340-1). Through color and black-and-white pictures and an extensive text, 76 species are described. [599.5]

10045 Matero, Robert. *The Birth of a Humpback Whale* (5–8). Illus. 1996, Simon & Schuster $16.00 (0-689-31931-2). A narrative with pencil drawings that covers the birth of a humpbacked whale and its journey from Hawaii to Alaska. (Rev: BL 4/1/96; SLJ 6/96) [599.5]

10046 Norris, Kenneth S. *Dolphin Days: The Life and Times of the Spinner Dolphin* (9–12). 1991, Norton $21.95 (0-393-02945-X). The author, a researcher, describes a dolphin society, explains the dolphin's language and navigational skills. Includes an unsettling eyewitness report of the deadly disorientation and fear caused by tuna netting. (Rev: BL 9/1/91) [599.5]

10047 Obee, Bruce. *Guardians of the Whales: The Quest to Study Whales in the Wild* (9–12). 1992, Alaska Northwest $34.95 (0-88240-428-8). Profiles the scientists largely responsible for saving whales from near extinction and explains how research on the marine mammals is conducted. (Rev: BL 10/15/92) [599.5]

10048 Paine, Stefani. *The World of the Arctic Whales: Belugas, Bowheads, Narwhals* (10–12). 1995, Sierra Club $26.00 (0-87156-378-9). Using many photographs, this book describes the diet, mating, birth, life, and death of whales and the impact of humans on their lives throughout history. (Rev: SLJ 3/96; VOYA 6/96) [599.5]

10049 Papastavrou, Vassili. *Whale* (5–9). (Eyewitness Books) 1993, Knopf LB $20.99 (0-679-93884-2). A heavily illustrated introduction to various kinds of whales, their habits, and where they live. (Rev: BL 10/1/93) [599.5]

10050 Pascoe, Elaine, adapt. *Animal Intelligence: Why Is This Dolphin Smiling?* (5–8). 1997, Blackbirch LB $17.95 (1-56711-226-9). This book reports on the scientific research on communication between dolphins and humans, with reports on such projects as one by John Lilly to create, via computer, dolphin equivalents of human words. (Rev: SLJ 12/97)

[599.5]

10051 Payne, Roger. *Among Whales* (9–12). 1995, Macmillan $24.00 (0-02-595245-5). An introduction to the anatomy, habits, and characteristics of whales by one of the world's leading marine mammal experts. (Rev: BL 4/15/95*) [599.5]

10052 Price-Groff, Claire. *The Manatee* (7–10). (Endangered Animals and Habitats) 1999, Lucent LB $53.88 (1-56006-445-5). This well-illustrated book describes this endangered sea mammal and tells about its habits, habitats, and appearance. (Rev: BL 9/15/99) [599.53]

10053 Pringle, Laurence. *Dolphin Man: Exploring the World of Dolphins* (5–9). Illus. 1995, Simon & Schuster $17.00 (0-689-80299-4). A fascinating photoessay about the world of dolphins as explored by marine biologist Randall Wells in a dolphin community in the Sarasota Bay area of Florida. (Rev: BL 1/1–15/96; SLJ 2/96) [599.5]

10054 Read, Andrew. *Porpoises* (5–8). (World Life Library) 1999, Voyageur paper $16.95 (0-89658-420-8). With many color illustrations, and large print, this book introduces porpoises, their characteristics, behavior, habitats, and how they are studied. (Rev: BL 8/99) [599.53]

Microscopes, Microbiology, and Biotechnology

10055 Bleifeld, Maurice. *Experimenting with a Microscope* (5–9). Illus. 1988, Watts LB $22.50 (0-531-10580-6). The story of the microscope plus many experiments and projects involving its use. (Rev: BL 1/15/89; BR 3–4/89) [578]

10056 Levine, Shar, and Leslie Johnstone. *The Microscope Book* (5–8). Illus. 1997, Sterling $19.95 (0-8069-4898-1); paper $10.95 (0-8069-4899-X). An excellent introduction to microscopes, with material on parts of the microscope, lenses, how to focus and produce slides, and tips on keeping a journal. (Rev: SLJ 7/97) [502]

10057 Margulis, Lynn, and Dorion Sagan. *What Is Life?* (9–12). 1995, Simon & Schuster $40.00 (0-684-81326-2). Explores the multifaceted answer to the question posed by the title. A microscopic complement to Stephen Gould's macroscopic paleobiology in his *Book of Life.* (Rev: BL 9/1/95) [577]

10058 Nachtigall, Werner. *Exploring with the Microscope: A Book of Discovery and Learning* (7–12). Trans. by Elizabeth Reinersmann. 1995, Sterling $19.95 (0-8069-0866-1). A thorough book about microscopes and their uses, with 100 color slides, diagrams, and black-and-white photos. (Rev: BL 10/1/95; SLJ 11/95) [578]

10059 Nardo, Don. *Germs: Mysterious Microorganisms* (6–8). (Encyclopedia of Discovery and Invention) 1991, Lucent LB $18.96 (1-56006-214-2). Explains the history of germ theory and "useful" germs as well as those that cause disease. (Rev: BL 12/1/91; SLJ 2/92) [616]

10060 Rainis, Kenneth G., and George Nassis. *Biotechnology Projects for Young Scientists* (9–12). (Projects for Young Scientists) 1998, Watts $25.00 (0-531-11419-8); paper $6.95 (0-531-15913-2). After a discussion of biotechnology and its applications in the areas of food, environment, industry, the courts, and genetic testing, a series of remarkable projects, such as cloning carrots, are presented for the advanced science student. (Rev: BR 1–2/99; SLJ 10/98) [620.8]

10061 Rainis, Kenneth G., and Bruce J. Russell. *Guide to Microlife* (7–12). Illus. 1996, Watts paper $40.00 (0-531-11266-7). A handbook to microscopic animals that describes habitats, the various groups of organisms, and projects. Each entry is accompanied by stunning photographs. (Rev: BL 2/15/97; SLJ 5/97) [576]

10062 Rogers, Kirsteen. *The Usborne Complete Book of the Microscope* (4–8). Illus. 1999, EDC paper $14.95 (0-7460-3106-8). Objects and organisms that can be viewed with a microscope are pictured and described in a series of double-page spreads, along with material on the parts and uses of different kinds of microscopes. (Rev: SLJ 7/99) [535]

10063 Ruiz, Andres L. *The Life of a Cell* (6–9). Illus. (Sequences of Earth and Space) 1997, Sterling $12.95 (0-8069-9741-9). This work describes the types of cells, their similarities and differences, their structures, and their functions. (Rev: BL 12/1/97) [574.87]

10064 Stwertka, Eve, and Albert Stwertka. *Microscope: How to Use It & Enjoy It* (6–9). Illus. 1989, Silver Burdett LB $11.95 (0-671-63705-3); paper $4.95 (0-671-67060-3). A fine introduction that covers such topics as the parts of the microscope, how they operate, techniques for use, and how to prepare slides. (Rev: BL 3/1/89; BR BR 9–10/89; SLJ 4/89) [502.8]

10065 Tomb, Howard. *MicroAliens: Dazzling Journeys with an Electron Microscope* (6–10). Illus. 1993, Farrar $16.00 (0-374-34960-6). An introduction to the development of the electron microscope, with black-and-white photos of ordinary objects as seen through its lens. (Rev: BL 12/1/93; SLJ 1/94) [574]

Pets

GENERAL AND MISCELLANEOUS

10066 Alderton, David. *101 Essential Tips: Caring for Your Pet Bird* (6–12). 1996, DK Publg. paper $4.95 (0-7894-1077-X). This book covers all the basics for first-time bird owners, from selection to feeding and maintaining health. (Rev: VOYA 4/97) [598]

10067 Barrie, Anmarie. *A Step-by-Step Book about Rabbits* (9–12). Illus. 1987, TFH paper $5.95 (0-86622-475-0). After a discussion of types of rabbits, this book tells how to feed and care for them. (Rev: BL 11/15/87) [636.9]

10068 Birmelin, Immanuel, and Annette Wolter. *The New Parakeet Handbook* (9–12). Illus. 1986, Barron's paper $9.95 (0-8120-2985-2). A manual on selecting and caring for parakeets, also known as budgerigars. (Rev: BL 5/15/86) [636.6]

10069 Garisto, Leslie, and Peg Streep. *The Best-Ever Book of Dog & Cat Names* (7–12). 1989, Holt paper $7.95 (0-8050-0775-X). Over 1,000 names for dogs and cats taken from history and literature are listed and explained. (Rev: BR 9–10/89) [636.08]

10070 Gerstenfeld, Sheldon L. *The Bird Care Book: All You Need to Know to Keep Your Bird Healthy and Happy*. Rev. ed. (8–12). Illus. 1989, Addison-Wesley paper $16.00 (0-201-09559-9). A basic handbook on the choosing, care, and feeding of both pet and wild birds. (Rev: BL 9/15/89) [636.6]

10071 Lantermann, Werner. *The New Parrot Handbook: Everything about Purchase, Acclimation, Care, Diet, Disease, and Behavior of Parrots* (9–12). Illus. 1986, Barron's paper $9.95 (0-8120-3729-4). A complete handbook that covers choosing and caring for a bird with information about species, breeding, and behavior. (Rev: BL 11/1/86) [636.6]

10072 Simon, Seymour. *Pets in a Jar: Collecting and Caring for Small Wild Animals* (7–10). Illus. 1975, Penguin paper $5.99 (0-14-049186-4). Valuable information is given on caring for such small pets as ants, crickets, crabs, and starfish. [639]

10073 Taylor, Michael. *Pot Bellied Pigs as a Family Pet* (9–12). 1993, TFH $35.95 (0-86622-081-X). Includes what to feed pot-bellies, how they are related to other swine, and legal restrictions on ownership. (Rev: BL 4/15/93) [636.4]

10074 Vriends, Matthew M. *Pigeons* (7–12). Illus. 1988, Barron's paper $6.95 (0-8120-4044-9). A brief but thorough guide to raising pigeons plus material on their behavior and how to breed them. (Rev: BL 2/1/89) [636.5]

CATS

10075 Altman, Roberta. *The Quintessential Cat* (9–12). 1994, Prentice Hall $27.50 (0-671-85008-3). Includes feline tales, trivia, and tips, specific breeds and their abilities, and cat-loving celebrities such as Robert De Niro. (Rev: BL 10/1/94) [599.74]

10076 Brown, Philip. *Uncle Whiskers* (9–12). Illus. 1980, Warner paper $2.95 (0-446-87108-7). The true story of a remarkable cat that was crippled in an accident. [636.8]

10077 Caras, Roger A. *The Cats of Thistle Hill: A Mostly Peaceable Kingdom* (9–12). 1994, Simon & Schuster $22.00 (0-671-75462-9). Anecdotes about the personalities and behaviors of the dozens of cats—and countless other animals—that share Caras's home and grounds. (Rev: BL 5/1/94) [636.8]

10078 Clutton-Brock, Juliet. *Cat* (5–9). (Eyewitness Books) 1991, Knopf LB $20.99 (0-679-91458-7). An illustrated introduction to the cat family and their habits. (Rev: BL 12/1/91) [599.74]

10079 Denny, D. Michael. *How to Get a Cat to Sit in Your Lap: Confessions of an Unconventional Cat Person* (9–12). 1995, Andiron paper $14.95 (0-9645799-0-1). Based on 30 years of living with cats, the author humorously tells of cat evolution, anatomy, behavior, naming, hunting, eating, and more. (Rev: BL 6/1–15/95) [636.8]

10080 Fogle, Bruce. *The Encyclopedia of the Cat* (6–12). 1997, DK Publg. $34.95 (0-7894-1970-X). This handsomely-illustrated volume contains excellent information about cats, their breeds, care and feeding, history, behavior, and place in world culture. (Rev: BL 11/15/97; VOYA 10/98) [636.8]

10081 Fogle, Bruce. *Know Your Cat: An Owner's Guide to Cat Behavior* (9–12). 1991, DK Publg. $24.95 (1-879431-04-1). A veterinarian provides insights into cat behavior, with 350 color photos. (Rev: BL 1/1/92) [636.8]

10082 Gerstenfeld, Sheldon L. *The Cat Care Book: All You Need to Know to Keep Your Cat Healthy and Happy*. Rev. ed. (8–12). Illus. 1989, Addison-Wesley paper $16.00 (0-201-09569-6). Tips on how to choose a cat and detailed information on taking care of cats as pets. (Rev: BL 9/15/89) [636.8]

10083 Hammond, Sean, and Carolyn Usrey. *How to Raise a Sane and Healthy Cat* (9–12). 1994, Howell Book House $22.95 (0-87605-797-0). Answers questions regarding the many facets of cat care and ownership, including choosing a cat, nutrition, and care of stray cats. (Rev: BL 7/94) [636.8]

10084 Herriot, James. *James Herriot's Cat Stories* (9–12). 1994, St. Martin's $17.95 (0-312-11342-0). A small collection of cat tales, ranging from the informative and scientific to the humorous and poignant. (Rev: BL 7/94) [636.8]

10085 McGinnis, Terri. *The Well Cat Book: The Classic Comprehensive Handbook of Cat Care*. 2nd ed. (9–12). 1993, Random $23.00 (0-394-58769-3). An authoritative guide by a veterinarian, covering feline anatomy, preventive medicine, diagnosis, home care, breeding, reproduction, and choosing a doctor. (Rev: BL 6/1–15/93) [636.808]

10086 Maggitti, Phil. *Owning the Right Cat* (9–12). 1993, Tetra $29.95 (1-56465-111-8). Provides information on feeding, grooming, breeding, showing, laws, history, health care, and genetics, with color photos and illustrations. (Rev: BL 11/1/93) [636.8]

10087 Morris, Desmond. *Catlore* (7–12). 1987, Crown $13.00 (0-517-56903-5). A rich collection of facts about cats and cat behavior that even analyzes the sounds cats make. (Rev: VOYA 10/88) [599.74]

10088 Morris, Desmond. *Catwatching* (8–12). 1987, Crown $13.00 (0-517-56518-8); paper $8.00 (0-517-88053-9). Using a question-and-answer approach, the author explores many facets of cat behavior. (Rev: BL 4/1/87) [636.8]

10089 Muller, Ulrike. *Long-Haired Cats* (10–12). 1984, Barron's paper $6.95 (0-8120-2803-1). A specialized book on the types of long-haired cats and how to care for them with a special chapter on cat psychology. [636.8]

10090 Pugnetti, Gino. *Simon and Schuster's Guide to Cats* (9–12). 1983, Simon & Schuster paper $14.00 (0-671-49170-9). A guide to the different breeds of cats and how to care for them with additional material on the history of cats and their personality. [636.8]

10091 Steiger, Brad. *Cats Incredible! True Stories of Fantastic Feline Feats* (9–12). 1994, NAL paper $9.95 (0-452-27159-2). An amusing cat miscellany of feline factoids and believe-it-or-not anecdotes. (Rev: BL 3/15/94) [636.8]

10092 Taylor, David. *You & Your Cat* (9–12). Illus. 1986, Knopf paper $16.95 (0-394-72984-6). Historical and anatomical information is followed by material on each breed and on the care and grooming of your cat. (Rev: BL 7/86; BR 11–12/86) [636.8]

10093 Zistel, Era. *A Gathering of Cats* (9–12). 1993, J. N. Townsend paper $11.95 (1-880158-00-0). Zistel tells the stories of various members of her pride of cats. (Rev: BL 11/1/93) [636.8]

DOGS

10094 American Kennel Club. *The Complete Dog Book*. 19th ed. (7–12). Illus. 1998, Howell $32.95 (0-87605-148-4). The standard manual for dog owners and guide to every AKC-recognized breed. The first edition appeared over 50 years ago. (Rev: BL 6/15/85) [636.7]

10095 Benjamin, Carol Lea. *The Chosen Puppy: How to Select and Raise a Great Puppy from an Animal Shelter* (10–12). Illus. 1990, Howell Book House paper $7.95 (0-87605-417-3). This is an informal guide to selecting and training a dog from an animal shelter; many humorous illustrations. (Rev: BL 9/1/90) [636.7]

10096 Benjamin, Carol Lea. *Dog Training for Kids*. Rev. ed. (5–8). Illus. 1988, Howell Book House $17.95 (0-87605-541-2). A simple guide to dog training that emphasizes the goal of having fun with a dog you are proud of. (Rev: SLJ 4/89) [636.7]

10097 Clutton-Brock, Juliet. *Dog* (5–9). (Eyewitness Books) 1991, Knopf LB $20.99 (0-679-91459-5). An introduction to various breeds of dogs and their habits, with many photographs. (Rev: BL 12/1/91) [599.74]

10098 Delmar, Diana. *The Guilt-Free Dog Owner's Guide: Caring for a Dog When You're Short on Time and Space* (10–12). Illus. 1990, Storey paper $10.95 (0-88266-575-8). A manual on how to keep a dog happy and well trained when you have to be away for hours each day. (Rev: BL 4/1/90) [636.7]

10099 Fogle, Bruce. *ASPCA Complete Dog Care Manual* (9–12). 1993, DK Publg. $24.95 (1-56458-168-3). Illustrated information and instructions for novice dog owners on diet, housebreaking, obedience, grooming, and health. (Rev: BL 5/1/93; SLJ 7/93) [636.7]

10100 Fogle, Bruce. *Cocker Spaniel: American and English* (6–12). Illus. (Dog Breed Handbook) 1996, DK Publg. $14.95 (0-7894-1065-6). This book introduces cocker spaniels, including their history, factors to consider in choosing one as a pet, housebreaking, training, health issues, and showing. A companion volume is *Golden Retriever* (1996). (Rev: VOYA 4/97) [636.7]

10101 Fogle, Bruce. *The Encyclopedia of the Dog* (8–12). 1995, DK Publg. $39.95 (0-7894-0149-5). Enhanced by outstanding photographs, this work identifies and describes over 400 breeds of dogs. Also use: *The Encyclopedia of the Cat* (1998). (Rev: BL 10/1/95; SLJ 3/96; VOYA 4/96) [636.7]

10102 Fogle, Bruce. *Know Your Dog: An Owner's Guide to Dog Behavior* (8–12). 1992, DK Publg. $24.95 (1-56458-080-6). Color photos enhance Fogle's introduction to dog characteristics and behavior in this large-format book. (Rev: BL 1/1/93) [636.7]

10103 Gerstenfeld, Sheldon L. *The Dog Care Book: All You Need to Know to Keep Your Dog Healthy and Happy*. Rev. ed. (8–12). Illus. 1989, Addison-Wesley paper $16.00 (0-201-09667-6). Tips on selecting a dog plus extensive material on care and feeding. (Rev: BL 9/15/89) [636.7]

10104 Hart, Benjamin, and Lynette Hart. *The Perfect Puppy: How to Choose Your Dog by Its Behavior* (9–12). 1988, Freeman paper $12.95 (0-7167-1829-4). A guide to choosing the right dog that outlines the characteristics of 56 different breeds. (Rev: BR 5–6/88) [599.74]

10105 Herriot, James. *James Herriot's Dog Stories* (9–12). Illus. 1986, St. Martin's $21.95 (0-312-43968-7). The famous veterinarian tells some of his favorite anecdotes about his 50 years working with dogs. (Rev: BL 4/15/86; SLJ 9/86) [636.7]

10106 Kay, William J., and Elizabeth Randolph, eds. *The Complete Book of Dog Health* (9–12). Illus. 1985, Howell Book House paper $15.00 (0-87605-455-6). This is a comprehensive account that covers all topics from diagnosing symptoms to choosing a veterinarian. (Rev: BL 6/1/85) [636.7]

10107 Klever, Ulrich. *The Complete Book of Dog Care: How to Raise a Happy and Healthy Dog* (9–12). Illus. 1989, Barron's paper $12.95 (0-8120-4158-5). The kinds of purebred dogs are profiled, plus information on how to select a dog and how to train and care for it. (Rev: BL 1/15/90) [636.7]

10108 Maggitti, Phil. *Owning the Right Dog* (8–12). 1993, Tetra $29.95 (1-56465-110-X). Provides information on feeding, grooming, breeding, showing, and training, with color illustrations. (Rev: BL 11/1/93) [636.7]

10109 Margolis, Matthew, and Catherine Swan. *The Dog in Your Life* (9–12). 1982, Random paper $16.00 (0-394-71174-2). This book covers selection, care, and training of dogs. [636.7]

10110 Morris, Desmond. *Dogwatching* (8–12). 1987, Crown $13.00 (0-517-56519-6). Why dogs act the way they do is explored in a question-and-answer format. (Rev: BL 4/1/87) [636.8]

10111 Paulsen, Gary. *My Life in Dog Years* (5–10). Illus. 1998, Delacorte $15.95 (0-385-32570-3). The famous novelist tells about 8 wonderful dogs that he has known and loved over the years. (Rev: BL 1/1–15/98; SLJ 3/98; VOYA 4/98) [636.7]

10112 Paulsen, Gary. *Puppies, Dogs, and Blue Northers: Reflections on Being Raised by a Pack of Sled Dogs* (6–10). Illus. 1996, Harcourt $16.00 (0-15-292881-2). In 7 short vignettes, Paulsen describes the life of his lead dog, Cookie, and how she raises her pups to race and pull sleds. (Rev: BR 3–4/97; SLJ 11/96; VOYA 2/97) [636.7]

10113 Scalisi, Danny, and Libby Moses. *When Rover Just Won't Do: Over 2000 Suggestions for Naming Your Puppy* (8–12). 1993, Howell Book House $9.95 (0-87605-691-5). This collection of names for dogs includes more than 2,000 ideas, from Fajita to Rocky and Bullwinkle. (Rev: BL 11/1/93) [636.7]

10114 Schuler, Elizabeth M. *Simon & Schuster's Guide to Dogs* (9–12). Illus. 1980, Simon & Schuster paper $14.00 (0-671-25527-4). A handbook that gives information on 324 breeds. [636.7]

10115 Silverstein, Alvin, and Virginia Silverstein. *Dogs: All About Them* (6–8). Illus. 1986, Lothrop $16.00 (0-688-04805-6). After a history of dogs from the Stone Age on, the authors cover such topics as breeds, uses, and care of dogs. (Rev: BL 3/1/86; SLJ 9/86; VOYA 2/86) [599.74]

10116 Smith, Ernie. *Warm Hearts & Cold Noses: A Common Sense Guide to Understanding the Family Dog* (9–12). 1987, Sunstone paper $10.95 (0-86534-109-5). A pet-care manual that covers topics such as feeding, housebreaking, and leash training. (Rev: BR 5–6/88) [636.7]

10117 Taylor, David. *The Ultimate Dog Book* (9–12). Illus. 1990, Simon & Schuster $29.95 (0-671-70988-7). An oversize book that discusses such topics as history, anatomy, breeds, and dog care. (Rev: BL 9/15/90) [636.7]

10118 Taylor, David, and Peter Scott. *You & Your Dog* (9–12). Illus. 1986, Knopf paper $17.00 (0-394-72983-8). Practical suggestions on choosing and caring for your dog are given along with information on history, anatomy, and a description of various breeds. (Rev: BL 7/86; BR 11–12/86; SLJ 9/86; VOYA 8/86) [636.7]

10119 Vine, Louis L. *The Total Dog Book: The Breeders' and Pet Owners' Complete Guide to Better Dog Care* (9–12). 1988, Warner paper $5.99 (0-446-31483-8). This complete handbook on maintaining healthy dogs stresses prevention of problems. [636.5]

10120 Widmer, Patricia P. *Pat Widmer's Dog Training Book* (9–12). 1980, NAL paper $3.95 (0-451-14468-6). A thorough manual on the care and training of a dog. [636.7]

10121 Woodhouse, Barbara. *Dog Training My Way* (10–12). 1985, Berkley paper $5.99 (0-425-08108-7). This is a print version of the television series on dog training given by the renowned British pet specialist. [636.7]

FISHES

10122 Emmens, Cliff W. *A Step-by-Step Book about Tropical Fish* (8–12). Illus. 1988, TFH paper $5.95 (0-86622-471-8). A brief, brightly illustrated introduction to various types of tropical fish, their care, and housing. (Rev: BL 1/1/89) [639.34]

10123 Harris, Jack C. *A Step-by-Step Book about Goldfish* (9–12). Illus. 1987, TFH $9.95 (0-86622-917-5). Topics covered in this guide include varieties, feeding, and health problems. (Rev: BL 5/1/88) [639.344]

10124 Mills, Dick. *Aquarium Fish* (6–12). Illus. 1996, DK Publg. paper $4.95 (0-7894-1074-5). A well-illustrated book that covers all aspects of fish as pets, from selecting healthy fish to maintaining a proper habitat and diet. (Rev: VOYA 4/97) [636.6]

HORSES

10125 Brady, Irene. *America's Horses and Ponies* (7–9). 1969, Houghton $17.95 (0-395-06659-X). Thirty-nine of the most popular breeds of horses are introduced and described. [599.72]

10126 Chapple, Judy. *Your Horse: A Step-by-Step Guide to Horse Ownership* (10–12). Illus. 1984, Garden Way paper $16.95 (0-88266-353-4). Starting with how to choose a horse, this guide supplies all kinds of information on caring for and training horses. [636.1]

10127 Clutton-Brock, Juliet. *Horse* (5–9). (Eyewitness Books) 1992, Knopf LB $20.99 (0-679-91681-4). An explanation of the origins of the horse, the various breeds, and care and handling procedures. (Rev: BL 6/1/92) [636.1]

10128 Edwards, Elwyn Hartley. *The Ultimate Horse Book* (9–12). 1991, Random $34.95 (1-879431-03-3). This illustrated guide introduces more than 80 breeds of horses and ponies, describes their relationship with humans, and discusses equine ownership and care. (Rev: BL 12/1/91) [636.1]

10129 Jurmain, Suzanne. *Once upon a Horse: A History of Horses and How They Shaped Our History* (5–9). Illus. 1989, Lothrop $15.95 (0-688-05550-8). A history of the horse and how it has been domesticated and used by humans. (Rev: BL 12/15/89; BR 3–4/90; SLJ 1/90; VOYA 4/90) [636.1]

10130 Meltzer, Milton. *Hold Your Horses! A Feedbag Full of Fact and Fable* (5–8). 1995, HarperCollins LB $14.89 (0-06-024478-X). This book, the last of Meltzer's trilogy on vegetable-mineral-animal and the 3 kingdoms of nature, focuses on how people have used horses in work, war, sports, and art. (Rev: BL 11/15/95; SLJ 12/95*) [636.1]

10131 Morris, Desmond. *Horsewatching* (10–12). Illus. 1989, Crown $15.00 (0-517-57267-2). Extensive answers are given to questions concerning the anatomy, habits, history, and behavior of the horse. (Rev: BL 5/1/89) [636.1]

10132 Roberts, Monty. *The Man Who Listens to Horses* (10–12). 1997, Random $23.00 (0-679-45689-9). The story of how the author, a child rodeo star, overcame abuse, rejection, and ridicule to become trainer of Queen Elizabeth II's horses, what he has learned about horses and their ways, and his unique, nonviolent methods of training. (Rev: SLJ 5/98) [636.1]

10133 Rosen, Michael J., ed. *Horse People: Writers & Artists on the Horses They Love* (9–12). Illus. 1998, Artisan $30.00 (1-885183-93-3). A delightful book of essays and artwork by such horse lovers as Dick Francis, Jane Smiley, and Rita Mae Brown, who describe their fascination with these animals and the thrill of working with them. (Rev: SLJ 9/98) [636.1]

10134 Ryden, Hope. *Wild Horses I Have Known* (4–8). 1999, Clarion $18.00 (0-395-77520-5). This photoessay about the wild mustangs that live around the Wyoming-Montana border was compiled by the author who spent years observing these animals and noting details of their behavior, social structure, and survival methods. (Rev: BL 4/15/99; SLJ 4/99) [636.1]

10135 Silverstein, Alvin, and Virginia Silverstein. *The Mustang* (4–8). (Endangered in America) 1997, Millbrook LB $22.40 (0-7613-0048-1). The life cycle and behavior of the mustang is examined, along with the reasons it has become endangered and techniques used to ensure survival. (Rev: BL 3/15/97; SLJ 6/97) [636.1]

10136 Twelveponies, Mary. *There Are No Problem Horses—Only Problem Riders* (10–12). 1982, Houghton paper $14.00 (0-395-33194-3). A book on horsemanship that stresses how horses think and how riders can communicate with them. [636.1]

10137 van der Linde, Laurel. *The White Stallions: The Story of the Dancing Horses of Lipizza* (6–8). 1994, Macmillan LB $22.00 (0-02-759055-0). The history of the famous Austrian Lipizzans, including how the horses were protected during World War II. (Rev: BL 5/1/94; SLJ 6/94) [636.1]

10138 Vogel, Colin. *The Complete Horse Care Manual* (6–12). 1995, DK Publg. $24.95 (0-7894-0170-3). This thorough explanation of caring for a horse covers such topics as housing, feed, disease prevention and treatment, and equipment needed. (Rev: VOYA 4/96) [636.1]

Zoos, Aquariums, and Animal Care

10139 Axelrod, Herbert R., et al. *Dr. Axelrod's Mini-Atlas of Freshwater Aquarium Fishes* (10–12). Illus. 1987, TFH $35.95 (0-86622-385-1). This large volume not only identifies freshwater aquarium fish but also covers setting up and maintaining an aquarium. (Rev: BL 12/1/87) [639]

10140 Barrie, Anmarie. *A Step-by-Step Book about Our First Aquarium* (9–12). Illus. 1987, TFH paper $5.95 (0-86622-454-8). This introductory guide covers all topics from choosing a tank to maintaining a balanced habitat. (Rev: BL 11/15/87) [639.34]

10141 McCormack, John. *A Friend of the Flock: Tales of a Country Veterinarian* (10–12). 1997, Crown $23.00 (0-517-70612-1). A funny and sad memoir by the first veterinarian of Chactaw County, Alabama. (Rev: BL 9/15/97; BR 3–4/98; SLJ 1/98) [636]

10142 Mills, Dick. *You & Your Aquarium* (9–12). Illus. 1986, Knopf paper $17.00 (0-394-72985-4). In addition to material on setting up an aquarium, this account features material on fish anatomy, feeding, and breeding. (Rev: BL 7/86; BR 11–12/86; SLJ 11/86) [639.4]

10143 Rinard, Judith E. *Zoos without Cages* (6–9). Illus. 1981, National Geographic LB $12.50 (0-87044-340-2). A description of the new kinds of zoos that strive to reproduce the natural habitat of the enclosed animals. [590.74]

10144 Sterba, Gunther, ed. *The Aquarium Encyclopedia* (10–12). Illus. 1983, MIT Pr. $45.00 (0-262-19207-1). An alphabetically arranged compendium of information on home aquariums and their upkeep. [639.3]

10145 Yancey, Diane. *Zoos* (5–8). (Overview) 1995, Lucent LB $16.95 (1-56006-163-4). Discusses the history of zoos, the controversy surrounding them, and species survival plans, from an ecologically friendly approach. (Rev: BL 6/1–15/95; SLJ 3/95) [590]

Chemistry

General and Miscellaneous

10146 Asimov, Isaac. *A Short History of Chemistry* (9–12). Illus. 1965, Greenwood LB $55.00 (0-313-20769-0). This is a readable account that stresses progress from the 18th century on to the modern age. [540.9]

10147 Blashfield, Jean F. *Calcium* (6–9). (Sparks of Life) 1998, Raintree Steck-Vaughn $27.12 (0-8172-5040-9). From seashells to human bone structure, this volume explores the nature of calcium and its importance in the world. (Rev: BL 1/1–15/99) [546]

10148 Blashfield, Jean F. *Carbon* (6–9). (Sparks of Life) 1998, Raintree Steck-Vaughn $27.12 (0-8172-5041-7). Carbon is a cornerstone of the elements. This book describes its uses and compounds, from the composition of proteins to the plant-based production of starches and sugars. (Rev: BL 1/1–15/99) [546]

10149 Blashfield, Jean F. *Hydrogen* (6–9). (Sparks of Life) 1998, Raintree Steck-Vaughn $27.12 (0-8172-5038-7). This volume explores the many different forms and uses of hydrogen, from its role as a primary component of water to its role in the hydrocarbons used to fuel the modern world. (Rev: BL 1/1–15/99) [546]

10150 Blashfield, Jean F. *Nitrogen* (6–9). (Sparks of Life) 1998, Raintree Steck-Vaughn $27.12 (0-8172-5039-5). The properties and value of nitrogen are explored, from its use in explosives to its role in fertilizers. (Rev: BL 1/1–15/99) [546]

10151 Blashfield, Jean F. *Oxygen* (6–9). (Sparks of Life) 1998, Raintree Steck-Vaughn $27.12 (0-8172-5037-9). This volume introduces oxygen, how it was discovered, its reaction with other elements to form compounds and mixtures, and its importance as the "breath of life." (Rev: BL 1/1–15/99) [546]

10152 Blashfield, Jean F. *Sodium* (6–9). (Sparks of Life) 1998, Raintree Steck-Vaughn $27.12 (0-8172-5042-5). This volume describes the history of sodium, its importance as an element, and its role as an ingredient in table salt, soaps, detergents, explosives, preservatives, and other common and not-so-common items. (Rev: BL 1/1–15/99) [546]

10153 Brock, William H. *The Norton History of Chemistry* (9–12). 1993, Norton paper $19.95 (0-393-31043-4). Historical highlights and development of the science of chemistry. (Rev: BL 7/93) [540.9]

10154 Challoner, Jack. *Visual Dictionary of Chemistry* (6–10). 1996, DK Publg. $18.95 (0-7894-0444-3). This beautifully illustrated introduction to chemistry contains material on the structure of atoms and molecules, the periodic table, chemical bonding, chemical reactions, groups of elements, organic chemistry, and chemical analysis. (Rev: BL 11/15/96; BR 3–4/97; SLJ 10/96; VOYA 2/97) [580]

10155 Cobb, Vicki. *Chemically Active! Experiments You Can Do at Home* (6–9). Illus. 1985, Harper-Collins LB $14.89 (0-397-32080-9). A group of scientific experiments that demonstrate chemical principles and can be performed with common household items. (Rev: BR 9–10/86; SLJ 8/85; VOYA 12/85) [507]

10156 Farndon, John. *Nitrogen* (5–8). (The Elements) 1998, Benchmark LB $22.79 (0-7614-0877-0). An informative science book that introduces nitrogen's properties, reactions, place in the periodic table, and importance in the human body and the environment, and environmental issues related to nitrogen such as pollution from noxious gases and acid rain. (Rev: SLJ 2/99) [540]

10157 Farndon, John. *Oxygen* (5–8). (The Elements) 1998, Benchmark LB $22.79 (0-7614-0879-7). Oxygen, its properties, uses, and various chemical reactions, are covered in this informative text that also introduces the periodic table and discusses air pollution and the thinning of the ozone layer. (Rev: SLJ 2/99) [540]

10158 Fitzgerald, Karen. *The Story of Iron* (5–8). (First Books: Chemical Elements) 1997, Watts LB $22.50 (0-531-20270-4). This volume outlines the discovery, uses, and chemistry of iron, with explanations of its importance throughout history and the role it plays in our lives today. (Rev: BL 9/1/97; SLJ 10/97) [669]

10159 Fitzgerald, Karen. *The Story of Nitrogen* (5–8). (First Books: Chemical Elements) 1997, Watts LB $22.50 (0-531-20248-8). Nitrogen is introduced, with information on its atomic structure, properties, uses, and production. (Rev: BL 9/1/97; SLJ 10/97) [546]

10160 Fitzgerald, Karen. *The Story of Oxygen* (5–8). 1996, Watts LB $22.50 (0-531-20225-9). A discussion of the discovery of oxygen, its role in nature, and its chemistry. (Rev: BL 10/15/96; SLJ 9/96) [546]

10161 Gardner, Robert. *Science Projects about Chemistry* (6–9). 1994, Enslow LB $19.95 (0-89490-531-7). Gardner conveys the fun of learning in this book about the uses of chemistry. (Rev: BL 1/1/95; SLJ 2/95) [540]

10162 Hess, Fred C. *Chemistry Made Simple*. Rev. ed. (10–12). Illus. 1984, Doubleday paper $12.95 (0-385-18850-1). An easily understood presentation of the basic concepts and facts in the area of chemistry. One of a large Made Simple series that covers many academic subjects. [540]

10163 Mebane, Robert C., and Thomas R. Rybolt. *Adventures with Atoms and Molecules, Vol. 5: Chemistry Experiments for Young People* (7–10). 1995, Enslow LB $18.95 (0-89490-606-2). A basic user's guide to start young people thinking scientifically, with ideas for science fair projects. (Rev: BL 12/1/95) [540]

10164 Stwertka, Albert. *A Guide to the Elements* (9–12). 1996, Oxford $49.95 (0-19-508083-1). A rundown on each of the elements, with material on symbols, history, uses, and compounds. (Rev: BL 12/1/96; BR 1–2/97; VOYA 6/97) [540]

10165 Stwertka, Albert. *The World of Atoms and Quarks* (7–12). (Scientific American Sourcebooks) 1995, Twenty-First Century LB $22.40 (0-8050-3533-8). Using profiles of important scientists, this work traces humankind's quest for an understanding of matter and its building blocks. (Rev: BL 12/1/95; BR 3–4/96; SLJ 2/96) [539.7]

Geology and Geography

Earth and Geology

10166 Campbell, Ann-Jeanette, and Ronald Rood. *The New York Public Library Incredible Earth: A Book of Answers for Kids* (7–10). Illus. 1996, Wiley paper $12.95 (0-471-14497-5). Using a question-and-answer approach, this book presents facts and theories about the origin of the earth, its structure, volcanoes, earthquakes, oceans, fresh water, and weather. (Rev: BL 9/15/96; SLJ 1/97) [551]

10167 Clifford, Nick. *Incredible Earth* (5–8). (Inside Guides) 1996, DK Publg. $15.95 (0-7894-1013-3). Earth's structure, composition, wind and water patterns, earthquakes, volcanoes, geysers, glaciers, the ocean floor, coral reefs, flood plains, deserts, and related topics are covered in a series of attractive double-page spreads. (Rev: SLJ 2/97) [550]

10168 Erickson, Jon. *Rock Formations and Unusual Geologic Structures: Exploring the Earth's Surface* (9–12). 1993, Facts on File $26.95 (0-8160-2589-4). A detailed explanation of the forces that created the earth's landscape, including the logistics of continental rift and drift. (Rev: BL 5/1/93) [550]

10169 Hartmann, William. *The History of the Earth: An Illustrated Chronicle of an Evolving Planet* (9–12). 1991, Workman $35.00 (1-56305-122-2); paper $19.95 (0-89480-756-0). Illustrated with paintings of often unseen sights, a story of Earth's coming of age. (Rev: BL 11/1/91) [525]

10170 Hehner, Barbara Embury. *Blue Planet* (7–12). (Wide World) 1992, Harcourt $17.95 (0-15-200423-8). An examination of the interdependent systems that make up the planet Earth, including plate tectonics, volcanoes, weather, satellites, and the ozone layer. (Rev: BL 11/15/92; SLJ 10/92) [508]

10171 Loeschnig, Louis V. *Simple Earth Science Experiments with Everyday Materials* (6–8). Illus. 1996, Sterling $14.95 (0-8069-0898-X). A well-organized book of activities and demonstrations that explore subjects like soil, time, earthquakes, glaciers, gravity, and conservation. (Rev: BL 10/15/96) [550]

10172 Macdougall, J. D. *A Short History of Planet Earth: Mountains Mammals Fire & Ice* (10–12). (Wiley Popular Science) 1996, Wiley $24.95 (0-471-14805-9). Full of charts, graphs, and illustrations, this is a concise introduction to geology. (Rev: SLJ 7/97) [551]

10173 Officer, Charles, and Jake Page. *Tales of the Earth* (9–12). 1993, Oxford $48.00 (0-19-507785-7). This introduction to earth science presents accounts of natural catastrophes: volcanoes, floods, earthquakes, meteorites and comets, profound climatic change, and mass extinctions. (Rev: BL 5/1/93) [550]

10174 O'Neill, Catherine. *Natural Wonders of North America* (7–12). Illus. 1984, National Geographic LB $12.50 (0-87044-519-7). Excellent color photographs complement the text and maps that describe such natural wonders as tundra regions, volcanoes, glaciers, and the Badlands of South Dakota. [557]

10175 Silverstein, Alvin. *Plate Tectonics* (5–8). (Science Concepts) 1998, Twenty-First Century LB $23.40 (0-7613-3225-1). Using many photographs, maps, and diagrams, this book introduces plate tectonics, the theory that the earth's surface moves, and explains the origins of volcanic eruptions and earthquakes. (Rev: BL 2/1/99; SLJ 5/99) [551.1 36]

10176 Smith, Norman F. *Millions and Billions of Years Ago: Dating Our Earth and Its Life* (8–12). (Venture) 1993, Watts LB $25.00 (0-531-12533-5). The history of attempts to date artifacts, the Earth, the moon, and the universe, including descriptions of dating methods. (Rev: BL 1/1/94; SLJ 11/93) [551.7]

10177 VanCleave, Janice. *Janice VanCleave's A+ Projects in Earth Science: Winning Experiments for Science Fairs and Extra Credit* (5–10). 1999, Wiley $27.95 (0-471-17769-5); paper $12.95 (0-471-17770-9). Thirty projects that vary in complexity and difficulty are included in this book that explores topography, minerals, atmospheric composition, the ocean floor, and erosion. (Rev: BL 12/1/98; SLJ 6/99) [550]

Earthquakes and Volcanoes

10178 Booth, Basil. *Earthquakes and Volcanoes* (5–8). 1992, Macmillan LB $13.95 (0-02-711735-9). The interrelationship between earthquakes and volcanoes is explored in picture-essay form. (Rev: BL 9/15/92; SLJ 10/92) [551.2]

10179 Carson, Rob. *Mount St. Helens: The Eruption and Recovery of a Volcano* (9–12). Illus. 1990, Sasquatch paper $19.95 (0-912365-32-3). With excellent photographs, this is the story of the Mount St. Helens eruption, its aftermath, and the condition today. (Rev: BL 6/15/90) [508.79]

10180 Christian, Spencer, and Antonia Felix. *Shake, Rattle & Roll: The World's Most Amazing Natural Forces* (6–10). (Spencer Christian's World of Wonders) 1997, Wiley paper $12.95 (0-471-15291-9). This book supplies good information and suitable projects involving earthquakes and volcanoes, with material on topics like plate tectonics, seismic waves, geysers, and hot springs. (Rev: SLJ 6/98) [551.2]

10181 Cox, James A., et al. *Our Violent Earth* (6–9). Illus. 1982, National Geographic LB $12.50 (0-87044-388-7). A discussion of such phenomena as earthquakes, volcanoes, and floods. [363.3]

10182 Erickson, Jon. *Quakes, Eruptions and Other Geologic Cataclysms* (9–12). 1994, Facts on File $26.95 (0-8160-2949-0). Describes the physical mechanisms that cause such geologic cataclysms as earthquakes, volcanoes, landslides, mudflows, and dust storms. (Rev: BL 8/94; SLJ 11/94) [550]

10183 Erickson, Jon. *Volcanoes and Earthquakes* (10–12). Illus. 1988, TAB $22.95 (0-8306-1942-9); paper $15.95 (0-8306-2842-8). In addition to general information on volcanoes and earthquakes the author gives a valuable introduction to plate tectonics and how planets were formed. (Rev: BL 1/1/89) [551.2]

10184 Levy, Matthys, and Mario Salvadori. *Earthquake Games* (5–8). Illus. 1997, Simon & Schuster

$16.00 (0-689-81367-8). A clear text plus games and experiments explain what causes earthquakes and volcanoes, and describes their effects. (Rev: BL 9/1/97; SLJ 12/97) [551.22]

10185 Levy, Matthys, and Mario Salvadori. *Why the Earth Quakes* (9–12). 1995, Norton $25.00 (0-393-03774-6). All about earthquakes and safety precautions. (Rev: BL 9/15/95) [551.2]

10186 Thro, Ellen. *Volcanoes of the United States* (7–10). 1992, Watts LB $25.00 (0-531-12522-X). Focuses on volcanic activity in Alaska, Hawaii, and the Pacific Northwest, including history, related thermal activities, environmental impact, and modern scientific methods of study. (Rev: BL 7/92; SLJ 8/92) [551.2]

10187 Van Rose, Susanna. *Volcano and Earthquake* (5–9). (Eyewitness Books) 1992, Knopf LB $20.99 (0-679-91685-7). A basic, well-illustrated book that explains the causes and effects of volcano eruptions and earthquakes. (Rev: BL 11/1/92) [551.2]

10188 *Volcanoes & Earthquakes* (5–8). (Nature Company Discoveries) 1995, Time-Life Books LB $16.00 (0-7835-4764-1). This handsome overview of volcanoes and earthquakes contains many attractive illustrations, including an 8-page foldout. (Rev: SLJ 1/96) [551.2]

Icebergs and Glaciers

10189 Erickson, Jon. *Glacial Geology: How Ice Shapes the Land* (10–12). (The Changing Earth) 1996, Facts on File $26.95 (0-8160-3355-2). With generous use of photos and line drawings, this is an exploration of the relationship between glaciers and the land or sea beneath them. (Rev: SLJ 7/96) [551.3]

Physical Geography

General and Miscellaneous

10190 Gold, John C. *Environments of the Western Hemisphere* (5–8). Illus. (Comparing Continents) 1997, Twenty-First Century $21.40 (0-8050-5601-7). This work compares the climates of South, North, and Central America and shows how they affect the environment and the way people live and work. (Rev: BL 2/1/98; SLJ 3/98) [363.7]

10191 Levinson, David. *Human Environments: Cross-Cultural Encyclopedia* (10–12). (Encyclopedias of the Human Experience) 1995, ABC-CLIO LB $49.50 (0-87436-784-0). This title examines the complex relationships that exists among climate, weather, land forms, and plants, and their interaction with humankind's physical environment. (Rev: SLJ 6/96) [573]

10192 Lisowski, Marylin, and Robert A. Williams. *Wetlands* (7–10). (Exploring Ecosystems) 1997, Watts LB $24.00 (0-531-11311-6). Once considered useless places, wetlands are revealed in this book to be areas that provide us with food and water, house a variety of wildlife, act as flood barriers, and provide protection against erosion. (Rev: BL 5/1/97; SLJ 6/97) [574.5]

10193 Niering, William A. *Wetlands* (9–12). Illus. 1985, Knopf paper $19.95 (0-394-73147-6). After identifying and describing the wetlands of North America, this account identifies each species living there. (Rev: BL 7/85; SLJ 9/85) [574.5]

10194 Rezendes, Paul, and Paulette Roy. *Wetlands: The Web of Life* (10–12). 1996, Sierra Club $40.00 (0-87156-851-9); paper $25.00 (0-87156-878-0). A variety of wetland environments such as bottomlands, swamps, mires, mud flats, and wet meadows are examined, showing the diversity of plant and animal life and the wetland systems' critical role in environmental health. (Rev: BL 11/15/96; SLJ 5/97) [574.5]

10195 Schultz, Ron. *Looking Inside Caves and Caverns* (5–8). (X-Ray Vision) 1993, John Muir paper $9.95 (1-56261-126-7). This introduction to spelunking covers the flora, fauna, and physical characteristics of caves. (Rev: BL 1/1/94; SLJ 2/94) [551.4]

Deserts

10196 MacMahon, James A. *Deserts* (9–12). Illus. 1985, Knopf paper $19.95 (0-394-73139-5). This volume not only describes the desert habitat but also, with pictures, describes the various species that live there. (Rev: BL 7/85; SLJ 9/85) [574.5]

10197 MacQuitty, Miranda. *Desert* (5–9). (Eyewitness Books) 1994, Knopf LB $20.99 (0-679-96003-1). A nicely illustrated book on the origins of deserts, where they are found, and their ecology. (Rev: BL 10/15/94) [910]

10198 Ruth, Maria Mudd. *The Deserts of the Southwest* (5–8). (Ecosystems of North America) 1998, Benchmark LB $27.07 (0-7614-0899-1). After an overview of the deserts of the Southwest and how they were formed, this book introduces desert plants and wildlife, how they interact, adaptions they have made to the desert environment, and the impact of human development. (Rev: BR 5–6/99; SLJ 2/99) [591]

10199 Steele, Philip. *Deserts* (5–8). (Pocket Facts) 1991, Macmillan LB $10.95 (0-89686-588-6). A concise introduction to deserts, featuring easily understand facts and photos. (Rev: BL 3/15/92) [508.315]

10200 Twist, Clint. *Deserts* (5–8). (Ecology Watch) 1991, Dillon LB $17.95 (0-87518-490-1). Traces the evolution of deserts, explains why they are threatened, and offers possible solutions to specific problems. (Rev: BL 3/1/92; SLJ 4/92) [574.5]

Forests and Rain Forests

10201 Aldis, Rodney. *Rainforests* (5–8). (Ecology Watch) 1991, Dillon LB $13.95 (0-87518-495-2). A study of how rain forests have developed, highlighting how plants and animals depend on each other for survival in this delicate ecosystem. (Rev: BL 3/1/92; SLJ 4/92) [574.5]

10202 Collard, Sneed B. *Monteverde: Science and Scientists in a Costa Rican Cloud Forest* (6–9). Illus. 1997, Watts LB $25.00 (0-531-11369-8). A stunning introduction to the amazing tropical cloud forest of Costa Rica, the town of Monteverde founded by Quakers, and the efforts to keep the paradise from disappearing. (Rev: BL 9/1/97; SLJ 9/97) [577.3]

10203 Cozic, Charles P. *Rainforests* (9–12). (At Issue) 1997, Greenhaven paper $17.25 (1-56510-694-6). An anthology of articles and essays by environmentalists, business people, scientists, and journalists presenting different viewpoints on the complex causes of and cures for deforestation of rain forests. (Rev: SLJ 5/98) [574.5]

10204 Goodman, Susan E. *Bats, Bugs, and Biodiversity: Adventures in the Amazonian Rain Forest* (4–8). Illus. 1995, Simon & Schuster $16.00 (0-689-31942-6). Some junior high students learn firsthand about the Amazon rain forest and its endangered ecology. (Rev: BL 12/1/97) [508]

10205 Kallen, Stuart A. *Life in the Amazon Rain Forest* (6–10). (The Way People Live) 1999, Lucent LB $35.92 (1-56006-387-4). A description of the Amazon rain forest and of the Yanomami people who live there, their traditions, food, shelter, religion, encounters with Europeans, and the continuous threats to their existence. (Rev: SLJ 7/99) [574.5]

10206 Lasky, Kathryn. *The Most Beautiful Roof in the World: Exploring the Rainforest Canopy* (5–8). 1997, Harcourt $18.00 (0-15-200893-4); paper $8.00 (0-15-200897-7). The canopy of plants and animals found in the rain forest of Belize is explored by the author, a biologist, who also explains the methods scientists use to conduct research in this environment, sometimes under extremely difficult conditions. (Rev: BL 4/1/97; SLJ 4/97) [574.5]

10207 Lewington, Anna. *Atlas of the Rain Forests* (6–12). 1997, Raintree Steck-Vaughn $32.83 (0-

8172-4756-4). Enhanced by maps and photographs, this work contains information on the plant and animal life found in rain forests, the cultures of the people who live in them, and how these environments are changed by economic development. (Rev: BL 5/15/97; SLJ 8/97) [574.5]

10208 McAllister, Ian. *The Great Bear Rain Forest* (9–12). 1998, Sierra Club $40.00 (1-57805-011-1). This magnificently illustrated volume describes the wonders of the west coast of Canada from the U.S. border to the Alaska Panhandle, the home of the coastal grizzly bear and the largest tract of intact temperate rain forest on earth, and makes a powerful case for the need protect it from overdevelopment. (Rev: SLJ 4/99) [971]

10209 Maynard, Caitlin, and Thane Maynard. *Rain Forests and Reefs: A Kid's-Eye View of the Tropics* (4–8). Illus. 1996, Watts LB $24.00 (0-531-11281-0). The flora and fauna of rain forests and coral reefs in Belize are described in text and stunning photos. (Rev: BL 2/15/97; SLJ 3/97*) [574.5]

10210 Morrison, Marion. *The Amazon Rain Forest and Its People* (5–8). (People and Places) 1993, Thomson Learning LB $24.26 (1-56847-087-8). After a general history and a description of the region's plants, animals, and people, the author discusses the current dangers developers pose to this rain forest. (Rev: BL 11/1/93) [333.75]

10211 Silcock, Lisa, ed. *The Rainforests: A Celebration* (9–12). 1990, Chronicle $35.00 (0-87701-790-5). Rain forest experts describe various aspects of life in this habitat, supplemented by illustrations. (Rev: BL 2/1/91) [508.315]

10212 Sutton, Ann, and Myron Sutton. *Eastern Forests* (9–12). Illus. 1985, Knopf paper $19.95 (0-394-73126-3). Although this book chiefly aims to identify species living in eastern forests, it also describes this habitat and their locations. (Rev: BL 7/85; SLJ 9/85) [574.5]

10213 Whitney, Stephen. *Western Forests* (9–12). Illus. 1985, Knopf paper $19.95 (0-394-73127-1). A description of each species, color illustrations, and a general introduction to this type of habitat are the highlights of this field guide. (Rev: BL 7/85; SLJ 9/85) [574.5]

Mountains

10214 Collinson, Alan. *Mountains* (5–8). (Ecology Watch) 1992, Dillon LB $17.95 (0-87518-493-6). A discussion of the formation of mountains and how they are gradually being eroded. (Rev: BL 11/1/92) [574.5]

10215 Cumming, David. *Mountains* (5–8). (Habitats) 1995, Thomson Learning LB $24.26 (1-56847-388-

5). Material includes the geology of mountains, their formation, the life they support, and the effects of industry, tourism, and transportation. (Rev: BL 2/1/96) [551.4]

10216 Steele, Philip. *Mountains* (5–8). (Pocket Facts) 1991, Macmillan LB $15.95 (0-89686-587-8). Easy-to-understand facts about mountains, with many photos. (Rev: BL 3/15/92) [910]

10217 Stronach, Neil. *Mountains* (4–8). (Endangered People and Places) 1996, Lerner LB $22.60 (0-8225-2777-4). Geological aspects of mountains are covered, as well as the adjustments people make to live in mountainous regions. (Rev: SLJ 11/96) [333.73]

Ponds, Rivers, and Lakes

10218 Beck, Gregor Gilpin. *Watersheds: A Practical Handbook for Healthy Water* (7–12). Illus. 1999, Firefly $19.95 (1-55037-330-1). This account highlights the importance of water in our lives, with special attention to pollution, flooding, and other environmental problems. (Rev: BL 9/1/99) [333.73]

10219 Cumming, David. *Rivers and Lakes* (5–8). (Habitats) 1995, Thomson Learning LB $22.78 (1-56847-389-3). The plant and animal life that is supported by lakes and rivers is introduced, with accompanying information on geology and pollution. (Rev: BL 2/1/96) [551.48]

10220 Ganeri, Anita. *Rivers, Ponds and Lakes* (5–8). (Ecology Watch) 1992, Dillon LB $17.95 (0-87518-497-9). A discussion of these water environments and how they are threatened by various forms of pollution. (Rev: BL 11/1/92) [574.5]

10221 Loewer, Peter. *Pond Water Zoo: An Introduction to Microscopic Life* (5–8). Illus. 1996, Simon & Schuster $16.00 (0-689-31736-0). Various life forms found in a drop of pond water are revealed by the microscope. (Rev: BL 9/15/96; SLJ 2/97) [576]

10222 Martin, Patricia A. *Rivers and Streams* (7–12). Illus. 1999, Watts $24.00 (0-531-11523-2). This book contains over 30 projects and experiments involving streams, rivers, and the life they support. (Rev: BL 6/1–15/99) [577.6]

10223 Palmer, Tim. *The Snake River: Window to the West* (9–12). 1991, Island Pr. $40.00 (0-933280-59-9). A history of the Snake River is combined with a detailed report on the ecological issues surrounding it. (Rev: BL 8/91) [333.91]

10224 Parker, Steve. *Pond & River* (6–8). Illus. 1988, Knopf LB $20.99 (0-394-99615-1). In 28 short, lavishly illustrated chapters, various aspects of pond and river ecology are explored. (Rev: SLJ 12/88) [551.48]

Prairies and Grasslands

10225 Brown, Lauren. *Grasslands* (9–12). Illus. 1985, Knopf paper $19.95 (0-394-73121-2). This volume describes grasslands in the United States and then identifies the species found there. (Rev: BL 7/85; SLJ 9/85) [574.5]

10226 Ormsby, Alison. *The Prairie* (5–8). (Ecosystems of North America) 1998, Benchmark LB $27.07 (0-7614-0897-5). A description of the prairie ecosystem and an examination of how the plants and animals in prairies affect one another and their environments. (Rev: BR 5–6/99; SLJ 2/99) [551.4]

Rocks, Minerals, and Soil

10227 Chesterman, Charles W., and Kurt E. Lowe. *The Audubon Society Field Guide to North American Rocks and Minerals* (7–12). Illus. 1978, Knopf $19.00 (0-394-50269-8). A key by color arrangement plus color illustrations of each rock and mineral are two features of this basic guide. [549]

10228 Dietrich, R. V., and Reed Wicander. *Minerals, Rocks and Fossils* (9–12). 1983, Wiley paper $9.95 (0-471-89883-X). For the amateur geologist, this is a guide to identifying and collecting rocks, minerals, and fossils. [552]

10229 Erickson, Jon. *An Introduction to Fossils and Minerals: Seeking Clues to the Earth's Past* (9–12). 1992, Facts on File LB $26.95 (0-8160-2587-8). An overview of how rocks, fossils, and minerals have moved naturally over the ages and how they can provide information to the earth's history. (Rev: BL 4/15/92) [560]

10230 Pellant, Christopher, and Roger Phillips. *Rocks, Minerals & Fossils of the World* (9–12). Illus. 1990, Little, Brown paper $25.00 (0-316-69796-6). An identification manual that contains photographs and data in three sections—one each on rocks, minerals, and fossils. (Rev: BL 6/15/90) [552]

10231 Pough, Frederick H. *A Field Guide to Rocks and Minerals*. 4th ed. (7–12). Illus. 1976, Houghton $21.95 (0-395-24047-6); paper $16.95 (0-395-24049-2). This volume in the Peterson Field Guide series gives photos and identifying information on 270 rocks and minerals. [549]

10232 Ricciuti, Edward R., and National Audubon Society, eds. *National Audubon Society First Field Guide: Rocks & Minerals* (5–8). Illus. 1998, Scholastic $17.95 (0-590-05463-5). A guide to equipment and techniques for observation and general information on geology, followed by an examination of 50 common rocks, their composition, texture, color, and environment. (Rev: SLJ 8/98) [552]

10233 VanCleave, Janice. *Janice VanCleave's Rocks and Minerals: Mind-Boggling Experiments You Can Turn Into Science Fair Projects* (6–8). (Spectacular Science Projects) 1996, Wiley paper $10.95 (0-471-10269-5). In easy-to-follow steps, a series of experiments and projects are outlined that illustrate the properties and uses of a number of rocks and minerals. (Rev: BL 3/15/96; SLJ 3/96) [552]

Mathematics

General and Miscellaneous

10234 Guillen, Michael. *Five Equations That Changed the World: The Power and Poetry of Mathematics* (9–12). 1995, Hyperion $22.95 (0-7868-6103-7). A philosophical, biographical, and historical trip through 2 centuries of changing scientific thought and 5 scientists who helped shaped the future: Newton, Bernoulli, Faraday, Clausius, and Einstein. (Rev: BL 9/1/95) [530.1]

10235 Haven, Kendall. *Marvels of Math: Fascinating Reads and Awesome Activities* (5–8). Illus. 1998, Teacher Ideas Pr. paper $21.50 (1-56308-585-2). This book chronicles 16 turning points in the history of mathematics, including the discovery of zero and the story of the first female to become a professor of mathematics. (Rev: BR 5–6/99; VOYA 4/99) [510]

10236 Hershey, Robert L. *How to Think with Numbers* (7–9). Illus. 1987, Janson paper $7.95 (0-939765-14-4). Elementary mathematical concepts such as percentage and interest are explained through a series of puzzles and problems. [510]

10237 Huff, Darrell. *How to Lie with Statistics* (10–12). Illus. 1954, Norton paper $3.95 (0-393-09426-X). A now-classic account of how numbers can be manipulated to produce desired results. [519.5]

10238 Kogelman, Stanley, and Joseph Warren. *Mind over Math* (10–12). Illus. 1978, McGraw-Hill paper $8.95 (0-07-035281-X). Based on the authors' many workshops, this is a course on how to overcome math anxiety. [510]

10239 Krieger, Melanie J. *Means and Probabilities: Using Statistics in Science Projects* (9–12). Illus. (Experimental Science) 1996, Watts LB $24.00 (0-531-11225-X). This is an excellent introduction to

elementary statistics and statistical methodology and how these principles can be applied in science projects. (Rev: BL 8/96; SLJ 9/96) [001.4]

10240 Lieberthal, Edwin M., and Bernadette Lieberthal. *The Complete Book of Fingermath* (7–12). Illus. 1979, McGraw-Hill $21.96 (0-07-037680-8). How hands and fingers can be turned into primitive computers. [513]

10241 Mandell, Muriel. *Simple Experiments in Time with Everyday Materials* (5–9). Illus. 1997, Sterling $14.95 (0-8069-3803-X). Through a series of well-organized experiments, this volume explores time and how we measure it, and presents facts about time in history. (Rev: BL 12/1/97) [529.7]

10242 Markle, Sandra. *Discovering Graph Secrets: Experiments, Puzzles, and Games Exploring Graphs* (4–8). 1997, Simon & Schuster $17.00 (0-689-31942-8). An entertaining and informative book that introduces 4 different graphs and their uses. (Rev: BL 2/15/98; SLJ 3/98) [511]

10243 Salvadori, Mario, and Joseph P. Wright. *Math Games for Middle School: Challenges & Skill-Builders for Students at Every Level* (5–8). Illus. 1998, Chicago Review paper $14.95 (1-55652-288-6). The concepts in arithmetic, geometry, graphs, linear equations, and probability are explained in separate chapters, each with a list of problems illustrating the concept for readers to solve. (Rev: BL 11/1/98) [510.7]

10244 Schwartz, David M. *G Is for Googol: A Math Alphabet Book* (6–10). Illus. 1998, Tricycle Pr. $15.95 (1-883672-58-9). A humorous romp through mathematical terms and concepts using an alphabetical approach and cartoon illustrations. (Rev: BL 10/15/98; SLJ 11/98) [510]

10245 Tobias, Sheila. *Succeed with Math: Every Student's Guide to Conquering Math Anxiety* (10–12).

Illus. 1987, College Entrance Examination Board paper $12.95 (0-87447-259-8). A book that helps readers develop problem-solving techniques as well as understand mathematical concepts. (Rev: BL 2/1/88; BR 3–4/88; SLJ 6/88; VOYA 4/88) [510]

10246 Vorderman, Carol. *How Math Works* (5–8). Illus. 1996, Reader's Digest $24.00 (0-89577-850-5). This book covers the history of mathematics and its major concepts, and includes a variety of interesting activities. (Rev: BL 11/1/96) [510]

Algebra, Numbers, and Number Systems

10247 Clawson, Calvin C. *The Mathematical Traveler: Exploring the Grand History of Numbers* (9–12). 1994, Plenum $25.95 (0-306-44645-6). A mathematical adventure examining the history of numbers as a reflection of the evolution of culture, from the Chinese, Mayans, and Greeks to the modern day. (Rev: BL 5/1/94) [513.2]

10248 Fisher, Leonard E. *Number Art: Thirteen 1 2 3s from around the World* (6–9). Illus. 1982, Macmillan $12.95 (0-590-07810-0). Different numbering systems from around the world (for example, Chinese, Arabic) are explained and illustrated. [513]

10249 Humez, Alexander, et al. *Zero to Lazy Eight: The Romance of Numbers* (9–12). 1993, Simon & Schuster $21.00 (0-671-74282-5). A collection of brain games using prime numbers, square roots, sequences, base-2 arithmetic, and other concepts. (Rev: BL 6/1–15/93) [513.2]

Mathematical Games and Puzzles

10250 Burns, Marilyn. *Math for Smarty Pants* (6–9). Illus. 1982, Little, Brown paper $12.95 (0-316-

11739-0). A series of games, puzzles, and tricks that use numbers. (Rev: BL 4/15/90) [513]

10251 Gardner, Martin. *Aha! Gotcha: Paradoxes to Puzzle and Delight* (7–12). Illus. 1982, W. H. Freeman paper $14.95 (0-7167-1361-6). A book of puzzles from *Scientific American* that involve mathematics and logic. [793.7]

10252 Gardner, Martin. *Hexaflexagons and Other Mathematical Diversions* (10–12). 1988, Univ. of Chicago Pr. paper $13.00 (0-226-28254-6). A collection of brain teasers and mathematical puzzles from the pages of *Scientific American*. (Rev: SLJ 5/89) [793.7]

10253 Gardner, Martin. *Time Travel and Other Mathematical Bewilderments* (10–12). Illus. 1987, W. H. Freeman paper $14.95 (0-7167-1925-8). Another collection of puzzles and explanatory descriptions from *Scientific American*. (Rev: BL 1/15/88) [793.7]

10254 Lobosco, Michael L. *Mental Math Challenges* (5–8). 1999, Sterling $16.95 (1-895569-50-8). An attractive book that contains 37 projects involving mathematical models of 2 and 3 dimensions using everyday materials. The projects vary in difficulty and each math concept that is demonstrated is explained fully. (Rev: SLJ 8/99) [510]

10255 Steinhaus, Hugo. *One Hundred Problems in Elementary Mathematics* (9–12). 1979, Dover paper $7.95 (0-486-23875-X). These are problems that illustrate basic operations in mathematics. [510]

10256 Tahan, Malba. *The Man Who Counted: A Collection of Mathematical Adventures* (9–12). 1993, Norton paper $14.95 (0-393-30934-7). Regales readers with delightful mathematical adventures featuring beautiful princesses, viziers, sultans, and Tahan himself. (Rev: BL 2/15/93*) [793.7]

10257 Vecchione, Glen. *Math Challenges: Puzzles, Tricks & Games* (6–10). Illus. 1997, Sterling $14.95 (0-8069-8114-8). A slim volume that contains a number of mathematical puzzles arranged by subjects and followed by the solutions. (Rev: SLJ 10/97) [510]

Meteorology

General and Miscellaneous

10258 Facklam, Margery, and Howard Facklam. *Changes in the Wind: Earth's Shifting Climate* (6–9). Illus. 1986, Harcourt $14.95 (0-15-216115-5). An excellent explanation of what causes climate and how and why it changes. (Rev: BL 8/86; SLJ 12/86) [551.6]

Air

10259 Gardner, Robert. *Science Project Ideas about Air* (5–8). (Science Project Ideas) 1997, Enslow LB $18.95 (0-89490-838-3). The properties of air are explored in a series of experiments and projects with easy-to-follow instructions. (Rev: BR 5–6/98; SLJ 4/98) [678.5]

Storms

10260 Allaby, Michael. *Hurricanes* (7–12). (Dangerous Weather) 1997, Facts on File $26.95 (0-8160-3516-4). An exhaustive introduction to hurricanes covering such topics as conditions that may lead to them, why they are common in particular areas, historic hurricanes, their naming and tracking, and how global climate changes will affect them. (Rev: BR 1–2/98; SLJ 4/98) [551.5]

10261 Allaby, Michael. *Tornadoes* (7–12). (Dangerous Weather) 1997, Facts on File $26.95 (0-8160-3517-2). This excellent book on tornadoes describes

how they begin, their structure, travel patterns, interiors, historic tornadoes, and when and where tornadoes occur. (Rev: BR 1–2/98; SLJ 4/98) [551.55]

10262 Erickson, Jon. *Violent Storms* (10–12). Illus. 1988, TAB $24.95 (0-8306-9042-5); paper $16.95 (0-8306-2942-4). In addition to a description of the nature and causes of storms, the author gives a general introduction to weather and such topics as the greenhouse effect and acid rain. (Rev: BL 1/1/89; VOYA 4/89) [551.5]

10263 Junger, Sebastian. *The Perfect Storm* (10–12). 1997, Norton $23.95 (0-393-04016-X). This bestselling book re-creates the last few hours of the swordfishing vessel *Andrea Gail* as it heads into "the perfect storm" and tragedy. (Rev: SLJ 11/97) [904]

10264 Lauber, Patricia. *Flood: Wrestling with the Mississippi* (5–8). Illus. 1996, National Geographic $18.95 (0-7922-4141-X). An introduction to floods that focuses on the great Mississippi River flood of 1993. (Rev: BL 10/15/96; SLJ 11/96*) [363.3]

10265 Lauber, Patricia. *Hurricanes: Earth's Mightiest Storms* (4–8). Illus. 1996, Scholastic $16.95 (0-590-47406-5). This photoessay gives details on important hurricanes and explains what causes hurricanes, how they can be tracked, and their effects. (Rev: BL 10/1/96; SLJ 9/96*) [363.3]

10266 Sherrow, Victoria. *Hurricane Andrew: Nature's Rage* (4–8). (American Disasters) 1998, Enslow $18.95 (0-7660-1057-0). The story of the storm that caused millions of dollars of damage to the Atlantic coast, told in dramatic text and pictures. (Rev: BL 1/1–15/99; BR 5–6/99; VOYA 4/99) [551.5]

10267 Sherrow, Victoria. *Plains Outbreak Tornadoes: Killer Twisters* (4–8). (American Disasters) 1998, Enslow $18.95 (0-7660-1059-7). The causes and effects of the giant tornadoes that occur in the Midwest, with details on some of the most horrendous. (Rev: BL 1/1–15/99; BR 5–6/99) [551.55]

10268 Simon, Seymour. *Tornadoes* (4–8). 1999, Morrow LB $15.93 (0-688-14647-3). Well-organized text discusses the weather conditions that give rise to tornadoes, how they form, where they are most likely to occur, and how scientists predict and track them, supplemented by large, riveting photographs showing meteorologists at work, a variety of tornadoes, and the devastation caused by major tornadoes in our history. (Rev: BL 5/99; SLJ 6/99) [551.55]

10269 Twist, Clint. *Hurricanes and Storms* (5–8). (Repairing the Damage) 1992, Macmillan LB $13.95 (0-02-789685-4). This book explores the causes and effects of severe storms and hurricanes. (Rev: BL 9/15/92; SLJ 10/92) [551.55]

Water

10270 Cossi, Olga. *Water Wars: The Fight to Control and Conserve Nature's Most Precious Resource* (6–12). 1993, Macmillan LB $16.95 (0-02-724595-0). Discusses the sources and uses of fresh water and examines the reasons for drought, water quality problems, and how to conserve water. (Rev: BL 11/1/93; SLJ 2/94; VOYA 4/94) [333.91]

10271 Gardner, Robert. *Experimenting with Water* (7–12). (Venture) 1993, Watts LB $24.00 (0-531-12549-1). The unusual properties of water are described in these simple experiments and "puzzlers" that provide clear explanations of scientific concepts. (Rev: BL 2/15/94; SLJ 4/94) [546]

10272 Ocko, Stephanie. *Water: Almost Enough for Everyone* (5–10). 1995, Atheneum $16.00 (0-689-31797-2). Ocko traces the interconnectedness of the earth's ecosystems and provides ways people can conserve water and care for the environment. (Rev: BL 6/1–15/95; SLJ 6/95; VOYA 12/95) [363.3]

10273 Zubrowski, Bernie. *Making Waves: Finding Out About Rhythmic Motion* (5–8). (Boston Children's Museum Activity Book) 1994, Morrow LB $14.93 (0-688-11787-2). Demonstrates how to observe waves in water, cloth materials, and string, and suggests ways to explore and experiment with waves, including instructions for building a simple wave machine. (Rev: BL 7/94; SLJ 8/94) [532]

Weather

10274 Allaby, Michael. *Droughts* (6–12). Illus. (Dangerous Weather) 1997, Facts on File $26.95 (0-8160-3519-9). Topics discussed in this comprehensive volume include how droughts are classified, droughts of the past, the Dust Bowl, irrigation, water storage, saving water, and jet streams and storm tracks. (Rev: BL 12/1/97) [551.55]

10275 Arnold, Caroline. *El Niño: Stormy Weather for People and Wildlife* (4–8). Illus. 1998, Clarion $16.00 (0-395-77602-3). A brief overview of El Niño, its causes, its history, present-day effects, and how tracking and forecasting are used to make predictions. (Rev: BL 10/1/98; BR 5–6/99; SLJ 12/98) [551.6]

10276 Dickinson, Terence. *Exploring the Sky by Day: The Equinox Guide to Weather and the Atmosphere* (7–10). Illus. 1988, Camden House $17.95 (0-920656-73-0); paper $9.95 (0-920656-71-4). A book about weather that explores such subjects as types of clouds and kinds of precipitation. (Rev: BL 3/1/89; SLJ 1/89) [551.6]

10277 Elsom, Derek. *Weather Explained: A Beginner's Guide to the Elements* (4–8). Illus. (Your World Explained) 1997, Holt $18.95 (0-8050-4875-8). Basic material on clouds and winds is followed by a discussion of the world's changing climate and the causes and effects of El Niño. (Rev: BL 3/1/98; SLJ 2/98) [551.5]

10278 Kahl, Jonathan D. *Weather Watch: Forecasting the Weather* (5–8). (How's the Weather?) 1996, Lerner LB $21.27 (0-8225-2529-1). This work provides basic information on weather systems, maps, and forecasting tools, the history of weather forecasting and keeping weather records, and directions for making a weather station. (Rev: BL 6/1–15/96; SLJ 6/96) [551.6]

10279 Lockhart, Gary. *The Weather Companion: An Album of Meteorological History, Science, Legend, & Folklore* (9–12). 1988, Wiley paper $17.95 (0-471-62079-3). From ancient myths to modern research, this book covers lore and facts concerning the weather. (Rev: BR 3–4/89; SLJ 6/89) [551.5]

10280 Ludlum, David M. *The American Weather Book* (10–12). 1990, American Meteorological Soc. paper $20.00 (0-933876-97-1). A collection of facts, myths, and figures all involving the weather. [551.6]

10281 Mogil, H. Michael, and Barbara G. Levine. *The Amateur Meteorologist: Explorations and Investigations* (6–10). Illus. (Amateur Science) 1993, Watts LB $21.40 (0531-11045-1). This book shows how to get started in weather observation and forecasting, with projects like making an anemometer, wind vane, barometer, and rain gauge. (Rev: BL 1/15/94) [551.5]

10282 National Audubon Society, eds. *Weather* (4–8). 1998, Scholastic $17.95 (0-590-05469-4); paper $10.95 (0-590-05488-0). Using many illustrations, this a basic guide to all kinds of weather, the causes, and effects. (Rev: SLJ 4/99) [551.5]

10283 Ramsey, Dan. *Weather Forecasting: A Young Meteorologist's Guide* (8–12). Illus. 1990, TAB $19.95 (0-8306-8338-0); paper $10.95 (0-8306-

3338-3). A detailed and often technical examination of the techniques of weather forecasting with many tables, charts, and diagrams. (Rev: BL 10/15/90) [551.6]

10284 Verkaik, Jerrine, and Arjen Verkaik. *Under the Whirlwind: Everything You Need to Know About Tornadoes But Didn't Know Who to Ask* (9–12). Illus. 1997, Whirlwind Books paper $20.00 (0-9681537-0-4). This book contains a wealth of information about tornadoes, with material on their development and structure, how to survive them, and how to deal with post-tornado trauma. (Rev: SLJ 7/98) [551.5]

Oceanography

General and Miscellaneous

10285 Dudley, William, ed. *Endangered Oceans* (8–12). (Opposing Viewpoints) 1999, Greenhaven LB $20.96 (0-7377-0063-7); paper $20.25 (0-7377-0062-9). This anthology of opinions about the spoiling of Earth's oceans debates such topics as the seriousness of the problem, the effectiveness of present practices, international policies, and how to save the whales. (Rev: BL 4/15/99; SLJ 8/99) [574.5]

10286 Erickson, Jon. *Marine Geology: Undersea Landforms and Life Forms* (10–12). (The Changing Earth) 1996, Facts on File $26.95 (0-8160-3354-4). This volume covers the entire realm of undersea landscapes and life forms, covering such topics as the seabed, the oceanic crust, undersea mountains and chasms, ocean circulation, and marine biology. (Rev: BL 12/1/95; SLJ 7/96) [551.46]

10287 Erickson, Jon. *The Mysterious Oceans* (9–12). Illus. 1988, TAB paper $15.95 (0-8306-9342-4). After discussing how oceans were formed, the author explores such topics as deep sea life, waves, food resources, and pollution. (Rev: VOYA 2/89) [551.46]

10288 Fleisher, Paul. *Our Oceans* (5–9). Illus. 1995, Millbrook LB $25.90 (1-56294-575-0). An attractive work that deals with such topics as seawater physics and chemistry, undersea geology, ocean currents, and undersea resources and their conservation. (Rev: BL 1/1–15/96; SLJ 3/96) [551.46]

10289 Groves, Don. *The Oceans: A Book of Questions and Answers* (9–12). Illus. 1989, Wiley paper $15.95 (0-471-60712-6). Information is given on the oceans and their exploration in a question-and-answer format. (Rev: BL 4/15/89; BR 11–12/90) [551.46]

10290 MacQuitty, Miranda. *Ocean* (5–9). (Eyewitness Books) 1995, Knopf LB $20.99 (0-679-97331-1). Two-page spreads with full-color photos introduce the oceans of the world. (Rev: BL 12/15/95; SLJ 12/95) [551.46]

10291 Simon, Seymour. *How to Be an Ocean Scientist in Your Own Home* (6–8). Illus. 1988, HarperCollins LB $14.89 (0-397-32292-5). A great deal of information about oceans and life in them is imparted through a series of simple experiments and activities. (Rev: BL 10/1/88) [551.46]

10292 Siy, Alexandra. *The Great Astrolabe Reef* (5–8). (Circle of Life) 1992, Dillon $14.95 (0-87518-499-5). Offers general information about the fragile coral ecosystem and the delicate interconnectedness of life on earth. (Rev: BL 9/1/92; SLJ 11/92) [574.5]

10293 Talbot, Frank H., ed. *Under the Sea* (5–8). (Nature Company Discoveries) 1995, Time-Life Books LB $16.00 (0-7835-4760-9). Marine life, both plant and animal, is introduced in this handsome book with lavish illustrations and a 4-page foldout. (Rev: SLJ 1/96) [551.46]

10294 Tesar, Jenny. *Threatened Oceans* (5–9). (Our Fragile Planet) 1991, Facts on File LB $19.95 (0-8160-2494-4). Basic material for general reading and for research on the oceans' vast resources, their role in land erosion, and marine ecosystems such as coral reefs and shorelines. (Rev: BL 12/1/91) [333.91]

10295 Twist, Clint. *Seas and Oceans* (5–8). (Ecology Watch) 1991, Dillon LB $21.00 (0-87518-491-X). Discusses how the seas and oceans evolved and how and why they are now threatened. (Rev: BL 3/1/92) [333.95]

10296 VanCleave, Janice. *Janice VanCleave's Oceans for Every Kid: Easy Activities that Make Learning*

Science Fun (5–10). Illus. (Science for Every Kid) 1996, Wiley paper $11.95 (0-471-12453-2). This volume gives good background information about oceans plus a number of entertaining and instructive projects and activities. (Rev: BL 4/15/96; SLJ 5/96) [551.46]

10297 Weber, Michael, and Judith Gradwohl. *The Wealth of Oceans* (9–12). 1995, Norton $25.00 (0-393-03764-9). New discoveries in marine ecology are discussed with regard to the stresses imposed by human societies. (Rev: BL 4/1/95) [333.71]

Underwater Exploration and Sea Disasters

10298 Ballard, Robert D. *Exploring the Titanic* (5–8). Illus. 1988, Scholastic $15.95 (0-590-41953-6). The story by the underwater explorer of his expeditions to explore the sunken *Titanic.* (Rev: BL 1/15/89; SLJ 11/88) [363.1]

10299 Ballard, Robert D., and Rick Archbold. *The Discovery of the Titanic* (9–12). Illus. 1987, Warner $35.00 (0-446-51385-7). An account of the complex, often frustrating but eventually successful quest for the wreck of the *Titanic.* (Rev: BL 12/1/87; VOYA 4/88) [622]

10300 Callahan, Steven. *Adrift: Seventy-Six Days Lost at Sea* (9–12). Illus. 1986, Ballantine paper $5.95 (0-345-34083-3). The incredible saga of a shipwrecked man who lived for 76 days on a rubber raft in the Atlantic Ocean. (Rev: BL 1/1/86; SLJ 9/86) [910]

10301 Cousteau, Jacques, and Frederic Dumas. *The Silent World* (7–12). Illus. 1987, Lyons Pr. paper $12.95 (0-941130-45-2). A description of how the aqualung was developed and how it has opened up the exploration of oceans and their sunken treasures. [551.46]

10302 Cussler, Clive, and Craig Dirgo. *The Sea Hunters* (10–12). 1996, Simon & Schuster $24.00 (0-684-83027-2). This is an account of 12 deep-sea wrecks, including how and why they happened and attempts to locate them. (Rev: SLJ 3/97) [940.4]

10303 Davie, Michael. *Titanic: The Death and Life of a Legend* (10–12). Illus. 1987, Knopf $19.95 (0-317-58565-7). A re-creation of the sinking of the *Titanic* that highlights the mysteries surrounding it that have not yet been solved. (Rev: BL 6/1/87) [363.1]

10304 Gaines, Richard. *The Explorers of the Undersea World* (6–9). Illus. (World Explorers) 1993, Chelsea LB $19.95 (0-7910-1323-5). A fully illus-

trated history of underwater exploration, with particular emphasis on the life and work of Cousteau. (Rev: BL 12/15/93; SLJ 2/94) [561.46]

10305 Hackwell, W. John. *Diving to the Past: Recovering Ancient Wrecks* (6–8). Illus. 1988, Macmillan LB $14.95 (0-684-18918-6). An introduction to the many riches contained in sunken ships and the dangers and excitement of salvaging them. (Rev: BL 3/1/88; SLJ 6/88) [930.1]

10306 Heyer, Paul. *Titanic Legacy: Disaster as Media Event and Myth* (9–12). 1995, Praeger $39.95 (0-275-95352-1). Traces the events surrounding the sinking of the *Titanic,* the heroes and villains, and how the media reported the disaster. (Rev: BL 12/1/95) [363.12]

10307 Kinder, Gary. *Ship of Gold in the Deep Blue Sea: The History & Discovery of America's Richest Shipwreck* (10–12). Illus. 1998, Grove Atlantic $27.50 (0-87113-464-0). An engrossing story of Tommy Thompson, an engineer from Ohio, and his determination to explore and salvage the cargo of the *SS Central America,* a ship that sank in 1857 off the coast of North Carolina. (Rev: BL 6/1–15/98; SLJ 10/98) [910.4]

10308 Lord, Walter. *A Night to Remember* (7–12). 1956, Bantam paper $5.99 (0-553-27827-4). A brilliant re-creation of the maiden and only voyage of the *Titanic.* (Rev: BL 3/15/98) [910.4]

10309 Marx, Robert F. *The Search for Sunken Treasure* (10–12). 1996, Key Porter paper $19.95 (1-55013-788-3). This is an exciting history of the world's most famous shipwrecks, beginning with the Phoenicians and ancient Greeks up to the more recent *Bismark* and *Edenburgh.* (Rev: SLJ 5/97) [910.4]

10310 Platt, Richard. *Shipwreck* (4–9). (Eyewitness Books) 1997, Knopf LB $20.99 (0-679-98569-X). An overview of the causes and consequences of the world's most famous maritime disasters. (Rev: BL 12/15/97; BR 1–2/98) [387.2]

10311 Ritchie, David. *Shipwrecks: An Encyclopedia of the World's Worst Disasters at Sea* (10–12). 1996, Facts on File $40.00 (0-8160-3163-0). Alphabetically arranged articles chronicle sea disasters, from the sinking of the Santa Maria in 1492 to a ferry tragedy in Haiti in 1993. (Rev: SLJ 2/97) [904]

10312 Sloan, Frank. *Titanic.* rev. ed. (5–8). 1998, Raintree Steck-Vaughn $25.69 (0-8172-4091-8). This thorough account of the *Titanic* and its sinking covers the structure of the ship, why it sank, the inquiries that followed, the many attempts to find and explore the wreckage, and movies and plays inspired by it. (Rev: BL 9/1/98; SLJ 2/99) [910]

10313 *Sunk! Exploring Underwater Archaeology* (5–8). (Buried Worlds) 1994, Lerner LB $23.93 (0-8225-3205-0). Provides a general overview of how archaeologists interpret underwater discoveries to learn about aspects of ancient trade, commerce, and history. (Rev: BL 10/15/94; SLJ 9/94) [930.1]

10314 *Titanic: Fortune & Fate* (9–12). 1998, Simon & Schuster $30.00 (0-684-85710-3). Letters, pictures, newspaper articles, and photos of memorabilia are logically arranged with explanatory captions and minimal text in this catalog of an exhibit that covers background information, life onboard the ship, the sinking itself, and the aftermath, with a detailed list of both passengers and crew that includes age, class, occupation, and whether or not they were lost or saved. (Rev: SLJ 2/99) [910]

10315 Van Dover, Cindy L. *Octopus's Garden* (10–12). 1996, Addison-Wesley $20.00 (0-201-40770-1). This is an autobiographical account of a woman pioneer in the field of oceanography and her experiences piloting the research submersible ALVIN, where she studied the ocean floor and the sea life that exists there. (Rev: BL 12/15/95; SLJ 9/96) [551.46]

Physics

General and Miscellaneous

10316 Barnett, Lincoln. *The Universe of Dr. Einstein* (8–12). 1980, Amereon $18.95 (0-8488-0146-6). A lucid explanation of Einstein's theory of relativity and how it is changing our ideas of the universe. [530.1]

10317 Challoner, Jack. *Visual Dictionary of Physics* (6–12). 1995, DK Publg. $18.95 (0-7894-0239-4). This oversize, heavily illustrated dictionary of terms and concepts related to physics is fun to browse through. (Rev: SLJ 12/95; VOYA 6/96) [530]

10318 Cooper, Christopher. *Matter* (5–8). (Eyewitness Science) 1992, DK Publg. $15.95 (1-879431-88-2). Clear explanations and color photos provide a wealth of information on the origins, principles, and history of the study of matter. (Rev: BL 1/15/93; SLJ 12/92) [530]

10319 Davies, Paul. *About Time: Einstein's Unfinished Revolution* (9–12). 1995, Simon & Schuster $24.00 (0-671-79964-9). Time warps, black holes, Einstein's theory of relativity, quantum time, and imaginary time are among the topics covered. (Rev: BL 3/1/95) [530.1]

10320 Davies, Paul, and John Gribbin. *The Matter Myth: Dramatic Discoveries That Challenge Our Understanding of Physical Reality* (9–12). 1992, Simon & Schuster paper $13.00 (0-671-72841-5). Astrophysicists reveal recent discoveries that make obsolete the traditional scientific notions of how the world works. (Rev: BL 1/15/92*) [530.2]

10321 Friedhoffer, Robert. *Physics Lab in a Hardware Store* (5–8). Illus. (Physical Science Labs) 1996, Watts LB $24.00 (0-531-11292-6). Using objects like nails, axes, and ladders, a number of principles in physics are introduced. (Rev: BL 12/1/96; SLJ 5/97) [621.9]

10322 Friedhoffer, Robert. *Physics Lab in a Housewares Store* (5–8). Illus. (Physical Science Labs) 1996, Watts LB $24.00 (0-531-11293-4). Various concepts in physics are demonstrated using such household items as a garlic press and a can opener. (Rev: BL 12/1/96; SLJ 1/97) [530]

10323 Friedhoffer, Robert. *Physics Lab in the Home* (6–9). Illus. (Physical Science Labs) 1997, Watts LB $24.00 (0-531-11323-X). Using such common household items as the refrigerator and the toilet, this book explains such concepts in physics as heat transfer and air and water pressure. (Rev: BR 5–6/98; SLJ 1/98) [530]

10324 Gardner, Robert. *Science Projects about Physics in the Home* (6–9). (Science Projects) 1999, Enslow $19.95 (0-89490-948-7). Ranging in difficulty from simple to complex, these projects about physics involving ideas from the living room, kitchen, playground, and bathroom are presented in a clear, straightforward way. (Rev: BR 5–6/99; SLJ 5/99) [530]

10325 Lafferty, Peter. *Heat and Cold* (4–8). Illus. (Let's Investigate Science) 1996, Benchmark LB $25.64 (0-7614-0033-8). The properties of heat and cold, their effects on living things, and how we use them are explained in this attractive science book that also contains many experiments. (Rev: SLJ 7/96) [536]

10326 Lafferty, Peter. *Light and Sound* (4–8). Illus. (Lets Investigate Science) 1996, Benchmark LB $25.64 (0-7614-0030-3). Through experiments and a clever, well-illustrated text, the properties of light and sound are covered, the nature of their waves explained, and the uses of mirrors and lenses discussed. (Rev: SLJ 7/96) [535]

10327 McGrath, Susan. *Fun with Physics* (5–9). Illus. 1986, National Geographic LB $12.50 (0-87044-581-2). An introduction to physics that uses everyday situations as examples and supplies a smattering of experiments. (Rev: SLJ 6/87) [530]

10328 Motz, Lloyd, and Jefferson Hane Weaver. *The Story of Physics* (10–12). Illus. 1989, Plenum $24.50 (0-306-43076-2). A clearly written history of physics that explores such topics as Newton's contributions, optics, relativity, and quantum mechanics. (Rev: BL 5/1/89) [530]

Energy and Motion

General and Miscellaneous

10329 Asimov, Isaac. *How Did We Find Out about Solar Power?* (6–9). Illus. 1981, Walker LB $22.90 (0-8027-6423-1). An explanation is given on how the sun's energy has been used from the earliest time until today. [621.47]

10330 Chandler, Gary, and Kevin Graham. *Alternative Energy Sources* (4–8). Illus. (Making a Better World) 1996, Twenty-First Century LB $20.40 (0-8050-4621-6). Many varieties of alternate energy, such as solar, are explored, with emphasis on using these resources in eco-friendly ways. (Rev: BL 12/15/96; SLJ 1/97) [333.79]

10331 DiSpezio, Michael. *Awesome Experiments in Force & Motion* (5–8). Illus. (Awesome Experiments) 1999, Sterling $17.95 (0-8069-9821-0). Inertia, buoyancy, surface tension, air pressure, and propulsion are covered in over 70 well-presented experiments using available materials and supplemented with background material on the concepts involved. (Rev: SLJ 7/99) [531]

10332 Doherty, Paul, and Don Rathjen. *The Cool Hot Rod and Other Electrifying Experiments on Energy and Matter* (4–8). Illus. (Exploratorium Science Snackbook) 1996, Wiley paper $10.95 (0-471-11518-5). Based on exhibits at the Exploratorium in San Francisco, this book supplies activities that demonstrate the properties of energy and matter. (Rev: BL 4/15/96; SLJ 7/96) [531]

10333 Doherty, Paul, and Don Rathjen. *The Spinning Blackboard and Other Dynamic Experiments on Force and Motion* (4–8). Illus. (Exploratorium Science Snackbook) 1996, Wiley paper $10.95 (0-471-11514-2). The many activities in this well-organized, attractive book reveal important characteristics of force and motion. (Rev: BL 4/15/96; SLJ 6/96) [531]

10334 Gardner, Robert. *Experiments with Motion* (6–9). (Getting Started in Science) 1995, Enslow LB $18.95 (0-89490-667-4). This book explains the laws of motion and describes animal and machine movements, with projects and experiments to illustrate each. (Rev: SLJ 2/96; VOYA 6/96) [531]

10335 Gutnik, Martin J., and Natalie B. Gutnik. *Projects That Explore Energy* (5–8). Illus. (Investigate) 1994, Millbrook LB $21.40 (1-56294-334-0). Through a series of simple experiments, the principles and properties of energy are explored and the concept of energy conservation explained. (Rev: BL 8/94; SLJ 6/94; VOYA 6/94) [333.79]

10336 Jacobs, Linda. *Letting Off Steam: The Story of Geothermal Energy* (7–12). Illus. 1989, Carolrhoda LB $21.27 (0-87614-300-1). A lucid account that tells about the sources and the use of geothermal energy. (Rev: BL 9/15/89; SLJ 9/89) [333.8]

10337 Kaufman, Allan. *Exploring Solar Energy: Principles & Projects* (9–12). 1989, Prakken paper $8.95 (0-911168-60-5). An account that explains the 3 aspects of solar energy and gives 8 projects of varying difficulty and sophistication. (Rev: BR 5–6/90) [621.47]

10338 Lafferty, Peter. *Force and Motion* (5–8). (Eyewitness Science) 1992, DK Publg. $15.95 (1-879431-85-8). This well-illustrated book explores force and motion. (Rev: BL 1/15/93; SLJ 12/92) [531]

10339 Parker, Edward. *Fuels for the Future* (5–8). 1998, Raintree Steck-Vaughn LB $25.68 (0-8172-4937-0). This work shows how fuels like coal, oil, and nuclear power have polluted the environment, and outlines possible alternate energy sources, such as solar, wind, and geothermal energy. Also use *Waste, Recycling, and Re-use* (1998). (Rev: BR 9–10/98; VOYA 12/98) [363.7]

10340 Woelfle, Gretchen. *The Wind at Work: An Activity Guide to Windmills* (4–8). 1997, Chicago Review paper $14.95 (1-55652-308-4). The history, types, and uses of windmills are covered, with many activities and a discussion of the future of wind power. (Rev: BL 9/1/97; SLJ 10/97*) [621.4]

Nuclear Energy

10341 Andryszewski, Tricia. *What to Do about Nuclear Waste* (7–12). 1995, Millbrook LB $22.40 (1-56294-577-7). An examination of this urgent problem, including discussion of the Manhattan Project, nuclear power's heyday in the 1950s, and the Three Mile Island and Chernobyl meltdowns, plus a review of controversial solutions. (Rev: BL 11/1/95; SLJ 12/95; VOYA 4/96) [363.72]

10342 Daley, Michael J. *Nuclear Power: Promise or Peril?* (7–12). Illus. (Pro/Con) 1997, Lerner LB $23.93 (0-8225-2611-5). This book examines conflicting opinions about nuclear power, the possibility of nuclear accidents, the demand for energy, and the problems involving storage of nuclear waste. (Rev: BL 11/1/97; SLJ 12/97) [333.792]

10343 Galperin, Anne. *Nuclear Energy/Nuclear Waste* (9–12). 1991, Chelsea LB $19.95 (0-7910-1585-8). The pros and cons of nuclear energy are examined, along with the political and technological problems of radioactive waste disposal. (Rev: BL 2/1/92) [333.792]

10344 Kidd, J. S., and Renee A. Kidd. *Quarks and Sparks: The Story of Nuclear Power* (7–12). 1999, Facts on File $19.95 (0-8160-3587-3). A history of the development of nuclear power, with good coverage on the nuclear race during World War II and its contemporary uses and problems. (Rev: BL 8/99; VOYA 10/99) [621.48]

10345 League of Women Voters Education Fund. *The Nuclear Waste Primer: A Handbook for Citizens* (10–12). 1994, Lyons Pr. paper $10.95 (1-55821-226-4). This concise handbook explains what nuclear wastes are, how they are presently being handled, and how to participate in making decisions involving them. (Rev: BL 12/15/85) [363.7]

10346 Wilcox, Charlotte. *Powerhouse: Inside a Nuclear Power Plant* (4–8). Illus. 1996, Carolrhoda LB $22.60 (0-87614-945-X); paper $7.95 (0-98714-979-4). The benefits and hazards of nuclear energy are explored along with details on how energy is produced, nuclear waste, and possible future developments. (Rev: BL 10/1/96; SLJ 9/96) [621.48]

Light, Color, and Laser Science

10347 Billings, Charlene W. *Lasers: The New Technology of Light* (9–12). (Science Sourcebooks) 1992, Facts on File LB $19.95 (0-8160-2630-0). A concise overview of lasers, their development, uses, types, and how they are revolutionizing communications, surgery, industry, scientific research, and other fields with coverage ending in 1991. (Rev: BL 1/15/93) [621.36]

10348 Burnie, David. *Light* (5–8). (Eyewitness Science) 1992, DK Publg. $15.95 (1-879431-79-3). Clear explanations and color photos provide a wealth of information on the origins, principles, and history of the study of light. (Rev: BL 1/15/93; SLJ 11/92) [535]

10349 Cobb, Vicki, and Josh Cobb. *Light Action: Amazing Experiments with Optics* (5–8). 1993, HarperCollins LB $14.89 (0-06-021437-6). Presents basic principles of optics, with experiments that demonstrate them. (Rev: BL 1/15/94; VOYA 6/94) [535]

10350 Hecht, Jeff. *Optics: Light for a New Age* (6–10). Illus. 1987, Macmillan $15.95 (0-684-18879-1). In this general discussion of light such topics as the human eye, optical instruments, and artificial light are also described. (Rev: BL 4/1/88; SLJ 3/88) [535]

10351 Heifetz, Jeanne. *When Blue Meant Yellow: How Colors Got Their Names* (7–12). 1994, Holt $14.95 (0-8050-3178-2). Explores the origins of 191 color terms—from apricot to zinnaber green. (Rev: BL 1/1/95; SLJ 2/95) [535.6]

10352 Levine, Shar, and Leslie Johnstone. *The Optics Book: Fun Experiments with Light, Vision & Color* (5–8). Illus. 1999, Sterling $21.95 (0-8069-9947-0). Divided into sections on such subjects as light rays and reflection, the speed of light and refraction, light and color, and optical instruments, this book presents 37 experiments and activities using easily obtained materials. (Rev: BL 3/1/99; SLJ 7/99) [535]

10353 Nassau, Kurt. *Experimenting with Color* (7–10). (Venture Books: Science Experiments and Projects) 1997, Watts LB $25.00 (0-531-11327-2). The general properties of light, the electromagnetic spectrum, color vision, and electron interactions are explored in this book of 17 easily performed experiments and projects. (Rev: SLJ 10/97; VOYA 6/98) [535]

10354 Wick, Walter. *Walter Wick's Optical Tricks* (4–8). 1998, Scholastic $13.95 (0-590-22227-9). A stimulating collection of photos that present unusual optical illusions, with their secrets revealed in subsequent pages. (Rev: BL 8/98; SLJ 9/98) [152]

Magnetism and Electricity

10355 DiSpezio, Michael. *Awesome Experiments in Electricity & Magnetism* (5–8). Illus. (Awesome Experiments) 1999, Sterling $17.95 (0-8069-9819-9). Using easily available materials and simple assembly, this clear, well-organized collection of over 70 experiments covers such fields as electrical charges, static electricity, currents, circuits, switches, and magnetism. (Rev: SLJ 7/99) [537]

10356 Gardner, Robert. *Electricity and Magnetism* (6–9). Illus. (Yesterday's Science, Today's Technology) 1994, Twenty-First Century LB $24.90 (0-8050-2850-1). Discusses magnets, electric charges, the future of electric power, and other topics. (Rev: BL 12/1/95; SLJ 11/94) [537]

10357 Parker, Steve. *Electricity* (5–8). (Eyewitness Science) 1992, DK Publg. $15.95 (1-879431-82-3). From the earliest discoveries to new technology, this heavily illustrated book explains how electricity has changed our lives. (Rev: BL 1/15/93) [537]

10358 Stwertka, Albert. *Superconductors: The Irresistible Future* (6–10). (Venture) 1991, Watts LB $22.00 (0-531-12526-2). A description of the history, development, and molecular activity of superconducting materials and an explanation of their potential use. (Rev: BL 6/15/91; SLJ 8/91) [621.3]

10359 Vecchione, Glen. *Magnet Science* (4–9). Illus. 1995, Sterling $14.95 (0-8069-0888-2). This book explains magnetism and electromagnetism and contains 26 experiments to illustrate these principles. (Rev: BL 12/1/95; SLJ 5/96) [528.4]

10360 Wong, Ovid K. *Experimenting with Electricity and Magnetism* (7–12). 1993, Watts LB $22.50 (0-531-12547-5). These experiments explain such basic concepts as Coulomb's Law, piezoelectricity, electrical induction, and electromagnetism, and include instructions for building an electroscope, galvanometer, and a copper-zinc battery. (Rev: BL 8/93; SLJ 7/93; VOYA 10/93) [537]

Nuclear Physics

10361 Taubes, Gary. *Bad Science: The Short Life and Very Hard Times of Cold Fusion* (9–12). 1993, Random $25.00 (0-394-58456-2). Documents the bizarre 1989 episode of 2 scientists who announced they had created a sustained nuclear-fusion reaction at room temperature and the ensuing scandal. (Rev: BL 5/15/93*) [539.7]

Technology and Engineering

General Works and Miscellaneous Industries

10362 Aaseng, Nathan. *Twentieth-Century Inventors* (7–10). (American Profiles) 1991, Facts on File $19.95 (0-8160-2485-5). Combines historical perspective with personal profiles of inventors to explain the events that influenced the development of such items as plastic, rockets, and television. (Rev: BL 11/1/91; SLJ 11/91) [609.2]

10363 Brackin, A. J. *Clocks: Chronicling Time* (6–10). (Encyclopedia of Discovery and Invention) 1991, Lucent LB $23.70 (1-56006-208-8). A history of the measurement of time and how time devices have changed the world. (Rev: BL 4/15/92) [681.1]

10364 Cardwell, Donald. *The Norton History of Technology* (9–12). (Norton History of Science) 1994, Norton paper $19.95 (0-393-31192-9). An overview of humankind's technological progress, from simple tools to computers and satellites, focusing on such key areas as transportation, medicine, and energy. (Rev: BL 8/94) [609]

10365 *Cds, Super Glue, and Salsa Series 2: How Everyday Products Are Made* (5–10). 1996, Gale $49.00 (0-7876-0870-X). This two-volume set tells how 30 everyday products are made, including air bags, bungee cords, contact lenses, ketchup, pencils, soda bottles, and umbrellas. (Rev: BR 1–2/97; SLJ 8/97) [6.5.8.5]

10366 Cohen, Leah H. *Glass, Paper, Beans: Revelations on the Nature and Value of Ordinary Things* (10–12). 1997, Doubleday $22.95 (0-385-47819-4). Starting with coffee in a glass cup and a newspaper, the author examines glass production, newspaper printing, and coffee manufacturing, and moves on from there to introduce individuals involved in those fields of work and their relationship to technology and the production economy. (Rev: SLJ 11/97) [620]

10367 Colman, Penny. *Toilets, Bathtubs, Sinks, and Sewers: A History of the Bathroom* (5–8). 1994, Atheneum $16.00 (0-689-31894-4). An interesting, well-written introduction to the history of technology and inventions related to personal cleanliness and hygiene. (Rev: BL 1/1/95; SLJ 3/95) [643]

10368 Crump, Donald J., ed. *How Things Are Made* (6–9). Illus. 1981, National Geographic LB $12.50 (0-87044-339-9). An inquiry into how such objects as baseballs and light bulbs are made. [670]

10369 Crump, Donald J., ed. *How Things Work* (7–9). Illus. 1983, National Geographic LB $12.00 (0-87044-430-1). An exploration of the principles on which such common objects as alarm clocks and bicycles work. [600]

10370 Crump, Donald J., ed. *Small Inventions That Make a Big Difference* (6–9). Illus. 1984, National Geographic LB $12.50 (0-87044-503-0). A book on inventions and inventors that covers such common items as the zipper. [608]

10371 Fox, Roy. *Technology* (9–12). 1985, David & Charles $19.95 (0-7134-3710-3). A survey of the developments in technology from the Industrial Revolution to today's frontiers in computers and atomic energy. (Rev: SLJ 11/85) [600]

10372 Friedel, Robert. *Zipper: An Exploration in Novelty* (9–12). (Perspectives) 1994, Norton $23.00 (0-393-03599-9). Describes the people who created and manufactured the zipper, and their marketing struggles and patent wars. (Rev: BL 3/15/94) [609]

10373 Galas, Judith C. *Plastics: Molding the Past, Shaping the Future* (6–10). (Encyclopedia of Discovery and Invention) 1995, Lucent LB $18.96 (1-56006-251-7). A description of how plastics were invented, the various types, and their many uses. (Rev: BL 4/15/95) [668.4]

10374 Hellman, Hal. *Beyond Your Senses: The New World of Sensors* (7–9). 1997, Dutton paper $16.99 (0-525-67533-7). Each of the senses is explained, with a focus on what scientists are doing to develop machines that duplicate and even surpass human functions, e.g., cochlear implants for the deaf. (Rev: BL 6/1–15/97; BR 1–2/98; SLJ 9/97) [681]

10375 *How Things Work in Your Home: And What to Do When They Don't* (9–12). Illus. 1985, Holt paper $22.50 (0-8050-0126-3). After a description of how common machines around the house operate, this book tells how to keep them working properly. (Rev: SLJ 9/85) [621.8]

10376 *Inventors and Discoverers: Changing Our World* (9–12). Illus. 1988, National Geographic $35.00 (0-87044-751-3). A capsule history of modern technology in words and pictures that highlights major inventions like the steam engine, cameras, and computers. (Rev: BL 3/15/89) [609]

10377 Lukas, Paul. *Inconspicuous Consumption: An Obsessive Look at the Stuff We Take for Granted, from the Everyday to the Obscure* (10–12). 1997, Crown paper $12.95 (0-517-88668-5). A look at 105 products on the market, some commonplace, others exotic, and how they are manufactured. (Rev: BL 10/15/96; SLJ 9/97) [608]

10378 Macaulay, David. *The Way Things Work* (7–12). Illus. 1988, Houghton $29.95 (0-395-42857-2). From the zipper to the computer, the author through his text and masterful drawings explains the wonders of technology. (Rev: BL 1/15/89; BR 5–6/89; SLJ 12/88; VOYA 4/89) [600]

10379 Macaulay, David, and Neil Ardley. *The New Way Things Work* (6–12). 1998, Houghton $35.00 (0-395-93847-3). With an emphasis on visual cutaways, this revision of a fascinating 1988 introduction to modern machines now includes more material on computers. (Rev: BL 12/1/98; SLJ 12/98) [600]

10380 *Machines and Inventions* (5–9). (Understanding Science and Nature) 1993, Time-Life Books $17.95 (0-8094-9704-2). Using a question-and-answer format, this covers historic inventions as well as modern machines and electronic equipment. (Rev: BL 1/15/94; SLJ 6/94) [621.8]

10381 Parker, Steve. *The Random House Book of How Things Work* (6–12). 1991, Random LB $19.99 (0-679-90908-7); paper $18.00 (0-679-80908-2). This well-illustrated book shows how everyday appliances and gadgets work. (Rev: BL 5/15/91; SLJ 7/91) [600]

10382 Paterson, Alan J. *How Glass Is Made* (5–9). Illus. 1985, Facts on File $14.95 (0-8160-0038-7). In this well-illustrated volume, a history of glass making is given with text and diagrams on the kinds of glass and the processes in existence today. (Rev: BL 6/15/85; SLJ 2/86) [666]

10383 Platt, Richard. *Inventions Explained: A Beginner's Guide to Technological Breakthroughs* (4–8). Illus. (Your World Explained) 1997, Holt $18.95 (0-8050-4876-6). An in-depth look at the changing world of technological innovations, covering systems of transportation, energy, medicine, machinery, and computing. (Rev: BL 3/1/98; SLJ 2/98) [609]

10384 Platt, Richard. *Stephen Biesty's Incredible Everything: How Things Are Made—From Chocolate to False Teeth and Race Cars to Rockets* (6–12). Illus. 1997, DK Publg. $19.95 (0-7894-2049-X). A profusely illustrated volume that explores such everyday technology as doughnut making, airplane construction, and newspaper publishing. (Rev: SLJ 1/98; VOYA 2/98) [609]

10385 Reid, Struan. *Inventions and Trade* (5–8). Illus. (The Silk and Spice Routes) 1994, Silver Burdett LB $15.95 (0-02-726316-9). A history of the trade between China and Europe that focuses on the technological advances that occurred because of cultural exchange. (Rev: BL 12/15/94) [382]

10386 Rubin, Susan G. *Toilets, Toasters, & Telephones: The How & Why of Everyday Objects* (5–8). Illus. 1998, Harcourt $20.00 (0-15-201421-7). In addition to the objects in the title, this book gives details on the invention and design of other familiar household items, such as stoves, vacuum cleaners, bathtubs, and pencils. (Rev: BL 11/1/98; SLJ 11/98) [683.8]

10387 Sandler, Martin W. *Inventors* (5–8). (Library of Congress Books) 1996, HarperCollins $24.95 (0-06-024923-4). Concentrating on the late 19th and 20th centuries, the book is divided into sections on inventors, transportation, communication, and entertainment. (Rev: SLJ 2/96) [608]

10388 Sobey, Ed. *How to Enter and Win an Invention Contest* (6–12). Illus. 1999, Enslow LB $19.95 (0-7660-1173-9). A book that not only describes how to invent a new product but also tells how to enter it in a local or national competition. (Rev: BL 9/1/99) [607.973]

10389 Streissguth, Thomas. *Communications: Sending the Message* (5–8). (Innovators) 1997, Oliver Pr. LB $19.95 (1-881508-41-2). A compact, easy-to-understand history of communication from earliest times, through Gutenberg, Edison, and Marconi, to the present "information highway." (Rev: BR 3–4/98; SLJ 2/98) [001.51]

10390 Sutton, Caroline, and Duncan M. Anderson. *How Do They Do That?* (10–12). 1982, Morrow paper $9.95 (0-688-01111-X). An explanation is given for a variety of present-day achievements. [600]

10391 Taylor, Barbara. *Be an Inventor* (5–9). Illus. 1987, Harcourt $11.95 (0-15-205950-4); paper $7.95 (0-15-205951-2). A discussion of the process of invention and some examples plus coverage of entries in a Weekly Reader invention contest. (Rev: BL 12/15/87; SLJ 3/88) [608]

10392 Tucker, Tom. *Brainstorm! The Stories of Twenty American Kid Inventors* (5–8). Illus. 1995, Farrar $15.00 (0-374-30944-2). Profiles of 20 young adult inventors, both known, such as Edison, Westinghouse, and Franklin, and unknown, from the 1770s to the 1990s, with an epilogue offering legal and financial advice. (Rev: BL 8/95; BR 1–2/96; SLJ 10/95; VOYA 2/96) [608]

10393 Vare, Ethlie A., and Greg Ptacek. *Women Inventors and Their Discoveries* (6–10). 1993, Oliver Pr. LB $18.95 (1-881508-06-4). A review of women who are known in the world of industry and technology for their unusual inventions. (Rev: BL 10/15/93; SLJ 1/94; VOYA 2/94) [609.2]

10394 Wilkinson, Philip, and Jacqueline Dineen. *Art and Technology Through the Ages* (5–8). Illus. (Ideas That Changed the World) 1995, Chelsea LB $19.95 (0-7910-2769-4). A survey of the evolution of art and communications, from cave paintings through advanced digital recording and computer graphics. (Rev: BR 5–6/96; SLJ 11/95; VOYA 2/96) [501.4]

10395 Wulffson, Don L. *The Kid Who Invented the Popsicle: And Other Surprising Stories About Inventions* (4–8). 1997, Cobblehill paper $13.99 (0-525-65221-3). An alphabetically arranged presentation of the stories behind such inventions as animal crackers and the zipper. (Rev: BL 2/15/97; SLJ 3/97) [609]

Building and Construction

10396 Adkins, Jan. *How a House Happens* (7–9). 1983, Walker paper $3.95 (0-8027-7206-4). From land selection to the completed building, this is how a house takes shape. [728]

10397 Bennett, David. *Skyscrapers: Form and Function* (9–12). 1995, Simon & Schuster $35.00 (0-684-80318-6). A look at the functions and interiors of skyscrapers plus an informative history of their evolution. (Rev: BL 10/15/95) [720]

10398 Darling, David. *Spiderwebs to Skyscrapers: The Science of Structures* (5–8). 1991, Dillon LB $13.95 (0-87518-478-2). Discusses foundations, building materials, and styles of construction, in both nature and advanced technology, using experiments and color illustrations. (Rev: BL 6/1/92; SLJ 3/92) [624.1]

10399 Hawkes, Nigel. *Structures: The Way Things Are Built* (9–12). 1990, Macmillan $39.95 (0-02-549105-9). An illustrated look at some of the marvels of civil engineering throughout the world. (Rev: BL 1/15/91) [624.09]

10400 Macaulay, David. *Underground* (7–12). Illus. 1976, Houghton $18.00 (0-395-24739-X); paper $9.95 (0-395-34065-9). The infrastructure of a large city is explored in drawings that show how building foundations and underground utility connections exist. [624]

10401 Platt, Richard. *Stephen Biesty's Incredible Cross-Sections* (6–12). Illus. 1992, Knopf $19.95 (0-679-81411-6). Highly detailed cross-sections of 18 buildings and other structures, such as the Queen Mary, a steam train, an oil rig, an automobile factory, and a 747 plane. (Rev: BL 9/1/92) [624]

10402 Wilkinson, Philip. *Building* (5–9). (Eyewitness Books) 1995, Knopf $19.00 (0-679-87256-6). The history of building techniques, materials, and philosophy through the years. (Rev: BL 8/95; SLJ 8/95) [690]

10403 Wilkinson, Philip. *Super Structures* (5–8). (Inside Guides) 1996, DK Publg. $15.95 (0-7894-1011-7). The interiors of oil rigs, skyscrapers, undersea tunnels, and other structures are illustrated and explained in double-page spreads. (Rev: BL 12/15/96; SLJ 2/97) [624.1]

10404 Wood, Tim. *Houses & Homes* (4–8). (See Through History) 1997, Viking $17.99 (0-670-86777-2). A well-illustrated examination of different kinds of houses, their variations through history, and their structure and parts. (Rev: BL 11/15/97; SLJ 4/98) [690]

Clothing, Textiles, and Jewelry

10405 Kennett, Frances. *Ethnic Dress* (10–12). 1995, Facts on File $40.00 (0-8160-3136-3). Beautiful photographs and text show contemporary fashions and clothing around the world. (Rev: BL 9/1/95; BR 3–4/96; SLJ 5/96) [355.1]

10406 Lawlor, Laurie. *Where Will This Shoe Take You? A Walk Through the History of Footwear* (5–8). Illus. 1996, Walker LB $18.85 (0-8027-8435-6). This is a history of footwear, from the sandals worn by the ancients to the sneakers popular today. (Rev: BL 11/15/96; BR 3–4/97; SLJ 5/97; VOYA 6/97) [391]

10407 Miller, Brandon M. *Dressed for the Occasion: What Americans Wore, 1620–1970* (5–8). 1999, Lerner $22.60 (0-8225-1738-8). A fascinating look at men's and women's fashions throughout history and how they reflect society's culture and values. (Rev: BL 4/1/99; SLJ 9/99) [391]

10408 O'Keeffe, Linda. *Shoes: A Celebration of Pumps, Sandals, Slippers & More* (10–12). 1996, Workman paper $12.95 (0-7611-0114-4). Divided by types of shoe, such as sandals and boots, this is an illustrated history of footwear and famous shoe designers, filled with quotes about shoes from celebrities, ordinary people, designers, and historical figures, quips, and historical oddities. (Rev: SLJ 4/97) [646]

10409 Ruby, Jennifer. *Underwear* (7–12). (Costumes in Context) 1996, Batsford $24.95 (0-7134-7663-X). This is a thoughtful, information-filled, illustrated history of underwear from 1066 through the 1990s. (Rev: SLJ 1/97) [646]

10410 Yue, Charlotte, and David Yue. *Shoes* (5–8). 1997, Houghton $14.95 (0-395-72667-0). An in-depth survey of footwear through the ages with emphasis on Western cultures. (Rev: BL 4/1/97; SLJ 4/97) [391]

Computers, Automation, and the Internet

10411 Billings, Charlene W. *Supercomputers: Shaping the Future* (7–12). (Science Sourcebooks) 1995, Facts on File $19.95 (0-8160-3096-0). A history of the silicon revolution—focusing on the megamachines that are the most powerful computers in the world. (Rev: BL 10/15/95; SLJ 4/96; VOYA 4/96) [004.1]

10412 Bortz, Fred. *Mind Tools: The Science of Artificial Intelligence* (7–12). 1992, Watts LB $25.00 (0-531-12515-7). A concise overview of the controversy surrounding the science of artificial intelligence and new computer technologies, with material on the field's pioneers. (Rev: BL 11/1/92) [006.3]

10413 Brunner, Laurel. *Introducing the Internet* (9–12). Illus. 1997, Totem paper $10.95 (1-874166-84-6). Though now somewhat out of date, this book gives valuable information on the origins of the Internet, introduces Internet language, servers, URLs, and browsers, and discusses the problems we face when we enter the year 2000. (Rev: SLJ 1/98) [004.6]

10414 Cooper, Brian, and Anna Milner, eds. *The Internet: How to Get Connected & Explore the World Wide Web, Exchange News & Email, Download Software, & Communicate On-Line* (10–12). 1996, DK Publg. $16.95 (0-7894-1288-8). Though dated, this is a good introduction to the Internet using Windows 95. (Rev: SLJ 4/97; VOYA 6/97) [001.6]

10415 Cooper, Gail, and Garry Cooper. *Virtual Field Trips* (8–12). 1997, Libraries Unlimited $24.00 (1-56308-557-7). This is a fantastic source of information on Web sites that contain inventive and entertaining material for young adults. (Rev: BL 3/1/98; BR 9–10/98; SLJ 5/98) [004.6]

10416 Cozic, Charles P., ed. *The Future of the Internet* (9–12). (At Issue) 1997, Greenhaven LB $18.70 (1-56510-659-8); paper $15.57 (1-56510-658-X). The popularity of the Internet and computer networks worldwide has led to businesses and governments proposing many changes and regulations. This book presents various viewpoints, both positive and negative, on these issues as well as on such concerns as invasion of privacy, security matters, excessive Internet use as a behavior disorder, and the impact of the Internet on the quality of life. (Rev: BL 9/1/97; SLJ 12/97) [004.67]

10417 Cozic, Charles P., ed. *The Information Highway* (9–12). 1996, Greenhaven LB $19.95 (1-56510-375-0); paper $16.20 (1-56510-374-2). Although a few years old, this book still provides a good introduction to the Internet and discusses still-timely questions such as filtering sites for children and who should pay for the infrastructure. (Rev: BL 6/1–15/96; SLJ 3/96) [384.3]

10418 Gay, Martin. *The New Information Revolution: A Reference Handbook* (10–12). 1996, ABC-CLIO LB $39.50 (0-87436-847-2). This guidebook to the Information Revolution gives a detailed chronology, definitions of key words, profiles of important figures, and a large bibliography of print and nonprint sources. (Rev: BR 9–10/97; SLJ 5/97) [004]

10419 Gay, Martin, and Kathlyn Gay. *The Information Superhighway* (7–12). Illus. 1996, Twenty-First Century $16.98 (0-8050-4741-7). This book traces the development of this vast electronic communication system, discusses uses of the Internet and the World Wide Web, both positive and negative, and examines possibilities for the future. (Rev: BL 7/96; SLJ 7/96; VOYA 8/96) [004.6]

10420 Godwin, Mike. *Cyber Rights: Defending Free Speech in the Digital Age* (10–12). 1998, Times Bks. $27.50 (0-8129-2834-2). This book explores the issue of freedom of expression on the Internet, presenting all sides, and comes out firmly for protecting First Amendment rights and adopting an anti-censorship stance. (Rev: BL 8/98; SLJ 2/99) [004.6]

10421 Goldberg, Matt, ed. *Tripod's Tools for Life: Streetsmart Strategies for Work, Life—and Everything Else* (10–12). 1998, Hyperion paper $16.00 (0-7868-8332-4). After a general introduction to the Internet, its use, and possible problems, this volume gives irreverent but useful information on topics like job hunting on the Net, health, cooking, and home finding and furnishing. (Rev: SLJ 1/99) [004.6]

10422 Grady, Sean M. *Virtual Reality: Computers Mimic the Physical World* (7–12). Illus. (Science Sourcebooks) 1998, Facts on File $19.95 (0-8160-3605-5). This book provides young readers with a working knowledge of virtual reality, how this technology developed, its uses, drawbacks, and the philosophical questions raised by the manufacture of "reality." (Rev: BL 4/15/98; BR 11–12/98; SLJ 7/98) [006]

10423 Gralla, Preston. *Online Kids: A Young Surfer's Guide to Cyberspace* (4–8). 1996, Wiley paper $14.95 (0-471-13545-3). An informal guide to online services that includes addresses for sites, rates sites for "usefulness" and "coolness," describes various resources, and includes information on chat for kids, kid-oriented newsgroups, and how to make home pages on the Web. (Rev: BL 7/96; SLJ 9/96) [025.04]

10424 Green, John. *The New Age of Communications* (10–12). 1997, Holt paper $10.95 (0-8050-4027-7). After a general history of communications, this account focuses on what computers will and will not be able to do in the future. (Rev: SLJ 8/97) [004.6]

10425 Henderson, Harry. *The Internet* (6–9). Illus. (Overview) 1998, Lucent $17.96 (1-56006-215-0). A survey of the history of the Net, its uses, its impact on our way of life, and problems and controversies associated with it. (Rev: BL 9/1/98; SLJ 8/98) [004.67 8]

10426 Henderson, Harry. *Issues in the Information Age* (7–12). (Contemporary Issues) 1999, Lucent LB $23.70 (1-56006-365-3). This work examines troubling questions in the new information age involving censorship on the Internet, loss of privacy, parental prerogatives, and human interaction. (Rev: BR 9–10/99; SLJ 7/99) [004.6]

10427 Kalbag, Asha. *Build Your Own Web Site* (4–8). (Usborne Computer Guides) 1999, EDC paper $8.95 (07460-3293-5). This thorough guide explains how, why, when, and where to create a Web site. (Rev: SLJ 6/99) [004.6]

10428 Lampton, Christopher. *Home Page: An Introduction to Web Page Design* (4–8). 1997, Watts LB $22.50 (0-531-20255-0); paper $6.95 (0-531-15854-3). The author explains to youngsters clearly and simply how they can design their own Web home pages using offline time. (Rev: BL 7/97; SLJ 2/98) [005.7]

10429 Lampton, Christopher. *The World Wide Web* (4–8). 1997, Watts LB $22.50 (0-531-20262-3). Aspects of the World Wide Web that would be of value and interest to children are covered, with practical suggestions for effective searching. (Rev: BL 7/97; SLJ 2/98) [025.04]

10430 Lindsay, Dave, and Bruce Lindsay. *Dave's Quick 'n' Easy Web Pages* (5–9). 1999, Erin $14.95 (0-9690609-7-1). Dave, the 14-year-old webmaster of the children's literature Redwall Abbey Homepage, gives simple, practical, easy-to-follow directions for creating a personal Web page. (Rev: BL 8/99) [005.7]

10431 McComb, Gordon. *The Robot Builder's Bonanza: 99 Inexpensive Robotics Projects* (10–12). Illus. 1987, McGraw-Hill paper $17.95 (0-8306-2800-2). For advanced students, an introduction to robotics plus projects involving many practical applications. (Rev: BL 12/1/87) [629.8]

10432 McCormick, Anita Louise. *The Internet: Surfing the Issues* (6–9). Illus. 1998, Enslow LB $19.95 (0-89490-956-8). Organized around issues like control, security, equity, and access, this volume explores the Internet and topics such as filters, pornography, viruses, and Web TV. (Rev: BL 10/1/98; SLJ 12/98) [004.67]

10433 Marshall, Elizabeth L. *A Student's Guide to the Internet: Exploring the World Wide Web, Gopherspace, Electronic Mail and More!* (6–12). Illus. 1996, Millbrook LB $23.90 (1-56294-923-3). Using a step-by-step approach, online searching is explained along with basic information about the Web and the Internet. (Rev: BL 12/15/96; BR 9–10/97) [004.6]

10434 Northrup, Mary. *American Computer Pioneers* (6–12). Illus. (Collective Biographies) 1998, Enslow LB $19.95 (0-7660-1053-8). This book profiles the people who revolutionized modern technology, along with a concise history of the evolution of computers and their capabilities. (Rev: BL 10/15/98; BR 11–12/98; SLJ 8/98) [004]

10435 Owen, Trevor, and Ronald Owston. *The Learning Highway: The Student's Guide to the Internet* (9–12). 1997, Key Porter paper $19.95 (1-55013-905-3). This well-written work explains how students can use the Internet to enhance classroom learning, with extensive material on connecting and searching and chapters detailing projects done on the Internet by different schools, plus exercises and programs at the back of the book. (Rev: SLJ 8/98; VOYA 8/98) [004.6]

10436 Peterson, Ivars. *Fatal Defect: Chasing Killer Computer Bugs* (9–12). 1995, Times Bks. $25.00 (0-8129-2023-6). Peterson, a reporter for *Science News*, describes the work of "bug hunters," software experts who investigate and analyze computer problems. (Rev: BL 6/1–15/95) [005.3]

10437 Ryan, Ken. *Computer Anxiety? Instant Relief!* (9–12). 1991, Castle Mountain Pr. paper $9.95 (1-879925-05-2). Using subtle humor, this work attempts to simplify an intimidating subject for novice users, with definitions of computer terms and illustrations of difficult concepts. (Rev: BL 9/1/91) [004]

10438 Salzman, Marian, and Robert Pondiscio. *Kids On-Line: 150 Ways for Kids to Surf the Net for Fun and Information* (5–9). 1995, Avon paper $5.99 (0-380-78231-6). A leap into cyberspace for both adults and youth, with valuable information plus etiquette for Internet users. (Rev: BL 10/15/95) [004.69]

10439 Smolan, Rick. *One Digital Day: How the Microchip is Changing Our World* (10–12). (Day in the Life) 1998, Digital Day $40.00 (0-8129-3031-2). The lowly microchip is celebrated in this history that reviews its many uses in computers, automobiles, telephones, refrigerators, medicine, and entertainment. (Rev: BL 5/15/98; SLJ 9/98) [004.6]

10440 Thro, Ellen. *Robotics: The Marriage of Computers and Machines* (7–12). (Science Sourcebooks) 1993, Facts on File LB $17.95 (0-8160-2628-9). Presents this complicated subject in interesting, understandable terms, covering artificial intelligence and the use of robots underground, in factories, and in space exploration. (Rev: BL 7/93) [629.8]

10441 Wallace, Mark. *101 Things to Do on the Internet* (4–8). Illus. (Usborne Computer Guides) 1999, EDC paper $9.95 (07460-3294-3). Double-page spreads focus on Internet activities, arranged according to themes such as space, sports, music, games, movies, and weather. (Rev: SLJ 6/99) [004.6]

10442 Weiss, Ann E. *Virtual Reality: A Door to Cyberspace* (7–12). Illus. 1996, Twenty-First Century LB $21.50 (0-8050-3722-5). This book describes the development of virtual reality and its accomplishments, applications, and uses, as well as the ethical issues surrounding its development. (Rev: BL 5/15/96*; SLJ 7/96; VOYA 10/96) [006]

10443 Wickelgren, Ingrid. *Ramblin' Robots: Building a Breed of Mechanical Beasts* (7–12). Illus. 1996, Watts LB $25.00 (0-531-11301-9). An exciting history of the development of robots with details on current developments. (Rev: BL 11/15/96; SLJ 1/97) [629.8]

10444 Winters, Paul A. *Computers & Society* (7–12). (Current Controversies) 1997, Greenhaven LB $20.96 (1-56510-564-8); paper $16.20 (1-56510-563-X). The articles in this anthology discuss the impact of computers on society and education, as well as problems involving privacy and censorship. (Rev: BL 7/97; SLJ 12/97) [303.48]

10445 Wright, David. *Computers* (5–8). (Inventors and Inventions) 1995, Benchmark LB $25.64 (0-7614-0064-8). The development of the computer is traced, with brief profiles of important people in its history and an examination of the uses of computers in the world today. (Rev: SLJ 6/96) [004]

Electronics

10446 Bonnet, Bob, and Dan Keen. *Science Fair Projects with Electricity and Electronics* (4–8). Illus. 1996, Sterling $16.95 (0-8069-1300-2). Details are given for 46 projects and experiments involving such topics as electric motors and resistance. (Rev: BL 12/1/96; SLJ 12/96) [507.8]

10447 Bridgman, Roger. *Electronics* (5–8). (Eyewitness Science) 1993, DK Publg. $15.95 (1-56458-324-4). Describes the changes in machines from pre-electric times to the modern world of computers and other technological innovations. (Rev: BL 11/15/93; VOYA 4/94) [621.381]

10448 Grob, Bernard. *Basic Electronics.* 6th ed. (10–12). 1988, McGraw-Hill $95.48 (0-07-025119-3). An introduction to the principles of electronics and their applications in radio, television, and other industrial areas. [621.38]

10449 Guzman, Andres. *33 Fun-and-Easy Weekend Electronics Projects* (10–12). Illus. 1987, TAB $14.95 (0-8306-0261-5); paper $8.95 (0-8306-2861-4). Using fairly simple circuitry, this is a good book for the novice electrician. (Rev: BL 4/15/88) [621.381]

10450 Traister, John E., and Robert J. Traister. *Encyclopedic Dictionary of Electronic Terms* (7–12). Illus. 1984, Prentice Hall $18.95 (0-13-276981-6). All of the basic terms in electronics are explained, usually in fairly simple terms. [621.381]

Telecommunications

10451 Coe, Lewis. *The Telegraph: A History of Morse's Invention and Its Predecessors in the United States* (9–12). 1993, McFarland LB $28.50 (0-89950-736-0). This concise history of the telegraph and its uses focuses on its impact on American society. (Rev: BL 3/1/93) [621.383]

10452 Fisher, Trevor. *Communications* (7–9). Illus. 1985, Batsford $19.95 (0-7134-4631-5). This is a clear history of communication from the development of language to today's sophisticated telecommunications networks. (Rev: SLJ 2/86) [302.2]

10453 Gardner, Robert. *Communication* (6–9). Illus. (Yesterday's Science, Today's Technology) 1994, Twenty-First Century LB $20.40 (0-8050-2854-4). Today's electronic methods of communication are introduced with about 20 activities that would make good science fair projects. (Rev: BL 3/15/95) [303.48]

10454 Webb, Marcus. *Telephones: Words over Wires* (6–10). (Encyclopedia of Discovery and Invention) 1992, Lucent LB $18.96 (1-56006-219-3). Covers the history of the telephone to present-day mass communication—including fax machines, communication satellites, and deregulation of the telephone industry—and looks to the future and the potential impact of such technologies as fiber optics. (Rev: BL 12/15/92) [621]

10455 Winters, Paul A., ed. *The Information Revolution* (8–12). (Opposing Viewpoints) 1998, Greenhaven LB $20.96 (1-56510-801-9); paper $16.20 (1-56510-800-0). This anthology of essays explores issues raised by the advances in telecommunication technology via the telephone, television, and computer, and discusses the impact of these advances on society and education. (Rev: BL 6/1–15/98) [384]

Television, Motion Pictures, Radio, and Recording

10456 DK Publishing, eds. *Special Effects* (5–10). 1998, DK Publg. $17.95 (0-7894-2813-X). Using double-page spreads illustrated with many movie stills, this is a dazzling look at how special effects are produced in movies. (Rev: SLJ 6/98) [791.43]

10457 Frantz, John P. *Video Cinema: Techniques and Projects for Beginning Filmmakers* (9–12). 1994, Chicago Review paper $14.95 (1-55652-228-2). This excellent handbook for the beginning video camera filmmaker discusses equipment, techniques, direction, and the finished product. (Rev: BL 11/15/94; SLJ 1/95) [791.43]

10458 Gottfried, Ted. *The American Media* (7–12). Illus. (Impact) 1997, Watts LB $24.00 (0-531-11315-9). This book provides a look at the history and present-day conditions of the U.S. media—the personalities, major events, the First Amendment and other important issues, and current trends. (Rev: BL 9/1/97; SLJ 6/97) [302.23]

10459 Hamilton, Jake. *Special Effects: In Film and Television* (4–8). Illus. 1998, DK Publg. $17.95 (0-7849-2813-X). This is an intriguing glimpse at special effects in film and television, using double-page spreads that each focus on a different aspect of production, such as storyboards, makeup, and stunts. (Rev: BL 8/98; VOYA 10/98) [791.43]

10460 Hampe, Barry. *Making Documentary Films and Reality Videos* (10–12). 1997, Holt paper $17.95 (0-8050-4451-5). A handy, practical manual for aspiring filmmakers on all aspects of film production, from arriving at an idea to distribution of the final product. (Rev: BL 1/1–15/97; SLJ 3/98) [791]

10461 Hampe, Barry. *Making Videos for Money: Planning and Producing Information Videos, Commercials, and Infomercials* (10–12). 1998, Holt paper $17.95 (0-8050-5441-3). From preshooting planning to postproduction promotion, this manual is filled with practical advice on how to make and market videos. (Rev: SLJ 5/99) [791.45]

10462 Lewis, Roland. *101 Essential Tips: Video* (6–12). 1995, DK Publg. paper $4.95 (0-7894-0183-5). This small-format book gives sound advice on using camcorders for video production and touches on equipment, techniques, composition, lighting, editing, and audio. (Rev: VOYA 6/96) [621]

10463 *Multimedia: The Complete Guide* (7–12). Illus. 1996, DK Publg. $24.95 (0-7894-0422-2). This introduction to the vast possibilities in the cybernetic world opens up an exploration of the many media forms available: text, video, animation, pictures, music, and narration. (Rev: BL 4/15/96; VOYA 10/96) [004.6]

10464 O'Brien, Lisa. *Lights, Camera, Action! Making Movies & TV from the Inside Out* (4–8). Illus. 1998, Greey dePencier Books $19.95 (1-895688-75-2); paper $12.95 (1-895688-76-0). Using a fictitious situation involving 2 teens who are cast in a movie, this book takes the reader behind the scenes, discusses auditions and the importance of agents, covers acting basics, and describes how movies are filmed and distributed. (Rev: BL 6/1–15/98; SLJ 7/98) [791]

10465 Oleksy, Walter. *Entertainment* (6–12). (Information Revolution) 1996, Facts on File $19.95 (0-8160-3077-4). This book describes the revolutionary changes in the entertainment industry, including satellite TV broadcasting, digital wide-screen TV, laser disk players, interactive CD-ROMs, and computer movies. (Rev: BL 2/15/96; SLJ 4/96; VOYA 10/96) [621]

Transportation

General and Miscellaneous

10466 Butterfield, Moira. *Look Inside Cross-Sections: Record Breakers* (4–8). Illus. (Look Inside Cross-Sections) 1995, DK Publg. paper $5.95 (0-7894-0320-X). The inner workings of a number of record-breaking speed machines are pictured in a series of cross-sectional diagrams that supply amazing details. (Rev: BL 9/15/95) [629.04]

10467 Gardner, Robert. *Transportation* (6–9). Illus. (Yesterday's Science, Today's Technology) 1994, Twenty-First Century LB $20.40 (0-8050-2853-6). This volume covers the technologies of transportation and suggests about 20 related projects for the young scientist. A glossary, table of units, and list of materials are appended. (Rev: BL 3/15/95) [629.04]

10468 Spangenburg, Raymond, and Diane Moser. *The Story of America's Bridges* (5–9). (Connecting a Continent) 1991, Facts on File LB $18.95 (0-8160-2259-3). History, descriptions of key technological innovations, and short stories are used to present a picture of the country's bridges. (Rev: BL 11/15/91) [624]

10469 Spangenburg, Raymond, and Diane Moser. *The Story of America's Roads* (5–9). (Connecting a Continent) 1991, Facts on File LB $18.95 (0-8160-2255-0). Short stories, biographies, and charts are used to trace the development of the nation's road system. Includes a discussion of Roman roads and Indian trails. (Rev: BL 11/15/96) [388]

10470 Spangenburg, Raymond, and Diane Moser. *The Story of America's Tunnels* (5–9). (Connecting a Continent) 1992, Facts on File LB $19.00 (0-8160-2258-5). The story of how the nation's great tunnels were built and the role they play in transportation. (Rev: BL 2/15/93) [624]

10471 Wilkinson, Philip, and Jacqueline Dineen. *Transportation* (5–8). Illus. 1995, Chelsea LB $19.95 (0-7910-2768-6). An informative, simple overview of inventions and changes that created the modern transportation systems of today. (Rev: BR 5–6/96; VOYA 2/96) [629]

10472 Wilson, Anthony. *The Dorling Kindersley Visual Timeline of Transportation: From the First Wheeled Chariots to Helicopters and Hovercraft* (4–8). 1995, DK Publg. $16.95 (1-56458-880-7). An illustrated history of transportation from ancient times, with advances in each period selected with both importance and fun for the reader in mind. (Rev: BL 12/15/95; SLJ 1/96; VOYA 4/96) [629.04]

Airplanes, Aeronautics, and Ballooning

10473 Aaseng, Nathan. *Breaking the Sound Barrier* (6–9). 1992, Messner LB $7.95 (0-671-74213-2). The events that led to the breaking of the sound barrier by Chuck Yeager in 1947, including the efforts of early pilots to achieve greater air speed. (Rev: BL 11/15/92) [626.132]

10474 Berliner, Don. *Aviation: Reaching for the Sky* (6–9). Illus. (Innovators) 1997, Oliver Pr. LB $18.95 (1-881508-33-1). The history of flight is covered in 7 chapters, each devoted to a single breakthrough, such as the Montgolfiers and hot-air ballooning, Giffard and the dirigible, the Wright brothers and the airplane, and Sikorky and the helicopter. (Rev: BL 5/1/97; BR 9–10/97; SLJ 7/97) [609]

10475 Bryan, C. D. B. *The National Air and Space Museum* (10–12). Illus. 1988, Abrams $75.00 (0-

8109-1380-1). A history of aeronautics and the airplane as reflected in the collection of the National Air and Space Museum. (Rev: BL 12/15/88) [629.13]

10476 Cole, Michael D. *TWA Flight 800: Explosion in Midair* (4–8). (American Disasters) 1999, Enslow $18.95 (0-7660-1217-4). The dramatic account of the terrible air tragedy that still leaves many unanswered questions. (Rev: BL 1/1–15/99) [629.136]

10477 Hart, Philip S. *Flying Free: America's First Black Aviators* (5–9). 1992, Lerner LB $22.60 (0-8225-1598-9). The contributions of African Americans who succeeded against great odds to become aerial performers, combat pilots, and aviation instructors. (Rev: BL 10/15/92; SLJ 1/93) [629.13]

10478 Jaspersohn, William. *A Week in the Life of an Airline Pilot* (5–9). 1991, Little, Brown $14.95 (0-316-45822-8). A description of the routine and work schedule of an airplane pilot during a typical week. (Rev: BL 3/15/91; SLJ 5/91) [629.132]

10479 Lindbergh, Charles A. *The Spirit of St. Louis* (10–12). 1975, Macmillan $60.00 (0-684-14421-2). An autobiographical account first published in 1954 of the first solo transatlantic flight. [629.13]

10480 Lopez, Donald S. *Aviation: A Smithsonian Guide* (9–12). (Smithsonian Guide) 1995, Macmillan $38.00 (0-02-860006-1). Looks at the history of aviation, aviation principles, and personalities with 2-page, full-color photos of famous planes. (Rev: BL 6/1–15/95) [629.13]

10481 Nader, Ralph, and Wesley J. Smith. *Collision Course: The Truth about Airline Safety* (9–12). 1993, TAB $21.95 (0-8306-4271-4). Outlines the development of the commercial aviation industry and examines each aspect of the "system" that controls safety measures and regulations. (Rev: BL 7/93) [363.12]

10482 Ryan, Craig. *The Pre-Astronauts: Manned Ballooning on the Threshold of Space* (9–12). 1995, Naval Institute Pr. $32.95 (1-55750-732-5). A chronicle of the achievements of people involved in the dangerous, manned balloon programs after World War II. (Rev: BL 5/1/95) [629.13]

10483 Sullivan, George. *Modern Fighter Planes* (7–12). (Military Aircraft) 1991, Facts on File LB $17.95 (0-8160-2352-2). The stories of 11 fighter planes conceived and tested between 1960 and 1990, with black-and-white photos and a glossary. (Rev: BL 1/15/92; SLJ 3/92) [358.4]

10484 Tessendorf, K. C. *Barnstormers and Daredevils* (6–9). Illus. 1988, Macmillan LB $14.95 (0-689-31346-2). The fascinating story of the fearless pioneers of flight including Lindbergh and Wiley Post. (Rev: BL 9/15/88; BR 1–2/89; SLJ 10/88) [797.5]

10485 Tessendorf, K. C. *Wings Around the World: The American World Flight of 1924* (5–9). 1991,

Atheneum LB $14.95 (0-689-31550-3). An account of the first plane flight around the world in 1924. (Rev: BL 1/15/92; SLJ 11/91) [910.4]

10486 Wilkey, Michael. *They Never Gave Up: Adventures in Early Airation* (5–8). Illus. 1998, Orca paper $9.95 (1-55143-077-0). This history of early aviation in North America emphasizes Canadian pioneers, their fortitude, setbacks, and lasting contributions. (Rev: SLJ 9/98) [629.133]

Automobiles and Trucks

10487 Italia, Bob. *Great Auto Makers and Their Cars* (6–10). Illus. (Profiles) 1993, Oliver Pr. LB $18.95 (1-881508-08-0). This is a history of automobiles with coverage of famous cars and biographies of famous engineers and automakers. (Rev: BL 10/15/93; SLJ 11/93) [629.2]

10488 Lukach, Justin. *Pickup Trucks: A History of the Great American Vehicle* (9–12). 1998, Black Dog & Leventhal $24.98 (1-57912-011-3). The history of America's most popular vehicle, the pickup truck, featuring full-color and vintage black-and-white photographs of antique and newer trucks. (Rev: BL 3/1/99; SLJ 9/99) [629.222]

10489 Makower, Joel. *The Green Commuter* (9–12). 1992, National Press Books paper $9.95 (0-915765-95-0). Tips on how to make a car less damaging to the environment, with lists of environmental organizations, government resources, and addresses of major U.S. car manufacturers. (Rev: BL 2/1/92) [363.73]

10490 Schleifer, Jay. *Corvette: America's Sports Car* (6–10). (Cool Classics) 1992, Macmillan LB $13.95 (0-89686-697-1). Presents information on styling, engine development, suspension and braking advances, and other technical matters, with color photos of various Corvette models. (Rev: BL 10/15/92) [629.222]

10491 Schleifer, Jay. *Ferrari: Red-Hot Legend* (6–10). (Cool Classics) 1992, Macmillan LB $17.95 (0-89686-700-5). Presents information on styling, engine development, suspension and braking advances, and other technical matters, with color photos of various Ferrari models. (Rev: BL 10/15/92; SLJ 1/93) [629.222]

10492 Schleifer, Jay. *Mustang: Power-Packed Pony* (6–10). (Cool Classics) 1992, Macmillan LB $13.95 (0-89686-699-8). Presents information on styling, engine development, suspension and braking advances, and other technical matters, with color photos of various Mustang models. (Rev: BL 10/15/92) [629.222]

10493 Schleifer, Jay. *Porsche: Germany's Wonder Car* (6–10). (Cool Classics) 1992, Macmillan LB

$21.00 (0-89686-703-X). Presents information on styling, engine development, suspension and braking advances, and other technical matters, with color photos of various Porsche models. (Rev: BL 10/15/92; SLJ 1/93) [629.222]

10494 Sikorsky, Robert. *From Bumper to Bumper: Robert Sikorsky's Automotive Tips* (9–12). 1991, TAB $16.95 (0-8306-2134-2). Practical advice on automobile maintenance, driving techniques, buying tips, and motoring information. (Rev: BL 11/1/91) [629.28]

10495 Volpe, Ren. *The Lady Mechanic's Total Car Care for the Clueless* (9–12). 1998, Griffin paper $13.95 (0-312-18733-5). A comprehensive guide (useful not just for women) that introduces all aspects of car care, as well as safety tips, advice on handling accidents, and discussions on buying and selling cars. (Rev: BL 7/98; SLJ 1/99) [629.222]

10496 Whitman, Sylvia. *Get Up and Go! The History of American Road Travel* (5–8). Illus. 1996, Lerner LB $22.60 (0-8225-1735-3). From primitive pathways to modern superhighways, this is a history of American roads and the vehicles that traveled them. (Rev: BL 10/15/96; SLJ 10/96; VOYA 2/97) [388.1]

10497 Willson, Quentin. *Classic American Cars* (9–12). 1997, DK Publg. $29.95 (0-7894-2083-X). Using full-color photos and clear text, this book features 60 cars, with historical, technical, and design information about each. (Rev: BL 12/1/97; SLJ 7/98) [629.222]

10498 Willson, Quentin. *The Ultimate Classic Car Book* (10–12). 1995, DK Publg. $29.95 (0-7894-0159-2). Over 90 classic cars are featured, each with a description and a color photograph, arranged by decade. (Rev: BL 1/1–15/96; SLJ 6/96) [629.2]

Cycles

10499 Wilson, Hugo. *Encyclopedia of the Motorcycle* (10–12). 1995, DK Publg. $39.95 (0-7894-0150-9). An encyclopedia that pictures more than 1,000 motorcycles and scooters and lists more than 3,000 manufacturers. (Rev: BL 11/15/95; BR 5–6/96; SLJ 2/96) [796.7]

Railroads

10500 Blumberg, Rhoda. *Full Steam Ahead: The Race to Build a Transcontinental Railroad* (6–12). Illus. 1996, National Geographic $18.95 (0-7922-2715-8). A realistic account that includes stories of the corruption, greed, exploitation, sacrifice, and heroism that went into the building of the first transcontinental railroad. (Rev: BL 6/1–15/96*; SLJ 8/96*) [365]

10501 Coiley, John. *Train* (5–9). (Eyewitness Books) 1992, Knopf LB $20.99 (0-679-91684-9). A history of trains, their parts, and their importance, supplemented by lavish illustrations. (Rev: BL 11/1/92) [625.1]

10502 Johnstone, Michael. *Look Inside Cross-Sections: Trains* (4–8). Illus. (Look Inside Cross-Sections) 1995, DK Publg. paper $6.95 (0-78894-0319-6). Cross-sectional drawings with descriptive text are given for 10 past and present locomotives. (Rev: BL 9/15/95) [625.1]

10503 Laughlin, Rosemary. *The Great Iron Link: The Building of the Central Pacific Railroad* (6–9). Illus. 1996, Morgan Reynolds LB $18.95 (1-883846-14-5). An interesting history of the Central Pacific Railroad that focuses on the 5 men who were responsible for its inception. (Rev: BL 10/15/96; BR 5–6/97; SLJ 4/97) [385]

10504 Levinson, Nancy S. *She's Been Working on the Railroad* (5–8). Illus. 1997, Dutton $16.99 (0-525-67545-0). A history of women's roles as railway workers, including the famous Harvey Girls of the late 1800s, who worked in restaurants that served train travelers out West, and nurses and hostesses on trains in the 1930s, when few occupations were open to women, enhanced by photographs and studies of individual women in each period. (Rev: BL 9/15/97; SLJ 12/97; VOYA 12/97) [331.4]

10505 Murphy, Jim. *Across America on an Emigrant Train* (6–12). 1993, Clarion $16.95 (0-395-63390-7). Using excerpts from Robert Louis Stevenson's journal and a variety of illustrations, Murphy paints a picture of the transcontinental railroad of the 1880s. (Rev: BL 12/1/93*; SLJ 12/93*) [625.2]

10506 Spangenburg, Raymond, and Diane Moser. *The Story of America's Railroads* (5–9). (Connecting a Continent) 1991, Facts on File LB $18.95 (0-8160-2257-7). This history of the railways incorporates stories, biographies, timelines, and charts to show their influence on the development of the nation. (Rev: BL 11/15/91) [625]

10507 Warburton, Lois. *Railroads: Bridging the Continents* (6–10). (Encyclopedia of Discovery and Invention) 1991, Lucent LB $23.70 (1-56006-216-9). The history of the nation's railroads. (Rev: BL 4/15/92) [385]

10508 Weitzman, David. *Superpower: The Making of a Steam Locomotive* (6–9). Illus. 1987, Godine $35.00 (0-87923-671-X). A step-by-step guide to the parts of a locomotive and how they are assembled. (Rev: SLJ 1/88) [625.2]

10509 Wormser, Richard. *The Iron Horse: How Railroads Changed America* (6–9). 1993, Walker LB $19.85 (0-8027-8222-1). The economic and social impact of the railroad between 1830 and 1900, from the robber barons to the gold rush and massive influx of immigrants. (Rev: BL 12/15/93; SLJ 1/94; VOYA 4/94) [385]

Ships and Boats

10510 Ballard, Robert D., and Rick Archbold. *Ghost Liners* (5–9). Illus. 1998, Little, Brown $18.95 (0-316-08020-9). The discoverer of the wreckage of the *Titanic* describes this adventure, with additional coverage of such ship disasters as the *Lusitania, Britannic, Andrea Doria,* and the *Empress of Ireland.* (Rev: BL 8/98; SLJ 9/98) [363]

10511 Humble, Richard. *Submarines & Ships* (4–8). (See Through History) 1997, Viking $17.99 (0-670-86778-0). A well-illustrated account that examines several historic ships and submarines and identifies different structures and uses. (Rev: BL 11/15/97) [387.2]

10512 Kentley, Eric. *Boat* (5–9). (Eyewitness Books) 1992, Knopf LB $20.99 (0-679-91678-4). A richly illustrated history of boats, their planning, design, construction, and operation. (Rev: BL 6/1/92) [623.8]

10513 Macaulay, David. *Ship* (5–8). 1993, Houghton $19.95 (0-395-52439-3). This narrative describes the recent discovery of and recovery of artifacts from a caravel that sank in the Caribbean 500 years ago. (Rev: BL 10/15/93*; SLJ 11/93) [387.2]

10514 Platt, Richard. *Stephen Biesty's Cross-Sections: Man-of-War* (6–12). Illus. 1993, DK Publg. $16.95 (1-56458-321-X). Detailed cutaways and text describe life at sea on an 18th-century British man-of-war. (Rev: BL 10/1/93; SLJ 1/94; VOYA 2/94) [359.1]

10515 Stillwell, Paul. *Battleship Arizona: An Illustrated History* (9–12). 1991, Naval Institute Pr. $65.00 (0-87021-023-8). The story of Pearl Harbor's most famous "victim." (Rev: BL 1/15/92) [359.3]

Weapons and Submarines

10516 Cheney, Glenn. *They Never Knew: The Victims of Nuclear Testing* (7–12). Illus. (Impact) 1996, Watts LB $24.00 (0-531-11273-X). The story of the innocent military members, workers, and local inhabitants who contracted fatal diseases as a result of nuclear testing programs in Nevada and in the South Pacific. (Rev: BL 1/1–15/97; SLJ4/97) [363.17]

10517 Clancy, Tom. *Submarine: A Guided Tour Inside a Nuclear Warship* (9–12). 1993, Berkley paper $16.00 (0-425-13873-9). An in-depth look at nuclear submarines, including their history, design, weapons, tactics, crew, and scenarios aimed at showing their continued value. (Rev: BL 9/15/93) [623.812]

10518 Cohen, Daniel. *The Manhattan Project* (7–12). 1999, Millbrook LB $22.95 (0-7613-0359-6). This account captures the spies, intrigue, politics, secrecy, and science that became part of the story of the first atomic bomb. (Rev: BL 7/99; SLJ 9/99) [355.8]

10519 Day, Malcolm. *The World of Castles and Forts* (5–8). 1997, Bedrick LB $19.95 (0-87226-278-2). This book covers a world history of fortification, from ancient walled cities to the modern Maginot Line and nuclear bastions. (Rev: BL 3/1/97; SLJ 2/97) [355.7]

10520 Diagram Group. *Weapons: An International Encyclopedia from 5000 B.C. to 2000 A.D.* (9–12). 1991, St. Martin's paper $21.95 (0-312-03950-6). From the clubs of cavemen to nuclear weapons, this account describes them all in pictures and text. [623.4]

10521 Gilbert, Adrian. *Arms and Armor* (4–8). Illus. (Then and Now) 1997, Millbrook LB $21.90 (0-7613-0605-6). In double-page spreads, a chronological history of armaments and weapons is covered, beginning with bows and arrows and ending with missiles and rockets. (Rev: SLJ 4/98) [355.02]

10522 Gonen, Rivka. *Charge! Weapons and Warfare in Ancient Times* (5–9). (Buried Worlds) 1993, Lerner LB $23.93 (0-8225-3201-8). Traces the evolution of weapons from sticks and stones for hunting to increasingly sophisticated tools for warfare and defense in ancient times. (Rev: BL 2/1/94; SLJ 2/94) [355.8]

10523 Grady, Sean M. *Explosives: Devices of Controlled Destruction* (6–10). (Encyclopedia of Discovery and Invention) 1995, Lucent LB $23.70 (1-56006-250-9). A history of explosives and their use

in war and peace through the ages. (Rev: BL 4/15/95) [662]

10524 Holmes, Richard. *Battle* (5–8). (Eyewitness Books) 1995, Knopf LB $20.99 (0-679-97333-8). Full-captioned photos and drawings are used in this introduction to warfare from ancient days to World War I, with descriptions of most aspects of war, including infantry, artillery, supply and transport, reconnaissance, etc. (Rev: BL 12/15/95; SLJ 1/96) [355]

10525 Hurley, Jennifer A., ed. *Weapons of Mass Destruction* (8–12). (Opposing Viewpoints) 1999, Greenhaven LB $21.96 (0-7377-0059-9); paper $20.25 (0-7377-0058-0). This collection of writings explores the possibility of a terrorist attack using weapons of mass destruction, domestic and foreign policies concerning these weapons, and ways to defend the country against such attacks. (Rev: BL 4/15/99) [355.02]

10526 Meltzer, Milton. *Weapons & Warfare: From the Stone Age to the Space Age* (5–9). Illus. 1996, HarperCollins LB $16.89 (0-06-024876-9). This work describes the evolution of weapons from clubs to the H-bomb, including how these weapons have been used and misused through the ages. (Rev: BL 12/1/96; SLJ 1/97) [355.02]

10527 Pangallo, Michelle. *North American Forts and Fortifications* (5–8). 1986, Cambridge Univ. Pr. $16.95 (0-521-26642-4). Thirteen forts such as those at Ticonderoga, Sumter, the Alamo, and McHenry are described. (Rev: BR 1–2/87) [623]

10528 Rhodes, Richard. *Dark Sun: The Making of the Hydrogen Bomb* (9–12). 1995, Simon & Schuster $32.95 (0-684-80400-X). Examines the history of the hydrogen bomb, from the race to be the first to develop it to the moral implications of its existence and use. (Rev: BL 7/95*) [623.4]

Recreation and Sports

Crafts, Hobbies, and Pastimes

General and Miscellaneous

10529 Adkins, Jan. *String: Tying It Up, Tying It Down* (5–8). 1992, Scribners LB $13.95 (0-684-18875-9). Entertaining step-by-step directions for tying knots. (Rev: BL 4/15/92; SLJ 6/92) [677]

10530 Albregts, Melisa, and Elizabeth Cape. *Best Friends: Tons of Crazy, Cool Things to Do with Your Girlfriends* (4–8). Illus. 1998, Chicago Review paper $12.95 (1-55652-326-2). Arranged by seasons, this activity book contains crafts, games, dances, snacks, and skits to amuse girls when they get together. (Rev: BL 3/1/99; SLJ 1/99) [796.083]

10531 Black, Penny. *The Book of Pressed Flowers* (10–12). Illus. 1988, Simon & Schuster $22.00 (0-671-66071-3). A fine craft book on pressing and arranging dried flowers and other plants. (Rev: BL 6/1/88) [745.92]

10532 Brown, Rachel. *The Weaving, Spinning, and Dyeing Book*. Rev. ed. (10–12). Illus. 1983, Knopf paper $40.00 (0-394-71595-0). Various kinds of weaving techniques and patterns are introduced through 50 different projects. [746.1]

10533 Brownrigg, Sheri. *Hearts and Crafts* (4–8). Illus. 1995, Tricycle Pr. paper $9.95 (1-883672-28-7). Clear instructions are given in this craft book on how to complete a variety of Valentine's Day projects, including making necklaces and candles. (Rev: BL 3/1/96; SLJ 3/96) [745.5]

10534 Cherry, Raymond. *Leathercrafting: Procedures and Projects*. 5th ed. (9–12). Illus. 1979, Glencoe paper $15.00 (0-02-672700-5). A how-to book that explains the basics of leather work with many sample projects. [745.53]

10535 Firestein, Cecily Barth. *Making Paper and Fabric Rubbings: Capturing Designs from Brasses, Gravestones, Carved Doors, Coins, and More*

(9–12). 1999, Lark $19.95 (1-57990-104-2). This introduction to the hobby of rubbings explains the basics of using pencil and paper, then tells how to create T-shirts, note paper, and framed pictures from the results. (Rev: SLJ 8/99) [760]

10536 Irving, Robert, and Mike Martins. *Pathways in Juggling* (7–12). Illus. 1997, Firefly paper $19.95 (1-55209-121-X). This book, heavily illustrated with photographs, shows how to juggle such objects as balls, clubs, devil sticks, and diabolos. (Rev: BL 2/15/98) [793.8]

10537 Jans, Martin. *Stage Make-up Techniques* (9–12). 1993, Players Pr. paper $24.00 (0-88734-621-9). A primer of basic makeup techniques, including children's makeup, with detailed illustrations of all aspects of the craft. (Rev: BL 11/1/92) [792]

10538 McCormick, Anita Louise. *Shortwave Radio Listening for Beginners* (9–12). 1993, TAB paper $10.60 (0-8306-4135-1). Explains shortwave reception, profiles major broadcasters, summarizes necessary equipment for hobbyists, and includes tables with band frequencies of stations. (Rev: BL 5/15/93) [621.3841]

10539 Maflin, Andrea. *Easy & Elegant Home Decorating: 25 Stylish Projects for Your Home* (10–12). Illus. 1998, Facts on File $24.95 (0-8160-3829-5). Using supplies available at crafts stores, this book outlines many projects like gilding various objects, stenciling, decoupage, printing, and making mosaics. A separate section of templates is included. (Rev: SLJ 9/98) [745]

10540 Merrill, Yvonne Y. *Hands-On Latin America: Art Activities for All Ages* (4–8). Illus. (Hands-On) 1998, K-ITS paper $20.00 (0-9643177-1-0). A collection of 30 interesting, affordable arts and crafts projects inspired by the ancient cultures of Latin America. (Rev: BL 9/1/98; SLJ 8/98) [980.07]

10541 *Nature Craft* (9–12). 1993, North Light paper $16.99 (0-89134-542-6). Projects in basketry, woodworking, flowers, and gardening, based on the British crafts magazine *Creative Hands*. (Rev: BL 11/15/93; SLJ 1/94) [745.5]

10542 Newman, Frederick. *Mouthsounds* (9–12). 1980, Workman paper $6.95 (0-89480-128-7). This is a guide to making all sorts of interesting sounds including tips on how to be a master at whistling. [620.2]

10543 Olson, Beverly, and Judy Lazzara. *Country Flower Drying* (8–12). 1988, Sterling paper $9.95 (0-8069-6746-3). A concise manual on raising and drying flowers plus tips on creating arrangements and other uses of dried flowers. (Rev: BR 11–12/88) [745.92]

10544 Purdy, Susan. *Christmas Gifts for You to Make* (7–9). 1976, HarperCollins LB $12.89 (0-397-31695-X). Instructions on how to make a wide variety of gifts including puppets, note pads, and aprons. [745.5]

10545 Reader's Digest, eds. *Reader's Digest Crafts & Hobbies* (9–12). Illus. 1979, Reader's Digest $27.95 (0-89577-063-6). Information on 37 popular crafts including leatherwork, jewelry making, and bookbinding. [745.5]

10546 Rhodes, Vicki. *Pumpkin Decorating* (4–8). 1997, Sterling $11.95 (0-8069-9574-2). Clear directions and full-color photos show how to decorate pumpkins with more than 80 different designs. (Rev: SLJ 12/97) [745.5]

10547 Ross, John, et al. *The Complete Printmaker: Techniques, Traditions, Innovations*. Rev. ed. (9–12). Illus. 1989, Free Pr. $49.95 (0-02-927371-4). A thorough introduction to various kinds of printmaking, necessary techniques, and the printmaking business—all well illustrated. (Rev: BL 1/15/90) [760]

10548 Sadler, Judy A. *Corking* (4–8). Illus. (Kids Can Easy Crafts) 1998, Kids Can paper $4.95 (1-55074-265-5). Simple instructions are given to create knit tubes, or corks, that can be used in making toys and headbands. (Rev: BL 5/15/98) [746.43]

10549 Sassoon, Rosemary. *The Practical Guide to Calligraphy* (9–12). 1982, Norton paper $10.95 (0-500-27251-4). A useful guide to calligraphy, from England. [745.6]

10550 Shepherd, Margaret. *Learning Calligraphy: A Book of Lettering, Design and History* (9–12). Illus. 1978, Macmillan paper $15.00 (0-02-015550-6). Basic material on calligraphy is logically presented in this volume that is continued in *Using Calligraphy* (1979). [745.6]

10551 Simons, Robin. *Recyclopedia* (6–8). 1976, Houghton paper $10.20 (0-395-24380-7). A craft book showing how to use materials that are usually thrown out. [745.5]

10552 Sloane, Paul, and Des MacHale. *Challenging Lateral Thinking Puzzles* (9–12). 1993, Sterling paper $6.95 (0-8069-8671-9). More than 90 brain-teasers, with clues leading the reader through a "lateral thinking" mode. (Rev: BL 5/1/93) [793.73]

10553 Summers, Kit. *Juggling with Finesse* (9–12). Illus. 1987, Finesse Pr. paper $19.95 (0-938981-00-5). Simple instructions, profusely illustrated, on how to juggle a variety of objects. (Rev: BL 10/1/87) [793.8]

10554 Taylor, Maureen. *Through the Eyes of Your Ancestors: A Step-By-Step Guide to Uncovering Your Family's History* (5–9). Illus. 1999, Houghton $16.00 (0-395-86980-3); paper $8.95 (0-395-86982-X). The book presents a series of steps to help budding researchers learn about their family history, from conducting interviews to visiting genealogical libraries. (Rev: BL 3/1/99; SLJ 5/99) [929.1]

10555 Treinen, Sara Jane, ed. *Better Homes and Gardens Incredibly Awesome Crafts for Kids* (5–8). 1992, Meredith paper $16.95 (0-696-01984-1). More than 75 projects are explained step-by-step and illustrated with color photos. (Rev: BL 4/15/92) [745.5]

10556 Van Dyke, Janice. *Captivating Cryptograms* (5–8). 1996, Sterling paper $5.95 (0-8069-4890-6). A collection of 400 cryptograms based on famous quotes, with the solutions and origins included. (Rev: SLJ 8/96) [793.73]

10557 *Working with Metal* (10–12). Illus. 1990, Silver Burdett LB $20.60 (0-8094-7388-7). With many illustrations and clear text, this volume covers the basic terms, tools, and practices in metalworking. Part of Time-Life's Home Repair and Improvement series. [684]

American Historical Crafts

10558 Greenwood, Barbara. *Pioneer Crafts* (4–8). Illus. 1997, Kids Can paper $5.95 (1-55074-359-7). This guide gives directions for 17 projects in such crafts as candle making, soap carving, and basket weaving. (Rev: BL 9/15/97; SLJ 9/97) [745.5]

10559 Merrill, Yvonne Y. *Hands-On Rocky Mountains: Art Activities about Anasazi, American Indians, Settlers, Trappers, and Cowboys* (4–8). Illus. 1996, K-ITS paper $20.00 (0-9643177-2-9). Historical groups from the Rocky Mountain region—early people, American Indians, trappers, settlers, and cowboys—are introduced and, for each, a series of craft projects is outlined. (Rev: BL 1/1–15/97; SLJ 4/97) [745.5]

Clay Modeling and Ceramics

10560 Cosentino, Peter. *The Encyclopedia of Pottery Techniques* (9–12). Illus. 1990, Running Pr. $24.95 (0-89471-892-4). Through many color illustrations, both the finished product and step-by-step instructions on how to create pottery are covered. (Rev: BL 9/15/90) [738]

10561 Kenny, John B. *The Complete Book of Pottery Making*. 2nd ed. (7–12). Illus. 1976, Chilton paper $29.95 (0-8019-5933-0). In easily followed instructions with many photographs, the steps in pottery making are outlined. [738.1]

10562 Nelson, Glenn C. *Ceramics: A Potter's Handbook* (9–12). Illus. 1984, Holt paper $64.00 (0-03-063227-7). A basic how-to guide for both the beginning and experienced potter. [738.1]

10563 Nicholson, Libby, and Yvonne Lau. *Creating with Fimo* (6–10). Illus. (Kids Can Crafts) 1999, Kids Can $12.95 (1-55074-310-4); paper $5.95 (1-55074-274-4). Using the nontoxic clay called Fimo (available in crafts stores) and the step-by-step instructions in this book, 25 projects suitable for experienced crafters, such as making necklaces, earrings, and pins, can be completed. (Rev: SLJ 5/99) [738]

Cooking

10564 Albyn, Carole Lisa, and Lois S. Webb. *The Multicultural Cookbook for Students* (6–9). 1993, Oryx paper $35.00 (0-89774-735-6). Provides 337 recipes from 122 countries, arranged geographically. (Rev: BL 2/15/94; SLJ 10/93) [641.59]

10565 Amari, Suad. *Cooking the Lebanese Way* (7–10). Illus. 1986, Lerner LB $19.93 (0-8225-0913-X). After a general introduction to Lebanon, this book introduces recipes for more than 20 native dishes. (Rev: BL 6/1/86) [641]

10566 Andreev, Tania. *Food in Russia* (6–9). Illus. 1989, Rourke LB $21.27 (0-86625-343-2). Both an introduction to Russia and a survey of foods and typical recipes. (Rev: SLJ 12/89) [641.5]

10567 Axcell, Claudia, et al. *Simple Foods for the Pack*. Rev. ed. (10–12). Illus. 1986, Sierra Club paper $9.00 (0-87156-757-1). For the outdoor person, here is a collection of recipes and food suggestions that can be either prepared beforehand or cooked over a campfire. [641.5]

10568 Bacon, Josephine. *Cooking the Israeli Way* (7–10). Illus. 1986, Lerner LB $19.93 (0-8225-0912-1). A brief history and geography of Israel is given

followed by more than 20 tempting native recipes. One of an extensive series. (Rev: BL 6/1/86) [641]

10569 Baggett, Nancy. *The International Cookie Cookbook* (9–12). Illus. 1988, Stewart, Tabori & Chang $30.00 (1-55670-041-5). An oversize volume of recipes from around the world, many pictured in lovely color photographs. (Rev: BL 3/15/89) [641.8]

10570 Bayless, Rick, and Deann Groen Bayless. *Authentic Mexican: Regional Cooking from the Heart of Mexico* (9–12). Illus. 1987, Morrow $28.50 (0-688-04394-1). A thorough guide to genuine Mexican cooking that also features bits of history and information about the country's culture. (Rev: BL 4/15/87) [641]

10571 *Better Homes and Gardens New Cook Book.* 11th ed. (9–12). Illus. 1996, Meredith $25.95 (0-696-20188-7); Bantam paper $7.99 (0-553-57795-6). A fine basic cookbook with easy-to-follow instructions and ample illustrations. (Rev: BL 11/1/89; BR 1–2/90) [641.5]

10572 *Betty Crocker's Great Chicken Recipes* (9–12). 1993, Prentice Hall paper $8.00 (0-671-84689-2). Contains more than 100 recipes, color photos, food ideas, boxed tips, and practical hints. (Rev: BL 3/1/93) [641.6]

10573 *Betty Crocker's Holiday Baking* (9–12). 1993, Prentice Hall paper $8.00 (0-671-86961-2). More than 100 simple recipes for the holiday season, including nutritional information for classic and revamped favorites. Color photos and sidebar tips make directions easy to follow. (Rev: BL 10/1/93) [641.7]

10574 *Betty Crocker's Low-Calorie Cooking* (9–12). 1993, Prentice Hall paper $8.00 (0-671-84690-6). Contains more than 100 recipes, color photos, food ideas, boxed tips, and practical hints. (Rev: BL 3/1/93) [641.5]

10575 *Betty Crocker's New Choices Cookbook* (9–12). 1993, Prentice Hall paper $25.00 (0-671-86767-9). More than 500 health-conscious recipes are labeled as low calorie, low fat, low cholesterol, low sodium, or high fiber to make eating right easy. (Rev: BL 10/1/93) [641.5]

10576 *Betty Crocker's Quick Dinners: In 30 Minutes or Less* (9–12). 1993, Prentice Hall paper $9.95 (0-671-84692-2). Contains more than 100 recipes, color photos, food ideas, boxed tips, and practical hints. (Rev: BL 3/1/93) [641.5]

10577 *Betty Crocker's Soups and Stews* (9–12). 1993, Prentice Hall paper $8.00 (0-671-86960-4). More than 100 soups and stews are presented, with color photos, sidebar explanations and tips, and nutritional information. (Rev: BL 10/1/93) [641.5]

10578 Bisignano, Alphonse. *Cooking the Italian Way* (7–9). Illus. 1982, Lerner LB $19.93 (0-8225-0906-

7). Like others in this extensive series on ethnic foods, this account gives recipes plus an introduction to the country and its culture. [641.5]

10579 Branson, Ann, ed. *The Good Housekeeping Illustrated Cookbook.* Rev. ed. (9–12). Illus. 1988, Hearst $27.00 (0-688-08074-X). A fine basic cookbook that contains about 1,500 recipes and many illustrations and drawings. (Rev: BL 1/15/89) [641.5]

10580 Claiborne, Craig. *Craig Claiborne's Kitchen Primer* (9–12). 1972, Knopf $12.95 (0-394-42071-3); paper $10.00 (0-394-71854-2). In this handy manual, the well-known chef explains basic cooking techniques and describes important utensils and their uses. [641.5]

10581 Coronado, Rosa. *Cooking the Mexican Way* (7–9). Illus. 1982, Lerner LB $19.93 (0-8225-0907-5). Mexican culture is highlighted as well as a few basic recipes. Part of an extensive series. (Rev: BL 6/87) [641.5]

10582 Cotler, Amy. *The Secret Garden Cookbook: Recipes Inspired by Frances Hodgson Burnett's The Secret Garden* (4–8). Illus. 1999, HarperCollins $17.95 (0-06-027740-8). A collection of 42 recipes that reflect the locales and characters of Burnett's classic tale, accompanied by fascinating bits of culinary and social history, and quotes from poems, various Victorian personages, and *The Secret Garden.* (Rev: SLJ 7/99) [641]

10583 Cox, Beverly, and Martin Jacobs. *Spirit of the Harvest: North American Indian Cooking* (9–12). 1991, Stewart, Tabori & Chang $35.00 (1-55670-186-1). Native American experts have helped the authors with recipes of various North American tribes, adapted for modern kitchens and substituting readily available ingredients when required. (Rev: BL 9/15/91) [641.59]

10584 Cunningham, Marion. *Learning to Cook with Marion Cunningham* (9–12). 1999, Knopf $29.95 (0-375-40118-0). Basic cooking techniques are shown and demonstrated, with 150 simple recipes for the beginning cook. (Rev: BL 5/15/99; SLJ 8/99) [641]

10585 Damerow, Gail. *Ice Cream! The Whole Scoop* (9–12). 1991, Glenbridge Publg. $26.95 (0-944435-09-2). This collection of recipes is also a thorough survey of all types of frozen desserts and includes technical information on ingredients, techniques, and special equipment. (Rev: BL 9/1/91) [641.8]

10586 D'Amico, Joan, and Karen Eich Drummond. *The Science Chef Travels Around the World: Fun Food Experiments and Recipes for Kids* (4–8). Illus. 1996, Wiley paper $12.95 (0-471-11779-X). A fun combination of simple science experiments and international cooking, with recipes from 14 countries and activities that demonstrate scientific principles

of various cooking and baking processes. (Rev: SLJ 3/96) [641.5]

10587 Delmar, Charles. *The Essential Cook* (9–12). Illus. 1989, Hill House $24.95 (0-929694-00-7). An excellent handbook on food preparation that includes such subjects as methods of cooking, equipment needed, and shopping tips. (Rev: BR 11–12/90; SLJ 7/89) [641.5]

10588 Diamond, Marilyn. *The American Vegetarian Cookbook: From the Fit for Life Kitchen* (9–12). 1990, Warner $28.00 (0-446-51561-2). As well as many tempting recipes, this book contains much information on nutrition and health. (Rev: BL 8/90) [641]

10589 Erdosh, George. *The African-American Kitchen: Food for Body and Soul* (6–9). Illus. (Library of African American Arts and Culture) 1999, Rosen $17.95 (0-8239-1850-5). This book traces the development of cooking associated with African Americans such as gumbo, chitlins, and corn pudding, with recipes and cooking tips. (Rev: BR 9–10/99; SLJ 8/99; VOYA 8/99) [641]

10590 Gaspari, Claudia. *Food in Italy* (6–9). Illus. 1989, Rourke LB $21.27 (0-86625-342-4). This account introduces Italy and its food and gives some recipes. (Rev: SLJ 12/89) [641.5]

10591 Gayler, Paul. *Ultimate Vegetarian Cookbook* (8–10). 1999, DK Publg. $24.95 (0-7894-4184-5). From soups to desserts, this book supplies delicious recipes for the vegetarian. (Rev: SLJ 8/99) [641]

10592 Gomez, Paolo. *Food in Mexico* (6–9). Illus. 1989, Rourke LB $21.27 (0-86625-341-6). As well as some typical recipes, this account introduces Mexico and its types of food. (Rev: SLJ 12/89) [641.5]

10593 Hadamuscin, John. *Special Occasions: Holiday Entertaining All Year Round* (9–12). 1988, Harmony $29.00 (0-517-57005-X). A collection of menus involving notable annual events plus interesting background information on the foods associated with them. (Rev: BL 7/88) [642]

10594 Hansen, Barbara. *Mexican Cookery* (9–12). Illus. 1988, Price Stern Sloan paper $14.95 (0-89586-589-0). Easily followed recipes and many illustrations highlight this guide to the food of many different regions of Mexico. [641.5]

10595 Herbst, Sharon Tyler. *The Food Lover's Tiptionary* (9–12). 1994, Morrow paper $15.00 (0-688-12146-2). Tips on buying, storing, cooking, preparing, and serving food and drink. (Rev: BL 3/15/94) [641.3]

10596 Kaur, Sharon. *Food in India* (6–9). Illus. 1989, Rourke LB $21.27 (0-86625-339-4). This illustrated book gives recipes, and introduces the foods and dining customs of India. (Rev: SLJ 12/89) [641.5]

10597 Kirlin, Katherine S., and Thomas Kirlin. *Smithsonian Folklife Cookbook* (9–12). 1991, Smithsonian paper $19.95 (1-56098-089-3). The contributors of these historical recipes, which have been demonstrated at the Smithsonian's Festival of American Folklife, show how they reflect bygone cultural mores and eating habits. (Rev: BL 9/15/91; SLJ 2/92) [641.5973]

10598 Krizmanic, Judy. *The Teen's Vegetarian Cookbook* (6–12). Illus. 1999, Viking $15.99 (0-670-87426-4). From breakfast items to desserts, this cookbook supplies recipes that involve no meat, milk, eggs, etc., as well as "fast-food," easy-to-prepare dishes. (Rev: BL 6/1–15/99; SLJ 6/99; VOYA 10/99) [641.5]

10599 Lemlin, Jeanne. *Quick Vegetarian Pleasures* (9–12). 1992, HarperCollins paper $17.00 (0-06-096911-3). Tasty, easy-to-prepare meatless recipes ranging from appetizers to entrees. (Rev: BL 3/1/92) [641.5]

10600 Lemlin, Jeanne. *Vegetarian Pleasures: A Menu Cookbook* (9–12). Illus. 1986, Knopf paper $20.00 (0-394-74302-4). From breakfast to dinner, here is a collection of 250 vegetarian recipes that are simple to prepare. (Rev: BL 5/1/86) [641.5]

10601 Levin, Karen A. *Twenty-Minute Chicken Dishes: Delicious, Easy-to-Prepare Meals Everyone Will Love!* (9–12). 1991, Contemporary paper $12.95 (0-8092-4033-5). This collection of quick, simple chicken dishes includes familiar favorites and ethnic specialties. (Rev: BL 12/1/91) [641.6]

10602 McCaffrey, Anne, and John Gregor Betancourt, eds. *Serve It Forth: Cooking with Anne McCaffrey* (9–12). 1996, Warner paper $12.99 (0-446-67161-4). This cookbook features tempting recipes from 80 science fiction and fantasy writers, like Starship Trooper Chili and Night of the Living Meatloaf. (Rev: VOYA 4/97) [641]

10603 Medearis, Angela Shelf. *The African-American Kitchen: Cooking from Our Heritage* (9–12). 1994, Dutton paper $23.95 (0-525-93834-6). Contains more than 250 recipes from Africa, the Caribbean, and the United States for such dishes as Tanzanian baked bananas, pumpkin meat loaf, and baked ham. (Rev: BL 9/15/94) [641.59]

10604 Medearis, Angela Shelf, and Michael R. Medearis. *Cooking* (5–8). Illus. 1997, Twenty-First Century $18.90 (0-8050-4484-1). This book traces the contributions of African Americans to cooking and to food. (Rev: BL 2/15/98; BR 1–2/98; SLJ 11/97) [641.59]

10605 Moll, Lucy. *Vegetarian Times Complete Cookbook* (9–12). 1995, Macmillan paper $29.95 (0-02-621745-7). A former editor of *Vegetarian Times* presents more than 600 recipes in what she hopes will be the standard vegetarian cookbook. Includes nutritional breakdowns for each recipe. (Rev: BL 11/15/95) [641.5]

10606 Moore, Marilyn M. *The Wooden Spoon Cookie Book: Favorite Home-Style Recipes from the Wooden Spoon Kitchen* (9–12). 1994, Atlantic Monthly $15.00 (0-87113-601-5). Over 100 recipes for cookies and sweets, from animal crackers to rosy rhubarb squares. (Rev: BL 7/94) [641.8]

10607 Nabwire, Constance, and Bertha Vining Montgomery. *Cooking the African Way* (5–10). Illus. 1988, Lerner LB $19.93 (0-8225-0919-9). Part of the extensive Easy Menu Ethnic Cookbook series, this volume describes the land and culture of East and West Africa and gives several recipes for native dishes. (Rev: BL 3/15/89) [394.1]

10608 Nguyen, Chi, and Judy Monroe. *Cooking the Vietnamese Way* (6–10). Illus. 1985, Lerner LB $19.93 (0-8225-0914-8). The authors introduce the land and people of Vietnam before giving recipes for regional dishes. Part of a lengthy series. (Rev: BL 9/15/85) [641]

10609 Norman, Jill. *The Complete Book of Spices* (9–12). 1991, Viking paper $25.00 (0-670-83437-8). Recipes are divided into 3 levels of difficulty and explore the world of spices. (Rev: BL 3/1/91) [641.3]

10610 Osseo-Asare, Fran. *A Good Soup Attracts Chairs: A First African Cookbook for American Kids* (5–9). 1993, Pelican $18.95 (0-88289-816-7). A basic cookbook for youngsters that explores the past and present world of African cooking. (Rev: BL 10/15/93) [641.5966]

10611 Peters, Colette. *Colette's Cakes: The Art of Cake Decorating* (9–12). 1991, Little, Brown $27.50 (0-316-70205-6). A guide to creative cake design and decorating, not just a cake cookbook, with step-by-step instructions for assembling elaborate baked desserts. (Rev: BL 9/1/91) [641.8]

10612 Raab, Evelyn. *Clueless in the Kitchen: A Cookbook for Teens & Other Beginners* (8–12). Illus. 1998, Firefly paper $12.95 (1-55209-224-0). Cooking and kitchen basics are explained and recipes for good traditional dishes are given in this beginner's cookbook, with emphasis on fresh over convenience and processed foods and a section of suggested menus designed for particular guests or occasions. (Rev: BL 7/98; BR 9–10/98; SLJ 9/98) [641.5]

10613 Rani. *Feast of India* (9–12). 1991, Contemporary paper $16.95 (0-8092-4095-5). This beginner's guide to Indian cuisine includes recipes for traditional Indian curries, kabobs, pilao, and dals, with modern cooking techniques. (Rev: BL 11/15/91) [641.5954]

10614 Rombauer, Irma S., and Marion Rombauer Becker. *Joy of Cooking* (7–12). Illus. 1997, Dutton $16.95 (0-452-27923-2); NAL paper $14.95 (0-452-27915-1). First published in 1931, this has through several editions become one of the standard basic American cookbooks. [641.5]

10615 Rosso, Julee, and Sheila Lukins. *The New Basics Cookbook* (10–12). Illus. 1989, Workman $29.95 (0-89480-392-1); paper $19.95 (0-89480-341-7). A beautifully designed cookbook that contains outstanding basic recipes plus many cooking tips. (Rev: BL 3/1/90) [641.5]

10616 Shaw, Maura D., and Synda Altschuler Byrne. *Foods from Mother Earth* (6–10). 1994, Shawangunk Pr. paper $9.95 (1-885482-02-7). A vegetarian cookbook in which most of the recipes can be prepared in 3 or 4 easy steps. (Rev: BL 1/15/95; SLJ 2/95) [641.5]

10617 Takeshita, Jiro. *Food in Japan* (6–9). Illus. 1989, Rourke LB $21.27 (0-86625-340-8). This book provides an introduction to Japan and its food plus supplying a few basic recipes. (Rev: SLJ 12/89) [641.5]

10618 Tan, Jennifer. *Food in China* (6–9). Illus. 1989, Rourke LB $21.27 (0-86625-338-6). Recipes are given plus general information on China, its food, and its people's eating habits. (Rev: SLJ 12/89) [641.5]

10619 Vezza, Diane S. *Passport on a Plate: A Round-the-World Cookbook for Children* (6–8). Illus. 1997, Simon & Schuster paper $19.95 (0-689-80155-6). One hundred recipes are given in this cookbook from 12 areas including Africa, Japan, Italy, Mexico, India, and Russia. (Rev: BL 11/1/97; SLJ 10/97) [641.59]

10620 Villios, Lynne W. *Cooking the Greek Way* (5–9). Illus. 1984, Lerner LB $19.93 (0-8225-0910-5). Along with traditional recipes, this account introduces the country and its people. [641]

10621 Warner, Margaret Brink, and Ruth Ann Hayward, comps. *What's Cooking? Favorite Recipes from around the World* (7–9). 1981, Little, Brown $16.95 (0-316-35252-7). A collection of recipes associated with various ethnic groups that have come to America. [641.5]

10622 Wayne, Marvin A., and Stephen R. Yarnall. *The New Dr. Cookie Cookbook: Dessert Your Way to Health with More Than 150 Scrumptious Cookies, Cakes, and Treats* (9–12). 1994, Morrow paper $14.00 (0-688-12222-1). Using substitutions and deletions for the health conscious, these 2 doctors present recipes for more than 150 desserts along with nutritional information such as calorie and fat counts. (Rev: BL 12/15/93) [641.8]

10623 Webb, Lois S. *Holidays of the World Cookbook for Students* (5–8). 1995, Oryx paper $35.00 (0-89774-884-0). This excellent cookbook contains 388 recipes for holidays in 136 countries, including

many from regions of the United States. (Rev: SLJ 1/96) [641]

10624 Wedman, Betty. *Quick and Easy Diabetic Menus: More Than 150 Delicious Recipes for Breakfast, Lunch, Dinner, and Snacks* (9–12). 1993, Contemporary paper $14.95 (0-8092-3853-5). These recipes are useful for both diabetics and anyone watching his or her weight. (Rev: BL 7/93) [641.5]

10625 Weiner, Leslie, and Barbara Albright. *Quick Chocolate Fixes: 75 Fast and Easy Recipes for People Who Want Chocolate . . . in a Hurry!* (9–12). 1995, St. Martin's paper $6.95 (0-312-13153-4). Describes 75 quick recipes, all loaded with chocolate, including flourless chocolate cake, gorp clusters, brownie cheese cake, and s'mores ice cream pie. (Rev: BL 7/95) [641.6]

10626 Woods, Sylvia, and Christopher Styler. *Sylvia's Soul Food: Recipes from Harlem's World-Famous Restaurant* (9–12). 1992, Hearst $18.00 (0-688-10012-0). A Harlem restaurateur and her chef present more than 100 recipes from her kitchen, all representative of African American culture. (Rev: BL 10/15/92) [641.59]

10627 Yu, Ling. *Cooking the Chinese Way* (7–9). Illus. 1982, Lerner LB $19.93 (0-8225-0902-4). Part of the Easy Menu Ethnic Cookbooks series, this gives information on Chinese life followed by a selection of recipes from soups to desserts. [641.5]

10628 Zalben, Jane Breskin. *Beni's Family Cookbook: For the Jewish Holidays* (4–8). Illus. 1996, Holt $19.95 (0-8050-3735-7). This entertaining collection of recipes is arranged around the Jewish calendar. (Rev: BL 9/15/96; SLJ 2/97) [641.5]

10629 Zamojska-Hutchins, Danuta. *Cooking the Polish Way* (7–9). Illus. 1984, Lerner LB $19.93 (0-8225-0909-1). Part of a lengthy series of ethnic cookbooks that give recipes and details about life in each individual country. [641.5]

10630 Zanzarella, Marianne. *The Good Housekeeping Illustrated Children's Cookbook* (5–8). Illus. 1997, Morrow $17.95 (0-688-13375-4). A visually appealing cookbook containing a number of excellent recipes, some of which require adult supervision. (Rev: BL 12/15/97; SLJ 1/98) [641.5]

Costume and Jewelry Making, Dress, and Fashion

10631 Busch, Marlies. *Friendship Bands: Braiding, Weaving, Knotting* (6–12). Illus. 1997, Sterling $7.95 (0-8069-0309-0). A collection of projects to create bracelets, necklaces, decorations, and hair wraps using basic braiding, knotting, and weaving techniques, plus more complicated projects, all with clear, easy-to-follow instructions. (Rev: BL 5/15/98) [746.42 22]

10632 Carnegy, Vicky. *Fashions of a Decade: The 1980s* (7–12). 1990, Facts on File $21.95 (0-8160-2471-5). This elegantly illustrated volume traces styles and trends in fashion for this decade, linking them to social and political developments. There are volumes in this set for each decade from the 1920s to the 1990s. (Rev: BL 2/15/91; SLJ 5/91) [391]

10633 Coles, Janet, and Robert Budwig. *The Book of Beads* (9–12). Illus. 1990, Simon & Schuster $22.95 (0-671-70525-3). An excellent book with many color illustrations on the kinds and nature of various beads and techniques of beadwork. (Rev: BL 8/90) [745.58]

10634 Cummings, Richard. *101 Costumes for All Ages, All Occasions* (5–9). Illus. 1987, Plays paper $12.00 (0-8238-0286-8). A variety of easily made costumes are described from Frankenstein and Captain Hook to Cleopatra and even a tube of toothpaste. (Rev: BL 1/1/88; BR 3–4/88) [792.026]

10635 Doney, Meryl. *Jewelry* (5–8). (World Crafts) 1996, Watts LB $22.00 (0-531-14406-2). A number of excellent jewelry-making projects from around the world are outlined with easy-to-follow directions and good background cultural information. (Rev: SLJ 1/97) [739.27]

10636 Feldman, Elane. *Fashions of a Decade: The 1990s* (7–12). (Fashions of a Decade) 1992, Facts on File $21.95 (0-8160-2472-3). This is the last of the 8-volume set that traces fashion trends and styles decade by decade in a historical context from the 1920s through the 1990s. (Rev: BL 12/15/92) [391]

10637 Gayle, Katie. *Snappy Jazzy Jewelry* (5–8). 1996, Sterling $14.95 (0-8069-3854-4). Making necklaces and earrings are 2 of the craft projects described, with many helpful photographs. (Rev: BL 5/15/96; SLJ 6/96) [745.594]

10638 Hunnisett, Jean. *Period Costume for Stage & Screen: Patterns for Women's Dress, 1500–1800* (9–12). Illus. 1991, Players Pr. $50.00 (0-88734-610-3). A discussion of historic costume plus over 20 patterns are given. (Rev: BL 3/1/87) [791.43]

10639 Jackson, Sheila. *Costumes for the Stage: A Complete Handbook for Every Type of Play* (9–12). Illus. 1988, New Amsterdam paper $14.95 (0-941533-36-0). A manual for junior and senior high students on creating costumes for their productions. [792]

10640 Kenzle, Linda Fry. *Dazzle: Creating Artistic Jewelry and Distinctive Accessories* (9–12). 1995, Chilton paper $19.95 (0-8019-8638-9). How to create 30 design patterns that customize and personalize outfits. (Rev: BL 10/1/95) [745.594]

10641 LaFerla, Jane. *Make Your Own Great Earrings: Beads, Wire, Polymer Clay, Fabric, Found Objects* (10–12). Illus. 1998, Lark $24.95 (1-57990-031-3); paper $14.95 (1-57990-014-3). Thirty-one artists present 45 different projects for making quality earrings, with simple directions, full-color photos, and a history of earring making. (Rev: SLJ 10/98) [745.594]

10642 Leuzzi, Linda. *A Matter of Style: Women in the Fashion Industry* (7–12). Illus. (Women Then—Women Now) 1996, Watts LB $25.00 (0-531-11303-5). The important part women have played in the fashion industry in such roles as designers, pattern-makers, merchandisers, buyers, and models. (Rev: BL 3/15/97; SLJ 2/97) [338.4]

10643 Lister, Margot. *Costume: An Illustrated Survey from Ancient Times to the Twentieth Century* (9–12). Illus. 1968, Plays $35.00 (0-8238-0096-2). A survey of dress from ancient times to 1914 with hints on how to make many of these costumes. [391]

10644 Litherland, Janet, and Sue McAnally. *Broadway Costumes on a Budget: Big Time Ideas for Amateur Producers* (7–12). Illus. 1996, Meriwether paper $14.95 (1-56608-021-5). Information about period costumes are given in this helpful manual with instructions for making costumes for nearly 100 Broadway plays and musicals. (Rev: BL 12/1/96) [792.6]

10645 Morgenthal, Deborah. *The Ultimate T-Shirt Book: Creating Your Own Unique Designs* (10–12). Illus. 1998, Lark paper $14.95 (1-57990-017-8). Providing more than 100 examples, this books offers instructions for 6 decorative techniques: batik, tie-dying, painting, marbling, stamping, and screen printing. (Rev: SLJ 9/98) [746]

10646 O'Donnol, Shirley Miles. *American Costume, 1915–1970: A Source Book for the Stage Costumer* (9–12). Illus. 1982, Indiana Univ. Pr. $39.95 (0-253-30589-6); paper $19.95 (0-253-20543-3). A nicely illustrated guide to 20th-century fashion that emphasizes women's clothes. [792]

10647 Parks, Carol. *Make Your Own Great Vests: 90 Ways to Jazz Up Your Wardrobe* (9–12). 1995, Sterling $27.95 (0-8069-0972-2). A showcase for tailoring unusual vests. (Rev: BL 4/15/95) [646.4]

10648 Peacock, John. *The Chronicle of Western Fashion: From Ancient Times to the Present Day* (9–12). 1991, Abrams $39.95 (0-8109-3953-3). A former BBC costume designer offers a quick review of Western fashion from ancient Egypt to 1980. (Rev: BL 6/1/91) [391]

10649 Rowland-Warne, L. *Costume* (5–10). (Eyewitness Books) 1992, Knopf $19.00 (0-679-81680-1). This is a history of dress and fashion with brief, clever text and excellent illustrations. (Rev: BL 8/92; SLJ 2/93) [391]

10650 Sadler, Judy A. *Beading: Bracelets, Earrings, Necklaces & More* (4–8). Illus. (Kids Can Easy Crafts) 1998, Kids Can paper $4.95 (1-55074-338-4). Using photographs and simple instructions, directions are given for making a simple beading loom and creating good-looking necklaces and bracelets. (Rev: BL 5/15/98) [745.594]

10651 Schnurnberger, Lynn. *Let There Be Clothes* (9–12). 1991, Workman paper $19.95 (0-89480-833-8). An overview of fashion history from cave dwellers to the present. (Rev: BL 1/15/92; SLJ 12/91) [391]

10652 Taylor, Carol. *Creative Bead Jewelry* (9–12). 1995, Sterling paper $18.95 (0-8069-1306-1). This book, with 70 examples from 38 bead artists, is guaranteed to send one off to the nearest bead emporium. (Rev: BL 11/15/95) [745.594]

10653 Walker, Mark. *Creative Costumes for Any Occasion* (9–12). Illus. 1984, Liberty paper $5.95 (0-89709-138-8). Ideas for 35 different easily made costumes as well as instructions and lists of materials needed. (Rev: BL 3/15/85) [391]

10654 Wilcox, R. Turner. *The Dictionary of Costume* (7–12). Illus. 1969, Macmillan $60.00 (0-684-15150-2). First published in 1969, this book describes in words and drawings over 3,000 articles of clothing. [391]

10655 Wilcox, R. Turner. *Five Centuries of American Costume* (9–12). Illus. 1963, Macmillan $40.00 (0-684-15161-8). Arranged in chronological order, this is a description of what people wore in America from the Vikings to 1960. [391]

10656 Wilcox, R. Turner. *Folk and Festival Costume of the World* (9–12). Illus. 1965, Macmillan $55.00 (0-684-15379-3). An illustrated survey of folk costumes around the world. [391]

10657 Yarwood, Doreen. *The Encyclopedia of World Costume* (9–12). Illus. 1986, Crown $16.99 (0-517-61943-1). A guide to dress from ancient times to the present in text and more than 2,000 drawings. [391]

Dolls and Other Toys

10658 King, Patricia. *Making Dolls' House Furniture* (9–12). 1993, Sterling paper $15.95 (0-946819-24-6). A how-to guide for using found household objects to create furnishings for every room of an English 19th-century dollhouse. (Rev: BL 5/15/93) [745.5]

10659 McClary, Andrew. *Toys with Nine Lives: A Social History of American Toys* (6–12). Illus. 1997, Linnet LB $35.00 (0-208-02386-0). After a general history of toys and how they have changed in format and manufacture through the centuries, this account

gives details on 8 kinds of toys, including building blocks, dolls, and marbles. (Rev: BL 2/15/97; BR 9–10/97; SLJ 1/98; VOYA 8/97) [790.1]

10660 McGraw, Sheila. *Dolls Kids Can Make* (5–8). 1995, Firefly LB $19.95 (1-895565-75-8); paper $9.95 (1-895565-74-X). This work gives directions for making dolls—out of washrags, gloves, and old fabrics—that kids will like. Many require skills in sewing, reading, organizing, and planning—or adult assistance. (Rev: BL 11/15/95; SLJ 3/96) [745]

10661 Newlin, Gary. *Simple Kaleidoscopes: 24 Spectacular Scopes to Make* (7–10). 1996, Sterling paper $14.95 (0-8069-3155-8). This book describes 24 projects that represent different kinds of kaleidoscopes, supplemented by background material on lenses, mirror systems, and eye pieces. (Rev: SLJ 8/97) [745]

10662 Wakefield, David. *How to Make Animated Toys* (9–12). Illus. 1987, Sterling paper $17.95 (0-943822-94-7). A how-to guide to making toys with movable parts such as a hopping kangaroo. (Rev: BL 2/1/87) [745.592]

Drawing and Painting

10663 Albert, Greg, and Rachel Wolf, eds. *Basic Watercolor Techniques* (9–12). 1991, North Light paper $16.99 (0-89134-387-3). An illustrated guide to basic painting methods, materials, and how to paint specific subjects, while also encouraging experimentation. (Rev: BL 10/1/91) [751.42]

10664 Allen, Anne, and Julian Seaman. *Fashion Drawing: The Basic Principles* (9–12). 1993, Trafalgar paper $24.95 (0-7134-7096-8). A large-format paperback that explains techniques in this stylized tradition, with traceable examples of clothing and accessories. (Rev: BL 9/15/93) [746.92]

10665 Arnosky, Jim. *Sketching Outdoors in Spring* (6–8). Illus. 1987, Morrow $12.95 (0-688-06284-9). A beautifully illustrated book on how to draw items such as trees, spring flowers, and some animals. There are companion volumes that cover the other seasons—*Autumn, Summer,* and *Winter* (all 1985). (Rev: BL 5/87; BR 9–10/87; SLJ 5/87) [741]

10666 Baron, Nancy. *Getting Started in Calligraphy* (7–9). 1979, Sterling $13.95 (0-8069-8840-1). How to draw letters with beauty and grace using few materials. [745.6]

10667 Bohl, Al. *Guide to Cartooning* (6–12). Illus. 1997, Pelican paper $13.95 (1-56554-177-4). Though actually a textbook, this work is a splendid guide to the history of cartooning as well as a practical guide to all the basics. (Rev: BL 9/15/97) [741.5]

10668 Clark, Roberta C. *How to Paint Living Portraits* (10–12). Illus. 1990, North Light $28.99 (0-89134-326-1). A guide with many illustrations on how to do portraits in various media such as watercolor, oil, and charcoal. (Rev: BL 9/1/90) [751.45]

10669 Clinch, Moira. *The Watercolor Painter's Pocket Palette: Instant, Practical Visual Guidance on Mixing and Matching Watercolors to Suit All Subjects* (9–12). 1991, North Light $17.99 (0-89134-401-2). A guide to mixing watercolors. (Rev: BL 1/1/92) [751.422]

10670 DK Publishing, eds. *Cartoons* (4–8). (You Can Draw) 1998, DK Publg. paper $4.95 (0-7894-2822-9). After introductory material on drawing techniques, this book covers specific topics and offers step-by-step instructions for each project. (Rev: SLJ 8/98) [741.2]

10671 DK Publishing, eds. *You Can Draw Sharks, Whales, & Sea Creatures* (4–8). (You Can Draw) 1998, DK Publg. paper $4.95 (0-7894-2888-1). This book contains introductory material on cartooning techniques as well as detailed information and instructions on drawing marine life. (Rev: SLJ 8/98) [741.2]

10672 DuBosque, Doug. *Draw Insects* (4–8). 1997, Peel Productions paper $8.95 (0-939217-28-7). A carefully constructed drawing book that gives simple directions for how to draw over 80 insects, including millipedes, ticks, and spiders. (Rev: SLJ 6/98) [741.2]

10673 Foster, Patience. *Guide to Drawing* (5–8). Illus. 1981, Usborne Hayes LB $14.95 (0-88110-025-0); paper $6.95 (0-86020-540-1). This book covers such topics as color, media, and perspective while dealing with a large number of subjects. Also use *Guide to Painting* (1981). [741]

10674 Gerberg, Mort. *Cartooning: The Art and the Business.* Rev. ed. (9–12). Illus. 1989, Morrow paper $15.00 (1-55710-017-9). In addition to basic techniques, this book shows how styles differ within the medium (e.g., comics, children's books) and how to sell the finished product. (Rev: BL 3/15/89) [741.5]

10675 Gordon, Louise. *How to Draw the Human Figure: An Anatomical Approach* (7–10). Illus. 1979, Penguin paper $15.95 (0-14-046477-8). This is both a short course on anatomy and a fine manual on how to draw the human body. [743]

10676 Graves, Douglas R. *Drawing Portraits* (10–12). Illus. 1974, Watson-Guptill paper $14.95 (0-8230-1431-2). An excellent guide to portraiture that covers such topics as posing positions, lighting, and drawing faces and hands. [743]

10677 Harris, David. *The Art of Calligraphy: A Practical Guide to the Skills and Techniques* (7–12). Illus. 1995, DK Publg. $24.95 (1-56458-849-1). After a brief history of the development of Western writing, this beautifully illustrated book shows how to produce intricate lettering and fanciful human figures. (Rev: BR 3–4/96; SLJ 9/95; VOYA 2/96) [741]

10678 Hart, Christopher. *Drawing on the Funny Side of the Brain* (7–12). Illus. 1998, Watson-Guptill paper $19.95 (0-8230-1381-2). This book describes how to create single and multipanel comic strips, with tips on joke writing, pacing, framing, color, and dialogue. (Rev: BL 7/98) [741.5]

10679 Hart, Christopher. *How to Draw Cartoon Dogs, Puppies & Wolves* (6–12). 1998, Watson-Guptill paper $9.95 (0-8230-2366-4). This book supplies a step-by-step approach to drawing both realistic and imagined canines and their relatives. Also use *How to Draw Comic Book Bad Guys and Gals* (1998). (Rev: BL 2/15/99; VOYA 8/99) [741.5 8]

10680 Hart, Christopher. *How to Draw Comic Book Heroes and Villains* (10–12). Illus. 1995, Watson-Guptill paper $18.95 (0-8230-2245-5). An excellent how-to book for older teens, with numerous sketches to demonstrate how to draw, costume, and equip comic book heroes, heroines, and villains. (Rev: BL 1/1–15/96) [741.5]

10681 Johnson, Cathy. *Painting Watercolors* (9–12). 1995, North Light paper $18.99 (0-89134-616-3). A book for beginners. (Rev: BL 9/15/95) [751.42]

10682 Lee, Stan, and John Buscema. *How to Draw Comics the Marvel Way* (9–12). 1984, Simon & Schuster paper $15.00 (0-671-53077-1). Step-by-step instructions are given for drawing cartoons like the Hulk and the Thing. [741.5]

10683 Lewis, Amanda. *Lettering: Make Your Own Cards, Signs, Gifts and More* (4–8). Illus. 1997, Kids Can paper $4.95 (1-55074-232-9). This book describes calligraphy and gothic lettering techniques, covering such topics as typefaces, displays, types of pens to purchase, how to determine pen size, and how to use pens, as well as explaining how to make letterhead stationery and newsletters on the computer. (Rev: BL 10/15/97; SLJ 1/98) [745.6]

10684 Lloyd, Elizabeth Jane. *Watercolor Still Life* (9–12). (DK Art School) 1994, DK Publg. $16.95 (1-56458-490-9). Practical advice for beginners and amateurs looking for fresh ideas and inspiration. (Rev: BL 12/15/94; SLJ 4/95) [751.42]

10685 McGill, Ormond. *Chalk Talks! The Magical Art of Drawing with Chalk* (4–8). Illus. 1995, Millbrook LB $24.90 (1-56294-669-2). This collection of tricks and projects shows how to create upside-down drawings, pictures that transform themselves, and artwork that appears and disappears. (Rev: SLJ 1/96) [741]

10686 McKenzie, Alan. *How to Draw and Sell Comic Strips for Newspapers and Comic Books* (9–12).

Illus. 1987, Writer's Digest $19.95 (0-89134-214-1). In addition to giving detailed instructions with examples on how to draw comics, the author gives a history of comics and tells students how to sell their products. (Rev: SLJ 4/88) [741.5]

10687 Nice, Claudia. *Creating Textures in Pen and Ink with Watercolor* (9–12). 1995, North Light $27.99 (0-89134-595-7). Instructions for rendering specific objects and materials, with a focus on texture. (Rev: BL 9/15/95) [751.4]

10688 Nicolaides, Kimon. *The Natural Way to Draw: A Working Plan for Art Study* (9–12). Illus. 1990, Houghton paper $15.00 (0-395-53007-5). Using illustrations from both old masters and students, this book demonstrates drawing basics. [741.2]

10689 Padubosque, Doug. *Draw 3-D: A Step-by-Step Guide to Perspective Drawing* (4–8). Illus. 1999, Peel Productions paper $8.95 (0-939217-14-7). Using easy-to-follow sketches, the author introduces the techniques of 3-D drawing, beginning with basic concepts involving depth and progressing to more difficult areas like multiple vanishing points. (Rev: SLJ 5/99; VOYA 8/99) [743]

10690 Pellowski, Michael M. *The Art of Making Comic Books* (4–8). Illus. 1995, Lerner LB $21.27 (0-8225-2304-3). A history of comic books, plus drawing techniques and advice on how to become a comic book artist. (Rev: BL 1/1–15/96; SLJ 1/96) [741.5]

10691 Petrie, Ferdinand, and John Shaw. *The Big Book of Painting Nature in Watercolor* (9–12). Illus. 1990, Watson-Guptill paper $29.95 (0-8230-0499-6). This book contains 135 separate lessons on techniques of painting subjects from nature using watercolors. (Rev: BL 9/1/90) [751.42]

10692 Reinagle, Damon J. *Draw Sports Figures* (4–8). Illus. 1997, Peel Productions paper $8.95 (0-939217-32-5). In 6 chapters arranged by sport or sports category, the author gives easy-to-follow instructions on how to draw action figures. (Rev: SLJ 6/98) [742]

10693 Sarnoff, Bob. *Cartoons and Comics: Ideas and Techniques* (9–12). Illus. 1988, Davis $20.75 (0-87192-202-9). A basic handbook with plenty of examples to help the novice. (Rev: BL 3/15/89) [741.5]

10694 Seslar, Patrick. *Wildlife Painting Step by Step* (9–12). 1995, North Light $28.99 (0-89134-584-1). A guide to the art of careful observation and meticulous execution as well as a celebration of nature. (Rev: BL 9/15/95) [751.4]

10695 Sheppard, Joseph. *Realistic Figure Drawing* (9–12). 1991, North Light paper $19.99 (0-89134-374-1). A guide to using different materials and

approaches to capture figures in rest and in motion. (Rev: BL 5/15/91; SLJ 10/91) [751]

10696 Smith, Ray. *The Artist's Handbook* (10–12). Illus. 1987, Knopf $40.00 (0-394-55585-6). A basic manual and guide to all forms of art techniques from etching to oil painting. (Rev: BL 3/15/88) [760]

10697 Smith, Ray. *Drawing Figures* (9–12). (DK Art School) 1994, DK Publg. $16.95 (1-56458-666-9). Provides many photos of materials, examples of techniques, and reproductions of portraits of the very young and the old. (Rev: BL 12/15/94; SLJ 4/95) [743]

10698 Smith, Ray. *How to Draw and Paint What You See* (9–12). Illus. 1984, Knopf paper $0.30 (0-394-72484-4). A comprehensive volume that covers drawing and painting in a variety of media including oil, acrylic, and watercolor. [750]

10699 Smith, Ray. *An Introduction to Perspective* (7–12). (DK Art School) 1995, DK Publg. $16.95 (1-56458-856-4). Using copious illustrations, diagrams, and reproductions of paintings, this book explains the concept of perspective and how it is created and manipulated in drawings and paintings. (Rev: VOYA 2/96) [741]

10700 Tate, Elizabeth. *The North Light Illustrated Book of Painting Techniques* (9–12). Illus. 1986, Writer's Digest $29.99 (0-89134-148-X). An alphabetically arranged guide to over 40 painting techniques explained in both text and illustrations. (Rev: BL 4/1/87; SLJ 3/87) [708]

10701 Wallace, Mary. *I Can Make Art* (4–8). (I Can Make) 1997, Firefly $17.95 (1-895688-64-7); paper $6.95 (1-895688-65-5). Art and crafts combine in these 12 projects involving such techniques as watercolor, still life, chalk drawing, print making, and collage. (Rev: SLJ 12/97) [741.2]

10702 Waters, Elizabeth, and Annie Harris. *Painting: A Young Artist's Guide* (5–8). (Young Artist) 1993, DK Publg. $14.95 (1-56458-348-1). Reproductions of art masterpieces are used to illustrate basic painting techniques and discussions about fundamental visual elements and design principles. (Rev: BL 1/15/94; SLJ 3/94; VOYA 8/94) [751.4]

10703 Welton, Jude. *Drawing: A Young Artist's Guide* (5–8). 1994, DK Publg. $14.95 (1-56458-676-6). The basics of drawing are covered in this well-organized, attractive book with copious illustrations. (Rev: BL 1/15/95; SLJ 3/95) [741.2]

Gardening

10704 Beard, Henry, and Roy McKie. *Gardening* (9–12). 1982, Workman paper $6.95 (0-89480-200-

3). This is a humorous but instructive guide to this pastime. [635]

10705 *Better Homes and Gardens New Garden Book* (9–12). Illus. 1990, Meredith $29.95 (0-696-00042-3). Forty years after its first edition, this remains one of the best general gardening books available. (Rev: BL 4/1/90) [635]

10706 Bremness, Lesley. *The Complete Book of Herbs: A Practical Guide to Growing & Using Herbs* (9–12). 1988, Viking paper $32.95 (0-670-81894-1). This is a directory of over 100 herbs, their characteristics, and cultivation plus 80 recipes for their use. (Rev: BL 1/1/89) [635.7]

10707 Chiusoli, Alessandro, and Maria Luisa Boriani. *Simon & Schuster's Guide to House Plants* (9–12). Illus. 1987, Simon & Schuster paper $14.00 (0-671-63131-4). This guide gives information on 243 plants and how to care for them. (Rev: BL 5/15/87) [635.9]

10708 Damrosch, Barbara. *The Garden Primer* (9–12). Illus. 1988, Workman paper $16.95 (0-89480-316-6). A multitude of facts and advice on all kinds of plants, including houseplants, with detailed information on about 300 specific varieties. (Rev: BL 11/15/88) [635]

10709 Reader's Digest, eds. *Reader's Digest Guide to Creative Gardening* (9–12). Illus. 1987, Reader's Digest $32.00 (0-276-35223-8). A comprehensive, richly illustrated volume that identifies individual plants and gives their growing requirements. [635]

10710 Rich, Libby. *Odyssey Book of Houseplants* (9–12). Illus. 1990, Plant Odyssey paper $19.95 (0-9625702-0-6). A guide to the characteristics and care of 150 different houseplants. (Rev: BL 3/15/90) [635.965]

10711 Rosen, Michael J., ed. *Down to Earth* (5–8). Illus. 1998, Harcourt $18.00 (0-15-201341-5). In this collection of stories, recipes, and projects, 41 children's authors and illustrators explore the world of gardening. (Rev: BL 4/1/98; SLJ 4/98) [635]

Home Repair

10712 Time-Life Books, eds. *The Home Workshop* (10–12). Illus. 1989, Silver Burdett LB $23.27 (0-8094-6281-8). A basic guide to setting up and maintaining a practical home workshop. This is part of a 36-volume set from Time-Life Books called the Home Repair and Improvement series that covers all sorts of projects from kitchens and bathrooms to porches and patios. [684]

Kite Making and Flying

10713 Schmidt, Norman. *The Great Kite Book* (6–10). 1997, Sterling $19.95 (1-895569-36-2). A stunning book that gives directions on how to make 19 different kites, accompanied by kite lore material. (Rev: SLJ 3/98) [929.133]

10714 Schmidt, Norman. *Marvelous Mini-Kites* (6–10). 1999, Sterling $19.95 (1-895569-29-X). Along with a description of the artistry and use of kites in Oriental culture, this book supplies a step-by-step guide to constructing 17 beautiful kites, some with intricate patterns. (Rev: SLJ 2/99) [796.1]

Magic Tricks and Optical Illusions

10715 Cobb, Vicki. *Magic . . . Naturally! Science Entertainments and Amusements* (7–9). Illus. 1976, HarperCollins $12.95 (0-397-31631-3). Thirty magic acts are described, each involving a scientific principle. [507]

10716 Ginn, David. *Clown Magic* (9–12). 1993, Piccadilly Books paper $20.00 (0-941599-21-3). Advice for new clowns, including skits, gags, magic tricks, and specifics on creating and using surprise-filled props. (Rev: BL 4/15/93) [793.8]

10717 Hay, Henry. *The Amateur Magician's Handbook.* 4th ed. (7–12). 1982, NAL paper $5.99 (0-451-15502-5). Tricks for magicians of all ages are given and at various levels of difficulty. [793.8]

10718 Jennings, Terry. *101 Amazing Optical Illusions: Fantastic Visual Tricks* (5–8). Illus. 1997, Sterling $17.95 (0-8069-9462-2). In a large-format book, easily followed instructions are given for optical illusions divided into 3 groups: sight, perception, and movement. (Rev: BL 9/15/97; SLJ 8/97) [152.14]

10719 Kaye, Marvin. *The Stein and Day Handbook of Magic* (9–12). Illus. 1973, Scarborough House paper $8.95 (0-8128-6203-1). Good background material on magic and magicians is given as well as a wide variety of magic tricks. [793.8]

10720 Paulsen, Kathryn. *The Complete Book of Magic and Witchcraft.* Rev. ed. (10–12). 1970, NAL paper $5.95 (0-451-15515-7). A history of magic and witchcraft through the ages. [793.8]

10721 Scarne, John. *Scarne on Card Tricks* (9–12). 1986, NAL paper $5.99 (0-451-15864-4). A description and explanation of 150 card tricks. [795.4]

10722 Severn, Bill. *Bill Severn's Best Magic: 50 Top Tricks to Entertain and Amaze Your Friends on All Occasions* (9–12). 1990, Stackpole paper $14.95 (0-

8117-2229-5). Instructions on how to perform over 50 tricks are given so simply that even the beginner can master them. (Rev: BL 3/15/90) [793.8]

10723 Tarr, Bill. *Now You See It, Now You Don't! Lessons in Sleight of Hand* (7–9). Illus. 1976, Random paper $18.00 (0-394-72202-7). Over 100 easy tricks to mystify one's friends. Each is graded by level of difficulty. [793.8]

Masks and Mask Making

10724 Sivin, Carole. *Maskmaking* (9–12). Illus. 1987, Davis $25.95 (0-87192-178-2). A history of maskmaking plus the techniques and materials needed to create your own. (Rev: BL 3/1/87) [731.75]

10725 Smith, Dick. *Dick Smith's Do-It-Yourself Monster Make-Up Handbook* (9–12). Illus. 1985, Imagine, Inc. paper $9.95 (0-911137-02-5). An Academy Award-winning makeup artist tells how to create several monster disguises and supplies photographs of the finished products. (Rev: BL 11/1/85) [792.027]

Model Making

10726 Spohn, Terry, ed. *Scale Model Detailing: Projects You Can Do* (9–12). 1995, Kalmbach paper $14.95 (0-89024-209-7). Modelers who have already developed their skills will find this a comprehensive resource for honing them. Includes 20 projects from *FineScale Modeler* magazine. (Rev: BL 9/1/95) [745.5]

Paper Crafts

10727 Ayture-Scheele, Zulal. *The Great Origami Book* (9–12). Illus. 1987, Sterling $24.95 (0-8069-6600-9); paper $12.95 (0-8069-6640-8). In easy-to-follow instructions and many illustrations, directions for folding 8 basic forms and 40 figures are given. (Rev: BL 11/15/87) [736]

10728 Botermans, Jack. *Paper Capers: An Amazing Array of Games, Puzzles, and Tricks* (9–12). Illus. 1986, Holt paper $16.95 (0-8050-0139-5). A collection of 40 different puzzles that can be made from paper or cardboard. (Rev: BL 12/1/86; SLJ 11/86) [745.54]

10729 Botermans, Jack. *Paper Flight* (9–12). 1984, Holt paper $19.95 (0-8050-0500-5). Simple directions are given on how to build 48 paper airplane models. [629.133]

10730 Diehn, Gwen. *Making Books That Fly, Fold, Wrap, Hide, Pop Up, Twist, & Turn: Books for Kids to Make* (4–8). Illus. 1998, Lark $19.95 (1-57990-023-2). Clear directions, diagrams, and many photographs are used to guide youngsters in 18 projects to produce folded, wrapped, and pop-up books. (Rev: BL 7/98; SLJ 8/98) [736.98]

10731 Doney, Meryl. *Papercraft* (4–8). (World Crafts) 1997, Watts LB $22.00 (0-531-14446-1). This book looks at the history of papercrafting and provides instructions for inexpensive projects using such techniques as origami, papier-mache, and collage. (Rev: SLJ 12/97) [745.592]

10732 Jackson, Paul. *The Encyclopedia of Origami and Papercraft* (9–12). 1991, Running Pr. $24.95 (1-56138-063-6). Provides technical information and instructions for 3-dimensional paper creations from simple folded forms to sculptures using papier-mache, paper pulp, and castings. (Rev: BL 12/1/91) [736.98]

10733 Kelly, Emery J. *Paper Airplanes: Models to Build and Fly* (4–8). Illus. 1997, Lerner LB $23.93 (0-8225-2401-5). This is a practical manual on making and flying paper airplanes, with good coverage of the principles of aerodynamics. (Rev: BL 12/1/97; SLJ 2/98) [745.592]

10734 Kline, Richard. *The Ultimate Paper Airplane* (9–12). Illus. 1985, Simon & Schuster paper $11.00 (0-671-55551-0). A new concept in airplane design is shown in this paper airplane and 7 variations. (Rev: BL 9/1/85) [745.592]

10735 Leland, Nita, and Virginia Lee Williams. *Creative Collage Techniques* (9–12). 1994, North Light $28.99 (0-89134-563-9). Step-by-step instructions for creating collages, with lists of materials that can be used, including fabric, photos, newspaper, ink, and acrylics. (Rev: BL 10/15/94) [702]

10736 *Paper Craft* (9–12). 1993, North Light paper $16.99 (0-89134-541-8). Taken from the British crafts publication *Creative Hands,* this explains marbling, making boxes and jewelry, and more, with drawings and photos. (Rev: BL 11/15/93; SLJ 1/94) [745.54]

10737 Schmidt, Norman. *Fabulous Paper Gliders* (6–12). 1998, Tamos Books $21.95 (1-895569-21-4). A history of glider development and the basic principles of aerodynamics are given along with patterns and step-by-step instructions for 16 gliders, all but one based on actual gliders. (Rev: BL 5/15/98; SLJ 6/98) [745.592]

10738 Schmidt, Norman. *Paper Birds That Fly* (5–8). 1997, Sterling $19.95 (1-895569-01-X); paper $12.95 (1-895569-11-7). Using the simplest of material—paper, patterns, pencils, ruler, scissors, and glue—this book shows how to make birds that fly. (Rev: SLJ 7/97) [745.5]

10739 Stoker, Andrew, and Sasha Williamson. *Fantastic Folds* (10–12). 1997, St. Martin's paper $16.95 (0-312-17095-5). This book on paper crafts for experienced hobbyists contains projects such as creating picture frames, bowls, boxes, and various free-standing forms. (Rev: SLJ 2/98) [745.592]

10740 Tuyen, P. D. *Wild Origami: Amazing Animals You Can Make* (5–8). 1996, Sterling paper $12.95 (0-8069-1380-0). This book contains diagrams of how to fold paper to create 18 creatures, from an ant to a dinosaur, with single sheets of origami paper. (Rev: SLJ 12/96) [745.5]

Photography, Video, and Film Making

10741 Alabiso, Vincent, and Chuck Zoeller, eds. *Flash! The Associated Press Covers the World* (10–12). Illus. 1998, Harry N. Abrams $39.95 (0-8109-1974-5). Arranged under subjects of Leadership, War, Struggle, and Moments, this is an impressive collection of memorable Associated Press news photographs that provide a history of 20th century events and personalities. (Rev: BL 6/1–15/98; SLJ 8/98; VOYA 12/98) [771]

10742 Czech, Kenneth P. *Snapshot: America Discovers the Camera* (6–9). Illus. 1996, Carolrhoda $22.60 (0-8225-1736-1). An account of the camera's long history in America and its influence on our culture. (Rev: BL 2/15/97; SLJ 12/96; VOYA 4/97) [770]

10743 Fitzharris, Tim. *Wild Bird Photography: National Audubon Society Guide* (10–12). 1996, Firefly paper $19.95 (1-55209-018-3). A complete guide to photographing birds, from choosing equipment, lighting, and closeup techniques to the final product, demonstrated with many excellent photographs. (Rev: SLJ 6/97) [771]

10744 Fitzharris, Tim, and Sierra Club Staff. *Close-Up Photography in Nature* (10–12). 1998, Sierra Club paper $20.00 (0-87156-913-2). Nature photography is covered thoroughly, with discussion of terms, equipment, settings, approaches, subjects, and lastly, digital techniques. (Rev: SLJ 8/98) [771]

10745 Gleason, Roger. *Seeing for Yourself: Techniques and Projects for Beginning Photographers* (7–12). 1993, Chicago Review paper $14.95 (1-55652-159-6). Emphasizes pinhole camera techniques and the basics of more advanced cameras. (Rev: BL 12/1/92; SLJ 6/93) [771]

10746 Grimm, Tom. *The Basic Book of Photography*. Rev. ed. (9–12). Illus. 1985, NAL paper $15.95 (0-452-26096-5). A complete, well-illustrated guide to modern photography. [770]

10747 Grimm, Tom, et al. *The Basic Darkroom Book*. Rev. ed. (9–12). Illus. 1986, NAL paper $9.95 (0-452-25892-8). A useful manual on techniques and skills involved in successful development of film in the darkroom. (Rev: BL 12/15/86) [770]

10748 Hedgecoe, John. *The Book of Photography: How to See and Take Better Pictures* (10–12). Illus. 1984, Knopf paper $29.95 (0-394-72466-6). An introduction to fine picture taking by a prolific writer in the field who has several other recommended titles in print on photography. [770.2]

10749 Henderson, Kathy. *Market Guide for Young Artists and Photographers* (9–12). 1990, Betterway paper $12.95 (1-55870-176-1). A manual for beginners with information on poster and art competitions as well as art submission policies and hints. (Rev: BL 1/1/91; SLJ 3/91) [706.8]

10750 Joyner, Harry M. *Roll 'em! Action! How to Produce a Motion Picture on a Shoestring Budget* (9–12). 1994, McFarland paper $30.00 (0-89950-860-X). Provides advice on producing and directing film and video projects on a low budget. (Rev: BL 3/15/94) [791.43]

10751 Levy, Edmond. *Making a Winning Short: How to Write, Direct, Edit, and Produce a Short Film* (9–12). 1994, Holt paper $15.95 (0-8050-2680-0). Gives advice and instructions on the creation of short films. (Rev: BL 10/1/94) [791]

10752 Morgan, Terri, and Shmuel Thaler. *Photography: Take Your Best Shot* (5–8). (Media Workshop) 1991, Lerner LB $21.27 (0-8225-2302-7). Includes basic information on cameras, film, developing, composition, lighting, special effects, and display, as well as discussing career opportunities. (Rev: BL 10/1/91; SLJ 11/91) [771]

10753 *101 Essential Tips: Photography* (9–12). 1996, DK Publg. paper $4.95 (0-7894-0174-6). A pocket-size book that covers photography essentials both for the beginner and the expert. (Rev: VOYA 6/96) [771]

10754 Price, Susanna, and Tim Stephens. *Click! Fun with Photography* (4–8). 1997, Sterling $14.95 (0-8069-9541-6). A fine introduction to photography that covers both beginning and advanced subjects, including the operation of various cameras, exposure, lighting, different types of photography, and filters. (Rev: SLJ 8/97) [771]

10755 Schaefer, John P. *Basic Techniques of Photography* (9–12). 1992, Little, Brown $50.00 (0-8212-1801-8); paper $35.00 (0-8212-1882-4). An introduction to photography, with information on techniques, film development, and equipment. (Rev: BL 2/15/92) [771]

Sewing and Other Needle Crafts

10756 Colton, Virginia, ed. *Reader's Digest Complete Guide to Needlework* (9–12). Illus. 1979, Reader's Digest $30.00 (0-89577-059-8). From applique to rug making, 10 different needlecrafts are presented. [746.4]

10757 Cream, Penelope, ed. *The Complete Book of Sewing: A Practical Step-by-Step Guide to Sewing Techniques* (9–12). Illus. 1996, DK Publg. $39.95 (0-7894-0419-2). A practical guide to sewing, including choosing patterns, selection of fabrics, basic stitches and seams, interfacings, and how to make darts, tucks, and pleats. (Rev: SLJ 10/96) [646.4]

10758 Hiatt, June Hemmons. *The Principles of Knitting: Methods and Techniques of Hand Knitting* (10–12). Illus. 1989, Simon & Schuster $35.00 (0-671-55233-3). A comprehensive overview of all sorts of knitting techniques with many explanatory drawings. (Rev: BL 4/1/89) [746.9]

10759 Ladbury, Ann. *The Sewing Book: A Complete Practical Guide* (9–12). Illus. 1990, Random $14.99 (0-517-00193-4). Everything that a beginner needs to know including how to run a sewing machine and details of dressmaking. (Rev: BL 3/1/86) [646.2]

10760 Ligon, Linda, ed. *Homespun, Handknit: Caps, Socks, Mittens, and Gloves* (10–12). Illus. 1987, Interweave paper $15.00 (0-934026-26-2). Simple enough for the beginner, this includes many styles for various age groups. (Rev: BL 2/15/88) [746.9]

10761 Margaret, Pat Maixner, and Donna Ingram Slusser. *Watercolor Quilts* (9–12). 1993, That Patchwork Place paper $24.95 (1-56477-031-1). A guide to using color values to achieve striking effects in the creation of quilts suitable for wall hanging. (Rev: BL 1/1/94) [746.3]

10762 Marston, Gwen, and Joe Cunningham. *Quilting with Style: Principles for Great Pattern Design* (9–12). 1993, American Quilter's Society $24.95 (0-89145-814-X). Methods of planning the cable, fan, and feather of a quilt are described, with more than 75 color photos of traditional quilts and traceable, full-size figures. (Rev: BL 11/1/93) [746.9]

10763 Mumm, Debbie. *Quick Country Quilting: Over 80 Projects Featuring Easy, Timesaving Techniques* (9–12). 1991, Rodale $27.95 (0-87857-984-2). An expert quilter offers 80 sewing projects for the enthusiast who has already mastered some of the basic techniques. (Rev: BL 2/1/92) [746.46]

10764 *Timesaving Sewing* (9–12). Illus. 1987, Contemporary $16.95 (0-86573-215-9). A fine guide to time-saving techniques from shopping for fabrics to producing dresses, draperies, and place mats. (Rev: BL 1/15/88) [646.2]

10765 Zieman, Nancy, and Robbie Fanning. *The Busy Woman's Sewing Book*. Rev. ed. (9–12). Illus. 1988, Open Chain paper $9.95 (0-932086-03-9). Sewing basics are covered in a time-efficient mode. Well-illustrated. (Rev: BL 5/1/88) [646.2]

Stamp, Coin, and Other Types of Collecting

10766 Dyson, Cindy. *Rare and Interesting Stamps* (5–8). (Costume, Tradition, and Culture: Reflecting on the Past) 1998, Chelsea $16.95 (0-7910-5171-4). The stories behind 25 rare and unusual stamps are told beginning with Britain's first one-penny stamp with a portrait of Queen Victoria on it. (Rev: BL 3/15/99) [769.56]

10767 Green, Paul, and Kit Kiefer. *101 Ways to Make Money in the Trading-Card Market* (9–12). 1994, Bonus paper $8.95 (1-56625-002-1). Advice on investing in, as opposed to collecting, trading cards, including information on identifying undervalued items and when to buy and sell. (Rev: BL 3/15/94) [790.132]

10768 Green, Paul, and Donn Pearlman. *Making Money with Baseball Cards: A Handbook of Insider Secrets and Strategies* (8–12). Illus. 1989, Bonus paper $7.95 (0-933893-77-9). A guide to the hobby that can be an investment for the future or simply a pleasant extension of one's love of baseball. (Rev: BL 3/15/89) [796.357]

10769 Hobson, Burton. *Coin Collecting for Beginners* (9–12). 1982, Wilshire paper $7.00 (0-87980-022-4). This account supplies solid basic information on how to begin and organize a coin collection. [737]

10770 Mackay, James. *The Guinness Book of Stamps: Facts and Feats* (7–12). Illus. 1989, Guinness $34.95 (0-85112-351-1). All sorts of curiosities about postage stamps such as the most valuable, the largest, and so on. (Rev: BL 4/15/89) [769.56]

10771 Owens, Thomas S. *Collecting Basketball Cards* (5–8). 1998, Millbrook $23.90 (0-7613-0418-5). An informative guide on all aspects of this hobby, including collection building, caring for cards, choosing a dealer, and even trading over the Internet. (Rev: BL 1/1–15/99; SLJ 3/99) [790.1]

10772 Owens, Thomas S. *Collecting Comic Books: A Young Person's Guide* (5–8). 1995, Millbrook LB $25.90 (1-56294-580-7). A beginner's guide to comic book collecting, with sections on kinds of collections, sources, and organizations. (Rev: BL 2/1/96; SLJ 1/96) [741.5]

10773 Owens, Tom. *Collecting Sports Autographs* (9–12). 1989, Bonus paper $6.95 (0-933893-79-5). A thorough introduction to this hobby that covers topics such as hobby shows, techniques of soliciting, autographing, and organizing collections. (Rev: BL 5/1/89) [929.99]

10774 Pellant, Christopher. *Collecting Gems & Minerals* (5–8). Illus. 1998, Sterling $14.95 (0-8069-9760-5). This book describes how minerals and gems are formed, defines important terms, describes different varieties, and gives sound advice on how to become a collector. (Rev: BL 6/1–15/98; SLJ 8/98) [553.8 075]

10775 *Postal Service Guide to U.S. Stamps* (7–12). Illus. 1988, U.S. Postal Service $5.00 (0-9604756-8-0). A well-illustrated history of U.S. postage stamps. [769.56]

10776 *Scott Standard Postage Stamp Catalogue: Countries of the World* (7–12). 1997, Scott paper $35.00 (0-89487-231-1). This is the most comprehensive stamp catalog in print. Volume 1 deals with stamps from the English-speaking world; the other 3 volumes cover alphabetically the other countries of the world. [769.56]

10777 Weston, Murray. *Collecting Fossils* (5–8). Illus. 1998, Sterling $14.95 (0-8069-9762-1). After a discussion of how fossils are formed, this work introduces different types of fossils, explains important terms, and tells how to collect fossils and organize the collections. (Rev: BL 6/1–15/98; SLJ 6/98) [560.75]

Woodworking and Carpentry

10778 Blandford, Percy W. *24 Table Saw Projects* (10–12). Illus. 1988, TAB paper $6.95 (0-8306-2964-5). Step-by-step instructions on how to make such items as cabinets and benches. (Rev: BL 5/1/88) [684]

10779 Brann, Donald R. *How to Build Outdoor Projects* (10–12). 1981, Easi-Bild paper $9.95 (0-87733-807-8). Easily followed directions are given to build all sorts of outdoor furniture. [684]

10780 De Cristoforo, R. J. *The Table Saw Book* (10–12). Illus. 1988, TAB paper $16.95 (0-8306-2789-8). An introduction to the table saw, the various types of cuts it can produce, and how to select and use one. (Rev: BL 5/1/88) [684]

10781 Higginbotham, Bill. *Whittling* (9–12). 1982, Sterling paper $11.95 (0-8069-7598-9). An introduc-

tion to this folk art is given plus 32 patterns for projects. [684]

10782 Key, Ray. *The Woodturner's Workbook* (9–12). 1993, Batsford $29.95 (0-7134-6667-7). A text for upgrading skills, rather than learning basic techniques, with sections on choosing wood, effects various woods display, and exotic woods. (Rev: BL 9/15/93) [684]

10783 Miller, Wilbur R., et al. *Woodworking* (9–12). Illus. 1978, Glencoe paper $9.33 (0-02-672800-1). A guide that covers basic tools, techniques, and materials in woodworking. [684]

10784 Nelson, John A. *52 Weekend Woodworking Projects* (9–12). 1991, Sterling paper $14.95 (0-8069-8300-0). A collection of short-term projects from the very simple to the intricate, including toys, mirrors, clocks, and furniture. (Rev: BL 11/1/91) [684]

10785 Self, Charles R. *Making Birdhouses and Feeders* (9–12). Illus. 1986, Sterling paper $13.95 (0-8069-6244-5). Over 40 projects are described that even a beginner with few tools can accomplish. (Rev: SLJ 5/86) [684]

10786 Self, Charles R. *Making Fancy Birdhouses & Feeders* (10–12). Illus. 1988, Sterling paper $13.95 (0-8069-6690-4). In addition to specific projects, the author discusses materials, tools, types of joints, and finishing methods. (Rev: BL 5/15/86) [690]

10787 Spielman, Patrick, and Patricia Spielman. *Scroll Saw Puzzle Patterns* (9–12). Illus. 1989, Sterling paper $14.95 (0-8069-6586-X). A total of 80 plans are included for puzzles involving the alphabet, animals, robots, and so on. (Rev: BL 1/15/89) [688.7]

10788 Tangerman, Elmer J. *Complete Guide to Wood Carving* (9–12). Illus. 1985, Sterling paper $17.95 (0-8069-7922-4). This beginner's guide describes the tools and materials needed plus details on how to carve faces, animals, and figures. (Rev: BL 2/15/85; BR 1–2/86) [731.4]

10789 Tangerman, Elmer J. *Whittling and Woodcarving* (9–12). 1936, Dover paper $9.95 (0-486-20965-2). This is a beginner's guide to these ancient crafts. [684]

10790 *Working with Wood* (9–12). Illus. 1979, Silver Burdett LB $20.60 (0-8094-2427-4). Basic woodworking skills, tools, and techniques are introduced in this volume from the Time-Life Home Repair and Improvement series. [694]

Jokes, Puzzles, Riddles, and Word Games

10791 Gleason, Norma. *Cryptograms and Spygrams* (10–12). 1981, Dover paper $5.95 (0-486-24036-3). This is a collection of over 100 puzzles and problems to solve. [793.7]

10792 Lewis, J. Patrick. *Riddle-icious* (4–8). Illus. 1996, Knopf $15.00 (0-679-84011-7). A collection of 28 delightful poem-riddles that are bound to please. (Rev: BL 6/1–15/96; SLJ 6/96) [818]

10793 Phillips, Louis, comp. *The Latin Riddle Book* (10–12). Trans. by Stan Schechter. Illus. 1988, Harmony $9.95 (0-517-56975-2). For Latin students a book of riddles that will keep them guessing. (Rev: SLJ 4/89) [470]

10794 Rosenbloom, Joseph. *Biggest Riddle Book in the World* (6–9). Illus. 1977, Sterling paper $6.95 (0-8069-8884-3). Very clever riddles collected by a children's librarian. [808.7]

10795 Rosenbloom, Joseph. *Dr. Knock-Knock's Official Knock-Knock Dictionary* (6–9). Illus. 1977, Sterling paper $4.95 (0-8069-8936-X). Over 500 knock-knock jokes in this very humorous collection. [808.7]

10796 Rosenbloom, Joseph. *The Gigantic Joke Book* (6–9). 1978, Sterling paper $6.95 (0-8069-7514-8). A large collection of jokes that span time from King

Arthur to the space age. Also use *Funniest Joke Book Ever* (1986). [808.7]

10797 Rosenbloom, Joseph. *Sports Riddles* (6–9). Illus. 1982, Harcourt $8.95 (0-15-277994-9). A delightful collection of riddles involving favorite sports such as baseball and basketball. [398]

10798 Salny, Abbie, and Burke Lewis Frumkes. *The Mensa Think Smart Book* (9–12). Illus. 1986, HarperCollins paper $10.00 (0-06-091255-3). A collection of word games, puzzles, and quizzes that are mind benders. (Rev: BL 4/1/86) [153]

10799 Schwartz, Alvin, comp. *Tomfoolery: Trickery and Foolery with Words* (6–9). Illus. 1973, HarperCollins $12.95 (0-397-31466-3). A collection of jokes and riddles from folklore and from children. [398]

10800 Schwartz, Alvin, comp. *Witcracks: Jokes and Jests from American Folklore* (6–9). Illus. 1973, HarperCollins LB $14.89 (0-397-31475-2). Tall tales, jokes, riddles, and humorous stories are included in this collection from our past. [398]

10801 Smullyan, Raymond. *To Mock a Mockingbird* (7–12). 1985, Knopf $14.95 (0-394-53491-3). A book of 200 puzzles—some fairly easy, others very difficult—but all with solutions given. (Rev: VOYA 12/85) [793.7]

10802 Aaseng, Nathan. *Science Versus Pseudoscience* (7–12). 1994, Watts LB $24.00 (0-531-11182-2). Explains the difference between true scientific theory and pseudoscience, discussing ESP, near-death experiences, creation science, and cold fusion. (Rev: BL 8/94; SLJ 9/94) [001.7]

10803 Allen, Eugenie. *The Best Ever Kids' Book of Lists* (5–8). 1991, Avon paper $2.95 (0-380-76357-5). Brief lists of the biggest, smallest, strangest, ugliest, etc., with humorous drawings. (Rev: BL 12/15/91) [031.02]

10804 Ash, Russell. *Factastic Book of 1001 Lists* (5–9). 1999, DK Publg. $19.95 (0-7894-3769-4); paper $14.95 (0-7894-3412-1). A collection of bizarre facts and unusual trivia organized under broad topics like space, the earth, science, countries, the arts, and sports. (Rev: BR 9–10/99; SLJ 7/99; VOYA 8/99) [031.04]

10805 Ash, Russell. *The Top 10 of Everything 1999* (6–10). Illus. 1998, DK Publg. paper $17.95 (0-7894-3523-3). The top 10 in a wide range of areas, such as speed records, sports records, animal records, and toys. (Rev: VOYA 8/99) [001.9]

10806 Ballinger, Erich. *Monster Manual: A Complete Guide to Your Favorite Creatures* (5–8). 1994, Lerner LB $19.95 (0-8225-0722-6). A survey of the great monsters of the world from mythology, literature, and the media. (Rev: BL 12/1/94; SLJ 3/95) [001.9]

10807 Berlitz, Charles. *The Bermuda Triangle* (9–12). Illus. 1987, Avon paper $5.99 (0-380-00465-8). An account that discusses the various mysterious disappearances of planes and ships that have occurred in this stretch of the Atlantic Ocean. [001.9]

10808 Bondeson, Jan. *A Cabinet of Medical Curiosities* (10–12). 1997, Cornell Univ. Pr. $35.00 (0-8014-3431-9). A carefully researched series of essays that deal with human curiosities, among them tailed peo-

ple, a giant, a two-headed boy, and an extremely hairy woman, some exaggerated, some documented, placing them in historical perspective. (Rev: BL 10/15/97; SLJ 4/98) [031.02]

10809 Brier, Bob. *Encyclopedia of Mummies* (10–12). Illus. 1997, Facts on File $35.00 (0-8160-3108-8). A topically arranged history of mummification that occurs both in nature and in various cultures, including such modern examples as John Paul Jones, who was preserved in whiskey, Eva Peron, whose body was infused with wax, and Lenin, whose corpse was chemically treated. (Rev: BL 3/15/98; SLJ 6/98) [001.9]

10810 Bunson, Matthew. *The Vampire Encyclopedia* (9–12). 1993, Crown paper $16.00 (0-517-88100-4). Enough ghoulish lore to satisfy the bloodthirstiest vampire enthusiast. (Rev: SLJ 3/94) [001.9]

10811 Burnam, Tom. *More Misinformation* (9–12). Illus. 1980, HarperCollins $16.95 (0-690-01685-9). An entertaining book that debunks popularly held beliefs. A sequel to *Dictionary of Misinformation* (1975). [001.9]

10812 Cavendish, Richard. *The World of Ghosts and the Supernatural* (9–12). 1994, Facts on File $24.95 (0-8160-3209-2). Describes encounters with the spirit world and other paranormal phenomena, including reports of ghosts haunting the Tower of London. (Rev: BL 8/94; SLJ 6/95) [133.1]

10813 Cohen, Daniel. *The Encyclopedia of Monsters* (9–12). 1990, Dorset $17.95 (0-88029-442-6). A guide to all sorts of monsters, including the vampire, abominable snowman, and giant sea creatures. [398]

10814 Cohen, Daniel. *The Encyclopedia of the Strange* (9–12). Illus. 1985, Avon paper $4.50 (0-380-70268-1). A collection of weird and often bizarre information on such topics as Atlantis, Jack the Ripper, levitation, and King Tut's tomb. (Rev: SLJ 11/85) [001.9]

10815 Cohen, Daniel. *Prophets of Doom: The Millennium Edition* (6–8). 1999, Millbrook $20.90 (0-7613-1317-6). An updated edition of the 1992 book on people and groups who through the ages have predicted the end of the world, with such additions as David Koresh of the Heaven's Gate cult and Shoko Ashara, the cultist who released nerve gas into a Tokyo subway. (Rev: BL 5/15/99; SLJ 6/99) [133.3]

10816 Cohen, Daniel. *Werewolves* (5–9). 1996, Dutton $14.99 (0-525-65207-8). The author traces the history of the werewolf from 16th-century France to the Internet of today. (Rev: BL 10/1/96; BR 1–2/97; SLJ 3/96) [398]

10817 Cohen, Daniel. *The World's Most Famous Ghosts* (7–9). Illus. 1989, Pocket Books paper $2.99 (0-671-69145-7). Accounts of many different ghosts—from Abraham Lincoln to the Flying Dutchman. [133.1]

10818 Cohen, Daniel. *Young Ghosts* (5–8). 1994, Dutton $13.99 (0-525-65154-3). "True" accounts of ghost children, such as Rosalie, who is summoned in seances by her mother. Also includes tales of ghosts that appear to children. (Rev: BL 9/1/94; SLJ 10/94) [133.1]

10819 Crawford, S., and G. Sullivan. *The Power of Birthdays, Stars & Numbers* (9–12). 1998, Ballantine paper $24.95 (0-345-41819-0). This introduction to astrology not only explains the effects of planets on personality, but also describes each day in the calendar in terms of the zodiac and numerology. (Rev: SLJ 4/99) [133.5]

10820 Crosse, Joanna. *The Element Illustrated Encyclopedia of Mind, Body, Spirit & Earth* (10–12). Illus. 1998, Element Books $24.95 (1-901881-10-5). This volume covers diverse topics like astrology, paranormal phenomena, fortune-telling, numerology, common religions or "belief systems," and health and fitness, organized under four main topics: The Mind, The Body, The Spirit, and The Earth. (Rev: SLJ 8/98) [133]

10821 Dinsdale, Tim. *Loch Ness Monster.* 4th ed. (9–12). Illus. 1982, Routledge paper $7.95 (0-7100-9022-6). An account of the search for Nessie, the monster that supposedly lives in this picturesque lake in the Scottish Highlands. [001.9]

10822 Drimmer, Frederick. *Incredible People: Five Stories of Extraordinary Lives* (9–12). 1997, Atheneum $16.00 (0-689-31921-5). The 5 lives retold here are of people who were placed on display as oddities, including a man over 7 feet tall, Siamese twins, an African pygmy, and a child reared in the wilds. (Rev: BL 6/1–15/97; BR 1–2/98; SLJ 5/97; VOYA 8/97) [001.9]

10823 Duncan, Lois, and William Rool. *Psychic Connections: A Journey into the Mysterious World of Psi* (6–10). 1995, Delacorte paper $12.95 (0-385-32072-8). After her daughter's murder, Duncan used psychics to learn more about it. Here she joins Psychical Research Foundation project director Rool in a comprehensive look at psychic phenomena. (Rev: BL 6/1–15/95; SLJ 5/95) [133]

10824 Floyd, E. Randall. *Great American Mysteries* (9–12). 1991, August House paper $9.95 (0-87483-170-9). Thirty-eight well-known mysteries, such as the Salem witchcraft trials, the Lizzie Borden case, the Bermuda Triangle, ghosts, and psychics. (Rev: BL 3/1/91; SLJ 8/91) [001.94]

10825 Garden, Nancy. *Devils and Demons* (7–9). 1976, HarperCollins $11.95 (0-397-31666-6). An international survey of the weird demons believed in by various cultures and peoples. [133]

10826 Gardner, Martin. *On the Wild Side: The Big Bang, ESP, the Beast 666, Levitation, Rain Making, Trance-Channeling, Seances and Ghosts, and More* (9–12). 1992, Prometheus $27.95 (0-87975-713-2). A collection of articles that examine, expose, and debunk many offbeat scientific theories, cults, and beliefs. (Rev: BL 2/15/92) [500]

10827 Gardner, Robert. *What's Super about the Supernatural?* (7–12). 1998, Twenty-First Century $25.90 (0-7613-3228-6). This book explores paranormal phenomena like ESP, psychokinesis, haunted houses, seances, and extraterrestrials, with a set of experiments to test the reader's psychic abilities. (Rev: BL 3/1/99; SLJ 4/99) [133]

10828 Guiley, Rosemary Ellen. *The Encyclopedia of Ghosts and Spirits* (9–12). 1993, Facts on File paper $19.95 (0-8160-2846-X). Comprehensive coverage—400 entries and many photos—of the spirit world. (Rev: SLJ 6/93*) [333.1]

10829 Harvey, Michael. *The End of the World* (6–10). (Great Mysteries: Opposing Viewpoints) 1992, Greenhaven LB $17.96 (0-89908-096-0). A review of many of the dire predictions that foretold the end of the world. (Rev: BL 1/15/93) [001.9]

10830 Hepplewhite, Peter. *Unexplained: Hauntings* (5–8). Illus. (The Unexplained) 1998, Sterling $14.95 (0-8069-3881-1). A well-researched account that describes 5 unexplained events involving hauntings, such as Lincoln's death premonition. (Rev: SLJ 10/98; VOYA 10/98) [133.1]

10831 Hill, Douglas. *Witches & Magic-Makers* (6–8). 1997, Knopf LB $20.99 (0-679-98544-1). This book introduces magical charms, talismans, and amulets from around the world, with a brief look at the history of witches and practitioners of magic, witches of fiction and film, and witch-hunting activities. (Rev: SLJ 8/97) [133.4]

10832 Innes, Brian. *Millennium Prophecies* (5–8). Illus. 1999, Raintree Steck-Vaughn $24.26 (0-8172-5486-2). All sorts of prophecies related to the calendar and the millennium are explored in this attractive volume. (Rev: BL 5/15/99; SLJ 9/99; VOYA 10/99) [001.7]

10833 Innes, Brian. *Mysterious Healing* (5–8). Illus. (Unsolved Mysteries) 1999, Raintree Steck-Vaughn $24.26 (0-8172-5489-7). Hands-on healing, acupuncture, iridology, and auras are some of the subjects discussed in this volume that also contains personal accounts of those that believe and those that don't. (Rev: SLJ 9/99; VOYA 10/99) [001.7]

10834 Jenkins, Martin. *Vampires* (6–8). (Informania) 1998, Candlewick $15.99 (0-7636-0315-5). Following a graphic-novel version of Bram Stoker's *Dracula,* there are sections on all sorts of animal bloodsuckers, like leeches and various parasitic insects (with photographs); a "history of bloodsucking," especially in Eastern and Central European tradition; a survey of vampire films and TV shows; and a tongue-in-cheek "Vampire Hunter's Survival Guide." (Rev: SLJ 2/99) [133.4]

10835 Kemp, Gillian. *Tea Leaves, Herbs, and Flowers: Fortune-Telling the Gypsy Way* (5–9). Illus. (Elements of the Extraordinary) 1998, Element Books paper $5.95 (1-901881-92-X). This book discusses the meaning of different tea-leaf clusters and how to read fortunes through tea leaves, followed by a description of the lore and language of flowers, with a chapter on ways to attract a lover, keep one, and even to repel unwanted attention using folk methods. (Rev: SLJ 1/99) [133.3]

10836 Krull, Kathleen. *They Saw the Future: Oracles, Psychics, Scientists, Great Thinkers, and Pretty Good Guessers* (5–9). Illus. 1999, Simon & Schuster $19.99 (0-689-81295-7). This chronological survey of people who professed to see into the future includes the Oracle at Delphi, Nostradamus, Jules Verne, Leonardo da Vinci, and Jeane Dixon. (Rev: BL 6/1–15/99; SLJ 7/99; VOYA 12/99) [133.3]

10837 McHargue, Georgess. *Meet the Werewolf* (6–9). 1976, HarperCollins $11.95 (0-397-31662-3). A factual account that explores the evidence concerning the existence of werewolves. Also use: *Meet the Witches* (1984). [133.4]

10838 Malone, John. *Predicting the Future: From Jules Verne to Bill Gates* (10–12). 1997, M. Evans $19.95 (0-87131-830-X). This book presents a series of predictions, dates of origin, material about each predictor, and material on whether or not the predictions came true. (Rev: BL 10/1/97; SLJ 5/98) [001.9]

10839 Myers, Arthur. *The Ghostly Register* (9–12). Illus. 1986, Contemporary paper $14.95 (0-8092-5081-0). A guide to 64 houses that are reputedly haunted. (Rev: SLJ 3/87) [133.1]

10840 Myers, Janet Nuzum. *Strange Stuff: True Stories of Odd Places and Things* (5–8). Illus. 1999, Linnet $19.50 (0-208-02405-0). A collection of curiosities—items about zombies, the dangers of quicksand, scorpions, poisonous snakes, black holes, Bigfoot, mermaids, voodoo, the Bermuda triangle, and feral children raised by wolves. (Rev: SLJ 7/99) [001.9]

10841 Netzley, Patricia. *Alien Abductions* (6–9). (Opposing Viewpoints Great Mysteries) 1996, Greenhaven LB $17.96 (1-56510-352-1). The truth or falsehood behind kidnappings by creatures from outer space is examined. (Rev: BL 4/15/96; SLJ 6/96) [001.9]

10842 Nickell, Joe, and John F. Fischer. *Secrets of the Supernatural: Investigating the World's Occult Mysteries* (9–12). Illus. 1988, Prometheus $28.95 (0-87975-461-3). The scientific investigation of 10 supernatural occurrences. (Rev: BL 9/1/88) [133]

10843 O'Connell, Margaret F. *The Magic Cauldron: Witchcraft for Good and Evil* (7–9). 1976, Phillips $37.95 (0-87599-187-4). In this history of witchcraft, the reader learns that witches can be agents of both good and evil. [133]

10844 O'Neill, Catherine. *Amazing Mysteries of the World* (7–12). Illus. 1983, National Geographic LB $8.50 (0-87044-502-2). UFOs, Bigfoot, and Easter Island are only 3 of the many mysteries explored. [001.9]

10845 Reid, Lori. *The Art of Hand Reading* (10–12). 1996, DK Publg. $24.95 (0-7894-1060-5). The history, physiology, and how-to of hand reading to learn about a person's health, personality, and background. (Rev: BL 10/15/96; SLJ 3/97; VOYA 8/97) [133.3]

10846 Reid, Lori. *Hand Reading: Discover Your Future* (5–9). Illus. (Elements of the Extraordinary) 1998, Element Books paper $5.95 (1-901881-82-2). Palmistry is explained in detail, including the meaning of the shape of the hand and nails, the relative length of fingers, fingerprints, and each line and curve, and how hand gestures or the way people shake hands reveal clues to their personalities. (Rev: SLJ 1/99) [133.6]

10847 Roberts, Nancy. *Southern Ghosts* (6–9). Illus. 1979, Sandlapper paper $7.95 (0-87844-075-5). Thirteen ghostly tales from the South are retold with photographs of their locales. [133]

10848 Rose, Carol. *Spirits, Fairies, Gnomes, and Goblins: An Encyclopedia of the Little People* (8–12). 1996, ABC-CLIO LB $75.00 (0-87436-811-1). An encyclopedia of fairies, angels, dwarfs, djinns, trolls, tricksters, and other otherworldly creatures. (Rev: BL 5/1/97; BR 9–10/97; SLJ 8/97) [001.9]

10849 Shermer, Michael. *Why People Believe Weird Things: Pseudoscience, Superstition and Other Confusions of Our Time* (10–12). 1997, W. H. Freeman $22.95 (0-7167-3090-1). The author applies scientific reasoning to disprove such phenomena as alien abduction, near-death experiences, and psychics. (Rev: SLJ 3/98) [133]

10850 Skal, David J. *V Is for Vampire: The A–Z Guide to Everything Undead* (8–12). 1996, NAL paper $15.95 (0-452-27173-8). This compendium of information about vampires examines the myths and beliefs surrounding them, the stories behind wooden stakes, zombies, and Dracula lore, and includes lists of vampire movies and novels. (Rev: BL 10/1/95; VOYA 2/97) [001.7]

10851 Snodgrass, Mary Ellen. *Signs of the Zodiac: A Reference Guide to Historical, Mythological, and Cultural Associations* (9–12). 1997, Greenwood $39.95 (0-313-30276-6). An interesting, browsable reference work that describes each zodiac sign, the history of astrology, its influences in art and the sciences, characteristics of each sign, and famous people born under each. (Rev: BR 3–4/98; SLJ 2/98) [133.5]

10852 Stein, Wendy. *Witches* (6–9). (Great Mysteries: Opposing Viewpoints) 1995, Greenhaven LB $17.96 (1-56510-240-1). A discussion of the real nature of witches. (Rev: BL 4/15/95; SLJ 3/95) [133.4]

10853 Tambini, Michael. *Future* (4–9). (Eyewitness) 1998, Knopf LB $20.99 (0-679-99317-7). The world of the future is explored in this oversize, richly illustrated book. (Rev: BL 8/98) [133.3]

10854 Tonge, Neil. *Unexplained: Mysterious Places* (5–8). Illus. (The Unexplained) 1998, Sterling $14.95 (0-8069-3863-3). Stonehenge and Easter Island are 2 of the unusual places described, followed by theories about their existence, ranging from scientific to the supernatural. (Rev: SLJ 10/98; VOYA 10/98) [001.9]

10855 Underwood, Peter. *Ghosts and How to See Them* (9–12). 1995, Trafalgar paper $16.95 (1-85470-194-0). Experiencing the paranormal and photographing it. (Rev: BL 2/15/95) [133.1]

10856 Varasdi, J. Allen. *Myth Information* (8–12). 1989, Ballantine paper $5.99 (0-345-35985-2). A fascinating collection of facts that challenge some popular beliefs such as the belief that the American buffalo is really a bison. (Rev: BL 11/1/89) [001.9]

10857 Wilson, Colin. *Mysteries of the Universe* (5–8). Illus. 1997, DK Publg. $14.95 (0-7894-2165-8). Such world mysteries as the Shroud of Turin, showers of fish, and life on Mars are explored. (Rev: BL 2/1/98; SLJ 2/98) [001.9]

10858 Windham, Kathryn Tucker. *Jeffrey Introduces 13 More Southern Ghosts* (7–10). 1978, Univ. of Alabama Pr. paper $13.00 (0-8173-0381-2). A total of 13 ghosts tell their weird stories. [133]

10859 Winters, Paul A. *Paranormal Phenomena* (8–12). Illus. (Opposing Viewpoints) 1997, Greenhaven LB $21.96 (1-56510-558-3); paper $20.25 (1-56510-557-5). This collection of articles explores such controversial topics as UFOs, life after death, and ESP. (Rev: BL 7/97; BR 1–2/98; SLJ 9/97; VOYA 12/97) [133]

10860 Wolf, Leonard. *Dracula: The Connoisseur's Guide* (9–12). Illus. 1997, Broadway Books paper $16.00 (0-553-06907-1). This book is filled with fascinating vampire lore and discussion of vampire fiction stemming from Bram Stoker's 19th century novel and the Dracula movies. (Rev: SLJ 6/98) [001.9]

Sports and Games

General and Miscellaneous

10861 Aaseng, Nathan. *The Locker Room Mirror: How Sports Reflect Society* (7–10). 1993, Walker LB $15.85 (0-8027-8218-3). Argues that problems in professional sports today—cheating, drug abuse, violence, commercialization, discrimination—are reflections of society at large. (Rev: BL 6/1–15/93; SLJ 5/93) [306.4]

10862 Allsen, Phillip E., and Alan R. Witbeck. *Racquetball*. 6th ed. (9–12). 1996, W. C. Brown & Benchmark $17.95 (0-697-25627-8). From the simple to the complex, this manual covers the techniques and strategies used in racquetball. [796.34]

10863 Banks, Mike. *Mountain Climbing for Beginners* (10–12). Illus. 1978, Scarborough House $8.95 (0-8128-2448-2). This is a guide for those who are interested in basic knowledge of this sport. [796.5]

10864 Barash, David P. *The Great Outdoors* (9–12). 1989, Lyle Stuart $17.95 (0-8184-0496-5). Outdoor pursuits such as horseback riding, backpacking, cross-country skiing, and stargazing are discussed. (Rev: BL 5/1/89) [796.5]

10865 Berlow, Lawrence H. *Sports Ethics* (7–12). (Contemporary World Issues) 1995, ABC-CLIO LB $39.50 (0-87436-769-7). A general introduction to the subject followed by discussion of questions concerning children in sports, college athletics, the Olympics, racism, women, drug abuse, and media relations. (Rev: BL 8/95; SLJ 1/96) [796]

10866 Borden, Fred, and Jay Elias. *Bowling: Knowledge Is the Key* (9–12). Illus. 1987, Bowling Concepts paper $19.95 (0-9619177-0-9). A straightforward instructional program that is simple to follow and thorough. (Rev: BL 6/15/87) [794.6]

10867 Burgett, Gordon. *Treasure and Scavenger Hunts: How to Plan, Create, and Give Them* (9–12). 1994, Communication Unlimited paper $11.75 (0-910167-25-7). Although this book focuses on adult recreation, it also includes suggestions for teens. (Rev: BL 3/15/94) [796.1]

10868 Cook, Ann Mariah. *Running North: A Yukon Adventure* (9–12). 1998, Algonquin $21.95 (1-56512-213-5). An exciting story of the Yukon Quest International Sled Dog Race and the Cook family who, with their 32 Siberian huskies, moved from New Hampshire to Alaska to train for the race and participate in it. (Rev: BL 9/1/98; SLJ 1/99) [798.8]

10869 Cooper, Michael. *Racing Sled Dogs: An Original North American Sport* (5–8). Illus. 1988, Clarion $13.95 (0-89919-499-0). A simple but fascinating account of this sport that focuses on the Iditarod Trail Race in Alaska. (Rev: BL 2/1/89; SLJ 3/89) [798]

10870 Currie, Stephen. *Issues in Sports* (7–12). Illus. (Contemporary Issues) 1997, Lucent LB $22.45 (1-56006-477-3). Issues in sports that are discussed include the use of steroids and other performance-enhancing drugs, drug testing, the commercialization of sports, sky-rocketing salaries, and athletes as role models. (Rev: BL 5/1/98) [306.4 83 0973]

10871 Dolan, Edward F. *In Sports, Money Talks* (6–9). 1996, Twenty-First Century LB $21.40 (0-8050-4569-4). Issues in this book about financial aspects of sports include athletes' salaries, labor disputes, the influence of money on college athletics, and the effect of TV on revenues. (Rev: BR 1–2/97; SLJ 1/97) [796]

10872 Doney, Meryl. *Games* (5–8). (World Crafts) 1996, Watts LB $22.00 (0-531-14405-4). Along with background cultural information on games played around the world, this book provides illustrated directions for making the games and playing them. (Rev: SLJ 1/97) [790.1]

10873 Dudley, William, ed. *Sports in America* (7–12). (Opposing Viewpoints) 1994, Greenhaven paper $16.20 (1-56510-104-9). A collection of essays that explore such diverse subjects as racism in sports, drug use, and commercialism. (Rev: BL 5/15/94; SLJ 7/94) [796]

10874 Egendorf, Laura K., ed. *Sports and Athletes* (7–12). Illus. (Opposing Viewpoints) 1999, Greenhaven LB $21.96 (0-7377-0057-2); paper $17.45 (0-7377-0056-4). The 30 essays in this critical anthology cover children in sports, college athletics reform, racial discrimination, gender inequality, and drugs. (Rev: BL 9/15/99) [796]

10875 Fair, Erik. *Right Stuff for New Hang Glider Pilots* (9–12). Illus. 1987, Publitec Editions paper $9.95 (0-913581-00-3). A collection of articles by Fair exploring many topics related to hang gliding. (Rev: BL 4/1/87) [797.5]

10876 Feinberg, Jeremy R. *Reading the Sports Page: A Guide to Understanding Sports Statistics* (7–10). 1992, Macmillan LB $21.00 (0-02-734420-7). Explains how to read baseball, basketball, football, hockey, and tennis statistics in newspaper sports pages. (Rev: BL 1/15/93; SLJ 1/93) [796]

10877 Finnigan, Dave. *The Joy of Juggling* (9–12). 1993, Jugglebug paper $5.95 (0-9615521-3-1). Describes and provides illustrations for 25 juggling routines, discusses plagiarism of others' acts, and gives performance tips for various audiences. (Rev: BL 12/15/93) [793.8]

10878 Flowers, Sarah. *Sports in America* (5–8). Illus. (Overview) 1996, Lucent LB $17.96 (1-56006-178-2). This book explores current controversies in the sports world like commercialism, huge salaries, endorsements, racism, sexism, steroids, and the conflict between education and sports in colleges. (Rev: BL 9/1/96) [306.5]

10879 Gay, Kathlyn. *They Don't Wash Their Socks! Sports Superstitions* (6–9). Illus. 1990, Walker LB $14.85 (0-8027-6917-9). A compendium of myths and superstitions that helps explain some of the unusual behavior of players and coaches. (Rev: VOYA 8/90) [796]

10880 Glowacz, Stefan, and Uli Wiesmeier. *Rocks around the World* (9–12). Trans. by Martin Boysen. Illus. 1989, Sierra Club $24.95 (0-87156-677-X). The thrilling experiences of Glowacz, an internationally known rock climber, are captured in his text and the impressive photographs of Wiesmeier. (Rev: BL 3/15/89) [796.5]

10881 Greenberg, Judith E. *Getting into the Game: Women and Sports* (9–12). (Women Then—Women Now) 1997, Watts LB $25.00 (0-531-11329-9).

From Native American ball games and colonial skating parties to today's tennis, wrestling, road-racing, and gymnastics, this is a history of women's involvement in sports at the amateur, student, and professional levels. (Rev: SLJ 9/97; VOYA 10/97) [796]

10882 Gryski, Camilla. *Super String Games* (6–8). Illus. 1988, Morrow paper $6.95 (0-688-07684-X). Directions for 26 string games from around the world are given in text and diagrams. (Rev: BL 3/1/88; BR 5–6/88; SLJ 6/88) [793]

10883 Hinkson, Jim. *Lacrosse Fundamentals* (9–12). 1993, Firefly paper $15.95 (1-895629-11-X). Tips and techniques for stick selection, cradling, grip, catching, passing, offense and defense, shooting, face-offs, and goal-tending. (Rev: BL 11/15/93) [796.34]

10884 Jenkins, Dan, ed. *The Best American Sports Writing, 1995* (9–12). 1995, Houghton paper $12.95 (0-395-70069-8). From short to lengthy essays, this collection has something for nearly every sports fan. (Rev: BL 9/15/95) [796.0973]

10885 Judson, Karen. *Sports and Money: It's a Sell-out!* (7–12). (Issues in Focus) 1995, Enslow LB $19.95 (0-89490-622-4). A straightforward presentation that uses first-person accounts concerning the profitable financial side of being in the sports business. (Rev: BL 11/15/95; SLJ 6/96) [796.0619]

10886 Krakauer, Jon. *Eiger Dreams: Ventures among Men and Mountains* (9–12). 1990, Lyons Pr. $25.00 (1-55821-057-1). The author writes in 12 different short pieces about the dangers and thrills of mountaineering. (Rev: BL 4/1/90; SLJ 8/90) [795.5]

10887 Krakauer, Jon. *Into Thin Air: A Personal Account of the Mt. Everest Disaster* (10–12). 1997, Villard $24.95 (0-679-45752-6). A history of Mount Everest expeditions is intertwined with the disastrous expedition the author was a part of, during which five members were killed by a hurricane-strength blizzard. (Rev: BL 4/1/97; BR 11–12/97; SLJ 11/97) [796.5]

10888 Kuntzleman, Charles T. *The Complete Book of Walking* (10–12). 1989, Pocket Books paper $5.99 (0-671-70074-X). Tips on how to get the most out of walking are given plus good information on training. [796.4]

10889 Langley, Andrew. *Sports and Politics* (9–12). (World Issues) 1990, Rourke LB $25.27 (0-86592-117-2). A look at how politics influence sports. (Rev: BL 1/1/91) [796]

10890 Loughman, Michael. *Learning to Rock Climb* (10–12). Illus. 1981, Sierra Club paper $14.00 (0-87156-281-2). A guide to mountaineering that stresses safety and sound techniques. [796.5]

10891 Macy, Sue. *Winning Ways: A Photohistory of American Women in Sports* (7–10). Illus. 1996, Holt

$15.95 (0-8050-4147-8). Beginning with the 1880s bicycle craze, this book vividly chronicles the history of women's sports in America. (Rev: BL 6/1–15/96*; SLJ 8/96*; VOYA 10/96) [796]

10892 Macy, Sue, and Jane Gottesman, eds. *Play like a Girl: A Celebration of Women in Sports* (5–9). 1999, Holt $15.95 (0-8050-6071-5). Using material from books, photo archives, newspapers, and magazines, this book celebrates women in sports. (Rev: BL 7/99; SLJ 9/99; VOYA 12/99) [796]

10893 Malafronte, Victor A. *The Complete Book of Frisbee: The History of the Sport & the First Official Price Guide* (9–12). 1998, American Trends paper $19.95 (0-9663855-2-7). After discussing various flying-disc objects, games associated with them such as quoits, hoops, and skittles, and the history of the frisbee, this book focuses on the modern-day frisbee and related memorabilia, collecting, especially the historical Frisbie pie pan, and a price guide for collectors. (Rev: SLJ 5/99) [796]

10894 Margolis, Jeffrey A. *Violence in Sports* (6–12). Illus. 1999, Enslow $19.95 (0-89490-961-4). Using extensive documentation and numerous recent incidents, the author traces the decline in sportsmanship and the effect that violence is having on sports. (Rev: BL 9/1/99) [796]

10895 Miller, Thomas. *Taking Time Out: Recreation and Play* (5–8). (Our Human Family) 1995, Blackbirch LB $22.45 (1-56711-128-9). This book, complete with many color photographs, shows how people around the world relax and enjoy themselves, revealing many similarities. (Rev: SLJ 1/96) [790]

10896 Mizerak, Steve, and Joel Cohen. *Steve Mizerak's Pocket Billiards: Tips and Trick Shots* (10–12). 1982, Contemporary paper $12.95 (0-8092-5779-3). An introduction to billiards and tips on how to build one's skills. Also use: *Inside Pocket Billiards* (1973). [794.7]

10897 Neil, Randy L., and Elaine Hart. *The All-New Official Cheerleader's Handbook* (9–12). Illus. 1986, Simon & Schuster paper $14.95 (0-671-61210-7). This guide covers cheerleading from basic movements to complex stunts. [791]

10898 Nelson, Mariah Burton. *The Stronger Women Get, the More Men Love Football: Sexism and the American Culture of Sports* (9–12). 1994, Harcourt $22.95 (0-15-181393-0). A hard-hitting account asserting that women are better athletes than men and capable of competing with men. (Rev: BL 5/15/94) [796]

10899 Nicholson, Lois. *The Composite Guide to Lacrosse* (4–8). (The Composite Guide) 1998, Chelsea LB $16.95 (0-7910-4719-9). This book includes a history of the sport and its connections to early Native Americans as well as the rules, tech-

niques, its greatest players, and the reasons for its continued growth. (Rev: SLJ 12/98) [796.34]

10900 Nuwer, Hank. *Sports Scandals* (7–12). 1994, Watts LB $24.00 (0-531-11183-0). Profiles contemporary sports stars who have fallen from grace because of scandals ranging from gambling to sexual misconduct. (Rev: BL 8/94; SLJ 8/94; VOYA 12/94) [796]

10901 Orlick, Terry. *Cooperative Sports and Games Book* (9–12). 1996, Kendall Hunt paper $15.00 (0-7872-1928-2). This book describes 100 games that depend on cooperation, rather than competition, for success. [798]

10902 Paulsen, Gary. *Winterdance: The Fine Madness of Running the Iditarod* (9–12). 1994, Harcourt $21.95 (0-15-126227-6). This survival adventure describes the author's experiences running with his dog team in the 1,180-mile Alaskan Iditarod race. (Rev: BL 2/15/94; VOYA 10/94) [798.8]

10903 Paulsen, Gary. *Woodsong* (7–12). Illus. 1990, Bradbury paper $16.00 (0-02-770221-9). Paulsen describes his experiences with sleds and dogs and his entry into the grueling Iditarod Sled Dog Race in Alaska. (Rev: BL 8/90; SLJ 10/90) [796.5]

10904 Pearl, Bill, and Gary T. Moran. *Getting Stronger: Weight Training for Men & Women* (9–12). Illus. 1986, Random paper $19.95 (0-936070-04-8). A comprehensive account that begins with programs for the novice and continues through high levels and also covers topics like equipment, exercise, and nutrition. (Rev: SLJ 5/87) [796.4]

10905 Pejcic, Bogdan, and Rolf Meyer. *Pocket Billiards: Fundamentals of Technique and Play* (9–12). Trans. by Elisabeth E. Reinersmann. 1994, Sterling paper $4.95 (0-8069-0458-5). An illustrated introduction to the sport of billiards, providing insight into equipment, rules, and playing techniques. (Rev: BL 2/15/94) [794.7]

10906 Porter, David L., ed. *African-American Sports Greats: A Biographical Dictionary* (8–12). 1995, Greenwood $59.95 (0-313-28987-5). This reference book contains realistic, readable profiles of all the African American sports greats, both well known and less well known, with information about their lives, who influenced them, and the challenges they faced on the road to success. (Rev: BR 9–10/96; VOYA 4/96) [796]

10907 Press, David P. *A Multicultural Portrait of Professional Sports* (7–12). (Perspectives) 1993, Marshall Cavendish LB $28.50 (1-85435-661-5). This work explores the number of different races represented in modern sports. (Rev: BL 3/15/94; SLJ 3/95) [306.4]

10908 Quirk, Charles F., ed. *Sports and the Law: Major League Cases* (10–12). (American Law and

Society) 1996, Garland $61.00 (0-8153-0220-7). Fifty essays explore legal cases involving such controversies as the rights and responsibilities of coaches, franchise owners moving their teams from one city to another, and access to locker rooms by female journalists. (Rev: BR 11–12/96; SLJ 10/96) [796]

10909 Rice, Wayne, and Mike Yaconelli. *Play It! Over 400 Great Games for Groups* (8–12). Illus. 1986, Zondervan paper $12.99 (0-310-35191-X). All kinds of games—indoor, outdoor, active, cerebral, and those involving few or more players—are described. (Rev: BL 1/15/87) [790.1]

10910 Savage, Jeff. *Fundamental Strength Training* (5–9). (Fundamental Sports) 1998, Lerner $22.60 (0-8225-3461-4). Along with a discussion of the uses, advantages, and disadvantages of weight machines, free weights, and training without weights, this book focuses on exercises to develop specific parts of the body, stressing safety and with equal treatment of women and girls. (Rev: SLJ 2/99) [796.4]

10911 Savage, Jeff. *A Sure Thing? Sports & Gambling* (7–12). (Sports Issues) 1996, Lerner LB $23.93 (0-8225-3303-0). After a brief history of gambling, this book looks at the many forms of gambling available today, from church bingo games to horse racing to Las Vegas casinos, with a focus on the connection between gambling and sports and emphasis on the dangers of gambling addiction. (Rev: BL 7/97; SLJ 11/97) [796]

10912 Schultz, Ron. *Looking Inside Sports Aerodynamics* (5–8). Illus. (X-Ray Vision) 1992, John Muir paper $6.95 (1-56261-065-1). Uses what scientists know about air (effects of gravity, turbulence, drag, lift) to explain what happens when we throw or hit all kinds of balls and other objects. (Rev: BL 1/15/93; SLJ 2/93) [796]

10913 Schwarzenegger, Arnold. *Arnold's Bodybuilding for Men* (10–12). Illus. 1981, Simon & Schuster paper $16.00 (0-671-53163-8). A guide to exercise and weight lifting that stresses a total fitness program. [613.7]

10914 Sherrow, Victoria. *Encyclopedia of Women and Sports* (7–12). 1996, ABC-CLIO LB $75.00 (0-87436-826-X). This alphabetically arranged book on women's involvement in sports from ancient Greece to modern times covers athletes, sports, organizations, and social issues such as discrimination, steroid use, pregnancy, and eating disorders. (Rev: BL 9/1/97; BR 9–10/97; SLJ 8/97) [796]

10915 Smith, Lissa. *Nike Is a Goddess: The History of Women in Sports* (9–12). 1998, Grove Atlantic $24.00 (0-87113-726-7). This is an excellent reference and an interesting read on the history of women in sports that covers not only the obvious ones like tennis and softball, but also the more esoteric like kayaking and equestrian sports. (Rev: BL 9/1/98; SLJ 4/99) [796]

10916 Steiner, Andy. *A Sporting Chance: Sports and Gender* (4–8). (Sports Issues) 1995, Lerner LB $22.60 (0-8225-3300-6). An overview of the hurdles that female athletes have had to overcome and the persistent inequality between men and women in sports at all levels, from Little League to the pros. (Rev: BL 1/1–15/96; SLJ 1/96) [796]

10917 Weiss, Ann E. *Money Games: The Business of Sports* (7–12). 1993, Houghton $14.95 (0-395-57444-7). Reviews the place of sports in history and examines the financial forces that shape sports today: profit motive, league control, TV rights, gambling, endorsement contracts, and others. (Rev: BL 4/1/93; SLJ 6/93; VOYA 8/93) [796]

10918 Wirth, Dick. *Ballooning: The Complete Guide to Riding the Winds* (9–12). Illus. 1984, Random paper $12.95 (0-394-72796-7). The parts of the balloon are fully described as well as navigational tips. [797.5]

10919 Woods, Karl Morrow. *The Sports Success Book: The Athlete's Guide to Sports Achievement* (9–12). Illus. 1985, Copperfield Pr. $17.95 (0-933857-00-4); paper $12.95 (0-933857-01-2). A guide to becoming a successful athlete from junior high through the Olympics to the pros. (Rev: BL 10/15/85; SLJ 4/86; VOYA 12/85) [796]

10920 Woolum, Janet. *Outstanding Women Athletes: Who They Are & How They Influenced Sports in America* (6–12). Illus. 1998, Oryx $65.00 (1-57356-120-7). This update of the 1992 edition on women in sports captures many of the recent advances that women have made, adds 26 new biographies and a new chapter on outstanding teams, and includes a sport-by-sport annotated bibliography and statistics. (Rev: BL 9/1/98; SLJ 11/98; VOYA 12/98) [796]

10921 Young, Perry D. *Lesbians and Gays and Sports* (8–12). (Issues in Lesbian and Gay Life) 1995, Chelsea $24.95 (0-7910-2611-6); paper $12.95 (0-7910-2951-4). Looks at homosexuals in sports, with biographies of Kopay, Tilden, King, and Navratilova. (Rev: BL 6/1–15/95) [796]

Automobile Racing

10922 Benson, Michael. *Crashes & Collisions* (5–8). (Race Car Legends) 1997, Chelsea $16.95 (0-7910-4435-1). This book focuses on multi-car pileups in car racing and people who have survived them. (Rev: SLJ 2/98) [629.228]

10923 Gaillard, Frye, and Kyle Petty. *200 M.P.H.: A Sizzling Season in the Petty/NASCAR Dynasty*

(9–12). 1993, St. Martin's $19.95 (0-312-09732-8). Petty describes NASCAR racing from the viewpoint of a third-generation driver, emphasizing the camaraderie among drivers, crews, and families. (Rev: BL 10/1/93) [796.72]

10924 Golenbock, Peter. *American Zoom: Stock Car Racing—from the Dirt Tracks to Daytona* (9–12). 1993, Macmillan $23.00 (0-02-544615-0). Presents the history of the sport from the mouths of drivers, mechanics, crew chiefs, and promoters. (Rev: BL 9/15/93*) [796.7]

10925 Parsons, Benny. *Inside Track: A Photo Documentary of NASCAR Stock Car Racing* (9–12). 1996, Artisan $24.95 (1-885183-59-3). This book examines the National Association of Stock Car Racing and NASCAR races, traveling stock car shows, the development of super speedways, and the top drivers of yesterday and today. (Rev: VOYA 10/97) [796.7]

10926 Perry, David, and Barry Gifford. *Hot Rod* (9–12). 1997, Chronicle paper $22.95 (0-8118-1593-5). The timeless, unique hot rod culture is captured in 80 sepia photographs of speed racers, drag cars, and souped-up automobiles of all kinds, along with their gearheads, greasers, dollies, and fans—tattoos, beards, shades, cigarettes, and all. (Rev: VOYA 4/98) [629.222]

10927 Rubel, David. *How to Drive an Indy Race Car* (7–12). (Masters of Motion) 1992, John Muir paper $6.95 (1-56261-062-7). Describes in detail diverse aspects of Indy car racing—and with a touch of comedy. (Rev: BL 2/1/93; SLJ 2/93) [796.7]

10928 Savage, Jeff. *Drag Racing* (4–8). (Action Events) 1996, Crestwood LB $14.95 (0-89686-890-7); paper $4.95 (0-382-39293-0). The thrill of drag racing is conveyed through many action photographs and a simple text. Also use: *Mud Racing* and *Super Cross Motorcycle Racing* (both 1996). (Rev: SLJ 2/97) [796.7]

10929 Taylor, Rich. *Indy: Seventy-Five Years of Racing's Greatest Spectacle* (9–12). 1991, St. Martin's $39.95 (0-312-05447-5). A detailed history of the great car racing event from its beginning in 1911 through its seventy-fifth running, with more than 500 photos. (Rev: BL 5/15/91) [796.7]

10930 Williams, Frank, and Flavio Briatore. *Renault Formula 1 Motor Racing Book* (5–8). Illus. 1996, DK Publg. $16.95 (0-7894-0440-0). A fascinating introduction to the world of Grand Prix racing, with material on car care and maintenance. (Rev: BL 12/15/96) [796.72]

Baseball

10931 Asinof, Eliot. *Eight Men Out* (9–12). 1981, Holtzman $24.95 (0-941372-00-6); Holt paper $14.00 (0-8050-0346-0). The story of a shameful incident in baseball history when 8 Chicago White Sox players in 1919 were bribed into losing the World Series. [796.357]

10932 Baker, Dusty, et al. *You Can Teach Hitting: A Systematic Approach to Hitting for Parents, Coaches and Players* (9–12). 1993, Bittinger paper $24.95 (0-940279-73-8). Presents systematic instruction on hitting a baseball, including drills and situational tips. (Rev: BL 12/1/92*) [796.357]

10933 Blake, Mike. *Baseball Chronicles: An Oral History of Baseball Through the Decades* (9–12). 1994, Betterway paper $16.95 (1-55870-350-0). Oral histories from 140 former and current major-league players, organized by decade through the early 1990s. (Rev: BL 4/15/94) [796.357]

10934 Cockcroft, James D. *Latinos in Béisbol* (9–12). (The Hispanic Experience in the Americas) 1996, Watts LB $25.00 (0-531-11284-5). This book points out that baseball had its roots in Latin America, where it is still very popular, examines the discrimination against Hispanics in the major leagues throughout the early part of the 20th century and their continued underrepresentation in management and coaching positions today, and cites outstanding Hispanic players. (Rev: SLJ 3/97) [796.357]

10935 Collins, Ace, and John Hillman. *Blackball Superstars: Legendary Players of the Negro Baseball Leagues* (6–9). 1999, Avisson LB $19.95 (1-888105-38-0). This book profiles 12 stars of the Negro Baseball Leagues, including Satchel Paige and Josh Gibson, all of whom are now in the National Baseball Hall of Fame. (Rev: SLJ 8/99) [796.357]

10936 Dixon, Phil, and Patrick J. Hannigan. *The Negro Baseball Leagues: A Photographic History* (9–12). 1992, Amereon $34.95 (0-8488-0425-2). Celebrates the defunct Negro Baseball Leagues with anecdotes, newspaper accounts, and hundreds of photos. (Rev: BL 10/1/92) [796.357]

10937 Eisenhammer, Fred, and Jim Binkley. *Baseball's Most Memorable Trades: Superstars Swapped, All-Stars Copped and Megadeals That Flopped* (8–12). 1997, McFarland paper $28.50 (0-7864-0198-2). The causes and effects of the top 25 baseball trades since the turn of the century are covered. (Rev: VOYA 10/97) [796.323]

10938 Fiffer, Steve. *How to Watch Baseball: A Fan's Guide to Savoring the Fine Points of the Game* (9–12). Illus. 1987, Facts on File paper $10.95 (0-8160-2001-9). A guide for spectators on how to enjoy the subtleties of baseball. (Rev: BL 3/15/87) [796.357]

10939 Forker, Dom. *Baseball Brain Teasers* (7–12). 1986, Sterling paper $6.95 (0-8069-6284-4). A baseball trivia book in which baseball situations are described and questions are asked about them. (Rev: BR 11–12/86; SLJ 12/86) [796.357]

10940 Fremon, David K. *The Negro Baseball Leagues* (7–12). (American Events) 1994, Silver Burdett paper $7.95 (0-382-24730-2). A history of baseball from the segregated Negro Baseball League's point of view. (Rev: BL 3/15/95) [796.357]

10941 Galt, Margot F. *Up to the Plate: The All American Girls Professional Baseball League* (6–9). (Sports Legacy) 1995, Lerner LB $23.93 (0-8225-3326-X). This history of the All-American Girls Professional Baseball League includes interviews with the players and their reactions to the movie *A League of Their Own*. (Rev: BL 7/95; SLJ 6/95) [796.357]

10942 Gardner, Robert, and Dennis Shortelle. *The Forgotten Players: The Story of Black Baseball in America* (5–8). 1993, Walker LB $13.85 (0-8027-8249-3). Description of the lives of players in the Negro Baseball Leagues. (Rev: BL 2/15/93) [796.357]

10943 Gay, Douglas, and Kathlyn Gay. *The Not-So-Minor Leagues* (5–8). Illus. 1996, Millbrook LB $22.40 (1-56294-921-7). A history of the minor leagues, unusual facts about them, and the reasons for their increased importance in the world of baseball. (Rev: BL 5/15/96; BR 11–12/96; SLJ 6/96) [796.357]

10944 Gilbert, Thomas. *Baseball at War: World War II & the Fall of the Color Line* (7–10). (The American Game) 1997, Watts LB $24.00 (0-531-11330-2). Beginning with Joe DiMaggio's winning streak in 1941, this book covers baseball history during World War II, including two chapters on how Branch Rickey and Jackie Robinson broke the color barrier. (Rev: BL 7/97; SLJ 7/97; VOYA 10/97) [796.357]

10945 Gilbert, Thomas. *Damn Yankees: Casey, Yogi, Whitey, and the Mick* (6–9). (The American Game) 1997, Watts $24.00 (0-531-11338-8). An exciting, partisan account of the New York Yankees under Casey Stengel, with material on Yankee greats Babe Ruth, Lou Gehrig, and Joe DiMaggio, and the stars between 1949 and 1964—Mickey Mantle, Whitey Ford, Yogi Berra, and Roger Maris. The author recounts each season, weaving in the rivalry with the then Brooklyn Dodgers and New York Giants and the dramatic story of Jackie Robinson. (Rev: BR 5–6/98; SLJ 12/97; VOYA 4/98) [796.357]

10946 Gilbert, Thomas. *Deadball: Major League Baseball before Babe Ruth* (8–12). Illus. (The American Game) 1996, Watts LB $24.00 (0-531-11262-4). In the deadball era before Babe Ruth changed the

game in 1920, baseballs were softer, ballparks larger, and contact hitters like Ty Cobb the stars. (Rev: BL 9/1/96; SLJ 9/96; VOYA 8/97) [796.357]

10947 Gilbert, Thomas. *The Good Old Days: Baseball in the 1930s* (6–9). (The American Game) 1996, Watts LB $24.00 (0-531-11278-0). Although sometimes called the "golden age of baseball," the author points out that the 1930s was a difficult time for the sport because of the Depression. The book summarizes changes such as as night games, radio broadcasts, the all-star game, and the Hall of Fame, and reviews each season, focusing on funny anecdotes and dramatic stories. (Rev: SLJ 2/97) [796.357]

10948 Gilbert, Thomas. *The Soaring Twenties: Babe Ruth & the Home-run Decade* (7–12). (The American Game) 1996, Watts LB $24.00 (0-531-11279-9). This book describes an era of spectacular sports stars and business tycoons who "owned" the newly evolving major leagues, widespread graft and game-fixing, beginning with the Black Sox gambling scandal, and the recovery of the game under Babe Ruth and other great players of the 1920s. Coverage is also given to race problems and the Negro Leagues. (Rev: SLJ 1/97) [796.357]

10949 Hammer, Trudy J. *The All-American Girls Professional Baseball League* (7–12). Illus. (American Events) 1994, Silver Burdett LB $18.95 (0-02-742595-9). The story of this pioneering effort to bring women into professional baseball and its eventual demise. (Rev: BL 3/15/95; SLJ 3/95; VOYA 5/95) [796.357]

10950 Isaacs, Neil D. *Innocence and Wonder: Baseball Through the Eyes of Batboys* (9–12). 1994, Masters Pr. paper $14.95 (1-57028-000-2). Major league batboys from 75 years of baseball history describe their memories of the game and its players. (Rev: BL 9/1/94) [796.357]

10951 James, Bill, and Mary A. Wirth. *The Bill James Historical Baseball Abstract* (9–12). 1988, Random $29.95 (0-394-53713-0); paper $15.95 (0-394-75805-6). This volume provides historical statistics and commentary on baseball. (Rev: BR 11–12/88; SLJ 8/88; VOYA 12/88) [796.357]

10952 Layden, Joe. *The Great American Baseball Strike* (5–8). (Headliners) 1995, Millbrook LB $23.40 (1-56294-930-6). A discussion of the issues that led to the 1995 baseball strike, with a review of the history of professional baseball and of the stormy relationship between the owners and players. (Rev: BL 11/15/95; SLJ 1/96) [796.357]

10953 Light, Jonathan F. *The Cultural Encyclopedia of Baseball* (7–12). 1997, McFarland $75.00 (0-7864-0311-X). This book contains entries on a broad range of baseball topics, such as alcoholism in baseball, baseball in different countries, and the dumbest players, as well as the standard information like famous players, managers, perfect games and no-hitters, statistics, ballparks, and important games. (Rev: BL 9/1/97; SLJ 2/98) [796.357]

10954 McCarver, Tim, and Danny Peary. *Tim McCarver's Baseball for Brain Surgeons & Other Fans: Understanding & Interpreting the Game so You Can Watch It Like a Pro* (10–12). 1998, Villard $23.00 (0-375-50085-5). For the learned baseball fan, this overview looks at the finer aspects of the game, subtle strategies, and complex interpretations. (Rev: SLJ 9/98) [796.357]

10955 McKissack, Patricia, and Fredrick McKissack. *Black Diamond: The Story of the Negro Baseball Leagues* (6–10). Illus. 1994, Scholastic $14.95 (0-590-45809-4). A history of African Americans in baseball and the Negro Baseball Leagues, until Jackie Robinson's entry into the major leagues. (Rev: BL 4/94; VOYA 10/94) [796.357]

10956 McRae, Michael. *Home Run: A Modern Approach to Baseball Skill Building* (8–12). 1998, Polestar Book Publishers paper $15.95 (1-896095-29-1). This book breaks down each of the fundamentals of baseball into small units, explaining and illustrating each thoroughly. Chapters cover such topics as throwing, receiving, hitting, fielding, and base running, each with a good selection of drills. (Rev: BR 1–2/99; VOYA 12/98) [796.357]

10957 Macy, Sue. *A Whole New Ballgame: The Story of the All-American Girls Professional Baseball League* (6–10). 1993, Holt $14.95 (0-8050-1942-1). Celebrates the women who played in the All-American Girls Professional Baseball League, started by P. K. Wrigley during World War II. (Rev: BL 3/15/93; SLJ 5/93*; VOYA 12/93) [796.357]

10958 Marazzi, Rich, and Len Fiorito. *Aaron to Zuverink* (10–12). 1984, Avon paper $4.50 (0-380-68445-4). More than 1,000 major league players of the 1950s are profiled. [796.357]

10959 Margolies, Jacob. *The Negro Leagues: The Story of Black Baseball* (7–12). (African American Experience) 1993, Watts LB $24.00 (0-531-11130-X). The history of African American baseball from the 1880s through the birth of the Negro Leagues in the 1920s and their demise in the 1950s. (Rev: BL 2/15/94; VOYA 6/94) [793.357]

10960 Meyer, Gladys C. *Softball for Girls & Women* (10–12). Illus. 1982, Macmillan paper $11.95 (0-684-18140-1). All facets of softball are explored in this guide geared to the specific needs of women. [796.357]

10961 Nash, Bruce, and Allan Zullo. *The Baseball Hall of Shame: Young Fans Edition* (5–8). Illus. 1990, Pocket Books paper $2.99 (0-671-69354-9). For younger readers, here is an edition of the authors' collection of baseball's worst moments. (Rev: SLJ 7/90) [796.357]

10962 Nash, Bruce, and Allan Zullo. *The Baseball Hall of Shame's Warped Record Book* (9–12). 1991, Macmillan paper $9.95 (0-02-029485-9). An amusing collection of unusual baseball "records," such as "longest time trapped in a bathroom during a game" and other weird or embarrassing incidents. (Rev: BL 9/15/91) [796.357]

10963 Ritter, Lawrence. *The Story of Baseball* (6–12). 1999, Morrow $16.00 (0-688-16264-9). This history of baseball from its origins to the McGwire-Sosa race for the record book in 1998 also contains material on elements of the game like pitching and fielding. (Rev: BL 4/1/99; SLJ 4/99; VOYA 10/99) [796.357]

10964 Schenin, Richard. *Field of Screams: The Dark Underside of America's National Pastime* (9–12). 1994, Norton paper $14.95 (0-393-31138-4). A chronologically arranged collection of items from the "underside" of baseball history. (Rev: BL 3/15/94) [796.357]

10965 Schmidt, Mike, and Rob Ellis. *The Mike Schmidt Study: Hitting Theory, Skills and Techniques* (9–12). 1994, McGriff & Bell $22.95 (0-9634609-1-9); paper $18.95 (0-9634609-2-7). Designed to help coaches teach Little Leaguers how to hit, Schmidt explains the 3 major systems and the mental aspects involved. (Rev: BL 12/15/93) [796.35726]

10966 Skipper, John C. *Umpires: Classic Baseball Stories from the Men Who Made the Calls* (8–12). 1997, McFarland paper $24.50 (0-7864-0364-0). Great, memorable moments in the careers of 19 umpires. (Rev: VOYA 12/97) [796.323]

10967 Sports Illustrated. *Home Run Heroes* (9–12). 1998, Simon & Schuster $20.00 (0-684-86357-X). Great photos and sports writing capture the exciting race in 1998 major league season to break the home-run records of baseball greats Babe Ruth and Roger Maris. (Rev: SLJ 4/99) [796.357]

10968 Stewart, John. *The Baseball Clinic: Skills and Drills for Better Baseball: A Handbook for Players and Coaches* (6–10). 1999, Burford paper $12.95 (1-58080-073-4). Written by a major league scout, this book contains useful tips for young baseball players in the areas of pitching, fielding, hitting, base running, and catching. (Rev: SLJ 7/99) [796.357]

10969 Stewart, Mark. *Baseball: A History of the National Pastime* (7–10). (Watts History of Sports) 1998, Watts $32.00 (0-531-11455-4). A solid overview of the history of baseball, with good coverage of off-the-field developments like labor-management conflicts and the influence of free agency. (Rev: SLJ 7/98) [796.357]

10970 Stewart, Mark, and Mike Kennedy. *Home Run Heroes: Mark McGwire & Sammy Sosa* (4–8). 1999, Millbrook LB $22.90 (0-7613-1559-4); paper $6.95 (0-7613-1045-2). This account captures the excitement of the home-run race between McGwire and Sosa during the 1998 season, with alternating chapters focusing on the contrasting backgrounds and personalities of the two stars. (Rev: SLJ 8/99) [796.357]

10971 Thorn, John. *Treasures of the Baseball Hall of Fame: The Official Companion to the Collection at Cooperstown* (9–12). 1998, Villard $39.95 (0-375-50143-6). A thrilling history of baseball as reconstructed through some of the exhibits and memorabilia found at the Baseball Hall of Fame in Cooperstown, New York. (Rev: SLJ 1/99) [796.357]

10972 Turner, Frederick. *When the Boys Came Back: Baseball and 1946* (10–12). 1996, Holt $27.50 (0-8050-2645-2). The story of the 1946 baseball season, when many major leaguers returned from the war and the Boston Red Sox and the St. Louis Cardinals played in the World Series. (Rev: BL 6/1–15/96; SLJ 2/97) [796.357]

10973 Ward, Geoffrey, and Ken Burns. *Baseball: An Illustrated History* (9–12). 1994, Knopf $60.00 (0-679-40459-7). A history of the game, published in conjunction with a PBS documentary, with essays, facts, and over 500 photos. (Rev: BL 7/94*) [796.357]

10974 Ward, Geoffrey, et al. *Who Invented the Game?* (4–8). Illus. (Baseball, the American Epic) 1994, Knopf LB $16.99 (0-679-96750-8). The story of the origins of baseball including the accomplishments of Abner Doubleday. (Rev: BL 12/15/94; SLJ 1/95) [796.357]

Basketball

10975 Anderson, Dave. *The Story of Basketball* (4–8). Illus. 1997, Morrow $16.00 (0-688-14316-4). An updated introduction to basketball history, rules, players, and teams. (Rev: BL 1/1–15/98; SLJ 10/97) [796.32]

10976 Bird, Larry. *Bird on Basketball: How-to Strategies from the Great Celtics Champion.* Rev. ed. (8–12). Illus. 1988, Addison-Wesley paper $16.00 (0-201-14209-0). The basketball star associated with the Boston Celtics gives advice to young players on basics. [796.32]

10977 Frey, Darcy. *The Last Shot: City Streets, Basketball Dreams* (9–12). 1994, Houghton $19.95 (0-395-59770-6). Chronicles a group of teenagers playing for one of the best high school teams in New York City. (Rev: BL 12/1/94) [796.323]

10978 Guffey, Greg. *The Greatest Basketball Story Ever Told: The Milan Miracle, Then and Now* (9–12). 1993, Indiana Univ. Pr. $29.95 (0-253-

32688-5); paper $14.95 (0-253-32689-3). The real-life events that inspired the movie *Hoosiers* are explored in this look at the 1954 Milan High School basketball team and changes since then. (Rev: BL 12/1/93) [796.323]

10979 Huet, John. *Soul of the Game: Images & Voices of Street Basketball* (10–12). 1997, Workman $30.00 (0-7611-1028-3). This book chronicles the history of street basketball as played in New York City, highlighting its players—both unsung and famous—and their feats, their lives, and their local tournaments that once drew not only the gifted amateurs but also the pro-basketball stars. (Rev: SLJ 4/98) [796.323]

10980 Jackson, Phil, and Hugh Delehanty. *Scared Hoops: Spiritual Lessons of a Hardwood Warrior* (9–12). 1995, Hyperion $22.95 (0-7868-6206-8). Jackson, head coach of the Chicago Bulls, offers the coaching philosophy that helped him get his team to pull together spiritually and attain a common goal. (Rev: BL 9/1/95) [796.323]

10981 Jeremiah, Maryalyce. *Basketball: The Woman's Game* (7–12). Illus. 1983, Athletic Inst. paper $5.95 (0-87670-069-5). The fundamentals of basketball as seen through the specific needs of female players. [796.32]

10982 Kessler, Lauren. *Full Court Press* (10–12). 1997, Dutton paper $23.95 (0-525-94035-9). The story of the low-rated Oregon Ducks, a university women basketball team, their heroic coach, Jody Runge, and how they battled their way to the 1994 NCAA tournament, including conflicts and emotional experiences, and their struggles for a share of the university's sports facilities, equipment, and honor they deserved. (Rev: BL 3/15/97; SLJ 2/98) [796.323]

10983 Lace, William W. *The Houston Rockets Basketball Team* (5–8). (Great Sports Teams) 1997, Enslow LB $18.95 (0-89490-792-1). A profile of the Houston Rockets, with sketches of their key players. (Rev: BL 10/15/97) [796.323]

10984 Lieberman-Cline, Nancy, and Robin Roberts. *Basketball for Women* (7–12). Illus. 1995, Human Kinetics paper $16.95 (0-87322-610-0). After a brief history of women's basketball, Lieberman-Cline, who has played in college, Olympics, and professional women's basketball, discusses the commitment required of a serious basketball player, how to formulate a plan for skill development, the recruitment process, and other concerns, and devotes 7 chapters to more than 100 drill exercises. (Rev: VOYA 6/96) [796.323]

10985 McKissack, Fredrick. *Black Hoops: African-Americans in Basketball* (6–10). 1999, Scholastic $15.95 (0-590-48712-4). This work gives a concise history of basketball from the early days to the present, documenting the contributions of black players and teams and placing the development of the sport in a social and historic context. The final chapter presents an overview of African American women's participation in basketball. (Rev: BL 2/15/99; BR 9–10/99; SLJ 3/99; VOYA 10/99) [796.323 089 96073]

10986 Miller, Reggie, and Gene Wojciechowski. *I Love Being the Enemy: A Season on the Court with the NBA's Best Shooter and Sharpest Tongue* (9–12). 1995, Simon & Schuster $23.00 (0-684-81389-0). Miller's diary kept during the 1994-1995 season reveals a side of him not often seen. (Rev: BL 12/1/95) [796.323]

10987 Morris, Greggory. *Basketball Basics* (7–9). Illus. 1976, TreeHouse $6.95 (0-13-072256-1). A fine book for the beginner that explains basic moves, shots, and skills. [796.32]

10988 Mullin, Chris. *The Young Basketball Player: A Young Enthusiast's Guide to Basketball* (4–8). 1995, DK Publg. $15.95 (0-7894-0220-3). Such basketball techniques and team tactics as dribbling, passing, and scoring are described, along with a summary of the history of the sport and an explanation of the rules. (Rev: BL 11/1/95; SLJ 1/96) [796.323]

10989 Nash, Bruce, and Allan Zullo. *The Basketball Hall of Shame* (9–12). (Hall of Shame) 1991, Pocket Books paper $10.00 (0-671-69414-6). Brief, humorous basketball stories, including battles with referees, strange shots, and weird happenings. (Rev: BL 11/1/91) [796.323]

10990 Owens, Thomas S. *The Chicago Bulls Basketball Team* (5–8). Illus. (Great Sports Teams) 1997, Enslow LB $18.95 (0-89490-793-X). A history of the Chicago Bulls, with emphasis on the stars who have made the team famous. (Rev: BL 10/15/97) [796.323]

10991 Pietrusza, David. *The Phoenix Suns Basketball Team* (5–8). (Great Sports Teams) 1997, Enslow LB $18.95 (0-89490-795-6). An introduction to the Phoenix Suns, their great games, and their star players. (Rev: BL 10/15/97) [796.323]

10992 Pluto, Terry. *Falling from Grace: Can Pro Basketball Be Saved?* (9–12). 1995, Simon & Schuster $22.50 (0-684-80766-1). An examination of a declining sport, with comments from 52 experts bolstering Pluto's assertion that a trash-talking, in-your-face culture of disrespect dominates pro basketball. (Rev: BL 11/15/95) [796.323]

10993 Ponti, James. *WNBA: Stars of Women's Basketball* (5–8). 1999, Pocket Books paper $4.99 (0-671-03275-5). This book introduces women's professional basketball teams and profiles key individual players. (Rev: SLJ 8/99) [796.323]

10994 Preller, James. *NBA Game Day: An Inside Look at the NBA* (4–8). Illus. 1997, Scholastic paper $10.95 (0-590-76742-9). A photo-collage of a day in the life of the NBA, from morning workout to cleanup after the game, with pictures of prominent players at work and play. (Rev: BL 1/1–15/98; VOYA 8/98) [796.323]

10995 Rogers, Glenn. *The San Antonio Spurs Basketball Team* (5–8). (Great Sports Teams) 1997, Enslow LB $18.95 (0-89490-797-2). Profiles of important players and stories behind important games are included in this introduction to the San Antonio Spurs. (Rev: BL 10/15/97) [796.323]

10996 Stewart, Mark. *Basketball: A History of Hoops* (6–10). (Watts History of Sports) 1999, Watts $32.00 (0-531-11492-9). A chronological history of basketball that gives alternating treatment to college and pro games and includes how basketball has been influenced by off-the-court financial and social pressures. (Rev: SLJ 8/99) [796.323]

10997 Sullivan, George. *All about Basketball* (5–8). 1991, Putnam paper $9.99 (0-399-21793-2). Surveys the history of basketball from its beginnings in 1891 through the NBA 1991 playoffs. (Rev: BL 1/1/92) [796.323]

11998 Vancil, Mark. *NBA Basketball Basics* (5–9). 1995, Sterling $16.95 (0-8069-0927-7). A book of basics for young people, loaded with full-color photos. (Rev: BL 4/15/95; SLJ 7/96) [796.323]

11999 Vancil, Mark. *NBA Basketball Offense Basics* (4–8). Illus. 1996, Sterling $17.95 (0-8069-4892-2). Action photos and lively text are used to demonstrate such techniques as dribbling, passing, and shooting. (Rev: BL 9/1/96; SLJ 7/96) [796.332]

11000 Vitale, Dick, and Dick Weiss. *Holding Court: Reflections on the Game I Love* (9–12). 1995, Masters Pr. $22.95 (1-57028-037-1). College basketball's voice on ESPN and a former coach himself, Vitale reflects on various aspects of the sport, including the intense pressure on coaches to win. (Rev: BL 12/1/95) [796.323]

11001 Weatherspoon, Teresa, et al. *Teresa Weatherspoon's Basketball for Girls* (7–12). 1999, Wiley paper $14.95 (0-471-31784-5). This manual, by the famous basketball star and Olympic gold medalist, gives wonderful, practical information about playing the game and becoming a healthy, happy athlete. (Rev: BL 7/99; SLJ 8/99) [796.323]

11002 Wilker, Josh. *The Harlem Globetrotters* (5–10). (African American Achievers) 1996, Chelsea LB $19.95 (0-7910-2585-3); paper $8.95 (0-7910-2586-1). This is a chronologically arranged history of the Harlem Globetrotters, the basketball team that has been entertaining crowds since 1927. (Rev: SLJ 3/97) [796.357]

Bicycling, Motorcycling, etc.

11003 Abt, Samuel. *Tour de France: Three Weeks to Glory* (9–12). 1991, Bicycle Books $22.95 (0-933201-40-0). Overview of the world's largest, most prestigious bicycle race, its origins, and the sport's leading riders with coverage ending in 1990. (Rev: BL 6/1/91) [796.62]

11004 Ballantine, Richard, and Richard Grant. *Richard's Bicycle Repair Manual* (9–12). 1994, DK Publg. paper $9.95 (1-56458-484-4). An illustrated handbook for the home bicycle mechanic, covering routine and preventive maintenance and emergency repairs. (Rev: BL 3/15/94; SLJ 9/94; VOYA 2/95) [629.28]

11005 Bennett, Jim. *The Complete Motorcycle Book* (9–12). 1995, Facts on File $27.95 (0-8160-2899-0). The definitive work on buying, riding, and caring for motorcycles. (Rev: BL 12/15/94; SLJ 6/95) [629.28]

11006 Bicycling Magazine, eds. *Cycling for Women* (9–12). Illus. 1989, Rodale paper $8.95 (0-87857-811-0). General tips for both sexes are interspersed with those specifically aimed at women's abilities and endurance levels. (Rev: BL 3/15/89) [796.6]

11007 Coombs, Charles. *All-Terrain Bicycling* (6–10). Illus. 1987, Holt $14.95 (0-8050-0204-9). After an introduction to various kinds of bicycles and their parts, Coombs gives tips that emphasize safety in all kinds of biking. (Rev: BL 3/15/87; BR 11–12/87; SLJ 8/87; VOYA 8/87) [796.6]

11008 Hautzig, David. *Pedal Power: How a Mountain Bike Is Made* (4–8). 1996, Lodestar $15.99 (0-525-67508-6). A fascinating account of the origins and birth of the mountain bike and the processes, materials, and machinery involved in making them, with pointers on how to choose and maintain one. (Rev: BL 4/15/96; SLJ 4/96) [629.227]

11009 King, Andy. *Fundamental Mountain Biking* (5–9). (Fundamental Sports) 1996, Lerner LB $22.60 (0-8225-3459-2). This introduction to mountain biking discusses its history, equipment, maneuvers, competitions, tricks, safety reminders, and repair tips. (Rev: SLJ 2/97) [796.64]

11010 LeMond, Greg, and Kent Gordis. *Greg LeMond's Complete Book of Bicycling* (9–12). Illus. 1987, Putnam paper $14.95 (0-399-51594-1). For both the beginner and specialist, this book covers equipment, techniques, and training. (Rev: BL 10/1/87) [796.6]

11011 Wilson, Hugo. *The Ultimate Motorcycle Book* (9–12). 1993, DK Publg. $29.95 (1-56458-303-1). Color photos of over 200 bikes illustrate this guide to U.S. and imported motorcycles, their history—including their use in World War II—racing, touring, motocross, and customizing. (Rev: BL 11/1/93) [629.227]

Camping, Hiking, Backpacking, and Mountaineering

11012 Boy Scouts of America. *Fieldbook* (5–9). Illus. 1985, Boy Scouts of America paper $16.25 (0-8395-3200-8). Though written specifically for the Boy Scouts, this is a fine guide for the outdoor person interested in camping, hiking, or related activities. (Rev: BL 8/85) [369]

11013 Bryson, Bill. *A Walk in the Woods: Rediscovering America on the Appalachian Trail* (10–12). 1998, Broadway Books $25.00 (0-7679-0251-3). An often hilarious, sometimes moving account of 2 inept, out-of-condition adventurers and their attempts to hike the Appalachian Trail. (Rev: BL 9/15/98; SLJ 10/98) [796.54]

11014 Cook, Charles. *The Essential Guide to Hiking in the United States* (9–12). 1991, Michael Kesend paper $19.95 (0-935576-41-X). Contains information on such hiking essentials as shoes, clothing, safety, and the best areas for hiking and the trails in each state. (Rev: BL 12/1/91) [996.5]

11015 Drake, Jane, and Ann Love. *The Kids Campfire Book* (4–8). Illus. 1998, Kids Can paper $9.95 (1-55074-539-5). This manual describes how to select a location, build safe campfires, and later douse them, suggests fireside activities, including some science demonstrations, and offers safe cooking tips. (Rev: BL 3/15/98; SLJ 4/98) [796.54]

11016 Fletcher, Colin. *The Complete Walker III: The Joys and Techniques of Hiking and Backpacking* (10–12). Illus. 1984, Knopf $22.95 (0-394-51962-0); paper $19.00 (0-394-72264-7). This readable, thorough guide to hiking and backpacking first appeared in 1969 and is in its third edition. [796.5]

11017 Logue, Victoria, et al. *Kids Outdoors* (5–9). Illus. 1996, McGraw-Hill paper $14.95 (0-07-038477-0). A guide for young campers and hikers that includes material on sleeping bags, tents, equipment, food preparation, wildlife, games, and even tips for backyard campers. (Rev: BL 9/15/96) [796.5]

11018 McManners, Hugh. *The Complete Wilderness Training Book* (9–12). 1994, DK Publg. $29.95 (1-56458-488-7). Survival techniques for the hardcore survivalist in familiar as well as extreme environments. This British import is more international in scope than American versions. (Rev: BL 5/15/94; VOYA 12/94) [613.6]

11019 Manning, Harvey. *Backpacking One Step at a Time*. Rev. ed. (9–12). Illus. 1986, Random paper $15.00 (0-394-72939-0). In addition to information on equipment and techniques, this book tells how to get the most enjoyment possible out of backpacking. (Rev: SLJ 9/86; VOYA 8/86) [796.5]

11020 Randall, Glenn. *The Backpacker's Handbook: An Environmentally Sound Guide* (9–12). 1994, Lyons Pr. paper $14.95 (1-55821-248-5). Tells "how to be comfortable in the wilderness while leaving it untouched for the enjoyment of the next visitor" by providing tips on clothing, packing, safety, and more. (Rev: BL 12/1/93) [796.5]

11021 Riviere, Bill. *The L. L. Bean Guide to the Outdoors* (10–12). Illus. 1981, Random $15.50 (0-394-51928-0). In addition to hiking, camping, and backpacking this general account includes some material on skiing and canoeing. [796.5]

11022 Seaborg, Eric, and Ellen Dudley. *Hiking and Backpacking* (9–12). 1994, Human Kinetics paper $12.95 (0-87322-506-6). An introduction to hiking and backpacking, covering safety gear, safe travel, and the best places to go. (Rev: BL 3/15/94; VOYA 12/94) [796.5]

11023 Waterman, Jonathan. *In the Shadow of Denali: Life and Death on Alaska's Mt. McKinley* (9–12). 1998, Lyons Pr. paper $14.95 (1-55821-726-6). This first-person narrative explores the psychology of climbers who attempt to scale the nation's highest mountain. (Rev: BL 3/1/94) [796.5]

Chess, Checkers, and Other Board and Card Games

11024 De Satnick, Shelly. *Bridge for Everyone: A Step-by-Step Text and Workbook* (10–12). 1982, Avon paper $9.95 (0-380-81083-2). An elementary but excellent introduction to bridge. [795.4]

11025 Frey, Richard. *According to Hoyle* (9–12). 1985, Fawcett paper $5.99 (0-449-21112-6). This handbook supplies instructions, rules, and regulations for over 200 games. [795.4]

11026 Gibson, Walter B. *Hoyle's Modern Encyclopedia of Card Games: Rules of All the Basic Games and Popular Variations* (10–12). Illus. 1974, Dolphin Books paper $12.95 (0-385-07680-0). The master of "according to Hoyle" fame describes a number of card games including poker and solitaire. [795.4]

11027 Holland, Tim. *Beginning Backgammon* (9–12). 1974, McKay paper $4.95 (0-679-14038-7). An elementary guide for the beginner in this board game that combines chance with skill. [794]

11028 Keene, Raymond. *The Simon & Schuster Pocket Book of Chess* (6–8). Illus. 1989, Simon & Schuster paper $8.95 (0-671-67924-4). An introduction to this game plus the mastery of more complicated moves are given through text, diagrams, and attractive photographs. (Rev: BL 6/1/89; BR 11–12/90; VOYA 12/89) [794.1]

11029 Morehead, Albert H., and Geoffrey Mott-Smith, eds. *Hoyle's Rules of Games*. 2nd rev. ed. (9–12). 1983, NAL paper $7.95 (0-452-26049-3). This is a guide on how to play over 200 card and parlor games. [794.4]

11030 Pike, Robert. *Play Winning Checkers: Official American Mensa Game Book* (8–12). 1999, Sterling paper $7.95 (0-8069-3794-7). After a history of the game, this book starts with the basics of checkers and continues through complex strategies. (Rev: SLJ 9/99) [794.2]

11031 Pritchard, D. B. *Begin Chess* (9–12). 1987, NAL paper $2.95 (0-451-14723-5). A fine introduction to this game with clear instructions for the beginner. [794.1]

11032 Redman, Tim, ed. *U.S. Chess Federation's Official Rules of Chess* (10–12). 1987, McKay paper $7.95 (0-679-14154-5). This is the official book of international chess rules and their interpretation. [794.1]

11033 Reinfeld, Fred. *Be a Winner at Chess* (9–12). 1986, Fawcett paper $5.99 (0-449-21257-2). This book presumes a basic knowledge of chess and describes many interesting strategies. Also use by this author: *Beginner's Guide to Winning Chess* (1982), *Chess in a Nutshell* (1989), *The Complete Chessplay* (1982), and *Win at Chess* (1945). [794.1]

11034 Reinfeld, Fred. *How to Win at Checkers* (9–12). 1982, Wilshire paper $7.00 (0-87980-068-2). A guide to this board game and popular pastime. [794]

11035 Sheinwold, Alfred. *101 Best Family Card Games* (6–12). Illus. 1993, Sterling paper $4.95 (0-8069-8635-2). Card games for all ages, from 5 to adulthood. (Rev: BL 2/15/93) [795.4]

Fishing and Hunting

11036 Bailey, John. *The Young Fishing Enthusiast: A Practical Guide for Kids* (5–8). 1999, DK Publg. $15.95 (0-7894-3965-4). The history of fishing, fish anatomy, gear and tackle, casting, lures, fly-fishing, and landing your catch are some of the topics covered in this richly illustrated book. (Rev: SLJ 7/99) [799.1]

11037 Capstick, Peter Hathaway. *Sands of Silence* (9–12). 1991, St. Martin's $35.00 (0-312-06459-4). The author muses on life and death in the wild in this story of elephant hunting near the edge of the African Kalahari desert, with an in-depth report on the lives of the region's natives. (Rev: BL 10/15/91) [799.2]

11038 Migdalski, Edward C. *The Inquisitive Angler* (9–12). 1991, Lyons Pr. $27.95 (1-55821-132-2). A serious fishing text, with information on taxonomy, habitat, limnology, and anatomy, designed to improve sports skills. (Rev: BL 12/15/91) [799.1]

11039 Patent, Dorothy Hinshaw. *A Family Goes Hunting* (5–8). Photos. 1991, Clarion $14.95 (0-395-52004-5). A balanced exploration of hunting, with information on weapons, licenses, gun cleaning, hunting dogs, and safety measures. (Rev: BL 12/15/91; SLJ 11/91) [799.29786]

11040 Paulsen, Gary. *Father Water, Mother Woods: Essays on Fishing and Hunting in the North Woods* (6–12). 1994, Delacorte $16.95 (0-385-32053-1). Essays reflecting the author's deep love for the wilderness, describing his adventures hunting, fishing, canoeing, and camping. (Rev: BL 7/94; SLJ 8/94; VOYA 10/94) [799]

Football

11041 Anastasia, Phil. *Broken Wing, Broken Promise: A Season Inside the Philadelphia Eagles* (9–12). 1993, Camino Books $18.00 (0-940159-20-1). Reporter Anastasia chronicles the Eagles' 1992 season, including Jerome Brown's death, mistrust of coach Kotite, and the division of team loyalty between 2 quarterbacks. (Rev: BL 10/1/93) [796.332]

11042 Anderson, Dave. *The Story of Football* (4–8). Illus. 1997, Morrow $16.00 (0-688-14314-8). This revision of the 1985 edition is a fine introduction to football, major teams and players, and the rules of the game. (Rev: BL 1/1–15/98; BR 1–2/98; SLJ 10/97) [796.48]

11043 Devaney, John. *Winners of the Heisman Trophy*. Rev. ed. (5–8). Illus. 1990, Walker LB $15.85 (0-8027-6907-1). A history of the award is given, plus profiles of 15 past winners. (Rev: SLJ 6/90) [796.332]

11044 DiLorenzo, J. J. *The Miami Dolphins Football Team* (5–8). (Great Sports Teams) 1997, Enslow LB $18.95 (0-89490-796-4). A history of the Miami Dolphins that focuses on their brightest stars and best moments on the field. (Rev: BL 10/15/97) [796.48]

11045 Harrington, Denis J. *The Pro Football Hall of Fame: Players, Coaches, Team Owners and League Officials, 1963–1991* (9–12). 1991, McFarland LB $35.00 (0-89950-550-3). Thumbnail profiles of football greats, organized by position through 1990. (Rev: BL 1/15/92) [796.332]

11046 Lace, William W. *The Dallas Cowboys Football Team* (5–8). Illus. (Great Sports Teams) 1997, Enslow LB $18.95 (0-89490-791-3). Opening with the Dallas championship in 1973, this book traces the history of the team, with plenty of sports action. (Rev: BL 10/15/97) [796.48]

11047 Mooney, Chuck. *The Recruiting Survival Guide* (10–12). 1991, 21st Century Pr. paper $9.95 (0-9630239-0-X). A former college ball player explains how recruiters work and the pitfalls and rewards that await the targeted athlete. (Rev: BL 4/15/92) [796.33]

11048 Nash, Bruce, and Allan Zullo. *The Football Hall of Shame* (9–12). 1990, Pocket Books paper $7.95 (0-671-69413-8). A recent collection that continues to bring into focus some of the low points of the game. (Rev: BL 9/15/90) [796.33]

11049 Peterson, Robert W. *Pigskin: The Early Years of Pro Football* (10–12). 1997, Oxford $48.00 (0-19-507607-9). An absorbing history of professional football from its beginnings in 1889 to the 1958 championship game between the Colts and the Giants. (Rev: BL 11/15/96; SLJ 6/97) [796.48]

11050 Sullivan, George. *Quarterbacks! 18 of Football's Greatest* (5–10). 1998, Simon & Schuster $18.00 (0-689-81334-1). The author chooses 18 of the great quarterbacks of all time, including Brett Favre, Troy Aikman, Sammy Baugh, and Sid Luckman, and explains why he chose them and their contributions to the game. (Rev: SLJ 9/98) [796.48]

Golf

11051 Anderson, Dave. *The Story of Golf* (4–8). 1998, Morrow $16.00 (0-688-15796-3); paper $7.95 (0-688-15797-1). A history of golf that highlights the careers of some of its great stars, plus material on the lure of the game, golf architecture, and caddies. (Rev: BL 5/15/98; SLJ 7/98) [796.352]

11052 Andrisani, John. *The Tiger Woods Way: Secrets of Tiger Woods' Power-Swinging Technique* (10–12). Illus. 1997, Crown $18.00 (0-609-60094-X). This is an in-depth look at the powerful swing of Tiger Woods and, through text and illustrations, provides tips on how readers can develop this technique themselves. (Rev: VOYA 10/97) [796.352]

11053 Campbell, Malcolm. *The Random House International Encyclopedia of Golf: The Definitive Guide to the Game* (9–12). 1991, Random $60.00 (0-394-58893-2). Though somewhat dated, this is a comprehensive reference for golf enthusiasts highlighting courses, equipment, and past tournament winners. (Rev: BL 1/15/92) [796.352]

11054 Donegan, Lawrence. *Maybe It Should Have Been a Three Iron: My Years As Caddy for the World's 438th Best Golfer* (9–12). 1998, St. Martin's $21.95 (0-312-18584-7). A caddy's eye view of the sport of golf told with wisdom, candor, and humor. (Rev: BL 5/15/98; SLJ 9/98) [796.352]

11055 Glenn, Rhonda. *The Illustrated History of Women's Golf* (9–12). 1991, Taylor $34.95 (0-87833-743-1). Examines the women's amateur golf circuit from the 1920s through the 1950s, with a complete list of golf records. (Rev: BL 1/1/92) [796.352]

11056 Grout, Jack. *On the Lesson Tee: Basic Golf Fundamentals* (9–12). 1982, Sterling paper $5.95 (0-87670-064-4). An informal guide to golf basics that is particularly good for the beginner. [796.352]

11057 Hogan, Ben. *Power Golf* (10–12). 1990, Pocket Books paper $6.50 (0-671-72905-5). Expert advice for people already familiar with the basics of golf. [796.352]

11058 Kaskie, Shirli. *A Woman's Golf Game* (10–12). 1983, Contemporary paper $12.95 (0-8092-5756-4). For both the beginner and the experienced female golfer, this is a fine guide. [796.352]

11059 Lopez, Nancy. *The Complete Golfer* (9–12). Illus. 1989, Contemporary paper $15.95 (0-8092-4711-9). This well-known golf professional gives her tips on the sport for both men and women. (Rev: BR 11–12/89) [796.352]

11060 Nash, Bruce, and Allan Zullo. *The Golf Hall of Shame* (9–12). 1991, Pocket Books paper $12.00 (0-671-74583-2). Golfing goofs from the caddies to the pros. (Rev: BL 11/15/89) [796.352]

11061 *101 Essential Tips: Golf* (9–12). 1996, DK Publg. paper $4.95 (0-7894-0172-X). This book covers such essentials of golf as equipment, club grips, stance, swing control, clothing, and rules. (Rev: VOYA 6/96) [796.352]

11062 Paulson, Carl, and Louis H. Janda. *Rookie on Tour: The Education of a PGA Golfer* (10–12). 1998, Putnam $23.95 (0-399-14378-5). This candid account of the challenges of a PGA tour will appeal to young golfers who wonder about the professional aspects of this sport. (Rev: BL 3/15/98; SLJ 9/98) [796.352]

11063 Penick, Harvey, and Bud Shrake. *For All Who Love the Game: Lessons and Teachings for Women* (9–12). 1995, Simon & Schuster $19.50 (0-684-

80058-6). Goal-directed tips for golf swings. (Rev: BL 4/15/95) [796.352]

Gymnastics

11064 Gutman, Dan. *Gymnastics* (5–8). Illus. 1996, Viking paper $14.99 (0-670-86949-X). In addition to presenting a history of gymnastics from the ancient Greeks to the 1996 Olympics, this book explains the different competitive events and how they are judged. (Rev: BL 5/1/96; BR 11–12/96; SLJ 8/96; VOYA 12/96) [796.44]

11065 Rutledge, Rachel. *The Best of the Best in Gymnastics* (5–8). (Women of Sports) 1999, Millbrook LB $22.90 (0-7613-1321-4); paper $6.95 (0-7613-0784-2). After a description and history of gymnastics, the author profiles 8 contemporary stars in this sport from around the world, including 3 on the successful U.S. women's team at the 1996 Olympics. (Rev: SLJ 7/99) [796.44]

Hockey

11066 Foley, Mike. *Fundamental Hockey* (4–8). (Fundamental sports) 1996, Lerner LB $22.60 (0-8225-3456-8). The basics of ice hockey are introduced, accompanied by a brief history of the sport and an explanation of what the various players do. (Rev: SLJ 3/96) [796.962]

11067 Hubbard, Kevin, and Stan Fischler. *Hockey America: The Ice Game's Past Growth & Bright Future in the U.S.* (8–12). 1998, NTC paper $24.95 (1-57028-196-3). This work traces the history of ice hockey in this country, introduces some key players, and speculates about the sport's future. (Rev: VOYA 10/98) [796.962]

11068 Hunter, Douglas. *A Breed Apart: An Illustrated History of Goaltending* (9–12). Illus. 1995, Triumph Books $28.95 (1-57243-048-6). A history of goaltending from its earliest years, but mostly after 1943, with portraits of the most renowned goalies. (Rev: BL 10/1/95*) [796.962]

11069 Jensen, Julie, adapt. *Beginning Hockey* (4–8). (Beginning Sports) 1996, Lerner LB $22.60 (0-8225-3506-8). An introduction to hockey that includes its history, teams, and the techniques and tricks used by its players. (Rev: SLJ 3/96) [796.964]

11070 Stevens, Julie, and Joanna Avery. *Too Many Men on the Ice: Women's Hockey in North America* (8–12). 1998, Polestar Book Publishers paper $16.95 (1-896095-33-X). From 19th-century tournaments to the inclusion of women's ice hockey in the 1998

Winter Olympics, this is a history of women's participation in this sport and their struggles to gain recognition. (Rev: VOYA 12/98) [796.962]

11071 Sullivan, George. *All about Hockey* (5–8). 1998, Putnam $15.99 (0-399-23172-6); paper $9.99 (0-399-23173-0). An efficient general introduction to hockey, with a brief history, coverage of basic rules and skills and defensive and offensive strategies, an examination of professional, Olympic and World Cup hockey, and profiles of players who have had a major impact on the sport. (Rev: SLJ 3/99) [796.962]

11072 Wimmer, Dick, ed. *The Fastest Game* (7–12). 1998, NTC paper $15.00 (1-57028-152-1). This work contains 23 excerpts from previous published works that describe great hockey moments and unforgettable participants over the years. (Rev: VOYA 4/98) [796.962]

11073 Wolfe, Bernie, and Mitch Henkin. *How to Watch Ice Hockey* (9–12). Illus. 1985, National Pr. paper $9.95 (0-915765-09-8). All of the rules of a hockey match are carefully explained plus a description of each position and the kinds of action one can expect at a typical game. (Rev: BL 12/15/85) [796.96]

Horse Racing and Horsemanship

11074 Best, David Grant. *Portrait of a Racetrack: A Behind the Scenes Look at a Racetrack Community* (9–12). 1992, Best Editions paper $24.95 (0-9634241-0-6). A black-and-white photoessay featuring the horses, jockeys, grooms, and trainers at a Seattle racetrack. (Rev: BL 12/1/92*) [798.4]

11075 Binder, Sibylle Luise, and Gefion Wolf. *Riding for Beginners* (5–9). Trans. by Elisabeth E. Reinersmann. 1999, Sterling $19.95 (0-8069-6205-4). This book uses beautiful color illustrations and an accessible text to cover the basics and intermediate stages of mastering horseback riding. (Rev: SLJ 8/99) [798.4]

11076 Kirksmith, Tommie. *Ride Western Style: A Guide for Young Riders* (5–8). 1991, Howell Book House $16.95 (0-87605-895-0). Background information and step-by-step instructions for youth interested in learning to ride horses western style. (Rev: BL 4/1/92; SLJ 7/92) [798.2]

Ice Skating

11077 Boo, Michael. *The Story of Figure Skating* (5–8). 1998, Morrow $16.00 (0-688-15820-X);

paper $7.95 (0-688-15821-8). A history of figure skating from its beginnings, when bones, antlers, and walrus teeth were used for blades, to the 20th century, with decade-by-decade coverage from the 1960s through the 1998 Olympics. (Rev: BL 11/1/98; SLJ 12/98; VOYA 4/99) [796.91]

11078 Brennan, Christine. *Inside Edge: A Revealing Journey into the Secret World of Figure Skating* (10–12). 1996, Scribners $22.50 (0-684-80167-1). A hard look at the realities of figure skating by a reporter who covered the sport for the *Washington Post* for 11 years, and including interviews with and profiles of skaters, coaches, parents, and judges. (Rev: BL 1/1–15/96; SLJ 7/96) [796.91]

11079 Foeste, Aaron. *Ice Skating Basics* (6–10). 1999, Sterling $17.95 (0-8069-9517-3). An excellent, well-illustrated introduction to ice skating that enthusiastically describes in detail easy to more difficult maneuvers, types of skates, their care and fit, and appropriate clothing. (Rev: SLJ 2/99) [796.91]

11080 Gutman, Dan. *Ice Skating: From Axels to Zambonis* (5–8). 1995, Viking $14.99 (0-670-86013-1). Chronicles the early history of skating, with biographies of famous skaters. (Rev: BL 10/1/95; SLJ 12/95; VOYA 2/96) [796.91]

11081 Sweet, Christopher. *Secrets of Skating* (10–12). 1997, Universe $29.95 (0-7893-0104-0). This book focuses on the life of figure skaters, focusing on Oksana Baiul, the Ukrainian gold medalist in the 1994 Olympics. (Rev: SLJ 3/98) [796.911]

11082 U.S. Figure Skating Association. *The Official Book of Figure Skating* (9–12). 1998, Simon & Schuster $30.00 (0-684-84673-X). This all-inclusive look at figure skating covers its history, past and present champions, skating techniques, fitness advice, tips on creating routines, and the judging system. (Rev: SLJ 3/99) [796.91]

In-Line Skating

11083 Dugard, Martin. *In-Line Skating Made Easy: A Manual for Beginners with Tips for the Experienced* (10–12). 1996, Globe Pequot Pr. paper $16.95 (1-56440-903-1). Tips for both the novice and expert are offered, along with information on equipment, competitions, and the dynamics of in-line skating. (Rev: SLJ 6/97) [796.2]

11084 Edwards, Chris. *The Young Inline Skater* (5–9). 1996, DK Publg. $15.95 (0-7894-1124-5). Double-page layouts cover such topics related to in-line skating as history, equipment, safety, techniques, and maneuvers. (Rev: BL 11/15/96; SLJ 11/96; VOYA 4/97) [796.2]

11085 Werner, Doug. *In-line Skater's Start-up: A Beginner's Guide to In-line Skating and Roller Hockey* (6–12). 1995, Tracks paper $9.95 (1-884654-04-5). Using many black-and-white photographs, this book is both a guide to in-line skating basics for beginners as well as an introduction to the growing sport of roller hockey. (Rev: BL 2/1/96) [796.2]

Martial Arts

11086 Atwood, Jane. *Capoeira: A Martial Art and a Cultural Tradition* (5–8). (The Library of African American Arts and Culture) 1999, Rosen $24.93 (0-8239-1859-9). Capoeira, a unique martial art developed by African slaves in Brazil, is described, along with its history and preparations for its debut in the 2004 Olympic games. (Rev: BR 9–10/99; SLJ 8/99) [796.8]

11087 Blot, Pierre. *Karate for Beginners* (5–8). Illus. 1996, Sterling $19.95 (0-8069-3874-9). After interesting background information, important karate techniques are covered in a readable text and clear illustrations. (Rev: BL 8/96; SLJ 7/96) [796.8]

11088 McFarlane, Stewart. *The Complete Book of T'ai Chi* (10–12). 1997, DK Publg. $22.95 (0-7894-1476-7). With numerous, clear illustrations, this book introduces the history of this ancient martial art form, and describes preparatory stretching exercises and its stances and flow of postures. (Rev: SLJ 1/98) [796.8]

11089 Metil, Luana, and Jace Townsend. *The Story of Karate: From Buddhism to Bruce Lee* (6–9). 1995, Lerner LB $23.93 (0-8225-3325-1). A history of this martial art from its origins in Oriental history to its present-day popularity. (Rev: BL 7/95) [796.8]

11090 Mitchell, David. *The Young Martial Arts Enthusiast* (5–9). 1997, DK Publg. $15.95 (0-7894-1508-9). Double-page spreads and plenty of full-color photos are used in this history of the martial arts, which explains how to perform various stances and other self-defense techniques. (Rev: SLJ 7/97) [796.8]

11091 Queen, J. Allen. *Learn Karate* (4–8). 1999, Sterling $17.95 (0-8069-8136-9). This excellent manual covers the basics of karate, like kicks, blocks, and stances, as well as stretches, meditation, safety, equipment, and sparring. (Rev: SLJ 5/99) [796.8]

11092 Rafkin, Louise. *The Tiger's Eye, the Bird's Fist: A Beginner's Guide to the Martial Arts* (5–8). 1997, Little, Brown paper $12.95 (0-316-73464-0). The author focuses on exploring the philosophy and history of martial arts fighting styles, with additional material on basics such as stances, self-defense,

sparring, and belt ranks, origins of major styles around the world, lore and legends associated with martial arts, and ancient masters and modern "warriors." (Rev: BL 6/1–15/97; SLJ 7/97; VOYA 10/97) [796.8]

11093 Tegner, Bruce. *Bruce Tegner's Complete Book of Jujitsu* (7–12). Illus. 1978, Thor paper $14.00 (0-87407-027-9). A master in the martial arts introduces this ancient Japanese form of self-defense and gives basic information on stances and routines. [796.8]

11094 Tegner, Bruce. *Bruce Tegner's Complete Book of Self-Defense.* New ed. (7–12). Illus. 1975, Thor paper $14.00 (0-87407-030-9). A basic primer on ways to defend oneself including hand blows and restraints. [796.8]

11095 Tegner, Bruce. *Karate: Beginner to Black Belt* (7–12). Illus. 1982, Thor paper $14.00 (0-87407-040-6). In an account that stresses safety and fitness, techniques for both the novice and the experienced are explained. [796.8]

11096 Tegner, Bruce, and Alice McGrath. *Self-Defense & Assault Prevention for Girls & Women* (7–12). Illus. 1977, Thor paper $10.00 (0-87407-026-0). Various defensive and offensive techniques are introduced in situations where they would be appropriate. [796.8]

11097 Tegner, Bruce, and Alice McGrath. *Solo Forms of Karate, Tai Chi, Aikido & Kung Fu* (9–12). Illus. 1981, Thor paper $10.00 (0-87407-034-1). Routines are described in copious pictures plus text that emphasize exercise and good training. [796.8]

11098 Yates, Keith D., and Bryan Robbins. *Tae Kwon Do for Kids* (4–8). 1999, Sterling paper $5.95 (0-8069-1761-X). A step-by-step manual that introduces and describes Tae Kwon Do, a Korean form of self-defense, with material on stances, blocks, exercises, and important pressure points. (Rev: SLJ 6/99) [796.8]

Olympic Games

11099 Currie, Stephen. *The Olympic Games* (8–12). (Overview) 1999, Lucent LB $23.70 (1-56006-395-5). Noting that controversies have surrounded the Olympic Games since their beginning, the author examines current controversies, such as commercialization and corporate sponsorship, politics, the use of drugs by athletes, and professional athletes in amateur competitions. (Rev: BL 9/15/99; SLJ 9/99) [796.4]

11100 DK Publishing, eds. *Chronicle of the Olympics, 1896–2000* (9–12). 1998, DK Publg. $29.95 (0-7894-2312-X). After a brief discussion of the ancient games, this account traces the history of the Olympics from 1896 in Athens to 1998 in Atlanta, including plans for Nagano in 1998 and Sydney, Australia, in 2000, with photographs capturing the spirit of the games, descriptions of each contest, and charts with statistics. (Rev: BL 2/15/98; SLJ 7/98) [796.4]

11101 Glubok, Shirley, and Alfred Tamarin. *Olympic Games in Ancient Greece* (7–10). 1976, HarperCollins LB $16.89 (0-06-022048-1). History and legend are combined in this account of the first Olympics. (Rev: BL 2/15/88) [796.4]

11102 Greenspan, Bud. *Frozen in Time: The Greatest Moments at the Winter Olympics* (7–12). 1997, General Publishing Group $24.95 (1-57544-027-X). The stories of nearly 60 stars of the Winter Olympics are told in 2- or 3-page accounts, many of them involving personal triumph and courage. (Rev: VOYA 6/98) [796.98]

11103 Kristy, Davida. *Coubertin's Olympics: How the Games Began* (5–8). 1995, Lerner LB $21.50 (0-8225-3327-8). How the Olympic games began and information about the life of Baron Pierre de Coubertin, their founder. (Rev: BL 8/95; SLJ 11/95) [338.4]

Running and Jogging

11104 Fixx, James F. *The Complete Book of Running* (10–12). Illus. 1977, Random $25.50 (0-394-41159-5). This book answers all kinds of questions one might have about running. A follow-up is *Jim Fixx's Second Book of Running* (1980). [796.4]

11105 Higdon, Hal. *Boston: A Century of Running* (9–12). 1995, Rodale $40.00 (0-87596-283-1). From the senior writer for *Runner's World* and a marathon runner himself, a history of the marathon and information on current runners. (Rev: BL 11/1/95) [796.42]

11106 Rutledge, Rachel. *The Best of the Best in Track and Field* (5–8). (Women of Sports) 1999, Millbrook LB $22.90 (0-7613-1300-1); paper $6.95 (0-7613-0446-0). A brief history of track and field is followed by profiles of 8 new stars in these events from the United States and other countries. (Rev: SLJ 7/99) [796.42]

Sailing, Boating, and Canoeing

11107 Adkins, Jan. *The Craft of Sail* (10–12). 1973, Walker paper $10.95 (0-8027-7214-5). A respected manual on small-boat craftsmanship. [797.1]

11108 Anderson, Scott. *Distant Fires* (8–12). Illus. 1990, Pfeifer-Hamilton paper $14.95 (0-938586-33-5). A journal of a 1,700-mile canoe trip from Minnesota to Canada's Hudson's Bay. (Rev: BL 1/15/91; SLJ 4/91) [797.122]

11109 Caswell, Christopher. *The Illustrated Book of Basic Boating* (9–12). Illus. 1990, Hearst paper $15.00 (0-688-08931-3). A step-by-step guide to power boating, from launching to tying up to a dock. (Rev: BL 7/90) [796.125]

11110 Conner, Dennis, and Michael Levitt. *Learn to Sail* (9–12). 1994, St. Martin's $22.95 (0-312-11020-0). A beginner's guide for the novice sailor. (Rev: BL 5/15/94) [797.1]

11111 Goodman, Di, and Ian Brodie. *Learning to Sail: The Annapolis Sailing School Guide for All Ages* (9–12). 1994, International Marine paper $12.95 (0-07-024014-0). Provides instruction for novices on how to begin recreational sailing, including nautical jargon, safety tips, and helpful drawings. (Rev: BL 7/94) [797.1]

11112 Kuhne, Cecil. *Whitewater Rafting: An Introductory Guide* (9–12). 1995, Lyons Pr. paper $16.95 (1-55821-317-1). An introduction to whitewater rafting, including pre-trip checklists and a list of classic whitewater rafting spots. (Rev: BL 2/15/95) [796.1]

11113 Lundy, Derek. *Godforsaken Sea: Racing the World's Most Dangerous Waters* (9–12). 1999, Algonquin $22.95 (1-56512-229-1). This is a gripping account of the Vendee Globe sailing race of 1996–97, a 4-month, single-handed ordeal that involves sailing to Antarctica and back. (Rev: BL 4/15/99; SLJ 9/99) [797.1]

11114 Ray, Slim. *The Canoe Handbook: Techniques for Mastering the Sport of Canoeing* (9–12). 1992, Stackpole paper $15.95 (0-8117-3032-8). A handbook covering canoeing fundamentals, including paddling techniques, styles, maneuvers, design, and equipment. (Rev: BL 2/15/92) [797.1]

11115 Riviere, Bill. *The Open Canoe* (9–12). Illus. 1985, Little, Brown paper $12.95 (0-316-74768-8). A fine handbook that is organized by different kinds of canoeing such as recreational and competitive. (Rev: BL 8/85) [797.1]

Skateboarding

11116 Andrejtschitsch, Jan, et al. *Action Skateboarding* (6–12). 1993, Sterling $16.95 (0-8069-8500-3). A handbook that provides a history of skateboarding, reviews equipment, and defines styles and terrains, with tips on tricks and maneuvers. (Rev: BL 6/1–15/93; SLJ 7/93) [795.2]

Snowboarding

11117 Bennett, Jeff, and Scott Downey. *The Complete Snowboarder* (9–12). 1994, McGraw-Hill paper $14.95 (0-07-005142-9). Presents tips for prospective snowboarders, with diagrams and illustrations. (Rev: BL 9/15/94) [796.9]

11118 Fabbro, Mike. *Snowboarding: The Ultimate Freeride* (10–12). Illus. 1996, McClelland & Stewart Tundra Books paper $12.99 (0-7710-3122-X). This is a comprehensive guide to this rising sport, with information on equipment, techniques, competitions, and complex maneuvers. (Rev: SLJ 4/97) [796.9]

11119 Iguchi, Bryan. *The Young Snowboarder* (5–8). Illus. 1997, DK Publg. $15.95 (0-7894-2062-7). Using middle schoolers as models in the photos, this book illustrates and describes basic skills, equipment, and techniques of snowboarding, freestyle riding, and slalom racing, with an emphasis on safety and mastering the basics. (Rev: BL 11/15/97; SLJ 2/98) [796.1]

11120 Jensen, Julie, adapt. *Beginning Snowboarding* (4–8). (Beginning Sports) 1996, Lerner LB $22.60 (0-8225-3507-6). An introduction to snowboarding, with material on equipment, basic maneuvers, types of competition, and advanced stunts. (Rev: SLJ 3/96) [796.9]

11121 Lurie, John. *Fundamental Snowboarding* (4–8). (Fundamental Sports) 1996, Lerner LB $22.60 (0-8225-3457-6). With eye-catching photos, the equipment and principles of snowboarding are covered, with material on basic and advanced maneuvers, skills, and stunts. (Rev: SLJ 3/96) [796.9]

Soccer

11122 Baddiel, Ivor. *The Ultimate Soccer Book* (5–9). Illus. 1998, DK Publg. $16.95 (0-7894-2795-8). A well-illustrated look at the history of soccer, winning teams and players, and rules, techniques, and tactics. (Rev: BL 9/1/98; SLJ 8/98; VOYA 8/98) [796.334]

11123 Bauer, Gerhard. *Soccer Techniques, Tactics and Teamwork* (9–12). 1993, Sterling paper $14.95 (0-8069-8730-8). Basic soccer training and skill development, with color photos. (Rev: BL 7/93*) [796.344]

11124 Chyzowych, Walter. *The Official Soccer Book of the United States Soccer Federation* (10–12). n.d., U.S. Soccer Federation paper $7.00 (0-318-16830-8). This manual covers topics such as training, physical fitness, and strategies. [796.334]

11125 Herbst, Dan. *Sports Illustrated Soccer: The Complete Player* (7–12). Illus. 1988, Sports Illustrated for Kids paper $9.95 (1-56800-038-3). Basic and advanced skills are explained plus a variety of game strategies. [796.334]

11126 Miller, Marla. *All-American Girls: The U.S. Women's National Soccer Team* (4–8). 1999, Pocket Books paper $4.99 (0-671-03599-1). A portrait of members of the U.S. Women's National Soccer Team, with advice for aspiring players. (Rev: SLJ 8/99; VOYA 8/99) [796.334]

11127 Rosenthal, Gary. *Soccer Skills and Drills* (10–12). 1978, Macmillan LB $14.95 (0-87460-258-0). In addition to a rundown on techniques, this manual includes a glossary and the official rules. [796.334]

11128 Scott, Nina S. *The Thinking Kids Guide to Successful Soccer* (5–8). 1998, Millbrook LB $18.90 (0-7613-0324-3). An insider's look at strategies for kids playing soccer, including topics not frequently addressed such as dealing with inexperienced coaches, unfair calls from referees, not getting enough playing time, and pressures of competition. The author encourages kids to have a good time and not worry about making mistakes. (Rev: BL 5/15/99; SLJ 4/99) [796..334]

11129 Stewart, Mark. *Soccer: An Intimate History of the World's Most Popular Game* (7–10). (Watts History of Sports) 1998, Watts $32.00 (0-531-11456-2). With clear text and photographs, this book traces the history of soccer in the United States, with interesting material on memorable games, famous players, related off-the-field developments, and a discussion of why soccer is not as popular as other sports in the United States. (Rev: SLJ 7/98) [796.334]

11130 Trecker, Jim, and Charles Miers, eds. *Soccer! The Game and the World Cup* (9–12). 1998, Universe paper $27.50 (0-7893-0145-8). A handsomely illustrated paperback on the history of soccer and highlights of World Cup games, with a whole section on women's soccer and women's World Cup games. (Rev: SLJ 1/99) [796.334]

11131 Woog, Dan. *The Ultimate Soccer Almanac* (6–12). Illus. 1998, Lowell House $14.95 (1-56565-951-1); paper $6.95 (1-56565-891-4). A review of the history of soccer, important players and teams, and rules of the game and how to play it. (Rev: BL 7/98) [796.334]

10932 Wukovits, John. *The Composite Guide to Soccer* (4–8). 1998, Chelsea LB $7.95 (0-7910-4718-0). A basic guide to the history, rules, positions, and playing techniques of this sport, with material on its European popularity. (Rev: SLJ 12/98; VOYA 6/99) [796.334]

Surfing, Water Skiing, and Other Water Sports

11133 Brems, Marianne. *The Fit Swimmer: 120 Workouts & Training Tips* (9–12). Illus. 1984, Contemporary paper $12.95 (0-8092-5454-9). For a person who has chosen swimming as a way of keeping fit, this book describes 120 workouts. [797.2]

11134 Counsilman, James E. *The Complete Book of Swimming* (9–12). 1979, Macmillan paper $10.00 (0-689-70583-2). This book for both the novice and the expert gives material on strokes, drills, and advanced techniques. [797.2]

11135 Grubb, Jake, et al. *The New Sailboard Book* (9–12). Illus. 1990, Norton paper $16.95 (0-393-30682-8). This guide to a fast-growing sport contains information on equipment, basic techniques, and types of competitions. (Rev: BL 5/1/85) [797.124]

11136 Werner, Doug. *Surfer's Start-Up: A Beginner's Guide to Surfing.* 2nd ed. (7–12). 1999, Tracks paper $11.95 (1-884654-12-6). A new edition of this standard instructional guide that covers basic instruction, surfing gear, safety, etiquette, and history. (Rev: SLJ 9/99) [797]

Tennis and Other Racquet Games

11137 Ashe, Arthur, and Alexander McNab. *Arthur Ashe on Tennis: Strokes, Strategy, Traditions, Players, Psychology, and Wisdom* (9–12). 1995, Knopf $20.00 (0-679-43797-5). An instructional guide that also expresses admiration for Ashe the man and his struggle with a heart condition and then with AIDS. (Rev: BL 3/1/95) [796.342]

11138 *International Book of Tennis Drills* (9–12). 1993, Triumph Books paper $14.95 (1-880141-36-1). The U.S. Professional Tennis Registry presents more than 100 tennis drills, with accompanying diagrams to build basic skills. (Rev: BL 11/15/93) [796.342]

11139 Jennings, Jay, ed. *Tennis and the Meaning of Life: A Literary Anthology of the Game* (9–12). 1995, Breakaway $24.00 (1-55821-378-3). A collection of tennis-related stories and poetry by well-known writers. (Rev: BL 5/15/95) [808.8]

11140 Kittleson, Stan. *Racquetball: Steps to Success* (9–12). 1991, Human Kinetics paper $15.95 (0-88011-440-1). An instructional text for beginning

players on mastering 18 basic racquetball skills, each with appropriate drills. (Rev: BL 10/1/91) [796.34]

11141 Lendl, Ivan, and George Mendoza. *Hitting Hot* (9–12). Illus. 1986, Random $14.95 (0-394-55407-8). A 14-day tennis clinic with a specific skill covered on each day. (Rev: BR 5–6/87; VOYA 2/87) [796.342]

11142 *101 Essential Tips: Tennis* (9–12). 1996, DK Publg. paper $4.95 (0-7894-0182-7). From equipment to clothing and from strokes to racquet positioning, this book covers the sport of tennis for both the beginner and the expert. (Rev: VOYA 6/96) [796.342]

11143 Singleton, Skip. *The Junior Tennis Handbook: A Complete Guide to Tennis for Juniors, Parents, and Coaches* (6–12). 1991, Betterway paper $12.95 (1-55870-192-3). A comprehensive tennis instruction guide for beginners 10 years old and up. (Rev: BL 8/91) [796.342]

11144 Turner, Ed, and Woody Clouse. *Winning Racquetball: Skills, Drills, and Strategies* (9–12). 1995, Human Kinetics paper $16.95 (0-87322-721-2). This handbook on racquetball includes drills to develop recommended shots, strategies, and tips on conditioning. (Rev: BL 12/1/95) [796.34]

Volleyball

11145 Lucas, Jeff. *Pass, Set, Crush: Volleyball Illustrated.* 3rd ed. (9–12). Illus. 1993, Euclid Northwest paper $24.95 (0-9615088-6-8). A guide for players who want to improve their volleyball skills. (Rev: BL 11/15/88) [796.32]

Wrestling

11146 Douglas, Bobby. *Take It to the Mat* (9–12). 1993, Sigler Pr. paper $15.95 (0-9635812-0-1). U.S. Olympic wrestler/coach Douglas presents an introductory guide to competitive wrestling, with photos of holds and escapes, as well as diet guidelines. (Rev: BL 9/15/93) [796.8]

11147 Jarman, Tom, and Reid Hanley. *Wrestling for Beginners* (7–12). Illus. 1983, Contemporary paper $12.95 (0-8092-5656-8). From a history of wrestling, this book moves on to skills, strategies, moves, and holds. [796.8]

Author Index

Authors are arranged alphabetically by last name. Authors' and joint authors' names are followed by book titles — which are also arranged alphabetically — and the text entry number. Book titles may refer to those that appear as a main entry or as an internal entry in the text. All fiction titles are indicated by (F), following the entry number.

Aamodt, Donald. *A Name to Conjure With*, 1562(F)
Aaron, Chester. *Lackawanna*, 1(F)
 Out of Sight, Out of Mind, 2(F)
Aaseng, Jay (jt. author). *Head Injuries*, 5921
Aaseng, Nathan. *American Dinosaur Hunters*, 7960
 Athletes, 7624
 Black Inventors, 7507
 Breaking the Sound Barrier, 10473
 Head Injuries, 5921
 Invertebrates, 9813
 The Locker Room Mirror, 10861
 Nature's Poisonous Creatures, 9863
 Navajo Code Talkers, 8241
 The O. J. Simpson Trial, 4643
 Paris, 8242
 Science Versus Pseudoscience, 10802
 Sports Great David Robinson, 7699
 Sports Great John Stockton, 7703
 Treacherous Traitors, 5127
 True Champions, 7625
 Twentieth-Century Inventors, 10362
 Yearbooks in Science: 1940–1949, 9569
 You Are the Corporate Executive, 5314
 You Are the General, 4702
 You Are the General II, 8030
 You Are the Juror, 4644
 You Are the President, 4614
 You Are the President II, 4615
 You Are the Senator, 4625
 You Are the Supreme Court Justice, 4645
Aaseng, Rolf E. *A Beginner's Guide to Studying the Bible*, 4460
Abbey, Lynn. *Unicorn & Dragon*, 1563(F)
Abdul-Jabbar, Kareem. *Giant Steps*, 7678
 Kareem, 7678
Abelove, Joan. *Go and Come Back*, 1513(F)
 Saying It Out Loud, 898(F)
Abraham-Podietz, Eva (jt. author). *Ten Thousand Children*, 8289
Abrahams, Roger D., ed. *African Folktales*, 4072

Afro-American Folktales, 4135
Abt, Samuel. *Tour de France*, 11003
Acatoz, Sylvio. *Pueblos*, 8920
Ackerman, Diane. *Bats*, 9864
Ackerman, Ned. *Spirit Horse*, 2236(F)
Adair, Gene. *George Washington Carver*, 7551
 Thomas Alva Edison, 7558
Adams, Ansel. *Ansel Adams*, 6437
 The Portfolios of Ansel Adams, 6438
Adams, Cynthia. *The Mysterious Case of Sir Arthur Conan Doyle*, 6842
Adams, Douglas. *Dirk Gently's Holistic Detective Agency*, 3385(F)
 The Hitchhiker's Guide to the Galaxy, 3384(F)
 Last Chance to See, 9960
 Life, the Universe, and Everything, 3384(F)
 The Long Dark Tea-Time of the Soul, 3385(F)
 Mostly Harmless, 3386(F)
 The Restaurant at the End of the Universe, 3384(F)
 So Long, Thanks for the Fish, 3384(F)
Adams, Florence. *Catch a Sunbeam*, 9716
Adams, John Winthrop, ed. *Stars and Stripes Forever*, 8867
Adams, Richard. *Ideas for Science Projects*, 9604
 More Ideas for Science Projects, 9605
 The Plague Dogs, 1564(F)
 Tales from Watership Down, 1565(F)
 Watership Down, 1565(F), 1566(F)
Adams, Simon. *Junior Chronicle of the 20th Century*, 8224
 Visual Timeline of the 20th Century, 8223
Adamson, Joe. *The Bugs Bunny Golden Jubilee*, 6520
Adamson, Joy. *Born Free*, 9893
Adamson, Lydia. *A Cat on Stage Left*, 2922(F)
Adeeb, Bonnetta (jt. author). *Nigeria*, 8491
Adeeb, Hassan. *Nigeria*, 8491
Adelson, Alan, ed. *The Diary of Dawid Sierakowiak*, 8243
Adkins, Jan. *The Craft of Sail*, 11107
 How a House Happens, 10396

Step by Step along the Pacific Crest Trail, 9528

What to Do about Nuclear Waste, 10341

Anema, Durlynn. *Harriet Chalmers Adams*, 6604

Anflick, Charles. *Resistance*, 8250

Angela, Alberto. *The Extraordinary Story of Human Origins*, 7992

Angela, Piero (jt. author). *The Extraordinary Story of Human Origins*, 7992

Angell, Judie. *The Buffalo Nickel Blues Band*, 1030(F)

Angelou, Maya. *All God's Children Need Traveling Shoes*, 6794

And Still I Rise, 3953

Gather Together in My Name, 6794

The Heart of a Woman, 6794

I Know Why the Caged Bird Sings, 6794

I Shall Not Be Moved, 3954

Just Give Me a Cool Drink of Water 'fore I Die, 3953

Now Sheba Sings the Song, 4390

Oh Pray My Wings Are Gonna Fit Me Well, 3953

Shaker, Why Don't You Sing? 3953

Singin' and Swingin' and Gettin' Merry Like Christmas, 6794

Angier, Bradford. *Field Guide to Medicinal Wild Plants*, 9789

Ansary, Mir T. *Afghanistan*, 8570

Ansell, Rod. *To Fight the Wild*, 8591

Antal, John F. *Proud Legions*, 11(F)

Anthony, Mark. *Beyond the Pale*, 1575(F)

Anthony, Piers. *Being a Green Mother*, 1576(F)

Blue Adept, 3395(F)

But What of Earth? 3396(F)

Castle Roogna, 1582(F)

Demons Don't Dream, 1577(F)

Faun & Games, 1578(F)

For Love of Evil, 3392(F)

Geis of the Gargoyle, 1579(F)

Golem in the Gears, 1580(F)

Heaven Cent, 3393(F)

If I Pay Thee Not in Gold, 1586(F)

Justaposition, 3395(F)

Man from Mundania, 3393(F)

On a Pale Horse, 1584(F)

Race Against Time, 3394(F)

Roc and a Hard Place, 1581(F)

Shade of the Tree, 2679(F)

The Source of Magic, 1582(F)

A Spell for Chameleon, 1582(F)

Split Infinity, 3395(F)

Total Recall, 3396(F)

Vale of the Vole, 3393(F)

Wielding a Red Sword, 1583(F)

With a Tangled Skein, 1584(F)

Zombie Lover, 1585(F)

Anthony, Suzanne. *West Indies*, 8821

Antle, Nancy. *Lost in the War*, 1032(F)

Aparicio, Frances R., ed. *Latino Voices*, 437(F)

Applegate, K. A. *Animorphs #1*, 3397(F)

Applegate, Katherine. *August Magic*, 3274(F)

July's Promise, 3274(F)

June Dreams, 3274(F)

See You in September, 3276(F)

Sharing Sam, 3275(F)

Applegate, Stan. *The Devil's Highway*, 2426(F)

Apt, Jay. *Orbit*, 9665

Aquila, Richard. *That Old Time Rock & Roll*, 6458

Archbold, Rick (jt. author). *The Discovery of the Titanic*, 10299

Ghost Liners, 10510

Archer, Chris. *Alien Blood*, 3398(F)

Alien Terror, 3399(F)

Archer, Jeffrey. *A Matter of Honor*, 12(F)

Shall We Tell the President? 13(F)

Archer, Jules. *The Incredible Sixties*, 9394

Special Interests, 4688

To Save the Earth, 7510

Winners and Losers, 4695

Archibald, Zofia. *Discovering the World of the Ancient Greeks*, 8104

Ardley, Neil. *Music*, 6495

A Young Person's Guide to Music, 6447

Ardley, Neil (jt. author). *The New Way Things Work*, 10379

Arduini, Paolo. *Simon & Schuster's Guide to Fossils*, 7961

Armor, John. *Manzanar*, 9395

Armstrong, Carole. *Women of the Bible*, 4463

Armstrong, Jennifer. *The Dreams of Mairhe Mehan*, 2373(F)

Mary Mehan Awake, 2511(F)

Shipwreck at the Bottom of the World, 8849

Steal Away, 2321(F)

Armstrong, Jennifer (jt. author). *In My Hands*, 8351

Armstrong, William H. *Sounder*, 438(F)

Sour Land, 438(F)

Arnest, Lauren Krohn. *Children, Young Adults, and the Law*, 4721

Arnold, Caroline. *Coping with Natural Disasters*, 6243

El Niño, 10275

Hawk Highway in the Sky, 9945

Pele, 7770

Stone Age Farmers Beside the Sea, 7993

Arnold, Elliott. *Blood Brother*, 2427(F)

Arnold, Katya. *Katya's Book of Mushrooms*, 9790

Arnold, Sandra M. *Alicia Alonso*, 6963

Arnoldi, Katherine. *The Amazing True Story of a Teenage Single Mom*, 6071

Arnosky, Jim. *Autumn*, 10665

Nearer Nature, 9503

Sketching Outdoors in Spring, 10665

Summer, 10665

Winter, 10665

Aronson, Virginia. *Literature*, 6660

Venus Williams, 7754

Arredia, Joni. *Sex, Boys, & You*, 6244

Arrick, Fran. *Steffie Can't Come Out to Play*, 901(F)

Arthur, Alex. *Shell*, 9999

Asante, Molefi K. *The African-American Atlas*, 4850

Berry, James. *Rough Sketch Beginning*, 3957
  A Thief in the Village and Other Stories, 618(F)
Berry, James, ed. *Classic Poems to Read Aloud*, 3933
Berry, James R. *Everywhere Faces Everywhere*, 4040
Berry, Liz. *The China Garden*, 1618(F)
Berry, Louise A. (jt. author). *Acid Rain*, 5106
  Air Alert, 5107
Berry, Michael. *Georgia O'Keeffe*, 6758
Berry, Richard. *Discover the Stars*, 9636
Bertrand, Diane Gonzales. *Lessons of the Game*, 3283(F)
  Sweet Fifteen, 445(F)
  Trino's Choice, 1043(F)
Beshore, George. *Sickle Cell Anemia*, 5729
Bessire, Aimee. *Sukuma*, 8409
Bessire, Mark. *Great Zimbabwe*, 8460
Bessire, Mark (jt. author). *Sukuma*, 8409
Besson, Jean-Louis. *October 45*, 8263
Best, David Grant. *Portrait of a Racetrack*, 11074
Betancourt, Jeanne. *Kate's Turn*, 1044(F)
Betancourt, John Gregor (jt. author). *Serve It Forth*, 10602
Bettmann, Otto L. *Johann Sebastian Bach As His World Knew Him*, 6948
Bial, Daniel. *Arnold Schwarzenegger*, 7098
Bial, Raymond. *Mist Over the Mountains*, 9553
  The Strength of These Arms, 9122
Bianchi, Anne. *C. Everett Koop*, 7587
Bicycling Magazine, ed. *Cycling for Women*, 11006
Biddle, Wayne. *Field Guide to Germs*, 5730
Biel, Timothy L. *The Age of Feudalism*, 8162
  Charlemagne, 7839
  Life in the North during the Civil War, 9166
Bierhorst, John. *The Mythology of North America*, 4140
  Native American Stories, 4141
  The Way of the Earth, 4142
  The White Deer and Other Stories Told by the Lenape, 4143
Biesele, Megan. *San*, 8461
Biggers, Jeff. *Transgenerational Addiction*, 5619
Bigler, Philip. *Washington in Focus*, 9505
Bilger, Burkhard. *Global Warming*, 5059
Billings, Charlene W. *Lasers*, 10347
  Supercomputers, 10411
Billings, Henry. *Antarctica*, 8850
Billingsley, Franny. *The Folk Keeper*, 1619(F)
  Well Wished, 1620(F)
Binchy, Maeve. *Evening Class*, 421(F)
  The Glass Lake, 3284(F)
Binder, Sibylle Luise. *Riding for Beginners*, 11075
Binkley, Jim (jt. author). *Baseball's Most Memorable Trades*, 10937
Binstock, R. C. *Tree of Heaven*, 2102(F)
Biracree, Tom. *Althea Gibson*, 7749
  Grandma Moses, 6756
  Wilma Rudolph, 7767
Birch, Beverley, retel. *Shakespeare's Stories*, 4371
  Shakespeare's Stories: Histories, 4371
  Shakespeare's Stories: Tragedies, 4371

Bird, Larry. *Bird on Basketball*, 10976
Birdseye, Debbie H. *Under Our Skin*, 4820
Birdseye, Tom. *Tucker*, 619(F)
Birdseye, Tom (jt. author). *Under Our Skin*, 4820
Birmelin, Immanuel. *The New Parakeet Handbook*, 10068
Bishop, Jack. *Ralph Ellison*, 6846
Bishop, Rudine Sims. *Presenting Walter Dean Myers*, 4293
Bisignano, Alphonse. *Cooking the Italian Way*, 10578
Biskup, Michael D., ed. *AIDS*, 5731
  Criminal Justice, 4648
Bisson, Terry. *Nat Turner*, 7248
  Talking Man, 1621(F)
Bitton-Jackson, Livia. *I Have Lived a Thousand Years*, 8264
  My Bridges of Hope, 7911
Bix, Cynthia O. *Animal Athletes*, 9814
Bjarkman, Peter C. *Sports Great Dominique Wilkins*, 7704
  Sports Great Scottie Pippen, 7696
Bjornlund, Lydia. *The U.S. Constitution*, 4596
Black, Beryl. *Coping with Sexual Harassment*, 6172
Black, Christine M. *The Pursuit of the Presidency*, 4617
Black, Eric. *Bosnia*, 8606
  Northern Ireland, 8653
Black, Penny. *The Book of Pressed Flowers*, 10531
Black, Veronica. *A Vow of Adoration*, 2949(F)
Black, Wallace B. (jt. author). *Oil Spills*, 5098
Blacklock, Dyan. *Pankration*, 2067(F)
Blackwood, Gary L. *Life on the Oregon Trail*, 9260
  Moonshine, 2555(F)
  Shakespeare Stealer, 2137(F)
Blades, Ann. *A Boy of Tache*, 23(F)
Blair, Clifford. *The Guns of Sacred Heart*, 2432(F)
Blair, Walter. *Tall Tale America*, 4159
Blake, Michael. *Airman Mortensen*, 3285(F)
Blake, Mike. *Baseball Chronicles*, 10933
Blake, Randolph (jt. author). *Star Trek on the Brain*, 5937
Bland, Celia. *The Mechanical Age*, 8654
  Osceola, Seminole Rebel, 7499
Bland, Joellen, adapt. *Stage Plays from the Classics*, 3788
Blandford, Percy W. *24 Table Saw Projects*, 10778
Blashfield, Jean F. *Calcium*, 10147
  Carbon, 10148
  Hydrogen, 10149
  Nitrogen, 10150
  Oil Spills, 5098
  Oxygen, 10151
  Sodium, 10152
Blassingame, Wyatt. *The Look-It-Up Book of Presidents*, 7132
Blauer, Ettagale. *South Africa*, 8462
  Swaziland, 8463
  Uganda, 8427
Bledsoe, Jerry. *The Angel Doll*, 620(F)

Exile's Song, 3429(F)
The Firebrand, 1632(F)
Ghostlight, 1633(F)
The Gratitude of Kings, 1634(F)
Hawkmistress! 1635(F)
Mists of Avalon, 1632(F)
Sword of Chaos, 1636(F)
Bradley, Marion Zimmer, ed. *Sword and Sorceress XIV*, 1637(F)
Bradshaw, Gillian. *The Beacon at Alexandria*, 2055(F)
The Dragon and the Thief, 1638(F)
Island of Ghosts, 2056(F)
The Land of Gold, 1638(F)
Brady, Irene. *America's Horses and Ponies*, 10125
Brager, Bruce L. *The Trial of Adolf Eichmann*, 8270
Bragg, Janet Harmon. *Soaring above Setbacks*, 7467
Bragg, Rick. *All Over but the Shoutin'*, 6812
Braithwaite, E. R. *To Sir, with Love*, 7913
Bramwell, Martyn. *Birds*, 9948
How Maps Are Made, 7953
Mammals, 9867
Mapping Our World, 7953, 7954
Mapping the Seas and Airways, 7955
Maps in Everyday Life, 7955
Brancato, Robin F. *Come Alive at 505*, 1060(F)
Facing Up, 1061(F)
Winning, 906(F)
Branch, Muriel M. *Juneteenth*, 4855
Pennies to Dollars, 7506
The Water Brought Us, 9554
Brand, Max. *Dan Barry's Daughter*, 25(F)
Way of the Lawless, 26(F)
Brandenburg, Jim. *Sand and Fog*, 8466
Brandon, Jay. *Rules of Evidence*, 2951(F)
Brandon, Ruth. *The Life and Many Deaths of Harry Houdini*, 7031
Branford, Henrietta. *Fire, Bed, and Bone*, 2138(F)
White Wolf, 262(F)
Brann, Donald R. *How to Build Outdoor Projects*, 10779
Branscum, Robbie. *Johnny May Grows Up*, 1062(F)
Branson, Ann, ed. *The Good Housekeeping Illustrated Cookbook*, 10579
Brantley, C. L. *The Princeton Review Write Smart Junior*, 5365
Brash, Sarah, ed. *World War II*, 8271
Braun, Barbara. *A Weekend with Diego Rivera*, 6772
Braun, Lilian Jackson. *The Cat Who Knew Shakespeare*, 2954(F)
The Cat Who Lived High, 2952(F)
The Cat Who Sang for the Birds, 2953(F)
The Cat Who Sniffed Glue, 2954(F)
The Cat Who Talked to Ghosts, 2955(F)
Bray, Rosemary L. *Unafraid of the Dark*, 6813
Bredeson, Carmen. *American Writers of the 20th Century*, 6666
The Battle of the Alamo, 9123
Texas, 9563
Breitenbucher, Cathy. *Bonnie Blair*, 7731

Bremness, Lesley. *The Complete Book of Herbs*, 10706
Brems, Marianne. *The Fit Swimmer*, 11133
Brener, Milton. *Opera Offstage*, 6485
Brenlove, Milovan S. *Vectors to Spare*, 5437
Brennan, Christine. *Inside Edge*, 11078
Brennan, J. H. *Shiva*, 2035(F)
Shiva Accused, 2035(F)
Shiva's Challenge, 2036(F)
Brennan, Kristine. *Diana, Princess of Wales*, 7846
Scott Hamilton, 7737
Brennan, Matthew (jt. author). *Top Guns*, 6595
Brenner, Barbara. *If You Were There in 1776*, 9084
Brenner, Joel Glenn. *The Emperors of Chocolate*, 5304
Bresee, Clyde. *How Grand a Flame*, 9555
Breslin, Rosemary. *Not Exactly What I Had in Mind*, 6814
Breton, Mary Joy. *Women Pioneers for the Environment*, 5060
Brett-Surman, Michael. *The World of Dinosaurs*, 7963
Breuilly, Elizabeth. *Religions of the World*, 4469
Brewer, James D. *No Escape*, 2956(F)
No Justice, 2435(F)
No Remorse, 2957(F)
Brewer, Paul. *Warfare in the Ancient World*, 8062
Warfare in the Renaissance World, 8163
Brewster, Hugh. *Anastasia's Album*, 7885
Brewster, Todd (jt. author). *The Century*, 8896
Brewton, Sara, ed. *My Tang's Tungled and Other Ridiculous Situations*, 3884
Briatore, Flavio (jt. author). *Renault Formula 1 Motor Racing Book*, 10930
Brickhill, Paul. *The Great Escape*, 8272
Bridal, Tessa. *The Tree of Red Stars*, 27(F)
Bridgers, Jay. *Everything You Need to Know about Having an Addictive Personality*, 6249
Bridgers, Sue Ellen. *All We Know of Heaven*, 1063(F)
Home Before Dark, 629(F)
Keeping Christina, 1064(F)
Notes for Another Life, 630(F)
Permanent Connections, 1065(F)
Bridgman, Roger. *Electronics*, 10447
Brier, Bob. *Encyclopedia of Mummies*, 10809
The Murder of Tutankhamen, 8075
Brill, Marlene T. *Extraordinary Young People*, 7777
Guatemala, 8779
Guyana, 8829
Illinois, 9488
Indiana, 9489
Mongolia, 8571
Women for Peace, 4724
Brimelow, Peter. *Alien Nation*, 4797
Brimner, Larry Dane. *Being Different*, 6127
Voices from the Camps, 9398
Brimner, Larry Dane, ed. *Letters to Our Children*, 6128
Brin, David. *Otherness*, 3430(F)

Burgess, Melvin. *The Baby and Fly Pie*, 31(F)
  Smack, 911(F)
Burgett, Gordon. *Treasure and Scavenger Hunts*,
  10867
Burke, Delta. *Delta Style*, 6250
Burke, Jan. *Hocus*, 2960(F)
Burke, Kathleen. *Louisa May Alcott*, 6792
Burke, Patrick. *Eastern Europe*, 8607
Burkert, Nancy Ekholm. *Valentine & Orson*, 4100
Burkett, Elinor. *And the Band Played On*, 5735
  The Gravest Show on Earth, 5735
  Myth of Heterosexual AIDS, 5735
Burks, Brian. *Runs with Horses*, 2240(F)
  Soldier Boy, 2436(F)
  Walks Alone, 2241(F)
  Wrango, 32(F)
Burleigh, Robert. *Black Whiteness*, 6606
  Hoops, 3960
  Who Said That? Famous Americans Speak, 7135
Burnam, Tom. *Dictionary of Misinformation*, 10811
  More Misinformation, 10811
Burnett, Carol. *One More Time*, 6980
Burnett, Frances Hodgson. *The Secret Garden*,
  360(F)
Burnham, Philip. *Gbaya*, 8428
Burnham, Robert. *Advanced Skywatching*, 9637
Burnie, David. *The Concise Encyclopedia of the
  Human Body*, 5904
  Light, 10348
  Plant, 9792
  Tree, 9779
Burns, Ken (jt. author). *Baseball*, 10973
Burns, Landon C. *Pat Conroy*, 4300
Burns, Marilyn. *Math for Smarty Pants*, 10250
Burns, Olive Ann. *Cold Sassy Tree*, 2512(F)
Burr, Claudia. *Broken Shields*, 8795
Burroughs, Edgar Rice. *At the Earth's Core*, 3436(F)
  The Chessmen of Mars, 3437(F)
  Gods of Mars, 3437(F)
  Pellucidar, 3436(F)
  A Princess of Mars, 3437(F)
  Tamar of Pellucidar, 3436(F)
  Tarzan of the Apes, 33(F)
  Warlord of Mars, 3437(F)
Burstein, Chaya M. *The Jewish Kids Catalog*, 4543
Burstein, Patricia (jt. author). *The Many Lives of
  Elton John*, 7040
Burt, William Henry. *A Field Guide to the Mammals*,
  9868
Buscema, John (jt. author). *How to Draw Comics the
  Marvel Way*, 10682
Busch, Frederick. *Girls*, 2961(F)
Busch, Kristen. *Golden Boy*, 6994
Busch, Marlies. *Friendship Bands*, 10631
Busch, Phyllis B. *Wildflowers and the Stories behind
  Their Names*, 9793
Busch, Robert. *The Wolf Almanac*, 9900
Busch, Robert, ed. *Wolf Songs*, 9901
Busenberg, Bonnie. *Vanilla, Chocolate and
  Strawberry*, 9759

Bush, Lawrence. *Rooftop Secrets*, 452(F)
Bush, Vanessa T. (jt. author). *Tyra's Beauty Inside &
  Out*, 5892
Butcher, Kristin. *The Runaways*, 422(F)
Butler, Charles. *The Darkling*, 2690(F)
Butler, Geoff. *The Hangashore*, 34(F)
Butler, Susan. *The Hermit Thrush Sings*, 3438(F)
Butler, William. *The Butterfly Revolution*, 35(F)
Butterfield, Moira. *Look Inside Cross-Sections*,
  10466
  Richard Orr's Nature Cross-Sections, 9573
Butts, Nancy. *Cheshire Moon*, 1655(F)
  The Door in the Lake, 3439(F)
Byalick, Marcia. *It's a Matter of Trust*, 636(F)
Byars, Betsy. *Bingo Brown, Gypsy Lover*, 2836(F)
  Bingo Brown's Guide to Romance, 2837(F)
  Coast to Coast, 36(F)
  The Glory Girl, 637(F)
Byers, Ann. *The Holocaust Camps*, 8273
  Jaime Escalante, 7480
Byers, Patricia. *The Kids Money Book*, 5569
Byman, Jeremy. *Andrew Grove and the Intel
  Corporation*, 7576
  Madam Secretary, 7357
  Ted Turner, 7618
Byrne, Synda Altschuler (jt. author). *Foods from
  Mother Earth*, 10616
Byrnes, Patricia. *Environmental Pioneers*, 7512

Cader, Michael, ed. *Saturday Night Live*, 6559
Cadnum, Michael. *Breaking the Fall*, 1076(F)
  Edge, 912(F)
  Heat, 3684(F)
  In a Dark Wood, 2140(F)
  Rundown, 1077(F)
  Taking It, 638(F)
  Zero at the Bone, 639(F)
Caduto, Michael J. *Earth Tales from around the
  World*, 4049
Cady, Edwin H. *Stephen Crane*, 4301
Caes, Charles J. *Studies in Starlight*, 9667
Cage, Elizabeth. *Spy Girls*, 37(F)
Cahill, Susan, ed. *Writing Women's Lives*, 6667
Cahill, Tim. *Jaguars Ripped My Flesh*, 6607
  A Wolverine Is Eating My Leg, 6607
Cain, Michael. *Mary Cassatt*, 6715
Calabro, Marian. *Great Courtroom Lawyers*, 4649
  Operation Grizzly Bear, 9886
  The Perilous Journey of the Donner Party, 9264
Calambokidis, John. *Blue Whales*, 10031
Calder, Nigel, ed. *On the Frontiers of Science*, 9574
Caldicott, Helen. *If You Love This Planet*, 5062
Calhoun, Dia. *Firegold*, 1656(F)
Callahan, Steven. *Adrift*, 10300
Callan, Jamie. *Over the Hill at Fourteen*, 1078(F)
Callander, Don. *Geomancer*, 1657(F)
Calloway, Colin G. *The Abenaki*, 8937
  Indians of the Northeast, 8938
Calvert, Patricia. *Bigger*, 2437(F), 2439(F)

Glennis, Before and After, 640(F)
Great Lives, 7136
The Hour of the Wolf, 3685(F)
Picking Up the Pieces, 913(F)
The Snowbird, 2438(F)
Sooner, 2439(F)
The Stone Pony, 1079(F)
Calvert, Roz. *Zora Neale*, 6871
Calvino, Italo, retel. *Italian Folktales*, 4101
Camenson, Blythe (jt. author). *Careers in Education*, 5520
Cameron, Ann. *The Kidnapped Prince*, 7920
Camp, Carole Ann. *American Astronomers*, 7513
Sally Ride, 6653
Campbell, Andrew (jt. author). *The Encyclopedia of Aquatic Life*, 10000
Campbell, Ann-Jeanette. *The New York Public Library Amazing Space*, 9668
The New York Public Library Incredible Earth, 10166
Campbell, Bebe Moore. *Singing in the Comeback Choir*, 641(F)
Campbell, Eric. *Papa Tembo*, 264(F)
The Place of Lions, 38(F)
The Shark Callers, 39(F)
Campbell, Malcolm. *The Random House International Encyclopedia of Golf*, 11053
Campbell, Patricia J. *Fade*, 4302
Presenting Robert Cormier, 4302
Candaele, Kerry. *Bound for Glory*, 9358
Canesso, Claudia. *South Africa*, 8467
Canfield, Jack. *Chicken Soup for the Teenage Soul*, 6223
Chicken Soup for the Teenage Soul II, 6224
Cann, Kate. *Diving In*, 3287(F)
Living in the World, 5001
Cannon, A. E. *The Shadow Brothers*, 1080(F)
Cantwell, Mary. *Manhattan, When I Was Young*, 7470
Cape, Elizabeth (jt. author). *Best Friends*, 10530
Capek, Michael. *Murals*, 6394
Caplan, Theresa. *The First Twelve Months of Life*, 6073
Capote, Truman. *A Christmas Memory*, 1081(F)
The Thanksgiving Visitor, 1081(F)
Capps, Walter, ed. *The Vietnam Reader*, 9447
Capstick, Peter Hathaway. *Sands of Silence*, 11037
Caraccilo, Dominic J. *The Ready Brigade of the 82nd Airborne in Desert Storm*, 9448
Caras, Roger A. *The Cats of Thistle Hill*, 10077
A Most Dangerous Journey, 9912
Roger Caras' Treasury of Great Cat Stories, 265(F)
Roger Caras' Treasury of Great Dog Stories, 266(F)
Carbone, Elisa. *Stealing Freedom*, 2331(F)
Card, Orson Scott. *Alvin Journeyman*, 3440(F)
The Call of Earth, 3441(F)
Children of the Mind, 3442(F)
Ender's Game, 3446(F)
Homebody, 2691(F)
The Memory of Earth, 3444(F)

Pastwatch, 3445(F)
Seventh Son, 1658(F)
Speaker for the Dead, 3446(F)
Card, Orson Scott, ed. *Future on Ice*, 3443(F)
Cardillo, Joe. *Pulse*, 423(F)
Cardozo, Arlene. *Jewish Family Celebrations*, 4544
Cardwell, Donald. *The Norton History of Technology*, 10364
Carey, D. L. *Distress Call 911*, 40(F)
Cargill, Linda. *Pool Party*, 2962(F)
The Surfer, 2692(F)
Carkeet, David. *Quiver River*, 2838(F)
Carle, Eric. *Flora and Tiger*, 6714
Carlin, Richard. *Jazz*, 6460
Carlip, Hillary (jt. author). *Zine Scene*, 5364
Carlish, Anne. *Divorce*, 6310
Carlon, Patricia. *The Souvenir*, 2963(F)
Carlson, Dale B. *Girls Are Equal Too*, 6251
Where's Your Head? 6216
Carlson, Hannah (jt. author). *Girls Are Equal Too*, 6251
Where's Your Head? 6216
Carlson, Judy. *Harriet Tubman*, 7247
Carlson, Lori M., ed. *American Eyes*, 453(F)
Barrio Streets Carnival Dreams, 4952
Cool Salsa, 3961
Carlson, Richard. *2020 Visions*, 5268
Carlson-Finnerty, La Vonne (jt. author). *Memory and Learning*, 6242
Carlsson, Bo Kage. *Sweden*, 8718
Carmean, Karen. *Ernest J. Gaines*, 4303
Carnegy, Vicky. *Fashions of a Decade*, 10632
Carnes, Jim. *Us and Them*, 5240
Caroli, Betty Boyd. *Immigrants Who Returned Home*, 4799
Carpenter, Angelica S. *Frances Hodgson Burnett*, 6823
Robert Louis Stevenson, 6913
Carr, Ian Digby Fairweather, ed. *Jazz*, 6461
Carr, Philippa. *The Changeling*, 3288(F)
Carrel, Annette. *It's the Law! A Young Person's Guide to Our Legal System*, 4650
Carrillo, Louis. *Oscar de la Renta*, 7918
Carrol, Rebecca. *Sugar in the Raw*, 4856
Carroll, Bob. *Napoleon Bonaparte*, 7882
Pancho Villa, 7905
Carroll, Joan. *The Black College Career Guide*, 5416
Carroll, Lenore. *One Hundred Girls' Mother*, 2513(F)
Carroll, Marilyn. *Cocaine and Crack*, 5621
Carrow, Robert. *Put a Fan in Your Hat!* 9609
Carson, Clayborne, ed. *The Eyes on the Prize Civil Rights Reader*, 4726
Carson, Mary Kay. *Epilepsy*, 5736
Carson, Rob. *Mount St. Helens*, 10179
Cart, Michael. *My Father's Scar*, 1082(F)
Presenting Robert Lipsyte, 4304
Cart, Michael, ed. *Tomorrowland*, 3447(F)

Cline, Don. *Alias Billy the Kid, the Man Behind the Legend*, 7465

Cline, Ruth K. J. *Focus on Families*, 6312

Clinton, Catherine, ed. *I, Too, Sing America*, 3962

Clinton, Susan. *Reading Between the Bones*, 7965

Close, Jessie. *The Warping of Al*, 652(F)

Clouse, Woody (jt. author). *Winning Racquetball*, 11144

Clucas, Richard A. *Encyclopedia of American Political Reform*, 4590

Clute, John. *The Illustrated Encyclopedia*, 4256

Clute, John, ed. *The Encyclopedia of Fantasy*, 4257

Clutton-Brock, Juliet. *Cat*, 10078
Dog, 10097
Horse, 10127

Cobain, Bev. *When Nothing Matters Anymore*, 5991

Cobb, Josh (jt. author). *Light Action*, 10349

Cobb, Richard, ed. *Voices of the French Revolution*, 8629

Cobb, Vicki. *Chemically Active! Experiments You Can Do at Home*, 10155
How to Really Fool Yourself, 5960
Light Action, 10349
Magic . . . Naturally! Science Entertainments and Amusements, 10715
More Science Experiments You Can Eat, 9610
Science Experiments You Can Eat, 9610
The Secret Life of Cosmetics, 9611
The Secret Life of Hardware, 9612
You Gotta Try This! 9613

Cochran, Molly. *The Broken Sword*, 1666(F)

Cochran, Thomas. *Roughnecks*, 3689(F)

Cochrane, Kerry. *Researching Colleges on the World Wide Web*, 5417

Cockcroft, James D. *Diego Rivera*, 6773
The Hispanic Struggle for Social Justice, 4954
Latinos in Béisbol, 10934

Cocke, William. *A Historical Album of Virginia*, 9557

Codell, Esmé Raji. *Educating Esmé*, 5339

Coe, Lewis. *The Telegraph*, 10451

Coe, Michael D. *Atlas of Ancient America*, 8940

Coel, Margaret. *The Story Teller*, 2992(F)

Coelho, Paulo. *The Alchemist*, 1667(F)

Coen, Patricia. *Beautiful Braids*, 5893

Cofer, Judith O. *An Island Like You*, 456(F)
The Latin Deli, 457(F)
The Year of Our Revolution, 458(F)

Cohall, Alwyn T. (jt. author). *The Watts Teen Health Dictionary*, 5582

Cohen, Barbara. *Canterbury Tales*, 361

Cohen, Daniel. *The Alaska Purchase*, 9327
Animal Rights, 5003
Cloning, 5878
Cults, 4559
The Encyclopedia of Monsters, 10813
The Encyclopedia of the Strange, 10814
Great Conspiracies and Elaborate Coverups, 8035
Joseph McCarthy, 7415
The Manhattan Project, 10518
The Modern Ark, 9961

Phantom Animals, 2695(F)
Prophets of Doom, 10815
Southern Fried Rat & Other Gruesome Tales, 4161
Werewolves, 10816
The World's Most Famous Ghosts, 10817
Young Ghosts, 10818

Cohen, Daniel (jt. author). *Teenage Competition*, 6253
Teenage Stress, 5992

Cohen, David (jt. author). *The African Americans*, 4858

Cohen, Joel (jt. author). *Inside Pocket Billiards*, 10896
Steve Mizerak's Pocket Billiards, 10896

Cohen, Leah H. *Glass, Paper, Beans*, 10366
Heat Lightning, 1096(F)

Cohen, Miriam. *Robert and Dawn Marie 4Ever*, 1097(F)

Cohen, Susan. *Teenage Competition*, 6253
Teenage Stress, 5992

Cohn, Amy L., comp. *From Sea to Shining Sea*, 4162

Cohodas, Nadine. *Strom Thurmond and the Politics of Southern Change*, 7456

Coil, Suzanne M. *Campaign Financing*, 4696
Harriet Beecher Stowe, 6916

Coiley, John. *Train*, 10501

Colbert, David, ed. *Eyewitness to America*, 8873

Colbert, Nancy A. *Lou Hoover*, 7274

Cole, Barbara. *Alex the Great*, 916(F)

Cole, Brock. *The Facts Speak for Themselves*, 653(F)
The Goats, 1098(F)

Cole, Carolyn Kozo. *Shades of L.A.*, 4800

Cole, Joanna, ed. *Best-Loved Folktales of the World*, 4051

Cole, Melanie. *Mariah Carey*, 6981

Cole, Michael D. *Bill Clinton*, 7260
The Los Angeles Riots, 4857
The Siege at Waco, 4560
TWA Flight 800, 10476

Cole, Sheila. *What Kind of Love?* 1099(F)

Cole, Wendy M. *Vietnam*, 8573

Coleman, Michael. *Weirdo's War*, 50(F)

Coleman, Ray. *Clapton!* 6988

Coleridge, Samuel Taylor. *The Rime of the Ancient Mariner*, 3935

Coles, Janet. *The Book of Beads*, 10633

Coles, Joan M. (jt. author). *Emily Post's Teen Etiquette*, 6236

Coles, Robert. *The Youngest Parents*, 6074

Collard, Sneed B. *Alien Invaders*, 5066
Monteverde, 10202

Collier, C. *Andrew Jackson's America, 1824–1850*, 9125
Hispanic America, Texas & the Mexican War, 1835–1850, 9126
The Jeffersonian Republicans, 1800–1823, 9127

Collier, Christopher. *The American Revolution*, 9085
Building a New Nation, 1789–1801, 9086
Clash of Cultures, Prehistory–1638, 9046
Creating the Constitution, 1787, 4597

Farish, Terry. *Talking in Animal*, 1149(F)
Farjeon, Eleanor. *The Glass Slipper*, 1706(F)
Farley, Steven (jt. author). *The Black Stallion*, 275(F)
　The Young Black Stallion, 275(F)
Farley, Walter. *The Black Stallion*, 274(F)
　The Young Black Stallion, 275(F)
Farlow, James O. *On the Tracks of Dinosaurs*, 7972
Farman Farmaian, Sattareh. *Daughter of Persia*, 7804
Farmer, Nancy. *The Ear, the Eye and the Arm*, 3489(F)
　A Girl Named Disaster, 2092(F)
Farmer, Penelope. *Penelope*, 688(F)
Farmer, Philip Jose. *The Dark Design*, 3492(F)
　Dayworld, 3490(F)
　Dayworld Breakup, 3490(F)
　Dayworld Rebel, 3490(F)
　Gods of Riverworld, 3491(F)
　The Gods of Riverworld, 3492(F)
　The Magic Labyrinth, 3492(F)
　To Your Scattered Bodies Go, 3492(F)
Farndon, John. *Nitrogen*, 10156
　Oxygen, 10157
Farnes, Catherine. *Snòw*, 929(F)
Farr, Judith. *I Never Came to You in White*, 1150(F)
Farrand, John. *Eastern Birds*, 9927
　How to Identify Birds, 9927
　Western Birds, 9927
Farrell, Jacqueline. *The Great Depression*, 9364
Farrell, Jeanette. *Invisible Enemies*, 5753
Farrell, Kate (jt. author). *Talking to the Sun*, 3905
Farrell, Mame. *Bradley & the Billboard*, 3707(F)
　Marrying Malcolm Murgatroyd, 1151(F)
Farro, Rita. *Life Is Not a Dress Size*, 6261
Farwell, Byron. *Ball's Bluff*, 9186
Fast, Howard. *April Morning*, 2303(F)
　The Immigrants, 2304(F)
Fasulo, Michael. *Careers for Environmental Types*, 5443
Faulk, Laura E. (jt. author). *The Modoc*, 8951
Faulk, Odie B. *The Modoc*, 8951
Faust, Drew Gilpin. *Mothers of Invention*, 9187
Favreau, Marc (jt. author). *Remembering Slavery*, 9121
Feder, Harriet K. *Mystery in Miami Beach*, 3033(F)
　Mystery of the Kaifeng Scroll, 3033(F)
Feelings, Tom. *The Middle Passage*, 4866
　Tommy Traveler in the World of Black History, 4867
Feelings, Tom (jt. author). *Now Sheba Sings the Song*, 4390
Feest, Christian F. *The Powhatan Tribes*, 8952
Feik, Luanne (jt. author). *Stars in Your Eyes . . . Feet on the Ground*, 5487
Feinberg, Barbara S. *Constitutional Amendments*, 4601
　Douglas MacArthur, 7411
　Harry S Truman, 7335
　Next in Line, 4629
Feinberg, Brian. *The Musculoskeletal System*, 5948
Feinberg, Jeremy R. *Reading the Sports Page*, 10876

Feintuch, David. *Fisherman's Hope*, 3493(F)
　Voices of Hope, 3494(F)
Felder, Deborah G. *The Black 100*, 6592
　The Jewish 100, 6592
　The 100 Most Influential Women of All Time, 6592
Felder, Leonard (jt. author). *Making Peace with Your Parents*, 6305
Feldman, Douglas A. *The AIDS Crisis: A Documentary History*, 5754
Feldman, Elane. *Fashions of a Decade*, 10636
Felgar, Robert. *Understanding Richard Wright's Black Boy*, 4318
Felix, Antonia (jt. author). *Is There a Dinosaur in Your Backyard?* 7964
　Shake, Rattle & Roll, 10180
Felleman, Hazel, ed. *Poems That Live Forever*, 3889
Fensch, Thomas, ed. *Oskar Schindler and His List*, 7887
Fenton, M. Brock. *Just Bats*, 9869
Ferber, Edna. *Cimarron*, 2454(F)
　Ice Palace, 2520(F)
　Saratoga Trunk, 2454(F)
　Show Boat, 2520(F)
　So Big, 2520(F)
Ferber, Elizabeth. *Diabetes*, 5755
　Steven Spielberg, 7107
　Yasir Arafat, 7799
Ferguson, Alane. *Overkill*, 3034(F)
　Show Me the Evidence, 3035(F)
Ferguson, Alane (jt. author). *Cliff-Hanger*, 217(F)
　Wolf Stalker, 3229(F)
Ferguson, Gary. *Spirits of the Wild*, 4057
Ferguson, J. G. *What Can I Do Now?* 5479
Ferguson, Kitty. *Stephen Hawking*, 7579
Ferguson Publishing, eds. *Careers in Focus—Arts & Entertainment*, 5480
　Careers in Focus—Medical Tech, 5530
Ferguson Publishing, ed. *Careers in Focus—Sports*, 5481
Ferlazzo, Paul J. *Emily Dickinson*, 4393
Fernandez, Ronald M. *Puerto Rico Past & Present*, 8822
Ferrell, Nancy W. *The Battle of the Little Bighorn*, 8953
　Destination Valdez, 9532
　The U.S. Coast Guard, 4705
Ferrie, Richard. *The World Turned Upside Down*, 9093
Ferris, Jean. *All That Glitters*, 76(F)
　Bad, 1152(F)
　Into the Wind, 2338(F)
　Invincible Summer, 930(F)
　Love Among the Walnuts, 2849(F)
　Relative Strangers, 689(F)
　Signs of Life, 1153(F)
　Song of the Sea, 77(F)
Ferris, Jeri. *Thomas Jefferson*, 7278
Ferry, Charles. *A Fresh Start*, 1154(F)
　Raspberry One, 2604(F)
Feuer, Elizabeth. *Lost Summer*, 690(F)

Japanese-American Internment in American History, 9407

The Negro Baseball Leagues, 10940

The Watergate Scandal in American History, 9408

Freund, David M. P. *Biographical Supplement and Index,* 4870

Frey, Darcy. *The Last Shot,* 10977

Frey, Richard. *According to Hoyle,* 11025

Fridell, Ron. *Amphibians in Danger,* 9817

Friedel, Robert. *Zipper,* 10372

Friedhoffer, Robert. *Physics Lab in a Hardware Store,* 10321

   Physics Lab in a Housewares Store, 10322

   Physics Lab in the Home, 10323

   Science Lab in a Supermarket, 9616

Friedlander, Mark P. *The Immune System,* 5761

Friedman, C. S. *Crown of Shadows,* 1711(F)

Friedman, Ina R. *Flying Against the Wind,* 7890

Friedman, Kinky. *God Bless John Wayne,* 3044(F)

Friedman, Norman. *Desert Victory,* 9457

Friel, Maeve. *Charlie's Story,* 1168(F)

Friesen, Gayle. *Janey's Girl,* 704(F)

Frissell, Susan. *Eating Disorders and Weight Control,* 5762

Fritz, Jean. *Bully for You, Teddy Roosevelt!* 7330

   China Homecoming, 6848

   China's Long March, 8529

   The Great Little Madison, 7310

   Harriet Beecher Stowe and the Beecher Preachers, 6917

   Homesick, My Own Story, 6849

   Make Way for Sam Houston, 7393

   Stonewall, 7394

   Traitor, 7359

   Why Not, Lafayette? 7874

Froehlich, Margaret W. *Hide Crawford Quick,* 936(F)

Frome, Keith (jt. author). *The Columbia Book of Civil War Poetry,* 4009

Fromental, Jean-Luc. *Broadway Chicken,* 1712(F)

Fromon, David K. *Running Away,* 6262

Fronval, George. *Indian Signs and Signals,* 8956

Frost, Helen, ed. *Why Darkness Seems So Light,* 5012

Frost, Mary Pierce. *The Mexican Revolution,* 8798

Frost, Robert. *A Swinger of Birches,* 3974

   You Come Too, 3975

Frost-Knappman, Elizabeth. *Women's Rights on Trial,* 4740

Frumkes, Burke Lewis (jt. author). *The Mensa Think Smart Book,* 10798

Fry, Annette R. *The Orphan Trains,* 9329

Fry, Ron. *"Ace" Any Test,* 5359

   How to Study, 5350

Fry, Stephen. *Making History,* 1713(F)

Fry, Virginia. *Part of Me Died, Too,* 5591

Frydenborg, Kay. *They Dreamed of Horses,* 5446

Fuchs, Thomas. *The Hitler Fact Book,* 7868

Fulbrook, Mary. *A Concise History of Germany,* 8639

Fulghum, Robert. *All I Really Need to Know I Learned in Kindergarten,* 4457

Fuller, Jamie. *The Diary of Emily Dickinson,* 2522(F)

Fuller, Kimberly. *Home,* 3503(F)

Fuller, Sarah B. *Hazelwood v. Kuhlmeier,* 4741

Fuller, Sarah B. (jt. author). *Brown v. Board of Education,* 4739

Fulton, Michael T. *Exploring Careers in Cyberspace,* 5546

Funderburk, Robert. *Winter of Grace,* 88(F)

Funk, Gary. *A Balancing Act,* 5419

Funk, Wilfred (jt. author). *Thirty Days to a More Powerful Vocabulary,* 5390

Fuqua, Jonathon Scott. *The Reappearance of Sam Webber,* 705(F)

Furbee, Mary R. *Women of the American Revolution,* 7143

Furey, Joan A. (jt. author). *Visions of War, Dreams of Peace,* 9478

Furgurson, Ernest B. *Ashes of Glory,* 9190

   Chancellorsville 1863, 9191

Furlong, Monica. *Juniper,* 1714(F)

   Wise Child, 2721(F)

Fynn, Anna. *Mister God, This Is Anna,* 5996

Fyson, Nance Lui. *Feeding the World,* 5221

   The 1940s, 9409

Gaar, Gillian. *She's a Rebel,* 6454

Gaarder, Jostein. *The Solitaire Mystery,* 706(F)

Gabhart, Ann. *Bridge to Courage,* 1169(F)

   Wish Come True, 2722(F)

Gable, Fred B. *Opportunities in Pharmacy Careers,* 5547

Gabriel, Mary. *Notorious Victoria,* 7458

Gaeddert, Louann. *Breaking Free,* 2307(F)

Gaer, Joseph. *What the Great Religions Believe,* 4477

Gaertner, Ursula. *Elmolo,* 8432

Gaffron, Norma. *Dealing with Death,* 5592

Gaillard, Frye. *If I Were a Carpenter,* 5270

   200 M.P.H., 10923

Gaiman, Neil. *Stardust,* 1715(F)

Gaines, Ann. *Entertainment and Performing Arts,* 6674

   Herodotus and the Explorers of the Classical Age, 8068

   The Panama Canal in American History, 8780

   Prisons, 5144

   Roseanne, 6969

   Sports and Activities, 7629

   Terrorism, 5295

   Whoopi Goldberg, 7017

Gaines, Ernest J. *The Autobiography of Miss Jane Pittman,* 469(F)

   A Gathering of Old Men, 470(F)

   A Lesson Before Dying, 3045(F)

Gaines, Richard. *The Explorers of the Undersea World,* 10304

Galang, M. Evelina. *Her Wild American Self,* 4658

Galas, Judith C. *Drugs and Sports,* 5631

Gay Rights, 4742

Plastics, 10373

Galbraith, Judy. *The Gifted Kids' Survival Guide*, 6239

Galbraith, Judy (jt. author). *What Teens Need to Succeed*, 6246

Galicich, Anne. *The German Americans*, 4979

Gall, Grant. *Apache*, 2249(F)

Gall, Susan B. (jt. author). *Asian American Chronology*, 4853

Gallagher, Gary, ed. *The Wilderness Campaign*, 9192

Gallagher, Hugh Gregory. *Black Bird Fly Away*, 7484

Gallagher, Jim. *Pedro Martinez*, 7665

Gallagher-Mundy, Chrissie. *The Essential Guide to Stretching*, 5974

Gallant, Roy A. *The Day the Sky Split Apart*, 9702

Earth, 9709

Earth's Vanishing Forests, 9783

The Peopling of Planet Earth, 5121

When the Sun Dies, 9722

Gallen, David. *Bill Clinton*, 7262

Malcolm X, 7227

Gallico, Paul. *The Snow Goose*, 276(F)

Gallman, J. Matthew. *The North Fights the Civil War*, 9193

Gallo, Donald R. *Presenting Richard Peck*, 4319

Gallo, Donald R., ed. *Center Stage*, 3830

Join In, 471(F)

No Easy Answers, 1170(F)

Sixteen, 1171(F)

Time Capsule, 3756(F)

Galloway, Priscilla. *Daedalus and the Minotaur*, 4210

The Snake Dreamer's Story, 1716(F)

Galloway, Priscilla, retel. *Aleta and the Queen*, 4209

Galperin, Anne. *Nuclear Energy/Nuclear Waste*, 10343

Galt, Margot F. *Up to the Plate*, 10941

Galvin, Irene F. *The Ancient Maya*, 8781

Galvin, Jack (jt. author). *Within Reach*, 6649

Gan, Geraldine. *Communication*, 9330

Ganeri, Anita. *Inside the Body*, 5906

Out of the Ark, 4478

Rivers, Ponds and Lakes, 10220

The Young Person's Guide to the Ballet, 6514

Ganesan, Indira. *Inheritance*, 2109(F)

Gann, Ernest K. *Fate Is the Hunter*, 89(F)

Gantos, Jack. *Heads or Tails*, 2221(F)

Jack's Black Book, 1172(F)

Jack's New Power, 2221(F)

Joey Pigza Swallowed the Key, 937(F)

Garassino, Alessandro. *Life, Origins and Evolution*, 7997

Plants, 9796

Garbarino, Merwyn S. *The Seminole*, 8957

Garcia, Cristina. *The Aguero Sisters*, 426(F)

Garcia, John. *The Success of Hispanic Magazine*, 4438

Garden, Nancy. *Devils and Demons*, 10825

The Door Between, 1717(F)

Dove and Sword, 2155(F)

Fours Crossing, 1717(F)

Good Moon Rising, 1173(F)

Lark in the Morning, 707(F)

Watersmeet, 1717(F)

The Year They Burned the Books, 1174(F)

Gardner, Helen, ed. *The New Oxford Book of English Verse, 1250–1950*, 3939

Gardner, Herb. *Conversations with My Father*, 3831

Gardner, Joann, ed. *Runaway with Words*, 3976

Gardner, John. *Grendel*, 1718(F)

Maestro, 3046(F)

Gardner, Martin. *Aha! Gotcha*, 10251

Hexaflexagons and Other Mathematical Diversions, 10252

On the Wild Side, 10826

Time Travel and Other Mathematical Bewilderments, 10253

Gardner, Mary. *Boat People*, 472(F)

Gardner, Richard. *The Boys and Girls Book about Stepfamilies*, 6322

Gardner, Robert. *Architecture*, 6382

Celebrating Earth Day, 5072

Communication, 10453

Crime Lab 101, 5145

Electricity and Magnetism, 10356

Experimenting with Water, 10271

Experiments with Motion, 10334

The Forgotten Players, 10942

Kitchen Chemistry, 9617

Science Project Ideas about Air, 10259

Science Project Ideas about Animal Behavior, 9850

Science Project Ideas about Trees, 9784

Science Projects about Chemistry, 10161

Science Projects about Kitchen Chemistry, 9618

Science Projects about Physics in the Home, 10324

Science Projects about Plants, 9797

Science Projects about the Environment and Ecology, 9966

Transportation, 10467

The Whale Watchers' Guide, 10036

What's Super about the Supernatural? 10827

Where on Earth Am I? 8039

Gardner, Robert (jt. author). *Ideas for Science Projects*, 9604

More Ideas for Science Projects, 9605

Garfield, Leon. *Shakespeare Stories*, 3816

Shakespeare Stories II, 4374

Garg, Samidha. *Racism*, 4823

Garisto, Leslie. *The Best-Ever Book of Dog & Cat Names*, 10069

Garland, Sherry. *Indio*, 2265(F)

Letters from the Mountain, 1175(F)

A Line in the Sand, 2456(F)

Rainmaker's Dream, 708(F)

Shadow of the Dragon, 473(F)

Song of the Buffalo Boy, 2110(F)

Garner, Joan. *Stagings*, 3832

Garretson, James D. *The Deadwood Conspiracy*, 90(F)

Garrett, Wendell, ed. *Our Changing White House*, 9512

Garrison, Webb. *A Treasury of Civil War Tales*, 9194

Gartner, Bob. *High Performance through Teamwork*, 6217

  Working Together Against the Destruction of the Environment, 5073

Garvey, Lonny D. *Opportunities in the Machine Trades*, 5519

Garwood, Julie. *A Girl Named Summer*, 3305(F)

Garza, Hedda. *African Americans and Jewish Americans*, 4824

  Barred from the Bar, 4659

  Frida Kahlo, 6739

  Pablo Casals, 6984

Gaskins, Pearl Fuyo, ed. *What Are You? Voices of Mixed-Race Young People*, 4825

Gaspari, Claudia. *Food in Italy*, 10590

Gates, Doris. *Blue Willow*, 709(F)

  A Fair Wind for Troy, 4211

Gates, Henry Louis, Jr. *Thirteen Ways of Looking at a Black Man*, 4871

Gatti, Anne, retel. *The Magic Flute*, 6488

Gavin, Thomas. *Breathing Water*, 3047(F)

Gay, Douglas. *The Not-So-Minor Leagues*, 10943

Gay, Kathlyn. *After the Shooting Stops*, 8885

  Air Pollution, 5103

  Child Labor, 5013

  Church and State, 4602

  Civil War, 9195

  Communes and Cults, 4561

  Getting Your Message Across, 4413

  I Am Who I Am, 4826

  Korean War, 9458

  Militias, 5014

  Neo-Nazis, 5015

  Persian Gulf War, 9459

  Pregnancy, 6080

  Revolutionary War, 9094

  The Right to Die, 5593

  Rights and Respect, 6183

  Saving the Environment, 5074

  Spanish-American War, 9331

  They Don't Wash Their Socks! Sports Superstitions, 10879

  Vietnam War, 9460

  War of 1812, 9130

  Who's Running the Nation? 4690

  World War I, 8235

  World War II, 8292

Gay, Kathlyn (jt. author). *The Information Superhighway*, 10419

  The Not-So-Minor Leagues, 10943

Gay, Martin. *The Information Superhighway*, 10419

  The New Information Revolution, 10418

Gay, Martin (jt. author). *After the Shooting Stops*, 8885

  Civil War, 9195

  Korean War, 9458

  Persian Gulf War, 9459

  Revolutionary War, 9094

  Spanish-American War, 9331

  Vietnam War, 9460

  War of 1812, 9130

  World War I, 8235

  World War II, 8292

Gayle, Katie. *Snappy Jazzy Jewelry*, 10637

Gayler, Paul. *Ultimate Vegetarian Cookbook*, 10591

Geary, Rick. *A Treasury of Victorian Murder*, 9332

Gee, Maurice. *The Champion*, 2111(F)

  The Fat Man, 3048(F)

  The Fire-Raiser, 3049(F)

Geier, Arnold. *Heroes of the Holocaust*, 8293

Gelb, Alan. *Real Life*, 1176(F)

Gelbspan, Ross. *The Heat Is On*, 5075

Gelinas, Paul J. *Coping with Weight Problems*, 6041

Gellman, Marc. *How Do You Spell God? Answers to the Big Questions from Around the World*, 4479

Genet, Donna. *Father Junipero Serra*, 6659

Genovese, Eugene D. *Roll, Jordan, Roll*, 4872

Gentry, Tony. *Elvis Presley*, 7080

  Jesse Owens, 7764

  Paul Laurence Dunbar, 6844

George, Jean Craighead. *The Case of the Missing Cutthroats*, 91(F)

  Frightful's Mountain, 277(F)

  Julie of the Wolves, 92(F)

  Julie's Wolf Pack, 93(F)

  My Side of the Mountain, 94(F)

  One Day in the Alpine Tundra, 95(F)

  Shark Beneath the Reef, 96(F)

  Summer of the Falcon, 278(F)

  The Talking Earth, 97(F)

  Water Sky, 98(F)

George-Kanentiio, Douglas M. (jt. author). *Skywoman*, 4154

Geraghty, Helen M. *Chris Burke*, 6979

Geras, Adèle. *Pictures of the Night*, 3306(F)

  The Tower Room, 3307(F)

Gerber, Merrill Joan. *Handsome as Anything*, 3308(F)

Gerber, Philip. *Robert Frost*, 4394

Gerberg, Mort. *Cartooning*, 10674

  The U.S. Constitution for Everyone, 4603

Gerdes, Louise, ed. *Battered Women*, 6323

  Sexual Harassment, 6184

Gerritsen, Tess. *Bloodstream*, 99(F)

Gerrold, David. *Chess with a Dragon*, 3504(F)

Gerstein, Mordicai. *Victor*, 2156(F)

Gerstenfeld, Sheldon L. *The Bird Care Book*, 10070

  The Cat Care Book, 10082

  The Dog Care Book, 10103

Gherman, Beverly. *E. B. White*, 6938

  Georgia O'Keeffe, 6759

  Robert Louis Stevenson, 6914

Giardino, Vittorio. *Adolescence*, 2157(F)

  A Jew in Communist Prague, 2157(F)

  Loss of Innocence, 2157(F)

Gibbons, Kaye. *Charms for the Easy Life*, 2523(F)

  On the Occasion of My Last Afternoon, 2389(F)

The American Media, 10458
Capital Punishment, 5148
Eleanor Roosevelt, 7320
Georges Clemenceau, 7843
Homelessness, 5222
James Baldwin, 6805
Pornography, 5245
Privacy, 4745
Gottlieb, Eli. *The Boy Who Went Away*, 711(F)
Goulart, Ron. *Groucho Marx*, 3054(F)
Gould, Lewis L., ed. *American First Ladies*, 7144
Gould, Marilyn. *Golden Daffodils*, 939(F)
The Twelfth of June, 939(F)
Gould, Steven. *Wild Side*, 3508(F)
Gourley, Catherine. *Beryl Markham*, 6644
Good Girl Work, 9333
Hunting Neptune's Giants, 10037
Sharks! 10023
Gourley, Catherine, ed. *Read for Your Life*, 104(F)
Gourse, Leslie. *Aretha Franklin, Lady Soul*, 7012
Blowing on the Changes, 6455
Deep Down in Music, 6467
Dizzy Gillespie and the Birth of Bebop, 7015
Mahalia Jackson, 7036
Striders to Beboppers and Beyond, 6468
Swingers and Crooners, 6677
Govignon, Brigitte, ed. *The Beginner's Guide to Art*, 6406
Gow, Catherine H. *The Cuban Missile Crisis*, 9411
Gowing, Lawrence. *Biographical Dictionary of Artists*, 6678
Grabish, Beatrice R. *Drugs and Your Brain*, 5638
Grabowski, John. *Canada*, 8774
The Death Penalty, 4661
Sports Great Emmitt Smith, 7724
Grace, C. L. *The Merchant of Death*, 3055(F)
Gradwohl, Judith (jt. author). *The Wealth of Oceans*, 10297
Grady, Sean M. *Explosives*, 10523
Virtual Reality, 10422
Graeber, Charlotte. *Grey Cloud*, 280(F)
Graff, Henry F., ed. *The Presidents*, 4618
Grafton, Sue. *"G" Is for Gumshoe*, 3056(F)
"M" Is for Malice, 3057(F)
Gragg, Rod. *The Civil War Quiz and Fact Book*, 9199
Graham, Andrew (jt. author). *Meteorites*, 9703
Graham, Kevin (jt. author). *Alternative Energy Sources*, 10330
Environmental Causes, 5063
Kids Who Make a Difference, 5064
Natural Foods and Products, 9760
Protecting Our Air, Land, and Water, 5065
Recycling, 5113
Graham, Kristen, ed. *The Great Monologues from the Women's Project*, 3836
Graham, Paula W. *Speaking of Journals; Children's Book Writers Talk about Their Diaries, Notebooks, and Sketchbooks*, 5374
Graham, Robin Lee. *Dove*, 6630

Graham-Smith, Francis. *Pathways to the Universe*, 9643
Gralla, Preston. *Online Kids*, 10423
Grambo, Rebecca L. *Eagles*, 9950
Grand, Gail L. *Student Science Opportunities*, 5411
Granfield, Linda. *Amazing Grace*, 7497
Circus, 6581
Grant, Cynthia D. *Mary Wolf*, 712(F)
Shadow Man, 713(F)
The White Horse, 940(F)
Grant, Donna (jt. author). *Tryin' to Sleep in the Bed You Made*, 462(F)
Grant, Janet. *The Young Person's Guide to Becoming a Writer*, 5375
Grant, John (jt. author). *The Encyclopedia of Fantasy*, 4257
Grant, Lesley. *Great Careers for People Concerned about the Environment*, 5548
Grant, Michael. *Myths of the Greeks and Romans*, 4212
Grant, R. G. *The Berlin Wall*, 8641
Genocide, 4579
Hiroshima and Nagasaki, 8298
The Holocaust, 8299
Grant, Richard (jt. author). *Richard's Bicycle Repair Manual*, 11004
Grattan-Dominguez, Alejandro. *Breaking Even*, 1183(F)
Grau, Andrea. *Dance*, 6515
Gravelle, Jennifer (jt. author). *The Period Book*, 6134
Gravelle, Karen. *The Period Book*, 6134
Soaring Spirits, 4963
Teenage Fathers, 6081
Teenagers Face to Face with Bereavement, 5594
Teenagers Face to Face with Cancer, 5764
What's Going on Down There? 6133
Where Are My Birth Parents? A Guide for Teenage Adoptees, 6327
Graves, Douglas R. *Drawing Portraits*, 10676
Graves, Robert. *Greek Gods and Heroes*, 4213
Gravett, Christopher. *Castle*, 8174
The World of the Medieval Knight, 8175
Gray, Heather. *Real Girl/Real World*, 6264
Gray, Keith. *Creepers*, 1184(F)
Gray, Mary L. *In Your Face*, 6135
Graymont, Barbara. *The Iroquois*, 8962
Greeley, Ronald. *The NASA Atlas of the Solar System*, 9673
Green, Carl R. *Allan Pinkerton*, 7433
Butch Cassidy, 7474
The Dalton Gang, 7478
David Robinson, 7700
Doc Holliday, 7392
Jackie Joyner-Kersee, 7759
Jesse James, 7488
Wyatt Earp, 7382
Green, Connie Jordan. *Emmy*, 2563(F)
Green, Jen. *Exploring the Polar Regions*, 8852
Green, John. *The New Age of Communications*, 10424

Green, Paul. *Making Money with Baseball Cards*, 10768

101 Ways to Make Money in the Trading-Card Market, 10767

Green, Peter. *Ancient Greece*, 8108

Green, Rayna. *Women in American Indian Society*, 8963

Green, Rebecca L. *Merina*, 8470

Green, Richard G. *Sing, like a Hermit Thrush*, 475(F)

Green, Robert. *China*, 8531

Hannibal, 7864

Julius Caesar, 7835

Green, Roger L. *Adventures of Robin Hood*, 4107

King Arthur and His Knights, 4108

The Tale of Troy, 4214

Tales of Ancient Egypt, 4075

Tales of the Greek Heroes, 4215

Green, Timothy. *Twilight Boy*, 3058(F)

Greenberg, Ellen. *The House and Senate Explained*, 4630

Greenberg, Jan. *The American Eye*, 6441

Chuck Close, up Close, 6724

Exercises of the Heart, 1185(F)

Just the Two of Us, 1186(F)

Greenberg, Joanne. *I Never Promised You a Rose Garden*, 941(F)

Greenberg, Judith E. *Getting into the Game*, 10881

Journal of a Revolutionary War Woman, 9095

Newcomers to America, 4805

Greenberg, Judith E., ed. *A Pioneer Woman's Memoir*, 6610

Greenberg, Keith E. *Family Abuse*, 6328

Out of the Gang, 5149

Runaways, 6329

Greenberg, Martin H. *Miskatonic University*, 2726(F)

Greenberg, Martin H., ed. *Civil War Women II*, 2391(F)

The Dean Koontz Companion, 6881

Elf Fantastic, 1724(F)

Great Writers & Kids Write Spooky Stories, 2727(F)

Lord of the Fantastic, 3509(F)

Wizard Fantastic, 1725(F)

Greenberg, Martin H. (jt. author). *Catfantastic*, 3602(F)

Catfantastic IV, 1873(F)

Hitchcock in Prime Time, 3145(F)

Sci-Fi Private Eye, 3652(F)

Sisters of the Night, 2730(F)

Werewolves, 2827(F)

Greenberg, Morrie. *The Buck Stops Here*, 7337

Greenberg, Morrie (jt. author). *Survival in the Square*, 7712

Greenblatt, Miriam. *Franklin D. Roosevelt*, 7326

The War of 1812, 9133

Greene, Constance C. *Monday I Love You*, 1187(F)

Nora, 714(F)

Your Old Pal, Al, 1188(F)

Greene, Harry W. *Snakes*, 9839

Greene, Jacqueline D. *Out of Many Waters*, 2276(F)

Greene, Katherine. *The Man Behind the Magic*, 6730

Greene, Meg. *Slave Young, Slave Long*, 4873

Greene, Rebecca L. *The Empire of Ghana*, 8498

Greene, Richard (jt. author). *The Man Behind the Magic*, 6730

Greene, Shep. *The Boy Who Drank Too Much*, 942(F)

Greenfeld, Barbara C. *The Kids' College Almanac*, 5420

Greenfeld, Howard. *The Hidden Children*, 8300

Paul Gauguin, 6733

Greenfield, Susan A., ed. *The Human Mind Explained*, 5930

Greeno, Gayle. *Mind Snare*, 3510(F)

Greenspan, Bud. *Frozen in Time*, 11102

Greenspon, Jaq. *Careers for Film Buffs and Other Hollywood Types*, 5483

Greenwald, Ted. *Music*, 5484

Greenwood, Barbara. *Pioneer Crafts*, 10558

Gregory, Diana. *Two's a Crowd*, 3309(F)

Gregory, Hugh. *A Century of Pop*, 6470

Gregory, Kristiana. *The Great Railroad Race*, 2458(F)

Jenny of the Tetons, 2277(F)

Jimmy Spoon and the Pony Express, 2459(F)

The Legend of Jimmy Spoon, 2250(F), 2459(F)

The Winter of Red Snow, 2308(F)

Grey, Zane. *The Last Trail*, 2460(F)

Riders of the Purple Sage, 2461(F)

The Wolf Tracker and Other Animal Tales, 281(F)

Gribbin, John (jt. author). *The Matter Myth*, 10320

Griffin, Adele. *Dive*, 715(F)

Other Shepards, 716(F)

Split Just Right, 717(F)

Griffin, Donald R. *Animal Thinking*, 9851

Griffin, Judith Berry. *Phoebe the Spy*, 7483

Griffin, Peni R. *Switching Well*, 1726(F)

Vikki Vanishes, 718(F)

Griffith, Helen V. *Foxy*, 282(F)

Journal of a Teenage Genius, 3511(F)

Grima, Tony, ed. *Not the Only One*, 943(F)

Grimes, Martha. *Biting the Moon*, 105(F)

Hotel Paradise, 1189(F)

Grimes, Nikki. *A Dime a Dozen*, 3985

Hopscotch Love, 3986

Jazmin's Notebook, 476(F)

Grimm, Tom. *The Basic Book of Photography*, 10746

The Basic Darkroom Book, 10747

Grimm Brothers. *The Complete Grimms' Fairy Tales*, 4109

Grinde, Donald A., Jr. (jt. author). *Encyclopedia of Native American Biography*, 8972

Grisham, John. *The Client*, 3059(F)

The Pelican Brief, 3060(F)

The Street Lawyer, 106(F)

Grob, Bernard. *Basic Electronics*, 10448

Grob, Gerald N. *The Mad among Us*, 5998

Grody, Carl W. *Sports Great Mitch Richmond*, 7697

Grollman, Earl A. *Straight Talk about Death for Teenagers*, 5595

Gross, Ernie. *The American Years*, 8887

The Middle Ages, 8182

Howarth, W. *America's Wild Woodlands*, 8892

Howe, Florence (jt. author). *Women Working*, 1529(F)

Howe, James. *Dew Drop Dead*, 3086(F)
The New Nick Kramer or My Life as a Baby-Sitter, 2857(F)
Stage Fright, 3087(F)
The Watcher, 953(F)
What Eric Knew, 3087(F)

Howe, Norma. *The Adventures of Blue Avenger*, 1530(F)
God, the Universe, and Hot Fudge Sundaes, 1221(F)

Hoxie, Frederick E. *The Crow*, 8968

Hoyt, Edwin. *Blue Skies and Blood: The Battle of the Coral Sea*, 8312
Hirohito, 7809
McCampbell's Heroes, 8312
Mussolini's Empire, 7881

Hoyt, Erich. *Meeting the Whales*, 10041

Hoyt-Goldsmith, Diane. *Potlatch*, 8969

Hrdlitschka, Shelley. *Beans on Toast*, 1222(F)
Disconnected, 1223(F)

Hronek, Pamela Claire (jt. author). *Doing What the Day Brought*, 9305

Hu, Evaleen. *A Level Playing Field*, 4754

Hubbard, Jim. *Lives Turned Upside Down*, 5225

Hubbard, Kevin. *Hockey America*, 11067

Hubbard-Brown, Janet. *The Shawnee*, 8970

Hubert, Cam. *Dreamspeaker*, 136(F)

Hudler, George W. *Magical Mushrooms, Mischievous Molds*, 9799

Hudson, Cheryl W. (jt. author). *In Praise of Our Fathers & Our Mothers*, 3762(F)

Hudson, W. H. *Green Mansions*, 342(F)

Hudson, Wade, ed. *In Praise of Our Fathers & Our Mothers*, 3762(F)

Huegel, Kelly. *Young People and Chronic Illness*, 5770

Huet, John. *Soul of the Game*, 10979

Huff, Darrell. *How to Lie with Statistics*, 10237

Huff, Tanya. *Summon the Keeper*, 1747(F)

Hughes, Christopher. *Antietam*, 9206

Hughes, Dean. *Family Pose*, 744(F), 1224(F)
Nutty's Ghost, 2737(F)
Team Picture, 744(F)

Hughes, Langston. *The Dream Keeper and Other Poems*, 3995

Hughes, Langston, ed. *The Collected Poems of Langston Hughes*, 3996

Hughes, Libby. *Colin Powell*, 7438
Nelson Mandela, 7798
Norman Schwarzkopf, 7443

Hughes, Meredith Sayles. *Cool as a Cucumber, Hot as a Pepper*, 9774
Glorious Grasses, 9762
Stinky and Stringy, 9775

Hughes, Monica. *Hunter in the Dark*, 954(F)
Invitation to the Game, 3539(F)

Hughes, Monica, ed. *What If . . . ?* 1748(F)

Hughes, Ted. *Moon-Whales and Other Moon Poems*, 3941
Season Songs, 3941

Hughes, Tracy. *Everything You Need to Know about Teen Pregnancy*, 6084

Hugo, Victor. *The Hunchback of Notre-Dame*, 343(F)
The Hunchback of Notre Dame, 344(F)
Les Miserables, 345(F)

Hull, Mary. *The Boston Tea Party in American History*, 9096
Ethnic Violence, 4829
Rosa Parks, 7235
Struggle and Love, 1972–1997, 9418

Hull, Mary (jt. author). *The History of Slavery*, 4898

Hull, Robert. *Aztecs*, 8803
Greece, 8110

Humble, Richard. *Submarines & Ships*, 10511

Humez, Alexander. *Zero to Lazy Eight*, 10249

Humphrey, Judy. *Genghis Khan*, 7807

Hunnisett, Jean. *Period Costume for Stage & Screen*, 10638

Hunt, Angela E. *Brothers*, 2046(F)
Dreamers, 2047(F)

Hunt, Angela E. (jt. author). *Listening with My Heart*, 7947

Hunt, Conover. *JFK for a New Generation*, 9419

Hunt, Irene. *No Promises in the Wind*, 2567(F)

Hunt, Jonathan. *Bestiary*, 8183

Hunter, Douglas. *A Breed Apart*, 11068

Hunter, Karen (jt. author). *Ladies First*, 7046

Hunter, Mollie. *The King's Swift Rider*, 2162(F)
The Mermaid Summer, 1749(F)
A Stranger Came Ashore, 1750(F)
You Never Knew Her As I Did! 2163(F)

Hunter-Gault, Charlayne. *In My Place*, 7486

Huntley, E. D. *Amy Tan*, 4322

Hurley, Bob. *Divided Loyalties*, 7631

Hurley, Jennifer A. *Animal Rights*, 5020

Hurley, Jennifer A., ed. *Child Abuse*, 6333
Mental Health, 6003
Racism, 4830
Weapons of Mass Destruction, 10525

Hurmence, Belinda. *Tancy*, 2527(F)

Hurmence, Belinda, ed. *Slavery Time When I Was Chillun*, 4884

Hurston, Zora Neale. *Their Eyes Were Watching God*, 495(F)

Hurwin, Davida Wills. *A Time for Dancing*, 955(F)

Hurwitz, Jane. *Choosing a Career in Animal Care*, 5452
High Performance through Effective Budgeting, 5577
Sally Ride, 6654

Hurwitz, Johanna. *Even Stephen*, 1225(F)
Leonard Bernstein, 6950

Hurwitz, Sue. *High Performance through Effective Scheduling*, 5341

Hurwitz, Sue (jt. author). *Sally Ride*, 6654

Huser, Glen. *Touch of the Clown*, 1226(F)

Jacobs, Thomas A. *What Are My Rights? 95 Questions and Answers about Teens and the Law*, 4755

Jacobs, William J. *Great Lives*, 7150
  Search for Peace, 4567
  They Shaped the Game, 7632

Jacques, Brian. *The Long Patrol*, 1753(F)
  Marlfox, 1754(F)
  Mattimeo, 1755(F)
  Mossflower, 1755(F)
  Outcast of Redwall, 1756(F)
  The Pearls of Lutra, 1757(F)
  Redwall, 1755(F)

Jacques, Geoffrey. *Free within Ourselves*, 9370

Jaffe, Nina. *The Cow of No Color*, 4059
  A Voice for the People, 6833

Jaffe, Sherril. *Ground Rules*, 746(F)

Jaffe, Steven H. *Who Were the Founding Fathers? Two Hundred Years of Reinventing American History*, 8895

Jah, Yusuf. *Uprising*, 5157

Jakobson, Cathryn. *Think about Teenage Pregnancy*, 6085

Jakoubek, Robert E. *Harriet Beecher Stowe*, 6919
  Joe Louis, 7713
  Martin Luther King, Jr., 7217

James, Barbara. *Animal Rights*, 5022

James, Bill. *The Bill James Historical Baseball Abstract*, 10951
  Take, 3089(F)

James, Cary. *Julia Morgan*, 6755

James, Elizabeth. *How to Write a Term Paper*, 5381

James, Elizabeth (jt. author). *The Holiday Handbook*, 5284

James, Laura. *Michelle Kwan*, 7739

James, Mary. *Frankenlouse*, 1758(F)

James, Naomi. *Courage at Sea*, 8042

James, P. D. *A Certain Justice*, 3090(F)
  Original Sin, 3091(F)

James, Roby. *Commencement*, 3541(F)

Jameson, W. C. *Buried Treasures of New England*, 9514
  Buried Treasures of the Atlantic Coast, 8019
  Buried Treasures of the Great Plains, 9490

Jamiolkowski, Raymond M. *Drugs and Domestic Violence*, 5651

Jancik, Wayne. *Cult Rockers*, 6472

Janda, Louis H. (jt. author). *Rookie on Tour*, 11062

Janeczko, Paul B. *How to Write Poetry*, 5382

Janeczko, Paul B., comp. *Poetry from A to Z*, 5383

Janeczko, Paul B., ed. *Looking for Your Name*, 3902
  Poetspeak, 3997
  Wherever Home Begins, 3904

Janeczko, Paul B., sel. *The Place My Words Are Looking For*, 3903

Janeczko, Paul B. (jt. author). *I Feel a Little Jumpy around You*, 3913

Janello, Amy, ed. *A Global Affair*, 4568

Janeway, Elizabeth. *The Vikings*, 8720

Jans, Martin. *Stage Make-up Techniques*, 10537

Janson, Anthony F. (jt. author). *History of Art for Young People*, 6414

Janson, H. W. *History of Art*, 6413
  History of Art for Young People, 6414

Jantzen, Steven. *Hooray for Peace, Hurrah for War*, 8236

January, Brendan. *The Dred Scott Decision*, 9136
  Science in Colonial America, 9061

Jarman, Tom. *Wrestling for Beginners*, 11147

Jarrow, Gail. *The Naked Mole-Rat Mystery*, 9873

Jarzyna, Dave. *Slump*, 3711(F)

Jaspersohn, William. *Senator*, 7369
  A Week in the Life of an Airline Pilot, 10478

Javna, Gordon (jt. author). *60s!* 9420

Javna, John. *60s!* 9420

Jay, Annie. *Stars in Your Eyes . . . Feet on the Ground*, 5487

Jaynes, Gregory. *The Killing Ground*, 9208

Jean, Georges. *Writing*, 4432

Jeffrey, Laura S. *American Inventors of the 20th Century*, 7522
  Barbara Jordan, 7400
  Simon Wiesenthal, 7826

Jenkins, A. M. *Breaking Boxes*, 1231(F)

Jenkins, Dan, ed. *The Best American Sports Writing, 1995*, 10884

Jenkins, Earnestine. *A Glorious Past*, 8126

Jenkins, Lyll Becerra de. *So Loud a Silence*, 2225(F)

Jenkins, Martin. *Vampires*, 10834

Jenkins, Robert. *The Biology of Star Trek*, 6533

Jenner, Bruce. *The Athletic Body*, 5975

Jennings, Coleman A., ed. *Theatre for Youth*, 3844

Jennings, Jay, ed. *Tennis and the Meaning of Life*, 11139

Jennings, Paul. *Uncovered! Weird, Weird Stories*, 2740(F)
  Undone! More Mad Endings, 2741(F)

Jennings, Peter. *The Century*, 8896

Jennings, Terry. *101 Amazing Optical Illusions*, 10718

Jensen, Julie, adapt. *Beginning Hockey*, 11069
  Beginning Snowboarding, 11120

Jensen, Marilyn. *Phyllis Wheatley*, 6936

Jeremiah, Maryalyce. *Basketball*, 10981

Jermyn, Leslie. *Mexico*, 8804
  Uruguay, 8831

Jerome, Judson. *The Poet's Handbook*, 4367

Jespersen, James. *Mummies, Dinosaurs, Moon Rocks*, 9582

Jeter, K. W. *The Mandalorian Armor*, 3542(F)

Jezer, Marty. *Rachel Carson*, 7549

Jiang, Ji-li. *Red Scarf Girl*, 7812

Jicai, Feng. *Let One Hundred Flowers Bloom*, 1531(F)

Jimenez, Francisco. *The Circuit*, 500(F)

Johannsson, Phillip. *Heart Disease*, 5773

Johansen, Bruce E. *Encyclopedia of Native American Biography*, 8972

John, Bertram A. (jt. author). *Teenagers Face to Face with Cancer*, 5764

Lachtman, Ofelia Dumas. *The Girl from Playa Bianca*, 3327(F)
Leticia's Secret, 964(F)
Lackey, Mercedes. *The Eagle and the Nightingales*, 1794(F)
Fiddler Fair, 1795(F)
The Fire Rose, 1796(F)
Firebird, 1797(F)
The Silver Gryphon, 1799(F)
Winds of Fate, 1798(F)
Lackey, Mercedes (jt. author). *If I Pay Thee Not in Gold*, 1586(F)
Reap the Whirlwind, 1662(F)
Lackman, Ron. *Same Time . . . Same Station*, 6565
Ladbury, Ann. *The Sewing Book*, 10759
La Farge, Ann. *Pearl Buck*, 6822
La Farge, Oliver. *Laughing Boy*, 2253(F)
Lafaye, Alexandria. *Edith Shay*, 2530(F)
Strawberry Hill, 767(F)
The Year of the Sawdust Man, 768(F)
LaFerla, Jane. *Make Your Own Great Earrings*, 10641
Lafferty, Peter. *Force and Motion*, 10338
Heat and Cold, 10325
Light and Sound, 10326
Laird, Christa. *But Can the Phoenix Sing?* 2619(F)
Shadow of the Wall, 2620(F)
Laird, Elizabeth. *Kiss the Dust*, 507(F)
Secret Friends, 965(F)
Laird, Marnie. *Water Rat*, 2287(F)
Lalich, Janja (jt. author). *Cults in Our Midst*, 4562
Lally, Soinbhe. *A Hive for the Honeybee*, 1800(F)
Lamb, Brian, comp. *Booknotes*, 7155
Lamb, Charles. *Tales from Shakespeare*, 3817
Lamb, Lawrence E. *The Weighting Game*, 6046
Lamb, Mary (jt. author). *Tales from Shakespeare*, 3817
Lamb, Nancy. *One April Morning*, 9491
Lamberg, Lynne. *Drugs & Sleep*, 5656
Lambert, David. *A Field Guide to Dinosaurs*, 7975
The Ultimate Dinosaur Book, 7976
Lamensdorf, Len. *The Crouching Dragon*, 150(F)
Lamott, Anne. *Crooked Little Heart*, 1270(F)
L'Amour, Louis. *Bendigo Shafter*, 151(F)
Lampton, Christopher. *Home Page*, 10428
The World Wide Web, 10429
Lancaster, Bruce. *The American Heritage Book of the Revolution*, 9100
Landau, Diana (jt. author). *Animal Athletes*, 9814
Landau, Elaine. *Alzheimer's Disease*, 5779
The Beauty Trap, 5895
Big Brother Is Watching, 4582
Bill Clinton and His Presidency, 7264
Hooked, 5657
Interracial Dating and Marriage, 6274
Living with Albinism, 6066
Parkinson's Disease, 5780
The Right to Die, 5598
Sexual Harassment, 6190
Stalking, 5164

Teenage Drinking, 5658
Tourette's Syndrome, 5781
Tuberculosis, 5782
The Warsaw Ghetto Uprising, 8323
We Survived the Holocaust, 8324
Why Are They Starving Themselves? Understanding Anorexia Nervosa and Bulimia, 5783
Your Legal Rights, 4761
Landis, Jill Marie. *Just Once*, 2344(F)
Landon, Margaret. *Anna and the King of Siam*, 7930
Landsman, Julie (jt. author). *Welcome to Your Life*, 3759(F)
Landsman, Susan. *Who Shot JFK?* 9425
Lang, Andrew. *The Arabian Nights Entertainments*, 4083
Lang, Denise V. *But Everyone Else Looks So Sure of Themselves*, 6275
Lang, Paul. *The English Language Debate*, 5028
Teen Fathers, 6088
Lang, Paul (jt. author). *Censorship*, 5248
Lang, Susan S. *Censorship*, 5248
Teens and Tobacco, 5659
Lang, Susan S. (jt. author). *Teen Fathers*, 6088
Langdon, William Chauncey. *Everyday Things in American Life, 1776–1876*, 9140
Langguth, A. J. *A Noise of War*, 8137
Langley, Andrew. *Medieval Life*, 8187
Renaissance, 8188
The Roman News, 8138
Sports and Politics, 10889
Langton, Jane. *Face on the Wall*, 3113(F)
Lanier, Virginia. *Blind Bloodhound Justice*, 3114(F)
Lanier-Graham, Susan D. *The Ecology of War*, 5080
Lannert, Paula. *Mexican Americans*, 4956
Lansche, Jerry. *Stan the Man Musial*, 7668
Lantermann, Werner. *The New Parrot Handbook*, 10071
Lantz, Francess. *Fade Far Away*, 966(F)
Rock, Rap, and Rad, 5489
Someone to Love, 769(F)
Stepsister from the Planet Weird, 2867(F)
Lapierre, Dominique (jt. author). *Freedom at Midnight*, 8546
La Pierre, Yvette. *Native American Rock Art*, 8021
Lapine, James (jt. author). *Into the Woods*, 6492
Larimer, Tamela. *Buck*, 1271(F)
Larrick, Nancy, ed. *Piping Down the Valleys Wild*, 3906
Larroche, Caroline. *Corot from A to Z*, 6725
Larsen, Rebecca. *Paul Robeson*, 7090
Richard Nixon, 7314
Larson, Gary. *There's a Hair in My Dirt!* 1801(F)
Larson, Mark (jt. author). *The Creative Writing Handbook*, 5361
Larson, Rodger. *What I Know Now*, 967(F)
Lasky, Kathryn. *Alice Rose & Sam*, 2397(F)
Beyond the Burning Time, 2288(F)
Beyond the Divide, 2472(F)
Dreams in the Golden Country, 2531(F)
Memoirs of a Bookbat, 770(F)

The Voyage of the Dawn Treader, 1817(F)

Lewis, Elizabeth Foreman. *Young Fu of the Upper Yangtze*, 2118(F)

Lewis, J. D. *Journeys in Art*, 6397

Lewis, J. Patrick. *Riddle-icious*, 10792

Lewis, John. *Walking with the Wind*, 7223

Lewis, Jon E. *Jim Morrison*, 7066

Lewis, Leonard (jt. author). *Bowie*, 2451(F)

Lewis, Linda. *Is There Life After Boys?* 1285(F)

Lewis, Naomi. *Stories from the Arabian Nights*, 4084

Lewis, Norman. *Thirty Days to a More Powerful Vocabulary*, 5390

Thirty Days to Better English, 5389

Lewis, Roland. *101 Essential Tips*, 10462

Lewis, Sinclair. *Babbitt*, 401(F)

Main Street, 402(F)

Libby, Megan M. *Postcards from France*, 8631

Libura, Krystyna. *What the Aztecs Told Me*, 8807

Lieberman, Susan A. *The Real High School Handbook*, 5412

Lieberman-Cline, Nancy. *Basketball for Women*, 10984

Liebermann, Randy (jt. author). *Blueprint for Space*, 9687

Lieberthal, Bernadette (jt. author). *The Complete Book of Fingermath*, 10240

Lieberthal, Edwin M. *The Complete Book of Fingermath*, 10240

Lifton, Betty Jean. *A Place Called Hiroshima*, 8329

Liggett, Cathy (jt. author). *The Complete Handbook of Songwriting*, 6474

Liggett, Mark. *The Complete Handbook of Songwriting*, 6474

Light, Jonathan F. *The Cultural Encyclopedia of Baseball*, 10953

Lightman, Marjorie (jt. author). *Ellis Island and the Peopling of America*, 4819

Ligon, Linda, ed. *Homespun, Handknit*, 10760

Lilley, Stephen R. *The Conquest of Mexico*, 8808

Fighters Against American Slavery, 7157

Hernando Cortes, 6615

Limón, Graciela. *Song of the Hummingbird*, 2227(F)

Lincoff, Gary. *The Audubon Society Field Guide to North American Mushrooms*, 9802

Lincoln, Frances. *A Family Treasury of Prayers*, 4515

Stories from The Old Testament, 4516

Lindbergh, Anne. *Three Lives to Live*, 1818(F)

Lindbergh, Charles A. *The Spirit of St. Louis*, 10479

Lindbergh, Reeve. *Under a Wing*, 7496

Lindop, Edmund. *Panama and the United States*, 8784

Political Parties, 4692

Presidents by Accident, 4620

Presidents versus Congress, 4631

Richard M. Nixon, Jimmy Carter, Ronald Reagan, 7158

Woodrow Wilson, Franklin D. Roosevelt, Harry S. Truman, 7159

Lindop, Laurie. *Athletes*, 7634

Champions of Equality, 7160

Political Leaders, 7161

Scientists and Doctors, 7525

Lindsay, Bruce (jt. author). *Dave's Quick 'n' Easy Web Pages*, 10430

Lindsay, Dave. *Dave's Quick 'n' Easy Web Pages*, 10430

Lindsay, Jeanne W. *Caring, Commitment and Change*, 6278

Challenge of Toddlers, 6090

Coping with Reality, 6344

Discipline from Birth to Three, 6095

Pregnant? Adoption Is an Option, 6091

Teen Dads, 6092

Teenage Couples Expectations & Reality, 6345

Your Baby's First Year, 6093

Your Pregnancy & Newborn Journey, 6094

Lindsay, William. *Prehistoric Life*, 7999

Lindwer, Willy. *The Last Seven Months of Anne Frank*, 7858

Ling, Amy (jt. author). *Imagining America*, 450(F)

Ling, Bettina. *Aung San Suu Kyi*, 7820

Linn, Ed. *Hitter*, 7677

Linnea, Sharon. *Princess Ka'iulani*, 7828

Lipinski, Tara. *Tara Lipinski*, 7741

Lipkowitz, Myron A. (jt. author). *Encyclopedia of Vitamins, Minerals and Supplements*, 6051

Lipman, Jean. *Alexander Calder and His Magical Mobiles*, 6713

Lippincott, Joseph W. *Wilderness Champion*, 305(F)

Lippman, Thomas W. *Understanding Islam*, 4537

Lipsitz, Alexis (jt. author). *Delta Style*, 6250

Lipson, Greta Barclay. *Romeo and Juliet*, 3818

Lipsyte, Robert. *The Brave*, 515(F)

The Chemo Kid, 1819(F)

The Chief, 516(F)

The Contender, 517(F)

One Fat Summer, 972(F)

Liptak, Karen. *Indians of the Southwest*, 8983

Lisandrelli, Elaine S. *Ignacy Jan Paderewski*, 7883

Maya Angelou, 6797

Lisle, Holly. *In the Rift*, 1820(F)

Lisowski, Marylin. *Wetlands*, 10192

Lister, Maree. *England*, 8663

Lister, Margot. *Costume*, 10643

Litherland, Janet. *Broadway Costumes on a Budget*, 10644

Littell, Mary Ann. *Heroin Drug Dangers*, 5663

LSD, 5664

Litteral, Linda L. *Boobies, Iguanas, and Other Critters*, 8835

Littke, Lael. *Haunted Sister*, 2760(F)

Loydene in Love, 1286(F)

Shanny on Her Own, 1287(F)

Trish for President, 2869(F)

Little, Elbert L. *The Audubon Society Field Guide to North American Trees: Eastern Region*, 9785

The Audubon Society Field Guide to North American Trees: Western Region, 9786

Little, Jean. *His Banner over Me*, 2570(F)

Sworn Enemies, 2177(F)

Matcheck, Diane. *The Sacrifice*, 2256(F)

Matero, Robert. *The Birth of a Humpback Whale*, 10045

Mathews, Eddie. *Eddie Mathews and the National Pastime*, 7666

Mathews, Nancy Mowll. *Mary Cassatt*, 6716

Mathis, Sharon. *Teacup Full of Roses*, 979(F)

Matthee, Dalene. *Fiela's Child*, 2095(F)

Matthew, Donald. *Atlas of Medieval Europe*, 8193

Matthews, Jill. *Hanson*, 7023

Matthews, John (jt. author). *Atlas of the Roman World*, 8133

Matthews, Leonard J. *Cowboys*, 9290
  Gunfighters, 9290
  Indians, 9291
  Pioneers, 9292
  Railroaders and Soldiers, 9292

Matthews, Phoebe. *The Boy on the Cover*, 3336(F)
  Switchstance, 1318(F)

Matthews, Rupert. *Explorer*, 7952

Mattison, Chris. *The Encyclopedia of Snakes*, 9840
  Frogs & Toads of the World, 9837
  Snakes of the World, 9841

Mattson, Mark T. (jt. author). *The African-American Atlas*, 4850

Maupassant, Guy de. *The Best Short Stories of Guy de Maupassant*, 346(F)

Maupin, Melissa. *The Ultimate Kids' Club Book*, 6376

Maurer, Richard. *The Wild Colorado*, 9340

Mauser, Pat Rhoads. *Love Is for the Dogs*, 3337(F)

Maxwell, Joe (jt. author). *Beautiful Braids*, 5893

Mayer, Marianna. *Turandot*, 4087
  Women Warriors, 4062

Mayfield, Katherine. *Acting A to Z*, 5493

Mayfield, Thomas Jefferson. *Adopted by Indians*, 8990

Maynard, Caitlin. *Rain Forests and Reefs*, 10209

Maynard, Meredy. *Blue True Dream of Sky*, 1319(F)

Maynard, Thane (jt. author). *Rain Forests and Reefs*, 10209

Mayne, William, ed. *Supernatural Stories*, 2773(F)

Mayo, Edith P., ed. *The Smithsonian Book of the First Ladies*, 7165

Mazer, Anne. *A Sliver of Glass*, 2774(F)

Mazer, Anne, ed. *America Street*, 1320(F)
  Going Where I'm Coming From, 6687
  A Walk in My World, 3766(F)
  Working Days, 1321(F)

Mazer, Harry. *The Dog in the Freezer*, 307(F)
  The Dollar Man, 1324(F)
  The Girl of His Dreams, 1322(F)
  Hey, Kid! Does She Love Me? 1323(F)
  I Love You, Stupid! 1324(F)
  The Island Keeper, 173(F)
  The Last Mission, 2628(F)
  Snow Bound, 174(F)
  The Solid Gold Kid, 175(F)
  The War on Villa Street, 1322(F)

Who Is Eddie Leonard? 795(F)
  The Wild Kid, 980(F)

Mazer, Harry (jt. author). *Bright Days, Stupid Nights*, 1536(F)

Mazer, Norma Fox. *After the Rain*, 796(F)
  Bright Days, Stupid Nights, 1536(F)
  D, My Name Is Danita, 797(F)
  Downtown, 798(F)
  Good Night, Maman, 2629(F)
  Missing Pieces, 799(F)
  Mrs. Fish, Ape, and Me, the Dump Queen, 800(F)
  Out of Control, 1325(F)
  Silver, 981(F)
  Someone to Love, 1326(F)
  Taking Terri Mueller, 801(F)
  When She Was Good, 1327(F)

Mazer, Norma Fox (jt. author). *The Solid Gold Kid*, 175(F)

Mazzio, Joann. *Leaving Eldorado*, 2479(F)
  The One Who Came Back, 527(F)

Meachum, Virginia. *Jane Goodall*, 7574
  Martha Stewart, 7614

Mead, Alice. *Adem's Cross*, 1537(F)

Meaney, Carron A. (jt. author). *Encyclopedia of Animal Rights and Animal Welfare*, 4998

Mebane, Robert C. *Adventures with Atoms and Molecules, Vol. 5*, 10163

Mech, L. David. *The Way of the Wolf*, 9907

Medawar, Mardi O. *Witch of the Palo Duro*, 2257(F)

Medearis, Angela Shelf. *The African-American Kitchen*, 10603
  Cooking, 10604
  Dance, 6519
  Music, 6456

Medearis, Michael R. (jt. author). *Cooking*, 10604
  Dance, 6519
  Music, 6456

Medeiros, Teresa. *Fairest of Them All*, 2076(F)

Mee, Susie, ed. *Downhome*, 3767(F)

Meeker, Clare Hodgson. *A Tale of Two Rice Birds*, 4088

Meer, Jeff. *Drugs & Sports*, 5671

Megna-Wallace, Joanne. *Understanding I Know Why the Caged Bird Sings*, 4334

Mehta, Gita. *Snakes and Ladders*, 8550

Meier, August (jt. author). *Black Leaders of the Nineteenth Century*, 7141, 7162
  Black Leaders of the Twentieth Century, 7141

Meinkoth, Norman A. *The Audubon Society Field Guide to North American Seashore Creatures*, 10007

Meiselas, Susan. *Kurdistan*, 8763

Mekler, Eva. *Sunrise Shows Late*, 3338(F)

Melder, Keith. *Hail to the Candidate*, 4699

Melford, Michael. *Big Sky Country*, 9501

Melling, Orla. *The Druid's Tune*, 1854(F)

Melody, Michael E. *The Apache*, 8991

Melton, H. Keith. *The Ultimate Spy Book*, 5166

Meltzer, Brad. *The Tenth Justice*, 176(F)

Meltzer, Milton. *Andrew Jackson and His America*, 7275
Bread and Roses, 5330
Brother, Can You Spare a Dime? The Great Depression, 1929–1933, 9373
Cheap Raw Material, 5032
Columbus and the World around Him, 9043
Crime in America, 5167
Food, 9766
Hold Your Horses! A Feedbag Full of Fact and Fable, 10130
Langston Hughes: A Biography, 6867
Langston Hughes: An Illustrated Edition, 6868
The Many Lives of Andrew Carnegie, 7548
Mark Twain, 6925
Never to Forget, 8338
Rescue, 8339
Ten Queens, 7782
Theodore Roosevelt and His America, 7331
Thomas Jefferson, 7279
Tom Paine, 7428
Weapons & Warfare, 10526
Who Cares? Millions Do . . . A Book about Altruism, 5277
Meltzer, Milton, ed. *The American Promise*, 9428
Frederick Douglass, 7197
Meltzer, Milton, ed. *Lincoln in His Own Words*, 7302
Mendelsohn, Jane. *I Was Amelia Earhart*, 177(F)
Mendheim, Beverly. *Ritchie Valens*, 7112
Mendoza, George (jt. author). *Hitting Hot*, 11141
Menez, Joseph F. (jt. author). *Summaries of Leading Cases on the Constitution*, 4595
Menzel, Donald H. *A Field Guide to the Stars and Planets*, 9714
Mercier, Cathryn M. *Presenting Avi*, 6804
Merino, Jose Maria. *Beyond the Ancient Cities*, 2228(F)
The Gold of Dreams, 2229(F)
Meriwether, Louise. *Daddy Was a Numbers Runner*, 528(F)
Fragments of the Ark, 2399(F)
Mernit, Susan. *Everything You Need to Know about Changing Schools*, 5344
Merrell, James H. *The Catawbas*, 8992
Merriam, Eve. *The Inner City Mother Goose*, 4011
Merrill, Jean. *The Pushcart War*, 2884(F)
Merrill, Yvonne Y. *Hands-On Latin America*, 10540
Hands-On Rocky Mountains, 10559
Merriman, Nick. *Early Humans*, 8001
Merritt, Russell. *Walt in Wonderland*, 6541
Meryman, Richard. *Andrew Wyeth*, 6790
Meschel, Susan V. (jt. author). *Young People Speak*, 8302
Metil, Luana. *The Story of Karate*, 11089
Mettger, Zak. *Reconstruction*, 9341
Metz, Melinda. *The Outsider*, 3590(F)
Metzger, Lois. *Barry's Sister*, 982(F)
Ellen's Case, 983(F)
Missing Girls, 802(F)
Meyer, Carolyn. *Drummers of Jericho*, 1328(F)

Gideon's People, 529(F)
In a Different Light, 9541
Jubilee Journey, 530(F)
Mary, Bloody Mary, 2178(F)
Where the Broken Heart Still Beats, 2480(F)
White Lilacs, 530(F)
Meyer, Gladys C. *Softball for Girls & Women*, 10960
Meyer, Rolf (jt. author). *Pocket Billiards*, 10905
Meyer, Susan E. *Edgar Degas*, 6729
Meyers, Jeffrey. *Robert Frost*, 6850
Meyers, Madeleine, ed. *The Cherokee Nation*, 8993
Forward into Light, 4766
Meyers, Odette. *Doors to Madame Marie*, 8340
Mgadla, Part T. (jt. author). *Batswana*, 8464
Michaels, Anne. *Fugitive Pieces*, 2630(F)
Michaels, Barbara. *Other Worlds*, 2775(F)
Shattered Silk, 3134(F)
Stitches in Time, 3135(F)
Michaels, Melisa C. *Far Harbor*, 1855(F)
Michener, James A. *The Bridges at Toko-Ri*, 2666(F)
Creatures of the Kingdom, 308(F)
Legacy, 1538(F)
South Pacific, 2631(F)
Mickle, Shelley Fraser. *Replacing Dad*, 803(F)
Middleton, Alex L. A. (jt. author). *The Encyclopedia of Birds*, 9929
Miers, Charles (jt. author). *Soccer!* 11130
Migdalski, Edward C. *The Inquisitive Angler*, 11038
Mikaelsen, Ben. *Countdown*, 531(F)
Petey, 984(F)
Rescue Josh McGuire, 309(F)
Stranded, 310(F)
Miklowitz, Gloria D. *After the Bomb*, 178(F)
Anything to Win, 1329(F)
Camouflage, 179(F)
Masada, 2049(F)
Past Forgiving, 985(F)
The War Between the Classes, 532(F)
Mikolaycak, Charles. *Orpheus*, 4217
Milan, Albert R. *Breast Self-Examination*, 5977
Miles, Bernard. *Favorite Tales from Shakespeare*, 3819
Robin Hood, 4115
Miles, Betty. *Just the Beginning*, 804(F)
Maudie and Me and the Dirty Book, 1539(F)
The Real Me, 1330(F)
The Trouble with Thirteen, 1331(F)
Miles, Keith. *Murder in Perspective*, 3136(F)
Milios, Rita. *Shopping Savvy*, 5322
Working Together Against Racism, 4837
Millar, Heather. *China's Tang Dynasty*, 8539
The Kingdom of Benin in West Africa, 8513
Spain in the Age of Exploration, 8728
Millard, Anne. *A Street Through Time*, 8048
Millay, Edna St. Vincent. *Edna St. Vincent Millay's Poems Selected for Young People*, 3944
Miller, Arthur. *The Crucible*, 3859
Death of a Salesman, 3860
Miller, Brandon M. *Dressed for the Occasion*, 10407
Just What the Doctor Ordered, 5861

Miller, Calvin C. *Boris Yeltsin*, 7894
  Mary Wollstonecraft and the Rights of Women, 7948
  Pete Sampras, 7751
  Spirit like a Storm, 6907
Miller, Christina G. *Acid Rain*, 5106
  Air Alert, 5107
Miller, Chuck (jt. author). *Kingdom of Fear*, 4357
Miller, Claudia. *Shannon Miller*, 7728
Miller, Dorothy R. *Home Wars*, 805(F)
Miller, Douglas T. *Frederick Douglass and the Fight for Freedom*, 7198
  Thomas Jefferson and the Creation of America, 7280
Miller, Frances A. *The Truth Trap*, 180(F)
Miller, J. Anthony. *Texas vs. Johnson*, 5250
Miller, Jonathan. *The Human Body*, 5910
Miller, Julia Wang (jt. author). *The AIDS Crisis: A Documentary History*, 5754
Miller, Lee, ed. *From the Heart*, 8994
Miller, Louise. *Careers for Animal Lovers and Other Zoological Types*, 5462
Miller, Marla. *All-American Girls*, 11126
Miller, Martha J. *Kidney Disorders*, 5796
Miller, Maryann. *Drugs and Date Rape*, 5672
  Drugs and Gun Violence, 5673
  Drugs and Violent Crime, 5674
  Everything You Need to Know About Dealing with the Police, 5033
Miller, Montana (jt. author). *Circus Dreams*, 6579
Miller, Nathan. *War at Sea*, 8341
Miller, Phyllis (jt. author). *House of Shadows*, 2782(F)
Miller, Reggie. *I Love Being the Enemy*, 10986
Miller, Sandy. *Smart Girl*, 3339(F)
Miller, Shannon. *Winning Every Day*, 7729
Miller, Thomas. *Taking Time Out*, 10895
Miller, Wilbur R. *Woodworking*, 10783
Miller-Lachmann, Lyn. *Hiding Places*, 1332(F)
Millmoss, A. B. (jt. author). *Backyard and Beyond*, 9741
Mills, Claudia. *What about Annie?* 2572(F)
Mills, Dick. *Aquarius Fish*, 10124
  You & Your Aquarium, 10142
Mills, Judie. *Robert Kennedy*, 7403
Mills, Kay. *From Pocahontas to Power Suits*, 8902
Mills, Nicolaus, ed. *Arguing Immigration*, 4810
Millspaugh, Ben. *Aviation and Space Science Projects*, 9683
Milman, Barbara. *Light in the Shadows*, 8342
Milne, Lorus. *The Audubon Society Field Guide to North American Insects and Spiders*, 9988
Milne, Margery (jt. author). *The Audubon Society Field Guide to North American Insects and Spiders*, 9988
Milner, Angela (jt. author). *Dinosaur*, 7984
Milner, Anna (jt. author). *The Internet*, 10414
Min, Anchee. *Red Azalea*, 7817
Mines, Jeanette. *Risking It*, 3340(F)

Minks, Benton (jt. author). *The Revolutionary War*, 9104
Minks, Louise. *The Revolutionary War*, 9104
  Traditional Africa, 8417
Minnis, Whitney. *How to Get an Athletic Scholarship*, 5424
Minor, Wendell. *Grand Canyon*, 9502
Mintz, Barbara (jt. author). *Hieroglyphs*, 8083
Miotto, Enrico. *The Universe*, 9733
Mirable, Lisa. *The Berlin Wall*, 8644
Mirault, Don. *Dancing . . . for a Living*, 5494
Mirriam-Goldberg, Caryn. *Sandra Cisneros*, 6830
Mitcham, Samuel W., Jr. *Rommel's Greatest Victory*, 8343
Mitchard, Jacquelyn. *The Most Wanted*, 806(F)
Mitchell, David. *The Young Martial Arts Enthusiast*, 11090
Mitchell, Graham. *The Napoleonic Wars*, 8665
Mitchell, Hayley R. *Teen Alcoholism*, 5675
Mitchell, Hayley R., ed. *Readings on a Doll's House*, 4369
  Readings on Wuthering Heights, 4266
Mitchell, Joseph B. *Decisive Battles of the American Revolution*, 9105
Mitchell, Margaret. *Gone with the Wind*, 2400(F)
Mitchell, Sara. *Trial of the Innocent*, 3137(F)
Mitton, Jacqueline. *Gems of Hubble*, 9647
Mitton, Jacqueline (jt. author). *Astronomy*, 9648
Mitton, Simon. *Astronomy*, 9648
Mizerak, Steve. *Inside Pocket Billiards*, 10896
  Steve Mizerak's Pocket Billiards, 10896
Moche, Dinah L. *Astronomy Today*, 9649
Modesitt, L. E., Jr. *Chaos Balance*, 3591(F)
  The Death of Chaos, 3592(F)
  The Soprano Sorceress, 1856(F)
Modley, Rudolf. *Handbook of Pictorial Symbols*, 4418
Moe, Barbara. *Coping with Eating Disorders*, 5797
  Coping with PMS, 5798
  Everything You Need to Know About PMS, 6149
  Inside Eating Disorder Support Groups, 5799
  A Question of Timing, 6099
Moe, Jörgen (jt. author). *Norwegian Folk Tales*, 4099
Moeyaert, Bart. *Bare Hands*, 1333(F)
Mogel, Leonard. *Making It in Advertising*, 5510
Mogil, H. Michael. *The Amateur Meteorologist*, 10281
Mohan, Kim, ed. *Amazing Stories*, 3593(F)
Mohr, Nicholasa. *El Bronx Remembered*, 533(F)
  Felita, 534(F), 535(F)
  Going Home, 535(F)
  Nilda, 536(F)
Moiles, Steven. *The Summer of My First Pediddle*, 1334(F)
Molitor, Graham T. T. (jt. author). *The 21st Century*, 5273
Moll, Lucy. *Vegetarian Times Complete Cookbook*, 10605
Molzahn, Arlene Bourgeois. *Top 10 American Women Sprinters*, 7635

Monath, Norman. *How to Play Popular Piano in Ten Easy Lessons*, 6499

Monfredo, Miriam G. *The Stalking Horse*, 2350(F)

Monnig, Judy (jt. author). *Coping with a Hospital Stay*, 5849

Monroe, Jean Guard. *First Houses*, 8995

Monroe, Judy. *Antidepressants*, 5676
  Inhalant Drug Dangers, 5677
  Nicotine, 5678
  The Nineteenth Amendment, 4767
  Phobias, 6017
  Steroid Drug Dangers, 5679

Monroe, Judy (jt. author). *Cooking the Vietnamese Way*, 10608

Monsarrat, Nicholas. *The Cruel Sea*, 2632(F)

Monseau, Virginia R. *Presenting Ouida Sebestyen*, 6905

Monson-Burton, Marianne, comp. *Girls Know Best 2*, 6284

Montgomery, Bertha Vining (jt. author). *Cooking the African Way*, 10607

Montgomery, L. M. *Anne of Avonlea*, 807(F)
  Anne of Green Gables, 807(F)
  Anne of Ingleside, 807(F)
  Anne of the Island, 807(F)
  Anne of Windy Poplars, 807(F)
  Anne's House of Dreams, 807(F)
  Emily Climbs, 808(F)
  Emily of New Moon, 808(F)
  Emily's Quest, 808(F)

Montgomery, Sy. *The Snake Scientist*, 9842
  Walking with the Great Apes, 9883

Montijo, Yolanda (jt. author). *Native Ways*, 8988

Montpetit, Charles, ed. *The First Time, vol. 1*, 6150

Moody, Anne. *Coming of Age in Mississippi*, 7932

Moody, Bill. *The Sound of the Trumpet*, 3138(F)

Moon, Elizabeth. *Remnant Population*, 3594(F)

Moon, Pat. *The Spying Game*, 986(F)

Mooney, Bel. *The Voices of Silence*, 2179(F)

Mooney, Bill. *Storyteller's Guide*, 5391

Mooney, Chuck. *The Recruiting Survival Guide*, 11047

Moorcroft, Christine. *The Taj Mahal*, 8551

Moore, Barbara (jt. author). *The Nine-Ton Cat*, 4642

Moore, David L. *Dark Sky, Dark Land*, 6377

Moore, Joseph Thomas. *Pride against Prejudice*, 7656

Moore, Marilyn M. *The Wooden Spoon Cookie Book*, 10606

Moore, Martha. *Under the Mermaid Angel*, 1335(F)

Moore, Patrick. *The New Atlas of the Universe*, 9650

Moore, Robin. *The Bread Sister of Sinking Creek*, 2481(F)

Moore, Ruth Nulton. *Mystery of the Missing Stallions*, 3139(F)

Moore, Yvette. *Freedom Songs*, 537(F)

Moragne, Wendy. *Attention Deficit Disorder*, 6018
  Dyslexia, 6019

Moran, Gary T. (jt. author). *Getting Stronger*, 10904

Moran, Tom. *The U.S. Army*, 4708

Morehead, Albert H., ed. *Hoyle's Rules of Games*, 11029

Morell, Virginia. *Ancestral Passions*, 7589

Morella, Joseph. *Simon and Garfunkel*, 7101

Morey, Eileen. *Eleanor Roosevelt*, 7321

Morey, Eileen, ed. *Readings on The Scarlet Letter*, 4335

Morey, Janet Nomura. *Famous Hispanic Americans*, 7166

Morey, Walt. *Angry Waters*, 181(F)
  Death Walk, 182(F)
  Gentle Ben, 311(F)
  Kavik the Wolf Dog, 312(F)
  The Year of the Black Pony, 313(F)

Morgan, Jill. *Blood Brothers*, 2776(F)

Morgan, Peggy. *Buddhism*, 4491

Morgan, Terri. *Junior Seau*, 7723
  Photography, 10752
  Steve Young, 7727

Morgenstern, Susie. *Secret Letters from 0 to 10*, 1336(F)

Morgenthal, Deborah. *The Ultimate T-Shirt Book*, 10645

Mori, Kyoko. *One Bird*, 809(F)
  Shizuko's Daughter, 1337(F)

Morin, Isobel V. *Impeaching the President*, 4621
  Our Changing Constitution, 4609
  Women of the U.S. Congress, 7167
  Women Who Reformed Politics, 7168

Morpurgo, Michael. *The Butterfly Lion*, 183(F)
  Joan of Arc, 2180(F)
  Little Foxes, 1857(F)
  Waiting for Anya, 2633(F)
  The War of Jenkins' Ear, 1858(F)

Morpurgo, Michael, ed. *Ghostly Haunts*, 2777(F)

Morra, Marion (jt. author). *Understanding Your Immune System*, 5809

Morrell, David. *Fireflies*, 810(F)

Morressy, John. *The Juggler*, 2077(F)

Morrill, John, ed. *The Oxford Illustrated History of Tudor & Stuart Britain*, 8666

Morris, Desmond. *Catlore*, 10087
  Catwatching, 10088
  Dogwatching, 10110
  Horsewatching, 10131

Morris, Gerald. *The Squire, His Knight, & His Lady*, 2078(F)
  The Squire's Tale, 2079(F)

Morris, Gilbert (jt. author). *Toward the Sunrising*, 2535(F)

Morris, Greggory. *Basketball Basics*, 10987

Morris, Jeffrey. *The FDR Way*, 7327
  The Jefferson Way, 7281
  The Reagan Way, 9429

Morris, Juddi. *The Harvey Girls*, 9293
  Tending the Fire, 6748

Morris, Lynn. *Toward the Sunrising*, 2535(F)

Morris, Norval, ed. *The Oxford History of the Prison*, 5168

Neufeld, John. *Boys Lie*, 1349(F)
 Edgar Allan, 549(F)
 Gaps in Stone Walls, 2537(F)
 Lisa, Bright and Dark, 990(F)
 A Small Civil War, 1541(F)
Neumann, Peter J. *Playing a Virginia Moon*, 3723(F)
Neville, Emily C. *The China Year*, 1542(F)
 It's Like This, Cat, 1350(F)
Nevin, David. *The Road to Shiloh*, 9222
 Sherman's March, 9223
Nevins, Francis M., ed. *Hitchcock in Prime Time*, 3145(F)
Newell, John (jt. author). *On the Frontiers of Science*, 9574
Newhall, Beaumont. *The History of Photography*, 6418
Newlin, Gary. *Simple Kaleidoscopes*, 10661
Newman, Amy. *The Nuremburg Laws*, 8344
Newman, Frederick. *Mouthsounds*, 10542
Newman, Gerald. *Martha Graham*, 7020
 PCP, 5683
 Racism, 4839
Newman, Robert. *The Case of the Baker Street Irregular*, 3146(F)
 The Case of the Threatened King, 3146(F)
 The Case of the Vanishing Corpse, 3146(F)
Newth, Mette. *The Dark Light*, 2181(F)
Newton, David E. *Black Holes & Supernovae*, 9651
 Drug Testing, 5684
 Making and Using Scientific Equipment, 9623
 Science/Technology/Society Projects for Young Scientists, 9624
 Teen Violence, 5169
 Tokyo, 8345
 Violence and the Media, 5251
 Yearbooks in Science: 1920–1929, 9590
Newton, David E. (jt. author). *Leukemia*, 5817
Ng, Fae Myenne. *Bone*, 550(F)
Ng, Franklin. *The Taiwanese Americans*, 4932
Nguyen, Chi. *Cooking the Vietnamese Way*, 10608
Ngwane, Zolani. *Zulu*, 8479
Nice, Claudia. *Creating Textures in Pen and Ink with Watercolor*, 10687
Nichelason, Margery G. *Homeless or Hopeless?* 5229
Nichol, John. *Bites and Stings*, 9854
Nichols, Janet. *Women Music Makers*, 6689
Nichols, Joan Kane. *Mary Shelley*, 6908
Nicholson, Dorinda M. *Pearl Harbor Child*, 8346
Nicholson, Libby. *Creating with Fimo*, 10563
Nicholson, Lois. *The Composite Guide to Lacrosse*, 10899
 Helen Keller, 7492
 Michael Jackson, 7037
 Oprah Winfrey, 7118
Nicholson, Stuart. *Billie Holiday*, 7030
Nickell, Joe. *Secrets of the Supernatural*, 10842
Nickson, Chris. *Mariah Carey*, 6982
Nicolaides, Kimon. *The Natural Way to Draw*, 10688
Nicolle, David. *Medieval Knights*, 8196

Niehaus, Theodore F. *A Field Guide to Pacific States Wildflowers*, 9803
Niering, William A. *The Audubon Society Field Guide to North American Wildflowers*, 9804
 Wetlands, 10193
Nies, Judith. *Native American History*, 8999
Nieuwsma, Milton J., ed. *Kinderlager*, 8347
Niles, Douglas. *A Breach in the Watershed*, 1865(F)
 Darkenheight, 1865(F)
Nilsen, Alleen P. *Presenting M. E. Kerr*, 6878
Nilsson, Jenny L. (jt. author). *The Sandy Bottom Orchestra*, 1241(F)
Nilsson, Lennart. *Behold Man*, 5911
Nimmo, Jenny. *Griffin's Castle*, 1866(F)
Nimoy, Leonard. *I Am Not Spock*, 7068
 I Am Spock, 7068
Nir, Yehuda. *The Lost Childhood*, 8348
Nirgiotis, Nicholas. *No More Dodos*, 9971
Nirgiotis, Theodore (jt. author). *No More Dodos*, 9971
Nisbet, Lee, ed. *The Gun Control Debate*, 5034
Nishi, Dennis. *Life During the Great Depression*, 9376
Niven, Larry. *Ringworld*, 3599(F)
 The Ringworld Engineers, 3599(F)
Niven, Larry, ed. *The Magic Goes Away*, 1867(F)
 The Magic May Return, 1867(F)
Nix, Garth. *Shade's Children*, 3600(F)
Nixon, Joan Lowery. *And Maggie Makes Three*, 1351(F)
 A Candidate for Murder, 3147(F)
 Circle of Love, 2485(F)
 A Dangerous Promise, 2403(F)
 The Dark and Deadly Pool, 3148(F)
 The Ghosts of Now, 3149(F)
 The Haunting, 2780(F)
 In the Face of Danger, 2486(F)
 The Island of Dangerous Dreams, 3150(F)
 Keeping Secrets, 2404(F)
 The Kidnapping of Christina Lattimore, 3151(F)
 Land of Dreams, 2538(F)
 Land of Hope, 2539(F)
 Land of Promise, 2540(F)
 Maggie Forevermore, 1351(F)
 Maggie, Too, 1351(F)
 Murdered, My Sweet, 3152(F)
 The Name of the Game Was Murder, 3153(F)
 The Other Side of Dark, 3154(F)
 The Seance, 3155(F)
 Search for the Shadowman, 3156(F)
 Shadowmaker, 3157(F)
 The Specter, 3158(F)
 Spirit Seeker, 3159(F)
 The Stalker, 3160(F)
 The Weekend Was Murder! 3161(F)
 Whispers from the Dead, 2781(F)
 Who Are You? 3162(F)
Njoku, Onwuka N. *Mbundu*, 8438
Nnoromele, Salome C. *Life among the Ibo Women of Nigeria*, 8515

The Reproductive System, 6153
Seashore, 10009
Parker, Steve (jt. author). *Birds*, 9921
Mammals, 9867
Parker, Thomas. *Day by Day*, 8406
Parkman, Francis. *The Oregon Trail*, 9296
Parks, Carol. *Make Your Own Great Vests*, 10647
Parks, Gordon. *Half Past Autumn*, 6761
The Learning Tree, 553(F)
Parks, Rosa. *Dear Mrs. Parks*, 4902
Rosa Parks, 7236
Parr, Jan. *Amelia Earhart*, 6624
The Young Vegetarian's Companion, 6052
Parramon Editorial Team. *The Human Body*, 5914
Parrinder, Geoffrey, ed. *World Religions from Ancient History to the Present*, 4493
Parrot, Andrea. *Coping with Date Rape & Acquaintance Rape*, 6199
Parsons, Benny. *Inside Track*, 10925
Partridge, Elizabeth. *Restless Spirit*, 6741
Pasachoff, Jay M. (jt. author). *A Field Guide to the Stars and Planets*, 9714
Pasachoff, Naomi. *Alexander Graham Bell*, 7543
Links in the Chain, 7784
Marie Curie and the Science of Radioactivity, 7552
Pascal, Francine. *Can't Stay Away*, 3342(F)
Get Real, 3343(F)
Paschall, Rod. *Witness to War*, 9471
Pascoe, Elaine. *America's Courts on Trial*, 4675
First Facts about the Presidents, 7169
Freedom of Expression, 4611
Mexico and the United States, 8813
The Pacific Rim, 8523
Racial Prejudice, 4841
Pascoe, Elaine, adapt. *Animal Intelligence*, 10050
Mysteries of the Rain Forest, 7608
Pasternak, Ceel. *Cool Careers for Girls in Computers*, 5559
Cool Careers for Girls in Sports, 5496
Cool Careers for Girls with Animals, 5464
Pateman, Robert. *Bolivia*, 8842
Patent, Dorothy Hinshaw. *Biodiversity*, 9747
A Family Goes Hunting, 11039
Fire, 9787
The Vanishing Feast, 9769
Paterson, Alan J. *How Glass Is Made*, 10382
Paterson, John. *Images of God*, 4494
Paterson, Katherine. *Come Sing, Jimmy Jo*, 821(F)
Jacob Have I Loved, 1359(F)
Jip, His Story, 2352(F)
Lyddie, 2353(F)
A Midnight Clear, 3771(F)
Parzival, 4118
Preacher's Boy, 2541(F)
Rebels of the Heavenly Kingdom, 2124(F)
Paterson, Katherine, ed. *Angels and Other Strangers*, 3770(F)
Paterson, Katherine (jt. author). *Images of God*, 4494
Patneaude, David. *Dark Starry Morning*, 2783(F)
Framed in Fire, 822(F)

The Last Man's Reward, 192(F)
Someone Was Watching, 3171(F)
Paton, Alan. *Cry, the Beloved Country*, 1544(F)
Paton-Walsh, Jill (jt. author). *Thrones, Dominations*, 3222(F)
Patrick, Denise Lewis. *The Adventures of Midnight Son*, 2354(F), 2490(F)
The Longest Ride, 2490(F)
Patrick, Diane. *The New York Public Library Amazing African American History*, 4903
Patterson, Charles. *Animal Rights*, 5037
The Civil Rights Movement, 4773
Patterson, Lillie. *Martin Luther King, Jr. and the Freedom Movement*, 7218
Patterson, Lily (jt. author). *Lewis Latimer*, 7588
Pattou, Edith. *Fire Arrow*, 1884(F)
Hero's Song, 1884(F), 1885(F)
Paul, Caroline. *Fighting Fire*, 5525
Paul, Richard. *A Handbook to the Universe*, 9591
Paulsen, Gary. *Alida's Song*, 1360(F)
The Boy Who Owned the School, 1361(F)
Brian's Winter, 193(F)
Call Me Francis Tucket, 2491(F)
Canyons, 194(F)
The Car, 1362(F)
The Crossing, 1363(F)
Dancing Carl, 1364(F)
Dogsong, 195(F)
Eastern Sun, Winter Moon, 6900
Father Water, Mother Woods, 11040
Harris and Me, 2894(F)
Hatchet, 196(F), 198(F)
The Haymeadow, 197(F)
The Island, 1365(F)
The Monument, 994(F)
Mr. Tucket, 2491(F), 2492(F)
My Life in Dog Years, 10111
Nightjohn, 2355(F)
Popcorn Days and Buttermilk Nights, 1366(F)
Puppies, Dogs, and Blue Northers, 10112
The Rifle, 1545(F)
The River, 198(F)
Sarny, 2405(F)
The Schernoff Discoveries, 2895(F)
Sentries, 1546(F)
Sisters/Hermanas, 1367(F)
Soldier's Heart, 2406(F)
The Tent, 823(F)
Tracker, 1368(F)
The Transall Saga, 3606(F)
The Voyage of the Frog, 199(F)
The Winter Room, 824(F)
Winterdance, 10902
Woodsong, 10903
Paulsen, Kathryn. *The Complete Book of Magic and Witchcraft*, 10720
Paulson, Carl. *Rookie on Tour*, 11062
Paulson, Timothy J. *Days of Sorrow, Years of Glory, 1831–1850*, 9147
Pausewang, Gudrun. *The Final Journey*, 2640(F)

Reuter, Bjarne. *The Boys from St. Petri*, 2643(F)

Revoyr, Nina. *The Necessary Hunger*, 3729(F)

Reybold, Laura. *Everything You Need to Know about the Dangers of Tattooing and Body Piercing*, 5899

Reynolds, David West. *Star Wars: Incredible Cross-Sections*, 6544

Star Wars: The Visual Dictionary, 6545

Star Wars Episode I, 6546

Reynolds, Marilyn. *Baby Help*, 842(F)

Beyond Dreams, 1390(F)

But What About Me? 1391(F)

Detour for Emmy, 1392(F)

If You Loved Me, 1393(F)

Telling, 1394(F)

Too Soon for Jeff, 1395(F)

Reynolds, Marjorie. *The Starlite Drive-in*, 843(F)

Reynolds, Quentin. *The Wright Brothers*, 7622

Rezendes, Paul. *Wetlands*, 10194

Rhoads, Rick (jt. author). *The Real Athletes Guide*, 5486

Rhodes, Lisa R. *Barbara Jordan*, 7401

Coretta Scott King—Humanitarian, 7213

Rhodes, Richard. *Dark Sun*, 10528

Rhodes, Vicki. *Pumpkin Decorating*, 10546

Rhue, Morton. *The Wave*, 1396(F)

Rhyne, Nancy. *More Tales of the South Carolina Low Country*, 4171

Ricchiardi, Sherry. *Bosnia*, 8618

Ricci, Vincent L. (jt. author). *Czars*, 8687

Ricciuti, Edward R., ed. *National Audubon Society First Field Guide*, 10232

Rice, Anne. *Interview with the Vampire*, 2791(F)

Rice, Bebe F. *The Year the Wolves Came*, 2792(F)

Rice, Dorothy M. *The Seventeenth Child*, 7501

Rice, Dorothy M. (jt. author). *Pennies to Dollars*, 7506

Rice, Earle, Jr. *The Attack on Pearl Harbor*, 8359

The Battle of Belleau Wood, 8237

The Battle of Britain, 8360

The Battle of Midway, 8361

The Final Solution, 8362

The Inchon Invasion, 9473

Life among the Great Plains Indians, 9007

Life during the Crusades, 8203

Life during the Middle Ages, 8202

Nazi War Criminals, 8363

The Nuremberg Trials, 8364

The Salem Witch Trials, 9069

The Tet Offensive, 9474

Rice, Tanya. *Mother Teresa*, 7825

Rice, Wayne. *Play It! Over 400 Great Games for Groups*, 10909

Rich, Libby. *Odyssey Book of Houseplants*, 10710

Richards, Arlene Kramer. *What to Do If You or Someone You Know Is Under 18 and Pregnant*, 6101

Richards, Colin. *Sheriff Pat Garrett's Last Days*, 9304

Richards, Roy. *101 Science Tricks*, 9627

Richards, Stanley, ed. *The Most Popular Plays of the American Theatre*, 3862

Richardson, Bob (jt. author). *Great Careers for People Interested in How Things Work*, 5561

Great Careers for People Interested in Math and Computers, 5562

Richardson, Joy. *Looking at Pictures*, 6421

Richardson, Nancy A. (jt. author). *Winning Every Day*, 7729

Richardson, P. Mick. *Flowering Plants*, 9809

Richardson, Peter. *Great Careers for People Interested in How Things Work*, 5561

Great Careers for People Interested in Math and Computers, 5562

Richardson, Susan. *Bob Dylan*, 7003

Richmond, Merle. *Phillis Wheatley*, 6937

Richter, Conrad. *The Light in the Forest*, 2494(F)

Richter, Hans Peter. *Friedrich*, 2644(F)

I Was There, 7941

Ridd, Stephen, ed. *Julius Caesar in Gaul and Britain*, 8153

Ride, Sally. *To Space and Back*, 9690

Ridgeway, James. *Blood in the Face*, 5039

Riefe, Barbara. *Westward Hearts*, 2495(F)

Riggs, Bob. *My Best Defense*, 2901(F)

Riley, Dick. *The Bedside, Bathtub & Armchair Companion to Sherlock Holmes*, 4276

Riley, Dick, ed. *The New Bedside, Bathtub & Armchair Companion to Agatha Christie*, 4277

Riley, Gail B. *Miranda v. Arizona*, 4679

Wah Ming Chang, 6722

Riley, Glenda. *The Life and Legacy of Annie Oakley*, 7072

Riley-Smith, Jonathan, ed. *The Oxford Illustrated History of the Crusades*, 8204

Rinaldi, Ann. *Acquaintance with Darkness*, 2545(F)

The Blue Door, 2359(F)

A Break with Charity, 2290(F)

Broken Days, 2359(F), 2360(F)

Cast Two Shadows, 2311(F)

The Coffin Quilt, 2546(F)

The Fifth of March, 2312(F)

Finishing Becca, 2313(F)

Hang a Thousand Trees with Ribbons, 2291(F)

In My Father's House, 2411(F)

Keep Smiling Through, 2645(F)

Mine Eyes Have Seen, 2361(F)

A Ride into Morning, 2314(F)

The Second Bend in the River, 2496(F)

The Secret of Sarah Revere, 2315(F)

A Stitch in Time, 2292(F)

Wolf by the Ears, 2316(F)

Rinard, Judith E. *Zoos without Cages*, 10143

Ring, Gertrude. *Careers in Finance*, 5514

Riordan, James. *King Arthur*, 4125

Stone, 7128

Tales from the Arabian Nights, 4090

Ripley, C. Peter. *Richard Nixon*, 7316

Ripley, S. Dillon. *Fire of Life*, 9725

Russell, Barbara T. *Blue Lightning*, 1921(F)
  The Taker's Stone, 1922(F)
Russell, Bruce J. (jt. author). *Guide to Microlife*, 10061
Russell, Francine (jt. author). *The Safe Zone*, 5002
Russell, Jeffrey B. *A History of Witchcraft*, 8056
Russell, P. Craig. *Fairy Tales of Oscar Wilde, Vol. 3*, 1923(F)
Russell, Sharmen Apt. *Frederick Douglass*, 7199
Russell, Sharon A. *Stephen King*, 4342
Russman, Edna R. *Nubian Kingdoms*, 8445
Russo, Monica. *Watching Nature*, 9823
Rutberg, Becky. *Mary Lincoln's Dressmaker*, 7929
Ruth, Maria Mudd. *The Deserts of the Southwest*, 10198
Rutherford, Edward. *London*, 2189(F)
Rutledge, Rachel. *The Best of the Best in Gymnastics*, 11065
  The Best of the Best in Track and Field, 11106
Ryan, Alan, ed. *Haunting Women*, 2796(F)
  The Reader's Companion to Alaska, 9543
Ryan, Bernard. *Caring for Animals*, 5278
  Expanding Education and Literacy, 5279
  Helping the Ill, Poor and the Elderly, 5280
  Participating in Government, 5282
  Promoting the Arts and Sciences, 5281
  Protecting the Environment, 5090
  Serving with Police, Fire, and EMS, 4641
Ryan, Craig. *The Pre-Astronauts*, 10482
Ryan, Elizabeth A. *How to Build a Better Vocabulary*, 5395
  How to Write Better Book Reports, 5396
  Straight Talk about Parents, 6356
Ryan, Ken. *Computer Anxiety? Instant Relief!* 10437
Ryan, Margaret. *How to Give a Speech*, 5397
  How to Write a Poem, 5398
Ryan, Mary C. *Frankie's Run*, 3354(F)
  Who Says I Can't? 2904(F)
Ryan, Mary E. *Alias*, 850(F), 3219(F)
  The Trouble with Perfect, 1405(F)
Ryan, Patrick J. *Organized Crime*, 5176
Rybolt, Thomas R. (jt. author). *Adventures with Atoms and Molecules, Vol. 5*, 10163
Ryden, Hope. *Lily Pond*, 9877
  Wild Horse Summer, 1406(F)
  Wild Horses I Have Known, 10134
Rydjord, John. *Indian Place-Names*, 9494
Rylant, Cynthia. *A Blue-Eyed Daisy*, 851(F)
  Every Living Thing, 323(F)
  A Fine White Dust, 1407(F)
  I Had Seen Castles, 2647(F)
  The Islander, 1924(F)
  Soda Jerk, 4020
  Something Permanent, 4021
  Waiting to Waltz, 4022
Ryskamp, George R. *A Student's Guide to Mexican American Genealogy*, 4960
Ryskamp, Peggy (jt. author). *A Student's Guide to Mexican American Genealogy*, 4960

Saavedra, Dane (jt. author). *The What's Happening to My Body? Book for Boys*, 6143
Saberhagen, Fred. *A Sharpness on the Neck*, 2797(F)
Sachar, Louis. *Holes*, 1408(F)
Sachs, Marilyn. *Almost Fifteen*, 1409(F)
  Another Day, 324(F)
  Baby Sister, 852(F)
  Class Pictures, 1410(F)
  Fourteen, 1411(F)
  Ghosts in the Family, 853(F)
  Just Like a Friend, 854(F)
  Peter and Veronica, 1412(F)
  Surprise Party, 1413(F)
  Thunderbird, 3355(F)
  The Truth about Mary Rose, 855(F)
Sacker, Ira M. *Dying to Be Thin*, 5814
Sacks, David. *Encyclopedia of the Ancient Greek World*, 8121
Sacks, Terrence J. *Careers in Medicine*, 5537
Sadeh, Pinhas, ed. *Jewish Folktales*, 4065
Sadler, A. E., ed. *The Environment*, 5091
  Family Violence, 6357
  Juvenile Crime, 5177
  Urban Terrorism, 5296
Sadler, Judy A. *Beading*, 10650
  Corking, 10548
Safage, Jeff. *Sports Great Juwan Howard*, 7686
Safir, Leonard (jt. author). *Good Advice on Writing*, 5399
Safire, William, ed. *Good Advice on Writing*, 5399
Sagan, Carl. *Comet*, 9704
  Cosmos, 9655
  Pale Blue Dot, 9692
Sagan, Dorion (jt. author). *Book of Life*, 10057
  What Is Life? 10057
Sagan, Miriam. *Malcolm X*, 7232
Saiko, Tatyana (jt. author). *Russia*, 8706
Saint-Exupery, Antoine de. *The Little Prince*, 1925(F)
St. George, Judith. *Crazy Horse*, 7377
  To See with the Heart, 7448
St. James, Renwick (jt. author). *Voyage of the Basset*, 1664(F)
St. Pierre, Stephanie. *Everything You Need to Know When a Parent Is in Jail*, 6358
  Everything You Need to Know When a Parent Is Out of Work, 6359
  Teenage Refugees from Cambodia Speak Out, 4935
Salak, John. *Drugs in Society*, 5695
  Violent Crime, 5178
Salinger, Adrienne. *In My Room*, 6218
Salinger, J. D. *The Catcher in the Rye*, 1414(F)
Salinger, Margaretta. *Masterpieces of American Painting in the Metropolitan Museum of Art*, 6446
Salisbury, Graham. *Blue Skin of the Sea*, 3776(F)
  Jungle Dogs, 1415(F)
  Shark Bait, 215(F)
  Under the Blood-Red Sun, 2648(F)

Siegel, Dorothy. *Ann Richards*, 7442
  Dental Health, 5954
  Leukemia, 5817
Siegen-Smith, Nikki, comp. *Welcome to the World*, 3923
Sienkiewicz, Henryk. *Quo Vadis*, 349(F)
Sierra, Patricia. *One-Way Romance*, 3357(F)
Sierra Club Staff (jt. author). *Close-Up Photography in Nature*, 10744
Sifry, Micah L., ed. *The Gulf War Reader*, 9476
Sigerman, Harriet. *Land of Many Hands*, 9311
  An Unfinished Battle, 9150
Sikorsky, Robert. *From Bumper to Bumper*, 10494
Silcock, Lisa, ed. *The Rainforests*, 10211
Siliotti, Alberto (jt. author). *Virtual Archaeology*, 8018
Sills, Leslie. *Visions*, 6426
Silver, Diane. *The New Civil War*, 6204
Silver, Larry. *Rembrandt*, 6770
Silverberg, Robert. *Lord Valentine's Castle*, 3626(F)
  Majipoor Chronicles, 3626(F)
  Valentine Pontifex, 3626(F)
Silverberg, Robert, ed. *Legends*, 1939(F)
  Robert Silverberg's Worlds of Wonder, 3627(F)
  SFFWA Fantasy Hall of Fame, 1940(F)
Silverman, Jerry. *Just Listen to This Song I'm Singing*, 6511
  Songs and Stories from the American Revolution, 6512
Silverman, Maida. *Israel*, 8751
Silverstein, Alvin. *Alcoholism*, 5704
  Allergies, 5824
  Asthma, 5818
  Chickenpox and Shingles, 5819
  Clocks and Rhythms, 9593
  Cystic Fibrosis, 5820
  Depression, 6027
  Diabetes, 5821
  The Digestive System, 5945
  Dogs, 10115
  Epilepsy, 6028
  Evolution, 8005
  The Excretory System, 5946
  Food Chains, 9751
  Glasses and Contact Lenses, 5963
  Heart Disease, 5940
  Heartbeats, 5941
  Measles and Rubella, 5825
  Mononucleosis, 5822
  The Muscular System, 5950
  The Mustang, 10135
  Overcoming Acne, 5900
  Photosynthesis, 9758
  Plants, 9810
  Plate Tectonics, 10175
  The Reproductive System, 6105
  The Respiratory System, 5958
  Runaway Sugar, 5826
  Saving Endangered Animals, 9973
  Sickle Cell Anemia, 5823

  The Skeletal System, 5951
  Sleep and Dreams, 5938
  So You're Getting Braces, 5955
  Symbiosis, 9752
Silverstein, Herma. *Kids Who Kill*, 5181
  Teenage and Pregnant, 6106
  Threads of Evidence, 5182
  Yearbooks in Science: 1990 and Beyond, 9594
Silverstein, Shel. *A Light in the Attic*, 4026
  Where the Sidewalk Ends, 4026
Silverstein, Virginia (jt. author). *Alcoholism*, 5704
  Allergies, 5824
  Dogs, 10115
  Epilepsy, 6028
  Evolution, 8005
  Food Chains, 9751
  Glasses and Contact Lenses, 5963
  Heart Disease, 5940
  Heartbeats, 5941
  Measles and Rubella, 5825
  The Mustang, 10135
  Photosynthesis, 9758
  Plants, 9810
  Runaway Sugar, 5826
  Sleep and Dreams, 5938
  So You're Getting Braces, 5955
  Symbiosis, 9752
Silverthorne, Elizabeth. *Sarah Orne Jewett*, 6876
Silvey, Anita, ed. *Help Wanted*, 1423(F)
Simmons, William S. *The Narragansett*, 9018
Simon, Neil. *Barefoot in the Park*, 3864
  Biloxi Blues, 3865
  Brighton Beach Memoirs, 3865, 3866
  Broadway Bound, 3865, 3866
  The Collected Plays of Neil Simon, 3867
  Lost in Yonkers, 3868
Simon, Nissa. *Good Sports*, 5980
Simon, Noel. *Nature in Danger*, 9974
Simon, Seymour. *How to Be an Ocean Scientist in Your Own Home*, 10291
  The Optical Illusion Book, 5964
  Pets in a Jar, 10072
  Poisonous Snakes, 9845
  Tornadoes, 10268
Simons, Robin. *Recyclopedia*, 10551
Simpson, Carolyn. *Careers in Medicine*, 5540
  Coping with an Unplanned Pregnancy, 6107
  Coping with Compulsive Eating, 5827
  Coping with Post-Traumatic Stress Disorder, 6029
  Coping with Sleep Disorders, 5828
  Everything You Need to Know about Asthma, 5829
  Everything You Need to Know about Living with a Grandparent or Other Relatives, 6365
  High Performance through Negotiation, 6241
  High Performance through Organizing Information, 5358
  Methadone, 5705
Simpson, Dwain (jt. author). *Coping with Post-Traumatic Stress Disorder*, 6029

Simpson, Nancy. *Face-to-Face with Women of the Bible*, 4499

Sinclair, April. *Coffee Will Make You Black*, 1424(F)

Singer, Beverly R. (jt. author). *Rising Voices*, 8965

Singer, Isaac Bashevis. *The Certificate*, 2580(F)
  A Day of Pleasure, 6909
  The Golem, 4126
  The Power of Light, 569(F)
  Stories for Children, 2195(F)
  The Topsy-Turvy Emperor of China, 1941(F)

Singer, Margaret. *Cults in Our Midst*, 4562

Singer, Marilyn. *The Course of True Love Never Did Run Smooth*, 1425(F)
  Deal with a Ghost, 1942(F)

Singer, Marilyn, ed. *Stay True*, 1426(F)

Singh, Nikky-Guninder Kaur. *Sikhism*, 4500

Singleton, Skip. *The Junior Tennis Handbook*, 11143

Sinnott, Susan. *Extraordinary Hispanic Americans*, 4961
  Lorraine Hansberry, 6856

Sioras, Efstathia. *Czech Republic*, 8623

Sirak, Ron. *Juwan Howard*, 7687

Sirof, Harriet. *Because She's My Friend*, 1007(F)
  Bring Back Yesterday, 1943(F)

Sis, Peter. *Tibet*, 8586

Siskel, Gene (jt. author). *The Future of the Movies*, 6526

Sisson, Mary Barr. *The Gathering Storm*, 9151

Sita, Lisa. *Worlds of Belief*, 4501

Sivananda, Swami. *Yoga Mind & Body*, 5981

Sivin, Carole. *Maskmaking*, 10724

Siy, Alexandra. *The Great Astrolabe Reef*, 10292

Skal, David J. *V Is for Vampire*, 10850

Skinner, David. *The Wrecker*, 1427(F)

Skipper, John C. *Umpires*, 10966

Skurzynski, Gloria. *Cliff-Hanger*, 217(F)
  Manwolf, 2196(F)
  Spider's Voice, 2085(F)
  Virtual War, 3628(F)
  Wolf Stalker, 3229(F)

Slade, Arthur G. *Draugr*, 2802(F)
  The Haunting of Drang Island, 2803(F)

Slaewicz, Chris (jt. author). *Bob Marley*, 7057

Slaight, Craig, ed. *Great Monologues for Young Actors*, 3801
  Great Scenes and Monologues for Children, 3802
  Great Scenes for Young Actors from the Stage, 3803
  Multicultural Monologues for Young Actors, 3804
  Multicultural Scenes for Young Actors, 3805
  New Plays from A.C.T.'s Young Conservatory, 3869
  New Plays from A.C.T.'s Young Conservatory, vol. II, 3870
  Short Plays for Young Actors, 3806

Slaughter, Charles H. *The Dirty War*, 2233(F)

Sleator, William. *The Beasties*, 2804(F)
  The Boxes, 1944(F)
  The Boy Who Reversed Himself, 3629(F)
  Dangerous Wishes, 2805(F)
  The Duplicate, 3630(F)
  House of Stairs, 3631(F)

Interstellar Pig, 3632(F)
  The Night the Heads Came, 3633(F)
  Rewind, 1945(F)
  Singularity, 3634(F)
  The Spirit House, 2805(F), 2806(F)
  Strange Attractors, 3635(F)

Slepian, Jan. *The Broccoli Tapes*, 1428(F)

Sloan, Frank. *Titanic*, 10312

Sloane, David E. *The Adventures of Huckleberry Finn*, 4344

Sloane, Paul. *Challenging Lateral Thinking Puzzles*, 10552

Sloate, Susan. *Abraham Lincoln*, 7307
  Amelia Earhart, 6625

Slote, Alfred. *My Robot Buddy*, 3636(F)

Slusser, Donna Ingram (jt. author). *Watercolor Quilts*, 10761

Small, David. *Fenwick's Suit*, 1946(F)

Smart, Paul. *Everything You Need to Know about Mononucleosis*, 5830

Smith, A. G. *Where Am I? The Story of Maps and Navigation*, 7958

Smith, Anne Warren. *Sister in the Shadow*, 864(F)

Smith, April. *North of Montana*, 3230(F)

Smith, Betty. *Joy in the Morning*, 1429(F)
  A Tree Grows in Brooklyn, 2550(F)

Smith, Brenda. *The Collapse of the Soviet Union*, 8708
  Egypt of the Pharaohs, 8095

Smith, Bruce G. (jt. author). *Space Science Projects for Young Scientists*, 9680

Smith, C. Fraser. *Lenny, Lefty, and the Chancellor*, 5706

Smith, Carter. *The Pyramid Builders*, 8096

Smith, Carter, ed. *The Arts and Sciences*, 9071
  Behind the Lines, 9234
  Daily Life, 9072
  The First Battles, 9235
  The Founding Presidents, 9110
  One Nation Again, 9236
  Prelude to War, 9237
  Presidents in a Time of Change, 9343
  Presidents of a Divided Nation, 9238
  Presidents of a Growing Country, 9238
  Presidents of a World Power, 9381
  Presidents of a Young Republic, 9344
  The Revolutionary War, 9111
  The Road to Appomattox, 9239

Smith, Charles R., Jr. *Rimshots*, 3734(F)

Smith, Chris. *Conflict in Southern Africa*, 8486

Smith, Cotton. *Dark Trail to Dodge*, 218(F)

Smith, Dick. *Dick Smith's Do-It-Yourself Monster Make-Up Handbook*, 10725

Smith, Doris Buchanan. *Return to Bitter Creek*, 1430(F)

Smith, Edwin R. *Blue Star Highway, Vol. 1*, 2905(F)

Smith, Elizabeth Simpson. *Coming Out Right*, 6611

Smith, Erica. *Anorexia Nervosa*, 5831

Smith, Ernie. *Warm Hearts & Cold Noses*, 10116

Smith, Gene. *Lee and Grant*, 7174

Stebbins, Robert C. *A Field Guide to Western Reptiles and Amphibians*, 9835

Steedman, Scott. *The Egyptian News*, 8097

Steel, Danielle. *Now and Forever*, 3361(F)
Once in a Lifetime, 3361(F)
Palomino, 3361(F)
The Promise, 3361(F)
The Ring, 3361(F)
Season of Passion, 3361(F)

Steel, Rodney. *Sharks of the World*, 10028

Steele, Allen. *The Jericho Iteration*, 3639(F)

Steele, Mary Q. *Journey Outside*, 222(F)

Steele, Philip. *Astronomy*, 9660
The Aztec News, 8817
Deserts, 10199
Little Bighorn, 9021
Mountains, 10216
Smuggling, 5186
Space Travel, 9695

Steele, William Paul. *Stay Home and Star! A Step-by-Step Guide to Starting Your Regional Acting Career*, 5503

Steffens, Bradley. *Censorship*, 5255
Emily Dickinson, 6841
Photography, 6427

Steffensen, James L., Jr., ed. *Great Scenes from the World Theater*, 3808

Stefoff, Rebecca. *Abraham Lincoln*, 7308
Accidental Explorers, 8059
The American Environmental Movement, 5093
Andrew Jackson, 7276
Charles Darwin and the Evolution Revolution, 8006
Children of the Westward Trail, 9313
Extinction, 9976
Ferdinand Magellan and the Discovery of the World Ocean, 6643
Finding the Lost Cities, 8028
Friendship and Love, 6238
Gloria Estefan, 7010
Independence and Revolution in Mexico, 1810–1940, 8818
Japan, 8567
John Adams, 7255
Mao Zedong, 7827
Oregon, 9547
The Oregon Trail in American History, 9314
Plácido Domingo, 7002
Raul Julia, 7044
Recycling, 5119
Saddam Hussein, 7811
Scientific Explorers, 6599
Tecumseh & the Shawnee Confederacy, 7454
Theodore Roosevelt, 7333
Vasco da Gama and the Portuguese Explorers, 6600
West Bank/Gaza Strip, 8752
Women of the World, 6601
Women Pioneers, 9315

Steger, Will. *Over the Top of the World*, 8861

Steiber, Ellen. *Shapes*, 3232(F)
The X-Files #4, 3232(F)

Steidl, Franz. *Lost Battalions*, 8382

Steig, Jeanne. *Alpha Beta Chowder*, 4030

Steiger, Brad. *Cats Incredible! True Stories of Fantastic Feline Feats*, 10091

Steiger, Gretchen (jt. author). *Blue Whales*, 10031

Stein, Joseph. *Fiddler on the Roof*, 3874

Stein, R. Conrad. *The Aztec Empire*, 8819
Cape Town, 8487
John Brown's Raid on Harpers Ferry in American History, 9153
The Mexican Revolution, 1910–1920, 8820
New Jersey, 9522
The Transcontinental Railroad in American History, 9348

Stein, Sara Bonnett. *The Body Book*, 5917
The Evolution Book, 8007

Stein, Stephen J. *The Shaker Experience in America*, 4523

Stein, Wendy. *Dinosaurs*, 7987
Witches, 10852

Steinbeck, John. *Of Mice and Men*, 2582(F)
The Pearl, 866(F)
The Red Pony, 332(F)
Tortilla Flat, 1556(F)

Steinberg, Margery. *Opportunities in Marketing Careers*, 5518

Steinberg, Michael. *The Symphony*, 6501

Steiner, Andy. *A Sporting Chance*, 10916

Steiner, Barbara. *Dreamstalker*, 3233(F)
Spring Break, 3234(F)

Steinhaus, Hugo. *One Hundred Problems in Elementary Mathematics*, 10255

Steins, Richard. *Alcohol Abuse*, 5708
The Allies Against the Axis, 8383
Censorship, 5256
The Death Penalty, 5187
The Nation Divides, 9243
A Nation Is Born, 9112
The Postwar Years, 9435

Stekler, Paul (jt. author). *Killing Custer*, 9032

Stemp, Jane. *Waterbound*, 3640(F)

Stepanek, Sally. *John Calvin*, 7837
Mary, Queen of Scots, 7879

Stephens, C. A. *Stories from Old Squire's Farm*, 2551(F)

Stephens, Tim (jt. author). *Click!* 10754

Stephenson, Karen F. (jt. author). *Scientists of the Ancient World*, 7509

Stepto, Michele, ed. *African-American Voices*, 575(F)

Sterba, Gunther, ed. *The Aquarium Encyclopedia*, 10144

Stering, Shirley. *My Name Is Seepeetza*, 576(F)

Sterman, Betsy. *Saratoga Secret*, 2319(F)

Stern, Dave. *Will Smith*, 7105

Stetter, Cornelius. *The Secret Medicine of the Pharaohs*, 8098

Stevens, Bernardine S. *Colonial American Craftspeople*, 9073

The Look of the Century, 8229

Tames, Richard. *Islam*, 4541
 Nazi Germany, 8650

Tan, Amy. *The Kitchen God's Wife*, 579(F)
 The Moon Lady, 580(F)

Tan, Jennifer. *Food in China*, 10618

Tanenhaus, Sam. *Louis Armstrong*, 6967

Tangerman, Elmer J. *Complete Guide to Wood Carving*, 10788
 Whittling and Woodcarving, 10789

Tanner, Helen Hornbeck. *The Ojibwa*, 9023

Tansey, Richard G. (jt. author). *Gardner's Art Through the Ages*, 6404

Tanskaya, Alissa (jt. author). *Love You to Bits and Pieces*, 7025

Taraborelli, J. Randy. *Michael Jackson*, 7038

Targ, Harry R. (jt. author). *Guatemala*, 8779

Tarr, Bill. *Now You See It, Now You Don't! Lessons in Sleight of Hand*, 10723

Tarr, Judith. *His Majesty's Elephant*, 1969(F)
 Lord of the Two Lands, 2053(F)
 Throne of Isis, 2063(F)

Tashjian, Janet. *Multiple Choice*, 1012(F)
 Tru Confessions, 1013(F)

Tate, Elizabeth. *The North Light Illustrated Book of Painting Techniques*, 10700

Tate, Sonsyrea. *Little X*, 7505

Tatum, Beverly. *Why Are All the Black Kids Sitting Together in the Cafeteria?* 4844

Taubes, Gary. *Bad Science*, 10361

Taulbert, Clifton L. *Eight Habits of the Heart*, 6298

Taylor, Barbara. *Arctic and Antarctic*, 8862
 Be an Inventor, 10391
 Incredible Plants, 9812

Taylor, Carol. *Creative Bead Jewelry*, 10652

Taylor, Charles. *The Oxford Children's Book of Science*, 9599

Taylor, David. *The Ultimate Dog Book*, 10117
 You & Your Cat, 10092
 You & Your Dog, 10118

Taylor, Diane (jt. author). *Coping with a Dysfunctional Family*, 6370

Taylor, Don. *Marley and Me*, 7059

Taylor, Kenny. *Puffins*, 9936

Taylor, Kimberly H. *Black Abolitionists and Freedom Fighters*, 7177
 Black Civil Rights Champions, 7178

Taylor, Leighton. *Creeps from the Deep*, 10011

Taylor, Marian W. *Chief Joseph*, 7402

Taylor, Maureen. *Through the Eyes of Your Ancestors*, 10554

Taylor, Michael. *Pot Bellied Pigs as a Family Pet*, 10073

Taylor, Mildred D. *Let the Circle Be Unbroken*, 581(F)
 The Road to Memphis, 581(F)
 Roll of Thunder, Hear My Cry, 581(F)

Taylor, Paul. *Coping with a Dysfunctional Family*, 6370

Taylor, Rich. *Indy*, 10929

Taylor, Richard L. *The First Flight*, 7623

Taylor, Theodore. *Battle in the English Channel*, 8389
 The Battle Off Midway Island, 8390
 The Bomb, 1558(F)
 The Cay, 232(F)
 The Flight of Jesse Leroy Brown, 7468
 H.M.S. Hood vs. Bismarck, 8391
 Rogue Wave and Other Red-Blooded Sea Stories, 233(F)
 The Trouble with Tuck, 334(F)
 The Weirdo, 234(F)

Taylor, Thomas. *Lightning in the Storm*, 9477

Taylor, William. *The Blue Lawn*, 1449(F)

Tchen, Richard (jt. author). *Spinners*, 1863(F)

Te Kanawa, Kiri. *Land of the Long White Cloud*, 4096

Teachman, Debra. *Understanding Pride and Prejudice*, 4287

Teague, Allison L. *Prince of the Fairway*, 7776

Tedards, Anne. *Marian Anderson*, 6964

Teens at Risk. *Teens at Risk*, 6229

Tegner, Bruce. *Bruce Tegner's Complete Book of Jujitsu*, 11093
 Bruce Tegner's Complete Book of Self-Defense, 11094
 Karate, 11095
 Self-Defense & Assault Prevention for Girls & Women, 11096
 Solo Forms of Karate, Tai Chi, Aikido & Kung Fu, 11097

Teitelbaum, Michael. *Grand Slam Stars*, 7645

Tekavec, Valerie. *Teenage Refugees from Haiti Speak Out*, 4991

Temple, Frances. *The Beduins' Gazelle*, 2099(F)
 Grab Hands and Run, 1559(F)
 The Ramsay Scallop, 2087(F)
 Taste of Salt, 2235(F)
 Tonight, by Sea, 335(F)

Ten Boom, Corrie. *The Hiding Place*, 8392

Tenquist, Alasdair. *Nigeria*, 8519

Terban, Marvin. *Checking Your Grammar*, 5404

Teresa, Mother. *Words to Love By*, 4527

Terhune, Albert Payson. *Lad*, 336(F)

Terkel, Studs. *Giants of Jazz*, 6699
 Hard Times, 9387

Terkel, Susan N. *Colonial American Medicine*, 9075
 The Drug Laws, 5713

Terris, Daniel. *Ripple of Hope*, 7404

Terris, Susan. *Nell's Quilt*, 1014(F)
 Octopus Pie, 3240(F)

Teruzzi, Giorgio (jt. author). *Simon & Schuster's Guide to Fossils*, 7961

Tesar, Jenny. *Endangered Habitats*, 9977
 Food and Water, 9770
 Threatened Oceans, 10294
 The Waste Crisis, 5111

Tessendorf, K. C. *Barnstormers and Daredevils*, 10484
 Over the Edge, 8863

Wood, Angela. *Being a Jew*, 4556
  Judaism, 4557
Wood, Beverly. *Dog Star*, 2008(F)
Wood, Chris (jt. author). *Dog Star*, 2008(F)
Wood, Geraldine. *Science of the Early Americas*,
  8770
Wood, June R. *The Man Who Loved Clowns*,
  1024(F), 1495(F)
  A Share of Freedom, 892(F)
  Turtle on a Fence Post, 1495(F)
  When Pigs Fly, 893(F)
Wood, Nancy. *Sacred Fire*, 9037
  Thunderwoman, 2263(F)
Wood, Nancy, ed. *The Serpent's Tongue*, 9038
Wood, Peter H. *Strange New Land*, 9079
Wood, Tim. *Ancient Wonders*, 8074
  Houses & Homes, 10404
  The Incas, 8847
  The Renaissance, 8209
Woodbury, Mary. *Brad's Universe*, 894(F)
Woodford, Susan. *The Parthenon*, 8124
Woodhead, Edward, ed. *The Woman's Way*, 9039
Woodhead, Henry. *Atlanta*, 9253
  Soldier Life, 9254
Woodhouse, Barbara. *Dog Training My Way*, 10121
Woodring, Carl. *The Columbia Anthology of British
  Poetry*, 3948
Woodruff, Joan L. *The Shiloh Renewal*, 1025(F)
Woods, Geraldine. *Heroin*, 5725
  Science in Ancient Egypt, 8102
Woods, Karl Morrow. *The Sports Success Book*,
  10919
Woods, Paula L., ed. *Spooks, Spies, and Private
  Eyes*, 3267(F)
Woods, Samuel G. *Everything You Need to Know
  about Sexually Transmitted Disease*, 5843
Woods, Stuart. *Orchid Beach*, 3268(F)
Woods, Sylvia. *Sylvia's Soul Food*, 10626
Woodson, Jacqueline. *The Dear One*, 597(F)
  From the Notebooks of Melanin Sun May, 598(F)
  The House You Pass on the Way, 1496(F)
  I Hadn't Meant to Tell You This, 895(F)
  If You Come Softly, 3381(F)
  Lena, 895(F)
  Maizon at Blue Hill, 599(F)
Woodson, Jacqueline, ed. *A Way out of No Way*, 4920
Woodward, Bob. *The Final Days*, 9441
Woodward, Fred. *Rolling Stone*, 4453
Woog, Adam. *The Beatles*, 6974
  Bill Gates, 7573
  Elvis Presley, 7082
  Harry Houdini, 7032
  The History of Rock and Roll, 6484
  Marilyn Monroe, 7064
  The 1900's, 9352
  Roosevelt & the New Deal, 9390
  Suicide, 6035
Woog, Dan. *The Ultimate Soccer Almanac*, 11131
Wooldridge, Susan Goldsmith. *Poemcrazy*, 5407

Woolley, Persia. *How to Write and Sell Historical
  Fiction*, 5408
  Queen of the Summer Stars, 2210(F)
Woolum, Janet. *Outstanding Women Athletes*, 10920
Wooten, Sara McIntosh. *Oprah Winfrey*, 7119
Wootton, Anthony. *Insects of the World*, 9997
Wormser, Richard. *American Childhoods*, 8918
  American Islam, 4542
  Growing Up in the Great Depression, 9391
  Hoboes, 8919
  The Iron Horse, 10509
  Juveniles in Trouble, 5207
  Three Faces of Vietnam, 9482
Worth, Richard. *Edith Wharton*, 6935
  Poverty, 5239
  Single-Parent Families, 6374
  Women in Combat, 4717
Wouk, Herman. *The Caine Mutiny*, 2663(F)
  War and Remembrance, 2664(F)
  The Winds of War, 2664(F)
Wrede, Patricia C. *Book of Enchantments*, 2009(F)
  Calling on Dragons, 2012(F)
  Magician's Ward, 2010(F)
  Searching for Dragons, 2011(F)
  Talking to Dragons, 2012(F)
Wren, Bonnie (jt. author). *Torn by the Issues*, 5031
Wright, Betty R. *The Summer of Mrs. MacGregor*,
  1497(F)
Wright, Bruce Lanier. *Yesterday's Tomorrows*, 6557
Wright, David. *Arthur Ashe*, 7747
  Brunei, 8588
  Computers, 10445
  John Lennon, 7052
  A Multicultural Portrait of Life in the Cities, 4847
  A Multicultural Portrait of the Vietnam War, 9484
  Paul Robeson, 7093
  Vietnam War, 9483
  War in Vietnam, 9485
  War in Vietnam, Book II: A Wider War, 9485
  War in Vietnam, Book III: Vietnamization, 9485
  War in Vietnam, Book IV: Fall of Vietnam, 9485
Wright, Joseph P. (jt. author). *Math Games for
  Middle School*, 10243
Wright, Lawrence. *Twins*, 6222
Wright, Mike. *What They Didn't Teach You about
  World War II*, 8399
Wright, Patricia (jt. author). *The Story of Painting*,
  6401
Wright, Peter (jt. author). *Manzanar*, 9395
Wright, Rachel. *The Viking News*, 8724
Wright, Richard. *Native Son*, 600(F)
  Rite of Passage, 601(F)
Wright, William (jt. author). *Pavarotti*, 7077
Writer's Digest. *The Writer's Digest Guide to Good
  Writing*, 5409
Wu, Priscilla. *The Abacus Contest*, 2130(F)
Wukovits, John. *Anne Frank*, 7860
  Annie Oakley, 7074
  The Composite Guide to Soccer, 11132
  The Importance of Martin Luther King Jr., 7222

Jesse James, 7490

Jim Carrey, 6983

Tim Allen, 6961

Wulffson, Don L. *Future Fright*, 3668(F)

The Kid Who Invented the Popsicle, 10395

Wunder, John R. *The Kiowa*, 9040

Wunderli, Stephen. *The Heartbeat of Halftime*, 3747(F)

Wunsch, Susi Trautmann. *The Adventures of Sojourner*, 9728

Wyeth, Sharon D. *Once on This River*, 2297(F)

Wyndham, John. *The Day of the Triffids*, 3669(F)

Wynne-Jones, Diana. *Fantasy Stories*, 2013(F)

Wynne-Jones, Tim. *Lord of the Fries*, 3782(F)

The Maestro, 251(F)

Some of the Kinder Planets, 2014(F)

Stephen Fair, 896(F)

Wyss, Johann. *The Swiss Family Robinson*, 354(F)

Yaconelli, Mike (jt. author). *Play It! Over 400 Great Games for Groups*, 10909

Yaeger, Don (jt. author). *Tiger in a Lion's Den*, 7681

Yalof, Ina. *Life and Death*, 5874

Yamaguchi, Yoji. *A Student's Guide to Japanese American Genealogy*, 4947

Yamazaki, James N. *Children of the Atomic Bomb*, 8400

Yancey, Diane. *The Hunt for Hidden Killers*, 5844

Life in a Japanese American Internment Camp, 9442

Life in Charles Dickens's England, 8672

Life in the Elizabethan Theater, 8673

Life in War-Torn Bosnia, 8625

Zoos, 10145

Yang, Margaret. *Locked Out*, 1498(F)

Yannuzzi, Della A. *Ernest Hemingway*, 6863

Zora Neale Hurston, 6875

Yans-McLaughlin, Virginia. *Ellis Island and the Peopling of America*, 4819

Yarbro, Chelsea Q. *Beyond the Waterlilies*, 2015(F)

Yarnall, Stephen R. (jt. author). *The New Dr. Cookie Cookbook*, 10622

Yarwood, Doreen. *The Encyclopedia of World Costume*, 10657

Yashinsky, Dan, ed. *Ghostwise*, 2825(F)

Yates, Diana. *Chief Joseph*, 7373

Yates, Elizabeth. *Amos Fortune, Free Man*, 7482

Yates, Janelle. *Woody Guthrie*, 6952

Yates, Keith D. *Tae Kwon Do for Kids*, 11098

Yates, Sarah. *Alberta*, 8778

Yeatts, Tabatha. *The Holocaust Survivors*, 8401

Yenawine, Philip. *Key Art Terms for Beginners*, 6399

Yeoman, John, retel. *The Seven Voyages of Sinbad the Sailor*, 4093

Yeomans, Donald. *Comets*, 9705

Yep, Laurence. *The Case of the Firecrackers*, 3269(F)

The Case of the Goblin Pearls, 252(F)

Child of the Owl, 603(F)

Dragon Cauldron, 2016(F), 2018(F)

Dragon of the Lost Sea, 2017(F)

Dragon Steel, 2016(F), 2017(F)

Dragon War, 2018(F)

Dragon's Gate, 2509(F)

Dragonwings, 604(F)

Mountain Light, 2131(F)

The Rainbow People, 4094

Ribbons, 897(F)

The Serpent's Children, 2131(F)

The Star Fisher, 605(F)

Thief of Hearts, 606(F)

Yep, Laurence, ed. *American Dragons*, 602(F)

Yetiv, Steve A. *The Persian Gulf Crisis*, 9486

Yolen, Jane. *Armageddon Summer*, 253(F)

Briar Rose, 2019(F)

Children of the Wolf, 1561(F)

The Devil's Arithmetic, 2020(F)

Dragon's Blood, 2024(F)

Heart's Blood, 2024(F)

Here There Be Ghosts, 2826(F)

Hobby, 2021(F)

Merlin, 2022(F)

The One-Armed Queen, 2023(F)

Sacred Places, 3931

A Sending of Dragons, 2024(F)

Sister Light, Sister Dark, 2025(F)

The Transfigured Hart, 2026(F)

Twelve Impossible Things Before Breakfast, 2027(F)

The Wild Hunt, 2028(F)

Yolen, Jane, ed. *Dragons & Dreams*, 2029(F)

Favorite Folktales from around the World, 4070

Mother Earth, Father Sky, 3930

Spaceships & Spells, 3671(F)

Werewolves, 2827(F)

Xanadu, 3670(F)

Xanadu 3, 3670(F)

Xanadu 2, 3670(F)

Yolen, Jane, sel. *Once Upon Ice*, 4039

Youmans, Marly. *Catherwood*, 2298(F)

Young, Ed. *Voices of the Heart*, 4427

Young, Judy Dockery (jt. author). *Ozark Ghost Stories*, 2828(F)

The Scary Story Reader, 2829(F)

Stories from the Days of Christopher Columbus, 4071

Young, Karen R. *The Beetle & Me*, 3382(F)

Young, Mary. *Testaments of Courage*, 9156

Young, Michael. *Architectural and Building Design*, 6383

Young, Patrick. *Mental Disturbances*, 6036

Schizophrenia, 6037

Young, Perry D. *Lesbians and Gays and Sports*, 10921

Young, Richard. *Ozark Ghost Stories*, 2828(F)

The Scary Story Reader, 2829(F)

Stories from the Days of Christopher Columbus, 4071

Young, Ronder T. *Moving Mama to Town*, 1499(F)

Title Index

This index contains both main entry titles and internal titles cited in the entries. References are to entry numbers, not page numbers. All fiction titles are indicated by (F), following the entry number.

A Is for Arctic: Natural Wonders of a Polar World, 8855
A. Lincoln: His Last 24 Hours, 7305
A. Philip Randolph: Labor Leader, 7238
Aaron to Zuverink, 10958
The Abacus Contest: Stories from Taiwan and China, 2130(F)
Abandoned, 3215(F)
The ABC-CLIO World History Companion to the Industrial Revolution, 8058
The Abductors: Conspiracy, 3502(F)
Abe Lincoln Grows Up, 7306
The Abenaki, 8937
Abigail Adams, 7254
Abigail Adams: Witness to a Revolution, 7253
Abortion, 6102
Abortion: A Positive Decision, 6097
Abortion: Debating the Issue, 6076
Abortion: Rights, Options, and Choices, 6070
The Abortion Battle: Looking at Both Sides, 6096
The Abortion Controversy, 6075
About the B'nai Bagels, 3715(F)
About Time: Einstein's Unfinished Revolution, 10319
The Abracadabra Kid: A Writer's Life, 6847
Abraham Lincoln, 7299
Abraham Lincoln: 16th President of the United States, 7308

Abraham Lincoln: The Freedom President, 7307
Abraham Lincoln: U. S. President, 7296
Absolutely Normal Chaos, 2845(F)
An Acceptable Time, 1811(F)
Accidental Explorers: Surprises and Side Trips in the History of Discovery, 8059
According to Hoyle, 11025
"Ace" Any Test, 5359
Acid and Hallucinogens, 5607
Acid Rain, 5105, 5112
Acid Rain: A Sourcebook for Young People, 5106
The Acorn Eaters, 2184(F)
Acorna: The Unknown Girl, 1824(F)
Acorna's Quest, 1824(F)
Acoustic Guitars and Other Fretted Instruments: A Photographic History, 6498
Acquaintance with Darkness, 2545(F)
Acquainted with the Night, 2736(F)
Across America on an Emigrant Train, 10505
Across Asia by Land, 8522
Across the Great River, 486(F)
Across the Lines, 2408(F)
Across the Plains in the Donner Party, 9295
Acting A to Z: The Young Person's Guide to a Stage or Screen Career, 5493
Acting Normal, 951(F)
Action Skateboarding, 11116

The Actor's Book of Contemporary Stage Monologues, 3800
The Actor's Book of Movie Monologues, 6552
Acts of Love, 3293(F)
An Actual Life, 3366(F)
Ada Byron Lovelace: The Lady and the Computer, 7593
Adam and Eve and Pinch-Me, 1233(F)
Addiction: The "High" That Brings You Down, 5667
Adem's Cross, 1537(F)
The Adept, 1792(F)
The Adept, No. 3: The Templar Treasure, 1793(F)
Admiral Hornblower in the West Indies, 2154(F)
Adolescence, 2157(F)
Adolescents and ADD: Gaining the Advantage, 6023
Adolf Hitler, 7867, 7870
Adopted by Indians: A True Story, 8990
Adopted from Asia: How It Feels to Grow Up in America, 6340
Adoption, 6314, 6330
Adoption: The Facts, Feelings, and Issues of a Double Heritage, 6320
Adrian Mole: The Lost Years, 2913(F)
Adrift: Seventy-Six Days Lost at Sea, 10300
Advanced Skywatching, 9637
Adventures in Archaeology, 8022
Adventures in the Wilderness, 9301

874

Genocide, 4579

Genocide: The Systematic Killing of a People, 4572

Gentle Ben, 311(F)

Gentlehands, 1245(F)

The Gentleman Outlaw and Me-Eli: A Story of the Old West, 2462(F)

The Genuine Half-Moon Kid, 250(F)

Geomancer, 1657(F)

George Balanchine: American Ballet Master, 6968

George Bush, 7256

George C. Marshall, 7418

George Eastman, 7557

George Lucas: Creator of Star Wars, 7054

George Washington, 7339, 7343

George Washington: 1st President of the United States, 7340

George Washington Carver, 7551

George Washington's World, 7341

Georges Braque, 6711

Georges Clemenceau, 7843

Georgia, 8710

Georgia: Then and Now, 8690

Georgia O'Keeffe: Painter, 6758

Georgia O'Keeffe: The Wideness and Wonder of Her World, 6759

The German-American Heritage, 4978

German Americans, 4977

The German Americans, 4979

Germany, 8636, 8642

Germany: United Again, 8649

Germany—in Pictures, 8640

Germany Then and Now, 8647

Germany's Lightning War: Panzer Divisions of World War II, 8332

Germs: Mysterious Microorganisms, 10059

Geronimo: Apache Freedom Fighter, 7388

Geronimo: His Own Story, 7387

Geryon, 4200

Get a Life, 1397(F)

Get It? Got It? Good! A Guide for Teenagers, 6285

Get It While It's Hot; or Not, 1214(F)

Get off My Brain: A Survival Guide for Lazy* Students (*Bored, Frustrated, & Otherwise Sick of School), 5352

Get Real, 3343(F)

Get Up and Go! The History of American Road Travel, 10496

Getting Even, 4225

Getting Help: Treatments for Drug Abuse, 5700

Getting into the Game: Women and Sports, 10881

Getting Started in Bird Watching, 9925

Getting Started in Calligraphy, 10666

Getting Stronger: Weight Training for Men & Women, 10904

Getting the Real Story: Nellie Bly and Ida B. Wells, 6671

Getting Unscrewed and Staying That Way: The Sourcebook of Consumer Protection, 5321

Getting Your Message Across, 4413

Getting Your Period: A Book about Menstruation, 6147

Gettysburg, 9196, 9210

Gettysburg: The Confederate High Tide, 9177

Ghana, 8497

Ghana, Mali, Songhay: The Western Sudan, 8510

Ghost Abbey, 2819(F)

Ghost Brother, 607(F)

Ghost Canoe, 127(F)

Ghost Dance: The Czar's Black Angel, 1898(F)

Ghost Horses, 2465(F)

The Ghost in the Noonday Sun, 78(F)

The Ghost in the Tokaido Inn, 1745(F)

Ghost Island, 146(F)

Ghost Liners, 10510

Ghost of a Chance, 1913(F)

The Ghost of the Stone Circle, 1775(F)

Ghost Song, 1899(F)

Ghost Stories from the American South, 2770(F)

Ghost Stories from the Pacific Northwest, 4168

Ghost Train, 3140(F)

The Ghost Wore Gray, 2699(F)

Ghostlight, 1633(F)

Ghostly Haunts, 2777(F)

The Ghostly Register, 10839

Ghosts and Bogles, 2810(F)

Ghosts and How to See Them, 10855

Ghosts in the Family, 853(F)

The Ghosts of Now, 3149(F)

Ghosts, Vampires, and Werewolves: Eerie Tales from Transylvania, 4127

Ghostwise: A Book of Midnight Stories, 2825(F)

Giant Bones, 1608(F)

The Giant Book of Bugs and Creepy Crawlies, 9990

The Giant Book of Snakes and Slithery Creatures, 9834

The Giant Panda, 9918

Giant Steps, 7678

Giants from the Past: The Age of Mammals, 7966

The Giant's House, 973(F)

Giants of Jazz, 6699

Gib Rides Home, 2581(F)

Gibbons v. Ogden: Controlling Trade between States, 4640

Gideon and the Mummy Professor, 2342(F)

Gideon v. Wainwright (1963): Right to Counsel, 4730

Gideon's People, 529(F)

The Gift of Changing Woman, 9015

A Gift of Magic, 3022(F)

The Gift of the Magi, 399(F)

The Gift of the Magi and Other Stories, 3761(F)

The Gift of the Pirate Queen, 710(F)

The Gifted Kids' Survival Guide: A Teen Handbook, 6239

The Gigantic Joke Book, 10796

Gimme a Kiss, 3181(F)

Giotto and Medieval Art, 6403

Girl Boss: Running the Show Like the Big Chicks, 5570

The Girl Death Left Behind, 1298(F)

The Girl from Playa Bianca, 3327(F)

A Girl from Yamhill: A Memoir, 6831

Girl Gives Birth to Own Prom Date, 2909(F)

The Girl in the Box, 3225(F)

A Girl Named Disaster, 2092(F)

A Girl Named Sooner, 914(F)

A Girl Named Summer, 3305(F)

The Girl of His Dreams, 1322(F)

Girl Talk: Staying Strong, Feeling Good, Sticking Together, 6265

The Girl Who Dreamed Only Geese and Other Stories of the Far North, 4152

The Girl Who Heard Dragons, 1829(F)

Yasir Arafat: The Battle for Peace in Palestine, 7799

Year by Year in the Rock Era, 9415

The Year My Parents Ruined My Life, 1167(F)

The Year of Impossible Goodbyes, 1092(F)

Year of Impossible Goodbyes, 2107(F)

The Year of Our Revolution, 458(F)

The Year of the Black Pony, 313(F)

The Year of the Sawdust Man, 768(F)

The Year of the Tiger, 9897

The Year the Wolves Came, 2792(F)

The Year They Burned the Books, 1174(F)

The Year They Walked: Rosa Parks and the Montgomery Bus Boycott, 7237

The Year Without Michael, 831(F)

Yearbooks in Science: 1940–1949, 9569

Yearbooks in Science: 1900–1919, 9586

Yearbooks in Science: 1990 and Beyond, 9594

Yearbooks in Science: 1970–1979, 9579

Yearbooks in Science: 1960–1969, 9587

Yearbooks in Science: 1920–1929, 9590

The Yearling, 322(F)

The Year's Best Fantasy & Horror: Tenth Annual Collection, 2705(F)

The Year's Best Science Fiction: Eleventh Annual Collection, 3483(F)

The Year's Best Science Fiction: Fifteenth Annual Collection, 3484(F)

Year's Best SF, 3517(F)

Yellow Blue Bus Means I Love You, 1199(F)

The Yellow House on the Corner, 3968

A Yellow Raft in Blue Water, 463(F)

Yellowstone, 9499

Yellowstone Country: The Enduring Wonder, 9564

Yemen—in Pictures, 8766

Yesterday's Child, 777(F)

Yesterday's Tomorrows: The Golden Age of Science Fiction Movie Posters, 1950–1964, 6557

Yitzhak Rabin: Israel's Soldier Statesman, 7818

Yo! 609(F)

Yoga Mind & Body, 5981

Yogi: It Ain't Over . . ., 7652

Yoruba, 8492

Yoruba Girl Dancing, 444(F)

Yorubaland: The Flowering of Genius, 8506

Yosemite: A Landscape of Life, 9540

You & Your Aquarium, 10142

You & Your Cat, 10092

You & Your Dog, 10118

You Are the Corporate Executive, 5314

You Are the General, 4702

You Are the General II: 1800–1899, 8030

You Are the Juror, 4644

You Are the President, 4614

You Are the President II: 1800–1899, 4615

You Are the Senator, 4625

You Are the Supreme Court Justice, 4645

You Can Call Me Worm, 722(F)

You Can Draw Sharks, Whales, & Sea Creatures, 10671

You Can Teach Hitting: A Systematic Approach to Hitting for Parents, Coaches and Players, 10932

You Come Too: Favorite Poems for Young Readers, 3975

You Gotta Try This! Absolutely Irresistible Science, 9613

You Mean I Have to Stand Up and Say Something? 5369

You Never Can Tell, 1103(F)

You Never Knew Her As I Did! 2163(F)

You Put Up with Me, I'll Put Up with You, 1110(F)

You Shouldn't Have to Say Goodbye, 1210(F)

You'll Never Guess the End, 2918(F)

The Young Actor's Book of Improvisation: Dramatic Situations from Shakespeare to Spielberg: Ages 12–16, 6576

The Young Astronomer, 9642

The Young Basketball Player: A Young Enthusiast's Guide to Basketball, 10988

Young, Black, and Determined: A Biography of Lorraine Hansberry, 6854

The Young Black Stallion, 275(F)

The Young Entrepreneur's Guide to Starting and Running a Business, 5571

Young Extraterrestrials, 3409(F)

The Young Fishing Enthusiast: A Practical Guide for Kids, 11036

Young Fu of the Upper Yangtze, 2118(F)

Young George Washington: The Making of a Hero, 7345

Young Ghosts, 10818

The Young Inline Skater, 11084

Young Joan, 2073(F)

The Young Landlords, 546(F)

The Young Martial Arts Enthusiast, 11090

The Young Oxford Book of Aliens, 3608(F)

The Young Oxford Book of Folk Tales, 4053

The Young Oxford Book of the Human Being: The Body, the Mind, and the Way We Live, 6212

The Young Oxford Companion to the Congress of the United States, 4634

The Young Oxford History of Britain & Ireland, No. 9, 8655

A Young Painter: The Life and Paintings of Wang Yani—China's Extraordinary Young Artist, 6782

A Young Patriot: The American Revolution as Experienced by One Boy, 9106

Young People and Chronic Illness: True Stories, Help, and Hope, 5770

Young People From Bosnia Talk about War, 8609

Young People Speak: Surviving the Holocaust in Hungary, 8302

The Young People's Book of Quotations, 4435

The Young Person's Guide to Becoming a Writer, 5375

A Young Person's Guide to Music, 6447

A Young Person's Guide to Philosophy, 4459

The Young Person's Guide to the Ballet: With Music from the Nutcracker, Swan Lake, & the Sleeping Beauty, 6514

Subject/Grade Level Index

All entries are listed within specific subjects and then according to grade level suitability (see the key at the foot of pages for grade level designations). Subjects are arranged alphabetically and subject heads may be subdivided into nonfiction (e.g., "Trucks") and fiction (e.g., "Trucks — Fiction"). References to entries are by entry numbers, not pages.

A

Aaron, Henry
JS: 7647

Abandoned children—Fiction
J: 787, 1163
JS: 799, 1453

Abbott, Jim
IJ: 7648

Abdul, Paula
IJ: 6959

Abdul-Jabbar, Kareem
JS: 7678

Abelard and Heloise—Fiction
JS: 2085

Abenaki Indians
JS: 8937

Abernathy, Ralph
JS: 7181

Abolitionists
See also Slavery
JS: 4891, 4910

Abolitionists—Biography
IJ: 7211, 7245
J: 7188, 7194
JS: 4858, 7157, 7187, 7189–90, 7197, 7208, 9153

Abolitionists—Fiction
IJ: 2349
J: 2330

Aborigines—Fiction
J: 3003

Aborigines—Folklore
JS: 4095

Abortion
JS: 4668, 4682, 4684, 6070, 6075–76, 6086, 6096–97, 6102–3
S: 6072

Abortion—Fiction
J: 3215
JS: 1269, 1509

Academic guidance
JS: 5352, 5412

Academy Award (motion pictures)—History
JS: 6531

Accidents
See also Safety
IJ: 6120
J: 6116

Accidents—Fiction
J: 205, 998, 2542
JS: 180, 3023, 3180

Accounting—Careers
JS: 5515

Acid rain
See also Environmental problems
IJ: 5105–6
JS: 5112

Acid rain—Experiments and projects
IJ: 5104

Acne
JS: 5900

Acting
IJ: 3809
J: 5505
JS: 3837, 6583, 6585

Acting—Careers
JS: 5493, 5503

Acting—Fiction
J: 913

Activism
See also Social action
J: 5063, 5835
JS: 5283

Actors—Biography
IJ: 6996, 7000, 7043, 7075, 7078
J: 6961, 6979, 6993, 6999, 7044, 7083, 7085, 7366
JS: 6962, 6983, 6990, 6994–95, 7001, 7034, 7042, 7067–68, 7084, 7095, 7099, 7103–4, 7116
S: 7092

Actors—Fiction
IJ: 2737, 2833
J: 14
JS: 516, 1473, 3176, 7105

Actresses—Biography
IJ: 6969, 7069
J: 6674, 7017, 7062, 7065

IJ = Intermediate-Junior High; J = Junior High; JS = Junior-Senior High; S = Senior High

IJ = Intermediate-Junior High; J = Junior High; JS = Junior-Senior High; S = Senior High

African Americans—Colleges and universities
JS: 5416

African Americans—Comedians
JS: 4230

African Americans—Cookbooks
J: 10589
JS: 5287, 10603, 10626

African Americans—Dance
JS: 6516

African Americans—Diseases
JS: 5729

African Americans—Explorers
J: 9042

African Americans—Family structure
JS: 6360

African Americans—Fiction
IJ: 32, 187, 460–61, 466, 477, 494, 496, 549, 555, 570, 596, 599, 1348, 1435, 1456, 1850, 2004, 2340, 2354, 2362, 2407, 2478, 2483, 2576, 2768, 3682, 7213
J: 232, 482–83, 489, 521, 530, 543–44, 562, 589, 597, 627, 686, 908, 1159, 1163, 1304, 2339, 2365, 2377, 2392, 2408, 2439, 2490, 3065, 3681, 3717, 4520, 7438
JS: 417, 420, 438, 440, 442, 446, 449, 454–55, 459, 469, 476, 478, 480, 485, 488, 490, 499, 501, 504, 510, 514–15, 517, 523, 528, 537–38, 540–42, 545–46, 548, 551, 566, 574–75, 581, 592–95, 598, 601, 728, 733, 747, 813, 910, 925–26, 956, 979, 987, 1015, 1200–1, 1341, 1358, 1381, 1424, 1442, 1471, 1487, 1723, 2111, 2255, 2291, 2316, 2320–21, 2329, 2331, 2334–35, 2346, 2355, 2364, 2366, 2380, 2399, 2521, 2527, 2578, 2667, 2731, 2911, 2951, 3045, 3061, 3267, 3722, 7105, 7746
S: 448, 462, 465, 470, 495, 502, 553, 567, 585, 600, 641, 749, 771, 784, 1122, 1213, 1230, 1455, 1560, 2533, 2948, 3258, 3729

African Americans—Folklore
IJ: 4163, 4166
J: 4164, 4167
JS: 4135, 4165

African Americans—Food
IJ: 10604

African Americans—Health
JS: 5585, 5971

African Americans—History
IJ: 4867–68, 4873, 4878–79, 8354, 9122, 9128, 9136–37, 9143, 9267, 9307, 9341
J: 4859, 4876–77, 4894–95, 4898, 4903, 4908, 5329, 7194, 9089, 9129, 9132, 9145, 9147, 9282–83, 9371, 9400, 9422–23
JS: 539, 4242, 4250, 4739, 4785, 4849–50, 4854, 4861–63, 4865, 4870, 4880–81, 4883–84, 4890–91, 4896–97, 4905, 4907, 4910, 4915–19, 4983, 7146, 7197, 8421, 8947, 9055, 9066, 9079, 9138, 9142, 9148, 9151, 9155–56, 9224, 9280–81, 9284, 9317, 9337, 9345, 9358, 9402, 9413, 9418, 9426, 9515
S: 4851, 4860, 4869, 4872, 4875, 4889, 4911, 9121

African Americans—Holidays
IJ: 4855
JS: 4888

African Americans—Inventors
JS: 7520

African Americans—Literature
IJ: 4306
JS: 4250

African Americans—Motion pictures
JS: 6535

African Americans—Music
IJ: 6448
J: 6466
JS: 6451, 6453, 6459, 6479, 6572

African Americans—Musicians
JS: 6955, 6967, 7006
S: 6965, 7005

African Americans—Newspapers
JS: 4448

African Americans—Plays
JS: 3828, 3841, 3848, 3880
S: 3861, 3879

African Americans—Poetry
IJ: 3986
J: 3998, 4520, 6696
JS: 504, 575, 592, 3914, 3914, 3950–51, 3955, 3968–69, 3978–81, 3995–96, 4000, 4390
S: 3953–54, 4008

African Americans—Poets
JS: 3967

African Americans—Politics
JS: 9414

African Americans—Publications
JS: 4882

African Americans—Quotations
JS: 4848

African Americans—Religion
JS: 4906

African Americans—Scientists
J: 7541
JS: 7539, 7542, 7551, 7556

African Americans—Sex education
S: 6157

African Americans—Singers
JS: 6964, 7029, 7089–91

African Americans—Slavery
IJ: 2307
S: 9118

African Americans—Songs
JS: 6511

African Americans—Teenagers
S: 4856

African Americans—Television
JS: 7119

African Americans—Tennis
JS: 7747, 7749

African Americans—Track and field
J: 7764
JS: 7767

African Americans—Women
J: 4719, 7133
JS: 4390, 4882, 5585, 7246

African Americans—World War II
J: 8305

African Canadians—Fiction
S: 857

African kingdoms—History
J: 8422, 8441, 8451, 8496, 8498, 8509, 8520

Africans—Biography
IJ: 7921

IJ = Intermediate-Junior High; J = Junior High; JS = Junior-Senior High; S = Senior High

Africans—Fiction
IJ: 2232
JS: 3394

Agassi, Andre
IJ: 7743–44

Aggression—Fiction
JS: 3631

Agikuyu (African people)
JS: 8436

Aging
See also Death; Elderly persons; Euthanasia
JS: 5124

Agriculture
See Farms and farm life

Agriculture—Careers
S: 5476

AIDS
See also HIV
IJ: 5790, 5795, 5816
JS: 5731, 5735, 5737, 5740, 5744, 5746, 5754, 5757–59, 5763, 5771, 5774–75, 5778, 5786, 5788, 5793, 5803, 5807, 5833, 5836

AIDS—Biography
IJ: 7689
J: 7745
JS: 7688, 7907

AIDS—Fiction
IJ: 826
J: 816, 922, 927, 1501
JS: 695, 833, 1535

Aikman, Troy
IJ: 7715

Air—Experiments and projects
IJ: 10259

Air Force (U.S.)—Biography
IJ: 7378, 7396

Air Force (U.S.)—Careers
JS: 5447

Air Force (U.S.)—Fiction
J: 10

Air pollution
See also Environmental problems; Pollution
IJ: 5105
J: 5107
JS: 5103, 5108, 5110

Air traffic controllers—Careers
JS: 5437

Airplane crashes
IJ: 10476

Airplane crashes—Fiction
JS: 54

Airplane pilots
IJ: 8863
J: 9538, 10478

Airplane pilots—African American
J: 10477

Airplane pilots—Alaska
JS: 9530

Airplane pilots—Biography
IJ: 6611–12, 6624–26, 7396
J: 6598, 6603, 6623, 7511, 10477
JS: 6595, 6627, 6640, 6644
S: 6622, 6645, 7467

Airplane pilots—Canada
IJ: 10486

Airplane pilots—Fiction
JS: 177, 6638

Airplane pilots—Women
IJ: 6611
J: 6603
JS: 6627

Airplanes—Armed forces
JS: 10483

Airplanes—Biography
IJ: 7622–23

Airplanes—Fiction
IJ: 36
J: 2659
JS: 2604, 2666

Airplanes—History
IJ: 10486
J: 10473–74, 10484–85
JS: 6621, 6639, 7621, 10480
S: 8269, 10479

Airplanes—Model
IJ: 10733
JS: 10729

Airplanes—Paper
JS: 10734

Airplanes—Safety
JS: 10481

Akamba (African people)
JS: 8452

Alabama
IJ: 9562

Alabama—Fiction
IJ: 460, 466

Alabama—Poetry
JS: 3998

Alamo (Texas)
IJ: 9123, 9152
JS: 9141

Alamo (Texas)—Fiction
S: 2451

Alaska
IJ: 8969, 9531, 9544, 10869
J: 9532, 9538, 9541
JS: 7926, 9529–30, 9537, 10868, 10903
S: 9543

Alaska—Fiction
IJ: 24, 98, 209, 244, 2008
J: 92, 190, 586
JS: 182, 3685

Alaska—History
IJ: 9327
JS: 6597

Alaska—Oil spills
IJ: 9545

Alaska—Poetry
JS: 4045

Alaska Gold Rush
See Gold Rush (Alaska and Yukon)

Alaska Purchase
IJ: 9131, 9327

Alateen
J: 5716

Alberta (Canada)
IJ: 8778

Albinism
IJ: 6066

Albinism—Fiction
J: 929
JS: 1319

Albright, Madeleine
JS: 7356–58

Alcatraz Island
IJ: 9542

IJ = Intermediate-Junior High; J = Junior High; JS = Junior-Senior High; S = Senior High

Alcatraz Island—Fiction
J: 29

Alcohol
IJ: 5639, 5650, 5666, 5696
J: 5619, 5641, 5652, 5688
JS: 5614, 5622, 5625, 5638, 5643,
    5645, 5655, 5669, 5675, 5724

Alcohol—Fiction
IJ: 2555
JS: 3367

Alcohol—Health problems
J: 5688

Alcohol—Teenagers
J: 5708
JS: 5658

Alcoholism
J: 5652, 5708, 5716
JS: 5613–14, 5617, 5643, 5658, 5675,
    5703–4, 5720

Alcoholism—Fiction
IJ: 464, 659, 734, 846, 892, 1146,
    1198, 1405
J: 597, 942
JS: 524, 613, 696, 836, 838, 875,
    1008, 1070, 1154, 1306, 1363,
    2894, 3687

Alcott, Louisa May
JS: 6792

Alexander, Sally Hobart
JS: 7460

Alexander the Great
IJ: 7829

Alexander the Great—Fiction
JS: 2053

Ali, Muhammad
J: 7709
JS: 7705–8, 7710, 9456

Alicea, Gil C.
JS: 7910

Aliens
See Ethnic groups;
    Extraterrestrial persons;
    Illegal aliens

**All-American Girls
    Professional Baseball
    League**
J: 10941
JS: 10949, 10957

***All Quiet on the Western
    Front*—Criticism**
S: 4272

Allen, Tim
J: 6961

Allen, Woody
JS: 6962

Allergies
JS: 5747, 5784, 5824

Alligators
JS: 9836

Alligators—Fiction
J: 298

Alomar, Roberto
JS: 7650

Alonso, Alicia
JS: 6963

Alou, Moises
JS: 7651

Alphabet
J: 4411
S: 4433

Alphabet—History
IJ: 4425–26
JS: 4432

Alternative energy
IJ: 10330

Alternative medicine
J: 5851, 5858
JS: 5866

Alvarez, Julia
S: 6793

Alzheimer's disease
JS: 5738, 5766, 5779

Alzheimer's disease—Fiction
IJ: 1485
J: 3324
JS: 141, 758

***Amazing Grace* (hymn)**
IJ: 7497

***Amazing Stories* (periodical)**
JS: 3593

Amazon River
IJ: 10204, 10210
JS: 8832–33, 10205

Amazon River—Exploration
J: 8828

Amazon River—Fiction
IJ: 235, 297

Ambulances
IJ: 5852

**America—Discovery and
    exploration**
JS: 9043

American-Cuban Relations
See Cuban-American relations

American English
S: 4412

**American literature—History
    and criticism**
JS: 4310, 4349–50

American Red Cross
J: 7361

American Revolution
See Revolutionary War (U.S.)

Ameru (African people)
JS: 8450

Amish
IJ: 4981
J: 4529
JS: 4525

Amish—Fiction
IJ: 778, 1283–84
J: 529
JS: 1058

Amish women
JS: 4525

***Amistad* mutiny**
IJ: 9137
J: 9145
JS: 6521, 9157
S: 2357

Amnesia—Fiction
JS: 162, 2688
S: 3314, 3626

Amphibians
IJ: 9834
J: 9830
JS: 9817, 9829, 9831–33, 9837

Amphibians—Evolution
IJ: 7979

Amputations—Fiction
JS: 1016

Amsterdam—History
JS: 8371

IJ = Intermediate-Junior High; J = Junior High; JS = Junior-Senior High; S = Senior High

IJ = Intermediate-Junior High; J = Junior High; JS = Junior-Senior High; S = Senior High

Anorexia
See also Eating disorders
IJ: 5752
J: 5741
JS: 5762, 5765, 5783, 5787, 5794, 5797, 5808, 5812, 5831–32
S: 5769

Anorexia—Fiction
J: 934
JS: 1000, 2588
S: 970, 1009, 3199

Antarctic
See also Polar regions; South Pole
IJ: 8848, 8850, 8853
J: 8862
JS: 8849, 8858

Antarctic—Fiction
JS: 3120

Antarctica
IJ: 8852, 8854, 8856

Anthony, Susan B.
IJ: 7182
JS: 7183–84

Anthony, Susan B.—Fiction
IJ: 2518

Anthropology
IJ: 7994–95, 8004, 8009, 8844
J: 5194, 8001
JS: 8002, 9055

Anthropology—Biography
IJ: 7590
JS: 7589, 7596–97

Anthropology—Careers
JS: 5550

Anthropology—Fiction
JS: 1513

Anti-Semitism
S: 4972

Anti-Semitism—Fiction
IJ: 2194
J: 452, 562, 1328
JS: 568, 1384, 2183, 2191–92, 2608, 2619, 3098

Anti-Semitism—History
JS: 8245

Antidepressants (drugs)
JS: 5676

Antietam, Battle of
IJ: 9206
JS: 9226

Antony, Mark—Fiction
JS: 2063

Ants—Fiction
IJ: 3549

Anxiety
JS: 6009, 6015

Apache Indians
IJ: 7935
JS: 8961, 8991
S: 7387

Apache Indians—Biography
J: 7388
JS: 7374

Apache Indians—Fiction
J: 2240–41, 3714
JS: 2246, 2249
S: 2427

Apache Indians—Women
IJ: 9015

Apartheid
IJ: 8484
JS: 8465

Apartheid—Biography
JS: 7797

Apartheid—Fiction
JS: 474, 2093
S: 1522, 1544

Apartheid—South Africa
JS: 7798

Ape family
See also Gorillas
JS: 9883

Apes—Fiction
JS: 3422

Apollo (space expedition)
J: 9676
JS: 9678

Appalachia
IJ: 9553

Appalachia—Fiction
IJ: 2526
J: 886
JS: 728, 1440, 2534, 3779

Appalachia—Poetry
J: 4022

Appalachian Mountains—Pollution
S: 9551

Appalachian Trail
IJ: 8869
S: 11013

Apple (computer)
J: 7620

Aqualung
JS: 10301

Aquariums
JS: 10140, 10142
S: 10139, 10144

Aquatic animals
JS: 10000
S: 10038

Aquirre, Hank
JS: 7649

Arab Americans
JS: 4986

Arab-Israeli relations
JS: 8736, 8743, 8747–48

Arab-Israeli relations—Fiction
JS: 2135

Arabia—Folklore
IJ: 4078
J: 4083–84, 4090

Arabian Nights
IJ: 4078, 4093
JS: 2044

Arabs
JS: 8457

Arabs—Biography
JS: 7799–800

Arafat, Yasir
JS: 7799–800

Arapaho Indians—Fiction
S: 2992

Arawak Indians—Fiction
J: 2218

Archaeology
IJ: 7993, 8012, 8014, 8020, 8022, 8061, 8066, 8069, 8943
J: 4430, 8013, 8025
JS: 8015, 8017, 8023–24, 8026–29, 8104, 9019, 9055
S: 4234, 8018

IJ = Intermediate-Junior High; J = Junior High; JS = Junior-Senior High; S = Senior High

Archaeology—Biography
JS: 7589

Archaeology—Fiction
J: 7, 1441
JS: 76
S: 3177

Architecture
See also Building and construction
J: 10402
JS: 6383

Architecture—Biography
J: 6675, 6788
JS: 6723, 6755, 6787, 6789

**Architecture—Experiments
and projects**
J: 6382

Architecture—Fiction
S: 1550

Architecture—Gothic
JS: 6389

Architecture—History
IJ: 6385
JS: 6388, 6390, 8064, 8139

Arctic
See also North Pole; Polar
regions
IJ: 8848, 8852, 8860–61, 8863,
8865–66, 9549
J: 8862
JS: 8857
S: 8855, 9890

Arctic—Exploration
J: 6648

Arctic—Fiction
IJ: 93
J: 135, 312
JS: 3231

Arctic Ocean
IJ: 8861

Argentina
IJ: 7969

Argentina—Fiction
J: 2233

**Aristide, Jean-Bertrand—
Fiction**
JS: 2235

Arizona—Fiction
IJ: 1521
S: 2007, 2502

Arizona—History
S: 9565

Arizona (battleship)
JS: 10515

Armed forces—Biography
IJ: 7413

Armed forces—Careers
JS: 5447, 5449–51

Armed forces—History
S: 8036

**Armed forces—Vocational
guidance**
JS: 5448

Armed forces—Women
JS: 4711

Armed forces (U.S.)
See also specific branches, e.g.,
Air Force (U.S.)
IJ: 4709–10
J: 4704
JS: 4702, 4715, 5080

**Armed forces (U.S.)—African
Americans**
IJ: 8275

**Armed forces (U.S.)—
Biography**
IJ: 7437
J: 7411, 7438
JS: 7441, 8349

Armed forces (U.S.)—Women
JS: 4714, 4716–17

Armenia
IJ: 8680

Armenia—History
S: 8605

Armenians—Biography
JS: 7927

Arms control
See also Gun control
J: 4578

Armstrong, Louis
J: 6966
JS: 6967
S: 6965

Army (U.S.)
See also Armed forces (U.S.)
IJ: 4708
JS: 9448

**Army (U.S.)—African
Americans**
JS: 7445

Army (U.S.)—Biography
IJ: 7440
JS: 7436, 7443
S: 7418, 7439

Army (U.S.)—Careers
JS: 5448

Army (U.S.)—History
IJ: 8354

Arnold, Benedict
J: 7359–60

Arnold, Benedict—Fiction
JS: 2313

Arson—Fiction
JS: 141, 2747, 3049

Art—American
J: 6445
JS: 4032, 6446

Art—Careers
JS: 5477, 5488, 5502

Art—Dictionaries
JS: 6399

Art—Egypt
J: 6432

Art—Fiction
JS: 51, 1514

Art—History
IJ: 6397–98, 6412, 6416, 6421, 6426,
8109, 8136, 8634, 8916, 9071,
10394
J: 6379–80, 6408, 6415, 6445, 8176
JS: 6378, 6395, 6401–6, 6409,
6413–14, 6420, 6422–23, 6436,
6446, 6669, 6749, 8161
S: 6407, 6417, 6425, 8165

Art—Mexican
JS: 6774

Art—Middle Ages
IJ: 6400

Art—United States
JS: 6441

Art appreciation
IJ: 6412, 6421
J: 6396, 6433
JS: 6395, 6422–23, 6429, 6441

Art deco
JS: 6381

IJ = Intermediate-Junior High; J = Junior High; JS = Junior-Senior High; S = Senior High

Art galleries
JS: 4642

Arthritis
JS: 5810

Arthur, King
IJ: 4125
J: 4108, 4122–24, 4129
JS: 4114, 4119
S: 4105

Arthur, King—Fiction
IJ: 2022, 2172
J: 1671
JS: 1676, 1931, 1960, 2001, 2003, 2086, 4134
S: 1803, 1886, 2002, 2144, 2209–10

Arthur, King—Plays
JS: 3853

Artificial intelligence
JS: 10412

Artists—American
JS: 6444

Artists—Biography
IJ: 6426, 6439, 6676, 6714, 6718–19, 6722, 6725, 6727, 6731–32, 6734–35, 6742, 6750, 6763, 6772, 6776, 6782, 6785–86, 6791
J: 6433–35, 6713, 6717, 6736, 6738–39, 6746, 6759, 6766–67, 6773, 6775
JS: 6661, 6669, 6678, 6681, 6704–5, 6711, 6715–16, 6720–21, 6724, 6729, 6733, 6737, 6743–44, 6747, 6751–54, 6756, 6758, 6760, 6764–65, 6768–71, 6779–81, 6784, 6790, 7852, 8161
S: 6712, 6783

Artists—Fiction
J: 994
JS: 966
S: 2197

Artists—Renaissance
J: 8176

Artists—Women
J: 6717
JS: 6716

Arts—Eighteenth century
J: 6379

Arts—Seventeenth century
J: 6380

Arts and entertainment— Careers
J: 5499

Asante (African people)
J: 8501

Ashanti (African kingdom)
JS: 8512

Ashe, Arthur
J: 7745
JS: 7746–47

Asia
See also specific countries, e.g., China
IJ: 8524
JS: 4245

Asia—Economy
JS: 8523

Asia—Folklore
JS: 4085

Asia—History
JS: 7807, 8522

Asian Americans
See also specific groups, e.g., Chinese Americans
IJ: 4931, 6340
J: 4853, 4937
JS: 4245, 4921–23, 4926–27, 4934–36, 4938–42, 4945–46, 9548
S: 4925

Asian Americans—Biography
JS: 4933, 6668, 7538

Asian Americans—Fiction
JS: 453, 493, 509, 512, 554, 579, 602, 2110, 2669

Asian Americans—History
JS: 4929

Asimov, Isaac
J: 6800–1

Assassination—Fiction
JS: 81
S: 13

Assertiveness
JS: 6283

Assyrian Empire
J: 8128

Asthma
J: 5829
JS: 5802, 5818

Astrology
JS: 10819, 10851

Astronauts
IJ: 6654
JS: 9690

Astronauts—Biography
IJ: 6655, 7595
J: 6598
JS: 6653

Astronomy
IJ: 9642, 9644, 9648, 9651, 9660, 9668, 9672, 9693, 9713, 9729
J: 9671, 9731
JS: 9591, 9635–36, 9639–40, 9643, 9646, 9649–50, 9652–55, 9658–59, 9661, 9663–64, 9714, 9734
S: 9637, 9641, 9667

Astronomy—Biography
IJ: 7584
J: 7513, 7600
JS: 7583, 7585

Astronomy—Experiments and projects
IJ: 9642
JS: 9657, 9715

Astronomy—History
S: 9645

Astrophysics
S: 9667

Ataturk, Kemal
JS: 7830

Athletes—Biography
J: 7629

Atlanta (Georgia)—Fiction
JS: 820

Atlanta (Georgia)—History
S: 9253

Atlantic coast
JS: 9736
S: 9737

Atlases
JS: 7956

Atmosphere
JS: 10276

Atmosphere—Problems
JS: 5078

Atomic bomb
JS: 8297–98, 8329, 8335–36, 8400, 10518

Atomic bomb—Biography
JS: 7566, 7819

IJ = Intermediate-Junior High; J = Junior High; JS = Junior-Senior High; S = Senior High

Atomic bomb—Fiction
JS: 1558

Atomic bomb—History
JS: 7605, 8373

Atomic structure
JS: 10165

Attention deficit disorder
See also Learning disabilities
IJ: 5987
J: 6018
JS: 5800, 6023

Attention deficit disorder—Biography
IJ: 7762

Attention deficit disorder—Fiction
IJ: 937

Audubon, John James
JS: 6704

Austen, Jane
JS: 6802

Austen, Jane—Criticism
JS: 4287
S: 4284, 4286

Austen, Jane—Fiction
S: 2933

Australia
IJ: 8599, 10013
J: 8593
JS: 8591
S: 8598

Australia—Animals
JS: 9917

Australia—Biography
S: 7025

Australia—Fiction
IJ: 17, 938, 1277, 1490, 2108, 2851, 2921
J: 69, 761, 3003
JS: 168–70, 255, 731, 875, 978, 1301, 1848, 2122, 2742, 2765, 2839–40, 3002, 3126
S: 2120, 2963, 3012

Australia—History
J: 8596

Austria—Fiction
J: 2204
JS: 2637

Austrian Americans—Biography
JS: 7099

Authors
S: 5386

Authors—African American
IJ: 4306
S: 4403

Authors—Biography
IJ: 6666, 6672, 6795, 6798, 6803, 6808–9, 6823, 6830, 6838, 6842, 6857, 6871, 6882, 6888–89, 6899, 6901, 6904, 6906, 6910, 6913–14, 6927, 6929, 6931, 6942
J: 6660, 6673, 6691, 6693, 6696, 6796, 6800–1, 6811, 6818, 6827, 6829, 6839, 6841, 6858, 6884–85, 6893, 6902, 6917, 6919, 6921, 6923, 6938
JS: 4265, 4271, 4328, 6662–64, 6667–68, 6680, 6686–87, 6700, 6792, 6799, 6802, 6804–7, 6810, 6816–17, 6819, 6821–22, 6824–26, 6828, 6831–37, 6840, 6844–45, 6847, 6852, 6854–56, 6859–64, 6866–70, 6872–73, 6875–76, 6878–79, 6881, 6883, 6886–87, 6891–92, 6894–98, 6900, 6903, 6905, 6907, 6912, 6915–16, 6918, 6920, 6924–25, 6928, 6932–34, 6939–40, 6945, 7428, 7463, 10505
S: 6665, 6793, 6813–14, 6850, 6865, 6890, 6908, 6911, 6922, 6926, 6930, 6935, 6941, 7470

Authors—Childhood
J: 5371

Authors—Criticism
JS: 4326

Authors—Fiction
IJ: 644, 1148, 6670
J: 808
JS: 1218

Authors—Latin American
JS: 6695

Authors—Renaissance
J: 8176

Authors—Science fiction
JS: 4338

Authors—Women
IJ: 6823, 6871, 6882
J: 6818, 6893, 6917
JS: 4328, 4346, 6671, 6702, 6810, 6825–26, 6832, 6837, 6853, 6859,
6872–73, 6876, 6894, 6898, 6905, 6916, 6918, 6944
S: 6935

Autism
JS: 6016

Autograph collecting
JS: 10773

Automation
JS: 10443

Automobile accidents—Fiction
IJ: 1056
JS: 632, 992, 1463

Automobile driving
JS: 10494

Automobile driving—Fiction
JS: 1105

Automobile industry—Careers
JS: 5455

Automobile racing
IJ: 10922, 10928, 10930
JS: 10923–25, 10927, 10929

Automobile racing—Biography
J: 7646

Automobile racing—Fiction
JS: 3676

Automobiles
JS: 10489–94, 10926

Automobiles—Fiction
J: 3382
JS: 2744

Automobiles—History
JS: 10487, 10497
S: 10498

Automobiles—Maintenance and repair
JS: 10494–95

Automobiles—Pollution
JS: 5108, 5110

Avalanches—Fiction
IJ: 2226

Avi (author)
IJ: 6803
JS: 6804

Aviation—Fiction
J: 604

Azerbaijan
IJ: 8681

IJ = Intermediate-Junior High; J = Junior High; JS = Junior-Senior High; S = Senior High

965

IJ = Intermediate-Junior High; J = Junior High; JS = Junior-Senior High; S = Senior High

Baseball—History
IJ: 10942, 10974
J: 10935, 10941, 10945, 10947
JS: 10931, 10933–34, 10936, 10940, 10944, 10946, 10948–50, 10955, 10957, 10959, 10969, 10971, 10973
S: 10972

Baseball—Statistics
JS: 10951

Baseball cards
JS: 10768

Basie, Count
JS: 6970

Basketball
IJ: 10975, 10983, 10988, 10990–91, 10994–95, 10999
J: 10987, 10998, 11002
JS: 7631, 10976–78, 10980, 10986, 10989, 10992, 11000
S: 10979, 10982

Basketball—Biography
IJ: 7628, 7641, 7660, 7679, 7682, 7685–87, 7689, 7692–93, 7695–97, 7699–704
J: 7626, 7639, 7684
JS: 7368–69, 7630, 7678, 7680–81, 7683, 7688, 7690–91, 7694, 7698

Basketball—Drugs
JS: 5706

Basketball—Fiction
IJ: 498, 1267
J: 573, 3681, 3706
JS: 545, 920, 1388, 3323, 3678, 3694, 3702, 3713, 3722
S: 3729

Basketball—History
IJ: 10997
JS: 10985, 10996

Basketball—Poetry
IJ: 3960
J: 3734
JS: 3983

Basketball—Short stories
J: 3734

Basketball—Women
IJ: 10993
JS: 10981, 10984, 11001

Basketball cards
IJ: 10771

Basotho (African people)
JS: 8489

Bass (musical instrument)
JS: 6467

Basuto (African kingdom)
JS: 8477

Bat mitzvah
IJ: 4553

Batboys
JS: 10950

Bathrooms—History
IJ: 10367

Bats
IJ: 9864
JS: 9869, 9878

Battered women—Fiction
J: 661

Battles (military)
See also specific battles, e.g., Bull Run, Battle of
J: 8030
JS: 8045, 8368, 9105, 9222

Bauer, Marion Dane
IJ: 5363

Baughman, Michael
JS: 8924

Bawden, Nina
JS: 6810

Bay of Fundy
IJ: 10005

Beads and beadwork
IJ: 10650
JS: 10633, 10652

Bearden, Romare
JS: 6705

Bears
IJ: 9886
J: 9888
JS: 9889, 9892
S: 9887, 9891

Bears—Fiction
IJ: 311
J: 309
JS: 234, 272, 290
S: 520

Beatles (musical group)
IJ: 6974
J: 6972
JS: 6971, 6973, 7050–52

Beauty and the Beast (musical)
JS: 6580

Beauty care
See also Grooming
JS: 5902
S: 5892

Beauty culture
See also Cosmetics
JS: 5895

Beavers
S: 9877

Bees—Fiction
JS: 1800

Beethoven, Ludwig Van
IJ: 6949

Beetles
JS: 9995
S: 9985

Behavior
JS: 6283

Behavioral problems— Children
JS: 6095

Beiderbecke, Bix
JS: 6975

Belarus
IJ: 8683

Belgium—Biography
JS: 7844

Belize
IJ: 8786, 10206, 10209

Bell, Alexander Graham
J: 7543

Belleau Wood, Battle of
JS: 8237

Beloved (motion picture)
S: 6556

Benin (African kingdom)
IJ: 8513
J: 8502, 8509
JS: 8512

Benin—Folklore
IJ: 4077

Beowulf—Criticism
S: 4288

Beowulf—Fiction
S: 1718

IJ = Intermediate-Junior High; J = Junior High; JS = Junior-Senior High; S = Senior High

Berbers
JS: 8457

Berg, Moe
J: 7461

Berland-Hyatt, Felicia
JS: 7831

Berlin—History
JS: 8253

Berlin Wall
IJ: 8644
JS: 8638, 8641

Bermuda—Fiction
JS: 260

Bermuda Triangle
JS: 10807

Bernstein, Leonard
IJ: 6950

Berra, Yogi
JS: 7652

Bethune, Mary McLeod
JS: 7185

Bettis, Jerome
IJ: 7716

Bible
IJ: 4494
JS: 4464, 4467, 4476, 4495
S: 4465

Bible—Biography
IJ: 4499

Bible—Fiction
IJ: 2045
JS: 2050

Bible—Geography
J: 8753

Bible—History and criticism
JS: 4460

Bible stories
IJ: 2349, 4470–71, 4484, 4516, 4521
J: 4490, 4526
JS: 4463

Biculturalism
JS: 4840, 4928, 6348

Bicycles
IJ: 11008
JS: 11004, 11007, 11010

Bicycles—Fiction
IJ: 2907

Bicycles—Racing
JS: 11003

Bicycles—Touring—Africa
J: 8410

Bicycles—Women
JS: 11006

Bielenberg, Christabel
IJ: 8379

Big-bang theory
IJ: 9729, 9735
JS: 9638

Big Bend National Park
IJ: 9864

Big cats
IJ: 9896

Bigfoot—Fiction
IJ: 220

Bikini Atoll—Fiction
JS: 1558

Bilingual education
JS: 5028

Bill of Rights
JS: 4610

Billiards
JS: 10905
S: 10896

Billy the Kid—Fiction
S: 2453

Binge eating
See also Eating disorders
JS: 5812

Bini (African people)
JS: 8493

Biochemistry
JS: 9742

Biodiversity
JS: 9747

Biofeedback
JS: 5929

Biographical writing
S: 7155

Biography
See also under specific occupations, e.g., Actors—Biography; specific sports, e.g., Baseball—Biography; and cultural groups, e.g.,

Hispanic Americans—Biography
IJ: 7135
S: 7040, 7137

Biography—Collective
IJ: 7908

Biological clocks
JS: 5912

Biology—Biography
IJ: 7592

Biology—Experiments and projects
JS: 9754

Biology—General
IJ: 9740
J: 9757
JS: 6533, 9742, 9745, 9747, 9750
S: 9707, 9711

Biomedical ethics
J: 5586
JS: 5583–84

Bionics and transplants
JS: 5867

Biotechnology
JS: 5867, 10060

Biracialism
JS: 4825, 4838, 4840

Biracialism—Fiction
IJ: 522
J: 530
JS: 420, 763, 833
S: 567

Bird watching
JS: 9955
S: 9925, 9953

Birdfeeders
JS: 9920, 9923

Birdhouses
JS: 9920, 9923, 9935, 10785
S: 10786

Birds
See also specific birds, e.g., Eagles
IJ: 9939, 9946
J: 9921, 9943, 9948
JS: 9539, 9920, 9922–24, 9926, 9929–31, 9935, 9940, 9942, 10070
S: 9927, 9937

Birds—Art
JS: 6704

IJ = Intermediate-Junior High; J = Junior High; JS = Junior-Senior High; S = Senior High

Birds—Behavior
JS: 9933, 9942

Birds—Endangered
IJ: 9932

Birds—Evolution
IJ: 9928

Birds—Extinct
JS: 9964

Birds—Feeding
JS: 9934

Birds—Fiction
IJ: 887, 1574
J: 525

Birds—Pets
JS: 10066

Birds—Photography
S: 10743

Birds—Poetry
IJ: 3970

Birds of prey
See also specific birds, e.g.,
Eagles
IJ: 9945–46
J: 9948

Birth
S: 6078

Birth control
JS: 4786, 6106

Bisexuality
JS: 1246, 6127, 6132, 6135, 6148,
6155

Bisland, Elizabeth
JS: 7463

***Bismarck* (battleship)**
IJ: 8333

Bitton-Jackson, Livia
JS: 7911

Black Americans
See African Americans

Black authors—Fiction
JS: 446

***Black Boy*—Criticism**
JS: 4318

Black Death
J: 8170

Black Hawk (Sac chief)
JS: 7363

Black Hawk War
JS: 7363

Black holes
IJ: 9651
J: 9730

Black magic—Fiction
S: 1607

Black Muslims—Biography
J: 7225
JS: 7224, 7227, 7229–30

**Black Panthers (political
organization)**
JS: 4914, 9414

Blackfeet Indians
J: 8776

Blackfeet Indians—Fiction
JS: 2260

Blackfeet Indians—History
J: 8980

Blacks—Biography
IJ: 7920

Blacks—Fiction
JS: 444, 558, 2093, 2235

Blacks—Great Britain
JS: 7913

Blacks—History
JS: 8421

Blacksmiths—Biography
IJ: 6777

Blackwell, Elizabeth
J: 7545
JS: 7544

Blades, Ruben
J: 6976–77

Blair, Bonnie
IJ: 7731

Blind—Biography
IJ: 7832
JS: 6986, 7460, 7814
S: 7495

Blind—Fiction
IJ: 334
J: 232
JS: 155, 1507, 1752
S: 957

Blue (color)
J: 6442

Blue whales
See also Whales
JS: 10031

Blues (music)
J: 6466
JS: 6452, 6459
S: 6478

Blume, Judy—Criticism
JS: 4358

Bly, Nellie
IJ: 7464
JS: 6671, 7462–63

Board of Education *v.* Pico
JS: 5244

Boats
See also Ships and boats

Body piercing
JS: 5899, 5901, 5916

Bodybuilders—Biography
JS: 7099

Bodybuilding
J: 10910
JS: 10904

Bodybuilding—Fiction
IJ: 2910
JS: 3326

Bogues, Tyrone "Muggsy"
JS: 7680

Boitano, Brian
IJ: 7732

Bolivar, Simon
JS: 7896

Bolivia
IJ: 8842

Bonds, Barry
IJ: 7653

Bones
JS: 5949

Bonilla, Bobby
J: 7654

Bonney, William
JS: 7465

Book making
See also Publishing
IJ: 10730

IJ = Intermediate-Junior High; J = Junior High; JS = Junior-Senior High; S = Senior High

IJ = Intermediate-Junior High; J = Junior High; JS = Junior-Senior High; S = Senior High

British Columbia—Fiction
IJ: 1924, 2226, 2803

Broadcasters—Biography
J: 6679, 7425
JS: 7614
S: 7055

Brontë, Charlotte
See also Brontë family
IJ: 6815
JS: 6816
S: 4252

Brontë, Charlotte—Criticism
JS: 4253

Brontë, Emily—Criticism
S: 4266

Brontë, Emily—Fiction
S: 3320

Brontë family
J: 6818
JS: 6817, 6819

Brontë family—Criticism
JS: 4271

Brooklyn (New York)—Fiction
JS: 2550
S: 556, 1557

Brooks, Geraldine
S: 7914

Brothers—Fiction
IJ: 1379

Brothers and sisters
JS: 6363

Brown, Claude
JS: 6820

Brown, Dale
JS: 7681

Brown, Helen Gurley
IJ: 7546

Brown, Jesse Leroy
S: 7468

Brown, John
J: 7188
JS: 7187, 7189–90, 9153

Brown, John—Fiction
J: 2330, 2358
JS: 2361

Brown, Tom, Jr.
S: 6605

Brown v. Board of Education
JS: 4654, 9436

Bruchac, Joseph
JS: 6821

Brunei
IJ: 8588

Bryan, William Jennings
JS: 9375

Bubble gum
IJ: 9772

Buck, Pearl S.
JS: 6822

Buck, Pearl S.—Criticism
S: 4316

Buddhism
IJ: 4492
J: 4504
JS: 4491

Buddhism—Biography
IJ: 7803

Budgets and budgeting
JS: 5322, 5577

Buffalo Bill
JS: 7072

Buffalo Soldiers
JS: 9317

Buffaloes
JS: 9271

Buffaloes—Fiction
IJ: 2504

Bugs Bunny cartoons
JS: 6520

Building and construction
See also Architecture;
Construction; and types of
buildings, e.g., Skyscrapers
IJ: 6384, 6386, 10398, 10403
J: 6387, 10396, 10402
JS: 10399–401

Bulfinch's *Age of Fable*
JS: 4193

Bulgaria
JS: 8614

Bulimia
See also Eating disorders
IJ: 5752
J: 5741

JS: 5734, 5762, 5783, 5794, 5797,
5808, 5812, 5832, 6036
S: 5769

Bulimia—Fiction
IJ: 969
J: 945

Bull Run, Battle of
JS: 9188

Bull Run, Battle of—Fiction
JS: 2386

Bull Run, Second Battle of
JS: 9231

Bullfighting—Fiction
IJ: 1493

Bullies—Fiction
IJ: 1273, 1437, 1461, 2609, 2891,
3677
J: 1027, 1159, 1427
JS: 508, 705, 1168, 3691, 3721

Bunche, Ralph
J: 7371

Burch, Jennings Michael
JS: 7915

Burial customs
IJ: 8077
JS: 5588

Buried treasure
IJ: 8019, 9490, 9514

Buried treasure—Fiction
IJ: 164
S: 206

Burke, Chris
J: 6979

Burkina Faso
JS: 8508

Burma—Biography
J: 7820, 7822
JS: 7821

Burnett, Carol
JS: 6980

Burnett, Frances Hodgson
IJ: 6823

Burns, Anthony
JS: 7191

Burroughs, John
IJ: 7547

Bush, George
JS: 7256

IJ = Intermediate-Junior High; J = Junior High; JS = Junior-Senior High; S = Senior High

Bush pilots—Alaska
J: 9538

Business
See also Capitalism; Corporate power; Economics and business
IJ: 5315
JS: 4690, 5309
S: 5336

Business—Biography
J: 7527, 7615–16
JS: 7519, 7530–31, 7548, 7614

Business—Careers
JS: 5314

Business—History
J: 9277, 9336

Business ethics
JS: 5310

Business management
JS: 5571

Business (U.S.)—History
J: 9312

Butterflies and moths
IJ: 9994
JS: 9991–92

Butterflies and moths—Fiction
IJ: 1742
JS: 429

Byrd, Admiral
IJ: 6606

Byrd Antarctic Expedition
S: 8864

Byzantine Empire
J: 8167
S: 8197

Byzantium—Fiction
JS: 2066

C

Cable television
JS: 7618

Cable television—Careers
JS: 5552

Caddying (golf)
JS: 11054

Caesar, Augustus
J: 8140
JS: 7833

Caesar, Julius
IJ: 7835–36, 8152–53
JS: 7834, 8142

Caffeine
JS: 5630, 5632

Cahill, Tim
JS: 6607

Cahokia Mounds (Illinois)
IJ: 8943

Cahuilla Indians—Fiction
JS: 1743

Cajuns—Fiction
IJ: 2382

Cajuns—Folklore
IJ: 4170

Cake decorating
JS: 10611

Calamity Jane
J: 7469

Calcium
J: 10147

Calder, Alexander
J: 6713
S: 6712

Calendars—Fiction
S: 2193

California
IJ: 9527, 9535

California—Fiction
IJ: 1351, 2446
J: 191, 205, 425, 1433, 2449, 2487, 2622, 3291, 3372
JS: 178, 295, 332, 762, 1286, 2466, 2476, 2989, 3262
S: 139, 479, 563, 1556, 2755

California—History
IJ: 9126, 9533
J: 6658–59, 9278

California Gold Rush
See Gold Rush (California)

California Indians
IJ: 8988

The Call of the Wild—**Criticism**
JS: 4313

Calligraphy
IJ: 10683
J: 4411, 10666
JS: 10549–50, 10677

Calusa Indians—Fiction
IJ: 44

Calvin, John
JS: 7837

Cambodia
IJ: 8572

Cambodia—Fiction
J: 2115

Cambodian Americans
JS: 4935

Camcorders
JS: 10462

Camcorders—Fiction
IJ: 668

Cameroon
JS: 8514

Campbell, Ben Nighthorse
IJ: 7372

Campfires
IJ: 11015

Camping
IJ: 11015
J: 11017
JS: 11040

Camping—Fiction
IJ: 224, 3062
JS: 774, 3236, 3353

Camps—Fiction
IJ: 184, 690, 1222, 2893
J: 299, 1098, 1459
JS: 35, 1209, 1293, 1383, 1447, 2838

Camus, Albert
JS: 6824

Canada
IJ: 8771, 8774, 8777–78
JS: 8769

Canada—Biography
S: 6890

Canada—Fiction
IJ: 464, 865, 2219, 2222–23, 2792, 2878
J: 23, 185, 196, 590, 807, 909, 1027, 2570

IJ = Intermediate-Junior High; J = Junior High; JS = Junior-Senior High; S = Senior High

IJ = Intermediate-Junior High; J = Junior High; JS = Junior-Senior High; S = Senior High

The Catcher in the Rye—
  Criticism
JS: 4317

Cathedrals
J: 6387
JS: 6389

Cather, Willa
JS: 6825–26

Catholicism—Biography
IJ: 4519
J: 7873
JS: 6891, 7838

Cats
J: 10078
JS: 10069, 10075–77, 10079–87,
  10090–93
S: 10089

Cats—Art
JS: 6422

Cats—Behavior
JS: 10088

Cats—Fiction
IJ: 142, 319, 1833
J: 1350
JS: 265, 1192, 1613, 1747, 1859,
  1873, 1915, 1968, 2952, 3602
S: 1777–78, 2953–55, 3141

Cats—Folklore
JS: 4054

Cats—Poetry
JS: 3938

Catskill Mountains—Fiction
IJ: 2699
J: 94

Cattle drives
IJ: 9297

Cattle drives—Fiction
J: 202

Cattle drives—History
J: 9359

Cave dwellers—Fiction
J: 2035

Cave painting
IJ: 6416

Caves
IJ: 10195

Caves—Biology
IJ: 9826

Caves—Fiction
JS: 231

Cells
J: 10063

Celts
IJ: 8192
JS: 8181

Celts—Fiction
S: 1689

Celts—Mythology
JS: 4180, 4188

Censorship
J: 4789, 5252, 5256
JS: 4607, 4611, 5243–44, 5248,
  5254–55, 5257, 5261

Censorship—Fiction
IJ: 1148, 1539
JS: 1174, 1525, 1541, 1547

Censorship—Internet
S: 10420

Central America—Fiction
S: 1538

Central America—History
IJ: 8770
JS: 8816

**Central Intelligence Agency
  (U.S.)**
JS: 4582

Central Pacific Railroad
J: 10503

Cerebral palsy
JS: 7936

Cerebral palsy—Fiction
IJ: 939
J: 948, 982, 984
JS: 983

Cervantes, Miguel de
J: 6827

Cezanne, Paul
IJ: 6719

Chagall, Marc
JS: 6720–21

Champlain, Samuel de
IJ: 8772

Chancellorsville, Battle of
JS: 9175, 9191

Chang, Michael
IJ: 7748

Chang, Wah Ming
IJ: 6722

Chaplin, Charlie
JS: 6985

Chapman, John
IJ: 7476

Charge of the Light Brigade
JS: 8211

Charlemagne, Emperor
IJ: 7839
J: 7840, 8190

**Charlemagne, Emperor—
  Fiction**
J: 1969

Charles, Ray
IJ: 6987
JS: 6986

**Charles II, King of England—
  Fiction**
S: 2139

Charleston, Siege of
JS: 9248

Chaucer—Adaptations
J: 361, 3934

Chaucer—Criticism
S: 4259

Chauvet cave (France)
IJ: 6416

Chavez, Cesar
JS: 7192

Cheating—Fiction
IJ: 1281
JS: 509

Checkers
JS: 11030, 11034

Cheerleading
JS: 10897

Cheerleading—Fiction
S: 3184

Cheetahs
IJ: 9899

Chekhov, Anton—Criticism
S: 4363

Chemical dependency
See also Drugs and drug abuse
JS: 5721

IJ = Intermediate-Junior High; J = Junior High; JS = Junior-Senior High; S = Senior High

Chemistry
JS: 10164–65
S: 10162

Chemistry—Biography
JS: 7607

Chemistry—Dictionaries
JS: 10154

Chemistry—Experiments and projects
J: 10155, 10161
JS: 9632, 10163

Chemistry—History
JS: 10146, 10153

Cherokee Indians
IJ: 8993
JS: 8967, 9002

Cherokee Indians—Biography
JS: 7417, 7444

Cherokee Indians—Fiction
J: 525
S: 2242

Cherokee Indians—History
JS: 9016

Chesapeake Bay—Fiction
J: 296
JS: 1359

Chesnutt, Charles
JS: 6828

Chess
IJ: 11028
JS: 11031, 11033
S: 11032

Chess—Fiction
J: 1967

Chewing gum
IJ: 9772

Cheyenne Indians
IJ: 4964, 7372
JS: 8966

Cheyenne Indians—Fiction
J: 2248, 2261
JS: 2254

Cheyenne Indians—History
S: 9013

Chicago—Fiction
J: 2540, 2557
JS: 2530
S: 600, 2898

Chicago—History
J: 7472, 9492
JS: 7471

Chicago Bulls (basketball team)
IJ: 10990

Chicago Fire, 1871
J: 9492

Chicken pox
JS: 5819

Chickens
J: 9941

Chickens—Fiction
IJ: 1712

Chief Joseph (Nez Perce Indian)
JS: 7373, 8925

Child abuse
See also Child sexual abuse; Physical abuse
IJ: 6325, 6352
J: 6328
JS: 5009, 5120, 6189, 6210, 6311, 6317, 6332–36, 6347
S: 5996, 6337

Child abuse—Fiction
IJ: 203, 658, 2518, 3214
J: 330, 718, 740, 977, 981
JS: 680, 820, 835, 876, 883, 921, 951, 953, 968, 1460, 1477
S: 1482

Child care
JS: 6073, 6081, 6088, 6090, 6092–93, 6098, 6100, 6344

Child care—Careers
J: 5439
JS: 5441–42

Child care—History
S: 6079

Child labor
IJ: 7397, 9325
JS: 5009, 5013, 5032, 5036, 5051, 7815, 9333

Child labor—Fiction
IJ: 2222, 2337

Child labor—History
J: 5011
JS: 9328

Child sexual abuse
See also Child abuse; Sexual abuse
JS: 6189, 6210

Child sexual abuse—Fiction
IJ: 894

Childbirth
JS: 6082, 6087

Childbirth—Poetry
S: 3923

Childhood
JS: 3759

Childhood—Poetry
IJ: 4014
JS: 3945, 3989, 3998
S: 3923

Childhood—United States
JS: 8918

Children—Civil rights
IJ: 4733, 4765
J: 7204
JS: 4721, 4761, 4782

Children—Exploitation
JS: 4782, 5009

Children—Fiction
JS: 57

Children—Pioneer
J: 9272

Children—Poetry
IJ: 3926
J: 3916, 3918

Children—World War II
JS: 8278

Children's literature—Biography
J: 6938
JS: 6832, 6939

Children's literature—History and criticism
J: 4361
JS: 4358

Children's rights
See Children—Civil rights

Chile
JS: 6896

Chimpanzees
JS: 7574, 9880

IJ = Intermediate-Junior High; J = Junior High; JS = Junior-Senior High; S = Senior High

China
IJ: 8530
JS: 6848, 7812, 8531, 8534, 8542
S: 8543

China—Animals
JS: 9919

China—Biography
JS: 6822, 7817, 7827

China—Cookbooks
J: 10618, 10627

China—Fiction
IJ: 580, 1542, 2118
J: 2124, 2509, 2600
JS: 1343, 1531, 2102, 2104, 2119,
  2129, 2131
S: 49

China—Folklore
IJ: 1896, 4087
JS: 4094
S: 4091

China—History
IJ: 8538
J: 8529, 8541, 8544
JS: 6849, 7817, 8533, 8535–37,
  8539–40
S: 8527–28

China-Japan War—Fiction
JS: 2102

China-United States relations
See United States-China relations

Chinese Americans
See also Asian Americans
JS: 4922, 4924, 4927, 4936, 4938,
  4944, 4946

**Chinese Americans—
  Biography**
IJ: 6722
JS: 6920

Chinese Americans—Fiction
IJ: 252, 519, 580, 606, 897, 3169,
  3269
J: 603–4
JS: 508–9, 547, 550, 579, 605, 1343
S: 891, 2513

Chinese language
IJ: 4427

Chinook Indians
J: 9025

Chinook Indians—Fiction
J: 505

Chippewa Indians
J: 8946, 9023

Chippewa Indians—Fiction
JS: 559, 1083

Chiropractics—Careers
JS: 5538

Chivalry, Age of
S: 4130

Chocolate
J: 9759
JS: 10625

Chocolate—Manufacture
S: 5304

Choctaw Indians
J: 8987

Choctaw Indians—Fiction
S: 2440

Choirs (music)
JS: 6451

Choreographers—Biography
IJ: 7019, 7021
JS: 7022

Choreography
JS: 6518

Christian Science
JS: 4530

Christianity
IJ: 4513, 4515–16
J: 4512
JS: 4482, 4517, 4527, 6257, 8172
S: 4509

Christianity—Biography
JS: 7837

Christianity—Fiction
JS: 2052

Christianity—History
J: 8194
JS: 8978
S: 4518

Christie, Agatha
J: 6829

Christie, Agatha—Criticism
JS: 4290
S: 4277

Christmas
J: 4520
JS: 4517, 4524, 4528

Christmas—Crafts
J: 10544

Christmas—Fiction
IJ: 1022
J: 399, 1684, 3770–71
JS: 365, 1107, 1300, 3758
S: 620

Christmas—Plays
JS: 3794

Christmas—Poetry
JS: 3897

Christmas—Songs and carols
IJ: 6508
JS: 6507

Christmas—Wales
S: 3947

Chumash Indians
IJ: 9533

**Church and state—United
  States**
JS: 4462, 4602, 4662

Churchill, Winston
IJ: 7842
JS: 7841

Cickamauga, Battle of
JS: 9249

Cid, El
J: 6609

Cid, El—Fiction
J: 2173

Cinderella—Fiction
IJ: 1813
J: 1706

Cinque, Joseph—Fiction
S: 2357

Circulation system
See also Heart
IJ: 5939
JS: 5909

Circus
IJ: 6581
JS: 6579, 7123
S: 7124

Circus—Biography
IJ: 7125, 7127

IJ = Intermediate-Junior High; J = Junior High; JS = Junior-Senior High; S = Senior High

IJ = Intermediate-Junior High; J = Junior High; JS = Junior-Senior High; S = Senior High

Clones and cloning—Fiction
IJ: 3547
JS: 3666

Close, Chuck
JS: 6724

Clothing and dress
See also Fashion design; United
States—Costume and dress
JS: 10638, 10646–47
S: 5896, 10405

Clothing and dress—History
IJ: 10407
J: 10649
JS: 9397, 10409, 10632, 10636,
10648, 10651

Cloud forest (Costa Rica)
J: 10202

Clowns
JS: 6588, 10716

Clowns—Fiction
JS: 1226

Clubs
IJ: 6376

CNN (Cable Network News)
JS: 7618

Coal mining—History
IJ: 9325

Coast Guard (U.S.)
JS: 4705

Coast Guard (U.S.)—Careers
JS: 5449

Coast Salish Indians
J: 9005

Cocaine
See also Crack cocaine; Drugs
and drug abuse
J: 5690
JS: 5618, 5621, 5649

Cochise (Apache chief)
JS: 7374

Cochran, Jacqueline
IJ: 6611

Cock fighting—Fiction
S: 791

Cocker Spaniels
JS: 10100

Codes
See also Cryptograms and cryp-
tography
J: 4421

Cody, Buffalo Bill
IJ: 7477

Coffee
S: 10366

Coin collecting
JS: 10769

Cold
IJ: 10325

Cold fusion
JS: 10361

Cold War
IJ: 9435
J: 9411
JS: 8405, 9439

Coleman, Bessie
IJ: 6612

Collage
JS: 10735

Collecting and collections
JS: 10769

College application essay
JS: 5421

College stories—Fiction
JS: 972, 1092, 1326, 2959
S: 1455, 2912

Colleges and universities
JS: 5416, 5418

**Colleges and universities—
Academic guidance**
JS: 5420, 5423

**Colleges and universities—
Admissions**
JS: 5338, 5421, 5423
S: 5422

**Colleges and universities—
World Wide Web**
S: 5417

Colombia—Fiction
JS: 2225

Colonial Period (U.S.)
IJ: 4868, 7367, 9046, 9051–53, 9067,
9070, 9087
J: 9062, 9068, 9511
JS: 7206, 9069
S: 9074

**Colonial Period (U.S.)—
Biography**
IJ: 6763, 7383
JS: 7386
S: 7385

Colonial Period (U.S.)—Crafts
IJ: 9073

**Colonial Period (U.S.)—
Everyday life**
IJ: 9050

Colonial Period (U.S.)—Fiction
IJ: 2276, 2278–80, 2285
J: 2267–68, 2271–74, 2283, 2287,
2289, 2293–94, 2296
JS: 398, 2269–70, 2281, 2286, 2288,
2290–92, 2297, 2299, 2312, 2320
S: 2242, 2284, 2298

Colonial Period (U.S.)—History
IJ: 9049, 9058–59, 9063, 9071–72,
9076
J: 9060, 9064
JS: 9054, 9056–57, 9077–79

**Colonial Period (U.S.)—
Medicine**
IJ: 9075, 9113

Colonial Period (U.S.)—Science
IJ: 9061

Color
JS: 10351

**Color—Experiments and pro-
jects**
IJ: 10352

Colorado
IJ: 9497
S: 9498

Colorado—Fiction
IJ: 2469, 2937
JS: 1404, 3130

Colorado River
IJ: 9502
J: 9340

Colosseum (Rome)
JS: 8149

Columbus, Christopher
IJ: 6614, 8159
JS: 6613, 9043

**Columbus, Christopher—
Fiction**
JS: 3445

IJ = Intermediate-Junior High; J = Junior High; JS = Junior-Senior High; S = Senior High

Comanche Indians
J: 9010
JS: 8989, 9124

Comanche Indians—Biography
JS: 7500

Comanche Indians—Fiction
IJ: 2431
JS: 2480

Comedians
JS: 6962, 6980
S: 6537

Comedians—Biography
IJ: 6969, 7018, 7069–70, 7102
J: 7017
JS: 6983, 6990, 7016, 7061, 7067, 7095, 7111
S: 6991

Comets
J: 9700
JS: 9704–5

Comets—Fiction
JS: 3463
S: 3657

Comic books
IJ: 4867, 10690
JS: 4444, 8380, 10686
S: 10680

Comic books—Collecting
IJ: 10772

Comic books—Fiction
IJ: 1758
JS: 3014

Comic strips
JS: 6213

Comic strips—Fiction
J: 1591

Commandos
JS: 4715

Commercial art
JS: 10664

Commonwealth of Independent States
See also specific states, e.g., Ukraine
IJ: 8685

Communication
IJ: 10389
J: 10452
JS: 4413
S: 10424

Communication—Careers
J: 5467, 5553
JS: 5512

Communication—Experiments and projects
J: 10453

Communication—History
IJ: 10394
J: 9330

Communication arts
JS: 5394

Communism
J: 7416
JS: 5317, 7415, 8616, 8619, 8641, 8699, 9439, 9443

Communism—Biography
JS: 7889

Communism—China
JS: 8535

Communism—Fiction
J: 2179

Comnena, Anna—Fiction
JS: 2066

Compassion
JS: 6227

Competition
JS: 6253

Composers
J: 6457

Composers—Biography
IJ: 6685, 6949–50, 6953
J: 6956–57
JS: 6529, 6689, 6948, 6954–55, 7003, 7006

Composers—Women
JS: 6689

Compulsive behavior
See also Mental disorders
JS: 6025

Compulsive eating
See also Eating disorders
JS: 5827

Computer games—Fiction
J: 3475

Computer report writing
JS: 5378

Computers
See also specific topics, e.g., Internet; World Wide Web
IJ: 10423, 10427–29, 10441, 10445
J: 10425, 10430, 10432, 10438
JS: 4439, 5309, 10411–13, 10416–17, 10419, 10422, 10435, 10437, 10440, 10444, 10463
S: 10414, 10418, 10421, 10424, 10439

Computers—Biography
IJ: 7572, 7593
J: 7573, 7620
JS: 7571, 7576, 10434

Computers—Careers
J: 5560
JS: 5546, 5555–57, 5559, 5562, 5565–66

Computers—Fiction
IJ: 3156, 3512
J: 2977
JS: 1837, 2976, 3408, 3444, 3465, 3474, 3507, 3555–56
S: 3568

Computers—History
JS: 10434

Computers—Medicine
JS: 5863

Computers—Social issues
JS: 10426

Computers—Software
JS: 10436

Con games
See also Crime and criminals
J: 5197
JS: 5193

Conflict resolution
JS: 6228

Confucianism
J: 4483

Confucius
IJ: 7801

Congo, Republic of the
J: 8499

Congress (U.S.)
See also United States— Government; Senate (U.S.); House of Representatives (U.S.)
IJ: 4632
J: 4635–36

IJ = Intermediate-Junior High; J = Junior High; JS = Junior-Senior High; S = Senior High

JS: 4626, 4631, 4634
S: 4628

Congress (U.S.)—Biography
JS: 4633, 7140, 7167, 7368–69,
7399–400, 7415, 7456

Congressional committees
J: 4635
S: 4628

Congressional Medal of Honor
J: 4704

Connecticut—Fiction
IJ: 2336
J: 2294

Connecticut—History
J: 9511

Conquistadores—Fiction
JS: 2265

Conrad, Joseph—Criticism
JS: 4283
S: 4285

Conroy, Pat—Criticism
S: 4300

Consciousness raising—Women
J: 6270

Conservation
See also Ecology;
Environment; Environmental
problems
IJ: 5065, 5079, 5092, 9760, 9969,
9971
J: 5063
JS: 5062, 5074, 5083–84, 5091, 5094
S: 5076, 5081

Conservation—Biography
IJ: 7602
J: 7549
JS: 7512, 7550, 7603, 7792
S: 5060

Conspiracies
JS: 8035

Constellations
See also Galaxies
IJ: 9713
JS: 9715

**Constitution of the United
States**
IJ: 4597, 9086
J: 4600

JS: 4596, 4598–99, 4602–3, 4605–7,
4610–11, 5248, 8895, 9108
S: 4595, 4683

**Constitution of the United
States—Amendments**
IJ: 4601, 4604, 4767, 5247
JS: 4594, 4608–9, 4612–13

Construction
See also Building and construc-
tion
IJ: 10403

Consumer protection
JS: 5321

Consumerism
J: 5323
JS: 5321

Consumerism—Biography
JS: 7426

Contests
JS: 5573

Cook, James
J: 8596

Cookbooks
IJ: 10582, 10586, 10623, 10630
J: 9068, 10564, 10566, 10578, 10581,
10590, 10592, 10596, 10607,
10610, 10617–18, 10620–21,
10627, 10629
JS: 5287, 6045, 9288, 10565, 10569,
10571–77, 10579, 10583–85,
10587–88, 10591, 10593, 10597,
10599–603, 10605–6, 10608–9,
10611–14, 10616, 10622,
10624–26
S: 10567, 10615

Cookbooks—African American
IJ: 10604
J: 10589

Cookbooks—Civil War (U.S.)
JS: 9241

Cookbooks—Ethnic
IJ: 10619, 10628
JS: 10568, 10570, 10594

Cookies
JS: 10606, 10622

Cooking
JS: 10580, 10595, 10609

Cooking—Africa
J: 10610

Cooking—Biography
S: 7939

Cooking—Careers
S: 5470

Cooking—Fiction
JS: 3309

Cooking—History
JS: 9288

Copts
JS: 8457

Coral reefs
IJ: 10012–13, 10209, 10292
J: 10014
S: 10015

Corking
IJ: 10548

Cormier, Robert—Criticism
JS: 4302

Cornwall (England)—Fiction
IJ: 2169

Corot, Jean Camille
IJ: 6725

Corporate executives
JS: 5314

Corporate power
JS: 4690

Corporations
JS: 4690, 5313

Cortes, Hernando
IJ: 6615, 8159, 8795
JS: 6616, 7901, 8810

Corvette (automobile)
JS: 10490

Cosby, Bill
JS: 6990
S: 6991

Cosmetics
See also Beauty culture
S: 5898

Cosmetics—Biography
IJ: 7580
J: 7619
JS: 7579

Cosmetics—History
JS: 5897

Costa Rica
J: 10202

IJ = Intermediate-Junior High; J = Junior High; JS = Junior-Senior High; S = Senior High

Costumes
See also Clothing and dress
J: 10634
JS: 10639, 10644, 10646, 10653–54,
10657

Costumes—Folk
JS: 10656

Costumes—History
JS: 10638, 10643, 10655, 10657

Cote d'Ivoire
IJ: 8507

Cougars
JS: 9894

Country music
JS: 6465

Country music—Biography
S: 6464

Country music—Fiction
JS: 821

Courlander, Harold
JS: 6833

Courts
JS: 4672

Courts (U.S.)
See also Jury system; Supreme
Court (U.S.)
J: 4643, 4651, 4675
JS: 4648, 4650, 4657, 4671, 4680,
4740
S: 4678

Courts (U.S.)—History
J: 4652

Cowboys
J: 9290, 9359
S: 9265, 9306

Cowboys—African Americans
IJ: 9267

Cowboys—Fiction
IJ: 32, 107, 1198, 1277, 2483, 2504
J: 848
JS: 218, 2484

Cowboys—History
J: 9294, 9316
JS: 9289

Cowboys—Mexico
IJ: 8792

Cowboys—Songs
J: 6503

Crack cocaine
See also Cocaine; Drugs and
drug abuse
J: 5690
JS: 5618, 5621, 5649

Crafts
See also specific crafts, e.g.,
Paper crafts
IJ: 10530, 10533, 10540, 10546,
10551, 10555, 10558–59
J: 10544
JS: 4524, 10541, 10545
S: 10539, 10645

Crafts—Historical
IJ: 9073

Crane, Stephen—Criticism
JS: 4324, 4354
S: 4301

Crazy Horse (Sioux chief)
JS: 7375–77

Creation—Mythology
IJ: 4060
S: 4189

Creationism
JS: 8008

Cree Indians—Art
J: 8984

Crichton, Michael—Criticism
S: 4356

Crick, Francis
JS: 5879

Crime and criminals
IJ: 5153, 5170, 5178, 5189, 7474,
7478, 9425
J: 4643, 5127, 5140, 5155, 5158,
5183, 5186–87, 5194, 5197
JS: 5002, 5133–35, 5139, 5143, 5152,
5154, 5157, 5160, 5165, 5167–68,
5172, 5176–77, 5180, 5193, 5198,
5203, 5205, 5207, 5644, 5648,
5674
S: 4678, 5137, 5163, 9332

**Crime and criminals—
Biography**
IJ: 7487–90
J: 7472, 7475
JS: 7471

Crime and criminals—Fiction
J: 15, 636
JS: 246, 432, 542
S: 208

Crime and criminals—History
S: 5129

Crime and Punishment—
Criticism
S: 4254

Crime laboratories
IJ: 5130

**Crime laboratories—
Experiments and projects**
J: 5145

Crimean War
JS: 8211–12

Criminal justice
IJ: 5130
J: 5145, 5155
JS: 4648, 4650, 4671, 5135, 5154,
5160, 5167–68, 5172
S: 4678

Criminal justice—Trials
JS: 4644

Criminals
See Crime and criminals

Crocodiles
JS: 9836

Cronkite, Walter
S: 6992

Crow Indians
J: 8968

The Crucible—**Criticism**
S: 4391, 4400

Cruise, Tom
J: 6993

Crusades
JS: 8203–4

Crusades—Fiction
JS: 2068–69, 2087

Crutcher, Chris
JS: 6834

**Cryptograms and cryptogra-
phy**
See also Codes
IJ: 10556
J: 8241

Cuba
JS: 7897, 8825

Cuba—Biography
JS: 6963, 7897, 7899, 7902

IJ = Intermediate-Junior High; J = Junior High; JS = Junior-Senior High; S = Senior High

Cuba—Fiction
JS: 22
S: 156

Cuba—History
S: 4955

Cuban-American relations
JS: 8825

Cuban Americans
See also Hispanic Americans
S: 4955

Cuban Americans—Biography
IJ: 7009
J: 7010

Cuban Americans—Fiction
IJ: 4951
JS: 3282
S: 426

Cuban Missile Crisis
J: 9411
JS: 9405

Cuffe, Paul
JS: 7193

Cults
IJ: 10815
J: 4560
JS: 4558, 4561–64

Cults—Fiction
J: 69, 427, 1540
JS: 253, 1135
S: 3106

Cults—History
JS: 4559

Cultural anthropology
S: 6215

Cultural Revolution (China)
JS: 7812

Cultural values
JS: 5259–60
S: 9434

Curie, Marie
JS: 7552–53

Curiosities
IJ: 10803, 10833, 10840, 10854, 10857
J: 10804
JS: 10802, 10805, 10811, 10814, 10822, 10824, 10826, 10829, 10844, 10848, 10856
S: 10808, 10820

Curses—Fiction
J: 189

Curtis, Edward S.
JS: 6726

Custer, George Armstrong
IJ: 9021, 9027
JS: 7377, 9032
S: 9012

Customs and rituals
IJ: 5294

Cyberspace—Careers
JS: 5546

Cyprus
IJ: 8601, 8604

Cystic fibrosis
JS: 5820

Czech Republic
IJ: 8608
JS: 8623

D

D-Day
IJ: 8265

D-Day—Fiction
J: 2634

d'Aboville, Gerard
JS: 6617

Dahl, Roald
JS: 6835–36

Dahomey (African kingdom)
IJ: 8503

Dakota Indians—Fiction
JS: 1997

Dakota Territory—Fiction
J: 2438

Dalai Lama
IJ: 4492, 7803
JS: 7802

Dallas Cowboys (football team)
IJ: 11046

Dalton gang
IJ: 7478

Daman, Hortense
JS: 7844

Damon, Matt
IJ: 6996
JS: 6994–95

Dance and dancers
IJ: 6515
JS: 6516, 6518

Dance and dancers—African American
J: 6519

Dance and dancers—Biography
IJ: 7019, 7021
J: 7020
JS: 6963, 7022

Dance and dancers—Careers
JS: 5494

Dance and dancers—Fiction
IJ: 1044
JS: 1503

Danzinger, Paula
JS: 6837

Darling, Grace—Fiction
JS: 2205

Darrow, Clarence
JS: 9375

Darwin, Charles
J: 7555
JS: 7554, 8006

Date rape
See also Rape
J: 6170
JS: 5044, 5672, 6176, 6193, 6196, 6199, 6203, 6209
S: 6205, 6208

Date rape—Fiction
JS: 985

Dating (science)
IJ: 9582
JS: 10176

Dating (social)
JS: 6176, 6278

Dating (social)—Violence
JS: 6186

Da Vinci, Leonardo
IJ: 6727

Davis, Benjamin, Jr.
IJ: 7378

Davis, Donald
S: 7479

IJ = Intermediate-Junior High; J = Junior High; JS = Junior-Senior High; S = Senior High

Davis, Jefferson
IJ: 7379
JS: 7380

Davis, Miles
JS: 6997–98

Dawson's Creek (television series)
JS: 6560

Day, Dorothy
JS: 7381

Day, Tom
IJ: 6728

de Soto, Hernando
JS: 6618

Dead Sea Scrolls
IJ: 4472

Deaf—Biography
S: 7947

Deaf—Fiction
J: 998
JS: 1003, 2075

Deafness
J: 6064

Death
IJ: 5591, 5597, 5603–4
JS: 5125–26, 5588–89, 5592–96, 5598, 5601–2, 5605–6, 5806, 7931
S: 7481

Death—Fiction
IJ: 283, 607, 716, 734, 751, 811, 907, 964–65, 986, 1018, 1024, 1056, 1072, 1093, 1161, 1238, 1348, 1495, 1945, 2132, 2929, 3677
J: 16, 324, 610, 787, 860, 1079, 1094, 1101, 1149, 1210, 1220, 1260, 1298, 1311, 1331, 1368, 1464, 1686, 2439, 2448, 2660, 3747
JS: 186, 424, 632, 639, 645, 680, 692, 713, 777, 783, 796, 810, 832, 834, 836, 863, 867, 883, 898, 917, 926, 954–55, 962, 1055, 1059, 1068, 1105, 1153, 1160, 1176, 1192, 1276, 1289, 1302, 1310, 1317, 1333, 1372, 1380–81, 1398, 1503, 1505, 1688, 1743, 2216, 2733, 3035, 3154, 3181, 3275, 3286, 3332
S: 664, 719–21, 1096, 1327, 1511, 3279, 3297

Death—Poetry
JS: 3888

Death of a Salesman—Criticism
S: 4398

Death penalty
See also Capital punishment
J: 5187
JS: 4661, 4665–66, 5148, 5150, 5179, 5188, 5204

Decathlon—Biography
IJ: 7762

Decision making
JS: 6286

Deer
JS: 9911

Deer—Fiction
J: 322, 1368

DeFerrari, Gabriella
S: 7917

Degas, Edgar
JS: 6729

de Gaulle, Charles
IJ: 7845

de la Renta, Oscar
IJ: 7918

Delaware Indians
J: 8964

Delaware Indians—Folklore
JS: 4143, 8986

Demeter (mythology)—Poetry
JS: 3967

Democracy
IJ: 4592, 8040
JS: 4573, 4591

Denali National Park
JS: 9537

Denmark—Fiction
IJ: 74
J: 2592
JS: 2643

Denmark—Folklore
JS: 4098

Dental care
See also Teeth
JS: 5954

Dentistry
J: 5953, 5955

Denver—Fiction
S: 2506

Depression, Great
IJ: 9356, 9383
J: 9372, 9384
JS: 4883, 9357, 9362–66, 9373–74, 9376, 9378, 9380, 9382, 9387, 9389, 9391
S: 9354, 9379, 9386

Depression, Great—Biography
S: 7933

Depression, Great—Fiction
IJ: 67, 257, 583, 2555–56, 2561, 2572, 2575
J: 1, 2567, 2583, 2585
JS: 528, 2559, 2571, 2577
S: 553, 859, 2582

Depression, Great—Poetry
JS: 4021

Depression (mental)
See also Mental disorders
J: 6006
JS: 5723, 5842, 5991, 6000, 6015, 6027, 6032–34

Depression (mental)—Fiction
IJ: 2563
J: 700, 1225
JS: 926, 2672

Deserts
IJ: 10198–200
J: 10197
JS: 10196

Deserts—Fiction
JS: 1555

Designer drugs
See also Drugs and drug abuse
JS: 5691

Desktop publishing
JS: 4439

Desktop publishing—Careers
JS: 5516

Desserts
JS: 10585, 10606, 10611, 10622, 10625

Detective stories—Fiction
See Mystery stories—Fiction

Detectives
IJ: 5130

Detectives—Biography
IJ: 7433

Devil (religion)
J: 4497

IJ = Intermediate-Junior High; J = Junior High; JS = Junior-Senior High; S = Senior High

IJ = Intermediate-Junior High; J = Junior High; JS = Junior-Senior High; S = Senior High

J: 10097, 10111
JS: 10069, 10094, 10099–109, 10112–14, 10116–20
S: 10095, 10098, 10121

Dogs—Behavior
JS: 10110

Dogs—Fiction
IJ: 19, 209, 282, 284, 288, 301–2, 304, 306, 315–16, 334, 1976, 2266, 2437, 2594
J: 267–68, 300, 303, 305, 307, 312, 324, 336–37, 403, 1149, 1419, 1788, 2138, 2858–59
JS: 266, 279, 326, 404, 406, 438, 731, 978, 1083
S: 287, 1564, 2745, 2993

Dogsled racing—Fiction
JS: 3685

Dollhouses—Fiction
J: 1911

Dollhouses—Furniture
JS: 10658

Dollmaking
IJ: 10660

Dolls—Fiction
JS: 2798
S: 620

A Doll's House—Criticism
S: 4369

Dolphins
IJ: 10050
J: 10053
JS: 10001, 10040, 10044, 10046
S: 10035

Dolphins—Fiction
IJ: 297, 3531
J: 949

Domestic helpers—History
J: 9277

Domestic violence
See also Family problems
JS: 5044, 5651, 6338, 6346, 6366, 6368, 6371

Domingo, Plácido
J: 7002

Dominican Republic
S: 6793

Dominican Republic—Fiction
JS: 2211
S: 609, 2215

Donner Party
IJ: 9264
JS: 9287, 9295

Dostoevsky, Fyodor—Criticism
S: 4254, 4262

Douglass, Frederick
J: 7194
JS: 7197–99
S: 7195–96

Down's syndrome
JS: 6005

Down's syndrome—Biography
J: 6979

Down's syndrome—Fiction
IJ: 893, 932, 980, 1024
J: 909

Doyle, Sir Arthur Conan
IJ: 6842
JS: 6843

Doyle, Sir Arthur Conan—Criticism
S: 4276

Dracula
JS: 10860

Drag racing
IJ: 10928

Dragons—Fiction
IJ: 1605, 1638, 2017
JS: 1601, 1772, 1986, 2016, 2018, 2024
S: 1828

Drake, Sir Francis
J: 6619
JS: 6620

Drama
See Plays

Drawing and painting
IJ: 10665, 10671–73, 10685, 10689, 10692, 10701–3
JS: 6440, 10663, 10667, 10669, 10674–75, 10681, 10684, 10686–88, 10691, 10693–95, 10697–700
S: 10668, 10676, 10680, 10696

Dreams
J: 5938
JS: 5933

Dreams—Fiction
IJ: 887

JS: 1223, 2103
S: 3561

Dred Scott Case
IJ: 9128, 9136
JS: 9135, 9142

Dress
See Clothing and dress

Dressmaking
JS: 10759

Drew, Charles
JS: 7556

Drinking and driving
See also Alcohol; Drunk driving
IJ: 5639

Dropouts
JS: 5414

Drought
J: 10272
JS: 10274

Drought—Fiction
JS: 2234

Drowning—Fiction
IJ: 1072
JS: 2943

Drucker, Olga Levy
JS: 7919

Drug testing
JS: 5684

Drug trade
IJ: 5189
JS: 5697, 5711, 5719

Drugs
See also Drugs and drug abuse
IJ: 5717
J: 5664, 6247
JS: 5630, 5632, 5692, 5698, 5712, 5724

Drugs—Fiction
JS: 46, 122–23, 386, 454, 545, 916, 979, 1329

Drugs—Legalization
JS: 5628, 5685, 5713

Drugs—Sports
IJ: 5631
JS: 5684

Drugs and drug abuse
See also Drugs and specific drugs, e.g., Cocaine

IJ = Intermediate-Junior High; J = Junior High; JS = Junior-Senior High; S = Senior High

IJ: 5189, 5607, 5626, 5642, 5650,
5663, 5679–80
J: 5619–20, 5623, 5633–34, 5641,
5661, 5677, 5686, 5690, 5693,
5695, 5699, 5701–2, 5705, 5708
JS: 5608–11, 5613, 5615, 5617–18,
5621, 5625, 5628–29, 5635–38,
5640, 5643–44, 5648–49, 5651,
5654, 5656–58, 5660, 5662, 5665,
5667, 5670–74, 5676, 5681–84,
5691, 5697, 5700, 5706–7,
5709–11, 5713–15, 5718–21, 5723,
5725, 5922, 9809

Drugs and drug abuse—Fiction
J: 16, 1027
JS: 940, 1157, 1393, 3230–31
S: 911

Drunk driving
See also Drinking and driving
JS: 5655, 5669

Drunk driving—Fiction
JS: 713, 926, 1176

Du Bois, W. E. B.
IJ: 7202
J: 7203
S: 7200–1

Ducks and geese
See also Water birds
JS: 9944

Ducks and geese—Fiction
IJ: 286
JS: 276

Dunbar, Paul Laurence
JS: 6844

Dunkerque, Battle of
JS: 276

Dust Bowl
IJ: 9383

Duvalier, François and Jean-Claude
J: 7898

Dylan, Bob
JS: 7003

Dysgraphia
IJ: 6803

Dyslexia
IJ: 5995
J: 6019
JS: 5961

Dyslexia—Biography
J: 6993, 7017

E

Eagles
IJ: 9945, 9950
JS: 9947

Earhart, Amelia
IJ: 6624–26
J: 6623
JS: 6621, 6627
S: 6622

Earhart, Amelia—Fiction
JS: 177

Earp, Wyatt
IJ: 7382

Earring making
See also Jewelry making
S: 10641

Earth
IJ: 9706, 10167
J: 9662
JS: 5057, 9708–9, 10166, 10169–70
S: 9665, 9707, 9711, 10172

Earth science
IJ: 7964
JS: 10173
S: 10189

Earth science—Experiments and projects
IJ: 10171
J: 10177
JS: 8039

Earthquakes
IJ: 9546, 10175, 10178, 10184, 10188
J: 10181, 10187
JS: 10180, 10182, 10185
S: 10183

Earthquakes—Fiction
S: 113

East Timor
JS: 8600

Easter
See also Holidays
IJ: 4513

Easter Island
S: 8597

Eastern Europe
IJ: 8607

JS: 8610, 8616, 8619–20
S: 8602

Eastman, George
JS: 7557

Eating disorders
See also specific disorders, e.g.,
Anorexia
IJ: 5752, 5847
J: 5701, 5741
JS: 5732, 5734, 5739, 5751, 5760,
5762, 5765, 5783, 5787, 5794,
5797, 5805, 5808, 5814, 5827,
5831–32, 5840, 5842, 5916
S: 5813

Eating disorders—Fiction
J: 752, 934
S: 970, 1009

Eating disorders—Support groups
JS: 5799

Ecology
See also Conservation;
Environment; Environmental
problems; Pollution
IJ: 5056, 5065, 5079, 5092, 9573,
9782, 10201
J: 5072
JS: 5071, 5073–74, 5085, 5091, 5093,
5096, 9783, 10211, 10223
S: 5081

Ecology—Careers
IJ: 5463

Ecology—Experiments and projects
J: 9966
JS: 5069

Ecology—Fiction
JS: 867
S: 3497

Economic forecasting
JS: 5268

Economics and business
See also Business, Capitalism,
Corporate power
IJ: 5315
JS: 5305–6, 5313, 5318

Economics and business—Careers
JS: 5514

Economics and business—International
JS: 5311

IJ = Intermediate-Junior High; J = Junior High; JS = Junior-Senior High; S = Senior High

Ecstasy (drug)
See also Drugs and drug abuse
JS: 5608

Ecuador
JS: 8843

Eddy, Mary Baker
JS: 4530

Edelman, Marian Wright
J: 7204

Edison, Thomas Alva
IJ: 7559, 7561
JS: 7558, 7560

Edmonds, Walter D.
JS: 6845

Education
See also Colleges and universities; Schools; Teachers
IJ: 5345
JS: 5344, 5414

Education—African Americans
JS: 4748

Education—Biography
JS: 6668, 7180, 7250

Education—Careers
JS: 5520

Education—Fiction
JS: 2156

Education—History
J: 9276, 9338

Education—United States
IJ: 5340
JS: 5342, 5348

Educational guidance
JS: 5413

Edwards, Honeyboy
S: 7004

Eggs
J: 9941

Egypt
IJ: 8737–38
J: 8455

Egypt—Antiquities
JS: 8027

Egypt—Biography
JS: 7793, 7795

Egypt—Fiction
IJ: 1638, 2045
J: 2043

JS: 51, 2053, 2063, 2966
S: 2046–47, 3177, 3207–8

Egypt—Folklore
J: 4075

Egypt—History
IJ: 8044, 8076–78, 8080, 8084–89, 8091, 8096–97, 8102, 8737
J: 6432, 8025, 8081, 8083, 8090, 8094–95
JS: 6392, 7793–95, 8092, 8098–101, 8126
S: 8075, 8079

Egypt—Mythology
See Mythology—Egypt

Eichengreen, Lucille
JS: 7848

Eichmann, Adolf
JS: 8270

Eighteenth century—History
JS: 8883

Einstein, Albert
J: 7563
JS: 7562, 7564, 10316

Eisenhower, Dwight D.
IJ: 7269
J: 7268
JS: 7270
S: 8249

El Niño
IJ: 10275

El Salvador—Fiction
JS: 1559

Elderly persons
See also Aging; Death; Euthanasia
JS: 5124

Elderly persons—Fiction
IJ: 1136, 1229, 1268
J: 649
JS: 1342, 1762

Eleanor of Aquitaine—Fiction
J: 2165

Elections
IJ: 4692, 4698, 9399
JS: 4617, 4695, 4701, 8894

Elections—Fiction
JS: 2874

Elections—Finances
JS: 4696

Elections—School
JS: 5343

Electricity
IJ: 10357
J: 10356
JS: 10358

Electricity—Biography
J: 7617

Electricity—Experiments and projects
IJ: 10355, 10446
JS: 10360

Electromagnetism—Experiments and projects
IJ: 10359

Electron microscopes
JS: 10065

Electronics
JS: 10450
S: 10448–49

Electronics—Careers
JS: 5563

Electronics—Experiments and projects
IJ: 10446

Electronics—History
IJ: 10447

Elements
See also specific elements, e.g., Carbon
JS: 10164

Elephants
IJ: 9912
J: 9916
JS: 9914–15

Elephants—Biography
IJ: 7601

Elephants—Fiction
IJ: 2515, 2552
JS: 264

Elizabeth I, Queen of England
IJ: 7849
J: 8651, 8668
JS: 8660

Elizabeth I, Queen of England—Biography
JS: 7850

IJ = Intermediate-Junior High; J = Junior High; JS = Junior-Senior High; S = Senior High

IJ = Intermediate-Junior High; J = Junior High; JS = Junior-Senior High; S = Senior High

Environment
See also Conservation;
Ecology; Environmental
problems; Pollution
JS: 5074
S: 10191

Environment—Careers
IJ: 5463
JS: 5443, 5466, 5548

Environment—Diseases
IJ: 5846

**Environment—Experiments
and projects**
J: 9966
JS: 5069

Environmental problems
See also Conservation;
Ecology; Environment;
Pollution; and specific problems, e.g., Acid rain
IJ: 5055–56, 5064, 5077, 5079, 5082,
5098, 5100, 5105, 5109, 9781,
10339
J: 5063, 5072, 5111, 9977
JS: 5057–59, 5061–62, 5066–68,
5070–71, 5073, 5078, 5080,
5083–91, 5093, 5095–97, 5099,
5103, 5108, 5110, 5112, 5118,
9738–39, 9749, 9962
S: 5075–76, 5081, 9974

**Environmental problems—
Biography**
JS: 7524
S: 5060

**Environmental problems—
Fiction**
IJ: 1521
J: 505, 1600, 1741, 1894
JS: 423, 1579

Environmental protection
JS: 5101

Environmental sciences
JS: 9738

Environmentalists—Biography
JS: 7512

Epic poetry
S: 3927

Epidemics
JS: 5746, 5763

Epidemics—Fiction
JS: 3585

Epilepsy
JS: 5736, 6028

Epilepsy—Fiction
J: 899

Equiano, Olaudah
IJ: 7920

Erie Canal
IJ: 9516

Escalante, Jaime
JS: 7480

Eskimo
See Inuit; Native Americans

ESP
See Extrasensory perception

Essays
JS: 1401, 2646, 3774, 4235, 4240,
5372, 9581, 9745–46
S: 4241, 4243–44, 4246

Essays—Humorous
S: 4227

Essays—Native Americans
IJ: 8965

Essence (periodical)
JS: 4882

Estefan, Gloria
IJ: 7009
J: 7008, 7010

Estonia
IJ: 8688
JS: 8709

Ethics and ethical behavior
See also Medical ethics;
Morals, public; Politics—
Ethics
J: 6231
JS: 4454, 4689, 6230, 6232

Ethiopia
J: 8437, 8446
JS: 8435

Ethiopia—Fiction
IJ: 2094

Ethiopia—History
J: 8441
JS: 8126

Ethnic cleansing
See also Genocide
S: 4577

Ethnic groups
See also Immigration (U.S.);
Minorities; and specific eth-
nic groups, e.g., Irish
Americans
IJ: 4820
J: 4833
JS: 4728, 4800, 4830, 4834–35, 4841,
4845, 4928
S: 4831, 4836, 4844

Ethnic groups—Fiction
IJ: 467, 1320
JS: 450

Ethnic groups (U.S.)—History
JS: 8898

Ethnic groups (U.S.)—Texas
IJ: 9568

Ethnic problems
See also Discrimination;
Prejudice; Racism
IJ: 4829
JS: 4846
S: 4577

Ethnology—Biography
IJ: 7575

Etiquette
JS: 6234–36

Eurasia
JS: 8682

Europe
IJ: 8048
JS: 8603

Europe—Fiction
S: 12

Europe—History
JS: 8162
S: 8193, 8219

Europe—Modern history
S: 8602

Euthanasia
See also Aging; Death; Elderly
persons; Right to die
JS: 5126, 5593, 5606
S: 5587

Evangelists—Fiction
JS: 823

Evans, Dale
S: 7481

Evans, Minnie
IJ: 6731

IJ = Intermediate-Junior High; J = Junior High; JS = Junior-Senior High; S = Senior High

Evardson, Cordelia
S: 8287

Everglades (Florida)—Fiction
J: 97

Evolution
See also Scopes trial
IJ: 7996–97, 8007, 8009, 9796
J: 8005, 9855
JS: 6212, 7992, 7998, 8006, 8008,
9375, 9749–50, 9965
S: 9707, 9711

Evolution—Biography
IJ: 7590
J: 7555
JS: 7554, 7589

Excretory system
See also Digestive system
IJ: 5946

Exercise
See also Health care; Physical
fitness
JS: 5973, 5976, 5978–80, 6062, 6294
S: 5974, 10913

Explorers
IJ: 6637, 6652, 8159, 8720
J: 6596, 6598–600, 6619, 6648, 6651,
6658, 7952, 8059, 8596, 8767,
8828, 9042, 9340
JS: 6617, 6620, 6631, 6635, 6641–43,
9041
S: 6650

Explorers—Biography
IJ: 6657
J: 6601
JS: 6616, 6618

Explorers—Fiction
J: 2488
JS: 18

Explosives
JS: 10523

Extinct species
See also Endangered species;
Environmental problems
IJ: 9968
JS: 9964–65, 9967, 9976

Extrasensory perception (ESP)
JS: 10823

**Extrasensory perception
(ESP)—Fiction**
IJ: 1816, 1852, 1954
J: 2, 1612, 1687, 2206, 2706, 3022,
3179, 3420

JS: 1276, 1826, 3025, 3264, 3651
S: 2743

Extraterrestrial persons
IJ: 9675, 9677
J: 10841
JS: 10859
S: 9697

**Extraterrestrial persons—
Fiction**
J: 3409, 3548, 3608
JS: 3458, 3500, 3562, 3611, 3615,
3632, 3646, 3655
S: 3530, 3532

***Exxon Valdez* oil spill**
See also Oil spills
IJ: 9545

Eyes
See also Senses
J: 5963

F

Fabergé, Carl
JS: 7852

Fables
JS: 4190–91

Factories—Fiction
JS: 2353

Fairs—Fiction
IJ: 140
J: 328

Fairy tales
IJ: 1813, 1923, 4055, 4169
J: 1706, 2164
JS: 1193, 1690, 1845, 1863, 2011–12,
4106
S: 1698, 1715

Fairy tales—Anthologies
S: 4109

Fairy tales—Denmark
JS: 4098

Falcons
See also Peregrine falcons
IJ: 9945
JS: 9952

Falcons—Fiction
IJ: 277

J: 278
S: 947

Family abuse
See Family problems

Family histories
J: 10554

Family life
IJ: 6318
S: 5970, 6215, 6351, 7479

Family life—African American
JS: 3762

Family life—Art
JS: 6423

Family life—Fiction
IJ: 570, 668, 703, 729, 797, 802, 841,
1344, 2221, 2429
J: 492, 752, 755, 761, 787, 909, 948,
982, 2229, 2455
JS: 445, 501, 512, 550, 554, 628, 679,
872, 956, 997, 1727, 2292, 4229
S: 609, 2551

Family life—Poetry
IJ: 4012

Family planning
JS: 6099

Family problems
See also specific problems, e.g.,
Divorce
IJ: 6319, 6326, 6352
JS: 666, 5120, 5599, 5703, 6109,
6295, 6306–7, 6309, 6312, 6317,
6320, 6323–24, 6327, 6329–30,
6332, 6335, 6339, 6341–42, 6344,
6346, 6349, 6356–60, 6363, 6365,
6368, 6370, 6373–74, 7915
S: 5745, 6305, 7481, 7933

Family problems—Fiction
IJ: 210, 269, 284, 291, 304, 422, 464,
582, 607, 614, 619, 623–24, 635,
637, 640, 644, 654–55, 658, 660,
669–70, 674, 687–88, 690, 693,
697, 699, 709, 714–17, 724, 734,
736–37, 739, 744, 748, 751, 756,
765, 767, 775, 778, 792, 804–5,
811–12, 814, 819, 826, 830, 844,
846, 851, 853, 865, 869, 882, 887,
892–94, 907, 932, 999, 1005, 1022,
1035, 1051–52, 1084, 1195, 1198,
1351, 1430, 1497, 1499, 1786,
1804, 2108, 2136, 2222, 2226,
2398, 2420, 2428, 2467, 2517,
2526, 2561, 2563, 2572, 2851,
2867, 3204, 3679, 3688
J: 204, 259, 296, 330, 531, 586, 608,

IJ = Intermediate-Junior High; J = Junior High; JS = Junior-Senior High; S = Senior High

610–11, 627, 636, 647–49, 651,
656, 672, 676–77, 686, 691, 698,
700, 704, 708, 710, 718, 722,
740–43, 753, 768, 770, 779, 794,
816, 822, 828, 837, 845, 847–48,
854, 860, 873, 877, 880, 884, 890,
895, 922, 927, 934, 945, 1255,
1265, 1350, 1448, 2233, 2333,
2430, 2524, 2524, 2557, 2813,
2885

JS: 59, 119, 179, 320, 420, 455, 473,
480, 499, 526, 547, 558, 587, 613,
615, 622, 626, 630–31, 633–34,
638–39, 642–43, 650, 652–53, 657,
665, 667, 673, 678, 680, 682, 684,
689, 692, 695–96, 701, 705,
712–13, 723, 725–26, 731, 733,
747, 754, 758–59, 762–63, 769,
772, 776–77, 780, 783, 785, 789,
793, 795–96, 798–99, 801, 803,
809, 813, 815, 817, 820, 823, 825,
831, 833–34, 836, 838, 840,
849–50, 852, 858, 862–63, 867–68,
871, 874–76, 878–79, 881, 883,
885, 889, 896, 912, 925, 966, 1013,
1032, 1064, 1067, 1076, 1116,
1121, 1183, 1185, 1192, 1200,
1214, 1216, 1218, 1291, 1301,
1310, 1319, 1339, 1342, 1345,
1352, 1357–59, 1389, 1392, 1444,
1471, 1486, 1547–48, 1732, 2095,
2122, 2133, 2543, 2549, 2573,
2587, 2589, 2742, 2909, 2959,
3194, 3219, 3257, 3260, 3284,
3684, 3710, 3718, 3724, 6364

S: 426, 567, 617, 621, 641, 663–64,
702, 706, 711, 719–21, 745–46,
749, 766, 771, 788, 790–91, 806,
839, 843, 857, 888, 961, 1090,
1520, 1528, 2116, 3329, 3344,
3366, 3370

Family problems—Plays
JS: 3831, 3868

Family stories
S: 4900

Family stories—Fiction
IJ: 288, 313, 535, 616, 683, 760, 786,
824, 855, 1040, 1409, 1574, 1668,
1962, 2213, 2371, 2486, 2498,
2507, 2556, 2835, 2855, 2926,
3313

J: 213, 530, 534, 646, 662, 764, 773,
781–82, 807–8, 886, 1501, 1942,
2147, 2570, 3417

JS: 237, 393, 487, 524, 592, 612, 629,
685, 694, 727–28, 730, 750, 774,
821, 856, 861, 898, 1049, 1211,
1215, 1276, 1355, 1452, 1487,
2523, 2584

S: 620, 859, 891, 1475, 2146, 2519,
2668, 3345

Family violence
See also Family problems
J: 6328
JS: 6332, 6357

Fantasy—Fiction
IJ: 3, 356, 382, 688, 1567, 1570,
1573–74, 1590, 1596–97, 1599,
1605, 1611, 1619–20, 1624, 1638,
1655, 1663, 1668, 1673, 1677,
1679, 1702, 1712, 1717, 1730,
1733, 1738, 1740, 1742, 1749,
1753–58, 1775, 1785–86, 1804,
1812–13, 1816–18, 1822, 1833,
1835, 1850–53, 1866, 1868, 1883,
1896, 1910, 1916–18, 1921, 1924,
1941, 1944–48, 1950–52, 1954–55,
1958, 1961–62, 1964–65, 1976,
1981–82, 2004, 2008–9, 2013–14,
2017, 2026, 2180, 2737

J: 383, 1568–69, 1571–72, 1591,
1600, 1603, 1612, 1649, 1652,
1671–72, 1684, 1686–87, 1693,
1696, 1699, 1701, 1706, 1708,
1726, 1734, 1741, 1750–51, 1759,
1763–64, 1769, 1776, 1787–88,
1814–15, 1821, 1836, 1838, 1843,
1857–58, 1861, 1864, 1869, 1879,
1887–89, 1891–92, 1894, 1898–99,
1904, 1911, 1913–14, 1919–20,
1925, 1942–43, 1949, 1967,
1969–70, 1972–73, 1984, 1987,
1988, 1994, 2027, 2690, 2863,
2873, 2902

JS: 261, 365, 392, 397, 415, 1562,
1565–66, 1575, 1577–79, 1581,
1585–86, 1592, 1594–95, 1598,
1601–2, 1604, 1609–10, 1613,
1616, 1618, 1622–23, 1625,
1627–29, 1634, 1637, 1641–42,
1646–48, 1650, 1653–54, 1656–57,
1660, 1662, 1665, 1667, 1669–70,
1675–76, 1678, 1681–83, 1685,
1688, 1690, 1694–95, 1700, 1703,
1705, 1707, 1709, 1711, 1714,
1716, 1719–25, 1729, 1731–32,
1735–37, 1739, 1743–48, 1752,
1760–62, 1765, 1767–68, 1770,
1772, 1780, 1782–84, 1790,
1792–95, 1798, 1800, 1802,
1805–8, 1810–11, 1819–20,
1823–27, 1829–30, 1832, 1834,
1837, 1839, 1841–42, 1844,
1846–48, 1854–56, 1859–60,
1862–63, 1871, 1873–78, 1881–82,
1884–85, 1890, 1893, 1895,
1900–3, 1908–9, 1915, 1922,
1926–39, 1953, 1956–57, 1959–60,
1963, 1966, 1968, 1974–75, 1977,
1979, 1983, 1985–86, 1989,

1991–93, 1995–98, 2000–1, 2003,
2005–6, 2010–12, 2015–16,
2018–20, 2023–24, 2028–32, 2077,
2636, 2686, 2705, 2722, 3595–96,
3616, 3654, 3670, 3732, 4116,
4134

S: 342, 706, 1563–64, 1576, 1580,
1582–84, 1587–89, 1593, 1606–8,
1614–15, 1617, 1621, 1626,
1630–33, 1635–36, 1639–40,
1643–45, 1651, 1658–59, 1661,
1664, 1666, 1680, 1689, 1691–92,
1697, 1704, 1710, 1713, 1715,
1718, 1728, 1766, 1771, 1773–74,
1777–79, 1781, 1789, 1791,
1796–97, 1799, 1801, 1803, 1809,
1828, 1831, 1840, 1849, 1865,
1867, 1870, 1872, 1886, 1897,
1905–7, 1912, 1940, 1978, 1980,
1990, 1999, 2002, 2007, 2025,
2054, 3141, 3592

Fantasy—History and criticism
JS: 4251, 4333, 4337–38
S: 4257–58

Faraday, Michael
JS: 7565

Farm workers—Biography
IJ: 7210
JS: 7192

Farman Farmaian, Sattareh
JS: 7804

Farms and farm life
IJ: 9761, 9768
JS: 9979

Farms and farm life—Fiction
IJ: 464, 756, 786, 824, 2222, 2307,
2371, 2429
J: 909, 1464, 2547
JS: 626, 643, 1134, 1338, 1360, 1727,
1739, 2501, 2894, 3743
S: 1489, 2551

Farms and farm life—History
J: 9274

Farrakhan, Louis
JS: 4862, 7205

Fascism
JS: 7880

Fashion—History
IJ: 10407
J: 10649
JS: 9368, 9396–97, 10632, 10636,
10648, 10651

IJ = Intermediate-Junior High; J = Junior High; JS = Junior-Senior High; S = Senior High

Fashion design
See also Clothing and dress
JS: 10664

Fashion design—Biography
IJ: 7918
S: 7470, 7577

Fashion industry
JS: 10642

Fashion industry—Careers
JS: 5477, 5507–8

Fashion photography—Careers
J: 5495

Father-son relationships—Fiction
J: 531
JS: 874

Fathers
JS: 6081, 6088, 6098

Faulkner, William—Criticism
S: 4351

Favre, Brett
IJ: 7717–18

Fear
IJ: 1415
J: 3172
JS: 6017

Federal Bureau of Investigation (U.S.)
JS: 5143

Federal Bureau of Investigation (U.S.)—Fiction
S: 3245

Feminism
J: 4064
JS: 4722, 4747, 4752

Feminism—Biography
JS: 7241–42

Feminism—Poetry
JS: 3887

Fermi, Enrico
JS: 7566

Ferrari (automobile)
JS: 10491

Feudalism
See also Middle Ages
JS: 8162

Fiction writing
IJ: 5363

J: 5362
JS: 5361, 5392, 5399, 5409

Fighter pilots—Biography
JS: 6595

Figure skating
IJ: 11077
JS: 11082
S: 11078, 11081

Figure skating—Biography
IJ: 7735, 7741
J: 7734, 7737, 7742
JS: 7738

Filipino Americans
JS: 4923, 4941
S: 4658

Filipovic, Zlata
JS: 7853

Finance—Careers
JS: 5514

Finances (personal)
JS: 5569

Fine arts—Careers
JS: 5480

Finland
IJ: 8719

Fire Island—Fiction
IJ: 3335
JS: 3067

Firefighters
JS: 4638

Firefighters—Careers
IJ: 9777
JS: 5525

Firefighters—History
JS: 4639

Firefighters—Women
JS: 5525

Fires—Fiction
IJ: 855
JS: 53

Fires—History
JS: 4638

First aid
See also Accidents, Safety
IJ: 6120

First aid manuals
JS: 6115, 6122

First Ladies (U.S.)—Fiction
S: 3210–13

Fish
J: 10018
JS: 10000–1, 10016–17, 10019, 10122–23, 10140, 10142
S: 10139, 10144

Fish—Fiction
IJ: 91

Fish—Pets
JS: 10124

Fishing
IJ: 11036
JS: 11038, 11040

Fishing—Fiction
J: 96
JS: 111

Fitness
See Physical fitness

Fitzgerald, F. Scott—Criticism
S: 4309, 4314

Flag burning
JS: 5250

Flags
IJ: 8888
J: 4408

Flags—History
JS: 8867

Flags—United States
JS: 8867, 8910

Fleischman, Sid
JS: 6847

Fleming, Alexander
JS: 7567

Flight—History
J: 10474

Flight attendants—Careers
JS: 5440, 5454

Flipper, Henry O.
IJ: 6629
S: 6628

Floods
IJ: 10264

Florida
IJ: 9556, 9558
JS: 8957

Florida—Fiction
IJ: 44, 203, 827

IJ = Intermediate-Junior High; J = Junior High; JS = Junior-Senior High; S = Senior High

IJ = Intermediate-Junior High; J = Junior High; JS = Junior-Senior High; S = Senior High

IJ = Intermediate-Junior High; J = Junior High; JS = Junior-Senior High; S = Senior High

J: 263, 293, 296, 299, 483, 505, 590,
779, 781, 800, 837, 902, 946, 952,
971, 981, 984, 1029, 1033, 1086,
1095, 1097, 1132, 1165, 1233,
1261, 1295, 1304, 1378, 1410–12,
1416, 1419, 1427, 1474, 2384,
2408, 2611, 2843

JS: 231, 474, 613, 735, 793, 820,
916–17, 921, 928, 931, 955, 958,
967, 995, 1007, 1030, 1057, 1061,
1080, 1106, 1137–39, 1166, 1175,
1185, 1211, 1214, 1217, 1226,
1231, 1236, 1271, 1312, 1318,
1340, 1358, 1383, 1422, 1442,
1449, 1472, 1492, 1536, 2100,
2119, 2133, 2577, 2671, 3693,
3697, 3727, 3739

S: 462, 556, 973, 1047, 1053, 1096,
1122, 1270, 1305, 1371, 1482,
2616, 2917

Frisbees
JS: 10893

Fritz, Jean
JS: 6848–49

Frogs and toads
IJ: 9838
JS: 9817, 9837

Frontier life (U.S.)
IJ: 7478, 8979, 9017, 9256, 9260,
9264, 9267–68, 9297–98, 9307,
9310, 9319
J: 9257, 9259, 9269–70, 9272–74,
9276–77, 9283, 9285, 9290,
9292–94, 9312–13, 9316, 9324
JS: 8989, 9261–63, 9275, 9279–80,
9284, 9286–87, 9289, 9295, 9299,
9301–4, 9308–9, 9311, 9314, 9317,
9323, 9329, 9348
S: 6656, 9265–66, 9296, 9300, 9306,
9318, 9322

Frontier life (U.S.)—African Americans
J: 9282
JS: 9281

Frontier life (U.S.)—Biography
IJ: 7136, 7382, 7392, 7474, 7487–90,
7935
J: 6610, 7365, 7469
JS: 7073, 7130, 7364, 7374, 7465,
7611, 9315, 9321
S: 7473

Frontier life (U.S.)—Cookbooks
JS: 9288

Frontier life (U.S.)—Crafts
IJ: 10558

Frontier life (U.S.)—Fiction
IJ: 2250, 2322, 2371, 2426, 2428–29,
2437, 2444, 2446, 2456, 2458–59,
2462, 2464, 2467–69, 2471,
2474–75, 2478, 2482, 2485–86,
2491, 2497–98, 2503–4, 2507,
2937
J: 2237, 2241, 2248, 2262, 2272,
2277, 2283, 2293, 2328, 2430,
2436, 2438–39, 2442–43, 2448–49,
2455, 2470, 2472, 2477, 2479,
2487, 2490, 2492, 2494, 2496,
3372
JS: 151, 218, 279, 395, 2260, 2423,
2425, 2432–34, 2445, 2447, 2450,
2454, 2457, 2461, 2463, 2466,
2473, 2476, 2481, 2484, 2489,
2499–501, 2505, 3373–74
S: 394, 2378, 2427, 2440–41,
2451–53, 2460, 2495, 2502, 2508,
2519

Frontier life (U.S.)—Medicine
IJ: 9320

Frontier life (U.S.)—Poetry
IJ: 4034
JS: 4033

Frontier life (U.S.)—Women
J: 9258
JS: 9305

Frost, Robert
S: 6850

Frost, Robert—Criticism
JS: 4392
S: 4394

Fulani (African people)
JS: 8504, 8514

Fungi
JS: 9799

Fur trade—Fiction
IJ: 2219, 2264

Futurism
IJ: 10853
JS: 5268, 5276

Futurism—Fiction
JS: 3425, 3488

G

Gaines, Ernest—Criticism
S: 4303

Galan, Nely
IJ: 7014

Galapagos Islands
JS: 8835

Galapagos Islands—Fiction
JS: 3380

Galapagos Islands Biosphere Reserve
JS: 8835

Galaxies
See also Stars
IJ: 9712

Galdikas, Biruté
JS: 9883

Galileo
JS: 7570

Gallagher, Hugh
S: 7484

Gallic Wars
JS: 8142

Gama, Vasco da
J: 6600

Gambia
IJ: 8521

Gambling
JS: 5006, 5016, 5019, 5021, 5041,
10911

Gambling—Fiction
JS: 1202

Game hunters—Fiction
S: 221

Games
See also specific games, e.g.,
Chess
IJ: 10872
JS: 10867, 10901, 10909, 11035

Gandhi, Mahatma
J: 7806
S: 7805

Gangs
IJ: 5146, 5149, 5170, 5195, 5200–2
JS: 5128, 5139, 5152, 5157, 5162,
5174, 5184–85, 5190–91, 5198,
5718

Gangs—Biography
JS: 7912

Gangs—Fiction
IJ: 75, 187, 1034, 2514

IJ = Intermediate-Junior High; J = Junior High; JS = Junior-Senior High; S = Senior High

J: 211, 425, 544, 1420
JS: 120–21, 155, 428, 538, 601,
1127–28, 1143, 3348

Garbage
IJ: 5116
J: 5111
JS: 5114, 5117–19

Gardening
IJ: 10711
JS: 10704–5, 10708–10

Gardens—Fiction
IJ: 467

Garfunkel, Art
JS: 7101

Garibaldi, Giuseppi
JS: 7862

Garlic
IJ: 9775

Garrett, Pat—Fiction
S: 2453

Garrett, Thomas
J: 9120

Garter snakes
IJ: 9842

Garvey, Marcus
JS: 7207

Gates, Bill
IJ: 7572
J: 7573
JS: 7571

Gaugin, Paul
JS: 6733

Gaulic Wars
JS: 8142

Gay men
See also Homosexuality
JS: 6132, 6138, 6145, 6164, 6169

Gay men—Biography
JS: 6806
S: 6941

Gay men—Civil rights
JS: 6201, 6204

Gay men—Fiction
J: 816, 922, 927
JS: 615, 695, 967, 2652

Gay men—Marriage
JS: 4779

Gay rights
J: 4742
JS: 4772, 4779, 6158

Gay youth
JS: 1246, 3749, 6127–28, 6131, 6135,
6148, 6155
S: 6156

Gay youth—Biography
S: 6161

Gay youth—Fiction
JS: 1045, 1091, 1174, 1231, 1251,
1418, 1449, 1470, 1480, 3691
S: 891, 943, 1489

Gaza Strip (Israel)
JS: 8752

Gbaya (African people)
JS: 8428

Geese
See Ducks and geese

Gehrig, Lou
JS: 7657

Gems—Collecting
IJ: 10774

Gender bias
JS: 6202

Gender roles
See also Sex roles
JS: 5266

Genealogy
IJ: 6318
J: 6350, 10554
JS: 4960, 4975, 4982, 4988, 6331

Genealogy—Irish
JS: 4985

Genealogy—Japanese Americans
JS: 4947

Genesis (Bible)
IJ: 4471

Genetic engineering
See also Clones and cloning
IJ: 5884
J: 5876
JS: 5878, 5880, 5885–86, 5890
S: 5887

Genetic engineering—Fiction
JS: 3472

Genetics
IJ: 5884

J: 5876–77, 9765
JS: 5584, 5878–83, 5885–86, 5888,
5890, 9769
S: 5887

Genetics—Biography
IJ: 7594, 7599

Genetics—Fiction
IJ: 3547

Genghis Khan
JS: 7807

Genocide
See also Ethnic cleansing
J: 4579
JS: 4572

Genocide—Armenians
S: 8605

Geography
IJ: 10190
JS: 8037
S: 8051

Geography—Experiments and projects
JS: 8039

Geology
IJ: 9706, 10167
JS: 9818, 10166, 10168–70,
10173–74, 10176, 10228–29
S: 9707, 10172, 10189

Geology—Experiments and projects
IJ: 10171
J: 10177
JS: 8039

Georgia
J: 9554

Georgia—Fiction
IJ: 570, 1075

Georgia (former Soviet Republic)
IJ: 8690
JS: 8710

Geothermal resources
JS: 10336

German Americans
IJ: 4979
JS: 4977–78

German Americans—Fiction
JS: 2621

IJ = Intermediate-Junior High; J = Junior High; JS = Junior-Senior High; S = Senior High

Germany
IJ: 8640, 8642, 8646
J: 8636, 8649
JS: 8641

Germany—Biography
IJ: 7867
J: 7941
JS: 7866, 7870

Germany—Fiction
IJ: 2161, 2661, 2790
J: 3728
JS: 835, 2192, 2590, 2642
S: 348, 3338

Germany—Folklore
IJ: 4118, 4131
S: 4109

Germany—History
IJ: 7867, 7888, 8332, 8379, 8644
J: 8286
JS: 4978, 7869–70, 7924, 8258, 8270,
  8290, 8308, 8384, 8638–39, 8645,
  8647, 8650
S: 7868, 8322, 8637, 8643

Germany, East—Fiction
J: 2147

Germs
S: 5776

Geronimo
J: 7388
S: 7387

Gestation
S: 6078

Gettysburg, Battle of
J: 9209–10
JS: 9165, 9177–78, 9196

Gettysburg Address
J: 9221

Ghana
J: 8497

Ghana Empire
J: 8498

Ghost stories—Fiction
IJ: 183, 607, 714, 1655, 1775, 1921,
  1962, 2699, 2735, 2737, 2768,
  2795, 2808, 2814–15, 3027
J: 1451, 1686, 1764, 1913, 1987,
  2695, 2695–96, 2753, 2777, 2782,
  2793, 2805, 2810, 2813, 2819,
  2826, 2829
JS: 365, 1623, 1723, 1727, 1847,
  1909, 2000, 2335, 2674, 2689,

2704, 2733, 2736, 2760, 2769–71,
2778, 2780, 2785, 2818, 2825,
2828
S: 1606, 2453, 2676, 2693, 2707–8,
  2732, 4168

Ghost stories—Folklore
J: 4158, 4173

Ghosts
IJ: 10818, 10830
J: 10817, 10847
JS: 10812, 10828, 10855, 10858

Giant Panda
JS: 9918

Gibson, Althea
JS: 7749

Gibson, Josh
JS: 7658

Gifted children
JS: 6239

Gilbert and Sullivan—Songs
IJ: 6493

Gillespie, Dizzy
JS: 7015

Ginsburg, Ruth Bader
IJ: 7389

Giotto di Bondine
JS: 6403

Glaciers
S: 10189

Gladiators (Rome)
J: 8158

Glasburg, Ruth
S: 7922

Glass
J: 10382
S: 10366

The Glass Menagerie—
  Criticism
S: 4401

Glasses
J: 5963

Glasses—Fiction
JS: 1653

Glassmaking—Biography
J: 6736

Global warming
  See also Environment problems

JS: 5087
S: 5075

Globe Theatre (London)
IJ: 4389
JS: 4375

Globe Theatre (London)—
  Fiction
IJ: 2137

Glorious Revolution (England)
JS: 8671

Gobi Desert
IJ: 7971

God
IJ: 4494

Gold Coast (Africa)
J: 8501

Gold Rush—Fiction
J: 2472

Gold Rush—Poetry
J: 4046

Gold Rush (Alaska and Yukon)
IJ: 9536, 9536
J: 8775
JS: 6597

**Gold Rush (Alaska and
  Yukon)—Fiction**
J: 403

Gold Rush (California)
IJ: 9256
J: 9278, 9285
JS: 9309

Goldberg, Whoopi
IJ: 7018
J: 7017
JS: 7016

Goldfish
JS: 10123

Golding, William—Criticism
S: 4255, 4281

Golem
J: 4126

Golf
IJ: 11051
JS: 11053–54, 11056, 11059–61,
  11063
S: 11052, 11057–58, 11062

Golf—Biography
J: 7773

JS: 7755, 7757, 7774, 7776
S: 7775

Golf—History
JS: 11055

Golf—Women
JS: 11055, 11063

Goodall, Jane
IJ: 7575
JS: 7574, 9880, 9883

Goode, W. Wilson
JS: 7390

Gordeeva, Ekaterina
IJ: 7735
J: 7734

Gorillas
See also Ape family
IJ: 9882, 9884
S: 7568

Gorman, R. C.
IJ: 6734

Gospel music—Biography
JS: 7036

Government (U.S.)—Biography
J: 7151

Government (U.S.)—Careers
J: 5523
JS: 5465, 5526

Graham, Katharine
JS: 7485

Graham, Martha
IJ: 7019, 7021
J: 7020
JS: 6518, 7022

Graham, Robin Lee
JS: 6630

Grains
IJ: 9762

Grammar
IJ: 5376, 5404
JS: 5401
S: 5380, 5389

Grand Canyon
IJ: 9502
J: 9340

Grand Canyon—Fiction
JS: 125, 129

Grandfathers—Fiction
IJ: 1437, 2136

J: 1196
JS: 762, 1236

Grandmothers—Fiction
IJ: 736, 844, 870, 1526, 2835
J: 698, 1517
JS: 547, 682, 1045

Grandmothers—Poetry
JS: 3979

Grandparents
IJ: 6372
JS: 6365

Grandparents—Fiction
J: 23, 603, 649, 662, 672, 1368
JS: 727, 758

Grant, Ulysses S.
J: 7271
JS: 7174, 7272

The Grapes of Wrath—
   Criticism
S: 4359

Graphic arts—Careers
JS: 5469

Graphs
IJ: 10242

Grasslands
See also Prairies
JS: 9951, 10225

Grateful Dead (musical group)
J: 6469

Gravity (theory)
JS: 7604

Gray wolves
IJ: 9910

Great Astrolabe Reef (Fiji)
IJ: 10292

Great Barrier Reef (Australia)
IJ: 10013

Great Britain
See also England; Northern
   Ireland; Scotland
IJ: 8657

Great Britain—Biography
IJ: 7842
JS: 7841, 7851, 7877
S: 7892

Great Britain—Fiction
JS: 2070, 3050

Great Britain—History
IJ: 8192, 8655
J: 8184, 8665
JS: 7841, 7847, 7891
S: 8666

Great Britain—Theater
JS: 6590

Great Depression
See Depression, Great

*Great Expectations—*Criticism
JS: 4260
S: 4263

Great Famine
S: 8185

*The Great Gatsby—*Criticism
S: 4314

Great Lakes
J: 8939

Great Sioux War
JS: 9009

Great Wall (China)
IJ: 8538
JS: 8537

Greece
IJ: 8674

Greece—Ancient
S: 8108, 8111

Greece—Architecture
JS: 8064

Greece—Art
IJ: 8109

Greece—Biography
IJ: 7829
JS: 8107

Greece—Cookbooks
J: 10620

Greece—Fiction
IJ: 2067, 2136
J: 1519, 1904, 2610
S: 2060, 2630

Greece—History
IJ: 7829, 8109, 8112, 8122, 9588
J: 4214, 8073, 8110, 8119
JS: 8104–6, 8113–18, 8120, 8124,
   11101
S: 8103, 8121, 8123

Greece—History—Theater
S: 4370

IJ = Intermediate-Junior High; J = Junior High; JS = Junior-Senior High; S = Senior High

Handicaps
See specific types of handicaps, e.g., Dyslexia; Mental handicaps

Hands
J: 10846

Hang gliding
JS: 10875

Hankins, Anthony M.
S: 7577

Hannam, Charles
JS: 7924

Hannibal
IJ: 7864
JS: 8148

Hansberry, Lorraine
IJ: 6857
JS: 6853–56

Hanson (musical group)
IJ: 7024
J: 7023

Hanukkah
See also Jewish holy days
IJ: 4550

Hanukkah—Fiction
JS: 569

Hardaway, Anfernee
IJ: 7682

Hardy, Thomas—Criticism
JS: 4265

Harlem Globetrotters
J: 11002

Harlem (New York City)
JS: 6820, 6851, 9519

**Harlem (New York City)—
Fiction**
IJ: 187
J: 543–44
JS: 476, 517, 528, 540, 546

Harlem Renaissance
IJ: 9361
JS: 6875, 9358, 9360, 9367, 9370

**Harlem Renaissance—
Biography**
IJ: 6871
JS: 6872–73

Harlem Renaissance—Fiction
J: 2569

Harper's Ferry Raid—Fiction
J: 2358
JS: 2361

Harriot, Thomas
JS: 7578

Harvey Girls
J: 9293

Hashish
See also Drugs and drug abuse
JS: 5627

Hastings, Battle of
IJ: 8670

Hate crimes
IJ: 5049
J: 5047, 5140
JS: 5015, 5205

Hate groups
IJ: 5049
J: 5047
JS: 4784, 4822, 5039

Hate groups—Fiction
JS: 1552

Hatfield-McCoy feud
JS: 2546

**Hatshepsut, Queen of Egypt—
Fiction**
J: 2043

Haunted houses
JS: 10839

Haunted houses—Fiction
JS: 2738

Hautzig, Esther
JS: 7925

Hawaii
IJ: 9534

Hawaii—Fiction
IJ: 522, 1415, 1428, 3143
J: 1220, 1474, 2648, 3359
JS: 215
S: 745

Hawaii—History
IJ: 7828, 8346
JS: 9548

Hawking, Stephen
IJ: 7580
JS: 7579

Hawkins, Dwight
JS: 7712

Hawks
See also Birds of prey
IJ: 9945
JS: 9949, 9951
S: 9953

Hawks—Fiction
J: 293
JS: 858

Hawthorne, Nathaniel
J: 6858
JS: 4350

**Hawthorne, Nathaniel—
Criticism**
S: 4292, 4325, 4335

Hayden, Lewis
JS: 7209

Hazing—Fiction
IJ: 1169

Hazing—Schools
JS: 6292

Headaches
JS: 5841

Health
IJ: 5581
J: 5894, 6060
JS: 5580, 5582, 5585, 5747–48,
5966–67, 5982, 6058, 6281, 6294
S: 5970, 6055

Health care
See also Exercise; Medical care
JS: 5859, 5868

Health care—Biography
JS: 7587

Health care—Careers
IJ: 5534
JS: 5478, 5501, 5529, 5532, 5537,
5539, 5541
S: 5542

Health insurance
See Insurance—Health

Heart
See also Circulation system
JS: 5940–41

Heart attacks—Fiction
J: 854

Heart disease
JS: 5773, 5940–41

Heart of Darkness—Criticism
JS: 4283

IJ = Intermediate-Junior High; J = Junior High; JS = Junior-Senior High; S = Senior High

Heat
IJ: 10325

Heaven—Fiction
S: 1771

Heinlein, Robert A.—Criticism
JS: 4347

Heisman Trophy
IJ: 11043

Helgoff, David
S: 7025

Hellman, Lillian
JS: 6859

Hemingway, Ernest
JS: 6860–63

Hemingway, Ernest—Criticism
S: 4294, 4308, 4355

Hendrix, Jimi
J: 7026–27

Henrietta Marie (slave ship)
S: 4860

Henry, Marguerite
JS: 6864

Henry VIII, King of England
JS: 7865

Henson, Jim
JS: 7028

Henson, Matthew
JS: 6631

Herbs
JS: 5637, 9801, 10706

Herero (African people)
JS: 8488

Herodotus
J: 8068

Heroes and heroism
JS: 5249

Heroes and heroism—Biography
IJ: 6593
JS: 6594

Heroes and heroism—Fiction
JS: 3775

Heroin
See also Drugs and drug abuse
IJ: 5663
JS: 5725

Herons—Fiction
IJ: 1035

Herriot, James
JS: 7581–82

Hershey Company
S: 5304

Hershiser, Orel
IJ: 7659

Herzl, Theodor
JS: 7808

Hieroglyphics
See also Egypt—History
J: 8083

High schools
JS: 5356

High schools—Handbooks
JS: 5412

Highways
JS: 8874

Highways—History
IJ: 10496

Hijacking—Fiction
JS: 73

Hiking
See also Walking
J: 11017
JS: 11014, 11018, 11020, 11022
S: 11013, 11016

Hill, Grant
IJ: 7685
J: 7684
JS: 7683

Hillary, Edmund
IJ: 6632

Hillesum, Etty
S: 8309

Himalaya Mountains
JS: 8525

Hindenburg, Paul von
JS: 7866

Hindenburg (air ship)
JS: 3298

Hinduism
IJ: 4485, 4489
J: 4466, 4505
JS: 4503

Hingis, Martina
JS: 7645

Hinton, S. E.—Criticism
JS: 4307

Hip-hop poetry
JS: 3952, 3955

Hippies—Fiction
J: 1266

Hirohito (emperor of Japan)
JS: 7809

Hiroshima
IJ: 8317
JS: 8297–98, 8329, 8335–36, 8373, 8400

Hiroshima—History
JS: 7819

Hispanic American literature
JS: 577

Hispanic Americans
See also specific groups, e.g., Cuban Americans
IJ: 4948, 4959, 5288, 7210
J: 4957
JS: 4950, 4953–54, 4956, 4960, 5174
S: 4955

Hispanic Americans—Art
JS: 4952

Hispanic Americans—Baseball
JS: 10934

Hispanic Americans—Biography
IJ: 6830, 6904, 7009, 7014, 7043, 7075, 7918, 7938
J: 4961, 6976, 7008, 7094, 7096, 7100, 7164, 7654, 7773
JS: 577, 7112, 7166, 7175, 7192, 7480, 7503, 7529, 7651, 7675, 7720
S: 6793

Hispanic Americans—Careers
S: 5430

Hispanic Americans—Fiction
IJ: 535, 572, 1172, 2907, 4951
J: 500, 533–34, 536, 573, 578, 1043, 1086, 1433, 2126
JS: 437, 439, 445, 456–58, 486–87, 518, 526–27, 561, 587, 735, 1434, 1470, 1516, 1559, 2694, 3282, 3780
S: 435, 571, 609

IJ = Intermediate-Junior High; J = Junior High; JS = Junior-Senior High; S = Senior High

Hispanic Americans—Folklore
JS: 4139

Hispanic Americans—History
JS: 4958

Hispanic Americans—Plays
IJ: 3873

Hispanic Americans—Poetry
JS: 561, 3961

History—Careers
JS: 5550

History—General
IJ: 8040
J: 8052
JS: 8045

History—Methodology
S: 8041

Hit-and-run accidents—Fiction
JS: 3149, 3180

Hitler, Adolf
IJ: 7867
JS: 7869–70, 8290, 8384, 8645
S: 7868

Hitler, Adolf—Fiction
JS: 247
S: 1713

Hitler Youth
JS: 8308

HIV
See also AIDS
JS: 5737, 5740, 5744, 5771, 5775, 5807, 5836

Hobbes, Anne
JS: 7926

Hockey
IJ: 11066, 11069, 11071
JS: 11067, 11072

Hockey—Biography
IJ: 7736, 7740
J: 7644, 7733

Hockey—Fiction
IJ: 3679–80, 3682–83
J: 3696
JS: 3708, 3718

Hockey—Goalies
J: 7644

Hockey—History
JS: 11068

Hockey—Women
JS: 11070

Holiday, Billie
JS: 7029–30

Holidays
See also specific holidays, e.g., Christmas
IJ: 5284
J: 5291, 5293
JS: 5286, 5292

Holidays—Cookbooks
IJ: 10623
JS: 10573, 10593

Holidays—Crafts
J: 10544

Holidays—History
IJ: 9063

Holidays—Plays
J: 3846

Holidays—Poetry
JS: 3890

Holistic medicine
JS: 5855

Holland
See Netherlands

Holliday, Doc
IJ: 7392

Hollywood—Fiction
J: 3325
S: 1626

Holmes, Sherlock—Fiction
JS: 3066

Holocaust
IJ: 7857, 7888, 8255, 8276, 8289, 8320
J: 2644, 8244, 8250–51, 8260, 8294, 8300, 8339, 8342, 8352, 8367, 8393
JS: 2606, 7787, 8245–47, 8254, 8256, 8258, 8261–62, 8264, 8266–67, 8270, 8288, 8291, 8295, 8299, 8302, 8311, 8318, 8323–24, 8326, 8328, 8330, 8338, 8344, 8347–48, 8351, 8357, 8365, 8370, 8372, 8375, 8378, 8380, 8385, 8387, 8392, 8396, 8401, 8403
S: 8243, 8257, 8259, 8279, 8293, 8309, 8321–22, 8340, 8362–63, 8374

Holocaust—Biography
J: 7826, 7945

Holocaust—Biography *(cont.)*
JS: 6686, 7831, 7848, 7854–56, 7858–61, 7887, 7911, 7919, 7924, 7940
S: 7922, 8287

Holocaust—Fiction
IJ: 2633, 2641, 2655, 2657, 2661, 8252
J: 971, 1984, 2586, 2596, 2601, 2624–25, 2629, 2638
JS: 1116, 2019–20, 2183, 2588, 2590, 2598, 2602, 2618–20, 2626–27, 2636, 2639–40, 2642, 2646, 2654, 2662, 3277, 8273
S: 2603, 2617, 2630, 2651

Holocaust—Museums
JS: 9525

Holocaust—Plays
JS: 3835

Holocaust—Poetry
JS: 3922

Holocaust—Resources
JS: 8377

Holocaust Museum (Washington, D.C.)
J: 8260
JS: 8262, 9525

Holy Grail—Fiction
S: 1587

Holy Land—History
IJ: 8735

Home pages (computers)
J: 10430

Homeless children
IJ: 5210, 5225
JS: 5212

Homeless people
See also Poverty
IJ: 5225, 5229, 5235
J: 5228, 5232–33
JS: 5215, 5222–23, 5230–31, 5234, 5236

Homeless people—Fiction
IJ: 422, 1146
J: 130, 877, 1163
JS: 712, 1514
S: 106

Homeless teens
JS: 5212, 5238

Homer—Criticism
S: 4267

IJ = Intermediate-Junior High; J = Junior High; JS = Junior-Senior High; S = Senior High

Homer, Winslow
IJ: 6735

Homesteading
See also Frontier life (U.S.)
J: 9292

Homework
IJ: 5355

Homophobia
JS: 6138

Homosexuality
See also Gay men; Gay youth;
Lesbians
JS: 1246, 3749, 6128, 6131–32, 6138,
6145, 6148, 6155, 6158, 6164,
6169, 6201
S: 6161

Homosexuality—Fiction
J: 816, 922, 927, 1501
JS: 598, 615, 695, 707, 967, 1045,
1048, 1082, 1091, 1173, 1217,
1251, 1258, 1275, 1418, 1445,
1449, 1470, 1480, 2652, 3691,
3721
S: 943, 1425, 1489, 2876

Homosexuality—Marriage
JS: 4779

Homosexuals—Biography
JS: 6806
S: 6941

Honesty
J: 6231

Honesty—Fiction
JS: 1064

Hong Kong
IJ: 8532

Hong Kong—Fiction
JS: 100

Hooks, Bell
S: 6865

Hoover, Herbert
IJ: 7273

Hoover, Lou
IJ: 7274

Hopi Indians—Fiction
JS: 3130

Horror stories—Fiction
IJ: 2727, 2740, 2766, 2774, 2792,
2816, 2823

J: 390, 2687, 2692, 2700, 2702, 2706,
2717, 2779, 2804, 2811, 2829,
3232
JS: 386, 388, 408–9, 1736, 2673,
2677, 2686, 2698, 2701, 2705,
2709, 2712, 2724–25, 2728–29,
2734, 2739, 2742, 2744, 2749,
2752, 2754, 2757, 2759, 2762–63,
2769, 2772, 2786–87, 2789, 2796,
2798, 2801, 2817, 2821–22, 2824,
2830–31, 2850, 4127
S: 391, 2678–79, 2697, 2718, 2720,
2726, 2732, 2743, 2745, 2748,
2750–51, 2755–56, 2758, 2761,
2784, 2791, 2794, 2797, 2799,
2995–96

Horror stories—Folklore
JS: 4161

**Horror stories—History and
criticism**
JS: 4274, 4342
S: 4291

Horse racing
JS: 11074

Horse racing—Fiction
IJ: 257
JS: 258
S: 3038, 3040, 3042

Horseback riding
IJ: 11076
J: 11075
S: 10136

Horseback riding—Fiction
IJ: 291

Horses
IJ: 10130, 10134–35, 10137
J: 10125, 10127, 10129
JS: 10128, 10133, 10138
S: 10126, 10131–32, 10136

Horses—Careers
J: 5446

Horses—Fiction
IJ: 184, 256, 274, 283, 285, 291, 313,
329, 331, 1277, 2172, 2236, 2808
J: 263, 270, 275, 296, 299, 321, 325,
327–28, 330, 1010, 2261, 3139
JS: 124, 258, 273, 317–18, 320, 332,
1830, 2314, 2473, 3064
S: 1635

Horses—Stories
IJ: 257, 294

Horses—Training
S: 10132

Hospitals
JS: 5849
S: 5874

Hospitals—Careers
JS: 5541

Hospitals—Fiction
JS: 1508

Hot rods
JS: 10926

Hotels—Fiction
JS: 1504

Houdini, Harry
IJ: 7032
JS: 7031

House of Representatives (U.S.)
See also United States—
Government
S: 4630

Houseplants
JS: 10707, 10710

Houses
IJ: 10404
J: 10396

Houses—History
IJ: 6385

Houston, James
J: 6736

Houston, Sam
J: 7393

Houston, Whitney
IJ: 7033

**Houston Rockets (basketball
team)**
IJ: 10983

Howard, Juwan
IJ: 7686–87

Howard, Ron
JS: 7034

Hoya, Oscar de la
IJ: 7711

Hubble, Edwin
IJ: 7584
JS: 7583, 7585

Hubble Space Telescope
IJ: 9693
S: 9647

Huckleberry Finn—**Criticism**
IJ: 6929

IJ = Intermediate-Junior High; J = Junior High; JS = Junior-Senior High; S = Senior High

Huerta, Dolores
IJ: 7210

Hughes, Langston
JS: 6866–70

Human body
See also various systems, e.g.,
  Circulation system, and spe-
  cific organs, e.g., Heart
IJ: 5905–6, 5913
J: 5903, 5914–15, 5917, 5920
JS: 5904, 5907, 5910–12, 5916,
  5918–19, 6212
S: 5977

**Human development and
  behavior**
See also Personal guidance;
  Psychology
JS: 5925, 6216, 6219

Human Genome Project
JS: 5881, 5883

Human rights
See also Civil rights
J: 4743
JS: 4775, 4777, 4781, 4791, 7160

Human rights—Biography
J: 7781

Hummingbirds
JS: 9938

Humor—Art
S: 6425

Humor—Quotations
S: 4237

Humor and satire
See also Wit and humor
JS: 4240
S: 11013

Humorous stories—Fiction
IJ: 6, 70, 616, 1158, 1161, 1172, 1186,
  1267, 1344, 1439, 1596, 1605,
  1712, 1961, 2221, 2343, 2446,
  2541, 2568, 2737, 2832–37, 2845,
  2851, 2853, 2855–56, 2864, 2867,
  2872, 2875, 2878–80, 2886–87,
  2889–91, 2893, 2895, 2897, 2900,
  2907–8, 2910, 2916, 2921, 3620,
  3716
J: 413, 691, 1131, 1259, 1408, 1751,
  2071, 2841–44, 2847, 2857–59,
  2862–63, 2870–71, 2873, 2881,
  2885, 2888, 2899, 2902, 2919,
  3191, 3747
JS: 642, 923, 1046, 1120, 1292–93,
  1296, 1460, 1507, 1915, 1971,

2754, 2838–40, 2846, 2848–50,
  2852, 2854, 2861, 2866, 2869,
  2874, 2877, 2882–84, 2892, 2894,
  2896, 2901, 2903–6, 2909, 2911,
  2913–15, 2918, 2920, 3302, 3337,
  3385, 3609, 4240
S: 430, 1789, 2860, 2865, 2868, 2876,
  2898, 2912, 2917, 3073, 3115–16,
  3195, 4233

Humpback whales
IJ: 10045
S: 10032

Hungary
IJ: 8613

Hungary—Biography
JS: 7943

Hungary—Fiction
J: 2202
JS: 2618

Hungary—History
JS: 8302

Hunger
See also Poverty
JS: 5211, 5220

Hunter, Clementine
JS: 6737

Hunter-Gault, Charlayne
JS: 7486

Hunting
IJ: 11039
JS: 11037, 11040

Hunting—Fiction
JS: 954

Huntington's chorea—Fiction
JS: 849

Huron Indians
J: 8926

Hurricane Andrew
IJ: 10266

Hurricanes
See also Storms
IJ: 10265–66, 10269
JS: 10260

Hurricanes—Fiction
J: 201
JS: 76

Hurston, Zora Neale
IJ: 6871
JS: 6872–75

Hussein, Saddam
JS: 7810–11

Hussein, Saddam—Fiction
JS: 84

Hutu (African people)
J: 8447

Hydrogen
J: 10149

Hydrogen bomb
JS: 10528

Hygiene
See also Health care
J: 5894
JS: 6303

Hypnotherapy
S: 5986

I

***I Know Why the Caged Bird
  Sings*—Criticism**
JS: 4298, 4334

Ibo (African people)
JS: 8515

Ibsen, Henrik—Criticism
S: 4369

Ice—Poetry
IJ: 4039

Ice ages
JS: 7966

Ice cream
JS: 10585

Ice hockey
JS: 11073

Ice skating
JS: 11079, 11082
S: 11078

Ice skating—Biography
IJ: 7731–32, 7739
J: 7734, 7737, 7742
JS: 7738

Ice skating—Fiction
J: 1364

Ice skating—History
IJ: 11080

IJ = Intermediate-Junior High; J = Junior High; JS = Junior-Senior High; S = Senior High

IJ = Intermediate-Junior High; J = Junior High; JS = Junior-Senior High; S = Senior High

Indians of North America
See Native Americans and specific groups, e.g., Cherokee Indians

Indians of South America
JS: 8833, 8843
S: 8837

Indians of South America—Fiction
IJ: 297

Indians of South America—Folklore
JS: 4181

Indians of South America—History
J: 8793
S: 8940, 8975

Indians of the West Indies—Fiction
J: 2218

Individualism—Fiction
S: 1549–50

Indonesia
IJ: 8584

Industrial Revolution
IJ: 9125
J: 8222, 9336
JS: 8058, 8213, 8654, 9333

Industrial Revolution—United States
IJ: 8901
JS: 8876

Industry
JS: 10384

Industry—History
J: 8222, 9336
JS: 7548, 8876

Infertility
JS: 6146

Influenza—Fiction
IJ: 2565
JS: 3585

Information handling
JS: 5358

Information Revolution
JS: 10455
S: 10418

Inhalants
J: 5677, 5702
JS: 5635

Inner cities
JS: 5303

Inquisition
S: 8729

Inquisition—Fiction
IJ: 2084, 2194

Insanity
See also Mental disorders
S: 5163

Insanity—Fiction
JS: 3474

Insects
IJ: 9990, 9996
J: 9794, 9987
JS: 9982, 9988–89, 9993, 9997
S: 9981, 9983–84, 9986

Insects—Drawing and painting
IJ: 10672

Insurance—Health
JS: 5872

Intel Corporation
JS: 7576

Intelligence
See also Human development and behavior
JS: 6239

Intelligence service
JS: 4582

International relations
JS: 4574–76, 4581, 4583, 4587–88

Internet
IJ: 10423, 10427–29, 10441
J: 10425, 10430, 10432, 10438
JS: 10413, 10415–17, 10419, 10433, 10435
S: 5417, 10414, 10418, 10420–21

Internet—Censorship
JS: 10426

Internment camps
S: 7946, 9430

Interracial dating
See also Dating (social)
JS: 6274

Interracial dating—Fiction
JS: 3381

Interracial marriage
JS: 4826, 6274

Interracial marriage—Fiction
J: 1496, 2333
JS: 558, 1083

Interventionism (international)
JS: 4589

Inuit
See also Native Americans
IJ: 8865–66
J: 8927, 9541
JS: 8851, 8859

Inuit—Fiction
IJ: 98
J: 92, 135, 190, 586, 794
JS: 195, 228, 333, 3231

Inuit—Folklore
IJ: 4152

Inuit—Poetry
J: 4042

Inuits—History
IJ: 8014

Inventions
IJ: 4510, 7523, 10386–87, 10395
J: 10370, 10391
JS: 10362, 10372, 10376, 10379, 10388
S: 10377

Inventions—History
IJ: 8011, 10385
J: 10380

Inventors
IJ: 7536, 7561, 10387, 10392
J: 7522, 7543
JS: 7558, 9597, 10362

Inventors—African American
IJ: 7536
JS: 7507

Inventors—Biography
IJ: 7526, 7559
J: 7617
JS: 6743–44, 7520, 7560, 7588

Inventors—Women
IJ: 7508, 7523
JS: 10393

Invertebrates
J: 9813
JS: 10007
S: 9984

IJ = Intermediate-Junior High; J = Junior High; JS = Junior-Senior High; S = Senior High

Invisibility—Fiction
JS: 3658
S: 3469

Invisible Man—**Criticism**
S: 4297

Iowa—Fiction
JS: 1211

Iran
IJ: 8761
JS: 8762

Iran—Biography
JS: 7804, 7814, 7823

Iran—Emigration
JS: 4990

Iran—Fiction
JS: 507

Iran-Iraq War
JS: 8762

Iranian Americans
JS: 4990

Iraq
See also Persian Gulf War
IJ: 8755
JS: 8733, 8762, 9457
S: 8763

Iraq—Biography
JS: 7810–11

Iraq—Fiction
J: 2206
JS: 84, 507

Ireland
JS: 8653

Ireland—Biography
S: 8664

Ireland—Fiction
J: 1701, 2153, 2190
JS: 643, 1168, 1854, 1930, 2142,
  3284
S: 2146, 2171, 3350

Ireland—Folklore
IJ: 4111–12
JS: 4102
S: 4110

Ireland—History
IJ: 8655
JS: 8658

Ireland—Mythology
IJ: 1883
JS: 4188

Ireland—Poetry
S: 3940

Ireland, Northern
See Northern Ireland

Irish Americans
IJ: 4993
JS: 4976, 4985, 4992

Irish Americans—Fiction
IJ: 2518
J: 2368, 2540
JS: 2373

Irish Brigade (Civil War)
JS: 9164

**Irish Republican Army—
  Fiction**
JS: 112

Iron
IJ: 10158

Iroquois Indians
JS: 8962

Islam
J: 4536, 4852
JS: 4535, 4539–42
S: 4537

Islam—Biography
JS: 7505

Islam—Fiction
IJ: 2145
JS: 754

Islam—History
IJ: 4534
S: 4538

Islands—Fiction
J: 191, 1420
JS: 103, 240, 1365, 3085

Israel
J: 8739–40, 8750, 8753
JS: 8742, 8747–48, 8752, 10568
S: 8749

Israel—Biography
IJ: 7813, 7816
JS: 7784, 7790, 7808, 7818

Israel—Fiction
IJ: 1375
J: 2586, 2624
JS: 243, 776, 2135, 2176

Israel—History
J: 4971, 8751
JS: 7808

Israel-U.S. relations
JS: 8744

Israeli-Arab relations
See Arab-Israeli relations

Italian Americans
JS: 4975, 4995

Italian Americans—Biography
JS: 7566

Italian Americans—Fiction
IJ: 2482

Italian Australians—Fiction
JS: 2122

Italy
IJ: 8679
J: 8675
S: 8677

Italy—Biography
JS: 7862, 7880–81

Italy—Cookbooks
J: 10578, 10590

Italy—Fiction
J: 2166
JS: 1417, 2080, 2598
S: 2193

Italy—Folklore
JS: 4101

Italy—History
JS: 7881, 8198
S: 8676

Italy—Plays
JS: 3824

Ivory Coast
See Cote d'Ivoire

Iwo Jima, Battle of
JS: 8285, 8368

J

Jackson, Andrew
IJ: 9125, 9139
J: 7276
JS: 7275, 9154

Jackson, Andrew—Fiction
S: 2356, 2367

Jackson, Mahalia
JS: 7036

IJ = Intermediate-Junior High; J = Junior High; JS = Junior-Senior High; S = Senior High

Jackson, Michael
IJ: 7037
JS: 7038

Jackson, Stonewall
IJ: 7395
JS: 7394

Jacobs, Harriet A.
IJ: 7211

Jacobs, Harriet A.—Fiction
JS: 2346

Jacobs, Lionel and Barron
J: 9312

Jaguars—Fiction
JS: 2234

Jails—Fiction
J: 1408

Jamaica—Biography
J: 7058
JS: 7057, 7059

Jamaica—Fiction
JS: 618

Jamaica—Poetry
JS: 4040

Jamaican Americans
JS: 4980

James, Daniel "Chappie"
IJ: 7396

James, Jesse
IJ: 7487–90

James I, King of England
JS: 7871

James II, King of England
JS: 8671

Jamestown (Virginia)—History
IJ: 9048

Jane Eyre—Criticism
IJ: 6815
JS: 4253

Japan
IJ: 8565, 8568
J: 8566, 8569
JS: 8563–64, 8567

Japan—Art
J: 6431

Japan—Biography
JS: 7809

Japan—Cookbooks
J: 10617

Japan—Crafts
IJ: 8560

Japan—Fiction
IJ: 2117, 2132
J: 2113, 2126
JS: 1337, 1681–82, 1745, 2114, 2123, 2125, 2128, 2133
S: 2121

Japan—Folklore
IJ: 4089
J: 4081
JS: 4086, 4092

Japan—History
IJ: 8317, 8557, 8562
JS: 7809, 8336, 8559, 8561
S: 8558

Japan—Mythology
JS: 1878

Japan—World War II
S: 8376

Japanese Americans
See also Asian Americans
IJ: 4931, 8565
J: 4937
JS: 4934, 4943, 4947, 8395, 9392, 9398, 9407, 9417, 9442
S: 7946, 8382, 9395, 9430

Japanese Americans—Biography
JS: 4929, 7944

Japanese Americans—Fiction
IJ: 582–83
J: 481, 584, 2648, 3746
JS: 497, 532, 551, 591
S: 745, 3729

Japanese Americans—History
JS: 8277, 9427

Japanese Canadians—Fiction
J: 590

Jazz
JS: 6450, 6455, 6460, 6467, 6480, 6482
S: 6461, 6965, 7005

Jazz—Biography
J: 6688, 6692
JS: 6468, 6699, 6970, 6975, 6997–98, 7015, 7060, 7076

Jazz—Fiction
J: 2557

Jazz—History
JS: 6463

Jefferson, Thomas
IJ: 7278, 7281–82, 9127
JS: 7279–80, 7283
S: 7277

Jefferson, Thomas—Fiction
JS: 2316, 2334

Jennings, Cedric
JS: 7491

Jerusalem
JS: 8747

Jerusalem—Biography
IJ: 7813

Jesus Christ—Fiction
S: 353

Jewel (singer)
JS: 7039

Jewelry—Ancient
IJ: 8066

Jewelry—Fiction
JS: 362

Jewelry making
See also Earring making
IJ: 10635, 10637, 10650
JS: 10631, 10633, 10640, 10652
S: 10641

Jewett, Sarah Orne
JS: 6876

Jewish Americans
IJ: 4968–69
J: 9312
JS: 4970, 9382
S: 4972

Jewish Americans—Biography
IJ: 4967

Jewish Americans—Civil rights
J: 4736

Jewish Americans—Fiction
IJ: 2531
J: 2548
JS: 2628

Jewish holy days
See also specific holy days, e.g., Hanukkah
J: 4543
JS: 4544, 4555

IJ = Intermediate-Junior High; J = Junior High; JS = Junior-Senior High; S = Senior High

Jewish holy days—Fiction
JS: 569

Jewish humor
JS: 4048

Jews
J: 4543
JS: 4556, 4824

Jews—Biography
IJ: 6909
J: 7615–16
JS: 7787–88, 7788, 7911

Jews—Cookbooks
IJ: 10628

Jews—Fiction
IJ: 498, 1019, 2094, 2186, 2194,
2276, 2564, 2633, 2641, 2655,
2657, 3715
J: 452, 529, 578, 884, 971, 1239,
1328, 1412, 1814, 2167, 2195,
2539, 2586, 2593, 2596, 2601,
2622, 2625, 2629, 2638
JS: 1385, 1534, 2048–49, 2051, 2177,
2191, 2588, 2598, 2602, 2618–21,
2626–28, 2636–37, 2639, 2642,
2649, 2654, 2903, 3277
S: 556, 941, 1557, 2617, 2630

Jews—Folklore
J: 4126, 4543
JS: 4048, 4065

Jews—History
IJ: 4547
J: 4554, 4971, 8127, 8300, 8342,
8367, 8393, 8726, 8751
JS: 4970, 7854, 7856, 7924, 8245–46,
8254, 8256, 8258, 8264, 8273,
8291, 8299, 8323–24, 8328, 8344,
8348, 8372, 8375, 8377–78, 8385,
8396, 8401, 8403
S: 2157, 4549, 4551, 4966, 8257,
8279, 8321, 8374, 8729

Jews—Musicals
JS: 3874

Jews—Plays
JS: 3831, 3868

Jews—Women
JS: 7788

Jiang, Ji-li
JS: 7812

Joan of Arc
IJ: 7872
JS: 8633

Joan of Arc—Fiction
IJ: 2180
JS: 2073
S: 2155

Job hunting
See also Occupational guid-
ance; Vocational guidance
JS: 5427, 5435, 5532, 5569

Jobs—Fiction
J: 1378
JS: 3148

John, Elton
JS: 7041
S: 7040

John Paul II, Pope
J: 7873

Johnson, Isaac
IJ: 7928

Johnson, James Weldon
JS: 6877

Johnson, Lyndon B.
IJ: 7285
JS: 7284, 7286–87

Johnson, Magic
IJ: 7689
JS: 7688

Jokes and riddles
IJ: 10792
J: 10794–97, 10799–800
S: 10793

Joliot-Curie, Irène
JS: 7553

Jones, Caroline
JS: 7586

Jones, James Earl
JS: 7042

Jones, Mother
IJ: 7397
JS: 7398, 9328

Jones, Mother—Fiction
IJ: 2469

Jones, Quincy
IJ: 6953

Joplin, Scott
JS: 6954–55

Jordan
IJ: 8756
J: 8765

Jordan, Barbara
IJ: 7401
JS: 7399–400

Jordan, Michael
JS: 7630, 7690–91

Joseph (Bible)—Fiction
S: 2046–47

Joseph (Nez Perce chief)
JS: 7402

**Joseph (Nez Perce chief)—
Fiction**
J: 2259

Journal keeping
IJ: 5374, 5402
JS: 5387, 5406

Journalism
JS: 4445–46

**Journalism—African
Americans**
JS: 4448

Journalism—Biography
IJ: 7115, 7464
J: 6679, 7425
JS: 4447, 6671, 6690, 6702, 7173,
7462–63, 7485–86, 7609–10
S: 6812, 6992, 7498

Journalism—Careers
JS: 5479

Journalism—Fiction
J: 2842, 3365
JS: 1399, 1458, 1536

Journalism—Women
JS: 7462

Journeys—Art
IJ: 6397

Joyner-Kersee, Jacqueline
IJ: 7759
JS: 7760

Judaism
See also Israel; Jews
IJ: 4516, 4546, 4548, 4557
J: 4545, 4552
JS: 4544, 4555–56
S: 4549

Judaism—Biography
JS: 7784

Judaism—Fiction
J: 3033
JS: 2051

IJ = Intermediate-Junior High; J = Junior High; JS = Junior-Senior High; S = Senior High

Juggling
JS: 10536, 10553, 10877

Jujitsu
JS: 11093

Julia, Raul
IJ: 7043
J: 7044

Julius Caesar (play)—Criticism
JS: 4373
S: 4377

Juneteenth
IJ: 4855

Jungles—Fiction
JS: 33

Junipero Serro, Father
J: 6659

Jury system
JS: 4644, 4657, 4687

Justice
J: 4651, 4675
JS: 4645

Justice—Folklore
IJ: 4059
JS: 4052

Juvenile delinquency
J: 5155
JS: 5207

Juvenile delinquency—Fiction
JS: 120–23, 200, 738

K

Kahlo, Frida
J: 6738–39

Kalahari (Africa)
IJ: 8472

Kaleidoscopes
JS: 10661

Ka'liulani, Princess
IJ: 7828

Kane, Bob
JS: 6740

Kansas—Fiction
J: 2843

Kansas—History
JS: 9494
S: 9318

Karate
See also Martial arts
IJ: 11087, 11091
J: 11089
JS: 11095

Karate—Fiction
IJ: 3744

Kayaks and kayaking
IJ: 9531

Kazakhstan
IJ: 8694

Keller, Helen
JS: 7492–93

Kelly, Jim
IJ: 7719

Kennedy, John F.
IJ: 7293
J: 7288
JS: 7289–92, 7294–95
S: 9419

**Kennedy, John F.—
  Assassination**
IJ: 9412, 9425

Kennedy, Robert F.
IJ: 7404
JS: 7403

**Kennedy Center (Washington,
  D.C.)—Fiction**
S: 3246

Kentucky—Fiction
IJ: 619, 2563
JS: 2546

Kenya
JS: 8432–33, 8435–36, 8450,
  8452–53

Kenya—Folktales
J: 4076

Kerr, M. E.
JS: 5384

Kerr, M. E.—Criticism
JS: 6878

Kherdian, Veron
JS: 7927

Kibbutz
J: 8740

Kibbutz life—Fiction
JS: 2135, 2176

Kidd, Jason
IJ: 7660

Kidnapping
J: 5053

Kidnapping—Fiction
IJ: 19, 78, 86, 110, 210, 2541, 3112,
  3249
J: 608, 718, 848, 2339, 2923, 3006,
  3151, 3171, 3241
JS: 31, 175, 387, 667, 801, 1380,
  1842, 2282, 2988, 3024, 3026,
  3061, 3068, 3225, 3631
S: 3114

Kidney diseases
JS: 5796

Kidney failure—Fiction
JS: 974

Kiley, Deborah Scaling
JS: 6633

Killer whales
JS: 10039
S: 10043

Kindertransport
IJ: 8289

King, Coretta Scott
IJ: 7213
JS: 7212, 7214

King, Martin Luther, Jr.
IJ: 4758, 7215, 7221
J: 4877, 7217, 7222
JS: 4759, 7212, 7216, 7218–20
S: 7502

King, Stephen
JS: 6879

King, Stephen—Criticism
JS: 4340, 4342
S: 4357, 4360

King Philip's War
JS: 7432

Kiowa Indians
J: 9040

Kiowa Indians—Fiction
S: 2257

Kites
JS: 10713–14

Kleckley, Elizabeth
JS: 7929

IJ = Intermediate-Junior High; J = Junior High; JS = Junior-Senior High; S = Senior High

Klein, Norma
JS: 6880

Knights
See also Middle Ages
IJ: 8196
J: 4124, 8175, 8184

Knights—Fiction
J: 2078–79, 2188
JS: 2006, 2074

Knitting
IJ: 10548
S: 10758, 10760

Knot tying
IJ: 10529

Knowles, John—Criticism
S: 4329

Koalas
JS: 9917

Kollek, Teddy
IJ: 7813

Kongo (African empire)
J: 8500

Kongo (African people)
JS: 8440

Kongo Ndongo (African kingdom)
JS: 8511

Koontz, Dean
JS: 6881

Koop, C. Everett
JS: 7587

Kordi, Gobar
JS: 7814

Korea—Fiction
JS: 2106–7, 2128
S: 11, 2116

Korea, South
IJ: 8580

Korean Americans
IJ: 6340
JS: 4940
S: 4930

Korean Americans—Fiction
IJ: 441
J: 511
JS: 512–13, 1092, 2669

Korean War
IJ: 9458

J: 9453
JS: 9450, 9461, 9463, 9471

Korean War—Battles
JS: 9473

Korean War—Fiction
JS: 2106, 2666

Kosovo—Fiction
JS: 1537

Kovic, Ron
JS: 7494
S: 9466

Ku Klux Klan—Fiction
IJ: 494, 2576

Kurdish Americans
IJ: 4987

Kurdistan
S: 8763

Kurds—Fiction
JS: 507

Kuusisto, Stephen
S: 7495

Kuwait
See also Persian Gulf War
J: 8757
JS: 8733, 9457

Kwakiutl Indians—History
J: 9030

Kwan, Michelle
IJ: 7739
JS: 7738

Kwanzaa
JS: 4888, 5287

L

Labor camps—Fiction
S: 1554

Labor problems
IJ: 9342

Labor problems—Fiction
IJ: 2469
J: 565

Labor unions
J: 5329
JS: 5326

Labor unions—Biography
J: 7238
JS: 7176

Labor unions—History
IJ: 7397, 9342
J: 5327, 5331
JS: 5328, 5330, 7398

La Brea Tar Pits (Los Angeles, California)
IJ: 7989

Lacrosse
IJ: 10899
JS: 10883

Ladybugs
J: 9987

Lafayette, Marquis de
IJ: 7874

Lake Superior—Fiction
IJ: 2574

Lakes
See also Ponds
IJ: 10219–20

Lakota Indians
JS: 9022
S: 9006

lang, k. d.
JS: 7045

Lange, Dorothea
JS: 6741

Language
J: 4421, 4424
JS: 4407
S: 4417

Language—Food
IJ: 4415

Laos
IJ: 8583

La Purisima Mission
IJ: 9533

Large women
See also Obesity; Weight problems
S: 6250

Lascaux caves (France)—Fiction
JS: 1153

Lasers
JS: 10347

IJ = Intermediate-Junior High; J = Junior High; JS = Junior-Senior High; S = Senior High

Lasky, Kathryn
JS: 6883

Latifah, Queen
S: 7046

Latimer, Lewis
JS: 7588

Latin
S: 10793

Latin America—Crafts
IJ: 10540

Latin America—Folklore
IJ: 4176–77

Latin America—History
IJ: 10540

Latin Americans
See Hispanic Americans

Latvia
IJ: 8697

Law
See also Legal system
J: 4643
JS: 4650, 4680
S: 8060

Law—Careers
IJ: 5522
J: 5523
JS: 5524

Law—History
J: 4652

Law—United States
J: 4649
JS: 4671

Law enforcement
JS: 5167

Law enforcement—Careers
JS: 5527

Law enforcement—History
S: 5129

Lawrence, Jacob
IJ: 6742

Lawyers—Biography
J: 4649
JS: 7138

Lawyers—Fiction
JS: 2981
S: 106

Lawyers—Women
JS: 4663
S: 4659

Leadership
JS: 6287

Leakey, Louis
JS: 7589

Leakey, Louis and Mary
IJ: 7590

Learning
See also Psychology
JS: 6242

Learning disabilities
See also specific disabilities,
e.g., Attention deficit disor-
der
IJ: 5987, 5995, 6001, 6008, 6065
J: 6018
JS: 5800, 5961, 5989, 6012

**Learning disabilities—
Biography**
IJ: 6803

Learning disabilities—Fiction
IJ: 937, 1375
J: 908, 1181
JS: 1380

Leather work
JS: 10534

Lebanese Americans
IJ: 4994

Lebanon
IJ: 8758
J: 8764

Lebanon—Cookbooks
JS: 10565

Lebanon—Fiction
S: 1090

Lee, Harper—Criticism
JS: 4296

Lee, Robert E.
IJ: 7406
JS: 7174, 7405, 7407–8

Lee, Spike
J: 7049
JS: 6535, 7047–48

Leeuwenhoek, Antoni Van
IJ: 7591

Legal system
See also Law; Law
enforcement
JS: 4680

Lemurs
IJ: 9881

Lenape Indians
J: 8964

Lenape Indians—Fiction
S: 3069

L'Engle, Madeleine
IJ: 6882

Lenin, Vladimir Ilich
JS: 7875–76

Leningrad—History
JS: 8303

Leningrad, Siege of
JS: 8303

Lennon, John
JS: 7050–52

Leonardo da Vinci
JS: 6743–44

Leonardo da Vinci—Fiction
J: 2166

Leonowens, Anna
JS: 7930

Leprosy—Fiction
JS: 2181

Lesbians
See also Homosexuality
JS: 3749, 6127–28, 6131–32, 6135,
6138, 6145, 6148, 6155, 6158,
6164, 6169
S: 6156

Lesbians—Biography
JS: 6825–26, 7045

Lesbians—Civil rights
JS: 6201, 6204

Lesbians—Fiction
J: 1496
JS: 598, 707, 1173–74, 1275, 1445,
1492
S: 943, 1698, 3729

Lesbians—Marriage
JS: 4779

Lesotho
JS: 8489

IJ = Intermediate-Junior High; J = Junior High; JS = Junior-Senior High; S = Senior High

Letter writing
JS: 5370

Letter writing—Fiction
IJ: 1133

Lettering
IJ: 10683

Letterman, David
J: 7053

Leukemia
JS: 5806, 5817, 7931

Leukemia—Biography
JS: 7819

Leukemia—Fiction
IJ: 1018
J: 975
JS: 930, 954

Lewin, Ted
J: 6746
JS: 6745

Lewis, C. S.
J: 6884–85

Lewis, Carl
JS: 7761

Lewis, Edmonia
JS: 6747

Lewis, John
S: 7223

Lewis, Meriwether
IJ: 6637
JS: 6635
S: 6634

Lewis and Clark Expedition
IJ: 6637, 9127
JS: 6635
S: 6634, 6636

**Lewis and Clark Expedition—
Fiction**
IJ: 2266
J: 2488

Libby Prison—Fiction
S: 2390

Liberia—Fiction
JS: 2100

Libraries
See School libraries

Libraries—Fiction
IJ: 2908, 3354
JS: 3355

Libya
IJ: 8456

Lies and lying—Fiction
IJ: 1072
JS: 3312

Life (biology)
JS: 10057

Life cycles
IJ: 9870

Light
IJ: 10326, 10348
JS: 10347, 10350

**Light—Experiments and pro-
jects**
IJ: 10349, 10352
JS: 10353

Lighthouses—Fiction
IJ: 2574
JS: 2205

Limericks
J: 4004

Lincoln, Abraham
IJ: 7307–8, 9513
J: 7296, 7298–99, 7302, 7306
JS: 7297, 7300–1, 7304–5, 9171,
9240
S: 7303

**Lincoln, Abraham—
Assassination**
JS: 9255

Lincoln, Abraham—Fiction
JS: 2412, 2545
S: 2350, 2414

Lincoln, Mary Todd
JS: 7929

**Lincoln Memorial
(Washington, D.C.)**
IJ: 9513

Lindbergh, Charles A.
JS: 6638–40
S: 7496

Lindbergh, Reeve
S: 7496

Lindow Man
IJ: 7994

Lindros, Eric
IJ: 7740

Linnaeus, Carl
IJ: 7592

The Lion King **(motion picture)**
JS: 6527

Lions
JS: 9893–94

Lions—Fiction
IJ: 183
J: 38

Lipinski, Tara
IJ: 7741

Lipizzaner horses
IJ: 10137

Lipsyte, Robert—Criticism
JS: 4304

Literacy programs
JS: 5279

Literature—Anthologies
JS: 3757; 3772

**Literature—History and criti-
cism**
J: 4247, 6380
S: 4248

Lithuania
IJ: 8698
JS: 8693

Little Bighorn, Battle of
IJ: 8979, 9021, 9027
J: 8953
JS: 7447, 7450, 9032
S: 9012

**Little Bighorn, Battle of—
Fiction**
J: 2436
JS: 1790

Livingstone, David
JS: 6641

Lizards
IJ: 9834

Lloyd George, David
JS: 7877

Lobbying
J: 4636
JS: 4688

Lobel, Anita
JS: 8330

Loch Ness monster
JS: 10821

Locksmiths
S: 4233

IJ = Intermediate-Junior High; J = Junior High; JS = Junior-Senior High; S = Senior High

Locomotives
J: 10508

Logging—History
J: 9324

London, Jack
JS: 6886

London, Jack—Criticism
JS: 4313

London (England)—Fiction
IJ: 3146
J: 1763, 1914, 2599
JS: 31, 55, 271, 643, 1180, 1900,
   2187, 2656, 3648
S: 1371, 2189

London (England)—History
JS: 8177, 8319

Loneliness—Fiction
J: 1506

Long, Huey
JS: 7409

Long Island—Fiction
IJ: 1054
JS: 1245

Longfellow, Henry Wadsworth
JS: 6887

Longitude—History
S: 8057

Loper, Joshua—Fiction
IJ: 2483

Lord of the Flies—**Criticism**
S: 4255, 4281

Los Angeles
J: 9400
S: 5137

Los Angeles—Biography
JS: 7912

Los Angeles—Ethnic groups
JS: 4800

Los Angeles—Fiction
JS: 53, 1286, 2694
S: 1230

Los Angeles riots
J: 4857

Loss—Poetry
JS: 3912

Louis, Joe
IJ: 7714
J: 7713

Louis XIV, King of France
JS: 8627

Louisiana
IJ: 9559, 9561

Louisiana—Biography
JS: 7409

Louisiana—Fiction
J: 741, 768, 2318
JS: 3045
S: 2344

Louisiana—Folklore
IJ: 4170

Louisiana Purchase
IJ: 9127, 9131
J: 9083

L'Ouverture, Toussaint
IJ: 7900

Louvre Museum
S: 6417

Love
JS: 6238

Love—Poetry
IJ: 3970–71, 3986, 4027
JS: 3894, 3899, 3910, 3973, 3993,
   4035
S: 3982

Lovelace, Ada Byron
IJ: 7593

Lowry, Lois
IJ: 6888–89

LSD
See also Drugs and drug abuse
J: 5664

Luba (African people)
JS: 8444

Lucas, George
IJ: 7054
JS: 6526

Lumbee Indians—History
J: 8944

**Lumber and lumbering—
   Fiction**
J: 2560

Lund, Eric
JS: 7931

Lungs
See also Respiratory system
JS: 5956

Lying
J: 6231

Lyme Disease
JS: 5839

Lymphoma—Fiction
JS: 955

M

MacArthur, Douglas
IJ: 7413
J: 7410–12
JS: 7414

Macbeth
IJ: 3814

Macbeth—**Criticism**
IJ: 4382
S: 4383

McCall, Bruce
S: 6890

McCandless, Chris
JS: 9537

McCarthy, Joseph
J: 7416
JS: 7415, 9443

McCarthyism—Fiction
J: 1334

McClintock, Barbara
IJ: 7594

McGwire, Mark
IJ: 7662, 10970
JS: 7661

Machiavelli, Niccolo
S: 4455

**Machine tool industries—
   Careers**
JS: 5554

Machine trades—Careers
JS: 5519

Machinery
JS: 10375, 10379

Machinery—History
J: 10380

Machines—Careers
JS: 5561

IJ = Intermediate-Junior High; J = Junior High; JS = Junior-Senior High; S = Senior High

McKay, Jim
S: 7055

McNair, Ronald E.
IJ: 7595

McTaggart, David
JS: 7510

Madagascar
IJ: 9881
JS: 8470

Maddux, Greg
IJ: 7663

Madison, Dolley
IJ: 7309

Madison, James
IJ: 7310
J: 7311

Madonna (singer)
JS: 7056

Mafia—Fiction
S: 208

Magazines
JS: 4438, 5364

Magellan, Ferdinand
JS: 6642–43

Magellan (space expedition)
JS: 9718

Magic
See also Tricks
IJ: 10685
J: 10715, 10723
JS: 10716–17, 10719, 10722

Magic—Fiction
IJ: 1611
JS: 1562, 1805, 1808, 2788
S: 1645, 1766

Magic—History
S: 10720

***The Magic Flute* (opera)**
IJ: 6488
J: 6956

Magic spells—Fiction
JS: 1998, 3235

Magicians—Biography
IJ: 7032
JS: 7031

Magicians—Fiction
S: 1589, 3279

Magicians—Folktales
IJ: 4068

Magnetism
J: 10356

Magnetism—Experiments and projects
IJ: 10359
JS: 10360

Magnifying glasses—Experiments and projects
JS: 9626

Maine—Fiction
IJ: 671, 882, 2552
J: 698
S: 2551

Makeup
See also Cosmetics
S: 5898

Makeup (stage)
JS: 10537, 10725

Malawi
JS: 8481

Malawi (African people)
JS: 8481

Malaysia
IJ: 8585

Malcolm X
J: 7225, 7231–32
JS: 7224, 7226–30

Mali
JS: 8454, 8514

Mali Empire
J: 8520

Malinche (Aztec)
JS: 7901

Malone, Karl
IJ: 7641

Mammals
IJ: 9871, 9875
J: 9819, 9855
JS: 9865–68, 9874, 9879

Mammals—Extinct
JS: 7966

Mammals—History
IJ: 8010

Manassas, Battle of
JS: 9188

Manatee
JS: 10052

Mandan Indians—History
J: 8955

Mandela, Nelson
IJ: 7796
JS: 7797–98

Manhattan Project
JS: 10518

Manitoba—Fiction
J: 2802
JS: 1488

Mankiller, Wilma
JS: 7417

Manners
See Etiquette

Mantle, Mickey
JS: 7664

Manufacturing
J: 10365, 10368

Maori people—Folklore
JS: 4096

Maoris—Fiction
JS: 564

Mapp *v.* Ohio
JS: 4676

Maps and globes
IJ: 7953–55, 7958
JS: 7956

Maps and globes—History
JS: 7957, 7959

Marathon, Battle of
JS: 8114

Marathon (race)—History
JS: 11105

Marco Polo
IJ: 8159

Marijuana
See also Drugs and drug abuse
IJ: 5607
JS: 5627, 5670, 5698

Marine biology
See also Marine life;
Oceanography
IJ: 10005
S: 10286

Marine Corps (U.S.)
S: 4703

IJ = Intermediate-Junior High; J = Junior High; JS = Junior-Senior High; S = Senior High

Marine Corps (U.S.)—Careers
JS: 5450

Marine life
IJ: 10006, 10011
JS: 10004

Marine life—Drawing and painting
IJ: 10671

Maritime history—Biography
J: 7466

Marketing
JS: 5337
S: 5336

Marketing—Careers
JS: 5518

Markham, Beryl
JS: 6644
S: 6645

Marley, Bob
J: 7058
JS: 7057, 7059

Marriage
JS: 4230, 6354

Marriage—Fiction
JS: 1014
S: 788, 1429

Mars
J: 9701, 9728
JS: 9698, 9717, 9724

Mars—Fiction
S: 3426

Mars Company
S: 5304

Mars Pathfinder mission
JS: 9724

Marsalis, Wynton
JS: 7060

Marshall, George C.
S: 7418

Marshall, Thurgood
IJ: 7423
J: 7421
JS: 7419–20, 7422, 7424

Martha's Vineyard—Fiction
IJ: 2537
JS: 593

Marti, Jose
JS: 7902

Martial arts
See also specific fields, e.g., Karate
IJ: 11086, 11091–92, 11098
J: 11089–90
JS: 11093–97
S: 11088

Martial arts—Fiction
IJ: 3744

Martians—Fiction
JS: 3661

Martinez, Maria
IJ: 6748

Martinez, Pedro
JS: 7665

Marvel Comics
JS: 4444

Marx, Groucho
JS: 7061

Marx, Groucho—Fiction
S: 3054

Mary, Queen of Scots
JS: 7878–79

Mary, Queen of Scots—Fiction
JS: 2163, 3050

Mary I, Queen of England—Fiction
J: 2178
S: 2150

Maryland—Fiction
J: 2384

Masada—Fiction
JS: 2049

Masih, Iqbal
JS: 7815

Masks and maskmaking
JS: 10724–25

Masks and maskmaking—Fiction
J: 2098

Mass media
See also Media studies
IJ: 4443
JS: 4450, 10465
S: 6567, 9434

Mass media—Careers
JS: 5512

Mass media—Censorship
JS: 5243

Mass media—Violence
J: 5242, 5253
JS: 5241, 5251, 5258

Massachusetts
IJ: 9517

Massachusetts—Fiction
IJ: 2337, 2359
JS: 2353, 2360

Mastodons
See also Prehistoric life
IJ: 6762

Mathematical puzzles
See also Puzzles
IJ: 10243
J: 10236, 10250
JS: 10249, 10251, 10255–57
S: 10252–53

Mathematics
IJ: 10242, 10246
J: 5576, 10236
JS: 10240, 10244
S: 10238, 10245

Mathematics—Biography
IJ: 7593
JS: 7514, 7521, 7564, 7570

Mathematics—Careers
JS: 5429, 5562

Mathematics—Experiments and projects
IJ: 10254

Mathematics—History
IJ: 10235
JS: 10234, 10247

Mathematics—Projects
IJ: 10246

Mathematics—Puzzles

Mathews, Eddie
JS: 7666

Mathewson, Christy
JS: 7667

Matisse, Henri
IJ: 6750
JS: 6749

Matter
IJ: 10318
JS: 10320

IJ = Intermediate-Junior High; J = Junior High; JS = Junior-Senior High; S = Senior High

Matter (physics)—Experiments and projects
IJ: 10332

Mayan Indians
IJ: 8781
J: 4949, 8793
JS: 8787, 8789, 8816

Mayan Indians—Fiction
IJ: 2220
J: 2230
JS: 1515, 2234

Mayflower—Fiction
J: 2268, 2296

Mbundu (African people)
JS: 8438

Mbuti (African people)
JS: 8439

Mead, Margaret
JS: 7596–97

Measles
JS: 5825

Media—Violence

Media studies
See also Mass media
IJ: 4443
J: 5661
JS: 4450–51, 4694, 5241, 5251, 6229, 10458

Mediation
JS: 6240

Medical care
See also Health care
JS: 5872

Medical ethics
See also Ethics and ethical behavior
J: 5876
S: 5587

Medical technology
JS: 5875

Medical technology— Biography
IJ: 7528

Medical technology—Careers
JS: 5530

Medicinal plants
IJ: 9806
JS: 5871, 9807
S: 9789

Medicine
See also Doctors
IJ: 5865
J: 5835, 5851, 5858
JS: 5855, 5859, 5862, 5867–68, 5871, 5875, 5967
S: 5848

Medicine—Biography
IJ: 5869, 7515, 7528
J: 7517

Medicine—Careers
JS: 5530, 5536–37, 5539–40
S: 5542

Medicine—Computers
JS: 5863

Medicine—History
IJ: 5853, 5861, 5870, 9036, 9075, 9113, 9320
J: 5801, 8928
JS: 5856, 8098, 8949
S: 5854, 5864

Mediterranean Sea—Fiction
JS: 82

Meir, Golda
IJ: 7816

Melville, Herman—Criticism
S: 4353

Memory
JS: 6242
S: 5351

Mendel, Gregor
IJ: 7599
JS: 7598

Mennonites
IJ: 4514

Mennonites—Fiction
JS: 1058

Menominee Indians
J: 9001

Menstruation
See also Puberty
IJ: 6166
J: 6124, 6144, 6147, 6160, 6247
JS: 6134, 6152

Mental disorders
See also Mental illness, and specific disorders, e.g., Compulsive behavior
JS: 5961

Mental handicaps
See also specific handicaps, e.g., Dyslexia
IJ: 5995
JS: 5791, 5985, 5989, 5998–99, 6016

Mental handicaps—Fiction
IJ: 34, 659, 999, 1006, 1024
J: 741, 902, 909, 915, 1464
JS: 900, 1023, 3242
S: 959

Mental health
JS: 6003

Mental illness
See also Mental disorders and specific disorders, e.g., Compulsive behavior
IJ: 5772, 6004, 6011
J: 5994, 6026
JS: 5985, 5990, 6000, 6003, 6013–14, 6025, 6036–37
S: 5986, 6021

Mental illness—Biography
S: 7025

Mental illness—Children
JS: 5999

Mental illness—Fiction
IJ: 1022, 3100
J: 946, 990, 2443
JS: 630, 849, 900, 935, 956, 978, 989, 991, 1004, 1014, 1074, 1340, 1352, 3026, 3266
S: 711, 941

Mental illness—History
JS: 5998

Mental illness—Teenagers
JS: 5999

Mental problems
See Mental disorders

Mental retardation
JS: 6005

Mental retardation—Fiction
IJ: 1006
JS: 2731

Merina (African people)
JS: 8470

Merlin—Fiction
IJ: 2022
J: 1603
JS: 1602, 2021

Mermaids—Fiction
IJ: 1749

IJ = Intermediate-Junior High; J = Junior High; JS = Junior-Senior High; S = Senior High

Mermaids—Folklore
IJ: 4050

Merton, Thomas
JS: 6891

**Mesa Verde National Park—
Fiction**
J: 217

Mesopotamia
IJ: 8071
J: 8093, 8128

Metalwork
S: 10557

Meteorites
J: 9701
JS: 9702–3

**Meteorology—Experiments
and projects**
JS: 10281

Methadone
See also Drugs and drug abuse
J: 5705

Methamphetamine (speed)
See also Drugs and drug abuse
J: 5699

Mexican-American War
IJ: 9123, 9126
J: 8812, 9146
JS: 9124

**Mexican-American War—
Fiction**
J: 2487

Mexican Americans
See also Hispanic Americans
JS: 4950, 4956, 4960, 5174

**Mexican Americans—
Biography**
J: 7096
JS: 7720

Mexican Americans—Fiction
IJ: 964, 2907
J: 468, 500, 2126
JS: 445, 518, 527, 561, 587, 735,
1183, 1470, 3780
S: 435, 563, 571

Mexican Americans—Folklore
J: 4157–58
JS: 4139

Mexican Revolution
J: 8820

Mexico
IJ: 8792, 8804–6, 8809
JS: 8799–800, 8815

Mexico—Biography
J: 6738, 6775, 7906
JS: 6760

Mexico—Cookbooks
J: 10581, 10592
JS: 10570, 10594

Mexico—Fiction
J: 96, 189, 2229–30, 3144
JS: 486, 866, 1215, 1363, 2216–17,
2227–28, 2231

Mexico—Folklore
JS: 4136

Mexico—History
IJ: 6615, 7905, 8795–96, 8807, 8814,
8819
J: 7906, 8798, 8803, 8808, 8812,
8820, 9146
JS: 8794, 8797, 8802, 8810–11, 8816,
8818

Mexico—Holidays
IJ: 8801

Mexico-U.S. relations
JS: 8813

Miami Dolphins (football team)
IJ: 11044

Michelangelo Buonarroti
JS: 6751–52

Michigan
S: 4892

Michigan—Fiction
IJ: 2370

Michigan—History
J: 5331

Mickey Mouse—Biography
IJ: 6549

Microbes
S: 5776

Microbiology
IJ: 10059, 10221
J: 10063
JS: 10057, 10061

Microbiology—Biography
IJ: 7591

Microchips
S: 10439

Microorganisms
IJ: 10059

Microscopes
IJ: 10056, 10062
J: 10064
JS: 10058, 10065

Microscopes—Biography
IJ: 7591

**Microscopes—Experiments and
projects**
J: 10055

Microsoft—Biography
IJ: 7572
JS: 7571

Middle Ages
See also Castles; Feudalism
IJ: 6400, 8164, 8180, 8182–83, 8187,
8196, 8199, 8208
J: 6387, 8166, 8174–75, 8184,
8189–90, 8194, 8200
JS: 8162, 8168, 8177–78, 8195,
8202–4, 8669
S: 4105, 8173, 8179, 8185, 8193,
8207

Middle Ages—Art
JS: 6403

Middle Ages—Biography
J: 7840

**Middle Ages—Books and read-
ing**
J: 4442

Middle Ages—Fiction
IJ: 2065, 2084
J: 2071, 2078–79, 2188, 2207
JS: 1695, 1714, 2021, 2064, 2068–70,
2072, 2075, 2077, 2080–81, 2083,
2086–87, 2089, 2140, 3055, 3178
S: 2076, 2082

Middle Ages—Literature
IJ: 347

Middle Ages—Poetry
S: 3932

Middle Ages—Wars
JS: 8191

Middle class—Fiction
S: 401

Middle East
See also specific countries, e.g.,
Israel
J: 8753
JS: 8733–34, 8736

IJ = Intermediate-Junior High; J = Junior High; JS = Junior-Senior High; S = Senior High

IJ = Intermediate-Junior High; J = Junior High; JS = Junior-Senior High; S = Senior High

Mississippi—Fiction
JS: 499, 2578

Mississippi River
IJ: 8907
S: 4238

Mississippi River—Biography
IJ: 7504

Mississippi River—Fiction
J: 2442
JS: 411, 1959, 2520, 2956
S: 2435

Mississippi River—Floods
IJ: 10264

Missouri—Fiction
IJ: 2393, 2555
S: 1482

Missouri River
J: 9500

Mitchell, Maria
J: 7600

Moceanu, Dominique
IJ: 7730

Model making
JS: 10726

Modeling—Careers
J: 5511

Modeling—Fiction
IJ: 904, 3707
J: 1078
JS: 1341

Modern history
IJ: 8223
J: 9409
JS: 8404

Modern history—United States
J: 9424

Modoc Indian War—Fiction
IJ: 2475

Modoc Indians
JS: 8951

Mohawk Indians—History
JS: 8924

Moldova
IJ: 8701

Mole-rats
See also Naked mole-rats
IJ: 9873

Mona Lisa—Fiction
J: 2166

Monasteries—Fiction
JS: 3178

Monet, Claude
JS: 6754

Money
IJ: 5315, 5332–33
JS: 5579

Money-making ideas
IJ: 5568, 5572, 5578
JS: 5567, 5570–71

Money management
IJ: 5572, 5578
JS: 5579

Mongolia
IJ: 8571

Mongolia—History
JS: 7807

Mongols
JS: 7824

Monkeys
See also Ape family

Monkeys—Fiction
IJ: 292

Monologues
IJ: 3802, 3809
JS: 3783–87, 3795–96, 3800–1, 3804,
3829, 3836, 6552
S: 3843

Monomatapa (African kingdom)
JS: 8477

Mononucleosis
J: 5830
JS: 5815, 5822

Monroe, James
JS: 7312

Monroe, Marilyn
J: 7062
JS: 7063–64

Monsters
IJ: 10806
JS: 10725, 10813, 10821

Monsters—Fiction
JS: 1736, 3634
S: 1718

Montana
S: 9501

Montana—Fiction
JS: 229
S: 520, 3190

Montezuma
IJ: 8795
JS: 8802

Montgomery, L. M.
J: 6893

Moody, Anne
S: 7932

Moon
J: 9676
JS: 9678
S: 9710

Moon—Fiction
J: 2847, 3523
JS: 61, 3485, 3525, 3649, 3655

Moon—Poetry
J: 3941

Morals, public
See also Ethics and ethical
behavior
JS: 5259, 6182, 6230, 6232

More, Sir Thomas—Plays
JS: 3811

Moreno, Rita
J: 7065

Morgan, Julia
JS: 6755

Morgan, Sir Henry
JS: 6646

Mormons
J: 4531

Mormons—Fiction
JS: 377

Morocco
IJ: 8458

Morrison, Jim
J: 7066

Morrison, Toni
JS: 6894–95

Mosaics—History
IJ: 8061

Moscow
JS: 8692

IJ = Intermediate-Junior High; J = Junior High; JS = Junior-Senior High; S = Senior High

Moscow—Fiction
S: 3095

Moses—Fiction
IJ: 2045

Moses, Grandma
JS: 6756

Moss, Cynthia
IJ: 7601

Mossi (African people)
JS: 8504, 8508

Mother-daughter relation-ships—Fiction
S: 788

Mother Goose—Parodies
JS: 4011

Motherhood
See also Parenting; Parents
S: 4244, 6089

Motherhood—Fiction
S: 806, 818

Motherhood—Poetry
IJ: 4038
JS: 3891

Motion (physics)
IJ: 10338

Motion (physics)—Experiments and projects
IJ: 10331, 10333
J: 10334

Motion pictures
IJ: 6530, 6546, 6549–50, 10464
J: 6543
JS: 4914, 6520–21, 6524, 6526–28, 6532, 6534–35, 6547, 6552, 6962, 10465, 10750–51
S: 6556

Motion pictures—Biography
IJ: 7000, 7014, 7054, 7098
J: 6730, 7049, 7094
JS: 6985, 7034, 7047–48, 7063, 7107, 7111, 7128, 7503

Motion pictures—Careers
JS: 5483

Motion pictures—Fiction
IJ: 2568, 2737
J: 1260, 2858, 2862, 3099
JS: 2854

Motion pictures—History
JS: 6522, 6531, 6539–41, 6548, 6553
S: 6537, 6542

Motion pictures—Musicals
JS: 6529

Motion pictures—Production
JS: 6525
S: 10460

Motion pictures—Science fiction
JS: 6551

Motion pictures—Scripts
JS: 6523, 6536

Motion pictures—Special effects
IJ: 10459
J: 10456

Motorcycles
JS: 11005, 11011
S: 10499

Motown (recording company)
JS: 6572

Mott, Lucretia
JS: 7233

Mount Everest
IJ: 6632
JS: 6649
S: 10887

Mount Everest—Fiction
JS: 43

Mount McKinley (Alaska)
JS: 11023

Mount St. Helens (Washington)
JS: 10179

Mountain bicycles
IJ: 11008

Mountain biking
J: 11009

Mountain life—Fiction
JS: 1021

Mountain lions
JS: 9894

Mountaineering
See also Rock climbing
JS: 10886, 11023
S: 10863, 10887, 10890

Mountaineering—Biography
IJ: 6632
JS: 6649

Mountaineering—Fiction
J: 242
JS: 43

Mountains
IJ: 10214–17

Mourning, Alonzo
IJ: 7693

Movie stars—Fiction
IJ: 3087

Moving—Fiction
IJ: 765, 1054, 1110, 1186, 2118
J: 779, 890, 1165, 1167
JS: 825

Mozart, Wolfgang Amadeus
J: 6956

Mozart, Wolfgang Amadeus—Plays
JS: 3863

Mughal Empire
JS: 8552

Muir, John
IJ: 7602
JS: 7510, 7603

Multiculturalism
JS: 4826, 4832, 4838, 4847, 5436

Multiculturalism—Fiction
JS: 471

Multimedia
JS: 10463

Multiple sclerosis—Fiction
JS: 1002

Mummies
IJ: 8016, 8044
J: 8090
S: 10809

Mummies—Fiction
IJ: 2342, 3131

Muñoz Marín, Luis
IJ: 7903

Muppets
JS: 7028

Murals—History
IJ: 6394

IJ = Intermediate-Junior High; J = Junior High; JS = Junior-Senior High; S = Senior High

Murphy, Eddie
JS: 7067

Murrow, Edward R.
J: 7425

Muscles
JS: 5948–49

Muscular system
IJ: 5947, 5950

Musculoskeletal system
See also Skeletal system
JS: 5948

Museums
JS: 4642

Museums—Fiction
IJ: 147

Museums—United States
JS: 9507, 9525

Mushrooms
IJ: 9790
JS: 9802

Musial, Stan
JS: 7668

Music—African American
IJ: 6448
J: 6456

Music—Biography
IJ: 6685, 6950, 6950, 6953, 6974,
  6987, 7082, 7097, 7497
J: 6684, 6692, 6957, 6966, 6972,
  6976–77, 6984, 7023
JS: 6699, 6948, 6952, 6960, 6967,
  6970, 6975, 6989, 6998, 7007,
  7015, 7050, 7052, 7057, 7059–60,
  7076, 7101, 7120–21
S: 6951, 7004, 7040

Music—Careers
IJ: 5490
JS: 5484–85, 5489, 5498, 5506
S: 5482

Music—Fiction
IJ: 819, 1456, 2108
J: 1451
JS: 1178, 1494

Music—History
J: 6457

Music—Poetry
JS: 3907, 4031

Music appreciation
IJ: 6447
JS: 6450

Musical instruments
See also Wind instruments
IJ: 6447
J: 6495
JS: 6496

Musicals
See also Motion pictures—
  Musicals
J: 2631
JS: 6489, 6491–92, 6580, 6958
S: 6490, 6582

Musicians—Fiction
S: 1483

Mussolini, Benito
JS: 7880–81

Mustang (automobile)
JS: 10492

Mustangs
IJ: 10135

Mutes—Fiction
IJ: 938, 2814

Mutiny
S: 8592

Myanmar
See Burma

Myers, Walter Dean—Criticism
JS: 4293

Mystery stories
See also Detective stories
IJ: 164
S: 3177

Mystery stories—Criticism
JS: 4336

Mystery stories—Fiction
IJ: 91, 252, 285, 329, 855, 1611,
  1742, 2169, 2347, 2774, 2815,
  2864, 2925–26, 2929, 2937, 3013,
  3016, 3027, 3062, 3070, 3086–87,
  3097, 3100, 3112, 3131, 3133,
  3142–43, 3146, 3153, 3156,
  3167–69, 3204–5, 3229, 3240,
  3249–50, 3269, 3551
J: 764, 1787, 1920, 2327, 2703, 2710,
  2806, 2923, 2977, 2994, 3000,
  3003, 3006, 3015, 3022, 3032–33,
  3052, 3065, 3099, 3119, 3139–40,
  3144, 3151–52, 3157, 3159, 3165,
  3171–73, 3179, 3196–97, 3206,
  3215, 3218, 3227, 3232, 3237,
  3241, 3253, 3255, 3259, 3270
JS: 100–1, 180, 362, 369, 372–78,
  417–18, 527, 750, 777, 1234, 1313,
  1592, 1859, 2447, 2688, 2781,
  2789, 2818, 2928, 2930, 2935,
  2941–46, 2951–52, 2956, 2959,
  2962, 2965–67, 2969–74, 2976,
  2979–85, 2987–91, 3001–2, 3004,
  3008, 3014, 3017–21, 3023–24,
  3026, 3028–31, 3034–35, 3039,
  3043, 3045–51, 3055, 3058–61,
  3063–64, 3066–68, 3071, 3074,
  3077, 3079–80, 3083, 3085,
  3088–89, 3091–92, 3094, 3096,
  3098, 3101–5, 3117, 3120–22,
  3124, 3126, 3126–28, 3130, 3132,
  3135, 3147–50, 3154–55, 3158,
  3160–62, 3170, 3176, 3178,
  3180–83, 3189, 3192–94, 3198,
  3202–3, 3216–17, 3219–20, 3225,
  3228, 3230–31, 3233–36, 3238–39,
  3242, 3251–52, 3254, 3256–57,
  3260–67, 3322, 3327, 3388, 3510,
  3567, 3652
S: 20, 88, 176, 363, 430, 1189, 2057,
  2082, 2150, 2203, 2212, 2257,
  2922, 2924, 2927, 2931–34, 2936,
  2938–40, 2947–50, 2953–55,
  2957–58, 2960–61, 2963–64, 2968,
  2975, 2978, 2986, 2992–93,
  2995–99, 3005, 3007, 3009–12,
  3036–38, 3040–42, 3044, 3053–54,
  3056–57, 3069, 3072–73, 3075–76,
  3078, 3081–82, 3084, 3090, 3093,
  3095, 3106–11, 3113–14, 3118,
  3123, 3125, 3129, 3134, 3136–38,
  3141, 3145, 3163–64, 3166,
  3174–75, 3184–88, 3190, 3195,
  3199–201, 3207–13, 3221–24,
  3226, 3243–48, 3258, 3268, 3619

Mystery stories—Poetry
JS: 3984

Mythology
IJ: 4185, 4187
J: 4183
JS: 4179–80, 4182, 4188, 4190–91

Mythology—Anthologies
JS: 4193

Mythology—Classical
JS: 4198, 4204–5, 4207, 4212

Mythology—Egypt
IJ: 4184, 8091

Mythology—General
IJ: 1883, 4186
S: 1664, 4189

IJ = Intermediate-Junior High; J = Junior High; JS = Junior-Senior High; S = Senior High

Mythology—Greece
IJ: 4192, 4195–97, 4209, 4213, 4218,
4220, 4222, 8112
J: 1904, 4194, 4199, 4208, 4210–11,
4214–15
JS: 1716, 1880, 2059, 4182, 4190–91,
4198, 4200–7, 4212, 4216–17,
4221, 4223
S: 2060

Mythology—Rome
IJ: 4192, 4218–9
JS: 4212, 4224

Mythology—Scandinavia
JS: 4182

N

Nader, Ralph
JS: 7426

Nagasaki
JS: 8298, 8400

Naked mole-rats
IJ: 9873

Names
JS: 4416

Names—Animal
JS: 10069

Namibia
IJ: 8476
J: 8466
JS: 8488
S: 8468

Namibia—Fiction
JS: 443

**Napoleon, Emperor of the
French**
IJ: 7882
J: 8215, 8665

Napoleonic Wars
J: 8665

Napoleonic Wars—Battles
JS: 8217

Narcotics
See also Drugs and drug abuse
J: 5634

Narrative poetry
J: 4046–47
JS: 4006

Nashville (Tennessee)
S: 4875

Nast, Thomas
JS: 6757

Natchez Trail—Fiction
IJ: 2426

Nation of Islam
J: 4852
JS: 4862

Nation of Islam—Biography
JS: 7205

**National Air and Space
Museum (U.S.)**
S: 10475

**National Association of Stock
Car Racing (NASCAR)**
JS: 10925

National debt
IJ: 4637

National Geographic (maga-
zine)
JS: 9589
S: 8051

**National Museum of American
Art (U.S.)**
JS: 6444

National parks (U.S.)
See also specific parks, e.g.,
Canyonlands National Park
JS: 8055, 8884

National parks (U.S.)—Art
JS: 6437

National Rifle Association
JS: 5007, 5048

National Storytelling Festival
JS: 3750, 3768

Nationalism
JS: 4584
S: 4577

Native Americans
See also specific groups, e.g.
Cherokee Indians
IJ: 4964, 7935, 8969, 8982, 8988,
8990, 8996, 8998, 9004, 9017,
9544
J: 8776, 9033
JS: 4962–63, 4965, 8925, 9011, 9024,
9029
S: 8950, 9006

**Native Americans—Armed
forces**
JS: 8285

Native Americans—Art
J: 8921, 8984

Native Americans—Biography
IJ: 6657, 6734, 6748, 7129, 7372,
7453, 7499
J: 7142, 7388, 7448–49
JS: 6681, 6747, 6821, 6944, 7252,
7363, 7373–77, 7417, 7432, 7434,
7444, 7447, 7450, 7452, 7500,
7624, 7768, 7923, 8976
S: 6656, 6665, 7387

**Native Americans—Burial
grounds**
JS: 8017

**Native Americans—
Communication**
JS: 8956

Native Americans—Cookbooks
JS: 10583

Native Americans—Crafts
JS: 6681

Native Americans—Dance
JS: 6517

Native Americans—Fiction
IJ: 44, 451, 2236, 2243, 2245, 2247,
2250, 2280, 2285, 2459, 2468,
2474, 2478, 2491, 2503
J: 475, 482, 505, 525, 576, 686, 1196,
1265, 1741, 2042, 2237, 2240–41,
2244, 2248, 2256, 2259, 2261–62,
2271–74, 2277, 2283, 2289, 2293,
2295, 2490, 2492, 2494, 2496,
2605, 3714, 8953
JS: 124, 194, 290, 395, 424, 484, 491,
515–16, 552, 557, 559, 588, 1068,
1080, 1083, 1743, 1790, 1929,
1963, 1997, 2238–39, 2246, 2249,
2251–55, 2258, 2260, 2263, 2265,
2282, 2286, 2360, 2425, 2450,
2473, 2480, 2499, 3079, 3189,
3198, 3353, 3780
S: 436, 463, 479, 2242, 2257, 2427,
2440, 2992, 3078, 3081–82,
3243–44

Native Americans—Folklore
IJ: 4144–45, 4148, 4154
J: 4149, 4157
JS: 2239, 4140–43, 4146, 4150–51,
4153, 4155–56, 8936, 8986
S: 4147

IJ = Intermediate-Junior High; J = Junior High; JS = Junior-Senior High; S = Senior High

Native Americans—History
IJ: 8941, 8965, 8993, 9021, 9027, 9046
J: 8922, 8926, 8930–33, 8939, 8944, 8946, 8954–55, 8958, 8964, 8968, 8970–71, 8980, 8987, 9000–1, 9005, 9007, 9010, 9014, 9023, 9025–26, 9028, 9030–31, 9035, 9040, 9291
JS: 4983, 6517, 6726, 7454, 8920, 8923–24, 8935–38, 8942, 8945, 8947–49, 8951–52, 8957, 8959, 8961–63, 8966–67, 8972–74, 8977, 8981, 8983, 8985, 8991–92, 8994, 8997, 8999, 9002–3, 9009, 9016, 9018–20, 9022, 9032, 9034, 9037–39, 9045, 9124, 9154, 9271
S: 8934, 8940, 8975, 9008, 9012–13

Native Americans—Houses
J: 8995

Native Americans—Literature
J: 8958

Native Americans—Medicine
IJ: 9036
J: 8928

Native Americans—Place names
JS: 9494, 9494

Native Americans—Poetry
JS: 3956, 4006

Native Americans—Religion
JS: 8929, 8978

Native Americans—Rights
JS: 9003

Native Americans—Sports
JS: 7769

Native Americans—Treaties
IJ: 8960

Native Americans—Women
IJ: 9015
JS: 8963, 9039

Natural disasters
JS: 6243

Natural history
See also Nature study
J: 9620
JS: 5094, 9748

Natural history—Essays
JS: 9581, 9745–46

Natural history—New England
S: 9737

Natural history—United States
JS: 9736

Naturalists—Biography
JS: 7524, 7574

Nature
See also Biology; Natural history; Nature study
IJ: 9740

Nature—Cycles
IJ: 9593

Nature—Drawing
IJ: 10665

Nature—Folklore
IJ: 4049

Nature—Poetry
IJ: 3957, 3959, 4024
J: 3972
JS: 4029

Nature crafts
JS: 10541

Nature study
J: 9819
JS: 9503, 9739, 9741, 9744, 9823

Nature study—Biography
IJ: 7547, 7575, 7602
JS: 7603

Navajo Arts and Crafts Enterprise (NACE)
JS: 5319

Navajo Indians
J: 8971
JS: 5319, 8315

Navajo Indians—Fiction
IJ: 683
J: 2605
JS: 124, 484, 2253, 2258, 3058, 3079
S: 3078, 3081–82, 3244

Navajo Indians—History
J: 8241

Navajo Indians—Poetry
JS: 3956

Naval Academy (Annapolis)
JS: 4707, 4712

Navratilova, Martina
JS: 7750

Navy (U.S.)
See also Armed forces (U.S.)
JS: 8312

Navy (U.S.)—African Americans
JS: 4713

Navy (U.S.)—Careers
JS: 5451

Navy (U.S.)—History
S: 9204

Navy (U.S.)—World War II
JS: 8341

Naylor, Phyllis Reynolds—Criticism
JS: 4348

Nazi Germany
See also Holocaust; World War II
JS: 8650
S: 8322

Nazi Germany—Biography
J: 7941

Nazism
See also Holocaust; Nazi Germany; World War II
JS: 8290

Nazism—Fiction
JS: 85, 158

Ndebele (African people)
JS: 8485

Nebraska—Fiction
IJ: 2515
J: 2443

Needlecrafts
See also Sewing
JS: 10756, 10761–63

Negotiation skills
JS: 6241

Negro Baseball Leagues
IJ: 10942
J: 10935
JS: 10936, 10940, 10955, 10959

Neo-Nazis
See also Militia movement
JS: 5015, 5039

Neo-Nazis—Fiction
JS: 1552, 2636

Nepal
IJ: 8578

Neptune (planet)—Fiction
JS: 3449

IJ = Intermediate-Junior High; J = Junior High; JS = Junior-Senior High; S = Senior High

Neruda, Pablo
JS: 6896–97

Nervous system
See also Brain and nervous system
IJ: 5932
J: 5923, 5936
JS: 5924, 5931, 5934–35
S: 5937

Netherlands—Art
JS: 6706

Netherlands—Biography
JS: 7940

Netherlands—Fiction
IJ: 2641, 2655
J: 2159, 2653
JS: 1139, 2589, 6768, 8313, 8396

Netherlands—History
JS: 8295

Neurology
S: 5937

Nevada—Fiction
J: 2397

New Deal
J: 9372, 9384
JS: 9363, 9374, 9390

New England
See also individual states, e.g., Maine
IJ: 9514
S: 9737

New England—Fiction
J: 828, 2793
JS: 1014, 1249, 2990
S: 1615

New England—History
JS: 6391

New England—Plays
S: 3877

New Guinea
JS: 8594

New Guinea—Fiction
JS: 39
S: 1520

New Jersey
IJ: 9522

New Jersey—Fiction
IJ: 2645
J: 2862

New Market, Battle of
IJ: 9163

New Mexico—Fiction
IJ: 870
J: 2479, 4157

New Mexico—History
S: 9565

New Orleans—Fiction
IJ: 2342

New Orleans, Battle of
IJ: 9139

New York City
IJ: 5297, 9523

New York City—Fiction
IJ: 147, 2531, 3335
J: 130, 533, 536, 611, 1132, 1350, 1887, 2544, 2562, 2569, 2583
JS: 454, 540, 546, 901, 1332, 1414, 2573
S: 208, 1550, 2940, 3187

New York City—History
JS: 9515, 9518

New York City—Plays
JS: 3864

New York City—Subway system
JS: 9518

New York State
IJ: 9521

New York State—Fiction
IJ: 2307, 2428, 2699
J: 1164, 2333
JS: 138, 400, 2309, 2332, 2511, 2543

New York Times
S: 4449, 7498

New Zealand
IJ: 8595

New Zealand—Conservation
IJ: 9969

New Zealand—Fiction
IJ: 624
JS: 119, 564, 1301, 1449, 2111, 3048–49

New Zealand—Folklore
JS: 4096

New Zealand—History
J: 8596

Newfoundland—Fiction
IJ: 34, 1238

Newspapers
JS: 4446
S: 4449

Newspapers—Fiction
JS: 1536

Newspapers—History
JS: 4448

Newton, Isaac
JS: 7604

Newton, John
IJ: 7497

Nez Perce Indians
JS: 7402, 8925

Nez Perce Indians—Biography
JS: 7373

Nez Perce Indians—Fiction
J: 2259

Nez Perce Indians—History
J: 9026

Niagara Falls
J: 9510

Nicaragua—Fiction
S: 1538

Nicaraguan Americans
JS: 4953

Nicotine
See also Smoking; Tobacco industry
JS: 5678

Nigeria
IJ: 8491, 8519
JS: 8492–93, 8514–16

Nigeria—Fiction
JS: 444

Nigeria—History
J: 8506

Nightmares—Fiction
JS: 3034, 3233

Nike (firm)
JS: 5308, 5312

Nimoy, Leonard
JS: 7068

Nitrogen
IJ: 10156, 10159
J: 10150

IJ = Intermediate-Junior High; J = Junior High; JS = Junior-Senior High; S = Senior High

Nixon, Richard M.
IJ: 7158
J: 7314–15, 7317
JS: 4656, 7313, 7316, 9408, 9416
S: 9441

Nobel Prize winners—Biography
JS: 7516

Norling, Donna Scott
S: 7933

North America—Biology
JS: 9748

North America—Birds
JS: 9940

North America—Exploration
IJ: 6614
J: 8767
JS: 6613, 9041

North America—Geography
JS: 10174

North Carolina
IJ: 9560

North Carolina—Biography
S: 7479

North Carolina—Fiction
IJ: 1430, 2340
JS: 537, 1134, 2549, 2848
S: 2533

North Dakota
S: 9501

North Pole—Exploration
J: 6648

Northern Ireland
IJ: 8667
JS: 8653
S: 8659

Northern Ireland—Fiction
IJ: 2597
J: 1420
JS: 112

Northhampton (Massachusetts)
S: 5300

Northwest Indians—Folklore
JS: 4150–51

Norway—Fiction
JS: 2181

Norway—Folklore
JS: 4099

Norwegian Americans—Fiction
JS: 694, 2501

Nova Scotia
IJ: 8777

Nova Scotia—Fiction
JS: 696

Nubia (Africa)
J: 8445

Nubia (Africa)—History
JS: 8126

Nuclear accidents
JS: 5792

Nuclear accidents—Fiction
JS: 82

Nuclear energy
IJ: 10346
JS: 10342–44

Nuclear holocaust—Fiction
JS: 1959

Nuclear medicine
JS: 5862

Nuclear physics
JS: 10165, 10361

Nuclear physics—Biography
JS: 7518

Nuclear testing
JS: 10516

Nuclear war—Fiction
IJ: 227
JS: 178, 1203, 1524, 1546, 3603

Nuclear waste
IJ: 10346
JS: 10341, 10343
S: 10345

Nuclear waste—Fiction
IJ: 1526
JS: 3120

Nuclear weapons
JS: 4576, 8297, 8335, 8373, 8400, 10516, 10525, 10528

Numbers
J: 10248
JS: 10249

Numbers—History
JS: 10247

Nunez, Tommy
JS: 7694

Nuns—Biography
IJ: 7825

Nupe (African people)
JS: 8504

Nuremberg trials
JS: 8364

Nurses
J: 5850

Nurses—Fiction
JS: 2672

Nursing—Careers
JS: 5531, 5535

Nutrition and diet
IJ: 5944
J: 6048, 6060
JS: 5580, 5973, 5975, 5980, 6042–44, 6053, 6056–58, 6061–62
S: 5927, 5968, 6055

Nye, Naomi Shihab
S: 7934

O

Oakley, Annie
IJ: 7071, 7074
JS: 7072–73

Oakley, Annie—Fiction
IJ: 2529

Oatman, Olive
IJ: 7935

Obesity
See also Large women; Weight problems
JS: 6041, 6047

Obesity—Fiction
IJ: 1461
J: 903, 946, 952, 1244
JS: 921, 1200, 1293, 1445, 1705

O'Brien, Dan
IJ: 7762

Observatories
JS: 9658

Obsessive-compulsive disorder—Fiction
J: 1012
JS: 950

IJ = Intermediate-Junior High; J = Junior High; JS = Junior-Senior High; S = Senior High

Occupational guidance
See also Vocational guidance
JS: 5428–29, 5431, 5433, 5435, 5459,
  5474, 5528, 5543, 5547
S: 5415, 5426

Ocean floor—Fiction
JS: 3611

Ocean liners—Fiction
J: 3119

Oceanography
See also Marine biology;
  Marine life; Underwater
  exploration
IJ: 10006, 10011, 10293
J: 10288, 10294, 10304
JS: 10287, 10289, 10301
S: 10286, 10315

Oceanography—Biography
J: 7532

**Oceanography—Experiments
  and projects**
IJ: 10291
J: 10296

Oceans
IJ: 10291, 10293, 10295
J: 10014, 10290, 10294
JS: 10285, 10297, 10807
S: 10286

Ochs, Adolph S.
S: 7498

O'Connor, Flannery
JS: 6898

O'Connor, Sandra Day
JS: 7427

Octopus
IJ: 10002

O'Donnell, Rosie
IJ: 7069–70

Odysseus
IJ: 4222
J: 4194

Odyssey—**Criticism**
S: 4267

Oedipus plays
JS: 3828

Oedipus plays—Criticism
S: 4364

Of Mice and Men—**Criticism**
S: 4330

Office occupations—Careers
S: 5458

O'Grady, Scott
JS: 6647

Ohio—Fiction
IJ: 729
J: 2448, 2455

Oil spills
See also Environmental problems, and specific oil spills,
  e.g., *Exxon Valdez* oil spill
IJ: 5098, 5109

Oil spills—Alaska
IJ: 9545

Ojibwa Indians—Fiction
IJ: 2247
JS: 559, 1083

Ojibwa Indians—History
J: 9023

O'Keeffe, Georgia
J: 6759
JS: 6758

Oklahoma
IJ: 9493

Oklahoma—Fiction
IJ: 2575
J: 337, 1196
JS: 2536
S: 1279

Oklahoma—History
S: 9118

Oklahoma City bombing (1995)
IJ: 9491, 9496

Old age—Fiction
IJ: 1136

The Old Man and the Sea—
  Criticism
S: 4355

Olmos, Edward James
IJ: 7075

Olympic Games
JS: 11099–102

Olympic Games—Biography
JS: 7766

Olympic Games—Fiction
IJ: 2067

Olympic Games—History
IJ: 11103

O'Neal, Shaquille
IJ: 7695

O'Neill, Eugene—Criticism
S: 4399

Onions
IJ: 9775

Ontario—Fiction
IJ: 251

Opera
IJ: 6488
J: 6956
JS: 6486–87
S: 6485

Opera—Biography
J: 7002
JS: 7077

Opera—Fiction
JS: 3228

Operetta
IJ: 6493

Oppenheimer, Robert
JS: 7605

Optical illusions
IJ: 10354, 10718
J: 5960, 5964
JS: 5959

Optics
JS: 10350

**Optics—Experiments and pro-
  jects**
IJ: 10349

Oral history
JS: 5366, 5387
S: 8041

Oregon
IJ: 9547, 9550

Oregon—Fiction
IJ: 2429, 2471
J: 1600, 2560

Oregon—History
J: 9313

Oregon Trail
IJ: 9260
JS: 9314
S: 9296

Oregon Trail—Fiction
IJ: 2444, 2491
J: 2492

IJ = Intermediate-Junior High; J = Junior High; JS = Junior-Senior High; S = Senior High

Organ transplants
JS: 5583

Organic gardening
IJ: 9768

Origami
IJ: 10740
JS: 10727, 10732

Orkney Islands
IJ: 7993

Orozco, Jose
JS: 6760

Orphans—Fiction
IJ: 248, 1456, 1954, 2581, 2833, 3214
J: 201, 773, 1857, 2035, 2352, 2569
JS: 622, 862, 1909, 2669

Orphans train
IJ: 9388
JS: 9329

Orpheus (mythology)
JS: 4217

Orwell, George—Criticism
JS: 4280
S: 4273

Osage Indians
J: 9035

Osceola
IJ: 7499

**Out-of-body experiences—
    Fiction**
S: 2934

Outdoor cooking
S: 10567

Outdoor life
J: 6375, 11012
JS: 6115, 10864, 10903, 11018–19
S: 11021

Outdoor life—Careers
JS: 5461, 5471

Owens, Jesse
J: 7764
JS: 7765–66
S: 7763

Owls
J: 9954
JS: 9955

Oxford—Fiction
S: 3107

Oxford English Dictionary
S: 4452

Oxygen
IJ: 10157, 10160
J: 10151

Oxymorons
J: 4405

Oyo (African kingdom)
JS: 8512

Ozarks—Fiction
JS: 2828, 3779

Ozone layer
IJ: 5077
JS: 5070

P

Pacific Crest Trail
IJ: 9528

Pacific Northwest—Fiction
JS: 1319, 3263

**Pacific Rim countries—
    Economy**
JS: 8523

Pacific States—Ecology
JS: 9539

Pacific States—Wildflowers
JS: 9803

Pacifists—Fiction
IJ: 2609

Paderewski, Ignacy
J: 7883

Pageants
IJ: 6574

Paige, Satchel
JS: 7669

Paine, Thomas
JS: 7428–29

Painters
See Artists

Painting—History
J: 6410

Paiute Indians
J: 8954

Paiute Indians—Biography
JS: 6944

Pakistan
J: 8555
JS: 7815

Pakistan—Fiction
JS: 1555, 2127

Pakistan—History
S: 8546

Paleontology
See also Dinosaurs; Fossils;
    Prehistoric life
IJ: 7962, 7964, 7968–74, 7977–78,
    7982, 7989, 10777
J: 7960, 7999
JS: 7961, 7963, 7965, 7967, 7976,
    7980, 7983, 7985, 7987–88
S: 7986, 7990

Paleontology—Biography
IJ: 6762

Paleontology—Careers
JS: 5550

Paleontology—Fiction
J: 2465
JS: 2039

Palestine
J: 8750
JS: 8746, 8752

Palestine—Biography
JS: 7799–800

Palestine—Fiction
JS: 2052, 2183

Palestinian Americans
S: 7934

Palestinians
S: 8745

Palindromes
IJ: 4404

Palmistry
See also Fortune-telling
J: 10846

Panama
IJ: 8784, 8791
JS: 8782

Panama—Biography
J: 6976–77

Panama—Fiction
J: 1086

IJ = Intermediate-Junior High; J = Junior High; JS = Junior-Senior High; S = Senior High

Panama Canal
IJ: 8780, 8784–85
JS: 8782, 8788

Pandas
JS: 9918–19

Panic attacks
JS: 6009

Panther (motion picture)
JS: 4914

Pantomime
JS: 6573

Paper
S: 10366

Paper airplanes
JS: 10734, 10737

Paper crafts
IJ: 10730–31, 10733, 10738, 10740
JS: 10728–29, 10732, 10735–36
S: 10739

Paraguay
IJ: 8839

Parakeets
JS: 10068

Paramedical careers
JS: 5533

Paranormal phenomena
JS: 10827

Parapsychology
JS: 10823

Parent-teenager relationships
See also Family problems
JS: 6324

Parental abuse—Fiction
JS: 789

Parenting
See also Motherhood
JS: 6074

Parents
JS: 6355–56

Parents—Drug use
JS: 5707

Parents—Fiction
IJ: 1148
J: 656, 675–76, 854, 1094, 1130,
1244, 1672, 2871, 2902
JS: 630, 652, 692, 989, 1055, 1115
S: 2865

Paris—History
JS: 8242

Parker, Charlie
JS: 7076

Parker, Cynthia Ann—Fiction
JS: 2480

Parker, John P.
S: 7234

**Parker, Quanah (Comanche
chief)**
JS: 7500, 8989

Parkinson's disease
JS: 5780

Parkman, Francis
IJ: 9017

Parks, Gordon
JS: 6761

Parks, Rosa
IJ: 4902, 7237
JS: 7235–36

Parliamentary practice
JS: 6237

Parrots
JS: 10071

Parthenon (Greece)
JS: 8116, 8124
S: 8123

Passover
See also Jewish holy days
IJ: 4548

Passover—Fiction
JS: 2020

Pasteur, Louis
IJ: 7606

Paterson, Katherine
IJ: 6899

Pathfinder (Mars mission)
J: 9728

Patriotism—United States
J: 8905

Patton, General George S.
J: 7430
S: 8356

Patton, Larry
JS: 7936

Paul Bunyan
JS: 4174

Pauling, Linus
JS: 7607

Paulsen, Gary
IJ: 6901
JS: 6900

Paulsen, Gary—Criticism
JS: 4343

Pavarotti, Luciano
JS: 7077

Pawnee Indians—Fiction
IJ: 2491
J: 2492

Pawtucket Indians—Fiction
JS: 2286

Payne, Lucille M. W.
JS: 7501

PCP (drug)
See also Drugs and drug abuse
JS: 5629, 5683

Pea Ridge, Battle of
JS: 9232

Peace movement—Women
JS: 4724

Peale, Charles Willson
IJ: 6762–63

The Pearl—Criticism
S: 4331

Pearl Harbor
IJ: 8346
JS: 8331, 8355, 8359, 10515

Pearl Harbor—Fiction
J: 2648

Pearl Harbor—History
JS: 8316

Peary, Robert E.
J: 6648
JS: 8857

Peck, Richard
J: 6902

Peck, Richard—Criticism
JS: 4319

Peer pressure
JS: 5682

Pele
IJ: 7770

IJ = Intermediate-Junior High; J = Junior High; JS = Junior-Senior High; S = Senior High

Penguins
JS: 9957–58
S: 9956, 9959

Penicillin
JS: 7567

Penn, William
JS: 7431

Pennsylvania—Fiction
IJ: 9526
J: 2267, 2542
JS: 625, 2269, 2481, 2571, 7431

Penpals
S: 7914

Perception
J: 5960, 5964

Peregrine falcons
See also Falcons
JS: 9952

Performing arts—Biography
J: 6694

Performing arts—Careers
JS: 5480

**Persephone (mythology)—
  Poetry**
JS: 3967

Persia—Biography
JS: 7804

Persia—Folklore
IJ: 4093

Persia—History
J: 8129
JS: 8131

Persian Empire
J: 8129

Persian Gulf War
IJ: 9459
J: 8757
JS: 8733, 9448, 9452, 9457, 9465,
  9476–77
S: 9486

Persian Gulf War—Biography
IJ: 7440
JS: 7436, 7443

Persian Gulf War—Fiction
J: 2206
JS: 1548

Personal finance
J: 5576
JS: 5579

Personal guidance
IJ: 5347, 6139, 6256, 6266, 6279,
  6284, 6293, 6302
J: 5269, 6140, 6244, 6247, 6254,
  6268–70, 6275, 6277, 6288–90,
  6300
JS: 4454, 5344, 5412, 5433, 5459,
  5585, 5983, 6123, 6126, 6177,
  6180, 6217, 6223–25, 6228,
  6240–41, 6243, 6245–46, 6252–53,
  6255, 6257–58, 6260, 6262–64,
  6267, 6271–74, 6278, 6280–83,
  6285, 6287, 6291, 6295–98, 6301,
  6303, 10919
S: 6250, 6259, 6261, 6299

Personal guidance—Fiction
JS: 1470

Personal guidance—Girls
J: 6251
JS: 6265, 6276

Personal problems
See also Personal guidance;
  Teenage problems
IJ: 6256
J: 1108
JS: 1454, 2112, 5120, 5992, 6280

Personal problems—Fiction
IJ: 50, 86, 251, 283, 310, 338, 360,
  451, 496, 503, 522, 596, 654, 660,
  716–17, 724, 765, 804, 829, 897,
  907, 933, 965, 986, 1026, 1034,
  1038, 1040, 1042, 1044, 1054,
  1062, 1075, 1084, 1093, 1104,
  1110, 1123, 1133, 1145, 1151,
  1162, 1169, 1172, 1186, 1188,
  1190–91, 1195, 1207, 1212, 1222,
  1238, 1241, 1263, 1268, 1272–73,
  1280–81, 1303, 1307, 1320, 1330,
  1336, 1348, 1369, 1374, 1403,
  1405–7, 1409, 1413, 1415, 1428,
  1431–32, 1435, 1443, 1465, 1476,
  1485, 1490–91, 1493, 1495, 1499,
  1539, 2161, 2214, 2223, 2555,
  2845, 2890, 3675, 3680, 3711,
  3735, 4951
J: 16, 150, 267, 278, 298, 324, 425,
  511, 576, 589, 610, 636, 647, 677,
  884, 908, 929, 942, 949, 1012,
  1017, 1027, 1033, 1037, 1041,
  1043, 1078–79, 1094, 1097–98,
  1101, 1103, 1118–19, 1124, 1130,
  1149, 1159, 1164, 1167, 1179,
  1181–82, 1196, 1208, 1210,
  1219–20, 1225, 1227, 1233,
  1239–40, 1255, 1259, 1261,
  1265–66, 1285, 1287, 1298–99,
  1304, 1311, 1316, 1331, 1334,
  1353, 1361–62, 1376–77, 1408,
  1416, 1427, 1441, 1448, 1451,

1459, 1466–68, 1496, 1506,
  1517–18, 1652, 1942, 2096, 2190,
  2650, 3681, 3700, 3730
JS: 128, 173, 212, 419, 431, 459, 490,
  497, 506, 545, 560, 595, 625, 634,
  645, 653, 665–66, 705, 730, 738,
  757, 817, 835, 840, 856, 858, 864,
  876, 896, 898, 912, 914, 918–20,
  923, 928, 931, 940, 950, 953, 960,
  963, 972, 974, 985, 987, 1001,
  1020, 1023, 1025, 1028, 1030,
  1036, 1039, 1046, 1048–49,
  1058–60, 1065–66, 1068–70, 1073,
  1076–77, 1082, 1087–89, 1100,
  1102, 1105–7, 1111–15, 1120,
  1127–29, 1134–35, 1137, 1140–44,
  1147, 1152, 1155, 1157, 1160,
  1166, 1168, 1170–71, 1175,
  1177–78, 1180, 1184, 1187, 1193,
  1197, 1201–3, 1205–6, 1209, 1216,
  1221, 1223, 1226, 1228, 1231–32,
  1234, 1245, 1247–50, 1252–54,
  1264, 1271, 1275, 1278, 1282,
  1286, 1288, 1291–92, 1297, 1300,
  1302, 1306, 1308–10, 1313–15,
  1317–18, 1322–26, 1332–33,
  1337–39, 1341, 1343, 1345–46,
  1349, 1352, 1354, 1357, 1360,
  1363, 1365–66, 1372–73, 1385–88,
  1390–91, 1393, 1395–402, 1404,
  1414, 1417, 1421–22, 1424, 1426,
  1434, 1438, 1440, 1442, 1444–45,
  1447, 1450, 1452–53, 1457–58,
  1460, 1463, 1469, 1471, 1473,
  1477–79, 1481, 1484, 1486–88,
  1492, 1500, 1502–4, 1507–9, 1512,
  1530, 1546, 1548, 1555, 1622,
  1660, 1971, 2092, 2100, 2181,
  2184, 2216, 2530, 2647, 2670,
  2689, 2698, 2733, 2801, 2840,
  2883, 2901, 2905, 2913–14, 3002,
  3293, 3308, 3347, 3360, 3368,
  3663, 3687, 3699, 3726–27, 3740,
  3743
S: 421, 462–63, 664, 681, 905, 947,
  957, 970, 1009, 1011, 1053, 1063,
  1081, 1085, 1096, 1189, 1213,
  1230, 1242–43, 1256–57, 1270,
  1274, 1279, 1294, 1305, 1327,
  1429, 1455, 1475, 1482–83,
  1510–11, 1538, 2121, 2356, 2506,
  2868

Personal problems—Plays
JS: 3849

Personal problems—Poetry
IJ: 3985

Perspective (art)
JS: 10699

Peru
IJ: 8834, 8841

IJ = Intermediate-Junior High; J = Junior High; JS = Junior-Senior High; S = Senior High

Physics—Dictionaries
JS: 10317

Physics—Experiments and projects
IJ: 10321–22
J: 10324

Pianists—Biography
JS: 6468
S: 7025

Pianists—Fiction
JS: 1178

Piano
S: 6499

Picasso, Pablo
J: 6766
JS: 6764–65

Pictograms
IJ: 4420

Pigeons
JS: 10074

Pigeons—Fiction
IJ: 280, 314

Pigs
JS: 10073

Pigs—Fiction
IJ: 1042

Pilgrims (New England)
IJ: 7367, 9049, 9053, 9087

Pilgrims (New England)—Fiction
J: 2268, 2296

Pilots
See Airplane pilots

Pima-Maricopa Indians
JS: 8945

Pinkerton, Allan
IJ: 7433

Pioneer life (U.S.)
See Frontier life (U.S.)

Pippen, Scottie
IJ: 7696
JS: 7630

Pirates
J: 8054
JS: 8043

Pirates—Biography
JS: 6646

Pirates—Fiction
IJ: 78, 161
JS: 245, 389, 2174

Pirates—Women
J: 6602

Pitchers (baseball)—Biography
JS: 7633

Pitt, Brad
IJ: 7078

Place names
J: 8032–33
JS: 9494

Plagues
JS: 5727, 5763

Plagues—Fiction
JS: 1832, 3471
S: 1617

Plains Indians
J: 8968, 9007

Planets
See also Solar system, and specific planets, e.g., Mars
IJ: 9721
J: 9719
JS: 9714
S: 9725

Planets—Fiction
JS: 3396, 3487, 3518, 3522, 3524, 3562, 3578, 3581, 3583, 3597, 3601, 3646
S: 3395, 3577

Plantation life—History
JS: 9555

Plants
IJ: 9796, 9800, 9806, 9808
J: 9792, 9795, 9805, 9812
JS: 9807, 9810
S: 9789

Plants—Experiments and projects
IJ: 9797

Plants—Fiction
JS: 1802
S: 3669

Plants—Medicinal
IJ: 5865
JS: 5856

Plastic surgery—Fiction
JS: 960

Plastics
JS: 10373

Plate tectonics
IJ: 10175
JS: 10168

Plays—African American playwrights
S: 3861

Plays—American
IJ: 3847
J: 3858
JS: 3806, 3828–29, 3831–33, 3841–42, 3848, 3850, 3852–55, 3857, 3862, 3864–67, 3869, 3871, 3874, 3876, 3880–81
S: 3792, 3834, 3838, 3845, 3851, 3859–60, 3877–79

Plays—Anthologies
IJ: 3873
J: 3788, 3844
JS: 3794, 3797, 3799, 3810–11, 3826, 3839, 3849, 3872
S: 3789–90, 3807, 3870

Plays—English
JS: 3813, 3820, 3823, 3863
S: 3792, 3812, 3821–22

Plays—Folktales
JS: 3798

Plays—Hispanic American
IJ: 3875

Plays—History and criticism
S: 4399

Plays—Holocaust
JS: 3835

Plays—Humorous
JS: 4225

Plays—Latin American
JS: 3825

Plays—Multicultural
JS: 3827

Plays—One-act
J: 3793, 3846
JS: 3830

Plays—Production
JS: 3832, 6585, 10644

Plays—Scenes
IJ: 3802
JS: 3791, 3803, 3805, 3837, 3840
S: 3808

IJ = Intermediate-Junior High; J = Junior High; JS = Junior-Senior High; S = Senior High

IJ = Intermediate-Junior High; J = Junior High; JS = Junior-Senior High; S = Senior High

Polar regions—Biography
IJ: 6606

Police
JS: 5033

Police—Careers
IJ: 5522
JS: 5527

Police—History
J: 4652

Police brutality
JS: 4646, 4681

Police questioning
JS: 4679, 6214

Polio—Biography
S: 7484

Polio—Fiction
IJ: 1195
S: 620

Polio vaccine—Biography
JS: 7612

Political liberty
IJ: 4753

Political parties
IJ: 4692
J: 4691

Political science
S: 4455

Politicians—Biography
IJ: 7401, 7404
J: 7442
JS: 7785

Politics
IJ: 4693
JS: 4590, 4690, 4694, 4696–97,
    4699–700
S: 8060

Politics—African Americans
JS: 4897

Politics—Ethics
JS: 4689

Politics—Fiction
JS: 2874, 3147, 3202

Politics—History
J: 9335

Politics—Women
JS: 7161

Pollination
J: 9794
S: 9983

Pollution
See also Environment;
    Environmental problems;
    and specific types of pollu-
    tion, e.g., Water pollution
IJ: 5055, 5065, 5082, 5098, 5100,
    5106, 5109, 9768, 10220, 10339
J: 5107, 5111
JS: 5061–62, 5067, 5080, 5086,
    5088–89, 5091, 5095, 5097, 5099,
    5101–3, 5108, 5110
S: 9551

**Pollution—Experiments and
    projects**
IJ: 5104

Pollution—Fiction
JS: 1819

Polo, Marco
S: 6650

Ponce de León, Juan
J: 6651

Ponds
See also Lakes
IJ: 10220–21, 10224

Ponies
J: 10125

Ponies—Fiction
J: 321

Pony Express
IJ: 9319
JS: 9303

Pony Express—Fiction
IJ: 2459
J: 2477

Pool—Fiction
IJ: 3677

Popes—Biography
J: 7873

Popular culture
S: 5290

Popular music—History
JS: 6470

Population
JS: 5121–23

Population problems
JS: 6080
S: 4836

Pornography
JS: 5245, 5257

Porpoises
IJ: 10054
JS: 10040
S: 10035

Porsche (automobile)
JS: 10493

Portrait painting
S: 10668, 10676

Portugal
IJ: 8725, 8730

Post, Mary Titus
JS: 9095

Post-traumatic stress disorder
J: 6010
JS: 6029
S: 6022

Posters—Motion pictures
JS: 6557

Posters—Science fiction films
JS: 6557

Postimpressionism
J: 6408

Pot-bellied pigs
JS: 10073

Potawatomi Indians
J: 8939

Potlatch
IJ: 8969

Pottery
JS: 10560–62

Pottery—Biography
IJ: 6748

Pottery—History
IJ: 8069

Poultry
S: 9980

Poverty
See also Homeless people,
    Hunger
IJ: 5235, 5239
J: 5232
JS: 5211, 5214, 5216–19, 5222, 5224,
    5227, 5236, 5238, 8919
S: 5209, 8664

Poverty—Biography
IJ: 4912

IJ = Intermediate-Junior High; J = Junior High; JS = Junior-Senior High; S = Senior High

Poverty—Fiction
IJ: 422, 572, 671, 709, 734, 827, 1062, 2108, 2118, 2576, 2581
J: 468, 565, 651, 899, 1518, 2567, 3717
JS: 428, 476, 552, 629, 712, 889, 889, 987, 1121, 1358, 2101, 2142, 2353, 2550, 2587
S: 1556, 1560

Poverty—Folklore
J: 4100

Powell, Colin
IJ: 7435, 7437, 7440
J: 7438
JS: 7436, 7441
S: 7439

Powell, John Wesley
IJ: 6652
J: 9340

Power boats
JS: 11109

Powhatan Indians
JS: 8952

Powhatan Indians—Biography
JS: 7434

Prague
S: 2157

Prairies
See also Grasslands
IJ: 10226

Prayers
IJ: 4515

Prayers—Africa
JS: 4502

Predictions
See also Fortune telling; Prophecies
IJ: 10815
J: 10836
JS: 5273, 9404, 10829
S: 10838

Pregnancy
JS: 6080, 6082, 6084–85, 6087, 6091, 6099, 6101, 6106–7, 6110, 6114
S: 6072

Pregnancy—Fiction
IJ: 1272
J: 816, 1208
JS: 440, 633, 1147, 1214, 1269, 1346, 1373
S: 988, 2758, 2876

Prehistoric animals
IJ: 7972, 7982, 7989
JS: 7983

Prehistoric art
IJ: 6416

Prehistoric life
See also Paleontology; Stone age
IJ: 7993, 8000, 8004, 8009–11, 8016, 8063, 8943
J: 7999, 8001, 8013
JS: 8003

Prehistoric life—Fiction
IJ: 2037–38, 2040
J: 2035–36, 2042, 3032
JS: 1932, 2039, 2041
S: 2033–34

Prejudice
See also Discrimination, Ethnic problems, Racism
IJ: 4771
J: 4842, 5001, 5140
JS: 4821–23, 4827, 4834–35, 4839, 4841, 4843, 4846, 5000, 5240
S: 4844, 4892, 4900

Prejudice—Fiction
IJ: 477, 498, 522, 549, 555, 599, 2094, 2576
J: 521, 562, 578, 590, 1814, 3746
JS: 101, 459, 473, 488, 513, 532, 537, 552, 559, 568, 581, 594, 605, 1462, 1534, 1656, 2536, 3381
S: 857

Premenstrual syndrome
JS: 5798, 6149

Presidency (U.S.)
JS: 4619, 8894

Presidents (U.S.)
IJ: 4622, 4624, 8906, 9399
J: 8897
JS: 4615–17, 4631, 7339
S: 4618

Presidents (U.S.)—Biography
IJ: 7154, 7158, 7169, 7261, 7264, 7269, 7273, 7278, 7281–82, 7285, 7293, 7307–8, 7310, 7318, 7326–27, 7329–30, 7332, 7340–43, 7345, 7348, 9110, 9238, 9343–44, 9381
J: 7132, 7159, 7255, 7258–60, 7268, 7271, 7276, 7288, 7296, 7298–99, 7302, 7306, 7311, 7314–15, 7317, 7333–34, 7337, 7349
JS: 4620, 7163, 7256, 7262–63, 7265, 7270, 7272, 7275, 7279–80, 7283–84, 7286–87, 7289–92, 7294–95, 7297, 7300, 7304–5, 7312–13, 7316, 7325, 7328, 7331, 7335–36, 7338, 7344, 7346, 7350
S: 7257, 7277, 7303, 9441

Presidents (U.S.)—Elections
JS: 4697, 4699–700

Presidents (U.S.)—Fiction
JS: 885

Presidents (U.S.)—History
JS: 4614

Presidents (U.S.)—Impeachment
JS: 4621

Presidents (U.S.)—Wives—Biography
IJ: 7266, 7274, 7309, 7320–21, 7324
J: 7267, 7319, 7347
JS: 7165, 7253–54, 7322–23
S: 7144

Presidents (U.S.)—Wives—Fiction
S: 2367

Presley, Elvis
IJ: 7082
J: 7079
JS: 7080–81

Presley, Elvis—Fiction
JS: 524

Press, freedom of the
See Freedom of the press

Pressed flowers
S: 10531

Price, Michelle
JS: 7937

***Pride and Prejudice*—Criticism**
JS: 4287
S: 4286

Prieto, Jorgé
JS: 7720

Primitive peoples
JS: 8002

Prince Edward Island—Fiction
J: 807
JS: 685

Printing
JS: 4439

IJ = Intermediate-Junior High; J = Junior High; JS = Junior-Senior High; S = Senior High

Printing—History
J: 4437
JS: 4440

Printmaking
JS: 10547

Prisoners of war
JS: 8272

Prisoners of war—Fiction
IJ: 2421

Prisons
IJ: 5153
JS: 5138, 5144, 5168, 5171–72, 5192, 5199, 6342, 6358

Prisons—Fiction
IJ: 302
J: 181, 1994
JS: 339, 813, 1152, 1387, 2030, 2163, 2231, 2595
S: 1213

Privacy
J: 4789

Privacy rights
JS: 4729, 4745
S: 4718

Private schools—Fiction
JS: 1112, 1400, 1436, 3021, 3103, 3328
S: 1256–57

Pro Football Hall of Fame
JS: 11045

Prohibition (U.S.)
JS: 4608, 9369

Prohibition (U.S.)—Fiction
J: 2585
JS: 2577

Prophecies
See also Predictions
IJ: 10832

Prostitution
JS: 5246

Prostitution—Fiction
JS: 901, 1367

Protests and demonstrations
JS: 5272

Prozac
J: 5686

Psychiatrists—Fiction
JS: 3034

Psychic abilities
JS: 10827
S: 10849

Psychic abilities—Fiction
J: 475

Psychoanalysis
S: 7569

Psychology
See also Human development and behavior
JS: 6212, 6216, 6219

Psychopaths—Fiction
JS: 2988

Puberty
See also Adolescence; Menstruation
J: 6140, 6167, 6211

Puberty—Boys
JS: 6136, 6143

Puberty—Girls
IJ: 6139
J: 6124
JS: 6142

Public speaking
IJ: 5393
JS: 5369, 5405

Public welfare
JS: 5216–17, 5227

Publishing
See also Book making
JS: 4438

Publishing—Biography
IJ: 7546

Publishing—Careers
JS: 5509, 5516

Publishing—Fiction
JS: 3091

Pueblo Indians
IJ: 8941, 8982
J: 9000
JS: 4156, 8920, 9037–38

Pueblo Indians—Fiction
JS: 2263, 2265

Pueblo Indians—Legends
JS: 4155

Puerto Rican—Fiction
JS: 458

Puerto Ricans
IJ: 4948

Puerto Ricans—Biography
IJ: 7903
J: 7044, 7065
JS: 7503, 7910

Puerto Ricans—Fiction
IJ: 535
J: 533–34, 536
JS: 456–57, 876

Puerto Rico
IJ: 8824
JS: 8822–23

Puerto Rico—Fiction
IJ: 2213

Puerto Rico—History
IJ: 7903, 8826

Puffins
J: 9936

Pulaski, Casimir
IJ: 7884

Pulitzer, Joseph
JS: 7609–10

Pullman strike (1894)
JS: 5328

Pumpkin decorating
IJ: 10546

Punic Wars
JS: 8148

Puns
JS: 5401

Puppeteers—Biography
JS: 7028

Puppets—Fiction
JS: 2686

Puritanism
IJ: 9087

Puritans—Fiction
JS: 2286

Puzzles
See also Games; Mathematical puzzles; Word games
JS: 10552, 10728, 10798, 10801
S: 10791

Pygmies—Fiction
IJ: 2516

Pyramids
See also Egypt—History

IJ = Intermediate-Junior High; J = Junior High; JS = Junior-Senior High; S = Senior High

IJ: 8084, 8096
J: 8025
JS: 6392, 8100

Q

Qatar
IJ: 8754

Quaaludes (drugs)
See also Drugs and drug abuse
JS: 5726

Quakers
JS: 4532

Quakers—Biography
JS: 7431

Quakers—Fiction
JS: 2364, 2417
S: 2519

Quapaw Indians
JS: 8923

Quapaw Indians—Fiction
JS: 1963

Quebec—Fiction
S: 857

Queens—Biography
IJ: 7782

Quilting
JS: 10761–63

Quilts—Fiction
JS: 2292, 3135

Quinn, Anthony
J: 7083

Quintanilla, Guadalupe
IJ: 7938

Quotations
J: 4435

**Quotations—African
Americans**
JS: 4848
S: 4886

R

Rabbits
JS: 10067

Rabbits—Fiction
JS: 1566, 3500

Rabin, Yitzhak
JS: 7818

Raccoons
JS: 9876

Race relations
J: 4833, 4877
JS: 4726, 4822, 4828, 4837, 4847,
    4874, 4905, 4909
S: 4831

Racism
See also Discrimination;
    Prejudice; Segregation
    (racial)
IJ: 4771, 4820
J: 4842, 5001, 7203–4, 9371, 9422–23
JS: 4572, 4738, 4821–23, 4827–28,
    4830, 4834–35, 4837, 4839, 4843,
    4846, 4874, 4885, 4896, 4909,
    4919, 5039, 6226, 8344
S: 4831, 4892

Racism—Biography
JS: 7923

Racism—Fiction
IJ: 466, 599, 606
J: 299, 492, 1474
JS: 459, 473, 485, 512, 524, 564, 566,
    574, 591, 598, 605, 1116, 1424,
    1525, 2093, 2110, 2380, 2578
S: 410, 571

Racism—Poetry
JS: 3963

Racquetball
JS: 10862, 11140

Racquetball—Technique
JS: 11144

Radiation
See also Nuclear energy
JS: 5792

Radio
JS: 10538

Radio—Careers
JS: 5504

Radio—History
S: 6565

Radioactive materials
See also Nuclear energy
JS: 4576

Radiology
IJ: 5873

Rafting
JS: 11112

Railroads
IJ: 10502

Railroads—Fiction
IJ: 2458
J: 2509
JS: 2553
S: 2356

Railroads—History
IJ: 10504
J: 9324, 10503, 10506, 10509
JS: 5328, 9348, 10500, 10505, 10507

Rain forests
See also Forests
IJ: 7608, 9782, 9808, 10201, 10204,
    10206, 10209–10
J: 10202
JS: 8833, 9783, 10203, 10205, 10207,
    10211

Rain forests—Canada
JS: 10208

Rain forests—Fiction
IJ: 235
JS: 731

Rainmaking—Fiction
S: 139

Raleigh, Sir Walter
JS: 9044

Rama (Hindu deity)—Fiction
J: 1734

Ranch life—Fiction
IJ: 184, 1379, 1403, 1406
J: 197, 2470
JS: 332, 491, 738

Ranches—History
J: 9274

Randolph, A. Philip
J: 7238

Rap music
JS: 6449, 6479

Rap music—Careers
JS: 5489

Rap music—Fiction
JS: 551

IJ = Intermediate-Junior High; J = Junior High; JS = Junior-Senior High; S = Senior High

Rape
See also Date rape; Sexual assault
J: 6170
JS: 6171, 6173, 6188, 6191, 6193, 6196, 6199, 6203, 6209
S: 6205, 6208

Rape—Fiction
JS: 510, 924, 985, 1015, 1028, 1031, 1077, 1091, 1349, 1370, 3351

Raphael (painter)
J: 6433

Raptors—Fiction
J: 254

Rats
S: 9872

Rattlesnakes
JS: 9844

Ray, James Earl
S: 7502

Reading
JS: 5349

Reading—Fiction
JS: 3425

Reagan, Ronald
IJ: 7158, 7318
J: 9429

***The Real World* (television program)**
JS: 6562

Ream, Vinnie—Fiction
JS: 2412

Reconstruction to World War I (U.S.)
See also United States (1865–1914)—History
IJ: 9326, 9334, 9341
J: 9338
JS: 4881, 9347

Reconstruction to World War I (U.S.)—Fiction
IJ: 2420, 2525–26, 2529
J: 413
JS: 2511, 2521, 2532, 9345
S: 2435, 2510, 2535

Recorders (music)
JS: 6502

Recreation—Careers
JS: 5491

Recreation and sports
IJ: 10530, 10895

Recycled materials—Crafts
IJ: 10551

Recycling
IJ: 5113, 5116
J: 5111
JS: 5095, 5117, 5119

***The Red Badge of Courage*— Criticism**
JS: 4324
S: 4320

Red Cross
IJ: 4566
J: 7362

Red Shirt, Delphine
S: 9006

Red wolves
See also Wolves
IJ: 9909

Reece, Gabrielle
JS: 7771

Reeve, Christopher
J: 7085
JS: 7084

Reformation
JS: 8172, 8206

Refugees
J: 4949
JS: 4585, 4815, 4939, 5050, 5223, 6377, 8783, 8800

Refugees—Fiction
J: 2115, 2593, 2611
JS: 335, 507, 1559, 2106, 2128
S: 3338

Refugees—Teenage
JS: 4935–36, 4945, 4953, 4990–91, 4996

Reggae music—Biography
JS: 7057, 7059

Reichl, Ruth
S: 7939

Reiss, Johanna
JS: 7940

Relatives—Fiction
IJ: 697, 2410
J: 211, 782
JS: 725, 1258

Relativity (physics)
JS: 10316, 10319

Religion
IJ: 4470, 4478–80, 4501
JS: 4454, 4460–61, 4469, 4473, 4475, 4477, 4482, 4491, 4496, 4498, 4506, 4527, 5592
S: 4468, 4486–87, 4507–8

Religion—Africa
JS: 4502

Religion—African Americans
JS: 4906

Religion—Biography
IJ: 7801
J: 7778
JS: 7837

Religion—Comparative
JS: 4469

Religion—Fiction
IJ: 1263, 2528, 2558
J: 770, 1353
JS: 1066, 1221, 1250, 1385, 1417, 1547
S: 1085

Religion—History
J: 9276
JS: 8172
S: 4493

Religion—Poetry
J: 3931

Religion—Schools
J: 4655

Religion—Stories
JS: 4488

Religious liberty
See also Freedom of religion
IJ: 4753

Remarque, Erich Maria
S: 4272

Remarriage—Fiction
IJ: 614, 1351
S: 961

Rembrandt van Rijn
J: 6434, 6767
JS: 6768–70

Renaissance
IJ: 8188, 8209
J: 8169, 8210
JS: 8161, 8198
S: 8160, 8165, 8171

IJ = Intermediate-Junior High; J = Junior High; JS = Junior-Senior High; S = Senior High

Renaissance—Art
JS: 6402, 6409

Renaissance—Biography
JS: 7570

Renaissance—Fiction
S: 2193

Renaissance—Wars
JS: 8163

Renoir, Auguste
JS: 6771

Report writing
IJ: 5357
J: 5396
JS: 5373, 5378, 5388, 5403

Reproduction
See also Sex education
S: 6078

Reproduction—Human
IJ: 6105
JS: 5584, 6113

Reproductive system
J: 6153
JS: 5908

Reptiles
See also specific reptiles, e.g.,
   Snakes
IJ: 9828
JS: 9827, 9829, 9831–33, 9835

Research—Guides
IJ: 5379

**Resistance Movement (World
   War II)**
JS: 8325

Respiratory system
See also Lungs
IJ: 5957–58
JS: 5909, 5956

Restaurants—Careers
JS: 5438

Resurrection—Fiction
S: 3491

Revenge
S: 6233

Revenge—Fiction
JS: 918

Revere, Paul—Fiction
J: 2306
JS: 2315

Revolutionary period (U.S.)
See also Revolutionary War
   (U.S.)
IJ: 9084, 9086, 9110
J: 9102
JS: 8883, 9080–81, 9096

**Revolutionary period (U.S.)—
   Biography**
J: 7143
JS: 7253

**Revolutionary period (U.S.)—
   Fiction**
IJ: 2302, 2307
J: 2305
JS: 2313, 2317

Revolutionary War (U.S.)
See also Revolutionary period
   (U.S.)
IJ: 9085, 9094, 9098–99, 9106,
   9111–12, 9114
J: 9065, 9082, 9089, 9091, 9093, 9103
JS: 8218, 8883, 9090, 9095, 9097,
   9100–1, 9104–5, 9107, 9109, 9115,
   9117
S: 9092

**Revolutionary War (U.S.)—
   African Americans**
JS: 9088

**Revolutionary War (U.S.)—
   Biography**
IJ: 7340, 7342, 7391, 7874, 7884,
   7942
J: 7351, 7359–60, 7483
JS: 7312, 7339, 7428–29

**Revolutionary War (U.S.)—
   Fiction**
IJ: 2275, 2308, 2310, 2319
J: 2244, 2300, 2306, 2311
JS: 2301, 2303–4, 2309, 2314–15

**Revolutionary War (U.S.)—
   Songs**
JS: 6512

**Revolutionary War (U.S.)—
   Women**
IJ: 9116

Rhine River
IJ: 8646

Rhinoceroses
S: 8468

Rhode Island—Fiction
J: 2547

Rice, Jerry
IJ: 7721

Richard III, King of England
J: 8662

Richards, Ann
J: 7442

Richmond, Mitch
IJ: 7697

Richmond (Virginia)—History
S: 9190

Richter, Hans Peter
J: 7941

Riddles
See Jokes and riddles

Ride, Sally
IJ: 6654–55
JS: 6653

Rifles—Fiction
J: 1545

Right to die
See also Euthanasia; Suicide
JS: 5593, 5598, 5606

Rimes, LeAnn
IJ: 7086–88

Rio de Janeiro—Fiction
JS: 428

Ripken, Cal, Jr.
IJ: 7670

Ritalin (drug)
See also Drugs and drug abuse
JS: 5615

Rivera, Diego
IJ: 6772
J: 6773, 6775
JS: 6774

Rivers
IJ: 10219–20, 10224
JS: 8832

**Rivers—Experiments and pro-
   jects**
JS: 10222

Rivers—Fiction
IJ: 222
JS: 2520

Rivers, Doc
JS: 7698

IJ = Intermediate-Junior High; J = Junior High; JS = Junior-Senior High; S = Senior High

Roads—History
IJ: 10496
J: 10469

Roanoke Colony
JS: 9044

Roanoke Colony—Fiction
J: 2295

Roanoke Island—History
JS: 7578

Robberies—Fiction
JS: 1076

Roberts, Monty
S: 10132

Robeson, Paul
J: 7093
JS: 7089–91
S: 7092

Robin Hood
J: 4107, 4115, 4121, 4132
JS: 4113

Robin Hood—Fiction
J: 4103
JS: 2088, 2140

Robinson, David
IJ: 7699–700

Robinson, Jackie
J: 7671
JS: 7672

Robotics
JS: 10440

Robots
JS: 10440, 10443
S: 10431

Robots—Fiction
IJ: 3411–12, 3636
JS: 3406–7, 3539
S: 3403, 3610

Rock and Roll Hall of Fame
JS: 6483

Rock carvings
IJ: 8021

Rock carvings—Fiction
IJ: 1521
JS: 3353

Rock climbing
See also Mountaineering
JS: 10880
S: 10890

Rock music
J: 6469, 6477, 6481, 6484
JS: 6458, 6462, 6471, 6483, 6494,
6971, 6973, 6988, 7051, 7112,
9415
S: 6472, 6475–76

Rock music—Careers
JS: 5485, 5489, 5498

Rock music—Fiction
J: 656
JS: 673, 834, 1046, 3265
S: 1243

Rock music—Women
JS: 6454

Rock musicians—Biography
IJ: 7037
J: 6684, 7079
JS: 6960, 6989, 6989, 7038, 7041,
7050, 7056, 7081, 7108, 7120–21
S: 7040

Rock paintings
IJ: 8021

Rockport (Maine)—Fiction
JS: 1444

Rocks and minerals
See also Minerals
IJ: 10232
JS: 10227–31

**Rocks and minerals—
Experiments and projects**
IJ: 10233

Rockwell, Norman
IJ: 6776

Rodman, Dennis
IJ: 7701–2

Rodriguez, Luis
IJ: 6904

Rodriguez, Robert
J: 7094

Roe *v.* Wade
JS: 4668, 4682, 4684, 6103

Rogers, Will
JS: 7095

Roller hockey
JS: 11085

***Rolling Stone* (magazine)**
JS: 4453

Rolling Stones (musical group)
JS: 7120–21

Roman Empire
See also Italy—History
IJ: 7835, 7864, 8138, 8152–53, 8156,
9588
J: 8073, 8140, 8144, 8155
JS: 8134–35, 8137, 8139, 8142–43,
8145–46, 8148–51, 8157
S: 8133

Roman Empire—Architecture
JS: 8064

Roman Empire—Art
IJ: 8136

Roman Empire—Biography
IJ: 7836
JS: 7833–34, 8132, 8154

Roman Empire—Fiction
IJ: 2061, 2172
JS: 2055, 2062
S: 349, 353, 2054, 2056–57, 3009

Roman Empire—Literature
JS: 4249

Roman Empire—Recreation
J: 8158

Roman Empire—Slavery
JS: 8147

Romance—Fiction
IJ: 256, 1019, 1283, 1490, 1526,
2370, 2385, 2387, 2444, 2834,
2837, 2872, 2872, 2879, 3294,
3313, 3330, 3335–36, 3343, 3354,
3375, 3773
J: 77, 543, 636, 755, 1208, 1260,
1299, 1356, 1411, 1467, 1913,
2159, 2327, 2844, 3280, 3287,
3289–91, 3299, 3305, 3324–25,
3333, 3340–41, 3359, 3363–65,
3372, 3376, 3382, 3590
JS: 87, 132, 134, 229, 355, 358–59,
478, 593, 750, 757, 867, 871, 930,
944, 1021, 1050, 1073, 1117, 1137,
1143, 1173, 1199, 1205–6, 1236,
1247–48, 1296, 1312, 1315, 1323,
1323–24, 1339–40, 1384, 1391,
1393, 1397, 1446, 1508–9, 1514,
1527, 1552, 1618, 1669, 1844,
1882, 2000, 2070, 2083, 2085,
2102, 2185, 2217, 2253, 2332,
2338, 2341, 2433–34, 2463, 2484,
2505, 2511, 2520, 2546, 2580,
2656, 2861, 2877, 2904, 3085,
3239, 3260, 3266, 3271–72,
3274–75, 3277–78, 3281–86, 3288,
3292–93, 3293, 3295–96, 3298,
3300, 3302–4, 3306–11, 3311–12,
3315–17, 3319, 3321–23, 3326–28,
3331–32, 3334, 3337, 3339, 3342,

IJ = Intermediate-Junior High; J = Junior High; JS = Junior-Senior High; S = Senior High

3346–49, 3351–52, 3352–53,
3355–58, 3360, 3362, 3367–68,
3371, 3373–74, 3377–81, 3383
S: 961, 1063, 1489, 1796, 2076, 2109,
2134, 2215, 2344, 2460, 2510,
2794, 3137, 3200, 3273, 3279,
3297, 3301, 3314, 3318, 3320,
3329, 3329, 3338, 3344–45, 3350,
3361, 3366, 3369–70

Romance—Poetry
JS: 4035

Romania
IJ: 8621
JS: 8622

Romania—Fiction
J: 2179
JS: 4127

Romanov, Anastasia
IJ: 7885

Rome
IJ: 8678

Rome—History
JS: 8141, 8146
S: 8676

Rome—Mythology
See Mythology—Rome

Rommel, General Erwin
S: 8343

Romeo and Juliet
S: 3818

Romeo and Juliet—**Criticism**
JS: 4380
S: 4378

Romeo and Juliet—**Retelling**
IJ: 3815

Ronstadt, Linda
J: 7096

Roosevelt, Eleanor
IJ: 7320–21, 7324
J: 7319
JS: 7322–23, 9410

Roosevelt, Eleanor—Fiction
S: 3210–13

Roosevelt, Franklin D.
IJ: 7326–27, 7329
J: 9372
JS: 7325, 7328, 9390, 9410

Roosevelt, Theodore
IJ: 7330, 7332

J: 7333–34
JS: 7331

Rosewood (Florida)—Fiction
J: 521

Roubickov, Eva
JS: 8370

Rowland, Mary Canaga
JS: 7611

Royalty—Fiction
IJ: 3667
J: 1925, 2165
JS: 47, 416
S: 1680

Royalty—Plays
S: 3834

Royce, Sarah
IJ: 9310

Rubbings (art)
JS: 10535

Rubella
JS: 5825

Rudolph, Wilma
JS: 7767

Runaways
JS: 5185, 5238, 6262, 6313, 6329,
6367

Runaways—Fiction
IJ: 1224, 1347
J: 130, 309, 505
JS: 173, 245, 574, 601, 707, 901,
1001, 1271, 1332, 1354, 1454,
1460, 1500, 2191

Running
S: 11104

Running—Fiction
JS: 878, 3710, 3723

Running—History
JS: 11105

Russia
IJ: 4968, 8612, 8684, 8686, 8702,
8705–6, 8708
J: 7894
JS: 7886, 7895, 8689, 8695–96,
8703–4, 8707, 8711, 8715–16
S: 8687, 8717

Russia—Biography
IJ: 7885
J: 7894
JS: 7886, 7895

Russia—Cookbooks
J: 10566

Russia—Fiction
IJ: 2186, 2564
J: 1898, 2167, 2208, 2593
JS: 216, 2177, 2191
S: 1797, 3007

Russia—Folklore
JS: 4097, 4133

Russian Americans
JS: 4996

Russian Americans—Fiction
J: 2539
JS: 1199

**Russian literature—History
and criticism**
S: 4363

Russian Revolution
IJ: 7885
JS: 8704, 8707, 8716

**Russian Revolution—
Biography**
JS: 7875–76

Russian Revolution—Fiction
IJ: 2186

Rustin, Bayard
IJ: 7239

Rwanda
J: 8448
JS: 8431

Ryan, Nolan
IJ: 7673

S

Sac and Fox Indians—History
J: 8930

Sac Indians—Biography
JS: 7363

Sacagawea
IJ: 6657
S: 6656

Sacagawea—Fiction
J: 2488

Safety
See also Accidents; First aid
IJ: 5860, 6119–21

IJ = Intermediate-Junior High; J = Junior High; JS = Junior-Senior High; S = Senior High

J: 6116
JS: 6177, 6180

Safety education
IJ: 6117

Safety education—Women
JS: 6118, 6174–75, 6178–79

Sailboarding
JS: 11135

Sailing and boating
See also Ships and boats
JS: 11110–11, 11113
S: 11107

Sailing and boating—Fiction
IJ: 199

St. Augustine (Florida)
J: 8921

***St. Louis Post-Dispatch* (news-paper)**
JS: 7609

St. Louis World's Fair, 1904
IJ: 2516

St. Patrick—Fiction
J: 2153

Saints
IJ: 4519
S: 4509

Salem witch trials
IJ: 9070
J: 9060, 9062
JS: 9054, 9057, 9069, 9078

Salem witch trials—Fiction
JS: 2288, 2290

Salinger, J. D.—Criticism
JS: 4317

Salk, Jonas
JS: 7612

Salsitz, Norman
JS: 7787

Salzburg Marionette Theater
J: 6956

Samburu (African people)
JS: 8433

Sampras, Pete
IJ: 7752
JS: 7751

Samuri
JS: 8559

Samurai—Fiction
IJ: 2117
J: 2113
JS: 1745, 2114

San (African people)
JS: 8461

San Antonio (Texas)
S: 7934

San Antonio (Texas)—Fiction
J: 1726
JS: 487

San Antonio Spurs (basketball team)
IJ: 10995

San Francisco
IJ: 9542, 9546

San Francisco—Fiction
IJ: 1910, 2517
J: 29, 603–4
S: 2513

San Juan (Puerto Rico)
IJ: 8824

Sanders, Barry
IJ: 7722

Sanitation—History
IJ: 10367

Santa Claus—Fiction
J: 1684

Santa Fe Trail—History
JS: 9124

Santee Sioux Indians
J: 8931

Santiago, Esmeralda
JS: 7503

Saratoga, Battle of
IJ: 9099

Sasaki, Sadako
JS: 7819

Satire
See Humor and satire

***Saturday Night Live* (television program)**
JS: 6559

Saudi Arabia
IJ: 8759

Saul, John—Criticism
S: 4291

Scandinavia—Folklore
JS: 4099

Scandinavia—History
IJ: 8720

Scandinavia—Mythology
See Mythology—Scandinavia

Scandinavian Americans
JS: 4988

***The Scarlet Letter*—Criticism**
S: 4292, 4325, 4335

Scavenger hunts
JS: 10867

Scavenger hunts—Fiction
JS: 2786

Schindler, Oskar
IJ: 7888
JS: 7887

Schizophrenia
See also Mental illness
JS: 6037

Schizophrenia—Fiction
JS: 935, 956
S: 941

Schoen, Allen M.
JS: 7613

Scholarships
JS: 5424

School libraries
JS: 5244

School of American Ballet—Fiction
IJ: 1435

School prayer
See also Freedom of religion
JS: 4462

School stories—Fiction
IJ: 338, 477, 496, 503, 596, 599, 616, 826, 1123, 1161, 1194, 1204, 1235, 1237, 1267, 1375, 1432, 1439, 1461, 1465, 1758, 2834, 2880, 2889, 2900, 2916, 3250, 3330, 3343, 3536, 3620
J: 268, 489, 573, 753, 1041, 1118, 1130–31, 1159, 1182, 1259, 1285, 1361, 1468, 1498, 1518, 1540, 1776, 1858, 2702, 2841–42, 2863, 2873, 2899, 3227, 3363, 3365, 3696, 3719
JS: 102, 238, 476, 554, 568, 594–95, 705, 976, 1036, 1039, 1088–89, 1100, 1102, 1105–6, 1111–12,

IJ = Intermediate-Junior High; J = Junior High; JS = Junior-Senior High; S = Senior High

1168, 1173–74, 1197, 1199, 1278, 1296, 1314, 1339, 1345–46, 1372, 1382, 1388, 1400, 1421, 1436, 1462, 1471, 1541, 2160, 2866, 2869, 2882, 2892, 2909, 2911, 2915, 3019, 3071, 3092, 3103, 3307, 3342, 3348, 3358, 3362, 3377, 3383, 3642, 3689, 3692, 3702, 3705, 3739, 3742, 7916, 8631

S: 421, 1256–57, 2860

School violence
JS: 5023–24

Schools
See also Education
IJ: 5340, 5345
JS: 5141, 5342, 5348

Schools—Censorship
J: 5252

Schools—History
J: 9064, 9339

Schools—Personal guidance
IJ: 5347
JS: 5344

Schools—Poetry
JS: 3983

Schools—Prayer
J: 4655

Schools—Segregation
JS: 4654, 4739

Schools—Violence
IJ: 5025
JS: 5043

Schubert, Franz
J: 6957

Schuman, Clara
IJ: 7097

Schwarzenegger, Arnold
IJ: 7098
JS: 6528, 7099

Schwarzkopf, Norman
JS: 7443

Science—Biography
IJ: 7528, 7534–35, 7592, 7606
J: 6599, 7509, 7517, 7533, 7541, 7555, 7563
JS: 7514, 7516, 7525, 7529, 7537–40, 7542, 7551–54, 7556, 7565–66, 7578, 7598, 7604–5

Science—Careers
J: 5549

JS: 5544
S: 5545

Science—Discoveries
JS: 9592

Science—Experiments and projects
IJ: 9607, 9611, 9613, 9625, 9627–30, 9633–34
J: 9609–10, 9612, 9615–20
JS: 9604–6, 9608, 9614, 9621–24, 9626, 9631, 10239

Science—General
IJ: 9569–70, 9573, 9577, 9579, 9586–87, 9593–94, 9599, 9625
J: 9576, 9601, 10715
JS: 4496, 9574, 9581, 9584, 9589, 9597, 9600, 9602–3
S: 9583, 9598

Science—History
IJ: 8102, 8553, 8770, 9061, 9071, 9571, 9585, 9588
J: 9580
JS: 8117, 9572, 9575, 9578, 9590, 9592, 9595–96

Science—Research
S: 9583

Science—Schools
JS: 5411

Science fairs
JS: 9606

Science fiction
IJ: 2867, 3397–99, 3410–12, 3431, 3438–39, 3456, 3468, 3470, 3482, 3495, 3511–13, 3520, 3531, 3534, 3536, 3538, 3547, 3549, 3551, 3554, 3572, 3587, 3612, 3620, 3636, 3643, 3667
J: 2847, 3409, 3417, 3420, 3435, 3453–54, 3475, 3480, 3506, 3523, 3537, 3542, 3548, 3550, 3570, 3573, 3590, 3598, 3608, 3625, 3628, 3633, 3662, 3668, 3671
JS: 351–52, 1674, 1731, 1748, 3384–89, 3393–94, 3396, 3400, 3402, 3404, 3406–8, 3413, 3415–16, 3418, 3422–25, 3427–28, 3430, 3433, 3436–37, 3441, 3443–45, 3447–50, 3455, 3457–58, 3460–61, 3463–67, 3471–74, 3476, 3478–79, 3481, 3483–89, 3494, 3498–504, 3507, 3509–10, 3516–18, 3521–22, 3524–29, 3539–41, 3543, 3546, 3552, 3555–56, 3558–60, 3562–64, 3567, 3569, 3571, 3574–76, 3578–86, 3588, 3593, 3595–97, 3600–7,

3609, 3611, 3614–18, 3621–24, 3627, 3629–32, 3634–35, 3637–40, 3642, 3645–46, 3648–55, 3658–61, 3663–66, 3670, 3672, 3674
S: 959, 1905, 3390–92, 3395, 3401, 3403, 3405, 3414, 3419, 3421, 3426, 3429, 3432, 3434, 3440, 3442, 3446, 3451–52, 3459, 3462, 3469, 3477, 3490–93, 3496–97, 3505, 3508, 3514–15, 3519, 3530, 3532–33, 3535, 3544–45, 3553, 3557, 3561, 3565–66, 3568, 3577, 3589, 3591, 3594, 3599, 3610, 3613, 3619, 3626, 3641, 3644, 3647, 3656–57, 3669, 3673

Science fiction—Biography
IJ: 6670

Science fiction—Films
JS: 6551

Science fiction—History and criticism
JS: 3627, 4275, 4338, 4341
S: 4256

Science fiction—Illustration
JS: 6393

Science fiction—Writing
JS: 5392

Science fiction films—Art
JS: 6557

Science projects
See Science—Experiments and projects

Scientific research
J: 9757

Scientific research—Fiction
S: 1564

Scientists—Fiction
J: 3570
JS: 154, 2763, 3609, 3658

Scoliosis
JS: 5750

Scoliosis—Fiction
IJ: 904

Scooters
S: 10499

Scopes trial
See also Evolution
JS: 9375

Scorsese, Martin
JS: 6526

IJ = Intermediate-Junior High; J = Junior High; JS = Junior-Senior High; S = Senior High

Scotland
See also Great Britain
JS: 7878, 10821

Scotland—Biography
JS: 7871, 7879

Scotland—Fiction
IJ: 223, 2721
J: 1750
JS: 79, 387, 1057, 1436, 2162–63, 2935
S: 2141, 2198

Scott, Dred
JS: 9135

Scott, Robert F.—Fiction
JS: 18

Scottish Americans
IJ: 4989
JS: 4982

Scottsboro trial (Alabama)
JS: 4670

Scouts and scouting
J: 6375, 11012
JS: 6377, 6506

Scuba diving—Fiction
IJ: 3531
JS: 76, 2785

Sculptors—Fiction
JS: 2412

Sculpture—Biography
J: 6713
JS: 6752
S: 6712

Sculpture—Fiction
IJ: 2853

Sculpture—History
J: 6411
JS: 6419, 6424

Sea disasters
JS: 10314
S: 10263, 10311

Sea mammals
S: 10038

Sea monsters—Fiction
J: 1838

Sea stories
See also Adventure stories—Fiction
JS: 261, 1389
S: 8471

Sea stories—Fiction
IJ: 249, 2348
J: 2168, 2566
JS: 22, 166, 188, 233, 260, 335, 381, 405, 2632
S: 145

Sea turtles
S: 9847

Sea voyages
S: 8042

Seafarers—Fiction
S: 2154

Seances—Fiction
JS: 3155

Search warrants
JS: 4676

Seashells
J: 9999
JS: 10003, 10008, 10010

Seashores
J: 10009
JS: 9998, 10007

Seattle (Washington)—Fiction
IJ: 3112
J: 2650
JS: 872, 2584
S: 3769

Seau, Junior
IJ: 7723

Sebestyen, Ouida
JS: 6905

***The Secret Garden*—Cookbooks**
IJ: 10582

***The Secret Garden*—Criticism**
IJ: 6823

Secretary of State (U.S.)—Biography
JS: 4627, 7356, 7358

Seeds
J: 9795

Segregation (racial)
See also Prejudice; Racism
JS: 4654, 4738–39, 9436
S: 4875

Segregation (racial)—Biography
IJ: 4912

Segregation (racial)—History
JS: 4907

Selena
J: 7100

Seles, Monica
IJ: 7753

Self-defense
IJ: 6117
JS: 11094, 11096

Self-defense—Women
JS: 6118

Self-esteem
See also Personal guidance
IJ: 6266
JS: 6255, 6267

Self-esteem—Women
J: 6270
S: 6261

Self-image—Fiction
JS: 1234

Self-mutilation
JS: 5990

Self-realization—Fiction
JS: 1609

Seminole Indians
IJ: 7499
JS: 8957

Seminole Indians—Fiction
J: 97
JS: 2255

Senate (U.S.)
See also Congress (U.S.);
United States—Government
JS: 4625
S: 4630

Senate (U.S.)—Biography
J: 7416

Senegal
IJ: 8494
JS: 8518

Senses
J: 5962

Sensors
J: 10374

***A Separate Peace*—Criticism**
S: 4329

Sequoyah (Cherokee chief)
IJ: 8993
JS: 7444

IJ = Intermediate-Junior High; J = Junior High; JS = Junior-Senior High; S = Senior High

**Serengeti Plain (Tanzania)—
Fiction**
J: 38

Sermons
S: 4889

Serra, Junípero
J: 6658

Sesame Street **(television program)**
JS: 6558

Seventh-Day Adventists
J: 4560

Sewage
IJ: 5115

Sewing
See also Needlecrafts
JS: 10757, 10759, 10761–65

Sex—Fiction
J: 1448
JS: 1050, 1157, 1324, 1473, 2838,
3311
S: 1274

Sex education
IJ: 6105, 6139, 6151, 6166
J: 5620, 6133, 6140, 6153, 6160,
6167, 6254
JS: 6077, 6084, 6123, 6125–26,
6129–30, 6137, 6141–43, 6146,
6154, 6159, 6162–63, 6165, 6168,
6199, 6252, 6264, 6297, 6303

**Sex education—African
Americans**
S: 6157

Sex education—Fiction
IJ: 1235

Sex roles
See also Gender roles
J: 5264
JS: 5262–63

Sex roles—Fiction
IJ: 3735
JS: 2127

Sex roles—Poetry
JS: 3913

Sexism
See also Sexual discrimination;
Sexual harassment
JS: 4663, 4714, 6183, 6185, 6190,
6202, 10898
S: 5434

Sexual abuse
See also Child sexual abuse
JS: 6171, 6181, 6187, 6191, 6197,
6200

Sexual abuse—Fiction
J: 981
JS: 763, 920, 925, 976, 1021, 1349,
1394, 1442
S: 766, 1489

Sexual assault
See also Date rape; Rape
JS: 6188

Sexual behavior
JS: 6226
S: 6150

Sexual discrimination
See also Sexism; Sexual harass-
ment
JS: 5265–66, 10898

Sexual ethics
JS: 6182

Sexual harassment
See also Sexism; Sexual dis-
crimination
J: 4742
JS: 6172, 6183–85, 6190, 6192,
6194–95, 6198, 6202, 6206

Sexual harassment—Fiction
JS: 1325, 1454

Sexual violence
See also Date rape; Rape
JS: 6207

Sexuality
S: 6150

Sexually transmitted diseases
JS: 5733, 5742–43, 5843

Shackleton, Sir Ernest
IJ: 8854
JS: 8849

Shakers (religion)
IJ: 4510–11
JS: 4523, 4533
S: 4522

Shakers (religion)—Fiction
IJ: 2464

Shakespeare, William
IJ: 3814–15, 6906

**Shakespeare, William—
Adaptations**
J: 3816–17, 4371
JS: 4374

**Shakespeare, William—
Collected works**
JS: 3820

**Shakespeare, William—
Criticism**
IJ: 4382, 4389
JS: 3813, 3819, 4373, 4379–81, 4388
S: 3818, 4372, 4376–78, 4383–84,
4386–87

Shakespeare, William—Fiction
IJ: 2137

Shakespeare, William—Poetry
JS: 3946

**Shakespeare, William—
Sonnets—Criticism**
S: 4385

Shakespeare, William—Theater
JS: 4375

Sharks
IJ: 10021, 10023
J: 10020, 10024
JS: 10022, 10025–26, 10028–29
S: 10027

Sharks—Fiction
JS: 39

Shaw, Robert Gould
JS: 7445

Shawnee Indians—Biography
JS: 7452

Shawnee Indians—History
J: 8970
JS: 7454

Sheep—Fiction
J: 197
JS: 1823

Shelley, Mary
JS: 6907
S: 6908

Shelters (homeless)
See also Homeless people;
Poverty
JS: 5230

Sherburne, Andrew
IJ: 7942

IJ = Intermediate-Junior High; J = Junior High; JS = Junior-Senior High; S = Senior High

Silk route
IJ: 10385
J: 8201

Silk route—Fiction
IJ: 2061

Simmons, Philip
IJ: 6777

Simon, Paul
JS: 7101

Simpson, O. J.
J: 4643
JS: 4885

Singer, Isaac Bashevis
IJ: 6909

Singers—Biography
IJ: 6959, 7009, 7024, 7033, 7037, 7086–88, 7106, 7117
J: 6981, 7002, 7008, 7010, 7026–27, 7035, 7058, 7066, 7093, 7096, 7100
JS: 6677, 6982, 6986, 7003, 7012–13, 7030, 7036, 7038–39, 7041, 7045, 7056–57, 7059, 7077, 7080–81, 7089–90, 7101, 7109–10

Single parents
JS: 6106, 6364, 6369, 6374

Single parents—Fiction
IJ: 737, 892, 1344, 2889, 2891
J: 755
JS: 889

Sioux Indians
IJ: 9021
J: 8931–32
JS: 7376, 9009, 9032

Sioux Indians—Biography
JS: 7377, 7447, 7450

Sioux Indians—Fiction
JS: 557

Sister cities
IJ: 7949

Sisters—Fiction
J: 2524
JS: 1398

Sitting Bull (Sioux chief)
J: 7448–49
JS: 7447, 7450

Skara Brae
IJ: 7993

Skateboarding
JS: 11116

Skeletal system
IJ: 5947, 5951
J: 9755
JS: 5948

Skeletons
JS: 5949

Skiing—Biography
JS: 7772

Skiing—Fiction
J: 3720

Skill development
JS: 5428

Skin care
JS: 5900
S: 5838

Skin disorders
S: 5838

Skinheads—Fiction
JS: 3323

Skyscrapers—History
JS: 10397

Slang
JS: 4428

Slavery
See also related topics, e.g., African Americans—History; Underground Railroad
IJ: 2525, 4868, 4873, 4878–79, 7245, 9048, 9122, 9128, 9134, 9136, 9143, 9149
J: 4876, 4894–95, 4898, 4908, 7188, 7194, 7482, 9120, 9129, 9132, 9145, 9147
JS: 4612, 4785, 4861, 4884, 4891, 4910, 4918, 7157, 7197, 7206, 7246, 7301, 8147, 8216, 9055, 9066, 9135, 9138, 9142, 9148, 9151, 9155–57, 9171, 9247
S: 4851, 4860, 4866, 4869, 4872, 4911, 7134, 7234, 8411, 9118, 9121

Slavery—Biography
IJ: 7211, 7247, 7497, 7920, 7928
J: 7249
JS: 7177, 7189, 7191, 7193, 7198, 7208–9, 7248, 7929

Slavery—Fiction
IJ: 1850, 2004, 2232, 2307, 2345, 2347, 2349, 2354, 2362, 2372, 2393, 2407, 3520
J: 2318, 2330, 2339, 2358, 2365, 2377, 2392, 2408
JS: 5, 411, 469, 514, 2258, 2297,

2316, 2320–21, 2326, 2329, 2331–32, 2335, 2346, 2355, 2364, 2366, 2399, 2405
S: 410, 2351, 2357, 2389, 2533

Slavery—History
JS: 9284

Slavery—Poetry
JS: 4000

Sled dog racing
See also Iditarod Sled Dog Race; Yukon Quest International Sled Dog Race
IJ: 10869
JS: 10868, 10902–3

Sled dogs
JS: 10112

Sleep
J: 5938
JS: 5656, 5928, 5933

Sleeping Beauty (fairy tale)—Adaptations
JS: 2019

Sleeping disorders
JS: 5828

Slovakia
IJ: 8624

Slovakia—Fiction
JS: 2662

Slugs—Fiction
JS: 3504

Slums
JS: 5303

Slums—Fiction
JS: 490

Small pox
JS: 5763

Smith, Emmitt
IJ: 7724–25

Smith, Will
IJ: 7102
JS: 7103–5

Smithsonian Institution (Washington, D.C.)
JS: 9507

Smokey Bear
JS: 9889

Smoking
See also Nicotine; Tobacco industry

IJ = Intermediate-Junior High; J = Junior High; JS = Junior-Senior High; S = Senior High

IJ = Intermediate-Junior High; J = Junior High; JS = Junior-Senior High; S = Senior High

South America—Mythology
JS: 4181

South Asian Americans
See also Asian Americans
JS: 4942

South Carolina
J: 9554
JS: 9555

South Dakota
S: 9006

South Dakota—Fiction
J: 648

South Pole
See also Antarctic; Polar
regions
S: 8864

South Pole—Fiction
JS: 18

South (U.S.)
See also specific states, e.g.,
Texas
S: 7932

South (U.S.)—Civil War
JS: 9245

South (U.S.)—Fiction
IJ: 494, 1075, 1430
J: 322
JS: 318, 510, 581, 2379, 2416, 2422,
2512, 2770
S: 410, 3767

South (U.S.)—Folklore
J: 4171

South (U.S.)—History
JS: 9208, 9223

Southwest (U.S.)
See also specific states, e.g.,
New Mexico
IJ: 10198
JS: 9141, 9566
S: 8950

Southwest (U.S.)—Biography
S: 6628

Southwest (U.S.)—Fiction
S: 435, 3078, 3244

Southwest (U.S.)—History
IJ: 8982, 9126
JS: 9567
S: 9008, 9565

Soviet Union
See also Russia, and other
separate states, e.g., Ukraine
IJ: 8684–85, 8708
JS: 8691, 8695, 8699, 8704
S: 8717

Soviet Union—Biography
JS: 7875–76

Soviet Union—Fiction
S: 1533, 1554

Space and time
JS: 10319

Space colonies
JS: 9656

Space colonies—Fiction
JS: 3404

Space exploration
See also Space travel
IJ: 9668–69, 9672, 9679, 9681,
9695–96
J: 9662, 9671, 9676
JS: 9653, 9656, 9666, 9673, 9678,
9685, 9687–88, 9690–92, 9694,
9698, 9708, 9717–18, 9726, 9734
S: 9665, 9710

Space exploration—Biography
J: 7511
JS: 6653

**Space exploration—
Experiments and projects**
JS: 9680, 9683

Space exploration—Fiction
JS: 3460

Space stations—Fiction
IJ: 3468
S: 3566

Space travel
See also Space exploration
IJ: 9669

Space travel—Fiction
J: 3523
JS: 3524, 3526–27, 3529

Spaceships—Fiction
JS: 3464, 3473, 3529
S: 3452

Spain
IJ: 8732
J: 8731

Spain—Biography
JS: 6616

Spain—Fiction
IJ: 2194
J: 2148, 2173
JS: 2087, 2184

Spain—Folklore
J: 4071

Spain—History
J: 6609, 8726, 8728
JS: 8205, 8727, 9043
S: 8729

Spanish American War
IJ: 9331

Spanish Armada
JS: 8186, 8727

Spanish Inquisition
JS: 8205

Spanish language
JS: 4414

Spanish language—Poetry
JS: 3989

Speaking skills
IJ: 5393
JS: 5394, 5397

Special effects (motion pictures)
IJ: 10459

Special interest groups (U.S.)
JS: 4688

Speech, freedom of
See Freedom of speech

Speeches—African Americans
JS: 4242

Speed (methamphetamine)
See also Drugs and drug abuse
J: 5699

Spelling bees—Fiction
JS: 487

Spice Girls (musical group)
IJ: 7106

Spices
JS: 10609

Spiders
IJ: 9990
JS: 9988

Spiders—Fiction
IJ: 1162
JS: 4079

IJ = Intermediate-Junior High; J = Junior High; JS = Junior-Senior High; S = Senior High

IJ = Intermediate-Junior High; J = Junior High; JS = Junior-Senior High; S = Senior High

States (U.S.)
IJ: 8912

States (U.S.)—Capitals
JS: 8879

States (U.S.)—Rights
JS: 4640

Statesmen (U.S.)—Biography
J: 7139, 7371

Statistics
JS: 6225, 10239
S: 10237

Statue of Liberty
J: 9506

Stealing—Fiction
J: 1240
JS: 1008

Steamboats—Biography
IJ: 7504

Steinbeck, John
JS: 4349, 6912
S: 6911

Steinbeck, John—Criticism
S: 4330–31, 4359

Steinem, Gloria
J: 7243
JS: 7241–42

Stepfamilies
See also Adoption
J: 6322

Stepfamilies—Fiction
IJ: 21, 614, 715, 744, 797, 1456
J: 890, 2328
JS: 146, 1067, 2411, 2728

Stepfathers—Fiction
J: 627

Stepsisters—Fiction
IJ: 3688

Steroids
IJ: 5679
J: 5693
JS: 5665

Stevenson, Robert Louis
IJ: 6913–14
JS: 10505

Stevenson, Robert Louis— Criticism
S: 4278

Stewart, Martha
JS: 7614

Still, William
J: 9120

Stine, R. L.—Criticism
JS: 4327

Stock market—Crash of 1929
JS: 9362

Stockton, John
IJ: 7641, 7703

Stoker, Bram
JS: 6915

Stone, Oliver
JS: 7128

Stone Age
See also Prehistoric life
IJ: 8000
JS: 8003

Stone Age—Fiction
IJ: 2038

Storms
See also Weather, and specific types of storms, e.g., Hurricanes
IJ: 10269
S: 10262–63

Storytelling
IJ: 5367
JS: 5391

Storytelling—Fiction
JS: 1453, 2044

Stowe, Harriet Beecher
J: 6917, 6919
JS: 6916, 6918

Strauss, Levi
J: 7615–16

Strawberries
J: 9759

Streams
See Rivers

Stress
IJ: 6030
J: 5988, 6010
JS: 5983, 5992, 6020
S: 6022

Stretching
S: 5974

String games
IJ: 10882

Stuart, Jeb
IJ: 7451

Stuart England
S: 8666

Study skills
IJ: 5355, 5357
J: 5360
JS: 5349–50, 5352, 5356, 5358–59, 5381, 5418
S: 5353

Stuttering—Fiction
IJ: 1005

Submarines
IJ: 10511
JS: 10517

Subterranean world—Fiction
JS: 3436

Suburban life
JS: 4232

Subways—Fiction
JS: 1342

Sudan
JS: 8449

Suicide
See also Physician-assisted suicide; Right to die
IJ: 5604, 6035
JS: 5590, 5593, 5599–600, 5984, 5993, 5997, 6002, 6007, 6024

Suicide—Fiction
IJ: 3214
J: 700, 1179, 1316
JS: 871, 910, 926, 995, 1074, 1192, 1337, 1477, 2335, 2736, 2942, 2952, 3310, 3685

Sukuma (African people)
IJ: 8409

Sullivan, Anne—Plays
JS: 3833

Summer, Donna
JS: 7109

Sun
JS: 9722
S: 9725

The Sun Also Rises
S: 4294

IJ = Intermediate-Junior High; J = Junior High; JS = Junior-Senior High; S = Senior High

IJ = Intermediate-Junior High; J = Junior High; JS = Junior-Senior High; S = Senior High

IJ = Intermediate-Junior High; J = Junior High; JS = Junior-Senior High; S = Senior High

5157, 5161, 5165, 5169, 5177, 5181, 5208, 6229

Teenage violence—Fiction
JS: 1117, 1381

Teenage violence—Poetry
JS: 3984

Teenage workers—Fiction
JS: 1321, 1423

Teenage writers
JS: 3774

Teenage writers—Essays
JS: 5372

Teenage writers—Fiction
JS: 3754

Teenagers—AIDS victims
JS: 5778

Teenagers—Alcohol use— Fiction
JS: 926

Teenagers—Civil rights
J: 4744
JS: 4721, 4727, 4751, 4755, 4761, 4770, 4776, 5033, 6192

Teenagers—Homeless
JS: 5234

Teenagers—Opinions
JS: 6221, 6226, 9432

Teeth
See also Dental care
IJ: 5952
J: 5953, 5955
JS: 5954

Telecommunications
JS: 10451, 10454–55

Telecommunications— Experiments and projects
J: 10453

Telegraph—History
JS: 10451

Telephones
JS: 10454

Telescopes
IJ: 9693
J: 9662
S: 9647

Telescopes—Biography
IJ: 7584
JS: 7585

Television
JS: 1250, 6560, 6562–63, 7618, 10465
S: 6568

Television—Biography
IJ: 7115, 7118
JS: 7119

Television—Careers
JS: 5492, 5558

Television—Criticism
JS: 4451
S: 6567

Television—Fiction
IJ: 3269
J: 1029, 1103, 1108, 3280
JS: 2987

Television—History
JS: 6569

Television—Journalism
JS: 4445, 4451, 4697

Television—Production
S: 10460

Television—Programs
JS: 6559, 6571

Television—Special effects
IJ: 10459

Temper—Fiction
IJ: 996

Temptations (musical group)
JS: 7110

Tennessee
S: 4972

Tennessee—Fiction
JS: 1025

Tennis
JS: 11137–39, 11141–43

Tennis—Biography
IJ: 7743–44, 7748, 7752–54
J: 7745
JS: 7645, 7746–47, 7749–51, 7755–56

Tennis—Fiction
IJ: 3675
JS: 3727, 3745
S: 1270

Teresa, Mother
IJ: 7825

Term papers
S: 5377

Terrorism
IJ: 5297, 9491
JS: 4997, 5295–96, 5298

Terrorism—Fiction
J: 3033
JS: 47, 55, 57, 66, 100, 117
S: 27, 90, 3037

Tesla, Nikola
J: 7617

Tests and test taking
J: 5360
JS: 5359

Tet Offensive
See also Vietnam War
J: 9481
JS: 9474

Teton Sioux Indians—History
J: 8932

Texas
IJ: 2456, 9563, 9568

Texas—Biography
J: 7393

Texas—Fiction
IJ: 2372, 2431, 2483, 2497, 2504, 2556
J: 1043, 1227, 2424, 2439, 2470
JS: 230, 279, 472, 1183, 1314, 1367, 3160
S: 2917

Texas—History
IJ: 9152
JS: 9141
S: 9386

Texas *v.* Johnson
JS: 5250

Textiles
JS: 6391

Thailand
J: 8576
JS: 7930

Thailand—Fiction
J: 2805
JS: 1527

Thailand—Folklore
IJ: 4088

Thanksgiving Day
IJ: 5289

IJ = Intermediate-Junior High; J = Junior High; JS = Junior-Senior High; S = Senior High

IJ = Intermediate-Junior High; J = Junior High; JS = Junior-Senior High; S = Senior High

IJ = Intermediate-Junior High; J = Junior High; JS = Junior-Senior High; S = Senior High

Twenty-first century
JS: 5273

Twins
JS: 6362
S: 6222

Twins—Fiction
IJ: 1307, 1596, 1818, 2776, 3343
J: 2, 1769, 2333, 3139, 3696
JS: 832, 1153, 1359, 2713, 3569,
3634

Twins—Folklore
J: 4100

Typing
JS: 5354

U

Ubar (Oman)
JS: 8015

Uchida, Yoshiko
S: 7946

UFOs
IJ: 9677, 9682, 9699
JS: 9670, 9689, 10859
S: 9697

Uganda
IJ: 8427, 9882
JS: 8429

Ukraine
IJ: 8713
JS: 8700

Ukraine—Fiction
JS: 2191

Umpires (baseball)
JS: 10966

Underground Railroad
See also African Americans—
History; Slavery
IJ: 9134
J: 9120, 9132, 9147
JS: 9148

**Underground Railroad—
Biography**
IJ: 7247
JS: 7209
S: 7234

**Underground Railroad—
Fiction**
IJ: 2340, 2345, 2362
J: 1987, 2365, 2377
JS: 2321, 2326, 2329, 2331–32, 2364,
2366

Underground Railroad—Poetry
JS: 4000

Underwater exploration
See also Oceanography
IJ: 10298, 10305, 10313, 10513
J: 10304
JS: 10299, 10301
S: 10315

**Underwater exploration—
Fiction**
JS: 64, 76, 352, 3473

Underwater salvage
S: 10302

Underwear—History
JS: 10409

Unemployment
JS: 6359, 8919

Unemployment—Fiction
J: 742

Ungerer, Tomi
JS: 6778

Unicorns
IJ: 1673

Unicorns—Fiction
JS: 1609, 1805–6

Unidentified flying objects
See UFOs

Uniforms
JS: 9203

United Nations
IJ: 4570
JS: 4567–69, 4571

United Nations—Biography
JS: 7863

**United Nations High
Commissioner for Refugees**
IJ: 4565

United States
IJ: 9433

United States—Atlases
JS: 7956

United States—Census, 1990
JS: 5123

United States—Civil War
See Civil War (U.S.)

United States—Congress
See Congress (U.S.)

United States—Constitution
See Constitution of the United
States

**United States—Costumes and
dress**
JS: 10655

United States—Culture
S: 9434

United States—Economics
JS: 5306

United States—Fiction
J: 708, 1545
S: 2351, 2363

United States—Folklore
IJ: 4169, 4172
J: 4171, 4173, 10799–800
JS: 3779, 4160, 4162, 4174–75
S: 4159, 4168

United States—Foreign policy
IJ: 8784
JS: 4574–75, 4581, 4627, 8405, 8813

**United States—Frontier and
pioneer life**
See Frontier life (U.S.)

United States—Geography
IJ: 8915
JS: 8769, 8874, 8892
S: 8917

United States—Government
See also House of
Representatives (U.S.),
Senate (U.S.)
IJ: 4593, 4622, 4632
J: 9335
JS: 4590–91, 4605, 4619, 4625, 4629,
4688, 4695, 4697, 4699–700
S: 4630

United States—Historic sites
JS: 8908

**United States—Historical docu-
ments**
S: 8868

United States—History
IJ: 8888, 8899, 8907, 8915–16, 9131

IJ = Intermediate-Junior High; J = Junior High; JS = Junior-Senior High; S = Senior High

J: 7139, 8897, 9371
JS: 4615, 6511, 7153, 8871, 8875–78,
 8882–83, 8885–87, 8889–91, 8893,
 8895, 8898, 8900, 8903–4, 8908–9,
 8911, 8918
S: 8873, 8881, 8914

United States—History—Plays
IJ: 3847

United States—Intelligence service
JS: 4581

United States—Literary history
IJ: 4306

United States—Modern history
IJ: 9421, 9435, 9446
J: 9349, 9385, 9422–23, 9429
JS: 7403, 9394, 9404–5, 9415, 9420,
 9426, 9428, 9431, 9443
S: 9353

United States—Poetry
S: 3958

United States—Politics
JS: 4615, 7335

United States—Politics—Fiction
S: 1543

United States—Presidents
See Presidents (U.S.)

United States—Revolutionary War
See Revolutionary War (U.S.)

United States—States
See States (U.S.)

United States—Wars
IJ: 8880

United States (1776–1876)—History
JS: 9140

United States (1789–1861)—Biography
JS: 7187

United States (1789–1861)—Fiction
IJ: 2336

United States (1789–1861)—History
IJ: 9119
JS: 9151

United States (1789–1876)—Fiction
IJ: 2359

United States (1800–1860)—History
JS: 9144

United States (1815–1861)—Fiction
JS: 2324

United States (1828–1860)—Fiction
S: 2350

United States (1828–1860)—History
IJ: 9125

United States (1865–1914)—Fiction
IJ: 2537
JS: 2512

United States (1865–1914)—History
See also Reconstruction to
 World War I (U.S.)
IJ: 9326
J: 9330

United States (1900s)—History
J: 9349
JS: 9352

United States (1910s)—History
JS: 9350

United States (1915–1945)—History
JS: 9355, 9377

United States (1920s)—History
J: 9385
JS: 9368

United States (1940s)—History
J: 9438
JS: 9397

United States (1950s)—History
IJ: 9406, 9421, 9435
JS: 9396, 9432

United States (1960s)—History
IJ: 9406
J: 9424
JS: 8406, 9394, 9403, 9420, 9431,
 9437

United States-China relations
JS: 8526, 8526

United States-Israel relations
See Israel-U.S. relations

United States-Mexico relations
See Mexico-U.S. relations

**United States Women's
 National Soccer Team**
IJ: 11126

Universe
IJ: 9732–33, 9735
J: 9662, 9730–31
JS: 9638, 9649–50, 9652, 9661

Universe—Fiction
JS: 3526

Universities and colleges
See Colleges and universities

Unmarried mothers—Fiction
JS: 2549

Uruguay
IJ: 8840
JS: 8831

Uruguay—Fiction
S: 27

USSR
See Soviet Union

Utah—Fiction
JS: 2671

Ute Indians—Fiction
JS: 290

Utopias—Fiction
S: 3613

Uzbekistan
IJ: 8714

V

V-E Day, 1945
See also World War II
JS: 8296

Valdez (Alaska)
J: 9532

Valens, Ritchie
JS: 7112

Valentine's Day—Crafts
IJ: 10533

Values
JS: 5260

IJ = Intermediate-Junior High; J = Junior High; JS = Junior-Senior High; S = Senior High

Vampires
IJ: 10834
JS: 10810, 10850, 10860

Vampires—Fiction
IJ: 2776
J: 390, 2717
JS: 2677, 2683, 2728–30, 2752,
2763–64, 2807, 2817, 3077
S: 391, 2784, 2791, 2797, 2809

Van Beek, Cato Bontjes
JS: 7890

Vancouver (Canada)
J: 8773

Van Gogh, Vincent
J: 6435
JS: 6779–81

Van Gogh, Vincent—Fiction
S: 2197

Vanilla
J: 9759

Vegetables
IJ: 9774
JS: 9776

Vegetarian cooking
JS: 6045, 6059, 10588, 10591,
10598–600, 10605, 10616

Vegetarianism
JS: 6045, 6052, 6054, 6059

Velazquez, Diego de—Fiction
J: 2148

Vendee Globe (sailing race)
JS: 11113

Venice—Fiction
J: 3341

Ventriloquism
JS: 6587

Venus (planet)
JS: 9718

Veracruz
IJ: 8809

Vermont
IJ: 9508
JS: 9503

Vermont—Fiction
IJ: 2541, 2565
J: 828, 2352, 2524
JS: 1249, 1254, 2831

Versailles, Palace of
JS: 8627

Vesey, Denmark
J: 7249

Vests
JS: 10647

Veterinarians
JS: 10105
S: 10141

Veterinarians—Biography
JS: 7581–82, 7613

Veterinarians—Fiction
JS: 1877

Veterinary medicine—Careers
JS: 5528

Vicario, Leona—Fiction
JS: 2217

Vice Presidency (U.S.)
JS: 4629

**Vice-presidents (U.S.)—
Biography**
JS: 4620

Vicksburg, Siege of
JS: 9250

Victimhood
JS: 5054

Victims' rights
JS: 4734

**Victoria, Queen of Great
Britain**
IJ: 7921
S: 7892

**Victoria, Queen of Great
Britain—Biography**
JS: 7891

Victorian Age
JS: 8656

Victorian Age—Biography
S: 7892

Victorian Age—Fiction
J: 327
JS: 207

Video—Careers
JS: 5558

Video recordings
JS: 10457, 10462, 10750
S: 10461

Vienna—Fiction
JS: 3176

Vietnam
IJ: 8577, 8587
JS: 8573
S: 8581

Vietnam—Cookbooks
JS: 10608

Vietnam—Fiction
JS: 2110

**Vietnam Veterans Memorial,
Washington, D.C.**
IJ: 9504

Vietnam War
IJ: 9446, 9460
J: 9481, 9485
JS: 9444–45, 9447, 9449, 9451,
9454–56, 9464, 9467, 9469, 9474,
9479, 9482–84
S: 9462, 9466, 9468, 9472, 9475,
9480

Vietnam War—Art
JS: 9470

Vietnam War—Biography
JS: 7494

Vietnam War—Fiction
IJ: 699, 869
J: 1362
JS: 289, 850, 878, 1032, 1317, 2667,
2670–72, 2736
S: 2665, 2668

Vietnam War—Women
JS: 9478

Vietnamese Americans
See also Asian Americans
JS: 4921, 4945

**Vietnamese Americans—
Fiction**
JS: 472–73

Viking (space expedition)
JS: 9698

Vikings
IJ: 8720, 8724
J: 8767
JS: 8722

Vikings—Fiction
IJ: 1238
JS: 1744, 2070, 2201

IJ = Intermediate-Junior High; J = Junior High; JS = Junior-Senior High; S = Senior High

Villa, Pancho
IJ: 7905
J: 7906

Violence
See also Teenage violence
IJ: 4829, 5025, 5146, 5149, 5195, 6352
J: 4857, 5253
JS: 5002, 5012, 5023–24, 5044, 5131, 5136, 5139, 5151–52, 5161, 5169, 5208, 5241, 5651, 5674, 6186, 6207, 6323, 6338, 6346, 6357, 6366, 6368, 6371, 10894

Violence—Mass media

Virginia
IJ: 9552, 9557

Virginia—Biography
JS: 7501

Virginia—Fiction
IJ: 2376
J: 562, 2289
JS: 2270

Virtual reality
JS: 10422, 10442

Virtual reality—Fiction
J: 3475, 3662
JS: 1837, 3507, 3555–56

Viruses
JS: 5730, 5804, 5811

Viruses—Fiction
J: 3598

Viruses (computers)
JS: 10436

Vision
J: 5963

Vitamins
JS: 6050
S: 6051

Vocabulary
J: 5395
S: 5390

Vocational education
S: 5415

Vocational guidance
See also Occupational guidance
J: 5439, 5446, 5495, 5511
JS: 5427, 5429, 5431, 5440–44, 5447–51, 5454–55, 5457, 5461–62, 5465, 5471–72, 5474, 5478, 5483–85, 5488–89, 5492, 5494,

5498, 5501–3, 5506–10, 5512–16, 5518–20, 5524, 5526, 5529, 5531–33, 5536–41, 5548, 5552, 5554–55, 5557–58, 5561–66
S: 5476, 5521, 5542, 5545

Voigt, Cynthia—Criticism
JS: 4339

Volcanoes
IJ: 10175, 10178, 10184, 10188
J: 10181, 10187
JS: 10179–80, 10182, 10186
S: 10183

Volcanoes—Fiction
IJ: 2017
JS: 39, 351

Volleyball
JS: 11145

Volleyball—Biography
JS: 7771

Volleyball—Fiction
IJ: 3688
JS: 1472

Volunteerism
See also Social action
IJ: 5064, 5271, 5275
JS: 4641, 5090, 5267, 5274, 5277–82
S: 5270

Volunteerism—Fiction
J: 1517
JS: 433, 1535

Von Trapp family
JS: 7113

Voting rights—African Americans
JS: 4594, 4897

Voting rights—Biography
S: 7458

Voting rights—Women
IJ: 4766
JS: 4769, 7240
S: 4787

Voyager (space expedition)
IJ: 9674, 9723

Voyages and travels
S: 6650

W

Waco, Texas, siege at
J: 4560

Wakeman, Sarah Rosetta
JS: 9172

Wales
S: 3947

Wales—Biography
JS: 6835

Wales—Castles
JS: 6388

Wales—Fiction
IJ: 1775
J: 2591
JS: 558, 2083, 2170, 3560

Wales—History
S: 8173

Walesa, Lech
JS: 7893

Walker, Madam C. J.
J: 7619

Walker, Maggie
IJ: 7506

Walking
See also Hiking
S: 10888

Wallenda, Delilah
JS: 7114

Walters, Barbara
IJ: 7115

Walton, Jenny
S: 6930

Wamesit Indians—Fiction
JS: 2286

Wampanoag Indians
J: 9031

Wampanoag Indians— Biography
JS: 7432

Wang Yani
IJ: 6782

War
IJ: 10524
J: 8030

IJ = Intermediate-Junior High; J = Junior High; JS = Junior-Senior High; S = Senior High

JS: 4580, 4588, 8885
S: 8050

War—Children
JS: 4586

War—Fiction
JS: 48, 434, 2920

War—History
JS: 8045, 8062, 8218, 8221, 8891

War—North America
JS: 8047

War—Poetry
J: 4018
JS: 3917
S: 3924

War—South and Central America
JS: 8047

War—United States
IJ: 8880

War crimes
JS: 4572

War games—Fiction
JS: 143

War of 1812
IJ: 9127, 9130, 9139
JS: 9133

War of 1812—Fiction
J: 2327, 2368–69
JS: 2338, 2360

War of the Roses—Fiction
JS: 385

Warhol, Andy
S: 6783

Warner Brothers cartoons
JS: 6522

Warren, Earl
JS: 7457

Warsaw—Ghetto uprising, 1943
JS: 8323, 8385

Warships—Fiction
JS: 166

Washington, Booker T.
JS: 7250–51

Washington, D.C.
IJ: 9509
JS: 9505, 9524

Washington, D.C.—Fiction
JS: 2373, 2545
S: 3134, 3245–48

Washington, D.C., March on (1963)
J: 9393

Washington, Denzel
JS: 7116

Washington, George
IJ: 7340–43, 7345
J: 9093
JS: 7339, 7344, 7346

Washington, George—Fiction
JS: 2317
S: 2284

Washington, Martha
J: 7347

Washington (state)—Fiction
IJ: 127, 1224

Waste recycling
IJ: 5113, 5115–16
JS: 5114

Watches
See Clocks and watches

Water
J: 9770, 10272
JS: 10218, 10270

Water—Experiments and projects
JS: 10271

Water birds
See also Ducks and geese
J: 9943

Water pollution
See also Environmental problems; Pollution
IJ: 10220
J: 9770
JS: 5102, 10270

Watercolor painting
JS: 10663, 10669, 10681, 10684, 10687, 10691

Watergate Affair
JS: 4656, 9408, 9416
S: 9441

Waterloo, Battle of
JS: 8217

Watson, James
JS: 5879

Watson, Lyall
IJ: 6931

Watts riot
J: 9400

Waves—Experiments and projects
IJ: 10273

Wayne, "Mad" Anthony—Fiction
JS: 2314

Weapons
IJ: 10524
J: 10526
JS: 10520

Weapons—History
IJ: 10521
J: 10522
JS: 10523

Weapons of mass destruction
JS: 10525

Weather
See also Storms
IJ: 10275, 10277, 10282
JS: 10276, 10279
S: 10262, 10280

Weather—Experiments and projects
JS: 10281

Weather—Fiction
IJ: 3538

Weather forecasting
IJ: 10278
JS: 10283

Weaving
S: 10532

Web pages
IJ: 10427–28

Webber, Andrew Lloyd
JS: 6958

Weddings—Fiction
J: 646

Weight control
See also Diet and dieting
JS: 6046

Weight lifting
J: 10910
JS: 10904
S: 10913

IJ = Intermediate-Junior High; J = Junior High; JS = Junior-Senior High; S = Senior High

Weight lifting—Biography
IJ: 7098

Weight-loss programs
JS: 6039

Weight problems
See also Eating disorders;
Obesity
J: 6048
JS: 6039, 6041, 6044, 6053
S: 6261

Weight problems—Fiction
IJ: 304, 1052, 1237
J: 1244, 1255, 1468
JS: 972, 1020, 1187, 1446

Welfare—United States
J: 6069
JS: 5213–14, 5219, 5224, 5226, 5237

Wells, H. G.
JS: 6932

Wells, Randell
J: 10053

Wells-Barnett, Ida B.
JS: 6671

Welsh Americans
JS: 4982

Welty, Eudora—Criticism
JS: 4295

Werewolves
J: 10816, 10837

Werewolves—Fiction
J: 2196, 2717, 2827
JS: 2824

Wersba, Barbara
JS: 6933

West Bank (Israel)
JS: 8752

West Indian Americans
JS: 4974

**West Indian Americans—
Fiction**
J: 492
JS: 506

West Indians—Emigration
JS: 4980

West Indies
JS: 8821

West Indies—Fiction
J: 2218

West (U.S.)
See also individual states, e.g.,
Montana
JS: 9275, 9303, 9786
S: 9266, 9306

West (U.S.)—Biography
JS: 7073, 9321

West (U.S.)—Birds
JS: 9931

West (U.S.)—Fiction
IJ: 95, 1224
J: 1287, 2465
JS: 25, 28, 151, 229, 491, 2461, 2493,
2852
S: 26, 167, 2441, 2508

West (U.S.)—History
J: 9258–59, 9269–70, 9272–73, 9282,
9290–92, 9316, 9351
JS: 4983, 9222, 9261–63, 9280, 9284,
9286, 9301–2, 9304–5, 9323
S: 8934, 9300, 9322

West (U.S.)—Poetry
JS: 4033

West Virginia—Fiction
IJ: 315–16, 851
JS: 2546

Westerns—Fiction
IJ: 107
JS: 25, 218, 2433–34, 2445, 2489,
3198

Wetlands
JS: 10192–93
S: 10194

Whales
IJ: 10033, 10037, 10042, 10045
J: 10041, 10049
JS: 10001, 10030–31, 10034, 10036,
10039–40, 10044, 10047, 10051
S: 10032, 10043, 10048

Whales—Fiction
IJ: 310, 2348
JS: 295

Whaling
IJ: 9119

Whaling—History
IJ: 10037
JS: 4899, 8768

Wharton, Edith
JS: 6934
S: 6935

Wheatley, Phillis
JS: 6936–37

Wheatley, Phillis—Fiction
JS: 2291

Whistler, James McNeill
JS: 6784

Whistling
JS: 10542

White, E. B.
J: 6938
JS: 6939

**White House Press Secretary—
History**
S: 4623

White House (U.S.)
IJ: 9520

White House (U.S.)—Fiction
S: 3247

White House (U.S.)—History
JS: 9512

White water rafting
JS: 11112

White water rafting—Fiction
JS: 1404

Whitestone, Heather
S: 7947

Whitman, Walt
J: 4001
JS: 4037, 6940

Whitman, Walt—Criticism
JS: 4402

Whitman, Walt—Poetry
JS: 4005

Whittling
JS: 10781, 10789

The Who (musical group)
JS: 6494

Wiesenthal, Simon
J: 7826

Wife abuse—Fiction
J: 661

Wild cats
J: 10078

Wild West shows
IJ: 7071
JS: 6578

IJ = Intermediate-Junior High; J = Junior High; JS = Junior-Senior High; S = Senior High

IJ = Intermediate-Junior High; J = Junior High; JS = Junior-Senior High; S = Senior High

Women—Careers
JS: 5464, 5475, 5559

Women—Folklore
IJ: 4062, 4163

Women—History
JS: 8870, 8902, 9346, 9401

Women—Occupations
IJ: 4749

Women—Pioneers
S: 9318

Women—Poetry
JS: 3980

Women—Poets
JS: 3887, 3895, 3899, 3967–68, 4041

Women—Scientists
S: 7568

Women—Self-defense
JS: 11096

Women—Sex roles
S: 3765

Women—Singers
JS: 7029

Women—Sports
JS: 10891, 10920, 10981, 11006,
11059
S: 10960, 11058

Women in art
IJ: 6426
S: 6407

Women in aviation
IJ: 6611
JS: 6621, 6627, 6644

Women in business
IJ: 7546
J: 7527, 7619
JS: 5307, 7531

Women in crime
J: 6602

Women in fashion
JS: 10642

Women in government
J: 7151
JS: 7357, 7783

Women in history
IJ: 7152, 7780, 7791, 8070
J: 5264, 6610, 7143, 8189, 9258, 9282

JS: 6592, 7130, 8890, 8900, 9090,
9150, 9305, 9311, 9315
S: 9187

Women in industry
J: 7527

Women in journalism
J: 6679
JS: 6690

Women in law
JS: 4663
S: 4659

Women in literature
J: 6660, 6691
JS: 4346, 6664

Women in mathematics
JS: 7514

Women in medicine
IJ: 5869
J: 7517
S: 5848, 5857

Women in music
JS: 6689
S: 6476

Women in photography
JS: 6682

Women in politics
IJ: 4767
J: 7151, 7779
JS: 4633, 4724, 7140, 7161, 7168,
7179, 7783, 7785

Women in science
IJ: 7508, 7535, 7593
J: 7511, 7517, 7600
JS: 7514, 7516, 7525, 7537, 7540,
7550, 7552–53

Women in sports
IJ: 10916, 10993, 11065, 11106
J: 5496, 7629, 10892, 10941
JS: 7634, 7771, 10881, 10914–15,
10920, 10949, 10957, 10984,
11001, 11055, 11070
S: 10982

Women in the arts
IJ: 6703
J: 6674
JS: 6697

Women in the military
J: 8402
JS: 4711, 4714, 4716, 8301, 9478

Women in the work force
IJ: 8853
JS: 5052, 5475, 8870
S: 5434

Women in the work place
JS: 5425

Women in transportation
IJ: 10504

Women in war
IJ: 9116
JS: 4717, 8911
S: 9440

Women's rights
See also Civil rights; Voting
rights—Women
IJ: 4749, 4766–67
J: 7243, 8913
JS: 4722, 4740, 4747, 4752, 4768–69,
4783, 7160, 7233, 9346
S: 4659, 4787

Women's rights—Biography
IJ: 7182
JS: 4750, 7183–84, 7186, 7208, 7240,
7242, 7459, 7948
S: 7458

Women's rights—Fiction
IJ: 2518

Wood, Grant
IJ: 6785

Wood, Michele
IJ: 6786

Wood block prints
J: 6431

Woodcarving
JS: 10788–89

Woodhull, Victoria
JS: 7459
S: 7458

Woods, Tiger
JS: 7774, 7776
S: 7775, 11052

Woodson, Carter G.
JS: 6945

Woodwork and woodworking
JS: 10782–85, 10787, 10790
S: 10778–80, 10786

Word games
See also Games; Puzzles
IJ: 4404, 10556

IJ = Intermediate-Junior High; J = Junior High; JS = Junior-Senior High; S = Senior High

IJ = Intermediate-Junior High; J = Junior High; JS = Junior-Senior High; S = Senior High

Wuthering Heights—Criticism
S: 4266

Wyeth, Andrew
JS: 6790

Wyoming
S: 9501

Wyoming—Fiction
IJ: 95, 1406
J: 2477
JS: 2484
S: 1528

X

X-Files (television series)
JS: 6561

Xhosa (African people)
J: 8473

Y

Yakima Indians
J: 9014

Yana Indians—Fiction
JS: 3198

Yanomami (people)
JS: 10205

Yellow fever—Fiction
J: 2305

Yellowstone National Park
IJ: 9886, 9910
JS: 9499, 9564
S: 9887

Yellowstone National Park—
Fiction
IJ: 3229

Yeltsin, Boris
J: 7894
JS: 7895

Yemen
IJ: 8766

Yep, Laurence—Criticism
JS: 4326

Yoga
JS: 5972
S: 5969, 5981

Yom Kippur—Fiction
J: 1239

Yorktown, Battle of
J: 9093

Yoruba (African people)
JS: 8492

Yoruba (African people)—
Fiction
J: 2098

Yorubaland (Africa)
J: 8506

Yosemite National Park
(California)
JS: 9540

Young, Neil
JS: 7120–21

Young, Steve
IJ: 7727

Young adult literature—
Biography
J: 6902
JS: 6837, 6905

Young adult literature—
Criticism
JS: 4302, 4304, 4307, 6851, 6878,
6880, 6947

Young adult literature—
History and criticism
J: 4361
JS: 4319, 4321, 4339, 4343, 4348

Young people—Biography
JS: 7777

Youth groups
IJ: 6376

Yugoslavia—Biography
JS: 7889

Yukon—History
JS: 6597

Yukon Quest International Sled
Dog Race
JS: 10868

Z

Zaharias, Babe Didrikson
JS: 7755–57

Zaire
JS: 8439, 8444

Zama, Battle of
JS: 8141

Zedong, Mao
JS: 7827

Zhang, Song Nan
IJ: 6791

Zimbabwe
J: 8490

Zimbabwe—Fiction
JS: 3489

Zimbabwe—History
J: 8460

Zindel, Paul
JS: 6947

Zippers
JS: 10372

Zitkala-Sa (Red Bird)
JS: 7252

Zoo animals
JS: 9978

Zoology
JS: 9825

Zoology—Experiments and
projects
JS: 9815

Zoos
IJ: 10145
J: 10143

Zulu (African kingdom)
JS: 8477

Zulu (African people)
IJ: 8479
J: 8474

Zuñi Indians—History
J: **8933**

IJ = Intermediate-Junior High; J = Junior High; JS = Junior-Senior High; S = Senior High

DATE DUE

SEP 1 5 2006